July 6-10, 2013
Amsterdam, The Netherlands

Association for
Computing Machinery

Advancing Computing as a Science & Profession

GECCO'13

VOL 2 of 2

Proceedings of the 2013

Genetic and Evolutionary Computation Conference

Sponsored by:

ACM SIGEVO

Supported by:

Third Millennium, Green Pocket, NVIDIA, OPTRAK, & JMP

Association for Computing Machinery

Advancing Computing as a Science & Profession

The Association for Computing Machinery
2 Penn Plaza, Suite 701
New York, New York 10121-0701

Notice to Past Authors of ACM-Published Articles
ACM intends to create a complete electronic archive of all articles and/or other material previously published by ACM. If you have written a work that has been previously published by ACM in any journal or conference proceedings prior to 1978, or any SIG Newsletter at any time, and you do NOT want this work to appear in the ACM Digital Library, please inform permissions@acm.org, stating the title of the work, the author(s), and where and when published.

ISBN: 978-1-4503-1963-8 (Digital)

ISBN: 978-1-4503-2701-5 (Print)

Additional copies may be ordered prepaid from:

ACM Order Department
PO Box 30777
New York, NY 10087-0777, USA

Phone: 1-800-342-6626 (USA and Canada)
+1-212-626-0500 (Global)
Fax: +1-212-944-1318
E-mail: acmhelp@acm.org
Hours of Operation: 8:30 am – 4:30 pm ET

Printed in the USA

Welcome from General Chair

It is my pleasure to welcome you to Amsterdam for the 2013 Genetic and Evolutionary Computation Conference (GECCO-2013). This year GECCO is being held in Europe, and we very much hope you enjoy the city of Amsterdam, as well as the many historical and modern places directly reachable from it. We hope to offer you an appealing combination of research and culture worth experiencing.

Organizing GECCO has been for me both a pleasure and an honor. A pleasure, because I have been involved in it since 1999: now a long trip, with this incredible community of skilled people and close friends. An honor, since I am having the possibility to give back to the community what I have got from GECCO, personally and in my own research. The high quality, the ideas, and the possibility to interact with GECCO's attendees had a profound impact in my students, my postdocs, and my actual research program.

Christian Blum served as the editor-in-chief this year, and did a superb job in maintaining the well-known high quality of this conference. GECCO-2013 accepted 204 full papers for oral presentation out of a total of 570 submitted. This large number of submissions accounts for the world interest in this year's GECCO. But also, it represents an acceptance rate of less than 36%, what tells on the expected quality of the accepted works. I am very thankful to Christian Blum, Leonardo Vanneschi (this year's Proceedings Chair), and all the track chairs for their hard work managing the review, selection, and scheduling process for the scientific papers. Thanks also to Linklings and Sheridan Printing for their assistance with the publication of the proceedings.

One of the highlights of every GECCO is the set of free tutorials and free workshops held during the first two days of the conference. I found these to be incredibly helpful when I was still learning about the field, and even now, to keep my knowledge fresh on specialized new trends. Thanks to Gabriela Ochoa for chairing the tutorials and Mike Preuss for chairing the workshops. Guys, you are great.

In addition to the main program, there are many other parts that make GECCO a special and meaningful experience. Evert Haasdijk and Peter Bosman served as Local Chairs, and were very helpful with planning our visit to Amsterdam. Xavier Llorà did an excellent job of publicity with the help of our webmaster and design consultant, Gerardo Valencia. Daniele Loiacono did a great job as the Competitions Chair and, as Student Chair, Emilia Tantar masterfully oversaw the process of awarding student travel grants. I would also like to thank Thomas Bartz-Beielstein and Joern Mehnen for their role as EC in Practice Chairs.

I could not have planned GECCO-2013 without the generous commitment of all the chairs mentioned above. I would also like to thank Marc Schoenauer and Darrell Whitley from the ACM SIGEVO Business Committee, as well as Franz Rothlauf and Wolfgang Banzhaf, for their encouragement and assistance navigating an enormous number of details, from budgets to planning and execution. Additionally, I would like to thank Roxane Rose and Cara Candler from Executive Events for their expert handling of the many logistical and registration-related details that are needed to make the conference a success.

Finally, I would like to thank you, the authors, presenters, reviewers, and all the other attendees. It is your participation that makes GECCO what it is, one of the premier conferences on evolutionary computation and a source of inspiration for the future of our community. Thank you all for your involvement.

Enrique Alba, Ph.D.

University of Málaga, Spain

A Word from the Chair of SIGEVO

Welcome to the Proceedings of GECCO-2013, the fifteenth GECCO, and a "recombination" of the 22nd International Conference on Genetic Algorithms (ICGA) and the 18th Genetic Programming Conference (GP). This year, Enrique Alba has acted as General Chair of GECCO-2013 with great enthusiasm. Christian Blum, the Editor-in-Chief of GECCO-2013 has done a terrific job at "keeping the tracks on track", the reviewing process going and leading the effort to select papers for publication. Finally, Leonardo Vanneschi has served as Proceedings Chair, an important job tending to the details of this year's proceedings. The results before you speak for themselves.

GECCO is the premiere venue for presenting papers in the area of Genetic and Evolutionary Computation world-wide. The quality of papers submitted to GECCO is very high, and GECCO has a rigorous paper selection process. This means that the best and most important work in Evolutionary Computation and on related topics is presented at GECCO.

If you were not able to attend GECCO-2013 in person, the Proceedings are in the ACM Digital Library; they are globally accessible and readily found, which benefits both readers and authors.

ACM SIGEVO

Members of ACM SIGEVO, sponsor of GECCO, continue to draw major benefits from joining ACM. First is a discount at SIGEVO sponsored conferences, at GECCO as much as $100 per registrant. Members have access to the ACM Digital Library, a large and continuously growing resource for research in computing. Another key benefit is the outstanding newsletter *SIGEVOlutions* produced by Pier Luca Lanzi and his excellent editorial board. If you are accessing these proceedings and are not a member of SIGEVO, please consider joining (for the low price of $25/year for non-students, and $10/year for student members). This will help us a lot in promoting our community.

Involvement in ACM SIGEVO

SIGEVO became a *Special Interest Group (SIG)* of the ACM in 2005. ACM considers its SIGs as the lifeblood of the organization. We are governed by bylaws available on the SIGEVO web pages. There, you also find a list of members of the 18-member Executive Committee.

Since 2011, I serve as chair of SIGEVO, together with a team of officers: Una-May O'Reilly (Vice-Chair), Marc Schoenauer (Secretary), and Franz Rothlauf (Treasurer). The Executive, its Officers and I are dedicated to continuously improve our organization. If you have any suggestions how to make GECCO or SIGEVO better, please let us know.

Wolfgang Banzhaf

Memorial University of Newfoundland, CA

SIGEVO Chair

Table of Contents

Track: Artificial Life/Robotics/Evolvable Hardware

Track: Biological and Biomedical Applications

Track: Digital Entertainment Technologies and Arts

Track: Estimation of Distribution Algorithms

Track: Evolution Strategies and Evolutionary Programming

Track: Evolutionary Combinatorial Optimization and Metaheuristics

Track: Evolutionary Multiobjective Optimization

Track: Generative and Developmental Systems

Track: Genetic Algorithms

Volumn 2

Track: Genetic Programming

Track: Genetics Based Machine Learning

Track: Integrative Genetic and Evolutionary Computation

Track: Parallel Evolutionary Systems

Track: Real World Applications

Track: Search-Based Software Engineering

Track: Self-* Search

Track: Theory

GECCO 2013 Proceedings Editors

Christian Blum *(IKERBASQUE and University of the Basque Country UPV/EHU, Spain)*

Enrique Alba *(University of Malaga, Spain)*

Anne Auger *(INRIA Saclay-Ile-de-France, France)*

Jaume Bacardit *(University of Nottingham, UK)*

Josh Bongard *(University of Vermont, USA)*

Juergen Branke *(University of Warwick, UK)*

Nicolas Bredeche *(Université Pierre et Marie Curie, France)*

Dimo Brockhoff *(INRIA Lille - Nord Europe, France)*

Francisco Chicano *(University of Malaga, Spain)*

Alan Dorin *(Monash University, Australia)*

René Doursat *(Drexel University, USA)*

Aniko Ekart *(Aston University, UK)*

Tobias Friedrich *(Friedrich-Schiller-Universität Jena, Germany)*

Mario Giacobini *(University of Torino, Italy)*

Mark Harman *(University College London, UK)*

Hitoshi Iba *(University of Tokyo, Japan)*

Christian Igel *(University of Copenhagen, Denmark)*

Thomas Jansen *(Aberystwyth University, UK)*

Tim Kovacs *(University of Bristol, UK)*

Taras Kowaliw *(ISC-PIF, CNRS, France)*

Manuel López-Ibáñez *(Université Libre de Bruxelles (ULB), Belgium)*

José A. Lozano *(University of the Basque Country UPV/EHU, Spain)*

Gabriel Luque *(University of Malaga, Spain)*

John McCall *(Robert Gordon University, UK)*

Alberto Moraglio *(University of Birmingham, UK)*

Alison Motsinger-Reif *(NC State University, USA)*

Frank Neumann *(University of Adelaide, Australia)*

Gabriela Ochoa *(University of Stirling, UK)*

Gustavo Olague *(CICESE, Mexico)*

Yew-Soon Ong *(Nanyang Technological University, Singapore)*

Michael E. Palmer *(Stanford University, USA)*

Gisele Lobo Pappa *(Federal University of Minas Gerais, Brazil)*

Konstantinos E. Parsopoulos *(University of Ioannina, Greece)*

Thomas Schmickl *(University of Graz, Austria)*

Stephen L. Smith *(University of York, UK)*

Christine Solnon *(LIRIS, CNRS / INSA de Lyon, France)*

Thomas Stützle *(Université Libre de Bruxelles (ULB), Belgium)*

El-Ghazali Talbi *(University of Lille, France)*

Daniel Tauritz *(Missouri University of Science and Technology, USA)*

Leonardo Vanneschi *(Universidade Nova de Lisboa, Portugal)*

GECCO 2013 Conference Organizers

General Chair: Enrique Alba *(University of Malaga, Spain)*

Editor-in-Chief: Christian Blum *(IKERBASQUE and University of the Basque Country UPV/EHU, Spain)*

Business Committee: Marc Schoenauer *(INRIA Saclay, France)*
Darrell Whitley *(Colorado State University, USA)*

Publicity Chair: Xavier Llorà *(Google Inc., USA)*

Proceedings Chair: Leonardo Vanneschi *(Universidade Nova de Lisboa, Portugal)*

Local Chairs: Peter A.N. Bosman *(Centrum Wiskunde & Informatica, The Netherlands)*
Evert Haasdijk *(Vrije Universiteit Amsterdam, The Netherlands)*

Tutorials Chair: Gabriela Ochoa *(University of Stirling, UK)*

Workshops Chair: Mike Preuss *(Münster University, Germany)*

Students Chair: Emilia Tantar *(University of Luxembourg, Luxembourg)*

Competitions Chair: Daniele Loiacono *(Politecnico di Milano, Italy)*

Evolutionary Computation in Practice Chairs: Jörn Mehnen *(Cranfield University, UK)*
Thomas Bartz-Beielstein *(Cologne University of Applied Sciences, Germany)*

GECCO 2013 Program Committee

Hussein Abbass *(UNSW@ADFA, Australia)*
Ashraf Abdelbar *(American University in Cairo, Egypt)*
Ajith Abraham *(Machine Intelligence Research Labs, USA)*
Tarek Abudawood *(King Abdulaziz City for Science & Technology, Saudi Arabia)*
Berry Adam *(CSIRO, Australia)*
Andrew Adamatzky *(University of the West of England, UK)*
Michael Affenzeller *(Upper Austrian University of Applied Sciences, Austria)*
Wasif Afzal *(Blekinge Institute of Technology, Sweden)*
Jesus S. Aguilar-Ruiz *(Pablo de Olavide University, Spain)*
Hernan Aguirre *(Shinshu University, Japan)*
Chang Wook Ahn *(Sungkyunkwan University, Republic of Korea)*
Barry Ahrens *(Nova Southeastern University, USA)*
Juan-Manuel Ahuactzin *(PROBAYES, Mexico)*
Youhei Akimoto *(INRIA Saclay, France)*
Ricardo Aler *(Universidad Carlos III de Madrid, Spain)*
Eva Alfaro-Cid *(Instituto Tecnologico de Informatica, Spain)*
Richard Allmendinger *(University College London, UK)*
Francisco Almeida *(La Laguna University, Spain)*
Lee Altenberg *(University of Hawai'i, USA)*
Ng Amos *(University of Skövde, Sweden)*
Gautham Anil *(University of Central Florida, USA)*
Giuliano Antoniol *(Ecole Polytechnique de Montreal, Canada)*
Ricardo Araujo *(Federal University of Pernambuco, Brazil)*
Andrea Arcuri *(Simula Research Laboratory, Italy)*
Alfredo Arias Montaño *(CINVESTAV-IPN, Mexico)*
Takaya Arita *(Nagoya University, Japan)*
Dirk V. Arnold *(Dalhousie University, Canada)*
Antonio D. Masegosa Arredondo *(University of Granada, Spain)*
Daniel Ashlock *(University of Guelph, Canada)*
Gideon Avigad *(Braude College of Engineering, Israel)*
Nizamettin Aydin *(Yildiz Technical University, Turkey)*
Raja Muhammad Atif Azad *(University of Limerick, Ireland)*
Vladan Babovic *(National University Singapore, Singapore)*
Jaume Bacardit *(University of Nottingham, UK)*
Mohamed Bader-el-den *(Portsmouth University, UK)*
Thomas Baeck *(Leiden University, The Netherlands)*
Rami Bahsoon *(The University of Birmingham, UK)*
Ruibin Bai *(University of Nottingham, UK)*
Carsten Baldauf *(Fritz-Haber-Institut der MPG, Germany)*
Pedro J. Ballester *(European Bioinformatics Institute, UK)*
Sunith Bandaru *(Indian Institute of Technology Kanpur, India)*
Sanghamitra Bandyopadhyay *(Indian Statistical Institute, India)*
Zorana Bankovic *(Technical University of Madrid, Spain)*
Wolfgang Banzhaf *(Memorial University of Newfoundland, Canada)*
Helio J.C. Barbosa *(LNCC, Brazil)*
Gregory J. Barlow *(Carnegie Mellon University, USA)*
Marcio Barros *(UNIRIO, Brazil)*
Thomas Bartz-Beielstein *(Cologne University of Applied Sciences, Germany)*
Marcio Basgalupp *(ICT-UNIFESP, Portugal)*
Jeffrey K. Bassett *(George Mason University, USA)*
Jacob Beal *(BBN Technologies, United States)*
Mohammad Behdad *(The University of Western Australia, Australia)*
Theodore C. Belding *(Belding Consulting, Inc., USA)*
Gerardo Beni *(University of California at Riverside, USA)*
Peter J. Bentley *(University College London, UK)*
Matthias Bernt *(University Leipzig, Germany)*
Rod Berry *(University of Technology Sydney, Australia)*
Tom Bersano *(University of Michigan, USA)*
Eva Besada-Portas *(Universidad Compluntense de Madrid, Spain)*
Hans-Georg Beyer *(Vorarlberg Univ. of Applied Sciences, Austria)*
Leonardo Bezerra *(IRIDIA, CoDE, ULB, Belgium)*
Bir Bhanu *(University of California at Riverside, USA)*

Clare Bates Congdon *(University of Southern Maine, USA)*
Brian D. Connelly *(BEACON Center for the Study of Evolution in Action, USA)*
Ademir Constantino *(Universidade Estadual de Maringá, Brazil)*
Oscar Cordon *(European Centre for Soft Computing, Spain)*
David Corne *(Heriot-Watt University, UK)*
Steven M. Corns *(Missouri University of Science and Technology, USA)*
Ernesto Costa *(University of Coimbra, Portugal)*
Lino António Costa *(University of Minho, Portugal)*
Carlos Cotta *(University of Málaga, Spain)*
Bart G.W. Craenen *(University of Birmingham, UK)*
Wei Cui *(University College Dublin, Ireland)*
Ronan Cummins *(University of Glasgow, Ireland)*
Dara Curran *(Cisco Systems, Ireland)*
Sylvain Cussat-Blanc *(University of Toulouse, France)*
Keshav Dahal *(, UK)*
Palle Dahlstedt *(University of Gothenburg / Chalmers University of Technology, Sweden)*
David B. D'Ambrosio *(University of Central Florida, USA)*
Christian Darabos *(Dartmouth College, USA)*
Angan Das *(Intel, USA)*
Swagatam Das *(Jadavpur University, India)*
Rituparna Datta *(IIT Kanpur, India)*
Patrick De Causmaecker *(KU Leuven, Belgium)*
Kenneth De Jong *(George Mason University, USA)*
Luis Gerardo de la Fraga *(CINVESTAV, Mexico)*
Luis de la Ossa *(Universidad de Castilla-La Mancha, Spain)*
Anthony G. Deakin *(The University of Liverpool, UK)*
Kalyanmoy Deb *(Indian Institute of Technology Kanpur, India)*
Kusum Deep *(Indian Institute of Technology, India)*
Antonio Della Cioppa *(Natural Computation Lab - DIIIE, University of Salerno, Italy)*
Eelco den Heijer *(VU University Amsterdam, The Netherlands)*
Clarisse Dhaenens *(LIFL / CNRS / INRIA, France)*
Medha Dhurandhar *(Centre for Dev. of Advanced computing, India)*
Gianni Di Caro *(IDSIA, Switzerland)*
Luca Di Gaspero *(University of Udine, Italia)*
Massimiliano Di Penta *(RCOST - University of Sannio, Italy)*
Ada Diaconescu *(Telecom ParisTech, France)*
Peter Dittrich *(Friedrich-Schiller-Universität Jena, Germany)*
Federico Divina *(Universidad Pablo de Olavide, Spain)*
Benjamin Doerr *(MPI Saarbruecken, Germany)*
Carola Doerr *(Max-Planck-Institut fuer Informatik, Germany)*
Stéphane Doncieux *(ISIR/UPMC, France)*
Bernabe Dorronsoro *(University of Lille, France)*
Rene Doursat *(Institut des Systemes Complexes, CNRS, France)*
León Dozal *(CICESE, México)*
Scott Draves *(Electric Sheep, USA)*
Jan Drugowitsch *(École normale supérieure, France)*
Haibin Duan *(Beihang University, China)*
Jérémie Dubois-Lacoste *(Université Libre de Bruxelles, Belgium)*
Frederick Ducatelle *(IDSIA, Switzerland)*
Marc Ebner *(Ernst-Moritz-Universität Greifswald, Germany)*
Arne Eigenfeldt *(Simon Fraser University, Canada)*
Aniko Ekart *(Aston University, United Kingdom)*
Mohammed El-Abd *(American University of Kuwait, Kuwait)*
Alice Eldridge *(University of the Arts London, UK)*
Michael T. M. Emmerich *(LIACS, The Netherlands)*
Andries P. Engelbrecht *(University of Pretoria, South Africa)*
Michael Epitropakis *(University of Stirling, UK)*
Anton V. Eremeev *(Omsk Branch of Sobolev Institute of Mathematics, Russia)*
Daryl Essam *(UNSW@ADFA, Australia)*
Lutton Evelyne *(INRIA Saclay, France)*
Richard Everson *(University of Exeter, UK)*
Patrick Fan *(Virginia Tech, USA)*
Muddassar Farooq *(National University of Computer and Emerging Sciences, Pakistan)*
Robert Feldt *(Chalmers University of Technology, Sweden)*
Serge Fenet *(Universite Lyon 1, France)*
Jose David Fernandez *(Universidad de Malaga, Spain)*
Francisco Fernández de Vega *(Universidad de Extremadura, Spain)*
Paola Festa *(Universitá degli Studi di Napoli, Italy)*
Jonathan Edward Fieldsend *(University of Exeter, UK)*

Jose Figueira *(Technical University of Lisbon, Portugal)*
Bogdan Filipic *(Jozef Stefan Institute, Slovenia)*
Steffen Finck *(FH Vorarlberg University of Applied Sciences, Austria)*
Peter Fleming *(University of Sheffield, UK)*
Gianluigi Folino *(ICAR-CNR, Italy)*
Carlos M. Fonseca *(University of Coimbra, Portugal)*
James A. Foster *(University of Idaho, USA)*
Maria Auxiliadora Franco Gaviria *(University of Nottingham, UK)*
Gordon Fraser *(University of Sheffield, UK)*
Regina Frei *(Cranfield University, UK)*
Bernd Freisleben *(Universität Marburg, Germany)*
Alex A. Freitas *(University of Kent, UK)*
Charlie Frowd *(University of Central Lancashire, UK)*
Alex Fukunaga *(University of Tokyo, Japan)*
Matteo Gagliolo *(VUB, Belgium)*
Christian Gagné *(Université Laval, Canada)*
Philip Galanter *(Texas A&M University, USA)*
Marcus R. Gallagher *(University of Queensland, Australia)*
Edgar Galvan *(Trinity College Dublin, Ireland)*
Leo Galway *(University of Ulster, United Kingdom)*
Luca Maria Gambardella *(IDSIA, Switzerland)*
Jose A. Gamez *(Universidad de Castilla-La Mancha, Spain)*
Xavier Gandibleux *(Université de Nantes, France)*
Yang Gao *(Nanjing University, China)*
Carlos García-Martínez *(Univ. of Córdoba, Spain)*
Alvaro Garcia-Piquer *(Institute of Space Sciences (IEEC-CSIC), Spain)*
Pablo García-Sánchez *(University of Granada, Spain)*
Ivan I. Garibay *(University of Central Florida, USA)*
Josep Maria Garrell-Guiu *(La Salle - Ramon Llull University, Spain)*
Deon Garrett *(Icelandic Institute for Intelligent Machines, Iceland)*
Antonio Gaspar-Cunha *(University of Minho, Portugal)*
Zong Woo Geem *(Gachon University, South Korea)*
Shahin Gelareh *(University of Artois/ LGI2A, France)*
Michel Gendreau *(École Polytechnique de Montréal, Canada)*
Vassilios Georgiou *(Technological Educational Institute of Patras, Greece)*
George Georgoulas *(TEI of Epirus, Greece)*
Osvaldo Gervasi *(University of Perugia, Italy)*
Marian Gheorghe *(University of Sheffield, UK, UK)*
Jean-Louis Giavitto *(CNRS - IRCAM, UPMC, Inria, France)*
Acampora Giovanni *(University of Salerno, Italy)*
Raul Giraldez Rojo *(Pablo de Olavide University of Seville, Spain)*
Tobias Glasmachers *(IDSIA, Switzerland)*
Chi Keong Goh *(Rolls-Royce, Singapore)*
Marco César Goldbarg *(Universidade Federal do Rio Grande do Norte, Brazil)*
Brian W. Goldman *(Michigan State University, USA)*
Juan A. Gomez-Pulido *(University of Extremadura, Spain)*
Erik Goodman *(Michigan State University, USA)*
Mario Graff *(Universidad Michoacana de San Nicolas de Hidalgo, Mexico)*
Uli Grasemann *(UT Austin, USA)*
Marde Greeff *(Council for Scientific and Industrial Research, South Africa)*
Gary Greenfield *(University of Richmond, USA)*
David Greiner *(Universidad de Las Palmas de Gran Canaria, Spain)*
Roderich Gross *(The University of Sheffield, UK)*
Paul Grouchy *(University of Toronto Institute for Aerospace Studies, Canada)*
Frederic Guinand *(University of Le Havre, France)*
Steven Gustafson *(GE Global Research, USA)*
Walter J. Gutjahr *(University of Vienna, Austria)*
Evert Haasdijk *(VU University Amsterdam, The Netherlands)*
Johan Hagelbäck *(Blekinge Tekniska Högskola, Sweden)*
Jennifer S. Hallinan *(Newcastle University, UK)*
Heiko Hamann *(University of Paderborn, Germany)*
Lutz Hamel *(University of Rhode Island, USA)*
Ali Hamzeh *(Shiraz University, Iran)*
Hisashi Handa *(Kindai University, Japan)*
Nikolaus Hansen *(INRIA, research centre Saclay, France)*
Jin-Kao Hao *(University of Angers, France)*
Simon Harding *(IDSIA, Switzerland)*
Emma Hart *(Napier University, UK)*
William Hart *(Sandia National Laboratories, USA)*
Geir Hasle *(SINTEF, Norway)*
Erin Hastings *(University of Central Florida, USA)*
Mark W. Hauschild *(University of Missouri-St. Louis, USA)*

Jun He *(University of Wales, Aberystwyth, UK)*
Verena Heidrich-Meisner *(IEAP, CAU Kiel, Germany)*
Tim Hendtlass *(Swinburne University of Technology, Australia)*
James Hereford *(Murray State University, USA)*
Arturo Hernández-Aguirre *(Centre for Research in Mathematics, Mexico)*
Alfredo G. Hernández-Díaz *(Pablo de Olavide University, Spain)*
Daniel Eduardo Hernandez *(CICESE, Mexico)*
Hugo Hernandez *(Technical University of Catalonia, Spain)*
Benjamín Hernández *(Uiversidad Nacional Autónoma de México, México)*
Francisco Herrera *(University of Granada, Spain)*
Malcolm Heywood *(Dalhousie University, Canada)*
J. Ignacio Hidalgo *(Complutense University of Madrid, Spain)*
Robert Mark Hierons *(Brunel University, UK)*
Ronald Hochreiter *(WU Vienna University of Economics and Business, Austria)*
Tim Hohm *(University of Lausanne, Switzerland)*
Ekaterina Holdener *(Exegy, Inc., USA)*
Kenneth Holladay *(Southwest Research Institute, USA)*
John Holmes *(University of Pennsylvania, USA)*
Amy K. Hoover *(University of Central Florida, USA)*
Jeffrey Horn *(Northern Michigan University, USA)*
Gregory S. Hornby *(UC Santa Cruz, USA)*
Gerard Howard *(University of the West of England, UK)*
Bin Hu *(Technische Universität Wien, Austria)*
Jianjun Hu *(University of South Carolina, USA)*
Ting Hu *(Dartmouth College, USA)*
Joost Huizinga *(University of Wyoming, USA)*
Phil Husbands *(Sussex University, UK)*
Frank Hutter *(UBC, Canada)*
Matthew Hyde *(University of East Anglia, UK)*
David Andrei Iclanzan *(Sapientia Hungaryan University of Transylvania, Romania)*
Fumiya Iida *(ETH Zurich, Switzerland)*
Takashi Ikegami *(University of Tokyo, Japan)*
Iñaki Inza *(University of the Basque Country, Spain)*
Manuel Iori *(University of Modena and Reggio Emilia, Italy)*
Pedro Isasi *(Universidad Carlos III de Madrid, Spain)*
Hisao Ishibuchi *(Osaka Prefecture University, Japan)*
Juhos Istvan *(University of Szeged, Hungary)*
David Jackson *(University of Liverpool, UK)*
Wilfried Jakob *(Karlsruhe Institute of Technology, Germany)*
Cezary Z. Janikow *(UMSL, USA)*
Thomas Jansen *(Aberystwyth University, UK)*
Yaochu Jin *(University of Surrey, UK)*
Daniel Johannsen *(Tel Aviv University, Israel)*
Colin Graeme Johnson *(University of Kent, UK)*
András Joó *(Sapientia University, Romania, Romania)*
Laetitia Jourdan *(INRIA Lille Nord Europe, France)*
Reyes Juarez *(UABC, Mexico)*
Bryant Arthur Julstrom *(St. Cloud State University, USA)*
George Kampis *(DFKI, Germany)*
Istvan Karsai *(East Tennessee State University, USA)*
Sindhya Karthik *(EMO, Finland)*
Ahmed Kattan *(Umm Al-Qura University, Saudi Arabia)*
Graham Kendall *(University of Nottingham, UK)*
Marouane Kessentini *(Missouri University of Science and Technology, USA)*
Yong-Hyuk Kim *(Kwangwoon University, Korea)*
Evan Kirshenbaum *(HP Labs, USA)*
Ronald Klazar *(University of Pretoria, South Africa)*
Joshua D. Knowles *(University of Manchester, UK)*
Mario Koeppen *(Kyushu Institute of Technology, Japan)*
Maciej Komosinski *(Poznan University of Technology, Poland)*
Lysimachos Kondi *(University of Ioannina, Greece)*
Anna Kononova *(Heriot-Watt University, UK)*
Ioannis Konstantaras *(University of Macedonia, Greece)*
Oliver Korb *(Cambridge Crystallographic Data Centre, UK)*
Ilias Kotsireas *(Wilfried Laurier University, Canada)*
Timo Kötzing *(MPI-INF, Germany)*
Taras Kowaliw *(ISC-PIF, CNRS, France)*
Oliver Kramer, *(University of Oldenburg, Germany)*
Jozef Kratica *(Mathematical Institute, Serbian Academy of Sciences and Arts, Serbia)*
Krzysztof Krawiec *(Poznan University of Technology, Poland)*
Stefanie Kritzinger *(Johannes Kepler University Linz, Austria)*
Jiri Kubalik *(CTU Prague, Czech Republic)*

Saku Kukkonen *(Lappeenranta University of Technology, Finland)*
Joerg Laessig *(Hochschule Zittau/Görlitz, Germany)*
Isaac Lagaris *(University of Ioannina, Greece)*
Gary Byron Lamont *(AF Institute of Technology, USA)*
Jouni Lampinen *(University of Vaasa, Finland)*
Dario Landa-Silva *(University of Nottingham, UK)*
Payam Langdon *(University of Graz, Austria)*
William B. Langdon *(University College London, UK)*
Pier Luca Lanzi *(Politecnico di Milano, Italy)*
Adriana Lara *(CINVESTAV-IPN, Mexico)*
Pedro Larranaga *(Technical University of Madrid, Spain)*
Antonio LaTorre *(Universidad Politécnica de Madrid, Spain)*
Hoong-Chuin Lau *(Singapore Management University, Singapore)*
Pierrick Legrand *(Université Bordeaux, France)*
Guillermo Leguizamon *(Universidad Nacional de San Luis, Argentina)*
Joel Lehman *(The University of Texas at Austin, USA)*
Per Kristian Lehre *(University of Nottingham, UK)*
Kenji Leibnitz *(Osaka University, Japan, Japan)*
Coromoto Leon *(Universidad de La Laguna, Spain)*
Kwong Sak Leung *(The Chinese University of Hong Kong, China)*
Matthew Lewis *(Ohio State University, USA)*
Peter R. Lewis *(University of Birmingham, UK)*
Hui Li *(Xi'an Jiaotong University, China)*
Xiaodong Li *(RMIT University, Australia)*
Zheng Li *(Beijing University of Chemical Technology, China)*
Jing Liang *(Zhengzhou University, China)*
Arnaud Liefooghe *(Université Lille 1, France)*
Steffen Limmer *(University Erlangen, Germany)*
Alain Lioret *(Universite Paris 8, France)*
Piotr Lipinski *(University of Wroclaw, Poland)*
Bo Liu *(Chinese Academy of Sciences, China)*
Daniel Lobo *(Tufts University, USA)*
Fernando G. Lobo *(University of Algarve, Portugal)*
Gisele Lobo Pappa *(Federal University of Minas Gerais - UFMG, Brazil)*
Daniele Loiacono *(Politecnico di Milano, Italy)*
Michael Lones *(University of York, UK)*
Heitor S. Lopes *(UTFPR, Brazil)*
Eunice Lopez-Camacho *(ITESM, Mexico)*
Manuel López-Ibáñez *(IRIDIA, Université Libre de Bruxelles, Belgium)*
Antonio López-Jaimes *(Centro de Investigación y de Estudios Avanzados (CINVESTAV), Mexico)*
ILYA Loshchilov *(INRIA, University Paris-Sud, France)*
Jose A. Lozano *(University of the Basque Country, Spain)*
Manuel Lozano *(University of Granada, Spain)*
Guanzhou Lu *(University of Birmingham, UK)*
Simon Lucas *(University of Essex, UK)*
Hervé Luga *(Université Toulouse 1, France)*
Martin Lukasiewycz *(University of Erlangen Nuremberg, Germany)*
Sean Luke *(George Mason University, USA)*
Francisco Luna *(University of Málaga, Spain)*
Monte Lunacek *(National Renewable Energy Lab, USA)*
Rodica Ioana Lung *(Babes-Bolyai University, Romania)*
Gabriel Luque *(University of Malaga, Spain)*
Thibaut Lust *(UPMC, France)*
Rob MacCurdy *(Cornell University, USA)*
Penousal Machado *(University of Coimbra, Portugal)*
Nuria Macia *(ETSEEI La Salle, Universitat Ramon Llull, Spain)*
Demetrio Macias *(Université de technologie de Troyes, France)*
Ana Maria Madureira *(Polytechnic Institute of Porto, Portugal)*
Domenico Maisto *(National Research Council of Italy (ICAR CNR), Italy)*
Luigi Malago *(Università degli Studi di Milano, Italy)*
Abhinav Malhotra *(NSIT, India)*
Andrea Mambrini *(University of Birmingham, UK)*
Spiros Mancoridis *(Drexel University, USA)*
Bernard Kamiel Manderick *(Vrije Universiteit Brussel, Belgium)*
Jacek Mandziuk *(Warsaw University of Technology, Poland)*
Gong Maoguo *(Xidian University, China)*
Elena Marchiori *(Radboud University, The Netherlands)*
Yannis Marinakis *(Technical University of Crete, Greece)*
Dietmar Maringer *(University of Basel, Switzerland)*

Robert E. Marmelstein *(East Stroudsburg University, USA)*
Marie-Eleonore Marmion *(Universite de Lille 1 - INRIA, France)*
Luis Marti *(Universidad Carlos III de Madrid, Spain)*
Andrew Martin *(Dept Biochem & Mol Biol, UCL, England)*
Hector P. Martinez *(IT-Universitetet i København, Denmark)*
Ivette C. Martinez *(Universidad Simon Bolivar, Venezuela)*
Franco Mascia *(Université Libre de Bruxelles, Belgium)*
Igor V. Maslov *(EvoCo Inc., Japan)*
Florence Massen *(Université Catholique de Louvain, Belgium)*
Shouichi Matsui *(SERL, CRIEPI, Japan)*
Nicolini Matteo *(University of Udine, Italy)*
Jorge Maturana *(Universidad Austral de Chile, Chile)*
Helmut A. Mayer *(University of Salzburg, Austria)*
John McCall *(IDEAS Research Institute, Scotland)*
Kent McClymont *(University of Exeter, UK)*
Sean McGarraghy *(University College Dublin, Ireland)*
Bob McKay *(Seoul National University, Korea)*
Phil McMinn *(University of Sheffield, UK)*
Nicholas Freitag McPhee *(University of Minnesota, Morris, USA)*
David Meignan *(University of Osnabrück, Germany)*
Nouredine Melab *(Université Lille 1, France)*
Alexander Melkozerov *(Tomsk State University of Control Systems and Radioelectronics, Russia)*
Drew Mellor *(The University of Newcastle, Australia)*
Rui Mendes *(CCTC/UM, Portugal)*
Alexander Mendiburu *(University of the Basque Country UPV/EHU, Spain)*
Juan-Julián Merelo-Guervós *(University of Granada, Spain)*
Daniel Merkle *(University of Southern Denmark, Denmark)*
Olaf Mersmann *(TU Dortmund, Germany)*
Bernd, Meyer, *(Monash University, Australia)*
Silja Meyer-Nieberg *(Universitaet der Bundeswehr Muenchen, Germany)*
Efren Mezura-Montes *(University of Veracruz, Mexico)*
Olivier Michel *(LACL - U-PEC, France)*
Martin Middendorf *(University of Leipzig, Germany)*
Risto Miikkulainen *(The University of Texas at Austin, USA)*
Julian F. Miller *(University of York, UK)*
Ali Minai *(University of Cincinnati, USA)*
Leandro Minku *(The University of Birmingham, UK)*
Luis Miramontes Hercog *(Self-Organizing Solutions, Mexico)*
Mustafa MISIR *(INRIA, France)*
Boris Mitavskiy *(Aberystwyth University, United Kingdom)*
George Mitchell *(CCKF Ltd, Ireland)*
Eric Mjolsness *(UC Irvine, USA)*
Hans Jonas Fossum Moen *(Norwegian Defence Research Estblishment, Norway)*
Chilukuri K. mohan *(Syracuse University, USA)*
Julian Molina *(University of Malaga, Spain)*
Nicolas Monmarche *(University of Tours, France)*
David Montana *(BBN Technologies, USA)*
Jean-Marc Montanier *(Université Paris-Sud, France)*
Marco A. Montes de Oca *(University of Delaware, USA)*
Jason Moore *(Dartmouth College, USA)*
Antonio Mora *(University of Granada, Spain)*
Eduardo Morales *(INAOE, Mexico)*
Christoph Möslinger *(Karl-Franzens-University Graz, Austria)*
Sanaz Mostaghim *(Karlsruhe Institute of Technology, Germany)*
Jean-Baptiste Mouret *(ISIR - UPMC/CNRS, France)*
Santiago Muelas *(Universidad Politécnica de Madrid, Spain)*
Christian Lorenz Müller *(ETH Zurich, Switzerland)*
Christine Lesley Mumford *(Cardiff University, UK)*
Nysret Musliu *(Vienna University of Technology, Austria)*
Yuichi Nagata *(Tokyo Institute of Technology, Japan)*
Amir Nakib *(Université Paris-Est Créteil, France)*
Boris Naujoks *(Cologne University of Applied Sciences, Germany)*
Antonio Nebro *(University of Málaga, Spain)*
Chrystopher L. Nehaniv *(University of Hertfordshire, UK)*
Ferrante Neri *(University of Jyväskylä, Finland)*
Huy Nguyen *(Misfit Wearables, USA)*
Trung Thanh Nguyen *(Liverpool John Moores University, UK)*
Hoai Nguyen Xuan *(Hanoi University, Vietnam)*

Julio Cesar Nievola *(PUCPR, Brazil)*
Yusuke Nojima *(Osaka Prefecture University, Japan)*
Nasimul Noman *(University of Tokyo, Japan)*
Ann Nowe *(Vrije Universiteit Brussel, Belgium)*
Mel Ó Cinnéide *(National University of Ireland, Dublin, Ireland)*
Gabriela Ochoa *(University of Stirling, UK)*
Choong Kun Oh *(U.S. Naval Research Laboratory, USA)*
Toby O'Hara *(University of the West of England, England)*
Markus Olhofer *(Honda Research Institute Europe GmbH, Germany)*
Pedro N. F. P. Oliveira *(University of Minho, Portugal)*
Pietro S. Oliveto *(University of Birmingham, UK)*
Mohammed Omran *(Gulf University for Science & Technology, Kuwait)*
Michael O'Neill *(University College Dublin, Ireland)*
Yew-Soon Ong *(Nanyang Technological University, South Korea)*
Una-May O'Reilly *(Massachusetts Institute of Technology, USA)*
Colm O'Riordan *(NUI, Galway, Ireland)*
Albert Orriols-Puig *(Universitat Ramon Llull, Spain)*
Julio Ortega *(University of Granada, Spain)*
Ender Özcan *(University of Nottingham, UK)*
Nikhil Padhye *(MIT, USA)*
Leon Palafox *(The University of Tokyo, Japan)*
Michael E. Palmer *(Stanford University, USA)*
Luis Paquete *(University of Coimbra, Portugal)*
Victor Parque *(Toyota Technological Institute, Japan)*
Konstantinos Parsopoulos *(University of Ioannina, Greece)*
Philippe Pasquier *(SIAT - Simon Fraser University, Canada)*
Castillo Pedro *(UGR, Spain)*
Martin Pelikan *(Google, USA)*
Paola Pellegrini *(IRIDIA-CoDE ULB, Belgium)*
David Pelta *(University of Granada, Spain)*
Jorge Peña *(University of Basel, Switzerland)*
Jose-Maria Peña *(Universidad Politécnica de Madrid, Spain)*
Juan Peralta *(Universidad Autónoma de Barcelona, Spain)*
Francisco Baptista Pereira *(Instituto Superior de Engenharia de Coimbra, Portugal)*
Leslie Perez Caceres *(Iridia - ULB, Belgium)*
Steve Phelps *(University of Essex, UK)*
Andrew Philippides *(University of Sussex, UK)*
Vassilis Plagianakos *(University of Central Greece, Greece)*
Petr Po ík *(Czech Technical University in Prague, Czech Republic)*
Daniel Polani *(University of Hertfordshire, UK)*
Silvia Poles *(EnginSoft, Italy)*
Riccardo Poli *(University of Essex, UK)*
Carlo Poloni *(Esteco, Italy)*
Petrica Pop *(North University of Baia Mare, Romania)*
Elena Popovici *(Icosystem Corp., USA)*
Daniel Porumbel *(Univ. Lille-Nord de France, UArtois, France)*
Walter Potter *(University of Georgia, USA)*
Simon Poulding *(University of York, UK)*
Steve Prestwich *(University College Cork, Ireland)*
Mike Preuss *(TU Dortmund, Germany)*
Kenneth Price *(Packard Bell, USA)*
Adam Prugel-Bennett *(University of Southampton, UK)*
Jakob Puchinger *(AIT - Austrian Institute of Technology, Austria)*
Cesar Puente *(Universidad Autónoma de San Luis Potosi, Mexico)*
Jose Miguel Puerta *(UCLM, Spain)*
William F. Punch *(Michigan State University, USA)*
Robin Purshouse *(University of Sheffield, UK)*
Kai Qin *(INRIA Grenoble Rhone-Alpes, France)*
Rong Qu *(University of Nottingham, UK)*
Günther R. Raidl *(Vienna University of Technology, Austria)*
Ranji S. Ranjithan *(North Carolina State Univ, USA)*
Khaled Rasheed *(University of Georgia, USA)*
Tapabrata Ray *(School of Aerospace, Civil and Mechanical Engineering, Australia)*
Tom Ray *(University of Oklahoma, USA)*
Patrick Michael Reed *(Pennsylvania State University, USA)*
Phill Kyu Rhee *(Inha University, Korea)*
J. Neal Richter *(Rubicon Project, USA)*
John Rieffel *(Union College, USA)*
Maria Cristina Riff *(UTFSM, Chile)*
Sebastian Risi *(Cornell University, USA)*
Marylyn Ritchie *(Penn State University, USA)*
Wille Robert *(University of Bremen, Germany)*
Denis Robilliard *(Univ Lille-Nord de France, France)*
Daniel Rodríguez *(The University of Alcala, Spain)*

Philipp Rohlfshagen *(SolveIT Software, Spain)*
Andrea Roli *(Alma Mater Studiorum Universita' di Bologna, Italy)*
Marc Roper *(University of Strathclyde, UK)*
Brian J. Ross *(Brock University, Canada)*
Peter M. Ross *(Napier University, UK)*
Franz Rothlauf *(University of Mainz, Germany)*
Jonathan Rowe *(University of Birmingham, UK)*
Rajkumar Roy *(Cranfield University, UK)*
Sarker Ruhul *(University of New South Wales, Australia)*
Ruben Ruiz *(Polytechnic University of Valencia, Spain)*
Thomas Runarsson *(University of Iceland, Iceland)*
Conor Ryan *(University of Limerick, Ireland)*
Ramon Sagarna *(University of the Basque Country, Spain)*
Erol Sahin *(Middle East Technical University, Turkey)*
Sancho Salcedo-Sanz *(Universidad de Alcala, Spain)*
Michael Sampels *(Université Libre de Bruxelles, Belgium)*
Luciano Sanchez *(Universidad de Oviedo, Spain)*
Rian Sanderson *(Carnegie Mellon West, USA)*
Roberto Santana *(University of the Basque Country (UPV/EHU), Spain)*
Iván Santibáñez Koref *(Technical Univ. Berlin, Germany)*
Federica Sarro *(University College London, UK)*
Hiroyuki Sato *(The University of Electro-Communications, Japan)*
Yuji Sato *(Hosei University, Japan)*
Fredéric Saubion *(University of Angers, France)*
Hideyuki Sawada *(Kagawa University, Japan)*
Hiroki Sayama *(SUNY Binghamton, USA)*
Andrea Schaerf *(University of Udine, Italy)*
Tom Schaul *(New York University, USA)*
Massimiliano Schillaci *(MGTech S.r.l., Italy)*
Lothar M. Schmitt *(The University of Aizu, Japan)*
Marc Schoenauer *(INRIA Saclay, France)*
Oliver Schuetze *(CINVESTAV-IPN, Mexico)*
Carlos Segura *(Universidad de La Laguna, Spain)*
Yann Semet *(Yakaz, France)*
Sandip Sen *(University of Tulsa, USA)*
Bernhard Sendhoff *(Honda Research Institute Europe, Germany)*
Kevin Seppi *(Brigham Young University, USA)*
Martin Serpell *(University of the West of England, UK)*
Travis Service *(Vanderbilt University, USA)*
Marc Sevaux *(Université de Bretagne-Sud - Lab-STICC, France)*
Kamran Shafi *(UNSW@ADFA, Australia)*
Fatima Shaheen *(Loughborough University, UK)*
Siddhartha Shakya *(Business Modelling & Operational Transformation Practice, BT, UK)*
Jonathan Lee Shapiro *(University of Manchester, UK)*
Yang Shengxiang *(De Montfort Unviersity, UK)*
Patrick Siarry *(University of Paris-Est Créteil, France)*
Outi Sievi-Korte *(Tampere University of Technology, Finland)*
Sara Silva *(INESC-ID Lisboa, Portugal)*
Kevin Sim *(Edinburgh Napier University, UK)*
Anabela Simões *(DEIS/ISEC - Coimbra Polytechnic, Portugal)*
Christopher L. Simons *(University of the West of England, UK)*
Ankur Sinha *(Aalto University School of Business, Finland)*
Moshe Sipper *(Ben-Gurion University, Israel)*
Konstantina Skouri *(University of Ioannina, Greece)*
Alexei N. Skurikhin *(Los Alamos National Laboratory, USA)*
Alice Smith *(Auburn University, USA)*
Jim Smith *(University of the West of England, UK)*
Tamara Smyth *(University of Califronia San Diego, USA)*
Andy Song *(RMIT University, Australia)*
Humberto Sossa *(Instituto Politécnico Nacional, Mexico)*
Jerffeson Souza *(State University of Ceara, Brazil)*
Lee Spector *(Hampshire College, USA)*
Giandomenico Spezzano *(ICAR-CNR, Italy)*
Antoine Spicher *(Universite Paris-Est Creteil, France)*
Giovanni Squillero *(Politecnico di Torino, Italy)*
Dipti Srinivasan *(National University of Singapore, Singapore)*
Patrick Oliver Stalph *(University of Tübingen, Germany)*
Kenneth Stanley *(University of Central Florida, USA)*
Chris Stephens *(Instituto de Ciencias Nucleares, UNAM, Mexico)*
Susan Stepney *(University of York, UK)*
Wolfgang Stolzmann *(Daimler AG, Germany)*
Forrest Stonedahl *(Northwestern University, USA)*
Daniel W. Stouch *(Charles River Analytics, USA)*
Umberto Straccia *(ISTI-CNR, Italy)*

Juergen Stradner *(University of Graz, Austria)*
Thomas Stützle *(Université Libre de Bruxelles, Belgium)*
Chrysostomos Stylios *(University of Patras, Greece)*
Dirk Sudholt *(University of Sheffield, UK)*
YI Sun *(IDSIA, Switzerland)*
Andrew Michael Sutton *(University of Adelaide, Australia)*
Reiji Suzuki *(Nagoya University, Japan)*
Jerry Swan *(University of Stirling, UK)*
Keiki Takadama *(The University of Electro-Communications, Japan)*
El-Ghazali Talbi *(INRIA Futurs, France)*
Kiyoshi Tanaka *(Shinshu University, Japan)*
Ivan Tanev *(Faculty of Engineering, Doshisha University, Japan)*
Ke Tang *(University of Science and Technology of China, China)*
Ernesto Tarantino *(ICAR - CNR, Italy)*
Daniel R. Tauritz *(Missouri University of Science and Technology, USA)*
Jorge Tavares *(Microsoft, Germany)*
Roberto Tavares *(UFSCAR, Brazil)*
Tim Taylor *(Goldsmiths, University of London, UK)*
Jürgen Teich *(University of Erlangen-Nuremberg, Germany)*
Hugo Terashima Marín *(ITESM - CSI, Mexico)*
German Terrazas Angulo *(University of Nottingham, UK)*
Andrea G. B. Tettamanzi *(Université de Nice Sophia Antipolis, France)*
Christof Teuscher *(Portland State University, USA)*
Fabien Teytaud *(University of Paris-Dauphine / HEC Paris, CNRS, France)*
Olivier Teytaud *(INRIA, France)*
Madeleine Theile *(TU Berlin, Germany)*
Ronald Thenius *(Karl-Franzens-University of Graz, Austria)*
Lothar Thiele *(ETH Zurich, Switzerland)*
Dirk Thierens *(Utrecht University, The Netherlands)*
Jonathan Timmis *(University of York, UK)*
Peter Tino *(University of Birmingham, UK)*
Ashutosh Tiwari *(Cranfield University, UK)*
Santosh Tiwari *(Vanderplaats Research & Development Inc., USA)*
Julian Togelius *(IT University of Copenhagen, Denmark)*
Marco Tomassini *(University of Lausanne, Switzerland)*
Alberto Paolo Tonda *(Politecnico di Torino, Italy)*
Alexander Topchy *(Nielsen Media Research, USA)*
Jim Torresen *(University of Oslo, Norway)*
Jose Torres-Jimenez *(CINVESTAV TAMAULIPAS, Mexico)*
Heike Trautmann *(TU Dortmund, Germany, Germany)*
Martin Trefzer *(The University of York, UK)*
Vito Trianni *(ISTC-CNR, Italy)*
Leonardo Trujillo *(Instituto Tecnológico de Tijuana, Mexico)*
Elio Tuci *(Aberystwyth University, UK)*
Gunnar Tufte *(Norwegian University of Science and Technology, Norway)*
Cem Celal Tutum *(Michigan State University, USA)*
Jamie Twycross *(University of Nottingham, UK)*
Man Chon U *(The University of Georgia, USA)*
Ryan Urbanowicz *(Dartmouth, USA)*
Neil Urquhart *(Edinburgh Napier University, UK)*
A. Sima Uyar *(Istanbul Technical University, Turkey)*
H. Jaap Van den Herik *(Tilburg University, The Netherlands)*
Leonardo Vanneschi *(University of Milano-Bicocca, Italy)*
Pieter Vansteenwegen *(KU Leuven, Belgium)*
Igor Vatolkin *(TU Dortmund, Germany)*
Kalyan Veeramachaneni *(MIT, USA)*
Nadarajen Veerapen *(LUNAM Université, Université d'Angers, LERIA, France)*
Sebastian Ventura *(Universidad de Cordoba, Spain)*
Phillip Verbancsics *(University of Central Florida, USA)*
Sebastien Verel *(university of Nice Sophia Antipolis, France)*
Silvia Vergilio *(Federal University of Paraná, Brazil)*
Konstantinos Voglis *(University of Ioannina, Greece)*
Christoph von der Malsburg *(Goethe University Frankfurt am Main, Germany)*
Tanja Vos *(Universidad Politecnica de Valencia, Spain)*
Michael N. Vrahatis *(University of Patras, Greece)*
Markus Wagner *(The University of Adelaide, Australia)*
Antony Waldock *(BAE Systems, UK)*
Paul Walsh *(Cork Institute of Technology, Ireland)*
Berend Weel *(VU Amsterdam, The Netherlands)*

Joachim Wegener *(Berner & Mattner Systemtechnik GmbH, Germany)*
Justin Werfel *(Harvard University, USA)*
Simon Wessing *(Technische Universität Dortmund, Germany)*
Peter Alexander Whigham *(University of Otago, New Zealand)*
David White *(University of Glasgow, UK)*
Darrell Whitley *(Colorado State University, USA)*
R. Paul Wiegand *(Institute for Simulation and Training / UCF, USA)*
Josh Wilkerson *(Missouri University of Science and Technology, USA)*
Stewart W. Wilson *(Prediction Dynamics, USA)*
Mark Wineberg *(University of Guelph, Canada)*
Alan F. T. Winfield *(University of the West of England, UK)*
Stephan Winkler *(Upper Austrian University of Applied Sciences, Austria)*
Carsten Witt *(Technical University of Denmark, Denmark)*
John Woodward *(Nottingham University, UK)*
Brian Woolley *(University of Central Florida, USA)*
Alden H. Wright *(University of Montana, USA)*
Jonathan Wright *(Loughborough University, UK)*
Borys Wrobel *(Adam Mickiewicz University, Poland)*
Annie S. Wu *(University of Central Florida, USA)*
Zheng Yi Wu *(Bentley Systems, USA)*
Huayang Xie *(Victoria University of Wellington, New Zealand)*
Takeshi Yamada *(NTT Communication Science Labs., Japan)*
Lidia Yamamoto *(University of Strasbourg, France)*
Georgios Yannakakis *(IT University of Copenhagen, Denmark)*
Zhang Yanqing *(Georgia State University, USA)*
Wei-Chang Yeh *(National Tsing Hua University, China)*
Shin Yoo *(University College London, UK)*
Jason Yosinski *(Cornell University, USA)*
Tian-Li Yu *(Taiwan Evolutionary Intelligence Lab, Taiwan)*
Tina Yu *(Memorial University, Canada)*
Yang Yu *(Nanjing University, China)*
Daniela Zaharie *(West University of Timisoara, Romania)*
Franco Zambonelli *(Universita degli Studi di Modena e Reggio Emilia, Italy)*
Michael Zapf *(University of Kassel, Germany)*
Saúl Zapotecas Martínez *(CINVESTAV-IPN, Mexico)*
Christine Zarges *(The University of Birmingham, UK)*
Andreas Zell *(University of Tübingen, Germany)*
Zhu Zexuan *(Shenzhen University, China)*
Jun Zhang *(Sun Yat-sen University, China)*
Mengjie Zhang *(Victoria University of Wellington, New Zealand)*
Qingfu Zhang *(University of Essex, UK)*
Yi Zhang *(IESD, De Montfort Univeristy, UK)*
Yuanyuan Zhang *(University College London, UK)*
Ming-Jie Zhao *(University of Manchester, UK)*
Zhi-Hua Zhou *(Nanjing University, China)*

Papers Nominated for Best Paper Award

GECCO 2013 Sponsors and Supporters

ACM SIGEVO
Association for Computing Machinery
Special Interest Group on Genetic and Evolutionary Computation

Benchmarking Pareto Archiving Heuristics in the Presence of Concept Drift: Diversity Versus Age

Aaron Atwater
Faculty of Computer Science,
Dalhousie University,
Halifax, NS. Canada
atwater@cs.dal.ca

Malcolm I. Heywood
Faculty of Computer Science,
Dalhousie University,
Halifax, NS. Canada
mheywood@cs.dal.ca

ABSTRACT

A framework for coevolving genetic programming teams with Pareto archiving is benchmarked under two representative tasks for non-stationary streaming environments. The specific interest lies in determining the relative contribution of diversity and aging heuristics to the maintenance of the Pareto archive. Pareto archiving, in turn, is responsible for targeting data (and therefore champion individuals) as appropriate for retention beyond the limiting scope of the sliding window interface to the data stream. Fitness sharing alone is considered most effective under a non-stationary stream characterized by continuous (incremental) changes. Fitness sharing with an aging heuristic acts as the preferred heuristic when the stream is characterized by non-stationary stepwise changes.

Categories and Subject Descriptors

I.2.6 [**Learning**]: Parameter Learning

General Terms

Algorithms, Experimentation, Performance

Keywords

Streaming data, Online learning, Pareto archiving, Coevolution, Genetic Programming

1. INTRODUCTION

Streaming data applications represent a requirement for online as opposed to offline evolution. Taken from the perspective of a classification or regression task this implies that it is not possible to assume that the data can be divided into independent training, validation and test partitions i.e., the underlying process (describing the data) is non-stationary. This means that evolution should be conducted as a continuous process. The principle interest is therefore with respect to how well a machine learning algorithm – genetic programming (GP) in this case – is capable of tracking / reacting to such changes.

Streaming applications appear frequently in financial environments (e.g., [7]), computer network applications (e.g., [28]) or 'big data' applications (e.g., [2]). The interface between data stream and evolutionary algorithm typically takes the form of a sliding window. At each training epoch (generation) only data within the window can be accessed and used for fitness evaluation. In this work, evolution under a Pareto archiving model is assumed (Section 3). The implication of this is that a formal framework exists for identifying and retaining the (hopefully) few instances from the stream that are most useful in promoting the identification of the fittest learners.

The explicit interest of this research is to characterize the suitability of heuristics used to maintain finite archiving constraints necessary to minimize computational overheads associated with Pareto archiving. Such heuristics have a direct impact on the capability of the system to operate within non-stationary environments. In particular, we are interested in quantifying the importance attributed to heuristics for diversity versus age. With this in mind, two artificial data generators will be employed to create multi-class classification benchmarks with stepped versus continuous variation of the underlying data generating process (Section 4). Section 2 will summarize related research in dynamic environments whereas Section 3 summarizes the approach to Pareto archiving and team based task decomposition in GP. The paper concludes with a discussion and an identification of future research in Section 5.

GECCO'13, July 6–10, 2013, Amsterdam, The Netherlands.

2. RELATED WORK

Unlike static tasks, dynamic or non-stationary tasks require convergence to be pursued only up to a point. Specifically, when the underlying task is dynamic, convergence potentially compromises the ability to react to change. It has been proposed that previous approaches investigated for applying evolutionary computation to dynamic environments fall into one of five forms [7]: memory, diversity, multi-populations, problem decomposition and evolvability. The following provides a short review of the contributions made and where necessary their relation to this work.

Memory: as reflected in the capability to return to a previously evolved solution. This implicitly assumes that the task is in some way periodic. Moreover, there is always a tradeoff in terms of the amount of resources made available for memory and the amount made available for supporting other properties, such as diversity. In this work we are interested in the utility of Pareto archiving as a candidate memory mechanism under explicit enforcement of finite archive sizes. Pareto archiving provides a much more formal basis for retaining both learners (GP individuals) and points (data 'distinguishing' between non-dominated learners). A previous article looked at the simplified case of Pareto archiving applied under a streaming data context, but with respect to an environment with a underlying dynamic that was stationary [2]. As such the earlier work was not able to draw any conclusions regarding the appropriateness of Pareto archiving to non-stationary environments.

Diversity: as in mechanisms for supporting multiple species within a population. The most typically assumed mechanism is to vary the rate of mutation or introduce a fixed number of entirely new individuals at each generation [13]. Niching (speciation) has been considered to resist favouring the same individuals [5]. Likewise, solution age has been proposed to bias the retention of the 'middle aged' as opposed to the old or new [12]. [20] introduced 'sentinel' individuals as those which are uniformly distributed through the representation space. Such individuals act as a diverse source of genotypic information for seeding the population on a continuous basis. The later benchmarking study conducted here will revisit and compare the advantages and disadvantages of assuming speciation and age heuristics in conjunction with Pareto archiving.

Multi-populations: associate different populations with different aspects of the search space. The basic assumption in this case is that genetic drift associated with the smaller subpopulations will encourage the investigation of new areas of the search space. Finding a suitable heuristic for controlling the exploration–exploitation tradeoff controlling the interaction between the multiple populations remains an ongoing research issue.

Problem decomposition: is taken to have been articulated first by Simon's watchmaker parable in which the capacity to configure quickly is attributed to having appropriate 'modules' available [27]. From the perspective of GP, task decomposition might be most synonymous with support for modularity, run–time libraries and teaming. Studies have shown the utility of each relative to static task domains— e.g., in the case of the teaming metaphor adopted here, see [18].

Evolvability: implies that a representation is assumed that supports the identification of fitter parents in changing environments. Geno- to phenotypic mappings have been proposed in this respect e.g., [24]. In this work we equate evolvability with the degree to which modularity is supported, and a symbiotic coevolutionary framework for teaming in GP specifically [18].

3. PARETO ARCHIVING IN GP

As noted in Sections 1 and 2, Pareto archiving will be assumed as the 'memory mechanism' by which the uniqueness of GP individuals (learners) is formally established. Potentially, Pareto archiving provides a scheme for identifying a subset of learners as being non-dominated relative to the rest of the population. To do so, training exemplars represent 'objectives' and are rewarded for distinguishing between the capability of different learners. Such a model is of interest in a streaming context, as a basis is then provided for identifying a small number of data instances for retention beyond the immediate content of the sliding window i.e., interface to the stream (Section 3.1). Hereafter, the specific form assumed for GP will be the Symbiotic bid-based (SBB) framework for cooperatively evolving GP teams [17, 8]. Such a framework supports task decomposition and multi-class classification from a single evolutionary cycle and is therefore potentially capable of supporting multiple factors significant to dynamic environments (as reviewed in Section 2). In the following we first develop the Pareto archiving methodology independent of GP (Section 3.2) and then summarize SBB (Section 3.3).

3.1 Streaming data and concept drift

The streaming data assumption used in this work is the same sliding window implementation used in previous work such as [2]. This implies that at any given generation t only a subset of the total training instances are available to be sampled from, and at generation $t+1$ some number of instances will have left the window and will never be accessible again, while simultaneously some previously inaccessible instances will also be added to the window and thus available for selection. As in previous cases, the GP system is provided time equivalent to 10% of the maximum number of generations, t_{max}, with access to the first 10% of the stream, in order to train an initial population of GP individuals.

Concept drift is introduced in the data sets used herein, in the incarnation of multiple distinct rulesets which partition the attribute space into separate classes being employed at different time points throughout the stream. Two distinct rulesets may or may not be conceptually related, and data representing both these cases is presented in Section 4.2. The challenge posed to an online learning system in such an environment is to not only correctly determine the correct class label for exemplars in the current environment, but also to quickly adapt to changes in the underlying concepts – something that cannot be explicitly trained upon in the sense of traditional supervised learning tasks.

3.2 Pareto archiving and fitness sharing

A two stage process is assumed consisting of Pareto dominance ranking and fitness sharing,[1] the latter representing a heuristic for promoting diversity when enforcing finite archiving constraints [25].

Pareto dominance ranking: The members of the point population, p_k are taken to represent 'objectives'. Fitness is only ever evaluated against the content of the point population. This decouples fitness evaluation from the cardinality of a data set. From a streaming data perspective P_{gap} points are replaced at each generation with a sample of new points taken from the current sliding window location [2]. Such objectives / points are used to distinguish between the capability of different GP learners under a pairwise test for Pareto dominance, or

$$\begin{aligned} &\forall p_k \in P : G(l_i, p_k) \geq G(l_j, p_k) \\ &\text{AND } \exists p_k \in P : G(l_i, p_k) > G(l_j, p_k) \end{aligned} \tag{1}$$

where P is the point population; l_i and l_j are two individuals (cf., learners) from the GP population currently under evaluation, and; $G(\cdot, \cdot)$ is the task specific reward function returning 0 on an incorrect classification and 1 on a correct classification (see Eqn (4) later).

[1]For a tutorial on Pareto archiving as applied to GP see [15].

Eqn (1) implies that learner l_i dominates learner l_j *iff* it performs as well on every point and better on at least one point. For a total of $|L|$ learners there are a total of $|L|^2 - |L|$ learner comparisons [6].[2] Moreover, for point p_k a comparison between learner l_i and l_j has the form of a distinction vector:

$$d_k[L \cdot i + j] = \begin{cases} 1 & if G(l_i, p_k) > G(l_j, p_k) \\ 0 & \text{otherwise} \end{cases} \quad (2)$$

Thus, when Eqn (2) returns a value of 1 then a *distinction* is said to have been made [10]. Points are penalized for defeating all learners or when it is defeated by all learners i.e., no distinctions result. Such points would therefore tend to be prioritized for removing from the point population. The fittest learners / GP individuals are naturally those promoted by the Pareto dominance expression – Eqn (1). One drawback of the Pareto approach is that as the number of objectives (points) increases, then comparatively weak overlapping behaviours may satisfy the Pareto archiving criteria [10, 21, 19]. SBB therefore adopts the following fitness sharing heuristic with the motivation of maintaining diversity in the points learners solve. This point will be revisited in Section 4 when we consider alternative heuristics that might be more appropriate to a data streaming context.

Fitness sharing: The reward function $G(l_i, p_k)$ establishes a vector of distinctions (Eqn. (2)) for each point. The point population can now be divided into two sets: those in the non-dominated front (the archive), $\mathcal{F}(P^t)$, versus those that are not, $\mathcal{D}(P^t)$. Naturally, the decision to limit the number of archives to two is motivated by a desire to balance the computational cost of archive construction against maintaining monotonic progress to an 'ideal' training trajectory [6].

Up to P_{gap} points are replaced at each generation from the current stream window using the process of Section 3.1 [2]. Points are targeted for replacement under two basic conditions [17, 8]:

- If $|\mathcal{F}(P^t)| \leq |P| - P_{gap}$ THEN: stochastically select points for replacement from $\mathcal{D}(P^t)$ alone.
- If $|\mathcal{F}(P^t)| > |P| - P_{gap}$ THEN: all the dominated points are replaced, plus some subset $P_{gap} - |\mathcal{D}(P^t)|$ of the Pareto archive. A fitness sharing heuristic is assumed for weighting members of the Pareto archive such that the more unique the distinction the greater the weight. Thus, relative to distinction vector d_k of point p_k, fitness sharing is defined as:

$$\sum_i \frac{d_k[i]}{1 + N_i} \quad (3)$$

where i indexes all distinction vector entries (Eqn (2)), and N_i counts the number of points in $\mathcal{F}(P^t)$ that make the same distinction.

[2]This is distinct from the number of fitness evaluations per generation, with fitness evaluation being a more costly process than establishing the comparison vector.

3.3 Symbiotic bid-based GP

Symbiotic bid-based GP as applied to classification – hereafter SBB – utilizes two populations: program and team (or symbiont and host), which are coevolved through symbiosis [17, 8]. The program (symbiont) population utilizes a bid-based GP representation [16], itself defining each individual in terms of a tuple $\langle c, b \rangle$. Here c declares a scalar class label selected from the set of labels associated with the task domain ($c \in C$); whereas b is the program that evolves a context for deploying its class label. The team (host) population identifies combinations of symbionts that attempt to coexist in a coevolutionary relationship. Members of the team population assume a variable length representation, wherein the number of symbionts per team are adapted as part of the evolutionary cycle. Indeed, [2] noted that hosts were first composed from symbionts representing the most frequent classes and only later were symbionts added representing the less frequent classes. Fitness evaluation is only ever performed at the 'level' of the hosts; thus, hosts represent the 'learner' in the above discussion of Pareto dominance (Section 3.2).

Evaluation of a host, $l_i \in L^t$, is repeated for each training instance as identified by the point population at generation t, $p_k \in P^t$. For all symbionts a member of the host, $s_j \in l_i$, execute their programs w.r.t. point p_k. The host identifies the symbiont with maximum output (the winning bid) or $s^* = arg_{s_j \in l_i} max[s_j.b]$. The winning symbiont gains the right to suggest the class label for the current point, or

$$G(l_i, p_k) = \begin{cases} 1 & if \text{ IF } s^*.c = p_k.t \\ 0 & \text{otherwise} \end{cases} \quad (4)$$

where $p_k.t$ is the target label for point p_k. Naturally, $G(l_i, p_k)$ is the reward function referred to in Section 3.2.

Algorithm 1 summarizes the breeder model of evolution defining the stepwise application of SBB to a data stream [2]. Initialization provides initial sliding window content, S^t from the data stream, τ, and then samples from S^t until $P - P_{gap}$ points have been selected (Section 3.1). Initialization of the host and symbiont population follows the original SBB algorithm [17, 8]. On entering the main loop the remaining P_{gap} and L_{gap} points and teams are initialized. The point population assumes the same stochastic sampled process as used during the initialization step. Additional L_{gap} hosts are added through application of the SBB variation operators. Variation operators include crossover between hosts and symbiont mutation. The latter implies symbionts are first cloned, with the content varied through appropriate GP mutation operators [17, 8].

The 'Evaluate' function (line 11) resolves values for $G(l_i, p_k)$. Once all hosts have been evaluated on all points then the location of the sliding window is incremented relative to the data stream S^t (line 14). Point replacement is performed under the Pareto archiving–fitness sharing heuristic of Section 3.2 (line 15). Likewise, a fixed number of hosts, L_{gap}, are removed at each generation (line 16) resulting in members of the host population being either non-dominated (Pareto archive), $\mathcal{F}(L^t)$, or dominated, $\mathcal{D}(L^t)$. Thus, hosts are identified for replacement. Should symbionts *no longer* receive any host indexes then this is taken to imply that they were only associated with the worst L_{gap} hosts and they therefore 'die'. The symbiont population size is therefore free to float.

Finally, the role of function 'Best' (line 19) is to return

Algorithm 1 Overview of the SBB training algorithm as applied to streaming data τ. S^t denotes the set of training instances associated with the sliding window at generation t; τ denotes the streaming data; $|P|$ and P^t are the size and content of the point population respectively; $|L|$ and L^t are the size and content of the host population respectively;.

```
procedure TRAIN
    t = 0                                        ▷ Initialization.
    S^t = INITSTREAM(τ(t))
    P^t = INITPOINTS(P, S^t)
    (L^t, L^t) = INITTEAMS(M)
    while t ≤ t_max do
        P^t = GENPOINTS(P^t, S^t)    ▷ Add 'gap' size points
        (L^t) = GENTEAMS(L^t)                    ▷ ... and hosts
        for all l_i ∈ L^t do
            for all p_k ∈ P^t do
                EVALUATE(l_i, p_k)               ▷ Evaluate fitness
            end for
        end for
        S^{t+1} = SHIFTSTREAM(τ(t + 1))          ▷ Resample
        P^{t+1} = SELPOINTS(P^t)
        (M^{t+1}) = SELTEAMS(L^t)
        t = t + 1
    end while
    return BEST(L^t, P^t)
end procedure
```

the champion host for evaluation against the test partition. Given the streaming context – or continuous evolution against the stream – all hosts currently in the Pareto archive are evaluated against the current content of the point population. The assumption being that if the Pareto archiving strategy is effective, then the points remaining in the point population should be the most appropriate for prioritizing the champion host. The metric assumed for champion identification is the average class-wise detection rate or:

$$avg.DR = \frac{1}{|C|} \sum_{c \in C} DR_c(l_i) \qquad (5)$$

where C is the set of class labels associated with this task and $DR_c(l_i)$ is the detection rate of host l_i relative to class c. Readers are referred to [17, 8] for additional SBB details e.g., instruction set and variation operators.

4. EVALUATION

4.1 Diversity versus aging heuristics

Relative to the Pareto archiving framework of Section 3.2, we note that at present a fitness sharing heuristic is used to promote the maintenance of diversity once the number of non-dominated points encounters the constraint imposed by a finite archive. Given that streaming applications are often of a real time nature, letting archive size increase to include all non-dominated points is not a desirable option [2]. Moreover, once a point provides a distinction it could potentially lie in the point population indefinitely i.e., the case of an outlier or mislabelled data. Under streaming applications this is also deemed to be undesirable as the underlying process determining stream content are frequently non-stationary. With this in mind, the fitness sharing heuristic of Equation 3 will be adjusted with the goal of evaluating its role in allowing the GP populations to interact more effectively with the current contents of the stream. To that end, the following three configurations will be explored:

1. Fitness sharing in its original, unmodified format. This case will serve as the base case for attempted optimizations to the fitness sharing heuristic. Hereafter this case is denoted **org**.

2. Fitness sharing scores multiplied by the normalized inverse of point archive ages; that is, $score = score \times (1 - age/age_{max})$. Naturally, this heuristic introduces an age bias, with the motivation being to make older points more likely to be replaced. Hereafter this case is denoted **age**.

3. Points with a fitness sharing score of 0 are considered to be ranked highest; after this, points are taken in the order of highest score first. This case is intended to address the issue of new points which **no** GP individuals are able to correctly classify being unable to enter the point archive. This prevents material that is currently entirely unclassifiable from being presented to the team population as a desirable problem to be solved. Hereafter this case is denoted **zero**.

Since online learning applications require an answer in the "here and now" of a data stream and not in a separately partitioned external environment, testing is performed at periodic intervals during training by extracting the current front-running GP individual and evaluating it separately across the previous interval, and the next (as-yet-unseen) interval. The evaluation metrics used will be the accuracy (total number correct versus the total number of exemplars in the interval) and average detection rate (Eqn (5)) as calculated across the interval. The relative variation between accuracy and average detection rate provide a characterization for how sensitive the resulting classifier is to class imbalance.

4.2 Datasets

Two methods of generating synthetic data for benchmarking streaming classification algorithms are employed:

1. Dataset Generator[3], a tool for generating benchmark data for data mining applications, is used to generate exemplars representing three separate concepts, C1, C2, and C3. These concepts are then mixed as in [31]: a stream of 7,000,000 total exemplars is divided into "chunks" containing 500,000 exemplars each, and containing representation from each of the three concepts in a tuple written in the form $\langle\%C1, \%C2, \%C3\rangle$. The entire stream can then be written as fourteen chunks expressed, in order, as follows: $\langle 100, 0, 0\rangle$ $\langle 100, 0, 0\rangle$ $\langle 100, 0, 0\rangle$ $\langle 90, 10, 0\rangle$ $\langle 80, 10, 0\rangle$ ... $\langle 10, 90, 0\rangle$ $\langle 0, 100, 0\rangle$ $\langle 0, 0, 100\rangle$. The resulting data set will be denoted **datgen**.

   The data is generated using the parameterization set forth in [31]. Five real-valued attributes are specified that are relevant to the class attribute, and a sixth attribute that is irrelevant. Datgen then creates a

[3]Gabor Melli. The datgen Dataset Generator. http://www.datasetgenerator.com/

decision tree-style list of rules that partitions the attribute space into 5 classes based on randomly generated threshold values, and assigns a class label to each of the tree branches. Exemplars are then created by randomly determining attribute values and evaluating them against the generated decision tree in order to assign a class label to the instance.

2. Two hyperplanes of the form $\Sigma_{i=1}^{d} a_i x_i = a_0$ are generated, as in [9], where the values of a_i represents the current state of the stream (initialized randomly), the values of x_i represent the attribute values of a given exemplar, and $d = 10$ represents the chosen dimensionality for the task domain. A stream of 150,000 exemplars is created, and concept drift is parameterized and simulated as follows: Every $N = 1,000$ exemplars, each entry in a vector $s = \{-1, +1\}^d$ (also initialized randomly) is given a 20% chance of inverting its value. The first 5 of 10 non-class attributes in a are then moved at a rate of $t = 10\%$ over the course of the next N exemplars, compounded every generation. This function is summarized in Equation 6 :

$$a_i = a_i + s_i \cdot \frac{a_i \cdot t}{N} \tag{6}$$

Exemplars are created by generating uniform random values for all non-class attributes. To determine the class label, the values a_0 for each hyperplane are first normalized by summing the rest of the entries in the vector and multiplying by a factor of 1/3 and 2/3 respectively, in order to keep the class distribution from becoming entirely one-sided. The class label is then equal to the number of hyperplanes for which $\Sigma_{i=1}^{d} a_i x_i < a_0$. The resulting dataset will be denoted **planar**.

This provides two basic scenarios for comparing the performance of the heuristics under different styles of concept drift. The first is a discrete case in which two different concepts cannot be interpolated between, and instead only the frequency of their appearance in the surrounding stream changes over time. The second is a continuous case in which two different concepts are related to each other by some randomly drifting function, and a given exemplar may exist on some fuzzy boundary between the two as the stream's make-up slowly drifts from being composed of one concept to another.

In keeping with established practice in generating synthetic data sets for classification, new exemplars are created by randomly choosing values for each attribute and then applying the generated ruleset to determine the exemplar's class attribute. This tends to lead to a natural class imbalance dependent on how much of the attribute space falls under the jurisdiction of each generated rule. The datasets are summarized in Table 1.

4.3 Parameterization

There are two parameters specific to the interface between SBB and the sliding window:

Maximum number of generations, t_{max}: This defines the number of generations conducted while making a single pass through the data set (Section 4.1), and is held constant across all datasets. The impact of this is that new training instances become eligible at the rate of ≈ 233 per generation under datgen and ≈ 5 per generation under planar (i.e., total training instance count $\div\ t_{max}$).

Window size, w, for the sliding window: This is set at 5% of the total dataset size, or 350,000 records for datgen and 7,500 for planar. A larger window size allows more data to be sampled for possible inclusion in the archive at a time (and thus more representation of the current concept distribution of the stream), at the cost of increased storage costs.

SBB parameters: are the same as the original study on Pareto archiving [2], and shown for convenience in Table 2).

In each case a total of 50 runs are performed per experiment.

Table 1: Characterization of benchmarking datasets. Attribute counts appear next to the respective dataset names.

Class	datgen (11)	planar (7)
1	2,615,747	14,055
2	1,801,055	120,167
3	1,643,327	15,778
4	635,629	–
5	304,242	–

Table 2: SBB parameterization.

	Description	Value
P_{size}	Point population size.	120
M_{size}	Team population size.	120
t_{max}	Number of generations.	30 000
p_d	Probability of learner deletion.	0.7
p_a	Probability of learner addition.	0.7
μ_a	Probability of action mutation.	0.1
ω	Maximum team size.	20
P_{gap}	Point generation gap.	20
M_{gap}	Team generation gap.	60

4.4 Results

As outlined in Section 4.1, a total of three scenarios are considered across the **datgen** and **planar** data sets: 1) Unmodified fitness sharing scores or the **org** configuration. 2) Fitness sharing scores multiplied by inverse normalized exemplar age, or the **age** configuration. 3) Fitness sharing scores left unmodified, except scores of 0 are changed to ∞, or the **zero** configuration.

The average detection rate metrics, as calculated across periodic intervals in the stream, are shown in Figure 1 for the datgen data set, and in Figure 2 for the planar dataset.

In the base case **org** for the **datgen** stream, performance hovers near unity for the first two intervals while the underlying concept C1 does not change, then begins to steadily decline as data points from the second concept C2 are gradually introduced. The decline in performance continues until the tenth chunk, at which point more than two-thirds of the stream is composed of representatives of C2, and only then does the algorithm begin adapting to the change in the underlying environment. Interestingly, the next-to-last chunk of data composed entirely of C2 exemplars caused the performance of the algorithm to drop the lowest, but the team population is able to easily adjust to a brand new concept C3 when it abruptly takes over the stream (last chunk of the sequence). Such behaviour would seem to imply a weakness in the current GP model for adapting to change spread out over a significant period of time, at least in the case of discrete concept representation. Conversely, sudden change appears to result in a more effective retraining and replacement of GP classifiers.

The other experiments **age** and **zero** in the **datgen** environment exhibit similar behaviour but appear to be able to start compensating for the gradual change in concept earlier in the stream. Thus, the quartile statistic is better at remaining above an average detection rate of 70% than under **org**. Of the three, the **age** case appears to adapt the quickest. This configuration, as described in Section 4.1, was intended to punish points that have spent more time in the archive – to the extent that the oldest point is deterministically removed at each generation.

In all cases for the **planar** stream, performance in terms of average detection rate appears to suffer initially from a pathological case of class imbalance. This is corroborated by the high accuracy metrics reported for that portion of the stream (Figure 3), and can be verified by looking at the class distribution of the point archive from an example run (not shown). In this case, the original diversity based heuristic appears to resist the incremental variation in the stream content better than either the explicitly age or 'disengaged point' biases or **age** and **zero** respectively. This is particularly true under the balanced detection rate metric of Figure 2. Note the different scales under the accuracy metric in Figure 3. In this case there is much more variation in the spread of the original heuristic (e.g., 1st quartile extends down to 50%) whereas the **age** and **zero** heuristics demonstrate less variance. However, in either metric, median performance never descends below 70% under **org** whereas both the alternative heuristics fail to do so.

The magnitude of the effect of the different fitness sharing heuristics on the archive policy's age bias can be clearly seen in Figure 4. The **org** heuristic constantly churns the contents of the point archive, whereas both **age** and **zero** provide an additional level of granularity to the score values that allow the archive to distinguish between points enough to single some out for more long-term archiving.

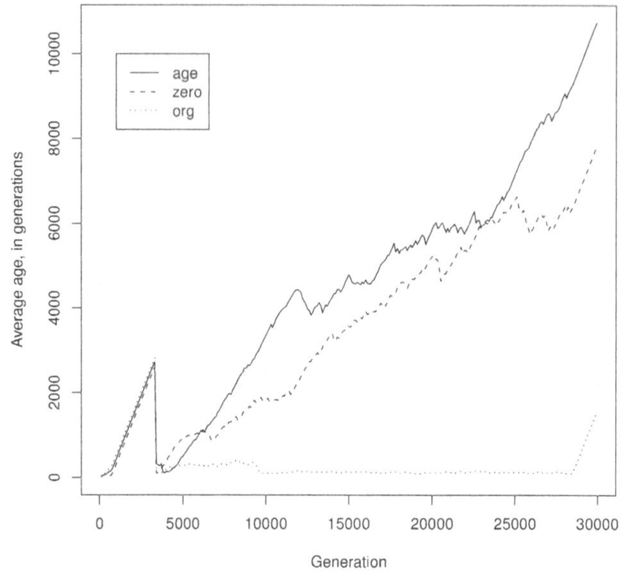

Figure 4: Average age of individuals in the point archive from single runs of experiments in the *planar* environment.

5. CONCLUSION

Pareto archiving and the development of GP teams through symbiosis are proposed as a general framework for supporting the multiple factors deemed to be of significance to continuous evolution in non-stationary environments. Specifically, the SBB algorithm supports task decomposition through speciation and bidding, whereas evolvability is addressed through the use of independent representations and variation operators for teams and programs. Pareto archiving provides a formal framework for retaining specific learners (GP teams) and the corresponding data points, or a memory mechanism. This study introduces two multi-class benchmarks of importance to streaming under non-stationary tasks. Specifically, the 'datagen' task assumes stepped changes to the underlying process whereas 'planar' adopts a continuously varying process. The resulting benchmark study indicates that diversity is more effective under the continuously varying process. Conversely, introducing an additional age bias that deterministically retires the oldest non-dominated learners / points is more effective in the non-stationary task with stepped changes.

In the case of future research we note that GP individuals are currently only evaluated with respect to a single exemplar. Conversely, data structures such as tapped delay lines [28] and evolved sliding window parameterizations [29] would further enhance the capability of GP individuals to characterize the time varying nature of the underlying task, and possibly introduce a method of dealing with cyclical concept drift behaviour which has not been examined here. We are also interested in the use of GP within active learning environments to perform change detection without the use of labeled data. This would imply that only when changes are detected would labels be requested.

Acknowledgements

The authors gratefully acknowledge support from NSERC scholarship and grant programs (Canada).

6. REFERENCES

[1] H. Abdulsalam, D. B. Skillicorn, and P. Martin. Classification using streaming random forests. *IEEE Transactions on Knowledge and Data Engineering*, 23(1):22–36, 2011.

[2] A. Atwater, M. I. Heywood, and A. N. Zincir-Heywood. Gp under streaming data constraints: A case for Pareto archiving? In *ACM Genetic and Evolutionary Computation Conference*, pages 703–710, 2012.

[3] P. Bruneau, F. Picarougne, and M. Gelgon. Incremental semi-supervised clustering in a data

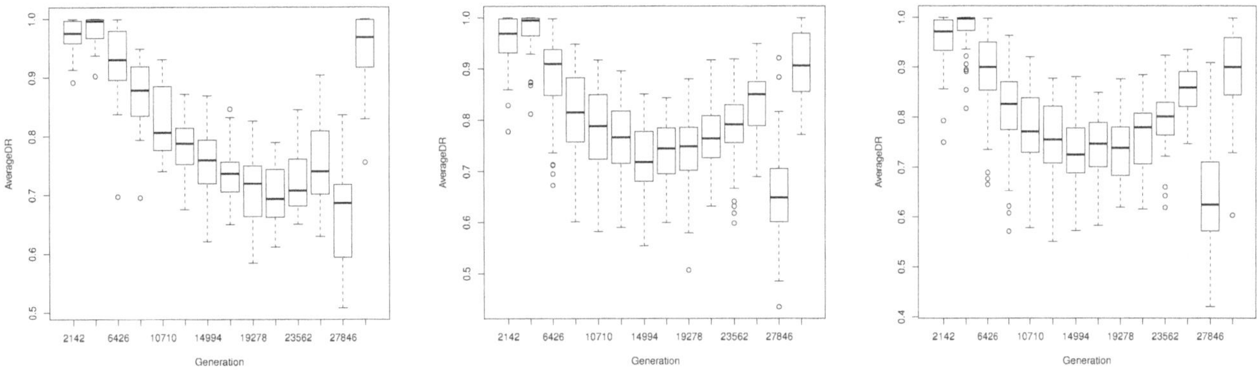

(a) org (b) age (c) zero

Figure 1: Average Detection Rate across previous chunks during training on the stream, using the *datgen* data set.

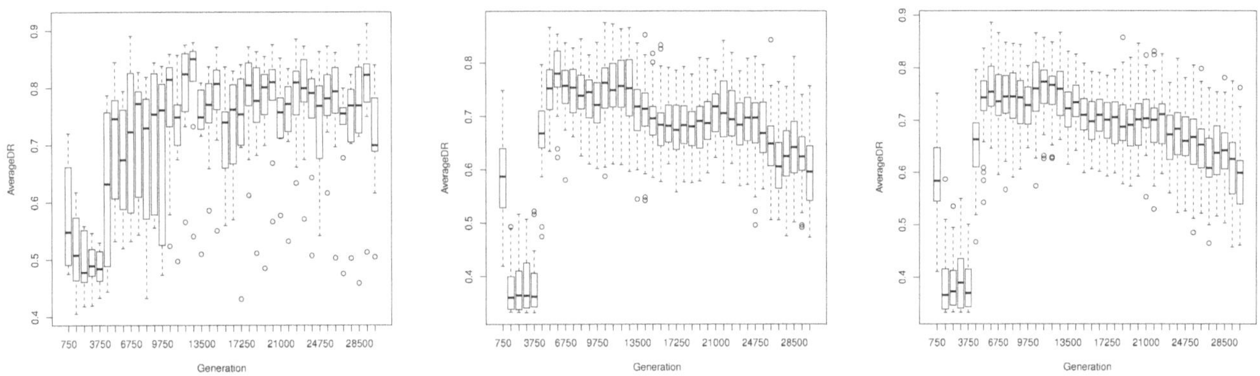

(a) org (b) age (c) zero

Figure 2: Average Detection Rate across previous chunks during training on the stream, using the *planar* data set.

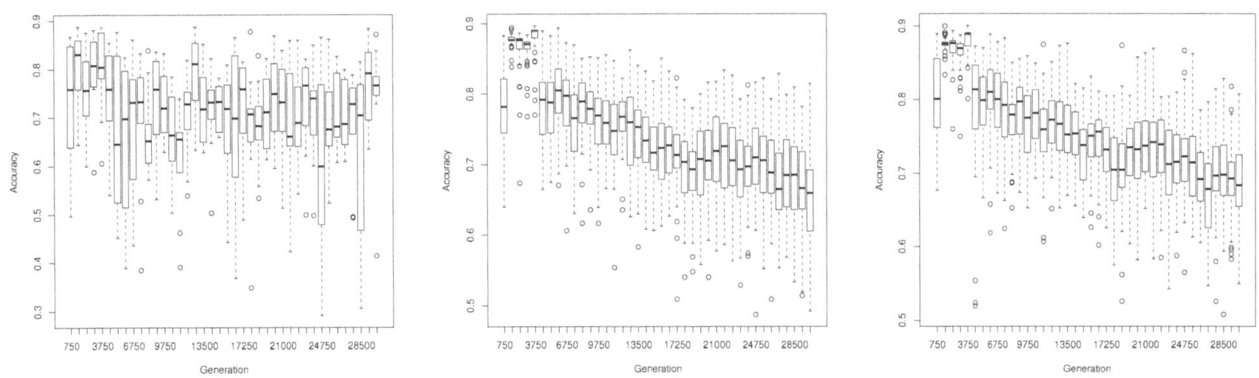

(a) org (b) age (c) zero

Figure 3: Accuracy across previous chunks during training on the stream, using the *planar* data set.

stream with a flock of agents. In *IEEE Congress on Evolutionary Computation*, pages 3067–3074, 2009.

[4] J. Cartlidge and D. Ait-Boudaoud. Autonomous virulence adaptation improves coevolutionary optimization. *IEEE Transactions on Evolutionary Computation*, 15(2):215–229, 2011.

[5] W. Cedeno and V. R. Vemuri. On the use of niching for dynamic landscapes. In *IEEE Congress on Evolutionary Computation*, pages 361–366, 1997.

[6] E. D. de Jong. A monolithic archive for pareto-coevolution. *Evolutionary Computation*, 15(1):61–93, 2007.

[7] I. Dempsey, M. O'Neill, and B. A. *Foundations in Grammatical Evolution for Dynamic Environments*, volume 194 of *Studies in Computational Intelligence*. Springer, 2009.

[8] J. A. Doucette, A. R. McIntyre, P. Lichodzijewski, and M. I. Heywood. Symbolic coevolutionary genetic programming: A benchmarking study under large attribute spaces. *Genetic Programming and Evolvable Machines*, 13:to appear, 2012.

[9] W. Fan, Y. Huang, H. Wang, and P. S. Yu. Active mining of data streams. In *Proceedings of the Fourth SIAM International Conference on Data Mining*, pages 457–461, 2004.

[10] S. G. Ficici and J. Pollack. Pareto optimality in coevolutionary learning. In *European Conference on Advances in Artificial Life*, pages 316–325, 2001.

[11] C. Gathercole and P. Ross. Dynamic training subset selection for supervised learning in genetic programming. In *Parallel Problem Solving from Nature*, pages 312–321, 1994.

[12] A. Ghosh, S. Tstutsui, and H. Tanaka. Function optimization in non-stationary environment using steady state genetic algorithms with aging of individuals. In *IEEE Congress on Evolutionary Computation*, pages 666–671, 1998.

[13] J. J. Greffenstette. Genetic algorithms for changing environments. In *Proceedings of Parallel Problem Solving from Nature*, pages 137–144, 1992.

[14] M. Kotanchek, G. Smits, and E. Vladislavleva. Exploiting trustable models via pareto GP for targeted data collection. In *Genetic Programming Theory and Practice VI*, pages 145–162. Springer, 2009.

[15] M. Lemczyk. Pareto-cevolutionary genetic programming classifier. Master's thesis, Faculty of Computer Science, Dalhousie University, 2006. http://web.cs.dal.ca/~mheywood/Thesis/MCS.html.

[16] P. Lichodzijewski and M. I. Heywood. Pareto-coevolutionary genetic programming for problem decomposition in multi-class classification. In *ACM Genetic and Evolutionary Computation Conference*, pages 464–471, 2007.

[17] P. Lichodzijewski and M. I. Heywood. Managing team-based problem solving with symbiotic bid-based genetic programming. In *ACM Genetic and Evolutionary Computation Conference*, pages 363–370, 2008.

[18] P. Lichodzijewski and M. I. Heywood. Symbiosis, complexification and simplicity under gp. In *ACM Genetic and Evolutionary Computation Conference*, pages 853–860, 2010.

[19] A. R. McIntyre and M. I. Heywood. Cooperative problem decomposition in pareto competitive classifier models of coevolution. In *European Conference on Genetic Programming*, pages 289–300, 2008.

[20] R. W. Morrison. *Designing evolutionary algorithms for dynamic environments*. Springer, 2004.

[21] J. Noble and R. A. Watson. Pareto coevolution: Using performance against coevolved opponents in a game as dimensions for pareto selection. In *ACM Genetic and Evolutionary Computation Conference*, pages 493–500, 2001.

[22] A. Orriols-Puig, J. Casillas, and E. Bernado-Mansilla. First approach toward on-line evolution of association rules with learning classifier systems. In *ACM Genetic and Evolutionary Computation Conference*, pages 2031–2038, 2008.

[23] V. Ramos and A. Abraham. Swarms on continuous data. In *IEEE Congress on Evolutionary Computation*, pages 1370–1375, 2003.

[24] J. Reisinger, K. O. Stanley, and R. Miikkulainen. Towards and empirical measure of evolvability. In *ACM Genetic and Evolutionary Computation Conference*, pages 257–264, 2005.

[25] C. D. Rosin and R. K. Belew. New methods for competitive coevolution. *Evol. Comput.*, 5(1):1–29, 1997.

[26] D. Saad, editor. *On-line learning in neural networks*. Cambridge University Press, 1998.

[27] H. A. Simon. *The sciences of the artificial*. MIT Press, 2nd edition, 1996.

[28] S. Song, M. I. Heywood, and A. N. Zincir-Heywood. Training genetic programming on half a million patters: An example from anomaly detection. *IEEE Transactions on Evolutionary Computation*, 9(3):225–239, 2005.

[29] N. Wagner, Z. Michalewicz, M. Khouja, and R. R. McGregor. Time series forecasting for dynamic environments: The DyFor genetic program model. *IEEE Transactions on Evolutionary Computation*, 11(4):433–452, 2007.

[30] S. X. Wu and W. Banzhaf. Rethinking multilevel selection in genetic programming. In *ACM Genetic and Evolutionary Computation Conference*, pages 1403–1410, 2011.

[31] X. Zhu, P. Zhang, X. Lin, and Y. Shi. Active learning from stream data using optimal weight classifier ensemble. *IEEE Transactions on Systems, Man, and Cybernetics–Part B*, 40(6):1607–1621, 2010.

Automatic Inference of Hierarchical Graph Models using Genetic Programming with an Application to Cortical Networks

Alexander Bailey
Brock University
St. Catharines, Canada

Beatrice Ombuki-Berman
Brock University
St. Catharines, Canada

Mario Ventresca
University of Toronto
Toronto, Canada

ABSTRACT

The pathways that relay sensory information within the brain form a network of connections, the precise organization of which is unknown. Communities of neurons can be discerned within this tangled structure, with inhomogeneously distributed connections existing between cortical areas. Classification and modelling of these networks has led to advancements in the identification of unhealthy or injured brains, however, the current models used are known to have major deficiencies. Specifically, the community structure of the cortex is not accounted for in existing algorithms, and it is unclear how to properly design a more representative graph model. It has recently been demonstrated that genetic programming may be useful for inferring accurate graph models, although no study to date has investigated the ability to replicate community structure. In this paper we propose the first GP system for the automatic inference of algorithms capable of generating, to a high accuracy, networks with community structure. We utilize a common cat cortex data set to highlight the efficacy of our approach. Our experiments clearly show that the inferred graph model generates a more representative network than those currently used in scientific literature.

Categories and Subject Descriptors

I.2.2 [**Artificial Intelligence**]: Automatic Programming—*Program synthesis*

General Terms

Algorithms,theory,design

Keywords

Complex networks, genetic programming, graph models, automatic inference, cortical networks

GECCO'13, July 6-10, 2013, Amsterdam, The Netherlands.

1. INTRODUCTION

The term *complex network* [23] refers to any set of interrelated elements where the pattern of connections is meaningful. The elements are the vertices in the network and their connections form the edges. Usually we are interested in network behaviour emergent from these patterns and by studying how these networks connect it is possible to learn the functional implication of these connections. In this paper we will focus our attention on the cortical network of a cat. The study of the brain as a complex network is relatively new, and began with the advent of modern technologies that facilitate the large-scale mapping of brain connectivity [30].

Numerous studies have focused on various aspects of brain connectivity and their implications on its functionality and health. These studies range from very large scale simulations of neuron growth and interaction requiring petascale computing power [19], to examining the connectivity of high-level regions of the brain associated with functional characteristics – in particular the cortex [20, 30, 31, 33, 36]. Existing human-designed graph models have provided valuable insights into the organization of cortical networks, and have even helped to refine methods of diagnosis for neurological diseases [5, 18]. However, existing commonly-used graph models do not describe the connectivity between functionally separate cortical areas, and there is some debate about which of these models is best to use given that none of them properly describe the network dynamics [36]. Simulations of the brain at the micro-level could potentially provide very accurate models of its large-scale organization, however, they are inaccessible to most researchers due to the computational resources required. Simulations of a rat cortical column consisting of about 10^3 neurons have successfully been constructed using modern supercomputing technology [19] – the scale of a full cortical simulation, the human cortex has an estimated 10^{10} neurons, making such a simulation currently impossible. Simple, accessible, and accurate models or methods of producing models of the high level organization of cortical networks are needed to further our understanding of their function.

Recently, it has been shown that Genetic Programming (GP) is a promising candidate for the automatic inference of graph models for complex networks [3]. We propose a model of hierarchical cortical connectivity inferred automatically via GP, and show that it performs at least as well or better than existing popular models of cortical structure.

2. BACKGROUND

Complex networks are usually studied in terms of their overall structure using statistical measures of connectivity. When considering cortical networks the *average geodesic path length*, as well as the *clustering coefficient* sometimes called *transitivity*, the *degree distribution*, and the *community structure* are of interest because of their effect on communication pathways ([1,16,24] provide a good overview of these terms). Various studies focusing on categorizing cortical networks include [8, 29, 30, 32]. Throughout this paper the assumed definition of a graph is $G = (V, E)$ where V is the vertex set and E is the edge set, the size of the vertex set $|V| = n$, and the degree of vertex i is k_i. The transitivity and the average geodesic path length will be referred to as C and l respectively.

2.1 Complex Network Models

Community structure [16] is a property found in many networks, in which there are subsets of nodes that are more connected to each other than the rest of the network. The densely connected subsets are known as communities. Community structure is apparent in cortical networks, is known to correspond to functional groups of cortical nodes, and injured and unhealthy brains have been shown to exhibit different community structures than healthy ones [5, 8, 11, 26, 32, 36].

A value affected by the community structure is the centrality of a vertex, which describes how important or connected they are within a network [24]. The *betweenness centrality* of a vertex is defined as the number of geodesic paths that run through it. The betweenness centrality describes a vertex's influence on the flow of information within a network and is expected to be an important property with respect to cortical networks [32].

Given information about a network with respect to the properties described above, algorithms can be designed that produce a potentially infinite set of graphs that mimic these properties, these algorithms are called *graph models*. Cortical networks, having a low average geodesic path length and a high clustering coefficient are often modelled with the Watts-Strogatz (WS) small-world model [26, 31, 32, 35]. However, the WS model does not produce highly connected hub nodes, an important feature of brain structure. The hub nodes present in cortical networks have given rise to the idea that the connectivity may follow a power law. Networks that possess this property are called *scale-free* (SF) and if it is necessary to model this property then a model such as the Barabási-Albert (BA) is usually used [4, 26, 32]. Both of these models have been important in the analysis of brain networks [32], however neither of them model both the degree distribution as well as the transitivity and path length properties.

2.2 Cortical Networks

The experiments in this paper will focus on the cortical connectivity within the brain of a cat because it has the most complete available data of its kind [36]. The dataset, representing a macro-scale network of grey matter sections, was created via a collation of tract-tracing experiments and literature reporting, supported by analytical treatment of the results [28]. It has been found that this network is dominated by paths of length one and two, that it contains a high density of connections, it has highly connected hubs, and that it is segregated into clusters (which closely align with the visual, auditory, somatosensory-motor, and frontolimbic centres) [36]. It is also speculated that the number of alternative pathways between cortical nodes plays an important role in the brain's ability to process complex information [36]. Cortical networks are often classified as small-world networks [31, 36]; however, there is also some debate as to whether or not they could be scale-free networks [17, 20, 33]. As such, these networks are often modelled or simulated using algorithms that generate scale-free or small-world networks. Although, it is known that the cortical data in the literature suggests neither model is quite suitable given that they do not describe the inter-community dynamics of the cortex well [36].

The proposed system for the automatic inference of graph models works only with undirected networks, and while cortical networks are thought to be directed networks, it has been shown that an undirected approximation is a reasonable relaxation because the majority of connections are reciprocal [22, 36]. The cat cortical network dataset [28] in its undirected form contains 52 cortical nodes and 515 edges. It has a clustering coefficient of $C_c = 0.585$ and an average geodesic path length of $l_c = 1.636$ and a diameter of $d_c = 3$. These simple properties are useful because they are known to be good classifiers of the behaviour of message propagation across a network [2]. If multiple paths are used for processing then it may be that the longest path is also of consequence, especially if the temporal aspect of these signals is important, so the diameter will also be considered.

3. GP SYSTEM

The GP system for automatically generating graph models for complex networks was built using *RobGP*, a Koza-style GP system [13]. All operations were strongly typed. The system generates hierarchical graph models given an initial set of input networks, called the *target networks*. The set can be any size, but they should all be related as only one algorithm will be generated that should approximate all targets in the set. Hierarchical models generated by the GP are meant to exhibit a strong community structure. This is achieved by breaking the target apart into two sets of subgraphs, which are used as target sets for two parallel evolving populations. These populations are distinct but use the same GP language, fitness functions, parameters, and are evaluated in the same way. This process is described in the following subsection.

The goal of the application of the GP system is to automatically infer a model of the cortex data which exhibits an accurate degree distribution, average geodesic path length, transitivity, and exhibits a community structure which mimics the structure of the cortex. Neither the BA nor WS model exhibit all of these features, and although it is a desirable property, none of them generate graphs with a community structure that matches the cortex [26].

3.1 Generation of Hierarchical Models

This paper does not focus on the problem of discovering communities directly with the GP system itself, although it may be an effort for future work. Instead, we endeavour to model communities that we are able to identify in a target network via an external algorithm (many exist [12]). We propose a system which represents the first effort to automatically infer graph models for networks which exhibit a

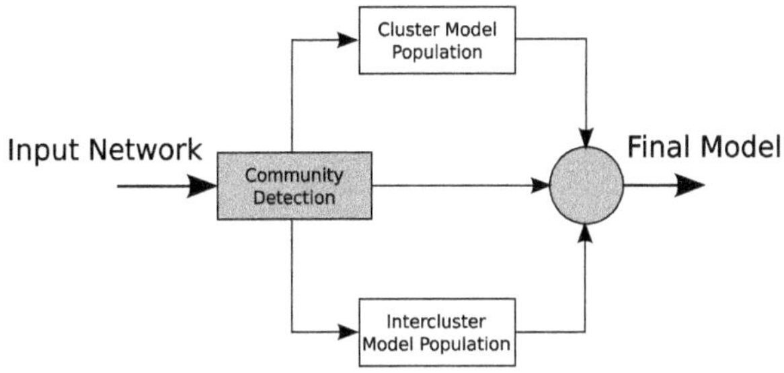

Figure 1: The process of generating hierarchical models.

hierarchical clustered organization for a defined community structure. It works as follows:

1. A black-box method is employed to identify the communities within the target network.
2. The communities are isolated and fed into the GP as the target set for the community model population.
3. The inter-community edges form a graph which is fed into the GP as the target for the inter-community model population.
4. Select two models, one evolved from each population, and combine them to create a hierarchical model.

Note that Steps 2 and 3 are performed in parallel. Step 4 is accomplished by using the community model to generate a number of small graphs $\{C_1, .., C_l\}$ that are combined into a graph G_C using a disjoint union. Next a graph, G_O, is generated by the inter-community model using an initially empty edge set, and the vertex set of G_C. The final graph is then constructed $G = \{V(G_C), E(G_C) \cup E(G_O)\}$ where $V(G_C)$, $E(G_C)$, and $E(G_O)$ are the vertex set for G_C, and the edge sets for G_C and G_O respectively. The process of selecting a model from each population for Step 4 will be described in Section 3.3, but some necessary definitions must first be made in Section 3.2. Figure 1 illustrates the steps above.

The community detection algorithm is responsible only for dividing the initial target graph and informing the final model about how many communities it should create. The evolved model is responsible for deciding how it initializes a graph, in what way it adds nodes, how to connect those nodes, and how many edges to do it with. It should also be noted that the community detection algorithm could be exchanged for any method which divides the original network. In this paper, the algorithm used is the leading eigenvector community detection algorithm [25].

There are some issues for further investigation in the proposed method, in particular the number of communities is dependent on a community detection algorithm external to the GP system. Secondly, the GP system is aware of how the community and inter-community models perform independently, but their interaction is not evaluated. Hence, while a future study will evaluate what the best method for hierarchical model generation is, and further address these issues, this paper represents the first effort at automatically generating these types of models and our preliminary results already outperform existing models.

3.2 Selection and Fitness Evaluation

The fitness functions were designed to compare a target network to the graphs produced by the evolved models, that we call the *active graphs*. Graph models are usually benchmarked by comparing how well they reproduce a particular *feature* of a set of complex networks [4, 23, 35]. There is evidence to suggest that the degree distribution (probability distribution of node degrees), the average geodesic (shortest) path length, and the clustering coefficient (number of triangles) are sufficient to describe nearly all of the diffusive behaviour on a network [2], thus our fitness functions are based on comparing these features between the active and target graph. Our system uses a multi-objective, weighted and normalized, *summed-ranks* strategy [6] to consider multiple features. This multi-objective strategy is simple to use, ranks are easy to compute, it has been shown to perform well in problems of high dimensionality [10], and recently it has been shown to work well on problems of low dimensionality [7, 14, 27].

Summed-ranks works by assigning each individual j a raw fitness value for each objective i. Individuals are then assigned a rank $Rank_{ji}$ with respect to each objective, such that zero is the worst rank. Assuming a maximization problem, the fitness F_j of an individual is defined as:

$$F_j = \frac{\sum_{i \in O} w_i \times Rank_{ji}}{\max(Rank_i)} \tag{1}$$

where O is the set of objectives and w_i is the weight placed at objective i. This is the same formulation given in [6] for their *Weighted Average Ranking* with the addition of a rank normalization by the maximum rank in each objective. The raw fitness objectives are defined as:

$$F_1Raw = |l(G_t) - l(G_a)| \tag{2}$$

$$F_2Raw = [C(G_t) - C(G_a)]^2 \tag{3}$$

$$F_3Raw = D_{G_t,G_a} \tag{4}$$

$$F_4Raw = \frac{1}{|H|}\sum_i \frac{(h_i^t - h_i^a)}{h_i^t + h_i^a} \tag{5}$$

where $l(G_t)$ is the average geodesic path length of the target graph, $l(G_a)$ is the average geodesic path length of an active graph, $C(G_t)$ and $C(G_a)$ are global clustering coefficients of the target and an active graph respectively, and $D_{t,a}$ is the K-S test [9] statistic comparing the degree distribution of the target graph to an active graph. $|H|$ is the number of discrete values in the degree distribution histogram, h_i^t and h_i^a are the ith values in the target network and active graph's degree distributions respectively.

The raw fitnesses are used during evolution in order to compute the ranks of each model. For presentation, they are adjusted to values in the range $[0, 1]$ with a value of 1 being the most desirable. These adjusted fitnesses are computed as follows:

$$F_1 = \left[1 + \left(\frac{F_1Raw}{n}\right)\right]^{-1} \tag{6}$$

$$F_2 = [1 + |C(G_t) - C(G_a)|]^{-1} \tag{7}$$

$$F_3 = 1 - \frac{F_3}{n} \tag{8}$$

$$F_4 = 1 - F_4Raw \tag{9}$$

An adaptive weighting scheme was used that dynamically

adjusts the weights during evolution in order to eliminate the need to manually search for useful objective weights. The rank weight for each objective $i \in O$ at generation t, denoted $w(t)_i$ was computed as:

$$w(t)_i = \frac{\sqrt{1.0 - \overline{F}(t-1)_i}}{\sum_{j \in O} \sqrt{1.0 - \overline{F}(t-1)_j}} \quad (10)$$

where O is the set of objectives, $\overline{F}(t-1)_i$ is the average adjusted fitness value for objective i at generation $t-1$. The value for $w(t)_i$ is used in place of w_i in (1).

When calculating the average geodesic path length, if there was no path between a vertex pair the length of the path was returned as the size of the vertex set, a value larger than any possible path. If the graph was empty, the worst possible fitness values were assigned. As a control to increase the quality of the models generated, evolved models may be executed more than once during evaluation, in this case the model is assigned the average fitness value per objective.

3.3 Construction of The Final Model

From the community and inter-community populations, a set of candidate community models, and a set of candidate inter-community models are evolved. Exactly one model from each pool of candidates is needed to construct the final model, in order to select these models from their respective pools, each candidate from each pool was used to create 30 graphs that were compared to their respective target graphs. The comparisons were used to assign a final fitness value to each candidate community and inter-community model with respect to each objective, i. The models were then ranked according to these values. The rankings were then automatically assigned a weight, α_i, according to:

$$\alpha_i = \frac{\max(\mu_{ji}) - \min(\mu_{ji})}{\sum_{i=1} \max(\mu_{ji}) - \min(\mu_{ji})} \quad (11)$$

where μ_{ji} is the average fitness objective produced by the jth evolved model. Each evolved model j was then assigned a final weighted rank sum, $RankSum_j$, which was used to automatically select a model from each pool to construct the final model (note that this value is used only for candidate model selection and not as a fitness value during evolution). $RankSum_j$ is computed as:

$$RankSum_j = \sum_i \alpha_i \times rank_{ji} \quad (12)$$

where $rank_{ji}$ is the rank of the jth individual with respect to the ith objective. Once the ranking process was completed the median, not the best, model was selected to be used for the final hierarchical model. Selection of the best model often led to selection of a model that was both over-fit, and not representative of the quality of the models the GP system was likely to produce. Thus, in selecting the median model we found our results improved.

3.4 Shape of the GP Tree and Language

Strong typing [21] was used to enforce a specific tree shape, which was evaluated in the following manner. The root node has three branches, each containing a list of actions. One branch for initialization, one branch which defines growth actions, and one branch which describes finalization actions. Operations in the *initialization* branch are responsible for

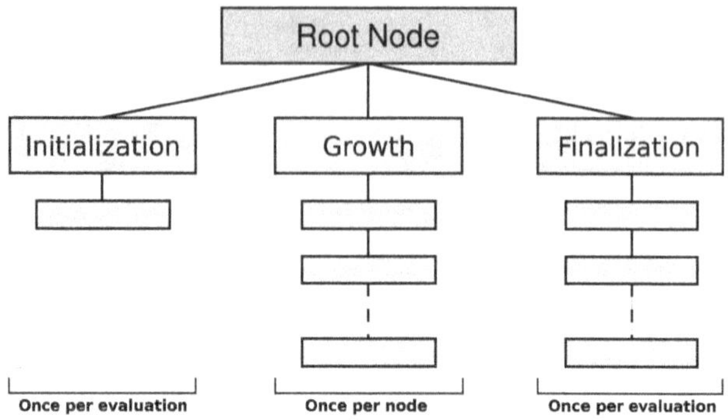

Figure 2: The shape of the trees used by the GP

adding vertices or specifying how vertices are to be added during the graph building process, these actions are executed once per evaluation. *Growth* operations are responsible for adding edges to the graph, and are executed n times per evaluation, where n is the desired number of vertices in the generated network. *Finalization* operations are any operations which require edges and vertices to be present in the graph, edge removal, for example. Figure 2 illustrates the tree structure.

The GP language includes a basic set of math operators, $\{+, -, *, \%\}$, Ephemeral random constants (ERC), boolean functions, $\{AND, OR, TRUE, FALSE\}$, IF structures, and the relational $<$ operator which takes two float arguments and returns a boolean (only the $<$ operator was included because swapping the arguments is equivalent to $>$). It also includes functions for adding and subtracting probabilities via the function $P(float)$ which accepts an argument of type *float*, and converting integer values to probabilities via $P(index)$ which accepts an argument of type *index*. These functions are defined at the end of this section. Initialization actions include a function to add all nodes to the network without any edges, one function to add all nodes and connect them in a ring, and one function to specify that one node is to be added per iteration. Finalization actions include a function to randomly rewire all edges in the network with an equal probability, a function to randomly rewire all edges, and a function to remove edges with a given probability. The terminal set includes *index* and *probability* types of fixed value, the value of the current node degree, the average degree of the active graph, the maximum degree of the active graph, the total vertex count, the final target vertex count, and the edge count of the active graph. There is one additional boolean function which returns true given a probability that can be used in any branch. The remaining growth actions are described below:

- `GROW CREATE_TRIANGLE`: Creates a triangle that includes the current node in the active graph.
- `GROW CONNECT_W_PROB(prob)`: Connect to each node with probability *prob*.
- `GROW CONNECT_RAND`: Connects the current node in the active graph to some random node in the active graph.
- `GROW CONNECT_STUB(prob, bool)`: Connects an edge from the current node to a node that has previously executed `CONNECT_STUB`. Connects nodes to others which have called this function. Nodes are connected to other

nodes probabilistically or randomly according to priority based on the degree of the node being connected to. Once a node has been connected to it is removed from the queue of available nodes. If no nodes were available to the calling node then it is entered into the request queue of nodes available for connection.

- `GROW CONNECT_STUB_PERSIST(Prob, bool)`: Connects an edge as `CONNECT_STUB` does, but it always adds its own request to the request queue and it does not remove any requests it satisfies from the request queue.

- `DUPLICATE(prob)`: Connects the current node to the neighbours of a randomly selected node. With probability p the current node is also connected to the selected node. This is based on models of protein interaction and this behaviour is known to generate an exponential degree distribution [34].

The function $P(index)$ takes an integer value as an argument and returns a floating point value from a pre-defined list at the location specified by $index\ MOD\ L$, where L is the length of the list. If the value of $index$ is negative then the absolute value is used. The function $P(float)$ takes a floating point value and returns a value between $[0, 1]$. If the argument's absolute value is already within that range, it simply returns the absolute value of the argument. If the absolute value of the argument is greater than one then it computes $\lfloor |float| \rfloor$ and behaves in the same way as $P(index)$.

4. EXPERIMENTATION AND RESULTS

In order to ascertain how well the evolved model compares to the WS model and the BA model, the parameters of these models were tuned to fit the given data as well as possible via the methods described in the next subsection. Once the models were fit to the data, they were compared to the cortical network with respect to the average geodesic path length, transitivity, number of paths of all lengths between all node pairs. To do these comparisons 50 graphs were generated with the evolved, BA, and WS models respectively, because graph models are probabilistic in nature.

4.1 Parameter Tuning

The Barabási-Albert model is primarily concerned with matching the degree distribution of real-world networks [4], and so this the feature that we will focus on tuning. There are two parameters that can be adjusted, the power of the preferential attachment α_{BA} and the number of edges added per iteration, m. By adjusting the power we can influence the shape of the degree distribution, and adjusting m will translate it. The two parameters were tuned by a linear search of parameter combinations beginning with $m = 1$, and $\alpha_{BM} = 0.1$ and incrementing them by 1 and 0.1 respectively. Fifty graphs were generated with each parameter combination and the tuning process was terminated when the difference between the cumulative average degree distribution histogram from the fifty graphs and the cortex network was minimized. The difference was measured via the K-S test statistic and the final values chosen were $\alpha_{BA} = 0.3$ and $m = 11$. This combination produced a K-S test statistic of $D = 0.1$ and a *p-value* of 0.9899, indicating this was a very good fit.

In tuning the small-world model the value $p_{rew} = 0.08$ was taken from [36] in which the authors were fitting the same model to the same data, and the number of neighbours for the initial lattice was set at 10 to most closely match the number of edges in the cortex network.

4.2 Evolving A Cortical Model

A hierarchical model was generated as described in Section 3.1. The parameters used to evolve the model are listed in Table 1.

Table 1: GP parameters.

Parameter	Value
Initialization Method	Koza's 'grow' method
Grow Min	3
Grow Max	5
Population Size	200
Generations	150
Selection	Tournament: k=3
Crossover	Subtree Crossover: 0.95
Mutation	Grow: 0.2, linearly decreasing, min depth $= 1$, max depth $= 4$
Runs	50

4.3 Performance of the Evolved Model

The final model constructs communities by initializing them with a ring of nodes, and then proceeds to create dense interconnections via the `DUPLICATE` function, as well creating some heavily connected hubs with the `CONNECT_STUB_PERSIST` function. It then probabilistically connects all pairs of nodes, and finally rewires a portion of the edges. The inter-community model, responsible for joining the communities, connects nodes by triangles and features hubs created again with a combination of the `DUPLICATE` and `CONNECT_STUB_PERSIST` functions, it also adds some edges probabilistically between all nodes. Finally, it probabilistically removes some edges. The combination of these models produces graphs with dense clusters, prominent hubs, and less dense inter-community connections which are joined with hubs. It also features short-cuts in the form of random edges between communities. The evolved model possess features of both WS model as well as the BA model. The average cumulative degree distributions of 50 graphs produced by each model are plotted against the cumulative degree distribution of the cat cortex in Fig. 3. The degree distribution of the WS graphs are clearly dissimilar to the cortical network, while the BA distribution and the evolved model distributions are very similar. A K-S test comparing the evolved model's average degree distribution to the cortical network's gives a test statistic of $D = 0.1053$, with *p-value* of 0.9844 which is similar to the fit of the BA model. Even more striking is how the degree distribution of a single evolved graph looks against the cortical degree distribution, as seen in Fig. 4. The cortical network distribution has degree frequencies which reoccur at almost regular intervals, which is different than the unimodal distributions produced by the BA and WS models. The evolved model is capable of producing these unusual distributions which have reoccurring degree frequencies, similar to the distribution observed in the cortical model.

Tables 2, 3, and 4 show how the models perform with respect to the size of the edge set $|E|$, transitivity (clustering

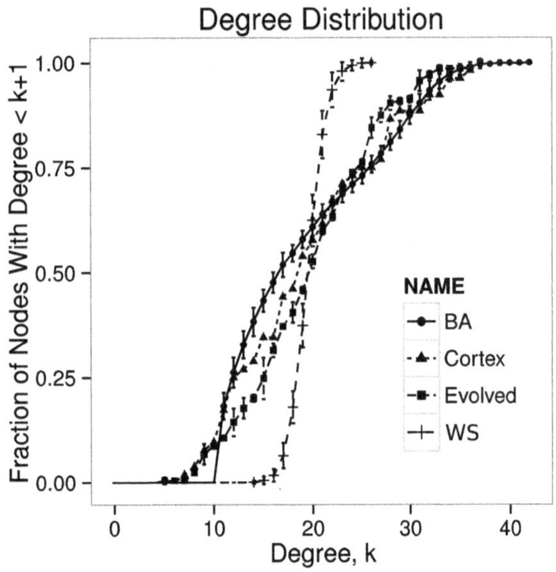

Figure 3: Cumulative degree distributions of the models compared to the cortical network

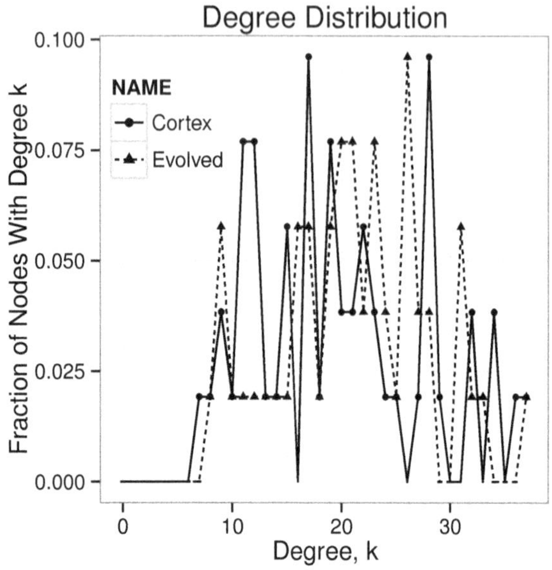

Figure 4: A single degree distribution produced by the evolved model vs. the cortical network

Table 2: Properties of graphs generated by the BA model compared to the cortical network, t.

	Min.	Q1	μ	Q2	Max.	$(\mu - t)^2$
$\|E\|$	506	506	**506**	506	506	$8.10 \cdot 10^{1}$
Trans.	0.47	0.48	**0.49**	0.49	0.50	$9.71 \cdot 10^{-3}$
Diam.	2	3	**2.92**	3	3	$6.40 \cdot 10^{-3}$
Avg. geo.	1.62	1.62	**1.62**	1.62	1.62	$2.48 \cdot 10^{-4}$
Comm.	2	3	**3.52**	4	5	$2.70 \cdot 10^{-1}$

Table 3: Properties of graphs generated by the WS model compared to the cortical network, t.

	Min.	Q1	μ	Q2	Max.	$(\mu - t)^2$
$\|E\|$	520	520	**520**	520	520	$\mathbf{2.50} \cdot 10^{1}$
Trans	0.47	0.52	**0.53**	0.54	0.56	$3.22 \cdot 10^{-3}$
Diam	3	3	**3**	3	3	**0**
Avg. geo.	1.61	1.61	**1.62**	1.62	1.62	$4.30 \cdot 10^{-4}$
Comm.	3	3	**3.72**	4	4	$5.18 \cdot 10^{-1}$

coefficient), diameter, average geodesic path lengths, and the number of communities in the graphs. The far right column shows the squared error between the average values and the values found in the cortical network t. If the error value is bold it means it is at least as small as the smallest error of any of the models. The BA model produces the greatest errors, while the WS model is the closest in terms of edges and is able to consistently match the diameter of the cortical network. However, the evolved model also consistently matches the diameter, and is more similar to the cortical network than the other models with respect to these properties than the other models except the edge count where it falls between the BA and WS models. For reference, the cortical network has $|E_c| = 515$ edges, a transitivity of $C_c = 0.585$, a diameter of 3, an average geodesic path length of $l_c = 1.636$ and 3 communities.

It is thought that the number of alternate shortest paths between any two node pairs (i, j) may have an important impact on information processing within the cortex [36], this value is called the multiplicity, $M_{i,j}$. A good cortical model should be capable of generating similar frequencies of geodesic paths between node pairs. Fig. 5 shows how the average frequency of multiplicity values in 50 graphs generated by each model compare to the cortical network. While all three models reasonably reproduce the frequencies of path lengths of one and two, only the evolved model produces a number of paths of length three comparable to those observed in the cortical network. Longer cortical pathways generally travel between different functional areas of the cortex [36], and in the evolved model graphs they travel between different communities. This is a feature the BA and WS models lack, and it is an important feature of the cortical networks given that these longer paths may be responsible for multisensory modulation and integration [36].

Another property which describes how elements of a network communicate is the betweenness centrality, it is affected by community structure and is an important property with respect to cortical networks [16, 32]. The mean betweenness was measured in the fifty graphs generated by each model, and the average of those scores was then taken. The BA and WS models both generate graphs with average

Table 4: Properties of graphs generated by the evolved model compared to the cortical network, t.

	Min.	Q1	μ	Q2	Max.	$(\mu - t)^2$
$\|E\|$	450	546	**523**	546	546	$6.40 \cdot 10^{1}$
Trans.	0.55	0.55	**0.55**	0.55	0.55	$\mathbf{1.04} \cdot 10^{-3}$
Diam.	3	3	**3**	3	3	**0**
Avg. geo.	1.61	1.61	**1.64**	1.61	1.72	$\mathbf{1.81} \cdot 10^{-5}$
Comm.	3	3	**3**	3	3	**0**

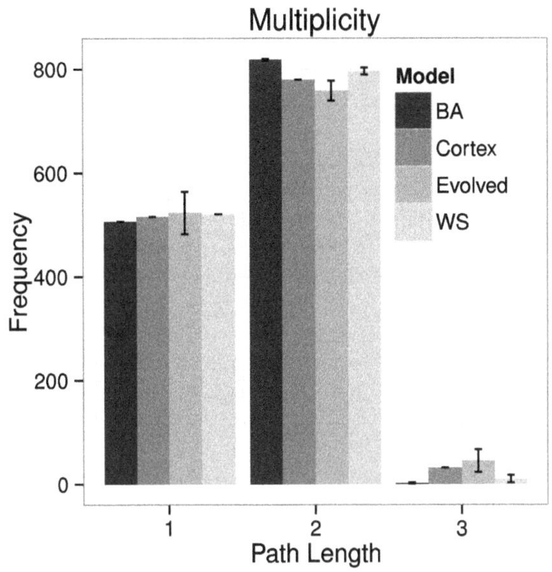

Figure 5: The number of shortest paths between all node pairs i, j in all models versus the cortical network.

betweenness scores more than twice as high as the cortical network, while the evolved model's average betweenness score is within one standard deviation of the cortical network. Table 5 lists the results.

Table 5: Betweenness centrality comparison

Model	μ	σ
Evolved	**16.31**	1.22
BA	37.85	0.144
WS	43.03	0.70
Cortex Mean Betweenness = **16.21**		

Lastly, Figures 6(a), 6(b), 6(c), and 6(d) show the cortical network, and examples of one randomly selected BA, WS and evolved model graph. The node sizes in the plots are proportional to their degree, and the nodes were positioned using the Fruchterman-Reingold algorithm [15]. It is possible to visually distinguish the clustered organization of the cortical network as well as the network generated by the evolved model and how they differ from the BA and WS graphs.

5. CONCLUSION

The cortex is a complicated structure which possesses an inhomogeneous distribution of connections to other cortical areas, with communities of nodes more densely connected than others. This is reflected in the number and length of communication paths through the cortex. The organization of the communication pathways is important to healthy brain function, and classification and modelling of this behaviour has led to advancements in identifying unhealthy or injured brains. However, the important community structure of the cortex is not modelled by existing algorithms in

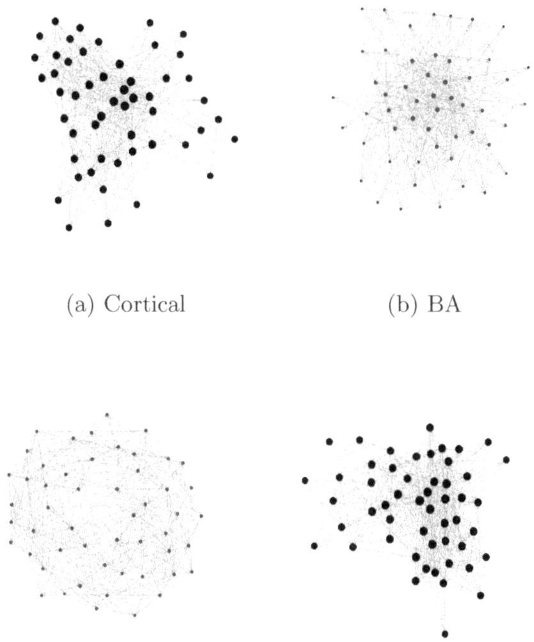

(a) Cortical (b) BA

(c) WS (d) Evolved

Figure 6: The cortical network and a graph generated by each model.

common use and it is unclear how to properly design or select better algorithms. Recent work has shown that GP is a promising method for automatically generating graph models robust to real-world data, such as cortical networks, especially in the case where good algorithms are unknown. This paper proposed the first GP system for the automatic inference of graph models capable of generating graphs which exhibit a strong community structure, and it was applied to infer a model of the cat cerebral cortex.

There are some challenges ahead to improving the process of inferring graph models which exhibit community structure, such as removing the dependence on an algorithm external to the GP. However, the proposed GP was able to evolve a model able to generate graphs more similar to the cortical network than existing models with respect to important features of the cortical network. Future work will focus on improving the process of inferring models of community structure, as well as exploring the breadth of applications which could benefit from the automatic inference of models.

Acknowledgement

The authors would like to thank the anonymous reviewers for their valuable comments.

6. REFERENCES

[1] R. Albert and A. Barabási. Statistical mechanics of complex networks. *Reviews of modern physics*, 74(1):47–97, 2002.

[2] G. M. Ames, D. B. George, C. P. Hampson, A. R. Kanarek, C. D. McBee, D. R. Lockwood, J. D. Achter, and C. T. Webb. Using network properties to predict disease dynamics on human contact networks. *Proc. R. Soc. B*, 2011.

[3] A. Bailey, M. Ventresca, and B. Ombuki-Berman. Automatic generation of graph models for complex networks by genetic programming. GECCO '12, pages 711–718, New York, NY, USA, 2012. ACM.

[4] A. L. Barabási and R. Albert. Emergence of scaling in random networks. *Science (New York, N.Y.)*, 286(5439):509–512, Oct. 1999.

[5] D. S. Bassett, E. Bullmore, B. A. Verchinski, V. S. Mattay, D. R. Weinberger, and A. Meyer-Lindenberg. Hierarchical organization of human cortical networks in health and schizophrenia. *The J. of Neurosci.*, 28(37):9239–9248, 2008.

[6] P. Bentley and J. Wakefield. Finding acceptable solutions in the pareto-optimal range using multiobjective genetic algorithms. In *Soft Computing in Engineering Design and Manufacturing*, pages 231–240. Springer, June 1997.

[7] S. Bergen and B. J. Ross. Aesthetic 3d model evolution. In *Evolutionary and Biologically Inspired Music, Sound, Art and Design*, volume 7247 of *LNCS*, pages 11–22. Springer, 2012.

[8] E. Bullmore and O. Sporns. Complex brain networks: graph theoretical analysis of structural and functional systems. *Nature Rev. Neurosci.*, 10(3):186–198, 2009.

[9] I. Chakravarti, R. Laha, and J. Roy. *Handbook of methods of applied statistics*, volume 1 of *Wiley series in probability and mathematical statistics*. Wiley, 1967.

[10] D. Corne and J. Knowles. Techniques for highly multiobjective optimisation: Some nondominated points are better than others. In *Proc. GECCO 2007*, pages 773–780. ACM Press, 2007.

[11] F. De Vico Fallani, R. Sinatra, L. Astolfi, D. Mattia, F. Cincotti, V. Latora, S. Salinari, M. Marciani, A. Colosimo, and F. Babiloni. Community structure of cortical networks in spinal cord injured patients. Proc. EMBS, pages 3995 –3998, 2008.

[12] S. F. Community detection in graphs. *Phys. Reports*, 486(3-5):75 – 174, 2010.

[13] R. Flack. The robgp genetic programming system, 2011. http://robgp.sourceforge.net/.

[14] R. W. J. Flack and B. J. Ross. Evolution of architectural floor plans. Proc. EvoApplications'11, pages 313–322. Springer-Verlag, 2011.

[15] T. M. J. Fruchterman and E. M. Reingold. Graph drawing by force-directed placement. *Softw. Pract. Exper.*, 21(11):1129–1164, Nov. 1991.

[16] M. Girvan and M. E. J. Newman. Community structure in social and biological networks. *Proceedings of the National Academy of Sciences*, 99(12):7821–7826, 2002.

[17] B. J. He, J. M. Zempel, A. Z. Snyder, and M. E. Raichle. The Temporal Structures and Functional Significance of Scale-free Brain Activity. *Neuron*, 66:353–369, 2000.

[18] Y. He, A. Dagher, Z. Chen, A. Charil, A. Zijdenbos, K. Worsley, and A. Evans. Impaired small-world efficiency in structural cortical networks in multiple sclerosis associated with white matter lesion load. *Brain*, 132(12):3366–3379, Dec. 2009.

[19] S. Hill, W. Y., R. I., S. F., and M. H. Statistical connectivity provides a sufficient foundation for specific functional connectivity in neocortical neural microcircuits. Sept 2012.

[20] M. Kaiser, R. Martin, P. Andras, and M. P. Young. Simulation of robustness against lesions of cortical networks. *Euro. J. of Neurosci.*, 10:3185–3192, 2007.

[21] D. J. Montana. Strongly typed genetic programming. *Evol. Comput.*, 3(2):199–230, June 1995.

[22] T. Nepusz, L. Négyessy, G. Tusnády, and F. Bazsó. Reconstructing cortical networks: Case of directed graphs with high level of reciprocity. In B. Bollobás, R. Kozma, and D. Miklós, editors, *Handbook of Large-Scale Random Networks*, volume 18 of *Bolyai Society Mathematical Studies*, pages 325–368. Springer, 2008.

[23] M. Newman. *Networks: An Introduction.* Oxford University Press, Inc., New York, NY, USA, 2010.

[24] M. E. J. Newman. The structure and function of complex networks. *SIAM Review*, 45:167–256, 2003.

[25] M. E. J. Newman. Modularity and community structure in networks. *PNAS*, 103(23):8577–8582, 2006.

[26] B. J. Prettejohn, M. J. Berryman, and M. D. McDonnell. Methods for generating complex networks with selected structural properties for simulations: A review and tutorial for neuroscientists. *Frontiers in Comp. Neurosci.*, 5:11, 2011.

[27] B. J. Ross. The evolution of higher-level biochemical reaction models. *Genetic Programming and Evolvable Machines*, 13(1):3–31, Mar. 2012.

[28] J. W. Scannell, C. Blakemore, and M. P. Young. Analysis of connectivity in the cat cerebral cortex. *J. of Neurosci.*, 15:1463, 1995.

[29] O. Sporns, C. J. Honey, and R. Kötter. Identification and classification of hubs in brain networks. *PLoS ONE*, 2(10):e1049, 10 2007.

[30] O. Sporns, G. Tononi, and R. Kötter. The human connectome: A structural description of the human brain. *PLoS Comput Biol*, 1(4):e42, 09 2005.

[31] O. Sporns and J. Zwi. The small world of the cerebral cortex. *Neuroinformatics*, 2:145–162, 2004.

[32] C. Stam and J. Reijneveld. Graph theoretical analysis of complex networks in the brain. *Nonlinear Biomedical Physics*, 1(1):3, 2007.

[33] C. J. Stam and E. A. de Bruin. Scale-free dynamics of global functional connectivity in the human brain. *Human Brain Mapping*, 22(2):97–109, 2004.

[34] A. Vazquez, A. Flammini, A. Maritan, and A. Vespignani. Modeling of protein interaction networks. *ComplexUs*, 1:38–44, 2003.

[35] D. J. Watts and S. H. Strogatz. Collective dynamics of 'small-world' networks. *Nature*, 393(6684):440–442, 1998.

[36] G. Zamora-López, C. Zhou, and J. Kurths. Graph analysis of cortical networks reveals complex anatomical communication substrate. *Chaos*, 19(1):015117, 2009.

Efficient Indexing of Similarity Models with Inequality Symbolic Regression

Tomáš Bartoš
Charles University in Prague
Faculty of Mathematics and Physics, SIRET Group
bartos@ksi.mff.cuni.cz

Tomáš Skopal
Charles University in Prague
Faculty of Mathematics and Physics, SIRET Group
skopal@ksi.mff.cuni.cz

Juraj Moško
Charles University in Prague
Faculty of Mathematics and Physics, SIRET Group
mosko@ksi.mff.cuni.cz

ABSTRACT

The increasing amount of available unstructured content introduced a new concept of searching for information - the *content-based retrieval*. The principle behind is that the objects are compared based on their content which is far more complex than simple text or metadata based searching. Many indexing techniques arose to provide an efficient and effective similarity searching. However, these methods are restricted to a specific domain such as the metric space model. If this prerequisite is not fulfilled, indexing cannot be used, while each similarity search query degrades to sequential scanning which is unacceptable for large datasets. Inspired by previous successful results, we decided to apply the principles of *genetic programming* to the area of database indexing. We developed the GP-SIMDEX which is a universal framework that is capable of finding precise and efficient indexing methods for similarity searching for any given similarity data. For this purpose, we introduce the *inequality symbolic regression* principle and show how it helps the GP-SIMDEX Framework to find appropriate results that in most cases outperform the best-known indexing methods.

Categories and Subject Descriptors

H.3 [**Information Storage and Retrieval**]: General; H.3.1 [**Content Analysis and Indexing**]: *Indexing Methods*

General Terms

Algorithms, Performance, Theory

Keywords

Genetic programming, Similarity search, Content based retrieval

1. INTRODUCTION

Finding the right information in large or growing databases within an acceptable time frame is crucial in almost every area. For structured data (e.g., relational databases) and simple unstructured content types such as text documents, the efficient querying methods are known for decades. On the other hand, the currently popular multimedia objects, social network data, biometric, medical or scientific databases, etc. are more difficult to search or explore due to the complexity of the objects stored. Therefore, we use *content-based retrieval* [3, 13], which for querying purposes converts the objects from their native formats to more appropriate forms. It extracts the important information and creates *object descriptors* usable for the searching models.

One of the popular searching methods is *similarity search* [22] which returns the relevant results (i.e., the most similar objects) for any sample query object. To properly rank the results, we need a model of how to specify the relevancy between any pair of objects. Using two object descriptors, we apply the appropriate similarity function that will produce a single numeric value which we can interpret as the degree of similarity between these objects. The choice of the similarity function (or similarity model) is dependent on the type of dataset and application we deal with.

For many applications, the widely known *metric space model* [22] has been considered as the best choice, mainly because of its simplicity and fixed properties such as *identity*, *positivity*, *symmetry*, and especially the *triangle inequality*. The combination of these properties enables to index any database using *metric access methods*, also known as metric indexes [2, 22, 15].

However, with the increased complexity of objects, there appeared similarity models in various domains for which the metric indexing is not sufficient either because it is not precise, lacks some of the anticipated features, or simply does not fit. We describe these models as *nonmetric* [18], as they typically involve some nonmetric similarity functions [20] that violate one or more metric properties.

And here we see the major challenge primarily in terms of querying efficiency. Compared to the metric space model, the nonmetric functions are typically designed to fit to a particular problem or to a specific area, focusing on the searching precision, effective retrieval, robustness or better object description (Figure 1 shows sample similarity models using local features for images [11] and protein structures [6]). As they usually do not contain explicit and fixed properties such as those in metric model, we cannot index the data easily. Because of the lack of a specific indexing technique, the result is that each query degrades to slow sequential scanning which is applicable only to small databases. For larger volumes of data, this approach is unacceptable, as users will not wait hours or days to get their results for a single query.

GECCO'13, July 6–10, 2013, Amsterdam, The Netherlands.

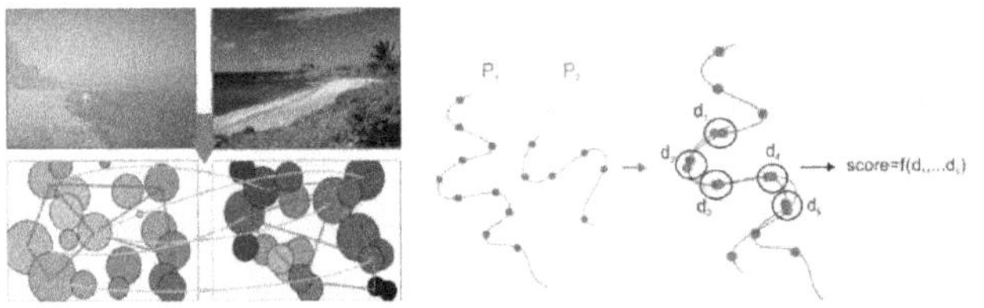

(a) Image similarity (b) Protein similarity

Figure 1: Sample similarity models

As this relates to our research interests, we declare our main objective to find alternative methods for indexing specific or unusual data. We get inspired by the previous research [17, 18, 7] that showed that it is possible to find other models that for some databases might increase the efficiency and provide better results than the metric space model. We also saw a great potential in our recent work [19] in which we suggested to explore the universe of expressions (so called axioms) with the proposed SIMDEX Framework in order to reveal new and unknown indexing possibilities.

We based our research on a similar idea, but we decided to leverage another principle for the exploration, more precisely the *genetic programming* (GP) which is useful for finding relatively good results within the limited time frame. Motivated by the success of Eureqa tool [16] and because a variety of other applications proved GP approach to be valid, we wanted to modify and enrich the previously proposed SIMDEX Framework and replace the exploration phase with the symbolic regression algorithm [9, 8] customized for finding inequalities (see Section 4.2).

Our contribution is twofold depending on the point of view. First, the most beneficial outcome is for the database research community, as we show how to discover new indexing methods for any data sample using GP-SIMDEX, the universal GP-based framework. Moreover, we also implemented the theoretical concept and developed a working prototype. Consequently, other domain experts such as computational biologists could benefit from this as they create models for practically oriented applications using database techniques. Secondly, for GP community we show a particular customized version of the symbolic regression applied to a new domain that delivered successful results.

In the following sections, we will describe the similarity search principles/challenges into more details (Section 2), add the previous related attempts to provide alternatives to the metric space model (Section 3), and precisely describe how GP-SIMDEX Framework differs from them (Section 4) together with the experimental evaluation (Section 5).

2. SIMILARITY SEARCHING

We already introduced similarity searching as one of the content-based retrieval methods applicable to various different areas. The whole concept is based on the extraction of important objects features (*object descriptors*) combined with the similarity measure (also called similarity function) used for querying.

The most popular queries are the *range query* that for a query object q returns all objects o from the database that are similar to the query to some extent (defined by the radius r), and the kNN queries that return k most similar objects to the query object.

The basic task concerning similarity search is to increase the performance of these queries by means of indexing. Compared to traditional relational databases where the I/O cost represents the standard measure of real-time performance, here the major component is assumed to be the number of distance computations used for ranking the database. In this context, distances and similarities are interchangeable – the higher the similarity (s), the lower the distance (δ) between any two objects. For normalized spaces with values in the interval $[0, 1]$, the relation is typically defined as $s = 1 - \delta$ or $\delta = 1 - s$ [22].

With strong focus on the number of distance evaluations, the indexing methods try to leverage the *lowerbounds* which are cheaper measures for distance value estimation. For any lowerbound LB it holds

$$LB(\delta(q,o)) \leq \delta(q,o) \tag{1}$$

where q is the query object, o is a database object, $\delta(q,o)$ is the computed distance between q and o, and LB is its estimation. The tighter (better) the lowerbound is, the more objects it filters out without computing the generally expensive distance $\delta(q,o)$ and thus saving a great amount of time during the query evaluation.

To compute the lowerbound, we very often use reference objects p_i called *pivots* and leverage the precomputed distances between objects and pivots. Several metric access methods such as the *pivot table* [12] apply this approach.

2.1 Metric and Nonmetric Models

Some lowerbounds are easy to compute if a set of preconditions holds. This is true for *metric space model* which assumes distance functions constrained by the metric axioms:

$\delta(x,y) = 0$	$\Leftrightarrow x = y$	identity
$\delta(x,y) > 0$	$\Leftrightarrow x \neq y$	positivity
$\delta(x,y) = \delta(y,x)$		symmetry
$\delta(x,y) + \delta(y,z) \geq \delta(x,z)$		triangle inequality

Table 1: Metric space postulates

Using a single pivot p, we define the Triangle (metric) lowerbound $LB_\triangle$ as

$$LB_\triangle(\delta(q,o)) = |\delta(q,p) - \delta(p,o)| \leq \delta(q,o) \tag{2}$$

The advantage is that the lowerbound is computed quickly, so it is a cheap method of estimating the distance and metric indexing. However, it is limited almost exclusively to metric distances.

Another specific approach is *Ptolemaic indexing* [7, 11], which uses *Ptolemy's inequality* to construct lowerbounds. *Ptolemy's inequality* defines for any four database objects x, y, u, and v the following relation

$$\delta(x,v) \cdot \delta(y,u) \leq \delta(x,y) \cdot \delta(u,v) + \delta(x,u) \cdot \delta(y,v) \tag{3}$$

In order to use this as a lowerbound, the distance function must be *Ptolemaic distance*. This applies when it holds the properties of *identity*, *positivity*, *symmetry*, and satisfies *Ptolemy's inequality*.

To construct the ptolemaic lowerbound ($\mathrm{LB}_{\mathtt{ptol}}$), we first define the candidate bound δ_{C} using two pivots p and s:

$$\delta_{\mathrm{C}}(q,o,p,s) = \frac{|\delta(q,p) \cdot \delta(o,s) - \delta(q,s) \cdot \delta(o,p)|}{\delta(p,s)} \tag{4}$$

For simplicity, we let $\delta_C(q,o,p,s) = 0$ if $\delta(p,s) = 0$. Considering a set of pivots $\mathbb{P}$, we maximize the candidate bound δ_C over all pairs of distinct pivots which results in the final Ptolemaic bound $\text{LB}_{\texttt{ptol}}$:

$$\text{LB}_{\texttt{ptol}}(\delta(q,o)) = \max_{p,s \,\in \mathbb{P}} \delta_C(q,o,p,s) \leq \delta(q,o) \quad (5)$$

The ptolemaic indexing was successfully used with *signature quadratic form distance* [11] that was proved to be suitable for effective matching of image signatures [1].

2.2 Indexing Challenges

If we knew about some specific properties of the given similarity model, it would be easier to propose or create the lowerbounding method for indexing and querying customized for the given scenario. We might or might not be able to achieve this as the similarity model could be really complex. Without any a priori constraints, picking the best indexing method for a general similarity model which assumes only a black-box similarity function with a former unknown universe of object descriptors is a challenging task. Here, the only valuable information we could use is the computed distance between any two arbitrary objects.

Having this in mind, we want to be able to derive insight and some information about the data only through the *distance matrix* – matrix which on ith row and jth column contains the distance $\delta(o_i, o_j)$ between two objects o_i and o_j. This would mean that no previous knowledge of the similarity model is required to provide a good indexing technique for any given data.

Therefore, inspired by the discovery of ptolemaic indexing, and recently introduced SIMDEX Framework, our major goal is to respond to this challenge and create GP-SIMDEX, a universal framework for the efficient similarity searching that will for any input data reveal the best indexing method (a specific lowerbounding inequality, respectively). To be successful means that we are able to provide insight from the data space of the given model only based on the distances between objects. In the later sections, we show the framework concept together with the promising results.

3. RELATED WORK

The idea to deal with the challenges outlined in the previous sections that the application of nonmetric similarity models brings is not completely new. We will describe the previous approaches starting with TriGen algorithm, through the mentioned Ptolemaic indexing, to the recently announced SIMDEX Framework. We also depict the way of how the symbolic regression might help in this situation.

3.1 TriGen Algorithm

One of the very first methods dealing with the nonmetric models was TriGen algorithm [17, 18] which tries to convert the nonmetric similarity spaces to semi-metric or metric ones. Based on a given database sample, the algorithm tunes the modified distance $g(\delta)$ with respect to the rate of non-triangular triplets (T-error). After a fixed number of iterations, the output is the T-modifier for which the intrinsic dimensionality ρ [2] is minimized.

The modified distance $g(\delta)$ determined by TriGen can be immediately employed by the pivot table [22] for exact but slower (T-error is zero; ρ gets bigger) or approximate but fast (T-error is positive, ρ gets smaller) similarity search in the same way as ptolemaic indexing was implemented [11]. Although this idea sounds almost perfect, it is not always the best-case scenario as it might lead to either large retrieval error or low indexability as was later discovered [20].

3.2 Ptolemaic Indexing

A slightly different perspective of how to deal with generally nonmetric distances and the most problematic triangle inequality is the recently introduced concept of Ptolemaic indexing [7, 11] and its fundamentals that we already described in Section 2.1. It shows the conceptual shift – instead of tuning and changing the distance or data to comply with metric space properties, authors find out that it is easier to replace the problematic triangle lowerbounding (Eq. 2) with ptolemaic lowerbounding (Eq. 5). Authors demonstrated its validity using *signature quadratic form distance* [11] for effective matching of image signatures [1]. In experiments, the pivot table with ptolemaic lowerbounding outperformed the corresponding triangle metric variant four times in real-time costs.

However, it is difficult to determine in general which preconditions must be met, so the ptolemaic technique will be better and more efficient than the triangle lowerbounding. This still remains as the open question for future research.

3.3 SIMDEX Framework

To unify and generalize the whole lowerbounding concept, we previously attempted to build a universal framework (called SIMDEX) for axiom exploration [19]. The framework iteratively searches the infinite space of axioms which correspond to expressions that might be used as potential lowerbounds. In the mentioned paper, we introduce the framework at the theoretical layer and show the first preliminary results. However, we do not provide any feedback on the obtained results – there is no verification of found expressions in terms of indexing efficiency. Also, the potential drawback of this approach is in the exploration's iterative method, as it could take long time to discover a meaningful and applicable lowerbound. The perfect situation would be if we were able to provide the exploration algorithm hints of how to quickly find good results.

3.4 Symbolic Regression

Dealing with numeric data together with mathematical expressions, we noticed that similar issues are solved by the *genetic programming* (GP) approach [9], namely the *symbolic regression* [9, 8]. Symbolic regression, also called function identification, is the example of evolutionary algorithms which were introduced to solve computationally intensive problems for which simpler algorithms or random optimizations do not work. In symbolic regression, we deal with independent and dependent variables together with a set of values. The main goal is to find the perfect fit – a perfect model that provides a linear combination of the independent variables with corresponding coefficients that minimizes the measured error rate. If we take the model as the mathematical expression, we can see the parallelism with the SIMDEX Framework mentioned above.

There already exists an implemented solution based on the concepts of symbolic regression which is the software tool Eureqa [16] that revealed and "reinvented" some interesting analytical laws mainly for physics. The idea that comes to the mind is to reuse this tool also for our purposes.

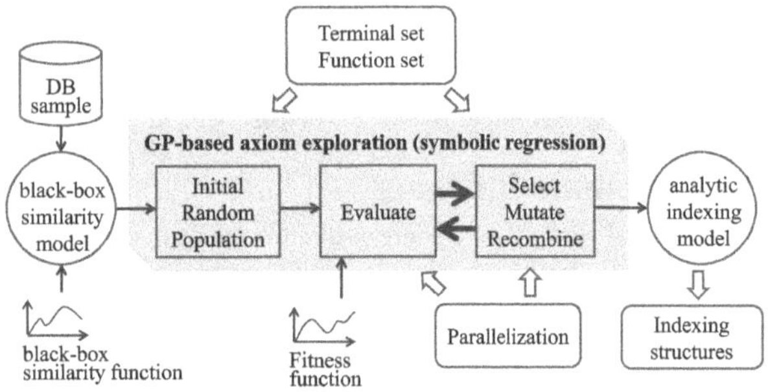

Figure 2: GP-SIMDEX Framework

4. GP-SIMDEX FRAMEWORK

Motivated by the innovation of SIMDEX Framework and inspired by the promising results from Eureqa tool, we decided to combine these two approaches.

However, there are two issues that prevent us from doing so straightforwardly. The first one is that based on the input values, Eureqa tries to find the equation $LB = f(\ldots)$ which will be in our terms a perfect distance estimation that is in most cases unreal to find. So, to be able to use it, we will need to modify it to consider also inequalities. Secondly, there is a problem with the error rate measurement. Generally, the symbolic regression takes the (mean) absolute error. However, during object filtering it is required that the lowerbound is smaller or equal to the real distance. Any occurrence of the situation when $LB(\delta(q,o)) > \delta(q,o)$ leads to incorrect filtering and thus the expression LB cannot be considered as the proper lowerbound.

In order to achieve this, we need to address these issues, and so we incorporate the required modifications. As the result, we develop GP-SIMDEX Framework which is the customized implementation of the original SIMDEX Framework's theoretical concept. It internally uses the inequality symbolic regression (see Section 4.2) to effectively search the infinite universe of lowerbound candidates. In the following sections, we will describe its concepts into more details showing also how it differs from the original SIMDEX.

4.1 Architectural Overview

Looking at Figure 2 which depicts the concept of the GP-SIMDEX we might notice that both the input and output remain unchanged compared to SIMDEX. The input is a particular similarity space which consists of (1) a *black-box similarity function* and (2) a *database sample*. Also, for the exploration purposes we use the corresponding distance matrix obtained by computing the pair-wise distances between objects in the database sample. The output is a set of expressions that might be immediately used as lowerbounds for indexing/filtering purposes. By this point, nothing changed compared to the original SIMDEX Framework.

The first modification is that the Grammar definition [19] is replaced by the terminal and the function set, so it better corresponds to the genetic programming principles [9]. As the terminal set, we choose real-valued and integer numeric constants together with distance expressions $\delta(\cdot,\cdot)$. The function set consists of unary (e.g., `abs`, `sqr`) and binary (e.g., `min`, `max`, `+`, `-`) operations.

4.2 Inequality Symbolic Regression (ISR)

The major difference is in the concept of the whole expression discovery method. The newly proposed exploration phase uses a customized algorithm of *inequality symbolic regression* while it still conforms to the rules of genetic programming. Starting with the initial population of randomly generated mathematical expressions $\{LB\}_i$ (with limited complexity), the resulting set evolves with each next generation (iteration of the program).

After a new generation is composed, it is evaluated using the evaluation function on the distance matrix. In our case, we implemented two different options: (a) evaluate all n-tuples for each candidate expression where n denotes number of variables within the expression; or (b) evaluate a fixed number of randomly selected n-tuples. The latter method does not fully cover the database sample but it is faster.

To quickly determine and dismiss inappropriate candidates, we check for *lowerbound correctness* which means that all results comply with $LB(\delta(q,o)) \leq \delta(q,o)$. We also do not consider and skip candidates for which $LB \leq 0$, as their power to filter out any objects during query evaluation is minimal or none.

To proceed, we need to implement a specific error measure. We try to minimize the average difference between the lowerbound value and the real (computed) distance for all tuples t in the set of tuples to be tested T:

$$\texttt{minimize}\left(\frac{1}{|T|}\sum_{t\in T}(\delta(q,o) - LB(t))\right) \qquad (6)$$

where $\delta(q,o)$ is the computed distance between the query q and object o variables for which we get values from a given tuple t. The expression $LB(t)$ corresponds to the lowerbound computed based on the values from the same tuple. However, any negative result should immediately inform us that the candidate LB must be dismissed from the result set, as it provides incorrect lowerbound.

Next, we provide three selection methods of how to determine which individuals will participate in the genetic operations. We implemented the *tournament selection* [9, 10] with enabled re-selection, *stochastic sampling with replacement* [21], and *stochastic universal sampling* [21] to build the intermediate population.

For the selection purposes, we use a specific version of the fitness function. The generic fitness value corresponds to:

$$fitness = \frac{\texttt{SuccessRatio}}{\texttt{AvgDifference}} \qquad (7)$$

where `SuccessRatio` is the percentage of successful tuple evaluations, and `AvgDifference` is the average difference between the real distance and the tested lowerbound (see Eq. 6). Because higher fitness values are better, it is easy to observe that we try to maximize the `SuccessRatio` while minimizing the `AvgDifference` which follows our interest.

After selecting the proper individuals (candidate expressions), we perform the genetic operations. We apply standard operations [10, 14] based on the given probabilities:

- **Mutation** (with probability $\mathcal{P}_M$) that picks a random node in the expression tree of an individual (except for the root) and replaces the node's subtree with a new random expression tree

- **Crossover** (with probability $\mathcal{P}_C$) that randomly selects two nodes in expression trees of two individuals (except for the root) and mutually swap their subtrees.
- **Reproduction** (with probability $\mathcal{P}_R$) that chooses the individual that will be reproduced without any further modifications to the next generation
- **Alter-Architecture** (with probability $\mathcal{P}_A$) that selects a random node in the expression tree of an individual and changes the operator in the unary/binary function or replaces the terminal (numeric constant or distance)

Outputs of these operations provide us the next generation which is ready for the next iteration of evaluation and selection processes.

At all times, we maintain a set[1] of top `10` individuals with the highest fitness values – the best-so-far results. After the given number of generations is processed, this set contains the best individuals that we validate with the indexing/querying tests and compare on the large datasets between each other and to the metric/ptolemaic methods.

Although not implemented yet, we plan to apply *island-population model* [4, 5] to further parallelize the computations and to implant it to multiple distributed servers. Currently, we operate in multi-threading environment only.

5. EXPERIMENTAL EVALUATIONS

The previously introduced concept of GP-SIMDEX Framework seems perfect in theory. However, to verify its usability in practice, we extensively tested it applying the implemented prototype to the real-world datasets. Although we focus our research primarily on similarity models in which indexing and querying with metric postulates produce notable errors, we employed similarity models which involved nonmetric distances and also show how the framework behaves in metric spaces.

During the experiments, we traced several parameters in order to find out how vital GP-SIMDEX is, namely

- **Fitness evolution** – how the fitness value of the best-so-far individual changes over time
- **Average Precision** – during the query evaluation using a chosen lowerbounding method, we study the precision averaged over all queries. We understand the precision as the *success rate* which is the number of items in the query result identical to items in the result from sequential (SEQ) scan divided by the total number of items in the query result.
- **Average DC ratio** – we take the average number of distance computations (DCs) compared to the DCs produced by the SEQ scanning. The reason why we select the average number of distance computations is that it is a relatively good measurement for query efficiency not dependent on the hardware used.

Note that in our paper, we do not study whether the similarity model is valid and whether the resulting items make any sense. We suppose that the SEQ scan always returns good results and take them as ground truth.

[1]For efficiency purposes we implemented the set as the heap with the minimal fitness value in the root

Regarding the datasets, we tested more than 10 different similarity models on different data. However, for presenting results, we pick two representational datasets that provided the most promising results. More precisely, we depict results for *PolygonSet* (a synthetic dataset of 250,000 polygons in 2D space, each consisting of 5 to 15 vertices) with Hausdorff distance using L_2 as the ground distance, and color histograms from *Corel Image Features*[2] with nonmetric Jeffrey Divergence distance measure [20]. While the first dataset is representational for metric similarity models, the other one belongs to nonmetric ones.

For the experimental evaluations, we created a distance matrix for each dataset by computing pair-wise distances between 1,000 randomly selected objects from the database.

5.1 Framework Settings

Before we present the results, we will provide background information about framework settings we used to get the results we are presenting.

The function set consists of unary functions (`abs`, `sqr`[3]) and the binary functions (`min`, `max`, `+`, `-`, `*`, `/`).

As the terminal set, we use distances between random pairs of six independent database objects (query q, object o, and pivots $p_1 - p_4$) and random numeric constants from the interval [-5,5].

Regarding ISR settings, we use the population size of 800 individuals with limited complexity (the maximal depth of all initial expression trees is six levels) that evolve in 1,000 generations using the standard tournament selection with reselection enabled as it provides the best results compared to others. The genetic operations occurred with probabilities: $\mathcal{P}_M = 5\%$, $\mathcal{P}_R = 10\%$, $\mathcal{P}_A = 10\%$, and $\mathcal{P}_C = 75\%$.

We generate the initial population iteratively by randomly building the expression trees with respect to the terminal and function sets together with limited complexity settings. We do not put any further restrictions on creating the expressions.

As the evaluation function, we apply the random sampling of n-tuples with a fixed number of 8,000 tuples for each n which corresponds to the number of independent variables in an expression. We enable the lowerbound correctness testing (see Section 4.2).

Because we are interested in tight lowerbounds (which we expect to be most powerful in the distance estimations and object filtering), we put a strong focus on the value of the average difference (see `AvgDifference` in Eq. 7). Therefore we define the fitness function as

$$fitness = \frac{\texttt{SuccessRatio}}{5 \cdot \texttt{AvgDifference}} \qquad (8)$$

For completeness, we accept only lowerbound candidates with 100% success ratio and use a maximal number of 100 threads for ISR evaluation.

5.2 Fitness Evolution

Our first task is to track how the candidates evolve during the time in subsequent generations. For this purpose, we log and audit the fitness values of the best-so-far candidate lowerbounds. This provides us a good feedback whether the evolution is converging to a better result, or whether it is just randomly testing lowerbound expressions.

[2]http://kdd.ics.uci.edu/databases/CorelFeatures/CorelFeatures

[3]$sqr(x) = x^2$

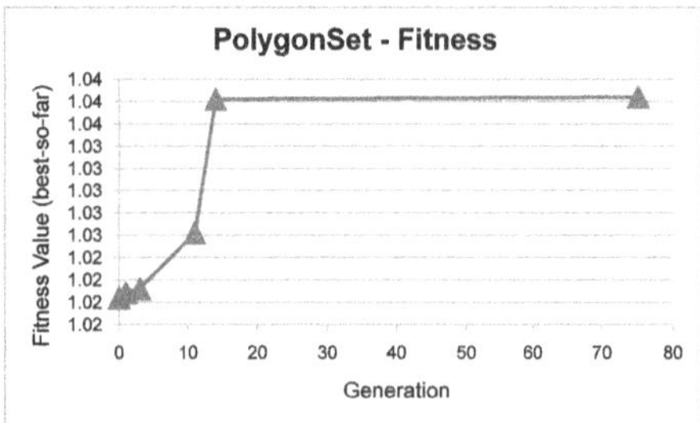

Figure 3: PolygonSet - best fitness value evolution

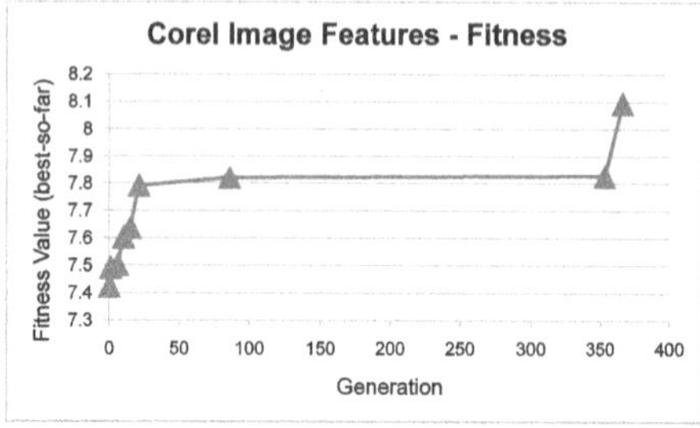

Figure 4: Corel Image Features - best fitness value evolution

5.2.1 PolygonSet Fitness Evolution

In Figure 3 we study the fitness evolution for the dataset *PolygonSet*. Although it might not be clear, we notice that in the 14th generation our framework rediscover (as the candidate #6) the triangle lowerbound $LB_{\triangle}$ (see Eq. 2) which is the best-known indexing method for general metric spaces.

However, in the 75th generation, it slightly improves the fitness value by finding the lowerbound #5:

$$\delta(q,o) \geq \left| min\left(2.3192, \frac{-4.9608}{\delta(o,p_1)^2}\right) - (\delta(o,p_2) - \delta(p_2,q)) \right|$$

Within the top 10 individuals, we might find also interesting lowerbound #10 with similar fitness value as $LB_{\triangle}$:

$$\delta(q,o) \geq |min\left(\delta(p_2,p_1) \cdot 3.2683, \delta(o,p_1) - \delta(p_1,q)\right)|$$

5.2.2 Corel Image Features Fitness Evolution

For the nonmetric similarity model represented by *Corel Image Features*, we depict the fitness evolution in Figure 4. We highlight two generations (21 and 366) in which the huge improvements occur.

The responsibility for these improvements hold the following candidates, namely the lowerbound #49:

$$\delta(q,o) \geq min\left(\frac{\delta(p_1,q) \cdot (\delta(o,p_2) - \delta(p_2,q))^2}{2.0993}, \delta(o,p_3)\right)$$

and the lowerbound #50:

$$\delta(q,o) \geq min\left(\left|\frac{\delta(o,p_1) - \delta(p_1,q)}{max(4.3194, \delta(p_2,q))}\right|, \delta(q,p_1)\right)$$

In the following section, we will explain how the previously discovered lowerbounds act in the indexing tasks.

5.3 Indexing Performance

To verify the outcomes (resulting lowerbounds), we run several indexing tests using Pivot Table indexing method with 10 pivots. We employ the lowerbounds in the same way as ptolemaic indexing has been applied [11].

To evaluate the effectiveness of the lowerbounds, we compared the newly found lowerbound expressions with traditional triangle and ptolemaic lowerbounds.

We focus our observation on (1) the number of distance computations of the lowerbound method, (2) the number of distance computations of the sequential scan, (3) the error rate, and (4) the precision (see Section 5).

We performed 100 randomly chosen kNN queries with $k = 10$ and averaged the results over three database sizes (100,000; 150,000; and 200,000) for *PolygonSet* and over two database sizes (10,000 and 20,000) for *Corel Image Features*.

5.3.1 PolygonSet Indexing

Because we use L_2 distance [22] as the ground distance for Hausdorff distance, the resulting similarity space is metric. We observe this fact in Figure 7 which shows how the precision relates to the average DC ratio. The Triangle lowerbounding provides 100% precision together with the dramatic improvement of the number of DCs. We admit that the Ptolemaic method is faster but it provides a critically low precision of 49%.

The newly discovered lowerbound #10 performs in our environment with the same results as the Triangle lowerbound. The other lowerbounding method #5 shows slightly better performance than the previous two techniques but the improvements are hardly noticeable (see Figure 6).

Due to these representational results and our previous experience, we give the research community the open question whether there is a way of finding any better indexing method for metric spaces than the Triangle lowerbounding. This seems to be very difficult especially for any metric L_p (Minkowski) distances [22].

5.3.2 Corel Image Features Indexing

Because *Corel Image Features* dataset with Jeffrey divergence distance is nonmetric, we also take into account the *TriangleFP* lowerbound which is the triangle lowerbounding modified by the TriGen algorithm. We use 100,000 triplets in 24 iterations to find the best Fractional Power (FP) modifier, and we get FP with the weight $w = 0.802037$; for further details about TriGen algorithm and its settings see [17, 18].

The results depicted in Figure 7 are more interesting than the previous ones. The similarity model is clearly nonmetric (triangle lowerbounding's precision of 48%) and the ptolemaic lowerbounding (with the precision of tiny 24%) does not work neither.

On the other hand, we discover the lowerbound #50 which gives 99.8% precision rate using less than 35% of SEQ scan's DCs. We acknowledge that this is not a perfect fit, however we obtain the lowerbound from a relatively small database sample which indicates a pretty good result.

The other lowerbound #49 acts in this case as the best solution. It provides 100% precision and at the same time it needs only 23.77% of DCs compared to SEQ scanning.

For completeness, we also provide a lowerbound expression which returned 100% success during the exploration phase, however it performs poorly while indexing. This false alarm causes the expression #47:

$$min(2.4454 + min(\delta(p,o), 0.841284 + \delta(q,p)), 0.0407)$$

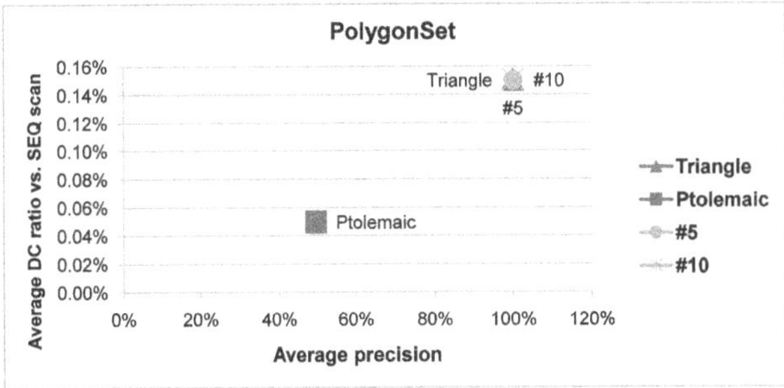

Figure 5: PolygonSet - Average DC ratio compared to Average precision

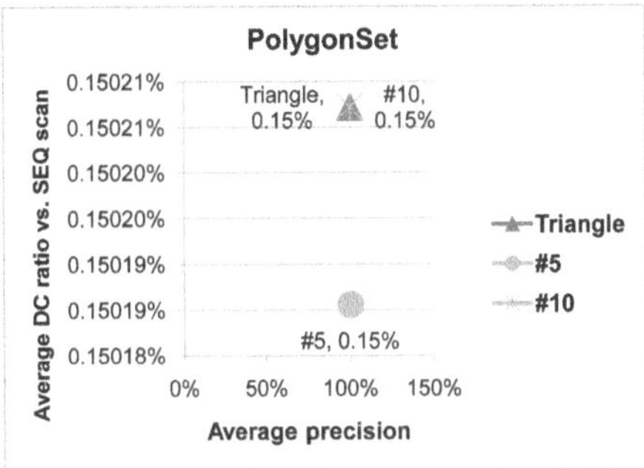

Figure 6: PolygonSet - Detailed Average DC ratio compared to Average precision

Studying Figure 7, we see that this lowerbound returns only 80.75% precision using more than 81% SEQ scan's DCs.

Therefore, the comparison of results from the exploration phase (expression #50 is better than #49 in terms of fitness value evaluations) and indexing test results (lowerbound #49 performs better than #50; inefficiency of #47) shows that the currently used fitness function is not ideal. We will need to make further enhancements to fitness function to disallow the occurrence of such cases.

To properly evaluate the results, we need to compare our results with TriangleFP lowerbounding. TriGen algorithm expressly works here, as this method gives 100% precision while using 24.01% of sequential DCs. This shows the validity of TriGen and that properly configured GP-SIMDEX is capable of finding better results.

6. CONCLUSIONS

In this paper, we deal with database indexing techniques for similarity searching to achieve the efficient and effective content-based retrieval. We focus on nonmetric similarity models in which the metric space postulates are violated, as they occur in multiple popular disciplines such as multimedia retrieval. Although there exist several methods that address the challenges of nonmetric spaces, none of them is a perfect fit for arbitrary data.

We generalize the task of searching for a valid and precise indexing approach to any similarity model, not limited to (non)metric ones. For this purpose, we leverage the principles of genetic programming together with the recently proposed SIMDEX Framework resulting in the implementation of GP-SIMDEX. Our universal framework is capable of

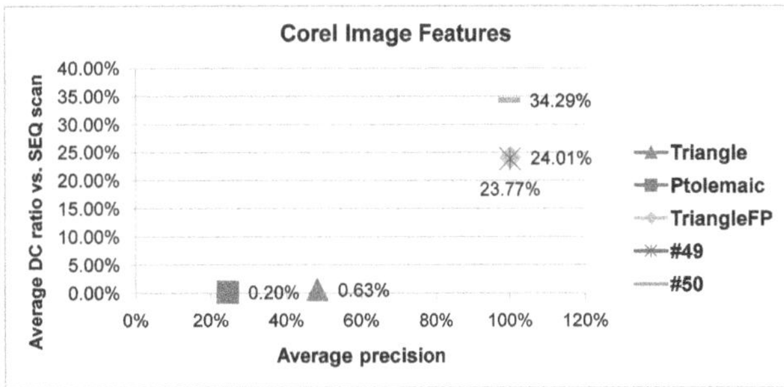

Figure 7: Corel Image Features - Average DC ratio compared to Average precision

exploring any similarity space based only on the given data and a similarity measure in order to provide insight to the model and reveal alternative indexing methods. It internally uses customized inequality symbolic regression algorithm to explore the space of all candidates efficiently. We show its validity by providing a set of discovered indexing methods for various datasets. As these new techniques in most cases outperform the best-known indexing methods, we see a great potential of applying our approach to much wider range of research areas.

6.1 Future Enhancements

All the previously presented results validated the proposed theoretical concept of GP-SIMDEX and verified its usability as the universal framework for finding suitable indexing methods for a given database.

However, we admit, that in order to provide the framework for wider usage, we need to make several enhancements. We would like to address challenges such as

- increase the **efficiency** by applying a higher degree of parallelization using *island-population model* [4, 5]. This will allow us to either evaluate more generations and find better results, or inflate the total size of the function set to be used.

- utilize **architecture scaling** to tens/hundreds of computers using modern Map-Reduce techniques to boost the performance.

- use third-party software tools such as Maxima system[4] to **simplify** all tested mathematical expressions and group them to equivalent classes. This could improve whole performance as we will disable retesting different forms of the same mathematical expression.

- find out how to efficiently **explore equivalent classes** of mathematical expressions and thus provide the feedback for genetic operations, for further evolution, or for next generations.

Nevertheless, we plan to release the beta version of GP-SIMDEX tool for general usage in the near future, so we could get feedback from end-users and to further propagate our research.

[4]http://maxima.sourceforge.net/

7. ACKNOWLEDGMENTS

This research has been supported by Czech Science Foundation (GAČR) project 202/11/0968 together with Grant Agency of Charles University (GAUK) project 567312 and project 910913.

8. REFERENCES

[1] C. Beecks, M. S. Uysal, and T. Seidl. Signature quadratic form distance. In *Proc. ACM International Conference on Image and Video Retrieval*, pages 438–445, 2010.

[2] E. Chávez, G. Navarro, R. Baeza-Yates, and J. L. Marroquín. Searching in metric spaces. *ACM Comp. Surveys*, 33(3):273–321, 2001.

[3] C. Faloutsos, R. Barber, M. Flickner, J. Hafner, W. Niblack, D. Petkovic, and W. Equitz. Efficient and Effective Querying by Image Content. *J. Intell. Inf. Syst.*, 3:231–262, July 1994.

[4] F. Fernandez, G. Spezzano, M. Tomassini, and L. Vanneschi. Parallel genetic programming. In E. Alba, editor, *Parallel Metaheuristics*, Parallel and Distributed Computing, chapter 6, pages 127–153. Wiley-Interscience, Hoboken, New Jersey, USA, 2005.

[5] C. Gagné, M. Parizeau, and M. Dubreuil. A robust master-slave distribution architecture for evolutionary computations. In *Late Breaking Papers, Genetic and Evolutionary Computation COnference (GECCO) 2003*, pages 80–87, July 12-16 2003.

[6] J. Galgonek, D. Hoksza, and T. Skopal. SProt: sphere-based protein structure similarity algorithm. *Proteome Science*, 9:1–12, 2011.

[7] M. L. Hetland. Ptolemaic indexing. `arXiv:0911.4384 [cs.DS]`, 2009.

[8] J.W.Davidson, D.A.Savic, and G.A.Walters. Symbolic and numerical regression: experiments and applications. *Information Sciences*, 150(1-2):95 – 117, 2003.

[9] J. R. Koza. *Genetic programming.* MIT Press, Cambridge, MA, USA, 1992.

[10] J. R. Koza and R. Poli. Genetic programming. In *Search Methodologies: Introductory Tutorials in Optimization and Decision Support Techniques*, chapter 5, pages 127–164. Springer, 2005.

[11] J. Lokoč, M. Hetland, T. Skopal, and C. Beecks. Ptolemaic indexing of the signature quadratic form distance. In *Proc. of the 4th Int. Conf. on SImilarity Search and APplications*, pages 9–16. ACM, 2011.

[12] G. Navarro. Analyzing metric space indexes: What for? In *IEEE SISAP 2009*, pages 3–10, 2009.

[13] W. Niblack, R. Barber, W. Equitz, M. Flickner, E. H. Glasman, D. Petkovic, P. Yanker, C. Faloutsos, and G. Taubin. The QBIC Project: Querying Images by Content, Using Color, Texture, and Shape. In *Storage and Retrieval for Image and Video Databases (SPIE)'93*, pages 173–187, 1993.

[14] R. Poli, W. B. Langdon, N. F. Mcphee, and J. R. Koza. Genetic programming an introductory tutorial and a survey of techniques and applications. Technical report, 2007.

[15] H. Samet. *Foundations of Multidimensional and Metric Data Structures.* Morgan Kaufmann Publishers Inc., USA, 2005.

[16] M. Schmidt and H. Lipson. Distilling free-form natural laws from experimental data. *Science*, 324(5923):81–5, 2009.

[17] T. Skopal. On fast non-metric similarity search by metric access methods. In *Proc. 10th International Conf. on Extending Database Technology (EDBT'06)*, LNCS 3896, pages 718–736. Springer, 2006.

[18] T. Skopal. Unified framework for fast exact and approximate search in dissimilarity spaces. *ACM Transactions on Database Systems*, 32(4):1–46, 2007.

[19] T. Skopal and T. Bartoš. Algorithmic Exploration of Axiom Spaces for Efficient Similarity Search at Large Scale. In *Similarity Search and Applications*, LNCS, 7404, pages 40–53. Springer, 2012.

[20] T. Skopal and B. Bustos. On nonmetric similarity search problems in complex domains. *ACM Comp. Surv.*, 43:1–50, 2011.

[21] D. Whitley. A genetic algorithm tutorial, 1993.

[22] P. Zezula, G. Amato, V. Dohnal, and M. Batko. *Similarity Search: The Metric Space Approach.* Advances in Database Systems. Springer-Verlag, USA, 2005.

Table 1: The dimensions of Tartarus test cases.

Dimension	Initial Placement Bounds of Agent	Blocks	Cases
4	2×2	2	120
5	3×3	3	5040
6	4×4	6	320,320
7	5×5	9	130,750,400
8	6×6	12	1.20×10^{11}
9	7×7	17	18.32×10^{14}
10	8×8	22	1.35×10^{19}

tal feedback [2, 4]. Alternatively, finite state machines have been used, often augmenting each state with classifiers to map the large input space into one more manageable for a finite state machine [1, 3, 5, 9]. More recent work has focused upon recurrent neural networks [7, 8] and gene regulatory networks [18] to model the decision making of the agent.

The best recorded performance on the Tartarus problem appears to through an agent-based solution that incrementally builds a map of the environment and uses this map to continually update a sequence of movements [6]. However, this approach uses additional information (specifically, the successful or failed movement of a block) that is not available in the standard definition of the Tartarus problem, so these results are not directly comparable. Of the examples that use sensory input as the only environmental feedback, ISAc lists appear to continually offer the best performance.

3. GENETIC PROGRAMMING AND THE TARTARUS PROBLEM

Previous work would suggest that genetic programming methods are not well-suited to solving the Tartarus problem [15, 16]. However, it is important to note that the goal of Teller's original work was not to find an 'optimal' agent for the Tartarus problem, but rather to demonstrate the ability of GP to manipulate state through indexed memory. As such, the true performance of genetic programming on Tartarus remains an open question. In this section, this original representation will be described, and the basic performance demonstrated.

3.1 Standard Parse Tree Representation

Teller's representation uses a fairly standard parse tree representation with an automatically defined function (ADF) with two arguments [11]. In addition to the parse tree, each individual has access to an indexed array of memory of length M=20. Each element in the array can take on values in the range [0,19], and can be retrieved and updated through operations embedded in the parse tree (see Table 2).

The available terminals for the parse tree are operators to access sensor state (Upper Middle, Upper Right, ... , Upper Left), or the constants 0..19. The operators are described in Table 2. For the most part, these are fairly typical operators for a GP representation. The READ and WRITE operators are the exception, in that they manipulate the indexed memory array. The WRITE operator alters the indexed memory, meaning that it imparts side-effects when executed, so care is needed with its use. Teller spends considerable time defining the actions of the WRITE operator, and makes particular emphasis of the fact that it returns the old value from memory before it is overwritten with the new value [15].

With a couple of exceptions, initialisation and offspring generation in Teller's representation operated in a manner typical of canonical GP [10]. Initialisation was through a ramped half and half process, however the probabilities attached to each operator varied: preference was given to calling the ADF in the main tree, and to the use of sensor terminals. In the ADF tree, the ADF arguments were biased over the other terminals. It was argued that this did not distort the initialisation of trees unfairly [15]. Although never expressly mentioned, it was assumed that crossover was performed with uniform selection of crossover points. Mutation was performed as a point mutation operator, which changed the operation performed at a given node with uniform probability. If the arity of the operation changed through mutation, subtrees were generated or deleted as required.

3.2 Performance of Teller's Representation

The original Teller representation was run under a configuration as close as possible to that defined in the original work. The population size was 800 individuals, and 100 generations per run were performed. Selection was via fitness proportionate methods, but the units of fitness were never clearly defined. For selection probability, we assumed the raw fitness of the individual in terms of its mean score on the applied training cases. No elitism was used, and 40 test cases were generated (without replacement) for each generation. New test cases are generated for each generation to avoid overfitting the agent's behaviour to a small sample of fixed cases.

The described GP configuration was run 100 times to form an average statistic. To provide a point of comparison, the same generational strategy was applied to the evolution of fixed patterns (similar to that in [2]) and ISAc lists. Also, a random agent, one that uses uniform sampling to pick its next action, was run to obtain a null model for performance. The fixed pattern representation consisted of a string of length 80 that contained the sequence of actions that the agent would execute upon any test case that it encountered. A two-point crossover was applied to the fixed pattern representation, and after crossover a mutation operator was applied (with probability 0.4) that picked a single element of the string at random and replaced it with a random action.

The average measurements of these runs are presented in Figure 2. The shaded area around each plot represents the 99% confidence interval around the measured statistic. Before proceeding with interpretation, it must be acknowledged that the results for Teller's representation appear to be slightly worse than those presented in [15]. It is assumed that this is a product of a larger sample size (100 runs versus 10) combined with the fact that some details about selection and fitness are missing from the original work [15]. As shown in §5.1, the framework used in this paper is able to recreate the results from other papers, so confidence is placed in the results presented here. Also, as the same framework is used across all the results, comparisons between them are valid (which is the main emphasis here).

The results presented in Figure 2 raise some interesting points; as expected, ISAc lists are able to significantly outperform Teller's original representation. What is surprising is that fixed patterns of behaviour also outperform Teller's

Table 2: The set of operators used in the original parse tree representation [15].

Operator	Description
ADD(x, y)	Returns the addition of the results of executing subtrees x and y. Addition is done with an upper limit of M-1.
SUB(x, y)	Returns the difference between the results of executing subtrees x and y. Subtraction is done with a lower limit of zero.
IF-THEN-ELSE(x, y, z)	If the result of executing subtree x is greater than zero, then return the result of executing subtree y, otherwise return the result of executing subtree z.
EQ(x, y)	Returns 1 if the result of executing subtree x is equal to the result of executing subtree y, otherwise returns 0.
LESS(x, y)	Returns 1 if the result of executing subtree x is less than the result of executing subtree y, otherwise returns 0.
OR(x, y)	Returns the larger result of executing subtrees x and y.
NOT(x)	Returns 1 if the result of executing subtree x is zero, otherwise returns 0.
READ(x)	Returns the current value in memory indexed by the result of executing subtree x.
WRITE(x, y)	Returns the current value in memory indexed by the result of executing subtree x, and then overwrites this value with the result of executing subtree y.

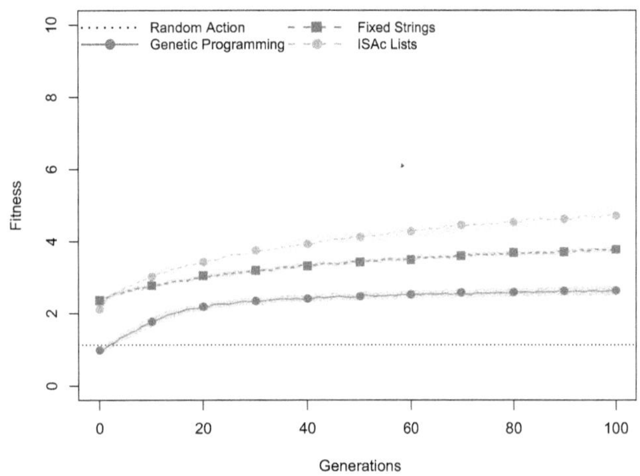

Figure 2: Relative performance of Teller's representation on the Tartarus problem.

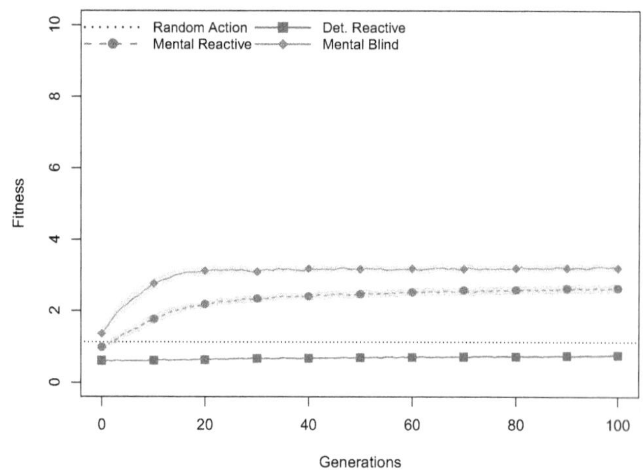

Figure 3: Performance of Teller's representation when memory or sensor information is removed.

representation. This is surprising because in [15] it is suggested that the agents being evolved are essentially developing generators for fixed patterns of behaviour. However, the results here suggest that they cannot reach the same level of fitness as a string-based genetic algorithm evolving fixed patterns, suggesting that something is hindering the ability of the agent to search for fixed pattern generators.

4. ANALYSIS OF GP REPRESENTATION

In addition to developing the 'mental reactive' agent representation, Teller explored several derivatives of the representation, where features were removed to explain their contribution to the overall behaviour. One of these configurations, the 'deterministic reactive' agent, removes the ability of the agent to access the indexed memory, forcing the agent to operate solely with sensor information. One configuration that was not tested, however, was the 'mental blind' agent, which is one stripped of any ability to access sensor information. Together these two agent types will help to explain the overall behaviour of the 'mental reactive' representation.

The experiments from the previous section were repeated for each of the deterministic reactive and mental blind configurations. All other parameters were held constant. The results of these experiments are shown in Figure 3. As expected, the deterministic reactive agents perform very poorly; without any state to keep track of their movements, they must treat every action as an isolated event. The results of the mental blind agent are interesting; it appears that removing the ability to access sensor information has allowed the agent to perform a better job of creating a fixed pattern generator. This suggests that the way that sensor information is handled in Teller's representation is inefficient: essentially, the sensors cannot contribute enough of a useful signal to overcome the noise that they would add to the fixed pattern generation component of memory.

In the experiments discussed above, the deterministic reactive agents are essentially attempting to evolve a function that maps the input space into a fixed set of actions. A simpler approach to this is to use a genetic algorithm to evolve a string that maps each possible input to a single action, much like evolving a string to generate a fixed pattern of actions. If this simpler approach is able to produce fitter solutions than the deterministic reactive representation, then it suggests that the representation used by Teller is not capable of fully exploiting sensory information.

Another set of experiments were run under the same parameters, but this time using a string representation to evolve a lookup table to respond to sensory input. This representation was a string of actions of length 6561, which corresponds to the number of unique sensory input configurations that they agent may encounter. Each unique combination of sensory input then maps to an index into this string to find the action to execute. Crossover and mutation were implemented as for the fixed pattern representation described earlier. The results presented in Figure 4 confirm our hypothesis; although the lookup table agent does not perform particularly well, it is still able to outperform the deterministic reactive agent by a considerable margin. Although this result suggests that the overall value of the sensor information is probably not as great as the contribution of internal memory, it still highlights the poor job that the Teller representation is doing in terms of extracting what information is available.

In the Tartarus problem discussed so far, sensor information is given arbitrarily as 0=Empty, 1=Block, and 2=Wall. The choice of these values presents some complications for the operators chosen in Teller's representation. For example, consider the parse tree shown in Figure 5. This parse tree considers four out of the eight sensor inputs, and adds them in pairs, then selects the maximum result of these two additions as its output. Problems arise with this parse tree when considering the range of inputs it will encounter. Take, for example, the sample inputs presented Figure 5. The first two inputs are rotations of each other, which may occur if the agent performs a turn action. The last two sets of inputs are also related, as the fourth example is the input the agent might receive after performing a move action after receiving the third input set. What is interesting is that all four configurations will return the same value (2). Therefore, not only can the parse tree not distinguish between vastly different examples of inputs, it also struggles to detect changes in the environment brought about through the agent's own actions. Even if this parse tree was a component in a larger program, it is unlikely that it will contribute much to the decision making process. While this is a somewhat manufactured example, it goes some way to highlighting the problems that Teller's representation may have when performing arithmetic on values that are essentially identifiers, rather than true numbers.

5. A REVISED GP REPRESENTATION FOR TARTARUS

The previous section demonstrates some crucial inadequacies in Teller's representation for the Tartarus problem. Again, it must be stressed that Teller's primary goal was not to find an optimal agent for the Tartarus problem. Nonetheless, an alternative representation is required for genetic programming approaches to Tartarus.

Table 3 presents a set of operators and terminals for an alternative parse tree representation for the Tartarus problem. Immediately, the similarities between this representation and that used for other GP planning problems (e.g., artificial ants) are obvious. Most importantly, the use of sensor information has moved from terminals and into the operators themselves — this is analogous to the IF-FOOD-AHEAD operator used in the artificial ant problem. In the previous section, it was shown that the indexed memory tended towards the chaining together of fixed sequences of behaviour. In the revised representation, this is served, in part, by the PROG2 operator. Unlike the artificial ant problem, the revised representation used here also has access to a memory structure, albeit smaller than the one used in the Teller representation. The reduced size was done in response to recommendations made in [1], which suggested that the memory size used by Teller is many orders

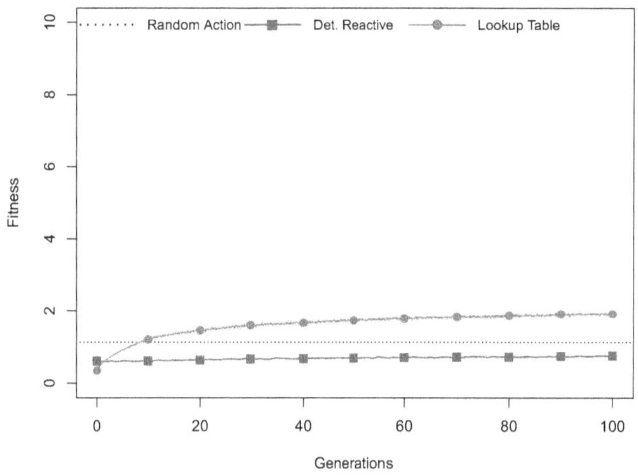

Figure 4: Comparison of the performance of Teller's 'deterministic reactive' agent with that of an agent that evolves a lookup table to determine the response to provided sensory information.

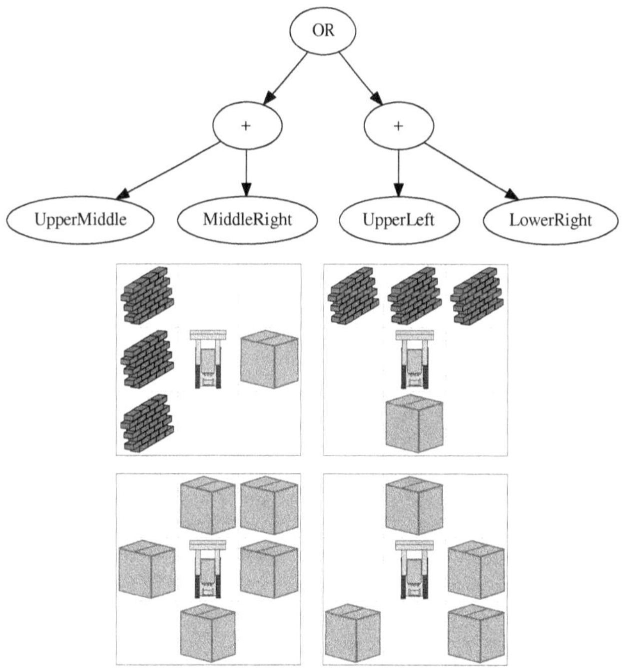

Figure 5: An example parse tree, along with four example configurations that, when supplied as inputs and executed, will produce the same output (2).

Table 3: The set of operators used in the revised parse tree representation.

Operator	Description
PROG2(x, y)	Executes the subtree x, and then returns the result of executing subtree y
IF-*C*-IS-*S*-THEN-ELSE(x, y)	Examines the current state of the sensor cell *C*, and executes the subtree x if this state equals *S*, otherwise the subtree y is executed. $C \in$ { UpperMiddle, UpperRight, MiddleRight, LowerRight, LowerMiddle, LowerLeft, MiddleLeft, UpperLeft } and $S \in$ { Empty, Block, Wall }.
IF-THEN-ELSE(x, y, z)	If the result of executing subtree x is greater than zero, then return the result of executing subtree y, otherwise return the result of executing subtree z.
EQ(x, y)	Returns 1 if the result of executing subtree x is equal to the result of executing subtree y, otherwise returns 0.
NOT(x)	Returns 1 if the result of executing subtree x is zero, otherwise returns 0.
STORE*i*(x)	Executes the subtree x, and stores the result in register *i*. $i \in$ { 1, 2, 3 }.
READ*i*()	Returns the current value in the register *i*. $i \in$ { 1, 2, 3 }.
TurnLeft()	Executes the turn left action on the agent and returns 0.
TurnRight()	Executes the turn left action on the agent and returns 1.
MoveForward()	Executes the move forward action on the agent and returns 2.
Zero()	Returns the constant value 0.
One()	Returns the constant value 1.
Two()	Returns the constant value 2.

of magnitude greater than is needed for the Tartarus problem. Additionally, the means by which memory is accessed is simplified, which is through STORE*i* and READ*i* operators that directly access the memory location *i* without having to execute a subtree to determine the address. In order to make the available memory useful, a mechanism is needed by which program execution can be branched in response to changes in state. To achieve this, the representation provides a simple IF-THEN-ELSE test, and two simple Boolean tests.

Due to the closure requirement in GP, the terminals related to Tartarus actions have their own return value. Ideally, this would not be needed, and a typed system, such as strongly-typed GP, or a grammar-based solution could structure the system in such a way that these return values are not required.

Execution of the revised representation follows a similar strategy to that of the artificial ant problem. While there is time left in the Tartarus environment, the tree is executed, and actions are performed as they are encountered in the tree. If the execution reaches the end of the tree, the pointer is moved back to the root and execution continues. Due to the fact that not all of the terminals perform an action in the Tartarus environment, there is the possibility to generate infinite loops in the execution. To counter this, we set an upper limit of ten complete iterations through the tree. When this limit is reached, the execution of the Tartarus environment halts, regardless of how much time is remaining, and a score for the environment is measured.

Figure 6 demonstrates the performance of the revised representation when evolved under the parameters used in the previous sections. As can be seen, the overall performance is still somewhat poor (this is addressed in the next section), but interestingly, the relative performance of the revised representation appears to be very good. In particular, the revised representation is slightly outperforming ISAc lists.

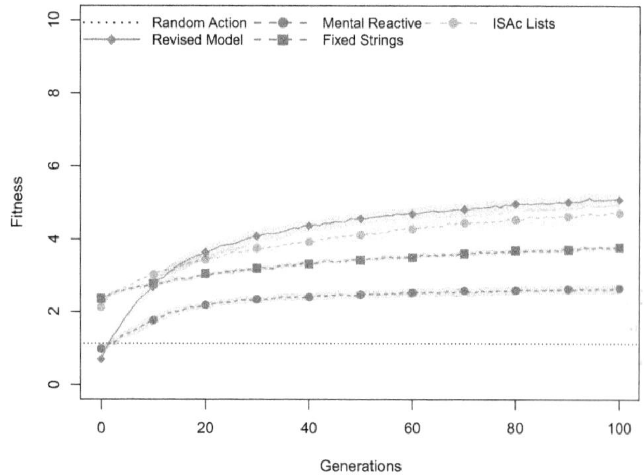

Figure 6: Performance of the revised genetic programming representation in relation to existing methods for the Tartarus problem.

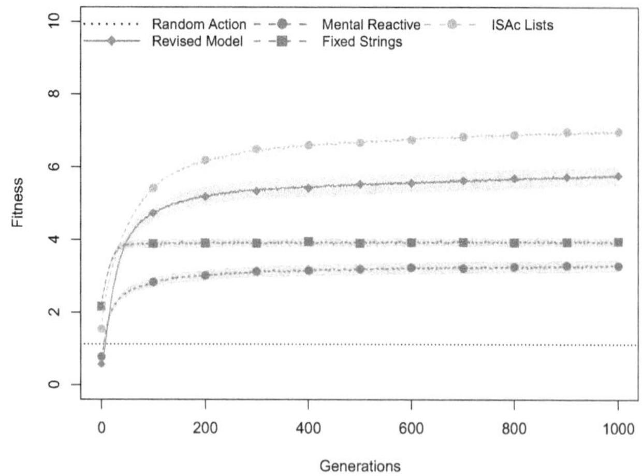

Figure 7: Performance of the revised genetic programming representation in relation to existing methods for the Tartarus problem. A revised generational strategy using a smaller population size and longer runs is adopted in line with previous work.

5.1 Relative Performance

So far, any runs have used the evolutionary strategy outlined in [15]. Subsequent work on Tartarus suggests that the problem is better suited to search using smaller populations running for longer generations. Therefore, the performance of the revised representation, along with that of ISAc lists, fixed action patterns, and Teller's original representation, were tested using a generational method used in [2] and [5].

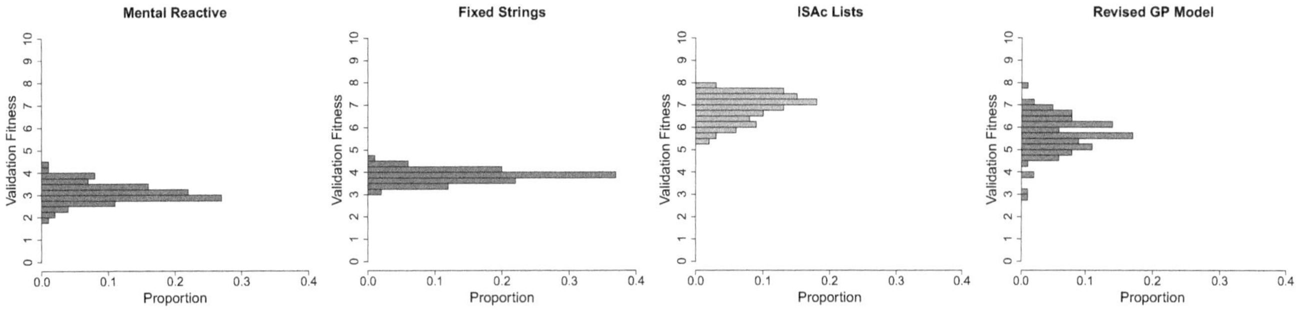

Figure 8: Comparison of validation fitness for each of the examined methods.

Table 4: The quartiles of the validation fitness for each of the examined methods.

Method	0%	25%	50%	75%	100%
Mental reactive	1.91	2.83	3.06	3.33	4.31
Fixed strings	3.23	3.63	3.81	4.01	4.62
ISAc Lists	5.33	6.41	6.98	7.33	7.89
Revised GP	2.95	5.16	5.66	6.23	7.76

Specifically, the following strategy was adopted: a population of 200 individuals was evolved for 1000 generations. Each generation, a set of 100 training cases is randomly selected (without replacement) from the pool of all possible Tartarus starting configurations. All population members are then evaluated on this training set. Then, the population is shuffled into 50 groups of four individuals, and the fittest two of each group are recombined and/or mutated to replace the weakest two. As before, this whole process is repeated 100 times for each algorithm.

The results of this alternative generational strategy are shown in Figure 7. This time, ISAc lists perform much more effectively, and surpass the performance of the revised GP representation. Although not presented here, the revised representation performs at a similar level to Tree-State Machines evolved through the same process [9], and somewhat greater than recurrent neural networks as used in [7, 8].

In each generation of the evolutionary process, 100 new training cases are selected (without replacement) from the pool of all starting configurations. It has been noted in previous work that the variance in fitness between generations using this approach can be large, and so the fitness of the best individual in the final generation may not accurately reflect their behaviour over the entire set of starting cases [2]. To obtain a more accurate measure of this behaviour, a validation fitness was measured for the best individual in the final generation of each run. This was done by applying the best individual to another set of 5000 examples, and reporting the mean fitness over these cases. The same 5000 cases were used across all runs and all algorithms to provide a more accurate comparison. The histograms of these validation fitnesses for each algorithm are shown in Figure 8, and the quartiles of these samples are shown in Table 4. The results demonstrate the superiority of the revised representation over Teller's original model. While the representation is not quite able to perform consistently at the level of ISAc lists, it should be noted that its best performing result is quite close to the best performing ISAc list. This suggests that the representation may have the capacity to perform better when an alternative generation strategy or crossover method is used.

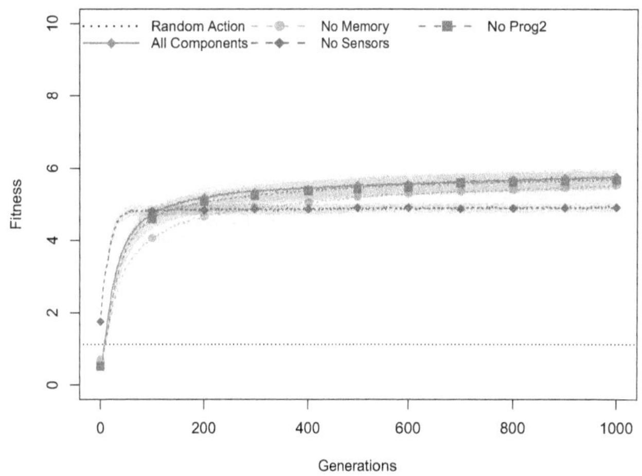

Figure 9: Behavioural contribution of the underlying components of the revised GP representation.

5.2 Contribution of Representation Components

The revised representation consists of three main components — internal state, sensory input, and the ability to concatenate sequences of actions through PROG2 commands. From the results shown in the previous section, it is unclear how much each component contributes to the overall performance of the representation. To determine this contribution, the experiments from the previous section were repeated three times, with each repeat removing one component from the representation. The results of this experimentation are shown in Figure 9. When sensor information is removed from the representation, the representation resorts to building fixed pattern generators, as with Teller's representation. However, this time the performance drop is smaller, relative to the results that include sensor information, suggesting that the representation is indeed making better use of the available environmental information. An interesting observation can be made about memory and PROG2: both of these components appear to be performing a similar job, and so removing either one has only a small impact on overall behaviour. One could make an argument then for removing the PROG2 operator, as it appears to offer slightly less of a contribution than indexed memory. However, the choice was made to keep the PROG2 as an option, as future work on higher dimension Tartarus instances may reveal its increased utility.

6. CONCLUSION

The Tartarus problem presents an interesting benchmark problem for evolutionary computation. Until now, there has been difficulty in identifying a useful representation for the Tartarus problem when using genetic programming. This paper presents a revised representation for GP that allows for reasonable searching of the search space. The representation demonstrates the utility of GP as a method for searching the Tartarus problem, and the results presented suggest that it is a viable candidate as a general purpose benchmark problem.

There are several interesting areas of future research. Obviously, the representation needs to be applied to higher dimension instances of the Tartarus problem. Also, using the representation within other GP models may provide useful insights into the representation's properties.

7. REFERENCES

[1] D. Ashlock and J. Freeman. A pure finite state baseline for tartarus. In *Proceedings of the 2000 Congress on Evolutionary Computation*, pages 1223–1230, 2000.

[2] D. Ashlock and M. Joenks. ISAc lists, A different representation for program induction. In J. R. Koza, W. Banzhaf, K. Chellapilla, K. Deb, M. Dorigo, D. B. Fogel, M. H. Garzon, D. E. Goldberg, H. Iba, and R. Riolo, editors, *Genetic Programming 1998: Proceedings of the Third Annual Conference*, pages 3–10, University of Wisconsin, Madison, Wisconsin, USA, 1998. Morgan Kaufmann.

[3] D. Ashlock and M. McRoberts. A gp-automata reprise of astro teller's bulldozer experiment. Technical report AM97-17, ISU Mathematics, 1998.

[4] D. Ashlock and E. Warner. The geometry of tartarus fitness cases. In J. Wang, editor, *2008 IEEE World Congress on Computational Intelligence*, Hong Kong, 2008. IEEE Computational Intelligence Society, IEEE Press.

[5] D. Ashlock, S. Willson, and N. Leahy. Coevolution and tartarus. In *Proceedings of the 2004 IEEE Congress on Evolutionary Computation*, pages 1618–1624, Portland, Oregon, 2004. IEEE Press.

[6] M. C. J. Bot, N. Urquhart, and K. Chisholm. Agent motion planning with gas enhanced by memory models. In L. Spector, E. D. Goodman, A. Wu, W. Langdon, H.-M. Voigt, M. Gen, S. Sen, M. Dorigo, S. Pezeshk, M. H. Garzon, and E. Burke, editors, *Proceedings of the Genetic and Evolutionary Computation Conference (GECCO-2001)*, pages 227–234, San Francisco, California, USA, 2001. Morgan Kaufmann.

[7] G. Cuccu and F. Gomez. When novelty is not enough. In C. Chio, S. Cagnoni, C. Cotta, M. Ebner, A. Ekárt, A. I. Esparcia-Alcázar, J. J. Merelo, F. Neri, M. Preuss, H. Richter, J. Togelius, and G. N. Yannakakis, editors, *Applications of Evolutionary Computation*, volume 6624 of *Lecture Notes in Computer Science*, pages 234–243. Springer Berlin Heidelberg, 2011.

[8] F. J. Gomez. Sustaining diversity using behavioral information distance. In *Proceedings of the 11th Annual conference on Genetic and evolutionary computation*, GECCO '09, pages 113–120, New York, NY, USA, 2009. ACM.

[9] D. Kim. Analyzing sensor states and internal states in the tartarus problem with tree state machines. In X. Yao, E. Burke, J. A. Lozano, J. Smith, J. J. Merelo-Guervós, J. A. Bullinaria, J. Rowe, P. T. A. Kabán, and H.-P. Schwefel, editors, *Parallel Problem Solving from Nature - PPSN VIII*, volume 3242 of *Lecture Notes in Computer Science*, pages 551–560, Birmingham, UK, 2004. Springer-Verlag.

[10] J. R. Koza. *Genetic Programming: On the Programming of Computers by Means of Natural Selection.* MIT Press, Cambridge, MA, USA, 1992.

[11] J. R. Koza. *Genetic Programming 2 - Automatic Discovery of Reusable Programs.* MIT Press, Cambridge, MA, USA, 1994.

[12] J. McDermott, U.-M. O'Reilly, S. Luke, and D. White. gpbenchmarks.org — problem classification (control/planning problems). `http://www.gpbenchmarks.org/wiki/index.php?title=Problem_Classification#Control.2FPlanning_problems`, Sept. 2012.

[13] J. McDermott, D. R. White, S. Luke, L. Manzoni, M. Castelli, L. Vanneschi, W. Jaskowski, K. Krawiec, R. Harper, K. De Jong, and U.-M. O'Reilly. Genetic programming needs better benchmarks. In *Proceedings of the fourteenth international conference on genetic and evolutionary computation*, GECCO '12, pages 791–798, New York, NY, USA, 2012. ACM.

[14] D. J. Montana. Strongly typed genetic programming. *Evol. Comput.*, 3(2):199–230, June 1995.

[15] A. Teller. The evolution of mental models. In K. E. Kinnear, Jr., editor, *Advances in Genetic Programming*, chapter 9, pages 199–219. MIT Press, 1994.

[16] A. Trenaman. Concurrent genetic programming, tartarus and dancing agents. In R. Poli, P. Nordin, W. B. Langdon, and T. C. Fogarty, editors, *Genetic Programming, Proceedings of EuroGP'99*, volume 1598 of *Lecture Notes in Computer Science*, pages 270–282, Goteborg, Sweden, 1999. Springer-Verlag.

[17] P. A. Whigham. Grammatically-based genetic programming. In J. P. Rosca, editor, *Proceedings of the Workshop on Genetic Programming: From Theory to Real-World Applications*, pages 33–41, Tahoe City, California, USA, 9 July 1995.

[18] P. Zahadat and S. D. Katebi. Tartarus and fractal gene regulatory networks with inputs. *Advances in Complex Systems*, 11(06):803–829, 2008.

Genetic Programming for Edge Detection using Multivariate Density

Wenlong Fu
School of Mathematics, Statistics and Operations Research
Victoria University of Wellington
New Zealand
Wenlong.Fu@msor.vuw.ac.nz

Mark Johnston
School of Mathematics, Statistics and Operations Research
Victoria University of Wellington
New Zealand
Mark.Johnston@msor.vuw.ac.nz

Mengjie Zhang
School of Engineering and Computer Science
Victoria University of Wellington
New Zealand
Mengjie.Zhang@ecs.vuw.ac.nz

ABSTRACT

The combination of local features in edge detection can generally improve detection performance. However, how to effectively combine different basic features remains an open issue and needs to be investigated. Multivariate density is a generalisation of the one-dimensional (univariate) distribution to higher dimensions. In order to effectively construct composite features with multivariate density, a Genetic Programming (GP) system is proposed to evolve Bayesian-based programs. An evolved Bayesian-based program estimates the relevant multivariate density to construct a composite feature. The results of the experiments show that the GP system constructs high-level combined features which substantially improve the detection performance.

Categories and Subject Descriptors

I.4.6.a [**Image Processing and Computer Vision**]: Edge and feature detection; I.2.m.c [**Artificial Intelligence**]: methodologies—*Evolutionary computing and genetic algorithms*

General Terms

Algorithms

Keywords

Genetic Programming, Edge Detection, Bayesian

1. INTRODUCTION

Edge detection has been developed for many years [20, 21, 24]. It is widely applied to computer vision and image analysis, such as object recognition [23], object tracking [28], and image retrieval [17]. Feature extraction is a very important stage in edge detection [22]. Features in edge detection are functions of raw pixel values in an image relative to a local point and are used in the process of classifying pixels as edge points or non-edge points. Since there does not exist a generic model for constructing features for all problems, many approaches have been developed to extract features for detecting edges [4, 21, 24].

Generally, one single feature is often not sufficient to fully identify the edges in an image, and multiple features are used to improve detection performance. For instance, it is difficulty for texture edges to be directly indicated by image gradients [1, 21, 24]. Since different features have their own advantages [24], a combination of features may bring the advantages of each basic feature together. Different machine learning algorithms have been used to combine local features [21]. However, how to efficiently and effectively combine features still needs to be investigated.

Genetic Programming (GP) has been employed for edge detection since at least 1996 [14, 25]. The work on edge detection using GP to construct low-level edge detectors shows that GP can successfully evolve good edge detectors [8, 16, 30]. The limited research in GP for edge detection mainly focuses on the use of directly predefined extracted features.

The overall goal of this paper is to propose a GP system to evolve Bayesian-based programs with multivariate density to construct features for edge detection. Multivariate density is a generalisation of the one-dimensional (univariate) distribution to higher dimensions. Instead of directly constructing composite features by GP, this GP system is proposed to evolve new programs which construct composite features using multivariate density. Here, a simple Bayesian model [5] is employed to do the initial investigation because of its popularity. The simple Bayesian model with a general multivariate normal density is proposed as a function to construct different Bayesian-based programs. Specifically, we would like to investigate the following research objectives:

- whether the evolved Bayesian-based programs are better than directly using the simple Bayesian model to construct edge features;
- what differences exist between the features constructed by GP and the basic features; and
- whether the evolved Bayesian-based programs can be reasonably interpreted.

In the remainder of the paper, Section 2 briefly describes the background. Section 3 proposes the GP system to evolve

GECCO'13, July 6–10, 2013, Amsterdam, The Netherlands.

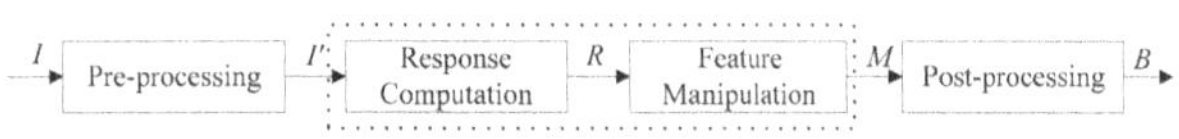

Figure 1: General edge detection flow.

Bayesian-based programs to construct features. After presenting the design of the experiments in Section 4, Section 5 describes the results with discussion. Section 6 draws conclusions and suggests future work directions.

2. BACKGROUND

2.1 Edge Detection

Edge detection usually contains three stages: pre-processing, feature extraction and post-processing [22, 24]. Figure 1 shows a general edge detection process flow. For an image I, an intermediate result I' will be obtained after pre-processing. The pre-processing stage mainly focuses on noise reduction and texture suppression while preserving edges and not blurring boundaries between different areas. The feature extraction stage is divided into two phases, namely response computation and feature manipulation. In the response phase, the computation can come from gradients, and also statistics [19], and a set of features R is obtained. Note that some edge detectors combine the pre-processing and response computation together, such as the image gradients after filtering noise by a Gaussian filter in the Canny detector [3]. In the feature manipulation phase, feature selection [4] and further feature construction [12, 21] are included, and the output is a set of features M. The feature extraction stage is the main and necessary stage in edge detection. The purpose of extracting features is to use them to classify pixels as edge points or non-edge points. After post-processing, a final edge map B is obtained. Post-processing mainly focuses on marking edge points, thinning edges, removing stand-alone edge points and linking broken edge points.

In order to evaluate a feature, different thresholds are used to obtain binary edge maps from the feature. Final edge maps obtained by post-processing techniques (applied to the binary edge maps) are measured by an evaluation method, such as the F-measure technique [21]. In general, the post-processing techniques can usefully follow most feature extraction approaches, such as the surround suppression [12] and non-maximum suppression [3] techniques, thinning operations [18], and linking approaches. The evaluation of the features without using suppression and linking techniques in edge detection is also very important [22] although the performance evaluation usually focuses on final edge maps.

For the sake of simplicity and ease of implementation, feature extraction mainly works on local features. Most local features are based on gradient computation, such as image derivatives [3, 12] or local histogram derivatives [21]. The image derivatives extracted from different directions have been widely applied to different edge detectors [24], such as the popular Canny edge detector [3]. The derivative of a Gaussian filter extracted in the horizontal direction (horizontal edges, not horizontal derivatives) is described in Equation (1), where (u, v) is the position of a point relative to a center pixel, and σ is the parameter. After the convolution ($\circledast$) of an image $I(x, y)$ with the derivative $g_\theta(u, v)$ ($\theta = 0°, 90°$) is performed, the image Gaussian filter derivative $T_{gg,\theta}$ is obtained (see Equation (3)). The rotation-invariant Gaussian gradient T_{gg}, combining the horizontal and vertical derivatives, is defined in Equation (4).

$$g_{0^\circ}(u,v) = -\frac{v}{2\pi\sigma^4}\exp\left(-\frac{u^2+v^2}{2\sigma^2}\right) \quad (1)$$

$$g_{90^\circ}(u,v) = -\frac{v}{2\pi\sigma^4}\exp\left(-\frac{u^2+v^2}{2\sigma^2}\right) \quad (2)$$

$$T_{gg,\theta}(x,y) = g_\theta(u,v) \circledast I(x,y) \quad (3)$$

$$T_{gg}(x,y) = \sqrt{T^2_{gg,0^\circ}(x,y) + T^2_{gg,90^\circ}(x,y)} \quad (4)$$

Image local histogram gradients have shown good performance for detecting edges [21]. The image local histogram gradient is extracted from a direction θ as defined in Equation (5), where pixels around pixel (x, y) in a local area are divided into two groups with the boundary in the direction θ, and $l_{\theta,i}$ and $r_{\theta,i}$ are the number occurrences for the pixels located in the bin i from the two groups, respectively. Since $h_\theta(x, y) \geq 0$, the local histogram gradient T_{hg} (see Equation (6)) is the sum of $h_\theta(x, y)$ in all possible directions. In this paper, the local histogram gradient T_{hg} is combined with the histogram derivatives from two directions as one invariant feature. Different from T_{gg} (constructed based on the horizontal and vertical directions), T_{hg} is constructed with $\theta = 45°, 135°$ so that different directional responses are used. A reason for only using the two directions is that the diagonal derivatives have been found to be more effective than the horizontal and vertical derivatives for detecting edges [7]. Also, for the test image dataset in the Berkeley Segmentation Dataset (BSD) [21], the performance on T_{hg} with $\theta = 45°, 135°$ is almost the same as T_{hg} with $\theta = 0°, 45°, 90°, 135°$.

$$h_\theta(x,y) = \tfrac{1}{2}\sum \frac{(l_{\theta,i} - r_{\theta,i})^2}{l_{\theta,i} + r_{\theta,i}} \quad (5)$$

$$T_{hg} = \sum_\theta h_\theta(x,y) \quad (6)$$

The normalised standard deviation is an indication of the image quality [27]. However, the normalised standard deviation is seldom used as a feature for edge detection in the literature. The local normalised standard deviation is utilised in this paper. It is extracted from a small moving window and is not affected by image rotation. The local normalised standard deviation T_{sd} is defined in Equation (7), where $SD(x, y)$ and $Mean(x, y)$ are the standard deviation and the mean of the pixel (x, y) intensities in a local area around (x, y), respectively.

$$T_{sd}(x,y) = \frac{SD(x,y)}{Mean(x,y)} \quad (7)$$

Image derivatives are popular to extract edge features [1]. However, the local features from derivatives include high responses on non-edge points which are affected by noise or textures. For instance, Figure 2 shows the features of detecting an image from the BSD image dataset with T_{gg}, T_{hg} and T_{sd}. Three different areas are marked with three colour ellipses in the image. The number 1 area includes a partial boundary with low contrast intensities, compared with the whole intensities of the image; the number 2 area includes noise and subjective edges for the different background; and number 3 area includes very low contrast intensities, compared with the intensities of the pixels nearby. Feature T_{gg}

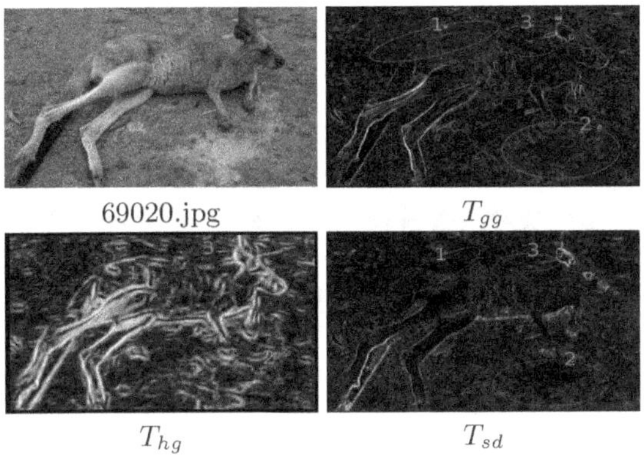

Figure 2: Detected image based on Gaussian gradients T_{gg}, histogram gradients T_{hg} and normalised standard deviations T_{sd}.

has a problem to give strong responses on the edges in the area 1, is affected by noise in the area 2, and only detects few edge points in the area 3. Feature T_{hg} improves the responses on the edges in the area 1, but is also strongly affected by noise in the area 2, and detects a few edge points in the area 3. Feature T_{sd} also has a problem to give strong responses on the edges in the area 1, but is weakly affected by noise in the area 2. T_{sd} finds partial edges in the area 3. Approaches, which efficiently manipulate these local features, need to be employed to improve the detection performance. For instance, the surround suppression technique reduces some texture responses on image gradients [12]. Therefore, we hypothesise that construction of features from basic local features can potentially improve the detection performance.

2.2 Related Work to GP for Edge Detection

Much work in image processing has been done by GP [26], but there is very little work on edge detection. The limited work on GP for edge detection focuses on approximating desired outputs, and finding good detection accuracy.

2.2.1 *Approximating Desired Outputs*

Like symbolic regression problems, GP has been used to approximate desired outputs in edge detection [14]. The first direction is to approximate ideal responses on edge signals. The desired outputs from a set of different step edge signals and noise were employed to evolve one-dimensional filters [14]. The second direction aims at approximating a target edge detector. Assuming the responses from a target edge detector as desired outputs, GP has been employed to evolve similar programs, such as the Sobel detector [15, 13] and a Canny detector [6].

Approximating existing edge detectors or desired signal responses can be considered as regression problems. However, the desired outputs are dependent on the human knowledge for understanding edge responses. Edge features learned from desired outputs (edge responses) only can represent the known (limited) edge information.

2.2.2 *Detection Accuracy*

Edge detection has been considered as a special binary classification problem when edge detectors determine each pixel as an edge point or a non-edge point. Zhang and Rockett [30] used 13×13 windows as patterns to extract features via multi-objective GP, with objectives of Bayesian error, classification error and the number of nodes. In [29], morphological operators erosion and dilation were used as the terminal set and the evolved detectors classify pixels as edge points or non-edge points. Different fitness functions based on the accuracy over all pixels, and the accuracy of training images, against desired outputs were investigated [9, 10].

GP has also been used to design edge detectors for some special tasks. Artificial images were designed to evolve 64-bit digital circuits as edge detectors by GP [11]. To detect object boundaries, some image operators were utilised to combine high-level detectors by GP [16]. In [2], GP programs were designed to find edge pixels in one image. These programs start at a pixel and then "walk" to find edge points.

In summary, the current research on GP for edge detection directly aims at evolving edge detectors or edge features. The limitations for these evolved programs are based on the training data. When the training data is changed, a GP system needs to evolve new programs. If we can evolve a new method based on parameter estimation, it is possible to only estimate the parameters of an evolved program when the training data is changed. In general, the computational cost for parameter estimation is lower than evolving a new program.

3. THE METHOD

This section describes the new GP system to evolve Bayesian-based programs for constructing composite features.

3.1 Terminal Set

In order to conduct an initial investigation on automatic construction of an edge feature using GP, three invariant features are employed as terminals. The three invariant features are the image Gaussian filter gradient T_{gg}, the normalised standard deviation T_{sd}, and the histogram gradient T_{hg} [21]. Since the three features have their own characteristics (see Figure 2), we expect GP to construct new composite features to improve detection performance. In this study, only grayscale images are used. Note that random constants are not included in the terminal set because an evolved program estimates the relevant multivariate density to construct a composite feature, rather than directly using its observations as a feature.

3.2 Function Set

The function set only contains three functions: a proposed Bayesian-based function, and two general algebraic operators.

3.2.1 *Bayesian-based Function*

Edge detection in this study is considered as a binary classification problem. We use j to indicate the class label. Let $j = 0$ be the class non-edge point, $j = 1$ be the class edge point, and x be a $d-$component vector-valued random variable. P_j is the prior probability for the class non-edge point or edge point. Let $p_{x|j}$ be the state-conditional probability density function for x (on the $j = 0$ or 1 being the true state). The posterior probability $p_{j|x}$ can be estimated from $p_{x|j}$ by the Bayesian Equation (8) [5], where the conditional probability density function $p_{x|j}$ is estimated by the general multivariate normal density (see Equation (9)). Here, $\hat{\mu}_j$ is the estimated d-component mean vector for class j, $\hat{\Sigma}_j$ is the estimated d-by-d covariance matrix, $|\hat{\Sigma}_j|$ is its determinant and $\hat{\Sigma}_j^{-1}$ is its inverse, and $(x - \hat{\mu}_j)^T$ is the transpose of $x - \hat{\mu}_j$.

$$p_{j|x} = \frac{p_{x|j} P_j}{\sum_{j=0}^{1} p_{x|j} P_j} \quad (8)$$

$$p_{x|j} = \frac{1}{(2\pi)^{\frac{d}{2}} |\hat{\Sigma}_j|^{\frac{1}{2}}} \exp\left(-\tfrac{1}{2}(x - \hat{\mu}_j)^T \hat{\Sigma}_j^{-1} (x - \hat{\mu}_j)\right) \quad (9)$$

The full terminal set is $\{T_{gg}, T_{sd}, T_{hg}\}$. In order to improve the performance of the standard Bayesian model, the proposed Bayesian-based function is defined in Equation (10). Here, s is its input variable, x is one of possible combinations from the full set $\{T_{gg}, T_{sd}, T_{hg}\}$, and $\{x, s\}$ is a multivariate including possible combinations from the full set $\{T_{gg}, T_{sd}, T_{hg}\}$ and the function argument s. Since the class edge point is the major class in edge detection, the output is a one-dimensional variable based on the probability of the class edge point. In edge detection, multiple outputs are not necessary, but the function can support multiple outputs, which is a future application of multiple classification problems.

$$b_{1|x}(s) = \frac{p_{1|x,s}}{\sum_{j=0}^{1} p_{j|x,s}} \quad (10)$$

The range of the output for the function $b_{1|x}(s)$ is from 0 to 1, and a composite feature from a standard Bayesian equation can be described as $b_{1|x_1}(T_{hg})$, where $x_1 = \{T_{gg}, T_{sd}\}$. Note that the argument s of the Bayesian-based function $b_{1|x}$ can be the output of another $b_{1|x}$, such as $b_{1|x}(b_{1|x}(s))$.

Therefore, the Bayesian-based function has three behaviours: (1) selecting basic features; (2) combining basic features and s (possibly as an intermediate combination); and (3) giving responses after estimating the relevant multivariate normal density.

3.2.2 General Algebraic Operators

In order to enrich the evolved Bayesian-based programs, the general algebraic operators $\{\oplus, \ominus\}$ are added into the function set. The operation of $\oplus$ is defined in Equation (11), and the operation of $\ominus$ is defined in Equation (12). Here, s_a and s_b are the arguments of the operators $\oplus$ and $\ominus$, and the operator $\ominus$ is the absolute value of difference of s_a and s_b. The ranges of s_a and s_b are from 0 to 1, so the range of the outputs of both operators is also from 0 to 1.

$$s_a \oplus s_b = \frac{s_a + s_b}{2} \quad (11)$$

$$s_a \ominus s_b = |s_a - s_b| \quad (12)$$

3.3 Fitness Function

From the set of terminals and functions, the range of outputs of a program is from 0 to 1, which is directly considered as the value of a composite feature. The aim of the new constructed features is to detect as many true edge points as possible, so recall r (the number of pixels on the edges correctly detected as a proportion of the total number of pixels on the edges) is a very important indicator. It is possible that non-edge points are incorrectly detected as edge points, therefore, specificity s (the number of pixels not on the edges correctly detected as a proportion of the total number of pixels not on the edges) is also considered in the fitness function. Therefore, we adopt the fitness function Fit as defined in Equation (13) in the training phase.

$$Fit = \frac{2rs}{r + s} \quad (13)$$

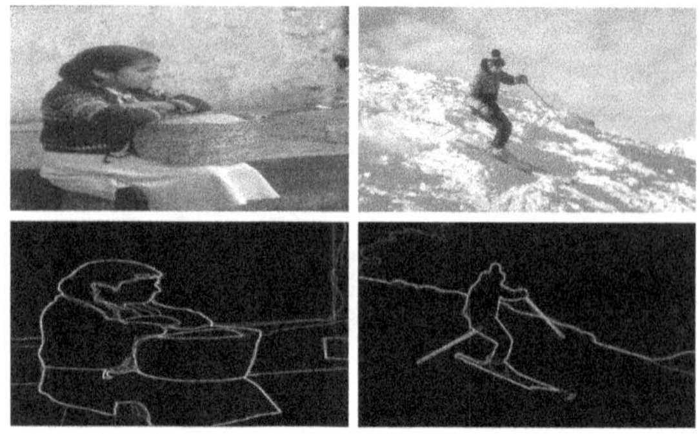

(a)23025.jpg (b)61060.jpg

Figure 3: Two example training images from BSD dataset and their ground truth.

In order to obtain r and s, three percentiles ($25th$, $50th$ and $75th$) are used as different thresholds for the outputs of a program. After the evaluation on the three percentiles, the maximum value of Fit is chosen as the fitness for the relevant program.

4. EXPERIMENT DESIGN

The Berkeley Segmentation Dataset consists of natural images (of size 481×321 pixels) with ground truth provided. The training dataset contains 200 images and the test dataset has 100 images. These natural images in this dataset are taken throughout the world. For fairness of judgement of edges, the ground truth images are combined from five to ten persons. Figure 3 shows two training images and their ground truth. To present the human observations, brighter edges in the ground truth mean that a larger number of persons marked them as edge points. Edges with lower intensities (not black), such as the edge in the top left of image 61060.jpg, mean that a smaller number of persons marked them. Note that the marked edges in the dataset are combined from different human observers, and they are not extracted by some interesting objects in these images. For simplicity, we sample image pixels with the same number of edge points and non-edge points as our training data. Approximately 250 edge points and 250 non-edge points are randomly sampled from each training image. Therefore, the training data is a balanced binary classification dataset, including approximately $100,000$ cases and the three invariant features.

The parameter values for GP are: population size 50; maximum generations 50; maximum depth (of a program) 5; and probabilities for mutation 0.15, crossover 0.80 and elitism (reproduction) 0.05. The window sizes for T_{gg}, T_{sd} and T_{hg} are 7×7, 3×3 and 13×13, respectively. These values are chosen based on common settings and initial experiments [8, 24]. There are 30 independent runs.

To obtain the test performance on a feature, it is directly evaluated without special post-processing techniques, such as non-maximum suppression. To measure the performance of these features constructed by GP, the F-measure is used in the testing phase [21, 4]. The F-measure (used in [21, 4] as $F = \frac{2rp}{r+p}$) is the combination of recall r and precision p (the number of pixels on the edges correctly detected as a proportion of the total number of pixels detected as edges). In the F-measure evaluation system, pixels are discriminated as edge points if the values of their features are larger than

Table 1: Comparison of F_{max} Values Among Constructed Features by Evolved Bayesian-based Programs from GP, Image Gaussian Gradients T_{gg}, Normalised Standard Deviations T_{sd}, Histogram Gradients T_{hg}, Sobel Edge Detector and the Simple Bayesian Model $b_{1|x_1}(T_{hg})$ for the 100 BSD Test Images.

	F_{max}
GP	**0.5591** $\pm$ 0.0150
T_{gg}	0.5153
T_{sd}	0.4968
T_{hg}	0.5434
Sobel	0.4832
$b_{1\|x_1}(T_{hg})$	0.5302

a threshold, and the predicted edges are simply thinned by the thinning operator [21]. After obtaining thinned prediction, an optimal matching operator will be used to match the prediction and the ground truth. Based on the threshold $\frac{k}{52}$ ($k = 0, 1, ..., 51$), a maximum F_{max} ($F_{max} = max\{F_k\}$) will be considered as the measurement for the feature, where F_k is the F value when the threshold $\frac{k}{52}$ is used.

For fair comparison, the F_{max} values of the three basic features (T_{gg}, T_{sd}, T_{hg}) also are given without non-maximum suppression, so their values are different from the final performance evaluation in [21]. In the feature performance evaluation, the Sobel edge detector has the same result as the final detection result evaluated in [21], because the Sobel edge detector does not contain special post-processing techniques.

5. RESULTS AND DISCUSSION

5.1 Overall Results

Table 1 presents the mean and standard deviation of F_{max} values from the 30 features constructed by GP, and F_{max} values from T_{gg}, T_{sd}, T_{hg}, the Sobel edge detector and the Bayesian model $b_{1|x_1}(T_{hg})$. The training time for each evolved program is around 124 seconds on a single machine with CPU 3.1 GHz, and the test time can be ignored (several milliseconds) because all basic features are loaded in the memory before executing a program. For simplicity, all input variables are considered as independent variables. "GP" indicates the relevant results from the Bayesian-based programs evolved by GP. The bold font means that the results from the evolved programs are significantly better than the others using the one sample t-test with significance level 0.05. In additional, the 95% confidence interval (based on the t-test) for the evolved programs is $(0.5533, 0.5648)$. These results show that the features constructed by GP significantly improve the detection performance. However, the F_{max} value from the simple Bayesian model $b_{1|x_1}(T_{hg})$ is lower than the basic feature T_{hg}, so it seems that the simple combination does not improve the detection performance (F_{max}). Therefore, GP is effective for automatic construction of new features.

In order to check the details of the performance on all evolved programs, Figure 4 gives the relevant F_{max} values for all 30 evolved Bayesian-based programs. Most of the evolved Bayesian-based programs have higher F_{max} than

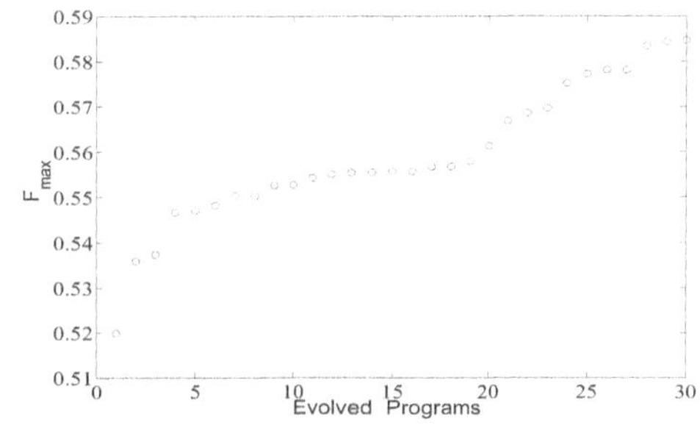

Figure 4: F_{max} values for the features constructed by the evolved 30 programs from GP.

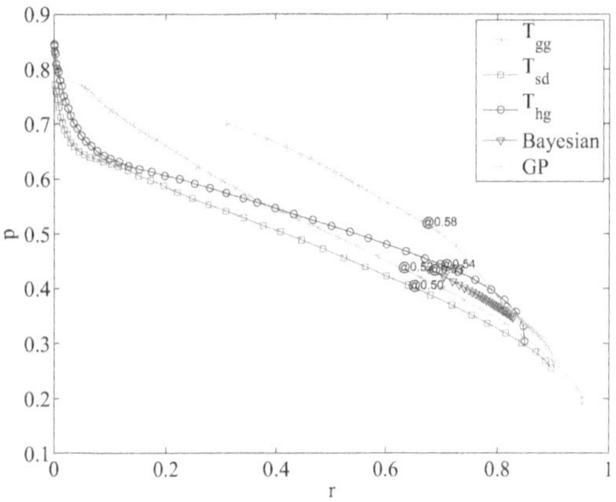

Figure 5: Recall and precision for T_{gg}, T_{sd}, T_{hg}, the simple Bayesian model $b_{1|x_1}(T_{hg})$, and an evolved program.

the best basic feature T_{hg}, and most of the evolved programs obtain good performance. However, the constructed features from three evolved programs are worse than T_{hg} (with F_{max}). The lowest F_{max} value of the constructed feature from the worst evolved program is only 0.52. How to improve the performance on the worst evolved program will be future work.

5.2 Recall and Precision of the Best Evolved Method By GP

Figure 5 shows different values of recall (r) and precision (p) for T_{gg}, T_{sd}, T_{hg}, the simple Bayesian model $b_{1|x_1}(T_{hg})$, and a program evolved by GP (with $F_{max} = 0.5847$). Here, "@" is the position for the F_{max}. From the different thresholds, it is clear that the evolved program has higher precision than the others when recall is not too low.

Another interesting observation from Figure 5 is that the simple Bayesian model $b_{1|x_1}(T_{hg})$ has a narrow range for recall and precision. A reason for this phenomenon is that the Bayesian Equation (8) gives very low probabilities for most non-edge points and very high probabilities for most edge points. Therefore, the change of the threshold does not strongly affect the detection performance. Compared with the basic features, the simple Bayesian method $b_{1|x_1}(T_{hg})$ and the evolved program have very high recall values for many thresholds. It seems that the composite features from the Bayesian model can easily discriminate pixels as edge points or non-edge points with a set of thresholds.

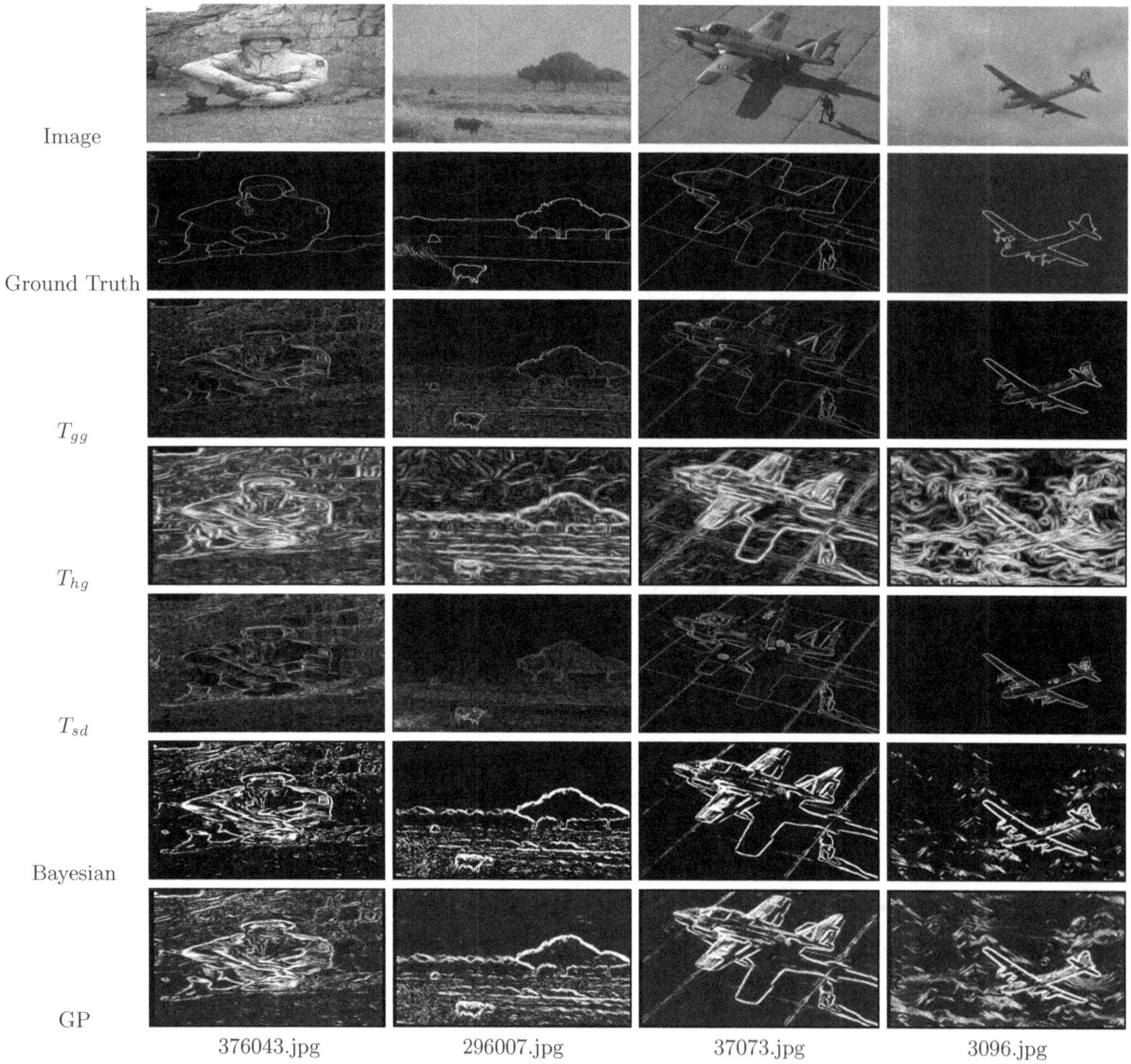

Figure 6: Four example images detected by T_{gg}, T_{hg}, T_{sd}, the simple Bayesian method $b_{1|x_1}(T_{hg})$, and the best evolved method from GP.

5.3 Detected Images

Figure 6 shows four example detected images from different methods. From the detected images, we can see that the detected images by the simple Bayesian method $b_{1|x_1}(T_{hg})$ and the evolved method have obviously strong responses on true edge points, which is similar to T_{hg}. The strong responses on non-edge points from T_{hg} are mostly suppressed by the simple Bayesian method $b_{1|x_1}(T_{hg})$ and the evolved method. However, some non-edge points with high responses from T_{hg} still have high responses in the simple Bayesian method $b_{1|x_1}(T_{hg})$. Comparing the responses from T_{sd} and T_{gg}, most of the non-edge points with high responses from T_{hg} in these four images are obviously decreased in the evolved program. Therefore, the evolved program effectively constructs a new composite feature.

Figure 7 shows the image 69020.jpg detected by the best evolved program from GP and the simple Bayesian model $b_{1|x_1}(T_{hg})$. As we can see, the detected image by the best evolved program from GP is improved in the areas 1 and 2. Also, the responses on edge points are obviously higher than the non-edge points. Most of the true non-edge points have very weak responses (very dark) for this image, which is the same with the detection result of the combination from the simple Bayesian model $b_{1|x_1}(T_{hg})$. Although the simple Bayesian model $b_{1|x_1}(T_{hg})$ decreases responses on most of the non-edge points, it wrongly strengthens responses on a few non-edge points.

5.4 Example of the Best Evolved Bayesian-based Program

The best evolved Bayesian-based program is described by Equation (14), where EB indicates an evolved Bayesian-based program, and subscript indices 0, 1 and 2 represent the basic features T_{gg}, T_{sd} and T_{hg}, respectively. Func-

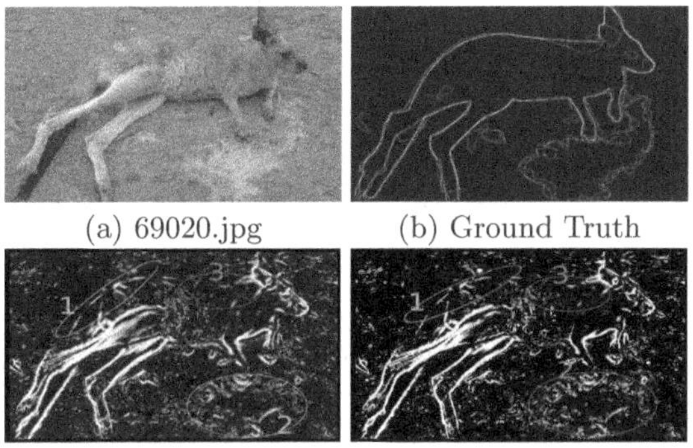

(a) 69020.jpg (b) Ground Truth

(c) GP (d) Bayesian

Figure 7: Image 69020.jpg detected by an evolved method from GP and the simple Bayesian model $b_{1|x_1}(T_{hg})$.

tion $b_{0,1}(T_{gg})$ is used to construct a model with the multivariate including T_{gg} and T_{sd}. Note that the proposed function accepts redundant variables. From the first part $b_{0,1,2}(b_{0,1}(b_{0,1}(T_{gg})))$, the formula aims at finding true edge points detected by T_{gg} and then constructing a feature with three basic variables. Since T_{gg} has high recall, this first part should be good at finding true edge points. The second part $b_2(b_2(b_2(T_{hg})))$ only includes the basic feature T_{hg}. After repeating estimation on true edge points (using the second part), the responses for those non-edge points with high responses in T_{hg} should be decreased. Since the output of the Bayesian-based function is based on the class edge point, the accuracy (precision) for the constructed feature should not be too low. Generally, the responses on clear boundaries (easily detected) are accurately given. Therefore, the second part possibly focuses on the boundary detection.

$$EB = b_{0,1,2}(b_{0,1}(b_{0,1}(T_{gg}))) \oplus b_2(b_2(b_2(T_{hg}))) \quad (14)$$

In order to visually present the characteristics from the two parts, Figure 8 shows two example images detected by the two parts of the best evolved method. "First" means the images detected by the first part $b_{0,1,2}(b_{0,1}(b_{0,1}(T_{gg})))$, and "Second" for the second part $b_2(b_2(b_2(T_{hg})))$. From the two example detected images, the second part appears to be better than the first part to detect true edge points. Since the first part focuses on finding edge points (possibly with low precision), the combination of both parts makes high responses on boundaries and low responses on non-edge points. The test performances (F_{max}) on the first part and second part for the 100 BSD test images are 0.5231 and 0.5436. Compared with T_{hg}, the second part does not improve the F_{max} value, but it decreases response magnitudes for non-edge points. Iteratively estimating a single feature might be helpful to improve detection performance, which is future work.

In order to further check the performance of both parts, Figure 9 reveals the details of recall and precision for the two parts of the evolved programs. From the curves, it is found that the recall and precision values of the second part are almost located on the curve of T_{hg}. Different from T_{hg}, the recall and precision values of the second part of the evolved program crowd in an area (with not too low recall and not too low precision). From the view of the performance based on different thresholds, repeating estimation of a single variable with its estimated outputs transforms the variable val-

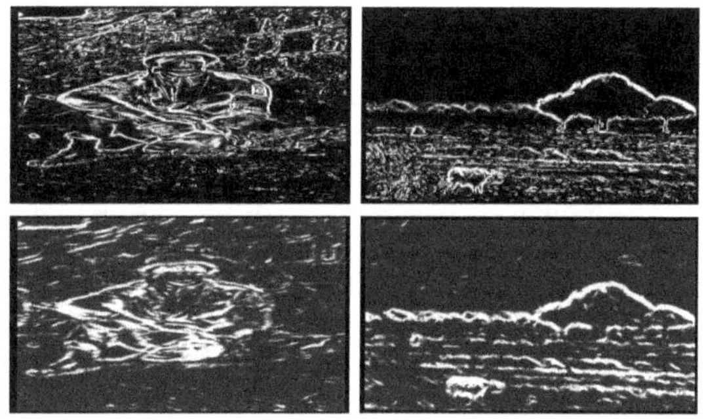

Figure 8: Two example images detected by two parts of the best evolved method from GP.

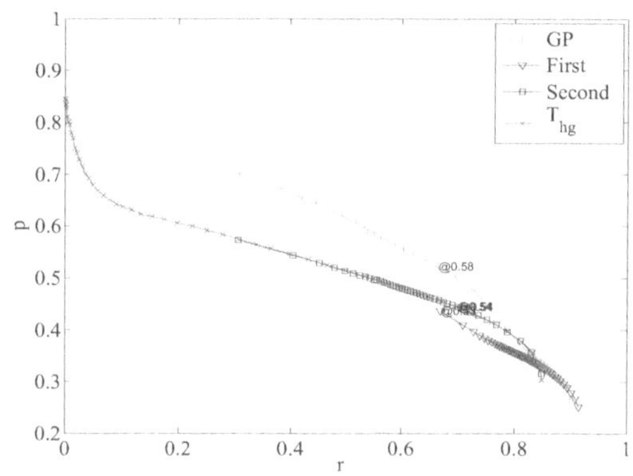

Figure 9: Recall and precision for an evolved program, its two parts and T_{hg}.

ues into a suitable range which is not strongly affected by the change of a threshold.

6. CONCLUSIONS

The goal of this paper was to investigate evolving Bayesian-based programs to construct edge features by a proposed GP system for edge detection. Based on a proposed special function set, the results of the experiment show that the goal of evolving new programs to construct composite features for edge detection was successfully achieved. The evolved programs using the general multivariate normal density is better than the simple Bayesian model $b_{1|x_1}(T_{hg})$ directly using basic features to construct composite features. The results on the BSD dataset show that GP effectively constructs features which take advantages from basic features and improve the detection performance. Further analysis of the best evolved program reveals that iteratively estimating a single feature may help to improve detection performance.

For future work, we will test the evolved programs on different image datasets. Also, more functions based on machine learning algorithms will be developed and applied in the function set. In addition, the improvement of effectively evolved programs will be investigated so that the features constructed by GP are better than the basic features.

7. REFERENCES

[1] M. Basu. Gaussian-based edge-detection methods: a

survey. *IEEE Transactions on Systems, Man, and Cybernetics, Part C: Applications and Reviews*, 32(3):252–260, 2002.

[2] E. Bolis, C. Zerbi, P. Collet, J. Louchet, and E. Lutton. A GP artificial ant for image processing: preliminary experiments with EASEA. In *Proceedings of the 4th European Conference on Genetic Programming*, pages 246–255, 2001.

[3] J. Canny. A computational approach to edge detection. *IEEE Transactions on Pattern Analysis and Machine Intelligence*, 8(6):679–698, 1986.

[4] P. Dollar, Z. Tu, and S. Belongie. Supervised learning of edges and object boundaries. In *Proceedings of the IEEE Computer Society Conference on Computer Vision and Pattern Recognition*, volume 2, pages 1964–1971, 2006.

[5] R. O. Duda, P. E. Hart, and D. G. Stork. *Pattern Classification (2nd Edition)*. Wiley-Interscience, 2000.

[6] M. Ebner. On the edge detectors for robot vision using genetic programming. In *Proceedings of Horst-Michael Groß, Workshop SOAVE 97 - Selbstorganisation von Adaptivem Verhalten*, pages 127–134, 1997.

[7] W. Fu, M. Johnston, and M. Zhang. Analysis of diagonal derivatives in edge detectors evolved by genetic programming. In *Proceedings of the Twenty-sixth International Conference on Image and Vision Computing New Zealand*, pages 345–350, 2011.

[8] W. Fu, M. Johnston, and M. Zhang. Genetic programming for edge detection: a global approach. In *Proceedings of the IEEE Congress on Evolutionary Computation*, pages 254–261, 2011.

[9] W. Fu, M. Johnston, and M. Zhang. Genetic programming for edge detection based on accuracy of each training image. In *Proceedings of the 24th Australasian Joint Conference on Artificial Intelligence*, pages 301–310, 2011.

[10] W. Fu, M. Johnston, and M. Zhang. Genetic programming for edge detection via balancing individual training images. In *Proceedings of the IEEE Congress on Evolutionary Computation*, pages 1–8, 2012.

[11] T. Golonek, D. Grzechca, and J. Rutkowski. Application of genetic programming to edge detector design. In *Proceedings of the International Symposium on Circuits and Systems*, pages 4683–4686, 2006.

[12] C. Grigorescu, N. Petkov, and M. A. Westenberg. Contour and boundary detection improved by surround suppression of texture edges. *Image and Vision Computing*, 22(8):609–622, 2004.

[13] S. Harding and W. Banzhaf. Genetic programming on GPUs for image processing. *International Journal of High Performance Systems Architecture*, 1(4):231–240, 2008.

[14] C. Harris and B. Buxton. Evolving edge detectors with genetic programming. In *Proceedings of the First Annual Conference on Genetic Programming*, pages 309–314, 1996.

[15] G. Hollingworth, S. Smith, and A. Tyrrell. Design of highly parallel edge detection nodes using evolutionary techniques. In *Proceedings of the Seventh Euromicro Workshop on Parallel and Distributed Processing*, pages 35–42, 1999.

[16] I. Kadar, O. Ben-Shahar, and M. Sipper. Evolution of a local boundary detector for natural images via genetic programming and texture cues. In *Proceedings of the 11th Annual Conference on Genetic and Evolutionary Computation*, pages 1887–1888, 2009.

[17] M. Kokare, P. K. Biswas, and B. N. Chatterji. Edge based features for content based image retrieval. *Pattern Recognition*, 36(11):2649–2661, 2003.

[18] L. Lam, S.-W. Lee, and C. Suen. Thinning methodologies-a comprehensive survey. *IEEE Transactions on Pattern Analysis and Machine Intelligence*, 14(9):869–885, 1992.

[19] D. H. Lim and S. J. Jang. Comparison of two-sample tests for edge detection in noisy images. *Journal of the Royal Statistical Society. Series D (The Statistician)*, 51(1):21–30, 2002.

[20] D. Marr and E. Hildreth. Theory of edge detection. *Proceedings of the Royal Society of London, Series B, Biological Sciences*, 207(1167):187–217, 1980.

[21] D. Martin, C. Fowlkes, and J. Malik. Learning to detect natural image boundaries using local brightness, color, and texture cues. *IEEE Transactions on Pattern Analysis and Machine Intelligence*, 26(5):530–549, 2004.

[22] R. Moreno, D. Puig, C. Julia, and M. Garcia. A new methodology for evaluation of edge detectors. In *Proceedings of the 16th IEEE International Conference on Image Processing (ICIP)*, pages 2157–2160, 2009.

[23] C. Olson and D. Huttenlocher. Automatic target recognition by matching oriented edge pixels. *IEEE Transactions on Image Processing*, 6(1):103–113, 1997.

[24] G. Papari and N. Petkov. Edge and line oriented contour detection: state of the art. *Image and Vision Computing*, 29:79–103, 2011.

[25] R. Poli. Genetic programming for image analysis. In *Proceedings of the First Annual Conference on Genetic Programming*, pages 363–368, 1996.

[26] R. Poli, W. B. Langdon, and N. F. McPhee. *A Field Guide to Genetic Programming*. Published via `http://lulu.com` and freely available at `http://www.gp-field-guide.org.uk`, 2008. With contributions by J. R. Koza.

[27] G. Rezai-Rad and H. H. Larijani. A new investigation on edge detection filters operation for feature extraction under histogram equalization effect. In *Proceedings of the Geometric Modelling and Imaging*, pages 149–153, 2007.

[28] J. Sullivan and S. Carlsson. Recognizing and tracking human action. In *Proceedings of the 7th European Conference on Computer Vision-Part I*, pages 629–644, 2002.

[29] J. Wang and Y. Tan. A novel genetic programming based morphological image analysis algorithm. In *Proceedings of the 12th Annual Conference on Genetic and Evolutionary Computation*, pages 979–980, 2010.

[30] Y. Zhang and P. I. Rockett. Evolving optimal feature extraction using multi-objective genetic programming: a methodology and preliminary study on edge detection. In *Proceedings of the Conference on Genetic and Evolutionary Computation*, pages 795–802, 2005.

An Efficient Distance Metric for Linear Genetic Programming

Marco Gaudesi
Politecnico di Torino
Corso Duca degli Abruzzi, 24
10129 Torino, Italy
marco.gaudesi@polito.it

Giovanni Squillero
Politecnico di Torino
Corso Duca degli Abruzzi, 24
10129 Torino, Italy
giovanni.squillero@polito.it

Alberto Tonda
INRA UMR 782, MALICES
1 Avenue Lucien Brétignères
78850 Thiverval-Grignon,
France
alberto.tonda@grignon.inra.fr

ABSTRACT

Defining a distance measure over the individuals in the population of an Evolutionary Algorithm can be exploited for several applications, ranging from diversity preservation to balancing exploration and exploitation. When individuals are encoded as strings of bits or sets of real values, computing the distance between any two can be a straightforward process; when individuals are represented as trees or linear graphs, however, quite often the user must resort to phenotype-level problem-specific distance metrics. This paper presents a generic genotype-level distance metric for Linear Genetic Programming: the information contained by an individual is represented as a set of symbols, using n-grams to capture significant recurring structures inside the genome. The difference in information between two individuals is evaluated resorting to a symmetric difference. Experimental evaluations show that the proposed metric has a strong correlation with phenotype-level problem-specific distance measures in two problems where individuals represent string of bits and Assembly-language programs, respectively.

Categories and Subject Descriptors

H.4 [**Information Systems Applications**]: Miscellaneous; D.2.8 [**Software Engineering**]: Metrics—*complexity measures, performance measures*

Keywords

Algorithms; Measurements; Linear Genetic Programming; Diversity Preservation; Distance Metric; Fitness Sharing; Experimental Analysis; Individual Encoding; Assembly; NK-Landscapes

1. INTRODUCTION

Defining a *distance metric* in an Evolutionary Algorithm (EA) is both theoretically sound and practically challenging – and ultimately useful. Being able to quantify the similarity of two individuals can be used to promote diversity inside the population's gene pool, to avoid the over-exploitation of niches in the fitness landscape, to balance exploration and exploitation, and ultimately to ease the premature convergence problem. Not surprisingly, the topic has been actively investigated by the evolutionary community for many years.

From the theoretical point of view, two different aspects must be examined when a distance is defined: the level at which it is calculated; and the purpose for calculating it. On the other hand, for the practitioner the complexity involved in the calculation is the key point.

The level at which a distance is defined may be: genotype, phenotype, or fitness. The first and the last are probably the most easily definable: the genotype corresponds to the internal representation of the candidate solution; the fitness is ultimately the number, or numbers, returned by its evaluation. In biology, the phenotype is the sum of all the observable characteristics of an organism that result from the interaction of its genotype with the environment. It is hard to translate the concept in Evolutionary Computation since the environment is missing, being indirectly defined by its effects through the fitness function. Yet, in several classical problems – where an individual is a fixed-length bit string, for instance – the need to distinguish between genotype and phenotype is reduced. As a consequence, several works assimilate the fitness to the phenotype.

In many other cases identifying phenotype and fitness is not an option. The fitness is a synthetic information, and may not be able to convey the necessary data to separate individuals. Even in the simplistic one-max problem two solutions may have the same fitness without sharing a single gene (e.g., "0011" and "1100"). Moreover, the very same solution can be encoded in different ways. If the individual is the movement of a robot, for instance, a single 90° turn could also be represented as two consecutive 45° ones. More generally, whenever the genotype cannot be evaluated directly by the fitness function, but needs to be transformed into something else, fitness and genotype should be distinguished. In such scenarios, the phenotype could be easily defined as the "something else" in which the genotype needs to be transformed into.

The final goal for measuring the distance between individuals plays an important role. If the distance metric is used to avoid that a region of the search space becomes overly populous, then it should be defined at the level of phenotype. However, phenotype-level distances are often difficult

GECCO'13, July 6–10, 2013, Amsterdam, The Netherlands.

to define or practically impossible to calculate. Remarkably, NSGA-II, the widely used multi-objective evolutionary optimizer, adopts a sharp and computationally efficient mechanism called *crowding distance* to scatter individuals [6]. Here, the crowding distance may rely exclusively on information from the fitness because the genotypes are fixed-length arrays of real numbers, requiring no transformation; and the fitness is composed of several different values, reducing the loss of information.

Conversely, if the distance metric is used to promote diversity in the gene pool, balancing exploration and exploitation, it could be based on the genotype. For example, in [13] solutions are encoded as fixed-length bit strings and a metric based on the hamming distance is used to assess the global diversity inside the population. When the phenotypes are sets of real values of fixed size, computing the distance between them is relatively straightforward, albeit not trivial [5]. However, phenotypes in Genetic Programming (GP) [11], Linear Genetic Programming (LGP) [3] and other complex EAs pose a harder challenge: calculating the similarity between two binary trees, linear graphs, or generic compound structures is an open problem.

This paper proposes a new distance metric easily usable in different types of LGPs. The distance is calculated quite efficiently at the level of genotype, yet it is able to convey a considerable amount of information about the individual. Thus, it may be used to reduce crowding in place of a phenotype-level distance. The proposed approach computes the *symmetric difference* [1] between the global information contained in two individuals; while the global information itself is evaluated resorting to the concept of n-grams [18].

Experimental results demonstrate that the proposed distance is highly correlated with other phenotype-level problem-specific distance measures, both where individuals are string of bits and Assembly language programs. Further experiments show that exploiting the proposed metric to perform fitness sharing in a sample problem produces results comparable to using a phenotype-level metric.

2. BACKGROUND

2.1 Linear Genetic Programming

LGP is a variant of GP that evolves computer programs as sequences of instructions. It was introduced by Markus Brameier and Wolfgang Banzhaf between the late 90s and the early 2000s [2] [3], after the seminal work of Friedberg [7]. A traditional, *Koza-style* GP encodes individuals as trees. Such tree GPs – or TGPs, as they are sometimes called – are commonly used to evolve mathematical expressions: leaves correspond to *terminals*, such as input values, constants or variables; inner nodes represent *functions*. Quite differently, LGP evolves a simplified list structure that represents a sequence of instructions in an imperative programming language. The resulting individuals represent real programs, although in a simplified language, that can grow to a significant complexity. Since their appearance, LGPs have been widely used to solve both practical problems and perform theoretical studies.

In LGP the difference between genotype and phenotype becomes fully apparent. The *genotype* is the internal, list-based representation; the *phenotype* is the actual program resulting from the interpretation of the genotype; the *fitness* is the final result of the evaluation of the program (Figure 1).

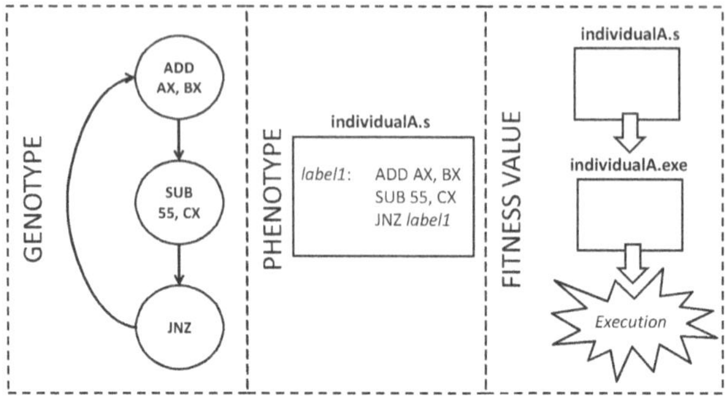

Figure 1: Distinction between genotype, phenotype and fitness value in an example with LGP used for Assembly language generation.

2.2 Symmetric Difference

In set theory, the symmetric difference [1] of two sets A and B is defined as

$$A \triangle B = A \cup B - A \cap B \tag{1}$$

In practice, the symmetric difference contains all elements which are in either of the sets and not in their intersection. The Venn diagram of the symmetric difference is reported in Figure 2.

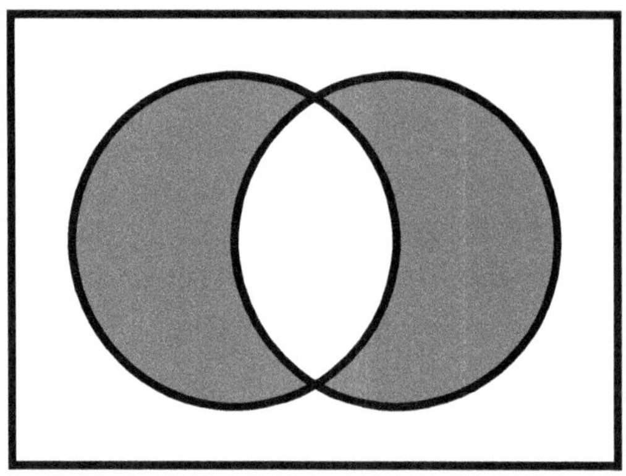

Figure 2: Venn diagram of the symmetric difference. The area corresponding to $A \triangle B$ is depicted in grey.

Considering the set as the *information* carried by an individual, the symmetric difference appears a plausible formalization of the intuitive idea of distance: when two sets are almost completely overlapping, their symmetric difference is very small; when they are completely separated, it is big.

Moreover, the symmetric difference exhibits useful properties for a distance: it is commutative ($A \triangle B = B \triangle A$); and the empty set is neutral ($A \triangle \emptyset = A$ and $A \triangle A = \emptyset$). The symmetric distance is also associative, but this fact is negligible in this application.

2.3 Fitness Sharing

When a reliable distance metric is defined, one useful application is to exploit it for *fitness sharing*, one of many methods to enforce diversity inside the population of an EA [16] [14].

The general idea of fitness sharing is to artificially decrease the fitness of individuals in crowded areas of the search space. The fitness f_i of an individual I_i is modified in a fitness $f'_i = f/m_i$, where m_i is dependent upon the number of individuals in a given radius σ_s from individual I_i, and their distance from the individual itself. In particular,

$$m_i = \sum_{j=0}^{N} sh(I_i, I_j) \quad (2)$$

where N is the number of individuals in the population, and $sh(I_i, I_j)$ is defined as

$$sh(I_i, I_j) = \begin{cases} 1 - (\frac{d(I_i,I_j)}{\sigma_s})^\alpha & d(I_i, I_j) < \sigma_s \\ 0 & d(I_i, I_j) \geq \sigma_s \end{cases} \quad (3)$$

where σ_s is once again a user-defined radius, and $d(I_i, I_j)$ is a distance measure applicable to the individuals' representation. α is a constant parameter that regulates the shape of the sharing function. In many practical cases $\alpha = 1$, with the resulting sharing function referred to as the triangular sharing function [8].

3. PROPOSED APPROACH

In LGP, Shannon entropy can be effectively used as a metric to assess the diversity in a population at a given generation [4]. The entire population is considered a message, and each allele appearing in an individual is a symbol: entropy is then computed on the basis of the number of different symbols and their occurrences.

In a preliminary work [17], a variant of this approach is sketched. Instead of considering just the alleles of each gene, their disposition inside the individual is also taken into account. A symbol is no longer considered equivalent to a single allele, but to the allele and its position inside the individual instead. Following the idea that recurring structures might possess meaning, *n-grams* of nodes are also regarded as symbols. An n-gram is a group of n items from a longer sequence. For example, `a b`, `b c` and `c d` are all 2-grams from the sequence `a b c d`, while `a b c` and `b c d` are 3-grams. Very often n-grams are used for the purpose of modelling the statistical properties of sequences, particularly natural language [18].

Building on the same principles, a generic genotypic *Universal Information Distance* (UID) for individuals in LGP is proposed. Considering two individuals I_i and I_j, the UID is defined as

$$UID(I_i, I_j) = |S(I_i) \bigtriangleup S(I_j)| \quad (4)$$

where $S(I)$ represents the set of symbols in individual I, $\bigtriangleup$ is the symmetric difference as defined in Equation 1, and the operator $|S|$ denotes the cardinality of set S.

In other words, the UID between two individuals is the number of distinct symbols they do not have in common. Intuitively, when two individuals share many common symbols, the UID will be small; on the contrary, if they have no symbols in common, their UID will be high. An example is reported in Figure 3.

When used in practice, symbols for each individual are computed resorting to a hash function of the n-grams and alleles. It is interesting to notice how the proposed UID, that acts at genotype level and is quite straightforward to compute, could provide the same information of more computationally intensive distance metrics that are evaluated at phenotype level: thus, UID could be used for fitness sharing, delivering the same results as problem-specific metrics.

4. EXPERIMENTAL EVALUATION

The correlation between the proposed UID and two phenotypic distance metrics is examined, in two problems where individuals are encoded as strings of bits, and as Assembly language programs, respectively. Experiments with an evolutionary toolkit that supports LGP [15] are then performed for the two problems, and the effectiveness of UID for fitness sharing is compared to the previously considered phenotypic distance metrics.

In the all the experiments, the computation of UID is limited to n-grams of order 2 and 3, as a trade-off between computational efficiency and thoroughness of the approach. Symbols are computed resorting to the DJB[1] hash function.

4.1 Considered Problems

The proposed approach is tested on two benchmarks: NK-landscapes, a NP-complete problem where individuals are represented a strings of bits, and a simple Assembly-language generation task.

4.1.1 NK-Landscapes

In the NK-landscapes problem [10], the individual is a string of bits of fixed length: both the overall size of the fitness landscape and the number of its local optima can be adjusted by tuning the two parameters, N and K. Generally speaking, values of K close to N create more irregular landscapes. Albeit simple, this benchmark is widely studied in the optimization community, because it is proven to be NP-complete [19]. In the following experiments, values of N and K are very close, in order to obtain a fairly rugged fitness landscape.

4.1.2 Assembly Language Generation

This second set of experiments targets a simple Assembly language generation problem: the fitness of a program is the number of bits set to 1 in registry $\%eax$ at the end of its execution.

During the Assembly-generation problem, the minimum length of the variable part of a program is set to 1 instruction, the while the maximum length is set to 1500 instructions. For the initial population, individuals are generated in order to possess an average of 70 instructions, with a large standard deviation of 60 in order to efficiently sample the search space. Table 1 recapitulates the possible genes (instructions) appearing in the individuals.

The fitness function used for this experiment is based on both the result of a candidate program's execution and the length of its code, and it is defined as

$$f(I) = 10^4 \cdot (\sum_{i=0}^{N=31} \%eax[i]) + max(0, 10^4 - length(I)) \quad (5)$$

where $\%eax[i]$ is the value of the ith bit of register $\%eax$, while $length(I)$ represents the number of instructions of candidate program I. Thus, the most important objective is to

[1] http://cr.yp.to/djb.html

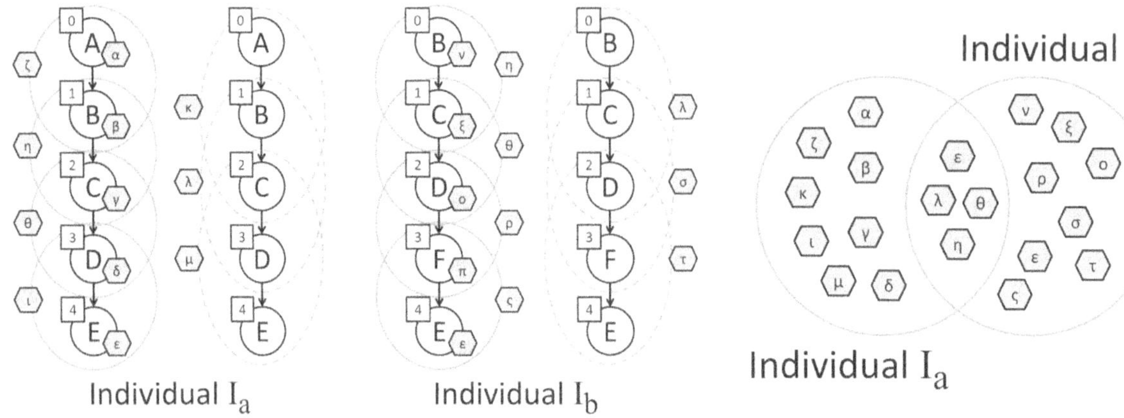

Figure 3: Example of symbols computed for alleles and $(2,3)$-grams for two individuals. Symbols are represented as Greek letters inside hexagons, alleles as Roman letters inside circles, while their position in the individual is reported in a square. The symbols common to the two individuals are ϵ (corresponding to allele E in position 4), η (2-gram $B-C$), θ (2-gram $C-D$) and λ (3-gram $B-C-D$). The UID between the two individuals is thus $|S(A) \triangle S(B)| = |S(A) \cup S(B) - S(A) \cap S(B)| = 16$

Gene	Parameters	Prob.
<ins> <sreg>, <dreg>	**ins**={addl, subl, movl, andl, orl, xorl, compl}, **sreg**={%eax, %ebx, %ecx, %edx}, **dreg**={%eax, %ebx, %ecx, %edx}	0.33
<ins> <scon>,<dreg>	**ins**={addl, subl, movl, andl, orl, xorl, compl}, **scon**={integer in (0,255)}, **dreg**={%eax, %ebx, %ecx, %edx}	0.33
<ins> <reg>	**ins**={incl, decl, notl}, **reg**={%eax, %ebx, %ecx, %edx}	0.33

Table 1: Possible genes appearing inside the individuals during the Assembly generation problem. For each gene, all variables and corresponding values are listed, as well as the probability of occurrence.

set to 1 bits in register *%eax*, while a small bonus is assigned to individuals that perform the task with a moderate number of instructions.

4.2 Correlation

An important result that it is possible to immediately esteem looking at the figures is how much the proposed UID distance is well correlated with problem-specific phenotype-level distances. Figure 4 plots the UID against the standard Hamming distance for 500 random 50-bit individuals[2]. The cloud of points does not stretch down to the origin, nor up to the maximum because it is quite unlikely to find two identical strings, or two completely different ones, in a random pool.

Figure 5, on the other hand, plots the same data for all

[2]Several values are overlapping.

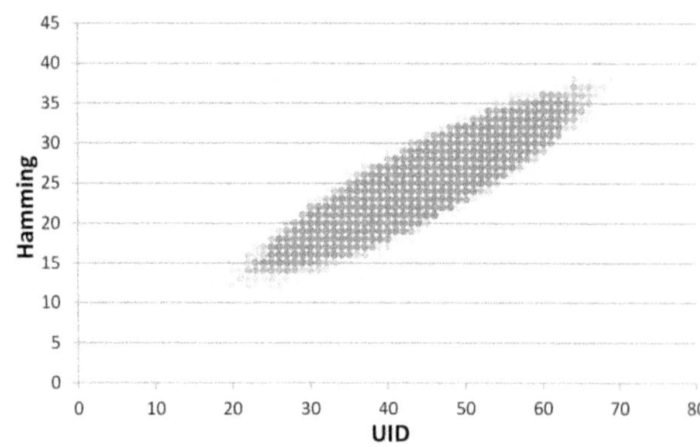

Figure 4: Correlation between the proposed UID distance and hamming distance in the standard One-Max problem (50 bits)– Sample of 500 random individuals.

individuals generated during a run, until the optimal solution is reached. Since there is a strong similarity between all individuals in the same parental group, the cloud stretches down to distance zero. The correlation is even more evident than in the preceding example.

Figure 6 plots the proposed distance against the Levenshtein, or *edit*, distance for 500 random programs on the Assembly OneMax problem. Here, differences are more subtle and the number of overlapping values is reduced compared to the previous case. The triangular shape of the cloud is indicative: the two distances are better correlated for low values – that is, exactly when they are more useful: distinguishing between closely related individuals is in fact quite harder than discriminating between very different ones. The Levenshtein distance is a computationally-expensive metric that can be computed only at the level of phenotype. The proposed UID, on the contrary, can be efficiently calculated at the level of genotype and it is effective in estimating the distance between *similar* individuals.

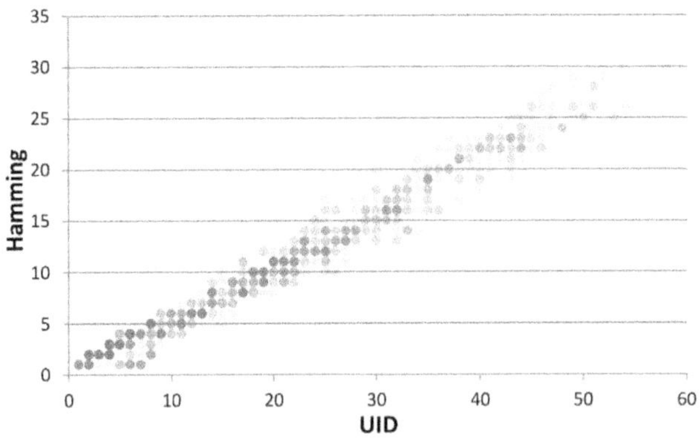

Figure 5: Correlation between the proposed UID distance and hamming distance in the standard OneMax problem (50 bits) – Individuals generated during a run.

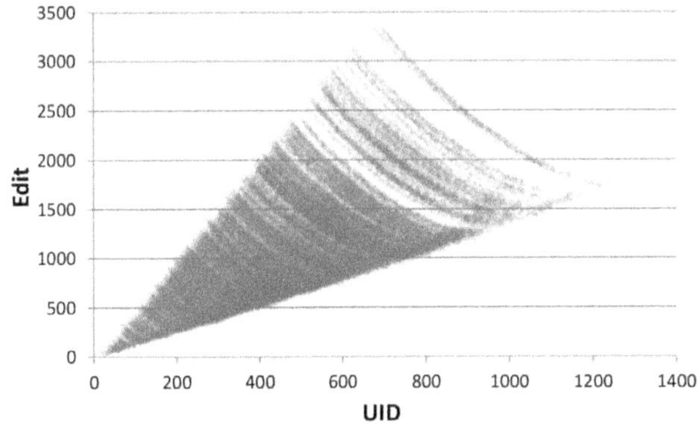

Figure 6: Correlation between the proposed UID distance and the Levenshtein distance in the Assembly OneMax problem (32 bits) – Sample of 500 random individuals.

4.3 Fitness Sharing

Since the proposed metric shows a heavy correlation with phenotypic distance metrics, its effectiveness can now be tested in multi-modal problems where a fitness sharing might help to spread the individuals over the search space. The aim of the following experiments is to show how using the proposed UID for fitness sharing delivers the same results as employing more rigorous problem-specific distance metrics, that are also more computationally expensive.

The first experiments are performed on the NK-landscapes (or NK-model) benchmark, tuned to obtain a rugged fitness landscape: the UID is compared to a classical Hamming distance [9]. A second set of experiments is then executed on a simple Assembly-language generation problem, where the objective is to obtain a program able to set all bits of register $\%eax$ to 1. In this latter tests, the UID is weighted against the Levenshtein distance [12].

In the LGP tool used for the experiments [15], μ is the population size; λ represents the number of genetic operators applied at each generation, rather than the offspring size; and σ is the *strength* of the mutation operators. Each time a mutation operator is applied to an individual, a random number r in the interval $(0, 1)$ is generated: if $r < \sigma$, the operator creates another mutation in the same individual, and a new r is generated.

It is important to notice that the parameters of the tool used in the trials have not been tuned to optimality, since the main objective of this experimental evaluation is to assess whether the fitness sharing mechanism behaves comparably when different distance metrics are applied with an equivalent radius, even with sub-optimal settings.

4.3.1 NK-landscapes

Parameters of the LGP tool used in the experiments are reported in Table 2. The mutation operator in this case simply changes the value of a random gene, while the one-point crossover selects a random cut point.

Parameter	Value	Parameter	Value
μ	32	P(one-point crossover)	0.5
λ	32	P(mutation)	0.5
σ	0.5	Max generations	50

Table 2: Parameters used during the experiments with fitness sharing in the NK-landscapes benchmark.

For each landscape, 10 experiments are run with the Hamming distance, and 10 with the UID, respectively, using equivalent radius measures derived from the correlation described in Subsection 4.2. At the end of the evolution, the fitness of the best individual (*online fitness*) and the average fitness of the final population (*offline fitness*) are compared.

From results in Table 3 it is noticeable how, for the same NK-landscape, the final online and offline fitness values are very close, as well as the average distance value between individuals in the population. In fact, running a two-sample Kolmogorov-Smirnov test on corresponding distributions for an equivalent radius reveals that the distributions are undistinguishable with $p < 0.01$.

4.3.2 Assembly OneMax

This second set of experiments targets a simple Assembly language generation problem: the fitness of a program is the number of bits set to 1 in registry $\%eax$ at the end of its execution. Table 4 summarizes the parameters used for the LGP tool in this experiment.

Parameter	Value	Parameter	Value
μ	10	P(crossover)	0.25
λ	7	P(mutation)	0.75
σ	0.7	Max generations	10

Table 4: Parameters used during the experiments with fitness sharing in the Assembly language generation problem.

The mutation operator, in this case, can add a random instruction; remove a random instruction; or change one or more parameters inside a random instruction, with equal probability. The crossover can operate on one or two cut points, with equal probability.

Table 5 shows the results over 10 experiments with each parameter configuration. At the end of the evolution, the fitness of the best individual (*online fitness*) and the average fitness of the final population (*offline fitness*) are compared.

Fitness sharing with Hamming distance					Fitness sharing with UID				
Radius (Hamming)	Online fitness (avg)	StDev	Offline fitness (avg)	StDev	Radius (UID)	Online fitness (avg)	StDev	Offline fitness (avg)	StDev
N=16, K=14, seed=1234567890									
5	0.6710	0.0167	0.3655	0.0256	10	0.6739	0.0326	0.3798	0.0391
N=16, K=14, seed=4242424242									
5	0.6774	0.0318	0.4094	0.0142	10	0.6948	0.0304	0.4099	0.0235
N=16, K=15, seed=1234567890									
5	0.6543	0.0228	0.3819	0.0124	10	0.6468	0.0109	0.3901	0.0137
N=16, K=15, seed=4242424242									
5	0.6770	0.0209	0.3912	0.0352	10	0.6671	0.0256	0.4067	0.0316

Table 3: Results for the set of experiments on the NK-landscapes benchmark. Experiments with fitness sharing with the Hamming distance (left) and the UID (right); experiments with a corresponding radius are reported on the same line.

Fitness sharing with Levenshtein distance					Fitness sharing with UID				
Radius (Levenshtein)	Online fitness (avg)	StDev	Offline fitness (avg)	StDev	Radius (UID)	Online fitness (avg)	StDev	Offline fitness (avg)	StDev
3	325,927	7,205.14	312,903	19,800.8	2	320,919	12,608.4	297,899	32,800.8
5	324,939	7,992.28	309,902	27,989.6	3	324,949	8,008.23	315,909	17,616.6
10	318,909	11,422.8	292,901	20,998.7	5	314,930	15,015.5	285,923	32014.3

Table 5: Results for the set of experiments on the Assembly-language generation benchmark. Experiments using fitness sharing with the Levenshtein distance (left) and the UID (right); experiments with a corresponding radius are reported on the same line.

Again, the results for an equivalent radius are indistinguishable through a two-sample Kolmogorov-Smirnov test with $p < 0.01$.

5. CONCLUSIONS

This paper presents a new distance metric for Linear Genetic Programming, based on the symmetric difference between the *information* contained in the genome, represented as symbols based upon n-grams and alleles. Experiments show a prominent correlation between the proposed method and phenotypic problem-specific distance measurements in two samples where individuals are radically different, NK-landscapes and Assembly language generation. The methodology is then successfully applied to two experiments with fitness sharing, showing again results comparable to more complex and computationally more demanding phenotypic fitness metrics.

Following the same general principles, a similar distance metric could also be defined for classical Genetic Programming, using for example a node and its children in place of n-grams. However, further studies are needed to assess the general validity of the proposed approach. Variations of the methodology need to be conceived in order to tackle individuals composed of both real values and constants, or individuals in combinatorial problems. Also, since the proposed approach relies upon the number of symbols encoded in each individual, its use for diversity preservation might implicitly benefit larger individuals, thus possibly contributing to the known issue of *bloating*.

6. ACKNOWLEDGEMENTS

The authors would like to thank Davide Barbieri (École des Hautes Études en Sciences Sociales, France) for his invaluable advice and stimulating conversation.

7. REFERENCES

[1] Symmetric difference. In E. J. Borowski and J. M. Borwein, editors, *The HarperCollins Dictionary of Mathematics*. HarperCollins, 1991.

[2] W. Banzhaf, P. Nordin, R. E. Keller, and F. D. Francone. Genetic programming: An introduction: On the automatic evolution of computer programs and its applications (the morgan kaufmann series in artificial intelligence). 1997.

[3] M. Brameier and W. Banzhaf. *Linear Genetic Programming*, volume 117. Springer, 2007.

[4] F. Corno, E. Sánchez, and G. Squillero. Evolving assembly programs: how games help microprocessor validation. *Evolutionary Computation, IEEE Transactions on*, 9(6):695–706, 2005.

[5] G. Corriveau, R. Guilbault, A. Tahan, and R. Sabourin. Review and Study of Genotypic Diversity Measures for Real-Coded Representations. *IEEE Transactions on Evolutionary Computation*, 16(5):695–710, Oct. 2012.

[6] K. Deb, A. Pratap, S. Agarwal, and T. Meyarivan. A fast and elitist multiobjective genetic algorithm: Nsga-ii. *Evolutionary Computation, IEEE Transactions on*, 6(2):182 –197, apr 2002.

[7] R. M. Friedberg. A learning machine: Part i. *IBM Journal of Research and Development*, 2(1):2–13, 1958.

[8] D. Goldberg. Genetic algorithms in search, optimization, and machine learning. 1989.

[9] R. Hamming. Error detecting and error correcting codes. *Bell System technical journal*, 29(2):147–160, 1950.

[10] S. Kauffman and E. Weinberger. The nk model of rugged fitness landscapes and its application to maturation of the immune response. *Journal of theoretical biology*, 141(2):211–245, 1989.

[11] J. R. Koza. *Genetic Programming, On the Programming of Computers by Means of Natural Selection. A Bradford Book.* MIT Press, Cambridge, MA, USA, 1992.

[12] V. Levenshtein. Binary codes capable of correcting deletions, insertions, and reversals. In *Soviet Physics-Doklady*, volume 10, 1966.

[13] M. Mauldin. Maintaining diversity in genetic search. In *Proceedings of the national conference on artificial intelligence (AAAI conference on artificial intelligence)*, volume 247, page 250, 1984.

[14] C. D. Rosin and R. K. Belew. New methods for competitive coevolution. *Evolutionary Computation*, 5(1):1–29, 1997.

[15] E. Sanchez, M. Schillaci, and G. Squillero. *Evolutionary Optimization: the µGP toolkit.* Springer, 2011.

[16] B. Sareni and L. Krahenbuhl. Fitness sharing and niching methods revisited. *Evolutionary Computation, IEEE Transactions on*, 2(3):97–106, 1998.

[17] G. Squillero and A. Tonda. A novel methodology for diversity preservation in evolutionary algorithms. In *Proceedings of the 2008 GECCO conference companion on Genetic and evolutionary computation*, pages 2223–2226. ACM, 2008.

[18] C. Suen. N-gram statistics for natural language understanding and text processing. *Pattern Analysis and Machine Intelligence, IEEE Transactions on*, (2):164–172, 1979.

[19] E. Weinberger. NP completeness of Kauffman nk model, a tuneably rugged fitness landscape. *Santa Fe Institute Technical Reports*, 1996.

Length Bias and Search Limitations in Cartesian Genetic Programming

[Genetic Programming Track]

Brian W. Goldman
BEACON Center for the Study of Evolution in Action
Michigan State University, U.S.A.
brianwgoldman@acm.org

William F. Punch
BEACON Center for the Study of Evolution in Action
Michigan State University, U.S.A.
punch@msu.edu

ABSTRACT

In this paper we examine how Cartesian Genetic Programming's (CGP's) method for encoding directed acyclic graphs (DAGs) and its mutation operator bias the effective length of individuals as well as the distribution of inactive nodes in the genome. We investigate these biases experimentally using two CGP variants as comparisons: *Reorder*, a method for shuffling node ordering without effecting individual evaluation, and *DAG*, a method for removing the concept of node position. Experiments were performed on four problems tailored to highlight potential search limitations, with further testing on the 3-bit multiplier problem.

Unlike previous work, our experiments show that CGP has an innate parsimony pressure that makes it very difficult to evolve individuals with a high percentage of active nodes. This bias is particularly prevalent as the length of an individual increases. Furthermore, these problems are compounded by CGP's positional biases which can make some problems effectively unsolvable. Both *Reorder* and *DAG* appear to avoid these problems and outperform *Normal* CGP on preliminary benchmark testing. Finally, these new techniques require more reasonable genome sizes than those suggested in current CGP, with some evidence that solutions are also more terse.

Categories and Subject Descriptors

I.2.8 [**Artificial Intelligence**]: Problem Solving, Control Methods, and Search; I.2.2 [**Artificial Intelligence**]: Automatic Programming

General Terms

Algorithms

Keywords

Cartesian Genetic Programming, Neutrality, Bloat

1. INTRODUCTION

In all black box search, search designers must make assumptions about the properties of the problem in order to outperform random search. When these assumptions match the application, search time can be greatly reduced. As such, understanding how design decisions effect search effectiveness or even prevent search from finding solutions is very important. In Cartesian Genetic Programming (CGP) the maximum genome size of an individual is set at initialization. While this requires the maximum genome size to be larger than the problem's solution needs, the question remains; how will the maximum genome size effect evolution's speed at finding solutions? As larger genomes inherently represent larger search spaces, intuition suggests that using the lowest possible maximum size will have the most efficient search. However, in CGP a mounting body of evidence suggests the optimal maximum size is much larger than the actual solutions evolved [7]. We examine the cause of this discrepancy by applying CGP and a few modified versions of CGP to problems which test specific edge cases in representation. The result is a better understanding of the search limitations of CGP.

2. CGP

In Cartesian Genetic Programming (CGP) individuals use a fixed length string of integers to encode directed acyclic graphs (DAGs). Each node in the DAG is encoded using multiple genes: one specifying a function and the rest specifying node input connections. Graph output is determined by additional genes which can connect to any node or program input. To prevent cycles, nodes may only connect to problem inputs or nodes that precede them in the genome. Early versions of CGP limited valid connections further through user specified graph topologies. While specifying topology is still useful when evolving circuits with known hardware limitations, the less restricted form allows CGP to represent all possible DAGs of size N, where N is the number of nodes in the genome.

The most common evolutionary mechanism in CGP is a $1 + \lambda$ population where each generation the best offspring replaces the parent if it is no less fit. CGP almost exclusively uses a form of point mutation to create offspring, with no form of crossover commonly being employed. As such, these are the methods considered in our analysis. For a more detailed description of CGP, see [6].

While CGP imposes a maximum graph size N, the minimum effective graph size is variable, as there can be unused portions of the genome. These inactive nodes exist because both output locations and internal connections can be changed by evolution. A trivial example is when all outputs are connected directly to problem inputs the entire genome becomes inactive. Thus the active nodes are those nodes used when computing output.

A pernicious problem in the Genetic Programming (GP) community is individual bloat, in which solutions become larger with time without substantive improvement in quality [4]. Experimental evidence has so far suggests that CGP is able to avoid bloat, as the evolved number of active nodes does not grow during evolution [5] nor does it grow significantly as the maximum number of nodes is raised [7].

The existence of inactive genes provides CGP with an explicit form of genetic introns, allowing the evolutionary process to perform neutral search. CGP's replacement strategy facilitates neutral space exploration by ensuring offspring replace their parents if they are no less fit. This allows the population to drift, which has been shown to be beneficial [10]. Furthermore, there is evidence that as much as 95% of the genotype should be inactive to allow for sufficient neutral search [7].

However, this approach to neutral search may have disadvantages. In response to a previous claim about neutrality's beneficial effects on needle in a haystack style problems, Collins [1] showed that on problems with no search gradient, efficient random sampling can significantly outperform CGP with neutral search. Collins argued that the benefits CGP claimed to be receiving through neutral search may be better attributed to higher maximum genome sizes causing an increase in the total number of active genes.

3. LENGTH AND POSITIONAL BIASING

Despite CGP's ability to represent all possible DAGs of size N, there is little evidence that it uniformly searches the space of DAGs. In fact, [9] showed that certain types of structures are more difficult to evolve than others. In particular, larger structures may be more difficult to evolve as they are less common in the search space. Tree based GP has similar issues, with strong evidence that specific types of trees are more difficult to evolve even though they are common in the search space [2]. We suggest that the mechanics used to initialize and evolve connection genes in CGP impose significant biases on the structures of the DAGs evolved, with more bias against larger genotypes than should be expected by just representation frequency.

When initializing and mutating a connection gene, its value is randomly set to either a preceding node in the genome or to an input. As was discussed in [1], this means the expected location of a new connection is $\frac{i}{2}$ where i is the number of nodes and inputs that precede the mutated node. If all nodes had a single connection gene, we would expect random individuals to have a length of $\log_2 N$. Precise calculation of the expected length when using more connection genes is made difficult due to node overlap, but the relationship will remain logarithmic to the total genome size.

The probability that a node is active changes greatly depending on where in the genome it is encoded. Consider nodes near the end of the genome. The highest index node expected to be active is given by Equation 1.

$$(N+I)\frac{O}{O+1} \tag{1}$$

Here, N is the number of nodes in the genome, I is the number of input locations, and O is the number of output locations. This equation is derived from the fact that if numbers are drawn uniformly at random and then ranked, the mean value for each rank will be evenly spaced in the range. As a result, the expected highest output location will be the same as if O locations were placed evenly on the range $N+I$. On problems with a single output (such as the commonly used parity problem) this means, on average, nodes in the second half of the genome are inactive. Some CGP implementations reduce this problem by fixing the output locations to the last O nodes in the genome, which has the effect of scaling O in Equation 1 by the arity of the nodes in use. However, this does not remove the probability for large sections of inactive nodes near the end of the genome.

Conversely, nodes near the beginning of the genome are almost always active. Equation 2 shows how the expected number of incoming connections increases as the number of nodes following node i increases and the arity (a) used increases. This relationship is non-linear monotonic, with input locations and nodes near the inputs likely to have more than one incoming connection while nodes near the output location will likely have less than one incoming connection.

$$\sum_{j=i+1}^{N} \frac{a}{j} \tag{2}$$

Equation 2 is derived from the fact that all nodes following i in the genome have a connections which each have a $\frac{1}{j}$ chance of connecting to i.

The probability that a node is active increases as the number of incoming connections increases, as each could potentially come from an active node. This creates a self reinforcing cycle: The closer a node is to the inputs the more incoming connections it can receive from other nodes with lots of incoming connections. As a result, nodes near the inputs are almost always active while nodes near the outputs are almost never active. Furthermore, the output of nodes near the inputs is likely to be used by multiple active nodes.

Having many active nodes near the start and few near the end has important implications on CGP's ability to perform neutral search. If there are no inactive nodes preceding a given node, it cannot benefit from neutral evolution. Nodes that have a high percentage of inactive nodes preceding them will conversely have a high probability of attaching to inactive nodes, but will likely be inactive themselves.

How this positional bias of active genes effects search can be examined using a thought experiment, shown in Figure 1. Each of the three Cases given are of the second best phenotype, in which Z takes its input from X, while in the optimal phenotype Y is applied on X's output before input to Z. In Case 1 there are inactive nodes between X and Z, so CGP is able to use drift to insert Y. Unfortunately, because active nodes cluster heavily near the start of the genome, this is unlike to happen if even a moderate percentage of the genome is active. In Case 2, X and Z are adjacent nodes, or equivalently all nodes between X and Z are active. CGP can only solve this case by recreating X and/or Z somewhere else in the genome using drift, converting this back to Case 1. That process is highly unlikely as it involves drift

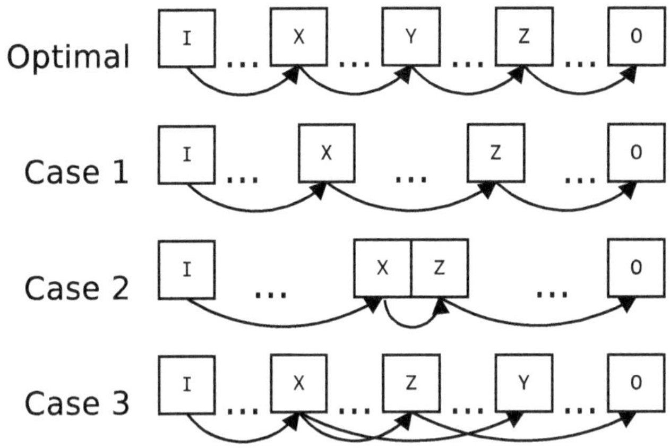

Figure 1: Thought experiment illustrating limitations in *Normal* CGP. Arrows represent the flow of information.

of active genes. In Case 3, Y already exists in the genome, but in the wrong order relative to Z. CGP can solve this by either reinventing Y as in Case 1 or moving Z as in Case 2. From a phenotypic standpoint, the first two cases should be equally difficult with the third being easier, as Y already exists. However, due to CGP's positional biases, Case 2 is much harder than Case 1, as active nodes must be reinvented before Y can be evolved and added between X and Z. Furthermore, Case 3 is just as hard as Case 1, as even though Y already exists, Z cannot connect to it. Case 2 and 3 become even more difficult if X, Y, and Z are thought of as collections of nodes used to produce a single output, as recreating these complex structures increases the difficulty. They also become more common as interwoven structures in the genome act the same as adjacent nodes in this experiment.

4. AVOIDING SEARCH LIMITATIONS

In order to experimentally examine how the mechanisms of CGP bias search, we propose two CGP variants. The first is *Reorder*, which attempts to mitigate positional bias by performing phenotypically neutral node shuffling. The second is *DAG*, which allows nodes to connect to any other node in the genome as long as no cycle is created. For clarity, we will refer to standard CGP as *Normal*. Note that both variants are capable of representing the exact same set of graphs as *Normal*. They only differ in how graphs can be modified by evolution.

4.1 Reorder

Reorder works identically to normal CGP with a single change: Before producing offspring, the parent's nodes are shuffled without changing the phenotype of the individual. That is, we perform neutral search on the parent's node ordering. This process begins by building bidirectional node dependency sets, such that each node's input and output sets can be easily accessed. First the set of *addable* nodes is created, which initially contains all of the inputs. The new node ordering is then determined iteratively using the following steps:

1. Select and remove a node α at random from the *addable* set.
2. If α is not an input, map it sequentially to the next genome location.
3. For each node β which takes output from α:
   (a) Mark β's dependency on α as satisfied.
   (b) If β's dependencies have all been satisfied, add it to *addable*.

Iteration ends when all nodes have been given new locations in the sequence. At this point, nodes can be moved into their new locations, with their connections being updated using the ordering map. Once reordered, nodes maintain the normal CGP requirement that all nodes must take their inputs from nodes preceding them in the genome, meaning that the mutation and evaluation process remains the same. As all connections and functions are preserved during this process, there is no change in the result obtained by executing an individual. *Reorder* is just a neutral permutation of the node ordering.

Repeating the thought experiment in Figure 1 with *Reorder* shows how it can differ from *Normal*. Because inactive nodes can be shuffled between X and Z, Case 1 and 2 become identical. Case 3 can be solved by *Reorder* without recreating Y, as it can be shuffled to precede Z.

Without breaking connections, a node can be moved forward such that it transitively depends on all preceding nodes. A node can also be moved back until all following nodes transitively depend on it. Furthermore, the distance between a node and its input with the highest amount of transitive dependency will be on average smaller than in *Normal*. This is illustrated when considering graphs with a node arity of one. In *Normal* and at initialization of *Reorder*, a node is on average $\frac{i}{2}$ indexes away from where it gets its input and $2i$ indexes from where its output goes. In *Reorder*, nodes will on average be equidistant to their their inputs and outputs. In this case, the expected distance is related to the total number of nodes in the dependency chain. This means that an increased number of active nodes can occupy higher index locations as they are pushed to the center between their inputs and outputs.

This does not directly translate into *Reorder* being able to create more active graphs, or mean that *Reorder* is without length bias. When creating new connections, the expected location is still $\frac{i}{2}$, which means given enough mutations, the individual can revert back to all of the expectations for *Normal*. In general however, *Reorder* will allow nodes on which many nodes transitively depend to increase how many nodes can connect to them, while simultaneously allowing nodes with only a few transitive dependencies to gain more dependencies.

A final artificial bias in both *Reorder* and *Normal* is that all connections in a node will tend to have the same transitive dependencies. This is because if node β is already transitively dependent on node α, then α is always a valid connection when generating new connections in β. This is because all transitive dependencies to a node always precede that node, even when using *Reorder*. Nodes that β is not already transitively dependent on have a probability of being unreachable, and therefore are connected to less frequently.

4.2 DAG

The concept behind *DAG* is to relax the requirement that nodes must connect forward in the genome. To accomplish this, only two portions of CGP have to be modified: connection gene mutation and evaluation ordering. In *Normal*, when a connection gene is mutated, its value is randomly changed to any input or node index less than the mutating node's index. In *DAG*, when a connection gene is chosen to be mutated, new connections are tried randomly and kept if they do not create a cycle.

At the start of each mutation, a mapping is developed to store which nodes are transitively dependent on the mutating node, and which are not. Initially this map stores that the input indexes are not dependent on the mutating node, and that the node is dependent on itself. Nodes are then tested in a random order for transitive dependence. This is performed by recursively applying the following rules:

- If the node's dependency is already known, return the stored information.
- If this node takes input from a dependent node, it is dependent.
- If none of its inputs are dependent, it is not dependent.

As information is collected, the map is updated to ensure a node is never checked for dependency twice. If the randomly chosen node is not dependent on the mutating node, it is used as the new connection value. While this algorithm can result in each mutation needing to traverse a large portion of the graph searching for dependencies, the growth is at worst linear. Furthermore, our reason for introducing *DAG* is to analyze limitations in *Normal*, not necessarily as a computationally efficient alternative.

To determine node ordering during evaluation, *DAG* performs a recursive walk of the active nodes starting from the output locations, recording for each node its bidirectional dependencies on other active nodes. Next, *DAG* builds the ordering of active nodes similar to the *Reorder* method in Section 4.1, ensuring only active nodes are added and that they are added only after all of their dependencies are in the list. Using this ordering, which is only built once for each individual, any number of input sequences can be evaluated with identical run time as *Normal*.

Removing the forward-only requirement found in *Normal* and *Reorder* allows *DAG* to avoid positional bias. This is because any node can connect to any structure that exists in the graph as long as its not already part of that structure. In contrast, *Reorder* can only connect to nodes currently shuffled in front of the mutating node, while in *Normal* structures may have to be reinvented to achieve the same connection. *DAG* can also insert inactive nodes between active nodes, as there is no concept of adjacency.

As to individual length, *DAG* has a much higher expected percentage of active nodes than *Normal* or *Reorder*. When mutating, a connection can be made to any non-dependent node and input. Using an arity of one as an example, the expected number of active nodes is $\frac{N}{I+1}$ where I is the number of inputs. Higher arity will increase the active proportion, but overlap makes precise estimations difficult. Note that unlike *Normal*, the number of active nodes in *DAG* scales linearly with the total number of nodes. Also, since *DAG* still uses *Normal*'s method of initialization, the actual individuals evolved may be less active than expected.

While *DAG*'s reduced search biases do not necessarily result in better results on specific problems, it should generally make *DAG* effective on a wider range of applications. Also note that while evolution of complete DAGs has been done previously [8], our *DAG* method mirror's CGP more faithfully and allows for more direct comparison.

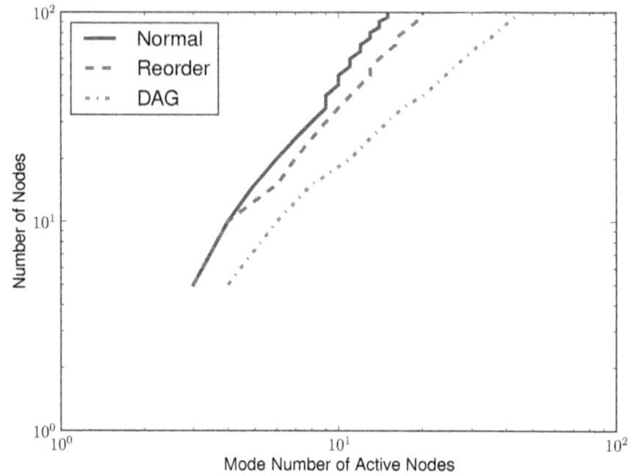

Figure 2: Genome sizes required to achieve different mode numbers of active nodes on the *Neutral* problem

5. TAILORED PROBLEMS

To test the search biases of CGP and our variants, we propose a few benchmark problems specifically tailored to highlight certain types of bias. The following experimental configuration is used across all experiments reported here. Keeping with existing CGP literature, we opted for a $1 + 4$ strategy using mutation as the only variation operator. To avoid tuning the mutation rate, we use the *Single* mutation method described in [3], which mutates genes at random until exactly one active gene is changed. Each run of each experiment used the same initial individual for all algorithms. All experiments were replicated 50 times, resulting in 50 different starting individuals per experiment. Having all algorithms start with the same initialization was done to reduce noise. Each run was given 10,000,000 evaluations before being terminated, and runs were stopped immediately on success.

For all problems except *Neutral* (Section 5.1), we provide a plot of the median evaluations until success using different problem sizes. If the median run was unsuccessful, no information is plotted. Note that both axes in these plots use a log scale. In order to ensure a good sample of scalability we used 20 evenly spaced problem sizes [5..100] at increments of 5. This information was then used to calculate each algorithms' order of complexity in regards to problem size, with results given in Table 2. A complete package of our results as well as the source code used in testing is available from our website.[1]

5.1 Neutral Exploration

To examine how CGP and our variants bias the active length of individuals based on the maximum genome size, we first experiment using the *Neutral* problem. Similar to the problems used in [5, 1], *Neutral* has a completely flat landscape, such that all individuals evaluate to the same fitness.

[1]`https://github.com/brianwgoldman/LengthBiasCGP`

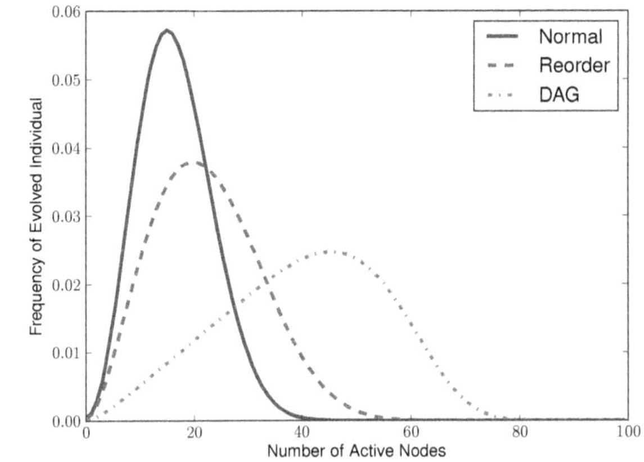

Figure 3: Frequency of evolving individuals of different active lengths on the *Neutral* problem

	Normal	*Reorder*	*DAG*
Mode	15	20	45
95% CI	[5, 31]	[6, 44]	[10, 67]
<99.99%	45	61	81
Longest	59	76	92

Table 1: Frequency of different length individuals on *Neutral*. Includes the most common length (mode), 95% confidence interval (CI), length that 99.99% of individuals were below, and the longest individual found.

In CGP this means parents are replaced each generation with a randomly chosen offspring. Thus there is no evolutionary pressure, only drift. This problem highlights what kinds of individuals each variant is biased toward creating, independent of the evolutionary pressure. In less complex representations, such as those in binary genetic algorithms, you would expect all representable search points to have an equal probability of being seen given enough evaluations. As CGP's representation involves complex decoding, *Neutral* can help examine the likelihood of searching different parts of the search space. In our experiments, *Neutral* has a single input and a single output, with a node arity of two. Furthermore, the function set used is of size one, meaning *Single* mutation must change an active node's connection gene or the output location in order to produce new offspring.

We performed two types of experiments on the *Neutral* problem. The first tests how each variant's evolved number of active nodes changes with genome size. The results provided in Figure 2 can be used to predict how large of a genome size should be used given a user's rough estimate of the number of active nodes required by the problem. This also assumes that search will perform best when the most commonly searched length is close to the optimal individual length. Figure 2 shows that *Normal* required the largest genome sizes to achieve each mode number of active nodes. In terms of scaling, *Normal* needs a genome size of $O(n^{1.79})$ with n the desired mode number of active nodes. While *Reorder* only reduced this to $O(n^{1.53})$, *DAG* scaled much better at $O(n^{1.18})$. This implies that as true problem size increases, we should expect *Normal* to require nearly quadratically increasing genome sizes, while *DAG* scales nearly linearly.

	Normal	*Reorder*	*DAG*
Breadth	3.24	2.06	2.09
Depth	7.72	3.66	4.17
Flat	1.86	1.87	1.94

Table 2: $O(n^x)$ for each variant on each problem, where n is problem size and x is given in the table.

The second experiment looked at the distribution of evolved lengths using a fixed genome size of 100. This information is shown in Figure 3 as a probability density curve, with numeric results in Table 1. The results for *Normal* match our predictions in Section 4.1; most individuals were highly inactive, with a mode number of active nodes of only 15. The probability of generating an individual drops quickly as the number of active nodes deviates from the mode, with none of the 0.5 billion generated individuals having more than 59 active nodes, and only one in 10,000 above 45. This is in contrast to the actual number of graphs of each size, which increases exponentially. This means that *Normal* is biased toward small graphs even more than Figure 3 indicates. *Reorder* and *DAG* show less of a bias, with *DAG*'s mode of 45 close to the prediction made in Section 4.2. The implications of these biases is that each is most likely to find solutions fastest when the number of active nodes desired by the problem best matches the algorithm's search bias, as otherwise the algorithm will add artificial pressure to search different sized graphs. The steepness of the bias reflects how much pressure will be applied. Combined with the length scaling results in Figure 2, we would predict *Normal* to both require a larger genome size than *Reorder* and *DAG*, as well as search a much smaller subset of the search space.

5.2 Breadth

The *Breadth* problem tests CGP's ability to evolve graphs that connect to all inputs using the minimum possible number of nodes. The landscape for this test is a problem with N nodes which has $N+1$ inputs and a single output. The optimal structure is a tree with all nodes in the genome active and all inputs used exactly once as leaves. To evaluate an individual, all nodes execute the binary *OR* function, and possible program inputs are all strings of length $N+1$ with exactly one bit set. As a result, the fitness of an individual is equal to the number of inputs connected to the output. This problem is similar to the tree graph proposed in [9], except the problem scales such that all nodes must always be active, multiple inputs are used, and the fitness function involves individual execution instead of graph edit distance.

Experimental results for the *Breadth* problem are given in Figure 4. This shows that both *Reorder* and *DAG* scale better than *Normal* when solving *Breadth*, but have similar behavior to each other. From Table 2 we see that the number of evaluations *Normal* requires to solve the *Breadth* problem increases cubically while the other variants scale quadratically. A likely cause of this growth discrepancy is that the solution to *Breadth* requires all nodes in the genome to be active, which *Normal* does with difficulty. The fact that *Reorder* does not share this issue even though its search bias on *Neutral* was relatively similar implies that *Reorder* is better able to adapt to problem pressures than *Normal*. While

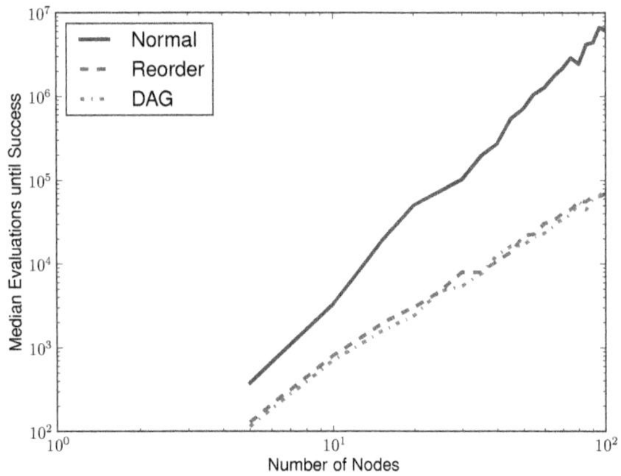

Figure 4: Median evaluations until success for different sizes of the *Breadth* problem

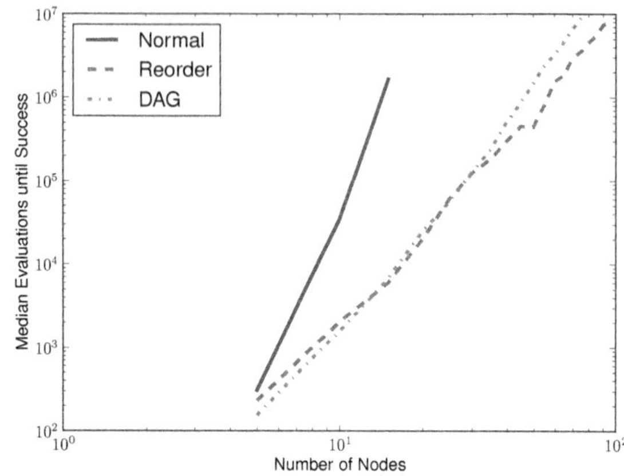

Figure 5: Median evaluations until success for different sizes of the *Depth* problem

DAG scaled slightly worse than *Reorder*, the difference is not significant.

5.3 Depth

The *Depth* problem requires CGP to evolve graphs with the maximum possible node reuse. In this problem, all nodes use the same function, which takes the minimum of their inputs, increments it by one, and returns that value. The fitness function is equal to the value returned, and each individual is tested on a single input of zero. As a result, the maximum fitness is achieved when all nodes are connected in a chain such that all nodes are active and all connections in each node go to the previous node in the graph. Where *Breadth* required no node reuse, *Depth* requires the maximum amount of node reuse. Also in contrast to *Breadth*, *Depth* has a unique solution for *Normal* and *Reorder*, with *DAG* having multiple ways of representing the same graph by encoding nodes in different orders. This problem is similar to the linear graph proposed in [9], except the problem scales such that all nodes must always be active and the fitness function involves individual execution instead of graph edit distance.

Figure 5 and Table 2 both show how *Normal* is effectively unable to solve this problem. *Normal* was only able to solve the smallest three problem sizes of the twenty tried, with an experimental growth rate of $O(n^{7.72})$. By comparison, *Reorder* and *DAG* solved all or almost all, respectively, of the problems tried, with far lower growth rates. As *Breadth* also required all nodes to be active, the reason for *Normal*'s breakdown must be something else about *Depth*. A likely explanation is that *Normal* requires structures to be evolved in a precise location in the genome, in that a node with all connections set to i is only part of the optimal solution if that node is at position $i + 1$. If it is not, it must be reinvented at $i + 1$ to move to optimality. This is especially problematic in the following case. Consider a fully optimal individual, except that $i+1$ is inactive and $i+2$ is active and all of its connections go to i. The only way to improve this individual is to set all of $i + 1$'s connections to i and change all of $i + 2$'s connections to $i + 1$. What makes this difficult is the absence of fitness gradient, meaning all changes can only happen by drift and that changes to $i+2$ can only happen after $i+1$ is relatively correct. Otherwise the individual will decrease in fitness. This problem is further exacerbated by *Normal*'s mutation method, which on average connects i to $\frac{i}{2}$, meaning high index nodes are rarely connected to adjacent indexes. *Reorder* avoids this problem by allowing structures to be moved to where they are needed, while simultaneously decreasing the length of connections. *DAG* has no concept of position, and therefore cannot have this problem.

While *Reorder* and *DAG* have very similar behaviors in Figure 5, Table 2 shows that *Reorder* scaled slightly better. A likely cause of this is that *Reorder* has a higher probability of making nodes with uniform connections as compared to *DAG*. This is true because nodes with no transitive dependency on the mutating node and can still sometimes be unreachable by mutation in *Reorder*. Conversely, nodes that the mutating node is transitively dependent on will always be reachable. In *DAG* there is no bias toward connecting to already transitively dependent nodes. As a result, *Reorder* is able to leverage this search bias to better make nodes with uniform connection genes, improving search speed.

5.4 Flat

As a counter point to *Breadth* and *Depth*, which require entirely active genomes, we propose *Flat*. Unlike the other problems, *Flat* evaluates an individual's genome directly, with the fitness of an individual equal to the number of connections made directly to the input. In this case the optimal individual is one where all nodes and the output location are connected to the only input location. This tests how well CGP is able to create genomes with the least amount of internal structure. Similar to *Depth*, *Flat* has exactly one solution. In [9] some evidence was found that solutions that appear less often in the search space may be harder to find. If this is the reason *Depth* was more difficult than *Breadth*, then *Flat* should also be difficult to solve. As all nodes now participate in evaluation regardless of connections, they are all considered active when performing *Single* mutation.

On this problem, all three algorithms have approximately the same overall shape, shown in Figure 6, and have similar complexities, shown in Table 2. *DAG* does appear to be slower than the other two, although the difference may just

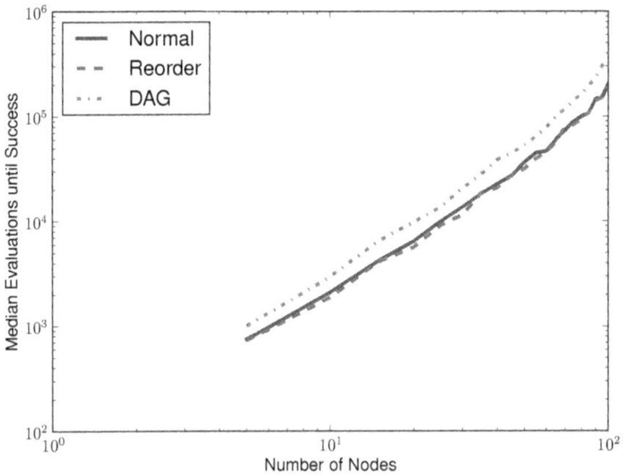

Figure 6: Median evaluations until success for different sizes of the *Flat* problem

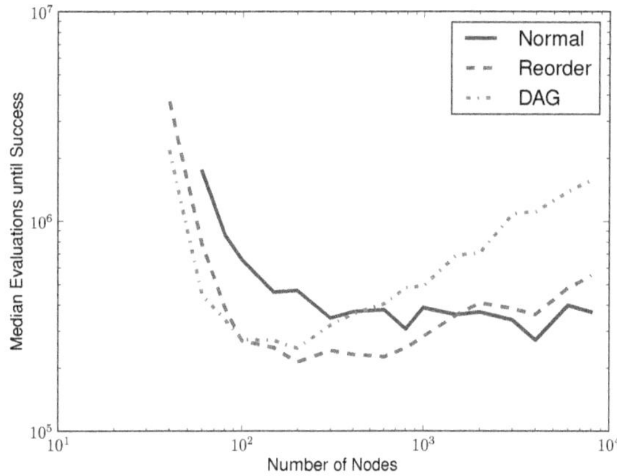

Figure 7: Median evaluations until success on the Multiply problem using different genome sizes

be by a constant scalar. This makes sense as the probability of a connection mutating to an input is $\frac{1}{N}$ for *DAG* and $\frac{1}{i}$ for *Normal* and *Reorder*, with $i \leq N$. In *DAG*, if there are nodes with transitive dependencies on the mutating node, then the probability of connecting to the input increases. However, it can never surpass that for *Normal* and *Reorder*. More generally, these results support the idea that *Reorder* and *DAG* do not have a harder time making highly unconnected structures than *Normal*, and that solution rarity in the search space is not why *Normal* did so poorly on *Depth*.

	Normal	*Reorder*	*DAG*
Genome	4000	200	200
MES	467,621	236,438	265,997
MAD	215,993	82,966	66,930
P-value	N/A	0.00012	0.00006
Active	245	115	116

Table 3: Best configuration of each algorithm on 3-bit Multiplier. Includes maximum genome size, Median Evaluations to Success (MES), Median Absolute Deviation (MAD) one tailed P value comparison with *Normal*, and median number of active nodes in the final solutions found.

6. BENCHMARKING

Understanding length biases and search limitations allows users to solve new search problems easier. In order to examine how our predicted search biases interact with standard CGP landscapes, we tested all three algorithms on the 3-bit multiplier problem. In this problem there are six inputs and six outputs with a function set of {AND, OR, NAND, NOR}. Instead of scaling problem difficulty as in Section 5, each algorithm was tested with scaling genome sizes. We used the range [10..8000], taking 21 points on an exponential scale. Other run parameters were kept the same. The median number of evaluations to success is shown in Figure 7 on a log-log scale. The runs using the best genome size for each algorithm were then repeated to allow for statistical comparison free from selection bias. The results from the repeated runs are given in Table 3.

As predicted, both the graphic and tabular results show that *Reorder* and *DAG* can perform effective search with much smaller genome sizes than *Normal*: The best tested genome size for both novel variants had lower median evaluations to success than *Normal*'s best, which also required a genome twenty times larger. A Kruskal-Wallis Test was first used to determine that at least one of the three algorithms had a different median than the others, with a resulting p-value of 0.00006. Both *Reorder* and *DAG* were statistically better than *Normal* under the single tailed Mann-Whitney U test, even after accounting for multiple comparisons using the Bonferroni correction. Beyond the difference in median evaluations to success, *Normal* also had a much higher median absolute deviation. We believe this deviation is caused by *Normal*'s occasional need to reinvent useful structures in different genome locations. In the unlikely event that active nodes are evolved with the right amount of inactive nodes between them, and in the right order relative to each other, *Normal* is likely going to receive far better results. In cases were these properties do not hold, *Normal* will have to recreate nodes in new locations, often with no fitness gradient, significantly increasing run time. As the number of nodes in the genome increases, the probability that inactive nodes exist between two active nodes increases. This may be part of the reason *Normal* requires such a large genome size to perform well. Also, more inactive space in the genome may facilitate structure recreation in new locations. The higher number of evaluations, higher deviation, and larger optimal genome size also combined to make *Normal* take almost three times more computational time than either of the other algorithms to complete all runs. As a final advantage to *Reorder* and *DAG*, we see that both evolved solutions with half as many median active nodes as *Normal*. A potential reason for this is *Normal*'s need to leverage introns in order to perform neutral search more than the other methods.

Reorder and *DAG* are not without drawbacks. In Figure 7 we see that *Normal* may underperform at peak performance and at lower genome sizes, but as the genome size increases it surpasses the other methods. *DAG* is especially sensitive to increasing genome sizes, performing worse than *Normal* on sizes above 600. *Reorder* also falls behind *Normal* once sizes exceed 2000. This could indicate that the novel methods are more sensitive to genome size. While this is true, we believe it to be less of a flaw and more of an unavoidable side effect of these techniques being able to evolve more complex graphs than *Normal*.

7. CONCLUSIONS AND FUTURE WORK

Existing literature suggests CGP performs best when the maximum genome size far exceeds the actual solution size [7], supported by evidence that inactive genes improve neutral search [10], and that CGP doesn't suffer from bloat [5]. We, however, find evidence that the need for highly inactive genomes is likely due to limitations in CGP's search mechanisms. When no selective pressure on size exists, CGP highly favors short individuals, with this search bias continuing even when the problem structure calls for longer individuals. Furthermore, when combined with CGP's use of node positioning, problems requiring significant proportions of the genotype to be active were found to be difficult or impossible for CGP to solve. We showed theoretical and experimental evidence that the blame for this problem lies with the way CGP's mutation interacts with its representation, as existing mechanisms impose artificial search limitations not inherent to the search problem. *Reorder*, which shuffled node positions without changing node expression, and *DAG*, which removed all concept of node position, were both able to avoid these limitations and more fully utilize genome space. As these methods were able to achieve better results with less inactive genes, we conclude that while inactive genes are useful, the number required by *Normal* CGP is a result of the inherent length bias and search limitations in its representation and evolutionary mechanisms, and not because that many inactive nodes are needed for neutral search. Similarly, CGP's resistance to bloat is likely no more than the work of a previously unexamined form of parsimony pressure, the strength of which is determined by the maximum number of nodes. The drawback of *Reorder* and *DAG* is that in removing this parsimony pressure, they are more able to utilize all genes in the genome, making them more sensitive to the genome size. Yet this may prove to be an advantage, as it may allow CGP to solve more complex problems without explosively increasing the genome size.

Further analysis of *Reorder* and *DAG* should be performed in light of the evidence found here. Both appear to be valid ways of making CGP more flexible and powerful, but wider testing needs to be performed to solidify that claim. As an important aspect of those tests, run time comparisons using equal genome sizes need to be performed, as both increase the computational expense of CGP, with *DAG* especially having the potential for significant overhead. It is also possible either could benefit from further modification, such as using different initialization or method for mutation.

More analysis on the tailored problems will likely improve the clarity of results. Specifically *Neutral* would likely benefit from further scalability testing to see how search frequencies change with respect to genome size, especially at larger genome sizes. Tests with *Breadth* and *Depth* to see how many inactive nodes are needed before *Normal* surpasses *Reorder* and *DAG*, if ever, may also help highlight exactly what proportion of inactive nodes *Normal* needs to solve problems.

8. REFERENCES

[1] M. Collins. Finding needles in haystacks is harder with neutrality. *Genetic Programming and Evolvable Machines*, 7(2):131–144, Aug. 2006. Special Issue: Best of GECCO 2005.

[2] J. M. Daida, H. Li, R. Tang, and A. M. Hilss. What makes a problem GP-hard? validating a hypothesis of structural causes. In *Genetic and Evolutionary Computation – GECCO-2003*, volume 2724 of *LNCS*, pages 1665–1677, Chicago, 12-16 July 2003. Springer-Verlag.

[3] B. W. Goldman and W. F. Punch. Reducing wasted evaluations in cartesian genetic programming. In *Proceedings of the 16th European Conference on Genetic Programming, EuroGP 2013*, volume 7831 of *LNCS*, pages 61–72, Vienna, Austria, 3-5 Apr. 2013. Springer Verlag.

[4] S. Luke and L. Panait. A comparison of bloat control methods for genetic programming. *Evolutionary Computation*, 14(3):309–344, Fall 2006.

[5] J. Miller. What bloat? cartesian genetic programming on Boolean problems. In *2001 Genetic and Evolutionary Computation Conference Late Breaking Papers*, pages 295–302, San Francisco, California, USA, 9-11 July 2001.

[6] J. F. Miller. Cartesian genetic programming. In *Cartesian Genetic Programming*, Natural Computing Series, chapter 2, pages 17–34. Springer, 2011.

[7] J. F. Miller and S. L. Smith. Redundancy and computational efficiency in cartesian genetic programming. *IEEE Transactions on Evolutionary Computation*, 10(2):167–174, Apr. 2006.

[8] J. Niehaus, C. Igel, and W. Banzhaf. Reducing the number of fitness evaluations in graph genetic programming using a canonical graph indexed database. *Evolutionary Computation*, 15(2):199–221, Summer 2007.

[9] A. J. Payne and S. Stepney. Representation and structural biases in CGP. In *2009 IEEE Congress on Evolutionary Computation*, pages 1064–1071, Trondheim, Norway, 18-21 May 2009. IEEE Computational Intelligence Society, IEEE Press.

[10] T. Yu and J. Miller. Neutrality and the evolvability of Boolean function landscape. In *Genetic Programming, Proceedings of EuroGP'2001*, volume 2038 of *LNCS*, pages 204–217, Lake Como, Italy, 18-20 Apr. 2001. Springer-Verlag.

Approximating Geometric Crossover by Semantic Backpropagation

Krzysztof Krawiec
krawiec@cs.put.poznan.pl

Tomasz Pawlak
tpawlak@cs.put.poznan.pl

Institute of Computing Science, Poznan University of Technology
Piotrowo 2, 60965 Poznań, Poland

ABSTRACT

We propose a novel crossover operator for tree-based genetic programming, that produces approximately geometric offspring. We empirically analyze certain aspects of geometry of crossover operators and verify performance of the new operator on both, training and test fitness cases coming from set of symbolic regression benchmarks. The operator shows superior performance and higher probability of producing geometric offspring than tree-swapping crossover and other semantic-aware control methods.

Categories and Subject Descriptors

I.2.2 [**Artificial Intelligence**]: Automatic Programming; I.2.8 [**Artificial Intelligence**]: Problem Solving, Control Methods, and Search—*Heuristic methods*

General Terms

Algorithms, Design, Experimentation, Performance

Keywords

genetic programming, program semantics, geometric crossover

1. INTRODUCTION AND MOTIVATIONS

The conventional search operators used in genetic programming (GP) are designed to be generic. Whether the domain is symbolic regression, Boolean function synthesis, or artificial ant, a standard operator like tree-swapping crossover and subtree-replacing mutation manipulates the code in the same way. Their actual impact on the *effect* of program execution (i.e., on program output) can be very complex and depend strongly not only on the code of the program that undergoes modification, but also on the choice of location at which the operator is applied. As a result, a mutated GP program yields output that is often very different from that of its parent. Similarly, an offspring solution resulting from GP crossover frequently cannot be said to be a 'mixture' of its parents in terms of the output it produces.

This is unfortunate as, in the end, it is the output of program execution that undergoes fitness assessment and drives the search process.

This issue was known since the early days of GP, and characterized from different perspectives. The convenient framing of this phenomenon involves the notion of *locality* [10], meant as the degree of distortion introduced by the genotype-phenotype mapping. Put in these terms, in GP genotypes (program code) map into phenotypes (program behavior) at low locality, so that even a small change of code can translate into huge difference in behavior.

This problem has been recently addressed in a systematic way using program *semantics*. The common feature of semantic-aware approaches in GP is consideration of the operational effects of code, which is usually realized by investigating the output values returned by programs or program fragments. Such semantic information can be exploited in different ways. It can be used as a means to design search operators with properties that are believed to be advantageous, e.g., crossover operators that swap only code fragments that have sufficiently similar effect [11]. But even more can be gained by noticing that semantic information induces certain geometric structure on the space of solutions and the fitness landscape [7, 4]. In this paper, following the recent studies on such operators [9], we propose a specific approximate realization of semantically geometric semantic crossover that exploits reversibility of instructions. This operator and its experimental validation are the main contributions of this study.

2. BACKGROUND

In GP, the objective is to evolve a program that produces desired output for a predefined set of program arguments, i.e. *inputs* (*examples, fitness cases*). The vector of desired outputs associated with particular examples forms the *target* for the search process. This process is driven by fitness function that usually aggregates the errors committed by a program on particular examples into single scalar value. Usually, fitness function is expressed as a distance between the vector of outputs produced by a program and the target, where the former one is known as *program semantics* (or sampling semantics) [1, 11]. The particular form of distance metrics depends on output data type and problem formulation: Euclidean or city-block distance are commonly used for real-valued programs (e.g., symbolic regression), and Hamming distance for Boolean domain. However, such a metric can also be defined for non-scalar data types, i.e., the Levenshtein distance for strings.

Formally, semantics $s(p)$ of program p is a vector of outcomes produced by p in a response to the given set of ex-

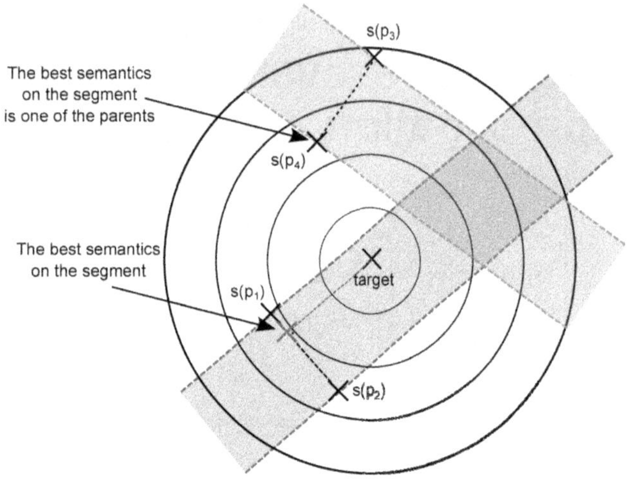

Figure 1: The conic fitness landscape defined by fitness function expressed as Euclidean distance from the given target semantics. The segments between parents show the range of semantics of geometric offspring. For p_1 and p_2 there exists a geometric offspring that is better than the best of the parents. For p_3 and p_4 there is no better offspring. It is the presence or absence of the target in the shaded area that distinguishes these cases.

amples. For instance, if p is a symbolic regression program tested on n fitness cases, its semantic $s(p)$ is the vector of n numbers it returns when applied to these cases. Denoting the above mentioned metric by d, the fitness f of a program p can be expressed as $f(p) = d(s(p), t)$, where t is the target. Importantly, the same metric can be used to measure the semantic proximity $d(s(p_1), s(p_2))$ of any pair of programs p_1 and p_2, and thus it endows the space of semantics (and indirectly the space of programs) with certain geometric structure.

An important consequence of defining fitness as a distance from the target t is that the fitness landscape spanning the space of all semantics is a cone centered at t. By the properties of metric, this landscape is unimodal, with the only one global minimum in t. If a program p is modified so that its semantics $s(p)$ becomes closer to the target t, the fitness $f(p)$ decreases (improves) too, because $f(p) = d(s(p), t)$. There is perfect correlation between f and the phenotypic distance d, because they are equivalent. If one could manipulate the semantics directly, the search on such landscapes would become trivial, with even the simplest local search algorithms guaranteed to find the target. However, typical search operators employed in GP operate only on program code, disregarding semantics, and such purely syntactic manipulations translate into changes of program semantics in a complex way.

The possibility of exploiting the properties of semantic fitness landscape propelled research on corresponding search operators. One of the most important concepts on this avenue of research is geometric crossover. According to Moraglio, a recombination operator is a geometric crossover under the metric d if all offspring are in the d-metric segment between its parents [8]. The offspring resulting from geometric crossover have certain attractive properties that we explain in the following for the special case of Euclidean metric.

Consider the space of programs represented by their semantics and the conical fitness landscape spanned over that space by the Euclidean fitness function (see Fig. 1). Choose any two programs from the space and cross them over. For the standard tree-swapping crossover, the semantics of the resulting offspring may be located almost anywhere on the cone, and that location is only weakly related to parents' semantics. However, the semantics of an offspring resulting from geometric crossover must lay somewhere on the segment between the parents, so its fitness must be not worse than the fitness of the worst of parents. Moreover, if it happens to be closer to the target than the semantics of the better parent, the offspring is more fit that both its parents.

This example illustrates that geometric offspring can outperform its parents. The main challenge for technical realization of such operators is that, in GP, there is no direct control on program semantics: the search operators change program code, and these changes translate into complex trajectories in the semantic space. Nevertheless, certain degree of 'geometricity' can be attained using simple means, e.g., by applying standard crossover multiple times and picking the offspring that is as geometric as possible [4]. However, the major recent advancement in studies on geometric crossover is [9], where Moraglio *et al.* have proposed a systematic way of designing *exact* mutation and crossover operators that exploit the conic shape of the semantic fitness landscape (geometric semantic genetic programming, GSGP). The key idea there is to use the instructions available to the GP search process to build an expression atop the parent(s) that modifies its semantics in a way that *guarantees* preserving of the geometric properties. In this way, a mutated program is guaranteed to be semantically similar to the parent, and crossover's offspring has to be located on the segment between the semantics of the parents. For instance, the semantically geometric crossover applied to a pair of symbolic regression parent programs (p_1, p_2) produces an offspring program of the form $\alpha p_1 + (1-\alpha)p_2$, where α is a constant. It is immediately obvious that such an offspring, being a linear combination of p_1 and p_2, has semantics located on the Euclidean segment connecting their semantics.

However, as Moraglio *et al.* report [9], bloat remains the main challenge for GSGP. Because the offspring solutions are syntactic aggregates of entire parent programs (offspring include parents as subprograms), every generation of offspring involves more code, and additional simplification is necessary to make the search process technically feasible. And simplification procedures incur also additional computational overhead. In this paper, we make an attempt to circumvent this problem by proposing an approximate geometric crossover operator. This operator, described in the subsequent section, does not guarantee to produce perfectly geometric offspring, but it is also less affected by bloat.

3. APPROXIMATE GEOMETRIC CROSSOVER

The main idea behind Approximate Geometric Crossover (AGX) is to replace subtrees in parents with such code fragments (subtrees) that the semantics of offspring lays in the middle of the segment connecting parents' semantics. The operator first calculates the semantics $s(p_1)$ and $s(p_2)$ of, respectively, parents p_1 and p_2[1]. Next, the midpoint m on the segment connecting $s(p_1)$ and $s(p_2)$ is determined. For

[1] If the programs have been previously evaluated, their semantics are already known.

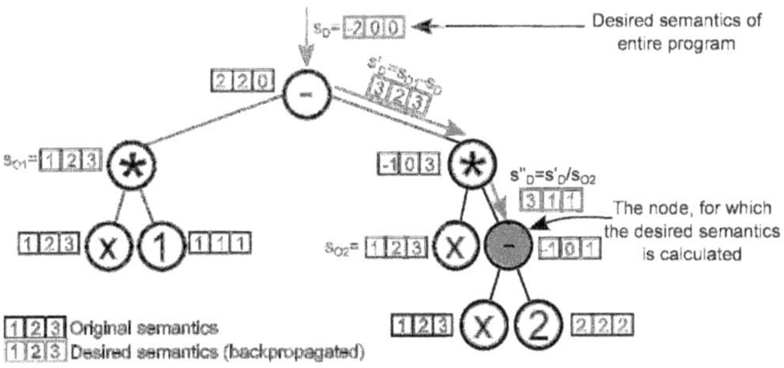

Figure 2: An example of semantic backpropagation. For a given desired program semantics, we calculate the desired semantics for each node on path from the root node to the crossover point (the blue one).

numerical semantics and Euclidean distance, this is the average of semantics of both parents. The calculated vector m becomes the desired semantics of offspring, as it corresponds to a 'perfect mixing' of parents' behaviors.

Next, AGX chooses two crossover points in p_1 and p_2. The subsequent steps apply to each parent independently, so for simplicity from now we focus on p_1 only. Then the operator executes all instructions on the path from program root to the chosen crossover point in a 'reverse manner'. The input data for this process is the semantics m. Compared to regular program execution, the order of execution is reversed (execution proceeds top-down in the tree), and at each step of this process an 'inverse' instruction is executed.

The details of reverse execution can be found in Section 3.1, and here we explain its objective. Let us consider the first stage of this process, i.e., the root node r and its direct child c on the path defined above. Reverse execution determines what should be the output of c in order for r to produce m. In other words, we calculate the *desired semantics* of the subprogram to replace c (desired in the sense that it would make the resulting offspring a perfect mixture of the parents). This process, continued along the path, allows us to propagate this information to the instruction located at the crossover point, and thus determine the desired semantics of the subtree to be replaced.

Once the operator determined the desired semantics for crossover point, it searches the previously prepared library of short programs (called 'procedures') for a procedure, that has the closest semantics to the desired one (see Section 3.2). Finally, the selected procedure replaces entire subtree under the crossover point, producing the offspring. The same steps are applied to the other parent.

3.1 Semantic backpropagation

We call the algorithm that calculates the desired semantics of an intermediate node *semantic backpropagation*. By analogy to error backpropagation in neural networks, we apply the desired value of semantics to program's root node and then propagate this value reversely, down the program tree (Fig. 2). The algorithm needs to know the semantics of all nodes in the program (subtrees) before performing the backpropagation, but this requirement is already fulfilled if the program has been previously evaluated (which is the case in the standard GP loop).

To explain the details, let us focus on a single tree node. Given the desired semantics of that node (desired output) and the actual semantics of all children of that node, we want to calculate the desired value of semantics of a specific child of this node. To do that, we need to execute the inversion of actual instruction in the node in context of the other children and the desired semantics of current node.

For the instructions characteristic to symbolic regression (considered in the experimental part), inversion can be implemented by using a *complementary operation* that reverts the actions performed by the actual instruction. For instance, consider subtraction instruction $output := child_1 - child_2$. Since subtraction is an asymmetric operation, the form of complementary operation depends on which child we propagate the desired semantics to. For the first child the complementary operation is $child_1 := output + child_2$, and for the second child it is $child_2 := child_1 - output$. The values calculated in this way for all elements of the vector that defines the desired semantics ($output$) form the semantics (vector shown in blue in Fig. 2) to be propagated further down the tree.

As long as an instruction implements a bijective function (transforms distinct arguments to distinct values in the codomain and vice versa) it can be safely inverted in the above way. However if an instruction is surjective (and not bijective), its inversion is ambiguous, since there are many arguments that cause it to return the same output value. In general, two types of ambiguity are possible, with a finite and infinite number of inversions. In the former case one can calculate, provided enough computational resources, all possible inversions and continue the semantic backpropagation in child node for each of these semantics. However for the latter case, the set of possible inversions can be only sampled.

To cope with the above problems while keeping computational cost at bay, in case of ambiguity we calculate at most two desired semantics for the child node. The subsequent part of the semantic backpropagation is then carried out for both desired semantics independently. Each of them can possibly lead to further ambiguities. Thus, even with this constraint, the number of backpropagated semantics may increase exponentially with node depth.

Another special case needs to be handled when inverting non-surjective instructions. For instance, $\forall x : \exp(x) > 0$, so for negative values of desired semantics no argument x exists that could be propagated down the tree. In other words, there is no semantics for the appointed crossover point (and thus no procedure in the library) that can move the semantics of the entire program to the midpoint of the segment. If this happens even for a single element of desired semantics, we discard it. However, this does not necessarily stop the entire semantic backpropagation: if the ancestor nodes had ambiguous inversions and thus led to alternative versions of desired semantics, the processing continues for them. Only when inversion fails for all versions of desired semantics, the algorithm gives up.

Note that, an instruction can be both ambiguously invertible and non-invertible. This is the case for, e.g. $y := x^2$, which maps exactly two x values to every *positive* value of y and no x value to every *negative* value of y. Therefore, the feasibility of instruction inversion is highly contextual: it may be possible to unambiguously invert an instruction at one location in a program but not at another. The ruling factor is the desired semantics of the instruction being inverted. In this sense, we may say that the instruction's desired semantics specifies (one unique inversion), underspecifies (multiple inversions), or overspecifies (no inversions) the desired semantics of instruction's argument (the selected child node).

Table 1: The benchmarks used in the experiment. $E[a,b,n]$ means n *equidistant* points from the range $[a,b]$. $U[a,b,n]$ means n random points chosen with *uniform* distribution from the range $[a,b]$.

Problem	Definition (formula)	Training set Test set
Nonic	$\sum_{i=1}^{9} x^i$	$E[-1,1,20]$ $U[-1,1,20]$
R1	$(x+1)^3/(x^2-x+1)$	$E[-1,1,20]$ $U[-1,1,20]$
R2	$(x^5-3x^3+1)/(x^2+1)$	$E[-1,1,20]$ $U[-1,1,20]$
Nguyen-7	$log(x+1)+log(x^2+1)$	$E[0,2,20]$ $U[0,2,20]$
Keijzer-1	$0.3xsin(2\pi x)$	$E[-1,1,20]$ $U[-1,1,20]$
Keijzer-4	$x^3e^{-x}cos(x)sin(x)(sin^2(x)cos(x)-1)$	$E[0,10,20]$ $U[0,10,20]$

In conclusion, due to possible ambiguities and non-invertibility of instructions, the outcome of the semantic backpropagation is a *set* of desired semantics for the given tree node. That set may contain zero, one, or many semantics.

3.2 Library of procedures

AGX makes use of the library of short programs, called *procedures* in following. Its purpose is to supply AGX with code fragments that match as close as possible the desired semantics resulting from semantic backpropagation. To provide high diversity of semantic, we populate the library with all possible program trees, up to an assumed height, composed of the elements of the assumed instruction set. Since it is only the semantic distance between the desired semantics and the semantic of a procedure that determines which procedure is fetched from the library, storing semantically identical procedures is pointless. Therefore, for any set of procedures that have the same semantics, the library stores only the shortest one. There are obviously many other ways in which the library could be populated, but here we limit our considerations to this straightforward method.

The size of the library is exponential in function of the height limit, so providing fast search for the closest semantics is essential. This process can be sped up by means of spatial (multidimensional) indexes, data structures originally designed for geographic databases. We tested wide range of spatial indexes and found out that for this particular task, characterized by high dimensionality of the search space, the KD-tree [2] works best. The nearest neighbor query to the index consisting of m elements takes on average $O(\log m)$ time, and $O(m^{1-1/k})$ in the worst case.

4. GEOMETRY OF OPERATORS

In general, AGX cannot guarantee the semantics of offspring to reach the midpoint of the segment connecting parents' semantics. There are two reasons for this. Firstly, the library is a finite set of procedures, which by definition do not implement all possible semantics. Therefore, in most crossover acts, the substituted procedure has a non-zero distance from the desired semantics, and that discrepancy propagates to the root node. Secondly, limited arithmetic precision makes the reversal process inherently inexact.

For these reasons we carry out a computational experiment aimed at quantitative assessment of the probability at which different operators produce geometric offspring. Technically, we ran evolution on six symbolic regression problems from Table 1 for 100 generations each and recorded each crossover act by AGX, standard subtree crossover (GPX) [3], and a comparable approach, locally geometric semantic crossover (LGX, [5]), that approximates geometric changes on the level of homologous program tree loci. Next, for each resulting offspring we checked whether it is located on the segment connecting parent's semantics according to the Manhattan distance. We chose this metric because it is characterized by the biggest size of segment between parents of all Minkowski distances $L_p, p \geq 1$. In other words, Manhattan distance defines geometric offspring in the most 'liberal' way.

Table 2: Fraction of geometric offspring (according to Manhattan distance) bred by AGX, LGX, GPX, and p-values of Z-test for the equality of two proportions. Best values in rows and the significant p-values ($\alpha = 0.05$, one-sided test) are in bold.

Depth of crossover	AGX	LGX	GPX	p-values AGX>GPX	p-values LGX>GPX	p-values AGX>LGX
1	.0155	**.1676**	.0035	**.0000**	**.0000**	1.000
2	**.0151**	.0100	.0031	**.0000**	**.0000**	**.0000**
3	**.0136**	.0031	.0018	**.0000**	**.0001**	**.0000**
4	**.0105**	.0016	.0020	**.0000**	.9570	**.0000**
5	**.0055**	.0014	.0011	**.0000**	.1219	**.0000**
6	**.0028**	.0009	.0007	**.0000**	.1521	**.0000**
7	**.0017**	.0006	.0005	**.0000**	.2899	**.0000**
8	**.0012**	.0004	.0003	**.0000**	.1944	**.0000**
9	**.0010**	.0007	.0003	**.0001**	**.0121**	.0558
10	**.0006**	.0005	.0003	**.0296**	.0766	.3660
11	**.0005**	.0002	.0003	.1214	.8050	.0529
12	**.0004**	.0001	.0003	.2305	.9037	**.0499**
13	**.0003**	.0002	.0002	.3577	.6258	.3114
14	.0002	.0000	**.0005**	.9526	.8704	.2298
15	.0000	.0000	**.0002**	.6843	.6582	.5000
16	.0000	.0000	**.0005**	.5979	.6968	.5000
17	.0000	.0000	.0000	.5000	.5000	.5000
Overall	**.0057**	.0035	.0008	**.0000**	**.0000**	**.0000**

Table 2 presents the probability of producing geometric offspring by all considered operators and the corresponding p-values of Z-test for the equality of two proportions. We present the overall outcome in the last row of the table, and for particular depths of crossover points. Each offspring is counted separately, thus two offspring resulting from the same crossover act may contribute to different rows in the table.

From the table, we see that in 12 of 17 cases AGX has the highest probability of producing geometric offspring. LGX dominates both other operators only in one case. GPX is most geometric in three cases, however the probabilities are very small and insignificant. AGX is significantly more geometric than GPX in 10 of 17 cases, while LGX is significantly better in only 4 cases. Taking into account overall result, both AGX and LGX are significantly more geometric than GPX, however the test also shows that AGX is significantly more likely to produce geometric offspring than LGX. No crossover act at depth 17 was geometric in this experiment.

The important observation is that, while the probability of producing geometric offspring drops with depth for all operators, AGX maintains the relatively highest probability for the widest range of depths. For AGX, the probability

Table 3: Experimental setup.

Parameter	AGX	LGX	GPX
Instruction set	$\{+,-,\times,/,sin,cos,exp,log,x\}$[a]		
Population size	1024		
Initial max tree depth	6		
Max tree height	17		
Selection	tournament selection		
Tournament size	7		
Trials per experiment	100 independent runs		
Termination condition	250 generations		
Crossover probability	0.9		
Mutation probability	0.1		
Max procedure height	$\{3,4\}$	$\{3,4\}$	—
Crossover point selection	linear	homologous	Koza-I [3]

[a]The / and log are protected. Division by 0 returns 0 and logarithm calculates absolute value of its argument.

decreases due to the growing number of instructions in the path from crossover point to the program root, causing multiple transformations of geometry of semantic space. Since the semantics of the procedure chosen from the library in general only approximates the desired semantics, the error of this approximation is propagated through the program structure, where it may be increased or decreased depending on instructions on the path. This complex process may affect each fitness case to a different extent, and apparently causes the changes on the level of program root to be 'less geometric'.

In conclusion, we observe that AGX is more likely to produce geometric offspring than LGX and GPX, however the probabilities are rather low. In the next section, we verify whether these properties have any significant impact on the effectiveness of evolutionary search.

5. PERFORMANCE OF OPERATORS

We use six univariate symbolic regression problems to assess the performance of AGX, comparing to the LGX [5] and subtree crossover (GPX) [3]. The problems, enumerated in Table 1, come from [3, 6] and represent four classes. There are problems with the target defined by a polynomial, rational, logarithmic and trigonometric functions. For each problem, we define a training set of fitness cases used by fitness function during evolution, and a disjoint test set of fitness cases for post-evolution assessment of generalization capability.

Evolution is allowed to use eight non-terminal instructions (see Table 3). The only terminal instruction is the independent variable x (there are no constants). Crossover operators are engaged with 0.9 probability and are supplemented by subtree-replacement mutation. Mutation is added to prevent premature convergence and to make competition with GPX more fair for the latter (without mutation, evolution run by GPX can irreversibly lose instructions from population). There is no reproduction.

AGX and LGX employ the same libraries of procedures. We consider two libraries: a small one containing all unique program trees of height up to 3, and a big one with height limit 4. The cardinalities of libraries are, respectively, 212 and 108520 (recall that semantic duplicates are discarded).

Table 4: Symmetry test. P-values represent probability of *erroneously* judging method in row as better than method in column. Values in bold are significant ($\alpha = 0.05$).

	AGX_3	AGX_4	GPX	LGX_3	LGX_4
AGX_3					
AGX_4	**0.002**		**0.048**	0.123	0.996
GPX	0.892				
LGX_3	0.705		0.996		
LGX_4	**0.009**		0.123	0.262	

The suffix following method name indicates the type of library (e.g. AGX_4).

Note that the operators use different methods for selection of crossover point. AGX uses linear selection, which assigns equal probability to each depth of tree. First the set of nodes on particular depth is chosen, then a crossover point is selected from this set. On the other hand LGX involves homologous selection and GPX uses Koza-style selection (with 0.9 probability an intermediate node is chosen, otherwise a leaf).

5.1 Search progress

Figure 3 shows the average of best-of-generation fitness achieved by AGX_3, AGX_4, LGX_3, LGX_4 and GPX for problems from Table 1, averaged over 100 runs, with confidence intervals marked by shading. AGX_4 is the unquestionable winner in terms of speed of convergence. On average, it leads from the beginning, and in less than 50 generations achieves fitness that is unbeatable by the other methods for long time. Only for two problems, Nonic and Nguyen-7, AGX_4 is overtaken by LGX_4 at the end of trial. However, these differences are statistically insignificant. The second best method is LGX_4, which achieves fitness at the level of AGX_4 or a bit worse, however it requires significantly more time to do so.

The situation is quite different for the methods equipped with the small library. AGX_3 is better than LGX_3 only on the R2 problem, and in the other cases the latter is noticeably better. We hypothesize that it is an effect of imperfect match of procedures to desired semantics. The big library is three orders of magnitude larger than the small one, therefore it can be expected to provide procedures that match the desired semantics more closely.

The relation of GPX to other methods is highly problem-dependent. It is significantly worse than the best of the other methods. However, for each problem there is at least one other method that does not outperform it. Usually it is the AGX_3, but for R2 it is LGX_3.

We performed Friedman's test for multiple achievements of series of subjects on the average of best-of-run fitness to assess significance of the differences between methods. The resulting p-value is 0.0024, so assuming $\alpha = 0.05$ there exists at least one statistically significant difference. Therefore we conducted post-hoc analysis using symmetry test to analyze significance between particular pairs of methods. The results, shown in Table 4, indicate that AGX_4 is significantly better than GPX and AGX_3.

5.2 Test-set performance

To assess the performance of generalization, we ran best-of-run individual on independent test-set data (Tab. 1) and averaged the results over 100 runs of GP. The values shown

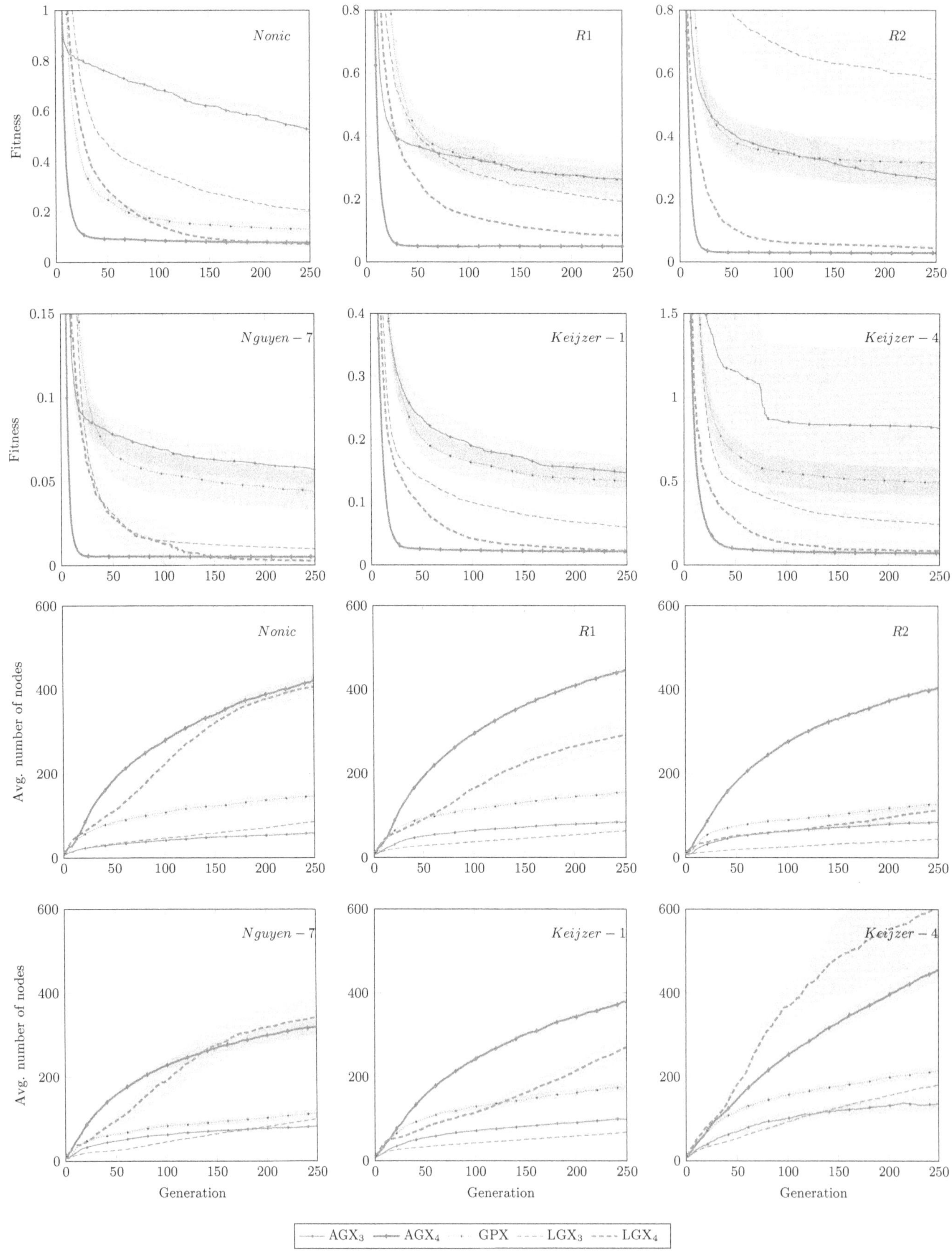

Figure 3: Performance of AGX, LGX and GPX. Rows 1 & 2: Best-of-run fitness. Rows 3 & 4: Number of nodes in programs. Values averaged over 100 runs.

Table 5: Error committed by best-of-run individual on test set (avg. of 100 runs). For values higher than 100 we left only an order of magnitude.

Problem	AGX_3	AGX_4	GPX	LGX_3	LGX_4
Nonic	0.359 ±0.036	**0.093** ±0.012	0.130 ±0.021	0.201 ±0.037	0.191 ±0.074
R1	0.224 ±0.025	**0.050** ±0.006	0.261 ±0.053	0.167 ±0.025	0.103 ±0.018
R2	$10^7 \pm 10^7$	**0.028** ±0.004	0.316 ±0.073	0.621 ±0.126	0.042 ±0.012
Nguyen-7	0.051 ±0.008	0.005 ±0.001	0.044 ±0.011	0.018 ±0.015	**0.004** ±0.003
Keijzer-1	0.190 ±0.032	**0.039** ±0.007	0.134 ±0.026	0.091 ±0.013	0.041 ±0.010
Keijzer-4	3.113 ±2.792	$10^{13} \pm 10^{13}$	**0.492** ±0.084	2.008 ±1.141	2.854 ±3.278

in the Table 5 demonstrate that AGX_4 generalizes the best for 4 out of 6 problems. In contrast, LGX_4 provides the best generalization for only one problem, however the difference compared to AGX_4 is insignificant in this case. GPX proves superior to other methods only on one problem.

Comparison of the errors obtained for the test set to the corresponding fitness values measured on the training set (Fig. 3) show that AGX_4 noticeably overfits only on the Keijzer-4 problem. On the other hand, there are no doubts that overfitting occurs also twice for AGX, once for LGX_3 and LGX_4. GPX turns out to be the most resistant to overfitting, which is however not surprising given its poor performance on the training set.

5.3 Impact on tree size

Figure 3 presents the average number of nodes of programs in evolutionary runs for AGX, LGX and GPX. The very first observation is that the size of solutions created by both AGX and LGX depends on the size of used library. Both methods, when equipped with the small library, produce solutions that are noticeably smaller than the solutions created by standard tree-swappinng crossover. With the big library, both produce significantly bigger trees.

Though the trees produced by AGX_4 at the end of runs are rather large, it is worth noticing that the method achieves its top fitness much earlier, typically in less than 50 generations (Fig. 3), and the remaining ~ 200 generations do not noticeably improve fitness. And when we consider the programs generated by AGX_4 in the 50th generation, their sizes can be claimed comparable to those evolved by, e.g., GPX.

At this point it is also desirable to compare AGX, an *approximate* geometric crossover, to the *exact* geometric crossover from [9]. The exact geometric crossover combines two parent programs into one offspring, by adding an additional structure as a new program root. Such a structure must consist of at least one node. Thus, the exact crossover on average doubles the size of programs in every generation. The rough estimate of the expected number of nodes in programs produced by this operator after g generations is $2^g \times avg_{p \in P_0}(size(p))$, where P_0 is the initial population. Even if P_0 contained single-node programs, for $g = 50$ this amounts to 1.1×10^{15}. Though the authors of [9] do not report tree sizes and claim that bloat can be kept at bay by employing simplification procedures, this analysis shows that the sizes of programs produced by AGX_4 when fitness saturates (~ 170 nodes on average) can be still attractive. In other words, compared to exact geometric crossover, AGX trades exactness for program size.

6. DISCUSSION

An observant reader has probably noticed the following. If the objective of semantic backpropagation is to 'shift' parent's semantic from its current location to specific other location (in our case: the midpoint of the segment spanning parents' semantics), then why not use the same procedure to shift the semantics *directly* to the target of the search process? In such a case, the semantic being backpropagated through the path of instructions would be simply the ultimate goal of the entire search process. Assuming that the semantic backpropagation is at least partially effective at changing the semantic in the right direction (and the above experiments suggest that it is), one may expect such search converge to the target faster than AGX.

Indeed, such *direct search* is a natural analog to AGX, and we investigate it in a separate study [12]. Note however that applicability of direct search is limited. Firstly, it requires the target to be explicitly given. This requirement is met in all typical symbolic regression tasks. However, there are conceivable scenarios in which this is not the case. Imagine for instance an application in which the target cannot be revealed due to privacy concerns or other issues (e.g., the target is a confidential historical time series). In such a case, even if the fitness function definition is fully conformant with the formalisms presented in Section 2, and fitness landscape is a unimodal cone, the target cannot be directly used. Contrary to direct search, AGX, for which the knowledge of target is irrelevant, can be still applied to such tasks.

There is also a much wider class of problems that can be approached with AGX, but not with the direct search. In this study, we assumed that fitness function is a *distance* from a *uniquely defined* target, which causes the fitness landscape to be conic and guarantees the offspring of geometric crossover to be not worse than the worse of its parents (Fig. 1). Many problems involve fitness function that cannot be expressed in that way, e.g., where fitness results from some simulation process (control problems like pole balancing, design problems, etc.). Consequently, unimodality is lost (or uncertain), and the above guarantee becomes void. Nevertheless, it is reasonable to expect that fitness landscapes for such problems are at least locally convex, and within such local basins AGX can still be effective at improve solutions (while, again, direct search is useless as the target is unknown). More specifically, as long as both parents dwell in the same basin of local optimum, AGX's operation is consistent with the reasoning presented in Section 2. Its effectiveness on such problems will be subject of our future studies.

Probably the strongest limitation of the approach proposed here is the requirement of instruction inversibility. Definitely, many instructions are in general irreversible, particularly those used in conventional programming languages. Nevertheless, we hypothesize that AGX can bring some benefits even if the inversion operations are imperfect in some sense (e.g., return multiple possible outcomes or do not return any outcome). Note that the library typically does not contain the procedure with exactly the desired semantics, so even if all instructions on the path would be perfectly inversible, the semantics of the modified individual is not guaranteed to shift to the prescribed location. Also, in the end, given the stochasticity of the other elements of evolutionary search (selection, mutation), the approximate nature of AGX can be of secondary importance.

In conclusion, the performance of AGX is clearly related to the contents of the provided library. If we could hypothetically equip AGX with an ideal library, that provides a perfectly matching procedure to the desired semantics, the AGX would operate almost identically on semantics level to the exact geometric crossover [9]. However we expect that the sizes of trees produced by AGX would remain smaller than exact crossover's. Note that the ideal library is virtually not possible to be built. Additionally one may consider such library as a form of an oracle, which returns a program for a given semantics. It is clear that having this form of an oracle, we need not any optimization algorithm anymore.

7. CONCLUSIONS

We presented AGX, a new GP crossover operator that is semantically approximately geometric. AGX exhibits superior performance compared to the locally geometric semantic crossover [5], and the canonic tree-swapping crossover [3]. It maintains this advantage on both training set and test set. Though it suffers from substantial bloat, particularly when allowed to run too long, the sizes of trees produced by AGX are significantly smaller than the theoretical expected tree size of non-simplified programs produced by exact geometric crossover [9].

Acknowledgment

Work supported by grant no. DEC-2011/01/B/ST6/07318.

8. REFERENCES

[1] L. Beadle and C. Johnson. Semantically driven crossover in genetic programming. In J. Wang, editor, *Proceedings of the IEEE World Congress on Computational Intelligence*, pages 111–116, Hong Kong, 1-6 June 2008. IEEE Computational Intelligence Society, IEEE Press.

[2] Bentley. Multidimensional binary search trees used for associative searching. *CACM: Communications of the ACM*, 18, 1975.

[3] J. R. Koza. *Genetic Programming: On the Programming of Computers by Means of Natural Selection.* MIT Press, Cambridge, MA, USA, 1992.

[4] K. Krawiec and P. Lichocki. Approximating geometric crossover in semantic space. In G. Raidl, et al., editors, *GECCO '09: Proceedings of the 11th Annual conference on Genetic and evolutionary computation*, pages 987–994, Montreal, 8-12 July 2009. ACM.

[5] K. Krawiec and T. Pawlak. Locally geometric semantic crossover: a study on the roles of semantics and homology in recombination operators. *Genetic Programming and Evolvable Machines*, 14(1):31–63, 2013.

[6] J. McDermott, D. R. White, S. Luke, L. Manzoni, M. Castelli, L. Vanneschi, W. Jaskowski, K. Krawiec, R. Harper, K. De Jong, and U.-M. O'Reilly. Genetic programming needs better benchmarks. In T. Soule, et al., editors, *GECCO '12: Proceedings of the fourteenth international conference on Genetic and evolutionary computation conference*, pages 791–798, Philadelphia, Pennsylvania, USA, 7-11 July 2012. ACM.

[7] A. Moraglio. *Towards a Geometric Unification of Evolutionary Algorithms.* PhD thesis, Department of Computer Science, University of Essex, UK, Nov. 2007.

[8] A. Moraglio. Abstract convex evolutionary search. In H.-G. Beyer and W. B. Langdon, editors, *Foundations of Genetic Algorithms*, pages 151–162, Schwarzenberg, Austria, 5-9 Jan. 2011. ACM.

[9] A. Moraglio, K. Krawiec, and C. G. Johnson. Geometric semantic genetic programming. In C. A. Coello Coello, et al., editors, *Parallel Problem Solving from Nature, PPSN XII (part 1)*, volume 7491 of *Lecture Notes in Computer Science*, pages 21–31, Taormina, Italy, Sept. 1-5 2012. Springer.

[10] F. Rothlauf. *Representations for genetic and evolutionary algorithms.* Springer, pub-SV:adr, second edition, 2006. First published 2002, 2nd edition available electronically.

[11] N. Q. Uy, N. X. Hoai, M. O'Neill, R. I. McKay, and E. Galvan-Lopez. Semantically-based crossover in genetic programming: application to real-valued symbolic regression. *Genetic Programming and Evolvable Machines*, 12(2):91–119, June 2011.

[12] B. Wieloch and K. Krawiec. Running programs backwards: Instruction Inversion for Effective Search in Semantic Spaces. In Christian Blum, et al., editor, *GECCO '13: Proceedings of the 15th annual conference on Genetic and evolutionary computation*, Amsterdam, The Netherlands, 2013. ACM.

Pattern-Guided Genetic Programming

Krzysztof Krawiec
Institute of Computing Science
Poznan University of Technology
Piotrowo 2, 60965 Poznań, Poland
kkrawiec@cs.put.poznan.pl

Jerry Swan
Computing Science and Mathematics
University of Stirling
Stirling FK9 4LA, Scotland
jsw@cs.stir.ac.uk

ABSTRACT

Online progress in search and optimization is often hindered by neutrality in the fitness landscape, when many genotypes map to the same fitness value. We propose a method for imposing a gradient on the fitness function of a metaheuristic (in this case, Genetic Programming) via a metric (Minimum Description Length) induced from patterns detected in the trajectory of program execution. These patterns are induced via a decision tree classifier. We apply this method to a range of integer and boolean-valued problems, significantly outperforming the standard approach. The method is conceptually straightforward and applicable to virtually any metaheuristic that can be appropriately instrumented.

Categories and Subject Descriptors

I.2.2 [**Artificial Intelligence**]: Automatic Programming; I.2.8 [**Artificial Intelligence**]: Problem Solving, Control Methods, and Search—*Heuristic methods*

General Terms

Algorithms, Design, Experimentation

Keywords

genetic programming, neutrality, program trace, MDL, Push

1. INTRODUCTION AND MOTIVATIONS

A Genetic Programming (GP) task is defined by a set of input data (fitness cases) and the desired program output for each of them. A GP algorithm is expected to infer the program only from these training examples. This can be very hard. When the task is challenging, it may be difficult for the search process to 'lift off', i.e. to make any progress. For instance, if exhibiting *any* nontrivial (non-constant) behavior leads to fitness deterioration, then it will locally pay off for a program in a population to return a constant output regardless of the input data.

This problem is not as severe in domains in which program performance on each test is assessed *quantitatively*. An example of such a domain is symbolic regression, where the error committed by a program on each fitness case is a continuous value, and thus can change gradually. Unfortunately, for more typical programing tasks, tests are *qualitative*: a program either passes a test or not. Synthesizing Boolean functions, sorting programs etc., belong to this category.

The key observation that motivates this study is that even programs which yield a completely useless output (meaning: output that does not match in any way the desired output) may produce some intermediate outcomes that can be relevant for solving the task. Take for instance the n-bit parity task. An initial part of program that correctly calculates the number of ones in half of the inputs (bits) provides a potentially useful capability. However, this partial outcome may be lost in the course of subsequent calculations carried out by the program, so that the ultimate output of the program is (for instance) the constant *true*. As a result, the program receives low fitness, and may not pass the selection process, so that its useful partial capability will be lost.

In standard GP, such intermediate results are not taken into account, because there is no singular means for assessing the quality of partial (intermediate) results produced by a program, given only the specification of the entire task. This is similar to a reinforcement learning setting, in which the agents are usually rewarded only *after* the entire task has been solved (i.e. once the goal state has been reached). For instance, an agent learning to play a game receives rewards only for complete games — there is no direct feedback about the quality of individual moves.

We postulate here that evaluation of partial program outcomes may yield better insight and is technically feasible. Since these partial results have ultimately been calculated from input data that came with the task and using an instruction set that also belongs to task formulation, they can represent useful pieces of knowledge of potential value in assembling a complete solution. In particular, the outcomes calculated for multiple inputs (fitness cases) can form some *patterns* that can be exploited to solve the task.

A skilled human programmer or mathematician is capable of discovering such patters and exploiting them to reach the goal, i.e. to design an algorithm that meets a prescribed specification. Moreover, humans are capable of defining what patterns are *desired* as an intermediate result. Consider designing an algorithm that calculates the median of a vector of numbers. A reasonable first stage of solving this task is sorting the elements of the input vector. Therefore, an intermediate memory state (pattern) containing sorted elements of the input vector is desired for this task (and anticipated by a human programmer).

Given that the distribution of problems considered in practice (including the problems approached with GP) is highly nonuniform, one might anticipate that some such patterns occur more frequently than others. In theory, it should be then possible to build an algorithm (system) which mimics the human programmer in that respect, i.e. in being capable of detecting the potentially useful patterns and rewarding the programs that produce them at intermediate execution stages. Hereafter, we use the term PANGEA (PAtterN Guided Evolutionary Algorithms) to describe this conceptual framework (as will be seen, there are no specific requirements that this approach be restricted to GP).

The specific approach proposed in this paper belongs to this framework and is based on the observation that, as a matter of fact, computational intelligence already provides automated pattern discovery tools that can capture the regularities in data. What we mean by this are the various machine learning and knowledge discovery algorithms. Thus, the key idea of the approach is to use a machine learning algorithm to search for such patterns by training it on the partial outcomes of program execution. Information on the resulting trained classifier (in particular its complexity and accuracy) is then used to augment the fitness function. If this approach is able to reveal meaningful dependencies between partial outcomes and the desired output, we may hope to thereby promote programs with the potential to produce good results in future, even if at the moment of evaluation the output they produce is incorrect.

2. THE BACKGROUND

We define a GP task as a set of n *fitness cases* (*tests*). A test is a pair (x_i, y_i), $i = 1, \ldots, n$, where x_i is the input to be fed into program, and y_i is the desired output. In general, x_is and y_is can be arbitrary objects.

Evaluation of an individual-program p assesses the quality of its mapping from inputs to desired outputs by applying it to all tests in turn. For each test, p is provided with input x_i and executed, returning output which we denote as $p(x_i)$. We say that p *solves test* (x_i, y_i) if it terminates and $p(x_i) = y_i$. The fitness of a program is simply the fraction of tests it does not solve, i.e.:

$$f(p) = \frac{1}{n}\left[n - |\{(x_i, y_i) : p(x_i) = y_i\}|\right]. \qquad (1)$$

Note that for the sake of simplicity, in this study we assume that only *perfect* matches between the desired output and the actual output are of interest. Therefore, only the equality relation in the space of program outputs needs to be defined (rather than more sophisticated relations like similarity). The fitness defined in this way is obviously minimized fitness, and a program p solves a task if $f(p) = 0$.

3. THE METHOD

The method proposed in this paper differs from standard GP only in the manner in which fitness is assigned to individuals. Therefore, given the formalization of the conventional fitness assessment in the previous section, we show here how we diverge from it. This process, illustrated in Fig. 1, can be split into four stages detailed in the following subsections.

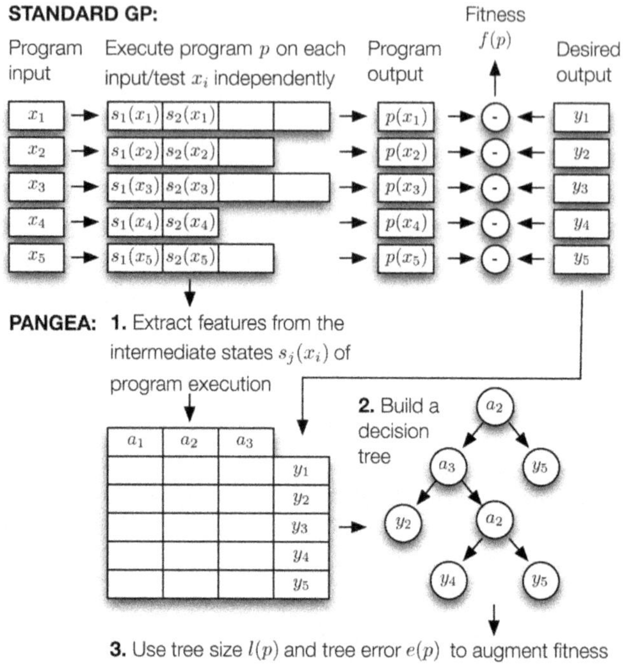

Figure 1: The outline of the proposed method. The top part illustrates the conventional GP evaluation procedure that results with fitness $f(p)$. The bottom part shows the components added by PANGEA.

3.1 Program trace acquisition

Our method works by gathering and exploiting information resulting from the intermediate stages of program execution. For this to be possible, we have to assume that (i) program execution is a stepwise process that can be paused, and that (ii) at such pauses, some information can be obtained from the execution environment. In virtually all genres of GP, these requirements are met by default. Concerning for instance the former, program is a discrete structure composed of symbols interpreted in certain order. These assumptions allow us to formalize certain notions, which we do below, abstracting from any specific form of GP.

Formally, let $s_j(p, x_i)$ denote the *state* of the execution environment when applying program p to test x_i after j steps have been executed. In side-effect free programming, relatively typical of tree-based GP, this would embrace a partial program (a subtree) and its outcome (the value returned by this subtree). For stateful execution environments, typical of programming languages with side-effects, this would be the state of the interpreter (its memory, instruction pointer, etc.). In other words, state is a 'snapshot' of the concrete process of program execution (i.e. pertaining to specific x_i). The sequence of states $(s_j(p, x_i) : j = 1, \ldots, l)$ resulting from entire program run forms its *trace*, where l is the number of steps, e.g., the number of instructions executed by a program, whether it terminated on its own or was forced to do so. The last state in a trace is the state of execution environment after program completion. We used a similar definition in our previous work on semantic analysis of program behavior [5].

In the proposed approach, the fitness assessment presented in Section 2 is accompanied by trace registration. As a result, we obtain a list of traces $(s_j(p, x_i) : j = 1, \ldots, l_i)$ for our n fitness cases (x_i, y_i). Let us note that, because in general program termination depends on its input, traces can vary in length, hence the index i in l_i.

3.2 Extracting trace features

The trace can be considered as a way of capturing program behavior. The key idea of PANGEA consists in analyzing the traces in search for patterns/regularities that reveal hidden qualities in the program and its partial outcomes. Various tools can be potentially used for this purpose, which we elaborate on in Section 7. In this paper, for the sake of simplicity, we aim at employing conventional machine learning algorithms that implement the paradigm of learning from examples and attribute-value representation [8].

To match the requirements of conventional machine learning algorithms with respect to input data, we transform the list of traces into a conventional machine learning dataset, where each row (example) corresponds to GP test, and every column is a feature derived in certain way from the traces. Each feature reflects certain syntactic or semantic information of all program traces at certain stage of program execution. Because the way the features are calculated from the states depends on state internals, this (and only this) stage of our approach varies depending on GP genre. In the subsequent section and experimental part, we detail it for Push [12], but in our pursuit of generality, we abstract from this technical detail in this section.

Crucially, we make this dataset define a *supervised* learning task. To this aim, we equip it with an extra column that defines a decision attribute. The value of this attribute is based on the desired output y_i of the corresponding test (x_i, y_i). In this paper we focus on GP tasks in which y_i is a single discrete value, in which case the decision attribute simply *is* y_i. This attribute will allow us to detect and capture patterns that are relevant for solving the task at hand.

3.3 Capturing patterns in features

The outcome of the above stage is a dataset of n examples, each described by the same number of features and labeled with a decision attribute that identifies the desired output. The purpose of the next step is to assess how useful these features are in predicting the desired output of the program. We achieve this by training a standard machine learning classifier, using the entire dataset as the training set. Specifically, we employ C4.5, a popular decision tree induction algorithm [9]. We anticipate that this choice is not critical; any inductive learning method could be applied here, as long as its outcomes can be analyzed with respect to the properties required in the next step.

We are interested in two characteristics of the induced classifier. Firstly, it has certain inherent *complexity*, which in the case of decision trees can be conveniently expressed as the number of tree nodes. Secondly, it commits a certain *classification error* on the training set, i.e. it erroneously classifies some of the examples. According to the *Minimum Description Length* principle (MDL [10]), the complexity of the mapping from the space of features onto the decision attribute may be expressed by summing the encoding length of the classifier (the 'rule') and the number of erroneously classified examples (the exceptions from the rule). In our context, this quantity tells us how easy it is to come up with the correct output of the program given the partial results gathered from its traces. This is the core element of the approach we propose here.

From another perspective, the role of the classifier is to complement the program's capability of solving the problem (i.e. producing the desired output value). If the features collected from the program trace form meaningful patterns, i.e. capture regularities in input data that are relevant to program output (decision class), then the induction algorithm should be able to build a compact tree that commits few classification errors (and thus has short description length).

To illustrate this, let us consider an extreme case of an ideal program p that solves the task, i.e. produces the desired output y_i for all tests ($y_i \equiv p(x_i)$). Since the final (post-execution) state is the last element of each trace, and the features are collected from trace elements, then one or more of the features in the training set will highly correlate with it. Assume for simplicity that the feature is perfectly correlated with y_i. In such a case, the induction algorithm will produce a decision tree composed of a single decision node (using that particular feature), and d leaves that correspond to the d decision classes. This is the smallest decision tree that can be built for such problem. This tree commits no classification errors, so the total length of the classifier encoding and the 'exceptions' will be minimal. In this scenario, the classifier does not augment the capabilities of the program.

If the program does not produce the desired output, the tree induction algorithm will be forced to make use of other features collected from the traces. The resulting tree will usually be larger than the minimal tree and/or commit some classification errors. In general, the less useful the features collected from the trace, the longer will be the total description length of the mapping. This shows that the total length of encoding expresses the usefulness of the intermediate results produced by the program (not only explicit results, reflecting, e.g. memory states, but also side-effects such as total number of execution steps). Most importantly, this length provides a meaningful way of assessing a program's 'prospective' capabilities, *even if the actual output of the program is completely useless from the point of view of the task being solved* (i.e. has nothing in common with the desired output).

3.4 Fitness calculation

Based on the above rationale, we define program fitness as follows. Let $l(p)$ denote the total number of tree nodes, and $e(p)$ the number of examples that are erroneously classified by the tree induced from the traces of individual-program p, $e(p) \in [0, n]$. In PANGEA, the fitness of p is the product of the standard fitness $f(p)$ ($0 \leq f(p) \leq 1$, Formula 1) and two terms that penalize the individual for, respectively, the complexity of mapping implemented by the induced classifier, and for the number of classification errors (exceptions from that mapping):

$$f_P(p) = f(p) \times \log_2(l(p) + 1) \times \frac{e(p) + 1}{n + 1}. \qquad (2)$$

The particular form of this equation results from preliminary experiments. The logarithm of the tree size is used so that model complexity is proportional to tree depth rather than to tree size. The +1 term in the second component (responsible for model complexity) prevents it from sinking to zero (the tree always has at least one node). The +1 term in the nominator of the third component (encoding length of exceptions) plays an analogous role. Therefore, the MDL-related components of fitness have an impact on program's fitness, but will never render it perfect. This can be achieved only by bringing the actual error committed by p on the tests, i.e., $f(p)$, to zero. Thus, a solution is optimal in PANGEA if and only if it is optimal w.r.t. the standard fitness definition (Formula 1).

4. RELATED WORK

There are numerous occasions in which the MDL principle has been used in GP. In most such cases, it has played a similar role to other machine learning techniques, i.e. as a means of controlling the trade-off between model complexity (sometimes referred to as *parsimony* in a ML context) and accuracy. In this spirit, Iba *et al.* [3] used it to prevent bloat in GP by designing an MDL-based fitness function that took into account the error committed by an individual as well as the size of the program. A few later studies followed this research direction (see, e.g. [14]).

By focusing mostly on the effects of program execution (the partial outcomes reflected in trace features) rather than on syntax, PANGEA can be seen as following the recent trend of semantic GP, initiated in [7]. Interestingly, it also resembles evolutionary synthesis of features for machine learning and pattern/image analysis tasks [6]. However, here the ML part serves only as a scaffolding for evolution; it is supposed to provide 'gradient' for evolution when the sole program output is not able to do so. The classifier is not the part of a solution.

5. IMPLEMENTING PANGEA WITH PUSH

In this section we explain how the process of feature extraction can be implemented for the programming language Push [12], which is also used in the experimental part of this paper. However, this choice is rather incidental, since program traces and their features can be easily acquired for other programming environments common in GP.

5.1 The fundamentals of Push

Push is a stack-based language, and its interpreter is equipped with a stack that holds the program to be executed, and a separate stack for each data type. For simplicity, we assume here that computation takes place in the Boolean and integer domains only, so only these three stacks (called EXEC, BOOLEAN and INTEGER in the following) will be of interest to us.

Push programs are lists of instructions that can be nested. To run a program, it is pushed onto the EXEC stack. Instructions are then popped from this stack and executed in turn. Every Push instruction manipulates one or more stacks. For instance, *integer.=* instruction pops two elements from the integer stack and pushes the result of their comparison atop the boolean stack. An instruction has no effect if the stack is too shallow. For details on this and other features of this programming framework, see [12].

When matching the notation introduced in Section 2 against Push, a task is a list of tests (x_i, y_i), where x_i determines the state of the execution environment (the stacks) before program execution, and y_i determines the analogous desired state after program completion. For inputs, 'determines' means in practice placing the elements of x_i onto the stacks of appropriate types. For outputs, y_i, usually a scalar value, specifies the desired value on the top of the stack of appropriate type.

For simplicity, we consider here only tasks with desired outputs y_i specified as scalars (atoms) of either integer or boolean type (depending on task type). We also assume that x_i is an arbitrary-length vector of integers that determines the initial state the INTEGER stack, and the output is the contents it leaves on the top the stack (INTEGER or BOOLEAN, depending on the type of desired output) after completion. We assume that a test has not been solved if the output stack is empty.

By way of example consider the task of verifying whether the input is a list of integers sorted ascedingly. In such task, each x_i would be a list of integers that would be placed on the INTEGER stack prior to program execution, while each y_i would be a Boolean value to be expected on the BOOLEAN stack.

5.2 Trace acquisition and feature extraction in Push

For Push, we implement the trace acquisition and feature extraction process introduced in general in Sections 3.2 and 3.1 as follows. We track program execution by pausing it after each instruction and storing the state of the interpreter. We do so until the program terminates or reaches a prescribed maximum number of steps. A state comprises all stacks that are relevant for the tasks considered in this paper, i.e., BOOLEAN, INTEGER, and EXEC. The list of states collected in this way for a specific test (x_i, y_i) forms the trace. Let us reiterate that, depending on input x_i, the number of executed instructions may vary, and hence the length of the resulting trace (see Fig. 1).

After tracing execution of the program on all n tests, we build a machine learning dataset by extracting features from selected elements of the history of program execution gathered in traces. Each trace gives rise to one example in the set. Starting from the last state of the trace, we iterate backwards over k last states, and from each of these states s_j we extract the following features:

- The sizes of all three stacks under consideration.
- The top elements of these stacks (if a stack is empty, we assume default values: zero for INTEGER stack, and a special value *Null* for the BOOLEAN and EXEC stacks).

In this process, we maintain the types of data: the integer-valued components of interpreter state (the sizes of all stacks and the top element of the INTEGER stack) translate into ordinal features, and the remaining components (the top elements of BOOLEAN and EXEC stacks) give rise to nominal (categorical) features.

Let us illustrate this process with a simple example, in which we focus exclusively on the INTEGER stack (feature extraction for the other stacks proceeds analogously). Assume we have three fitness cases and $k = 2$. A program was applied to these cases, and the top elements on the INTEGER in the corresponding traces were as follows:

- For test #1: `1 2 3 4`
- For test #2: `5 6 7`
- For test #3: `8 9`

The lengths of traces range from four to two, which tells us that the program terminated after executing different number of instructions for each fitness case. This is quite common for Push programs and may result from, e.g., the presence of loops. Because $k = 2$, two features (apart from the features reflecting the sizes of stacks) will be extracted from these traces: $a_1 = [3, 6, 8]$ and $a_2 = [4, 7, 9]$. As shown, they are 'aligned' with the ends of traces, because, in the end, a program may be expected to produce meaningful output in the final steps of its execution.

Nevertheless, it may be the case that meaningful patterns emerge also when stack contents are traced and converted into features by aligning them with respect to *beginning* of traces. This leads us to introduce also other features, which we build by merging into the feature vectors the top stack elements from the states that have the same index when counted from the beginning of programs. In our example, where $k = 2$, such forward-aligned features are: $a_3 = [3, 7, 0]$ and $a_4 = [4, 0, 0]$, where the zeroes are the default values.

In general, three stacks (each giving rise to two features, the top element and the size), and two methods of feature building total to $12 \times k$ features for horizon of length k. This set is supplemented with another feature: the number of execution steps t_i carried out by the interpreter for the ith test. Thus, the complete dataset forms a table of n rows (examples) and $12k + 1$ columns (features), $8k$ of which are ordinal and $4k+1$ nominal. Finally, we provide each example with a class label, which is simply the actual output of the program, i.e., z_i. Therefore, the number of distinct output values in the set of fitness cases is also the number of decision classes in the extracted dataset.

The dataset constructed in this way forms the result of feature extraction process, and is subject to further processing presented in Sections 3.3 and 3.4.

6. EXPERIMENT

The main objective of the experiment is to determine if pattern-based evaluation of individuals can be beneficial for evolutionary search. To this end, we compare the PANGEA approach to the control method of standard PushGP. More specifically, we compare GP running two fitness definitions, given by Formula (1) and Formula (2).

In all the test problems we consider, listed in Table 1, the input data is a table (one or more elements placed on the integer stack prior to program execution), and the desired output is a scalar value. In most problems (AEQ, CNF, ISO, MAJ), the task is to verify certain properties of the input (the output type is boolean). Two problems (COZ, MAX) are of a more arithmetic nature (the output type is integer).

The choice of this particular suite of tasks deserves justification. The tool we use for capturing patterns in traces and assessing their relevance is a decision tree inducer. As any machine learning algorithm, it brings with it certain *biases*, which in practice means that it prefers discovering certain types of patterns to others. Decision tree inducers like C4.5 are particularly good at discovering nontrivial patterns that engage *multiple* features. Therefore, it is suitable mostly for problems for which the traces are likely to give rise to multiple noncorrelated features, which, when used in combination, allow the tree to capture valuable input-output dependencies (patterns).

To illustrate this characteristic, let us shortly mention that in a preliminary experiment, we tested this approach on the problem of evolving a factorial function. In this problem, the tests (x_i, y_i) take the form $(m, m!)$, $m = 1, \ldots, n$. Because the input includes only one scalar datum m, many features collected from traces will be highly correlated with it (not mentioning the fact that most likely m itself will become one of the features). Secondly, because factorial is an injective function, there is one-to-one correspondence between the inputs x_i and the desired outputs y_i. As a result, each input (m) corresponds to a unique output ($m!$), and in such a case building a tree that perfectly maps inputs to outputs becomes trivial. The classification error $e(p)$ is zero for most individuals in the run, and the MDL-related components of the fitness function cease to drive evolution in a useful direction.

For all tasks, the training set of cases contains all possible tables of lengths $2 \ldots m$, filled with all possible combinations of integers from the interval $[0, m-1]$. Thus, for the two values of n considered in this experiment, i.e., $m = 3$ and $m = 4$, the numbers of tests are $2^2 + 3^3 = 31$ and $2^2 + 3^3 + 4^4 = 286$, respectively. The only exception is the MAJ task, in which the input tables can contain only zeroes and ones; for this problem, there are $2^2 + 2^3 = 12$ and $2^2 + 2^3 + 2^4 = 28$ tests, respectively. We denote problem size by suffixing its name, e.g., MAX3.

Let us note two facts for which these tasks should be considered nontrivial. Firstly, the input tables are of variable size, so the evolved programs have to be general in this respect. In other words, evolving a simple sequence of instructions that individually and in turn pop the elements from the stack may be insufficient to solve a task, as such a program may reach the bottom of the stack too early for short tables, or ignore some elements on the stack for long tables. Secondly, because of that varying input size, we are not using the *type.input.k* instruction, which fetches the kth element from the input vector of the corresponding type (e.g., *integer.input.2* fetches the third element of the input data). This instruction is present in the original Push to provide *permanent* access to particular input data for the entire program runtime; without it, the initial instructions of a program can quickly empty the stacks. In absence of the *input* instruction, programs cannot access input data directly, and must therefore solve the tasks only by stack manipulation.

We evolve a population of 1000 individuals for 100 generations, using evolutionary parameters typical for Push: viz. mutation probability 0.2, crossover probability 0.7, probability of reproduction 0.1, and a tournament size of 7. The Instruction set, presented in Table 2, consists of control structures, integer arithmetic, and boolean operations. The set of constants is limited to *true*, *false*, 0, 1, 2. To avoid interference of other factors, we do not use any additional mechanisms (*input* instruction, code stack), nor do we simplify programs (in contrast to many other studies on Push). Our implementation is based on a Push interpreter *PshGP* written by Jon Klein [4].

The maximal number of instructions in a newly-generated program is 20. However, the programs can grow much larger as a result of mutation and recombination.

The only difference between the standard Push (STD) and the proposed approach (PANGEA) is the manner in which individuals are evaluated. Fitness is minimized in both cases. In STD, it is Formula 1, and in PANGEA it is calculated according to Formula 2. PANGEA gathers fea-

Table 1: The definitions of tasks.

Symbol	Short explanation	Output type	Desired output
AEQ	All Equal	Boolean	*true* iff all elements on INTEGER stack are equal
CNF	Contains First	Boolean	*true* iff the element on top of INTEGER stack occurs also
COZ	Count Zeroes	Integer	The number of zeroes on the INTEGER stack
ISO	Is Ordered	Boolean	*true* iff the elements on the INTEGER stack are ordered non-descendingly
MAJ	Majority	Boolean	*true* iff more than half of the elements on the INTEGER stack are ones
MAX	Maximum	Integer	The maximum element on the INTEGER stack

Table 3: Success rate of compared methods (100 runs of each method and task).

Method	AEQ3	CNF3	COZ3	ISO3	MAJ3	MAX3	AEQ4	CNF4	COZ4	ISO4	MAJ4	MAX4	Rank
STD	0.93	0.17	0.47	0.20	0.46	0.07	0.32	0.00	0.02	0.00	0.20	0.00	3.67
PANGEA	**1.00**	**0.61**	**0.76**	**0.76**	0.97	**0.22**	**1.00**	0.00	0.04	0.00	**0.70**	0.00	**1.92**
PANGEA-E	**1.00**	0.18	0.42	0.46	**1.00**	0.00	**1.00**	0.00	0.02	0.00	0.67	0.00	2.50
PANGEA-M	**1.00**	0.32	0.40	0.67	**1.00**	0.22	0.99	0.00	**0.07**	0.00	0.50	0.00	4.04
PANGEA-X	0.97	0.12	0.46	0.03	0.46	0.01	0.42	0.00	0.00	0.00	0.09	0.00	2.88

Table 2: The instruction set.

boolean.and boolean.or boolean.xor boolean.= boolean.not boolean.dup boolean.flush boolean.pop boolean.rot boolean.stackdepth boolean.swap
integer.+ integer.- integer.* integer./ integer.% integer.< integer.= integer.> integer.dup integer.flush integer.pop integer.rot integer.stackdepth integer.swap
exec.= exec.dup exec.flush exec.pop exec.rot exec.stackdepth exec.swap exec.if exec.do*count exec.do*range exec.do*times
boolean.frominteger integer.fromboolean integer.erc true false

tures from the last three states of the interpreter ($k = 3$) before program termination (the upper limit on executed instructions is 150 instructions per test). This particular value of k was determined by preliminary experiments. The number of features then totals to $12k + 1 = 37$ (see Section 5). However, the tree does not have to use all of them (as a matter of fact, it is often the case that many of those features are constant). The decision tree is induced using an improved implementation of the C4.5 algorithm, known as J48 in WEKA package [2]. The algorithm builds an unprunned tree, i.e. no postpruning is employed.

We remind the reader that the decision trees are induced as part of an individual's evaluation process and do not become part of the resulting solutions. A tree is built to assess the quality of an individual, and is destroyed as soon as that assessment is completed.

6.1 The performance of methods

Given the nature of the benchmarks considered, we are interested only in perfect solutions, i.e. programs that solve *all* training tests. For this reason, success rate (i.e. the fraction of runs that yield perfect solutions), is our primary performance indicator.

The upper part of Table 3 reports the success rate of the two compared algorithms on all problems, based on 100 runs per each setup and benchmark. Overall, the proposed approach has a much higher success ratio, often several times greater than standard Push. The AEQ3 problem turns out to be very easy for pure Push, so it is unsurprising that PANGEA cannot do much better. As expected, the 'big' problems with four-element tables are substantially harder, and three of them (CNF4, ISO4, MAX4) have not been solved even once by either of the compared methods. Nevertheless, PANGEA outperforms STD on the remaining big problems.

One of the factors that can affect these results is the number of distinct desired outputs. For the AEQ, CNF, ISO, and MAJ, there are two desired values only: *true* and *false*. However, for the COZ and MAX tasks, there are, respectively, $m + 1$ and m distinct output values, where m is the size of the input table. This property of the problem determines the number of decision classes in the dataset used for tree induction.

6.2 The role of fitness components

The interplay of the components of the fitness function defined by Formula (2) can be expected to be very complex, so it is worth investigating the extent to which they all contribute to the performance of PANGEA. In other words: could it be that PANGEA fares better only because the MDL-related components introduce pseudo-random noise into the evaluation criterion and so help the evolution to escape stagnation?

To verify this, we ran a series of experiments with fitness based on Formula (2), but devoid of single components:

- PANGEA-E: formula (2) devoid of the program error (first) component,
- PANGEA-M: formula (2) devoid of the model length (second) component,
- PANGEA-X: formula (2) devoid of the classification error (third) component.

The performance of these methods is shown in the lower part of Table 3. As it turns out, all three components of Formula (2) are vital. Removal of any of them typically results in a lower success ratio than PANGEA. The only exceptions are AEQ3 and AEQ4, which apparently can be solved with near certainty even with such 'crippled' fitness functions. This result shows that for the fitness assessment scheme followed by PANGEA, it is important to take into account not only the complexity of the model (tree), but also the classification errors it commits.

To provide an overall perspective on these results, in the last column of Table 3 we report the average rank for each of the five setups. PANGEA clearly ranks as best. We validate the statistical significance of ranks using the Friedman test, the outcome of which is positive ($p \approx 0.0005$), i.e. at least one of the has success ratio significantly different from the others. Shaffer's post-hoc analysis procedure allows us to determine that PANGEA is significantly better ($p < 0.05$) than STD and PANGEA-M.

6.3 Dynamics of the search process

To illustrate the working principle of PANGEA, in this section we shortly analyze an exemplary evolutionary run for MAJ3 problem. That particular run lasted for 20 generations, in which an ideal solution has been found.

The chart in Fig. 2 summarizes the dynamics of that search process by plotting the important parameters of the best-of-generation individuals. For each such individual p, we show in parallel the essential components of PANGEA fitness (Formula 2): program fitness $f_P(p)$, the actual error $f(p)$ committed by the program on the fitness cases, the size $l(p)$ (the number of nodes) of the associated decision tree induced from trace features, and the classification error $e(p)$ committed by the tree. Because of different magnitudes, the former two are plotted against the left-hand ordinate axis, and the latter against the right-hand ordinate axis.

In the first five generations of the run evolution does not seem to make progress and all the parameters of the best-of-generation solutions remain unchanged. In this period, the decision trees comprise only three nodes and commit 8.4 classification errors (in general, the classification error of C4.5 is defined on a continuous scale), i.e. roughly eight of 12 fitness cases that constitute the MAJ3 task get misclassified. Let us emphasize that the fixing of this parameters may be purely incidental, i.e. it does not imply that the trees corresponding to these five best-of-generation individuals use the same features. The very small tree size in connection with relatively large number of classification errors suggests that the traces are scant in useful features, and that decision trees that accurately and succinctly map them onto the desired output cannot be built.

In generation 6 evolution manages to make progress and the best-of-generation fitness $f_P(p)$ substantially improves. The reason for this is however not a better match of program output with the desired output; just the opposite, $f(p)$ actually *deteriorates*. The cause for fitness improvement lies elsewhere: what actually happened is that the classification error committed by the tree $e(p)$ dropped from 8.4 to 3.5, while the size of the tree $l(p)$ increased from 3 to 5. Apparently, at some stage of execution of the best-of-generation program, a new pattern emerged in its traces (new w.r.t. to the best programs from previous generations). That feature (one or more) allowed building a more accurate decision tree that has only two more nodes. As a result, the product of the two MDL-related terms in Formula 2 decreased, and brought down the overall fitness $f_P(p)$ despite actual deterioration of the final output produced by the program as measured by the standard fitness $f(p)$ (Formula 1).

In the subsequent 7th generation the induction algorithm manages to build an even smaller tree, bringing its size back to three nodes, while maintaining the same classification error $e(p) = 3.5$. This results in further improvement of overall fitness, even given that $f(p)$ remains unchanged.

Generation 8 is the first time when program trace allows building a perfect decision tree ($e(p) = 0$). This is also the generation in which the mismatch between the program's output and the desired output ($e(p)$) is maximal in this run. This however does not prevent this program to outperform the best-of-run of the previous generation in terms of fitness $f(p)$.

The tree found in generation 8 is large: it comprises 21 nodes. Nevertheless, the very next generation sees a large decrease of this value: the tree has five nodes again, and classifies all examples perfectly. With minor fluctuations, this state is maintained in the remaining part of the run, while the evolution clearly works on the output of the program, gradually bringing $f(p)$ to zero.

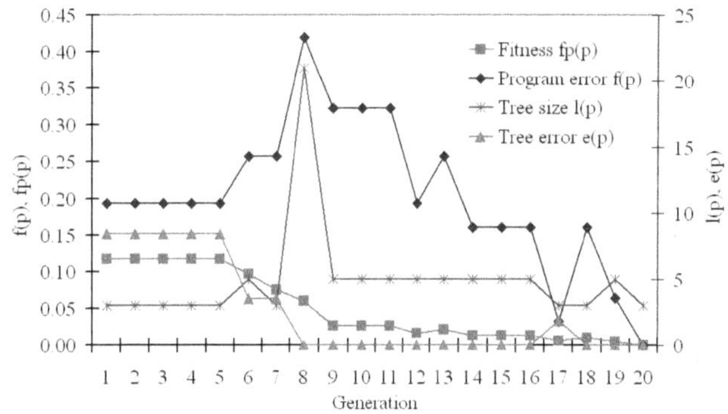

Figure 2: The changes of parameters of best-of-genration programs for an exemplary evolutionary run solving MAJ3 task.

This illustration confirms our rationale behind PANGEA's design, which we expressed in Section 3.3: the MDL-related components in fitness definition protect the individuals that discover meaningful patterns in the task and display those patterns in their behavior (written down in program traces). Without this mechanism, the individual like the that became best-of-generation 6 would most probably get lost in the selection process, as its error $f(p)$ is noticeably worse than the error of the best individual from the previous generation.

PANGEA enables even more insightful analysis, which we are forced to omit in this short contribution. For instance, it would be fascinating to see *what* are the features that led to the major transitions observable in runs like the one here, and also the code that generated it. Such investigations could help us for instance to determine whether, in the example above, evolution, after discovering the meaningful patterns around generations 5 to 8, kept the initial parts of programs roughly unchanged (to preserve the patterns), while working mostly on the final instructions (responsible for producing the final program output).

7. DISCUSSION

Our approach relies on a three-stage process: the recognition of patterns, the explicit description of such patterns in 'working memory', and the exploitation of these patterns to guide the search process. In the approach described here, the patterns are written down as decision trees, which in turn augment the fitness function. Of course, such classifiers might be incapable of capturing the specific form of patterns that are relevant for solving a particular task.

We have adopted the intentionally evocative term 'pattern' rather than feature in order to emphasize the potential for algorithmic sophistication and nontrivial computational effort in detecting and exploiting any aspects of the search process. We might therefore hope to mine for such patterns in problem description, genotype-to-phenotype mapping, solution-state trajectory, algorithm-state trajectory, or operator-sequence trajectory. It is clearly possible to combine these modalities, e.g. as in the current article which works with the combined trajectories of algorithm state, solution state and operator sequence.

We give here some possible 'use cases' for pattern detection that illustrate the potential for future work within this abstract framework:

1. One of the well-known properties of GP is that it is a 'model-agnostic' approach - assuming that we apply the function set {+,-,*,/,exp, log, sin, cos, tan} to a function that is actually linear, then we expect the transcendental non-terminals to be dropped and the resulting best program to be a linear expression.

However, the detection of linearity is merely implicit in GP - this activity is not explicitly directed by any features of the problem. GP may find out at some point of evolution that using a linear model is profitable, but does not 'sanction, mandate or suggest' it. The detection of linear relationships between features is of course a relatively trivial computational task, but the ability to explicitly recognize such patterns and inject the corresponding (sub)programs into the population can be viewed as a special case of a more general recognition-exploitation strategy [13].

2. Consider a training set T over a function $f(x,y)$, in which $f(x,y) = f(y,x) \forall f \in T$. Even in the absence of prior domain knowledge, a human presented with sufficient samples from the raw training data for this task would in all probability notice that the function is symmetric. Algorithms for online induction of symmetries in the context of search and optimization is given in [1, 11]. Such symmetry is of course a very specific case of (what is provisionally conjectured to be) an invariant of the function. Presented with such a regression task, a 'pattern-sensitive' human being would likely proceed to synthesize a function that respects this invariant. A partial synthesis might of course break the invariant, but activity is subject to the implicit understanding that ultimately restoring it is imperative. There are a number of ways in which one might attempt to incorporate the invariant into the subsequent search process, perhaps the most obvious of which is to add it as a soft constraint of the heuristic function.

8. CONCLUSIONS

PANGEA imposes a gradient on the fitness function of a metaheuristic (in this case, Genetic Programming) via a metric (Minimum Description Length) obtained from patterns detected in the trajectory of program execution (trace). The success of this method was demonstrated on a range of integer and Boolean-valued problems. The method is conceptually straightforward and applicable to virtually any genre of GP. The computational overhead it imposes in comparison to conventional fitness assessment is reasonable, because trace acquisition is done on the fly during program execution (which has to be carried out in regular GP as well). The only substantial additional cost results from training the classifier, however simple symbolic classifiers like C4.5 learn quickly.

It is increasingly being acknowledged that EC approaches are not a "one size fits all" approach. In particular, it is now understood that the initially popularized crossover and mutation operators do not enjoy the universality that were once ascribed to them. There is therefore in general a requirement in current EC practice for human ingenuity in the design and application of domain-specific operators, penalty functions etc. This work is an initial attempt to circumvent this requirement via the exploitation of regularity. In this case, regularity was determined by a statistical machine learning approach, i.e. the induction of a decision tree. In future work, we seek to extend the both the pattern detection methodology and the means by which it influences the subsequent search process.

Acknowledgments

K. Krawiec acknowledges financial support from grant no. 91507. J. Swan acknowledges support from grant EP/J017515/1.

9. REFERENCES

[1] J. Crawford, M. Ginsberg, E. Luks, and A. Roy. Symmetry-breaking predicates for search problems. In *5th International Conference on Principles of Knowledge Representation and Reasoning*, pages 148–159. Morgan Kaufmann, 1996.

[2] M. Hall, E. Frank, G. Holmes, B. Pfahringer, P. Reutemann, and I. H. Witten. The weka data mining software: an update. *SIGKDD Explor. Newsl.*, 11(1):10–18, Nov. 2009.

[3] H. Iba, T. Sato, and H. de Garis. System identification approach to genetic programming. In *Proceedings of the 1994 IEEE World Congress on Computational Intelligence*, volume 1, pages 401–406, Orlando, Florida, USA, 27-29 June 1994. IEEE Press.

[4] J. Klein. Psh - java implementation of the push programming language. Avalable from https://github.com/jonklein/Psh, 2010.

[5] K. Krawiec. On relationships between semantic diversity, complexity and modularity of programming tasks. In T. Soule et al., editors, *GECCO '12: Proceedings of the fourteenth international conference on Genetic and evolutionary computation conference*, pages 783–790, Philadelphia, Pennsylvania, USA, 7-11 July 2012. ACM.

[6] K. Krawiec and B. Bhanu. Visual learning by evolutionary and coevolutionary feature synthesis. *IEEE Transactions on Evolutionary Computation*, 11(5):635–650, Oct. 2007.

[7] N. F. McPhee, B. Ohs, and T. Hutchison. Semantic building blocks in genetic programming. In M. O'Neill et al., editors, *Genetic Programming*, volume 4971 of *LNCS*, pages 134–145. Springer, 2008.

[8] T. M. Mitchell. *Machine Learning*. McGraw-Hill, Inc., New York, NY, USA, 1 edition, 1997.

[9] J. Quinlan. *C4.5: Programs for machine learning*. Morgan Kaufmann, San Mateo, 1992.

[10] J. Rissanen. Modeling By Shortest Data Description. *Automatica*, 14:465–471, 1978.

[11] I. Shlyakhter. Generating effective symmetry-breaking predicates for search problems. *Discrete Appl. Math.*, 155(12):1539–1548, June 2007.

[12] L. Spector and A. Robinson. Genetic programming and autoconstructive evolution with the push programming language. *Genetic Programming and Evolvable Machines*, 3(1):7–40, Mar. 2002.

[13] J. Swan, J. Woodward, E. Özcan, G. Kendall, and E. Burke. Searching the hyper-heuristic design space. *Cognitive Computation*, February 2013.

[14] B.-T. Zhang and H. Mühlenbein. Balancing accuracy and parsimony in genetic programming. *Evolutionary Computation*, 3(1):17–38, 1995.

Self-adaptive Mate Choice for Cluster Geometry Optimization

António Leitão
CISUC, Department of Informatics Engineering
University of Coimbra, 3030
Coimbra, Portugal
apleitao@dei.uc.pt

Penousal Machado
CISUC, Department of Informatics Engineering
University of Coimbra, 3030
Coimbra, Portugal
machado@dei.uc.pt

ABSTRACT

Sexual Selection through Mate Choice has, over the past few decades, attracted the attention of researchers from various fields. They have gathered numerous supporting evidence, establishing Mate Choice as a major driving force of evolution, capable of shaping complex traits and behaviours. Despite its wide acceptance and relevance across various research fields, the impact of Mate Choice in Evolutionary Computation is still far from understood, both regarding performance and behaviour.

In this study we describe a nature-inspired self-adaptive mate choice model, relying on a Genetic Programming representation tailored for the optimization of Morse clusters, a relevant and widely accepted problem for benchmarking new algorithms, which provides a set of hard test instances. The model is coupled with a state-of-the-art hybrid steady-state approach and both its performance and behaviour are assessed with a particular interest on the replacement strategy's acceptance rate and diversity handling.

Categories and Subject Descriptors

I.2.8 [**Artificial Intelligence**]: Problem solving, Control Methods, and Search—*Heuristic Methods*

General Terms

Algorithms, Design

Keywords

Evolutionary Algorithms, Genetic Programming, Sexual Selection, Mate Choice, Self-adaption, Cluster Geometry Optimization

1. INTRODUCTION

Darwin has proposed two complementary theories accounting for the evolution of species: Natural Selection [5] and Sexual Selection [6]. Natural Selection was described as the result of competition within or between species affecting its individuals rate of survival, while Sexual Selection resulted from the competition between individuals of the same species affecting their relative rate of reproduction.

While Natural Selection was widely accepted and endorsed by the scientific community, Sexual Selection was discredited as a curiosity rather than an influential theory. However, interest arose in the 1970s through the works of Fisher [9, 10] and Zahavi [30] and an increasing number of researchers have put their efforts on exploring the subject of Sexual Selection. Among the processes that compose Sexual Selection, Darwin was most focused on Mate Choice [6] as were some of his most preeminent followers [9, 10, 30] and many present day researchers. Nowadays, Mate Choice is highly regarded across various research fields and widely accepted as a major force in evolution [1, 2]. While it has come a long way on other research fields, the effects of Mate Choice on Evolutionary Computation are still far from understood, requiring further research on both performance and behaviour.

Cluster geometry optimization (CGO) has important applications in Nanoscience, Physics, Chemistry and Biochemistry [32]. Finding the geometry of a cluster such that its potential energy is minimized is a NP-hard task [4]. Moreover, the problem provides a large set of difficult test instances and has been widely used for benchmarking the efficiency of global optimization algorithms [4, 7, 12, 14, 23, 24, 25]. The most relevant models are Lennard-Jones clusters [17] and Morse clusters [21], mostly because their modeling functions depend solely on the distance between every pair of particles in the cluster. Optimization of Morse clusters is regarded as a particularly tough problem, specially if used to model short range interactions between particles [8].

Evolutionary Algorithms (EA) have been first applied to CGO problems in the early 1990s [14] and are currently considered state-of-the-art approaches. Several breakthroughs have been achieved since then, such as coupling the algorithms with local-search methods to relax individuals into the nearest local optima [7, 12, 14, 25]. The base algorithm adopted in this study has been proposed by Pereira et al. [24], who suggested that maintenance of diversity may be a key-point to efficiency when tackling CGO [23, 24].

In this study we apply Sexual Selection through Mate Choice to the optimization of Morse clusters using an unbiased hybrid steady-state EA combined with a single phase local-search method. The study aims at two goals: assessing performance on a hard optimization problem; getting insight

GECCO'13, July 6–10, 2013, Amsterdam, The Netherlands.

on how Mate Choice affects the behaviour of the algorithm in terms of diversity and acceptance rate.

The following section introduces the subject of Mate Choice, briefly covering its background and reviewing related work in EAs. Section 3 introduces Morse clusters optimization, examines important contributions and describes a hybrid steady-state EA tailored for tackling the problem. It finally describes a Mate Choice approach for the optimization of Morse clusters. Section 4 covers the experimental setup and the results are thoroughly analyzed and discussed. Section 5 presents our conclusions and future work.

2. SEXUAL SELECTION THROUGH MATE CHOICE

Since publishing his theory of Natural Selection, Darwin was intrigued with animal ornamentation and courtship behaviours. Natural Selection would only favor traits that benefit the survivability of individuals and therefore could not explain the emergence of costly and complex traits that he observed across different species and which seemed to make no contribution to survival. He knew however that such traits had to bring evolutionary advantage in order to spread along the generations. Considering that these traits appeared to be related to mating behaviour, Darwin envisioned that there must be a trait-shaping selection feature other than Natural Selection accounting for the emergence of traits that bring advantage in mating rather than survival.

While Natural Selection adapts species to their environment [5], Sexual Selection adapts individuals in relation to others in a competition for mating partners [6]. Failing to find suitable mate(s) results in few or no offspring rather than death. However, from an evolutionary perspective, failing to reproduce or to survive have mostly the same outcome: the long term survivability of the genes is jeopardized.

Darwin described two main processes in Sexual Selection: male competition and female mate choice, the latter being the scope of this study. Darwin's ideas on Mate Choice explained the emergence of traits in males through adaption to female mating preferences [6]. Males that are better adapted to the tastes of females attain a higher reproduction rate. Various contributions followed, the most important arguably by Fisher, who explained how mating preferences evolve and are heritable the same way as physical traits [9, 10]. He also introduced the idea that ornamentations evolve as indicators of fitness (health, energy, etc.), and that females who are able to choose males with good genetic quality will produce healthier offspring that will reinforce both the inherited mating preferences and physical traits [9]. Finally, he showed how mating preferences and physical traits influence each other through a positive feedback loop [10].

Over the years, a number of publications have arisen covering different ideas regarding the design and implementation of Mate Choice in EAs. We are interested in models that follow three nature-inspired rules:

1. individuals must choose who they mate with based on their perception of others and on their own mating preferences;
2. mating preferences are heritable the same way as physical traits;
3. mate selection introduces its own selection pressure but is subject to selection pressure itself [11];

Several publications fall into this scope.

Hinterding and Michalewicz [16] tackle the constrained optimization of a nonlinear programming problem. Instead of relying on traditional methods for constrained optimization, they propose using a Mate Choice approach that promotes the feasibility of individuals. The first parent is selected using a tournament that favors feasible individuals. It will then select a mate from a candidate pool by preferring mates that, in conjunction with itself, violate the least number of constraints. Therefore, individuals that best complement the first parent are promoted in hope of increasing feasibility. The approach was compared with standard constraint optimization methods achieving comparable results.

Smorokdina and Tauritz have proposed a self-adaptive approach where each individual encodes its own Mate selection function in addition to a candidate solution for the working problem [28]. The Mate selection function is represented using Genetic Programming (GP). The terminal nodes of the trees are, exclusively, the remaining individuals in the population. The non-terminals are a set of selection operators such as *tournament selection*, *biggest hamming distance*, etc. Constraints are enforced to make sure the operators are applied correctly. Mate selection functions are inherited from parents to offspring following one of two proposed rules: given that the new offspring show improvements they inherit the function that was actively used; otherwise, the function attributed to new offspring is the result of the recombination of those from both parents. Results on a set of test problems were slightly worse than a traditional approach.

Guntly and Tauritz [13] propose a Learning Individual Mating Preferences (LIMP) approach with two variants: using a centralized mating preferences vector (C-LIMP) and a decentralized approach (D-LIMP). LIMP is tailored for problems with binary representation, using a real-valued preference vector, with the same size as the genotype, to encode in each position how desirable it is that the corresponding gene is set to one. In D-LIMP each individual encodes its own preference vector, used to evaluate others. Offspring inherit their parents' preferences so that they match the genes inherited from each parent. In addition, the preference vectors are updated based on the relative success of the offspring. The C-LIMP uses 2 preference vectors common to the whole population, the first relative to genes set to 0 and the second to genes set to 1. When an individual assess others, it checks either vector based on its own genotype. At each reproduction step, the vectors are updated in a similar way as in D-LIMP. Both approaches were compared with a traditional GA and a variable dissortative mating GA, achieving better results in part of the test set.

Machado and Leitão [20] have addressed self-adaption of mate evaluation functions on the Circle Packing in Squares (CPS) problem. In this problem, candidate solutions to a given instance also encode candidate solutions to smaller instances. How an individual performs on smaller instances of the CPS problem can be used as indicators of genetic quality, carrying information about how they may contribute to healthy offspring. Apart from a candidate solution to the problem, each individual encodes an extra chromosome representing its own mating preferences. Two models were tested either relying on Genetic Algorithms (GA) or GP. The GA mate evaluation function was designed as a weighted sum matching the weights on the first individual with the fitness values obtained by each candidate on smaller instances of the problem and evolving only the weights. The GP approach evolves whole evaluation functions that are built using the fitness values from each candidate on smaller instances as the terminal set and a set of arithmetic operators as the function set. Results achieved by the GA approach were poor when compared to a standard approach. On the other hand, the GP approach was able to improve upon the results obtained with a classical approach.

3. MORSE CLUSTERS OPTIMIZATION

The Morse potential is the N-particle additive function defined by Eq. 1. As in previous studies [22, 24, 4] we have adopted a scaled version of the Morse potential by setting both the bond dissociation energy, ϵ, and the equilibrium bond length, r_0, to 1. The range exponent of the potential, β, has a strong influence on the character of the potential energy surface (PES), the multidimensional function that describes the interactions between the particles in the cluster. As the value of β is increased, the PES is much more likely to assume a multiple-funnel character with an increasing number of local minima [22, 8]. In this study we have set $\beta = 14$ which corresponds to short range interactions [8], regarded as particularly tough. Therefore, r_{ij} is left as the only variable in Eq. 1, resulting on a function that depends only on the distance between particles.

$$V_{Morse} = \epsilon \sum_{i}^{N-1} \sum_{j>i}^{N} \{exp[-2\beta(r_{ij} - r_0)] - 2exp[-\beta(r_{ij} - r_0)]\} \quad (1)$$

3.1 Related Work

This section covers key achievements on CGO. An overview of EA approaches has been published by Hartke [15].

Morse clusters optimization was first tackled by Doyes and Wales [22] who applied a basin-hopping algorithm and report finding all but 12 putative optima on clusters ranging up to 80 atoms. Roberts et al. [27] applied an EA which combined a real-valued representation [31] with a Cut and Splice crossover operator (C&S) [7] and Lamarckian local optimization [7]. They achieved most of the putative optima on Morse clusters consisting of 19 to 50 atoms.

Locatelli and Schoen proposed using a two-phase local search algorithm designed to tackle multi-funnel charactered PESs [19]. Their algorithm would on a first phase perform local optimization on a modified potential function combining knowledge from the true PES and the geometric structure of the putative solution thus biasing the search toward local optima with specific proprieties and helping search on the true PES during the second step. The algorithm was coupled with a basin-hopping approach and applied to Morse clusters [8], finding all putative optima on clusters ranging from 41 to 80 atoms. The two-phase algorithm has also been combined with a population-based algorithm [12].

Despite the success of these approaches, they depend on a number of parameters that need to be set a priori and that rely on information regarding the target solution. This raises questions concerning bias and their performance when such information is unknown. Two self-adaptive approaches have been proposed to overcome this setback. Cassioli et al. [3] presented a population basin-hopping algorithm where the required parameters are encoded in each individual as weight factors that undergo self-adaptation. Pereira and Marques [23] proposed encoding in each individual the parameters to be applied in their own local-search method, starting with random values that adjust online. These approaches successfully remove the need of setting the parameters beforehand despite causing a reduction on the success rate when applied to Morse clusters ranging up to 80 atoms.

On the same study, Pereira and Marques discussed that the success of their approach was mostly the result of an increased diversity induced by the self-adaption of parameters. A later study by Pereira et al. [24] applied an unbiased hybrid steady-state EA coupled with an unbiased single-phase local optimization procedure and reports finding all putative optima on Morse clusters consisting from 41 to 80 atoms. They show that an unbiased hybrid EA can successfully tackle such problems and that maintenance of diversity is a key-factor in doing so.

3.2 A hybrid steady-state EA for Morse clusters optimization

The aforementioned study by Pereira et al. [24] introduced the base algorithm of this research. The Mate Choice approach applied in this study introduces however some changes as it relies on individuals composed of two chromosomes. The first chromosome encodes a candidate solution for the optimization of Morse Clusters while the second chromosome represents each individual's function for assessing mating candidates. The remaining of this section relates to the first chromosome and other components of the algorithm. Specifics of the Mate Choice approach and the second chromosome are introduced in Sect. 3.3.

3.2.1 *Representation*

A cluster with N atoms on the *3D* space is represented as a $3 \times N$ real valued array that encodes the Cartesian coordinates of the particles. Each gene ranges between *0* and $N^{1/3}$ which is widely accepted to allow the correct scaling of the cluster volume with N [24, 31]. Restrictions are enforced on the distance between each pair of particles during initialization and when genetic operators are applied as to avoid excessively repulsive potentials that result from too small distances. Only solutions where distances are larger than a pre-specified parameter, $\delta = 0.5$, are allowed.

3.2.2 *Genetic operators*

Both crossover and mutation operators specifically tailored for CGO are applied. A generalized C&S operator, proposed by Pereira et al. [26] ensures that parents contribute with particles that are placed close together while sigma mutation [26], applied to offspring, acts on one particle at each time. The new location is obtained by disrupting its coordinates on the *3D* space with values sampled from a Normal distribution with mean *0* and standard deviation σ.

3.2.3 *Local optimization*

The limited memory Broyden-Fletcher-Goldfarb-Shanno (L-BFGS) method, which relies on first order derivative information, guides individuals into the nearest local optimum. The generic element n of the Morse potential gradient is obtained through Eq. 2 where x_{ni} represents the difference between the Cartesian coordinates of particles n and i, $x_{ni} = x_n - x_i$. Similar expressions apply to the y and z axis. L-BFGS is applied to every generated individual prior to evaluation and executes until it finds a local optimum or until it reaches a maximum number of iterations, the Local Search Length (LSL). The accuracy of the method as been set to $1.0E-8$.

$$g_n = -2\beta\epsilon \sum_{i \neq n}^{N} \left(\frac{x_{ni}}{r_{ni}}\right) \{exp[-2\beta(r_{ni} - r_0)] - exp[-\beta(r_{ni} - r_0)]\} \quad (2)$$

3.2.4 *The population*

Individuals evolve as a steady-state model where two offspring are generated at each step and compete with the remaining individuals for a place in the population. This procedure is repeated until a termination criterion is met. Such a model requires a replacement strategy that controls which offspring are allowed in the population and which individuals perish in return. The one applied in this study is a fitness-based strategy that includes mechanisms which aim at maintaining diversity [18]. Briefly, given an individual X already locally optimized and evaluated, if the population contains an individual Y that is closer to X than a predefined value d_{min}, then only the best one is kept. Otherwise, X is different from all other solutions and will replace the worst one, given that X is better. In order to perceive if individuals are close, a distance measure $d(X, Y)$ is required, reflecting the similarity between individuals.

3.2.5 *The diversity measure*

This study relies on a measure based on the distances of particles to the cluster's center of mass, as first proposed by Grosso et al. [12], which expresses the structural dissimilarity between individuals. The choice was made based on the analysis by Pereira et al. [24]. Briefly, for each cluster, the distances from the particles to the center of mass are ordered in a vector in a non-decreasing fashion. Given two clusters and the respective ordered vectors Ord_X and Ord_Y, $d(X,Y)$ is given by Eq. 3. To estimate d_{min}, information provided by the initial population is used according to Eq. 4 where Pop represents the size of the population, $d(X, Y)$ the distance between individuals X and Y and ζ corresponds to the proportion among the average distance calculated with a set of randomly generated individuals and the minimum allowed distance between each pair. ζ has been set to 0.25.

$$d_{ord}(X,Y) = \frac{1}{10}\sum_{i=1}^{N} |(Ord_X(i) - Ord_Y(i))|^3 \quad (3)$$

$$d_{min} = \zeta \times \frac{\sum_{X=1}^{Pop-1}\sum_{Y=X+1}^{Pop} d(X,Y)}{\frac{1}{2}(Pop^2 - Pop)} \quad (4)$$

3.3 A mate choice approach to the optimization of Morse Clusters

As introduced in Sect. 3.2.1, each individual is composed of two chromosomes. The first is a GA vector that represents a candidate solution to the optimization of Morse clusters. The second is a GP tree that represents the function used by each individual to assess its mating candidates. The selection process is succinctly described in Alg. 1. *Parent 1* is selected using a fitness based tournament selection ad a set of mating candidates is selected randomly. *Parent 1* evaluates each of the candidates using its own evaluation function. The candidate that seems the most attractive, i.e. the one for which the GP tree of *Parent 1* returns the lowest value, is selected for mating. Since CGO is a minimization problem, we have opted to select the candidate with the lowest attractiveness value as the best one. When reproduction occurs, offspring inherit genetic material from both parents, resulting from GA operators acting on the first chromosomes and GP operators acting on the second ones.

Algorithm 1 Parent selection using Sexual Selection through Mate Choice

```
mate selection {
    parent1 = parent_selection(Pop)
    candidates = mating_candidates_selection(Pop)
    evaluate_mating_candidates(parent1,candidates)
    parent2 = select_best(candidates)
}
```

In order for individuals to assess others, they perceive problem-specific information regarding their phenotype. As described in sect. 3.2, when tackling the optimization of clusters of size N, individuals encode the positions of N particles, meaning that they also encode candidate solutions to each $N-1$ smaller clusters. How an individual performs on each of these clusters is an indicator of gene quality, showing how they may contribute to the optimization of N sized clusters. However, optimal solutions to clusters with different sizes can correspond to different geometric motifs. Thus, performing well on a $N-i$ sized cluster does not necessarily translate into good genes for the optimization of the N sized cluster. Without access to the cluster motifs it is difficult to build a function that uses this information in an appropriate way. We expect to self-adapt functions that do so in a meaningful way for the purpose of selecting mating partners.

Coupling a self-adaptive Mate Choice approach with a steady-state EA raises an interesting discussion point. Both mating preferences and physical traits evolve in a feedback loop, promoting those that bring reproductive advantage and causing individuals to continuously adapt to each other. The replacement strategy will however discard individuals that do not meet its constraints. Mating preferences that are unable to select adequate mating partners and produce offspring that are accepted into the population will therefore be incapable of spreading and gaining evolutionary advantage. On the other hand, accepted individuals will inherit and successfully promote both mating preferences and physical traits. Ultimately, the replacement strategy guides the evolution process. We expect mate evaluation functions to evolve accordingly and promote offspring that successfully integrate the population, therefore contributing to progress.

4. EXPERIMENTAL RESULTS

This section firstly describes the test setup applied in this study, followed by an analysis of both behaviour and performance.

4.1 Experimental Setup

The standard approach evolves a population of 100 individuals for 5.000.000 evaluations. Each iteration of the L-BFGS method counts as one evaluation. LSL is set to

1.000. Selection of both parents is done through a tournament of size 5, followed by crossover, applied with a rate of 70%, and mutation, applied with a rate of 5% [24]. Also $\sigma = 0.05 \times N^{1/3}$. Experiments were repeated 30 times for Morse clusters ranging from 41 to 80 particles. Finally, for analysis purposes, for every 100 individuals bred a generation counter is incremented.

In the Mate Choice approach, the first parent is selected through a tournament of 5 individuals. Then, a pool of 5 mating candidates is randomly selected from the population and the second parent is chosen following Alg. 1. Reproduction occurs by means of operators applied independently to each chromosome. The operators described in sect. 3.2.2 are applied to the first chromosome and crossover and mutation are applied to the second chromosome with the rates of 85% and 5% respectively. The terminal set of the GP trees is composed by the constants $\{-1, 2\}$ and 5 dynamic terminals. These dynamic terminals correspond to smaller instances of the target cluster so that they are equally spaced in the interval $[1, N-1]$. When a mating candidate is assessed, the dynamic terminals in the active function translate to the fitness obtained by the candidate on the corresponding instance. The non-terminal set consists on the following arithmetic functions: $\{+, -, *, /\}$. Experiments were repeated 30 times for Morse clusters ranging from 41 to 80 particles.

Performance of state-of-the-art approaches for tackling CGO problems is often measured based on the success rate of the runs [24, 8, 12], therefore, we register the number of runs where the putative optima was found for each instance of the problem. Also, in order to analyze the behaviour of our approach, the following elements were registered on each run: best fitness, average fitness, number of substitutions and average dissimilarity between individuals.

4.2 Analysis and Results

The success rates obtained by the studied approaches can be found in Table 1, where the label *Sexual Sel.* corresponds to our approach and the label *Standard* corresponds to the results reported in the study by Pereira et al. [24]. Our approach was able to find all putative optima on Morse clusters ranging from 41 to 80 atoms as well as outperform the Standard approach in 20 instances of the problem. On the other hand it achieved smaller rates in 13 instances and 7 ties. The pairwise proportions test proposed by Taillard et al. [29] was conducted with a significance level of *0.01* and significant differences were found on 4 instances which have been emphasized in Table 1. There is an obvious evolutionary overhead introduced by the evolution of Mate Choice functions: unless good mating choice functions are found, the ability of individuals to select appropriate mates is hindered, which could significantly delay evolution. While no significant differences were found on the majority of the instances, the proposed approach was able to attain competitive and sometimes better results than the standard approach, which indicates that the algorithm, in spite of the aforementioned overhead, is able to evolve mate choice functions that assess individuals in meaningful and advantageous ways.

The means by which the algorithm is able to take advantage of the mate choice process are not straightforward to analyze. Figure 1 shows an example of a GP tree evolved for the purpose of selecting mating partners. While the algorithm has evolved much larger trees, the presented one still serves the purpose of showing that interpreting the meanings

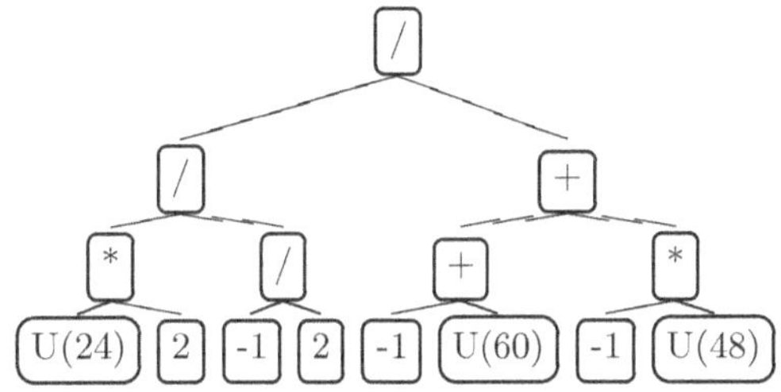

Figure 1: Example of a GP tree evolved for mating selection

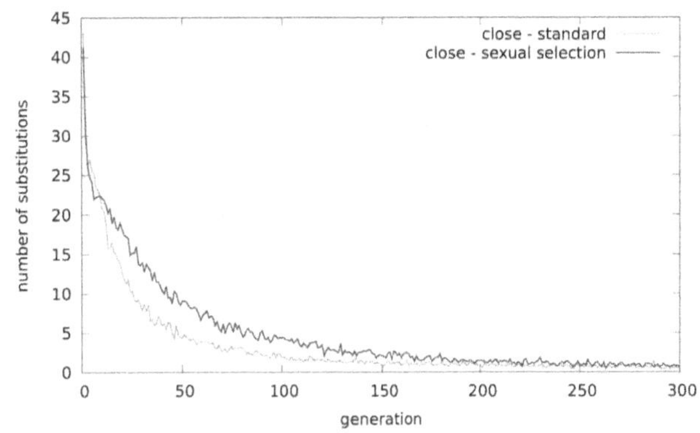

Figure 2: Average substitution rate from 30 runs with clusters of size 61, where *close* corresponds to individuals replacing a similar one in the population.

of the evolved trees is not an easy task. An analysis of the example in Fig. 1 leads us to conjecture that how individuals perform on the optimization of clusters sizing 24, 48 and 60 atoms is relevant for the individual owning this tree. However, how these terminals relate with each other and how much they weigh in the process of choosing a mate depends on how non-terminals act on them, which often prevents us from attributing meaning to the terminals. This makes the analysis of the evolved mate selection functions an often frustrating task, specially on larger trees. Still, we can draw two conclusions from the obtained results and tree analysis: the provided terminal and non-terminal sets can be combined in useful ways for mate selection; evolved functions allow individuals to choose their partners in unforeseeable ways which we would unlikely be able to design on our own.

While the inner workings of Mate Choice are difficult to analyze, its impact on the behaviour of the algorithm is quite noticeable. Experiments were conducted in order to measure the impact of Mate Choice on the acceptance rate as well as on the structural diversity of the population, two relevant aspects on the Standard approach. The following discussion will focus on Morse clusters consisting of 61 atoms, an instance that is considered particularly tough [8, 12].

Figures 2 and 3 compare the acceptance rates of individuals on both approaches. The replacement strategy has a powerful role in the steady-state model since it determines which of the offspring are allowed in the population. Ultimately, the progress of the evolution process is determined by how well it is able to adapt to the restrictions imposed by the replacement strategy and its capabilities to continuously produce offspring that are included in the population. Fur-

Table 1: Success rate obtained by the Standard and the Mate Choice approaches on clusters of size N

N	41	42	43	44	45	46	47	48	49	50	51	52	53	54	55	56	57	58	59	60
Sexual Sel.	**24**	**21**	18	**18**	12	14	6	16	16	2	2	9	4	7	7	11	9	5	3	**7**
Standard	15	12	14	7	5	9	2	14	18	5	7	6	5	12	6	11	8	4	2	0

N	61	62	63	64	65	66	67	68	69	70	71	72	73	74	75	76	77	78	79	80
Sexual Sel.	1	6	8	8	9	10	5	3	6	6	6	3	6	5	5	3	3	4	2	5
Standard	1	12	6	11	8	8	5	4	6	8	6	7	6	1	2	4	7	3	6	5

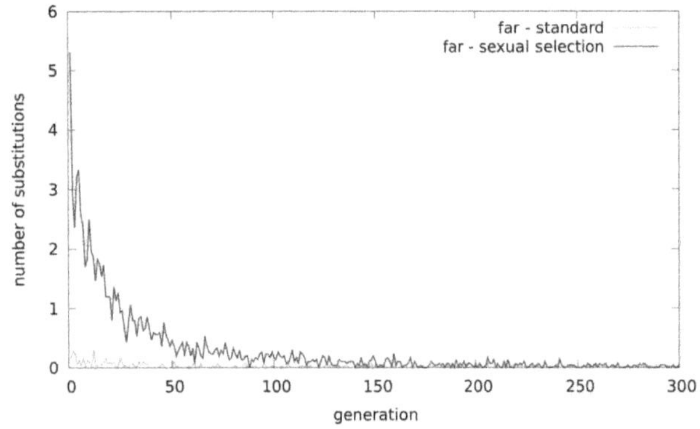

Figure 3: Average substitution rate from 30 runs with clusters of size 61, where *far* corresponds to individuals replacing worst one in the population.

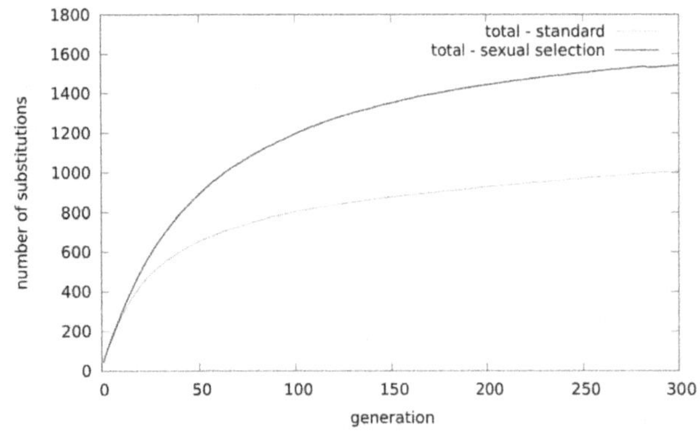

Figure 4: Cumulative average number of substitutions obtained in 30 runs with clusters of size 61.

thermore, on the proposed model, the replacement strategy not only controls what genes are allowed to spread through the population of candidate solutions but also which mating preferences will disseminate.

Figure 2 shows that the Mate Choice approach is able to successfully contribute with offspring that are better than the most structurally similar individuals in the population. Also, it does so at a fairly higher average rate than the Standard approach since the early stages of the runs. A similar behaviour is displayed in Fig. 3 regarding offspring that while being structurally different from the individuals in the population, are better than the worst one. These substitution rates are much lower, than the ones of Fig. 2 since the algorithms are more likely to produce offspring similar to individuals in the population, an effect that seems more pronounced in this particular instance. Still, differences between the two approaches are quite visible.

Although an increase in the acceptance rate doesn't necessarily translate into a better performance, it does show an aptitude to adapt to the replacement strategy. While the Standard approach is bound to give advantage to fittest individuals, the Mate Choice approach, despite selecting one of the parents through a tournament operator, may adopt different strategies to select the second one. Also, these strategies vary and self-adapt on the individual level. Adaption occurs as the replacement strategy discards unfit offspring, therefore giving an advantage not only to individuals that are fit but also to those that are able to select mating partners that contribute positively to the quality of their offspring. By means of inheritance, good mating evaluation functions are bound to spread through the population and further contribute to an increase of the acceptance rate observed in Figs. 2 and 3. Results in Table 1 suggest that such an increase in the acceptance rate contributes to competitive and sometimes better success rates.

A possible setback on the application of our mate choice approach is the extra computational overhead created by the evaluation of mating candidates. While this is not the scope of the study, it is relevant to note that such an analysis is not straightforward due to a number of reasons. Firstly, mating candidates do not undergo local optimization while being evaluated on smaller instances of the problem, which is responsible for the largest part of the computational effort required for evaluating individuals. Secondly, the effort needed to calculate the potential energy of a cluster varies with its size. Thirdly, mechanisms may be easily included in the algorithm to ensure that individuals are not repeatedly evaluated on the same instances of the problem, which is particularly relevant on steady-state models where individuals may have a considerably long life. Fourthly, which individuals are evaluated and on what instances is highly dependent on the mating preferences present in the population, which are subject to adaptation along the run. Finally, as Fig. 4 shows, the Mate Choice approach produces an increase of roughly 50% on the cumulative average number of substitution, reaching the average number of substitutions attained by the Standard approach still early in the evolution process. By reducing periods of stasis, our approach may reach the putative optima on a smaller number of generations thus reducing the number of required evaluations.

Even though the Mate Choice approach results on a much larger number of substitutions along the evolution process, their impact is quite different from those on the Standard approach. Figure 5 shows the average distance between individuals and how it is influenced by substitutions in each approach. The measure is calculated through Eq. 3 and evaluates the structural dissimilarity between individuals in

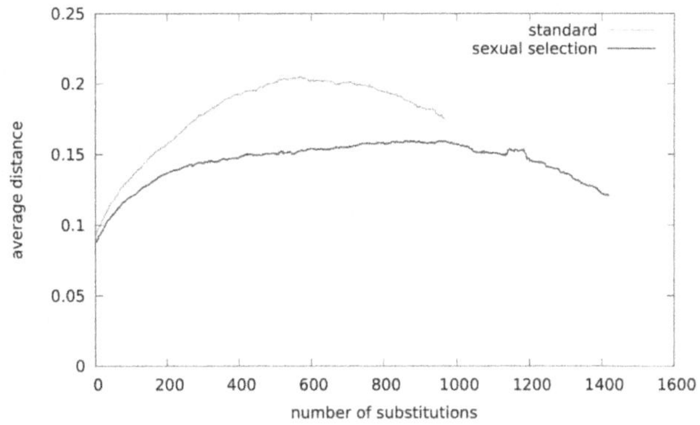

Figure 5: Average distance between individuals obtained from 30 runs with clusters of size 61.

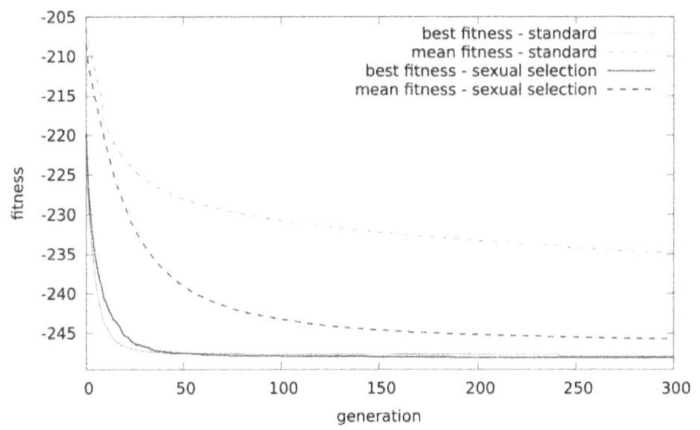

Figure 6: Average fitness obtained from 30 runs with clusters of size 61.

the population. Both approaches start with nearly the same dissimilarity value, however, the Standard approach, while producing a smaller number of offspring, is able to introduce new individuals in the population that have a much stronger impact on its average dissimilarity. These results may appear contradictory with the ones reported in Fig. 3, which shows that Mate Choice generates more replacements by dissimilar individuals. This can be explained as follows: the number of substitutions resulting from the introduction of dissimilar individuals is low in both strategies and hence unnoticeable in terms of average distance.

Our approach shares some characteristics with the Standard one, with a period where the average dissimilarity between individuals increases, followed by stagnation and a period where it slowly downfalls. There are however inherent differences between the impact of new individuals. While unable to reach an average dissimilarity as high as the Standard approach, Mate Choice causes a slower yet longer increase in the population's dissimilarity, suggesting that offspring cause a smaller but steadier impact on the progress of the evolution process. Nonetheless, despite the gradual decrease of dissimilarity toward the end of the run, both approaches are able to keep diversity above initial levels, promoting a good mixture of individuals along each run.

Based on the number of substitutions in Figs. 2 and 3 as well as on the impact new individuals have on the population as reported in Fig. 5, Mate Choice seems to produce offspring that share a higher structural similarity with individuals in the population. Such an effect is most likely the result of how mating preferences evolve along the run, suggesting that they adapt in a way that favours reproduction between structurally similar individuals, thus producing offspring that have less impact on the average dissimilarity of the population while still being valuable to the evolution process. However, as Fig. 3 shows, this does not prevent the discovery of individuals that are structurally dissimilar and, yet, reasonably fit – in the sense that they are at least better than the worst individual of the population. Thus, even when generating dissimilar individuals the Mate Choice approach behaves more robustly than the Standard approach, eventually leading to a higher number of substitutions by both similar and dissimilar individuals. This indicates that individuals tend to chose "compatible" mating partners.

The promotion of structurally similar individuals shown by Fig. 2 and the resulting impact on the average dissimilarity between individuals illustrated by Fig. 5 may indicate that the higher rate of substitutions caused by the evolved mating evaluation functions contributes to a slower search for the optimal solution as Mate Choice generates individuals that cause a smaller impact and possibly smaller gains in performance. However, Fig. 6 seems to contradict this assumption, showing that Mate Choice actively contributes to performance gains, a behaviour that is repeatedly found on the other instances of the problem.

5. CONCLUSIONS

This study proposes a Mate Choice approach to the optimization of Morse clusters. Major breakthroughs on CGO are reviewed and a hybrid steady-state EA coupled with a local-search method is thoroughly described. Mate Choice is introduced and state of the art approaches applied to a variety of problems are presented. A Mate Choice model for Morse clusters optimization is described and coupled with the aforementioned EA.

Morse clusters ranging from 41 to 80 atoms are tackled, the results compared and discussed with a particular interest on diversity handling as well as on the replacement strategy's acceptance rate. The results show a significant increase on the success rate on 4 instances of the problem and a slightly more robust behaviour on the global level. It is discussed that the evolved mating functions are difficult to analyze and seem to evolve in unforeseeable yet useful ways. The acceptance rate is analyzed and it is suggested that the Mate Choice approach is able to produce valuable individuals at an higher rate than the Standard approach, showing an adaption to the replacement strategy. Also, the analysis of diversity handling suggests that the Mate Choice model promotes mating between structurally similar individuals, therefore producing offspring that have a smaller yet longer impact on the population's diversity, and that individuals appear to choose compatible mating partners. It is also shown that the model is able to contribute to performance gains in the population. Finally, difficulties in studying the overhead caused by Mate Choice are discussed.

Future work may include applying Mate Choice to a set of Morse clusters ranging up to 160 atoms as well as studying how different mating preferences, representations, and varying mutation and crossover probabilities affect the behaviour and performance of Mate Choice on hybrid steady-state approaches to CGO.

6. ACKNOWLEDGMENTS

This work was partially funded by the Portuguese Foundation for Science and Technology (FCT) under project INO164-PTDC/EIA-EIA/102212/2008, High-Performance Computing over the Large-Scale Internet.

7. REFERENCES

[1] D. Buss. *Evolutionary psychology*. Washington, DC, US: American Psychological Association; New York, NY, US: Oxford University Press, 2000.

[2] J. Cartwright. *Evolution and human behavior: Darwinian perspectives on human nature*. The MIT Press, 2000.

[3] A. Cassioli, M. Locatelli, and F. Schoen. Global optimization of binary lennard-jones clusters. *Optimization Methods Software*, 24:819–835, 2009.

[4] L. Cheng, Y. Feng, J. Yang, and J. Yang. Funnel hopping: Searching the cluster potential energy surface over the funnels. *The Journal of Chemical Physics*, 130(21):214112, 2009.

[5] C. Darwin. The origin of species, 1859.

[6] C. Darwin. *The descent of man and selection in relation to sex*. John Murray London, 1906.

[7] D. M. Deaven and K. M. Ho. Molecular Geometry Optimization with a Genetic Algorithm. *Physical Review Letters*, 75:288–291, 1995.

[8] J. P. K. Doye, R. H. Leary, M. Locatelli, and F. Schoen. Global optimization of morse clusters by potential energy transformations. *INFORMS J. on Computing*, 16:371–379, 2004.

[9] R. Fisher. The evolution of sexual preference. *The Eugenics Review*, 7(3):184, 1915.

[10] R. Fisher. The genetical theory of natural selection. 1930.

[11] R. Fry, S. Smith, and A. Tyrrell. A self-adaptive mate selection model for genetic programming. In *Evolutionary Computation, 2005. The 2005 IEEE Congress on*, volume 3, pages 2707–2714. IEEE, 2005.

[12] A. Grosso, M. Locatelli, and F. Schoen. A population-based approach for hard global optimization problems based on dissimilarity measures. *Mathematical Programming*, 110:373–404, 2007.

[13] L. Guntly and D. Tauritz. Learning individual mating preferences. In *Proceedings of the 13th annual conference on Genetic and evolutionary computation*, pages 1069–1076. ACM, 2011.

[14] B. Hartke. Global geometry optimization of clusters using genetic algorithms. *The Journal of Physical Chemistry*, 97(39):9973–9976, 1993.

[15] B. Hartke. Application of evolutionary algorithms to global cluster geometry optimization. In R. L. Johnston, editor, *Applications of Evolutionary Computation in Chemistry*, volume 110 of *Structure & Bonding*, pages 33–53. Springer Berlin / Heidelberg, 2004.

[16] R. Hinterding and Z. Michalewicz. Your brains and my beauty: parent matching for constrained optimisation. In *Evolutionary Computation Proceedings, 1998. IEEE World Congress on Computational Intelligence., The 1998 IEEE International Conference on*, pages 810–815. IEEE, 1998.

[17] J. E. Jones. On the Determination of Molecular Fields. II. From the Equation of State of a Gas. *Royal Society of London Proceedings Series A*, 106:463–477, 1924.

[18] J. Lee, I.-H. Lee, and J. Lee. Unbiased global optimization of lennard-jones clusters for $n \leq 201$ using the conformational space annealing method. *Phys. Rev. Lett.*, 91:080201, Aug 2003.

[19] M. Locatelli and F. Schoen. Fast global optimization of difficult lennard-jones clusters. *Computational Optimization and Applications*, 21:55–70, 2002.

[20] P. Machado and A. Leitão. Evolving fitness functions for mating selection. *Genetic Programming*, pages 227–238, 2011.

[21] P. M. Morse. Diatomic Molecules According To Wave Mechanics. II. Vibrational Levels. *Phys. Rev.*, 1929.

[22] J. P. K. Doye and D. J. Wales. Structural consequences of the range of the interatomic potential a menagerie of clusters. *J. Chem. Soc., Faraday Trans.*, 93:4233–4243, 1997.

[23] F. Pereira and J. Marques. A self-adaptive evolutionary algorithm for cluster geometry optimization. In *Hybrid Intelligent Systems, 2008. HIS '08. Eighth International Conference on*, pages 678 –683, 2008.

[24] F. Pereira and J. Marques. A study on diversity for cluster geometry optimization. *Evolutionary Intelligence*, 2:121–140, 2009.

[25] F. Pereira, J. Marques, T. Leitao, and J. Tavares. Analysis of locality in hybrid evolutionary cluster optimization. In *Evolutionary Computation, 2006. CEC 2006. IEEE Congress on*, pages 2285 –2292, 2006.

[26] F. B. Pereira, J. Marques, T. Leitao, and J. Tavares. Designing efficient evolutionary algorithms for cluster optimization: A study on locality. In P. Siarry and Z. Michalewicz, editors, *Advances in Metaheuristics for Hard Optimization*, Natural Computing Series, pages 223–250. Springer Berlin Heidelberg, 2008.

[27] C. Roberts, R. L. Johnston, and N. T. Wilson. A genetic algorithm for the structural optimization of morse clusters. *Theoretical Chemistry Accounts: Theory, Computation, and Modeling (Theoretica Chimica Acta)*, 104:123–130, 2000.

[28] E. Smorodkina and D. Tauritz. Toward automating ea configuration: the parent selection stage. In *Evolutionary Computation, 2007. CEC 2007. IEEE Congress on*, pages 63–70. IEEE, 2007.

[29] E. D. Taillard, P. Waelti, and J. Zuber. Few statistical tests for proportions comparison. *European Journal of Operational Research*, 185(3):1336 – 1350, 2008.

[30] A. Zahavi. Mate selection–a selection for a handicap. *Journal of theoretical Biology*, 53(1):205–214, 1975.

[31] Y. Zeiri. Prediction of the lowest energy structure of clusters using a genetic algorithm. *Phys. Rev. E*, 51:R2769–R2772, 1995.

[32] J. Zhao and R.-H. Xie. Genetic algorithms for the geometry optimization of atomic and molecular clusters. *Journal of Computational and Theoretical Nanoscience*, 1(2):117–131, 2004.

Genetic Programming with Genetic Regulatory Networks

Genetic Programming

Rui L. Lopes
Centro de Informática e Sistemas da Universidade de Coimbra
Polo II - Pinhal de Marrocos
3030-290 Coimbra, Portugal
rmlopes@dei.uc.pt

Ernesto Costa
Centro de Informática e Sistemas da Universidade de Coimbra
Polo II - Pinhal de Marrocos
3030-290 Coimbra, Portugal
ernesto@dei.uc.pt

ABSTRACT

Evolutionary Algorithms (EA) approach differently from nature the genotype - phenotype relationship, and this view is a recurrent issue among researchers. Recently, some researchers have started exploring computationally the new comprehension of the multitude of regulatory mechanisms that are fundamental in both processes of inheritance and of development in natural systems, by trying to include those mechanisms in the EAs.

One of the first successful proposals was the Artificial Regulatory Network (ARN) model. Soon after some variants of the ARN, including different improvements over the base model, were tested. In this paper, we combine two of those alternatives, demonstrating experimentally how the resulting model can deal with complex problems, including those that have multiple outputs. The efficacy and efficiency of this variant are tested experimentally using two benchmark problems that show how we can evolve a controller or an artificial artist.

Categories and Subject Descriptors

I.2.8 [**Problem Solving, Control Methods, and Search**]: Heuristic Methods

General Terms

Algorithms

Keywords

artificial regulatory network, genetic programming, inverted pendulum, artificial art

1. INTRODUCTION

Nature-inspired algorithms are used extensively today to solve a multitude of learning, design, and optimisation problems, giving rise to a new research area called Evolutionary Computation (EC) [1]. Over time many variants of a basic algorithm especially tuned for some problems and/or situations were proposed (e.g., algorithms for dealing with noisy, uncertain or dynamic environments, for evolving rather than designing the algorithm's parameters or some of its components, algorithms with local search operators or for multi-objective optimisation). Typically, the objects manipulated by the evolutionary algorithms are represented at two different levels. At a low level (the genotype) the representations are manipulated by the variation operators; at a high level (the phenotype) the objects are evaluated to determine their fitness and are selected accordingly. Because of that, we need a mapping between these two levels. The issue of the relationship between the genotype and the phenotype is as old as the area itself, with many experts claiming that the standard approach is too simplistic, and advocating that it is worth trying to close the gap between EC and Biology, introducing more complex relationships between the genotype and the phenotype, and evaluate if they are responsible for an improvement in both robustness and evolvability [2, 3]. For example, typically in an EA, the two phases of transcription and translation (that exist in nature) are merged into just one and the regulatory processes are missing. At a larger scale, we could add the lack of epigenetic phenomena that contribute to the evolution and all the mechanisms involved in the construction of an organism.

During the last years we saw the appearance of novel representations and the corresponding genotype to phenotype mapping: grammatical evolution [4], self-modifying cartesian genetic programming [5], gene expression programming [6], or enzyme programming [7]. Along a different path, W. Banzhaf et al. [3], suggested that one should enrich the artificial model of evolution with the inclusion of feedback regulatory mechanisms. Earlier, in [8] the author had proposed an artificial gene regulatory network(ARN) model and showed how it could be used computationally in different settings [9]. Later, the ARN model was extended by [10] with the inclusion of extra input proteins and dividing the gene's products in transcription factors and non-regulatory proteins. The latter are used as outputs. More recently [11] presented another variant of the ARN, enlarging its applicability, by transforming the regulatory gene network into a computable graph, with or without feedback edges, similarly to what is done in GP. In this work we merge these two approaches and explore further its capabilities.The combined model is tested with two benchmark problems, one involving the evolution of a controller and the other an artificial artist. The latter is developed as a proof-of-concept for the model's multiple output capabilities.

The paper is organised as follows. Section 2 is a brief overview of the concepts behind regulation at the transcriptional and translational levels, the types of models that have been proposed, and the contribution of evolutionary computation to the problem of inferring GRNs from data. Section 3 describes the original ARN model as originally proposed by the author. Then, Section 4 describes an extension of that model, elucidating in particular how a program can be extracted from a network. In Section 5 we briefly refer to the problems used and we present the experimental setup in Section 6. The results are presented and analysed in Section 7. Finally, in Section 8 we draw some conclusions and present ideas for future work.

2. GENE REGULATORY NETWORKS

For a long time it was believed that the DNA was transcribed into RNA, which in turn was translated into proteins in a one-way process. Today, we know that the process of gene expression into proteins is more complex, and relies on a network of interactions (known as regulatory network) between genes and many other molecules including proteins, the very products of gene expression (see Fig. 1).

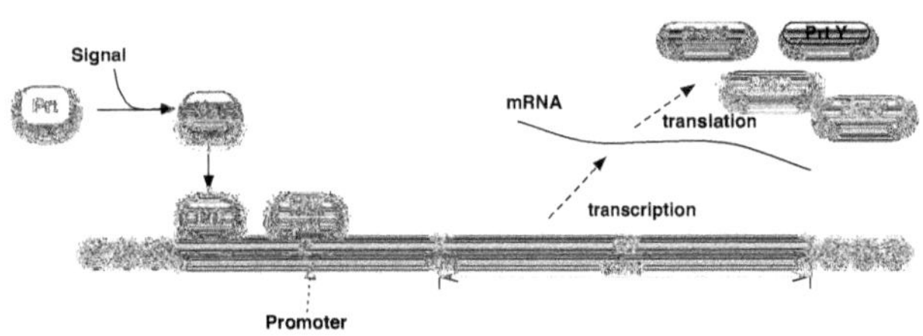

Figure 1: Gene Regulation: the transcription of a gene is driven by a protein called RNA polymerase, which binds to a special regulatory region of the DNA called the promoter. Other proteins (transcription factors) control the accessibility of the promoter to RNA polymerase. These proteins are activated by external signals and bind in the vicinity of the promoter. They can enhance the production of a protein by a gene, as in the figure, or inhibit its production.

A correct understanding of the behaviour of gene regulatory networks (GRN) is of paramount importance in many areas of application, like personalised medicine, epidemic prevention, energy production, bio-remediation or synthetic biology [12].

Various approaches for formally modelling gene regulatory networks appeared in the last decades. The proposed models can be classified according to the following aspects: variables such as product concentrations are discrete, continuous or mixed; time is discrete and the update of the variables is either synchronous or asynchronous (there are, however, cases where time is continuous); space is discrete, continuous or absent. Examples of models include directed graphs, bayesian networks, ordinary and partial differential equations, random boolean networks, neural networks, and rule-based formalisms [13, 12, 14, 15]. Since these regulatory networks are highly non-linear and have several thousand variables obtaining a model is a complex task. Computational approaches to this problem try to reconstruct the GRN from experimental data, for instance, gene expression data obtained from microarrays. Within this perspective devising a GRN is viewed as a reverse engineering problem, where one builds a model from data. Some attempts were made to use evolutionary algorithms to solve this problem for some of the formal models. In particular, there have been proposed solutions based on genetic algorithms [16], genetic programming [17], evolution strategies [18], and differential evolution [19].

Researchers have been interested in GRNs from different points of view, besides the biological one. For example, the different artificial models have been studied from a system's perspective, trying to understand its topological and dynamics properties [20, 21, 22, 9]. In a different path, some computational explorations have been proposed that reflect our comprehension about regulatory mechanisms and how they mediate between evolution and development, i.e., that try to incorporate those mechanisms into artificial evolutionary systems. For example, in [23, 24, 25, 26, 27] GRNs are explored in the context of artificial 3D morphogenesis. In [28, 29] regulation is explored to evolve real-time controllers for a robot, and to the task of automatically designing robots in a physical-based virtual environment. In [20] the authors proposed a model of an artificial genome and studied the implications for artificial ontogeny, while [30] also proposed a model of gene expression and regulation in an artificial cellular organism and speculates about its application to evolutionary computation. There is a third perspective for studying artificial GRNs: using them as a computational device. To the best of our knowledge, the unique proposal of an artificial regulatory network used for problem solving, was the one proposed in [8] (ARN). Due to its importance for our work it will be detailed in the next section.

3. THE ARN MODEL

The Artificial Regulatory Network (ARN) [8] is an attempt to incorporate regulatory mechanisms between the genotype and the phenotype. There are no other products, i.e., DNA, and processes in between these two levels. The genome has fixed length and is constructed by simple duplication with mutation events. Regulation between genes is a mediated process, achieved by means of a binding process between proteins (i.e., transcription factors) and special zones in the genome that appear upstream of the promoter of a gene. The remaining of this section will describe this with more detail.

Genome

The model presented in this paper uses a binary genome and implements a simple algorithm to transcribe and then translate it into proteins. The genome can be generated randomly or by a process of duplication with mutation, also called *DM*, that is considered the driving force for creating new genes in biological genomes and has an important role in the growth of gene regulatory networks [31]. In the latter case we start with a random 32-bit binary sequence, that is followed by several DM episodes. As we will see later the number of duplications is an important parameter. So, if we have 10 duplication events then the final length of the genome is $2^5 \times 2^{10} = 32768$. The mutation rate is typically of 1%. The genome is divided in several regions, namely a regulatory site, the promoter, and the gene itself. The first

32 bits of the regulation zone are the enhancer site, while the following 32 bits are the inhibitory site. The promoter is located downstream and has the form $XYZ01010101$.The first 24 bits (the sequence represented by XYZ) can be either 0 or 1, while the last 8 bits are fixed. This way, the probability for a promoter to occur is $2^{-8} = 0,39\%$. The idea is to model what happens in nature, where we have a small consensus sequence where the RNA polymerase binds (in our case 01010101), inside a larger promoter. A gene is composed of five 32-bit long sequences, i.e., a 160-bit string. The choice of the method to obtain the genome, including the values for the parameters, is guided by what happens in the natural world.

Gene expression

The genotype - phenotype mapping is defined by expressing each 160-bit long gene, resulting in a 32-bit protein. A gene expresses a protein by a majority rule: if we consider a gene, for example G^m, divided into 5 parts of size 32 each, G_1^m to G_5^m, at position i, say, the protein's bit will have a value corresponding to the most frequent value in each of these 5 parts, at the same position, i.e.,

$$P_i^m = majority(G_{ki}^m, \quad \forall k = 1, \ldots, 5), \quad \forall i = 1, \ldots, 32$$

Figure 2 show a simple illustrative example.

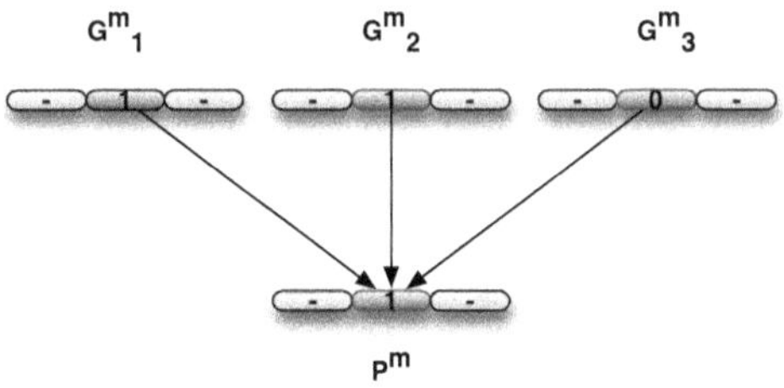

Figure 2: The majority rule: a simple example for a gene with three regions of size three and the corresponding protein. Here just the process for the second position.

Figure 3 gives an idea of the representation. P is the promoter region, that indicates the beginning of the gene; G1 to G5 are the five parts of a gene; E is the gene activation binding site (enhancer) for the protein, and H is the repression binding site for the protein (inhibitor).

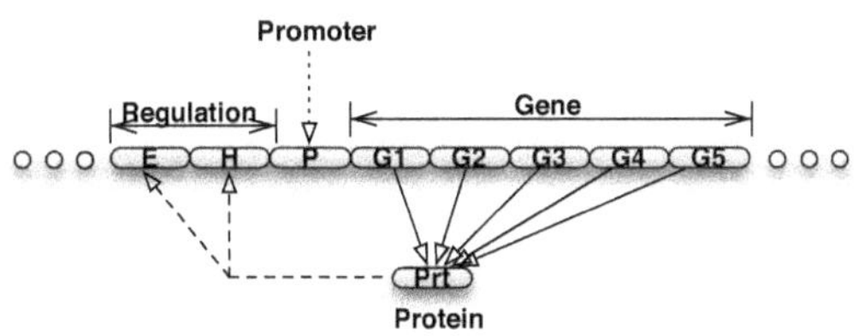

Figure 3: A genome element in the ARN model.

Regulation

Genes interact mediated by proteins, which bind to the regulatory region of each gene. If, say, gene **A** expresses protein p_A and that protein contributes to the activation of gene **B**, we say that gene **A** regulates **B** (see Fig. 4).

Notice that in order for a link to exist between any two genes, the concentration of the corresponding protein must attain a certain level, and that depends on the strength of the binding. The strength of the binding is computed by calculating the degree of complementarity between the protein and each of the regulatory regions, according to formula 1:

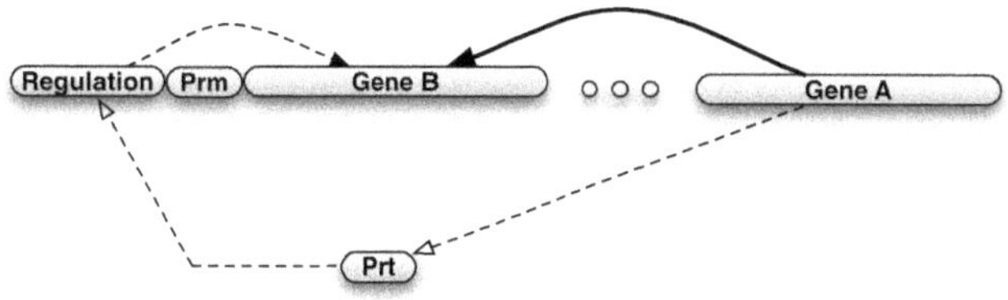

Figure 4: Gene - Protein - Gene interaction

$$x_i = \frac{1}{N} \sum_{j=1}^{N} c_j e^{\beta(\mu_{ji} - \mu_{max})} \tag{1}$$

where x_i represents the binding strength of the enhancer (e_i) or the inhibitory (h_i) region, N is the number of proteins, c_j the concentration of protein j, μ_{ji} is the number of bits that are different in the protein (j) and in the regulation site (r_i), that is,

$$\mu_{ji} = \sum_{k=1}^{32} j_k \oplus r_{i_k} \tag{2}$$

μ_{max} is the maximum match achievable, and β is a scaling factor. The production of a protein over time depends on its concentration, which in turn is a function of the way each protein binds to that gene's regulatory regions. It is defined by the differential equation

$$\frac{dc_i}{dt} = \delta(e_i - h_i)c_i \tag{3}$$

where e_i and h_i are defined by equation 1, and δ is a scaling factor.

Computational Device

Using this process we can build for each genome the corresponding artificial gene regulatory network. From a problem-solving perspective we want to transform an ARN into a computational problem-solver.To that end we need to clarify what we put into the system, what we extract from the system, and how we define the semantics, that is, the meaning of the computation in which the network is engaged. Finally, and as a consequence of the points just identified, it is also fundamental to determine if we are interested in the input/output relationship or if what we want is just the output. A solution for the latter situation was proposed in [32] in the context of optimization problems. The idea is to define (randomly) two new contiguous 32-bit sequences in the genome. The first one being a new inhibitory site (h_i), and the second one a new activation site (e_i). All generated proteins can bind to these sites. The levels of activation and inhibition can be computed as before (Equation 1), but there is no gene (thus no protein) attached.

The state of this site is just the sum of all bindings (see Eq. 4) and is defined as the output. This additional binding is thus a method to extract a meaning from the variation of the proteins' concentrations over time.

$$s(t) = \sum_{i}(e_i - h_i) \tag{4}$$

To use the model as a representation formalism for genetic programming one needs to define what are the inputs and what are the outputs. For that purpose the ARNs model was extended in two directions [10]. First, some extra proteins, not produced by genes but contributing to regulation, were introduced and act as inputs. Second, the genes were divided into two sets, one producing proteins that are used in regulation (i.e., transcriptional factors), and a second one with proteins without regulatory function which are used as outputs. These two types of genes are distinguished by having different promoters (see Fig. 5).

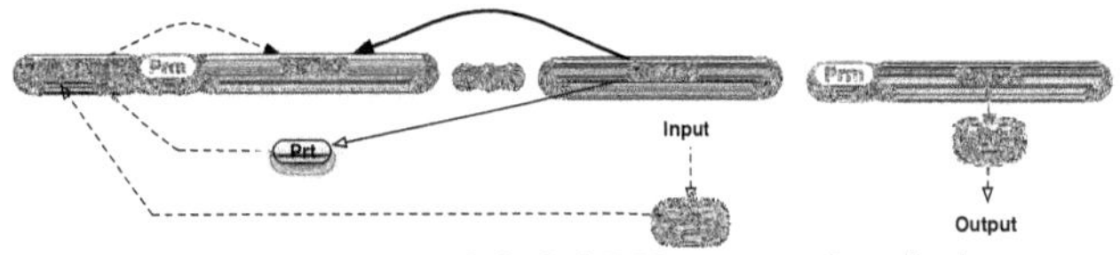

Figure 5: The modified ARN proposed in [10].

This model has been successfully used to solve different problems, namely, the cart-pole balancing [10] and to predict time-series [33]. A different approach presented in [11], called ReNCoDe, employs the original ARN architecture as the genotypical representation, without using the proteins' concentrations, and proposed an algorithm to extract a program from the regulatory network. Moreover, new biologically inspired genetic operators were introduced, which improved the performance of the algorithm. In particular the *transposon* operator, which copies a section of the genome and inserts it into a new random location. In the current paper we propose to merge these approaches. We keep the fundamental aspects of ReNCoDe, i.e., the transformation of the GRN in a program that ignores the protein's concentrations, and the new genetic operators, but introduce extra input proteins and output proteins. This reformulation will be described in the following sections.

4. GENETIC PROGRAMMING WITH ARNS

The merge of ReNCoDe [11] with the extended ARN model presented in [10] involves three aspects: the definition of the inputs and the outputs, the algorithm for extracting the program from the network, and the mapping of proteins to functions.

4.1 Input and Output

Extra proteins are introduced to represent the inputs and the proteins coded in the genome are distinguished between transcription factors and products, based on using two promoters $XYZ00000000$ and $XYZ11111111$, respectively. The extra proteins have distinct 32-bit signatures. The products are regulated by all proteins but do not regulate, while the inputs participate in the regulatory process but are not regulated. This means that, in the resulting network, there are not connections towards the inputs, nor from the output(s) towards other proteins (see Fig. 5).

4.2 Building the graph

First the ARN of the individual is built, composed of multiple links (inhibition and excitation) between different nodes (genes). In order to extract a graph from this network it must first be reduced. This is achieved by transforming every pair of inhibition (h) and excitation (e) connections into a single link with the difference between both ($e - h$). Connections whose weight is less than or equal to zero are ignored.

The graph is constructed in a top-down fashion, starting from the output node(s). Recursively, the inputs of each protein in the circuit will be added until only the extra proteins (inputs) are left aside. The order of inclusion in the graph is defined by the corresponding connection weight (see Eq. 2), that is, the strongest connections (with higher binding strength) will be added first. Finally, to avoid recursion, if a node has input connections from others already in the circuit, those are discarded.

When only one output is necessary each product is tested as the graph output (a graph is built and tested for each product). If one wants N outputs from the graph, then the first N products are used as outputs and the graph is built from these in the same fashion (there are no connections amongst the outputs since they do not regulate). Note that the initial individuals usually have fewer proteins and products. If there are not enough products in a network, 0 will be returned for the missing outputs.

4.3 Mapping Proteins to Functions

A mapping is needed to translate nodes (i.e., genes/proteins) to functions. The terminals are mapped sequentially using the input proteins (disregard of their signature). For the remaining nodes we use the gene-protein correspondence.

The protein's signature is used to obtain the function by a majority vote process (each protein codifies a function). As an example, to code the function set `{ +, -, *, / }` only two bits are necessary. The protein's signature is split into sixteen two-bit chunks. Then we obtain the function set index (two bits) by applying the majority vote rule over each bit (two positions) of the sixteen chunks (since the number of chunks is even, in case of a tie the result holds 1). If the function set length is not a power of two, it is either used circularly, or dummy functions may be added.

It is possible for some node to be included in the graph, while not having any input connection available. In this case the proteins' signature is mapped to an integer and wrapped by the hyperbolic tangent function (producing one of the constants -1.0 or 1.0).

5. PROBLEMS

In this section we present the problems used to assess the capabilities of this model. First, we show that the approach is capable of evolving a controller for the inverted pendulum (where only one product is necessary). Second, we test the evolution of graphs with multiple outputs in the context of symbolic expression for Artificial Art.

5.1 The Inverted Pendulum

In this problem there is a cart with an inverted pendulum, the pole, in a finite length 1D track. The goal is to keep the pole balanced and the cart inside the track limits by successively applying a constant force in either direction (left or right) [34].

The function set used was `{ +, -, *, / }`. The terminal set is composed by the position and velocity of the cart, as well as the angle and angular velocity of the pole. Using these building-blocks a controller is constructed whose output is translated into a push to the left if negative, or to the right if positive.

Each individual was tested over 10 randomised trials, returning the mean fitness of the set. A trial ends when either the cart goes off the track boundaries ($\pm 2.4m$) or the pole falls below 12°. The individual fitness of each trial is defined as in [10]:

$$F(x) = \frac{120000}{\text{number\_of\_successful\_steps}}$$

The evolutionary run terminates when the an individual is found that successfully balances the pole for 120000 steps for each trial, or the maximum number of evaluations is reached. After the evolutionary process the controller is tested for generalisation over $5^4 = 625$ trials (the four input variables, combined using five different rates for each {0.05, 0.275, 0.5, 0.725, 0.95}), during 1000 steps, as described in [34].

5.2 Artificial Art

Evolutionary Art is a growing research field which gathers nowadays researchers from the most varied areas. One of the favourite techniques used to generate evolutionary artifacts is symbolic expression [35]. In the context of GP, it consists in evolving trees (or graphs) that generate for each pixel a colour value which is a function of its coordinates. It is not a goal of the present work to fully describe and improve on the state of art of this field, but rather to provide a proof-of-concept of the use of the model for generating multiple outputs.

The function set used varies amongst researchers, depending on the specific approach/goals. The terminal set is commonly composed of $\{x, y\}$, although variations can be found (for instance, one can use also the distance to the centre, or information from a target image). Fitness can be interactive or automated, both presenting advantages and disadvantages [35].

In this work we intend to test the applicability of the new computational model to this type of problem, by evolving coloured images. The function set that we used was $\{+, -, *, /, sin, cos, sinh, cosh\}$, and the available inputs are the coordinates (x, y), and the distance to the centre r. The colour space used was RGB, so each graph will have three outputs (one for each colour dimension). Fitness automation was not implemented.

Every round the population is displayed on a grid, ordered by fitness score. The run starts with equal fitness for each individual and each time the user chooses one (a mouse click on the interface), its score is increased.

6. EXPERIMENTAL SETUP

The experimental setup for both applications described in the previous section is detailed in Table 1. In the inverted pendulum case the experiment was repeated 50 times, for comparability with results on the literature (as the evaluation is interactive for the artificial artist, a number of runs is not specified). The runs for evolving images lasted from 40 to 60 iterations. The evolution strategy used was an ES-(250+250), while for the artist the strategy used was ES-(25+5). with the initial population generated by a random 32-bit seed submitted to 8 DM-events. The mutation rate used for generating the initial population was 0.02%. For the bit-flip mutation operator a 0.01% rate was applied. In order to allow variable length genomes (aimed at improving efficiency [11]), the *transposon* operator was used in conjunction with the *delete* operator, using 64-bit length sections. The crossover operator is not used in any experiment.

Table 1: Experimental Setup.

Problem	Pendulum	Artificial Art
Number of Runs	50	-
Evolution Strategy	(250+250)	(25+5)
Num. Iterations	10^3	40-60
Number of DMs	8	
DM Mutation Rate	0.02	
Mutation Operator Rate	0.01	
Protein Bind Thresh.	16	
Genome Length	Variable	
Operator Type	Transposon	
Operator Length	64	

7. RESULTS

In the following sections we present the results for both applications. Firstly, we present the results for the pole balancing and compare with other approaches in the literature. Secondly, we display distinct images evolved with the artificial artist.

7.1 Inverted Pendulum

The experiments show that the present model is capable of evolving solutions for the single-output problem of balancing an inverted pendulum. Table 2 averages the generalisation results of the 50 runs, indicating the performance of the best solution found, as well as known results from the literature. Although the approaches are not directly comparable, one can see that this model performs as well as other methods [10, 36], displaying better average over the runs and smaller standard deviation. Also, when compared to [11] there is some deterioration, although the fitness functions used in the present work uses less random initialisations.

Table 2: Summary of the generalisation tests for the cart-pole problem, by number of successful trials out of 625 (see Sect. 5.1). Results from the literature are also transcribed.

Reference	N	Best	Mean	Std. Dev.
ARN-GP	50	434	373.8	48.3
[10]	50	422	202.18	110.01
[36]	50	406	203.18	116.05
[11]	50	497	478	12.63

Figure 6 shows the best circuit found. The output is identified by the hexagonal shape while the inputs are squared. The oval nodes correspond to the transcription factors. It is clear the re-use of functions (nodes) that are used simultaneously as inputs to various other nodes.

7.2 Artificial Artist

In order to test the multiple output features of the model we tried to evolve genomes capable of generating interesting images, by outputting the RGB values for each pixel given the input set {x,y,r}. In this section we present some of

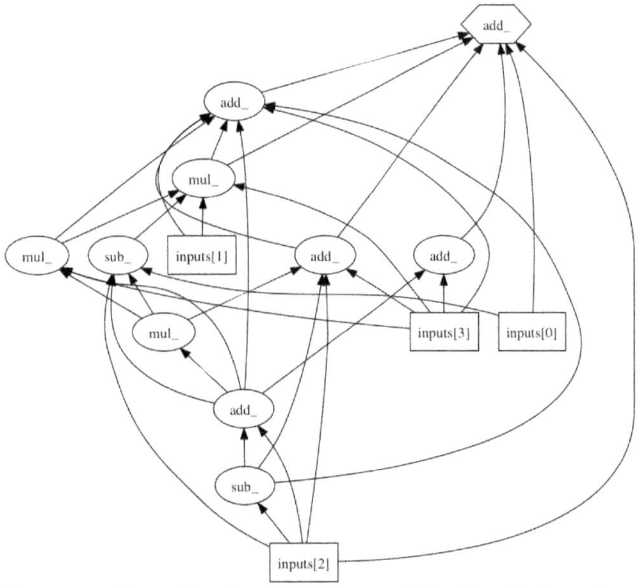

Figure 6: Controller for the best run of the Cart-Pole problem. The output is distinguished by the hexagonal shape, the inputs by the square shape. Oval nodes correspond to the transcription factors. The function set is composed by the arithmetic functions. The input indexes represent, respectively, cart position, pole angle, velocity, and angular velocity.

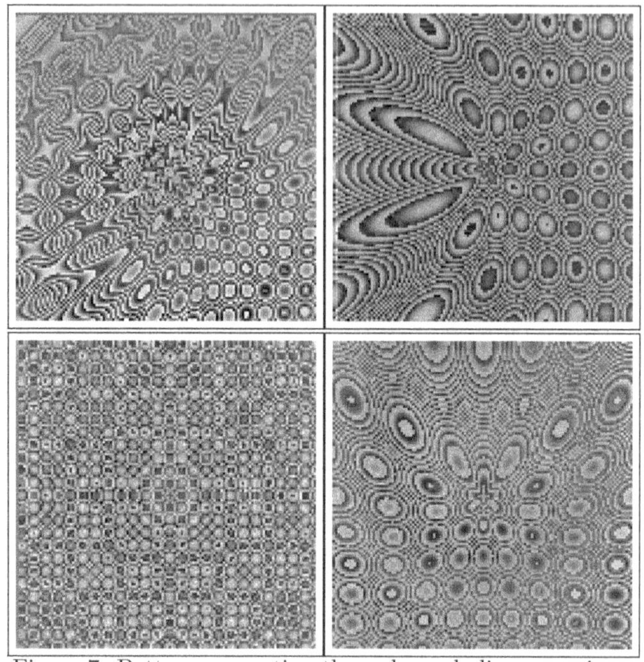

Figure 7: Pattern generation through symbolic expression.

those images, although the corresponding graphs are too big to be displayed in the present format.

In Figure 7 we can see the four most fit individuals of an experiment where the evolutionary process was driven towards images with patterns, composed of circular shapes. A higher resolution version of the picture on the bottom left is presented in Figure 8. The display of patterns and symmetries is clear and one can see some resemblance with fractal images.

Driving the experiment to less complex, but more colourful images we obtained individuals like those presented in Figure 9. A higher resolution version of the picture on the bottom left is presented in Figure 10. Despite the simplicity of this image some symmetries and patterns are also present.

These experiments demonstrate the use of the present model to generate parallel outputs. Although only interactive evolution was used, we have shown the ability of the approach to generate solutions with different properties. It is our believe that it provides a proof-of-concept for future applications of this hybrid.

8. CONCLUSION

A fusion between the ReNCoDe and the extended ARN models was presented, aimed at solving a different class of problems. This method allows the extraction of executable graphs with one or more outputs from an artificial regulatory network. Moreover, the algorithm for the graph extraction is more clear with the ordering based on the protein binding strengths.

We have tested the hybrid in a typical GP benchmark problem - the inverted pendulum - showing that the approach is competitive with others in the literature, including the original ReNCoDe. In the domain of multiple output

Figure 8: Augmented rendering of the individual on the bottom left of Fig. 7.

Figure 9: Abstract symbolic expression.

Figure 10: Augmented rendering of the individual on the bottom left of Fig. 7

applications, we provided a proof-of-concept for the methodology by testing it in an artificial art context. The evolved images display complex repetitive patterns and symmetries, as well as simpler forms, more colourful, also displaying symmetries and repetition with variation.

Future work will test the model's ability to evolve solutions for complex binary problems, such as the full adder and binary multipliers of different input sizes.

Acknowledgements

The work of the first author was partially funded by Fundação para a Ciência e Tecnologia, grant ref. SFRH / BD / 69106 / 2010.

9. REFERENCES

[1] A. E. Eiben and J. E. Smith, *Introduction to Evolutionary Computing*. Springer Verlag, 2003.

[2] M. O'Neill, L. Vanneschi, S. Gustafson, and W. Banzhaf, "Open issues in genetic programming," *Genetic Programming and Evolvable Machines*, vol. 11, pp. 339–363, 2010.

[3] W. Banzhaf, G. Beslon, S. Christensen, J. Foster, F. Képès, V. Lefort, J. Miller, M. Radman, and J. Ramsden, "From artificial evolution to computational evolution: a research agenda," *Nature Reviews Genetics*, vol. 7, no. 9, pp. 729–735, 2006.

[4] M. O'Neill and C. Ryan, *Grammatical Evolution: Evolutionary Automatic Programming in a Arbitrary Language*. Genetic programming, Kluwer Academic Publishers, 2003.

[5] J. F. Miller, *Cartesian Genetic Programming*. Natural Computing Series, Springer, 2011.

[6] C. Ferreira, *Gene Expression Programming (2nd Edition)*. Springer, 2006.

[7] M. A. Lones and A. M. Tyrrell, "Biomimetic representation with genetic programming enzyme," *Genetic Programming and Evolvable Machines*, vol. 3, pp. 193–217, June 2002.

[8] W. Banzhaf, "Artificial regulatory networks and genetic programming," in *Genetic Programming Theory and Practice* (R. L. Riolo and B. Worzel, eds.), ch. 4, pp. 43–62, Kluwer, 2003.

[9] P. Dwight Kuo, W. Banzhaf, and A. Leier, "Network topology and the evolution of dynamics in an artificial genetic regulatory network model created by whole genome duplication and divergence.," *Bio Systems*, vol. 85, no. 3, pp. 177–200, 2006.

[10] M. Nicolau, M. Schoenauer, and W. Banzhaf, "Evolving Genes to Balance a Pole," in *Proceedings of the 13th European Conference on Genetic Programming, EuroGP 2010* (A. I. and others Esparcia-Alcazar, ed.), vol. 6021 of *LNCS*, (Istanbul), pp. 196–207, Springer, 2010.

[11] R. Lopes and E. Costa, "The regulatory computational device," *Genetic Programming and Evolvable Machines*, vol. 13, no. 3, pp. 339–375, 2012.

[12] H. Bolouri, *Computational modeling of gene regulatory networks: a primer*. Imperial College Press, 2008.

[13] H. de Jong, "Modeling and simulation of genetic regulatory systems: a litterature review," *Journal of Computational Biology*, vol. 9, no. 1, pp. 67–103, 2002.

[14] Â. Gonçalves and E. Costa, "A model for an heterogeneous gene regulatory network," in *Handbook of Research on Computational Methodologies in Gene Regulatory Networks* (S. Das, D. Caragea, S. M. Welch, and W. H. Hsu, eds.), ch. Chapter 12, IGI Global, 2009.

[15] M. Hecker, S. Lambeck, S. Toefler, E. van Soemren, and R. Guthke, "Gene regulatory network inference: data integration in dynamic models - a review," *BioSystems*, vol. 96, no. 1, pp. 86–103, 2009.

[16] D. Marbach, C. Mattiussi, and D. Floreano, "Bio-mimetic evolutionary reverse engineering of gene regulatory networks," in *5th European Conference on Evolutionary Computation,Machine Learning and Data Mining in Bioinformatics, EvoBIO2007* (E. Marchiori, J. H. Moore, and J. C. Rajapakse, eds.), vol. 4447 of *LNCS*, pp. 155–165, Springer, 2007.

[17] E. Sakamoto and H. Iba, "Inferring a system of differential equations for a gene regulatory network by using genetic programming," in *Proceedings of the Congress on Evolutionary Computation*, pp. 720–726, IEEE Press, 2001.

[18] F. Streichert, H. Planatscher, C. Spieth, H. Ulmer, and A. Zell, "Comparing genetic programming and evolution strategies on inferring gene regulatory networks," in *Proceeding of Genetic and Evolutionary computation Conference (GECCO2004)*, vol. 3102 of *LNCS*, pp. 471–480, 2004.

[19] N. Noman and H. Iba, "Inferring gene regulatory networks using differential evolution with local search heuristics," *Computational Biology and Bioinformatics, IEEE/ACM Transactions on*, vol. 4, pp. 634 –647, oct.-dec. 2007.

[20] T. Reil, "Dynamics of gene expression in an artifical genome - implications for biological and artificial ontogeny," in *Proceedings of the 5th European conference on Artificial Life* (D. Floreano, J.-D. Nicoud, and F. Mondada, eds.), pp. 457–466, Springer, 1999.

[21] S. Kauffman, *The origins of order: self-organization and selection of evolution*. Oxford University Press, 1993.

[22] H. de Jong, J.-L. Gouzé, C. Hernandez, M. Page, T. Sari, and J. Geiselmann, "Hybrid modeling and simulation of genetic regulatory networks," in *Proceedings of the 6th international conference on Hybrid systems: computation and control*, HSCC'03, (Berlin, Heidelberg), pp. 267–282, Springer-Verlag, 2003.

[23] P. Eggenberger, "Evolving morphologies of simulated 3D organisms based on differential gene expression," in *Fourth European Conference of Artificial Life* (P. Husbands and I. Harvey, eds.), pp. 205–213, MIT Press, 1997.

[24] D. Roggen, D. Federici, and D. Floreano, "Evolutionary morphogenesis for multi-cellular systems," *Genetic Programming and Evolvable Machines*, vol. 8, pp. 61–96, Mar. 2007.

[25] M. Joachimczak and B. Wrobel, "Evo-devo in silico: a model of a gene network regulating multicellular development in 3d space with artificial physics," in *Artificial Life XI: Proceedings of the Eleventh International Conference on the Simulation and Synthesis of Living Systems* (S. Bullock, J. Noble, R. Watson, and M. A. Bedau, eds.), pp. 297–304, MIT Press, 2008.

[26] J. Knabe, M. Schilstra, and C. Nehaviv, "Evolution and morphogenesis of differential multicellular organisms: autonomously generated diffusion gradients for positional information," in *Artificial Life XI: Proceedings of the Eleventh International Conference on the Simulation and Synthesis of Living Systems* (S. Bullock, J. Noble, R. Watson, and M. A. Bedau, eds.), pp. 321–328, MIT Press, 2008.

[27] M. Kessler, *Analysis of the dynamics of a GRN-based Evo-devo system*. PhD thesis, University of Zurich, September 2009.

[28] J. Bongard, "Evolving modular genetic regulatory networks," in *IEEE 2002 Congress on Evolutionary Computation (CEC2002)*, pp. 1872–1877, IEEE Press, 2002.

[29] T. Quick, C. Nehaviv, K. Dautenhahn, and G. Roberts, "Evolving embodied genetic regulatory network-driven control systems," in *Proceedings of the European Conference on Artificial Life (ECAL 2003)* (W. Banzhaf, ed.), vol. 2801 of *Lecture Notes in Artificial Intelligence*, pp. 266–277, 2003.

[30] P. Kennedy and T. Osborn, "A model of gene expression and regulation in an artificial cellular organism," *Complex Systems*, vol. 13, no. 1, pp. 33–59, 2001.

[31] S. A. Teichmann and M. M. Babu, "Gene regulatory network growth by duplication.," *Nature Genetics*, vol. 36, pp. 492–6, May 2004.

[32] P. Kuo, A. Leier, and W. Banzhaf, "Evolving dynamics in an artificial regulatory network model," *Lecture Notes in Computer Science*, pp. 571–580, 2004.

[33] M. Nicolau, M. O'Neill, and A. Brabazon, "Applying Genetic Regulatory Networks to Index Trading," *Parallel Problem Solving from Nature-PPSN XII*, pp. 428–437, 2012.

[34] D. Whitley, S. Dominic, R. Das, and C. W. Anderson, "Genetic reinforcement learning for neurocontrol problems," *Machine Learning*, vol. 13, no. 2, pp. 259–284, 1993.

[35] P. Machado, J. J. Romero, and A. Carballal, *Evolutionary and Biologically Inspired Music, Sound, Art and Design*. First International Conference, EvoMUSART 2012, Málaga, Spain, April 11-13, 2012, Proceedings, Springer-Verlag New York Incorporated, Mar. 2012.

[36] E. Murphy, M. Nicolau, E. Hemberg, M. O'Neill, and A. Brabazon, "Differential Gene Expression with Tree-Adjunct Grammars," *Parallel Problem Solving from Nature-PPSN XII*, pp. 377–386, 2012.

GEARNet: Grammatical Evolution with Artificial Regulatory Networks

Genetic Programming

Rui L. Lopes
Centro de Informática e Sistemas da Universidade de Coimbra
Polo II - Pinhal de Marrocos
3030-290 Coimbra, Portugal
rmlopes@dei.uc.pt

Ernesto Costa
Centro de Informática e Sistemas da Universidade de Coimbra
Polo II - Pinhal de Marrocos
3030-290 Coimbra, Portugal
ernesto@dei.uc.pt

ABSTRACT

The Central Dogma of Biology states that genes made proteins that made us. This principle has been revised in order to incorporate the role played by a multitude of regulatory mechanisms that are fundamental in both the processes of inheritance and development. Evolutionary Computation algorithms are inspired by the theories of evolution and development, but most of the computational models proposed so far rely on a simple genotype to phenotype mapping. During the last years some researchers advocate the need to explore computationally the new biological understanding and have proposed different gene expression models to be incorporated in the algorithms.Two examples are the Artificial Regulatory Network (ARN) model, first proposed by Wolfgang Banzhaf, and the Grammatical Evolution (GE) model, introduced by Michael O'Neill and Conor Ryan. In this paper, we show how a modified version of the ARN can be combined with the GE approach, in the context of automatic program generation. More precisely, we rely on the ARN to control the gene expression process ending in an ordered set of proteins, and on the GE to build, guided by a grammar, a computational structure from that set. As a proof of concept we apply the hybrid model to two benchmark problems and show that it is effective in solving them.

Categories and Subject Descriptors

I.2.8 [**Problem Solving, Control Methods, and Search**]: Heuristic Methods

General Terms

Algorithms

Keywords

genetic regulatory network, grammatical evolution, artificial ant, symbolic regression

1. INTRODUCTION

Long ago researchers saw the potential of using nature-inspired algorithms to solve learning, design, and optimisation problems, giving rise to a new research area called Evolutionary Computation [1]. There are a plethora of different algorithms each of them tuned for a specific problem or class of problems, yet they all rely on a similar approach: (1) randomly define an initial population of solution candidates; (2) select, according to fitness, some individuals for reproduction with variation; (3) define the survivors for the next generation; (4) repeat steps (2) and (3) until some condition is fulfilled. Typically, the objects manipulated by the algorithms are represented at two different levels. At a low level (the genotype) the representations are manipulated by the variation operators; at a high level (the phenotype) the objects are evaluated to determine their fitness and are selected accordingly. Because of that, we need a mapping between these two levels.

During the last years some researchers have advocated the need to explore computationally the new biological understanding [2, 3, 4] and have proposed different solutions centred on the use of specific representations associated with indirect mappings from the genotype to the phenotype. Some examples are Linear Genetic Programming [5], Cartesian Genetic Programming (CGP) and Self-Modifying CGP [6], Gene Expression Programming [7], Enzyme Genetic Programming [8], and Fractal Proteins [9]. Two other approaches important for our work must be mentioned. In [10] the author proposed an artificial gene regulatory (ARN) model as a novel representation for genetic programming, and showed how it could be used computationally in different settings [11, 12]. Recently, some modifications to the ARN model were proposed, which try to expand its capabilities and improve its performance [13, 14, 15]. On the other hand, Michael O'Neill and Conor Ryan proposed a computational model of gene expression, called Grammatical Evolution (GE), and described how the corresponding evolutionary algorithm can be used for the automatic generation of programs [16]. GE uses a grammar to transform a linear genome into an executable program. It has been used with success in different domains.

In this paper, we present a hybrid model that links together the ARN approach with the GE model. More precisely, we use the ARN to transform a linear genotype into an **ordered set** of expressed proteins, which in turn is transformed into a computational structure, i.e., a program, by means of a grammar. As a proof of concept we apply the hybrid model to two benchmark problems and show that it is effective in solving them.

The paper is organized as follows. Section 2 describes gene regulatory networks and the basics of the ARN model and of the GE. Then, Section 3 describes how we combine the two ideas in a hybrid model. In Section 4 we briefly refer to the problems used and the experimental setup. The results are presented in Section 5. Finally, in Section 6 we draw some conclusions and present some ideas for future work.

2. BACKGROUND

2.1 Gene Regulatory Networks

For a long time it was believed that the DNA was transcribed into RNA, which in turn was translated into proteins in a one-way process. Today, we know that the process of gene expression into proteins is more complex, and rely on a network of interactions, known as regulatory networks, between genes and many other molecules including proteins, the very products of gene expression (see Figure 1).

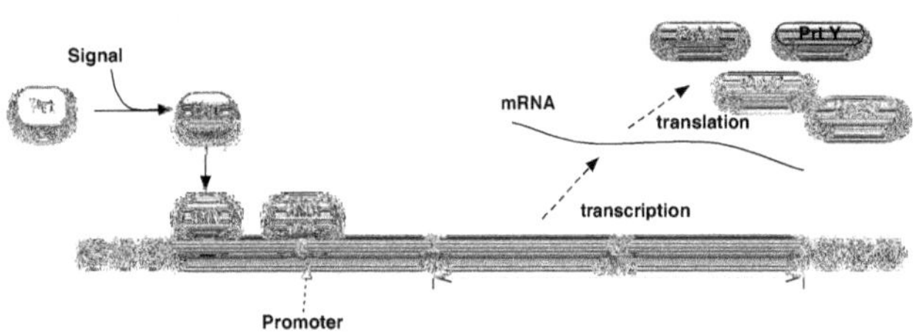

Figure 1: Gene Regulation: the transcription of a gene is driven by a protein called RNA polymerase, which binds to a special regulatory region of the DNA called the promoter. Other proteins (transcription factors) control the accessibility of the promoter to RNA polymerase. These proteins are activated by external signals and bind in the vicinity of the promoter. They can enhance the production of a protein by a gene, as in the figure, or inhibit its production.

A correct understanding of the behavior of gene regulatory networks (GRN) is of paramount importance in many areas of application, like personalized medicine, epidemic prevention, energy production, bioremediation or synthetic biology [17].

Researchers have been interested in GRNs from different points of view, besides the biological one. For example, the different artificial models have been studied from a system's perspective, trying to understand its topological and dynamics properties [18, 19, 20, 21]. In a different path, some computational explorations have been proposed that reflect our comprehension about regulatory mechanism and how they mediate between evolution and development, i.e., that try to incorporate those mechanisms into artificial evolutionary systems. For example, in [22, 23, 24, 25, 26] GRNs are explored in the context of artificial 3D morphogenesis. In [27, 28] regulation is explored to evolve real-time controllers for a robot, and to the task of automatically designing robots in a physical-based virtual environment. In [18] the authors proposed a model of an artificial genome and studied the implications for artificial ontogeny, while [29] also proposed a model of gene expression and regulation in an artificial cellular organism and speculates about its application to evolutionary computation. There is a third perspective for studying artificial GRNs: using them as a computational device. Using artificial regulatory network for problem solving was first proposed by Wolfgang Banzhaf [10].

2.2 ARN

The Artificial Regulatory Network (ARN) [10] is an attempt to incorporate regulatory mechanisms between the genotype and the phenotype. There are no other products, i.e., those corresponding to RNA, and processes in between these two levels. The genome has fixed length and is constructed by simple duplication with mutation events. Regulation between genes is a mediated process, and is achieved by means of a binding process between proteins (i.e., transcription factors) and special zones in the genome that appear upstream of the promoter of a gene.

Genome

The genome can be generated randomly or by a process of duplication with mutation, also called *DM*. In the latter case we start with a random 32-bit binary sequence, that is followed by several duplication episodes. So, if we have 10 duplication events then the final length of the genome is $32 \times 2^{10} = 32768$. The mutation rate is typically of 1% and may occur only in the duplicate. Figure 2 illustrates the process with a simple example.

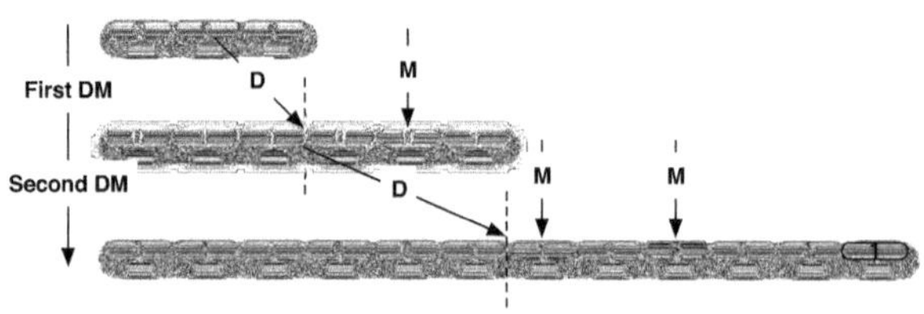

Figure 2: The process of duplication with mutation

The genome has several functional elements, each one divided in a coding region and a regulatory region. The former is the gene, which is expressed in a protein, while the latter includes the promoter and the binding sites. In the ARN model, the first 32 bits of the regulatory zone are the enhancer site (e), while the following 32 bits are the inhibitory site (h). The promoter itself is located downstream and has the form $XYZ01010101$. This means that only the last 8 bits are fixed (XYZ are arbitrary bytes). A gene is a five 32-bit long sequence, i.e., a 160-bit string. Only the promoters cannot overlap. Figure 3 gives an idea of the representation.

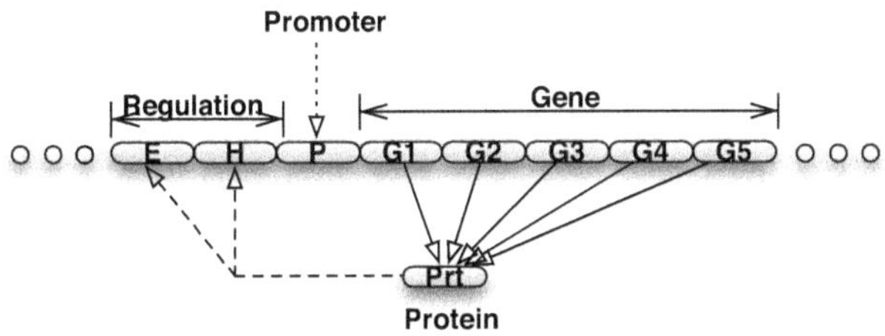

Figure 3: Artificial Regulatory Network, after W. Banzhaf

Gene expression

The genotype - phenotype mapping is defined by expressing each 160-bit long gene, resulting in a 32-bit protein. A gene expresses a protein by a majority rule: if we consider a gene, for example G^m, divided into 5 parts of size 32 each, G_1^m to G_5^m, at position i, say, the protein's bit will have a value corresponding to the most frequent value in each of these 5 parts, at the same position, i.e.,

$$P_i^m = majority(G_{ki}^m, \quad \forall k = 1, \ldots, 5), \quad \forall i = 1, \ldots, 32$$

Regulation

Genes interact mediated by proteins, which bind to the regulatory region of each gene. If, say, gene **A** expresses protein p_A and that protein contributes to the activation of gene **B**, we say that gene **A** regulates **B** (see Fig. 4).

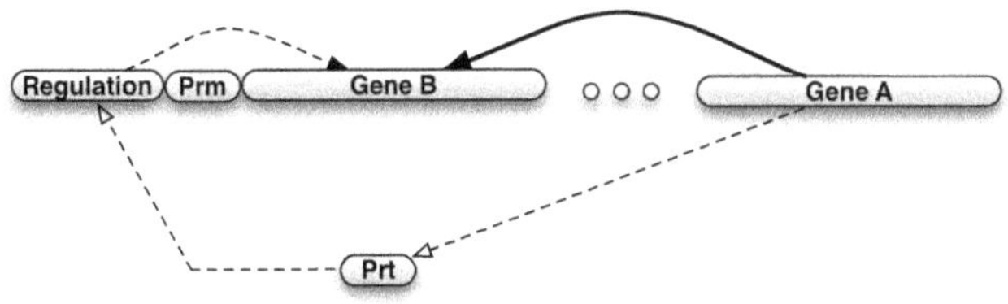

Figure 4: Gene - Protein - Gene interaction

Notice that in order for a link to exist between any two genes, the concentration of the corresponding protein must attain a certain level, and that depends on the strength of the binding. The strength of the binding is computed by calculating the degree of complementarity between the protein and each of the regulatory regions, according to formula 1:

$$x_i = \frac{1}{N} \sum_{j=1}^{N} c_j e^{\beta(\mu_{ji} - \mu_{max})} \tag{1}$$

where x_i represents the binding strength of the enhancer (e_i) or the inhibitory (h_i) region, N is the number of proteins, c_j the concentration of protein j, μ_{ji} is the number of bits that are different in the protein (j) and in the regulation site (r_i), that is,

$$\mu_{ji} = \sum_{k=1}^{32} j_k \oplus r_{i_k} \tag{2}$$

μ_{max} is the maximum match achievable, and β is a scaling factor. The production of a protein over time depends on its concentration, which in turn is a function of the way each protein binds to that gene's regulatory regions. It is defined by the differential equation

$$\frac{dc_i}{dt} = \delta(e_i - h_i)c_i \tag{3}$$

where e_i and h_i are defined by equation 1, and δ is a scaling factor.

Computational Device

The ARN can be used as a computational device in different ways. For example, in the context of optimisation problems, in [30] the authors define (randomly) two new contiguous 32-bit sequences in the genome. The first one, being a new inhibitory site and, the second one, a new activation site. All generated proteins can bind to these sites. The levels of activation and of inhibition can be computed as before (see equation 1) , but now there is no gene (thus no protein) attached. The state of this new site is just the sum of all bindings and it is defined as the output. This additional binding is thus a method to extract a meaning from the variation of the proteins' concentrations along time. In another approach, the ARN is used as a representation formalism for genetic programming, leading to the extension of Banzhaf's model in two different directions. In the first one [12], some extra proteins, not produced by genes but contributing to regulation, were introduced and act as inputs. Also, the genes were divided into two sets, one producing proteins that are used in regulation (i.e., transcriptional factors), and a second one with proteins with no regulatory function which are used as outputs. These two types of genes are distinguished by having different promoters. The model was tested with the classic control problem known as the pole balancing problem. In the second one [13, 15], the regulatory network itself is used as a starting point, and then it is transformed by a reduction algorithm, that simplifies the network into an executable genetic programming-like structure. Differently from [12], in this approach the concentrations of the proteins are fundamental to define the regulatory network but do not play a role in its transformation into the executable program. Moreover, new biologically inspired genetic operators were introduced, besides standard flip mutation, which improved the performance of the algorithm. In particular the *transposon* operator, which copies a section of the genome and inserts it into a new random location. No crossover is used. This approach was successfully tested with several benchmark problems, like, for example, regression, n-bit parity, and the Santa Fe ant trail.

2.3 Grammatical Evolution

Grammatical Evolution (GE) is a form of Grammar-Guided Genetic Programming (GGGP). In simple terms, GGGP is a class of population-based stochastic search techniques applied to a specific class of context-free grammar-based representations [31]. A context-free grammar is a tuple $G = (N, T, S, P)$, where N is a non-empty set of non terminal symbols, T is a non-empty set of terminal symbols, S is an element of N called axiom, and P is a set of production rules of the form $A ::= \alpha$, with $A \in N$ and $\alpha \in (N \cup T)^*$. N and T are disjoint. A language associated with a grammar G, $L(G)$, is the set of all sequences of terminal symbols that can be derived from the axiom, that is $L(G) = \{w : S \overset{*}{\Rightarrow}$

$w,\ w \in T^*\}$.

Being an example of GP, in Grammatical Evolution, once the representation of individuals (at the genotype and phenotype levels) is decided, one has to define how the population is initialised, which genetic operators will be used to manipulate the genotype, how the fitness of an individual is calculated, which values will be used for the different parameters (e.g., population size, maximum generations, maximum individuals size, and operator probabilities). The genotype is a linear binary string, while the phenotype structure depends on the grammar. Here, we consider the case where the phenotype is a tree expression. Genetic operators for linear structures are used (see [32] and [33] for a discussion related with this issue). The fitness is evaluated in a standard way by executing the tree expression. A key issue in GE is the separation between the genotype and the phenotype and, as a consequence, the need of a mapping between these two structures.

GE introduces a genotype to phenotype mapping in successive steps (see figure 5). Initially the genome is a binary

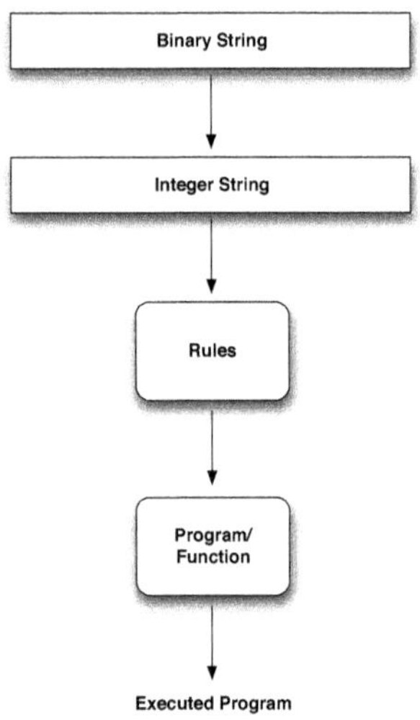

Figure 5: GE: from a binary string to a program (adapted from [16])

linear sequence. The binary string is transcribed onto a sequence of integers, each one called a codon. Then translation starts: a derivation tree (the phenotype) is obtained from the axiom of the grammar, and will be further decoded to an expression tree, the program. Each codon is used to determine the rule for a non-terminal symbol when it is expanded.

Suppose that we have the following production rule,

$$
\begin{aligned}
< expr > ::= \; & < expr >< op >< expr > && (0)\\
& |(< expr >< op >< expr >) && (1)\\
& | < pre - op > (< expr >) && (2)\\
& | < var > && (3)
\end{aligned}
$$

where there are four options to rewrite its left hand side symbol $< expr >$. In the beginning we have our genome transcribed into a string of integers and a syntactical form equal to the axiom $< expr >$. We want to rewrite the axiom and must choose which alternative will be used. We take the first integer and divide it by the number of options for $< expr >$. The remainder of that operation will indicate the option to be used. In the example above, if we admit that the integer is 9 then we will have $9\%4 = 1$ and the axiom will be rewritten in $(< expr >< op >< expr >)$. Then we read the second integer and apply the same method to the left most non-terminal of the derivation. We iterate this process, that stops when we don't have more non-terminals to rewrite. But what happens if we run out of integers, because we arrive to the end of the genome, and still have non-terminals to expand? This is when we use a wrapping mechanism: we restart from the beginning of the string of integers. The existence of redundancy is also worth noting, for different integers may correspond to the same alternative due to the nature of the operation remainder. In the example above, the integers $5, 9, 13, \ldots$ all codify the same production alternative for $< expr >$. With GE three main innovations were introduced that led to improved performance: individuals have variable length, redundancy, and wrapping is allowed. GE has been applied with success to different problems. For an in-depth recent review of GGGP see [31].

3. ARCHITECTURE

As described in Section 2.2, the ARN provides a model of gene regulatory networks by which the genome is translated into a set of proteins with differentiated concentrations. Both the transcription and the translation processes are implicit, and the result of the gene expression is reflected in the proteins' concentrations. In sum, this model translates the genotype into a set of proteins with a determined concentration, which is a function of the interactions between the genes/proteins in the system.

In order to be usable in problem solving, a mapping is needed for the expressed phenotype. In this work we create a hybrid algorithm and investigate whether a grammatical-evolution-like technique is a suitable mapping, capable of generating solutions for the benchmark problems presented in Section 4. In fact, the grammatical evolution algorithm will be applied to the sequence of proteins expressed by the ARN, analogously to the development of an organism, which is a function of the gene expression.

As mentioned in the previous section, the GE algorithm uses a linear binary genome, transcribed into a linear integer sequence, which is then translated to an expression by means of a grammar. In the hybrid model presented here, the integer stream is generated from the ARN proteins' signatures. Firstly, the proteins are ordered by concentration. Secondly, each protein signature is split into four 8-bit integers. Finally, the sequence of integers is used to derive an expression using the given grammar.

Often the integer sequence is not entirely used to derive an expression, hence the lowest concentration proteins (corresponding to genes that were not expressed) are not used in the mapping. This way gene expression is solely dictated by the ARN model and is naturally reflected on the resulting programs. In other words, instead of starting from a random generated binary string, the GE will have as input a sequence of integers, which are the result of the evolution by the ARN. Figure 6 demonstrates the hybridisation method just described.

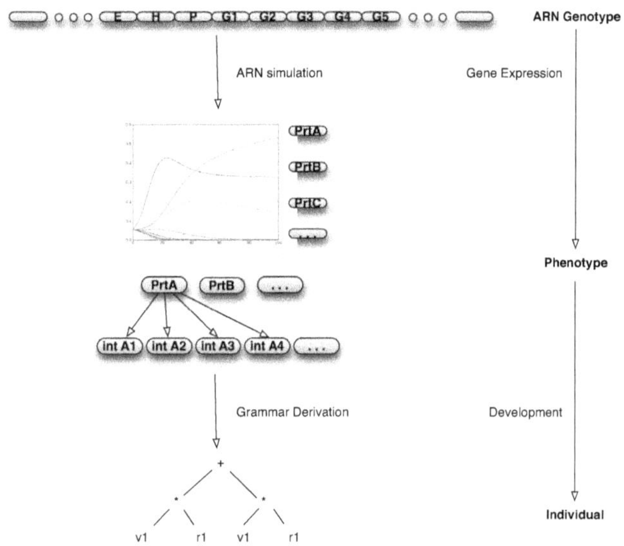

Figure 6: GEARNet summary diagram.

In this representation we can see a chart of the concentrations of the proteins in a typical ARN throughout the simulation time. In the next section we describe experiments that were setup to analyse the influence of this time. In the case of a tie, the positional order in the genome is used.

4. PROBLEMS AND EXPERIMENTAL SETUP

In order to evaluate the algorithm's effectiveness it was applied to two benchmark problems: symbolic regression [34], and artificial ant[34, 35]. These will be described in the next subsections, followed by the experimental setup.

4.1 Symbolic Regression.

The symbolic regression problem consists of evolving a mathematical formula to fit a polynomial expression to a set of points over some range. Table 1 summarizes how a grammatical evolution system is applied to the problem [36].

Target Polynomial	$x^4 + x^3 + x^2 + x$
Terminal Operands	x
Terminal Operators	$\{+, -, *, /, sin, cos, exp, log\}$
Fitness Cases	The given sample of 20 data points in the interval $[-1, 1]$
Raw Fitness	The sum of the error taken over the 20 fitness cases

Table 1: Grammatical Evolution Tableau for Symbolic Regression.

The terminal operators set includes all the arithmetic operators `{+, -, *, /}`, as well as the unary operators `{sin, cos, exp, log}`, while the terminal operands set has only the input $\{x\}$. The protected division operator is used, returning 1 whenever the denominator is 0. Also, the protected *log* operator is used returning 1 if the input is 0.

As an example, the expression $x^4 + x^3 + x^2 + x$ over the range $[-1, 1]$, with a 0.1 step was used as the target. The fitness function used was the sum of the absolute error over the set of points.

The production rules for the grammar used in this problem are presented below.

$$
\begin{aligned}
< expr > &::= < expr >< op >< expr > \\
&|(< expr >< op >< expr >) \\
&| < pre - op > (< expr >) \\
&| < var > \\
< op > &::= + \mid - \mid * \mid / \\
< pre - op > &::= sin|cos|exp|log \\
< var > &::= x
\end{aligned}
$$

4.2 Artificial Ant.

The goal in the artificial ant problem is to evolve a strategy that an agent will follow to collect food along a trail in a toroidal 2D grid. The artificial ant will be placed at the upper left corner facing east, in this grid of 32x32 cells where there is a specific trail of food pellets with a few gaps in between, in this case the Santa Fe Ant trail.

Table 2 summarizes how a grammatical evolution system is applied to the problem [37]. The terminal operators set is composed of only `{if_food_ahead()}` and the terminal operands set consists of `{left(), right(), move()}`. The function `if_food_ahead` allows the ant to check whether there is food in the cell directly in front of it and perform some action or group of actions according to this result. The operands allow the agent to turn 90 degrees left or right without moving, and to move to the adjacent cell it is facing. If a cell contains a food pellet it is immediately eaten when the ant stands on it.

Target	Find a program that controls an artificial ant so that it can collect the 89 food pellets located on the Santa Fe trail
Terminal Operands	left(), right(), move()
Terminal Operators	if_food_ahead()
Fitness Cases	One artificial ant
Raw Fitness	Number of pieces collected in 600 operations
Standardized Fitness	The total number of food pellets less the raw fitness

Table 2: Grammatical Evolution Tableau for the Artificial Ant.

Using the described terminals a foraging strategy is derived and each ant is given a determined number of steps, 600 in this case, to apply it repeatedly in the search of the 89 food pellets available in the trail. The fitness function used for this problem is the remaining number of food pellets, after the foraging strategy is applied.

The production rules for the grammar used in this problem are presented below.

$$\begin{aligned}
< code >&::= < line > \mid < line >< code > \\
< line >&::= < op > \mid < condition > \\
< line2 >&::= < op >< line2 > \mid \\
&\quad < condition < line2 > \mid \\
&\quad < op > \\
< condition >&::= if_food_ahead()\{ \\
&\qquad < line2 > \\
&\quad \} \\
&\quad else\{ \\
&\qquad < line2 > \\
&\quad \} \\
< op >&::= left() \mid right() \mid move()
\end{aligned}$$

4.3 Experimental Setup.

A standard evolutionary strategy was used for every experiment that will be described: (50+500)-ES. The process selects the best 50 solutions generating ten new individuals from each by applying the bit-flip mutation operator.

Parameter	Value
Number of Runs	30
Initial Population	500
Number of DMs	5
Mutation Rate	0.01
Protein Bind Threshold	14
Genome Length	Fixed

Table 3: Parameter values for the benchmark problems.

Table 3 summarizes the parameterizations used to solve the described problems. For both the problems 30 runs were executed, initialized with 500 genomes created from a 32-bit seed by duplication-and-mutation (see Sect. 2.2). These individuals were generated with 5 DM events, and a mutation rate of 1%. As the only operator applied was the bit-flip mutation, the genomes' size is fixed ($32 * 2^5 = 1024 bits$).

The goal of these experiments is to make the proof of concept of the hybridization method described. The experiments were given a determined time limit of execution, halting when a correct solution was found. Because the underlying artificial networks vary in size, so does the time of each evaluation. For this reason some runs were able to evaluate more individuals than others. In order to investigate the influence of the ARN simulation time, first a set of experiments were run varying the simulation time from 10 to 20000 iterations, for the artificial ant problem. Then, the approach was tested on the symbolic regression, using the best performing value in the artificial ant. Moreover, we investigate the influence of the mutation rate, varying it from .1% to 20%, with the Santa Fe trail problem.

The results of these experiments will be presented and briefly discussed in the following section, together with examples of solutions to the problems.

5. RESULTS

As mentioned earlier, the goal of these experiments is to assess the effectiveness of the approach. As such, we are mainly interested in the success rates obtained. The results are summarized in Tables 4 and 5 (artificial ant), and Table 6 (regression). We present the minimum and average effort as well as the success rates for each value of the ARN simulation time on the artificial ant problem. For the regression problem we present the results for only the best simulation time.

Problem	Artificial Ant			
Sim.Time	10	50	100	1000
Success (%)	96.6	83.3	93.3	83.3
Min. Eval.	14099	15837	28697	6164
Avg. Eval.	1181563	569605	612097	718840
Std. Dev.	1542440	727011	891694	7567744

Table 4: Summary of the results for each simulation time for the artificial ant problem.

Problem	Artificial Ant			
Sim.Time	3000	5000	10000	20000
Success (%)	66.6	63.3	43.3	30
Min. Eval.	78561	71212	18842	27363
Avg. Eval.	479247	369348	294934	96180
Std. Dev.	419629	287180	324989	75253

Table 5: Summary of the results for each simulation time for the artificial ant problem (continuation).

Problem	Regression
Sim.Time	10
Success (%)	66.6
Min. Eval.	46476
Avg. Eval.	739965
Std. Dev.	983721

Table 6: Summary of the results for the regression problem.

As we can see the algorithm is successful in finding solutions to both problems. The increasing success rates with lower simulation times tell us, first, that the simulation time does not affect the efficacy of the algorithm (as long as it is a deterministic process), and second, that many runs need a big amount of evaluations to find a solution, fact that is corroborated by the average number of evaluations.

In Table 7 the results with varying mutation rates are presented. First, the success rate shows that if there is not enough variation solutions cannot be found. Then, looking at the mean effort reported one can see that the mutation rate has to be moderated (between 1% and 5%), otherwise the effort needed increases with the mutation rate.

Examples of solutions are presented in Equations (4) and (5), and Listing 1 for the regression and the artificial ant, respectively. The results are slightly encouraging and it should be noted that only the bit-flip mutation was used, without crossover or other operators. Moreover, there was no special tuning of the parameters.

$$x + x * x + x + x - x + x * x * x + x * x * x * x - x \quad (4)$$

$$(x * x + x * x * x + x * x * x * x + x) \quad (5)$$

Problem	Artificial Ant			
Mut. Rate	0.001	0.05	0.1	0.2
Success (%)	3.3	93.3	96.6	96.6
Min. Eval.	2348494	1947	14652	310276
Avg. Eval.	-	669061	1330401	1614059
Std. Dev.	-	593511	1091191	1170977

Table 7: Summary of the results varying the mutation rate for the artificial ant problem (for 1%, see table 4, with a simulation time of 10.).

```
if _food_ahead():
    move()
else:
    left()
    if _food_ahead():
        right()
    else:
        left()
        left()
    if _food_ahead():
        move()
    else:
        left()
    move()
```

Listing 1: Solution program for the Artificial Ant

6. CONCLUSION AND FUTURE WORK

In this work we explored the capabilities of a hybrid algorithm that uses an ARN as the genotypic representation and develops the phenotype using GE. In sum, the ARN representation is used to obtain an ordered set of proteins with varying concentrations, which is then derived in a GE-fashion until a syntax-tree, i.e., an individual) is obtained.

We have shown experimentally that this hybridization is able to solve the two proposed benchmarks. A standard Evolution Strategy was used, without crossover, being only applied the bit-flip mutation. The exploratory results obtained still have to be improved, but they provide a proof of the concept.

This is admittedly a preliminary work, and in the future we must do comparisons with recent and similar work and outside our model[38, 39]. Some other avenues of research include the exploration of different operators (crossover, pruning and others), as well as different selection mechanisms and evolution strategies. Moreover, taking the direction of GE, different types of grammars can be explored (for instance, context-dependent grammars, annotated grammars). Having an artificial gene regulatory network underlying the process of development may confer advantages in different problem domains. As an example, if the environment changes it may be reflected on the underlying dynamic ARN, altering the phenotype development, possibly resulting in individuals that are more adaptable.

Acknowledgements

We thank the anonymous reviewers for the constructive comments. The work of the first author was partially supported by grant ref. SFRH/BD/69106/2010 from the portuguese Foundation for Science and Technology (FCT).

7. REFERENCES

[1] A. E. B. Eiben and J. E. Smith, *Introduction to Evolutionary Computing.* Springer Verlag, 2003.

[2] W. Banzhaf, G. Beslon, S. Christensen, J. Foster, F. Képès, V. Lefort, J. Miller, M. Radman, and J. Ramsden, "From artificial evolution to computational evolution: a research agenda," *Nature Reviews Genetics*, vol. 7, no. 9, pp. 729–735, 2006.

[3] D. S. Burke, K. A. De Jong, J. J. Grefenstette, C. L. Ramsey, and A. S. Wu, "Putting more genetics into genetic algorithms," *Evolutionary Computation*, vol. 6, no. 4, pp. 387–410, 1998.

[4] S. Luke, S. Hamahashi, and H. Kitano, ""genetic" programming," in *Genetic and Evolutionary Computation-GECCO 1999*, pp. 1098–1105, 1999.

[5] P. Nordin, "A Compiling Genetic Programming System that Directly Manipulates the Machine Code," in *Advances in Genetic Programming* (K. E. Kinnear, Jr., ed.), ch. 14, pp. 311–331, MIT Press, 1994.

[6] J. F. Miller, *Cartesian Genetic Programming.* Natural Computing Series, Springer, 2011.

[7] C. Ferreira, *Gene Expression Programming (2nd Edition).* Springer, 2006.

[8] M. Lones and A. Tyrrell, "Biomimetic representation with genetic programming enzyme," *Genetic Programming and Evolvable Machines*, pp. 193–217, 2002.

[9] J. Krohn, P. Bentley, and H. Shayani, "The challenge of irrationality: fractal protein recipes for PI," *of the 11th Annual conference on Genetic and Evolutionary Computation*, pp. 715–722, 2009.

[10] W. Banzhaf, "Artificial Regulatory Networks and Genetic Programming," in *Genetic Programming Theory and Practice* (R. L. Riolo and B. Worzel, eds.), ch. 4, pp. 43–62, Kluwer, 2003.

[11] P. Dwight Kuo, W. Banzhaf, and A. Leier, "Network topology and the evolution of dynamics in an artificial genetic regulatory network model created by whole genome duplication and divergence.," *Bio Systems*, vol. 85, no. 3, pp. 177–200, 2006.

[12] M. Nicolau, M. Schoenauer, and W. Banzhaf, "Evolving Genes to Balance a Pole," in *Proceedings of the 13th European Conference on Genetic Programming, EuroGP 2010* (A. I. Esparcia-Alcazar, A. Ekart, S. Silva, S. Dignum, and A. S. Uyar, eds.), vol. 6021 of *LNCS*, (Istanbul), pp. 196–207, Springer, 2010.

[13] R. L. Lopes and E. Costa, "ReNCoDe: A Regulatory Network Computational Device," in *EuroGP '11: Proceedings of the 13th annual conference on Genetic and Evolutionary Computation* (S. Silva, J. A. Foster, M. Nicolau, M. Giacobini, and P. Machado, eds.), vol. 6621 of *LNCS*, (Turin, Italy), pp. 143–154, Springer Verlag, 2011.

[14] R. L. Lopes and E. Costa, "Using Feedback in a Regulatory Network Computational Device," in *GECCO '11: Proceedings of the 13th annual conference on Genetic and Evolutionary Computation*, 2011.

[15] R. Lopes and E. Costa, "The regulatory computational device," *Genetic Programming and Evolvable Machines*, vol. 13, no. 3, pp. 339–375, 2012.

[16] M. O'Neill and C. Ryan, *Grammatical Evolution: Evolutionary Automatic Programming in a Arbitrary Language*, vol. 4 of *Genetic programming*. Kluwer Academic Publishers, 2003.

[17] H. Bolouri, *Computational modeling of gene regulatory networks*. Imperial College Press, 2008.

[18] T. Reil, "Dynamics of gene expression in an artifical genome - implications for biological and artificial ontogeny," in *Proceedings of the 5th European conference on Artificial Life* (D. Floreano, J.-D. Nicoud, and F. Mondada, eds.), pp. 457–466, Springer, 1999.

[19] S. Kauffman, *The origins of order: self-organization and selection of evolution*. Oxford University Press, 1993.

[20] H. de Jong, J.-L. Gouzé, C. Hernandez, M. Page, T. Sari, and J. Geiselmann, "Hybrid modeling and simulation of genetic regulatory networks," in *Proceedings of the 6th international conference on Hybrid systems: computation and control*, HSCC'03, (Berlin, Heidelberg), pp. 267–282, Springer-Verlag, 2003.

[21] P. Dwight Kuo, W. Banzhaf, and A. Leier, "Network topology and the evolution of dynamics in an artificial genetic regulatory network model created by whole genome duplication and divergence.," *Bio Systems*, vol. 85, no. 3, pp. 177–200, 2006.

[22] P. Eggenberger, "Evolving morphologies of simulated 3d organisms based on differential gene expression," in *Fourth European Conference of Artificial Life* (P. Husbands and I. Harvey, eds.), pp. 205–213, MIT Press, 1997.

[23] D. Roggen, D. Federici, and D. Floreano, "Evolutionary morphogenesis for multi-cellular systems," *Genetic Programming and Evolvable Machines*, vol. 8, pp. 61–96, Mar. 2007.

[24] M. Joachimczak and B. Wrobel, "Evo-devo in silico: a model of a gene network regulating multicellular development in 3d space with artificial physics," in *Artificial Life XI: Proceedings of the Eleventh International Conference on the Simulation and Synthesis of Living Systems* (S. Bullock, J. Noble, R. Watson, and M. A. Bedau, eds.), pp. 297–304, MIT Press, 2008.

[25] J. Knabe, M. Schilstra, and C. Nehaviv, "Evolution and morphogenesis of differential multicellular organisms: autonomously generated diffusion gradients for positional information," in *Artificial Life XI: Proceedings of the Eleventh International Conference on the Simulation and Synthesis of Living Systems* (S. Bullock, J. Noble, R. Watson, and M. A. Bedau, eds.), pp. 321–328, MIT Press, 2008.

[26] M. Kessler, *Analysis of the dynamics of a GRN-based Evo-devo system*. PhD thesis, University of Zurich, September 2009.

[27] J. Bongard, "Evolving modular genetic regulatory networks," in *IEEE 2002 Congress on Evolutionary Computation (CEC2002)*, pp. 1872–1877, IEEE Press, 2002.

[28] T. Quick, C. Nehaviv, K. Dautenhahn, and G. Roberts, "Evolving embodied genetic regulatory network-driven control systems," in *Proceedings of the European Conference on Artificial Life (ECAL 2003)* (W. Banzhaf, ed.), vol. 2801 of *Lecture Notes in Artificial Intelligence*, pp. 266–277, 2003.

[29] P. Kennedy and T. Osborn, "A model of gene expression and regulation in an artificial cellular organism," *Complex Systems*, vol. 13, no. 1, pp. 33–59, 2001.

[30] P. Kuo, A. Leier, and W. Banzhaf, "Evolving Dynamics in an Artificial Regulatory Network Model," in *Proc. of the Parallel Problem Solving from Nature Conference (PPSN-04)* (X. Yao, E. Burke, J. A. Lozano, J. Smith, J. J. Merelo-Guervós, J. A. Bullinaria, J. Rowe, P. Tino, A. Kabán, and H.-P. Schwefel, eds.), pp. 571–580, Springer, 2004.

[31] R. McKay, N. Hoai, P. Whigham, and M. O'Neil, "Genetic representation and genetic neutrality in gene expression programming," *Genetic Programming and Evolvable Machines*, vol. 11, no. 31, pp. 365–396, 2010.

[32] J. Byrne, M. O'Neill, and A. Brabazon, "Structural and nodal mutation in grammatical evolution," in *GECCO '09: Proceedings of the 11th Annual conference on Genetic and evolutionary computation* (G. Raidl, F. Rothlauf, G. Squillero, R. Drechsler, T. Stuetzle, M. Birattari, C. B. Congdon, M. Middendorf, C. Blum, C. Cotta, P. Bosman, J. Grahl, J. Knowles, D. Corne, H.-G. Beyer, K. Stanley, J. F. Miller, J. van Hemert, T. Lenaerts, M. Ebner, J. Bacardit, M. O'Neill, M. Di Penta, B. Doerr, T. Jansen, R. Poli, and E. Alba, eds.), (Montreal), pp. 1881–1882, ACM, 2009.

[33] M. O'Neill, C. Ryan, M. Keijzer, and M. Cattolico, "Crossover in Grammatical Evolution," *Genetic Programming and Evolvable Machines*, vol. 4, pp. 67–93, Mar. 2003.

[34] J. R. Koza, *Genetic Programming: On the Programming of Computers by Means of Natural Selection*. Cambridge, MA, USA: MIT Press, 1992.

[35] W. B. Langdon and R. Poli, "Why ants are hard," *Cognitive Science Research Papers*, pp. 193–201, Jan. 1998.

[36] C. Ryan and M. O'Neill, "Grammatical Evolution: A Steady State Approach," in *Second International Workshop on Frontiers in Evolutionary Algorithms*, vol. 2, (Research Triangle Park, NC, USA), pp. 419–423, 1998.

[37] M. O'Neill and C. Ryan, "Grammar based function definition in grammatical evolution," *Genetic Programming*, no. 3, 2000.

[38] E. Murphy, M. Nicolau, E. Hemberg, M. O'Neill, and A. Brabazon, "Differential gene expression with tree-adjunct grammars," *Parallel Problem Solving from Nature-PPSN XII*, pp. 377–386, 2012.

[39] M. Nicolau, M. O'Neill, and A. Brabazon, "Applying genetic regulatory networks to index trading," *Parallel Problem Solving from Nature-PPSN XII*, pp. 428–437, 2012.

Accelerating Convergence in Cartesian Genetic Programming by Using a New Genetic Operator

Andreas Meier
Group Research
Volkswagen AG
38436 Wolfsburg, Germany
andreas.meier1@volkswagen.de

Mark Gonter
Group Research
Volkswagen AG
38436 Wolfsburg, Germany
mark.gonter@volkswagen.de

Rudolf Kruse
Faculty of Computer Science
University of Magdeburg
39114 Magdeburg, Germany
kruse@iws.cs.uni-magdeburg.de

ABSTRACT

Genetic programming algorithms seek to find interpretable and good solutions for problems which are difficult to solve analytically. For example, we plan to use this paradigm to develop a car accident severity prediction model for new occupant safety functions. This complex problem will suffer from the major disadvantage of genetic programming, which is its high demand for computational effort to find good solutions. A main reason for this demand is a low rate of convergence. In this paper, we introduce a new genetic operator called *forking* to accelerate the rate of convergence. Our idea is to interpret individuals dynamically as centers of local Gaussian distributions and allow a sampling process in these distributions when populations get too homogeneous. We demonstrate this operator by extending the *Cartesian Genetic Programming* algorithm and show that on our examples convergence is accelerated by over 50% on average. We finish this paper with giving hints about parameterization of the forking operator for other problems.

Categories and Subject Descriptors

I.2.2 [**Artificial Intelligence**]: Automatic Programming—*Program synthesis*; I.2.8 [**Artificial Intelligence**]: Problem Solving, Control Methods, and Search

General Terms

Algorithms, Design, Performance

Keywords

Cartesian Genetic Programming, optimization, genetic operator

1. INTRODUCTION

In the field of evolutionary algorithms, genetic programming (GP) is a paradigm which enables automatic derivation of programs that solve problems. In contrast to other algorithms like artificial neural networks, GP algorithms learn interpretable models so that e.g. safety applications may be realized more easily. GP got significant attention after Koza has applied it to solve complex problems [8]. One of these problems is called *symbolic regression*, which seeks to find mathematical expressions describing the relation between input and output data. In contrast to parametrical regression, symbolic regression builds up complex formulae automatically by combining variables, basic operators (+,-,*,/) and functions (for example sin, cos or tan). Recently, Schmidt and Lipson used symbolic regression to discover natural laws describing kinematics of different oscillators [16].

Although GP is able to solve difficult problems, its major disadvantage is low efficiency. We define *efficiency* as the required computational effort for an evolutionary algorithm to achieve convergence. One measure for efficiency is the average number of generations it takes to find a solution. Another approach is to measure computation time until convergence is achieved. Schmidt and Lipson used a 32-core implementation which needs 30 to 40 hours to learn a solution for a specific oscillator problem [16]. Since they optimized their algorithm to require only 7 to 8 hours, we consider the original algorithm as being less efficient.

In contrast to accelerating execution by parallelization [9], we focus on increasing efficiency of GP algorithms by introducing the *forking* operator. This operator uses population statistics to interpret individuals dynamically as distributions in solution space. In that way, the forking operator samples new individuals when populations get too homogeneous. As a result, diversity is increased, which may lead to better convergence behavior. We demonstrate this improved convergence behavior by extending the *Cartesian Genetic Programming* (CGP) algorithm with the forking operator. As Miller describes, CGP represents programs as graphs in which nodes perform functions and the connection between the nodes controls the data flow [12]. Thus, the learning task consists of assigning functions to nodes and connecting the nodes with each other.

In this paper, we explain the background and relevant literature at first. Next, we give reasons for low efficiency of real-valued CGP and explain the forking operator. Afterwards, we present and discuss results for four symbolic regression problems used to measure efficiency of our extended CGP algorithm. We finish this paper with discussing conclusions and suggestions for future research questions.

GECCO'13, July 6–10, 2013, Amsterdam, The Netherlands.

2. BACKGROUND

In this section, we explain Cartesian Genetic Programming, which is the GP algorithm that we extended with the forking operator. Furthermore, we give an overview of relevant literature.

2.1 Cartesian Genetic Programming

GP is a data-driven paradigm that seeks to evolve programs by applying genetic operators to individuals. Although first steps towards GP have already been taken in the 1970s [4, 15], this paradigm gained significant attention after Koza applied it to complex optimization and search problems [8]. Koza represented programs as LISP parse trees, which combine multiple simple functions to more complex functions. In 2000, Miller and Thomson introduced another algorithm for GP called *Cartesian Genetic Programming* (CGP) [14].

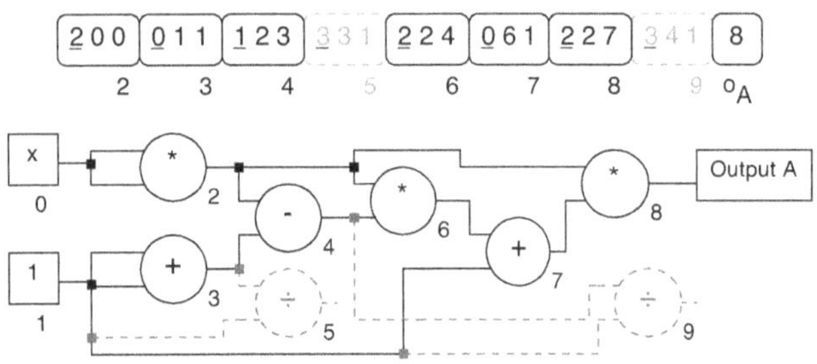

Figure 1: Genotype and phenotype for CGP individuals, source: Clegg et al.[2]

CGP represents programs as indexed, acyclic and directed graphs via genotype-phenotype-mapping. Originally, these graphs were structured as a rectangular grid, but later work focused on a graph with only one row [2]. In figure 1, we show an example of a genotype and its corresponding phenotype. The sequence of numbers at the top of the figure represents the genotype, in which each group maps to one node of the graph except for the last group. These numbers are indexes and either describe the function to perform (underlined number) or the index of the inputs to work on (non-underlined number). The index in the last group specifies the output of the program. The algorithm evaluates a program via recursive backward search through the directed graph. It starts from program output and processes all nodes directly or indirectly linked to it. In that way, only active nodes are processed whereas inactive nodes, which are not connected to the output, remain untouched. Thus, the given example specifies the function $x^6 - 2x^4 + x^2$.

2.2 Related work

The presented genotype-phenotype-mapping offers some properties, which were investigated in more detail. At first, we note that the genotype can encode functionality that is not relevant for the phenotype. In figure 1, the dashed groups and the corresponding dashed, inactive nodes do not have any direct or indirect connection to the output. Therefore, these genes can be arbitrarily set, the phenotype will not change. Miller and Thomson described this property as an example of *neutrality* and published work emphasizing its importance [14]. This genotype redundancy can improve efficiency when unused genes are altered and used in future individuals. Another important property is that integer-based CGP usually only uses mutation but not crossover operators. Koza underlined the importance of crossover operators for his tree-based program representation [8]. According to him, no run on his experiments, which used only a mutation operator and a fitness-proportionate reproduction, has ever produced a solution to any problem. In contrast, Clegg et al. showed that omitting a crossover operator and relying only on a mutation operator can produce a solution in a CGP algorithm [2]. Clegg et al. also evaluated different crossover operators, but reasoned that swapping integers as crossover operator influences efficiency negatively. Therefore, they changed gene encoding to real values from the interval [0, 1] as shown in figure 2. For receiving indexes for the lookup tables, gene values are multiplied with the function or input count. This modification of gene encoding enables the use of a weighted average crossover operator. Without a crossover operator, integer-based and real-valued CGP achieve similar efficiency. In contrast, adding a weighted average crossover operator to real-valued CGP improves efficiency significantly.

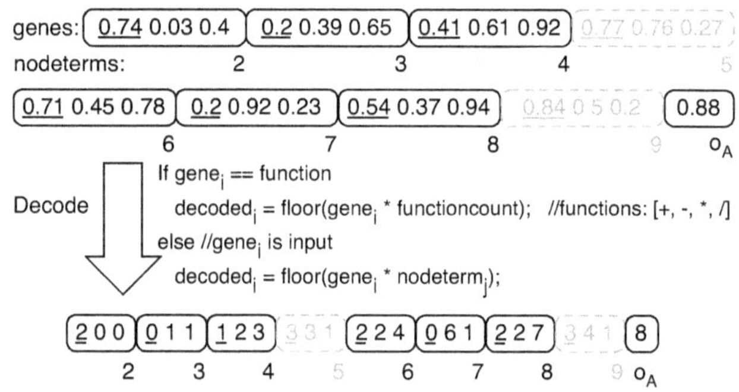

Figure 2: Decoding from real-valued to integer-based genotype, bases on: Clegg et al.[2]

Other approaches have also been investigated to improve efficiency of CGP. Miller analyzed the population size of a CGP algorithm, but also show node count influences efficiency [11]. With one exception out of 12 Boolean symbolic regression problems, lower population sizes tend to improve efficiency. It also improves when node count is increased. However, Miller stated that these findings may be limited to this type of problems. In a later publication, Miller and Smith investigated the correlation between efficiency and node count in more detail [13]. The authors presented a 2-bit multiplier problem and showed that with increasing node count, efficiency increases as well. According to them, the reason for this correlation is increased redundancy utilized by the mutation operator. Since a larger CGP individual can hold multiple inactive programs in parallel, the mutation operator may change the active program by deactivating or activating nodes. According to Miller, this behavior is a confirmation for the importance of neutrality [12].

Low efficiency is also related to *premature convergence*. Premature convergence is caused by decreasing population diversity and describes the effect that a population converges too early, thus getting stuck in local optima [3]. Despite increasing mutation rate [1], another solution is to continuously create new random individuals. Hornby introduced the *Age-Layered Population Structure* (ALPS) which tracks the age of each individual and allows genetic operations only to work on individuals of similar age [5]. Hornby showed that this paradigm helps to improve the fitness significantly for an antenna design problem. Later, Slaný combined the ALPS paradigm with CGP and demonstrated a better performance for the evolution of image operators [17]. However, for more complex problems, the performance gain appears to be less superior. Lehman and Stanley replaced the fitness function in a GP algorithm with a novelty function, which helps to maintain population diversity [10]. Although the novelty function leads to better and smaller solutions in the presented experiments, algorithms using a fitness function may find a solution faster.

Tu and Lu presented a genetic algorithm, which interprets individuals not only as points but also as stochastic regions in solution space [18]. They consider each individual as mean of a Gaussian distribution with an adaptable variance and sample over this distribution to produce and evaluate new individuals. In that way, each individual also covers slight modifications, which helps to improve efficiency. In their experiments, Tu and Lu showed a large increase in efficiency due to this sampling. Four years later, they have published a correction because of a mistake in their original implementation [19]. This mistake lead to much better results, but was originally not discovered due to a special behavior of the example problems. Although the corrected implementation does not achieve satisfactory efficiency, sampling likely good genes during evolution may be beneficial anyway. Thus, we use and modify this idea for our forking operator.

3. FORKING OPERATOR

In this section, we present our preliminary considerations that lead to the development of the new genetic operator called *forking*. Afterwards, we explain the operator and show how it integrates into the evolutionary process.

3.1 Preliminary considerations

In the previous section, we present approaches to improve efficiency of evolutionary algorithms, especially for CGP. Even for real-valued CGP, which we use as base for our operator, we often note low efficiency. At the beginning of evolution, the population converges fast towards good solutions whereas the rate of convergence decreases notably in the end. One way to avoid this low rate of convergence is to define an easily reachable convergence threshold. For most problems, we want to find very good or even perfect solutions so that this threshold must be kept very low. Therefore, other solutions have to be found to improve efficiency.

From our experience, the main reason for this convergence behavior is that individuals are getting more and more similar during evolution. Thus, the algorithm evaluates (nearly) identical individuals over and over again so that fewer regions of solution space are covered. This reduces the gene pool significantly so that crossover operators work less efficiently. From our perspective, real-valued CGP even intensifies this problem due to its genotype-phenotype-mapping.

The problem of genotype-phenotype-mapping is its large difference in complexity of genotype and phenotype spaces. Although all individuals in one population have most likely different genotypes, the probability of sharing the same phenotype is much higher. To underline this statement, we consider a example given in figure 3.

The example consists of one node with four possible functions, two inputs and one program output. Each gene is encoded by a 32-bit floating-point variable, which is a common size in modern programming languages like C [7]. According to IEEE 754 standard, a 32-bit floating-point variable encodes $2^{32} - 2^{25}$ different normal numbers [6]. Thus, the combination of four genes leads to $(2^{32} - 2^{25})^4$ =~3,298e+38 possible genotypes. However, there are only 48 possible phenotypes. That means ~3,298e+38 possible genotypes encode only 48 possible phenotypes, which prove the mapping as being very robust. Even if we use a more efficient encoding and pack all genes into one 32-bit floating-point variable, we still have $2^{32} - 2^{25} = 4,261,412,864$ possible genotypes. Naturally, this is a very simplified example to emphasize the disparity between phenotype and genotype spaces. Usually, CGP programs consist of more nodes, have more node functions and also more inputs. Furthermore, the gene encoding may be more efficient, but for real-valued CGP genotype and phenotype spaces will likely still maintain a large difference in complexity. However, CGP phenotype complexity prevents an exhaustive search for the best solution.

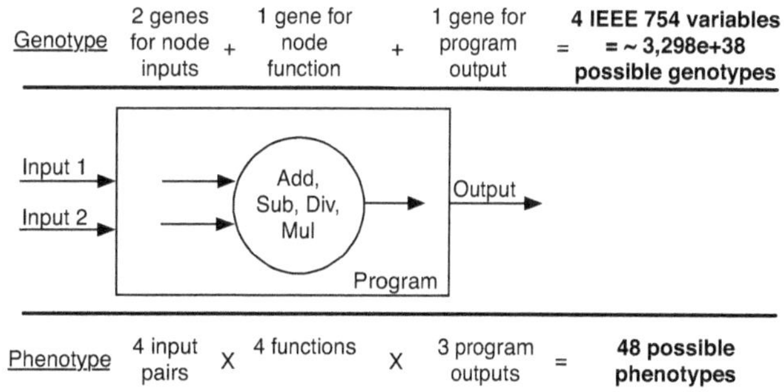

Figure 3: Example for difference in complexity of genotype and phenotype spaces

This large difference in complexity of genotype and phenotype spaces leads to different problems, which common genetic operators cannot easily address. Crossover operators usually work best when individuals differ notably. However, CGP individuals that differ in genotype may have the same phenotype with a reasonable probability. This property can render crossover operators useless if individuals focus on one region of genotype space and thus represent the same point in phenotype space. Mutation operators usually modify genotypes slightly by altering some genes. For real-valued CGP, mutation operators must perform larger modifications to genotypes. Otherwise changes in genotype will most likely not reflect to phenotype. Thus, the mutation rate may have to be increased or mutation operators must alter genes relevantly, which may slow convergence down when individuals are changed too much.

3.2 Introducing the forking operator

All these considerations lead to the development of a new genetic operator that we call *forking*. As base for forking, we use an idea similar to the approach published by Tu and Lu [18]. This idea states that an individual should not only represent a point but may also span a region in genotype space as a multivariate Gaussian distribution. For this distribution, the individual is the mean whereas specified standard deviations for each dimension define the region's size. In that way, new individuals can be created by drawing a sample from this distribution. In contrast to the work done by Tu and Lu [18], we apply this idea to GP. Furthermore, our algorithm decides dynamically whether it interprets an individual as a point or as a distribution.

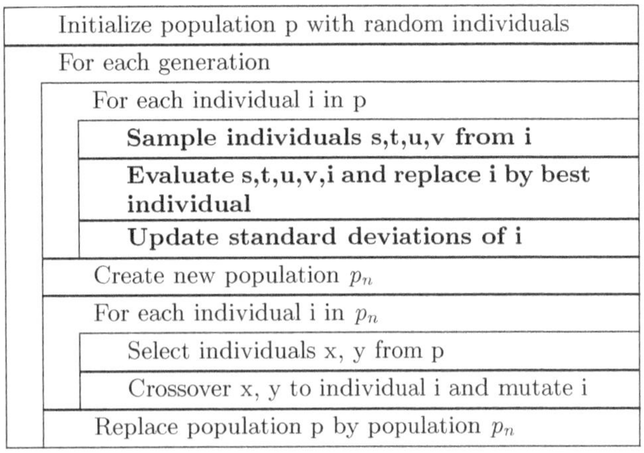

Figure 4: Structure chart of augmented algorithm

In our first implementation, we augmented real-valued CGP presented by Clegg et al.[2] with the stochastic algorithm described by Tu and Lu [18]. In figure 4 we show the augmented algorithm in which differences to the original algorithm are marked in bold. Since genotypes of real-valued CGP individuals consist only of floating-point numbers, the stochastic algorithm of Tu and Lu is applied without any modifications. As Tu and Lu described, we sample four individuals s, t, u and v in the distribution defined by each individual i and adapt the standard deviations of i as proposed. We compare this algorithm with a real-valued CGP algorithm similar to the one from Clegg et al., but grant the augmented algorithm to have only one fifth of the population size of the real-valued CGP algorithm. This adaptation is necessary for a fair comparison, because the augmented algorithm evaluates four additional individuals per each original individual so that its population size is virtually increased by factor five. In our experiments, real-valued CGP performs much better because it utilizes its larger real population size for covering more regions of genotype space in parallel. Even after reducing population size for the real-valued CGP algorithm and keeping the augmented algorithm untouched, real-valued CGP converges faster. Furthermore, we observed that when individuals are spread in genotype space, it is more efficient to interpret them as points. However, if they focus on few regions in genotype space, it is better to interpret them as distributions, because the sampling process leads to less redundant phenotypes.

Based on our first experiments, we conclude that it is better to combine both algorithms in a different way. In figure 5, we show real-valued CGP extended with the forking operator that realizes a dynamic combination of both algorithms. Again, modifications to real-valued CGP are marked in bold. Depending on current state of evolution, the forking operator decides for each individual whether it is interpreted as a point or as a distribution in genotype space. For this decision, forking uses population statistics. The central elements of these statistics are *fingerprints* stored in a hash map. As fingerprints, we use textual representations of phenotypes, e.g. a mathematical term like $x_0 + x_1 * x_0$, where x_0 and x_1 are inputs of the encoded program. The hash map stores the frequency of every fingerprint in the current population. Based on this frequency, the operator calculates a fork probability for an individual. The *amplifier* is a parameter and controls how a relative fingerprint frequency should be transformed into a fork probability. If the fork probability exceeds an adjustable *probability limit*, the fork probability will be set to this limit. Afterwards, the operator uses a uniform distribution to sample a random number and if this number is below the fork probability, the current individual will be interpreted as distribution. In this case, a new individual is sampled from current individual's distribution and it replaces the current individual. The next step is the evaluation of the individual. After all individuals have been evaluated, the population for the next generation is created. During this step, the hash map is updated with new fingerprint frequencies.

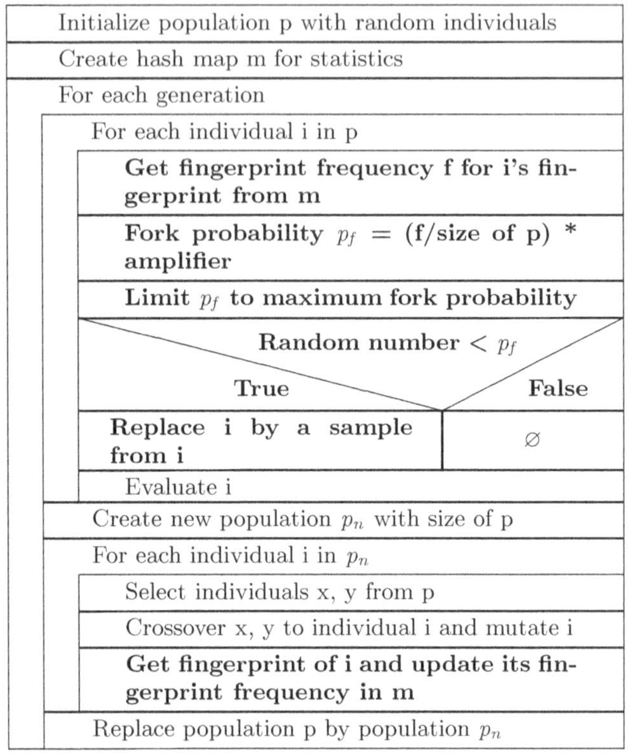

Figure 5: Structure chart of extended algorithm

We realize sampling of new individuals from existing ones in a different way than Tu and Lu [18]. Similar to their work, we use the genotype of an individual as the mean of a multivariate Gaussian distribution. However, we do not use a separate standard deviation for each dimension. Instead, we perform sampling as shown in equation 1 and 2

$$G_{n,i} \sim \mathcal{N}\left(G_i, \sigma^2_{input}\right), \forall G_i \in \textit{input genes} \tag{1}$$

$$G_{n,f} \sim \mathcal{N}\left(G_f, \sigma^2_{function}\right), \forall G_f \in \textit{function genes} \tag{2}$$

, where $G_{n,i}$ represents a gene for an input, which is sampled from the Gaussian distribution defined by the current gene G_i as mean and σ_{input} as standard deviation for inputs. $G_{n,f}$ is a gene for a node function, which is sampled from the Gaussian distribution defined by the current gene G_f as mean and $\sigma_{function}$ as standard deviation for functions. By sampling in all genes G_i and G_f of an existing individual, the genotype of a new individual is created. Additionally to *amplifier* and *probability limit*, input deviation σ_{input} as well as function deviation $\sigma_{function}$ are parameters of the forking operator. In contrast to Tu and Lu, our two standard deviations are neither part of the genotype nor altered during evolution. Instead, standard deviations have to be defined carefully. As our example in figure 3 outlines, phenotype space is much smaller than genotype space. Since forking samples in genotype space, standard deviations have to be large enough so that genotypes may be created that map on different phenotypes. Setting standard deviations too large may lead to completely randomly initialized individuals so that any similarities to original individuals get lost. The choice of standard deviations depends also on program input and node functions count so that for many inputs and node functions, standard deviations should be smaller.

Population statistics are the key to decide dynamically between the two interpretations of individuals. When the current individual's phenotype and thus fingerprint is rare in the population, the forking operator likely interprets this individual as a point. This is usually the case in the beginning of evolution so that the algorithm behaves like real-valued CGP proposed by Clegg et al. [2]. With ongoing evolution, individuals focus on fewer regions so that the current individual's phenotype may be shared by other individuals as well. In this case, its fingerprint frequency increases and the forking operator will more likely interpret the current individual as a distribution. We also experimented with updating statistics, when a sampled individual replaces the original, but we did not see any significant differences in our experiments. The *amplifier* and *probability limit* influence the decision between both interpretations of an individual. It depends on the problem whether these parameters should be raised to increase likelihood of forking.

In addition to crossover and mutation, the forking operator is another genetic operator that modifies the genotype of individuals. Whereas mutation operators alter individuals due to a specified mutation rate, the forking operator always considers population statistics. These statistics base on phenotype and not on genotype, so that forking pays attention to the robust genotype-phenotype-mapping. Thus, forking is a dynamic genetic operator as it only reacts when phenotypes of individuals get too homogeneous. Furthermore, the forking operator performs a full sampling in all dimensions of the distribution and thus, in all genes. Although this sampling likely modifies all genes, it does not guarantee that a sampled individual will have another phenotype than distribution's mean. Instead, the probability of changes in individual's phenotype depends mostly on the standard deviations for node inputs and functions.

4. EVALUATION

In this section, we compare the efficiency of real-valued CGP and the algorithm using the forking operator. After describing our methodology, we present and discuss results for four symbolic regression experiments. Furthermore, we give hints for configuring the parameters of the forking operator and discuss the usage with other GP representations.

4.1 Methodology

For evaluating efficiency, we apply the real-valued CGP algorithm and the algorithm using the forking operator on the following symbolic regression problems.

$$f_1(x) = x^6 - 2 * x^4 + x^2$$
$$f_2(x) = x^5 - 2 * x^3 + x$$
$$f_3(x, y) = (x^2 * y^2)/(x + y)$$
$$f_4(x, y) = x^5/y^3$$

Function f_1 and f_2 are also used by Clegg et al. [2]. We use the other functions to consider functions with multiple inputs as well as functions that also include the save division operator. As training data, we sample 50 random data points from the interval $[-1, 1]$. Like Clegg et al., we use the sum of absolute differences between expected and calculated outputs as cost function and require it to be smaller than 0.01. Since the implementations of real-valued CGP differ the results presented in this paper are not directly comparable to results published by Clegg et al.. Furthermore, we do not use variable crossover rates as proposed by Clegg et al., because their values were problem specific.

In our experiments, we use the same configuration for all algorithms, which is also similar to the configuration used by Clegg et al.. In table 1, we show this configuration.

Table 1: Basic configuration of all algorithms

Property	Value
Maximum node count	10
Function lookup table	+ (0), - (1), * (2), / (3)
Population size	50
Maximum Generations	20,000
Crossover operator	Weighted average
Crossover rate	0.75, not adaptive
Mutation operator	Reset gene to value $\in [0,1]$
Mutation rate	0.20, not adaptive
Tournament selection size	20
Elitism size	2

The optimal configuration of parameters of the forking operator, *amplifier*, *probability limit*, *input deviation* and *function deviation*, depends on the problem to be solved so that we list it for each experiment separately. We also performed a meta-evolution on all four problems. This meta-evolution found a general set of parameters, which minimizes the number of generations to converge on all four problems. In table 2, we show this general set.

Table 2: General set of forking parameters

Parameter	Value
Amplifier	5
Probability limit	1.0
Input deviation	0.8
Function deviation	0.0

As measures for efficiency, we use the number of processed generations and also the required computation time until convergence. For every problem, we average these efficiency measures over 1,000 runs, which are performed with different seeds for the pseudo-random number generator. For each measure, e.g. 140 ± 316, the first number denotes the average value and the second the standard deviation. Our evaluation guarantees that all algorithms work on the same seeds. Furthermore, all algorithms process exactly the same input data. The algorithms are implemented in Java 6 (64-Bit) and not optimized for speed. They were run on a laptop equipped with an Intel Core i5-2520M CPU clocked at 2.50 GHz, 4 GB RAM and Microsoft Windows 7 Enterprise x64.

4.2 Results

Table 3: Efficiency for problem $f_1(x) = x^6 - 2 * x^4 + x^2$

Algorithm	Avg. number of generations	Avg. computation time in ms
Real-valued CGP	140 ± 316	837 ± 2,186
Best general	61 ± 91	330 ± 542
Best specific	60 ± 64	330 ± 391

In table 3, we show results for the first problem. *Real-valued CGP* is the equivalent to the algorithm proposed by Clegg et al.[2] and *Best general* represents the general set of forking parameters found by the meta-evolution. *Best specific* represents the optimal configuration of the forking operator for this problem and uses the following parameter values: amplifier = 5, probability limit = 1.0, input deviation = 0.4, function deviation = 0.1. Compared with real-valued CGP, this optimal configuration needs 57% fewer generations and 61% less computation time per run to converge on average. The general set of parameters is negligibly slower as it needs 56% fewer generations and also 61% less computation time per run.

In figure 6 and 7, we show plots summarizing convergence behaviors for the first problem. Figure 6 presents the average fitness of all 1,000 runs over the first 500 generations. Figure 7 shows the number of generations to converge for the sorted, slowest 500 runs. As visible, the forking operator enables notably faster convergence especially due to avoiding very slow runs. For the remaining problems, we will use the plot style as shown in figure 7. One main reason for this decision is that some of the presented problems use high polynomials, which lead to very high fitness values. Due to space limitations, it is not possible to plot these graphs as a whole in a good readable fashion. Furthermore, we are interested in finding perfect solutions so that the detailed development of convergence is not as important as the final number of generations to converge.

As visible in the tables 4-6 and their corresponding figures 8-10, the forking operator converges much faster for the other three problems as well. The configurations for the best specific configuration differ notably for amplifier, input and function deviation. Only the forking probability is always the same with 0.9 or 1.0.

Table 4: Efficiency for $f_2(x) = x^5 - 2 * x^3 + x$

Algorithm	Avg. number of generations	Avg. computation time in ms
Real-valued CGP	900 ± 1,882	5,720 ± 13,280
Best general	248 ± 294	1,431 ± 1,765
Best specific	244 ± 220	1,354 ± 1,231

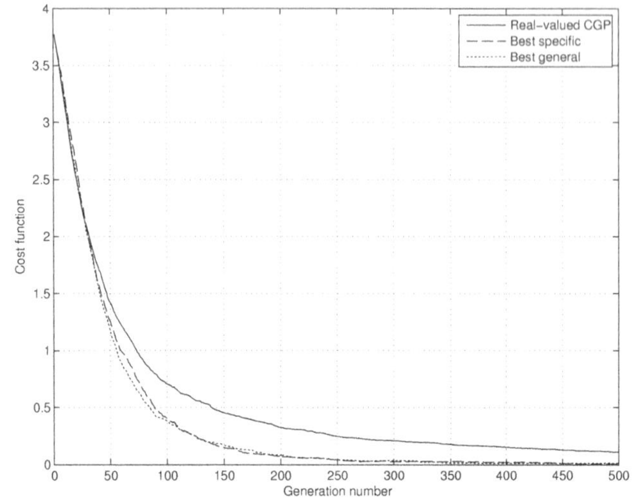

Figure 6: Average convergence for problem $f_1(x) = x^6 - 2 * x^4 + x^2$ covering multiple algorithms

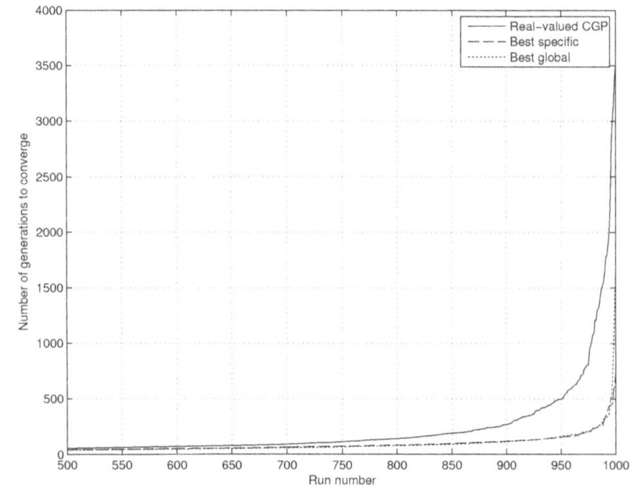

Figure 7: The number of generations to converge over the slowest 500 runs for $f_1(x) = x^6 - 2 * x^4 + x^2$

4.3 Discussion

Efficiency evaluations for the presented problems show that forking can accelerate convergence significantly. Although best specific parameter sets and best general set partly differ, their difference in efficiency is negligible. In comparison to the real-valued CGP algorithm, the forking operator configured with the best general parameter set reduces the number of necessary generations by 54% on average. Computation time per run is reduced by 61% on average. The reason for the difference between these speedups is that often not all individuals of the last generation are evaluated. Furthermore, the similar speedups for generation count and computation time in each experiment demonstrate that the additional operations of the forking operator do not affect computation time notably.

For number of generations to converge but also computation time, the standard deviations are significantly reduced in comparison to real-valued CGP. This fact is also underlined by the presented figures. As we have shown in the figures, the forking operator based algorithms do not accelerate all problem runs, but avoid very slow runs. Furthermore, all

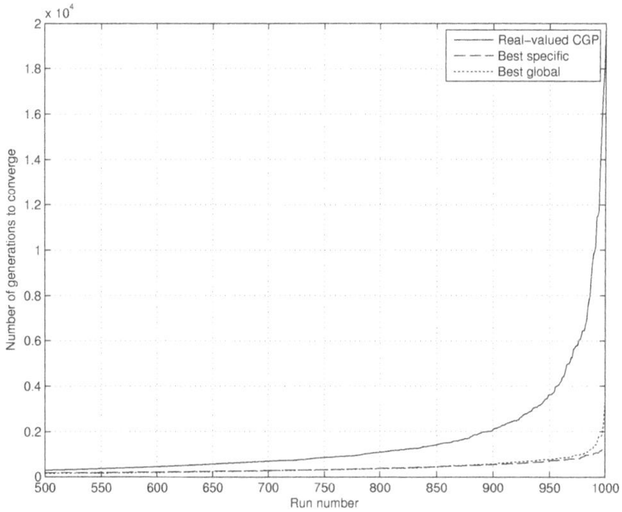

Figure 8: The number of generations to converge over the slowest 500 runs for $f_2(x) = x^5 - 2 * x^3 + x$

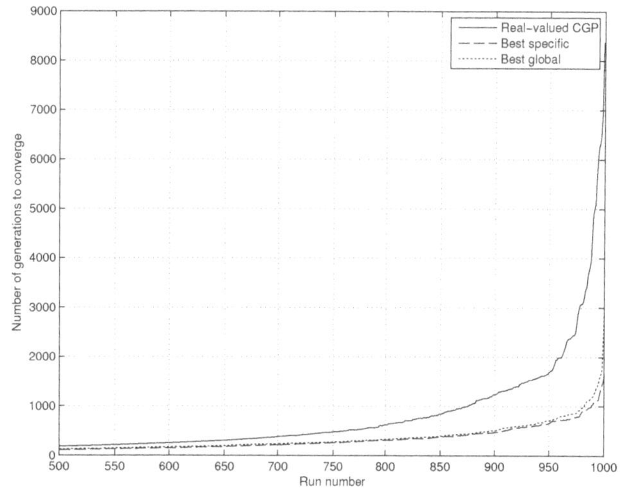

Figure 9: The number of generations to converge over the slowest 500 runs for $f_3(x, y) = (x^2 * y^2)/(x + y)$

Table 5: Efficiency for $f_3(x, y) = (x^2 * y^2)/(x + y)$

Algorithm	Avg. number of generations	Avg. computation time in ms
Real-valued CGP	466 ± 863	2,251 ± 4,366
Best general	216 ± 264	881 ± 1,131
Best specific	194 ± 224	741 ± 894

Table 6: Efficiency for $f_4(x, y) = x^5/y^3$

Algorithm	Avg. number of generations	Avg. computation time in ms
Real-valued CGP	411 ± 1,187	2,352 ± 7,563
Best general	260 ± 583	1,181 ± 2,705
Best specific	240 ± 471	1,128 ± 2,303

runs of the algorithm with the forking operator found the correct solution, so that premature convergence did not occur. However, it cannot be generalized that forking will not lead to premature convergence in some cases.

Although the forking operator demonstrated its ability to accelerate convergence, the introduction of new parameters without supplying a well-founded description of how to initialize them is a disadvantage. If we take the best general set of parameters for guidance, it seems that probability limit should always be set to the maximum value of 1.0 so that this parameter can be removed. Setting amplifier to 5 seems to be a good general choice, so that input and function deviations remain as most difficult parameters. According to their values in the best general set, the main problem is rather the correct connection between nodes, but not which function is associated to each node. However, we only used four possible node functions and ten nodes per CGP program. For other problems, which use more possible node functions, importance of the function deviation may increase. One solution for this problem could be the increase of available nodes per CGP program. As Miller and Smith outlined, increasing node count increases efficiency, too [13]. As a side effect, we assume that this change will likely cause every possible node function to be present in the graph. Thus, the problem could be reduced to finding the correct connection between nodes so that only the input deviation is of importance. However, both deviations should not be set close to 1.0 at the same time, because this may lead to a completely randomly initialized individual.

For using forking with other GP representations, effective methods for creating fingerprints and sampling new individuals from existing individuals have to be found. Basically, fingerprinting offers a way to detect *behavioral equivalence* in the population. Since every GP representation should offer a textual representation of a program, this is the simplest form to realize fingerprinting. However, especially for large programs, a fingerprint mechanism that finds semantical instead of only textual equivalence may be beneficial. Sampling new individuals can be realized easily when the genotype space is continuous. However, GP representations like Koza's parse trees have a discrete genotype space so that sampling using a Gaussian distribution requires a mapping from real-valued space to discrete genotype space. This mapping has to be considered, when standard deviations for each distribution are defined. Maybe, CGP's mapping from real-valued genotype to its discrete phenotype space can be modified to work with other GP representations as well.

5. CONCLUSIONS AND FUTURE WORK

Genetic programming is a powerful paradigm for solving difficult problems, but its algorithms often demand high computational effort to converge. In this paper, we introduced the forking operator, which samples new individuals from existing ones when populations get too homogeneous. Experimental results on four symbolic regression problems showed that forking can improve efficiency by over 50% on average. Despite evaluating the operator for other problems the choice of parameters for a specific problem in advance remains as an important research question. Furthermore, developing an improved fingerprint mechanism may be beneficial, so that syntactically different but semantically equivalent phenotypes could be recognized. Besides the forking operator, we think combining population statistics upon fingerprints with other genetic operators is an interesting research topic. For instance, the variable crossover rate pro-

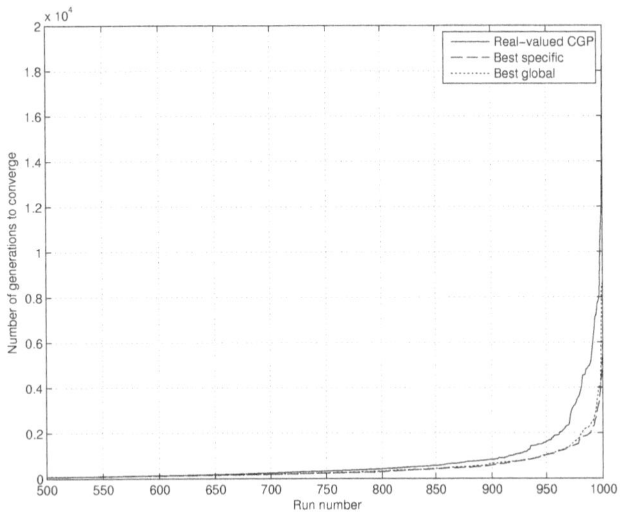

Figure 10: The number of generations to converge over the slowest 500 runs for $f_4(x, y) = x^5/y^3$

posed by Clegg et al. [2] may be realized with these statistics in a problem-independent way.

Another interesting research question could be extending forking to evolutionary algorithms. In contrast to GP applications, phenotype spaces for evolutionary algorithms are often continuous and not discrete. Thus, identifying individuals with the same phenotype is not as easy as for discrete spaces. A possible solution may be a metric that describes similarity of individuals in a problem-independent fashion.

For future research, our main focus will rely on further accelerating GP algorithms. Additionally, we will use these algorithms to realize a prediction model for car accident severity so that new intelligent occupant safety functions could be developed. By improving convergence behavior, we believe that we find better solutions for this particular problem as larger solution spaces could be covered.

References

[1] Wolfgang Banzhaf, Frank D Francone, and Peter Nordin. The Effect of Extensive Use of the Mutation Operator on Generalization in Genetic Programming Using Sparse Data Sets. In *Proceedings of the 4th International Conference on Parallel Problem Solving from Nature*, pages 300–309. Springer-Verlag, 1996.

[2] Janet Clegg, James Alfred Walker, and Julian Frances Miller. A New Crossover Technique for Cartesian Genetic Programming. In *Proceedings of the 9th annual conference on Genetic and evolutionary computation*, GECCO '07, pages 1580–1587. ACM, 2007.

[3] Lawrence Davis et al. *Handbook of Genetic Algorithms*, volume 115. Van Nostrand Reinhold New York, 1991.

[4] John H. Holland. *Adaptation in Natural and Artificial Systems: An Introductory Analysis with Applications to Biology, Control, and Artificial Intelligence.* University of Michigan Press, April 1975.

[5] Gregory S Hornby. ALPS: The Age-Layered Population Structure for Reducing the Problem of Premature Convergence. In *Proceedings of the 8th annual conference on Genetic and evolutionary computation*, pages 815–822. ACM, 2006.

[6] IEEE Task P754. IEEE Standard for Floating-Point Arithmetic. Technical report, Microprocessor Standards Committee of the IEEE Computer Society, August 2008.

[7] ISO. ISO C Standard 1999. Technical report, ISO, 1999. ISO/IEC 9899:1999 draft.

[8] John R. Koza. *Genetic Programming: A Paradigm for Genetically Breeding Populations of Computer Programs to Solve Problems.* Stanford University, Department of Computer Science, 1990.

[9] W. B. Langdon. A Many Threaded CUDA Interpreter for Genetic Programming. In *Proceedings of the 13th European Conference on Genetic Programming*, volume 6021 of *LNCS*, pages 146–158. Springer, 2010.

[10] Joel Lehman and Kenneth O. Stanley. Efficiently Evolving Programs Through the Search for Novelty. In *Proceedings of the 12th annual conference on Genetic and evolutionary computation*, GECCO '10, pages 837–844. ACM, 2010.

[11] Julian F. Miller. An Empirical Study of the Efficiency of Learning Boolean Functions using a Cartesian Genetic Programming Approach. In *Proceedings of the Genetic and Evolutionary Computation Conference*, volume 2, pages 1135–1142. Morgan Kaufmann, 1999.

[12] Julian F. Miller, editor. *Cartesian Genetic Programming.* Springer Berlin Heidelberg, 1st edition. edition, September 2011.

[13] Julian F. Miller and Stephen L. Smith. Redundancy and Computational Efficiency in Cartesian Genetic Programming. *Transactions on Evolutionary Computation*, 10(2):167–174, September 2006.

[14] Julian F. Miller and Peter Thomson. Cartesian Genetic Programming. In *Proceedings of the Third European Conference on Genetic Programming*, volume 1802, pages 121–132. Springer-Verlag, 2000.

[15] Ingo Rechenberg. *Evolutionsstrategie : Optimierung technischer Systeme nach Prinzipien der biologischen Evolution.* Number 15 in Problemata. Frommann-Holzboog, Stuttgart-Bad Cannstatt, 1973.

[16] Michael Schmidt and Hod Lipson. Distilling Free-Form Natural Laws from Experimental Data. *Science*, 324 (5923):81–85, 2009.

[17] Karel Slanỳ. Comparison of CGP and Age-Layered CGP Performance in Image Operator Evolution. *Genetic Programming*, pages 351–361, 2009.

[18] Zhenguo Tu and Yong Lu. A Robust Stochastic Genetic Algorithm (StGA) for Global Numerical Optimization. *Transactions on Evolutionary Computation*, 8(5):456–470, October 2004.

[19] Zhenguo Tu and Yong Lu. Corrections to "A Robust Stochastic Genetic Algorithm (StGA) for Global Numerical Optimization". *Transactions on Evolutionary Computation*, 12(6):781–781, December 2008.

Runtime Analysis of Mutation-Based Geometric Semantic Genetic Programming for Basis Functions Regression

Alberto Moraglio & Andrea Mambrini
CERCIA, University of Birmingham, Birmingham B15 2TT, UK
{a.moraglio,a.mambrini}@cs.bham.ac.uk

ABSTRACT

Geometric Semantic Genetic Programming (GSGP) is a recently introduced form of Genetic Programming (GP) that searches the semantic space of functions/programs. The fitness landscape seen by GSGP is *always* – for any domain and for any problem – unimodal with a linear slope by construction. This makes the search for the optimum much easier than for traditional GP, and it opens the way to analyse theoretically in a easy manner the optimisation time of GSGP in a *general setting*. Very recent work proposed a runtime analysis of mutation-based GSGP on the class of *all* Boolean functions. We present a runtime analysis of mutation-based GSGP on the class of *all* regression problems with generic basis functions (encompassing e.g., polynomial regression and trigonometric regression).

Categories and Subject Descriptors

F.2.2 [**Analysis of Algorithms and Problem Complexity**]: Nonnumerical Algorithms and Problems

Keywords

Genetic programming, semantics, geometric crossover, runtime analysis

1. INTRODUCTION

Traditional Genetic Programming searches the space of functions/programs by using search operators that manipulate their syntactic representation, regardless of their actual semantics/behaviour. For instance, subtree swap crossover is used to recombine functions represented as parse trees, regardless of trees representing Boolean expressions, mathematical functions, or computer programs. Although this guarantees that offspring are always syntactically well-formed, it is unclear why such a blind syntactic search should work well for different problems and across domains.

In recent literature, there are a number of approaches that use the semantics of programs in various ways to guide the search of GP [1, 4, 17, 6, 7]. Whereas these semantically aware methods are promising, their implementations are very wasteful as they are heavily based on trial-and-error: search operators are implemented via acting on the syntax of the parents to produce offspring, which are accepted only if some semantic criterion is satisfied. More importantly from a theoretical perspective, these implementations do not provide insights on how syntactic and semantic searches relate to each other. Is a *direct* implementation of semantic operators possible? That is, can we act on the syntax of the parent programs and produce offspring that are *guaranteed* to respect some semantic criterion/specification by construction?

Geometric Semantic Genetic Programming [12] is a novel form of genetic programming that answers this question in the affirmative. GSGP uses geometric crossover and geometric mutation [14, 11] to search *directly* the semantic space of functions/programs. Informally, semantic geometric crossover and semantic geometric mutation generate offspring that are guaranteed to be, respectively, "semantically intermediate" and "semantically near" their parents. These search operators can be directly implemented for different domains following a *simple formal recipe* [12], which was used to derive specific forms of GSGP for a number of classic GP domains (i.e, Boolean functions, arithmetic functions and classifiers).

The fitness landscape seen by the semantic geometric operators is *always* unimodal with a linear slope (cone landscape) by construction, as the fitness of an individual is by definition its *semantic distance* to the optimum individual. This suggests that GSGP performs better than standard GP. GSGP was compared with standard GP on several well-known problems across domains (finding Boolean functions, polynomial regressions, and classification tasks) and it consistently found much better solutions with the same budget of fitness evaluations [12]. Furthermore, GSGP has been found more efficient and generalising better than standard GP on some initial studies on real-world problems [2].

Genetic programming has been hard to analyse theoretically. The current literature on GP theory is heterogeneous. Perhaps the most developed theory of GP is the schema theory [8]. There is also some work on Markov models of GP search [10]. There are theory-laden methods to combat bloat based on an exact formalisation of the dynamics of average program size [16]. Other works focus on the analysis of some static structural features of the search space of GP programs (e.g., proportions of programs encoding the same function for different program sizes), and experimen-

GECCO'13, July 6–10, 2013, Amsterdam, The Netherlands.

tal hardness studies of fitness landscapes [8]. There is also some theoretical works on GP from a semantic perspective. In [15], a notion of geometric mutation based on a semantic distance was used to show that the No Free Lunch theorem does not apply to GP. Furthermore, the work [9] analyses traditional subtree crossover in terms of "semantic building blocks" in Boolean functions, reporting that most of the time this crossover does not make useful search in the semantic space.

Runtime analysis is the standard approach to analyse analytically algorithmic performance. In the last decade it has been applied, with an ever increasing success, to randomised search heuristics and it is establishing itself as a leading theory. Despite its success, the analysis is done on a per-algorithm-and-per-problem basis. Obtaining interesting, general runtime results holding on a large class of problems for non-trivial search algorithms would be a major progress. Due to the difficulty of analysing GP, there is only very initial work on its runtime analysis. Durrett et al. [3] present the runtime analysis of a mutation-based GP with a tree representation on very simplified problems (the ORDER and MAJORITY problems).

The cone landscape seen by GSGP makes it very attractive from a theoretical point of view. When GSGP is applied to search the space of Boolean functions, the GSGP search is equivalent to a GA search on OneMax-like problems. Based on this, very recently [13], a runtime analysis of GSGP with various types of mutations on the class of *all* Boolean functions has been possible by simply extending known runtime results for GAs. Remarkably, it was found that GSGP finds the optimum Boolean function in polynomial time on most of the Boolean problems. We continue this line of investigation and present a runtime analysis of GSGP on the class of *all* regression problems with generic basis functions (encompassing e.g., polynomial regression and trigonometric regression). This is a large class of regression problems, which is, however, only a subclass of general symbolic regression that is the natural target class of traditional GP. This work is the first step towards the analysis of more general regression problems.

2. GEOMETRIC SEMANTIC GENETIC PROGRAMMING

A search operator $CX : S \times S \to S$ is a *geometric crossover* w.r.t. the metric d on S (set of candidate solutions) if for any choice of parents p_1 and p_2, any offspring $o = CX(p_1, p_2)$ is in the segment $[p_1, p_2]$ between parents, i.e., it holds that $d(p_1, o) + d(o, p_2) = d(p_1, p_2)$. A search operator $M : S \to S$ is a *geometric ϵ-mutation* w.r.t. the metric d if for any parent p, any of its offspring $o = M(p)$ is in the ball of radius ϵ centered in the parent, i.e., $d(o,p) \leq \epsilon$. Given a fitness function $f : S \to \mathbb{R}$, the geometric search operators induce or see the fitness landscape identified by the triple (f, S, d). Many well-known recombination operators across representations are geometric crossovers [11].

For most applications, genetic programming can be seen as a supervised learning method. Given a training set made of fixed input-output pairs $T = \{(x_1, y_1), ..., (x_N, y_N)\}$ (i.e., fitness cases), a function $h : X \to Y$ within a certain fixed class H of functions (i.e., the search space specified by the chosen terminal and function sets) is sought that interpolates the known input-output pairs. I.e., for an optimal solution h^* it holds that $\forall (x_i, y_i) \in T : h^*(x_i) = y_i$. The fitness function $F_T : \mathrm{H} \to \mathbb{R}$ measures the error of a candidate solution h on the training set T. Compared to other learning methods, two distinctive features of GP are (i) it can be applied to learn virtually any type of functions, and (ii) it is a *black-box method*, as it does not need explicit knowledge of the training set, but only of the errors on the training set.

We define the *genotype-phenotype mapping* as the function $P : \mathrm{H} \to Y^{|X|}$ that maps a representation of a function h (i.e., its genotype) to the vector of the outcomes of the application of the function h to all possible input values in X (i.e., its phenotype), i.e., $P(h) = (h(x_1), ..., h(x_{|X|}))$. We can define a *partial* genotype-phenotype mapping by restricting the set of input values X to a given subset X' as follows: $P_{X'} : \mathrm{H} \to Y^{|X'|}$ with $P_{X'}(h) = (h(x_1), ..., h(x_{|X'|}))$ with $x_i \in X'$. Let $I = (x_1, ..., x_N)$ and $O = (y_1, ..., y_N)$ be the vectors obtained by splitting inputs and outputs of the pairs in the training set T. The output vector of a function h on the training inputs I is therefore given by its partial genotype-phenotype mapping $P_I(h)$ with input domain restricted to the training inputs I, i.e., $P_I(h) = (h(x_1), ..., h(x_N))$. The training set T identifies the partial genotype-phenotype mapping of the optimal solution h^* restricted to the training inputs I, i.e., $P_I(h^*) = O$.

Traditional measures of error of a function h on the training set T can be *interpreted as distance* between the target output vector O and the output vector $P_I(h)$ measured using some suitable metric D, i.e., $F_T(h) = D(O, P_I(h))$ (to minimise). For example, when the space H of functions considered is the class of Real functions, the input and output spaces are $X = \mathbb{R}^n$ and $Y = \mathbb{R}$, and the output vector restricted to the training inputs is a real vector of size N (i.e., size of training set). A suitable metric D to measure the error as a distance between real vectors is e.g. the Euclidean distance (ED), or also the Manhattan distance (MD).

We define *semantic distance SD* between two functions $h_1, h_2 \in \mathrm{H}$ as the distance between their corresponding output vectors measured with the metric D used in the definition of the fitness function F_T, i.e., $SD(h_1, h_2) = D(P(h_1), P(h_2))$. The semantic distance SD is a genotypic distance induced from a phenotypic metric D, via the genotype-phenotype mapping P [1].

We define *semantic geometric crossover and mutation* as the instantiations of geometric crossover and geometric mutation to the space of functions H endowed with the distance SD. E.g., semantic geometric crossover SGX on Real functions represented e.g. as trees returns offspring Real functions (i.e., trees) such that the output vectors of the offspring are in the Euclidean segment between the output vectors of the parents (w.r.t. all $x_i \in X$).

When the training set covers all possible inputs, the *semantic fitness landscape* seen by an evolutionary algorithm with semantic geometric operators is, from the definition of semantic distance, a unimodal landscape in which the fitness of a solution is its distance in the search space to the optimum. This holds for any domain of application of GP (e.g., Boolean, Arithmetic, Program), any specific problem

[1] P is generally non-injective (i.e., different genotypes may have the same phenotype), but it can be made bijective by interpreting a genotype as a representation of a semantic class (i.e., of all functions with the same semantics) without affecting the subsequent analysis (see [13]).

within a domain and for any choice of metric for the error function. Naturally, in practice, the training set covers only a fraction of all possible input-output pairs of a function. This has the effect of *adding a particular form of neutrality* to the cone landscape, as only the part of the output vector of a function corresponding to the training set affects its fitness, the remaining large part is "inactive".

GP search with geometric operators w.r.t. the semantic distance SD on the space of functions H (represented e.g. as trees) is formally equivalent to EA search with geometric operators w.r.t. the distance D on the space of output vectors. This is because: (i) semantic classes of functions are in bijective correspondence with output vectors, as "functions with the same output vector" is the defining property of a semantic class of function; (ii) semantic geometric operators on functions (i.e., trees) are isomorphic to geometric operators on output vectors, as SD is induced from D via the genotype-phenotype mapping P (see also diagram (1) and explanation in the next section). Despite this formal equivalence, actually encoding a function in an EA using its output vector instead of, say, a parse tree, is futile: in the end we want to find a function represented in an *intensive form* (i.e., as a tree) that can represent concisely "interesting" functions and that allows for meaningful generalisation of the training set.

The commutative diagram below illustrates the relationship between the semantic geometric crossover GX_{SD} on genotypes (e.g., trees) on the top, and the geometric crossover (GX_D) operating on the phenotypes (i.e., output vectors) induced by the genotype-phenotype mapping P, at the bottom. It holds that for any $T1, T2$ and $T3 = GX_{SD}(T1, T2)$ then $P(T3) = GX_D(P(T1), P(T2))$.

$$\begin{array}{ccccc} T1 & \times & T2 & \xrightarrow{GX_{SD}} & T3 \\ \downarrow{\scriptstyle P} & & \downarrow{\scriptstyle P} & & \downarrow{\scriptstyle P} \\ O1 & \times & O2 & \xrightarrow{GX_D} & O3 \end{array} \qquad (1)$$

The problem of finding an algorithmic characterization of semantic geometric crossover can be stated as follows: given a family of functions H, find a recombination operator GX_{SD} (unknown) acting on elements of H that induces via the genotype phenotype mapping P a geometric crossover GX_D (known) on output vectors. E.g., for the case of Real functions with fitness measure based on Euclidean distance, output vectors are real vectors and GX_D is a line crossover that returns offspring vectors on the (Euclidean) line segment between parent vectors. We want to derive a recombination operator acting on Real functions that corresponds to a line crossover on their output vectors. Note that there is a different type of semantic geometric crossover for each choice of space H and distance D. Consequently, there are different semantic crossovers for different GP domains.

DEFINITION 1. *Given two parent functions $T1, T2 : \mathbb{R}^n \to \mathbb{R}$, the recombinations SGXE and SGXM return the real function $T3 = (T1 \cdot TR) + ((1 - TR) \cdot T2)$ where TR is a random real constant in $[0, 1]$ (SGXE) (see Fig. 1), or a random real function with codomain $[0, 1]$ (SGXM). Given a parent function $T : \mathbb{R}^n \to \mathbb{R}$, the mutation SGMR with mutation step ms returns the real function $TM = T + ms \cdot (TR1 - TR2)$ where $TR1$ and $TR2$ are random real functions.*

THEOREM 1. *SGXE and SGXM are semantic geometric crossovers for the space of real functions with fitness function based on Euclidean and Manhattan distances, respectively, for any training set and any real problem. SGMR is a semantic ϵ-geometric mutation for real functions with fitness function based on Euclidean and Manhattan distances. The mean of its probability distribution is the parent, and ϵ is proportional to the step ms.*

Table 1: Training set for the polynomial regression problem (first 2 columns). Output vectors of trees in Figure 1 (last 4 columns): of parents T1 and T2, of random value TR, and of offspring T3.

X	Y	$P(T1)$	$P(T2)$	$P(TR)$	$P(T3)$
-1	1	0	0	0.5	0
-0.5	0.75	0.5	-0.75	0.5	-0.125
0	1	1	-1	0.5	0
+0.5	1.75	1.5	-0.75	0.5	0.375
+1	3	2	0	0.5	1

The proof of the previous theorem can be found in [12]. In the following, we give an example to illustrate the theorem for the SGXE crossover. Let us consider the simple symbolic regression problem, in which, we want to find an expression whose values match those on the quadratic polynomial x^2+x+1 in the range $[-1, +1]$. Let us say the target function values for $x \in \{-1, -0.5, 0, +0.5, +1\}$ are given as training set (see two leftmost columns of Table 1, X inputs and Y outputs). The target output vector Y is the real vector $(1, 0.75, 1, 1.75, 3)$ (column 2 of Table 1). For each tree representing a real function, one can obtain its output vector by querying the tree on the inputs X. The output vectors of the trees in Figure 1 are in the last 4 columns of Table 1. The fitness $f(T)$ of a tree T (to minimise) is the Euclidean distance between its output vector $P(T)$ and the target output vector Y (restricted to the outputs of the training set), e.g., the fitness of parent $T1$ is $f(T1) = ED(P(T1), Y) = ED((0, 0.5, 1, 1.5, 2), (1, 0.75, 1, 1.75, 3)) \simeq 1.436$. The semantic distance between two trees $T1$ and $T2$ is the Euclidean distance between their output vectors $P(T1)$ and $P(T2)$, e.g., the semantic distance between parent trees $T1$ and $T2$ is $SD(T1, T2) = ED(P(T1), P(T2)) = ED((0, 0.5, 1, 1.5, 2), (0, -0.75, -1, -0.75, 0)) \simeq 3.824$. Let us now consider the relations between the output vectors of the trees in Table 1. This crossover on output vectors is a geometric crossover w.r.t. Euclidean distance, as $P(T3)$ is in the Euclidean segment between $P(T1)$ and $P(T2)$ as $P(T3)$ is obtained as a convex combination of $P(T1)$ and $P(T2)$. We can also verify this on the example using the distance relation for the line segment:
$ED((0, 0.5, 1, 1.5, 2), (0, -0.125, 0, 0.125, 1)) +$
$ED((0, -0.125, 0, 0.125, 1), (0, -0.75, -1, -0.75, 0)) =$
$1.912 + 1.912 = 3.824 =$
$ED((0, 0.5, 1, 1.5, 2), (0, -0.75, -1, -0.75, 0))$.
This shows that the crossover on trees in Figure 1 is a semantic geometric crossover w.r.t. Euclidean distance.

As the syntax of the offspring of semantic operators contain at least one parent, the size of individuals grows quickly in the number of generations. To keep their size manageable during evolution, we need to *simplify algebraically* offspring sufficiently and efficiently *without changing the computed*

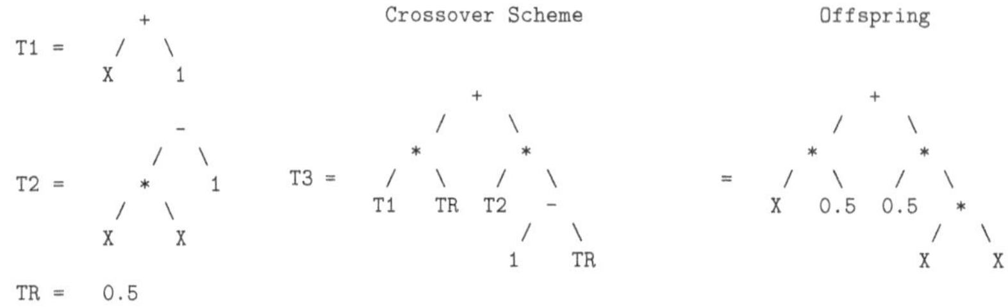

Figure 1: T1 and T2 are parent functions and TR is a random value in $[0, 1]$. The offspring T3 is obtained by substituting T1, T2 and TR in the crossover scheme and simplifying algebraically.

function. The search of semantic crossover and semantic mutation is unaffected by the simplification, which can then be done at any moment and in any amount. In practice, we need to work with "well-behaved" families of functions whose offspring can be easily simplified. Furthermore, as the semantic operators generate offspring as a functional combination of their parents, *it does not matter how functions are actually represented* (e.g., trees, graphs, sequences) as the representation does not affect the search behaviour. We have represented functions as trees only to contrast this framework with traditional GP. The following analysis focuses on linear combinations of basis functions as family of functions, which can be represented as fixed-length vectors of coefficients, and GP with mutation only.

3. RUNTIME ANALYSIS

3.1 Problem Definition

The problem class we consider is a general form of regression – basis functions regression – defined as follows. Let $g_j : \mathbb{R}^n \to \mathbb{R}$ be a family of m basis functions, and H be the class of functions expressible as linear combination of the basis functions $\{g_j\}$. Let $p : \mathbb{R}^n \to \mathbb{R}$ be an unknown target function, and $T = \{(i_1, o_1), ..., (i_k, o_k)\}$ be a fixed set of input/output pairs of p. The aim is to find a function $h \in H$ that best approximates p on the training examples. I.e., $h^* = argmin_{h \in H}\{ED(P_I(h), O)\}$. By using different families of basis functions, one obtains well-known specific regression classes such as simple linear regression, polynomial regression, splines regression, trigonometric regression and more. E.g., for polynomial regression with a single input variable, one can choose $g_j = x^j$.

The general problem class can be solved directly, without search, using the *least squares method.* A function $h \in H$ can be written as $h(x_1, \ldots, x_n) = c_1 \cdot g_1(x_1, \ldots, x_n) + \ldots + c_m \cdot g_m(x_1, \ldots, x_n)$ and it is identified in H, given $\{g_j\}$, by the vector of coefficients $C = (c_1, \ldots, c_m)$. The optimal vector of coefficients can be determined solving the system of simultaneous linear equations obtained by using the training set T, i.e., $o_z = c_1 \cdot g_1(i_z) + \ldots + c_m \cdot g_m(i_z)$ with $z = 1, \ldots, k$. In matrix form is $O' = GC'$ with O is the vector of training set outputs and G is the matrix $\{g_j(i_z)\}_{j,z}$. The solution is $C' = G^+ O'$ where G^+ is the Moore-Penrose pseudoinverse of G that is a generalisation of inverse matrix that returns a well-defined result when the system is underdetermined ($m > k$) or overdetermined ($m < k$). The optimal approximating function so computed *minimises the Euclidean distance* to the target output vector.

Symbolic regression is more flexible and general than basis functions regression as it allows to search variable length functions and functions obtained by arbitrary functional compositions of a base set of functions, not only linear combinations. Furthermore, traditional GP solves symbolic regression problems in a black-box setting: it does not use the knowledge of the training set, but only the errors of candidate solutions on the training set. GSGP goes beyond the least square method as it can solve the basis function regression problem in the black-box setting (Sections 3.3 and 3.4), and it can search the space of variable length linear combinations of basis functions.

3.2 Mutation Design

In [5], a runtime analysis of 1+1-ES with adaptive isotropic Gaussian mutation on the sphere function is reported showing that 1+1-ES is efficient on the sphere. This analysis applies unchanged to the Euclidean cone landscape.

We *reduce* the runtime analysis of GSGP for *any* basis functions regression problem, i.e., any choice of basis functions g_j, any choice of function to approximate p, and any choice of training set T, to the above settings. This is achieved by designing a sematic mutation operator for real functions that on the output vector space *always* corresponds to an isotropic Gaussian mutation.

The semantic mutation we consider is of the form $o(x) = p(x) + ms \cdot r(x)$ where $p(x) \in H$ is the parent function, $ms \in \mathbb{R}^+$ is the mutation step, $r(x)$ is the perturbing function which is sampled according to some probability distribution over H. As $o(x)$ is a linear combination of elements of H it is also in H. For a fixed number of basis functions m, we can represent functions in H by their (fixed-length) vectors of coefficients in the linear combination. The semantic mutation on this representation becomes $c_o = c_p + ms \cdot c_r$ where $c_o, c_p, c_r \in \mathbb{R}^m$ denote the vectors of coefficients of $o(x)$, $p(x)$ and $r(x)$. Simplification of the offspring in this representation is implicitly achieved by algebraic operations on real vectors. The genotype-phenotype mapping on this representation becomes a function $P : \mathbb{R}^m \to \mathbb{R}^k$ that maps vectors of coefficients to output vectors.

LEMMA 1. *The genotype-phenotype mapping P is a linear map. So, it holds that $P(c_1 + c_2) = P(c_1) + P(c_2)$ and $P(\lambda c) = \lambda P(c)$ for all $c_1, c_2, c \in \mathbb{R}^m$ and $\lambda \in \mathbb{R}$.*

PROOF. The mapping P from C to O can be expressed in matrix form as $O' = GC'$ (see Section 3.1). From linear algebra, we know that this is a linear map. □

Consequently, line segments and circles on the space of

vectors of coefficients (genotypes) are projected via P to, respectively, line segments and (possibly rotated and rescaled) ellipses on the output vectors space (phenotypes). To obtain a circle on phenotype space, one needs an ellipse in the genotype space that compensates for the transformation P. In terms of semantic operators, this means that a line crossover on genotypes induces a line crossover on phenotypes. A carefully chosen non-isotropic Gaussian mutation on the space of genotypes corresponds to an isotropic Gaussian mutation on the space of phenotypes. We prove the last statement formally.

THEOREM 2. *The non-isotropic Gaussian mutation on genotypes* $c_o = c_p + ms \cdot c_r$ *with* $c_r \sim N(0, G^+IG'^+)$ *induces the isotropic Gaussian mutation on phenotypes* $P(c_o) = P(c_p) + ms \cdot P(c_r)$ *with* $P(c_r) \sim N(0, I)$.

PROOF. $c_o = c_p + ms \cdot c_r$; $P(c_o) = P(c_p + ms \cdot c_r)$; For linearity of P: $P(c_o) = P(c_p) + ms \cdot P(c_r)$; $P(c_r)' = Gc_r'$ is a linear transformation of the multivariate Gaussian c_r: $P(c_r) \sim N(0, G \cdot G^+IG'^+ \cdot G') = N(0, I \cdot I \cdot I') = N(0, I)$ □

The implementation of the semantic mutation requires to sample c_r from $N(0, G^+IG'^+)$. This can be done by multiplying G^+ by a vector formed by sampling k times the normal distribution $N(0,1)$.

3.3 Analysis with Known Training Inputs

In [5], an asymptotic runtime analysis to obtain an approximated solution within ϵ from the optimum [2] of the standard (1+1)-ES with the 1/5-rule (Algorithm 1) on the Euclidean cone is reported. It was found that it takes $\Theta(n)$ generations (where n is the dimension of the search space) to halve the distance $|c|$ from the initial point c to the optimum. Consequently, it takes $\Theta(n \log_2(\frac{|c|}{\epsilon}))$ generations to find an approximated solution within ϵ from the optimum. When the search space is a hyper-box with length of the sides constant in n and ϵ, the maximum distance of the initial point to the optimum is given by the length of the longest diagonal of the hyper-box, which is $\Theta(\sqrt{n})$. The runtime then becomes $\Theta(n \log_2(\frac{\sqrt{n}}{\epsilon}))$. The algorithm is very efficient both in n for any fixed ϵ, as the runtime is $\Theta(n \log n)$, and in $\frac{1}{\epsilon}$ for a fixed n, as the runtime is $\Theta(\log(\frac{1}{\epsilon}))$.

Algorithm 1 (1+1)-ES with 1/5-rule for adaptation

```
initialise curr ∈ ℝ^n with a starting point
σ := f(curr)/n; gen := 0; succ := 0
while f(curr) > ε do
    choose mutation vector mut ∈ ℝ^n randomly ~ N(0, I)
    create offspring vector off := curr + σ · mut
    if f(off) ≤ f(curr) then curr := off; succ := succ+1 endif
    if gen%n = 0 then
        if succ < n · 1/5 then σ := σ/2 else σ := σ · 2 endif
        succ := 0
    end if
    gen := gen + 1
end while
return curr
```

The GSGP algorithm that corresponds to Algorithm 1 on the space of output vectors can be obtained from it with the following modifications. The search space is the space of functions in H represented by vectors of coefficients, so $curr, mut \in \mathbb{R}^m$, and n is m. The fitness function $f(x)$ returns the Euclidean distance of the output vector of the function x to the target output vector. The mutation vector mut is sampled from $N(0, G^+IG'^+)$. The pseudo-inverse matrix G^+ is needed to sample mut, which is pre-computed in the initialisation of the algorithm. *This algorithm is only partly black-box because it uses knowledge of the inputs of the training set (but not of the outputs) in the computation of* G^+. In the next Section, a complete black-box algorithm is presented.

When the unknown target function p belongs to the search space H or when the number of basis functions m is larger or equal to the number of points in the training set k, GSGP may in the limit find a function h^* that passes through all points of the training set, i.e., $f(h^*) = 0$. When $p \notin H$ and $m < k$, the best approximating function $h^* \in H$ has non-zero fitness on the training set. This fitness value is the smallest error ϵ_{min} GSGP searching H can achieve.

From a runtime viewpoint, the search done by (1+1)-GP is equivalent to the search of (1+1)-ES on the output vector space. The dimension of the space is the size k of the training set, which is therefore a natural definition of problem size. The size of the hyper-box delimiting the output vector space depends on the endpoints of the interval co-domains of the basis functions $\{g_j\}$, the endpoints of the ranges of the coefficients of linear combinations, which we consider both constant w.r.t. k and ϵ, and on the number of basis functions m, which we consider to be some function of k (e.g., $m = k$ to find an interpolating function). The length of the sides of the hyper-box is therefore $\Theta(m)$, and the runtime to find a function h with $f(h) - f(h^*) < \epsilon$ is $\Theta(k \log_2(\frac{m\sqrt{k}}{\epsilon}))$. In particular, the runtime is constant in the number of input variables n of the functions searched.

3.4 Analysis with Random Training Inputs

In Machine Learning, when one can choose the training examples, they are normally selected to cover evenly the input domain X of the functions $h \in H$ so that the distance between any pair of closest training inputs in X is the same (i.e., they form a grid covering the input domain). In this case, the training inputs are known, and the GSGP analysis in the previous section applies. When one cannot choose the training examples, the standard assumption is that they were sampled uniformly at random on the input domain X. We present an analysis for the second case, in which the sampled training inputs are not known (i.e., *full black-box* scenario).

The idea behind the analysis is as follows. As the number of sampled input points grows, their spatial distribution tends to approximate better and better a grid on X. Asymptotically, GSGP with random training inputs behaves as GSGP with a grid of training inputs covering X. The grid can be determined from the geometry of the domain X. Hence, we can *reduce* the asymptotic runtime analysis of GSGP with *unknown* random training inputs to that of GSGP with a *known* grid of points.

3.4.1 Uni-dimensional Case

Let A and B be collections of points of $X = \mathbb{R}$ with $|A| = |B| = n$. We say that the spatial distribution of A approximates that of B within tolerance ϵ if there is a bijective assignment $\sigma : A \to B$ such that the distance be-

[2]In continuous domains, there is zero probability of hitting exactly the optimum.

tween corresponding points via σ is never greater than ϵ, i.e., $\max_{a \in A} |a - \sigma(a)| \leq \epsilon$.

Let us consider $X = [0, 1]$. Let $A = \{\frac{1}{n+1}, \frac{2}{n+1}, \ldots, \frac{n}{n+1}\}$ be a grid on X and B be a set of n points sampled uniformly at random in X. Let σ be the assignment obtained by ordering B in ascending order and pairing its elements with elements of A also considered in ascending order, i.e., the smallest element in B corresponds to $\frac{1}{n+1}$, the second smallest to $\frac{2}{n+1}$, and so on.

The elements of A have been chosen to coincide with the expected values of the order statistics of B. The order statistics of B are the random variables $b(1), b(2), \ldots, b(n)$ obtained by ordering in ascending order the independent random variables $b_1, b_2, \ldots, b_n \sim U([0, 1])$. E.g., $b(1) = \min\{b_1, b_2, \ldots, b_n\}$ and $b(n) = \max\{b_1, b_2, \ldots, b_n\}$. As n grows, the order statistics concentrate towards their expected values. This means that uniformly sampled points become closer and closer to the points of the grid for larger n. We make this precise.

THEOREM 3. *The random points B are approximated by the grid A within an arbitrarily small error $\epsilon > 0$ with overwhelming probability w.r.t. n.*

PROOF. The order statistics of B are $b(k) \sim Beta(k, n - k + 1)$ for $k = 1 \ldots n$, with means $m(k) = \frac{k}{n+1}$. The cdf of $Beta(\alpha, \beta)$ is the regularised incomplete beta function $I(x; \alpha, \beta)$.

The grid A approximates the random points B with tolerance $\epsilon > 0$, when $|b(k) - m(k)| < \epsilon$ for all $k = 1 \ldots n$. We want a lower-bound of $P = Pr(|b(k) - m(k)| < \epsilon, \forall k = 1 \ldots n)$. Note that $b(k)$ are not independent. We can estimate P using the union bound: $P \geq 1 - \sum Pr(|b(k) - m(k)| > \epsilon)$.

As $b_i \sim U([0, 1])$, the distributions of $b(k)$ and of $b(n - k + 1)$ are mirror images of each other w.r.t. the mid-point of $[0, 1]$. $\sum_{k=1,n} Pr(|b(k) - m(k)| > \epsilon) = \sum_{k=1,n}(Pr(b(k) > m(k) + \epsilon) + Pr(b(k) < m(k) - \epsilon)) = \sum_{k=1,n} Pr(b(k) > m(k)+\epsilon)+\sum_{k=1,n} Pr(b(k) < m(k)-\epsilon) = 2\sum_{k=1,n} Pr(b(k) > m(k) + \epsilon)$ by mirror symmetry.

The cdf I is related to the cdf $F(x; q, p)$ of the binomial distribution $Bin(q, p)$ as follows: $F(x; q, p) = 1 - I(p; x + 1, q - x)$. So, $Pr(b(k) > m(k) + \epsilon) = 1 - I(\frac{k}{n+1} + \epsilon; k, n - k + 1) = F(k - 1; n, \frac{k}{n+1} + \epsilon)$.

The Hoeffding's inequality gives an upper-bound for the cdf of the binomial: $F(x; q, p) \leq \frac{1}{2}\exp(-2\frac{(qp-x)^2}{q})$.

Hence $Pr(b(k) > m(k) + \epsilon) \leq \frac{1}{2}\exp(-2\frac{(n(\frac{k}{n+1}+\epsilon)-(k-1))^2}{n})$.

Let us write the index $k \in \{1, \ldots, n\}$ as $k = r \cdot n$ with $r \in [0, 1]$ a constant w.r.t. n. We have then $Pr(b(k) > m(k) + \epsilon) \leq \frac{1}{2}\exp(-2\frac{(n(\frac{r \cdot n}{n+1}+\epsilon)-r \cdot n+1))^2}{n})$. For $n \to \infty$, for any k: $Pr(b(k) > m(k) + \epsilon) \leq \frac{1}{2}\exp(-2n\epsilon^2)$. Then $P = 1-2\sum_{k=1,n} Pr(b(k) > m(k)+\epsilon) \geq 1-n\exp(-2n\epsilon^2)$ i.e., overwhelming probability of success for any choice of $\epsilon > 0$. □

THEOREM 4. *With overwhelming probability, the GSGP algorithm with* unknown *uniformly random training inputs with* continuous *basis functions that uses a regular grid as a surrogate for the inputs has the same asymptotic runtime of GSGP with knowledge of the inputs.*

PROOF SKETCH. Let us consider a function F that maps the set of training inputs I to the runtime T of GSGP with the inputs I, i.e., $T = F(I)$. Let I_r be the set of the actual training inputs, and I_g be the surrogate input grid. The runtime of GSGP on these two input sets is $T_r = F(I_r)$ and $T_g = F(I_g)$. As $I_r \to I_g$ w.o.p., then $T_r \to T_g$ w.o.p. provided the function F is continuous. We show that when the basis functions are continuous, F is continuous.

The random inputs I_r converge w.o.p. to the input grid I_g. For the continuity of the basis functions g_j, the matrix $G_r = \{g_j(i_z)\}_{j,z}$ with $i_z \in I_r$ converges w.o.p. to the matrix $G_g = \{g_j(i_z)\}_{j,z}$ with $i_z \in I_g$. For the continuity of the operator of matrix inversion, G_r^{-1} converges w.o.p. to G_g^{-1}. For continuity of matrix product, the mutation vector $mut_r = G_r \cdot rv$ converges w.o.p. to $mut_g = G_g \cdot rv$ with $rv \sim N(0, I)$. The distribution of the offspring $off_r = curr + \sigma \cdot mut_r$ converges w.o.p. to the distribution $off_g = curr + \sigma \cdot mut_g$. The fitness distribution $f(off_r) = ED(G_g \cdot off_r, O)$ converges w.o.p. to the fitness distribution $f(off_g) = ED(G_g \cdot off_g, O)$. Then the probability of improvement over the parent and the expected improvement in fitness also converge. Consequently, the runtime T_r converges w.o.p. to the runtime T_g. □

3.4.2 Multi-dimensional Case

Analogously to the uni-dimensional case, we will choose a grid of points A on the input domain $X = \mathbb{R}^d$, define a bijective assignment σ from A to B, and then show that for any $\epsilon > 0$ asymptotically w.o.p. $dist(A, B) = \max_{a \in A} \|a - \sigma(a)\|_\infty \leq \epsilon$.

Given the vectors $a, b \in \mathbb{R}^d$, $\|a - b\|_\infty = \max(|a_1 - b_1|, \ldots, |a_d - b_d|)$. Hence $dist(A, B) \leq \epsilon$ is equivalent to requiring the maximum absolute difference *in each coordinate* of all points of A to corresponding points in B is $\leq \epsilon$.

Let us consider $X = [0, 1]^d$. Let $|A| = |B| = n^d$ for n integer. Let $A = \{\frac{1}{n+1}, \frac{2}{n+1}, \ldots, \frac{n}{n+1}\}^d$ be a grid on X and B be a set of points sampled uniformly at random in X.

We create the assignment σ from A to B as follows. We order all points of B in ascending order on the *first coordinate* regardless of the values on the other coordinates. Then we make n groups, putting in group B_1 the first n points in the ordered list, in group B_2 the following n points, and so on. For each group B_i, we order all its points in ascending order on the *second coordinate*. Then we make n subgroups, putting in group $B_{i,1}$ the first n points of B_i, in group $B_{i,2}$ the following n points of B_i, and so on. We continue to form new nested levels of subgroups until all d coordinates have been considered. Now, each group of the last level contains exactly a single point of B, which is uniquely identified by the d-dimensional index of its group. The assignment σ put into correspondence points of B to points of A with the same index, interpreting A as a d-dimensional matrix.

THEOREM 5. *The points B tend to the grid A w.o.p.*

PROOF. Let us consider a bi-dimensional input space i.e., $d = 2$, and let B be a set of $N = n^2$ points sampled uniformly at random in $[0, 1]$.

We first determine the joint probability distributions of the coordinates of the ordered points $B_{i,j}$ on $[0, 1]^2$. The coordinates of the points in B are i.i.d. r.v. $x, y \sim U([0, 1])$. The set of points obtained ordering B on the x-coordinate have their x-coordinates distributed as the order statistics $u_{1:N}, u_{2:N}, \ldots, u_{N:N}$ of $U([0, 1])$, and their y-coordinates i.i.d. $\sim U([0, 1])$. The ordered points are then grouped in n groups with the distributions:

$B_1 = \{(u_{1:N}, U([0,1])), \ldots, (u_{n:N}, U([0,1])),$
$B_2 = \{(u_{n+1:N}, U([0,1])), \ldots, (u_{2n:N}, U([0,1])), \ldots,$
$B_n = \{(u_{N-n+1:N}, U([0,1])), \ldots, (u_{N:N}, U([0,1])).$
The points of each group B_i are ordered on the y-coordinate and split in n subgroups obtaining the distributions:
$B_{1,1} = (U(\{u_{1:N}, \ldots, u_{n:N}\}), u_{1:n}), \ldots,$
$B_{1,n} = (U(\{u_{1:N}, \ldots, u_{n:N}\}), u_{n:n}),$
$\ldots$
$B_{n,1} = (U(\{u_{N-n+1:N}, \ldots, u_{N:N}\}), u_{1:n}), \ldots,$
$B_{1,n} = (U(\{u_{N-n+1:N}, \ldots, u_{N:N}\}), u_{n:n}).$
Using the law of total probability, the cdf of the compound distribution $U(\{u_{1:N}, \ldots, u_{n:N}\})$ can be determined explicitly: $Pr(U(\{u_{1:N}, \ldots, u_{n:N}\}) \leq z) = \frac{\sum_{i=1,n} Pr(u_{i:N} \leq z)}{n}$, and $E[U(\{u_{1:N}, \ldots, u_{n:N}\})] = \frac{\sum_{i=1,n} E[u_{i:N}]}{n}$.
We can now verify that $E[B_{i,j}] \to A_{i,j}$ for $n \to \infty$.

The means of the distributions $u_{1:N} \ldots u_{n:N}$ are evenly distributed in the interval $[0, 1/n]$ at locations $\frac{1}{n^2+1}, \ldots, \frac{n}{n^2+1}$. These distributions concentrate around their means for growing n in the same way (see proof of Theorem 3). As the interval $[0, 1/n]$ converges towards a single point for $n \to \infty$, the means of $u_{1:N} \ldots u_{n:N}$ converge to the mean of $U(\{u_{1:N}, \ldots, u_{n:N}\})$, and asymptotically $U(\{u_{1:N}, \ldots, u_{n:N}\})$ concentrates around its mean in the same way as $u_{1:N} \ldots u_{n:N}$.

For a given $\epsilon > 0$, the probability that a point in B is not within ϵ from the corresponding point in A in the x-coordinate is $\leq \exp(-2N\epsilon^2) \leq \exp(-2N^{1/2}\epsilon^2)$, and in the y-coordinate is $\leq \exp(-2N^{1/2}\epsilon^2)$. By the union bound, the probability that all points in B are within ϵ in both coordinates is $\geq 1 - 2N \exp(-2N^{1/2}\epsilon^2)$. Generalising the reasoning to d dimensions we obtain a probability of success $\geq 1 - d \cdot N \exp(-2N^{1/d}\epsilon^2)$. □

4. EXPERIMENTS

We have provided analytical asymptotical runtime results for GSGP for the black-box basis functions regression problem. In the following, we compare experimentally GSGP and the standard (1+1)-ES with 1/5-rule for adaptation on the vector of coefficients to search the space of functions (hereinafter (1+1)-ES). These algorithms differ only on the mutation operator used, i.e, GSGP uses the semantic mutation and (1+1)-ES uses the isotropic Gaussian mutation. Unlike GSGP, (1+1)-ES (to search the space of functions) is difficult to analyse theoretically as its mutation operator is distorted by the genotype-phenotype mapping, and it corresponds to a non-isotropic mutation on the space of output vectors. We also compare GSGP, that uses the knowledge of training inputs in the mutation operator, with GSGPg that replaces it with a surrogate regular grid of inputs points covering the input space. The asymptotical runtime of GSGP and GSGPg are the same, but they may be different for finite training set size k. Comparison with standard GP is not included here. In [12], it was shown that (1+1)-ES (to search the space of functions) is much faster than standard GP on polynomial regression.

We test the algorithms on randomly generated problem instances. A random problem p is a polynomial of a single input variable x of degree m with coefficients generated uniformly at random in $[-1, 1]$. A random instance of the problem p is a set T of k input/output pairs obtained by querying p with inputs sampled uniformly at random in $[-1, 1]$. Each point in the graphs in Figure 2 reports the average number of generations of 100 runs, each on a new random instance of a new random problem. The basis functions are powers of x, i.e., $g_i(x) = x^i$ for $i = 0 \ldots m$. We always choose the degree of the polynomial p equal to the number of basis functions.

Figure 2(left) compares GSGP and (1+1)-ES in terms of the number of generations (on the ordinates) to get a solution within tolerance $\epsilon = 0.05$ from the optimum, for increasing size of the training set k (data points for $k = 8, 12, 16, 20$ on the abscissa). The number of basis functions m is set to k. GSGP is much faster and scales in k much better than (1+1)-ES. Standard deviations are not reported on the graph. (1+1)-ES has very large standard deviations, almost equalling the average, GSGP has much smaller standard deviations. This suggests that the performance of (1+1)-ES is much strongly affected by the specific problem instance. The performance curve of GSGP is approximately fitting a $k \log k$, in line with the theoretical analysis.

Figure 2(centre) compares GSGP and (1+1)-ES in terms of the number of generations (on the ordinates) to get increasingly better approximations to the optimum, measured as $\log(\frac{1}{\epsilon})$ on the abscissa (data points for $\epsilon = 1, 0.5, 0.1, 0.05$). The size of the training set k and the number of basis functions m are kept fixed as $m = k = 20$. GSGP scales linearly in $\log(\frac{1}{\epsilon})$, in line with the theory. (1+1)-ES reaches a certain approximation to the optimum quickly, after that it takes increasingly longer time to get better approximations, i.e., its approximation performance does not scale well.

Figure 2(right) shows the effect on the performance of GSGP and GSGPg of the number of basis functions m (data points for $m = 4, 6, 8, 10$) for a fixed training set size $k = 18$, and a fixed approximation ϵ. GSGP and GSGPg have similar performances, as they have asymptotically by the theory, when k is large w.r.t. m. Their performance difference becomes marked as m gets closer to k. However, asymptotically the theory predicts that this effect should vanish as the continuity of the basis functions guarantees the continuity of G. The reason for this discrepancy is not entirely clear, and further experiments are needed to cast light on it.

5. SUMMARY AND FUTURE WORK

Geometric semantic genetic programming is a formal framework to design search operators that act directly on the semantic space of functions. The landscape seen by these operators is *always* a cone by construction. This makes the search potentially more effective than traditional GP, and allows us to easily derive *general* runtime results, an important open challenge.

We have considered GSGP for Basis Functions Regression, which is a large class of regression problems. Problems in this class can be solved directly by the least squares method. However, GSGP can solve them in a black-box setting. We have shown a tight link between GSGP for real functions and Evolutionary Strategy. In particular, we have designed a semantic mutation operator that makes the search of GSGP for *any* basis functions regression problem equivalent to standard (1+1)-ES with isotropic mutation on the sphere function. We could then transfer known runtime results for the (1+1)-ES to GSGP with this semantic mutation, in both partial and complete black-box scenarios. GSGP is very efficient in terms of scalability in both the size of the training set k ($\Theta(k \log k)$) and the target approximation to the optimum ϵ ($\Theta(\log(\frac{1}{\epsilon}))$). Preliminary experiments have shown that GSGP with the new semantic mutation performs well in practice.

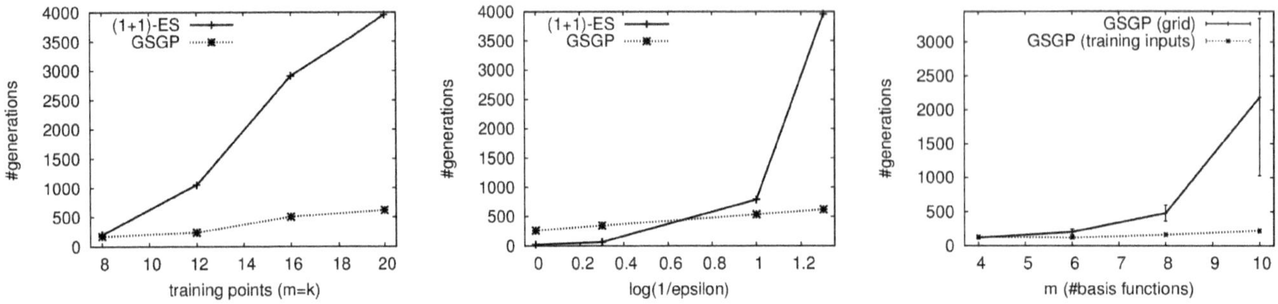

Figure 2: Comparison of GSGP and (1+1)-ES to reach an approximation $\epsilon = 0.05$ (left). Comparison of GSGP and (1+1)-ES with $m = k = 20$ to reach different levels of approximation (centre). Comparison of GSGP using grid and GSGP using the training input for $k = 18$ and different values of m (right).

There is plenty of future work. Two defining characteristics of GP are those of working with variable-length functions, and searching more complex families of functions. We would like to extend this work to variable length linear combinations of basis functions, which is within reach, and explore the possibility of working with more general combinations of functions, like in symbolic regression. Also, we would like to do further experimental investigations of GP with the new semantic operators on standard GP benchmarks, to see how they perform on more practical problems. At present, how functions trained by GP generalise on unseen inputs is a big mystery. As the effect of semantic operators on the output vectors is transparent, this may allow us to explicitly characterise the dependencies between training and testing sets reveling exactly what the inductive bias of GSGP is. Finally, we want to analyse GSGP on other domains. This seems to be within reach as, e.g., semantic operators for classifiers give rise to cone landscapes on integer vectors, which have been studied already for traditional GA, and whose analysis may be extended to GSGP.

6. ACKNOWLEDGMENTS

Alberto Moraglio was supported by EPSRC grant EP/I010297/1.

7. REFERENCES

[1] L. Beadle and C. G. Johnson. Semantic analysis of program initialisation in genetic programming. *Genetic Programming and Evolvable Machines*, 10(3):307–337, 2009.

[2] M. Castelli, L. Manzoni, and L. Vanneschi. An efficient genetic programming system with geometric semantic operators and its application to human oral bioavailability prediction. *arXiv:cs.NE/1208.2437v1*, 2012.

[3] G. Durrett, F. Neumann, and U.-M. O'Reilly. Computational complexity analysis of simple genetic programming on two problems modeling isolated program semantics. In *Workshop on Foundations of Genetic Algorithms*, 2011.

[4] D. Jackson. Phenotypic diversity in initial genetic programming populations. In *Proc. of EuroGP 2010*, pages 98–109, 2010.

[5] J. Jägersküpper. Analysis of a simple evolutionary algorithm for minimization in euclidean spaces. *Theoretical Computer Science*, 379(3):329–347, 2007.

[6] K. Krawiec and P. Lichocki. Approximating geometric crossover in semantic space. In *Proc. of GECCO '09*, pages 987–994, 2009.

[7] K. Krawiec and B. Wieloch. Analysis of semantic modularity for genetic programming. *Foundations of Computing and Decision Sciences*, 34(4):265–285, 2009.

[8] W. Langdon and R. Poli. *Foundations of Genetic Programming*. Springer-Verlag, 2002.

[9] N. F. McPhee, B. Ohs, and T. Hutchison. Semantic building blocks in genetic programming. In *European Conference on Genetic Programming*, 2008.

[10] B. Mitavskiy and J. Rowe. Some results about the markov chains associated to GPs and to general EAs. *Theoretical Computer Science*, 361(1):72–110, 2006.

[11] A. Moraglio. *Towards a Geometric Unification of Evolutionary Algorithms*. PhD thesis, University of Essex, 2007.

[12] A. Moraglio, K. Krawiec, and C. Johnson. Geometric semantic genetic programming. In *Proceedings of Parallel Problem Solving from Nature*, 2012.

[13] A. Moraglio, A. Mambrini, and L. Manzoni. Runtime analysis of mutation-based geometric semantic genetic programming on boolean functions. In *Foundations of Genetic Algorithms*, 2013. (to appear).

[14] A. Moraglio and R. Poli. Topological interpretation of crossover. In *Proc. of GECCO '04*, pages 1377–1388, 2004.

[15] R. Poli, M. Graff, and N. McPhee. Free lunches for function and program induction. In *Workshop on Foundations of Genetic Algorithms*, 2009.

[16] R. Poli and N. F. McPhee. Parsimony pressure made easy: Solving the problem of bloat in gp. In Y. Borenstein and A. Moraglio, editors, *Theory and Principled Methods for Designing Metaheuristics*, chapter 9. Springer, 2012.

[17] N. Q. Uy, N. X. Hoai, M. O'Neill, R. McKay, and E. Galván-López. Semantically-based crossover in genetic programming: Application to real-valued symbolic regression. *Genetic Programming and Evolvable Machines*, 12(2):91–119, 2011.

Structural Difficulty in Grammatical Evolution versus Genetic Programming

Ann Thorhauer
Dept. of Information Systems and Business Administration
University of Mainz, Germany
thorhauer@uni-mainz.de

Franz Rothlauf
Dept. of Information Systems and Business Administration
University of Mainz, Germany
rothlauf@uni-mainz.de

ABSTRACT

Genetic programming (GP) has problems with structural difficulty as it is unable to search effectively for solutions requiring very full or very narrow trees. As a result of structural difficulty, GP has a bias towards narrow trees which means it searches effectively for solutions requiring narrow trees. This paper focuses on the structural difficulty of grammatical evolution (GE). In contrast to GP, GE works on variable-length binary strings and uses a grammar in Backus-Naur Form (BNF) to map linear genotypes to phenotype trees. The paper studies whether and how GE is affected by structural difficulty. For the analysis, we perform random walks through the search space and compare the structure of the visited solutions. In addition, we compare the performance of GE and GP for the Lid problem. Results show that GE representation is biased, this means it has problems with structural difficulty. For binary trees, GE has a bias towards narrow and deep structures; thus GE outperforms standard GP if optimal solutions are composed of very narrow and deep structures. In contrast, problems where optimal solutions require more dense trees are easier to solve for GP than for GE.

Categories and Subject Descriptors

I.2.8 [**Artificial Intelligence**]: Problem Solving, Control Methods, and Search—*Heuristic methods*

General Terms

Algorithms

Keywords

grammatical evolution, structural difficulty, bias, random walk, Lid problem

GECCO'13, July 6–10, 2013, Amsterdam, The Netherlands.

1. INTRODUCTION

In standard genetic programming (GP) [9], solutions are represented as trees. Daida and co-workers studied the influence of the standard GP representation on the search process and found that not only crossover and selection, but also the representation itself influences GP search behavior [2, 3, 4, 6]. Standard tree-based GP has problems with structural difficulty as it is unable to search effectively for solutions requiring very full or very narrow trees [6]. Using the Lattice-Aggregate model [2, 3], which models the tree growth process in GP, it can be found that the standard GP tree representation introduces a bias, making it difficult for GP to solve problems where optimal solutions require very full or very narrow trees.

To study how GP performance depends on the structure of the optimal solutions, Daida and co-workers introduced the Lid problem [4]. For the Lid problem, only the structure of the represented tree and not the content (type of node) is relevant. The Lid problem searches for a tree with a predefined size and shape. The fitness of a solution increases with its similarity to the pre-defined optimal solution. The structure of the optimal solution is defined by its tree depth and number of nodes.

In contrast to standard GP, grammatical evolution (GE) [11] uses binary strings to encode trees and uses a grammar in Backus-Naur Form (BNF) to map the binary genotypes to the tree phenotypes. Thus, GE applies standard genetic search operators to linear bit strings and not to trees. This paper studies whether the structural difficulty also holds for GE. Daida claimed that "*structural difficulty is a consequence of the large step size of the operators in standard genetic programming, which is itself a consequence of the fixed-arity property embodied in its representation*" *[6]*. As the problem representation is different between GP and GE, and GE applies standard search operators to linear bit strings, it is possible that GE is not at all or differently affected by the bias of the tree construction process. We follow two different approaches to study differences in structural difficulty between GE and GP:

1. First we remove selective pressure from the search and perform random walks with standard GP and GE. If the representation itself does not introduce a bias into search (no structural difficulty), random search would visit all possible structures with equal probability. If some structures are visited with higher probability, we have a problem with structural difficulty as some solutions are over-represented during the random walk.

2. In the second experiment, we follow Daida's approach and study GE performance for the Lid problem [4]. Here, we can control the structure of optimal solutions. Using the Lid problem, we study whether search performance depends on the structure of the optimal solution.

Our results show that structural difficulty also exists for GE, however, there are some differences between GP and GE. As GE is biased towards very narrow and deep structures, it outperforms GP if optimal solutions require such a tree shape. In contrast, in a specific depth range, GP outperforms GE for more dense or full trees, which are underrepresented using the GE representation.

Section 2 introduces GE; section 3 reviews structural difficulty in GP and discusses bias in GE. Experiments and results are presented in Sect. 4. The paper ends with a discussion and some concluding remarks.

2. GRAMMATICAL EVOLUTION

GE [11] is a variant of GP that can evolve complete programs in an arbitrary language using a variable-length binary string. In GE, phenotype expressions are created from binary genotypes by using a complex genotype-phenotype mapping. The mapping selects production rules in a BNF grammar and thereby creates a phenotype. In contrast to standard GP [9], the genotypes are not parse trees but binary strings of variable length. A genotype consists of groups of eight bits (denoted as codons) that select production rules from a BNF grammar.

The functionality of GE follows standard evolutionary algorithm approaches using binary genotypes. As binary strings are used as genotypes, no specific crossover or mutation operators are necessary. Therefore, standard crossover operators like one-point or uniform crossover and standard mutation operators like bit-flipping can be used.

2.1 Mapping Process

Standard GP creates parse trees from a terminal and a function set. GE defines a grammar in BNF to generate the phenotypes from the genotypes. Therefore, the grammar contains all production rules to produce a program. In BNF, it can be distinguished between terminals, which are equivalent to leaf nodes in trees, and non-terminals, which can be interpreted as interior nodes in a tree and can be expanded. A grammar in BNF is defined by the quadruple $\{N, T, P, S\}$, where N is a set of non-terminals, T is a set of terminals, P is a set of production rules that maps N to a set of elements of T and N, and $S \in N$ is the start symbol.

To apply GE to a problem, it is necessary to define the BNF grammar for the problem. The BNF grammar must be defined in such a way that the optimal solution for a specific problem can be created from the elements defined by the grammar. In GE, a phenotype is created from a binary genotype in two steps. In a first step, integer values are calculated from codons of eight bits. Therefore, from a binary genotype $x^{g,bin}$ of length $8l$ we get an integer genotype $x^{g,int}$ of length l, where each integer $x_i^{g,int} \in \{0, \dots, 255\}$, for $i \in \{0, \dots, l-1\}$. Beginning with the start symbol $S \in N$, the integer value $x_i^{g,int}$ is used to select production rules from the BNF grammar. n_P denotes the number of production rules in P. To select a rule, we calculate the number of the used rule as $x_i^{g,int} mod\ n_P$, where mod denotes the modulo

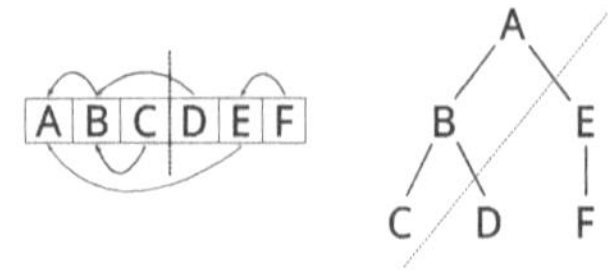

Figure 1: Effect of GE crossover (taken from Keijzer et al. [7]). GE does not exchange single subtrees but larger parts of a tree.

operation. In this manner, the mapping process traverses the genotype beginning from the left hand side ($x_0^{g,int}$) until one of the following situations arises:

- A complete program is created. Unused codons (introns) are not considered any more.
- The end of the genotype is reached. In this case, a wrapping operator reads the genotype once again, trying to solve the remaining non-terminals, beginning at the first codon.
- The upper limit of wrapping events is reached and the mapping-process has not yet finished. Then the individual receives the worst possible fitness value.

The mapping process is deterministic, as the same genotype always results in the same phenotype.

2.2 Search Operators

The effect of the crossover operator is different for GP versus GE, because in GP crossover is applied to trees, whereas in GE standard crossover operators for linear structures are applied to binary strings. We review existing studies on the differences between recombination operators.

The standard GE one-point crossover operator is similar to the cut and splice operator as described by Goldberg et al. [5]. After selecting two parents, a crossover-point is selected randomly and independently for each parent. Then, the genetic material after this points is changed between the parents. As a result, the length of a genotype is not fixed but changes during the search.

Ryan [16] compared GE and GP crossover operators. In contrast to standard GP, crossover in GE can exchange more than one subtree between two parent solutions (compare Fig. 1). As on average half of the genetic material is exchanged using GE crossover [7], GE does not get stuck so easily in global optima in comparison to standard GP.

GE re-uses existing genetic material, if the genotype string is too short to generate a complete solution. Thus, some of the genetic material is used multiple times in a different context resulting in polymorphism [12, 7]. Due to polymorphism, codons choose production rules in a context-sensitive way. As a consequence it could be possible that after the mapping-process a newly created subtree differs completely from the parent subtree. In contrast to GP, where the offsprings consist of original parts of their parents, the effect of GE crossover is difficult to predict. Fig. 2 shows an example on how the first codon (the integer 1) can be used to solve various non-terminals with different outcome (illustration is taken from Keijzer et al. [7]).

Inspired by biology, GE uses a duplication operator which copies genotype sequences and inserts them at the end of the binary string. This operator is motivated by the goal

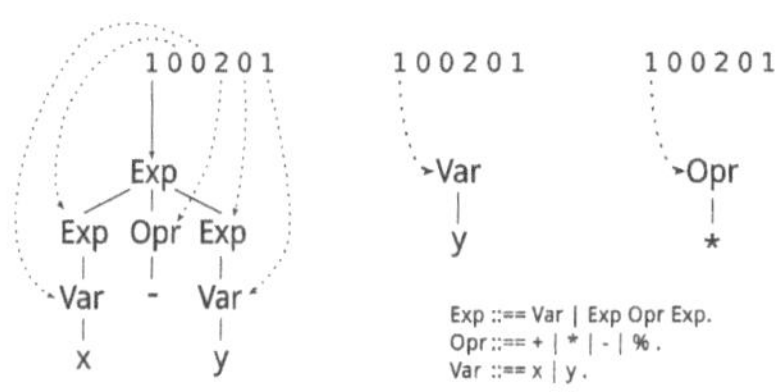

Figure 2: Polymorphism in GE (taken from Keijzer et al. [7])

to protect high-quality genetic material and to make it less vulnerable by mutation or recombination [10].

For GE, the duplication operator starts with selecting a random position in the genotype string $x^{g,int}$. Then, a random number of codons is copied and inserted after the second last codon $x^{g,int}_{l-2}$ in the genotype.

3. STRUCTURAL DIFFICULTY

Due to structural difficulty, GP search performance depends on the structure of the optimal solution and there are regions in the search space of tree structures that are not accessible by standard GP approaches [6]. Structural difficulty is closely related to a bias of search methods. A bias exists if some solutions or solution structures are visited more often than others by a search procedure, or certain actions are performed more frequently than others. In general, all factors that influence the search process are referred to as bias [17]. The existence of a bias may be advantageous or disadvantageous for the search [14]. For example, a bias of the search operators may be used to guide the search into a certain direction where promising solutions are presumed; this would be a desired bias. Unwanted bias would occur if there is an interaction between the used search operators and the chosen representation in such a way that the problem would become deceptive [1].

In GP and GE, desired bias results from the selection process. By selecting highly-fit individuals for the next generation, selection drives a population in the direction of fitter individuals. In addition, by using problem-specific crossover or mutation operators, GP performance can be improved [17].

Search bias can also be a result of redundant encodings [15]. Encodings are redundant if there are phenotypes that are encoded by more than one genotype. A redundant encoding is biased (non-uniformly redundant) if not all phenotypes are encoded by the same number of genotypes but some phenotypes are represented by a larger number. When using GE, we have a redundant representation as there are more than one genotype representing the same phenotype. Non-uniform redundancy, where the phenotypes are non-uniformly represented by the genotypes, leads to a bias and causes structural difficulty as some solution structures are under-represented. A standard approach to study the bias of a representation is using random walks.

3.1 Bias of Genetic Programming

Daida and Hilss [3] studied if there are any other mechanisms besides selection which influence GP search behavior. They were interested whether GP search performance is affected by the structure of the optimal solution. They found a bias of GP denoted as structural difficulty. For binary trees, they identified four different regions in the search space (see Fig. 3 [3]):

- Region I: If the structure of optimal solutions lies in this region, the problem is easy for GP. Most of the solutions found by GP are here.
- Region II (II_a and II_b): Problems, whose optimal solutions lie in this area, are more difficult to solve.
- Region III (III_a and III_b): Optimal solutions lying in this area could practically not be found.
- Region IV (IV_a and IV_b): There are no binary trees that exist in these areas.

To empirically verify that these regions actually occur in GP problems, Daida and Hilss [3] verified that the optimal solutions of well-known test-problems, which can be solved using GP, lie inside the boundaries of region I. This finding confirmed their assumption that the use of tree structures results in additional mechanisms which influence GP search behavior besides selection. They argue that not the content of structures is responsible for the bias but the the structures themselves.

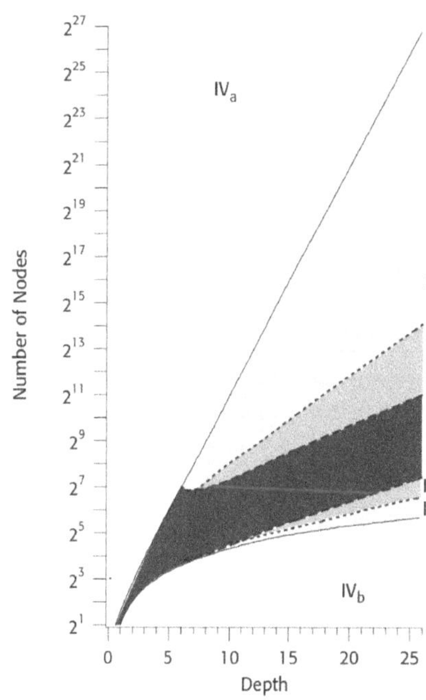

Figure 3: Predicted regions of search (taken from Daida et al. [3]).

To further study the bias of GP, Daida et al. [4] introduced the Lid problem. In contrast to most of the other well-known problems for GP, only structure and not the content of structures is relevant. The goal of the Lid problem is to build a tree structure of a predefined size and depth. The non-terminal set consists of an arity-2 function ("join"), the terminal set consists of only one terminal ("X"). Thus, only binary trees can be created. Tree fitness varies between 0 and 100. The more similar a tree structure is to the target structure, the higher its fitness. The maximum fitness is 100 if the structure of the individual is equal to the pre-defined

Table 1: GP parameters

pop size	500
initialization	ramped-half-and-half method (range 2-6)
crossover p_c	0.9 (with internal node-bias: 90% functions, 10% terminals)
reproduction p_r	0.1
selection	fitness-proportionate selection

Table 2: GE parameters

pop size	500
initialization	random
string length	80 (10 codons)
crossover p_c	0.9
mutation p_m	0.01
duplication p_d	0.01
selection	tournament selection, (steady state)

target structure. In their experiments, Daida et al. [4] varied the target depth while holding target size constant and vice versa to detect which problems are easy to solve for GP and which are not.

3.2 Bias of Grammatical Evolution

There is no work on structural difficulty for GE. O'Neill and Ryan studied the influence of the used grammar on the selection probability of rules [13]. They found that the probability of selecting a specific rule to solve a non-terminal depends on the number of possible rules for this non-terminal, the number of bits that form one codon, and the order of the single rules. A bias exists if rules are selected with different probabilities. Rules are selected with different probabilities if the number of available rules is not a divisor of 2^{l_c}, where l_c is the number of bits that form one codon. In case the number of rules is not a divisor of 2^{l_c}, the first rules are used with higher probability. An approach to overcome this bias is to use introns.

4. EXPERIMENTS AND RESULTS

In comparison to GP, GE uses a different representation and applies its search operators to strings of variable length instead of parse trees with variable size. This section studies the differences in structural difficulty between GE and GP. We perform two different types of experiments. First, we perform random walks on binary trees and study the probability of visiting specific tree structures. Second, we solve the Lid problem [4] using GP and GE and compare the resulting performance.

For both types of experiments, we use a standard parameter setting for GE and GP. Details can be found in Tables 1 and 2. To be comparable to existing studies on GP [4], we define the terminal and function set as $T = \{X\}$ and $F = \{+\}$, respectively. When using GE, we need to define a BNF that correspond to the binary tree problem defined for GP. Figure 4 defines the resulting production rules.

4.1 Random walk

By performing a random walk (a GP or GE run without selection) we can study whether there are differences in the

```
<expr>  ::= (<expr> + <expr>)
          | <var>
<var>  ::= X
```

Figure 4: Production rules in BNF

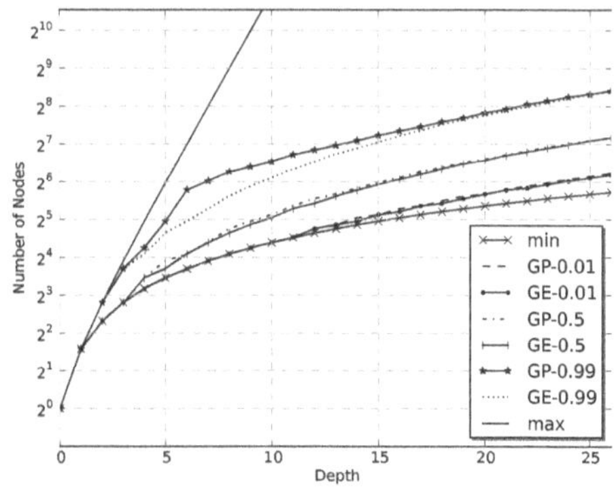

Figure 5: Solutions visited during random walks for GP versus GE.

probabilities of visiting particular solutions. If all possible solutions are visited with equal probability, the representation/operator combination is unbiased; otherwise, the used combination of representation and operator leads to a bias of search.

Consequently, we remove the selection operator from GE and GP. In addition, we remove the constraint of the maximal tree depth for GP and the wrapping-operator for GE, as we do not need it for the chosen grammar. As we set the number of generations to 1000, each random walk visits 500,000 solutions. In addition to the parameter settings listed in Tables 1 and 2, we performed the same experiments for other parameter combinations. In particular, we used different initialization methods for GP. For GP, we used the full method with $d = 6$ and $d = 3$, the grow method with $d = 6$ and $d = 3$, and the ramped-half-and-half method with $d = 3$. For GE, we used a different codon length of 20. As the results for these different configurations are similar, details are omitted and we only present results for the parameter settings from Tables 1 and 2. For each parameter setting, we perform 250 runs.

Inspired by the work of Daida and Hills [3], we want to identify the predicted regions of difficulty for GE and compare it to GP. Thus, we analyzed the properties (number of nodes and tree depth) of all solutions visited during random walks. Figure 5 presents the results and shows the different regions in the space of tree structures that are visited using GP versus GE. We plot the 1st and 99th percentile as well as the median. All visited structures lie in the regions I and II_b of Daida's Lattice-Aggregate model (Fig. 3). The lines max and min are the boundaries of possible solution structures which can be represented by binary trees.

We can observe the same effects as described by the Lattice-Aggregate model [3]. With high probability, random search visits relatively deep and narrow tree structures. Very full or very narrow trees are not visited at all during a random walk. The large area above the 99th percentile indicates that random walks do not visit very full structures. This

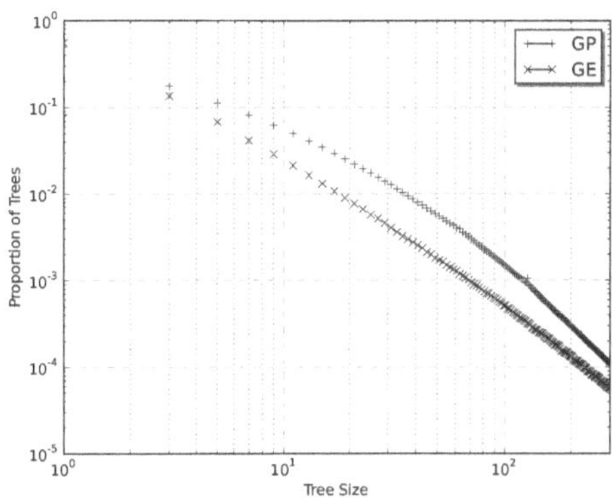

Figure 6: Distribution of structural length for GP and GE

area of non-visited solutions is greater than region III_a (see Fig. 3) of the Lattice-Aggregate model [3]. This difference is a result of different experimental settings: Using the Lattice-Aggregate model, Daida and Hilss [4] studied and predicted tree growth for GP; the experiments here study the bias of random walks. More interesting is the comparison between GE and GP. First of all, GE is affected by the same problems of structural difficulty as GP, although the search operators as well as the representation are quite different. Second, the 99th percentile of GP includes more tree structures meaning that a GP random walk finds a larger number of different tree structures in comparison to GE. Thus, GP random walks visit a higher number of dense tree structures. We can interpret this as a stronger bias of GE towards narrow tree structures in comparison to GP.

To gain deeper insights into the structure of the solutions visited during the random walks, Fig. 6 shows the distribution of the tree size. For GE versus GP, we plot the proportion of visited solutions over their size. The size of a tree is calculated as the sum of the functions and the number of terminals. For GP, structures of length 3 were found most frequently. As 50% of the structures visited during a GE random walk consist of only one terminal, the bias towards very short structures is higher for GE than for GP. GP as well GE have a strong bias towards short structures; in exchange, the probability of visiting trees of larger size is higher for GP.

To study the influence of the initialization method, we compare the properties of solutions visited during the first 50 generations with the final generations of all random walks (generation 950 to 1000). Figure 7 compares the median (for a particular depth, 50% of the visited solutions have a lower number of nodes) for GE and GP for the different stages of the random walks. At the beginning of a random walk, the initialization methods have a strong and different effect on the median. There is a significant difference between GP and GE. At the beginning of a walk (Fig. 7, left), GP visits more dense structures in comparison to GE. The influence of the initial population is reduced during the random walk. For the last 50 generations (Fig. 7, right), the influence of the initialization is neglectable and there are no significant differences between GE and GP.

Responsible for this effect are the different initialization methods of GP versus GE. The ramped-half-and-half method

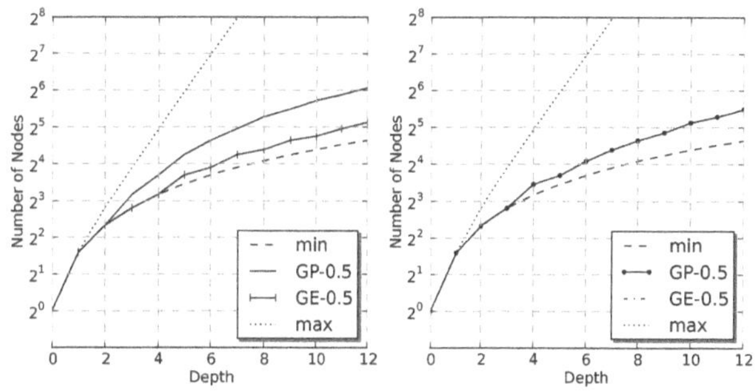

Figure 7: Median of GE and GP for the beginning (left) and end (right) of random walk s.

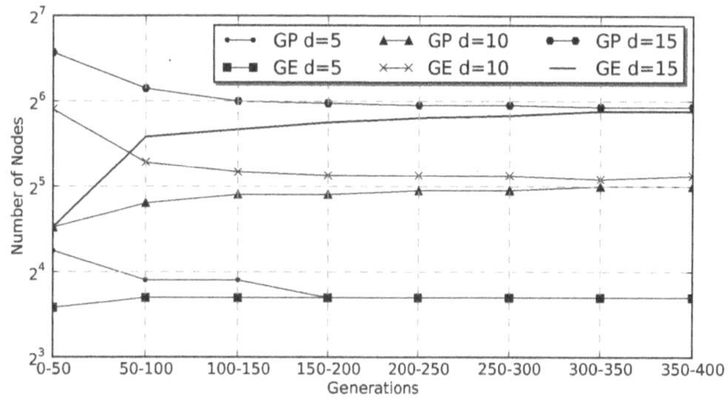

Figure 8: Median over number of generations for different tree depths d.

used in GP is able to produce full structures of depth 6 with a tree size of 128, whereas GE can only build structures with a maximal tree size of nine (codon size 10). Furthermore, due to the used grammar defining binary trees, half of the structures created with GE consist of only one terminal (all solutions, where $x_7^{g,bin} = 1$).

To more closely study how fast the effect of different initialization methods for GE versus GP diminishes, we analyze how the median develops over time. Figure 8 plots the median values for different depths (5, 10 and 15) over the number of generations. We observe large differences between GP and GE at the beginning of random walks. Due to the initialization method (ramped-half-and-half), GP visits more dense structures than GE in the first generations. For GP, the median values become lower in the first 200 generations, which means that the solution structures visited become more sparse. After 200 generation, the median stays constant. For GE, the median curves show the opposite behavior. In the first generations, the median increases and more dense structures are visited over time. After a few hundred generations, this trend stabilizes, the effect of the initialization diminishes, and there are no differences between GE and GP.

In summary, GP is not able to preserve the dense tree structures generated by the initialization method (ramped-half-and-half), but the tree structures become more sparse. On the long run, both approaches (GE and GP) visit the same structures; differences only exist in the beginning of a random walk due to different initialization methods.

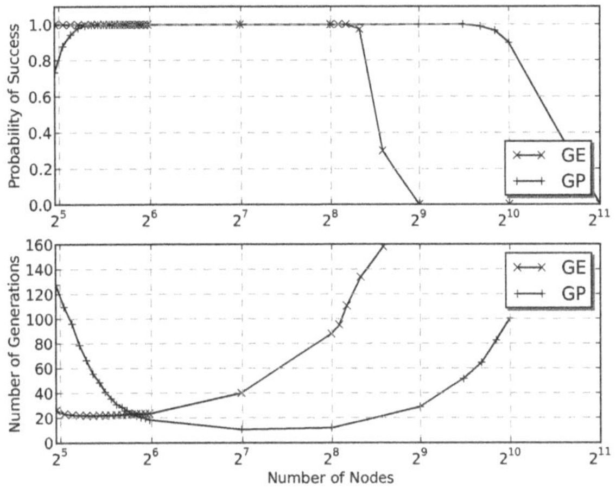

Figure 9: Success probability (top) and average number of generations until target tree is found (bottom) over target size. The depth of the target tree is fixed at 15.

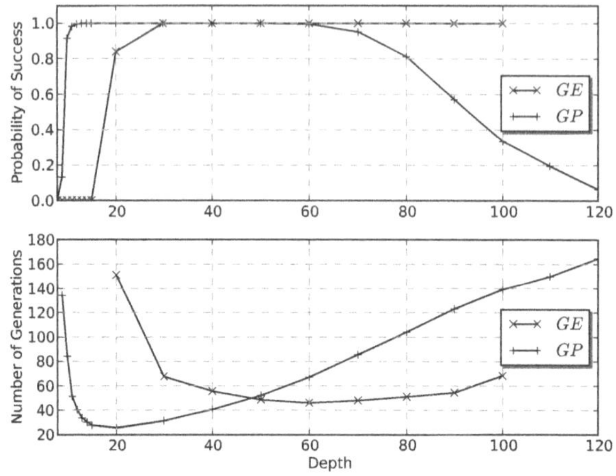

Figure 10: Success probability (top) and average number of generations until target tree is found (bottom) over d_{target}. The size of the target tree is fixed at 511.

4.2 GE versus GP performance

We compare the performance of GE versus GP for the Lid problem. We want to study if GE is affected by the same problems of structural difficulty as GP and confirm our results from random walks analysis presented in the previous section.

For GE and GP, we use the parameters from Tables 1 and 2. As we want to compare search performance, we use a selection operator. With the depth d_{target} and number of terminals t_{target} of the pre-defined optimal tree, the fitness of a solution to the Lid problem is calculated as $f = metric_d + metric_t$, where $metric_d = W_d\left(1 - \left(\frac{|d_{target} - d_{actual}|}{d_{target}}\right)\right)$ and $metric_t = W_t\left(1 - \left(\frac{|t_{target} - t_{actual}|}{t_{target}}\right)\right)$ if $metric_d = W_d$, otherwise $metric_t = 0$ [4]. We assume $W_d + W_t = 100$ and set $W_d = 30$ and $W_t = 70$ [4]. For the experiments, we set the maximal number of generations to 200 and the maximum depth of a GP tree to 512 [4].

In the first experiments, we vary the size $size_{target}$ of the target tree between 31 and 2047 while holding the depth d_{target} of the target trees fixed at 15. Second, we vary d_{target} between 8 and 120, while setting its size to 511. We perform 1000 runs for each target tree.

Fig. 9 compares the GE and GP success probability and average number of generations over $size_{target}$ for a fixed $d_{target} = 15$. A run is successful if it finds the target tree. For very small optimal structures (sparse trees, low $size_{target}$), GE outperforms GP as it finds optimal solutions with higher probability and faster. For more dense trees (larger $size_{target}$), the situation changes and GP outperforms GE as it needs less number of generations to find the optimal solutions and is able to solve problems where the optimal solutions have a larger structural size. The results indicate that GP covers a larger area where optimal solution structures can be found. For $size_{target} \gtrsim 500$, GE fails finding optimal solutions. In summary, for $d_{target} = 15$, GE outperforms GP if the target tree is very small; for medium sized trees ($50 \lesssim size_{target} \lesssim 500$), both GE and GP find the optimal tree; for larger trees ($size_{target} \gtrsim 500$), GP outperforms GE.

Analogously, Fig. 10 plots the success probability and average number of generations over d_{target} for $size_{target} = 511$. Both GE and GP are not able to solve the problem if the target tree is the full tree ($d_{target} = 8$). For slightly deeper target trees ($8 < d_{target} < 20$), GP is able to find the optimal tree, whereas GE still fails. For $20 \lesssim d_{target} \lesssim 80$, GE as well as GP are able to find the optimal solution. For very deep target trees ($d_{target} \gtrsim 60$), only GE can find optimal solutions. The results for the number of generations are analogous, as for $d_{target} \gtrsim 50$, GE needs less generations than GP.

In summary, GE outperforms GP if optimal solutions require very narrow tree structures. On the other side, in a specific depth range, for more dense or fuller tree structures, GP outperforms GE. The performance results are in accordance with the random walk results where a GP random walk visits more dense structures in comparison to GE (compare 99% percentile in Fig. 5).

5. DISCUSSION

The results of our random walk experiments reveal that with increased number of generations existing differences between visited structures of GP and GE disappear. At the beginning of a random walk, GE has a bias towards small and sparse individuals. A reason for this bias lies in the low number of codons used in GE in the first generations. With 10 codons, only trees with a maximum size of 9 can be encoded. During the random walk, solutions with more codons are created by recombination and duplication leading to a higher probability of finding tree structures with greater size.

Due to the use of a grammar allowing only binary trees (Fig. 4) together with the GE mapping process, random GE solutions consist with a probability of 50% of only one terminal. All solutions where $x_7^{g,bin} = 1$ decode to a tree with only one node. Therefore, using GE for solving binary tree problems leads to a non-uniform redundant representation overrepresenting very small tree structures. Nevertheless, GE shows similar performance to GP for larger tree sizes. This can be attributed to the used search operators (including duplication) and the mapping-process. As not all genetic material is used in every single mapping-process, a large amount of unused material can exist in a GE individual. With a simple bit-flipping mutation, this genetic material can be reactivated with the effect of a totally different phenotype. This behavior of GE is in accordance with the neutral theory [8], which assumes that the random fixation of neutral mutations is a driving force of molecular evolution.

Our results for the Lid problem [4] reveal differences between GE and GP performance depending on the structure of the target solution. GP performance is high, if the optimal solution requires small and not deep tree structures. GE performance is high, if the optimal solution requires very sparse and deep trees. One explanation of the differences is the non-uniform GE representation. The probability of a random GE solution to encode a tree of size one is 50%, whereas full trees are encoded with much lower probability. For example, a full tree of depth two can only be encoded by a genotype which selects the production rules in the order 0-0-1-1-0-1-1 (for the decoding rules see Fig. 4). Thus, the probability of a random GE solution encoding a full tree is only $0.5^7 = 0,78\%$. Thus, fuller tree structures are more difficult to find for GE as such structures are encoded by a lower number of genotypes. In contrast, sparse or very narrow trees are overrepresented by the GE representation making it more likely to find such optimal solutions.

6. CONCLUSIONS

This work studies the structural difficulty of GE. Structural difficulty is a result of a bias of the tree construction process. Search performance depends on the structure of the optimal solution and there are regions in the search space of tree structures that are not accessible by standard GP approaches [6]. We follow two different approaches to study the bias/structural difficulty of GE. First, we perform random walks on binary tree structures. Second, we compare GE and GP performance for the Lid problem.

We find differences in the bias between GP and GE. The random walk experiments for binary trees reveal that GE has a stronger bias towards narrow tree structures than GP. In exchange, a random GP walk finds more dense tree structures. Furthermore, although the used initialization method leads to an overrepresentation of some tree types (GP with ramped-half-and-half creates more dense trees whereas GE creates sparser trees) on the long run there are no differences between GE and GP.

For the Lid problem, GE outperforms GP if optimal solutions require very narrow and deep tree structures. For a specific depth range, if the target tree is very dense or full, GP outperforms GE. The performance results are in accordance with the random walk results where a GP random walk visits more dense structures in comparison to GE.

7. REFERENCES

[1] R. A. Caruana and J. D. Schaffer. Representation and hidden bias: Gray vs. binary coding for genetic algorithms. In *Proceedings of the 5th International Conference on Machine Learning*, pages 153–161, Los Altos, CA, June 1989. Morgan Kaufmann Publishers.

[2] J. M. Daida. Limits to expression in genetic programming: Lattice-aggregate modeling. In D. B. F. et al, editor, *Proceedings of the 2002 Congress on Evolutionary Computation CEC2002*, pages 273–278. IEEE Press, 2002.

[3] J. M. Daida and A. M. Hilss. Identifying structural mechanisms in standard genetic programming. In E. Cantú-Paz, J. A. Foster, K. Deb, D. Davis, R. Roy, U.-M. O'Reilly, H.-G. Beyer, R. Standish, G. Kendall, S. Wilson, M. Harman, J. Wegener, D. Dasgupta, M. A. Potter, A. C. Schultz, K. Dowsland, N. Jonoska, and J. Miller, editors, *Genetic and Evolutionary Computation – GECCO-2003*, volume 2724 of *LNCS*, pages 1639–1651, Chicago, 2003. Springer-Verlag.

[4] J. M. Daida, H. Li, R. Tang, and A. M. Hilss. What makes a problem GP-hard? validating a hypothesis of structural causes. In E. Cantú-Paz, J. A. Foster, K. Deb, D. Davis, R. Roy, U.-M. O'Reilly, H.-G. Beyer, R. Standish, G. Kendall, S. Wilson, M. Harman, J. Wegener, D. Dasgupta, M. A. Potter, A. C. Schultz, K. Dowsland, N. Jonoska, and J. Miller, editors, *Genetic and Evolutionary Computation – GECCO-2003*, pages 1665–1677, Berlin, 2003. Springer-Verlag.

[5] D. E. Goldberg, B. Korb, and K. Deb. Messy genetic algorithms: Motivation, analysis, and first results. *Complex Systems*, 3(5):493–530, 1989.

[6] N. X. Hoai, R. I. B. McKay, and D. Essam. Representation and structural difficulty in genetic programming. *IEEE Transactions on Evolutionary Computation*, 10(2):157–166, Apr. 2006.

[7] M. Keijzer, C. Ryan, M. O'Neill, M. Cattolico, and V. Babovic. Ripple crossover in genetic programming. In J. F. Miller, M. Tomassini, P. L. Lanzi, C. Ryan, A. G. B. Tettamanzi, and W. B. Langdon, editors, *Genetic Programming, Proceedings of EuroGP'2001*, volume 2038 of *LNCS*, pages 74–86, Lake Como, Italy, 2001. Springer-Verlag.

[8] M. Kimura. *The Neutral Theory of Molecular Evolution*. Cambridge University Press, 1983.

[9] J. R. Koza. *Genetic programming: On the programming of computers by natural selection*. MIT Press, Cambridge, Mass., 1992.

[10] J. R. Koza. Evolving the architecture of a multi-part program in genetic programming using architecture-altering operations. In *Evolutionary Programming*, pages 695–717, 1995.

[11] M. O'Neill and C. Ryan. Grammatical evolution. *IEEE Transactions on Evolutionary Computation*, 5(4):349–358, 2001.

[12] M. O'Neill, C. Ryan, M. Keijzer, and M. Cattolico. Crossover in grammatical evolution: The search continues. In J. F. Miller, M. Tomassini, P. L. Lanzi, C. Ryan, A. G. B. Tettamanzi, and W. B. Langdon, editors, *Genetic Programming, Proceedings of EuroGP'2001*, volume 2038 of *LNCS*, pages 337–347, Lake Como, Italy, 18-20 Apr. 2001. Springer-Verlag.

[13] M. O'Neill, C. Ryan, and M. Nicolau. Grammar defined introns: An investigation into grammars, introns, and bias in grammatical evolution. In

L. Spector, E. D. Goodman, A. Wu, W. B. Langdon, H.-M. Voigt, M. Gen, S. Sen, M. Dorigo, S. Pezeshk, M. H. Garzon, and E. Burke, editors, *Proceedings of the Genetic and Evolutionary Computation Conference (GECCO-2001)*, pages 97–103, San Francisco, California, USA, 7-11 July 2001. Morgan Kaufmann.

[14] F. Rothlauf. *Design of Modern Heuristics*. Natural Computing Series. Springer, 2011.

[15] F. Rothlauf and D. E. Goldberg. Redundant representations in evolutionary computation. *Evolutionary Computation*, 11(4):381–415, 2003.

[16] C. Ryan. Grammatical evolution tutorial. In M. Pelikan and J. Branke, editors, *GECCO (Companion)*, pages 2385–2412. ACM, 2010.

[17] P. A. Whigham. Grammatically-based genetic programming. In J. Rosca, editor, *Proceedings of the Workshop on Genetic Programming: From Theory to Real-World Applications*, pages 33–41, San Mateo, 1995. Morgan Kaufmann.

Cartesian Genetic Programming encoded Artificial Neural Networks: A Comparison using Three Benchmarks

Andrew James Turner
University of York
Department of Electronics
Heslington, York
YO10 5DD, UK
at568@york.ac.uk

Julian Francis Miller
University of York
Department of Electronics
Heslington, York
YO10 5DD, UK
julian.miller@york.ac.uk

ABSTRACT

Neuroevolution, the application of evolutionary algorithms to artificial neural networks (ANNs), is well-established in machine learning. Cartesian Genetic Programming (CGP) is a graph-based form of Genetic Programming which can easily represent ANNs. Cartesian Genetic Programming encoded ANNs (CGPANNs) can evolve every aspect of an ANN: weights, topology, arity and node transfer functions. This makes CGPANNs very suited to situations where appropriate configurations are not known in advance. The effectiveness of CGPANNs is compared with a large number of previous methods on three benchmark problems. The results show that CGPANNs perform as well as or better than many other approaches. We also discuss the strength and weaknesses of each of the three benchmarks.

Categories and Subject Descriptors

I.2.2 [**ARTIFICIAL INTELLIGENCE**]: Automatic Programming; I.2.6 [**ARTIFICIAL INTELLIGENCE**]: Learning—*Connectionism and neural nets*

General Terms

Algorithms

Keywords

Genetic programming, Neural networks, Machine learning

1. INTRODUCTION

Neuroevolution (NE) is the application of evolutionary algorithms to the training of artificial neural networks (ANNs). NE has many advantages over traditional gradient based methods. These include: decreased likelihood of becoming trapped in local optima, not requiring gradient information which can be computationally expensive to obtain and is suited to applications without a precise fitness function [47].

GECCO'13, July 6–10, 2013, Amsterdam, The Netherlands.

NE methods which evolve weights and topologies also have the advantage of not requiring the user to assume a suitable topology, something which is often not known in advance.

A popular general class of techniques which employ evolutionary techniques is Genetic Programming (GP) [22]. GPs traditionally arrange nodes in a tree structure. This tree structure, however, is not suited to ANNs which are commonly arranged in much less limited graph structures. For example, graph structures allow the reuse of nodes, a key property of ANNs and something which is not possible when directly using tree structures. Cartesian Genetic Programming (CGP) [28], is a form of GP whereby the nodes are arranged in a graph structure, making it much more suited to ANNs. CGP also has many advantages over traditional GP, including redundancy in the chromosomes [29] and natural resilience to bloat [27]. Another previous study of applying a graph-based GP to ANNs was undertaken using PDGP [38]. Although PDGP showed promising results, further published research on its application to ANNs is not found in the literature.

This paper reports the application of CGP to ANNs (CGPANN) on a number of benchmark problems and presents the results in comparison to other NE and machine learning (ML) techniques. The benchmarks chosen cover two large areas of ML, control and classification.

An interesting aspect of CGPANN is that it allows multiple connections between pairs of nodes. This artifact could also be present in other NE methods, such as NEAT [41] or SANE [31], but is not discussed in the literature. This behaviour enables CGPANN to evolve each node's arity. This combined with the ability to evolve weights, topology, number of nodes and the nodes transfer functions means CGPANN has complete control over the evolved ANNs. Other possible consequences of allowing multiple connections between two nodes are also discussed in this paper.

An analysis of the utility of the benchmarks themselves for comparing ML techniques is also discussed. There is nothing wrong with the benchmarks, but often their usefulness is undermined because many published methods use slightly different implementations. This raises the questions about whether or not differences in implementation are significant in the comparisons between different algorithms. For instance, when Stanley et al. published their results of applying NEAT to the double pole experiment [41], they used a slightly modified sigmoidal transfer function. So when comparing NEAT to other NE techniques, which do not use their modified sigmoidal transfer function, it is not known if the

Figure 1: A general form of CGP with chromosome given beneath, taken from [28]

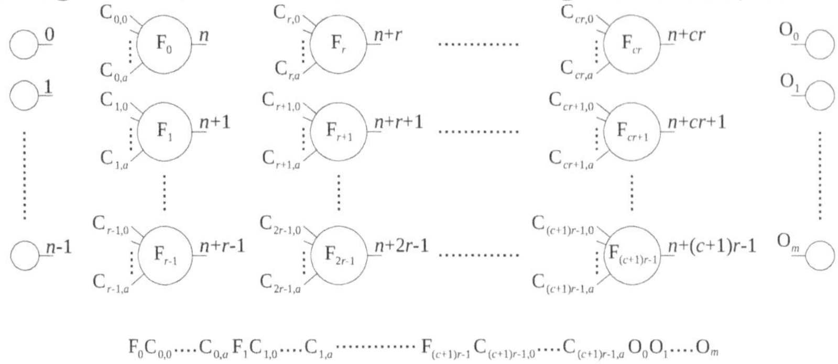

differences between results are due to the NE techniques, the use of the modified sigmoidal transfer function, or both.

2. CARTESIAN GENETIC PROGRAMMING

CGP [28, 30] is a form of GP in which computational structures are organised as directed, often acyclic graphs indexed by their Cartesian coordinates. Each node may take its inputs from any previous node or program input (although recurrent graphs can also be implemented). The program outputs are taken from the output of any internal node or program input. This structure leads to many of the nodes described by the CGP chromosome not contributing to the final operation of the phenotype, these inactive, or "junk", nodes have been shown to greatly aid the evolutionary search [29, 44, 50]. The representational feature of inactive genes in CGP is also closely related to the fact that it does not suffer from bloat [27].

The nodes described by CGP chromosomes are arranged in a rectangular $r \times c$ grid of nodes, where r and c respectively denote the user-defined number of rows and columns. In CGP, nodes in the same column are not allowed to be connected together (as in multi-layer perceptrons). CGP also has a connectivity parameter l called "levels-back" which determines whether a node in a particular column can connect to a node in a previous column. For instance if $l = 1$ all nodes in a column can only connect to nodes in the previous column. Note that levels-back only restricts the connectivity of nodes; it does not restrict whether nodes can be connected to program inputs (terminals). It was later realised however that any architecture (limited by the number of nodes) could be constructed by arranging the nodes in a $1 \times n$ format where the n represents the maximum number of nodes (columns) and choosing $l = n$. Using this representation the user does not need to specify the topology, which is then automatically evolved along with the program.

Figure 1 gives the general form of a CGP showing that a CGP chromosome can describe multiple input multiple output (MIMO) programs with a range of node transfer functions and arities. In the chromosome string, also given in Figure 1, F_i denote the function operation at each node, C_i index where the node gathers its inputs and each O_i denote which nodes provide the outputs of the program. It should be noted that CGP is not limited to only one data type, it may be used for Boolean values, floats, images, audio files, videos etc. CGP uses a $(1 + \lambda) - ES$, the mutation operator and rank selection; no crossover operator is used. The λ value used by CGP is commonly set as four, which is the value used throughout this paper. The connection genes in the chromosomes are initialised with random values that obey the constraints imposed by the three CGP structural parameters, r, c, l. The function genes are randomly chosen from the allowed values in the function lookup table. The output genes O_i are randomly initialised to refer to any node or input in the graph. The standard mutation operator in CGP is very simple, it is point mutation [28]. It works by randomly choosing a valid allele at a randomly chosen gene location. The reason why both a simple operator and a simple evolutionary algorithm are so effective is related to the presence of non-coding genes. Simple mutations can connect or disconnect whole sub-programs, thus this operator, during evolution explores a distribution of program topologies. Also the algorithm navigates the search space using neutral drift. For a more detailed description of CGP and these issues see [28].

2.1 Encoding Neural Networks

ANNs are a natural application for CGP as both are structured using directed acyclic graphs. CGP can also evolve cyclic graphs as used in recurrent ANNs. When CGPANNs are used to encode ANNs, the inputs are the same as used for CGP, the connections are also left unchanged, the functions are those suited to ANNs (sigmoid, hyperbolic tangent etc) and the outputs are taken as the output of any hidden node or input node. The only alteration necessary is an additional gene for each connection in order to encode the connection weights, as used by ANNs. These weights are real values within a range specified by the user; set as $[-1, 1]$ throughout this paper.

As a direct result of the encoding method used by CGPANN it is possible, and indeed probable, that there will be multiple connections between two nodes. This possibly novel behaviour is due to the fact that the inputs to each node are evolved and no interference is made to ensure they do not connect to the same node multiple times. The presence of these multiple connections has three consequences. The first is that the maximum effective weight range set by the user (often $[-1, 1]$) can be exceeded. This is due to the multiple connections between nodes being equivalent to one connection with the sum of the weights, see Figure 2. Secondly, having multiple connections between two nodes results in less connections to other nodes; this has the effect of variable arity, again see Figure 2. Thirdly having multiple connections between nodes could create resilience to future mutations, as removing one connection does not remove the

Figure 2: Depiction that multiple inter-node connections (above) can be simplified as one (below)

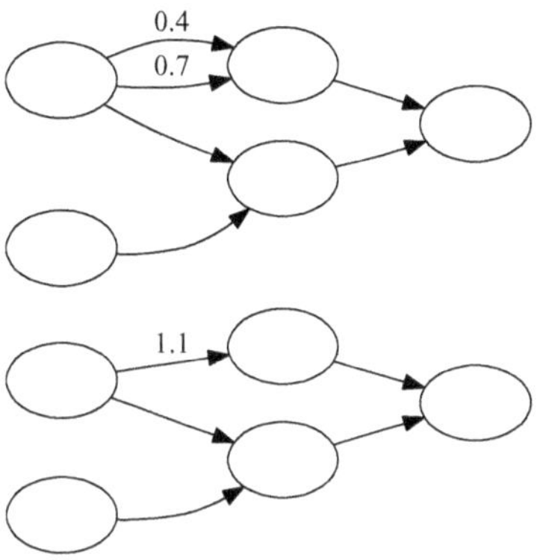

effect of the previous node on the latter. This ability to have multiple connections between nodes maybe possible in many NE methods which evolve topologies. However methods such as NEAT [42] or SAIN [31], which appear may be able to evolve multiple connections between nodes unless actively prevented, do not discuss the matter.

The user defined basic parameters which govern the operation of a CGPANN are: maximum number of generations, mutation percentage, maximum number of nodes (i.e. colummns with rows set to one), connection weight range and maximum arity. Other parameters can also include: rows and columns, "levels-back" and transfer functions. In this paper, for simplicity, only the basic parameters are used with the "levels-back" parameter set as the number of nodes (columns). Although CGPANN (and CGP in general) can use many types of mutation operands, a simple point mutation is used throughout this paper; where each gene in the chromosome is changed to a new random value with a given probability.

In summary the advantages of evolving ANN using CGPANN include: MIMO networks, recurrent and non-recurrent networks, evolvable topology, evolvable arity, evolvable transfer functions, evolvable weights, no bloat and the presence of redundancy in the chromosomes aiding evolution.

3. RECENT RELATED WORK

To date there is very little published work on the application of CGP to ANN; what has been published we discuss here.

M. Khan et al. published [19, 20] describing the application of CGPANN to both the single and double pole balancing benchmarks. They showed remarkable results for both tasks, solving them faster (in terms of number of evaluations) than any other NE published method. M. Khan et al. also implemented a recurrent form of CGPANN [18] which was again applied to the double pole balancing problem. The reason for repeating the double pole balancing benchmark is to offer a fairer comparison with other published results. When M. Khan et al. conducted their experiments they allowed the transfer functions used within the nodes to also be evolved, by choosing between sigmoid and hyperbolic tangent. Although the ability to evolve the transfer function, along with the weights and topology, is one of the many advantages of NE methods, it was not used by other reported NE methods and so weakens the comparison. They also used a "bang-bang" control system, whereas most reported results for this benchmark use a continuous force. Additionally they added connection switches to the connections between nodes; these switches were evolved within the chromosomes as binary values indicating whether a connection is made between the nodes. Although this additional gene may be advantageous to the evolutionary process, this paper uses CGP in its original form; further alterations will be researched in the future.

Another application of CGP to ANN was published by G. Khan et el. who used CGP to evolve a multi-chromosome representation of realistic neurons to create neural networks which more closely mimic the biological brain. Their method was applied to the classic artificial intelligence problems wumpus world [16] and the game of checkers [17], where they showed their solution was capable of continuous learning within the task environment.

4. THE BENCHMARKS

The three benchmarks chosen to assess the effectiveness of CGPANN cover a range of different applications to which NE can be applied. They include the well known double[1] pole balancing [45], the relatively new ball throwing [21] and Cancer1 taken from the Proben1 set of benchmarks for ANNs [37]. The first two benchmarks are control based problems. The double pole balancing is a continuous (balancing) single output control problem and the ball throwing is a multiple output problem which includes a one off event (throwing) aspect. The final benchmark is a popular, and well used, classification problem.

4.1 Double Pole Balancing

The double pole balancing benchmark has been used for many decades in the artificial intelligence literature and is simply the task of balancing two poles attached to a cart with all components limited to one degree of freedom; see [45] for diagrams and additional information. The equations which govern the dynamics of the double pole experiment are given in Equations 1, 2, 3 and 4 with the symbol definitions and values given below.

$$\ddot{x} = \frac{F - \mu_c sgn(\dot{x}) + \sum_{i=1}^{N} \tilde{F}_i}{M + \sum_{i=1}^{N} \tilde{m}_i} \tag{1}$$

$$\ddot{\theta}_i = -\frac{3}{4l_i}\left(\ddot{x}\cos\theta_i + g\sin\theta_i + \frac{\mu_{pi}\dot{\theta}_i}{m_i l_i}\right) \tag{2}$$

$$\tilde{F}_i = m_i l_i \dot{\theta}_i^2 \sin\theta_i + \frac{3}{4} m_i \cos\theta_i \left(\frac{\mu_{pi}\dot{\theta}_i}{m_i l_i} + g\sin\theta_i\right) \tag{3}$$

$$\tilde{m}_i = m_i\left(1 - \frac{3}{4}\cos^2\theta_i\right) \tag{4}$$

Where x is the carts position limited to $[-2.4, 2.4]m$, θ_i is the ith poles angle from virtual limited to $[-36, 36]deg$, F is the force applied to the cart limited to $[-10, 10]N$, l_i is the half length of the ith pole with $l_1 = 0.5m$ and $l_2 = 0.05m$, M is the cart mass set as $1.0kg$, m_i is the mass of the ith pole with $m_1 = 0.1kg$ and $m_2 = 0.01kg$, μ_c is the cart-track

[1]There is also a single pole version but it appears be less standardised (different initial conditions, parameters and limits are used), and is also very easy for modern methods to solve, weakening any comparison.

friction set as 0.0005 and μ_{pi} is the ith pole-cart friction set as 0.000002.

The simulations are run using Euler integration with a time step of $0.01sec$ and the controller outputs were updated every $0.02sec$; the simulations were run for 100000 time steps in each experiment. The simulations were always initialised with the cart in the center of the track, the longer pole at $1deg$ from vertical and the short pole at vertical.

The fitness of the solutions are determined by the number of time steps that the controller can keep both poles within the range $[-36, 36]deg$. Some implementations used by others, such as [5], penalise rapid swinging[2]; this was not used in the experiments presented here. The inputs to the controller were the usual cart position, cart velocity, both pole positions and both pole velocities.

The inputs are scaled to be within $[-1, 1]$ by assuming their values would always be in the following ranges: cart position $[-2.4, 2.4]m$, cart velocity $[-1.5, 1.5]m/s$, pole positions $[-36, 36]deg$ and pole velocities $[-115, 115]deg/s$.

The output of the controller is also in the range $[-1, 1]$ which is then scaled to be between $[-10, 10]N$ in what is commonly called "continuous force" as opposed to the binary "bang-bang force" which is sometimes used. A restriction placed on the controller, also used by [6, 8, 45], is to limit the magnitude of the applied force to always be greater than $\frac{1}{256} \times 10N$; this ensures the controller cannot position the poles to be almost at the point of balance and then do nothing until they fall.

4.2 Ball Throwing

The Ball Throwing experiment is taken from [21] where it was used as a comparison between CoSyNE and Compressed CoSyNE training algorithms. The goal of the task is to throw a ball, initially attached at the end of a swinging arm, a distance of $9.50m$; slightly below the maximum possible distance of $10.202m$. The arm is attached to a pivot and initially hangs downwards under gravity; with the ball located at the lower end. The controller can only *see* two variables: the angle of the arm from vertical and the arm's angular speed. The controller also has two outputs: the torque applied to the arm and whether or not to release the ball.

Equation 5 describes the arm dynamics with the released ball obeying regular Newtonian mechanics until the ground is reached.

$$\left(\dot{\theta}, \dot{\omega}\right) = \left(\omega, -c \cdot w + \frac{g \cdot \sin(\theta)}{l} + \frac{T}{m \cdot l^2}\right) \quad (5)$$

Where θ is the arm angle, ω is the arms angular speed, c is a constant to control the friction set as $2.5s^{-1}$, l is the arm length set as $2m$, g is the gravity set as $9.81ms^{-2}$, m is the mass of the ball set as $0.1kg$, and finally, T is the torque applied to the arm whose value is limited to $[-5, 5]Nm$.

Figure 3 shows the set up of the benchmark with θ and l labelled. It can also be seen in Figure 3 how d, the distance the ball is thrown, is measured. The value of d is then used as the fitness assigned to each possible solution.

An additional constraint is that ω is set to zero when $|\theta| \geq \pi/2$. The simulation is run using Euler integration with a time step of $0.01s$ and the controller outputs are also updated every $0.01s$.

[2]In these experiments [5] also removed velocity information.

Figure 3: Depiction of the Ball Throwing Benchmark taken from [21]

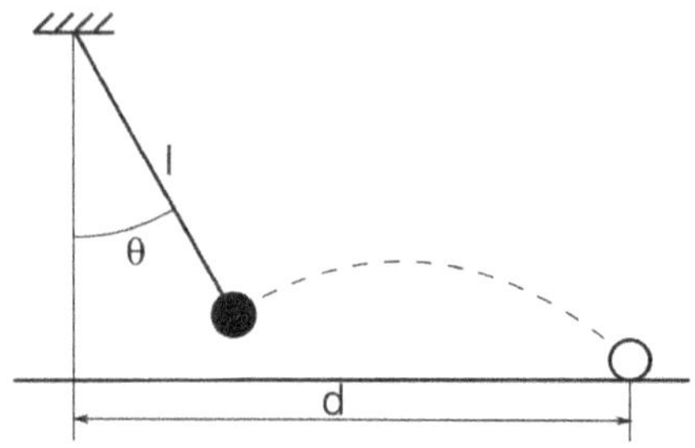

The inputs to the ANN are scaled to fit the range $[0, 1]$ by knowing that θ can never exceed $\pm\pi/2$ and by the fact that ω can never exceed $\pm 5rad/s$ (found through simulation; actual maximum value $\pm 4.4915rad/s$). The torque output of the ANNs is also scaled to meet the range $[-5, 5]Nm$. The ball is released when the release output is greater than 0.5.

As the original paper [21] did not state the transfer function used, it was assumed to be a regular sigmoid. The values used to scale the inputs into a $[0, 1]$ range were also not provided by the original paper and so logical choices were made.

4.3 Proben1: Cancer1

The Proben1 [37] document is a collection of many, mainly real world, classification benchmark problems for ANNs; along with best practices concerning how to report and compare results. Cancer1 is one of the fifteen classification benchmark problems and was originally constructed at the University of Wisconsin Hospital [24]; the '1' refers to the permutation of the data as described in [37].

There are a total 699 entries in the breast cancer data set each with the following details (scaled between $[0, 1]$): clump thickness, uniformity of cell size, uniformity of cell shape, marginal adhesion, single epithelial cell size, bare nuclei, bland chromatin, normal nuclei and mitosis. Each data set also contains two classification flags; benign and malignant. The data set contains 458 (66%) benign cases and 241 (34%) malignant. The first 525 entries are used for training and the following 174 are used for testing. In some cases the testing set is further divided into testing and validation so the generalisation ability can be assessed during the search for a solution; this was not done in this paper. As suggested in [37] the squared error percentage was used for the fitness function, Equation 6. Where o_{min} and o_{max} are the minimum and maximum output values form the ANN, N is the number of outputs from the ANN, P is the number of training examples, o_{pi} are the actual output values from the ANN and t_{pi} are the target outputs. The produced classifier is then tested on the test data set, producing a test error percentage which is then used to compare different techniques. The training error percentage is also often given for comparison.

$$E = 100 \cdot \frac{o_{max} - o_{min}}{N \cdot P} \sum_{p=1}^{P} \sum_{i=1}^{N} (o_{pi} - t_{pi})^2 \quad (6)$$

The evolved ANNs have two outputs corresponding to whether the condition is benign or malignant. The output with the highest value is taken as the predicted class; in the case of a draw the entry is classified as benign.

5. RESULTS

When applying CGPANN to the benchmarks, the transfer function was fixed as unipolar sigmoid (Equation 7) in the case of the ball throwing and Proben1 Cancer1 and as bipolar sigmoid (Equation 8) for the pole balancing. Although CGPANN can use evolution to dictate which transfer functions are used, this was not undertaken here to strengthen the comparison with other results in the literature. The weight values used between nodes were limited to the range $[-1, 1]$ for all of the experiments. Additionally for each benchmark the following parameters were varied so as to be suitable in each case: mutation rate, maximum arity and maximum number of nodes.

$$f(x) = \frac{1}{1+e^{-x}} \tag{7}$$

$$f(x) = \frac{1-e^{-x}}{1+e^{-x}} \tag{8}$$

The number of runs was set as one hundred for the pole balancing and ball throwing and as fifty for Proben1 Cancer1. Each run used different initial random chromosomes and was averaged to produce the results presented in this paper. In cases where a run failed to find a solution it was assumed that a solution was found on the last evaluation and the number of failed runs stated.

5.1 Double Pole Balancing

For this benchmark, the CGPANN parameters found which produced the best results were as follows: a mutation rate of five percent, a maximum of one hundred nodes each with a maximum arity of thirty. Using these parameters all of the one hundred runs found a solution in the allowed 16001 evaluations.

The results of applying CGPANN to the double pole balancing benchmark are given in Table 1 where they are compared to other NE methods. As can be seen in Table 1, CGPANN compares very well, outperforming popular methods SAIN, ESP and NEAT, being comparable to CoSyNE and CMA-ES but requiring significantly more evaluations than DirE.

Unfortunately the benchmark used by some of the other NE methods was implemented slightly differently, and so a true comparison is not possible. These differences include: NEAT used their own modified sigmoid function, DirE included an extra unit bias input, ESP used a weight range of $[-6, 6]$ and CoSyNE $[-10, 10]$ (the others used a range of $[-1, 1]$). It is likely that the transfer function, extra bias input and connection weight ranges will have an effect on the difficulty of this benchmark, but to what extent is not known.

5.2 Ball Throwing

For this benchmark, the CGPANN parameters found which produced the best results were as follows: a mutation rate of ten percent, a maximum of forty nodes each with a maximum arity of ten. Using these parameters ninety-two of the one hundred runs found a solution in the allowed 20001 evaluations.

Table 1: Comparison of Results for the Double Pole Balancing Benchmark

Method	Evaluations	Std. Dev	Avg'ed Over
EP [45]	307200	-	-
CE [8]	34000	-	>30
CNE [7]	22100	-	50
EuSAIN [35]	≈ 19000	-	100
SAIN [7]	12600	-	50
-MPL [7]	10583	-	50
ESP [7]	3800	-	50
NEAT [41]	3578	2704	120
NEvA [43]	2177	-	50
CGPANN	**1111**	**1476**	**100**
CoSyNE [6]	954	-	50
CMA-ES [12]	895	-	50
DirE [8]	410	-	>30

Table 2: Comparison of Results for the Ball Throwing Benchmark

Method	Evaluations	Std. Dev.
CoSyNE [21]	10224	-
Compressed CoSyNE [21]	8220	-
CGPANN	**6069**	**5990**

The results of applying CGPANN to the ball throwing benchmark are given in Table 2. It can be seen from Table 2 that CGPANN outperforms both of the given forms of CoSyNE.

5.3 Proben1: Cancer1

When studying which CGPANN parameters were suited to the Proben1 Cancer1 benchmark, the well know curse of over-training was observed; whereby a ANN can correctly classify more of the training set at the expense of its ability to correctly classify the testing set. Therefore two results are presented for this benchmark: the best result obtained in terms of the training error percentage and also in terms of the testing error percentage. Both of these results are given in Table 3, where "Tr" is the best training error percentage case and "Te" is the best testing error percentage case.

For this benchmark the lowest testing error percentage of 1.89% was found using the following parameters: a mutation rate of eight percent, a maximum of one hundred nodes each with a maximum arity of twenty-five. These parameters produced a training error percentage of 2.68%. The lowest training error percentage of 2.34% was found using the following parameters: a mutation rate of one percent, a maximum of one hundred nodes each with a maximum arity of forty. These parameters produced a testing error percentage of 2.18%. For all of the Cancer1 experiments the number of evaluations was 20001.

Most of the results published in the literature, given in Table 3, do not conform to the strict rules laid out in the Proben1 documentation [37]; which weakens the comparison. Of the results which do not follow the methodology of the Proben1 document, the methods used vary and are not standardised. The differences include: size of the data set, preprocessing of the data, sizes of training, validation

Table 3: **Comparison of Results for the Proben1: Cancer1 Benchmark**

Method	Proben Compliant	% Train Err	% Test Err
LM [9]	No	5.5	12.2
MLP [39]	No	-	6
SCG [9]	No	0.2	5.4
MLP [32]	No	-	5.18
RAIC [10]	No	-	5.01
NEFCLASS [32]	No	-	4.94
SFC [1]	No	-	4.43
C4.5 [10]	No	-	4
LLS [9]	No	4.0	4.0
Fuzzy-GA [33]	No	3.00	3.98
CMAC ANN [46]	Yes	0.59	3.94
RBFNN-Kalman [40]	No	-	3.6
BP [34]	Yes	-	3.506
GDX [9]	No	2.3	3.3
RBFNN-RLS [40]	No	-	3.2
LLWNN-RLS [40]	No	-	2.8
AR + ANN [14]	No	-	2.6
SBS-BP-PSO [11]	No	-	2.49
ACS [34]	Yes	-	2.184
CGPANN (Tr)	**Yes**	**2.34**	**2.18**
MFNNCA[3] [13]	Yes	24.86	2.00
GA-MOO-ANN [3]	Yes	-	1.9
CGPANN (Te)	**Yes**	**2.68**	**1.89**
M-RAN [49]	Yes	-	1.72
LP MSM [23]	No	0.0	1.7
LS-SVM [36]	No	-	1.47
MFN [49]	Yes	-	1.38
EPNet [48]	No	3.773	1.376
LSA machine [4]	No	-	1.2
SBS-BP-LM [11]	No	-	1.17
HS [15]	No	-	0.71

and test sets, different permutations of the data set and the fitness functions used. Of the results which do follow the Proben1 document, some split the testing dataset into testing and validation; this is allowed and documented by the Proben1 standards. This validation dataset can then be used to test how well each solution has generalised and is used as an early stopping criteria. An early stopping criteria was not used by the CGPANN presented here; however CMAC ANN, MFNNCA and GA-MOO-NN did use an early stopping criteria.

6. DISCUSSION

As can be seen by the results given in Tables 1, 2 and 3, CGPANN preformed very well on the double pole balancing compared to other NE methods, outperformed both forms of CoSyNE on the ball throwing and performed well on the Proben1: Cancer1 benchmark compared to a wide range of ML methods. It should be noted that many of the methods used as comparison were not topology optimising techniques; therefore decisions including the number of nodes to be used and their arrangement must be made prior to their use. CGPANN, in contrast, does not need the user to specify a topology, and only requires a maximum number of nodes to be defined. Although not undertaken in this paper, CGPANN can also evolve the transfer functions to be used within the nodes; networks containing many different node types could then be generated without increased complexity to the implementation. Therefore when creating ANNs using CGPANN the user does not need to make decisions about the number, arrangement or even type of nodes to be evolved; information which is often not available in real world tasks. On the other hand if a specific topology or transfer function is known to be suitable, CGPANN can then be restrained to these conditions, leaving evolution to only operate on the unknowns; again making it very suited to real world tasks where some domain knowledge is available.

From the double pole balancing and the Proben1: Cancer1 results sections, it is clear that there is an issue with non-standardised use of these benchmarks. The majority of the double pole balancing did follow the same standards, with the exceptions stated. This was not the case however for the Proben1: Cancer1 benchmark. It should be noted that this does not reflect poorly on the published papers, for example, some of the Cancer1 results pre-date the Proben1 document and others were not concerned with the comparison and simply wanted to show that medical diagnosis is an application for a given method. It should be stated however that there are enormous benefits of following the same standards, such as being able to repeat experiments, truly compare methods/ results and then being able to accurately investigate why different methods perform differently on different tasks.

Allowing multiple connections between nodes could be interpreted as another example of slightly different ways in which a benchmark could be implemented; this is not the case. When CGP was originally applied to Boolean circuits [26] it was perfectly reasonable, for example, for both inputs to a two input AND gate to be connected to the same point. As the implementation of CGPANN presented here is CGP in its original form but applied to ANN, no extra criteria was made to prevent multiple connection between nodes. This is an artefact of CGP and not an example of a difference in benchmark implementation. However, if it was decided that exceeding a given weight range was undesirable, it could easily be prevented whilst maintaining the ability of CGPANN to evolve the arity of the nodes'. For example, only the first connection could be decoded into the phenotype, or the average of the weights could be used.

The presence of multiple connections between nodes allows CGPANN to evolve the arity of each node. Therefore CGPANN can evolve the arity, weights, topology and transfer functions of ANNs, everything necessary to fully describe an ANN. It is not known currently whether the ability to evolve arity in this way offers an advantage. It is known however that it was extensively utilised by the generated ANNs, as many instances of multiple connections were found in every final ANN inspected for all three benchmarks. If it is found that multiple connections between nodes is beneficial it could be utilised by other topology evolving NE methods. On the other hand if it is found to be insignificant or detrimental it can easily be removed from CGPANN with no impact to its operation.

The average number of evaluations (or epochs) required

[3]The experiment was repeated for a range of epochs and the best result given.

to find a solution is not often given when ML methods are applied to classification problems. This however has the issue that different methods may require significantly more evaluations to achieve their result. As an extreme, a truly random search given infinite time will always find the best solution but is clearly not the best search method. It is also true that some methods get trapped in local optima and, regardless of the amount of time available, will never find better solutions. A significant advantage of NE methods is that they are much less susceptible to getting trapped in local optima and will often continue to find better solutions with additional time. It is therefore recommended that when applying ML methods to classification probelms, the number of trial solutions tested before a solution is reached is stated.

Between submission and acceptance of this paper there were two publications very closely related to the research presented in this paper. The first is the use of CGPANN on a range of medical diagnosis problems [2] including the breast cancer dataset taken from the University of Wisconsin Hospital [24]; as used in this paper. The second is an implementation of CGPANN which uses the crossover evolutionary operator and radial bias functions within the nodes [25]; this paper also used the breast cancer dataset to evaluate performance.

7. CONCLUSION

CGP is naturally suited to the evolution of ANNs due to its ability to describe every aspect of a ANN; weights, topology, number of nodes, arity and transfer function. This complete description means that very few assumptions concerning the form of solutions need to be made prior to applying CGPANN to a problem. Additionally, a CGPANN can be constrained when domain knowledge is available, making CGPANN suited to real world problems. The results presented in this paper show that CGPANN compares strongly to many other NE and ML techniques; many of which require the user to select suitable topologies prior to training. CGPANN has many of the advantages associated with other NE methods, resilience to local optima, not requiring gradient information and being suited to reinforcement learning, coupled with advantages more specific to CGP, resilience to bloat and redundancy in the chromosomes.

8. REFERENCES

[1] J. Abonyi and F. Szeifert. Supervised fuzzy clustering for the identification of fuzzy classifiers. *Pattern Recognition Letters*, 24(14):2195–2207, 2003.

[2] A. M. Ahmad and G. M. Khan. Bio-signal processing using cartesian genetic programming evolved artificial neural network (cgpann). In *Frontiers of Information Technology (FIT), 2012 10th International Conference on*, pages 261–268. IEEE, 2012.

[3] F. Ahmad, N. Mat Isa, Z. Hussain, and S. Sulaiman. A genetic algorithm-based multi-objective optimization of an artificial neural network classifier for breast cancer diagnosis. *Neural Computing & Applications*, pages 1–9, 2012.

[4] A. Albrecht, G. Lappas, S. Vinterbo, C. Wong, and L. Ohno-Machado. Two applications of the LSA machine. In *Proceedings of the 9th International Conference on Neural Information Processing*, volume 1, pages 184–189. IEEE, 2002.

[5] F. Gomez and R. Miikkulainen. Solving non-markovian control tasks with neuroevolution. In *International Joint Conference on Artificial Intelligence*, volume 16, pages 1356–1361, 1999.

[6] F. Gomez, J. Schmidhuber, and R. Miikkulainen. Accelerated neural evolution through cooperatively coevolved synapses. *The Journal of Machine Learning Research*, 9:937–965, 2008.

[7] F. J. Gomez and R. Miikkulainen. *Robust non-linear control through neuroevolution.* PhD thesis, 2003.

[8] F. Gruau, D. Whitley, and L. Pyeatt. A comparison between cellular encoding and direct encoding for genetic neural networks. In *Proceedings of the First Annual Conference on Genetic Programming*, pages 81–89. MIT Press, 1996.

[9] B. Guijarro-Berdiñas, O. Fontenla-Romero, B. Pérez-Sánchez, and P. Fraguela. A linear learning method for multilayer perceptrons using least-squares. *Intelligent Data Engineering and Automated Learning*, pages 365–374, 2007.

[10] H. Hamilton, N. Shan, and N. Cercone. RIAC: A rule induction algorithm based on approximate classification. Technical report, University of Regina, 1996.

[11] M. Huang, Y. Hung, and W. Chen. Neural network classifier with entropy based feature selection on breast cancer diagnosis. *Journal of medical systems*, 34(5):865–873, 2010.

[12] C. Igel. Neuroevolution for reinforcement learning using evolution strategies. In *Evolutionary Computation*, volume 4, pages 2588–2595. IEEE, 2003.

[13] S. Kamruzzaman, A. Hasan, A. Siddiquee, M. Mazumder, and E. Hoque. Medical diagnosis using neural network. In *Proceedings of the International Conference on Electrical and Computer Engineering (ICECE-2004)*, pages 537–540, 2004.

[14] M. Karabatak and M. Ince. An expert system for detection of breast cancer based on association rules and neural network. *Expert Systems with Applications*, 36(2):3465–3469, 2009.

[15] A. Kattan, R. Abdullah, and R. Salam. Harmony search based supervised training of artificial neural networks. In *International Conference on Intelligent Systems, Modelling and Simulation (ISMS)*, pages 105–110. IEEE, 2010.

[16] G. Khan, J. F. Miller, and D. Halliday. A developmental model of neural computation using cartesian genetic programming. In *Genetic And Evolutionary Computation Conference: Proceedings of the 2007 GECCO conference companion on Genetic and evolutionary computation*, volume 7, pages 2535–2542, 2007.

[17] G. Khan, J. F. Miller, and D. Halliday. Developing neural structure of two agents that play checkers using cartesian genetic programming. In *Proceedings of the 2008 GECCO conference on Genetic and evolutionary computation*, pages 2169–2174. ACM, 2008.

[18] M. Khan, G. Khan, and J. F. Miller. Efficient representation of recurrent neural networks for markovian/non-markovian non-linear control problems. In *Intelligent Systems Design and*

Applications (ISDA), 2010 10th International Conference on, pages 615–620. IEEE, 2010.

[19] M. Khan, G. Khan, and J. F. Miller. Evolution of optimal ANNs for non-linear control problems using cartesian genetic programming. In *Proceedings of International Conference on Artificial Intelligence (ICAI 2010)*, 2010.

[20] M. M. Khan, G. M. Khan, and J. F. Miller. Evolution of neural networks using cartesian genetic programming. In *Proceedings of IEEE World Congress on Computational Intelligence*, 2010.

[21] J. Koutník, F. Gomez, and J. Schmidhuber. Evolving neural networks in compressed weight space. In *Proceedings of the Conference on Genetic and Evolutionary Computation (GECCO-10)*, 2010.

[22] J. R. Koza. *Genetic Programming: On the Programming of Computers by Means of Natural Selection.* The MIT Press, 1992.

[23] K. Mangasarian. Neural network training via linear programming. *Advances in Optimisation and Parallel Computing*, pages 56–67, 1992.

[24] O. Mangasarian, R. Setiono, and W. Wolberg. Pattern recognition via linear programming: Theory and application to medical diagnosis. *Large-scale numerical optimization*, pages 22–31, 1990.

[25] T. Manning and P. Walsh. Improving the performance of cgpann for breast cancer diagnosis using crossover and radial basis functions. In *Evolutionary Computation, Machine Learning and Data Mining in Bioinformatics*, pages 165–176. Springer, 2013.

[26] J. F. Miller. An empirical study of the efficiency of learning boolean functions using a cartesian genetic programming approach. In *Proceedings of the Genetic and Evolutionary Computation Conference*, volume 2, pages 1135–1142. Citeseer, 1999.

[27] J. F. Miller. What bloat? cartesian genetic programming on boolean problems. In *2001 Genetic and Evolutionary Computation Conference Late Breaking Papers*, pages 295–302, 2001.

[28] J. F. Miller, editor. *Cartesian Genetic Programming.* Springer, 2011.

[29] J. F. Miller and S. Smith. Redundancy and computational efficiency in cartesian genetic programming. *Evolutionary Computation, IEEE Transactions on*, 10(2):167–174, 2006.

[30] J. F. Miller and P. Thomson. Cartesian genetic programming. In *Proceedings of the Third European Conference on Genetic Programming (EuroGP2000)*, volume 10802, pages 121–132. Springer-Verlag, 2000.

[31] D. Moriarty and R. Mikkulainen. Efficient reinforcement learning through symbiotic evolution. *Machine learning*, 22(1):11–32, 1996.

[32] D. Nauck and R. Kruse. Obtaining interpretable fuzzy classification rules from medical data. *Artificial intelligence in medicine*, 16(2):149, 1999.

[33] C. Pena-Reyes and M. Sipper. A fuzzy-genetic approach to breast cancer diagnosis. *Artificial intelligence in medicine*, 17(2):131–155, 1999.

[34] N. Pokudom. Determine of appropriate neural networks structure using ant colony system. In *ICCAS-SICE, 2009*, pages 4522–4525. IEEE, 2009.

[35] D. Polani and R. Miikkulainen. Fast reinforcement learning through eugenic neuro-evolution. Technical report, University of Texas at Austin, Austin, TX, 1999.

[36] K. Polat and S. Güneş. Breast cancer diagnosis using least square support vector machine. *Digital Signal Processing*, 17(4):694–701, 2007.

[37] L. Prechelt. Proben1: A set of neural network benchmark problems and benchmarking rules. *Fakultät für Informatik, Univ. Karlsruhe, Karlsruhe, Germany, Tech. Rep*, 21:94, 1994.

[38] J. Pujol and R. Poli. Evolving the topology and the weights of neural networks using a dual representation. *Applied Intelligence*, 8(1):73–84, 1998.

[39] A. Raad, A. Kalakech, and M. Ayache. Breast cancer classification using neural network approach: MLP and RBF. *Networks*, 7(8):9, 2012.

[40] M. Senapati, A. Mohanty, S. Dash, and P. Dash. Local linear wavelet neural network for breast cancer recognition. *Neural Computing & Applications*, pages 1–7, 2011.

[41] K. Stanley and R. Miikkulainen. Efficient evolution of neural network topologies. In *Evolutionary Computation, 2002. CEC'02. Proceedings of the 2002 Congress on*, volume 2, pages 1757–1762. IEEE, 2002.

[42] K. O. Stanley. *Efficient evolution of neural networks through complexification.* PhD thesis, The University of Texas at Austin, 2004.

[43] Y. Tsoy and V. Spitsyn. Using genetic algorithm with adaptive mutation mechanism for neural networks design and training. In *Science and Technology. Proceedings. The 9th Russian-Korean International Symposium on*, pages 709–714. IEEE, 2005.

[44] V. K. Vassilev and J. F. Miller. The Advantages of Landscape Neutrality in Digital Circuit Evolution. In *Proc. International Conference on Evolvable Systems*, volume 1801 of *LNCS*, pages 252–263. Springer Verlag, 2000.

[45] A. Wieland. Evolving neural network controllers for unstable systems. In *Neural Networks, 1991., IJCNN-91-Seattle International Joint Conference on*, volume 2, pages 667–673. IEEE, 1991.

[46] J. Wu. MIMO CMAC neural network classifier for solving classification problems. *Applied Soft Computing*, 11(2):2326–2333, 2011.

[47] X. Yao. Evolving artificial neural networks. *Proceedings of the IEEE*, 87(9):1423–1447, 1999.

[48] X. Yao and Y. Liu. A new evolutionary system for evolving artificial neural networks. *Neural Networks, IEEE Transactions on*, 8(3):694–713, 1997.

[49] L. Yingwei, N. Sundararajan, and P. Saratchandran. Performance evaluation of a sequential minimal radial bass function (RBF) neural network learning algorithm. *Neural Networks, IEEE Transactions on*, 9(2):308–318, 1998.

[50] T. Yu and J. F. Miller. Neutrality and the evolvability of boolean function landscape. *Genetic programming*, pages 204–217, 2001.

Running Programs Backwards: Instruction Inversion for Effective Search in Semantic Spaces

Bartosz Wieloch
bwieloch@cs.put.poznan.pl

Krzysztof Krawiec
kkrawiec@cs.put.poznan.pl

Institute of Computing Science, Poznan University of Technology
Piotrowo 2, 60965 Poznań, Poland

ABSTRACT

The instructions used for solving typical genetic programming tasks have strong mathematical properties. In this study, we leverage one of such properties: invertibility. A search operator is proposed that performs an approximate reverse execution of program fragments, trying to determine in this way the desired semantics (partial outcome) at intermediate stages of program execution. The desired semantics determined in this way guides the choice of a subprogram that replaces the old program fragment. An extensive computational experiment on 20 symbolic regression and Boolean domain problems leads to statistically significant evidence that the proposed Random Desired Operator outperforms all typical combinations of conventional mutation and crossover operators.

Categories and Subject Descriptors

I.2.2 [**Artificial Intelligence**]: Automatic Programming; I.2.8 [**Artificial Intelligence**]: Problem Solving, Control Methods, and Search—*Heuristic methods*

Keywords

genetic programming, program semantics, desired semantics, search operators, instruction inversion

1. INTRODUCTION

The conventional search operators used in genetic programming (GP) make little or no assumptions about the properties of instructions from the programming language of consideration. Essentially, the only attribute of instruction that such operators have to be aware of is its arity (and the types of instruction's inputs and outputs, if types are considered). A common argument for this attitude is generality: by abstracting from the internals of instructions, operators like tree-swapping crossover or subtree-replacement mutation can be indeed regarded as universal.

GECCO'13, July 6–10, 2013, Amsterdam, The Netherlands.

This argument is however strikingly inconsistent with the GP practice, which to great extent focuses on symbolic regression, Boolean function synthesis, and other programming domains with instruction sets strongly rooted in mathematical foundations. These foundations bestow the instructions with formal properties that can be potentially exploited.

Following this observation, this paper proposes a straightforward method for exploiting the property of (partial or complete) invertibility of instructions. This property, shared by most arithmetic and logic instructions, enables us to determine the desired semantics at any arbitrary location (locus) in a program. This ability is leveraged in a new GP search operator that is the main contribution of this paper, and which turns out to significantly outperform the conventional operators.

2. GENERAL IDEA

In this paper, for simplicity we concentrate on the canonical tree-based GP as proposed by Koza [6]. We assume that subprograms (subtrees) in programs can be replaced by independently generated subtrees (procedures). This assumption is not constraining as it is also required by standard GP search operators. Procedures can be executed independently from the rest of a program. Moreover, execution of a subprogram returns a certain result, exactly in the same manner as the execution of the entire program does.

However, let us emphasize that our approach can be likewise adopted for other variants of GP, like Linear GP [1] or Cartesian GP [10]. Moreover, the proposed general idea may be used even in non evolutionary metaheuristics. For example, it may be applied as an operator for generating a neighbor solution in local search.

In the following, we limit our considerations only to such GP tasks in which fitness calculation is based on fitness cases, meant as a list of pairs composed of input data and the corresponding desired (correct) output. In such case, following [8], we may define the *program semantics* as a list of outputs that are actually produced by the program for all fitness cases. Additionally, by the *target semantics* we mean the semantics of an ideal solution (i.e., target semantics equals to a list of the desired outputs defined in the list of fitness cases). Obviously, the closer the semantics of a program to the target semantics, the better it is. Therefore, the distance between the semantics of an individual and the target semantics can be treated as a minimized fitness value. In practice, most benchmark problems considered in the literature define the fitness value in the above way, even if the term 'program semantics' is not used explicitly.

Now, let us imagine that we have an oracle that can tell us what should any given fragment (called *part* in the following) of a program return for a given fitness case to make the entire program yield the correct output. Because oracle's verdicts do not depend on the actual part in question, only the rest of the entire program (called *context*) is relevant. In the case of tree-based GP we will identify *context* with an incomplete tree that misses a single branch (*part*). Thus, an entire program can be assembled by combining a context with a part (subtree). We will say that a context *accepts* a part if the entire program returns the correct output.

For a given context, the list of values obtained from the oracle for each fitness case constitutes the *desired semantics of a context* (*desired semantics* for short). The rather obvious yet important observation for this study is that finding a part (subprogram) with semantics equal to the desired semantics of some context is equivalent to solving the entire GP task, as such a part combined with the context will form the ultimate, optimal solution. In this way, the ideal solution could be created in just a single step. Because it is not always possible (or technically feasible) to find a part with semantics equal to the desired semantics, we are interested here in minimizing this discrepancy. Our hypothesis is that decreasing the distance between the desired semantics and the semantics of a part can at least bring us *closer* to solving the problem.

Now, to apply this idea in practice, we need two things: (1) the oracle (i.e., a computationally feasible method to calculate the desired semantics), and (2) the source of parts which will be matched to a given context. In the next section, we will present an algorithm for calculating the approximate desired semantics for two different domains of problems: real-valued functions (symbolic regression problems) and the Boolean domain (synthesis of logic functions). In relation to the second requirement, there are many possible ways to provide the set of parts to match the context (called *library* in the following). It may be a library of intentionally designed subprograms, a sample of random subprograms, or even an exhaustive set of all programs within certain constraints (e.g., maximal size [7]). In this paper we shall present an efficient and uncontroversial form of library, suitable for working with population-based approaches. Specifically, the library of parts is constructed from all parts of individuals from the current population. Apart from computational efficiency, this approach avoids, among others, human biases — the library contains only code fragments that have already evolved.

3. DESIRED SEMANTICS

In this section we describe the concept of desired semantics in more detail. Firstly, we show the possible types of oracle's answers. These considerations dictate to some extent the representation of desired semantics used in this paper, which we describe subsequently. Finally, we present a simple method for calculating the desired semantics for so-called partially invertible instructions.

3.1 Possible Situations

In general, it is convenient for us to assume that the oracle, when queried with a specific context, returns a *set* of desired

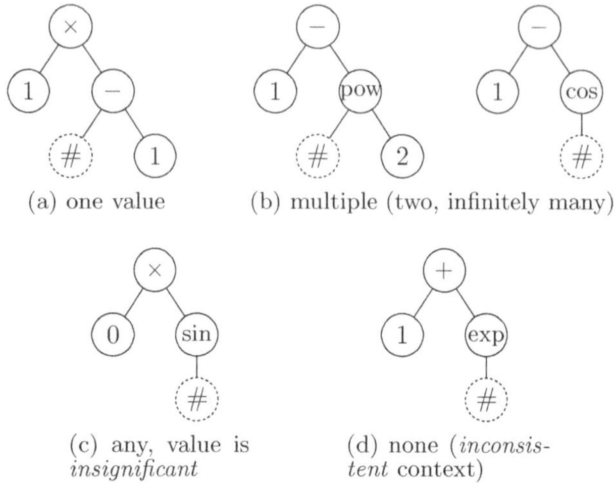

Figure 1: Examples of the four situations concerning oracle's answer for a zero-valued target (i.e., $t = 0$). The subtitles report the number of accepted values. The dotted circle (node '#') represents a missing subtree of the context.

values. The reason for this choice is the fact that we have to consider the following four possible situations:

1. There exists exactly one value which causes the context to return the correct output.
2. There exist more than one such values (either finite or infinite number of them).
3. Any value fed into the context causes the semantics of entire program to reach the target. In other words, the missing part in this context is an intron and does not have any influence on the final behavior of the program.
4. No matter what is fed into the context, the resulting program will not attain the target. In such a case, the context has to be changed to make it possible.

To illustrate the above situations let us assume that the task is to evolve a real-valued mathematical expression which identically equals zero, i.e., its target semantics $t = 0$. For this problem, we can easily design contexts that represent the above categories, shown in Figure 1. The first context encodes expression $1 \times (\# - 1)$, where # is the missing subtree, and accepts exactly one semantics — only by replacing # with a subtree returning 1 we can obtain an expression which equals 0. The next two contexts accept more than one value. However, the context $1 - \#^2$ accepts only two possible semantics: -1 and 1, whereas the context $1 - cos(\#)$ accepts any subtree returning $2\pi n$, $n \in \mathbb{Z}$ (thus, infinitely many values are accepted in this case). In the next example, where the context is $0 \times \sin(\#)$, whatever subtree is pasted in place of #, the whole expression will return zero anyway. Finally, the last example shows a situation in which the resultant expression is always greater than 1, disregard the semantic substituted in place of #. That context cannot be used to construct a solution to our toy problem.

Because the desired semantics contains the oracle's answers for each fitness case, then its every element should be able to express all of the four considered situations. However, the situation where a context accepts many values

Algorithm 1 Calculating the *desired semantics of a context.*

```
procedure DesiredSemantics(c, t)          ▷ for context c and target semantics t
    L ← list of nodes on the path from the root of c
        to the subtree missing in c (to the '#' node)
    d ← t                ▷ desired semantics of an empty context
    for all n ∈ L do
        S ← semantics of all child subtrees x
            of node n such that x ∉ L
        d ← n^{-1}(d, S)     ▷ calculate the desired values
                               using the inverse of instruction n
    return d
end procedure
```

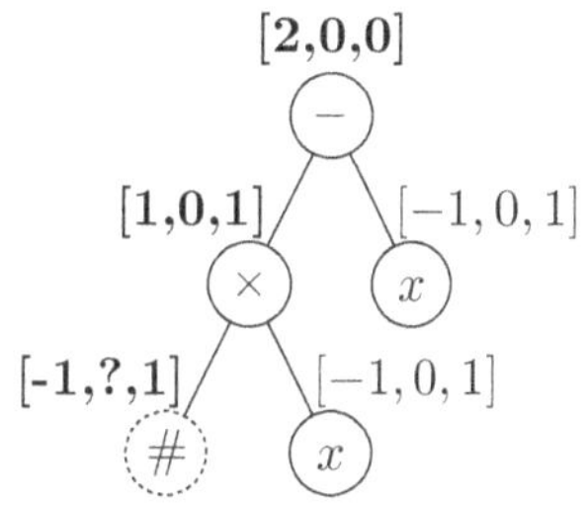

Figure 2: Exemplary context with calculated desired semantics (in bold). The target semantics of a task is $[2, 0, 0]$, the semantics of an independent variable is $[-1, 0, 1]$, and the context desired semantics is $[-1, ?, 1]$.

(in particular, infinitely many) is not convenient to encode. Moreover, this may lead to exponential growth of memory demand and complexity of the required computations by a method calculating the desired semantics. To avoid such problems, from now on we adopt a technically feasible but formally incomplete solution where the desired semantics stores for each fitness case at most one arbitrary chosen value from the set returned by the oracle.

The elements of such *simplified desired semantics* are allowed to express one of three situations (instead of four):

- Only one concrete value is acceptable (possibly an arbitrarily chosen one).
- Any value is acceptable (i.e., 'don't care') — such elements will be called *insignificant* in the following.
- No value is acceptable — such element is *inconsistent.*

The simplified desired semantics can be expressed as a list (similarly to conventional program semantics as introduced in Section 2), where each element of the list is a concrete value or one of two special values used to encode the undefined elements: *insignificant* ('don't care'), and *inconsistent.* In the following we will identify desired semantics with this simplified version of it, which does not require encoding of alternative values.

It is important to notice that switching to simplified desired semantics can introduce certain bias and omit potentially good parts. To illustrate this, let us continue the example presented earlier, where the goal was to evolve an expression returning zero (see Figure 1b). For the context $1 - \#^2$, our simplified desired semantics will contain either -1 or 1 (the other value will be discarded). Similarly, for the context $1 - cos(\#)$, the simplified desired semantics will contain a specific multiplicity of 2π (e.g., 0), and a part returning a different multiplicity of 2π (e.g., -2π) will be treated as committing some error.

3.2 Calculating the Desired Semantics

Let us assume for a while that a method calculating the desired input value for a single instruction is given. In such a case, it becomes straightforward to design an algorithm that calculates the desired semantics of the entire context. The algorithm starts from the root node and proceeds along the path to the missing subtree (#) of the context. In each step, the desired semantics of a subsequent node on the path is calculated. Thus, at the beginning, the desired argument for the instruction located at the root node is calculated (the given target semantics is simultaneously the desired semantics of the root). Then, recursively, all consecutive nodes on the path are processed. For each node, the semantics of all its subtrees (arguments) are known, therefore the only unknown for each node is the quested desired semantics. The last calculated value forms the unknown desired semantics of the context. Algorithm 1 presents the pseudocode of this procedure. In this process of 'semantic backpropagation', the special *insignificant* and *inconsistent* values of calculated desired semantics are directly propagated.

To calculate the desired semantics of a context, all instructions on the abovementioned path should be invertible. When we have a invertible instruction, the inversion of it will have the same properties as an inverse function in mathematics. This means that it must be possible to calculate the desired input for each of the used functions (instructions), given the values of all the other inputs (remaining arguments of a function) and the expected output (the result of the function). For functions that are partially invertible, some elements of the calculated desired semantics can be ambiguous or inconsistent (cf. the example in Fig. 1). It should be also noticed that the invertibility requirement means that the used functions cannot be blackboxes — we must know how to calculate the desired argument to get an expected function value (i.e., we must know the inverse functions).

As an example of calculations conducted by Algorithm 1, let us consider the symbolic regression task of evolving the expression $x^2 - x$ (or, to be precise, of evolving an expression with *semantics* equivalent to that of $x^2 - x$). The only input variable is x, and there are three fitness cases, for which x assumes values $-1, 0$, and 1, respectively. Thus, the semantics of the terminal node x equals $[-1, 0, 1]$ and the semantics of the target is $[2, 0, 0]$. Figure 2 shows an exemplary context $(\# \times x - x)$ with semantics of all subtrees denoted in plain text (here only terminals). The desired semantics, computed for the consecutive nodes on the path from the root node to the missing part of the context are marked in bold. Starting from the root node, $[2, 0, 0]$ is both the desired semantics of an empty context (empty program) and simultaneously the target semantics of the problem. The desired semantics for the context $(\# - x)$ is $[1, 0, 1]$. Finally, the desired semantics of the context $(\# \times x - x)$ is $[-1, ?, 1]$, with the question mark denoting insignificant value. It does not matter what is the second element of the semantics of the missing subtree, because any value of this element is multiplied by zero and always yields zero.

Table 1: Symbolic regression tasks used in the experiment. The columns present the number of independent variables and their domains.

	Target program (expression)	Variables	Range
F03	$x^5+x^4+x^3+x^2+x$	1	$[-1;1]$
F04	$x^6+x^5+x^4+x^3+x^2+x$	1	$[-1;1]$
F05	$\sin(x^2)\cos(x)-1$	1	$[-1;1]$
F06	$\sin(x)+\sin(x+x^2)$	1	$[-1;1]$
F07	$\log(x+1)+\log(x^2+1)$	1	$[0;2]$
F08	$\sqrt{x}$	1	$[0;4]$
F09	$\sin(x)+\sin(y^2)$	2	$[0.01;0.99]$
F10	$2\sin(x)\cos(y)$	2	$[0.01;0.99]$
F11	x^y	2	$[0.01;0.99]$
F12	$x^4-x^3+y^2/2-y$	2	$[0.01;0.99]$

4. RANDOM DESIRED OPERATOR

The previous sections presented the conceptual framework of desired semantics. Here, we embed them into the evolutionary context by designing a concrete search operator, called *Random Desired Operator* (RDO) in the following.

Desired semantics determines the preferred semantic properties at a specific location in a program, but is incapable to synthesize the suitable part (subtree). Rather than synthesizing such a part, RDO relies on a dynamically changing repository of ready-to-use parts, which we call *library*, containing subtrees extracted from individuals in the present population. Technically, in every generation, all subtrees from all current individuals are first collected. Next, semantic duplicates are eliminated: if two or more subtrees have the same semantics, only the one with the smallest subtree depth[1] remains in the set, while the others are discarded. This reduction to minimal subtrees with unique behaviors drastically decreases the library size. There are two reasons to it. Firstly, the majority of program fragments in the whole evolved population exists in many copies. Secondly, different genotypes often map to equivalent phenotypes, i.e., syntactically different program can have the same semantics.

To create new solutions, RDO combines a selected context extracted from a single parent individual and the best matching subtree from the library built anew in every generation. RDO is then somehow similar to the standard subtree-replacing mutation operator [6]. Specifically, RDO removes a *randomly* chosen subtree from the parent, but instead of generating a new random subtree in place of the old one, it looks for a subtree in the library. From the parts available there, it chooses the one that has semantics that is most similar to the desired semantics of the context arising from removing the old subtree (see Algorithm 2).

The *undefined* (i.e., both insignificant and inconsistent) elements in desired semantics are ignored when calculated the semantic distance.

Note that, given the method in which the library is built, the RDO is most likely to insert a subtree from *other* individuals. Therefore, RDO may be seen as a specialized crossover operator (tossing the second child) which performs certain mate selection with respect to the 'semantic utility' of partner's subtrees.

[1]We use subtree depth criterion because we apply the same type of constraint to the evolutionary process., i.e., we limit the maximal tree depth. Other measures, e.g., the maximal number of nodes, might be more appropriate as well.

Algorithm 2 *Random Desired Operator* (RDO)

```
procedure RDO(p)
    r ← random node in program p
    c ← CONTEXT(p, r)        ▷ extract the context by removing subtree r from p
    s ← DESIREDSEMANTICS(c, t)
    r' ← SEARCHLIBRARY(s)     ▷ find a subtree that best matches semantics s
    return tree obtained from p by replacing subtree r with r'
end procedure
```

5. THE EXPERIMENT

5.1 The Benchmarks

In the following experiment, we aim at comparing RDO with standard GP search operators. To this aim, we test them on problems from two different domains: real-valued functions and logic functions. In each domain, we have ten problem instances (tasks).

Symbolic Regression Problems

The set of symbolic regression problems is presented in Table 1. Problems F03–F12 are taken from Nguyen *et al.* paper [12], half of which originate from [6, 3, 5, 4]. The table shows the 'hidden' equation to discover (*Target program*), the number of independent variables (*Vars*), and the range from which they are chosen (*Range*). The number of fitness cases (points) for univariate (F03–F08) and for bivariate (F09–F12) problems is 20 and 100, respectively.

A program is considered an optimal solution if it returns correct (target) values for each fitness case within a $1.11 \cdot 10^{-15}$ tolerance. This tolerance threshold is necessary to handle the floating point imprecision. Without it, even an expression mathematically equivalent to the target program could be found non-optimal (i.e., would have a non-zero value of our minimized fitness function).

The fitness cases are evenly distributed in variable domain(s). More precisely, the values are evenly spaced in a given closed interval from Table 1, with the extreme values placed on the interval boundaries. For univariate problems, this implies that the spans between any two consecutive points equal $(b-a)/(k-1)$ for k points in range $[a;b]$.

In case of bivariate functions the values of both variables in fitness cases lie on an evenly spaced square grid. This, however, may cause problems. For that instance, if the variable ranges were $[0;1]$ for F11, then a substantial number of fitness cases (nearly 40%) would fall on values that constitute special cases, i.e. 0^y, 1^y, x^0, or x^1. This may render evolution unable to escape from even very simple local optima. Therefore, we slightly narrowed the original $[0;1]$ interval to $[0.01;0.99]$. The problem mentioned above does not exist in the original problem formulation with $[0;1]$ interval as in paper [12] because Nguyen *et al.* (as most researchers) have used randomly selected points uniformly distributed in this range. However, we have strong evidence that such a selection of fitness cases is not a good practice, because GP is highly sensitive to the choice of fitness cases. In other words, the precise values of fitness cases should be always considered as part of a GP task.

Table 2: Boolean tasks used in the experiment.

Problem	Instance	Bits	Fitness cases
even parity	PAR4	4	16
	PAR5	5	32
	PAR6	6	64
multiplexer	MUX6	6	64
	MUX11	11	2048
majority	MAJ5	5	32
	MAJ6	6	64
	MAJ7	7	128
comparator	CMP6	6	64
	CMP8	8	256

For univariate problems, the terminal set contains two elements, x, the independent variable, and a constant 1.0. For bivariate problems there are two terminals, x and y, the independent variables, without the constant 1.0. Though the lack of constants for bivariate problems may seem surprising, let us note that it has been shown many times that GP fares pretty well without any constants at all, as evolution can easily come up with the idea of filling in for them using subexpressions like x/x or $x - x$.

The set of non-terminal instructions consists of eight functions: $+$, $-$, $\times$, / (protected), sin, cos, exp, log (protected). The protected version of division returns 1.0 if the denominator equals zero, irrespective of the numerator. log(x) returns 0.0 if $x = 0$, and $log(|x|)$ otherwise.

Let us note that the provided set of instructions allows expressing all target functions presented in Table 1. In other words, for every benchmark problem, an optimal solution is present in the considered solution space.

Boolean Problems

In the Boolean domain, four different problems are studied here: even parity, multiplexer, majority, and comparator. The first three of them come from [6], and the last one is a simplified version of a digital comparator proposed by Walker and Miller [13]. In the following, we will use the terms 'argument' and 'bit' in the same meaning as 'independent variable' was used in the symbolic regression context.

The objective of the *even parity* (PAR) problem is to synthesize a function which returns *true* if and only if an even number of its arguments are *true*. PAR can be alternatively seen as a generalization of the Not-Exclusive-Or function to more than two arguments. We consider instances with 4, 5, and 6 bits (i.e. with 4, 5, or 6 input arguments), denoted as PAR4, PAR5, and PAR6, respectively.

In the *multiplexer* problem (MUX), program arguments are divided into two blocks: address bits and data bits. The goal is to interpret the address bits as a binary number and use that number to index and return the value of the appropriate data bit. We consider two variants of this problem — 6-bit (MUX6) and 11-bit (MUX11). In the former we have 2 address bits and 4 data bits. In the latter — 3 and 8 bits, respectively.

The task in *majority* (MAJ) problem is to create a function that returns *true* if more than half of input arguments are *true*. Note that for an even number of arguments, the function should return *false* if exactly half (or less) of them are *true*. We consider three variants of this problem: with 5 bits (MAJ5), 6 bits (MAJ6), and 7 bits (MAJ7).

The last Boolean problem used in this paper is *comparator*. The objective here is to interpret the input bits as two binary integers, and return *true* only if the first number is greater than the second one. We used six (CMP6) and eight (CMP8) bits variants, which means that we compare 3-bits numbers (CMP6) or 4-bits numbers (CMP8).

In Table 2, all ten problems are shown together with the number of fitness cases on which solutions will be evaluated. A solution is considered as an ideal only if it returns the correct result for all fitness cases.

The set of terminals used in Boolean domain experiments comprises one terminal for each input bit ($D1 \ldots D11$ depending on the number of bits). The non-terminal instructions are: AND, OR, NAND, and NOR. Similarly to regression problems, also for this domain solutions to all aforementioned problems can be found in the assumed solution space.

5.2 The Setups

To verify the performance of RDO, we conduct a series of experiments involving RDO, standard crossover (X), and standard mutation (M) individually, and every combination of two of them. The setup that uses standard crossover and standard mutation serves as control experiment.

For each pair of operators we test different proportions of their probabilities varying from 0.0 to 1.0 with step 0.1, which results in ten different setups with RDO and eleven different control setups. Setups are generally denoted as $O_1 + O_2\,\beta$, where O_1 and O_2 are symbols of used operators, and β is the probability of operator O_2 (i.e., $\Pr(O_1) = 1-\beta$). For example, in the setup X+RDO 0.2 crossover is applied with 0.8 probability and RDO with 0.2. Whenever $\beta = 0$ or $\beta = 1$, the notation simplifies to O_1 1.0 or O_2 1.0, respectively (e.g., X 1.0 or RDO 1.0).

In total, we have 30 setups, with 19 of them involving RDO ($2 \times 9 + 1$, i.e., $X + RDO\,\beta$ and $M + RDO\,\beta$ with $\beta = 0.1 \ldots 0.9$, and $RDO\,1.0$) and 11 control experiments ($X + M\,\beta$ with $\beta = 0.1 \ldots 0.9$, $X\,1.0$, and $M\,1.0$).

The parameters of the evolutionary algorithm used in our experiments, shown in Table 3, are based on Nguyen's work [11]. The parameters not mentioned there are taken from ECJ [9] package and are based on the values originally used by Koza [6].

Every setup was tested on all 20 problems. To arrive at statistically significant results, every setup was run independently 200 times with different seeds of a pseudo random number generator, which give us $30 \times 20 \times 200 = 120{,}000$ evolutionary runs in total.

6. RESULTS

Rather than presenting detailed results for every combination of method and benchmark, we provide a global, ranking-based perspective. For statistical validation, we perform the Friedman test comparing success ratio of all setups tested on our benchmark problems. The null hypothesis of this nonparametric test says that medians of all samples (corresponding to setups in our case) are equal, and the alternative hypothesis says that this is not true.

Tables 4a-c present the computed ranks for success rate performance measured on all 20 problems, and for problems from the two domains separately. In each table, of all setups that use the same combination of operators, the one marked

Table 3: Evolutionary parameters.

Parameter	Value
Generations	100
Population size	500
Initialization method	Ramped Half-and-Half algorithm
Initial minimal depth	2
Initial maximal depth	6
Duplicate retries	100 (before accepting a syntactic duplicated individual)
Selection method	Tournament
Tournament size	3
Operators probability	Varying from 0 to 1 with step 0.1
Maximal program depth	15
Node selection	Probability of terminal nodes: 10% Probability of non-terminal nodes: 90%
Mutation method	Subtree mutation
Subtree builder	Grow algorithm
Subtree depth	5
Crossover method	Subtree swapping
Instructions	*Symbolic regression*: x, either 1 or y, $+$, $-$, $\times$, / (protected), sin, cos, exp, log (protected) *Boolean domain*: D1...D11 (inputs depend on a problem instance), AND, OR, NAND, NOR
Success	*Symbolic regression*: error on each fitness case $< 1.11 \cdot 10^{-15}$ *Boolean domain*: perfect reproduction of all fitness cases
Number of runs	200

Table 4: Friedman ranks of *success ratio* performance measure.

(a) on all 20 problems

Setup	Rank	Setup	Rank
M+RDO 0.7	**8.63**	X+RDO 0.2	11.70
M+RDO 0.3	8.78	**RDO 1.0**	**13.40**
X+RDO 0.5	**8.90**	X+RDO 0.1	14.28
M+RDO 0.5	9.15	M+RDO 0.1	14.58
X+RDO 0.4	9.20	**X 1.0**	**20.55**
X+RDO 0.8	9.23	**X+M 0.1**	**21.30**
M+RDO 0.4	9.25	X+M 0.2	22.53
X+RDO 0.6	9.75	X+M 0.3	23.10
M+RDO 0.6	9.88	X+M 0.4	23.55
X+RDO 0.3	9.95	X+M 0.5	23.85
X+RDO 0.7	9.95	X+M 0.6	24.53
M+RDO 0.8	10.08	X+M 0.7	25.73
M+RDO 0.2	10.65	X+M 0.8	25.85
X+RDO 0.9	11.15	**M 1.0**	**27.18**
M+RDO 0.9	11.20	X+M 0.9	27.18

(b) on 10 symbolic regression problems

Setup	Rank	Setup	Rank
X+RDO 0.4	**7.60**	X+RDO 0.9	13.70
X+RDO 0.5	8.00	M+RDO 0.9	14.25
M+RDO 0.3	**8.20**	**X 1.0**	**17.10**
M+RDO 0.7	8.80	M+RDO 0.1	17.60
X+RDO 0.8	9.20	**RDO 1.0**	**17.60**
X+RDO 0.3	9.25	**X+M 0.1**	**19.50**
M+RDO 0.4	9.30	X+M 0.2	21.05
M+RDO 0.5	9.30	X+M 0.3	22.40
X+RDO 0.7	10.45	X+M 0.4	23.20
X+RDO 0.2	10.60	X+M 0.5	23.40
X+RDO 0.6	10.60	X+M 0.6	23.95
M+RDO 0.2	10.85	X+M 0.8	25.05
M+RDO 0.6	11.00	X+M 0.7	26.10
X+RDO 0.1	11.35	**M 1.0**	**26.70**
M+RDO 0.8	11.70	X+M 0.9	27.20

(c) on 10 Boolean domain problems

Setup	Rank	Setup	Rank
M+RDO 0.9	**8.15**	X+RDO 0.4	10.80
M+RDO 0.7	8.45	M+RDO 0.1	11.55
M+RDO 0.8	8.45	X+RDO 0.2	12.80
X+RDO 0.9	**8.60**	X+RDO 0.1	17.20
M+RDO 0.6	8.75	**X+M 0.1**	**23.10**
X+RDO 0.6	8.90	X+M 0.3	23.80
M+RDO 0.5	9.00	X+M 0.4	23.90
M+RDO 0.4	9.20	**X 1.0**	**24.00**
RDO 1.0	**9.20**	X+M 0.2	24.00
X+RDO 0.8	9.25	X+M 0.5	24.30
M+RDO 0.3	9.35	X+M 0.6	25.10
X+RDO 0.7	9.45	X+M 0.7	25.35
X+RDO 0.5	9.80	X+M 0.8	26.65
M+RDO 0.2	10.45	X+M 0.9	27.15
X+RDO 0.3	10.65	**M 1.0**	**27.65**

Table 5: Friedman ranks of *median error*.

(a) on all 20 problems

Setup	Rank	Setup	Rank
M+RDO 0.7	**8.83**	X+RDO 0.2	12.45
M+RDO 0.6	8.98	X+RDO 0.1	12.63
M+RDO 0.5	9.00	**RDO 1.0**	**13.18**
M+RDO 0.4	9.35	M+RDO 0.1	13.25
M+RDO 0.8	9.38	**X 1.0**	**20.70**
X+RDO 0.7	**9.75**	**X+M 0.1**	**20.70**
M+RDO 0.3	9.78	X+M 0.2	20.85
X+RDO 0.8	10.05	X+M 0.3	22.25
X+RDO 0.6	10.18	X+M 0.4	22.53
X+RDO 0.5	10.33	X+M 0.5	23.45
X+RDO 0.4	10.35	X+M 0.6	23.93
X+RDO 0.3	10.53	X+M 0.7	25.90
M+RDO 0.9	11.08	X+M 0.8	25.95
M+RDO 0.2	11.50	X+M 0.9	26.85
X+RDO 0.9	11.73	**M 1.0**	**29.63**

(b) on 10 symbolic regression problems

Setup	Rank	Setup	Rank
M+RDO 0.7	**6.80**	X+RDO 0.2	13.20
M+RDO 0.6	7.10	X+RDO 0.1	13.35
M+RDO 0.5	7.15	M+RDO 0.1	14.70
M+RDO 0.4	7.85	**RDO 1.0**	**15.50**
M+RDO 0.8	7.90	**X+M 0.1**	**19.85**
X+RDO 0.7	**8.65**	**X 1.0**	**20.15**
M+RDO 0.3	8.70	X+M 0.2	20.75
X+RDO 0.8	9.25	X+M 0.3	23.20
X+RDO 0.6	9.50	X+M 0.4	23.20
X+RDO 0.5	9.80	X+M 0.5	24.80
X+RDO 0.4	9.85	X+M 0.6	25.20
X+RDO 0.3	10.20	X+M 0.8	27.40
M+RDO 0.9	11.30	X+M 0.7	27.70
M+RDO 0.2	12.15	X+M 0.9	27.90
X+RDO 0.9	12.60	**M 1.0**	**29.30**

(c) on 10 Boolean domain problems

Setup	Rank	Setup	Rank
M+RDO 0.2	**10.85**	X+RDO 0.9	10.85
M+RDO 0.3	10.85	X+RDO 0.2	11.70
M+RDO 0.4	10.85	M+RDO 0.1	11.80
M+RDO 0.5	10.85	X+RDO 0.1	11.90
M+RDO 0.6	10.85	**X+M 0.2**	**20.95**
M+RDO 0.7	10.85	**X 1.0**	**21.25**
M+RDO 0.8	10.85	X+M 0.3	21.30
M+RDO 0.9	10.85	X+M 0.1	21.55
RDO 1.0	**10.85**	X+M 0.4	21.85
X+RDO 0.3	**10.85**	X+M 0.5	22.10
X+RDO 0.4	10.85	X+M 0.6	22.65
X+RDO 0.5	10.85	X+M 0.7	24.10
X+RDO 0.6	10.85	X+M 0.8	24.50
X+RDO 0.7	10.85	X+M 0.9	25.80
X+RDO 0.8	10.85	**M 1.0**	**29.95**

in bold is the best (however, not necessarily in a statistically significant manner).

These tables show that the M+RDO 0.7 setup fares the best. Moreover, the Holm's post-hoc analysis (as suggested by Derrac *et al.* in [2]) reveals that the best control setup (X 1.0) is statistically worse (p-value < 0.01) than the best 13 setups from this ranking — only X+RDO 0.2 and setups with RDO 0.1, 0.9, 1.0 are not statistically better than it.

However, there is also clear difference between the performance of setups when considering particular domains separately (Tables 4b-c). The best setups for symbolic regression are those that employ RDO with lower probability than in case of Boolean problems, which may suggest that RDO is not as advantageous in the former domain. The differences are even more visible in the qualitative comparison: for symbolic regression problems, the best control setup (also X 1.0) is not statistically worse than any other setup. The best setup, X+RDO 0.4, is statistically better than X+M 0.3, and following setups (the worst 8 setups from the ranking). However, for the Boolean problems the best control setup (X+M 0.1) is statistically worse than the best 12 setups.

In Table 5 we show the rankings of median error committed by each setup. When considering both regression and Boolean domain together, the best setup is the same as comparing success ratio, M+RDO 0.7. For symbolic regression, it seems more beneficial to use bit higher probability of RDO than when maximizing success ratio. For the Boolean problems little can be concluded, as they are almost always solved by RDO, so the median error is zero and does not differentiate the setups (16 of its setups rank equally well at the top).

Table 6 presents more detailed results for the globally best setup M+RDO 0.7 (the best success rate and the lowest median error on all problems) and the best control setup (X 1.0). The table shows the achieved success rate, the mean generation when the ideal solution was found (calculated only over the successful runs), the median error of the best-of-run individuals, and the time required by a single evolutionary process (averaged over 200 runs). The last column says how many successes are expected if an algorithm would be allowed to run for one hour, starting a new evolutionary run every time the previous one has been completed (with success or not). We find this efficiency measure convenient, because a method that executes very fast does not necessary score many successes. On the other hand, it can be run more times within a fixed computational budget. However, if a method is actually bad, the successive runs do not help much, and this performance indicator will show that. Last but not least, fixing the time budget allows us to take into account the overhead of searching for procedures in the library, which causes RDO to be substantially slower in absolute terms.

To provide another reference point, in the rows named 'best' we present the best value of each objective achieved by any setup. Therefore, each value in each 'best' row may come from a different setup.

Table 6 confirms our earlier finding that RDO is very beneficial for all Boolean problems. For instance, only 1% of runs for the quite challenging PAR6 problem fail. All other runs of M+RDO 0.7 succeeded, while standard GP failed to solve PAR6 even once. For this reason, the efficiency measured as success per hour for the Boolean domain can be even several orders of magnitude higher.

For symbolic regression problems, the results are not so firm. For seven out of ten problems (F05–F11), the success ratio achieved by M+RDO 0.7 is better. However, in terms of the number of successes per hour, this setup can have up to two orders of magnitude worse performance — only for 5 problems (F05, F08–F11) RDO is more efficient than the control setup.

One of the possible reasons for inferior performance of RDO in the regression domain is the way in which the errors, committed by the inserted procedures with respect to desired semantics, propagate through the programs. In the Boolean domain, when a perfectly matching procedure cannot be found (which is most often the case), a mismatch on a single element of desired semantics causes unitary loss of fitness (one incorrect output bit). In the regression domain however, even a relatively small discrepancy between the semantics of the inserted procedure and the desired semantics may translate into arbitrarily large error of the entire program (consider, e.g., the context $(1/\#)$).

Apart from that,we anticipate that the RDO performance for symbolic regression can be substantially improved by using a more efficient implementation of the algorithm that searches the library for the best matching subtree.

7. CONCLUSIONS

The speedup and the overall improvement in quality provided by the presented approach result from exploiting certain properties of a given problem, more specifically, the properties of instructions that form the programming language of consideration. We demonstrated that taking into account such implicit, but often easily available, features can help to overcome some weaknesses of genetic programming, at least in certain domains and applications.

As we already mentioned in Introduction, it is surprising to see that such supplementary[2] and easily exploitable properties are rarely considered in the genetic programming. The "one fits all" attitude prevails, particularly when it comes to operator design, which is puzzling in the light of the No Free Lunch theorem heritage. Therefore, we believe that this innovative approach is an important contribution to GP and that other methods developed in this spirit will lead to essential breakthrough in the field of genetic programming.

There are several directions in which this research can develop. In the variant of RDO presented here, we used the desired semantics in a very strict way, searching the library for the part that *exactly* matched the desired values (i.e., the values that made the entire program return the correct output). However, to exploit the presented idea, an omniscient oracle is not necessary. It may be enough to only narrow the space of the considered parts in such way that the genetic operators can faster choose the part to be inserted into the parent individual. Therefore, our approach can be also applied to problems where the instructions are not easily invertible, which we plan to investigate in the future research.

Acknowledgment

Work supported by grant no. DEC-2011/01/B/ST6/07318.

[2]Supplementary in the sense that the invertibility of, e.g., the multiplication operator is not required for program execution.

Table 6: Detailed comparison of the best setup with RDO (M+RDO 0.7) with the best control setup (X 1.0). The shown best values (in italic) for each problem and each column may come from different setups.

(a) symbolic regression

	Setup	Success rate	Success gen.	Median error	Time [ms]	Success per hour
F03	RDO	0.335	3.9	0.001	4268.8	282.5
	X 1.0	0.680	19.0	0.000	101.9	24014.6
	best:	*0.680*	*2.7*	*0.000*	*101.9*	*24014.6*
F04	RDO	0.185	4.4	0.001	4631.4	143.8
	X 1.0	0.270	30.5	0.174	216.4	4492.3
	best:	*0.400*	*4.0*	*0.001*	*216.4*	*4492.3*
F05	RDO	0.480	4.7	0.000	3042.4	568.0
	X 1.0	0.015	18.3	0.096	278.6	193.8
	best:	*0.580*	*2.4*	*0.000*	*278.6*	*1384.7*
F06	RDO	0.615	3.5	0.000	2760.2	802.1
	X 1.0	0.460	24.2	0.054	122.2	13547.7
	best:	*0.925*	*2.6*	*0.000*	*122.2*	*19369.3*
F07	RDO	0.360	2.3	0.000	3133.4	413.6
	X 1.0	0.070	20.4	0.049	217.8	1157.0
	best:	*0.405*	*1.9*	*0.000*	*217.8*	*1157.0*
F08	RDO	0.440	8.0	0.000	2848.4	556.1
	X 1.0	0.000	—	0.216	287.4	0.0
	best:	*0.535*	*3.4*	*0.000*	*287.4*	*1390.0*
F09	RDO	0.995	2.8	0.000	209.1	17130.9
	X 1.0	0.250	32.2	1.967	409.9	2195.9
	best:	*1.000*	*1.5*	*0.000*	*67.7*	*53207.3*
F10	RDO	0.975	2.4	0.000	439.9	7979.3
	X 1.0	0.190	24.6	0.894	422.2	1620.0
	best:	*0.990*	*1.6*	*0.000*	*310.6*	*11474.4*
F11	RDO	1.000	1.4	0.000	76.5	47052.2
	X 1.0	0.170	13.4	2.578	509.6	1200.9
	best:	*1.000*	*1.3*	*0.000*	*48.4*	*74443.4*
F12	RDO	0.000	—	0.145	13193.4	0.0
	X 1.0	0.005	92.0	1.890	582.4	30.9
	best:	*0.005*	*8.0*	*0.141*	*582.4*	*30.9*

(b) Boolean domain

	Setup	Success rate	Success gen.	Median error	Time [ms]	Success per hour
CMP6	RDO	1.000	5.3	0.000	73.4	49060.3
	X 1.0	0.100	71.1	2.000	553.4	650.5
	best:	*1.000*	*5.0*	*0.000*	*68.3*	*52717.4*
CMP8	RDO	1.000	11.2	0.000	449.7	8005.6
	X 1.0	0.000	—	14.000	431.5	0.0
	best:	*1.000*	*11.0*	*0.000*	*119.2*	*8428.4*
MAJ5	RDO	1.000	3.1	0.000	34.2	105407.9
	X 1.0	0.870	33.9	0.000	206.1	15195.5
	best:	*1.000*	*3.0*	*0.000*	*28.4*	*126854.7*
MAJ6	RDO	1.000	4.7	0.000	97.7	36836.3
	X 1.0	0.360	69.1	1.000	608.9	2128.4
	best:	*1.000*	*4.4*	*0.000*	*87.2*	*41294.6*
MAJ7	RDO	1.000	7.6	0.000	309.7	11623.2
	X 1.0	0.000	—	5.000	768.2	0.0
	best:	*1.000*	*6.8*	*0.000*	*190.1*	*12486.8*
MUX11	RDO	1.000	9.8	0.000	1404.9	2562.5
	X 1.0	0.000	—	334.500	615.1	0.0
	best:	*1.000*	*8.7*	*0.000*	*117.4*	*3147.2*
MUX6	RDO	1.000	3.6	0.000	56.6	63639.3
	X 1.0	0.730	56.5	0.000	382.8	6865.2
	best:	*1.000*	*3.4*	*0.000*	*47.9*	*75164.4*
PAR4	RDO	1.000	4.1	0.000	44.1	81600.1
	X 1.0	0.365	55.0	1.000	557.5	2356.8
	best:	*1.000*	*3.7*	*0.000*	*41.7*	*86394.4*
PAR5	RDO	1.000	8.7	0.000	250.2	14391.3
	X 1.0	0.005	82.0	6.000	772.0	23.3
	best:	*1.000*	*7.4*	*0.000*	*211.3*	*17037.0*
PAR6	RDO	0.990	21.3	0.000	1576.8	2260.3
	X 1.0	0.000	—	18.000	682.5	0.0
	best:	*1.000*	*15.9*	*0.000*	*224.8*	*3153.9*

8. REFERENCES

[1] W. Banzhaf et al. *Genetic Programming – An Introduction; On the Automatic Evolution of Computer Programs and its Applications.* Morgan Kaufmann, San Francisco, CA, USA, January 1998.

[2] J. Derrac et al. A practical tutorial on the use of nonparametric statistical tests as a methodology for comparing evolutionary and swarm intelligence algorithms. *Swarm and Evolutionary Computation*, 2011.

[3] N. X. Hoai et al. Solving the symbolic regression problem with tree-adjunct grammar guided genetic programming: The comparative results. In D. B. Fogel et al., editors, *Proceedings of the 2002 Congress on Evolutionary Computation CEC2002*, pages 1326–1331. IEEE Press, 12-17 May 2002.

[4] C. Johnson. Genetic programming crossover: Does it cross over? In *Proceedings of the 12th European Conference on Genetic Programming, EuroGP 2009*, volume 5481 of *LNCS*, pages 97–108, Tuebingen, April 15-17 2009. Springer.

[5] M. Keijzer. Improving symbolic regression with interval arithmetic and linear scaling. In C. Ryan et al., editors, *Genetic Programming, Proceedings of EuroGP'2003*, volume 2610 of *LNCS*, pages 70–82, Essex, 14-16 April 2003. Springer-Verlag.

[6] J. R. Koza. *Genetic Programming: On the Programming of Computers by Means of Natural Selection.* MIT Press, Cambridge, MA, USA, 1992.

[7] K. Krawiec and T. Pawlak. Approximating geometric crossover by semantic backpropagation. In C. Blum et al., editor, *GECCO '13: Proceedings of the 15th annual conference on Genetic and evolutionary computation*, Amsterdam, The Netherlands, 2013. ACM.

[8] K. Krawiec and B. Wieloch. Analysis of semantic modularity for genetic programming. *Foundations of Computing and Decision Sciences*, 34(4):265–285, 2009.

[9] S. Luke. *The ECJ Owner's Manual – A User Manual for the ECJ Evolutionary Computation Library*, zeroth edition, online version 0.2 edition, October 2010.

[10] J. F. Miller. An empirical study of the efficiency of learning boolean functions using a cartesian genetic programming approach. In *Proceedings of the Genetic and Evolutionary Computation Conference*, volume 2, pages 1135–1142, Orlando, Florida, USA, 13-17 July 1999. Morgan Kaufmann.

[11] Q. U. Nguyen et al. Semantic aware crossover for genetic programming: The case for real-valued function regression. In *Proceedings of the 12th European Conference on Genetic Programming, EuroGP 2009*, volume 5481 of *LNCS*, pages 292–302, Tuebingen, April 15-17 2009. Springer.

[12] Q. U. Nguyen et al. Self-adapting semantic sensitivities for semantic similarity based crossover. In *2010 IEEE World Congress on Computational Intelligence*, pages 4034–4040, Barcelona, Spain, 18-23 July 2010. IEEE Computational Intelligence Society, IEEE Press.

[13] J. A. Walker and J. F. Miller. Investigating the performance of module acquisition in cartesian genetic programming. In H.G. Beyer et al., editors, *GECCO 2005: Proceedings of the 2005 conference on Genetic and evolutionary computation*, volume 2, pages 1649–1656, Washington DC, USA, 25-29 June 2005. ACM Press.

Prioritized Grammar Enumeration: Symbolic Regression by Dynamic Programming

Tony Worm
Binghamton University
worm@binghamton.edu

Kenneth Chiu
Binghamton University
kchiu@cs.binghamton.edu

ABSTRACT

We introduce Prioritized Grammar Enumeration (PGE), a deterministic Symbolic Regression (SR) algorithm using dynamic programming techniques. PGE maintains the tree-based representation and Pareto non-dominated sorting from Genetic Programming (GP), but replaces genetic operators and random number use with grammar production rules and systematic choices. PGE uses non-linear regression and abstract parameters to fit the coefficients of an equation, effectively separating the exploration for form, from the optimization of a form. Memoization enables PGE to evaluate each point of the search space only once, and a Pareto Priority Queue provides direction to the search. Sorting and simplification algorithms are used to transform candidate expressions into a canonical form, reducing the size of the search space. Our results show that PGE performs well on 22 benchmarks from the SR literature, returning exact formulas in many cases. As a deterministic algorithm, PGE offers reliability and reproducibility of results, a key aspect to any system used by scientists at large. We believe PGE is a capable SR implementation, following an alternative perspective we hope leads the community to new ideas.

Categories and Subject Descriptors

I.2.8 [**Problem Solving, Control Methods, and Search**]: [Dynamic Programming, Graph and tree search strategies]; G.2.1 [**Combinatorics**]: [Generating functions]; I.6.5 [**Model Development**]: [Modeling methodologies]

General Terms

Algorithms, Performance, Reliability

Keywords

Symbolic Regression, Genetic Programming, Representation, Grammar Enumeration

GECCO'13, July 6–10, 2013, Amsterdam, The Netherlands.

1. INTRODUCTION

Symbolic Regression (SR) is a subproblem of Genetic Programming (GP) which evolves equations to model observational data [19]. Despite two decades of research, SR still has not become a mainstream technology the way linear and non-linear regression have. GP, as the de facto algorithm for SR, suffers from two limitations. First, state-of-the-art GP implementations often fail to return the original formula from which the input data was generated [17]. Second, the results returned are inconsistent and difficult to reproduce. A user who is not an expert in GP will not likely trust an algorithm which cannot reliably reproduce the same results with each invocation and leaves them to decide whether or not to keep the results. GP's difficulties stem from its non-deterministic behavior and use of random number generation. To become a technology, SR will have to overcome the issues brought on by non-determinism while reliably returning correct answers to known problems.

This work introduces Prioritized Grammar Enumeration (PGE), a deterministic SR algorithm. PGE reconsiders the SR problem as an exploration within an abstract grammar. Working with a grammar's production rules, PGE prioritizes the enumeration of expressions in that language. Starting from simple basis functions, PGE searches by expanding the best candidates into increasingly complex equations. Candidates are selected from a Pareto Priority Queue to balance the trade-off between accuracy and parsimony. New equations are generated from the current best through recursive application of the grammar's production rules, resulting in all possible offspring within one production rule application. PGE extends the SR search tree without the use of any random number generation.

PGE drastically reduces the size of the search space, avoiding invalid expressions and merging isomorphic representations with simplification and partial ordering. It memoizes equations as it searches and discards equations which have been previously encountered. PGE fits and evaluates each unique equations once, fully optimizing each equation form the first time it is discovered. By fitting abstract parameters (placeholder coefficients without value) using non-linear regression, PGE finds the 'best' version of an equation. This effectively separates the search for form, from the optimization of that form.

PGE's foundations in dynamic programming and deterministic execution result in an algorithm which will traverse the same search path when given the same inputs. In doing so, PGE offers exactly reproducible results with the reliability of getting those results. We demonstrate PGE's capabilities on 22 benchmarks documented in[24]. PGE shows good accuracy and returns exact expressions in many cases. We postulate that PGE, in conjunction with standardized benchmark problems, can be a benchmark against which SR implementations can measure themselves.

2. RELATED WORK

Since Koza's initial formulation of GP and SR [19], there has been a plethora of research from generalized implementation enhancements to improvements addressing the issues of disruptiveness of crossover, bloat, population diversity, and premature convergence among many others. We cover material which has relevance to our discussion, though it will necessarily be abridged due to space limitations.

Selection is arguably the most important aspect of GP, determining which solutions continue contributing to the search and which results will ultimately be returned. The Pareto non-dominated sort, or Pareto front, balances the trade-off between opposing goals in multi-objective optimization [5, 9, 33, 21, 30]. Various methods improve the diversity along the Pareto front, and/or maintain archives of good solutions: NSGA-II [2], SPEA2 [35], SPEA2+ [12], and PESA-II [1]. These algorithms all aim to improve the quality of solutions in a population. Age Layered Population Structure (ALPS) [10] partition the population by age to restrict competition and breeding interactions, combating premature convergence.

At the individual genome level, changes to representation, crossover, and coefficient optimization have been explored. Tree-based representation is standard, others include linear, grammar-based [25], and graph or Cartesian GP [27]. Invalid mathematical operations are removed in [11, 18] and restricted by the grammar in TAG3P [8, 7, 6]. Additionally, TAG3P only allows crossover points to be of the same s-expression type. Context-aware crossover [22] selects a snip in one tree and substitutes it at all valid locations in the other parent. [15] extends this to include all possible valid snip replacements from both parents. Semantically Aware Crossover (SAC) [28] biases crossover to exchange semantically different material and Semantic Similarity-based Crossover (SSC) [32] extends this, by limiting the size of material to small, manageable snips. Real-valued coefficient optimization, a known difficulty for GP, has been improved by local gradient search, non-linear regression, and swarm intelligence [31, 29, 3].

Abstract Expression Grammar (AEG) [16], uses several concurrent searches with state-of-the-art GP implementations. AEG replaces functions, variables, and coefficients with abstract place-holders. These place-holders enable different optimization methods to focus on restricted subsections of the search space or parts of an expression. Parameters and restrictions to a SR method are encapsulated into a SQL-like language, providing high level specifications and fine-grained search control. Opening book rules allow each island to be tailored to search a reduced area of the search space, while closing book rules enable AEG to update the constraints on islands which have stagnated. The author states that designing closing book rules is time consuming, were arrived at empirically, and often need to be tailored to the SR system and problem at hand. AEG was shown to make many problems tractable with current techniques [17]. Additionally, almost any SR algorithm can be used within the AEG framework.

On a new front, Fast Function eXtraction (FFX) [23] is a recently purposed SR implementation which does not use genetic operators or a tree based representation. Instead, FFX uses a Generalized Linear Model (GLM) of the form:

$$y = F(\vec{x}, \vec{w}) = \sum_{b}^{B} w_b f_b(\vec{x})$$

FFX learns a linear combination of b basis functions, from $1 \rightarrow B$, by applying pathwise regularized learning. Basis functions are incrementally included and fit until the number of functional bases equals the desired model complexity. The GLM is linear in coefficients, w.r.t. the terms of the summation, though trigonometric, logarithmic, and other non-linear functions are permitted. FFX is deterministic, making no use of random number generation and is also computationally efficient. FFX, however, suffers from two significant limitations: (1) there are no coefficients or parameters within the bases, meaning more difficult, non-linear relationships are beyond its abilities. This issue could be addressed by using non-linear regression and abstract coefficients. (2) individual terms of the summation are limited in complexity to a pair-wise combination of uni-variate and bi-variate bases determined at initialization. Seeding with increased basis functions could become prohibitive as the number of terms grows through pair-wise basis combinations. In the 13 variable example provided, the initial number of GLM basis functions was 7100.

Candidate fitness metrics, methods for comparing implementations, and benchmark problems vary widely across the GP field. Last year, [24] surveyed three years of literature from EuroGP and GECCO GP track, bringing this issue to the forefront of the community. Their aim was to start a discussion on unifying and standardizing the evaluation process in GP. We agree with these ideals and use 22 of their SR target functions for the evaluation of PGE. Further, we believe PGE can contribute to this effort, as a deterministic, base-line algorithm, against which evolutionary methods can measure themselves. We do, however, disagree with the assumption in [24], that results should not be expected to be repeatable, and thus unverifiable by a third party. A non-GP practitioner will not likely use a tool which gives different answers each time it is used. This has been partially addressed by *rate of convergence* (how often an implementation finds an answer) and *cumulative probability of success* (the prob-

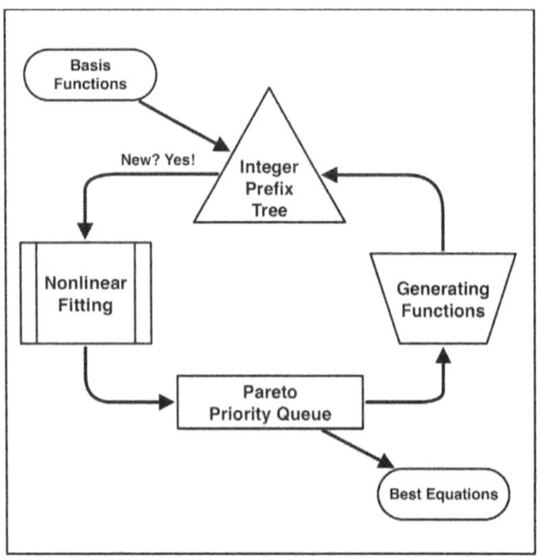

Figure 1: The PGE Search Process

Figure 2: Grammar for Mathematical Equations

```
START -> E
E -> E + T | E * T | T
T -> T - N | T / N | N
N -> Cos(E) | Sin(E) | Tan(E) |
     Log(E) | Exp(E) | Sqrt(E) | L
L -> (E) | -(E) | (E)^(E) | TERM
TERM -> Constant | Variable
```

ability that an ideal solution would be found on or prior to generation i). Both of these methods require many trials. Nevertheless, we agree that the optimum is less obtainable and that a consensus needs to be reached on unbiased methods for comparison between different implementations.

3. PRIORITIZED GRAMMAR ENUMERATION

Prioritized Grammar Enumeration (PGE) is a deterministic, dynamic programming algorithm for SR. Being largely influenced by GP, PGE maintains the parse tree representation for equations and incorporates the Pareto non-dominated sort. PGE diverges in how it organizes, explores, and processes the search space. PGE replaces the genetic operators with grammar production rules and random selections with well defined choices. In doing so, PGE becomes an algorithm offering reliability and reproducibility that a non-deterministic implementation cannot.

Figure 1 shows a pictorial representation of the PGE algorithm. It is presented now to serve as a reference point as the details are unveiled. Psuedocode is provided, at the end of the section, after the necessary material has been covered.

3.1 Organizing the Search Space

Figure 2 is a grammar for mathematical equations and the one we use in this work. A grammar, such as this one, defines the search space which a SR implementation will explore. The terminals, non-terminals, and production rules form the building blocks from which valid equations may be constructed. Equations are composed of these basic components to form the 'DNA' of an expression, a functional genome that mirrors the parse tree for an equation. Operators (+ - * / sin exp etc.) are the internal nodes to the tree. Operands are the terminals or leaves representing state variables, constants, and real-valued numbers. PGE, like AEG, uses indexed coefficients, enabling these abstract parameters to be optimized separately from the search for form.

PGE uses n-ary trees, where operands can have a variable number of children. In the n-ary tree representation, the associative operators can have n sub-trees, flattening and reducing the tree's size. This is a slight modification from the usual binary tree; only affecting the associative operators addition and multiplication. The n-ary tree does not change the modeling ability of the equation, but will effect the trade-off between parsimony and accuracy. This in turn effects the selection operation of any SR implementation, though we do not investigate this issue here.

In addition to the reductions in parse tree size, the n-ary representation eases the design of sorting and simplification algorithms. These algorithms, detailed next, work within the parse tree to reshape equivalent trees into a canonical form. This effectively merges isomorphic equations, reducing the size of the search space, while simultaneously adding structure to the search space.

Reducing the Search Space

The size of the space defined by a grammar is infinite, even when disregarding the increase brought by considering real valued coefficients. This is the result of a grammar's production rules being applicable recursively and indefinitely. Adding to the multiplicity, an equation will usually have several derivations for each parse tree and isomorphs through manipulations with basic algebra techniques. Consider the equation $a \cdot b \cdot c$ (Figure 3). This equation has 12 different binary tree representations, from six leaf permutations and two shape permutations. If we use both addition and multiplication, this number of trees is 48.

As the number of operations, operands, and tree complexity are increased, the size of the search space undergoes a combinatorial explosion. To consolidate this space, PGE imposes operator restrictions, simplifies equations, and partially orders sub-expressions. When combined, these methods only allow syntactically valid equations to be considered, merge isomorphic equations into a canonical form, reduce the overall size of the search space, and create a structural ordering to the search space.

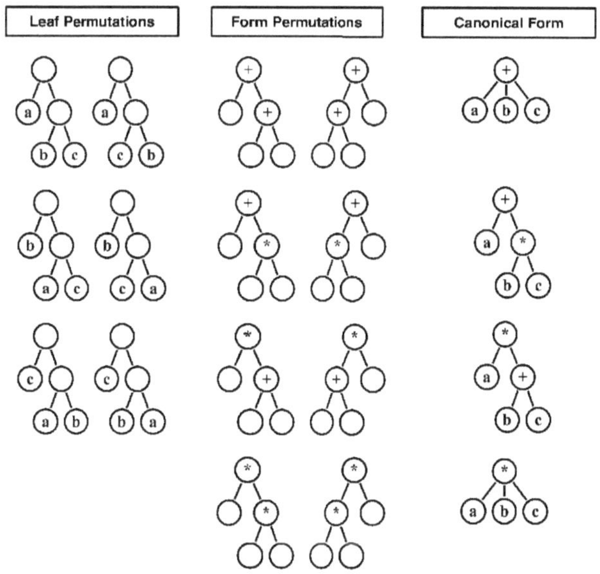

Figure 3: Equation Tree Permutations

Operator restrictions, or interval arithmetic [11], disallow invalid mathematics such as dividing by zero or taking the logarithm of a negative number. In general, we wish to only consider valid equations, however, there may be instances when an invalid equation is an intermediary to a valid equation ($log(x) \rightarrow log(abs(x))$). Though this issues is beyond the scope of this paper, it deserves further investigation.

Simplifications group like terms together ($x + x$), replace sub-expressions which evaluate to a constant value ($\sin \pi$, $\frac{x}{x}$, or $x - x$), and reduce unnecessarily complex expressions such as $\frac{1}{\frac{1}{x}}$. The resulting equations are equivalent, simpler forms. There is debate as to how simplification effects the SR process [14, 13, 26]. Certainly, changing the tree effects the Pareto trade-off which in turn has consequences on selection and therefore search progress. Questions still remain as to how much and which simplifications should be applied, which forms of the equation should be kept, and the overall effects simplification has on the search process.

Despite these questions, PGE still employs the use of the aforementioned simplifications. This is done to eliminate those sub-expressions which unnecessarily complicate equation and the overall search space. If they were not replaced, many equivalent variations of a good equation could crowd out other potential solutions, as they would be selected more often. This would result in the algorithm stagnating in a local optima of the search space. Simplifications effectively trim out parts of the search space which are redundant, and also return results which are more comprehensible.

Partial ordering of sub-expressions provides the necessary machinery for comparing and thus sorting terms of associative operators. In PGE, partial ordering is created by placing a relative order on each building block type. Terminals are less than non-terminals, variables are less than constants, and unary functions are less than binary functions. Since addition and multiplication are the only associative operators, they are the only building blocks affected by sorting of sub-expressions. Figure 3, right column, shows the canonical form of $a \cdot b \cdot c$ with a n-ary tree and sorting. If $a < b < c$, then there is only one representation for each of the expressions, reducing the original 48 to just 4. The savings created by sorting become larger as equations become more complex.

Partial ordering, coupled with the n-ary tree representation and simplifications, yields many-fold reductions of the search space. Invalid and ineffectual expressions are removed, variations of associative forms are limited, and isomorphs are combined, shrinking the number of representable equations that need to be explored by a SR implementation. PGE takes reductionism one step further, fully optimizing an equation in the search space the first time it is encountered and remembering which equations it has discovered thus far. These features enable PGE to discard equations it has already seen and is described next.

3.2 Evaluating Forms Once

At its core, PGE is a dynamic programming algorithm which aims to evaluate each sub-problem once. In PGE and SR, a sub-problem is a particular equation form, namely the parse tree and its parameters or coefficients. The key to evaluating forms once is to fully optimize a form the first time it is seen and to remember the forms which have already been explored. PGE optimizes forms by fitting abstract parameters with non-linear regression and by recording which equations it has already seen with a lookup trie.

Non-Linear Regression

Non-linear regression is not unique to PGE, or GP for that matter, but it is a central component of PGE's ability to evaluate an equation form once. As PGE encounters new equation forms, it fits the abstract parameters using non-linear regression, resulting in the 'best' version of that form on the training data. PGE uses the Levmar C library implementation of the Levenberg-Marquardt optimization algorithm [20]. The analytical Jacobian version is used by symbolically calculating the derivations of an equation w.r.t. each coefficient. In cases were an equation is linear to the coefficients, the Levmar library returns in one iteration by using singular value decomposition (SVD). Training performance is used as the metric for fitness comparison, along with equation size, as is usual when using Pareto fronts. The fully optimized form is later evaluated on unseen testing data to provide an unbiased measure of accuracy.

PGE's treatment of coefficients is in direct contrast to the probabilistic optimization GP uses through its genetic operators. Abstract parameters and non-linear regression enables the separation of search for equation form, from optimization of a form's parameters. This separation, in turn, enables an equation form to be fully evaluated once, removing duplication of effort that GP experiences when using genetic operators to optimizing the coefficients of an equation form.

Memoization of Equation Forms

In PGE, a sub-problem is equivalent to a particular equation form. Sub-problems are encountered when an equation has several parse derivations and isomorphs to an equation exist through algebraic manipulations. This means there are multiple orderings of the production rules which result in the same equation and that each equation may appear in more than one form, as several equivalent points within a grammar's representable space.

Detecting previously encountered equations is the key to the dynamic programming approach taken by PGE. The memoization of form allows PGE to consider a form just once. PGE matches equations by comparing the serialized representation of the equations. Serialization transforms an equation into a sequence of integers by assigning a unique value to each node type. The resulting integer sequence is equivalent to the prefix notation of the equation. Also, since PGE uses abstract coefficients, they are all converted to the same value. This means PGE only memoizes their existence and location.

PGE uses a trie structure, implemented as an integer prefix tree (IPT), for the lookup table of currently explored equations. An equation serial is the key that the IPT uses to return a boolean value, indicating if the respective equation is new or not. The IPT was inspired by the suffix tree algorithm for string matching [34, 4]. The suffix tree algorithm gives log-time lookup for string existence in a piece of text. Similarly, the IPT provides log-time determination, w.r.t. the size of the equation alphabet (terminals & non-terminals), and linear-time to the length of the serial (a sequence of integers), as to whether an equation has been encountered before. If the IPT is reasonably balanced, then it has log-time w.r.t. the number of equations encountered thus far, with worst case being linear-time.

Listing 4 provides the psuedocode for the IPT. The IPT is a recursive structure which is iteratively built as new equations are encountered. To perform a lookup, and possible insertion, a serial S and the root *memoNode* are passed to the *Insert* function. At each recursive call, equivalently each *memoNode* of the IPT and position in the serial S, the first element of S (the current node type) is looked up in a balanced binary tree (*memoNode.next*). If the node does not exist, it implies that this serial has not been seen before, and thus, that this is a new equation. When this happens, a new *memoNode* is created and each successive recursive call will produce a new *memoNode*. Recursion continues until the serial has been completely traversed. If no new nodes have been inserted, then it means that this equation has been encountered before, and is subsequently discarded.

The IPT also tracks the number of total unique visits. This allows PGE to report the total number of unique equa-

Figure 4: Memoziation Tree

```
struct memoNode {
  int                curr_type
  map[int,memoNode]  next

  int unique
}

func Insert(S []int, N memoNode) bool {
  inserted = false
  in = N.next[S[0]]

  // does this branch exist?
  if in == nil
    in = new(memoNode)
    in.curr_type = S[0]
    N.next[S[0]] = in
    inserted = true

  // recursive call to insert
  if len(S) > 1
    inserted = Insert(S[1:], in) || inserted

  // visitation accounting
  if inserted == true
    N.unique++

  return inserted
}
```

tions evaluated, which is the same as the total number of equations evaluated in PGE. Due to the reductions of isomorphs to a canonical form, the reported amount of space explored by PGE is much larger in the original, unreduced search space. To our knowledge, no one has before reported the unique number of equations evaluated. The IPT is easily incorporated into almost any SR implementation, and we believe that it can improve the reporting of the extent to which the search space was explored, as well as the amount of effort expended on searching for form versus optimizing forms.

3.3 Removing Non-Determinism

Removing sources of non-determinism was a central theme to the development of PGE. The aim was to produce an algorithm which would give the same results with each invocation. To achieve this deterministic behavior, PGE makes no use of random number generation. It performs the exact same algorithmic steps given the same parameters and same training data. PGE replaces the initialization, breeding and selection mechanisms of GP. The first two are detailed here and the selection policy is described in Section 3.4.

To determine the SR starting points, GP uses methods like grow, full, and ramped half-and-half to randomly generate initial equations. In contrast, PGE initializes a search with a set of basis functions, such as $c_0 * x_i$, $c_0 + c_1 * x_i$, $\frac{c_0}{x_i}$, and $c_0 * f(x_i)$. These starting points are the simplest functions and are predetermined by the usable building blocks. Instead of growing equations at the beginning, PGE starts with simple functions, expanding them to reach new, unseen areas of the search space.

To expand a candidate equation, PGE uses generating functions derived from the grammar's production rules. Generating functions are the deterministic replacement for the non-deterministic genetic operators, crossover and mutation. Each generation function corresponds to one or more of the grammar's production rules. The generation functions are policies for how to expand and modify an equation's parse tree to obtain functions 'close' to the current one. New equations are produced by recursively applying the generating functions over the parse tree. From a single tree, this process produces a set of reachable equations within one step of the input equation. As the production rules are applied recursively, the current node's type determines the appropriate generation function(s) to apply. Listing 5 shows some example generation functions. *AddTerm* increases the number of terms in a summation, such as $aX + bY \Rightarrow aX + bY + cZ$. *WidenTerm* increases the number of terms in a multiplication, such as $aXY^2 \Rightarrow aX^2Y^2$ or $aXY^2 \Rightarrow aXY^2Z$. *DeepenTerm* increases the complexity of a term, such as $aXY \Rightarrow a(X + bZ)Y$ or $aSin(X) \Rightarrow aSin(X + Y)$.

Figure 5: PGE Expansion Functions

```
func AddTerm(E Expr) {
  E  →  E + c*TERM
  E  →  E + c*N(TERM)
}
func WidenTerm(T Expr) {
  T  →  T * TERM
  T  →  T * N(TERM)
  T  →  T / TERM
  T  →  T / N(TERM)
}
func DeepenTerm(N Expr) {
  N  →  N + c*TERM
  N  →  N + c*N(TERM)
  N  →  (c*TERM) / N
  N  →  N / (c*TERM)
}
```

Variations on the PGE expansion algorithm can be created by parameterizing where and which generation functions are applied to a candidate. By modifying the productions applied at each node, we can reduce or increase the set of equations generated at each node of the tree, and thus each point in the search space. In this paper, we used three different expansion methods. The basic method (PGE-1) restricts the grammar by removing productions which result in non-distributed expressions like $ax * (b + cx * (d + x^2))$. It only uses *AddTerm* and *WidenTerm* during the recursive expansion. The second method (PGE-2) adds back the previously mentioned restriction, using all three generation functions from Listing 5. This results in isomorphs which are too 'far' apart for simplification rules to consider the same. Despite being equivalent, these isomorphic forms can produce very different offspring, and represent separate areas of the search space. The third method (PGE-3) is FFX inspired, but starts with only a set of univariate bases. These bases are iteratively grown into a summation of multiplications by applying *AddTerm* and *WidenTerm*, creating candidates with more and increasingly complex bases. PGE-3 differs from the PGE-1 method by explicitly defining the root node to be addition and placing stricter limitations on the complexity of each term in the summation.

The initialization and generating functions, determine the set of reachable expressions in a SR search. As with the equations themselves, there is a trade-off between space and complexity; how wide and how deep a search can explore. The expansion methods discussed above enable PGE to remove non-determinism at the individual level. To fully remove non-determinism, and give direction to the search, the selection strategy still needs to be replaced.

3.4 Directing the Search

SR seeks to optimizes both the parsimony and accuracy of equations. PGE uses a priority queue to express which points in the search space to expand next. By incorporating the Pareto non-dominated sort into a priority queue, the PGE search can exploit and optimize the trade-off between competing objectives in a deterministic order.

The Pareto Priority Queue

The Pareto Priority Queue (PPQ) is the deterministic mechanism for controlling the search direction of PGE. The PPQ replaces selection for mating with prioritized equations for expansion (selection for survival is unnecessary since all equations are remembered). The PPQ is what its name implies, a priority queue built on the Pareto non-dominated sorting. The PPQ prioritizes expansion towards those branches of the search space which balance size and accuracy best. The PPQ removes the need for generations, survivors, and mating pools, storing all explored equations which have not been expanded. Our experimentations have not shown this to be prohibitive. Consumed memory never exceeded 500Mb, even in the face of hundreds of thousands of unique equations.

To construct the PPQ, successive Pareto frontiers are appended onto a linear structure. Thus, the smallest equation from the first Pareto front is at the head of the queue. The next elements are the remainder of the first Pareto front in increasing size. The remaining Pareto fronts follow a similar pattern. Priority is first given to the Pareto frontier and then to size within the frontier. This is the same as Pareto sorted array that results from the GP Pareto sort during selection.

During processing, PGE removes the top p equations from the PPQ in order to select the next areas to expand. By doing so, PGE selects the p smallest equations from the first Pareto frontier. This gives variation across the trade-offs for which equations to expand, exploiting multiple paths in the space simultaneously. If only the first (smallest) equation is removed, search would progress through the space by size. If p is too large, then overly complex equations are produced, over fitting the data and causing bloat to ensue. Bloat in PGE is the result of good solutions crowding the front of the PPQ. As the search progresses, extraneous material is added to candidates which has little effect on the accuracy of the equation. This has a compounding effect, whereby the extra material increases the number of expansion points of the tree, creating even more similarly accurate expressions with ineffectual sub-expressions.

PGE's selection policy is deterministic. With each independent PGE invocation, and each iteration, the same equations will be at the front of the queue. This means the same equations will be expanded, the same productions will be applied, and the same results will be returned.

Processing in PGE

In PGE, processing follows a deterministic execution path. It uses no random number generation. Given a parameter setting and training data, PGE will execute the same way every time. Further, the PGE search algorithm only has to be run once in order to obtain conclusive results. This is an advantage over GP implementations, which are run multiple times to produce statistically significant results for the number of successful trials. PGE has no analogue to the percentage of successful trials that GP has.

The PGE search proceeds as follows. Initialization generates a set of basis functions for each variable. These basis functions are then memoized by the IPT, fit to the training data, evaluated on the testing data, and pushed into the PPQ. The main PGE loop iteratively pops p equations from the top of the PPQ for processing. Each of these equations is expanded through recursive application of the generation functions. The resulting equations are memoized using the IPT. If the equation has been encountered before, it is discarded. The remaining unique equations are fit to the training data with non-linear regression, evaluated on the testing data, and pushed into the PPQ. PGE continues until a model of desired accuracy is discovered or a computational threshold is reached. Theoretically, PGE could explore the entire space of representable equations given infinite space and unlimited time.

Figure 6: The PGE Search Loop

```
PPQ = ∅
memoTree = ∅
func PGE_Search(int p, GenerationFunc gFuncs,
                Data trainData, Data testData ) {
  bases = createBasisFunctions()
  memoTree.insert(bases)
  bases.FitCoefficents(trainData)
  PPQ.push(bases)
  bases.Evaluate(testData)

  while (check_stopping_criteria() != stop)
    new_eqns = ∅
    for i=0; i < p; i++
      top_eqn = PPQ.pop()
      new_eqns += Expand(top,gFuncs)

    for e in new_eqns
      did_ins = memoTree.insert(e)
      if did_ins
        e.FitCoefficents(trainData)
        PPQ.push(e)
        e.Evaluate(testData)
}
```

Parameters

PGE is nearly a parameter free algorithm, requiring only that the building blocks, generating functions, the value of p, and termination criteria be established prior to beginning an equation search. Since building blocks are generally established by the benchmarks, and stopping criteria are relatively common across SR implementations, PGE has only two unique parameters: (1) p, the number equations to remove from the PPQ and (2) which generation functions to use. This is a substantial advantage over GP, which requires many parameters to be set, a notoriously difficult task.

4. EXPERIMENTAL RESULTS

We evaluate PGE on 22 benchmarks from [24] and compare results with the published results[17, 32]. We used 200 training points, 2000 testing points, and operator parameters established in [24]. We performed our model searches using a single core running on an Intel i5-2500k @ 3.30GHz with 8 GB of memory. The PGE results in Table 1 were obtained from 400 iterations with a $p = 4$. The PGE results in Table 2 were obtained from 200 iterations with a $p = 3$. Source code is available at github.com/user/project.

We compare PGE against published results of the SSC and AEG algorithm described in Section 2. The SSC-T6 and SSC-T7 errors in Table 1 are taken from Tables 6 and 7 in [32]. The numbers are the average absolute error, obtained

Table 1: Benchmarks results for Nguyen problems

Problem		SSC-T6	SSC-T7	PGE-1			PGE-2			PGE-3		
Name	Equation	error	error	error	time	eqns	error	time	eqns	error	time	eqns
Nguyen-01	$x^3 + x^2 + x$	0.0035	0.003	**0.000003**	0.1s	67	**0.000003**	0.2s	131	**0.000003**	0.1s	73
Nguyen-02	$x^4 + x^3 + x^2 + x$	0.0075	0.007	**0.000004**	1.2s	464	**0.000004**	0.6s	218	**0.000004**	0.3s	124
Nguyen-03	$x^5 + x^4 + x^3 + x^2 + x$	0.009	0.0095	**0.000003**	9.0s	2138	0.094944	9.8s	2240	**0.000003**	1.0s	386
Nguyen-04	$x^6 + x^5 + x^4 + x^3 + x^2 + x$	0.013	0.011	0.107365	12.5s	2428	0.000005	12.2s	2361	**0.000004**	3.8s	1308
Nguyen-05	$sin(x^2) * cos(x) - 1$	0.0045	0.0045	0.000068	46.5s	10164	0.000014	278.1s	10032	**0.000001**	450.1s	18399
Nguyen-06	$sin(x) + sin(x + x^2)$	0.0045	0.0035	0.011798	3.8s	2947	0.000446	805.5s	32079	**0.000036**	68.1s	6196
Nguyen-07	$ln(x + 1) + ln(x^2 + 1)$	0.003	0.0035	0.002571	0.2s	131	0.000351	329.4s	25597	**0.000251**	1078.4s	23499
Nguyen-08	$sqrt(x)$	0.0065	0.005	**0.000001**	0.1s	21	**0.000001**	0.1s	116	**0.000001**	0.1s	78
Nguyen-09	$sin(x) + sin(y^2)$	0.0264	0.0099	0.003898	1.0s	868	**0.000001**	60.0s	6519	0.000270	1461.5s	53721
Nguyen-10	$2 * sin(x) * cos(y)$	0.0122	0.0066	**0.000002**	1.5s	1233	0.000004	1.9s	461	0.000004	0.1s	174

Table 2: Benchmarks results for Korns problems

Problem		AEG-T2		AEG-T4		PGE-1		PGE-2		PGE-3		Testing
Name	Equation	NLSE	eqns	NLSE	eqns	error	eqns	error	eqns	error	eqns	StdDev
Korns-01	$1.57 + 24.3v$	0.00	.15K	0.00	.06K	0.000000	.17K	0.000000	.47K	0.000000	.35K	709
Korns-02	$0.23 + 14.2(v + y)/3w$	0.00	3.26K	0.00	113.00K	0.027277	25.05K	0.0055	34.07K	0.1135	2.30K	165
Korns-03	$-5.41 + 4.9(v - x + y/w)/3w$	0.00	804.49K	0.00	222.46K	0.498	0.36K	0.0065	29.00K	0.1245	1.96K	1810
Korns-04	$-2.3 + 0.13sin(z)$	0.00	.59K	0.00	.86K	0.000000	.17K	0.000000	10.95K	0.000000	28.06K	0.093
Korns-05	$3 + 2.13ln(w)$	0.00	.25K	0.00	.16K	0.000000	.17K	0.000000	.48K	0.000000	.35K	2.154
Korns-06	$1.3 + 0.13sqrt(x)$	0.00	.13K	0.00	.01K	0.000000	.17K	0.000000	.48K	0.000000	.35K	0.215
Korns-07	$213.809408(1 - e^{-0.547237x})$	0.00	187.26K	0.00	4.10K	0.031941	8.37K	0.0075	53.08K	0.058696	9.45K	11487
Korns-08	$6.87 + 11sqrt(7.23xvw)$	0.00	5.99K	0.00	11.00K	0.021827	19.34K	0.000000	9.86K	0.069829	54.18K	2034
Korns-09	$(sqrt(x)/ln(y)) * (e^z/v^2)$	0.00	97.24K	0.00	116.81K	0.1855	1.87K	0.000000	7.14K	0.0615	.70K	8735
Korns-10	$0.81 + 24.3\frac{2y+3z^2}{4v^3+5w^4}$	0.99	763.53K	0.00	1.34 M	0.055193	4.42K	0.008	78.19K	0.107	1.65K	2763
Korns-11	$6.87 + 11cos(7.23x^3)$	1.00	774.89K	0.00	4.7 M	0.493	.17K	0.0055	8.33K	0.1195	2.62K	7.794
Korns-12	$2 - 2.1cos(9.8x)sin(1.3w)$	1.04	812.79K	1.00	16.7 M	0.117404	34.34K	0.0065	44.27K	0.124	1.67K	1.056

by selecting the best summed absolute error and dividing by the number of sample points. This was done so that runs with different number of sample points could be compared. The errors in Table 2 here, for AEG-T2 and AEG-T4 are from [17], Tables 2 and 4 respectively. These numbers are the least squared errors normalized to the standard deviation of the output variable. Since the errors in Table 2 are not directly comparable due to differing error calculations, we included the standard deviation of the output variable from our testing data. Equations listed for AEG are total number of equations evaluated before a solution was found as reported in [17].

PGE-(1,2,3) are the three expansion variations discussed in Section 3.3 The reported error numbers for PGE in both tables are the average absolute error on the testing data. The times reported in Table 1 are the amount of elapsed time from the initial invocation of the PGE implementation until the minimal error is reached. Reported equation counts are the number unique equations evaluated when the minimum was reached.

PGE solved all cases were the error was less than 0.0001, meaning PGE returned the *exact* formula in the first Pareto front. Numerical accuracy limitations and minor variations in coefficient values preclude this error from reaching zero. The amount of improvement in error is several orders of magnitude over SSC, demonstrating PGE's ability to hone in on solutions. For the single and bimodal Nguyen problems, PGE solved all but one. For the five-variable Korns problems PGE solves 6 exactly, but did not solve the other 6. PGE had difficulty with nested addition and non-linear coefficients within non-linear functions. AEG required larger numbers of equations for the same problems, so is not surprising that PGE's error values were larger for these problems. Performance, however, is still good on the simple problems and shows they are tractable even with noisy channels.

Comparing number of equations examined is more difficult. AEG equations reported are the total evaluated, while PGE is the unique count. Due to PGE's use of sorting and canonical forms, the number of equations evaluated by PGE would be much larger in an equivalent, unreduced space. It is also likely that PGE overlooks portions of the expression space through its simplifications and search space ordering. We hope to determine the extent to which this happens and further characterize the search space in future work.

PGE is also efficient, not only from the space reduction but also in time. All searches ran to completion in under 30 minutes. Beyond this, the simple equations from both test suites were often found very early in the search, and in many cases finding the correct solution in just a few seconds. These times are comparable to AEG which was reported as taking 1-60 minutes to complete. In comparison, FFX runs very quickly, returning results on 13 variable problems in just 5-60 seconds. As was discussed in Section 2, its limitations render it unable to find many of these benchmarks, so we omitted further analysis. SSC times were not reported, however, the reported errors were averaged over 100 trials. Because PGE is deterministic, it does not have to be run multiple times in this manner, creating a relative savings in time.

5. CONCLUSIONS

As we aim for an algorithm that solves the SR problem we must consider alternative implementations to the usual GP. PGE is a deterministic SR implementation with exactly reproducible results, using no random number generation. PGE replaces evolutionary methods with well defined expansion rules and prioritizes the search with the Pareto Priority Queue. PGE consolidates the space of equations by merging isomorphs with sorting and simplification algorithms. PGE further avoids duplication of effort by considering form once, through the use of abstract parameters, non-linear regression, and memoization. This also allows PGE to separate the search for form, from the optimization of that form. PGE is effective, providing accurate results and returning many exact solutions in a short amount of time. Additionally, PGE only needs to be run once to provide statistically significant results.

As a deterministic algorithm, PGE may be useful for characterizing the difficulty of problems, and the IPT can provide a new metric for measuring the search coverage. PGE may also bring new insites on the nature of non-convexity in SR problems.

We believe further progress can be made by incorporating the use of all-valid s-expression crossover and embedding PGE into the AEG framework to make use of abstract variables and functions. Speedups may be realized, while maintaining deterministic behavior by parallelizing the evaluation of equations. We hope to provide validation on more of the benchmarks as well as differential equations, invariants, and other problems from domains beyond equations which can be represented by an abstract grammar.

6. REFERENCES

[1] D.W. Corne, N.R. Jerram, J.D. Knowles, M.J. Oates, et al. Pesa-ii: Region-based selection in evolutionary multiobjective optimization. In *Proceedings of the Genetic and Evolutionary Computation Conference (GECCO'2001.* Citeseer, 2001.

[2] K. Deb, S. Agrawal, A. Pratap, and T. Meyarivan. A fast elitist non-dominated sorting genetic algorithm for multi-objective optimization: Nsga-ii. *Lecture notes in computer science*, 1917:849–858, 2000.

[3] R.C. Eberhart, Y. Shi, and J. Kennedy. *Swarm intelligence.* Morgan Kaufmann, 2001.

[4] M. Farach. Optimal suffix tree construction with large alphabets. In *Proceedings of the 38th Annual Symposium on Foundations of Computer Science*, FOCS '97, pages 137–, Washington, DC, USA, 1997. IEEE Computer Society.

[5] C.M. Fonseca, P.J. Fleming, et al. Genetic algorithms for multiobjective optimization: Formulation, discussion and generalization. In *Proceedings of the fifth international conference on genetic algorithms*, volume 1, page 416. San Mateo, California, 1993.

[6] N. Hoai, R.I. McKay, and HA Abbass. Tree adjoining grammars, language bias, and genetic programming. *Genetic Programming*, pages 157–183, 2003.

[7] N.X. Hoai. Solving the symbolic regression problem with tree-adjunct grammar guided genetic programming: The preliminary results. In *In Proceedings of Congress on Evolutionary Computation (CEC-2002), Hawai.* Citeseer, 2002.

[8] N.X. Hoai and RI McKay. A framework for tree adjunct grammar guided genetic programming. In *Proceedings of the Post-graduate ADFA Conference on Computer Science (PACCS-2001)*, pages 93–99, 2001.

[9] J. Horn, N. Nafpliotis, and D.E. Goldberg. A niched pareto genetic algorithm for multiobjective optimization. In *Evolutionary Computation, 1994. IEEE World Congress on Computational Intelligence., Proceedings of the First IEEE Conference on*, pages 82–87. IEEE, 1994.

[10] G.S. Hornby. Alps: the age-layered population structure for reducing the problem of premature convergence. In *Proceedings of the 8th annual conference on Genetic and evolutionary computation*, pages 815–822. ACM, 2006.

[11] Maarten Keijzer. Improving symbolic regression with interval arithmetic and linear scaling. In Conor Ryan, Terence Soule, Maarten Keijzer, Edward Tsang, Riccardo Poli, and Ernesto Costa, editors, *Genetic Programming, Proceedings of EuroGP'2003*, volume 2610 of *LNCS*, pages 70–82, Essex, 14-16 April 2003. Springer-Verlag.

[12] M. Kim, T. Hiroyasu, M. Miki, and S. Watanabe. Spea2+: Improving the performance of the strength pareto evolutionary algorithm 2. In *Parallel problem solving from nature-PPSN VIII*, pages 742–751. Springer, 2004.

[13] D. Kinzett, M. Johnston, and M. Zhang. How online simplification affects building blocks in genetic programming. In *Proceedings of the 11th Annual conference on Genetic and evolutionary computation*, pages 979–986. ACM, 2009.

[14] D. Kinzett, M. Zhang, and M. Johnston. Using numerical simplification to control bloat in genetic programming. *Simulated Evolution and Learning*, pages 493–502, 2008.

[15] M.F. Korns. Large-scale, time-constrained symbolic regression-classification. *Genetic Programming Theory and Practice V*, pages 53–68, 2008.

[16] M.F. Korns. Abstract expression grammar symbolic regression. *Genetic Programming Theory and Practice VIII*, pages 109–128, 2011.

[17] M.F. Korns. Accuracy in symbolic regression. *Genetic Programming Theory and Practice IX*, pages 129–151, 2011.

[18] M. Kotanchek, G. Smits, and E. Vladislavleva. Trustable symbolic regression models: using ensembles, interval arithmetic and pareto fronts to develop robust and trust-aware models. *Genetic Programming Theory and Practice V*, pages 201–220, 2008.

[19] J Koza, R. *Genetic Programming: On the Programming of Computers by Means of Natural Selection.* MIT Press, Cambridge, MA, 1992.

[20] M.I.A. Lourakis. levmar: Levenberg-marquardt nonlinear least squares algorithms in C/C++. [web page] `http://www.ics.forth.gr/~lourakis/levmar/`, Jul. 2004. [Accessed on 13 July. 2012.].

[21] S. Luke, L. Panait, et al. Lexicographic parsimony pressure. In *Proceedings of the Genetic and Evolutionary Computation Conference*, pages 829–836, 2002.

[22] H. Majeed and C. Ryan. Using context-aware crossover to improve the performance of gp. In *Proceedings of the 8th annual conference on Genetic and evolutionary computation*, pages 847–854. ACM, 2006.

[23] Trent McConaghy. Ffx: Fast, scalable, deterministic symbolic regression technology. In Rick Riolo, Ekaterina Vladislavleva, and Jason H. Moore, editors, *Genetic Programming Theory and Practice IX*, Genetic and Evolutionary Computation, pages 235–260. Springer New York, 2011. 10.1007/978-1-4614-1770-5-13.

[24] James McDermott, David R. White, Sean Luke, Luca Manzoni, Mauro Castelli, Leonardo Vanneschi, Wojciech Jaskowski, Krzysztof Krawiec, Robin Harper, Kenneth De Jong, and Una-May O'Reilly. Genetic programming needs better benchmarks. In *Proceedings of the fourteenth international conference on Genetic and evolutionary computation conference*, GECCO '12, pages 791–798, New York, NY, USA, 2012. ACM.

[25] R.I. Mckay, N.X. Hoai, P.A. Whigham, Y. Shan, and M. OâĂŹNeill. Grammar-based genetic programming: a survey. *Genetic Programming and Evolvable Machines*, 11(3):365–396, 2010.

[26] R.K. McRee. Symbolic regression using nearest neighbor indexing. In *Proceedings of the 12th annual conference companion on Genetic and evolutionary computation*, pages 1983–1990. ACM, 2010.

[27] J.F. Miller and P. Thomson. Cartesian genetic programming. *Lecture Notes in Computer Science*, pages 121–132, 2000.

[28] Q. Nguyen, X. Nguyen, and M. OâĂŹNeill. Semantic aware crossover for genetic programming: the case for real-valued function regression. *Genetic Programming*, pages 292–302, 2009.

[29] G.R. Raidl. A hybrid gp approach for numerically robust symbolic regression. *Genetic Programming*, pages 323–328, 1998.

[30] G. Smits and M. Kotanchek. Pareto-front exploitation in symbolic regression. *Genetic programming theory and practice II*, pages 283–299, 2005.

[31] A. Topchy and W.F. Punch. Faster genetic programming based on local gradient search of numeric leaf values. In *Proceedings of the Genetic and Evolutionary Computation Conference (GECCO-2001)*, pages 155–162, 2001.

[32] N.Q. Uy, N.X. Hoai, M. O'Neill, RI McKay, and E. Galván-López. Semantically-based crossover in genetic programming: application to real-valued symbolic regression. *Genetic Programming and Evolvable Machines*, 12(2):91–119, 2011.

[33] D.A. Van Veldhuizen and G.B. Lamont. Evolutionary computation and convergence to a pareto front. In *Late Breaking Papers at the Genetic Programming 1998 Conference*, pages 221–228, 1998.

[34] Peter Weiner. Linear pattern matching algorithms. In *Proceedings of the 14th Annual Symposium on Switching and Automata Theory (swat 1973)*, SWAT '73, pages 1–11, Washington, DC, USA, 1973. IEEE Computer Society.

[35] E. Zitzler, M. Laumann, L. Thiele, E. Zitzler, E. Zitzler, L. Thiele, and L. Thiele. Spea2: Improving the strength pareto evolutionary algorithm, 2001.

Comparing Multi-objective and Threshold-moving ROC Curve Generation for a Prototype-based Classifier

Ricardo Aler
Computer Science Department
Universidad Carlos III de Madrid, Spain
aler@inf.uc3m.es

Julia Handl
Manchester Business School
University of Manchester, UK
julia.handl@mbs.ac.uk

Joshua D. Knowles
School of Computer Science
University of Manchester, UK
j.knowles@manchester.ac.uk

ABSTRACT

Receiver Operating Characteristics (ROC) curves represent the performance of a classifier for all possible operating conditions, i.e., for all preferences regarding the tradeoff between false positives and false negatives. The generation of a ROC curve generally involves the training of a single classifier for a given set of operating conditions, with the subsequent use of threshold-moving to obtain a complete ROC curve. Recent work has shown that the generation of ROC curves may also be formulated as a multi-objective optimization problem in ROC space: the goals to be minimized are the false positive and false negative rates. This technique also produces a single ROC curve, but the curve may derive from operating points for a number of different classifiers. This paper aims to provide an empirical comparison of the performance of both of the above approaches, for the specific case of prototype-based classifiers. Results on synthetic and real domains shows a performance advantage for the multi-objective approach.

Categories and Subject Descriptors

I.5.m [**Pattern Recognition**]: Miscellaneous

General Terms

Experimentation

Keywords

ROC curves, Multi-objective Machine Learning

1. INTRODUCTION

Receiver Operating Characteristic (ROC) curves are an important tool in classification problems, especially in applications that involve dynamic or imprecise operating conditions [19], where the class distributions and the misclassification costs of future data may differ from those of the data available at the time of training. More concretely, a ROC curve is a graphical plot of the True Positive Rate (TPR) versus the False Positive Rate (FPR) of a binary classifier (although ROC analysis can be extended to multi-class problems, see [5]).

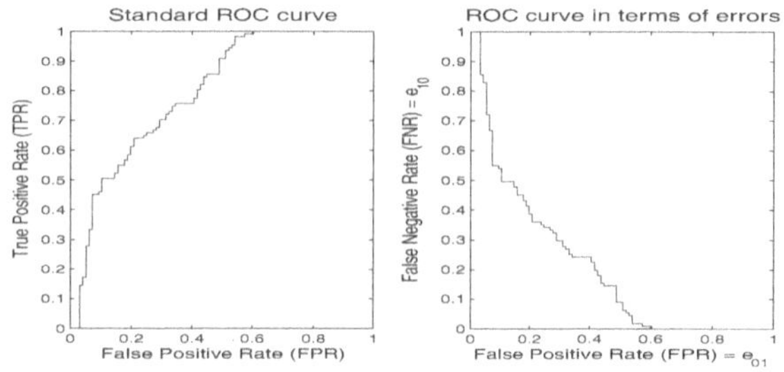

Figure 1: Standard ROC curve (left) and ROC curve in terms of errors FNR and FPR (right)

A ROC curve is typically constructed in two steps. First a classifier capable of ranking or scoring instances (e.g. a neural network) is trained for a particular set of operating conditions, using a standard learning algorithm. For instance, backpropagation optimizes neural network weights by minimizing training error, assuming equal missclassification costs and the class distribution present in the training data. The resulting classifier is then evaluated, which produces a single point in ROC space.

Second, the output threshold of the classifier is varied to obtain a range of different points (TPR, FPR) in ROC space [5]. The resulting ROC curve represents the classifier's performance for different operating conditions, which allows for the selection of an optimal operating point (threshold) for this classifier once the operating conditions become known. Figure 1 displays a standard ROC curve on the left. ROC curves can also be represented in terms of errors (FNR and FPR), as will be shown later in the paper and it is pictured in Figure 1 on the right.

Interestingly, points in ROC space obey the principle of Pareto dominance. This allows the formulation of ROC curve generation as a multi-objective (MO) optimization problem, where the objective space corresponds to the ROC space and the decision space corresponds to the parameters (e.g. neural network weights) and the thresholds of the classifiers employed. A complete formulation of this approach was presented by Everson and Fieldsend, who used PAES

GECCO'13, July 6–10, 2013, Amsterdam, The Netherlands.

for evolving the parameters of neural network-based classifiers [4]. In contrast to the approach of threshold-moving (where a single classifier is obtained), the MO approach may produce a number of different classifiers (e.g. a set of different weights for the neural networks used in [4]), each one optimized for different operating conditions. This set of classifiers maps to an approximation of the Pareto front (PF) in ROC space, which may be used in the same way as a ROC curve. In short, a threshold-moving ROC curve involves learning the parameters of a classifier and then moving the threshold, while a MO ROC curve basically involves learning a non-dominated collection of parameters.

Given that classifiers are optimized for individual operating conditions, one may expect the MO approach to provide better ROC curves than the curves produced using standard thresholding, in theory. However, there has been only limited empirical evaluation regarding the actual practical performance differences between the two approaches. This paper focuses on the specific case of prototype-based classifiers and carries out an empirical comparison across several data sets.

The structure of this paper is as follows. Section 2 defines key concepts about ROC curves, including the generation methods based on threshold-moving and MO optimization. Section 3 introduces prototype-based classifiers and describes the generation of ROC curves for these classifiers. It also sets out the methodology employed for the comparison of ROC curves. Section 4 presents and discusses the results of the experiments. Finally, Section 5 draws conclusions and discusses future research directions.

2. BACKGROUND

The aim of this Section is to define key concepts about classifiers, ROC curves and the multi-objective and threshold-moving methods to generate them.

2.1 Basic terminology

We consider binary classification, and two-class ROC analysis. A binary classifier maps instances into two classes $\{C_0, C_1\}$ commonly referred to as the negative and the positive class. Discrete classifiers return a class prediction only, whereas rankers, scorers, and probability estimators output a numerical value that is linked to the degree of membership of instances to specific classes [7]. More concretely, rankers sort all instances from the negative to the positive class. Scorers go beyond this and provide a continuous output that measures the degree of membership of instances to one of the classes. Probability estimators are specific types of scorers that estimate class memberships using probabilities (e.g. $p(C_i|x)$, for every instance x). It is clear that both probability estimators and scorers can be easily transformed into rankers, which in turn can be transformed into discrete classifiers by setting a threshold. Most work in classification and ROC analysis deals with scorers and this will also be the focus of this manuscript.

In binary classification, classifiers are commonly evaluated by estimating the True Positive Rate (TPR) and the False Positive Rate (FPR). TPR is the number of instances classified as positive divided by the number of instances that are actually positive, whereas FPR is the number of negative instances classified as positive, divided by the number of negative instances. More generally, the performance of a classifier can be measured by the set of probabilities e_{ij} that measure the probably of mistakenly assigning instances in class C_i to class C_j. This formulation is more homogeneous (it only uses errors), can be extended to multi-class problems, and, for binary classifiers, is equivalent to the above, as $TPR = 1 - e_{1,0}$ and $FPR = e_{0,1}$.

For two-class problems, ROC curves (ROCs) are two-dimensional graphs in which TPR is plotted on the Y axis and FPR rate is plotted on the X axis. If the errors e_{ij} are used instead, the result is an inverted (but equivalent) ROC curve, where $e_{1,0}$ is plotted against $e_{0,1}$. For $q > 2$ classes, ROC space has $q * (q-1)$ coordinates (e_{ij} with $i \neq j$) [4].

2.2 Threshold-moving

A given (trained) discrete classifier can be represented in ROC space as a point $(e_{1,0}, e_{0,1})$. Furthermore, a given (trained) ranker, scorer, or probability estimator can be represented by a ROC curve, which is generated by moving the classifier's threshold t. If $s(x)$ is the score assigned to instance x by the scorer s, all instances with a score of $s(x) > t$ will be classified as positive, and all others as negative. For any choice of the threshold t, a point $(e_{1,0}, e_{0,1})$ of the ROC curve can be generated. For $q > 2$ classes, scorers usually output q scores. In this case, threshold-moving becomes impractical (NP-hard), because each threshold has to be paired with all possible thresholds for the rest of the classes [15]. Therefore, there is potential for heuristic optimization approaches [4].

2.3 Multi-objective approaches for ROC generation

Based on the observation that Pareto dominance holds in ROC space, an "optimal" ROC curve can be defined more generally as the result of the multi-objective optimization of $s_{w,t}$ where s_w is a scorer defined by the set of parameters or weights $w = \{w_1, w_2, \ldots\}$ and $s_{w,t}$ is the discrete classifier that results from applying a particular threshold t to the scorer s_w. For instance, $s_{w,t}$ could be a neural network with the weights w and the output threshold t. The decision space of this multi-objective optimization problem is (w, t) and the objective space is $(e_{0,1}, e_{1,0})$ (e_{ij} in general, with $i \neq j$). In this formulation, a multi-objective optimizer can be used to find an approximation to the real Pareto front, which can be interpreted as a ROC curve. However, in contrast to threshold-moving, the optimal operating points in this ROC curve may correspond to different scorers $s_{w,t}$ (i.e. classifiers that have been discretized at different values of the threshold t, but may also differ in terms of their actual parameters w). This multi-objective formulation was first suggested in [22], tested in [13] using a Niched-Pareto Genetic Algorithm, and generalized to multi-class problems in [4], using the algorithm PAES [12].

2.4 Differences between the two approaches

The multi-objective approach provides a more general formulation for the problem of generating ROC curves. A further motivation of the approach is the observation that it provides classifiers that are optimized for all possible operating conditions [13]. In contrast to this, threshold-moving trains a classifier for a single operating point only. The ROC curve derived from threshold-moving is likely to be optimal for this particular operating point, but possibly not optimal for very different operating conditions.

Despite these conceptual and theoretical considerations,

there is currently only limited empirical evidence for an actual practical advantage of the multi-objective approach. Initial work on this topic [13] showed that, for neural networks, the ROC curves obtained using multi-objective optimization improved upon those obtained from standard threshold-moving. However, the study was limited to a single XOR synthetic domain and neural networks with two hidden units only. Everson and Fieldsend [4] focused on the extension of the multi-objective approach to multi-class problems. The resulting method was applied to a number of different domains, but, due to the focus of the work, an empirical comparison to threshold-moving was not provided. Finally, [8] used NSGA-II for the direct evolution of neural networks in ROC space and compared them to a single-objective approach based on threshold-moving. The results on three different 2-class UCI domains showed that anti-overfitting measures worked better for the multi-objective than for the threshold-moving approach. However, if no anti-overfitting measures were used, the ROC curves obtained from both approaches were quite similar. In principle, this work did not exclude the possibility that the threshold-moving approach could have been competitive, if other anti-overfitting measures had been used.

As mentioned in Section 2.2, standard threshold-moving becomes NP-hard for more than two classes. Therefore, two-class domains offer a good setting for comparison, because simple thresholding is still efficient, so it can be checked whether the additional conceptual advantages for the MO approach hold in this simple case.

2.5 Research question

Given the above, the principal aim of this manuscript can be formalized as follows. Let $s_w(x) : X \to \Re$ be a scorer whose parameters or weights are $w = \{w_1, w_2, \ldots\}$, that maps instances $x \in X$ to a continuous value, indicating the degree of membership to the positive class. Let $s_{w,t}(x) : X \to \{0, 1\}$ be the discrete classifier obtained from $s_w(x)$ by setting a threshold t, that classifies instances x as positive if $s_w(x) > t$ and negative otherwise.

The multi-objective approach generates a ROC curve by optimizing the two objectives $(e_{0,1}, e_{1,0})$ over the decision space (w, t). As will be explained in Section 3.3, a population-based multi-objective evolutionary algorithm will be used, and the ROC curve generated can potentially contain all members of the population. The threshold-moving approach optimizes some single-objective (scalar) criterion (such as the mean squared error or the classification accuracy) over the decision space w and, subsequently, generates the ROC curve by moving the threshold t. In this paper, the threshold-moving approach will also be referred to as "single objective" (SO) approach, given that a scalar value is optimized.

The hypothesis to be tested in our experiments is whether the multi-objective approach generates ROC curves that are consistently better than those returned by simple thresholding. If this is not the case, the single objective would be preferable, in principle, due to its smaller computational expense.

3. METHODOLOGY

3.1 Prototype-based classifiers

Prototype-based classifiers generally show good classification performance and tend to generate very simple models [9]. They are intuitive since they represent their decisions in terms of the prototypes in feature space and have a direct geometrical representation, which is useful for the visualization of classification boundaries. Finally, the classification procedure used in prototype-based classifiers generalizes to more than two classes.

A prototype-based classifier consists of a set of p prototypes, where p indicates the complexity of the classifier. A prototype is represented by its coordinates in feature space, as well as its class. A prototype-based classifier classifies instances by computing the distance to each of the prototypes and returning the class of the closest prototype. To obtain a classifier that returns a score rather than a class, we can score instances x based on the difference between the distances of the two nearest different-class prototypes p_0 and p_1 [17]. This is done in the following way: let p_0 and p_1 be the closest prototypes to x belonging to class 0 and 1, respectively. The score of instance x is $s_w(x) = d(x, p_1) - d(x, p_0)$, where d is the Euclidean distance. Scores range from $-\infty$ (class 1) to ∞ (class 0). It can be seen threshold $t = 0$ corresponds to the actual prototype-based classifier. Scores can be normalized to [0,1] by means of the sigmoid function. In that case, the default threshold becomes $\frac{1}{2}$.

3.2 Objective function

In order for the comparison between the SO and MO approach to be meaningful, the scalar criterion or loss function to be optimized by the SO approach should guarantee that the optimal classifier is part of the Pareto optimal set of the multi-objective formulation. Otherwise, the MO approach might outperform the SO approach just because the SO criterion does not return solutions that are optimal in the Pareto sense. Certain classification training criteria, such as the mean-squared error, do not meet this condition. A scalar criterion of the form $S_{A,B} = A * e_{0,1} + B * e_{1,0}$ guarantees that s_w will be on the front, for any values of A and B. If A and B were set to the proportion of negative and positive instances (respectively), then $S_{A,B}$ would provide the classification error (i.e. 1−accuracy). In this paper, the setting $A = B = 1$ has been chosen, so that the SO criterion does not depend on class proportions and gives equal importance to both classes. Also note that the Area under the Curve (AUC) of a discrete classifier with TPR and TNR (true positive and negative rates) is $\frac{(TPR+TNR)}{2}$[1]. Therefore, the minimization of $e_{0,1} + e_{1,0}$ is equivalent to the maximization of the AUC of the corresponding discrete classifier.

3.3 Optimization method

A further experimental choice are the algorithms used for the MO and SO optimization. For the MO case, MSOPS-II will be used [10]. MSOPS-II is one of the best algorithms for multi-objective optimization for many-objective problems. In this article, only two-class problems have been tested, but given that ROC space dimensionality grows as the square of the number of classes, future research is expected to require an optimizer capable of dealing with many objectives. For the SO optimization, Learning Vector Quantization (LVQ)

[1]The ROC curve of a discrete classifier is made of three points: the discrete classifier itself (TPR, TNR) and the two trivial classifiers at (TPR=1, TNR=0) and (TPR=0, TNR=1). The AUC of this ROC curve is made of a triangle and a trapezoid, whose areas can be added to compute the AUC [6].

is a well-known family of training algorithms for prototype-based systems [21]. However, LVQ does not guarantee that solutions are Pareto optimal in ROC space. In addition, if different algorithms are used for the MO and SO optimization, then differences between the two approaches may be due to differences in the effectiveness of the particular optimizers used. This problem can be avoided by using MSOPS-II for the implementation of both approaches. Specifically, the Pareto front (PF) approximation obtained from the MO approach is directly filtered to select the specific solution that optimizes the SO criterion $e_{0,1} + e_{1,0}$ (also referred to as the $fp + fn$ solution). In this way, the influence of optimizer performance and statistical variation are reduced.

3.4 Encoding

Prototype-based classifiers are directly encoded in the MSOPS-II chromosome, by encoding their coordinates. The class of the prototypes is encoded indirectly: prototypes are distributed uniformly among the classes, with the first prototype assigned to class 0, the second to class 1, the third to class 0, and so on. All classifiers in the MSOPS-II population contain the same number of prototypes. This is similar to the approach in [13] and [4], where all neural networks in the population had the same number of hidden units. (Differently to this, the work reported in [8] used classifiers of varying complexity within the same population.)

In previous paragraphs we have assumed that the MO approach operates in the decision space (w, t) (optimizing both the classifier's parameters w and its threshold t). In the present study, a further simplication was made, as the decision space was restricted to the set of feature vectors w only. More specifically, the scorers were used as discrete classifiers with a fixed (default) threshold of $t = \frac{1}{2}$. This approach reduces the dimensionality of the decision space, by removing one degree of freedom from the scorer. The empirical results in Section 4 show that the optimization of feature vectors alone is sufficiently powerful to obtain good classification results in all of the domains tested. The reason for this is that changes in the location of prototypes can account for the lack of changes in the threshold. In other words, $s_{w,t}$ represents a boundary in feature space (i.e. a discrete classifier), which may also be approximated by a discrete classifier $s_{w',t'}$ with different set of parameters w', but a default threshold of $t' = \frac{1}{2}$.

4. EMPIRICAL COMPARISON

4.1 Methodology

This section describes the methodology applied for comparing the ROC curves generated using the MO and the SO approach. We describe a metric based on cost-curves, as well as the cross-validation procedure used in the experiments.

4.1.1 Average expected cost

The ROC curves obtained by MSOPS-II and threshold-moving are learned on the training set, and do then need to be compared on independent test data. A popular scalar measure to evaluate ROC curves is the area under the curve (AUC) computed on the test set, which can also be interpreted as the probability that the score for positive instances is larger than the score for negative ones. The AUC provides a natural way of quantifying the ranking abilities of the scorer associated to the ROC, but it does not entirely reflect the way ROC curves are typically used. ROC curves can be used in classification when future operating conditions are not known at training time and the operating point must be selected once the target operating conditions have become known [19]. If there are few data points available, it is likely that there will be significant mismatches between the ROC curves obtained on the training and testing data (most likely as a result of overfitting on the training data). This mismatch can introduce additional errors because the operating point is selected based on the ROC curve on training data, but this may not accuractely reflect the best operating point from the perspective of the ROC curve on the testing data.

The following (simplistic) example is designed to illustrate this:

- Case 1: The ROC curve on the training data contains just two $(e_{0,1}, e_{1,0})$ points: (0.35, 0.25) and (0.25, 0.35). When tested on the test data, the corresponding classification performance for the corresponding operating points is (0.25, 0.35) and (0.35, 0.25), respectively. In other words, the training errors on these data fail to represent accurately the testing errors, a problem that commonly occurs with small data sets.

- Case 2: The ROC curve on the training data contains the two points (0.25, 0.35) and (0.35, 0.25), and the ROC curve obtained for the testing data is identical to this ROC curve on the training data. This situation would be expected to be the case for large data sets.

In both cases, the AUC obtained from testing will be identical because the ROC curves on the test data are identical. However, in the first case, the selection of an operating point based on the training ROC may be misleading, due to the mismatch between the ROC curves on the training and testing data. This problem is absent in the second case. Evaluation based on the testing AUC only does not reflect the difference between the two situations.

To avoid this limitation of the AUC, this paper adopts a different approach to the comparison of ROC curves , which is inspired by the average expected cost metric (TEC) suggested by Drummond and Holte [3]. TEC essentially repeats the operating point selection process for every possible operating condition, computes the corresponding cost, and averages across all conditions [3] [2]. Thus, TEC measures the expected cost (the average over all possible operating conditions) of the ROC curve on a given data set. Here, we propose to use the testing data for computing TEC, but carrying out the operating point selection on the ROC built from the training set, to ensure that the effect of mismatches between training and testing ROCs on operating point selection can be taken into account.

We refer to this measure as 'average expected cost' (AEC) and it is computed by Eq. 1, where E is the expectation operator, and $\mathbf{P} = (P_0, P_1)$ (class distribution) and $\mathbf{C} = (C_{10}, C_{01})$ (misclassification costs) represent the operating conditions. The expression $\hat{\mathbf{e}}_{(\mathbf{P},\mathbf{C})}$ represents the errors on the testing set of the optimal point $\mathbf{e}_{(\mathbf{P},\mathbf{C})}$ selected from the training ROC for operating conditions $(\mathbf{P}, \mathbf{C})$. It is assumed that all possible operating conditions are equally likely:

[2]Details are slightly more complicated as this computation is done in terms of cost curves, as will be explained later.

$$AEC = E_{(\mathbf{P},\mathbf{C})}[Cost(\hat{\mathbf{e}}_{(\mathbf{P},\mathbf{C})}, \mathbf{P}, \mathbf{C})] \quad (1)$$

where $Cost(\hat{\mathbf{e}}_{(\mathbf{P},\mathbf{C})}, \mathbf{P}, \mathbf{C})$ in Eq. 1 is computed in three steps: first select the minimum cost point $\mathbf{e}_{(\mathbf{P},\mathbf{C})}$ from the training ROC, second compute its errors $\hat{\mathbf{e}}_{(\mathbf{P},\mathbf{C})}$ on the test set, third compute its expected cost.

Under the operating conditions $\mathbf{P} = (P_0, P_1)$ and $\mathbf{C} = (C_{10}, C_{01})$, the expected cost of any point $\mathbf{e}$ (from the training ROC) can be computed as shown in Eq. 2 (assuming that correct classification has no costs):

$$Cost(\mathbf{e}, \mathbf{P}, \mathbf{C}) = e_{10}P_1C_{10} + e_{01}P_0C_{01} \quad . \quad (2)$$

Operating point selection is carried out by selecting the point from the training ROC that minimizes the expected cost. In short, $\mathbf{e}_{(\mathbf{P},\mathbf{C})} = \arg\min_{e \in \mathrm{ROC}} Cost(\mathbf{e}, \mathbf{P}, \mathbf{C})$. Eq. 2 is then used to compute the testing cost, once the errors $\hat{\mathbf{e}}_{(\mathbf{P},\mathbf{C})}$ on the testing set have been evaluated.

A minor technical point about the testing cost is that in principle, $\mathbf{P}$ should describe the class distribution of the testing set. In practice, this is not important, since the operating conditions $(\mathbf{P}, \mathbf{C})$ are never used independently. Rather, the products P_1C_{10} and P_0C_{01} are employed. Given that missclassification costs can have any positive value, it does not really matter the actual values of $\mathbf{P}$.

It turns out that the average expected cost of Eq. 1 can be given a geometrical interpretation by means of cost curves [3] (just like AUC being equivalent to the probability of ranking instances correctly). Cost curves were introduced by Drummond and Holte in 2006 [3] as an alternative way of visualizing ROC curves, but focusing on expected cost. For two-class problems, cost curves display (normalized) expected cost on the y-axis for all possible (normalized) operating conditions on the x-axis. [3] shows that TEC is equivalent to the area under the cost curve. [3] should be consulted for the technical details. This provides an elegant way of computing Eq. 1 that has been used in the present paper: for every possible normalized operating condition, select the operating point on the training ROC and compute its normalized expected cost. Finally, determine the area under this curve.

A graphical representation of what is computed in Eq 1 can be seen in Figures 4 and 5, later in the paper. For instance, the top left figure of Figure 4 displays the ROC curves obtained by the SO and MO approach on the training data. These would be used to select operating points (i.e. classifiers from the MO ROC curve, or thresholds from the SO ROC curve) once the operating conditions become known. The top right figure of Figure 5 displays the cost curve computed by simulating each operating point selected on the training ROC curve, on the test data. The average expected cost of Eq. 1 is equivalent to the area under the cost curve in the top right figure of Figure 5. It must be stressed that the top right figure of Figure 5 is not the testing cost curve, but the curve obtained by selecting operating points on the training ROC and computing the cost on the testing data.

4.1.2 *Cross-validation procedure and statistical significance*

In order to obtain statistically significant conclusions, several training/testing partitions were employed for each domain, according to the following procedure:

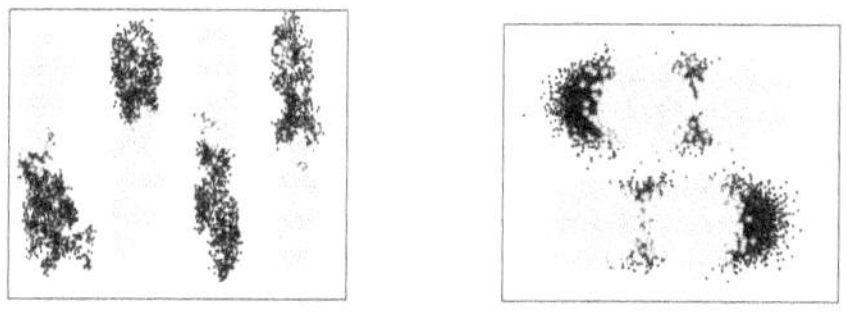

Figure 2: Irregular chess domain (left) and Gaussian chess domain (right).

- If the size of the dataset is large, overfitting should not pose a significant problem, and, therefore, the following training/testing procedure was followed: 40% of the data were used for training, and 60% were used for testing. This was repeated 5 times with different training/testing partitions. In order to take into account the stochastic nature of MSOPS-II, five independent runs of the optimizer were used for each partitions. Therefore, for these domains, MO was run 5x5=25 times, and the results are averages over these 25 runs. This approach was used for the two synthetic domains where sufficient data was available.
- In the real domains, a 5x2(x2) cross-validation procedure [2] was used using the optimally balanced stratified cross-validation [16]. For every training/testing partition, MSOPS-II was run twice (with different random seeds) and the results were averaged. In total, MSOPS-II was run 5x2x2=20 times, and the results displayed in the tables are averages over these 20 runs.
- Given that the multi-objective and fp+fn solutions are obtained from the same run, under exactly the same conditions, a paired t-test was used to test for statistical significance, with $\alpha = 0.05$, following the procedure described in [24] (chapter 5.3).

4.2 Domains and parameters

Two synthetic domains and four real domains (from the UCI database [1]) have been tested. All domains are 2-class problems with numerical attributes. The synthetic domains are: irregular chess and gaussian chess (see Figure 2). Irregular chess (8590 instances) is a two-attribute problem drawn by hand with the MLdemos tool [18] with 8 irregular overlapping clusters. Gaussian chess contains 8 symmetrical and identical gaussians. The four real domains are: Blood (748 instances, 5 attributes), Diabetes (768 instances, 8 attributes), German Number (1000 instances, 24 attributes), Estate (5322 instances, 12 attributes).

Distance-based classifiers are known to be very sensitive to irrelevant attributes. Therefore, prior to running MSOPS-II, a correlation-based filter method (CFS + best-first search [24]) was used to reduce the number of attributes.

4.3 Parameter settings

Table 1 displays the main MSOPS-II parameters used in the runs. In order to help MSOPS-II to converge more quickly, 25% of the individuals of the initial population were generated using a stochastic gradient descent algorithm called Generalized Learning Vector Quantization (GLVQ) [20], using the MATLAB implementation of [23]. GLVQ may converge to local optima [9], which was seen as an advantage in

Parameter	Value
Population size	100
Iterations	1000
Tau	0.001
Aggregation method	weighted min-max
Number of target vectors	**50** (default)
Number of decision space targets	**20** (default)
Crossover rate	**0.5** (default)
Probability of mutation	**0.9** (default)

Table 1: MSOPS-II parameter settings

this context, since a set of diverse initial solutions was generated. The remaining 75% of the initial population were generated randomly. Both the MO and SO approach were tested across a range of classifier complexities (number of prototypes).

4.4 Results

Figure 3 displays the results for the synthetic domains: irregular chess (top) and gaussian chess (bottom). The y-axis shows how the average expected cost changes as the number of prototypes increases. The solid line represents the results obtained for the MO approach while the dashed one corresponds to the SO solution. A circle means that the difference between the MO and SO results is statistically significant. Despite the fact that these two synthetic data sets are structurally similar, the results obtained are markedly different. For the irregular chess domain, it can be seen that the MO approach outperforms the SO approach, for all classifier complexities. The differences are significant on both the training and testing data. It can be seen that after 8 prototypes, there is almost no improvement in the expected cost. This is reasonable because the domain contains 8 irregular clusters. Contrariwise, in the gaussian chess domain, for complexities equal or larger than 8, the average expected cost is comparable for the SO and MO approach.

The different behavior of the SO and MO approach in both domains might be explained because in the gaussian chess domain there is a unique optimal ranking of instances (or ROC curve): this is the classification obtained by locating 8 prototypes in the gaussian centers. It is therefore not possible for the MO approach to identify solutions that outperform this optimal classifier. In the irregular case, there is either no unique optimal ranking (ROC curve) that can be represented by prototypes (due to the irregularity of the domain) or it is very hard for MSOPS-II to locate it. So, in this case, the MO approach achieves an advantage over the SO approach through the inclusion of different classifiers in the Pareto approximation set; each one of these will be appropriate for a different range of operating conditions. A visual inspection of all 25 runs for the Irregular Chess domain with 12 prototypes shows that the solutions returned by the MO and SO approaches fall into one of the two categories illustrated in Figures at the top (first category) and figures at the bottom (second category) of Figure 4 (which has been zoomed to $[0, 0.3] \times [0, 0.3]$). It can be observed that the MO approach outperforms the SO method either because it obtains better results for operating conditions near the x-axis (first category, figures at the top in Figure 4) or for operating conditions close to the y-axis (second category, figures at the bottom in Figure 4). Contrariwise, in the Gaussian Chess domain, the ROC curves returned from the MO and SO approach are very similar in all runs (results not shown).

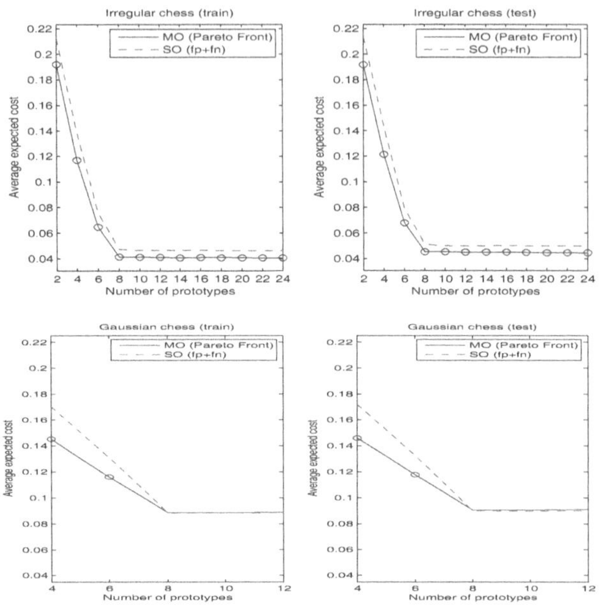

Figure 3: Average expected cost for the synthetic domains (training data on the left, testing data on the right): irregular chess (top) and gaussian chess (bottom).

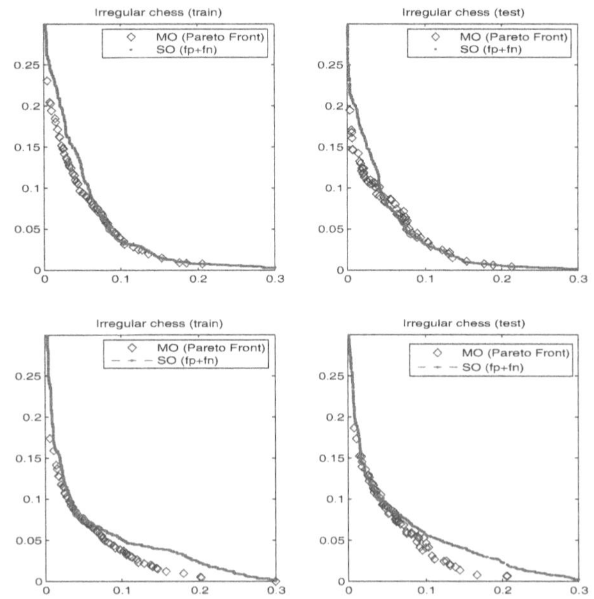

Figure 4: MO (diamonds) vs SO (dots) for the Irregular Chess domain with 12 prototypes. Category 1 (top). Category 2 (bottom).

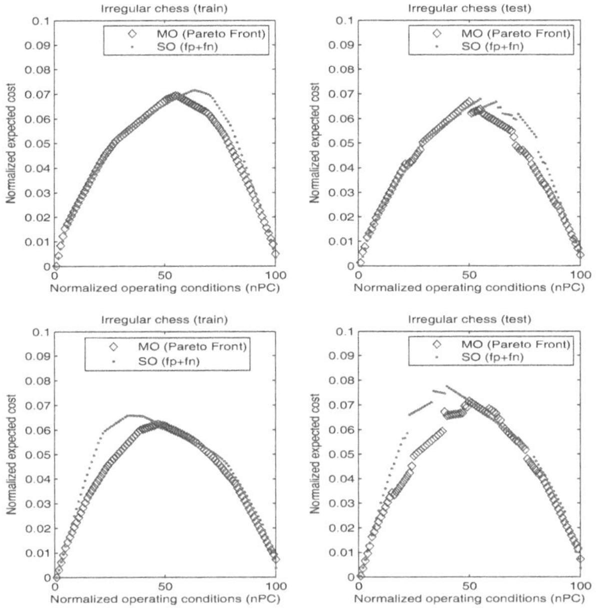

Figure 5: Cost curves corresponding to ROC curves of figures in Figure 4. Category 1 (top). Category 2 (bottom).

As an illustration, Figure 5 show the cost curves corresponding to the ROC curves in Figure 4. The area under the cost curve is equivalent to the average expected cost computed in Section 4.1.

Figures 6 and 7 display the results obtained for the real domains. It can be seen that, on the training data, the solutions returned by the MO approach perform significantly better than those from the SO approach, for all of the domains tested. This result continues to hold for the testing data. Specifically, the solutions returned by the MO approach have a lower cost than those for the SO approach, for the entire range of complexities tested. This includes the number of prototypes that leads to the best performance on the test set.

5. CONCLUSIONS

This paper extends previous investigations regarding multi-objective approaches to ROC curve generation, by providing empirical results concerning the performance of a multi-objective approach to ROC curve generation in comparison to a standard threshold-moving approach. In particular, the Pareto front approximations generated by MSOPS-II are compared with the ROC curves generated through threshold-moving for a single solution selected from MSOPS-II solution set. Results on a number of synthetic and real domains show that the multi-objective approach consistently provides ROC curves that are superior to those obtained from standard threshold-moving. The experiments are limited to the use of a prototype-based classifiers and future research may extend this analysis to more powerful classification techniques.

The experimental design of this study included a couple of aspects that warrant some further discussion.

First, MSOPS-II is able to approximate concave Pareto fronts, in principle. Given that only the convex hull of the

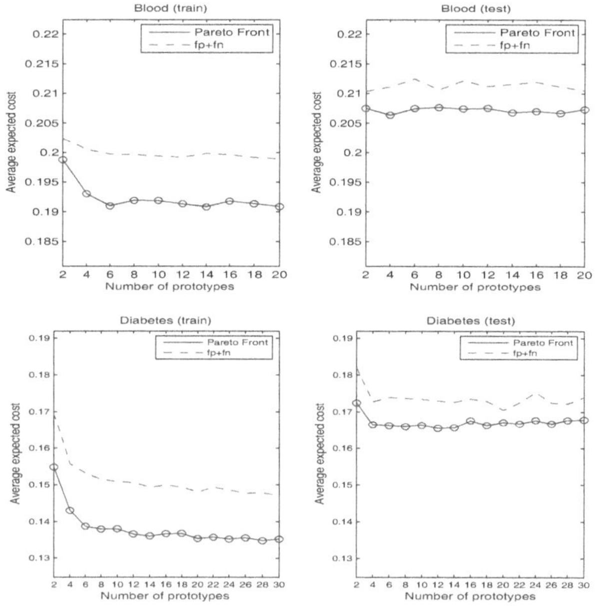

Figure 6: Average expected cost for domains Blood (top) and Diabetes (bottom). Training data on the left, testing data on the right.

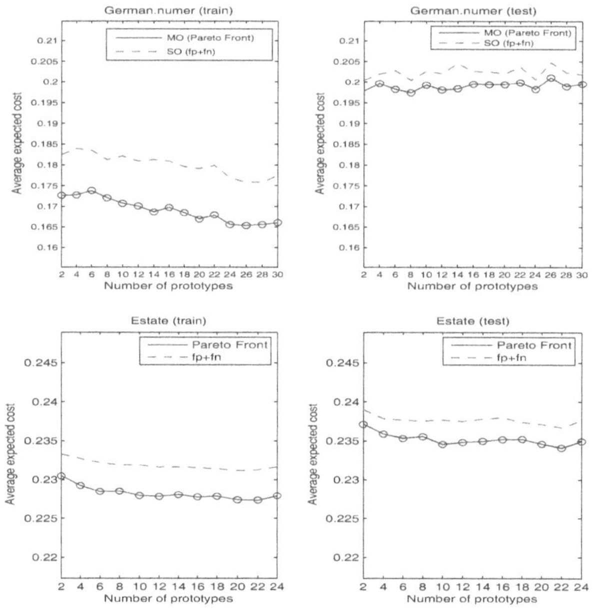

Figure 7: Average expected cost for domains German Number (top) and Estate (bottom). Training data on the left, testing data on the right.

fronts is important in ROC curve generation, it would be interesting to study if simpler aggregated weighted functions, which can only approximate convex fronts, may be able to improve the efficiency of the search.

Second, the paper has developed a novel methodology to compare the ROC curves obtained from the MO and SO approaches. In order to account for possible discrepancies between the ROC curves obtained on testing and training data, the ROC curves are compared by computing the average expected cost (or equivalently, the area under the cost curve) on the test set, while selecting operating the conditions based on the training ROC curve.

Third, by selecting solutions for threshold-moving from MSOPS-II's solution set, we have tried to ensure that the MO approach and the threshold-moving ROC are obtained under the same conditions. This means that differences observed between the MO and SO approach are not due to differences in the optimization algorithm used. It is, however, possible that the multi-objective formulation of the problem may also be advantageous in the sense of changing the difficulty of the search. Dependent on the formulation of the problem, a SO optimizer may sometimes get stuck in local optima, where a MO optimizer can escape [11]. In the context of ROC curves, some evidence for this is given in [13] for a simple NN example, and it may be worth exploring this issue further.

Two-class domains have been used in this paper because simple thresholding becomes NP-hard for more than two classes. In the future, it is intended to extend the comparison for more than two classes by using heuristic approximations to threshold-moving (such as hill-climbing [14]).

Acknowledgements

This work has been funded by the Spanish Ministry of Science under contract TIN2011-28336 (MOVES project).

6. REFERENCES

[1] D.J. Newman A. Asuncion. UCI machine learning repository, 2007.

[2] Thomas G. Dietterich. Approximate statistical tests for comparing supervised classification learning algorithms. *Neural Computation*, 10:1895–1923, 1998.

[3] Chris Drummond and Robert C. Holte. Cost curves: An improved method for visualizing classifier performance. *Machine Learning*, 65(1):95–130, 2006.

[4] Richard M. Everson and Jonathan E. Fieldsend. Multi-class ROC analysis from a multi-objective optimisation perspective. *Pattern Recogn. Lett.*, 27(8).

[5] Tom Fawcett. An introduction to ROC analysis. *Pattern Recogn. Lett.*, 27(8).

[6] Tom Fawcett. ROC graphs: Notes and practical considerations for researchers. Technical report, 2004.

[7] Peter A. Flach and Edson Takashi Matsubara. On classification, ranking, and probability estimation. In *Probabilistic, Logical and Relational Learning - A Further Synthesis*, 2007.

[8] Lars Gräning, Yaochu Jin, and Bernhard Sendhoff. Generalization improvement in multi-objective learning. In *IJCNN*, pages 4839–4846, 2006.

[9] Barbara Hammer, Marc Strickert, and Thomas Villmann. Relevance LVQ versus SVM. In *Artificial Intelligence and Soft Computing, Volume 3070 of Springer Lecture Notes in Artificial Intelligence*, pages 592–597. Springer, 2004.

[10] Evan J. Hughes. MSOPS-II: A general-purpose many-objective optimiser. In *IEEE Congress on Evolutionary Computation*, pages 3944–3951, 2007.

[11] J. Knowles, R. Watson, and D. Corne. Reducing local optima in single-objective problems by multi-objectivization. In *Evolutionary Multi-Criterion Optimization*, pages 269–283. Springer, 2001.

[12] Joshua D. Knowles and David Corne. Approximating the nondominated front using the pareto archived evolution strategy. *Evolutionary Computation*, 8(2):149–172, 2000.

[13] Matthew A. Kupinski and Mark A. Anastasio. Multiobjective genetic optimization of diagnostic classifiers with implications for generating receiver operating characteristic curves. *IEEE Transactions on Medical Imaging*, 18:675–685, 1999.

[14] Nicolas Lachiche and Peter Flach. Improving accuracy and cost of two-class and multi-class probabilistic classifiers using ROC curves, 2003.

[15] Thomas C. W. Landgrebe and Robert P. W. Duin. Approximating the multiclass ROC by pairwise analysis. *Pattern Recogn. Lett.*, 28(13).

[16] Jose G. Moreno-Torres, José A. Sáez, and Francisco Herrera. Study on the impact of partition-induced dataset shift on k -fold cross-validation. *IEEE Trans. Neural Netw. Learning Syst.*, 23(8):1304–1312, 2012.

[17] E. Mwebaze, P. Schneider, F.M. Schleif, JR Aduwo, JA Quinn, S. Haase, T. Villmann, and M. Biehl. Divergence-based classification in learning vector quantization. *Neurocomputing*, 74(9):1429–1435, 2011.

[18] Basilio Noris. Mldemos, 2011. `http://mloss.org/software/view/278/`.

[19] Foster Provost and Tom Fawcett. Robust classification for imprecise environments. *Mach. Learn.*, 42(3).

[20] Atsushi Sato. Discriminative dimensionality reduction based on generalized LVQ. In *ICANN*, pages 65–72, 2001.

[21] Panu Somervuo and Teuvo Kohonen. Self-organizing maps and learning vector quantization for feature sequences. *Neural Processing Letters*, 10(2):151–159, 1999.

[22] Ashwin Srinivasan. Note on the location of optimal classifiers in n-dimensional ROC space. Technical report, 1999.

[23] Marc Strickert. Generalized matrix relevance learning vector quantization grlvq, 2011. `http://mloss.org/software/view/323/`.

[24] Ian H. Witten, Eibe Frank, Len Trigg, Mark Hall, Geoffrey Holmes, and Sally Jo Cunningham. Weka: Practical machine learning tools and techniques with java implementations, 1999.

Evolving Artificial Neural Networks for Nonlinear Feature Construction

Tobias Berka
University of Cambridge & University of Salzburg
15 JJ Thomson Avenue, William Gates Building
Cambridge CB3 0FD
United Kingdom
tobias.berka@cl.cam.ac.uk

Helmut A. Mayer
University of Salzburg
Jakob-Haringer-Str. 2
5020 Salzburg
Austria
helmut@cosy.sbg.ac.at

ABSTRACT

We use neuroevolution to construct nonlinear transformation functions for feature construction that map points in the original feature space to augmented pattern vectors and improve the performance of generic classifiers. Our research demonstrates that we can apply evolutionary algorithms to both adapt the weights of a fully connected standard multi-layer perceptron (MLP), and optimize the topology of a generalized multi-layer perceptron (GMLP). The evaluation of the MLPs on four commonly used data sets shows an improvement in classification accuracy ranging from 4 to 13 percentage points over the performance on the original pattern set. The GMLPs obtain a slightly better accuracy and conserve 14% to 54% of all neurons and between 40% and 89% of all connections compared to the standard MLP.

Categories and Subject Descriptors

G.1.6 [**Optimization**]: Stochastic Optimization

General Terms

Experimentation

Keywords

Multi-layer perceptron, Evolutionary algorithm, Nonlinear dimensionality reduction, Feature construction, Classification

1. INTRODUCTION

Feature construction is currently a very active research area. And indeed, the promise of automated or black-box methods which can improve the geometric properties of virtually any supervised learning problem is a tempting goal. While this may seem far-fetched at first, it is the objective of a range of methods in machine learning, pattern recognition, and data mining. Feature selection is structurally the most simple problem in this area. It consists of the selection of those features, which can make a meaningful contribution to the discrimination of pattern vectors that belong to different classes. However, the actual methods used to solve the underlying combinatorial problem effectively are often far from simple. A slightly more complex task is feature weighting, where we go beyond a simple, binary selection, and scale the respective features based on their ability to create a differentiated view of the data. Some of the most prominent methods in computational statistics, such as multi-dimensional scaling, principal component analysis or factor analysis construct linear combinations of features. But as with all linear techniques, the limits of their expressive power surface quickly in a variety of applications.

Consequently, the focus has shifted to nonlinear methods. One of the most popular means to introduce nonlinearity is the *kernel trick* [2], where a nonlinear function is applied to the original pattern vectors. It is used in conjunction with a metric to make a transition into a kernel space, in the hope that the problem is more easily solved in the transformed domain. But there is of course a catch: the choice of this transition function is often more or less arbitrary. There are two main research directions in response to this problem. The first approach is to choose a default kernel function out of a limited set, such as polynomials or radial basis functions. Every new component in a vector in the kernel space is the result of applying the kernel function to a pair of components of the original vector. For a binary kernel function ϕ,

$$\phi : \mathbb{R}^2 \to \mathbb{R} \tag{1}$$

and d features $f_1, ..., f_m$ we thereby construct d^2 new features $f'_1, ..., f'_{d^2}$ by letting

$$f'_{id+j} := \phi(f_i, f_j) \text{ for all } i, j \in \{1, ..., d\} \ . \tag{2}$$

Unfortunately, an exhaustive construction of new features involves all pairs of components in the source vectors. The result is a quadratic increase in dimensionality. For low-dimensional problems, which suffer from poor separation of data points, this can actually be an advantage, and support vector machines explicitly exploit that fact [30]. The dimensionality problem can be mitigated to some extent by using feature selection, where relevant features are identified from the initially computed range of candidate features. In any case the increase in dimensionality is the exact opposite of the desirable dimensionality reduction. The second approach is to attempt to construct a kernel function specifically for the task at hand. In order to obtain a nonlinear

GECCO'13, July 6-10, 2013, Amsterdam, The Netherlands.

function that leads to a reduction in dimensionality, we decided to follow this direction in our work. We are using an evolutionary algorithm (EA) [3] to construct nonlinear transformation functions implemented by a standard multi-layer perceptron (MLP) and, more effectively, by a generalized multi-layer perceptron (GMLP) [6]. Neural networks generated by EAs have been studied extensively for the construction of classifiers (e.g. [31, 8, 21]). However, we are not evolving a neural classifier, but a multi-layer perceptron that maps the original input patterns to a transformed space of reduced dimensionality. This gives us additional flexibility in the choice of the classification system and potentially allows us to use the transformation for other applications, such as similarity-based search and retrieval.

Our key contribution is the following: We are using standard and generalized multi-layer perceptrons as structural templates for nonlinear functions for feature construction. We use a genetic algorithm to adapt the weights of the standard MLPs and the topology of the GMLPs using the classification accuracy as a fitness function to steer the evolution. We have conducted an experimental leave-one-out evaluation on four data sets with a K-nearest-neighbor (K-NN) classifier and compared the classification accuracy of the best solution against the performance of the same classifier on the raw (untransformed) data set. The best solution is the fittest MLP obtained in 50 independent runs over 2,000 generations with 50 individuals each. In our experiments, the standard MLPs improved the base classification accuracy by 4, 5, 12, and 13 percentage points (pp) on the data sets used for comparison. The GMLPs provide a slightly better improvement in classification accuracy but are dramatically smaller, omitting 14% to 54% of all neurons and between 40% and 89% of all connections. We also give a comparison to the related work, however, the literature on related approaches does not give all the details on performance assessment. Therefore, all of these comparisons must be taken with a grain of salt. Nonetheless, the results indicate the potential of evolutionary neural feature construction.

The remainder of this article is structured as follows. Section 2 gives a brief outline of the related work. Section 3 describes our approach, including the adaptation of weights in standard MLPs, and the evolution of the topology and weights of the GMLPs. In Section 4, we discuss the experimental evaluation, and compare the performance of the MLPs and GMLPs. Lastly, we summarize our findings and draw conclusions in Section 5.

2. RELATED WORK

Today, we have a very broad spectrum of methods for feature construction or dimensionality reduction, and a comprehensive survey of all of these techniques is beyond the scope of this article. Therefore, we will focus on the literature that is more closely related to our approach. The references given here contain further pointers to, and quantitative comparisons with, the state of the art in feature construction and dimensionality reduction.

Spectral, singular value or eigenvalue techniques are perhaps the most common family of methods for feature space transformations. These are the classic foundation of linear projection methods for dimensionality reduction by projection onto the principal axes. Related to the evolutionary aspects of our approach, a linear dimensionality reduction can also be constructed with evolutionary algorithms [1]. In short, evolution generates a low-dimensional hyper-plane, on which the original data are projected. These projected points are then presented to a classifier for computing the fitness and evaluating the overall quality. The dimensionality of the reduced space can be adjusted by the user, but the algorithm may occasionally go lower.

In digital image processing, the principal component analysis (PCA) traditionally used for dimensionality reduction has been combined with the kernel trick to form the nonlinear component analysis [25], which corresponds to solving an eigenvalue problem in the kernel space. It can be used to construct nonlinear features for feature extraction [7] or various image enhancement tasks [19].

More closely related to our approach, genetic programming (GP) has also been successfully used for nonlinear feature construction [22, 27]. Here, features are constructed by evolved programs using a pre-defined set of arithmetical operators and the raw features as program input. A recent article on multi-objective optimization of feature selection for multi-class classification problems gives a very good overview of the past work [32]. Some approaches are closely related to our own work, because they use operators commonly used as activation functions in neural networks [12]. In this case, the resulting program trees can be translated into a neural network. A related approach is based on the construction of nonlinear decision trees [17] using polynomial functions to restrict the search space.

Naturally, prior work in neuroevolution is highly relevant for our approach. Evolution of neural networks for classification tasks can lead to highly competitive classifiers [10]. The task of feature construction has been carried out implicitly in any neural classifier, where it is not trivially possible to discriminate the processing of the classifier from the feature construction that takes place before it. Regarding the issue of neural encodings, we point to the discussion of the related work together with our own approach in Section 3.2.

Several developments in the domain of neural networks share some structural similarities with our approach. Extreme learning machines (ELMs) use a purely random, single layer neural network, which provides an input to a linear least-squares regression module or regression-based classifier [14, 15]. This approach differs from our method in three principle ways. Firstly, the nonlinear part of the neural network has only a single layer, which limits the expressiveness. Secondly, the input weights are configured purely at random in the hope that the configuration will introduce a suitable nonlinearity into the representation, which is substantially different from the directed randomness provided by evolutionary optimizations. And thirdly, ELMs are inherently based on least-squares regression as a second stage. Our own approach does not make any assumptions about the classifier (or other predictor) it is deployed with in actual, productive use.

To solve the problems associated with the random input layer in ELMs, a hybrid learning approach for ELMs with a differential evolutionary algorithm can be used to adapt the weights of the input layer [33]. This is structurally similar to a combination of ELMs and evolutionary methods for linear dimensionality reduction [1].

Deep belief networks [13], and other new approaches to the training of deep, multi-layered neural network architectures such as auto-encoders [4, 23] proceed by training networks

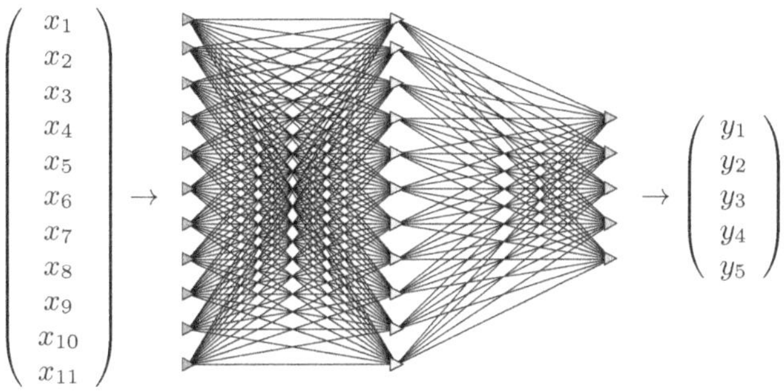

Figure 1: Using neural networks for feature construction.

layer-by-layer. They typically exploit various unsupervised machine learning techniques to train the initial layers in the hope that this will subsequently lead to improved application performance. This approach has been met with some success, but a full survey is beyond the scope of this article. The key differences between deep belief networks and our approach is that they attempt to perform certain unsupervised learning tasks in the hope that the underlying optimization provides an improvement in the classification accuracy, while we are performing a supervised training by evolution and directly optimize the figure of merit. With the use of GMLPs, we also go beyond the tuning of weights and perform an adaptation of the topology of the network.

3. NEUROEVOLUTIONARY FEATURE CONSTRUCTION

Before we discuss the details of our work, let us take an analytic look at the basic problem that we are trying to solve. Feature construction can be decomposed into a number of individual tasks:

- Feature selection: The lowest tier of the hierarchy is the selection of atomic features. Individual features may not make a meaningful contribution to the separation of classes, and we can make the decision to disregard a feature entirely.
- Feature weighting: A generalization of feature selection is feature weighting, which is extensively used in information retrieval. We compute and apply weights to scale the respective coordinates to reflect their discriminatory strength, in the hope that the distances between points in the transformed space are more meaningful for our purposes. A feature weighting using only the values zero and one formally corresponds to feature selection.
- Linear feature construction: If we use d features f_1, ..., f_d and weights $\omega_1, ..., \omega_k$, we can compute a linear combination

$$\sum_{j=1}^{d} \omega_j f_j \ .$$

  This form of feature construction enjoys a prominent role in classical statistics. We encounter it in many forms, including the principal component and factor analysis. All forms of linear dimensionality reduction conform to this type of feature construction. Linear feature construction corresponds to feature weighting if only one weight is non-zero.
- Translation: An affine function may also shift the origin.

Modern non-linear methods often combine these classic operations with a non-linear transition function, which serves as a source of nonlinearity:

- Nonlinear transformation: an elementary nonlinear function is used to introduce nonlinearity into a combination of otherwise linear or affine feature constructions.

The multi-layer perceptron has the ability to provide all of these transformations. If out_j is the activation of neuron j, $\omega_{j,i}$ the weight of the connection from neuron i to j, and b_j the bias for neuron j, we can define a multi-layer perceptron with n neurons as

$$\text{in}_j := \sum_{i=1}^{n} \omega_{j,i}\,\text{out}_i + b_j \ , \qquad (3)$$

$$\text{out}_j := \text{act}(\text{in}_j) \ , \qquad (4)$$

where act is a suitable activation function. The properties of the individual neurons and the network can model all of these individual operations:

- Feature selection: By connecting or disconnecting an input neuron to or from the next layer, we can control the presence or absence of the corresponding feature in the construction process. If an input neuron k has all outgoing weights set to zero,

$$(\forall j \in \{1, ..., n\}) \ (\omega_{j,k} = 0) \ ,$$

  the corresponding feature has effectively been deselected.
- Feature weighting: The weights of the outgoing connections of a neuron allow us to weigh the contribution, and thereby the feature weighting, of the underlying feature. Formally, the weighting for a feature k is contained in the weights for all outgoing connections $\omega_{*,k}$.
- Linear feature construction: For the standard and generalized MLP, the input of every neuron is defined as a linear combination of the output values of the previous layer(s). Therefore, every neuron computes a linear combination of the features provided by the inputting neurons.

Formally, this operation is expressed in the sum

$$\sum_{i=1}^{n} \omega_{j,i} \, \text{out}_i \ .$$

- Translation: At every neuron, we add a bias to the linear combination of the input values. This provides a mechanism for translation at every neuron.The bias values of the input layer, b_k for every input neuron k, correspond to a translation of the input pattern vectors.

- Nonlinear transformation: The activation function act which is applied to a neuron's input value serves as a source of nonlinearity for our neural networks.

In addition, the multi-layer perceptron has another important feature, which is not present in many other feature construction methods:

- Layering: We can repeat all operations by adding more layers, thereby increasing the computational capacity of the network and the corresponding feature construction function.

Formally, we can describe our approach as thus. We have a set X of d-dimensional, real-valued pattern vectors,

$$(\forall x \in X) \left(x \in \mathbb{R}^d \right) \ .$$

We construct a transformation function

$$f_T : \mathbb{R}^d \rightarrow \mathbb{R}^{d'}$$

to perform feature construction. The function f_T is implemented by a neural network with d input neurons and d' output neurons. The weights of the connections and biases of the individual neurons are encoded in a bit genome. Starting with a randomly initialized population of MLPs, we compute a fitness score based on the performance of the constructed features, select the fitter individuals, and apply standard operators for mutation and two-point crossover during reproduction. This process is repeated until a sufficiently good solution has been found.

3.1 Evolving MLP Weights

Initially, we use conventional multi-layer perceptrons, so only neurons within adjacent layers are connected. For a data set with d features and a user-specified reduced dimensionality of d' components, we have chosen a network topology with d input neurons, d hidden neurons and d' output neurons. This can also be referred to as a $d - d - d'$ topology. Hence the d-dimensional input pattern is transformed to a d'-dimensional output pattern. This topology has been determined experimentally and performed well for all of our benchmark experiments. We thus recommend it as a starting point for other data sets as well.

The choice of a suitable d' is not easy. For our evaluation, we have chosen d' according to experiments reported in related literature. This was necessary in order to draw a meaningful performance comparison between our method and the related work. In general, we recommend using an SVD to compute the singular values of the data matrix and plotting them on a logarithmic scale to reveal potential cutoff thresholds for a rank reduction. This threshold should also serve as a reasonable value for d'.

We are not using any learning algorithms – the optimization of the weights is the sole responsibility of the EA. This evolution of weights can be viewed as *evolutionary training* of a network. Conventionally, this strategy is used in scenarios where training patterns are not or scarcely available, such as the evolution of robotic neurocontrollers [34]. However, our own work also showed that evolutionary training may even outperform conventional training algorithms in problems with given input/output patterns [20].

The activation function of all hidden neurons is the standard sigmoid function, which is responsible for the nonlinearity provided by the neural network. The input and output neurons have linear activation functions (i.e., the identity function), to allow free scaling without a limiting activation function.

The choice of the output neuron's activation function is based on the fact that certain classes of patterns may already be arranged in distinct clusters within a certain interval, which might be collapsed to points because the sigmoid function limits output values to the unit interval.

The genotype of the network simply consists of all the network's weights and biases encoded in a bit string. We restrict each weight to the interval $[-10, +10]$ and use eight bits to encode a single weight or bias. All neurons except the input neurons have a bias value, as translating the input vectors did not produce any improved results. For a network with 90 weights and 10 biases, the length of the chromosome is 800 bits.

The two genetic operators comply with the usual choices without any specific adaptations. The standard bit-flip mutation is applied with a mutation rate of $\frac{1}{l}$, where l is the chromosome length. This means that mutation on average alters a single bit of the chromosome. The crossover rate p_c – the probability with which parents exchange genetic information during reproduction – was chosen to be $p_c = 0.6$.

As a selection mechanism, we used binary tournament selection without replacement. The constant population size was 50, and the number of generations was set to 2,000 for all experiments. Overall, these settings constitute a basic evolutionary algorithm without problem-specific algorithmic adjustments.

The evaluation of the fitness of the individual neural networks adheres to a technique commonly used in determining the quality of a feature subset. For the latter there are two basic approaches, namely, the *filter* and the *wrapper* approach [18]. With the filter approach a statistical measure is used to assess the quality of a feature subset, while the wrapper approach employs the accuracy of a classifier. As usual, both approaches have their advantages and drawbacks.

Essentially, the filter approach would allow fast computation of the fitness, however, there is no general guideline, which measures should be used to achieve good classification performance for a specific classifier. In preliminary experiments, we used the standard *Fisher criterion* [12] in a filter approach giving some improvement in classification performance. The wrapper approach directly uses the classifier's accuracy, leading to an improved classifier performance. However, this comes at the price of increased computational cost and classifier specificity. Using a K-NN classifier, the wrapper method produced better results with acceptable computational cost. We use a value of $K = 1$, or a single-nearest-neighbor classifier, because it led to the best accuracy in our preliminary evaluation.

A more detailed discussion of our initial work on evolving standard MLPs for feature selection in classification problems has been published in [5].

A problem with our approach stems from the fact that the number of connections increases with the square of the number of neurons. Since we have to encode a weight for every connection, the length of the bit string may exceed feasible values as the number of connections increases. This poses a problem, as the number of input neurons is dictated by the number of features in a given data set. Consequently, we believe that the specific approach presented here is currently only applicable to data sets with a moderate number of features. However, it should be noted that the best results in this article have been achieved with the largest network encoded with a hefty 11,752 bits.

3.2 Evolving GMLP Topology

To overcome these limitations we also investigated the evolution of the topology of GMLPs for nonlinear feature construction. These do not have a strictly layered structure, as connections are allowed between any neurons as long as no loops are introduced, i.e., GMLPs are feed–forward networks. A specific property of this network type are direct connections from input to output neurons, which may put special emphasis on features being very (ir)relevant for a specific class represented by the output neuron. Moreover, neurons and groups of neurons do not have to be fully connected, which paves the way for an evolutionary elimination of superfluous connections.

In principal, connections (and neurons) could also be removed by evolution if weights assume a value near zero (or close to it). However, it is very unlikely that a considerable number of connections is removed in this evolutionary setting. Hence, in the evolution of GMLPs the presence or absence of connections and neurons is encoded and evolved explicitly.

In our experiments we used a simple, direct encoding for GMLPs, as presented in [20]. In addition to the bits encoding the weights, there are two more bit fields, which represent the hidden neurons and all possible connections. Each neuron and each connection is encoded by a single bit indicating the presence or absence of a neuron or a connection. The connection bit field is built from a linearized, binary adjacency matrix. The order of the bit fields on the chromosome is neurons, connections, and weights. The order of weights strictly corresponds to the order of connections.

This structure of the genotype implies that the maximal number of hidden neurons has to be set in advance. To restrict the size of the network, but enable a better adaptation of these fewer neurons and connections, we set the maximum number for the GMLPs to the smallest number of hidden neurons used with the MLPs (eleven for the experiments described below). This is a very simple measure to bias the evolutionary search towards (rather) small networks, which are known to generalize well [24].

When a neuron becomes deactivated, all associated connections are also removed from the network. Moreover, all the weight values for the pruned connections become irrelevant, i.e., their bit representations effectively become non–coding regions in the genotype. Hence, a single bit–flip mutation may result in removal or addition of a neuron with a number of connections to the network, or may have no effect in the case of mutating a bit of an unused weight.

4. EVALUATION

We have obtained four data sets from the UCI Machine Learning Repository [11] whose kind support we wish to acknowledge. Table 1 summarizes the data sets used in the following experiments. The reduced dimensionalities are identical to those published in the related work to ensure that our results are comparable. The reduced dimensionalities and the neural network topology used in our experimental evaluations are listed in Table 2.

To compare the performance of our approach with the feature construction by genetic programming [12], we are using the *Breast Cancer Wisconsin (Diagnostic)* data set [29], which contains features extracted from fine needle aspirates of breast mass for the discrimination of benign and malignant tissue. It contains 569 patterns with 32 features, which are uniquely labeled to belong to one of two classes.

We have selected two data sets for comparison with the evolution of representative patterns for linear dimensionality reduction [1]. The *Ionosphere* data set [28] contains radar return signals. Here, we are instructed to discriminate between "good" and "bad" radar return signals. Good return signals may be used to reveal some structures in the ionosphere, whereas bad signals merely pass through it. This data set contains 351 instances with 34 features.

We are also using the *Image Segmentation* data set [26], which consists of 2,310 patterns with 19 features. It is based on an image processing task and contains instances of seven real-world image region categories for machine vision (brick face, cement, foliage, grass, path, sky, and window).

A data set that usually requires some pre-processing is a collection of chemical data for wine samples [9], which are categorized into six quality classes. It presents an interesting feature construction challenge because the individual features have disparate scales. This data set allows us to demonstrate the ability of our approach to operate on raw, unprocessed and unnormalized data. The red wine subcollection, with 1599 patterns and 11 features, completes the data sets used in the experiments.

We experimentally determined some evolution parameters by conducting trial runs on the data sets. We use a population size of 50 individuals and execute 2,000 generations. For all experiments, we have conducted 50 independent runs. The optimal result reported is always the single best solution found for a given data set in all of these runs.

The Java software implementing the evolution of neural networks and the K-NN classifier has been developed at our institution, and is mainly based on the *JEvolution* package, written by one of the authors, and the neural network package *Boone*[1]. A single run as specified above required approximately 30 minutes on an Intel Nehalem i7 960 CPU running at 3.2 GHz with 6 GB of memory.

To visualize the evolutionary progess, Figure 2 depicts the development of the fitness scores over the number of generations. These plots contain two measures to illustrate the development of the populations across all runs. The *mean average fitness* is the average of the fitness score over all runs and individuals within the same generation. The *best overall* fitness score is the highest fitness score found for any individual in all runs up to that generation.

These measurements reveal that most of the evolutionary progress is achieved within the first 200 generations. Appar-

[1]All credits for Boone go to our colleague August Mayer.

Name	Full Name	Reference(s)	Patterns	Features	Classes
Cancer	Breast Cancer Wisconsin (Diagnostic)	[12, 29]	569	32	2
Ionosphere	Ionosphere	[1, 28]	351	34	2
Segmentation	Image Segmentation	[1, 26]	2310	19	7
Wine	Red Wine	[9]	1599	11	6

Table 1: Overview of the data sets used for evaluation.

ently, the problem of constructing a suitable transformation function has sufficiently many sound solutions, so that the genetic algorithm can make immediate and substantial improvements. The rather sharp transition to a small rate of progress is typical for artificial evolution, but improvements may be found along the entire interval of measurement.

In any case, the ultimate measure of success is the classification accuracy in the transformed space compared to that on the original data, and in relation to the performance reported in the literature. It should be noted that comparisons to related work are more of a qualitative manner, as not all necessary details are given, e.g., random subsets of the original data sets are used for the evolution of the linear hyperplanes [1]. The leave-one-out classification accuracy performance evaluation on the raw data and the transformed data generated by the best MLP are summarized in Table 2.

For comparability with related approaches, we have taken the following performance figures from the related work: 99% for the cancer set [12], 92% for the ionosphere set [1], 78% for the segmentation set [1] and 62% for the wine set [9]. The baseline accuracy is the performance of our k-NN classifier on the original, unmodified data sets.

With the evolution of GMLPs we have attempted to reduce the size of the networks while preserving the classification performance by adapting the topology together with the weights of the connections. The resulting classification accuracies are comparable to those achieved by MLP evolution, as shown in Table 3. We obtain about one percentage point of improvement for three of the four data sets when looking at the best evolved networks. Naturally, the optimal MLP result of 100% for the ionosphere data set could not be surpassed, instead a slight performance decrease to 99.71% has been observed.

However, as shown in Table 3, the reduction in the number of neurons and connections compared to the MLP topology is considerable, as the GMLPs have 14% to 68% fewer neurons and 40% to 89% fewer connections. Together, the savings in neurons and connections make for much smaller and computationally more efficient neural networks.

It has to be stressed that these reductions are governed by our restriction of the maximal number of hidden neurons (11). However, it is not unlikely that the complexity of the GMLPs could be further reduced by using regularization parameters in the fitness function biasing evolution towards preferring smaller networks [16]. Thus, the benefit of using GMLPs is not mainly in terms of classification performance, but especially in computational efficiency.

5. SUMMARY AND CONCLUSIONS

In this article we have introduced the use of multi-layer perceptrons as nonlinear functions for feature construction in classification tasks. Our key contribution is that we evolve the standard and generalized MLPs as transformation functions and not for immediate use as predictors. An evolutionary algorithm is used to evolve weights and biases of the neural networks directly encoded in a bit string. The classification accuracy of a K-nearest-neighbor classifier with $K = 1$ has been used to determine the fitness of the neural networks transforming the original feature vectors to a lower dimension. Plots of the development of the fitness values over time indicate that this approach is able to find excellent solutions, and that a stable optimization does take place. We have evaluated this approach on four commonly used data sets using a leave-one-out evaluation of the classification accuracy. To the extent possible we compared the performance of our approach with related work. In addition we measured a performance baseline on the raw (untransformed) data. The evolutionary adaptation of weights in standard MLPs delivers performance improvements of 4, 5, 12, and 13 percentage points over these baseline figures, outperforming the related work in three out of four cases. Using GMLPs the classification performance differs by -0.28 pp, 0.95 pp, 1.05 pp and 1.87 percentage points on the data sets used in our evaluation. However, they allow us to conserve 14%, 38%, 41% and 54% of all neurons and 40%, 73%, 83% and 89% of all connections, resulting in a significant reduction in network size. The result of using GMLPs is a clear gain in computational efficiency, which comes at a small loss or even a minor gain in predictive accuracy.

It seems that the performance is limited for data sets that have either a very high or low classification accuracy. Our explanation is that trivial data sets with small error rates leave very little margin for improvement because it is difficult to evolve a neural network that can improve on these few patterns and preserves correct classification for all others. Data sets with a low classification accuracy may be hard to improve upon due to the continuous nature of the neural networks used in our experiment. The smooth activation functions cannot disentangle points if they are close together, and the resulting transformation thus preserves the confusion in local neighborhoods. The highest improvements were achieved on data sets that fall between these extremes, because they provide plenty of room for improvement, but the local neighborhoods contain enough consistently labeled points for our approach to succeed.

The presented technique has some limitations when the dimensionality of the input space is very large, as the number of neurons and connnections of the networks increases with the number of features (even with GMLPs). Hence, future research will address this problem by extending the evolutionary process to explicitly control and reduce the number of input and output neurons. A reduction of input neurons is equivalent to an integrated process of feature selection. The evolution of output neurons could lead to a further reduction of dimensionality that is more feasible for evolutionary optimization.

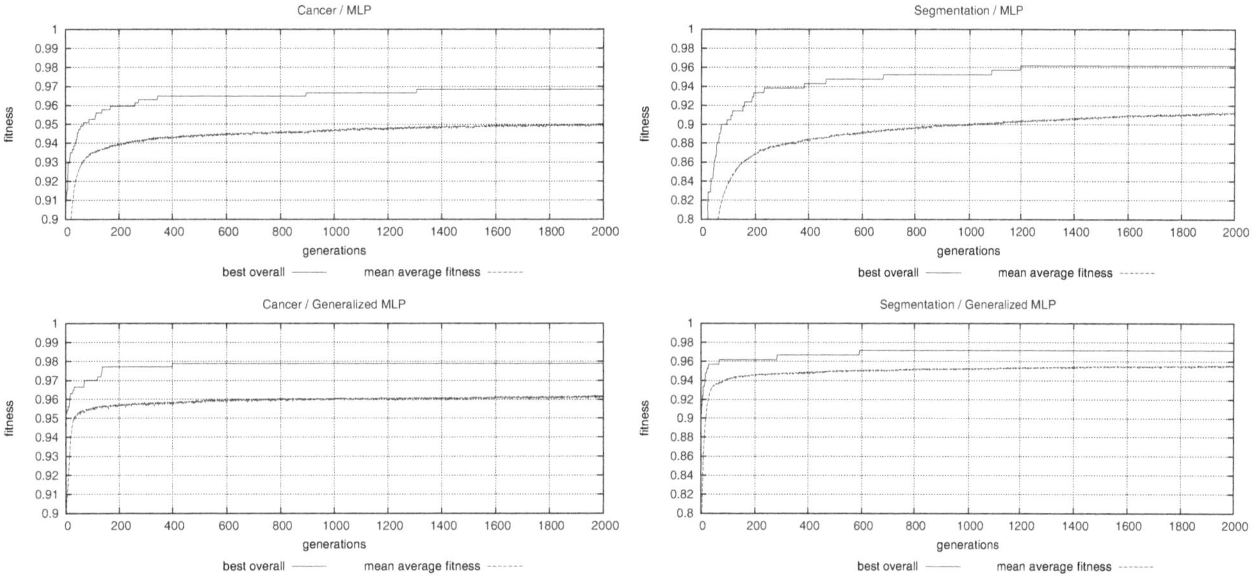

Figure 2: Fitness scores of 50 independent experimental runs with 50 individuals over 2,000 generations using the cancer (left) and segmentation (right) data set using standard MLPs (top) and GMLPs (bottom) showing the best and mean average scores across all runs and individuals.

Data Set	Features	Topology	Reduced Features	Neurons	Connections	Baseline Accuracy	Related Work	Best MLP
Cancer	30	$30-30-3$	3	63	990	93%	99%	97%
Ionosphere	34	$34-34-7$	7	75	1394	87%	92%	100%
Segmentation	19	$19-19-4$	4	42	437	84%	78%	96%
Wine	11	$11-11-5$	5	27	176	62%	62%	70%

Table 2: Multi-layer perceptron topology and resulting classifier performance. Comparisons to related work should be viewed as qualitative trends, as performance measurement could not be reproduced in full detail. The number of dimensions in the reduced space is based on the related literature.

Data Set	Topology	Neurons	Neurons Saved	Connections	Connections Saved	Accuracy MLP	Accuracy GMLP
Cancer	30-4-3	37	-26 (-41%)	107	-883 (-89%)	96.84%	97.89%
Ionosphere	34-5-7	46	-29 (-38%)	226	-1168 (-83%)	100.00%	99.71%
Segmentation	19-6-4	29	-13 (-54%)	114	-323 (-73%)	96.19%	97.14%
Wine	11-7-5	23	-4 (-14%)	104	-72 (-40%)	70.61%	72.48%

Table 3: Evolved GMLP topologies and savings in neurons and connections compared to the MLPs.

6. REFERENCES

[1] C. Aggarwal. The Generalized Dimensionality Reduction Problem. In *Proc. SDM*, pages 607–618. SIAM, 2010.

[2] A. Aizerman, E. M. Braverman, and L. I. Rozoner. Theoretical Foundations of the Potential Function Method in Pattern Recognition Learning. *Automat. and Rem. Contr.*, 25:821–837, 1964.

[3] T. Bäck. *Evolutionary Algorithms in Theory and Practice*. Oxford University Press, 1996.

[4] Y. Bengio, P. Lamblin, D. Popovici, and H. Larochelle. Greedy Layer-Wise Training of Deep Networks. In *Proc. NIPS*, pages 153–160, 2006.

[5] T. Berka and H. A. Mayer. Nonlinear Feature Construction with Evolved Neural Networks for Classification Problems. In *Proc. ICPRAM*. INSTICC, 2012.

[6] C. M. Bishop. *Neural Networks for Pattern Recognition*. Oxford University Press, Inc., USA, 1995.

[7] T.-J. Chin and D. Suter. Incremental Kernel PCA for Efficient Non-linear Feature Extraction. In *Proc. BMVC*, pages 939–948. BMVA, 2006.

[8] A. Coelho, D. Weingaertner, and F. J. von Zuben. Evolving Heteregeneous Neural Networks for Classification Problems. In *Proc. GECCO*, pages 266–273, USA, July 2001. Morgan Kaufmann.

[9] P. Cortez, A. Cerdeira, F. Almeida, T. Matos, and J. Reis. Modeling Wine Preferences by Data Mining from Physicochemical Properties. *Decis. Support Syst.*, 47(4):547–553, 2009.

[10] M. Dragoni, A. Azzini, and A. Tettamanzi. A Neuro-Evolutionary Approach to Electrocardiographic Signal Classification. In *Proc. WIVACE*, pages 1–11, Italy, 2012. Università degli Studi di Parma, Dipartimento di Scienze Sociali.

[11] A. Frank and A. Asuncion. UCI Machine Learning Repository, 2010.

[12] H. Guo and A. K. Nandi. Breast Cancer Diagnosis using Genetic Programming Generated Feature. *Pattern Recogn.*, 39(5):980–987, 2006.

[13] G. E. Hinton, S. Osindero, and Y. W. Teh. A Fast Learning Algorithm for Deep Belief Nets. *Neural Comput.*, 18:1527–1554, 2006.

[14] G.-B. Huang, D. H. Wang, and Y. Lan. Extreme Learning Machines: A Survey. *Int. J. Mach. Learn. & Cyber.*, 2(2):107–122, 2011.

[15] G.-B. Huang, H. Zhou, X. Ding, and R. Zhang. Extreme Learning Machine for Regression and Multiclass Classification. *IEEE Trans. Syst. Man Cybern. B. Cybern.*, 42(2):513–529, 2012.

[16] R. Huber, R. Schwaiger, and H. A. Mayer. On the Role of Regularization Parameters in Fitness Functions for Evolutionary Designed Artificial Neural Networks. In *Proc. WCNN*, pages 1063–1066. INNS, Lawrence Erlbaum Associates, September 1996.

[17] A. Ittner and M. Schlosser. Discovery of Relevant New Features by Generating Non-Linear Decision Trees. In *Proc. KDD*, pages 108–113. AAAI, 1996.

[18] G. H. John, R. Kohavi, and K. Pfleger. Irrelevant Features and the Subset Selection Problem. In *Proc. ICML*, pages 121–129, 1994.

[19] K. I. Kim, M. O. Franz, and B. Schölkopf. Iterative Kernel Principal Component Analysis for Image Modeling. *IEEE Trans. Pattern Anal. Mach. Intell.*, 27(9):1351–1366, 2005.

[20] A. Mayer and H. A. Mayer. Multi–Chromosomal Representations in Neuroevolution. In *Proc. CI*. ACTA Press, November 2006.

[21] H. A. Mayer and R. Schwaiger. Differentiation of Neuron Types by Evolving Activation Function Templates for Artificial Neural Networks. In *Proc. WCCI*, pages 1773–1778. IEEE, May 2002.

[22] K. Neshatian, M. Zhang, and P. Andreae. A Filter Approach to Multiple Feature Construction for Symbolic Learning Classifiers Using Genetic Programming. *IEEE Trans. Evol. Comput.*, 16(5):645–661, Oct. 2012.

[23] M. Ranzato, Y.-l. Boureau, S. Chopra, and Y. Lecun. A Unified Energy-Based Framework for Unsupervised Learning. In *Proc. AISTATS*, volume 2, pages 860–867, 2007.

[24] D. E. Rumelhart, B. Widrow, and M. A. Lehr. The Basic Ideas in Neural Networks. *Comm. ACM*, 37(3):87–92, March 1994.

[25] B. Schölkopf, A. Smola, and K.-R. Müller. Nonlinear Component Analysis as a Kernel Eigenvalue Problem. *Neural Comput.*, 10(5):1299–1319, 1998.

[26] M. J. J. Scott, M. Niranjan, and R. W. Prager. Realisable Classifiers: Improving Operating Performance on Variable Cost Problems. In *Proc. BMVC*. BMVA, 1998.

[27] J. R. Sherrah, R. E. Bogner, and A. Bouzerdoum. The Evolutionary Pre-Processor: Automatic Feature Extraction for Supervised Classification using Genetic Programming. In *Proc. GP*, pages 304–312. Morgan Kaufmann, July 1997.

[28] V. G. Sigillito, S. P. Wing, L. V. Hutton, and K. B. Baker. Classification of Radar Returns from the Ionosphere using Neural Networks. *Johns Hopkins APL Tech. Dig.*, 10:262–266, 1989.

[29] W. N. Street, W. H. Wolberg, and O. L. Mangasarian. Nuclear Feature Extraction for Breast Tumor Diagnosis. In *Proc. Electronic Imaging*, volume 1905, pages 861–870. SPIE, 1993.

[30] V. N. Vapnik. *The Nature of Statistical Learning Theory*. Springer, USA, 1995.

[31] X. Yao. Evolving Artificial Neural Networks. *Proc. IEEE*, 87(9):1423–1447, 1999.

[32] Y. Zhang and P. I. Rockett. A Generic Optimising Feature Extraction Method Using Multiobjective Genetic Programming. *Appl. Soft Comput.*, 11(1):1087–1097, Jan. 2011.

[33] Q.-Y. Zhu, A. Qin, P. Suganthan, and G.-B. Huang. Evolutionary Extreme Learning Machine. *Pattern Recognition*, 38(10):1759–1763, 2005.

[34] T. Ziemke, J. Carlsson, and M. Bodén. An Experimental Comparison of Weight Evolution in Neural Control Architectures for a 'Garbage-Collecting' Khepera Robot. In *Proc. Khepera Workshop*. HNI–Verlagsschriftenreihe, 1999.

Extending Learning Classifier System with Cyclic Graphs for Scalability on Complex, Large-Scale Boolean Problems

Muhammad Iqbal
Victoria University of Wellington, NZ
muhammad.iqbal@

Will N. Browne
Victoria University of Wellington, NZ
will.browne@

Mengjie Zhang
Victoria University of Wellington, NZ
mengjie.zhang@ecs.vuw.ac.nz

ABSTRACT

Evolutionary computational techniques have had limited capabilities in solving large-scale problems, due to the large search space demanding large memory and much longer training time. Recently work has begun on automously reusing learnt building blocks of knowledge to scale from low dimensional problems to large-scale ones. An XCS-based classifier system has been shown to be scalable, through the addition of tree-like code fragments, to a limit beyond standard learning classifier systems. Self-modifying cartesian genetic programming (SMCGP) can provide general solutions to a number of problems, but the obtained solutions for large-scale problems are not easily interpretable. A limitation in both techniques is the lack of a cyclic representation, which is inherent in finite state machines. Hence this work introduces a state-machine based encoding scheme into scalable XCS, for the first time, in an attempt to develop a general scalable classifier system producing easily interpretable classifier rules. The proposed system has been tested on four different Boolean problem domains, i.e. even-parity, majority-on, carry, and multiplexer problems. The proposed approach outperformed standard XCS in three of the four problem domains. In addition, the evolved machines provide general solutions to the even-parity and carry problems that are easily interpretable as compared with the solutions obtained using SMCGP.

Categories and Subject Descriptors

F.1.1 [**Models of Computation**]: Genetics-Based Machine Learning, Learning Classifier Systems

General Terms

Algorithms, Performance

Keywords

Learning Classifier Systems, XCS, Finite State Machines, Genetic Programming, Scalability, Pattern Recognition

1. INTRODUCTION

A learning classifier system (LCS) is a rule-based learning system that adaptively learns a task by interacting with an unknown environment and uses evolutionary computing to evolve the rules according to the reinforcement received. The LCS technique can scale in a problem domain, but as the problem increases in dimensionality, resulting in increased search space, it becomes difficult to solve due to the needed resources. By explicitly feeding domain knowledge to an LCS, scalability can be achieved, but it adds bias and restricts use in multiple domains [11].

A main research direction is to develop an autonomously scalable classifier system that can provide general solutions, i.e. solutions that can be scaled to any problem size in the domain. A code-fragment based XCS system has been developed by Iqbal et al. [15], using a genetic programming (GP) like rich encoding scheme and a layered learning approach. Although the system has shown scalability beyond standard XCS [25], the solutions found were not scalable in general at the domain level due to the large sized nested tree structures.

The self-modifying cartesian genetic programming (SMCGP) is a developmental graph-based GP system where a computer program is evolved that can generate an arbitrary sequence of computer programs (see section 2.3). The graph-based representation has benefits of implicitly reusing the nodes in the graph. Harding et al. [10] have evolved programs using SMCGP that were proved to provide general solutions for a number of problems. The issue with SMCGP is that the size of the obtained graphical solutions to Boolean problems can increase for every next level problem in the domain. This makes the visualization and interpretation of the solution difficult for large scale problems in such domains.

A finite-state-machine (FSM) is a cyclic mathematical model that can be used to represent any finite-state system (see section 2.1). The advantage of cyclic representations is that they can map repeated patterns in a compact form, so this work introduces a state-machine based rich encoding scheme into scalable XCS, for the first time, in an attempt to develop a general scalable classifier system producing concise and easily interpretable classifier rules.

The proposed system is to be tested on four different Boolean problem domains, i.e. even-parity, majority-on, carry, and multiplexer problems. These are complex problem domains having overlapping, niche imbalance, and epistatic properties (see section 4). The results are to be compared with standard numeric action based XCS and SMCGP to test the scalability of the proposed system.

2. BACKGROUND

2.1 Finite State Machines

A finite state machine (FSM), also known as finite state automaton (FSA), is a mathematical model of computation that can be used to model any finite-state system. FSMs have been used to design sequential logic circuits as well as algorithms for different computational tasks such as pattern matching, sequence prediction, communication protocols, and parsing [2]. In general, a finite state machine consists of a set of finite states and can be in only one state at any given time, called the *current state*. On receiving an input, the machine can change its current state and/or cause an action or output to take place for any given change. One of the states is labeled as *start state*, which is used as the current state in the beginning while processing the input.

There are many state machine modeling techniques, e.g. deterministic finite automata (DFA), non-deterministic finite automata (NFA), Mealy machines, Moore machines, pushdown automata, and Turing machines. The state machine used in the work presented here is the Moore machine [23], as it is simple and suitable for modeling classification problems. A Moore machine is formally defined as a six-tuple $M = (Q, \Sigma, \Delta, \delta, \lambda, q_0)$ where Q is a finite set of states, Σ is a finite set of input symbols, Δ is a finite set of output symbols, δ is a transition function from a state $p \in Q$ and an input $x \in \Sigma$ to a next state $q \in Q$, λ is an output function from a state $p \in Q$ to an output $y \in \Delta$, and $q_0 \in Q$ is the *start state*.

For example, the state machine shown in Fig. 1 is described as $Q = \{q_0, q_1, q_2\}$, $\Sigma = \{0, 1\}$, $\Delta = \{0, 1\}$, *start state* $= q_0$, λ defined as: $\lambda(q_0) = 1$, $\lambda(q_1) = 1$, and $\lambda(q_2) = 0$, and δ defined as: $\delta(q_0, 0) = q_2$, $\delta(q_0, 1) = q_1$, $\delta(q_1, 0) = q_1$, $\delta(q_1, 1) = q_0$, $\delta(q_2, 0) = q_1$, and $\delta(q_2, 1) = q_2$. Here a circle denotes a state along with the corresponding output value, and an arc represents a transition.

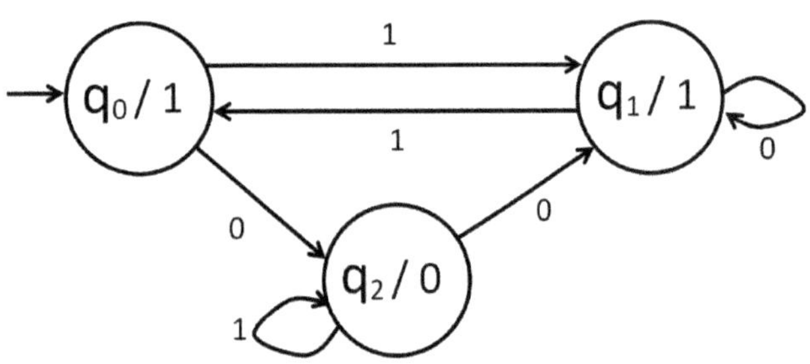

Figure 1: A Moore state machine with three states q_0, q_1, and q_2 where q_0 is the start state.

Usually, a Moore machine outputs a string of symbols from Δ on receiving an input string of symbols from Σ, e.g. if the input is '10100' then the Moore machine depicted in Fig. 1 will produce '11101' as the output string. In the work presented here, it is adapted for classification problems. To use a Moore machine for classification, the value of the last state visited while processing the input string is taken as the only output, instead of a whole output string. Therefore the class of input string '10100' will be 1 whereas the string '10101' will belong to class 0, if processed via the machine shown in Fig. 1.

2.2 Learning Classifier Systems

Traditionally, an LCS represents a rule-based agent that incorporates evolutionary computing and machine learning to solve a given task by interacting with an unknown environment. After observing the current state of the environment, the agent performs an action and the environment provides a reward.

XCS [25] is a formulation of LCS that uses accuracy-based fitness to learn the problem by forming a complete mapping of states and actions to rewards. In XCS, the learning agent evolves a population $[P]$ of classifiers, where each classifier consists of a rule and a set of associated parameters estimating the quality of the rule. Each rule is of the form 'if *condition* then *action*', having two parts: a condition and the corresponding action. Commonly, the condition is represented by a fixed length bitstring defined over the ternary alphabet $\{0, 1, \#\}$ where '#' is the 'don't care' symbol which can be either 0 or 1; and the action is represented by a numeric constant.

XCS operates in two modes, explore and exploit. In the explore mode, the agent attempts to obtain information about the environment and describes it by creating the decision rules, using the following steps:

- observes the current state s of the environment, usually represented by a fixed length bitstring defined over the binary alphabet $\{0, 1\}$.
- selects classifiers from the classifier population $[P]$ that have conditions matching the state s, to form the match set $[M]$.
- performs covering: for every action $a_i \in A$ in the set of all possible actions, if a_i is not represented in $[M]$ then a random classifier is generated with a given generalization probability such that it matches s and advocates a_i, and added to the set $[M]$ as well as to the population $[P]$.
- forms a system prediction array, $P(a_i)$ for every $a_i \in A$ that represents the system's best estimate of the payoff should the action a_i be performed in the state s.
- selects an action a to explore (probabilistically or randomly) and selects all the classifiers in $[M]$ that advocated a to form the action set $[A]$.
- performs the action a, records the reward r received from the environment, and uses r to update the associated parameters of all classifiers in $[A]$.
- when appropriate, implements rule discovery by applying an evolutionary mechanism (commonly a genetic algorithm) in the action set $[A]$, to introduce new classifiers to the population.

Additionally, the explore mode may perform subsumption deletion to merge specific classifiers into any more general and accurate classifiers. Subsumption deletion is a way of biasing the genetic search towards more general, but still accurate, classifiers [4]. It also effectively reduces the number of classifier rules in the final population [18].

In contrast to the explore mode, in the exploit mode the agent does not attempt to discover new information and simply performs the action with the best predicted payoff. The exploit mode is also used to test learning performance of the agent in the application. Various richer encoding schemes have been investigated to represent high level knowledge in LCS in an attempt to obtain compact classifier rules [8, 13, 14], to reach the optimal performance faster [19, 20], to approximate functions [5, 26], to develop useful feature extractors [1], and to identify and process building blocks of knowledge [6, 15].

2.3 Scalable Evolutionary Computation

A main research direction is to develop an autonomously scalable classifier system to obtain general solutions for any problem size in the domain. To achieve this goal, Iqbal et al. [16] used GP-like rich encoding scheme to identify building blocks of knowledge. Then they extracted building blocks of knowledge, in the form of tree-like code fragments, from smaller problems and reused them to learn more complex problems of the domain [12]. The system having ability to reuse the extracted domain knowledge [15] has shown scalability beyond the standard XCS, but the solutions found were not scalable in general at the domain level. The reason behind this limitation is that the code fragments extracted from smaller problems were reused as terminals in the code fragments of larger problems of the domain, resulting in large sized acyclic nested tree structures that increased the search space and eventually restricted the system to a limit in problem size.

Cartesian genetic programming (CGP) is a flexible graph-based version of GP that allows a program to be evolved with more than one output [22]. The graph-based representation has benefit of implicitly reusing the nodes in the graph. SMCGP is a developmental form of CGP where an evolved individual computer program can be iterated to produce an infinite sequence of computer programs using a set of self-modifying functions [9]. It allows programs to take more inputs and give more outputs during each iteration so that each of the generated programs solves a particular problem in the domain. Using SMCGP, Harding et al. [10] have evolved programs that can provide general solutions to a number of problems including an n-bits parity problem and an adder to add two n-bits binary numbers. The limitation of SMCGP is that cycles were not allowed[1] in the graphical programs to avoid infinite loops. Therefore, the size of the obtained solutions to Boolean problems increases for every next level problem in the domain (e.g. see Fig. 6), due to the application of self-modifying operators, especially the duplication operator that duplicates a part of the graph in it. So for very large scale Boolean problems, solutions are very long making visualization and interpretation difficult.

3. XCS WITH STATE-MACHINE ACTION

In the work presented here, the typical static numeric action in XCS will be replaced by an FSM in an attempt to develop a general scalable learning classifier system having concise and easily interpretable classifier rules.

In the proposed approach of XCS with state-machine action, called XCSSMA, the static binary action is replaced by a Moore state machine [23] retaining the ternary alphabet in the condition of a classifier rule. Each state machine consists of n states, where some of the states may be deactivated. A linear representation is used to encode a machine. Each state $p \in Q$ is encoded as a three-tuple $\{v, active, T\}$ where $v \in \Delta$ is the output value of the state p, *active* is a Boolean flag determining whether the state p is activated, and T is a transition function from an input symbol $x \in \Sigma$ to a next state $q \in Q$.

For example the state machine shown in Fig. 2, where a deactivated state q_1 is represented by a dashed circle, will be encoded as '$11q_1q_210q_2q_101q_2q_0$'. Here $Q = \{q_0, q_1, q_2\}$, $\Sigma = \{0, 1\}$, $\Delta = \{0, 1\}$, $startstate = q_0$, λ is defined as: $\lambda(q_0) = 1$, $\lambda(q_1) = 1$, and $\lambda(q_2) = 0$, and δ is defined as: $\delta(q_0, 0) = q_1$, $\delta(q_0, 1) = q_2$, $\delta(q_1, 0) = q_2$, $\delta(q_1, 1) = q_1$, $\delta(q_2, 0) = q_2$, and $\delta(q_2, 1) = q_0$.

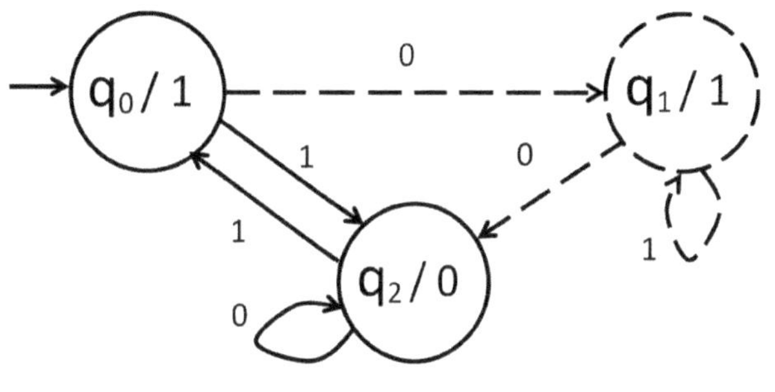

Figure 2: A Moore state machine with a deactivated state q_1. This machine will be encoded as '$11q_1q_210q_2q_101q_2q_0$'.

If a state q_j has been deactivated and an activated state q_i has a transition to q_j, then that transition will be changed to any activated state in the machine, chosen uniformly randomly, as suggested by Spears and Gordon-Spears [24], e.g. in Fig. 2 the transition $\delta(q_0, 0) = q_1$ will be set to $\delta(q_0, 0) = q_0$ or $\delta(q_0, 0) = q_2$. For simplicity, the first state in the state-machine action is set to be the *start state*. To avoid the creation of any junk machine in the evolutionary process, the *start state* will always be activated.

The proposed XCSSMA approach extends standard XCS, described in section 2.2, in the following cases: the action value, the covering operation, the rule discovery operation, the procedure comparing equality of two classifiers, and the subsumption deletion mechanism.

3.1 State-Machine Action Value

The action value of a classifier is determined by processing the current input string s via the state-machine action in the classifier. The processing starts from the *start state* in the state-machine action, and the value of the last state visited is taken as the action value. For example, consider the classifier shown in Fig. 3. If the input string s is '100101' then the action value will be 0.

Condition	Action
10#10#	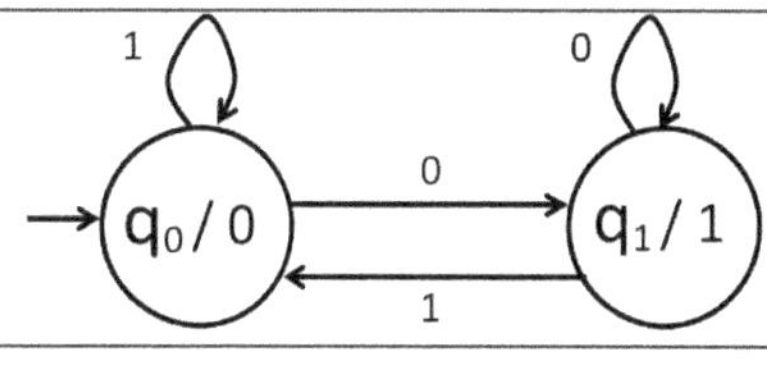

Figure 3: A classifier rule with state-machine action.

3.2 Covering Operation

Covering occurs if an action a is missing in the match set $[M]$. If so, a random classifier is created whose condition matches the current environmental state s and contains

[1] In principle SMCGP could have cycles as can CGP.

'don't care' symbols with probability $P_{\#}$. The state-machine action is randomly generated until the output is a.

3.3 Rule Discovery Operation

In the rule discovery operation, a genetic algorithm is applied in the action set $[A]$ to produce two offspring. First of all, two parent classifiers are selected from $[A]$ based on fitness and the offspring are created out of them. Next, the conditions and state-machine actions of the offspring are separately crossed, with probability χ, by applying GA crossover operation. After that, each symbol in the conditions of the resulted children by crossover are mutated with probability μ, such that both children match the currently observed state s. In the mutation of conditions, a 'non-don't care' symbol is replaced by the 'don't care' symbol '#', and a 'don't care' symbol is replaced by the corresponding bit in the state s. Then, the state-machine actions of the children are mutated with probability μ.

3.4 Comparing Equality of Two Classifiers

If a newly created classifier in the rule discovery operation is not subsumed and there is no classifier equal to it in the population, then it will be added to the population. Two classifiers are considered to be equal if and only if both have the same conditions and genotypically the same state-machine (i.e. identically the same state-machine encoding) in their actions.

3.5 Subsumption Deletion

A classifier cl_1 can subsume another classifier cl_2 if both have the same action and cl_1 is accurate, sufficiently experienced, and more general than cl_2 [7]. It is to be noted that due to the multiple genotypes to a single phenotype issue caused by using state-machines in place of numeric values in the actions of classifier rules, subsumption deletion is less likely to occur. Subsumption deletion is still made possible, albeit limited, by matching the state-machine descriptions on a character by character basis.

4. EXPERIMENTAL DESIGN

4.1 The Problem Domains

The problem domains used in the experimentation are the even-parity, majority-on, carry, and multiplexer problems which have been often studied using the LCS and GP approaches.

In even-parity problems, the output depends on the number of ones in the input instance. If the number of ones is even, the output will be one, and zero otherwise. Using the ternary alphabet based conditions with the static numeric action, no useful generalizations can be made for the even-parity problems.

The majority-on problems are similar to even-parity problems in that the output depends on the number of ones in the input instance. If the number of ones is greater than the number of zeros, the problem instance is of class one, otherwise class zero. In majority-on problem domain, the complete solution consists of strongly overlapping classifiers, so is therefore difficult to learn. For example, '1##11:1' and '11#1#:1' are two maximally general and accurate classifiers, but they overlap in the "11*11" subspace.[2]

[2]Here, * can be 0, 1, or #.

In the carry problem, two binary numbers of the same length are added. If the result triggers a carry, then the output is one otherwise zero. For example, in case of three bits numbers 101 and 010, the output is 0, whereas for the numbers 110 and 100 the output is 1. Similar to majority-on problems, the complete solution in carry problem domain consists of overlapping classifiers, and in addition it is a niche imbalance problem domain.

A multiplexer is an electronic circuit that accepts input strings of length $n = k + 2^k$, and gives one output. The values of k so-called address bits are used to select one of the 2^k remaining data bits to be given as output. For example in 6-bits multiplexer, if the input is 011101 then the output will be 1 as the first two bits 01 represent the index 1 (in base ten), which is the second bit following the address. Multiplexer problems are highly non-linear and have epistasis, i.e. importance of data bits is dependent on address bits.

4.2 Experimental Setup

The system uses the following parameter values, commonly used in the literature, as suggested by Butz and Wilson in [7]: learning rate $\beta = 0.2$; fitness fall-off rate $\alpha = 0.1$; prediction error threshold $\epsilon_0 = 10$; fitness exponent $\nu = 5$; threshold for GA application in the action set $\theta_{GA} = 25$; two-point crossover with probability $\chi = 0.8$; mutation probability $\mu = 0.04$; experience threshold for classifier deletion $\theta_{del} = 20$; fraction of mean fitness for deletion $\delta = 0.1$; classifier experience threshold for subsumption $\theta_{sub} = 20$; probability of 'don't care' symbol in covering $P_{\#} = 0.5$; reduction of the fitness $fitnessReduction = 0.1$; number of states $n = 5$; input alphabet $\Sigma = \{0, 1\}$; output alphabet $\Delta = \{0, 1\}$; and the selection method is tournament selection with tournament size ratio 0.4. Both GA subsumption and action set subsumption are activated. The number of classifiers used is 2000 and the number of training examples is half a million, in all the experiments conducted here. Explore and exploit problem instances are alternated. The reward scheme used is 1000 for a correct classification and 0 otherwise. All the experiments have been repeated 30 times with a known different seed in each run. Each result reported in this work is average of the 30 runs.

In all graphs presented here, the X-axis is the number of problem instances used as training examples, the Y-axis is the performance measured as the percentage of correct classification during the last 100 exploit problem instances, and the error bars show standard deviation in the 30 runs.

5. RESULTS

5.1 The Even-Parity Problem Domain

The largest solved parity problem, directly from training data, reported in literature is 24-bits even-parity problem, by Harding et al. [10] using SMCGP. The performance of standard XCS and XCSSMA in learning 24-bits even-parity problem is shown in Fig. 4. It is observed that standard XCS cannot learn the 24-bits even-parity problem, whereas XCSSMA has solved it using approximately $5,000$ training examples.

The even-parity domain does not allow generalizations if the standard ternary alphabet based encoding scheme is used with static numeric action. So each bit must be specific for a rule to be accurate, requiring 2^{25} such rules for the 24-

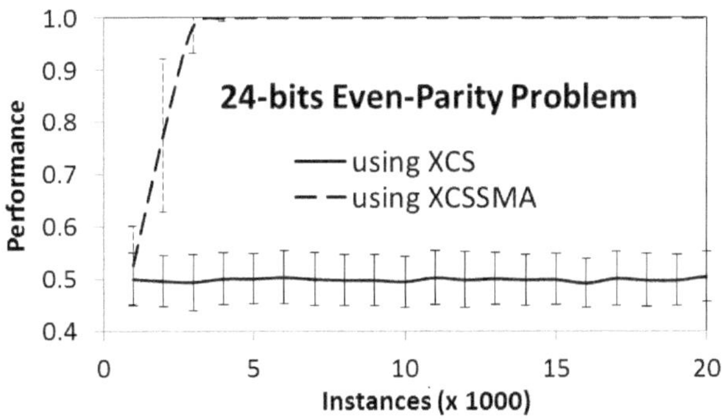

Figure 4: Results of 24-bits even-parity problem.

bits even-parity problem. The standard XCS technique was not able to evolve enough accurate rules, even using a larger population of classifiers. However, the proposed XCSSMA approach not only solved the 24-bits even-parity problem, but the obtained solutions are compact, easily understandable[3], and general for any n-bits even-parity problem.

One of the classifier rules from the final solution obtained using XCSSMA is shown in Fig. 5. This is a maximally general and accurate classifier covering the whole problem space. The FSM action in this rule is general to solve any n-bits even-parity problem. It is to be noted that state q_3 is not active, so there is no transition from any active state to q_3. The state q_4 is active, but not reachable from the start state q_0. It means only three states, i.e. q_0, q_1 and q_2, are the working states in this FSM action.

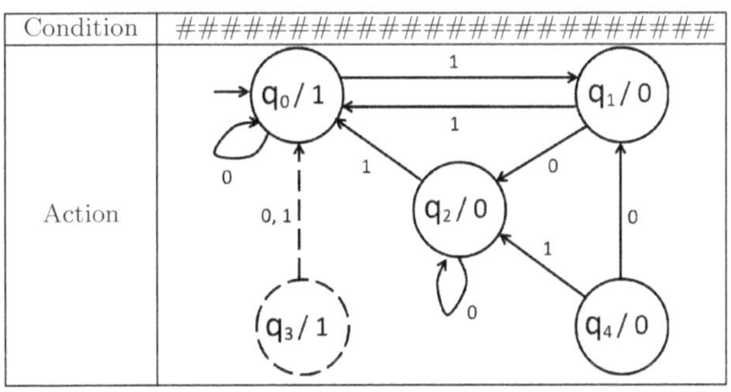

Figure 5: A sample classifier rule from final solution of 24-bits even-parity problem in XCSSMA.

The solutions found by Harding et al. [10] using SMCGP were also general, but not as compact and easily interpretable as the classifier rules obtained using XCSSMA here. For example, an evolved program using SMCGP is shown in Fig. 6 that provides a solution for the 4-bits even-parity problem after two iterations of the evolved program. Here x_0, x_1, x_2, and x_3 represent input symbols; INPP and OUTPUT are input and output nodes respectively; BNOR, BAND, BOR, and BNAND are the Boolean operators; and DUP is a duplication operator that duplicates a section of the graph. To obtain the solution for 24-bits even-parity problem, twenty more iterations will need to be performed. One can imagine the resulting solution for the 24-bits even-parity problem, but it is impractical to draw it.

[3]Assuming the reader understand how state machines work.

5.2 The Majority-on Problem Domain

The complete solution of the majority-on problem domain consists of strongly overlapping classifiers, which makes it a hard problem to learn. The largest attempted majority-on problem in literature is a 7-bits problem, by Jackson and Gibbons [17] using layered learning in genetic programing and the reported success rate is 90%. The performance of standard XCS and XCSSMA in learning 7-bits majority-on problem is shown in Fig. 7. It is observed that standard XCS reached approximately 94% performance, but could not completely solve the 7-bits majority-on problem, whereas XCSSMA has solved it using approximately 25,000 training examples.

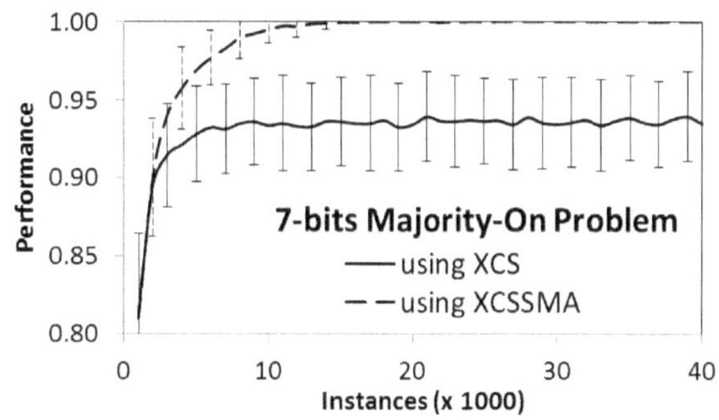

Figure 7: Results of 7-bits majority-on problem.

A sample accurate classifier rule for 7-bits majority-on problem is shown in Fig. 8. This is an interesting rule covering eight problem instances, four of which belong to class 0 and the other four are of class 1. This form of classifier rule is not expressible using the standard numeric action based XCS with ternary conditions.

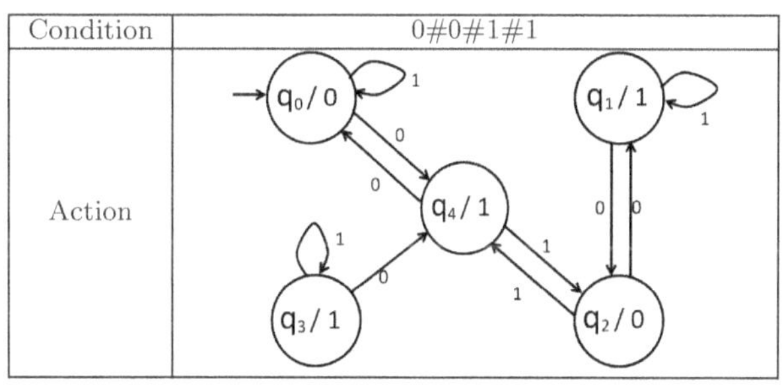

Figure 8: A sample classifier rule from final solution of 7-bits majority-on problem in XCSSMA.

5.3 The Carry Problem Domain

The largest solved carry problem, directly from training data, reported in literature is 6+6 bits carry problem, by Harding et al. [10] using SMCGP. The performance of standard XCS and XCSSMA in learning 6+6 bits carry problem is shown in Fig. 9.

The complete solution in the carry problem domain consists of overlapping classifiers, in addition it is a niche imbalance domain, which makes it very difficult to learn. However, XCSSMA successfully learned the 6+6 bits carry problem, whereas standard XCS failed. In addition, the obtained solutions in XCSSMA are compact, easily understandable, and general for any n+n bits carry problem.

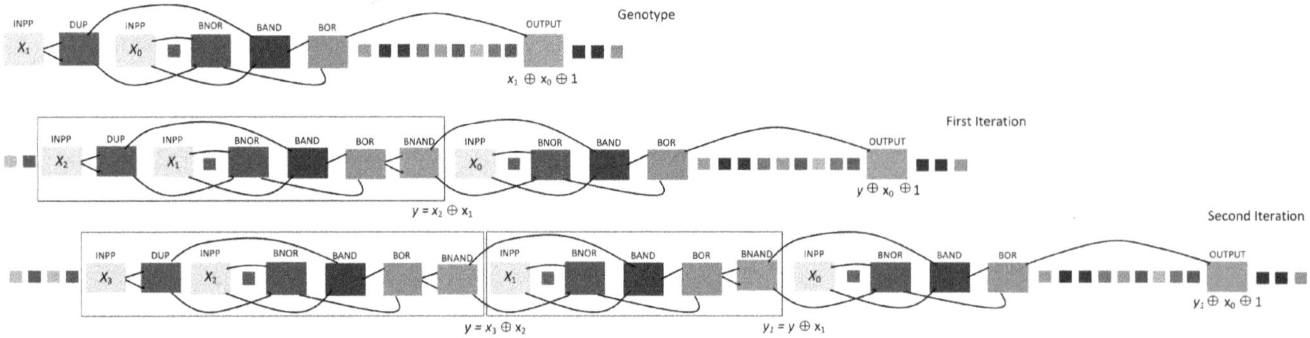

Figure 6: An evolved genotype, using SMCGP [10], iterated twice that provides solution for the 4-bits even-parity problem. Here x_0, x_1, x_2, and x_3 represent input symbols and $\oplus$ denotes XOR operator. This is a colored figure and is adapted by kind permission of the author.

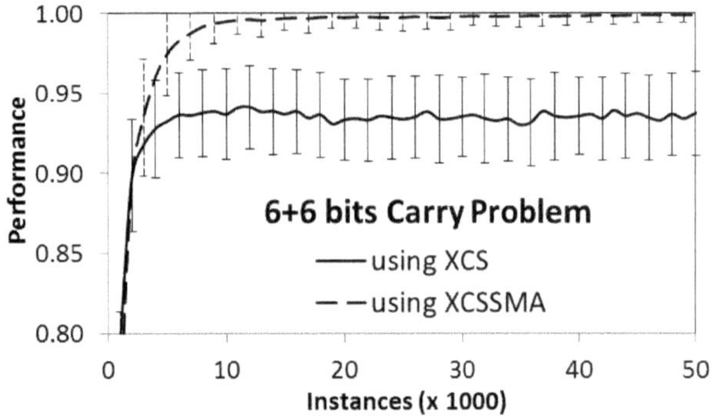

Figure 9: Results of 6+6 bits carry problem.

One of the classifier rules from the final solution obtained using XCSSMA is shown in Fig. 10. This is a maximally general and accurate classifier covering the whole problem space. The FSM action in this rule is general to solve any n+n bits carry problem. It is to be noted that state q_1 and state q_2 are not active, so there is no transition from any active state to these deactivated states. The state q_3 is active, but not reachable from the start state q_0. It means only two states, q_0 and q_4, are the working states in this FSM action.

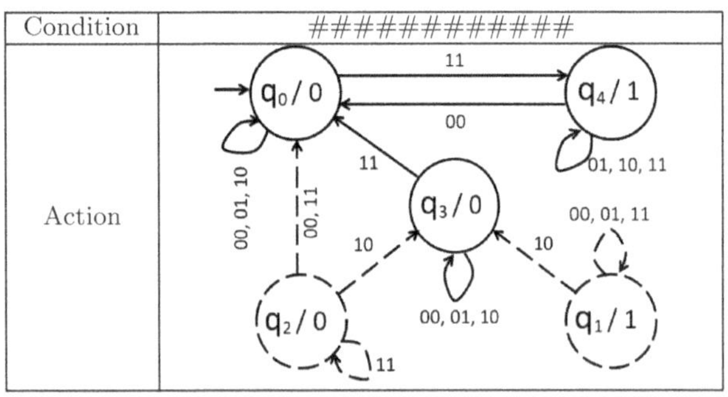

Figure 10: A sample classifier rule from final solution of 6+6 bits carry problem in XCSSMA.

The solutions found by Harding et al. [10] using SMCGP were also general, but not as compact and easily interpretable as the classifier rules obtained using XCSSMA here. For example, an evolved program using SMCGP is shown in Fig. 11 that provides solution for the 3+3 bits carry problem after two iterations. Here (x_0, y_0), (x_1, y_1), and (x_2, y_2) represent input-pair symbols; c_0 and c_1 denote the carry bits; INPP and OUTPUT are input and output nodes respectively; BF0, BF1, BF2, ... BF15 are the 16 Boolean operators of two variables; and DUP is the duplication operator. To obtain the solution for 6+6 bits carry problem, three more iterations will be performed resulting in a long chaining phenotype.

5.4 The Multiplexer Problem Domain

The results of standard XCS and XCSSMA for the 20-bits multiplexer problem are shown in Fig. 12. XCSSMA successfully solved it, but took more instances as compared with the standard XCS to reach a similar performance level.

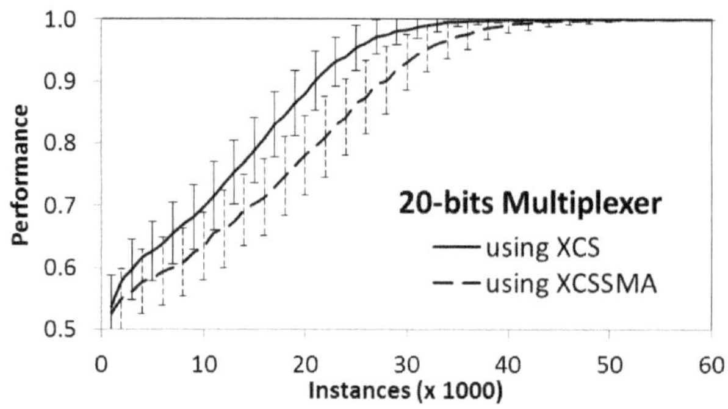

Figure 12: Results of 20-bits multiplexer problem.

The multiplexer is a niche balanced problem domain and there exists a complete solution for multiplexer problems that does not contain any overlapping classifier rules. So, standard XCS effectively solved the 20-bits multiplexer problem. The XCSSMA approach used more training examples, due to the increased search space as a result of the state-machine based actions.

A sample classifier rule for 20-bits multiplexer problem is shown in Fig. 13. This rule is equivalent to numeric action based XCS rule '0011###0############ : 0'. The states q_1 and q_4 are not reachable from the start state q_0 in the FSM action of this rule. The processing of any matched input message ends at the state q_3 that have output value 0, therefore action value of this rule will be 0.

6. DISCUSSION

Although SMCGP solutions are large, they compute parity in a conceptually parallel fashion. Standard XCS computes condition matching in parallel, but the action is a

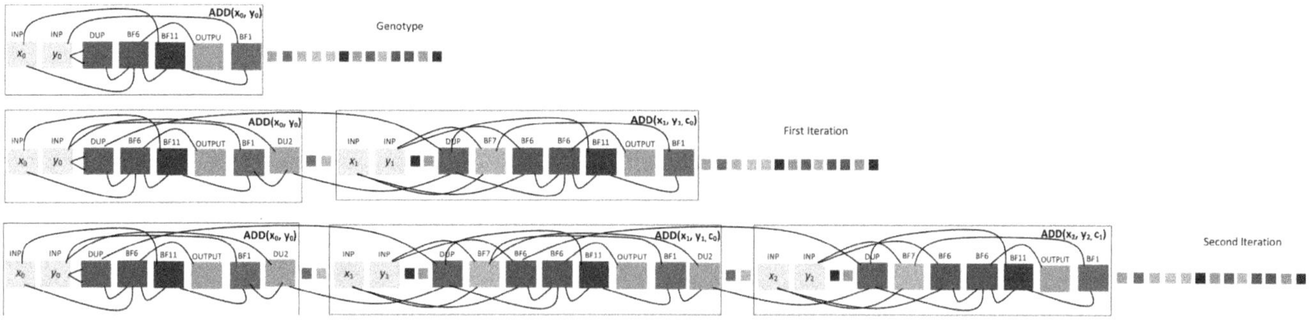

Figure 11: An evolved genotype, using SMCGP [10], iterated twice that provides solution for the 3+3 bits carry problem. Here (x_0, y_0), (x_1, y_1), and (x_2, y_2) represent input-pair symbols; c_0 and c_1 denote the carry bits. This is a colored figure and is adapted by kind permission of the author.

Condition	0011###0############
Action	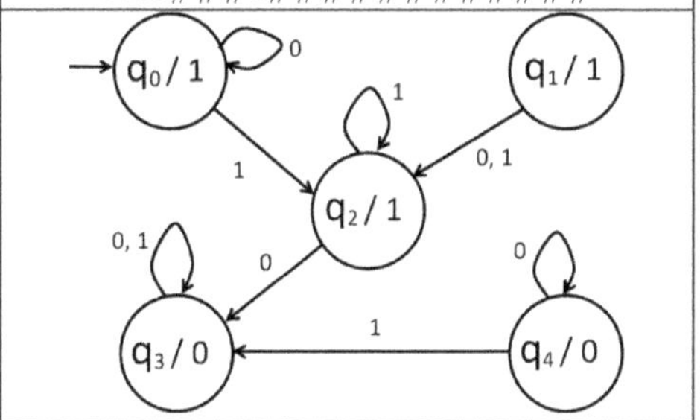

Figure 13: A sample classifier rule from final solution of 20-bits multiplexer problem in XCSSMA.

single scalar. By introducing XCSSMA the action is computed by a sequential process, which trades compactness for execution speed, which is still fast. It is to be noted that condition matching is still in parallel so that the division of search space may be computed efficiently.

The developed system, XCSSMA, can be viewed from two different perspectives. First, it can be regarded as a system to evolve finite state machines. If a general state machine M can be created for the problem at hand with the given machine configuration parameters (i.e. the number of states, input alphabet, output alphabet, etc.), then the system produces a rule of the form '###...# : M'. This rule will cover the whole problem space and classify each input instance accurately using the machine M as the action, e.g. the classifier rules shown in Fig. 5 and Fig. 10 for 24-bits even-parity problem and 6+6 bits carry problem respectively. Second, if a single general FSM cannot be created for the problem then the system behaves like a typical XCS and evolves a set of rules that collectively solve the problem, e.g. in majority-on and multiplexer problem domains.

An FSM is an abstract model that can represent a finite-state system in a compact form, but the evolution of FSMs is a hard task. Usually, FSMs are evolved using supervised learning so for large scale problems some form of subsampling and/or incremental testing is needed [3,21,24]. The online learning, niche based breeding, and generalization properties of XCS implicitly provides incremental testing and subsampling of the training data set. So, the developed system, as a combination of XCS and FSMs, rapidly evolved the general FSMs for the even-parity and carry problems.

It is to be noted that using an FSM as the action of a classifier rule, in place of a static numeric action, the size of the search space increases. This was compensated by improving the generalization ability of standard XCS in even-parity, carry, and majority-on problems. This improvement is obvious in the accurate rules shown in Fig. 5, Fig. 10, and Fig. 8 that match all the problem instances from 24-bits even-parity, all the problem instances from 6+6 bits carry, and eight problem instances from 7-bits majority-on problems respectively. The generalization to this level is beyond the ability of standard XCS using ternary alphabet based conditions along with the numeric action.

The FSM based action could not improve the generalization beyond numeric action based XCS for the multiplexer domain because the state machines needed for this domain are more complex than the other domains. The inherent property of indexing to a certain position according to the address bits in the input problem makes the creation of a state machine really hard in the multiplexer domain. So in the multiplexer problem domain, XCSSMA takes more training examples, due to the increased search space, to reach a performance level similar to standard XCS. It is to be noted that the code-fragment based XCS techniques [12, 14, 15] can scale in the multiplexer domain beyond 20-bits MUX, and using XCS with code-fragment conditions [15] 135-bits MUX have been solved.

In summary, if a proper representation scheme is used in XCS to encode the classifier rules, then the system can evolve maximally general and accurate classifiers, possibly just one classifier rule covering the whole problem space, e.g. XCSSMA for the even-parity and carry problems here and a code-fragment based XCS for the frog problem in [13]. It is also possible that the obtained solutions will be general to solve any problem from the domain, e.g. the solutions obtained in XCSSMA for the even-parity and carry problems.

The suite of scalable-XCS techniques and SMCGP are very promising systems that use rich encoding schemes to address the problem of scalable learning, but in different ways. SMCGP produces an individual as a 'single' solution, whereas the XCS classifier systems evolve a co-operative set of rules. SMCGP generally requires supervised learning with the whole training set, rather than on-line, reinforcement learning as in an XCS classifier system. Scalable-XCS can produce more compact solutions, but needs human selection for encoding schemes, i.e. code fragments or FSMs. SMCGP is more flexible as it evolves a computer program that can generate a sequence of programs, each of which solves a particular problem in the domain. However, XCS can divide up problem space using co-operative classifiers, which is advantageous in certain domains.

7. CONCLUSIONS

The proposed XCSSMA technique successfully solved four difficult Boolean problems, i.e. even-parity, majority-on, carry, and multiplexer problems. Further XCSSMA evolved, for the first time, compact and easily interpretable general solutions for the even-parity and carry problem domains. The XCSSMA technique is expected to be most useful when problems contain cyclic regularity in the problem input that is useful for deciding the answer to the problem.

Future work includes simplifying the final solution obtained by removing the deactivated and non-reachable states. Also two FSMs could be compared semantically, instead of syntactically as present, to fully enable the subsumption deletion mechanism in XCSSMA.

In the work presented here, only binary classification problems were tested. It would be interesting to apply the proposed system to the problems having more than two classes. It is anticipated that the implemented system can be extended to learn sequence prediction and multi-step tasks. There are advanced forms of state machines that have memory component such as pushdown automata and Turing machines, which could be used in XCSSMA for problems needing memory.

8. REFERENCES

[1] M. Ahluwalia and L. Bull. A Genetic Programming Based Classifier System. In *Genetic and Evolutionary Computation Conference*, pages 11–18, 1999.

[2] J. A. Anderson. *Automata Theory with Modern Applications*. Cambridge University Press, 2006.

[3] K. Benson. Evolving finite state machines with embedded genetic programming for automatic target detection. In *Congress on Evolutionary Computation*, pages 1543–1549, 2000.

[4] M. V. Butz, T. Kovacs, P. L. Lanzi, and S. W. Wilson. Toward a Theory of Generalization and Learning in XCS. *IEEE Transactions on Evolutionary Computation*, 8(1):28–46, 2004.

[5] M. V. Butz, P. L. Lanzi, and S. W. Wilson. Function Approximation With XCS: Hyperellipsoidal Conditions, Recursive Least Squares, and Compaction. *IEEE Transactions on Evolutionary Computation*, 12(3):355–376, 2008.

[6] M. V. Butz, M. Pelikan, X. Llorà, and D. E. Goldberg. Automated Global Structure Extraction for Effective Local Building Block Processing in XCS. *Evolutionary Computation*, 14(3):345–380, 2006.

[7] M. V. Butz and S. W. Wilson. An Algorithmic Description of XCS. *Soft Computing*, 6(3-4):144–153, 2002.

[8] H. H. Dam, H. A. Abbass, C. Lokan, and X. Yao. Neural-based learning classifier systems. *IEEE Transactions on Knowledge and Data Engineering*, 20(1):26–39, 2008.

[9] S. Harding, J. F. Miller, and W. Banzhaf. Self-Modifying Cartesian Genetic Programming. In *Genetic and Evolutionary Computation Conference*, pages 1021–1028, 2007.

[10] S. Harding, J. F. Miller, and W. Banzhaf. Developments in Cartesian Genetic Programming: self-modifying CGP. *Genetic Programming and Evolvable Machines*, 11(3-4):397–439, 2010.

[11] C. Ioannides and W. N. Browne. Investigating Scaling of an Abstracted LCS Utilising Ternary and S-Expression Alphabets. In *Genetic and Evolutionary Computation Conference*, pages 2759–2764, 2007.

[12] M. Iqbal, W. N. Browne, and M. Zhang. Extracting and Using Building Blocks of Knowledge in Learning Classifier Systems. In *Genetic and Evolutionary Computation Conference*, pages 863–870, 2012.

[13] M. Iqbal, W. N. Browne, and M. Zhang. XCSR with Computed Continuous Action. In *Australasian Joint Conference on Artificial Intelligence*, pages 350–361, 2012.

[14] M. Iqbal, W. N. Browne, and M. Zhang. Evolving Optimum Populations with XCS Classifier Systems. *Soft Computing*, 17(3):503–518, 2013.

[15] M. Iqbal, W. N. Browne, and M. Zhang. Reusing Building Blocks of Extracted Knowledge to Solve Complex, Large-Scale Boolean Problems. *IEEE Transactions on Evolutionary Computation*, 2013. under review.

[16] M. Iqbal, M. Zhang, and W. N. Browne. Automatically Defined Functions for Learning Classifier Systems. In *Genetic and Evolutionary Computation Conference (Companion)*, pages 375–382, 2011.

[17] D. Jackson and A. P. Gibbons. Layered Learning in Boolean GP Problems. In *European Conference on Genetic Programming*, pages 148–159, 2007.

[18] T. Kovacs. Evolving Optimal Populations with XCS Classifier Systems. Technical Report CSR-96-17 and CSRP-9617, University of Birmingham, UK, 1996.

[19] P. L. Lanzi. XCS with Stack-Based Genetic Programming. In *Congress on Evolutionary Computation*, pages 1186–1191, 2003.

[20] D. Loiacono, A. Marelli, and P. Lanzi. Support Vector Machines for Computing Action Mappings in Learning Classifier Systems. In *Congress on Evolutionary Computation*, pages 2141–2148, 2007.

[21] S. M. Lucas and T. J. Reynolds. Learning finite-state transducers: Evolution versus heuristic state merging. *IEEE Transactions on Evolutionary Computation*, 11(3):308–325, 2007.

[22] J. F. Miller and P. Thomson. Cartesian Genetic Programming. In *European Conference on Genetic Programming*, pages 121–132, 2000.

[23] E. F. Moore. Gedanken-experiments on Sequential Machines. In *Automata Studies: Annals of Mathematics Studies*, pages 129–153. Princeton University Press, 1956.

[24] W. M. Spears and D. F. Gordon-Spears. Evolution of strategies for resource protection problems. In *Advances in Evolutionary Computing: Theory and Applications*, pages 367–392. Springer, 2003.

[25] S. W. Wilson. Classifier Fitness Based on Accuracy. *Evolutionary Computation*, 3(2):149–175, 1995.

[26] S. W. Wilson. Classifiers that Approximate Functions. *Natural Computing*, 1:211–233, 2002.

An Analysis of a Spatial EA Parallel Boosting Algorithm

Uday Kamath
Dept. of Computer Science
George Mason University
Fairfax, USA
ukamath@gmu.edu

Carlotta Domeniconi
Dept. of Computer Science
George Mason University
Fairfax, USA
carlotta@cs.gmu.edu

Kenneth A. De Jong
Dept. of Computer Science
George Mason University
Fairfax, USA
kdejong@gmu.edu

ABSTRACT

The scalability of machine learning (ML) algorithms has become a key issue as the size of training datasets continues to increase. To address this issue in a reasonably general way, a parallel boosting algorithm has been developed that combines concepts from spatially structured evolutionary algorithms (SSEAs) and ML boosting techniques. To get more insight into the algorithm, a proper theoretical and empirical analysis is required. This paper is a first step in that direction. First, it establishes the connection between this algorithm and well known density estimation and mixture model approaches used by the machine learning community. The paper then analyzes the algorithm in terms of various theoretical and empirical properties such as convergence to large margins, scalability effects on accuracy and speed, robustness to noise, and connections to support vector machines in terms of instances converged to.

Track: Genetic Based Machine Learning

Categories and Subject Descriptors

I.2.6 [**Computing Methodologies**]: Artificial Intelligence—*Learning*[Knowledge acquisition]

General Terms

Algorithms

Keywords

spatially structured evolutionary algorithms, machine learning, ensemble learning, boosting.

1. INTRODUCTION

The most common applications of machine learning (ML) involve supervised learning, where a learned model is induced from training data and is used for prediction of unseen future instances. The scalability of these ML algorithms has become increasingly important for many applications like real-time systems, bioinformatics, and web data mining, where the training dataset sizes are in millions or even larger. Many current ML techniques have scalability issues, either because they require the entire training set to be in memory for learning the model, or because the learning time during model induction grows exponentially with training set size, or both [6]. Basic solutions like reducing the size of the training datasets via sampling can be used, but they can introduce sampling errors [4]. Another approach is to employ complex changes specific to the desired ML algorithm for running on parallel and distributed architectures [9]. Boosting techniques are designed to boost training instances that are hard, but do so either by making multiple passes over the training data [13] or via incremental methods [10], affecting time and space complexity for large datasets.

To develop a solid general framework that tackles the scalability issue of supervised ML techniques, in this paper we analyze an alternative approach, that combines concepts from spatially structured evolutionary algorithms (SSEAs) [24, 29] for parallelization with the techniques of ensemble learning and boosting [19, 27]. This parallel spatial boosting algorithm (PSBML) has been shown to be a general approach for parallelizing ML methods [16]. It achieves this goal by partitioning the training data and by parallelizing the boosting step. The algorithm learns from the entire training data without changing the underlying learning techniques, and yet performs comparably to standard boosting and ensemble methods in terms of prediction accuracy.

In this paper, we show an equivalence between PSBML and well-established machine learning properties. Drawing this connection enables us to derive important properties of the PSBML method, and to achieve a better understanding of the extent of its applicability and its limitations. Theoretical models to study the distributions generated by SSEAs have been previously developed [24, 29]. Here we deal with an SSEA that runs an EA and a machine learner at each node of its grid. Each learner has access to only locally distributed subsets of training data (the current population of the local EA) and identifies the hardest instances to be classified. That information is used by the EA to define the fitness of training instances in terms of their classification difficulty, and then redistribute locally the most difficult instances via fitness proportionate selection. This parallel process causes an iterative change of the underlying training data distribution to increase the frequency of the difficult instances (as in boosting).

In this paper, we draw a clear connection between this procedure and statistical techniques that aim to find the

GECCO'13, July 6–10, 2013, Amsterdam, The Netherlands.

modes (i.e. local maxima) of Gaussian mixture models. By virtue of this connection, we can show that PSBML converges to a distribution whose modes are centered around the *margin*, i.e. around the hardest points as defined by the classification problem at hand. As a consequence, the PSBML algorithm preserves the main feature of boosting: convergence to the hard-to-classify instances.

In addition, we perform an empirical study to investigate the scalability of PSBML in terms of speed and accuracy, a crucial aspect of any parallel algorithm from a practitioner standpoint. Finally, we conduct an empirical analysis of the effects of noise on the parallel boosting framework as implemented in PSBML.

2. RELATED WORK

SSEAs have been theoretically analyzed using diffusion models [1, 14, 25]. In particular, various important properties such as how the shape and the structure of spatial topography affect diversity, the distribution of the best individuals, and convergence have been analyzed [24, 29]. Some of these findings constitute an important foundation for our theoretical and empirical analysis.

In statistical learning theory, a formal relationship between the notion of *margin* and the generalization classification error has been established [30]. As a result, classifiers that converge to a large margin have better performance in terms of generalization error. One of the most popular examples of such classifiers is support vector machines (SVMs). A trained SVM satisfies the maximum margin property, i.e. the decision boundary it represents has the maximum minimum distance from the closest training point. In addition, a formal analysis of the AdaBoost technique, and many of its variants, has derived theoretical bounds on the margin distribution to which the approach converges [26].

The AdaBoost technique, and boosting in general, is an example of a learning methodology known as ensemble learning [19], in which multiple classifiers are generated and combined to make the final prediction. Ensemble learning has been shown to be effective with unstable classifiers, by improving upon the performance of the base learners. Semi-supervised ensemble methods have also been introduced that select the collection of learners that make consistent prediction on the unlabeled data. It has been shown that this approach is equivalent to maximizing the margin in function space of both the labeled and unlabeled data [5]

Estimation of Distribution Algorithms (EDAs) is a well known methodology in the EA community that maps evolutionary algorithms to statistical distribution models [17, 18]. Various previous studies have established relationships between evolutionary algorithms and multivariate distribution models [2, 23].

3. THE PSBML FRAMEWORK

The algorithm for parallelizing boosting (PSBML) has at its core a standard SSEA [24], where training instances are distributed over a two-dimensional toroidal grid with a common machine learning algorithm running at each node of the grid. A node in the grid, as in SSEA, interacts with only its neighbors as predefined by the neighborhood structure (see Figure 1). From Boosting perspective, the balance between maintaining the diversity of instances in the training set and eliminating easy instances is very important. Selection

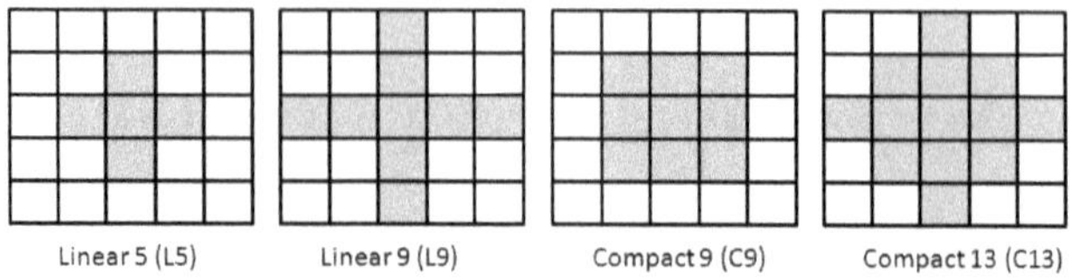

Figure 1: Two dimensional grid with various neighborhood structures.

pressure in SSEA performs this task and it depends on two elements: the survival selection method used by the EA in the node of the grid, and the size and shape of the neighborhood structure defined for the grid.

Each node in the grid starts with a uniformly stratified distribution of the training data. The local EA running in a node updates its training data during the generational cycle. Each node of the grid also has a pluggable ML classifier (e.g., a naive Bayes classifier, a decision tree learner, or support vector machine). During each generation, a node in the grid performs a standard training procedure using its own data, and performs testing using the combined training examples of neighboring nodes. In addition to classifying the test examples, the models output a confidence value for each prediction. These confidence values are used to assign a fitness to the instance, allowing the local EA in the node to subsequently select the most difficult instances for the next generation. Since each instance is a member of the neighborhood of multiple nodes, an ensemble assessment of difficulty is performed, similar to boosting the margin in AdaBoost [26]. Namely, the fitness v_i of an instance i is set equal to the smallest confidence value obtained from any node and for any class:

$$v_i = \min_{n \in N_i} c_{ni}$$

where N_i is a set of indices defined over the neighborhoods to which instance i belongs, and c_{ni} is the confidence credited to instance i by the learner corresponding to neighborhood n. A normalized weight v_i^{norm} with value in the interval [0,1] is obtained from v_i through linear re-scaling:

$$v_i^{norm} = \frac{v_i - v_{min}}{v_{max} - v_{min}}$$

where v_{min} and v_{max} are the smallest and largest fitness values obtained across all the nodes, respectively. The selection probability w_i associated to instance i is then set to:

$$w_i = 1 - v_i^{norm}$$

w_i is used in fitness proportionate selection, so that, the smaller the confidence credited to an instance i is (i.e., the harder to learn instance i is), the larger the probability for instance i to be selected will be. Instead of deterministically replacing the entire pool of local data at a given generation, a replacement probability P_r was introduced. Experimentally, it was determined that overlapping-generation model for the local EAs was more effective and the most effective value for P_r was found to be 0.20 [16] which we will be using in all the experiments.

The pseudo-code of PSBML is given in Algorithm 3.1. Various parameters for grid configuration, such as width/height, replacement probability, and maximum iterations (or epochs), are all included in *GridParam*.

Algorithm 3.1: PARBOOST(*Train*, *Test*, *GridParam*)

```
INITIALIZEGRID(Train, GridParam)
comment: distribute the instances over the nodes in grid
currentMin ← 100
Pr ← GridParam.pr
comment: Probability of replacement
for i ← 0 to GridParam.iter
  do
  hardData ← Train
  comment: hardData initialized to all train
  { TRAINNODES(GridParam)
  { comment: Train all nodes
  { TESTANDWEIGHNODES(GridParam);
  { comment: Test using neighborhood and assign weight
  { PrunedData ← {}
  { for j ← 0 to GridParam.nodes
  {   do
  {   { NeighborData ← COLLECTNEIGHBORDATA(j);
  {   { NodeData ← NodeData + NeighborData
  {   { ReplaceData ← FITNESSPROPSEL(NodeData, Pr)
  {   { PrunedData ← UNIQUE(PrunedData, ReplaceData)
  {   { comment: Unique keeps 1 copy of instance in set
  { error ← TESTCLASSIFIER(PrunedData, Test)
  { comment: Perform Validation step for the model
  { if error < currentMin
  {          { currentMin ← error
  {    then  { bestClassifier ← SAVECLASSIF(PrunedData)
  {          { hardData ← PrunedData
  {          { comment: hardData set reduced
return (bestClassifier, hardData)
```

4. ANALYSIS OF PSBML

We utilize Gaussian Mixture Models (GMMs) combined with mean-shift to show that the PSBML algorithm iteratively changes the underlying data distribution, and converges to a distribution whose modes are centered around the margin, i.e. around the hardest points as defined by the classification problem at hand.

4.1 Background on Gaussian Mixture Models and Mean-shift

A Gaussian mixture model (GMM) is a parametric probabilistic model consisting of a linear combination of Gaussian distributions with unknown parameters. Typically the parameter values are estimated so that the resulting model is the one that best fit the data [21]. Gaussian mixtures have been widely used to model clustering applications, to classifying complex data, and segmenting images [22].

Mean-shift is a local search algorithm whose aim is to find the modes (i.e. local maxima) of a distribution. It achieves this goal by performing kernel density estimation, and iteratively locating the local maxima of the kernel mixture as the zeros of the corresponding gradient function [8]. Convergence to local maxima is guaranteed from any starting point. Furthermore, it has been shown that, when combined with GMMs, mean-shift is equivalent to an expectation-maximization (EM) algorithm [7]. Mean-shift can be used as a nonparametric clustering approach, and has been successfully applied in many computer vision problems [8]. The key advantage of using the mean-shift algorithm on a given density for mode finding is two-fold: (1) The approach is deterministic and nonparametric, since based on kernel density estimation; and (2) It poses no a priori assumptions on the number of the modes [7, 8].

4.2 Connection between GMMs with Mean-shift and PSBML

The PSBML algorithm, through the fitness proportionate selection process driven by the replacement probabilities associated to instances, effectively performs, locally at each node, a change of the underlying data distribution. Such local changes are reflected in an overall shift of the distribution. We argue here that the iterative process of changing the underlying data distribution converges to a distribution whose modes are centered around the margin, i.e. around the hardest points as defined by the classification problem at hand. In virtue of this argument we'll be able to demonstrate interesting properties of the PSBML algorithm at convergence. Our argument makes use of GMMs combined with the mean-shift procedure.

The mean-shift procedure is used in Gaussian mixture models to find the modes of a given distribution, irrespective of the starting location [7]. As we'll see, this is a desirable property that maps nicely to the PSBML framework, thus providing convergence properties which are independent of the sampling process used to distribute the data through the nodes of the grid.

In a classification problem, a common approach to assess the confidence of a prediction for an instance is to measure its distance from the estimated decision boundary: the smaller the distance, the smaller the confidence will be. Each node of the grid, along with its neighborhood structure, can be visualized as a sample, where each point is weighed according to its hardness, and on which a distribution can be fit. The underlying classifier trained on a node, and tested on the whole neighborhood, plays the role of estimating the distance of the corresponding points from the boundary, and weighting them accordingly. If we fit a Gaussian mixture model using mean-shift on the data assigned to a node and on its neighbors, at a given instance of time, it can be argued that the modes closer to the boundary, corresponding to points with larger weights, will be the ones visited by mean-shift, irrespective of the starting point. Since each node in the wraparound grid behaves similarly, in this scenario every node, in parallel, fits a Gaussian mixture model on its neighborhood. At each successive iteration of learning, sampling is performed at each node according to the new distribution, and therefore it's biased towards the peaks previously found, and instances are re-weighted based on the current estimation of the boundary. Thus, inductively, aggregating the local behavior of each node, it can be argued that the whole data distribution would converge to a distribution with peaks around the boundary, since the points at this location hold larger weights. Our findings through an empirical analysis, presented in Section 5, corroborate this argument.

From the above discussion, it can be seen that the mean-shift procedure, which is an iterative search algorithm used to locate the modes of a distribution, is similar to a local EA running on a node of the grid. The local classifier assigns confidence to data based on the current estimated boundary. The confidence acts as an instance weight, interpreted as a fitness by the EA, where the harder instances are the most

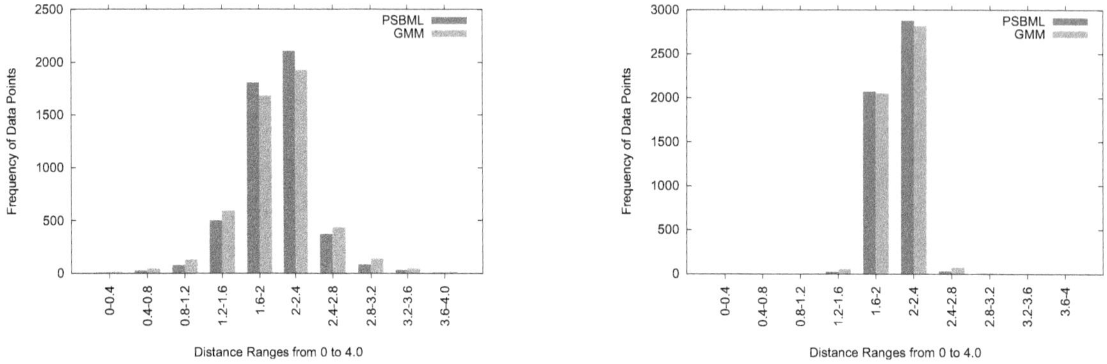

Figure 2: Linearly separable dataset: Data distribution at epochs 25 (Left) and 50 (Right) using PSBML and GMMs.

fit. Fitness proportionate selection, which makes copies of highly fit points, is thus equivalent to performing a weighted sampling of the data. As a result, through the iterations, the peaks of the data density gradually move towards the boundary, in a way simulating successive estimations of the modes via mean-shift, with convergence at the margin.

5. EXPERIMENTS

All the experiments were run on an Intel Core2 Duo machine with 8GB RAM and 3.2GHz CPU. The PSBML algorithm implementation and the comparative classifier runs were all run using Java with max heap size of 4GB and and WEKA ML software [15]. LibSVM and LibLinear were run using native implementation in C++ for performance comparisons [11, 12].

5.1 Empirical Equivalence between GMMs with Mean-shift and PSBML

To empirically verify the above hypothesis and the relationship between PSBML and GMMs, a detailed step by step process was employed. First, synthetic datasets were crafted to have known boundaries/margins on which we ran the experiments. The experiments ranged from running PSBML with a machine learner in a grid, to eventually running GMMs with mean-shift on the whole dataset without any grid or learner. This change was done gradually in three steps, detailed below with justification of their intent. The focus of these experiments was to validate the comparison between GMMs and PSBML in terms of distribution of instances. At this stage classifier accuracy comparisons were not the focus.

1. Run the PSBML algorithm using a 5×5 spatial grid with the C9 neighborhood (see Fig. 1) and a large margin classifier on the synthetic dataset to observe the population distribution change over time.

2. Replace each local classifier with a GMM with mean-shift, while keeping the grid structure and neighborhood interaction unchanged. Each data instance is weighted a-priori according to its distance from the known boundary (the smaller the distance, the larger the weight). We run GMM with mean-shift on each node and perform sampling iteratively at every training epoch exactly as in PSBML. We observe the population distribution change over time. The assumption of the relationship between PSBML and GMMs with mean-shift is confirmed if the distributions generated in the two cases are similar.

3. Delete the grid structure and run GMMs with mean-shift estimation on the whole dataset, with each instance weighted according to its distance from the known boundary as above. We observe the data distribution and final modes at convergence, and compare them with those obtained in the previous setting.

5.1.1 *Experiment on a Linearly Separable Dataset*

A linearly separable one dimensional dataset of size 5000 is generated by uniformly sampling in the interval $[0, 4]$. The instances between 0 and 2 are labeled as negative, and the instances between 2 and 4 are labeled as positive. We run the three experiments as described in the previous section. For experiment 1, the large margin classifier used at each node fits a line to its training set by placing it at the location corresponding to the average distance between the smallest positive and the largest negative instances. The confidence associated to a point is its distance from the estimated edge.

To compare the data distributions obtained in experiments 1 and 2, we recorded the number of points at various intervals at generations 25 and 50. The resulting histograms are reported in Figure 2. We can clearly observe that the two methodologies, PSBML and GMMs with mean-shift, provide a practically identical distribution at both generations, and they converge to a distribution with modes centered on the points closest to the actual boundary ($x = 2$).

For experiment 3, we run GMMs with mean-shift estimation 30 times on the whole weighted data. The means of the modes at convergence were 1.973 and 2.012, with a very small standard deviation of 0.046. Again, the distribution at convergence was very close to those obtained in experiments 1 and 2. Interestingly, when the weights were removed, and therefore, implicitly the role performed by the classifier was also removed, the means of the modes at convergence moved to 1.03 and 2.98. This result corroborates the fact that the weights credited to points by PSBML proportionally increase their mass, so that the modes of the resulting distributions are centered on those points with the largest weights.

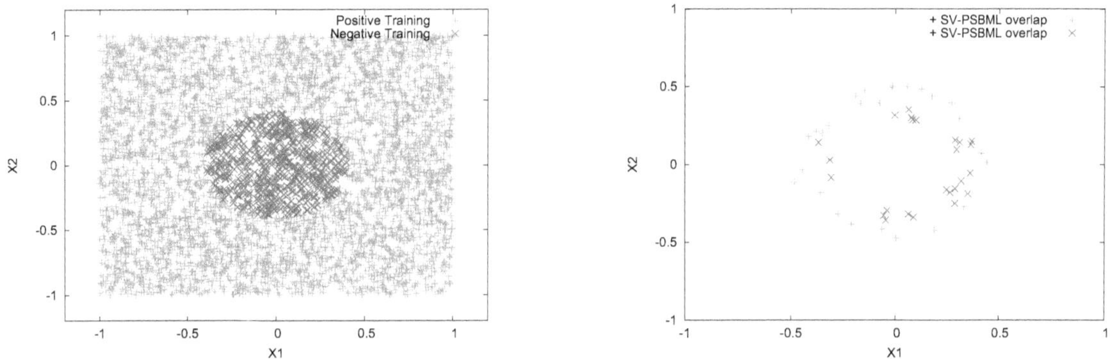

Figure 3: (Left) Circle dataset; (Right) Points that are both support vectors and hard instances selected by PSBML.

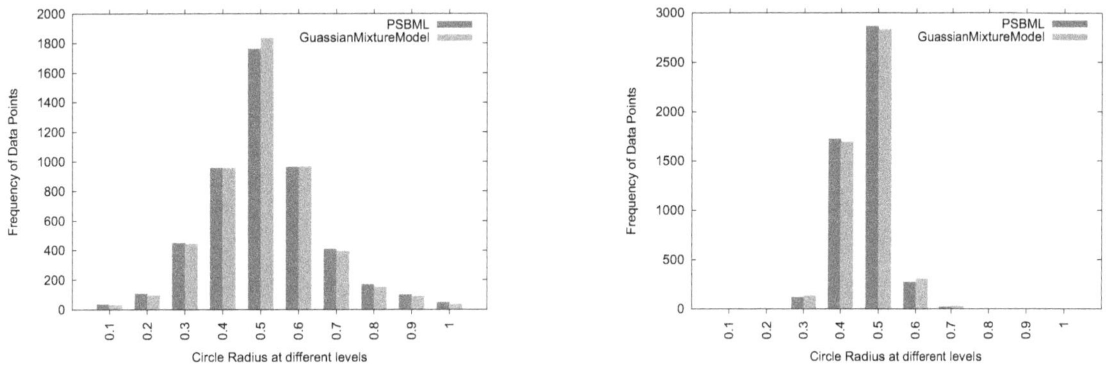

Figure 4: Circle dataset: Data distribution at epochs 25 (Left) and 50 (Right) using PSBML and GMMs.

5.1.2 Experiment on a Non-linearly Separable Dataset

Instances were drawn at random within a square centered at the origin and with side of length two. Points with a distance smaller than 0.4 from the origin are labeled as negative, and those with a distance greater or equal than 0.4 are labeled as positive (see Figure 3). Again, we run the three experiments as described in Section 5.1. For experiment 1, the large margin classifier used at each node fits a circle to its training set by setting its radius to the average distance of the origin from the smallest positive and the largest negative instances. For testing, the learner outputs "−" when the instance falls within the circle, and "+" otherwise. The confidence of the prediction is the distance of the instance from the circled boundary.

To compare the data distributions obtained in experiments 1 and 2, we recorded the number of points at various intervals of distances from the origin at generations 25 and 50. The resulting histograms are reported in Figure 4. We can observe again that the two methodologies, PSBML and GMMs with mean-shift, provide a practically identical distribution at both generations, and they converge to a distribution with modes centered on the points closest to the boundary.

For experiment 3, we run GMMs with mean-shift estimation 30 times on the whole weighted data. The means of the modes at convergence were $(-0.01, 0.38)$ and $(0.01, -0.41)$, with a very small standard deviation of 0.03. Again, the distribution at convergence was very close to those obtained in experiments 1 and 2. Similarly to the one dimensional dataset, removing the weights from the instances during the runs with GMMs results in a change of means of modes at convergence; they are $(-0.03, 0.51)$ and $(0.03, -0.49)$.

5.1.3 Support Vectors and Hard Instances in PSBML

We also analyzed the data distribution at convergence by comparing the hard instances identified by PSBML with the support vectors of a trained SVM. Table 1 shows the percentage of overlap for the two simulated datasets. The support vectors of the trained SVMs with the highest α (i.e. weight) values correspond to the hard instances with the top 10% largest weights identified by the PSBML algorithm. The points that are identified both as hard instances and as support vectors for the circle dataset are shown in Figure 3.

Datasets	1D Linear	2D Circle
SV overlap	92%	90%

Table 1: Support vectors and PSBML hard instances overlap.

5.1.4 Weight Distribution Changes

One important property of boosting is to scale the weights of data as a function of its distance from the margin. SSEAs have similar behavior where the *takeover* curves exhibit a logistic function with time [1, 14, 25]. To observe the effect

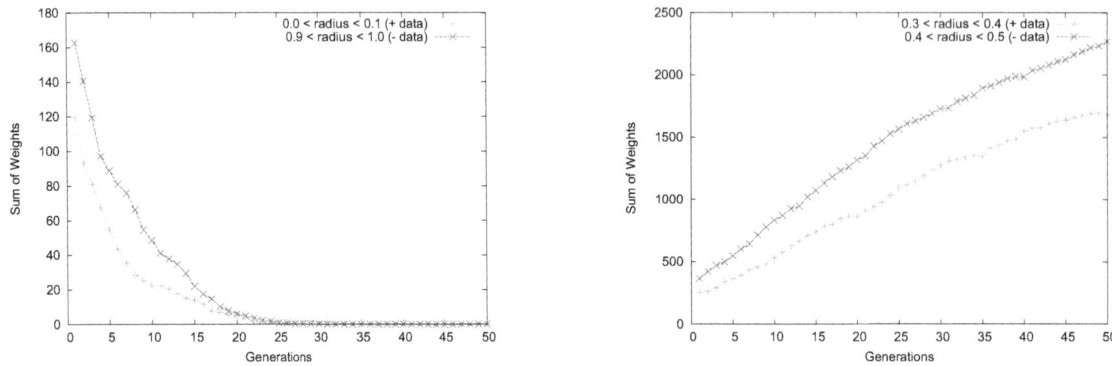

Figure 5: Changes in weight distribution as function of time: (Left) exponential decay; (Right) logistic increase.

of weight changes, in Figure 5 we plotted the weights of all points at different radii for the circle dataset at different generations. We can clearly see the exponential decay and the logistic increase based on the data points closeness to the margin. For positive points, when the radius is between 0.3 and 0.4, and for negative points, when the radius is between 0.4 and 0.5, an increase is seen with time, and for the rest there is exponential decay, confirming the behavior analogous to boosting.

5.2 Scalability and Accuracy Experiments

To evaluate how PSBML would behave in terms of scalability of data, we created three different non-linear and complex decision boundary datasets with functions normally used for optimization experiments. In each case, the points above the surface defined by the function were designated as positive examples, and the points below were negative examples.

The first dataset was a two dimensional decision boundary based on a sine wave generated by the function

$$f(\mathbf{x}) = 2sin(2\pi x_1) \quad (1)$$

The dimension x_1 was sampled from $[0, 6.28]$ and the $y = f(\mathbf{x})$ dimension was randomly sampled from $[0, 2]$.

A three dimensional decision boundary was generated using the Rastrigin function

$$f(\mathbf{x}) = 20 + (x_1^2 - 10cos(2\pi x_1)) + (x_2^2 - 10cos(2\pi x_2)) \quad (2)$$

The two dimensions x_1 and x_2 were sampled between $[-1, 1]$, and the $y = f(\mathbf{x})$ dimension was sampled between $[0, 40]$.

Another three dimensional decision boundary was generated using the Rosenbrock function

$$f(\mathbf{x}) = (1 - x_1^2)^2 + 100(x_2 - x_1^2)^2 \quad (3)$$

The two dimensions x_1 and x_2 were sampled between $[-3, 3]$ and the $y = f(\mathbf{x})$ dimension was sampled between [0,2500].

In each case we generated a training dataset with a million instances. However, this was too large for an SVM (LIBSVM) with a non-linear kernel (RBF kernel). We kept reducing the data and found that at 10% (i.e. around $100K$ sample points) the non-linear SVM could run in reasonable time. We thus performed 25×10 times a bootstrap approach of sampling with replacement from the whole dataset, and computed the best performance from the runs. For comparison, we also ran the liblinear SVM, which has been optimized to scale on large datasets but constrained to linear models only. The trade-off of speed for model simplification results in reduced performance, exaggerated here because of the highly non-linear datasets.

Finally, we ran PSBML with decision trees (J48) [20] as the base classifier with a 3×3 grid for 25 generations to approximate the budget in terms of data sampled. A decision tree classifier was used as it had an intermediate training speed relative to the other classifiers we tested initially (fast LibLinear and the kernel estimated Naive Bayes) [16]. PSBML takes advantage of multi-threading and parallelizing the node learning on a multi-processor machine. The whole setup was run 10 times to get the average auROC of all the runs and paired t-test for significance comparisons. Table 2 summarizes the findings. We also measured the speed and show comparative runs in Table 3. We clearly see that, while maintaining good accuracy, the parallelization using SSEA helped reducing the training time significantly.

To further evaluate the scalability of PSBML on training times with different sizes of the training set, we used the real-world KDDCup-99 intrusion detection dataset with close to 4.9 million training data, 42 features, and 24 classes. The training data was sampled in various sizes from $50K$, $100K$, $500K$ and 1 Million, and 10 runs were performed with standard PSBML with decision trees, a 3×3 grid, and the C9 neighborhood. The training times are shown in Figure 6, which clearly shows almost linear scalability with training data sizes.

Datasets	Sinewave	Rossenbrock	Rastrigin
SVM (Sampled 111k)	70.3	97.2	85.1
LibLinear (1M)	68.8	51.1	69.3
PSBML (1M)	**84.2**	**99.6**	**92.2**

Table 2: Accuracy (auROC) comparisons with SVMs.

Datasets	Sinewave	Rossenbrock	Rastrigin
LibSVM 111K	356.23	243.2	367.8
LibSVM 1M	3611.23	2512.2	2713.4
PSBML-Node 111K	25.8	28.3	22.3
PSBML-Grid 1M	26.2	28.6	22.6

Table 3: Average speed (secs) comparisons with SVMs.

5.3 Accuracy Comparison on a Large Real-world Dataset

The goal of this experiment is to perform a statistical analysis comparing PSBML to known classifiers and meta-classifiers on a sufficiently large real-world dataset with non-overlapping train/test distributions. We used the NSL-KDD dataset with approximately $120K$ training data and $22K$ test data [28]. The NSL-KDD dataset retained all the important statistical characteristics of KDDCup-99, but it's smaller so that performance can be evaluated on a variety of algorithms. We ran the PSBML algorithm with a 3×3 grid, the C9 neighborhood, and Naive Bayes as the base classifier. We obtained similar performance using other classifiers like decision trees, but to reduce experimental computation time we used Naive Bayes. We used the top ranking competitive methods (as shown in [28]), performed 30 runs of 10-fold cross validation, and compared the results using a paired t-test for significance. The results are shown in Table 4. Boosting and PSBML are very close in performance. However, in this case, PSBML is statistically significantly better, illustrating the ability of PSBML to perform well on a large dataset, while maintaining the advantage of parallelization.

Algorithms	Accuracy (auROC)
DecisionTee (J48)	81.02
NaiveBayes	80.67
NB-Tree	82.8
NeuralNetwork	77.42
SVM (RBF)	60.12
RandomForest	80.67
RandomTree	81.5
AdaBoost	90.77
PSBML (NaiveBayes)	**93.5**

Table 4: Performance on NSL-KDD.

5.4 Noise Impact Analysis

Classification problems with medium-to-large datasets from the UCI ML repository [3] were chosen to perform an additional empirical analysis of PSBML in presence of noise. The purpose of this experiment was to compare the impact of noise on the behavior of boosting on a whole dataset and PSBML in parallel mode. The datasets are described in Table 5 in terms of numbers of training and testing instances, number of features, and number of classes.

We first performed a comparison between the PSBML algorithm and standard AdaBoost to show their accuracy measured as area under ROC which is a reliable measure when data is imbalanced.

Adding noise to the class values in the training set and validating it on the hold-out test set gives a good empirical robustness measure of an algorithm to noise. We performed an analysis with noise level at 10% and ran the train/test 30 times, using 90-10 split for train-test in WEKA-experimenter. We ran AdaBoost with the same underlying classifier (Naive Bayes) and with the same settings so that we can draw conclusive results in the comparisons. We used a paired t-test for significance comparison. The results are shown in Table 6, where statistically significant accuracy values are shown in boldface. PSBML achieved statistically significant

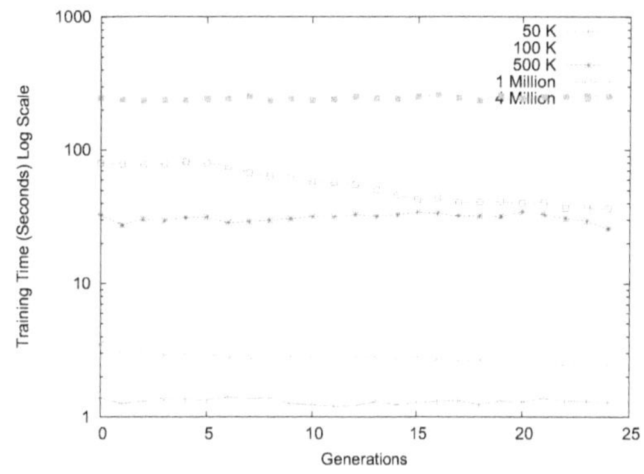

Figure 6: Mean training times with varying dataset sizes.

improvements compared to AdaBoost in most datasets. Similar results were obtained for 10% level of noise, showing advantages of PSBML.

6. CONCLUSION AND FUTURE WORK

In this paper we take an important first step in analyzing PSBML, an SSEA-based parallel boosting framework for improving the scalability of ML techniques. By establishing an equivalence between PSBML and GMMs using mean-shift analysis, important properties regarding convergence to large margins are obtained and verified empirically. In addition, it was also shown that the scalability achieved by PSBML is obtained without compromising on accuracy or performance, an important feature from a practitioner's perspective. Finally, the spatial topology of PSBML was shown to provide a level of robustness to noise that is lacking in standard ML techniques.

The experimental studies in this paper were done on a single multi-threaded machine. An interesting extension of this work would be to analyze it for parallel and distributed computational architectures like the Beowulf-style clusters. Also, the focus of this paper was on analyzing ML properties. However, the GMM approach is more general than that and could be a useful analysis tool for other more optimization-oriented EC areas such as SSEAs and EDAs.

7. REFERENCES

[1] E. Alba and G. Luque. Growth curves and takeover time in distributed evolutionary algorithms. In *Proc. of GECCO-2004*, pages 864–876, 2004.

[2] S. J. Arnold. Multivariate inheritance and evolution: a review of concepts. *Quantitative Genetic Studies of Behavioral Evolution*, pages 17–48, 1994.

[3] A. Asuncion and D. Newman. UCI machine learning repository, 2007.

[4] J. Bacardit and X. Llorà. Large scale data mining using genetics-based machine learning. In *Proc. of GECCO-2012*, pages 1171–1196, 2012.

[5] K. P. Bennett, A. Demiriz, and R. Maclin. Exploiting unlabeled data in ensemble methods. In *In Proc. ACM Int. Conf. Knowledge Discovery and Data Mining*, pages 289–296. ACM Press, 2002.

[6] A. Bordes, L. Bottou, and P. Gallinari. Sgd-qn: Careful quasi-newton stochastic gradient descent. *J. of Machine Learning Research*, 10:1737–1754, 2009.

Dataset	Chess	Spam	Digit	Magick	Adult	W8A	Cod	Cover	KDD99
#Train	3196	4600	10992	19020	32560	49749	271617	581012	4898431
#Test	319	460	1099	1902	16279	14951	59535	58102	311027
#Feat	36	57	256	10	14	300	8	54	42
#Class	2	2	10	2	2	2	2	7	24

Table 5: UCI datasets used in the experiments.

No Noise	Chess	Spam	Digit	Magick	Adult	W8A	Cod	Cover	KDD99
AdaBoost	92.83	93.89	86.9	83.22	85.13	97.45	92.43	78.72	99.14
PSBML	**93**	**94**	**90**	83.1	**89.01**	**98.1**	90.01	**85.1**	**99.65**
10%Noise									
AdaBoost	81.80	76.6	81.9	80.22	82.13	96.45	**92.13**	76.72	98.14
PSBML	**84.38**	**81.8**	79.21	**81.9**	**83.7**	96.9	90.20	**78.1**	99.18

Table 6: Comparison with AdaBoost with and without Noise (10%).

[7] M. Á. Carreira-Perpiñán. Gaussian mean shift is an em algorithm. *IEEE Trans. on Pattern Analysis and Machine Intelligence*, 29:2007, 2005.

[8] M. Á. Carreira-Perpiñán and C. K. I. Williams. On the number of modes of a gaussian mixture. In *Proc. of Scale-Space 2003*, pages 625–640, 2003.

[9] P. Domingos, G. Hulten, P. C. W. Edu, and C. H. G. W. Edu. A general method for scaling up machine learning algorithms and its application to clustering. In *In Proceedings of the Eighteenth Int'l Conference on Machine Learning*, pages 106–113, 2001.

[10] N. U. Edakunni, G. Brown, and T. Kovacs. Boosting as a product of experts. In *Proc. of UAI-2011*, pages 187–194, 2011.

[11] R.-E. Fan, K.-W. Chang, C.-J. Hsieh, X.-R. Wang, and C.-J. Lin. LIBLINEAR: A library for large linear classification. *J. Machine Learning Research*, 9:1871–1874, 2008.

[12] R.-E. Fan, P.-H. Chen, and C.-J. Lin. Working set selection using the second order information for training SVM. *J. Machine Learning Research*, 6(1532-4435):1889–1918, 2005.

[13] Y. Freund and R. E. Schapire. Experiments with a new boosting algorithm. In *Proc. of ICML-1996*, pages 148–156, 1996.

[14] M. Giacobini, M. Tomassini, A. Tettamanzi, and E. Alba. Selection intensity in cellular evolutionary algorithms for regular lattices. *IEEE Trans. Evolutionary Computation*, 9(5):489–505, 2005.

[15] M. Hall, E. Frank, G. Holmes, B. Pfahringer, P. Reutemann, and I. H. Witten. The WEKA data mining software: an update. *SIGKDD Explor. Newsl.*, 11(1):10–18, 2009.

[16] U. Kamath, J. Kaers, A. Shehu, and K. A. De Jong. A spatial EA framework for parallelizing machine learning methods. In *Parallel Problem Solving from Nature — PPSN XII*, volume 7491 of *Lecture Notes in Computer Science*, pages 206–215. Springer, 2012.

[17] H. Mühlenbein, J. Bendisch, and H.-M. Voigt. From recombination of genes to the estimation of distributions: II. continuous parameters. In *Parallel Problem Solving from Nature — PPSN IV*, pages 188–197, Berlin, 1996. Springer.

[18] H. Mühlenbein and G. Paaß. From recombination of genes to the estimation of distributions: I. Binary parameters. In *Parallel Problem Solving from Nature — PPSN IV*, pages 178–187, Berlin, 1996. Springer.

[19] D. Opitz and R. Maclin. Popular ensemble methods: An empirical study. *Journal of Artificial Intelligence Research*, 11:169–198, 1999.

[20] R. Quinlan. *C4.5: Programs for Machine Learning.* Morgan Kaufmann Publishers, San Mateo, CA, 1993.

[21] C. E. Rasmussen. The infinite gaussian mixture model. In *In Advances in Neural Information Processing Systems 12*, pages 554–560. MIT Press, 2000.

[22] D. A. Reynolds, T. F. Quatieri, and R. B. Dunn. Speaker verification using adapted gaussian mixture models. *Digital Signal Processing*, 10:19–41, 2000.

[23] S. H. Rice. *Evolutionary Theory: Mathematical and Conceptual Foundations.* Sinauer Associates, Inc., 2004.

[24] J. Sarma and K. De Jong. An analysis of the effects of neighborhood size and shape on local selection algorithms. In *Parallel Problem Solving from Nature — PPSN IV*, pages 236–244. Springer-Verlag, 1996.

[25] J. Sarma and K. De Jong. An analysis of local selection algorithms in a spatially structured evolutionary algorithm. In *Proc. ICGA-1997*, pages 181–187, 1997.

[26] R. E. Schapire, Y. Freund, P. Bartlett, and W. S. Lee. Boosting the margin: A new explanation for the effectiveness of voting methods. *The Annals of Statistics*, 26(5):1651–1686, 1998.

[27] R. E. Schapire and Y. Singer. Improved boosting algorithms using confidence-rated predictions. *Machine Learning*, 37(3):297–336, 1999.

[28] M. Tavallaee, E. Bagheri, W. Lu, and A. A. Ghorbani. A detailed analysis of the KDD CUP 99 data set. In *Proceedings of the Second IEEE international conference on Computational intelligence for security and defense applications*, CISDA'09, pages 53–58, Piscataway, NJ, USA, 2009. IEEE Press.

[29] M. Tomassini. *Spatially structured evolutionary algorithms: artificial evolution in space and time.* Natural Computing series. Springer, 2005.

[30] V. N. Vapnik. *The nature of statistical learning theory.* Springer-Verlag New York, Inc., New York, NY, USA, 1995.

Evolving Large-Scale Neural Networks for Vision-Based Reinforcement Learning

Jan Koutník Giuseppe Cuccu Jürgen Schmidhuber Faustino Gomez
IDSIA, USI-SUPSI
Galleria 2
Manno-Lugano, CH 6928
{hkou, giuse, juergen, tino}@idsia.ch

ABSTRACT

The idea of using evolutionary computation to train artificial neural networks, or *neuroevolution* (NE), for reinforcement learning (RL) tasks has now been around for over 20 years. However, as RL tasks become more challenging, the networks required become larger, so do their genomes. But, scaling NE to large nets (i.e. tens of thousands of weights) is infeasible using direct encodings that map genes one-to-one to network components. In this paper, we scale-up our "compressed" network encoding where network weight matrices are represented indirectly as a set of Fourier-type coefficients, to tasks that require very-large networks due to the high-dimensionality of their input space. The approach is demonstrated successfully on two reinforcement learning tasks in which the control networks receive visual input: (1) a vision-based version of the octopus control task requiring networks with over 3 thousand weights, and (2) a version of the TORCS driving game where networks with over *1 million* weights are evolved to drive a car around a track using video images from the driver's perspective.

Categories and Subject Descriptors

I.2.6 [**Artificial Intelligence**]: Learning—*Connectionism and neural nets*

Keywords

neuroevolution; indirect encodings; vision-based TORCS; reinforcement learning; games

1. INTRODUCTION

Neuroevolution (NE), has now been around for over 20 years. The main appeal of evolving neural networks instead of training them (e.g. backpropagation) is that it can potentially harness the universal function approximation capability of neural networks to solve reinforcement learning (RL) tasks without relying on noisy, nonstationary gradient information to perform temporal credit assignment.

Early work in NE focused on evolving rather small networks (hundreds of weights) for RL benchmarks, and control problems with relatively few inputs/outputs. However, as RL tasks become more challenging, the networks required become larger, as do their genomes. The result is that scaling NE to large nets (i.e. tens of thousands of weights) is infeasible using a straightforward, direct encoding where genes map one-to-one to network components. Therefore, recent efforts have focused increasingly on *indirect* encodings [2, 3, 6, 7, 13] where relatively small genomes are transformed into networks of arbitrary size using a more complex mapping.

In previous work [4, 8, 9, 14], we presented a new indirect encoding where network weight matrices are represented as a set of coefficients that are transformed into weight values via an inverse Fourier-type transform, so that evolutionary search is conducted in the frequency-domain instead of weight space. The basic idea is that if nearby weights in the matrices are correlated, then this regularity can be encoded using fewer coefficients than weights, effectively reducing the search space dimensionality. For problems exhibiting a high-degree of redundancy, this "compressed" approach can result in an two orders of magnitude fewer free parameters and significant speedup [8].

With this encoding, networks with over 3000 weights were evolved to successfully control a high-dimensional version of the Octopus Arm task [16], by searching in the space of as few as 20 Fourier coefficients (164:1 compression ratio) [10]. In this paper, the approach is scaled up to two tasks that require networks with up to over *1 million weights*, due to their use of high-dimensional, vision inputs: (1) a visual version of the aforementioned Octopus Arm task, and (2) a visual version of the TORCS race car driving environment. In the standard setup for TORCS, used now for several years in reinforcement learning competitions (e.g. [11]), a set of features describing the state of the car is provided to the driver. In the version used here, the controllers do not have access to these features, but instead must drive the car using only a stream of images from the driver's perspective; no task-specific information is provided to the controller, and the controllers must compute the car velocity internally, via feedback (recurrent) connections, based on the history of observed images. To our knowledge this the first attempt to tackle TORCS using vision, and successfully evolve neural network *controllers* of this size.

The next section describes the compressed network encod-

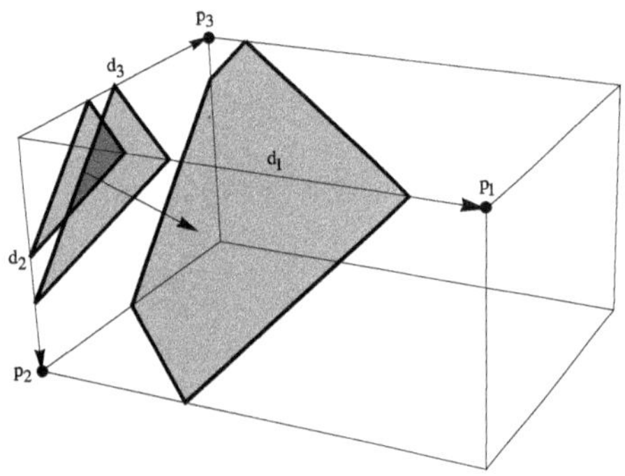

Figure 1: Mapping the coefficients: The cuboidal array (top) is filled with the coefficients from chromosome g one simplex at a time, according to Algorithm 1, starting at the origin and moving to the opposite corner one simplex at a time.

Algorithm 1: Coefficient mapping(g, d)

$j \leftarrow 0$
$K \leftarrow \text{sort}(\text{diag}(d) - \mathbb{I})$
for $i = 0$ **to** $|d| - 1 + \sum_{n=1}^{|d|} d_n$ **do**
  $l \leftarrow 0$
  $s_i \leftarrow \{e | \sum_{k=1}^{|d|} e_{\xi_j} = i\}$
  while $|s_i| > 0$ **do**
    $ind[j] \leftarrow \underset{e \in s_i}{\text{argmin}} \| e - K[l\text{++} \bmod |d|] \|$
    $s_i \leftarrow s_i \setminus ind[j\text{++}]$
  end
end
for $i = 0$ **to** $|ind|$ **do**
  if $i < |g|$ **then**
    coeff_array$[ind[i]] \leftarrow c_i$
  else
    coeff_array$[ind[i]] \leftarrow 0$
  end
end

ing in detail. Section 3 presents the experiments in the two test domains, which are discussed in section 4.

2. COMPRESSED NETWORKS

Networks are encoded as a string or *genome*, $\boldsymbol{g} = \{g_1, \ldots, g_k\}$, consisting of k substrings or *chromosomes* of real numbers representing DCT coefficients. The number of chromosomes is determined by the choice of network architecture, Ψ, and data structures used to decode the genome, specified by $\Omega = \{D_1, \ldots, D_k\}$, where D_m, $m = 1..k$, is the dimensionality of the coefficient array for chromosome m. The total number of coefficients, $C = \sum_{m=1}^{k} |g_m| \ll N$, is user-specified (for a compression ratio of N/C, where N is the number of weights in the network), and the coefficients are distributed evenly over the chromosomes. Which frequencies should be included in the encoding is unknown. The approach taken here restricts the search space to *band-limited* neural networks where the power spectrum of the weight matrices goes to zero above a specified limit frequency, c_ℓ^m, and chromosomes contain all frequencies up to c_ℓ^m, $g_m = (c_0^m, \ldots, c_\ell^m)$.

Figure 2 illustrates the procedure used to decode the genomes. In this example, a fully-recurrent neural network (on the right) is represented by $k = 3$ weight matrices, one for the input layer weights, one for the recurrent weights, and one for the bias weights. The weights in each matrix are generated from a different chromosome which is mapped into its own D_m-dimensional array with the same number of elements as its corresponding weight matrix; in the case shown, $\Omega = \{3, 3, 2\}$: 3D arrays for both the input and recurrent matrices, and a 2D array for the bias weights.

In [8], the coefficient matrices were 2D, where the simplexes are just the secondary diagonals; starting in the top-left corner, each diagonal is filled alternately starting from its corners. However, if the task exhibits inherent structure that cannot be captured by low frequencies in a 2D layout, more compression can potentially be gained by organizing the coefficients in higher-dimensional arrays [10].

Each chromosome is mapped to its coefficient array according to Algorithm 1 (figure 1) which takes a list of array dimension sizes, $d = (d_1, \ldots, d_{D_m})$ and the chromosome, g_m, to create a total ordering on the array elements, $e_{\xi_1, \ldots, \xi_{D_m}}$. In the first loop, the array is partitioned into $(D_m - 1)$-simplexes, where each simplex, s_i, contains only those elements e whose Cartesian coordinates, $(\xi_1, \ldots, \xi_{D_m})$, sum to integer i. The elements of simplex s_i are ordered in the `while` loop according to their distance to the corner points, p_i (i.e. those points having exactly one non-zero coordinate; see example points for a 3D-array in figure 1), which form the rows of matrix $K = [p_1, \ldots, p_m]^T$, sorted in descending order by their sole, non-zero dimension size. In each loop iteration, the coordinates of the element with the smallest Euclidean distance to the selected corner is appended to the list ind, and removed from s_i. The loop terminates when s_i is empty.

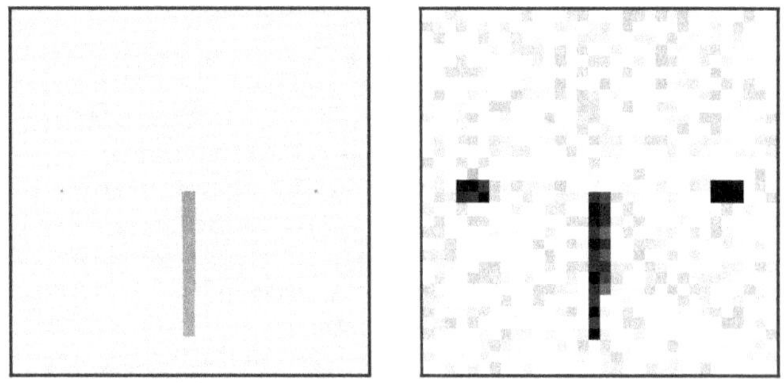

(a) (b)

Figure 3: Visual Octopus Arm. (a) The arm has to reach the goal (red dot) using a noisy visualization of the environment (b).

After all of the simplexes have been traversed, the vector ind holds the ordered element coordinates. In the final loop, the array is filled with the coefficients from low to high frequency to the positions indicated by ind; the remaining positions are filled with zeroes. Finally, a D_m-dimensional inverse DCT transform is applied to the array to generate the weight values, which are mapped to their position in the corresponding 2D weight matrix. Once the k chromosomes have been transformed, the network is complete.

3. EXPERIMENTS

Two vision-based control tasks were used to scale-up the

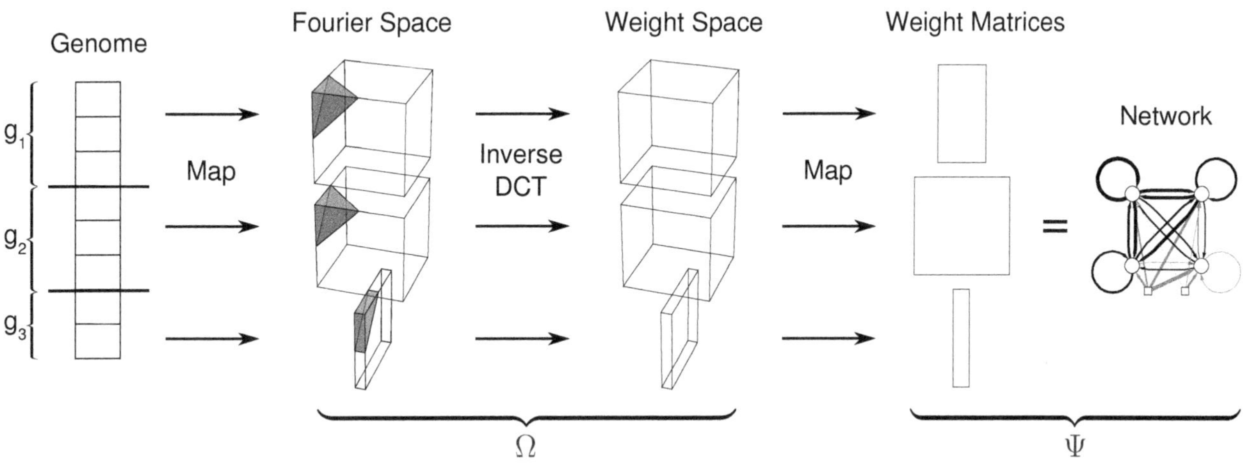

Figure 2: Decoding the compressed networks. The figure shows the three step process involved in transforming a genome of frequency-domain coefficients into a recurrent neural network. First, the genome (left) is divided into k chromosomes, one for each of the weight matrices specified by the network architecture, Ψ. Each chromosome is mapped, by Algorithm 1, into a coefficient array of a dimensionality specified by Ω. In this example, an RNN with two inputs and four neurons is encoded as 8 coefficients. There are $k = |\Omega| = 3$, chromosomes and $\Omega{=}\{3, 3, 2\}$. The second step is to apply the inverse DCT to each array to generate the weight values, which are mapped into the weight matrices in the last step.

compressed network encoding, the Visual Octopus Arm and Visual TORCS. All neural network controllers were evolved using the Cooperative Synapse NeuroEvolution (CoSyNE; [5]) algorithm.

3.1 Visual Octopus Arm

The octopus arm (see figure 3) consists of p compartments floating in a 2D water environment. Each compartment has a constant volume and contains three controllable muscles (dorsal, transverse and ventral). The state of a compartment is described by the x, y-coordinates of two of its corners plus their corresponding x and y velocities. Together with the arm base rotation, the arm has $8p + 2$ state variables and $3p + 2$ control variables. In the vision-based version used here, the control network does not have access to the state variables. Instead it receives a noisy 32×32 pixel gray-scale image of the arm from a the perspective shown in figure 3(b). The goal of the task to reach a target position with the tip of the arm, from the starting position (arm hanging down) by contracting the 32 muscles appropriately at each 1s step of simulated time. Figure 3(a) shows the standard visualization the environment with the arm hanging down and two target positions shown in red. The idea of modifying an existing RL benchmark to use visual inputs dates back to the adaptive "broom balancer" of **(author?)** [15], and more recently the vision-based mountain car in [1].

3.1.1 Setup

An evaluation consists of two trials, one with the target on the left, the other on the right, see figure 3. In each trial the target disappears after the first time-step, so that the network must remember which target is active throughout trial in order to solve the task. Having two target positions forces the controller to use the visual input instead of just outputting a fixed action sequence (i.e. open-loop control).

The controllers were represented by fully-connected recurrent neural networks with 32 neurons, one for each muscle in the 10 compartment arm, for a total of 33,824 weights organized into 3 weight matrices. Twenty simulations were run with networks encoded using the following numbers of DCT coefficients: {10,20,40,80,160,320,640,1280,2560}. In all case the coefficients were mapped into 3 coefficient arrays using mapping $\Omega{=}\{4, 4, 2\}$: (1) a 4D array encodes the input weights from the 2D input image to the 2D array of neurons, so that each weight is correlated (a) with the weights of adjacent pixels for the same neuron, (b) with the weights for the same pixel for neurons that are adjacent in the 3×11 grid, and (c) with the weights from adjacent pixels connected to adjacent neurons; (2) a 4D array encodes the recurrent weights, again capturing three types of correlation; (3) a 2D array encodes the hidden layer biases (see [10] for further discussion of higher-dimensional coefficient matrices).

CoSyNE was used to evolve the coefficient genomes, with a population size of 128, a mutation rate of 0.8, and fitness computed as the average of the following score over the two trials:

$$\max\left[1 - \frac{t}{T}\frac{d}{D}, 0\right], \tag{1}$$

where t is the number of time-steps before the arm touches the target, T is a number of time-steps in a trial, d is the final distance of the arm tip to the target and D is the initial distance of the arm tip to the goal. Each trial lasted for $T = 200$ time-steps.

3.1.2 Results

Figure 6 compare the performance of the various compressed encoding with the direct encoding in which evolution is conducted in 33,824-dimensional weight space. Using only 10 coefficients performs poorly but almost as well as the direct approach. With just 20 coefficient performance increases significantly, and after 40 coefficients, near optimal performance is achieved. For a video demo of the evolved behavior go to `http://www.idsia.ch/~koutnik/images/octopusVisual.mp4`

(a) (b) (c)

Figure 4: Visual TORCS environment. (a) The 1st-person perspective used as input to the RNN controllers (figure 5) to drive the car around the track. (b), a 3rd-person perspective of car. The controllers were evolved using a track (c) of length of 714.16m and road width of 10m, that consists of straight segments of length 50 and 100m and curves with radius of 25m. The car starts at the bottom (start line) and has to drive counter-clockwise. The track boundary has a width of 14m.

3.2 Visual TORCS

The goal of the task is to evolve a recurrent neural network controller that can drive the car around a race track using only vision. The challenge for the controller is not only to interpret each static image as it is received, but also to retain information from previous images in order to compute the velocity of the car internally, via its feedback connections.

The visual TORCS environment is based on TORCS version 1.3.1. The simulator had to be modified to provide images as input to the controllers. At each time-step during a network evaluation, an image rendered in OpenGL is captured in the car code (C++), and passed via UDP to the client (Java), that contains the RNN controller. The client is wrapped into a Java class that provides methods for setting up the RNN weights, executing the evaluation, and returning the fitness score. These methods are called from Mathematica which is used to implement the compressed networks and the evolutionary search.

The Java wrapper allows multiple controllers to be evaluated in parallel in different instances of the simulator via different UDP ports. This feature is critical for the experiments presented below since, unlike the non-vision-based TORCS, the costly image rendering, required for vision, cannot be disabled. The main drawback of the current implementation is that the images are captured from the screen buffer and, therefore, have to actually be rendered to the screen.

Other tweaks to the original TORCS include changing the control frequency from 50 Hz to 5 Hz, and removing the "*3-2-1-GO*" waiting sequence from the beginning of each race. The image passed in the UDP is encoded as a message chunk with *image* prefix, followed by *unsigned byte* values of the image pixels. Each image is decomposed into the HSB color space and only the saturation (S) plane is passed in the message.

3.2.1 Setup

In each fitness evaluation, the car is placed at the starting line of the track shown in figure 4(c), and its mirror image, and a race is run for 25s of simulated time, resulting in a maximum of 125 time-steps at the 5Hz control frequency. At each control step (see figure 5), a raw 64×64 pixel image, taken from the driver's perspective is split into three color planes (hue, saturation and brightness). The saturation plane is passed through Robert's edge detector [12] and then fed into a Elman (recurrent) neural network (SRN) with $16 \times 16 = 256$ fully-interconnected neurons in the hidden layer, and 3 output neurons. The first two outputs, o_1, o_2, are averaged, $(o_1 + o_2)/2$, to provide the steering signal, and the third neuron, o_3 controls the brake and throttle (-1 = full brake, 1 = full throttle). All neurons use sigmoidal activation functions.

With this architecture, the networks have a total of 1,115, 139 weights, organized into 5 weight matrices. The weights are encoded indirectly by 200 DCT coefficients which are mapped into 5 coefficient arrays using mapping $\Omega=\{4, 4, 2, 3, 1\}$: (1) a 4D array encodes the input weights from the 2D input image to the 2D array of neurons in the hidden layer, so that each weight is correlated (a) with the weights of adjacent pixels for the same neuron, (b) with the weights for the same pixel for neurons that are adjacent in the 16×16 grid, and (c) with the weights from adjacent pixels connected to adjacent neurons; (2) a 4D array encodes the recurrent weights in the hidden layer, again capturing three types of correlations; (3) a 2D array encodes the hidden layer biases; (4) a 3D array encodes weights between the hidden layer and 3 output neurons; and (5) a 1D array with 3 elements encodes the output neuron biases.

CoSyNE was used to evolve the coefficient genomes, with a population size of 64, a mutation rate of 0.8, and fitness being computed by:

$$f = d - \frac{3m}{1000} + \frac{v_{max}}{5} - 100c \; , \qquad (2)$$

where d is the distance along the track axis, v_{max} is maximum speed, m is the cumulative damage, and c is the sum of squares of the control signal differences, divided by the

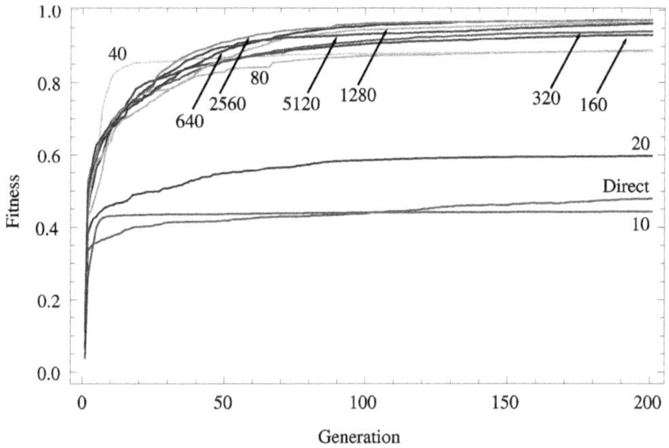

Figure 6: Performance on Visual Octopus Arm Task. Each curve is the average of 20 runs using a particular number of coefficients to encode the networks.

number of control variables, 3, and the number simulation control steps, T:

$$c = \frac{1}{3T}\sum_{i}^{3}\sum_{t}^{T}[o_i(t) - o_i(t-1)]^2. \tag{3}$$

The maximum speed component in equation (2) forces the controllers to accelerate and brake efficiently, while the damage component favors controllers that drive safely, and c encourages smoother driving. Fitness scores roughly correspond to the distance traveled along the race track axis.

Each individual is evaluated both on the track and its mirror image to prevent the RNN from blindly memorizing the track without using the visual input.[1] The original track starts with a left turn, while the mirrored track starts with a right turn, forcing the network to use the visual input to distinguish between tracks. The fitness score is calculated as the minimum of the two track scores.

3.2.2 Results

Table 1 compares the distance travelled and maximum speed of the visual RNN controller with that of other, hard-coded controllers that come with the TORCS package. The performance of the vision-based controller is similar to that of the other controllers which enjoy access to the full set of pre-processed TORCS features, such as forward and lateral speed, angle to the track axis, position at the track, distance to the track side, etc.

Figure 7 shows the learning curve for the compressed networks (upper curve). The lower curve shows a typical evolutionary run where the network is evolved *directly* in weight space, i.e. using chromosomes with 1,115,139 genes, one for each weight, instead of 200 coefficient genes. Direct evolution makes little progress as each of the weights has to be set individually, without being explicitly constrained by the values of other weights in their matrix neighborhood, as is the case for the compressed encoding.

As discussed above, the controllers were evaluated on two tracks to prevent them from simply "memorizing" a single

[1]Evolution can find weights that implement a dynamical system that drives around the track from the same initial conditions, even with no input.

Table 1: Maximum distance, d, in meters and maximum speed, v_{max}, in kilometers per hour achieved by the selected hard-coded controllers that enjoy access to the state variables, compared to the visual RNN controller which does not.

controller	d [m]	v_{max} [km/h]
olethros	570	147
bt	613	141
berniw	624	149
tita	657	150
inferno	682	150
visual RNN	**625**	**144**

sequence of curves. In the initial stages of evolution, a suboptimal strategy is to just drive straight on both tracks ignoring the first curve, and crashing into the barrier. This is a simple behavior, requiring no vision, that produces relatively high fitness, and therefore represents local minima in the fitness landscape. This can be seen in the flat portion of the curve until generation 118, when the fitness jumps from 140 to 190, as the controller learns to turn both left and right. Gradually, the controllers start to distinguish between the two tracks as they develop useful visual feature detectors, and from then on the evolutionary search refines the control to optimize acceleration and braking through the curves and straight sections. For a video demo go to
`http://www.idsia.ch/~koutnik/images/torcsVisual.mp4`

4. DISCUSSION

The compressed network encoding reduces the search space dimensionality by exploiting the inherent regularity in the environment. Since, as with most natural images, the pixels in a given neighborhood tend to have correlated values, searching for each weight independently is overkill. Using fewer coefficients than weights sacrifices some expressive power (some networks can no longer be represented), but constrains the search to the subspace of lower complexity, but still sufficiently powerful networks, reducing the search space dimensionality by, e.g. a factor of more than 5000 for the car-driving networks evolved here.

Figure 8(a) shows the weights from the input layer of a successful car-driving network. Each 64×64 square corresponds to the input weight values of a particular neuron in the 16×16 hidden layer. The pattern in each square indicates the part of the input image to which the neuron responds. Because of the 4D structure of the input coefficient matrix, these feature detectors vary smoothly across the layer. This regularity is apparent in all five of the network matrices. Figures 8(b) and 8(c) show the activation of the hidden layer while driving through a left and right curve on the track, respectively. The two curves produce very different activation patterns from which the network computes the control signal. The highly activated neurons (in orange) form contiguous regions due to the correlation between the feature detectors of adjacent neurons.

Further experiments are needed to compare the approach with other indirect or generative encodings such as HyperNEAT [2]; not only to evaluate the relative efficiency of each algorithm, but also to understand how the methods differ in

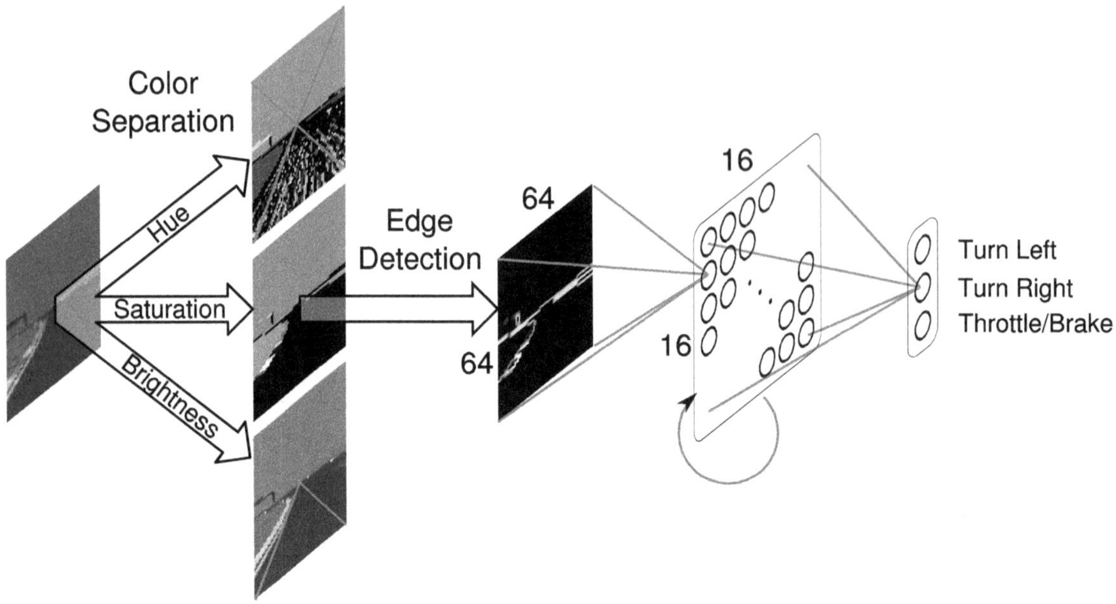

Figure 5: Visual TORCS network controller pipeline. At each time-step a raw 64×64 pixel image, taken from the driver's perspective, is split into three planes (hue, saturation and brightness). The saturation plane is then passed through Robert's edge detector [12] and then fed into the 164×16=256 recurrent neurons of the controller network, which then outputs the three driving commands.

the type of solutions they produce. Part of that comparison should involve testing the controllers in different conditions from those under which they were evolved (e.g. on different tracks) to measure the degree to which the ability to generalize benefits from the low-complexity representation, as was shown in [10].

In this work, the size of the networks was decided heuristically. In the future, we would like to apply Compressed Network Complexity Search [4] to simultaneously determine the number of coefficients *and* the number of neurons (topology) by running multiple evolutionary algorithms in parallel, one for each topology-coefficient complexity class, and assigning run-time to each based on a probability distribution that is adapted on-line according to the performance of each class. This approach has so far only been applied to much simpler control tasks than those used here, but should produce solutions for harder tasks that are both simple in terms of weight matrix regularity, and model class, to evolve potentially more robust controllers.

The compressed network encoding used here assumes band-limited networks, where the matrices can contain all frequencies up to a predefined limit frequency. For networks with as many weights as those used for visual TORCS, this may not be the best scheme as the limit has to be chosen by the user, and if some specific high frequency is needed to solve the task, then all lower frequencies must be searched as well. A potentially more tractable approach might be Generalized Compressed Network Search (GCNS; [14]) which uses a messy GA to simultaneously determine which arbitrary subset of frequencies should be used as well as the value at each of those frequencies. Our initial work with this method has been promising.

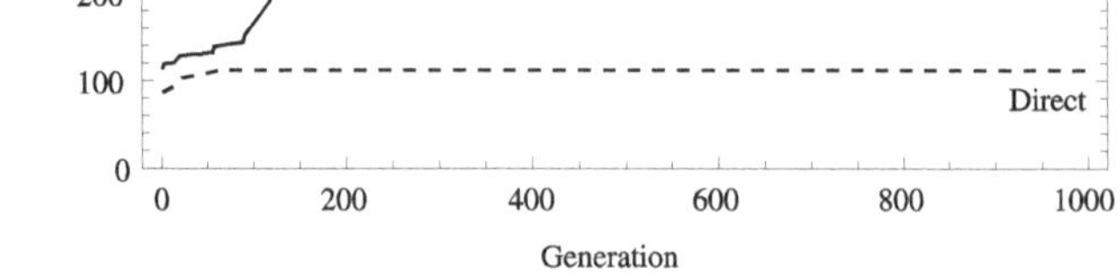

Figure 7: Visual TORCS results. Typical fitness evolution of a compressed (upper curve) and directly encoded (lower curve) controller during 1000 generations. The compressed controller escapes from the local minima at generation 118, but the directly encoded network never learns to distinguish between left and right curve from the visual features.

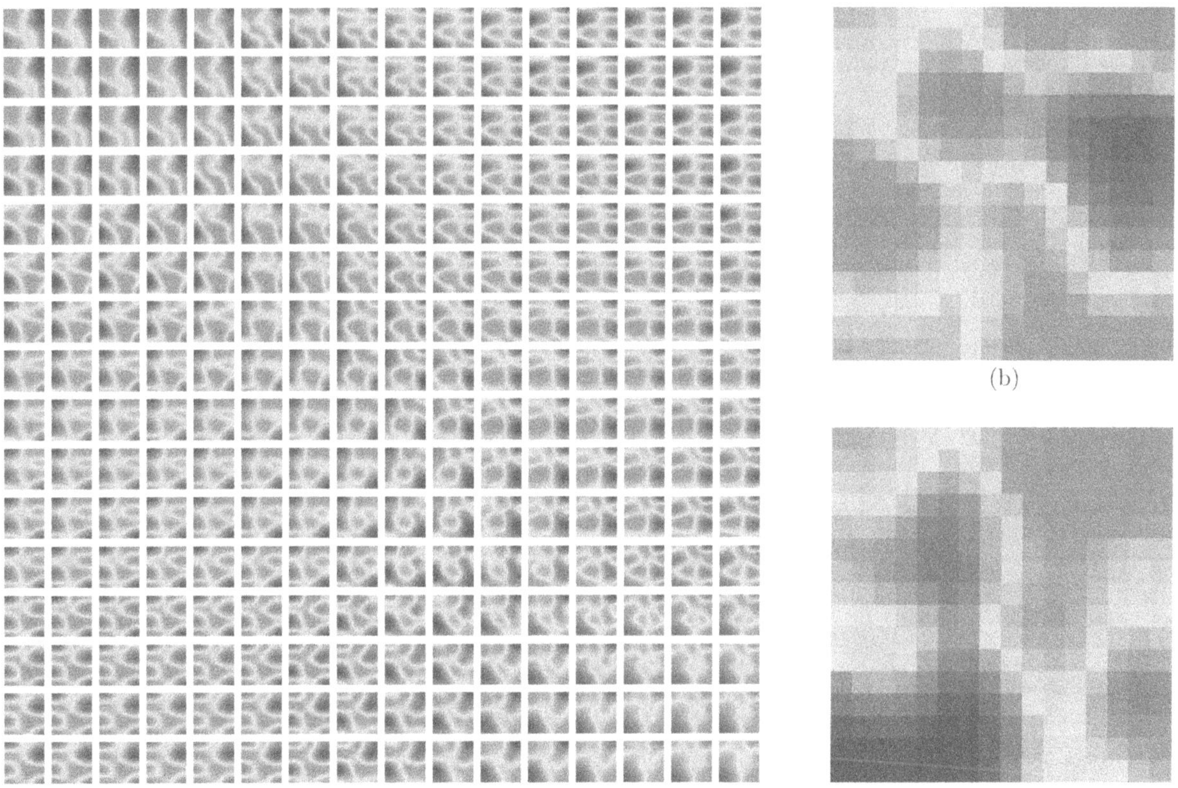

(a) (b) (c)

Figure 8: Evolved low-complexity feature detectors. (a) each square shows the 64×64 input weight values corresponding to one of the neurons in 16×16 hidden layer. Colors indicate weight value: orange = large positive; blue = large negative. (b) the activation of each neuron in the hidden layer while the car is being driven through and left curve, and (c) during a right curve.

Acknowledgements

This research was supported by Swiss National Science Foundation grants #137736: "Advanced Cooperative NeuroEvolution for Autonomous Control" and #138219: "Theory and Practice of Reinforcement Learning 2". Koutník implemented the compressed networks based on original ideas from our previous work cited here, and conducted the experiments. Schmidhuber supervised Koutník. Cuccu devised and implemented the extensive modifications to the TORCS simulator. Gomez directed this research, and wrote most of the paper.

References

[1] G. Cuccu, M. Luciw, J. Schmidhuber, and F. Gomez. Intrinsically motivated evolutionary search for vision-based reinforcement learning. In *Proceedings of the IEEE Conference on Development and Learning, and Epigenetic Robotics*, 2011.

[2] D. B. D'Ambrosio and K. O. Stanley. A novel generative encoding for exploiting neural network sensor and output geometry. In *Proceedings of the 9th annual conference on Genetic and evolutionary computation*, (GECCO), pages 974–981, New York, NY, USA, 2007. ACM.

[3] J. Gauci and K. Stanley. Generating large-scale neural networks through discovering geometric regularities. In *Proceedings of the Conference on Genetic and Evolutionary Computation*, pages 997–1004, New York, NY, USA, 2007. ACM.

[4] F. Gomez, J. Koutník, and J. Schmidhuber. Compressed network complexity search. In *Proceedings of the 12th International Conference on Parallel Problem Solving from Nature (PPSN XII, Taormina, IT)*, 2012.

[5] F. Gomez, J. Schmidhuber, and R. Miikkulainen. Accelerated neural evolution through cooperatively coevolved synapses. *Journal of Machine Learning Research*, 9(May):937–965, 2008.

[6] F. Gruau. Cellular encoding of genetic neural networks. Technical Report RR-92-21, Ecole Normale Superieure de Lyon, Institut IMAG, Lyon, France, 1992.

[7] H. Kitano. Designing neural networks using genetic algorithms with graph generation system. *Complex Systems*, 4:461–476, 1990.

[8] J. Koutník, F. Gomez, and J. Schmidhuber. Evolving neural networks in compressed weight space. In *Proceedings of the Conference on Genetic and Evolutionary Computation (GECCO)*, 2010.

[9] J. Koutník, F. Gomez, and J. Schmidhuber. Searching for minimal neural networks in fourier space. In *Proceedings of the 4th Annual Conference on Artificial General Intelligence*, 2010.

[10] J. Koutník, J. Schmidhuber, and F. Gomez. A frequency-domain encoding for neuroevolution. Technical report, arXiv:1212.6521, 2012.

[11] D. Loiacono, P. L. Lanzi, J. Togelius, E. Onieva, D. A. Pelta, M. V. Butz, T. D. Lönneker, L. Cardamone, D. Perez, Y. Sáez, M. Preuss, and J. Quadflieg. The 2009 simulated car racing championship, 2009.

[12] L. G. Roberts. *Machine Perception of Three-Dimensional Solids.* Outstanding Dissertations in the Computer Sciences. Garland Publishing, New York, 1963.

[13] J. Schmidhuber. Discovering neural nets with low Kolmogorov complexity and high generalization capability. *Neural Networks*, 10(5):857–873, 1997.

[14] R. K. Srivastava, J. Schmidhuber, and F. Gomez. Generalized compressed network search. In *Proceedings of the 12th International Conference on Parallel Problem Solving from Nature (PPSN XII, Taormina, IT)*, 2012.

[15] V. V. Tolat and B. Widrow. An adaptive "broom balancer" with visual inputs. In *Proceedings of the IEEE International Conference on Neural Networks (San Diego, CA)*, pages 641–647. Piscataway, NJ: IEEE, 1988.

[16] Y. Yekutieli, R. Sagiv-Zohar, R. Aharonov, Y. Engel, B. Hochner, and T. Flash. A dynamic model of the octopus arm. I. biomechanics of the octopus reaching movement. *Journal of Neurophysiology*, 94(2):1443–1458, 2005.

Analysis of the Niche Genetic Algorithm in Learning Classifier Systems

Tim Kovacs
University of Bristol
kovacs@cs.bris.ac.uk

Robin Tindale
University of Bristol
rt9200@my.bristol.ac.uk

ABSTRACT

Learning Classifier Systems (LCS) evolve IF-THEN rules for classification and control tasks. The earliest Michigan-style LCS used a panmictic Genetic Algorithm (GA) (in which all rules compete for selection) but newer ones tend to use a niche GA (in which only a certain subset of rules compete for selection at any one time). The niche GA was thought to be advantageous in all learning tasks, but recent research suggests it has difficulties when the rules composing the solution overlap. Furthermore, the niche GA's effects are implicit, making it difficult study, and fixed, which prevents tuning its performance. Given these issues, we set out on a long-term project to reevaluate the niche GA. This work is our starting point and in it we address the implicit and unquantified effects of the niche GA by building a mathematical model of the probability of rule selection. This model reveals a number of insights into the components of rule fitness, particularly the bonus for rule generality and penalty for overlaps, both previously unquantified. These theoretical results are our primary contribution. However, to demonstrate one way to apply this theory, we then introduce a new variant of the UCS algorithm, which uses a hybrid panmictic/niche GA. Preliminary results suggest, unexpectedly, that the niche GA may have even more drawbacks than previously thought.

Categories and Subject Descriptors

I.2.6 [**Artificial Intelligence**]: Learning—*Concept Learning*; I.2.8 [**Artificial Intelligence**]: Problem Solving, Control Methods, and Search—*Heuristic methods*

General Terms

Algorithms

Keywords

Learning Classifier Systems; Niche Genetic Algorithm

GECCO'13, July 6–10, 2013, Amsterdam, The Netherlands.

1. INTRODUCTION

Learning Classifier Systems (LCS) are a family of machine learning algorithms introduced by Holland in 1975 [7] which combine rule evaluation methods with genetic search. An LCS learns a set of *IF... condition THEN... action* rules which specify what action the system should take when presented with particular input conditions. The success of a rule's suggested action is judged by a payoff received from the environment, and this payoff goes on to inform the rule's suitability or *fitness* when it comes to the periodic genetic breeding of rules. In this paper, we look primarily at UCS [1], but also XCS [12], both of which are LCS which evaluate rules based on their ability to accurately predict the level of payoff, good or bad (accuracy-based fitness), whereas earlier LCS, such as ZCS [11], tended to focus on developing high-payoff rules (strength-based fitness; see [12, 9]). In an LCS, rules can match multiple inputs (that is, they have some degree of generality) and we are searching for rules which not only suggest the correct action for training inputs, but which are also suitably general.

The Genetic Algorithm (GA) explores the rule space in a heuristic manner: it periodically crosses two parents to form offspring (crossover), or copies and slightly alters individuals (mutation). Higher-fitness rules are more likely to be selected for reproduction and the set, or *population*, of rules has a fixed size, which is maintained by culling lower fitness rules. This creates a *survival of the fittest*-style competition, encouraging fit (accurate) rules in the population and discouraging unfit (inaccurate) ones.

In Holland's LCS the GA selected parents from the whole population, that is, *panmictically*, and many subsequent LCS followed suit. Booker [2] introduced a *niche GA* in which, at any given time, only a subset of the rule population is eligible for selection as parents. This subset is called a niche and is defined as the set of rules matching the current input (and, sometimes, as having a certain action). Wilson adopted the niche GA in his seminal XCS system and almost all subsequent LCS research has used XCS or a variant of it; the niche GA is now a standard part of current LCS.

Nonetheless, a growing body of work has suggested shortcomings of the niche GA. Kovacs [9] noted that XCS penalises rules which overlap with other rules, and Ioannides et al. [8] suggests that as a result XCS fails to find optimally general rules for many problems. In addition, we observe that the niche GA's effects are implicit and it has an inherent lack of tunability: it is a fixed algorithm with no parameters to adapt its behaviour to suit different tasks.

The aim of this work is to model rule selection probability in the niche GA in order to make it explicit, and to identify and quantify components, including the known but unquantified generality bonus and fitness penalty. This is therefore a theory paper. We see this paper as a first step toward a thorough exploration of the effects of the niche GA and a reevaluation of its utility. Ultimately this may lead to new algorithms which avoid the niche GA's difficulty with overlapping rules, which are parameterisable, and which, ideally, are more analytically tractable (for example, all the fitness bonuses and penalties are known and quantified) and theoretically justified than the current niche GA.

We begin with background on the niche GA and on XCS and UCS, two widely-used LCS which incorporate a niche GA. We cover why the niche GA was introduced in section 2 and then describe problems with it, including both issues uncovered by previous research and some original points of our own (section 2.3). An analysis of the inner workings of the niche GA follows (section 3), which goes on to inform a number of experimental results (see section 5). Finally, we summarise our experimental findings and make suggestions for future work (see section 6).

2. BACKGROUND

Here we review the origins of the niche GA (section 2.1), present an analogy which may help give intuition about it (section 2.2), and discuss issues with it (section 2.3).

2.1 Niche GA LCS

We begin by outlining the process by which an LCS interacts with a learning problem or 'environment'. Each iteration, the environment presents the system with an input and the LCS finds the set of rules in its population which *match* that input (meaning the IF part of the rule is satisfied by the input). This set of matching rules is called the *match set*. Within the match set, rules may suggest different actions to take, and the LCS chooses one, typically by a fitness-weighted vote among matching rules. The subset of rules in the match set which advocate the chosen action is now found. This is called the *action set*. The action is taken by the system, and the environment returns a payoff, which is used to update the fitness of rules in the action set. The genetic algorithm can now run, selecting parents using a particular method, such as a roulette wheel based on fitness. In the earliest LCS, all rules in the population eligible to be selected; the GA was panmictic.

The niche GA was first introduced in LCS by Booker [2, 3, 4] as a way of focusing genetic search. Booker reasoned that since the rules in a match set were related (in that they apply to the same input), crossover among them would be more productive than crossover between unrelated rules. The niche GA is hence a form of mating restriction. In XCS, the GA originally ran in the match set [12] but was moved to the action set when this was found more effective [13].

By 1994, Stewart Wilson felt the increasing complexity of LCS was detrimental, hindering analysis and preventing quick improvements. To counter this, he introduced ZCS (Zeroth order Classifier System) as a minimal, back-to-basics LCS [11]. A year later, he introduced XCS [12], a derivative of ZCS in which he addressed shortcomings of ZCS. XCS also drew on Booker's GOFER-1 [4] from which it inherited the niche GA, an interest in rule accuracy ([12] p. 32), and a deletion scheme which encourages the distribution of rules throughout the environment. The first two are considered the key features of XCS and they contribute two powerful dynamics in its evolutionary search.

The first dynamic is pressure toward more general rules. Wilson observed that the panmictic GA provides no incentive for rules to generalise [12]. In contrast, only a certain subset of rules participate in each niche GA event, which encourages generality as more general rules appear in more niches, and therefore have more opportunities to be selected. This is captured by Wilson's XCS generalization hypothesis [12] and it provides a powerful fitness bonus for more general rules. Note, however, that it is an implicit bonus, which occurs due to the mating restriction of the niche GA. This bonus does not appear in the fitness updates used by XCS. To date it has not been fully quantified but some progress has been made by making simplifying assumptions. Kovacs [9] (section 3.3.2) derived a schema theorem for the niche GA, and Butz et al. derived the specificity equation of [6] (section III-F). Butz et al. also extended the generalization hypothesis with the concept of "set pressure": assuming all rules have the same fitness, the expected average generality of the whole population is lower than that of an action set, and since deletion occurs in the former and reproduction in the latter, their combined effect generalises the population. The current work is similar to [9, 6] in that we will make simplifying assumptions in order to explore the generalisation bonus, and ultimately obtain qualitative insights into it which do not reply on these simplifying assumptions (see section 4). We also address, the overlap penalty mathematically which [9, 6] do not. (See section 4.2.)

The second dynamic is a strong penalty against rules which are overgeneral (i.e. which match too many inputs – see [9]). In ZCS, a rule's fitness is based on the magnitude of the payoffs it received. By contrast, a rule's fitness in XCS is based on its accuracy in predicting its payoff, and this has the very important effect of inhibiting overgeneral rules. Wilson realised that in ZCS a very general rule, which on some inputs receives a very low payoff and on others receives a very high payoff, will have a respectable average fitness, and will therefore be seen as relatively fit. However, if we base fitness on the accuracy of rule predictions, overgenerals lose out because their average prediction is close to neither the higher nor the lower payoffs they receive [12, 9]. While there are others, this is one important reason why Wilson chose to adopt accuracy-based fitness in XCS [12].

The joint effect of these two dynamics is that XCS strongly favours more general (yet accurate) rules, and strongly penalises overgeneral rules. [6] discusses these and various other dynamics or "pressures".

An additional reason for adopting the niche GA in XCS was to prevent high fitness regions in the input space from dominating the population. In a panmictic GA, rules in a particularly high-fitness region will more often be selected as parents than rules in lower-fitness regions. Rules tend to produce children in their own region which means search becomes focused in the higher-fitness regions to the detriment of others. While it might seem useful to focus on the most rewarding parts of the search space, we must recall that in classification tasks we seek to classify all inputs correctly, not just some, and in reinforcement learning we seek to act optimally in all states of the world, not just some. With the niche GA there is healthy competition *within* regions and search progresses within each region.

XCS and its many variations are today the most popular LCS. UCS is a version of XCS adapted for supervised learning [1]. We will use UCS in our experimental work later in this paper, but our findings are intended to be generally applicable to all LCS which use the niche GA.

2.2 An Analogy

Here we present an analogy for the niche and panmictic GAs which aims to build intuition on the subject. Imagine we have a species in which only the dominant pair in any group is able to mate. Perhaps dominance is determined by fighting, or perhaps through a less dangerous weightlifting championship. Now imagine this species is divided into a number of geographically separated tribes.

In a panmictic scenario, we gather all the tribes together and have a species-wide weightlifting contest, with two winners who will be allowed to reproduce. Now suppose one tribe inhabits a particularly fertile region, and its members tend to grow larger and stronger as a result. This tribe will often win the contest and be rewarded with children (who may be even fitter than their fit parents), while other tribes are deprived of children. It is easy to imagine the weaker tribes collapsing in such a situation. In a niche scenario, we would hold regional weightlifting contests within each tribe, rather than a single global contest. In this case, competition is within tribes and we avoid the situation where one tribe excessively deprives the others of children.

To extend this analogy to cover generality, let's pretend that some mischievous members can sneak into other tribes' contests. The more contests they attend, the more opportunities they have to win and breed. As a result, an individual of average fitness but great generality can expect to reproduce more than an individual of the same fitness but lower generality. Hence generality provides a fitness bonus. Note, however, that the bonus is implicit. Generality buys more opportunities to reproduce, but does not directly affect the outcome of any one competition – an individual's fitness in any one competition is unchanged. We will return to the idea of an implicit fitness bonus later when we analyse the niche GA in section 4.

A corollary of the above is that if an individual is very weak it will not win very often, even if it is very general. Hence, generality does not guarantee reproductive success. Indeed, an individual who is too weak to ever win will never do so, regardless of its generality. These observations hold for the niche GA just as they do for the weightlifters.

2.3 Issues with the niche GA

While the niche GA was introduced to solve problems with the panmictic approach, it eventually emerged that it has shortcomings of its own. XCS and UCS have performed well on a range of classification tasks, but Ioannides et al. [8] suggest they do not perform optimally general rules on a wide range of problems, due to a fitness penalty on overlapping rules first noted by Kovacs [9].

In addition to this problem, we note that the niche GA has a number of other issues. i) It was incorporated in XCS in part to introduce a fitness bonus for general rules [12] but this bonus is implicit and has never been fully quantified, which makes it difficult to build theory about it ii) Similarly, the fitness penalty is implicit and unquantified. iii) Another motivation was to help ensure the even distribution of rules in the input space. This too is unquantified. iv) Of these effects, only the third is tunable (using the GA trigger threshold θ_{GA}). v) These effects are implicit in the algorithm and not immediately obvious and it is possible there are other as-yet unknown effects. vi) Finally, it seems we either have a niche and all of its effects, or we have a panmictic GA and none of the niche GA's effects. In this sense the niche GA seems to be atomic or all-or-nothing. This makes it difficult to study the system. We cannot, for example, turn off or otherwise manipulate one effect (e.g. the overlap penalty), in isolation from the others in order to determine how each effect changes the performance of the system. (We could in fact produce different kinds of niche GA by defining niches in different ways. XCS has used the match set and action set as niches and we could define them in other ways. We could also alternate between a niche and panmictic GA. But it is not clear to us that this would allow us to study some effects of the niche GA in isolation from others. We do however find a partial solution in section 3.2.)

Given that this defining feature of XCS and UCS has so many issues we believe that further study of the niche GA is overdue.

3. SELECTION PROBABILITY

In this section we derive and analyse the probability of selecting a rule as a parent under various conditions, and these are the main results of this work. A rule's probability of selection is a crucial factor in evolutionary search, as it determines how likely a rule is to survive and to contribute to new rules. Hence, we are modelling a central part of the evolutionary system.

Although there are many techniques to select parents (e.g. roulette wheel, tournament selection, rank selection ...), evolutionary search depends on fitter individuals being more likely to be selected as parents. Note that the previous statement refers to both a rule's fitness and its probability of being selected. In LCS, the two are related but distinct. Each rule has a fitness parameter which is adjusted according to its performance and these fitness values are then used to weight the probability of selecting rules as parents. These probabilities may be computed explicitly, as in a roulette wheel, or may be implicit, as in tournament selection.

The same set of fitness values may result in different selection probabilities when using different selection methods or different parameters (e.g. altering the tournament size). The fitnesses of other rules also affect the selection probability of a rule. This makes sense intuitively, since your likelihood of being selected depends on what competition you have.

A slight complication is that in the steady-state GA used by some LCS, rules are explicitly selected for deletion, to keep the population size constant when adding new rules. Consequently, each rule has a probability of selection for both deletion and reproduction. For simplicity, we will not deal with deletion, but in the simplest case it is uniform [12].

3.1 Terminology

As an aside on terminology, a rule's selection and deletion probabilities, rather confusingly, define its fitness in the biological sense: an individual's ability to survive and to reproduce. Unlike rules, living organisms are not labelled with an estimate called fitness, but nonetheless organisms have some implicit probability of "selection" and "deletion": their fitness. Our aim is thus to compute, explicitly, the fitness of rules in the biological and evolutionary computation sense of the word "fitness". However, as our readers are likely to be LCS users, to avoid confusion with the rule fitness parameter we will refer to "selection probability" as such rather than "fitness". Note, however, that a given rule's selection probability in a niche is not the same as it is panmictically, and that the term "selection probability" may refer to either, depending on the context. We will refer to the panmictic selection probability (the evolutionary fitness) of a rule in a niche GA as its Global Selection Probability (GSP).

3.2 Aim

Our aim is to develop an *explicit* formula for GSP, which can then be analysed to reveal what factors affect selection probability and to what extent each is important. For example, we know from Wilson's XCS generalization hypothesis [12] that generality plays a role in a rule's selection probability, but its role is entirely implicit: generality is not even a factor in a rule's fitness parameter. A formula for selection probability would make generality explicit and quantify interactions between generality and other factors. In addition to analysing the formula, we could actually implement a panmictic GA which mimics the niche GA by *explicitly calculating the selection probabilities the niche GA* implicitly uses. The remaining difference between the two would be that the panmictic version does not restrict mating. We could then compare the versions with and without mating restriction in order to determine what effects are due to mating restriction alone. To borrow a term from genetics, this gives us a knockout model, in which a component is removed and the effect of its absence is evaluated. This is a workaround to the all-or-nothing nature of the niche GA noted in section 2.3. We implement it in section 5.

3.3 Selection Probability in a Panmictic GA

Here we give the selection probability when using panmictic GA, in which all rules are eligible for selection. We will assume use of a roulette wheel to select parents, although it would be straightforward to compute selection probabilities for other methods. Using a roulette wheel, a rule's probability of selection is its proportion of the total fitness among the rules which are eligible for selection. The selection probability $SP()$ of a rule i is then:

$$SP(i) = \frac{F[i]}{\sum\limits_{\text{all rules } j} F[j]} \tag{1}$$

where $F[j]$ is the fitness of rule j, and j ranges across the entire population as we select panmictically. In XCS and UCS, each rule has a *numerosity* [12], which indicates the number of virtual rules with the same condition and action it represents. (Numerosity is a run-time optimisation which also yields interesting statistics of the state of the population.) By denoting the numerosity of rule i as $|i|$ we can add it explicitly to eq. (1) to yield:

$$SP(i) = \frac{F[i] \times |i|}{\sum\limits_{\text{all rules } j} F[j] \times |j|} \tag{2}$$

This formula gives us the panmictic selection probability for an individual rule in a particular population and describes an explicit relationship between the rule fitness parameter and the likelihood of being selected as a parent.

3.4 Selection Probability in a Niche GA

Here we derive the selection probability in a niche GA, in which only a subset of rules (the current niche) are eligible for selection. Here, selection probability is more complex than in a panmictic GA. To begin with there are two probabilities, which we will call the *Within-niche Selection Probability* (WSP) and the *Global Selection Probability* (GSP). The former is the probability that a rule in the current niche is selected and, continuing to assume use of a roulette wheel, it is given by eq. (2), except that we sum over the rules in the current niche rather than over the entire population:

$$WSP(i) = \frac{F[i] \times |i|}{\sum\limits_{\substack{\text{all rules} \\ j \text{ in niche}}} F[j] \times |j|} \tag{3}$$

Eq. (3) only gives the selection probability in any one particular niche at a time. However, while the niche GA runs in one niche at a time, the behaviour of the LCS in the long run is determined by how rules perform in all niches in which they occur. In other words, we would like to know the global selection probability of a rule, not just its within-niche selection probability. The global selection probability of rule i is obtained by weighting each within-niche probability (eq. (3)) by the probability of the GA occurring in that niche, and summing over all niches:[1]

$$\underset{\text{niches}}{\text{sum over}} \left(\begin{matrix}\text{probability of} \\ \text{GA in niche}\end{matrix} \times \begin{matrix} i\text{'s within-niche} \\ \text{selection probability}\end{matrix} \right) \tag{4}$$

Note that we can sum either only over the niches a rule occurs in, or over all niches. Since the probability of selection in a niche in which a rule does not occur is zero, it does not affect the sum. This global selection probability is well-defined but it is *implicit* in the definition of the niche GA. It has never been written explicitly, nor even discussed in the LCS literature. In statistical terms, the within-niche probability is a conditional probability distribution (conditional on the niche occurring) while the global probability is a joint probability distribution (joint over all niches).

The global probability tells us how likely a rule is to be selected on average across its niches (where the average is weighted by niche frequency). As noted in section 3.1, this is a rule's fitness in the evolutionary sense (as opposed to the LCS rule fitness parameter), and hence it can be used to analyse the behaviour of the system, as we do in section 4. As an aside, since the global probability explicitly includes the probability of each niche occurring, we can also interpret it as the probability of a rule being selected given that we do not know the current niche, only a distribution over niches. Since niche probabilities are defined in part by the distribution over inputs, we can also use the global probability when we have only a distribution over inputs, rather than knowing the current input. We will exploit this last interpretation in section 5 when we use the selection probabilities to implement an executable algorithm.

3.4.1 *Exploring the Probability of the GA Occurring in a Niche using Simplifying Assumptions*

The allocation of GA events to niches in XCS and UCS (the middle term in eq. (4)) has a complex distribution which depends on the training data and the population of rules.

[1] We use a minimum of mathematical notation in this equation as the concepts seem clearer in English.

Both, except in special cases, have high Kolmogorov complexity and hence are not easily specified so rather than attempting to model them in the general case we will make some simplifying assumptions. These assumptions will allow us to gain some insights into the niche GA by adding more detail to the "probability of GA in niche" term of eq. (4). These details (that is, the quantitative results) are naturally only valid given our simplifying assumptions, but nonetheless they shed much light on the general case by revealing many dynamics (qualitative results).

First, the distribution of GA events to niches depends on the distribution of inputs in the training data. Let us use an analytically tractable type of problem which is often used when analysing XCS: we learn some Boolean function in which the training set contains all inputs, which all occur with equal probability. A Boolean function of length l has 2^l inputs, and, when equally likely, each has probability:

$$1/2^l \tag{5}$$

The second factor affecting the distribution of GA events to niches is the rule population. This occurs due to the GA timing mechanism used in XCS and UCS, which triggers a GA event in a niche when a threshold θ_{GA} is exceeded by the average time since each rule in the niche was last in a GA event [12]. Hence, in general, to determine whether a GA will occur in a given niche, we must know what rules it contains and how long it has been since each was last in a GA. However, if we set $\theta_{GA} = 1$, then the niche GA is triggered on every time step regardless of the population, which greatly simplifies our analysis. We note, however, that this is *not* how XCS and UCS are normally parameterised, and it may be there are effects which arise under the normal parameterisation of the GA allocation mechanism which we overlook due to our simplification. Nonetheless, this simplification allows us to derive some concrete figures for the second term of eq. (4). We now do this for XCS, then UCS.

In XCS the niche GA runs within action sets (subsets of the match set which advocate the same action). When training, XCS customarily selects actions uniform randomly in order to explore the space of rewards. Since there are two possible actions in a Boolean function, and each defines it own action set, and as XCS selects them with equal probability, the action sets for a given input occur with probability 1/2. Multiplying this 1/2 by the probability of any given input from eq. (5) we obtain the probability of any given niche: $1/2 \times 1/2^l = 1/2^{l+1}$. Since $\theta_{GA} = 1$ this is also the probability of the GA occurring in any given niche, the second term in eq. (4). Expanding the rightmost term of eq. (4) using eq. (3) we obtain the XCS global selection probability:

$$GSP(i) = \sum_{\substack{\text{all rule } i\text{'s} \\ \text{action sets}}} \frac{1}{2^{l+1}} \times \frac{F[i] \times |i|}{\sum_{\substack{\text{all rules } j \\ \text{in action set}}} F[j] \times |j|} \tag{6}$$

Of course, this GSP only applies when our simplifying assumptions hold.

In UCS the niche GA runs within the correct set, the subset of the match set which advocates the correct action. Since the GA only occurs in the correct sets, the probability of the GA occurring in the correct set of any given input is the same as the the probability of that input occurring, as given by eq. (5). Replacing the second term of eq. (6) with eq. (5) and summing over correct sets rather than action set yields the UCS global selection probability:

$$GSP(i) = \sum_{\substack{\text{all rule } i\text{'s} \\ \text{correct sets}}} \frac{1}{2^{l}} \times \frac{F[i] \times |i|}{\sum_{\substack{\text{all rules } j \\ \text{in correct set}}} F[j] \times |j|} \tag{7}$$

Conversely, the probability of a rule participating in a GA event when it matches but is not in the correct set is 0. Hence in UCS a rule which is never in a correct set has 0 probability of being selected as a parent.

A Unified Notation for Global Selection Probability.

We can express the global selection probability for both XCS and UCS as one equation by introducing a ruleInSet(rule,action-set) operator, which returns 1 if a rule belongs to an action set and 0 otherwise. We can represent an action set as A(input:action), e.g. A(100:1) denotes the set of rules in the population which match input 100 and have action 1. As examples, ruleInSet(10#:1,A(100:1)) returns 1 whereas ruleInSet(100:0,A(100:1)) returns 0 as the actions don't match. We can now unify equations (6) and (7) by summing over all relevant sets, using ruleInSet() to only include those rules relevant to the current summation. Note that with UCS, we only include correct sets as incorrect action sets are not eligible for the GA, whereas in XCS any action set may be eligible as there is no supervision oracle. Given this, the global selection probability in either XCS or UCS can be written:

$$\frac{1}{2^l} \sum_{\substack{\text{all relevant} \\ \text{sets } A(k)}} \frac{F[i] \times |i| \times \text{ruleInSet}(i, A(k))}{\sum_{\text{all rules } j} F[j] \times |j| \times \text{ruleInSet}(j, A(k))} \tag{8}$$

with "all relevant sets A(k)" being action sets for XCS and correct sets for UCS.

4. ANALYSIS OF GLOBAL SELECTION PROBABILITY

We now analyse the equations from the previous section to see what we can learn about the niche GA. The equations define the global selection probability or a rule (i.e. its fitness, in the evolutionary, rather than rule parameter sense). Hence they must capture every factor which affects a rule's odds of reproduction. Two known factors are the generality of a rule [12] and whether it overlaps with other rules [9, 8].

4.1 Fitness Generality Bonus

General rules participate in more than one niche, increasing their selection opportunities and giving them an implicit fitness bonus. This bonus is implicit because it is not part of the rule fitness parameter in XCS or UCS, nor does it appear in the within-niche selection probability (eq. (3)). It occurs only because general rules participate in more niches, so it is captured in the global selection probability by the leftmost term in eq. (4) the "sum over niches". We can quantify this bonus by considering how rule generality increases the number of niches participated in but, unfortunately, this relationship depends entirely on the training data. Imagine for instance a dataset which contains only one input. No matter how general a rule is, it can match at most only one input. This highlights two different definitions of generality: the *syntactic generality* of a rule, which defines how many inputs it could match, and what we could call its *actual gen-*

erality; the number of inputs it does match. (These concepts were discussed in section 4.2 of [13].)

Although the actual generality of a rule depends on the training data, we can calculate its syntactic generality without reference to the training data (other than its cardinality), or indeed other rules. Let us assume we are learning a Boolean function and are using the ternary rule condition language often used with LCS (see e.g. [9]). In this language, conditions are drawn from the alphabet $\{0, 1, \#\}$ where # is a wildcard which matches both 0 and 1 in a binary input string. The number of # symbols in a condition determines a rule's syntactic generality. Specifically, a rule with g # symbols can match up to 2^g inputs, out of the 2^l possible inputs for a Boolean function of length l.

This bound was first obtained in [9] (section 3.3.2). We will now give a number of related results, and to emphasise them we number them, starting with the result above, which we restate as: i) The generality fitness bonus due to the niche GA has an upper bound of 2^g. ii) If, as in section 3.4.1, we assume all inputs are present in the training set, then the generality bonus does in fact meet this upper bound. iii) We note this bound is exponential in the number of # symbols.

iv) As noted above, this fitness bonus is captured by the leftmost term in eq. (4), which sums over niches. Note that this bonus is *not* added to the selection probability, but is itself the addition of probability-weighted within-niche probabilities. In other words, the bonus does not add to selection probability, but merely gives the rule extra chances to gain probability in extra niches. If we return to the tribe analogy, imagine our mischievous individual is going to multiple weight-lifting contests, but everyone at these contests is much stronger than him and he has 0 probability of winning (0 within-niche selection probability). No matter how many contests he attends, his global selection probability remains 0 – the fitness bonus does him no good. This means the bonus is only potential; nothing is guaranteed.

v) The example above illustrates that within-niche probability depends entirely on what other rules occur within each niche, that is, on the state of the rule population. It is therefore not possible to compute the within-niche selection probability, let alone the global selection probability, without knowing the contents of the rule population. This means it is not possible to write equations for these probabilities which do not contain variables to describe the state of the population. It is also not possible to totally remove these variables without fully specifying the population.

vi) Since the fitness bonus due to generality depends on the contents of the rule population (i.e. is co-evolutionary), the niche GA applies a different bonus to the same rule when it is part of different populations. vii) Since rule fitness parameters depend on training data, the niche GA also applies different bonuses depending on the training data. Consequently, the niche GA may apply a different generality bonus on different experiments with the same training data, as well as on different data.

Because the generality bonus is a function of the population and training data it is not a simple matter to characterise or analyse it. In contrast, we could imagine a system in which the generality bonus 2^g was *added* to the rest of the global selection probability for a rule i. That is, adding 2^g to eq. (4), we obtain:

$$2^g + \underset{\text{over niches}}{\text{average}} \left(\begin{matrix}\text{probability of}\\ \text{GA in niche}\end{matrix} \times \begin{matrix}i\text{'s within-niche}\\ \text{selection probability}\end{matrix} \right) \tag{9}$$

where g refers to this particular rule i, and we would need to normalise these SP values to obtain probabilities. Note that in this case the generality bonus is not co-evolutionary; a rule receives it regardless of what other rules are in the population. In fact, a rule gains fitness by gaining generality regardless of how accurate it is, which seems undesirable. However, our point is that it would be simpler to analyse a bonus such as the one in eq. (9), than the existing bonus.

To conclude, the niche GA's generality bonus is complex. It is unclear whether this complexity is necessary. Perhaps a simpler bonus would be more effective, or perhaps there is something about the niche GA's particular bonus which contributes to the success of XCS and UCS.

4.2 Fitness Overlap Penalty

In the niche GA overlapping rules inhibit each other's fitness [9] (sections 3.5.2 and 4.2.6). Intuitively, this occurs because they participate in the same GA selection events, and when one rule is selected the others simultaneously fail to be selected. In contrast, rules which do not overlap do not participate in the same selection events, so when a rule is selected, that does not represent a lost opportunity for rules which do not overlap with it. We can locate the pressure against overlapping rules in the within-niche selection probability eq. (3). The within-niche probability of a rule i decreases if we add another rule j to the niche, assuming j's fitness is non-zero, because j's fitness increases the denominator. (Similarly, i decreases j's fitness.) Since equation eq. (3) appears as a term in later equations for the global selection probability the overlap penalty is included in this probability. In contrast, although in a panmictic GA all rules compete in all selection events, there is no fitness penalty for overlaps in eq. (7). This is because all rules compete for selection and hence all rules inhibit each other regardless of whether they overlap or not; in terms of eq. (7), all rules in the entire population have the same denominator in their within-niche probability (regardless of which rules they overlap with). In addition to the niche GA, [9] (section 4.2.6) suggests the relative accuracy update and some deletion methods also penalise overlaps.

4.3 Empirical Validation of Equations

To confirm that eq. (7) for the global selection probability in UCS is correct when given the assumptions of section 3.4.1, we created the example population of rules shown in Table 1. We then modified an implementation of UCS to record the actual number of selection events for each rule, which we then converted into estimates of their selection probabilities by dividing them by the total number of selection events. We inserted the example population in UCS and disabled the genetic operators so that although parents were selected the rule population never changed. We then ran the system for 10,000 time steps to count the number of selections per rule, replicated the experiment 20 times, and averaged the results, which are shown in Table 1. We also manually computed the selection probabilities given by eq. (7) for this example population. Worked examples of this computation are available in [10]. The absolute differences between predicted and actual selections were small, and the

Condition:Action	Fitness	Numerosity	Avg. Selects in 20 Runs	Observed SP	Predicted SP	Absolute Difference	t-test p value
##1:1	0.3	2	4084.1	0.204205	0.204545	0.000340	0.56913
#01:0	0.8	4	2500.9	0.125045	0.125000	0.000045	0.95107
#00:0	0.7	4	4241.35	0.212068	0.212500	0.000432	0.55721
010:1	0.8	5	2242.6	0.112130	0.111111	0.001019	0.09211
1##:0	0.4	3	3255.45	0.162773	0.162500	0.000272	0.75723
###:1	0.5	1	3675.6	0.183780	0.184343	0.000563	0.37562

Table 1: Comparison of Selection Probabilities (SP) as estimated by running a UCS system with a static population, and as predicted by the UCS global selection probability (eq. (7)).

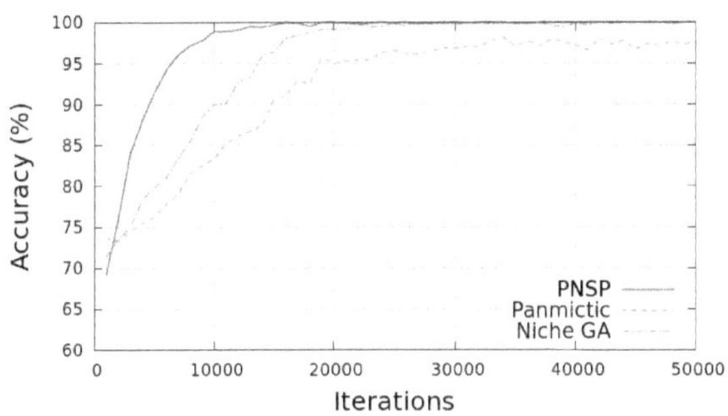

Figure 1: Accuracy on the 11-mux. Mating restriction in the niche GA reduces accuracy compared to PNSP.

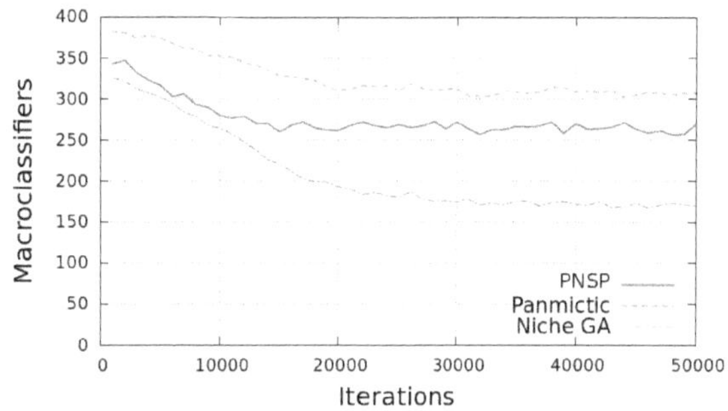

Figure 2: Macroclassifier counts on the 11-mux. Mating restriction in the niche GA reduces macroclassifiers compared to PNSP.

t-tests revealed no statistical significance to them at the 95% level, suggesting that the derivation of eq. (7) is sound.

5. EVALUATING MATING RESTRICTION

In section 2.3 we noted that one of the difficulties of studying the niche GA is its all-or-nothing nature, but here we demonstrate that this difficulty can be avoided. Specifically, we isolate the effects of the niche GA's mating restriction from its selection probability. We do this by creating an executable version of UCS with a panmictic GA, but in which rules have the same expected selection probabilities as in the niche GA, as given by eq. (7).[2] We call this version of UCS "Panmictic with Niche Selection Probability" (PNSP).

We now have a system which does not have the mating restriction effects of the niche GA (since any rule can cross with any other), but in which the selection probabilities are the same as in a niche GA. In particular, the generality bonus and overlap penalty are the same in PNSP as they would be in a niche GA. The following Table compares the three types of GA we now have.

Case	GA Type	Selection Probability	Mating
1	Niche	Niche GA	Restricted
2	Panmictic	Panmictic	Panmictic
3	PNSP	Niche GA	Panmictic

[2]Of course, in the niche GA, given a particular input, the selection probability of rules which do not match is 0. Here, however, we model the expected behaviour of the niche GA on one time step (given a uniform distribution over inputs because that is how inputs are selected).

This partially fulfils our aim from section 3.2 to be able to switch the components of the niche GA on and off independently in order to study them. A thorough comparison of these 3 GAs is beyond the scope of this paper but as a preliminary study we evaluated them in UCS as implemented in [5] (note: for simplicity, this is without fitness sharing).

The panmictic UCS simply uses the standard UCS rule fitness parameter in a panmictic GA. To implement the PNSP version we modified UCS so that every time there is a GA event we recalculate the UCS GSP (eq. (7)) of all rules as specified by the pseudocode in figure 3, then run a panmictic GA using the relevant GSP value as the fitness of its rule. Otherwise UCS is unchanged. Full implementation details are available in [10]. The GSP calculation is very time-consuming as it iterates through all training set instances in order to calculate all rules' selection probabilities in all possible niches (note that niches are defined by training set instances). Run-time could be significantly optimised by recomputing the GSP only for rules whose fitness has changed since the last GSP calculation, but we have not done so.

We tested our 3 versions of UCS on the 11 multiplexer (11-mux) Boolean function, in which an 11-bit binary input string is treated as having 3 address bits and 8 data bits and the class of the input is the value of the addressed data bit. For example, using the first 3 bits as the address, the value of 01000100000 is 1 as the third data bit is indexed. Of the 2048 possible strings we selected a training set of 900 uniform randomly and used the remaining 1148 as a test set.

To give a fair comparison, we allowed each algorithm approximately 25,000 GA events by setting the GA timing threshold $\theta_{GA} = 25$ for the niche GA, and for the other two algorithms triggering the GA on every second time step. (This latter was necessary because the action set size esti-

```
gsp(i) = 0 for each rule i in the population
probOfNiche = 1 / num of training examples
for each training example k
    fitnessSum = 0
    for each rule i in population
        if ruleInSet(i, k, correctAction(k))
            fitnessSum += fitness(i)
            setMembers.add(i)
    for each rule j in setMembers
        withinNicheProb = fitness(j) / fitnessSum
        gsp(j) += withinNicheProb * probOfNiche
```

Figure 3: Pseudocode to calculate GSP in PNSP

mates used to trigger the GA [12] were not computed in the panmictic and PNSP versions; an alternative would have been to do that.) Other parameters (see [1, 5]) were: population size limit 400, $\nu = 20, \mu = 0.05, \chi = 0.8, \gamma_{exp} = 0.01, P_{\#} = 0.3333, \theta_{sub} = 20, acc_0 = 0.99, \theta_{del} = 20, \delta = 0.1$ Experimental results were averaged over 5 replications.

The accuracy of the three algorithms is shown in figure 1. The panmictic UCS performs poorly on the test set, but this is not surprising as it has no incentive to generalise rules. (This makes the comparison unfair to the panmictic GA, but it does provide a baseline.) The niche GA outperforms the panmictic GA, but, surprisingly, it is outperformed by PNSP. In terms of macroclassifiers, shown in figure 2, PNSP is between the panmictic and niche GAs. In short, the comparison of niche and PSNP suggests mating restriction reduces both accuracy and population size.

Our main aim with this experiment was to demonstrate how GSP could be used to model the niche GA in a panmictic GA and hence factor out mating restriction while retaining the other effects of the niche GA. The results we have are limited to a single and not very difficult problem but we will briefly analyse them nonetheless. That PNSP has better accuracy than the niche GA was unexpected. We have two hypotheses. The first is that PNSP's better performance may result from greater diversity in the pool of potential parents. Although crossing very different parents often results in lethals (low-fitness offspring), it can also result in offspring which improve on their parents. The larger macroclassifier counts of PNSP compared to the niche GA may reflect this greater diversity. In contrast, the niche GA has a less diverse pool of candidate parents, since they must all overlap. If the diversity in the niche is too low, the niche GA will stagnate and generate too many clones of existing rules to perform an effective search. Our first hypothesis is that this may be occurring. Our second hypothesis is that the parameter settings for the various algorithms were somehow more favourable to PNSP than to the niche GA. In any case, a more extensive study would be needed to account for these preliminary results.

6. CONCLUSIONS

We have studied the niche GA, a defining component of the XCS and UCS classifier systems, by deriving a model of the Global Selection Probability (GSP) for rules in the niche. Analysis of this formula generated insight into the fitness calculation in these systems and some of their subtle effects, namely the bonus for general rules and the penalty for overlapping rules. One of the simplifications in section 3.4.1 was to factor out the GA timing mechanism by setting the timing threshold so that the GA runs in every niche. This simplification should be removed and the effect of the timing mechanism on selection probability should be studied. We intend to continue this work and to produce a more complete model of the niche GA.

We turned the GSP equation into an executable version of UCS we called PNSP which has the selection probability but not the mating restriction of the niche GA. Initial results suggest mating restriction may reduce population size at the cost of reduced accuracy, although the results are very preliminary. Much more work is also needed to isolate and study the niche GA's many other effects.

The long-term aim of this work is to ultimately design better Learning Classifier Systems.

7. REFERENCES

[1] E. Bernadó-Mansilla and J. M. Garrell-Guiu. Accuracy-Based Learning Classifier Systems: Models, Analysis and Applications to Classification Tasks. *Evolutionary Computation*, 11(3):209–238, 2003.

[2] L. B. Booker. *Intelligent Behavior as an Adaptation to the Task Environment.* PhD thesis, The University of Michigan, 1982.

[3] L. B. Booker. Improving the performance of genetic algorithms in classifier systems. In J. J. Grefenstette, editor, *Proc. of the 1st Int. Conf. on Genetic Algorithms and their Applications (ICGA85)*, pages 80–92. Lawrence Erlbaum Associates, 1985.

[4] L. B. Booker. Triggered rule discovery in classifier systems. In J. D. Schaffer, editor, *Proceedings of the 3rd International Conference on Genetic Algorithms (ICGA89)*, pages 265–274. Morgan Kaufmann, 1989.

[5] G. Brown, T. Kovacs, and J. Marshall. UCSpv: Principled Voting in UCS Rule Populations. In H. Lipson et al., editors, *GECCO'07: the Genetic and Evolutionary Computation Conference*, pages 1774–1781. ACM, 2007.

[6] M. Butz, T. Kovacs, P. L. Lanzi, and S. W. Wilson. Toward a Theory of Generalization and Learning in XCS. *IEEE Transactions on Evolutionary Computation*, 8(1):8–46, 2004.

[7] J. H. Holland. *Adaptation in Natural and Artificial Systems.* University of Michigan Press, Ann Arbor, 1975. Republished by the MIT press, 1992.

[8] C. Ioannides, G. Barrett, and K. Eder. XCS Cannot Learn all Boolean Functions. In *Proc. of the 13th Annual Conf. on Genetic and Evolutionary Comp.*, GECCO '11, pages 1283–1290. ACM, 2011.

[9] T. Kovacs. *Strength or Accuracy: Credit Assignment in Learning Classifier Systems.* Springer, 2004.

[10] R. Tindale. Investigation into improving niche genetic algorithm LCS. BSc Thesis, U. of Bristol, 2012.

[11] S. W. Wilson. ZCS: A Zeroth Level Classifier System. *Evolutionary Computation*, 2(1):1–18, 1994.

[12] S. W. Wilson. Classifier Fitness Based on Accuracy. *Evolutionary Computation*, 3(2):149–175, 1995.

[13] S. W. Wilson. Generalization in the XCS classifier system. In J. R. Koza, eta al., editors, *Genetic Programming 1998: Proceedings of the Third Annual Conference*, pages 665–674. Morgan Kaufmann, 1998.

Networks of Transform-Based Evolvable Features for Object Recognition

Taras Kowaliw
ISC-PIF, CNRS,
Paris, France
taras@kowaliw.ca

Wolfgang Banzhaf
Memorial University,
St. John's, Canada
banzhaf@mun.ca

René Doursat
Drexel University,
Philadelphia, USA
rene.doursat@drexel.edu

ABSTRACT

We propose an *evolutionary feature creator* (EFC) to explore a non-linear and offline method for generating features in image recognition tasks. Our model aims at extracting low-level features automatically when provided with an arbitrary image database. In this work, we are concerned with the addition of algorithmic *depth* to a genetic programming (GP) system, hypothesizing that it will improve the capacity for solving problems that require high-level, hierarchical reasoning. For this we introduce a *network superstructure* that co-evolves with our low-level GP representations. Two approaches are described: the first uses our previously used "shallow" GP system, the second presents a new "deep" GP system that involves this network superstructure. We evaluate these models against a benchmark object recognition database. Results show that the deep structure outperforms the shallow one in generating features that support classification, and does so without requiring significant additional computational time. Further, high accuracy is achieved on the standard ETH-80 classification task, also outperforming many existing specialized techniques. We conclude that our EFC is capable of data-driven extraction of useful features from an object recognition database.

Categories and Subject Descriptors

I.5.4 [**Computing Methodologies**]: Pattern Recognition—*Computer Vision*; I.2.8 [**Computing Methodologies**]: Artificial Intelligence—*Problem Solving, Control Methods, and Search*; I.2.2 [**Artificial Intelligence**]: Automatic Programming—*Program synthesis*

General Terms

Algorithms, Design, Experimentation

Keywords

pattern recognition, computer vision, object, genetic programming, TEF, deep learning

GECCO'13, July 6–10, 2013, Amsterdam, The Netherlands.

1. INTRODUCTION

In order to achieve greater autonomy in pattern recognition, we need the ability to extract representations directly from databases. This is especially true for computer vision, where large dimensionality is the norm, and sample distributions tend to be dense and noisy. Operating directly on the original, *raw pixel space* allows for the extraction of useful low-level patterns and features not captured by traditional vision-based routines. This is now an active area of research, with many strategies being explored, including wavelets, histograms, and others [27, 26, 8, 35, 24].

Our present work concentrates on evolutionary computation (EC). There is a long history of the use of EC in image processing tasks [1, 2, 11, 12, 15, 19, 34, 36, 32]. Genetic programming (GP), in particular, is known to generate versatile and self-adapting solution structures [29, 10]. Flexible, rather than intuitive, representations are especially critical in applications for which techniques inspired by human vision might be suboptimal, such as satellite, multispectral, or medical imagery [30, 13, 31].

One approach to evolutionary image classification is our design and use of *transform-based evolvable features* (TEFs), the key ingredient in a larger *evolutionary feature creator* (EFC). Here, a collection of genetic programs are evolved as transformations on the space of images, which are evaluated for their ability to create descriptions of the images. This approach was first introduced in [17], then applied to various challenges such as the recognition of artistic styles [18], or a form of muscular dystrophy in biological cell images [16]. In the latter case, our technique matched the state of the art. The advantages of using TEFs are four-fold:

- the discovered transforms and their descriptions can be computed in a single pass over the image;
- transforms are easily visualized and interpreted;
- transforms are represented as a simple mathematical expressions, easily interrogated or modified;
- we can evolve any number of distinct features in a natural way.

Here we will apply our system to an object recognition benchmark, the ETH-80 dataset [22]. Object recognition involves learning to classify objects from any of several perspectives (for instance, an image of a mug from the top looks like a circle, while from the side it looks like a cylinder with a handle). As such, higher-level representations are generally beneficial, allowing for more primitive features to be recombined in non-linear ways. For this reason, object recognition is a common target of *deep learning* systems [4], a branch of neural computation often applied to computer vision. Neural networks are considered "deep" if there are more steps between the inputs and outputs—implying a greater capacity for abstraction—as opposed to "shallow" representations, where a dictionary of sub-representations are combined simply (e.g. as in support vector machines, SVM). In deep learning, a network will implicitly create low-level and high-level features simultaneously while learning, expressing them as sub-networks. For a wide class of problems, deeper representations are known to be exponentially more effective than shallower representations, but are also known to contain more local minima [5]. Deep representations have been highly successful recently in vision problems [21, 7].

Here we consider a new, deep version of our evolutionary system. In addition to our evolving sub-representations (the TEFs), we also co-evolve a *network superstructure* connecting those TEFs. This new superstructure will allow for the re-use of existing TEFs as inputs to more specialized (i.e. deeper) TEFs. We will contrast this new system against our original, "shallow" setup. It is not obvious that this addition of depth to a shallow GP-based system will be useful: GPs are more malleable than perceptrons or SVM kernels, and are innately capable of representing hierarchical knowledge. Yet, while GPs can theoretically recreate some depth on their own, our intuition is that such a representation will not be evolvable. Rather, our reasoning is that an imposed two-level system will allow for more primitive features to co-evolve with higher-level representations while retaining interim information as a working output.

We are not the first to use a deep network representation for GP-based image processing. GP-based network systems have already generated successful image segmentation methods [33, 23], which are partial inspiration for this work. There are several important differences with our model, however: firstly, we aim for feature extraction for classification; secondly, our system co-evolves both network structure and the component sub-representations simultaneously; and thirdly, our system uses a classifier as a wrapper, meaning that the extracted features need to support a classifier rather than solve the problem directly. This last point allows for different, specialized classifiers to be swapped in and out as desired—as we shall demonstrate—and for expertise to be located at a later stage.

2. THE DATA

The ETH-80 database, created by Leibe and Schiele [22], is an object database composed of eight categories (typically toys, mugs or fruits), each consisting of ten instances or "objects", photographed from 41 views. This makes $8 \times 10 \times 41 = 3280$ images in total. Figure 1 shows one particular view for each object, all from the same angle (here we preprocess the images by scaling them to 80×80 pixels and converting to grayscale). A typical recognition task consists of predicting the category of a previously unseen object.

For each run, we divide our data into three sets: a *training* set, which is used to train a classifier; a *validation* set, used by the fitness function to evaluate any particular classifier; and a *test* set to evaluate the final result of the evolutionary process. Each set contains a certain number of objects, where each object means a series of 41 images.

Initially (Section 4.1), we choose 24 objects as validation objects (i.e., $24 \times 41 = 984$ images), and 8 objects as test objects (i.e., $8 \times 41 = 328$ images). First, we evolve a good solution using the validation data as a fitness function. Then,

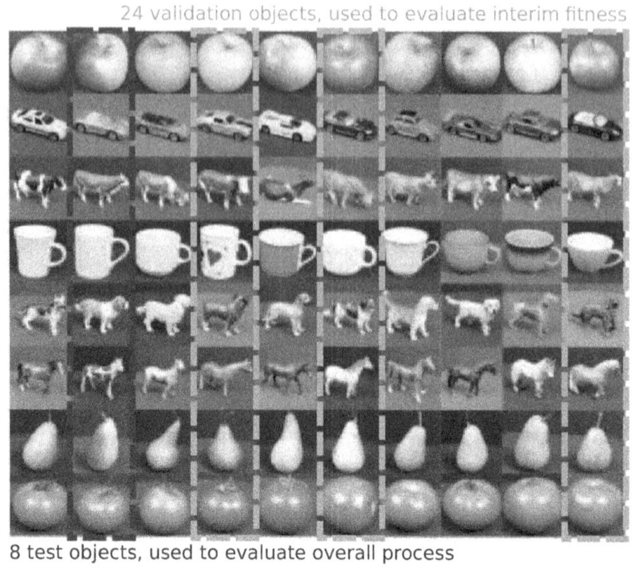

Figure 1: Samples from the ETH-80 database. There are 8 categories of 10 objects each. Each image shows a single view (from 41) of one object. One set of test objects (*column in dark red frame*) and three sets of validation objects (*columns in light green frames*) are highlighted. Each column contains a total of 8 × 41 views (other 40 not shown).

we evaluate the highest fitness solution on the test data to obtain our test accuracy.

Later (Section 4.2), we also choose 24 objects as validation objects, leaving 8 test objects aside. Evolution proceeds as above, using the validation set to compute fitness. However, once evolution is complete and we have extracted our highest fitness solution, we compute the test accuracy for each of the 8 test objects separately. That is, for each test object, we take the remaining 79 objects to create a new training pool, and evaluate the accuracy on that test object. This latter measure, called the *leave-one-object-out accuracy*, is the traditional evaluation metric for the ETH-80 database.

3. THE MODEL

We begin with a high-level overview of our original model (the interested reader should consult [16] for details). Next, we discuss the new features.

Our model, the EFC, operates on a provided database of images, divided into a finite number of classes. The ultimate output of the system will be a collection of easily computed features well-suited for classification of the database by some particular classifier. The EFC consists of two parts: an evolutionary algorithm, and a collection of *feature-extracting individuals* or simply "individuals".

An individual is a tuple: $(n, T_1, ..., T_k, M, \sigma)$ where n is a neighbourhood size, T_i is a transform-based evolvable feature, M is a dimensionality-reducing function, and σ is a classifier. When presented with an input image, an individual will process it as follows (Figure 2):

1. compute a collection of transformations of the image using its TEFs T_i;
2. convert the transformed images to a *feature vector* via the moment function M;
3. feed the feature vector to classifier σ, which will return a class label.

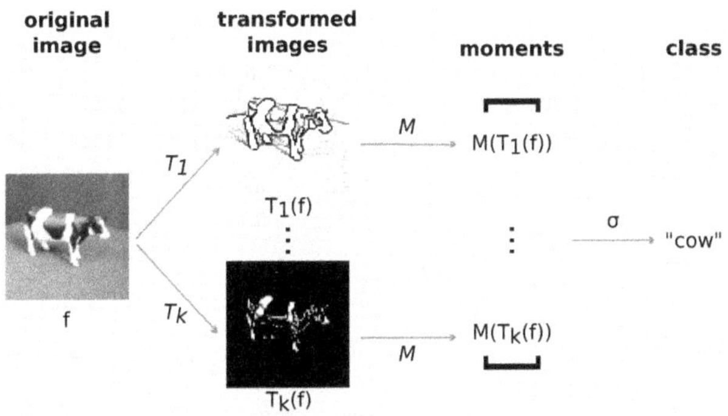

Figure 2: Overview of a feature-extracting individual. First, the original image is transformed by a collection of TEFs T_i. Next, each transform is converted to numerical values via the moment function M. Finally, the feature vector of moments is classified.

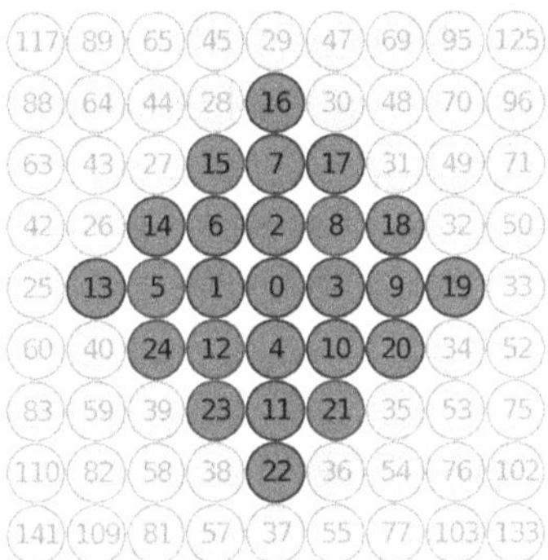

Figure 3: The neighbourhood of a pixel, VN-25, is mapped to a prioritized one-dimensional representation, which is fed to a genetic program.

A TEF is a genetic program which operates on the pixel space of the image as a sliding window. For each pixel in the source image, a neighbourhood is collected and passed to the TEF, which returns a real value in $[0, 1]$. This new value is used to define the intensity of the corresponding output image pixel. While neighbourhoods may vary (there is evidence that the EFC can self-select an appropriate neighbourhood size), here we simply use a neighbourhood of type VN-25 (Figure 3).

We use a single dimensionality-reducing function M, the first geometric moment. As in much previous work, informal experimentation convinced us that this was the best choice.

Our present work diverges from previous versions of the EFC in two ways: the chief modification is the inclusion of a *network superstructure* organizing the relations between TEFs. This allows for the generation of *depth* in the resulting transforms, as some TEFs can build upon the lower-level results of previous TEFs. A second change is the usage of Linear Genetic Programming (LGP) as the representation of the TEFs.

3.1 LGP representation for TEFs

There are two main motivations for using LGP: first, LGP is known to be naturally parsimonious, which is a desirable trait for our transforms; second, LGP is very easily converted to computer code—including, potentially, assembly code—which allows for the easy conversion of an LGP program to a compilable and fast machine-independent code listing. For reasons of verification and export of results from the system, this is also a desirable property.

Table 1: Pool of functions and actions on inputs (a, b).

func.	action	func.	action
plus	$a + b$	max	$\max\{a, b\}$
minus	$a - b$	min	$\min\{a, b\}$
times	ab	abs	$\|a\|$
sqrt	$\sqrt{\|a\|}$	square	a^2
inv	$1/a$, or 1 if $\|a\| < 0.0001$	thresh	1 if $a > b$, 0 otherwise
pow	a^b, if defined 1 otherwise	log	$\log a$, if defined 1 otherwise
dist	$\sqrt{a^2 + b^2}$		

Our implementation of LGP closely follows [6]. An LGP program consists of

- 25 initial registers, for the inputs from the VN-25 neighbourhood
- 5 additional registers, initialized to genetically controlled values in $[0, 1]$
- between 2 and 100 binary program statements
- a return statement, returning the contents of the first register (if necessary, the return statement is forced into the range $[0, 1]$ by using the closest extreme value).

Our pool of functions is shown in Table 1.

We can mutate an LGP program through two forms: micro-mutation and macro-mutation, where the former reinitializes existing elements with probability p_M, and the latter adds or removes a program statement. When mutating an LGP program, we choose macro-mutation with probability p_{mut}, otherwise we apply micro-mutation.

We will refer to the *effective size* of an LGP program as the number of non-neutral program statements. Note that this is an over-estimate of the complexity of a program, since some non-neutral program statements might be ineffective (e.g., $a = a + 0$). The *mean effective size* of an individual is the mean of the effective size of each of its transforms.

3.2 OrigEFC

We will refer to our original EFC system with LGP representation as OrigEFC. Like previous version, this is a *shallow* application of a series of transforms to the database.

As in previous work, we use four genetic operators: mutation, crossover, merger, and pruning. All are identical to previous work, except that intra-transform mutation now mutates an LGP program.

3.3 DeepEFC

Our primary extension of the EFC model will be termed DeepEFC, where we add a network structure to the original EFC representation. In this case, we view each transform as a linear list of functions, which is applied either to the raw images or to the outputs of previous transforms.

Thus, a DeepEFC individual can be written as

$$I = (n, (t_1, T_1), ..., (t_k, T_k), M, \sigma),$$

where n is a neighbourhood size, M is a statistical moment, σ is a classifier, and (t_i, T_i) is a target-TEF pair. The target t_i is a positive integer, interpreted either as the index of a preceding TEF T_j (in which case $t_i = j$) or as an indicator of the original image.

Given an image, denoted by f, a DeepEFC individual:

- applies the first TEF directly to f, producing image $f_1 = T_1(f)$
- for each subsequent target-TEF pair (t_i, T_i):
  - renormalizes the index: $j = (t_i \bmod i)$, so that it points to a preceding TEF T_j, where $j \in [0, i-1]$
  - gets the source image f_j to be used:
    * if $j = 0$, f_j is the original image f
    * if $j > 0$, f_j is as defined by previous iteration
  - applies the TEF to the source image:
    * $f_i = T_i(f_j)$
- computes the complete feature vector: $v = \{M(f), M(f_1), ..., M(f_k)\}$
- returns the class label $\sigma(v)$.

Thus, an individual now has its TEFs organized in a network, where one TEF might operate on the output of a previous TEF. By chaining the computation of the TEFs, we can compute a deep individual in the same amount of time as a shallow individual, assuming an equivalent complexity in terms of number and composition of TEFs.

A DeepEFC individual can be *initialized* in the same manner as an OrigEFC individual, with a random, positive integer chosen for each t_i value. With probability 0.5 we set $t_i = 0$ under the assumption that the majority of representations should be shallow.

All *genetic operators* applied to a DeepEFC individual are the same as for OrigEFC, where target-TEF pairs are always treated as a single unit. Thus, the crossover operator will swap target-TEF pairs between individuals, a merger will create an individual with a large list of target-TEF pairs from two source individuals, and pruning will delete a target-TEF pair from an individual. We can *mutate* a DeepEFC individual in the same manner as an OrigEFC individual, except that we also have some chance of mutating each t_i value. In these cases, the t_i value is reinitialized randomly.

3.4 Evolutionary Algorithm

Our system is driven by a steady-state evolutionary algorithm. A population of n_{pop} individuals is initialized and evaluated for fitness. Next, for $n_{\text{eval}} - n_{\text{pop}}$ iterations, we

(a) select an individual via a tournament of two randomly chosen individuals;
(b) select an operator from crossover, merger, or pruning, with probability p_{cross}, p_{merge}, and p_{prune} respectively. If none was selected, we choose mutation with strength p_{mut} (see [16] for operator definitions);
(c) in the case of crossover or merger, we select a second individual via tournament;
(d) we replace the worst individual from the initial tournament in (a) with the result of the operation.

Thus, we execute exactly n_{eval} evaluations in total.

The complexity of the training is linear in $O(n_{\text{eval}}\, n_{\text{im}} |f|)$, where n_{im} is the number of images in the training and validation sets, and $|f|$ is the number of dimensions in an image.

The *fitness* F of an individual I is the generalized sensitivity-specificity:

$$F(I, V) = \prod_{\text{categories } c} (1 - \text{FPR}(I, V, c))$$

where V denotes the set of validation images, and FPR is the False Positive Rate of the classifier over the images of category c. We use this product—rather than, say, simple classification accuracy—to discourage local minima when a classifier learns to recognize a single category but not others. To report results, however, we will use the classification accuracy. The winner of a tournament between individuals I_1 and I_2 is:

$$\text{win}(I_1, I_2) = \begin{cases} \arg\min_I n_T(I) & ; \text{if } |F(I_1) - F(I_2)| < \delta_{\text{pars}} \\ \arg\max_I F(I) & ; \text{otherwise} \end{cases}$$

where δ_{pars} is a parsimony threshold and $n_T(I)$ is the number of TEFs in individual I.

Following an informal parameter search of approximately 50 trial runs, we found the following parameter set to maximize the test fitness:

max number of initial TEFs	3	nbhd.	VN-25
max number of TEFs	20	δ_{pars}	0.001
n_{pop}	800	n_{eval}	15 000
p_{mut}	0.025	p_{cross}	0.33
p_{merge}	0.01	p_{prune}	0.025

Unless otherwise stated, these parameters will be used for all following experiments. Note that this choice was made based on the expected maximization of the OrigEFC model, not the DeepEFC, and hence, if any advantage exists, we expect it to favour the original technique.

4. RESULTS AND ANALYSIS

4.1 Model comparison

Initially, we compare the result from OrigEFC and DeepEFC on the ETH-80 database. For this section, we limited the test set to include the objects indexed "1" in each category (the second column in Figure 1), while the validation objects were randomly picked for each run. Constraining our choice of test objects to these particular ones is a setting we believe to be of greater than average difficulty based on the classifier accuracies that we computed in our early explorations. We do so to limit the variance due to selection of the test object and better see the stochasticity resulting from the use of an evolutionary algorithm. Note that this implies lower test accuracies than is generally possible, due to both the choice of test objects and less training data ($80 - 8 = 72$ left for training, instead of 79).

First, we looked at the performance of OrigEFC. The evolution of the classification accuracies for one typical run is shown in Figure 4. In general, evolution was successful, with individuals steadily increasing in fitness over time. Over about 15 independent runs, final test accuracies had a mean of 0.809 (s.d. 0.033) using the original first nearest neighbour (1-NN) classifier.

Generally speaking, test accuracy increased with training fitness, although there were occasional exceptions. The system did not, in general, overfit: on the contrary, generally there was substantial underfitting, with test accuracy approximately 20% higher than training accuracy. This means that our choice of validation technique (24 objects) was robust; it also suggests that running the experiments for more time might generate better results.

Next, we performed identical experiments on DeepEFC, using the same parameters as above, and again constraining the choice of test objects. In this case, evolution followed

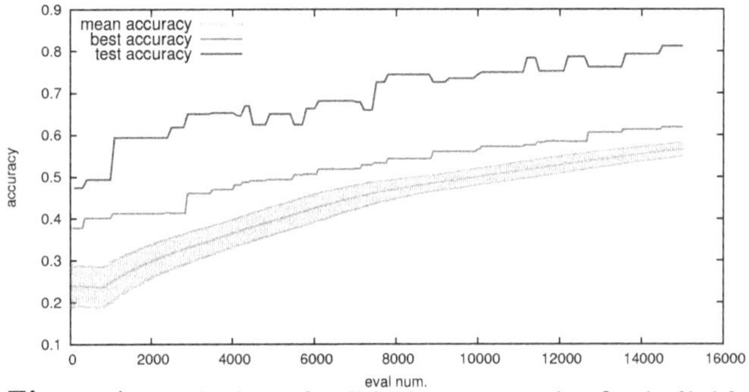

Figure 4: Evolution of validation accuracies for individuals in a typical OrigEFC run (*green*: mean, *red*: best). Test accuracy (*blue*) also computed to track overfitting.

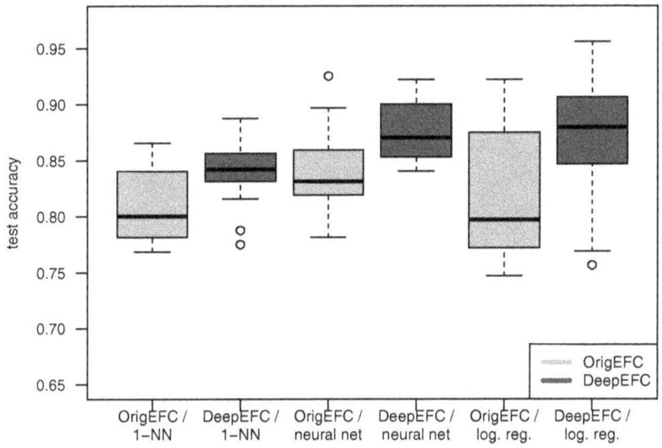

Figure 5: Comparison of test accuracies for several independent runs of OrigEFC (*orange*) and DeepEFC (*blue*) using several classifiers.

a very similar course, that is, a steadily increasing fitness over time, and substantial underfitting. The final mean test accuracy for about 15 independent runs of the DeepEFC system was 0.838 (s.d. 0.029) using the 1-NN classifier.

A comparison of the test accuracies achieved by OrigEFC and DeepEFC can be seen in Figure 5. We also consider the results re-evaluated via two additional classifiers: logistic regression and a neural network. Both are implemented via Weka [37] using default values. For all classifiers, a Welsch's two-value t-test confirms that the difference between mean values is significant ($p < 0.05$ in all cases), therefore that DeepEFC is an improvement over OrigEFC.

A second question we had was about the *complexity* of the evolved LGP programs. The mean effective size of the most

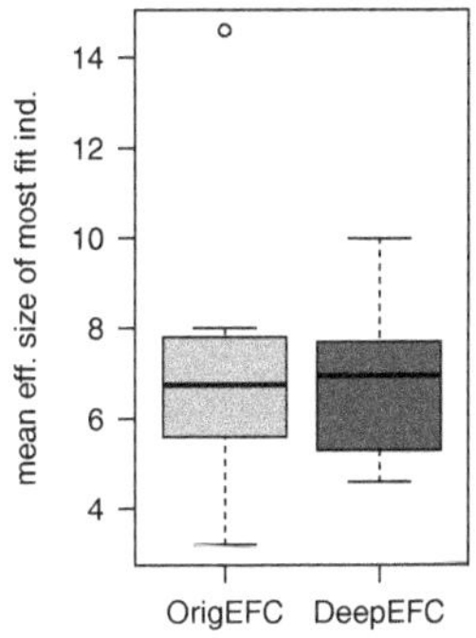

Figure 6: Comparison of the mean effective size of the TEFs in the most fit individual for several independent runs of OrigEFC and DeepEFC.

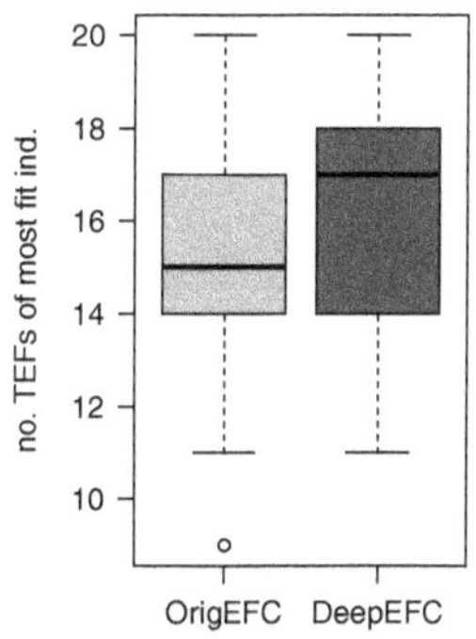

Figure 7: Comparison of the number of TEFs in the most fit individual for several independent runs of OrigEFC and DeepEFC.

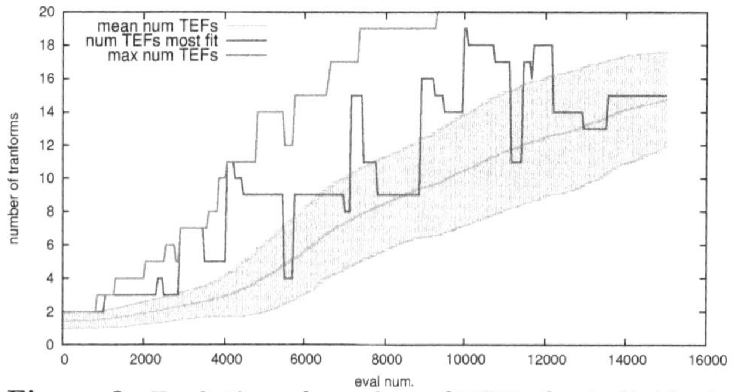

Figure 8: Evolution of number of TEFs for individuals in our example OrigEFC run.

fit individuals for each run is shown in Figure 6. Our first note is that our intuition regarding LGP was correct, the programs are parsimonious with an average size of six or seven program statements (see the appendix for samples): programs of this size can easily be analyzed by a human. This is a natural consequence of the use of LGP, as we did not put any pressure toward small LGP programs like we did toward a small number of TEFs.

A second note regarding the mean effective size is that there is no substantial difference between the OrigEFC and the DeepEFC program sizes. Indeed, with a mean program length of approximately six or seven statements, it is highly unlikely that the TEFs themselves are performing any computation that might be reasonably considered "deep". Thus if either system is capable of hierarchical reasoning, it most certainly comes from the network structure or the classifier.

A final note concerns the resulting size of the solutions. Since each TEF must be computed for each image, more TEFs imply greater computational complexity. We plot the number of TEFs of the most fit individuals for both groups in Figure 7. There seems to be some pressure toward larger solutions for DeepEFC than for OrigEFC, but this difference is not obviously significant ($p > 0.3$ by a Welsch's two-value t-test). Complicating this picture, it appears that our runs were constrained not by evolutionary pressure, but instead by our artificially imposed maximum number of TEFs. Figure 8 shows the evolution of the number of TEFs for our example run with OrigEFC. In this case, it is evident that evolution was pressing for larger solutions. Hence, it is difficult to predict what would happen if our solution size was fully unconstrained. We conclude that in this particular case, there was no significant additional computational cost to running DeepEFC compared with OrigEFC, but note that less restrained parameters might lead to different results.

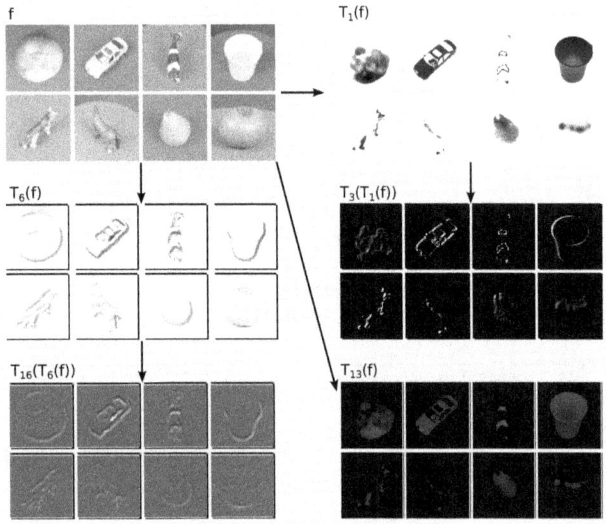

Figure 9: Illustration of part of the network comprising our exemplar individual: transforms T_6 and T_{16} show increasingly specialized edge detectors; transform T_1 generally serves to emphasize lighter areas of the image; transform T_3 reveals sharp diagonal transitions in the already segmented lighter areas.

4.2 Evaluation of DeepEFC using all objects

Here we re-evaluate the DeepEFC technique using randomly chosen test objects. As before, a collection of features is created having kept eight randomly chosen objects as test objects, one from each category. Once evolution is complete, however, we use the resulting collection of features to classify one test object, having re-trained the classifier using the other 79 test objects as training data. Thus, each run allows us to evaluate eight of the 80 test objects.

Since our technique is stochastic, we launched 20 independent runs (i.e. 160 evaluations in total, including at least one of each object). All parameters were the same as above, except for longer runs ($n_{\text{eval}} = 20\ 000$). As before, these trials showed some underfitting, and generally increasing test accuracies with time (again, it is possible that running the algorithm for more time might yield better results). The mean leave-one-object-out classification accuracy using the original 1-NN classifier, a neural network, and logistic regression, are:

classifier	mean test accuracy	s.d. test accuracy
1-NN	0.839	0.201
neural net	0.890	0.171
logist. reg.	**0.902**	0.168

It should be noted that the ETH-80 contains several particularly difficult objects, which bring down the mean values. The *median* classification accuracy, using logistic regression as a classifier, is **0.950**.

4.3 Exemplar individual

Here we analyze one exemplar individual, drawn from one DeepEFC after 15 000 evaluations. A full listing of the exemplar individual's genome is in the appendix.

It is clear that although depth is used, it is not extensively used. No transform is more than two steps deep, and most transforms operate on the original images. This is typical of our DeepEFC runs.

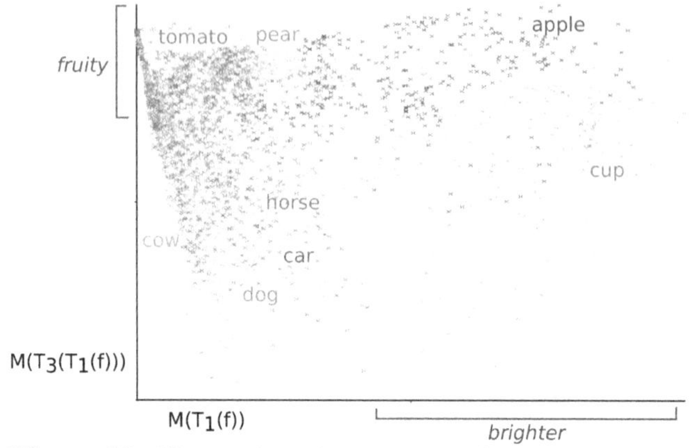

Figure 10: Illustration of the spread of values for transforms T_1, T_3. Best viewed in colour.

Figure 9 shows a sub-network of the exemplar individual, containing a couple of depth-two pathways. The benefits of increased specialization via depth can be seen here.

For instance, T_1 is a transform which (loosely) extracts the light-coloured sections of an image. Doing so discriminates between cups and apples on the one hand (the two brightest categories), and the remainder of the objects on other hand. The deeper T_3 transform highlights subregions from the bright regions already extracted, marking sharp transitions in the diagonal direction. This increased specialization serves to discriminate objects without sharp transitions in light-coloured regions, i.e. the fruits (Figure 10).

Similarly, T_6 is a rather general edge detector. While it has some discriminatory power, it does not favour any particular class. The deeper T_{16} transform, however, highlights a subset of these edges, which is effective at distinguishing between cars and pears.

As in our previous work with the EFC, TEFs range from very general to very specific. Edge detectors are common, as one would expect in an object recognition task. But some TEFs are also highly specialized: for the ETH-80, distinguishing between horses, dogs, and cows is the most difficult sub-problem. Our exemplar individual discovered a transform, T_{10}, which serves no other purpose than highlighting the spots on certain cow objects (Figure 11).

5. COMPARISON TO PREVIOUS WORK

The ETH-80 is a well-studied benchmark database with many results reported. Recent years, in particular, have seen rapid improvements in accuracy. Table 2 displays a subset of significant works on this database, including the most recent and the best, and contextualize our results. In all comparisons, however, it should be stressed that the EFC is a general-purpose system, and thus our application to this domain is rather naive. In particular, it should be remembered that our results are emergent, i.e., our model includes no preprogrammed low-level features or descriptors, no preselection of features, and no cognitive model of 3D objects. Our image sources were also constrained to grayscale.

Nilsback and Caputo utilized a multi-voting system under a decision tree classifier [28]. Bajramovic *et al.* considered several variants of nearest neighbour search in the context of optimizing an accuracy/runtime trade-off [3]. Ling and Ja-

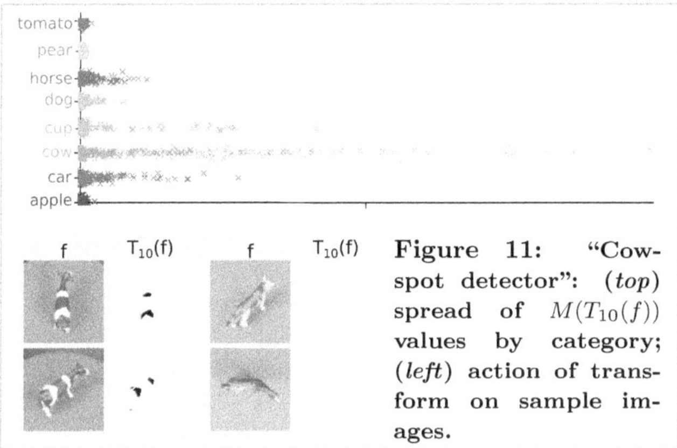

Figure 11: "Cow-spot detector": (*top*) spread of $M(T_{10}(f))$ values by category; (*left*) action of transform on sample images.

Table 2: Comparison of reported category recognition accuracies for the ETH-80 database by increasing values.

features (+ classifier)	accuracy
LDA [20]	0.652
biased discriminant analysis [20]	0.741
texture histograms + dec. tree [22]	0.798
nearest-neighbour variants [3]	0.840
colour, contour + dec. tree [22]	0.864
morphological + LCDP [14]	0.880
inner-distance, textures + dec. tree [25]	0.881
DeepEFC + logist. reg. (this work)	**0.902**
active sampling, metric learning + 1-NN [9]	0.903
colour, contour + multi-cue dec. tree [22]	0.930
Multivoting + dec. tree [28]	0.971
Complex histograms + SVM [24]	0.977

cobs designed a measure of inner distance in shapes, extracting a new means of representing the shape and augmenting with a texture description [25]. Kwak and Oh apply several forms of linear feature extraction techniques to PCA-reduced features [20]. Hu *et al.* use several morphological strategies to improve shape retrieval [14]. Ebert *et al.* rely on a combination of active sampling and metric learning. Their metric improves performance for many classifiers [9]. The best results to date come from Linde and Lindeberg, who defined a collection of low-level descriptors, which led to the definition of a multi-dimensional basis for histograms, further reduced by PCA. These histogram descriptions were then optimized via SVM [24].

6. CONCLUSIONS

In this paper, we applied a GP-based evolutionary feature creator to a benchmark object recognition problem. Our results were less than state-of-the-art, yet higher than many specialized techniques. Given that our system is a naively applied, general purpose machine, and that our features are entirely emergent from the original data source, we consider this to be a striking demonstration of the *capacity for artificial evolution to automatically extract features.*

Further, we contrasted a "shallow" and "deep" approach, showing that the latter generated improved results using the same computational time and solution complexity. This suggested that GP might benefit from deep representations in the same way that neural networks do, promising applicability to a wider range of problems.

In deep learning, however, it is well understood that increasing the depth of a chain of representations can generate more local optima. This problem almost certainly exists in the present system. It is an intriguing and unexplored question whether or not the solutions from the neural network community (e.g., pretraining via auto-association or sparse coding) could be applied to GP-based approaches as well.

7. REFERENCES

[1] E. Ahn, T. Mullen, and J. Yen. Evolutionary based feature extraction with dynamic mutation. In *IEEE Congress on Evolutionary Computation (CEC)*, pages 409–416, 2011.

[2] H. Al-Sahaf, K. Neshatian, and M. Zhang. Automatic feature extraction and image classification using genetic programming. In *Conference on Automation, Robotics and Applications (ICARA)*, pages 157–162, 2011.

[3] F. Bajramovic, F. Mattern, N. Butko, and J. Denzler. A comparison of nearest neighbor search algorithms for generic object recognition. In J. Blanc-Talon *et al.*, editor, *Advanced Concepts for Intelligent Vision Systems (ACIVS)*, pages 1186–1197. Springer-Verlag, 2006.

[4] Y. Bengio. Learning deep architectures for AI. *Foundations and Trends in Machine Learning*, 2(1):1–127, 2009.

[5] Y. Bengio and Y. LeCun. Scaling learning algorithms towards AI. In *Large Scale Kernel Machines*. MIT Press, 2007.

[6] M. Brameier and W. Banzhaf. *Linear Genetic Programming*. Springer, 2006.

[7] D. Ciresan, U. Meier, and J. Schmidhuber. Multi-column deep neural networks for image classification. In *Conference on Computer Vision and Pattern Recognition (CVPR)*, pages 3642–3649, 2012.

[8] N. Dalal and B. Triggs. Histograms of oriented gradients for human detection. In *IEEE Conference on Computer Vision and Pattern Recognition (CVPR)*, pages 886–893, 2005.

[9] S. Ebert, M. Fritz, and B. Schiele. Active metric learning for object recognition. In *DAGM-OAGM*, 2012.

[10] P. Espejo, S. Ventura, and F. Herrera. A survey on the application of genetic programming to classification. *IEEE Transactions on Systems, Man and Cybernetics — Part C*, 40(2):121–144, 2010.

[11] W. Fu, M. Johnston, and M. Zhang. Genetic programming for edge detection: a global approach. In *IEEE Congress on Evolutionary Computation (CEC)*, pages 254–261, 2011.

[12] H. Guo, L. Jack, and A. Nandi. Feature generation using genetic programming with application to fault classification. *IEEE Transactions on Systems, Man and Cybernetics — Part B*, 35(1):89–99, 2005.

[13] D. Howard, S. Roberts, and C. Ryan. Pragmatic genetic programming strategy for the problem of

vehicle detection in airborne reconnaissance. *Pattern Recognition Letters*, 27(11):1275–1288, 2006.

[14] R.-X. Hu, W. Jia, Y. Zhao, and J. Gui. Perceptually motivated morphological strategies for shape retrieval. *Pattern Recognition*, 45(9):3222–3230, 2012.

[15] N. Kharma, T. Kowaliw, E. Clement, C. Jensen, A. Youssef, and J. Yao. Project CellNet: Evolving an autonomous pattern recognizer. *International Journal of Pattern Recognition and Artificial Intelligence*, 18(6):1039–1056, 2004.

[16] T. Kowaliw and W. Banzhaf. The unconstrained automated generation of cell image features for medical diagnosis. In *Conference on Genetic and evolutionary computation (GECCO)*, pages 1103–1110, 2012.

[17] T. Kowaliw, W. Banzhaf, N. Kharma, and S. Harding. Evolving novel image features using genetic programming-based image transforms. In *IEEE Congress on Evolutionary Computation (CEC)*, pages 2502–2507, 2009.

[18] T. Kowaliw, J. McCormack, and A. Dorin. Evolutionary automated recognition and characterization of an individual's artistic style. In *IEEE Congress on Evolutionary Computation (CEC)*, 2010.

[19] K. Krawiec, D. Howard, and M. Zhang. Overview of object detection and image analysis by means of genetic programming techniques. *Frontiers in the Convergence of Bioscience and Information Technologies*, 0:779–784, 2007.

[20] N. Kwak and J. Oh. Feature extraction for one-class classification problems: Enhancements to biased discriminant analysis. *Pattern Recognition*, 42:17–26, 2008.

[21] Q. Le, M. Ranzato, R. Monga, M. Devin, K. Chen, G. Corrado, J. Dean, and A. Ng. Building high-level features using large scale unsupervised learning. In *International Conference in Machine Learning*, 2012.

[22] B. Leibe and B. Schiele. Analyzing contour and appearance based methods for object categorization. In *IEEE Conference on Computer Vision and Pattern Recognition (CVPR)*, 2003.

[23] J. Leitner, S. Harding, M. Frank, A. Förster, and J. Schmidhuber. An integrated, modular framework for computer vision and cognitive robotics research (icVision). In *Biologically Inspired Cognitive Architectures 2012*, pages 205–210. Springer, 2013.

[24] O. Linde and T. Lindeberg. Composed complex-cue histograms: An investigation of the information content in receptive field based image descriptors for object recognition. *Computer Vision and Image Understanding*, 116(4):538–560, 2012.

[25] H. Ling and D. Jacobs. Shape classification using the inner-distance. *IEEE Transactions on Pattern Analysis and Machine Intelligence*, 29:286–299, 2007.

[26] G. Malathi and V. Shanthi. Wavelet based features for ultrasound placenta images classification. In *Conference on Emerging Trends in Engineering and Technology (ICETET)*, pages 341–345, 2009.

[27] D. Maturana, D. Mery, and A. Soto. Learning discriminative local binary patterns for face recognition. In *IEEE Conference on Automatic Face Gesture Recognition and Workshops (FG)*, pages 470 –475, 2011.

[28] M. Nilsback and B. Caputo. Cue integration through discriminative accumulation. In *IEEE Conference on Computer Vision and Pattern Recognition (CVPR)*, 2004.

[29] R. Poli, W. Langdon, and N. McPhee. *A Field Guide To Genetic Programming*. Lulu Enterprises, 2008.

[30] P. Rosin and J. Hervas. Image thresholding for landslide detection by genetic programming. In *Analysis of multi-temporal remote sensing images,*, pages 65–72. World Scientific, 2002.

[31] B. Ross, A. Gualtieri, F. Fueten, and P. Budkewitsch. Hyperspectral image analysis using genetic programming. *Applied Soft Computing*, 5(2):147–156, 2005.

[32] L. Sekanina, S. Harding, W. Banzhaf, and T. Kowaliw. Image processing and CGP. In *Cartesian Genetic Programming*, pages 181–215. Springer, 2011.

[33] S. Shirakawa, S. Nakayama, and T. Nagao. Genetic image network for image classification. In *Applications of Evolutionary Computing*, pages 395–404, 2009.

[34] A. Song and V. Ciesielski. Texture segmentation by genetic programming. *Evolutionary Computation*, 16(4):461–481, 2008.

[35] A. Torralba, K. Murphy, W. Freeman, and M. Rubin. Context-based vision system for place and object recognition. In *IEEE Conference on Computer Vision (ICCV)*, page 273, 2003.

[36] L. Trujillo and G. Olague. Automated design of image operators that detect interest points. *Evolutionary Computation*, 16(4):483–507, 2008.

[37] H. Witten and E. Frank. *Data Mining: Practical Machine Learning Tools and Techniques*. Morgan Kaufman, 3rd edition, 2011.

APPENDIX

Mathematical form of all target-TEF pairs from our exemplar individual. Note that some redundancy has been removed, including a redundant and an empty transform. Transforms are listed in order of the information gain of the resulting features.

TEF	source	expression
T_{13}	orig.	$\log(\lvert i_3 - 0.614\rvert + i_9)$
T_1	orig.	$\frac{(1-i_{22})}{(0.611-i_{22})}$
T_{17}	T_2	$(i_{19})^{(i_{24})^{0.749}}$
T_5	orig.	$thresh\left(\sqrt{\lvert i_5\rvert}, i_{12}\right) - (1 - i_{17}) + \log(i_{21})$
T_3	T_1	$\left(\frac{i_{24}}{i_0} - 0.958\right) i_{18}$
$\emptyset$	–	Id
T_{12}	T_3	$i_{14} + \sqrt{(i_2)^2 + (i_{16})^2 \cdot i_1}$
T_{14}	orig.	$\left(thresh\left(\sqrt{\lvert i_5\rvert}, i_{21}\right) - (1 - i_{17}) + \log(i_{21})\right)$
T_{16}	T_6	$\frac{\log(\log(i_0))}{\left(\lvert 0.333+i_{21}\rvert - \log(0.333)\cdot\frac{i_4}{i_7}\right)}$
T_4	orig.	$\min\{i_{16}, 0.595\}$
T_9	orig.	$\max\{0.406 + \lvert i_3\rvert, i_{13}\}$
T_6	orig.	$\frac{\min\{i_6, i_9\}}{i_{23}}$
T_7	orig.	$\lvert(1 - \max\{i_2, i_{24}\})\rvert - \max\{i_3, i_0\}$
T_{10}	orig.	$\sqrt{\left\lvert 1 - \frac{1}{i_{23}}\right\rvert + \left(\log(i_{20})^{\frac{1}{i_{10}}}\right)^2}$
T_2	orig.	$\lvert\min\{i_9, i_{19}\} - i_{10}\rvert^{i_{14}}$
T_{15}	T_{11}	$\left\lvert \min\{i_6, thresh(i_{16}, i_{20})\} - \min\left\{\min\{\log(i_{20}), (i_{14} - i_7)\}, \sqrt{(i_3)^2 + (i_{19})^2}\right\}\right\rvert$

Selection Strategy for XCS with Adaptive Action Mapping

Masaya Nakata
Dept. of Informatics
The University of Electro-Communications
1-5-1, Chofugaoka, Chofu-shi
Tokyo, Japan
m.nakata@cas.hc.uec.ac.jp

Pier Luca Lanzi
Dipartimento di Elettronica, Informazione e Bioinformatica
Politecnico di Milano
I-20133
Milano, Italy
pierluca.lanzi@polimi.it

Keiki Takadama
Dept. of Informatics
The University of Electro-Communications
1-5-1, Chofugaoka, Chofu-shi
Tokyo, Japan
keiki@inf.uec.ac.jp

ABSTRACT

XCS with Adaptive Action Mapping (XCSAM) evolves solutions focused on classifiers that advocate the best action in every state. Accordingly, XCSAM usually evolves more compact solutions than XCS which, in contrast, works toward solutions representing complete state-action mappings. Experimental results have however shown that, in some problems, XCSAM may produce bigger populations than XCS. In this paper, we extend XCSAM with a novel selection strategy to reduce, *even further*, the size of the solutions XCSAM produces. The proposed strategy selects the parent classifiers based both on their fitness values (like XCS) and on the effect they have on the adaptive map. We present experimental results showing that XCSAM with the new selection strategy can evolve more compact solutions than XCS which, at the same time, are also maximally general and maximally accurate.

Categories and Subject Descriptors

I.2.6 [**Artificial Intelligence**]: Learning—*knowledge acquisition, concept learning*

General Terms

Algorithms, Experimentation, Performance

Keywords

Learning Classifier System, XCS classifier system, XCS with Adaptive Action Mapping, Best action mapping, Genetic Algorithm, Selection strategy

GECCO'13, July 6–10, 2013, Amsterdam, The Netherlands.

1. INTRODUCTION

Learning Classifier Systems [11] combine reinforcement learning [20] and genetic algorithms [10] to solve classification [2], regression [9], and sequential decision making problems [7]. XCS [21] is probably the most popular classifier system model so far that has been successfully applied to a wide range of problem domains [2]. XCS evolves solutions that provide an evaluation of the expected payoff of all the available actions in every situation, i.e., they represent complete (state-action) mappings of the problem solutions. Because it evolves complete mappings, XCS can learn optimal solutions for very difficult problems and because of its intrinsic genetic pressure toward generalization, XCS generates solutions that are maximally accurate and maximally general.

Complete mappings are often considered redundant since in most applications (e.g., classification, stock market prediction) only the actions with the highest return really count. Complete mappings are also very expensive both in terms of memory (since they allocate classifiers to non-optimal actions) and in terms of time required to achieve optimal performance (since they require a more thoroughly exploration to the problem space); Accordingly, to avoid complete mappings, Bernado et al. introduced the UCS classifier system [1] which, like XCS, exploits accuracy-based evolution, to produce maximally accurate maximally general solutions, but employs supervised learning (instead of reinforcement learning) to distribute incoming feedback to the classifiers accountable for it. Thus, UCS only evolves classifiers that advocate the best action but can solve only classification problems (since it does not apply reinforcement learning as XCS), therefore its approach cannot generalized to broader machine learning applications.

To overcome the limitations of UCS, we introduced XCS with Adaptive Action Mapping (XCSAM) [19, 18] a classifier system that (i) can evolve mappings mainly focused on the best action, with the highest payoffs, like UCS; at the same time, XCSAM (ii) can tackle both classification and sequential decision making problems using reinforcement learning like XCS. XCSAM [19, 18] mainly works like XCS and mainly selects parents classifiers based on their relative accuracy encoded in the classifiers' fitness [21].

In XCS, plain accuracy-based fitness results in the evolution of complete mappings but in XCSAM it produces solutions with more classifiers than XCS, even if, XCSAM tries to delete classifiers that do not represent the highest rewarded actions.

To reduce the size of the solutions evolved by XCSAM, in this paper we firstly analyzes the effect of accuracy-based selection in XCSAM; then, we introduce a more effective selection strategy for XCSAM; finally, we compare XCS, the original XCSAM, and the improved XCSAM to the hidden parity and multiplexer problems. Our results show that the improved version of XCSAM can produce solutions that are more compact than those evolved by XCS and the original XCSAM.

2. THE XCS CLASSIFIER SYSTEM

The XCS classifier system maintains a population of rules (the classifiers) which represents the solution to a reinforcement learning problem [13]. Classifiers consist of a condition, an action, and four main parameters [21, 6]: (i) the prediction p, which estimates the relative payoff that the system expects when the classifier is used; (ii) the prediction error ε, which estimates the error of the prediction p; (iii) the fitness F, which estimates the accuracy of the payoff prediction given by p; and (iv) the numerosity *num*, which indicates how many copies of classifiers with the same condition and the same action are present in the population.

At time t, XCS builds a *match set* [M] containing the classifiers in the population [P] whose condition matches the current sensory input s_t; if [M] does not contain all the feasible actions *covering* takes place and creates a set of classifiers that matches s_t and cover all the missing actons. This process ensures that XCS can evolve a complete mapping so that in any state it can predict the effect of every possible action in terms of expected returns.

For each possible action a in [M], XCS computes the *system prediction* $P(s_t, a)$ which estimates the payoff that the XCS expects if action a is performed in s_t. The system prediction $P(s_t, a)$ is computed as the fitness weighted average of the predictions of classifiers in [M] which advocate action a:

$$P(s_t, a) = \sum_{cl_k \in [M](a)} p_k \times \frac{F_k}{\sum_{cl_i \in [M](a)} F_i} \quad (1)$$

where, [M](a) represents the subset of classifiers of $[M]$ with action a, p_k identifies the prediction of classifier cl_k, and F_k identifies the fitness of classifier cl_k. Then, XCS selects an action to perform; the classifiers in [M] which advocate the selected action form the current *action set* [A]. The selected action a_t is performed, and a scalar reward r_{t+1} is returned to XCS together with a new input s_{t+1}. When the reward r_{t+1} is received, the estimated payoff $P(t)$ is computed as follows:

$$P(t) = r_{t+1} + \gamma \max_{a \in [M]} P(s_{t+1}, a) \quad (2)$$

where γ is the discount factor [20]. Next, the parameters of the classifiers in [A] are updated in the following order [6]: prediction, prediction error, and finally fitness. Prediction p is updated with learning rate β $(0 \leq \beta \leq 1)$:

$$p_k \leftarrow p_k + \beta(P(t) - p_k) \quad (3)$$

Then, the prediction error ϵ and classifier fitness are updated as,

$$\epsilon_k \leftarrow \epsilon_k + \beta(|P(t) - p_k| - \epsilon_k) \quad (4)$$

$$F_k \leftarrow F_k + \beta(\kappa'_k - F_k). \quad (5)$$

where κ'_k is the *raw accuracy* of classifier k computed from the classifier error ϵ_k [21].

On regular basis (dependent on parameter θ_{ga}), the genetic algorithm is applied to classifiers in [A]. It selects two classifiers, copies them, with probability χ performs crossover on the copies, and with probability μ it mutates each allele. The resulting offspring classifiers are inserted into the population and two classifiers are deleted to keep the population size constant.

3. XCS WITH ADAPTIVE ACTION MAPPING

The XCS classifier system [21] evolves solutions that map every possible situation (state) and action pair in its corresponding expected return. The maintenance of a complete mapping makes XCS robust to local optima and guarantees that, given an adequate amount of resources [8, 15], XCS can learn an optimal solution made of maximally accurate and maximally general classifiers. A complete mapping is however considered redundant in several domains (for instance, in classification we are not interested in the expected payoff of wrong classes) and very expensive to maintain both in terms of memory (since it keeps information on *all* available actions) and time (since it requires a thoroughly exploration of the space). Accordingly, Bernardo with colleagues introduced UCS [1] a classifier system specifically designed for classification tasks that applies supervised learning (instead of reinforcement learning as XCS) to evolve solutions containing only classifiers advocating the best actions.

XCS with Adaptive Action Mapping (XCSAM) [19, 18] represents a trade-off between XCS and UCS. Like XCS, it can solve both reinforcement learning (multi-step) and supervised classification (one-step) problems; similarly to UCS, XCSAM does not evolve a complete mapping but tries to focus on the best actions while the learning proceeds. To accomplish this, XCSAM extends the original XCS by adding mechanisms (i) to adaptively identify redundant actions and (ii) to get rid of them while still exploring the space of viable optimal solutions.

3.1 Identifying Best Action Mappings

To focus on the classifiers with the highest expected return, XCSAM examines the expected payoff at the current state $maxP(s_t, a)$ (Equation 2) against the payoff expected at the previous state ($maxP(s_{t-1}, a)$). Note that in general the former ($maxP(s_t, a)$) tends to be higher than the latter ($maxP(s_{t-1}, a)$) (because of the discount factor γ). Accordingly, since the action corresponding to a higher reward also corresponds to a shorter state sequence, the best actions will tend to have a value of $maxP(s_t, a)$ larger than $maxP(s_{t-1}, a)$. More precisely, $maxP(s_{t-1}, a)$ converges to $\gamma maxP(s_t, a)$ at the next state, while $maxP(s_t, a)$ converges to $maxP(s_{t-1}, a)/\gamma$. Thus, in XCS the prediction of the accurate classifiers in $[A]$ tends to converge to

$maxP(s_{t-1}, a)/\gamma$. For this reason, XCSAM can identify the actions that are likely to be part of the best mapping by comparing $maxP(s_t, a)$ against $\zeta \times maxP(s_{t-1}, a)/\gamma$ (where ζ is a learning rate added to guarantee convergence). If $maxP(s_t, a)$ is greater than the threshold $\zeta \times maxP(s_{t-1}, a)/\gamma$, then a is a good candidate and should be maintained.

After having identified good candidate actions for the best action mapping, XCSAM needs to adaptively identify classifiers that may be good candidate for the final best mapping. For this purpose, a parameter *eam* (effect of adaptive mapping) is added to the classifiers of XCSAM, and updated as,

$$eam_i \leftarrow \begin{cases} eam_i + \beta(1 - eam_i) \\ \quad \text{if } \; maxP(s_t, a) \geq \zeta \times maxP(s_{t-1}, a)/\gamma \\ eam_i + \beta(nma - eam_i) \quad \text{otherwise.} \end{cases}$$

where *nma* represents the number of available actions. The value of *eam* of classifiers advocating the selected action converges to 1 if the classifier is a good candidate for the final best action mapping; otherwise, *eam* converges to *nma*. Therefore, classifiers with an *eam* close to one are good candidates to represent the final best action mapping while classifiers with an *eam* close to *nma* are less likely to be maintained as they are probably advocating actions with lower expected return.

3.2 Focusing Evolution on the Best Actions

To focus evolution on the best actions, XCSAM acts on the covering operator to prevent the generation of classifiers that are not likely to be included in the final solution. In particular, XCSAM tunes the activation threshold of the genetic algorithm θ_{nma} using the actions' predicted reward and the *eam* parameters. Initially, θ_{nma} is set to the number of feasible actions (the same value used in XCS). When $[M]$ is generated, XCSAM computes the prediction array before the covering is applied (whereas XCS computes it only after covering). Then, XCSAM computes the current θ_{nma} as the average *eam* of the classifiers in [M] weighted for the expected future return $maxP(s_t, a)$. If the number of different actions in $[M]$ is smaller than the computed θ_{nma}, covering is called and the prediction array is computed again. After action selection is performed, XCSAM generates both the action set [A] (as XCS) and also the *not action set* $[\bar{A}]$ consisting of the classifiers in $[M]$ not advocating the selected action. When the executed action is considered a candidate best action, during the genetic algorithms, (i) the parent classifiers are selected from $[A]$ to promote the evolution of classifiers that are likely to be in the final best action mapping; instead, (ii) the deleted classifiers are selected from $[\bar{A}]$ to get rid of classifiers that are not likely to be part of the final solution. Otherwise, if there is not enough information about the executed action, or $[\bar{A}]$ is empty, XCSAM applies deletion in $[P]$ as done in XCS. When the executed action is not identified as a candidate best action, the parents are selected from $[\bar{A}]$ to explore the solution space even further and deletion is applied to the population as in XCS.

4. ANALYSIS OF SELECTION IN XCSAM

We analyzed the effect of pure accuracy-based selection in XCSAM by studying the characteristics of selected parent classifiers. For this purpose, we applied XCS and XCSAM to the hidden parity problem $\texttt{HP}_{20,5}$ and compared the characteristics of parents classifiers in the two models.

4.1 Hidden Parity problem

This class of Boolean functions has been first used with XCS in [12] to relate the problem difficulty to the number of accurate maximally general classifiers needed by XCS to solve the problem. They are defined over binary strings of length n in which only k bits are relevant; the hidden parity function ($\texttt{HP}_{n,k}$) returns the value of the parity function applied to the k relevant bits, that are *hidden* among the n inputs. For instance, given the hidden parity function $\texttt{HP}_{6,4}$ defined over inputs of six bits ($n = 6$), in which only the first four bits are relevant ($k = 4$), then we have that $\texttt{HP}_{6,3}(110111) = 1$ while $\texttt{HP}_{6,3}(000111) = 1$.

In this analysis, we applied the standard parameter settings for XCS [16]: $N = 2000$, $\epsilon_0 = 1$, $\mu = 0.04$, $P_\# = 1.0$, $P_{explr} = 1.0$, χ=1.0, $\beta = 0.2$, α=0.1, $\delta = 0.1$, $\nu = 5$, $\theta_{GA} = 25$, $\theta_{del} = 20$, $\theta_{sub} = 20$, GA subsumption is applied but Action set subsumption is not applied, in addition, we use the tournament selection with $\tau = 0.4$; for XCSAM, we applied the same parameters of XCS and in addition we set $\zeta = 0.99$.

4.2 Accuracy-Based Selection in XCS

Figure 1 shows the characteristics of parents classifiers selected by accuracy-based fitness in XCS. In particular, Figure 1a and Figure 1b show the relation between the prediction and the fitness of selected parents and the iteration when its parent has been selected. For instance, a parent is plotted at the upper right corner of Figure 1a, (with prediction 1000) if it was selected at iteration 150000. Figure 1c shows the relations between the prediction and the fitness of classifiers in [P] after 150000 iterations, that is, the final solutions. In XCS, to ensure a complete mapping, selection is designed to focus toward maximally accurate classifiers. Therefore, in classification problems with a 1000/0 reward scheme, the classifiers which should be selected as parent have a prediction of 1000 or 0. Figure 1a and Figure 1b show that the genetic algorithm in XCS selects classifiers with a prediction between between 100 and 900 until problem 60000; then, XCS gradually focuses on classifiers with a 0 or 1000 prediction. Similarly, selected classifiers have a low fitness until iteration 70000; then, XCS gradually focuses selection on classifiers with higher fitness values (near to 1). This behavior is coherent to what we should expected in XCS however the same strategy has a different effect in XCSAM.

4.3 Accuracy-Based Selection in XCSAM

In classification problems with a 1000/0 reward scheme, XCSAM should tend to focus mainly on accurate classifiers with high (near 1000) prediction values, which represent the best action mappings. Thus, XCSAM should behave differently than XCS and should not select accurate classifiers wih low, near 0, prediction values, which represent redundant classifiers for XCSAM.

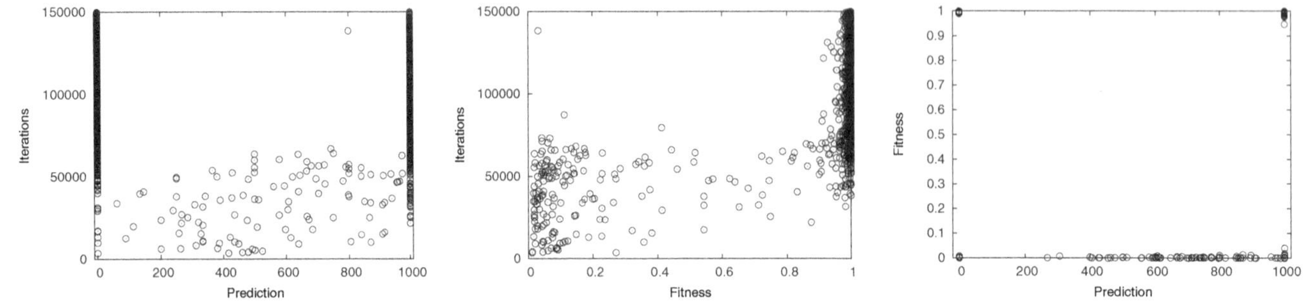

a) Prediction of selected parents and iteration that its parent are selected

b) Fitness of selected parents and iteration that its parent are selected

c) Prediction and Fitness of classifiers in [P] as final solutions

Figure 1: Characteristics of parents selected by accuracy-based selection in XCS (a & b) and characteristics of the final solutions (c).

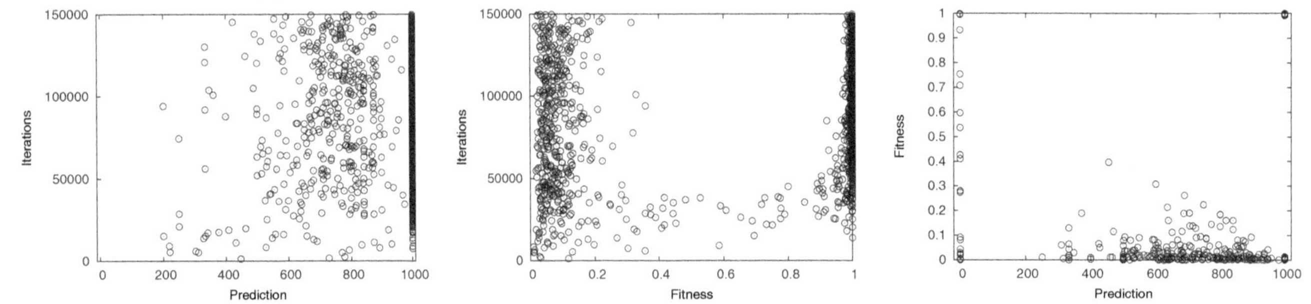

a) Prediction of selected parents and iteration that its parent are selected

b) Fitness of selected parents and iteration that its parent are selected

c) Prediction and Fitness of classifiers in [P] as final solutions

Figure 2: Characteristics of parents selected by accuracy-based selection in XCSAM (a & b) and characteristics of the final solutions (c).

Figure 2 shows the characteristics of selected classifier parents in XCSAM using plain accuracy-based fitness. Figure 2a and Figure 2b show that XCSAM selects most promising parent classifiers for a best action mapping (in fact, it tends to select classifiers with high fitness values). However, at the same time, the genetic algorithm still selects inaccurate classifiers until iteration 150000 (Figure 2b). XCSAM keeps selecting classifiers with low fitness (Figure 2c) therefore the final solutions evolved by XCSAM contain a large number of inaccurate classifiers. Thus, plain accuracy-based selection in XCSAM select the proper classifiers but also keeps a large number of inaccurate classifiers and thus produces solutions with more classifiers than needed (in fact, the system should still get rid of inaccurate classifiers).

5. IMPROVED XCSAM

We propose a new selection strategy for XCSAM to ensure that XCSAM evolves compact solutions containing mainly classifiers advocating the actions with the highest payoff. As shown by previous analysis, XCSAM with plain accuracy-based selection fails to select good parents that represent the best action mappings. To understand how we designed an adequate selection strategy for XCSAM, we analyzed the *eam* parameter in XCSAM. Figure 3 shows the relations between the prediction and effect of adaptive mapping (*eam*) of the classifiers in the final solutions.

As can be noted, classifiers with a low prediction (a near zero prediction) tend to have the high *eam* (which converges to *nma*); classifiers with a high prediction (a near 1000 prediction), have the low *eam* (which converges to 1). This suggests that XCSAM should select parents with a small value of *eam* and a high fitness. Accordingly, we introduce the *selection vote* which is used to decide parents. In detail, we compare the selection vote of each classifiers in [A] to select parents. In particular, we modify tournament selection [4] by defining the selection vote as:

$$selection\ vote = \frac{cl.F}{cl.num} \times \frac{1}{cl.eam - 1} \tag{6}$$

Note that the selection vote is equal to $cl.F/cl.num$ that is original selection pressure of the tournament selection [3], i.e., we only add $1/(cl.eam - 1)$ to the original selection vote. This means that XCSAM selects parents based on not only fitness but also based on the *eam* value so that XCSAM detects accurate parents that should be included in the best action mappings (because they have a low *eam*). We select the classifier which has maximum selection vote in the tournament with tournament size τ as done [4].

5.1 Analysis of New selection strategy

To analyze the characteristics of selected parent classifiers by the proposed selection strategy in XCSAM, we applied XCSAM on the 20/5 Hidden parity problem.

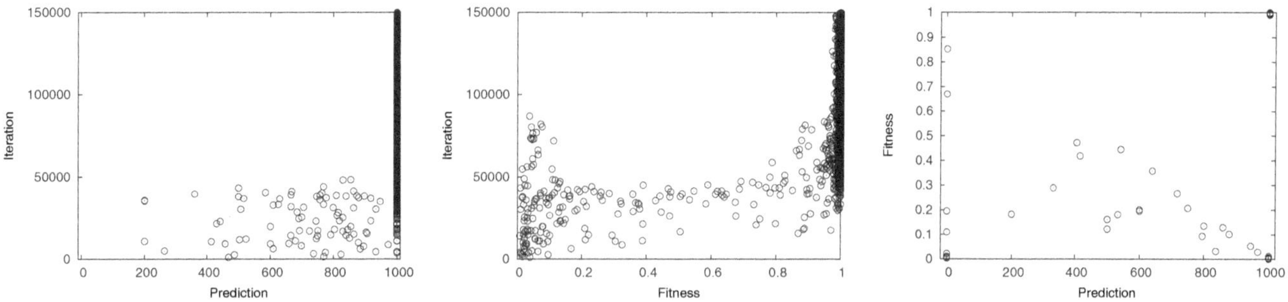

a) Prediction of selected parents and iteration that its parents are selected

b) Fitness of selected parents and iteration that its parents are selected

c) Prediction and Fitness of classifiers in [P] as final solutions

Figure 4: Characteristics of parents selected by the new selection strategy in XCSAM (a & b) and characteristics of the classifiers in the final solution.

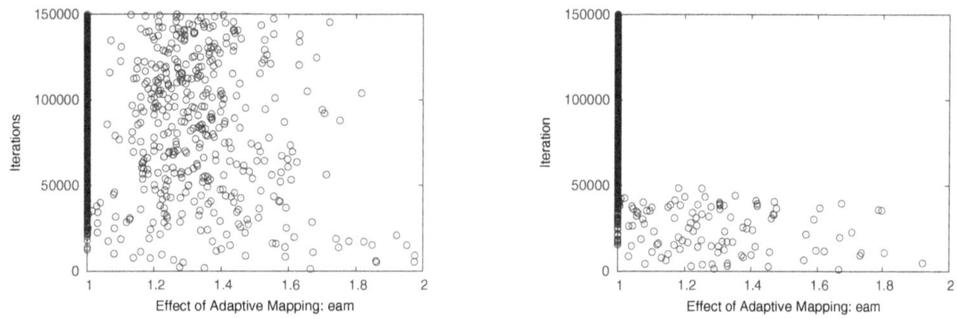

a) XCSAM with XCS's selection strategy

b) XCSAM with proposed selection strategy

Figure 5: Effect of adaptive mapping (*eam*) of parents selected by accuracy-based selection strategy and the new selection strategy in XCSAM.

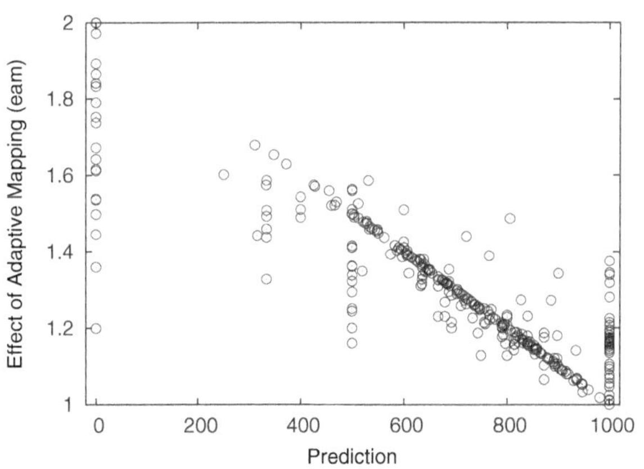

Figure 3: Relation between prediction and effect of adaptive mapping (eam) of classifiers in the final solution.

Figure 4 compares the characteristics of selected parent using accuracy-based selection and the new selection strategy. Figure 5 shows the relation between the iteration that parents are selected and the *eam* parameter of selected parents by both selection strategi in XCSAM.

Figure 4a shows that with the proposed selection strategy XCSAM selects inaccurate classifiers that have prediction $= 100 \sim 900$ till iteration 50000; then, it clearly focus only on good candidates with high accuracy and a high (near 1000) prediction. Similarly, Figure 4b shows that XCSAM still selects maximally accurate classifiers. Therefore, as shown in Figure 4c, final solutions contain very few inaccurate or redundant classifiers and thus represent the best mapping XCSAM should generate. Additionally, Figure 5 shows that the proposed selection strategy correctly focuses on classifiers with a low *eam* whereas pure accuracy-based fitness cannot stably select such classifiers.

Overall, these results suggest that the proposed selection strategy promotes accurate classifiers that mainly advocate the best actions in every situation and prevent the selection of inaccurate classifiers.

6. EXPERIMENTAL RESULTS

We applied XCS, the original XCSAM [19, 18], and XCSAM with the new selection strategy to the hidden parity problem and to the Boolean multiplexer. We compared the three models in terms of learning performance, population size, and evolved mapping.

Design of Experiments. Each experiment consists of a number of problems that the system must solve. Each problem is either a *learning* problem or a *test* problem.

During *learning* problems, the system selects actions randomly from those represented in the match set. During *test* problems, the system selects the action with highest expected return. When the system performs the correct action, it receives a 1000 reward, otherwise it receives 0. The genetic algorithm is enabled only during *learning* problems, and it is turned off during *test* problems. The covering operator is always enabled, but operates only if needed. Learning problems and test problems alternate. The performance is reported as the moving average over the last 5000 test problems. All the plots are averages over 10 experiments.

Hidden Parity. In the first set of experiments, we applied XCS, XCSAM, and the improved XCSAM with the new selection strategy to $\mathtt{HP}_{20,5}$ (see Section 4) using the standard parameter settings used in [17, 14].

Figure 6 compares the performance and population size of XCS, XCSAM, and the improved XCSAM. As can be noted XCS reaches optimal performance after 110000 problems (Figure 6a) and evolves solutions containing an average of 120 classifiers (Figure 6b). XCSAM learns faster and reaches optimality after 70000 iterations (Figure 6a) but produces larger solutions than XCS (an average of 580 classifiers, Figure 6b). In contrast, the improved version of XCSAM, using the new selection strategy, reaches optimality a bit faster than the original XCSAM but needs less classifiers than XCS (an average of 79 classifiers).

Boolean Multiplexer. In the second set of experiments, we compared the three models on the Boolean multiplexer [21]. These are are defined over a binary string of $k + 2^k$ bits; the first k bits represent an address pointing to the remaining 2^k bits. For instance, the 6-multiplexer function ($k = 2$) applied to the input string 110001 will return 1, while when applied to 110110 it will return 0. We compared the three XCS models using the 20-multiplexer ($k = 4$) and the 37-multiplexer ($k5$) using the standard parameter settings [5]: $N = 2000(k = 4)$, $5000(k = 5)$, $\epsilon_0 = 10$, $\mu = 0.04$, $P_{\#} = 0.5(k = 4)$, $0.65(k = 5)$, P_{explr} =1.0, $\chi = 0.8$, $\beta = 0.2$, $\alpha = 0.1$, $\delta = 0.1$, $\nu = 5$, $\theta_{GA} = 25$, $\theta_{del} = 20$, $\theta_{sub} = 20$, tournament selection is applied, $\tau = 0.4$, GA subsumption is turned on while AS subsumption is turned off; in XCSAM, we set $\zeta = 0.99$. Figures 7 and 8 compare the performance and population size of XCS, the original XCSAM, and the improved XCSAM using the new selection strategy on the 20-multiplexer and the 37-multiplexer. As can be noted, in the 20-multiplexer, XCS reaches optimal performance after 40000 problems (Figures 7a) and evolved solutions that on the average contain around 340 classifiers (Figures 7b). XCSAM learns a little bit faster than XCS but it produce larger solutions of about 630 classifiers (i.e., more than twice the size of the solutions evolved by XCS). In contrast, the improved XCSAM reaches optimality a little bit faster than XCS, while producing very compact solutions containing an average of 180 classifiers (Figures 7b), i.e., almost half the size of the solutions evolved by XCS. In the 37-multiplexer, XCS needs to train over 400000 problems before it can reach optimality and evolves solutions containing an average of 1200 classifiers. The original XCSAM [19, 18] learns much faster than XCS and reaches optimal performance just after 200000 problems; however, the final population size is about 2300 classifiers (almost twice what XCS needs).

In contrast, our improved XCSAM is even faster than the original XCSAM and reaches optimality after 170000 problems and produces solutions that are half of what XCS needs (just 570 classifiers).

Overall our results show that by focusing only on the actions with the highest reward, the original XCSAM [19, 18] can learn faster than XCS but requires more classifiers than XCS. The improved XCSAM combines the best of the two worlds and ensures fast learning and more compact solutions. The improved XCSAM in fact evolves solution that are around half of what XCS produces (as it should be expected).

7. CONCLUSIONS

XCSAM [19, 18] is an extension of XCS [21] that generates solutions mainly containing classifiers that advocate the actions with the highest returns. While XCS [21] learns the expected payoff of the available actions in every possible situation, XCSAM only concentrates on the most promising actions and therefore it can learn faster than XCS [19, 18]. However, XCSAM can often produces solutions that are larger than those evolved by XCS. Accordingly, in this paper, we extended XCSAM by introducing a novel selection strategy that could reduce the size of the solutions evolved by XCSAM. The proposed selection strategy enables XCSAM to select the parents classifiers based both on their fitness (as done in XCS) and also on the effect they have on the mapping (encoded by the parameter *eam*). We applied XCS, the original XCSAM, and the improved XCSAM to the 20/5 hidden parity problem [17, 14], to the 20-multiplexer and to the 37-multiplexer [21]. Our results show that the improved XCSAM can evolve solutions that are around half of the size of the solutions produced by XCS while also reaching optimal much smaller than XCS. Thus, the improved XCSAM opens up new opportunity to tackle much complex problems in acceptable time.

Acknowledgment

This work was supported by the JSPS Institutional Program for Young Researcher Overseas Visits.

8. REFERENCES

[1] E. Bernadó-mansilla and J. M.Garrell-Guij. Accuracy-based Learning Classifier Systems: Models, Analysis and Applications to Classification Tasks. *Evolutionary Computation*, 11:209–238, 2003.

[2] Larry Bull, Ester Bernadó-Mansilla, and John H. Holmes, editors. *Learning Classifier Systems in Data Mining*, volume 125 of *Studies in Computational Intelligence*. Springer, 2008.

[3] M. V. Butz. *Rule-Based Evolutionary Online Learning Systems*. Springer, 2006.

[4] M. V. Butz, D. E. Goldberg, and K. Tharakunnel. Analysis and Improvement of Fitness Exploitation in XCS: Bounding Models, Tournament Selection, and Bilateral Accuracy. *Evolutionary Computation*, 11(3):239–277, 2003.

[5] M. V. Butz, T. Kovacs, P. L. Lanzi, and S. W. Wilson. Toward a Theory of Generalization and Learning in XCS. *IEEE Transactions on Evolutionary Computation*, 8(1):28–46, February 2004.

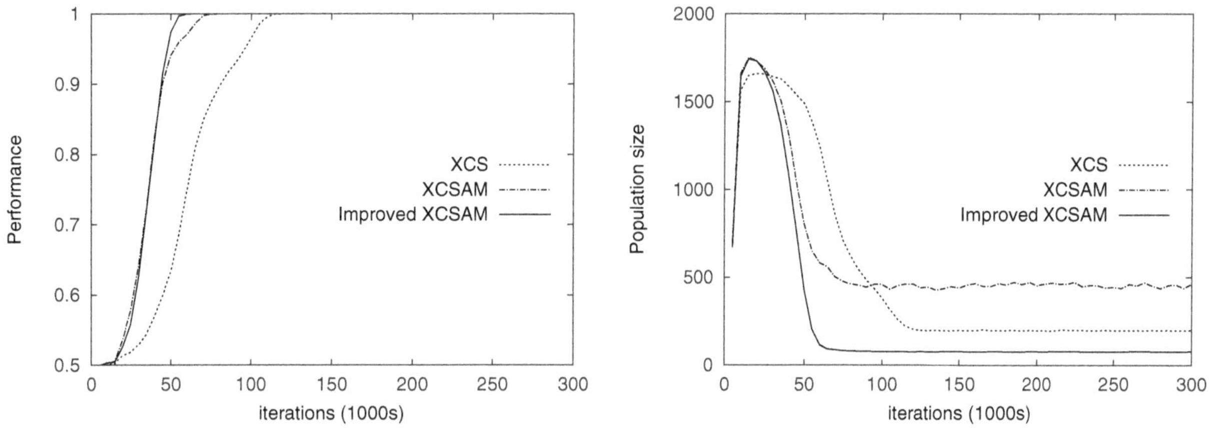

a) Performance b) Population size

Figure 6: Performance and population size on 20/5 Hidden parity problem

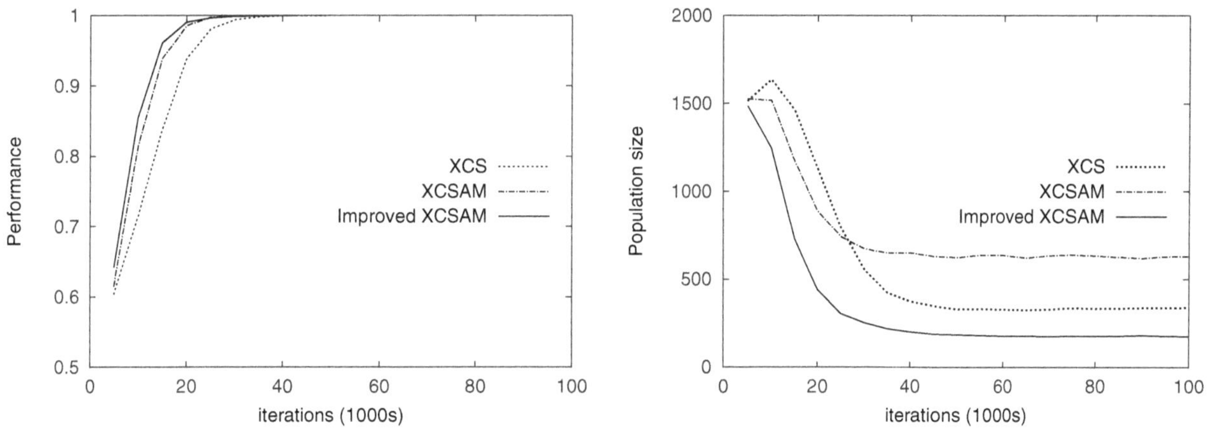

a) Performance b) Population size

Figure 7: Performance and population size on the 20-multiplexer.

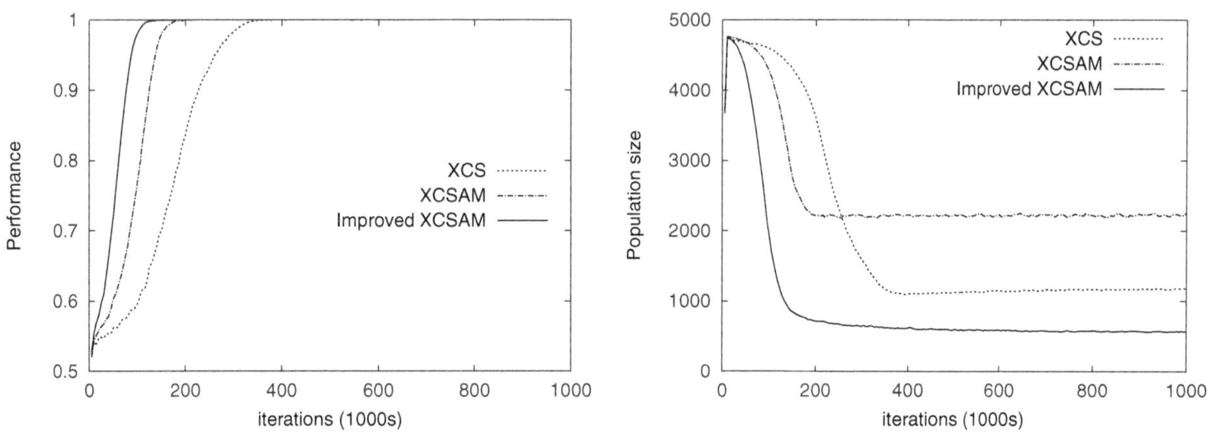

a) Performance b) Population size

Figure 8: Performance and population size on the 37-multiplexer.

[6] M. V. Butz and S. W. Wilson. An algorithmic description of xcs. *Journal of Soft Computing*, 6(3–4):144–153, 2002.

[7] Martin V. Butz, David E. Goldberg, and Pier Luca Lanzi. Gradient descent methods in learning classifier systems: Improving xcs performance in multistep

problems. *IEEE Transaction on Evolutionary Computation*, 9(5):452–473, October 2005.

[8] Martin V. Butz, Tim Kovacs, Pier Luca Lanzi, and Stewart W. Wilson. Toward a theory of generalization and learning in xcs. *IEEE Transaction on Evolutionary Computation*, 8(1):28–46, February 2004.

[9] Martin V. Butz, Pier Luca Lanzi, and Stewart W. Wilson. Function approximation with xcs: Hyperellipsoidal conditions, recursive least squares, and compaction. *IEEE Trans. Evolutionary Computation*, 12(3):355–376, 2008.

[10] D. E. Goldberg. Genetic Algorithms in Search, Optimization, and Machine Learning. *Addison Wesley*, 1989.

[11] J. H. Holland. Escaping Brittleness: The Possibilities of General Purpose Learning Algorithms Applied to Parallel Rule-based system. *Machine Learning*, 2:593–623, 1986.

[12] Tim Kovacs and Manfred Kerber. What makes a problem hard for xcs? In Pier Luca Lanzi, Wolfgang Stolzmann, and Stewart W. Wilson, editors, *IWLCS*, volume 1996 of *Lecture Notes in Computer Science*, pages 80–102. Springer, 2000.

[13] Pier Luca Lanzi. Learning classifier systems from a reinforcement learning perspective. *Soft Computing - A Fusion of Foundations, Methodologies and Applications*, 6(3):162–170, 2002.

[14] Pier Luca Lanzi, Daniele Loiacono, Stewart W. Wilson, and David E. Goldberg. XCS with computed prediction for the learning of boolean functions. In *Proceedings of the IEEE Congress on Evolutionary Computation – CEC-2005*, pages 588–595, Edinburgh, UK, September 2005. IEEE.

[15] Pier Luca Lanzi, Luigi Nichetti, Kumara Sastry, Davide Voltini, and David E. Goldberg. Real-coded extended compact genetic algorithm based on mixtures of models. In Ying-Ping Chen and Meng-Hiot Lim, editors, *Linkage in Evolutionary Computation*, volume 157 of *Studies in Computational Intelligence*, pages 335–358. Springer, 2008.

[16] P.L. Lanzi, D. Loiacono, S.W. Wilson, and D.E. Goldberg. XCS with computed prediction for the learning of Boolean functions. In *Evolutionary Computation, 2005. The 2005 IEEE Congress on*, volume 1, pages 588 –595, 2005.

[17] Martin V. Butz and David E. Goldberg, K. Tharakunnel. Analysis and Improvement of Fitness Exploitation in XCS: Bounding Models, Tournament Selection, and Bilateral Accuracy. *Evolutionary Computation*, 11(4):239–277, 2003.

[18] Masaya Nakata, Pier Luca Lanzi, and Keiki Takadama. Enhancing learning capabilities by xcs with best action mapping. In Carlos A. Coello Coello, Vincenzo Cutello, Kalyanmoy Deb, Stephanie Forrest, Giuseppe Nicosia, and Mario Pavone, editors, *PPSN (1)*, volume 7491 of *Lecture Notes in Computer Science*, pages 256–265. Springer, 2012.

[19] Masaya Nakata, Pier Luca Lanzi, and Keiki Takadama. Xcs with adaptive action mapping. In Lam Thu Bui, Yew-Soon Ong, Nguyen Xuan Hoai, Hisao Ishibuchi, and Ponnuthurai Nagaratnam Suganthan, editors, *SEAL*, volume 7673 of *Lecture Notes in Computer Science*, pages 138–147. Springer, 2012.

[20] R. S. Sutton and A. G. Barto. *Reinforcement Learning – An Introduction*. MIT Press, 1998.

[21] S. W. Wilson. Classifier fitness based on accuracy. *Evolutionary Computation*, 3(2):149–175, June 1995.

Searching for Novel Clustering Programs

Enrique Naredo
Leonardo Trujillo*
Doctorado en Ciencias de la Ingeniería
Instituto Tecnológico de Tijuana
Tijuana, B.C., México
enriquenaredo@gmail.com
leonardo.trujillo@tectijuana.edu.mx

ABSTRACT

Novelty search (NS) is an open-ended evolutionary algorithm that eliminates the need for an explicit objective function. Instead, NS focuses selective pressure on the search for novel solutions. NS has produced intriguing results in specialized domains, but has not been applied in most machine learning areas. The key component of NS is that each individual is described by the behavior it exhibits, and this description is used to determine how novel each individual is with respect to what the search has produced thus far. However, describing individuals in behavioral space is not trivial, and care must be taken to properly define a descriptor for a particular domain. This paper applies NS to a mainstream pattern analysis area: data clustering. To do so, a descriptor of clustering performance is proposed and tested on several problems, and compared with two control methods, Fuzzy C-means and K-means. Results show that NS can effectively be applied to data clustering in some circumstances. NS performance is quite poor on simple or easy problems, achieving basically random performance. Conversely, as the problems get harder NS performs better, and outperforming the control methods. It seems that the search space exploration induced by NS is fully exploited only when generating good solutions is more challenging.

Categories and Subject Descriptors

I.2.2 [**Artificial Intelligence**]: Automatic Programming—*program synthesis*

General Terms

Performance,Theory,Experimentation

Keywords

Novelty Search, Genetic Programming, Clustering

*Corresponding Author

1. INTRODUCTION

Natural evolution, as an open-ended process, is different from the conventional engineering approach towards search and optimization. Nevertheless, evolutionary algorithms (EAs) are abstractions of Neo-Darwinian evolution that are guided by an objective function and mostly lack the open-ended feature of their natural inspiration. Nonetheless, many EAs have distinguished themselves as innovative search techniques that frequently solve difficult problems in diverse domains [10]. Moreover, since the search is guided by fitness, most of the traditional algorithms tend to converge on local optima unless proper heuristic methods are integrated into the search for diversity preservation.

On the other hand, it is illustrative to consider that some of the earliest EAs were open-ended techniques [4]. Recently, other EAs have been developed that share this feature, but are mostly aimed at specialized domains, such as artificial life environments [19] and interactive search [9]. In particular, this paper studies the algorithm proposed by Lehman and Stanley called novelty search (NS) [11, 12, 13], an EA that abandons an explicit fitness function. Instead, NS focuses the selective pressure on finding unique solutions; i.e., individuals that introduce novel information into the search process with respect to the current search progress.

The core requirement in NS is that instead of relying on the genotype, phenotype or fitness to describe individuals, they are described based on their behavior. Therefore, a domain dependent behavior descriptor must be proposed to apply NS successfully. Most of the published works on NS have been in evolutionary robotics (ER), where the concept of robot behavior has a strong history in the field [3, 18, 23, 24, 16]. Conversely, the concept of behaviors is not common in other domains. In GP, for instance, resent research has incorporated the concept of semantics [15, 25]; however, behaviors are a broader concept, incorporating contextual information, as discussed in the following section.

Therefore, the goal of this paper is to present an application of NS on a common problem in machine learning and pattern recognition. In particular, unsupervised data clustering is solved with a NS-based GP system, using a domain specific behavioral descriptor. This work is an extension of recent research where NS was applied to supervised data classification [17]. Results are encouraging, the NS algorithm is indeed capable of solving clustering problems and in some cases outperforming standard clustering techniques. In particular, NS seems better suited for difficult cases, where the explorative abilities of the algorithm can be fully leveraged.

The remainder of this paper is organized as follows. Section 2 describes the concept of behavioral space and the NS algorithm. In Section 3 the clustering problem is defined and related work is discussed. Afterwards, Section 4 presents the proposed NS-based GP algorithm for data clustering and the proposed behavioral descriptor for evolved clustering programs. Then, Section 5 presents the experiments and an analysis of the results. Finally, a summary of the paper and concluding remarks are given in Section 6.

2. BEHAVIOR-BASED SEARCH

It is well understood that an EA concurrently samples three different spaces during a search. First, genotypic space, which corresponds to the encoding used to represent each valid solution. Second, phenotypic space, which represents the problem space where solutions are expressed. Finally, objective or fitness space, that corresponds to the space of performance criteria. In some cases these spaces are clearly distinct, but for some representations it is not [6].

While these three spaces have been the focus of most research, other spaces have recently been considered within the field. First consider that fitness gives a coarse and global evaluation of an individual's performance, averaging out differences in program quality on different fitness cases. Considering this, some researchers have proposed a finer grained approach to analyze the performance of each individual.

One approach is known as semantics in GP literature [15, 25], with its corresponding semantic space, which corresponds to the space of possible program outputs. Semantics is an important concept in GP because many genetically different programs can share the same semantic representation. However, only analyzing program outputs might not be the best approach to analyze performance in some domains. For instance, consider ER problems, where evolutionary algorithms are used to search for robust controllers of autonomous robots [18]. The goal of the ER approach, is to find high quality solutions introducing as little prior knowledge as possible into the objective function. In this scenario, the correspondence between program inputs, outputs and induced actions is much less clear. Moreover, evolution in an ER system is performed within real or simulated environments, where noisy sensors and the physical coupling between actuators and the real (simulated) world can produce a non-injective and non-surjective relation between program output and the actions performed by a robot.

Therefore, another approach towards describing performance in ER research is to focus on the behavioral space of a problem [23, 16]. The concept of behaviors in robotics dates back to the seminal works of Brooks from the 1980's [3]. A behavior is a description β of the way an agent K (robot in ER and program in the GP case) acts in response to a particular stimulus within a particular context $\mathcal{C}$. A context $\mathcal{C}$ includes the internal description the agent has of its environment and its own internal state [1]. Stated in another way, a behavior β is produced by the interactions of an agent K, the output $\mathbf{y}$ and a context $\mathcal{C}$. In behavior-based robotics, for instance, behaviors are described at a very high level of abstraction by the system designer. In ER, on the other hand, researchers have recently proposed domain-specific numerical descriptors that describe each behavior, allowing them to explicitly consider behavioral space during evolution[16]. The justification for this is evident, given that the objective function is stated as a high-level goal, then population management should take into account the behavioral aspect of the solutions.

A behavior, defined in this way, is a higher-level description of the semantics of a program. An individual's behavior is described in more general terms, accounting not only for the program output but the context in which the output was produced. If contextual information is not relevant, then semantics and behaviors could be regarded as equivalent. Therefore, in essence, fitness, program semantics, and behavior provide different levels of abstraction of a program's performance. At one extreme of this scale of analysis, fitness provides a coarse grained look at performance, a single value (for each criteria) that attempts to provide a global evaluation. At the other end of the analysis scale, semantics describe program performance in great detail. On the other hand, behavioral descriptors lie in between fitness and semantics, providing either a finer or coarser level of description, depending on how behaviors are meaningfully characterized within a particular domain.

2.1 Novelty Search

Lehman and Stanley proposed NS, an EA that eliminates the need for an explicit objective function [11, 12, 13]. Evolution is not guided by a measure of *quality*, but by the a measure of *uniqueness*. To measure the novelty an individual introduces into the evolutionary process, the NS algorithm describes each individual within behavioral space.

A limitation of most EAs is their tendency to converge on local optima, a common result in many real-world problems with multimodal and irregular fitness landscapes. Within EC, diversity preservation is usually incorporated into an EA to overcome this shortcoming. However, most proposals can be regarded as ad-hoc solutions that must continuously attempt to balance exploration and exploitation during the search. Conversely, through the search for novelty alone, diversity preservation introduces the sole selective pressure during evolution. The core assumption behind NS, that suggests why it can find high-fitness solutions, is that at the beginning of a search, most random solutions will exhibit behaviors with bad fitness values. Therefore, as NS progresses and it leads the search towards novel regions in the search space, this should also lead towards better behaviors and thus better fitness values; i.e., when initial random solutions have low performance then the search for novelty could lead towards quality during evolution.

In summary, instead of using fitness to guide the search, NS uses a measure of *novelty* to characterize each individual. More precisely, a sparseness measure establishes how novel an individual is within behavioral space, with respect to the current population and novel solutions generated in previous generations. Such a measure of novelty is dynamic; i.e., it can produce different results for the same individual depending on the population state and search progress. In NS, the sparseness ρ around each individual K, described by its behavioral descriptor $\boldsymbol{\beta}$, using the average distance to the k-nearest neighbors in behavioral space, with k an algorithm parameter, is given by

[1]McPhee et al. [15] describe context as the root node of a tree. This might be appropriate for some problems, but here context is given by external conditions of the problem.

$$\rho(\boldsymbol{\beta}) = \frac{1}{k}\sum_{i=0}^{k} dist(\boldsymbol{\beta}, \boldsymbol{\alpha}_i) , \quad (1)$$

where $\boldsymbol{\alpha}_i$ is the behavioral descriptor of the ith-nearest neighbor of K in behavioral space with respect to distance measure $dist$, a domain-dependent measure that depends on how descriptors are expressed. If the average distance is large then the individual lies within a sparse region of behavioral space and it lies in a dense region when the measure is small. Fitness is only considered at the end of the search, when the individual with the best fitness score is selected as the final solution produced by the NS algorithm.

An important aspect is to determine which individuals should be considered when sparseness in computed, since the population changes with every generation, and the sparseness value for the same individual can vary over time. In NS, the proposal is to consider individuals in the current population as well as individuals that were considered to be novel in previous generations; hence, an individual has an intra and inter-generational neighborhood. Therefore, individuals with a sparseness value above a minimal threshold ρ_{min}, the second parameter of NS, are added to a population archive. The archive stores novel individuals, and the individuals in the archive are used along with the population to compute the sparseness value. An advantage of using the archive is that it can mitigate backtracking during the search, serving as a memory of the search progress.

Since its original proposal [11], and in later works [12, 13], most applications of NS have focused on ER, such as navigation [11, 12, 13], morphology design [14] and gait control [13]. As stated before, search algorithms that explicitly contemplate behaviors seem well suited for robotics, since most high-level robotic tasks can usually be solved in structurally different ways, thus guaranteeing a multimodal search.

In spite of these good results, NS has still not been used in most other domains. One exception is found in [26], where NS is integrated with an interactive evolutionary system, combining the strengths of both strategies. Another recent example is found in [17], where NS is used for supervised classification. However, in general applying NS to mainstream problems, to the authors' knowledge, is not yet commonly done. Thus, the present work proposes the use of NS for a common machine learning problem: data clustering, extending the proposal in [17] to a more difficult domain.

3. CLUSTERING WITH GP

Data classification is one of the most common tasks in machine learning. Posed as a learning problem, classification can be either supervised or unsupervised. Unsupervised classification is also referred to as data clustering, where the goal is to organize a set of unlabeled elements into distinct groups using little or no prior knowledge [27].

Clustering has been studied in various domains, such as computer vision and web development [8]. Given the variety of areas where clustering is applied, a multitude of clustering methods have been developed. Most of the clustering techniques are objective driven, such as the well known K-means (KM) that uses a hard partitioning of feature space [27] or the the Fuzzy C-means (FC) algorithm that instead uses a soft partitioning [1].

It is commonly expected that a cluster must present internal homogeneity and external separation from other clusters; i.e., patterns in the same cluster should be similar to each other, while patterns from different clusters should be different (in some sense). Generally in a clustering problem is given a set of patterns $\mathcal{T} = \{\mathbf{x}_1, ..., \mathbf{x}_j, .., \mathbf{x}_m\}$, where each pattern is described by a vector of features $\mathbf{x}_j = (x_{j,1}, x_{j,2}, ..., x_{j,n}) \in \mathcal{R}^n$. Then, a clustering algorithm must assign each pattern to a unique cluster; where the number of clusters is normally set a priori.

GP has been used extensively for data classification, see for instance [28]. In particular, several GP-based clustering systems have been proposed, using grammar based evolution [5], theoretic probabilistic interpretations [2] and hybrid multiobjective algorithms [21]. However, one underlying characteristic that previous methods share, is that they all rely on an explicit fitness function, just like any evolutionary search. Instead, in this paper fitness is substituted by a behavior-based search based on the novelty criteria. Nevertheless, a measure of clustering performance is presented next, since it is required to compare different results and to select the final solution returned by the NS algorithm.

3.1 Cluster Distance Ratio

The cluster distance ration (CDR) compares the within cluster dispersion with the gap between clusters [7]. Here, only problems with two clusters will be considered. The intra-cluster dispersion is computed using the Euclidean distance of each pattern $\mathbf{x} \in \mathbb{R}^n$ to its nearest neighbor within the cluster. The average of this distance, for elements in the data set, measures the intra-cluster dispersion, given by

$$IntraCluster = \frac{1}{N}\sum_{i=1}^{K}\sum_{x \in C_i} ||\mathbf{x} - \mathbf{u}_i|| , \quad (2)$$

where N is the number of data elements, K is the number of clusters, and $\mathbf{u}_i$ is the nearest neighbor within the same cluster of $\mathbf{x}$. Then, the inter-cluster separation is computed similarly, but now considering the closest neighbor from the other cluster, given by

$$InterCluster = \frac{1}{N}\sum_{i=1}^{K}\sum_{x \in C_i} ||\mathbf{x} - \mathbf{v}_i|| , \quad (3)$$

where $\mathbf{v}_i$ is the closest neighbor of $\mathbf{x}$ from the other cluster. Finally, the CDR is defined as

$$CDR = \frac{IntraCluster}{InterCluster} . \quad (4)$$

The CDR value provides a good measure of clustering quality, where the goal is to achieve the highest value.

4. CLUSTERING WITH NS-GP

The proposal of this paper is to develop a NS-based GP system for unsupervised data clustering, hereafter referred to as NS-GP. The algorithm is a modification of the GP classifier that uses a static range selection [28] that functions as follows. Let us consider two clusters ω_1 and ω_2, a set of patterns $\mathbf{x} \in \mathbb{R}^n$, and a GP functions (programs) $K : \mathbb{R}^n \mapsto \mathbb{R}$. Then, data pattern $\mathbf{x}$ is assigned to cluster ω_1 if $K(\mathbf{x}) > 0$ and it is assigned to cluster ω_2 otherwise. To apply NS to clustering, a behavioral descriptor for each program K is required; the proposed descriptor is presented below.

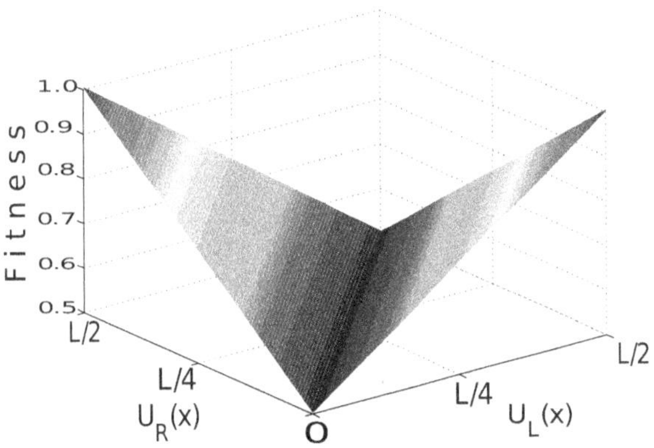

Figure 1: Fitness landscape in behavioral space for the proposed clustering descriptor.

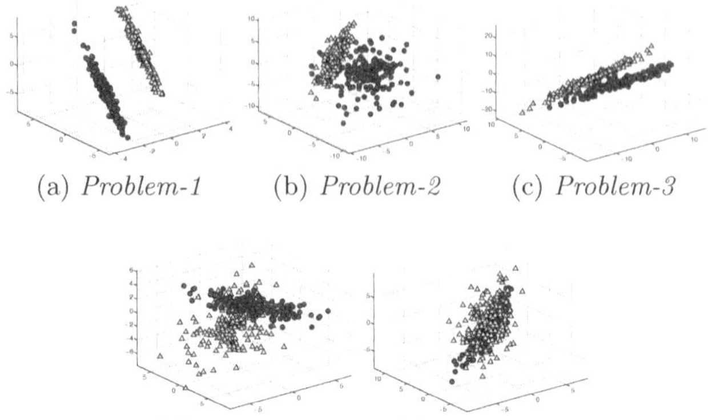

(a) *Problem-1* (b) *Problem-2* (c) *Problem-3*

(d) *Problem-4* (e) *Problem-5*

Figure 2: Five synthetic clustering problems; the observed clusters represent the ground truth data.

4.1 Clustering Descriptor

For a clustering problem a training set is not given since it is unsupervised, so the entire dataset $\mathcal{T}$ is treated as testing data, which contains sample patterns from each cluster. For a two-cluster problem with data set $\mathcal{T} = \{\mathbf{y}_1, \mathbf{y}_2, ..., \mathbf{y}_L\}$, and clusters ω_1 and ω_2, the cluster descriptor $\boldsymbol{\beta}^C$ is proposed, where for each GP clustering program K_i the descriptor is a binary vector $\boldsymbol{\beta}^{C_i} = (\beta_1, \beta_2, ..., \beta_L)$ of size L, where each vector element β_j is set to 1 if clustering function K_i assigns label ω_1 to pattern $\mathbf{y}_j$ and is set to 0 otherwise.

4.2 Behavioral Landscape

For a better explanation lets consider a synthetic problem where a ground truth clustering is provided. Then, suppose that the number of samples from each cluster is $\frac{L}{2}$, and that they are ordered in such a way that the first $\frac{L}{2}$ elements in $\mathcal{T}$ have a ground truth label of ω_1. Let $\mathbf{x}$ represents a binary vector, and function $u(\mathbf{x})$ returns the number of 1s in $\mathbf{x}$. Moreover, let K_O be the *optimal* clustering program that achieves a perfect accuracy on the data set based on the ground truth labeling. Then, the descriptor of K_O is given by $\boldsymbol{\beta}^{C_0} = (1_1, 1_2, ..., 1_{\frac{L}{2}}, 0_{\frac{L}{2}+1}, ..., 0_L)$. Moreover, for a two-cluster problem, an equally useful solution is to take the opposite (complement) behavior and invert the clustering, such that a 1 is converted to a 0 and vice-versa. This mirror behavior is defined by the descriptor $\boldsymbol{\beta}^{C_*} = (0_1, 0_2, ...0_{\frac{L}{2}}, 1_{\frac{L}{2}+1}, ..., 1_L)$. The complete fitness landscape in behavioral space, with fitness given by clustering accuracy, is depicted in Figure 1.

For a two-cluster problem with a reasonable degree of difficulty, the initial generations of a GP search should be expected to contain random clustering programs. For the cluster descriptor, behavioral space is organized on a two dimensional surface, such that one axis u_L considers the number of ones on the left hand side, first $\frac{L}{2}$ bits, of a behavior descriptor $\boldsymbol{\beta}^C$, and the other axis u_R considers the remaining $\frac{L}{2}$ bits; see Figure 1. Notice that the middle valley of the fitness landscape corresponds to basically random clustering functions, with worst case scenario performance. Hence, NS will push the search towards either of the two global optima, $\boldsymbol{\beta}^{C_0}$ and $\boldsymbol{\beta}^{C_*}$ Finally, given the above binary descriptor, a natural *dist*() function for Equation 1 is the Hamming distance, which counts the number of bits that differ between two binary sequences.

Table 1: Parameters for the NS-GP.

Parameter	Description
Population size	200 individuals.
Generations	100 generations.
Initialization	*Ramped Half-and-Half*, with 6 levels of max. depth.
Operator probabilities	Crossover $p_c = 0.8$, Mutation $p_\mu = 0.2$.
Function set	$(+ , - , \times , \div , \lvert\cdot\rvert , x^2 , \sqrt{x} , log , sin , cos , if)$.
Terminal set	$\{x_1, ..., x_i, ..., x_n\}$,where x_i is a dimension of the data patterns $\mathbf{x} \in \mathbb{R}^n$.
Bloat control	Dynamic depth control.
Initial dynamic depth	6 levels.
Hard maximum depth	20 levels.
Selection	Tournament.
Archive	No Limit on archive size.

5. EXPERIMENTS

The performance of the NS-GP clustering algorithm is compared against two well known clustering methods; K-means (KM) and Fuzzy C-means (FC). The NS-GP is tested in two different versions, each with a different behavioral threshold ρ_{min}: NS-GP-20 with $\rho_{min} = 20$ and NS-GP-40 with $\rho_{min} = 40$; in both cases parameter the number of neighbors k is set to 15 to compute sparseness.

5.1 Problems and GP Parameters

Synthetic clustering problems were generated using two randomly generated Gaussian functions in $\mathbb{R}^3$ for each problem, following a similar strategy to [22]. From each function, 160 data points were randomly generated. Then, an additional 40 data points were generated by triplicating the standard deviation of each, to get disperse clusters with some outliers. Table 2 shows the five selected test problems of increased difficulty, where each figure represents the ground truth data.

The NS-GP algorithms use a Koza style GP with subtree crossover and subtree mutation. Table 1 summarizes the

Table 2: A comparison of all of the clustering methods on each problem. The data shows the CDR values and the clustering error score; for NS these values are averages over all runs.

Problem	Clustering Distance Ratio					Clustering Error			
	GT	KM	FC	NS-GP-20	NS-GP-40	KM	FC	NS-GP-20	NS-GP-40
Problem-1	9.17	10.22	10.25	9.20	9.21	0.10	0.10	0.45	0.46
Problem-2	4.46	5.51	5.46	5.38	4.47	0.07	0.07	0.24	0.25
Problem-3	5.55	5.37	5.29	4.51	4.53	0.30	0.26	0.20	0.22
Problem-4	4.10	6.21	6.11	5.51	5.45	0.36	0.35	0.10	0.19
Problem-5	1.59	4.54	4.52	3.64	3.22	0.45	0.45	0.19	0.27

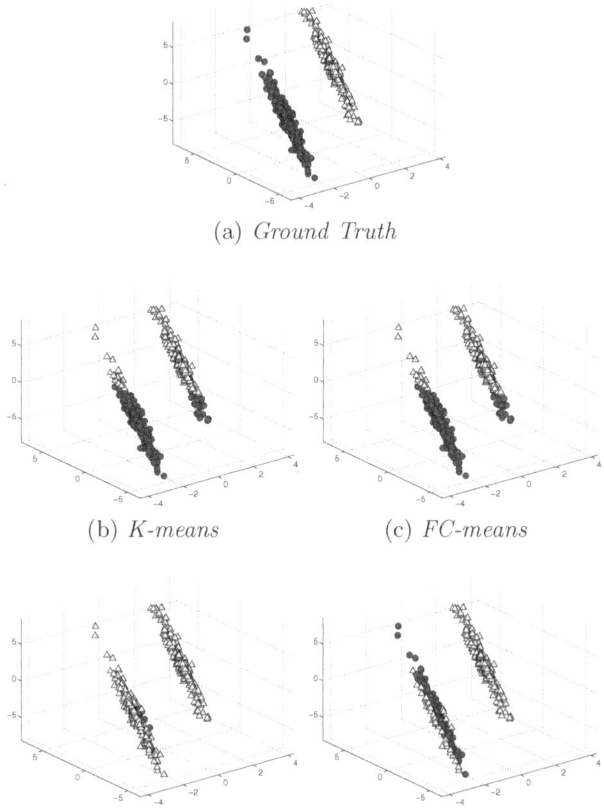

(a) *Ground Truth* (b) *K-means* (c) *FC-means* (d) *NS-GP-20* (e) *NS-GP-40*

Figure 3: Comparison of clustering performance on Problem No.1.

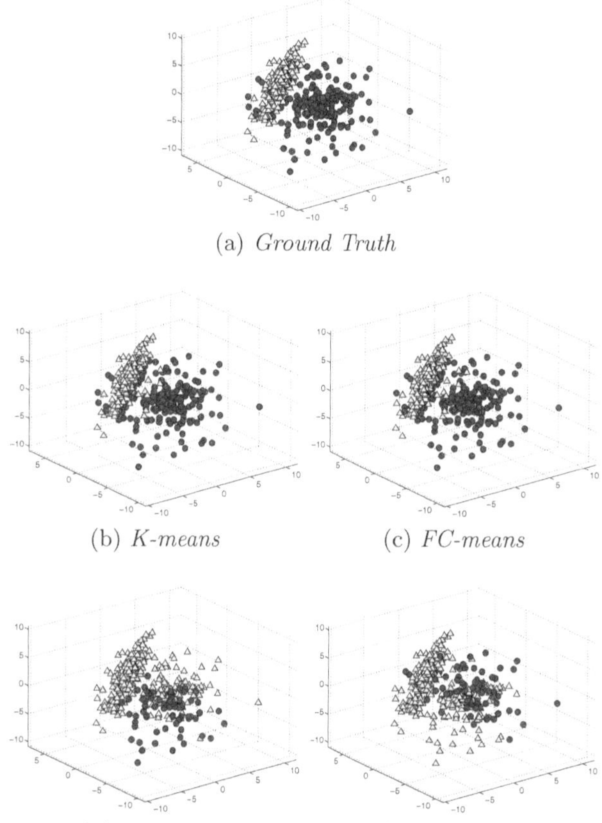

(a) *Ground Truth* (b) *K-means* (c) *FC-means* (d) *NS-GP-20* (e) *NS-GP-40*

Figure 4: Comparison of clustering performance on Problem No.2.

parameters of the algorithm, which was coded using Matlab 2012b and the GPLAB toolbox [20].

5.2 Results

This section presents an experimental evaluation of NS-GP clustering. All of the clustering algorithms were executed 30 times to find statistically significant results. Table 2 compare the performance of NS-GP with two baseline methods, KM and FC. The table presents two comparative views of average performance over all runs. First, the algorithms are compared based on their CDR score, and the CDR of the ground truth of each problem is also presented. Additionally, using the ground truth, a classification error was computed, based on the ordering suggested by each clustering method. In general, the results indicate two noteworthy trends. First, NS performs much worse on the simpler problems, it seems like it is basically doing a random search. On the other hand, NS noticeably outperforms the control methods on the harder problems, this is especially true for the hardest, Problem 5. Second, it seems that a lower ρ_{min} encourages better performance in most cases. A detailed view of how the data is being clustered can provide a different analysis of the results. Figures 3 - 7 present a graphical illustration of the clustering output achieved by each method. All figures show the ground truth clusters for visual comparison, along with a typical clustering output from each method. These figures confirm the data presented in Table 2, NS-GP performs worse on the easy problems and performs better on the difficult ones.

Figures 8 and 9 examine how sparseness evolves during the NS-GP search, for NS-GP-20 and NS-GP-40 respec-

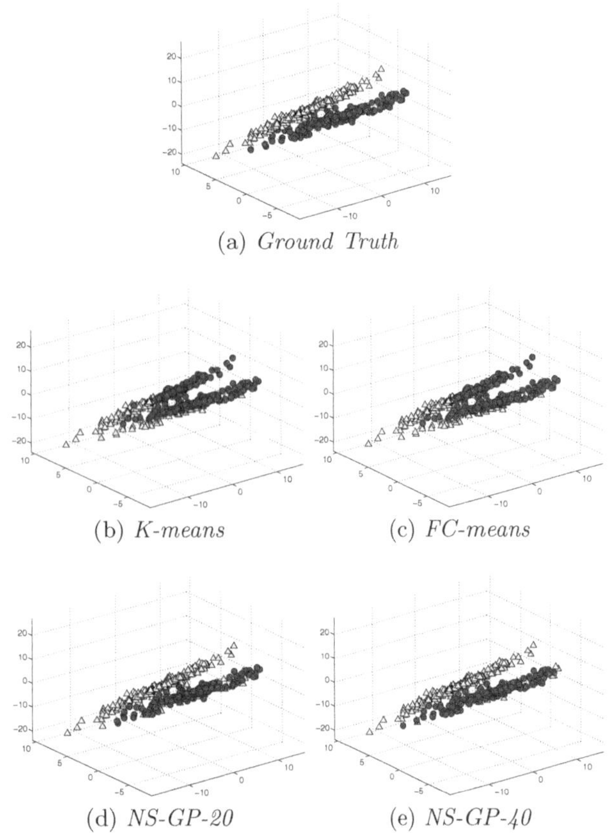

(a) *Ground Truth* (b) *K-means* (c) *FC-means* (d) *NS-GP-20* (e) *NS-GP-40*

Figure 5: Comparison of clustering performance on Problem No.3.

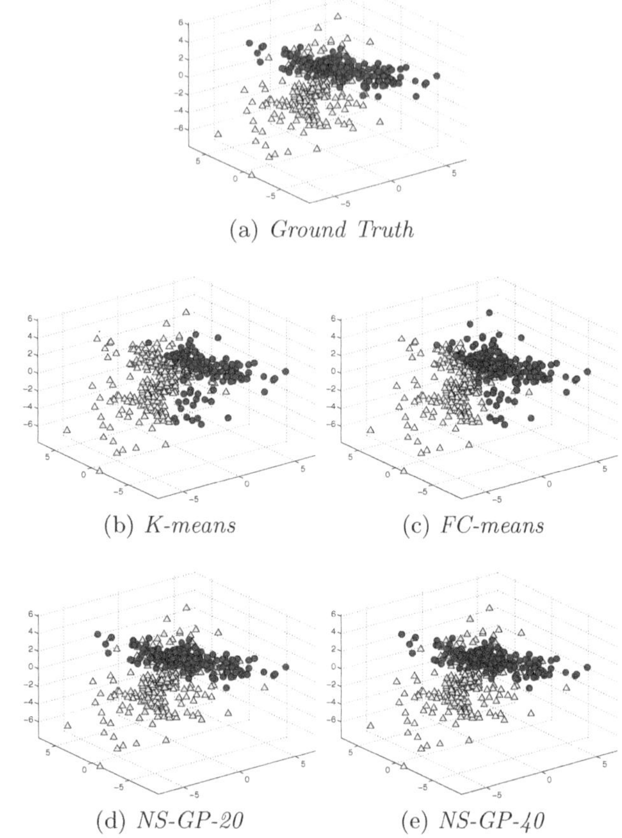

(a) *Ground Truth* (b) *K-means* (c) *FC-means* (d) *NS-GP-20* (e) *NS-GP-40*

Figure 6: Comparison of clustering performance on Problem No.4.

tively. Each figure presents a similar plot that shows how the sparseness of the best individual (based on fitness) evolves over each generation. The plots are averages of the 30 runs of each experiment and present a curve for each problem. A horizontal line shows the corresponding threshold value for each configuration, set to 20 in Figure 8 and set to 40 in Figure 9. In both cases it is possible to observe a similar pattern. For the easy problems (1, 2 and 3) the sparseness value of the best individual at each generation does not reach the threshold, and is therefore not included in the population archive. This means that the individual is lost, and maybe it is never found again. This explains the reason why NS fails to produce good results on the easy problems. It appears that since the problems are not difficult, then novelty does not necessarily lead to quality, and NS is not influencing the search as desired. On the other hand, for the more difficult problems (4 and 5) it is clear that good solutions almost always correspond with novel solutions; i.e., the solutions that are being introduced into the archive of novel solutions also exhibit good fitness values. In these cases, the search for novelty is indeed guiding evolution towards solutions that perform better. This is reasonable, since for difficult problems the initial (random) programs will mostly exhibit bad performance, and novelty can lead towards quality.

Finally, to illustrate how evolution progresses with the NS-GP clustering algorithm, Figure 10 presents four snapshots of NS-GP-40 applied to Problem 5. Each plot shown in the figure represents the best NS solution (taken from the current population and population archive) based on the CDR value at four different generations. For this difficult problem, it is clear that NS is progressively exploring the search space, and finding better solutions.

6. CONCLUSIONS

This work presents a NS-based GP algorithm for automatic data clustering. To the authors knowledge, the work represents the first attempt to leverage NS to solve this common problem in pattern recognition and machine learning, since previous applications of NS were primarily focused on robotics. This paper develops the idea of program behaviors and how they relate to semantics, and suggests that behavior based search, such as the NS algorithm, can be applicable to many problem domains. For the clustering problem addressed here, a domain-specific behavioral descriptor was proposed and its fitness landscape was analyzed. The NS-GP algorithm was also compared with two standard clustering methods, K-means and Fuzzy C-means. Initial results are informative and encouraging. The experiments suggest that NS is not well suited to solve easy problems, failing drastically on the examples given here. However, this is not discouraging for researchers from real-world domains, easy problems such as these rarely come up. Conversely, the NS-based GP exhibits very good results on the difficult test cases, outperforming the control methods. It seems that for easy problems, the exploration capacity of NS is mostly

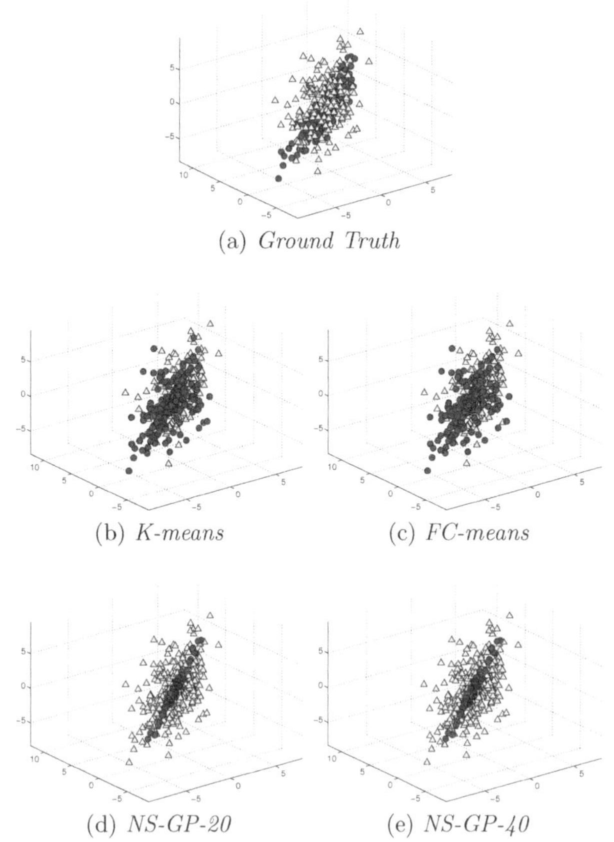

(a) *Ground Truth*

(b) *K-means* (c) *FC-means*

(d) *NS-GP-20* (e) *NS-GP-40*

Figure 7: Comparison of clustering performance on Problem No.5.

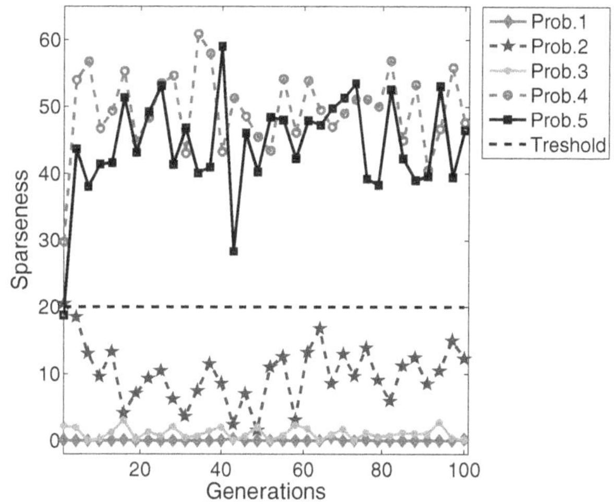

Figure 8: Evolution of sparseness for NS-GP-20, showing the average sparseness of he best individual at each generation.

unexploited or maybe even limits the search; i.e., if random solutions have a high fitness then novelty could easily lead the search towards worse results. On the other hand, since randomly generating a high-performance solution is less probable for difficult problems, then the incentive for behavioral exploration is incremented and the search for novelty can indeed lead towards quality during evolution. Future work will center on exploring further experiments in this domain, comprehensively testing different parametrizations of the NS-GP search, evaluating performance on real problems, and comparing the algorithm with other GP systems for data clustering.

Acknowledgments.

This research is funded by CONACYT (Mexico) Basic Science Research Grant No. 178323; and the first author supported by doctoral scholarship No. 232288 from CONACYT.

7. REFERENCES

[1] J. Bezdek, R. Ehrlich, and W. Full. Using direct competition to select for competent controllers in evolutionary robotics. *Fcm: The fuzzy c-means clustering algorithm*, 10(2-3):191–203, 1984.

[2] N. Boric and P. Estevez. Genetic programming-based clustering using an information theoretic fitness measure. In *Proceedings of the 2007 IEEE Congress on Evolutionary Computation*, pages 31–38. IEEE Press, 2007.

[3] R. A. Brooks. *Cambrian intelligence: the early history of the new AI.* MIT Press, Cambridge, MA, USA, 1999.

[4] R. Dawkins. *Climbing Mount Improbable.* W.W. Norton & Company, 1996.

[5] I. De Falco, E. Tarantino, A. D. Cioppa, and F. Fontanella. A novel grammar-based genetic programming approach to clustering. In *Proceedings of the 2005 ACM symposium on Applied computing*, SAC '05, pages 928–932, New York, NY, USA, 2005. ACM.

[6] E. Galván-López, J. Mcdermott, M. O'Neill, and A. Brabazon. Defining locality as a problem difficulty measure in genetic programming. *Genetic Programming and Evolvable Machines*, 12(4):365–401, 2011.

[7] T. K. Ho and M. Basu. Complexity measures of supervised classification problems. *IEEE Trans. Pattern Anal. Mach. Intell.*, 24(3):289–300, 2002.

[8] A. Jain, M. Murty, and P. Flynn. Data clustering: a review. *ACM Computing Surveys*, 31(3):264?323, 1999.

[9] T. Kowaliw, A. Dorin, and J. McCormack. Promoting creative design in interactive evolutionary computation. *Evolutionary Computation, IEEE Transactions on*, 16(4):523 –536, 2012.

[10] J. Koza. Human-competitive results produced by genetic programming. *Genetic Programming and Evolvable Machines*, 11(3):251–284, 2010.

[11] J. Lehman and K. O. Stanley. Exploiting open-endedness to solve problems through the search for novelty. In *Proceedings of the Eleventh International Conference on Artificial Life, Cambridge, MA*, ALIFE XI. MIT Press, 2008.

[12] J. Lehman and K. O. Stanley. Efficiently evolving programs through the search for novelty. In *Proceedings of the 12th annual conference on Genetic*

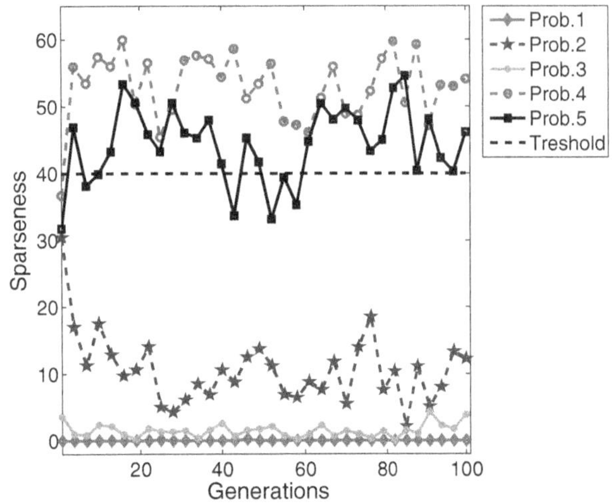

Figure 9: Evolution of sparseness for NS-GP-40, showing the average sparseness of he best individual at each generation.

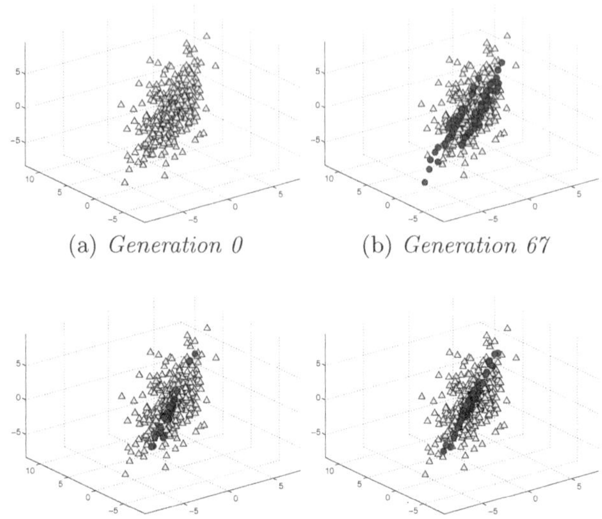

(a) *Generation 0* (b) *Generation 67*

(c) *Generation 134* (d) *Generation 200*

Figure 10: Evolution of the best solutions found at progressive generations for Problem 5 with NS-GP-40.

and evolutionary computation, GECCO '10, pages 837–844. ACM, 2010.

[13] J. Lehman and K. O. Stanley. Abandoning objectives: Evolution through the search for novelty alone. *Evol. Comput.*, 19(2):189–223, 2011.

[14] J. Lehman and K. O. Stanley. Evolving a diversity of virtual creatures through novelty search and local competition. In *Proceedings of the 13th annual conference on Genetic and evolutionary computation*, GECCO '11, pages 211–218. ACM, 2011.

[15] N. F. McPhee, B. Ohs, and T. Hutchison. Semantic building blocks in genetic programming. In *Proceedings of the 11th European conference on Genetic programming*, EuroGP'08, pages 134–145, Berlin, Heidelberg, 2008. Springer-Verlag.

[16] J. B. Mouret and S. Doncieux. Encouraging behavioral diversity in evolutionary robotics: An empirical study. *Evol. Comput.*, 20(1):91–133, 2012.

[17] E. Naredo, L. Trujillo, and Y. Martínez. Searching for novel classifiers. In *Proceedings from the 16th European Conference on Genetic Programming, EuroGP 2013*, volume 7831 of *LNCS*, pages 145–156. Springer-Verlag, 2013.

[18] S. Nolfi and D. Floreano. *Evolutionary Robotics: The Biology,Intelligence,and Technology.* MIT Press, Cambridge, MA, USA, 2000.

[19] C. Ofria and C. O. Wilke. Avida: a software platform for research in computational evolutionary biology. *Artif. Life*, 10(2):191–229, 2004.

[20] S. Silva and J. Almeida. Gplab–a genetic programming toolbox for matlab. In L. Gregersen, editor, *Proceedings of the Nordic MATLAB conference*, pages 273–278, 2003.

[21] J. Sun, W. Sverdlik, and S. Tout. Parallel hybrid clustering using genetic programming and multi-objective fitness with density (pyramid). In *Proceedings of the 2006 International Conference on Data Mining, DMIN 2006*, pages 197–203, 2006.

[22] L. Trujillo, Y. Martínez, E. Galván-López, and P. Legrand. Predicting problem difficulty for genetic programming applied to data classification. In *Proceedings of the 13th annual conference on Genetic and evolutionary computation*, GECCO '11, pages 1355–1362, New York, NY, USA, 2011. ACM.

[23] L. Trujillo, G. Olague, E. Lutton, and F. F. De Vega. Discovering several robot behaviors through speciation. In *Proceedings of the 2008 conference on Applications of evolutionary computing*, Evo'08, pages 164–174. Springer-Verlag, 2008.

[24] L. Trujillo, G. Olague, E. Lutton, F. Fernández de Vega, L. Dozal, and E. Clemente. Speciation in behavioral space for evolutionary robotics. *Journal of Intelligent & Robotic Systems*, 64(3-4):323–351, 2011.

[25] N. Q. Uy, N. X. Hoai, M. O'Neill, R. I. Mckay, and E. Galván-López. Semantically-based crossover in genetic programming: application to real-valued symbolic regression. *Genetic Programming and Evolvable Machines*, 12(2):91–119, 2011.

[26] B. G. Woolley and K. O. Stanley. Exploring promising stepping stones by combining novelty search with interactive evolution. *CoRR*, abs/1207.6682, 2012.

[27] R. Xu and I. Wunsch, Donald. Survey of clustering algorithms. *Neural Networks, IEEE Transactions on*, 16(3):645–678, may 2005.

[28] M. Zhang and W. Smart. Using gaussian distribution to construct fitness functions in genetic programming for multiclass object classification. *Pattern Recogn. Lett.*, 27(11):1266–1274, 2006.

An Evolutionary Data-Conscious Artificial Immune Recognition System

Darwin Tay[1,2], Chueh Loo Poh[2,*], Richard I. Kitney[1]

[1] Department of Bioengineering, Imperial College London, UK

[2] Division of Bioengineering, Nanyang Technological University, Singapore

Email: darwintay@imperial.ac.uk, clpoh@ntu.edu.sg, r.kitney@imperial.ac.uk

ABSTRACT

Artificial Immune Recognition System (AIRS) algorithm offers a promising methodology for data classification. It is an immune-inspired supervised learning algorithm that works efficiently and has shown comparable performance with respect to other classifier algorithms. For this reason, it has received escalating interests in recent years. However, the full potential of the algorithm was yet unleashed.

We proposed a novel algorithm called the evolutionary data-conscious AIRS (EDC-AIRS) algorithm that accentuates and capitalizes on 3 additional immune mechanisms observed from the natural immune system. These mechanisms are associated to the phenomena exhibited by the antibodies in response to the concentration, location and type of foreign antigens. Bio-mimicking these observations empower EDC-AIRS algorithm with the ability to robustly adapt to the different density, distribution and characteristics exhibited by each data class. This provides competitive advantages for the algorithm to better characterize and learn the underlying pattern of the data. Experiments on four widely used benchmarking datasets demonstrated promising results – outperforming several state-of-the-art classification algorithms evaluated. This signifies the importance of integrating these immune mechanisms as part of the learning process.

Categories and Subject Descriptors

I.2.6 [**Artificial Intelligence**]: Learning – *Concept learning, Induction, Knowledge acquisition, Parameter learning.*

Keywords

Artificial immune recognition system, Classification algorithm, Evolutionary computation.

*Corresponding author

1. INTRODUCTION

The human immune system is a highly sophisticated, distributed, complex and powerful natural defense mechanism that comprises of several functional mechanisms, positioned in strategic locations, conferring resistance against viruses and foreign pathogens. It has the ability to learn the characteristics of the foreign antigens and contrive a defense strategy to detect and neutralize them. Specifically, the immune system possesses properties such as the capability of recognition, memory acquisition, diversity and self-regulation, making it highly suitable for learning patterns that underlie a data. On this note, it has inspired the development of the artificial immune system capable of solving many problems related to computer science and engineering (e.g. computer security, anomaly detection, optimization, machine learning, etc.) [1, 2]. One such algorithm that has received escalating interests is the Artificial Immune Recognition System version 2 (AIRS2) [3].

Although AIRS2 algorithm has shown to be an effective classification algorithm, some useful immune mechanisms are yet to be exploited by the algorithm. For instance, artificial recognition balls (ARBs) are used in AIRS2 algorithm to denote a representative subset of B-Cells. They would compete for survival based on the idea of resource limited system [4]. However, the creation and elimination of the ARBs do not correspond to the density of the data in which they cover (i.e. a larger number of ARBs do not survive in regions that are more densely populated with data). This contradicts with the natural immune system where macrophages would flood the extracellular space of the infected regions (attempting to eliminate the harmful agents) and B-Cells would proliferate and secrete antibodies profoundly in response to pathogenic agents. In other words, a larger concentration of defense agents would be present in regions that has received intense invasion from harmful antigens. Another area that the original AIRS2 algorithm did not explore and exploit is the distributed diversity exhibited by the lymph nodes found in the natural immune system. The AIRS2 algorithm uses a common parameter set to model the distribution of different data classes. This is undesirable in cases where the distribution of different data classes differ by a considerable degree. Observation of the strategic positioning of the lymph nodes in human bodies (which promotes better immune defense) advocates for the need of a more specific and distinct parameter set (e.g. affinity threshold scalar, density and total resources parameters) to model each data class (i.e. instances that belong to a specific class). Finally, it is important to generate B-Cells that can affiliate/bind well with the antigens. This is realized biologically through the production of highly specific surface receptors on the B-Cells which facilitates the detection and eradication of the foreign antigens. To mimic this concept computationally, feature selection can be performed where highly informative features that can describe the underlying association were identified and used for classification.

This paper presents a novel algorithm called the evolutionary data-conscious AIRS (EDC-AIRS) algorithm, which extends the existing AIRS2 algorithm by contextualizing the immune response to the concentration, distribution and characteristics of the antigens and is no longer a global centralized response.

GECCO'13, July 6–10, 2013, Amsterdam, The Netherlands.

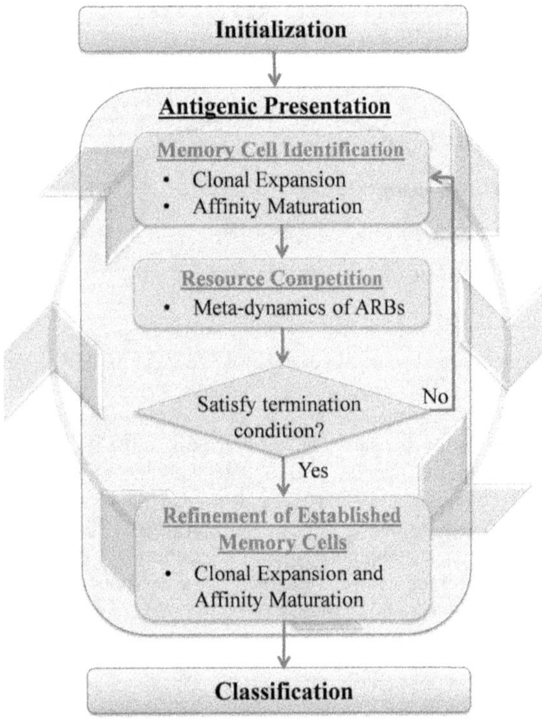

Figure 1: Canonical Flow of the AIRS2 Algorithm
The AIRS2 algorithm consists of 4 stages during the learning phase, namely the initialization, memory cell identification, resource competition and refinement of established memory cells stages. The last 3 stages will repeat for every data instance presented. After learning the underlying pattern of the data, classification is performed on the unseen data using K-nearest neighbor.

When evaluated using 4 widely used benchmarking datasets, our method has exhibited improved learning ability and classification accuracy.

The rest of the paper is organized as follows. Section 2 provides a brief introduction to the AIRS2 algorithm. A description of the proposed EDC-AIRS algorithm is presented in Section 3. The experimental results are offered in Section 4 and discussed in Section 5. Finally, conclusion is drawn in Section 6.

2. ARTIFICIAL IMMUNE RECOGNITION SYSTEM

The natural immune system is a highly rapid and efficient biological self-defense mechanism that protects a given host against infections, for example, from foreign antigens or pathogens. The immune system functions by detecting a wide variety of agents and distinguish the foreign antigens (e.g. viruses) from the organism's own healthy cells or molecules (also known as self-antigens). The immune system consists of a number of components. Two examples are macrophages and lymphocytes (e.g. B-cell ad T-Cell) which are responsible for the recognition and elimination of the determined infectious agents. The lymphocytes have highly specific surface antigenic receptors to a given antigenic determinant, in which they would only proliferate in response to a specific infection. Therefore, the type of antibodies present in an individual could reflect the infections to which they are infected with.

The antibody's polypeptide chains composed of a highly variable amino-terminal region (V-region) and a carboxy-terminal region (C-region) that can be of a few types. The V-region is responsible for the antigenic detection while the C-region is responsible for a variety of effector functions. The polypeptide chain of an antibody is formed through the genetic recombination and somatic hyper-mutation of multiple gene segments scattered along the chromosome of the genome. Such formation mechanism used to generate antibodies introduces diversity into the underlying immune defense [2], ameliorating the ability of the antibodies to recognize/bind to the antigens.

Inspired by the robustness exhibited by the natural immune system, the AIRS2 algorithm [3] - a novel one-shot incremental supervised learning algorithm was developed and applied to solve classification problems. It has several attractive characteristics such as the ability to (1) adaptively develop an appropriate architecture during the learning process, (2) achieve competitive accuracy compared to other classification algorithms, (3) develop a generalized model by generating a representative set of memory cells and (4) achieve accuracy comparable to those obtained with the optimal parameter set when experimented over a wide range of parameter values [5].

The AIRS2 algorithm consists of 4 stages during the process of learning the underlying patterns of the data. They are the initialization, memory cell identification, resource competition and refinement of established memory cells stages. The canonical flow of the AIRS2 algorithm is presented in Figure 1.

The initialization stage is responsible for normalization of the data, parameter discovery and seeding of memory cells. The data items found in the dataset is first normalized so that the Euclidean distance between the feature vectors of any 2 data items is in the range [0, 1]. Affinity threshold, the average Euclidean distance between each data item in the training dataset, is then calculated. This value controls the quality of the memory cells maintained and utilized for classification. The mathematical expression for computing the affinity threshold is as follow:

$$\text{affinity threshold} = \frac{\sum_{i=1}^{n}\sum_{j=i+1}^{n}\text{affinity}(ag_i, ag_j)}{\frac{n(n-1)}{2}} \quad (1)$$

where n is the number of training instances (antigens), ag_i and ag_j are the ith and jth training antigens in the training data, and affinity(ag_i,ag_j) returns the Euclidean distance between the two antigens. The initial memory cell pool (MCP), a collection of classifier cells that will be used for classification at the end of the training lifecycle, is then seeded by randomly selecting data item(s) from the training dataset.

A process known as the antigenic presentation is then undertaken where each training instance is subsequently presented to the AIRS2 algorithm. For each training instance presented, it first undergoes the memory cell identification stage where its affinity with the memory cells in MCP (that reside in the same class) is computed. The most stimulated memory cell (also known as matched memory cell) is then selected and cloned in proportion to its stimulation value (i.e. clonal expansion phase). This value is calculated based on the following equation:

$$\text{stimulation}(x, y) = 1 - \text{affinity}(x, y) \quad (2)$$

where x is the presented training instance and y is the memory cell. These cloned memory cells forms the artificial recognition ball (ARB) pool where an ARB [4] is a single representation for a number of similar memory cells. This allows a reduction in duplication and manages the survival of classifier cells within the population. The cloned ARBs are then mutated at a rate inversely proportional to the antigenic affinity, introducing diversity into the system (i.e. affinity maturation phase).

```
CandStim ← stimulation(ag, mc_candidate)
MatchSim ← stimulation(ag, mc_match)
CellAff ← affinity(mc_candidate, mc_match)
if (CandStim > MatchSim)
    if (CellAff < AT * ATS)
        MC ← MC - mc_match
    end
    MC ← MC U mc_candidate
end
```

Figure 2: Pseudo-code for Memory Cell Introduction used in AIRS2 Algorithm – adopted from [3]
CandStim (and MatchSim) denotes the stimulation level between the presented antigen and the candidate (and matched) memory cell. CellAff refers to the affinity between the candidate and matched memory cell. MC represents the memory cell pool.

The range of the maturated value assigned to a selected attribute is centered at the attribute's initial value and spanned over the difference between 1 and the ARB's stimulation value. In other words, mutated ARB offspring of highly stimulated cells are only allowed to explore and mutate to a value near its initial state while less stimulated ARB offspring are allowed to mutate over a lager range.

Next, the ARBs will compete for survival based on the concept of resource allocation mechanism [4], where the ARBs are allocated a number of resources proportional to their normalized stimulation values. The resulting ARBs with insufficient resources are subsequently pruned (i.e. meta-dynamic phase). The average simulation level for the ARBs is then computed based on the following equation:

$$\text{avg\_stimulation}_i = \frac{\sum_{j=1}^{|AB_i|} ab_j.stimulation}{|AB_i|}, \; ab_j \in AB_i \quad (3)$$

where AB refers to the ARB pool, ab ε AB; $|AB_i|$ is the number of ARBs in class i. The average stimulation is then compared with the user-defined stimulation threshold. If it is greater than the user-defined threshold, the training cycle stops for that training instance. Otherwise, the training cycle repeats.

Once the termination condition is satisfied, the most stimulated ARB is selected as the candidate memory (CM) cell. If this CM cell's stimulation level is higher than all the memory cells in the established memory (EM) set (i.e. collection of ARBs that have survived the resource competition stage), then it is added into the EM set. Otherwise, this CM cell is discarded. Finally, replacement of the EM cells is carried out first by computing the memory cell replacement cutoff value as defined as:

$$\text{Cutoff} = \text{AT} * \text{ATS} \quad (4)$$

where AT refers to affinity threshold and ATS denotes affinity threshold scalar. If the affinity between this CM cell and the best affiliated memory cell found previously (i.e. EM cell) is below the cutoff value, the EM cell will be removed and replaced with the CM cell. Consequently, the next training instance is deployed to the AIRS2 algorithm until all the training instances are presented. This process ultimately identifies a set of representative memory cells that provides a generalized representation of the pattern that underlies the data, which will then be used for classification. The classification algorithm employed is K-nearest neighbour (KNN) where the classification outcome for each unseen data instance is determined by taking the majority vote of the k most stimulated EM cells. For a more detailed description of the algorithm, readers can refer to [3, 6].

```
CellAff ← affinity(mc_candidate, mc_match)
Density_count ← 0
foreach (ag_i in AG)
do
    AntigenAff ← affinity(ag_i, mc_candidate)
    if (AntigenAff < AT*Radius_density)
        Density_count ← Density_count + 1
    end
done
Density_ratio ← Density_count / Density_max
if (CellAff < (1- Density_ratio) * AT * ATS)
    MC ← MC - mc_match
end
MC ← MC U mc_candidate
```

Figure 3: Pseudo-code for Memory Cell Introduction used in EDC-AIRS Algorithm
$Density_{count}$ represents the number of antigens that is proximal to the candidate memory cell. $Density_{max}$ denotes the maximum number of antigen present in the training data.

3. Material & Methods

3.1 Evolutionary Data-Conscious AIRS (EDC-AIRS) Algorithm

This study formulates a novel immune-inspired (EDC-AIRS) algorithm that employs several natural immune mechanisms. In particular, how antibodies evolve and adapt to the different concentration, location and type of foreign antigens are being mimicked in addition to those proposed by the AIRS2 algorithm. This, when implemented as a high fidelity computational technique, empowers the algorithm with the ability to independently adapt to the distinct (1) density, (2) distribution and (3) characteristics of each data class.

Firstly, the ability to adapt to the different (local) density present in the data was addressed by the observation of the rapid growth of macrophages and B-Cells in response to the invasion of foreign antigens (particularly, at the regions of infection). More specifically, a relative proportion of antibodies to antigens were necessary to neutralize the harmful agents. This mechanism was incorporated in the EDC-AIRS algorithm by allowing a relatively larger number of ARBs to survive in regions that are more densely populated with training data. Implementation was carried out by removing and modifying some of the criteria present in the original AIRS2 algorithm. In particular, the way the memory cells are introduced into the system is modified. The original pseudo-code for memory cell introduction [3] used in AIRS2 algorithm is shown in Figure 2. The criterion that requires the candidate memory cell ($mc_{candidate}$) to be more stimulated (by the training antigen, ag) than the matched memory cell (mc_{match}) before it was added to the memory cell pool was first removed. The reason for doing so is to encourage new ARBs that are highly stimulated (ensured by the high stimulation threshold adopted) to survive within the system. Secondly, computation of the density ($Density_{count}$) proximal to $mc_{candidate}$, based on the initial set of training antigens (AG), was implemented in the algorithm. The degree of proximity was determined by a user-defined parameter, $Radius_{density}$. Additionally, the maximum density ($Density_{max}$) present in AG was also computed based on the same approach. However, another user-defined parameter ($Radius_{max}$) was used to determine the size of the region to be considered.

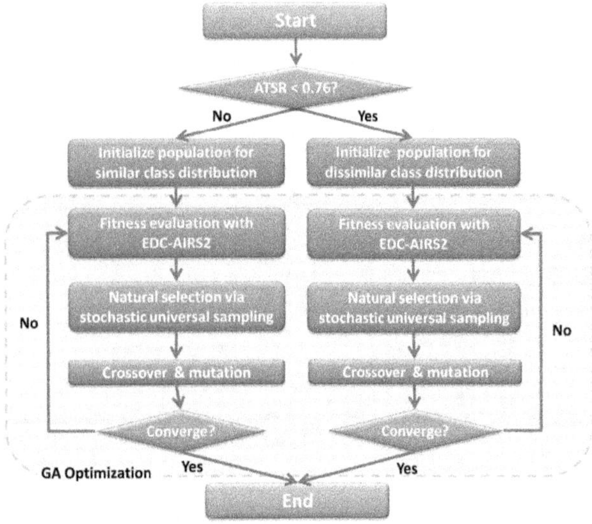

Figure 4: Proposed Methodology for Optimization of Parameter Set for Binary Class Classification Problems

The ATSR of the dataset was first computed. If it was smaller than the empirically derived threshold (0.76), an independent set of parameters for each data class was created. Otherwise, a common parameter set was used for all data classes. These parameters were then optimized (with respect to classification accuracy) using GA.

Finally, a weighting coefficient ($\text{Density}_{\text{ratio}}$) was derived based on the following equation:

$$\text{Density}_{\text{ratio}} = \frac{\text{Density}_{\text{count}}}{\text{Density}_{\text{max}}} \quad (5)$$

This weighting coefficient was subsequently multiplied with the product of affinity threshold (AT) and the affinity threshold scalar (ATS) to determine whether the new memory cell should be introduced into the memory cell pool. The revised pseudo-code for memory cell introduction used in EDC-AIRS algorithm is depicted in Figure 3.

The strategy that was delved into next is associated with the distribution characteristic of different data classes. This is vital according to the mechanism observed in the natural immune system, where lymph nodes are located in strategic positions – producing antibodies that could detect and eradicate the foreign antigens more efficiently. The spatial independency of the lymph nodes [7] and the circulatory networks in the immune system is of significant importance as it enables decentralized immune defense while protecting the human body in a global fashion. Therefore, if the distribution of different data classes differs by too much, this could indicate that the location at which the antibodies are produced (i.e. the position of the lymph nodes) would need to be adjusted so that the antibodies produced could detect and eradicate the antigens found in each data class in a more efficient manner. On the contrary, if the distribution of different data classes is near symmetry, this could indicate that no additional lymph nodes are required for more efficient neutralization of antigens; mitigating the required search effort as a result. This was empowered within the EDC-AIRS algorithm by having an independent set of parameters for evolving the memory cells if the distribution similarity between the data classes was below an empirically derived threshold, known as the Affinity Threshold Similarity Ratio (ATSR). Otherwise, a common set of parameters was used for all data classes. The ATSR was calculated by first computing the affinity threshold (i.e. the average affinity value over all training data) associated with each data class.

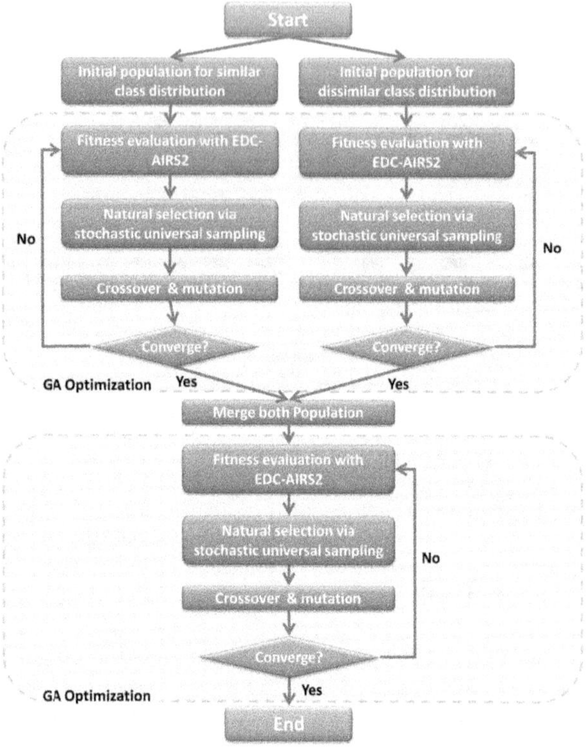

Figure 5: Proposed Methodology for Optimization of Parameter Set for Multiclass Classification Problems

Both similar and dissimilar populations were initialized and optimized concurrently. Upon convergence, these populations were merged and re-optimized by GA.

After which, the minimum affinity threshold found among the different data classes was divided by the maximum affinity threshold found. The mathematical expression is given below:

$$ATSR = \frac{\boldsymbol{min}_{i=1,\dots,C}(\boldsymbol{affinity}_{\boldsymbol{threshold}_i})}{\boldsymbol{max}_{j=1,\dots,C}(\boldsymbol{affinity}_{\boldsymbol{threshold}_j})} \quad (6)$$

where C is the total number of classes. This provides a yardstick to determine how similar the distributions of different data classes were. The parameters that orchestrate the evolution, survival and existence of the memory cells include the total resources, affinity threshold scalar (ATS), $\text{Radius}_{\text{density}}$ and $\text{Radius}_{\text{max}}$ parameters. Therefore, these parameters were duplicated and optimized independently for each data class if the ATSR computed for the dataset was below the pre-defined threshold value. All parameters were optimized using Genetic Algorithm (GA) [8], a search heuristic that imitates the process of natural evolution. The optimization algorithm was developed using MATLAB GA toolbox [9] and was executed in parallel over a high performance computer (HPC) cluster.

Figure 4 and 5 illustrate the canonical flow of the proposed methodology used for binary and multiclass classification problems respectively. For binary classification problem, we assume either a similar or dissimilar distribution based on the calculated ATSR and optimize that parameter set only (i.e. distinct parameter set for each data class if the computed ATSR is below the pre-defined threshold and a common parameter set if ATSR is above the pre-defined threshold). In contrast, both similar and dissimilar distributions were assumed for multiclass classification problems. In other words, both set of parameters were optimized concurrently by GA for multiclass datasets. Upon convergence of both runs (i.e. no improvement after 10 generations or the maximum number of generations has been reached), both the populations were merged and re-optimized by GA once again.

Finally, the ability to adapt to the characteristics of the data was performed by mimicking the genetic recombination and somatic hyper-mutation of gene segments scattered along the chromosome of the genome when forming a natural antibody. This process produces highly specific surface receptors of B-Cell necessary to recognize and bind to a certain type of antigen (that possess distinct structure). From a computational perspective, this was achieved through feature selection where a subset of informative features, that could capture the true patterns underlying the particular dataset, was selected for the learning process. GA was selected to perform this feature selection task as it has the potential to generate the optimal feature subset [10]. The GA parameters were determined experimentally and kept constant between benchmarks. The setup details of GA are as follow: population size: 100; maximum generation: 100; natural selection: stochastic universal sampling; crossover type: discrete recombination; crossover probability: 0.8; mutation rate: 1/P, where P is the number of parameters. The value of the EDC-AIRS parameters that was either assigned (i.e. given as a constant value) or tuned by GA (i.e. given as a range of value) are as follow: seed: 1; clonal rate: 10; hyper-mutation rate: 2; stimulation threshold: 0.9; initial memory pool size: [0, 200]; K-nearest neighbor value: [1, 15]; affinity threshold scalar: [0, 1]; total resource: [150, 300]; $Radius_{density}$ = [0, 3]; $Radius_{max}$ = [0, 3].

The performance of EDC-AIRS algorithm was evaluated with 4 benchmarking datasets, namely the Fisher's Iris, Ionosphere, Pima Indians Diabetes and Sonar Datasets. Hold-out validation was performed on the Ionosphere dataset while cross-validation was performed on the remaining 3 datasets. More specifically, the first 200 data items of the Ionosphere dataset was selected as the training data and was tested on the remaining 151 data items. As for the Iris, Pima Indians Diabetes and Sonar datasets, 5, 10 and 13-fold cross-validation was carried out respectively. The reason for choosing such validation strategy was to remain comparable to other experiments reported in the literature. Further details about the validation procedures applied on these benchmarking datasets can be found in [11].

3.2 Dataset

Four benchmarking datasets obtained from [12] were used to evaluate the performance of the novel EDC-AIRS algorithm. A brief description of these datasets is as follow:

1. Fisher's Iris Dataset – Consists of 4 features that describe the length and width of the sepal and petal. Three classes exist which represent the type of the iris plant (i.e. Iris Sentosa, Iris Vericolour and Iris Virginica). It has a sample size of 150 with 50 instances per class. The Iris Sentosa class is linearly separable from the other 2 classes while the Iris Vericolour and Iris Virginica classes are not linearly separable from each other.
2. Ionosphere Dataset – A binary class classification problem that contains 351 instances and 34 features. The 2 classes represent "good" or "bad" radar returns. The "good" radar returns refer to those that show some types of structure in the ionosphere while "bad" radar returns have their signals passed through the ionosphere.
3. Pima Indians Diabetes Dataset – Patients in this dataset are all females who are at least 21 years of age and are of Pima Indian heritage. It is a binary class classification problem that aims to distinguish between patients tested positive for diabetes and those who are not. It contains 768 instances and 8 features.
4. Sonar Dataset – The objective of this experiment is to determine whether an object is a mine (metal) or rock by bouncing sonar signal off the object at various angles and conditions. It contains 208 instances and 60 features.

In order to investigate on how different data class distribution affects the performance of the classification algorithm, several additional benchmarking datasets were acquired from [12]. Both similar and dissimilar distributions among the data classes were assumed for these datasets. Experiments were then conducted using these 10 datasets, with different degree of data class distribution (as determined by the computed ATSR value), to determine the impact of data class distribution on the algorithm's classification performance.

Table 1: Empirical Experiments with ATSR based on Datasets with Different Data Class Distribution

Measurement	Ionosphere	Iris	Wine	ks_yr50611	MAGIC	Pima Indians Diabetes	Hill-Valley	Bupa-Liver Disorder	Sonar	Statlog Heart
#Instances	200	100	178	270	19020	768	606	345	208	270
#Attributes	34	4	13	253	10	8	100	6	60	13
#Classes	2	3	3	2	2	2	2	2	2	2
#Class1 Instances	99	50	59	135	12332	268	305	145	97	120
#Class2 Instances	101	50	71	135	6688	500	301	200	111	150
#Class3 Instances	-	50	48	-	-	-	-	-	-	-
Validation Type	Holdout	5-CV	LOO	10-CV	5-CV	10-CV	Holdout	10-CV	13-CV	10-CV
Class 1 AT	0.437	0.106	0.162	0.308	0.160	0.217	0.121	0.157	0.271	0.427
Class 2 AT	0.266	0.129	0.223	0.408	0.209	0.183	0.107	0.167	0.283	0.408
Class 3 AT	-	0.152	0.185	-	-	-	-	-	-	-
Overall AT	0.371	0.288	0.266	0.366	0.187	0.202	0.114	0.164	0.283	0.448
ATSR	**0.609**	**0.698**	**0.727**	**0.756**	**0.764**	**0.842**	**0.885**	**0.937**	**0.957**	**0.957**
Acc. for Similar Distribution	96.7%	99.0%	98.9%	65.9%	**83.1%**	**77.3%**	**56.3%**	**69.9%**	**88.5%**	**84.8%**
Acc. for Dissimilar Distribution	**97.4%**	**99.6%**	**99.6%**	**67.0%**	82.8%	77.1%	55.7%	69.6%	87.0%	83.7%

Accuracy (Acc.) was used to evaluate how datasets with varying degree of data class distribution affects the performance of the algorithm. The dataset 'ks_yr50611', which uses the CHS dataset, predicts the occurrence of MI (from year 6 to 11) based on a balanced case-control sample obtained in year 5. AT means affinity threshold, CV denotes cross-validation and LOO refers to leave-one-out cross-validation.

Table 2: Classification Performance of the Benchmarking Datasets with Different Issues Addressed

Experiment	Description	Iris	Ionosphere	Pima Indians Diabetes	Sonar
1	AIRS2	96.0%	95.6%	74.2%	84.9%
2	GA-AIRS2	98.7%	97.4%	**77.3%**	86.5%
3	Density	98.7%	96.7%	**77.3%**	88.5%
4	Density & Distribution	**99.6%**	97.4%	**77.3%**	88.5%
5	Density, Distribution and Characteristics (EDC-AIRS)	**99.6%**	**98.0%**	**77.3%**	**90.9%**

Using GA-AIRS2 as the base algorithm, the techniques described in experiments 3, 4 and 5 are implemented respectively.

A succinct description of these datasets is as follow:

1. Wine Dataset – Contains results obtained from the chemical analysis of 3 different cultivars grown in the same region in Italy. It is a tri-nary classification problem that consists of 178 instances and 13 features.
2. Magic Dataset – This dataset, obtained from the Major Atmospheric Gamma Imaging Cherenkov (MAGIC) Telescope project, is a Monte Carlo generated data that aims to simulate the registration of high energy gamma particles in a ground-based atmospheric Cherenkov gamma telescope. It is a binary class classification problem which contains 19020 instances and 10 features.
3. Hill-Valley Dataset – This dataset consists of 606 instances, 100 features and 2 classes. Each instance represents 100 data points. When plotted (in the given order) on a 2-dimensional graph, the resultant plot would represent either a hill (a "bump" in the terrain) or a valley (a "dip" in the terrain).
4. Bupa Liver Disorder Dataset – This dataset contains examination results (e.g. quantity of alcoholic beverages consumed per day and blood tests) of males which are used to investigate liver disorders. It has a total of 345 instances and 6 features.
5. Statlog Heart Dataset – Investigation of the presence or absence of heart disease in an individual is carried out based on various medical diagnoses. This result is dictated in this dataset, which contains 270 instances and 13 features.
6. Cardiovascular Health Study (CHS) Dataset – This dataset, as described in [13], is an epidemiology study of risk factors for cardiovascular diseases in elderly aged 65 and above.

Table 3: Performance Comparison of Different Classification Algorithms – Modified from [3]

	Iris		Ionosphere		Pima Indians Diabetes		Sonar	
Rank	Algorithm	Acc	Algorithm	Acc	Algorithm	Acc	Algorithm	Acc
1	Grobian (rough)	100%	3-NN + Simplex	98.7%	Logdisc	77.7%	TAP MFT Bayesian	92.3%
2	**EDC-AIRS**	**99.6%**	**EDC-AIRS**	**98.0%**	IncNet	77.6%	**EDC-AIRS**	**90.9%**
					DIPOL92	77.6%		
3	SSV	98.0%	3-NN	96.7%	**EDC-AIRS**	**77.3%**	Nave MFT Bayesian	90.4%
	C-MLP2LN	98.0%	IB3	96.7%	Linear Disc. Analysis	77.5 – 77.2%	SVM	90.4%
	PVM 2 rules	98.0%					Best 2-layer MLP + BP, 12 hidden	90.4%
4	PVM 1 rule	97.3%	MLP + BP	96.0%	SMART	76.8%	AIRS2	84.9%
					GTO DT (5xCV)	76.8%		
5	AIRS	96.7%	AIRS2	95.6%	ASI	76.6%	MLP+BP, 12 hidden	84.7%
	FuNe-I	96.7%						
	NEFCLASS	96.7%						
6	AIRS2	96.0%	AIRS	94.9%	Fischer Disc. Analysis	76.5%	MLP+BP, 24 hidden	84.5%
	CART	96.0%	C4.5	94.9%				
7	FUNN	95.7%	RIAC	94.6%	MLP+BP	76.4%	1-NN, Manhanttan	84.2%
8			SVM	93.2%	LVQ	75.8%	AIRS	84.0%
					LFC	75.8%		
9			FSM + rotation	92.8%	RBF	75.7%	FSM	83.6%
10			1-NN	92.1%	kNN, k=22, Manh	75.5%		
					MML	75.5%		
					NB	75.5 – 73.8%		
…					… …			
n					AIRS2	74.2%		
n+1					AIRS	74.1%		

'Acc' denotes the classification accuracy.

The cohort consists of elderly subjects from four U.S. communities, namely Forsyth County, North Carolina; Sacramento County, California; Washington County, Maryland; and Pittsburgh, Pennsylvania. Data collected in year 5 of the CHS study was utilized. The balanced case-control sample size consists of 270 instances and 253 features. It is a binary class classification problem (i.e. with or without myocardial infarction).

4. EXPERIMENTAL RESULTS

EDC-AIRS algorithm was developed by extending AIRS2 algorithm. Three areas of optimization were carried out, each addressing an aspect of the phenomenon observed in the natural immune system (i.e. the concentration, distribution and characteristics of the antigens). In order to better generate a set of representative memory cells, it is necessary to empirically determine the ATSR threshold first. To perform this investigation, 10 datasets with different degree of data class distribution were evaluated. The ATSR value of these datasets ranges from 0.609 to 0.957, where a lower value indicates that the distribution of the data classes differs by a larger degree. Both classification with a common set of parameter (assuming similar distribution among data classes) and a distinct set of parameters for each data class (assuming dissimilar distribution among data classes) were performed. Based on the results shown in Table 1, it is indicative that with an ATSR value of 0.756 and below, a distinct parameter set for each data class is capable of achieving a higher accuracy. Therefore, an ATSR threshold of 0.76 was used for the rest of the experiments.

The performance of the proposed EDC-AIRS algorithm was evaluated using 4 benchmarking datasets. The algorithm was evaluated 3 times with consistent classification result obtained each time (i.e. standard deviation of 0). The classification accuracy for the incremental implementation of the 3 aforementioned mechanisms is given in Table 2. Baseline comparison was made with GA-AIRS2 algorithm - an AIRS2 algorithm with its parameters tuned via GA. It is noteworthy that GA-AIRS2 performs better than AIRS2 for all 4 benchmarking datasets.

With the implementation to address the density issue (Table 2 – experiment 3), ameliorated performance was observed for the Sonar dataset. However, the performance on the Ionosphere dataset exacerbates while the performance for the rest of the datasets remains comparable. With the additional implementation to amortize the impact of different distribution exhibited by each data class (Table 2 – experiment 4), the deterioration in performance observed previously on the Ionosphere dataset vanished. Moreover, the accuracy obtained for the Iris dataset improved while the accuracy for both Pima Indians Diabetes and Sonar datasets remain the same. Finally, when the characteristic of the dataset was delved into (Table 2 – experiment 5), further improvement in accuracy for Ionosphere and Sonar datasets was obtained. Accuracy for Iris and Pima Indians Diabetes datasets remains unchanged, probably due to the limited features available for selection (i.e. 4 and 8 features respectively).

A comparison of EDC-AIRS algorithm with other well-known classifiers (as presented in [3]) is provided in Table 3. The EDC-AIRS algorithm has shown promising results, clinching a place in the top 3 positions for all the datasets evaluated.

5. Discussion

We have developed an immune-inspired supervised classification algorithm called EDC-AIRS that have shown improved learning and classification capability. The success of the algorithm is primarily due to the recognition of the importance of additional immune metaphors, namely the ability to adapt to the different concentration, distribution and characteristics of the antigens. However, the EDC-AIRS algorithm did not achieve ameliorated performance for all classification problems investigated in this study (e.g. Pima Indian Diabetes dataset). This is not surprising as every learning algorithm has an inductive bias that would work reasonably well for some, but not all, datasets or application domains [1]. This phenomenon has been described as the selective superiority problem [14].

The AIRS2 parameters reported in [3] has been tuned manually. This apparently hinders the true potential of the AIRS2 algorithm. As demonstrated, the employment of GA to optimize the AIRS2 parameters (i.e. GA-AIRS2) improved the classification accuracy (ranging from 1.6% to 3.1% improvement) for all the 4 benchmarking datasets investigated. Clearly, this indicates that optimization of parameters with an evolutionary computing algorithm (e.g. GA) that is capable of dynamically searching through the defined search space is invaluable in discovering the optimal parameter setting. This is especially so when dealing with datasets from various application domains where the patterns that underlie these data would be very different, causing exhaustive manual tuning of the parameters to flounder as it would be very time consuming to carry out this task.

The EDC-AIRS algorithm, when juxtaposed with the AIRS2 algorithm, has several distinctive strengths when learning the underlying patterns within the data. Firstly, by adopting a mechanism to handle the different data density exhibited at different regions, it is capable of producing representative memory cells that could better characterize and capture the real data pattern. As a result, it is at an advantage when applied on datasets (such as Sonar dataset) that have data density which tends to fluctuate at different regions. Secondly, the EDC-AIRS algorithm is more capable at dealing with difference in distribution among data classes, generating representative memory cells for each data class. The ability to do so is important because it is unlikely for different data classes to have the same distribution and even more unlikely for a classifier to recognize and robustly adapt to such deviation without explicitly allowing for it. Efforts were therefore taken in this work to calculate the ATSR value and to determine whether to optimize a common or distinct parameter set. Ten datasets from diverse domains with different characteristics were used to evaluate the importance of implementing this technique. Results shown that for datasets with ATSR value lesser than 0.76 (e.g. Iris and Ionosphere datasets), it is more desirable to have a distinct parameter set for each data class. The need to compute the ATSR value and differentiate them into similar or dissimilar distribution is not an essential step but is advantageous to do so. This is because it is theoretically possible for GA to tune the parameter set meant for dissimilar distribution to one suitable for similar distribution. However, it is computationally intensive to do so. Therefore, by performing this simple step of differentiation, it can help to alleviate the complexity involved when tuning the parameters with GA. This complexity is introduced by the (linear) increase in the number of parameters that needs to be tuned, which in turn contributed to an exponential increase in the search space. This makes the task of discovering the optimal value for the parameters very challenging. This problem is commonly referred to as the 'curse of dimensionality' [15].

Finally, the EDC-AIRS algorithm is capable of selecting features that are highly informative and relevant. This avoids some of the difficulties when dealing with datasets (e.g. Ionosphere and Sonar datasets) that have irrelevant or redundant features which often jeopardize the algorithm's ability to learn and generalize. Moreover, it has the crucial advantage of identifying important features that best associate with an outcome, building a parsimonious classification model as a result. This property is highly desirable in accordance to the law of parsimony (Occam's razor principle [16]) where a simpler model with minimal complexity is preferred.

When EDC-AIRS algorithm was benchmarked with 4 datasets, promising results were obtained consistently. It outperforms AIRS2 algorithm in all the 4 cases. The increase in classification accuracy is 3.6%, 2.4%, 3.1% and 6% for Iris, Ionosphere, Pima Indians Diabetes and Sonar dataset respectively. This suggests that EDC-AIRS algorithm is a robust learner that is capable of adapting to different profound data patterns and structures.

6. CONCLUSION

Further inspired by the characteristics of the natural immune system, we have developed an adaptive and robust supervised classification algorithm called the EDC-AIRS algorithm. The performance of the proposed algorithm was evaluated with 4 benchmarking datasets. When ranked with other classifiers, the classification performance of EDC-AIRS algorithm is in the top 3 positions for all the datasets evaluated. Ameliorated performance achieved by the algorithm signifies the importance of empowering an algorithm with the ability to independently adapt to the distinct density, distribution and characteristics of each data class. However, this approach does not guarantee improved performance for all classification problems in face of the selective superiority problem.

7. ACKNOWLEDGMENTS

Darwin Tay would like to express his sincere gratitude for his scholarship funding provided by the Nanyang Technological University-Imperial College London Joint PhD programme.

The authors wish to acknowledge the support of The Engineering and Physical Science Research Council (EPSRC) in this study.

Dr. Chueh Loo Poh and Darwin Tay would also like to thank the Ministry of Education (Singapore) for the support in this work.

8. REFERENCES

[1] A. Freitas, and J. Timmis, "Revisiting the Foundations of Artificial Immune Systems for Data Mining", *IEEE Transactions on Evolutionary Computation,* vol. 11, no. 4, pp. 521-540, 2007.

[2] L. N. D. Castro, and J. Timmis, *Artificial Immune Systems: A New Computational Intelligence Approach.* Springer, 2002, pp. 398.

[3] A. Watkins, J. Timmis, and L. Boggess, "Artificial Immune Recognition System (AIRS): An Immune-Inspired Supervised Learning Algorithm", *Genetic Programming and Evolvable Machines,* vol. 5, no. 3, pp. 291-317, 2004.

[4] J. Timmisa1, and M. Nealb, "A Resource Limited Artificial Immune System for Data Analysis", *Knowledge-Based Systems,* vol. 14, pp. 121-130, 2001.

[5] A. Watkins and L. Boggess, "A New Classifier Based on Resource Limited Artificial Immune Systems", *Proceedings of Congress on Evolutionary Computation, 2002,* Honolulu, USA: 2002.

[6] J. Brownlee, "Artificial Immune Recognition System (AIRS). A Review and Analysis", Technical Report No. 1-02, Centre for Intelligent Systems and Complex Processes (CISCP), Faculty of Information and Communication Technologies (ICT), Swinburne University of Technology (SUT), Victoria, Australia: 2005

[7] M. Moses and S. Banerjee, "Biologically Inspired Design Principles for Scalable, Robust, Adaptive, Decentralized Search and Automated Response (RADAR)", *IEEE Symposium on Artificial Life (ALIFE),* 2011.

[8] J. Holland, "Genetic Algorithms", *Sci Am,* pp. 66-72, 1992.

[9] A.J. Chipperfield and P.J. Fleming, "The MATLAB Genetic Algorithm Toolbox", *IEE Colloquium on Applied Control Techniques Using MATLAB,* 1995.

[10] C. L. Huanga, and C. J. Wangb, "A GA-based Feature Selection and Parameters Optimization for Support Vector Machines", *Expert Systems with Applications,* vol. 31, no. 2, pp. 231-240, 2006.

[11] A. Watkins, "AIRS: A Resource Limited Artificial Immune Classifier," Master's Thesis, Mississippi State University, United States, 2001.

[12] C.L. Blake and C.J. Merz, "UCI Repository of Machine Learning Databases," Available at: http://www.ics.uci.edu/~mlearn/MLRepository.html. Accessed 8/11/2012.

[13] L. Fried, N. Borhani, P. Enright, and C. Furberg *et al.*, "The Cardiovascular Health Study: Design and Rationale", *Ann Epidemiol.,* vol. 1, no. 3, pp. 263-276, 1991.

[14] C. Brodley, "Addressing the Selective Superiority Problem: Automatic Algorithm/Model Class Selection", *In Proc. 10th Machine Learning Conf.,* 1993.

[15] R. Bellman, *Adaptive Control Processes.* Princeton New Jersey: Princeton University Press, 1961, pp. 274.

[16] A. Blumer, A. Ehrenfeucht, D. Haussler, and M. K. Warmuth, "Occam's Razor", *Information Processing Letters,* vol. 24, no. 6, pp. 377-380, 1987.

Self Organizing Classifiers and Niched Fitness

Danilo V. Vargas
Graduate School of Information Science and Electrical Engineering, Kyushu University
Fukuoka, Japan
vargas@cig.ees.kyushu-u.ac.jp

Hirotaka Takano
Faculty of Information Science and Electrical Engineering, Kyushu University
Fukuoka, Japan
takano@cig.ees.kyushu-u.ac.jp

Junichi Murata
Faculty of Information Science and Electrical Engineering, Kyushu University
Fukuoka, Japan
murata@cig.ees.kyushu-u.ac.jp

ABSTRACT

Learning classifier systems are adaptive learning systems which have been widely applied in a multitude of application domains. However, there are still some generalization problems unsolved. The hurdle is that fitness and niching pressures are difficult to balance. Here, a new algorithm called Self Organizing Classifiers is proposed which faces this problem from a different perspective. Instead of balancing the pressures, both pressures are separated and no balance is necessary. In fact, the proposed algorithm possesses a dynamical population structure that self-organizes itself to better project the input space into a map. The niched fitness concept is defined along with its dynamical population structure, both are indispensable for the understanding of the proposed method. Promising results are shown on two continuous multi-step problems. One of which is yet more challenging than previous problems of this class in the literature.

Categories and Subject Descriptors

I.2.11 [**Artificial Intelligence**]: Distributed Artificial Intelligence—*intelligent agents, languages and structures, multi-agent systems*; I.2.6 [**Artificial Intelligence**]: Learning

General Terms

Algorithms, Performance

Keywords

Self Organization, Self Organizing Systems, Self Organizing Map, Learning Classifier Systems, Reinforcement Learning, Structured Evolutionary Algorithms

1. INTRODUCTION

The importance of classifiers to maximize their reward (decrease the error in supervised learning problems or increase reward in reinforcement learning problems) with at the same time specializing to their best suited position (niching) were demonstrated by many articles about learning classifier systems (LCS) [29, 22]. Throughout the LCS history, there has been an initial focus on strength based systems (e.g., ZCS [33]) which highlight the focus on reward. Later, however, it was realized that much of the niching capability may be lost in strength based systems, because over-general classifiers dominate and high payoff niches become crowded. Accuracy based systems, on the other hand, (e.g., XCS [34, 10], XCSF [35]) try a middle ground between niching and reward. By rewarding the accuracy of the reward prediction, accuracy based systems have justifiably better niching than strength based systems (the accuracy-based fitness is more uniform over different niches). For this reason, recent articles have focused more on accuracy-based systems.

However, it is known for some time that XCS systems (and in general, accuracy-based systems) may have problems with generalization [19, 8]. Solutions have been proposed for some environments [21], but the hindrance is that different pressures are acting together and balancing them properly for every environment is difficult [13]. In other words, the balance between specialized (niched) and generic classifiers is still unsolved.

This article propose to face the dilemma from a different perspective. What if we separate completely the niching problem from the fitness problem? Suppose we could divide the input space into small niches [1] and evolve the solutions for each niche. By doing this, the fitness for each niche can be strength based because the niches are small and independently defined (not defined by the chromosome and thus not affected by evolution). Moreover, there is not any balance necessary, since niching and fitness pressures were separated from each other.

But then, two questions need to be solved:

1. How can we divide the input space automatically and compactly?

2. How can we compare individuals? Notice that the fitness defined above is relative to the niche!

The answer to the first question lies in using Self Organizing Map (SOM). Self Organizing Map is an unsupervised

[1]Concerning the proposed method, the term niche follows the Hutchinsonian niche definition [15]. Hutchinsonian niche is an n-dimensional hyper-volume composed of environmental features.

GECCO'13, July 6–10, 2013, Amsterdam, The Netherlands.

artificial neural network [18]. It is an algorithm capable of projecting high dimensional spaces into a map. In other words, by using SOM, a multidimensional input space can be divided automatically into the cells of a compact map. In fact, the projection done preserves the topological properties and retains many other relevant information (e.g., data frequency) of the input space.

The second question has a simple answer: they can not be compared. With relative fitness, there is not any easy way of comparing individuals from different niches. Therefore, regarding the fitness selection, the evolutionary algorithm (EA) should be constrained to each niche. Genetic operators, however, are not constrained and may benefit from any population structure present.

Actually, the proposed approach is evaluated at two continuous multi-step problems with promising results. The experiments conducted on two continuous labyrinths demonstrate the capabilities of the proposed approach. One of which is more challenging than the continuous multi-step problems solved by state of the art LCS.

2. LEARNING CLASSIFIER SYSTEMS IN MULTI-STEP AND/OR CONTINUOUS PROBLEMS

Learning classifier systems are evolutionary based systems capable of solving problems by the mutual competition and/or cooperation of their solutions. There is a wide and diverse literature. Here we will confine to a brief review of LCS applied to multi-step and/or continuous problems. For a detailed review of the literature, please refer to [29, 22].

LCS with continuous actions were applied to many problems. To begin with, XCSF has been applied to function approximation [35, 9, 28]. Other works in function approximation include the LCS with fuzzy logic [30, 6, 11], neural-based LCS algorithms [5, 6] and genetic programming-based [17]. The success of LCS also span the control of robotic arms [25, 7] and navigation problems [4, 14].

However, applications to multi-step problems with continuous actions restrict to the mobile robot in a corridor [4] and the empty room with noise [14]. Complex multi-step problems were solved only for **discrete outputs** [20].

3. STRUCTURED EVOLUTIONARY ALGORITHMS

Structured evolutionary algorithms does not possess a panmictic population. Instead they organize the individuals into a structured population [27, 1].

Two types of structured EAs will be given as examples which are somewhat related to the structure of the proposed method.

The first type is island models (also called distributed genetic algorithms) [3]. Figure 1 shows the structure. Basically, the population is divided into a number of subpopulations ("islands") with few genetic information exchanged between them.

The second type, cellular algorithms are structured evolutionary algorithms where individuals are usually positioned in a vertex of a lattice graph (Figure 2 shows a common cellular structure). They interact solely with adjacent individuals defined by the a neighborhood function [23, 2].

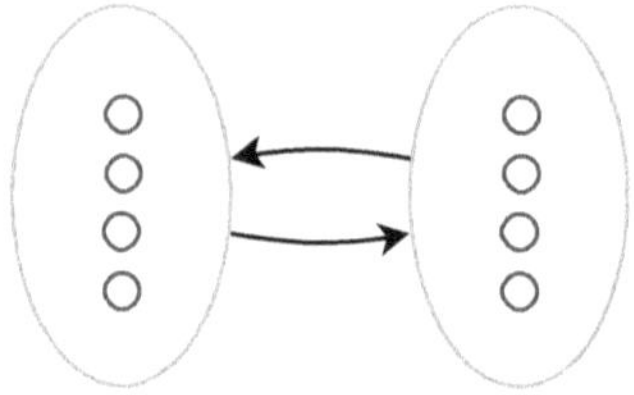

Figure 1: Island model structure. Arrows indicate the infrequent immigration procedure, the circles are the individuals and the oval shapes are the subpopulations.

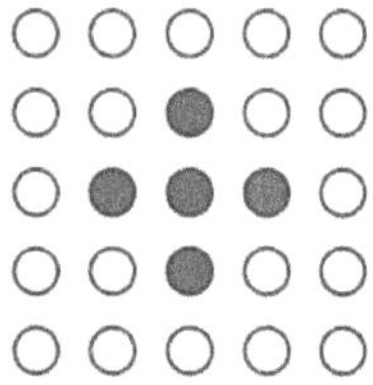

Figure 2: Cellular algorithm structure. Shaded area indicates an example of neighborhood for the central individual.

4. NEW CONCEPTS

First, in order to present the proposed method, it is necessary to explain some new concepts and their related literature.

4.1 Niched Fitness

A fitness which is relative to a given place or circumstance is called **niched fitness**. Thus, it does not possess a meaning when compared with another fitness out of this place or circumstance.

This is a new concept. At first glance, it may appear unwise to use niched fitness, because the comparison between individuals from different niches becomes impossible. But there is the benefit of avoiding competition between tasks different in nature. Therefore, every niche existence is protected from other more rewarding and/or more voluminous and/or more frequently accessed niches.

Moreover, niched fitness can be thought as a multiobjectivization procedure [24], because each niched fitness becomes a separate fitness. In fact, niching and multi-objective search are related subjects. The Pareto front created allows the existence of multiple non-dominated individuals (different niches). We consider this a relevant aspect which deserves to be mentioned. The remaining of this article, however, will ignore this aspect and treat the search as a single objective one.

4.2 SOM Population

This Section aims to define the SOM population concept. SOM population is a 2D grid with each cell in the grid having a subpopulation. Moreover, the 2D grid is a projection map which is not static, i.e., it is part of a SOM which is always self-organizing itself. Figure 3 illustrates the SOM population (SOM's weight vectors are excluded for simplification). Generally speaking, this structure can be seen as a mixture of both island models and cellular algorithms, with

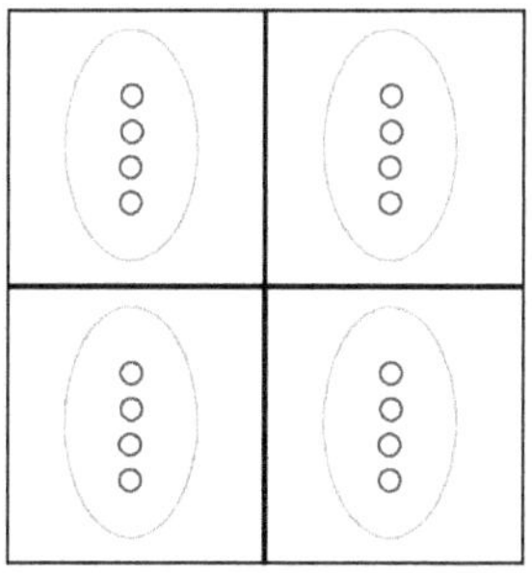

Figure 3: SOM population structure. A self organizing map grid with populations inside each cell.

the additional feature that the structure also changes its properties in relation to the input.

The SOM population's behavior is described below. When an input is given to a SOM population, a competition takes place between the cells of the map. The cell which is closer wins the competition to the input and the SOM cells in the neighborhood are updated (the update make the SOM cell's weight vectors get closer to the input). Then, an individual inside the winner cell acts on the environment and is consequently evaluated by a subsequent reward. The individual chosen to act inside the winner cell is based on a selection procedure which is algorithm specific. (here we use a random selection procedure, see Section 5).

5. SELF ORGANIZING CLASSIFIERS

Figure 4 shows a schematic of the overall procedure of **Self Organizing Classifiers** (SOC). It follows the classic schematic style used in ZCS, XCS and many other papers of the LCS literature [33]. Simple classifiers are used. They are made up of action parameters represented by an array of real numbers.

SOC uses a Q-learning based reinforcement scheme with niched fitness. The fitness update of each individual is done using the Widrow-Hoff rule [32]:

$$F = F + \eta(\hat{F} - F), \tag{1}$$

where η is the learning rate, F is the current fitness and $\hat{F}$ is a new fitness estimate. The fitness estimate of cell *cell* and classifier c which were activated at time $t-1$ is given by the following equation:

$$\hat{F}(c, cell)_{t-1} = R_{t-1} + \gamma \max_{c' \in cell'} \{F(c', cell')\}, \tag{2}$$

where R is the reward received, γ is the discount-factor and $\max_{c \in cell} \{F(t)\}$ is the maximum fitness of classifier c' inside the activated cell $cell'$ at the current cycle t.

Similar to learning classifier systems, to decrease computation resources, the structure of the SOM population is implemented as a single array of classifiers with a given numerosity indexed by the SOM population structure. In this manner, the numerosity is defined by the number of indexes a given individual possess.

This article uses a particular SOM population where the subpopulation inside each cell is divided into two groups: one of best individuals and the other of novel individuals. Best and novel individuals have a fixed size of β and ν respectively. Considering EA's cycle is an algorithm cycle when the EA is called, the following rules take place:

- Best individuals are the best fitted individuals inside the subpopulation in the last EA's cycle.
- Novel individuals are renewed every EA's cycle (the detailed process is described in the next Section).

The SOM population begins without any classifiers. Classifiers are created when the respective cell wins the competition inside the SOM. In one hand, novel individuals are created as random classifiers. On the other hand, best individuals, when possible, are set equal to another cell's best individuals from the neighborhood[2] which maximize $\frac{experience}{chebishevDistance^2}$. If not possible, best individuals are initialized in the same way as the novel individuals.

The system has, as usual in reinforcement learning, cycles of exploration and exploitation. Within the SOM's winning cell in a giving exploration or exploitation cycle a random individual from respectively the novel or best individuals are chosen to act. Moreover, cycles of exploration and exploitation are always alternated (a cycle of exploration is followed by an exploitation cycle and so on).

5.1 Evolution

For every cycle that a cell's individual acts, this cell has its experience counter increased. The evolutionary algorithm is called locally on each cell when the cell's experience is greater than ιS. Where S is the number of subpopulation individuals (novel plus best individuals) present on each cell. The parameter ι defines an experience per individual, above which they should have an accurate fitness evaluation.

By applying the evolutionary algorithm locally, it respects the niched fitness concept. Its procedure consists of sorting the individuals of the given cell according to their fitness. The current best β individuals substitute the previous best individuals and the remaining individuals are discarded (the index is removed and the individual numerosity decrease, if the numerosity reaches 0 it is deleted). Novel ν individuals are created using either:

1. Indexing - A copy from (index to) a randomly selected individual of the entire population;
2. Reproduction - Created by a genetic operator.

The two procedures above have equal probabilities.

Motivated by some comparison articles and robustness tests, the differential evolution is chosen as the genetic operator [26, 31, 16]. It compares well to even complex optimization algorithms (e.g., Estimation of Distribution Algorithms) [12]. The differential evolution's mutant vector is created by randomly choosing three vectors from the SOM's entire population of individuals (individuals with numerosity bigger than one are counted as one).

6. EXPERIMENTS

6.1 Environments

The experiments were conducted on both Empty Room and One-Wall Maze environments. They are respectively

[2]Neighborhood is defined as the cells within a Chebishev distance of less or equal to four

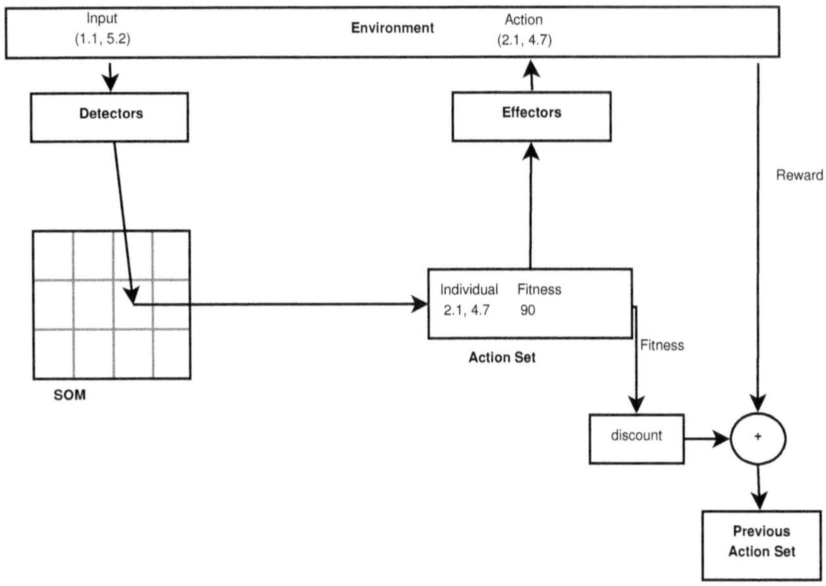

Figure 4: Self Organizing Classifier Schematic

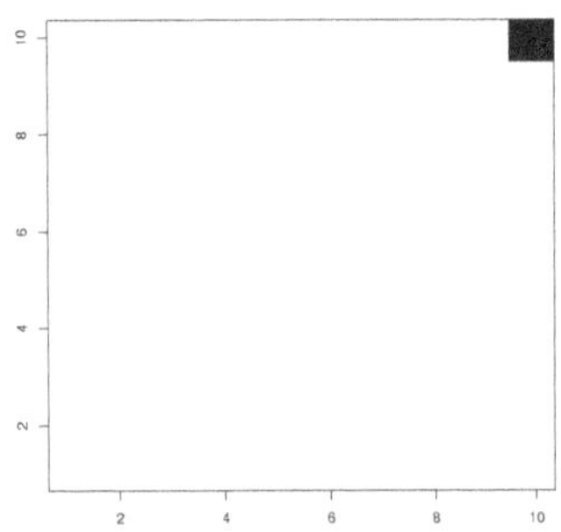

Figure 5: Empty room environment. The black position represents the goal.

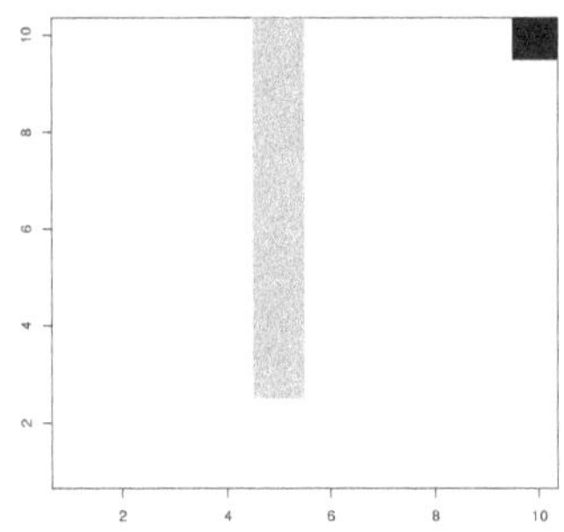

Figure 6: One-Wall Maze environment. Grey positions are obstacles and the black position is the goal.

depicted in Figures 5 and 6. All environments require continuous actions. The variable observed by the agent is the agent's position which is also continuous.

At every trial, the agent starts at a random position on the environment. Naturally, starting inside a wall is not possible. Reaching the goal would give the agent a reward of 1000, hitting an obstacle would return -20 and any other action would return -10. Additionally, agents can not move more than 1.0 in any direction. The collision system is simply implemented (which makes it harder than a real system). If an agent tries to move inside a wall, the system detects the infraction, sets the agent in the previous position and returns the reward. In other words, an agent constantly hitting the wall will not move at all. However, an agent that hits the limits of a maze will have its final position limited by the environment. Therefore, it is possible to move sideways when hitting the limit of the environment.

6.2 Settings and Design of Experiments

The parameters of the algorithm are fixed and described in Table 1. Here, it means the SOM iteration number, $chebyshevDistance()$ is the Chebyshev distance between the current cell and the cell which won the SOM's competition and $random(a, b)$ is a function which returns a uniform random value between a and b. The cells of the SOM are only updated if the neighborhood function multiplied by the learning restraint surpasses the cell update threshold.

Following the design of [20] the performance is computed as the average steps to reach the goal during the last 100 trials. The trials can not last more than 500 steps. Any trial which last more than 500 is terminated and a new trial is started with the agent, as usual, in a random position. All statistics, when not stated otherwise, are averaged over 20 experiments.

6.3 Empty Room

Empty Room is a well known problem, in continuous [14] as well as discrete action spaces [20]. The evaluation focus here is on the overall functionality of the system. Although not complicated in nature, this problem may expose strong instabilities and other undesired phenomena.

Figure 7 shows the average behavior obtained. To construct this figure, the action of the agent was sampled 100 times and averaged in a given environment area of size 1x1. The resulting matrix have a dimension of 10x10 averaged ac-

Table 1: Parameters

Differential Evolution	CR	0.2
	F	$random(0, 1)$
Self Organizing Map	Matrix Size	10×10
	Weight's initial value	$random(0, 1)$
	Learning restraint	$0.1(0.999999)^{it}$
	Neighborhood function	$\exp(-chebyshevDistance()^2)$
	Cell update threshold	0.005
Self Organizing Classifiers	η	0.2
	β	5
	ν	10
	ι	20
	γ	0.9
	$InitialFitness$	0

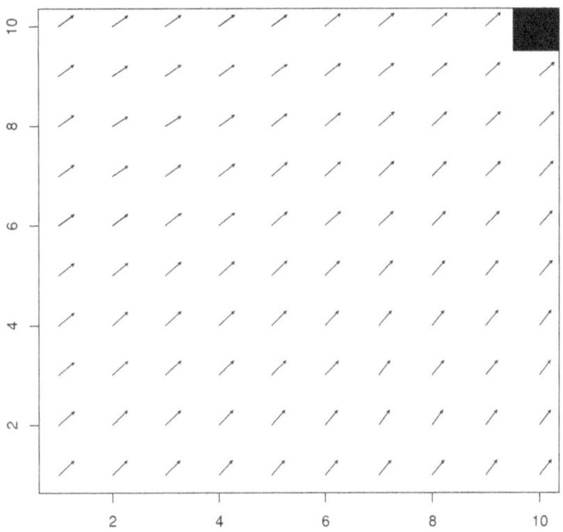

Figure 7: Behavior evolved in the Empty Room environment.

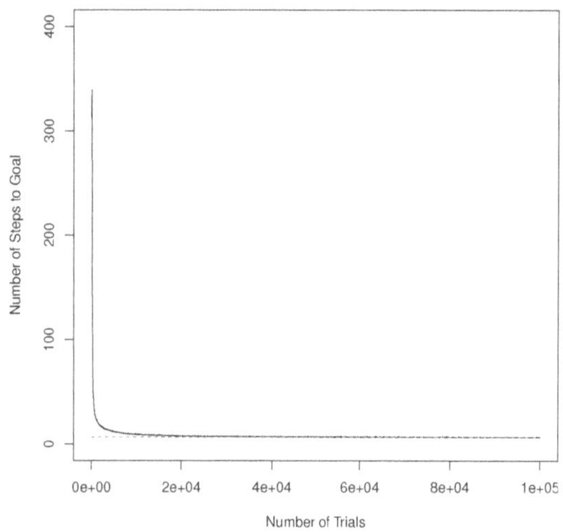

Figure 8: Performance over the Empty Room environment (continuous line). For guiding purposes a dashed line is drawn at 6.5 of distance to the x-coordinate.

tions. Subsequently, the matrices of 20 experiments in the same environment were averaged.

The SOC's developed behavior is optimal, in spite of the fact that inside the SOM structure each cell must arrive at the best solution (fitness is not global). The justification lies in the fact that the ability of the SOC algorithm to share and improve solutions between cells make the development very fast and stable. Figure 8 shows the performance. The fitness distribution is calculated in the same way as the matrix of actions, but instead of action vectors the maximum fitness of the cell is measured. The result is shown on Figure 9.

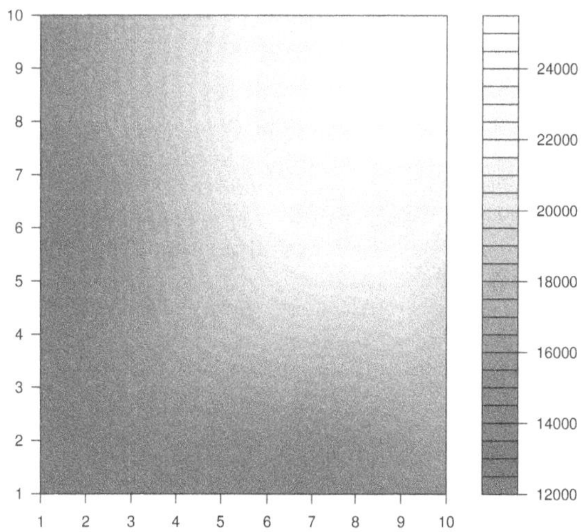

Figure 9: Average distribution of fitness in the Empty Room environment.

6.4 One-Wall Maze

This second problem is different from the previous one. It makes necessary the use of different actions for different places of the environment. Note that the classifiers used are very simple. Therefore, this experiment evaluates specifically the dynamical population structure's niching capabilities.

Figure 10 shows the behavior of the agent in the One-Wall Maze environment. This figure was obtained in the same manner of Figure 7.

One-Wall Maze is a difficult problem. Even so, the behavior observed is accurate and stable. This is justifiable by the SOM population capability of first self-organizing to the

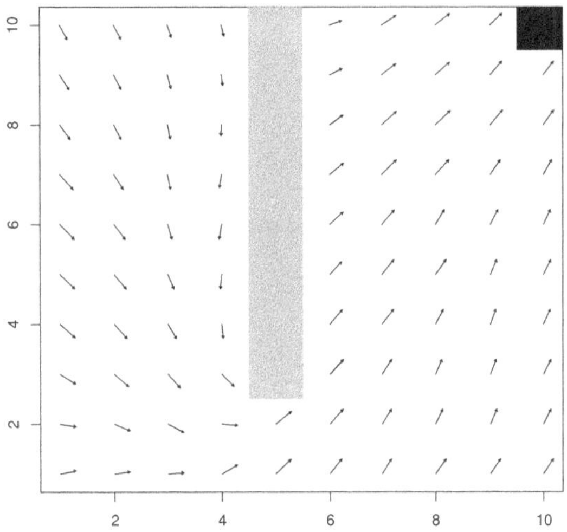

Figure 10: Behavior evolved in the One-Wall Maze environment.

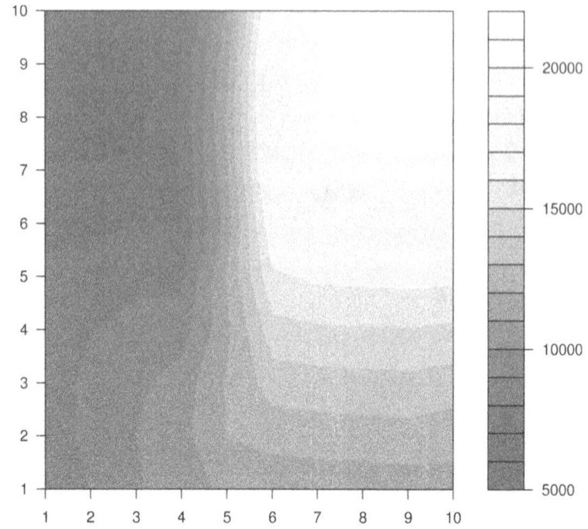

Figure 12: Average distribution of fitness in the One-Wall Maze environment.

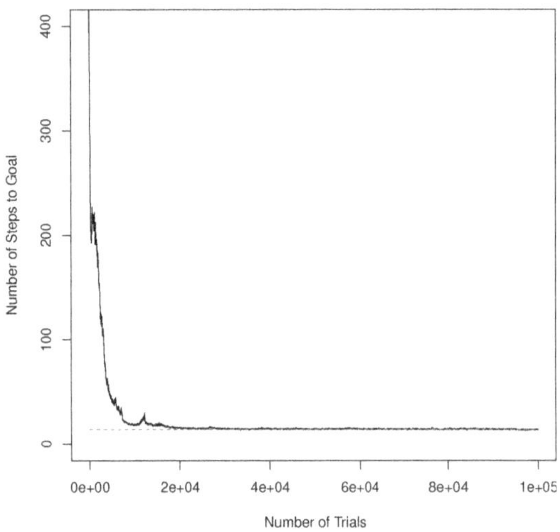

Figure 11: Performance over the One-Wall Maze environment (continuous line). Dashed-line is drawn for guiding purposes parallel to the x-coordinate at 14 **of distance.**

environment's input distribution. Projecting and dividing the input space respecting its topology. And secondly, the ability of developing different behavior at different parts of the space (niches) with their own subpopulation.

Note that the SOM used was initialized to values between zero and one as weight vectors. Therefore, it was not in any way biased to the environment's inputs range (environment values range from zero to ten). Additionally, Figures 11 and 12 show respectively the performance and fitness distribution.

6.5 Population Analysis

But what is the cost of running a SOC? Solving a problem is often not enough, it is required that a method uses reasonably its resources. The aim of this section is to evaluate briefly the population requirements of SOC. All tests are run over the One-Wall Maze.

Foremost, SOC's maximum possible population size can be computed by the following equation:

$$MaximumPopulationSize = cells * (\beta + \nu), \tag{3}$$

where $cells$ is the number of cells present in the SOM map. Taking the parameters found in Table 1 it is possible to compute a maximum population size of 1500 for the previous experiments. However, as shown in Figure 13 this value is never reached. The population grows rapidly to around 1100 and remains stable below this value.

Moreover, Figure 13 shows the population growth of two other variations of the same algorithm. Test A has $\beta = 2$ and $\nu = 5$ resulting in a maximum population size of 700, while Test B has a 7×7 SOM map and therefore having 735 of maximum population size. Note that they reach around 500 individuals and after that the population size remains approximately constant.

Figures 14 and 15 show respectively the behavior of Test A and Test B. Both achieve similar actions to the original algorithm with a bigger population. Although, Test A have places with high direction variations which result in vectors with smaller magnitude. This happens because smaller population sizes enable frequently accessed cells to evolve faster which makes even more infrequent the access of spots near the wall. Consequently, the SOM may not have any cells mapping those infrequent spots near the wall.

Tests A and B performance is also similar (see Figure 16). Actually, Tests A and B achieves the optimum faster than the original, because their populations are smaller, however, Test B presents small deviations from the optimum.

Thus, the cost in terms of population size is small. Besides, as shown above, smaller populations have similar results. Recall that a neural based LCS needed a maximum population size of 16000 individuals to solve a continuous Empty Room problem [14]. And XCS required on average 404 macroclassifiers to solve a similar problem though with **discrete output** called Side 10 [20]. Therefore, SOC's results are promising when compared with the literature.

7. CONCLUSIONS

This paper proposed the algorithm named Self Organizing

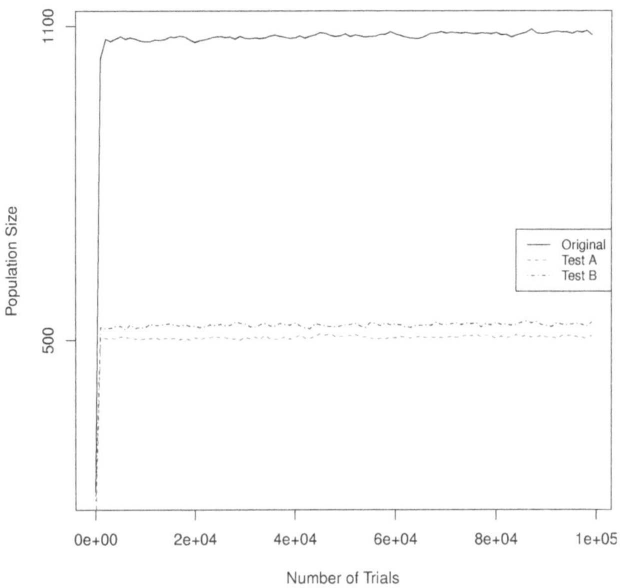

Figure 13: Population dynamics for the original and two additional tests with smaller maximum populations.

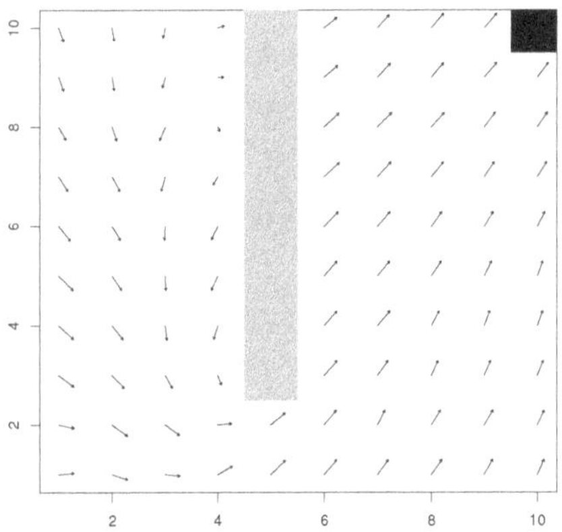

Figure 14: Behavior for the algorithm with a smaller population, i.e., $\beta = 2$ and $\nu = 5$ (Test A).

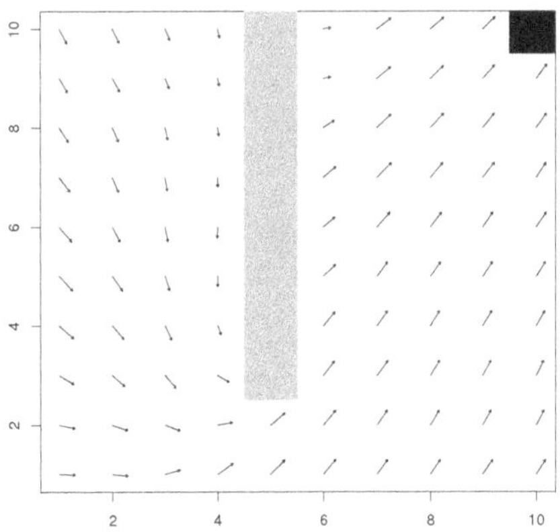

Figure 15: Behavior for the algorithm with a smaller population, i.e., a 7×7 SOM population (Test B).

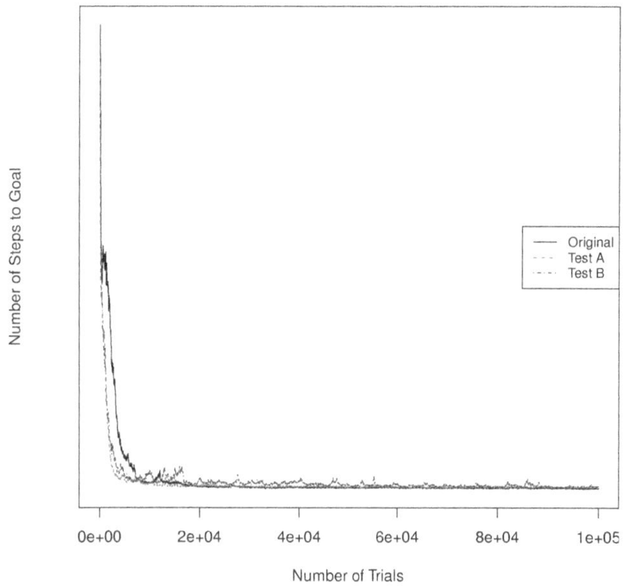

Figure 16: Performance comparison between the original parameters and the smaller population versions (Tests A and B).

Classifiers which possess a different perspective on how to face the balance of generalized and specialized classifiers.

We showed that with a self-organizing structured population, the separation of niching and fitness pressures is possible. Experiments on continuous multi-step problems showcased the capabilities of the approach. Note that this article presented a problem which is more difficult than previous continuous multi-step problems. This is just the first article about this type of algorithm and the difficulty of the problems solved shows a promising horizon for this line of algorithms.

Additionally, two new concepts were introduced:

- Niched Fitness - a fitness relative to the niche;
- SOM Population - a dynamical structured population based on the SOM's dynamics.

Both concepts are fundamental to understand the SOC algorithm.

Thus, with the promising results accomplished by the novel concepts and the algorithm introduced here, they will, hopefully, aid the development of other algorithms and theories specially in the area of genetics based machine learning or evolutionary computation in general.

8. REFERENCES

[1] E. Alba and M. Tomassini. Parallelism and evolutionary algorithms. *Evolutionary Computation, IEEE Transactions on*, 6(5):443–462, 2002.

[2] E. Alba and J. Troya. Cellular evolutionary algorithms: Evaluating the influence of ratio. In *Parallel Problem Solving from Nature PPSN VI*, pages 29–38. Springer, 2000.

[3] T. Belding. The distributed genetic algorithm revisited. In *Proceedings of the Sixth International Conference on Genetic Algorithms: University of*

Pittsburgh, July 15-19, 1995, page 114. Morgan Kaufmann Pub, 1995.

[4] A. Bonarini, C. Bonacina, and M. Matteucci. Fuzzy and crisp representations of real-valued input for learning classifier systems. *Learning Classifier Systems*, pages 107–124, 2000.

[5] L. Bull. On using constructivism in neural classifier systems. *Parallel problem solving from nature-PPSN VII*, pages 558–567, 2002.

[6] L. Bull and T. O'Hara. Accuracy-based neuro and neuro-fuzzy classifier systems. In *Proceedings of the Genetic and Evolutionary Computation Conference*, pages 905–911. Morgan Kaufmann Publishers Inc., 2002.

[7] M. Butz and O. Herbort. Context-dependent predictions and cognitive arm control with XCSF. In *Proceedings of the 10th annual conference on Genetic and evolutionary computation*, pages 1357–1364. ACM, 2008.

[8] M. Butz, T. Kovacs, P. Lanzi, and S. Wilson. Toward a theory of generalization and learning in XCS. *Evolutionary Computation, IEEE Transactions on*, 8(1):28–46, 2004.

[9] M. Butz, P. Lanzi, and S. Wilson. Function approximation with XCS: Hyperellipsoidal conditions, recursive least squares, and compaction. *Evolutionary Computation, IEEE Transactions on*, 12(3):355–376, 2008.

[10] M. Butz and S. Wilson. An algorithmic description of XCS. *Advances in Learning Classifier Systems*, pages 267–274, 2001.

[11] J. Casillas, B. Carse, and L. Bull. Fuzzy-XCS: A michigan genetic fuzzy system. *Fuzzy Systems, IEEE Transactions on*, 15(4):536–550, 2007.

[12] S. García, D. Molina, M. Lozano, and F. Herrera. A study on the use of non-parametric tests for analyzing the evolutionary algorithms' behaviour: a case study on the CEC'2005 special session on real parameter optimization. *Journal of Heuristics*, 15(6):617–644, 2009.

[13] J. Horn, D. Goldberg, and K. Deb. Implicit niching in a learning classifier system: Nature's way. *Evolutionary Computation*, 2(1):37–66, 1994.

[14] G. Howard, L. Bull, and P. Lanzi. Towards continuous actions in continuous space and time using self-adaptive constructivism in neural XCSF. In *Proceedings of the 11th Annual conference on Genetic and evolutionary computation*, pages 1219–1226. ACM, 2009.

[15] G. Hutchinson. Concluding remarks. In *Cold Spring Harbor Symposia on Quantitative Biology 22*, pages 415–427, 1957.

[16] A. Iorio and X. Li. Solving rotated multi-objective optimization problems using differential evolution. *AI 2004: Advances in Artificial Intelligence*, pages 861–872, 2005.

[17] M. Iqbal, W. N. Browne, and M. Zhang. Xcsr with computed continuous action. In *AI 2012: Advances in Artificial Intelligence*, pages 350–361. Springer, 2012.

[18] T. Kohonen. The self-organizing map. *Proceedings of the IEEE*, 78(9):1464–1480, 1990.

[19] P. Lanzi et al. A study of the generalization capabilities of XCS. In *Proceedings of the Seventh International Conference on Genetic Algorithm*, pages 418–425, 1997.

[20] P. Lanzi, D. Loiacono, S. Wilson, and D. Goldberg. XCS with computed prediction in multistep environments. In *Proceedings of the 2005 conference on Genetic and evolutionary computation*, pages 1859–1866. ACM, 2005.

[21] P. Lanzi, D. Loiacono, S. Wilson, and D. Goldberg. Generalization in the XCSF classifier system: Analysis, improvement, and extension. *Evolutionary Computation*, 15(2):133–168, 2007.

[22] P. Lanzi and R. Riolo. A roadmap to the last decade of learning classifier system research (from 1989 to 1999). *Learning Classifier Systems*, pages 33–61, 2000.

[23] B. Manderick and P. Spiessens. Fine-grained parallel genetic algorithms. In *ICGA'89*, pages 428–433, 1989.

[24] J. Mouret. Novelty-based multiobjectivization. *New Horizons in Evolutionary Robotics*, pages 139–154, 2011.

[25] P. Stalph and M. Butz. Learning local linear jacobians for flexible and adaptive robot arm control. *Genetic programming and evolvable machines*, 13(2):137–157, 2012.

[26] R. Storn and K. Price. Differential evolution–a simple and efficient heuristic for global optimization over continuous spaces. *Journal of global optimization*, 11(4):341–359, 1997.

[27] M. Tomassini. *Spatially structured evolutionary algorithms*. Springer, 2005.

[28] H. Tran, C. Sanza, Y. Duthen, and T. Nguyen. XCSF with computed continuous action. In *Genetic And Evolutionary Computation Conference: Proceedings of the 9 th annual conference on Genetic and evolutionary computation*, volume 7, pages 1861–1869, 2007.

[29] R. Urbanowicz and J. Moore. Learning classifier systems: a complete introduction, review, and roadmap. *Journal of Artificial Evolution and Applications*, 2009:1, 2009.

[30] M. Valenzuela-Rendón. The fuzzy classifier system: A classifier system for continuously varying variables. In *Proceedings of the Fourth International Conference on Genetic Algorithms pp346-353, Morgan Kaufmann I*, volume 991, pages 223–230, 1991.

[31] J. Vesterstrom and R. Thomsen. A comparative study of differential evolution, particle swarm optimization, and evolutionary algorithms on numerical benchmark problems. In *Evolutionary Computation, 2004. CEC2004. Congress on*, volume 2, pages 1980–1987. IEEE, 2004.

[32] B. Widrow and M. E. Hoff. Adaptive Switching Circuits. In *1960 IRE WESCON Convention Record, Part 4*, pages 96–104, New York, 1960. IRE.

[33] S. Wilson. ZCS: A zeroth level classifier system. *Evolutionary computation*, 2(1):1–18, 1994.

[34] S. Wilson. Classifier fitness based on accuracy. *Evolutionary computation*, 3(2):149–175, 1995.

[35] S. W. Wilson. Classifiers that approximate functions. 1(2-3):211–234, June 2002.

Learning Regression Ensembles with Genetic Programming at Scale

Kalyan Veeramachaneni
Massachusetts Institute of Technology
Cambridge, MA
kalyan@csail.mit.edu

Owen Derby
Massachusetts Institute of Technology
Cambridge, MA
ocderby@csail.mit.edu

Dylan Sherry
Massachusetts Institute of Technology
Cambridge, MA
dsherry@csail.mit.edu

Una-May O'Reilly
Massachusetts Institute of Technology
Cambridge, MA
unamay@csail.mit.edu

ABSTRACT

In this paper we examine the challenge of producing ensembles of regression models for large datasets. We generate numerous regression models by concurrently executing multiple independent instances of a genetic programming learner. Each instance may be configured with different parameters and a different subset of the training data. Several strategies for fusing predictions from multiple regression models are compared. To overcome the small memory size of each instance, we challenge our framework to learn from small subsets of training data and yet produce a prediction of competitive quality after fusion. This decreases the running time of learning which produces models of good quality in a timely fashion. Finally, we examine the quality of fused predictions over the progress of the computation.

Categories and Subject Descriptors

I.2.6 [**Artificial Intelligence**]: Learning

Keywords

Large scale data mining; Machine learning; Ensemble methods

1. INTRODUCTION

Growth in the sizes of both computing resources and datasets have prompted us to scale machine learning using regression supported by genetic programming (GP). On-demand computational resources are now accessible in quantities several orders of magnitude greater than have previously been available. Similarly, the increased availability and cost effectiveness of data storage has allowed the collection of many large datasets for learning algorithms. GP symbolic regression continues to mature as a technique, with the emergence of products such as DataModeler [13] and Eureqa [27].

However, accompanying the emergence of on-demand computation are the establishment of large training datasets. This represents a challenge in the context of GP for two reasons. First, the size of the training dataset may now exceeding the capacity of main memory. And second, the computational expense of the GP learner scales with the quantity of training data, as each member's fitness calculation depends on that member's error on the data.

When exploited by a thoughtfully designed parallelization framework together with efficient scalable decomposition of the computation required for learning, large computational resources can provide the strength to handle large sizes of data. One such method decomposes the data into multiple subsets and learns a large quantity of models via independent learners. This allows the computation to execute on many instances in parallel and is known as a data-parallel approach [17]. Each model is used to make a prediction and a meta-model is developed to fuse these predictions.

In this paper we present a framework which generates ensembles of regression models for large datasets by utilizing large quantities of computational resources teamed with a parallelization framework. We focus on regression through tree-based GP, which generates non-linear symbolic expressions. Our contributions and the challenges we address are:

- **Ensemble Fusion Methods**: We describe and evaluate a suite of different fusion methods for developing an ensemble which fuses multiple continuous-valued predictions. These range from simple averaging to building a meta model. Fusion approaches for both parametric and non-parametric regression approaches are rare in contrast with a plethora of well-explored approaches for classification.

- **Collaborative Solution Building**: We demonstrate how to address a large data problem through factoring. We do so by creating subsets of explanatory variables or by dividing the dataset into smaller datasets, thereby reducing the computational burden on each learner. To improve speed and address memory limitation, we reduce the data size at each instance by a

GECCO'13, July 6–10, 2013, Amsterdam, The Netherlands.

factor of 100 or even 1000. We explore whether factoring generates weak learners which can be fused into an ensemble which overcomes individuals' weaknesses. Additionally, we demonstrate how parameters of tree based GP can be diversified to generate multiple models. Finally, we consider whether factoring contributes ensemble members which improve fused accuracy.

- **Cloud-Scale Ensemble Learning**: We develop a cloud scale regression ensemble learning system. Models are generated by multiple cloud-backed virtual machines each supporting an independent parameterized GP learner. Under this scenario we create a fused model (ensemble) on demand at different points in time while the individual GP learners are evolving. The stochasticity of GP and the varying computation speed of virtual machines on the cloud induces variability in the learning rate of each learner. We examine how the performance of the fused models changes in real time. Finally, we discuss treating the convergence of the fusion methods' performance as a stopping criterion for GP.

The remainder of this paper is structured as follows. Section 2 discusses previous and related work. Sections 3 and 4 detail how we generate models and ensembles of models, respectively. Section 5 describes the datasets and parameters of our system used to run the experiments. Finally, Section 6 presents the results of our experiments and Section 7 concludes with some thoughts for future work.

2. RELATED WORK

Collections of multiple models are called "ensembles", whether the models are trained on different subsamples of the data, developed using different parameters of the same learner or simply obtained by different learners pursuing the same prediction task.

2.1 Ensembles in Machine Learning

Over the past two decades numerous researchers in the machine learning community have pursued the idea of generating a great quantity of models for the same data [7,8,22, 25,26]. Similarly, the task of combining predictions from an ensemble of models has attracted attention in recent years. This follows from two observations: there is usually not a single explanation for the data, and multiple models cover the observation space in a more robust manner than a single model can. Initially researchers focused on methods which generated multiple models from the same data irrespective of what kind of learner was being used. These methods relied on repeated subset sampling methods with replacement, e.g. bagging [4] and iterative sampling methods, e.g. boosting [11]. Other examples include random forests [5] and Adaboost. [12]. In this work, we focus on how the changing the parameters of the base learner can generate multiple models.

2.2 GP-based Machine Learning Ensembles

When looking at ensembles built using GP, most of the work has focused on classification [2,10,15,16,23,24]. In classification with GP, models are either built to output discrete class labels or are constructed to yield a continuous number which leads to a class label when converted into class probabilities. Multiple class labels can be fused via majority vote or a sophisticated criterion [19].

Conversely, there has been very little research on regression ensembles [14, 20, 29]. In regression, due to the unconstrained nature of GP models one must perform multiple tests which can guarantee models' outputs are within a reasonable range for any unseen data point before the model is admitted into an ensemble. To build regression ensembles, most current approaches use simple averaging techniques (discussed in Section 4.2). Many examine methods for combining ensembles of parametric models. These methods attempt to understand the differences in the models based on their parameters and/or produce a fused model by fusing the parameters.

3. GENERATION OF MODELS

The availability of massive on-demand computational resources via the cloud enables us to learn many models in parallel. Bagging, boosting or simple parameter variation are now feasible at an unprecedented scale. We use our distributed GP system, FlexGP, to run many instances of GP in parallel in the cloud, thus generating many models [6]. Below we discuss the specifics of the local learner and the factoring settings we used with FlexGP.

3.1 Local learner

Our local learner is based on tree based GP. We built a simple GP system with subtree mutation, single point cross over and tournament selection. We incorporated linear scaling [18,31] to allow GP to learn the shape of the regression function and implemented dynamic operator equalization to control bloating [28]. More parameters of our local learner are listed in Section 5.1.

3.2 Factoring

FlexGP has a probabilistic, user guided means of varying the parameters with which each GP learner executes. It establishes a large scale set of factored learners in a decentralized manner, thus working in parallel to learn a diverse set of models.

We define the parameters of a GP learner running at instance i as $\{L, O, D^i_{tr}, F\}$. L is the operator set provided to GP. O is the objective function used for fitness evaluations in GP. D^i_{tr} is the set of training cases presented to the learner, as defined in Table 2. F is the set of data features used for learning. Different options are available for these parameters and are summarized in Table 1.

Table 1: GP parameters and their possible values and definitions.

Parameter	Value	Definition
Operator Set (L)	W	$\{+, -, /, *\}$
	X	$\{exp, ln\}$
	Y	$\{sqrt, x^2, x^3, x^4\}$
	Z	$\{sin, cos\}$
Objective Function (O)	Norm	Mean absolute error
	Norm-2	Mean squared error
	Norm-inf	Max error
Training Cases (D^i_{tr})	n	Subset of D_{gp}, of size n
Feature Set (F)	m	Subset of features, of size m

Despite the massive number compute resources available to us in the cloud, it is still infeasible to exhaustively try every combination of these factoring settings. Instead, FlexGP assumes a distribution over each of these parameters to probabilistically bias how each instance chooses a value for that parameter when it starts the local GP. For example, one learner could choose $\{W, Norm2, \{d_{1...3000}\}, \{x_1, x_2\}\}$ and another might select $\{W \cup X, Norm2, \{d_{1...3000}\}, \{x_1, x_4\}\}$.

4. COMBINING REGRESSION MODELS

As described in Section 2, most previous work which focuses on regression ensembles examines the fusion of parametric models. Since GP produces non-parametric models, we must develop different methods. This requires us to rely on predictions for analyzing the model performance. Each GP learner produces an output $\hat{y}_{mj} = f_m(\overline{\mathbf{x}}_j)$ for each input data point $\overline{\mathbf{x}}_j$, where m and other notational conventions are defined in Table 2. An example of a GP model m is

$$\hat{f}_m(\overline{\mathbf{x}}) = log(x_1) + x_4x_5 + \frac{x_6}{e^{x_9}}$$

We propose and define six methods for combining ensembles of GP models for regression problems. These methods fall into two distinct categories: selection methods, which select a single model from the ensemble (4.1), and fusion methods, which produce predictions by fusing the predictions from a mixture of models in the ensemble (4.2). Probabilistic methods of fusion are discussed in Section 4.3

Table 2: Problem Notation

Variable	Notation	Definition
Data	D_{gp}	GP training data
	D^i_{tr}	Subset of D_{gp} used by instance i for training
	D^i_{val}	Subset of D_{gp} used by instance i for validation
	D_f	Fusion training data
	D_t	Testing data
Data point	$\overline{\mathbf{x}}_j$	$\overline{\mathbf{x}}_j = \{x_l \| l = 1...\gamma\}$
Output variable	z_j	$z_j \in \mathbb{R}$, for $\overline{\mathbf{x}}_j$
Model	m	Model m
Prediction	$\hat{y}_{mj} = f_m(\overline{\mathbf{x}}_j)$	Model m's prediction, non-linear in $\overline{\mathbf{x}}_j$
Candidate models	Ω	Set of models for fusion
Predictions for $\overline{\mathbf{x}}_j$	$\overline{\mathbf{y}}_j$	$\overline{\mathbf{y}}_j = \{\hat{y}_{mj} \| \forall m \in \Omega\}$
Predictions of model m, given D	$\overline{Y}^m_D$	$\overline{Y}^m_D = \{\hat{y}_{mj} \| \forall \overline{\mathbf{x}}_j \in D\}$
Output estimate	$\hat{z}_j$	ensemble's estimate of z_j

4.1 Selection Methods

Average Model Prediction (AMP)

The simplest selection method is to pick a random model from the ensemble. For each new query, this method would select a model at random and use that to produce a prediction. We measure the effectiveness of this method by measuring the average performance of every model in the ensemble on D_t.

Best A Priori Model (BAM)

As a slight improvement to AMP, we propose BAM: Best A priori Model selection. For predicting the output of new queries, we use the best model from the ensemble based on its MSE on D^i_{val}.

4.2 Fusion Methods

Fusion methods combine multiple models from the ensemble for prediction. They vary in how they mix the models and combine those models' predictions.

Average Ensemble Prediction (AVE)

The simplest fusion method is to generate $\overline{\mathbf{y}}_j$ for a new query $\overline{\mathbf{x}}_j$ and then report the average of those predictions. That is, $\hat{z}_j = \frac{1}{m}\sum_{i=1}^m \hat{y}_{ij}$ for each test point $\overline{\mathbf{x}}_j$ [20,30].

Median Average Model (MAD)

A variant of AVE, MAD finds the *median* prediction among $\overline{\mathbf{y}}_j$ and a prediction for a new query is computed as the average of the prediction of this median model and those of its two neighbors in the prediction space [31].

Adaptive Regression Mixing (ARM)

In Adaptive Regression by Mixing (ARM), each model m is assigned a weight, W_m, which is used to compute $\hat{z}_j$ via a weighted average [33]. The weights are computed in the following manner. Let $r = |D_f|$ and $o = |\Omega|$. First the data D_f is randomly partitioned into two equally sized parts $D^{(1)}$ and $D^{(2)}$. To identify the weights for each model, we assume that the errors for each model are normally distributed. We then use the variance in these errors to identify the weights by executing the following steps:

Step 1: Evaluate σ_m^2 which is the maximum likelihood estimate of the variance of the errors, $\overline{e}_m = \{\hat{y}_{mj} - z_j | \overline{\mathbf{x}}_j, z_j \in D^{(1)}\}$. Compute the sum of squared errors on $D^{(2)}$, $\beta_m = \sum_{j=\frac{r}{2}+1}^{r}(\hat{y}_{mj} - z_j)^2$.

Step 2: Estimate the weights using:

$$W_m = \frac{(\sigma_m)^{-r/2} exp(-\sigma_m^{-2}\beta_m/2)}{\sum_{j=1}^{o}(\sigma_j)^{-r/2} exp(-\sigma_j^{-2}\beta_j/2)} \quad (1)$$

Step 3: Redraw subsets $D^{(1)}$ and $D^{(2)}$ and repeat steps 1 and 2. Continue this process for a fixed number of times[1]. Average the weights to get the final weights for the models.

Given a test point $\overline{\mathbf{x}}_j$, predict $\hat{z}_j$ as the weighted average of model predictions: $\hat{z}_j = \sum_{m=1}^{o} W_m \hat{y}_{mj}$.

Transformation for large r: For large values of r, the calculation of the weights as given by equation 1 encounters an underflow error. To avoid this problem we equivalently compute the weights using equations 2 and 3.

$$A_m = -\frac{r}{2}log(\sigma_m) + log(\frac{-\sigma_m{}^{-2}\beta_m}{2}) \quad (2)$$

$$W_m = exp(A_m - log(\sum_{q=1}^{o} A_q)) \quad (3)$$

4.3 Probabilistic Fusion Methods

In meta-model based approaches, given the training data D_f, the joint probability density function $f_{Y,Z}(y,z)$ is built for $\{\overline{\mathbf{y}}_j, z_j | \forall \overline{\mathbf{x}}_j, z_j \in D_f\}$. $f_{Y,Z}(y,z)$ is then used to predict $\hat{z}_j$ for a new input $\overline{\mathbf{x}}_j$ by first computing $\overline{\mathbf{y}}_j$ via the GP generated models and then evaluating the conditional density function for $f_{Z|Y}(\hat{z}_j|\overline{\mathbf{y}}_j)$. An advantage of this approach is the availability of uncertainty information. In our current

[1] An intelligent stopping criteria could be used as well.

contribution, we focus on a non-parametric version of the probabilistic model which does not need any training.

Our model is a non-parametric multivariate kernel density (KDE) estimator, using a gaussian kernel [9, 32]. Let $n = |D_f|$ and $o = |\Omega|$. The multivariate kernel density function is given by

$$f_{Y,Z}(w,v) = \frac{1}{n}\sum_{j=1}^{n}\prod_{m=1}^{o} K_h(w_m - \hat{y}_{mj})K_h(v - z_j)$$

where $K_h(x) = \frac{1}{h}\phi(\frac{x}{h})$, $\phi(x)$ is the standard normal density function and h is the bandwidth. To compute $\hat{z}_k$ for a test point $\overline{\mathbf{x}}_k$, we first compute $\overline{\mathbf{y}}_k$ and then find the expected value of the conditional density function $f_{Z|Y}(z|\overline{\mathbf{y}}_k)$:

$$\begin{aligned}
\hat{z}_j &= E(Z|Y = \overline{\mathbf{y}}_k) \\
&= \int_Z z f_{Z|Y}(z|\overline{\mathbf{y}}_k)dz = \int_Z z\frac{f_{Z,Y}(z,\overline{\mathbf{y}}_k)}{f_Y(\overline{\mathbf{y}}_k)}dz \\
&= \frac{\sum_{j=1}^{n}\prod_{m=1}^{o} K_h(\hat{y}_{mk} - \hat{y}_{mj})\int_Z zK_h(z - z_j)dz}{\sum_{j=1}^{n}\prod_{m=1}^{o} K_h(\hat{y}_{mk} - \hat{y}_{mj})\int_Z K_h(z - z_j)dz} \\
&= \frac{\sum_{j=1}^{n} z_j\prod_{m=1}^{o} K_h(\hat{y}_{mk} - \hat{y}_{mj})}{\sum_{j=1}^{n}\prod_{m=1}^{o} K_h(\hat{y}_{mk} - \hat{y}_{mj})}
\end{aligned}$$

4.4 Advantages and limitations

Each of the fusion approaches we presented above has certain advantages and limitations. AVE is the simplest of all but could bias the estimation because many correlated models producing similar outputs for a training point. It could also be affected by outliers. MAD, though robust to outliers, ignores a lot more information embedded in more than a few models. Both of these techniques do not differentiate between different models based on their performance on the training data and consider the models themselves to be independent.

ARM presents a unique way of identifying the weights for each model however it can become computationally intensive. In our experiment we resample (according to step 3) 100 times to estimate the weights. The approach is also sensitive to the amount of data presented for training the weights. Once the weights are identified, real time execution of the deployed model is extremely efficient.

ARM, AVE and MAD require an outlier detection algorithm to remove any outliers before fusion. The outlier detection algorithm has to be run in real time. In our approach we estimate the minimum and maximum values for the output variable $z = (z_{min}, z_{max})$ and any model producing predictions that are outside these5C bounds are removed before fusion. For ARM, the weights are renormalized after removing the weights that correspond to the outlier models.

On the other hand, KDE is non-parametric and so is not sensitive to outliers. However the method has two weaknesses. First, the method requires the user to set the bandwidth parameter for the kernel. The performance of the algorithm is sensitive to this parameter and setting this value might require training. In this contribution we choose a bandwidth parameter heuristically. Second, the method requires us to carry the data to deployment scenario, and as the predictions are made in real time, this data is queried to make the calculations. This makes predicting outputs for new input computationally expensive.

5. EXPERIMENTAL SETUP

To demonstrate the efficacy of GP regression ensembles we experimented with 2 datasets, summarized in Table 3. In the first dataset, a number of settings in a power plant are used to predict the NOx emissions [3]. These settings (features) are continuous-valued and are known to have a non-linear relation with the NOx emissions. We abbreviate this problem as NOx.

Table 3: Summary of dataset statistics.

Dataset	$\lvert D_{gp}\rvert$	$\lvert D_f\rvert$	$\lvert D_t\rvert$	Total	$\lvert\overline{\mathbf{x}}_j\rvert$	Range of z
NOx	4,017	310	900	5,227	18	[0.270 0.654]
MSD	398,924	67204	49436	515564	90	[1922 2011]

Our second problem comes from the *music information retrieval* (MIR) community where a dataset of one million song tracks has been created to push the focus towards solving large scale MIR problems [1]. We set out to study the *year prediction problem*, where the task is to predict the release year of a song, given a set of track features. Of the million tracks in the dataset, roughly half have year data. We abbreviate this problem as MSD.

5.1 GP and FlexGP settings

Our experiments use a GP based learner described in Section 6. We use the same GP configuration as described by Koza with select differences [21]. The learner is set with a population of size 1000. The mutation rate is 0.1, the crossover rate is 0.6, and the max depth is set to 12 for the NOx experiments and is set to 8 in the MSD experiments. The tournament selection size is 7 and we used ramped-half-and-half as the algorithm for tree growth. The learners were allowed to run until stopped in the NOx experiments, but were terminated after 20 generations in the MSD experiments. Our method for advancing to the next generation is Silva's dynamic equalization with a bin width of 5 [28]. We ran multiple experiments with each dataset, each time with different amounts of training data or GP learner settings. Table 4 presents the settings for different runs.

Table 4: Settings of different experiments

Dataset	Exp.	$\frac{\lvert D^i_{tr}\rvert}{\lvert D_{gp}\rvert}$	# Nodes	Parameter Factored
NOx	1	67%	150	None
	2	67%	150	F
	3	67%	150	D
	4	67%	150	D & L
	5	67%	150	D & O
MSD	1	10%	75	ALL
	2	1%	150	ALL
	3	0.1%	150	ALL

For every experiment, except MSD1, we use 150 virtual machines, each with a single core and 2GB of RAM. In MSD1, each node required 3.4 GB of memory to load D_{gp}^{tr} into Java. Thus each node ran a virtual machine with two cores and 4GB of RAM, which forced us to halve the number of virtual machines used (we are core-limited).

Due to the variance in starting times across our nodes, each node runs for a different number of generations (up to a total of 20 generations in the MSD experiments). We collect the best model for each generation from each node. On average, we obtain about 30 models (20 models in the

Table 5: MSE and PG_{MSE} on the NOx experiments for all fusion methods. Note that the MSE value for AMP on NOx1 is used for the baseline in PG_{mse} calculations in all NOx experiments.

		AMP	BAM	AVE	MAD	ARM	KDE
NOx1	MSE	1.97E-3	1.37E-3	1.42E-3	1.65E-3	1.30E-3	6.63E-4
	PG_{MSE}	0.0%	30.4%	28.0%	16.4%	34.2%	66.4%
NOx2	MSE	2.35E-3	1.33E-3	1.54E-3	1.92E-3	1.29E-3	5.60E-4
	PG_{MSE}	-19.2%	32.4%	22.2%	2.8%	34.6%	71.6%
NOx3	MSE	2.10E-3	1.38E-3	1.41E-3	1.43E-3	1.31E-3	6.40E-4
	PG_{MSE}	-6.4%	30.0%	28.6%	27.5%	33.5%	67.6%
NOx4	MSE	1.66E-3	1.51E-3	1.26E-3	1.27E-3	1.22E-3	6.82E-4
	PG_{MSE}	15.8%	23.7%	36.0%	35.5%	38.2%	65.5%
NOx5	MSE	2.15E-3	1.30E-3	1.44E-3	1.54E-3	1.29E-3	6.53E-4
	PG_{MSE}	-9.0%	33.9%	26.8%	21.7%	34.6%	66.9%

MSD experiments) from each node giving us approximately 5000 models in the NOx experiments and around 2000-3000 models for the MSD experiments.

5.2 Data splits

We divide each dataset into three parts: for training GP models (D_{gp}), for training the fusion model (D_f) and for testing (D_t). Within D_{gp}, each node selects a random subset for training the GP models (D^i_{tr}) and reserves the rest for validation (D^i_{val}). Tables 3 and 4 report the size of these splits for both datasets.

For MSD data, the MIR commmunity has established a standardized train/test split to facilitate comparisons across different approaches [1]. This split ensures that no artist is present in both subsets. In this paper, we further split the provided MIR training dataset to produce D_{gp} and D_f. When constructing this split and when each node splits D_{gp} into D^i_{tr} and D^i_{val}, we continue to ensure that no artists appear in more than one subset.

6. RESULTS AND DISCUSSION

To measure the performance of our fusion strategies, we compute their MSE on D_t. To aid in comparing the performance of these strategies, we need to construct a comparative performance measurement. To do this, we establish the performance of a single method on a single experiment within each problem as a baseline performance value, $baseline_{MSE}$, which all other methods are measured against. Given the performance of a method in an experiment, $method_{MSE}$, we compute its *performance gain* as

$$PG_{MSE} = \frac{baseline_{MSE} - method_{MSE}}{baseline_{MSE}}$$

This number is positive if we achieved a better performance and negative otherwise.

For the NOx experiments, we set our basline as the performance of AMP in the NOx1 experiment. Because we executed NOx1 without any factorings, we ran an identical learner with the same data in parallel at each instance. This corresponds to what a standard run of classic GP would yield. Which is a good baseline for the NOx experiments, where we are concerned with how factoring affects fusion performance.

Our focus with the MSD experiments is the effects of the size of D^i_{tr} (see Section 6.3) on ensemble performance. To provide a similar measure of performance gain for the MSD experiments, we set the baseline to be the MSE of AMP on D_t for the MSD1 experiment. This baseline effectively highlights the impact of decreasing training set size on fusion performance.

Table 6: MSE and PG_{MSE} on the MSD experiments for all fusion methods, except KDE. The MSE value for AMP from MSD1 is used as the baseline for the computation of each PG_{MSE}

		AMP	BAM	AVE	MAD	ARM
MSD1	MSE	122.7	105.2	111.6	111.7	103.9
	PG_{MSE}	0.0%	14.3%	9.0%	9.0%	15.4%
MSD2	MSE	117.3	106.5	112.6	113.4	104.7
	PG_{MSE}	4.4%	13.2%	8.2%	7.6%	14.7%
MSD3	MSE	123.6	111.4	109.7	114.4	107.8
	PG_{MSE}	-0.7%	9.2%	10.6%	6.8%	12.1%

We present the results of implementing the fusion strategies from Section 4 to the NOx and MSD problems in Tables 5 and 6, respectively. There are no results for KDE in Table 6 because we could not compute KDE due to the MSD dataset size.

In Figure 1, we have computed the PG_{MSE} for each model considered for fusion in each experiment from Table 4 and plotted the resulting distribution as a box plot. For each box, the central line is the median of the distribution and the edges mark the 25th and 75th percentiles. The whiskers extend to the most extreme points which are not considered as outliers, and all outliers are marked by an 'x'. The circles indicate the highest performance gain achieved by any fusion strategy for each experiment.

We spend the next several paragraphs investigating a variety of questions. First, we examine the performance improvements which could be achieved by generating and fusing an ensemble of models. We also examine the efficacy of various problem factorizations. Next, we consider the performance of fusion with a relatively small sample of training data at each instance. This allows the minimization of both the overall GP training time and the memory requirements of each individual learner. Finally, we examine the performance of our system's predictions in real-time, and we detail the behavior and characteristics of several fusion strategies when considered in this setting.

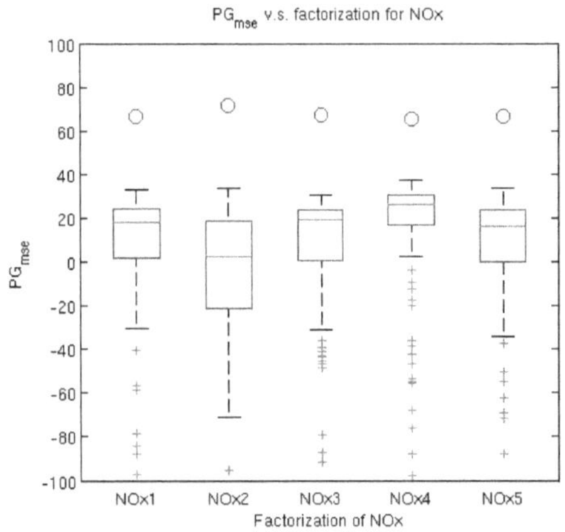

(a) NOx

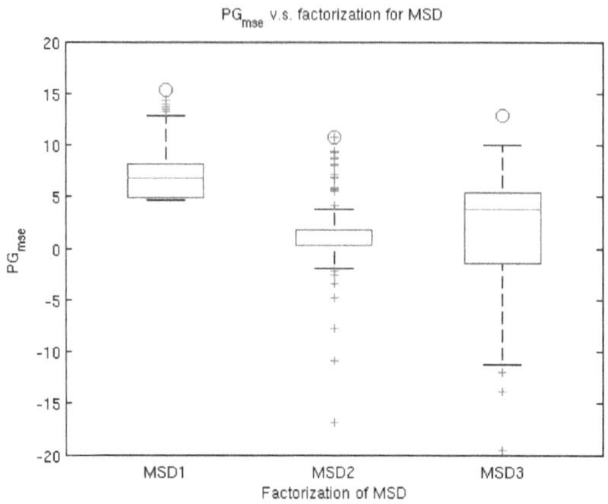

(b) MSD

Figure 1: The quartile distribution of PG$_{MSE}$ of models used for fusion in each experiment. The circles represent the best PG$_{MSE}$ from fusion. *Left* Results for NOx experiments; KDE was the best fusion method. *Right* Results for MSD experiments; ARM was the best fusion method.

6.1 Performance of Fusion Strategies

For the NOx dataset, KDE performs the best in all trials. ARM provides the second best performance gains. Selecting the best model among the ensemble based on their performance provides reasonably good performance gains. To our surprise MAD, which was most commonly used in previous GP-based regression ensemble work, did not perform well. This is because median average utilizes very few predictions around the median, thus ignoring the bulk of the predictions.

For MSD experiments the three factorings simply reduce the amount of the data used for training. We generally see the performance gain values fall as less data is provided to the GP learners. The exception is the AVE ensemble performance. Interestingly, AVE produces the best results MSD3, when each learner is given only 400 training points. We hypothesize this is because as data size is reduced to such small size each learner specializes in a different region of the input space and makes different errors. Thus, the models have uncorrelated errors and taking the average prediction becomes a good strategy for combining models [25].

6.2 Impact of Different Factorings

With the NOx experiments, we examine the impact of different factorings on ensemble performance. Looking at the NOx results in Figure 1, we notice models learned in the NOx4 experiment are generally better and the distribution is tighter than the rest (although there is a long tail of outliers). Conversely, we see that the models from NOx2 have less consistent results and perform worse than the rest. This is understandable since NOx2 is built with subset of features.

We first examine the performance gain of the AMP method across experiments. AMP results in worse performance than the classic GP baseline in all experiments except NOx4. This suggests that factoring the operator set (L) could be the linchpin in seeing performance gains from fusion. However, this merits further study as this result isn't observed across other the other fusion strategies.

Finally, we note that KDE and ARM result in consistently good performance gains, irrespective of factoring. This suggests that factor settings may not have such a large impact on ensemble performance.

6.3 Reducing the Size of the Data

In our experiments we examine how reducing the size of the data used by each local learner affects ensemble performance. Reducing the training data directly decreases the time taken to evaluate an individual, allowing for faster learning overall. However, learning on less data typically comes at the cost of decreased performance.

When decreasing the size of data in the MSD experiments, we see that while individual model performance drops, the fusion results remain better than baseline. As reported in Table 3, we experimented with using 10%, 1%, and 0.1% (40K, 4K and 400 data points, respectively) for training. As we can see in Figure 1 right, the resulting individual models perform less reliably as the number of training cases decreases. This is shown by the increased variance in the model performance. However, as reported in Table 6 the ensemble performance shows only slight decrease in performance. Indeed, ARM fusion performs better than the baseline in all cases. This demonstrates that decreasing the amount of training data used by a factor of 100 still allows for improved performance of the ensemble.

6.4 Analyzing Real-Time Fusion

In this section we assess how the performance of the fusion strategiess perform as time progresses and the GP models evolve more generations. Figure 2 presents the performance of the different fusion strategies in real time on the NOx problem. At each time step we collect the models so far, construct ensembles using the proposed methods, compute their predictions on D_t and report their performance gain. Plots for NOx2, NOx3 and NOx5 were omitted as they are highly similar to the three shown.

The plots in Figure 2 illustrate a couple interesting points. First, notice BAM is not robust and can give arbitrarily poor performance at different points in time. This is because BAM might select a model which has overfit on D^i_{tr} in such a way that it still does well on D^i_{val} but performs poorly

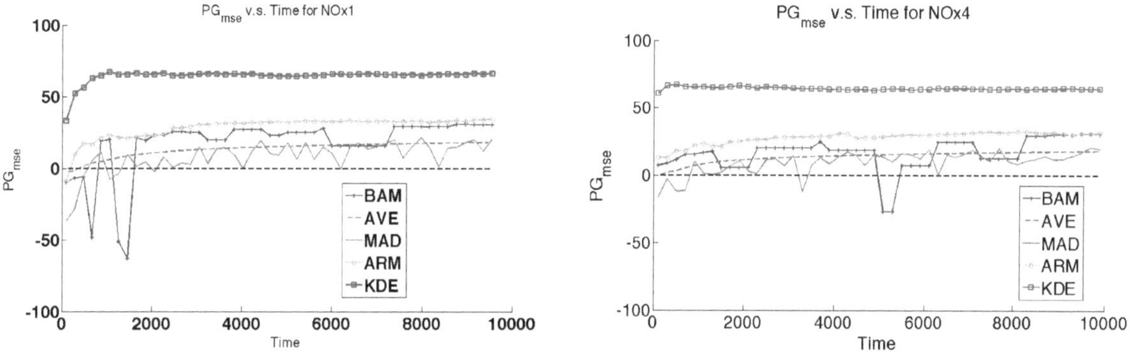

(a) NOx1 (b) NOx4

Figure 2: Improvements achieved over the baseline (no fusion) methodology as generations are executed and time (in seconds) progresses in our framework for NOx data.

on D_t. Thus, even though it achieves similar performance gains to ARM at some points, it is not a reliable strategy. Second, notice that ARM, KDE and AVE have stable and incremental performance. That is, as time progresses they either improve or remain at their last attained performance. This sort of performance stabilization over time suggests we could use the fused performance as a stopping criteria for the entire system.

7. CONCLUSIONS AND FUTURE WORK

In this paper we have presented a regression ensemble system which produces model ensembles by relying on a GP-based learner. Our system pairs the stochastic nature of GP with a probabilistic parameter factoring method and the variable computation speed of the cloud to produce many diverse models for fusion. We presented multiple robust strategies for fusing predictions from these ensembles of models. We also explored the affect of this probabilistic factoring method on the generation of model ensembles. A discussion of other results and suggested follow-on work follows.

Informed Factoring Distributions In our current implementation, we set all distributions for factoring to be static, uniform distributions. However, since these distributions are retrieved from the parent node, they could change dynamically as new nodes are launched. For example, a node could modify $p(D^i_{tr})$ to decrease the chance any node it starts will select the same training cases it did. Alternatively, if new nodes are to be brought up after the system has been running, $p(D^i_{tr})$ could be modified to weight difficult training cases more and $p(F)$ could be modified to weight features with little apparent informative power less. We hope to explore such possibilities in the future.

Data Challenge: We challenged ourselves to give each learner as little data as possible while still retrieving fused performance equivalent to the case where multiple learners are given large amounts of data. This enables our iterative learning mechanism to learn quickly from large data. We have been particularly successful in this challenge. For one of our problems we have provided as little as 400 training data points from a total of 400,000 available points. Under these constraints we achieved comparable performance to the case where 40,000 data points were made available. We also achieved comparable performance to the benchmark available in literature for this dataset, which utilises all data for training. As part of the future work we intend to further explore this aspect of our system and to seek answers to the following questions: How much data at each learner is enough? How many models, where each is trained on a small subset, are enough?

Repeating experiments While the results presenting are compelling, little attention has been paid to how robust they are. Ensembles are built from thousands of models, which should be sufficiently large enough to ensure we have used a representative sampling of possible models. However, a more rigorous and extensive experimental design incorporating cross-validation and repeated trials is needed before any deeper conclusions can be drawn.

Multiple Fusion Approaches: We have chartered the largely unexplored territory of how to fuse multiple continuous-valued predictions of regression ensembles. We presented multiple strategies with different complexities. We show conventionally used methods of average and median average do not yield good results.

Ensemble Learning at Scale: Finally, we presented a system which factors the data and the genetic programming learner in multiple ways. We demonstrated our system's capability to provide accurate intermediate fused answers as time progresses. As part of our future work we intend to demonstrate our system's capacity to leverage the power of thousands of nodes by testing the system on larger datasets where many learners build models independently.

Acknowledgements

This work was supported by the GE Global Research center. Any opinions, findings, and conclusions or recommendations expressed in this material are those of the authors and do not necessarily reflect the views of General Electric Company.

8. REFERENCES

[1] T. Bertin-Mahieux, D. Ellis, B. Whitman, and P. Lamere. The million song dataset. In *ISMIR 2011: Proceedings of the 12th International Society for Music Information Retrieval Conference, October 24-28, 2011, Miami, Florida*, pages 591–596. University of Miami, 2011.

[2] U. Bhowan, M. Johnston, M. Zhang, and X. Yao. Evolving diverse ensembles using genetic programming

for classification with unbalanced data. *Evolutionary Computation, IEEE Transactions on*, 2012.

[3] P. Bonissone. Lazy meta-learning: creating customized model ensembles on demand. *Advances in Computational Intelligence*, pages 1–23, 2012.

[4] L. Breiman. Bagging predictors. *Machine learning*, 24(2):123–140, 1996.

[5] L. Breiman. Random forests. *Machine learning*, 45(1):5–32, 2001.

[6] O. Derby, K. Veeramachaneni, and U.-M. OâĂŹReilly. Cloud driven design of a distributed genetic programming platform. In A. Esparcia-AlcÃązar, editor, *Applications of Evolutionary Computation*, volume 7835 of *Lecture Notes in Computer Science*, pages 509–518. Springer Berlin Heidelberg, 2013.

[7] T. Dietterich. Ensemble methods in machine learning. *Multiple classifier systems*, pages 1–15, 2000.

[8] T. Dietterich. An experimental comparison of three methods for constructing ensembles of decision trees: Bagging, boosting, and randomization. *Machine learning*, 40(2):139–157, 2000.

[9] V. A. Epanechnikov. Non-parametric estimation of a multivariate probability density. *Theory of Probability & Its Applications*, 14(1):153–158, 1969.

[10] G. Folino, C. Pizzuti, and G. Spezzano. Mining distributed evolving data streams using fractal gp ensembles. *Genetic Programming*, pages 160–169, 2007.

[11] Y. Freund and R. Schapire. Experiments with a new boosting algorithm. In *Machine learning international conference*, pages 148–156. Morgan Kauffman Publishers, Inc., 1996.

[12] Y. Freund and R. E. Schapire. A decision-theoretic generalization of on-line learning and an application to boosting. *Journal of computer and system sciences*, 55(1):119–139, 1997.

[13] M. Friese, O. Flasch, K. Vladislavleva, T. Bartz-Beielstein, O. Mersmann, B. Naujoks, J. Stork, and M. Zaefferer. Ensemble-based model selection for smart metering data. In *Proceedings 22 Workshop Computational Intelligence*, page 215, dec 2012.

[14] H. Iba. Bagging, boosting, and bloating in genetic programming. In *Proceedings of the genetic and evolutionary computation conference*, volume 2, pages 1053–1060, 1999.

[15] K. Imamura, T. Soule, R. Heckendorn, and J. Foster. Behavioral diversity and a probabilistically optimal gp ensemble. *Genetic Programming and Evolvable Machines*, 4(3):235–253, 2003.

[16] U. Johansson, T. Löfström, R. König, and L. Niklasson. Genetically evolved trees representing ensembles. *Artificial Intelligence and Soft Computing–ICAISC 2006*, pages 613–622, 2006.

[17] A. J. Keane, A. Choudhury, P. B. Nair, A. J. K. F. Choudhury, and P. Nair. A data parallel approach for large-scale gaussian process modeling. In *in Proc. the Second SIAM International Conference on Data Mining*. Citeseer, 2002.

[18] M. Keijzer. Improving symbolic regression with interval arithmetic and linear scaling. In C. Ryan, T. Soule, M. Keijzer, E. Tsang, R. Poli, and E. Costa, editors, *Genetic Programming*, volume 2610 of *Lecture Notes in Computer Science*, pages 275–299. Springer Berlin / Heidelberg, 2003. 10.1007/3-540-36599-0_7.

[19] J. Kittler, M. Hatef, R. Duin, and J. Matas. On combining classifiers. *Pattern Analysis and Machine Intelligence, IEEE Transactions on*, 20(3):226–239, 1998.

[20] M. Kotanchek, G. Smits, and E. Vladislavleva. Trustable symbolic regression models. *Genetic Programming Theory and Practice V, Genetic and Evolutionary Computation*, pages 203–222, 2007.

[21] J. R. Koza. *Genetic Programming: On the Programming of Computers by Means of Natural Selection*. MIT Press, Cambridge, MA, USA, 1992.

[22] A. Krogh and J. Vedelsby. Neural network ensembles, cross validation, and active learning. *Advances in neural information processing systems*, pages 231–238, 1995.

[23] W. Langdon, S. Barrett, and B. Buxton. Combining decision trees and neural networks for drug discovery. *Genetic Programming*, pages 76–89, 2002.

[24] P. L. Lanzi. XCS with stack-based genetic programming. In R. Sarker, R. Reynolds, H. Abbass, K. C. Tan, B. McKay, D. Essam, and T. Gedeon, editors, *Proceedings of the 2003 Congress on Evolutionary Computation CEC2003*, pages 1186–1191, Canberra, 8-12 Dec. 2003. IEEE Press.

[25] M. Perrone and L. Cooper. When networks disagree: Ensemble methods for hybrid neural networks. Technical report, DTIC Document, 1992.

[26] J. Quinlan. Bagging, boosting, and c4. 5. In *Proceedings of the National Conference on Artificial Intelligence*, pages 725–730, 1996.

[27] M. Schmidt and H. Lipson. Distilling free-form natural laws from experimental data. *Science*, 324(5923):81–85, 2009.

[28] S. Silva. Handling bloat in GP. In *Proceedings of the 13th annual conference companion on Genetic and evolutionary computation*, GECCO '11, pages 1481–1508, New York, NY, USA, 2011. ACM.

[29] K. Veeramachaneni, K. Vladislavleva, M. Burland, J. Parcon, and U. O'Reilly. Evolutionary optimization of flavors. In *Proceedings of the 12th annual conference on Genetic and evolutionary computation*, pages 1291–1298. ACM, 2010.

[30] K. Veeramachaneni, K. Vladislavleva, M. Burland, J. Parcon, and U. M. O'Reilly. Evolutionary optimization of flavors. In J. Branke and et al, editors, *GECCO '10: Proceedings of the 12th annual conference on Genetic and evolutionary computation*, pages 1291–1298, Portland, Oregon, USA, 7-11 July 2010. ACM.

[31] C. Vladislavleva and G. Smits. Symbolic regression via genetic programming. *Final Thesis for Dow Benelux BV*, 2005.

[32] M. P. Wand and M. C. Jones. *Kernel smoothing*, volume 60. Chapman & Hall/CRC, 1995.

[33] Y. Yang. Regression with multiple candidate models: selecting or mixing? *Statistica Sinica*, 13(3):783–810, 2003.

Solving Satisfiability in Fuzzy Logics by Mixing CMA-ES

Tim Brys
Artificial Intelligence Lab, VUB
Pleinlaan 2
1050 Brussels, Belgium
timbrys@vub.ac.be

Madalina M. Drugan
Artificial Intelligence Lab, VUB
Pleinlaan 2
1050 Brussels, Belgium
mdrugan@vub.ac.be

Peter A. N. Bosman
Centrum Wiskunde & Informatica (CWI)
P.O. Box 94079
1090 GB Amsterdam, The Netherlands
peter.bosman@cwi.nl

Martine De Cock
Dept. of Applied Math., Comp. Sc. and Stat., UGent
Krijgslaan 281 (S9)
9000 Gent, Belgium
martine.decock@ugent.be

Ann Nowé
Artificial Intelligence Lab, VUB
Pleinlaan 2
1050 Brussels, Belgium
anowe@vub.ac.be

ABSTRACT

Satisfiability in propositional logic is well researched and many approaches to checking and solving exist. In infinite-valued or fuzzy logics, however, there have only recently been attempts at developing methods for solving satisfiability. In this paper, we propose new benchmark problems and analyse the function landscape of different problem classes, focussing our analysis on plateaus. Based on this study, we develop Mixing CMA-ES (M-CMA-ES), an extension to CMA-ES that is well suited to solving problems with many large plateaus. We empirically show the relation between certain function landscape properties and M-CMA-ES performance.

Categories and Subject Descriptions

G.1 [**Numerical Analysis**]: Optimization

General Terms

Algorithms, Performance

Keywords

CMA-ES, Fuzzy Satisfiability, Mixing

1. INTRODUCTION

A logical formula, or a set of formulas, is said to be satisfiable if there exists a truth assignment to its variables that makes every formula true. Satisfiability checking is verifying whether such an assignment exists, and satisfiability solving means finding such an assignment. This problem is known as SAT in propositional logic and is of interest to researchers from various domains, as many problems can be reformulated as a SAT problem and subsequently solved by a state-of-the-art SAT solver.

In fuzzy logics – logics with an infinite number of truth degrees – the same principle of satisfiability exists (SAT_∞). Like its classical counterpart, it is useful for solving a variety of problems. Indeed, many fuzzy reasoning tasks can be reduced to SAT_∞, including reasoning about vague concepts in the context of the semantic web [11], fuzzy spatial reasoning [9] and fuzzy answer set programming [7], which in itself is an important framework for non-monotonic reasoning over continuous domains (see e.g. [8, 13]). Importantly, the transition into fuzzy logics makes SAT_∞ a problem on a continuous domain, instead of a discrete (boolean) domain.

Solving satisfiability in fuzzy logics has however received much less attention than its counterpart in classical logics. In [4], Hähnle proposes a mixed integer programming (MIP) approach for Łukasiewicz logic, which unfortunately suffers from scalability issues that are inherent to MIP. Schockaert et al. also propose a solver for SAT_∞ in Łukasiewicz logic [10], which reduces the infinite-valued logic to a finite-valued one and then applies a constraint satisfaction solver to check satisfiability. This approach suffers from an exponential complexity in the granularity of the truth values in a problem. Recently, we proposed a new solver [2] that models satisfiability as an optimization problem over a continuous domain and has the advantage of being independent of the underlying logic and its operators, as well as not suffering from the complexity issues associated with analytical solvers, as our results showed. The disadvantage of this approach is that it cannot be a complete solver, i.e. deciding both SAT_∞ and $UNSAT_\infty$, unless the optimization algorithm is proven to converge to the global optimum. The currently best performing optimization algorithm on these problems is the Covariance Matrix Adaptation Evolution Strategy (CMA-ES), which is considered state-of-the-art in black-box optimization on a continuous domain.

In this paper, we define an objective function for SAT_∞ and intuitively show that optimizing this function equals solving SAT_∞. We incrementally describe the generation of a set of challenging benchmark problems representing different problem classes from different logics and motivate our choices. Using landscape analysis, we identify certain properties from these problem classes and use this knowledge to propose an extension to CMA-ES, aimed to improve its performance. In Sections 2 and 3, we introduce Fuzzy Logics and CMA-ES respectively. Subsequently, in Section 4, we introduce the first problem classes and perform a landscape analysis. In Section 5, we propose an extension to CMA-ES and evaluate it on the benchmark problems, and in Section 6, we introduce two new problem classes and perform the same analysis.

2. FUZZY LOGIC AND SAT$_\infty$

In fuzzy logics [5], truth is expressed as a real number taken from the unit interval $[0, 1]$. Essentially, there are an infinite number of truth degrees possible. A formula in fuzzy logics is built from a set of variables $\mathcal{V}$, constants taken from $[0, 1]$ and n-ary connectives for $n \in \mathbb{N}$. An interpretation is a mapping $\mathcal{I} : \mathcal{V} \to [0, 1]$ that maps every variable to a truth degree. We can extend this fuzzy interpretation $\mathcal{I}$ to formulas as follows:

- For each constant c in $[0, 1]$, $[c]_\mathcal{I} = c$.
- For each variable v in $\mathcal{V}$, $[v]_\mathcal{I} = \mathcal{I}(v)$.
- Each n-ary connective f is interpreted by a function $\mathtt{f} : [0, 1]^n \to [0, 1]$. Furthermore we define

  $$[f(\alpha_1, \ldots, \alpha_n)]_\mathcal{I} = \mathtt{f}([\alpha_1]_\mathcal{I}, \ldots, [\alpha_n]_\mathcal{I})$$

  for formulas α_i with $1 \leq i \leq n$.

The connectives in fuzzy logics typically correspond to connectives from classical logic, such as conjunction, disjunction, implication and negation, which are interpreted respectively by a t-norm, a t-conorm, an implicator and a negator. A triangular norm or t-norm $\mathtt{T}$ is an increasing, associative and commutative $[0, 1]^2 \to [0, 1]$ mapping that satisfies the boundary condition $\mathtt{T}(1, x) = x$ for all x in $[0, 1]$. Similarly, a triangular conorm or t-conorm $\mathtt{S}$ is an increasing, associative and commutative $[0, 1]^2 \to [0, 1]$ mapping that satisfies the boundary condition $\mathtt{S}(0, x) = x$. An implicator $\mathtt{I}$ is a $[0, 1]^2 \to [0, 1]$ mapping that is decreasing in its first argument, increasing in its second argument and that satisfies the properties $\mathtt{I}(0, 0) = \mathtt{I}(0, 1) = \mathtt{I}(1, 1) = 1$ and $\mathtt{I}(1, 0) = 0$. A negator $\mathtt{N}$ is a decreasing $[0, 1] \to [0, 1]$ mapping that satisfies $\mathtt{N}(0) = 1$ and $\mathtt{N}(1) = 0$.

As an example of a particularly popular fuzzy logic, in Łukasiewicz logic, negation $\neg$, conjunction $\otimes$, disjunction $\oplus$ and implication $\to$ are interpreted as follows:

- $[\neg\alpha]_\mathcal{I} = 1 - [\alpha]_\mathcal{I}$
- $[\alpha \otimes \beta]_\mathcal{I} = \max([\alpha]_\mathcal{I} + [\beta]_\mathcal{I} - 1, 0)$
- $[\alpha \oplus \beta]_\mathcal{I} = \min(1, [\alpha]_\mathcal{I} + [\beta]_\mathcal{I})$
- $[\alpha \to \beta]_\mathcal{I} = \min(1 - [\alpha]_\mathcal{I} + [\beta]_\mathcal{I}, 1)$

for formulas α and β.

An interpretation $\mathcal{I}$ is said to be a model of a set of formulas Θ iff $\forall \alpha \in \Theta : l \leq [\alpha]_\mathcal{I} \leq u$, given lower and upper bounds l and u for that formula (usually u is 1, and in classical logic even both l and u are 1). An example of a formula with three variables v_1, v_2, and v_3 in Łukasiewicz logic, with bounds is:

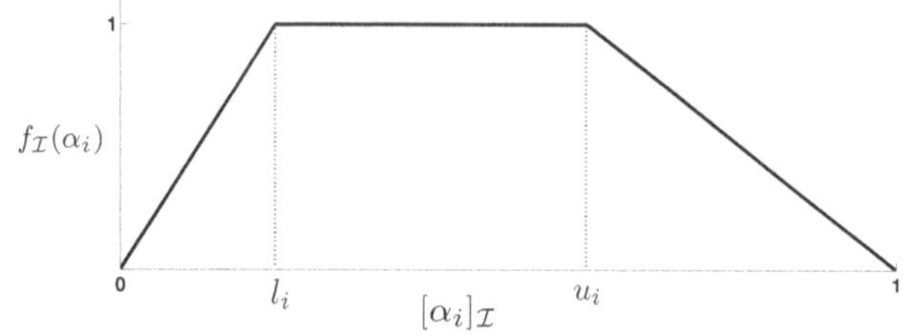

Figure 1: $f_\mathcal{I}(\alpha_i)$ for a formula α_i with lower bound l_i, upper bound u_i and degree of satisfaction $[\alpha_i]_\mathcal{I}$.

$$0.5 \leq \neg(v_1 \otimes v_2 \otimes \neg v_3) \leq 1 \tag{1}$$

One can easily verify that $\mathcal{I}_1$ with $\mathcal{I}_1(v_1) = 0$, $\mathcal{I}_1(v_2) = 0$ and $\mathcal{I}_1(v_3) = 1$ is a model of this formula as $[\neg(v_1 \otimes v_2 \otimes \neg v_3)]_{\mathcal{I}_1} = 1$. Similarly, $\mathcal{I}_2$ with $\mathcal{I}_2(v_1) = 0.6$, $\mathcal{I}_2(v_2) = 0.7$ and $\mathcal{I}_2(v_3) = 0.2$ is a model too because $[\neg(v_1 \otimes v_2 \otimes \neg v_3)]_{\mathcal{I}_2} = 0.9$. Even though the formula is not perfectly satisfied under interpretation $\mathcal{I}_2$, the degree of satisfaction is still high enough to meet the lower bound $l = 0.5$. The existence of the models $\mathcal{I}_1$ and $\mathcal{I}_2$ show that formula (1) is satisfiable. Solving SAT$_\infty$ amounts to finding a model for the set of formulas given, or deciding that there is no interpretation that satisfies all formulas and that the set is UNSAT$_\infty$.

2.1 SAT$_\infty$ as an optimization problem

As we will investigate an optimization approach to solving satisfiability in fuzzy logics, we need to reformulate SAT$_\infty$ instances as optimization problems, i.e. defining a function over the solution space such that optimizing this function corresponds to solving the SAT$_\infty$ instance. A SAT$_\infty$ problem consists of a set Θ of formulas α_i, each of which must be satisfied to a certain degree, as defined by an upper and lower bound per formula. Given these m formulas α_i, bounds (l_i, u_i), and an interpretation $\mathcal{I}$, we define the objective function f as follows:

$$f(\mathcal{I}) = \frac{\sum_{i=1}^{m} f_\mathcal{I}(\alpha_i, l_i, u_i)}{m} \tag{2}$$

and,

$$f_\mathcal{I}(\alpha_i, l_i, u_i) = \begin{cases} 1 & \text{if } l_i \leq [\alpha_i]_\mathcal{I} \leq u_i \\ \frac{[\alpha_i]_\mathcal{I}}{l_i} & \text{if } [\alpha_i]_\mathcal{I} < l_i \\ \frac{1-[\alpha_i]_\mathcal{I}}{1-u_i} & \text{if } [\alpha_i]_\mathcal{I} > u_i \end{cases} \tag{3}$$

with $[\alpha_i]_\mathcal{I}$ representing the degree of satisfaction of formula α_i under interpretation $\mathcal{I}$. Each $f_\mathcal{I}$ is a trapezoid function, with a plateau of value 1 when formula α_i's degree of satisfaction lies between the given bounds, and a slope leading to the plateau when the satisfaction lies outside these bounds, as visualised in Figure 1.

This function is formulated such that the global maxima will always have a function value 1 if the SAT$_\infty$ instance is satisfiable. In that case, every global maximum corresponds to a model of the problem.

3. CMA-ES

The Covariance Matrix Adaptation-Evolution Strategy (CMA-ES)[6] is an algorithm belonging to the class of Evolution Strategies, and is considered to be state-of-the-art in black-box optimization on a continuous domain. CMA-ES is a $(\mu/\mu, \lambda)$-ES with the addition of de-randomized adaptation of the multivariate distribution that generates candidate solutions. This additional mechanism allows CMA-ES to efficiently explore promising search directions by adapting the distribution to the local shape of the search space. For a full description of this algorithm, we refer the reader to [6].

In [3], we determined that the restart strategy proposed by Auger and Hansen [1] does not perform well on the problems considered in this paper. Therefore, we use the simple restart strategy that was found to increase performance, i.e. restart after $i \times \lambda$ function evaluations without improvement. It was previously found that $i = 1000$ gives good results.

Furthermore, since we are dealing with box-constraints ($[0, 1]^n$), we need to handle constraint violations. We use a penalty function when the constraint is violated. The penalty is dependent on the distance between the candidate solution and the box. The new objective function is:

$$f(\mathcal{I}) = \begin{cases} \frac{-\sum_{i=1}^{m} f_{\mathcal{I}}(\alpha_i, l_i, u_i)}{m}, & \text{if } \mathcal{I}(\mathcal{V}) \in [0,1]^n \\ 10^4 \sum_{i=1}^{m} \theta(|(\mathcal{I}(v_i) - 0.5)| - 0.5)(\mathcal{I}(v_i) - 0.5)^2, & \\ & \text{if } \mathcal{I}(\mathcal{V}) \notin [0,1]^n \end{cases} \quad (4)$$

with θ the heaviside function (0 for negative input, otherwise 1) and n the number of variables.

We make the new function conditional instead of adding the penalty to the objective function as is commonly done, because numbers beyond [0,1] have no meaning in fuzzy logics and prevent the formulas from being evaluated. Since CMA-ES is a minimization technique, we negate the objective function.

4. PROBLEM CLASSES AND LANDSCAPE ANALYSIS

To evaluate the performance of the proposed algorithms for solving SAT_∞, we need a set of challenging problem instances. In this section we first describe how we built a set of benchmark problems and then perform landscape analysis to identify properties that may give insights into algorithm performance.

4.1 Problem instances

Schockaert et al. [10] propose a procedure to generate satisfiability problems in Łukasiewicz logic; a somewhat different process than what is usual in classical SAT. This is due to the fact that not all formulas in Łukasiewicz logic can be converted to conjunctive-normal form, and that, when restricted to formulas in conjunctive-normal form (in the sense that only lower bounds are used, formulas are composed of conjunctions and negations, and all negations occur immediately in front of atoms), the satisfiability problem in Łukasiewicz logic can be reduced to linear programming, and can thus be decided in polynomial time. Hence, to generate interesting test problems, it is crucial to consider formulas which are not in conjunctive-normal form.

The recursive procedure *form*(p) is defined to generate logical formulas with a fixed number of variable occurrences. The base case, i.e. one variable in a formula, is as follows:

$$\mathit{form}(1) = \begin{cases} v_i & \text{probability } 0.5 \\ \neg v_i & \text{probability } 0.5 \end{cases} \quad (5)$$

where v_i is a randomly chosen variable from a predefined set of variables $\mathcal{V} = \{v_1, v_2, ..., v_m\}$.

The general case, for $p > 1$, is:

$$\mathit{form}(p) = \begin{cases} \mathit{form}(p_1) \otimes \mathit{form}(p_2) & \text{probability } 0.5 \\ \neg(\mathit{form}(p_1) \otimes \mathit{form}(p_2)) & \text{probability } 0.5 \end{cases} \quad (6)$$

with p_1 a random integer between 1 and $p - 1$, and $p_2 = p - p_1$.

The creation of challenging problems depends very much on the selection of bounds for formulas. Schockaert et al. propose the following procedure to select bounds for formula α:

- Let λ_1 be the largest value from $\mathbb{T}_4 = \{0, \frac{1}{4}, \frac{2}{4}, \frac{3}{4}, 1\}$ smaller than $[\alpha]_{\mathcal{I}_1}$.
- Let λ_2 be the smallest value from $\mathbb{T}_4$ larger than $[\alpha]_{\mathcal{I}_2}$.
- With probability 0.5, add $\lambda_1 \leq \alpha \leq 1$ to the set of formulas, otherwise add $\lambda_2 \leq \alpha \leq 1$.

The set of benchmark problems used in [10] was generated using this method, with the additional constraint that any variable can occur at most once in every formula. Each problem instance consists of 100 formulas ($n = 100$), with five variable occurrences per formula ($p = 5$), so we can say we are solving 5-SAT_∞. 50 problem instances were generated with 40 variables each.

In [2], we generated an additional set of problem instances, with problem bounds drawn from $\mathbb{T}_{100}$, i.e. $\{0, \frac{1}{100}, \frac{2}{100}, ..., 1\}$ instead of $\mathbb{T}_4$[1]. We distinguish between problems with formula bounds drawn from $\mathbb{T}_4$ and $\mathbb{T}_{100}$, as we have shown that this difference has a strong impact on the performance of current analytical solvers, and might also influence our optimization algorithms. That aside, the use of sets $\mathbb{T}_k$ is purely artificial; in reality, formula bounds are problem dependent and will usually not be directly derived from some set $\mathbb{T}_k$. Determining the smallest k such that $\mathbb{T}_k$ includes all bounds in an instance may not be trivial and will typically yield very large k, which is problematic for the analytical solver from [10]. Still, we use these sets to analyse the impact of granularity on algorithm performance, and because there is no other method known to generate hard SAT_∞ instances.

The two problem classes discussed will from now on be refered to as L_4 and L_{100} respectively.

4.2 Plateaus analysis

A plateau is a collection of points in the search space that span an ℓ-dimensional manifold, with the same fitness for all points. Since most optimization algorithms, including CMA-ES, use gradient information to optimize an objective function, plateaus, which provide zero gradient information,

[1]These benchmark problems, others, and Java code to interpret them can be downloaded here: http://ai.vub.ac.be/members/tim-brys

can hinder performance. We have seen that our objective function is built to yield a plateau for each formula when its degree of satisfaction lies between the bounds specified, and furthermore, the conjunction operator in Łukasiewicz logic calculates the maximum of two values, which also returns a plateau for a range of the input values. Therefore, we can expect our objective function to contain plateaus. We will analyse the two defined problem classes, looking for plateaus.

This analysis is performed by generating random walks. Specifically, for each of the 100 problem instances we have, we perform 10 random walks of 10^6 steps. One step consist of adding ± 0.01 to a randomly picked variable. This value is the smallest granularity in the problems.

Using these random walks, we estimate the size of plateaus by counting the number of subsequent steps of the same fitness. Figure 2(a) plots the relation between plateau size and the number of times they were encountered, which is an estimation of their overall frequency. Both Łukasiewicz problem classes have similar numbers of plateaus, which decrease with plateau size, i.e. there are many more small plateaus than there are large ones.

The relation between plateau size and plateau fitness is plotted in Figure 2(b). Interestingly, fitness increases much with plateau size on $Ł_4$ problems, which means that in general, the larger a plateau, the closer in function value it will be to optimal solutions. We expect this property to ensure that escaping large plateaus needs only be done a few times. This trait is shared with regular SAT landscapes. On the contrary, plateau fitness does not rise much with plateau size on the $Ł_{100}$ problems, which means that escaping from a plateau does not guarantee nearness to optimal solutions, that large plateaus are more distributed with respect to optimal solutions. Note that the plots become more noisy for large plateaus simply because fewer of such plateaus were found.

Given this analysis, we expect that CMA-ES's performance on these problem classes, and specifically on the $Ł_{100}$ problems, may be hindered by these plateaus. Therefore, we propose an additional mechanism for CMA-ES that may help it escape from plateaus.

5. MIXING CMA-ES

The idea we use in this paper for the plateau-escaping mechanism is an application of optimal mixing evolutionary algorithms [12] on the multi-population level: we have multiple CMA-ES populations running in parallel, and we recombine their distributions if this leads to improvements. We call this Mixing CMA-ES or M-CMA-ES. This recombination of distributions is executed by exchanging elements, i.e. variable assignments, between the means of the two populations. Pseudocode describing this mixing can be found in Algorithms 1 and 2.

We start with multiple CMA-ES algorithms running in parallel. When all populations have executed a regular CMA-ES iteration, we pair each one with another and apply mixing to the means of their distributions. The mean is used to evaluate the population's fitness during mixing, as it is the best estimator for the optimum in the population. Mixing goes as follows:

- For each pair of populations, the set of problem variables is randomly divided into s disjunct sets of variables of roughly the same size (the number of variables divided by s is not always a natural number).
- The variables of one of the sets are exchanged between the two population means.
- If at least one of the two new means has greater fitness than both parent means, the exchange is accepted. This ensures global improvement through mixing, avoiding local oscillations when optimized substructures go back and forth between populations.
- This exchange is performed for each disjunct variable set, each time continuing with the accepted means from the previous step.

Algorithm 1 Mixing CMA-ES

```
procedure M-CMA-ES
    populations ← InitializeCMAESPopulations(n)
    while !stopcriterion do
        for i ∈ {0, 1, .., n} do
            ExecuteCMAESIteration(population_i)
        end for
        for i, j ∈ {0, 1, .., n} do
            Mixing(populations_i, populations_j)
        end for
    end while
end procedure
```

Algorithm 2 Mixing Two Populations

```
procedure MIXING(MEAN1, MEAN2)
    variableSets ← DisjunctVariableSets(s)
    fp1 ← fitness(mean1)
    fp2 ← fitness(mean2)
    child1 ← mean1
    child2 ← mean2
    for each set ∈ variableSets do
        for each variable ∈ set do
            child1[variable] ← mean2[variable]
            child2[variable] ← mean1[variable]
        end for
        fc1 ← fitness(child1); fc2 ← fitness(child2)
        if (fc1 < fp1 and fc1 < fp2) or
            (fc2 < fp1 and fc2 < fp2) then
            mean1 ← child1; mean2 ← child2
            fp1 ← fc1; fp2 ← fc2
        else
            for each variable ∈ set do
                child1[variable] ← mean1[variable]
                child2[variable] ← mean2[variable]
            end for
        end if
    end for
    RecombineCovAndEvPaths(mean1, mean2)
end procedure
```

This is basically optimal mixing with the Marginal Product structure [12], although without structure learning. This is not feasible due to the small number of populations that is practically possible.

Besides the mean of the distribution, CMA-ES also maintains a covariance matrix and evolution paths for the sampling and updating of this distribution. In our mixing, we

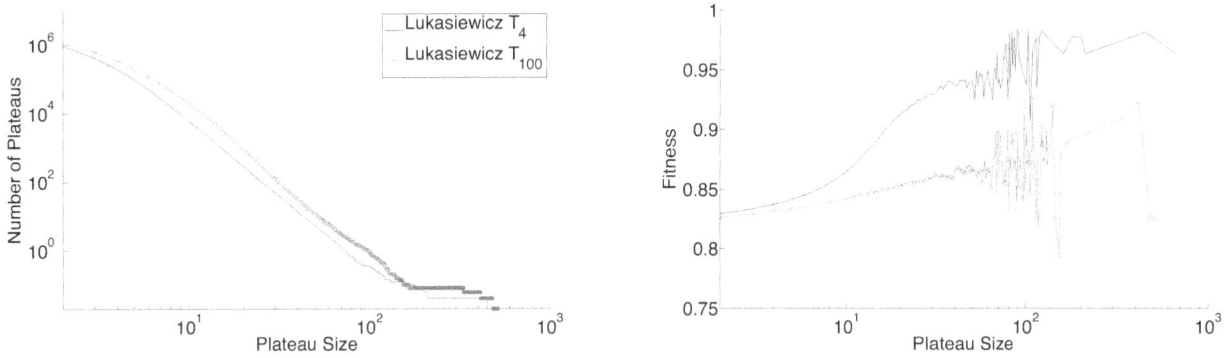

(a) (b)

Figure 2: (a) The number of plateaus as a function of plateau size, as estimated by the number of random steps at the same fitness value. (b) The fitness of plateaus as a function of plateau size.

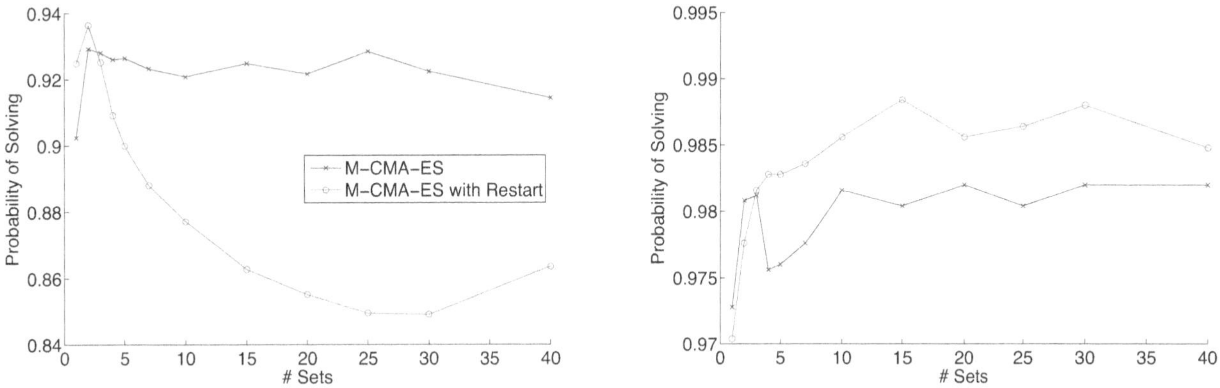

Ł$_4$ Ł$_{100}$

Figure 3: Success ratio achieved given a budget of 10^7 function evaluations as a function of the number of marginal product sets used in mixing on the Łukasiewicz problem classes.

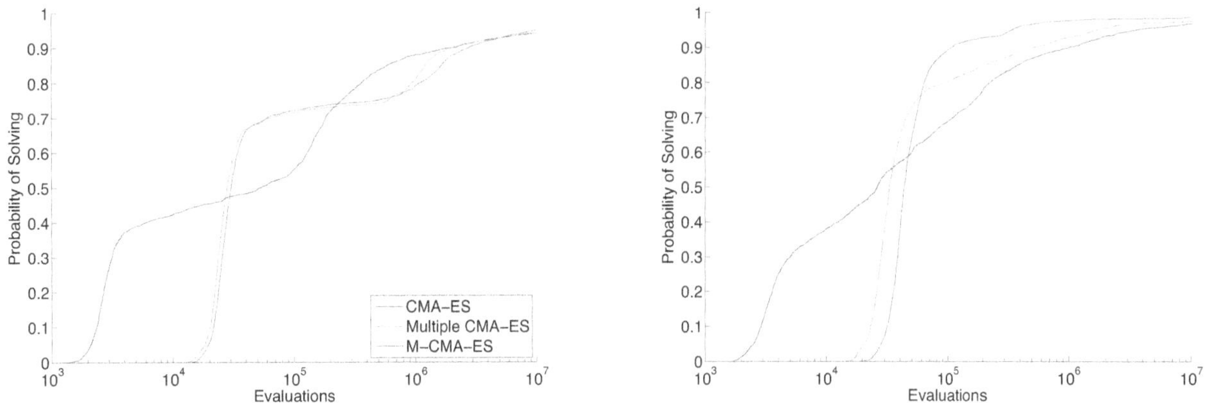

Ł$_4$ Ł$_{100}$

Figure 4: Run length distributions of CMA-ES, multiple CMA-ES and M-CMA-ES on the Łukasiewicz problem classes.

recombine these as described below, under the assumption that we should keep CMA-ES as intact as possible, since these parameters are adapted to the variable values in the mean that are exchanged. Still, we do not test whether this assumption really holds and whether mixing these parameters as well is necessary.

The recombination of the evolution paths is trivial, as these are represented by vectors in which the corresponding values can simply be exchanged. The recombination of the covariance matrix is less simple, as it encodes information between variables that may or may not be kept together during recombination. The way the matrix crossover is implemented is as follows: if variables v_i and v_j stay together, the covariance information for element (i, j) comes from the corresponding parent. If the variables come from different solutions, the average of the covariance information from both solutions is calculated and stored. This covariance matrix recombination can only take place after every variable set is exchanged, since only then can we know of all variables whether they stay together or not.

5.1 Empirical validation

Before we empirically evaluate and compare CMA-ES with M-CMA-ES on the given problem classes, we optimize the parameter governing the number of disjunct sets used for mixing. We run two variants of M-CMA-ES , one with and one without the restarting strategy described before. 50 runs of maximum 10^7 evaluations are performed for each instance, resulting in 5000 runs per parameter setting. 10 populations are used, and each population has $\mu = 2$ and $\lambda = 20$, as determined to be near-optimal settings for a single population on these problems [3]. Figure 3 shows the results of this experiment. Note that setting the sets parameter to 1 reduces M-CMA-ES to 10 independent CMA-ES populations (no extra evaluations are performed for mixing). Increasing the number of sets means more evaluations spent on mixing as compared to the standard sampling in CMA-ES, and also finer granularity in the mixing. Either of these can have a positive or negative impact on the performance, depending on the problem. For example, granularity of the sets in mixing should ideally be tuned to the linkage between variables in the problem, if any. Too fine grained mixing may disrupt optimized substructures, while too coarse grained mixing may not achieve the optimal possible performance increase.

To our surprise, the non-restarting M-CMA-ES dominates the restarting M-CMA-ES on the first problem class for all parameter settings (the observed difference for 2 sets is not significant). Note that for single CMA-ES and multiple independent CMA-ES (# sets = 1), the restarting does contribute to achieve better performance, see [3] and Figure 3. On the $Ł_{100}$ problems, restarting M-CMA-ES dominates the non-restarting variant as expected – the observed differences are only significant for 4 sets and more.

On both problem classes, the non-restarting variant remains fairly consistent in performance across the range of tested parameter settings, with only few statistically significant differences, while restarting makes the mixing more sensitive to parameter settings.

From this experiment, we select the restarting M-CMA-ES with 2 sets for $Ł_4$ problems (even though the difference is statistically insignificant, the observed performance of the restarting variant is highest). For the $Ł_{100}$ problems, we select the restarting variant with 15 sets. Furthermore, we

	Success		Evaluations	
	$Ł_4$	$Ł_{100}$	$Ł_4$	$Ł_{100}$
CMA-ES	94.24%	96.72%	297142	266974
10 CMA-ES	94.29%	97.44%	366655	178673
M-CMA-ES	95.06%	98.6%	478158	101670

Table 1: Success percentage after 10^7 evaluations, and average number evaluations in successful runs. All observed differences with the best are significant (Wilcoxon signed-rank test, confidence 95%).

will also compare with independent parallel CMA-ES populations, to isolate the effect of having multiple populations, and the effect of the mixing mechanism. We select the restarting and non-restarting variants for the $Ł_4$ and $Ł_{100}$ problems respectively.

As we compare standard CMA-ES with multiple independent CMA-ES and M-CMA-ES, we use the same population sizes ($\mu = 2$, $\lambda = 20$) in each, meaning that the latter two algorithms effectively perform an order of magnitude more evaluations each generation. There is no need to compare these with the performance of CMA-ES with population size times 10, since we previously showed that increasing population size by this amount on these problems does not improve performance, given a budget of 10^7 function evaluations [3]. Figure 4 shows the run-length distributions of these three variants of CMA-ES, and Table 1 summarizes these results.

We observe that, in agreement with our hypothesis based on the landscape analysis, using mixing when solving the $Ł_{100}$ problems has more effect than on the $Ł_4$ problems. The performance on the more granular problems increases both in terms of probability of solving an instance, and average number of evaluations required to solve an instance. On the coarse-grained problems, there is an increase in success probability, but at the cost of a much higher average number of evaluations. Note that not only having multiple populations improves performance, but also the mixing mechanism in itself. Furthermore, the single CMA-ES starts solving instances almost an order of magnitude faster, simply because these easy problems do not require the extra populations, nor the mixing to be solved efficiently, and therefore the algorithms that have these mechanisms spend too much evaluations on redundant mechanisms.

6. OTHER LOGICS

Since our objective function formulation is essentially independent of the underlying logic and its operators, we will now briefly evaluate two new problem classes with a different conjunction operator. Similar to how we generated the $Ł_4$ and $Ł_{100}$ problems, we build two new problem classes, replacing the conjunction ($\otimes$) from the Łukasiewicz logic with that from the Product logic[2] ($[\alpha \otimes \beta]_{\mathcal{I}} = [\alpha]_{\mathcal{I}} \times [\beta]_{\mathcal{I}}$), again with bounds from $\mathbb{T}_4$ and $\mathbb{T}_{100}$. We refer to these problem classes as P_4 and P_{100}. Since the Product logic conjunction is a smooth function, we can expect a decrease in the number of plateaus as compared to the $Ł_k$ problems. This is confirmed in Figure 5 (a). The P_k problems have orders

[2]The mixing of operators from different logics is justified as the formulation of any problem as SAT_∞ leaves open the choice of operators; their choice depends on the desired problem properties.

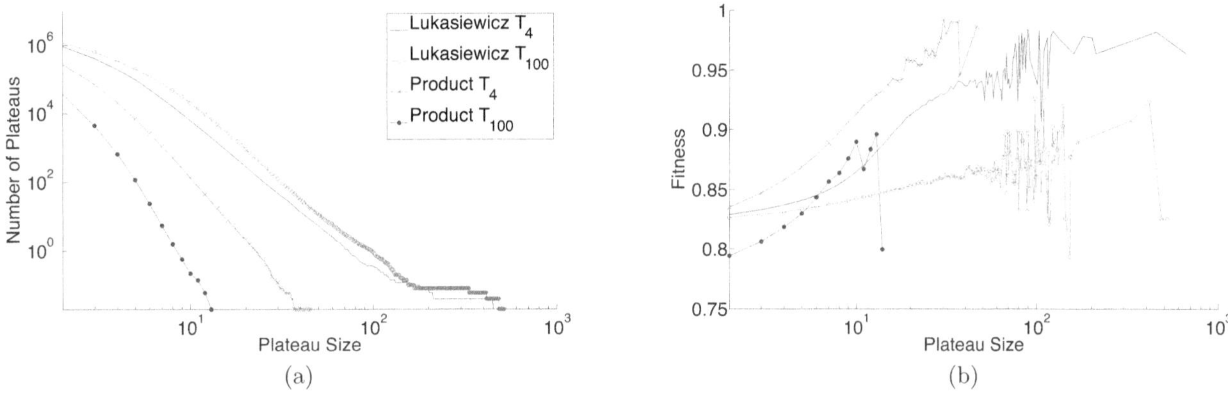

Figure 5: (a) The number of plateaus as a function of plateau size, as estimated by the number of random steps at the same fitness value. (b) The fitness of plateaus as a function of plateau size.

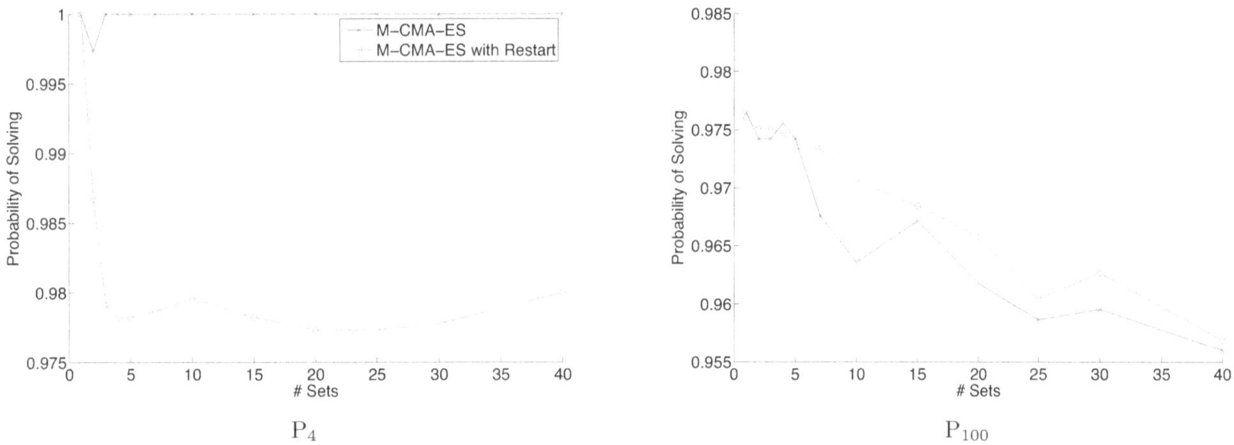

Figure 6: Success ratio achieved given a budget of 10^7 function evaluations as a function of the number of marginal product sets used in mixing on the Product problem classes.

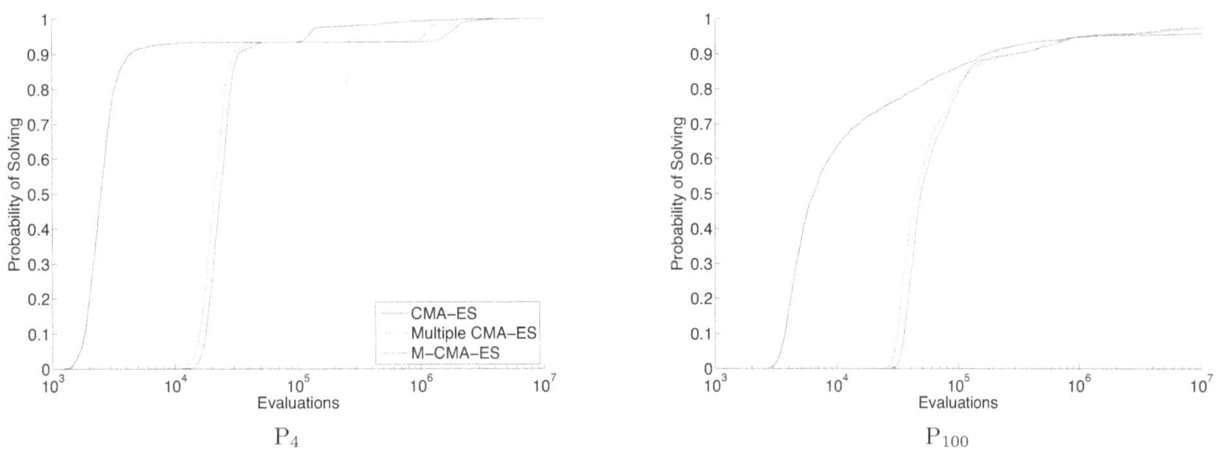

Figure 7: Run length distributions of CMA-ES, multiple CMA-ES and M-CMA-ES on the Product problem classes.

	Success		Evaluations	
	P_4	P_{100}	P_4	P_{100}
CMA-ES	100%	95.78%	26434	66056
10 CMA-ES	100%	97.78%	117490	186221
M-CMA-ES	100%	97.33%	149006	176690

Table 2: Success percentage after 10^7 evaluations, and average number evaluations in successful runs. All observed differences with the best are significant (Wilcoxon signed-rank test, confidence 95%). Note that in this case 100% means 45 instances solved, since in both classes, only 45 out of 50 instances are known to us to be satisfiable.

of magnitude less plateaus, and of much smaller size. Also, the average fitness of plateaus rises greatly with plateau size on both new classes (Figure 5 (b)). These two properties combined lead us to the expectation that the mixing mechanism will provide little to no improvement over standard CMA-ES.

As we will evaluate M-CMA-ES on these new problem classes, we again first optimize the parameter controlling the number of disjunct sets used in mixing. Figure 6 shows the results of this optimization, performed with the same experimental setup as in Section 5.1. Note that the relative performance of the restarting and non-restarting variant is very similar on these problem classes as on the first two problem classes. The non-restarting variant again dominates in performance on the first problem class, achieving much better performance, suggesting that the restart-mechanism, when combined with mixing, kicks in too soon and prevents the mixing to achieve its full potential. When no restarts are executed, mixing has the chance of trying many different mixes, since for each mix, variables are randomly distributed over the sets, and mixing partners are randomly selected.

We selected for both problem classes and both mixing and independent CMA-ES the non-restarting variant, M-CMA-ES with 2 and 4 sets on the two classes respectively. Figure 7 shows the run-length distributions of CMA-ES, multiple CMA-ES and M-CMA-ES on the P_k problem classes, and Table 2 summarises these results. It is clear that the mixing only worsens performance by spending precious evaluations on a mechanism that is not necessary. Having multiple CMA-ES populations makes a difference on the P_{100} problems in terms of probability of solving an instance (on the P_4 problems, success is already 100%), but the average number of evaluations is on both problem classes much higher than for a single CMA-ES population.

7. CONCLUSION

In this paper, we proposed an extension to CMA-ES, called M-CMA-ES, based on the landscape analysis of satisfiability problems in the Łukasiewicz fuzzy logic. M-CMA-ES incorporates two types of mechanisms: the standard CMA-ES model-based optimization at population level, and the recombination optimization at the meta-population level. The number of evaluations that go to either mechanism can be controlled and needs to be balanced for optimal effect. Product logic problems clearly benefit more from the standard CMA-ES optimization, and have no need for population recombination. Łukasiewicz problems on the other hand have many plateaus and benefit much from spending part of the evaluations on recombination. In future work, we will consider other mixing operators besides simple variable exchange, and will analyse their effect on inter-population diversity, as well as how this affects performance.

8. ACKNOWLEDGEMENT

This work was partially funded by a joint VUB-UGent Research Foundation-Flanders (FWO) project. Also, Tim Brys is funded by a Ph.D grant of the Research Foundation Flanders (FWO).

9. REFERENCES

[1] A. Auger and N. Hansen. Performance Evaluation of an Advanced Local Search Evolutionary Algorithm. In *IEEE Congress on Evolutionary Computation*, pages 1777–1784, 2005.

[2] T. Brys, Y.-M. De Hauwere, M. De Cock, and A. Nowé. Solving satisfiability in fuzzy logics with evolution strategies. In *Proceedings of the 31st Annual North American Fuzzy Information Processing Society Meeting*, 2012.

[3] T. Brys, M. M. Drugan, P. A. N. Bosman, M. De Cock, and A. Nowé. Local search and restart strategies for satisfiability solving in fuzzy logics. In *Proceedings of the IEEE Symposium Series on Computational Intelligence - SSCI-2013*. 2013.

[4] R. Hähnle. Many-valued logic and mixed integer programming. *Annals of Mathematics and Artificial Intelligence*, 12:231–263, 1994.

[5] P. Hájek. *Metamathematics of Fuzzy Logic*. Springer, 1998.

[6] N. Hansen. The CMA evolution strategy: a comparing review. In *Towards a new evolutionary computation. Advances on estimation of distribution algorithms*, pages 75–102. Springer, 2006.

[7] J. Janssen, S. Schockaert, D. Vermeir, and M. De Cock. Reducing fuzzy answer set programming to model finding in fuzzy logics. *CoRR*, 2011.

[8] N. Madrid and M. Ojeda-Aciego. Measuring inconsistency in fuzzy answer set semantics. In *Transactions on Fuzzy Systems*, volume 19, pages 605–622, 2011.

[9] S. Schockaert, M. De Cock, and E. E. Kerre. Spatial reasoning in a fuzzy region connection calculus. *Artificial Intelligence*, 173(2):258 – 298, 2009.

[10] S. Schockaert, J. Janssen, and D. Vermeir. Satisfiability checking in Łukasiewicz logic as finite constraint satisfaction. *Journal of Automated Reasoning*, 2012.

[11] U. Straccia and F. Bobillo. Mixed integer programming, general concept inclusions and fuzzy description logics. *Mathware & Soft Computing*, 2007.

[12] D. Thierens and P. A. N. Bosman. Optimal mixing evolutionary algorithms. In N. Krasnogor and P. L. Lanzi, editors, *GECCO*, pages 617–624. ACM, 2011.

[13] D. Van Nieuwenborgh, M. De Cock, and D. Vermeir. An introduction to fuzzy answer set programming. *Annals of Mathematics and Artificial Intelligence*, 50:363–388, 2007.

Using Representative Strategies for Finding Nash Equilibria

Chih-Yuan Chou
Department of Electrical Engineering
National Taiwan University
r00921082@ntu.edu.tw

Tian-Li Yu
Department of Electrical Engineering
National Taiwan University
tianliyu@cc.ee.ntu.edu.tw

ABSTRACT

Since the existence of at least one mixed Nash equilibrium (NE) for any game was proved by Nash, finding NE has been an important issue in the field of game theory. However, polynomial-time algorithms for such task have not yet been discovered, and one of the difficulties is the infinite search space. In this paper, we define the so-called ϵ-representative strategy to reduce the search space. In general, the equilibria on these representative strategies are not the original equilibria but approximations. To find such approximate equilibria, we then propose a two-level method, which firstly uses co-evolutionary algorithms to co-evolve the representative strategies for each player and then the approximate equilibria. The computational time can be controlled by the parameters of the co-evolutionary algorithms. Empirical results show that our method finds the approximate NE in a reasonable time. Finally, the definitions developed in this paper help define the co-evolvability of NE.

Categories and Subject Descriptors

F.2.m [**Analysis of Algorithms and Problem Complexity**]: Miscellaneous

General Terms

Algorithms

Keywords

Game Theory, Nash equilibrium, Bimatrix Game, Co-evolution

1. INTRODUCTION

The theory of games has been well studied in mathematical and economical aspects [2, 9, 19, 20, 26, 35]. The Nash equilibrium (NE), named after Nash [19], plays an important role in game theory and microeconomics. Furthermore, NE is also the standard notion of rationality and has served as the open computational problem in the emerging area at the interface between game theory and algorithms. Recent researches [4, 6, 7, 10, 23] have shown that computing a mixed NE is PPAD-complete, even in a two-person game. It is generally believed that $PPAD \neq P$. In the worst case, the time of computing an NE for the state-of-the-art algorithm grows exponentially with the game size [30].

GECCO'13, July 6–10, 2013, Amsterdam, The Netherlands.

(Prisoner 1, Prisoner 2)	Defect	Cooperate
Defect	(-5, -5)	(0, -20)
Cooperate	(-20, 0)	(-1, -1)

Table 1: The payoff matrix of prisoner's dilemma.

This paper focuses on finite normal-form games, where the payoff is usually represented by a matrix. For example, in the prisoner's dilemma [16], each prisoner can either *cooperate* or *defect.* The payoff matrix of the prisoner's dilemma is shown in Table 1. For example, if Prisoner 1 chooses *defect* and Prisoner 2 chooses *cooperate*, the payoffs of Prisoner 1 and 2 are 0 and -20, respectively.

To find NE in normal-form games, several algorithms have been proposed over the past half century, but all of them are either of unknown complexity, or known to be exponential in the worst case [7, 14, 15, 21]. In this paper, we introduce the concept of the *representative strategies* that are used to define the difficulty for finding NE. In addition, we develop a two-level method for finding NE. A definition of representative strategies and A definition of the *strengths* of the representative strategies are also given in this paper. Furthermore, two methods for finding the representative strategies of games and two methods for finding NE after obtaining the representative strategies are provided. Two reasons for finding the representative strategies of games are as follows. First, the representative strategies reduce the computing time for finding NE. Second, the representative strategies can help define the difficulty for finding NE.

The rest of this paper is organized as follows. Section 2 lists the basic definitions which are used in this paper. Section 3 presents the previous work on NE computation and some techniques we use in this paper. Section 4 shows the details of the representative strategies. The methods for finding NE by using the representative strategies, and the definition of the difficulty for finding NE, are both in Section 5. The experimental results are in Section 6. Conclusions and future works are in Section 7.

2. DEFINITION

In this section, the properties of games that considered in this paper are formally addressed. The concepts of pure strategies and mixed strategies are reviewed at first, and following by the introduction of NE as an optimal solution.

2.1 The Normal-Form Game

In game theory, the normal form is a common description of a game. Unlike the extensive form [32], the normal-form representation is usually represented by matrix [20]. In addition, The normal-form representation does not incorporate any notion of sequence, or time, of the actions of the players. A normal-form game consists of a set of players, a set of strategies for each player, and the corresponding payoffs for each player.

DEFINITION 1. *A **normal-form game** is a triple* (P, S, U). $P = \{1, 2, \cdots, n\}$ *is a set of **players**, and*

$$S = \{S_i | S_i = \{{s_i}^1, {s_i}^2, \cdots, {s_i}^{k_i}\}, 1 \leq i \leq n\}$$

*is the set that contains all **strategy** sets* S_i *for any player* i.

$$U = \{u_1, u_2, \cdots, u_n\}$$

*is the set of the **payoff** function* u_i *for each player* i, *where the payoff function*

$$u_i : S_1 \times S_2 \times \cdots \times S_n \rightarrow \mathbb{R}$$

gives the payoff of player i *with the strategies of all players given.*

2.2 Pure Strategies and Mixed Strategies

Each strategy in S_i is called a *pure strategy*. A player i with a strategy set S_i can also play with probability. A probabilistic combination of pure strategies is called a *mixed strategy*.

DEFINITION 2. *A **mixed strategy** on a strategy set* S_i *is a probability vector*

$$\vec{x_i} = ({x_i}^1, {x_i}^2, \cdots, {x_i}^{k_i})$$

where the pure strategy ${s_i}^j$ *is played with a probability of* ${x_i}^j$.

Obviously, the sum of probability is $\sum_{j=1}^{k_i} {x_i}^j = 1$ for player i. A pure strategy is a special case of mixed strategies because it always plays one single strategy with a probability of 1 and others with a probability of 0. Since a mixed strategy is a random variable, the payoff functions are defined by the expectation of the original payoffs.

DEFINITION 3. *Let* $\vec{x_i}$ *be the mixed strategy of player* i, *and mixed strategy profile* $\vec{x} = (\vec{x_1}, \vec{x_2}, \cdots, \vec{x_n})$. *The **expected payoff*** π_i *of player* i *is written as the following equation:*

$$\pi_i(\vec{x}) = \sum_{k_1, k_2, \cdots, k_n} (\prod_{j=1}^{n} x_j^{k_j}) \cdot u_i(s_1^{k_1}, s_2^{k_2}, \cdots, s_n^{k_n})$$

Furthermore, the *support* of a mixed strategy is the subset of the pure strategies that are assigned positive probabilities in the mixed strategy.

DEFINITION 4. *Let* $\vec{x_i} = ({x_i}^1, {x_i}^2, \cdots, {x_i}^{k_i})$ *be a mixed strategy on a pure strategy set* S_i *of player* i. *The **support** of the mixed strategy* $\vec{x_i}$ *is written as the following equation:*

$$support(\vec{x_i}) = \{{s_i}^j \in S_i \mid {x_i}^j > 0\}$$

2.3 Nash Equilibrium

A Nash equilibrium is a strategy profile that all rational players do not change their strategy.

DEFINITION 5. *Let* $(\vec{x_1}, \vec{x_2}, \cdots, \vec{x_n})$ *be a mixed strategy profile, where* $\vec{x_i}$ *is a mixed strategy of player* i. *This profile is a **Nash equilibrium** if*

$$\pi_i(\vec{x_1}, \cdots, \vec{x_i}, \cdots, \vec{x_n}) \geq \pi_i(\vec{x_1}, \cdots, \vec{x_i}', \cdots, \vec{x_n})$$

for all player i *and for all* $\vec{x_i}' \neq \vec{x_i}$.

All players are assumed to be rational, meaning that each player maximizes only its own payoff. In a NE, each player chooses not to change its strategy since it does not yield a higher payoff. Furthermore, if the strategies of all players are pure strategies, the NE of the strategy profile is called a *pure strategy Nash equilibrium* (pure NE); if not, it is called a *mixed strategy Nash equilibrium* (mixed NE).

3. RELATED WORK

Since the existence of NE in any finite game has been proved [19], finding NE became an important issue in game theory. Over the last several decades, many algorithms have been proposed for finding NE. In this section, the state-of-the-art algorithms for finding NE are reviewed, and some techniques we use in our algorithm are introduced.

3.1 the State-of-the-art Algorithms

The Lemke-Howson algorithm [13] has been the most commonly used algorithm to find an NE in two-player games. This algorithm utilized a linear complementarity problem for finding NE. More descriptions of the Lemke-Howson algorithm can be found in some recent articles [29, 34]. Furthermore, Codenotti *et al.* developed their own implementation of the Lemke-Howson algorithm [5]. Their experiments showed that the implementation was faster than other state-of-the-art software.

PNS, which is named after Porter, Nudelman, and Shoham, is a simple search method for finding NE [25]. PNS provides an algorithm that enumerates all the players' supports and for each joint support checks the existence of an NE by solving a linear feasibility problem. Although that idea has been previously described [8, 18], the paper improved on the basic idea by adding dominance checks and a well-motivated search bias.

Sandholm *et al.* introduced search algorithms based on mixed integer program (MIP) formulations for finding NE in two-player normal form games [28]. They studied different design dimensions of search algorithms that are based on those formulations. They also provided several methods to improve the computational efficiency.

Each of the above three algorithms outperforms the others in some specific settings: PNS outperforms MIP and Lemke-Howson algorithm for almost all the games generated by GAMUT [22]; Lemke-Howson algorithm outperforms PNS and MIP for games with medium-large support equilibria (this class of games is developed in [28]); MIP outperforms PNS and Lemke-Howson algorithm when one searches for an optimum equilibrium [3]. GAMUT [22] is the leading test suite of game generators. That library of 24 game generators is constructed from the descriptions of many different kinds of games in the literature. Also, GAMUT is the data that was used in the prior PNS and MIP experiments [25, 28].

In this paper, some of the experiments also use the games which are generated from GAMUT.

3.2 Techniques of Evolution

Evolution strategy (ES) [27] is based on the ideas of self-adaptation and evolution. (1+1) ES is one of the simplest ES which uses only one parent and one child. This paper uses (1+1) ES with the one-fifth rule [27] for finding representative strategies and for finding NE.

Since many games have more than one NE, we have to avoid being trapped in local optima. Pelikan *et al.* proposed a replacement method called restricted tournament replacement (RTR) [24]. RTR reserves the best individuals from previous population and still keeps diversity. Therefore, this paper uses the co-evolutionary genetic algorithms (co-evolutionary GA) with RTR for finding representative strategies.

In co-evolution, the fitness evaluation is based on interactions between multiple individuals. Therefore, the fitness of an individual in the population changes depending on other individuals. Co-evolutionary algorithms are used in the field of game theory [1,12,16,31]. Axelrod and Hamilton conducted experiments on the repeated prisoner's dilemma game [1,11]. Miller also used co-evolution to evolve a finite automaton as the strategy for playing the repeated prisoner's dilemma game [16,17]. Smith discussed co-evolution in connection with discovering strategies for games [31].

4. REPRESENTATIVE STRATEGY

Since finding all NE in every game is difficult [4,6,7,23], most of the algorithms [13,25,28] only focused on finding one of NE instead of finding all of NE. Therefore, we introduce the *representative strategies* that are used to help finding NE and to define the difficulty for finding NE. In this section, we provide a definition of the representative strategy and a definition of the strength of the representative strategy. In addition, two algorithms are provided for finding representative strategies in normal-form games, and an algorithm is provided for computing the strengths of the representative strategies.

4.1 Definition of the Representative Strategy

The representative strategy is the *best* response to a subset of the strategies of the other players. For example, the payoff matrix of a 3×3 two-player game is given in Table 2. This is a children's game which is known as the Rock-Scissors-Paper game: ROCK beats SCISSORS, SCISSORS beats PAPER, and PAPER beats ROCK. In this game, the best-reply strategies of Player 1 against all of the possible strategies of Player 2 is shown in Figure 1. In Figure 1, the three best-reply strategies (BR) are the representative strategies of Player 1. In other words, the pure strategies ROCK, SCISSORS, and PAPER are the representative strategies of Player 1, because these strategies are the best response to a subset of the mixed strategies of Player 2.

Since the mixed strategy is a set of real numbers, the algorithm for finding the representative strategies is real-coded. Therefore, our definition of the representative strategies has a tolerance ϵ.

DEFINITION 6. *Let $\vec{x_i} = ({x_i}^1, {x_i}^2, \cdots, {x_i}^{k_i})$ be a mixed strategy on the strategy set S_i of player i, where k_i is the number of pure strategies of player i. Let $\vec{R}_{-i}$ be the set of all the mixed strategies profiles of the remaining players. Let $\vec{\Delta}_\delta = (y^1, y^2, \cdots, y^{k_i})$, where y^j is a random uniform real number in $[-\delta, \delta]$ for all j and $\sum_{j=1}^{k_i} y^j = 0$. Given $\epsilon > 0$, $\vec{x_i}$ is an ϵ-**representative strategy** for player i if*

$$\exists \vec{r}_{-i} \in \vec{R}_{-i}\ \forall \delta \geq \epsilon\ \forall \vec{\Delta}_\delta \quad \pi_i(\vec{x_i} + \vec{\Delta}_\delta, \vec{r}_{-i}) \leq \pi_i(\vec{x_i}, \vec{r}_{-i}),$$

where $\vec{x_i} + \vec{\Delta}_\delta$ is a mixed strategy of player i.

(Player 1, Player 2)	Rock	Scissors	Paper
Rock	(0, 0)	(1, -1)	(-1, 1)
Scissors	(-1, 1)	(0, 0)	(1, -1)
Paper	(1, -1)	(-1, 1)	(0, 0)

Table 2: The payoff matrix of the Rock-Scissors-Paper game.

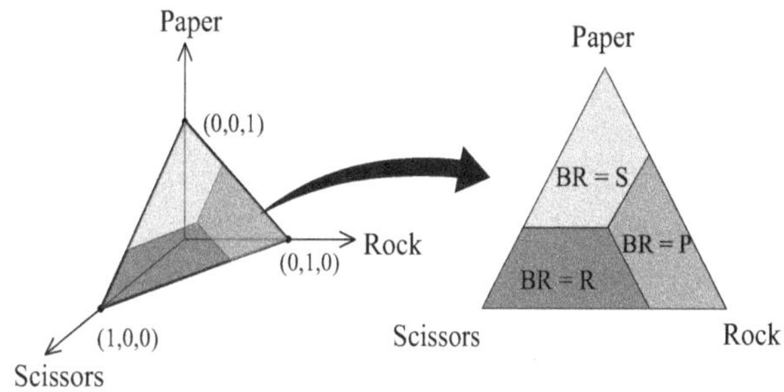

Figure 1: The best-reply strategy regions of Player 1 in the Rock-Scissors-Paper game. Each point in the triangle represents a mixed strategy of Player 2.

In Definition 6, the reason for restricting $\vec{x_i} + \vec{\Delta}_\delta$ to be a mixed strategy of player i is that otherwise the strategy may has a probability greater than 1, or a probability less than 0 of playing some pure strategies. Furthermore, if the value of ϵ is 0 in Definition 6, the ϵ-representative strategy is called a representative strategy for simplicity.

4.2 Definition of the Strengths of Representative Strategies

By Definition 6, every representative strategy of a player *dominates* a subset of the strategies of the other players. The term 'dominate' means that the player will not change its strategy with the subset of the strategies of the remaining players. Therefore, the *strength* of a strategy (not only for the representative strategy) can be defined as the ratio of the strategies of the remaining players which it dominates.

DEFINITION 7. *Let X_i be the set of all of the possible mixed strategies of player i, $\vec{R}_{-i}$ be the set of all the mixed strategies profiles of the remaining players, and $\pi_i^*(\vec{r}_{-i}) = \max_{\vec{x_i} \in X_i} \pi_i(\vec{x_i}, \vec{r}_{-i})$ be the highest expected payoff of player i with the strategies of the remaining players $\vec{r}_{-i}$, where $\vec{r}_{-i} \in \vec{R}_{-i}$. Given a mixed strategy $\vec{x_i}$ of player i, the **strength** of the mixed strategy $\vec{x_i}$ is given by:*

$$strength(\vec{x_i}) = \frac{\left|\{\vec{r}_{-i} \in \vec{R}_{-i} | \pi_i(\vec{x_i}, \vec{r}_{-i}) = \pi_i^*(\vec{r}_{-i})\}\right|}{\left|\{\vec{r}_{-i} \in \vec{R}_{-i}\}\right|}$$

By Definition 7, the strength of every strategy is in close interval $[0, 1]$. Moreover, the strength of each representative strategy is greater than 0, because the representative strategy must dominate some strategies.

4.3 The Algorithms for Finding Representative Strategies

Although the representative strategy is defined in Definition 6, finding representative strategies is not trivial. This paper provides two algorithms for finding representative strategies. One is the co-evolutionary GA, the other is the 1–to–1 iterative algorithm.

4.3.1 Co-evolutionary GAs

The first method for finding representative strategies is a co-evolutionary GA. In co-evolutionary GAs, each player has two populations: *the learner population* P_i and *the evaluator population* EP_i. The learner population is used to generate strategies as learners, while the evaluator population is used to record the representative strategies as evaluators. Each chromosome in the population P_i is a mixed strategy of player i for each player. Therefore, the length of the chromosomes (ℓ) of player i is equal to the number of pure strategies of player i. In addition, each gene in the chromosomes is encoded as a real number, which represents the probability of the respective pure strategies of the mixed strategy. Furthermore, the population size of the learner populations is fixed, but the population size of the evaluator populations grows when running the co-evolutionary GA. Detailed procedures of the co-evolutionary GA are shown in Algorithm 1.

Algorithm 1 The co-evolutionary GA for finding representative strategies.

1: Randomly initialize one chromosome to the evaluator population EP_i of player i for each player.
2: Randomly initialize the learner population P_i of player i for each player.
3: Evaluate the fitness of each chromosome in P_i.
4: For each player, generate the new learner population nP_i.
5: Evaluate the fitness of each chromosome in nP_i.
6: For each offspring x in nP_i, perform the RTR with P_i: Find $y \in S$ such that minimizes the distance between x and y, where $S \subseteq P_i$ is a random sample set and $|S|$ is equal to the window size w. Replace y with offspring x if x has a higher fitness.
7: If there is a chromosome c in P_i which has a fitness higher than all of the chromosomes in EP_i, add c to the evaluator population EP_i.
8: Stop if the terminal condition is satisfied, otherwise go to step 3.

In the above co-evolutionary GA, the fitness function is defined as the maximum payoff from matching up with all of the strategies in the evaluator population of the opponents: Let C_{-i} be the set of all the permutations of the chromosomes in the evaluator population of every player except player i, and R_{-i} be the set of the strategies which is represented by C_{-i}. Given a chromosome c_i of player i, and let x_i be the strategy which is represented by c_i, the fitness of c_i is defined as the equation

$$fitness_i(c_i) = \max_{r_{-i} \in R_{-i}} \pi_i(x_i, r_{-i}).$$

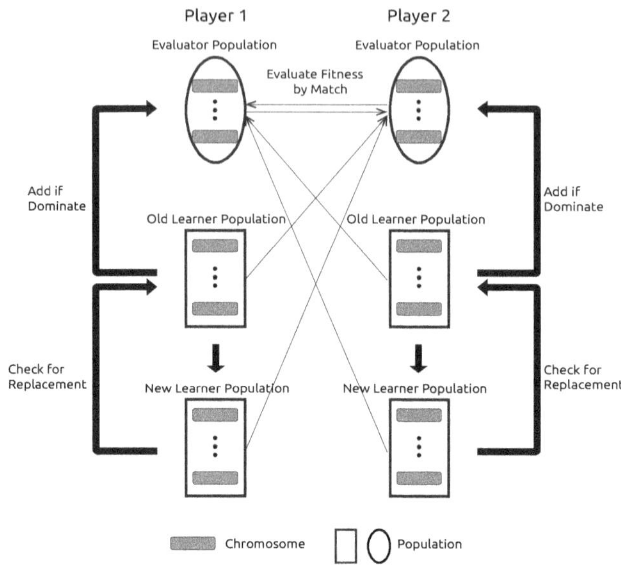

Figure 2: The implementation schemes of the co-evolutionary GA for finding representative strategies in two-player games.

In addition, the distance between two chromosomes (step 6 in Algorithm 1) is defined as the Manhattan distance: Let x and y be the chromosomes in the learner population, $x_1, x_2, \cdots, x_n$ be the genes of x, and $y_1, y_2, \cdots, y_n$ be the genes of y. The Manhattan distance between x and y is defined as the equation $dist(x, y) = \sum_{i=1}^{n} |x_i - y_i|$. Furthermore, the co-evolutionary GA has two terminal conditions (step 8 in Algorithm 1). One is that it can not find any strategy in the learner population which dominates all the strategies in the evaluator population for all of the players, and the other is that the generation is greater than the maximum limited generation. Our implementation schemes of two-player game is shown in Figure 2.

However, although the chromosomes of the evaluator population EP_i may be the representative strategies of player i, these strategies have a bias due to the randomly initialized chromosome of the evaluator population of each player. Therefore, we have to run the co-evolutionary GA several times for finding all of the representative strategies of each player.

4.3.2 The 1–to–1 iterative algorithm

The second method for finding representative strategies is called the 1–to–1 iterative algorithm. In the 1–to–1 iterative algorithm, each player has a representative strategy pool RP_i and a population P_i which has only one chromosome, where i is the index of players. Each chromosome represents a mixed strategy, which is the same as the chromosome in 4.3.1. In addition, the size of the representative strategy pools grows when running the 1–to–1 iterative algorithm. Detailed procedures of the 1–to–1 iterative algorithm are shown in Algorithm 2.

In the 1–to–1 iterative algorithm, the fitness function of the (1+1) ES of player i (step 2 in Algorithm 2) is the expected payoff π_i: Let p_i be the only chromosome of the population P_i of player i for each player. Let s_i be the

Algorithm 2 The 1–to–1 iterative algorithm for finding representative strategies.

1: Randomly initialize the chromosome of the population P_i of player i for each player.
2: Run the (1+1) ES to P_i for each player iteratively.
3: For player i, add the chromosome of the population P_i to the representative strategy pool RP_i when (1+1) ES of player i is over in step 2.
4: Stop if the terminal condition is satisfied, otherwise go to step 2.

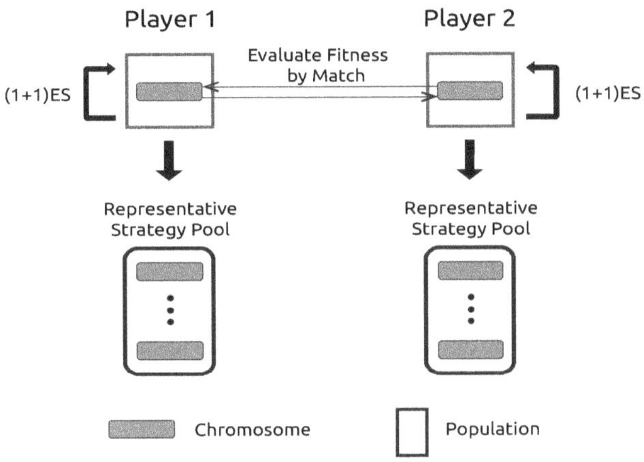

Figure 3: The implementation schemes of the 1–to–1 iterative algorithm for finding representative strategies in two-player games.

strategy which p_i represents for all $i = 1, 2, \cdots, n$, where n is the number of players. Given a chromosome c_i, which represents the mixed strategy x_i of player i, the fitness of c_i is defined as the equation

$$fitness_i(c_i) = \pi_i(s_1, \cdots, s_{i-1}, c_i, s_{i+1}, \cdots, s_n).$$

Our implementation schemes of two-player game is shown in Figure 3.

4.4 The Method of Computing Strengths of Representative Strategies

In this subsection, we provide an algorithm for computing the strengths of the strategies. By Definition 7, the strength of a strategy of player i is defined by matching up with all of the possible mixed strategies profiles of the remaining players R_{-i}, but it is not possible to compute in finite steps for any algorithm. Therefore, the algorithm for computing the strength of the strategy of player i uses a finite set which is random sampled from the possible mixed strategies profiles of the remaining players R_{-i} as the opponents.

The algorithm for computing strengths of the strategies is shown in Algorithm 3. In Algorithm 3, s_i^* means the best-response pure strategy of player i to q_{-i} in step 4.

Algorithm 3 The algorithm for computing strengths of the strategies.

Require: The strategy for computing the strength, s_i; The sample size, w;
Ensure: The strength of the strategy s_i, $strength(s_i)$;
1: $count = 0$;
2: Randomly sample a set of possible mixed strategies profiles of the remaining players $r_{-i} \subseteq R_{-i}$, where $|r_{-i}|$ is equal to the sample size w.
3: **for** each $q_{-i} \in r_{-i}$ **do**
4: **if** $\pi_i(s_i, q_{-i}) = \pi_i(s_i^*, q_{-i})$ **then**
5: $count = count + 1$;
6: **end if**
7: **end for**
8: $strength(s_i) = \frac{count}{w}$;

5. FINDING NASH EQUILIBRIA

In this section, we provide two methods for finding NE by using the representative strategies, and give a definition of the difficulty for finding NE. Both methods for finding NE use the (1+1) ES, and the main difference between them is the fitness functions. The first method for finding NE is called the max-min method, and the second method is called the difference method. Due to the minmax theorem [33] only holds in two-player zero-sum games, the max-min method, which has the fitness function based on the minmax theorem, can only use in two-player zero-sum games. Furthermore, the max-min method finds only one NE of the games, while the difference method finds as more NE as possible.

5.1 The Max-Min Method

The fitness function of the max-min method is defined as follows: Let $T_1 = \{t_1^1, t_1^2, \cdots, t_1^{n_1}\}$ be the representative strategies of player 1, and $T_2 = \{t_2^1, t_2^2, \cdots, t_2^{n_2}\}$ be the representative strategies of player 2. Given a strategy x_1 of player 1, the fitness function of player 1 is defined as the equation

$$f_1(x_1) = \min_{t_2 \in T_2} \pi_1(x_1, t_2).$$

Similarly, given a strategy x_2 of player 2, the fitness function of player 2 is defined as the equation

$$f_2(x_2) = \min_{t_1 \in T_1} \pi_2(t_1, x_2).$$

This method finds NE when the game is a two-player zero-sum game. It is because that if one player has the higher payoff to a strategy profile, the other player has the lower payoff to that strategy profile. Therefore, the max-min method do not promise to find NE if the game is not a two-player zero-sum game, because the minmax theorem [33] only holds in two-player zero-sum games. Detailed procedures of the max-min method are shown in Algorithm 4.

Algorithm 4 The max-min method for finding NE.

Randomly initialize a strategy x_1 of player 1, and a strategy x_2 of player 2.
Run the (1+1) ES with f_1 to obtain x_1.
Run the (1+1) ES with f_2 to obtain x_2.
return the NE, (x_1, x_2).

5.2 The Difference Method

The fitness function of the difference method is defined by the *distance* to the best-reply strategies. That is, to a mixed strategy profile $x = (x_1, x_2, \cdots, x_n)$ of n-player games, the fitness of x is defined as the sum of the weighted difference between x_i and x_i^* for all $i = \{i \in \mathbb{N} | 1 \leq i \leq n\}$, where x_i^* is the best-reply pure strategy of player i.

Given $x = (x_1, x_2, \cdots, x_n)$ as a mixed strategy profile of a n-player game. Let $r_{-i} = (x_1, \cdots, x_{i-1}, x_{i+1}, \cdots, x_n)$ denotes this same profile excluding the strategy of player i, so that (x_i, r_{-i}) forms a complete profile of strategies. Let x_i^* be the best-reply pure strategy of player i when playing the game against r_{-i}. Let $\pi_i^* = \pi_i(x_i^*, r_{-i})$ be the highest expected payoff of player i when playing the game against r_{-i}. The fitness of x is defined as the following equation:

$$fitness(x) = \sum_{i=1}^{n} \sum_{j=1}^{n_i} x_i^j \cdot (\pi_i(x_i^j, r_{-i}) - \pi_i^*)$$

With the above definition, the closer a player's strategy is to best reply strategy, the higher fitness the strategy profile gets. Furthermore, if a strategy profile is a NE, its fitness will be the highest and equal to 0. Detailed procedures of the difference method for finding NE are shown in Algorithm 5. In Algorithm 5, the terminal condition in step 8 is satisfied either when the generation of (1+1)ES exceeds the maximum limited generation, or when NE is found in step 5.

Algorithm 5 The difference method for finding NE.

Require: The set of the strategy profiles with the representative strategies of the players, $S = S_1 \times S_2 \times \cdots \times S_n$, where $S_i = \{ s_i^1, s_i^2, \cdots, s_i^{n_i}\}$ is the set of the representative strategies of player i for all $i = \{i \in \mathbb{N} | 1 \leq i \leq n\}$;
Ensure: The set of NE, $setE$;
1: **for** each $s \in S$ **do**
2: Initialize a strategy profile $x = s$.
3: **repeat**
4: mutate x for the (1+1) ES procedure.
5: **if** (x is an NE) **then**
6: Insert x to $setE$.
7: **end if**
8: **until** the terminal condition is satisfied
9: **end for**
10: **return** $setE$.

5.3 Definition of the difficulty for finding NE

With the observation of strengths of the representative strategies, the more the strength that a strategy has, the more representative the strategy is. Therefore, finding NE is easier when more high-strength strategies are found. Here we defined the ϵ-approximate NE first: Given a real number ϵ, and let $S_i = \{S_i^1, S_i^2, \cdots, S_i^{n_i}\}$ be the set of ϵ-representative strategies of player i for each players. Each NE which is found by using the representative strategies $S_1, S_2, \cdots, S_n$ is an ϵ-approximate NE.

In addition, if $\epsilon = 0$, then the ϵ-approximate NE is a real NE. Therefore, with the previous observation, the difficulty for finding the ϵ-approximate NE can be defined as follows.

DEFINITION 8. *Let $S_i = \{S_i^1, S_i^2, \cdots, S_i^{n_i}\}$ be the set of ϵ-representative strategies of player i for each players. Let $strength(S_i^j)$ be the strength of S_i^j for all $i = \{i \in \mathbb{N} | 1 \leq i \leq n\}$ and $j = \{j \in \mathbb{N} | 1 \leq j \leq n_i\}$. The* ***difficulty*** *for finding the ϵ-approximate NE is*

$$diff(S_1, S_2, \cdots, S_n) = \frac{\sum_{i=1}^{n} \sum_{j=1}^{n_i} strength(S_i^j)}{n}.$$

By this definition, higher $diff(S_1, S_2, \cdots, S_n)$ indicates that finding NE is easier by using the representative strategy sets $S_1, S_2, \cdots, S_n$.

(Player 1, Player 2)	Straight	Swerve
Straight	(-10,-10)	(1,-1)
Swerve	(-1,1)	(0,0)

Table 3: The payoff matrix of the chicken game.

6. EXPERIMENTS

In this section, we discuss the experiments of several famous games and of some games which are generated from GAMUT [22]. To each game, the experiments of finding the representative strategies and computing strengths of these representative strategies are conducted at first, and followed by the experiments of finding NE by using these representative strategies. Since most of these games are non zero-sum, the only method for finding NE by using representative strategies is the difference method in our experiments.

6.1 Famous Games

The experiments are conducted on many famous games, including the matching pennies game, the prisoner's dilemma, the chicken game, the tennis problem, the market entry game, the sealed bid auction, and the Rock-Scissors-Paper game. Although the experiments are conducted on all of these games, this paper only shows the results of the prisoner's dilemma (Table 1), the chicken game (Table 3), and the Rock-Scissors-Paper game (Table 2), since the other games' results are similar to these three games. All of the NE can be found either by using the co-evolutionary GA method or by using 1–to–1 iterative method in these games except for the chicken game (the special case of the chicken game would be explained later in this subsection). Therefore, this subsection focuses on the representative strategies and strengths of these games.

Tables 4, 5, and 6 show the representative strategies and the strength of each game. By definition 8, in the prisoner's dilemma, $diff(\{(1,0)\}, \{(1,0)\}) = 1$. In the chicken game, $diff(\{(1,0),(0,1)\}, \{(1,0),(0,1)\}) = 1$. Similarly, $diff(\{(1,0,0),(0,1,0),(0,0,1)\}, \{(1,0,0),(0,1,0),(0,0,1)\})$ also equals to 1 in the Rock-Scissors-Paper game. Besides, some representative strategies are not found in the chicken game sometimes. This special case is shown in table 7. In this case, $diff(\{(0,1)\}, \{(1,0)\}) \approx 0.5$, and it means that finding NE by using these representative strategies is harder than using $\{(1,0),(0,1)\}, \{(1,0),(0,1)\}$. By using the representative strategy set $\{(0,1)\}$ of Player 1 and the representative strategy set $\{(1,0)\}$ of Player 2, our algorithm only finds one NE $((0,1),(1,0))$ in the chicken game. Nevertheless, by using the representative strategy set $\{(1,0),(0,1)\}$ of Player 1 and the representative strategy set $\{(1,0),(0,1)\}$

	Representative Strategy	Theoretical Strength	Experimental Strength
Player 1	(1.0000,0.0000)	1	1.0000
Player 2	(1.0000,0.0000)	1	1.0000

Table 4: The representative strategies and their strengths for the prisoner's dilemma.

	Representative Strategy	Theoretical Strength	Experimental Strength
Player 1	(0.0000,1.0000)	9/10	0.8993
	(1.0000,0.0000)	1/10	0.1007
Player 2	(1.0000,0.0000)	1/10	0.0993
	(0.0000,1.0000)	9/10	0.9007

Table 5: The representative strategies and their strengths for the chicken game.

of Player 2, our algorithm finds all of NE $((0,1),(1,0))$, $((1,0),(0,1))$, and $((0.1,0.9),(0.1,0.9))$ in the chicken game. This shows that the number of NE that the algorithm finds is related to the difficulty of the representative strategy sets.

6.2 Random Games from GAMUT

In this subsection, the experiments are conducted on the random games which are generated from GAMUT [22]. Since the representative strategies and their strengths are easily observed in large-size games, we merely compare the execution time of our algorithm to the state-of-the-art algorithm [5]. In these experiments, our algorithm uses the 1–to–1 iterative algorithm for finding representative strategies and the difference method for finding NE, because random games may not be zero-sum.

For each size, five random games are generated from GAMUT. Then we compute the average execution time of these five games. The comparison of execution time is shown in Figure 4. Although our algorithm consumes more time for finding NE, the execution time grows very slowly with the game size. Therefore, when dealing with the games with larger size, our algorithm is expected to find the representative strategies in a shorter period of time, and compute the difficulty of the problem as well.

Our algorithms consume more time since all of the combination of the representative strategies of each player are used for co-evolving NE. Nevertheless, our algorithms obtain extra information from the game. When other players' strategies are unknown, we know the winning chance of each representative strategy through their strengths. Therefore, if all of the players are rational, we know which NE has a higher probability to be reached under co-evolution.

	Representative Strategy	Theoretical Strength	Experimental Strength
Player 1	(1.000,0.000,0.000)	1/3	0.3321
	(0.000,1.000,0.000)	1/3	0.3357
	(0.000,0.000,1.000)	1/3	0.3322
Player 2	(0.000,1.000,0.000)	1/3	0.3342
	(0.000,0.000,1.000)	1/3	0.3324
	(1.000,0.000,0.000)	1/3	0.3334

Table 6: The representative strategies and their strengths for the Rock-Scissors-Paper game.

	Representative Strategy	Theoretical Strength	Experimental Strength
Player 1	(0.0000,1.0000)	9/10	0.8998
Player 2	(1.0000,0.0000)	1/10	0.1000

Table 7: The representative strategies and their strengths for the chicken game in the failed case. In this case, not all of the representative strategies are found.

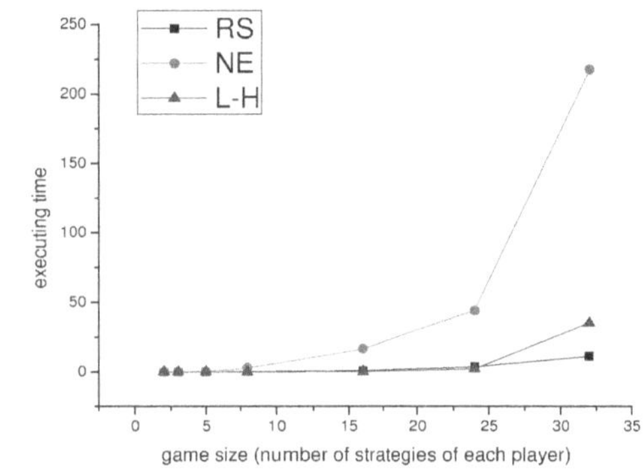

Figure 4: Comparison of execution time. RS is the execution time of finding representative strategies by using the 1–to–1 iterative method. NE is the execution time of finding NE by using the difference method. L-H is the execution time of finding NE by using the Lemke-Howson algorithm.

7. CONCLUSION AND FUTURE WORK

In this paper, we provided a two-level method for finding NE. To reduce the search space, we defined representative strategies and their strengths. By using those definitions, the difficulty for finding (co-evolving) NE was also defined. Then we proposed two methods for finding the representative strategies. To find the approximate NE of the game defined by representative strategies, two additional methods were proposed, where one applies only to zero-sum games, while the other applies to any games. Although our algorithms consume more time than the state-of-the-art algorithm [5] for finding NE, finding representative strategies is relatively fast. We believe that finding representative strategies and their strengths is important when dealing with complex games. The information gained from our algorithms also shed some lights on defining the co-evolvability of NE in the field of co-evolutionary game theory. Some other directions for future work include speeding up the methods for finding NE by using representative strategies and testing our algorithms on higher-dimensional games.

In this paper, we use the representative strategies to reduce the search space for finding NE. Further investigations concerning the proper way to reduce the search space is essential when dealing with complex games. The reduced space can be used directly to find approximate NE. In addition, the dimension of the reduced space may provide some hints to estimate the difficulty for finding the true NE.

ACKNOWLEDGMENTS

This work was sponsored by the National Science Council of Taiwan under grant NSC-101-2221-E-002-198. The authors would also like to thank Maggie Man-Tin Yung for writing consultation.

8. REFERENCES

[1] R. Axelrod. The evolution of strategies in the iterated prisonerĄfs dilemma. *Genetic algorithms and simulated annealing*, 3:32–41, 1987.

[2] T. D. H. Cau and E. J. Anderson. A co-evolutionary approach to modelling the behaviour of participants in competitive electricity markets. In *Power Engineering Society Summer Meeting, 2002 IEEE*, volume 3, pages 1534–1540. IEEE, 2002.

[3] S. Ceppi, N. Gatti, G. Patrini, and M. Rocco. Local search techniques for computing equilibria in two-player general-sum strategic-form games. In *Proceedings of the 9th International Conference on Autonomous Agents and Multiagent Systems: volume 1-Volume 1*, pages 1469–1470. International Foundation for Autonomous Agents and Multiagent Systems, 2010.

[4] X. Chen and X. Deng. Settling the complexity of two-player nash equilibrium. In *FOCS*, pages 261–272. IEEE Computer Society, 2006.

[5] B. Codenotti, S. De Rossi, and M. Pagan. An experimental analysis of lemke-howson algorithm. *CoRR, abs/0811.3247*, 2008.

[6] C. Daskalakis, Y. Cai, et al. *The complexity of Nash equilibria in multiplayer zero-sum games and coordination games*. PhD thesis, Massachusetts Institute of Technology, 2010.

[7] C. Daskalakis, P. W. Goldberg, and C. H. Papadimitriou. The complexity of computing a nash equilibrium. In *Proceedings of the thirty-eighth annual ACM symposium on Theory of computing*, pages 71–78. ACM, 2006.

[8] J. Dickhaut and T. Kaplan. A program for finding nash equilibria. *The Mathematica Journal*, 1(4):87–93, 1991.

[9] P. K. Dutta. *Strategies and games: theory and practice*. MIT press, 1999.

[10] P. W. Goldberg and C. H. Papadimitriou. Reducibility among equilibrium problems. In *Proceedings of the thirty-eighth annual ACM symposium on Theory of computing*, pages 61–70. ACM, 2006.

[11] W. D. Hamilton and R. Axelrod. The evolution of cooperation. *Science*, 211(27):1390–1396, 1981.

[12] J. R. Koza. Genetic evolution and co-evolution of computer programs. *Artificial life II*, 10:603–629, 1992.

[13] C. E. Lemke and J. T. Howson Jr. Equilibrium points of bimatrix games. *Journal of the Society for Industrial and Applied Mathematics*, 12(2):413–423, 1964.

[14] L. Mallozzi. An application of optimization theory to the study of equilibria for games: a survey. *Central European Journal of Operations Research*, pages 1–17, 2012.

[15] A. Migdalas, P. M. Pardalos, and P. Värbrand. *Multilevel optimization: algorithms and applications*, volume 20. Springer, 1997.

[16] J. H. Miller. The evolution of automata in the repeated prisoner's dilemma. In *Two Essays on the Economics of Imperfect Information*, Ph.D. dissertation, Ann Arbor, 1988. University of Michigan.

[17] J. H. Miller. The coevolution of automata in the repeated prisoner's dilemma. *Journal of Economic Behavior & Organization*, 29(1):87–112, 1996.

[18] R. B. Myerson. *Game theory: analysis of conflict*. Harvard University Press, 1997.

[19] J. F. Nash. *Non-cooperative Games*. PhD thesis, Princeton University, Princeton, NJ, May 1950.

[20] J. Neumann and O. Morgenstern. Theory of games and economic behavior. *Princeton University, Princeton*, 1947.

[21] N. Nisan, T. Roughgarden, E. Tardos, and V. V. Vazirani. *Algorithmic game theory*. Cambridge University Press, 2007.

[22] E. Nudelman, J. Wortman, Y. Shoham, and K. Leyton-Brown. Run the gamut: A comprehensive approach to evaluating game-theoretic algorithms. In *Proceedings of the Third International Joint Conference on Autonomous Agents and Multiagent Systems-Volume 2*, pages 880–887. IEEE Computer Society, 2004.

[23] C. H. Papadimitriou. *Algorithmic Game Theory*, chapter The Complexity of Finding Nash Equilibria, pages 29–51. Cambridge University Press, 2007.

[24] M. Pelikan and D. E. Goldberg. Escaping hierarchical traps with competent genetic algorithms. *Proceedings of the Genetic and Evolutionary Computation Conference (GECCO-2001)*, pages 511–518, 2001.

[25] R. Porter, E. Nudelman, and Y. Shoham. Simple search methods for finding a nash equilibrium. *Games and Economic Behavior*, 63(2):642–662, 2008.

[26] T. C. Price. Using co-evolutionary programming to simulate strategic behaviour in markets. *Journal of Evolutionary Economics*, 7(3):219–254, 1997.

[27] I. Rechenberg. *Evolutionsstrategie 94*, volume 1 of *Werkstatt Bionik und Evolutionstechnik*. Frommann-Holzboog, Stuttgart, 1994.

[28] T. Sandholm, A. Gilpin, and V. Conitzer. Mixed-integer programming methods for finding nash equilibria. In *Proceedings of the National Conference on Artificial Intelligence*, volume 20, page 495, 2005.

[29] L. S. Shapley. A note on the lemke-howson algorithm. *Pivoting and Extension*, pages 175–189, 1974.

[30] Y. Shoham and K. Leyton-Brown. *Multiagent systems: Algorithmic, game-theoretic, and logical foundations*. Cambridge University Press, 2008.

[31] J. M. Smith. *Evolutionary genetics*. Oxford University Press, 1989.

[32] F. Thompson. Equivalence of games in extensive form. *Classics in game theory*, page 36, 1997.

[33] J. Von Neumann. Zur theorie der gesellschaftsspiele. *Mathematische Annalen*, 100(1):295–320, 1928.

[34] B. Von Stengel. Computing equilibria for two-person games. *Handbook of game theory with economic applications*, 3:1723–1759, 2002.

[35] J. D. Weber and T. J. Overbye. A two-level optimization problem for analysis of market bidding strategies. In *Power Engineering Society Summer Meeting*, volume 2, pages 682–687. IEEE, 1999.

Improving Coevolution by Random Sampling

Wojciech Jaśkowski, Paweł Liskowski, Marcin Szubert and Krzysztof Krawiec
Institute of Computing Science, Poznan University of Technology
Piotrowo 2, 60965 Poznań, Poland
{wjaskowski,pliskowski,mszubert,kkrawiec}@cs.put.poznan.pl

ABSTRACT

Recent developments cast doubts on the effectiveness of coevolutionary learning in interactive domains. A simple evolution with fitness evaluation based on games with random strategies has been found to generalize better than competitive coevolution. In an attempt to investigate this phenomenon, we analyze the utility of random opponents for one- and two-population competitive coevolution applied to learning strategies for the game of Othello. We show that if coevolution uses two-population setup and engages also random opponents, it is capable of producing equally good strategies as evolution with random sampling for the expected utility performance measure.

To investigate the differences between analyzed methods, we introduce *performance profile,* a tool that measures the player's performance against opponents of various strength. The profiles reveal that evolution with random sampling produces players coping well with mediocre opponents, but playing relatively poorly against stronger ones. This finding explains why in the round-robin tournament, evolution with random sampling is one of the worst methods from all those considered in this study.

Categories and Subject Descriptors

I.2.6 [**Artificial Intelligence**]: Learning; I.2.8 [**Artificial Intelligence**]: Problem Solving, Control Methods, and Search—*Heuristic methods*

General Terms

Algorithms, Experimentation

Keywords

Competitive Coevolution, Solution Concepts, Othello, Maximization of Expected Utility, Strategy Learning, Performance Profile

1. INTRODUCTION

For two decades coevolutionary learning (CEL) has been perceived as a method-of-choice for learning in interactive domains such as game playing. It has attracted substantial interest and has been successfully applied to many games [1, 13, 12] mainly because it does not require handcrafted opponents or game databases to learn from. Coevolution is a knowledge-free method [21]: the process of strategy learning is driven solely by playing games between individuals and by the survival of the fittest.

Recently, Chong *et al.* proposed Improved Coevolutionary Learning [5] and showed that it significantly surpasses coevolutionary learning on the game of Othello. Their method is a straightforward knowledge-free variant of evolution strategy, in which individuals are evaluated through playing games against random players. Since the individuals do not confront each other, the use of the term 'coevolution' for this method is disputable, so within this study we refer to it as Random Sampling Evolutionary Learning (RSEL).

CEL has been known for its self-adapting capabilities [1], thus the experimental evidence that such a simple algorithm as RSEL performs better might have surprised not only the authors of this paper. In response, this study attempts to understand this phenomenon and show in which respects coevolution can outrank RSEL.

Our main contribution is demonstrating that CEL can be as effective as RSEL at finding good Othello players with respect to the performance measure of expected utility, but it is better at playing against the strong opponents. We show that this is possible for a two-population variant of CEL that additionally uses random players. We do not limit our attention to players' overall performance, but also scrutinize how they fare against opponents of different strength. To illustrate this, we propose *performance profile* plots, a new tool that gives insight into this characteristics.

2. BACKGROUND

An essential prerequisite for comparing algorithms that learn to play games is deciding what the goal of learning is. Simply saying that the goal is to learn the 'best strategy' is vague. The best strategy could be the one that maximizes the expected game outcome or the one that minimizes the worst possible loss. In order to be unambiguous in this respect, one has to choose a formal *solution concept* [9], which precisely defines which candidate solutions are solutions to the problem and which are not.

Ficici [9] postulated that solution concept is a part of a problem, and that in order to solve the problem while avoiding coevolutionary pathologies, an algorithm must *implement* the assumed solution concept. This holds when an algorithm monotonically approximates the concept, i.e., candidate solutions do not get worse with time with respect to an *performance measure* related to the assumed solution concept. Due to the nature of interactive domains and solution concepts, providing such a guarantee usually requires an unbounded archive of candidate solutions. Thus, the practically useful algorithms formally do not implement any solution concept, but are *designed for* one of them, yet without any formal guarantees of monotonic approximation. In this spirit, de Jong proposed the MaxSolve algorithm [6], which was designed for the Maximization of Expected Utility (MEU) solution concept [24], but does not implement it[1].

MEU, as opposed to other solution concepts such as Pareto-optimal set [7], has a natural real-valued performance measure: the player's expected utility, which is the expected game outcome against all possible opponents from a given search space. This measure can be easily estimated: one generates a number of random strategies from the search space and calculates the average result of games played against them. Clearly, this performance measure is consistent with the way the individuals are evaluated in RSEL, since RSEL was designed for MEU.

In contrast, CEL, a straightforward coevolutionary learning used recently as a control approach for RSEL [5], does not implement any known solution concept, nor it was designed for any, in particular not for MEU. From this perspective, the RSEL supremacy over CEL should not astound, because the two algorithms have been compared using a measure known as generalization performance in machine learning, which is merely a different name for expected utility.

However, the fact RSEL is better than CEL against an average opponent does not imply it can beat every opponent defeated by CEL and vice versa. Opponents vary in strength, and some methods may be more apt to produce players that win against, e.g., strong opponents than the weak ones. In MEU, such differences can cancel each other or become neglected because of the very uneven distribution of opponent strength, causing the methods to be apparently similar. One of the objectives of this paper is to investigate these deficiencies of MEU and obtain a more adequate picture of method performance.

3. RELATED WORK

The game of Othello is a simple but challenging testbed that has been widely used to analyze and compare different learning methods and player representations. Most approaches to develop Othello-playing programs were based on external domain knowledge (e.g., in the form of expert-labeled game databases) and efficient game tree search algorithms [3]. However, recent research has seen the advent of methods that learn autonomously, without any help of external domain knowledge. Typical examples of such methods are CEL and Temporal Difference Learning, which were applied to Othello separately [4, 19, 28] as well as in combination [27, 22]. Our work follows this direction of knowledge-free methods and focuses on CEL.

Apart from the learning algorithm, an important aspect that influences the strength of Othello strategies is player representation. A good overview of different representations and their performance is provided by the Othello Position Evaluation Function League [17]. Besides the simplest weighted piece counter (WPC) representation, more complex ones include: a symmetric n-tuple network [18], a multi-layer perceptron (MLP) [2], and a spatial MLP [4]. League rankings indicate that of these representations, n-tuple networks can achieve the highest performance against the predefined heuristic player. Nonetheless, in this work we decided to use the WPC encoding, because our goal is to consistently confront a few learning methods in fair conditions rather than to develop a player that is strong in absolute terms.

The players trained by particular methods have to be objectively compared. Most related studies use a score against a single benchmark opponent as a performance measure. Typical examples of such opponents are the heuristic player introduced by Yoshioka *et al.* [29], the positional and mobility strategies from Iago program [25], and the random player which makes a random legal move in each turn. An alternative approach was employed by Chong *et al.* [5] who compared CEL and RSEL with respect to their *generalization performance* measured as an average score against a very large number of random WPC-encoded players. Yet another method is direct confrontation of the players produced by compared methods in, e.g., a round-robin tournament [14]. In this paper, we use expected utility, head-to-head tournament, and a novel tool of performance profiles to assess the quality of players.

4. METHODS

The conceptual framework of this study consists of three elements: the definition of the game, the representation of strategies, and the algorithms that learn to play the game. We detail them in the following.

4.1 Othello and WPC encoding

The game of Othello is a deterministic, perfect information, zero-sum board game played by two players on an 8×8 board. There are 64 identical pieces which are white on one side and black on the other, with the colors representing players. The game starts with the four central squares of the board occupied with two black and two white pieces. Players make moves alternately by placing their pieces on the board until it is completely filled or until neither of them is able to make a legal move. The location to place a piece on has to fulfill two conditions. Firstly, it must be adjacent to an opponent's piece. Secondly, the new piece and some other piece of the current player must form a vertical, horizontal, or diagonal line with a continuous sequence of opponent's pieces inbetween. After placing the piece, all such opponent's pieces are flipped. A legal move requires flipping at least one of the opponent's pieces. The objective of the game is to have the majority of pieces on the board at the end of the game. If both players have the same number of pieces on the board, the game ends in a draw.

When designing an algorithm that learns to play Othello, one of several strategy representations that vary in complexity may be adopted (see Section 3). Here we focus on the

[1]To be precise, de Jong uses the same name MaxSolve for two algorithms: one with formal guarantees of monotonicity and its bounded version without them [6].

arguably simplest of them, position-weighted piece counter (WPC). WPC is a linear weighted board evaluation function which implements the state evaluator concept, i.e., it is explicitly used to evaluate how desirable a given board state is. It assigns a weight w_i to a board location i and uses scalar product to calculate the utility f of a board state $\mathbf{b}$:

$$f(\mathbf{b}) = \sum_{i=1}^{8\times 8} w_i b_i,$$

where b_i is 0 in the case of an empty location, +1 if a black piece is present or −1 in case of a white piece. The players interpret $f(\mathbf{b})$ conversely: the black player prefers moves leading towards states with a higher value, whereas lower values are favored by the white player.

All methods considered in this paper employ WPC as a state evaluator in a 1-ply setup: given the current state of the board, the player generates all legal moves and applies f to the resulting states. The state gauged as the most desirable determines the move to be made. Ties are resolved at random.

4.2 Random Sampling Evolutionary Learning (RSEL)

The approach we refer to here as Random Sampling Evolutionary Learning (RSEL), proposed by Chong *et al.* [5] under the name of Improved Coevolutionary Learning, is a $(\mu+\lambda)$ generational evolution strategy. The algorithm starts with a population of μ randomly generated players (vectors of 64 real-valued weights of WPC strategies in our case). In every generation, each of the μ fittest individuals produces λ/μ offspring through a mutation operator (thus, all populations except for the initial one consist of μ parents and λ offspring of those parents).

Fitness calculation in RSEL is straightforward. A sample of random WPC strategies is generated, the individual plays against each of them, and the average game result determines its fitness. Thus, individual's fitness in RSEL is an estimate of the expected utility of the strategy it encodes.

4.3 Coevolutionary Learning (CEL)

While coevolutionary algorithms borrow the overall mechanics from evolutionary algorithms, their distinctive feature is an explicit use of interactions between individuals for fitness assessment. By interacting, individuals in population directly influence each other's fitness, as opposed to evolutionary algorithms, where their evaluation is independent (and in this sense external and objective). From a few variants of this scheme proposed in past studies, we employ *competitive coevolution*, which is particularly useful when an objective evaluation function is difficult to compute. This is the case when learning game strategies: exact calculation of individual's performance requires playing a large or an infinite number of games, thus it is infeasible. However, it can be conveniently substituted by a rough assessment based on interactions within a population. The outcomes of such interactions determine fitness, called *competitive fitness* in this context. By engaging players in the mutual pressure to outperform each other, coevolutionary learning intends to provide an adaptive learning gradient that might otherwise be hard to obtain [23].

An important choice in designing coevolutionary algorithms is the interaction scheme. For symmetrical problems such as the game of Othello, the typical approach is *one-population coevolution* [20] which consists in evolving individuals in a single population, making them compete directly with each other. Although one-population coevolution has been intensely exploited in the context of games, some research [15, 8] suggests that it is worth to separately maintain two types of individuals: *candidate solutions* or *learners*, which are expected to improve over time as evolution proceeds, and *tests* or *trainers*, which main purpose is to differentiate the candidate solutions by defeating some of them and losing against the others. Thereby, coevolution is allowed to adaptively select the tests used for evaluation.

To ensure comparability with RSEL, coevolutionary learning (CEL) in this study is a $(\mu+\lambda)$ evolutionary strategy equipped with competitive fitness, calculated either via a round-robin tournament among individuals for one-population coevolution, or by confronting all candidate solutions with all tests in case of two-population coevolution. Therefore, the only difference between CEL and RSEL lies in the method of fitness assessment.

5. THE EXPERIMENT

The objectives of the experiment are twofold. Firstly, we want to determine which of the considered methods (RSEL, various configurations of CEL, and hybrids thereof) yields better Othello players given a fixed computational budget. To this aim, we employ the expected utility performance measure and round-robin tournament. Our second goal is to explain the anticipated differences by profiling the strategies using opponents of varying difficulty.

In order to fairly compare the algorithms, we set them up so that the total computational effort as well as the computational effort per one generation are equal between methods. Following other studies [16, 6], we identify the computational effort with the number of games played in interactions among individuals.

A single interaction is a double game, where both individuals play one game as black and one game as white player. In each game, one point is divided between players: the winner gets 1 point and the loser 0 points, or they get 0.5 points each in case of a draw. Each evolutionary run consists of 200 generations, and 5,000 games are played in each of them (2,500 double games), which adds up to the total effort of 1,000,000 games per run.

All methods start with an initial population filled with individuals whose weights are randomly drawn from $[-0.2, 0.2]$. The only search operator used by all algorithms is a simple mutation that perturbs all the weights with additive noise. The WPC weight w_i' of the offspring is obtained by adding a small random value to the corresponding WPC weight of the parent:

$$w_i' = w_i + 0.1 \cdot U[-1, 1],$$

where $U[-1, 1]$ is a real number drawn uniformly from the interval $[-1, 1]$. Weights resulting from mutation are clamped to the interval $[-10, 10]$. Consequently, the space of strategies we consider is a $[-10, 10]^{64}$ hypercube.

Some of the setups and performance assessment methods employ *random WPC players*. Each such player is obtained independently by drawing weights uniformly from the interval $[-10, 10]$. In the following, by 'random player/opponent' we mean a WPC player obtained in this way.

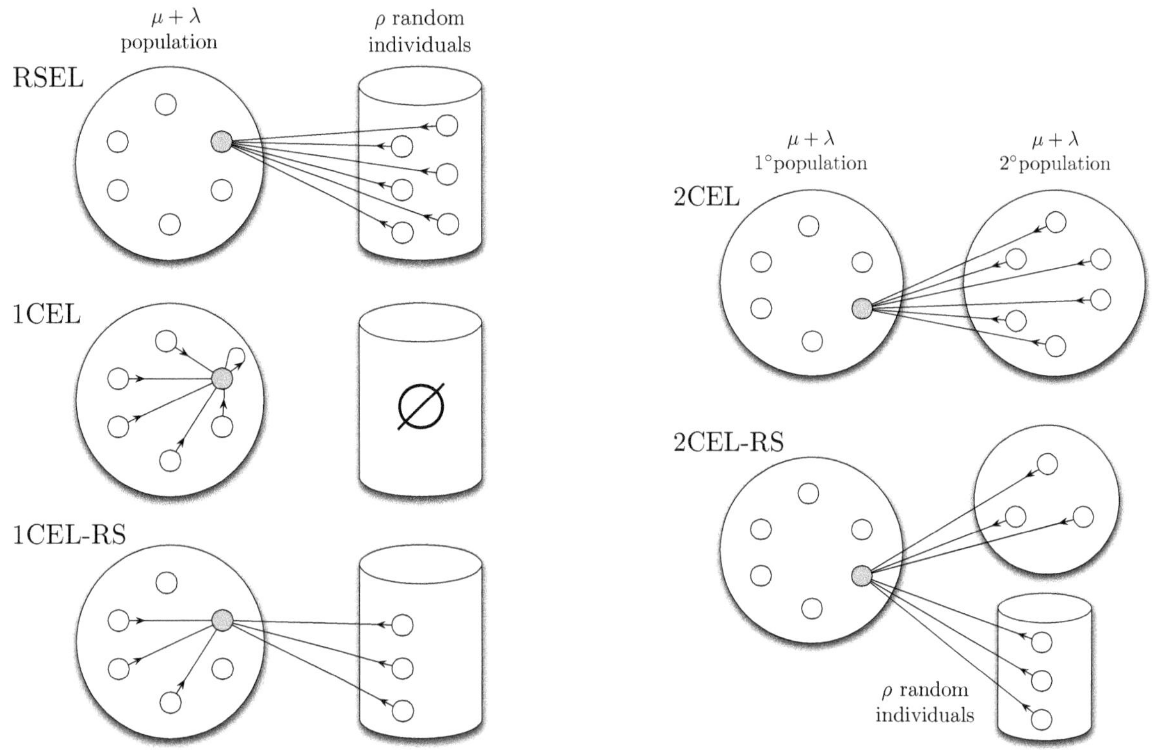

(a) RSEL and 1CEL

(b) 2CEL

Figure 1: The visualization emphasizes differences in fitness assignment among methods considered in the paper. An arrow means that a game is played between two players.

We emphasize that all setups use the same evolutionary operators of selection and mutation and differ only in the way fitness is assigned to individuals. In the following subsections we detail the setups of particular algorithms, and Figs. 1a and 1b illustrate their interaction schemes.

5.1 RSEL Setup

RSEL is a straightforward implementation of Random Sampling Evolutionary Learning algorithm described in Section 4.2, where $\mu = 25$ and $\lambda = 25$. During the evaluation phase, each individual is evaluated against a set of ρ random opponents. To fix the effort at 5,000 games per generation, we set $\rho = 50$ ($50 \times 50 \times 2 = 5000$). Figure 1a illustrates this configuration. We emphasize that a collection of random opponents is drawn anew in every generation.

5.2 1CEL Setups

1CEL is a one-population coevolutionary algorithm which implements the competitive $(\mu + \lambda)$ evolutionary strategy scheme outlined in Section 4.3. All individuals in population play double games with each other (round-robin tournament). In each generation, $\mu = 25$ best performing strategies produce via mutation $\lambda = 25$ children. The nature of this competitive fitness assessment is illustrated in Fig. 1a.

The second method, **1CEL-RS**, is a hybrid of 1CEL and RSEL that combines the competitive fitness with random sampling. Technically, each individual is evaluated on the basis of double games with 25 randomly selected individuals from the population (as in 1CEL) and $\rho = 25$ random opponents (as in RSEL). This configuration is illustrated in Fig. 1a.

5.3 2CEL Setups

2CEL is a two-population competitive coevolutionary algorithm in which individuals are bred in two separate populations. The first population contains candidate solutions, while the second one maintains tests, which here take the form of opponent strategies that challenge candidate solutions. The fitness of a candidate solution is the sum of points it obtains in double games with all tests.

Tests, in turn, are rewarded for making *distinctions* between candidate solutions [11]. The test's fitness is the weighted sum of points it receives for making distinctions. A test makes a distinction for a given pair of candidate solutions if the games played with it give different outcomes. To maintain diversity in the population, we employ *competitive fitness sharing* [26]; each point for distinction is weighted by the inverse of the number of tests that make this distinction. Consequently, genetic novelty is preferred, since tests that make unique distinctions are rewarded more than the ones that make the same distinctions as other tests in the population.

To guarantee fair comparison among the studied algorithms, the selection scheme in the population of candidate solutions remains the same as in 1CEL. The population of tests uses $(\mu + \lambda)$ evolutionary strategy, where $\mu = 25$ and $\lambda = 25$. Figure 1b illustrates how the fitness is assigned to a candidate solution in 2CEL.

Table 1: Performance comparison of best-of-run players. All t-Student tests have been performed against RSEL.

Algorithm	Performance [%]	t-value	p-value
RSEL	.86.46 ± 0.25	-	-
2CEL-RS	.86.44 ± 0.26	-20.30	3.73×10^{-54}
1CEL-RS	.83.63 ± 0.37	-12.63	1.29×10^{-28}
1CEL	.80.34 ± 0.54	-20.53	6.62×10^{-55}
2CEL	.79.97 ± 0.58	-0.09	0.46

The last method, **2CEL-RS**, is 2CEL enhanced by random sampling. While the population of candidate solutions still consists of 50 individuals, the population of tests is limited to 25 individuals. The fitness of a candidate solution is the sum of points obtained in 25 double games with the tests and 25 double games with the random opponents (cf. Fig. 1b).

6. RESULTS

We performed 120 runs for each method. In the following, the best-of-generation individual is the individual with the highest fitness in the population. By the best-of-run player we mean the best-of-generation player of the last generation.

6.1 Performance Comparison

To assess the individuals we use the approximated measure of expected utility. To calculate it, we let every individual play 25,000 double games (50,000 games in total) against random WPC players, obtained by drawing weights uniformly from the interval $[-10, 10]$. With one point for winning the game, zero for losing, and 0.5 for a draw, the expected utility of a player is in the range of $[0, 1]$, but for clearer presentation we report it in percent points. From now on, the term 'performance' refers to this measure.

Figure 2 shows how the performance of each method changes as a function of computational effort (which is here proportional to the number of generations). Each point on the plot is the performance of method's best-of-generation player averaged over 120 runs. Table 1 compares the methods in terms of the average performance of the best-of-run individuals accompanied by 95% confidence intervals, t-Student test values and p-values. The two-tail t-test compares RSEL with other methods.

Our results confirm Chong's *et al.* conclusion that evolution with fitness purely based on random sampling (RSEL) is significantly better than one-population coevolution [5]. The new result is that it is also much better than two-population coevolution. Although the difference between 2CEL and 1CEL is not statistically significant and some parts of the curves in Fig. 2 overlap, the comparison of setups that mix coevolution with random sampling, i.e. 2CEL-RS and 1CEL-RS, shows that separating learners from trainers in two-population setup pays off with respect to the expected utility.

The 1CEL-RS setup can be viewed as a hybrid of RSEL and 1CEL, thus it is not surprising to see its performance falling in between those two [5]. What is not obvious, however, is that a similar effect is cannot be observed in the case of 2CEL: RSEL and 2CEL-RS produce equally good strategies on average.

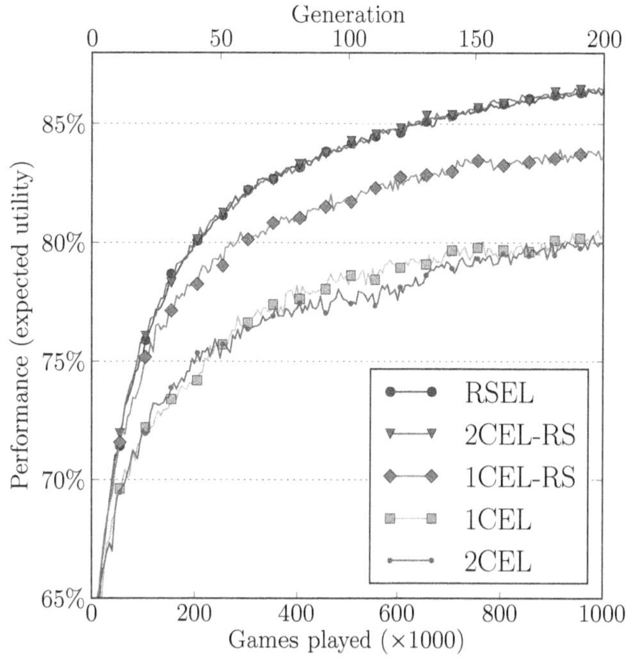

Figure 2: Comparison of methods over time in terms of expected utility performance measure.

However, while having roughly the same expected performance against opponents, do 2CEL-RS and RSEL differ in their capability of winning against opponents of different strength? In an attempt to answer this question, we will break down the performance value with performance profiles.

6.2 Analysis with Performance Profiles

To better understand characteristics of particular methods we devise *performance profile*. This tool gives us better insight into how a strategy copes with opponents of different strength.

To prepare a performance profile, we randomly generate 500,000 players (opponents) by sampling WPC weights uniformly and independently from the $[-10, 10]$ interval. Next, the performance of each opponent is estimated by playing 1,000 double games with random WPC strategies. The range of possible performance values, i.e., $[0, 1]$, is then divided into 100 bins of equal width, and each opponent is assigned to one of these bins based on its performance.

Building the opponents database is computationally expensive: here it required playing $500{,}000 \times 1{,}000 \times 2 = 1{,}000{,}000{,}000$ games. However, once created, it can be reused[2].

The ensemble of opponents partitioned into bins forms the basis for building the profile. The assessed player plays double games with all the opponents from each bin, and the average game outcome is plotted against the bins.

We apply performance profiling to inspect the best-of-run individuals of all algorithms considered in this paper and present them in Fig. 3. Since we have 120 runs per method, we average the profiles over 120 best-of-run players. A point of coordinates (x, y) in a plot means that the

[2]The data and Java code for creating performance profiles for Othello are available at `http://www.cs.put.poznan.pl/wjaskowski/projects/performance-profiles`.

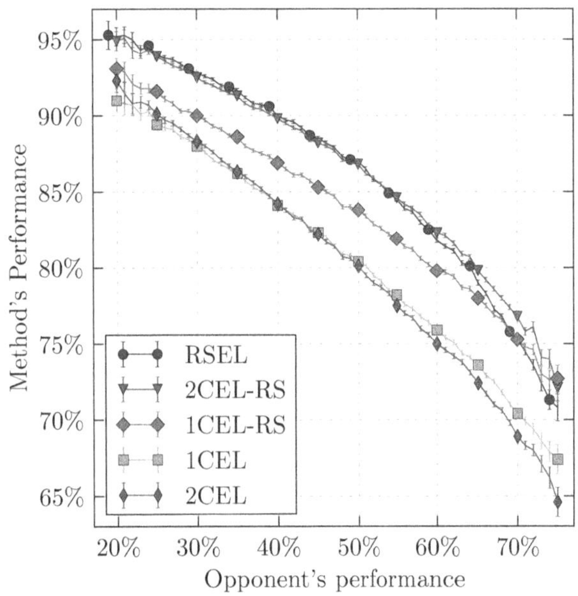

Figure 3: Performance profiles of five analyzed methods. Each point (x, y) means performance y over opponents of performance x. The whiskers mark 95% confidence interval.

best-of-run individuals have on average performance y when playing against opponents of performance x. For example, the performance of RSEL is about 90% for opponents with performance of 40%.

The whiskers in the plots mark 95% confidence intervals. Notably, they tend to widen towards the ends of plots. This is because it is hard to randomly generate opponents that are very strong or very weak, so the extreme bins contain relatively few opponents. For the same reason we removed the points with confidence intervals that were larger than 20% or were computed on a basis of 120 or fewer double games.

The decreasing trend in each data series confirms an obvious fact that it is harder to win with stronger opponents than with the weaker ones. We can also see that some methods are dominated by others, e.g., 1CEL and 2CEL are dominated by 2CEL-RS. Although 2CEL-RS is most of the time significantly better than 1CEL-RS (which is why it has a much higher performance), the difference between them decreases with the increasing opponent strength and it is hard to tell which one fares better against the strongest players.

What is however clearly visible in the plots is that while RSEL copes well with weak opponents (performance similar to 2CEL-RS), it fares worse when confronted with stronger ones (performance worse than 1CEL-RS and 2CEL-RS). Interestingly, 1CEL-RS has a complementary characteristics, so its plot and RSEL's plot cross at roughly 68% opponent strength. However, since the strong opponents are infrequent, the advantage of 1CEL-RS over RSEL on them cannot compensate its inferior position when it comes to weaker opponents, and its overall performance is still worse (cf. Table 1).

Table 2: The results of the round-robin tournament (percents).

Algorithm	1CEL-RS	2CEL-RS	1CEL	RSEL	2CEL	**Overall**
1CEL-RS	-	53.4%	53.3%	56.3%	56.7%	**54.9%**
2CEL-RS	46.6%	-	51.2%	53.2%	53.9%	**51.3%**
1CEL	46.7%	48.8%	-	51.8%	52.7%	**50.0%**
RSEL	43.7%	46.8%	48.2%	-	52.0%	**47.7%**
2CEL	43.3%	46.1%	47.3%	48.0%	-	**46.2%**

6.3 Round-Robin Tournament Comparison

Our final experiment is a round-robin tournament among all methods. This assessment determines a relative ranking of methods [13] by playing matches between teams of players. Every team consists of 120 best-of-run players produced by an algorithm. Thus, a single match in the tournament involves $120 \times 120 = 14400$ double games. Winning all games gives the round-robin-performance of 100%.

Table 2 presents the results of the tournament. Evolutionary learning with random sampling loses to all other methods except 2CEL in head-to-head matches and its aggregated round-robin-performance is significantly lower than 1CEL-RS, 2CEL-RS, and 1CEL. However, the difference between RSEL and 2CEL is too small to conclude anything for sure. Adding a random sampling component improves both one- and two-population coevolution (1CEL-RS vs. 1CEL and 2CEL-RS vs. 2CEL). Also, one-population variants are consistently better than two-population ones (2CEL vs. 1CEL and 2CEL-RS vs. 1CEL-RS). 1CEL-RS wins against all other algorithms and is clearly the best in terms of round-robin performance.

The ranking in terms of expected utility presented in Table 1 is different than the one resulting from the round-robin tournament. Do the rankings contradict each other?

In order to explain this discrepancy, notice that, contrary to the previous assessments which involved random opponents, here each individual in a team plays only with the players from the opponent teams, and those players (co)evolved to be strong. According to Table 1, the performance of team members is in the range of 79–87% and, as we have seen in Section 6.2, the methods differ in performance profiles. Figure 3 does not provide reliable data on how methods behave for very strong opponents because they are too scarce, but the trends are evident and can be extrapolated. As we already pointed out, RSEL, for instance, matches the performance of 1CEL-RS at opponent strength of 68%, where their curves cross, and then keeps on heading downwards. This explains why it ranks low in the round-robin tournament.

Similarly, performance profile plot shows that 1CEL-RS's curve is the most leveled, matching 2CEL-RS's plot at around 75% opponent performance and, presumably, surpassing it for the stronger opponents. We hypothesize that this may account for the former one scoring 3.6% more in the final tournament ranking.

7. DISCUSSION

Most of our findings confirm the results reported by Chong *et al.* [5]. When gauged with the performance measure of expected utility, evolutionary learning with random sampling indeed provides significantly better results than simple one-

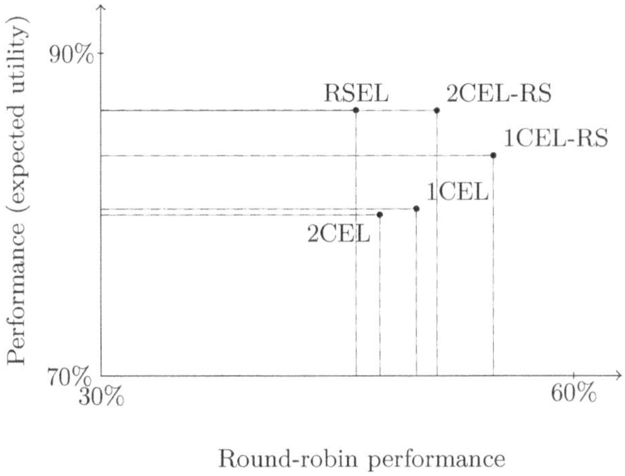

Figure 4: Methods compared in a two-objective manner. The objectives are: i) expected utility performance, and ii) round-robin tournament result.

population coevolution. However, as we have shown, this comes at a price: performance profiles reveal that RSEL, while being able to play well with easy opponents, has troubles when facing the stronger ones. This was further confirmed in the round-robin tournament, where RSEL, faced only with the highly-skilled opponents evolved by competitive methods, finished in the last but one place.

The beneficial role of hybridization with random sampling is puzzling. As we found out when preparing the performance profiles, drawing a strong opponent at random is very unlikely. From the 500,000 random opponents drawn, all had performance lower than 80%. Moreover, most of them are mediocre, so they cannot be challenging for the individuals that were evolving in the population for many generations. Thus, it is not obvious how they could form a useful training gradient. Yet coevolution obtains better results when coupled with random sampling. This effect is especially interesting for 1CEL-RS, which has indisputably won the round-robin tournament. Explaining this effect in detail requires further investigation, but we speculate that random sampling might play a role in preventing forgetting [10], a coevolutionary pathology that hampers learning.

Despite the fact that 1CEL-RS and 2CEL-RS rank among the top three algorithms both for the expected utility criterion and the round-robin tournament, we observe a trade-off of their performance against weak and strong players. This trade-off manifests in the performance profile plot (Fig. 2), but we can alternatively visualize it by plotting all methods against two objectives: the (estimated) expected utility and the round-robin-performance. Figure 4 shows that no method dominates all others on both criteria, however 2CEL-RS is close to dominate RSEL, 1CEL dominates 2CEL, and remarkably, coevolution with random sampling dominates coevolution without it.

This raises a question: which performance measure (and which solution concept in general) is more *practically useful*? Are strategies that play well on average preferable to those which can cope with strong opponents, but sometimes lose with the weak ones? Unfortunately, this question cannot be answered without assuming certain probability distribution of strategies as they occur in the real world, which is in general difficult.

8. CONCLUSIONS

This study presented an evidence that coevolution can offer advantage over evolution with random sampling for learning game strategies. In the particular case of the game of Othello and WPC strategy representation, this advantage was observable in head-to-head confrontation of generated solutions. An algorithm that autonomously and dynamically redefines its own fitness function (CEL) can produce strategies which are better in such confrontation than those produced by an algorithm that relies on (approximately) stationary fitness function (RSEL). However, pure coevolution is not sufficient to attain that, and additional means are required (here: two-population setup and random opponents). It remains to be seen whether analogous conclusions may be drawn for interactive domains other than Othello.

To provide detailed insight into the performance of players considered in this study, we proposed performance profiles. We used this straightforward tool to explain, among others, the differences between the results of the round-robin tournament and the comparison in terms of expected utility. However, it can be potentially useful also for explaining other phenomena, the dynamics of the search process, behavior of other algorithms, and helping design the new ones. Nevertheless, we must admit that in the preliminary variant presented here this tool suffers from certain limitations. First and foremost, the very strong (or very weak) opponents are hard to generate randomly. As a result, performance profile plots show only a partial picture and their reliability on the extremes of performance is low. This could be improved by adding players of certain performance, possibly generated in a non-random fashion (e.g., the strategies learned by CEL or RSEL), at the price of introducing a bias of unknown characteristic. Secondly, more powerful strategy representations, like n-tuples [18], may provide players with performance near 100% against all random opponents. In such cases, performance profiles would cease to differentiate the methods, so it is hard to anticipate how useful they would be in such contexts.

9. ACKNOWLEDGMENT

This work has been supported by grant no. N N519 441939. W. Jaśkowski has been supported by Polish Ministry of Science and Education, grant no. 91-550/DS. M. Szubert has been supported by Polish Ministry of Science and Education, grant no. 2012/05/N/ST6/03152.

10. REFERENCES

[1] R. Axelrod. The evolution of strategies in the iterated prisoner's dilemma. In L. Davis, editor, *Genetic Algorithms in Simulated Annealing*, pages 32–41. Pitman, London, 1987.

[2] K. J. Binkley, K. Seehart, and M. Hagiwara. A Study of Artificial Neural Network Architectures for Othello Evaluation Functions. *Transactions of the Japanese Society for Artificial Intelligence*, 22(5):461–471, 2007.

[3] M. Buro. The evolution of strong othello programs. *Entertainment Computing-Technology and Applications*, pages 81–88, 2003.

[4] S. Y. Chong, M. K. Tan, and J. D. White. Observing the evolution of neural networks learning to play the game of othello. *Evolutionary Computation, IEEE Transactions on*, 9(3):240–251, 2005.

[5] S. Y. Chong, P. Tino, D. C. Ku, and Y. Xin. Improving Generalization Performance in Co-Evolutionary Learning. *IEEE Transactions on Evolutionary Computation*, 16(1):70–85, 2012.

[6] E. D. de Jong. The maxsolve algorithm for coevolution. In H.-G. B. et al., editor, *GECCO 2005: Proceedings of the 2005 conference on Genetic and evolutionary computation*, volume 1, pages 483–489, Washington DC, USA, 25-29 June 2005. ACM Press.

[7] E. D. de Jong. A Monotonic Archive for Pareto-Coevolution. *Evolutionary Computation*, 15(1):61–93, Spring 2007.

[8] E. D. de Jong and A. Bucci. DECA: dimension extracting coevolutionary algorithm. In M. C. et al., editor, *GECCO 2006: Proceedings of the 8th annual conference on Genetic and evolutionary computation*, pages 313–320, Seattle, Washington, USA, 2006. ACM Press.

[9] S. G. Ficici. *Solution concepts in coevolutionary algorithms*. PhD thesis, Waltham, MA, USA, 2004. Adviser-Pollack, Jordan B.

[10] S. G. Ficici. Multiobjective Optimization and Coevolution. In J. Knowles, D. Corne, and K. Deb, editors, *Multi-Objective Problem Solving from Nature: From Concepts to Applications*, pages 31–52. Springer, Berlin, 2008.

[11] S. G. Ficici and J. B. Pollack. Pareto optimality in coevolutionary learning. In J. Kelemen and P. Sosík, editors, *Advances in Artificial Life, 6th European Conference, ECAL 2001*, volume 2159 of *Lecture Notes in Computer Science*, pages 316–325, Prague, Czech Republic, 2001. Springer.

[12] D. B. Fogel. *Blondie24: Playing at the Edge of AI*. Morgan Kaufmann Publishers, Sept. 2001.

[13] W. Jaśkowski, K. Krawiec, and B. Wieloch. Evolving strategy for a probabilistic game of imperfect information using genetic programming. *Genetic Programming and Evolvable Machines*, 9(4):281–294, 2008.

[14] W. Jaśkowski, K. Krawiec, and B. Wieloch. Winning ant wars: Evolving a human-competitive game strategy using fitnessless selection. In M. O. et al., editor, *Genetic Programming 11th European Conference, EuroGP 2008, Proceedings*, volume 4971 of *Lecture Notes in Computer Science*, pages 13–24. Springer-Verlag, mar 2008.

[15] H. Juillé and J. B. Pollack. Coevolving the "ideal" trainer: Application to the discovery of cellular automata rules. In *University of Wisconsin*, pages 519–527. Morgan Kaufmann, 1998.

[16] K. Krawiec, W. Jaśkowski, and M. Szubert. Evolving small-board go players using coevolutionary temporal difference learning with archive. *International Journal of Applied Mathematics and Computer Science*, 21(4):717–731, 2011.

[17] S. Lucas and T. P. Runarsson. Othello Competition; http://algoval.essex.ac.uk:8080/othello/League.jsp.

[18] S. M. Lucas. Learning to play Othello with N-tuple systems. *Australian Journal of Intelligent Information Processing Systems, Special Issue on Game Technology*, 9(4):1–20, 2007.

[19] S. M. Lucas and T. P. Runarsson. Temporal difference learning versus co-evolution for acquiring othello position evaluation. In *IEEE Symposium on Computational Intelligence and Games*, pages 52–59. IEEE, 2006.

[20] S. Luke and R. P. Wiegand. When coevolutionary algorithms exhibit evolutionary dynamics. In A. M. Barry, editor, *GECCO 2002: Proceedings of the Bird of a Feather Workshops, Genetic and Evolutionary Computation Conference*, pages 236–241, New York, 2002.

[21] J. Mandziuk. *Knowledge-Free and Learning-Based Methods in Intelligent Game Playing*, volume 276. Springer, 2010.

[22] E. P. Manning. Using resource-limited nash memory to improve an othello evaluation function. *Computational Intelligence and AI in Games, IEEE Transactions on*, 2(1):40–53, 2010.

[23] J. B. Pollack and A. D. Blair. Co-evolution in the successful learning of backgammon strategy. *Machine Learning*, 32(3):225–240, 1998.

[24] E. Popovici, A. Bucci, R. P. Wiegand, and E. D. de Jong. *Handbook of Natural Computing*, chapter Coevolutionary Principles. Springer-Verlag, 2011.

[25] P. Rosenbloom. A world-championship-level othello program. *Artificial Intelligence*, 19(3):279–320, 1982.

[26] C. D. Rosin and R. K. Belew. New methods for competitive coevolution. *Evolutionary Computation*, 5(1):1–29, 1997.

[27] M. Szubert, W. Jaśkowski, and K. Krawiec. Coevolutionary temporal difference learning for othello. In *IEEE Symposium on Computational Intelligence and Games*, pages 104–111, Milano, Italy, 2009.

[28] S. van den Dries and M. A. Wiering. Neural-Fitted TD-Leaf Learning for Playing Othello With Structured Neural Networks. *IEEE Transactions on Neural Networks and Learning Systems*, 23(11):1701–1713, Nov. 2012.

[29] T. Yoshioka, S. Ishii, and M. Ito. Strategy acquisition for the game "othello" based on reinforcement learning. In *ICONIP*, pages 841–844, 1998.

Shaping Fitness Function for Evolutionary Learning of Game Strategies

Marcin Szubert, Wojciech Jaśkowski, Paweł Liskowski and Krzysztof Krawiec
Institute of Computing Science, Poznan University of Technology
Piotrowo 2, 60965 Poznań, Poland
{mszubert,wjaskowski,pliskowski,kkrawiec}@cs.put.poznan.pl

ABSTRACT

In evolutionary learning of game-playing strategies, fitness evaluation is based on playing games with certain opponents. In this paper we investigate how the performance of these opponents and the way they are chosen influence the efficiency of learning. For this purpose we introduce a simple method for shaping the fitness function by sampling the opponents from a biased performance distribution. We compare the shaped function with existing fitness evaluation approaches that sample the opponents from an unbiased performance distribution or from a coevolving population. In an extensive computational experiment we employ these methods to learn Othello strategies and assess both the absolute and relative performance of the elaborated players. The results demonstrate the superiority of the shaping approach, and can be explained by means of performance profiles, an analytical tool that evaluate the evolved strategies using a range of variably skilled opponents.

Categories and Subject Descriptors

I.2.6 [**Artificial Intelligence**]: Learning—*Connectionism and neural nets, Parameter learning*; I.2.8 [**Artificial Intelligence**]: Problem Solving, Control Methods, and Search—*Heuristic methods*; J.m [**Miscellaneous**]:

General Terms

Algorithms

Keywords

Shaping, Fitness Evaluation, Coevolution, Othello

1. INTRODUCTION

The main motivation for this study originates from the question: what can be done to improve the results of an optimization algorithm on a given problem with respect to a specific performance measure? A typical approach is to modify the algorithm by tuning the parameters that affect its behavior. In particular, evolutionary algorithms involve numerous settings (including population size, variation operators, selection scheme) that need to be configured properly to attain satisfactory performance. Since devising such a configuration manually is usually nontrivial, various 'rule-of-thumb' recommendations, good practices and several techniques of automated parameter tuning have been proposed in the past [8]. Ultimately, if the configured algorithm still does not achieve the expected performance, it can be entirely replaced by a different one. Such a choice between a number of algorithms can also be done automatically by hyper-heuristics [3].

It may seem that, apart from searching the space of algorithms and/or their parameters, there are no alternative answers to the question posed in the beginning. Indeed, of the three abovementioned elements (algorithm, problem, performance measure), only the first one appears to be in experimenter's control. However, there is another option: instead of adjusting the algorithm for a particular problem, we can take a complementary approach and modify the problem to make it easier to solve by a particular algorithm. Such approach corresponds to the idea of *shaping* — a core concept of behavioral psychology [24] that already proved useful in, among others, reinforcement learning [21]. Shaping consists in a meaningful modification of the learning problem that brings the learner closer to reaching the behavior of ultimate interest [9]. We adopt shaping here as an umbrella term that characterizes our approach.

In case of evolutionary algorithms and optimization problems, shaping can be applied to two elements of problem definition. First, the search space, which can be shaped by, for instance, adjusting genetic encoding of solutions. Second, the fitness function, which may be purposefully different from the original objective performance measure in order to distort the evaluation of individuals and drive evolution through advantageous paths in the search space.

In this paper, we focus on shaping fitness function for evolutionary learning of game-playing strategies where the objective is to maximize the *expected utility*, i.e. the average outcome against all possible opponents. We investigate three different fitness assessment methods. Two of them are commonly used for such problems and employ random sampling of opponents [5] and coevolution [20]. The third method is a straightforward shaping approach, which we introduce in this paper. The idea is to shape the fitness function by sampling the opponents used for evaluation from a biased performance distribution. We show that using such

GECCO'13, July 6–10, 2013, Amsterdam, The Netherlands.

a function leads to more effective learning and results in stronger players both in absolute and relative terms. In order to verify whether it is actually shaping that drives the evolution towards better solutions, we also consider hybrid fitness evaluation methods which combine the three above approaches. This investigation is conducted with *performance profiles* [13], a novel tool that allows us to analyze the performance of a player with respect to opponents of different strength.

2. METHODS

Learning game-playing strategies is an example of a test-based problem [2, 11], in which candidate solutions are evaluated on a number of test cases such as environments, opponents or examples. In most real-world problems of this class, the large number of possible tests precludes computationally feasible calculation of objective performance measure. For this reason, solving test-based problems with evolutionary computation requires substituting the original performance measure with a computationally cheaper counterpart that drives the search process towards a possibly similar (and preferably the same) goal.

In the case of games, fitness is usually computed by averaging the results achieved against a limited number of tests, i.e., opponent strategies. The question that one needs to answer when designing such a fitness function is: how to choose the opponent strategies? The answer to this question is of utmost importance, as it is exactly the choice of these opponents that allows us to shape the fitness function and, accordingly, guide the learning process.

The set of evaluating opponents and the corresponding fitness function can be either static or dynamic. A static function employs a fixed pool of predefined players (e.g., expert strategies), and thus remains constant throughout evolution. A dynamic function, in contrast, uses a set of opponents that changes in every generation. By exposing players to different opponents each generation, learning algorithms that use dynamic evaluation function can be expected to produce players that win against a wider range of opponents. Here we confront three ways of dynamic opponent selection: random sampling, coevolution, and shaped sampling, the last being the main conceptual contribution of this study.

Before we discuss the algorithms that employ these methods, we need to present the game of Othello, which we use as our testbed, and the representation of strategies for this game. The latter is particularly important, since it directly determines the spaces of possible solutions and tests.

2.1 Othello and the WPC representation

The game of Othello is a deterministic, perfect information, zero-sum board game played by two players on an 8×8 board. There are 64 identical pieces which are white on one side and black on the other, with the colors representing players. The game starts with the four central squares of the board occupied with two black and two white pieces (see Fig. 1). Players make moves alternately by placing their pieces on the board until it is completely filled or until neither of them is able to make a legal move. The position to place a piece on has to fulfill two conditions. Firstly, it must be adjacent to an opponent's piece. Secondly, the new piece and some other piece of the current player must form a vertical, horizontal, or diagonal line with a continuous sequence of opponent's pieces inbetween. After placing the piece, all such opponent's pieces are flipped. A legal move requires flipping at least one of the opponent's pieces. The objective of the game is to have the majority of own pieces on the board at the end of the game. If both players have the same number of disks, the game ends in a draw.

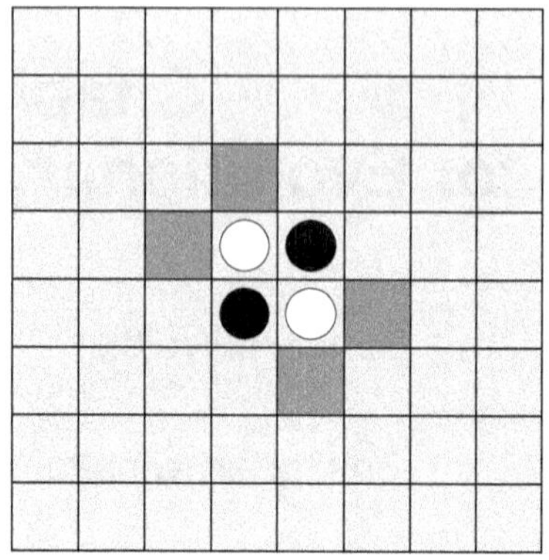

Figure 1: The initial board state of Othello

From the previously applied Othello-playing strategy representations such as multi-layer neural networks [1], spatial neural networks [4], and n-tuple networks [17, 16], we employ the simplest of them, the position-weighted piece counter (WPC) [18, 23]. WPC is a linear weighted board evaluation function which implements the state evaluator concept, i.e., it is explicitly used to evaluate how desirable a given board state is. It assigns weight w_i to board location i and uses scalar product to calculate the value f of a board state $\mathbf{b}$:

$$f(\mathbf{b}) = \sum_{i=1}^{8\times 8} w_i b_i,$$

where b_i is 0 in case of an empty location, +1 if a black piece is present or −1 in case of a white piece. The players interpret $f(\mathbf{b})$ in a complementary manner: the black player prefers moves leading towards states with a higher value, whereas lower values are favored by the white player.

All methods considered in this paper employ WPC as a state evaluator in 1-ply setup: given the current state of the board, the player generates all legal moves and applies f to the resulting states. The state gauged as the most valuable determines the move to be made. Ties are resolved at random. WPC is used to represent the candidate solutions to the learning problem as well as the opponent strategies employed by a fitness function.

2.2 Random Sampling Evolutionary Learning

The approach we refer here to as Random Sampling Evolutionary Learning (RSEL) was proposed by Chong *et al.* [5] under the name of Improved Coevolutionary Learning. This learning procedure is inspired by a $(\mu + \lambda)$ generational evolutionary strategy. The algorithm begins with a population of μ randomly generated individuals (vectors of 64 real-valued weights of WPC strategies in our case). In every generation, each of the μ fittest individuals produces λ/μ offspring through a mutation operator (thus, all populations except for the initial one consist of μ parents and λ offspring of those parents).

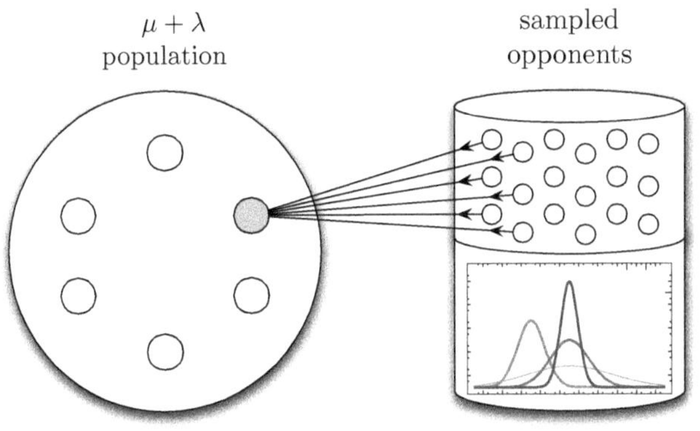

Figure 2: Fitness evaluation based on sampling opponents from a set with certain performance distribution.

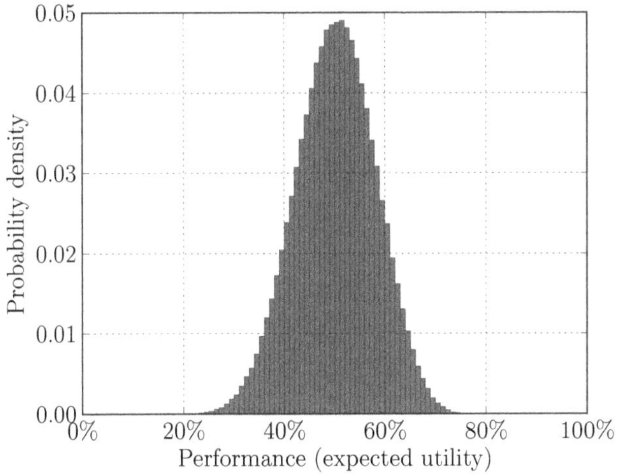

Figure 3: Performance distribution of randomly sampled WPC opponents

The fitness function used in RSEL is based on random sampling of opponents. A sample is drawn once per evaluation phase (i.e., once per generation for a generational evolutionary algorithm) by generating a set of WPC strategies. Afterwards, each individual in the population plays against all the opponents in the sample, and the average score determines its fitness. Consequently, the fitness calculated in RSEL is an unbiased estimator of the expected utility objective function.

Figure 2 schematically illustrates this type of fitness evaluation procedure. The figure highlights the fact that the performance in the population (statistical population), from which the sample is drawn, has certain distribution. This distribution affects the expected strength of evaluating opponents in the sample.

We conducted a preliminary experiment to estimate this distribution. Illustrated in Fig. 3, it was obtained by sampling 500,000 random strategies (in the same way as in RSEL) and calculating their performance as the average game outcome against another set of 1,000 random opponents. Clearly, the performance distribution resembles a normal one with a mean value of 50.2% and a standard deviation of 7.91%.

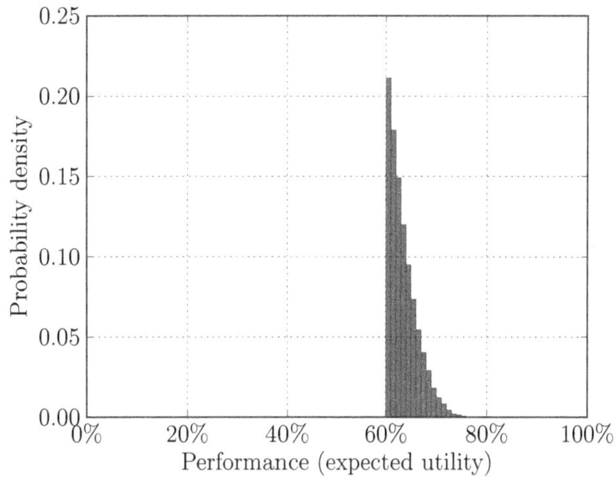

Figure 4: Performance distribution of shaped opponents

2.3 Shaped Sampling Evolutionary Learning

The performance distribution of evaluating opponents in RSEL (Fig. 3) indicates that the majority of WPC strategies achieve mediocre performance. Strong strategies are few and far between. As RSEL samples the opponents uniformly from this distribution, it is unlikely for an individual to face a strong opponent in the evaluation phase. For this reason, fitness function will be often unable to differentiate between two strategies that, e.g., play equally well against the average players but one of them is much better at beating the strong ones. This is unfortunate as, preferably, we would like to lead the evolution towards the strategies that are able to win with skilled players without losing the capability of winning with the opponents of average strength.

Therefore, we propose a method called Shaped Sampling Evolutionary Learning (SSEL), which operates largely like RSEL. The only exception is the fitness assessment phase (cf. Fig. 2), which uses a *biased* sample of opponents, i.e., a sample that is drawn from a different performance distribution. Here, such a shaped sample contains only the opponents that achieve the performance of more than 60%. We populate it in a similar manner in which Fig. 3 was obtained. Its performance distribution is shown in Fig. 4. In each fitness assignment phase, the set of evaluating opponents is randomly selected from the pool.

SSEL's rationale is to shape the fitness function in such a way that it promotes game-playing skills needed for defeating the strong opponents. In this context, RSEL can be considered as a reference, unshaped approach, where the set of evaluating opponents is an unbiased sample of the entire set of WPC strategies, and the performance distribution in the sample follows the the performance distribution of all WPC strategies.

2.4 Coevolutionary Learning

In both evolutionary approaches presented above, the fitness function is designed to reflect individual's *absolute* performance (whether using an unbiased or biased sample of opponents). Individual's absolute performance is, by definition, independent of other individuals in the population. In coevolutionary algorithms, by contrast, fitness function measures the *relative* performance of individuals with respect to other evolving individuals. From many variants of this scheme proposed in past studies, we employ competitive coevolution, which is particularly useful when an objective evaluation function is unknown or difficult to compute. This is the case when learning game strategies: it is computationally infeasible to objectively assess the quality of a strategy, but it is easy to let the individuals interact by playing games. The outcomes of such games determine fitness, which in this context is often called *competitive fitness*.

An important aspect of fitness evaluation in coevolution is the interaction scheme that determines which individuals should interact. For symmetrical problems such as the game of Othello, a popular approach is *one-population coevolution* [19] which consists in evolving individuals in a single, homogeneous population, making them compete directly with each other. Although one-population coevolution has been praised for problem solving advantages and intensely exploited in the context of games, some results suggest that it can be useful to maintain simultaneously two populations of strategies [7, 14]. Each population contains the opponents used for evaluating strategies in the other population — the interactions occur only between individuals that belong to different populations.

In this paper, CEL employs the two-population interaction scheme illustrated in Fig. 5. In contrast to RSEL and SSEL, where fitness assessment involved sampling opponents from a fixed, predefined distribution, here the set of evaluating opponents is coevolving with the population of solutions. Thus, apart from the initial opponent population which is sampled randomly (i.e., from the performance distribution shown in Fig. 3), the distribution of opponents in CEL is not explicitly defined and may vary across generations. Because this influence is reciprocal, the resulting competitive fitness function is thus not only dynamic but also adaptive (details on fitness definition in both population will be provided in the experimental part).

From the shaping perspective, coevolution can be considered as a form of *autonomous shaping* performed on the basis of the current state of the candidate solution population. This stays in contrast to SSEL, where shaping is realized by manual and permanent modification of the opponent pool, and consequently, its performance distribution.

Since mixing multiple learning gradients can speed up learning and make the resulting solutions generalize better [15], we consider also a hybrid fitness evaluation method (see Fig. 5) that combines the competitive fitness employed in CEL with the fitness based on sampling opponents from the performance distributions used in RSEL or SSEL (cf. Figures 3 and 4). These approaches are referred to as CEL-RS and CEL-SS, respectively.

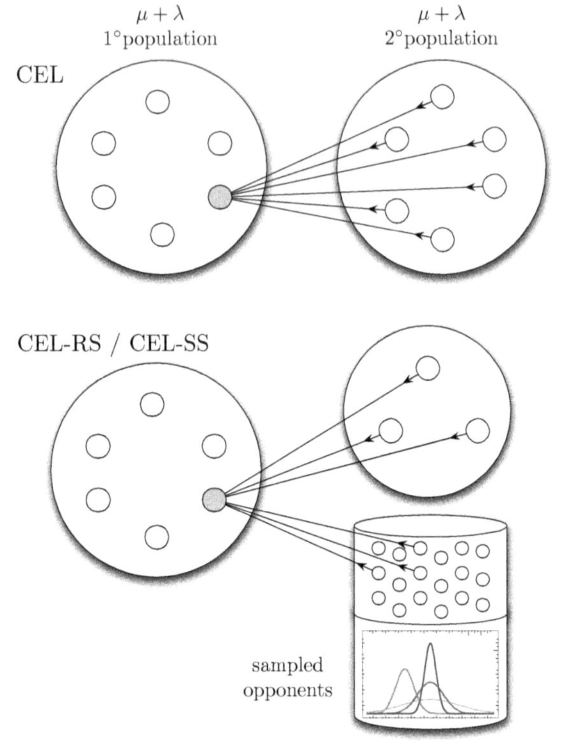

Figure 5: Fitness evaluation employed in coevolutionary learning and in the hybrid approach.

3. THE EXPERIMENT

The objectives of the experiment are twofold. Firstly, we want to determine which of the considered methods (RSEL, SSEL, various configurations of CEL, and hybrids thereof) yields best performing Othello players given a fixed computational budget. To this aim, we employ the expected utility performance measure and a round-robin tournament. Our second goal is to explain the anticipated differences by profiling the behavior of strategies using opponents of varying difficulty.

In order to fairly compare the algorithms, we set them up so that their total computational effort as well as the computational effort per one generation are equal among methods. Following other studies [7, 6, 15], we identify the computational effort with the number of games played in interactions among individuals.

A single interaction is a double game, where both individuals play one game as black and one game as white player. In each game, one point is to be divided between players: the winner gets one point and the loser zero points, or they get 0.5 point each in the case of draw. Each evolutionary run consists of 200 generations, in each of them 5,000 games are played (2,500 double games), which adds up to the total effort of 1,000,000 games per run.

All methods start with an initial population filled with individuals whose weights are randomly drawn from $[-0.2, 0.2]$. They also share the same simple mutation operator that perturbs all the weights using additive noise. The WPC weight $w_i^{'}$ of the offspring is obtained by adding a small random value to the corresponding WPC weight of the parent:

$$w_i^{'} = w_i + 0.1 \cdot U[-1, 1],$$

where $U[-1, 1]$ is a real number drawn uniformly from the interval $[-1, 1]$. Weights resulting from mutation are clamped to the interval $[-10, 10]$, effectively making the value equal to the respective bound. Consequently, the space of strategies we consider is a $[-10, 10]^{64}$ hypercube.

Some of the setups and performance assessment methods employ *random WPC players*. Each such player is obtained independently by drawing weights uniformly from the interval $[-10, 10]$. In the following, by 'random player/opponent' we mean a WPC player generated in this way.

We emphasize that in all setups the evolutionary operators of selection and mutation and their parameters are the same. The differences between them lie only in the way fitness is assigned to individuals. In the following subsections we detail the setups of particular algorithms while Figs. 2 and 5 illustrate their interaction schemes.

3.1 RSEL setup

RSEL is a straightforward implementation of Random Sampling Evolutionary Learning algorithm described in Section 2.2, where $\mu = 25$ and $\lambda = 25$. During the evaluation phase, each individual is evaluated against a set of ρ random WPC opponents obtained through random sampling of the space of strategies. The outcomes of these double games are summed to determine individual's fitness. To fix the effort at $5,000$ games per generation, we set $\rho = 50$ ($50 \times 50 \times 2 = 5000$). Figure 2 illustrates this configuration. We emphasize that a collection of random opponents is drawn anew every generation.

3.2 SSEL setup

SSEL works in the same way as RSEL. The only difference between them lies in the fitness evaluation phase (cf. Fig. 2) which uses a different, biased distribution of opponent strategies. The modified player performance distribution contains exclusively the opponents that achieve performance of more than 60%. In order to acquire the strategies that meet this condition, we filtered a set of $500,000$ randomly sampled players, which resulted in a *shaping pool* of $54,454$ players, with performance distribution illustrated in Fig. 4. Individual's fitness is determined on the basis of outcomes of double games with the set of $\rho = 50$ opponents randomly selected from the pool. Note that the computational cost of creating the shaping pool is not included in our results.

3.3 CEL setup

CEL is a two-population competitive coevolutionary algorithm in which individuals are bred in two separate populations. The first population contains candidate solutions, while the second one maintains tests. Here, tests take the form of opponent strategies that challenge players from the candidate solutions population.

The fitness of a candidate solution is the sum of points it obtains in double games with all tests. Tests, in turn, are rewarded for making *distinctions* between candidate solutions [10]. Test's fitness is the weighted number of points it receives for making distinctions. A test makes a distinction for a given pair of candidate solutions if the games it played against them gave different outcomes. To maintain diversity in the population, we employ a variant of *competitive fitness sharing* [22]; each point awarded for a distinction is weighted by the inverse of the number of tests that made that distinction. This extension promotes diversity in population, since a test that uniquely makes a distinction is rewarded more than the one that shares its distinction with many other tests.

To guarantee a fair comparison among all the studied algorithms, the selection scheme in the population of candidate solutions is the same as in RSEL and SSEL. The population of tests uses $(\mu+\lambda)$ evolutionary strategy, where $\mu = 25$ and $\lambda = 25$. Figure 5 illustrates how the fitness is assigned to a candidate solution in CEL.

3.4 Hybrid setups

The hybrid setups, referred to as **CEL-RS** and **CEL-SS**, combine the competitive fitness with the fitness based on sampling opponents from the performance distribution used in RSEL and SSEL respectively. Technically, each individual is evaluated on the basis of double games played against 25 individuals from the population of tests (as in CEL) and 25 random opponents drawn either from a uniform distribution (CEL-RS) or from the shaping pool (CEL-SS). This configuration is illustrated in Fig. 5. Note that while the population of candidate solutions still consists of 50 individuals, the population of tests is limited to 25 individuals.

4. RESULTS

We performed 120 runs for each method. In the following, the best-of-generation individual is the individual with the highest fitness in the population. By the best-of-run player we mean the best-of-generation player of the last generation. We identify method's performance with the performance of its best-of-generation players.

4.1 Absolute Performance

To objectively assess the individuals we use the approximate measure of expected utility. This performance measure is the percentage of points (with 1.0 point for winning the game and 0.5 for a draw) obtained in $25,000$ double games ($50,000$ games in total) against the random WPC players, generated by drawing weights uniformly from the interval $[-10, 10]$. From now on, the term 'performance' refers to this absolute measure.

Figure 6 shows the performance of each method as a function of computational effort (which is here proportional to the number of generations). Each point in the plot is the performance of method's best-of-generation players averaged over 120 runs. Additionally, Table 1 compares the methods to RSEL in terms of average performance of the best-of-run individuals accompanied by 95% confidence intervals.

The results demonstrate that CEL is definitely the worst algorithm on this performance measure — it struggles to reach the level of 80% while all the other methods easily go beyond 85%. Moreover, its best-of-run players' performance varies the most, which we attribute to its adaptive fitness function. As anticipated from the previous research [5], RSEL performs significantly better than CEL on the expected utility criterion because it employs an unbiased estimator of this measure as a fitness function. Intuitively, the hybrid of CEL and RSEL constructed by averaging their fitness functions (cf. Fig. 5) could be expected to result in averaging their performances as well. However, it turns out that CEL-RS is able to keep up with RSEL, even though it employs a smaller number of random opponents in the fitness evaluation phase.

Both shaping-based approaches (SSEL and CEL-SS) stay very close to each other throughout the entire evolution, and are the best methods in the comparison.

Although the shaped fitness function employed by SSEL is designed to encourage winning against stronger opponents, it appears that such redefinition allowed evolution to find the strategies that are generally better with respect to the expected utility measure. This is somewhat surprising because, technically, it is RSEL that is tailored to maximize this measure by utilizing the precise estimate of expected

Table 1: Performance comparison of best-of-run players

Method	Performance [%]	t-value	p-value
SSEL	87.30 ± 0.23	4.94	7.41×10^{-7}
CEL-SS	87.20 ± 0.26	4.10	2.79×10^{-7}
RSEL	86.46 ± 0.25	-	-
CEL-RS	86.44 ± 0.26	-0.9	0.46
CEL	79.97 ± 0.58	-20.53	6.62×10^{-7}

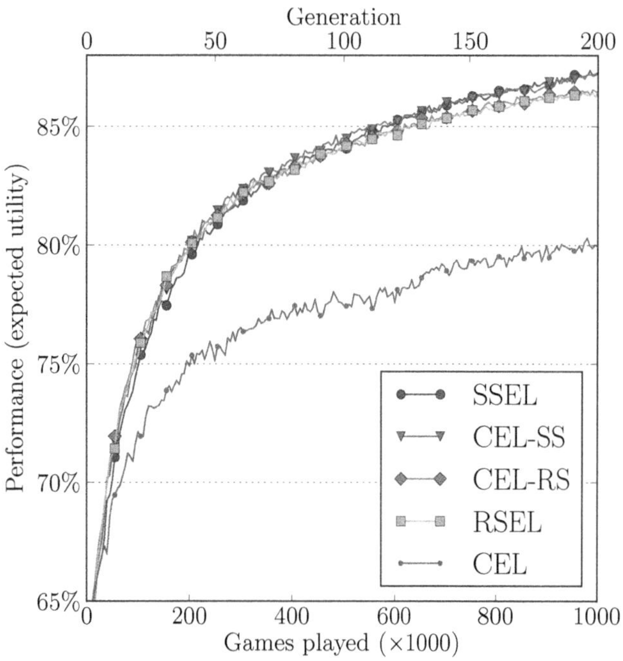

Figure 6: Performance of players over time.

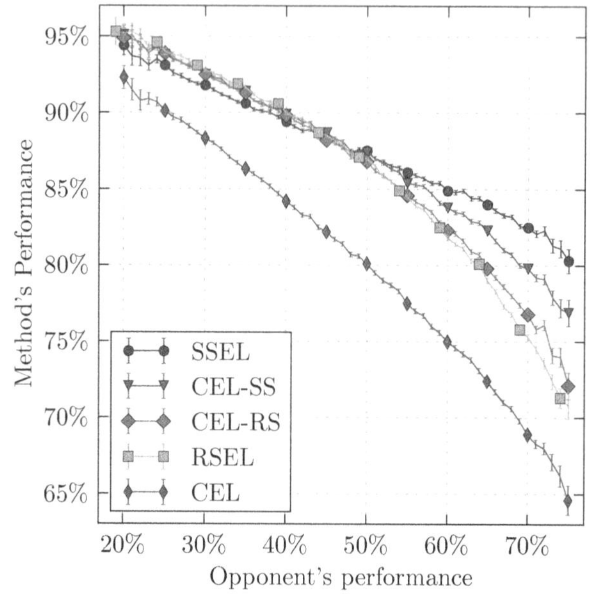

Figure 7: Performance profile plot illustrating the average percentage score against opponents of different performance.

utility to steer evolution — it learns from the same distribution of opponents on which it is later assessed. Yet it fares significantly worse than SSEL which employs a hand-crafted, biased probability distribution of opponents during learning. Thereby, it may be beneficial to distort the fitness function of the learning problem, even if the objective function is known and can be precisely approximated. This observation forms major rationale for shaping.

4.2 Performance Profiles

To understand the characteristics of particular methods we use *performance profiles* [13] that break down the expected utility measure into more detailed information on how a strategy copes with the opponents of different strength. To prepare a performance profile, we randomly generate $500,000$ players (opponents) using the same method as for generalization performance, i.e., by sampling WPC weights uniformly and independently from the $[-10, 10]$ interval. Next, the performance of each opponent is estimated by playing $1,000$ double games with random WPC strategies (generated on the fly). The range of possible performance values, i.e., $[0, 1]$, is then divided into 100 bins of equal width, and each opponent is assigned to one of these bins according to its performance.

The ensemble of opponents partitioned into bins forms the basis for building the profile. The assessed strategy plays double games against all opponents from each bin, and the average game outcome is plotted against the bins.

We apply the performance profiling to inspect the best-of-run individuals of all algorithms considered in this paper and present them in Fig. 7. Since we have 120 runs per method, we average the profiles over 120 best-of-run players. A point of coordinates (x, y) in a plot means that the best-of-run individuals have on average performance y when playing against the opponents of performance x. For example, the performance of most methods is about 90% for the opponents with performance of 40%.

In Fig. 7 the whiskers mark 95% confidence interval. Noticeably, they tend to widen towards the ends of plots. This is because it is hard to randomly generate the opponents that are very strong or very weak, so the extreme bins contain relatively few opponents. For the same reason we removed the points with the confidence intervals that were larger than 20% or were computed on a basis of less than 120 double games played. The decreasing trend in each data series demonstrates that it is generally harder to win with the stronger opponents than with the weaker ones.

The performance profile plots shed a new light on comparison between RSEL and CEL conducted by Chong et al. [5] and reproduced in Section 4.1. The plot explains the reason of the observed significant difference between these methods with respect to the expected utility measure. RSEL plays much better with the weak and mediocre opponents that occur frequently among the random WPC players. CEL, in contrast, learns to play against the strong opponents but at the same time underperforms against the weaker ones. The performance profile of CEL shows that it is the worst method in the entire space of considered opponents. We suppose that the performance distribution in a coevolving population of tests is biased even more than in SSEL — as solutions get better, their opponents (tests) must acquire more competence to distinguish between them. This challenges the solutions to perform even better, and so the feedback loop closes. Investigating how the performance distribution of opponents, and consequently the fitness function, is adaptively shaped by coevolution is an interesting direction for the future work.

Apart from CEL, all other methods perform similarly when evaluated against the players of performance lower than 50% (Fig. 7). Above this value, the profiles start to diverge and RSEL is the method that loses the most when the opponents get more challenging. To explain this fact, let us recall that the performance distribution of random WPC players (see Fig. 3) contains mainly the mediocre players. For this reason, RSEL can be seen as specialized to play with the opponents of average skills. Given the shaped performance distribution of opponents used for fitness evaluation (see Fig. 4), SSEL is analogously focused on defeating the highly skilled players. However, this method manages to maintain also the capability to play with the weaker players, albeit not as well as, e.g., RSEL. This is particularly interesting, knowing that SSEL's learners never meet players weaker than 60%. This may suggest that, at least for the game of Othello, it is enough to learn from the master opponents to obtain a well-playing strategy.

4.3 Relative Performance

In our final experiment we perform a round-robin tournament among all methods. This assessment determines a relative ranking of methods [12] by playing matches between the teams of players. Here, each team consists of 120 best-of-run players produced by an algorithm. Thus, a single match in the tournament involves $120 \times 120 = 14400$ double games. Winning games against all opponent teams gives a method the round-robin performance of 100%.

In order to gain better insight into the results, let us first explain the nature of the round-robin tournament. In contrast to the absolute performance measure (Section 4.1) which evaluates an individual on a set of random opponents, in a round-robin tournament each individual faces only the individuals from the other teams. And, judging from the expected utility attained by particular methods (see Table 1), these players tend to be strong.

Table 2 presents the results of the tournament. SSEL is clearly the best algorithm in the relative comparison. Thanks to employing a handcrafted pool of evaluating opponents with shaped performance distribution, it is substantially biased towards competing with the highly skilled opponents. Considering the fact that the tournament is held between the relatively strong players, such a good result of SSEL could be anticipated. Furthermore, RSEL, which is specialized at beating mediocre opponents, inevitably loses in head-to-head matches to all other methods except CEL.

The benefits of using a shaped performance distribution of opponents can be also observed when comparing CEL-RS with CEL-SS. According to Table 1, the difference in absolute performance between these methods is minor. However, in the round-robin tournament there is a 5% performance gap in favor of CEL-SS. This fact can be explained by analyzing Fig. 7 which demonstrates that the performance profile of CEL-SS is considerably more leveled than that of CEL-RS. Certainly, this results in better play against the strong tournament opponents.

Table 2: Round robin tournament

Method	SSEL	CEL-SS	CEL-RS	CEL	RSEL	**Final result**
SSEL	-	55.4%	62.0%	60.6%	65.6%	**60.9%**
CEL-SS	44.6%	-	56.3%	57.3%	58.8%	**54.3%**
CEL-RS	38.0%	43.7%	-	53.9%	53.2%	**47.2%**
CEL	39.4%	42.7%	46.1%	-	48.0%	**44.0%**
RSEL	34.4%	41.2%	46.8%	52.0%	-	**43.6%**

Another interesting observation is that the hybrid method of CEL-RS wins in direct confrontation with its both constituents — CEL and RSEL. This raises the question about the ratio between the random and population opponents that are sampled in the CEL-RS method. The presented results may suggest that sampling half of the evaluating opponents from the coevolving population is enough to learn to defeat strong players (RS-based opponents are on average much weaker than the population ones). However, whether a lower fraction would suffice as well, and what would happen if that fraction would be greater than 0.5, remains to be verified.

5. CONCLUSIONS

Let us rephrase here the original research question with which we began this paper: how can we improve the results of evolutionary algorithms on a problem of learning Othello-playing strategies with respect to the performance measure of expected utility? In this study we have attempted to answer this question by referring to the concept of shaping, borrowed from behavioral psychology. Specifically, we have modified the fitness function in the learning problem by changing the selection of the opponents used for strategy evaluation. By doing so we expected to shape the function and make it easier for an algorithm to explore the particularly desirable areas in the solution space.

The goal of improving the final learning results was attained. Both investigated methods of fitness function shaping — modifying the distribution of opponent performance a priori (SSEL) and autonomously by coevolution (CEL) — proved to influence the learning process and lead to significantly different results than the reference RSEL method.

An interesting direction for the future work is to investigate the performance distribution of opponents bred in coevolutionary learning. Knowing how this distribution evolves across generations could better explain the reported results and help to design a more effective method of adaptive fitness function shaping. Moreover, the analysis of opponent performance distributions provided by coevolution could help with understanding the coevolutionary pathologies [25]. Currently, our focus is on extending the algorithms considered in this paper with archives of historical opponents [22]. We anticipate that such long-time memory will sustain the learning progress and prevent forgetting the game-playing skills that allow defeating the weaker opponents.

6. ACKNOWLEDGMENT

This work has been supported by grant no. N N519 441939. M. Szubert has been supported by Polish Ministry of Science and Education, grant no. 2012/05/N/ST6/03152. W. Jaśkowski has been supported by Polish Ministry of Science and Education, grant no. 91–550/DS.

7. REFERENCES

[1] K. J. Binkley, K. Seehart, and M. Hagiwara. A Study of Artificial Neural Network Architectures for Othello Evaluation Functions. *Transactions of the Japanese Society for Artificial Intelligence*, 22(5):461–471, 2007.

[2] A. Bucci, J. B. Pollack, and E. de Jong. Automated extraction of problem structure. In K. D. et al., editor, *Genetic and Evolutionary Computation – GECCO-2004, Part I*, volume 3102 of *Lecture Notes in Computer Science*, pages 501–512, Seattle, WA, USA, 26-30 June 2004. Springer-Verlag.

[3] E. K. Burke, M. Hyde, G. Kendall, G. Ochoa, E. Ozcan, and J. R. Woodward. A classification of hyper-heuristics approaches. In M. Gendreau and J.-Y. Potvin, editors, *Handbook of Metaheuristics*, volume 57 of *International Series in Operations Research & Management Science*, chapter 15, pages 449–468. Springer, 2nd edition, 2010.

[4] S. Y. Chong, M. K. Tan, and J. D. White. Observing the evolution of neural networks learning to play the game of othello. *Evolutionary Computation, IEEE Transactions on*, 9(3):240–251, 2005.

[5] S. Y. Chong, P. Tino, D. C. Ku, and Y. Xin. Improving Generalization Performance in Co-Evolutionary Learning. *IEEE Transactions on Evolutionary Computation*, 16(1):70–85, 2012.

[6] E. D. de Jong. The maxsolve algorithm for coevolution. In H.-G. B. et al., editor, *GECCO 2005: Proceedings of the 2005 conference on Genetic and evolutionary computation*, volume 1, pages 483–489, Washington DC, USA, 25-29 June 2005. ACM Press.

[7] E. D. de Jong and J. B. Pollack. Ideal Evaluation from Coevolution. *Evolutionary Computation*, 12(2):159–192, Summer 2004.

[8] A. Eiben and S. Smit. Parameter tuning for configuring and analyzing evolutionary algorithms. *Swarm and Evolutionary Computation*, 1(1):19–31, 2011.

[9] T. Erez and W. Smart. What does shaping mean for computational reinforcement learning? In *Development and Learning, 2008. ICDL 2008. 7th IEEE International Conference on*, pages 215 –219, aug. 2008.

[10] S. G. Ficici and J. B. Pollack. Pareto optimality in coevolutionary learning. In J. Kelemen and P. Sosík, editors, *Advances in Artificial Life, 6th European Conference, ECAL 2001*, volume 2159 of *Lecture Notes in Computer Science*, pages 316–325, Prague, Czech Republic, 2001. Springer.

[11] W. Jaśkowski and K. Krawiec. Formal analysis, hardness and algorithms for extracting internal structure of test-based problems. *Evolutionary Computation*, 19(4):639–671, 2011.

[12] W. Jaśkowski, K. Krawiec, and B. Wieloch. Evolving strategy for a probabilistic game of imperfect information using genetic programming. *Genetic Programming and Evolvable Machines*, 9(4):281–294, 2008.

[13] W. Jaśkowski, P. Liskowski, M. Szubert, and K. Krawiec. Improving coevolution by random sampling. In *GECCO'13: Proceedings of the 15th annual conference on Genetic and Evolutionary Computation*, Amsterdam, The Netherlands, July 2013. ACM.

[14] H. Juillé and J. B. Pollack. Coevolving the "ideal" trainer: Application to the discovery of cellular automata rules. In *University of Wisconsin*, pages 519–527. Morgan Kaufmann, 1998.

[15] K. Krawiec, W. Jaśkowski, and M. Szubert. Evolving small-board go players using coevolutionary temporal difference learning with archive. *International Journal of Applied Mathematics and Computer Science*, 21(4):717–731, 2011.

[16] K. Krawiec and M. Szubert. Learning n-tuple networks for othello by coevolutionary gradient search. In N. K. et al, editor, *GECCO 2011 Proceedings*, pages 355–362. ACM, ACM, 2011.

[17] S. M. Lucas. Learning to play Othello with N-tuple systems. *Australian Journal of Intelligent Information Processing Systems, Special Issue on Game Technology*, 9(4):1–20, 2007.

[18] S. M. Lucas and T. P. Runarsson. Temporal difference learning versus co-evolution for acquiring othello position evaluation. In *CIG*, pages 52–59, 2006.

[19] S. Luke and R. P. Wiegand. When coevolutionary algorithms exhibit evolutionary dynamics. In A. M. Barry, editor, *GECCO 2002: Proceedings of the Bird of a Feather Workshops, Genetic and Evolutionary Computation Conference*, pages 236–241, New York, 2002.

[20] E. Popovici, A. Bucci, R. P. Wiegand, and E. D. de Jong. *Handbook of Natural Computing*, chapter Coevolutionary Principles. Springer-Verlag, 2011.

[21] J. Randløv and P. Alstrøm. Learning to drive a bicycle using reinforcement learning and shaping. In *Proceedings of the Fifteenth International Conference on Machine Learning*, pages 463–471. Morgan Kaufmann, San Francisco, CA, 1998.

[22] C. D. Rosin and R. K. Belew. New methods for competitive coevolution. *Evolutionary Computation*, 5(1):1–29, 1997.

[23] S. Samothrakis, S. Lucas, T. Runarsson, and D. Robles. Coevolving Game-Playing Agents: Measuring Performance and Intransitivities. *IEEE Transactions on Evolutionary Computation*, (99):1–15, 2012.

[24] B. Skinner. *The behavior of organisms: An experimental analysis*. Appleton-Century, 1938.

[25] R. A. Watson and J. B. Pollack. Coevolutionary dynamics in a minimal substrate. In L. S. et al., editor, *Proceedings of the Genetic and Evolutionary Computation Conference (GECCO-2001)*, pages 702–709, San Francisco, California, USA, 7-11 July 2001. Morgan Kaufmann.

A Parallel Evolutionary Approach to Solve the Relay Node Placement Problem in Wireless Sensor Networks

Jose M.Lanza-Gutierrez
Dept. of Computers and Communications Technologies
Univ. of Extremadura (Spain)
jmlanza@unex.es

Juan A.Gomez-Pulido
Dept. of Computers and Communications Technologies
Univ. of Extremadura (Spain)
jangomez@unex.es

Miguel A.Vega-Rodriguez
Dept. of Computers and Communications Technologies
Univ. of Extremadura (Spain)
mavega@unex.es

Juan M.Sanchez-Perez
Dept. of Computers and Communications Technologies
Univ. of Extremadura (Spain)
sanperez@unex.es

ABSTRACT

At this time, Wireless Sensor Networks (WSNs) are widely used in many fields. This kind of network has some attractive features that have promoted their use, such as the absence of wires and the use of low-cost devices. However, WSNs also have important shortcomings that affect some features like energy cost and quality of service. In this paper, we optimize traditional static WSNs (a set of sensors and a sink node) by means of adding routers to simultaneously optimize a couple of important factors: energy consumption and average coverage. This multiobjective optimization problem was solved in a previous work using two genetic algorithms (NSGA-II and SPEA2) which had an important limitation: the computing time was very high and then, to address complex instances was difficult. In this paper, both algorithms are parallelized using OpenMP in order to reduce the computing time, and a more realistic data set is included. The results obtained are analyzed in depth from both multiobjective and parallel viewpoints. A Quite good efficiency is obtained with a wide range of processing cores, observing that NSGA-II provides the best results in small and medium instances, but in the largest ones the behavior of both algorithms is similar.

Categories and Subject Descriptors

C.2.1 [**Network Architecture and Design**]: Wireless communication; G.1.6 [**Optimization**]: Constrained optimization; I.2.8 [**Problem Solving, Control Methods, and Search**]: Heuristic methods; D.1.3 [**Concurrent Programming**]: Parallel programming

General Terms

Algorithms

Keywords

Evolutionary algorithms, NSGA-II, OpenMP, parallelism, relay node, SPEA2, wireless sensor networks

1. INTRODUCTION

Nowadays, Wireless Sensor Networks (WSNs) are increasingly used. We can find examples of applications in many fields, such as precision agriculture, environmental monitoring, fire detection, traffic control, rescue operations, robotic, and home automation, among others [22].

Traditionally, these networks are composed of a set of sensors that capture information from the environment and a sink node that collects this information. Sensors have some important features that promote the use of WSNs, because they are small, cheap, wireless, autonomous, battery-powered, able to capture different kind of physical measures in a same device, etc. These aspects allow using WSNs in environments where other kinds of networks would be very expensive or impossible to be deployed. Nevertheless, WSNs also have important shortcomings that affect issues like network lifetime, Quality of Service (QoS) and maintenance costs.

Habitually, sensors use traditional batteries as an energy source in order to get cheaper and smaller devices, which implies that lifetime of sensors is subject to the life of these batteries. The energy wear suffered by these batteries is not only due to sensing tasks, but by the communication tasks among devices when they are poorly distributed. This way, an unbalanced energy wear will lead to a premature failure of some sensors which will affect the network behavior.

This paper is focused on a new approach in which a new kind of device, specialized in communication tasks, is added to WSNs in order to alleviate the workload of the sensors, allowing to deploy larger networks. This new device is known as relay node or router.

The efficient deployment of a traditional WSN depends on many factors, even more if we add these new devices. This is the reason why some authors [4][5] have defined this issue as a NP-hard optimization problem, hence it cannot be solved by means of traditional techniques due to its high computation cost.

We have studied how to optimize traditional static WSNs adding relay nodes subject to two important factors: the average energy consumption suffered by the sensors and the average coverage provided by the network. With this aim, we have used a couple of well-known multiobjective evolutionary algorithms (MOEAs) based on Genetic Algorithms (GAs) in order to solve this optimization problem, that is known as *the Relay Node Placement Problem (RNPP)*. These algorithms are NSGA-II [7] and SPEA2 [32].

This problem has been partially tracked in [17]. Now, in this paper we present the following new contributions:

- As in previous works, we use freely available synthetic data sets [16], allowing this work to be replicated and improved by other authors, now with a a more realistic approach by means of a new greater instance.
- In previous works, we had an important limitation: computing times were too high, so addressing more complex instances was difficult. In this paper we propose a parallelization of both algorithms using OpenMP, a known Application Programming Interface (API) for shared-memory programming.
- The obtained results have been analyzed from two viewpoints. On the one hand, we have used both hypervolume [33] (it was also used in [17]) and set coverage [31] multiobjective quality indicators; and on the other hand, we have used both efficiency and speedup from Amdhal's law [10] as parallelism quality metrics.
- We have used a widespread statistical methodology to analyze what algorithm is better at each test case, as well as a parallel scalability study using different numbers of cores: 2, 4, 8, 16 and 32.

The remaining of this paper is structured as follows. In the next section we discuss about the related work. In section III, the RNPP is defined. The evolutionary parallel approach used in this paper is described in section IV. Performance comparisons appear in section V. Finally, the conclusions and future works have been left for section VI.

2. RELATED WORK

In the literature, most WSN optimization papers can be classified into one of two research lines. On the one hand, optimization of traditional WSNs (a set of sensors and one or more sink nodes), and on the other hand optimization of traditional WSNs in which relay nodes have been added.

If we focus on the first line, we can distinguish some papers that use heuristics like Cheng et al. [4] (they assign different transmission power levels to the sensors with the purpose of optimizing the power consumption), Cardei et al. [2] (they split the WSN in disjoint sets of sensors, deciding which must be active at each time), Chang and Tassiulas [3] (they try to optimize the network lifetime in random WSNs) and Liu et al. [19] (they optimize the energy consumption, the coverage and the connectivity splitting the network in a similar way than Cardei et al.[2]).

In addition, other authors have also used Evolutionary Algorithms (EAs), like Martins et al. [21] (they assign different transmission power levels to optimize the network lifetime), Hu et al [11] (they maximize the network lifetime through splitting the WSN in sets of sensors like [2]), and Konstantinidis et al. in [15] and [13] (where they assign different transmission power levels to optimize the network lifetime and the coverage) or in [14] (where they propose to maintain a certain k-connectivity). Most of the works in this line have an important disadvantage: they use a greater number of sensors that is strictly necessary, with the aim of increasing the network lifetime, but the network cost increases.

The second research line appeared later, trying to solve the disadvantages mentioned before. Like the first line, we can find some works that use heuristics, such as Xu. et al. [28] (they propose random positioning methods of routers in order to optimize the network lifetime), Wang. et al. [27] (they add relay nodes with processing limitations in random WSN in order to minimize the energy consumption) or Han et al.[8] (they study how to add routers with the purpose of optimizing network fault tolerance).

We can also find other works where EAs are considered for this second research line, like Zhao and Cheng [30] (they add relay nodes to optimize both the energy consumption and the path average length) or Perez et al. [23] (they propose a MOEA to deploy a WSN optimizing the number of relay nodes and the energy dissipation).

As we have previously said, in this paper we optimize traditional static WSNs adding relay nodes, using for this purpose a couple of well-known EAs, so this work is located in the second research line. It is important to note that most of the authors use randomly generated data set or non-public ones, so we cannot directly compare our results with them, having to focus on collateral aspects. This situation led us to use our own publicly available data set [16] as we did in [17], allowing other authors to compare their results with those obtained by us.

3. RELAY NODE PLACEMENT PROBLEM

A wireless sensor network as we consider in this paper is composed of three kind of static wireless devices (M sensors, N routers and a sink node), which are placed on a bi-dimensional surface of size $D_x \times D_y$.

The sensors capture information about its environment with a sensitivity radius R_s on a regular basis and simultaneously, being powered by batteries. All the captured information by the sensors must be immediately sent to the sink node which collects this information. It is important to assure that the sink node has updated information, because it is the only connection point of the WSN to the outside. The sensors and the sink node are usually at a distance greater than one hop, thus the packets will have to pass through several sensors to arrive to the sink node. This situation involves that the sensors are submitted to a high energy consumption, so the WSN lifetime will have a strong dependence of the energy wear suffered by the sensors.

With the purpose of reducing the workload of the sensors in communication tasks, the routers or relay nodes are added. These devices only relay all the received information to the sink node. In contrast to the sensors, both routers and the sink node have an unlimited power supply.

In this model, the routing protocol is provided by Dijkstra's algorithm [6] using as measure the minimum distance among devices, where two devices can be directly linked if the distance is lower than R_c. This routing causes an in-

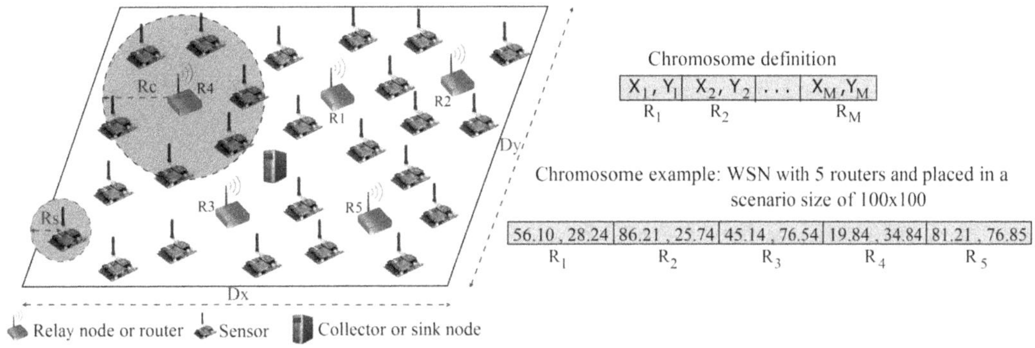

Figure 1: Representation of the network model used in this work.

creased traffic in some areas, which means a unbalanced greater energy consumption and consequently an important bottleneck. This handicap has led us to study how to optimally place routers in order to alleviate this inconvenience.

With the purpose of simulating the energy wear suffered by the sensors, we have used a well-known energy model [15] that is suitable for this kind of environments, since it incorporates packet loss, that is a common feature. Besides, we assume that there will be no collisions among devices in communication tasks, as S-MAC [29] protocol defines, as well as a perfect synchronization among them.

This way, all the sensors start with the same energy charge (EC) in their batteries, that will be decreased while the sensors send packets to other devices. We can define the residual energy of a sensor i at time t as (1), where $r_i(t)$ is the number of incoming packets from other sensors that sensor i has to relay to the sink node at this time, the $+1$ term is due to the sensor i, because it has to send the information packet that is captured by itself at this time, K is the information packet size (in bits), amp is the energy consumption per bit of the power amplifier, and P is the power transmission that i needs to reach j. This power transmission is defined in (2), where α is the path loss exponent, β is the transmission quality parameter and $d_{i,j}$ is the distance between i and j. As we can observe, the energy consumption due to processing, capturing and reception tasks is considered negligible, as the energy model defines.

$$E_i(t) = E_i(t-1) - [(r_i(t)+1) \times P_i * amp * K] \qquad (1)$$

$$P_i = \beta \times d_{i,j}^{\alpha} \qquad (2)$$

There is an essential concept in this problem: the network lifetime (LF). This is the amount of time units during which the network is able to provide adequate information. Usually, a coverage threshold (CV) is used to make this decision, that is to say, at least a certain percentage of the surface must be covered by the network in order to consider that this amount of information is enough. The covered surface will be decreased as long as the sensor batteries are going flat, so the coverage threshold could be reached.

In this way, we can define the RNPP as a NP-hard multiobjective problem given the following parameters:

- the position of the collector node (C),
- the N routers,
- the M sensors,
- the size of the 2D-surface ($D_x \times D_y$),
- the information packet size (K),
- the sensitivity and communication radius (R_s and R_c),
- the coverage threshold (CV),
- the initial energy charge (EC),
- several energy parameters (α, β and amp).

This problem will consider the following fitness functions:

- Average Energy Consumption (AEC), to be minimized: It is the average energy consumption of the sensors along the network lifetime. In this function (3), the parameter $sensorsAlive(t)$ is the number of sensors having an energy charge greater than zero at time t.

$$f_1 = LF^{-1} \times \sum_{t=1}^{LF} \sum_{i=1}^{M} \left(\frac{E_i(t-1) - E_i(t)}{sensorsAlive(t)} \right) \qquad (3)$$

- Average Coverage (AC), to be maximized: It is the average coverage provided by the WSN along the network lifetime. In the literature, we can find two ways to obtain the coverage provided by the sensors at a certain time [26]. On the one hand, some authors say that a sensor covers a circumference of radius R_s, and then its covered area is $\pi \times R_s^2$. This way, the full coverage is the intersection of all the sensors over the surface area defined by $D_x \times D_y$. On the other hand, the full coverage can be obtained using a binary matrix of $D_x \times D_y$ points which will be activated whether they are at a distance lower than R_s from some alive sensor; finally, the activated points are counted. We have decided to use the second way, since this approach is less hard to compute, although it is less accurate than the first one. In (4), $R_{x,y}(t)$ is the position (x,y) of the binary matrix at time t.

$$f_2 = LF^{-1} \times \sum_{t=1}^{LF} \sum_{x=1}^{D_x} \sum_{y=1}^{D_y} \left(\frac{R_{x,y}(t)}{D_x \times D_y} \right) \qquad (4)$$

4. A PARALLEL EVOLUTIONARY APPROACH

As we have previously said, the RNPP is a NP-hard problem, and then to solve it by means of exact techniques involves an unaffordable computation time. This reason has moved us to consider Evolutionary Computation [1], in order to allow us to obtain approximate solutions in a reduced computing time. In this paper, we have used two well-known multiobjective genetic algorithms, NSGA-II and SPEA2, using as chromosome definition a 2D-coordinate list of M routers. Figure 1 shows an example of this codification.

With the aim of being fair in the comparatives between both algorithms, we have used the same crossover and mutation operators. We have selected as crossover operator the habitual one-point crossover. As mutation, we have decided to randomly change the router positions, but following a greedy strategy: only the changes that provide better fitness values will be accepted. Some other implementations details of both algorithms can be found in [17].

In this paper we have decided to use a more realistic data set; the increased number of sensors and routers implies a higher computational cost, and hence a higher computing time. This situation makes it difficult for us to deal with even more realistic data set in the future. This is the reason that we have decided to address the parallelization of both algorithms, using for this purpose OpenMP, a known API for shared-memory parallel programming. This library has been used to perform a coarse-grained parallelism, using for this purpose a dynamic schedule.

Next section analyzes this approach from two viewpoints. First, we will study both algorithms in multiobjective terms, using the hypervolume and set coverage metrics. Next, we will determine the quality of this parallelization using both efficiency and speedup measures.

5. EXPERIMENTAL RESULTS

We have defined some data sets or experimental instances for the problem with the purpose of comparing the performance of both algorithms. These instances are traditional static WSNs that both algorithms will have to optimize by means of adding relay nodes. These data sets have been defined by ourselves, making them available to the scientific community by web [16], because we have not found any instance that fits for this definition of the problem.

The synthetic instances (a set of sensors and a collector node located on a bi-dimensional scenario) have dimensions of 100×100, 200×200 and 300×300, each of them with the minimum possible number of sensors to cover all the surface (see Table 1). This way, whether the area covered by a sensor is $\pi \times R_s^2$ and the area of the surface is $D_x \times D_y$, it will be necessary to have a number of sensors M defined by (5). These sensors have been placed at each scenario using a monoobjective classical genetic algorithm that maximizes the coverage provided by the sensors, being the stop criterion a coverage value of 90%.

For each instance, we have decided to place the collector node in the center of the scenario. The information packet size is a fixed value equal to $128KB$ and the coverage threshold is 70%. The remaining parameters have been taken from other papers: R_c (30 and 60 meters) and R_s (15 meters) take habitual values from [21], the energy values $\alpha = 2$, $\beta = 1$, $EC = 5J$ and $amp = 100pJ/bit/m_2$ are taken from [14].

Table 1: Data set used in this paper.

Instance	$D_x \times D_y$	M	R_c	*Ref AEC*		*Ref AC*	
				ideal	*nadir*	*ideal*	*nadir*
100x100_15_30	100x100	15	30	0.02	0.1	100%	60%
100x100_15_60	100x100	15	60	0.02	0.1	100%	60%
200x200_15_30	200x200	57	30	0.10	0.30	100%	60%
200x200_15_60	200x200	57	60	0.10	0.30	100%	60%
300x300_15_30	300x300	128	30	0.04	0.50	100%	60%

$$M = \lceil (D_x \times D_y)/(\pi \times R_s^2) \rceil \quad (5)$$

We have taken into account that to include routers involves an important cost, therefore we have decided not to include more than 20% of these devices with respect to the number of sensors. This way, we have defined 16 different test cases, as Tables 2, 3, 4 and 5 shown, where the number of routers are enclosed in parenthesis following the next notation: instance_name(number_of_routers). The instance name uses the following naming convention: $D_x \times D_y\_R_s\_R_c$. These test cases are arranged in an increasing order of complexity.

All the runs for each experiment have been performed with a population size of 100 individuals, considering a probability of 50% for mutation and crossover. These adjusted configurations were obtained in [17].

5.1 Multiobjective Performance

With the aim of obtaining statistical conclusions, we have performed 30 independent runs (as some authors recommend [9]) for each test case, using several stop criteria to study the convergence of the algorithms. These stop criteria have been fixed experimentally, taking into account that the computing times are high (as we will see in next subsection), and assuring they are large enough to observe the behavior of algorithms. Table 2 shows average hypervolumes and standard deviation obtained for each algorithm, instance, number of routers and stop criterion. The hypervolume needs a couple (as many as objectives are) of reference points that must be calculated. These reference points were experimentally established by ourselves, being shown in Table 1: *RefAEC* and *RefAC*.

We have used a widespread statistical methodology in order to determine what algorithm is better at each case. First, we have studied if the hypervolume data follow a gaussian distribution using Shapiro – Wilk's [25] and Kolmogórov – Smirnov – Lilliefors's [18] tests, proposing the following statistical hypotheses: data follow a normal distribution (H_0) and data do not follow it (H_1). P-values lower than 0.05 have been obtained for all cases, hence data do not follow a normal distribution. This fact forces us to use the mean (Me) as average value for the hypervolume.

The next step is to determine the differences between both algorithms, using for this purpose the Wilcoxon – Mann – Whitney's test [20] because, as we have shown before, data do not follow a normal distribution and the samples are independent. With this aim, the following hypotheses are considered: NSGA-II provides worse hypervolume values than SPEA2 (H_0) and NSGA-II provides better hypervolume values than SPEA2 (H_1). The p-values obtained are shown in Table 4, where values higher than 0.05 (we cannot reject H_0) are highlighted. If we observe the highest stop criterion, we can see as NSGA-II provides better results in 100×100 and

Table 2: Hypervolume measure for each algorithm

	NSGA-II (avg hypervolumes%, std dev)					SPEA2 (avg hypervolumes%, std dev)				
Evaluations	50 000	100 000	200 000	300 000	400 000	50 000	100 000	200 000	300 000	400 000
100x100_15_30(2)	**42.40%** 0.0029	42.45% 0.0030	**42.67%** 0.0002	**42.69%** 0.0002	**42.69%** 0.0002	42.11% 0.0036	42.45% 0.0028	42.65% 0.0004	42.66% 0.0002	42.66% 0.0001
100x100_15_30(3)	**55.02%** 0.0044	**55.37%** 0.0023	**55.53%** 0.0027	**55.55%** 0.0024	**55.66%** 0.0004	53.71% 0.0085	53.78% 0.0080	53.94% 0.0072	54.24% 0.0067	53.87% 0.0065
100x100_15_60(2)	**31.60%** 0.0019	**31.80%** 0.0012	**31.82%** 0.0014	**31.86%** 0.0010	**31.94%** 0.0000	31.35% 0.0027	31.57% 0.0018	31.78% 0.0014	31.82% 0.0012	31.87% 0.0008
100x100_15_60(3)	**58.97%** 0.0035	**59.25%** 0.0035	**59.69%** 0.0019	**59.73%** 0.0022	**59.91%** 0.0016	57.96% 0.0068	58.63% 0.0056	58.97% 0.0078	58.84% 0.0072	59.36% 0.0041
200x200_15_30(2)	34.39% 0.0193	**35.39%** 0.0175	**36.33%** 0.0152	**37.06%** 0.0103	**37.42%** 0.0050	34.08% 0.0139	34.35% 0.0137	34.72% 0.0140	34.85% 0.0113	34.99% 0.0109
200x200_15_30(4)	43.41% 0.0435	44.46% 0.0454	46.45% 0.0509	**47.22%** 0.0519	**47.48%** 0.0537	44.14% 0.0328	44.71% 0.0383	45.31% 0.0382	45.49% 0.0385	45.63% 0.0385
200x200_15_30(6)	53.70% 0.0792	59.27% 0.0643	**64.61%** 0.0087	**65.01%** 0.0094	**65.26%** 0.0110	57.93% 0.0139	61.62% 0.0160	63.22% 0.0188	63.80% 0.0164	64.07% 0.0165
200x200_15_30(9)	**73.67%** 0.0173	**76.16%** 0.0114	**77.56%** 0.0117	**78.14%** 0.0117	**78.47%** 0.0109	70.79% 0.0075	74.49% 0.0101	75.63% 0.0106	75.97% 0.0118	76.35% 0.0111
200x200_15_60(2)	**23.40%** 0.0048	**23.92%** 0.0046	**23.93%** 0.0037	**23.94%** 0.0028	**24.00%** 0.0032	22.91% 0.0036	23.29% 0.0036	23.65% 0.0030	23.81% 0.0024	23.94% 0.0017
200x200_15_60(4)	**58.16%** 0.0086	**58.72%** 0.0070	**59.94%** 0.0056	**60.08%** 0.0046	**60.15%** 0.0045	57.43% 0.0074	58.57% 0.0061	59.30% 0.0043	59.74% 0.0051	59.98% 0.0033
200x200_15_60(6)	**71.79%** 0.0098	**74.11%** 0.0076	**75.42%** 0.0093	**75.93%** 0.0103	**76.37%** 0.0096	71.24% 0.0067	72.69% 0.0060	73.59% 0.0076	74.04% 0.0087	74.35% 0.0112
200x200_15_60(9)	**85.98%** 0.0105	**88.38%** 0.0086	**90.05%** 0.0074	**90.51%** 0.0079	**90.94%** 0.0079	84.22% 0.0050	86.45% 0.0037	88.19% 0.0096	89.27% 0.0102	89.71% 0.0102
300x300_15_30(6)	38.22% 0.0114	39.41% 0.0086	40.31% 0.0094	40.77% 0.0097	41.11% 0.0102	**39.13%** 0.0109	**40.15%** 0.0105	**40.89%** 0.0114	41.12% 0.0118	41.21% 0.0117
300x300_15_30(12)	44.50% 0.0148	46.39% 0.0116	47.87% 0.0105	48.11% 0.0123	48.71% 0.0102	**45.56%** 0.0145	**47.03%** 0.0120	47.99% 0.0101	48.46% 0.0070	48.63% 0.0083
300x300_15_30(18)	47.01% 0.0242	50.02% 0.0209	52.53% 0.0184	53.39% 0.0167	**54.10%** 0.0201	**48.67%** 0.0135	50.89% 0.0084	52.11% 0.0067	52.96% 0.0092	**53.19%** 0.0106
300x300_15_30(24)	48.00% 0.0213	52.52% 0.0187	56.67% 0.0363	58.86% 0.0401	59.99% 0.0419	**52.39%** 0.0277	**56.93%** 0.0335	**59.44%** 0.0345	60.34% 0.0340	60.86% 0.0344

Table 3: Efficiency, speedup and sequential times

SPEA2	1 core	2 cores			4 cores			8 cores			16 cores			32 cores		
	T_s	T_p	E_p	S_p	T_p	E_p	S_p	T_p	E_p	S_p	T_p	E_p	S_p	T_p	E_p	S_p
100x100_15_30(2)	10100.00	5074.67	99.51%	1.99	2570.00	98.25%	3.93	1320.00	95.64%	7.65	700.13	90.16%	14.43	400.14	78.88%	25.24
100x100_15_30(3)	11680.95	5853.64	99.78%	2.00	3022.00	96.63%	3.87	1525.33	95.72%	7.66	810.69	90.05%	14.41	462.79	78.88%	25.24
100x100_15_60(2)	6884.64	3480.00	98.92%	1.98	1760.00	97.79%	3.91	904.13	95.18%	7.61	482.47	89.19%	14.27	274.33	78.42%	25.10
100x100_15_60(3)	11000.00	5535.33	99.36%	1.99	2798.00	98.28%	3.93	1446.00	95.09%	7.61	779.13	88.24%	14.12	449.20	76.52%	24.49
200x200_15_30(2)	10157.50	5088.00	99.82%	2.00	2659.33	95.49%	3.82	1287.33	98.63%	7.89	689.00	92.14%	14.74	409.83	77.45%	24.78
200x200_15_30(4)	13136.11	7240.83	90.71%	1.81	3654.29	89.87%	3.59	1777.69	92.37%	7.39	1001.77	81.96%	13.11	571.25	71.86%	23.00
200x200_15_30(6)	16769.23	8510.00	98.53%	1.97	4291.33	97.69%	3.91	2217.69	94.52%	7.56	1172.31	89.40%	14.30	661.08	79.27%	25.37
200x200_15_30(9)	19963.64	10350.00	96.44%	1.93	5079.33	98.26%	3.93	2654.62	94.00%	7.52	1422.11	87.74%	14.04	796.17	78.36%	25.07
200x200_15_60(2)	13133.33	6721.82	97.69%	1.95	3341.33	98.26%	3.93	1741.67	94.26%	7.54	925.07	88.73%	14.20	532.14	77.13%	24.68
200x200_15_60(4)	20936.36	10530.77	99.41%	1.99	5288.00	98.98%	3.96	2712.67	96.47%	7.72	1463.57	89.41%	14.30	832.07	78.63%	25.16
200x200_15_60(6)	24133.33	12153.33	99.29%	1.99	6210.00	97.16%	3.89	3134.00	96.26%	7.70	1683.75	89.58%	14.33	953.07	79.13%	25.32
200x200_15_60(9)	38883.33	19092.31	99.90%	2.00	9943.00	97.77%	3.91	5086.00	95.56%	7.65	2618.67	92.80%	14.85	1561.33	77.82%	24.90
300x300_15_30(6)	17400.00	8861.00	98.18%	1.96	4514.17	96.36%	3.85	2296.32	94.72%	7.58	1223.57	88.88%	14.22	699.31	77.76%	24.88
300x300_15_30(12)	20300.00	10342.14	98.14%	1.96	5254.29	96.59%	3.86	2804.00	90.50%	7.24	1427.69	88.87%	14.22	821.20	77.25%	24.72
300x300_15_30(18)	23270.00	13693.33	84.97%	1.70	6223.08	93.48%	3.74	3487.33	83.41%	6.67	1639.33	88.72%	14.19	948.38	76.68%	24.54
300x300_15_30(24)	33914.29	16953.33	99.90%	2.00	8990.00	94.31%	3.77	4762.00	89.02%	7.12	2717.33	78.00%	12.48	1496.14	70.84%	22.67
Average	-	-	**97.53%**	**1.95**	-	**96.57%**	**3.86**	-	**93.84%**	**7.51**	-	**88.37%**	**14.14**	-	**77.18%**	**24.70**

NSGA-II	1 core	2 cores			4 cores			8 cores			16 cores			32 cores		
	T_s	T_p	E_p	S_p	T_p	E_p	S_p	T_p	E_p	S_p	T_p	E_p	S_p	T_p	E_p	S_p
100x100_15_30(2)	10120.00	5065.83	99.88%	2.00	2564.67	98.65%	3.95	1372.67	92.16%	7.37	742.07	85.23%	13.64	442.73	71.43%	22.86
100x100_15_30(3)	11340.00	6397.33	88.63%	1.77	2854.67	99.31%	3.97	1504.00	94.25%	7.54	797.23	88.90%	14.22	500.87	70.75%	22.64
100x100_15_60(2)	6488.67	3331.54	97.38%	1.95	1664.62	97.45%	3.90	860.31	94.28%	7.54	504.29	80.42%	12.87	294.73	68.80%	22.02
100x100_15_60(3)	10381.33	5634.67	92.12%	1.84	2649.29	97.96%	3.92	1384.67	93.72%	7.50	761.93	85.16%	13.62	465.87	69.64%	22.28
200x200_15_30(2)	10141.33	5295.39	95.76%	1.92	2663.85	95.18%	3.81	1366.00	92.80%	7.42	723.67	87.59%	14.01	461.87	68.62%	21.96
200x200_15_30(4)	11362.67	6736.67	84.33%	1.69	3313.08	85.74%	3.43	1534.00	92.59%	7.41	931.31	76.25%	12.20	582.58	60.95%	19.50
200x200_15_30(6)	15910.00	8001.33	99.42%	1.99	4096.00	97.11%	3.88	2064.67	96.32%	7.71	1143.33	86.97%	13.92	681.18	72.99%	23.36
200x200_15_30(9)	20250.00	10236.67	98.91%	1.98	4999.33	99.99%	4.00	2652.67	95.42%	7.63	1474.74	85.82%	13.73	811.93	77.94%	24.94
200x200_15_60(2)	12485.71	6186.67	99.99%	2.00	3174.00	98.34%	3.93	1608.67	97.02%	7.76	907.53	85.99%	13.76	566.64	68.86%	22.03
200x200_15_60(4)	19866.67	9968.00	99.65%	1.99	5021.33	98.91%	3.96	2602.00	95.44%	7.64	1388.57	89.42%	14.31	858.53	72.31%	23.14
200x200_15_60(6)	22728.57	11478.57	99.00%	1.98	5826.67	97.52%	3.90	2955.33	96.13%	7.69	1550.00	91.65%	14.66	956.53	74.25%	23.76
200x200_15_60(9)	34100.00	18278.57	93.28%	1.87	9221.33	92.45%	3.70	4813.33	88.56%	7.08	2491.33	85.55%	13.69	1543.64	69.03%	22.09
300x300_15_30(6)	16162.50	4506.90	99.50%	1.99	2348.83	99.75%	3.99	2165.24	93.31%	7.46	1113.33	90.73%	14.52	698.00	72.36%	23.16
300x300_15_30(12)	17600.00	9360.67	94.01%	1.88	4863.33	90.47%	3.62	2487.50	88.44%	7.08	1268.00	86.75%	13.88	798.53	68.88%	22.04
300x300_15_30(18)	25633.33	11969.29	99.99%	2.00	6598.57	97.12%	3.88	3534.00	90.67%	7.25	1915.46	83.64%	13.38	1134.71	70.59%	22.59
300x300_15_30(24)	38750.00	21975.00	88.17%	1.76	10667.86	90.81%	3.63	5763.64	84.04%	6.72	2754.29	87.93%	14.07	1762.50	68.71%	21.99
Average	-	-	**95.63%**	**1.91**	-	**96.05%**	**3.84**	-	**92.82%**	**7.43**	-	**86.13%**	**13.78**	-	**70.38%**	**22.52**

Table 4: P-values of the Wilcoxon – Mann – Whitney's test.

	NSGA-II vs SPEA2				
Evaluations	50 000	100 000	200 000	300 000	400 000
100x100_15_30(2)	0.0002	0.1520	0.0027	0.0000	0.0000
100x100_15_30(3)	0.0000	0.0000	0.0000	0.0000	0.0000
100x100_15_60(2)	0.0001	0.0000	0.0466	0.0163	0.0000
100x100_15_60(3)	0.0000	0.0000	0.0000	0.0000	0.0000
200x200_15_30(2)	0.2014	0.0034	0.0000	0.0000	0.0000
200x200_15_30(4)	0.9235	0.7157	0.2138	0.0388	0.0106
200x200_15_30(6)	0.8080	0.2904	0.0008	0.0017	0.0018
200x200_15_30(9)	0.0000	0.0000	0.0000	0.0000	0.0000
200x200_15_60(2)	0.0075	0.0045	0.0075	0.0015	0.0009
200x200_15_60(4)	0.0075	0.0005	0.0001	0.0002	0.0001
200x200_15_60(6)	0.0075	0.0000	0.0000	0.0000	0.0000
200x200_15_60(9)	0.0000	0.0000	0.0000	0.0000	0.0000
300x300_15_30(6)	0.9978	0.9974	0.9669	0.8829	0.6402
300x300_15_30(12)	0.9926	0.9873	0.7304	0.7715	0.3206
300x300_15_30(18)	0.9975	0.9116	0.0916	0.1386	0.0215
300x300_15_30(24)	1.0000	1.0000	0.9993	0.9235	0.7658

Table 5: Set coverage measure among algorithms for 400 000 evaluations

A	NSGA-II	SPEA2
B	SPEA2	NSGA-II
100x100_15_30(2)	96.49%	72.97%
100x100_15_30(3)	100.00%	50.50%
100x100_15_60(2)	91.87%	80.80%
100x100_15_60(3)	74.60%	39.80%
200x200_15_30(2)	100.00%	20.81%
200x200_15_30(4)	100.00%	0.00%
200x200_15_30(6)	100.00%	0.00%
200x200_15_30(9)	100.00%	0.00%
200x200_15_60(2)	54.55%	67.39%
200x200_15_60(4)	0.00%	47.06%
200x200_15_60(6)	28.57%	41.12%
200x200_15_60(9)	100.00%	0.00%
300x300_15_30(6)	0.15%	87.05%
300x300_15_30(12)	4.94%	92.82%
300x300_15_30(18)	100.00%	0.00%
300x300_15_30(24)	0.00%	100.00%
Average	**65.70%**	**43.77%**

200×200 instances, but there are not significant differences between the algorithms in the new instance 300×300, except in $300 \times 300(18)$ in which NSGA-II is the best. If we observe the remaining stop criteria, we can see as this behavior is similar, except in some cases (200×200 with 2, 4 and 6 routers) where NSGA-II has needed more evaluations to obtain better values than SPEA2. This behavior can be observed in Table 2, where significantly different hypervolumes are highlighted. As we have seen, using several stop criteria has allowed us to define the behavior of both algorithms in a best way.

In this work, we have also decided to use the set coverage measure, a complementary quality indicator based on the dominance concept. To obtain these values, we have compared the median Pareto fronts obtained with each algorithm, test case and stop criterium of 400, 000 evaluations. The comparative between both algorithms appears in Table 5 in the way Coverage(algorithm A, algorithm B), that is the percentage of solutions from B that are dominated by A. If we observe these values, we can see as NSGA-II weakly dominates SPEA2 in 100×100 and 200×200_15_30; however, as the complexity of test cases are increased, SPEA2 seems to provide better or similar coverage than NSGA-II. In this table, we can also see as NSGA-II is better in average with 65.70%, instead of 43.77% that SPEA2 dominates.

In the curse of this multiobjective performance study, we have reached similar conclusions using the two quality indicators. We can check as NSGA-II provides better results than SPEA-2 in both small and medium instance sizes, but in large ones there not a clear advantage.

5.2 Parallel performance

We have used shared-memory parallelism in order to reduce the execution times, using for this purpose a number of cores equal to 2, 4, 8, 16 and 32. To determine the quality of the parallelization, we have use a couple of well-known measures: efficiency and speedup, which are defined in (6) and (7), where p is the number of used cores, a is the code that we want to analyze, $T_s(a)$ is the sequential time that a needs to execute, $T_p(a)$ is the execution time that a needs when p cores are used, and then $S_p(a)$ and $E_p(a)$ are respectively the speedup and efficiency obtained when the code a is executed using p cores.

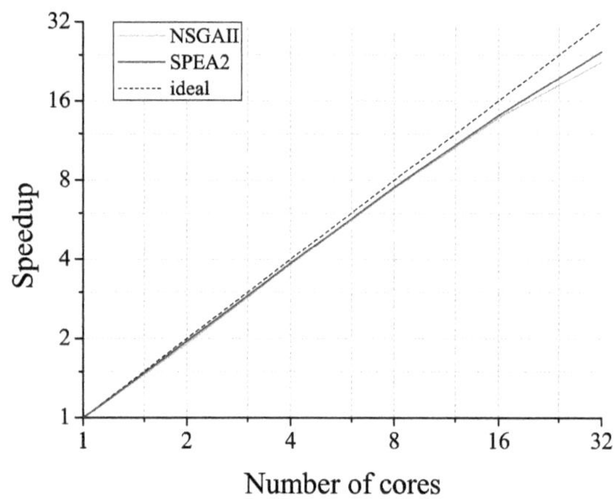

Figure 2: Speedup metric.

$$S_p(a) = \frac{T_s(a)}{T_p(a)} \tag{6}$$

$$E_p(a) = \frac{S_p(a)}{p} \tag{7}$$

With the aim of studying the efficiency of this parallelization, we have performed 30 independent runs (to obtain statistical conclusions) with a stop criterion of 400, 000 evaluations, for each combination of algorithm, test case and number of cores. This way, in Table 3 we can find the average sequential times (in seconds) for each test case and algorithm, as well as the average values of time, speedup and efficiency for each number of used cores. As we did with the hypervolume, we have studied what kind of average value we must use; for this purpose, Shapiro – Wilk's [25] and Kolmogórov – Smirnov – Lilliefors's [18] tests have been used, obtaining that data do not follow a normal distribution, and then we consider the mean as average value.

Observing this table, we can conclude we have obtained a quite good average efficiency, where SPEA2 provides better efficiency values than NSGA-II. In average, we have obtained values higher than 90% for 2, 4 and 8 cores, around 80% for 16, and 70% for 32 cores. This behavior can be observed in the speedup figure (Figure 2), where the differences among ideal performance and the obtained one are shown. These results lead us to conclude that both algorithms are suitable to be parallelized to solve this problem, reducing the execution times up to 25.39 times with 32 cores.

All the executions have been performed in a multiprocessor with the following features: 4 AMD Opteron 6176 2.3Ghz processors (each of them with 12 cores), 48GB RAM and operating system Scientific Linux 6.2. The OpenMP version was 3.1 and the C compiler was GCC 4.4.5.

6. CONCLUSIONS

We have used a couple of well-known multiobjective evolutionary algorithms (NSGA-II and SPEA2) in order to optimize traditional static WSNs adding relay nodes, analyzing the performance of both algorithms by means of a more realistic data set that considers a scenario with a higher number of both sensors and routers.

In previous works we had an important limitation: the computing times were very high, therefore addressing greater instances was more difficult. With the aim of solving this handicap, we have parallelized both algorithms using the shared-memory API OpenMP. The obtained results have been analyzed in depth from two viewpoints. On the one hand, the hypervolume and set coverage metrics have been used to determine the quality of both algorithms in multiobjective terms, and on the other hand, the efficiency and speedup from Amdhal's law have been considered to analyze the scalability of the parallelization.

In previous works, NSGA-II provided better performance than SPEA-2, but considering larger data sets we have seen that this advantage is blurred. This situation moved us to propose the use of a higher number of realistic instances, with the purpose of analyzing the multiobjective performance of both algorithms in a wide range of scenarios. The difficulty of tackling these instances comes from the very high computing times, so we have parallelized the algorithms, obtaining quite good efficiency values (around 70% with 32 cores) which will allow us to tackle more ambitious instances.

As future work, since in this work we have analyzed the behavior of a couple of standard algorithms from the evolutionary computation, it would be interesting to consider other techniques like swarm intelligence algorithms, such as Artificial Bee Colony (ABC) [12] or Gravitational Search Algorithm (GSA) [24], among others.

7. ACKNOWLEDGMENTS

This work was partially funded by the Spanish Ministry of Economy and Competitiveness and the ERDF (European Regional Development Fund), under the contract TIN2012-30685 (BIO project), and by the Government of Extremadura, with the aid GR10025 to the group TIC015.

8. REFERENCES

[1] T. Back. *Evolutionary Algorithms in Theory and Practice: Evolution Strategies, Evolutionary Programming, Genetic Algorithms.* Oxford University Press, USA, 1996.

[2] M. Cardei and D.-Z. Du. Improving wireless sensor network lifetime through power aware organization. *Wireless Networks*, 11:333–340, 2005. 10.1007/s11276-005-6615-6.

[3] J.-H. Chang and L. Tassiulas. Maximum lifetime routing in wireless sensor networks. *Networking, IEEE/ACM Transactions on*, 12(4):609 – 619, aug. 2004.

[4] X. Cheng, B. Narahari, R. Simha, M. Cheng, and D. Liu. Strong minimum energy topology in wireless sensor networks: Np-completeness and heuristics. *Mobile Computing, IEEE Transactions on*, 2(3):248 – 256, july-sept. 2003.

[5] A. E. F. Clementi, P. Penna, and R. Silvestri. Hardness results for the power range assignmet problem in packet radio networks. In *Proceedings of the Third International Workshop on Approximation Algorithms for Combinatorial Optimization Problems: Randomization, Approximation, and Combinatorial Algorithms and Techniques*, RANDOM-APPROX '99, pages 197–208, London, UK, 1999. Springer-Verlag.

[6] T. H. Cormen, C. E. Leiserson, R. L. Rivest, and C. Stein. *Introduction to Algorithms(Third Edition)*, page 1292. The MIT Press, 2009.

[7] K. Deb, A. Pratap, S. Agarwal, and T. Meyarivan. A fast elitist multi-objective genetic algorithm: Nsga-ii. *IEEE Transactions on Evolutionary Computation*, 6:182–197, 2000.

[8] X. Han, X. Cao, E. L. Lloyd, and C.-C. Shen. Fault-tolerant relay node placement in heterogeneous wireless sensor networks. *IEEE Transactions on Mobile Computing*, 9:643–656, May 2010.

[9] W. Hays and R. Winkler. *Statistics; probability, inference, and decision.* Number v. 1 in International series in decision processes. Holt, Rinehart and Winston, 1970.

[10] M. D. Hill and M. R. Marty. Amdahl's law in the multicore era. *Computer*, 41:33–38, 2008.

[11] X.-M. Hu, J. Zhang, Y. Yu, H.-H. Chung, Y.-L. Li, Y.-H. Shi, and X.-N. Luo. Hybrid genetic algorithm using a forward encoding scheme for lifetime maximization of wireless sensor networks. *Evolutionary Computation, IEEE Transactions on*, 14(5):766 –781, oct. 2010.

[12] D. Karaboga and B. Basturk. A powerful and efficient algorithm for numerical function optimization: artificial bee colony (abc) algorithm. *J. of Global Optimization*, 39(3):459–471, Nov. 2007.

[13] A. Konstantinidis and K. Yang. Multi-objective energy-efficient dense deployment in wireless sensor networks using a hybrid problem-specific moea/d. *Applied Soft Computing*, 11(6):4117 – 4134, 2011.

[14] A. Konstantinidis and K. Yang. Multi-objective k-connected deployment and power assignment in wsns using a problem-specific constrained evolutionary algorithm based on decomposition. *Computer Communications*, 34(1):83 – 98, 2011.

[15] A. Konstantinidis, K. Yang, and Q. Zhang. An evolutionary algorithm to a multi-objective deployment and power assignment problem in wireless sensor networks. In *Global Telecommunications*

Conference, 2008. IEEE GLOBECOM 2008. IEEE, pages 1 –6, 30 2008-dec. 4 2008.

[16] J. M. Lanza-Gutierrez, J. A. Gomez-Pulido, M. A. Vega-Rodriguez, and J. M. Sanchez-Perez. Instance sets for optimization in wireless sensor networks. http://arco.unex.es/wsnopt, Dec. 2011.

[17] J. M. Lanza-Gutierrez, J. A. Gomez-Pulido, M. A. Vega-Rodriguez, and J. M. Sanchez-Perez. Relay node positioning in wireless sensor networks by means of evolutionary techniques. In M. Kamel, F. Karray, and H. Hagras, editors, *Autonomous and Intelligent Systems*, volume 7326 of *Lecture Notes in Computer Science*, pages 18–25. Springer Berlin / Heidelberg, 2012.

[18] H. W. Lilliefors. On the kolmogorov-smirnov test for normality with mean and variance unknown. *J Amer Statistical Assoc*, 62(318):399–402, 1967.

[19] L. Liu, B. Hu, and L. Li. Energy conservation algorithms for maintaining coverage and connectivity in wireless sensor networks. *Communications, IET*, 4(7):786 –800, 30 2010.

[20] H. B. Mann and D. R. Whitney. On a test of whether one of two random variables is stochastically larger than the other. *Annals of Mathematical Statistics*, 1947.

[21] F. Martins, E. Carrano, E. Wanner, R. Takahashi, and G. Mateus. A hybrid multiobjective evolutionary approach for improving the performance of wireless sensor networks. *Sensors Journal, IEEE*, 11(3):545 –554, march 2011.

[22] J. Y. B. Mukherjee and D. Ghosal. Wireless sensor network survey. *Computer Networks*, 52(12):2292 – 2330, 2008.

[23] A. Perez, M. Labrador, and P. Wightman. A multiobjective approach to the relay placement problem in wsns. In *Wireless Communications and Networking Conference (WCNC), 2011 IEEE*, pages 475 –480, march 2011.

[24] E. Rashedi, H. Nezamabadi-pour, and S. Saryazdi. Gsa: A gravitational search algorithm. *Information Sciences*, 179(13):2232 – 2248, 2009. Special Section on High Order Fuzzy Sets.

[25] S. S. Shapiro and M. B. Wilk. An analysis of variance test for normality (complete samples). *Biometrika*, 52(3/4):591–611, Dec. 1965.

[26] B. Wang. Coverage problems in sensor networks: A survey. *ACM Comput. Surv.*, 43:32:1–32:53, Oct. 2011.

[27] Q. Wang, K. Xu, G. Takahara, and H. Hassanein. Transactions papers - device placement for heterogeneous wireless sensor networks: Minimum cost with lifetime constraints. *Wireless Communications, IEEE Transactions on*, 6(7):2444 –2453, july 2007.

[28] K. Xu, H. Hassanein, G. Takahara, and Q. Wang. Relay node deployment strategies in heterogeneous wireless sensor networks. *Mobile Computing, IEEE Transactions on*, 9(2):145 –159, feb. 2010.

[29] W. Ye, J. Heidemann, and D. Estrin. An energy-efficient mac protocol for wireless sensor networks. In *INFOCOM 2002. Twenty-First Annual Joint Conference of the IEEE Computer and Communications Societies. Proceedings. IEEE*, volume 3, pages 1567 – 1576 vol.3, 2002.

[30] C. Zhao and P. Chen. Particle swarm optimization for optimal deployment of relay nodes in hybrid sensor networks. In *Evolutionary Computation, 2007. CEC 2007. IEEE Congress on*, pages 3316 –3320, sept. 2007.

[31] E. Zitzler. Evolutionary algorithms for multiobjective optimization: Methods and applications, 1999.

[32] E. Zitzler, M. Laumanns, and L. Thiele. Spea2: Improving the strength pareto evolutionary algorithm. Technical report, 2001.

[33] E. Zitzler and L. Thiele. Multiobjective evolutionary algorithms: a comparative case study and the strength pareto approach. *Evolutionary Computation, IEEE Transactions on*, 3(4):257 –271, nov 1999.

Accelerating Population-Based Search Heuristics by Adaptive Resource Allocation

Joachim Lepping
INRIA Rhône-Alpes
51 Av. Jean Kuntzmann
38330 Montbonnot-St-Martin, France
joachim.lepping@udo.edu

Panayotis Mertikopoulos
French National Center for Scientific Research (CNRS), Laboratoire d'Informatique de Grenoble (LIG), France
panayotis.mertikopoulos@imag.fr

Denis Trystram
LIG, Grenoble University, IUF
51 Av. Jean Kuntzmann
38330 Montbonnot-St-Martin, France
denis.trystram@imag.fr

ABSTRACT

We investigate a dynamic, adaptive resource allocation scheme with the aim of accelerating the convergence of multi-start population-based search heuristics (PSHs) running on multiple parallel processors. Given that each initialization of a PSH performs differently over time, we develop an exponential learning scheme which allocates computational resources (processors) to each variant in an online manner, based on the performance level attained by each initialization. For the well-known example of $(\mu + \lambda)$–evolution strategies, we show that the time required to reach the target quality level of a given optimization problem is significantly reduced and that the utilization of the parallel system is likewise optimized. Our learning approach is easily implementable with currently available batch management systems and provides notable performance improvements without modifying the employed PSH, so it is very well-suited to improve the performance of PSHs in large-scale parallel computing environments.

Categories and Subject Descriptors

I.2.8 [**Artificial Intelligence**]: Problem Solving, Control Methods, and Search—*Scheduling; Heuristic methods*

General Terms

Algorithms; Performance

Keywords

exponential learning; online algorithms; cluster- and grid-computing

1. INTRODUCTION

For massively complex industrial problems (such as large parameter optimization or design optimization), exact solution methods are rarely applicable: the search space is often too large to be fully explorable and/or a mathematical model of the optimization problem is hard to obtain. In such cases, population-based randomized search heuristics (PSH) like evolutionary algorithms or particle swarms have become very popular because they do not require a specific mathematical model of the optimization problem. For instance, when using computational fluid dynamics in order to optimize the aerodynamic properties of a vehicle's shape, it is impossible to define a formal fitness expression and one uses simulations in order to determine the fitness function of a candidate solution.

In this context, a widely used class of population-based randomized search strategies are the so-called evolution strategies (ES): at each iteration, an ES (see also Section 3.2) provides certain solution candidates (which are commonly denoted as *individuals*), and selects the best ones based on selection-recombination mechanisms inspired by evolutionary biology. In this way, the next generation of individuals will be biased towards regions of the search space where better solutions have already been found, so the quality of the solution is improved at each iteration of the ES until a termination criterion is fulfilled.

Of course, this iterative process requires the fitness evaluation of every newly generated individual, a calculation which involves very complex simulations in an industrial setting: for instance, since the 1990s, aerodynamic optimization of real-world design objects requires extremely demanding computational fluid dynamics simulations that are all but impossible to execute in individual machines [1]. On the other hand, recent developments in high performance computing and clusters allow the evaluation of increasingly complex models on comparatively cheap hardware by virtue of parallelization. As a result, the performance of a PSH depends not only on its internal structure and convergence properties, but also on the efficient scheduling of the parallel machines – a factor which becomes even more important if the evaluations are time-consuming and the simulation times vary. More importantly, if one employs several different initializations of a PSH in order to reduce the risk of getting stuck in a local optimum (the so-called *multi-start* approach), allocating computational resources between better- and worse-performing initializations becomes a crucial issue.

In this paper, we seek to reduce the time required to reach a certain fitness value for a given optimization problem using multi-start PSHs by optimizing the allocation of computational resources to different variants of the PSH in an online, adaptive way. In contrast to cooperative problem-solving strategies [2] which require a significant level of interaction and coordination between different heuristics (or multiple initializations of the same heuristic), we consider here a fully decentralized setting where no such central coordination is possible; in a similar vein, any modifications of the PSH that would have to be performed by a central coordinator (such as model-assisted evaluations [3]) are likewise not considered. Instead, we only adjust the amount of resources assigned to each PSH over time based on its performance record: inspired by

GECCO'13, July 6–10, 2013, Amsterdam, The Netherlands.

the process of natural selection, variants with fitter individuals obtain more resources, allowing them to spread faster and explore the more profitable regions of the problem's search space. More precisely, we compare the best fitness value achieved by each heuristic at arbitrary timestamps, and depending on the fitness progress of each PSH so far (normalized by the number of already evaluated individuals), we reassign resources by means of an exponential stimulus-response scheme which is intimately related to the replicator dynamics of evolutionary game theory [4, 5].

In particular, the dynamic resource allocation scheme that we propose has the following pleasant properties:

- It is easy to implement in existing batch scheduling systems (such as Torque/PBS, LSF, etc.).
- It applies to every PSH that could benefit from a multi-start approach.
- No modifications in the internal algorithmic structure are required, so the original search heuristics remain untouched.
- There are no cooperation and/or central control requirements beyond the resource allocation policy of the batch scheduler.

In this framework, our evaluation with simulations of well-known test functions (see Section 6) shows that we achieve a better utilization of the parallel system and that we significantly speed up the convergence to the predefined quality level.

In the next section, we detail our resource allocation problem in the light of well-studied learning problems and we motivate the choice of our methodology. In Section 3, we present the precise formulation of our problem and we point out certain parallelization and convergence issues that appear in PSHs. Our proposed learning scheme is then presented in detail in Section 4, and its performance is examined and assessed in Sections 5 and 6.

2. BACKGROUND

The parallelization of PSHs has been extensively addressed in the literature – for instance, see Alba and Tomassini [6] for a good survey on existing approaches and technical solutions. Most of these works however modify the internal structure of the PSHs to take advantage of parallel resources and parallel communication models; in particular, the usage of parallel agents is often realized as collaborative or competitive search [7, 8].

On the other hand, from a learning point of view, our resource allocation problem bears close ties to the class of discrete choice problems known as "learning with expert advice" [9]. In this class of problems, a decision-maker (agent) is asked to choose between the advice of K "experts", and his reward is based on how good each expert's advice is. Of course, the performance of each expert is not constant over time, so the agent seeks to maximize his long-term payoff by selecting with higher probability the advice of experts who seem to be performing well and assigning lower probability to the rest. Accordingly, in our context, we will seek to devise a learning scheme for the allocation of computational resources so that the PSH variant which seems to be closer to reaching the target quality level gets more resources than others that lag consistently behind.

To that end, an approach which has met with particular success is that of Boltzmann-driven learning [10] where one keeps and updates a score variable for each expert by aggregating the expert's performance over time, and then choosing an expert at each instance with probability that is exponentially proportional to these scores – for a detailed account of this "exponential learning" process and its ties to evolutionary biology, see, e.g. [11, 12, 13, 9] and references therein. That said, a tacit assumption that underlies this "expert advice" literature is that the decision of the agent does *not* affect the performance of each expert: experts are not swayed in their predictions by what the agent does. In our computational setting however, this assumption fails spectacularly and for an unavoidable reason: by allocating more resources to a heuristic, this heuristic *will* run faster (and hence perform better), so we can no longer assume that the agent's decision-making does not interfere with the expert's advice.

Accordingly, the main challenge that needs to be overcome is how to estimate the speedup in the performance of a PSH variant that has been afforded extra resources, and how to compare the performance of different variants on an even keel. To overcome this challenge of spurious speedups, we introduce in Section 4.1 an unbiased estimator which compensates the performance profile of a heuristic by normalizing the fraction of resources allocated to it, and in so doing, we manage to compare the various PSH variants on an even keel.

3. PROBLEM FORMULATION

In this section, we describe the basic system model for a general multi-start PSH; for the sake of concreteness however, we will mostly focus on the widely used class of $(\mu + \lambda)$–Evolution Strategies (see Section 3.2).

3.1 System Model

We consider a set $\mathcal{K} = \{1, \dots, K\}$ of K realizations of a population-based randomized search heuristic. In each generation $i = 1, 2 \dots$, a heuristic must evaluate λ individuals in order to determine the objective values of its population – themselves representing the values of a global objective function f that we seek to minimize. Obviously, a new generation (i.e. the submission of λ new individuals to be simulated) can only start if all individuals of the incumbent generation have been completed, so each heuristic generates a set of λ jobs in each generation i. The simulation performed to determine an individual's objective will be regarded as a job and indexed by j, and we will also assume that the internal creation of the next generation (i.e., the process of selection, mutation, and recombination) requires negligible time compared to the actual job execution time.

We further consider a set of M identical machines (e.g., processors of a cluster) where evaluations can be performed in parallel.[1] Since we consider an online problem where the execution time of a job is only known after its completion, the scheduling on uniform or related parallel machines may only be done heuristically [14], and is beyond the scope of this paper. Here, the execution time of a job only depends on its processing time p_j (and thus not on a particular machine allocation), and the internal machine scheduling is realized (as in most batch scheduling systems) in a First-Come-First-Served fashion.

For a heuristic $k \in \mathcal{K}$, the best found value of the objective function f in generation i will be denoted by $f_k(i)$. As mentioned before, we assume the minimization of f throughout this paper, and we also assume that each generation improves on the previous one, i.e. $f_k(i-1) \geq f_k(i)$ (an assumption which is actually the evolutionary drive behind $(\mu+\lambda)$–evolutionary strategies). Additionally, we consider the best found objective value at a timestamp t and we again guarantee that $f_k(t') \geq f_k(t)$ whenever $t' \leq t$; on the other hand,

[1]Our resource adaption approach can be realized in arbitrary machine environments, so the restriction to parallel machines is hardly restrictive. We restrict ourselves to this model because it does not require the explicit modeling of machine-dependent job execution times.

since we are not considering cooperation and communication between heuristics we might well have $f_k(t') > f_\ell(t')$ and $f_k(t) < f_\ell(t)$ for two heuristics $k, \ell \in \mathcal{K}$, and $t' < t$.

Since all evaluations of a population within a generation are independent of each other, they can be executed in parallel. Thus, PSHs are well-suited to be executed on multi-core systems, clusters, or cloud-computing systems. The generation-based nature of these heuristics creates barriers in the parallel execution schedule. The problem occurs if the processing time for simulating an individual's fitness vary. Since new individuals are created by selection and variation depending on the fitness properties of the previous generation, the parallel evaluation of an generation i can only start if all λ individuals of the previous generation $i-1$ have been evaluated.

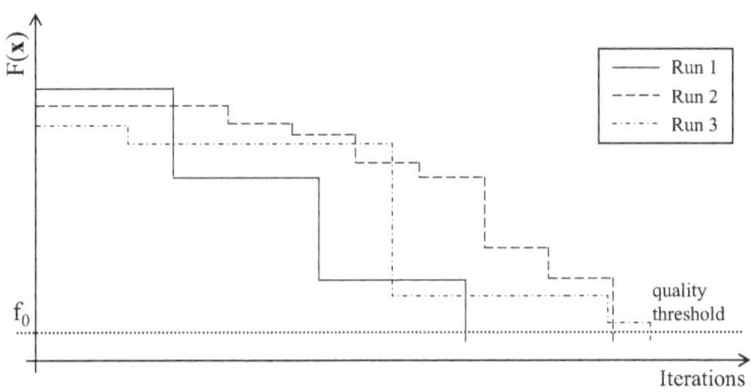

Figure 1: Typical fitness progress for a multiple runs of a PSH.

The convergence behavior of randomized search heuristics is only hardly predictable but it can be influenced by several algorithm parameters such as selection pressure or mutation rates. Once however the algorithm configuration is fixed, the heuristic's convergence behavior is determined by the random operators of the algorithms. Thus, the number of generations required to reach a solution below a predefined fitness values may well vary between two runs of otherwise identically configured PSH (cf. Figure 1).

3.2 $(\mu + \lambda)$–Evolution Strategies

As we mentioned before, our approach applies to any PSH that is amenable to multiple initializations. However, for the sake concreteness, we will focus in what follows on the popular class of PSHs known as $(\mu + \lambda)$–evolution strategies (ES) – for a detailed description and examples of other popular and practically relevant PSHs, see [15]. As all PSHs, an ES searches within a "population" of solutions wherein each individual represents a certain candidate solution of the optimization problem. The quality of this solution is called the "fitness" of an individual, and it is determined by evaluating the individual on the optimization problem. Following Schwefel and Rudolph [15], μ denotes here the number of *parents* while λ denotes the number of all offspring created by these parents within one synchronized generation. In the $(\mu + \lambda)$-ES the offspring and their λ parents are merged before the μ fittest individuals are selected from the $\mu + \lambda$ population (in particular, fitness never decreases), so each generation calls for the evaluation of λ individuals, and all these evaluations are independent.

4. ONLINE RESOURCE ALLOCATION

Before we start our adaptive resource allocation scheme, all heuristics must be initialized since the first parent population of μ individuals must be evaluated. We do not perform any update step during this phase and assume that at the initial timestamp $t = 0$ the μ progenitors have completed their evaluation. Once the K heuristics are initialized, we execute them in parallel assigning initially an equal portion of $m_k(0) = M/K$ resources to each heuristic. The jobs are assigned in a LIST-scheduling fashion to the machines, and as soon as a machine idles, it is assigned to a new job from any of the heuristics. Besides the already described dependencies between iterations and the resulting availability of jobs, we ensure that at no time more than $m_k(t)$ jobs are simultaneously executed for every heuristic k.

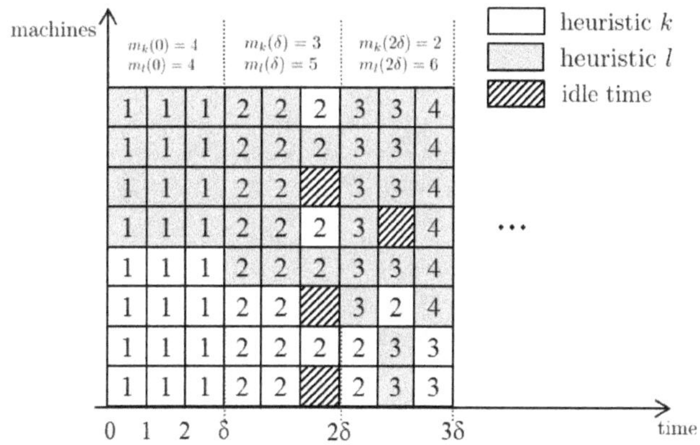

Figure 2: Scheduling and resource allocation concept for two PSHs and identical processing times in each evaluation. Each PSH has to evaluate $\lambda = 12$ individuals per generation and the cluster consists of $M = 8$ machines. The numbers denote the generation the evaluation belongs to.

In Figure 2, we illustrate a typical scheduling and resource assignment concept assuming for simplicity identical processing times for all evaluations. From timestamp δ and onwards, PSH k gets three of the eight resource assigned while PSH ℓ is allowed to use five resources at a time. At timestamp $t = 5$ heuristic ℓ has to finish generation 2 before it can start the next generation. The assigned resources cannot be entirely utilized by heuristic ℓ and the machines become idle. It would be possible to use idle resource to perform evaluations of other heuristics. However, we want to ensure that the updated resource allocations can be fulfilled during the next interval. This might become impossible if machines get occupied by other heuristics in a work-stealing like fashion.

4.1 Updating the allocation of resources

To optimize the allocation of resources per heuristic, we will score each heuristic's performance over time and then assign to each heuristic an amount of resources which is (roughly) exponentially proportional to this score. Specifically, at time t (counted every δ units of time), we measure the fitness values $f_k(t)$ of each heuristic $k \in \mathcal{K}$ and we iteratively define the heuristic's score as

$$U_k(t+\delta) = \eta_k(t)\left(U_k(t) - \frac{f_k(t)}{\max_{\ell \in K}\{f_l(t)\}}\right) \tag{1}$$

with $U_k(0) = 0$ for all heuristics. In the above, $\eta_k(t)$ is a normalization factor defined as

$$\eta_k(t) = \frac{n_k(t)}{\max_{\ell \in K}\{n_\ell(t)\}} \tag{2}$$

where $n_k(t)$ represents the overall number of evaluations that heuristic k has executed by timestamp t. This factor weighs the performance of a heuristic based on the number of evaluations it has already performed, so η_k compensates for the fact that the more evaluations a heuristic has executed, the better its objective value will be. As such, this aggregation method can be seen essentially as a moving average between the (normalized) performance history of heuristic k and its current fitness.

Indeed, by a slight rearrangement of terms, we obtain:

$$U_k(t+\delta) - U_k(t) = (\eta_k(t) - 1)U_k(t) - \frac{\eta_k(t) f_k(t)}{\max_{l \in K}\{f_l(t)\}}, \quad (3)$$

or, descending to continuous time for simplicity:

$$\dot{U}_k(t) = (\eta_k(t) - 1)U_k(t) - \overline{f}_k(t), \quad (4)$$

where $\overline{f}_k$ denotes the rightmost term of Equation (3), i.e. the relative performance of a heuristic normalized with regards to the fraction of resources that were allocated to it. Thus, if we set $\tau(t) = \int_0^t (1 - \eta_k(s))ds$ and then multiply both sides of this expression with the integrating factor $e^{\tau(s)}$, a simple integration yields:

$$U_k(t) = -\int_0^t e^{-(\tau(t)-\tau(s))}\overline{f}(s)ds. \quad (5)$$

This last expression (which can also be verified by differentiating under the integral sign) shows that the scores $U_k(t)$ can be interpreted as exponential moving averages of the heuristic's normalized performances, taken with respect to a non-uniform time-scale that accounts for the fact that the amount of resources allocated to a heuristic changes over time (and, thus, the time that it takes a heuristic to reach a given performance level should be scaled commensurately). Importantly, this is a different kind of averaging than the one induced by η in (1): η represents a normalization average over resources whereas the exponential factor in the integral of (3) represents a discounting of past information in order to construt an exponentially moving average over time.

Needless to say, better-scoring heuristics should be getting more resources; hence, inspired by its widespread use in the theory of learning [9], we will assign computational resources based on the Boltzmann–Gibbs stimulus-response scheme:

$$X_k(t) = \frac{\exp\{\alpha U_k(t)\}}{\sum_{\ell=1}^{K} \exp\{\alpha U_\ell(t)\}}, \quad (6)$$

where $X_k(t)$ is the fraction of resources appointed to heuristic k at time t. In this equation, the factor $\alpha < 1$ represents the inverse temperature of the Boltzmann distribution and will control the exploration/exploitation tradeoff of the dynamic policy (6). Since a small α induces a high temperature the learning speed is decreased as the behavior of (6) becomes less greedy. A pre-experimental study revealed that $\alpha = 5$ is a reasonable choice to ensure both fast learning and more-than-adequate adaptivity over a wide range of experimental parameters.

Now, following (6) the actual number of allocated resources will be determined using the expression:

$$m_k(t+1) = \lfloor X_k(t) \cdot (M - K) \rfloor + 1, \quad (7)$$

which guarantees that at least one resource is assigned to every heuristic at all times. To further guarantee that all resources are used for every instance we assign the remaining

$$\bar{M}(t+1) = M - \sum_{k=1}^{K} m_k(t+1) \quad (8)$$

resources to the $\bar{M}(t+1)$ currently best performing heuristics – and to avoid initialization issues, we set $\bar{M}(0) = 0$. Finally, to ensure the numerical stability of the discrete updating scheme in Equation (1) during the following steps, we shift the scores to zero level for all heuristics and actually use the updating rule:

$$U_k(t+\delta) \leftarrow U_k(t+\delta) - \max_{\ell \in K}\{U_\ell(t+\delta)\}. \quad (9)$$

Thanks to the exponential updating rule (6), this transformation does not affect the actual allocation profile because only differences in scores matter for the updating step.

Remark. It should be noted that this resource allocation scheme does *not* boil down to a "winner-takes-all" policy, whereby the "best" heuristic gets all computational resources. Thanks to the normalization of execution times, underperforming heuristics still get a share of the resources, so if they start performing well, the online learning scheme will re-allocate resources accordingly.

5. ASSESSING EVALUATION RESULTS

Our implementation of the $(\mu+\lambda)$-ES follows closely the detailed description in [16]. We thus consider different population sizes (a parameter which has a strong influence on the convergence behavior and also influences the resource adaptation process), and based on Schwefel's recommendation [17], we took a ratio of $\mu/\lambda \approx 1/7$ for all simulations. The parameter settings above may well be improved on for specific cases, but this parameter range leads to a better overall convergence rate on average [17]. More to the point, since we will show that it is possible to accelerate the algorithm performance by improved resource assignments the actual convergence behavior is only of minor importance – it only serves as an example which can be substituted by any other population-based randomized search heuristic.

5.1 Definition of Performance Criteria

As noted before, we are interested in minimizing the overall time it takes to reach a predefined level of our objective function. Thus, in order to evaluate our results, we consider the following performance metrics (for a single run of all experiments with the same configuration):

- T_l : Amount of time that the online learning approach required to reach the predefined quality threshold f_0.
- T_u : Amount of time that the fastest heuristic would have taken to reach the predefined quality threshold f_0 assuming uniform resource allocation: $m_k(t) = M/K$.
- T_b : Amount of time that the fastest heuristic (i.e., the heuristic that requires fewest iterations to reach f_0) would have taken if all M resource had been exclusively assigned to it.
- T_w : Amount of time that the slowest heuristic (i.e., the heuristic that requires most iterations to reach f_0) would have taken if all M resource had been exclusively assigned to it.

To measure the improvements of the online learning approach over a static uniform allocation, we define the average gain G over uniform resource allocation in Equation (10).

$$G = \frac{T_u - T_l}{T_u} \quad (10)$$

Furthermore, we define the average efficiency E_u of the uniform allocation, see Equation (11),

$$E_u = \frac{T_w - T_u}{T_w - T_b} \quad (11)$$

and the average efficiency E_l of the online learned allocations, see Equation (12).

$$E_l = \frac{T_w - T_l}{T_w - T_b} \quad (12)$$

In all cases, we compare the required time with the discrepancy between the worst and best heuristics: if we observe a negative efficiency, then simply choosing a heuristic at random and assigning all resources to it would have been the better choice (naïve as this might seem). In such cases, neither uniform allocation nor online learning is reasonable, so a sophisticated approach seems meaningless (the uncertainty is just too high).

Importantly, a standard evaluation criterion that is used in the learning literature to assess the performance of a dynamic learning scheme is its *regret series*:

$$R_k(t) = \frac{1}{t}\left[\sum\nolimits_{n=1}^{t} (f_k^*(n) - f(n))\right]_+ \tag{13}$$

where $f(n)$ is the value achieved at step n of the process, $f_k^*(n)$ is the value that would have been achieved by heuristic k at stage n if all resources had been allocated to heuristic k for all $n \leq t$ (see, e.g., Cesa-Bianchi and Lugosi [9] and references therein). In other words, the regret series R_k simply measures how much has been lost in terms of performance by not using heuristic k all the time: if k is consistently worse than all possible resource allocation to other heuristics then R_k will be identically equal to 0, whereas if k consistently outperforms all other heuristics, R_k will vanish if and only if all available resources are allocated to k. As a result, the standard objective in learning is to devise a learning scheme which is asymptotically *consistent* in the sense that $\lim_{t\to 0} R_k(t) = 0$ for all k (for an extended discussion of this issue, see [9, 18, 19] and references therein).

Nonetheless, the regret series as defined above suffers from two very important drawbacks in our setting: First of all, it is a *fictitious* criterion in the sense that R_k cannot be calculated unless we know the value $f_k^*(n)$ that the k-th heuristic *would* have achieved at each $n \leq t$ *if* all resources had been assigned to it. Even more importantly, consistency is an *unbalanced* criterion in the sense that R_k could stay unboundedly positive for perfectly reasonable resource allocation policies. To illustrate this last point, assume the following example which, despite its simplicity, captures the essence of the problem: we are given two heuristics, A and B with A two times slower than B, so that $f_A^*(n) = 2f_B^*(n) = 2n$ for all n; assume further for simplicity that the performance of each heuristic depends linearly on the fraction of alloted resources. Then, if we allocate resources with a ratio 2 : 1 in favor of the *slow* heuristic A, we will have $f(n) = \max\{2/3 \times n, 1/3 \times 2n\} = 2n/3$. In turn, this yields a *positive* and bounded away from zero regret series R_A for the slower heuristic, indicating (quite falsely!) a regret for not giving all resources to the slow heuristic A.

In view of the above, we see that regret-based consistency is not a suitable performance evaluation criterion for our resource allocation scheme, so, in all our experiments, our analysis will be focused on the runtime evaluation criteria defined at the beginning of this section.

6. SIMULATION SETUP AND RESULTS

To investigate the performance of our approach in challenging optimization problems with wildly varying convergence behaviors, we focused our experiments on two well-known test problems for evolutionary algorithms, the Ackley and Rastrigin functions [20, 21]. Of course, real-world problems might exhibit different behavior than these artificially constructed functions; the reason that we chose to focus on these highly challenging problems is that they represent the worst-case scenarios that could arise in real-world conditions, and they are also precisely the type of problems that require a massively parallel computing environment to boot.

Specifically, the first test problem that we are considering is the *Ackley function* [20] in its standard variant. The problem is finding a string $\vec{x} = \{x_1, x_2, \ldots, x_N\}$, with $x_i \in (-32.768, 32.768)$, that

μ	λ	K	M	δ	p_j
3	21	4/6/8	40/60/80	7/5	$\sim \mathcal{U}(1,5)/\mathcal{E}(2)$
4	30	4/6/8	40/60/80	9/6	$\sim \mathcal{U}(1,5)/\mathcal{E}(2)$
5	35	4/6/8	40/60/80	11/7	$\sim \mathcal{U}(1,5)/\mathcal{E}(2)$
6	40	4/6/8	40/60/80	12/8	$\sim \mathcal{U}(1,5)/\mathcal{E}(2)$
15	100	4/6/8	40/60/80	30/20	$\sim \mathcal{U}(1,5)/\mathcal{E}(2)$

Table 1: Detailed configuration of the discussed experiments. Note that δ is independent of the number of heuristics since we always chose $M = 10K$. It depends only on the processing time estimate and the population size. Here we use $\bar{P}(\mathcal{U}(1,5)) = 3$ and $\bar{P}(\mathcal{E}(2)) = 2$.

minimizes Equation (14).

$$F_1(\vec{x}) = 20\left(1 - e^{-0.2\sqrt{\frac{1}{N}\sum_i x_i^2}}\right) + e - e^{\frac{1}{N}\sum_i \cos(2\pi x_i)} \tag{14}$$

Next, we also consider the *Rastrigin function* first proposed in [21] as a typical example of a (2-dimensional) non-linear multimodal function:

$$F_2(\vec{x}) = 20 + \sum\nolimits_{i=1}^{2} \left(x_i^2 - 10\cos(2\pi x_i)\right), \quad x_i \in (-5.12, 5.12). \tag{15}$$

6.1 Experimental setup

In our experiments, we run each ES until it falls below an objective quality threshold of $f_0 = 10^{-4}$ and we simulate a compute cluster with $M = 10K$ computational resources (reflecting a reasonable load/resource scaling). The details of our experimental setup are shown in Table 1; in what follows, we will simply give a short account of some important experimental issues.

To begin with, in real batch-systems like PBS/Torque, the scheduler is only triggered at discrete timestamps. Due to performance issues the number of scheduling decisions is limited (although it might slightly reduce the utilization), so we submit new jobs only at integer time units ($t = 1, 2, \ldots$) while the online resource allocation is updated every δ units of time with

$$\delta = \left\lceil \bar{P} M^{-1} \lambda K \right\rceil, \tag{16}$$

where $\bar{P}$ involves the estimated mean execution time of an evaluation. Of course, in an online scheduling context the processing times of jobs are not known n advance, so we determine this value by a rough estimation based on pre-experimental reasoning; however, experiments showed that even a very coarse estimate is already sufficient, so we will not elaborate further on this issue.

Another important aspect of our simulations is the distribution of the jobs' execution times. Unfortunately, there exists no standard model for the processing times of sequential jobs submitted to clusters. The closest results that we could find was the analysis of [22] where the authors show that the runtimes in common workload traces follows a hyper-gamma distribution – however, the model of [22] refers to parallel workloads *only*. In light of the above, we chose instead to sample processing times $p_j \sim \mathcal{U}(a, b)$ for each evaluation form a uniform distribution over the interval $[a, b]$, and from an exponential distribution $p_j \sim \mathcal{E}(\rho)$ with mean ρ (in the displayed experiments, we chose $\rho = 2$). Our simulations showed that our approach is fairly indifferent to the processing time distributions, see Figures 3 and 4, so knowledge of the exact distribution of processing times does not seem to be particularly important.

6.2 Experimental results

Figure 3(a) shows the improvement of the online learning approach over a static uniform allocation for several population size configurations. Since the median gain is positive for all settings, the exponential learning scheme is superior to a static uniform resource assignment. For smaller populations, improvements lie between 7.5 % ($3+21$ and $k = 8$) and 15.23 % ($3+21$ and $k = 4$), but for larger populations, our adaptive resource allocation scheme is particularly advantageous: we observe a gain in convergence time between 30.47 % (15 + 100 and $k = 8$) and 36.6 % (15 + 100 and $k = 8$) over the simpler uniform allocation scheme.

However, the larger population configurations also highlight the only drawback that we were able to identify in our adaptive resource allocation scheme. Figure 3(b) shows the efficiency of a uniform allocation scheme and it reveals that resource sharing and a multi-start variant is not advantageous in those cases: apparently, the evolution strategy converges faster to the desired quality level if all resources are assigned to any arbitrary heuristic. One possible explanation of this phenomenon is that the explorative power of a (15 + 100)-population is so large that any multi-start variant will converge quickly to the optimal solution. In our approach, we always have to share the resource among the multi-start variant. for large populations, giving all resources to a single start of the PSH would have been obviously advantageous. Even the online adaption of the resource can not ameliorate this tendency entirely although results are slightly improved, see Figure 3(c).

In this way, a natural question that emerges is the following: do multi-start variants with online resource sharing lead to advantages in optimization time? To answer this question, we present the averaged absolute optimization durations (in seconds) in Table 3. Results are given for the Rastrigin function ($F_2(\vec{x})$) over 40 runs and for both uniformly and exponentially sampled processing times (we only present the results of $F_2(\vec{x})$ due to space limitations). Qualitatively, the results for $F_2(\vec{x})$ which would correspond to Figure 3, are similar. First, using multi-start variants on the parallel resources pays off in any case, since T_u becomes always smaller with increasing values of K. The learning (T_l) improves these values in every case over static shares T_u. This tendency is even stronger if the processing times are exponentially distributed (cf. Table 3).

7. CONCLUSION

We presented an approach to accelerate the convergence of any kind of population-based randomized search heuristic (PSH) that is executed on parallel computing installations. Taking a multi-start approach, we executed multiple initializations of the same PSH to solve the same optimization problem and used an exponential learning technique in order to adapt the fraction of computational resources assigned to each heuristic based on its performance envelope. The novelty of the approach lies in that the overall optimization process revolves exclusively around resource assignment: in particular, the actual PSH does not need to be modified and any kind of optimizer that is able to deliver intermediate results (to compare the current progress) may be improved with the approach presented in this paper. Our resource adaption scheme is particularly suited for evolutionary algorithms: evaluations with two common test functions and randomly generated processing times show that our online learning scheme yielded significant performance improvements and was robust to the processing time distribution.

An open (but orthogonal) question for further research is whether it really pays off to have a multi-start variant with online resource adaptation instead of a significantly larger population size – a question which we did not address due to space limitations. Indeed, this investigation requires a thorough look into the quality/speed tradeoff between exploring greater regions of the state space (multi-start) and potential premature convergence in local optima (single run of PSH with large explorative power). In this context, we also have to investigate self-adaptation of the mutation step-size for the large population ES and alternative PSHs like particle swarms or population-based ant colony optimization algorithms.

8. REFERENCES

[1] W. D. Gropp and E. B. Smith, "Computational fluid dynamics on parallel processors," *Computers & Fluids*, vol. 18, no. 3, pp. 289–304, 1990.

[2] L. Panait and S. Luke, "Cooperative multi-agent learning: The state of the art," *Autonomous Agents and Multi-Agent Systems*, vol. 11, pp. 387–434, 2005.

[3] M. Emmerich, A. Giotis, M. Özdemir, T. Bäck, and K. Giannakoglou, "Metamodel-assisted evolution strategies," in *In Parallel Problem Solving from Nature VII*. Springer, 2002, pp. 361–370.

[4] P. D. Taylor and L. B. Jonker, "Evolutionary stable strategies and game dynamics," *Mathematical Biosciences*, vol. 40, no. 1-2, pp. 145–156, 1978.

[5] W. H. Sandholm, *Population Games and Evolutionary Dynamics*, ser. Economic learning and social evolution. Cambridge, MA: MIT Press, 2011.

[6] E. Alba and M. Tomassini, "Parallelism and evolutionary algorithms," *IEEE Transactions on Evolutionary Computation*, vol. 6, no. 5, pp. 443–462, 2002.

[7] H. Mühlenbein, *Computational Intelligence*, ser. Intelligent Systems Reference Library. Springer, 2009, vol. 1, ch. Evolutionary Computation: Centralized, Parallel or Collaborative, pp. 561–595.

[8] C. Grimme, J. Lepping, and A. Papaspyrou, "Parallel predator-prey interaction for evolutionary multi-objective optimization," *Natural Computing*, vol. 11, no. 3, pp. 519–533, 2011.

[9] N. Cesa-Bianchi and G. Lugosi, *Prediction, Learning, and Games*. Cambridge University Press, 2006.

[10] D. Fudenberg and D. K. Levine, *The Theory of Learning in Games*, ser. Economic learning and social evolution. Cambridge, MA: The MIT Press, 1998, vol. 2.

[11] A. Rustichini, "Optimal properties of stimulus-response learning models," *Games and Economic Behavior*, vol. 29, pp. 230–244, 1999.

[12] R. Cominetti, E. Melo, and S. Sorin, "A payoff-based learning procedure and its application to traffic games," *Games and Economic Behavior*, vol. 70, pp. 71–83, 2010.

[13] P. Mertikopoulos and A. L. Moustakas, "The emergence of rational behavior in the presence of stochastic perturbations," *The Annals of Applied Probability*, vol. 20, no. 4, pp. 1359–1388, 2010.

[14] M. Pinedo, *Scheduling: Theory, Algorithms, and Systems*, 2nd ed. Prentice-Hall, 2002.

[15] H.-P. Schwefel and G. Rudolph, "Contemporary evolution strategies," in *Proceedings of the 3rd European Conference on Artificial Life*, F. Morán, A. Moreno, J. J. Merelo, and P. Chacón, Eds. Springer, 1995, pp. 893–907.

[16] T. Bäck, *Evolutionary algorithms in theory and practice*. New York: Oxford University Press, 1996.

[17] H.-P. Schwefel, *Evolution and Optimum Seeking*. John Wiley & Sons, 1995.

[18] S. Hart and A. Mas-Colell, "A simple adaptive procedure leading to correlated equilibrium," *Econometrica*, vol. 68, no. 5, pp. 1127–1150, September 2000.

[19] S. Sorin, "Exponential weight algorithm in continuous time,"

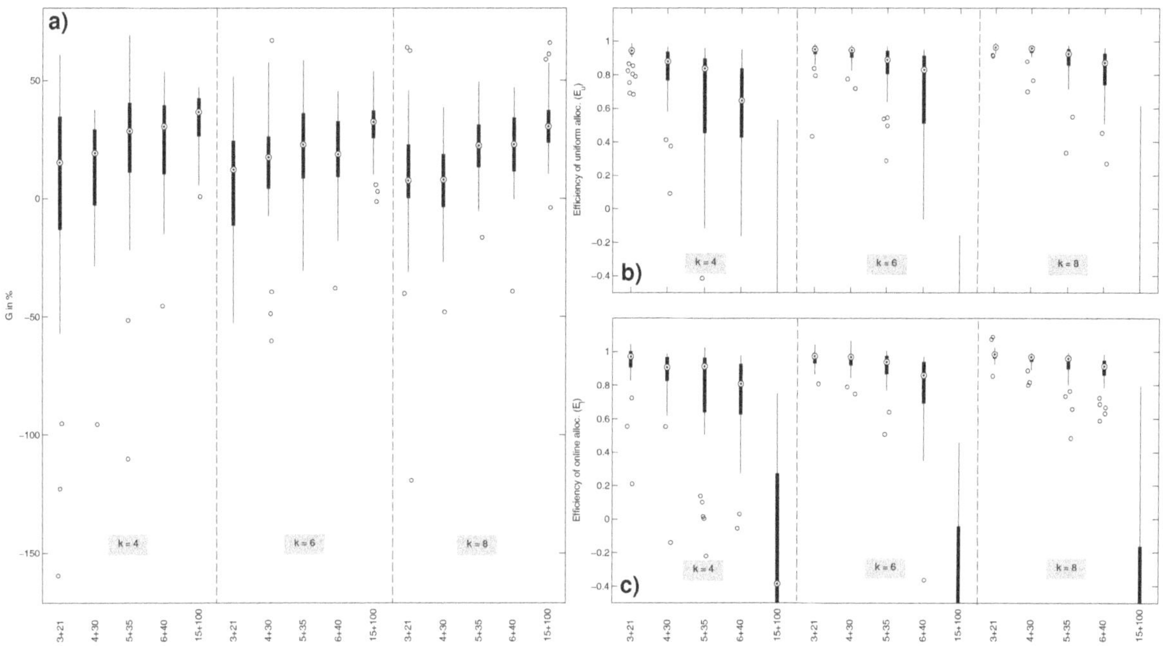

Figure 3: Boxplots of population-based search heuristic configurations over 40 runs on problem $F_1(\vec{x})$ with uniformly sampled processing times ($\mathcal{U}(1,5)$). The configurations comprise various population sizes ($\mu + \lambda$) and number of heuristics ($k = 4, 6, 8$). Figure (a) shows the gain of the online learning over uniform allocation in %. Figure (b) shows the efficiency of uniform allocation and Figure (c) the efficiency of the online learning approach.

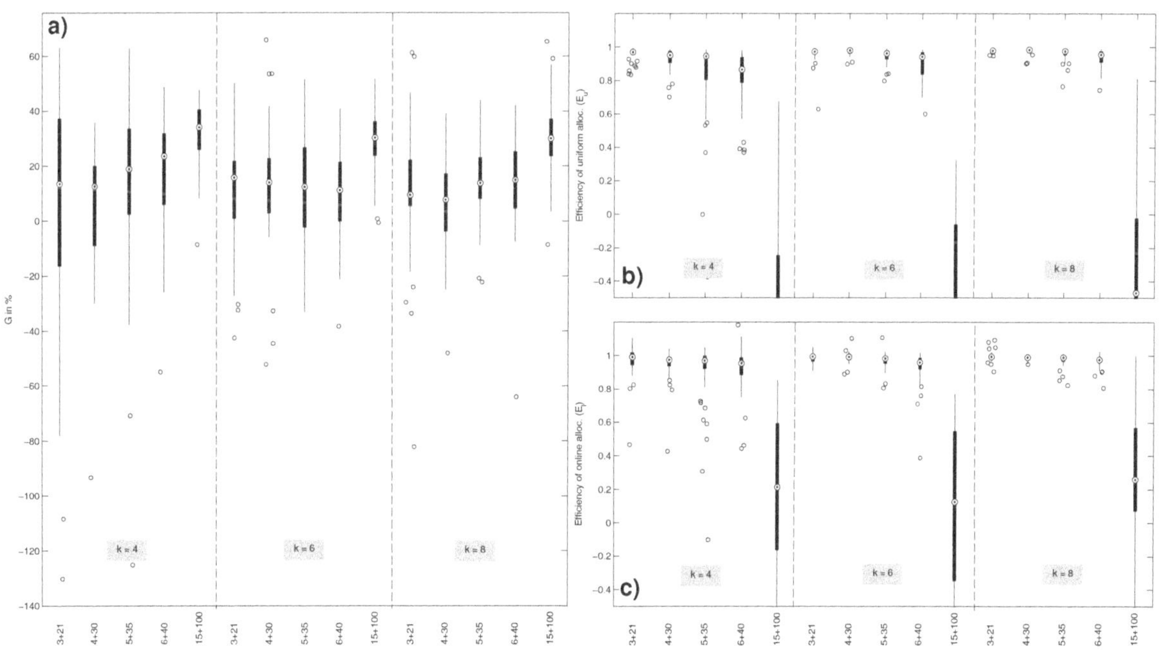

Figure 4: Boxplots of population-based search heuristic configurations over 40 runs on the $F_1(\vec{x})$ with exponentially sampled processing times ($\mathcal{E}(2)$). The configurations comprise various population sizes ($\mu + \lambda$) and number of heuristics ($k = 4, 6, 8$). Figure (a) shows the gain of the online learning over uniform allocation in %. Figure (b) shows the efficiency of uniform allocation and Figure (c) the efficiency of the online learning approach.

Processing Time ~ $\mathcal{U}(1,5)$					
$\mu+\lambda$	3+21	4+30	5+35	6+40	15+100
Average T_b					
K=4	1270.33	643.58	535.76	373.73	459.85
K=6	909.24	513.11	415.12	329.23	340.49
K=8	683.02	449.49	359.86	329.66	279.06
Average T_w					
K=4	9447.47	6070.25	5193.26	3362.32	922.88
K=6	8846.67	8394.89	6237.05	4213.93	744.49
K=8	9512.00	8716.71	7045.93	5217.18	787.73
Average T_u					
K=4	1872.82	1298.05	1318.86	1016.13	1429.19
K=6	1332.73	988.12	996.75	882.23	1350.82
K=8	993.22	856.79	848.25	862.34	1345.67
Average T_l					
K=4	1809.38	1122.08	1083.63	784.58	947.58
K=6	1223.73	831.80	775.60	738.83	928.75
K=8	872.40	800.28	671.08	691.35	917.18

Processing Time ~ $\mathcal{E}(2)$					
$\mu+\lambda$	3+21	4+30	5+35	5+35	6+40
Average T_b					
K=4	2185.64	1189.02	1013.96	728.44	643.79
K=6	1563.15	952.45	788.95	643.63	534.36
K=8	1185.85	828.04	683.09	642.75	504.45
Average T_w					
K=4	16239.86	11229.63	9876.43	6550.66	1288.59
K=6	15244.93	15499.63	11856.80	8223.91	1168.56
K=8	16330.41	16094.16	13428.35	10170.93	1421.76
Average T_u					
K=4	2752.20	1652.56	1533.94	1185.03	1556.82
K=6	1987.23	1286.34	1164.10	1016.80	1472.83
K=8	1500.02	1109.70	996.65	995.02	1465.85
Average T_l					
K=4	2552.45	1524.03	1439.48	984.83	1062.55
K=6	1769.90	1104.13	989.05	922.90	1044.15
K=8	1250.70	1035.00	855.78	867.30	1016.35

Table 2: Absolute results values (time in seconds) for the Ackley function ($F_1(\vec{x})$) over 40 runs.

Processing Time ~ $\mathcal{U}(1,5)$					
$\mu+\lambda$	3+21	4+30	5+35	6+40	15+100
Average T_b					
K=4	726.87	561.31	388.96	339.26	333.73
K=6	685.71	345.14	308.59	250.56	244.30
K=8	511.64	286.01	262.56	217.19	190.32
Average T_w					
K=4	8269.21	6326.30	6066.77	4951.90	748.49
K=6	9235.50	8458.56	7228.31	5699.95	1516.46
K=8	9593.47	9431.75	7707.12	7182.11	1366.91
Average T_u					
K=4	1074.58	1130.26	956.03	922.98	1035.93
K=6	1004.99	670.11	742.15	672.31	970.96
K=8	747.36	547.97	618.11	570.55	916.25
Average T_l					
K=4	1097.50	1002.13	737.48	775.18	727.40
K=6	964.88	566.60	577.28	543.45	620.78
K=8	689.13	458.08	504.40	445.58	618.83

Processing Time ~ $\mathcal{E}(2)$					
$\mu+\lambda$	3+21	4+30	5+35	6+40	15+100
Average T_b					
K=4	1106.01	920.56	667.02	593.53	376.75
K=6	1033.57	561.38	523.75	437.34	331.11
K=8	772.53	470.61	445.73	380.79	307.20
Average T_w					
K=4	12493.72	10370.81	10291.12	8658.72	860.73
K=6	13966.17	13873.15	12269.04	9941.66	2053.86
K=8	14507.25	15462.75	13084.37	12552.53	2204.08
Average T_u					
K=4	1352.06	1189.07	882.53	833.81	801.79
K=6	1309.81	723.13	691.49	606.01	757.23
K=8	995.53	605.05	590.84	521.74	714.76
Average T_l					
K=4	1377.85	1160.00	814.63	796.00	607.13
K=6	1214.33	658.45	650.30	559.43	522.28
K=8	854.48	544.48	546.45	479.33	516.58

Table 3: Absolute results values (time in seconds) for the Rastrigin function ($F_2(\vec{x})$) over 40 runs.

Mathematical Programming, vol. 116, no. 1, pp. 513–528, 2009.

[20] D. H. Ackley, *A connectionist machine for genetic hillclimbing*. Boston: Kluwer, 1987.

[21] A. Törn and A. Zilinskas, *Global Optimization*, ser. Lecture Notes in Computer Science. Springer, 1989, vol. 350.

[22] U. Lublin and D. G. Feitelson, "The workload on parallel supercomputers: Modeling the characteristics of rigid jobs." *Journal of Parallel and Distributed Computing*, vol. 63, no. 11, pp. 1105–1122, 2003.

The Asynchronous Island Model and NSGA-II: Study of a New Migration Operator and its Performance

Marcus Märtens
Advanced Concepts Team
European Space Agency (ESTEC)
Noordwijk, The Netherlands
marcus.maertens@esa.int

Dario Izzo
Advanced Concepts Team
European Space Agency (ESTEC)
Noordwijk, The Netherlands
dario.izzo@esa.int

ABSTRACT

This work presents an implementation of the asynchronous island model suitable for multi-objective evolutionary optimization on heterogeneous and large-scale computing platforms. The migration of individuals is regulated by the crowding comparison operator applied to the originating population during selection and to the receiving population augmented by all migrants during replacement. Experiments using this method combined with NSGA-II show its scalability up to 128 islands and its robustness. Furthermore, the proposed parallelization technique consistently outperforms a multi-start and a random migration approach in terms of convergence speed, while maintaining a comparable population diversity. Applied to a real-world problem of interplanetary trajectory design, we find solutions dominating an actual NASA/ESA mission proposal for a tour from Earth to Jupiter, in a fraction of the computational time that would be needed on a single CPU.

Categories and Subject Descriptors

I.2.8 [**Artificial Intelligence**]: Problem Solving, Control Methods, and Search; G.1.6 [**Optimization**]: Global Optimization

General Terms

Algorithms

Keywords

multi-objective optimization; island model; migration; distributed algorithms; evolutionary algorithms

1. INTRODUCTION

The need for algorithms exploiting parallel architectures has become more important than ever before. Today, supercomputers are not the only platforms having multiple CPUs: every modern PC is a parallel machine to be exploited. Connecting these machines via the internet creates another gigantic parallel computing platform whose potentials are still largely unexplored.

Due to their inherent suitability to such multiple CPU architectures, evolutionary optimization algorithms have been extensively studied in various parallel frameworks [1]. The main ideas to parallelize an optimization task are a) the master-slave model, b) the island model and c) the diffusion model. Past studies, mainly focused on homogeneous CPUs and static networks, proved clear benefits of all these schemes. However, in large, dynamic and heterogeneous CPU networks a coarse-grained approach like the island model is arguably most promising. For single-objective problems, a generalized version of the asynchronous island model has been recently studied in connection to a large number of islands (up to 1024), proving the importance of migration in general [12] and its topology (migration paths) in particular [16].

For multi-objective evolutionary algorithms (MOEA) the implementation on modern computing platforms is, instead, rather unexplored as noted also in [17]. While most works focus only on small numbers of homogeneous CPUs, a few groups [14, 15, 19] looked into grid computing architectures, heavily multithreaded environments or GPGPU computing. Some works study simple multi-start strategies as they are inherently scalable, asynchronous, robust to churn, well suited for heterogeneous environments and easy to implement, making them also the first choice for most practitioners. Besides, it can always be argued how having multiple runs with different initial seeds of an evolutionary algorithm may be more valuable than one single longer run. However, such an argument is already flawed in the case of single objective continuous optimization as shown in [12].

This work presents an implementation of the asynchronous island model suitable for multi-objective evolutionary optimization on heterogeneous and large-scale computing platforms. The main idea is that by using the crowding comparison operator [8] during migration we select solutions from a non crowded area of the Pareto-front of one population and inject them on a different population only when this improves its diversity. The importance of selecting suitable migration policies was already discussed in general by Coello et al. [5] whereas our goal is to give a analysis of the crowding comparison operator in particular. Unlike past implementations of the island model for multi-objective optimization [20, 10, 17], we do not assign a particular part of the search space nor of the Pareto-front to each island.

All islands are identical as they search the same space and focus on the entire the Pareto-front. This allows computational resources to be added and removed easily (during the optimization) and thus to be less sensitive to churn and heterogeneity. At Second, we make another contribution by finding the Pareto-front for the EJSM interplanetary trajectory (the NASA/ESA proposal for an Europa Jupiter System Mission), proving our approach suitable for real world applications.

2. ASYNCHRONOUS ISLAND MODEL

The island model is a coarse-grained model for parallel optimization, where N subpopulations $P_1, \ldots, P_N$ are distributed onto N islands $I_1, \ldots, I_N$ and evolve using algorithm A. An island is an abstraction of any basic parallel entity, i.e. a CPU-core, a thread or a computer in a large network. Islands evolve mostly independent, but are allowed to exchange individuals after a certain number of iterations, a process called *migration*. Migration is only allowed on migration paths between certain islands which are defined by a graph commonly called *migration topology*. By restricting these paths, each island maintains a niche where evolution can proceed (exploitation) but might also get new genetic material, which helps to maintain diversity and prevent premature convergence (exploration).

Migration has been shown to be helpful in improving and speeding up optimization in a more general context than evolutionary algorithms, i.e. when connected to different techniques such as simulated annealing, artificial bee colony, improved harmony search and many more meta-heuristics [12, 16]. The set of all islands together with the migration topology is what we call *archipelago*. Every individual in an archipelago corresponds to a solution to the optimization problem (decision vector) forming the *global Pareto-front* in contrast to the *local Pareto-front* consisting just of the solutions on a single island.

2.1 Migration

Migration is determined per island by several parameters: the migration frequency m_f is the number of iterations of the algorithm between two migrations and the migration rate m_r determines how many members of the subpopulations are selected and exchanged. Selection and replacement of migrants are governed by a selection policy m_{sel} and a replacement policy m_{rep}. Finally, a topology $\mathcal{T}$ defines the migration paths on which islands are allowed to exchange individuals.

Migration is often implemented as a synchronization point so that an island has to wait until all other islands have finished their iterations to migrate and proceed. Instead of this, we use an asynchronous implementation of the island model that is better suited for large-scale and heterogeneous computing architectures: each island I_i stores a list L_i containing the migration candidates. Before starting iterations of algorithm A, the replacement policy m_{rep} modifies the current population by taking into account all individuals in the list L_j of a randomly selected island I_j connected directly to I_i in the topology $\mathcal{T}$. According to the underlying computing architecture, shared memory (protected by the necessary mutexes), MPI or XMPP can be used by island I_i to access the information contained in L_j. Then, the algorithm A is executed for m_f iterations on the modified population. After that, the selection policy m_{sel} selects individuals from the current population, empties L_i and copies them into the list. This process repeats until a termination criterion is satisfied. Algorithm 1 summarizes the whole process for a single island.

Algorithm 1 Migration and evolution on an Island I_i

```
Initialize initial population P_i
Initialize L_i to an empty list
repeat
    Select a random island I_j directly connected by T
    P_i = m_rep(P_i ∪ L_j)
    for k = 1 → m_f do
        P_i = A(P_i)
    end for
    L_i = m_sel(P_i)
until termination criterion is satisfied
```

2.2 The island model for MOEAs

The asynchronous island model described in the previous subsection can be applied to parallelize any evolutionary algorithm as a generic scheme. According to the type of optimization problem to be solved (i.e. single/multiple objective continuous/integer, constrained/unconstrained) different choices for the selection and the replacement policy influence the archipelagos performance significantly. A common approach for MOEAs is to select and replace individuals randomly, which has the advantage of a straightforward implementation (see [20, 10]).

Instead of this, we suggest the use of a partial order $\prec$ to rank and select individuals both in m_{rep} and m_{sel}. The selection policy m_{sel} of an island I_i orders all p individuals in its current population with respect to $\prec$ and puts the first m_r into L_i. The replacement policy m_{rep} works on the union of the current population with the individuals in the selected list L_j and sorts it with respect to $\prec$. Afterwards, the first p individuals become the new population whereas the last m_r individuals are discarded. For $\prec$ we use the *crowding comparison operator* described and used in the popular non-dominated sorting genetic algorithm NSGA-II [8]. Let i_{rk} and i_{cd} be the non-domination rank and the crowding distance of individual i. Then $\prec$ is defined as:

$$i \prec j \text{ if } (i_{rk} \leq j_{rk}) \vee (i_{rk} = j_{rk} \wedge i_{cd} \geq j_{cd})$$

This partial order favours at first members with high non-domination ranks and, if individuals belong to the same front, members with the highest crowding distances. When used in the replacement and selection policies detailed above, it has the advantage that it incorporates individuals which help to improve the spreading of the Pareto-front: because a migrant that would be inserted in an already densely populated area would have a very small crowding distance, it is thus much more likely that by using $\prec$ it will be discarded in comparison to a replacement policy that discards just uniformly at random. Vice versa, the acceptance of a migrant in a sparsely populated area becomes more likely.

3. EXPERIMENTS

In this section we describe the experimental setups used to evaluate the performance of our new migration strategy in the asynchronous island model. As noted before, our scheme

problem	dimen-sion	objec-tives	problem properties
ZDT1	30	2	convex
ZDT2	30	2	concave
ZDT3	30	2	disc. fronts, multimodal
ZDT4	10	2	convex, multimodal
ZDT6	10	2	concave, multimodal, biased
DTLZ1	30	3	linear, multimodal
DTLZ2	90	3	concave
DTLZ3	30	3	concave, multimodal
DTLZ4	90	3	concave, biased
DTLZ7	90	3	disc. fronts, multimodal

Table 1: Properties and used parameters of the benchmark problems.

Figure 1: Example of a Barabasi-Albert topology with 64 nodes, generated with $m_0 = 3$ and 3 new random connections per added node. The size of a node is proportional to its degree.

can be used in connection to any multi-objective optimization algorithm, but here we only establish its performances when all islands are running an instance of NSGA-II. In this respect our result can also be seen as a study on coarse-grained parallelization of NSGA-II, implementing a research idea similar to one proposed by Coello et al. [5]. All experiments were conducted on a platform having sixteen Intel(R) Xeon(R) CPU - X5560 @ 2.80GHz with 8192 KB of cache. As we will simulate archipelagos with up to 128 islands, there are unpredictable effects on the wall-clock time due to cache efficiency considerations, especially when running more islands than cores (i.e. 32, 64, 128). In all comparative results, these effects are all factored out. The asynchronous island model, the new migration operator and the NSGA-II implementation used are all open source contributions to the parallel optimization platform PyGMO[1] under development at the European Space Agency.

3.1 Benchmark Problems

We use selected problems out of two well-known benchmark suites, namely the ZDT [21] and the DTLZ [9] problems. These problems cover various features like concave geometries, disconnected Pareto-fronts, biased and multimodal problems (see Table 1). The problem dimensions were chosen as to create an interesting complexity level.

3.2 Performance measures

Each of our test-problems is constructed as a composition of functions that describe the position and the shape of the Pareto-front, which is thus known beforehand. One of these functions, which we call *distance function* and indicate with g, is minimized by any Pareto-optimal solution. This fact can be used to define a convergence metric as follows: let g be the distance function of a problem, P a set of solutions and x^* any Pareto-optimal decision vector, we define

$$\Upsilon(P) = \frac{1}{|P|} \sum_{x \in P} g(x) - g(x^*) \quad (1)$$

as *convergence metric* of the corresponding problem. The lower the $\Upsilon(P)$, the closer the solutions of P are to solutions of the Pareto-front. Although there are already well-established convergence metrics in literature, Υ has the advantage of not relying on a reference set of Pareto-optimal solutions which allows for a more efficient computation while reflecting the same behaviour as most of the other convergence metrics.

For the ZDT problems we also use the diversity metric Δ introduced by Deb et. al [8, 6] and defined as:

$$\Delta = \frac{d_f + d_l + \sum_{i=1}^{p-1} |d_i - \bar{d}|}{d_f + d_l + (p-1)\bar{d}}$$

where p is the population size, d_i is the Euclidean distance between two consecutive solutions $i-1, i$ in the fitness space, $\bar{d}$ the average distance over all these distances, and d_l, d_f are the distances from the border solutions to the known extreme solutions of the Pareto-front.

3.3 The archipelago setups

To illustrate the effect of migration in experiments, different underlying migration topologies $\mathcal{T}$ can be considered. The extreme cases are the unconnected graph which does not include any migration paths at all. We call the setup based on the unconnected graph the *unconnected setup*. It corresponds to a multi-start strategy where an algorithm is executed several times on different initial populations and using different random seeds. In contrast to this, one can consider the fully-connected graph as a topology, which allows migration between arbitrary islands directly. While preliminary experiments with NSGA-II showed that the best results were achieved by using this topology, there are some heavy drawbacks. By using a fully-connected topology, each new island has to be linked to any existing island, producing a large communication overhead and a rather inefficient scalability. To be more applicable in practice, we decided to base our migration experiments on another graph instead, which is called the Barabasi-Albert network [2]. This network is a scale-free network observed in many growing systems including the internet, citation networks and social networks. Its degree of separation is in general small enough to allow a quick migration between any two islands but keeps the communication overhead much lower than a fully-connected topology. Moreover, this topology is known for its robustness against random node failures, characteristics of particular interest for heterogeneous large CPU networks. We grow our Barabasi-Albert networks by starting with $m_0 = 3$ nodes and adding 3 new random connections for each additional node. Figure 1 depicts an example of an archipelago with 64 islands. Based on the Barabasi-Albert network topology, we examine two other setups: in the *random migration*

[1] http://pagmo.sourceforge.net/pygmo/index.html

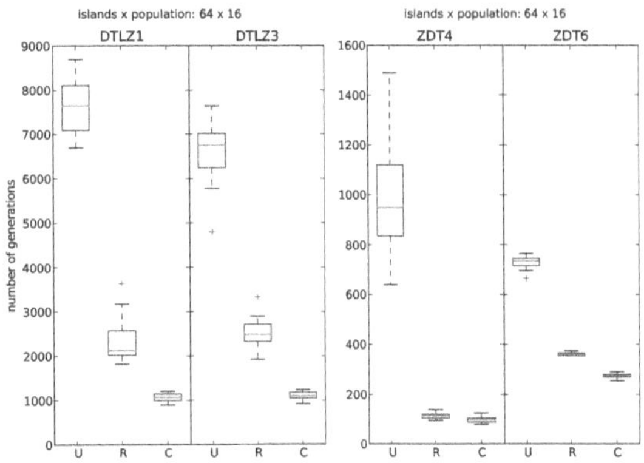

Figure 2: Number of generations till one island reaches τ for unconnected setup U, random migration setup R and crowding migration setup C.

setup selection and replacement of individuals happens uniformly at random and in the *crowding migration setup* we use our suggested scheme $\prec$ based on the crowding distance operator.

For each setup, the initial population is initialized at random, but is kept the same for all three setups. We always apply NSGA-II with a cross-over probability of $p_c = 0.9$, a mutation probability of $p_m = 0.01$ and distribution indices $\eta_c = 10$ and $\eta_m = 10$. The migration frequency is set to $m_f = 5$ generations and the migration rate to $m_r = 0.2 \cdot p$, rounded accordingly. No significant qualitative difference on the reported results was, though, observed when experimenting with different values.

The termination criterion is based on Υ and a problem-dependent threshold τ. We stop all islands in a setup as soon as there is one island with population P for which $\Upsilon(P) < \tau$ holds, where the τ is 0.01 for the ZDT and 0.1 for the DTLZ problems, taking into account their higher number of objectives. Reaching the threshold means that all individuals of a population in one island have converged close enough to a Pareto-optimal solution of the Pareto-front. We say that the population has *converged* to the Pareto-front in this case. While being important, note that Υ does not make any statement about whether the converged population is well-spread over the whole front or not.

3.4 Results

We conducted our experiments for all three setups, varying the number of islands $N \in \{16, 32, 64, 128\}$ and the number of individuals per island $p \in \{8, 16, 32, 64, 128\}$, using 25 repetitions for every combination of p and N as to accumulate enough statistical significance. During our experiments we recorded, for each of the 25 runs of every setup, wall-clock times (per island) and the generations necessary to converge. For the ZDT problems we also computed Δ. We report a summary of the whole experimental campaign, highlighting the most interesting results and observations. Statistical significance for all experiments was consistently found as standard deviations are all very small, which is why we omit an exhausting statistical analysis at this point.

First, we looked at the comparison between the unconnected setup and the migration setups. On every combination of p and N the migration setups clearly outperform the unconnected setup both in terms of generations and of wall-clock time. This effect was strongest for multimodal problems like ZDT4, ZDT6, DTLZ1 or DTLZ3 and for small population sizes p as shown in Table 2. Multi-start approaches for NSGA-II can thus be improved by exchanging information among independent runs. The question of whether to migrate or not thus always has a positive answer. We extend thereby the result acquired for single-objective algorithms [12] to NSGA-II.

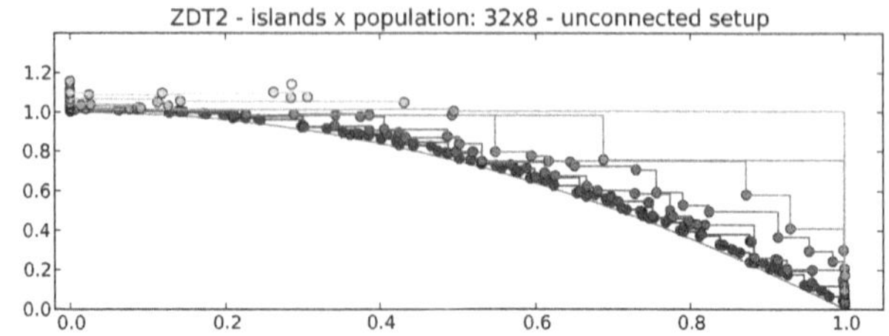

Figure 3: Sample of the solutions of an archipelago in an unconnected setup when $\tau = 0.01$ was reached by one island. Convergence after 170 generations, $\Delta = 0.680254$. Clearly, some islands need additional generations to converge.

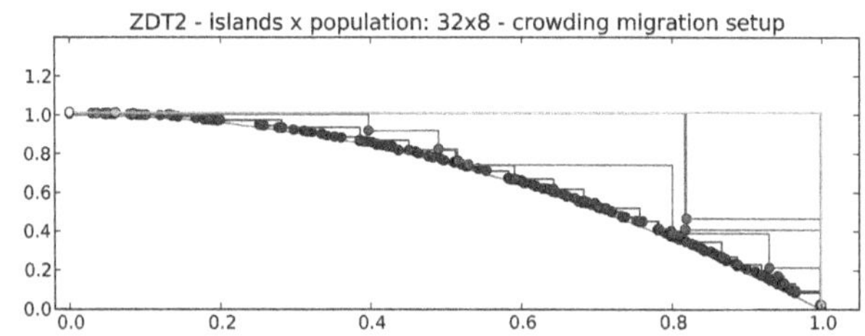

Figure 4: Sample of the solutions of an archipelago in a crowding migration setup when $\tau = 0.01$ was reached by one island. Convergence after 175 generations, $\Delta = 0.638917$. All islands approach the Pareto-front with a similar convergence speed.

Afterwards, we looked at the comparison between the two migration setups as to assess the performance of our proposed migration strategy based on $\prec$. We observed that the crowding migration setup outperforms by a factor of 2-3 the random migration setup in terms of average number of generations for the harder DTLZ1 and DTLZ3 problems and by smaller amounts for the easier ZDT problems. For the latter it does not need many less generations on average to converge as shown in Figure 2 for an archipelago with $p = 16$ and $N = 64$. Random migration may even have a slightly smaller average wall-clock runtime in those cases (such as ZDT4) where almost the same number of generations is needed for convergence. This is due to the implementation overhead of the crowding migration operator compared to the more easier random migration operator.

We then looked at the diversity of the global Pareto-front (i.e. $\Delta(\bigcup_{i=1}^{N} P_i)$) when convergence was reached. No significant difference was found between all the setups. The only exception is ZDT2 for small p where migration appears to help in finding the border solutions (observed for all but $p = 128$). Figure 3 and 4 show the global Pareto-fronts for the unconnected and crowding migration setup as an example. One can clearly see how in the unconnected setup many islands proceed slower and their individ-

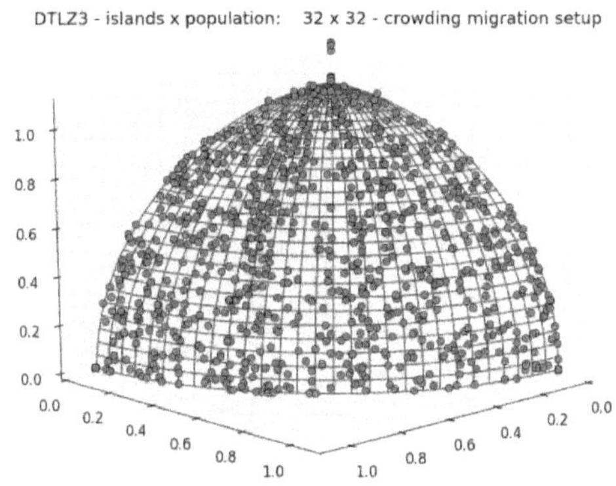

Figure 5: Sample of a global Pareto-front of a crowding migration setup till $\tau = 0.01$ was reached by one island after 970 generations.

uals have higher domination ranks on the archipelago level. Figure 5 shows the spreading of the global convergence over the Pareto-front for the DTLZ3 problem after one island reached $\tau = 0.01$. All in all, the diversity at the archipelago level is maintained when migrating, while migration helps islands in dominated areas to proceed faster towards the Pareto-front as they would by themselves.

Table 3 shows the generations and wall-clock times per island (averaged over the 25 runs) for all combinations of p and N in the crowding migration setup. By looking at the anti-diagonals we are comparing runs where the population number is equal (constant $N \cdot p$). When a fixed population size at the archipelago level is desired, the crowding migration setup encourages to have setups with a high number of islands evolving small populations. Reading the table by column we note how there is mostly just a very small speed-up in adding islands to an already existing archipelago. However, The advantage in this case is, that by increasing the product $p{\cdot}N$ we are getting more solutions at the archipelago level allowing for a finer approximation of the actual Pareto-front in roughly the same amount of time.

We finally observed that NSGA-II occasionally produces degenerated fronts on DTLZ4. The algorithm is known to perform in that way on this particular problem (see [9]) which will result in approximations consisting of just a single point or only a line of the border from the spherical shape of the Pareto-front. Using more than $N > 32$ islands, we observed that the island that reached τ first always had such a degenerated front in the unconnected setup but never in the crowding migration setup. We thus conclude that the crowding migration helps NSGA-II to deal better with strongly biased problems like DTLZ4.

4. TRAJECTORY OPTIMIZATION

The design of an interplanetary trajectory with deep space manoeuvres and multiple fly-bys is a challenging task. In order to maximize the payload of the on-board scientific instruments, the propellant mass has to be minimized. On the other hand, the transfer time needs to be short as to allow the mission to reach its objectives without having years of unnecessary delay.

NSGA-II has already been applied by Deb et. al [7] to a simplified version of this problem, allowing only 3 planetary

problem	number of islands N				population
	16	32	64	128	per island p
DTLZ1	6.29	8.46	9.15	11.14	8
	4.98	5.70	7.21	7.83	16
	4.01	4.74	5.37	5.74	32
	3.12	3.38	3.70	3.88	64
	2.53	2.59	2.78	2.84	128
DTLZ3	5.62	6.68	7.76	7.98	8
	4.29	5.43	6.02	6.54	16
	3.30	3.70	4.00	4.20	32
	2.57	2.69	2.88	2.98	64
	1.94	2.15	2.12	2.24	128
ZDT4	10.74	16.61	22.68	22.31	8
	7.44	8.67	9.68	10.07	16
	3.08	4.47	4.65	4.78	32
	2.50	2.55	3.20	3.19	64
	1.90	1.86	2.05	1.99	128
ZDT6	2.94	3.28	3.68	3.86	8
	2.19	2.46	2.67	2.77	16
	1.79	1.94	2.05	2.12	32
	1.51	1.60	1.69	1.78	64
	1.35	1.43	1.58	1.69	128

Table 2: Ratio of average number of generations until τ between unconnected and crowding migration setup.

parameter	unit	lower bound	upper bound
t_0	MJD2000	6210	8400
T	days	1000	3000
u	-	0	1
v	-	0	1
V_∞	km/s	1.0	3.5
$\eta^1, \ldots, \eta^\ell$	-	$1 \cdot 10^{-5}$	0.99999
$\alpha^1, \ldots, \alpha^\ell$	-	$1 \cdot 10^{-5}$	0.99999
$r_p^1, \ldots, r_p^{\ell-1}$	Planet Radii	1.1	100
$\beta^1, \ldots, \beta^{\ell-1}$	rad	-2π	2π

Table 4: Encoding of a MGA-1DSM tour with ℓ legs.

fly-bys and using a simplified dynamics not allowing for deep space manoeuvres. In this section, we use the MGA-1DSM trajectory model [11] to design a planetary tour using a predefined fly-by sequence of an arbitrary length and allowing the spacecrafts propulsion system to perform up to one DSM between each two planetary encounters. By the aid of our asynchronous island model, we construct approximating Pareto-fronts for various different sequences starting with Earth and ending with Jupiter and compare these results with the actual mission baseline of the NASA/ESA joint proposal for an Europa Jupiter System Mission (EJSM) [4].

4.1 Problem Description

Fixing a sequence S of planets for fly-by manoeuvres, we divide our trajectory into ℓ legs, where each leg corresponds to a transfer between two successive planets in S. We use the encoding and bounds described in Table 4 to model our optimization problem allowing for up to one DSM on each leg as follows.

The parameter t_0 describes the date of launch, u, v the launch direction and V_∞ is the departure velocity of the spacecraft. The parameter η^i describes the fraction of the

problem	number of islands N				population per island p
	16	32	64	128	
ZDT1	222.0 / 0.15	190.6 / 0.12	168.8 / 0.10	150.0 / 0.08	8
	186.6 / 0.21	167.0 / 0.17	151.0 / 0.13	138.4 / 0.10	16
	154.4 / 0.34	144.0 / 0.26	133.8 / 0.18	125.8 / 0.14	32
	125.0 / 0.51	121.0 / 0.38	112.6 / 0.30	104.4 / 0.25	64
	100.4 / 0.81	98.0 / 0.65	88.4 / 0.52	80.4 / 0.45	128
ZDT2	208.2 / 0.15	178.0 / 0.12	156.6 / 0.10	138.6 / 0.08	8
	172.4 / 0.20	153.0 / 0.16	138.0 / 0.12	126.2 / 0.10	16
	136.2 / 0.31	128.0 / 0.24	118.4 / 0.17	109.4 / 0.13	32
	110.8 / 0.47	103.8 / 0.33	96.0 / 0.26	89.0 / 0.22	64
	88.6 / 0.71	86.6 / 0.59	76.2 / 0.48	66.6 / 0.40	128
ZDT3	229.8 / 0.16	199.4 / 0.13	179.0 / 0.11	159.4 / 0.09	8
	189.8 / 0.23	174.6 / 0.18	158.2 / 0.15	145.8 / 0.11	16
	154.8 / 0.35	144.6 / 0.27	133.4 / 0.19	124.8 / 0.14	32
	133.0 / 0.55	129.0 / 0.41	118.6 / 0.32	108.8 / 0.26	64
	115.4 / 0.90	114.0 / 0.76	103.6 / 0.62	93.2 / 0.53	128
ZDT4	591.2 / 0.36	423.0 / 0.25	198.6 / 0.11	137.8 / 0.07	8
	292.2 / 0.30	183.4 / 0.16	154.4 / 0.13	95.8 / 0.07	16
	169.2 / 0.35	111.4 / 0.19	91.6 / 0.12	76.8 / 0.09	32
	117.6 / 0.49	82.2 / 0.26	73.2 / 0.18	65.0 / 0.16	64
	76.2 / 0.65	69.8 / 0.51	59.4 / 0.40	53.8 / 0.34	128
ZDT6	426.0 / 0.24	371.0 / 0.21	322.8 / 0.17	290.0 / 0.15	8
	363.4 / 0.34	325.8 / 0.27	293.0 / 0.23	270.6 / 0.18	16
	309.2 / 0.57	286.2 / 0.44	263.0 / 0.31	248.0 / 0.25	32
	250.8 / 0.98	236.6 / 0.68	221.6 / 0.50	204.0 / 0.42	64
	203.2 / 1.57	195.4 / 1.23	173.2 / 0.98	157.8 / 0.85	128
DTLZ1	2632.4 / 2.61	1844.0 / 1.60	1383.0 / 1.10	1140.4 / 0.78	8
	1878.2 / 3.33	1321.0 / 1.93	1091.6 / 1.27	889.8 / 0.88	16
	1312.2 / 4.32	1079.6 / 2.53	896.6 / 1.63	794.2 / 1.37	32
	1076.4 / 5.49	898.8 / 3.66	775.8 / 2.86	666.0 / 2.38	64
	757.8 / 9.09	686.0 / 6.71	624.4 / 5.58	596.8 / 4.61	128
DTLZ2	543.4 / 0.71	464.2 / 0.52	416.2 / 0.42	386.4 / 0.31	8
	368.4 / 0.83	335.2 / 0.60	311.6 / 0.43	294.0 / 0.34	16
	264.8 / 1.02	250.2 / 0.70	236.4 / 0.53	219.2 / 0.43	32
	200.8 / 1.19	194.2 / 0.95	182.6 / 0.78	168.8 / 0.69	64
	157.8 / 1.85	154.8 / 1.55	145.2 / 1.36	133.4 / 1.18	128
DTLZ3	2883.2 / 3.02	2045.4 / 1.86	1637.0 / 1.37	1311.2 / 0.93	8
	1780.8 / 3.26	1383.2 / 2.07	1144.2 / 1.38	931.2 / 0.94	16
	1091.8 / 3.77	970.8 / 2.36	853.2 / 1.59	745.6 / 1.33	32
	809.4 / 4.28	748.2 / 3.20	656.2 / 2.52	602.2 / 2.12	64
	589.6 / 6.14	582.2 / 5.49	516.6 / 4.35	480.6 / 3.81	128
DTLZ4	363.8 / 0.49	320.2 / 0.37	278.4 / 0.29	255.4 / 0.21	8
	293.2 / 0.69	269.8 / 0.50	245.6 / 0.34	222.2 / 0.26	16
	226.6 / 0.90	210.8 / 0.59	194.4 / 0.44	183.0 / 0.37	32
	176.8 / 1.07	170.2 / 0.86	158.4 / 0.69	144.2 / 0.60	64
	139.6 / 1.72	136.6 / 1.40	128.2 / 1.22	116.0 / 1.04	128
DTLZ7	495.6 / 0.62	420.6 / 0.46	358.0 / 0.35	321.2 / 0.25	8
	373.2 / 0.82	327.6 / 0.57	301.0 / 0.41	279.8 / 0.32	16
	300.0 / 1.12	276.4 / 0.76	255.4 / 0.56	234.8 / 0.45	32
	238.6 / 1.38	229.4 / 1.11	214.0 / 0.89	196.8 / 0.79	64
	201.0 / 2.33	195.6 / 1.94	182.6 / 1.67	168.4 / 1.45	128

Table 3: Average number of generations until τ for the crowding migration setup / average wall-clock time per island until τ for the crowding migration setup.

i-th leg on which the DSM is taken, whereas β^i, r_p^i model the fly-by radius and the orientation of the fly-by plane during the i-th fly-by. Thus we have in total $3 + 4 \cdot \ell$ decision variables by using this encoding. The upper bound on V_∞ is set to the maximum velocity allowed by the EJSM proposal. Also t_0 and T are bounded in a way that the EJSM solution with $t_0^* = 7364$ and $T^* = 2122$ is in the decision space.

Our first objective is to minimize the cumulative velocity change Δv, which is linked to the fraction of mass used for propellant via the Tsiolkovsky rocket equation [18]. The second objective is the total transfer time T, which we directly encode as a decision variable into the chromosome. The transfer times $T_1, \ldots, T_\ell$ per leg can be computed by the parameters $\alpha^1, \ldots, \alpha^\ell$ using the following equation:

$$T_i = \frac{\alpha^i \cdot T}{\sum_{j=1}^{\ell} \alpha^j} \qquad i = 1, \ldots, \ell.$$

4.2 Optimization Technique and Results

We observed that by using NSGA-II on any fixed planetary sequence with a random initialization, we only achieve poor results that miss large parts of the fitness space, especially in the area of low Δv that is of particular interest in the domain. To overcome this limitation, we initialized the population with solutions obtained by running a single-objective optimizer optimizing for low Δv only. We have chosen jDE [3] for this purpose which we also embedded into the asynchronous island model in order to improve the speed of computation and quality of solution, using $N = 8, p = 40, m_f = 100, m_r = 2$ and a ring topology, migrating the individuals with the best fitness values, replacing the ones with the worst. We also used a minor modification in the encoding of the problem. Instead of using T and $\alpha_i, \ldots, \alpha_\ell$ we put the transfer times per leg $T_1, \ldots, T_\ell$ directly into the chromosome, setting appropriate bounds. This produces better fitness values as with the original encoding, which is, however, better suited for multi-objective optimization allowing to have box bounds on the total time of flight (i.e. one of the objectives).

Evolution of jDE was stopped after the Δv did not decrease by more than 0.1 during 1000 generations and the best solution was extracted. In order to maintain a diverse set of solutions, this procedures was repeated 1024 times. Running NSGA-II for at least 10000 generations on this population produced better results than our first attempt, but took us more than $4h$ to be completed[2]. By using the island model in a crowding migration setup with $N = 16$, $p = 64$ we were able to lower this time dramatically to 140s per 10000 generations on average.

To allow for a stronger exploitation in the NSGA-II algorithm, we used $m_f = 10$ whereas all other parameters of the setup were the same as in subsection 3.1. As a final step, we put all individuals from all islands into one population and used NSGA-II for just 50 more generations on them, allowing every individual to advance to a single non-dominated front while maintaining a good spread of solutions.

[2]The original implementation of NSGA-II we used scales quadratically with the number of individuals of a population. Using a more sophisticated implementation like in [13] could improve the runtime, but would not change the quality of the overall solution. Moreover, we still need a fairly large amount of generations as NSGA-II is just making small improvements for every evolutionary step.

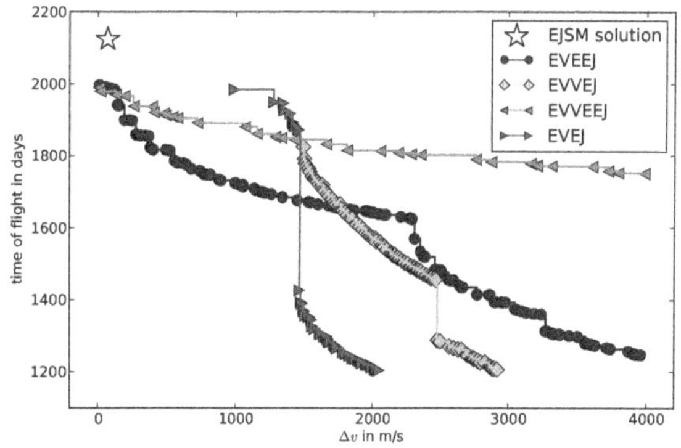

Figure 6: Pareto-fronts for different fly-by sequences (E=Earth, V=Venus, J=Jupiter) between 1200 and 2200 days of transfer using at most $\Delta v = 4000$ m/s. Solutions outside these bounds are excluded.

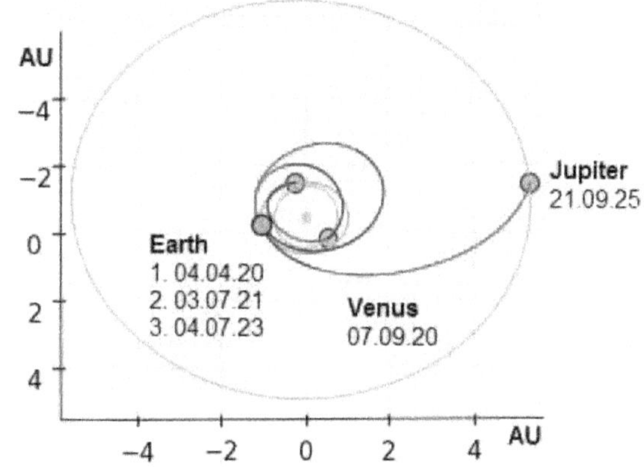

Figure 7: Alternative EVEEJ transfer found by NSGA-II with $\Delta v \approx 9.33$ m/s and a transfer time of 1996 days.

Using the outlined method, we analyzed several different sequences of planets (encoded with E for Earth, V for Venus and J for Jupiter) to obtain alternative trajectories from Earth to Jupiter[3]. Combining all trajectories we found creates a comprehensive overview on possible interplanetary transfer options in the given launch window of 6 years (01.01.2017 - 31.12.2022) and the possible trade-offs, shown in Figure 6. It turns out that the solutions of EVEEJ and the EVEJ trajectories dominate all other solutions, where at $\Delta v = 1452$ m/s a change between these two sequences can help saving over 249 days. Also, having an additional flyby on Venus is an alternative for very low Δv trajectories, as there are EVVEEJ solutions here that dominate a small part of the EVEEJ front.

Surprisingly, our optimization was able to find solutions for EVEEJ and EVVEEJ sequences that dominate the EJSM from NASA/ESA, which is also based on an EVEEJ sequence. The trajectory of the lowest Δv solution of our EVEEJ Pareto-front is shown in Figure 7 as an example. It uses a Δv of 9.33 m/s and a total transfer time of 1996

[3]We also analyzed sequences containing Mars but omit these results here as they are far less competitive as sequences using Earth and Venus only.

days instead of the EJSM proposal that uses a Δv of 67.95 m/s in 2122 days. A further investigation showed that this was coming at the price of a higher arrival velocity at the Jupiter system of 6.08 km/s instead of 5.5 km/s as in the EJSM. It would be interesting to look into the arrival velocity as a third objective to further explore the quality of the solution.

5. CONCLUSIONS

Motivated by the emergence of large heterogeneous computational networks, we have outlined how MOEAs can be embedded in the asynchronous island model while proposing a novel migration operator to select and replace solutions in sparsely populated areas. The experiments indicate that we can use a high number of islands with small populations to speed up convergence while maintaining a good diversity of the global solution. Furthermore, our approach is scalable and helps NSGA-II to not converge in degenerated fronts. As a second contribution, we have shown how our asynchronous island model together with an appropriate initialization technique can be used to produce a Pareto-front for a difficult interplanetary trajectory optimization task.

Future research might include additional MOEAs and new migration policies. Also combining different MOEAs in a single crowding migration setup could give interesting results. Using more sophisticated performance indicators might show how migration not only affects convergence speed but also the overall quality of the global approximation. Moreover, it would be interesting to see how the island model performs on more difficult problems that are non-separable or have a deceptive fitness landscape. We also think that the island model can be helpful in solving many-objective optimization problems with a high number of objectives. Algorithms for these problems usually need very large populations to construct a meaningful approximation of the Pareto-front. Since our experiments indicate that migration can help NSGA-II to converge even with small populations we can be optimistic.

6. REFERENCES

[1] E. Alba and M. Tomassini. Parallelism and evolutionary algorithms. *Evolutionary Computation, IEEE Transactions on*, 6(5):443–462, 2002.

[2] A. Barabási and R. Albert. Emergence of scaling in random networks. *science*, 286(5439):509–512, 1999.

[3] J. Brest, V. Zumer, and M. Maucec. Self-adaptive differential evolution algorithm in constrained real-parameter optimization. In *Evolutionary Computation, 2006. CEC 2006. IEEE Congress on*, pages 215–222. IEEE, 2006.

[4] K. Clark, T. Magner, R. Pappalardo, M. Blanc, R. Greeley, J. Lebreton, C. Jones, and J. Sommerer. Jupiter europa orbiter mission study 2008: Final report. *The NASA Element of the Europa Jupiter System Mission Technical Document, Task Order# NMO710851*, 2009.

[5] C. A. C. Coello, G. B. Lamont, and D. A. V. Veldhuizen. *Evolutionary algorithms for solving multi-objective problems*. Springer, 2007.

[6] K. Deb. Multi-objective optimization. *Multi-objective optimization using evolutionary algorithms*, pages 13–46, 2001.

[7] K. Deb, N. Padhye, G. Neema, and V. Adimurthy. Interplanetary trajectory optimization with swing-bys using evolutionary multi-objective optimization. *Lecture Notes in Computer Science*, 4683:26–35, 2007.

[8] K. Deb, A. Pratap, S. Agarwal, and T. Meyarivan. A fast and elitist multiobjective genetic algorithm: NSGA-II. *Evolutionary Computation, IEEE Transactions on*, 6(2):182–197, 2002.

[9] K. Deb, L. Thiele, M. Laumanns, and E. Zitzler. Scalable test problems for evolutionary multiobjective optimization. *Evolutionary Multiobjective Optimization*, pages 105–145, 2005.

[10] K. Deb, P. Zope, and A. Jain. Distributed computing of pareto-optimal solutions using multi-objective evolutionary algorithms. In *Proceedings of the Second Evolutionary Multi-Criterion Optimization (EMO-03) Conference, 8-11 April, Faro, Portugal*, pages 535–549. Proceedings of the Second Evolutionary Multi-Criterion Optimization (EMO-03) Conference, 8-11 April, Faro, Portugal, 2003.

[11] D. Izzo. *Global optimization and space pruning for spacecraft trajectory design*. Cambridge University Press, New York, NY, USA, 2010.

[12] D. Izzo, M. Ruciński, and F. Biscani. The generalized island model. *Parallel Architectures and Bioinspired Algorithms*, pages 151–169, 2012.

[13] M. Jensen. Reducing the run-time complexity of multiobjective EAs: The NSGA-II and other algorithms. *Evolutionary Computation, IEEE Transactions on*, 7(5):503–515, 2003.

[14] N. Melab, M. Mezmaz, and E. Talbi. Parallel cooperative meta-heuristics on the computational grid.: A case study: the bi-objective flow-shop problem. *Parallel computing*, 32(9):643–659, 2006.

[15] S. Mostaghim, J. Branke, A. Lewis, and H. Schmeck. Parallel multi-objective optimization using master-slave model on heterogeneous resources. In *Evolutionary Computation, 2008. CEC 2008.(IEEE World Congress on Computational Intelligence). IEEE Congress on*, pages 1981–1987. IEEE, 2008.

[16] M. Ruciński, D. Izzo, and F. Biscani. On the impact of the migration topology on the island model. *Parallel Computing*, 36(10):555–571, 2010.

[17] E. Talbi, S. Mostaghim, T. Okabe, H. Ishibuchi, G. Rudolph, and C. Coello Coello. Parallel approaches for multiobjective optimization. *Multiobjective Optimization*, pages 349–372, 2008.

[18] D. Vallado. *Fundamentals of astrodynamics and applications*, volume 12. Springer, 2001.

[19] M. Wong. Parallel multi-objective evolutionary algorithms on graphics processing units. In *Proceedings of the 11th Annual Conference Companion on Genetic and Evolutionary Computation Conference: Late Breaking Papers*, pages 2515–2522. ACM, 2009.

[20] N. Xiao and M. Armstrong. A specialized island model and its application in multiobjective optimization. In *Genetic and evolutionary computation GECCO 2003*, pages 213–213. Springer, 2003.

[21] E. Zitzler, K. Deb, and L. Thiele. Comparison of multiobjective evolutionary algorithms: Empirical results. *Evolutionary computation*, 8(2):173–195, 2000.

A Parallel Memetic Algorithm on GPU to Solve the Task Scheduling Problem in Heterogeneous Environments

Sayyed Ali Mirsoleimani
School of Electrical and Computer Engineering
Shiraz University
Shiraz, Iran
alimirsoleimani@gmail.com

Ali Karami
School of Electrical and Computer Engineering
Shiraz University
Shiraz, Iran
karami@cse.shirazu.ac.ir

Farshad Khunjush
Department of Electrical and Electronics Engineering
Hormozgan University
Bandar Abbas, Iran
School of Electrical and Computer Engineering
Shiraz University
Shiraz, Iran
khunjush@cse.shirazu.ac.ir

ABSTRACT

Hybrid metaheuristics have shown their capabilities to solve NP-hard problems. However, they exhibit significantly higher execution times in comparison to deterministic approaches. Parallel techniques are usually leveraged to overcome the execution time bottleneck for various metaheuristics. Recently, GPUs have emerged as general purpose parallel processors and have been harnessed to reduce the execution time of these algorithms. In this work, we propose a novel parallel memetic algorithm which is fully offloaded onto GPUs. In addition, we propose an adaptive sorting strategy in order to achieve maximum possible speedups for discrete optimization problems on GPUs. In order to show the efficacy of our algorithm, a task scheduling problem for heterogeneous environments is chosen as a case study. The output of this problem can have a tangible impact on overall performance of parallel heterogeneous platforms. The achieved results of our approach are promising and show up to 696x speedup in comparison to the sequential approach for various versions of this problem. Moreover, the effects of key parameters of memetic algorithms in terms of execution time and solution quality are investigated.

Categories and Subject Descriptors

G.1.0 [**Numerical Analysis**]: General—*Parallel algorithms*; F.2.2 [**Analysis OF Algorithms And Problem Complexity**]: Nonnumerical Algorithms and Problems—*Sequencing and scheduling*

General Terms

Algorithms

Keywords

Memetic algorithms, Task scheduling, GPU computing, Parallel algorithms

1. INTRODUCTION

Metaheuristic algorithms have been increasingly used to solve NP-hard problems. This is mainly because of the flexibility and effectiveness of these algorithms in comparison to heuristic methods. There are two main classes of metaheuristics: the trajectory and population-based classes. Trajectory methods only use a single solution to find the problem's answer while the population-based ones deal with a set of solutions in each iteration of the algorithm. Hybridization of these approaches has provided more powerful search techniques called *Memetic Algorithms* (MAs). The efficacy of hybrid algorithms has been demonstrated in many practical academic optimization problems [8]. These approaches usually deliver better solution qualities compared to heuristic methods. Nevertheless, their execution times remain limiting factors to using them in practical applications. One proper solution for tackling the execution time problem is to use parallel computing. Therefore, we have chosen the GPU architecture to propose a parallel memetic algorithm.

In order to evaluate the effectiveness of our parallel algorithm, a multiprocessor task scheduling problem is chosen as a case study. Given a set of tasks and a set of processors in a parallel computing system, the main objective of this problem is to map these tasks to the processors in such a way that the entire tasks complete at the earliest time. In general, there exist two types of task scheduling: *static* and *dynamic*[3]. In a static scheduling, a scheduler assigns tasks to available processors with prior knowledge of the tasks processing times, their precedence relationships, and their related communication costs. On the other hand, in a dynamic scheduling the states of the tasks are only known during the execution. In this paper, only the static scheduling problem is addressed.

The task scheduling problem remains to be NP-hard[17]. Several heuristic-based methods (e.g., Heterogeneous Earliest-Finish-Time (HEFT) [15] etc) have been proposed to solve this problem instantly. However, as these solutions lack high qualities, metaheuristic algorithms such as Ant Colony Optimization [16], Artificial Immune System [20], Genetic Algorithm (GA) [19], MA [18] and other evolutionary algorithms have been increasingly leveraged to reach high quality solutions, but the execution times of these methods remain challenging concerns in comparison to heuristic methods. The execution time of any algorithm to find an effective scheduling is an important efficiency metric, which means the one with a minimum running time could be the most practical implementation [15]. The proposed approach in this paper is mainly inspired by the fact that parallel MAs might find high quality solutions in a reasonable and practical time.

The main contribution of this paper is to propose a novel and efficient parallel MA on GPU architectures to solve a combinatorial optimization problem, that is, task scheduling. To the best of our knowledge, there is no any result in the literature regarding parallelizing the heterogeneous multiprocessors task scheduling problem on GPUs. The key features of our work include: first, running the whole search process of the MA on the GPU side; therefore, it does not require any computation on the CPU side. Thus, unnecessary data transfers between CPU and GPU are eliminated. Second, it speeds up the search process considering the existence of fast GPU's memories. Third, it proposes an efficient problem representation that is specially designed for the task scheduling problem. Finally, it introduces an adaptive sorting strategy based on population sizes in order to achieve higher speedups for small instances of the problem. The achieved results of our method are promising and reveal that higher quality solutions for the task scheduling problem could be reached in a reasonable amount of time as compared to deterministic methods.

The remainder of this paper is organized as follows. Section 2 surveys the literature. The task scheduling problem and its sequential hybrid evolutionary solution alongside GPU programming are provided in Section 3. Section 4 describes our proposed parallel method for accelerating MAs. The results are presented and discussed in Section 5. Finally, we conclude the paper in Section 6.

2. RELATED WORK

Nesmachnow et. al. [9] proposed GPU implementations of two heuristics for solving the scheduling of the independent tasks problem. Pinel et. al. [13] also proposed a parallel cellular genetic algorithm and a heuristic method for solving the same problem on GPUs. The selected problem and approaches of these two papers are different from our work.

Luong et. al. [6] proposed and implemented several schemes for island GA on GPUs. Although, they claimed considerable speedup in comparison to a single CPU implementation for continuous optimization problems, the proposed approaches could not be applicable for combinatorial optimization problems such as task scheduling due to shortage of shared memory space on GPUs. Luong et. al. [7] also proposed a cooperative CPU-GPU model to implement a hybrid genetic algorithm for solving uadratic Assignment Problem (AP). The major bottleneck in this model is the communication between the CPU and GPU, which degrades the performance of the algorithm. Kruger et. al. [5] implement a MA which is a combination of an evolutionary algorithm and a simple deterministic local search. They did not consider the efficiency of algorithm in finding the best solution. In this approach the evolutionary engine is kept on the CPU and the evaluation function and local search operations are transferred to the GPU for execution. However, to overcome the overhead of data transfers between the CPU and GPU large population sizes are required. On the contrary to these approaches, our proposed parallel MA is fully offloaded onto a GPU and as a result no inter-processor data transfer is necessary. Furthermore, we show that it is possible to reach orders of magnitude speedup even for small populations by using an efficient algorithm.

3. BACKGROUND

In this section we provide the required background on the problem description and GPU programming.

3.1 Problem Description

In this part, we provide a formal description of the static multiprocessor scheduling problem. In this problem, we are given m heterogeneous processors (j=1,...,m), which are fully connected through a network. Furthermore, a parallel program, decomposed into n smaller tasks with dependencies representing the precedence constraints (i=1,...,n), is also provided. These dependencies are usually shown by *Directed Acyclic Graphs* (DAGs), which we call them as *Task Precedence Graphs* (TPGs). A TPG consists of a set of nodes (V) as tasks and a set of edges (E) as the precedence constraints among the tasks. In this graph, the starting node of an edge is called *predecessor* and the ending node of the edge is called *successor*. The precedence constraints between two tasks mean that the result of the predecessor task must be transferred to the successor task before starting its execution. When two dependent tasks are assigned to two different processors, communication cost should be paid to transfer the required data from the predecessor to the successor task. The ultimate goal is to run tasks on available processors in parallel with focus on minimizing the *makespan*.

As we are dealing with heterogeneous systems, there are various types of processing elements with different computational capabilities. In our representation, the computation costs of tasks on processors are stored in a matrix called W. This matrix has dimensions of $n \times m$ and the value of W_{ij} represents the computation cost of task T_i on processor P_j. The weights associated with edges of the TPG are also stored in a communication cost matrix (C). The matrix C has dimensions of $n \times n$ and the value of C_{ij} is the communication cost between task T_i and task T_j. Consider an instance with n=10 tasks, and m=4 processors, computation costs are presented in Table 1, and a sample TPG, representing associated communication costs to its edges, is shown in Figure 1. A possible schedule is also illustrated in Figure 2.

In order to solve the task scheduling problem several attributes should be defined. First, the earliest time when a processor will be available for executing a new task is called *Earliest Start Time* (EST), which can be measured by (1).

$$\begin{aligned} EST(T_i, P_j) = max\{ &\max_{T_k \in run(P_j)} \{AFT(T_k)\}, \\ &\max_{T_l \in Pred(T_i)} \{AFT(T_l + C_{li})\}\} \end{aligned} \tag{1}$$

In the first step, the maximum of *Actual Finish Time* (AFT) for all tasks that have already been assigned to processor P_j ($run(P_j)$) is found. This value shows when processor P_j is available to execute a new task T_i. Next, in order to execute T_i on processor P_j, the maximum time needed for

Table 1: Computation cost matrix

	P_1	P_2	P_3	P_4
T_1	33	47	42	31
T_2	33	44	32	38
T_3	33	39	31	30
T_4	40	43	34	51
T_5	44	31	41	35
T_6	35	38	57	38
T_7	41	38	36	40
T_8	42	37	41	42
T_9	31	31	37	57
T_{10}	38	37	44	43

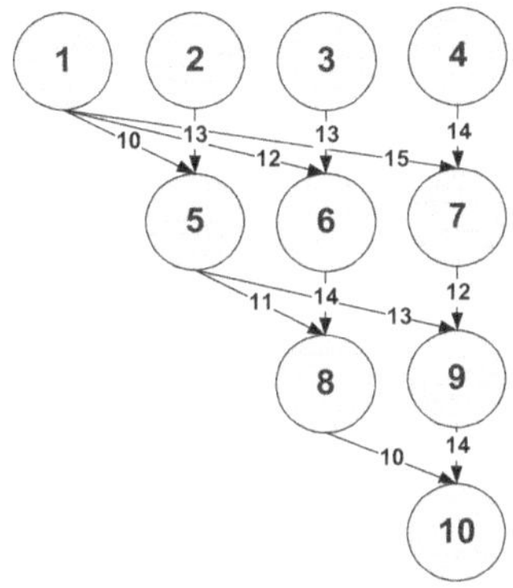

Figure 1: TPG graph

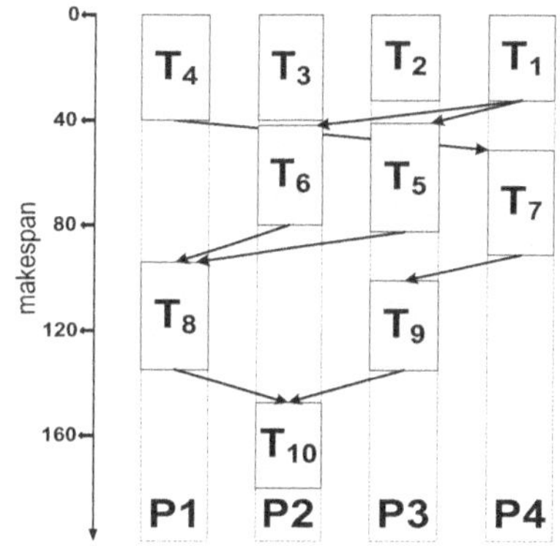

Figure 2: Sample schedule

transferring all required data from the predecessors of T_i to processor P_j is calculated. As mentioned before, this time is equal to 0 if both tasks are assigned to the same processor. *Earliest Finish Time* (EFT) of task T_i is equal to the time that the execution of task T_i on processor P_j is finished and is defined as follow:

$$EFT(T_i, P_j) = EST(T_i, P_j) + W_{ij} \tag{2}$$

When task T_i is explicitly allocated to processor P_j the EFT of all tasks are assigned to AFT. The *makespan* of the schedule is the largest AFT among all tasks and defined by (3).

$$makespan = \max_{T_i \in V} \{AFT(T_i)\} \tag{3}$$

In the next section, a sequential hybrid metaheuristic for solving the task scheduling problem will be briefly surveyed.

3.2 Sequential Algorithm

In order to evaluate our proposed parallel algorithm for MAs, a hybrid metaheuristic method proposed by Wen et. al. [18] for solving task scheduling problem is selected. This hybrid algorithm combines two metaheuristics: GA and VNS. GAs are population-based and stochastic search techniques in order to model the natural evolution. These algorithms are powerful in exploration of the search space, but their exploitation of found solutions are weak. In order to tackle this problem, a VNS metaheuristic is integrated with GA, which has a desirable exploitation feature. VNS is a single-point metaheuristic designed to search for an optimal point by swapping different neighborhood structures around a single solution.

This algorithm starts by initializing a population of randomly generated individuals. Each individual is an encoded version of a candidate schedule. Afterward, it generates new solutions by applying a crossover operator on selected individuals from the current generation as parents. Then, the mutation operator is applied on these newly created solutions with certain probabilities. To evaluate the completion time of each solution, the existing precedence constraints among scheduled tasks create challenges that should be addressed. Therefore, an upward-rank heuristic has been utilized to prioritize the assignments of tasks in TPG to processors [20]. The rank calculation of each task is defined as follow:

$$rank(T_i) = \begin{cases} W_{ij} & \text{if } succ(T_i) = \varnothing \\ W_{ij} + \max\limits_{T_k \in succ(T_i)} & \\ \{rc(T_i, T_k) + rank(T_k)\} & \text{if } succ(T_i) \neq \varnothing \end{cases} \tag{4}$$

where $succ(T_i)$ is a list containing the successors of task T_i, and $rc(T_i, T_k)$ represents the communication cost between task T_i and task T_k. If both tasks are scheduled on the same processor (P_j), this value is equal to 0; otherwise, it is equal to C_{ik}. In the evaluation function, in order to calculate the AFT of all tasks, the assignment order of each task to a processor in a schedule is chosen based on the rank of the task. Thereafter, the *makespan* of each solution is evaluated based on Sect 3.1 as its fitness value. After offspring production, only a subset of the population is selected for use by the VNS procedure because the VNS operation is time consuming . The size of this sub population is equal to the sampling rate parameter of the whole population. If an offspring's *makespan* is improved during the VNS process, it will be replaced. At the final stage, the algorithm combines the offspring with the current population, sorts them in an increasing order, and selects the first set of solutions, which are equal to the population size, to create the next population. This process continues until a desired termination criterion is satisfied.

3.3 GPU Programming

GPUs are processors with hundreds of processing cores which provide high throughput and high memory-bandwidth. The CUDA programming model [12] is developed by NVIDIA in order to run sequential programs on GPUs. The basic component of the CUDA programming model is a *thread*. A group of these basic elements creates a *Thread Block* (TB). Threads within the same TB can cooperate with each other to execute a piece of code on different data. There is a well-defined memory hierarchy in CUDA. Threads within a thread block can share data among themselves using a shared memory. TBs within a grid can also share data through a memory space called global memory. There are also data caches in the Fermi architecture to reduce the latency of accesses to the global memory [10]. In the following, we propose our parallel memetic algorithm based on the CUDA programming model, focusing both on design and implementation aspects.

4. PROPOSED PARALLEL ALGORITHM

The execution time of MAs is a challenging barrier to leveraging them in practical applications. As they have iterative identical operations on different individuals (that can be considered as different data), the realization of a parallel approach seems promising in achieving real-time solutions. In addition, the execution flow of these algorithms fits *Single Instruction Multiple Data* (SIMD) processors like GPUs, which are capable of executing the same instruction on different data.

Figure 3 illustrates the general scheme of the proposed parallel algorithm for MAs and the interactions between a CPU and a GPU. The main reasons for presenting this algorithm include: first, to accelerate the search process of MAs while having no adverse impact on the semantics of the algorithm itself; second, to take best advantage of these processors without becoming so bogged down in communication time between CPU and GPU by executing the whole process of evolution and local search on the GPU; third, to remove the restriction on the problem size; finally, to utilize efficiently the GPU's high-bandwidth memory subsystem and its computation power. As the heart of the selected MA is a GA, we describe the proposed parallel GA algorithm step by step in the following section. Afterward, the parallel VNS approach will be presented.

4.1 Parallel Genetic Algorithms

In a rough classification, parallel GAs can be classified into *master-slave*, *island*, and *cellular* models [4]. These models have different approaches in running GAs in order to accustom to different parallel executing platforms. We describe these models in the following.

The first model in this category is the master-slave model. The main objective of this approach concerns parallelizing the most time consuming operation, which is the evaluation of individuals. A master processor stores the population, executes the evolution engine, and divides the evaluation of individuals among several slave processors. However, the data transfer between CPU and GPU is the main bottleneck, which makes this model an unattractive choice. The second model is the island model in which a population is divided into multiple sub-populations (islands). The islands are evolved mostly isolated from each other and occasionally exchange individuals, which is called *migration*. This model is usually implemented on distributed systems. The main idea behind this model is to improve the search diversity along with the acceleration of the GA process. Nevertheless, the main bottleneck in front of porting this model to GPUs is the lack of sufficient shared memory for storing islands, especially in combinatorial optimization problems that need a large amount of memory [6]. Moreover, as local search is often used in MA to overcome the shortcoming of GA exploitation, improving the solution quality by applying this model seems to be unnecessary. The cellular model is the last parallel approach which considers a large number of small populations. Each of these small populations is assigned to a processor, and the crossover operator is restricted to use the neighborhood individuals. This model is a natural fit for massively parallel computers. However, this model is not naturally suitable to be used in the proposed parallel MA. To overcome the above-mentioned limitations as much as possible, a single population GA is selected to implement the proposed parallel algorithm. We have also decided to fully offload the GA operations onto the GPU side.

4.1.1 Problem Encoding

In this section, we elaborate the problem representation in our parallel algorithm. A solution is encoded in an array called *schedule list*. As shown in Figure 4 the cell index represents task number and its value determines the corresponding processor number. Along with this representation, all solutions in a population are also stored consecutively in the GPU's global memory, as shown in Figure 4. This strategy provides an efficient usage of the GPU's memory bandwidth through allowing coalesced accesses to the global memory. In coalesced accesses, consecutive memory blocks are fetched using one memory transaction. Furthermore, as the TPG is a sparse matrix, we propose a novel representation for storing TPG in the GPU's memory as efficiently as possible. In this encoding, the successors of all tasks are stored consecutively into the *successor array*. Then, the total number of successors of each task, equal to the out-degree of the task, is stored in *count array*. This allows retrieving the appropriate successors of a task. The same representation is used to store predecessors. Figure 4 shows this representation for TPG in Figure 1. This method enables storing large TPGs along with W and C matrices inside Fermi's small caches which consequently reduces the retrieval time of this read-only data.

4.1.2 Initialization

After allocating the required memory on the GPU and transferring the prerequisite data, a kernel initializes the population of the first generation. The *Generate Population* kernel is run with $PopSize \times Tasks$ number of threads. Each thread of a TB initializes one cell in a schedule list by assigning a randomly generated processor number to a task with a uniform distribution. A device RNG function from *curand* [11] library produces the required random numbers. This library provides the host and device sides with high quality random number generators.

4.1.3 Evaluation

Evaluation of candidate solutions is one of the most time consuming operations and requires to be parallelized. First, the *Task Priority* kernel calculating the ranks based on Section 3.2 is executed with *PopSize* number of threads. Here, each thread in a TB is responsible for calculation of all tasks in a schedule list, and precedence constraints among tasks avoids any further parallelism. As the rank calculation is a recursive operation, a kernel is implemented to find the ranks of the tasks of TPG in a bottom-up manner. Next, the *Evaluation* kernel is run with *PopSize* number of threads. A thread in a TB calculates the *makespan* of each solution of the population. This approach results in better GPU utilization by enlarging the population size.

4.1.4 Selection, Crossover and Mutation

In our implementation, genetic operators are also executed on the GPU to improve the performance by removing data transfers between the two processors (i.e., CPU and GPU). In addition, the *selection* and *crossover* operations could be integrated into a single GPU kernel. This integration decreases the overhead of costly global memory accesses because the selected solutions as parents are stored in the

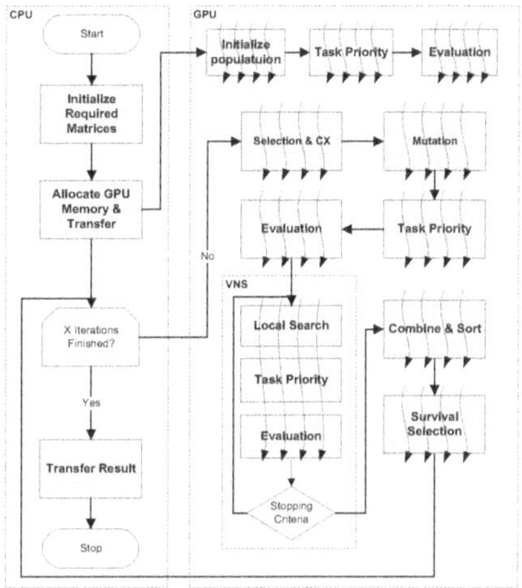

Figure 3: Parallel memetic algorithm

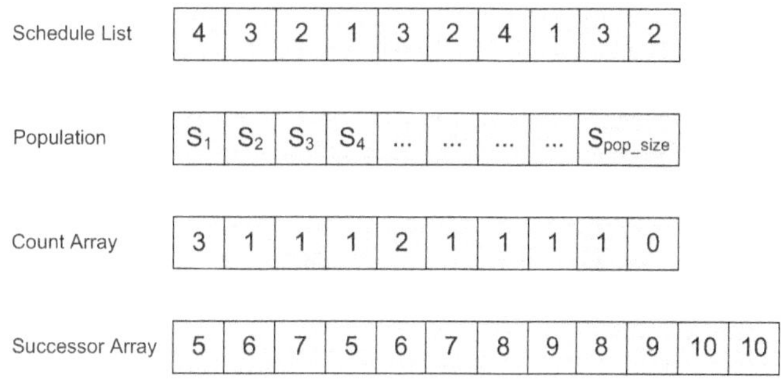

Figure 4: Problem representation for GPU

GPU's *shared memory*. The *Selection and CX* kernel is run with *PopSize* number of threads. Each thread in TB selects one parent from the population and copies it into the *shared memory*. Having selected all required parents, the thread selects two of them and applies crossover between them to generate a new solution. Finally, all the new generated solutions will be transferred into the global memory. After that, a mutation operator with a predefined probability (i.e., *mutation rate*) is applied on these solutions. The mutation operator assigns a random processor to a task. The expected number of mutations per solution is equal to the *mutation rate* multiplied by the *Tasks*. The *Mutation* kernel is run with *PopSize* number of threads. Each thread in a TB is responsible for applying the mutation operator on one solution. At this stage, the new solutions are ready for the next operation in the MA process which is VNS. This operation is explained in Section 4.2.

4.1.5 Survival Selection

The last stage of GA is the replacement of the current population with the new solutions. In this phase, the current population and new solutions are merged and sorted based on their *makespans*. For solving many discrete optimization problems small-size populations are sufficient; on the other hand, increasing the population size results in a better solution quality for complex ones. In our experiments, we have learned that the time elapsed in the sorting section, which is proportional to the population size, has a profound impact on the whole execution time of the parallel algorithm. Therefore, the selection of an efficient GPU-based sorting algorithm is vital to improve the execution time. Consequently, we use an adaptive sorting strategy to choose sorting mechanism based on the input population size. In this strategy, a single-TB bitonic sort algorithm is selected when the population size is less than a specific threshold, which is half of the TB size. Moreover, a multi-TB merge sort algorithm is leveraged to address the large populations. This adaptive approach makes it possible to achieve noticeable speedups even for small-size populations.

4.2 Parallel Variable Neighborhood Search

One of the most time consuming sections of the hybrid algorithm is VNS which makes the parallel execution of this part important to reaching a high performance algorithm. The kernel's algorithm is shown in Algorithm 1. The *VNS* kernel is run with *PopSize * sampling rate* number of threads. The *sampling rate* parameter is a criterion for selecting candidate solutions for the VNS operation. As shown in Algorithm 1, the VNS kernel has a complex control flow; therefore, this kernel is run by many TBs that each of them has few number of threads. As a result of this approach, we reduced adverse effects of thread divergence which decreases the performance of the parallel algorithms on GPUs. In the *VNS* kernel a set of neighborhood structures is chosen in the initialization step. Here, we have two neighborhood structures. Then, a certain number of solutions from the newly generated ones in the global memory are randomly selected and transferred to the *shared memory*, and the index of the neighborhood structure (k) is set. Each thread in a TB executes four device kernels: *Shaking*, *Local Search*, *Task Priority*, and *Evaluation*. These kernels are executed iteratively on the GPU for a single solution which is resided in the *shared memory* until a termination condition is met. This explains why we call this approach *massively parallel VNS* (MPVNS). In the *Shaking* device kernel, a new solution x' is randomly generated based on the selected neighborhood of the x solution. In literature, different strategies exist for neighborhood structures of the task scheduling problem, from fully randomized [2] to problem-specific [18]. We use two neighborhood structures which are proposed in [18]. One of the neighborhood structures is used to improve the load balancing of processors. First, the computational load of each processor should be calculated:

$$comp(P_j) = \sum_{T_i \in run(P_j)} W_{ij} \tag{5}$$

where $run(P_j)$ denotes the set of tasks that have been scheduled on processor P_j. Afterward, the processor with maximum computational load is found ($P_{maxcomp}$). Then, a task is selected randomly from the solution x' which is scheduled on this processor. Finally, the task is assigned to a new randomly generated processor number other than $P_{maxcomp}$. The goal of the second neighborhood structure is to reduce communication costs. First, the communication costs for all

Algorithm 1 Massively Parallel Variable Neighborhood Search (MPVNS)

```
Select a set of neighborhood structures N_k, for k = 1,...,k_max
Move solutions from global memory to shared memory, do (x ← x_global)
for all threads in a thread block do
    repeat
        function SHAKING(x',x,k) Generate a solution x' at random from the k^th neighborhood of x
        end function
        function LOCAL SEARCH(x'',x',k) Apply local search method with x' as initial point; denote x" the so obtained local optimum
        end function
        function TASK PRIORITY(x'') Apply upward-ranking heuristic on x'' solution.
        end function
        function EVALUATION(x'') Calculate the makespan of the x'' solution.
        end function
        if x" makespan is less than x makespan then
            x ← x"
            k ← 1
        else
            k ← k + 1
        end if
    until k ≤ k_max
end for
x_global ← x
```

processors are calculated as follow:

$$comm(P_j) = \max_{T_i \in run(P_j)} AFT(T_i) - comp(P_j) \quad (6)$$

where the $AFT(T_i)$ denotes when the task T_i actually finishes its execution on processor P_j. After that, a processor with a maximum communication cost is selected ($P_{maxcomm}$). Then, the predecessors of all assigned tasks on this processor ($T_i \in run(P_j)$ which are scheduled on other processors are found. Finally, a task randomly is chosen from this predecessors set and assigned to the $P_{maxcomm}$ processor.

The *Local Search* device kernel starts to proceed by using solution $x^{'}$ as its starting point and generating a new solution $x^{''}$. This solution is used by *Task Priority* and *Evaluation* device kernels in order to calculate its *makespan*. Finally, if the *makespan* of solution $x^{"}$ is less than that of x, it replaces x in *shared memory* and the algorithm continues with current neighborhood structure. Otherwise, k is incremented by one for using the next neighborhood structure. Due to existing dependencies between consequent phases of VNS there are no more rooms for extra parallelisms. However, this approach will be efficient on GPUs because of using the *shared memory* for storing solutions, intermediate results, and caches for prerequisite data such as W and C matrices. The final solution and its *makespan* will be stored back to the global memory for next operations.

5. EXPERIMENTAL WORK

In this section, we present a comparative evaluation between sequential and parallel versions of GVNS execution times. To show the effectiveness of our parallel algorithm, Gauss-Jordan elimination (GJ) with 15 and 21 tasks, Fast Fourier Transformation (FFT) with 15 tasks, and Laplace equation solver (L) with 16 and 36 tasks are chosen as the benchmarks [18]. Figure 1 shows a TPG of GJ as a well-known parallel application for 10 tasks. We randomly generate 10 computation cost matrices for each benchmark graph. The values of matrix entries are driven by Poisson distribution with an average computation time of 40 [20]. The value of all required parameters is shown in Table 2. The communication to computation ratio (CCR) is set to 0.25 for all tests, and the data transfer time between dependent tasks on different processors are the same, which is equal to $40 * 0.25 = 10$ in our experiments. The sequential algorithm has been executed on a system which is equipped by an Intel Xeon processor with 8 cores and 8 GBs of RAM. The GPU card used in our experiments is a GTX480 with 480 CUDA cores.

Table 2: Parameters

Parameter Name	Value
Generations Count	100
Population Size (PopSize)	128-8192
Crossover Rate	1
Mutation Rate	0.1
Sampling Rate	0.1
TPG Kind	GJ,FFT,L
Tasks	(21,45)(15)(16,36)
Processors Count	8

5.1 Performance Evaluation Metrics

The metrics to measure performance of parallel metaheuristics involve both computational effort and solution quality. The first and the most important metric is the *relative computational speedup* ($speedup_c$). The relative speedup is the ratio of serial execution time (T_s) to parallel execution time (T_p) of a program [1]. We have tried to satisfy two conditions in order to make fair comparisons: first, the serial code should be the most efficient one; second, the parallel time should include any overhead such as data transfers since the objective of parallelism is to reduce the real time of execution. As the execution times of non-deterministic algorithms vary for different runs, the average of execution times of 50 runs for each of 10 different configurations are considered as the expected execution time of the algorithm. The relative computational speedup is defined as follow:

$$speedup_c = \frac{E[T_s]}{E[T_p]} \quad (7)$$

After measuring the efficiency of our approach; the last important metric to evaluate is the quality of the obtained solutions. As explained, the goal of the algorithm is to find a schedule of tasks that its parallel execution time ($makespan_p$) is less than the serial execution time of all tasks' ($makespan_s$). By serial execution we mean to execute all tasks on a single processor instead of multiple processors. The ratio of these two values is the quality metric of the algorithm and is denoted by $speedup_q$:

$$speedup_q = \frac{makespan_s}{makespan_p} \quad (8)$$

As the optimum $makespan_p$ is unknown, the mean of the *makespans* of the best solutions over all predefined number of algorithm runs is measured. The $makespan_s$ is also computed as:

$$makespan_s = \min_{P_j \in P} \left\{ \sum_{T_i \in V} W_{ij} \right\} \quad (9)$$

In the context of discrete optimization, the overall goal is not full GPU utilization but to develop powerful parallel algorithms to find better solutions in a shorter time [14]. As the scheduling problem is a combinatorial optimization problem, the $speedup_q$ is increasing until the algorithm reaches a convergence point and after that no further improvement is observed and higher GPU utilization is not useful. Therefore, it would not be fair to report the $speedup_c$ of the parallel algorithm below and above of this certain point. Hence, we define *effective* $speedup_c$ as the measured computational speedup when the algorithm achieves the maximum $speedup_q$ for the first time with no further improvement after that.

5.2 Results and Discussion

In this part, we provide our experimental results for the sequential and parallel implementations. For the sequential algorithm, as we expect the increase in number of iterations results in better solution qualities but causes longer execution times as illustrated in Figure 5(a). Therefore, finding a solution with less number of iterations with a reasonable quality is a desirable goal. However, enlarging population size provides the same or better quality solutions while keeping a small number of iterations with much less execution time, as shown in Figure 5(b). Therefore, we choose the latter paradigm to achieve better qualities for 100 iterations in our parallel experiments.

As shown in Table 3, increasing the population size improves the solution quality of the algorithm. The maximum $speedup_c$ for GJ-21, GJ-45, FFT-15, L-16, and L-36 are 343, 696, 254, 272, and 568 respectively for population size of 512. However, this speedup may not be the *effective* $speedup_c$ of the parallel algorithm. Hence, we continue the execution of the algorithm by enlarging the population size in order to achieve the maximum $speedup_q$. As explained earlier, we have employed a multi-TB merge sort algorithm when the population size is more than 512. By changing the sorting algorithm the $speedup_c$ of the algorithm suddenly falls to much lower values, as shown in Table 3. However, when the population size becomes sufficiently large the overhead of sorting algorithm is amortized and large computational speedups are observed. The *effective* $speedup_c$ for GJ-21, GJ-45, FFT-15, L-16, and L-36 are 181, 40, 220, 13, and 42 for population sizes of 8192, 8192, 8192, 1024, and 4096 respectively. It is obvious that the *effective* $speedup_c$ depends on the problem size and complexity.

Table 3 shows speedups of 568 for L-36 and 696 for GJ-45 in population size of 512. The reason for this superlinear speedup is the fact that sequential algorithm requires more memory access in comparison to parallel one. As mentioned, we use a single-TB bitonic sort to remove memory accesses to global memory for population sizes of less than 1024. By increasing the size of the population more memory accesses are required; therefore, the execution times of the sequential algorithms increase while the execution times of the parallel implementations remain unchanged due to usage of single-TB sort.

Table 3: The average execution time and solution quality for parallel and sequential algorithms on different benchmarks for various population sizes.

TPG	*Pop.*	Avg. Time (Sec.) *Par.*	*Seq.*	$Speedup_q$	$Speedup_c$
GJ-21	128	0.003	0.183	3.30	61
	256	0.003	0.415	3.35	138
	512	0.003	1.028	3.38	343
	1024	0.238	2.832	3.39	12
	2048	0.289	8.758	3.39	30
	4096	0.384	29.899	3.39	78
	8192	0.603	109.268	3.40	181
GJ-45	128	0.003	0.447	4.32	149
	256	0.003	0.948	4.40	316
	512	0.003	2.088	4.47	696
	1024	0.798	4.993	4.53	6
	2048	0.945	13.243	4.58	14
	4096	1.183	39.558	4.61	33
	8192	3.247	131.446	4.64	40
FFT-15	128	0.003	0.118	2.77	39
	256	0.003	0.287	2.78	96
	512	0.003	0.763	2.79	254
	1024	0.166	2.268	2.80	14
	2048	0.209	7.539	2.80	36
	4096	0.286	27.059	2.80	95
	8192	0.464	102.022	2.81	220
L-16	128	0.003	0.131	2.20	44
	256	0.003	0.306	2.20	102
	512	0.003	0.815	2.20	272
	1024	0.178	2.379	2.21	13
	2048	0.226	7.763	2.21	34
	4096	0.307	27.49	2.21	90
	8192	0.495	102.879	2.21	208
L-36	128	0.003	0.335	3.03	110
	256	0.003	0.728	3.05	233
	512	0.003	1.646	3.08	568
	1024	0.564	4.089	3.09	7
	2048	0.673	11.444	3.10	17
	4096	0.844	35.85	3.12	42
	8192	1.883	123.422	3.12	66

Sampling rate is one of the most important parameters in the VNS algorithm. For example, higher sample rates are appropriate for complex search spaces to reach better solution quality. On the other hand, higher sample rates increase the execution time dramatically [18]. However, as shown in Figure 5(c), increasing sampling rate for improving the solution quality has a minimum impact on the execution time of the proposed algorithm because our parallel algorithm is highly scalable with regards to population size.

6. CONCLUSION

In this work, a parallel memetic algorithm has been proposed and implemented on GPUs. The proposed algorithm has been used to solve a task scheduling problem for heterogeneous multiprocessor systems as a case study. Furthermore, an especial encoding method has been designed for this case study to utilize the GPU's memory efficiently. In addition, we have shown that different sorting strategies

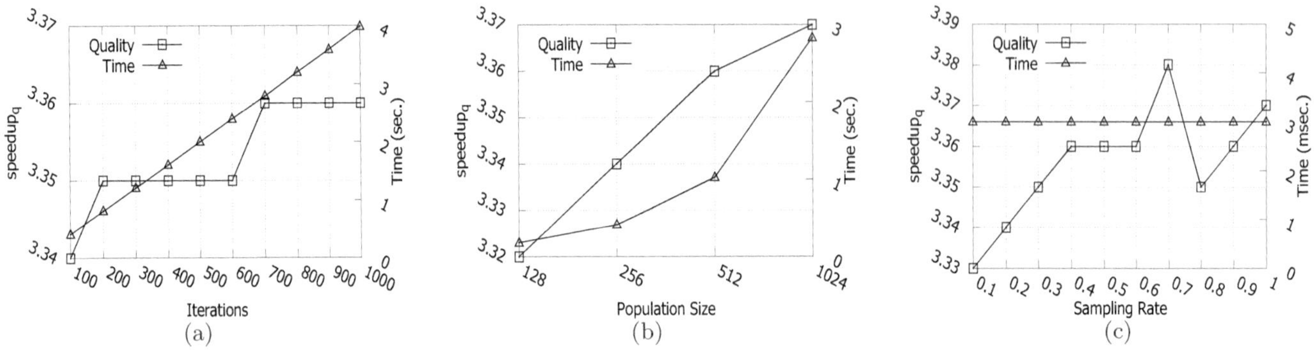

Figure 5: The effect of parameters on time and quality for GJ-21 : (a)different iterations for population of 256 individuals; (b)various population sizes for 100 iterations; (c)different sampling rates in parallel algorithm for population of 256 individuals

could be beneficial in terms of running times for various population sizes. As a result, an adaptive sorting policy has been proposed in our parallel algorithm. By using this method, we have achieved up to 696 computational speedup even for small populations. In the future, we plan to extend this algorithm into a general framework that can be leveraged by users in parallelizing different kinds of hybrid metaheuristics on GPUs with minimum effort.

6.1 Acknowledgments

The authors would like to thank Ali Hamze for his helpful comments on this work. This work was supported in part by Institute for Research in Fundamental Sciences (IPM) under grant number CS1391-4-03.

7. REFERENCES

[1] R. S. Barr and B. L. Hickman. Reporting Computational Experiments with Parallel Algorithms: Issues, Measures, and Experts' Opinions. *INFORMS Journal on Computing*, 5(1):2–18, Jan. 1993.

[2] T. Davidovic, P. Hansen, and N. Mladenovic. Permutation-based Genetic, Tabu and Variable Neighborhood Search Heuristics for Multiprocessor Scheduling with Communication Delays. *Asia-Pacific Journal of Operational Research*, 22(03):297–326, 2005.

[3] H. El-Rewini, T. G. Lewis, and H. H. Ali. *Task Scheduling in Parallel and Distributed Systems.* Prentice Hall, 1994.

[4] R. L. Haupt and S. E. Haupt. *Practical Genetic Algorithms.* John Wiley & Sons, 2 edition, 2004.

[5] F. Krüger, O. Maitre, S. Jiménez, L. Baumes, and P. Collet. *Applications of Evolutionary Computation*, volume 6024 of *Lecture Notes in Computer Science.* Springer Berlin Heidelberg, Berlin, Heidelberg, Apr. 2010.

[6] T. V. Luong, N. Melab, and E.-G. Talbi. GPU-based island model for evolutionary algorithms. In *GECCO'10*, page 1089, New York, New York, USA, 2010. ACM Press.

[7] T. V. Luong, N. Melab, and E.-G. Talbi. Parallel hybrid evolutionary algorithms on GPU. In *IEEE CEC*, pages 18–23. IEEE, 2010.

[8] F. Neri, C. Cotta, and P. E. Moscato. *Handbook of Memetic Algorithms, Studies in Computational Intelligence, Vol. 379.* Springer, 2011.

[9] S. Nesmachnow and M. Canabé. GPU implementations of scheduling heuristics for heterogeneous computing environments. In *Proceedings of the XVII Congreso Argentino de Ciencias de la Computación,*, pages 1563–1570, 2011.

[10] NVIDA. Whitepaper NVIDIA's Next Generation CUDA Compute Architecture: Fermi, 2009.

[11] NVIDIA. CUDA Toolkit 4 . 1 CURAND Guide, 2012.

[12] NVIDIA. NVIDIA CUDA C Programming Guide, 2012.

[13] F. Pinel, B. Dorronsoro, and P. Bouvry. Solving very large instances of the scheduling of independent tasks problem on the GPU. *J. Parallel Distrib. Comput.*, 73(1):101–110, Jan. 2013.

[14] C. Schulz. Efficient local search on the GPU - Investigations on the vehicle routing problem. *J. Parallel Distrib. Comput.*, 73(1):14–31, 2013.

[15] H. Topcuoglu, S. Hariri, and M.-Y. W. M.-Y. Wu. Performance-effective and low-complexity task scheduling for heterogeneous computing. *IEEE Transactions on Parallel and Distributed Systems*, 13(3):260–274, 2002.

[16] A. Tumeo, C. Pilato, F. Ferrandi, D. Sciuto, and P. L. Lanzi. Ant colony optimization for mapping and scheduling in heterogeneous multiprocessor systems. In *2008 International Conference on Embedded Computer Systems: Architectures, Modeling, and Simulation*, pages 142–149. IEEE, July 2008.

[17] J. D. Ullman. NP-complete scheduling problems. *Journal of Computer and System Sciences*, 10(3):384–393, 1975.

[18] Y. Wen, H. Xu, and J. Yang. A heuristic-based hybrid genetic-variable neighborhood search algorithm for task scheduling in heterogeneous multiprocessor system. *Information Sciences*, 181(3):567–581, 2011.

[19] A. S. Wu, H. Yu, S. Jin, K. C. Lin, and G. Schiavone. An incremental genetic algorithm approach to multiprocessor scheduling. *IEEE Transactions on Parallel and Distributed Systems*, 15(9):824–834, 2004.

[20] H. Yu. Optimizing task schedules using an artificial immune system approach. In *GECCO'08*, page 151. ACM Press, 2008.

ParadisEO-MO-GPU: a Framework for Parallel GPU-based Local Search Metaheuristics

Nouredine Melab
Inria Lille, CNRS-LIFL
Université Lille 1
Villeneuve d'Ascq - France
Nouredine.Melab@lifl.fr

Thé Van Luong
HEIG-VD
Yverdon-les-Bains
Switzerland
the-van.luong@heig-vd.ch

Karima Boufaras
Inria Lille, CNRS-LIFL
Université Lille 1
Villeneuve d'Ascq - France
boufaras.karima@gmail.com

El-Ghazali Talbi
Inria Lille, CNRS-LIFL
Université Lille 1
Villeneuve d'Ascq - France
El-Ghazali.Talbi@lifl.fr

ABSTRACT

In this paper, we propose a pioneering framework called ParadisEO-MO-GPU for the reusable design and implementation of parallel local search metaheuristics (S-Metaheuristics) on Graphics Processing Units (GPU). We revisit the ParadisEO-MO software framework to allow its utilization on GPU accelerators focusing on the parallel iteration-level model, the major parallel model for S-Metaheuristics. It consists in the parallel exploration of the neighborhood of a problem solution. The challenge is on the one hand to rethink the design and implementation of this model optimizing the data transfer between the CPU and the GPU. On the other hand, the objective is to make the GPU as transparent as possible for the user minimizing his or her involvement in its management. In this paper, we propose solutions to this challenge as an extension of the ParadisEO framework. The first release of the new GPU-based ParadisEO framework has been experimented on the permuted perceptron problem. The preliminary results are convincing, both in terms of flexibility and easiness of reuse at implementation, and in terms of efficiency at execution on GPU.

Categories and Subject Descriptors

D.2.13 [**Software Engineering**]: Reusable Software

Keywords

Local search, Metaheuristics, Parallel computing, GPU

1. INTRODUCTION

In practice, combinatorial optimization problems become more and more CPU time consuming and their modeling is continuously evolving. Therefore, there is a clear need to a software framework providing efficient parallel near-optimal optimization methods to solve large size problems. Using near-optimal search methods such as metaheuristics is a popular and efficient approach to deal with the highly combinatorial nature of industrial problems. Even if metaheuristics allow to significantly reduce the size of the search space of large problem instances, the search time remains prohibitive.

Massively parallel computing, based for instance on GPU accelerators, is required. Using a software framework is on the one hand a flexible way to deal with the evolution of modeling minimizing the design and implementation effort [3, 10]. On the other hand, it is an efficient mean to provide a transparent access to parallelism.

Metaheuristics are either single-solution namely S-Metaheuristics (e.g. local search methods) or population-based namely P-Metaheuristics (e.g. evolutionary algorithms). The focus in this paper is on S-Metaheuristics. During these two last decades, different parallel approaches and implementations have been proposed for S-Metaheuristics using Massively Parallel Processors [4], Networks or Clusters of Workstations [5] and Shared Memory or SMP machines [6]. These contributions have been later revisited for large-scale computational grids [15].

Recently, GPU accelerators have emerged as a new powerful support for massively parallel computing. A pioneering work on GPU-based S-Metaheuristics [8] has been proposed. Such experience has shown that parallel combinatorial optimization on GPU is not straightforward and requires a huge effort at design as well as at implementation level. The design of GPU-aware S-Metaheuristics often involves the cost of a sometimes painful apprenticeship of parallelization techniques and GPU computing technologies. In order to free from such burden those who are unfamiliar with those advanced features, optimization frameworks must integrate the up-to-date parallelization techniques and allow their transparent exploitation and accelerators. There exist some frameworks for the reusable design and implementation of S-Metaheuristics. However, these frameworks are often dedicated to a specific method [2] and are rarely parallel.

To the best of our knowledge, there does not exist any software framework for GPU-based S-Metaheuristics. In [3], the authors have proposed a framework called ParadisEO dedicated to the reusable design of parallel and distributed metaheuristics for only dedicated parallel hardware platforms. Later, they have extended the framework in [10] to dynamic and heterogeneous large-scale environments using Condor-MW middleware and in [14] to computational grids using Globus.

In this paper, we extend ParadisEO-MO[1] (ParadisEO for S-Metaheuristics) to deal with GPU accelerators. The challenges and contributions consist in (1) rethinking the parallel models provided into the framework to manage efficiently the hierarchical organization of the memories (different latencies and sizes) of the GPU device as well as the interaction of this latter with the CPU ; (2) making the GPU as transparent as possible for the user minimizing his or her involvement in its management. In this paper, we propose solutions to these challenges as an extension of the ParadisEO framework.

The focus is on the iteration-level parallel model of S-Metaheuristics which consists in exploring in parallel the neighborhood of a problem solution. The first release of the new GPU-based ParadisEO framework has been implemented using C++ and CUDA [11] and then experimented on the permuted perceptron problem (PPP). The preliminary results are convincing, both in terms of flexibility and easiness of reuse at implementation, and in terms of efficiency at execution on GPU.

The remainder of the paper is organized as follows. Section 2 highlights the principles of parallel iteration-level S-Metaheuristics and their challenges when using GPU computing. In Section 3, we first describe the major design features and architecture of ParadisEO. We then present the design and implementation of ParadisEO-MO on top of GPU called ParadisEO-MO-GPU. Section 4 shows and comments some experimental results obtained with ParadisEO-MO-GPU on the PPP. In Section 5, we conclude the paper and draw some perspectives of the presented work.

2. PARALLEL GPU-BASED S-METAHEURISTICS

In this section, we first present the principles of S-Metaheuristics and their associated parallel models focusing on the parallel exploration of the neighborhood. After that, we present the challenging issues to be dealt with for the GPU-acceleration of this latter.

2.1 Principles of S-Metaheuristics

S-Metaheuristics could be viewed as "walks through neighborhoods" meaning search trajectories through the exploration space of the problem being solved. Starting from an initial solution, the "walks" are performed by an iterative procedure (see Algorithm 1) that improves the current solution until a stopping criterion is met.

Algorithm 1 Local search pseudo-code

Generate(s_0);
Specific LS pre-treatment
$t := 0$;
repeat
  $m(t) :=$ SelectMove($s(t)$);
  $s_{t+1} :=$ ApplyMove($m(t), s(t)$);
  Specific LS post-treatment
  $t := t + 1$;
until Termination_criterion($s(t)$)

At each iteration of the procedure, the neighborhood of the current solution is generated and evaluated. The evaluation of solutions is performed using a cost function. This latter associates a fitness value to each solution indicating its suitability to the problem. Based on the evaluation of the neighborhood, the best solution is selected to become the current solution. The process is repeated until a stopping criterion is found. This criterion could be a fixed number of iterations or a convergence criterion.

The design of an efficient and effective S-Metaheuristic requires the definition of at least a solution representation or encoding scheme, a cost function, a neighborhood model and the iterative procedure. According to the problem to be solved, three major solution encodings may be used: binary encoding (e.g. Knapsack, SAT), vector of discrete values (e.g. location problem, assignment problem) and permutation (e.g. TSP, scheduling problems). The cost function allows to evaluate the quality of the visited solutions. The neighborhood model determines the regions of the search space to be visited during the exploration. The iterative procedures (see Algorithm 1) have a common generic part but they have some specific (pre and post-treatment) features.

For instance, for the Tabu Search S-Metaheuristic (implemented and experimented in this work) [13] a specific list called *tabu list* is used. In Tabu Search, the best solution in the neighborhood is selected as the new current solution even if it is not improving the current solution. This policy may generate cycles, i.e. previous visited solutions could be selected again. To avoid these cycles, the algorithm maintains a short-term memory (tabu list) of the moves (solutions) recently applied (visited). In Algorithm 1, the specific pre-treatment consists in initializing the tabu list and post-treatment is an update of the tabu list with the most recently visited solutions.

2.2 Parallelism of S-Metaheuristics

Solving efficiently large size problems using S-Metaheuristics requires the use of parallel computing. Three major parallel models can be used separately or together in a hierarchical way: *algorithmic-level model*, *iteration-level model* or *solution-level model*. The first model consists in deploying and executing in parallel several S-Metaheuristics in a (non-)cooperative way with the objective to improve the robustness and effectiveness of the exploration. The iteration-level model consists in generating and/or evaluating the neighborhood in parallel at each iteration of the algorithm. The third model is based on the parallel evaluation of the cost function. Unlike the two first models, the solution-level model is

[1]ParadisEO-MO (http://paradiseo.gforge.inria.fr) is an open source framework originally intended to the design and deployment of parallel hybrid local search metaheuristics on dedicated clusters and networks of workstations, shared-memory machines and computational grids.

problem-dependent. It is exploited when the cost function is CPU-time intensive and can be parallelized.

The iteration-level model, addressed in this paper, is a low-level Master-Worker model that does not alter the behavior of the heuristic. At the beginning of each iteration, the master generates the neighborhood of the current solution. Each worker receives from the master a set of neighbors (partition of the neighborhood). These neighbors are evaluated and returned back to the master. The neighbors can also be generated by the workers. In this case, each worker receives a copy of the current solution, generates one or several neighbor(s) to be evaluated and returned back to the master. A challenge of this model is to determine the granularity of each partition of neighbors to be allocated to each worker according to the communication delays of the network. In terms of genericity, as the model is problem-independent, it is generic and reusable.

2.3 GPU-accelerated S-Metaheuristics

For large-scale combinatorial optimization problems, the neighborhood of a solution is often extremely large. Therefore, massively parallel computing is required to generate and evaluate it. The parallel generation and evaluation of the neighborhood is a master-worker and problem independent regular data-parallel application. GPU computing is very well-suited for this kind of parallel application. In the GPU (e.g. CUDA-based) model, the master is the CPU and the workers are threads executed by the processing cores of the GPU. Using GPU computing is not straightforward especially for non-experts in parallel computing. Indeed, a GPU accelerator provides a hierarchy of memories with different sizes and access latencies. Exploiting efficiently such a hierarchy is particularly challenging in terms of data management and thread control.

The challenge is to re-think the design of the parallel exploration and evaluation of the neighborhood taking into account the GPU characteristics. Different issues have to be dealt with: (1) defining an efficient cooperation between CPU and GPU, which requires to share the work and to optimize the data transfer between the two devices; (2) GPU computing is based on hyper-threading (massively parallel multi-threading) and the order in which the threads are executed is not known. Therefore, an efficient mapping has to be defined between each neighboring candidate solution and a thread designated by a unique identifier assigned by the GPU runtime; (3) the neighborhood has to be placed efficiently on the different memories taking into account their sizes and access latencies.

In [8], the authors have proposed the design and the implementation of the parallel evaluation of the neighborhood model on GPU. The implementation of the proposed approaches has been performed outside our ParadisEO framework. From an implementation point of view, the challenge is to provide solutions to these issues in ParadisEO in a way as transparent as possible for the user.

The parallel iteration-level model is designed according to the data-parallel single program multiple data model of CUDA. In this model, a function code called kernel is sent to the GPU to be executed by a large number of threads grouped into blocks. As illustrated in Figure 1, the CPU-GPU task partitioning is such that the CPU hosts and executes the whole serial part of the local search method. The GPU is in charge of the evaluation of the neighborhood of

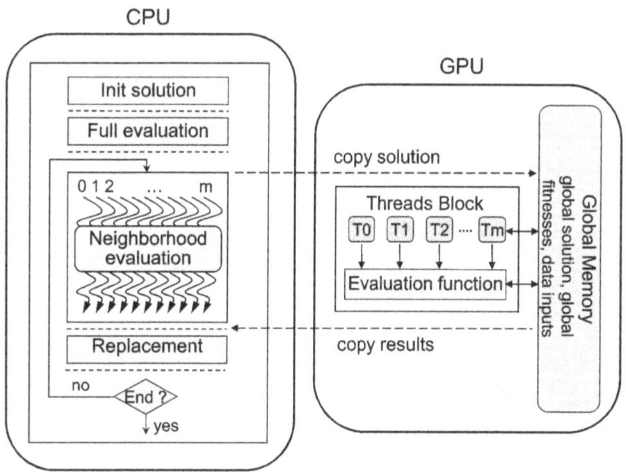

Figure 1: Parallel evaluation of the neighborhood on GPU (iteration-level). In this scheme, one thread is associated with one neighboring solution.

the current solution at each iteration. In order to minimize the cost of the data transfer from the CPU to GPU, the neighboring solutions are generated on GPU rather than on CPU. Indeed, only the current solution is sent to the GPU and each thread executes the same kernel. This is highly efficient for large neighborhoods.

The kernel consists in generating and evaluating a neighbor. A mapping function is required to allow each thread to find its corresponding (set of) neighboring solution(s). In [8], the mapping function is user-defined. In this work, we propose inside ParadisEO-MO an automatic mapping mechanism which can be exploited in a transparent way by the user application. Once all the neighboring solutions are generated and evaluated on GPU they are sent back to the CPU where the best solution is selected. The process is iterated until a stopping criterion is satisfied.

3. GPU-ENABLED PARADISEO

3.1 The ParadisEO-MO framework

ParadisEO-MO is part of ParadisEO dedicated to S-Metaheuristics such as Hill Climbing, Simulated Annealing, Tabu Search, Iterated Local Search, etc. ParadisEO [3] is a framework dedicated to the reusable design of parallel hybrid metaheuristics by providing a broad range of features including evolutionary algorithms (ParadisEO-EO), local search heuristics (ParadisEO-MO), parallel and distributed models (ParadisEO-PEO), different hybridization mechanisms, etc.

ParadisEO is a C++ LGPL extensible open source framework based on a clear conceptual separation of the metaheuristics from the problems they are intended to solve. ParadisEO is one of the rare frameworks that provide the most common parallel and distributed models. These models are portable on distributed-memory machines and shared-memory multi-processors as they are implemented using standard libraries such as MPI and Pthreads. The models can be exploited in a transparent way. One has just to instantiate their associated ParadisEO components.

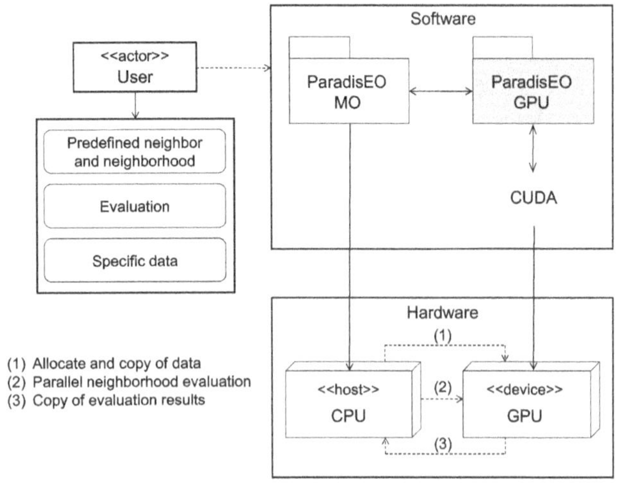

Figure 2: A layered architecture of ParadisEO-MO-GPU.

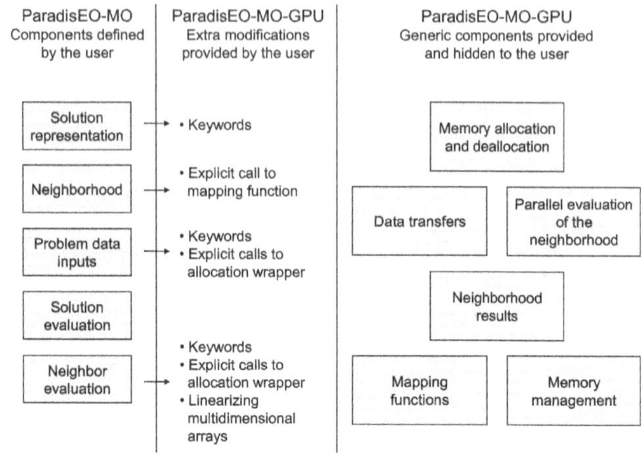

Figure 3: The major components of ParadisEO-MO-GPU

3.2 Architecture of ParadisEO-MO-GPU

ParadisEO-MO-GPU is a framework which is a coupling between ParadisEO-MO and CUDA for the design and implementation of reusable S-Metaheuristics on GPU. It is composed by a set of new C++ abstract and predefined classes that enables an easy and transparent development of S-Metaheuristics on GPU accelerators. The architecture of ParadisEO-MO-GPU is layered as illustrated in Figure 2.

The user layer indicates the different problem-dependent components that must be defined: input data, the evaluation function, neighbor and neighborhood representations. The software layer supplies the ParadisEO-MO components including optimization solvers embedding S-Metaheuristics. The ParadisEO-GPU module provides a CUDA interface allowing the transparent interaction with the hardware layer. The hardware layer supplies the different transparent tools provided by ParadisEO-GPU such as the allocation and copy of data or the parallel generation and evaluation of the considered neighborhood. In addition, the platform offers predefined neighborhood and mapping wrappers adapted to hardware characteristics to deal with binary and permutation problems.

The layered architecture of ParadisEO-MO-GPU has been designed in such a way that the user does not need to build his or her own CUDA code for the specific problem to be solved. Indeed, ParadisEO-GPU provides facilities for automatic execution of S-Metaheuristics on GPU. The only thing that must be user-managed is the different components described in the user level quoted above.

3.3 ParadisEO-MO-GPU Components

Figure 3 illustrates the major components of the platform. The advantage of the decomposition into components is to separate the components that must be defined by the user and those which are generic and provided in ParadisEO-MO-GPU.

Initially, to implement a sequential S-Metaheuristic, the user must overload required classes of ParadisEO-MO. The classes coding the problem-specific part are abstract classes to be specialized and implemented by the user. To GPU-enable their S-Metaheuristics, users need to derivate their own classes with a bench of new provided ones. In the following components, the main modifications to take into account are detailed:

- *Solution representation.* Some keywords must be specified by the user to indicate which part of the structure will be executed on GPU. Some predefined extensions for binary or permutation representations are already provided in the ParadisEO-GPU module.
- *Neighborhood.* According to the neighborhood used in the S-Metaheuristic, the user needs to make an explicit function call to a predefined mapping function. It will automatically allow to find the right association between a neighbor and a GPU thread.
- *Problem data inputs.* The user must specify which inputs of the problem to be solved will be allocated on GPU. This can be achieved by introducing additional keywords.
- *Solution evaluation.* The solution which generates the neighborhood is currently evaluated on CPU. Therefore, this component does not need to be extended.
- *Neighborhood evaluation.* In this component, structures which are likely to be allocated and managed on GPU must be indicated by the user. Every private structures specific to a neighbor (such as an array) must be declared in a static way. Furthermore, the user might translate multidimensional arrays into one-dimensional ones.

To summarize, regarding the new user-defined classes, the user must indicate the structures which are likely to be accessed on the GPU device. This strict restriction enables more efficiency and flexibility. Indeed, on the one hand, unnecessary structures for the generation and evaluation of the neighborhood should not be automatically allocated on GPU to reduce the complexity memory space. On the other hand, some additional structures required for the neighborhood evaluation might be copied for each iteration of the S-Metaheuristic whilst some others are transferred only once during the program. Such a restriction makes it possible to avoid undesirable transfers which would lead to a performance decrease.

Regarding the components supplied in the software framework, the associated classes constitute a hierarchy of classes implementing the invariant part of the code. The different features of these generic components are the following:

- *Memory allocation and deallocation.* According to the specification made by the user, this generic component enables the automatic allocation on GPU of the different structures used for the problem. Type inference and size detection are managed by this component. The same goes on for the deallocation.

- *Data transfers.* At each iteration, the transfer of the candidate solution which is used to generate the neighborhood is automatically performed from CPU to GPU. Moreover, this component also ensures the transparent copy of the neighborhood results (fitnesses) from GPU to CPU. Type inference and size detection of the different structures are also supported.

- *Parallel evaluation of the neighborhood.* This component manages the kernel of the neighborhood evaluation. Concepts involving kernel such as thread blocks and block grids are completely hidden to the user.

- *Neighborhood resulting evaluations.* This structure is manipulated in a transparent manner to store the results of the neighbors evaluated on GPU (fitnesses structure). Afterwards, this structure is sent back to the CPU to continue the local search process in a sequential manner.

- *Mapping functions.* Predefined mapping functions control the generation of the neighborhood on GPU. They consist in associating one thread with a specific neighbor. Such a mapping differs according to the used neighborhood.

- *Memory management.* Based on the user specifications, this component manages all the previous structures which are stored on global memory. This management is performed in a transparent way to the user.

The decomposition of the components in ParadisEO-MO-GPU allows to separate the features specific to S-Metaheuristics (ParadisEO-MO) from those which are related to the GPU code. This separation of concerns makes it possible to split the software framework into distinct features that overlap in functionality as little as possible.

3.4 A Case Study: Parallel Evaluation of a Neighborhood

The ParadisEO-MO-GPU execution is illustrated in Figure 4 through an UML sequence diagram. The scenario shows the design and implementation of the parallel neighborhood evaluation on GPU. At each iteration, the different stages of the parallel evaluation process on GPU are the following:

1. The neighborhood component *moCudaNeighborhood* prepares all the steps for the parallel generation of the neighborhood on GPU. The initialization consists in setting a mapping table between GPU threads and neighbors. Thereafter, the associated data are sent only once to the GPU global memory since the mapping structure does not change during the execution process of S-Metaheuristics. The last step relies on the evaluation kernel invocation. It will be informed later on its termination to retrieve the pre-computed fitnesses structure.

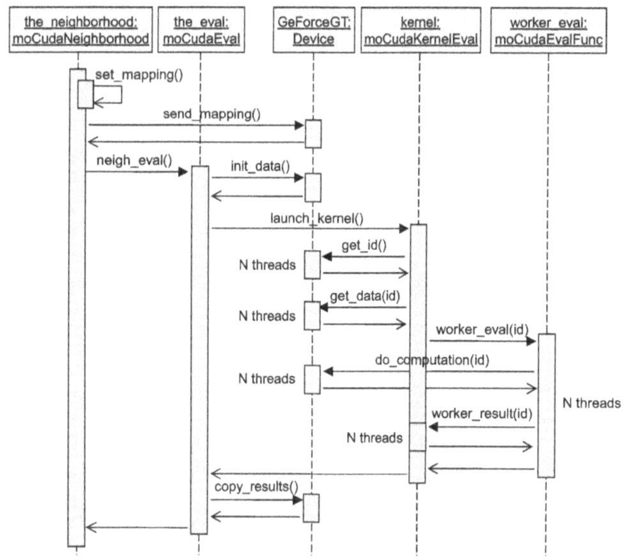

Figure 4: The parallel generation and evaluation of a neighborhood provided in ParadisEO-MO-GPU.

2. Before proceeding to the parallel evaluation, the component *moCudaEval* configures the kernel with m threads such that each thread is associated exactly with one neighbor evaluation (m designates the neighborhood size). During the first iteration, the component allocates the neighborhood fitnesses structure in which the result of the evaluated neighbors will be stored. Otherwise, in any case, it only sends to the GPU device the candidate solution which generates the neighborhood.

3. The component *moCudaKernelEval* modelizes the main body which will be executed by m concurrent threads on different input data. A first step consists in getting the thread identifier then the set of its associated data. This mechanism is done through the mapping table previously mentioned. The second step calculates the evaluation of the corresponding neighbor. Finally, the resulting fitness is stored in the corresponding index of the fitnesses structure.

4. The worker component *moCudaEvalFunc* is the specific object with computes on the GPU device the neighbor evaluation and returns back the produced result to the CPU.

Once the entire neighborhood has been carried out in parallel on GPU, the pre-calculated fitness structure is copied back to the CPU and given as input to the ParadisEO-MO module. In this way, the S-Metaheuristic continues the neighborhood exploration (iteration) on the CPU side. Instead of reevaluating each neighbor, the corresponding fitness value will be retrieved from the pre-computed fitnesses

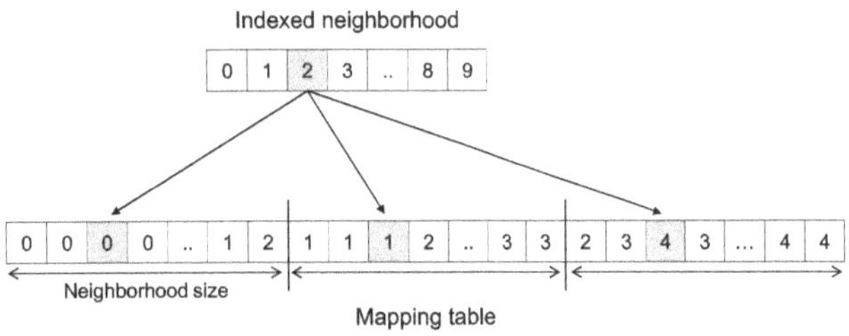

Figure 5: Automatic construction of the mapping function.

structure. Hence, this mechanism has the advantage of allowing both the deployment of any S-Metaheuristic and the use of toolboxes provided in ParadisEO-MO (e.g. statistical or fitnesses landscape analysis, checkpoint monitors, etc.)

3.5 Automatic Construction of the Mapping Function

As previously said, the advantage of generating the neighborhood on GPU is to reduce drastically the data transfers since the whole neighborhood does not have to be copied. However, the main difficulty is to find an efficient mapping between a GPU thread and neighbor candidate solution(s). In other words, the issue is to say which solution must be handled by which thread. The answer is dependent of the solution representation. In [8, 9], we provided some mappings for the main neighborhood structures of the literature. However, from an implementation point of view, they are still user-managed. Indeed, the neighborhood structure strongly depends on the target optimization problem representation.

To deal with these issues, mappings for different neighborhoods could be hard-coded in the software framework. However, such a solution does not ensure any flexibility. Hence, we propose to add a supplementary layer in terms of transparency for the deployment of S-Metaheuristics on GPU. The main idea is to find a generic mapping which is common for a set of neighborhoods. To achieve this, we provide an automatic construction of the mapping function for k-swaps and k-Hamming distance neighborhoods. Figure 5 depicts such a construction of a mapping table. In this example, each neighbor associated to a particular thread can retrieve its three corresponding indexes from the mapping table.

Considering a given vector of size n and a given neighborhood whose neighbors are composed of k indexes with k in $\{1, 2, 3, ...\}$, the size of the associated neighborhood is exactly $m = \frac{n \times (n\text{-}1) \times ... \times (n\text{-}k+1)}{k!}$. The resulting mapping table associates each thread id with a set of k indexes. Each index can be respectively retrieved from the mapping table with the access pattern:

$$\{id, id + m, ..., id + (k\text{-}2) \times m, id + (k\text{-}1) \times m\}$$

The corresponding mapping table will be used at each iteration of the local search. This table is dynamically constructed on CPU according to the neighborhood size and transferred only once to the GPU global memory during the program execution.

4. APPLICATION TO THE PERMUTED PERCEPTRON PROBLEM

4.1 Problem Formulation and Resolution

In [12], Pointcheval introduced a cryptographic identification scheme based on the perceptron problem, which seems to be suited for resource constrained devices such as smart cards. An ϵ-vector is a vector with all entries being either +1 or -1. Similarly, an ϵ-matrix is a matrix in which all entries are either +1 or -1. The PPP is defined as follows:

Definition 1. *Given an ϵ-matrix A of size $m \times n$ and a multi-set S of non-negative integers of size m, find an ϵ-vector V of size n such that $\{\{(AV)_j / j = \{1, \ldots, m\}\}\} = S$.*

A PPP solution can be represented with a binary encoding. Part of the full evaluation of a solution can be seen as a matrix-vector product. Therefore, the evaluation of a neighbor can be performed in linear time. As the iteration-level parallel model does not change the semantics of the sequential S-Metaheuristic, the effectiveness in terms of quality of solutions is not addressed here. In [9], the authors have investigated how the increase of the size of neighborhood allows to improve the quality of the solutions. Indeed, theoretical and experimental studies have shown that the increase of the neighborhood size may improve the quality of the obtained solutions [1]. Nevertheless, as it is generally CPU time-consuming, this mechanism is not often fully exploited in practice. Indeed, experiments using large neighborhoods are often stopped without reached. Thereby, in designing S-Metaheuristics, there is often a trade-off between the size of the neighborhood to use and the computational complexity to explore it. To deal with such issues, only the use of massive parallelism allows to design methods based on large neighborhood structures.

In this paper, the objective is to assess the impact in terms of efficiency of an implementation done with ParadisEO-MO-GPU compared with an optimized version done outside the software framework. To measure such a difference, three neighborhoods based on increasing Hamming distances are considered for the experiments. In such neighborhoods, a neighbor is produced by flipping respectively 1, 2 and 3 bits of the candidate solution.

4.2 Experimentation with ParadisEO-MO-GPU

The considered PPP instances are the challenging ones presented in [12] for cryptanalysis applications. A Tabu Search S-Metaheuristic has been implemented in four different versions: 1) a ParadisEO-MO implementation on CPU and its counterpart on GPU; 2) an optimized CPU implementation and its associated GPU version. ParadisEO versions are pure object-based implementations whilst the optimized ones are pointer-based made outside the software framework.

Experiments have been carried out on top of an Intel Core i7 970 3.2 Ghz with a GTX 480 card (15 multiprocessors with 32 cores). To measure the acceleration factors, only a single-core CPU has been considered using the Intel i7 turbo mode (3.46 Ghz). For the two first neighborhoods, 30 executions for each different version are considered. The stopping criterion of the S-Metaheuristic has been set to 10000 iterations. The average time has been measured in

Table 1: Measures in terms of efficiency of a ParadisEO-MO-GPU implementation with an optimized version made outside the platform. The permuted perceptron problem has been considered with a neighborhood based on a Hamming distance of one (n neighbors).

Instance	ParadisEO-MO			Optimized version		
	CPU	GPU	Acc.	CPU	GPU	Acc.
73-73	0.5	1.1	×0.4	0.3	0.8	×0.4
81-81	0.6	1.2	×0.5	0.4	1.0	×0.4
101-117	1.0	1.4	×0.7	0.7	1.2	×0.6
121-137	1.4	1.5	×0.9	1.1	1.3	×0.8
151-167	2.1	1.7	×**1.2**	1.7	1.5	×**1.1**
171-187	2.7	1.9	×**1.4**	2.3	1.7	×**1.4**
201-217	3.8	2.2	×**1.7**	3.3	1.9	×**1.7**

seconds. The standard deviation is not represented since its value is pretty low. The Kolmogorov-Smirnov's test has been applied to check the normal distribution of the data set.

Table 1 reports the results obtained for the Tabu Search based on a Hamming distance of one. From the instance $m = 171$ and $n = 187$, both GPU versions start to yield positive accelerations (from ×1.1 to ×1.2). As long as the instance size increases, the acceleration factor grows accordingly (from ×1.3 to ×1.7). The acceleration factor for this implementation is not really significant. This can be explained by the fact that since the neighborhood is relatively small (n threads), the number of threads per block is not enough to fully cover the memory access latency. Furthermore, since the execution time for CPU versions is not meaningful, one can also argue on the use of GPU computing in that case. To measure the efficiency of the GPU-based implementation of this neighborhood, bigger PPP instances such as the ones used in [8] should be considered.

An experiment on larger scale concerns a Tabu Search using a neighborhood based on a Hamming distance of two. For this neighborhood, the evaluation kernel is executed by $\frac{n\times(n-1)}{2}$ threads. The obtained results from experiments are reported in Table 2.

For the first instance ($m = 73$, $n = 73$), acceleration factors are already significant (from ×8.2 and ×13.1). As long as the instance size increases, the acceleration factor grows accordingly. A peek performance is obtained for the last instance (efficient speed-ups varying from ×29.5 to ×41.8). A thorough examination of the acceleration factors points out that the performance obtained with ParadisEO-MO-GPU are not so far from an optimized implementation. The performance degradation which occurs is certainly due to the additional cost provided by ParadisEO-MO.

Indeed, regarding the two CPU versions, initially, there is already a performance gap regarding the execution time (between 68% and 86%). This difference can be explained by the overhead caused by the creation of generic objects in ParadisEO whereas the optimized version on CPU is a pure pointer-based implementation. Indeed, the Tabu Search in ParadisEO-MO is a specialized instantiation of a common template to any S-Metaheuristic whilst the optimized version is a specific Tabu Search implementation. This may also clarify the performance difference between the two different GPU counterparts in which the same phenomenon occurs. However, for such a transparent exploitation and flexibility, the obtained results are really convincing. A conclusion of this experiment indicates that the performance results of the GPU version provided by ParadisEO are not much degraded compared to the GPU pointer-based one.

As previously said, the definition of the neighborhood is a major step for the performance improvement of the algorithm. Indeed, the increase of the neighborhood size may improve the quality of the obtained solutions. However, its exploitation for solving real-world problems is possible only by using a great computing power. The next experiment illustrates that for a very large neighborhood obtained with a Hamming distance of 3. For such neighborhood, the evaluation kernel is executed by $\frac{n\times(n-1)\times(n-2)}{6}$ threads. Since the execution was too much CPU time consuming, only 5 executions have been performed. Table 3 presents the obtained results for such a large neighborhood.

In general, for the same problem instance, the obtained acceleration factors are much more important than for the previous neighborhoods. For example, for the first instance, the obtained speed-up already varies from ×17.7 to ×19.8. GPU keeps accelerated the process as long as the size grows. A very significant acceleration alternates from ×34.1 to ×53 for the biggest instance ($m = 201$, $n = 217$). Regarding the difference between ParadisEO-MO implementations and the optimized ones, the performance degradation is more important between the CPU versions (from 53% to 70%). Indeed, the increase of the neighborhood size may induce more creations of objects. This is also the same case for the performance degradation regarding the GPU counterparts. Nevertheless, according to the reported time measurements, the performance results of ParadisEO-MO-GPU are still satisfactory for such allowed transparency.

5. CONCLUSIONS AND FUTURE WORK

In this paper, we have presented a step towards a ParadisEO framework for the reusable design and implementation of the GPU-based parallel metaheuristics. The focus is set on S-Metaheuristics and the iteration-level parallel exploration of the neighborhood of a solution. We have revisited the design and implementation of this last model in ParadisEO-MO to allow its efficient execution and its transparent use on GPU. In order to minimize the cost of the data transfer between CPU and GPU the neighborhood of the current solution is generated and evaluated on GPU at each iteration. To do that mapping functions are defined and implemented into ParadisEO-MO allowing to assign a thread identifier to each neighboring solution. These mapping functions may be used in a fully transparent way for binary and permutation-based problem representations.

The implementation in ParadisEO-MO using CUDA has been experimentally validated on a cryptographic application and compared to the same implementation realized outside ParadisEO. The experimental results show that the performance degradation that occurs between the two implementations is satisfactory. Indeed, for such a flexibility and an easiness of reuse at implementation, the results obtained with ParadisEO-MO-GPU are really promising (accelerations up to ×34). S-Metaheuristics based on large neighborhoods are unpractical on traditional machines because of their high computational cost. Hence, the use of ParadisEO-MO-GPU is a viable solution. Furthermore, we are strongly convinced that the overall performance provided by

Table 2: Measures in terms of efficiency of a ParadisEO-MO-GPU implementation with an optimized version made outside the platform. The permuted perceptron problem has been considered with a neighborhood based on a Hamming distance of two ($\frac{n\times(n-1)}{2}$ neighbors).

Instance	ParadisEO-MO			Optimized version			Perf. degradation	
	CPU	GPU	Acc.	CPU	GPU	Acc.	CPU	GPU
73-73	19.8	2.4	×**8.2**	17.1	1.3	×**13.1**	86%	54%
81-81	26	2.8	×**9.3**	22	1.6	×**13.8**	84%	57%
101-117	61	3.9	×**15.6**	51	2.2	×**23.2**	83%	56%
121-137	106	5.2	×**20.4**	91	2.9	×**31.3**	86%	56%
151-167	193	8.0	×**24.1**	134	4.1	×**32.7**	69%	51%
171-187	305	11.3	×**26.9**	208	5.6	×**37.1**	68%	49%
201-217	455	17.6	×**29.5**	343	8.2	×**41.8**	75%	46%

Table 3: Measures in terms of efficiency of a ParadisEO-MO-GPU implementation with an optimized version made outside the platform. The permuted perceptron problem has been considered with a neighborhood based on a Hamming distance of three ($\frac{n\times(n-1)\times(n-2)}{6}$ neighbors).

Instance	ParadisEO-MO			Optimized version			Perf. degradation	
	CPU	GPU	Acc.	CPU	GPU	Acc.	CPU	GPU
73-73	565	32	×**17.7**	303	15.3	×**19.8**	54%	47%
81-81	877	44	×**19.9**	464	21	×**22.1**	53%	47%
101-117	2468	99	×**24.9**	1375	50	×**27.5**	56%	50%
121-137	4887	182	×**26.8**	3137	89	×**35.2**	64%	48%
151-167	11983	401	×**29.9**	7781	190	×**41.0**	65%	49%
171-187	20239	612	×**33.1**	13089	288	×**45.4**	64%	47%
201-217	37956	1111	×**34.1**	26706	504	×**53.0**	70%	45%

ParadisEO-MO-GPU will be much better for other problems requiring more computational calculations (e.g. in [7]).

The first release of ParadisEO-MO on GPU is available on the ParadisEO website[2]. Tutorials and documentation are provided to facilitate its reuse. This release is dedicated to parallel S-Metaheuristics based on the iteration-level parallel model. In the short run, this release will be first extended to the algorithmic (multi-start) and solution-level parallel models. Second, it will be extended to other problem representations such as discrete representation and other solution methods. Third, it will be validated on a wider range of problems. In the long run, ParadisEO will be revisited following the same roadmap for population-based metaheuristics (P-Metaheuristics) such as evolutionary algorithms on GPU.

6. REFERENCES

[1] R. K. Ahuja, J. Goodstein, A. Mukherjee, J. B. Orlin, and D. Sharma. A very large-scale neighborhood search algorithm for the combined through-fleet-assignment model. *INFORMS Journal on Computing*, 19(3):416–428, 2007.

[2] M. Blesa, L. Hernande, and F. Xhafa. Parallel Skeletons for Tabu Search Method. In *In Proc. of ICPADS'01*, 2001.

[3] S. Cahon, N. Melab, and E.-G. Talbi. ParadisEO: A Framework for the Reusable Design of Parallel and Distributed Metaheuristics. *J. of Heuristics*, 10(3):357–380, 2004.

[4] J. Chakrapani and J. Skorin-Kapov. Massively Parallel Tabu Search for the Quadratic Assignment Problem. *Annals of Operations Research*, 41:327–341, 1993.

[5] T. Crainic, M. Toulouse, and M. Gendreau. Parallel Asynchronous Tabu Search for Multicommodity Location-Allocation with Balancing Requirements. *Annals of Operations Research*, 63:277–299, 1995.

[6] T. James, C. Rego, and F. Glover. A cooperative parallel tabu search algorithm for the quadratic assignment problem. *European Journal of Operational Research*, 195:810–826, 2009.

[7] T. Luong, N. Melab, and E.-G. Talbi. Parallel Hybrid Evolutionary Algorithms on GPU. In *IEEE Congress on Evolutionary Computation*, pages 1–8. IEEE, 2010.

[8] T.-V. Luong, N. Melab, and E.-G. Talbi. Local Search Algorithms on Graphics Processing Units. A Case Study: the Permutation Perceptron Problem. In *EvoCOP'2010*, volume 6022 of *LNCS*, pages 264–275. Springer, 2010.

[9] T. V. Luong, N. Melab, and E.-G. Talbi. Neighborhood Structures for GPU-Based Local Search Algorithms. *Parallel Processing Letters*, 20(4):307–324, 2010.

[10] N. Melab, S. Cahon, and E.-G. Talbi. Grid computing for parallel bioinspired algorithms. *J. Parallel Distributed Computing*, 66(8):1052–1061, 2006.

[11] J. Nickolls, I. Buck, M. Garland, and K. Skadron. Scalable Parallel Programming with CUDA. *ACM Queue*, 6(2):40–53, 2008.

[12] D. Pointcheval. A new identification scheme based on the perceptrons problem. In *EUROCRYPT*, pages 319–328, 1995.

[13] É. D. Taillard. Robust tabu search for the quadratic assignment problem. *Parallel Computing*, 17(4-5):443–455, 1991.

[14] A.-A. Tantar, N. Melab, C. Demarey, and E.-G. Talbi. Building a Virtual Globus Grid in a Reconfigurable Environment - A case study: Grid5000. In *INRIA Research Report, HAL INRIA*, 2007.

[15] A.-A. Tantar, N. Melab, and E.-G. Talbi. A Comparative Study of Parallel Metaheuristics for Protein Structure Prediction on the Computational Grid. In *IEEE NIDISC/IPDPS'2007, Long Beach, California, March 26*, 2007.

[2] http://paradiseo.gforge.inria.fr

Speeding Up Model Building for ECGA on CUDA Platform

Chung-Yu Shao
Department of Electrical Engineering
National Taiwan University
r00921046@ntu.edu.tw

Tian-Li Yu
Department of Electrical Engineering
National Taiwan University
tianliyu@cc.ee.ntu.edu.tw

ABSTRACT

Parallelization is a straightforward approach to enhance the efficiency for evolutionary computation due to its inherently parallel nature. Since NVIDIA released the compute unified device architecture (CUDA), graphic processing units have enabled lots of scalable parallel programs in a wide range of fields. However, parallelization of model building for EDAs is rarely studied. In this paper, we propose two implementations on CUDA to speed up the model building in the extended compact genetic algorithm (ECGA). The first implementation is algorithmically identical to original ECGA. Aiming at a greater speed boost, the second implementation modifies the model building. It slightly decreases the accuracy of models in exchange for more speedup. Empirically, the first implementation achieves a speedup of roughly 359 to the baseline on 500-bit trap problem with order 5, and the second implementation achieves a speedup of roughly 506 to the baseline on the same problem. Finally, both of our implementations scale up to 9,800-bit trap problem with order 5 on one single Tesla C2050 GPU card.

Categories and Subject Descriptors

D.1.3 [**Programming Techniques**]: Concurrent Programming - *Parallel programming*

General Terms

Algorithms, Performance, Experimentation

Keywords

CUDA, GPU, Estimation of Distribution Algorithms, ECGA, Model Building, Efficiency Enhancement

1. INTRODUCTION

The extended compact genetic algorithm (ECGA) [5] belongs to one of the evolutionary computations (ECs) called the estimation of distribution algorithms (EDAs) [1, 10, 8]. EDAs are stochastic optimization techniques that utilize the relations among genes to guide the search process via probabilistic models. Probabilistic models summarize the information of related genes from the promising candidate solutions. EDAs then generate offspring via sampling these models.

EDAs have been regarded as *competent* [4] that solve boundedly difficult problem in subquadratic number of function evaluations. However, for large-scale problems, the subquadratic number of function evaluations can still be time consuming. Therefore, efficiency enhancement techniques [18] are developed for large-scale, complex problems. Since ECs are inherently parallel, parallelization is a straightforward approach to enhance the efficiency [2].

Nowadays, the graphic processing unit (GPU) is a widely affordable parallel processor to solve massively parallel computation tasks. Since NVIDIA released the compute unified device architecture (CUDA) in 2007 [16], lots of scalable parallel programs have been developed in a wide range of fields. CUDA is not only a minimal extension of the C/C++ programming, but also a parallel computing platform that unifies graphics and general-purpose parallel computing applications. Developers write serial program that calls parallel *kernel* functions. When called, the kernel function is executed T times in parallel, where T is the number of CUDA threads defined by the programmer. The remaining portion of program is then executed sequentially on the central processing unit (CPU). Therefore, CUDA facilitates a heterogeneous computing between CPUs and GPUs. Although CUDA is friendly for a programmer familiar with C to start with, the performance of the program relies on the comprehension of several software and hardware properties, which are defined by CUDA's *compute capability*.

Researchers have implemented many ECs on CUDA, such as differential evolution [7], genetic algorithm (GA) [21, 11] and particle swarm optimization [13]. However, to the best of our knowledge, there are comparatively fewer researches related to EDAs with CUDA. Munawar *et al.* [12] proposed CUDA-based parallel Bayesian optimization algorithm (BOA). In their implementation, the Bayesian network construction in BOA [17] is implemented on CUDA, and the implementation speeds up a 192-bit test problem 13 times.

In this paper, we propose two CUDA-based implementations aiming at speeding up model building for ECGA. We first introduce a table-lookup method to speed up the process of counting the occurrences of schemata. This technique is then implemented on GPU with maximum utilization of

GECCO'13, July 6–10, 2013, Amsterdam, The Netherlands.

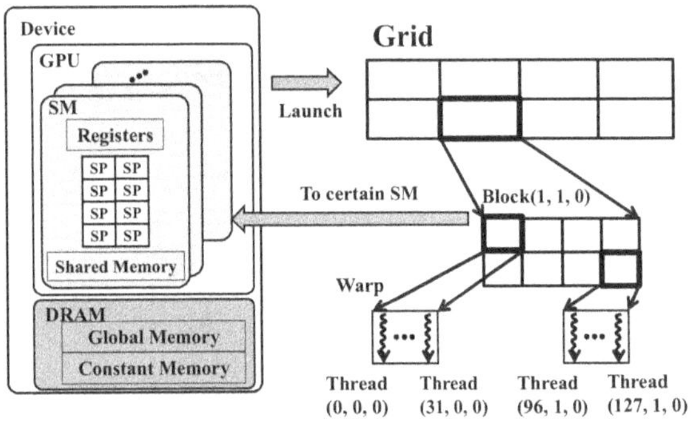

Figure 1: The GPU device lunches a grid with dimension (2, 4, 1) of thread blocks. In each thread block, there are 256 threads, which are divided into 8 warps.

available shared memory. Based on the first implementation, the second implementation modifies the greedy model-searching algorithm to obtain more speedup. The remainder of the paper is divided into five sections. In Sections 2 and 3, we describe the background of CUDA and ECGA in greater detail and review previous work on parallelism on ECGA. The proposed implementations are described in Section 4, and the empirical results are discussed in Section 5. Finally, we conclude this paper in Section 6.

2. GPU AND CUDA

In this section, the background of CUDA is discussed, followed by the programming model of CUDA. The CUDA design constraints are emphasized because these constraints affect how we design our algorithms. The section is mainly reorganized and summarized from [14, 15, 16].

2.1 Background

GPU was originally designed to support graphics rendering tasks. Specifically, a program for one thread drew one vertex or shaded one pixel fragment. Thousands of independent threads executed concurrently in a fine-grained, data-parallel sense on GPU. Because GPU was specialized for such highly parallel tasks with intensive computation, more transistors were devoted to data processing rather than caching and flow control.

The design made GPU well-suited to problems that could be expressed as data-parallel computations. The memory access latency could be hidden by many data elements that were executed at the same time. Traditionally, researchers had to explore a mapping between the non-graphics computations and the graphics rendering in order to utilize the resource of GPU. The need for general purpose computation on GPU hence motivated NVIDIA to develop CUDA.

2.2 CUDA Programming Model

Three key abstractions form the core of the CUDA programming model: (1) a hierarchy of thread groups, (2) shared memories, and (3) barrier synchronization. The hierarchy of thread groups enables programmers to control all the threads launched by kernel function, which is illustrated in Figure 1. A kernel executes across a set of threads parallely, and the set of threads is organized as a hierarchy of *grid* of *thread blocks*. Specifically, a grid is formed by several three-dimensional thread blocks. Each thread block contains a three-dimension of threads. Each thread in a given thread block has its unique thread index number. Threads in same thread block cooperate through the per-block shared memory and synchronize with __SYNCTHREADS(). Threads in different blocks cooperate through the global memory and synchronize through terminating the current kernel.

When a kernel launches, GPU automatically distributes the thread blocks to the streaming multiprocessors (SMs). SM creates, manages, schedules, and executes threads in *warp*, which is a group of 32 parallel threads. When given one or more thread blocks to execute, SM partitions each block to warps. Each warp is then scheduled by a warp scheduler for execution. A warp executes one common instruction at a time, which is called the single instruction multiple threads parallel programming model. The compute capability of the device defines the maximal number of resident warps on a SM. The resident blocks on a SM are divided into resident warps, and the resident warps are executed concurrently. When blocks terminate, GPU launches new blocks on the vacated SMs.

2.3 Design Constraints

There are many constraints for CUDA programming due to the GPU architecture. Below we describe three constraints in greater detail. The first constraint is the memory latency issue. As previously mentioned, threads in same block communicate through the on-chip shared memory. Due to the GPU architecture, the shared memory is expected to be a low-latency (few cycles) memory near each SM which provides high performance communication. In contrast, threads in different blocks or sequentially dependent grids communicate via the high-latency (hundreds of cycles) global memory. Nevertheless, if consecutive threads access consecutive memory addresses, all of the threads in a half-warp access the global memory at the same time. This process is called *coalesced memory* transaction.

The second constraint is the memory bandwidth. GPU has hundreds of cores that provide high arithmetic throughput. However, memory traffic in the global memory happens because we can't keep the input coming to GPU fast enough to sustain such high rates of computation. Specifically, when too many threads are acquiring data from the global memory, GPU might prevent all but few of threads from accessing. Many SMs are therefore idle. To evaluate the efficiency of how we utilize the limited bandwidth, the *compute to a global memory access* (CGMA) ratio is defined as the number of floating-point calculations performed for each access to the global memory within a region of a CUDA program. For example, the peak computation of NVIDIA GeForce 8800 GTX is 367 GFLOPS, and the memory bandwidth is 86.4GB/s. A program achieves the peak computation of this GPU until CGMA is above $\frac{367\times4}{86.4} \simeq 16.99$.

The last constraint with lower optimization priority is to maintain sufficient number of active threads per SM so that GPU can hide the memory latency. The ratio of the number of active warps per SM to the maximum number of possible active warps per SM is defined as the *occupancy* metric. This occupancy metric shows the degree to which we keep GPU busy. Unfortunately, a trade-off exists between occupancy and the resource of the shared memory per block. Table 2.3 indicates that to achieve full occupancy on a Tesla C2050

	GT8000	Tesla C2050
Compute capability	1.1	2.0
Shared memory size per MP (byte)	16K	48K
Maximum # resident blocks per SM	8	8
Shared memory when full occupancy	2K	6K

Table 1: The shared memory for 2 architecture of GPUs with 100% occupancy.

GPU card, one block only has 6,000 bytes of the shared memory. For a GPU card with lower compute capability, the amount of the shared memory per block is less.

To conclude, five policies are keys for high-performance CUDA program: (1) using the shared memory instead of the global memory, (2) using the global memory as coalesced as possible, (3) minimizing data transfer through the global memory between CPU and GPU, (4) keeping CGMA high, and (5) trying to keep GPU busy so that the latency can be hidden. For further information, please refer to [14, 15, 16].

3. ECGA

The section first describes EDAs and ECGA. ECGA, one of EDAs, models the population with the marginal product model. The model is decided by the combined complexity criteria that represents the description length of the model. The overall model building in ECGA and a previous work on ECGA with parallelism are described in greater detail.

3.1 Introduction to EDAs and ECGA

In the GA field, the term *linkage* refers to the relations among variables. A group of related variables can be seen as a *building block* (BB). Since Holland [6] addressed the importance of BBs, many different linkage-learning techniques have been developed for GAs. Studies have shown that losing linkage results in disruptive mixing and decreases the success of GAs dramatically [19]. Linkage learning capability is therefore a key that makes GAs competent [4].

EDAs, a branch of GAs, do not adopt the crossover operator and the mutation operator. The core idea behind EDAs is to build a probabilistic model that represents the promising solutions found so far. The offspring is then generated based on the model. The way that EDAs model the linkage significantly influences the complexity and the performance.

ECGA [5], one of EDAs, models the linkage as groups of variables and assumes that each group is mutually independent. This model, known as the marginal product model (MPM), consists of two components: (1) a partition that defines mutually independent groups over all variables, and (2) a probabilistic distribution for each group. Assumptions behind ECGA are that a good probability distribution is equivalent to the linkage learning and the 'good' distribution is based on two criteria. The criteria are the compressed representation of the population under the given distribution, and the distribution's representation given the problem's encoding. These two criteria form the combined complexity criteria (CCC), which is expressed as

$$CCC = N\sum_i Entropy(M_i) + \log_2(N+1)\sum_i(2^{S_i}-1), \quad (1)$$

where N is the population size and the i-th group of an MPM has S_i variables with marginal distribution M_i over this group. $Entropy(M_i)$ is defined as $\sum_k -p_k \log_2(p_k)$, where p_k is the probability of observing the k-th outcome. The entropy of each group means the average number of bits it takes to represent these S_i genes in the population with optimal compression. Therefore, the first term is named the compressed population complexity. The second term represents the memory required to store the MPM structure. It is called the model complexity because, given the MPM structure, one has to record $(2^{S_i}-1)$ frequency values, and each value requires $\log_2(N+1)$ bits. The sum of two terms can be regarded as the description length of the MPM model. To prevent from over-fitting, the minimum description length principle is taken under the philosophy of Occam's razor. To sum up, the overall objective is to find an MPM model that minimizes CCC to represent the selected population. ECGA uses a greedy algorithm as the search approach to decide the MPM model. The algorithm for model building is listed as Algorithm 1. The complexity of the model-building algorithm is $\Theta(\ell^3)$, where ℓ is the problem size. Using a cache structure that records CCC for each pair of groups, the complexity for model building is reduced to $\Theta(\ell^2 \log \ell)$, as implemented by Lobo *et al.* [9]

Algorithm 1: Model building in ECGA

```
begin
    Each variable is mutually independent. MPM has ℓ
    groups, each group contains one variable, where ℓ is
    the problem size.
    while Exist a pair that reduces CCC do
        Greedily find the best pair that reduces CCC
        most
        Merge the best pair
```

3.2 Previous Work on ECGA with Parallelism

Verma *et al.* [20] divided ECGA into three MapReduces [3]. The first Map phase evaluated the population and finished selection in the Reduce phase. In the model-building step, they partitioned individuals among multiple mappers. Each mapper calculated the marginal probability for every possible pairs of groups and sent the values to the reducers. A single reducer aggregated all the marginal probabilities, greedily found the best pair to merge and updated the model to a file for next model-building MapReduce. After building the model, the third MapReduce was applied to generate offspring. They performed the MapReduce-based ECGA on a cluster of 62 nodes, each with dual Intel Quad cores (8 cores), 16GB RAM and 2TB hard disks. The implementation scaled up to the 1,024-bit trap problem [4] with order 4 under the constraint of memory required to maintain marginal probability. However, the speedup between the MapReduce-based ECGA with cache structure and the sequential version of ECGA with cache structure was not mentioned in the paper.

4. CUDA-BASED ECGA

This section introduces the proposed implementations. A technique that speeds up the process of counting the occurrences of schemata is first described. The way that we utilize the technique to our implementations on GPU and the algorithm of our implementations are then introduced.

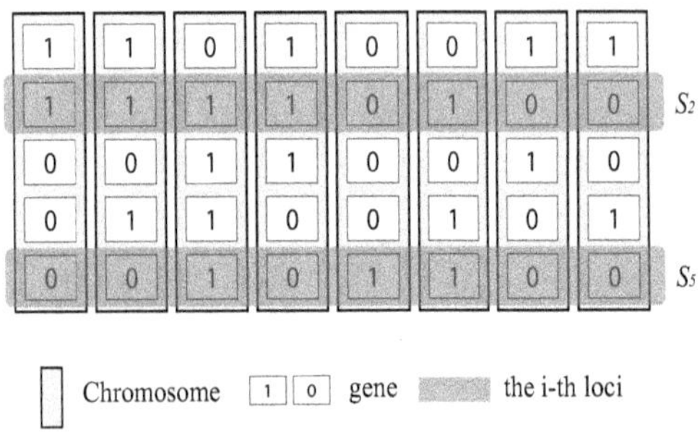

Figure 2: Counting schemata in the second and the fifth loci for the population

4.1 A Table-look-up Method to Speed Up Counting Distribution

A bit-wise table-look-up method is utilized in our implementation to count the occurrences of schemata in the population. For convenience, we call the method FASTCOUNT. The core of FASTCOUNT is a pre-calculated counting table. The counting table of x-bit binary string records the number of ones in each enumerated value that the x-bit binary string generates. For example, 2-bit binary string generates $\{0, 1, 2, 3\}$, and the corresponding ones are stored to the table as $\{0, 1, 1, 2\}$. For convenience, the table is called unity table afterwards.

The method is applied to EDAs as the following example. Suppose that we want to get the distribution of the second and the fifth loci from a population of size 8 as illustrated in Figure 2. Alleles for the second and the fifth loci among population form two bit stings: $S_2 = 11110100$ and $S_5 = 00101100$. Assume that the values from the i-th position of the two bit-strings form a pair P_i. For example, P_3 is $(1, 1)$. We use n_{xy} to denote the occurrences of the pair (x, y) in the population. Because each bit from $(\neg S_2 \& \neg S_5)$ is 1 only when $(x = 0 \; \& \; y = 0)$, n_{00} can be counted from the resulting bit-string of $(\neg S_2 \& \neg S_5)$. The result of $(\neg S_2 \& \neg S_5)$ is 00000011, or 3 in decimal. By looking up the unity table, we know that the number of ones in the resulting bit-string is 2. Similarly, n_{01} is derived from $(\neg S_2 \& S_5)$, and n_{10} is derived from $(S_2 \& \neg S_5)$. For a larger population, the occurrences can be accumulated from the results of every eight individuals.

We utilize this technique to ECGA when computing compressed population complexity. In the implementation, the selected population is transformed into UNSIGNED INT array, with each value representing 32 bits for a certain locus among the 32 individuals. The unity table in CPU is for a 16-bit binary string, which implies that we count the unity from 16 individuals at a time. For memory reason, the unity table in GPU is for a 8-bit binary string.

4.2 gECGA: CUDA-based Implementation

This section introduces our first implementation on GPU, which is called gECGA for convenience. The entire flow chart of gECGA is illustrated in Figure 3, and the overall kernel of the model building is listed in Algorithm 2. The section is followed by the redesign of the cache and the model, the allocation of the memory space, tasks for each thread block and how we update the cache and the model.

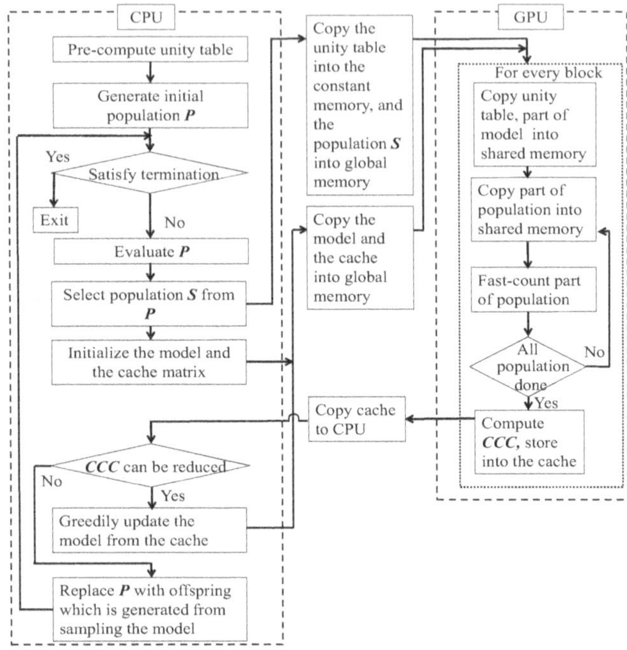

Figure 3: Block diagram of gECGA

Global Memory	Constant Memory	Shared Memory
entire population entire model matrix entire cache matrix status array	unity table	unity table merged group model part of population count array

Table 2: Memory space allocation of gECGA

4.2.1 *Cache and model structure*

Due to the separated memory spaces of a CPU and a GPU, we need to transfer the data from CPU to GPU. Harik *et al.* mentioned that ECGA could be optimized significantly by caching delta values for all pair combinations at each step [5]. The implementation can be found in [9]. In the implementation, the cache and the MPM model are divided into several C STRUCTURES. However, passing STRUCTURE to GPU is troublesome, let alone passing STRUCTURE inside another STRUCTURE. As the result, we redesign the cache and the MPM model.

The cache and the MPM model we use are simply two matrices. The cache is an ℓ-by-ℓ matrix, where ℓ is the problem size. Entry (i, j) stores CCC of a group which is merged from $group_i$ and $group_j$. If $i = j$, the entry stores CCC of the $group_i$. The loci in each group are stored in the model matrix. The model is an ℓ-by-L_{row} matrix, where $L_{row} = MAX_L + 1$ and MAX_L is hypothetically the maximum size of a group. L_{row} is equal to $MAX_L + 1$ because the first column stores the size of each group. In all the experiments, MAX_L is set to 10. In addition to the first column, the i-th row of the model matrix stores the loci inside $group_i$. We simultaneously initialize CCC for each group and copy the selected population to GPU.

4.2.2 *Memory space allocation*

Following the design constraints discussed in Section 2.3,

structure	data type	quantity	cost (bytes)
unity table	CHAR	2^8	256
merged group model	INT	L_{row}	44
count array	INT	$2^{MAX_L} - 1$	4092

Table 3: Memory costs except for the population in the shared memory

the strategy of making the global memory coalesced is to store data that might be accessed by the same warps of threads to contiguous memory. Additionally, the strategy of enhancing CGMA is to store those values that will be frequently used to the shared memory. Consequently, processing the global memory once can be applied to several operations.

The overall allocation is listed in Table 2. In Table 2, status array stores which group just being merged in the previous step, and count array stores the number of occurrences of every schemata. The unity table is invariant and is stored to the constant memory instead of the global memory.

In Table 2.3, the shared memory is 6KB per block under full occupancy on a Tesla C2050 card, which means that GPU can only afford 120 individuals for a 50-bit problem. Even if we transform the population into an UNSIGNED INT array, a block can only process $\frac{6000\times 64}{8\times 50} = 960$ individuals. It is not enough to solve a GA-hard problem like trap [4]. Therefore, separating the population in the shared memory is needed. In addition to the population, Table 3 lists the memory costs required to store the other structures in the shared memory. The sum is 4,392 bytes. As the result, we still have $(6,000 - 4,392)$ bytes per block, and the amount is equal to 12,864 bits. Given a merged group, we only keep the alleles in this group, and the quantity is not greater than MAX_L. The number of individuals a block can cover at once is therefore derived as $\lfloor \frac{12,864}{MAX_L} \rfloor = 1,286$. When computing CCC, every block sequentially iterates $\lceil \frac{population\ size}{1,286} \rceil$ times to go over the entire population.

4.2.3 Tasks allocation

We partition the model-building process to coarse subproblems that are solved independently in parallel by blocks of threads. We also partition each subproblem to finer pieces that are solved cooperatively in parallel by all threads within the block as the programming guide [16] suggests.

Each iteration of finding the group to merge greedily is called a model-searching step. In every model-searching step, a $|g|$-by-$|g|$ grid which consists of thread blocks is lunched, where $|g|$ is the number of groups in the current MPM model. The (x, y)-th block in the grid calculates CCC of the merging group from $group_i$ and $group_j$. Threads within the block cooperatively finish the following tasks in parallel:

1. Copy the entire unity table from the constant memory to the shared memory.
2. Copy the loci in the merged group from the model matrix in the global memory to the shared memory.
3. Initialize an array to store the distribution.
4. Copy alleles in these loci in the next 1,286 individuals from the global memory to the shared memory.
5. Sequentially count each enumerated value in these individuals by FASTCOUNT.
6. Repeat Step 4 and 5 until the whole population is covered.

When the step of counting the occurrences of schemata is done, one thread in the block calculates the resulting CCC and updates the value to the cache matrix in the global memory. After all the blocks finish updating the cache, the cache matrix is copied back to CPU. The entire algorithm is listed in Algorithm 2.

Algorithm 2: CUDA CCC kernel

Get the block coordinate (x, y) in the grid of threads CUDA launch. The (x, y)-block in the grid is responsible to calculate CCC for the merged group $group_{xy}$ from $group_x$ and $group_y$.
$tIdx \leftarrow$ the index of the thread in the block.
$L \leftarrow$ (size of $group_x$ + size of $group_y$)
if BORDERCHECK$(x, y, L) = False$ **then**
  return
COPYTOSHARED$(x, y, L, tIdx)$
Synchronize threads in the block.
for *each partition of population* **do**
  Parallely copy part of population from the global memory to the shared memory.
  Synchronize threads in the block.
  Parallely count the occurrences of schemata in the partition and store to distribution array.
  Synchronize threads in the block.
if $tIdx = 1$ **then**
  Calculate CCC from the distribution array and store to cache.

Function BORDERCHECK(x, y, L) **begin**
  if $(x \geq y) \vee group_x$ *is deleted* $\vee\ group_y$ *is deleted* $\vee (L > MAX_L)$ **then**
    return False
  else
    return True
Function COPYTOSHARED$(x, y, L, tIdx)$ **begin**
  Copy the $tIdx$ element of the unity table from the constant memory to the shared memory
  if $tIdx < L$ **then**
    Copy the $tIdx$ index in the $group_{xy}$ from the global memory to the shared memory
  $i \leftarrow tIdx$
  for $i < 2^L$ **do**
    i-th element of the distribution array $\leftarrow$ zero
    $i \leftarrow i$+total thread number in the block

4.2.4 Update cache and model

The updating step is illustrated in Figure 4. Assume that $\{1, 2, 3, 4\}$ is the merged group which minimizes the description length of the model. Numbers in the braces represent the loci in the group. The cache is updated by replacing the merged group with the last group in the current model. Steps (a) and (b) in the figure illustrate this goal. In step (c), we need to update CCC of $\{1, 2, 3, 4\}$ to the $(0, 0)$-entry, which stores CCC of $\{1, 2\}$ originally. When updating the model matrix, the group with the greater index in the merged group appends to the one with the less index, and the last row of the model replaces the row which

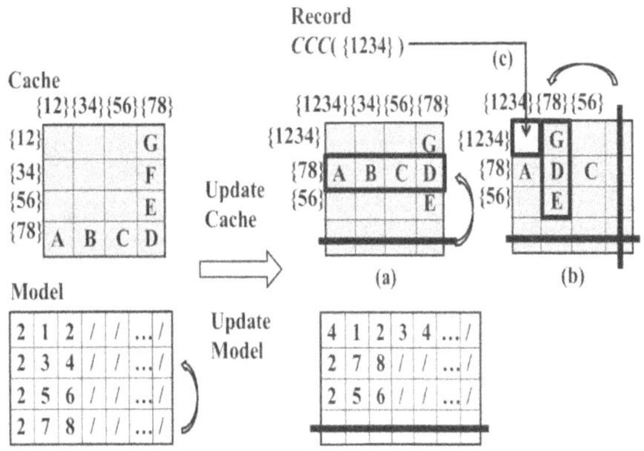

Figure 4: Update cache and model. The model is updated from $\{\{1,2\},\{3,4\},\{5,6\},\{7,8\}\}$ to $\{\{1,2,3,4\},\{5,6\},\{7,8\}\}$.

represents the merged group. The whole updating step is completed in CPU.

4.3 GM Search: The Modified Model-searching Algorithm

In the original ECGA, more than $\frac{\ell(\ell-1)}{2}$ CCC values are calculated in every generation, where ℓ is the problem size. However, for each model-searching step, only one CCC value is utilized from the greedy process. Our method records a group that minimizes the description length for each specific group, instead of finding one among all pairwise candidates greedily. After recording, pairs of groups merge only if they are the best companions to minimize the description length for each other. Therefore, we call this method the greedy mating (GM) search. In each model-searching step, at most half of the groups are merged to the other groups. As the result, GM search needs fewer model-searching steps to find the final model than the original greedy algorithm.

5. EXPERIMENTS

In this section, the hardware specification and general experiment setting are first described. The speedup from FastCount, gECGA and gECGA with GM search are then shown. The scalability of our implementation is also discussed.

5.1 Hardware Specification

We conduct the experiments on a computer with an 8 cores Intel XEON W3530 CPU at 2.8 GHz, and a NVIDIA Tesla C2050 GPU with 3 GB of DDR5 global memory. The GPU card has 448 cores at 1.15GHz. Cores cluster to 14 SMs. The operating system is Gentoo with kernel version 3.4.9. The driver version is NVIDIA-DRIVERS 295.71 with CUDA toolkit 4.0.

5.2 General Experiment Setting

The baseline comparison is the implementation from Lobo *et al.* [9] The test problem is the concatenated traps [4], where the order is 5. The fitness function of each subproblem is defined as

$$f_{trap5}(x) = \begin{cases} 5 & \text{if } x = 5 \\ 4 - x & \text{otherwise.} \end{cases} \quad (2)$$

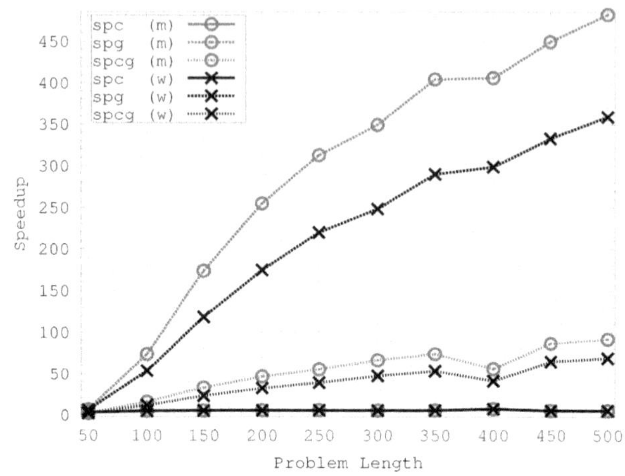

Figure 5: Speedup of FastCount on CPU is denoted as *spc*, speedup of gECGA is denoted as *spg*, and speedup between gECGA and FastCount on CPU is denoted as *spcg*. For the notation after speedup, (m) represents the duration for the entire model-building process, and (w) represents the duration for the whole ECGA process.

The test problem is called (m,k)-trap afterward, where m is the number of subproblems, and k is the order of a subproblem. The minimum population size required to correctly solve at least $m-1$ subproblems is obtained from the average over 30 independent bisection [18] runs, which is listed in Table 5. For problems with ℓ greater than 350, we use the theoretical values instead of running bisection method. Tournament selection is used, and the selection pressure is 8. Previous population is fully replaced by the offspring. The program terminates when all the individuals converge. The unity table on CPU is for 16-bit binary string while the unity table on GPU is for 8-bit binary string due to the memory limit. We assume that the maximum size of a group (MAX_L) is 10, which is also applied to the baseline implementation. Finally, the number of threads per block is set to 256 in the entire experiment.

5.3 Speedups

We show the speedups in Figure 5. The speedup between FastCount on CPU and baseline is defined as the ratio of execution time of baseline over the execution time of FastCount method on CPU, which is denoted as *spc*. Similarly, *spg* denotes the speedup between gECGA and baseline, which is defined as the ratio of execution time of baseline over the execution time of gECGA. The speedup between gECGA and FastCount on CPU is denoted as *spcg*. Two different execution periods are shown in Figure 5. The first one is the speedup for model building, and the second one is the speedup for the whole execution time to solve the problem. Each point in the figure is an average over 30 independent runs.

Although FastCount speeds up the counting step, the complexity of model building does not change. We still need to calculate CCC from the resulting distribution after FastCount. Consequently, the overall speedup from FastCount is limited, which is shown as *spc*. The speedups from

structure	data type	cost (byte)
entire population	UNSIGNED INT	$8(\frac{N\ell}{64})$
model matrix	INT	$4\ell L_{row}$
cache matrix	INT	$4\ell^2$
status array	BOOL	ℓ

Table 4: Global memory costs

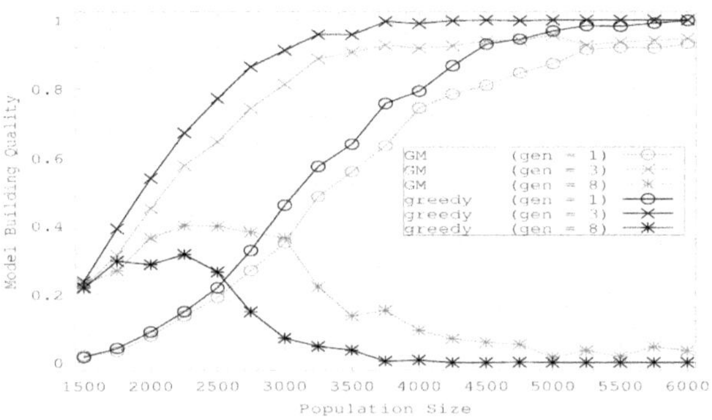

(a) Model-building quality

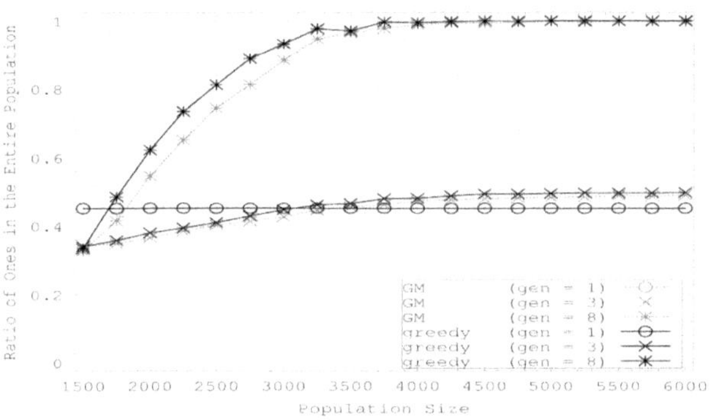

(b) Ratio of ones in the population

Figure 6: Model-building quality and ratio of ones in the population for the original ECGA and ECGA with GM search under different population size and different generations (gen).

gECGA can be seen in *spg* and *spcg*. We show the speedup on problems with ℓ up to 500.

Figure 5 shows that gECGA speeds up the model-building process 482.28 times on 500-bit problem, which results to a speedup of 358.97 times faster to solve the problem. The corresponding *spcg* is 68.56, which means that the implementation for FASTCOUNT on CUDA is 68.56 times faster than FASTCOUNT on CPU using single core.

5.4 Scalability

The only scalability constraint is that the memory which the entire population occupies should be less than the global memory. The shared memory is not a constraint in our implementations. For a Tesla C2050 card, a CUDA program can utilize at most 2.687 GBs of global memory. In Table 2, four structures need to be copied to the global memory. Assume that the population size is N, and the problem size is ℓ. The global memory costs are listed in Table 4. Using the theoretical population size [22], one C2050 GPU card can afford to solve a (2040, 5)-trap problem, where $\ell = 9,800$ and $N = 1,912,315$.

ℓ	50	100	150	200	250	300	350
greedy	2376	6670	11781	17160	21907	29890	36992
GM	2616	6670	12248	19008	24667	30530	39296

Table 5: Population size required to solve $m-1$ subproblems for ECGA with greedy search and ECGA with GM search respectively.

5.5 Experiments of GM Search

The speedup of GM search is not shown in Figure 5 because we suspect that the model-building quality in the new approach is lower than the original method. It is unfair to compare the speedup between the two methods without discussing the model-building quality first. The model-building quality is defined as the number of linkage group that is completely identical with the definition of the subproblem over the number of the subproblems. Figure 6(a) shows the model-building quality under different population sizes and different generations when solving a (10, 5)-trap. The third generation is the generation that achieves the maximum average model quality. The eighth generation is the last generation that program terminates. The figure shows that the overall model-building quality of ECGA with greedy search is greater than with GM search except for the last generation. A possible reason is that the relation between genes is hard to detect when the population is about to converge, and the model-building quality therefore drops in the last generations. Figure 6(b) presents the corresponding ratio of ones in the population after selection. The figure indicates that ECGA with greedy search converges earlier than with GM search, and the model-building quality might therefore drops more quickly.

Due to the loss of model-building quality, the minimum population sizes required to solve the problems are greater, which are listed in Table 5. The speedup from GM search is shown in Figure 7. The population sizes for gECGA with greedy search and gECGA with GM search are different. Although gECGA with GM search needs larger population, the execution time for gECGA with GM search is less than gECGA with the original greedy search.

6. CONCLUSION

In this paper, two implementations were proposed to speed up model building for ECGA. The first implementation was algorithmically identical with ECGA, but solved the problem with a speedup of 358.97 compared with the baseline implementation on a 500-bit trap problem with order 5. The key was to utilize thread blocks in CUDA by separating the model building in ECGA to coarse subproblems that were solved independently in parallel by blocks of threads. Furthermore, each subproblem was separated to finer pieces so that it was solved cooperatively in parallel by all threads within the block. On the basis of the first implementation, our second implementation modified the model building in ECGA. The second implementation solved the same problem with a speedup of 505.6 times faster compared with the baseline. The two implementations scaled up to 9,800-bit trap problem with order 5 on one single Tesla C2050 GPU card.

EDAs have shown the ability to solve many complex problems, and GPUs solve massively parallel computation tasks under relatively lower price than CPUs. To extend the ap-

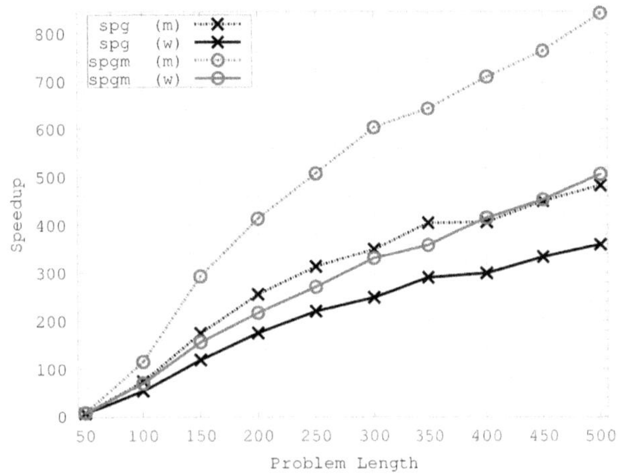

Figure 7: Speedup of gECGA is denoted as *spg*, **and speedup of gECGA wit GM search is denoted as** *spgm*. **For the notation after speedup, (m) represents the duration for the entire model-building process, and (w) represents the duration for the whole ECGA process.**

plicability of EDAs to large-scale problems, we believe that EDA researchers need to bear in mind the utilization of GPU features during their designs.

ACKNOWLEDGMENTS

This work was sponsored by the National Science Council of Taiwan under grant NSC-101-2221-E-002-198. The authors would also like to thank Maggie Man-Tin Yung for writing consultation.

7. REFERENCES

[1] S. Baluja. Population-based incremental learning: A method for integrating genetic search based function optimization and competitive learning. Technical report, Carnegie Mellon University, Pittsburgh, PA, 1994.

[2] E. Cantú-Paz. *Efficient and accurate parallel genetic algorithms*. Kluwer Academic Publishers, Boston, MA, 2000.

[3] J. Dean and S. Ghemawat. Mapreduce: simplified data processing on large clusters. *Communications of the ACM*, 51(1):107–113, 2008.

[4] D. E. Goldberg. *The design of innovation: Lessons from and for competent genetic algorithms*. Kluwer Academic Publishers, Boston, MA, 2002.

[5] G. R. Harik, F. G. Lobo, and K. Sastry. *Linkage Learning via Probabilistic Modeling in the Extended Compact Genetic Algorithm (ECGA)*. 2006.

[6] J. H. Holland. *Adaptation in natural and artificial systems*. Ann Arbor, MI: University of Michigan Press, 1975.

[7] P. Krömer, V. Snásel, J. Platos, and A. Abraham. Many-threaded implementation of differential evolution for the cuda platform. *Proceedings of the 13th annual conference on Genetic and evolutionary computation*, pages 1595–1602, 2011.

[8] P. Larrañaga and J. A. Lozano, editors. *Estimation of Distribution Algorithms: A New Tool for Evolutionary Computation*. Kluwer Academic Publishers, Boston, MA, 2002.

[9] F. Lobo, K. Sastry, and G. Harik. Extended compact genetic algorithm in C++: Version 1.1. IlliGAL Report No. 2006012, University of Illinois at Urbana-Champaign, 2006.

[10] H. Mühlenbein and G. Paaß. From recombination of genes to the estimation of distributions I. Binary parameters. In *Parallel Problem Solving from Nature*, pages 178–187. Springer-Verlag, 1996.

[11] A. Munawar, M. Wahib, M. Munetomo, and K. Akama. Hybrid of genetic algorithm and local search to solve max-sat problem using nvidia cuda framework. *Genetic Programming and Evolvable Machines*, 10(4):391–415, 2009.

[12] A. Munawar, M. Wahib, M. Munetomo, and K. Akama. Theoretical and empirical analysis of a gpu based parallel bayesian optimization algorithm. In *Parallel and Distributed Computing, Applications and Technologies, 2009 International Conference on*, pages 457–462. IEEE, 2009.

[13] L. Mussi, F. Daolio, and S. Cagnoni. Evaluation of parallel particle swarm optimization algorithms within the $CUDA^{TM}$ architecture. *Information Sciences*, 181(20):4642–4657, 2011.

[14] J. Nickolls, I. Buck, M. Garland, and K. Skadron. Scalable parallel programming with CUDA. *Queue*, 6(2):40–53, 2008.

[15] C. Nvidia. C best practices guide. *NVIDIA, Santa Clara, CA*, 2012.

[16] C. Nvidia. CUDA C Programming Guide 4.2. *NVIDIA, Santa Clara, CA*, 2012.

[17] M. Pelikan, D. E. Goldberg, and E. Cantú-Paz. BOA: The Bayesian optimization algorithm. *Proceedings of the Genetic and Evolutionary Computation Conference (GECCO-1999)*, I:525–532, 1999.

[18] K. Sastry. Evaluation-relaxation schemes for genetic and evolutionary algorithms. Master thesis, University of Illinois at Urbana-Champaign, Urbana, IL, 2002.

[19] D. Thierens. Scalability problems of simple genetic algorithms. *Evolutionary computation*, 7(4):331–352, 1999.

[20] A. Verma, X. Llorà, S. Venkataraman, D. E. Goldberg, and R. H. Campbell. Scaling eCGA model building via data-intensive computing. *Urbana*, 51:61801, 2010.

[21] P. Vidal and E. Alba. Cellular genetic algorithm on graphic processing units. *Nature Inspired Cooperative Strategies for Optimization (NICSO 2010)*, pages 223–232, 2010.

[22] T.-L. Yu, K. Sastry, D. E. Goldberg, and M. Pelikan. Population sizing for entropy-based model building in discrete estimation of distribution algorithms. *Proceedings of the Genetic and Evolutionary Computation Conference (GECCO-2007)*, pages 601–608, 2007.

A Novel Movable Partitions Approach with Neural Networks and Evolutionary Algorithms for Solving the Hydroelectric Unit Commitment Problem

Pedro de Lima Abrão
Centro Federal de Educação Tecnológica de Minas Gerais
CEFET-MG
Av. Amazonas, 7675
Belo Horizonte, Brazil
plabrao@lsi.cefetmg.br

Elizabeth F. Wanner
Centro Federal de Educação Tecnológica de Minas Gerais
CEFET-MG
Av. Amazonas, 7675
Belo Horizonte, Brazil
efwanner@decom.cefetmg.br

Paulo E. M. Almeida
Centro Federal de Educação Tecnológica de Minas Gerais
CEFET-MG
Av. Amazonas, 7675
Belo Horizonte, Brazil
pema@lsi.cefetmg.br

ABSTRACT

This paper presents a method based on Neural Networks and Evolutionary Algorithms to solve the Hydroelectric Unit Commitment Problem. A Neural Network is used to model the production function and a novel approach based on movable partitions is proposed, which makes it easier to model the desired power output equality constraint in the optimization modeling. Three evolutionary algorithms are tested in order to find optimized operation points: differential evolution DE/best/1/bin, a balanced version of DE and Particle Swarm Optimization algorithm (PSO). The results show that the proposed method is effective in terms of water consumption, reaching in some cases more than 1% of economy whether compared to the traditional commitment strategy.

Categories and Subject Descriptors

G.1.6 [**Optimization**]: [Constrained optimization] ; I.2.6 [**Learning**]: [Connectionism and neural nets]; J.2 [**Phisical Sciences and Engineering**]: [Engineering]

Keywords

Optimization algorithms, Operations research, Neural systems, Energy generation and storage, Renewable energy

1. INTRODUCTION

The hydro unit commitment (UC) problem aims to determine, for a time stage, the status of the generating units and their respective dispatch (in MW) in a hydroelectric generation plant, so that the total power demand is satisfied, the operating cost is minimized and the set of constraints is guaranteed. This work presents an optimum dispatch model which adopts, as the performance criteria, the minimum consumption of hydro resources. The main idea behind this study is that the water is a scarce resource, for which the generation units are competing.

In Brazil, the hydro generation is the main source of electric energy, corresponding to 81.7% of the total production. The energy generation grid is predominantly connected. Only 3.4% of its electric production capacity is out of the national system. In this way, there are centers which are responsible to imply the operation points in MW for each generation plant. From that, each plant must commit its generation units in order to meet the required demand.

The dispatch can be divided into long, medium and short-term planning [1]. The focus here will be in the short-term planning, which involves, in this case, to find for a specific time slice the respective dispatch for each generation unit in order to produce the desired total power output. Normally in a hydroelectric plant, the control system performs an equal division of the power demand in MW among its generation units. However, this approach does not take into consideration if each unit is operating at its particular efficient point. Considering the non-linearity of the production function and the high number of continuous and discrete constraints involved, this problem can be considered complex. In this way, many approaches have been developed around the world trying to solve it.

Lagrangian Relaxation (LR) is one of the most widely used methods to solve the UC problem, mainly over thermal plants [3] [15] [8]. This approach is very attractive, specially because of the possibility to relax the problem constraints, such as the spinning reserve and demand supply requirements, which makes possible to solve multiple independent subproblems, one for each generating unit, without any explicit coupling between them. However, the solution to UC problem by LR is sensitive to changes of the Lagrangian multipliers and highly dependent upon the size of the duality gap [11], which in large power systems such as the Brazilian one, can increase dramatically.

Another possible approach is to use decomposition techniques. Finardi and Silva proposed a solution in which two subproblems were created [7]. The first one corresponding to a linear programming which main purpose was to establish the total volume of water to be discharged by each hydro plant, in each time stage, without considering the units individually. The second problem, with respect to the nonlinearity, is associated with the hydro units and the combinatorial nature of the commitment. Forbidden zones constraints

GECCO'13, July 6–10, 2013, Amsterdam, The Netherlands.

were considered and the Branch and Bound method was used to determine feasible states. Thus, due to the various steps needed, this strategy becomes complex and harder to employ in systems that require small response times.

Considering the difficulties stated before, an alternative approach consists of heuristic methods since they have the merits of being more flexible while handling nonlinear and discrete variables, in addition to easy coding and implementation whether compared to classical optimization methods. Pancholi e Swarup [14] used the Particle Swarm Optimization (PSO) evolutionary technique to solve the economic dispatch problem taking into consideration security constraints. The results were compared to other techniques such as linear programming and quadratic programming achieving reduced computational costs.

Yalcinoz and Short [17] presented a solution for the economic dispatch problem based on a modified Hopfield Neural Network to deal with transmission capacity constraints. The proposed method achieved efficient solutions to power systems up to 120 units. When compared to a classical optimization program based on quadratic programming, the solution obtained the same results (operation cost [\$ / h]) while demanding less time to run.

Liu and Li [11] proposed an approach that establishes the hydro dispatch for T time stages. It was taken into consideration the desired power demand, operation regions and costs to start and to shutdown turbines. An enhanced version of the PSO was also used to search for optimal solutions. According to the results, the method outperformed the classical PSO algorithm and other methods such as genetic algorithms and dynamic programming in relation to the water consumption. However, the modelling applied did not explain in details the relation among the involved variables to establish the production function.

This paper presents a method based on a Neural Network to model the production function and the novel movable partition approach which makes it easier to model the desired power output equality constraint in the optimization problem. Three evolutionary algorithms are tested in order to find optimized operation points: differential evolution DE/best/1/bin, a balanced version of DE and Particle Swarm Optimization algorithm (PSO).

This paper is organized as follows. In section 2 the applied model is presented. Section 3 presents the evolutionary algorithms which will be applied. Section 4 shows the application of the proposed solution, the results obtained and some analysis among the algorithms tested and section 5 concludes the paper.

2. MODELING THE PROBLEM

Hydropower plants use the hydraulic potential to generate energy. A common installation is composed by a dam, responsible to hold back water, creating the reservoir. The gravity pulls the water to the penstock, a pipeline that leads to the turbine. Water builds up pressure as it flows through this pipe. Then the water strikes and turns the large blades of a turbine, which is attached to a generator above it by way of a shaft. Figure 1 shows a schematic representation of a hydroeletric plant.

The vertical distance between the forebay level and the tailrace level (intake to turbine) influences the resulting pressure at the bottom. This measure is called gross head of the turbine. However, when water is flowing, the pressure

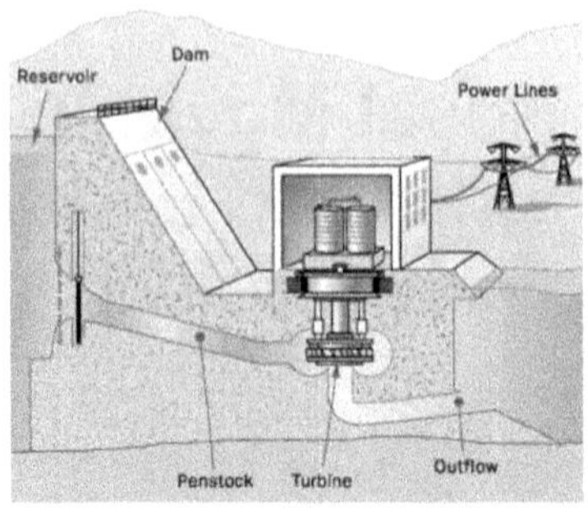

Figure 1: Hydroelectric plant representation

at the bottom of the penstock will be always less than the gross head due to energy losses within the pipeline. This measure, which takes into consideration the penstock losses, is called net water head [8].

Different generation units even operating with the same kind of turbine can have different net water heads associated when discharging the same amount of water. This happens mainly since their penstocks have different geometries, which leads to different losses, having a direct influence on the unit efficiency.

The production function of a hydro generating unit is dependent on the turbine-generator efficiency, the net water head, and the turbine water discharge. Both net water head and efficiency are described as nonlinear functions, which are dependent on the control variables (turbine water discharge and spillage) and the state variables (volumes at the beginning and end of each stage) [7]. The relationship among these variables can be described by curves known as Hill Diagram.

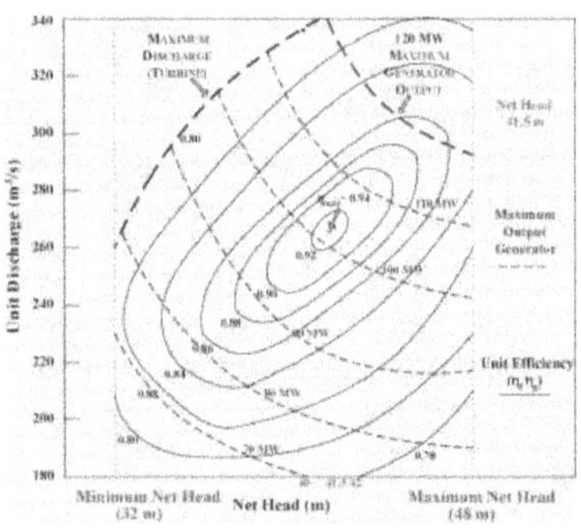

Figure 2: Hill Diagram Example. Adapted from [7].

As can be seen in Figure 2, the Hill Diagram provides basically two kinds of curves for a generation unit: one representing the relationship among the net water head, discharge and the efficiency, represented in %, and the other representing the relationship among the net water head, discharge and power output, normally represented in MW. Both curves are related since it is possible to define power output from the turbine efficiency [1].

A common approach to estimate the production function is to use the information provided by the Hill Diagram. Thus, since the Hill Diagram only provides specific curves to represent the relationships among the involved variables, further techniques have to be implemented to create a continuous function. Finardi represented this function using a polynomial function of degree seven. The coefficients were obtained using a multivariable nonlinear regression technique [7]. The problem of this technique is that losses of precision can occur during the definition of a specific degree for the polynomial and during the process of estimation of the coefficients.

In this paper, an Artificial Neural Network (ANN) approach is proposed with the same purpose. The major benefit of a ANN is its ability to learn and therefore to generalize. Generalization refers to the capacity of producing reasonable outputs for inputs not encountered during training (learning) phase [9]. This ability make it possible for neural networks to solve complex problems. From the extracted points in the Hill Diagram a multilayer perceptron was used to estimate the production function. The objective of this ANN is to estimate the relationship among variables net water head, power output and unit discharge. Considering that it is necessary to calculate the water discharge for each unit, the production function has to be represented in terms of this last variable.

The set of available points was separated randomly in two subsets: 80% for training and 20% for validation [9]. Then the points were normalized in the interval [-1, 1]. The network with 2 hidden layers having 4 and 7 neurons respectively was trained using the Levenberg-Marquadt method [2], with fixed learning rate 0.3 and momentum constant 0.6.

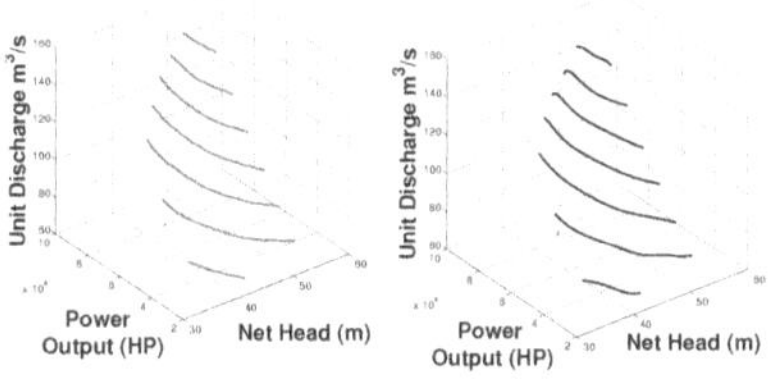

Figure 3: Hill Diagram and Neural Network Points

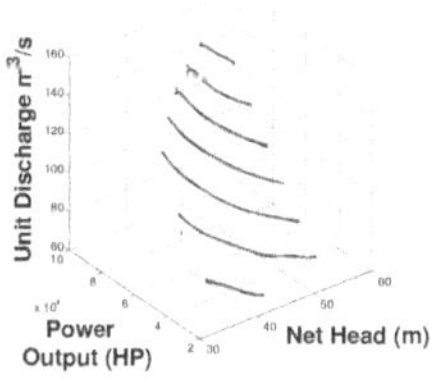

Figure 4: Neural Network Recall over Hill Diagram Points

Figure 3 shows the graphical representation of the original points extracted from the Hill Diagram and the corresponding points obtained through the neural network recall. Figure 4 shows both sets of points plotted together. Testing the validation set the mean error encountered was 0.3182 m^3/s with standard deviation 0.0910 m^3/s, which is very acceptable considering the precision of the hydro plants control systems. The mean squared error is 0.1934 m^3/s.

As mentioned before, the problem addressed in this paper can be stated as: given a power demand to be met by the hydro plant p, the units must be committed so that the total hydro plant discharge is minimized. Thus, each unit has power output forbidden zones which must be avoided during the dispatch. In addition, some plants need to establish that each unit and the plant as a whole are discharging water within a predetermined range. Formally, the problem can be mathematically modelled as follows:

$$Minimize\ C = \sum_{i=1}^{N(p)} q_i \tag{1}$$

$$q_i = Q_{NN}(p_i, hl_i) \tag{2}$$

subject to:

$$P^t = \sum_{i=1}^{N(p)} p_i \tag{3}$$

$$p_i^{min} \le p_i \le p_i^{max} \tag{4}$$

$$q_i^{min} \le q_i \le q_i^{max} \tag{5}$$

$$Q_p^{min} \le \sum_{i=1}^{N(p)} q_i \le Q_p^{max} \tag{6}$$

in which:

$N(p)$	number of generation units in the hydro plant p;
q_i	water discharge of unit i (m^3/s);
Q_{NN}	water discharge function calculated using the proposed artificial neural network (m^3/s);
p_i	production of unit i (MW);
hl_i	net water head of unit i (m);
P^t	required power demand for plant p (MW);
p_i^{min}	minimum power output allowed to unit i (MW);
p_i^{max}	maximum power output allowed to unit i (MW);
q_i^{min}	minimum discharge allowed to unit i (m^3/s);
q_i^{max}	maximum discharge allowed to unit i (m^3/s);
Q_p^{min}	minimum discharge allowed to hydro plant p (m^3/s);
Q_p^{max}	maximum discharge allowed to hydro plant p (m^3/s).

3. EVOLUTIONARY ALGORITHMS

3.1 Overview of Classical DE Algorithm

Differential evolution (DE) has recently proven to be an efficient method for optimizing real-valued multi-modal objective functions. Besides its good convergence properties and suitability for parallelization, DE's main assets are its conceptual simplicity and ease of use. The first written article on DE appeared as a technical report by R. Storn and K. V. Price in 1995 [16]. One year later, the success of DE was demonstrated at the First International Contest on Evolutionary Optimization in May 1996, which was held in conjunction with the 1996 IEEE International Conference on Evolutionary Computation (CEC). Thereafter, DE emerged as a very competitive form of evolutionary computation, turning out as one of the best among important competitions [4].

DE searches for a global optimum point in a D-dimensional real parameter space. The classical algorithm begins with a randomly initiated population of D-dimensional real-valued parameter vectors of size NP. In one of the simplest forms of DE-mutation, to create the donor vector for each ith target vector from the current population $X_t = \{x_{t,i}; i = 1, ..., NP\}$, three other distinct individuals, say $\vec{x}_{r_1^i}$, $\vec{x}_{r_2^i}$ and $\vec{x}_{r_3^i}$ are sampled randomly. The indices r_1^i, r_2^i and r_3^i are mutually exclusive integer random numbers from the range [1, NP]. Then, a differential vector is created, which is the difference between $\vec{x}_{r_2^i}$ and $\vec{x}_{r_3^i}$ scaled by a number F (that typically lies in the interval [0.4, 1]). The differential vector is then added to $\vec{x}_{r_1^i}$, that is named base vector [4]. This generates a mutant vector. The process at the generation t can be expressed as follows:

$$\vec{v}_{t,i} = \vec{x}_{t,r_1^i} + F(\vec{x}_{t,r_2^i} - \vec{x}_{t,r_3^i}) \quad (7)$$

The mutant population generated $V_t = \{v_{t,i}; i = 1, ..., NP\}$ is then combined to the current population producing the offspring $U_t = \{u_{t,i}; i = 1, ..., NP\}$. In the classic version of the algorithm, for each dimension j of each individual i of the population a discrete recombination with probability $C \in [0, 1]$ is applied, as follows:

$$u_{t,i,j} : \begin{cases} v_{t_{i,j}}, & \text{if } rand_{i,j}[0,1] \leq C \vee j = \delta_i \\ x_{t,i,j}, & \text{otherwise} \end{cases} \quad (8)$$

in which $rand_{i,j}[0, 1]$ is a uniformly distributed random number, which is called anew for each jth component of the ith generated individual. $\delta_i \in [1, 2, ..., D]$ is a randomly chosen index, which ensures that U_t gets at least one component from V_t.

The next step of the algorithm calls for selection to determine whether the parent or the mutant vector survives to the next generation, i.e., at $T = T + 1$. The selection operation is described as:

$$\begin{aligned} \vec{X}_{i,T+1} &= \vec{U}_{i,T} \quad \text{if } f(\vec{U}_{i,t}) \leq f(\vec{X}_{i,t}) \\ &= \vec{X}_{i,T} \quad \text{if } f(\vec{U}_{i,t}) > f(\vec{X}_{i,t}) \end{aligned} \quad (9)$$

in which $f(\vec{X})$ is the objective function to be minimized (minimization is considered). As each generated vector only replaces the corresponding parent vector in the next generation if its fitness is better, then it's guaranteed that population either gets better (with respect to the minimization of the objective function) or remains the same in fitness status, but never deteriorates [4].

3.2 Balanced Approach of the DE Algorithm

DE has shown to be effective on a large range of classical optimization problems, and it showed to be more efficient than other well known evolutionary algorithms [4] [16]. In addition to classical DE, many other mutation operators have been proposed to improve its convergence capabilities. However, not all of the DE mutation operators are equally efficient. Some favor the exploration of the search space, while some other operators favor its fast exploitation. Explorative mutation operators have a greater possibility of locating the minima of the objective function, but generally need more iterations (generations). On the other hand, the exploitive mutation operators rapidly converge to a minimum of the objective function. In this case, there exists the risk of premature convergence to a suboptimal solution.

Epitropakis et al proposed a hybrid approach that makes a linear combination between an explorative and exploitive mutation operator [12]. More specifically, the mutant individual $\vec{v}_{t,i}$ is generated using the following equation:

$$\vec{v}_{t,i} = \xi.v_{t,i}^a + (1 - \xi).v_{t,i}^b \quad (10)$$

in which ξ determines the influence of the explorative over the exploitive mutation operator, $v_{t,i}^a$ denotes a explorative mutation operator, while $v_{t,i}^b$ denotes a exploitive mutation operator. For example, $v_{t,i}^a$ can represent the mutation operator of the algorithm DE/rand/1/bin, $(\vec{x}_{t,r_1^i} + F(\vec{x}_{t,r_2^i} - \vec{x}_{t,r_3^i}))$ and $v_{t,i}^b$ can represent the mutation operator of the algorithm DE/best/1/bin $(\vec{x}_{t,best} + F(\vec{x}_{t,r_3^i} - \vec{x}_{t,r_2^i}))$. The parameter ξ can be calculated using one of the following equations:

$$\xi_1 = (1 + \rho).2^{-c.g}, \quad (11)$$

$$\xi_2 = \rho.2^{-c.g}, \quad (12)$$

$$\xi_3 = \frac{\xi_1 + \xi_2}{2}, \quad (13)$$

where g is the current generation, $\rho \in [0, 1]$ is a random number from the uniform distribution, and c, the noise decay constant, is calculated as one tenth of the maximum allowed number of generations. According to the author, this scheme can lead to reliable optimization of unknown objective functions, since it alleviates problems generated by poor selection of the user defined parameters, such as decreased rate of convergence, or even divergence and premature saturation [12].

3.3 Particle Swarm Optimization (PSO)

PSO was introduced by Kennedy and Eberhart in 1995. It was inspired by the swarm behaviour as is displayed by a flock of birds, a school of fish, or even human social behaviour being influenced by other individuals [10].

PSO consists of a swarm of particles moving in an N-dimensional, real-valued search space of possible problem solutions. Every particle has a position vector $\vec{x}$ encoding a candidate solution to the problem, a velocity vector $\vec{v}$ and a small memory that stores its own best position so far $\vec{p}$. Moreover, a global best position among the swarm $\vec{g}$ is stored. In the classical version of the algorithm the velocity and position of the particles are updated as follows:

$$\begin{aligned} v_{i,k} = \omega.v_{i,k-1} + c_1.R_1^k.[p_{i,k-1} - x_{i,k-1}] + \\ c_2.R_2^k.[g_{k-1} - x_{i,k-1}], \end{aligned} \quad (14)$$

$$x_{i,k} = v_{i,k} + x_{i,k-1}, \quad (15)$$

in which ω is a inertia weight factor, $v_{i,k}$ is the velocity of particle i at kth iteration, c_1 is the cognitive factor, c_2 is the social factor, R_1^k and R_2^k are two random numbers uniformly distributed in the range of [0, 1], $x_{i,k}$ is the current position of particle i at iteration k, $p_{i,k}$ is the position of particle i at kth iteration and g_k is the best position in the swarm at kth iteration.

3.4 Problem Model

As described before, the proposed model used in this paper defines four constraints: one regarding to the plant to meet the desired power output, one to ensure that each unit is respecting its output limits, one to evaluate if each unit is demanding discharges in accordance to the plant capabilities and the last one to evaluate if the total discharge is within a predetermined range.

The most popular range constraint handling strategy in evolutionary algorithms is to use a penalty function (PF) added to the individuals fitness values. Obviously, the individuals will avoid getting close to prohibited areas due to bigger fitness values that they reach when they do not meet the constraints established.

3.4.1 *Movable Partition Approach*

It is also possible to use the PF approach to satisfy equality constraints. However, it can make it harder for the optimization technique in the process of finding global minimum values because the fitness of the individuals can change very quickly for each difference between the current value of the equality variable and the required constant for it.

Here a movable partitions approach is proposed to deal with the desired power output equality constraint. This modelling consists of, instead of using a variable to represent the power output for each one of the $N(p)$ production units, define a compartment with fixed size representing the total power output for the plant separated by $N(p) - 1$ movable partitions. Using this approach, in addition to eliminate the equality constraint of the problem, one less dimension is required to represent the plant what improves the search capabilities of the algorithm. Figure 5 illustrates this technique.

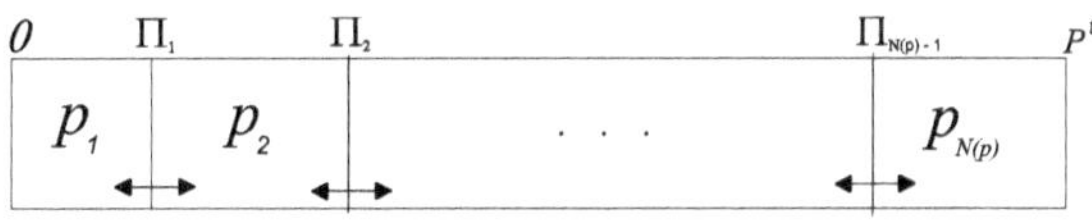

Figure 5: Movable Partitions Approach illustration

Observing Figure 5, $N(p) - 1$ partitions are used to determine $N(p)$ unit power outputs. In this way, the objective of the algorithm is to move these $N(p) - 1$ partitions over the space to find optimized solutions. The conversion calculus from partitions to power output is performed by a simple subtraction, as below:

$$p_i = \Pi_i - \Pi_{i-1}, \qquad 1 \le i \le N(p), \tag{16}$$

in which Π_i represents the partition i, $\Pi_0 = 0$ and $\Pi_{N(p)} = P^t$.

From this approach, the partition overpassing problem can occur. If one partition overpasses others during the algorithm processing then the power demand dispatched would be different from the desired. In this case, a possible solution is to sort the partitions according to their new indexes to ensure the commitment to this constraint, what is simple to implement and does not cause any issues to the algorithm behavior.

3.4.2 *Fitness Function*

After the range constraints be treated by PF method, the equality constraint be solved using the movable partition approach and based on the fitness function proposed by Liu and Li [11] the initial objective (Equation 1) can be turned into an unconstrained optimization problem, which can be formulated as:

$$Minimize\ F = \sum_{i=1}^{N(p)} \{\ q_i + \sum_{j=1}^{N(c)} [\ |\varphi_{i,j}|\ .\ \lambda_j\ ]\ \} \tag{17}$$

- $\varphi_{i,1} = \max(p_i^{max}, p_i^t) - p_i^{max}$
- $\varphi_{i,2} = \min(p_i^{min}, p_i^t) - p_i^{min}$
- $\varphi_{i,3} = \max(q_i^{max}, q_i) - q_i^{max}$
- $\varphi_{i,4} = \min(q_i^{min}, q_i) - q_i^{min}$
- $\varphi_{i,5} = \max(Q_p^{max}, \sum_{i=1}^{N(p)} q_i) - Q_p^{max}$
- $\varphi_{i,6} = \min(Q_p^{min}, \sum_{i=1}^{N(p)} q_i) - Q_p^{min}$

in which F is the fitness value of the individuals, $N(c)$ is the number of constraints (in this case 6), λ_j is the penalty operator of jth constraint and $\varphi_{i,j}$ represents the jth constraint according to the individual i.

4. APPLICATION OF THE OBTAINED SOLUTION

4.1 Plant and Algorithms Information

The proposed model was applied to the hydroelectric plant of Três Marias in Brazil. This plant has 6 units on the upstream of the São Francisco River but only 5 are fully operational at the moment. The power output interval tested for each unit was (35 to 61)MW which enables the power rating of 305MW (5 × 61MW). The turbines are identical, but they have different net heads due to their different geometries in the penstocks. The gross head used for the the units was 56m. The water dispatch interval allowed for each turbine used was (60 to 150)m^3/s and the total plant dispatch interval used was (320 to 700)m^3/s. Six different typical power demands for the plant were tested: 210MW, 230MW, 250MW, 270MW, 290MW and 300MW.

In order to optimize the proposed model, three evolutionary algorithms, the DE/best/1/ bin (DE_1), the balanced version of the DE proposed by Epitropakis ($DE_{2,1}$) and the classical Particle Swarm Optimization (PSO) algorithm, were tested. The only stop criteria used was number of generations which was equals to 50. It was chosen the DE/rand/1/bin and DE/best/1/bin as the explorative and exploitive mutation operations, respectively, in the balanced version of the DE algorithm. The parameter ξ_3 was used to perform the balancing. All the other parameters used in this algorithm were the same used in the DE_1 mentioned above. The PSO used a self-adaptive decreasing inertia weight schema [11]. The number of particles used was also 50. The parameters cognitive factor c_1, social factor c_2, maximum inertia weight w_{max}, minimum inertia weight w_{min}, as well as DE parameters are shown in table 1.

Table 1: Algorithms Parameters

DE Parameters			
F	C	NP	-
0.4	0.6	50	-
PSO Parameters			
c_1	c_2	w_{max}	w_{min}
2.0	3.5	0.9	0.4

The constraint penalties adopted and net water heads for each unit are contained in the table 2. They were found empirically.

Table 2: Model Parameters

Constraint Penalties Values					
λ_1	λ_2	λ_3	λ_4	λ_5	λ_6
6.0	6.0	5.0	5.0	5.0	5.0
Net Water Heads (hl_i)					
hl_1	hl_2	hl_3	hl_4	hl_5	-
52.5	54.0	55.0	54	52.5	-

4.2 Results

Each algorithm tested was executed 30 times for each power demand. Table 3 shows the best solutions encountered by each algorithm through the executions. In addition, it is shown the equal division of the power demand among the units available, what is the common practice of the plant studied. As can be seen in the table 3 all algorithms reached the same best fitness value. The best discharge gain happened for the demand of 230MW, reaching 4.95 less m^3/s what represents 1.05% of water economy.

Table 3: Unit Commitment Results

Load Demand (MW)	Method	Unit Power Output (MW) #1	#2	#3	#4	#5	Water Disch. (m^3/s)
210	DE_1	39.8	40.0	50.3	40.0	39.8	426.45
	$DE_{2,1}$	39.8	40.0	50.3	40.0	39.8	426.45
	PSO	39.8	40.0	50.3	40.0	39.8	426.45
	=	42.0	42.0	42.0	42.0	42.0	427.85
230	DE_1	40.3	53.6	54.8	40.8	40.3	465.40
	$DE_{2,1}$	40.3	40.8	54.8	53.6	40.3	465.40
	PSO	40.3	53.6	54.8	40.8	40.3	465.40
	=	46.0	46.0	46.0	46.0	46.0	470.35
250	DE_1	40.5	56.2	56.2	56.2	40.5	505.23
	$DE_{2,1}$	40.5	56.2	56.2	56.2	40.5	505.23
	PSO	40.5	56.3	56.2	56.3	40.5	505.23
	=	50.0	50.0	50.0	50.0	50.0	508.57
270	DE_1	40.7	57.1	56.8	57.1	58.0	546.87
	$DE_{2,1}$	58.0	57.1	56.8	57.2	40.7	546.87
	PSO	58.1	57.1	56.8	57.15	40.7	546.87
	=	54.0	54.0	54.0	54.0	54.0	547.67
290	DE_1	58.5	57.7	57.3	57.7	58.5	588.64
	$DE_{2,1}$	58.5	57.7	57.3	57.7	58.6	588.64
	PSO	58.5	57.7	57.3	57.7	58.6	588.64
	=	58.0	58.0	58.0	58.0	58.0	588.73
300	DE_1	60.5	59.8	59.3	59.8	60.5	613.19
	$DE_{2,1}$	60.5	59.8	59.3	59.8	60.4	613.19
	PSO	60.5	59.8	59.3	59.8	60.4	613.19
	=	60.0	60.0	60.0	60.0	60.0	613.74

4.3 Algorithm Analysis

As said before, all algorithms reached the same best solution at least once during their executions. In this section, the three algorithms will be compared in order to determine which of them is the most suitable to optimize the optimization problem.

4.3.1 Results Analysis

In order to analyse the results found for each algorithm during their executions, a box plot was generated for each power demand tested. Box plot is a compact representation that encodes the minimum, maximum, mean, median, and quartile information of a distribution [5]. The outliers are the observations that present greater distances to the rest of the distribution. Figure 6 shows the results distribution box plot for the the 290MW power demand. The x-axis represents the three algorithms tested and the y-axis represents the fitness value. The filled point is the mean of the distribution and the unfilled points are the outliers. The other box plots will not be shown in this paper because they had similar forms.

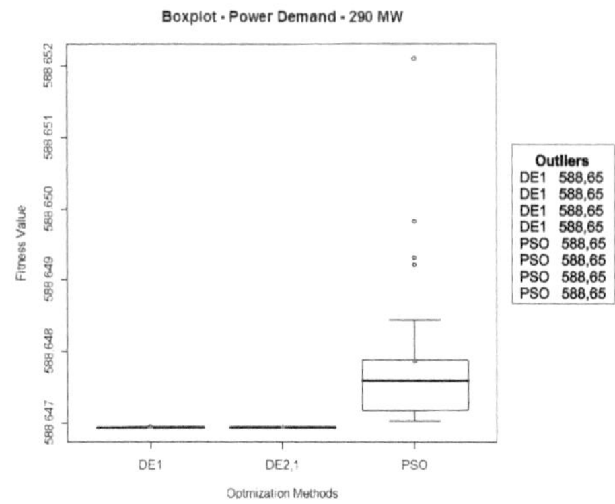

Figure 6: Box Plot - Demand 290MW

Analysing that box plot, it is possible to say that the algorithms had similar results. It is valid to notice that y-axis scale precision in Figure 6 is 10^{-3}, what makes the differences among the samples very discrete. Only a line was observed for the algorithms DE_1 and $DE_{2,1}$ in the box plot because the quartiles are very close to the medians. In the PSO algorithm, the difference between the upper and lower quartiles are also very subtle. All the outliers are very close to the rest of the distribution (differences less than 10^{-1}). Hence, there are indications that the algorithms are executing with robustness and usually find similar results during all the executions.

To testify the conclusions provided by the box plots, a Permutation Test was also applied to the algorithm results. Permutation tests are non-parametric statistical methods which estimate a reference distribution by calculating all possible values (or at least a considerably large set) of a statistic test rearrangements of the labels on a set of observed data points [13]. Any performance index can be chosen as the test statistic object. For the comparison of each pair of different algorithms, the following null and alternative hypothesis are formulated:

- Null hypothesis H_0: there is no performance difference between the two algorithms;
- Alternative hypothesis H_1: there is a performance difference between the two algorithms.

In other words, the null hypothesis states that *There is no evidence that one of the algorithms is intrinsically better than the other one, since the difference between their performance indices could be explained as being a realization of an underlying probability distribution of the test ob ect that is neutral (the distribution does not favor any algorithm).* The central assumption of the method is that, if the observed result has arisen by chance, then this value will not seem unusual in a distribution of results obtained through many random relabellings of the samples.

Permutation tests can be used for building a reference distribution in which it is possible to determine if the difference which has been observed between the sample means is enough to reject H_0. That test can be performed as follows [6].

1. Find the sample means $\overline{A}$ and $\overline{B}$.
2. Find the observed difference $d = \overline{A} - \overline{B}$.
3. Arrange the observations of A and B in a single vector $S = [a_1, a_2, \ldots a_{n_A}, b_1, b_2, \ldots b_{n_B}]$.
4. Make i $\leftarrow = 1$.
5. For a high pre-determined number of times:
   a) Shuffle the elements of S to create S'.
   b) Calculate $\overline{x_a} = \frac{1}{n_A} \sum_{i=1}^{n_A} S'_i$.
   c) Calculate $\overline{x_b} = \frac{1}{n_B} \sum_{i=n_A+1}^{n_B} S'_i$.
   d) Make $X_i \leftarrow \overline{x_a} - \overline{x_b}$.
6. Sort X in ascendant order
7. Calculate $p_{value}(d) = P(X \leq d)$.
8. If $p_{value}(d) \leq \frac{\alpha}{2}$ or $p_{value}(d) \geq 1 - \frac{\alpha}{2}$ then reject H_0 and accept H_1. Otherwise, keep H_0 as a non-discarded possibility.

In step 8, the parameter α is an user-defined confidence level for the rejection of the null hypothesis.

In the algorithms results case, A stands for the results distribution of one algorithm and B stands for the results distribution of another algorithm. It is worthwhile to notice that the Permutation Test is applied between two distributions. H_0 indicates that there are no sufficient statistic evidences that enable the rejection of the null hypothesis, which means that it can not be evaluated that the algorithm A is better or worse than the algorithm B. H_1 indicates that the results are different. In this case, if d is positive then it can be noticed that B has better results on average (the problem stands for minimization). The same way, if d is negative then it can be noticed that A has better results on average. The confidence level defined α is 0.05 (95%) and the number of times that the statistical object were performed (step 5) is 5000. The Permutation Test was performed for all the power demands tested using the following A vs. B: DE_1 vs. $DE_{2,1}$, DE_1 vs. PSO and $DE_{2,1}$ vs. PSO.

In the first part of the test, the difference of the objective function means was used as the statistical object. For all the tests performed, the hypothesis H_0 was true, indicating that there is no evidence that one of the algorithms is intrinsically better than the other one. Figure 7 shows the histogram of the test for the 210MW power demand, DE_1 vs. PSO. Notice that the observed result is not statistically significant since it is located inside the confidence interval. The other histograms will not be shown in this paper because they had similar forms.

4.3.2 Convergence Analysis

Figure 8 shows the mean convergence lines for each power demand tested. Each graph shows, for all evolutionary algorithms, the mean of the fitness value encountered at each generation among the 30 executions.

Table 4 shows the mean number of generations that each algorithm executed until find the best fitness value. It was just considered fitness value improvements higher than 5×10^{-3} in relation to the best previous fitness value encountered.

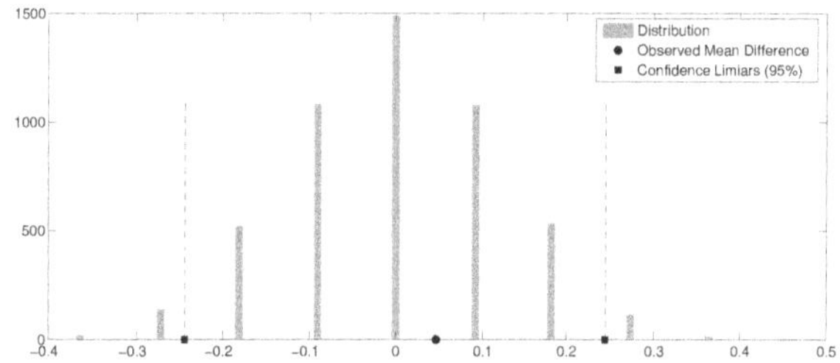

Figure 7: Permutation Test Histogram - DE_1 vs. PSO - 270MW

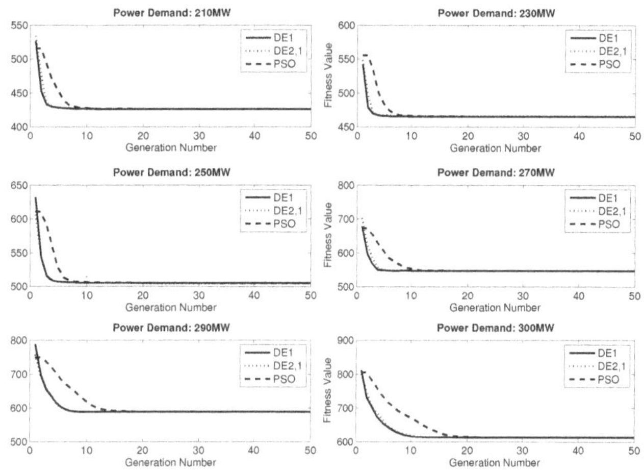

Figure 8: Mean Convergence Lines

Table 4: Mean Number of Generations to Converge

Method	Load Output (MW)	Mean # of Gen.	Stand. Dev.	General Mean # of Gen.	General Stand. Dev.
DE_1	210	14.0	1.9	14.8	2.4
	230	13.4	1.1		
	250	15.3	1.3		
	270	13.4	2.5		
	290	14.9	1.8		
	300	17.8	2.4		
$DE_{2,1}$	210	15.4	1.6	16.4	2.5
	230	15.2	1.5		
	250	16.7	1.5		
	270	16.2	3.1		
	290	15.7	1.6		
	300	19.7	2.2		
PSO	210	23.9	7.0	25.6	8.8
	230	23.8	4.8		
	250	24.7	7.8		
	270	18.1	5.8		
	290	24.0	5.2		
	300	39.1	5.1		

The algorithm DE_1 demanded less generations on average to find the results than the other methods tested, but its results were close to $DE_{2,1}$ algorithm. To better evaluate the convergence of the algorithms, another Permutation Test was applied. In this case, the number of generations required to algorithm convergence was used as statistical object. In this case, H_0 indicates that there are no sufficient statistic evidences to reject the hypothesis that the algorithm A converges demanding less generations than the algorithm B and vice versa. H_1 with d negative indicates that the algorithm A converges faster with 95% confidence level. The same way, H_1 with d positive indicates that the algorithm B converges faster with the same confidence level. Table 5 shows the results for the disputes A vs. B.

Table 5: Permutation Test Applied to the Algorithms Convergence

Power Output (MW)	DE_1 vs. $DE_{2,1}$	DE_1 vs. PSO	$DE_{2,1}$ vs. PSO
210	H_0	H_1-	H_1-
230	H_1-	H_1-	H_1-
250	H_1-	H_1-	H_1-
270	H_1-	H_1-	H_0
290	H_0	H_1-	H_1-
300	H_1-	H_1-	H_1-

At Table 5 H_1- indicates that d has a negative value. According to the results, it can be said that H_1 is predominant. DE_1 converged before that $DE_{2,1}$ in 4 of the 6 tested power demands and before the PSO for all power demands. Furthermore, $DE_{2,1}$ converged faster than PSO for 5 of the 6 tested demands. Figure 9 shows the histograms for DE_1 vs $DE_{2,1}$ for the demands 210 and 230 MW, which means H_1- and H_0, respectively.

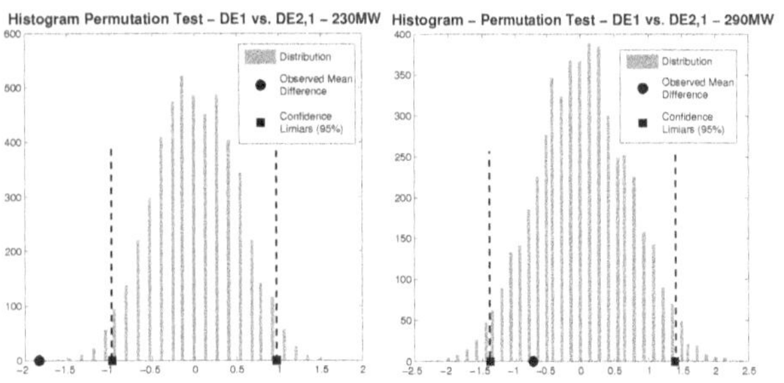

Figure 9: Permutation Results - Convergence

5. CONCLUSIONS

This paper presented a proposal for optimizing the unit commitment of hydroelectric generating units of a single plant. The proposed method is based on a Neural Network to model the discharge function and the novel movable partitions approach to meet the required power demand, which avoids an equality constraint in the model and requires one less dimension to represent it. Three evolutionary methods were tested to optimize the objective function modeled: DE/best/1/bin, a balanced version of DE and the PSO algorithm. All the three algorithms encountered similar best fitness values for all the demands tested and it was not possible to say if an algorithm is better than another. From the convergence test analysis, the algorithm DE/best/1/bin presented a higher performance for this problem comparing to the other two, in terms of number of generations required to reach the best solution. The balanced version of DE also manifested faster convergence when compared to PSO in most of cases.

6. REFERENCES

[1] T. O. A. Arce and S. Soares. Optimal dispatch of generating units of the itaipú hydroelectric plant. *IEEE Transactions on Power Systems*, 17:154–158, Feb 2002.

[2] N. Ampazis and S. Perantonis. Levenberg-marquadt algorithm with adaptive momentum for the efficient training of feedforward networks. In *IEEE International Joint Conference on Neural Networks*, volume 1, pages 126–131, Jul 2000.

[3] A. Conejo and N. J. Redondo. Short-termhydro-thermal coordination by relaxation lagrangian: Solution of the dual problem. *IEEE Trans on Power Systems*, 14(1):89–95, February 1999.

[4] S. Das and P. N. Suganthan. Differential evolution: A survey of the state-of-the-art. *IEEE Transactions on Evolutionary Computation*, 15:4–31, Feb 2011.

[5] J. L. D. David Kao, Alison Luo and A. Pang. Visualizing spatially varying distribution data. *Proceedings of the Sixth International Conference on Information Visualisation*, pages 219–225, Nov 2002.

[6] E. F. W. Eduardo G. Carrano and R. H. C. Takahashi. A multicriteria statistical based comparison methodology for evaluating evolutionary algorithms. *IEEE Transactions of Evolutionary Computation*, 15:848–870, Dec 2011.

[7] E. C. Finardi and E. L. da Silva. Unit commitment of single hydroelectric plant. *Electric Power Systems Research*, 75:116–123, May 2005.

[8] E. C. Finardi and E. L. da Silva. Solving the hydro unit commitment problem via dual decomposition and sequential quadratic programming. *IEEE Transactions on Power Systems*, 21(2):835–844, May 2006.

[9] S. Haykin. *Neural Networks - A Comprehensive Foundation*. Pearson Prentice Hall, 2nd edition, 1999.

[10] J. Kennedy and R. C. Eberhart. Particle swarm optimization. *Proceedings of the 1995 IEEE International Conference on Neural Networks*, 4:1942–1948, 1995.

[11] S. Liu and X. Li. Hydroelectric unit commitment by enhanced pso. In *IEEE E-Product E-Service and E-Entertainment*, pages 1–4, 2010.

[12] V. P. M.G Epitropakis and M. Vrahatis. Balancing the exploration and exploitation capabilities of the differential evolution algorithm. In *IEEE Congress on Evolutionary Computation*, pages 2686–2693, Jun 2008.

[13] D. S. Moore and G. P. McCabe. *Introduction to the Practice of Statistics*. Freeman, 5th edition, 2005.

[14] R. K. Pancholi and K. S. Swarup. Particle swarm optimization for security constrained economic dispatch. In *IEEE Intelligent Sensing and Information Processing*, pages 7–12, 2004.

[15] X. G. . Zhai and J. Cui. Unit commitment with identical units: Successive subproblem solving method based on lagrangian relaxation. *IEEE Trans on Power Systems*, 17(4):1250–1257, November 2002.

[16] R. Storn and K. V. Price. Differential evolution: A simple and efficient adaptive scheme for global optimization over continuous spaces. *ICSI, USA Technical Report TR-95-012*, Mar 1995.

[17] T. Yalcinoz and M. Short. Neural networks approach for solving economic dispatch problem with transmission capacity constraints. *IEEE Transactions on Power Systems*, 13:307–313, May 1998.

Searching for the Minimum Failures that Can Cause a Hazard in a Wireless Sensor Network

Iain Bate[1,2]
[1] Mälardalen Real-Time Research Centre
Mälardalen University
Västerås, Sweden
iain.bate@cs.york.ac.uk

Mark Louis Fairbairn[2]
[2] Department of Computer Science
University of York
York, UK
mlf@cs.york.ac.uk

ABSTRACT

Wireless Sensor Networks (WSN) are now being used in a range of applications, many of which are critical systems, e.g. monitoring assisted living facilities or for fire detection systems which is the example used in this paper. For critical systems it is important to be able to determine the minimum number of failures that can cause a hazard to occur. This is normally a manual, human intensive, task. This paper presents a novel application of search to both the WSN and safety domains; searching for combinations of failures that can cause a hazard and then reducing these to the minimum possible using a combination of automated search and manual refinement. Due to the size and complexity of the search problem, a parallel search algorithm is designed that runs on available compute resources with the results being processed using *R*.

Categories and Subject Descriptors

H.4 [**Performance of Systems**]: Reliability, availability, and serviceability; Performance attributes; Fault tolerance

General Terms

Performance

Keywords

stress-based testing; search-based testing; safety and dependability; wireless sensor networks

1. INTRODUCTION

Wireless Sensor Networks (WSN) are a fast growing area of research and are now being commercially deployed. Systems are normally composed from many simple nodes that autonomously deliver the overall functionality needed for the application. Uses of WSNs include, assisted living facilities to monitor patients, fire detection systems in building or forests, or within oil refineries to monitor stages of production. A typical deployment would consist of tens, if not hundreds, of autonomously-operating nodes. The combination of humans being central to the system, their mission critical nature and the fact functionality is delivered largely by software-based processing make them a classic example of a Cyber Physical System (CPS) where a complex computing system provides essential services to its human operators in order to make the operators more efficient and effective. The essential nature of the services extend beyond merely the functional or real-time properties but also encompass safety and dependability. At the same time there is growing evidence that deployments of WSNs have dependability issues [21, 22, 6].

WSNs use adaptive communications protocols which establish reliable ad-hoc networks, and minimise energy usage by reducing the number of message hops and aggregating information into fewer packets. The result is individual nodes having complex software in terms of how they are written and the algorithms encoded. These algorithms include signal processing from the sensors, data aggregation based on data being fed in from a range of nodes, and systems software including the operating system and network stack. Due to the low resources available, these algorithms tend to be written in a highly optimised device-specific manner. Clearly their behaviour is dependent on their software. However added difficulty is introduced as they are also dependent on, and interact with, other nodes in the WSN, as well as other wireless devices and physical objects in the collective shared environment. To this end, it is important to understand how many node failures can lead to the WSN not delivering the expected functionality. It is also important to know the physical area in which the failures may occur, i.e. there should be no more than M failures within area N. This information allows the designers to decide whether the design is sufficiently dependable, i.e. reliable or available. The designer can then either add more nodes or make the individual nodes more reliable. We only need to know why the individual nodes fail if there is a need to understand the cause of a failure, i.e. to prevent it having effect in the future [11].

There are two key approaches to understand the safety of systems, analysis and testing. Static analysis can work well for more constrained systems in terms of the design principles used and the configurations deployed [12, 2]. However even where these are highly-automated, they still require a model of the system to exist and then the results from this model are validated against the final system. It is our thesis that using search to manipulate the failures within a simulation can find similar results. Simulated models are used

GECCO'13, July 6–10, 2013, Amsterdam, The Netherlands.

as large-scale evaluation is not possible on "real" WSNs and for every trial (i.e. move of the search) all the nodes may need re-programming, and trials would consume much of the already limited power. The simulated models have been shown to be close to reality [5], however any inaccuracies do not matter to the results obtained. The reason is that we aim to determine the minimum number of node failures that can lead to a hazard without trying to understand what might have cause the nodes to fail. Of equal importance to the fact any inaccuracy should have a negligible effect is that the results obtained using a simulated model can easily be validated.

Even though simulation is easier to perform than large-scale trials with real hardware, each simulation can still take minutes, if not hours, [16] making search more difficult. Even though, for a particular system design, determining the minimum number of failures does not need to be determined often, there are still benefits that this is done as quickly as possible. One such benefit is the possible evaluation of many proposed designs. For this reason, a parallel search approach is proposed. This has the secondary advantage that the risk of premature convergence can be reduced by each of the individual searches swapping partial solutions at appropriate points in time [9]. It is assumed that most organisations have a reasonable number of computers that can be used to perform the simulations, e.g. as part of their background processing using frameworks like BIONC (http://boinc.berkeley.edu), or there are plenty of relatively cheap cloud computing facilities, e.g. Amazon EC2 (http://aws.amazon.com/ec2/). However these "commodity" solutions tend to larger variations in completion time due to the need to fairly share the resources across users or machines. This necessitates a parallel search algorithm where the individual search algorithms are not too tightly coupled.

The contributions of this paper include:

1. Presenting a search-based method for WSNs to determine the minimum number of failures that could lead to hazards.
2. Defining the size and complexity of the search problem.
3. Designing a search algorithm that can deal with these complexities despite the evaluation being time intensive.

The structure of the paper is as follows. Firstly, our approach to making WSNs dependable is presented including an example application that is to be used throughout this paper. Next, the search framework is designed showing the choices of the search algorithm itself, the fitness function that guides the search towards the desired solution, and the moves that the search algorithm makes to achieve an efficient and effective solution. Finally there is an evaluation of the approach followed by conclusions.

2. THE USE OF DEPENDABLE WSNS

The purpose of this section is to do the following: provide an overview of how WSNs are used as part of dependable systems; a description of the fire detection system used in this paper; and details of our approach based on the use of Health Monitoring (HM), specifically Safety Policy Monitoring (SPM).

2.1 WSNs for Dependability

An important feature of WSNs to consider is that nodes have highly restricted resource availability, owing to the requirement for small physical size and low unit cost. Limited availability of energy resources are particularly significant. When a node runs out of energy it cannot participate in the WSN. Eventually a state is reached in which there are insufficient active nodes for the distributed application to function correctly; at this stage the entire WSN is effectively useless for the application. WSN designs must therefore be sufficiently optimised to ensure correct operation for at least the specified operational lifetime. One approach that may be taken is to make them reactive. A reactive system will only transmit messages when there is something of interest to communicate. By contrast, a traditional approach taken in hard-wired systems would use many more messages and hence energy to provide similar functionality, due to the sensors continuously reporting back to the application. A quandary for the designer is that a silent network could indicate nothing of interest is happening or that the network has failed, e.g. due to a lack of energy. Therefore appropriate means, e.g. HM, are need to ensure that the network can still function correctly should the need arise that balances resource usage against the need to know if the WSN is still capable of delivering the intended application semantics [21]. The purpose of HM is to periodically check key aspects of the WSN's operation in order to ensure dependability [1]. In this paper, the attributes of dependability of considered are; reliability, availability, maintainability and safety.

One technique to improve the dependability is to use HM. HM approaches are split into centralised systems such as MANNA [14], and distributed systems where typically decisions are made based upon the local neighbourhood, with the global network improving as a more emergent behaviour. The main issue with these approaches is they simply detect failed nodes and do not check the WSN's ability to deliver the expected application semantics. A consequence of this is that maintenance may be ordered before it is needed, for example if sufficient replicas still exist to report information.

Wu et al [21] proposed RTA, which aims to verify the application level semantics of the system by simulating certain behaviours in the WSN. The approach is motivated by WSNs often being reactive which means for long periods the WSN may be quiet indicating there is no sensed data worth reporting, however it could also mean that the WSN has failed. Wu used the example of a fire detection system. Firstly omission of a fire detection is the only hazard considered, and secondly maintenance is only ordered when the WSN can no longer detect a fire. In [4], an improved type of RTA was introduced that specifically targets the mitigation of hazards and hence improving the safety of systems. The approach is referred to here as SPM and the tests that are periodically performed Safety Policy Tests (SPT). SPM is based on the concepts of Safety Policies [15] and Safety Kernels [20]. SPM is used in this paper as it is the only known example of an approach targeting safety of WSNs.

2.2 Fire Detection System

The purpose of this section is to introduce a case study, a firefighting system which is used throughout this paper, and the WSN design that has been produced to deliver dependability.

The firefighting system [21] is intended for use on larger buildings, e.g. skyscrapers, with each room having a number of different sensors, e.g. temperature and humidity. Based on these sensors a decision is made as to whether there is a fire in the building. Should a fire be detected then a signal is sent to a central monitoring station where information from all the rooms is then used to initiate and control appropriate firefighting measures. As part of the firefighting system it is envisaged the firefighters themselves will receive information on which rooms have a fire and in the case of evacuation what the best route out of the building would be. Other users of the information would be the buildings supervisor who would have responsibility for ensuring an operational fire fighting system, the people who have to maintain the WSN, and the fire chief(s) with responsibility for coordinating the firefighting. The reasons we feel this system is an appropriate example are as follows:

1. The system has clear hazards associated with it, for example not detecting a fire, not warning a firefighter of hazards within a room they are about to enter, or not providing or providing an incorrect egress route.
2. The system is sufficiently complex as it features heterogeneous sensors, data aggregation, communications that will be subject to interference and voids, and multiple categories of users. As such the failure conditions leading to the hazards are not straightforward.

In our WSN-based implementation of a fire detection system, there are five rooms. Each room has four nodes of which a minimum of two are needed to detect a fire. Each node would have a cpu with an application, network stack and a micro-kernel. The software has three distinct purposes. Firstly to sense the environment with some of the available sensors that each node might have, e.g. temperature or humidity, and then process it accordingly, e.g. to reduce the data size. The processed information is then sent to a sink node which collects it together, and then either processes the data or uploads it to remote computers for remote processing. This sink node is assumed to be hard-wired to the operators console, so is less likely to experience failures and is also mains powered. Secondly as most WSNs are multi-hop, a node commonly acts as a routing node. Its software is therefore responsible for receiving information from other nodes and forwards it to the next node en-route towards the sink. Unlike most traditional critical systems, WSNs operate in environments that are not well understood even after deployment and failures are more common place. These failures are more common due to node hardware being unreliable and also the possibility that new interference sources may be introduced during use. To counter these problems WSNs are often designed using adaptive algorithms and protocols which makes verification more challenging [17, 18, 19]. Finally it has system software which is responsible for scheduling, security, HM etc..

A hazard analysis was performed that determined a late fire detection is potentially unsafe, which leads to a DSR being specified. That is, DSR2 - *The fire detection system should detect a fire in a room within Z time units, where Z is dependent on the building's safety case and the need to evacuate the building within a given amount of time.* Therefore due to the reactive nature of WSNs, periodic simulated fire signals are raised at all nodes. These periodic signals are referred to as *Safety Policy Tests* (SPT). They allow the system to determine whether the DSR is in fact met. The test to cover DSR2 is to check whether any SPT message indicating a simulated fire has been delayed by more than Z time units from each and every node in the network. In the fire scenario Z is assumed to be 1 minute, as this is an early indication of either a node failure, node communications being dropped, or messages simply taking too long to reach the operator node. All of these should be handled by maintenance procedures. These failures could be for a large variety of reasons including: environmental noise effecting the chance of successful transmission, the number of hops to traverse the network, or the latency of other messages. The test looking for DSR2 failures is performed on the operator(s) consoles.

If problems are detected then maintenance is planned.

1. *Replacement maintenance* is scheduled if more than P nodes within a room have a permanent fail silent failure or a fail noisy failure indicating that the node is faulty and must be replaced.
2. *Communications maintenance* is scheduled by the presence of a DSR2 failure (transient fail silent failure) being raised on a node without the presence of a DSR1 failure (permanent fail silent failure). Should this be an isolated case then it's most likely a communication hardware failure, and thus the node should be replaced. If many nodes exhibit this behaviour then this form of maintenance does not physically replace the failed nodes, as this would not fix the issue, instead requiring that the network parameters are tuned to decrease the number of collisions, e.g. increasing communications jitter (decreasing the likelihood of a collision occurring during the sending of messages).

Further details on the methods by which the DSRs and SPTs are derived and used are contained in [8].

2.3 Assessing the Search Landscape

Each injected failure is considered to be within a specific node and is transient for a given period and given duration. Durations can be up to and including the length of the period at which point the failure becomes permanent. Each time a failure is triggered, it is assumed that with a given probability it will lead to a total failure of the node, i.e. the node will no longer sense information, communicate its own sensed data or act as a routing node for others. Where this does not happen it is assumed the failure is either not significant to these functions or it is tolerated. It is noted that other (not-injected) failures will occur as part of the simulation, e.g. communication failures due to packet collisions.

Variable	Min	Max	Step
Failure Period (hours)	1	4	1
Failure Duration (mins)	1	Period	1
Failure Offset (hours)	0	Period	0.25
Failure Probability (%)	0	100	5
Maintenance Period (hours)	2	8	2

Table 1: Variables to be Manipulated

The variables, their ranges and the step function used in this paper are described in Table 1. The step function assumes not all values might be chosen, i.e. a variable can take values min_value, min_value+step_value, min_value+2·step_value, ··, max_value. Without a step function, i.e. if all real values were assumed in the range, then the search space would be significantly larger. An important (related) issue is that the search landscape is not smooth. This means that search approaches, e.g. hill climbing, will struggle to find getting good solutions harder. Reducing the search size helps, however it is at the possible expense of the *best* possible solutions not being found. Initial trials show that too small a *step_value*, including not having a *step_value*, meant that none of the search algorithms could cause the hazard to occur within the time allowed. Too large a *step_value* meant the failure state of the nodes tended to be too regular, e.g. binary between not failed or permanently failed. This would be unrealistic for a WSN. The minimum and maximum values in Table 1 were chosen as they are realistic for the application. The step values were chosen, roughly following a binary search, to best show the differences in the algorithms.

The size of the search space is therefore 20!·307200·5, which equals $3.7\text{x}10^{24}$, based on the following.

1. There are 20! combinations of node failures that can occur if physical position is ignored. If physical position is taken into account then the number of combinations would be much larger, however 20! is sufficiently large to illustrate the significant complexity of the search problem.
2. There are $4 \cdot 240 \cdot 16 \cdot 20$ (=307,200) combinations for each node failure from the period, duration, offset and probability respectively.
3. The maintenance periods give 5 further options.

2.4 Simulation Used for Evaluation

To measure the fitness of a specific solution it was necessary to run a full simulation of the fire detection system using co-simulation between the application simulator and Network Simulator 2 (NS-2). The application was implemented using a custom built application level simulator which defines the behaviour of the nodes and the node failures. NS-2 (www.isi.edu/nsnam/ns/) was used to simulate the transport and lower network levels of the nodes as it is widely used, well tested and allows for high fidelity simulation. NS-2 was configured for a typical WSN application, Ad hoc On-Demand Distance Vector (AODV) protocol [13] for the transport layer, and 802.15.4 for the MAC protocol used in combination with the two-ray ground model for the physical radio model (a typical WSN setup). The failures injected into NS-2 are communications failures, whereby the node simply has its radio turned off, stopping the node communicating its own messages, or relaying messages for others. Further details on the simulation framework are in [8].

```
-PARAMETERS
SimulationTime, MaintenancePeriod
86400, 28800

-FAILURES
Type,NodeID,Probability,Offset,Period,Duration
1,4,0.350000,4560,14400,15840
1,19,0.950000,3840,14400,14880
```

Figure 1: Sample Search Solution

The failures are defined in each search solution, an example of a search solution is shown in figure 1. The figure shown in the figure defines the *SimulationTime*, which is not manipulated by the search algorithm, and the *MaintenancePeriod*. Then the failures are defined, with each row represent one failure. *Type* distinguishes between a comms failure (=0) and a node failure (=1). Node failures then have a *nodeID*, *Probability*, *Offset*, *Period* and *Duration*. Whilst the failure shown is simple, it represents much of the complexity of WSNs that are hard to analyse as discussed within in this paper such as sporadic interference or faulty hardware.

3. DESIGN OF THE SEARCH FRAMEWORK

The purpose of this section is to describe how the parallel search algorithm was implemented to manage the size and complexity of the search problem, how the fitness function was designed to guide the algorithm towards the desired solution, and the moves made by the search algorithm to efficiently and effectively transition the search landscape.

3.1 Parallelising the Search

Two main approaches of conducting the search were considered, genetic algorithms and simulated annealing. Genetic algorithms were considered good at dealing with large complex landscape and is easily parallelisable. Simulated annealing also has these characteristics as it is a local search algorithm. This means once it has got within the proximity of a good result, i.e. caused a hazard, it should be good at then exploring how to minimise the failures needed to cause the hazard. One of the benefits of a meta-heuristic search like simulated annealing is that, other than the definition of the neighbourhood, the heuristics for a good solution are not built into the algorithm but into the cost function. This makes it easy to move between goals such as achieving a load balanced system or minimising differences to an existing solution. One *individual simulated annealing algorithm* in the *parallel simulated annealing algorithm* is described in Figure 2 which is based on a standard algorithm from [10].

```
Γ = {γ_0, ..., γ_N}          /* Set of parallel simulated algorithms*/
ω*(i) = {ω*_1, ..., ω*_N}/* Best configuration for each γ_i algorithms*/
Ω = {ω_0, ..., ω_N}          /* Solution space */
f : Ω → [0, 1]               /* Cost function */
ψ ∈ Ω                        /* Initial configuration */
ω* = ψ                       /* Best configuration for this algorithm*/
ω = ψ                        /* Current configuration */
t = t_0                      /* Set initial temperature */
α = c_0                      /* Cooling factor */
λ = T_0                      /* Cooling period */
θ = R_0                      /* Re-seed period */
φ = S_0                      /* Swap period */
do
  i = 0
  do
    if (j mod φ) = 0 then
      ω' = ω*(rnd(Γ))
    else
      if (j mod θ) = 0 then
        ω' = ω*
        ω' = modify_config(ω)
      endif
      fork calculate_fitness_function(f(ω'))
      wait for all simulated annealing algorithms
      δ = f(ω') − f(ω)
      R = random value ∈ [0, 1]
      if (R < e^(−δ/t)) then ω = ω' endif
      if (f(ω) ≤ f(ω*)) then ω* = ω, j = 0 endif
      i = i + 1
      j = j + 1
    endif
  until (i = M or (stopping condition))
  if (i mod λ) = 0 then t = αt endif
until (stopping condition)
```

Figure 2: Parallel Simulated Annealing

3.1.1 Parallel Simulated Annealing Algorithm

Parallelisation is achieved by executing multiple simulated annealing algorithms, as described in 2. Specifically, each individual simulated annealing algorithm will **fork** the calculation of the fitness function every move and then it continues when it can **join** every individual simulated annealing algorithm (i.e. they all complete the calculation of the fitness function). The reason for doing this every move is any individual simulated annealing algorithm may wish to swap solutions at a particular move. This join does result in an increase in the elapsed time of the algorithm, however in our work this was not found to be significant and the computational resources were not wasted as they were free for other users to use.

An individual simulated annealing algorithm swaps in a new solution when no improvement has been found its current solution within 50 moves. The new solution is selected by taking the best solution from one of the other individual simulated annealing algorithms chosen at random. This new solution is then used as the current solution and the algorithm continues as normal. This value was found by trial and error, again approximately following a binary search. Twenty parallel versions were used as early trials found that the greater the level of parallelism the faster the completion, in terms of elapsed time, and for our cluster there was usually at least this many cores available. The individual jobs were executed via a Sun Grid Engine (SGE) upon which at least 20 cores should normally be available.

3.1.2 *Individual Simulated Annealing Algorithm*

For each individual simulated annealing algorithm, the initial temperature was set at 1000 with a cooling factor of 0.99. Cooling is performed every 10 moves and if no improved solution has been found within 25 moves the current solution is returned to the previous best. Each simulated annealing algorithm concludes when there has been a total of 250 moves. Future work could investigate the choice of search algorithms and perform parameter tuning of the algorithm, including what level of parallelism gives the most efficient and effective solution in terms of CPU time, and then trading this off against the desire to finish the search in the minimum elapsed time.

3.2 Evaluating the Fitness Function

In this work the fitness function has the usual purposes of guiding the search towards meeting the primary objective, which in this case is the hazard of an undetected fire, and then to achieve this with the minimum number of failures. Thus the fitness function has the following components. Each component is normalised to return a value between 0 and 1. This means that the overall cost value can also be in the range $[0, 1]$ as the final step is to sum the product of each component's result and its corresponding weight and then divide the result by the sum of the weights, shown in equation 6.

1. *Number of undetected fires* - This component maximises the number of undetected failures or hazards associated with a simulation. It is calculated to give a normalised value using equation (1). This objective is considered the most important. A challenge is to decide on the value for the $Maximum(\#undetectedfires)$ - assuming that multiple fires at the same time in a single room is treated as one. The maximum is not known apriori. An upper bound equivalent to the number of rooms could be taken, however this has two distinct issues. Firstly it is unlikely that all rooms have an undetected fire so the value of g_1 may only take a very small part of the $[0, 1]$ possible range. Secondly each room could theoretically have more than one undetected fire, i.e. there is an undetected fire, the WSN is repaired and then there is another one etc.. Therefore the preferred approach, referred to as a *dynamic fitness function* is to set $Maximum(\#undetected\,fires)$ based on the maximum observed during the particular search. Our previous work, e.g. [3, 7], and initial trials showed the negative aspects of such a dynamic fitness function were found to be better than the bias found with an un-normalised fitness function.

$$g_1 = \frac{\#undetected\,fires}{Maximum(\#undetected\,fires)} \tag{1}$$

2. *Number of node failures* - This component attempts to minimise the number of nodes required to achieve a hazard. Its value is zero unless a hazard occurs. Otherwise it is calculated using equation (2). Again, for similar reasons to equation (1), a dynamic fitness function is used. The purposes of the value found with equation (2) are to fulfil the secondary objective, of minimising the failures that cause the hazard, but also to moderate the above objectives which would otherwise drive the search towards failing all nodes in the network in a permanent fashion. The designer may be interested in inspecting failure combinations, other than the minimum node failure, that lead to a hazard to see if any improvements in the design are needed, in which case the weight of this component could be raised. An important point to note is that the fitness function has been encoded with no knowledge of what failure combinations could lead to a hazard, i.e. the nature of the likely best solution is not included.

$$g_2 = \begin{cases} \frac{Maximum\ failures\ (=20)-\#Failures)}{Maximum\ failures} & \text{, if } g_1 \geq 1 \\ 0 & \text{, otherwise} \end{cases} \tag{2}$$

3. *Number of SPT failures* - The purpose of this component is to maximise the number of failed SPTs in order to guide the search towards situations where the primary objective is met as a SPT failure indicates that we are starting to lose more nodes (but we may currently still be able to detect fires). A larger number will indicate an unhealthy network. To normalise the value the actual component is calculated using equation (3). Again, for similar reasons to equation (1), a dynamic fitness function is used.

$$g_3 = \frac{\#SPT\ Failures}{Maximum(\#SPT\ Failures)} \tag{3}$$

The cost function f is calculated from the scalar product of a vector of the cost function components and a weightings vector.

$$\vec{g} = (g_1, \ldots, g_n)^T \tag{4}$$

$$\vec{w} = (w_1, \ldots, w_n)^T \text{where } w_i \in \mathbb{R}\ \forall i \tag{5}$$

$$f = \frac{\vec{g} \cdot \vec{w}}{\sum_1^n w_i} \tag{6}$$

The weights, including the reasons for their relative sizes, are given below. Part of the reason for the ratios between the weights are the relative values of the fitness function elements, which tended to have quite different ranges despite being normalised.

1. w_1 was given a value of 10 which makes it more important than the number of SPT failures but less important than minimising the number of hazards.
2. w_2 was given a value of 100. Remembering that g_2 only has a non-zero value when a hazard has been found, then the concentration of the search moves to minimising the value of g_2.
3. w_3 was given a value of 1 as it was least important

3.3 Moving Through the Search Landscape

To move from one solution to another, a randomly modified version of the existing solution is chosen by the function $modify\_config()$. If a move takes the parameters outside of the ranges defined in Table 1 then no change is performed. A move is taken by randomly choosing a single action from the following list.

1. A node can be added with the random failure characteristics based on the ranges in Table 1.
2. A node failure can be removed.
3. A randomly chosen node can have its period increased or decreased by one hour.
4. A randomly chosen node can have its duration increased or decreased by one hour.
5. The maintenance period can have its duration increased or decreased by one hour.
6. The probability of a randomly chosen node failure can be increased or decreased by 5%.

An initial solution for each individual simulated annealing algorithm is generated as follows:

1. A random number of node failures in the range [1,20]
2. Each failed node has the following characteristics:
   (a) A random integer failure period in the range [1,12], all time units are hours
   (b) A random integer failure duration in the range [1,12] but not greater than the period
   (c) A random probability in the range [0,100] selected at multiples of 5, i.e. 0, 5, 10, ··, 100. Each time a node is due to next fail, the probability is used to decide whether an actual failure occurs, i.e. a random value is generated in the range [0,100] and if its less than or equal to the probability then it occurs
3. A random integer maintenance period in the range [4,24]

4. EVALUATION

The objective of this evaluation is to understand the feasibility of the proposed search-based approach in the context of the original motivating problem: finding the minimum number of failures that can lead to a hazardous fault. These requirements are expressed as three experimental questions:

1. **EQ1** - Is it possible to search for failure conditions that lead to a hazardous fault?
2. **EQ2** - Can the minimum number of failures be found?
3. **EQ3** - How does the approach compare to other possible approaches?

For this problem it is known that a hazard may be detected, subject to there being a real or simulated fire, when there is not a sufficient number nodes left in a single room to detect the event. This means there must be less than two nodes for the hazard to occur. If the starting position is four nodes per room, then the *best* solution (i.e. a hazard occurs with the minimum number of node failures) is three failures within the entire network as any more is unnecessary.

4.1 Experimental Method

The experimental method employed is to run fifty trials for each of the three following methods:

1. *Parallel simulated annealing algorithm* - as described in section 3.
2. *Sequential simulated annealing algorithm* - The parallel simulated annealing algorithm described in section 3, however instead of twenty parallel searches there is only one. This is equivalent the sequential version of simulated annealing in Figure 2. This is aimed at providing an understanding of whether the parallel search is making reasonable usage of the available resources. The only difference to the algorithm in section 3 is that different parameters are used. The ones that are different are the total moves is ($= 20 \cdot 250 = 5000$), the cooling factor ($= 0.995$) and the number of moves before the current solution is returned to the last best ($= 20 \cdot 25 = 500$). The parameters are chosen to give this algorithm the same number of moves as the parallel version and to maintain a higher level of divergence allowing for the larger number of moves. Clearly with this algorithm there is no swapping of best results between individual simulated annealing algorithms as there is only one
3. *Random search* - This again takes 5000 moves in order to give the same number of moves as the parallel simulated annealing algorithm. For each move it chooses a random solution in the same fashion as the initial solution for the simulated annealing algorithm. This search is sequential however this can be parallelised as each of the 5000 moves are independent

The metrics to be used for the evaluation are the fitness functions outlined in section 2.4 and the following:

1. *#Haz* - How many times each search method manages to find a hazard, i.e. an undetected fire, across each of the fifty repeated trials.
2. *#FH* - The number of moves to find the first hazard, i.e. an undetected fire. To give a reasonably fair comparison, the results for the parallel search are multiplied by 20 (To calculate the number of simulated evaluations performed).
3. *#Mo* - The number of moves to find the best solution. Again for the parallel search the number of moves is multiplied by twenty.
4. *Cl* - How close each approach gets to the *best* solution as shown in the equation below, where *trial* is an individual trial, mf is the minimum failures that can lead to a hazard, and f_x is the number of node failures associated with trial x, and pt is the set of positive trials, where for each trial there is at least one undetected fire. In most cases mf would not be known, however in the case of this paper an exact value is known as it is when there are too few nodes in a single room to detect a fire. For this paper five rooms with four sensors in each is used, which means mf is equal to 3. The results for this metric are examined across a number of repeated runs using the median and inter-quartile ranges as well as the minimum and maximum values.

$$
\begin{aligned}
closeness_{trial} &= \frac{f_{trial} - mf}{mf} &&\text{, if trial} \in pt \\
&= 2 \cdot max_{\forall i \in pt} f_i &&\text{, otherwise}
\end{aligned}
$$

4.2 Experimental Results

The parallel search algorithm was executed on a SGE and the fifty repeated trials took 8 days. It is noted that this time was dependent on what other work the SGE was doing. The random and uniprocessor search algorithms were run concurrently, i.e. all 100 trials at once, on a 64 core linux machine with 128 GB of memory. These trials took 4 days, however again the machine was not solely dedicated to this task. The results were processed using scripts written in *R*.

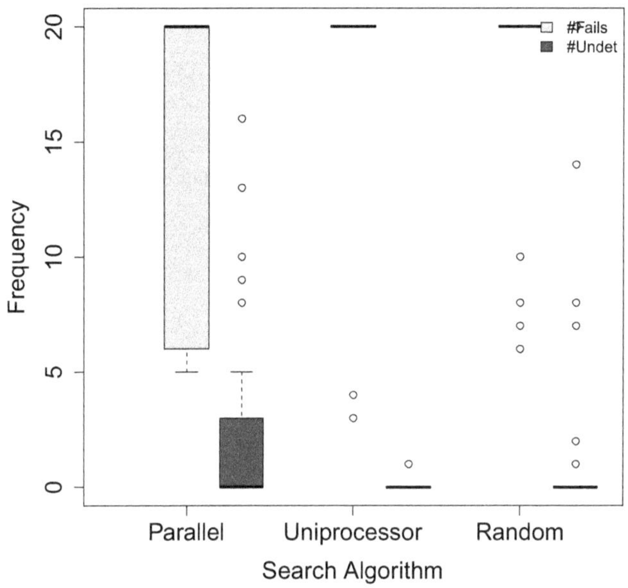

Figure 3: Comparison of Results

The results are summarised in Figure 3. The box plot shows the results for all three search algorithms against the three metrics introduced in section 4.1. A box plot is used as the box clearly shows the range of values between the upper and lower quartiles, the circles outliers, and the thicker black lines the minimum and maximum values.

1. *#Fails* - This indicates the minimum number of failures for which an undetected fire occurred. Where no undetected fire was found, the value of 20 is given as this is equivalent to every node failing. The box plot shows the parallel search algorithm found a large number of situations, 17, where there was an undetected fire. The best result was to have an undetected fire with 5 failures. In contrast the uniprocessor only twice created the undetected fire hazard, however it did it with fewer failures. These are considered random chance. The random case created an undetected fire more times, five, however it was with more failures than the uniprocessor case. A further trial was run with 500 moves for the parallel simulated annealing algorithm instead of 250. This time an undetected fire was reached with only two failures, i.e. the minimum number, which shows the approach is successful. This situation was found after 353 moves. Overall the results suggest the problem is in fact complex to solve and the parallel search algorithm was more reliable at solving the problem. It also showed given enough cases random search could do well. If failures were made less likely however, it is unlikely to succeed.
2. **#SPT** - This is not shown in the graph as the non-parallel search algorithms' best solution often features many failures, e.g. all the nodes in a single room at the same time. These situations lead to extremely high numbers of SPT failures, e.g. 10K+, which would skew the scale of the graphs. At the same time these are not good solutions as the aim of the work is to reach the hazardous state of an undetected fire with minimal failures. It is noted that the non-parallel search algorithms only reached the hazardous state when there were many failures for long durations in the same room, however this was always for a larger number of failures.
3. **#Undet** - The parallel search algorithm's best solution often had fewer undetected fires. This is seen as a positive result as assessing the detailed logs showed that there were solutions with more undetected fires, however this was at the expense of more node failures. The search then reduced the failures at the expense of less undetected fires,

Algorithm	#Haz	#FH	#Mo	Cl
Parallel	86.4	794.8	3972.4	14.42
Sequential	8.62	513.54	186.04	18.5
Random	9.6	651.64	1802.02	16.58

Table 2: Summary of the Search Algorithms

Table 2 presents a summary of how each of the three search algorithms perform against the metrics outlined in section 4.1. The table gives the mean for each of them. The results show parallel search is significantly better than the other two algorithms in terms of the number of hazards found and the closeness to the best possible result. The time to find the first hazard (when one is found) for the parallel approach is a little worse than the other approaches. However as the figures reported are multiplied by 20, the results show given a parallel computing platform then there is an almost linear speed up in terms of elapsed time to find the first solutions. For hard to reach hazards and with the abundance of processing cores then this is significant. Further investigation is needed to understand the precise relationship between cores available and the elapsed time to the first hazard being found. The final metric, *Mo*, indicates the parallel and sequential approaches tend to find their best solution after the same amount of steps through the algorithm (or elapsed time assuming sufficient processing cores are available) remembering the figures reported are multiplied by 20. Analysis of the results support the earlier claim the parallel search is less likely to suffer premature convergence. The analysis also show the parallelism allowed more diverse parts of the search space to be examined.

4.3 Manual refinement of the results

Two methods of manual refinement were used with equal effect. The first method was manual inspection. For the system considered and a result close to the best possible solution, this approach is possible. However in more complicated systems, this will be more difficult and prone to errors. The second is consider combinations of failures in the best found solution by feeding them back into the simulator. The mechanism for this is outlined below. The algorithm is guaranteed to give the minimum number of failures, based on the best solution found, that lead to a hazard. As stated in section 4.1, for the system used in this paper the minimum number of failures is an exact known value.

1. Step 1 - N is initialised to 1
2. Step 2 - For each combination of N failures from the best found solution, simulate the system
3. Step 3 - if no hazard found then increase N by 1 and repeat Step 2

4.4 Summary

The experimental questions posed at the start of this section are now re-visited.

1. **EQ1** - Is it possible to search for failure conditions that lead to a hazardous fault?
   The result for this question is clearly yes.
2. **EQ2** - Can the minimum number of failures be found?
   The result for this question is possibly yes. The exact value was found. The parallel search algorithm was shown to be much more effective at both creating the hazards and doing so with fewer failures. The "best" result was a hazard with five failures. This was sufficiently few failures for the designer to determine that only two of these were in fact needed. Three of the failures were deleted from the configuration, the test re-run and the hazard still found. The more failures there are the harder this manual step becomes.
3. **EQ3** - How does the approach compare to other possible approaches?
   The results show that a parallel search algorithm outperforms both sequential simulated annealing and random searches in terms of ability to find solutions. As each simulation takes minutes, if not hours, to perform, then the benefits of parallelisation are significant. Future work could look at stress testing other DSRs, and at how different search parameters and algorithms could improve efficiency and effectiveness.

5. CONCLUSIONS

This work has shown search-based testing can obtain a good estimate of the minimal failures that can cause a hazard. This technique can be used ahead of deployment allowing the designer then to make targeted (cost effective) changes to the WSN to make it more dependable. The designers can also use the results to validate the findings on the real system as once the situations have been established they would need less work to check. Parallel search was used which had the dual benefit of speeding up the evaluation and improving the results. Our belief is that the techniques proposed here are useful for more general problems related to WSNs and other complex software-based systems. Future work will examine whether this is true.

Acknowledgement

We thank Tiong Hoo Lim for his help analysing the results. We acknowledge the Swedish Foundation for Strategic Research (SSF) SYNOPSIS Project for supporting this work.

6. REFERENCES

[1] A. Avizienis, J.-C. Laprie, and B. Randell. Dependability and its threats - a taxonomy. In *Proceedings of the IFIP 18th World Computer Congress*, pages 91–120, 2004.

[2] I. Bate and A. Burns. An integrated approach to scheduling in safety-critical embedded control systems. *Real-Time Systems Journal*, 25(1):5–37, 2003.

[3] I. Bate and P. Emberson. Incorporating scenarios and heuristics to improve flexibility in real-time embedded systems. In *Proceedings of the 12th IEEE Real-Time And Embedded Technology And Applications Symposium*, pages 221– 230, 2006.

[4] I. Bate, Y. Wu, and J. Stankovic. Developing safe and dependable sensornets. In *Proceedings of the 37th Euromicro Conference on Software Engineering and Advanced Applications*, pages 279–282, 2011.

[5] D. Curren. A survey of simulation in sensor networks. Project report (CS580), University of Binghamton, 2005.

[6] J. Decotignie. The real-time and wireless sensor networks: are they compatible? Keynote at Euromicro Conference on Real-Time Systems, 2012.

[7] P. Emberson and I. Bate. Minimising task migrations and priority changes in mode transitions. In *Proceedings of the 13th IEEE Real-Time And Embedded Technology And Applications Symposium (RTAS)*, pages 158–167, 2007.

[8] M. Fairbairn, I. Bate, and J. Stankobic. Improving wireless simulation through noise modeling. In *Proceedings of the 9th International Conference on Distributed Computing in Sensor Systems*, page To Appear, 2013.

[9] S. Gordon and D. Whitley. Serial and parallel genetic algorithms as function optimizers. In *Proceedings of the Fifth International Conference on Genetic Algorithms*, pages 177–183, 1993.

[10] S. Kirkpatrick, C. D. Gelatt, and M. P. Vecchi. Optimization by simulated annealing. *Science*, 220(4598):671–680, 1983.

[11] J. Laprie. Dependable computing: concepts, limits, challenges. In *Proceedings of the Twenty-Fifth International Conference on Fault-tolerant computing*, pages 42–54, 1995.

[12] J. McDermid, M. Nicholson, D. Pumfrey, and P. Fenelon. Experience with the application of HAZOP to computer-based systems. In *Proceedings of the 10th Annual Conference on Computer Assurance*, pages 37–48, 1995.

[13] C. Perkins and E. Royer. Ad-hoc on-demand distance vector routing. In *Proceedings of the Workshop on Mobile Computing Systems and Applications*, pages 90–100, 1997.

[14] L. Ruiz, J. Nogueira, and A. Loureiro. Manna: A management architecture for wireless sensor networks. *IEEE Communications Magazine*, 41(2):116–125, 2003.

[15] J. Rushby. *Kernels for Safety?*, chapter 13, pages 210–220. Blackwell Scientific Publications, 1989.

[16] J. Tate and I. Bate. YASS: A scaleable sensornet simulator for large scale experimentation. In *Proceedings of Communicating Process Architectures*, 2008.

[17] J. Tate and I. Bate. Sensornet protocol tuning using principled engineering methods. *The Computer Journal*, 53(7):991–1019, 2010.

[18] J. Tate, B. Woolford-Lim, I. Bate, and X. Yao. Comparing design of experiments and evolutionary approaches to multi-objective optimisation of sensornet protocols. In *Proceedings of the 10th IEEE Congress on Evolutionary Computation*, pages 1137–1144, 2009.

[19] J. Tate, B. Woolford-Lim, I. Bate, and X. Yao. Evolutionary and principled search strategies for sensornet protocol optimization. *IEEE Transactions on Systems, Man, and Cybernetics, Part B*, 42(1):163–180, 2012.

[20] K. Wika and J. Knight. On the enforcement of software safety policies. In *Proceedings of the 10th Annual IEEE Conference on Computer Assurance*, June 1995.

[21] Y. Wu, K. Kapitanova, J. Li, J. Stankovic, S. Son, and K. Whitehouse. Run time assurance of application-level requirements in wireless sensor networks. In *Proceedings of the ACM/IEEE International Conference on Information Processing in Sensor Networks (IPSN 2010)*, pages 197–208, 2010.

[22] F. Zhao. Challenge problems in sensornet research. Keynote at NSF NOSS PI meeting and Distinguished Lectures at Johns Hopkins and Princeton, 2005.

Evolutionary Multiobjective Optimization for Selecting Members of an Ensemble Streamflow Forecasting Model

Darwin Brochero[1,2], Christian Gagné[2], and François Anctil[1]
[1] Chaire de recherche EDS en prévisions et actions hydrologiques, Dép. de génie civil et de génie des eaux
[2] Laboratoire de vision et systèmes numériques, Département de génie électrique et de génie informatique
Université Laval, Québec (Québec), Canada G1V 0A6
darwin.brochero.1@ulaval.ca, christian.gagne@gel.ulaval.ca, francois.anctil@gci.ulaval.ca

ABSTRACT

We are proposing to use the Nondominated Sorting Genetic Algorithm II (NSGA-II) for optimizing a hydrological forecasting model of 800 simultaneous streamflow predictors. The optimization is based on the selection of the best 48 predictors from the 800 that jointly define the "best" ensemble in terms of two probabilistic criteria. Results showed that the difficulties in simplifying the ensembles mainly originate from the preservation of the system reliability. We conclude that Pareto fronts generated with NSGA-II allow the development of a decision process based explicitly on the trade-off between different probabilistic properties. In other words, evolutionary multiobjective optimization offers more flexibility to the operational hydrologists than *a priori* methods that produce only one selection.

Categories and Subject Descriptors

I.2.8 [**Artificial Intelligence**]: Problem Solving, Control Methods, and Search—*Heuristic methods*; I.6.6 [**Simulation and Modelling**]: Simulation Output Analysis

Keywords

Evolutionary multiobjective optimization, Probabilistic forecasting, Streamflow forecasting, Hydrological ensemble prediction system, Uncertainty cascade model

General Terms

Experimentation

1. INTRODUCTION

The physics of hydrological processes inevitably leads us to different sources of uncertainty when forecasting their outcomes. First comes the uncertainty associated with meteorological variables. In this regard, in recent years, Meteorological Ensemble Prediction Systems (MEPS) have become increasingly popular. Second comes the uncertainty in the conceptualization of the hydrological processes such as evapotranspiration and the interactions among vegetation, land surface, and groundwater. Finally comes hydraulic routing conceptualization and parametric uncertainty in both the hydraulic and hydrological models. This uncertainty chain propagation model has been called *uncertainty cascade model* [24].

In recent years, the hydrometeorological community has focused on the development of Hydrological Ensemble Prediction Systems (HEPS) taking into account the uncertainty process chain evaluation as an important part of the decision making stage [7, 26, 28]. Consequently, hydrological response is seen as a pool of multiple probable scenarios, accepting the paradigm of complementarity (diversity) for forecasting purposes.

The classical evaluation of multiple forecast scenarios leads to the use of reductionist decision schemes based on combining functions such as average or more elaborated combination functions, ignoring the importance of uncertainty evaluation. In this context, the hydrometeorological community has developed probabilistic performance metrics, called scores, used not only to evaluate the most likely prediction, but also its uncertainty. Probabilistic response properties such as reliability, resolution, sharpness, and consistency have been highlighted as complex features in HEPS [3, 31].

However, the HEPS complexity may become an operational burden when one has to evaluate several hundreds of scenarios at each time step, a situation easily achieved with the increasing computational resources and the advancements of each component of the uncertainty chain presented above. As a result, simplification of such a HEPS becomes a mandatory step from an operational standpoint [5].

At this complexity level, represented by the number of scenarios and its probabilistic properties interaction, an "overproduce and select" mechanism appears as a natural procedure of simplification into the so-called *combiner response level* of a multiple classifier system [20]. So, in this work, the overproduce step is a consequence of evaluating multiple prediction scenarios from a pool of hydrological models, while the selection step is tackled with the NSGA-II algorithm. At this point, it is important to note the analogy between the classical problem of finding the inputs that give us the most information for training a given forecasting model (i.e. features selection) and selecting the predictors making the ensembles, which is investigated here. Henceforth we will refer to predictors selection as the effect of applying a features selection tool for selecting members at the response predictors level.

GECCO'13, July 6–10, 2013, Amsterdam, The Netherlands.

Features selection algorithms, as well as predictors selection, can roughly be grouped into two categories depending on their application model, that is *filter* methods and *wrapper* methods. Filter methods allow the selection to be made without involving the chosen learning/combining system, using instead some other measures, generally statistical ones. In contrast, wrapper methods use the performance of the chosen learning/combining system to guide the selection [1]. It is generally accepted that wrapper methods lead to higher performance [18] at the expense of high computational cost compared to filter approaches. It is frequently categorized as a "brute force" method, although it is not necessarily so [16]. Meta-heuristic procedures such as Genetic Algorithms (GA) have been proposed [9, 30, 36] as a wrapper method for features selection, with the advantage of reducing the computational cost, but also showing a capacity to find better solutions given its global search capabilities.

Another remarkable aspect in predictors selection based on wrapper methods is the central role played by the performance measures guiding the optimization process. Moreover, depending on the application, one might want to use several measures of different nature available for selecting the predictors. In that context, a common approach consists in aggregating these performance measures into a scalar global criterion, which has been called by some a global criterion method [21]. That approach has its drawback, foremostly requiring to articulate the trade-off between the performance measure beforehand, and being inefficient at handling an aggregation of objectives that have non linear (non convex) relations. Thus, a multiobjective framework emerges as a more natural and practical model of predictors selection with several performance measures. Indeed, in such a context, it may be more efficient to resort to an *a posteriori* multiobjective technique such as the Nondominated Sorting Genetic Algorithm II (NSGA-II) [8], where the optimization is generating as output a group of solutions that represents various trade-offs between the objectives, corresponding to the so-called Pareto front. An example of such an application, but in a deterministic context and with two UCI datasets, is presented in Waqas et al. [33].

In our work, based on the concepts outlined above, we apply NSGA-II in a multi-*score* framework for the selecting of the best predictors (better complementarity) in a real world application, that is a pool of 800 streamflow forecasting models. The remainder of the paper is organized as follows. Sec. 2 provides a presentation of the HEPS of reference and the cases studied. Sec. 3 summarizes the basic concepts underlying the scores to evaluate the performances of the HEPS. Follows in Sec. 4 a presentation of the working hypothesis used for our experiments. Sec. 5 details the experimental setup, while results and the corresponding analysis are presented in Sec. 6. Finally, some conclusions and a guideline for future work are given in Sec. 7.

2. HEPS SETUP AND LOCATIONS

The HEPS under study is formed of 16 hydrological models combined with 50 meteorological inputs given by the ECWMF EPS, leading to a grand ensemble of 800 members, usable for 1 to 9 days ahead forecasting. The precipitation inputs are *a priori* assumed to be equally likely [15]. Another important aspect of the HEPS at hand is the short duration of the series, from March 2005 to July 2006. This HEPS was implemented over 28 French catchments with an average response time of 3.2 days, representing a large range

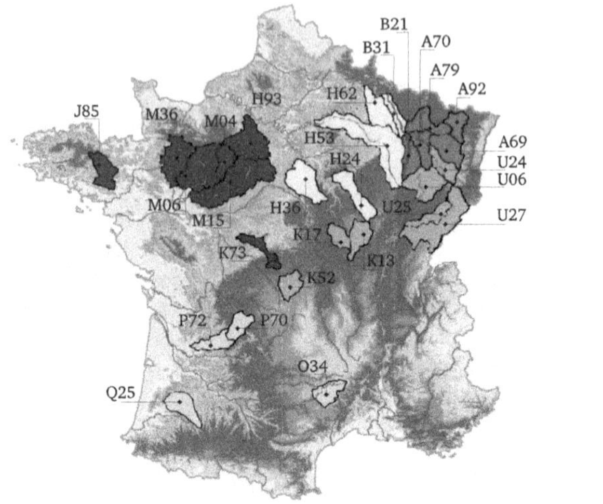

Figure 1: Catchments location.

of hydro-climatic conditions (Fig. 1). The results presented here are based on a selection of four basins that show different behaviours according to simplification. Basins H24, H93, M06, and P70 are used for training, whereas corresponding neighbouring basins H36, M04, M15, and P72 are used for testing.

The high performance of the 800-member HEPS for the 9-th day Forecast Time Horizon (FTH), and a lesser extent in the other FTHs, has been demonstrated in [31]. However, preliminary analysis has shown the high redundancy of the models response, opening the way to the hydrological model selection and precipitation clustering as an efficient simplification idea.

3. PERFORMANCE EVALUATION

In the machine learning community, the evolution of the bias-variance dilemma [12] to the accuracy-diversity breakdown [19], and the bias-variance-covariance decomposition [29], naturally supports the multiple classifier systems approach and, more generally speaking, the evaluation of multiple scenarios. However, this is frequently reduced to a single response to use in a scalar objective function. But in a probabilistic context, it is imperative to use the distribution-oriented approach (scores) that reveals more details about the response uncertainty.

The distribution-oriented approach reveals that forecast quality is inherently multifaceted in nature [7, 23]. In the following, we quote two of the properties commonly evaluated in probabilistic forecasting, that is the bias and the reliability. The reader is referred to Wilks [35] for a more detailed description of these and other features. Note that we use Gaussian distributions in the following examples for the sole purpose of facilitating the explanations.

The **bias**, also called unconditional bias or systematic bias, measures the correspondence between the mean forecast and the mean observation. In Fig. 2 we illustrate two cases regarding *pdf A*. The observation o^t first occurs near the mean forecast[1] (case 1), i.e. a system with low bias. Second, the observation o^t is located further from the central value (case 2), i.e. a highly biased system.

[1]Note that mean, median, and mode coincide with the peak of the Gaussian distribution.

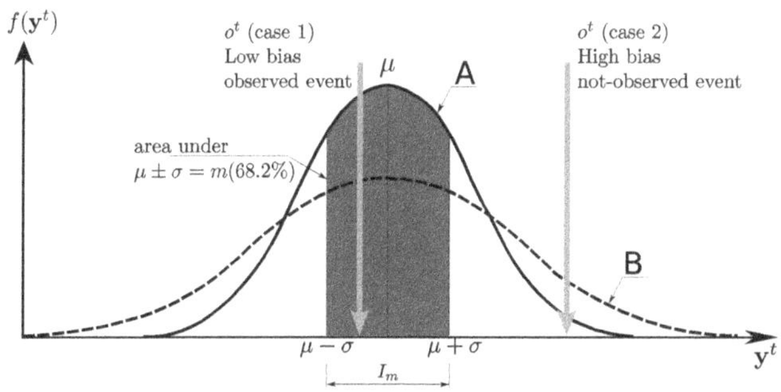

Figure 2: Probabilistic forecasting evaluation.

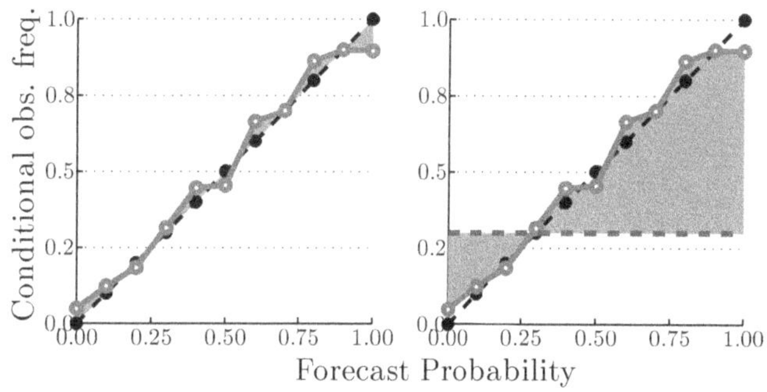

Figure 3: Reliability diagram.

The **reliability** relates to the occurrence of event o^t given a probability threshold m, averaged over all N observation - forecast pairs. In Fig. 2, the reliability evaluation of a threshold probability equal to 68.2% in *pdf A*. So, at each time step, it must be determined whether the event falls or not into the I_m region bounded by this probability value. Subsequently, the conditional observed frequency $\bar{o}_m$ is evaluated for the N observation - forecast pairs by Eq. 1:

$$\bar{o}_m = \frac{1}{N}\sum_{t=1}^{N} r^t, \text{ where } r^t = \begin{cases} 1 & \text{if } o^t \in I_m \\ 0 & \text{otherwise} \end{cases}. \quad (1)$$

Finally, for this probability threshold, the system is perfectly reliable if $\bar{o}_m$ is equal to m. For instance, in a perfectly reliable system with a probability threshold of 68.2%, we can imagine that for 1000 cases the event fell 682 times within the intervals evaluated. We say that the system is overforecasting if $\bar{o}_m$ is less than m, and underforecasting otherwise.

Given that m denotes the different M thresholds of probability to assess, the reliability of the system can be directly measured from the comparison of these thresholds with the M observed conditional probabilities. The goal is to have well-calibrated forecast systems for which the relative frequency is essentially equal to the probability of the forecast, i.e. $\bar{o}_m = m$.

In the following, we present two scores that represent bias and reliability, that is the ignorance score and the reliability diagram. Note that this antagonistic behaviour can be easily seen as another dimension of the bias-variance dilemma.

3.1 Ignorance score

Proposed by Good [14] as the logarithmic score, the IGNorance Score (IGNS), given in Eq. 2, is defined as the logarithm of the ensemble probability density function $f(\mathbf{y}^t)$ at the point corresponding to the observation o^t, all evaluated at time t:

$$\text{IGNS}\left(\mathbf{y}^t,\, o^t\right) = -\log_2\left[f\left(\mathbf{y}^t\right)_{o^t}\right]. \quad (2)$$

Note that this score can take negative values because the *pdf* may be larger than one[2]. Smaller values indicate better performance. The IGNS is a local measure that severely penalizes the bias because positioning the observation in forecast regions of low probability leads to values that tend to infinity. The logarithmic score involves a harsh penalty for low probability events and therefore is highly sensitive to extreme cases [13]. To rule out the possibility that the results solely reflect the effect of a few outliers, we analyzed trimmed means of the IGNS series excluding the highest and lowest 2% data values, following Weigend and Shi [34]. Infinite values were replaced by the next worst non-infinite value, following Boucher et al. [2].

3.2 Reliability diagram

The reliability diagram or attributes diagram is a graphical representation of the joint distribution of the forecasts and observations. For its construction, we define M probability thresholds, often deciles, then we compute the conditional observed frequency for each of these M thresholds. Finally, we illustrate the relationship between forecast probabilities and conditional observed frequency. In a perfectly reliable system, $\bar{o}_m$ will be equal to m, i.e. the distance or area between the 1:1 line and computed pairs $(m, \bar{o}_m)$, will be very small (left panel of Fig. 3). Consequently we can evaluate the reliability of the system from a distance measure such as the Mean Square Error (MSE):

$$\text{RD}_{\text{MSE}}(\mathbf{Y},\, \mathbf{o}) = \frac{1}{M}\sum_{i=1}^{M}\left(\bar{o}_{m_i} - m_i\right)^2, \quad (3)$$

where $m_i \in [0, 1]$.

Note that Eq. 3 corresponds to the reliability as defined in the Brier score decomposition [35]. It is clear that to maximize the reliability, one seeks at minimizing Eq. 3. The reliability diagram proposes a direct assessment of reliability and resolution of a probability forecast. Regarding the resolution (ability of the forecast to distinguish situations with different frequencies of occurrence), its measure is given by the difference between each of conditional observed probabilities $\bar{o}_m$ and the overall unconditional mean observation $\bar{o}$ (see No-resolution line in right panel of Fig. 3).

Finally, a reliability diagram diagnosis leads to determining overforecasting or underforecasting. For example if the curve is below the 1:1 line, that indicates that the average forecast is larger than the average observation (overforecasting). But, if the curve is above the 1:1 line (underforecasting), the average forecast is smaller than the average observation.

4. BASIC ASSUMPTIONS

A subtle but key aspect in the simplification scheme is the equiprobability condition of the precipitation inputs. Note that while meteorological members are interchangeable, the occurrence of each hydrological model within HEPS stays invariable. For all time steps, the first 50 hydrological members correspond to the combination of 50 precipitation members and the hydrological model #1. Similarly the last

[2] *pdf* values denotes an intensity of probability or a probability rate.

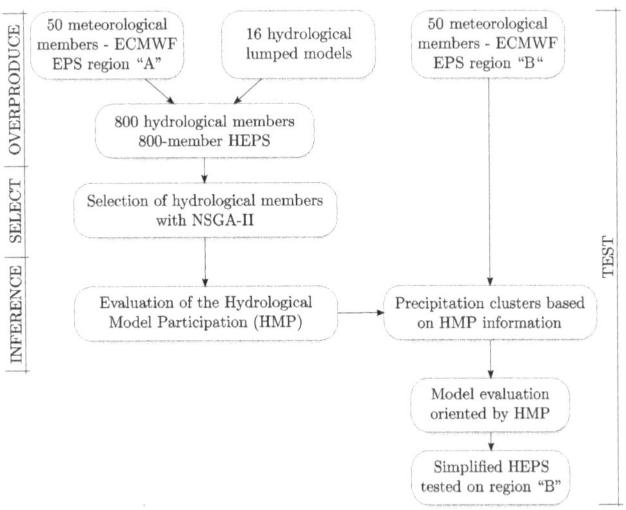

Figure 4: HEPS simplification based on clustering and different HMP.

50 hydrological members (751-800) correspond to the same combination with the hydrological model #16. It is clear that hydrological models act as non-linear filters in which one of the variables is precipitation. We assume that the hydrological models that form the HEPS of reference reflect different conceptualizations of the hydrological process. In this way, the removal of a member only represents a loss of model weight in the proposed simplified scheme that is based on the Hydrological Models' Participation (HMP) as a key concept of HEPS simplification.

In conclusion, we hypothesize that considering each hydrological member as a variable is not in conflict with the proposed methodology, because the selection of members, for subsequent interpretation in terms of HMP, is not made on members of the ECMWF EPS but rather on the 800-member hydrological response. The empirical validity of these assumptions will be evaluated particularly in Sec. 6 from the evaluation of multiple random predictors selections.

Beside that, Brochero et al. [3] and Velázquez et al. [31] showed that the 800-member HEPS has a high performance on the 9-th day FTH. Consequently, we apply the simplification process on the database corresponding to this lead time. This decision about the FTH is justified since the hydrological model participation as a method of simplifying HEPS should be unique regardless of the FTH.

5. EXPERIMENTAL SETUP

In Fig. 4 we illustrate the scheme of simplification and test. This procedure consists of four stages: overproduce, select, inference, and test. In this figure we outline how to train and test systematic selection results. For training, an 800-member HEPS database of a given catchment is analyzed for the 9-th day lead time. For testing, we use a neighbouring basin and other forecast time horizons.

5.1 Overproduce

The HEPS under study is formed of 16 hydrological models combined to one of the 50 meteorological inputs of the ECWMF EPS, leading to a grand-ensemble of 800 members. The MEPS members are *a priori* assumed to be equally likely [15]. Another important feature of the HEPS

Representation	Truncated permutations
Recombination	Partially mapped crossover (PMX)
Recombination probability	90%
Mutation	Swap
Mutation probability	2% for each allele
Parent selection	Best 2 out of random 4
Survival selection	Pareto-front rank and crowding distance
Population size	100
Initialization	Random
Termination condition	300 generations

Table 1: NSGA-II setup.

at hand is the short duration of the series, from March 2005 to July 2006. This has been highlighted by several authors as a negative point in the evaluation of system performance in the case of extreme events [7, 25]. However, other studies that focused on periods of analysis very similar to the one used here have also proven the usefulness of the ECMWF EPS. For example Rousset et al. [27] evaluated hundreds of French catchments from 4 September 2004 to 31 July 2005 showing that the information given by the ensemble forecast is useful for flood warning and water management agencies.

5.2 Predictors Selection

5.2.1 Schemes to analyze

Following [3, 4], who demonstrated in this same database that the best balance of scores is achieved with a number of selected members fluctuating between 30 and 100, here we use NSGA-II to select the best 48 predictors based on the scores presented in Sec. 3. This allows a fair comparison to be made with two reference models: i) a naive model that consists in a uniform participation of three forecasts for each of the sixteen hydrological models, resulting in a 48-member HEPS called 48UP, and ii) the Median of 200 Random member selections, scheme called 48MR.

5.2.2 NSGA-II setup

This technique uses a permutation representation GA following the NSGA-II algorithm. It has received the most attention because of its simplicity and demonstrated superiority over other multiobjective optimization methods [32]. A detailed description of the NSGA-II algorithm appears in [8]. Like any evolutionary algorithm, its configuration is given by way of representing potential solutions (genotype), evaluation function (or fitness function), population, initialization, parent selection mechanism, variation operators, survivor selection, and termination condition. Table 1 presents a summary of the configuration evaluated here.

Truncated permutation as representation is defined by the following guidelines: i) the individual should represent 48 *unique* members in order to compare solutions with other methods, and ii) in terms of selection of variables, the permutation of the same group of members does not represent a new solution. Thus, the representation of each individual (candidate solution) is a permutation of a set of 800 integers. However, only the first 48 alleles (string positions) represent the solutions to be tested. The other 752 alleles are reserved for the application of the variation operators presented in Table 1.

Moreover, with the goal of comparing NSGA-II with the other two selections schemes, a representative solution of the Pareto-front is necessary, in which case we orient this

30-member HEPS subset	800-member HEPS		HMP	HM weight(%)
	HM $\#i$	Members interval $[50i-49, 50i]$		
10, 12, 23, 25, 34,	1	1 – 50	7	23.3
42, 45, 55, 63, 70,	2	51 – 100	3	10.0
245, 247, 345, 350,	5	201 – 250	2	6.7
654, 680, 690, 700,	7	301 – 350	2	6.7
701, 710, 751, 753,	14	651 – 700	4	13.3
755, 757, 759, 760,	15	701 – 750	2	6.7
778, 780, 785, 800	16	751 – 800	10	33.3

Table 2: Hypothetical example to show the HMP.

selection with the post-Pareto front analysis proposed by Chaudhari et al. [6]. Therefore, the procedure consists in the following steps:

- Obtain a subset of solutions that represent the Pareto-optimal front.
- Apply k-means clustering on that Pareto front. For that purpose a normalization space is needed to avoid problems arising from the scale of the scores. Here we normalize each variable so that they will have zero mean and unit standard deviation. To find the "optimal" number of clusters, we evaluate the number of clusters that maximizes the mean silhouette value. The silhouette is a measure of how close each point forming a cluster is to others in the neighbouring clusters.
- For each cluster, select a representative solution. To do this, the solution that is closest to its respective cluster centroid is chosen as a good representative solution.
- Analyze the "knee" cluster or the k representative solutions. In this study the "knee" cluster is considered as the most interesting solution because we do not propose an operational scenario in which one could decide which of the two functions to minimize is more relevant at a given time.

5.3 Inference

Following the assumptions made in Sec. 4, the simplification of the 800-member HEPS is based on the direct systematic selection of certain hydrological members, which indirectly leads us to determine the hydrological models participation (HMP) as the base criterion of the simplification task.

Consider the example given in Table 2 for a simplified HEPS of 30 members presented in the first column. Assuming that this simplified scheme provides at least equal performance than the 800-member HEPS, Table 2 shows that the evaluation and posterior combination of Hydrological Models (HM) can be reduced substantially (7 instead of 16). Note that the last two columns show the apparent higher relevance of models 1 and 16; however, other models of less weight can be important to describe the uncertainty of the process with opposing views to those of the most relevant models.

5.4 Test

To assess hydrological models with representative precipitation members (RM), as proposed by several authors [17, 22] and following the trend of recent clustering products produced directly at ECMWF EPS [10], the HMP directly orients the evaluation of representative precipitation members at each time step to subsequently propagate them into

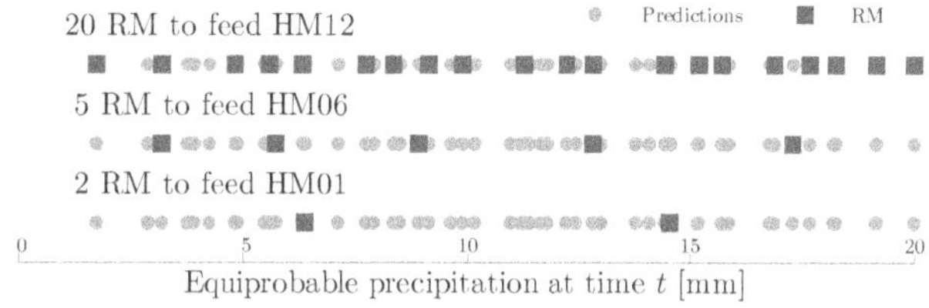

Figure 5: Representative members for simplification testing.

its respective hydrological model. For this, we rely on the k-means technique configured with the Euclidean distance as the similarity measure, and the HMP to define the number of clusters, so the EPS member closest to its cluster centroid will define the representative member.

Consider the following example to clarify the previous concepts: we have a HMP, of 16 elements that represent the 16 hydrological models, after applying a particular selection technique and evaluating the final number of members corresponding to each HM.

$$\mathrm{HMP} = \{\overbrace{2}^{\mathrm{HM01}}, 0,0,0,0, \overbrace{5}^{\mathrm{HM06}}, 0,0, \overbrace{16}^{\mathrm{HM09}}, 0,0, \overbrace{20}^{\mathrm{HM12}}, 0, \overbrace{5}^{\mathrm{HM14}}, 0,0\}$$

So, for test purposes, at each time step we evaluate the two precipitation members closest to two cluster centroids and we propagate them into the hydrological model HM01. We continue so on to evaluate the five representative precipitation members into the HM14. Fig. 5 presents a visual exploration of Representative precipitation Members (RM).

Finally, we compare the HMP results based on the NSGA-II, the 48MR and the 48UP schemes. For comparison purposes, each score in the selected ensemble of hydrological members (se subscript) is normalized by dividing it with the corresponding score in the initial 800-member ensemble (ie subscript), therefore using a similar scale for each component. Also we estimated a normalization threshold for the IGNS equal to -3 to manipulate the negative values of this score:

$$\text{normalized } \overline{\mathrm{IGNS}} = \frac{-3 - \overline{\mathrm{IGNS}}_{\mathrm{se}}}{-3 - \overline{\mathrm{IGNS}}_{\mathrm{ie}}}, \tag{4}$$

$$\text{normalized } \mathrm{RD_{MSE}} = \frac{\mathrm{RD_{MSE_{se}}}}{\mathrm{RD_{MSE_{ie}}}}. \tag{5}$$

6. RESULTS AND ANALYSIS

Table 3 compares results of the initial 800-member HEPS and the two reference schemes: a naive model of a Uniform HMP (48UP) and the Median of 200 Random member selections (48MR). Hereafter, $\mathrm{RD_{MSE}}$ values are expressed on a 10^{-3} basis.

With reference to 48-member schemes, it is noteworthy that in all cases the IGNS of reference is improved, at the expense of reliability. Specifically the uniform HMP scheme is the most efficient in minimizing IGNS, while the median of random evaluations is a little less inefficient in terms of reliability ($\mathrm{RD_{MSE}}$), but not yet matching the performance of reference (800 members). Consequently, simplification stands out as an optimization task involving hydrological models in a weight assignment problem.

In an effort to visualize explicitly the trade-off between the scores, Fig. 6 presents such a Pareto-type analysis of results

Training catchments	HEPS members	Scores		Testing catchments	HEPS members	Scores	
		RD_{MSE}	IGNS			RD_{MSE}	IGNS
H24	800	7.08	0.41	H36	800	3.50	−0.09
	48UP	8.20	−0.49		48UP	5.00	−0.75
	48MR	7.82	−0.46		48MR	4.67	−0.74
H93	800	2.59	−0.27	M04	800	1.74	−0.03
	48UP	4.47	−0.98		48UP	4.31	−0.72
	48MR	3.84	−0.95		48MR	3.50	−0.70
M06	800	1.42	−0.14	M15	800	1.61	0.28
	48UP	4.25	−0.77		48UP	3.37	−0.64
	48MR	3.19	−0.74		48MR	2.62	−0.61
P70	800	4.14	3.29	P72	800	4.39	0.89
	48UP	5.22	−0.06		48UP	5.28	−0.39
	48MR	4.51	0.06		48MR	4.51	−0.33

Table 3: Performance for a 9-day FTH in different schemes.

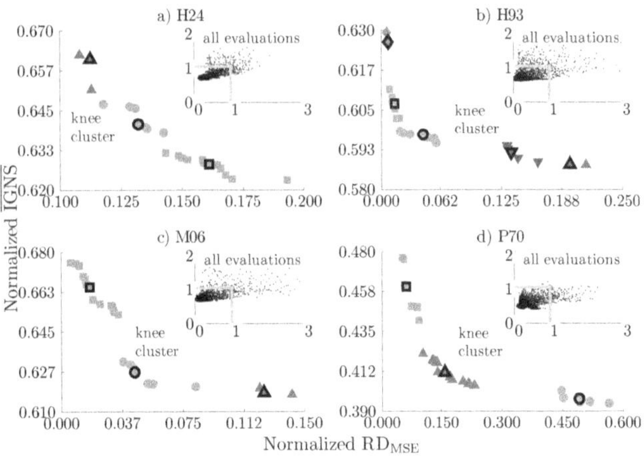

Figure 6: Evaluations of different selections with NSGA-II.

obtained with NSGA-II. Each panel illustrates the behaviour of different selections for each basin. The inset figure in the upper right corner of each panel shows the 30 000 tested selections in the optimization process. In these figures, we can see that the reliability of the system is the principal component of the variability of the results. Similarly, from the density of points outside the bounding rectangle, limited by unit normalized scores, we have evidence that the optimization process converges rapidly in the initial performance of the reference HEPS. Thus, the simplification process is shown primarily as a process of scores optimization, hence it may be referred to as a post-processing step.

The Pareto front obtained in the optimization is drawn in each panel, along with their respective clusters and centroids identification (symbols in bold). The scale of normalized scores of each panel is similar, except for basin P70 where the IGNS and the RD_{MSE} exhibit larger Pareto ranges, between 0.39 and 0.48, and between 0 and 0.6, respectively. This difference could be related to two factors specific to this basin: its lower drainage area and its higher relative flow. However, it is necessary to perform more experiments to identify the relationship of these factors.

Importantly, the Pareto front or simplification based on the centroid of each cluster offers a descriptive version of the optimization process, which allows the development of a decision process based on the characteristics of each score and the properties we want to prioritize in a particular case. In other words, NSGA-II offers more flexibility to the operational hydrologists than a single subset of predictors obtained with *a priori* multiobjective optimization methods.

However, a rigorous test requires evaluating the simplification model against new information. Thus, the above results are really optimistic indicators. Accordingly, Fig. 7 shows the results of different selection techniques in a framework of extrapolation in both time and space – executed on a nearby catchment at different forecast time horizons. bp-rand corresponds to box-plots of the 200 random selections executed.

As for the reliability of the system (left panels in Fig. 7), these results demonstrate again that the main difficulty lies in the preservation of this property. Furthermore, random selections show that the situation is more dramatic in FTH over 6 days, except in the basin P72 where the median of the random selections is around one. This behaviour is especially important if one considers that the benefits of the 800-member HEPS is focused primarily on these lead times. Also note that the interquartile range (length of the box-plots) exhibits an important dispersion in relation to the results observed with respect to IGNS (right panels in Fig. 7). Concerning the 48UP scheme, it is important to note that the tendency is similar than for the random selections. However, it is remarkable that in the initial FTHs (1 to 6 days) uniform selection is generally better than the first quartile of the 200 random selections tested. The high performances achieved with NSGA-II are obvious.

7. CONCLUSION

Given the singularity of HEPS in evaluation, where its 800 hydrological members come from the propagation of 50 interchangeable meteorological members, simplification scheme and/or scores optimization of the system based on the Hydrological Models Participation (HMP) has proven to be highly efficient. Clearly, the methodology presented here combines the HMP and the meteorological clustering stage as additional filters that facilitate the interpretation of the hydrological member selection. However, in the case of a HEPS conceived from non-interchangeable meteorological members (in Canada, for example), the selection task would

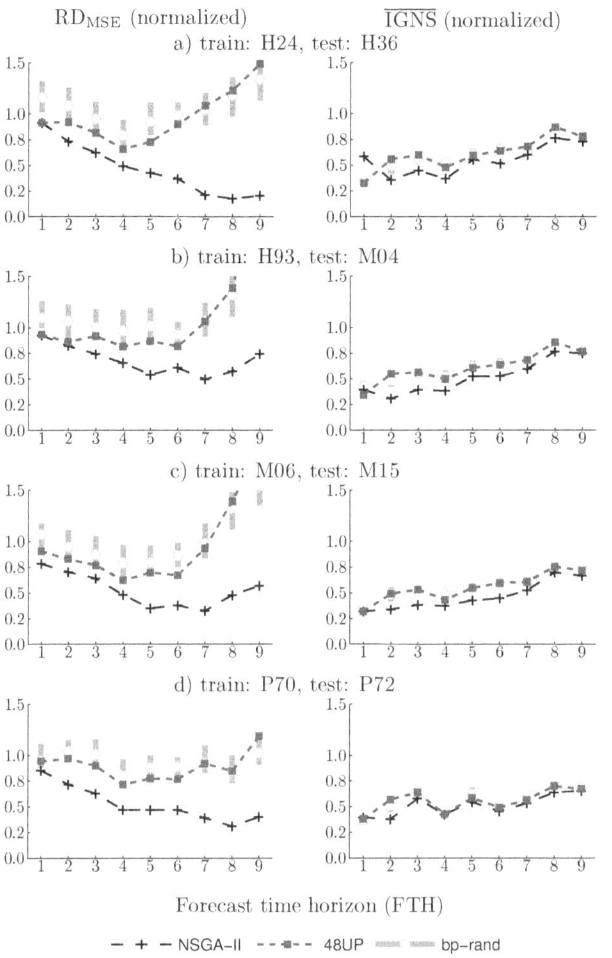

Figure 7: Test of different HEPS simplification schemes of 48 members.

then directly identify the importance of certain members in the propagation of uncertainty in flow prediction.

With respect to the reliability of the system, this property is notoriously the most difficult to maintain in the simplification scheme. The results of a uniform HMP and random selections show such difficulty. In this work, without loss of reference bias, it is important to note the high efficiency of the NSGA-II, which we consider to be the best choice among the techniques evaluated. At this point, operational hydrologists can highlight the following aspects:

- **Computational complexity** Although the Backward selection suggested in [3] is more intuitive, its complexity is the order of $O\left(d^2\right) = O\left(800^2\right)$ while the NSGA-II has a computational complexity of $O\left(s \cdot p^2\right)$, where s is the number of scores and p is the population size. Moreover, there are several open source user-friendly frameworks that include an efficient implementation of NSGA-II [11].
- **Trade-off between bias and reliability** Local optimization methods with a global criterion, as suggested in [3], do not allow a direct visualization of the relationship between multiple objectives. Although in the literature has proposed the manipulation of objectives weight to build a Pareto Front, the NSGA-II shows directly the different simplification schemes that highlight the trade-off among the evaluated objectives.
- **Optimization of the number of members to retain** Because the objective of our methodology is focused on a comparison of techniques with the same number of members, solution representation (genotype) with NSGA-II was established by permutations. However, a binary encoding would be more intuitive in order to optimize at the same time the number of members to hold out.
- **Search procedure** Finding the optimal subset is not guaranteed with a local search procedure [21]. For example, y_i and y_j by themselves may not be good, but taken together, they may decrease significantly the error. But because these algorithms are local or greedy and remove members one by one, they may not be able to detect this. In contrast, the NSGA-II has the capability to find the global optimum in its evolutionary search process in such a deceptive setting, although there is no absolute guarantee that it will find it.

Finally, we propose various directions for future research:

- Explore more probabilistic features through other scores as the δ ratio or the CRPS.
- Further research with longer databases is needed in order to identify the HEPS value in several type of events, e.g. peak events.
- Explore using an even larger number of basins in order to evaluate the relation between the selection performance and physiographic and hydro-climatological properties.
- Furthermore the diversity, evaluated from deterministic performance of each model, should be considered as an approximation to the true structural diversity of hydrological models, in this sense an explicit analysis of the relationship between the structural diversity of a group of hydrological models and their relevance in a probabilistic scheme should be studied in more detail.

Acknowledgements

The authors acknowledge NSERC (Canada) and the Institute EDS for financial support, CEMAGREF and ECWMF for making the databases available. We also thank J. Vrugt for providing a Matlab version of NSGA-II and A. Schwerdtfeger for proofreading this manuscript.

References

[1] E. Alpaydin. *Introduction to Machine Learning*. 2nd ed. The MIT Press, 2010.

[2] M.-A. Boucher, J.-P. Laliberté, and F. Anctil. "An experiment on the evolution of an ensemble of neural networks for streamflow forecasting". In: *Hydrol. Earth Syst. Sci.* 14.3 (2010), pp. 603–612.

[3] D. Brochero, F. Anctil, and C. Gagné. "Simplifying a hydrological ensemble prediction system with a backward greedy selection of members – Part 1: Optimization criteria". In: *Hydrol. Earth Syst. Sci.* 15.11 (2011), pp. 3307–3325.

[4] D. Brochero, F. Anctil, and C. Gagné. "Simplifying a hydrological ensemble prediction system with a backward greedy selection of members – Part 2: Generalization in time and space". In: *Hydrol. Earth Syst. Sci.* 15.11 (2011), pp. 3327–3341.

[5] D. Brochero, F. Anctil, and C. Gagné. *An experience on the selection of members for simplifying a multimodel hydrological ensemble prediction system.* In: *CSHS Workshop: Operational River Flow and Water Supply Forecasting.* 2011.

[6] P. Chaudhari, R. Dharaskar, and V. M. Thakare. "Computing the Most Significant Solution from Pareto Front obtained in Multi-objective Evolutionary". In: *IJACSA* 1.4 (2010), pp. 63–68.

[7] H. L. Cloke and F. Pappenberger. "Ensemble flood forecasting: A review". In: *J. Hydrol.* 375.3-4 (2009), pp. 613–626.

[8] K. Deb, A. Pratap, S. Agarwal, and T. Meyarivan. "A fast and elitist multiobjective genetic algorithm: NSGA-II". In: *IEEE Trans. Evol. Comp.* 6.2 (2002), pp. 182–197.

[9] A. Eiben and J. Smith. *Introduction to evolutionary computing.* 1, Corr. 2nd printing. Springer, 2003.

[10] L. Ferranti and S. Corti. "New clustering products". In: *ECMWF Newsl.* 127 (2011), pp. 6–12.

[11] F.-A. Fortin, F.-M. D. Rainville, M.-A. Gardner, M. Parizeau, and C. Gagné. "DEAP: Evolutionary Algorithms Made Easy". In: *Journal of Machine Learning Research* 13 (2012), pp. 2171–2175.

[12] S. Geman, E. Bienenstock, and R. Doursat. "Neural networks and the bias variance dilemma". In: *Neural Comput.* 4.1 (1992), pp. 1–58.

[13] T. Gneiting and A. E. Raftery. "Strictly proper scoring rules, prediction, and estimation". In: *J. Am. Statist. Assoc.* 102.477 (2007), pp. 359–378.

[14] I. J. Good. "Rational Decisions". In: *J. R. Stat. Soc.* 14.1 (1952), pp. 107–114.

[15] B. T. Gouweleeuw, J. Thielen, G. Franchello, A. P. J. De Roo, and R. Buizza. "Flood forecasting using medium-range probabilistic weather prediction". In: *Hydrol. Earth Syst. Sci.* 9.4 (2005), pp. 365–380.

[16] I. Guyon and A. Elisseeff. "An introduction to variable and feature selection". In: *The Journal of Machine Learning Research* 3 (2003), pp. 1157–1182.

[17] S. Jaun, B. Ahrens, A. Walser, T. Ewen, and C. Schär. "A probabilistic view on the August 2005 floods in the upper Rhine catchment". In: *Nat. Hazards Earth Syst. Sci.* 8 (2008), pp. 281–291.

[18] R. Kohavi and G. H. John. "Wrappers for feature subset selection". In: *Artif. Intell.* 97.1–2 (1997), pp. 273–324.

[19] A. Krogh and J. Vedelsby. *Neural Network Ensembles, Cross Validation, and Active Learning.* In: *Advances in Neural Information Processing Systems 8.* MIT Press, 1995, pp. 231–238.

[20] L. I. Kuncheva. *Combining Pattern Classifiers: Methods and Algorithms.* Wiley-Interscience, 2004.

[21] R. Marler and J. Arora. "Survey of multi-objective optimization methods for engineering". In: *Struct. Multidiscip. O.* 26 (6 2004), pp. 369–395.

[22] F. Molteni, R. Buizza, C. Marsigli, A. Montani, F. Nerozzi, and T. Paccagnella. "A strategy for high-resolution ensemble prediction. I: Definition of representative members and global-model experiments". In: *Q. J. R. Meteorolog. Soc.* 127 (2001), pp. 2069–2094.

[23] A. H. Murphy. "What is a good forecast? An essay on the nature of goodness in weather forecasting". In: *Wea. Forecasting* 8 (1993), pp. 281–293.

[24] F. Pappenberger, K. J. Beven, N. M. Hunter, P. D. Bates, B. T. Gouweleeuw, J. Thielen, and A. P. J. de Roo. "Cascading model uncertainty from medium range weather forecasts (10 days) through a rainfall-runoff model to flood inundation predictions within the European Flood Forecasting System (EFFS)". In: *Hydrol. Earth Syst. Sci.* 9.4 (2005), pp. 381–393.

[25] M. Renner, M. Werner, S. Rademacher, and E. Sprokkereef. "Verification of ensemble flow forecasts for the River Rhine". In: *J. Hydrol.* 376.3-4 (2009), pp. 463–475.

[26] E. Roulin. "Skill and relative economic value of medium-range hydrological ensemble predictions". In: *Hydrol. Earth Syst. Sci.* 11.2 (2007), pp. 725–737.

[27] F. Rousset, F. Habets, E. Martin, and J. Noilhan. "Ensemble streamflow forecasts over France". In: *ECMWF Newsl.* 111 (2007), pp. 21–27.

[28] J. C. Schaake, T. M. Hamill, R. Buizza, and M. Clark. "HEPEX: The Hydrological Ensemble Prediction Experiment". In: *Bull. Am. Meteorol. Soc.* 88.10 (2007), pp. 1541–1547.

[29] N. Ueda and R. Nakano. *Generalization error of ensemble estimators.* In: *IEEE International Conference on Neural Networks.* Vol. 1. 1996, pp. 90–95.

[30] H. Vafaie and K. De Jong. *Genetic algorithms as a tool for feature selection in machine learning.* In: *Fourth International Conference on Tools with Artificial Intelligence.* 1992, pp. 200–203.

[31] J. A. Velázquez, F. Anctil, M. H. Ramos, and C. Perrin. "Can a multi-model approach improve hydrological ensemble forecasting? A study on 29 French catchments using 16 hydrological model structures". In: *Adv. Geosci.* 29 (2011), pp. 33–42.

[32] J. Vrugt and B. Robinson. *Improved evolutionary optimization from genetically adaptive multimethod search.* In: *Proceedings of the National Academy of Sciences of the United States of America.* Vol. 104. 3. 2007, pp. 708–711.

[33] K. Waqas, R. Baig, and S. Ali. *Feature subset selection using multi-objective genetic algorithms.* In: *IEEE International Multitopic Conference (INMIC).* 2009, pp. 1–6.

[34] A. S. Weigend and S. Shi. "Predicting daily probability distributions of S&P500 returns". In: *J. Forecast.* 19.4 (2000), pp. 375–392.

[35] D. S. Wilks. *Statistical Methods in the Atmospheric Sciences.* 3rd ed. Vol. 100. Academic Press, 2011.

[36] J. Yang and V. Honavar. "Feature subset selection using a genetic algorithm". In: *IEEE Intell. Syst.* 13.2 (1998), pp. 44–49.

Human Action Recognition Optimization Based on Evolutionary Feature Subset Selection

Alexandros Andre Chaaraoui
Department of Computing Technology
University of Alicante
P.O. Box 99
E-03080, Alicante, Spain
alexandros@dtic.ua.es

Francisco Flórez-Revuelta
Faculty of Science, Engineering and Computing
Kingston University
Penrhyn Road, KT1 2EE
Kingston upon Thames, United Kingdom
F.Florez@kingston.ac.uk

ABSTRACT

Human action recognition constitutes a core component of advanced human behavior analysis. The detection and recognition of basic human motion enables to analyze and understand human activities, and to react proactively providing different kinds of services from human-computer interaction to health care assistance. In this paper, a feature-level optimization for human action recognition is proposed. The resulting recognition rate and computational cost are significantly improved by means of a low-dimensional radial summary feature and evolutionary feature subset selection. The introduced feature is computed using only the contour points of human silhouettes. These are spatially aligned based on a radial scheme. This definition shows to be proficient for feature subset selection, since different parts of the human body can be selected by choosing the appropriate feature elements. The best selection is sought using a genetic algorithm. Experimentation has been performed on the publicly available MuHAVi dataset. Promising results are shown, since state-of-the-art recognition rates are considerably outperformed with a highly reduced computational cost.

Categories and Subject Descriptors

I.4.8 [**Image Processing and Computer Vision**]: Scene Analysis; I.5.2 [**Pattern Recognition**]: Design Methodology—*Feature evaluation and selection*

General Terms

Algorithms, Experimentation

Keywords

feature subset selection, genetic algorithm, human action recognition, multi-view recognition, bag-of-key-poses

1. INTRODUCTION

Recently, human behavior analysis (HBA) has become of great interest in the field of artificial intelligence. The outlook of smart environments recognizing human actions and intentions, and understanding the scene and the context in which these occur opens a wide range of possible applications. Among these, video surveillance, human-computer interaction, but also gaming, ambient-assisted living and ageing well can be found. Cameras are one of the most popular sensors used in order to monitor people's behavior, since video images contain rich information about the scene to analyze. Specifically, human action recognition deals with the detection and classification of basic human motion in short temporal intervals, as, for instance, walking, jumping or falling. Through video analysis, the spatio-temporal properties of the human shape are learned and classified by means of computer vision and machine learning techniques [25].

Current efforts rely on achieving the required robustness to instance-, actor- and view-variance [26], as well as real-time suitability [27], which is essential in most of the applications of HBA. Therefore, the current goal is to improve existing approaches in order to reach high and stable recognition rates, and, at the same time, simplify the classification algorithm and feature extraction process, thus minimizing the involved computational cost. In this sense, in this work we propose and evaluate novel visual feature-related improvements which especially address these goals.

The feature subset problem arises when using feature vectors, since these might contain irrelevant or redundant information that could negatively affect the accuracy of a classifier [7]. In fact, irrelevant and redundant features interfere with useful ones, and most classifiers are unable to discriminate them [20, 18]. Also, identifying relevant features is of great importance for classification tasks, as it improves accuracy and reduces the computational costs involved [8, 36].

In this paper, a human action recognition optimization based on evolutionary feature subset selection is proposed. Using the contour points of the human silhouette, a radial scheme is applied so as to obtain a feature vector made up of summary values. These represent the shape of the silhouette with respect to each of the radial bins. This feature is especially suitable for feature subset selection, because its spatial definition is inherently related to the parts of the human body. Arms, legs, hip and head, might be or not be necessary to be considered, or they may even introduce noise to the feature descriptor. With this in mind, an evolutionary feature subset selection by means of a genetic algorithm is introduced. This proposal is evaluated using a human action recognition approach based on the one from Chaaraoui et al. [9], and performing an experimentation on the publicly available MuHAVi dataset [29]. The obtained results are very promising, since state-of-the-art recognition rates are significantly outperformed.

The remainder of this paper is organized as follows: Section 2 summarizes related work with respect to evolutionary feature subset selection and human action recognition. In section 3, the proposed radial summary feature, and evolutionary feature subset selection method are detailed. Section 4 briefly summarizes the employed human action recognition method which is used as fitness function in the genetic algorithm. Experimentation and results are analyzed in section 5. Finally, we present conclusions and discussion in section 6.

2. RELATED WORK

In this section, the most recent and relevant works related to evolutionary feature subset selection, and its application to human action recognition based on vision techniques are summarized.

2.1 Evolutionary Feature Subset Selection

Evolutionary feature subset selection has been used for decades [28]. The basic approach is to consider a binary vector where each gene represents the further consideration or not of a specific feature. Two main models are presented to implement this [7, 8]: the *wrapper* model [17], and the *filter* model. The latter selects the features based on *a priori* decisions on feature relevance according to some measures (information, distance, dependence or consistency) [22], but it ignores the learning algorithm underneath. In the former and on the contrary, the feature selection algorithm exists as a *wrapper* around the learning algorithm; in the search of a feature subset, the learning algorithm itself is used as part of the evaluation function [17]. The main disadvantage of the wrapper approach is the time needed for the evaluation of each feature subset [20]. On the other hand, filter-based approaches, although faster, find worse subsets in general [7].

Evolutionary feature subset selection has been broadly used in computer vision applications including: gender recognition from facial images [31], object detection (faces and vehicles) [30], human action recognition with RGB-D devices [12], target detection in synthetic aperture radar (SAR) images [2], image annotation [23, 21], and seed discrimination [11]. For a complete review of feature subset selection see the work of Casado Yusta [8].

2.2 Human Action Recognition

In the research field of human action recognition, machine learning and its application to computer vision and pattern recognition come together. This results in a research area that can be observed from multiple points of view. Since this paper focuses on the level of features extracted from binary human silhouettes, existing works from this area will be summarized.

A considerable number of works employ features based on human silhouettes (e.g. [4, 3, 34, 35, 33, 15]). These type of input data simplifies the amount of relevant data to a single region of interest (ROI) with binary shape data. Silhouettes can be obtained with traditional segmentation techniques, by more advanced human body detection algorithms, or even with depth or infra-red cameras. Bobick and Davis [4] proposed a feature which encodes the temporal evolution and the location of the motion with respect to sequences of silhouettes. In [35], this idea has been extended to a free-viewpoint representation, i.e. a model generated from view-invariant motion descriptors which are obtained from different viewpoints. The feature descriptor is based on Fourier analysis in cylindrical coordinates. Tran and Sorokin [34] developed a feature using both the shape of the silhouette, and the vertical and horizontal optical flow together with the context of 15 surrounding frames. In the case of [15], a histogram of the oriented rectangular patches extracted over the human silhouette is employed in a bag-of-words and dynamic time warping (DTW) based approach. For a complete review of previous work, we refer to the popular surveys from Moeslund et al. [25] and Poppe [26].

Regarding the specific application of feature selection to human action recognition, little can be found in the literature. The approach of Jhuang et al. [16] uses a zero-norm support vector machine (SVM) for feature selection of position-invariant spatio-temporal features, and concluded that feature density could be reduced up to 24 times without sacrificing accuracy. A multi-class delta latent Dirichlet allocation model for feature selection is introduced in [6], where collaborative feature selection is performed by taking into account the correlation between feature samples. Feature selection can also be performed based on a different criteria than highest classification accuracy. In this sense, in [19] multiple kernel learning (MKL) is applied in order to reach the most discriminative neighborhoods among interest points. Similarly, feature selection based on entropy is used in [14]. In this work, a new shape descriptor is defined based on the distribution of border lines which are histogrammed over 15° orientations. Selecting the bins with the highest entropy, the regions in which most of the motion occurs are found. In this way, feature size could be reduced by a factor of three.

3. FEATURE SUBSET SELECTION

In this section, both the characteristic feature based on human silhouettes, as well as the genetic algorithm used in order to apply binary feature subset selection are presented. As mentioned in the introduction, several data and data type related constraints need to be taken into account when applying feature subset selection. For instance, an appropriate level of granularity needs to be found. It needs to be fine-grained enough to successfully exclude the redundant or noisy elements and, at the same time, preserve the most characteristic data, but also coarse-grained enough in order to limit the problem scale to a moderate level. Furthermore, the size of the resulting feature set is particularly important in human action recognition due to the real-time requirement of multiple related applications. For this reason, we propose a low-dimensional feature with a highly reduced computational extraction cost, which in addition to the reduction due to feature subset selection, leads to a visual descriptor which is very optimized in both its size and the characteristic quality of its data.

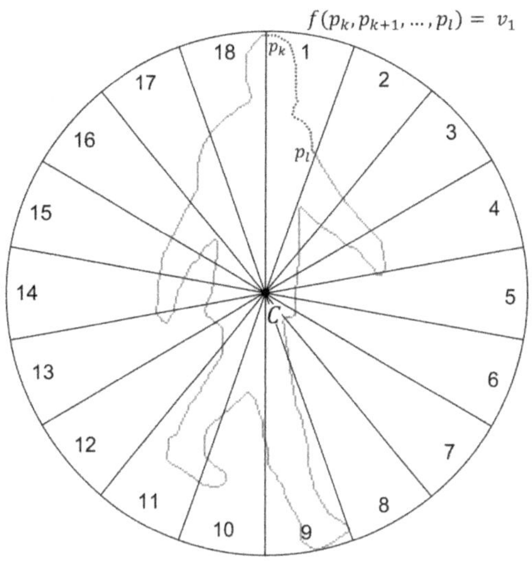

Figure 1: Application of the radial scheme. In this example, C indicates the centroid of the silhouette. Considering the centroid as origin, a radial scheme is applied in order to determine the radial bin of each point. Then, a summary value is obtained for the points of each of the radial bins ($S = 18$ in this case).

3.1 Radial Summary Feature

As shown in section 2, human silhouettes are widely used in human action recognition. This is due to multiple reasons. Firstly, they are relatively simple to obtain through background segmentation or human detection techniques. Secondly, they contain rich shape information which, when considering its evolution over time, can be sufficient in order to recognize complex human activities based on motion. And, finally, the silhouette can be simplified to an array of points using border following algorithms [32]. This leads to a silhouette contour which shows certain robustness to lighting changes and small viewpoint variations [1] using a reduced amount of elements.

Relying on the contour points $\boldsymbol{P} = \{p_1, p_2, ..., p_n\}$, where $p_i = (x_i, y_i)$, we divide the silhouette contour in S radial bins of the same size with the purpose of generating a summary value for each of them (see figure 1 for an overview).

First, the centroid $C = (x_c, y_c)$, with $x_c = \frac{\sum_{i=1}^{n} x_i}{n}, y_c = \frac{\sum_{i=1}^{n} y_i}{n}$, is computed. Then, the contour points $\boldsymbol{P}$ are re-ordered starting with the uppermost point with equal x-axis than the centroid, and following a clockwise order.

Secondly, using the centroid as the origin, the specific bin s_i of each contour point p_i can be assigned as follows (for the sake of simplicity $\alpha_i = 0$ is considered as $\alpha_i = 360$):

$$\alpha_i = \begin{cases} \arccos(\frac{y_i - y_c}{d_i}) \cdot \frac{180}{\pi} & \text{if } x_i \geq 0, \\ 180 + \arccos(\frac{y_i - y_c}{d_i}) \cdot \frac{180}{\pi} & \text{otherwise,} \end{cases} \quad (1)$$

$$s_i = \left\lceil \frac{S \cdot \alpha_i}{360} \right\rceil, \quad \forall i \in [1...n], \quad (2)$$

where d_i stands for the Euclidean distance between each contour point and the centroid.

Finally, the summary value of each radial bin is obtained based on the statistical range of the distances corresponding to the bin's points. These summary values are then concatenated to a normalized feature vector $\bar{\boldsymbol{V}}$.

$$\begin{aligned} v_j = &\max(d_k, d_{k+1}, ..., d_l) - \min(d_k, d_{k+1}, ..., d_l) \\ &/ \; s_k ... s_l = j \wedge k, l \in [1...n], \quad \forall j \in [1...S], \end{aligned} \quad (3)$$

$$\bar{v_j} = \frac{v_j}{\sum_{j=1}^{S} v_j}, \quad \forall j \in [1...S], \quad (4)$$

$$\bar{\boldsymbol{V}} = \bar{v_1} \parallel \bar{v_2} \parallel ... \parallel \bar{v_S}. \quad (5)$$

In result, the feature vector encodes the local shape properties of the individual radial bins. Then, feature subset selection can be applied with the purpose of filtering the unnecessary radial bins which may correspond to redundant, noisy or irrelevant body parts, and retaining the most important and characteristic ones.

3.2 Evolutionary feature subset selection

In this work, an evolutionary wrapper approach with a steady-state reproduction scheme is proposed for feature subset selection. Therefore, a binary selection approach is employed in which, through evolution of individuals, the optimal choice of feature elements is sought.

Specifically, an individual of the population is encoded as a binary array $\boldsymbol{U}$ whose elements $u_j, \forall j \in [1...S]$ represent whether ($u_j = 1$) or not ($u_j = 0$) a radial bin is selected. Having fixed the population size I, the following steps are performed:

1. The population is initialized with one individual with $u_j = 1, \forall j \in [1...S]$, so as to consider the default feature from the first iteration on. The values of the remaining individuals are set randomly.

2. Evaluate the fitness value of each individual. The aptitude of each of the generated feature subset selections is tested using the human action recognition approach detailed in section 4, and the fitness value of the individual is set to the returned success rate.

3. The population is ordered by descending fitness value. In the case that two individuals present the same fitness value, the one with the lowest number of selected elements ($u_j = 1$) comes first. Hence, among the fittest individuals those are preferred that result in a higher temporal and spatial efficiency.

4. Create a new individual using one-point crossover. Parents are chosen using the ranking selection method. The new individual is built up by the elements 1 to z from the first parent and $z + 1$ to S from the second parent (z denotes the randomly selected crossover point).

5. Each gene of the new individual is mutated according to a probability P_{mut}. This mutation consists in changing the binary value of the gene.

6. The fitness value for the new individual is obtained. If it does not exist in the current population, it is added to the population. Otherwise, the fitness of

the equivalent individual already in the population is updated with the new fitness in case it is improved. Note that the non-deterministic behavior of the classification process, which is caused by the random initialization of the K-means algorithm, leads to obtain different fitness values for the same feature vector.

7. Remove from the population the individual with the lowest fitness value.

8. Return to step 3 until the best-performing individual does not increase its fitness value for a specified number of generations max_{gen}.

4. HUMAN ACTION RECOGNITION

With the purpose of evaluating the proposed evolutionary feature subset selection method, the multi-view human action recognition approach from [9] has been chosen. With a simple yet effective algorithm, this work shows proficiency in both action recognition and speed. The method is based on: 1) a contour-based distance signal feature, 2) a bag-of-key-poses which serves as dictionary of the most common and characteristic key poses involved in action performances seen from multiple views, and 3) classification by means of key pose sequence matching. The employed learning and classification approach from [9] is briefly summarized in this section, where we want to point out that, in this case, the proposed visual feature from section 3.1 is used as input.

4.1 Learning based on Bag-of-Key-Poses

Using the radial summary feature detailed in section 3.1 and applying the feature subset selection, the required silhouette-based pose representations are obtained. These pose representation samples are reduced to a representative subset of key poses, with the purpose of decreasing the scale of the problem of exemplar-based classification and removing redundant data. This is achieved using K-means clustering and taking the cluster centers as representative values. K key poses are generated separately for each combination of action class and view, and joined building a so-called bag-of-key-poses. Then, the capacity of discrimination of each key pose is computed by finding the nearest neighbor key pose of each pose representation, and using the ratio of within-class matches as the final weight of the key pose. In this manner, very common poses which can be found across several classes will have a very low weight, whereas a key pose which can only be found in a specific class, and is therefore more discriminative, will have a higher weight.

4.2 Sequence recognition

So as to take into account the temporal evolution between key poses, sequences of key poses are built. For each of the training sequences, its pose representations are replaced with the corresponding nearest neighbor key pose. In this way, the temporal order between key poses is learned, and, at the same time, noise and outlier values are filtered. Thus, this specific step achieves to significantly improve the algorithm's robustness to actor-variance.

In order to perform classification, the learned sequences of key poses are compared with an analogous sequence of key poses retrieved from a sequence to recognize. Sequence matching is performed using dynamic time warping (DTW), which supports significant differences with respect to length, accelerations and decelerations, and consequently takes into account the different pace at which humans perform actions.

When comparing individual elements in the DTW algorithm, a distance is provided that takes into account the Euclidean distance between features, as well as the relevance of the specific match of key poses. This relevance is based on the previously obtained weights. It indicates how important a specific match is relying on its capacity of discrimination, and if its distance should be therefore carefully considered in the sequence alignment algorithm. We refer to [9] for more details.

Finally, multi-view sequences in the recognition phase are handled by evaluating the sequences recorded from each view, and returning the label of the best match, i.e. the sequence with the lowest DTW distance.

5. EXPERIMENTATION

The proposed approach has been evaluated on the MuHAVi [29] dataset. Since this multi-view human action recognition benchmark has been used in [9], it allows us to compare the obtained performances. The MuHAVi-MAS dataset provides the required silhouettes for two camera views. The action performances from two actors have been recorded up to four times. MuHAVi-14 includes 14 different action classes, among which actions as $CollapseLeft$, $GuardToPunch$ and $RunLeftToRight$ can be found. In MuHAVi-8 the different directions in which the actions occur have been ignored, merging the classes into eight different actions. In this sense, this second version does not require to distinguish the direction, and therefore it includes a higher number of samples for each class. Nonetheless, it also requires the human action recognition approach to be able to learn these actions which are performed differently.

The following tests have been performed:

1. Leave-one-sequence-out (LOSO): In this cross validation test, all but one sequence are used for training, while the remaining sequence is used for evaluation. This procedure is repeated for all the available sequences and the average recognition rate is determined.

2. Leave-one-actor-out (LOAO): In this cross validation test, actor-invariance is specifically tested by training with all but one actor, and testing the method with the unseen one. This is repeated for all actors, averaging the returned accuracy scores. As actors may differ in clothes, body build and how they perform the actions, this test presents an additional difficulty which usually leads to lower recognition rates.

With respect to the constant parameters of the method, the present results have been obtained with $S \in [12, 30]$ and $K \in [9, 100]$. In the genetic algorithm, a population of $I = 10$ individuals and a single offspring have been employed. The remaining parameters have been set as follows: $P_{mut} = 0.1$ and $max_{gen} = 250$. These values have been obtained based on experimentation. Note that using the specified data, convergence has been reached in a limited number of generations (under $\sim$900), and therefore no alternative stopping criteria has been applied.

Table 1: **Benchmark results obtained with the proposed radial summary feature and the corresponding binary feature subset selection. Results are compared with the ones published in [9], where the original human action recognition approach is used. Both LOSO and LOAO cross validations are performed.**

Dataset	Test	Chaaraoui et al.[9]	$u_j = 1, \forall j \in [1...S]$	Feature Subset Selection
MuHAVi-14	LOSO	94.1%	95.6%[a]	**98.5%**
MuHAVi-14	LOAO	86.8%	91.2%[b]	**94.1%**
MuHAVi-8	LOSO	98.5%	**100%**[c]	**100%**
MuHAVi-8	LOAO	95.6%	97.1%[d]	**100%**

Table 2: **Analysis of variance test for the LOAO cross validations. The results of 20 replicates have been compared between the method from Chaaraoui et al.[9] and the proposed feature subset selection. A confidence level of 99% ($\alpha = 0.01$) is considered.**

Output Measure	Source of variation	Sum of Sq.	DOF	Mean Sq.	F	p-value
MuHAVi-14 LOAO test	Between groups	0,229537	1	0,229537	947,862652	0.000000
	Within groups	0,009202	38	0,000242		
MuHAVi-8 LOAO test	Between groups	0,165585	1	0,165585	1630,778024	0.000000
	Within groups	0,003858	38	0,0001015		

5.1 Results

In table 1, the recognition rates are shown for both types of cross validation tests. The second last and last column represent the accuracy before and after optimization, respectively. It can be seen that when using the radial summary feature (individual with $u_j = 1, \forall j \in [1...S]$), the originally obtained recognition rates are improved. It seems obvious that starting with an adequate accuracy level is essential if we want to perform feature subset selection successfully. Furthermore, besides the low dimensionality of the feature, its definition, which is directly related to the parts of the body, leads to an inherent proficiency for feature subset selection. This is confirmed in the returned fitness values for the best evolved individuals. In both type of tests, significant performance improvements are shown.

In order to analyze the statistical significance of the obtained performance gain over the original method from [9], an analysis of variance (ANOVA) test has been performed for the results of the MuHAVi LOAO tests. In table 2, it can be seen that for both datasets highly statistically significant (.01 level) improvements have been obtained. In both cases, a *large* effect size has been measured indicating that these improvements are also practically significant (for MuHAVi-14 and MuHAVi-8, Cohen's d = 9.86 and 12.94 respectively).

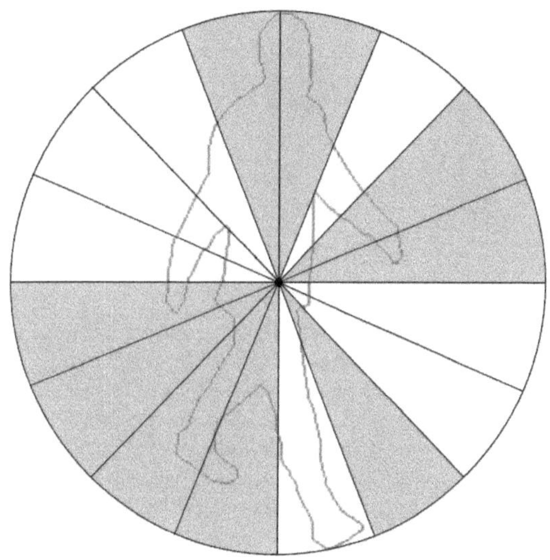

Figure 2: **Resulting feature subset selection of the MuHAVi-14 LOSO cross validation test (dismissed radial bins are shaded in gray). Through genetic selection, 7 out of 16 radial bins have been selected, as these provided the best result.**

Table 3: **The values $u_j, \forall j \in [1...S]$ of the final individuals of each of the run tests.**

Dataset	Test	Individual
MuHAVi-14	LOSO	*0100110100001110*
MuHAVi-14	LOAO	*011110101111*
MuHAVi-8	LOSO	*000111000011*
MuHAVi-8	LOAO	*00001011101111101011000100 1011*

Further details about the generated feature subset selections are specified in table 3, where the values of the best individuals are shown. It can be observed that several radial bins may be ignored, and that by doing so not only the feature size is reduced removing unnecessary elements, but also the recognition accuracy is increased as these bins introduced noise. Interestingly, although perfect recognition has been obtained in the MuHAVi-8 LOSO cross validation test using the default feature, the applied evolutionary feature subset selection maintains this rate with less than half of the feature vector elements. In average, in our tests we achieved to improve or preserve the highest recognition rate reducing ~47% of the feature elements. Figure 2 shows one of the selections on a sample silhouette.

Finally, our results are compared with other state-of-the-art recognition rates. As table 4 shows, very considerable improvements have been attained, especially regarding the actor-invariance tests. To the best of our knowledge, these are the highest rates reported so far for this dataset.

Table 4: Comparison of recognition rates obtained on the MuHAVi dataset with other state-of-the-art approaches.

	MuHAVi-14		MuHAVi-8	
Approach	**LOSO**	**LOAO**	**LOSO**	**LOAO**
Singh et al. [29] (baseline)	82.4%	61.8%	97.8%	76.4%
Martínez-Contreras et al.[24]	-	-	98.4%	-
Cheema et al. [10]	86.0%	73.5%	95.6%	83.1%
Eweiwi et al. [13]	91.9%	77.9%	98.5%	85.3%
Our method	**98.5%**	**94.1%**	**100%**	**100%**

5.2 Temporal Evaluation

So as to verify the computational cost of the proposed approach, we tested our method on a standard PC with an Intel Core 2 Duo CPU at 3 GHz and 4 GB of RAM with Windows 7 64-bit. The implementation has been developed with the .NET Framework and the OpenCV library [5]. All tests have been performed using the 720x576 px silhouette images from the MuHAVi-14 dataset (7941 frames) as input data, without any further hardware optimizations.

Regarding the feature extraction stages, most of the time, i.e. 76.36s, is spent processing the contour points of the image. The remaining feature extraction and classification stages are performed in only 1.50 and 5.86s respectively. Applying feature subset selection this time is reduced by 14%. With respect to the overall recognition speed, whereas in [9] a rate of 51 frames per second (FPS) is stated, here 96 FPS are reached.

6. CONCLUSION

In the present work, an optimization of a human action recognition algorithm has been introduced. Human silhouettes are used as input data out of which a contour-based feature is extracted. In particular, the shape of the silhouette is represented in a radial fashion, by summary values based on the point-wise distances to the centroid. This results in a very low-dimensional feature vector, whose elements encode the shape of the human silhouette, taking into account spatial alignment. This is due to the fact that, instead of directly reducing the array of contour points, the spatial distribution is considered applying a radial scheme. This approach results in a feature that is well-suited for feature subset selection. In order to find the best selection of radial bins to consider, an evolutionary feature subset selection has been applied. In result, the recognition rates of the original human action recognition approach have been increased, and new reference rates have been established for the MuHAVi dataset.

In conclusion, the main contributions of this paper can be summarized as follows:

1. An appropriate feature for feature subset selection has been presented. As the experimental results show, the radial summary feature successfully encodes the shape of the boundary of the human silhouette in order recognize human actions. This is achieved with a reduced computational complexity and a low-dimensional descriptor.

2. An evolutionary feature subset selection approach is proposed for the binary selection of feature elements. A genetic algorithm is used as search heuristic so as to provide the best possible solution in a limited amount of time. The obtained optimization achieved perfect recognition on the MuHAVi-8 LOSO and LOAO cross validation tests, reducing the number of necessary feature elements by ~47% in average.

Regarding future works, it would be interesting to consider a feature selection based on real-valued weights, so that a feature element could be taken into account more or less than others without completely discarding it. This would open a wider search space with potential solutions for more fine-grained optimizations. Furthermore, the optimal selection of features may change for the different types of actions to recognize. Walking, running and jogging may affect mostly the legs and the arms, whereas in bending, the upper part of the body may be the most relevant. Therefore, an action class-specific feature subset selection should be obtained. Multiple optimization objectives, as both the highest recognition rate and the least number of selected feature elements, could also be considered. Other future research lines include experimentation on more extensive datasets, usage of images which present occlusions, and a study of applicability to recognition of activities of daily living (ADL).

7. ACKNOWLEDGEMENTS

This work has been partially supported by the European Commission under project "caring4U - A study on people activity in private spaces: towards a multisensor network that meets privacy requirements" (PIEF-GA-2010-274649) and by the Spanish Ministry of Science and Innovation under project "Sistema de visión para la monitorización de la actividad de la vida diaria en el hogar" (TIN2010-20510-C04-02). Alexandros Andre Chaaraoui acknowledges financial support by the Conselleria d'Educació, Formació i Ocupació of the Generalitat Valenciana (fellowship ACIF/2011/160). The funders had no role in study design, data collection and analysis, decision to publish, or preparation of the manuscript.

8. REFERENCES

[1] M. Ángeles Mendoza and N. Pérez de la Blanca. HMM-based action recognition using contour histograms. In J. Martí, J. Benedí, A. Mendonça, and J. Serrat, editors, *Pattern Recognition and Image Analysis*, volume 4477 of *Lecture Notes in Computer Science*, pages 394–401. Springer Berlin / Heidelberg, 2007.

[2] B. Bhanu and Y. Lin. Genetic algorithm based feature selection for target detection in SAR images. *Image and Vision Computing*, 21(7):591 – 608, 2003. Computer Vision beyond the visible spectrum.

[3] M. Blank, L. Gorelick, E. Shechtman, M. Irani, and R. Basri. Actions as space-time shapes. In *Computer Vision, 2005. ICCV 2005. Tenth IEEE International Conference on*, volume 2, pages 1395 -1402 Vol. 2, oct. 2005.

[4] A. Bobick and J. Davis. The recognition of human movement using temporal templates. *Pattern Analysis and Machine Intelligence, IEEE Transactions on*, 23(3):257 -267, mar 2001.

[5] G. Bradski. The OpenCV Library. *Dr. Dobb's Journal of Software Tools*, 2000.

[6] M. Bregonzio, J. Li, S. Gong, and T. Xiang. Discriminative topics modelling for action feature selection and recognition. In *Proceedings of the British Machine Vision Conference*, pages 8.1–8.11. BMVA Press, 2010. doi:10.5244/C.24.8.

[7] E. Cantú-Paz. Feature subset selection, class separability, and genetic algorithms. In K. Deb, editor, *Genetic and Evolutionary Computation - GECCO 2004*, volume 3102 of *Lecture Notes in Computer Science*, pages 959–970. Springer Berlin Heidelberg, 2004.

[8] S. Casado Yusta. Different metaheuristic strategies to solve the feature selection problem. *Pattern Recognition Letters*, 30(5):525–534, 2009.

[9] A. A. Chaaraoui, P. Climent-Pérez, and F. Flórez-Revuelta. An efficient approach for multi-view human action recognition based on bag-of-key-poses. In A. A. Salah, J. Ruiz-del Solar, C. Meriçli, and P.-Y. Oudeyer, editors, *Human Behavior Understanding*, volume 7559 of *Lecture Notes in Computer Science*, pages 29–40. Springer Berlin Heidelberg, 2012.

[10] S. Cheema, A. Eweiwi, C. Thurau, and C. Bauckhage. Action recognition by learning discriminative key poses. In *Computer Vision Workshops (ICCV Workshops), 2011 IEEE International Conference on*, pages 1302–1309, 2011.

[11] Y. Chtioui, D. Bertrand, and D. Barba. Feature selection by a genetic algorithm. application to seed discrimination by artificial vision. *Journal of the Science of Food and Agriculture*, 76(1):77–86, 1998.

[12] P. Climent-Pérez, A. A. Chaaraoui, and F. Flórez-Revuelta. Optimal feature selection for skeletal data from RGB-D devices using a genetic algorithm. In *11th Mexican International Conference on Artificial Intelligence*, San Luis Potosí, Mexico, 2012.

[13] A. Eweiwi, S. Cheema, C. Thurau, and C. Bauckhage. Temporal key poses for human action recognition. In *Computer Vision Workshops (ICCV Workshops), 2011 IEEE International Conference on*, pages 1310–1317, 2011.

[14] N. Ikizler, R. Cinbis, and P. Duygulu. Human action recognition with line and flow histograms. In *Pattern Recognition, 2008. ICPR 2008. 19th International Conference on*, pages 1 -4, dec. 2008.

[15] N. İkizler and P. Duygulu. Human action recognition using distribution of oriented rectangular patches. In A. Elgammal, B. Rosenhahn, and R. Klette, editors, *Human Motion Understanding, Modeling, Capture and Animation*, volume 4814 of *Lecture Notes in Computer Science*, pages 271–284. Springer Berlin / Heidelberg, 2007.

[16] H. Jhuang, T. Serre, L. Wolf, and T. Poggio. A biologically inspired system for action recognition. In *Computer Vision, 2007. ICCV 2007. IEEE 11th International Conference on*, pages 1 -8, oct. 2007.

[17] G. John, R. Kohavi, and K. Pfleger. Irrelevant features and the subset selection problem. In *Proceedings of the 11th International Conference on Machine Learning*, pages 121–129, San Francisco, CA, 1994. Morgan Kaufmann.

[18] K. Kira and L. A. Rendell. The feature selection problem: traditional methods and a new algorithm. In *Proceedings of the tenth national conference on Artificial intelligence*, AAAI'92, pages 129–134. AAAI Press, 1992.

[19] A. Kovashka and K. Grauman. Learning a hierarchy of discriminative space-time neighborhood features for human action recognition. In *Computer Vision and Pattern Recognition (CVPR), 2010 IEEE Conference on*, pages 2046 -2053, june 2010.

[20] P. Lanzi. Fast feature selection with genetic algorithms: a filter approach. In *Evolutionary Computation, 1997., IEEE International Conference on*, pages 537–540, apr 1997.

[21] R. Li, J. Lu, Y. Zhang, and T. Zhao. Dynamic adaboost learning with feature selection based on parallel genetic algorithm for image annotation. *Knowledge-Based Systems*, 23(3):195 – 201, 2010.

[22] H. Liu and H. Motoda. *Feature Selection for Knowledge Discovery and Data Mining*. Kluwer Academic Publishers, Boston, 1998.

[23] J. Lu, T. Zhao, and Y. Zhang. Feature selection based-on genetic algorithm for image annotation. *Knowledge-Based Systems*, 21(8):887 – 891, 2008.

[24] F. Martínez-Contreras, C. Orrite-Urunuela, E. Herrero-Jaraba, H. Ragheb, and S. Velastin. Recognizing human actions using silhouette-based HMM. In *Advanced Video and Signal Based Surveillance, 2009. AVSS '09. Sixth IEEE International Conference on*, pages 43–48, 2009.

[25] T. B. Moeslund, A. Hilton, and V. Krüger. A survey of advances in vision-based human motion capture and analysis. *Comput. Vis. Image Underst.*, 104(2):90–126, Nov. 2006.

[26] R. Poppe. A survey on vision-based human action recognition. *Image and Vision Computing*, 28(6):976 – 990, 2010.

[27] J. Shotton, A. Fitzgibbon, M. Cook, T. Sharp, M. Finocchio, R. Moore, A. Kipman, and A. Blake. Real-time human pose recognition in parts from single depth images. In *Computer Vision and Pattern Recognition (CVPR), 2011 IEEE Conference on*, pages 1297 -1304, june 2011.

[28] W. Siedlecki and J. Sklansky. A note on genetic algorithms for large-scale feature selection. *Pattern Recognition Letters*, 10(5):335 – 347, 1989.

[29] S. Singh, S. Velastin, and H. Ragheb. MuHAVi: A multicamera human action video dataset for the evaluation of action recognition methods. In *Advanced Video and Signal Based Surveillance (AVSS), 2010*

Seventh IEEE International Conference on, pages 48–55, 29 2010-sept. 1 2010.

[30] Z. Sun, G. Bebis, and R. Miller. Object detection using feature subset selection. *Pattern Recognition*, 37(11):2165 – 2176, 2004.

[31] Z. Sun, G. Bebis, X. Yuan, and S. Louis. Genetic feature subset selection for gender classification: a comparison study. In *Applications of Computer Vision, 2002. (WACV 2002). Proceedings. Sixth IEEE Workshop on*, pages 165 – 170, 2002.

[32] S. Suzuki and K. Abe. Topological structural analysis of digitized binary images by border following. *Computer Vision, Graphics, and Image Processing*, 30(1):32 – 46, 1985.

[33] C. Thurau and V. Hlaváč. *n*-grams of action primitives for recognizing human behavior. In W. Kropatsch, M. Kampel, and A. Hanbury, editors, *Computer Analysis of Images and Patterns*, volume 4673 of *Lecture Notes in Computer Science*, pages 93–100. Springer Berlin / Heidelberg, 2007.

[34] D. Tran and A. Sorokin. Human activity recognition with metric learning. In D. Forsyth, P. Torr, and A. Zisserman, editors, *Computer Vision - ECCV 2008*, volume 5302 of *Lecture Notes in Computer Science*, pages 548–561. Springer Berlin Heidelberg, 2008.

[35] D. Weinland, R. Ronfard, and E. Boyer. Free viewpoint action recognition using motion history volumes. *Comput. Vis. Image Underst.*, 104(2):249–257, Nov. 2006.

[36] J. Yang and V. Honavar. Feature subset selection using a genetic algorithm. *Intelligent Systems and their Applications, IEEE*, 13(2):44 –49, mar/apr 1998.

Self-Adjusting Focus of Attention by Means of GP for Improving a Laser Point Detection System

Eddie Clemente
CICESE -
Tecnológico de Estudios
Superiores de Ecatepec,
Avenida Tecnológico S/N
Valle de Anáhuac, Ecatepec
de Morelos
eddie.clemente@gmail.com

Francisco Chávez
University of Extremadura
C/. Santa Teresa de Jornet, 38
06800, Mérida. Spain
fchavez@unex.es

León Dozal
CICESE
Carretera Ensenada-Tijuana
No. 3918, Zona Playitas
C.P. 22860, Ensenada, B.C.
México
leon.dozal@gmail.com

Francisco Fernández de Vega
University of Extremadura
C/. Santa Teresa de Jornet, 38
06800, Mérida. Spain
fcofdez@unex.es

Gustavo Olague *
CICESE
Carretera Ensenada-Tijuana
No. 3918, Zona Playitas
C.P. 22860, Ensenada, B.C.
México
gustavo.olague@gmail.com

ABSTRACT

This paper introduces the application of a new GP based Focus of Attention technique capable of improving the accuracy level when using a Laser Pointer as an interactive device. Laser Pointers have been previously employed in combination with environment control systems as interaction devices, allowing users to send orders to devices. Accurate detection of laser spots is required for sending correct orders; moreover, false offs must be eradicated, thus preventing devices to autonomously activate/deactivate when orders have not been sent by users. The idea here is to apply a self-adjusting process to a GP based algorithm capable of focusing the attention of a visual recognition system on a narrow area of an image, where laser spots will be then located. Images are taken by video cameras working on users' environment. The results show that the new approach improves significantly the accuracy level when laser spots are present -users sending orders- while maintains the extremely low values of false offs provided by previous techniques.

Categories and Subject Descriptors

H.5.2 [**User Interfaces**]: Input devices and strategies—*Interaction styles, User interface management systems*; I.4 [**Image Proceesing and Computer Vision**]: General—*Image processing software*

*Corresponding Author

General Terms

Algorithms

Keywords

Self-Adjusting, Focus of Attention, Laser Pointer, Environment Control Systems

1. INTRODUCTION

Citizens face nowadays an immersive process in a technological world: since birth, human beings are surrounded by hundred of electronic devices that will be part of their life. Technology helps everyday activities, and smart homes are particularly helpful for elderly and handicapped people: they are benefited by a proper application of technology in the users' environments. In this context, interaction systems are a main component. An interaction system can be defined as: *set of interrelated objects neatly exercising an interplay between them.* This concept can be applied to smart homes [1, 2, 3, 16] obtaining an *Environment control system.*

Among the different approaches available, several authors have already considered the use of laser pointers as a mean of interaction [13, 14, 17, 21]. We have already studied that possibility, and improved the technique, that allows the application of commercial laser pointers as an interaction system in combination with off-shelf cameras in users' homes. The idea is to provide the users with the ability of sending orders by projecting laser spots onto home devices in combination with domotic control systems [4, 5, 6, 7]. In this initial system status, the orders sent to devices must be only turn on/off. By applying computer vision techniques the system is capable of detecting laser spots and converting them to domotic control orders. In [4, 6, 7] we analyzed the application of Fuzzy Rules-Based Systems (FRBS) that in combination with Template Matching (TM) techniques provide good accuracy for the problem of laser spot detection. In that study, we confirmed the suitability of FRBS while also shown the problems that arise when applying TM techniques in combination with Dynamic Umbralization (DU) for a pre-filtering process on images that are then fed to the FRBS. The main sources for the incorrect classification processes -conducting to False Negatives or False Positives- where thus found on the $TM + DU$ processes. Nevertheless, FRBS needs a previous process for properly identifying main parameters to be classified as belonging to two specific sets: Images with or without a laser spot projected.

This paper presents a complete study for improving the first step of the image analysis. Instead of trying to enhance the classification provided by a FRBS properly trained, we attempt to improve the extraction of the main features required for a FRBS in order to accurately decide whether the laser spots are present or not - thus allowing a domotic system to send a turn on/off order to a specific device. We describe a Genetic Programming (GP) based approach called Brain Programming [19, 20] that emulates and self-adjust a Focus of Attention (FOA) method, capable of providing better areas of images and features extracted. We present a comparison with previous methods, and show a noticeable improvement on correct detection of user actions, while maintaining the extremely low level of false offs, highly undesired on such a system.

The rest of the paper is organized as follows: Section 2 describes our previous work, while the new technique -Focus of Attention- is presented in section 3. Section 4 shows the results obtained for a set of experiments that tries to compare the new approach with the previous one. Finally section 5 summarizes our main conclusions.

2. PREVIOUS WORK

As detailed below, we consider here laser pointers that allow to interactively control home devices. In combination with off-the-shelf video-cameras and image processing techniques, the whole system (i) analyzes environment images, (ii) detects laser spot on these images -when present- and (iii) automatically recognizes the device selected as well as the order desired by the user, thus sending the necessary orders to control the home device by means of a domotic system.

In our case, the whole system is made up of three sections (see figure 1):

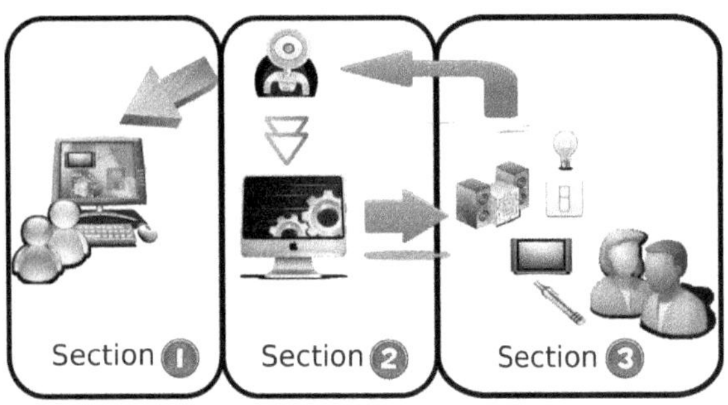

Figure 1: Environment control system

- 1st *Section*: The configuration tool allows users to select the home devices that will be controlled by the system. This tool allows advanced users to select the active zone for each of the home device by using the images sent by the video camera. This set up step is required for the system to properly work afterwards.
- 2nd *Section*: In this section the system uses different techniques in order to analyze the image sent by the video camera and to locate the position of the laser spot. The algorithm must thus follow a real-time approach.
- 3rd *Section*: KNX/EIB architecture [15] let the system control different home devices. Once the laser spot is found in an active zone, the system sends to the domotic system the necessary orders to turn on/off the device selected.

The contribution presented in this paper is focused on the 2nd *Section*, with the idea of improving the laser spot detection ability, which becomes one of the most important tasks in these kind of systems. The algorithms we previously employed to detect the laser spot on an image are the following ones, as described in [8]:

1. Algorithms using classical techniques for feature extraction:
   - Dynamic Umbralization (DU)
   - Template Matching (TM)
   - Template Matching + Dynamic Umbralization (TM + DU)
2. Algorithms using FRBS techniques for decision making:
   - Template Matching + FRBS design from Expert's Experience and automatic evolutionary tuning (TM + $\text{FRBS}_{\text{tuned-GA}}$).
   - Template Matching + evolutionary learning FRBS (TM + $\text{FRBS}_{\text{learning-GA}}$)

With the algorithms described above we try to design the best system to detect a laser spot in an image. The goal of this work is to obtain a system that can be used in a future real environment.

TM and DU are the initial algorithms employed to extract the main features that are later considered by FRBS to make a decision. FRBS can provide good decisions when good features are extracted. Previous analysis demonstrated the weakness of TM+DU, which were the main source for bad decisions taken by FRBS [5] and this is what we analyze here and try to improve: how to extract better information from images, with the help of GP based techniques.

In the next subsection we describe both DU and TM techniques previously employed for image analysis and feature extraction. They are our starting point.

2.1 Dynamic Umbralization

Dynamic Umbralization was the first algorithm considered. The idea was to detect high energy pixels within the images -that could probably belong to a laser spot. This algorithm calculates a threshold value, by means of which, the pixels under this value are eliminated. The threshold value is calculated by means of an empirical expression detailed in [5, 8]. As a consequence of this umbralization, the resultant image has laser spot's candidate pixels selected. Unfortunately, DU cannot be employed alone, given the high number of false offs detected (pixels that are not part of laser spots).

2.2 Template Matching

In order to improve the system performance Template Matching was considered instead. The idea was to detect rounded forms as candidates for laser spots. The algorithm that uses TM is based on convolution techniques. By means of this algorithm, an image named template is searched on the image sent by the video camera. A template is a laser spot image previously stored. Figure 2 shows a template image example.

Figure 2: Laser spot template

Each image sent by the video camera may have a section similar to the used template. The TM algorithm searches for such template on the obtained environment image. This algorithm obtains the probability of coincidence between the analyzed image sections and the template image. This probability is known as Zero Mean Normalized Cross Correlation (ZMNCC). The value obtained with this kind of correlation is normalized between -1 and 1. The expression is as follows:

$$\Phi(I_r, I_l) = \frac{\sum_{i,j\in[-w,w]} AB}{\sqrt{\sum_{i,j\in[-w,w]} A^2 \sum_{i,j\in[-w,w]} B^2}},$$

$$A = I_r(x+i, y+j) - \overline{I_r(x,y)},$$

$$B = I_l(x'+i, y'+j) - \overline{I_l(x',y')}, \quad (1)$$

where A contains the set of pixels which are in the main image section, and B contains the set of laser template pixels (see [5, 8] for more information on how this formula can be applied). The TM algorithm proposes the image section with the highest correlation since the laser spot should be found in the position of the obtained image section with the highest correlation. ZMNCC is also used as threshold value, if the highest correlation value calculated is under a specific value, the algorithm considers that there is not a laser spot in the analyzed image, and the result is a black image section. Nevertheless, TM working alone features the same problem as DU, a number of templates found that are not laser spots.

2.3 Template Matching + Dynamic Umbralization

Trying to improve the algorithms and eliminate the false offs, both techniques were considered to work together in [5, 8]. The first step aims at selecting the image section with highest correlation, by using the TM algorithm. The second step checks whether the section provided by TM is a laser spot image by applying the DU algorithm. In this step, if the image calculated has pixels with high energy, these pixels will not be eliminated, and the algorithm can thus conclude that the image filtered is a laser spot image. Results showed the interest of the combined approach, but still a number of false offs were present.

3. METHODOLOGY

After a careful study of the techniques described above, we concluded that TM was the main source for the false negatives, since this algorithm tends to find image sections which do not correspond with the laser spot. Although in combination with other more advanced techniques we were able of improving the accuracy, given that TM was still part of the whole system, we noticed the need for alternatives. For this reason, in this paper we have considered the possibility of improving the results obtained by TM + DU. We thus introduce a new algorithm that employs a GP based FOA which tries to reduce the section of the image on which TM has to find the laser spot. FOA is capable of self-adapting the section of the image where the laser spot must be located, thus reducing the search space for TM and also the false offs detected.

In the next section we describe FOA, as the technique used to improve the whole laser spot detection system FOA + TM + DU.

3.1 FOA algorithm

Nowadays, challenging computer vision problems are increasingly receiving interest from the evolutionary computing community, see [18]. Thus, it is said that humans are unable to create a complete mental representation of everything in their visual field; hence, in order to process visual information the person must focus on a region of the environment at a time. The idea behind focus of attention is to find a part of the scene that contains prominent information for solving a given task. The first explanations related to the ideas described in this section can be found in [9, 11, 12]. In this way, a basic phenomenon that defines the visual attention is selectivity, which is understood as the ability to filter unwanted information [10]. Therefore, the FOA algorithm is an abstraction of the natural process which can be applied to find the location of the laser spot in the image and reduce the detection of false positives during the TM stage.

The FOA algorithm is based on the feature-integration theory [23], which states that the visual attention is divided in two main stages: feature extraction and feature integration. Next, the computational implementation of the FOA is explained giving special emphasis on the aspects that make the self-adjusting process possible.

3.1.1 Extraction

In this stage the scene is perceived through a camera. Then, the extraction of the visual features is performed through, what we call, evolved visual operators (EVO). In this way, there are three different EVOs each one specialized in the detection of a single feature that are: orientation (EVO_O), color (EVO_C), and shape (EVO_S). There is a fourth visual operator that is not evolved; i.e., the intensity feature dimension. Such operators can be applied over the image in a parallel manner resulting in a visual map (VM) per feature dimension, see Fig. 3. In summary, we propose to use a GP based algorithm to obtain these artificial visual operators. The EVOs utilized within the FOA are generated by artificial evolution based on the functions and terminals listed in Table 1. Note that these functions and terminals are empirically proposed as is normally applied in the GP-strategy. The functions and terminals definition are provided in [9, 11, 19, 20, 12].

Table 1: Functions and terminals for EVOs building

Operator	Functions	Terminals
EVO_O	$+$, $-$, $\times$, $\div$, $\lvert + \rvert$, $\lvert - \rvert$, $\sqrt{I_{T_O}}$, $I_{T_O}^2$, $log_2(I_{T_O})$, $G_{\sigma=1}$, $G_{\sigma=2}$, $\lvert I_{T_O} \rvert$, $\frac{I_{T_O}}{2}$, D_x, D_y	I_r, I_g, I_b, I_c, I_m, I_y, I_k, I_h, I_s, I_v, $G_{\sigma=1}(I_r)$, $G_{\sigma=2}(I_r)$, $D_x(I_r)$, $D_y(I_r)$, $D_{xx}(I_r)$, $D_{yy}(I_r)$, $D_{xy}(I_r)$, ...
EVO_C	$+$, $-$, $\times$, $\div$, $\lvert + \rvert$, $\lvert - \rvert$, $\sqrt{I_{T_C}}$, $I_{T_C}^2$, $log_2(I_{T_C})$, $Exp(I_{T_C}$, $Complement(I_{T_C})$	I_r, I_g, I_b, I_c, I_m, I_y, I_k, I_h, I_s, I_v, RG_{oppn}, YB_{oppn}
EVO_S	$+$, $-$, $\times$, $\div$, $round(I_{T_S})$, $\lfloor I_{T_S} \rfloor$, $\lceil I_{T_S} \rceil$, $dilation_{diamond}(I_{T_S})$, $dilation_{square}(I_{T_S})$, $dilation_{disk}(I_{T_S})$, $erosion_{diamond}(I_{T_S})$, $erosion_{square}(I_{T_S})$, $erosion_{disk}(I_{T_S})$, $skeleton(I_{T_S})$, $boundary(I_{T_S})$, $hit - miss_{diamond}(I_{T_S})$, $hit - miss_{square}(I_{T_S})$, $hit - miss_{disk}(I_{T_S})$, $top - hat(I_{T_S})$, $bottom - hat(I_{T_S})$, $open(I_{T_S})$, $close(I_{T_S})$	I_r, I_g, I_b, I_c, I_m, I_y, I_k, I_h, I_s, I_v
EFI	$+$, $-$, $\times$, $\div$, $\lvert + \rvert$, $\lvert - \rvert$, $\sqrt{I_{T_{fi}}}$, $I_{T_{fi}}^2$, $Exp(I_{fi})$, $G_{\sigma=1}$, $G_{\sigma=2}$, $\lvert I_{T_{fi}} \rvert$, $round(I_{T_{fi}})$, $\lfloor I_{T_{fi}} \rfloor$, $\lceil I_{T_{fi}} \rceil$, D_x, D_y	CM_I, CM_O, CM_C, CM_S, $D_x(CM_I)$, $D_y(CM_I)$, $D_{xx}(CM_I)$, $D_{yy}(CM_I)$, $D_{xy}(CM_I)$, ...

Once the VMs are obtained, the next step is to compute the conspicuity maps (CMs). The CMs are obtained through a center-surround function that is applied in order to simulate the center-surround receptive fields in the natural visual system. The CMs are obtained as in Walther and Koch's model [24]. Finally, the CMs are combined to obtain a single saliency map as explained in the next section.

3.1.2 Integration

The following step is the fusion of the CMs into a single map of salient information with the aim of determining the location, in the visual field, where attention should be directed at a given time. The saliency map (SM) defines the place of the most prominent image regions; given the characteristics of intensity, orientation, color, and shape. In other words, the objective of this stage is to decide where attention should be directed within the image.

In this work, the task of the FOA algorithm is to find the laser spot. Hence, the criterion defined below is in accordance with the proposed task to guide the process towards the best combination of several extracted features that are integrated into a single saliency map. Therefore, we decided to evolve the integration of CMs through a function that we called Evolved Feature Integration (EFI), see Fig. 3. Thus, the self-adjusting process considers different combinations of CMs to approach the goal. The evolutionary method uses the set of functions and terminals listed in Table 1, to create a fusion operator to highlight the features of the laser spot.

Afterwards, the integration of features is performed an optimized saliency map (OSM) is obtained by indicating the location of the most prominent region of the original image. This is known as the proto-object P_t, measured at time t.

3.2 Self-adjusting FOA process

In this section, the central aspects for the evolution of the FOA are described in order to explain the self-adjusting process applied for the location of the laser spot around the image region. Thus, the exposition is divided in two main steps, first we start by outlining the training process, and we continue by providing the definition of the fitness function.

The first stage of the evolutionary algorithm refers to the training process. In this phase, the self-adjusting FOA

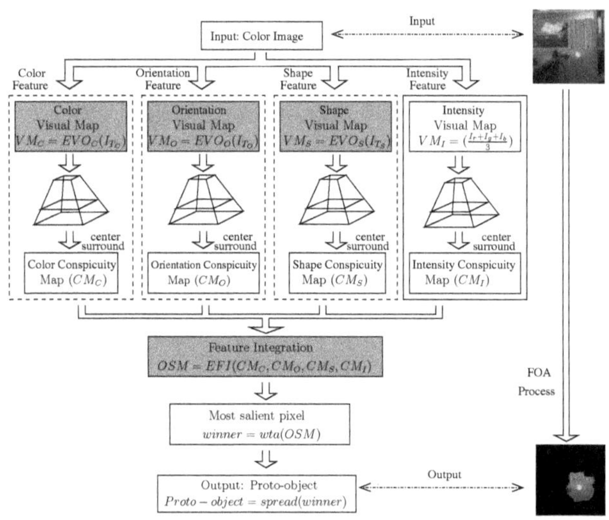

Figure 3: Focus of attention

learns to focus into a prominent region of the image, with the aim of characterizing the laser spot using an image database as reference. The FOA algorithm needs a flexible computational structure to encourage the self-adjustment of the general algorithm, depicted in Figure 3, through a simple yet robust code. In this work, we propose that the visual attention programs encoded as the genotype are defined by four different operators in the form of GP-trees; three of them focus on a particular image feature such as: color, orientation, and shape, and the fourth one is applied to integrate the information from the feature dimensions. These trees are evolved using their own specialized set of operations, which are integrated through another operation. Hence, the four trees have their own independent set of functions and terminals, turning into a higher complex programming environment with respect to classical GP. In this way, the functions and terminals sets are listed in Table 1. Thus, the genotype is a tree array and is constructed as follows: the first-tree encodes the orientation operator EVO_O; the second-tree EVO_C encodes a color function working over the image; the third-tree models the shape on the image region EVO_S. Finally, the fourth-tree encodes the integration of the extracted features with the aim of obtaining the saliency map using the operator EFI. In this manner, each tree is initialized with a ramped half-and-half technique with a maximum-depth of 9 levels. Given the complexity of the genotype structure there are two kinds of crossover operators, as well as two mutation operators, which are used to vary the programming of the chromosomes to create the visual attention program. Along these lines, since each element of the chromosome is represented as a tree, then, at a low level of variation mechanism, the crossover and mutation operators function similar as in a classic GP; nevertheless, as the structure of the chromosome should be understood as a complex array embedded within a software template defining the FOA, there is a high level variation operations, where the individuals are combined at an operator level, instead of a tree level, see Figure 3. These conditions define the self- adjusting system.

After initialization, the self-adjusting FOA relies on a well-posed fitness function in order to achieve the task at hand. In this manner, we propose the F-measure as score to tests the accuracy between the region selected by the FOA and the location of the laser spot within the image region, see [22]. The F-measure considers both the precision ρ and the recall ϑ to determine the number of pixels that conform the intersection between the proto-object P_t and the region where the laser spot is located; in this way, ρ is the number of pixels that match both regions divided by the number of proto-object pixels, and ϑ is the number of pixels that correspond to the intersection of both regions divided by the number of pixels from laser spot region. Then, the F-measure is defined as follows:

$$F_{measure} = 2 * \frac{\rho \times \vartheta}{\rho + \vartheta} \quad (2)$$

4. EXPERIMENTS AND RESULTS

As described in Section 2 the classic techniques used to detect the laser spot has a specific problem when TM is applied: a large number of false offs are passed to the following step, DU, thus inducing a low accuracy. The idea here is to include the FOA algorithm as a help for TM.

FOA, as presented in the above section, is an algorithm capable of focusing the visual attention on a certain area of the image considered, the area with the highest probability for including the searched object. Using this feature, we decided to let FOA to search the unique laser spot present in an image.

We must first notice that the GP based FOA algorithm needs to be fed first with a large number of images featuring the object to be searched. Thus, in the FOA self-adjusting process we used a set of 480 images taken from several real homes, with a laser spot included in each image. The image dataset was build considering three important features:

- Type of surface onto which lasers are projected.
- Distance between the laser pointer and the surface where the laser spot is projected.
- Type of environment light.

The set of 480 images used to self-adapt FOA to laser spot detection has been randomly divided into 5 subsets, with 20 % of the images each. Applying a 5-fold cross-validation method we obtained 5 different sets of images with 384 images for training and 96 images for test each. Six different runs have been repeated for each set, so that we obtained statistical data for the adjusting process. After checking the statistical validity of data obtained, we consider to use the results provided by FOA in combination with the other techniques. We first analyze the evolutionary process and then the best result obtained.

The results presented below are thus the average of 30 runs. Figure 4 shows the evolution of fitness values (best / avg / median for the 30 experiments). We see how fitness values improve along generations, which means that GP allows FOAs to adapt and focus on laser spot as the evolution goes forward. Given that experiments required several hours, we decided to stop them after 30 generations. Yet, we see in the figure that the improvement continues until the last generation, which could allow in the future run longer experiments trying to even improve the results presented below.

On the other hand, Figure 5 depicts how the number of unique operators was decreasing; the loss of population's diversity along the evolutionary process is a common feature that is also observed here. Diversity was measured by using the Hamming distance between individuals, in this case employing individuals' fitness values. This measure shows that even when the uniqueness decreases the difference among the performance of the FOAs remain almost the same. On the other hand, owing to the flexible representation of genotypes in GP, solutions may grow too big without any improvement of their performance and generalization ability. However, Figures 6 and 7 show that for this experiment the complexity stays almost the same during the evolutionary process while the fitness increases.

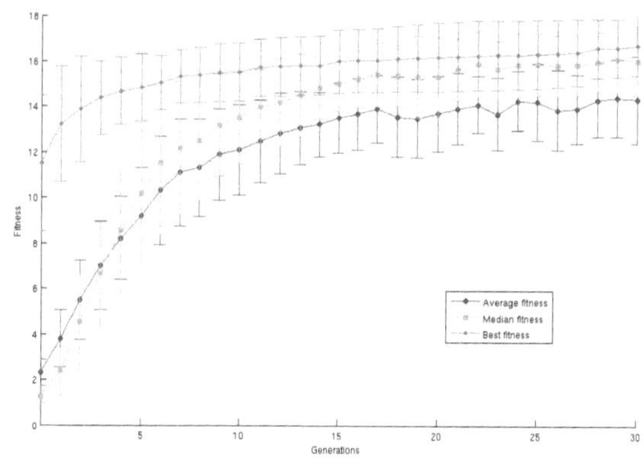

Figure 4: Fitness evolutions

The best individual found along the runs was the following one:

$$EVO_O = D_Y(C)$$

$$EVO_C = \frac{Complement(C)^2}{Exp(M)}$$

$$EVO_S = R$$

$$EFI = \lfloor CM_C \rfloor^2 \quad (3)$$

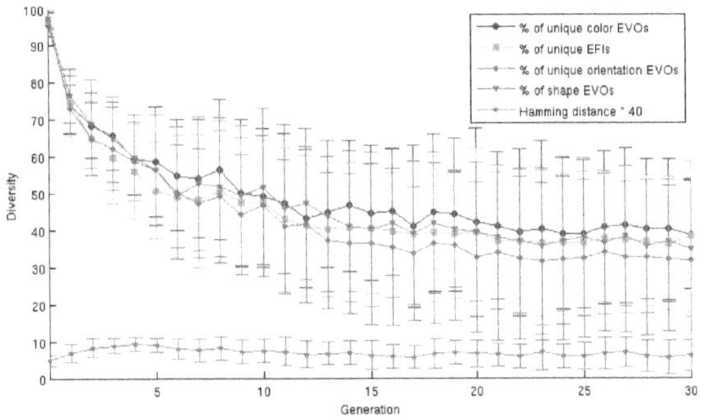

Figure 5: Diversity

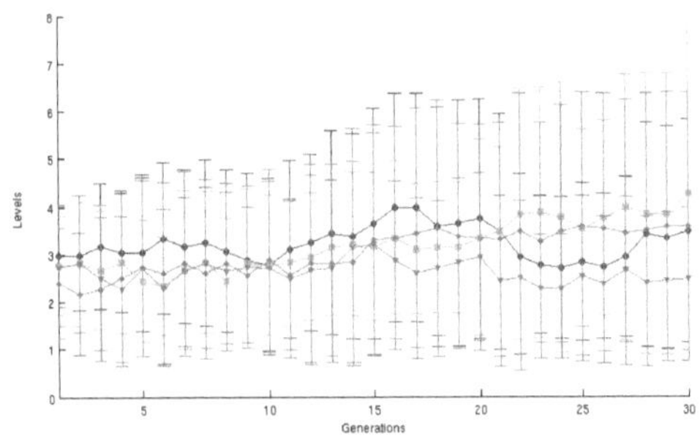

Figure 6: Complexity Level

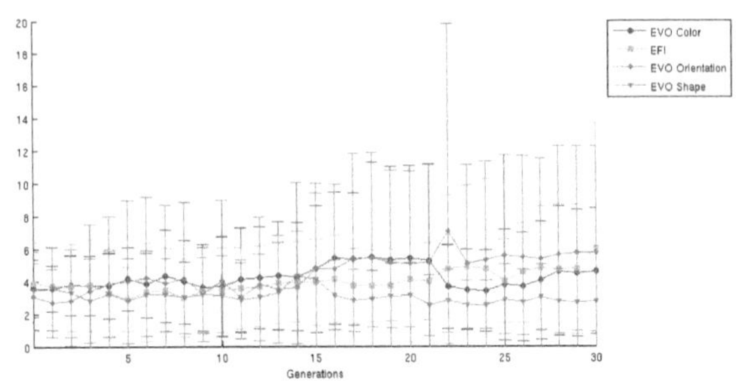

Figure 7: Complexity nodes

The idea is to apply this individual to focus the attention on a narrower area of the image, as a candidate for laser spot. We must point out that this best individual found only employed the color operator as can be seen in EFI equation. The evolutionary process has thus discarded other available features that we had consider in previous research. Once again, we can learn from evolution the important features to be studied.

Figure 8 presents an example where FOA has detected the area where the laser spot is located. Later on, this image region is marked by FOA and provided to be used by TM algorithm to find the laser spot. TM has then to extract the subsection of the image that better matches the template used (See Figure 2).

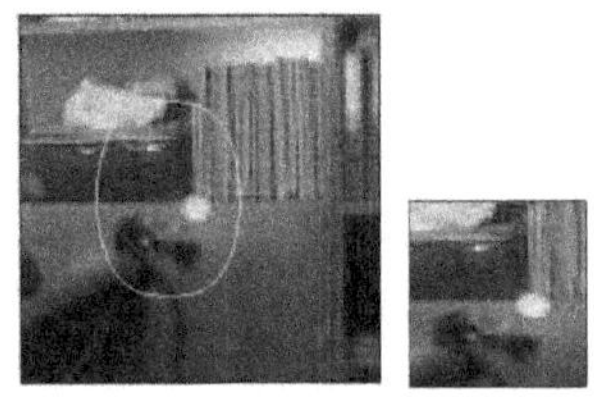

Figure 8: Image with a laser spot (right) Section extracted with the laser spot detected with FOA (left)

When the whole algorithm were run in a real home environment, most of the times no laser spot will be present in the images captured by the cameras, given that usually no orders are sent by users. Yet FOA will always detect and provide a region of interest, as shown in Figure 9. Likewise, a similar area will be extracted and analyzed by TM algorithm, with or without a laser spot. Therefore it is still necessary an algorithm to determine if the image extracted by FOA+TM has or not the laser spot included. DU will thus be used to determine whether the laser spot is found in the analyzed image.

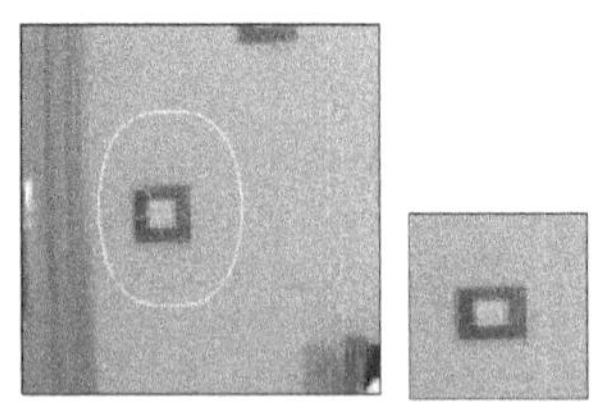

Figure 9: Image without a laser spot (right) Section extracted without the laser spot detected with FOA (left)

Next section analyzes how the new approach helps to reduce the false offs, thus to improve the success rate of the system using FOA + TM + DU.

4.1 Combining FOA+TM+DU

We present now the results obtained when FOA is added to the previous algorithm, and compared with results obtained when only using TM + DU. We have first allowed FOA algorithm to self-adjust and select the best operators to build a good individual allowing focus of attention on good areas of images provided. We have thus used a set of

480 images divided in 5 subset -that allows a cross-validation process, and repeated each of the 5 groups of experiments 6 times, for statistical purposes -giving thus rise to 30 different executions. This process employed is known as 5-fold cross-validation. The summary of these results is shown in Table 2.

Table 2: Results Training-Test FOA

FOA	Training	Test
$\bar{x}$	84.36 %	83.92 %
σ	0,0545	0,0708

Given that a 5-fold cross-validation is employed, we present results obtained in both training and test steps. We can see that the results obtained when FOA has been added to the system amounts to 83.92 % in test step (even better for training). This result shows us that the individuals obtained in the process have a high accuracy level. We have compared these results - FOA + TM + DU- with those obtained when FOA is not used - TM + DU-. Table 3 presents the comparison using different ZMNCC values in TM algorithm, which allows to see the improvement provided by FOA. Thanks to the ZMNCC threshold value it is possible to directly reject the images in which the highest ZMNCC value is under the threshold value established. When an image is analyzed, if the ZMNCC value is under a threshold, TM algorithm considers that is not a laser spot image, and the image section resulting is a black image.

We can see that the new approach - FOA + TM + DU- presents the best results in every situation -any of the values tried for ZMNCC. Other conclusion that we can obtain is that while with TM + DU has a good accuracy when no laser spot is present, the opposite is the case when laser spot is in the image, and detection level is poor, close to the 60%. However, FOA + TM + DU maintains the false offs reduction and notably increases the detection of the laser spot. FOA is thus a perfect complement for the detection of laser spots.

On the other hand, in previous works (see [4, 6, 7]) had addressed the idea of replacing DU algorithm by a FRBS, which helped to improve the quality of results . Table 4 shows us how the new approach presented in this paper, using FOA outperforms those obtained by means of TM+FRBS in the previous works -using the same conditions in both experiments. This results allow us to affirm that the combination of FOA with TM+FRBS could even offer better results. This will be addressed in a future research.

5. CONCLUSIONS

This paper shows the interest of a self-adjusting GP-based Focus of Attention technique for working in collaboration with classic computer vision techniques for a specific problem: the accurate detection of laser spots. The main goal is to offer a reliable user interface with standard domotic systems based on laser pointers and video cameras which are capable of detecting user actions and sending the appropriate orders to devices, such as turn on/off.

The paper has presented the addition of a GP based algorithm capable of properly focusing the attention of a visual recognition system in small areas of images from the environment, that are then analyzed by means of Template Matching and Dynamic Umbralization, in the search for laser spot. The GP-based FOA algorithm is first self-adjusted on a set of training images; then the filter obtained is applied in collaboration with TM + DU on real environments. The results presented show the advantages of the approach: the general accuracy level increase by (1) maintaining the extremely low level of false negative already provided by simply applying the classic techniques, and (2) increasing the detection level of laser spots when users do project laser pointer on devices; with the new technique we increase detection level from an initial 67,7% to 75,78% more than 8%, with a threshold value of ZMNCC equal to 0.5.

We plan to combine in the future the new GP-based FOA with other Soft Computing techniques with the aim of even increasing the good results presented here.

6. ACKNOWLEDGMENTS

This work has been supported by the Spanish Ministry of Science and Innovation under project TIN2011-28627-C04-03, regional government Gobierno de Extremadura, Consejería de Economía-Comercio e Innovación and FEDER, project GRU10029. This work is also sponsored by CONACyT México through the project 155045 - "Evolución de Cerebros Artificiales en Visión por Computadora". First author supported by scholarship 164884 from CONACyT. This research was also supported by TESE through the project DIMI-MCIM-004/08.

7. REFERENCES

[1] Alexander and Peine. Understanding the dynamics of technological configurations: A conceptual framework and the case of smart homes. *Technological Forecasting and Social Change*, 76(3):396 – 409, 2009.

[2] M. Chan, E. Campo, D. Estève, and J.-Y. Fourniols. Smart homes-current features and future perspectives. *Maturitas*, 64(2):90 – 97, 2009.

[3] M. Chan, D. Estève, C. Escriba, and E. Campo. A review of smart homes-present state and future challenges. *Comput. Methods Prog. Biomed.*, 91(1):55–81, 2008.

[4] F. Chávez, F. Fernández, R. Alcalá, J. Alcalá-Fdez, and F. Herrera. Evolutionary learning of a laser pointer detection fuzzy system for an environment control system. In *Fuzzy Systems (FUZZ), 2011 IEEE International Conference on*, pages 256–263. IEEE, 2011.

[5] F. Chávez, F. Fernández, R. Alcalá, J. Alcalá-Fdez, G. Olague, and F. Herrera. Hybrid laser pointer detection algorithm based on template matching and fuzzy rule-based systems for domotic control in real home environments. *Applied Intelligence*, pages 1–17, 2010. 10.1007/s10489-010-0268-6.

[6] F. Chávez, F. Fernández, J. Alcalá-Fdez, R. Alcalá, F. Herrera, and G. Olague. Genetic tuning of a laser pointer environment control device system for handicapped people with fuzzy systems. In *IEEE International Conference on Fuzzy Systems (FUZZ-IEEE 2010)*, pages 1 –8, 2010.

[7] F. Chávez, F. Fernández, M. Gacto, and R. Alcalá. Automatic laser pointer detection algorithm for environment control device systems based on template matching and genetic tuning of fuzzy rule-based

Table 3: Results TM+DU vs FOA+TM+DU

System	General	Images with Laser	Images without Laser	ZMNCC Evolution
TM+DU	83,43%	67,70%	98,42%	ZMNCC > 0.3
FOA+TM+DU	86,46%	78,88%	93,69%	
TM+DU	83,43%	67,70%	98,42%	ZMNCC > 0.4
FOA+TM+DU	86,46%	78,26%	94,28%	
TM+DU	83,43%	67,70%	98,42%	ZMNCC > 0.5
FOA+TM+DU	86,77%	75,78%	97,24%	
TM+DU	80,40%	60,04%	99,80%	ZMNCC > 0.6
FOA+TM+DU	82,53%	64,18%	100,00%	
TM+DU	72,83%	44,31%	100,00%	ZMNCC > 0.7
FOA+TM+DU	73,13%	44,93%	100,00%	

Table 4: Results TM+DU, FOA+TU+DU, TM+FRBS$_{\text{tuned-GA}}$

System	General	Images with Laser	Images without Laser
TM+DU	83,43%	67,70%	98,42%
TM+FRBS$_{\text{tuned-GA}}$	85,99%	72,75%	98,74%
FOA+TM+DU	86,77%	75,78%	97,24%

systems. *International Journal of Computational Intelligence Systems*, 5(2):368–386, 2012.

[8] F. Chávez, F. Fernández, G. Olague, and J. Llano. An independent and non-intrusive laser pointer environment control device system. In *Proceedings of the 5th international conference on Pervasive services (ICPS'08)*, pages 37–46, Sorrento, Italy, 2008. ACM.

[9] E. Clemente, G. Olague, L. Dozal, and M. Mancilla. Object Recognition with an Optimized Ventral Stream Model Using Genetic Programming. EvoApplications 2012: 315-325.

[10] R. Desimone and J. Duncan. Neural mechanisms of selective visual attention. *Annual Reviews*, 18:193–222, 1995.

[11] L. Dozal, G. Olague, E. Clemente, and M. Sánchez. Evolving Visual Attention Programs through EVO Features. EvoApplications 2012: 326-335.

[12] D. E. Hernández, G. Olague, E. Clemente, L. Dozal. Evolving a conspicuous point detector based on an artificial dorsal stream: SLAM system. GECCO 2012: 1087-1094.

[13] C. Kemp, C. Anderson, H. Nguyen, A. Trevor, and Z. Xu. A point-and-click interface for the real world: laser designation of objects for mobile manipulation. In *Proceedings of the 3rd ACM/IEEE international conference on Human robot interaction (HRI'08)*, pages 241–248, Amsterdam, The Netherlands, 2008. ACM.

[14] N. W. Kim, S. J. Lee, B.-G. Lee, and J.-J. Lee. Vision based laser pointer interaction for flexible screens. In J. A. Jacko, editor, *Human-Computer Interaction. Interaction Platforms and Techniques*, volume 4551 of *Lecture Notes in Computer Science*, pages 845–853. Springer, 2007.

[15] KNX/EIB. *http://www.knx.org.*

[16] H. Nakashima, H. Aghajan, and J. Augusto. *Handbook of Ambient Intelligence and Smart Environments.* Springer, 2010.

[17] J.-Y. Oh and W. Stürzlinger. Laser pointers as collaborative pointing devices. In *Proceedings of Graphics Interface*, pages 141–150, Calgary, Alberta, 2002.

[18] G. Olague. Evolutionary Computer Vision - The First Footprints -. Springer, to appear.

[19] G. Olague, E. Clemente, L. Dozal, and D. E. Hernández. Evolving an Artificial Visual Cortex for Object Recognition with Brain Programming. Studies in Computational Intelligence, Springer, to appear.

[20] G. Olague, L. Dozal, E. Clemente, and A. Ocampo. Optimizing an Artificial Dorsal Stream on Purpose for Visual Attention. Studies in Computational Intelligence, Springer, to appear.

[21] K.-H. Park, Z. Bien, J.-J. Lee, B. K. Kim, J.-T. Lim, J.-O. Kim, H. Lee, D. H. Stefanov, D.-J. Kim, J.-W. Jung, J.-H. Do, K.-H. Seo, C. H. Kim, W.-G. Song, and W.-J. Lee. Robotic smart house to assist people with movement disabilities. *Autonomous Robots*, 22(2):183–198, 2007.

[22] C. B. Pérez, and G. Olague. Evolutionary learning of local descriptor operators for object recognition. GECCO 2009: 1051-1058.

[23] A. M. Treisman and G. Gelade. A feature-integration theory of attention. *Cognitive psychology*, 12(1):97–136, January 1980.

[24] D. Walther and C. Koch. Modeling attention to salient proto-objects. *Neural Networks*, 19(9):1395–1407, 2006.

Multi- user Detection in Multi-Carrier CDMA Wireless Broadband System Using a Binary Adaptive Differential Evolution Algorithm

Swagatam Das
Electronics and Communications Sciences Unit, Indian Statistical Institute, Kolkata, India.
swagatam.das@isical.ac.in

Rohan Mukherjee
Department of Electronics and Telecommunication Engineering, Jadavpur University, Kolkata, India
rohan.mukherjii@gmail.com

Rupam Kundu
Department of Electronics and Telecommunication Engineering, Jadavpur University, Kolkata, India
rupam2422@gmail.com

Thanos Vasilakos
Department of Computer Science
Kuwait University
vasilako@ath.forthnet.gr

ABSTRACT

Multi-Carrier Code Division Multiple Access (MC-CDMA) is an emerging wireless communication technology that incorporates the advantages of Orthogonal Frequency Division Multiplexing (OFDM) into the original Code Division Multiple Access (CDMA) technique. But it suffers from the inherent defect called Multiple Access Interference (MAI) due to inappropriate cross-correlation possessed by the different user codes. To reduce MAI, the multi-user detection (MUD) technique has already been proposed in which MAI is treated as noise. Due to high computational cost incorporated by the optimal MUD detector with increasing number of users, researchers are looking for sub-optimal MUD solutions. This paper proposes a binary adaptive Differential Evolution algorithm with a novel crossover strategy (MBDE_*p*BX) for multi-user detection in a synchronous MC-CDMA system. Since MUD detection in MC-CDMA systems is a problem in binary domain, a binary encoding rule is introduced which converts a binary domain problem of any number of dimensions into a 4-dimensional continuous domain problem. The simulation results show that this new binary Differential Evolution variant can achieve superior bit error rate (BER) performance within much lower optimum solution detection time outperforming its competitors as well as achieving 99.62% reduction in computational complexity as compared to the MUD scheme using exhaustive search.

Categories and Subject Descriptors

I.2.8 [Artificial Intelligence]: Problem Solving, Control Methods, and Search–Heuristic Methods; G.1.6 [Numerical Analysis]: Optimization

General Terms

Algorithm. Theory, Experimentation.

Keywords

Code Division Multiple access, Multi-carrier CDMA, Multi-user detection, Multiple Access Interference, MBDE-*p*BX.

1. INTRODUCTION

Code division multiple access [1] is a very popular broadband wireless transmission technique used in numerous mobile radio communication technologies. CDMA falls in the category of spread-spectrum signaling, due to the reason that the modulated coded signal occupies a much larger bandwidth than the data being communicated. One of the most important advantages of CDMA over time domain [2] and frequency domain [2] counterparts is that it can utilize the spectrum more efficiently in mobile telephony applications.

In recent times, the concept of CDMA is extended to a Multi-Carrier Code Division Multiple Access (MC-CDMA) [3-4] where Orthogonal Frequency Division Multiplexing (OFDM) technique is incorporated in CDMA to improve the performance of CDMA as well as accomplishing high frequency diversity gain. However, for an ideal CDMA system, the spreading sequences ascribed to each specific user should be perfectly orthogonal possessing no cross-correlation between them. But if the cross-correlation values are finite, it can give rise to Multiple Access Interference (MAI) between the different users. In second generation CDMA systems, specifically in the Qualcomm IS-95 CDMA standard [5], the multiple access interference (MAI) is regarded as a noise. To mitigate MAI, an idea regarding joint detection of all users in a CDMA system has been put forward where MAI has been estimated as a part of information, not noise. This idea is regarded as multi-user detection (MUD) [6]. But the optimal MUD detector recommended by Verdu [7] has to scrutinize every possible sequence of the bit vector transmitted. Practically when the situation arises that there are huge number of users, the optimal MUD detector becomes inefficient as it induces large computational complexity which is not desirable. So, recent research work is focused on searching for a suitable MUD detector that can search sub-optimal solutions with low complexity.

The Differential Evolution (DE) [8] algorithm has emerged as a very competitive form of evolutionary computing more than a decade ago. Since MUD detection in MC-CDMA systems is a binary-valued problem an encoding rule is presented to generate a bit vector in the binary domain to compute the objective function value for the MUD detector from the continuous domain DE operation. This rule basically converts the binary domain problem into a 4-dimensional continuous domain problem. In this article the proposed innovative binary Differential Evolution algorithm named MBDE-*p*BX has been shown to serve as a suitable MUD detector with huge reduction in computational complexity and extensive improvement in performance comparison. The results obtained with the proposed algorithm as a MUD detector for the MC-CDMA system has been illustrated in various ways with superior convergence performance that can be attributed to the proposed modifications in the algorithmic components of MBDE_pBX ensuring massive reduction in computational cost in comparison with the exhaustive search algorithm.

The remainder of the paper is as follows: Section 2 gives an overview of CDMA, MUD detection and MC-CDMA system, Section 3 discusses the Synchronous CDMA system model and extends the problem formulation to MC-CDMA model. Section 4 gives the description of the MBDE_pBX algorithm and Section 5 shows the simulation strategies and results obtained. Finally Section 6 concludes the paper and Section 7 considers the references

2. OVERVIEW OF CDMA, MULTI-USER DETECTION AND MC-CDMA SYSTEM

Spread spectrum [9] modulation is a new emerging modulation technique in digital communication by which a signal occupying a particular bandwidth is intentionally spread to cover a broad range of the frequency spectrum. In CDMA the goal is to permit several customers to send information simultaneously over a single physical channel. CDMA applies spread spectrum technology where a distinct pseudo random sequence attributed to each user is used to spread the information signal to the assigned frequency bandwidth. The pseudo random code of each user is either orthogonal to the codes of the remaining users or the code may possess appropriate cross-correlation values that attenuates the problem regarding multiple access interference (MAI).This code acts as a modulator on the information signal, making the signal appear noise-like to the other users sharing the same spectrum. This can be achieved by using a random spreading code having an infinite repetition time, but the spreading codes must be deterministic known only to the intended transmitter and receiver. So, it has the capability to appear like random noise to non-intended receivers, generally known as Pseudo-noise (PN) sequences. This then allows the sharing of the same frequency bandwidth by multiple customers without causing excessive MAI. It also guarantees information privacy due to the uniqueness property possessed by the PN sequence. In comparison to frequency and time domain systems, CDMA systems suffer more multiple access interference which arises as a result of imperfect cross-correlation properties possessed by the PN-sequences. The wideband mobile channel damages the orthogonality property possessed by the codes. Traditionally, powerful error correcting codes are utilized to mitigate this defect. Recent research on CDMA based receivers includes multi-user detection (MUD) in order to reduce the MAI.

Conventional CDMA detectors such as the matched filter [10] are optimized for detecting the signal of a single desired user. The outputs from the matched filters are then systematically combined based on a diversity combining methods. These conventional detectors are quite inefficient because the interference is treated as noise and there is no utilization of the accessible knowledge about the spreading codes of the interfering users. Higher the cross-correlation higher is the MAI. Another defect regarding the conventional CDMA detectors is an event known as the "near-far effect" [11] or a condition in which a receiver captures a strong signal and thereby makes it impossible for the receiver to detect a weaker signal. For conventional detectors to operate in an efficient manner all the user's signals have to reach the receiver with almost the same power. In order to mitigate the problem of MAI regarding the conventional CDMA detectors the optimum MUD has been proposed. The optimum detector detects all the possible bit combinations in order to find out the sequence that maximizes the correlation metric. This optimum detector significantly outperforms the conventional detector and it is near-far resistant. Orthogonal frequency division multiplexing (OFDM) [12] is a parallel data transmission scheme in which high data rates can be achieved by transmitting several orthogonal subcarriers. OFDM systems diminish the inter symbol interference (ISI) as well as the inter channel interference (ICI) by inserting guard intervals. Recently CDMA systems based on the combination of CDMA schemes and OFDM signaling, which are referred to as multi-carrier CDMA systems, have attracted much attention. In a MC-CDMA system the serial input data stream spread by a pseudo-random code is transformed into parallel chip sequences with each chip modulating a different subcarrier. Thus the number of subcarriers is equivalent to the number of chips per data symbol. MC-CDMA system basically combines robustness of orthogonal modulation with the flexibility of the CDMA schemes [13].

3. SYNCHRONOUS CDMA SYSTEM MODEL

3.1 Synchronous CDMA System Model

In this article we are dealing with a bit-synchronous CDMA system as depicted in Figure 1, where K users transmit equal length data packets to a single receiver at the same time. The modulation technique adopted here is Binary Phase Shift Keying (BPSK). The transmitted signal of the kth user can be represented in the following manner:

$$\hat{s}_k(t)=\sqrt{\xi_k}\sum_{m=0}^{M-1} b_k^{(m)} a_k(t-mT_b), \forall k=1,........,K \quad (1)$$

Where ξ_k is the k-th user's signal energy per bit, $b_k^{(m)} \in \{-1,1\}$ denotes the m-th data bit of the k-th user, $a_k(t)$ is the k-th user's signature sequence, T_b is the data bit duration and M is the number of data bits transmitted in a packet. Here the synchronous system experiences no multipath interference, so the focus should be to observe the signal over single bit duration as there is no interference from symbols outside this duration. Hence without loss of generality, we can omit the superscript (m) from all the equations encountered below.

The k-th user's signature sequence $a_k(t)$ may be written as:

$$a_k(t)=\sum_{h=0}^{N_C-1} a_k^{(h)}\Gamma_{T_c}(t-mT_C), 0\le t\le T_b, \forall k=1,.........,K \quad (2)$$

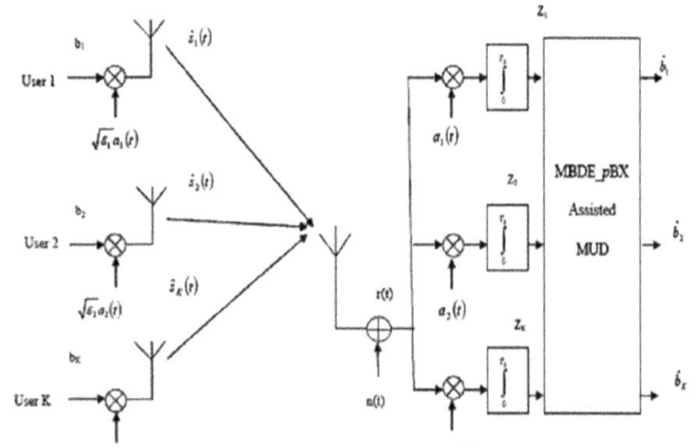

Fig. 1: Block diagram of the K-user synchronous CDMA model

Here, T_c is the chip duration, $a_k^{(h)} \in \{-1,1\}$ denotes the h-th chip, N_c is the spreading factor, which refers to the number of chips per data bit duration T_b such that $N_c = T_b / T_c$ and $\Gamma_{T_c}(t)$ is the chip pulse shape. For the sake of simplicity in our simulation, we assume that $\Gamma_\tau(t)$ is a rectangular pulse defined as:

$$\Gamma\tau(t) = \begin{cases} 1, & 0 \le t \le \tau \\ 0, & otherwise \end{cases} \tag{3}$$

We assume that the energy of the signature sequence $a_k(t)$ of all users is unity defined as: $\int_0^{T_b} a_k^2(t)\,dt = 1, \forall\, k = 1,........,K$ (4)

Each user's signal $\hat{s}(t)$ is assumed to travel through a channel having the following characteristics: single-path, frequency-nonselective, slowly Rayleigh fading channel, as shown in Figure 1 and the fading of each path is statistically independent for all users. The complex low-pass channel impulse response (CIR) for the link between the kth user's transmitter and the receiver, as shown in Figure 1, can be described as:

$$h_k(t) = \alpha_k(t) e^{j\varphi_k(t)} \delta(t), \forall k = 1,........,K \tag{5}$$

Here the amplitude $\alpha_k(t)$ is a Rayleigh distributed random variable and the phase is uniformly distributed between $[0,2\pi)$. Hence, when the k-th user's spread spectrum signal $\hat{s}_k(t)$ given by equation (1) propagates through a slowly Rayleigh fading channel having an impulse response given by equation (5), the resulting output signal $s_k(t)$ over a single bit duration can be written as: $s_k(t) = \sqrt{\xi_k}\,\alpha_k b_k a_k(t) e^{j\varphi_k}, \forall k = 1,........,K$ (6)

Upon combining equation (6) for all É users, the received signal at the receiver, which is denoted by $r(t)$ in Figure 1, can be written as: $r(t) = \sum_{k=1}^{K} s_k(t) + n(t),$ (7)

where $n(t)$ is the Additive zero-mean complex White Gaussian Noise (AWGN).The noise being complex, the real and imaginary components are independent of each other, each having a double-sided power spectral density of $\sigma^2 = N_o/2$ W/Hz. At the receiver, the output of a bank of filters matched to the corresponding set of the users' signature sequences is sampled at the end of the bit interval. The output of the l-th user's matched filter, denoted as z_l in Figure 1 can be written as:

$$z_l = \int_0^{T_b} r(t) a_l(t)\,dt = \int_0^{T_b} \sum_{m=0}^{M-1} \sqrt{\xi_k}\,\alpha_k b_k a_k(t) e^{j\varphi_k} a_l(t)\,dt + \int_0^{T_b} n(t) a_l(t)\,dt$$
$$= \underbrace{\sqrt{\xi_l}\,\alpha_l b_l e^{j\varphi_l}}_{Desired\ Signal} + \underbrace{\sum_{\substack{k=1 \\ K\neq l}}^{K} \sqrt{\xi_k}\,\alpha_k b_k \rho_{lk} e^{j\varphi_k}}_{Multiple\ Access\ Interference} + \underbrace{n_l}_{noise}, \tag{8}$$

where $$\rho_{lk} = \int_0^{T_b} a_l(t) a_k(t)\,dt \tag{9}$$

Eqn. (9) is the cross-correlation of the l-th and k-th user's signature sequence and,

$$n_l = \int_0^{T_b} n(t) a_l(t)\,dt \tag{10}$$

As seen in equation (8), apart from the Gaussian noise n_l, there is a MAI arising due to the signals coming from the other users. Assuming that the receiver has perfect knowledge of the l-th user's CIR coefficients $\alpha_l e^{j\varphi_l}$, the detected bit $\hat{b}_{l,MF}$ of the l-th user based on the conventional coherent single-user detector will be given by the sign of the matched filter output in equation (8) as:

$$\hat{b}_{l,MF} = \mathrm{sgn}\left[\Re\left(z_l \alpha_l e^{-j\varphi_l}\right)\right] \tag{11}$$

Multiplication by $\alpha_l e^{j\varphi_l}$ is mandatory in coherent detection, because the channel incorporates a phase rotation which needs to be eliminated. By approximating the MAI as a Gaussian distributed random variable in accordance with the central limit theorem [14], the Bit Error Probability (BEP) of the desired user can be given by [8]: $P_l = \frac{1}{2}\left(1 - \sqrt{\frac{\xi_l}{N_0/2 + \sum_k \xi_k \rho_{lk}}}\right)$ (12)

Hence from equation (12), we can see that unless the pseudo-random sequences unique to each of the interfering users are orthogonal to that of the desired user, yielding $\rho_{lk} = 0$ for $k = \{1,2,...,K\}$, $k \neq l$, i.e. no multiple access interference the BEP performance of the desired user will be inferior to that achieved in a single-user situation accompanied by a single-user matched filter. Furthermore, as the number of users is increased the BEP performance will decay and the conventional single-user detector will be exposed to near-far effects [15]. For our application, the associated signals should be expressed in discrete-time format for convenience. Taking equation (6) denoting the transmitted signal of each user, the sum of the transmitted signals of all users can be formulated in vector notation as shown below:

$$s(t) = \sum_{k=1}^{K} \hat{s}_k(t) = aC\xi b \tag{13}$$

where: $a = [a_1(t),....,a_K(t)], C = diag\left[\alpha_1 e^{j\varphi_1},....,\alpha_K e^{j\varphi_K}\right]$

$\xi = diag\left[\sqrt{\xi_1},....,\sqrt{\xi_K}\right], b = [b_1,....,b_K]^T$

Hence the received signal of equation (7) can be expressed as:

$$r(t) = s(t) + n(t) \tag{14}$$

Based on equations (13) and (14), the output vector Z from the bank of matched filters as depicted in Figure 1 can be written as:

$$Z = [Z_1,....,Z_K]^T = RC\xi b + n \tag{15}$$

$$R = \begin{bmatrix} 1 & \rho_{12} & \cdot & \cdot & \cdot & \rho_{1K} \\ \rho_{21} & 1 & \cdot & \cdot & \cdot & \rho_{2K} \\ \cdot & \cdot & \cdot & \cdot & \cdot & \cdot \\ \cdot & \cdot & \cdot & \cdot & \cdot & \cdot \\ \cdot & \cdot & \cdot & \cdot & \cdot & \cdot \\ \rho_{K1} & \rho_{K2} & \cdot & \cdot & \cdot & 1 \end{bmatrix} \tag{16}$$

is the $K \times K$ dimensional user signature sequence cross-correlation matrix having elements given by equation (9) and

$$n = [n_1,....,n_K]^T \tag{17}$$

is a zero-mean Gaussian noise vector with a covariance matrix $R_n = 0.5 N_0 R$. Based on this synchronous discrete-time model, we are going to derive the optimum multiuser detector based on the maximum likelihood criterion for the synchronous CDMA system considered here [16].

3.2 Optimum Multiuser Detector for Synchronous CDMA System Model

In this section we are going to deduce the joint optimum decision rule for a K-user CDMA system based on the synchronous system model described in the Section 3.1. Actually we are aiming to maximize the probability of jointly correct decisions of the K users supported by the system based on the received signal $r(t)$ of equation (14). Equation (13) reveals that there are $m = 2^K$ possible combinations or sequences of $\boldsymbol{b}$. We will refer the i-th combination as $\boldsymbol{b}_i$ and the combined transmitted signal of all users in equation (13) corresponding to the i-th combination as $b_i \leftrightarrow s_i(t)$. Based on the above notations, we can formulate the joint maximum *a posteriori* probability (MAP) criterion as [10]: $\hat{b} = \arg\left\{ \max_{b_i}\left[P\left(s_i(t) \middle| r(t)\right)\right]\right\}$, (18)

where $\hat{b}$ denotes the detected bit sequence. Using Bayes' rule, the *a posteriori* probability expression of equation (18) can be stated as [10]:

$$P\left(s_i(t)\middle|r(t)\right) = \frac{p\left(r(t)\middle|s_i(t)\right)P\left(s_i(t)\right)}{p\left(r(t)\right)}, \tag{19}$$

where $p\left(r(t) \mid s_i(t)\right)$ is the conditional joint probability density function (pdf) of the received signal $r(t)$ in equation (14), $p\left(s_i(t)\right)$ is the *a priori* probability of the signal containing the ith bit combination and $p\left(r(t)\right)$ is the pdf of the received signal. Since the transmitted data bits of the K users are independent, the *a priori* probability $p\left(s_i(t)\right) = 1/2^K$ is equal for all $m = 2^K$ bit combinations. Furthermore, the received signal pdf $p\left(r(t)\right)$ is independent of which of the $m = 2^K$ bit combinations is transmitted. Consequently, the decision rule based on finding the signal that maximizes $p\left(r(t) \mid s_i(t)\right)$ is equivalent to finding the signal that maximizes $p\left(r(t) \mid s_i(t)\right)$.This decision criterion based on the maximum of $p\left(r(t) \mid s_i(t)\right)$ is termed as the Maximum Likelihood (ML) criterion and $p\left(r(t) \mid s_i(t)\right)$ is referred to as a likelihood function [10]. According to equation (7), the received signal $r(t)$ is a Gaussian distributed random variable having a mean equal to that of $s(t)$ given by equation (13). Hence the likelihood function $p\left(r(t) \mid s_i(t)\right)$ is given by [7]:

$$\begin{aligned} p(Z|s) &= \exp\left(-\frac{1}{2\sigma^2}\int_0^{T_b}\left|r(t)-s(t)\right|^2 dt\right) \\ &= \exp\left(-\frac{1}{2\sigma^2}\int_0^{T_b}\left|r(t)-\sum_{k=1}^{K}\sqrt{\xi_k}\,\alpha_k b_k a_k(t)e^{j\phi_k}\right|^2 dt\right) \end{aligned} \tag{20}$$

Now, we take the natural logarithm of the likelihood function of equation (20) to express the resulting so-called Log-Likelihood Function (LLF) as:

$$\ln p(Z|s) = -\frac{1}{2\sigma^2}\left\{\int_0^{T_b}\left|r(t)\right|^2 dt + \int_0^{T_b}\left|\sum_{k=1}^{K}\sqrt{\xi_k}\,\alpha_k b_k a_k(t)e^{j\varphi_k}\right|^2 dt - 2\Re\left[\int_0^{T_b} r(t)\sum_{k=1}^{K}\sqrt{\xi_k}\,\alpha_k b_k a_k(t)e^{-j\varphi_k}dt\right]\right\} \tag{21}$$

The term $|r(t)|^2$ ý is common to all decision metrics, and hence it is ignored during the maximization. Similarly, the constant term $1/2\sigma^2$ will not affect the maximization and thus it is also ignored. Thus we can formulate the log-likelihood function of equation (21) in the form of a correlation metric as [10]:

$$\begin{aligned} \Omega(b) &= 2\Re\left[\int_0^{T_b} r(t)\sum_{k=1}^{K}\sqrt{\xi_k}\,\alpha_k b_k a_k(t)e^{-j\varphi_k}dt\right] - \int_0^{T_b}\left|\sum_{k=1}^{K}\sqrt{\xi_k}\,\alpha_k b_k a_k(t)e^{j\varphi_k}\right|^2 dt \\ &= 2\Re\left[\sum_{k=1}^{K}\sqrt{\xi_k}\,\alpha_k b_k e^{-j\varphi_k} z_k\right] - \sum_{l=1}^{K}\sum_{k=1}^{K}\sqrt{\xi_l}\sqrt{\xi_k}\,b_l b_k \alpha_l \alpha_k e^{j\varphi_l}e^{-j\varphi_k}\rho_{lk} \end{aligned} \tag{22}$$

Here z_k and ρ_{lk} are given by equation (8) and equation (9), respectively. Employing our discrete-time model discussed in section 3.1, the correlation metric of equation (22) can be stated in vector form as [7]:

$$\Omega(b) = 2\Re\left[b^T \xi C^* Z\right] - b^T \xi C R C^* \xi b \tag{23}$$

Hence the decision rule for the optimum CDMA multiuser detection scheme based on the maximum likelihood criterion is to choose the specific bit combination b which maximizes the correlation metric of equation (23). Hence,

$$\hat{b} = \arg\left\{\max_b\left[\Omega(b)\right]\right\} \tag{24}$$

The maximization of equation (23) is basically a combinatorial optimization problem, which demands an exhaustive search for each of the $m = 2^K$ combination of $\boldsymbol{b}$ in order to detect the sequence that maximizes the correlation metric of equation (23). But the exhaustive search incurs huge computational burden. Since there are $m = 2^K$ possible combinations of b, the optimum multiuser detection has a complexity that grows exponentially with the number of users K .

3.3 Extending the Problem Formulation to MC-CDMA Model

In this section, we consider a bit-synchronous MC-CDMA system where K users simultaneously transmit their bits over an idealized AWGN channel. The number of chips is equal to the number of sub-carriers where each user bit is first spread in the frequency spectrum by a specific pseudo-noise sequence and then modulated by "M" available sub-carriers by means of OFDM. The kth user's transmitted signal is given by,

$$s_k(t) = \sqrt{\frac{2E_k}{M}}\sum_{m=1}^{M} c_{k,m}(t)\cdot b_k(t)e^{j\omega_{m,t}} \tag{25}$$

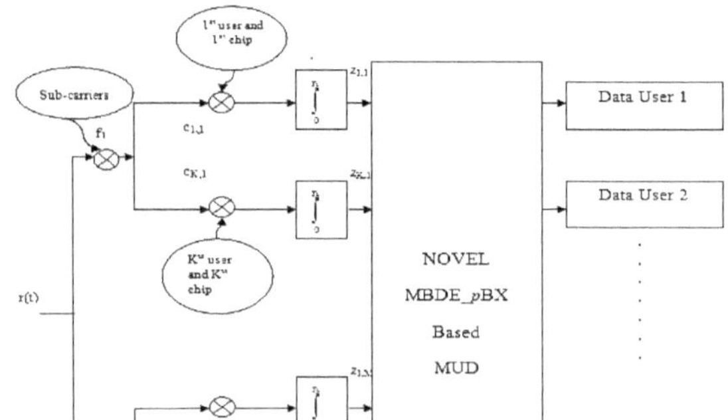

Fig. 2: A typical MC-CDMA receiver model

Here, E_k : The transmit power of the kth user, *M*: Number of sub-carriers, T_b : Data bit duration, $b_k(t)$: The transmitted bit sequence of the kth user, $c_{k,m}(t)$: Time-domain representation of the kth user's spreading sequence on the mth sub-carrier, $c_k(t)$: Time-domain representation of the kth user's spreading code over all sub-carriers. $\omega_m = 2\pi f_m$, where $f_m(m = 1,......., M)$ are the subcarrier frequencies and $f_m = f_1 + (m-1)\Delta f$, where frequency spacing is $\Delta f = 1/T_b$. After the action of the pseudo-noise sequence and OFDM modulation, the signal is then transmitted over the AWGN channel. The Figure 2 shows a simple MC-CDMA receiver followed by a binary DE based MUD. The data carried by each subcarrier is firstly demodulated. The demodulated data on the sub-carrier frequency f_1 yields a composite part of the spreading signals of all users, contributed by the 1st chips of their respective spreading sequences. Similarly, for the sub-carriers f_2 till f_M, the contribution is from the set of the 2nd chips till the last set of chips of the pseudo-random sequences from all users respectively. The received signal on the mth sub-carrier is,

$$r_m(t) = \sum_{k=1}^{K}\left[\sqrt{\frac{2E_k}{M}}c_{k,m}(t)\cdot b_k(t)\right] + n(t) \tag{26}$$

Here $n(t)$ is the AWGN noise added to the signal with two-sided power spectrum density $N_0/2$. Now, the joint optimum decision rule for a K user discrete-time synchronous CDMA model can be easily extended to a K – user multi-carrier CDMA (MC-CDMA) system model where the data is transmitted over M number of orthogonal subcarriers. So, the contribution of all the likelihood functions will yield the optimum vector $\hat{b}$.

$$\Omega(b) = \sum_{m=1}^{M}\Omega_m(b) = \sum_{m=1}^{M}\left\{2\Re\left[b^T\xi C^* Z_m\right] - b^T\xi CR_m C^*\xi b\right\}, \tag{27}$$

where $\Omega_m(b)$ denotes the discrete-time correlation metric on the mth sub-carrier. Our aim is to search for the specific bit sequence b out of 2^K possible combinations that maximizes the correlation metric of equation (27).

4. MODIFIED BINARY DIFFERENTIAL EVOLUTION WITH *P*-BEST CROSSOVER

The multi-user detection (MUD) mechanism in a synchronous multi-carrier CDMA system is a combinatorial maximization problem. But the continuous nature of DE does not permit the algorithm to apply to combinatorial optimization problems. Recently a powerful DE variant MDE_pBX [17] has been proposed which incorporates modifications in all the algorithmic components of classical DE-mutation, crossover and parameter adaptation. Firstly a less greedy and more explorative variant of the DE/current-to-best/1 mutation strategy, DE/current-to-gr_best/1 (*gr* stands for group) is projected. Unlike DE/current-to-best/1 that always uses the fittest (hence best) member of the entire current population to perturb a target (parent) vector, DE/current-to-gr_best/1 forms a group, corresponding to each target vector, by randomly selecting population members to form a group whose size is say *q*% of the total population size. The best member of this dynamic group is used to perturb the target vector. Secondly an exploitative crossover scheme called "*p*-best crossover" is proposed. Under this scheme a mutant vector is allowed to exchange its components not with the parent at the same index, but with a randomly selected member from the *p* top-ranked individuals from the current generation through uniform (binomial) crossover. Thirdly novel parameter adaptation schemes for scale factor *F* and crossover probability *Cr* had been proposed to update the values of these control parameters in each generation, guided by the knowledge of the successful values of *F* and *Cr* that were able to generate better offspring (trial vectors) in the last generation. In this article a novel binary version of MDE_*p*BX is designed to solve the optimum K-user MUD detection problem in MC-CDMA system. MUD detection demands fast convergence towards near-optimal solutions without incorporating large amount of computational complexity. The proposed binary Differential Evolution additionally emphasizes on the initialization of the population and encoding of variables for application in binary domain. The type of mutation, scale factor adaptation, and crossover probability adaptation are kept intact as discussed in [17].

4.1 Initial Population

The appropriate selection of initial population is necessary for any evolutionary algorithm to approach optimal fitness. Here, we present the excellent concept of orthogonal array to uniformly initialize population vectors within the search bound [0, 1]. If, in certain design purpose there are m factors and each factor have n levels then to find appropriate setting of each factor's level, m× n experiments must be done. So, the orthogonal arrays were developed to generate a brief but representative sample of combinations for testing. An orthogonal array (*OA*) is an array with *m* rows and *n* columns satisfying the condition that for each factors in a column, every level occurs the same number of times. For each column of $[OA]_{m\times n}$, a random permutation of $\{1,\ldots,m\}$ is generated and denoted as sequence *Z*. Then the elements in *Z* are picked sequentially one by one and filled randomly in the column. When all elements in *Z* were picked, the process starts once again from the beginning of sequence. So in every column of $[OA]_{m\times n}$, each of *m* elements will appear the same number of times.

4.2 Encoding of Variables

The original DE algorithm is a real coded continuous domain optimization algorithm. However, in this MUD detector based MC-CDMA we have to deal with the transmitted bits which has to be detected in the receiving end through multi-user detector which is a completely binary domain problem. So, the vectors which are evolving by the generations in the DE have to be encoded in to a binary domain, i.e. logic (1) and logic (0). In the encoding rule, we propose to evolve solutions to binary-valued optimization problems, without having to alter the operation of the original DE. This is accomplished by using a homomorphous mapping [18] to draw out a problem (in binary domain) into a simpler problem (defined in continuous domain), and then to solve the problem in the abstracted space. The solution obtained in the abstracted space is then transformed back into the original space in order to solve the problem. It utilizes the concept of angle modulation (AM), used to transmit signals in the telecommunication domain, to achieve such a homomorphous mapping between binary-valued and continuous-valued space. The intention is to evolve, in the abstracted space, a bit-string generating function, which will be

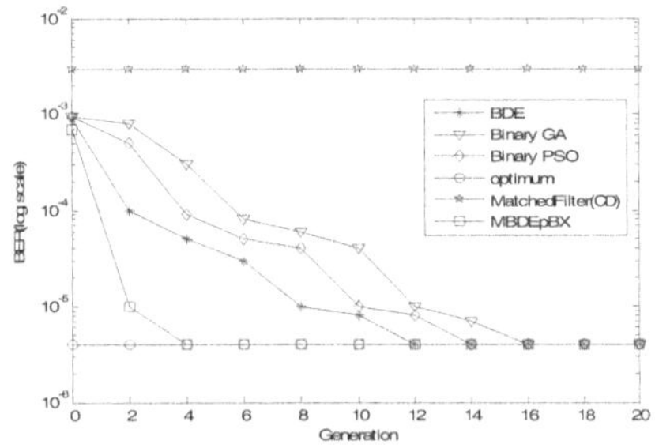

Fig. 3: Median Convergence comparison of MBDE_*p*BX vs. BDE, Binary GA, Binary PSO and Matched Filter Conventional Detector (CD) for a 10-user synchronous MC-CDMA system under 9dB SNR.

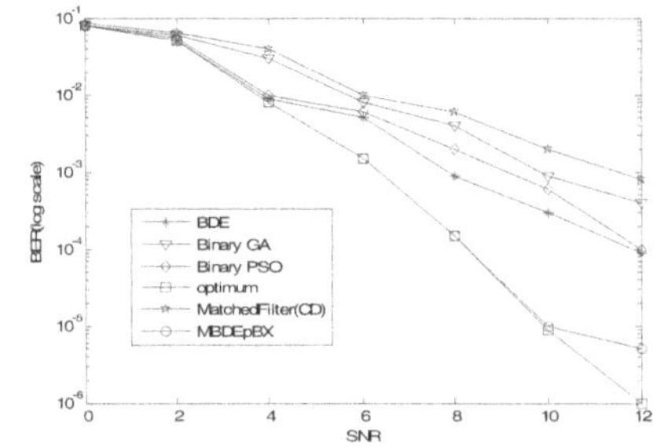

Fig. 4: Median BER comparison of MBDE_*p*BX vs. BDE, Binary GA, Binary PSO and. Matched Filter CD under the same computational burden (population size=25 and generation=5) for a 15-user MC-CDMA system with increasing SNR.

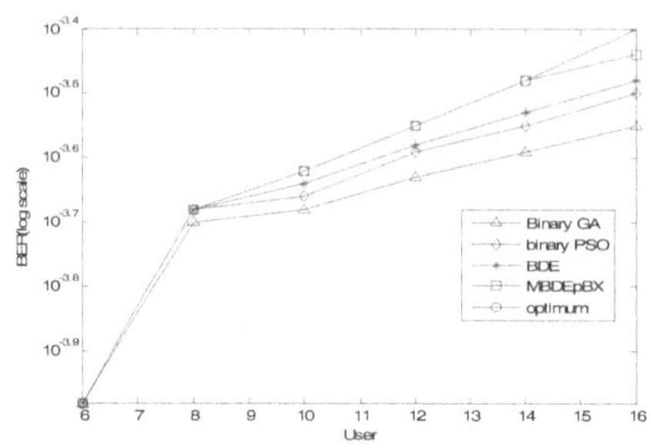

Fig. 5: Median BER performance of MBDE_*p*BX and its competitors for increasing number of users in a MC-CDMA system under 7dB SNR (population size=25 and generation=5).

employed in the original space to produce bit-vector solutions. The generating function as used in AM is

$$g(x)=\sin\left[2\pi(x-a)\times b\times\cos\left(2\pi(x-a)\times c\right)\right]+d \tag{28}$$

where x is a single element from a set of evenly spaced intervals determined by the required number of bits that need to be generated in order to satisfy the dimension of the original, binary-valued space. The coefficients $(a,b.c,d)$ in equation (28) determine the shape of the generating function: a represents the horizontal shift of the generating function, b represents the maximum frequency of the *sin* function, c represents the frequency of the *cos* function, and d represents the vertical shift of the generating function. The proposed DE algorithm evolves values for the four coefficients, *a, b, c, and d.* In this way, solving a problem in binary domain for as many dimensions as possible is equivalent to solving the problem in the continuous domain for 4 dimensions. After each generation the fitness of each vector in the population is determined by substituting the evolved values for the coefficients (which are basically the dimensions of the vectors) into equation (28). The resulting function is sampled at equally spaced points and a bit value is recorded for each point. Here, in this article we take $x\in[-1,+1]$ .If the function in equation (28) takes a positive value, a bit-value of logic (1) is recorded; otherwise, a bit-value of logic (0) is recorded. In this way, we generate the bit string or bit vector which is subjected into the MC-CDMA performance metric as shown in the equation (27). It is to be noted that this encoding rule does not directly evolve a binary string solution. Instead, it associates a function which is utilized to generate the bits that form the solution. The task of solving a binary-valued problem of any dimension diminishes to a 4-dimensional problem, where 4 floating-point parameters need to be optimized in continuous domain.

5. Simulation Strategies And Results

The modulation type used in this experiment is BPSK. The energy of the spreading sequence over a bit period T_b for each user is assumed to be 1.We assumed that perfect power control is invoked by all users so that on average signals arrive at the receiver with same power. The channel is idealized to be an AWGN one such that $\alpha_k=1$ and $\varphi_k=0$ for all the users i.e. there are no fading. All graphical results reported are median characteristics out of 25 independent runs. The simulation results are taken based on the three main performance criteria: Bit Error Rate (BER), optimum solution detection time and the associated computational burden. The detection time is given by the number of generations required to converge to a reliable decision. The computational complexity is governed by the total number of the objective function evaluations required for complete convergence.

5.1 Comparison of BER Performance with Binary GA and Binary PSO

In this section the BER performance of MBDE_*p*BX is compared with Binary DE referred to as BDE, Binary GA[19] and Binary PSO[20] for a 10-user MC-CDMA system under 9 dB signal-to-noise-ratio (SNR). The same binary encoding scheme as discussed in section 4.2 is applied to BDE, Binary GA and Binary PSO, employing the best-suited parametric set up chosen with guidelines from their respective literatures. A close scrutiny of figure 3 reveals that MBDE_*p*BX can converge to the optimum within only 4 generations in the median convergence characteristics for a 10-user synchronous MC-CDMA system whereas BDE, Binary PSO and Binary GA converges to the optimal solution within 12,14 and 16 generations under the same conditions. For a 15-user system MBDE_*p*BX can converge to the near-optimal solution within only 5 generations. This superior convergence performance of MBDE_*p*BX can be attributed to its unique features, especially the novel exploitative *p*-best crossover scheme ensuring good convergence speed. In figure 4, we have investigated the median BER performance of the 5th generation for all the algorithms with increasing SNR values for a 15-user MC-CDMA system. There is a problem associated with increasing SNR that the MAI gets enhanced. The simulation results in Figure 4 indicate that with increasing SNR values, MBDE_*p*BX still closely inosculates the optimum solution. When SNR increases it is evident that the multiple access interference gets elevated. Subsequently, for high SNR values it becomes very difficult to converge to the optimal solutions. Since the crossover scheme is exploitative it happens that the algorithm may be stuck at local maxima at high SNR values. The less greedy mutation scheme (DE/current-to-gr_best/1) and adaptive scale factor F and crossover probability Cr ensure significant amount of diversity in the newly created offspring so that the performance of MBDE_*p*BX does not get hampered for high SNR values as evident in Figure 4. MBDE_*p*BX is robust with the increasing number of users in a MC-CDMA system up to near about 14 users as can be seen from the Figure 5 unlike other approaches that start deteriorating from much lower user level. Even when the number of users is increased further MBDE_*p*BX is able to converge to the near-optimal solution as computational complexity increases.

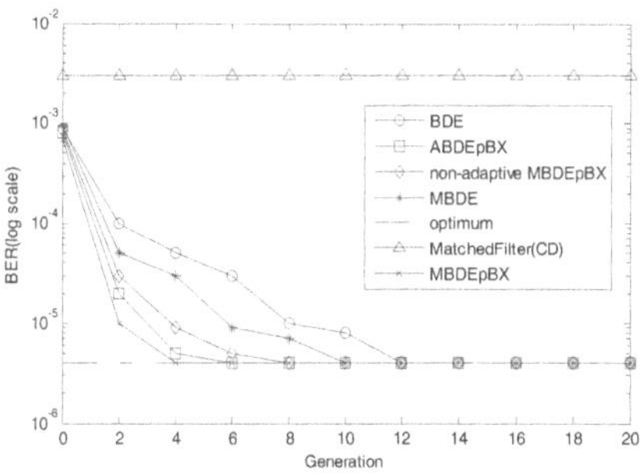

Fig. 6: Median Convergence comparison of MBDE_*p*BX vs. BDE, MBDE, non-adaptive MBDE_*p*BX, ABDE_*p*BX and Matched Filter Conventional Detector (CD) for a 10-user MC-CDMA system under 9dB SNR

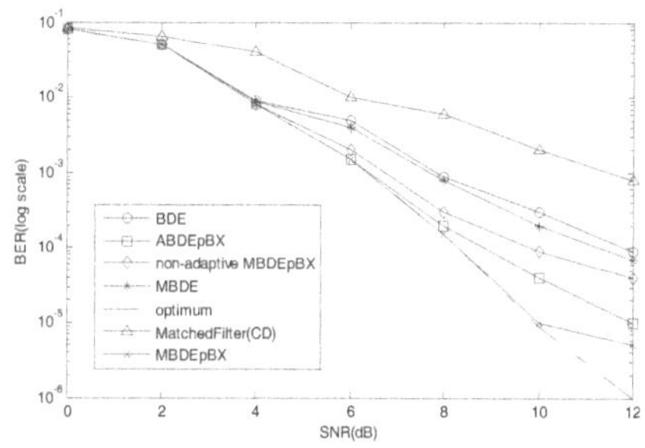

Fig. 7: Median BER comparison of MBDE_*p*BX vs. BDE, MBDE, non-adaptive MBDE_*p*BX, ABDE_*p*BX and Matched Filter CD under the same computational burden (population size=25 and generation=5) for a 15-user MC-CDMA

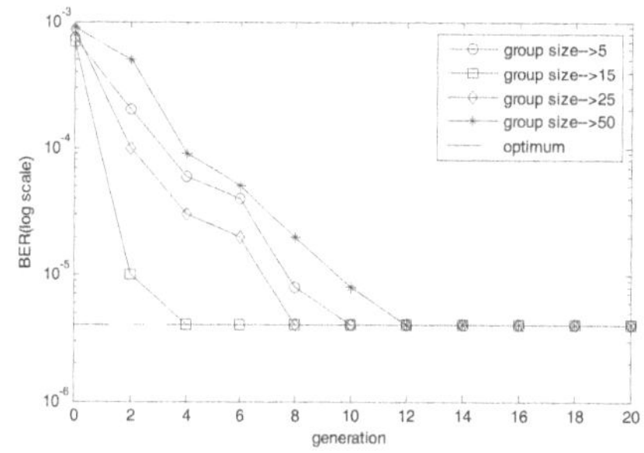

Fig. 8: Median BER performance of MBDE_*p*BX for different values of group size (q) in the mutation scheme DE/current-to- gr_best/1 for a 9dB 10-user MC-CDMA system

5.2 Effectiveness of Different Components of MBDE_*p*BX

To demonstrate the effectiveness of the modifications implemented in MBDE_*p*BX, experimental results are conducted where MBDE_*p*BX is compared with the following four variants-Binary DE, MBDE_*p*BX without *p*-best crossover (MBDE), MBDE_*p*BX without proposed adaptation schemes of F and Cr (i.e. we set $F_m = 0.8$ and $Cr_m = 0.9$ throughout the evolution process) named as non-adaptive MBDE_*p*BX and MBDE_*p*BX with the mutation strategy DE/current-to-best/1 instead of DE/current-to-gr_best/1 referred to as ABDE_*p*BX.

Figures 6 and 7 reveal that the BER performance of MBDE_*p*BX deteriorates when any of the three proposed modifications is eliminated but the performance is affected most when the novel crossover scheme *p*-best crossover is removed due to the fact that it is exploitative in nature eliminating which the convergence speed of the algorithm is affected in a worst way.

5.3 Effect on BER performance due to variation in the parameters of MBDE_*p*BX

Figures 8, 9 and 10 show the BER performance of the MBDE_*p*BX for different values of the parameters associated with the proposed modifications-group size (q), p in *p*-best crossover and the population size. A close scrutiny of Figure 9 shows that the BER performance of the MBDE_*p*BX-assisted MUD detector improves with increasing number of population. But the computational cost also increases at the same time. In order to nullify that, we adopt a fixed population size of $pop\_size = 25$ for all our simulations in this section. It is to be noted that while varying each parameter of MBDE_*p*BX to observe the BER performance the other two parameters are set to their optimum values. The performance of MBDE_*p*BX is dependent on the selection of group size q. If the value of q is large (near about population size), the proposed mutation scheme DE/current-to-gr_best/1 basically becomes identical to the current-to-best scheme. This hampers the explorative power and the algorithm may be trapped at some local optimum that is not the actual global optimum. The reason is that if q is on par with population size, the probability that the best of randomly chosen q% vectors is similar to the globally best vector of the entire population will be high. This drives most of the vectors towards a specific point in the search space resulting in premature convergence. Again, too small a value of q runs the risk of losing the exploitative capacity of the algorithm. This is due to the fact that the value of q being small, the best of randomly chosen q% vectors may not be a fitter agent of the population resulting in creation of poor donor vectors and the convergence performance may get hampered. Figure 8 indicates that keeping the group size (q) equal to 15% of the population size MBDE_*p*BX usually performs the best as far as the MUD detection in MC-CDMA system.

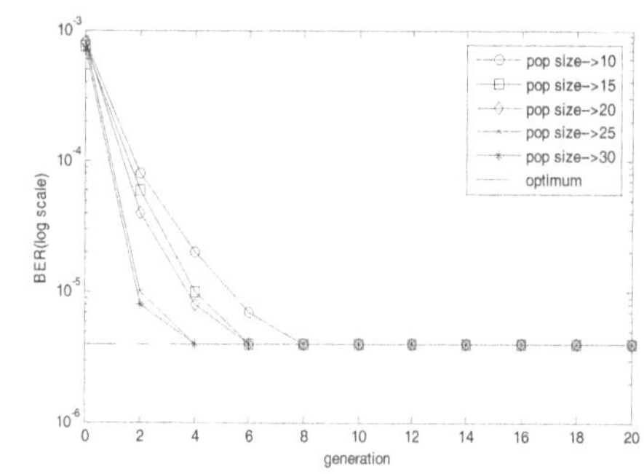

Fig. 9: Median BER performance of MBDE_*p*BX for different population size for a 9dB 10-user MC-CDMA

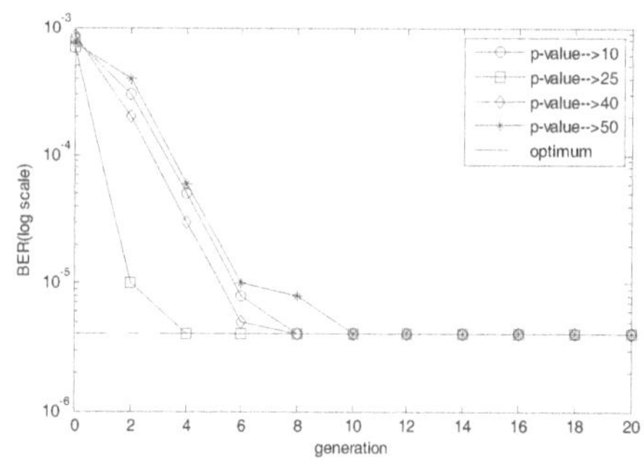

Fig. 10: Median BER performance of MBDE_*p*BX for different values of the parameter p in the exploitative *p*-best crossover scheme for a 9dB 10-user MC-CDMA system.

The convergence performance of MBDE_*p*BX is dependent on the selection of the parameter p in *p*-best crossover. The concept of this novel exploitative crossover scheme is that the useful genetic information contained in the fitness-wise best individuals is to be injected into the trial vector to improve the convergence speed. If the value of p is taken too large, it becomes ineffective as the randomly selected *p*-best vector with whom the donor vector exchanges its components may not be a top-ranking individual of the population. Again for too small a value of p the algorithm suffers from a tremendously greedy exploitation and thus there is a chance of premature convergence. Figure 10 reveals that keeping p equal to 25% of the population size offers the best performance of MBDE_*p*BX.

5.4 Reduction in Computational Complexity achieved by MBDE_*p*BX

The computational complexity is defined as the number of the cost function evaluation needed to reach the optimal solution. The exhaustive search method will require 2^K number of function evaluations to search for the optimal solution where K is the number of users. On the other hand, the number of cost function evaluations taken by MBDE_*p*BX is the product of the population size and the number of generations required to give the optimum solution. So the percentage of the complexity involved is $pop\_size \times Gen / 2^K \times 100\%$ where Gen is the number of generations involved. Now for $K=15$, MBDE_*p*BX can approach the near-optimum fitness within only 5 generations. So the number of cost functions involved is $25 \times 5 = 125$ as population size (*pop_size*) used is 25. So, percentage in computational complexity involved achieved by MBDE_*p*BX as compared to the traditional exhaustive search is given by $(125/2^{15}) \times 100\% = 0.38\%$. So, MBDE_*p*BX can attain 99.62% significant reduction in complexity as compared to the conventional exhaustive search.

6. CONCLUSION

MC-CDMA has emerged as a popular wireless broadband transmission technique combining the advantages of both OFDM and CDMA. Nowadays, the numbers of users are gradually escalating as well as the complexity of the optimal MUD detector in MC-CDMA. The proposed algorithm MBDE_*p*BX has successfully emerged itself as a potential sub-optimal MUD by carrying out a balanced ratio of exploration and exploitation throughout the evolutionary stages. It is to be noted that the algorithmic components do not incur any additional computational complexity. A close scrutiny of the simulation result reveals that MBDE_*p*BX offers excellent performance in terms of BER as well as optimum solution detection time. MBDE_*p*BX has been able to ensure huge reduction in computational complexity (99.62%). The performance of MBDE_*p*BX is verified with increasing SNR values as well as increasing the number of users in MC-CDMA system. We conclude that MBDE-*p*BX can serve as a superior MUD detector in MC-CDMA systems. Future research may focus on adapting MBDE_*p*BX for MUD detection with much higher number of users and under adverse SNR conditions.

7. REFERENCE

[1] R. Prasad and S. Hara, “Multicarrier Techniques For 4G Mobile Communications”, *IEEE Press/Wiley*, June 2003.

[2] R. Steele and L. Hanzo, Mobile Radio Communications. IEEE Press-John Wiley, 2 ed., 1999.

[3] S. Moshavi, “Multiuser Detection for DS-CDMA Communications”, *IEEE Communications Magazine*, October 1996.

[4] S. L. Miller and B. J. Ranbolt, “MMSE Detection of Multi-carrier CDMA,” *IEEE Journal on Selected Areas in Communications*, vol. 18, pp. 2356-2362, Nov 2000.

[5] A. J. Viterbi, *CDMA: Principles of Spread Spectrum Communication*. Addison-Wesley Publishing Company, 1995.

[6] T.J. Lim, L.K. Rasmussen, and H. Sugimoto, “An asynchronous multiuser CDMA detector based on the kalman filter,” *IEEE Journal of Selected Areas in Communications*, vol. 16, pp. 1711–1722, December 1998.

[7] S. Verdu, “Multiuser Detection”, New York, USA: Cambridge University Press, 1998.

[8] R. Storn and K. Price, “Differential evolution – A simple and efficient heuristic for global optimization over continuous spaces”, *Journal of Global Optimization*, 341–359, 1997.

[9] M. K. Simon, J. K. Omura, R. A. Scholtz, and B. K. Levitt, *Spread Spectrum Communications Handbook*. McGraw Hill, 1994.

[10] J. G. Proakis, *Digital Communications*. Mc-Graw Hill International Editions, 3rd ed., 1995.

[11] S. G. Glisic and P. A. Lepp¨annen, *Wireless Communications TDMA versus CDMA*. Kluwer Academic Publishers 1997.

[12] I. Kalet, “The multitone channel,” *IEEE Transactions on Communications*, vol. 37, pp. 119–124, February 1989.

[13] X Gui and T.-S. Ng, “Performance of asynchronous orthogonal multicarrier CDMA system in frequency selective fading channel,” *IEEE Transactions on Communications*, vol. 47, pp. 1084–1091, July 1999.

[14] J. M. Holtzman, “A simple, accurate method to calculate spread-spectrum multiple-access error probabilities,” *IEEE Transactions on Communications*, vol. 40, pp. 461–464, March 1992.

[15] M. K. Varanasi and B. Aazhang, “Near-optimum detection in synchronous code-division multiple-access systems,” *IEEE Transactions on Communications*, vol. 39, pp. 725–736, May 1991.

[16] S. Verdu, “Minimum probability of error for asynchronous Gaussian multiple-access channel,” *IEEE Transactions on Communications*, vol. 32, pp. 85–96, January 1986.

[17] S.M. Islam, S. Das, S. Ghosh,; S. Roy, P.N. Suganthan ; "An Adaptive Differential Evolution Algorithm With Novel Mutation and Crossover Strategies for Global Numerical Optimization," *Systems, Man, and Cybernetics, Part B: Cybernetics, IEEE Transactions on* , vol.42, no.2, pp.482-500, April 2012 doi: 10.1109/TSMCB.2011.2167966.

[18] S. Koziel and Z. Michalewicz, “Evolutionary algorithms, homomorphous mappings, and constrained parameter optimization,” *Evolutionary Computation*, vol. 7, no. 1, pp. 19–44, 1999.

[19] W. Kosi´nski, S. Kotowski, and J. Socala, “On Asymptotic Behaviour of a Binary Genetic Algorithm”, XXI Autumn Meeting of Polish Information Processing Society Conference Proceedings pp. 139–144, 2006.

[20] J.Kennedy, R.C. Eberhart ; , "A discrete binary version of the particle swarm algorithm," *Systems, Man, and Cybernetics, 1997. Computational Cybernetics and Simulation., 1997 IEEE International Conference*, vol.5, no., pp.4104-4108 vol.5, 12-15 Oct 1997

Automatic String Replace by Examples

Andrea De Lorenzo
DIA - University of Trieste
Italy
andrea.delorenzo@phd.units.it

Eric Medvet
DIA - University of Trieste
Italy
emedvet@units.it

Alberto Bartoli
DIA - University of Trieste
Italy
bartoli.alberto@units.it

ABSTRACT

Search-and-replace is a text processing task which may be largely automated with regular expressions: the user must describe with a specific formal language the regions to be modified (search pattern) and the corresponding desired changes (replacement expression). Writing and tuning the required expressions requires high familiarity with the corresponding formalism and is typically a lengthy, error-prone process.

In this paper we propose a tool based on Genetic Programming (GP) for generating automatically both the search pattern and the replacement expression based only on examples. The user merely provides examples of the input text along with the desired output text and does not need any knowledge about the regular expression formalism nor about GP. We are not aware of any similar proposal. We experimentally evaluated our proposal on 4 different search-and-replace tasks operating on real-world datasets and found good results, which suggests that the approach may indeed be practically viable.

Categories and Subject Descriptors

I.5.4 [**Pattern Recognition**]: Applications—*text processing*; H.4.1 [**Information Systems Applications**]: Office Automation—*word processing*

Keywords

Search-and-replace, Genetic Programming

1. INTRODUCTION

Techniques for automated text processing are becoming increasingly important due to the uninterrupted growth and diffusion of text sources that are unstructured or loosely structured, e.g., logs—which exist in many different forms and application domains, including server administration, web access, phone calls, intrusion detection—web catalogs, email messages, social networking sites and so on. A specific text processing task potentially suitable to being automated is *search-and-replace*, where all text regions matching a given pattern should be replaced according to a given scheme. Many tools offer powerful support for this task based on the usage of *regular expressions*, which are a way of specifying a pattern using a formal language. The user must specify a *search pattern* for identifying the text regions to be modified and a separate *replacement expression* for describing the changes to be applied. The replacement expression usually include references to specific subregions of the region to be modified and the description of these subregions must be encoded in the search pattern appropriately. This framework requires the involvement of technically savvy users because defining the expressions required for solving a specific search-and-replace task requires high familiarity with the corresponding formalism. Furthermore, tuning the expressions is usually a time-consuming, error-prone process.

In this paper, we propose a tool based on Genetic Programming (GP) that is capable of *automatically* generating both the search pattern and the replacement expression, only by means of *examples*. The user merely provides a set of examples of the search-and-replace task, each example consisting of the text before and after the desired replacement without any further annotation. The tool then generates automatically both the search pattern and the replacement expression for fulfilling the task. The output can be used with popular processing engines, e.g., Java, PHP and so on. We emphasize that the user does not need to have any knowledge about GP nor is she required to provide any hints about the structure of the search pattern or replacement expressions to be obtained. We are not aware of any other method capable of automatically defining the required expressions, based solely on examples.

Our tool internally works in three phases. In the first phase, it executes a GP search for generating a regular expression able to localize the text regions to be processed. This regular expression defines a single pattern across all the provided examples, usually including the text to be modified and some surrounding text, thereby defining a sort of *context* for characterizing the scope of the desired replacements. For instance, consider the anonimization of Twitter usernames (e.g., `@GECCO2013` $\rightarrow$ `@xxxxxxxxx`): a letter should be replaced by `x`, but only when it is part of a Twitter username—which is the context. This phase is essential for making the user experience as simple as possible: the user merely specifies the input text t and the desired output text t'; she does not need to annotate t for indicating which of its portions have to be modified. The regular expression produced in the

GECCO'13, July 6–10, 2013, Amsterdam, The Netherlands.

first phase is required internally in the next phases and is not visible to the user. In the second phase, the tool builds the replacement expression by identifying the subregions to be modified and using references to those subregions appropriately, i.e., according to the provided examples. In the third and final phase, the tool executes a further GP search for generating the search pattern to be used along with the replacement expression generated at the previous step.

We evaluated our proposal on 4 search-and-replace tasks executed on different real-world datasets, each including several hundreds of manually-labelled examples. The tasks consist of anonymization of usernames in tweets, partial anonymization of IP addresses, format change of dates and phone numbers. The experimental evaluation shows that our tool is indeed able to define an effective search-and-replace task with only few tens of examples. Even leaving aside the potential of our tool for non technically savvy users, this result also suggests that evolutionary computing, coupled with the power of modern computing resources, may increasingly become a surrogate for some specific technical expertise of human specialists.

2. RELATED WORKS

Automatic generation of regular expressions from examples of the desired behavior may be useful in a variety of problems. We categorize these problems in increasing order of difficulty, as follows. (1) The *flagging* problem consists in assigning a binary label to a text: true, if some region of the text matches the regular expression, false otherwise. The examples consist of text regions, each accompanied by the respective desired label. (2) The *text extraction* problem consists in extracting from a text each region which matches the regular expression. The examples consist of texts, each accompanied by the annotation of the region to be extracted or the indication that nothing has to be extracted. (3) The *search-and-replace* problem is a generalization of the text extraction problem: the extracted regions have to be modified according to the specification encoded into an additional replacement expression. The examples consist of texts, each accompanied by the corresponding modified text or the indication that nothing has to be modified.

To the best of our knowledge, no method for automatic generation of expressions suitable for search-and-replace has been proposed before. Accordingly, we briefly review in this section: (i) approaches suitable for the flagging problem or the text extraction problem; (ii) proposals not based on regular expressions for facilitating users while performing search-and-replace tasks.

The authors of [5] propose an evolutionary approach for generating regular expressions for the flagging problem. Their approach is based on grammatical evolution and individuals are specified in the Backus-Naur Form. The method effectiveness is assessed on the task of identifying those lines of HTML documents which contain hyperlinks.

Several earlier works addressed the text extraction problem with evolutionary approaches, such as Genetic Algorithms (GA) [2, 9] and Genetic Programming (GP) [19, 7, 18, 3]. In [2], after an initial evolution, individuals are recombined and then selected to obtain the final regular expression. In [9], the alphabet for regular expressions is chosen after a preliminary frequency analysis on the set of examples. Both proposals are evaluated on the task of URL extraction (composition and size of training and testing sets are not provided in [9]). Methods based on GP encode regular expressions as GP trees and evolve the corresponding individuals—each individual being a candidate expression—to maximize effectiveness according to some metric [19, 7, 18].

The large computing power widely available today revamped GP-based solutions, allowing them to outperform earlier proposals and solve practically relevant problems [3]. In this work we solve a more general problem than in [3]—search-and-replace, rather than mere text extraction. Our proposal generates automatically, in the first and third phase, regular expressions for text extraction. The corresponding procedures are built according to the proposal in [3] but extend that proposal in several key aspects. First, part of the initial population contains individuals generated directly from the examples, rather than randomly. Second, we generate regular expressions including capturing groups, a feature which is needed for solving the search-and-replace problem (we describe this feature in the next section). Third, we use fitness definitions tailored to the specific requirements of search-and-replace. In the first phase, the evolutionary search promotes individuals describing a suitable context across all the examples, which is usually larger than the region to be extracted and modified. In the third phase, the fitness of an individual depends on the behavior of that individual when coupled with the replacement expression found in the second phase.

The scenario considered in [20] concerns criminal justice information systems and the goal consists in minimizing human effort for data mining. The proposed approach starts from a single example and produces a reduced form of regular expression exploiting the operator interventions during the learning process, which is hence not fully automatic. A similar scheme for regular expression generation which involves the human operator is presented in [10]: here an active learning algorithm is proposed which starts from a single example and then requires an external operator to respond to membership queries about candidate expressions. In our work, instead, we just require a set of examples and never require human involvement during the search.

Other promising proposals for the text extraction problem which are not based on evolutionary approaches have been presented in [11, 1, 4]. In [11] the user is required to provide a set of examples and an initial regular expression: the algorithm then applies successive transformations until it reaches a local optimum in terms of precision and recall. The system proposed in [1] works similarly but the authors focus on noisy data. The method proposed in [4] does not rely on an initial regular expression: instead, it identifies relevant patterns in the set of examples and then combines the most promising pattern into a single regular expression. The proposal is evaluated on several business-related text extraction tasks, e.g., phone numbers and invoice numbers.

Concerning proposals for facilitating users in automated text editing that are not based on regular expressions, the authors of [14] propose a system (LAPIS) based on a pattern language. This pattern language, previously proposed by the same authors [16], can replace regular expressions in many common tasks, including simple forms of search-and-replace. Since some skill is still required to use the language, LAPIS offers an assisted mode in which an initial pattern is inferred from a set of positive and negative examples. Differently from our work, the assisted mode addresses only the search portion of the search-and-replace task. Furthermore, the results produced by our tool are not bound to a specific text processing system but can be used in a wealth of different environments. A similar scheme for inferring a pattern from examples is used in [15]: the goal here is to guess multiple selections for simultaneous editing.

A method for assisting the user in executing a search-and-replace tasks is proposed in [13]. The authors consider a scenario where, in order to mitigate the difficulty of defining a search pattern—which is the point we address in this paper—users often work with less precise patterns and then manual check each suggested match. They propose to cluster the suggested matches so as to reduce the number of manual checks, since the user approve or reject the whole cluster instead of inspecting each single match.

3. OUR APPROACH

The user provides a set of examples T. Each example is composed by a pair of strings $\langle t, t' \rangle$, where t is a string to be modified in t'. An example in which $t' = t$ is called a *negative* example.

The output of our system is a pair of strings $\langle s, r \rangle$, where s is the regular expression which defines the search pattern and r is the replacement expression.

The regular expression s may contain zero or more *capturing groups*. A capturing group is a substring of s enclosed between round parentheses. A capturing group is itself a regular expression: when a string t matches a regular expression s containing a capturing group, a substring of t matches the capturing group. The substring matched by a capturing group can be referenced in the replacement expression. The corresponding syntax is $\$n$[1], where n is the index of occurrence of the capturing group in the regular expression—e.g., `$1` indicates the substring matched by the first capturing group. For example, suppose the user needs to change the date format from month-date-year to day-month-year: a suitable search pattern, which includes three capturing groups, is the regular expression `(\d+)-(\d+)-(\d+)` and the corresponding replacement expression is `$2-$1-$3`.

Solving the search-and-replace problem by means of regular expressions requires a notion of *context*. In general, a single pattern identifying only the substrings to be replaced might not exist. That is, it might not exist a single regular expression which, for each example $\langle t, t' \rangle$, exactly matches the shortest substring of t including the characters which have to be modified in order to obtain t'. In practice, however, a pattern may often be found for superstrings of the strings to be replaced: we call these superstrings the *context* and this pattern the *context pattern*.

To clarify, the first two columns of Table 1 show a few examples related to three different search-and-replace tasks (the other columns show intermediate results discussed later). The third column illustrates the substring of t that is to be replaced: it is apparent that, for each of the three tasks, there is not any pattern identifying these substrings. On the other hand, a context pattern as defined above does exist for each of the three tasks: column c_k contains the contexts—i.e., superstrings of the substring to be replaced—extracted by the context pattern in column s_c.

[1]Some regular expression engines (e.g., Python, .NET, Ruby) use the $\backslash n$ notation, instead of the $\$n$ notation used, e.g., in Java, JavaScript, PHP, ...)

The context thus describes portions of input that do have to be replaced and where replacements have to be confined. An essential component of our approach is that we do *not* require the user to specify the context. On the contrary, the context is discovered automatically by the system. For instance, in the third row in Table 1, we do not require that the user specifies that `ic` has to be replaced by `xx` only when `ic` is part of the Twitter username `@Toxic`, but not when is part of `Sick`. It is up to the system to extract that information from the examples. The user only describes the input text and the desired output.

Note that, for a given set of examples, the context pattern may not be determined unambiguously—e.g., in Table 1, each context could also start with the space character, or with multiple arbitrary characters followed by a space. A given set of examples might thus be associated with 0, 1 or more context patterns and finding those patterns is not straightforward.

Our proposal consists of three phases, described in the next sections in full detail: (i) generate a context pattern s_c, (ii) build the replacement expression r, (iii) generate the search pattern s which works with r. We remark that phase 1 is necessary because we decided to not rely on the user for specifying the context of the desired changes. The result s_c of this phase is not exposed to the user and is only an input for the next phase.

4. IMPLEMENTATION

4.1 Generating the context pattern

In this phase we aim at generating the context pattern s_c. To this end, we build from T a learning set T_c suitable for a text extraction problem: for each example $\langle t, t' \rangle$ in T we construct exactly one example $\langle t, D(t, t') \rangle$ for T_c, where $D(t, t')$ is the substring of t to be replaced and is determined as described below. Then, we run a GP search for generating a regular expression that attempts to satisfy the examples in T_c.

The string $D(t, t')$ is the shortest substring of t which includes all characters that have to be modified in order to obtain t' (see also the third column in Table 1). Formally, let t^i be the i-th character in t and let $\mathcal{L}(t)$ be the length of t. Then $D(t, t') = t^i t^{i+1} \dots t^{\mathcal{L}(t)-j}$, where $i \geq 1$ is the lowest integer for which $t^i \neq t'^i$ and $j \geq 0$ is the lowest integer for which $t^{\mathcal{L}(t)-j} \neq t'^{\mathcal{L}(t')-j}$; if $t = t'$, $D(t, t') = \emptyset$.

For the purpose of the GP search, we partition the learning set T_c in a training set T_c^t and a validation set T_c^v. We form these two sets so as to distribute the negative examples evenly.

We then run a GP search on T_c^t, as follows. Every individual is a tree which represents a regular expression. The *function set* consists of (we assume the reader has some familiarity with regular expressions [8]): (i) the *concatenator*, that is a binary node that concatenates other nodes or leaves, (ii) the *character class* operators `[·]` and `[^·]`, (iii) the *capturing group* `(·)` and the *non-capturing group*[2] `(?:·)` operators, (iv) the *possessive quantifiers* (`·*+`, `·++`, `·?+`, `{·,·}+`). The *terminal set* consists of: (i) *constants*—i.e., a single character, a number or a string, (ii) *ranges*—i.e., `a-z` or `A-Z` and (iii) *character classes*, i.e., `\w` or `\d`.

[2]A non-capturing group is a group which cannot be referenced in the replacement expression.

Table 1: Three sets of synthetic examples and corresponding intermediate and final results: ∅ indicates the empty string.

t_k	t'_k	$D(t_k, t'_k)$	s_c	c_k	c'_k	r_k	s	r
I like @GECC013 conf	I like @GExxxx conf	CC013		@GECC013	@GExxxx	$1xxxx		
RT @MaleLabTs New paper	RT @Maxxxx New paper	leLabTs	@\w\w(\w+)	@MaleLabTs	@Maxxxx	$1xxxx	(@\w\w)\w+	$1xxxx
Sick of @Toxic chatter	Sick of @Toxxxx chatter	ic		@Toxic	@Toxxxx	$1xxx		
nothing new here	nothing new here	∅		∅	∅	∅		
today is 1-23-13	today is 23/01/13	1-23-		1-23-13	23/1/13	$2/$1/$3		
he left on 3-13-12	he left on 13/3/12	3-13-	\d+-\d+-\d+	3-13-12	13/3/12	$2/$1/$3	(\d+)-(\d+)-(\d+)	$2/$1/$3
great 1-1-13 party!	great 1/1/13 party!	-1-		1-1-13	1/1/13	$1/$2/$3		
he is Nick	he is *Nick*	Nick	[A-Z]\w+	Nick	*Nick*	*$1*	([A-Z]\w+)	*$1*
John was here	*John* was here	John		John	*John*	*$1*		

We build the initial population of P individuals so that half of them are generated directly from the examples, rather than randomly. If the number of examples is smaller than $\frac{P}{2}$, then we use them all and generate the remaining individuals randomly. In detail, let $P_E = \min\left(\frac{P}{2}, 2|T_c^t|\right)$, where $|T_c^t|$ is the size of T_c^t, and let $\langle t_k, D(t_k, t'_k)\rangle$ denote the k-th example in T_c^t. Then, the initial population consists of: $\frac{P_E}{2}$ individuals, each representing one of the strings $D(t_k, t'_k)$; $\frac{P_E}{2}$ individuals, each representing one of the strings $D(t_k, t'_k)$ where each digit is replaced with a \d and each alphabetical character with a \w; the remaining $P - P_E$ individuals are generated at random with a Ramped half-and-half method. We chose this strategy because we found, after preliminary experimentation, that it greatly speeds up the convergence toward good solutions.

The *fitness* function to be minimized during the search is the sum of the Levenshtein distances[3], across all the examples in the training set, between the string to be extracted and the string actually extracted by the first capturing group:

$$f_E(s_c) = \sum_{k=1}^{|T_c^t|} L(D(t_k, t'_k), E_1(t_k, s_c)) \quad (1)$$

where s_c is the evaluated individual, $L(x, y)$ is the Levenshtein distance between strings x and y, $E_1(t_k, s_c)$ is the substring of t_k matched by the first capturing group of s_c—if s_c does not contain a capturing group, we set $f_E(s_c) = +\infty$. We designed the fitness based on the key requirement of this phase, that is, automatic generation of a single pattern capable of extracting a superstring of the substring to be modified. For this reason, we promote individuals with at least one capturing group and such that this group matches $D(t_k, t'_k)$. We did not include in the fitness any component depending on what is extracted beyond $D(t_k, t'_k)$ because, as discussed in the previous section, we have no explicit information about what the whole expression should extract, i.e., about the context.

We run N_1 independent GP searches, differing only for the random seed. We evaluate on the validation set T_c^v each of the N_1 resulting regular expressions, and select as output s_c of this phase the one which minimizes f_E.

4.2 Building the replacement expression

In this phase we aim at generating the replacement expression r. To this end, we generate a candidate replacement expression r_k for each positive example $\langle t_k, t'_k\rangle$ in T, as follows.

Let c_k be the substring of t_k extracted by the context pattern s_c; let b, e be the integers such that $c_k = t_k^b t_k^{b+1} \dots t_k^{\mathcal{L}(t_k)-e}$; let c'_k be the substring of t'_k delimited in the same way by b and e, i.e., $c'_k = {t'}_k^b {t'}_k^{b+1} \dots {t'}_k^{\mathcal{L}(t'_k)-e}$ (if $b \geq \mathcal{L}(t'_k) - e$, then $c'_k = \emptyset$). We set the candidate replacement expression r_k for the example $\langle t_k, t'_k\rangle$ by executing Algorithm 1, which takes as input c'_k and the list of tuples C_k constructed with the following steps. Intuitively, C_k describes the boundaries of all the (maximal) substrings of c_k which appear in c'_k. In detail, we (i) construct the list C_k containing all tuples $\langle i, j, i', j'\rangle$ such that $c_k^i \dots c_k^j = {c'}_k^{i'} \dots {c'}_k^{j'}$; (ii) remove from C_k each tuple $\langle i, j, i', j'\rangle$ for which there exists another tuple $\langle i^*, j^*, i'^*, j'^*\rangle$ such that $i \geq i^*$ and $j \leq j^*$; (iii) sort C_k according to index i, in ascending order, and insert into each tuple an increasing integer n that represents the position of the tuple in C_k; (iv) sort C_k according to index i', in ascending order. At this point, we set $r_k = \mathcal{R}(c'_k, C_k)$ where $\mathcal{R}$ is defined in Algorithm 1. As pointed out above, C_k describes the boundaries of the substrings of c_k which appear in c'_k—in brief, of the common substrings. Algorithm 1 builds r_k by concatenating the substrings of c'_k between two common substrings, replacing common substrings by tokens $\$n$, after an appropriate sorting—see Figure 1 for an example.

Algorithm 1 Algorithm for building a candidate replacement expression r_k.

function $\mathcal{R}(c', C = \{\langle i_1, j_1, i'_1, j'_1, n_1\rangle, \dots\})$
  $r \leftarrow \emptyset$
  $b \leftarrow 1$
  $e \leftarrow i'_1 - 1$
  for $h \leftarrow 1, |C| - 1$ **do**
    $r \leftarrow r{c'}^b \dots {c'}^e \$n_h$ ▷ concatenation
    $b \leftarrow j'_h + 1$
    $e \leftarrow i'_{h+1} - 1$
  end for
  $r \leftarrow r{c'}^b \dots {c'}^e \$n_{|C|}{c'}^{j'_{|C|}+1} \dots {c'}^{\mathcal{L}(c')}$ ▷ concatenation
  return r
end function

Different examples might generate different replacement expressions, owing to conflicting or ambiguous examples. For

[3]The Levenshtein distance measures the difference between two strings: informally, it corresponds to the minimum number of single-character edits required to change one string into the other.

Figure 1: **Example of execution of $\mathcal{R}(c'_k, C_k)$ where C_k has been constructed from c_k, c'_k**

$$c_k = \texttt{07-14-1789}$$

$$c'_k = \texttt{<b>14/07/1789</b>}$$

$$C_k = \begin{array}{cccccl} i, & j, & i', & j', & n & \\ \langle 4, & 5, & 4, & 5, & 2\rangle & \texttt{14} \rightarrow \texttt{\$2} \\ \langle 1, & 2, & 7, & 8, & 1\rangle & \texttt{07} \rightarrow \texttt{\$1} \\ \langle 7, & 10, & 10, & 13, & 3\rangle & \texttt{1789} \rightarrow \texttt{\$3} \end{array}$$

$$r_k = \texttt{<b>\$2/\$1/\$3</b>}$$

instance, in Table 1, the third example generates a replacement expression `$1xxx` different from the one corresponding to the first and second example `$1xxxx`. The reason is the ambiguity associated with the `x` character, which is both part of the input text to be modified (`Toxic`) and of the text to be obtained (`Toxxxx`).

We select as output of this phase the replacement expression r which occurs most frequently among all the examples. In case two or more candidates occur the same number of times, we choose one of them at random.

4.3 Generating the search pattern

In this phase, we aim at generating the search pattern s. To this end, we partition the set of examples T in a training set T^t and a validation set T^v, by distributing negative examples evenly, and execute a GP search similarly to Section 4.1 with a crucial difference in the fitness definition. In this case we associate with each individual, i.e., regular expression, s two objective functions to be minimized:

$$f_R(s) = \sum_{k=1}^{|T^t|} L(t'_k, R(t_k, s, r)) \tag{2}$$

$$f_G(s) = |G_s(s) - G_r(r)| \tag{3}$$

where $R(t_k, s, r)$ is the string obtained by performing on t_k the search-and-replace task defined by the regular expression s and the replacement expression r (found in the previous phase), $G_s(s)$ is the number of capturing groups defined in s and $G_r(r)$ is the number of capturing groups defined in r. We minimize this multi-objective fitness by means of NSGA-II [6].

We run N_2 independent GP searches, differing only for the random seed, thereby obtaining N_2 search patterns s_h. Finally, we evaluate on the validation set T^v each of the N_2 candidate solutions $\langle s_h, r\rangle$ for the search-and-replace task, and select as final result the one which minimizes f_R and f_S by means of NSGA-II.

5. EXPERIMENTS

We experimentally evaluated our proposal on real-world datasets that we manually annotated for 4 search-and-replace tasks:

Twitter anonymization Replace each username found in a tweet corpus with `@xxxxxx`—e.g., `@GECCO2013` becomes `@xxxxxx`. The tweet corpus has been taken from [12];

Table 2: **GP parameters**

Parameter	Settings
Population size (phase 1)	500
Population size (phase 3)	3000
Number of generations (phase 1)	1000
Number of generations (phase 3)	200
Selection	Tournament of size 7
Initialization depths	1–5
Max depth after crossover	15
Reproduction rate	10%
Crossover rate	80%
Mutation rate	10%

IP partial anonymization Replace the second two digit groups of each IP address (expressed in dot-decimal notation) found in a web server log with `xxx.xxx`—e.g., `127.0.0.1` becomes `127.0.xxx.xxx`.

Date format change Change each date found in the web server log of the previous task from the Gregorian little-endian slash separated format to the Gregorian big-endian dash separated format—e.g., `31/Dec/2012` becomes `2012-Dec-31`.

Phone number format change Change each phone number found in an email collection by removing the parenthesis around the area code and adding a dash—i.e, `(555) 555-5555` becomes `555-555-5555`. The email corpus has been taken from [17] and was used by [11, 4].

The dataset consists of 1000 examples for each task, i.e., 1000 pairs $\langle t, t'\rangle$, of which 500 are negative. We executed three experiments for each task, varying the size of the set of examples.

We executed each experiment as follows: (i) we randomly split the dataset in two subsets T and T^e; each subset is balanced, i.e., contains the same number of positive and negative examples; (ii) we generated a solution $\langle s, r\rangle$ using T and evaluated the solution on T^e—i.e., T is the learning set and T^e is the testing set (during phases 1 and 3 the learning set is further split in training and validation, as discussed in the previous sections). We report results obtained with 5-fold cross-validation, i.e., we repeated the two steps above 5 times and averaged the performance indexes exhibited by the 5 solutions on the testing set of the corresponding experiment. We set the parameters for the GP searches as in Table 2. We chose the number of generations and the population size, which are different between phase 1 and phase 3, after some preliminary experimentation. We chose an equal number of independent searches in phase 1 and phase 3: $N_1 = N_2 = 32$.

We evaluated each generated solution $\langle s, r\rangle$ by means of two metrics. The *distance error rate* ϵ_d quantifies the percentage of characters that have not been processed correctly, i.e., it averages on T^e pairs the distance between the expected string and the string actually obtained, divided by the length of the former. The *count error rate* ϵ_c quantifies the percentage

Table 4: Experiment execution times, averaged across the 5 repetitions: third to fifth columns show the average execution of the three phases.

Task	$\|T^t\| + \|T^v\|$	Time (min) 1	2	3	Overall
Twitter anonymization	20	0	0	1	1
	25	0	0	1	1
	50	0	0	2	2
IP partial anonymization	20	2	0	10	12
	25	7	0	26	33
	50	4	0	39	43
Date format change	20	3	0	15	18
	25	7	0	29	36
	50	13	0	65	78
Phone number format change	20	7	0	28	35
	25	17	0	63	80
	50	27	0	105	132

of T^e pairs that have not been processed correctly. In detail:

$$\epsilon_d = \frac{1}{|T^e|} \sum_{i=1}^{|T^e|} \frac{L(t'_k, R(t_k, s, r))}{\mathcal{L}(t'_i)} \quad (4)$$

$$\epsilon_c = \frac{1}{|T^e|} \sum_{i=1}^{|T^e|} \mathbb{1}(t'_k, R(t_k, s, r)) \quad (5)$$

where $\mathbb{1}(x, y)$ is a function whose value is 1 if x and y are equal, 0 otherwise.

5.1 Results

The salient results are summarized in Table 3. Each row corresponds to one experiment and reports the results in terms of ϵ_d and ϵ_c, with average μ and standard deviation σ across the 5 repetitions. For ϵ_d, we show also the values for each repetition. We remark that the learning set $T = T^t \cup T^v$ is always a small portion of the dataset, less than 10%.

It seems fair to claim that the approach does provide very good performance. A set of 50 examples suffices to execute the "IP partial anonymization" and "Date format change" tasks without any mistake, which seems to be a remarkable result. Furthermore, 50 examples for the "Twitter anonymization" task suffice to achieve correct processing of 96.9% of the testing set instances. Concerning the "Phone number format change" task, the percentage of testing instances processed correctly is 92%, again as long as 50 or more examples are available for the learning procedure. To place this result in perspective we observe that the dataset for this task has been used in earlier works addressing automatic generation of solutions for the text extraction problem from examples [11, 4]. The cited works used training sets much bigger than ours. The results were provided in terms of F-measure and range in 85%–87% with 4100–33400 learning examples for [11] and 65%–92% with 400–52000 learning examples for [4]. Although our indexes cannot be compared directly to F-measure, which is not meaningful in our context, our ability of processing more than 92% of the testing instances correctly, even with a learning set smaller by one order of magnitude or more, seems to be a good result.

The previous results are the average performance across 5 repetitions of each experiment, where the result of each experiment is the best solution (on the learning set) across the 32 independent GP searches in phase 3. Further insights can be obtained by analyzing the performance of all the $5 \times 32 = 160$ solutions found for each task. To this end, Figure 3 plots the number of solutions with $\epsilon_d < 10\%$ and $\epsilon_c < 10\%$ (on the testing set). Each bar corresponds to an experiment repetition. It can be seen that our approach does generate a number of good solutions systematically, that is, the good performance is not the result of a single lucky individual.

It is also interesting to point out that there is a clear correlation between performance of an individual on the validation set T^v and its performance on the testing set T^e: Figure 2 shows ϵ_d on the two sets, for each of the $5 \times 32 = 160$ solutions found in our experiments (one plot per task). This outcome demonstrates that the relative performance on individuals on the validation set is a good predictor of their relative performance on the testing set.

Table 4 reports the execution time for each experiment, averaged across the 5 repetitions, with the indication of the time taken by each of the three phases. Each experiment has been executed in parallel on 4 identical machines powered with a quad-core Intel Xeon X3323 (2.53 GHz) and 2GB of RAM. The execution times are, in most cases, too high to devise a possible interactive use of our approach. On the other hand, they seem to be sufficiently low to be practical, especially in a not far away future. Besides, the corresponding computing effort might be leased at 1 or 2 USD per hour[4]—a less accurate but much cheaper surrogate for the specific skills of a specialist.

6. CONCLUDING REMARKS

We have considered the feasibility of solving a search-and-replace task described solely through examples by means of regular expressions. The motivation for this problem follows from the ever increasing wealth of unstructured or loosely structured text sources, along with the need of automated techniques for their processing.

We have presented the implementation of a tool able to generate the required search pattern and replacement expression automatically. The user merely provides examples of the input text coupled with the desired output text, without any further annotation or hints about the expected results. We are not aware of any other proposal with these features.

We assessed the performance of our tool on challenging search-and-replace tasks executed on real-world datasets. The experimental evaluation provided very good results and suggests that the approach may indeed be practically viable.

7. REFERENCES

[1] R. Babbar and N. Singh. Clustering based approach to learning regular expressions over large alphabet for noisy unstructured text. In *Proceedings of the fourth workshop on Analytics for noisy unstructured text data*, AND '10, pages 43–50, New York, NY, USA, 2010. ACM.

[2] D. Barrero, D. Camacho, and M. R-Moreno. Automatic Web Data Extraction Based on Genetic Algorithms and Regular Expressions. *Data Mining and Multi-agent Integration*, pages 143–154, 2009.

[3] A. Bartoli, G. Davanzo, A. De Lorenzo, M. Mauri, E. Medvet, and E. Sorio. Automatic generation of

[4] `http://aws.amazon.com/ec2/pricing/`

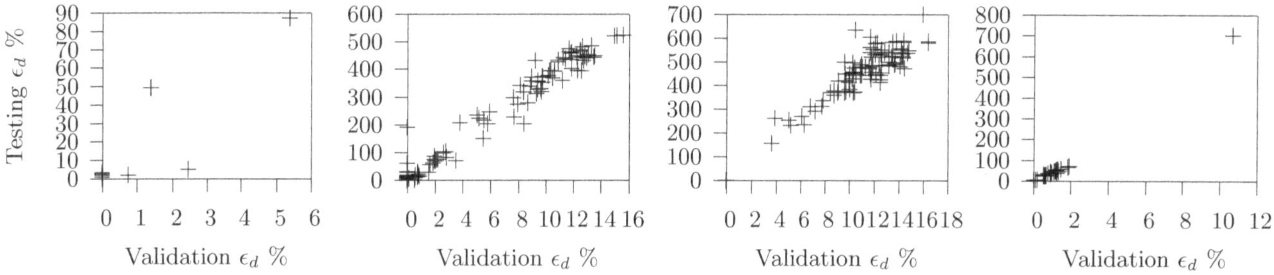

(a) Twitter anonymization (b) IP partial anonymization (c) Date format change (d) Phone n. format change

Figure 2: Validation ϵ_d vs. testing ϵ_d.

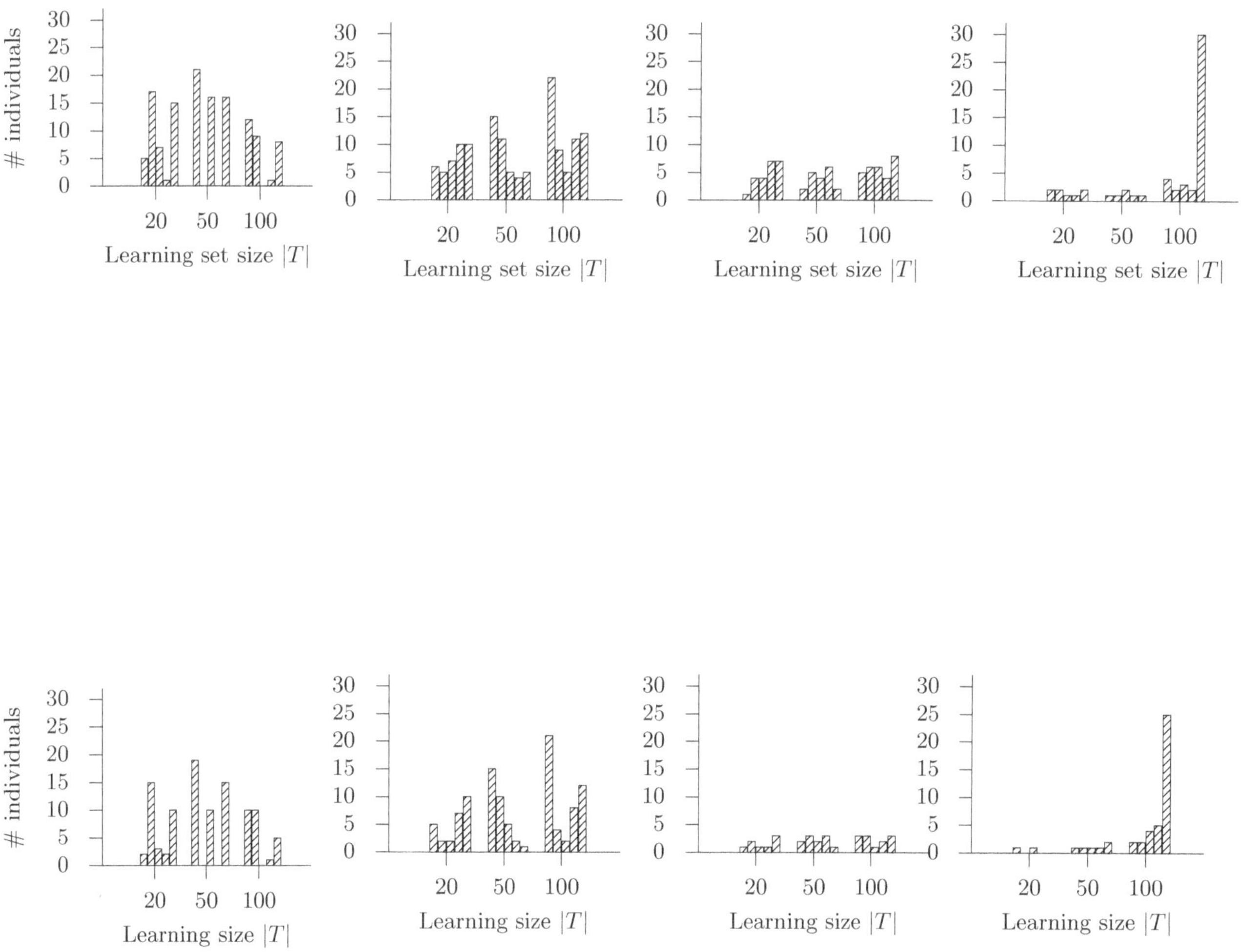

(a) Twitter anonymization (b) IP partial anonymization (c) Date format change (d) Phone n. format change

Figure 3: Number of generated solutions with $\epsilon_d \leq 10\%$ (above) and $\epsilon_c \leq 10\%$ (below). Each bar corresponds to a repetition.

Table 3: Experiment results

Task	Dataset			Repetition (ϵ_d %)					Overall (ϵ_d %)		Overall (ϵ_c %)	
	$\|T^t\|$	$\|T^v\|$	$\|T^e\|$	1	2	3	4	5	μ	σ	μ	σ
Twitter anonymization	10	10	980	1.7	0.0	7.7	10.7	0.0	4.0	4.9	5.5	10.5
	25	25	950	0.0	53.9	0.0	14.0	0.0	13.6	23.3	3.1	3.7
	50	50	900	0.0	0.0	14.0	9.5	0.0	4.7	6.6	2.0	1.6
IP partial anonymization	10	10	980	0.0	0.0	0.0	0.0	0.0	0.0	0.0	0.5	0.7
	25	25	950	0.0	0.0	0.0	0.0	0.0	0.0	0.0	0.0	0.0
	50	50	900	0.0	0.0	0.0	0.0	0.0	0.0	0.0	0.0	0.0
Date format change	10	10	980	32.7	58.5	58.1	0.0	0.0	29.9	29.2	60.0	54.8
	25	25	950	0.0	0.0	0.0	0.0	0.0	0.0	0.0	0.0	0.0
	50	50	980	0.0	0.0	0.0	0.0	0.0	0.0	0.0	0.0	0.0
Phone number format change	10	10	980	7.2	4.7	6.7	6.2	7.1	6.4	1.0	52.4	4.13
	25	25	950	1.9	0.9	0.0	0.0	12.9	3.2	5.5	8.2	10.8
	50	50	900	12.3	0.0	0.0	2.8	0.0	3.0	5.3	6.6	11.2

regular expressions from examples with genetic programming. In *Proceedings of the 14th GECCO conference companion*, pages 1477–1478. ACM, 2012.

[4] F. Brauer, R. Rieger, A. Mocan, and W. Barczynski. Enabling information extraction by inference of regular expressions from sample entities. In *Proceedings of the 20th ACM international conference on Information and knowledge management*, pages 1285–1294. ACM, 2011.

[5] A. Cetinkaya. Regular expression generation through grammatical evolution. In *Proceedings of the 2007 GECCO conference*, GECCO '07, pages 2643–2646, New York, NY, USA, 2007. ACM.

[6] K. Deb, A. Pratap, S. Agarwal, and T. Meyarivan. A fast and elitist multiobjective genetic algorithm: Nsga-ii. *Evolutionary Computation, IEEE Transactions on*, 6(2):182 –197, apr 2002.

[7] B. Dunay, F. Petry, and B. Buckles. Regular language induction with genetic programming. In *Evolutionary Computation, 1994. IEEE World Congress on Computational Intelligence., Proceedings of the First IEEE Conference on*, volume 1, pages 396–400. IEEE, 1994.

[8] J. Friedl. *Mastering Regular Expressions*. O'Reilly Media, Inc., 2006.

[9] A. González-Pardo, D. Barrero, D. Camacho, and M. R-Moreno. A case study on grammatical-based representation for regular expression evolution. In Y. Demazeau, F. Dignum, J. Corchado, J. Bajo, R. Corchuelo, E. Corchado, F. Fernández-Riverola, V. Julián, P. Pawlewski, and A. Campbell, editors, *Trends in Practical Applications of Agents and Multiagent Systems*, volume 71 of *Advances in Intelligent and Soft Computing*, pages 379–386. Springer Berlin / Heidelberg, 2010.

[10] E. Kinber. Learning regular expressions from representative examples and membership queries. *Grammatical Inference: Theoretical Results and Applications*, pages 94–108, 2010.

[11] Y. Li, R. Krishnamurthy, S. Raghavan, S. Vaithyanathan, and A. Arbor. Regular Expression Learning for Information Extraction. *Computational Linguistics*, (October):21–30, 2008.

[12] E. Medvet and A. Bartoli. Brand-related events detection, classification and summarization on twitter. In *Proceedings of the 2011 IEEE/WIC/ACM International Conferences on Web Intelligence and Intelligent Agent Technology - Volume 01*, WI-IAT '12. IEEE Computer Society, 2012, to appear.

[13] R. Miller and A. Marshall. Cluster-based find and replace. In *Proceedings of the SIGCHI conference on Human factors in computing systems*, pages 57–64. ACM, 2004.

[14] R. Miller and B. Myers. Lapis: Smart editing with text structure. In *CHI'02 extended abstracts on Human factors in computing systems*, pages 496–497. ACM, 2002.

[15] R. Miller and B. Myers. Multiple selections in smart text editing. In *Proceedings of the 7th international conference on Intelligent user interfaces*, pages 103–110. ACM, 2002.

[16] R. Miller, B. Myers, et al. Lightweight structured text processing. In *Proceedings of 1999 USENIX Annual Technical Conference*, pages 131–144, 1999.

[17] E. Minkov, R. C. Wang, and W. W. Cohen. Extracting personal names from email: applying named entity recognition to informal text. In *Proceedings of the conference on Human Language Technology and Empirical Methods in Natural Language Processing*, HLT '05, pages 443–450, Stroudsburg, PA, USA, 2005. Association for Computational Linguistics.

[18] B. Svingen. Learning Regular Languages Using Genetic Programming. In J. R. Koza, W. Banzhaf, K. Chellapilla, K. Deb, M. Dorigo, D. B. Fogel, M. H. Garzon, D. E. Goldberg, H. Iba, and R. Riolo, editors, *Genetic Programming 1998 Proceedings of the Third Annual Conference*, pages 374–376. Morgan Kaufmann, 1998.

[19] M. Tomita. Dynamic construction of finite automata from examples using hill-climbing. *Proceedings of the fourth annual cognitive science conference*, pages 105–108, 1982.

[20] T. Wu and W. Pottenger. A semi-supervised active learning algorithm for information extraction from textual data. *Journal of the American Society for Information Science and Technology*, 56(3):258–271, 2005.

Hybrid Discrete Harmony Search Algorithm for Scheduling Re-processing Problem in Remanufacturing

Kaizhou Gao
School of Electrical and Electronic Engineering
Nanyang Technological University, Singapore
kzgao@ntu.edu.sg

Ponnuthurai Nagaratnam Suganthan
School of Electrical and Electronic Engineering
Nanyang Technological University, Singapore
EPNSugan@ntu.edu.sg

Tayjin Chua
Singapore Institute of Manufacturing Technology, Singapore
tjchua@SIMTech.a-star.edu.sg

Tianxiang Cai
Singapore Institute of Manufacturing Technology, Singapore
txcai@SIMTech.a-star.edu.sg

Chinsoon Chong
Singapore Institute of Manufacturing Technology, Singapore
cschong@SIMTech.a-star.edu.sg

ABSTRACT

This paper proposes a hybrid discrete harmony search algorithm for solving the re-processing scheduling problem in pump remanufacturing. The process of pump remanufacturing and the scheduling problem of re-processing for pump subassembly are modeled. An experience based strategy is proposed for solving the unpredictability of subassembly re-processing time in remanufacturing. Hybrid discrete harmony search algorithm and local search are employed for scheduling re-processing of pump subassembly. The objectives of pump subassembly re-processing scheduling are minimization of the maximum completion time (makespan), and the mean of earliness and tardiness (E/T). These objectives are considered individually as well as together as a multi-objective problem. Computational experiments are carried out using real data from a pump remanufacturing enterprise. Computational results show that the objectives makespan and E/T can be optimized and the resulting schedules can be used in practice.

Categories and Subject Descriptors

J.1 [Administrative Data Processing]: Manufacturing;
I.2.8 [Problem Solving, Control Methods, and Search]: Scheduling

Keywords

Discrete harmony search; scheduling; remanufacturing; re-processing.

1. INTRODUCTION

The first one to define and discuss the remanufacturing problem was Lund [1]. Krupp [2, 3] perfected the concept of remanufacturing and predicted the future of remanufacturing engineering. In recent years, many researchers have focused on the remanufacturing scheduling problem. Guide [4] analyzed the capacity planning in remanufacturing environment. Guide [5] also examined the impact of product structure complexity on other managerial and operational decisions in a remanufacturing environment. Depuy [6] proposed a methodology for production planning within facilities involved in the remanufacturing of products. Teunter [7] developed a polynomial-time dynamic programming heuristic for the minimization of cost in manufacturing and remanufacturing engineering. Grubbstrom [8] proposed a model to analyze how labor costs, material costs and budget influence the optimal production decisions in remanufacture engineering. Denizel [9] considered the production planning when inputs have different and uncertain quality levels and discussed different decision variables in remanufacturing engineering.

Harmony search (HS) is a meta-heuristic method presented by Geem et al [10] for solving optimization problems. Compared to the earlier meta-heuristics, HS algorithm imposes fewer mathematical requirements. Numerical comparisons show that the process of evolution in harmony algorithm is faster than GA [11, 12]. During the past few years, HS algorithm has been successfully employed to solve problems, such as structural optimization [11], vehicle routing [13], water network design [14], multiple dam operation [15], Sudoku puzzle [16], blocking flow shop scheduling problem [17], lot-streaming flow shop scheduling problem [18], no-wait flow shop scheduling problem [19-20]. Following these successful applications of the HS algorithm, this paper develops a hybrid discrete harmony search algorithm (HDHS) to solve the pump re-processing scheduling problem in remanufacturing system with makespan, the mean of earliness and tardiness. The purpose is to obtain satisfying results for these two objectives individually and also together in a multi-objective framework. The rest of this paper is organized as follows: Section 2 introduces the scheduling problem of re-processing in pump remanufacturing system; Section 3 gives the details of the HDHS algorithm for the re-processing scheduling problem in remanufacturing; Section 4 is devoted to computational results obtained with real data from a remanufacturing enterprise. We conclude the paper in Section 5.

GECCO '13, July 06 – 10, 2013, Amsterdam, Netherlands

2. RE-PROCESSING SCHEDULING PROBLEM IN REMANUFACTURING

The process of pump remanufacturing is shown in Fig.1which is developed from the remanufacturing model in literature [4]. The process of re-processing operations for subassemblies is an important part in actual remanufacturing system. For pump remanufacturing, each pump has a set of subassemblies. After testing each subassembly, it can be classified into one of the three groups: (1) can be reused, (2) to be discarded or (3) to be re-processed. A subassembly of one pump can be re-processed by one machine or machine unit out of a set of candidate machines. Each subassembly of a pump must be re-processed only on one machine or machine unit at a time while each machine or machine unit can process only one subassembly at a time. It is difficult to obtain the disassembly or re-processing time for every received pump. For different pumps, the extent of the damage is also different. In addition, when the pumps were manufactured, they may not have integrated features for disassembly or re-processing. For different received products, the disassembly or re-processing time is different and not exactly known. The purpose of re-processing scheduling is to assign each subassembly of each pump to one machine or machine unit and sequence the subassembly on each machine or machine unit.

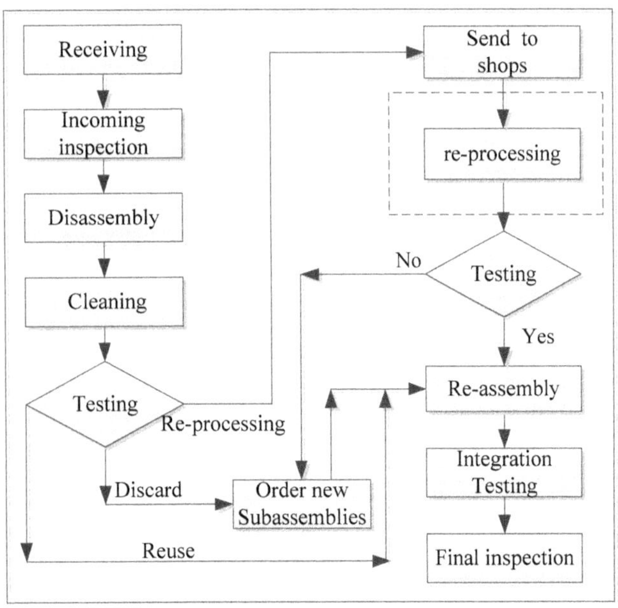

Figure 1. The flow chart of remanufacturing system for pump

Table 1 and Fig. 2 show an example of subassembly re-processing in pump remanufacturing system. In Table 1, there are two Volutes and three Impellers subassemblies. The same subassemblies may have different types and have different processing time on different machine or machine units. When the pumps are received, the same type subassembly may be of different quality. So, for one subassembly, its re-processing time on one machine or machine unit is uncertain. However, we can estimate the re-processing time in a range by experience. For example, the first operation of Volute 1 can be processed on Unit 1 or Unit 2 of Milling machine. The processing time is 6-8 minutes and 5-6 minutes respectively. The first operation of Volute 2 can only be processed by Unit 1 of Milling machine. The processing time is 3-4 minutes. For the three Impeller subassemblies, there are different selectable machines or machine units and the processing times on different machines or machine units are also in different ranges. Fig. 2 shows one scheduling solution of data in Table 1. In this solution, Unit 1 of Milling machine processes the first operation of volute 1, Impeller 2 and Impeller 3 while Unit 2 of Milling machine processes the first operation of Volute 1 and Impeller 1. Other operations of all subassemblies are processed by corresponding machines or machine units. In Fig. 2, the re-processing time of all subassemblies is taken as the upper bound of the corresponding re-processing time range in order to improve the robustness of scheduling process.

In manufacturing and remanufacturing, the makespan criterion has been considered by many researchers and enterprises [5, 7-9]. The due date related criterion may be important for many manufacturing and remanufacturing enterprises. The motivations for implementing optimized production schedules are to reduce inventories and improve response times and customer satisfaction. In production, earliness means more inventory while tardiness leads to un-satisfied customers. Hence, we consider minimizing the makespan and mean of earliness and tardiness of re-processing in pump remanufacturing. The makespan, mean of earliness and tardiness and multi-objective formulation of pump re-processing scheduling can be shown as follows:

Makespan, denoted by C_M , is the maximum completion time of all re-processing subassemblies.

$$\text{Min } C_M = \max_{1\le i\le n}\{c_i\}$$

Mean of earliness and tardiness, denoted by E/T , is the mean of ahead of or delay completion time of one subassembly compare to the due date d_i .

$$\text{Min } E/T = \frac{\sum_{i=1}^{n}|c_i - d_i|}{n}$$

where the c_i is the completion time of subassembly i and d_i is the due date of subassembly i. The multi-objective formulation can be described as follows:

$$\text{Min } f(x) = (C_M, E/T)\,,\ x \in \Omega\,,\ f(x) \in R^n$$

where x is the decision vector in space Ω and $f(x)$ is the objective vector.

Pareto domination states that solution A dominates solution B when all objectives in solution A are not worse than that in solution B and at least one objective in solution A is better than that in solution B. Solution A is an optimal solution in the Pareto sense if there is not any solution B which dominates A. Pareto optimal set is the collection of all Pareto optimal solutions and the corresponding image in the objective space is the Pareto front. In addition, an archive set (AS) is used to record the non-dominated solutions during the iterations. During the search process, the AS is updated iteratively.

Table 1. An example of subassembly processing in pump remanufacturing system

Sub-assembly	O 1 Milling unit1	Milling unit2	O 2 Metal building	O 3 Turning unit1	turning unit2
Volute					
1	6-8	5-6	6-8	6-7	3-5
2	3-4		9-10	5-6	3-4
Impeller					
1	5-7	5-6	6-8	4-6	2-4
2	1-4	5-8		2-3	4-5
3	5-7	4-6	2-3	11-12	7-9

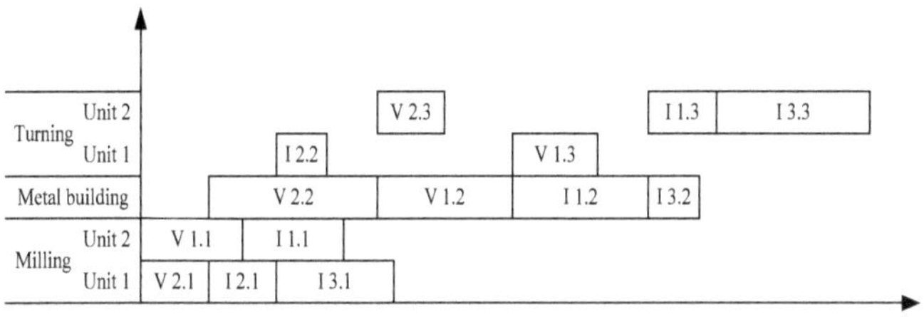

Figure 2. One solution's Gantt chart of the data in Table 1

3. HYBRID DISCRETE HARMONY SEARCH ALGORITHM

3.1 Harmony search algorithm

HS algorithm was proposed by Geem [10] who was inspired by the natural musical performance process whereby a musician searches for a better state of harmony. In HS algorithm, each solution is called a 'harmony'. And a harmony is an n dimensional solution vector. The computational procedure of basic HS algorithm can be summarized as follows:

Step 1: Initialization

The harmony vector or solution is generally represented as an n-dimensional real-valued vector $X = \{x(1), x(2), ..., x(n)\}$, where each dimension $x(k)$ denotes a decision variable of the optimization problem. In this step, the aims are to set parameters and fill the harmony memory (HM) with a population of initial harmonies. Parameters include the harmony memory size (HMS), the rate of choosing a value from the harmony memory (HMCR), the rate of choosing a neighboring value (PAR) and distance bandwidth (BW).

Step 2: Improvising a new harmony

The process to produce a harmony vector X_{new} is called improvisation. X_{new} is produced by applying three rules, i.e., a memory consideration, a pitch adjustment and a random selection.

Step 3: Update the HM

The HM will be updated if X_{new} is better than the worst harmony vector X_w in the HM. In this case, X_{new} will replace X_w and become a new member of the HM.

Step 4: Stopping condition

If a termination criterion is met, return the best harmony vector X_B in the HM; otherwise go to Step 2.

3.2 Hybrid Discrete Harmony search algorithm

3.2.1 Coding

A solution in HS algorithm consists of two vectors corresponding to the machine or machine unit assignment and operation scheduling sub-problems in pump subassembly re-processing scheduling problem. Using harmony search terminology, a harmony is therefore composed of two parts:

- Machine or machine unit assignment vector (hereafter called MA).
- Operation sequence vector (hereafter called OS).

Fig. 3 (a) illustrates a machine assignment vector while Fig. 3 (b) shows the corresponding operation sequence. In MA, each element represents the machine or machine unit selected for the corresponding operation. In OS, the same elements represent the different operations of the same subassembly [10]. For example, the first "1.3" in MA means that unit 3 of machine 1 is selected for operation $O_{1,1}$, and the second "4" in OS is the second operation of subassembly 4.

Therefore, in the hybrid discrete harmony search algorithm, a harmony includes two parts: one part is the machine or machine unit assignment which is the machine permutation and another is the operation sequence which is the subassembly permutation.

3.2.2 HM dynamic grouping

The small-sized HM works better than a large one for HS algorithm [21] and dynamic subpopulation can effectively balance the fast convergence and large diversity. Hence, hybrid discrete harmony search (HDHS) algorithm employs multiple small-sized dynamic sub-HMs. More specifically, the whole HM of HDHS algorithm is grouped into small-sized sub-HMs randomly in first iteration. Then, each sub-HM uses its own members to search for better solution. After this step, these sub-HMs form a whole HM which will be regrouped into small-sized sub-HMs randomly and the sub-HMs restart their search independently. This process, shown in Figure 4, is continued until the termination criterion is met.

3.2.3 Improvising a new harmony

In HDHS algorithm, each harmony includes machine or machine unit assignment and operation sequence. In MA part, each element represents a machine or machine unit selected for processing corresponding subassembly. From different harmonies, the elements at the same position are for the same subassembly in MA part while the elements at the same position may mean the different operations of different subassemblies in OS part. Therefore, we improve a new harmony for the machine assignment part and operation sequence part, respectively. The process of improvising the new MA part is shown in Fig. 5. The parameters HMCR and PAR affect the performance of HS algorithm.

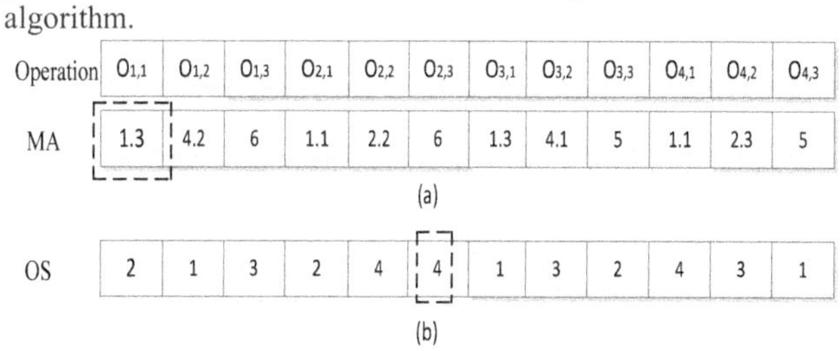

Figure 3. Illustration of MA and OS

According to the characteristic of FJSP and the coding strategies, we use crossover operators for the OS part of a new harmony. There are several crossover operators proposed during the past decades, such as partial-mapped crossover, order crossover, cycle crossover and so on [22]. In this study, we employ a crossover operator based on order crossover. We obtain two new harmonies from the current two harmonies. The employed crossover operator works for the OS part as follows:

Step1: Generate a random number *R* from 1 to number of jobs;

Step2: Copy the values from the OS part of Harmony1 to the corresponding positions in New Harmony1 where the values are less than or equal to *R*.

Step3: Copy the values from the OS part of Harmony2 to the corresponding positions in New Harmony2 where the values are larger than *R*.

Step4: From the OS part of Harmony2, copy the values which do not appear in New Harmony1 to the vacant positions in New Harmony1 from left to right according to the order of the sequence in Harmony2.

Step5: From the OS part of Harmony1, copy the values which do not appear in New Harmony2 to the vacant positions in New Harmony2 from left to right according to the order of the sequence in Harmony1.

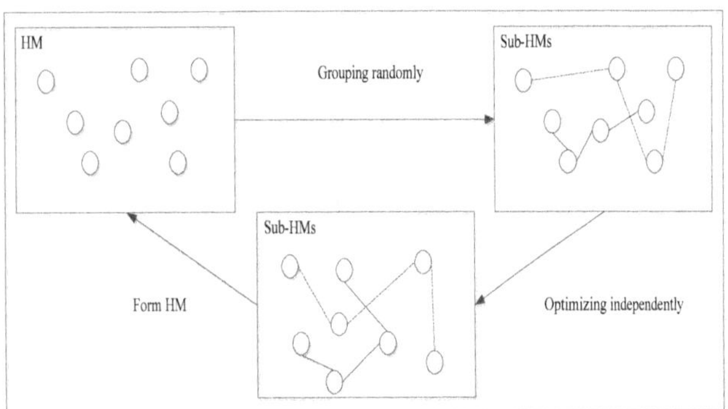

Figure 4. HM dynamic grouping

3.2.4 Local search

In this section, we propose a local search method for improving the performance of HDHS in the re-processing scheduling of pump remanufacturing. In the local search method, if the operation has two or more machines available for selection, we will assign a machine different from the current one. For the subassemblies in the same machine, we exchange their positions using insert and swap operators. The process of the local search algorithm is shown in Fig. 6.

```
Procedure: Improving the MA part for new harmony
  For each subassembly i
    For each operation j of subassembly i
      If Rand1(0-1)<HMCR                // memory consideration
        select a machine or machine unit k for Oi,j from the same position in harmony memory randomly
        If rand2(0-1)<PAR               // pitch adjustment
          If k is the last machine in the set of candidate machines
            select the first machine or machine unit k' in the set of candidate machines for Oi,j
          else
            select the next machine or machine unit knext of machine k in the set of candidate machines for Oi,j
        Endif
      Else
        randomly select a machine or machine unit kr from the set of dandidate machines for Oi,j
    Endfor
  Endfor
```

Figure 5. The Process of improvising MA of a new harmony

3.2.5 Computational procedure of HDHS

The flow of HDHS algorithm is shown in Fig. 7. After initialization, the HM is divided into several groups. Each small harmony group performs the optimization respectively. Each new harmony is subjected to the local search. When all groups complete the optimization process, all harmonies in HM are re-grouped for next optimization process. When the termination criterion is satisfied, the final solution and results are output.

```
Procedure: local search algorithm
  For each subassembly operation
    If two or more machines or machine unit can be selected for this operation
      Select a machine with least finally release time to replace current one;
    Endif
    Evaluation each solution and record the best one
  Endfor
  For each subassembly operation on the same machine
    exchange the position using insert and swap operators;
    Evaluation each solution and record the best one
  Endfor
```

Figure 6. Illustration of local search algorithm

4. SCHEDULING EXPERIMENT AND RESULTS

4.1 Experimental setup

HDHS algorithm was coded in C++.net and run on Intel 2.8GHz PC with 1 GB memory. The parameters HMS, HMCR and PAR affect the performance of HS algorithm. The HMS should be small. Omran and Mahdavi [21] suggested that it was generally better to use a large value of HMCR (i.e., >=0.9). A large PAR value enhances the local exploitation ability of the algorithm while a small PAR value enlarges the search area and diversity of the HS algorithm. In this paper, the parameters are fixed as follows: HMS=1000, HMCR=0.95 and PAR=0.5. The number of Sub-HM is 50.

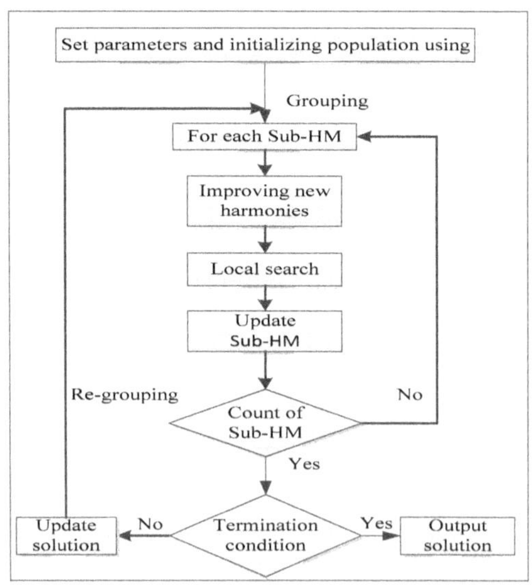

Figure 7. Flow chart of HDHS algorithm

Table 2 shows the subassemblies which will be re-processed. The subassemblies include two Volutes, three Impellers, two Shafts, three Shaft sleeves, four Case wear rings, three Impeller wear rings and three Impeller keys. The range of re-processing time of each subassembly is estimated in advance by experience. The corresponding range of re-processing time is also shown in Table 2. The first row of one subassembly is the lower bound of the re-processing time range while the second row is the upper bound of the range. For all subassemblies, the upper bound of the re-processing time range is used in this paper. If the processing time is smaller than the upper bound of the range, the time gap can be considered as the robustness of scheduling system in actual processing.

4.2 Scheduling results

In this section, the maximum completion time (makespan), the mean of earliness and tardiness, and Pareto-based multi-objective criterions are considered. The size of this re-processing problem is 20 subassemblies, 5 machines with 12 machine units, and 91 operations. Our purpose is to obtain the satisfactory scheduling solutions for both criteria.

Table 2. The ranges of re-processing times of all subassemblies

Subassembly	Operation 1			Operation 2		Operation 3			Operation 4		Operation 5	
	Milling			Metal		Turning			Welding		coating subcon	
	1	2	3	building1	2	1	2	3	1	2	1	2
Volute												
1	7	4	6	8	7	4	4		5	8	3	3
	8	6	8	10	8	6	5		6	10	5	6
2	8	7	9	10	7		6	7		6	4	1
	11	10	12	12	11		8	9		9	6	4
3	2	2		6	3	6	5	5	8	7	2	
	4	3		9	6	7	6	7	10	8	4	
Impeller												
1	5	5		7	6	7	5	5			6	5
	7	8		8	7	9	8	6			7	6
2		4	7		6	3	5	5			4	5
		6	9		7	5	7	6			5	6
3	6		5	4		9		9			2	4
	7		6	6		12		11			3	5
Shaft												
1	5	4			7		5	6	1	3	2	2
	6	5			9		6	8	2	4	3	3
2		5	6		8	5	7		2	2	1	1
		7	7		10	6	9		3	3	3	3
Shaft sleeve												
1		5					5	6	2		3	4
		6					7	7	3		4	5
2	4		6	4	5	6	5		3		3	3
	6		7	5	6	7	7		5		4	5
Case wear ring												
1		7	5	7	10	4		3		4	1	1
		8	7	8	12	6		5		5	2	2
2		6	6	8	8		5	2	1	3	4	4
		7	7	10	9		6	4	3	4	5	6
3		2	5	5			3	2	4	5	7	5
		4	7	7			4	3	5	6	8	7
4		4	2		9	3			2	3	4	5
		5	3		11	4			4	4	6	6
Impeller wear ring												
1	3	1				6		6			3	4
	4	2				8		7			4	5
2	3		2			4	5	8			2	3
	4		3			6	6	9			3	5
3		3					5	5			3	
		4					7	6			4	
Impeller key												
1	5	4		5	3	3	5		7	5	3	6
	6	5		6	5	4	6		8	6	4	7
2		4	4	3	6		4	6	5	4		6
		5	5	4	7		5	8	7	6		7
3		2	4	5	6	5	6		3	4		4
		4	5	6	7	6	7		5	5		5

4.2.1 Makespan criterion

For the subassemblies and corresponding re-processing times in Table 2, the value of makespan with iteration times is shown in Fig. 8. It can be seen from Fig. 8 that HDHS algorithm can obtain the best result of makespan when the iteration count is 115. The HDHS algorithm has a good convergence for makespan criterion. The scheduling result is satisfactory and the value of the best makespan is 80.

Table 3 shows a comparison of completion time of all subassemblies. The first column is the number of subassemblies. The second column is the completion time of all subassemblies with best makespan (80). Each operation of all subassemblies is assigned to one machine or machine unit 10 times randomly. The third column is the average completion time of each subassembly in 10 runs. The last column shows the improvement of subassembly complete time. The values are calculated as follows:

$$I_i = \frac{C_i^{best} - ac_i^{random}}{ac_i^{random}}$$

where I_i is the value of improvement of subassembly i, C_i^{best} is the complete time of subassembly i with best makespan (80), ac_i^{random} is the average completion of subassembly i in 10 runs random assignments. It can be easily seen from Table 3 that the completion times of all subassemblies are improved. The values of improvement is from 0.049 to 0.679 in which 0.049 is the improvement value of subassembly Shaft 2 and 0.679 is the improvement value of subassembly Impeller key 2. After scheduling, the average of completion time of all subassemblies is 59 while the corresponding value for randomized schedules is 90. The improvement for average completion time is 0.336. The makespan after scheduling is 80 while the average makespan for randomized schedules is 123. The improvement for makespan is 0.350.

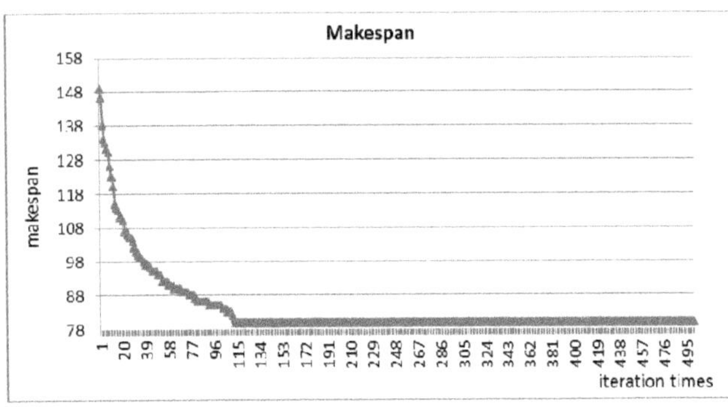

Figure 8. The value of makespan with iteration

4.2.2 E/T scheduling results

The due date related criterion may be important for many manufacturing and remanufacturing enterprises. The purposes of most enterprises are to reduce inventories and improve response times and customer satisfaction. Earliness means more inventory while tardiness leads to un-satisfied customers. Hence, we discuss mean of earliness and tardiness criterion of re-processing scheduling in this section.

The due dates of all subassemblies are shown in Table 4. The due date is based on the processing time of each operation on each machine or machine unit. So, different subassemblies have different due date. The value of E/T with iteration times is shown in Fig. 9. It can be seen from Fig. 9 that our HDHS algorithm achieves the best E/T when the iteration count is 361. The HDHS algorithm also has a good convergence for E/T criterion. Because the due date of all subassemblies is based on processing time on machine or machine unit and is not a single fixed time for the whole project. Although the value of the best E/T is 14 and is not approximately 0, the scheduling result is satisfactory. The Gantt chart of all subassemblies is shown in Fig. 10 when the value of E/T is 14.

Table 3. Comparison of complete time of all subassemblies

subassembly	complete time by HDHS	Ave complete time by random	improving
Volute 1	37	91	-0.592
2	76	95	-0.203
3	48	100	-0.521
Impeller 1	67	72	-0.071
2	38	91	-0.582
3	42	80	-0.475
Shaft 1	70	84	-0.162
2	80	84	-0.049
Shaft sleeve 1	52	88	-0.408
2	75	97	-0.229
Case wear ring 1	80	95	-0.154
2	62	78	-0.209
3	33	98	-0.665
4	54	96	-0.439
Impeller wear ring 1	67	81	-0.168
2	78	87	-0.108
3	56	88	-0.363
Impeller key 1	60	96	-0.376
2	30	93	-0.679
3	72	99	-0.269
Average	59	90	-0.336
Makespan	80	123	-0.350

4.2.3 Pareto-based multi-objective scheduling

For multi-objective optimization, the purpose is to obtain more non-dominated solutions that satisfy multiple objectives with good proximity and diversity [23] with respect to the Pareto front.

Table 5 shows 8 Pareto-based non-dominated solutions for the re-processing scheduling problem in Table 2. It can be seen from Table 2 that the best value of makespan (80) and the best value of E/T (14) are included in the non-dominated solutions Non-D-S1 and Non-D-S8. Fig. 11 shows 8 Pareto-based non-dominated solutions and 20 multi-objective solutions generated randomly. It is clear that the scheduling result is satisfactory. The Pareto-based non-dominated solutions are much better than solutions generated randomly. For real-world problems, ideal Pareto optimal solutions may not be known.

Hence, the re-processing scheduling problem of pump remanufacturing in Table 2 can be solved with different single objective criteria and Pareto-based multi-objective criteria. The results for all these cases are satisfactory.

Table 4. The due dates of all subassemblies

subassembly	due date	subassembly	due date
Volute 1	51	Case wear ring 1	43
2	66	2	43
3	43	3	40
Impeller 1	40	4	43
2	37	Impeller wear ring 1	21
3	40	2	21
Shaft 1	40	3	21
2	45	Impeller key 1	40
Shaft sleeve 1	30	2	43
2	40	3	39

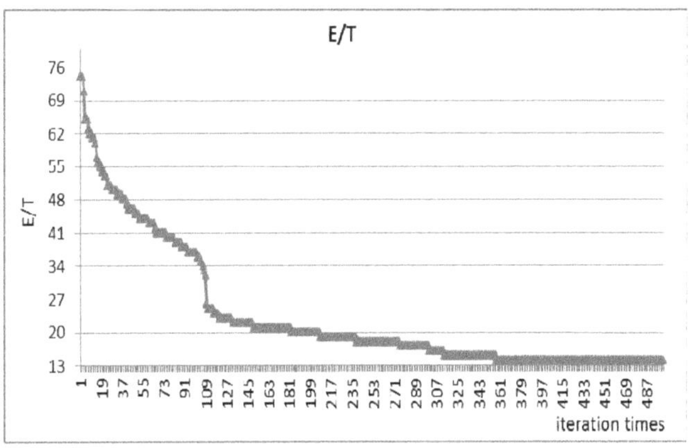

Figure 9. The value of E/T with iteration

Table 5. Pareto-based non-dominated solutions

Multi-objective	Non-D-S1	Non-D-S2	Non-D-S3	Non-D-S4
Makespan	90	87	86	85
E/T	14	15	16	17
	Non-D-S5	Non-D-S6	Non-D-S7	Non-D-S8
Makespan	83	82	81	80
E/T	18	19	32	43

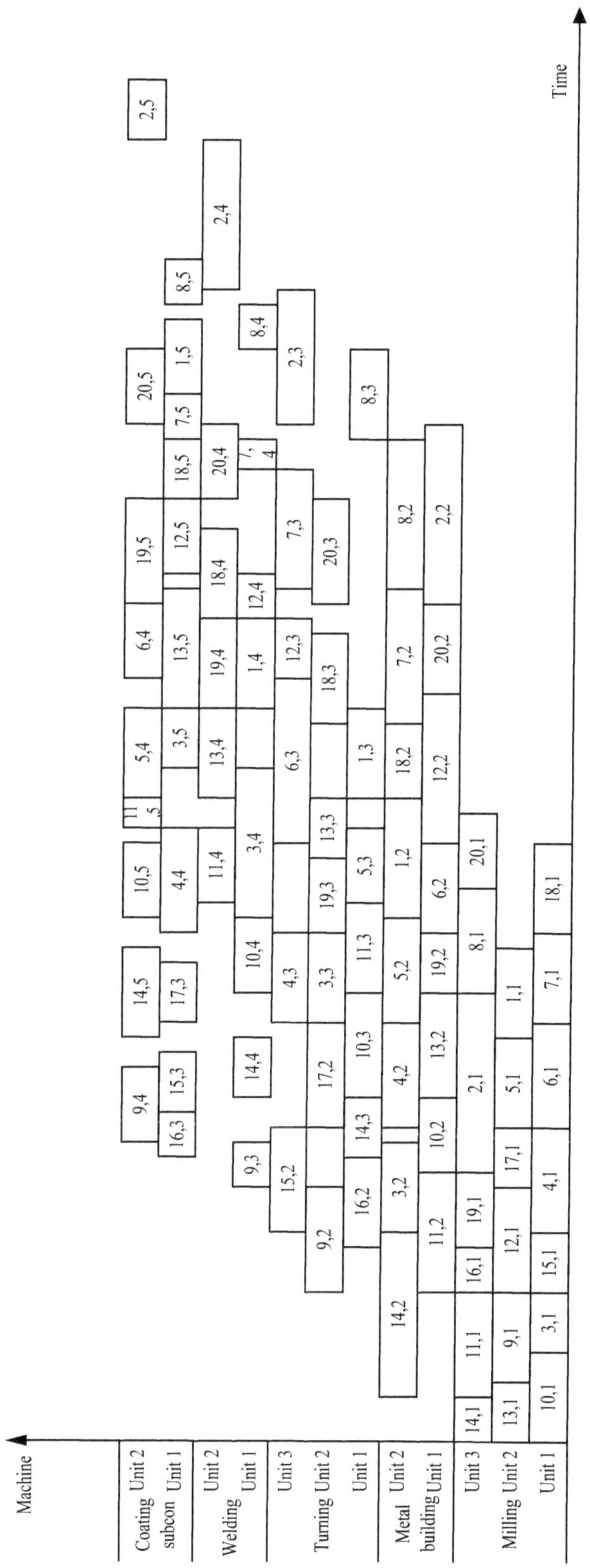

Figure 10. The Gantt chart with E/T=14

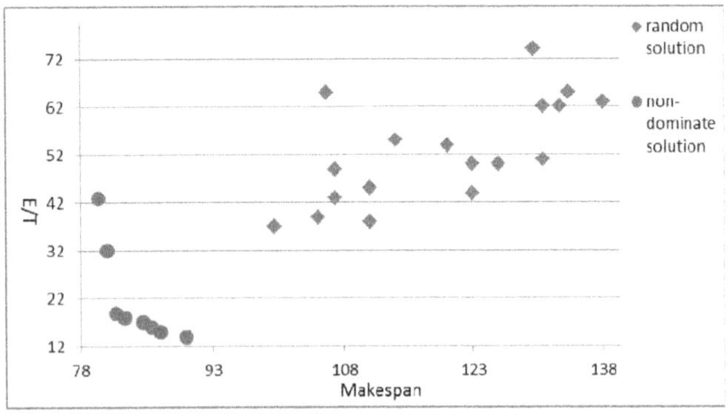

Figure 11. Pareto-based non-dominated solutions

5. Conclusions

This paper investigates the re-processing scheduling problem in a pump remanufacturing system. Pump remanufacturing and the scheduling problem of re-processing for pump subassembly are modeled. Considering the processing time of each subassembly is unpredictable, the processing time of subassembly is estimated in a range by experience. To increase the robustness of scheduling, the upper bound of the time range is considered as the processing time. Makespan, mean of earliness and tardiness, both criteria are considered in this paper. The scheduling results are satisfactory for all three cases.

Our future research will improve the algorithm to be able to handle the dynamic re-processing scheduling problem with unpredictable processing time in remanufacturing system. This approach will be able adapt the schedule if a particular re-processing takes too much time or too less time. Other heuristics and intelligence algorithms will also be employed for solving scheduling problem in remanufacturing system and they will be compared with HDHS. We will also investigate other related problems such as large-scale scheduling problems, man power scheduling problem, in the context of remanufacturing.

References

[1] LUND, R. I. 1984, Remanufacturing. *Technology Review*, 87(2), 18-23.

[2] KRUPP, J. A. 1993, Structuring bills of material for automotive remanufacturing. *Production and Inventory Management Journal*, 34(4), 46-52.

[3] KRUPP, J. A. 1992, Core obsolescence forecasting in remanufacturing. *Production and Inventory Management Journal*, 33(2), 12-17.

[4] GUIDE JR, V.D.R., SRIVASTAVA, R. and SPENCER, M.S. 1997, An evaluation of capacity planning techniques in a remanufacturing environment. *International Journal of Production Research*, 35:1, 67-82.

[5] GUIDE JR, V. D. R., SRIVASTAVA, R. and KRAUS, M. E. 1997, Product structure complexity and scheduling of operations in recoverable manufacturing, *International Journal of Production Research*, 35: 11, 3179-3200.

[6] DePuy, G. W., Usher, J. S., Walker, R. L. and Taylor, G. D. 2007, Production planning for remanufactured products, *Production Planning & Control*, 18: 7, 573-583.

[7] Teunter, Ruud H. , Bayindir, Z. Pelin and Heuvel, Wilco Van Den 2006, Dynamic lot sizing with product returns and remanufacturing, *International Journal of Production Research*, 44: 20, 4377-4400.

[8] Grubbström, R. W. and Tang 2006, O. Optimal production opportunities in a remanufacturing system, *International Journal of Production Research*, 44: 18, 3953-3966.

[9] Meltem, Denizel, Mark Ferguson and Gilban "Gil"C. Souza 2010. Multi-period remanufacturing planning with uncertain quality of inputs. *IEEE transactions on engineering management*, vol. 57, No. 3, 394-404.

[10] Geem ZW, Kim JH, Loganathan GV 2001, A new heuristic optimization algorithm: harmony search. Simulation, 76(2): 60–68.

[11] Lee KS, Geem ZW, Lee SH, Bae KW 2005, The harmony search heuristic algorithm for discrete structural optimization. Eng. Optimiz, 37(7): 663–684.

[12] Mahdavi M, Fesanghary M, Damangir E 2007, An improved harmony search algorithm for solving optimization problems. Appl Math and Comput, 188(2): 1567–1579.

[13] Geem ZW, Lee KS, Park Y 2005, Application of harmony search to vehicle routing. Am J Appl. Sci, 2(12): 1552–1557.

[14] Geem ZW 2006, Optimal cost design of water distribution networks using harmony search. Eng. Optimiz, 38(3): 259–280.

[15] Geem ZW 2007, Optimal scheduling of multiple dam system using harmony search algorithm. LNCS, 4507:316–323.

[16] Geem ZW 2007, Harmony search algorithm for solving Sudoku. LNAI, 4692: 371–378.

[17] Wang L, Pan QK, Tasgetiren MF, Minimizing the total flow time in a flow shop with blocking by using hybrid harmony search algorithms. Expert Syst. Appl, 37(12): 7929-7936. (2010)

[18] Pan QK, Suganthan PN, Liang JJ, Tasgetiren MF, A local-best harmony search algorithm with dynamic sub-harmony memories for lot-streaming flow shop scheduling problem. Expert Syst. Appl, 38(4): 3252-3259. (2011)

[19] Gao KZ, Pan QK, Li JQ Discrete harmony search algorithm for the no-wait flow shop scheduling problem with total flow time criterion. Int. J Adv. Manuf. Technol, 56: 683-692. (2011),

[20] Gao KZ, Pan Q.K, Li JQ etc al, A hybrid harmony search algorithm for the no-wait flow shop scheduling problems, Asia-Pacific J of Operational research, 29(2): 1250012 (23pages). (2012)

[21] M.G.H. Omran,, M. Mahdavi 2008, Global-best harmony search, Applied Mathematics and Computation, 198, 643–656.

[22] J. Gao, L. Sun, M. Gen 2008, A hybrid genetic and variable neighborhood descent algorithm for flexible job shop scheduling problems, Computers and Operations Research, 35, 2892–2907.

[23] L. Wang, G. Zhou, Y. Xu, M. Liu 2012. An enhanced Pareto-based artificial bee colony algorithm for the multi-objective flexible job shop scheduling, International Journal of Advanced Manufacturing Technology, 60, 1111-1123.

Stochastic Volatility Modeling with Computational Intelligence Particle Filters

Ayub Hanif
Intelligent Systems Group
University College London
Gower Street, London, WC1E 6BT
ayub.hanif@ucl.ac.uk

Robert E. Smith
Intelligent Systems Group
University College London
Gower Street, London, WC1E 6BT
robert.elliott.smith@gmail.com

ABSTRACT

Stochastic volatility estimation is an important task for correctly pricing derivatives in mathematical finance. Such derivatives are used by varying types of market participant as either hedging tools or for bespoke market exposure. We evaluate our adaptive path particle filter, a recombinatory evolutionary algorithm based on the generation gap concept from evolutionary computation, for stochastic volatility estimation of three real financial asset time series. We calibrate the Heston stochastic volatility model employing a Markov-chain Monte Carlo, enabling us to understand the latent stochastic volatility process and parameters. In our experiments we find the adaptive path particle filter to be superior to the standard sequential importance resampling particle filter, the Markov-chain Monte Carlo particle filter and the particle learning particle filter. We present a detailed analysis of the results and suggest directions for future research.

Categories and Subject Descriptors

G.3 [**Probability and Statistics**]: Probabilistic algorithms - *sequential Monte Carlo*; J.4. [**Social and Behavioral Sciences**]: Economics

General Terms

Algorithms, economics

Keywords

Nonlinear filters, sequential Monte Carlos, particle filters, recursive Bayesian estimation, evolutionary computation, stochastic volatility estimation, Heston model.

1. INTRODUCTION

Common derivative securities pricing involves assumptions of constant volatility, either as a known constant or a known deterministic function. Empirically, such assumptions are incorrect and lead to mispricing which in turn offers arbitrage opportunities to sophisticated market participants. Various measures of volatility show it to be unstable and variable leading to stochastic volatility models. These models address and allay the inconsistencies of common pricing measures. As the volatility measure of an underlying security is latent, estimation is a non-trivial undertaking. In this paper we are aiming to correctly model the volatility process of an underlying security through the calibration of a common stochastic volatility model.

Sequential Monte Carlo methods (commonly known as particle filters) are extensively applied to the stochastic volatility estimation problem. Particle filters are population based metaheuristics. The synergy between their statistical foundations and computational intelligence (evolutionary computation (EC) and genetic algorithms) has led to a number of ever-powerful computational intelligence particle filters. Kwok, et al. [23] propose a hybrid particle filter which includes an evolutionary stochastic universal sampling step. Simulated on the gambler's ruin problem they find their particle filter to outperform traditional particle filters. Han, et al. [18] embed an immune genetic algorithm into the traditional particle filter which effectively controls diversity as tested on the univariate non-stationary growth model from economics. Uosaki, et al. [34] combine evolutionary computation into their evolutionary strategies particle filter, which is used for fault detection. Duan & Cai [11] build an evolutionary particle filter for robust simultaneous localization and map building tasks of autonomous mobile robots. Hanif & Smith [20] employed an evolutionary computation particle filter to simulated univariate log-stochastic volatility series, where it excelled and outperformed contemporary and state-of-the-art particle filters.

In this paper, we apply sequential Monte Carlo methods to the stochastic volatility estimation problem. We compare our computational intelligence particle filter to contemporary filters across a number of real asset time series and find our method provides enhanced estimation accuracy.

2. BAYESIAN REASONING

To facilitate probabilistic reasoning over time we will be adopting state space representations under a Bayesian framework. Stochastic models overcome shortcomings of deterministic models and enable postulation of ideas encompassing uncertainty. A state space model of a time series $\{\mathbf{y}_t : t = 1, 2, ...\}$ is composed of two equations: the state equation and the observation equation. The observation equation relates the observed data $\{\mathbf{y}_t\}$ to the latent states $\{\mathbf{x}_t : t = 1, 2, ...\}$.

GECCO'13, July 6–10, 2013, Amsterdam, The Netherlands.

Consider the discrete time estimation problem with the system model

$$\mathbf{y}_t = h_t(\mathbf{x}_t, \mathbf{v}_t) \quad (1)$$

$$\mathbf{x}_{t+1} = f_t(\mathbf{x}_t, \mathbf{w}_t) \quad (2)$$

in which we represent the observation vector at time t by $\mathbf{y}_t \in \mathbb{R}^p$, which satisfies (1) where $h_t : \mathbb{R}^n \times \mathbb{R}^r \to \mathbb{R}^p$ is the observation function and $\mathbf{v}_t \in \mathbb{R}^r$ is the state error term of which the known distribution is independent of both system noise and time. Similarly, we represent the state vector at time t by $\mathbf{x}_t \in \mathbb{R}^n$, which satisfies (2) where $f_t : \mathbb{R}^n \times \mathbb{R}^m \to \mathbb{R}^n$ is the system transition function and $\mathbf{w}_t$ is an error term whose known distribution is temporally independent.

There are very few system models for which an analytic solution is available. Consider the linear Gaussian model

$$\mathbf{Y}_t = H_t\mathbf{X}_t + \mathbf{W}_t \quad (3)$$

$$\mathbf{X}_{t+1} = F_t\mathbf{X}_t + \mathbf{V}_t \quad (4)$$

where (3) is the measurement equation with $\{\mathbf{W}_t\} \sim \mathcal{N}(\mathbf{0}, R_t)$ observation errors; and (4) is the state equation with $\{\mathbf{V}_t\} \sim \mathcal{N}(\mathbf{0}, Q_t)$ state description errors. We assume that the observation errors and state errors are uncorrelated. That is $\forall s, \forall t : \mathbb{E}[\mathbf{W}_s\mathbf{V}_t] = 0$. Finally, the initial state $\mathbf{X}_0$ is assumed to be uncorrelated with all errors $\{\mathbf{V}_t\}$ and $\{\mathbf{W}_t\}$.

The principal foundation of stochastic filtering lies in recursive Bayesian estimation where we are essentially trying to compute the joint posterior. This is an inverse statistical problem: you want to find inputs as you are given outputs [8]. There are two key assumptions in deriving the recursive Bayesian filter: (i) that the state process follows a first-order Markov process

$$(\mathbf{x}_n|\mathbf{x}_{0:n-1}, \mathbf{y}_{0:n-1}) = p(\mathbf{x}_n|\mathbf{x}_{n-1})$$

and (ii) that the observations and states are independent

$$(\mathbf{y}_n|\mathbf{x}_{0:n-1}, \mathbf{y}_{0:n-1}) = p(\mathbf{y}_n|\mathbf{x}_n).$$

For simplicity, we shall denote $\mathcal{Y}_n$ as the set of observations $\mathbf{y}_{0:n} := \{\mathbf{y}_0, ..., \mathbf{y}_n\}$ and $p(\mathbf{x}_n|\mathcal{Y}_n)$ as the conditional pdf of $\mathbf{x}_n$. From Bayes rule we have

$$p(\mathbf{x}_n|\mathcal{Y}_n) = \frac{p(\mathbf{y}_n|\mathbf{x}_n)p(\mathbf{x}_n|\mathcal{Y}_{n-1})}{p(\mathbf{y}_n|\mathcal{Y}_{n-1})}, \quad (5)$$

the calculation and or approximation of which is the base of Bayesian filtering and inference.

3. SEQUENTIAL MONTE CARLO METHODS

There are two approaches to obtain the posterior distribution of concern defined in (5): parametric Gaussian approximation or non-parametric approximation using Monte Carlo techniques [32]. Though they are computationally efficient, parametric techniques such as the Kalman filter and its extensions do not reliably compute states and cannot be used to learn stochastic problems where the underlying process is non-linear and non-Gaussian. Some applications of Kalman filtering techniques are highlighted by [2] though, conversely, they highlight difficulties in calculating closed-form solutions to distribution approximations and propose application of numerical methods to overcome these difficulties.

Sequential Monte Carlo approximation, a numerical method, of optimal estimation problems in non-linear non-Gaussian settings is commonly performed using particle methods [8, 17, 22, 27, 6, 5, 9, 29]. The main advantage of these methods is that they do not rely on any local linearization or abstract functional approximation. This is at the cost of increased computational expense though given breakthroughs in computing technology and the related decline in processing costs, this is not considered a barrier except in extreme circumstances.

Monte Carlo approximation using particle methods calculates the expectation of the pdf by importance sampling (IS) [8]. The state space is partitioned, into which particles are filled with respect to some probability measure. The higher this measure the denser the particle concentration. The state space evolves temporally and the particle system evolves around this. Specifically, from (5) and [32]

$$p(x_t|\mathbf{y}_{0:t}) = \frac{p(y_t|x_t)p(x_t|\mathbf{y}_{0:t-1})}{p(y_t|\mathbf{y}_{0:t-1})}$$

where $p(x_t|\mathbf{y}_{0:t})$ is the state posterior (filtering distribution), $p(y_t|x_t)$ is the likelihood, $p(x_t|\mathbf{y}_{0:t-1})$ is the state prior (predictive distribution) and the denominator $p(y_t|\mathbf{y}_{0:t-1})$ is the evidence. The state prior is defined by

$$p(x_t|\mathbf{y}_{0:t-1}) = \int p(x_t|x_{t-1}, \mathbf{y}_{0:t-1})p(x_{t-1}|\mathbf{y}_{0:t-1})dx_{t-1}$$

where $p(x_t|x_{t-1}, \mathbf{y}_{0:t-1})$ is the transition density and $p(x_{t-1}|\mathbf{y}_{0:t-1})$ is the previous filtering distribution.

We approximate the state posterior by $f(x_t)$ with i samples of $x_t^{(i)}$. To find the mean $\mathbb{E}[f(x_t)]$ of the state posterior $p(x_t|\mathbf{y}_{0:t})$ at t, we generate the state samples $x_t^{(i)} \sim p(x_t|\mathbf{y}_{0:t})$. Though theoretically plausible, empirically we are unable to observe and sample directly from the state posterior. We replace the state posterior by the proposal state distribution (importance distribution) π which is proportional to the true posterior at every point $\pi(x_t|\mathbf{y}_{0:t}) \propto p(x_t|\mathbf{y}_{0:t})$. We are thus able to sample sequentially i.i.d. draws from $\pi(x_t|\mathbf{y}_{0:t})$ giving us

$$\mathbb{E}[f(x_t)] = \int f(x_t)\frac{p(x_t|\mathbf{y}_{0:t})}{\pi(x_t|\mathbf{y}_{0:t})}\pi(x_t|\mathbf{y}_{0:t})dx_t$$
$$\approx \frac{\sum_{i=1}^{N} f(x_t^{(i)})w_t^{(i)}}{\sum_{i=1}^{N} w_t^{(i)}}.$$

When increasing the number of draws N this average converges asymptotically to the expectation of the true posterior according to the central limit theorem [14]. This convergence is the primary advantage of sequential Monte Carlo methods as they provide asymptotically consistent estimates of the true distribution $p(x_t|\mathbf{y}_{0:t})$ [10].

IS allows us to sample from complex highly-dimensional distributions though exhibits linear increases in complexity upon each subsequent draw [10]. To admit fixed computational complexity we can use sequential importance sampling (SIS). The SIS approach is sensitive to the choice for the proposal density, with typical choices being the transition probability of states [22, 13]. This choice minimizes the variance of weights critical to the asymptotic convergence of the algorithm. However, SIS suffers from a debilitating problem: the variance of the estimates increases exponentially with n leading to fewer and fewer non-zero importance weights in a problem known as weight degeneracy. To alleviate the issue, states are resampled to retain the most pertinent contributors in a method known as sequential importance resampling

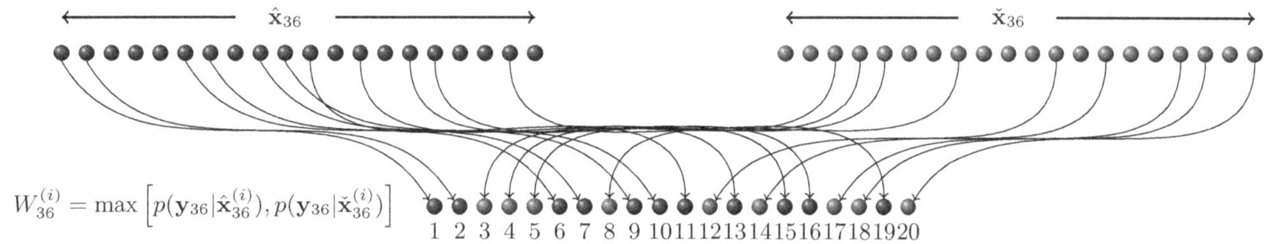

Figure 1: APPF weight update fitness assessment through inter-generational competition for $N = 20$ at $t = 36$

(SIR - also referred to as the particle filter (PF)). We provide the SIR algorithm using the transition prior as the proposal distribution [8] in Table 4, in Appendix A.

SIR attempts to address weight degeneracy by replacing particles with high weight with many particles with high inter-particle correlation [17, 8]. Frequent resampling leads to the marginal distribution $\hat{p}(\mathbf{x}_{0:t}|\mathbf{y}_{0:n})$ collapsing onto a few or single unique particle(s) in a problem similar to weight degeneracy. The samples are impoverished and resampling has not helped.

There are a number of schemes proposed to address weight degeneracy and sample impoverishment simultaneously. The Markov-chain Monte Carlo particle filter (MCMC-PF) attempts to reduce degeneracy by jittering particle locations, using Metropolis-Hastings to accept moves, whilst the particle learning particle filter (PLA) performs an MCMC after every 50 iterations. Details of the MCMC step embedded into the MCMC-PF and applied in the PLA every 50 iterations can be found in Table 5, in Appendix B..

The adaptive path particle filter (APPF) uses techniques from computational intelligence to alleviate weight degeneracy and sample impoverishment together [20]. It maintains diversity through embedding a generation based adaptive path switching step into the particle filter weight update, making use of previously discarded particles if their discriminatory power is higher than the current particle set. The complete APPF algorithm is detailed in Table 1.

Upon closer inspection we can see that the APPF is essentially a recombinatory evolutionary algorithm. In the example given in Figure 1 we have $N = 20$ particles: at $t = 36$ upon evaluation of the fitness function select 11 particles from the current importance samples $\hat{\mathbf{x}}_{36}$ (marked as the blue particles) and 9 particles from importance samples based on the previously resampled out set $\check{\mathbf{x}}_{36}$ (marked as the red particles). For example we can see $W_{36}^{(1)}$ is assigned as $\hat{\mathbf{x}}_{36}^{(1)}$, similarly $W_{36}^{(8)}$ is assigned as $\check{\mathbf{x}}_{36}^{(8)}$. As can be seen in the resultant particle set W_{36} we are leveraging the fittest particles amongst and across the two generations.

At the level of the representation of the probability distribution (the primary output of a sequential Monte Carlo method), APPF is using a fitness-based recombination of a past representation with a current representation. In this sense, we believe the algorithm draws upon the body of EC experience and theory. Admittedly, this is in essence a EC algorithm with a population of size 2. A natural extension (which would make APPF appear to be a more traditional EC algorithm) would be the maintenance and fitness-based recombination of several past iterations particles (and thus a larger population). However, note that due to the nature of the PF process itself - that of the state process being a

Table 1: APPF Algorithm

1. Initialization - forming the initial population: for $i = 1, ..., N_p$, sample

$$\boldsymbol{x}_0^{(i)} \sim p(\boldsymbol{x}_0)$$
$$\boldsymbol{\psi}_0^{(i)} \sim p(\boldsymbol{x}_0)$$

with weights $W_0^{(i)} = \frac{1}{N_p}$.

For $t \geq 1$

2. Importance sampling - selection: for $i = 1, ..., N_p$, draw samples

$$\hat{\mathbf{x}}_t^{(i)} \sim p(\mathbf{x}_t|\mathbf{x}_{t-1}^{(i)})$$
set $$\hat{\mathbf{x}}_{0:t}^{(i)} = \{\mathbf{x}_{0:t-1}^{(i)}, \hat{\mathbf{x}}_t^{(i)}\}$$
and draw $$\check{\mathbf{x}}_t^{(i)} \sim p(\mathbf{x}_t|\boldsymbol{\psi}_{t-1}^{(i)})$$
set $$\check{\mathbf{x}}_{0:t}^{(i)} = \{\mathbf{x}_{0:t-1}^{(i)}, \check{\mathbf{x}}_t^{(i)}\}$$

3. Weight update: assess fitness

$$W_t^{(i)} = \max\left[p(\mathbf{y}_t|\hat{\mathbf{x}}_t^{(i)}), p(\mathbf{y}_t|\check{\mathbf{x}}_t^{(i)})\right]$$

evaluate - recombination through inter-generational competition:

if $p(\mathbf{y}_t|\check{\mathbf{x}}_t^{(i)}) > p(\mathbf{y}_t|\hat{\mathbf{x}}_t^{(i)})$ **then**
$\hat{\mathbf{x}}_t^{(i)} = \boldsymbol{\psi}_t^{(i)}$
end if

4. Normalize weights:

$$\tilde{W}_t^{(i)} = \frac{W_t^{(i)}}{\sum_{j=1}^{N_p} W_t^{(j)}}$$

5. Commit (generation gap) pre-resample set of particles to memory:

$$\{\boldsymbol{\psi}_t^{(i)}\} = \{\hat{\mathbf{x}}_t^{(i)}\}$$

6. Resampling: Generate N_p new particles $\mathbf{x}_t^{(i)}$ from the set $\{\hat{\mathbf{x}}_t^{(i)}\}$ according to importance weights $\tilde{W}_t^{(i)}$.

7. Repeat from importance sampling step 2.

Markov process by assumption (i) in Section 2, the immediate previous particle set contains information about those previous representations explicitly. In this sense, the recombination of only these two sets of particles in APPF contains the implicit schema average fitness information upon which much of EC theory is based [16]. Thus, we feel that the dramatic improvements in performance the APPF offers (as shown in the following sections, and in other applications [19]) is directly related to EC theory and practice, and can be built on further using EC ideas.

4. STOCHASTIC VOLATILITY ESTIMATION PROBLEM

Understanding the dynamics of the volatility process in tandem with the dynamics of the underlying asset in the same timescale enable us to measure the stochastic volatility process. The most popular stochastic volatility model is the Heston model which uses both square-root and Ornstein-Uhlenbeck dynamics. We shall proceed to describe and estimate this model. Recent reformulations of the original Fourier integrals of the Heston stochastic volatility model [21] have led to numerically stable and efficient computations of derivative prices [1, 25, 26, 7, 24]. The Heston model to estimate stochastic volatility is defined by the coupled two-dimensional stochastic differential equation:

$$\mathrm{d}X(t)/X(t) = \sqrt{V(t)}\mathrm{d}W_X(t) \quad (6)$$

$$\mathrm{d}V(t) = \kappa(\theta - V(t))\mathrm{d}t + \varepsilon\sqrt{V(t)}\mathrm{d}W_V(t) \quad (7)$$

where κ, θ, ε are strictly positive constants, and where W_X and W_V are scalar Brownian motions in some probability measure; we assume that $\mathrm{d}W_X(t)\cdot\mathrm{d}W_V(t) = \rho\mathrm{d}t$, where the correlation measure ρ is some constant in $[-1,1]$. $X(t)$ represents an asset price process and is assumed to be a martingale in the chosen probability measure. $V(t)$ represents the instantaneous variance of relative changes to $X(t)$ - the stochastic volatility - and is modeled as a mean-reverting square-root diffusion, with Ornstein-Uhlenbeck dynamics (a continuous-time analogue of the discrete-time first-order autoregressive process).

Recognizing that the asset price process $X(t)$ is relatively close to geometric Brownian motion, it is sensible to work with logarithms of $X(t)$. By Ito's lemma we have:

$$d\ln X(t) = -\frac{1}{2}V(t)\mathrm{d}t + \sqrt{V(t)}\mathrm{d}W_X(t) \quad (8)$$

$$\mathrm{d}V(t) = \kappa(\theta - V(t))\mathrm{d}t + \varepsilon\sqrt{V(t)}\mathrm{d}W_V(t) \quad (9)$$

Euler discretization of the stochastic differential equation (8)-(9) takes the form:

$$\ln\hat{X}(t+\Delta) = \ln\hat{X}(t) - \frac{1}{2}\hat{V}(t)\Delta + \sqrt{\hat{V}(t)}Z_X\sqrt{\Delta} \quad (10)$$

$$\hat{V}(t+\Delta) = V(t) + \kappa(\theta - \hat{V}(t))\Delta + \varepsilon\sqrt{\hat{V}(t)}Z_V\sqrt{\Delta} \quad (11)$$

where $\hat{X}$ and $\hat{V}$ are discrete-time approximation to X and V, respectively, and where Z_X and Z_V are Gaussian random variables with correlation ρ. Z_X and Z_V are drawn as independent uniform samples from the inverse cumulative Gaussian distribution function.

A critical problem with the naive Euler discretization above enables the discrete process for V to become negative with non-zero probability, which makes the computation of $\sqrt{\hat{V}}$ impossible. A full truncation scheme produces the smallest discretization bias [28], leading to the dynamics:

$$\ln\hat{X}(t+\Delta) = \ln\hat{X}(t) - \frac{1}{2}\hat{V}(t)^+\Delta + \sqrt{\hat{V}(t)^+}Z_X\sqrt{\Delta} \quad (12)$$

$$\hat{V}(t+\Delta) = V(t) + \kappa(\theta - \hat{V}(t)^+)\Delta + \varepsilon\sqrt{\hat{V}(t)^+}Z_V\sqrt{\Delta} \quad (13)$$

where the operator $x^+ = \max(x,0)$ enables the process for V to go below zero thereafter becoming deterministic with an upward drift $\kappa\theta$, and where $\hat{X}(t)$ is the observed price process and $\hat{V}(t)$ is the stochastic volatility process to be estimated. In addition we need to calibrate the parameters κ, θ, ε to run the recursive Bayesian estimators.

5. EXPERIMENTAL RESULTS

We ran state estimation experiments on three assets' daily closing prices from the beginning of 2010 till the end of 2012: two common stocks, General Electric (GE) and Citigroup (C), and one index, the S&P500 (SPX). Prior to running the filters we ran a 10,000 iteration MCMC calibration to build an understanding of the prices process (observation equation) and volatility process (state equation). The price process is the evolution of log returns which for SPX can be seen in Figure 2. Our Heston model stochastic volatility calibration for SPX can be seen in Figure 3, where we can see the full truncation scheme forcing the SV process to be positive, and the associated parameter evolution can be seen in Figure 4. This process was repeated for the remaining securities.

Of note, we can see ε is a small constant (this is the same throughout all the securities). This is attributable to the fact ε represents the volatility of volatility. If it were large and or varying across the securities we would not observe the coupling between and amongst securities in these markets as we do. This coupling, referred to as trend/momentum in finance, can be seen as the measure of similarity between the return processes. There are large periods of activity which are similar across the securities indicative of an underlying trend within the market.

Given the price process we estimate the latent stochastic volatility process using the SIR, MCMC-PF, PLA and APPF particle filters run with 1,000 particles and systematic resampling. Furthermore, we shall explore the effects of increasing the number of particles. We take the joint maximum a posteriori (MAP) estimates of κ and θ from our MCMC calibration and calculate the root-mean-square error (RMSE) between the estimated volatility and actual stochastic volatility process for each particle filter. Furthermore, we explore the effects of increasing the number of particles. Our experiments were run on an Intel Core i7-2600k @ 3.4GHz processor with 16GB of DDR3 memory. Our results can be seen in Table 2, noting the RMSE and execution time in seconds, and visually in Figures 5 - 7.

We can clearly see the APPF providing more accurate estimates of volatility compared to the other particle filters. In estimation of SPX SV in Figure 5 we observe noticeably worse estimation by the MCMC-PF RMSE = 0.05393 and PLA RMSE = 0.05317 compared to the SIR PF RMSE = 0.05282 with the APPF RMSE = 0.04961 outperforming all these filters by a significant margin, a 7% improvement on SIR with moderate computational expense in reference to the other filters.

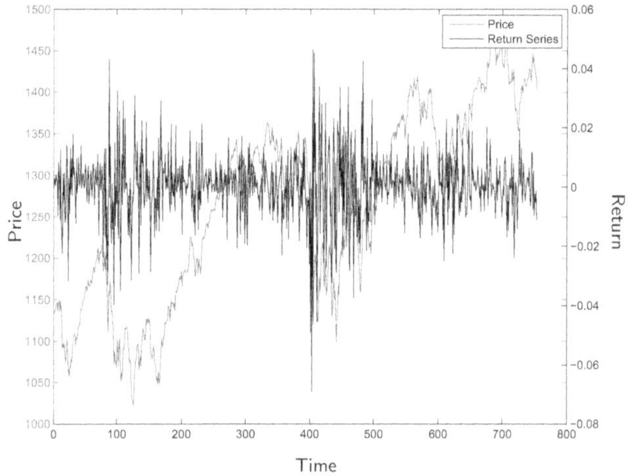

Figure 2: SPX daily closing price process [04-Jan-2010 – 28-Dec-2012]

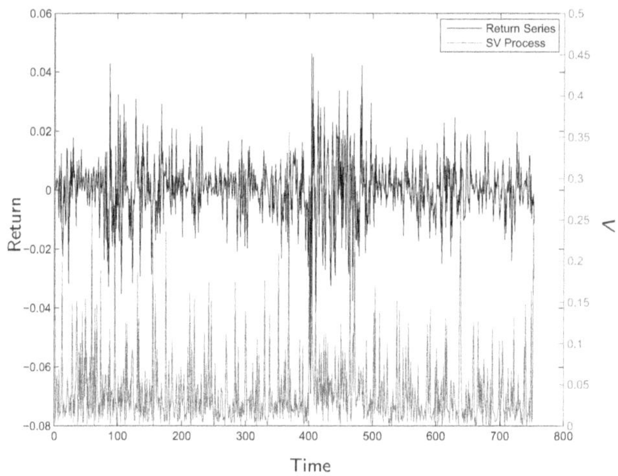

Figure 3: Heston model SPX daily closing stochastic volatility calibration [04-Jan-2010 – 28-Dec-2012]

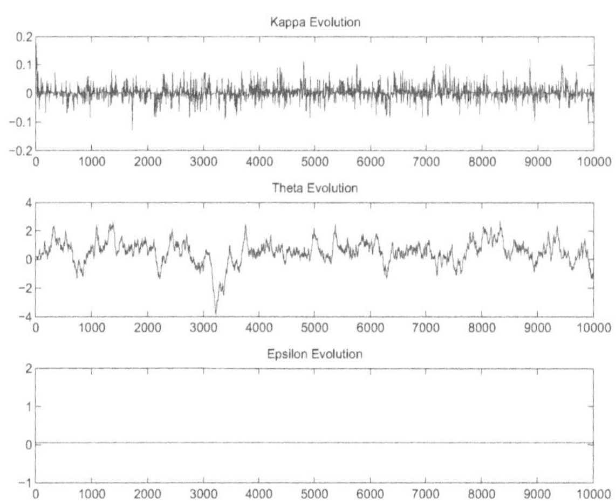

Figure 4: Heston model SPX daily closing stochastic volatility calibration, parameter estimates and evolution [04-Jan-2010 – 28-Dec-2012]

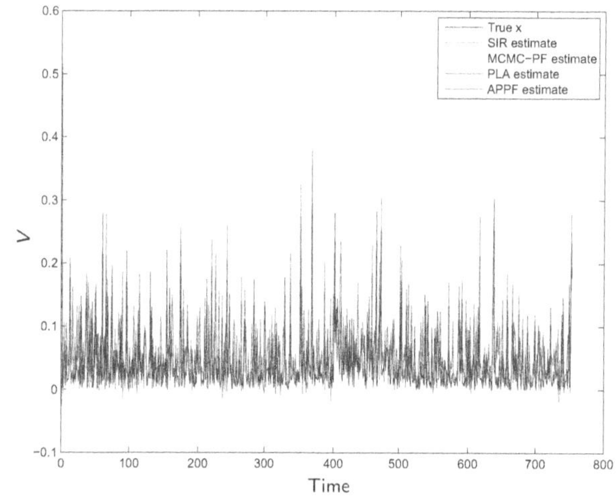

Figure 5: Heston model estimates for SPX - filter estimates (posterior means) vs. true state

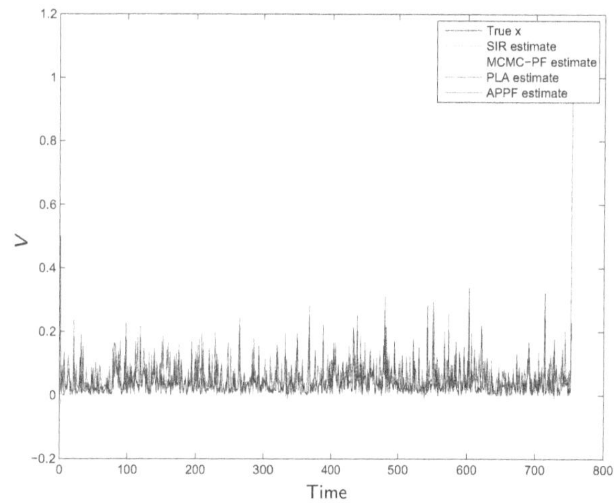

Figure 6: Heston model estimates for GE - filter estimates (posterior means) vs. true state

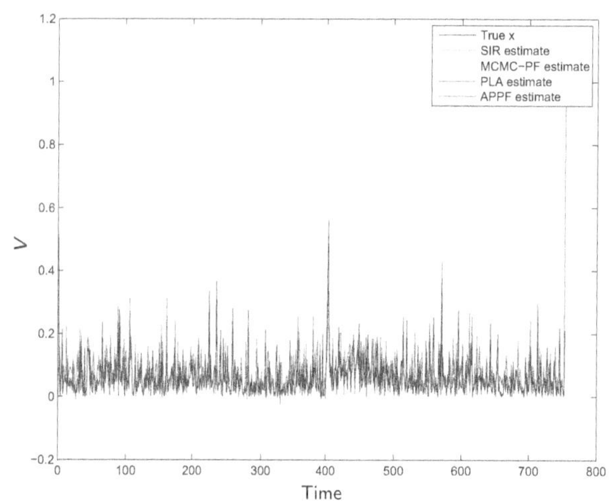

Figure 7: Heston model estimates for C - filter estimates (posterior means) vs. true state

Table 2: Heston model experimental results. RMSE mean and execution time in seconds using 1,000 particles and systematic resampling

SPX	RMSE	Exec. (s)
PF	0.05282	3.79
MCMC-PF	0.05393	59.37
PLA	0.05317	21.30
APPF	0.04961	39.33

GE	RMSE	Exec. (s)
PF	0.06121	3.79
MCMC-PF	0.06166	58.34
PLA	0.06095	20.91
APPF	0.05108	38.90

C	RMSE	Exec. (s)
PF	0.06162	3.88
MCMC-PF	0.06233	59.32
PLA	0.06175	21.33
APPF	0.05887	39.65

This trend continues upon estimation of the two common stocks. Estimating GE SV in Figure 6 the MCMC-PF RMSE = 0.06166 and PLA RMSE = 0.06095 perform comparably to the SIR PF RMSE = 0.06121, however the APPF RMSE = 0.05108 markedly outperforms all three of these displaying a 16% improvement in performance. In estimation of C SV in Figure 7, the MCMC-PF RMSE = 0.06233 and PLA RMSE = 0.06175 perform worse than the SIR PF RMSE=0.06162, with the APPF RMSE = 0.05887 outperforming all these filters once again with a 4.5% improvement in estimation accuracy compared to SIR with a similar computational expense gain as before. Such impairments across the board by filters other than the APPF can lead to both problematic trading and mispricing compared to derivatives factoring in the APPF SV estimates. The APPF provides a marked and statistically significant increase in performance.

Estimating the stochastic volatility for GE using 5,000 particles we find similar results to the above. Please see Table 3 noting the RMSE and execution time in seconds. By taking the MAP estimate we reduced the parameter estimation problem to a 2-dimensional, deterministic control function and as such this enables us to focus our efforts on state estimation. We observe similar results as in the literature with only the PF showing any discernible increase in estimation performance. It is evident that increasing the number of particles does not increase APPF performance and as such we can say it provides robust performance with a limited particle set in comparison to the PF, MCMC-PF and PLA.

Table 3: Heston model experimental results - particle size experiment. RMSE mean and execution time in seconds using 5,000 particles and systematic resampling

GE	RMSE	Exec. (s)
PF	0.06001	3.84
MCMC-PF	0.06154	58.80
PLA	0.06110	21.22
APPF	0.05108	39.22

Building on [20] the evolutionary computation step that is embedded in the APPF is successfully addressing sample impoverishment and weight degeneracy of sequential Monte Carlos. Maintaining diversity amongst the particle system allows the APPF to provide more accurate estimates compared to the the other filters. The execution time is slightly increased for the APPF however given compute resources will not prove a hindrance in the real-world.

6. CONCLUSIONS

We have proposed an evolutionary computation based particle filter for the estimation of stochastic volatility of indices and stocks. We have compared our method, the APPF with the traditional SIR particle filter, and the more advanced MCMC-PF and PLA. We find our filter to perform better in all state estimation experiments compared to these other filters, with marked and statistically significant improvements in places. Additionally, performance does not increase when increasing the number of particles indicating we can get optimal results with a small number of particles.

These results go some one way in showing that selective pressure from our generation-gap and distribution-recombination method does not lead to premature convergence. However, the inclusion of various evolutionary computation schemes to mitigate this should be considered in the future. Such schemes include fitness sharing [3, 15], crowding [30, 12], niche specialization [4] and triggered hypermutation [31] which aim to preserve diversity in populations and across generations providing further avenues of potential enhancement of the APPF. In addition, we hope to look into incorporating recombination at the state (particle) level as in the on-going, parallel effort [33], as well as at the distribution level, to yield even more enhanced performance through the exploitation of evolutionary computation ideas in sequential Monte Carlo methods.

7. ACKNOWLEDGMENTS

This work is supported by an EPSRC studentship under the RCUK Digital Economy program.

8. REFERENCES

[1] L. Andersen. Simple and efficient simulation of the heston stochastic volatility model. *Journal of Computational Finance*, 11(3):42, 2008.

[2] B. Anderson and J. Moore. Optimal filtering. *Prentice-Hall Information and System Sciences Series, Englewood Cliffs: Prentice-Hall, 1979*, 1, 1979.

[3] M. Arulampalam, S. Maskell, N. Gordon, and T. Clapp. A tutorial on particle filters for online nonlinear/non-gaussian bayesian tracking. *Signal Processing, IEEE Transactions on*, 50(2):174–188, 2002.

[4] D. Ashlock. *Evolutionary computation for modeling and optimization*, volume 200. Springer-Verlag New York Inc, 2006.

[5] L. Bauwens, M. Lubrano, and J. Richard. *Bayesian inference in dynamic econometric models*. Oxford University Press, USA, 1999.

[6] J. Carpenter, P. Clifford, and P. Fearnhead. Improved particle filter for nonlinear problems. In *Radar, Sonar*

and Navigation, IEE Proceedings-, volume 146, pages 2–7. IET, 1999.

[7] P. Carr and D. Madan. Option valuation using the fast fourier transform. *Journal of Computational Finance*, 2(4):61–73, 1999.

[8] Z. Chen. Bayesian filtering: From Kalman filters to particle filters. Technical report, and beyond. Technical report, Adaptive Systems Lab, McMaster University, 2003.

[9] A. Doucet, N. De Freitas, and N. Gordon. *Sequential Monte Carlo methods in practice*. Springer Verlag, 2001.

[10] A. Doucet and A. Johansen. A tutorial on particle filtering and smoothing: Fifteen years later, 2008.

[11] Z. Duan and Z. Cai. Evolutionary particle filter for robust simultaneous localization and map building with laser range finder. In *Natural Computation, 2008. ICNC'08. Fourth International Conference on*, volume 1, pages 443–447. IEEE, 2008.

[12] A. Eiben and J. Smith. Introduction to evolutionary computing (natural computing series). 2008.

[13] J. Freitas, M. Niranjan, A. Gee, and A. Doucet. Sequential monte carlo methods to train neural network models. *Neural computation*, 12(4):955–993, 2000.

[14] J. Geweke. Bayesian inference in econometric models using monte carlo integration. *Econometrica: Journal of the Econometric Society*, pages 1317–1339, 1989.

[15] D. Goldberg and J. Richardson. Genetic algorithms with sharing for multimodal function optimization. In *Proceedings of the Second International Conference on Genetic Algorithms on Genetic algorithms and their application*, pages 41–49. L. Erlbaum Associates Inc., 1987.

[16] D. E. Goldberg and J. H. Holland. Genetic algorithms and machine learning. *Machine Learning*, 3(2):95–99, 1988.

[17] N. Gordon, D. Salmond, and A. Smith. Novel approach to nonlinear/non-Gaussian Bayesian state estimation. In *Radar and Signal Processing, IEE Proceedings F*, volume 140, pages 107–113. IET, 1993.

[18] H. Han, Y. Ding, K. Hao, and X. Liang. An evolutionary particle filter with the immune genetic algorithm for intelligent video target tracking. *Computers & Mathematics with Applications*, 62(7):2685–2695, 2011.

[19] A. Hanif and P. Protopapas. Recursive bayesian estimation of regularized and irregular astrophysical time series. *Monthly Notices of the Royal Astronomical Society*, 2013.

[20] A. Hanif and R. Smith. Generation path-switching in sequential monte-carlo methods. In *Evolutionary Computation (CEC), 2012 IEEE Congress on*, pages 1–7. IEEE, 2012.

[21] S. Heston. A closed-form solution for options with stochastic volatility with applications to bond and currency options. *Review of Financial Studies*, 6(2):327–343, 1993.

[22] G. Kitagawa. Monte carlo filter and smoother for non-gaussian nonlinear state space models. *Journal of computational and graphical statistics*, 5(1):1–25, 1996.

[23] N. Kwok, G. Fang, and W. Zhou. Evolutionary particle filter: re-sampling from the genetic algorithm perspective. In *Intelligent Robots and Systems, 2005.(IROS 2005). 2005 IEEE/RSJ International Conference on*, pages 2935–2940. IEEE, 2005.

[24] R. Lee. Option pricing by transform methods: extensions, unification and error control. *Journal of Computational Finance*, 7(3):51–86, 2004.

[25] A. Lewis. Option valuation under stochastic volatility. *Option Valuation under Stochastic Volatility*, 2000.

[26] A. Lipton. The vol smile problem. *Risk*, 15(2):61–66, 2002.

[27] J. Liu and R. Chen. Sequential monte carlo methods for dynamic systems. *Journal of the American statistical association*, 93(443):1032–1044, 1998.

[28] R. Lord, R. Koekkoek, and D. Van Dijk. A comparison of biased simulation schemes for stochastic volatility models. *Quantitative Finance*, 10(2):177–194, 2006.

[29] S. Maskell. An introduction to particle filters. *State Space and Unobserved Component Models, Theory and Applications, editors Harvey, AC and Koopman, SJ and Shephard, N*, 2004.

[30] O. Mengshoel and D. Goldberg. The crowding approach to niching in genetic algorithms. *Evolutionary computation*, 16(3):315–354, 2008.

[31] R. Morrison and K. De Jong. Triggered hypermutation revisited. In *Evolutionary Computation, 2000. Proceedings of the 2000 Congress on*, volume 2, pages 1025–1032. IEEE, 2000.

[32] N. Nikolaev and E. Smirnov. Stochastic volatility inference with monte carlo filters. *Wilmott Magazine, John Wiley and Sons, July*, pages 72–81, 2007.

[33] R. Smith and M. Hussain. Hybrid metaheuristic particle filters for stochastic volatility estimation. In *Proceedings of the fourteenth international conference on Genetic and evolutionary computation conference*, pages 1167–1174. ACM, 2012.

[34] K. Uosaki, Y. Kimura, and T. Hatanaka. Nonlinear state estimation by evolution strategies based particle filters. In *Evolutionary Computation, 2003. CEC'03. The 2003 Congress on*, volume 3, pages 2102–2109. IEEE, 2005.

APPENDIX

A. PARTICLE FILTER ALGORITHM

Table 4: SIR Algorithm

1. Initialization: for $i = 1, ..., N_p$, sample
$$\boldsymbol{x}_0^{(i)} \sim p(\boldsymbol{x}_0)$$
with weights $W_0^{(i)} = \frac{1}{N_p}$.

For $t \geq 1$

2. Importance sampling: for $i = 1, ..., N_p$, draw samples
$$\hat{\boldsymbol{x}}_t^{(i)} \sim p(\boldsymbol{x}_t|\boldsymbol{x}_{t-1}^{(i)})$$
set $$\hat{\boldsymbol{x}}_{0:t}^{(i)} = \{\boldsymbol{x}_{0:t-1}^{(i)}, \hat{\boldsymbol{x}}_t^{(i)}\}$$
3. Weight update: calculate the importance weights
$$W_t^{(i)} = p(\boldsymbol{y}_t|\hat{\boldsymbol{x}}_t^{(i)})$$
4. Normalize weights:
$$\tilde{W}_t^{(i)} = \frac{W_t^{(i)}}{\sum_{j=1}^{N_p} W_t^{(j)}}$$
5. Resampling: Generate N_p new particles $\boldsymbol{x}_t^{(i)}$ from the set $\{\hat{\boldsymbol{x}}_t^{(i)}\}$ according to importance weights $\tilde{W}_t^{(i)}$.
6. Repeat from importance sampling step.

B. MARKOV-CHAIN MONTE CARLO ALGORITHM STEP

Table 5: Metropolis-Hastings Step

⋮

6. Smoothing Metropolis-Hastings Step
   i) Sample:
$$v \sim \mathcal{U}(0, 1)$$
   ii) Sample proposal candidate:
$$\mathbf{x}_t^{\star(i)} \sim p(\mathbf{x}_t|\mathbf{x}_{t-1}^{(i)})$$
   iii) If
$$v \leq \min\left[\frac{p(\mathbf{y}_t|\mathbf{x}_t^{\star(i)})}{p(\mathbf{y}_t|\tilde{\mathbf{x}}_t^{(i)})}, 1\right]$$
accept move: $\mathbf{x}_{0:t}^{(i)} = (\tilde{\mathbf{x}}_{0:t-1}^{(i)}, \mathbf{x}_t^{\star(i)})$

else reject move: $\mathbf{x}_{0:t}^{(i)} = \tilde{\mathbf{x}}_{0:t}^{(i)}$

⋮

Evolutionary Path Generation for Reduction of Thermal Variations in Thermal Spray Coating

Daniel Hegels
TU Dortmund University
Department of Computer Science VII
Otto-Hahn-Str. 16
D-44227 Dortmund, Germany
hegels@ls7.cs.tu-dortmund.de

Heinrich Müller
TU Dortmund University
Department of Computer Science VII
Otto-Hahn-Str. 16
D-44227 Dortmund, Germany
mueller@ls7.cs.tu-dortmund.de

ABSTRACT

Thermal spraying is a production process which consists of spraying hot material onto a workpiece surface in order to form a coating of a desired thickness. This paper describes a path generation algorithm for industrial robot-based thermal spraying which generates the desired coating as well as keeps the thermal variation on the object surface during the process low. The problem is formulated as a discrete optimization problem which includes the quality of the particle coating and the physics of heat induction, heat diffusion and cooling of the surface. The optimization problem is solved by an Evolutionary Algorithm. By specific mutation operators, self-adaptation, and dropping the concept of generations, an improvement of the quality of the results of over 25 % compared to standard operations is achieved. The evolutionary results overall outperform the solutions generated by the often-used strategy of direction-parallel paths.

Categories and Subject Descriptors

G.1.6 [**Numerical Analysis**]: Optimization—*Global Optimization*; I.2.8 [**Artificial Intelligence**]: Problem Solving, Control Methods, and Search—*Heuristic methods*; I.6.3 [**Simulation and Modeling**]: Applications; J.6 [**Computer Applications**]: Computer-aided Engineering—*Computer-aided manufacturing*

General Terms

Algorithms

Keywords

Path planning; Spray coating; Optimization; Evolutionary Algorithms

1. INTRODUCTION

Thermal spraying is a generic term for several techniques that are used to coat workpiece surfaces with materials [5].

GECCO'13, July 6–10, 2013, Amsterdam, The Netherlands.

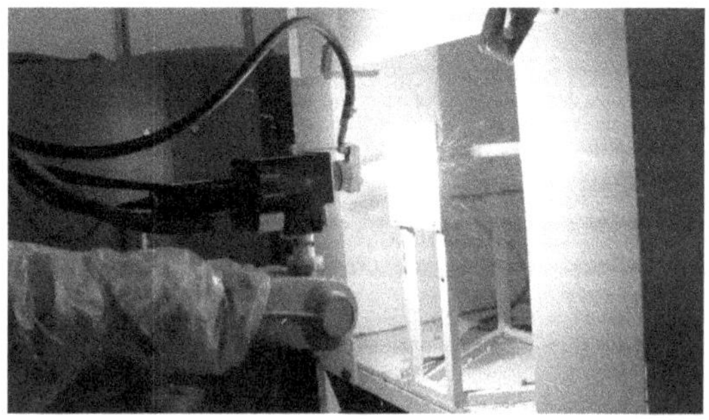

Figure 1: Thermal spraying process executed by an industrial robot.

A spray gun heats the coating material until it liquefies and sprays it onto the workpiece surface. Different methods of spraying exist, but the main idea is to feed the spray material into the spray gun as a wire or powder where it is heated. Using the gases of combustion or another kind of gas stream, the molten material droplets are accelerated towards the object surface to be coated. The deposited droplets cool down when the spray gun moves on so that the material solidifies. The gun is moved so that coatings of a desired thickness are produced. Depending on the material, these coatings can be used for wear protection, protection against corrosion etc. Due to new material technologies, thermal coating gains increasing importance in production.

Thermal spraying is related to paint spray processes. The main difference, however, is that the material in thermal spraying is extremely hot. When the hot particles reach the surface, they induce a great amount of heat energy. Thus, the location of particle impacts heats up, while other regions of the surface cool down. This may result in a thermal variance on the surface that leads to tensions in the material with negative effects on the coating quality. For that reason the tensions should be avoided by minimizing the thermal variance during the process.

A particular flexibility concerning the shapes of workpieces that can be coated is achieved by guiding the spray gun by an industrial robot. Figure 1 shows an industrial robot moving a spray gun over a workpiece. For this purpose a path is required on which the robot moves the spray gun so that the desired coating thickness is achieved. A common approach of path generation in practice is to choose a fixed path pattern. An example are direction-parallel paths which means to move a tool, in this case the spay gun, along a surface-covering family of curves of a same, given direction, see figure 2(a). Such solutions, however, are problematic with respect to heat variance. This paper follows the approach of algorithmic generation of adaptive tool paths which has been used before for other path-based production technologies, in particular for NC-controlled milling.

The contribution of this paper is an evolutionary solution to the problem of finding a spray gun path that simultaneously minimizes the coating thickness deviation and heat variation for a new, more general class of paths, the so-called contour-to-contour-paths, see figure 2(b), for a non-trivial physical macro-model of thermal spray coating.

Contour-to-contour-paths generalize the mirrorbox paths of Jones et al. [7, 6]. They allow more general planar shapes than rectangles, and may be extended to curved surfaces. Furthermore, they have more degrees of freedom thus offering more flexibility for optimization. All those benefits dominate the drawback that, in contrast to the approach of Jones et al., an analytical solution seems no longer to be possible.

The physical model presented in the paper is oriented at similar models, in particular at the model of Jones et al. [7, 6], and incorporates well-known laws of physics modeling heat induction, heat diffusion and surface cooling. It is coded in an objective function specifying the path planning problem as an optimization problem. The Evolutionary Algorithm presented for its solution includes several problem-specific operators and strategies to increase the quality of the results and to speed up the computations. The best effect is achieved by problem specific mutation operators and self-adaptation. They improve the quality of the results compared to the straightforward approach by over 25 %. Dropping the concept of generations improves the quality of the results up to 7 %. Furthermore, it allows in a straightforward way the parallelized implementation of the algorithm. The parallelization results in a speed-up of the computations scaling roughly with the number of processor cores used.

Section 2 gives an overview over related work. Section 3 sets up the problem specification as a discrete optimization problem and section 4 presents the Evolutionary Algorithm. Section 5 reports about results of an experimental evaluation of the algorithm. Section 6 concludes the paper.

2. RELATED WORK

Algorithmic path generation for thermal spray coating that takes thermal variations into account has not been investigated much in the past. Jones et al. [7, 6] restrict the problem to a rectangular surface and so-called mirrorbox paths. These paths consist of straight lines which are reflected at the surface contour. The spray gun moves with a constant velocity during the whole process. By these restrictions it is possible to find an optimal path with the starting point, the gun velocity and the gun scan angle as degrees of freedom analytically.

From the algorithmic point of view, there is a relation to covering path problems. Covering path problems have gained recent interest due to autonomous service robots e.g. for cleaning [4]. A special type of covering problem is to demand that every surface point is reached just once. This also is a common soft constraint of milling paths, a topic which also has found notable research interest in the past [8]. For these problems a relation to the traveling salesman problem (TSP) may be recognized. Indeed this view has opened the door to the variety of existing algorithmic paradigms for the TSP [1], some of which have led to methods of solutions to the aforementioned types of problem.

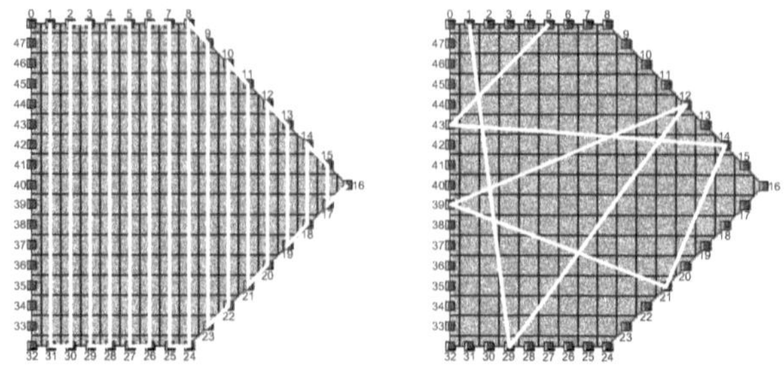

(a) Direction-parallel (b) Contour-to-contour

Figure 2: A pentagonal surface with 48 contour nodes, a sampling grid (black), and exemplary paths (white).

One difference of the path generation problem of coating to other path covering problems is the objective of a desired coating thickness and not just to traverse every surface point. This, however, does not have a severe impact on the problem structure, in contrast to the objective of minimizing heat variation. The main difference is that the latter objective concerns every initial subpath of a solution, because of heat diffusion, and not just the final result. The resulting objective function is considerably more complex and seems to include an issue of scheduling, not just the covering aspect. This has motivated to employ the paradigm of Evolutionary Algorithms for the solution of the problem in this paper. The paradigm of Evolutionary Algorithms is known to be well suited for the TSP, and it offers a superior flexibility of extension to further problem versions, as required here.

3. PROBLEM SPECIFICATION

The input of the path planning problem of spray coating consists of a spray gun and a workpiece surface. The spray gun delivers material at a constant rate. Its behavior is given by a model of material deposition and a heat flow model which specify its effect on the surface depending on its location relative to the surface. Furthermore, a thickness of the desired coating at every surface point is specified. The task is to determine a path of the spray gun, i.e. a motion of the spray gun over the surface, which achieves the desired coating thickness according to the material deposition model and an as low as possible thermal variance on the surface according to the thermal model. In the following these ingredients and objectives of the problem are formalized into a discretized specification suitable for a computational treatment.

In the setting here, the workpiece surface is represented by a flat, convex polygon. This type of surface represents the problem in a sufficiently general way with respect to algorithmic issues. The approach can be generalized to non-convex flat polygons, but also to curved surfaces with boundaries e.g. represented by triangle meshes. Closed surfaces without boundaries need a special treatment and are excluded from the considerations.

For the spray path representation, a concept of so called contour-to-contour paths is used. A contour-to-contour spray path is defined over a so-called impact path which is a polygonal chain on the surface connecting a sequence of nodes out of a finite set of equally spaced nodes on the contour of the surface, see figure 2. The spray path itself results by conducting the spray gun along the impact path, perpendicularly to the surface, in a fixed distance. The gun is moved at a constant velocity. Furthermore, for the purpose of calculation, the motion is discretized into time steps of equal length Δt. Hence a contour-to-contour spray path may be specified by a sequence of indices of contour nodes, according to a given enumeration, a distance of the gun, a velocity, and the time interval Δt.

The contour-to-contour paths are similar to the mirrorbox paths by Jones et al. [7, 6]. A major difference is that the reflection rule defining the continuation of a path at the surface contour is given up. This extends the variety of feasible paths. Both concepts have in common that gun turns in the inner of the surface are completely avoided. Because of their dynamic constraints a robot might not achieve the necessary velocity at sharp turns, what may cause complications for robot-based spray coating. Contour-to-contour paths move this problem to the boundary of the surface. In practice, the boundary may be chosen outside of the real surface so that a gun turn does not affect the surface. In our computations the effect of turns is taken into account by restricting the evaluation of the objective function to a subregion resulting by a shrinking of the contour of the surface by the radius of the spray cone on the surface.

The constant gun distance and velocity is more limited than in a practical setting. However, it is not a principle restriction with respect to algorithmic considerations, but it helps to focus on the principal strengths and weaknesses of the approach.

The evaluation of the coating thickness and of the heat variance uses a formal objective function. The objective function needs the state of coating thickness and heat distribution on the surface at different time steps. This information is stored in a discretized way at a finite set of sample points spread over the workpiece surface. In the setting of the paper the vertices of a regular grid in the inner of the surface polygon are used as these so-called *surface points* p_i, $i = 0, \ldots, P-1$, see figure 2.

The *objective function* is composed of three parts. They concern the coating thickness error, the thermal variance, and the waste of spray material.

The *coating thickness error* is specified by

$$E_s = \sqrt{\frac{1}{P}\sum_{i=0}^{P-1}(z(t_f, p_i) - z_s)^2},$$

where z_s denotes the desired coating thickness which is chosen to be constant over the surface. $z(t_f, p_i)$ is the coating thickness achieved at surface point p_i at the last time step t_f, i.e. after the execution of the spray path. Hence E_s is the root mean square deviation between the coating achieved and the desired coating.

The coating thickness generated by a spray path is determined by simulating the material deposition on the surface at every time step. The material deposition at a time step t is calculated by

$$\Delta z(t, p_i) = n_f \cdot f(d_x(t, p_i), d_y(t, p_i)).$$

$\Delta z(t, p_i)$ is the new deposited coating thickness at surface point p_i and time t. The right side of the equation is the gun deposit model. Analogously to [6], it uses a footprint $f(.,.)$ which describes the coating produced on a flat surface when the gun is not moved. The shape of the footprint depends on the specific spray gun. In our setting a Gaussian shape is used to approximate the footprint, but other, more realistic shapes may be employed without changing the algorithmic principle. $d_x(t, p_i)$ and $d_y(t, p_i)$ are the distances of the surface point p_i to the center of the projected location of the spray gun at time step t in x- and y- direction, respectively. n_f is a scaling factor which controls the amount of material sprayed at a time step depending on the speed of the spray gun and the material mass feed into the spray gun per second.

The *thermal variance* which has to be minimized is given by

$$E_t(t) = \frac{1}{P}\sum_{i=0}^{P-1}(\Theta(t, p_i) - \overline{\Theta}(t))^2.$$

$\Theta(t, p_i)$ denotes the temperature at surface point p_i, $i = 0, \ldots, P-1$, at time step t.

$$\overline{\Theta}(t) = \frac{1}{P}\sum_{i=0}^{P-1}\Theta(t, p_i)$$

is the mean temperature on the surface at time t.

$\Theta(t, p_i)$ is calculated by the simulation model which takes into account the heat induction from hot particles reaching the surface, the heat diffusion in the material, and the cooling of the material at its surface.

The *heat induction* takes place when new, hot particles are deposited on the surface. The thermal energy merges with the already existent energy at this surface point. This process can be described by the well-known *Richmann mixture rule.* Denoting the temperature of the new particles with Θ_n, the temperature at the surface point after merging is calculated as

$$\Theta(t + \Delta t, p_i) = \frac{\Theta(t, p_i)z(t, p_i) + \Theta_n \Delta z(t, p_i)}{z(t, p_i) + \Delta z(t, p_i)}.$$

Herein $\Theta(t + \Delta t, p_i)$ is the temperature at surface point p_i after merging. $z(t, p_i)$ and $\Delta z(t, p_i)$ are the coating thickness at surface point p_i and the change of the coating thickness, respectively.

The primary reason for *cooling* is the energy loss due to the heat transfer to the cool air above the surface [7]. This cooling can be described by a differential equation for the loss of heat at a surface [12]. Its discretization leads to

$$\Theta(t + \Delta t, p_i) = \Theta(t, p_i) - \frac{\alpha(\Theta(t, p_i) - \Theta_a)\Delta t}{c\rho z(t, p_i)}.$$

In this formula the temperature of the air is denoted by Θ_a. α is the heat transfer coefficient, c the heat capacity, and ρ the density of the material. The remaining heat $\Theta(t+\Delta t, p_i)$ at the next time step is therefore calculated by subtracting the energy transferred to the air from the current heat energy.

The last component of the heat model is the *heat diffusion* in the material. The thermal energy diffuses from hotter areas into the cooler ones. This process can be described by a differential equation [7]. By discretizing this equation, the heat at a surface point p_i at the next time step can be calculated as

$$\Theta(t+\Delta t, p_i) = \Theta(t, p_i) + \frac{\Delta t k}{c\rho(\Delta x)^2}\left(\Theta(t, p_i + p_{\Delta x}) - 2\Theta(t, p_i) + \Theta(t, p_i - p_{\Delta x})\right) + \frac{\Delta t k}{c\rho(\Delta y)^2}\left(\Theta(t, p_i + p_{\Delta y}) - 2\Theta(t, p_i) + \Theta(t, p_i - p_{\Delta y})\right).$$

In this formula k denotes the heat conductivity of the material. Δx and Δy are the x- and y- distances of two neighboring surface points in their grid and $p_{\Delta x}$ and $p_{\Delta y}$ are defined as $\begin{pmatrix}\Delta x\\0\end{pmatrix}$ and $\begin{pmatrix}0\\\Delta y\end{pmatrix}$ respectively. c and ρ denote again the heat capacity and the density of the material.

Altogether the temperature at time step $t + \Delta t$ results from temperatures at time step t by

$$\begin{aligned}&\Theta(t+\Delta t, p_i)\\&= \Bigg(\bigg(\frac{\Delta t k}{c\rho(\Delta x)^2}\left(\Theta(t, p_i + p_{\Delta x}) - 2\Theta(t, p_i) + \Theta(t, p_i - p_{\Delta x})\right)\\&+ \frac{\Delta t k}{c\rho(\Delta y)^2}\left(\Theta(t, p_i + p_{\Delta y}) - 2\Theta(t, p_i) + \Theta(t, p_i - p_{\Delta y})\right)\\&+ \Theta(t, p_i) - \frac{\alpha(\Theta(t, p_i) - \Theta_a)\Delta t}{c\rho z(t, p_i)}\bigg) \cdot z(t, p_i) + \Theta_n \Delta z(t, p_i)\Bigg)\\&\cdot \frac{1}{z(t, p_i) + \Delta z(t, p_i)}. \qquad (1)\end{aligned}$$

A canonical start value for the evaluation of this iteration is a constant temperature $\Theta(0, .)$, like the room temperature or a surface temperature after preheating the workpiece.

The last component of the objective function concerns the *amount of wasted spray material*. Material is wasted when it is sprayed outside the surface. This usually happens at the boundary of the sprayed region. To formulate an error value for wasted material, the difference between the emitted spray material and the material deposited on the workpiece surface is measured. With $V(s)$ describing the mass of sprayed material at a time step, the amount of wasted material is specified by

$$E_w = \left(\sum_{l=0}^{t_f/\Delta t}\left(V(s) - \sum_{i=0}^{P-1}\Delta z(l\cdot\Delta t, p_i)\cdot A\right)\right)\cdot\rho.$$

For every surface point and every discrete time step ranging from the start time 0 to the final time t_f, the thickness $\Delta z(l\cdot\Delta t, p_i)$ of the newly deposited material is measured and converted into a volume using A. A is the surface area of a surface point and is defined by the cell size of the grid used. The difference to the sprayed material $V(s)$ is calculated and the volume is converted into a mass using ρ, the material density.

The *overall objective function* which has to be minimized is chosen as a weighted sum of the sub-objectives,

$$E = E_s + \lambda_t \frac{1}{t_f}\sum_{l=0}^{t_f/\Delta t} E_t(l\cdot\Delta t) + \lambda_w E_w.$$

E_s, $E_t(t)$ and E_w are the functions given above, and λ_t, λ_w are appropriate weights. A reasonable alternative to taking the sum of $E_t(l\cdot\Delta t)$ could be to consider the maximum value over all time steps.

4. SOLUTION

In the following, an Evolutionary Algorithm for minimizing the objective function of the preceding chapter is presented.

Evolutionary Algorithms usually start with a number of initial solutions called individuals that form the first generation of evolution. Then operations of recombination and mutation are used to generate new individuals for the following generation. Selection processes based on the fitness of individuals decide which individuals survive and which are used for recombination and mutation. Beyond this basic principle, specific techniques, often application-depending, are usually employed to improve the solutions and the convergence speed. Details about the concept of Evolutionary Algorithms may be found e.g. in the book by Bäck [3].

In the solution presented here, an *individual* represents a contour-to-contour path by its defining sequence of contour nodes as genes. The objective function of the optimization problem to be solved is used as *fitness function*.

The population is *initialized* by generating a number of individuals that form the first population. Motivated by the fact that the individuals should be uniformly distributed over the complete solution space to guarantee a good exploration of the space, they are not generated completely randomly. Each dimension of the solution space, i.e. the index range of contour points, is subdivided into as many intervals as there are individuals in the population, and each individual is assigned to one of these intervals [11]. No two individuals are assigned to the same interval per dimension. A representative index is chosen in each interval and is inserted at the respective position in the individual.

The *recombination* is performed by the well-known one-point crossover, where two individuals are cut into two parts and recombined to form a new individual [3]. This operator works very well for contour-to-contour-paths. The parent paths are only cut at one position and therefore most of the path is not affected. This way large parts of the parents are inherited to the child which is the aim of the crossover operator.

A number of different *mutation operators* are used for an additional modification of the recombined individuals. The aim of these operators is to alter a small part of the individual so that new genes are introduced to the gene pool. The following operators are used in the algorithm (see also [9]):

Shift mutation: A gene is chosen uniformly distributed and then altered by adding or subtracting a small number to or from this gene. This number is taken out of a Gaussian distribution with mean 0 and standard deviation σ, which is a parameter of the algorithm. If the resulting number does not fall into the index range of contour nodes, the maximum index of the contour nodes is subtracted or added, respectively.

Displacement mutation: A subsequence of genes is selected uniformly at random which is dislocated in the individual.

Exchange mutation: Two genes are chosen uniformly distributed and their values are exchanged.

Insertion mutation: One gene in the individual is selected uniformly at random, deleted and inserted at a new location in the remaining individual.

Inversion mutation: Like for displacement mutation, a subsequence of genes is relocated in the individual. In addition, the genes in this subsequence are inverted so that the subpath represented by the subsequence is inverted, too.

Scramble mutation: This operator selects uniformly at random a subsequence in the individual and randomly reorders the genes in this sequence.

Simple inversion mutation: The genes in a subsequence of the individual are inverted. In contrast to the inversion mutation the subsequence is not relocated.

Add mutation: Due to the fact that the optimal length of the spray path and therefore the length of the individual are not known from the beginning, an operator has to be introduced that alters the length of the individual. The add mutation chooses a random but uniformly distributed position in the individual and adds a gene corresponding to a contour node. The length of the path is thereby increased by one contour node.

Delete mutation: In contrast to the add mutation, this operator deletes a single gene in the individual. This operator only works if the individual is at least two genes long.

These operators alter small parts of the individual in order to explore the search space. Every operator has its own probability of being used. The difficulty is the selection of these probabilities. The concept of self-adaptation is used for finding good parameters as discussed below.

Two *selection processes* are employed [3]. For the *survival selection*, which is used for selecting the individuals for the next population, a simple *survival of the fittest* approach is used. The advantage of this operator is that the best individual will never be discarded and that it can easily be adopted for the algorithm not using the concept of generations, which is described below. The *parent selection* selects two parents for the recombination and mutation process. The selection probability of an individual is proportional to its fitness so that fitter individuals have a higher selection probability. The less fit individuals have a selection probability greater than zero, which is useful to maintain a certain amount of genetic diversity in the population.

Beside these standard techniques of Evolutionary Algorithms, some more advanced techniques are used. The task of the first technique called *prohibition of clones* is to raise the genetic diversity in the population [10, 13]. Without such a technique, the individuals eventually will be very similar or even clones. If this happens, the recombination operator is completely useless. Hence, a method to maintain minimal genetic diversity is employed that strictly forbids clones to be gathered into the population.

Furthermore, the *concept of generations is dropped.* This means that, after a new child has been created using two parents and the recombination and mutation operators, it is instantly written back into the population if it is fit enough. If the fitness is not sufficient, the child is discarded. This way, new individuals enter the evolutionary process earlier than by using the concept of generations. This results in a slightly better convergence speed. In experiments, the best individual after 500000 evaluations has been about 7% better than the one generated by the algorithm using generations (section 5).

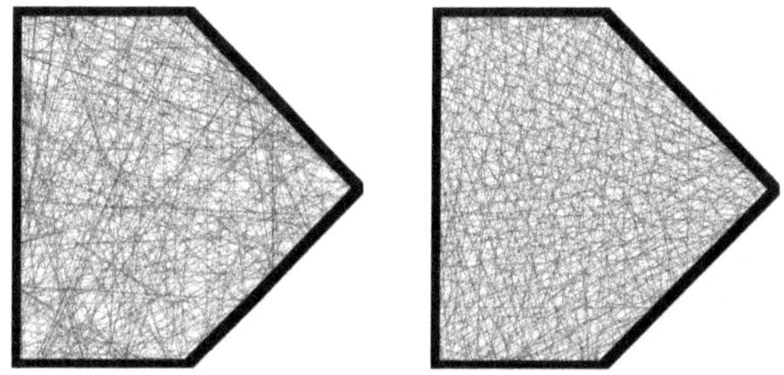

(a) Path at the beginning of the calculations. (b) Path at the end of the calculations.

Figure 3: Paths at the beginning and at the end of the evolutionary optimization process.

An additional benefit of this concept is that it is well suited for parallel computations. The creation process of children, consisting of the selection of parents, recombination, mutation and evaluation, can be done for every child independently. Therefore a number of threads can be used for these computations. Only the reading of the parents and the writing of the child in the population has to be done sequentially. Hence, the speed-up of the parallel approach scales approximately with the number of processor cores used.

The Evolutionary Algorithm relies on a number of parameters controlling the course of the algorithm. The choice of these parameters is crucial for the quality and convergence speed of the algorithm. A big problem is given when some parameter values, which provide good results at the beginning of the calculations, prevent the algorithm from further progress later on. Instead of using a function over time that defines the parameter values, it is more beneficial to use a technique called self-adaptation [3]. *Self-adaptation* is achieved by encoding the parameters as genes. Hence, every individual has its own set of parameters. Here, the mutation probabilities are used for self-adaptation. Right before a mutation, the probabilities are mutated using these probabilities. The new parameter values are then used for the actual mutation process. This way the algorithm itself evaluates the best parameter values. According to our experiments this technique in combination with the mutation operators has a significant positive effect, see section 5.

5. EXPERIMENTS AND RESULTS

The Evolutionary Algorithm has been evaluated by investigating the effectiveness of all the operators and methods described above. The results presented in the following base on experiments with a flat pentagonal workpiece surface of 334 mm horizontal and 334 mm vertical extension, like the one of figure 2(b). Coating thickness and heat is sampled at the vertices of a regular grid of 9 mm cell width, in a region resulting from shrinking the surface contour by the radius of the spray cone. The desired coating thickness is 0.2 mm. The contour-to-contour paths considered consist of line segments between pairs of 996 equally spaced contour nodes. The velocity of the spray gun is 200 mm/s, the interval between two time steps is $\Delta t = 0.025$ s. The radius

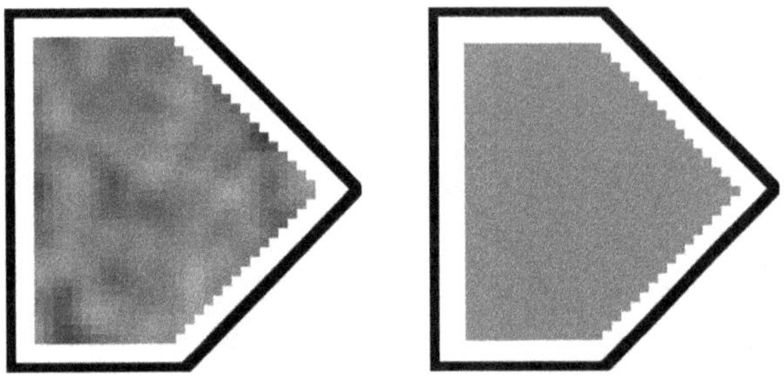

(a) Coating error at the beginning of the calculations. (b) Coating error at the end of the calculations.

Figure 4: Coating error at the beginning and at the end of the calculations using the Evolutionary Algorithm. Bright areas: Not enough material. Dark areas: Too much material.

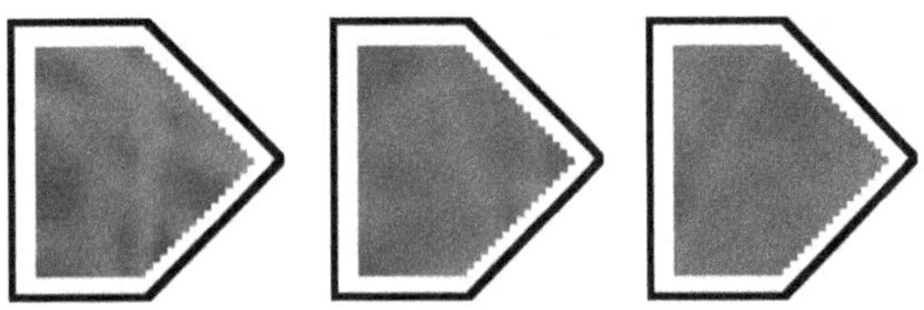

(a) After 35 seconds (b) After 70 seconds (c) After 105 seconds

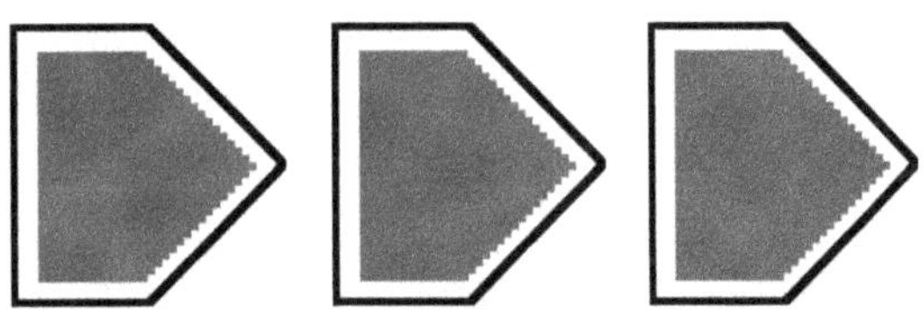

(d) After 140 seconds (e) After 175 seconds (f) After 210 seconds

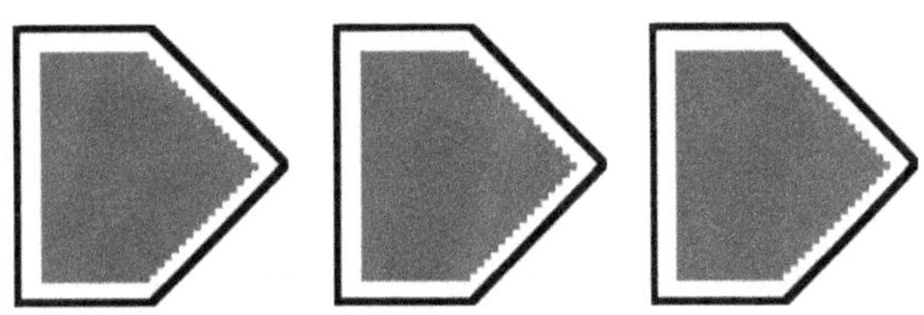

(g) After 245 seconds (h) After 280 seconds (i) After 315 seconds

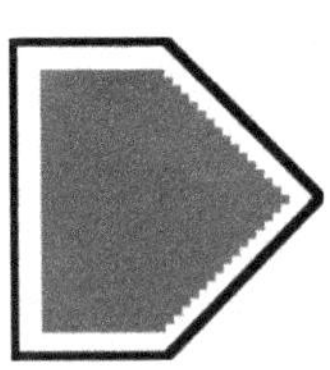

(j) After 350 seconds

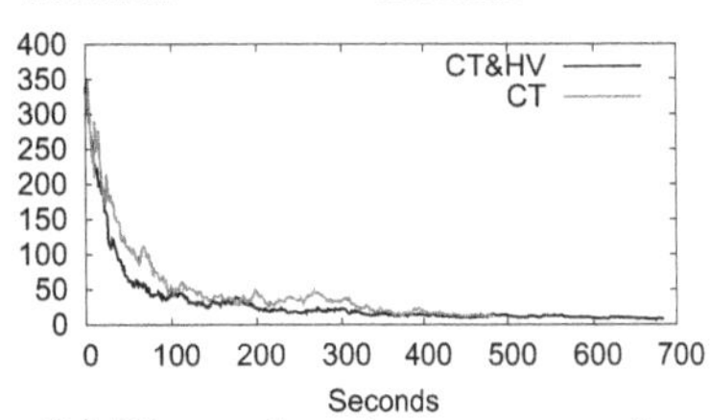

(k) Thermal variances as graph

Figure 5: Snapshots of the thermal variances on the workpiece during the spraying process for the CT&HV experiment. Red: Hot Areas. Blue: Cold Areas. The graph shows the thermal variances of this and the CT experiment.

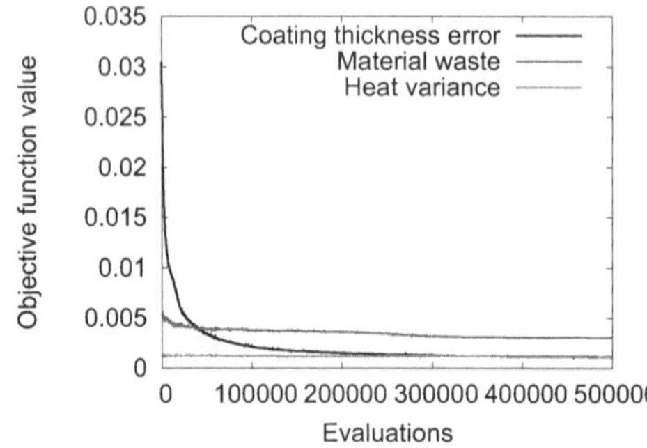

Figure 6: Development of the components of the objective function, scaled with their weight factors, during evolutionary optimization.

of the spray cone of the gun on the surface is 25 mm. The footprint modeling the material deposition of the spray gun at a time step has a Gaussian shape of mean 0 and variance 10, and a thickness scaling factor of $n_f = 0.5$. The heat parameters, cf. section 3, are $\rho = 14950\,\mathrm{kg/m^3}$, $c = 340\,\mathrm{J/kgK}$, $k = 70\,\mathrm{W/m{\cdot}K}$, $\alpha = 3\,\mathrm{W/m^2K}$, $\Theta_n = 1000\,°\mathrm{C}$, $\Theta_a = 20\,°\mathrm{C}$ and $\Theta(0,.) = 0\,°\mathrm{C}$.

The experiments with Evolutionary Algorithms use a population size of 50. The path lengths of the initial population are between 450 and 550.

The evaluation uses four main experiments conducted with the Evolutionary Algorithm approach and these settings, and one with direction-parallel paths:

CT&HV: Evolutionary Algorithm with adaptation, without generations. The weights $\lambda_t = 0.0001$ and $\lambda_w = 0.00001$ have been chosen so that the weighted components of the objective function are in the same order of magnitude, and thus of approximately equal influence on the result.

CT&HV$_{\mathrm{with-gen}}$: Like CT&HV, but with the concept of generation.

CT&HV$_{\mathrm{non-adapt}}$: Like CT&HV, but with a fixed setting of the crossover and mutation probabilities to 10%.

CT: Like CT&HV, but excluding the optimizing of heat variation, i.e. $\lambda_t = 0.0$, $\lambda_w = 0.00001$.

DP: Direction-parallel paths like in figure 2(a), starting on the left, with an inter-path-distance of 0.82812 mm and the same velocity as for the other experiments.

Figure 3 shows paths generated by CT&HV at the beginning and after 500000 evolutionary steps. Figure 4 visualizes the corresponding coating thickness error of the two paths. Figure 5 depicts the development of thermal variance during the execution of the optimized path. Obviously, a quite uniform thickness and a quickly decreasing thermal variance are achieved by the optimized path. Figure 6 plots the scaled components of the objective function during one evolutionary process of the best generated individual so far against the number of evaluations. The objective values improve quickly at the beginning, but decrease slower the longer the algorithm works. The magnitude of improvement for every component is depending on the weights, but generally all components improve simultaneously. In addition to this example, twenty further independent runs of the algorithm have been performed. They all were showing the basically

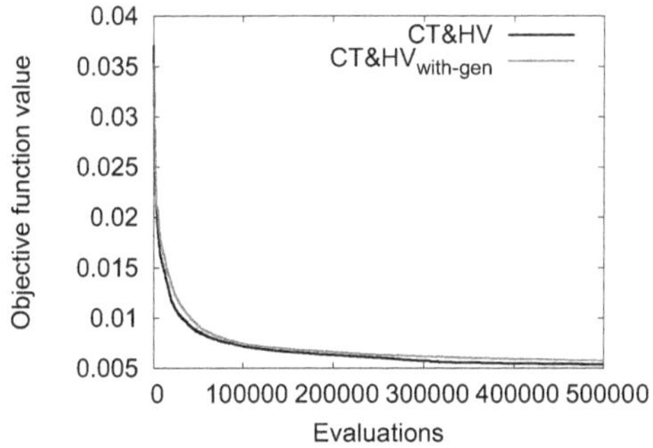

Figure 7: Development of the objective values of the best individual using the Evolutionary Algorithm with and without the concept of generations.

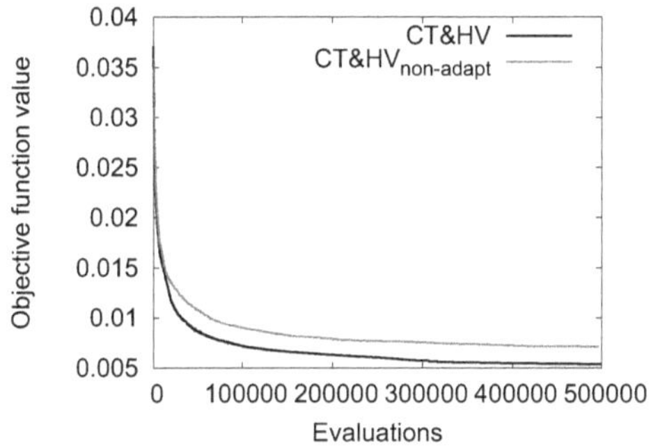

Figure 8: Development of the objective values of the best individual using the Evolutionary Algorithm with and without the concept of self-adaptation.

same behavior. The mean final objective value over all runs was 0.0054, with a variance of $3.27 \cdot 10^{-8}$. This underlines a stable behavior of the algorithm.

Figure 7 shows the development of the objective values for CT&HV and CT&HV$_{\text{with-gen}}$. The objective value of the best individual so far is plotted at every step of evolution, so that the values are monotonously decreasing. The path of the version without generations is about 7 % better.

Concerning the importance of the different evolutionary operators, many experiments have shown that the usage of crossover produces paths with objective function values about 38 % better than without crossover. Interestingly it is not essential what value the probability has as long as it is at least 10 %. A number of experiments have been executed to evaluate the mutation operators. Therefore one of every operator was varied while all others were switched off. The only exceptions were the add- and delete-mutation which cannot be omitted. The finding was that all operators perform very much the same if they are used on their own.

Using all the operators together with self-adapted parameter control results in about 25 % better individuals after the same amount of evaluations. Figure 8 shows the development of the objective values of the best individual using the Evolutionary Algorithm with (CT&HV) and without (CT&HV$_{\text{non-adapt}}$) the concept of self-adaptation.

The comparison of simultaneous optimization of all three objectives (CT&HV) with optimization of just the coating thickness error (CT) in figure 5(k) shows a significantly better behavior of the heat variance for the simultaneous case. Note that the behavior over the whole time range is relevant here. As could be expected, the coating error is worse for simultaneous optimization. This can be seen by the following

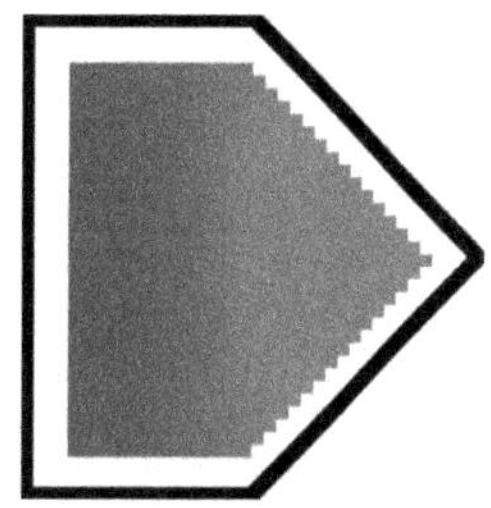

Figure 9: Thermal situation on the workpiece after using direction-parallel paths for the spraying process. Red: Hot Areas. Blue: Cold Areas.

comparison of the minimum, the maximum, and the mean relative absolute error, as well as of the coating thickness error according to the objective function which is comparable to the standard deviation, for CT&HV and CT after 500000 steps of evolution and direction-parallel paths (DP):

Coating error	max.	min.	mean	objective
CT&HV	0.081	$2.9 \cdot 10^{-5}$	0.007	0.001139
CT	0.088	$2.2 \cdot 10^{-6}$	0.006	0.001101
DP	0.018	$1.8 \cdot 10^{-6}$	0.002	0.000596

As can be seen, the loss of coating thickness quality caused by an optimized heat variance is acceptable. The coating error of evolutionary optimization is worse than of direction-parallel paths. However, the objective value is less than twice as high as those of direction-parallel paths. Further, the path of the CT&HV induces much lower thermal variance than direction-parallel paths, see figures 5 and 9. The images show the thermal situations on the workpiece surface during a spraying process using the Evolutionary Algorithm and direction-parallel paths, respectively. For the evolutionary generated path there are strong heat variations at the beginning of the process which cannot be avoided. Further experiments not presented here have shown that even if the execution order of the direction-parallel paths is permuted, what is not realistic in practice, the thermal variations are much higher than those of the evolutionary calculated paths.

The paths generated by the Evolutionary Algorithm seem to be still quite random, see figure 3(b). For a better understanding of the edge distribution, the path is plotted in a dual view in figure 10. The dual view depicts the adjacency of the path nodes. The horizontal and vertical axes list the nodes sequentially along the surface contour. A point (i, j) represents a path edge from node i to node j. The first quarter of the edges along the path are black, and the points of the succeeding quarters are successively brighter. The arrangement of the points seems to be quite random except a cumulation along the diagonal. These points represent short edges following the surface boundary. In order to get more insight in this observation, figure 11 shows the number of points of distance at most $d = 10$ from the diagonal relative to the number of all points. Obviously, the number of points near the diagonal increases, the longer the algorithms runs. Hence it seems that optimized paths often are not bounced back immediately into the interior of the surface when reaching the contour, but slightly move along the contour before they re-enter the interior.

A further aspect of the path structure is the development of the path length over the evolutionary process. The path length grows from about 525 to 686 nodes after 500000 it-

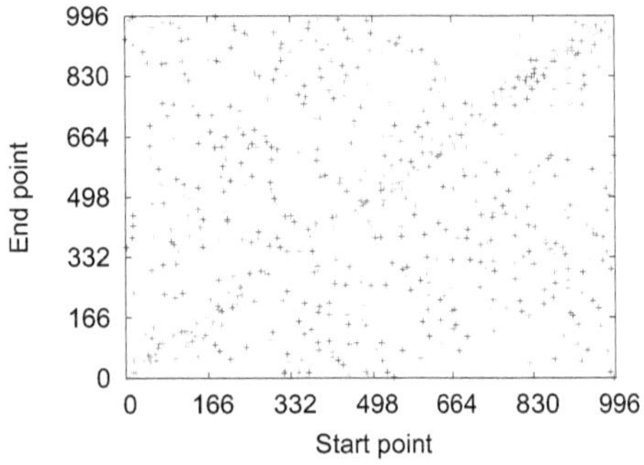

Figure 10: Path edges plotted by points where the horizontal coordinate represents the starting point and the vertical coordinate the end point of an edge. The first quarter of the path is drawn in black, the next quarters are drawn successively brighter.

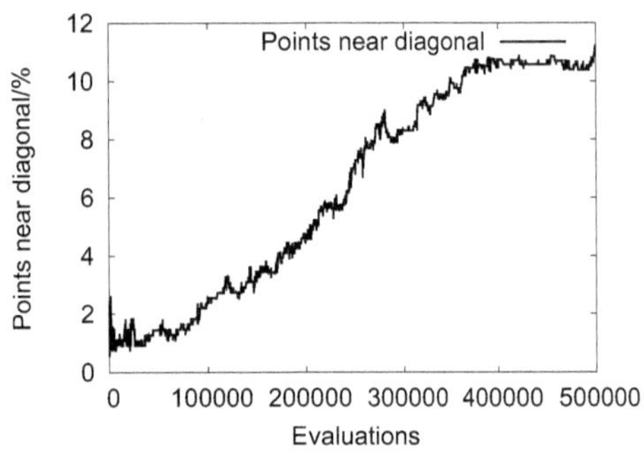

Figure 11: Development of diagonal cumulation of a path, represented by the relative number of points of distance at most $d = 10$ from the diagonal.

erations. An explanation of this effect may be the observed growing number of short edges along the boundary of the object that do not contribute much to the coating.

The experiment CT&HV, evaluating 500000 individuals using 4 processor cores on a core i5 processor with 2.67 GHz needs over 23 hours, with fully loaded cores due to dropping the principle of generations. This time requirement looks considerable, but the following table shows that useful results are already achieved within reasonable run time:

Coating error	10%	5%	2.5%	2%	1%
Iterations	1448	8335	27337	40303	113510
Run time (s)	257	1448	4893	7166	19749

Some other techniques were analyzed in order to find out if they are capable of further improving the results or convergence speed, however with minor effect. For example, two different approaches for raising the genetic diversity in the population were evaluated [10, 13]. Both failed to improve the algorithms convergence speed. The island approach [2] improved the results by approximately 2%, but at worse run times growing with the number of islands used.

6. CONCLUSION AND FUTURE WORK

An Evolutionary Algorithm has been presented which is capable to generate coating paths simultaneously reaching a desired coating thickness within error bounds adequate for technical applications and low heat variance at still practicable calculation times. Contour-to-contour paths have been used as a special path type. An interesting insight gained is that optimized paths do not seem to bounce back immediately at the contour. In future research, this could already be considered in the definition of new classes of paths which might avoid extensive calculations to reach this path structure. Further, simplified versions of the path planning problem of thermal spray coating more appropriate for basic algorithmic research might be derived. And, in opposite direction, after the successful proof-of-concept by this paper, the approach may now be transferred to curved workpiece surfaces occurring in practice.

Acknowledgment

This research was funded by the German Research Foundation (DFG) as part of the collaborative research center 708 "3D-Surface Engineering of Tools for Sheet Metal Forming – Manufacturing, Modeling, Machining", subproject B4.

7. REFERENCES

[1] D. Applegate, R. Bixby, V. Chvatal, and W. Cook. *The traveling salesman problem: a computational study.* Princeton University Press, 2007.

[2] M. Aydin and T. Fogarty. A distributed evolutionary simulated annealing algorithm for combinatorial optimisation problems. *Journal of Heuristics*, 10(3):269–292, 2004.

[3] T. Bäck. *Evolutionary Algorithms in Theory and Practice.* Oxford University Press, 1996.

[4] M. Dakulović, S. Horvatić, and I. Petrović. Complete coverage d* algorithm for path planning of a floor-cleaning mobile robot. *Preprints of the 18th IFAC World Congress*, 18(1):5950–5955, 2011.

[5] J. Davis. *Handbook of Thermal Spray Technology.* Asm International, 2004.

[6] P. Jones, S. Duncan, T. Rayment, and P. Grant. Control of temperature profile for a spray deposition process. *IEEE Transactions on Control Systems Technology*, 11(5):656–667, 2003.

[7] P. Jones, S. Duncan, T. Rayment, and P. Grant. Optimal robot path for minimizing thermal variations in a spray deposition process. *IEEE Transactions on Control Systems Technology*, 15(1):1–11, 2007.

[8] Y. Koren and R. Lin. Efficient tool-path planning for machining free-form surfaces. *ASME Trans. Journal of Engineering for Industry*, pages 20–28, 1996.

[9] P. Larranaga, C. Kuijpers, R. Murga, I. Inza, and S. Dizdarevic. Genetic algorithms for the travelling salesman problem: A review of representations and operators. *Artificial Intelligence Review*, 13(2):129–170, 1999.

[10] M. Mauldin. Maintaining diversity in genetic search. In *Proceedings of the National Conference on Artificial Intelligence*, volume 247, page 250, 1984.

[11] M. McKay, R. Beckman, and W. Conover. A comparison of three methods for selecting values of input variables in the analysis of output from a computer code. *Technometrics*, 21:239–245, 1979.

[12] Thirumaleshwar. *Fundamentals of Heat and Mass Transfer.* Pearson Education, 2006.

[13] R. Ursem. Diversity-guided evolutionary algorithms. *Parallel Problem Solving from Nature - PPSN VII*, pages 462–471, 2002.

Estimating MLC NAND Flash Endurance: A Genetic Programming Based Symbolic Regression Application

Damien Hogan
Computer Science & Information Systems,
University of Limerick,
Ireland.
damien.t.hogan@ul.ie

Tom Arbuckle
Computer Science & Information Systems,
University of Limerick,
Ireland.
tom.arbuckle@ul.ie

Conor Ryan
Computer Science & Information Systems,
University of Limerick,
Ireland.
conor.ryan@ul.ie

ABSTRACT

NAND Flash memory is a multi-billion dollar industry which is projected to continue to show significant growth until at least 2017. Devices such as smart-phones, tablets and Solid State Drives use NAND Flash since it has numerous advantages over Hard Disk Drives including better performance, lower power consumption, and lower weight. However, storage locations within Flash devices have a limited working lifetime, as they slowly degrade through use, eventually becoming unreliable and failing. The number of times a location can be programmed is termed its *endurance*, and can vary significantly, even between locations within the same device. There is currently no technique available to predict endurance, resulting in manufacturers placing extremely conservative specifications on their Flash devices. We perform symbolic regression using Genetic Programming to estimate the endurance of storage locations, based only on the duration of program and erase operations recorded from them. We show that the quality of estimations for a device can be refined and improved as the device continues to be used, and investigate a number of different approaches to deal with the significant variations in the endurance of storage locations. Results show this technique's huge potential for real-world application.

Categories and Subject Descriptors

I.2.8 [**Artificial Intelligence**]: Problem Solving, Control Methods and Search — *Heuristic methods*; B.3.1 [**Semiconductor memories**]

General Terms

Experimentation, Performance, Reliability

Keywords

Genetic programming, Symbolic regression, Flash memory, NAND, Endurance.

1. INTRODUCTION

Flash memory is the fastest growing product in the history of semiconductor technology [7]. The Flash market was forecast to surpass $30 billion in 2012 [15], with the market for NAND Flash (the type of Flash investigated in this research) projected to grow by 14% each year between 2012 and 2017. NAND Flash [21] is a key component in personal devices such as smart-phones, tablets, and digital cameras, and is also the core component in Solid State Drives (SSDs) [22], with SSD based Ultra-books providing one of the fastest growing areas for the NAND Flash market.

NAND Flash storage provides many advantages over hard-disk drives (HDDs) including faster performance, lower power consumption, greater durability (due to the absence of moving parts), lower noise emission, and lower weight. However, Flash remains significantly more expensive per gigabyte than traditional forms of storage.

A key operational characteristic of Flash memory is the degradation of storage locations through repeated use. This results in these storage locations having a finite lifetime, with the number of times they can be programmed being referred to as their *endurance*. The endurance is specified in terms of *p/e cycles*, or the number of times a block (the smallest erasable area, see Section 2) can be programmed and then erased. Both program and erase operations are part of this quantifier because locations must first be erased before they can be programmed.

The endurance of Flash memory poses difficulties for manufacturers since locations degrade at different rates; both from chip to chip, and even within the same Flash chip. Currently, no technique is available to successfully estimate the varying endurance values encountered across chips. This results in manufacturers placing extremely conservative endurance specifications on their devices in order to account for the worst performing storage blocks.

A feature of the degradation of storage locations through repeated use is that they become easier (lower voltage required) to program and erase as they degrade (see Section 2). This leads to the duration of the program and erase operations decreasing (because current flows for a shorter time) as the storage location continues to be p/e cycled. We show it is possible to use this characteristic of Flash memory to generate solutions which use the program and erase times to estimate the actual endurance of a storage block.

In collaboration with partners in industry, Genetic Programming (GP) [17] is used to perform symbolic regression, producing *expressions* which map the supplied input data to an estimated endurance. The data used by GP for training and testing the evolved expressions was accumulated over the course of three months through the destructive testing of NAND Flash chips.

The primary objective of this research is to investigate the potential to evolve accurate expressions which take, as inputs, the durations of program and erase operations recorded from test blocks and produce, as an output, an estimation of the block's endurance in p/e cycles. A secondary goal is to examine whether the accuracies of the estimates for each block improve as additional p/e cycles are completed, further into the lifetime of the block. Finally, the third objective focuses on the required generality of the solutions. A number of approaches are compared including the possibility of using a single expression to estimate endurance for blocks from all chips. Another approach considered is the use of an ensemble of expressions, with each member responsible for dealing with particular kinds of blocks, such as those from a particular production batch. The final approach proposes the use of classification and symbolic regression together and reports on the potential shown by the regression phase of this technique.

The remainder of this paper comprises the following sections. Section 2 provides background information about Flash memory while Section 3 introduces other research related to this topic. Section 4 details the hardware phase of the research and the GP configuration with Section 5 outlining the results achieved. Section 6 details our plans for future work and Section 7 concludes the paper.

2. BACKGROUND

Flash is currently the dominant non-volatile memory technology, although there are several others competing to replace it [18]. Flash memory stores information in *cells*. The main operational component of each cell is a particular type of transistor. Current through these transistors is controlled by the presence or absence of charge on a gate, called a *floating gate* [20], which is electrically isolated by an oxide layer from the rest of the transistor. The transistors' principle of operation relies on the placing and removal of charge on the floating gate. Fowler-Nordheim [8] tunnelling, a quantum mechanical effect, is used to force electrons through the insulating oxide layer and on to the gate (programming) or off the gate (erasing), the quantity of charge on the gate then being a representation of the information stored in the cell.

A difficulty with Flash memory arises because the oxide layer that maintains the charge on the floating gate degrades as the cell is repeatedly programmed and then erased [27]. With use, it becomes easier to program and erase the cells and each of these operations therefore requires less time. However, eventually the gate can no longer retain its charge and the memory location becomes unreliable.

In NAND Flash memory, the type under study in this paper, bits are represented by charge stored in cells. Read and program operations operate on groups of cells known as a *page* while erase operations take place on groups of pages referred to as *blocks*. Blocks must be erased before their pages can be programmed.

Early implementations of Flash memory store one bit per cell. A threshold is used to decide whether a gate stores sufficient charge to be considered programmed. Such cells are termed Single-Level Cells (SLC). Current Flash technologies use three thresholds so that a single gate can store four patterns representing two bits. These are termed Multi-Level Cells (MLC) and seven threshold/three bit chips are also available as Three-Level Cells (TLC). This increase in the number of bits stored per cell increases the difficulty in correctly placing precise amounts of charge and in determining the bit pattern stored in the cell. In addition, the time for which the pattern can be stored without the charge leaking away (its *retention*) decreases.

To compensate for these difficulties, Flash memory (on-chip) controllers implement Error Correcting Codes (ECC) [23]. Supplementary information is retained in extra cells (unavailable to users) that make it possible to detect and correct errors in the data stored. Once the number of errors passes a critical threshold, however, errors can no longer be corrected and the controller marks the block as bad and removes it from service. ECC is expensive, both in terms of silicon real estate and processing time, so there is a limit to how much can be implemented practically. The devices used in this work are capable of detecting and correcting 12 bits in each 512 byte *sector*, or part of a page.

Equipment manufacturers who use Flash in their devices need to know and rely on their endurance specifications. However, determining the endurance of a chip is both expensive and time consuming because blocks on the chip need to be repeatedly p/e cycled to destruction. Chips with the same nominal specification but manufactured from different wafers or in different manufacturing runs have differing behaviours. This leads chip manufacturers to place extremely conservative specifications on their chips. More accurate specifications of chip endurance would save users and manufacturers money. Moreover, the effective capacity of devices using Flash chips would be increased since less additional capacity to allow for the decreasing number of available blocks (*over-provisioning*) would be required.

3. RELATED WORK

In particular, Desnoyers [6] and Grupp et al. [10] provide good overviews of NAND performance and also include observations of the change in program and erase operation durations as storage locations are cycled. Other related papers include analysis of endurance [4] and proposals for improved performance including endurance [25, 24].

There have recently been a small number of publications reporting the use of Evolutionary Algorithms with Flash memory. Sullivan and Ryan [26] reported on their use of Genetic Algorithms to extend the endurance of NOR Flash memory by optimising some of the Flash device's internal control parameters. Hogan et al. constructed a successful technique to perform binary classification on NAND Flash blocks according to their endurance [12, 13], that is, predicting whether or not a block would survive past a particular number of cycles. This group also examined the potential use of retention classifiers [14]. Arbuckle et al. provide overviews of this and related work [2, 1] and also compare a number of statistical and machine learning techniques for the purpose of endurance classification [3].

Our research is concerned with performing symbolic regression using GP to estimate the endurance values of NAND Flash blocks. We have not found any previous reports of this approach to the endurance problem in the literature.

Finally, as an alternative view to that in which Flash market dominance will soon come to an end [9], we note that

Chiu [5] has reported endurance of up to 100 million cycles which may signify a new beginning for Flash memory.

4. EXPERIMENTAL SETUP

In order to generate endurance estimation expressions, GP was utilised together with data acquired from the destructive cycling of blocks on a number of MLC NAND Flash chips. Data recorded from each block included the durations of the program and erase times at regular intervals, and also the total number of p/e cycles successfully completed by the block prior to failure. The primary goal of this research was to evolve expressions to estimate the number of p/e cycles that a block would complete based only on its program and erase timing information. We will now provide an overview of the data acquisition process, followed by an analysis of the accumulated data, and a discussion of the GP configuration used in these experiments.

4.1 Data Acquisition

A distinguishing characteristic of this research is the use of data collected from the destructive testing of Flash chips. A Flash test platform was acquired which facilitated precise chip control, such as reading, programming, and erasing particular locations. Each platform contained the MLC NAND Flash chip under test, and also a single-board computer running a lightweight Linux distribution, accepting commands in the form of plain text strings from a test server.

Blocks were p/e cycled by programming all bits in each of their 128 pages to contain '0' and then immediately erasing the entire block so that all bits were reset to '1'. Every 1,000 cycles, the condition of the block was evaluated by calculating the number of errors occurring in data stored within the block. This process was performed by first programming each page within the block to contain a specific data pattern. The data stored in all of the block's pages was then immediately read, counting the number of bit differences occurring between the retrieved data and the programmed information. The number of bit differences is referred to as the *error count*. Error counts were obtained every 1,000 cycles until the number of errors exceeded the maximum number of errors correctable through ECC. The number of p/e cycles completed at the point of failure was the actual endurance of the block.

As well as calculating the error counts and determining the endurance, the durations of program and erase operations were also recorded at intervals of 1,000 cycles. Since each of the 128 pages needed to be programmed for each block, the program time stored was the average of the 128 recorded values, while the erase time was simply the duration of the single erase operation required to reset all cells within the block (because all pages are erased in a single operation).

In total, 96 blocks were p/e cycled to destruction on each of six chips, with three chips being tested in parallel through the use of three Flash test platforms. These chips were all produced by the same manufacturer to the same specification. Three chips from each of two different production batches, or manufacturing runs, were examined. This data acquisition phase of the research was extremely costly in terms of the time taken, since it took almost three months to accumulate just 576 data points.

Data points are required to train and test supervised machine learning systems by providing inputs to the system (operation durations) together with the corresponding output (endurance). Each data point represented a single block, and contained the duration of program and erase times at 1,000 p/e cycle intervals up to 15,000 p/e cycles together with the endurance value, or number of p/e cycles completed by the block.

Table 1: Endurance Statistics. The minimum, mean, maximum, and standard deviations for blocks evaluated on each individual chip are listed, together with combined information for groups of chips.

Chip	Min	Mean	Max	Std. Dev.
1 (A)	22,000	29,417	46,000	6,044
2 (A)	23,000	28,771	39,000	3,598
3 (A)	31,000	41,188	57,000	7,545
4 (B)	64,000	85,240	119,000	12,404
5 (B)	60,000	77,073	114,000	10,632
6 (B)	115,000	158,031	225,000	31,312
Batch A	22,000	33,125	57,000	8,249
Batch B	60,000	106,781	225,000	41,715
All	22,000	69,953	225,000	47,544

4.2 Data Analysis

The error counts and timing data recorded from the test blocks change in a predictable way as each block is p/e cycled. Through the degradation of the insulating oxide layer in each cell (see Section 2), errors become more likely, increasing the error count as the block is cycled. The degradation of the oxide also makes it easier to program and (initially, see below) erase the cells, resulting in the durations of these operations decreasing through repeated cycling.

The difficulty posed in evolving an expression to estimate the endurance of test blocks is illustrated in Table 1. This table highlights the fact that even though all chips are of the same make and model, the endurance of their blocks varies significantly. The range of endurance values across all chips is 203,000 cycles with a standard deviation of 47,544 cycles making the task of estimating a particular block's endurance very difficult.

Figures 1 and 2 display violin plots [11] which demonstrate the change in program and erase durations as the number of cycles completed increases. The violin plots show the distribution of data, with the widest areas of the plot, shaded grey in this case, showing the areas where most data points occur. The top of the plot represents the maximum value while the bottom is the minimum point. The black rectangle marks all points occurring within the second and third quartiles while the white dot marks the median of the data.

The durations of program operations slowly decrease as blocks are cycled. After 1,000 cycles, the fastest block had an average page program time of approximately 716μs while the slowest block required almost 830μs to program each page. As well as initially having a wide range of program durations, these times decrease at different rates, as can be seen in the violin plots in Figure 1. After 15,000 cycles, the difference between the minimum and maximum values clearly exceeds its initial value, meaning that the range of times recorded from blocks has increased.

The durations of erase operations initially decrease by up to 35%, then remain around a minimum value, before later sharply increasing to values up to 30% longer than the initial recorded times. However, this research will only use timing

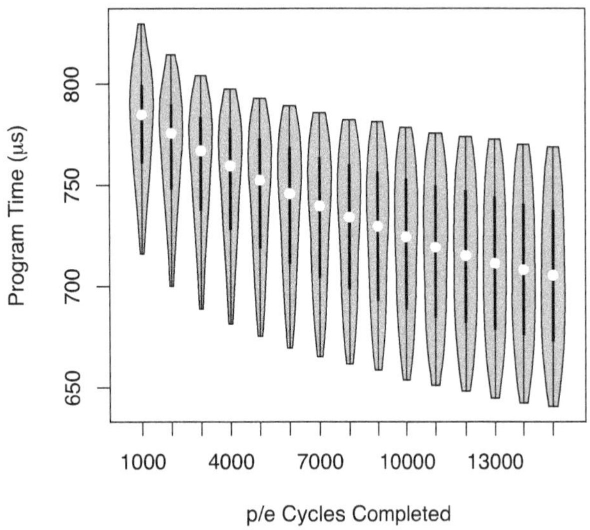

Figure 1: Distributions of Program Durations. The duration of program operations decreases as the number of p/e cycles increases.

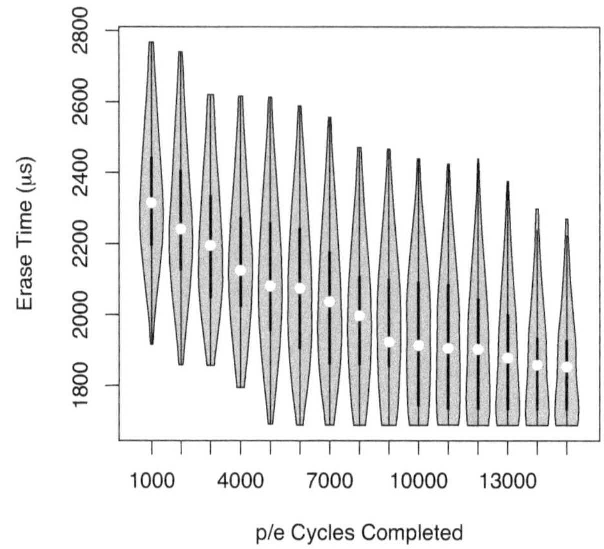

Figure 2: Distributions of Erase Durations. The duration of erase operations decreases (until it reaches a minimum value) as the number of cycles increases.

data recorded during the first 15,000 p/e cycles. This range of cycles was chosen since it is large enough to facilitate 15 different tests while also being less than 22,000 cycles, which is the point at which the first blocks fail. This means the previously described increase in erase time will not be applicable here since it occurs later in the blocks' lifetimes. Having quickly decreased to a minimum value, or fastest erase time, the duration of the erase operation then remains relatively static for a significant number of cycles. This phenomenon is apparent in the violin plots representing higher numbers of cycles in Figure 2. The quick decrease in erase time is easily identifiable but it is also noticeable from the violin plots that many of the erase times decrease towards a particular minimum value. Initially, after 1,000 cycles the bottom of the violin plot forms a point, but this later becomes a flatter, wider surface as the same erase times are recorded from more and more blocks.

It must be emphasised that the program and erase times change at different rates from block to block with stronger, higher endurance blocks showing slower changes and weaker, lower endurance blocks decreasing more quickly. As discussed above, the erase durations of many blocks had decreased to a minimum value within the 15,000 cycles illustrated in the violin plot. These lower erase times are recorded from the weaker blocks since the erase durations recorded from blocks with higher endurance values do not decrease to the minimum value until later in their lifetime.

4.3 Genetic Programming

The objective of this research is to establish a technique to estimate the endurance of blocks within Flash chips. In particular, the aim is to show that the quality of each estimation can be improved as more timing data becomes available from the relevant test block.

GP was used to perform symbolic regression to evolve expressions that took as inputs, program and erase times, and produced as the output, an estimated endurance value. The fitness of each GP individual was evaluated by calculating the mean error between the actual and estimated endurance values for each data point in the data set.

The data set for use by GP comprised 576 data points and was created using the process described in Section 4.1. Each data point represented the information captured from a single block and contained the durations of program and erase operations recorded at 1,000 cycle intervals up to 15,000 cycles. Combinations of this timing data formed the inputs for each generated expression throughout the evolution process. The total number of cycles successfully completed by the block was included in each data point and represented the output, or target result, for each expression.

In order to evaluate the ability of the evolved expressions to generalise to previously unseen data, five fold cross–validation was used, requiring the division of the data set into five equally sized parts. However, the first fold contained an extra data point since 576 is not divisible by five. Each single GP run then used four folds as training data (during evolution), and reserved the fifth fold for use as test data to evaluate the generalisation ability of the best performing expression. This resulted in approximately an 80% training and 20% testing split for each GP run. This cross validation process allowed five different compositions of the data set since five different folds could be used as the testing portion of the data set. Thirty GP runs were performed on each different data set composition, giving 150 runs in total for each set of inputs.

During initialisation of the population and throughout the evolutionary process, expressions which resulted in invalid values were discarded as proposed by Keijzer [16], rather than using guarded operations. The ephemeral random constant, also proposed in Keijzer's paper, which randomly chooses constants maintaining a mean of 0 and a standard deviation of 5, was also used. GP runs that evolved expressions producing results greater than five standard deviations from the mean test error for each set of inputs were removed from the result set. This filtering was performed since these anomalous results significantly affected the mean

Table 2: Sets of Inputs Used. Experiments were performed using data recorded at intervals of 1,000 cycles up to the completion of 15,000 cycles.

Test	Input 1	Input 2	Input 3	Input 4
1	pt1000	et1000		
2	pt1000	et1000	pt2000	et2000
...	...	...	...	...
10	pt1000	et1000	pt10000	et10000
...	...	...	...	...
15	pt1000	et1000	pt15000	et15000

Table 3: Tableau showing GP parameters.

Parameter	Details		
Objective	Accurately estimate the endurance for each test block.		
Function Set	+, -, *, /		
Terminal Set	Program and erase timing information as listed in Table 2. Keijzer ERC, where the ephemeral random constant ($\Re$) has a mean of 0 and a standard deviation of 5.		
Fitness	The mean error between estimated endurance and actual endurance across all points in the data set.		
Generations	100	Population	1000
Crossover	0.9	Mutation	0.1
Elitism	2	Max Tree Depth	10
Selection	Tournament selection, size = 7.		

results achieved, and accounted for approximately 1.07% of the total runs performed.

Fifteen different sets of inputs to the GP system were evaluated, each utilising timing information following the completion of an increased number of cycles as can be seen in Table 2. Each set of inputs was tested across 150 GP runs. This facilitated investigation into the change in quality of the estimations as timing information recorded later in the lifetime of blocks was supplied. The sets of inputs were formed, in turn, from the program and erase times recorded after 1,000 cycles together with those recorded at each of the remaining cycling intervals up to 15,000 cycles. The first of the 15 tests comprised just two inputs – the program and erase times after 1,000 cycles – while, for example, the inputs for the fifth test were formed from the times after 1,000 cycles together with the times recorded after 5,000 cycles. Providing the GP system with two pairs of program and erase inputs, recorded at different intervals, allowed the potential for learning from the rate of change of the program and erase times.

ECJ, a Java-based evolutionary computation research system [19] was utilised to perform the GP runs described above. Initially, trial runs were performed to assess GP parameter settings such as the function set operators, maximum tree depth, and a number of crossover / mutation rate combinations. Table 3 provides details of the resulting GP parameters which were used throughout the experiments. A population of 1,000 individuals evolves for 100 generations, using tournament selection together with sub-tree crossover and point mutation.

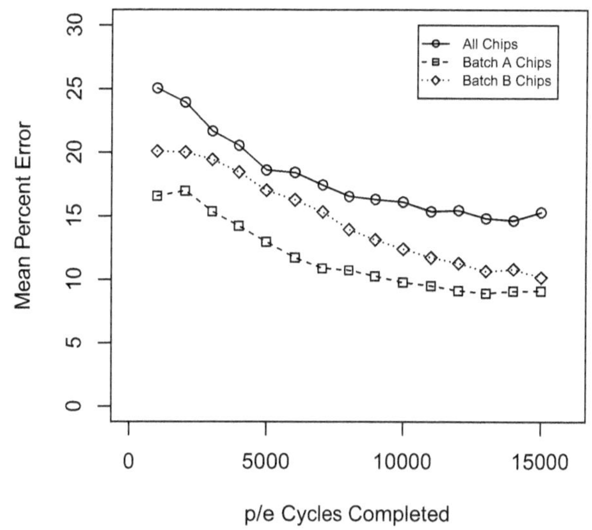

Figure 3: Batch Level Results. Each point represents the mean best test error for runs upon completion of increasing numbers of p/e cycles.

5. RESULTS

Each batch of tests examined 15 different sets of inputs in order to establish how the accuracy of the endurance estimation changes as more cycles are completed. Initially, the data set comprised all available data points from the six test chips. Following this, the same experiments were performed, but with smaller data sets, in which the data was divided according to the production batch of the chips. Finally, the potential for combining the use of classification and symbolic regression was considered, with regression performed on three groups of data points of similar endurance.

As mentioned in Section 4.3, prior to starting the GP runs, the entire data set was randomly subdivided into five partitions, or folds, ensuring that each fold contained roughly the same number of data points from each chip. Care was also taken to ensure that each fold contained a similar distribution of endurance values. The results presented in the following sections refer to the mean percentage error achieved on the test data by the single best training expression from each GP run.

5.1 Data Set Comprising All Data

Ideally, a single expression would be evolved to estimate the endurance of any block on any chip and from any production batch. The first set of tests examined the potential for achieving this, since the data from all six test chips was included in the data set. Referring back to Table 1, we can see that this data set ranged across 203,000 endurance values and had a standard deviation of 47,544 cycles. As can been seen in Figure 3, having initially reported a mean error for the endurance estimation of approximately 25%, the accuracy of the evolved solutions continually improves, achieving a minimum value of around 15%.

Figure 4 plots the mean best training fitness per generation for four tests performed using all data points. The plots for only four of the 15 tests are provided since it becomes difficult to distinguish them from each other as more are added to the diagram. These plots confirm that the evolved

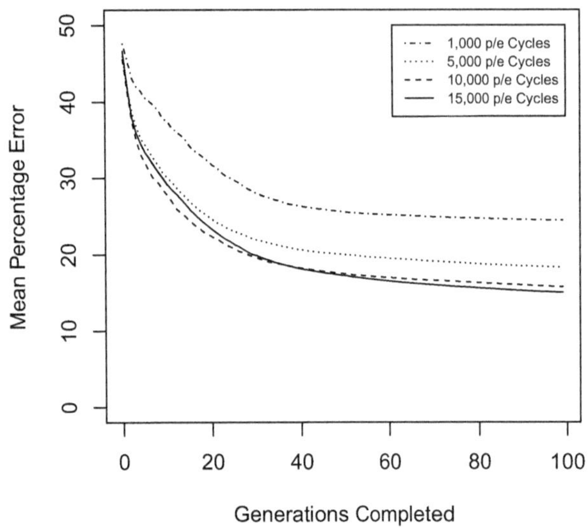

Figure 4: Mean Best Training Fitness. The mean data for four sample tests is presented showing that GP initially learns at a fast pace before later slowing.

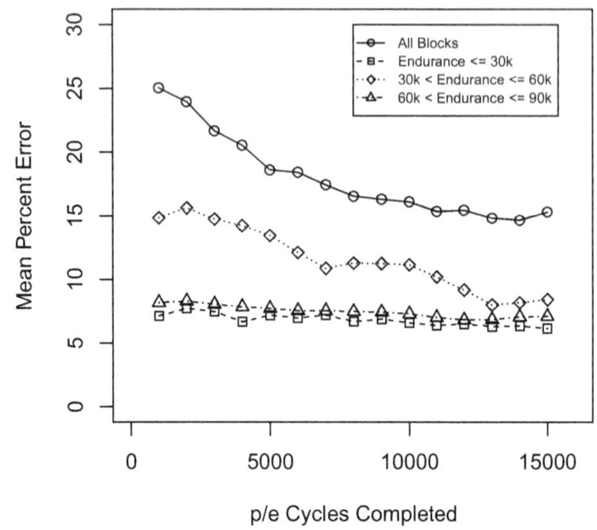

Figure 5: Block Level Results. Each point represents the mean best test error for runs upon completion of increasing numbers of p/e cycles.

expressions are improving as the number of generations increases meaning that GP is learning as evolution proceeds.

The huge performance difference between blocks within this data set had a significant effect on the results achieved. In order to investigate further, the next step in this research divided the available data points into two data sets; one comprising only chips from production batch A, with the other only containing data from production batch B.

5.2 Batch Level Division of Data

The data set comprising only blocks from batch A had a standard deviation of 8,249 cycles, implying that the blocks performed more similarly than those in the previous data set. However, batch B had a significantly larger standard deviation of 41,715 cycles, since chip six hugely outperformed the other two chips sampled from that production batch.

The results of the batch level tests are plotted in Figure 3. As expected, based on the standard deviations of the two data sets, more accurate expressions were evolved for the data points from batch A than from batch B. It is also significant that both sets of tests outperformed those from the initial data set. The results for batch A decreased from a mean error of 16.57% after 1,000 cycles to 9.10% after 15,000 cycles. Meanwhile, the more varied, and thus more difficult, batch B data set reported an initial mean error of 20.07% but this decreased to 10.17% after 15,000 cycles.

These batch level results are a significant improvement on the experiments comprising all available data. However, this approach requires evolution of expressions for all (including future) production batches, requiring the time consuming data acquisition phase (see Section 4.1) to be performed on chips from each extra batch. It would be preferable to evolve a fixed number of expressions, rather than having to evolve new expressions for each additional production batch. With the aim of evolving a fixed number of endurance estimation expressions capable of working with all production batches, the next stage of this research divided the original data set into a number of smaller, more targeted sets.

5.3 Block Level Division of Data

The block level division of data approach is based on the use of both classifiers (such as those proposed by Hogan et al. [12, 13]) *and* symbolic regression. Firstly a collection of binary classifiers are required to group the data points, or test blocks, by endurance, using the timing information recorded early in the block's lifetime. Secondly, expressions should be evolved using symbolic regression for each of the groups created in the first step. These groups of relatively similar blocks could then be treated as distinct data sets with symbolic regression providing more refined endurance estimations, with each expression targeting a specific category of blocks. Having completed these initial two steps, test blocks from the entire data set can be classified using an ensemble of binary classifiers. This step essentially predicts that the endurance of the block lies between two boundaries. Finally, the corresponding regression expression, for the data points lying within these boundaries, can be used to provide an accurate estimation of the endurance.

Since the focus of this research is the application of symbolic regression, only step two is performed in order to evaluate the potential of this hybrid technique. Three similarly sized data groups were created at boundaries of 30,000 cycles since this resulted in relatively equal numbers of blocks in each division. The first group contained all blocks with an endurance less than or equal to 30,000 cycles. The second group contained all blocks having endurance values between 31,000 and 60,000 cycles while the third group comprised those blocks that had an endurance of between 61,000 and 90,000 cycles. Blocks having endurance above 90,000 cycles were not used for this initial, proof-of-concept experiment.

Since the classification phase of this approach has not been completed, and would likely introduce some classification error, the results cannot be directly compared with those from the earlier two approaches. However, they can be used as an indication of the potential of this technique. The results plotted in Figure 5 show that all three block level groups perform better than the original, larger data set. In particular, the 30,000 and 90,000 groups perform extremely well, achieving mean error estimations of just 7.14% and 8.18% respectively after the completion of only 1,000 cycles. These values remain relatively consistent as the number of cycles completed increases, decreasing by only 1%.

Upon examination of the division of the data sets, the first sub group (up to 30,000 cycles) is expected to perform well. The data points in this group come from just two chips, and all contain very similar values since the lowest endurance in the entire data set is 22,000 cycles.

The data points in the third subgroup are also formed from two chips. However, unlike the first data group, these data points do vary across the available range from 61,000 to 90,000 cycles. Taking this into account, this sub set of the data performs extremely well.

Finally, the second set of data points, those achieving between 31,000 and 60,000 cycles, initially perform adequately, although noticeably not as well as the other two block based sub-groups. However, as the number of cycles completed increases, the results show significant improvement, achieving almost the same accuracy level as the other two sub-groups after 13,000 cycles. Having examined the program and erase times (inputs) for these tests, there is no clear explanation for this difference in performance between the second sub-group and the other sub-groups.

5.4 Discussion

The characteristic described in Section 4.2, whereby the erase time passes through three different operational phases, affects the results achieved. The duration of the erase time decreases (quickly in weaker blocks) to a minimum level, and then remains relatively static for a significant number of cycles (of the order of thousands) before later sharply increasing to a maximum level. During the period when the erase time settles around its minimum value, the GP system has no way of differentiating between different levels of cycling based on the erase time and, in turn, cannot learn from the rate of change. This explains the decreased rate of improvement as more cycles are completed, especially in the tests using the complete data set, and also the slight increase toward the right hand side (13,000 to 15,000) of a number of the results plots.

The block level division of data (classification/regression hybrid approach) suggests that, not surprisingly, having more specialised regression expressions yields better results. Since it has been shown by Hogan et al. [12] that it is possible to classify blocks as being of a particular performance group, this type of partitioning of the data can also be performed. The pilot investigation into this approach focuses only on the initial training of the symbolic regression expressions, and did not attempt to train or test the system using the required classifiers. However, this hybrid technique has shown significant potential and will be comprehensively evaluated in future work.

6. FUTURE WORK

We propose to continue our collaboration with partners in industry and construct a larger data set, providing more data points for training and testing, allowing construction of more robust endurance estimation tools. Having accumulated a larger data set, the research will proceed to verify that the classification and regression approaches can be used together to produce the most accurate estimations.

Initially, a series of binary classifiers will be evolved using GP to predict whether each test block will successfully complete a predefined number of cycles. Each classifier will be trained to identify a different portion of the data set. As with the regression results reported in this paper, we expect that the classifications will become more accurate as more timing data is supplied. GP based symbolic regression will then be utilised, together with a block level division of data points, to evolve a series of expressions to estimate the endurance for blocks within each of the classification groups. This process will result in the evolution of a number of classification and regression expressions.

We will proceed to evaluate the entire process, firstly classifying each block in order to select the most suitable regression expression, and then estimating the number of cycles the block will complete. Following this comprehensive set of tests, we will be in a position to directly compare the results achieved with those from the approaches discussed in Sections 5.1 and 5.2 above.

7. CONCLUSIONS

The overall goal of this research was to examine the potential of utilising symbolic regression techniques through GP to generate expressions to estimate endurance. These expressions should only use the program and erase timing information recorded from the block under test.

In response to the primary research question posed in Section 1, we have shown that symbolic regression can be successfully used to estimate the actual endurance of blocks. We have also shown that this can be achieved after the completion of relatively small numbers of cycles. Previous approaches to this problem (as discussed in Section 3) had focused on classification but our technique achieves far greater accuracy (predicting the point of failure) using symbolic regression. This is due to the continual refinement of estimations as more cycles are completed and the fact that regression is not limited to classifying within predefined boundaries such as iterative steps of 50,000 cycles.

Secondly, the accuracy of the estimates was also shown to improve as data is recorded from increasing numbers of cycles, essentially allowing the system to continually refine its estimation for any test block as more data becomes available. The rate of refinement is fast over the first few thousand cycles, before slowing down, which we expect is related to the properties of the change in erase time as the number of p/e cycles increases.

The third, and final research question queried the ability, or necessity, to create a general expression capable of working with all chips. Results show that a general solution is possible, producing reasonable estimations with a mean error of around 25% after only 1,000 cycles, and decreasing to around 15% later. These results are acceptable considering the range of endurance values and variance of the data set. Evolving expressions for each production batch was also investigated but the area which showed most potential was division of the data set at block level. The theory behind this approach was that, combining the classification and symbolic regression approaches, each block would first be classified based on the program and erase information in order to select the most suitable symbolic regression generated expression. In this paper, only the initial symbolic regression training was performed, with the entire classification/regression process to be evaluated in future work.

The techniques described in this paper show huge potential for real-world application. Currently, the endurance specifications for Flash chips are extremely conservative estimates based on worst-case performance of blocks. The research reported here will allow manufacturers increase the specified endurance of Flash chips since they can now predict the quality of blocks within chips after the completion of a relatively small number of cycles.

8. ACKNOWLEDGMENTS

The authors would like to thank the reviewers for their helpful comments.This research was funded by an Enterprise Ireland Innovation Partnership Grant, contract number IP/2008/0591.

9. REFERENCES

[1] T. Arbuckle, D. Hogan, and C. Ryan. Optimising Flash memory for differing usage scenarios: Goals and approach. In *Proc. Int. Conference on Convergence and Hybrid Information Technology*, pages 137–140, August 2012.

[2] T. Arbuckle, D. Hogan, and C. Ryan. Optimising Flash non-volatile memory using machine learning: A project overview. In *Proc. 5th Balkan Conference on Informatics*, pages 235–238, September 2012.

[3] T. Arbuckle, D. Hogan, and C. Ryan. Learning predictors for Flash memory endurance: A comparative study of alternative classification methods. *International Journal of Computational Intelligence Studies*, 2013. To appear.

[4] S. Boboila and P. Desnoyers. Write endurance in Flash drives: Measurement and analysis. In *8th USENIX Conference on File and Storage Technologies*, pages 115–128, February 2010.

[5] Y.-T. Chiu. Forever Flash. *IEEE Spectrum*, 49(12):11–12, 2012.

[6] P. Desnoyers. Empirical evaluation of NAND Flash memory performance. *SIGOPS Oper. Syst. Rev.*, pages 50–54, March 2010.

[7] Flash Memory Summit. Flash memory backgrounder. http://www.flashmemorysummit.com/English/Conference/FM_Backgrounder.html. Accessed January 28th, 2013.

[8] R. H. Fowler and L. Nordheim. Electron emission in intense electric fields. *Proceedings of the Royal Society of London. Series A*, 119(781):173–181, 1928.

[9] L. Grupp, J. Davis, and S. Swanson. The bleak future of NAND Flash memory. In *Proc. 10th USENIX conference on File and Storage Technologies*, pages 17–24, February 2012.

[10] L. M. Grupp, A. M. Caulfield, J. Coburn, S. Swanson, E. Yaakobi, P. H. Siegel, and J. K. Wolf. Characterizing Flash memory: Anomalies, observations, and applications. In *Proc. 42nd Annual IEEE/ACM International Symposium on Microarchitecture*, pages 24–33, 2009.

[11] J. L. Hintze and R. D. Nelson. Violin plots: A box Plot-Density trace synergism. *The American Statistician*, 52(2):181–184, 1998.

[12] D. Hogan, T. Arbuckle, and C. Ryan. Evolving a storage block endurance classifier for Flash memory: A trial implementation. In *Proc. 11th IEEE Int. Conference on Cybernetic Intelligent Systems*, pages 12–17, August 2012.

[13] D. Hogan, T. Arbuckle, and C. Ryan. How early and with how little data? Using genetic programming to evolve endurance classifiers for MLC NAND Flash memory. In *Proc. 16th European Conference on Genetic Programming*, pages 253–264, April 2013.

[14] D. Hogan, T. Arbuckle, C. Ryan, and J. Sullivan. Evolving a retention period classifier for use with Flash memory. In *Proc. 4th Int. Conf. on Evolutionary Computation Theory and Applications*, pages 24–33, October 2012.

[15] ICInsights. Total Flash memory market will surpass DRAM for first time in 2012. http://www.icinsights.com/news/bulletins/Total-Flash-Memory-Market-Will-Surpass-DRAM-For-First-Time-In-2012, December 2012. Accessed 27th Jan., 2013.

[16] M. Keijzer. Improving symbolic regression with interval arithmetic and linear scaling. In *Proc. 6th European Conference on Genetic Programming*, pages 70–82, 2003.

[17] J. R. Koza. *Genetic Programming: On the Programming of Computers by Means of Natural Selection.* The MIT press, 1992.

[18] H. Li and Y. Chen. An overview of non-volatile memory technology and the implication for tools and architectures. In *Design, Automation Test in Europe*, pages 731–736, April 2009.

[19] S. Luke. ECJ 20. A Java-based evolutionary computation research system. *http://cs.gmu.edu/~eclab/projects/ecj/*, October 2010.

[20] F. Masuoka and H. Iizuka. Semiconductor memory device and method for manufacturing the same, 1980. US Patent 4,531,203.

[21] R. Micheloni, L. Crippa, and A. Marelli. *Inside NAND Flash Memories.* Springer, 2010.

[22] R. Micheloni, A. Marelli, and K. Eshghi. *Inside Solid State Drives (SSDs)*, volume 37 of *Springer Series in Advanced Microelectronics.* Springer, 2012.

[23] R. Micheloni, A. Marelli, and R. Ravasio. *Error Correction Codes for Non-Volatile Memories.* Springer, 2010.

[24] V. Mohan, T. Siddiqua, S. Gurumurthi, and M. R. Stan. How I learned to stop worrying and love Flash endurance. In *Proc. 2nd USENIX conference on Hot topics in storage and file systems*, 2010.

[25] Y. Pan, G. Dong, and T. Zhang. Exploiting memory device wear-out dynamics to improve NAND Flash memory system performance. In *Proc. 9th USENIX conference on File and storage technologies*, 2011.

[26] J. Sullivan and C. Ryan. A destructive evolutionary algorithm process. *Soft Computing – A Fusion of Foundations, Methodologies and Applications*, 15:95–102, 2011.

[27] J. Witters, G. Groeseneken, and H. Maes. Degradation of tunnel-oxide floating-gate EEPROM devices and the correlation with high field-current-induced degradation of thin gate oxides. *IEEE Transactions on Electron Devices*, 36(9):1663–1682, September 1989.

Controlling Tensegrity Robots through Evolution

Atil Iscen
Oregon State University
Corvallis, OR, 97331, USA
iscena@onid.orst.edu

Adrian Agogino
UC Santa Cruz / NASA Ames
MS 269-3, Moffett Field, CA 94035, USA
Adrian.K.Agogino@nasa.gov

Vytas SunSpiral
SGT Inc. / NASA Ames
MS 269-3, Moffett Field, CA 94035, USA
vytas.sunspiral@nasa.gov

Kagan Tumer
Oregon State University
Corvallis, OR, 97331, USA
kagan.tumer@oregonstate.edu

ABSTRACT

Tensegrity structures (built from interconnected rods and cables) have the potential to offer a revolutionary new robotic design that is light-weight, energy-efficient, robust to failures, capable of unique modes of locomotion, impact tolerant, and compliant (reducing damage between the robot and its environment). Unfortunately robots built from tensegrity structures are difficult to control with traditional methods due to their oscillatory nature, nonlinear coupling between components and overall complexity. Fortunately this formidable control challenge can be overcome through the use of evolutionary algorithms. In this paper we show that evolutionary algorithms can be used to efficiently control a ball shaped tensegrity robot. Experimental results performed with a variety of evolutionary algorithms in a detailed soft-body physics simulator show that a centralized evolutionary algorithm performs 400% better than a hand-coded solution, while the multiagent evolution performs 800% better. In addition, evolution is able to discover diverse control solutions (both crawling and rolling) that are robust against structural failures and can be adapted to a wide range of energy and actuation constraints. These successful controls will form the basis for building high-performance tensegrity robots in the near future.

Categories and Subject Descriptors

I.2.6 [**Artificial Intelligence**]: Learning

General Terms

Algorithms, Design

Keywords

Evolution, Robotics, Tensegrity

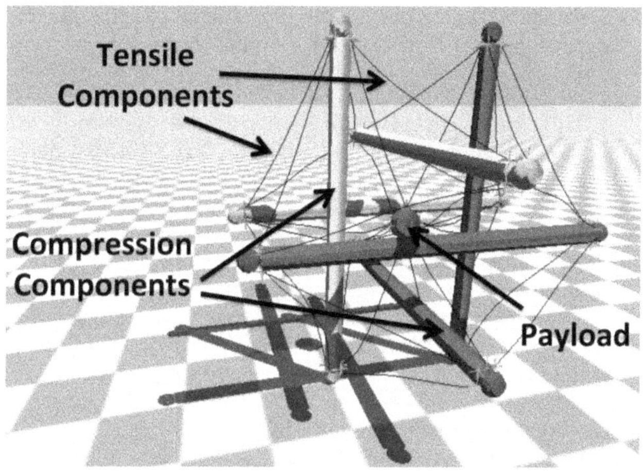

Figure 1: **Tensegrity Structure.** *Tensegrities are composed of pure tension and pure compression elements (e.g. cables and rods). They can be light-weight, energy-efficient and robust to failures.*

1. INTRODUCTION

Tensegrity robots are part of an exciting emerging field of soft-body robotics that are entirely composed of pure tension and compression elements (cables and rods - see Figure 1). These structures are made of axially loaded compression elements encompassed within a network of tensional elements, and thus each element experiences either pure linear compression or pure tension. As a result, individual elements can be extremely lightweight as there are no bending or shear forces that must be resisted. A unique property of tensegrity structures is how they can internally distribute forces. As there are no lever arms, forces do not magnify into joints or other common points of failure. Rather, externally applied forces distribute through the structure via multiple load paths, creating a system level robustness and tolerance to forces applied from any direction. Thus tensegrity structures can be easily reoriented and are ideally suited for operation in dynamic environments where contact forces cannot always be predicted.

Tensegrities have a number of beneficial properties including:

- **Light-weight**: Forces align axially with components and shocks distribute through the tensegrity, allowing tensegrities to be made of light-weight tubes/rods and cables/elastic lines.

- **Energy efficient**: Through the use of elastic tensile components and dynamical gaits, efficient movement is possible.
- **Robust to failures**: Tensegrities are naturally distributed systems and can gracefully degrade performance in the event of actuation or structural failure.
- **Capable of unique modes of locomotion**: Tensegrities can roll, crawl, gallop, swim or flap wings depending on construction and need.
- **Impact tolerant and compliant**: Since forces are distributed upon impact, they can fall or bump into things at moderate speed. In addition, their compliance ensures that they do minimal damage to objects they contact.
- **Naturally distributed control**: Characteristics of force propagation in tensegrities allows effective local controllers.

The last property is the most subtle but important. In "traditional" robots, distributed controls becomes messy due to the need to communicate global state information to all the controllers with high precision, and thus often undermines the very promise of distribution. Fundamentally, this stems from the fact that a rigidly connected structure will magnify forces internally through leverage, and will accumulate force into joints. Thus, the actions of a local distributed controller can have disproportionate global consequences. These consequences can require a certain amount of global coordination and state management, undermining the value of the local controller. Tensegrity structures are different, due to the tension network, there is no leverage in the structure. Thus, forces *diffuse* through the structure, rather than accumulate in joints. As a result, actions by a local controller diffuse through the structure, integrating with all the other local controllers. While any one local controller will impact the structure globally, that impact is locality relevant and not magnified via leverage. Thus, the structure enables true distributed control, because local actions stay (predominately) local.

Despite these desirable properties, tensegrity robots have remained mostly a novelty for many years due to difficult control properties that make them hard to control with traditional control algorithms such as:

1. **Complex oscillatory motions**: Tensegrity robots tend to have oscillatory motions influenced by their interactions with their environment.
2. **Elastic Nonlinear distributed interactions**: A force generated on one part of the tensegrity propagates in a nonlinear way through the entire tensegrity, causing shape changes, which further change force propagations.

Fortunately the combinatorial optimization capabilities of evolutionary algorithms combined with the distributed properties of multiagent systems are a natural match to these problems. Evolutionary algorithms can learn complex control policies that maximize a performance criterion without needing to handle the oscillatory motions and distributed interactions explicitly. In addition, increased performance can be achieved by assigning evolving agents to different control points throughout the tensegrity. Then as a multiagent system, the agents can co-evolve to create a unified control policy.

In this paper, we present how both centralized evolution as well as cooperative coevolutionary algorithms (CCEA) can be used to learn control policies that allow a six segment tensegrity to roll through its environment. We present different approaches for fitness and test the best one against different environmental conditions. This paper is organized as follows: Section 2 gives background on tensegrity robots and previous work. Section 3 gives details about the tensegrity robot used in this paper. Section 4 shows different approaches to evolving a control policy for the tensegrity robot. Section 5 presents experimental results. Section 6 discusses hardware details and Section 7 ends the paper with conclusions and future work.

2. BACKGROUND AND PREVIOUS WORK

Tensegrity structures are a fairly modern concept, having been initially explored in the 1960's by Buckminster Fuller [6] and the artist Kenneth Snelson [19]. For the first few decades, the majority of tensegrity related research was concerned with form-finding techniques [25, 9, 20, 15, 26, 12, 14] and the design and analysis of static structures [1, 7, 18]. Research into control of tensegrity structures was initiated in the mid-1990's, with initial efforts at formalizing the dynamics of tensegrity structures only recently emerging [18, 10, 24]. The very properties that make tensegrities ideal for physical interaction with the environment (compliance, multi-path load distribution, nonlinear dynamics, etc.) also present significant challenges to traditional control approaches. A recent review [22] shows that there are still many open problems in actively controlling tensegrities.

There are several approaches that have been taken to control tensegrity robots. Most related to the work in this paper are approaches to locomotion of tensegrity robots using evolutionary algorithms [5]. Paul et al [13] shows two different tensegrity robots that can perform a locomotion movement. These robots perform motion mostly by alternating between different configurations and doing small hops and crawling. Being able to successfully evolve these gaits is impressive given that one of the tensegrities uses only three rods, while the other uses four. However, such simple tensegrities are not able to achieve efficient rolling motion or complex dynamical movements mainly due to shape constraints of the structure used.

Instead of evolving control policies for tensegrities, more recent work has been done on engineering control algorithms that leverage key features of locomotion [17, 2]. There has also been recent work involving hand tuning of controls for rolling tensegrity robots by body deformation [16, 8, 21, 4]. While this work is able to produce stable smooth dynamics, they are not designed to address the oscillatory nature of tensegrities that come up at high speeds, on uneven terrain, or upon collisions with other objects that occurs in many domains. Instead, with our evolutionary approach, these oscillatory complexities of the tensegrity are implicitly incorporated into the fitness evaluation function generated from the physics simulations, and therefore we are able to create dynamical control that can incorporate complexities of the domain as they arise.

3. TARGET TENSEGRITY PLATFORM

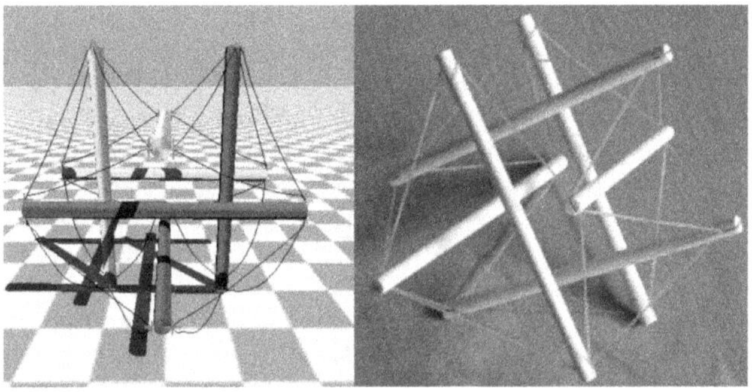

Figure 2: **Structure for Tensegrity Robot.** *This six-rod design is one of the simplest designs that can behave as a "ball." It is capable of rolling, changing shapes, and can be robust against failures.*

In this paper we show how controls can be evolved on a ball shaped tensegrity capable of a large range of movement. To do this we choose as our experimental platform, a 6-rod, 24-cable tensegrity as shown in Figure 2. It is chosen since it is one of the simplest tensegrity platforms that can exhibit the following complex behaviors:

- **Many modes of locomotion**: They can crawl, "gallop" and roll, with rolling being an especially efficient and fast mode of locomotion.
- **Robust against failures**: They exhibit enough redundancy that they can recover from hardware failure.
- **Shape changing**: They can change shape to "peer" over things, get unstuck or to move sensors located on tensegrity structure.

These "ball" tensegrities can be useful in many domains, especially those in which a tensegrity has to navigate rugged terrains that can be difficult for wheeled vehicles.

3.1 Structure

The structure of the tensegrity used in this paper is shown in Figure 2. Rods do not connect directly with other rods, instead, rods are indirectly connected through cables, resulting in a continuous tension network as the primary load transfer system of the structure. In the orientation shown in Figure 2 (left) one pair of the rods are parallel to x-axis, another pair is parallel to y axis and the last pair is parallel to z-axis. Each end of a rod is connected to the ends of other non parallel rods via 4 different cables. When the structure is in balance, it is symmetrical and convenient for a rolling motion. On the other hand, when an external force is applied, it easily deforms and distributes the force to every component of the structure.

In addition to the base tensegrity, we attached a ball shaped payload to the center of the tensegrity via an additional 8 payload cables. The payload represents the essential parts of the robot, such as computing, sensors, batteries, or other instruments. As opposed to the 24 outer cables, these 8 payload cables have constant length and are not actively controlled in this work (Figures 1,6).

3.2 Controls

The tensegrity is controlled by changing the lengths of the cables. Many hardware implementations do this by using a motor to wind the cable onto a spool that is either interior to the tensegrity or inside a rod. Other concepts involve using dynamic cable twisting or elastomers to change the length of the cable. In this paper we do not consider the hardware implementation, though we do limit our abstract model of actuation to reasonable performance characteristics for velocity, acceleration, and string elasticity.

The control of the robot is done via sinusoidal control of the lengths of the cables. The lengths of the cables change over time according to a sinusoidal signal, and the parameters of the signal are the output of the evolutionary algorithm. The length of each cable is calculated with the formula:

$$y(t) = C + A * sin(\omega t + \phi) \tag{1}$$

where,

- C represents the center position of the sine wave.
- A, the amplitude, is the peak deviation of the function from its center position.
- ω, the angular frequency, is how many oscillations occur in a unit time interval
- ϕ, the phase, specifies where in its cycle the oscillation begins at t = 0.

By using 24 sinusoidal signals for 24 cables, overall control of the tensegrity is based on 96 ($24 * 4$) parameters.

3.3 Simulation

Our tensegrity simulator is built on top of the open-source Bullet Physics Engine [3]. Bullet was chosen because of its built in support for soft-bodied physics, and has been used previously in tendon-driven robotics simulators such as Wittmeier et al's CALIPER software [23]. The simulated tensegrity structure has a size of 10 meters for each rod due to the fact that the physics engine is more precise for objects approximately that size. Cables are represented as nodes with Hooke's-law-like stiffness between them. Therefore our "cables" are actually somewhat elastic and exert a force dependent on their length. We keep our model of actuation abstract in order to explore the best control solutions and then drive requirements back into real hardware design requirements. To enforce additional realism, we prevent the cables being actuated when stretched more than 25%, as an upper limit on the hypothetical motor force. This approach allows us to find the types of control and requirements that will be driven into actuation selection.

4. EVOLUTIONARY ALGORITHMS

While the control parameters of our tensegrity platform are relatively straightforward, the relationship between these parameters is highly complex. In this section we explore how we can use the simulation combined with a fitness evaluation to implement an evolutionary algorithm that can evolve a set of control parameters that leads to the desired behavior.

4.1 Evaluation Function

We measure the performance of a simulated tensegrity based on how far it can travel from a starting location within 60 seconds:

$$f = d(C_1, A_1, \omega_1, \phi_1, \cdots, C_{24}, A_{24}, \omega_{24}, \phi_{24}) , \quad (2)$$

where, d is the distance travelled, which is a function of the 96 parameters of the control policy. Note that the decomposition of the distance function d is not readily obtainable in closed form. Instead it must be computed from observing simulations or measured from a physical implementation. Also note that our evaluation does not explicitly take any behavior into account besides distance moved. Tensegrities can exhibit many different gaits, ranging from hopping to rolling, and many different paths, ranging from spirals to straight lines. However, tensegrities that maximize our fitness function tend to roll in fairly straight lines. Deviations from this pattern tend to hurt performance.

4.2 Centralized Evolutionary Algorithms

In this paper, we perform both centralized evolution and multiagent coevolution. In the centralized case, a single control policy is evolved for the entire tensegrity robot. This control policy sets the 96 parameters for the sinusoidal controllers. The algorithm is a simple evolutionary algorithm designed to maximize our fitness function. At the beginning of training, a population of n random policies is created and evaluated based on our fitness function f. After each round of evolution, the worst k policies are removed, and are replaced by mutated versions of the best k policies. Mutation is uniformly random for each parameter. For experiments that use crossover, we use a simplest basic single point crossover. For single point crossover algorithm, in addition to mutation, new k policies are assigned to teams of two, and for each team, those two policies exchange part of their parameters. The crossover point is a randomly selected number between 1 and 96 (number of parameters) and all the parameters after this point are exchanged. In both cases (crossover and no crossover), as evolution progresses, the population tends to converge to higher performance policies.

4.3 Cooperative Coevolutionary Algorithms

While centralized approaches often produce good results, evolving a centralized controller can be slow due to the size of the search space. If the control parameters are tightly coupled, then the centralized approach may be the best we can hope for. However, control of a tensegrity robot is not necessarily tightly coupled. While changing the length of a cable will strongly affect neighboring components, it will have less of an effect on components on the opposite side of the tensegrity. Therefore decentralized control is possible and can greatly reduce the search space for each component in the decentralized controller.

In this paper, we introduce such a decentralized controller as a cooperative coevolutionary system, using principles derived from multiagent systems. In this paradigm each of the 24 cables is controlled by an individual agent. The job of each agent i is to control the four parameters of the sinusoid controlling its cable: C_i, A_i, ω_i and ϕ_i. To do this, each agent i will have its own population of control parameters, p_i, where each member of the population, $p_{i,j}$ specifies the four control parameters. Each agent then evolves its population to produce good values of control parameters in the context of the control choices of the other agents. The goal of these coevolutionary agents is still the same as the centralized evolutionary algorithm: Maximize the global fitness evaluation, f.

The advantage of this paradigm is that each agent now only has to search through four parameters. The difficulty is the value of each agent's choice of control parameters now depends on the choices of the other agents. The exact same choice may be good or bad, depending on what other agents are doing. One way to address this is to evaluate every possible team existing at the current generation. In this paper, this is not possible due to the number of possible cooperators. We attempt to handle this issue by taking a fixed number of samples of the population at each generation of evolution. Between two generations, each agent's population is sampled s time and they are put together to form s complete control policies. Each of these control policies is then evaluated with respect to our global fitness evaluation function, f, producing s evaluations. Typically the number of samples s will be many times larger than the size of the population, therefore each individual member of a population will typically be part of multiple control policies. The main issue is how we evaluate a member of a population $p_{i,j}$ which has participated in multiple control policies, when each control policy has received a different global fitness evaluation f.

In this paper, we address this issue in the following three ways:

1. Generational Average - Assign the mean value of the global fitness evaluations for control policies in which the member participated during this generation.
2. Leniency - Assign the highest value of the global fitness evaluations for control policies in which the member participated in.
3. Historical Average - Assign the mean value of global fitness evaluations, averaging across all the generations that the member survived.

Taking average and leniency are commonly used methods with cooperative coevolution [11]. To improve performance, we augment this approach by taking historical averaging. Historical averaging uses all the samples that the members had been part of, not only the current generation but also the ones with previous generations with previous teammates (Algorithm 1). Every surviving agent carries its history to the new generation and uses that information to calculate its average score.

4.4 Hand-Coded Solution

In addition to creating control policies through evolutionary algorithms, we explore how to hand-code a control solution using the same parameters available to the evolutionary system. The goal here is to explore the challenges of hand-coding a solution and to see how well our best effort compares to our learned solutions. It turns out that creating a control policy by hand using our 96 parameters is extremely difficult, so we created 8 control groups with 3 cables in each group. These 3 cables form a triangle that have the same length, making it easier to write a hand-coded controller. Even with this simpler approach, the best achieved solution barely moved. This problem will only get more difficult

Algorithm 1: Cooperative coevolutionary Algorithm with Historical Average

```
Data: Population of n elements for each agent
for i=1..15 do
    random team ← ∅ ;
    forall the Populations do
        random team ← random agent;
    end
    score = evaluate random team ;
    forall the agents ∈ random team do
        agent.history ← agent.score ;
    end
end
forall the Populations do
    forall the agents do
        agent.fitness = average(agent.history) ;
    end
    order the population;
    eliminate last k;
    copy first k to last k;
    set score of last k to MIN;
    mutate last k;
    clear history for last k;
end
```

as we scale the tensegrity robots to more complex versions with more elements. To improve performance, we reduced the parameter space by hand coding the amplitudes of each group and making the oscillation frequency the same for all groups. The results shown later in this paper are for this second, better-performing hand-coded solution.

5. EXPERIMENTAL RESULTS

In this section, we present experiments evaluating the performance of our evolution-based methods to control tensegrity robots in the physics simulator described in Section 3.3. The goal of our experiments is to evaluate whether evolutionary systems can be successfully applied to tensegrity robots under nominal conditions, and how robust these solutions are to limitations in the range of actuation, to actuator noise and to a physical breakage in a cable of the tensegrity. For the nominal condition case we test the following methods of creating the controller:

- **Hand Coded** Control policy is developed by hand to try to achieve maximum performance.
- **Centralized Evolution** A single control policy is learned for the entire tensegrity robot.
- **Decentralized Evolution** Cooperative Coevolutionary Algorithms (CCEA) approach.

We then test different fitness methods for CCEAs: Average, Leniency, Historical Average. We test the robustness of our highest performance solution (historical average) in the following ways:

- **Actuation Noise** We add noise to how far cables are actually moved as compared to how far they are being requested to move.
- **Cable Failure** We test performance when a single cable in the robot breaks.
- **Obstacles** We randomly place half sphere obstacles into the environment.

All experiments start with a stationary tensegrity robot on the ground. For each experiment, the robots are created on a flat surface, and after 5 seconds of stabilization time, active control of the cables starts. The agents are given a fixed amount of time (60 seconds) to move the robot as far as possible. The evaluation function is the distance between the starting position and the position at the end of the given time period. The population size in the policy search is set to $n = 10$ and the selection parameter is set to $k = 5$. We perform 10 statistical runs for each type of experiment. Using a t-test we confirm that our conclusions are statistically significant. All our major results are $p<0.95$.

5.1 Centralized, Decentralized and Hand-Coded

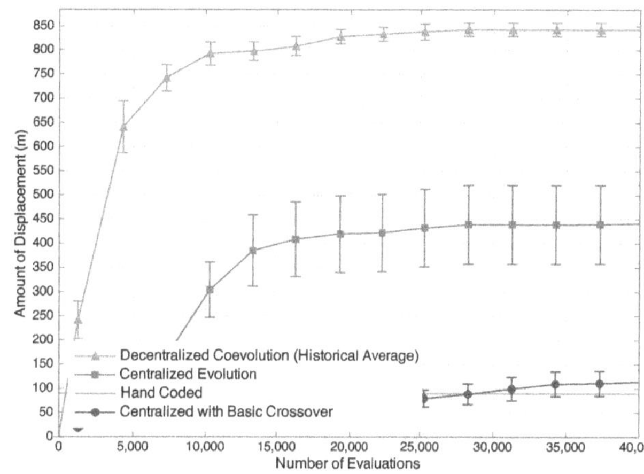

Figure 3: **Performance of Control Algorithms.** *Multiagent coevolution performs significantly better than other methods since it is able to take advantage of distributed nature of tensegrity control.*

The first experiment compares three different control policies: Hand-coded, centralized evolution and multiagent coevolution. Figure 3 shows that both evolution-based approaches can easily outperform the hand coded solution. Looking at the converged policies, the multiagent evolution approach provides the best performance by moving 100% more quickly than the single agent and 400% more than our hand coded agent. Both centralized and decentralized evolution are able to achieve smooth rolling motions as shown in Figure 6. Note that while our hand coded tensegrity is not able to achieve a rolling motion, we are not trying to imply that this problem is impossibly complex for non-evolving algorithms. In fact there have been several successful algorithms to do this [16, 8, 21, 4]. Instead we are illustrating that it is in fact quite difficult to create these controls, and that the centralized and multiagent evolutionary algorithms are creating complex, non-trivial control solutions. In addition a multiagent framework has the potential to be adapted to many different complex tensegrities with less effort than hand coding an algorithm for each new tensegrity.

It can be seen that the tensegrity controlled by policies evolved from coevolution reaches a performance around 900 meters in 60 seconds. By observing the behavior, we confirmed that the movement is established by smooth rolling motion as illustrated in Figure 6. This rate corresponds to the tensegrity moving at approximately 28 revolutions per minute.

5.2 Historical Average, Average and Leniency

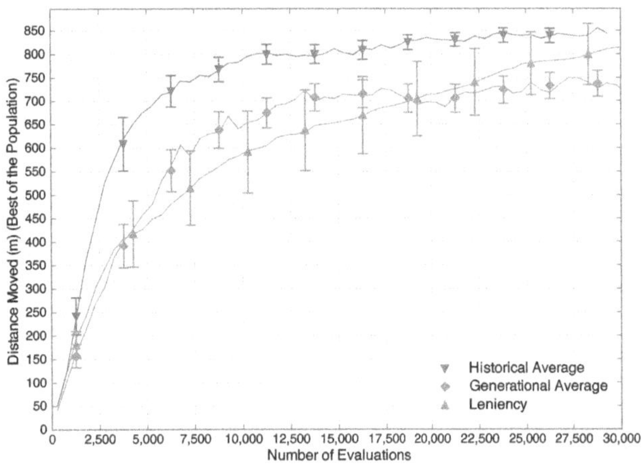

Figure 4: **Evaluation Methods.** *Using a historical average reaches best score and it is consistent. Lenient learners have bigger error bars.*

The second experiment compares different fitness assignment methods for CCEAs. As it can be seen, using a historical average performs better than every other method. Moreover, the small error bars signifies that using the historical average consistently provides similar performance. We are further analyzing historical average as a future research. Looking at the error bars of the lenient learners, it can be seen that standard deviation is high: It also reaches very good policies in some of the statistical runs, but the average success is lower.

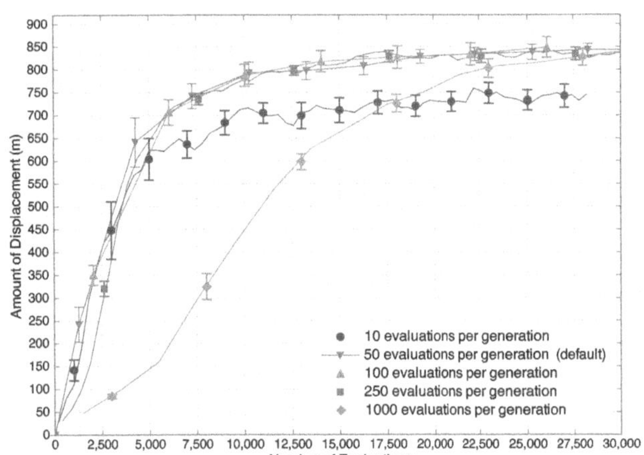

Figure 5: **Sample Size.** *Taking more samples for each trial improves stability but takes more time reach better behavior*

To make sure that the sample size that we chose does not significantly affect the results, we tested the historical average method with different sample size between each generation (s). Figure 5 shows that the sample size affects performance when it is too low such as 10, on the other hand,

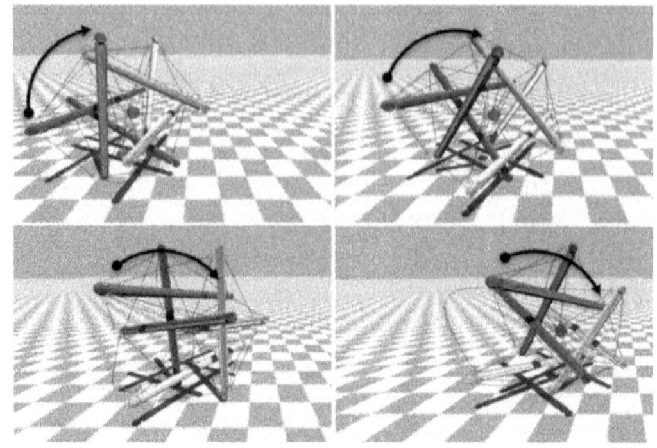

Figure 6: **Tensegrity Dynamics.** *Tensegrity is able to achieve smooth rolling motion. This rolling is accomplished solely by changing the length of the cables. Our learned control policies produce rolling that is also dynamical as the tensegrity does not stop to setup next roll action. This type of rolling can be fast and highly efficient.*

a sample size as high as 1000 decreases the learning speed. Considering this result, we used 50 as the default value for the rest of the experiments.

5.3 Actuation Noise

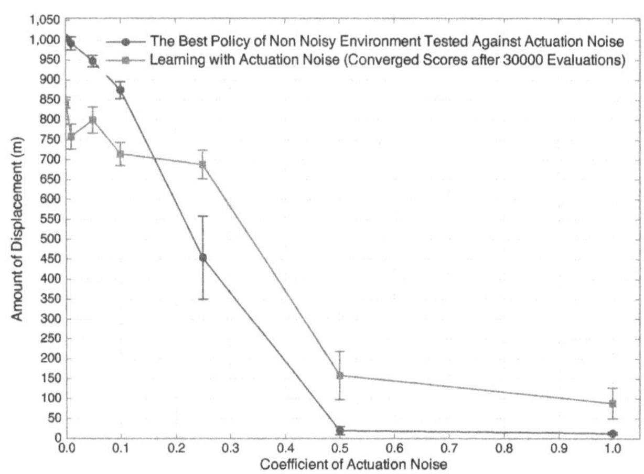

Figure 7: **Actuation Noise.** *The best policy can take up to 25% noise, evolving in a noisy environment scores better in higher noise environments.*

To measure the robustness of our evolutionary algorithm against noise, we test the multiagent tensegrity robot in an environment with different levels of actuation noise. Actuation noise is applied at every time step to the sinewave that the evolutionary algorithm generate to control the cables. At every time step, a random value from a normal distribution is directly added to the value of the Equation 1. To test different levels of noise, we use different environments where the standard deviation of the noise is set to $1\%, 2\%, 5\%, 10\%, 25\%, 50\%, 100\%$ of the amplitude of the sine wave for each cable.

In this experiment, we test two different policies in our noisy environment: 1) Policies from a multiagent system that had learned in an environment without noise, and 2) Policies that are learned in an environment with the same amount of noise they are tested in. Figure 7 shows that tensegrities trained both with and without noise can perform remarkably well when the level of noise is below 15%. This is an impressive result, as it shows that the solutions generated in a non-noisy environment are not highly specific to an exact model of a tensegrity and exact environmental conditions. Instead the solutions appear highly generalizable. Beyond this level of noise performance goes down significantly. However, while performance is low, a tensegrity trained with a high level of noise can still perform at a baseline level while subjected to high levels of noise, which could be very useful in many situations.

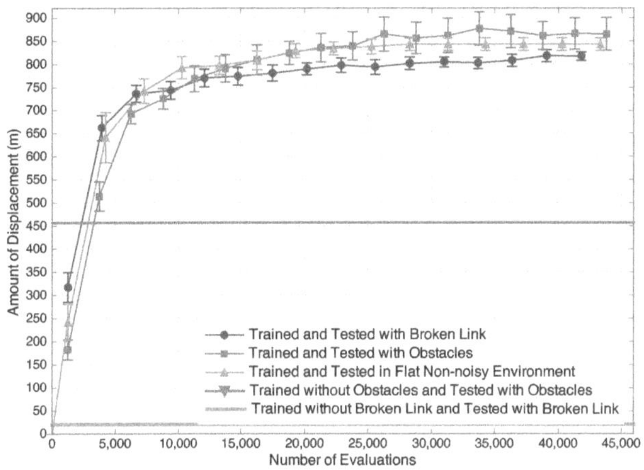

Figure 8: **Robustness Tests with Obstacles and Broken Link.** *Coevolutionary Algorithms can overcome both obstacles and broken link scenarios*

5.4 Broken Cable and Obstacles

The fourth experiment tests the robustness of the structure and the controller. In our first experiment we remove one of the cables, which decreases controllability and also disrupts the balance of the structure. With the cable removed, the structure is no longer symmetrical and it can not keep its ball shape by default. In our second experiment we place the normal tensegrity in an environment containing randomly placed half sphere obstacles. When we test our best policy trained in a perfect environment in these two conditions, the performance drops to 50% with obstacles and it cannot roll with a broken link (Figure 8). On the other hand, if we perform evolution in these conditions, the evolutionary algorithm can still find successful locomotion policies for a tensegrity with broken cable, or in an environment with obstacles.

This result shows that under adverse conditions we can evolve a controller that takes advantage of the large range of motion inherent in tensegrity robots to effectively maintain locomotion. Note that this result does not show that the evolved control policy dynamically adapts to problems, since in this experiment we retrain our policy after the breakage. However, it does show the flexibility of the evolution process and the ability to pre-evolve controls associated with potential failure modes.

Figure 9: **Tensebot, our Experimental Tensegrity Robot Prototype.** *This 6-rod tensegrity robot is designed to test hardware implementation and shape-changing abilities of tensegrities. We are in the process of building 6-rod tensegrity that can roll.*

6. HARDWARE ROBOT

With the actuation requirements explored in simulation, and building on our experience with prior prototype tensegrity robots, we will be spending this year researching appropriate actuation technologies and building a prototype of the rolling tensegrity robot discussed in this paper. Our existing prototype tensegrity robot uses position controlled spooled-cable actuation, and we will explore two new approaches: Impedance Controlled (Tension and Position) Spooled Cable actuation, and Twisted Cable Actuation. Our existing prototype robot is already designed for spooled cable actuation and we will retrofit it with new sensors and controls to support Impedance Control. In parallel we will evaluate a novel "twisted cable" actuation approach that we believe will allow for the use of significantly smaller and energy efficient motors due to the decoupling of motor torque output from actuator tension output. Finally these two actuator approaches will be evaluated for design simplicity, power efficiency, and total system mass, and the best approach will be used on our new rolling tensegrity robot. This new robot is designed to validate the controls approaches explored here and to show that these tensegrity robots can be used as landing and mobility systems.

7. CONCLUSIONS AND FUTURE WORK

Tensegrity robotics matched with multiagent evolutionary systems have a promising future. The structural properties of tensegrities give them many beneficial properties, while their distributed nature makes them a perfect match for multiagent systems. In this paper, we introduce a first step to this promise. We first show that, in simulation, evolutionary algorithms are able to come up with an effective controller that allows a moderately complex tensegrity ball to roll. Then we show how performance can be improved by applying a multiagent coevolutionary system to this same tensegrity robot. To handle fitness assignment problems in coevolution, we use sampling, introduce a new method based on the historical average and compare it with average and lenient learners. For future work, we are working on a detailed analysis of this method compared to averaging and leniency.

Not only is the coevolutionary approach able to produce a smooth rolling motion for the tensegrity robot, it is able to do so under a wide range of adverse conditions, including actuation noise, obstacles and cable breakage. These results show that multiagent evolutionary systems are a strong candidate for tensegrity control. In addition, the high level of robustness may allow our framework now used in simulation to be used on our physical tensegrities now in development.

The multiagent evolutionary system used in this paper represents just a glimpse of what may be possible for tensegrity control. While the distributed nature of a tensegrity makes it a natural match to the distributed nature of a multiagent system, the multiagent system we use in this paper is actually not as distributed as it could be. While all the agents take independent actions, they all try to maximize the same global system fitness evaluation function. Their use of this global evaluation function can cause agents to take into account too much information and limit their ability to evolve quickly. In contrast, future research may show that it is possible to use agent-specific evaluation functions that are more relevant to an agent's particular action. Such changes could allow coevolving systems to be used for even more complex tensegrities and achieve more sophisticated control behaviors.

Acknowledgments

This research was partially supported by the NASA Innovative Advanced Concepts (NIAC) Program. Tensebot constructed with support from Idaho Space Grant Consortium

8. REFERENCES

[1] N. Bel Hadj Ali, L. Rhode-Barbarigos, A. Pascual Albi, and I. Smith. Design optimization and dynamic analysis of a tensegrity-based footbridge. *Engineering Structures*, 32(11):3650–3659, 2010.

[2] V. Böhm, A. Jentzsch, T. Kaufhold, F. Schneider, F. Becker, and K. Zimmermann. An approach to locomotion systems based on 3d tensegrity structures with a minimal number of struts. In *Robotics; Proceedings of ROBOTIK 2012; 7th German Conference on*, pages 1–6. VDE, 2012.

[3] BulletPhysicsEngine. http://www.bulletphysics.org/.

[4] M. Calisti, A. Arienti, F. Renda, G. Levy, B. Hochner, B. Mazzolai, P. Dario, and C. Laschi. Design and development of a soft robot with crawling and grasping capabilities. In *Robotics and Automation (ICRA), 2012 IEEE International Conference on*, pages 4950–4955. IEEE, 2012.

[5] M. Fujiia, S. Yoshiia, and Y. Kakazub. Movement control of tensegrity robot. *Intelligent Autonomous Systems 9: IAS-9*, 9:290, 2006.

[6] B. Fuller. Tensegrity. *Portfolio and Art News Annual*, 4:112–127, 1961.

[7] H. Klimke and S. Stephan. The making of a tensegrity tower. In *IASS Symposium*, Montpellier, 2004.

[8] Y. Koizumi, M. Shibata, and S. Hirai. Rolling tensegrity driven by pneumatic soft actuators. In *Robotics and Automation (ICRA), 2012 IEEE International Conference on*, pages 1988–1993. IEEE, 2012.

[9] M. Masic and et al. Algebraic tensegrity form-finding. *International Journal of Solids and Structures*, 42:4833–4858, 2005.

[10] R. Motro. *Tensegrity: structural systems for the future*. Butterworth-Heinemann, 2003.

[11] L. Panait, K. Tuyls, S. Luke, and P. Kaelbling. Theoretical advantages of lenient learners: An evolutionary game theoretic perspective. *Journal of Machine Learning Research*, page 2008.

[12] C. Paul, H. Lipson, and F. J. V. Cuevas. Evolutionary form-finding of tensegrity structures. In *Proceedings of the 2005 conference on Genetic and evolutionary computation*, GECCO '05, pages 3–10, New York, NY, USA, 2005. ACM.

[13] C. Paul, F. Valero-Cuevas, and H. Lipson. Design and control of tensegrity robots for locomotion. *Robotics, IEEE Transactions on*, 22(5):944–957, 2006.

[14] A. Pugh. *An introduction to tensegrity*. Univ of California Press, 1976.

[15] J. Rieffel, F. Valero-Cuevas, and H. Lipson. Automated discovery and optimization of large irregular tensegrity structures. *Comput. Struct.*, 87(5-6):368–379, Mar. 2009.

[16] M. Shibata and S. Hirai. Moving strategy of tensegrity robots with semiregular polyhedral body. In *Proc. of the 13th Int. Conf. Climbing and Walking Robots (CLAWAR 2010), Nagoya*, pages 359–366, 2010.

[17] M. Shibata, F. Saijyo, and S. Hirai. Crawling by body deformation of tensegrity structure robots. In *Robotics and Automation, 2009. ICRA'09. IEEE International Conference on*, pages 4375–4380. IEEE, 2009.

[18] R. E. Skelton and M. C. Oliveria. *Tensegrity Systems*. Springer, New York, 2009.

[19] K. Snelson. Continuous tension, discontinuous compression structures. united states patent 3169611, Feburary 1965.

[20] Tibert and et al. Review of form-finding methods for tensegrity structures. *International Journal of Space Structures*, 18:209–223, 2003.

[21] J. Tur. On the movement of tensegrity structures. *International Journal of Space Structures*, 25(1):1–14, 2010.

[22] J. M. M. Tur and S. H. Juan. Tensegrity frameworks: Dynamic analysis review and open problems. *Mechanism and Machine Theory*, 44:1–18, 2009.

[23] S. Wittmeier, J. Michael, K. Dalamagkidis, and M. Rickert. CALIPER : A Universal Robot Simulation Framework for Tendon-Driven Robots. In *2011 IEEE/RSJ International Conference on Intelligent Robots and Systems*, pages 1063–1068, 2011.

[24] A. Wroldsen, M. de Oliveira, and R. Skelton. A discussion on control of tensegrity systems. In *Decision and Control, 2006 45th IEEE Conference on*, pages 2307–2313. IEEE, 2006.

[25] J. Y. Zhang and M. Ohsaki. Adaptive force density method for form-finding problem of tensegrity structures. *International Journal of Solids and Structures*, 43:5658–5673, 2006.

[26] L. Zhang and et al. Form-finding of nonregular tensegrity systems. *Journal of Structural Engineering*, 132:1435–1440, 2006.

Search for a Grand Tour of the Jupiter Galilean Moons

Dario Izzo
European Space Agency
dario.izzo@esa.int

Luís F. Simões
VU University Amsterdam
luis.simoes@vu.nl

Marcus Märtens
European Space Agency
marcus.maertens@esa.int

Guido C. H. E. de Croon
TU Delft
g.c.h.e.decroon@tudelft.nl

Aurelie Heritier
European Space Agency
relieheritier@gmail.com

Chit Hong Yam
Hong Kong University of Science and Technology
chithongyam@gmail.com

ABSTRACT

We make use of self-adaptation in a Differential Evolution algorithm and of the asynchronous island model to design a complex interplanetary trajectory touring the Galilean Jupiter moons (Io, Europa, Ganymede and Callisto) using the multiple gravity assist technique. Such a problem was recently the subject of an international competition organized by the Jet Propulsion Laboratory (NASA) and won by a trajectory designed by aerospace experts and reaching the final score of 311/324. We apply our method to the very same problem finding new surprising designs and orbital strategies and a score of up to 316/324.

Categories and Subject Descriptors

I.2.8 [**Artificial Intelligence**]: Problem Solving, Control Methods, and Search—*Graph and tree search strategies, Heuristic methods*

General Terms

Algorithms

Keywords

Self-adaptation, Differential Evolution, multi-criteria tree-search, interplanetary trajectory optimization

1. INTRODUCTION

The design of interplanetary trajectories can be profitably approached as a global optimization problem. In the last decade, a number of researchers [1, 9, 5, 14, 13, 10] have successfully applied different automated search techniques to these type of problems, helping to define a new approach to interplanetary mission design. In this context, the international Global Trajectory Optimization Competition (GTOC) series[1], was born with the objective of fostering research in this area by letting different methods compete on one, difficult, well-defined, problem. During the competition, standard design methods based on a profound domain knowledge and on human-in-the-loop procedures, compete with more or less automated design techniques. Interestingly, evolutionary search techniques have been used by many of the competition participants, but have never obtained results that are competitive to those found by other types of optimization procedures. For an example of the complex and diverse solution strategies employed in the first edition of the competition one can refer to [7]. In this paper we describe an automated search procedure based on evolutionary techniques that is able to design multiple fly-by interplanetary trajectories and apply it to the latest problem released in the GTOC series, the sixth edition problem.

[1]See `http://sophia.estec.esa.int/gtoc_portal/`

1.1 Brief problem description

The sixth edition of the GTOC series was organized by the Jet Propulsion Laboratory (JPL), and the problem was released on the 10th September 2012. The 33 international teams who registered to the event were given one month time to find a solution to arguably one of the most difficult problems ever formalized in the context of these competitions: mapping globally the four Galilean Jupiter moons (Io, Ganymede, Europa and Callisto) using multiple fly-bys and an electric propulsion spacecraft. The formal mathematical description (problem statement) can be found in [12]. Here we repeat some of the details to facilitate the reader. The inertial Jupiter centric frame $\mathcal{F}_i$ is indicated with $\hat{\mathbf{i}}, \hat{\mathbf{j}}, \hat{\mathbf{k}}$. On each moon, a body frame $\mathcal{F}_b$ is defined and indicated with $\hat{\mathbf{b}}_1, \hat{\mathbf{b}}_2, \hat{\mathbf{b}}_3$. In such a body frame, the moon surface is considered to be divided into 32 faces $F_i, i = 1..32$, similarly to the division used to stitch soccer balls (see Figure 1), defined by their cartesian coordinates in $\mathcal{F}_b$. We write $F_i := \{\hat{\mathbf{p}}_j, j = 1..n_i\}$ where n_i is the number of vertices of the i-th face (either 5 or 6), and $\hat{\mathbf{p}}_j$ are the j-th vertex coordinates in $\mathcal{F}_b$. Each face, according to its scientific interest, is assigned a score ranging from 1 to 3 points. Each face on Europa is assigned double scores because of the higher scientific interest of this particular Jupiter moon. A face F_i on a moon is visited, and thus its score added to the total trajectory score, when a fly-by around that moon is performed having its closest approach vector $\mathbf{r}_p$ passing through that particular face[2]. At each successive fly-by over

[2]More formally, this happens when $\mathbf{r}_p$ lies within the pyramid having the face F_i as a basis and the moon center as a vertex.

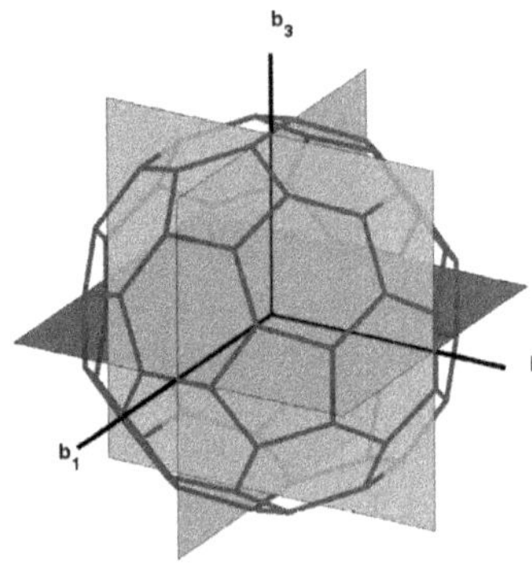

Figure 1: Visualization of the moon surface division into polygonal faces. Reproduced from the original problem description from JPL [12].

the same face, no further score is accounted. This scoring mechanism was used by the organizers in an attempt to represent numerically as an objective function the scientific value of imaging-experiments carried out on-board the spacecraft during each of its closest passages over the moons. This creates a trajectory design problem with a maximum score of 324 points, which corresponds to all faces of the four Galilean moons being visited. The spacecraft has a starting mass $M_0 = 2000$ kg of which half can be used as propellant for the spacecrafts electric engine, able to deliver continuously a maximum thrust $\tau_{max} = 0.1$ N. At each of its close Jupiter passages the available propellant mass decreases by a penalty value to account for added shielding necessary to protect the electronics from the strong Jupiter magnetic field. The functional form of this penalty is given in the JPL problem description [12]. Applying our technique, we find many different trajectories scoring up to 316/324 points and employing very different strategies from the one designed by the winners of this international competition.

The sixth edition of the GTOC series was won by a joint team from the University of Rome and Turin Polytechnic, who designed their winning trajectory scoring 311 out of the maximum 324 points. Their interplanetary trajectory made a clever use of orbital mechanics to first map Callisto partially, then all Ganymede, then all of Europa and to finish with a full mapping of Io.

The paper is organized as follows: in Section 2 and in Section 3 we introduce two global optimization problem ($\mathcal{P}_1$ and $\mathcal{P}_2$) which form the building blocks of our proposed method. In both cases, solutions represent interplanetary multiple gravity assist trajectories in the Jupiter system. In Section 4 we describe and comment upon the evolutionary strategy that we use for solving generic instances of both problems. We then show, in Section 5, how to build incrementally a tree $\mathcal{T}$ of solutions to the GTOC6 problem juxtaposing multiple $\mathcal{P}_1$ and $\mathcal{P}_2$ solutions. In the same section we discuss the tree search strategy that is employed to find the best possible tour. In Section 6 we report on the experimental set-up used and the results produced. Finally, in Section 7, we describe the best found trajectory that improves the previously known best.

2. PROBLEM $\mathcal{P}_1$: THE JUPITER CAPTURE

In this section the first part of the trajectory, i.e. the Jupiter capture, is described as a global optimization problem and is indicated with $\mathcal{P}_1(\mathbf{m})$. Formally, we define problem $\mathcal{P}_1$ as a global optimization problem:

$$\mathcal{P}_1(\mathbf{m}): \quad \begin{array}{rl} \text{find:} & \mathbf{x} \in R^{16} \\ \text{to minimize:} & \Delta V(\mathbf{x}, \mathbf{m}) = \sum_{i=0}^{3} \Delta V_i \\ \text{subject to:} & \mathbf{lb} \leq \mathbf{x} \leq \mathbf{ub} \\ & \Delta V_i < cT_i a_{max} \end{array}$$

Consider the set $\mathcal{M} := \{i, e, g, c\}$ containing the four Galilean moons i=Io, e=Europa, g=Ganymede, c=Callisto. Given a sequence $\mathbf{m} \in \mathcal{M}^4$ we want to find a vector $\mathbf{x}$ encoding an interplanetary trajectory that visits, in sequence, the moons $\mathbf{m}$ making use of maximum one deep space maneuver between two successive moons and one at the very beginning (at 1000 Jupiter Radii (JR) where the spacecraft is prescribed to start its journey [12]). The cumulative strength of the four allowed deep space maneuvers $\Delta V = \sum_{i=0}^{3} \Delta V_i$ is minimized and a maximum acceleration constraint on each ΔV_i is considered to account for the maximum acceleration a_{max} defined as τ_{max}/M, where M is the spacecraft mass. A detailed description of the decision vector $\mathbf{x}$ (here also called trajectory encoding), of the objective function $\Delta V(\mathbf{x}, \mathbf{m})$ and of the problem constraints follows.

2.1 Trajectory encoding

The capture trajectory is encoded into $\mathbf{x}$ using a modification of the MGA-1DSM encoding described in [8]. The modification is necessary to account for the fact that the spacecraft starts its journey from a point at $R_s = 1000$ Jupiter Radii (JR) from Jupiter center and not from a planet as assumed in the original MGA-1DSM encoding. Using the concatenation operator "+" to highlight the four separate trajectory legs[3], a capture trajectory is encoded as follows: $\mathbf{x} = [t_0, u, v, T_0] + [\beta_1, h_1, \eta_1, T_1] + [\beta_2, h_2, \eta_2, T_2] + [\beta_3, h_3, \eta_3, T_3]$, where all symbols are explained below.

2.1.1 1st leg

The launch date is encoded into t_0 as a continuous variable using the Modified Julian Date 2000 (MJD2000), defined as the number of days passed since 2000-01-01 at 00:00:00 hours. The starting position vector $\mathbf{r}_0$ of the spacecraft is encoded by the next two variables u, v as follow:

$$\mathbf{r}_0 = 1000R_s(\cos\theta\cos\phi\hat{\mathbf{i}} + \sin\theta\cos\phi\hat{\mathbf{j}} + \sin\phi\hat{\mathbf{k}})$$

where R_s is the Jupiter average radius and

$$\theta = 2\pi u, \phi = \cos^{-1}(2v - 1) - \pi/2$$

The use of the variables, u and v, is motivated by the need to have the position vector $\mathbf{r}_0$ uniformly distributed over the starting sphere of radius R_s when the encoding variables are sampled at random. The distribution would not be uniform if we were using directly θ and ϕ. Finally the total duration of the first leg is encoded in T_0.

2.1.2 Following legs

For each of the following three legs, the starting velocity $\mathbf{v}_{out}$ (outgoing spacecraft velocity at the moon m in $\mathcal{F}_i$), is encoded by the first two variables β, h as follows:

$$\begin{aligned} \mathbf{v}_{out} = \mathbf{v}_m + \\ |\mathbf{v}_{in}|(\cos(\delta)\hat{\mathbf{e}}_1 + \cos(\beta)\sin(\delta)\hat{\mathbf{e}}_2 + \sin(\beta)\sin(\delta)\hat{\mathbf{e}}_3) \end{aligned} \quad (1)$$

[3]A trajectory leg is a part of the whole trajectory between two consecutive moons.

Table 1: Lower and upper bounds, lb and ub, for the generic instance of $\mathcal{P}_1$.

	Lower	Upper
t_0 [MJD 2000]	7305	11323
u	0	1
v	0	1
T_0 [days]	190	210
β_i	-2π	2π
h_i [km]	50	2000
η_i	-2π	2π
T_1 [days]	0.1	5
T_2 [days]	5	100
T_3 [days]	20	55

where $\mathbf{v}_m$ is the velocity of the moon m at the beginning of the leg[4], $\mathbf{v}_{in}$ is the spacecraft velocity at the end of the previous leg (incoming velocity at the moon) and:

$$\begin{aligned} &\tilde{\mathbf{v}}_{in} = \mathbf{v}_{in} - \mathbf{v}_m \\ &e = 1 + ((h + R_m)/\mu_m)\,\tilde{v}_{in}^2 \\ &\delta = 2\sin^{-1}(1/e) \\ &\hat{\mathbf{e}}_1 = \tilde{\mathbf{v}}_{in}/|\tilde{\mathbf{v}}_{in}| \\ &\hat{\mathbf{e}}_2 = (\hat{\mathbf{e}}_1 \times \mathbf{v}_m)/|\hat{\mathbf{e}}_1 \times \mathbf{v}_m| \\ &\hat{\mathbf{e}}_3 = \hat{\mathbf{e}}_1 \times \hat{\mathbf{e}}_2 \end{aligned} \tag{2}$$

where R_m is the moon radius and μ_m its non dimensional gravity parameter. Next, the variable η_i encodes the position of a deep space maneuver which occurs at $t = t_0 + \sum_{j=0}^{i-1} T_j + \eta_i T_i$ and T_i encodes the total leg duration.

2.2 Objective function

The objective function for problem $\mathcal{P}_1$ is computed as follows. A single revolution Lambert's problem [2] is solved between $\mathbf{r}_0$ and $\mathbf{r}_1$ with transfer time T_0. $\mathbf{r}_1$ is the position of the first encountered moon at $t_0 + T_1$. The solution to the Lambert's problem returns $\mathbf{v}_0$ and $\mathbf{v}_{in}^1$, i.e. the velocities at the beginning and at the end of the first trajectory leg. From these results, we compute $\Delta V_0 = abs(|\overline{\mathbf{v}}_0| - |\mathbf{v}_0|)$, where $\overline{\mathbf{v}}_0$ is the magnitude of the prescribed starting velocity (i.e. 3.5 [km/s]). For each successive leg we then compute the velocity increments ΔV_i corresponding to the deep-space maneuver location encoded in $\mathbf{x}$ using the standard procedure employed by the MGA-1DSM encoding [8]. The final objective function is the sum of all computed velocity increments, i.e., $\Delta V = \sum_{i=0}^{3} \Delta V_i$.

2.3 Constraints

The box bounds **lb** and **ub** used in problem $\mathcal{P}_1$ are reported in Table 1. The most important bounds are those on the transfer times T_i. They, alone, select the type of capture we are looking for. In our case, we want to be captured in the Jupiter system in the shortest possible time and we aim to acquire a short orbital period to increase the frequency we will be able to score points with. We achieve this goal by forcing two moons to be visited on the very first revolution in a rapid succession and we thus select a very small upper bound on T_1. The possibility to have these types of "multiple-satellite-aided Jupiter capture trajectories" is discussed thoroughly in [11]. We then force the following orbit to have a relatively small period with an upper bound of 100 days on T_2, thus allowing, in the second leg, a 13:1 resonance with the Ganymede orbit or a 5:1 with Callisto. The upper bound on T_3, is then selected to be lower, i.e. 55 days, to complete the spacecraft insertion in the Galilean moon system (allowing only 3:1 resonances with the outer moon Callisto[5]).

The non linear constraint on the spacecraft ΔV_i accounts for the maximum acceleration τ_{max} allowed by the on-board spacecraft electric propulsion system. A constant c, here set to be 0.1, is also introduced to account for orbital effects while biasing the search towards purely ballistic captures (corresponding to $\Delta V = 0$)[6].

[4]The ephemerides of the moons are detailed in the original JPL problem statement [12]

3. PROBLEM $\mathcal{P}_2$: SINGLE TRANSFER BETWEEN MOONS

A fundamental building block to our overall strategy is a second global optimization problem we here indicate as $\mathcal{P}_2$. This represents the problem of finding a minimum ΔV transfer between two moons m_s and m_{next} fixing the starting conditions. The transfer starts at t_0 from m_s with a known absolute velocity $\mathbf{v}_{in}$ and makes a fly-by over the F_i face of m_s.

$$\mathcal{P}_2(F_i, m_{next}): \quad \begin{aligned} \text{find:} &\quad \mathbf{x} \in R^4 \\ \text{to minimize:} &\quad \Delta V(\mathbf{x}) \\ \text{subject to:} &\quad \mathbf{lb}_i(F_i) \le \mathbf{x} \le \mathbf{ub}_i(F_i) \end{aligned}$$

where $\mathbf{x} = [\beta, h, \eta, T]$ and, most importantly, the box bounds $\mathbf{lb}_i$ and $\mathbf{ub}_i$ depend on the face F_i to be visited. While any particular instance of the problem $\mathcal{P}_2$ depends on F_i, m_{next}, m_s, $\mathbf{v}_{in}$ and t_0, we write $\mathcal{P}_2(F_i, m_{next})$, neglecting those variables ($m_s, \mathbf{v}_{in}, t_0$) that are fixed when a previous part of the trajectory exists (e.g. a solution to $\mathcal{P}_1$ or to $\mathcal{P}_2$)

The objective function $\Delta V(\mathbf{x})$ is computed by first computing $\mathbf{v}_{out}$ from $\mathbf{v}_{in}$ using Eq.(1-2), and then by propagating those initial conditions with Keplerian dynamics for the time ηT. Finally, a single revolution Lambert's problem [2] is solved to get to the target moon position in $t_0 + T$.

3.1 Face-targeting

When instantiating $\mathcal{P}_2(F_i, m_{next})$ we need to specify the lower and upper bounds on the four variables β, h, η, T. The choice on the bounds on η, i.e. the position of the deep space maneuver, is rather simple: $\eta \in]0, 1[$ is set to allow small correction maneuvers at any points of the trajectory leg. For the transfer time, we use $T \in [0.1, min(4T_m, 40)]$ (days), where T_m is the largest period between the starting and final moon orbit. The maximum of 40 (days) on the upper bound avoids to consider long multiple revolution transfers when Callisto is either the starting or the targeted moon ($4T_m$ would then be roughly 64 days). The bounds on the remaining two variables, β and h are, instead, decided to have the resulting solution visit the chosen moon face F_i. The procedure to find these bounds is what we call face-targeting and it is based on the following results:

[5]The orbital period of Callisto is 16.7 days, while the orbital period of Ganymede is 7.15 days.

[6]The coefficient c is often referred to gravity loss and, coarsely, accounts for the difference between having to accumulate a given velocity difference in a flat space or in a central gravity field.

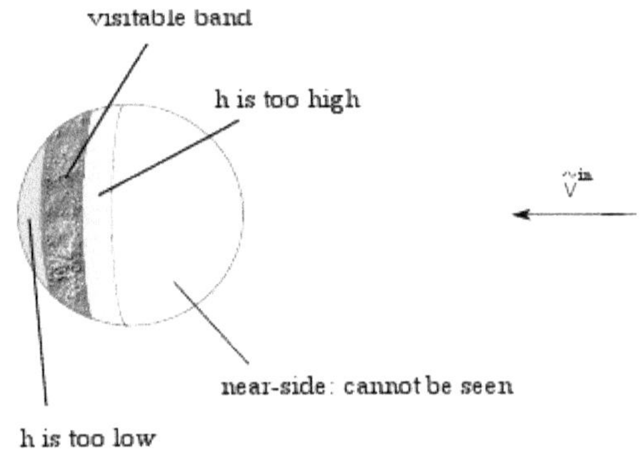

Figure 2: Visualization of the visitable band.

Definition 1. A point $\hat{\mathbf{p}}$ on the moon surface of radius R_m is visitable during a fly-by with incoming relative velocity $\tilde{\mathbf{v}}_{in}$ if and only if $\tilde{\mathbf{v}}_{in} \cdot \hat{\mathbf{p}} \geq 0$ and $h \in [h_{min}, h_{max}]$, where:

$$h + R_m = \mu_m/(\tilde{\mathbf{v}}_{out} \cdot \tilde{\mathbf{v}}_{out})(1/\sin(\delta/2) - 1)$$
$$\tilde{\mathbf{v}}_{out} = \tilde{\mathbf{v}}_{in} - 2(\tilde{\mathbf{v}}_{in} \cdot \hat{\mathbf{p}})\hat{\mathbf{p}}$$
$$\delta = \operatorname{acos}\left(\frac{\tilde{\mathbf{v}}_{out} \cdot \tilde{\mathbf{v}}_{in}}{\tilde{\mathbf{v}}_{out} \cdot \tilde{\mathbf{v}}_{out}}\right)$$

and h_{min}, h_{max} were prescribed by the JPL problem statement [12] as the minimum and maximum fly-by altitude on each moon. If $\tilde{\mathbf{v}}_{in} \cdot \hat{\mathbf{p}} < 0$ the vertex is said to be in the near side of the moon. For the cases in which $\tilde{\mathbf{v}}_{in} \cdot \hat{\mathbf{p}} \geq 0$, if $h < h_{min}$ the vertex is said to be above the visitable band, if $h > h_{max}$ it is said to be below.

If a point is visitable according to the above definition, then a moon-centric hyperbola exists and has its closest approach radius $\mathbf{r}_p$ aligned with $\hat{\mathbf{p}}$. Essentially, at each fly-by the moon surface can be represented as in Figure 2, where the area made by all visitable points is shown to form a band (the visitable band) that is symmetric with respect to the incoming relative velocity and that is placed in the far side of the moon.

Definition 2. A face $F := \{\hat{\mathbf{p}}_j, j = 1..n\}$ defined by its n vertices is visitable if and only if $a_j \geq 0, j = 1..n$ exist such that the point $\sum_{j=1}^{n} a_j \hat{\mathbf{p}}_j$ is visitable

In other words, a face is visitable if at least one of its points is visitable. In order to compute the set L containing all visitable faces, one can use the following algorithm:

Algorithm 1 Find visitable faces

$L := \emptyset$
for all F_i in the moon m **do**
  for all $\hat{\mathbf{p}}_j \in F_i$ **do**
    check if $\hat{\mathbf{p}}_j$ is in the near side or above, below or in the visitable band.
  end for
  if (at least one vertex is visitable) or (at least one, but not all vertices are above the band) **then** set $L = L \cup \{F_i\}$
  end if
end for
return L

Given a face $F_i \in L$, we may now find the lower and upper bounds β_m, β_M, h_m, h_M that bracket such a face and bias the solution of the problem $\mathcal{P}_2$ to fly over F_i and thus to score that face (if not scored already). We do so by using algorithm 2.

Algorithm 2 Face bracketing

Let $F_i \in L$
for all $\hat{\mathbf{p}}_j \in F_i$ **do**
  If $\hat{\mathbf{p}}_j$ is on the near side, project it to the far side.
  Compute $h_j = \mu_m/(\tilde{\mathbf{v}}_{out} \cdot \tilde{\mathbf{v}}_{out})(1/\sin(\delta/2) - 1) - R_m$
  Compute $\beta_j = \operatorname{atan2}(\tilde{\mathbf{v}}_{out} \cdot \hat{\mathbf{e}}_3, \tilde{\mathbf{v}}_{out} \cdot \hat{\mathbf{e}}_2)$
end for
set $\beta_m = \min_j \beta_j$, $\beta_M = \max_j \beta_j$
set $h_m = \max(\min h_j, h_{min})$, $h_M = \min(\max_j h_j, h_{max})$

4. SOLVING $\mathcal{P}_1$ AND $\mathcal{P}_2$

All problems that derive from different instances of $\mathcal{P}_1(\mathbf{m})$ and $\mathcal{P}_2(F_i, m_{next})$ are single objective, continuous global optimization problems that we solve by exploiting one powerful idea rooted in evolutionary computations: self-adaptation. By using self-adaptation we are able to not care about tuning algorithmic parameters, while still obtaining solutions for all different problems with an acceptable efficiency. This is a fundamental advantage as for each instance of $\mathcal{P}_1(\mathbf{m})$ or $\mathcal{P}_2(F_i, m_{next})$ we are, essentially, creating a much different objective function landscape. Resonant transfers, multiple revolution transfers and very short transfers may or may not exist according to the particular instance, drastically changing the fitness landscape.

In the case of $\mathcal{P}_1$ (a more difficult problem with a higher dimensionality with respect to $\mathcal{P}_2$ and a much larger search space mainly determined by the wide bounds on the t_0, the launch window), we also make use of a second tool: the asynchronous island model. This allows us to achieve a coarse-grained parallelization while introducing a migration operator that further accelerates evolution.

We tested three algorithms employing self-adaptation as a principle, a) differential evolution with self adaptation strategy (jDE) [3], the Corana's Adaptive Neighbourhood Simulated Annealing (SA-AN) [4], and Covariance Matrix Adaptation Evolutionary Strategy (CMA-ES) [6]. We do not have space here to discuss the performances of these algorithms in connection with our problems, but we did perform extensive test sessions and our final decision converged on jDE as for its clear superiority in the context of $\mathcal{P}_1$, where a good interaction with the asynchronous generalized island model is necessary to actually find any good solutions, and for its low run time in general.

It is worth anticipating here that, as explained in detail in a later section, to assemble one entire solution of the Jupiter's moon tour, up to 1,000,000 different instances of $\mathcal{P}_2$ need to be solved and one good solution to $\mathcal{P}_1$ has to be determined. To give an idea of the performances of our chosen set up, we report, preliminarily, some results on the resulting computational efficiency[7]. Figure 3 illustrates the results of 50 runs on three different instances of $\mathcal{P}_1(\mathbf{m})$, which consistently resulted in good final results: a) $\mathbf{m} = [g, c, c, c]$, b) $\mathbf{m} = [c, g, g, g]$, c) $\mathbf{m} = [g, i, i, i]$. Each run is made up to convergence, which we check every 40 generations and is defined by two criteria: fitness variability and chromosomic

[7]Our experiments are done on a Intel(R) Xeon(R) CPU - X5355 @ 2.66GHz

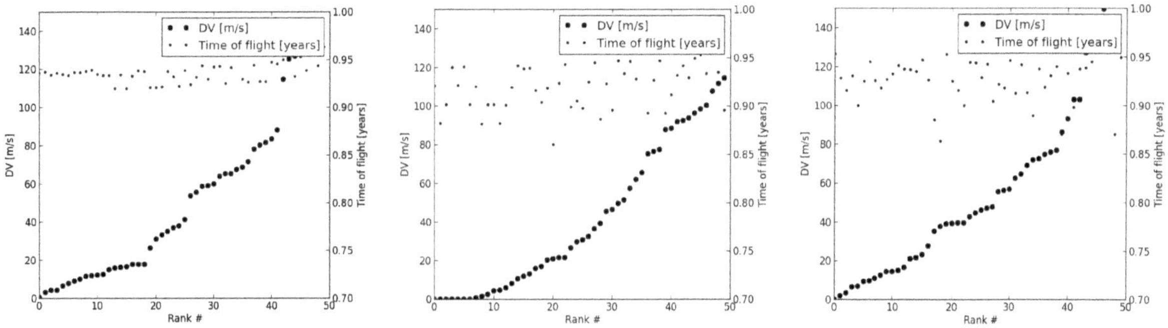

Figure 3: Performance of jDE in the asynchronous island model along 50 runs on different instances of problem $\mathcal{P}_1$. Left: $\mathbf{m} = [g, c, c, c]$. Center: $\mathbf{m} = [c, g, g, g]$. Right: $\mathbf{m} = [g, i, i, i]$. in the plots, the solutions are ranked with respect to their fitness.

variability $f_{tol} \leq 1e^{-2}$ and $x_{tol} \leq 1e^{-3}$. Eight islands are used and one individual is migrated along a ring topology each 100 generations. Each island evolves a population of 20 individuals. The asynchronous migration model implementation and the jDE implementation are made available via the open source PaGMO/PyGMO project[8]. In the case of $\mathcal{P}_2$, where one single island is used (i.e. no migration), we report that our set-up is able, on average, to solve 10 problem instances each second.

5. ASSEMBLING ONE MOON TOUR

Our overall strategy to solve the GTOC6 problem consists of assembling in cascade multiple solutions to problems $\mathcal{P}_1$ and $\mathcal{P}_2$. We start with a trajectory that captures our spacecraft in the Jupiter system (i.e. one solution to $\mathcal{P}_1(\mathbf{m})$), and we append to it, one by one, solutions to $\mathcal{P}_2(F_i, m_{next})$. As there are four moons and, on average, 15 visitable faces, the average branching factor is 60. This means that at the nth step a full search tree contains 60^n trajectories. This creates a tree $\mathcal{T}$ of possibilities that soon becomes intractable.

In our notation, the generic tree node is defined by $\mathcal{N} := \{m, t, \mathbf{v}_{in}, \Delta V, \mathbf{f}\}$ and represents an interplanetary trajectory (solution to the GTOC6 problem), that at the epoch t visits the moon m with an incoming velocity $\mathbf{v}_{in}$, having cumulated a velocity change of ΔV and having previously visited all moon faces in $\mathbf{f}$. Each node can thus be assigned a score that is computed as a function of $\mathbf{f}$. The root node of the tree, i.e. a Jupiter capture trajectory, is determined using Algorithm 3.

Algorithm 3 Find a capture trajectory $\mathcal{N}_{root}$

while $\Delta V \geq 100$ (m/s) and $\Delta T = t - t_0 \geq 0.9$ (years) **do**
  pick a random $\mathbf{m} \in \mathcal{M}^4$
  solve $\mathcal{P}_1(\mathbf{m})$
end while
  let m be the last moon in $\mathbf{m}$,
  let t be the epoch at the last moon,
  let $\mathbf{v}_{in}$ be the spacecraft velocity at t,
  let ΔV be the cumulative velocity increment,
  let $\mathbf{f}$ the set of all moon faces visited,
  let $\mathcal{N}_{root} := \{m, t, \mathbf{v}_{in}, \Delta V, \mathbf{f}\}$

5.1 The lazy race tree search

As explained above, starting from a root node $\mathcal{N}_{root}$ that is an outcome of Algorithm 3, we define a tree $\mathcal{T}$ where each node $\mathcal{N}$ represents a solution (i.e. a trajectory) to our problem. The tree depth, defined as d, represents the number of fly-bys performed (after capture). The tree dimension make a complete search intractable. We thus need to deploy a different strategy. A first attempt could be to search the tree implementing a depth first search by adding pruning criteria to make sure to trim uninteresting branches and to complete the search in a reasonable time. The advantage would be to prioritize an early exploration of the tree leaves. The problem with this approach is that it is impossible to estimate how much of the tree would be pruned out by a certain criterium, and thus each search could easily be too short or too long. A breadth first search strategy, carrying over to the next depth a constant number of nodes that is selected by a ranking criteria, solves this problem having a time complexity that grows linearly with the tree depth, which is a characteristic that is highly desirable in our case. In such an algorithm, nodes that have equal depth (i.e. number of fly-bys) need to be ranked and we would then be forced to compare trajectories that possess different times of flight, cumulative ΔV and score using an aggregated objective function, which introduces a lot of greediness in the search[9]. We thus introduce a novel algorithm that we call Lazy Race Tree Search (LRTS) able to overcome the problems mentioned above. The basic idea, outlined in Algorithm 4, is to only rank (and eventually select and prune) nodes that have similar time of flight, not equal tree depth. Introducing the set $\mathcal{U}$ containing all unbranched nodes, initialized to a set containing only the root node $\mathcal{N}_0$, at each iteration we look in $\mathcal{U}$ for nodes having time of flight smaller than the minimum time of flight T_0 among them plus a small ϵ. We then select bf (branching factor) nodes to branch, using the ranking criteria, and we remove all selected nodes from $\mathcal{U}$. The algorithm stops when T_0 is larger than the 4 years allowed by the problem definition.

6. TREE SEARCH RESULTS

In order to assess the performance of LRTS on our problem, while also trying to beat the best solution known for

[8]http://pagmo.sourceforge.net/pygmo/index.html

[9]In a preliminary implementation of this algorithm we could not reach the score threshold of 300

Algorithm 4 Lazy Race Tree Search

$\mathcal{U} := \{\mathcal{N}_{root}\}$ (the set of unbranched nodes)
let t_0 be the starting epoch of the trajectory
while $T_0 \leq 4$ years **do**
  let $T_0 := \min_{\mathcal{U}}(t - t_0)$,
  let $\mathcal{S} := \{\mathcal{N} \in \mathcal{U} | (t - t_0) \in [T_0, T_0 + \epsilon]\}$,
  select bf nodes in $\mathcal{S}$ and branch them,
  remove from $\mathcal{U}$ all nodes in $\mathcal{S}$
end while

the GTOC6 problem (i.e. the trajectory scoring 311 found by the group at Polytechnic of Turin and La Sapienza, University of Rome), we launch a large number (360) of tree searches. The LRTS uses a branching factor $bf = 50$, a time of flight bin of $\epsilon = 5$ days and a ranking method defined by the trajectory score augmented by the maximum potential number of points scored on the current moon m (with ties broken by a secondary ranking method defined as the number of non scoring fly-bys). A gravity loss coefficient of $c = 0.1$ is used when instantiating the various $\mathcal{P}_2$. Each search starts from a different root node $\mathcal{N}_{root}$ found by running once Algorithm 3. The results are summarized in Figure 4. Most trajectories found are above the threshold of 300 points, some (34 to be exact) have a higher score than the currently known best of 311. We here note that the overall trajectory ΔV is consistently very small thanks to the pruning at 100 m/s in Algorithm 3 and to the very small gravity loss coefficient c selected. As a consequence, all solutions found by LRTS can be transformed into low-thrust trajectories (i.e. trajectories that can be flown by an electric propulsion system such as that prescribed by the Jet Propulsion Laboratory problem statement). On average, one tree search is completed in 16.8 hours. The average depth of the searched tree is 132. Using 32 CPUs, the whole run lasts 7.87 days. During the entire run an estimated number of half a billion (500,000,000) different global optimization problems (of type Multiple Gravity Assist with one Deep Space Maneuver MGA-1DSM) are solved by the self-adaptive jDE deployed in our asynchronous island model. It is interesting to note how only the sequences $\mathbf{m} = [c, g, g, g]$, $\mathbf{m} = [g, i, i, e]$, $\mathbf{m} = [g, i, i, g]$, $\mathbf{m} = [g, i, i, i]$, $\mathbf{m} = [c, g, c, c]$, $\mathbf{m} = [c, i, c, c]$, $\mathbf{m} = [g, c, c, c]$ were found to be able to define a suitable capture trajectory and, in any case, all best trajectories used the Callisto, Ganymede, Ganymede, Ganymede sequence, indicating that such an entry strategy results in particularly good root nodes for LRTS.

7. OUR SOLUTION

In this section, we describe in more details the solution with the highest score found by our tree search (i.e. the left most point in Figure 4). It has a total score of 316 out of the maximum score of 324, visiting 120 moon faces against the 115 faces visited by the previously best known solution (winner of the 6th edition of the GTOC which scores 311). From Table 2, we note that our solution almost maps all faces on three of the four moons: full scores on Europa and Ganymede and one point less on Io. The solution was sent according to the required competition format to the Jet Propulsion Laboratory experts (the GTOC6 organizers) who kindly validated the new solution using their trajectory analysis tools.

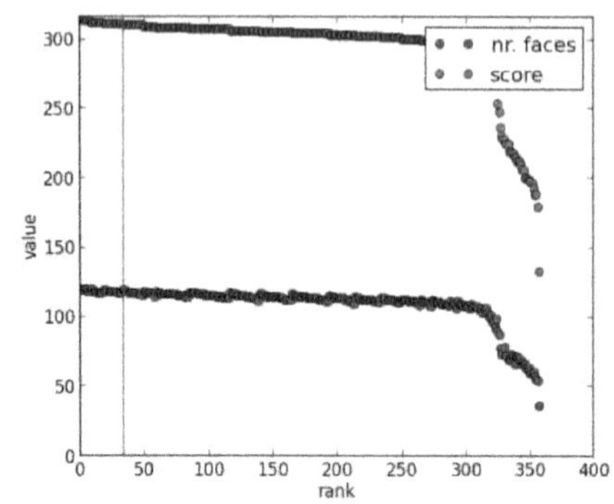

Figure 4: Results after 360 tree searches. The vertical line corresponds to the previous best known solution. The best score (most left point) is 316.

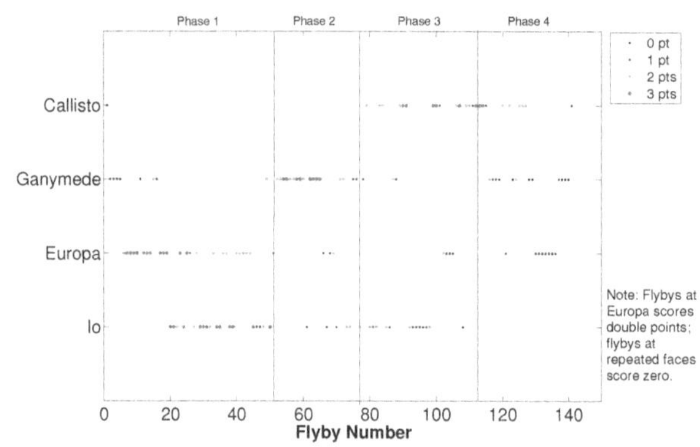

Figure 5: Scores obtained at each flyby of the four moons.

The scores on each flyby of the moons are plotted in Fig. 5, in which different colors indicates the points received: 3, 2, 1, or 0 for flyby on faces visited before, while Europa receives double points. From the plot, we notice that the flyby sequence and scores obtained are quite well structured instead of scattered evenly. The flybys on the same moon and scores are clustered together. They are also mostly ordered from first visiting the high score faces then the low score faces. From the dynamical point of view, visiting the same moon repeatedly implies the use of a resonance transfer (i.e. integer ratio of the orbital periods of the spacecraft and the moon) and is rather easy to obtain, while switching between moons may result in a time gain, but it is subject to stricter planetary phasing consideration and may thus cost more ΔV or just be not possible. Our solution clearly makes use of both possibilities trying to take advantage of quick moon

Table 2: Summary of our Jovian tour.

Moon	No. of Flybys	Scores Obtained/Max. Score
Io	37	67/68
Europa	39	136/136
Ganymede	40	60/60
Callisto	25	53/60
Total	141	316/324

switches as much as possible and otherwise mapping the same moon on resonances. This overall strategy, which we call moon-hopping, is very different from that employed by the GTOC6 winning trajectory that, instead, mapped one moon at a time.

From Fig. 5 we observe how the whole trajectory can be divided into four phases. In Phase 1, starting from a fast Callisto-Ganymede flyby using a 2.3 days long transfer, the spacecraft is captured in the Jovian system. A few more flybys at Ganymede are then able to further reduce the orbital period, allowing a visit to the high-score faces of the inner moons, Io and Europa. Phase 2 consists of mostly high-score flybys at Ganymede, mixed with flybys at the mid-score faces of Io. In the 3rd phase, the spacecraft visits Callisto and Io on faces with high and low scores, respectively. The remaining low-scores faces in Europa, Ganymede, and Callisto are visited in the final phase. The trajectories of the 4 phases are plotted in Figure 6.

Solutions from the tree searches are under an impulsive MGA-1DSM model, which is a good approximation of the low-thrust propulsion model. In the MGA-1DSM model, our solution has a total ΔV of 83 m/s, which is mostly used in the first leg for the capture and that implies the rest of the trajectory is basically ballistic. We optimized this solution for final mass in a continuous low-thrust model [15], as required by the problem. As the trajectories coming out from the search are mainly ballistic (i.e. very little ΔV is used) we did not encounter any problem in such a low-thrust conversion. The final mass of the trajectory is 1036 kg and the total time of flight is 3.9 years. The final mass is mainly accounting for the mass penalty that needs to be assigned at each successive Jupiter close encounter as described in the JPL problem statement [12]. We did not check such a penalty during the tree search, only at the end. As a consequence some of the trajectories (roughly one out of ten) in Figure 4 are actually infeasible for the GTOC6 problem (luckily not the highest ranked one).

8. CONCLUSIONS

The design of extremely complex interplanetary trajectories including dozens of multiple gravity assists may be performed autonomously by computers with the aid of carefully planned searches powered by evolutionary algorithms. We consider the case of the GTOC6 challenge proposed by the Jet Propulsion Laboratory and improve significantly over the best known solution (winner of the competition) using a new completely automated scheme that makes extensive use of self-adaptation and of the asynchronous island model. Compared to the previous best solution the trajectory found by our computers appears to be using a quite different orbital strategy, frequently hopping between moons, which is of interest to interplanetary trajectory designers.

9. ACKNOWLEDGMENTS

We thank Dr. Anastassios Petropoulos from Jet Propulsion Laboratory (the organizer of GTOC6) for having numerically validated our trajectory to be a solution to the GTOC6 problem.

10. REFERENCES

[1] B. Addis, A. Cassioli, M. Locatelli, and F. Schoen. A global optimization method for the design of space trajectories. *Computational Optimization and Applications*, 48(3):635–652, 2011.

[2] R. H. Battin. *An introduction to the mathematics and methods of astrodynamics*. American Institute of Aeronautics and Astronautics, revised edition, 1999.

[3] J. Brest, V. Zumer, and M. S. Maucec. Self-adaptive differential evolution algorithm in constrained real-parameter optimization. In *IEEE Congress on Evolutionary Computation, CEC 2006*, pages 215–222. IEEE, 2006.

[4] A. Corana, M. Marchesi, C. Martini, and S. Ridella. Minimizing multimodal functions of continuous variables with the "simulated annealing" algorithm Corrigenda for this article is available here. *ACM Transactions on Mathematical Software (TOMS)*, 13(3):262–280, 1987.

[5] K. Deb, N. Padhye, and G. Neema. Interplanetary trajectory optimization with swing-bys using evolutionary multi-objective optimization. In L. Kang, Y. Liu, and S. Zeng, editors, *Advances in Computation and Intelligence*, volume 4683 of *Lecture Notes in Computer Science*, pages 26–35. Springer, 2007.

[6] N. Hansen, S. D. Müller, and P. Koumoutsakos. Reducing the time complexity of the derandomized evolution strategy with covariance matrix adaptation (CMA-ES). *Evolutionary Computation*, 11(1):1–18, 2003.

[7] D. Izzo. 1st ACT global trajectory optimisation competition: Problem description and summary of the results. *Acta Astronautica*, 61(9):731–734, 2007.

[8] D. Izzo. Global Optimization and Space Pruning for Spacecraft Trajectory Design. In B. Conway, editor, *Spacecraft Trajectory Optimization*, Cambridge Aerospace Series, chapter 7, pages 178–201. Cambridge University Press, 2010.

[9] D. Izzo, V. M. Becerra, D. R. Myatt, S. J. Nasuto, and J. M. Bishop. Search space pruning and global optimisation of multiple gravity assist spacecraft trajectories. *Journal of Global Optimization*, 38(2):283–296, 2007.

[10] X. Liu, H. Baoyin, and X. Ma. Five special types of orbits around Mars. *Journal of guidance, control, and dynamics*, 33(4):1294–1301, 2010.

[11] A. E. Lynam, K. W. Kloster, and J. M. Longuski. Multiple-satellite-aided capture trajectories at Jupiter using the Laplace resonance. *Celestial Mechanics and Dynamical Astronomy*, 109(1):59–84, 2011.

[12] A. E. Petropoulos. Problem description for the 6th global trajectory optimisation competition. `http://goo.gl/FmrOc`. Accessed: 01/01/2013.

[13] M. Rosa Sentinella and L. Casalino. Cooperative evolutionary algorithm for space trajectory optimization. *Celestial Mechanics and Dynamical Astronomy*, 105(1–3):211–227, 2009.

[14] M. Vasile and M. Locatelli. A hybrid multiagent approach for global trajectory optimization. *Journal of Global Optimization*, 44(4):461–479, 2009.

[15] C. H. Yam, D. Izzo, and F. Biscani. Towards a high fidelity direct transcription method for optimisation of low-thrust trajectories. In *4th International Conference on Astrodynamics Tools and Techniques*, May 2010.

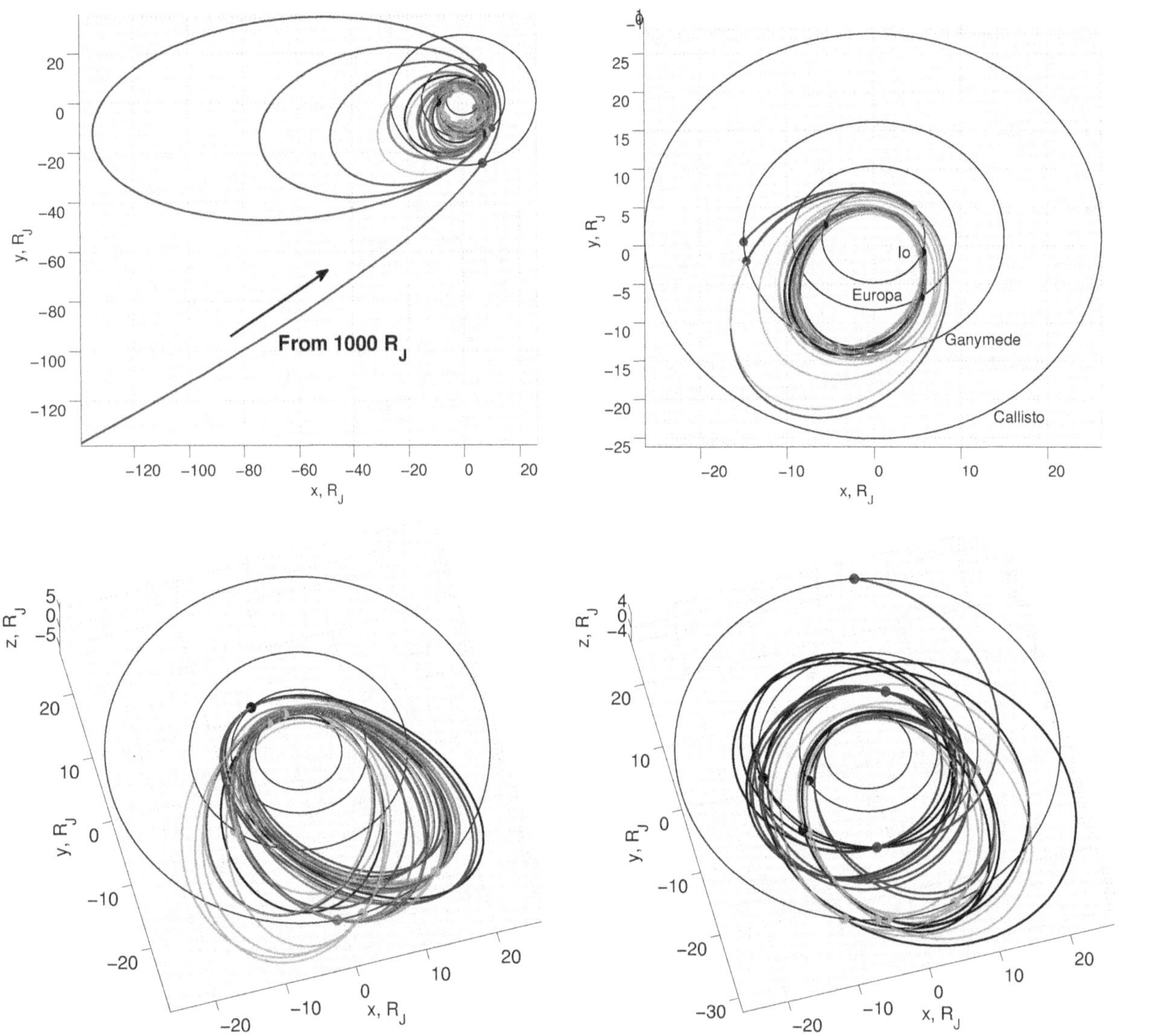

Figure 6: Visualization of the four phases of the moon tour. Phase 1: leg 1-51 (top-left); Phase 2: leg 52-78 (top-right); Phase 3: leg 79-115 (bottom-left); Phase 4: leg 116-141 (bottom-right). Colors on the trajectory represent scores obtained on the upcoming flyby (same color scheme as Fig. 5).

Pipe Smoothing Genetic Algorithm for Least Cost Water Distribution Network Design

Matthew B. Johns
University of Exeter
Harrison Building, North Park Road
Exeter EX4 4QF
+44(0) 1392 723909
mbj202@exeter.ac.uk

Edward Keedwell
University of Exeter
Harrison Building, North Park Road
Exeter EX4 4QF
+44(0) 1392 724014
E.C.Keedwell@exeter.ac.uk

Dragan Savic
University of Exeter
Harrison Building, North Park Road
Exeter EX4 4QF
+44(0) 1392 723637
D.Savic@exeter.ac.uk

ABSTRACT

This paper describes the development of a Pipe Smoothing Genetic Algorithm (PSGA) and its application to the problem of least cost water distribution network design. Genetic algorithms have been used widely for the optimisation of both theoretical and real-world non-linear optimisation problems, including water system design and maintenance problems. In this work we propose a pipe smoothing based approach to the creation and mutation of chromosomes which utilises engineering expertise with the view to increasing the performance of the algorithm compared to a standard genetic algorithm. Both PSGA and the standard genetic algorithm were tested on benchmark water distribution networks from the literature. In all cases PSGA achieves higher optimality in fewer solution evaluations than the standard genetic algorithm.

Categories and Subject Descriptors

G.1.6 [**Numerical Analysis**]: Optimization – *Constrained Optimization.*

Keywords

Water Distribution, Genetic Algorithm, Heuristic, Optimisation

1. INTRODUCTION

Evolutionary algorithms (EAs) are widely used for the optimisation of both theoretical and real-world problems. These problems tend to be highly complex and incorporate one or more constraints that limit the feasible space to be searched. One such problem is that of optimising a water distribution network where the task is to determine the optimally least-cost network design that still meets the requirements of the network (typically the provision of the required pressure at each of the points of demand). EAs have been shown to be excellent tools for optimising such networks, but many formulations fail to take into account engineering expertise. As such, the solutions they propose can be excellent from an objective function perspective, but are not able to be implemented in the real-world without considerable modification.

In this work, we propose the use of a heuristic based approach for the initialization and mutation of chromosomes based on human engineering expertise and demonstrate this method on some water distribution network design problems. Although the heuristic used is specific to the problem, the method of constraining the solutions could be applied to other network problems in the literature including sewer networks, communications networks etc. The heuristic-based 'pipe smoothing' approach is shown to perform better than a standard evolutionary algorithm on all water distribution network design problems tested, both in terms of outright performance and engineering feasibility.

1.1 Water Distribution Network Design Problem

Water distribution network (WDN) design is a complex non-linear optimisation problem, commonly involving a large number of different network components and hydraulic constraints. Due to the inherent complexity of WDN design, a simplified formulation of the problem is commonly employed when applied to optimisation techniques. This method is commonly comprised of the allocation of a diameter to each pipe in a given network layout, with the objective of minimising cost whilst satisfying pressure constraints at the nodes [1]. In this simplified version, design considerations such as water quality and network reliability are not included in the formulation of the problem. This method provides the designer with a base from which to solve the overall problem and allows the comparison of new optimisation techniques with the large amount of literature that employs this technique of problem formulation.

The optimal design of a water distribution network is presented here using the following mathematical statement. The objective function is defined as the total cost of the network with regard to pipe length and diameter

$$f(D_1, \dots, D_n) = \sum_{i=1}^{N} c(D_i, L_i)$$

where $c(D_i, L_i)$ = cost of pipe i with diameter D_i and length L_i with N = number of pipes in the network. This function is to be minimised whilst satisfying the following constraints. For each junction (excluding the source) the following continuity constraint has to be satisfied

$$\sum Q_{in} - \sum Q_{out} = Q_e$$

where Q_{in} = inflow to the junction, Q_{out} = outflow from the junction and Q_e = external flow or junction demand which in this case is always positive. The pressure drop due to friction or head loss h_f for a specific pipe i is calculated using the following equation

$$h_f = \omega \frac{L_i}{C_i^a D_i^b} Q_i^a$$

where C_i = Hazen-Williams roughness coefficient, Q_i = flow and a, b, and ω are parameters of the equations.

The minimum head constraint for each junction in the network is as follows

$$H_j \geq H_j^{min}; j = 1, \ldots, M$$

where H_j = hydraulic head (water pressure) at junction j, H_j^{min} = minimum head requirement at junction j and M = total number of junctions present in the network.

In the case of this formulation of the WDN design problem the optimisation is exclusively concerned with the selection of pipe diameters. Each individual problem has a set of available pipe diameters which can be selected for each decision pipe in the network. These decisions are encoded as a binary bit sub-string with a length dictated by the number of pipe sizes available. The substrings are then concatenated to form the chromosome to represent the entire solution.

1.2 Previous Work on WDN Optimisation

The optimal design of water distribution networks is considered a NP-hard problem [2] and has been solved with a number of approaches, such as classic methods that include linear and dynamic programming [3][4][5][6][7] and various heuristic algorithms. Due to the discrete nature of the decision space and the advent of effective hydraulic solvers, the application of global stochastic optimisation algorithms has been proven to be a good approach to the WDN design problem. These approaches, although effective can induce a large number of hydraulic evaluations which in the case of large, real world WDNs can become extremely computationally expensive. Over the last two decades a considerable amount of research has been applied to the problem of WDN design especially in the field of EAs such as Genetic Algorithms (GAs) [8][9][10][11][12], Simulated Annealing[13], Shuffled Complex Evolution [14], Ant Colony Optimisation [15] and Harmony Search [16]. These techniques have proven to be effective on a number of benchmark WDN design problems.

1.3 Constraint Handling In EAs

In their basic form, EAs are unconstrained optimisation procedures. However, many problems have constraints imposed upon them especially in real-world optimisation problems. A common approach to dealing with constrained optimisation problems is to incorporate the constraints into the fitness function of the EA by adding a penalty function to the fitness function, where the value obtained from the penalty function represents the solution's distance from feasibility. A frequently used approach is the static penalty [17], where the penalty factors remain constant throughout the evolutionary process. Another approach is the use of a dynamic penalty where the penalty function is varied over time, commonly tightening the constraints as the EA's population develops. The notion of allowing an EA to explore the search space unimpeded before increasing the focus of the search and therefore potentially improving the scope of the search has lead some researchers to argue that dynamic penalties perform better than a static penalty approach. However, it has been found that deriving an effective dynamic penalty function is as difficult to achieve as producing good penalty factors for static functions [18].

Another approach when handling the constraints of a problem is to employ a repair algorithm. The repair algorithm has proven a popular choice for many combinatorial optimisation problems as it is often relatively easy to 'repair' an infeasible solution through the iterative modification of individual decision variables. When a solution can be transformed from infeasible to feasible at a low computational cost, repair algorithms have proven to be effective. However, it is not always possible to repair an infeasible solution at an acceptable computational cost and in some cases the algorithm can harm the evolutionary process by introducing a strong bias in the search [19].

A further method is to use an indirect representation where the genes do not code for variables in the problem directly, but via a heuristic that determines the phenotype given the genotype developed by the algorithm. These approaches have been shown to work well in timetabling problems [20] but the relationship between the genotype and phenotype is more complex leading to a more multimodal fitness landscape.

1.4 Pipe Smoothing Approach

This paper describes the development of a Pipe Smoothing Genetic Algorithm (PSGA) and its application to the least cost WDN design problem. This method actively promotes engineering feasibility by directly influencing chromosome construction and mutation. PSGA is based upon a standard genetic algorithm and incorporates a modified population initialiser and mutation operator which directly targets elements of a network with the aim to increase network smoothness (in terms of progression from one diameter to the next) using network element awareness and an elementary heuristic. Experiments are conducted to compare a standard genetic algorithm and PSGA for a number of benchmark WDN design problems. The results show that the PSGA approach exhibits improved performance over the standard GA, especially for parallel expansion WDN design problems.

2. PIPE SMOOTHING GENETIC ALGORITHM

The Pipe Smoothing Genetic Algorithm (PSGA) is based around the principle that in a gravity fed WDN the diameter of any pipe is never greater than the sum of the diameter(s) of the directly upstream pipes. Networks that adhere to this rule can be seen to 'smoothly' transition from large to small diameters from source to the extremities of the network. This rule is routinely and implicitly applied by engineers when designing such networks as it makes little sense to follow a smaller diameter pipe with a larger one in the majority of circumstances. The larger pipe will cost more to install and will not add to the hydraulic capability of the system as it will be constrained by the smaller diameter pipe upstream. One further negative aspect of this arrangement is that velocities will be lower in the larger pipe and high water age can become an issue. A standard GA of course will mutate some of these inconsistent pipe selections from the final solution as they have a corresponding improvement in the cost function and no hydraulic penalty. However extensive experimentation has shown that even well-optimised solutions after hundreds of thousands of generations of a standard EA still contain significant numbers of incorrectly sized pipes in larger networks.

PSGA applies the rule described above directly to the genotype without evaluating the effect this process has on the phenotype. The heuristic employed by PSGA is developed from the network topology of a specific problem and remains constant throughout the evolutionary process. The heuristic is applied to a solution at initialization and through the mutation operator; where the probability of the heuristic being applied is defined by a preset algorithm parameter. It is the aim of the heuristic to guide the algorithm's search to the engineering feasible solution space to locate smoother WDN designs whilst maintaining the performance of a standard genetic algorithm. The PSGA mutation operator does not perform any additional partial or full fitness evaluations, except a single hydraulic simulation at initialisation to determine flow directions. This was an important consideration when developing PSGA as additional fitness evaluations would require further hydraulic evaluations, increasing algorithm run time.

PSGA is essentially a standard GA (SGA) which incorporates some additional features; these include a pipe smoothing initialiser heuristic based mutation operator. The standard GA used was a steady-state GA with tournament selection with tournament size t and single-point crossover with probability c. A Gray-coded binary string comprising of N sub-strings was employed where each sub-string represents the diameter of each pipe in the WDN. Mutation was conducted as a random bitwise mutation with probability m.

2.1 Pipe Smoothing Initialiser

The initial population of solutions is constructed by the pipe smoothing initialiser which applies a basic rule where the diameter of any pipe is never greater than the sum of the diameters of the pipes directly upstream. The operator first sets the diameter of all pipes directly connected to a reservoir to the maximum allowable diameter for the specific problem. The algorithm then selects each remaining downstream pipe in turn to allocate a diameter. The operator achieves this by calculating the maximum allowable diameter for the given pipe and randomly selecting a pipe diameter so as not to violate this constraint. Although the diameter selection is random, a skewed roulette wheel approach is employed to prioritise the selection of larger diameters. This results in larger allowable diameters having a greater probability of being chosen from the available list. It is later shown that when this operator is used to generate all chromosomes in the initial population this has a detrimental effect on the subsequent search of the genetic algorithm due to lack of diversity in the population. Therefore a mechanism was introduced to allow the probability of the pipe smoothing initialiser chromosome application to be varied.

2.2 Pipe Smoothing Mutation Operator

The pipe smoothing mutation operator randomly selects a pipe to be mutated. The sum of all the diameters of the directly upstream pipes is set as the maximum allowable diameter the current pipe can be. Much the same as the pipe smoothing initialiser, this operator employs a skewed roulette wheel approach to the random selection of the pipe diameter. This is achieved be weighting the larger pipe diameters that fall within the maximum allowable size so that the larger the diameter, the higher the probability there is of selection. Upon selection the pipe being mutated is changed to the selected diameter.

To function correctly both the pipe smoothing initialiser and mutation operator require each pipe in the network to be 'aware' of the pipes directly up and down stream of their location. When changes are made to a WDN there is a possibility that flow direction could change in some pipes hence swapping up & down stream pipes relative to the pipe in question. The flow direction is logged at each hydraulic evaluation of the network, therefore to preserve this hydraulic data the pipe smoothing mutation operator precedes the crossover operator. This is illustrated in figure 1.

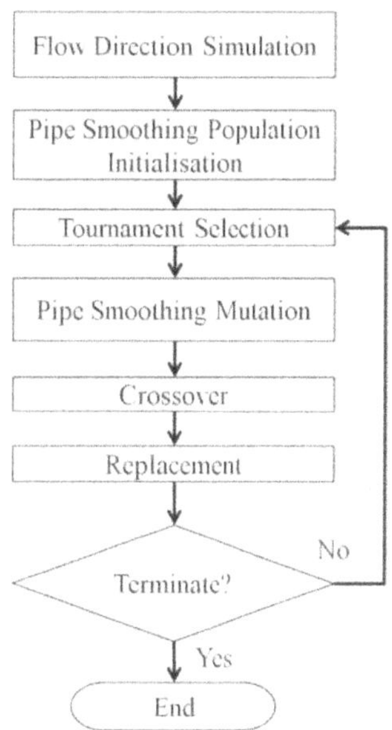

Figure 1. Flow diagram illustrating the structure of PSGA

3. COMPUTATIONAL RESULTS

PSGA was coded in C++ and run on an Intel Core i7 3.07GHz PC. The test problems used to evaluate the algorithm including a number of benchmark networks from the literature. The following test cases can be found at *emps.exeter.ac.uk/engineering/research/cws/downloads/benchmarks*. In all test cases both PSGA and SGA are run using identical common parameters.

3.1 Algorithm Development - Hanoi Problem

PSGA was applied to the Hanoi problem; a single reservoir, gravity fed water distribution network consisting of 32 junctions and 34 pipes organised in 3 loops. The Hanoi problem was used in this case to explore the effectiveness of the pipe smoothing operators when the probability of application to a standard GA was varied. The current best known solution for this specific benchmark is $6.081 million, achieved with a GA variant[21].

3.1.1 Probability of Pipe Smoothing Mutation

The probability that the pipe smoothing mutation operator was employed was varied throughout a number of experiments. When the pipe smoothing mutation operator was not employed, the standard bitwise mutation operator was used instead. The pipe smoothing initialisation operator was not employed for this first set of runs.

The base algorithm used in the following runs was built on a simple single objective steady state genetic algorithm with a mutation rate of 0.05 and tournament size of 0.05N where N is the population size which in this case is 100. The probability of pipe smoothing mutation was varied between 0% and 100% at 25% intervals. For each parameter set the algorithm was run a total of 20 times for 10,000 iterations (20,000 fitness evaluations) with different initial random seeds on the Hanoi problem with a penalty factor of 1,000,000 $/m head deficit. Below are the average results from these experiments.

Table 1. Pipe Smoothing Rate Results for PSGA on Hanoi

Probability of Pipe Smoothing Mutation	Mean Best Feasible Solution Cost ($)	Mean Best Feasible Solution Cost Standard Deviation ($)
0%	6,344,188	132,334
25%	6,308,339	111,084
50%	**6,297,480**	113,869
75%	6,303,149	**102,811**
100%	6,380,882	141,364

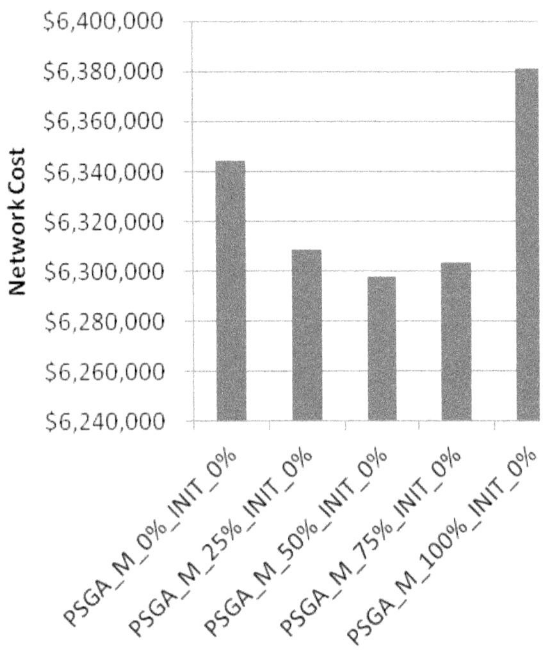

Figure 2. Mean Best Feasible Solution Cost

The preceding results show that PSGA appears to perform best when pipe smoothing mutation and standard bitwise mutation are applied in equal proportions. The results do however suggest that when the pipe smoothing mutation operator is applied continually the algorithm prematurely converges on a suboptimal solution compared to that of the standard genetic algorithm. The following figure (Figure 3) show the comparison between the standard genetic algorithm (PSGA_M_0%) and PSGA with 50% probability of pipe smoothing mutation. Note that this figure shows the average feasible solution (i.e. a solution that meets all hydraulic constraints) cost for all 20 runs.

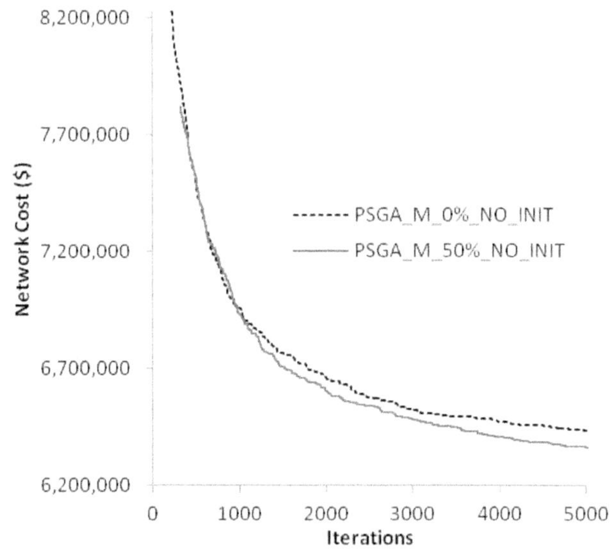

Figure 3. Mean Best Feasible Solution Cost- PSGA-Hanoi

Figure 3 shows that the standard genetic algorithm has a faster initial rate of convergence in the first 250 iterations compared to the Pipe Smoothing Genetic Algorithm (PSGA). However PSGA does surpass the standard GA beyond 1000 iterations.

3.1.2 Pipe Smoothing Population Initialiser

Instead of generating a population of random solutions, the pipe smoothing initialisation operator uses a heuristic based approach that ensures no pipe is larger than that total diameter of pipes directly upstream whilst retaining a random element. In this set of experiments the proportion of the initial population which employs the pipe smoothing initialisation operator is varied between 0% and 100% at 25% intervals. When the pipe smoothing initialisation operator is not employed, the solution is generated randomly.

The base algorithm used in the following runs is as described in section 3.1.1. Below are the average results from these experiments.

Table 2. Pipe Smoothing Initialisation Rate Results for PSGA on Hanoi

Probability of Pipe Smoothing Initialisation	Mean Best Feasible Solution Cost ($)	Mean Best Feasible Solution Cost Standard Deviation ($)
0%	6,344,188	132,334
25%	6,321,749	103,841
50%	**6,316,813**	110,051
75%	6,335,983	117,362
100%	6,380,001	**99,466**

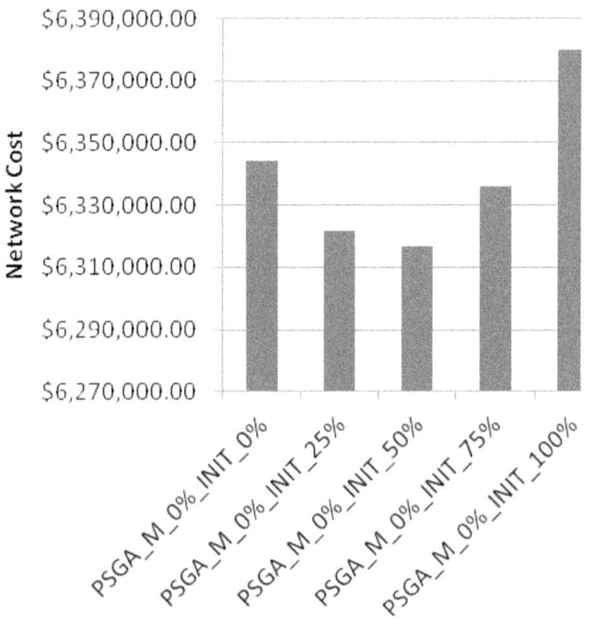

Figure 4. Pipe Smoothing Initialisation Rate Results for PSGA on Hanoi, Mean Best Feasible Solution Cost

These results suggest there is a performance increase when the pipe smoothing initialisation operator is applied to 25%, 50% and 75% of the population. However, at 100% pipe smoothing initialisation the algorithm performs worse than the standard genetic algorithm (PSGA_M_0%_INIT_0%).

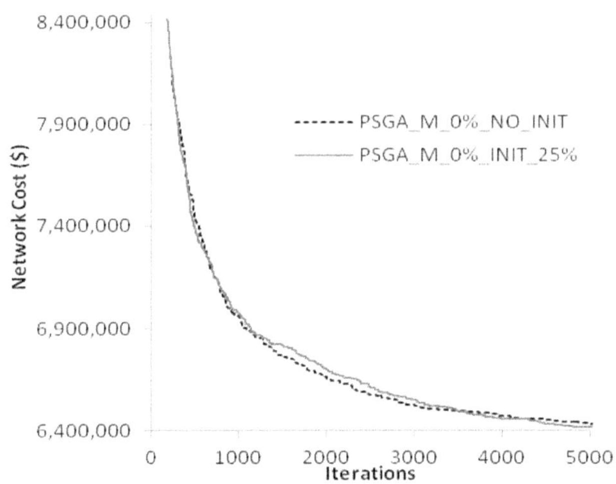

Figure 5. Mean Best Feasible Solution Cost- PSGA Initialisation – Hanoi

Figure 5 shows the comparison between the standard genetic algorithm with standard population initialisation and the standard GA with 25% pipe smoothing initialisation. The standard GA with pipe smoothing initialisation finds feasibility slightly sooner than the standard GA with standard initialisation, however there is not a notable difference in the convergence of the two algorithms.

To further explore the effect of the pipe smoothing initialisation operator, this next experiment uses the best performing version of PSGA (PS mutation at 50%) and varies the pipe smoothing initialisation rate between 0% and 100% again at 25% intervals.

Table 3. Pipe Smoothing Initialisation Rate Results for PSGA on Hanoi

Probability of Pipe Smoothing Initialisation	Mean Best Feasible Solution Cost ($)	Mean Best Feasible Solution Cost Standard Deviation ($)
0%	6,297,480	113,869
25%	6,290,517	119,694
50%	**6,279,120**	**111,130**
75%	6,298,693	120,991
100%	6,353,617	142,785

The results shown in table 3 and figure 6 indicate that PSGA with a pipe smoothing mutation rate of 50% benefits from the pipe smoothing initiation operator up to 50% population application.

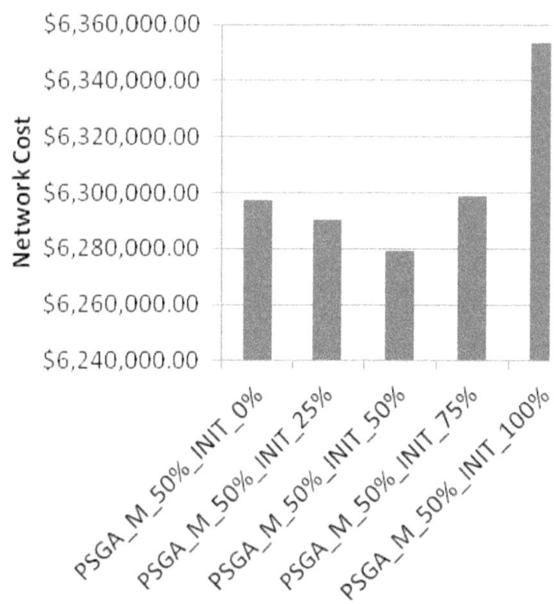

Figure 6. Pipe Smoothing Initialisation Rate Results for PSGA M 50% on Hanoi, Mean Best Feasible Solution Cost

As with the previous set of results, when pipe smoothing initialisation is applied to the whole starting population, the algorithm suffers premature convergence, achieving a suboptimal solution compared to the other algorithms.

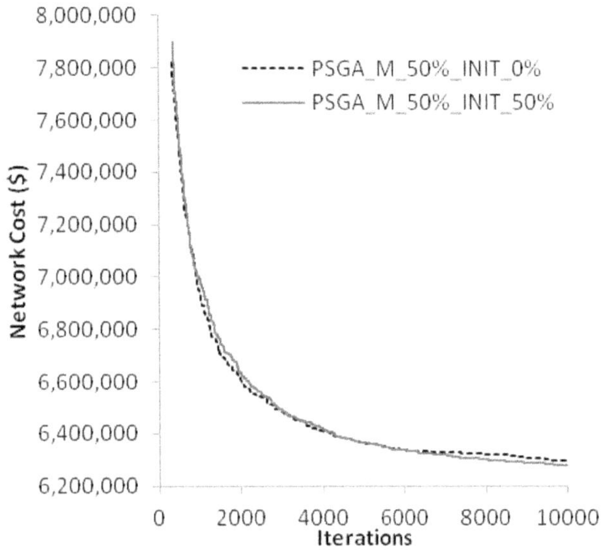

Figure 7. Mean Best Feasible Solution Cost- PSGA M50% Initialisation – Hanoi

Figure 7 shows the comparison between PSGA M50% with no pipe smoothing initialisation and the same algorithm with a pipe smoothing rate of 50%. The plots show that PSGA without pipe smoothing initialisation displays faster initial convergence, however it is outperformed in the later stages of the search by PSGA with pipe smoothing initialisation.

These initial experiments suggest that the pipe smoothing genetic algorithm benefits from an equal mix of the pipe smoothing heuristic mutation and standard bitwise mutation. Also the pipe smoothing initialisation operator adds additional performance when used to generate a moderate proportion of the initial population.

The following results show a direct comparison between the standard genetic algorithm and the best performing version of the pipe smoothing genetic algorithm.

Table 4. Standard GA vs. PSGA on Hanoi

Algorithm	Mean Best Cost ($)	Standard Deviation of Best Cost ($)
Standard GA	6,344,188	132,334
PSGA_M_50%_INIT_50%	**6,279,120**	**111,130**

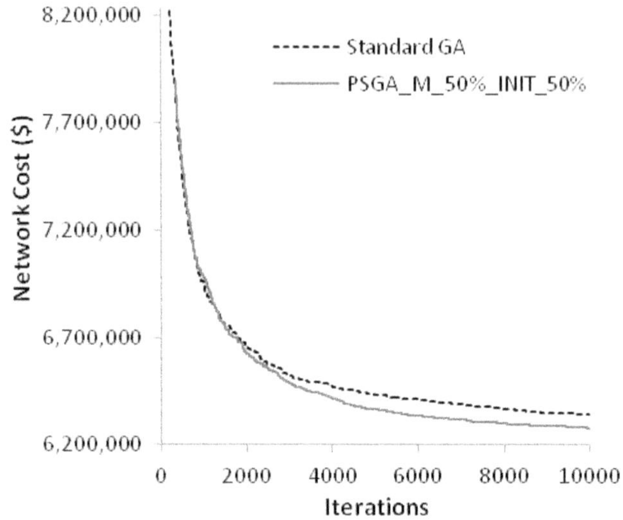

Figure 8. Mean Best Feasible Solution Cost- Standard GA vs. PSGA – Hanoi

Although the standard algorithm displays faster initial convergence over PSGA in the first 300 iterations (600 fitness evaluations), PSGA starts to outperform the standard GA after 1200 iterations (2400 fitness evaluations). PSGA achieves a better mean best feasible solution cost and with a lower standard deviation over the results of the standard GA although neither algorithm achieves the best known feasible solution ($6.081). This is not unexpected due to the number of solution evaluations allowed.

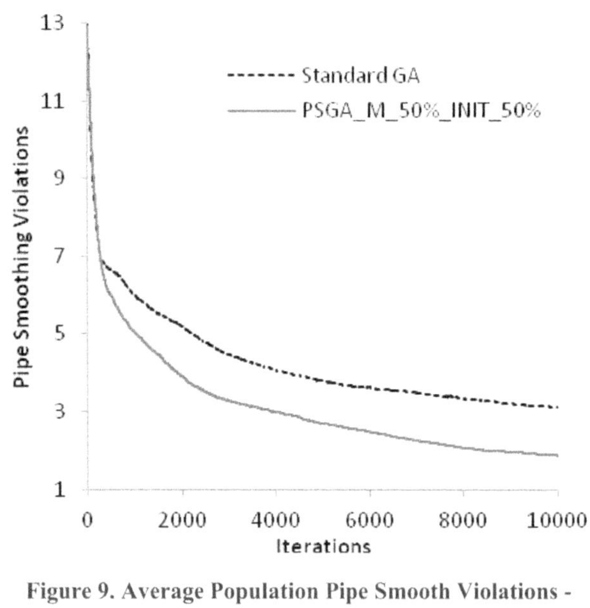

Figure 9. Average Population Pipe Smooth Violations - Standard GA vs. PSGA – Hanoi

Figure 9 shows the average population pipe smoothing violations. A violation occurs when a pipe's diameter is larger than the sum of diameters of the directly upstream pipes. From these results it is apparent that PSGA out performs the standard genetic algorithm with regard to pipe smoothing violations resulting in a population with smoother solutions and better performance. A network with fewer smoothing violations is more likely to be accepted by the engineer for implementation. The results in Figure 9 show that the PSGA solutions have approximately half the violations of those from the standard GA.

3.2 New York Tunnels Problem

The New York Tunnels Problem [3] is a parallel expansion problem consisting of 21 existing pipes and 20 junctions fed by a fixed head reservoir. The objective is to find the least cost configuration of pipes that could be installed parallel to the existing pipes to meet the head constraints of the problem. There are 16 available pipe diameters ranging from 0in to 804.0in therefore no encoding redundancy is required.

PSGA was then applied to the New York Tunnels problem and compared again to the standard GA. The base algorithm used in the following runs is built on a simple single objective steady state genetic algorithm with a mutation rate of 0.05 and tournament size of 0.05N where N is the population size which in this case is 100. For each parameter set the algorithm was run a total of 20 times for 10,000 iterations (20,000 fitness evaluations) with different initial random seeds. A penalty factor of 7,000,000 $/m head deficit was used. Below are the average results from these experiments.

Table 5. Standard GA vs. PSGA on New York Tunnels

Algorithm	Mean Best Cost ($)	Standard Deviation of Best Cost ($)
Standard GA	41,465,945	922,076
PSGA_M_50%_INIT_50%	**38,935,400**	**530,145**

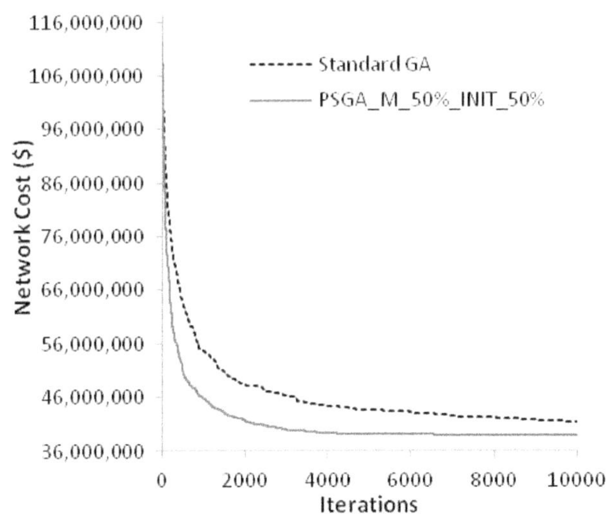

Figure 10. Mean Best Feasible Solution Cost- Standard GA vs. PSGA – New York Tunnels

In this set of runs, PSGA drastically outperforms the standard GA both in convergence rate and solution quality. It suggests that the heuristics used in PSGA directly complement the nature of the New York Tunnels problem as a parallel expansion problem. Figure 10 shows the PSGA reducing the feasible cost very close to the current best-known minimum [15] of $38.64 million in approximately 12000 fitness evaluations.

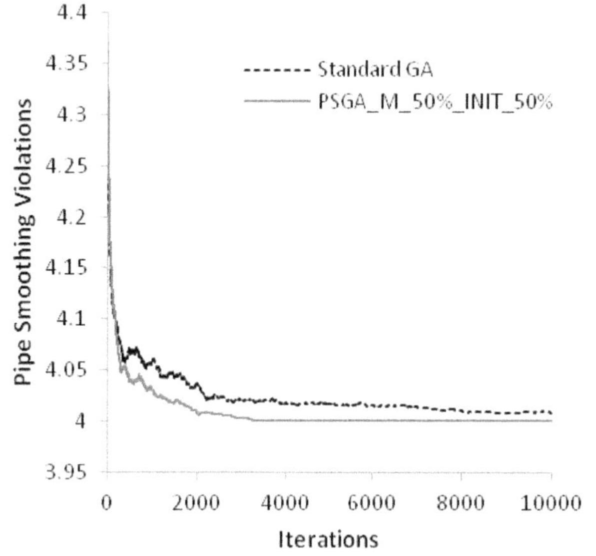

Figure 11. Average Population Pipe Smooth Violations - Standard GA vs. PSGA – New York Tunnels

Figure 11. shows the average pipe smoothing violation present in the population of both PSGA and the Standard GA. Although there is little difference between the two algorithms, PSGA does tend to outperform the Standard GA in terms of network smoothness after around 200 iterations (400 evaluations).

4. CONCLUSIONS

A 'pipe-smoothing' genetic algorithm has been created and tested on well-known benchmarks from the literature. Utilising a heuristic, PSGA encodes engineering expertise into a standard genetic algorithm with the view to improving the performance of the algorithm. The influence of the pipe smoothing initialisation and mutation operators of PSGA has proven to outperform a standard genetic algorithm on all benchmark problems tested in this paper without incurring additional fitness evaluations and hence computational complexity. For both problems tested in this paper, PSGA achieved lower cost solutions in less fitness evaluations than the standard genetic algorithm.

These experiments show PSGA will outperform a standard genetic algorithm for benchmark problems as used in this study, although further, more extensive experiments should be performed to verify the effectiveness of the new algorithm on larger real-world networks. It is also apparent that PSGA achieves a smoother solution than that of the standard genetic algorithm, making the PSGA solutions more engineering feasible for real-world application. However, the smoothness of a solution is not taken into account when assessing the network due to the nature of the fitness function which only computes the infrastructure cost and the head deficit information, thus it is most likely that smooth solutions are disregarded upon replacement. Also if we observe the behaviour of both the standard GA and the PSGA it is apparent that there is a potential correlation between the fitness of a solution and its smoothness. This leads to a question: Can search performance be improved by integrating a pipe smoothing violation component into the fitness function or separate objective in a multi-objective algorithm? Although this question falls outside the scope of this paper, this would be the natural direction to take this research in future work.

5. REFERENCES

[1] E. Alperovits and U. Shamir, "Design of optimal water distribution systems," *Water Resources Research*, vol. 13, no. 6, p. 885, 1977.

[2] D. F. Yates, A. B. Templeman, and T. B. Boffey, "The computational complexity of the problem of determining least capital cost designs for water supply networks," *Engineering Optimization*, vol. 7, no. 2, pp. 143–155, Jan. 1984.

[3] J. C. Schaake Jr. and D. Lai, "Linear Programming and Dynamic Programming Application to Water Distribution Network Design," Cambridge, MA, 1969.

[4] A. Kessler and U. Shamir, "Analysis of the linear programming gradient method for optimal design of water supply networks," *Water Resources Research*, vol. 25, no. 7, p. 1469, 1989.

[5] O. Fujiwara and D. B. Khang, "Correction to 'A Two-Phase Decomposition Method for Optimal Design of Looped Water Distribution Networks' by Okitsugu Fujiwara and Do Ba Khang," *Water Resources Research*, vol. 27, no. 5, pp. 985–986, 1991.

[6] H. D. Sherali, S. Subramanian, and G. V. Loganathan, "Effective Relaxations and Partitioning Schemes for Solving Water Distribution Network Design Problems to Global Optimality," *Journal of Global Optimization*, vol. 19, no. 1, pp. 1–26, Jan. 2001.

[7] C. Bragalli, C. D. Ambrosio, J. Lee, A. Lodi, and P. Toth, "Water Network Design by MINLP," 2008.

[8] G. C. Dandy, A. R. Simpson, and L. J. Murphy, "An Improved Genetic Algorithm for Pipe Network Optimization," *Water Resources Research*, vol. 32, no. 2, p. 449, 1996.

[9] D. A. Savic and G. A. Walters, "Genetic Algorithms for Least-Cost Design of Water Distribution Networks," *Journal of Water Resources Planning and Management*, vol. 123, no. 2, pp. 67–77, 1997.

[10] Z. Wu and A. Simpson, "Competent genetic-evolutionary optimization of water distribution systems," *Journal of Computing in Civil Engineering*, vol. 15, no. April, pp. 89–101, 2001.

[11] M. S. Kadu, R. Gupta, and P. R. Bhave, "Optimal design of water distribution networks using genetic algorithm with reduction in search space," in *One-Day National Conference Geotechnical and Environmentally Sustainable Development*, 2005, pp. 182–189.

[12] S. Artina, C. Bragalli, G. Erbacci, A. Marchi, and M. Rivi, "Contribution of parallel NSGA-II in optimal design of water distribution networks," *Journal of Hydroinformatics*, vol. 14, no. 2, p. 310, Apr. 2012.

[13] M. da C. Cunha and J. Sousa, "Water Distribution Network Design Optimization: Simulated Annealing Approach," *Journal of Water Resources Planning and Management*, vol. 125, no. 4, pp. 215–221, Jan. 1999.

[14] S. Liong and M. Atiquzzaman, "Optimal design of water distribution network using shuffled complex evolution," *Journal of The Institution of Engineers, Singapore*, vol. 44, no. 1, pp. 93–107, 2004.

[15] H. Maier, A. Simpson, A. Zecchin, W. Foong, K. Phang, H. Seah, and C. Tan, "Ant colony optimization for design of water distribution systems," *Journal of Water Resources Planning and Management*, vol. 129, no. June, pp. 200–209, 2003.

[16] Z. Geem, J. Kim, and G. Loganathan, "Harmony search optimization: application to pipe network design.," *International Journal of Simulation Modelling*, vol. 22, no. 2, pp. 125–133, 2002.

[17] A. K. Morales and C. V. Quezada, "A universal eclectic genetic algorithm for constrained optimization," in *Proceedings of the 6th European Congress on Intelligent Techniques and Soft Computing*, 1998, pp. 518–522.

[18] W. Siedlecki and J. Sklansky, "Constrained genetic optimization via dynamic reward-penalty balancing and its use in pattern recognition," in *Proceedings of the third international conference on genetic algorithms*, 1989, pp. 141–150.

[19] A. Smith and D. Coit, "Constraint handling techniques – penalty functions," in *Handbook of Evolutionary Computation*, T. Baeck, D. . Fogel, and Z. Michalewicz, Eds. Taylor & Francis, 1997.

[20] B. Paechter, R. Rankin, A. Cumming, and T. Fogarty, "Timetabling the classes of an entire university with an evolutionary algorithm," in *5th International Conference on Parallel Problem Solving from Nature (PPSN V)*, 1998, pp. 865–874.

[21] J. Reca and J. Martínez, "Genetic algorithms for the design of looped irrigation water distribution networks," *Water Resources Research*, vol. 42, no. 5, May 2006.

Cluster Energy Optimizing Genetic Algorithm

Vera A. Kazakova
Department of EECS
University of Central Florida
Orlando, Florida 32816
rusky.cs@gmail.com

Annie S. Wu
Department of EECS
University of Central Florida
Orlando, Florida 32816
aswu@eecs.ucf.edu

Talat S. Rahman
Department of Physics
University of Central Florida
Orlando, Florida 32816
talat.rahman@ucf.edu

ABSTRACT

Nanoclusters are small clumps of atoms of one or several materials. A cluster possesses a unique set of material properties depending on its configuration (i.e. the number of atoms, their types, and their exact relative positioning). Finding and subsequently testing these configurations is of great interest to physicists in search of new advantageous material properties. To facilitate the discovery of ideal cluster configurations, we propose the Cluster Energy Optimizing GA (CEO-GA), which combines the strengths of Johnston's BCGA [18], Pereira's H-C&S crossover [25], and two new mutation operators: Local Spherical and Center of Mass Spherical. The advantage of CEO-GA is its ability to evolve optimally stable clusters (those with lowest potential energy) without relying on local optimization methods, as do other commonly used cluster evolving GAs, such as BCGA.

Categories and Subject Descriptors

I.2.1 [**Artificial Intelligence**]: Applications and Expert Systems—*medicine and science*; J.2 [**Computer Applications**]: Physical Sciences and Engineering—*physics*

General Terms

Algorithms, design, performance, experimentation.

Keywords

Cluster energy optimization, Gupta potential, genetic algorithm, nanocluster, CEO-GA, global minimization

1. INTRODUCTION

In this paper, we introduce the Cluster Energy Optimization Genetic Algorithm (CEO-GA) derived from the Birmingham Cluster Genetic Algorithm (BCGA) [18]. The CEO-GA uses H-C&S crossover [25], atom permutation mutation, and incorporates two new operators: the Local Spherical mutation (Local-S) and the Center of Mass Spherical mutation (CoM-S). The CEO-GA, while not itself depending on local minimization like its predecessors, achieves results comparable to those previously obtained only via combining a GA with local optimization techniques.

Bulk solids typically have a periodic arrangement of atoms (unless they are amorphous), with well defined separations between the atoms (lattice constant) and characteristic geometry. For example, bulk Gold (Au) and Copper (Cu) are members of the so-called face-centered-cubic crystals. The percentage of atoms on the surface of a bulk material is negligible in relation to the total number of atoms in the bulk. Nanoclusters, on the other hand, are clusters of a few to a few hundred atoms that can be either homogeneous (composed entirely of atoms of a single material) or heterogeneous(containing atoms of two or more materials). A nanocluster is a unit in itself and decomposing it would alter its physical properties, effectively transforming it into several different clusters. The atoms on the surface of a nanocluster (which are responsible for any interactions with the environment) constitute a considerable percentage of the total cluster size. Since these surface atoms have lost some neighbors, they are under-coordinated and thus may serve as active sites for chemical reactions. Examples of Au, Cu, and Au-Cu nanoclusters are shown in figure 1.

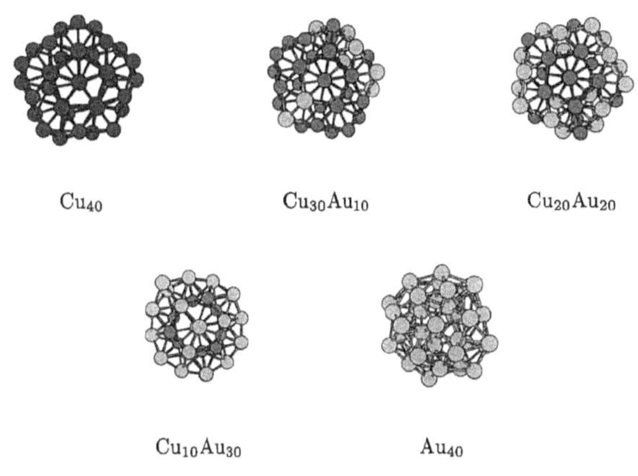

Figure 1: Examples of Au, Cu, and Au-Cu clusters. Dark and light sphere represent Cu and Au atoms, respectively.[1]

[1]Reprinted with permission from S. Darby, T. V. Mortimer-Jones, R. L. Johnson, and C. Roberts. Theoretical study of Cu-Au nanoalloy clusters using a genetic algorithm. *Journal of Chemical Physics*, 116(4):1536-1550, 2002. Copyright 2013, American Institute of Physics.

GECCO'13, July 6–10, 2013, Amsterdam, The Netherlands.

Materials science, which investigates the relation between the structure of a material and its physical properties, has in the past mostly dealt with bulk materials. Recent efforts have, however, turned to nanomaterials, which offer promising novel properties that could lead to technological advances such as stronger and lighter metals, self purifying liquids, or new catalysts. The variety of properties of metallic clusters can be drastically expanded through the creation of nanoalloy clusters, i.e. those formed by two or more metals [18]. One of the most interesting aspects of nanoalloys is the way their physical and chemical properties can be altered through varying the types of atoms in the cluster, their ordering, and their number [7]. Additionally, nanoalloys offer the opportunity to test properties of the combination of certain elements that are immiscible when combined in bulk [1].

So how do these special nanostructures behave? In order to answer this question we must first discover the most stable geometric configuration of atoms for a cluster of a specific size and composition. Clusters whose total energy corresponds to the global minimum for the given cluster composition (number and types of atoms) are more likely to be formed during a cluster experiment [12]. Once the optimal cluster has been evolved, we must construct this structure in a wet lab (by placing atoms onto a substrate, following the desired configuration). Finally, we must test the obtained structure so as to learn about its physical properties. In this paper we focus on the first step of this process, i.e. finding the exact relative atom locations for clusters with the lowest potential energy, given a specific number of atoms and their types. Starting with a search space of all possible cluster geometries, we use a GA to find those with minimal potential energy as calculated by the Gupta potential [5]. The Gupta potential has been previously shown to provide reasonably accurate results when assessing nanocluster energy [7], and thus has become a widely used heuristic employed to avoid computationally intensive ab initio calculations.

One of the difficulties with discovering lowest energy nanoclusters is the existence of "homotops", i.e. clusters that, despite being composed of the same number and types of atoms, and having identical cluster geometries, display different properties due to their atoms being arranged differently within said geometries [15]. Consequently, and although some research has been previously conducted through time consuming ab initio calculations [16], the majority of nanocluster formation research uses heuristics, such as genetic algorithms (GAs).

A GA will search for the optimum configuration of a cluster, given the desired composition (i.e. the number and types of atoms in the cluster), guided by an approximation of the interatomic interaction potential of each candidate cluster-configuration [18]. Examples of such interaction potentials are the Gupta potential ([5], [2], [21]) and the Lennard-Jones potential ([8], [12],[25]). Additionally, an energy-optimizing GA is generally combined with a local minimization method, such as the quasi-Newtonian conjugate gradient minimization L-BFGS (Limited-memory Broyden-Fletcher-Goldfarb-Shanno) [20].

Current cluster optimizing GAs rely heavily on local optimization techniques, being unable to successfully evolve low energy clusters when used without them. The purpose of a local optimization is to get from the current position to the nearest local optima. However, if diversity in the population is not maintained, a GA will be unable to continue exploring the search space for potentially better solutions, effectively getting stuck. The BCGA, proposed by Johnston [18], uses high selection pressure, causing the entire population to converge within a few generations, thus decreasing the chance of finding global optima.

In this work, the BCGA is stripped of its external local minimization procedure, L-BFGS [20], and subsequently augmented with a version of Deaven and Ho's C&S crossover developed by Pereira [25]: the H-C&S crossover. Additionally, the CEO-GA ensures population diversity by decreasing selection pressure, and incorporates two new mutation operators: Local-S mutation and CoM-S mutation. These improvements allow the CEO-GA to evolve clusters with energy values comparable to those obtained by the BCGA as reported by Darby et al. [7]. This represents a large improvement over the performance of cluster energy optimizing GAs without local optimization, as the CEO-GA is able to evolve the optimal known structures without local minimization (which may endanger the diversity of structures examined during the search process).

2. BACKGROUND

Below we review the history of cluster evolving GAs in general, as well as discuss the direct predecessor of the proposed CEO-GA: Johnston's BCGA [18]. In addition, we describe in detail Pereira's H-C&S crossover [25] and the Gupta many-body potential [5], both used in the CEO-GA.

2.1 History of cluster evolving methods

As the cluster size increases linearly, the number of minima increases exponentially. Ab initio methods for calculations of total energy, such as those based on density functional theory (DFT) [19], become increasingly computationally demanding. Approaches such as the Monte Carlo methods and Simulated Annealing for molecular dynamics have trouble finding global minima for certain types of interatomic interactions [23]. Random search algorithms also struggle to find the optimum even after thousands of searches [28]. As an alternative approach to cluster optimization, researchers have been turning to GAs, which have generally been able to evolve optimal clusters after a relatively small number of energy evaluations and local optimizations [28].

Hartke [11] and, independently, Xiao and Williams [31] conducted the first attempts to use GAs for the optimization of cluster geometries. The devised GAs used a binary encoding with corresponding genetic operators that modify the binary strings that represent each candidate cluster configuration. Zeiri improved this approach through the use of real-valued Cartesian coordinates to represent the location of each atom in the cluster [32]. Deaven and Ho further improved GA cluster optimization by using a gradient driven local minimization to optimize each configuration discovered by the GA during its run [8]. Yet another significant step pioneered by Deaven and Ho was to improve the crossover genetic operator by crossing the parents' phenotypes (the physical three dimensional cluster) instead of their genotypes (a string of Cartesian coordinates) [8]. The reason this change was so significant (leading them to discover numerous new minima [8]) is due to the fact that in 3D space, a section of the cluster would contain only neighboring atoms. In a string of numbers, consecutive coordinates do not necessarily correspond to nearby atoms, and thus cutting a piece of such string would likely not correspond to cutting a continuous section of the cluster, thus leading to a less principled crossover recombination. Deaven and Ho's crossover is often referred to as "Cut and Splice" (C&S) [26] or "Cut and Paste" [13].

The BCGA is a well known and widely used cluster-optimizing GA designed by Johnston [18]. The BCGA has been used to optimize clusters of different types and sizes, and has been combined with different energy optimization methods over the years ([17], [24], [13], [14], [9], [4], [30], [6]). When it comes to bimetallic clusters, the lack of atom relocating mutations in the BCGA causes it to rely heavily on the L-BFGS local minimization procedure [20] to find the lowest energy clusters. The CEO-GA proposed in this paper (and detailed in section 3) borrows BCGA's atom permutation mutation [18], cluster energy calculation (Gupta potential), dynamic energy scaling (equation 4), and exponential fitness function (equation 5), while excluding BCGA's local optimization procedure (L-BFGS), and incorporating two new mutations operators (Local-S and CoM-S).

2.2 Gen-C&S and H-C&S crossovers

In the aforementioned Deaven and Ho's C&S, given two parent clusters, two random planes are chosen, each passing through the center of mass of one of the parents, and the clusters are split in half. A child is generated by combining the top half of one parent with the bottom half of the other. If the resulting child does not have the correct number of atoms, the parent clusters are translated by the same amount in opposite directions, perpendicular to their cutting plane, and splicing is repeated [8]. The BCGA uses a variation of C&S, where each parent cluster is randomly rotated about two perpendicular axis before being cut by a horizontal plane, and subsequently spliced to form a child cluster [18].

In 2008, Pereira proposed a modified version of C&S [8], named the Generalized Cut and Splice (Gen-C&S) crossover [26], and showed it to outperform the C&S when tested on a steady-state GA evolving Morse clusters [27]. Pereira also successfully applied this crossover to a generational GA [26]. The main advantage of Gen-C&S is that it removes an artificial constraint imposed by C&S: the cutting plane creates an arbitrary division between atoms, such that an atom that is further from some other atom might be grouped with it during crossover because a closer atom ended up on the opposite side of the dividing plane. Additionally, Gen-C&S does not require rotating the parents prior to crossover.

In Gen-C&S crossover for two clusters (P1 and P2) of size μ, a cut point (CP) is chosen as one of the atom locations in P1. A random number S (between 1 and $\mu - 1$) is chosen, and the S atoms in P1 closest to CP are copied into a child cluster. Then, the remaining $\mu - S$ atoms are copied into that child from P2, starting with those closest to CP. After all atoms in P2 have been considered for inclusion, if the child cluster still has less than μ atoms, it is completed with randomly placed atoms. For a graphic depiction of this operator, please refer to [26].

To adapt the Gen-C&S to bi-metallic clusters, Pereira devised the H-C&S crossover and used it to evolve Binary Lennard-Jones clusters [25]. H-C&S behaves almost identically to Gen-C&S with one distinction: after copying the first S atoms from P1, an atom from P2 is copied only if the child cluster still requires atoms of that type, thus maintaining the desired cluster composition [25].

Parameter	Cu-Cu	Cu-Au	Au-Au
A	0.0855	0.1539	0.2061
p	10.960	11.050	10.229
r_0	2.556	2.556	2.884
ζ	1.2240	1.5605	1.7900
q	2.2780	3.0475	4.0360

Table 1: Gupta potential parameters for Cu-Au clusters.

The minimum allowed inter-atomic distance is half of the ideal distance as defined by the r_0 Gupta potential value, provided in section 2.3. If any two atoms are much closer than their ideal distance, the potential repulsive energy becomes too large [27], which confounds the evolutionary process. Thus no atoms closer than $0.5 * r_0$ to any other atom already in the cluster can become part of said cluster. H-C&S crossover observes this rule when creating a child cluster, only allowing new atoms into the cluster if their location is further than $0.5 * r_0$ away from every atom already in the cluster [27].

2.3 Gupta Potential

As mentioned earlier, the Gupta many-body potential [5] is a widely used heuristic for modeling the inter-atomic interactions within a cluster and for calculating its potential energy in order to avoid the computationally expensive ab initio calculations. The Gupta parameters are strictly dependent on the types of atoms composing the cluster, and are derived empirically based on the second moment approximation to tight-binding theory [24].

The Gupta potential energy of a cluster, designated as (V_{clus}), is composed of a repulsive (V^r) and an attractive (V^m) terms, which are obtained via summing over the interactions of each pair of atoms in the cluster, as defined in equations 1, 2, and 3.

$$V_{clus} = \sum_i^N \{V^r(i) - V^m(i)\}, \tag{1}$$

$$V^r(i) = \sum_j^N {}' A(a,b) exp\left(-p(a,b)\left(\frac{r_{ij}}{r_0(a,b)} - 1\right)\right) \tag{2}$$

$$V^m(i) = \left[\sum_j^N {}' \zeta^2(a,b) exp\left(-2q(a,b)\left(\frac{r_{ij}}{r_0(a,b)} - 1\right)\right)\right]^{1/2} \tag{3}$$

$\sum{}'$ in equations 2 and 3 indicates that the summation is to be performed over all atoms j, except for $j = i$ [7] i and j are atoms and a and b are their types. N is the number of atoms in the cluster. The values of the Gupta parameters A, p, r_0, ζ, and q used in this work were obtained from [5], and are listed in table 1. Thus $A(Cu, Au)$, for example, is the value of the Gupta parameter A for the interaction between an atom of Copper and another of Gold, as experimentally fitted for the reference bulk structure.

3. CLUSTER ENERGY OPTIMIZING GENETIC ALGORITHM (CEO-GA)

The CEO-GA is derived from the BCGA, which (in conjunction with other techniques) has proven capable of correctly discovering previously known optimal energy configurations [18]. The CEO-GA makes use of the successful genetic operators present in the BCGA, while also improving upon some of BCGA's shortcomings. We aim to increase the efficacy of the underlying GA itself so as to decrease its dependence on potentially detrimental local optimization techniques.

The CEO-GA is a $(\mu + \lambda)$ generational GA, in which a population of μ parents generate λ children, which (alongside their parents) become candidates for the next generation. Only parent clusters are eligible for mutation. Newly generated offspring do not get mutated, thus allowing the GA to assess clusters generated by crossover before further alternation. Once all the candidate clusters are collected, the next population is chosen via modified roulette-wheel selection [10]: a cluster is chosen at random and accepted for mating if its dynamically scaled fitness (see equations 4 and 5 in section 3) is greater than a randomly generated value between 0 and 1. The same method is also used selecting parents for CEO-GA's H-C&S crossover [25]. The CEO-GA explicitly incorporates elitism by copying the best two candidate clusters into the next generation.

The bounding box is the legal area that atoms can occupy, i.e. any time an atom location is randomly generated, the new coordinate values are chosen between 0 and length of the box edge. Following Johnston's and Darby's work [7][18], for a cluster of N atoms, each edge of the bounding box is set to be $N^{1/3}$ scaled by the ideal distance between two atoms (Gupta Parameter r_0), ensuring that the volume of the box increases linearly with cluster size. Bimetallic clusters usually have three different values for r_0, one per each type of interaction (e.g. Cu-Cu, Cu-Au, Au-Au). Consequently, the bounding box in this work is set to $0.05N^{1/3} * largestR_0$, where $largestR_0$ is the maximum ideal distance between two atoms of the present types. In Cu-Au clusters, that distance is the r_0 between two atoms of Gold and is equal to 2.884 (view table 1). Following Pereira's work [27], all atoms in the first generation are ensured to be at least $0.5 * r_0$ away from each other. This rule is also observed when filling a cluster with random atom locations after an incomplete H-C&S crossover operation.

The CEO-GA uses a modified atom permutation mutation [18], which has been shown to lead to a higher chance of finding the global minimum and to increase the reproducibility of the obtained results [18]. The atom permutation mutation consists of swapping the types of one or more pairs of atoms. In CEO-GA, the number of atom-type swaps per mutated cluster corresponds to 20% of the cluster size, instead of BCGA's 30%. This change results in a more gradual evolution, allowing the GA to assess the value of smaller changes one at a time.

Additionally, the CEO-GA incorporates two new mutation operators inspired by the spherical nature of nanoalloy clusters: the Center of Mass Spherical mutation (CoM-S) and the Local Spherical mutation (Local-S).

1. The **Center of Mass Spherical mutation (CoM-S)** is designed to quicken the search for optimum configurations by rotating an atom about the cluster's center of mass (CoM). The CoM is calculated as the weighted sum of its atoms' coordinates, divided by the total mass of the cluster[2]. The vector from the CoM to the atom is calculated and converted to spherical coordinates (ρ, θ, ϕ)[3]. The distance between the atom and the CoM is preserved by keeping ρ constant, while selecting some combination of θ and ϕ angles to rotate the atom about the CoM. Once the new angles are obtained, the vector $(\rho, \theta_{new}, \phi_{new})$ is converted to its Cartesian equivalent and added to the CoM location. The atom is then relocated to this new position.

2. The **Local Spherical mutation (Local-S)** is designed to make small changes to the locations of 10% of a cluster's atoms. A small vector of spherical coordinates (ρ, θ, ϕ) is created, and its Cartesian equivalent is added to the current location of an atom. Angle θ can take on any value in the range of $0° - 180°$, ϕ can be $0° - 360°$, while distance ρ is the absolute of a random value obtained from a Gaussian distribution with a mean of 0 and a standard deviation equal to 5% of the side of the bounding box.

Given the spherical and fairly tight nature of Cu-Au cluster geometries (as can be seen in figure 1), ensuring that the "greater than $0.5 * r_0$" rule is observed can be difficult. A GA could get stuck repeatedly selecting new random coordinates, as most locations would be disqualified for being too close to pre-existing cluster atoms. To avoid re-selecting indefinitely, for a cluster of N atoms, we cap the number of tries at $N * 10$ per each newly generated location. Once the maximum tries have been exhausted, a Local-S mutation is repeatedly performed on each new atom that is too close to atoms already in the cluster, until the minimum distance is satisfied. Note that while the Local-S mutation uses the bounding box to calculate the increment ρ, it does not itself obey the boundaries of said box in order to quicken compliance with the minimum distance rule. Thus, the resulting atom coordinates may place the atom outside of $[0, N^{1/3} * largestR_0]$ range.

The CEO-GA mutation rates are as follows: for any given cluster of size N, an atom permutation mutation has a 10% chance to occur, in which case $0.2 * N$ label swaps are performed. The CoM-S mutation also has a 10% chance to occur, and causes each of the atoms to have a 10% chance to rotate about the CoM. The Local-S mutation has a 20% chance to happen, producing a 10% chance to cause a small spherical permutation of the location of each of the atoms in the cluster. A cluster can be mutated by all or none of these mutations. When a mutation does occur, each operator produces a separate mutant cluster, which becomes one of the candidates for the next generation. This ensures that the GA will be able to assess potential benefits of each mutation individually.

An optional cluster relocation mechanism was designed for the CEO-GA, such that the entire cluster is re-centered around the origin, i.e. the CoM of the cluster ends up at

[2]The atomic mass of Cu is 63.546, and the atomic mass of Au is 196.96655.

[3]In this paper, spherical coordinates (ρ, θ, ϕ) are used as is customary in the physics field: ρ indicates radial distance, θ indicates polar angle, and ϕ indicates azimuthal angle.

(0,0,0). While the mechanism did not provide any advantage for the tested clusters, it could be beneficial for more sparse cluster geometries that require more spacious bounding boxes. Re-clustering around the origin would ensure that atoms from parent clusters are combined in a principled and correlated manner during crossover.

Energy (V_{clus}) is calculated using the Gupta potential [5] as detailed in section 2.3. Energy is scaled dynamically according to equation 4, where ρ_i is the scaled energy of a cluster i, V_{min} is the lowest V_{clus} in the current population, and V_{max} is the highest.

$$\rho_i = (V_i - V_{min})/(V_{max} - V_{min}) \quad (4)$$

This results in a ρ value of 0 for the best cluster, and 1 for the worst cluster in the population.

The fitness of a cluster (f_i) is calculated using the exponential fitness function, as defined by Johnston [18] and provided in equation 5.

$$f_i = exp(-\alpha\rho_i) \quad (5)$$

Parameter α determines how fast fitness drops as energy increases, and is set to $\alpha = 3$ as in the original work [18].

4. EXPERIMENTAL SETUP

All experiments in this paper are performed on Cu-Au clusters. Ample data is available on the best known configurations of Cu-Au clusters ([7], [18], [9], [3], [22]), thus making them a suitable basis for comparison between cluster evolving GAs. Of particular relevance to this paper is the research conducted by Darby et al. [7], as it allows a direct comparison between Cu-Au clusters evolved with BCGA and those evolved with CEO-GA. However, as Pereira has already shown the Gen-C&S to outperform Deaven and Ho's C&S [27], the CEO-GA's performance is tested directly against our own implementation of the BCGA, from here forward referred to as BCGA$^-$: a BCGA without L-BFGS local optimization and augmented with Gen-C&S crossover. These modifications are made in order to verify that the CEO-GA offers benefits beyond the inclusion of Pereira's crossover.

Given the lack of location-changing mutations in the standard implementation of BCGA for bimetallic clusters [18], we also conducted tests on the BCGA$^-$ augmented with Pereira's Sigma mutation (from here forward referred to as the BCGA$^+$). In the Sigma mutation, the new position of an atom is the sum of its current position and a random value obtained from a Gaussian distribution with a mean of 0 and a standard deviation σ, which, following Pereira's example, is set to 5% of the length of any one of the edges of the bounding box (defined in section 3)[27].

In this work, the BCGA$^-$, BCGA$^+$, and CEO-GA are tested on their ability to evolve the best known pure ($Cu_{(N)}$, $Au_{(N)}$) and doped ($CuAu_{(N-1)}$, $Cu_{(N-1)}Au$) clusters. Following the example of [7] and [18], we also evolve stoichiometric nanoalloy clusters with the composition of common stable bulk Cu-Au alloy phases, i.e. those with Cu to Au atom ratios of 3, 1, and 1/3 [7]. The three GAs are tested with a population size μ=75 and a crossover rate of 0.8. The CEO-GA has a mutation rate of 0.1 for its atom permutation mutation as well as for its CoM-S mutation, and a mutation rate of 0.2 for its Local-S mutation. In order to provide an equal number of mutation children to both the CEO-GA and the BCGA$^-$, the BCGA$^-$'s atom permutation mutation rate was increased to 0.4. As the BCGA$^+$ incorporates an additional mutation type (sigma), its mutation rates were set to 0.2 for the atom permutation mutation and 0.2 for the sigma mutation. All experiments were subjected to 50 runs of 25000 generations each. The findings are presented in table 2 and consist of the best and average cluster energies for each of the three tested GAs, as well as their success rates. Success rate is defined as the percentage of the 50 runs that evolved a cluster whose energy is within 0.1 of the minimum cluster energy reported by Darby et al. [7], also presented in table 2 for ease of comparison.

5. RESULTS AND DISCUSSION

We summarize our results in table 2: BCGA$^-$ results are shown in columns 3, 4, and 5, BCGA$^+$ in columns 6, 7, and 8, and CEO-GA in columns 9, 10, and 11. Results from the original BCGA (with L-BFGS optimization) provided by Darby et al. in Table II of [7] are displayed in column 2 of table 2. In figure 2 we provide an example of a 3D visualization of the lowest potential energy clusters evolved by the CEO-GA, as well as the corresponding cluster evolved by the BCGA and reproduced from Darby et al. [7].

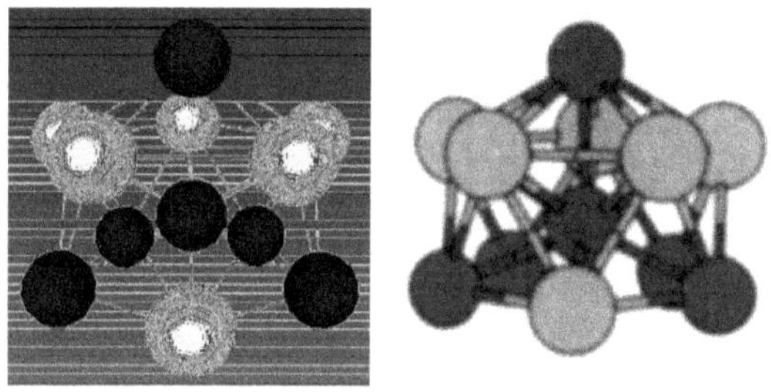

(a) CEO-GA Best (b) BCGA's Best [7]

Figure 2: Comparison of Cu_6Au_6 clusters evolved by the CEO-GA and the BCGA[4] Dark and light spheres represent atoms of Cu and Au, respectively. Both GAs evolved Cu_6Au_6 clusters with potential energy equal to -35.40, as can be seen in table 2. The depicted atomic radii are arbitrary, as only the atoms' centers are taken into account during the search.

As can be seen in table 2, the best structures reported by Darby et al. are consistently found accurate to two decimal places by the CEO-GA (column 9) within the span of 50 runs. Notice that since we are minimizing potential energy, lower (more negative) values are better. For example, for the Cu_3Au_9 cluster Darby reports the best found energy to be -37.725549, while the energy of the best cluster found by the CEO-GA is -37.724 (which is only 0.00155 away). Values that differ from the known minimum by up to 0.1 (and thus represent successful runs) were found by 26% of the CEO-GA runs. It is unknown, however, how often values near the optimum were found by Darby's implementation of the BCGA.

[4]Reprinted with permission from S. Darby, T. V. Mortimer-Jones, R. L. Johnson, and C. Roberts. Theoretical study of Cu-Au nanoalloy clusters using a genetic algorithm. *Journal of Chemical Physics*, 116(4):1536-1550, 2002. Copyright 2013, American Institute of Physics.

Cluster	BCGA	BCGA$^-$			BCGA$^+$			CEO-GA		
	Best	Best	AvgBest (stdv)	S.R.	Best	AvgBest (stdv)	S.R.	Best	AvgBest (stdv)	S.R.
Cu_{12}	-30.277969	-3.651	26.6296 (9.66)	0%	-30.233	-29.6094 (0.39)	24%	**-30.277**	-29.9218 (0.37)	50%
Au_{12}	-38.922569	110.389	190.2884 (30.76)	0%	-38.844	-38.5477 (0.19)	18%	**-38.921**	-38.6899 (0.18)	36%
$CuAu_{12}$	-	94.326	228.0147 (36.67)	0%	-43.055	-41.8591 (0.62)	14%	**-43.130**	-42.1157 (0.65)	20%
$Cu_{12}Au$	-	32.701	54.61392 (10.48)	0%	-34.973	-33.8937 (0.69)	22%	**-35.042**	-34.4089 (0.72)	52%
Cu_3Au_9	-37.725549	50.125	95.94986 (21.84)	0%	-37.671	-36.8992 (0.39)	10%	**-37.724**	-37.1537 (0.38)	26%
Cu_9Au_3	-33.112689	14.136	43.24580 (11.52)	0%	-33.080	-32.5323 (0.32)	14%	**-33.112**	-32.7186 (0.33)	38%
Cu_6Au_6	-35.402163	24.458	63.69496 (15.46)	0%	-35.341	-34.7210 (0.31)	8%	**-35.401**	-35.0093 (0.30)	28%

Table 2: GA performance comparison between BCGA (as reported by Darby et al. [7]), BCGA$^-$ (BCGA without L-BFGS and using Pereira's H-C&S crossover [25]), and BCGA$^+$ (BCGA without L-BFGS, using Pereira's H-C&S crossover and Sigma mutation), and the proposed CEO-GA. An evolved cluster is considered a success if by the end of a run its energy corresponds to BCGA's 'Best' energy (lowest cluster energy obtained by Darby et al. [7]) up to the first decimal place. Success rate (S.R.) represents a percentage of the 50 runs that evolved successful clusters (those with values within 0.1 of the minimum cluster energy reported by Darby et al. [7]) after 25000 generations of the GA. The best and average-best cluster potential energies, as well as standard deviation (stdv), are also reported out of 50 runs. Minimum energy values for doped clusters were not provided in the original work by Darby et al. [7]; therefore, the success cases for $CuAu_{12}$ and $Cu_{12}Au$ are estimated to be those within 0.1 of CEO-GA's best, given that in all other tested cases these values matched BCGA's 'Best' (column 2) up to the first two decimal places.

While not every run finds the known global optimum configurations, the CEO-GA success rates are much higher than those of BCGA$^-$ and BCGA$^+$, indicating that it approximates the global optimum significantly more frequently (1.4 to 3.5 times more), and the average best energies are closer to the known global optimum. The ability of the CEO-GA to accurately find global optima without the help of local optimization tools such as the L-BFGS is valuable because local optimization techniques can often cause premature convergence on a local optimum. GAs, on the other hand, are generally better suited for finding global optima. The CEO-GA relies solely on crossover and mutation for its search, lowering the risk of getting trapped in local optima (as can be seen by the higher success rates in table 2), while steadily approaching the global best, potentially paving the road for finding previously unknown global minima.

The BCGA$^-$ is included for reference only, as in absence of local minimization BCGA becomes unable to evolve even approximate solutions. This is a result of two of its characteristics: (1) the BCGA always picks the best μ solutions to become members of the next generation, which may cause premature convergence; (2) the BCGA does not itself possess the ability to make small adjustments to atom locations, and thus cannot narrow in specific coordinates, relying on H-C&S crossover for any atoms relocation away from its original randomly generated coordinates.

6. CONCLUSIONS

In this paper, a new cluster potential energy minimizing GA is presented: the Cluster Energy Optimization Genetic Algorithm. The CEO-GA is designed to improve upon the shortcomings of its predecessor, the BCGA, which requires a local minimization as it does not itself offer any atom relocating mutations. Additionally, the BCGA always picks the best μ solutions from amongst parent clusters, crossover offspring, and mutations, causing fast but often premature convergence such that every cluster in the population becomes identical to every other after just a few generations. These heavy-handed techniques cause high selection pressure, promptly pruning the population of all but the best-so-far cluster, making the BCGA highly susceptible to dangers of the low hanging fruit that is local optima. The CEO-GA combines BCGA's atom permutation mutation [18], Pereira's H-C&S crossover [25], and two new mutation operators designed to slowly move atoms closer to their idea location, thus paving a steady evolutionary path to the global optimum.

The CEO-GA is tested on pure, doped, and stoichiometric Cu-Au clusters, and is shown to outperform both the BCGA$^-$ (Johnston's BCGA without L-BFGS local minimization and with Devon and Ho's C&S crossover [8] replaced by Pereira's H-C&S crossover [25]) as well as the BCGA$^+$ (i.e. the BCGA$^-$ combined with Pereira's Sigma mutation [27]) in terms of success rate and ability to evolve the best known configurations. These results show that the CEO-GA, while not itself depending on local minimization, achieves results comparable to those previously obtained only via combining a GA with local optimization techniques. Since relying on local optimization can often lead to getting stuck on suboptimal clusters, a self-sufficient GA may not only possess a higher chance of finding global optima, but may also allow for the discovery of yet unknown lower energy cluster configurations. The CEO-GA's higher success rates (compared to other cluster evolving GAs without local optimization) also improve the reliability of finding a good cluster within fewer runs.

7. FUTURE WORK

Johnston devised an optional mechanism for maintaining diversity in BCGA's population through removing clusters whose energy was not sufficiently different from other clusters in the population [18], although it was unclear what effect this mechanism had on the GA's performance. CEO-GA could benefit from a similar diversity mechanism. However, we propose considering a clusters' geometric qualities as a measure of similarity instead of the clusters' potential energy. One approach could be to implement "speciation" based on clusters' atomic configuration, similar to that devised by Stanley for the NeuroEvolution of Augmenting Topologies (NEAT) algorithm for evolving structure [29]. Additionally it would be interesting to test the proposed optional relocation of the center of mass to the origin before crossover-recombination on materials with less tight clusters. We hypothesize that having large empty sections of the bounding box could hinder crossover if the parents' centers of mass are distant.

It is possible that while the CEO-GA was able to find the known optima for the tested clusters, when evolving larger clusters, not using an external (to the GA itself) local optimization method such as the L-BFGS could prohibitively slow down evolution. On the other hand, using such local optimization combined with an improved base genetic algorithm could produce results quicker than previously used methods. To test this theory, the authors intend on applying the CEO-GA in conjunction with L-BFGS to clusters of sizes up to 50 atoms. It would also be interesting to compare the structures evolved with the CEO-GA with those obtained through ab initio calculations.

References

[1] M. P. Andrews and S. C. O'Brien. Gas-phase "molecular alloys" of bulk immiscible elements: iron-silver (Fe_xAg_y). *The Journal of Physical Chemistry*, 96(21):8233–8241, 1992.

[2] F. Baletto, R. Ferrando, A. Fortunelli, F. Montalenti, and C. Mottet. Crossover among structural motifs in transition and noble-metal clusters. *Journal of Chemical Physics*, 116:3856 – 3863, 2002.

[3] G. Barcaro, A. Fortunelli, G. Rossi, F. Nita, and R. Ferrando. Electronic and structural shell closure in AgCu and AuCu nanoclusters. *The Journal of Physical Chemistry B*, 110(46):23197–23203, 2006.

[4] F. Y. Chen and R. L. Johnston. Structure and spectral characteristics of the nanoalloy Ag_3Au_{10}. *Applied Physics Letters*, 90(15):153123, 2007.

[5] F. Cleri and V. Rosato. Tight-binding potentials for transition metals and alloys. *Physical Review B*, 48:22–33, 1993.

[6] B. C. Curley, G. Rossi, R. Ferrando, and R. L. Johnston. Theoretical study of structure and segregation in 38-atom Ag-Au nanoalloys. *The European Physical Journal D*, 43:53–56, 2007.

[7] S. Darby, T. V. Mortimer-Jones, R. L. Johnson, and C. Roberts. Theoretical study of Cu-Au nanoalloy clusters using a genetic algorithm. *Journal of Chemical Physics*, 116(4):1536–1550, 2002.

[8] D. M. Deaven and K. M. Ho. Molecular geometry optimization with a genetic algorithm. *Physical Review Letters*, 75(2):288–291, 1995.

[9] R. Ferrando, A. Fortunelli, and R. L. Johnston. Searching for the optimum structures of alloy nanoclusters. *Physical Chemistry Chemical Physics*, 10:640–649, 2008.

[10] D. E. Goldberg. *Genetic Algorithms in Search, Optimization and Machine Learning.* Addison-Wesley Longman Publishing Co., Inc., Boston, MA, USA, 1st edition, 1989.

[11] B. Hartke. Global geometry optimization of clusters using genetic algorithms. *The Journal of Physical Chemistry*, 97(39):9973–9976, 1993.

[12] B. Hartke. Global cluster geometry optimization by a phenotype algorithm with niches: Location of elusive minima, and low-order scaling with cluster size. *Journal of Computational Chemistry*, 20(16):1752–1759, 1999.

[13] S. Heiles, A. J. Logsdail, R. Schäfer, and R. L. Johnston. Dopant-induced 2D-3D transition in small Au-containing clusters: DFT-global optimisation of 8-atom Au-Ag nanoalloys. *Nanoscale*, 4:1109–1115, 2012.

[14] R. Ismail and R. L. Johnston. Investigation of the structures and chemical ordering of small pd-au clusters as a function of composition and potential parameterisation. *Physical Chemistry Chemical Physics*, 12:8607–8619, 2010.

[15] J. Jellinek and E. B. Krissinel. *Theory of Atomic and Molecular Clusters.* Springer, 1999.

[16] D. R. Jennison, P. A. Schultz, and M. P. Sears. Ab initio calculations of Ru, Pd, and Ag cluster structure with 55, 135, and 140 atoms. *Journal of Chemical Physics*, 106(5):1856–1862, 1997.

[17] R. L. Johnston. *Atomic & Molecular Clusters.* CRC Press, 2002.

[18] R. L. Johnston. Evolving better nanoparticles: Genetic algorithms for optimising cluster geometries. *Dalton Transactions*, 0:4193–4207, 2003.

[19] W. Kohn, A. D. Becke, and R. G. Parr. Density functional theory of electronic structure. *The Journal of Physical Chemistry*, 100(31):12974–12980, 1996.

[20] D. C. Liu and J. Nocedal. On the limited memory BFGS method for large scale optimization. *Mathematical Programming*, 45(3):503–528, 1989.

[21] A. J. Logsdail and R. L. Johnston. Interdependence of structure and chemical order in high symmetry $(PdAu)_N$ nanoclusters. *RSC Advances*, 2:5863–5869, 2012.

[22] R. A. Lordeiro, F. F. Guimarães, J. C. Belchior, and R. L. Johnston. Determination of main structural compositions of nanoalloy clusters of $Cu_xAu_y(x + y \leq 30)$ using a genetic algorithm approach. *International Journal of Quantum Chemistry*, 95(2):112–125, 2003.

[23] J. P. K. Doye and D. J. Wales. Structural consequences of the range of the interatomic potential a menagerie of clusters. *Journal of the Chemical Society, Faraday Transactions*, 93:4233–4243, 1997.

[24] L. O. Paz-Borbon, A. Gupta, and R. L. Johnston. Dependence of the structures and chemical ordering of pd-pt nanoalloys on potential parameters. *Journal of Materials Chemistry*, 18:4154–4164, 2008.

[25] F. Pereira and J. Marques. Towards an effective evolutionary approach for binary lennard-jones clusters. In *Proceedings of the 2010 IEEE Congress on Evolutionary Computation (CEC)*, pages 1–7, 2010.

[26] F. B. Pereira, J. Marques, T. Leitão, and J. Tavares. Designing efficient evolutionary algorithms for cluster optimization: A study on locality. In P. Siarry and Z. Michalewicz, editors, *Advances in Metaheuristics for Hard Optimization*, Natural Computing Series, pages 223–250. Springer Berlin Heidelberg, 2008.

[27] F. B. Pereira and J. M. C. Marques. *Analysis of Crossover Operators for Cluster Geometry Optimization*, volume 46 of *Computational Intelligence for Engineering Systems Intelligent Systems, Control and Automation: Science and Engineering*, pages 77–89. Springer Netherlands, 2011.

[28] C. Roberts, R. L. Johnston, and N. T. Wilson. A genetic algorithm for the structural optimization of morse clusters. *Theoretical Chemistry Accounts*, 104:123–130, 2000.

[29] K. O. Stanley and R. Miikkulainen. Evolving neural networks through augmenting topologies. *Evolutionary Computation*, 10(2):99–127, 2002.

[30] D. T. Tran and R. L. Johnston. Theoretical study of $Cu_{38-n}Au_n$ clusters using a combined empirical potential-density functional approach. *Physical Chemistry Chemical Physics*, 11:10340–10349, 2009.

[31] Y. Xiao and D. E. Williams. Genetic algorithm: a new approach to the prediction of the structure of molecular clusters. *Chemical Physics Letters*, 215(1-3):17–24, 1993.

[32] Y. Zeiri. Prediction of the lowest energy structure of clusters using a genetic algorithm. *Physical Review E*, 51:R2769–R2772, 1995.

A Hybrid Genetic Approach for Stereo Matching

Eliyahu Kiperwasser
Department of Computer Science
Bar-Ilan University
Ramat-Gan 52900, Israel
elikip@gmail.com

Omid David*
Department of Computer Science
Bar-Ilan University
Ramat-Gan 52900, Israel
mail@omiddavid.com

Nathan S. Netanyahu†
Department of Computer Science
Bar-Ilan University
Ramat-Gan 52900, Israel
nathan@cs.biu.ac.il

ABSTRACT

In this paper we present a genetic algorithm (GA)-based approach for the stereo matching problem. More precisely, the approach presented is a combination of a simple dynamic programming algorithm, commonly used for stereo matching, with a practical GA-based optimization scheme. The performance of our scheme was evaluated on standard test data of the Middlebury benchmark [1]. Specifically, the number of incorrect disparities on these data decreases by approximately 20% in comparison to the original approach (without the use of a GA).

Categories and Subject Descriptors

I.2.10 [**Artificial Intelligence**]: Vision and Scene Understanding—*3D/stereo scene analysis*.

Keywords

Computer Vision, Genetic Algorithm, Stereo Matching

1. INTRODUCTION

Stereo vision has been extensively studied by the computer vision community for the last three decades. Robust stereo vision algorithms have many applications, including vehicle/robot obstacle detection, aerial topography acquisition, virtual reality, graffiti detection, and many more.

Stereo vision data are acquired by two (or more) cameras with separate perspectives and are used to determine the depth of an object or a particular point in a scene. The depth information is computed by applying the triangulation principle [20] to the position differences between corresponding points in the (two) images. The latter is referred

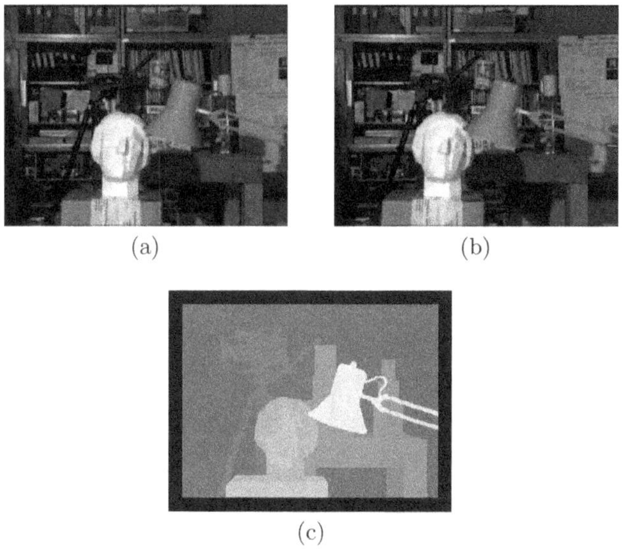

Figure 1: Stereo matching example: (a) The image taken by the left camera, (b) the image taken by the right camera, and (c) the ground truth disparity map.

to as the *image disparity* (at a pixel in question). Before determining the degree of disparity, the most difficult and time-consuming task is to identify corresponding points in the two images. This is the so-called *stereo matching* problem.

The input images to the stereo matching algorithm are assumed to be rectified, i.e., corresponding pixels must lie on the same horizontal line in both images. The output is called the disparity map (see Figure 1), where each pixel contains a displacement value, called the disparity and measured in pixels (from its location in the reference image to its corresponding location in the target image). The maximum distance between corresponding pixels, called the disparity range, is assumed to be known. Pixels in the target image that are occluded will be assigned an interpolated value or some special value encoding their occluded state.

Many algorithms for the stereo correspondence problem have been developed over time. This paper presents a novel evolutionary "boosting" scheme that draws on the well-known scan-line algorithm [14] for the stereo matching problem. We demonstrate that the use of our approach results in approx-

*Web: http://www.omiddavid.com

†Nathan Netanyahu is also affiliated with the Center for Automation Research, University of Maryland, College Park, MD 20742 (e-mail: nathan@cfar.umd.edu).

imately 20% increase in accuracy, compared to the performance of the scan-line algorithm without a GA. In principle, the framework can be used to boost other algorithms as well to enhance their performance.

The paper is organized as follows. In Section 2 we survey past work related to the problem of stereo matching. In Section 3 we present in detail our proposed hybrid approach, including the specification of various GA operators, and in Section 4 we present our empirical results. Section 5 makes concluding remarks.

2. PREVIOUS WORK

The most basic approach to the stereo correspondence problem compares each pixel from the reference image to its possible matches in the target image and takes the one with the minimum color difference as a match (see Figure 2). Since the input is assumed to be rectified, the only possible matches lie on the same horizontal line within a limited range of pixels specified a priori as the disparity range. This trivial approach does not perform well, as it is very error prone in dealing with smooth surfaces for which all color differences are roughly the same. Furthermore, when taking a picture from two different angles, the color of a certain pixel can change due to lighting conditions, a transparent object in the scene, etc. Such problems render this approach impractical for most cases.

Figure 2: Illustration of the naive approach: The method takes a pixel from one image and compares it to possible matches in the other image; the pixel with the closest color similarity is declared a match.

In order to overcome some of the problems of the naive approach, cost-aggregation methods were proposed [12]. The simplest of these methods are window-based, which apply the above mentioned naive approach with respect to a neighborhood of pixels (instead of a pixel-wise comparison). When considering an assignment to a pixel in the reference image, a window around this pixel is compared to other windows around relevant pixels in the target image. The displacement yielding the minimal window difference (using sum of squared differences, for example) is assigned as the pixel's disparity. The advantage of this approach over the naïve method lies in the greater amount of data considered when assigning a certain disparity to a given pixel.

Window-based methods advocate a tradeoff between accuracy and the sharpness of the resulting disparity map. The larger the neighborhood is, the more information is used to accurately determine the disparity. However, this leads to blurry edges, due to the attempt to incorporate information from both sides of the edge in determining the pixel's disparity. On the other hand, the smaller the neighborhood is, the less information is used and the less accurate the result is, although the sharper the edges are. (A very small neighborhood amounts practically to the naïve approach covered above.)

It is possible to consider a three-dimensional matrix whose dimensions are the length and width of the images and the disparity range. Each matrix cell will contain the local cost associated with the disparity assigned to it. Simple cost-aggregation methods apply a blurring mechanism to incorporate data from neighboring pixels, under the assumption that the disparity map is smooth. Advanced cost-aggregation methods apply more sophisticated aggregation / blurring, such as the use of a bilateral filter which assigns more weight to neighboring pixels with the same color. This improves the performance since neighboring pixels with roughly the same color tend to belong to the same object, whose depth map is relatively smooth.

Another cost-aggregation method is based on image segmentation [7]. This image processing operation splits an image into (fairly) homogeneous regions, each belonging to a single object whose depth map is assumed relatively smooth. Segmentation could have assisted in stereo matching, provided it was sufficiently accurate. Assuming exact object segments are given, cost-aggregation could be used with respect to each segment, independently, to compute more accurately the disparity value of a pixel. (Each segment is used as a kernel instead of a standard window.) Unfortunately, segmentation is still considered an open problem, and it usually results in "under-segmentation" / "over-segmentation" of objects and in "leaking" segments (see Figure 3). Also, the segmentation process is very sensitive to the parameters used and, in general, it is not robust to the input scene.

(a) (b) (c)

Figure 3: Illustration of segmentation artifacts [11]: (a) Under-segmentation, (b) over-segmentation, and (c) leaking segmentation.

The above discussed techniques determine a pixel's disparity based on its local neighborhood, independently of the disparity of other pixels. To achieve better results, most state-of-the-art algorithms incorporate a global optimization scheme as a vital part of the algorithm [10, 13, 19]. The global optimization attempts to minimize an objective function that receives as input the disparity map and outputs a fitness score. A most notable objective function is of the form [3]

$$E_{Data}\left(DisparityImage\right) + E_{Smooth}\left(DisparityImage\right),$$

where $E_{Data}(DisparityImage)$ denotes the local pixel disparity assignment cost (similarly to previously described local approaches) and $E_{Smooth}(DisparityImage)$ is associated with the cost of maintaining a piecewise smooth disparity image (by adding a penalty inversely proportional to the smoothness of the disparity image).

The above formulation is common in various machine learning teachniques, where we seek a fitting component (i.e., E_{Data}) and a regularization term (i.e., E_{Smooth}) to ensure an overall simple, non-overfitting solution. As in commonly used machine learning techniques, even the global minimum solution might be mistaken in comparison to the ground truth. The proximity of this model to ground truth is dependent on the objective function picked, in particular the regularization and data term.

As demonstrated in [3], minimizing this function can be mapped to the multi-way cut problem, which is known to be NP-complete [4]. Therefore, solving the problem is intractable (unless P = NP). Several approximation techniques for this minimization problem were suggested [3, 6, 19]. Some of these approximation methods result in an objective function score that is not greater than a certain factor times the global minimum. However, this does not ensure an approximation bound regarding the disparity errors, since satisfying the objective function used may not necessarily be compatible to ground truth.

A common objective function, according to the above formulation, sets the local data term to the absolute color difference between pixels in the reference image and their (hypothesized) counterparts in the target image. The smoothness term adds a constant for every spatially neighboring pixels having different disparities.

Another family of approximation algorithms uses dynamic programming to solve the minimization problem presented above [5, 17, 8]. Since solving the exact problem is intractable, these algorithms try to solve accurately a relaxed version of the problem, which is no longer NP-complete. Instead of solving the problem in a 2-D grid, the idea is to solve, independently, several relaxed sub-problems, each of which is concerned with the optimization of an objective function with respect to only part of the data, e.g., a 1-D row. Ignoring inter-line dependencies, one may thus apply repeatedly the common stereo scan-line technique [14] (which our method will attempt to improve) for solving the various (relaxed) 1-D problem instances. Optimization in the 1-D case is obtained due to Viterbi's well-known algorithm [18].

The latter is a dynamic programming algorithm for finding the most likely sequence of hidden states. In this case, the hidden states are the disparity assignments for each pixel. The scan-line technique can be employed in the framework of Viterbi's algorithm, with the possible disparities as the possible hidden states, a cost function for assigning a hidden state to a specific pixel, and a smoothness function penalizing two neighboring pixels on the line, provided their hidden states are unrelated.

The Viterbi algorithm maps the problem to finding the shortest path in a weighted graph generated as follows. Each pixel is represented by k vertices symbolizing its possible hidden states, i.e., the number of possible disparity assignments. Also, there is an edge between two vertices belonging to neighboring pixels, whose weight is given by the expression

$$E_{Data}\left(NextPixelDisparity\right) +$$
$$E_{Smooth}\left(PrevPixelDisparity, NextPixelDisparity\right)$$

(Note that summing the above expression over all line pixels gives the objective function minimized by the scan-line method.) The graph consists also of two dummy vertices, the "Start" and "End" vertices. These vertices are connected to each of the labeled vertices corresponding to the first and last pixels in the chain, respectively, as shown in Figure 4. The data term and smooth term involving the dummy vertices are set to zero. It can be easily verified that each path from the Start vertex to the End vertex is associated with a sequence of hidden state assignments (i.e., disparity values), such that its corresponding total weight is the cost of the objective function (presented in [3]) for those specific hidden states (or disparities). Thus, the shortest path (from Start to End) yields the optimal disparity assignment for this relaxed problem instance.

Realizing that there are k^2 edges between neighboring pixels, it can be shown that the time complexity of the scan-line algorithm is $O(n \cdot k^2)$, where n is the number of pixels in the chain and k is the number of possible disparity assignments for each pixel. For some objective functions, the time complexity can be reduced to $O(n \cdot k)$.

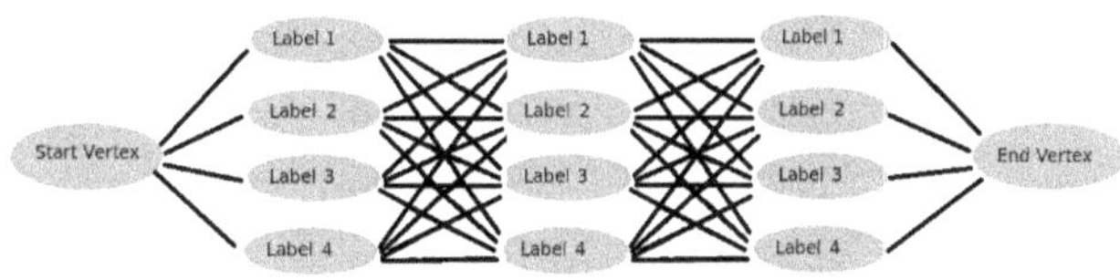

Figure 4: Graph for 1-D scan-line.

The 1-D scan-line technique ignores various constraints in order to achieve an efficient polynomial time solution. Considering each scan-line independently results, for example, in "striding" effects caused by the fact that no information from one scan-line is used to optimize another scan-line (see Figure 5). An important observation is that the less relaxed the problem is, the more suitable the solution becomes. In [17], a less relaxed version was treated by considering a tree induced by the image grid graph (i.e., a graph whose vertices are associated with the pixels and where an edge connects two vertices corresponding to 4-neighboring pixels), and optimizing the objective function with respect to this tree. The time complexity in this case was shown to be the same, i.e., $O(n \cdot k^2)$.

3. PROPOSED APPROACH

Our proposed approach explores the possibility of drawing on some of the above methods, in a relatively novel manner, for the stereo disparity problem. Specifically, we propose a hybrid GA-based optimization scheme, which combines

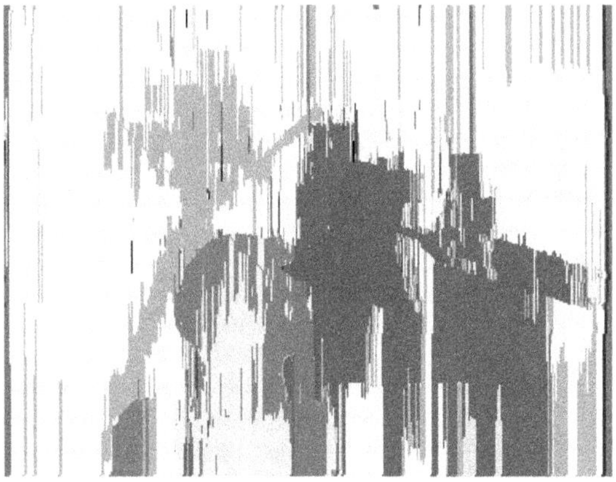

Figure 5: Result due to vertical scan-line.

the global search properties of genetic algorithms with the powerful properties of a local search.

Various components of a GA framework (such as initialization, crossover, mutation, and fitness function) will be specified by adapting relevant, previously described techniques. This adaptation focuses on the crossover operation, and involves effective "local" optimization that can cope with the very large dimensionality of the problem. (See detailed discussion below.) We believe that this hybrid approach will yield a practically sound scheme for the stereo matching problem.

3.1 Genetic Operators

This subsection describes the adaptation of each operator of the genetic scheme to fit the stereo correspondence problem, by incorporating also knowledge from the problem domain itself.

3.1.1 Chromosome Representation

Chromosome representation and encoding have a great impact on the performance of a genetic algorithm. A compact representation can significantly reduce the dimensionality and the search space. However, it also introduces difficulties in other aspects of the genetic algorithm, such as the crossover and fitness. A sparse image representation, on the other hand, such as contours or edge lists, requires sophisticated, time-consuming decoding and crossover mechanisms which often degrade the performance of the algorithm either by ignoring relevant data or by increasing significantly the algorithm's time complexity.

A chromosome representation of the problem at hand (with respect to some set of pixels) consists merely of plain disparity values assigned to these pixels. The dimensionality is quite large and the search space contains $DisparityRange^{|Pixels|}$ assignment possibilities. Despite this large search space, we show how the crossover routine can exploit domain knowledge in a clever manner to construct from this representation an improved solution.

3.1.2 Population Initialization

Selecting the initial population is important to the convergence of the genetic algorithm. In particular, a large diverse population of initial solutions would result in a broader perspective of the search space and would thus prevent convergence to a local minimum.

Our approach offers a compromise between a large diverse space and a small, highly adapted population. Natural images are mostly smooth with respect to the depth map, i.e., it is not likely for a pixel to have a different depth than its neighbor unless an edge is crossed. Therefore it is reasonable to assume that a bunch of spatially close pixels have roughly the same disparity value. We exploit this property to produce initial solutions by assigning a disparity value at random to a bunch of close pixels and repeating this process until no pixels are left unassigned. This creates a well-distributed initial population, and at the same time it enforces the assumption of a depth-smooth map by assigning the same disparity to small spatially contiguous regions.

3.1.3 Solution Mutation

This operator mutates the chromosomes, so as to generate new solutions that otherwise might not have been produced from the current population. Introducing mutation helps to diversify the population in each generation and avoid hopefully a local minimum. This operation is also guided by a tradeoff between less likely local minima and fast convergence, depending on the degree of mutation.

The "headless chicken" [9] was applied in our case. The crossover operation is applied to a given disparity map and a disparity map generated by the initialization described above. We consider the result from this crossover as a mutated chromosome. Using the hybrid crossover procedure as described in the next subsection ensures that the solution produced adds to the population diversity with little negative effect on the chromosome's fitness. Consequently, the time of convergence does not increase much in comparison to other mutation schemes.

This mutation procedure is applied to all chromosomes except the elite ones, that are passed as is to the next generation. Applying this mutation constantly to almost every chromosome (with mutation rate of 1.0), helps keep the population diverse and gain a better solution at the expense of losing valuable information. The likelihood of occurrences of the latter is smaller since the crossover operator incorporates knowledge of the domain.

3.1.4 Crossover Operator

The crossover operator is meant to merge two different solutions into a new solution in the next generation. The idea is that merging two solutions often evolves an improved solution. However, because of the curse of dimensionality in stereo matching, this is almost never the case. Thus, a powerful crossover technique is required.

The crossover proposed is based on the dynamic programming technique of the scan-line method. But instead of feeding the algorithm with all possible disparities, the disparity assignment to each pixel is limited to two possible values at most, one from the first solution and the other from the second. This procedure forces the algorithm to choose the globally optimal line assignments for each line, independently of another line, where an assignment is made either from the first or the second solution. Obviously, these assignments are optimal for each line independently, and they form a local/semi-optimal crossover solution.

Note that we choose horizontal and vertical scan-lines interchangeably (where the decision is made at random). Every two chromosomes are merged in a manner that is "optimal" with respect to the line direction chosen. Adding more lines in various orientations should improve the bottom-line result, as the crossover would accommodate many more orientations, i.e., it is more likely that the optimum of the global fitness (defined below) could be satisfied.

Finally, it is important to note that although the crossover is applied to global optimization, it is very efficient. Recall that the time complexity of the original scan-line algorithm is $O(n \cdot k^2)$. Since by construction, our crossover operator considers only two possible values (i.e., $k = 2$ in our case), its time complexity is linear in the number of pixels.

3.1.5 Solution Fitness

The fitness function is at the heart of a genetic algorithm's scheme. It is used to measure the quality of a solution. The fitness has of course a great impact on the algorithm's convergence and the solution accuracy.

We employ the well-known fitness function of the form

$$E_{Data}(DisparityImage) + E_{Smooth}(DisparityImage)$$

used by the scan-line algorithm. (The function was suggested in [3] and explained in Section 2.) The data term can simply be the absolute color difference between a pixel from the left image and its hypothesized corresponding pixel in the right image. The smoothness term between two neighboring pixels can be simplified to zero if they have the same disparity. Otherwise, if the absolute difference between the two disparities is 1, the smoothness term is assigned some $\alpha > 0$. If the disparity difference is greater than 1, the penalty is β, where $\beta > \alpha$.

Finding a global minimum to the fitness function yields a stereo disparity map whose agreement with the ground truth is highly dependent on the specific smoothness and data functions chosen. Even with the same functions above, the accuracy of the results could vary greatly for different values of α and β. Finding a set of parameters that satisfy all images is difficult if not impossible. We managed to fix all of the parameter values for the benchmark datasets we experimented with (see Section 4). Although we obtained promising overall performance, the performance for each image pair could have been improved by fine tuning the parameter values to fit each of the datasets experimented with.

3.2 Intuitive Rationale

The dynamic programming scan-line algorithm is a commonly used stereo matching algorithm. It instantly provides the global minimum over a chosen line. Note, though, that the global minimum for each line is essentially a local minimum for the complete, non-relaxed fitness function, since inter-line constraints are not taken into account.

The proposed crossover procedure is applied to two possible solutions (i.e., chromosomes); it obtains a better local solution over a random line direction by applying a scan-line optimization in the direction picked, selecting – for each pixel – one of the (two) assignments offered by the parents. Although this building block may yield an improved solution over a specific line direction, it is restricted to local optima (global optima regarding the line direction picked), as it only considers the parents' assignments and not the entire search space. However, by repeating the crossover procedure for various line orientations, it is expected that chromosomes will slowly improve with each orientation, and that a solution will eventually emerge that conforms to the relaxed fitness function over many line directions (meaning that if the solution "fits" many relaxed fitness functions with respect to many variations of partial data – this implies, hopefully, that it minimizes the non-relaxed fitness function over the entire data is minimized as well).

Table 1: Parameter values used by the hybrid algorithm

Algorithm Parameters	
Population size	80
Mutation probability	1.0
Elitism	3
Epochs	500
α	4
β	10

The crossover procedure quickly eliminates irrelevant assignment candidates, but it may eliminate relevant assignments as well, since they are not optimal over the line direction picked. To ensure that the global fitting assignments are not permanently removed, mutation is applied so that all of the assignments are considered. Furthermore, the fitness function used to score each chromosome is the complete non-relaxed function, which adds another "fail-safe" against the removal of pixel assignments that do fit the global function.

This procedure can be viewed as analogous to the well-known line search optimization [2]. In each phase of the algorithm, we optimize with respect to a specific line direction. The method's progress is limited, since only two selected chromosomes are considered (i.e., not all possibilities). Integrating the line search approach with the GA framework tends to avoid local minima and achieve improved results.

The algorithm quickly converges to a solution despite the vast search space due to the local optimization used in our hybrid approach. The solution also yields higher accuracy over the generations due to the genetic algorithm's mechanism of escaping local minima.

4. EMPIRICAL ANALYSIS

The performance of our approach was assessed on the Middlebury benchmark site [1][15][14], which is well recognized and widely used by the computer vision community. The site contains standard datasets for researchers to experiment with using an on-line interface. Also, it contains results for the most current algorithms and their relative ranking.

Figures 6—9 below present some preliminary results. The top three images in each figure are the left input image, right input image and ground truth (of the disparity map). Also, the bottom two images in each figure (from left to right) correspond to the disparity maps obtained (on the Middlebury site) by our approach and the dynamic programming scan-line approach (we have set out to improve). All of the performance evaluations were conducted on-line on the Middlebury evaluation site [1], according to the benchmark protocol and the test datasets (of 4 stereo pairs) agreed upon. The error rates obtained in this evaluation were 13.5% and 16.6%, respectively, for our approach and the scan-line method. Thus, the number of pixels assigned with a disparity different from the ground truth decreased by about 20% in comparison with the original scan-line method. Note that all disparity maps were obtained for the same parameter values of Table 1, used in all of the evaluation test data on the Middlebury site.

A main evaluation criterion used is the number of incorrect pixels, i.e., pixels for which the absolute disparity difference between the solutions provided and the ground truth is greater than 1. Table 2 shows the percentage of incorrect pixels obtained via the Middlebury evaluation site for our approach and the scan-line optimization method over non-occluded areas.

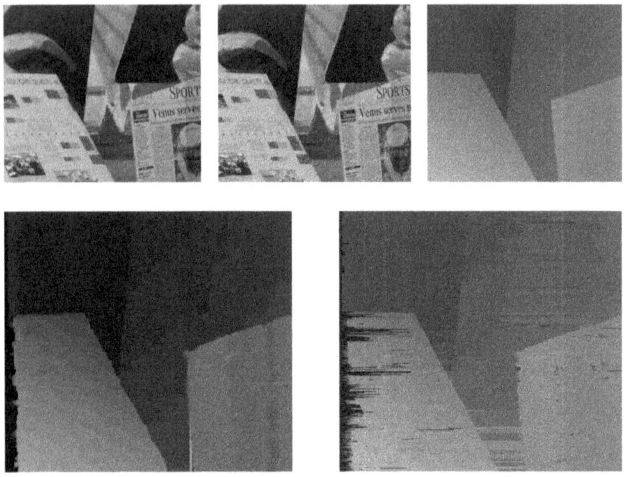

Figure 6: Top row shows the Venus stereo pair and its ground truth; bottom row shows (from left to right) the resulting disparity maps of our approach and the original scan-line algorithm)

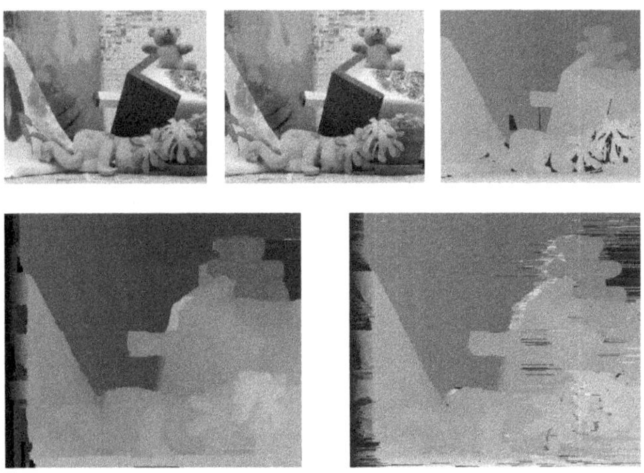

Figure 7: Top row shows the Teddy stereo pair and its ground truth; bottom row shows (from left to right) the resulting disparity maps of our approach and the original scan-line algorithm

5. CONCLUSION

We presented in this paper a novel scheme for the stereo matching problem. The algorithm presented yields a significant improvement in accuracy relative to the original scan-line approach it is based upon. In particular, the empirical results show a relative improvement of roughly 20%. Our scheme also enables to "boost" a weak local optimization

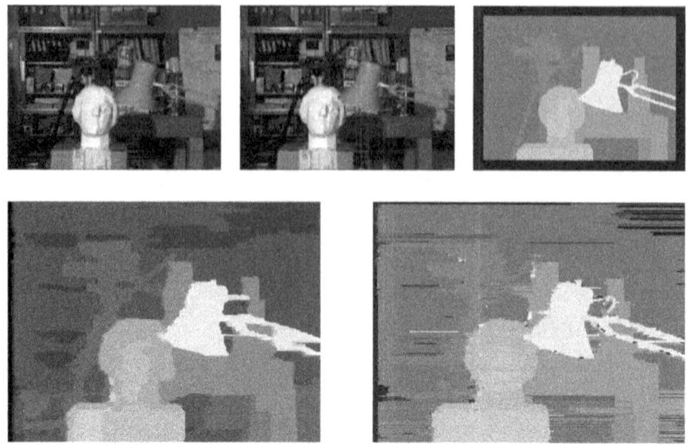

Figure 8: Top row shows the Tsukuba stereo pair and its ground truth; bottom row shows (from left to right) the resulting disparity maps of our approach and the original scan-line algorithm

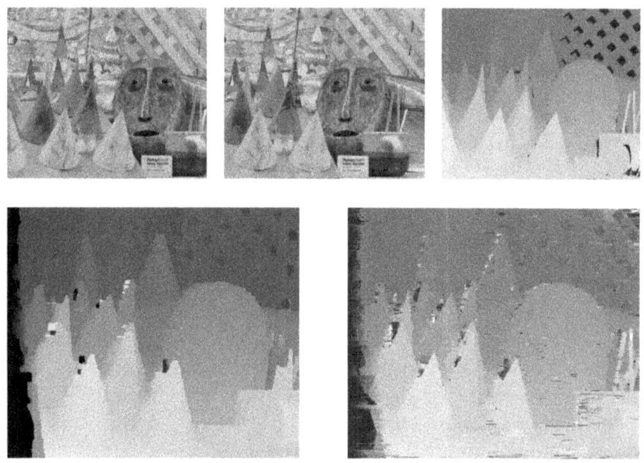

Figure 9: Top row shows the Cones stereo pair and its ground truth; bottom row shows (from left to right) the resulting disparity maps of our approach and the original scan-line algorithm

Table 2: Comparison of incorrect pixels, according to the Middlebury evaluation site for our approach vs. the scan-line algorithm

	Tsukuba	Venus	Teddy	Cones
Our approach	2.98%	2.71%	13.9%	6.53%
Scanline Opt	5.08%	9.44%	19.9%	13.0%

scheme via a genetic algorithm. Specifically, it could replace scan-line optimization modules in state-of-the-art algorithms (that achieve higher accuracy than that of our hybrid algorithm) [16, 13] to further enhance their performance.

Further research regarding the fitness function can contribute a great deal to the accuracy of the algorithm. Also, it would be of interest to investigate the impact on the convergence rate of the algorithm and the overall performance when taking in consideration the k-shortest path in the crossover operator.

6. REFERENCES

[1] Middlebury stereo vision page (http://vision.middlebury.edu/stereo).

[2] M.J. Box, D. Davies, and W.H. Swann. Non-linear optimization techniques. *Mathematical and statistical techniques for industry monograph*, 5:60, 1969.

[3] Y. Boykov, O. Veksler, and R. Zabih. Fast approximate energy minimization via graph cuts. *In Proceedings of the IEEE International Conference on Computer Vision*, pages 377—384, 1999.

[4] E. Dahlhaus, D.S. Johnson, C.H. Papadimitriou, P.D. Seymour, and M. Yannakakis. The complexity of multiway cuts. *In Proceedings of the ACM Symposium on Theory of Computing*, pages 241–251, 1992.

[5] Y. Deng and X. Lin. A fast line segment based dense stereo algorithm using tree dynamic programming. *In Proceedings of the European Conference on Computer Vision*, 3953:201–212, 2006.

[6] P.F. Felzenszwalb and D.P. Huttenlocher. Efficient belief propagation for early vision. *In Proceedings of the IEEE Conference on Computer Vision and Pattern Recognition*, 70:41–54, 2004.

[7] M. Gerrits and P. Bekaert. Local stereo matching with segmentation-based outlier rejection. *In Proceedings of the IEEE 3rd Canadian Conference on Computer and Robot Vision*, page 66, 2006.

[8] H. Hirschmuller. Stereo vision in structured environments by consistent semi-global matching. *In Proceedings of the IEEE Conference on Computer Vision and Pattern Recognition*, 2:2386–2393, 2006.

[9] T. Jones. Crossover, macromutation, and population-based search. *In Proceedings of the Sixth International Conference on Genetic Algorithms*, pages 73–80, 1995.

[10] A. Klaus, M. Sormann, and K. Karner. Segment-based stereo matching using belief propagation and a self-adapting dissimilarity measure. *In Proceedings of the International Conference on Pattern Recognition*, 3:15–18, 2006.

[11] D. Martin, C. Fowlkes, D. Tal, and J. Malik. A database of human segmented natural images and its application to evaluating segmentation algorithms and measuring eological statistics. *In Proceedings of the IEEE International Conference on Computer Vision*, 2:416–423, 2001.

[12] S. Mattoccia, E. Addimanda, and L. Di Stefano. Classification and evaluation of cost aggregation methods for stereo correspondence. *In Proceedings of the IEEE Conference on Computer Vision and Pattern Recognition*, pages 1–8, 2008.

[13] X. Mei, X. Sun, M. Zhou, S. Jiao, H. Wang, and X. Zhang. On building an accurate stereo matching system on graphics hardware. *In Proceedings of the International Conference on Computer Vision Workshops*, pages 467–474, 2011.

[14] D. Scharstein and R. Szeliski. A taxonomy and evaluation of dense two-frame stereo correspondence algorithms. *International Journal of Computer Vision*, 47:7–42, 2002.

[15] D. Scharstein and R. Szeliski. High-accuracy stereo depth maps using structured light. *In Proceedings of the IEEE Conference on Computer Vision and Pattern Recognition*, 1:195–202, 2003.

[16] X. Sun, X. Mei, S. Jiao, M. Zhou, and H. Wang. Stereo matching with reliable disparity propagation. *In proceedings of the IEEE International Conference on 3D Imaging, Modeling, Processing, Visualization and Transmission*, pages 132–139, 2011.

[17] O. Veksler. Stereo correspondence by dynamic programming on a tree. *In Proceedings of the IEEE Conference on Computer Vision and Pattern Recognition*, 2:384–390, 2005.

[18] A. Viterbi. Error bounds for convolutional codes and an asymptotically optimum decoding algorithm. *In Proceedings of the IEEE Transactions on Information Theory*, 13:260–269, 1967.

[19] Z. Wang and Z. Zheng. A region based stereo matching algorithm using cooperative optimization. *In Proceedings of the IEEE Conference on Computer Vision and Pattern Recognition*, pages 1–8, 2008.

[20] W.Y. Yau and H. Wang. Fast relative depth computation for an active stereo vision system. *Real-Time Imaging*, 5:189–202, 1999.

Optimization of a Supersonic Airfoil Using the Multi-Objective Alliance Algorithm

Valerio Lattarulo
University of Cambridge
Department of Engineering
Engineering Design Center
Cambridge, Trumpington Street, CB2 1PZ, UK
vl261@cam.ac.uk

Pranay Seshadri
University of Cambridge
Department of Engineering
Engineering Design Center
Cambridge, Trumpington Street, CB2 1PZ, UK
ps583@cam.ac.uk

Geoffrey T. Parks
University of Cambridge
Department of Engineering
Engineering Design Center
Cambridge, Trumpington Street, CB2 1PZ, UK
gtp10@cam.ac.uk

ABSTRACT

A baseline NACA0012 two-dimensional (2D) airfoil is optimized for supersonic flight conditions using a recently introduced optimization algorithm: the multi-objective alliance algorithm (MOAA). The efficacy of the algorithm is demonstrated through comparisons with NSGA-II for 300, 600 and 1000 function evaluations. Through epsilon/hypervolume indicators and the Mann-Whitney statistical test, we show that MOAA outperforms NSGA-II on this problem.

Categories and Subject Descriptors

G.1.6 [**Mathematics of Computing**]: Optimization—*Unconstrained Optimization*; G.4 [**Mathematics of Computing**]: Mathematical Software—*Algorithm design and analysis*

Keywords

MOAA; Multi-objective Optimization; Airfoil; Real-World problem

1. INTRODUCTION

In the recent past interest in the design of the next generation of civilian supersonic aircraft has renewed [14]. This movement within the aerodynamics community has been reignited by the capabilities of high fidelity computational fluid dynamics (CFD) codes coupled with state-of-the-art optimization algorithms. The focus is to use these codes to create new wing designs with minimum shock-induced losses — reduced wave drag and acoustic signatures — whilst maximizing the lift produced over the range of in-flight Mach numbers. The first step towards designing these wings is typically to optimize the 2D airfoil topology using potential flow or Euler solvers within an optimization routine.

Such real-world optimization problems are generally characterized by several conflicting objectives. Airfoil performance metrics such as the lift coefficient, C_l, the drag coefficient, C_d, and the aerodynamic moment coefficient, C_m, are prime examples of this as optimizing one of these parameters may cause a deterioration in the others. Such problems are often tackled using metaheuristic approaches, which have proved to be more successful than deterministic gradient-based methods for multi-objective (MO) problems. A variety of metaheuristics have been created for this purpose: the best-known were inspired by Darwinian evolution, e.g. Genetic Algorithms [13] and Differential Evolution [24], by metallurgical treatments, e.g. Simulated Annealing [17], by animal swarm behaviour, e.g. Particle Swarm Optimization [16] and Ant Colony Optimization [6], or by pragmatic common sense, e.g. Tabu Search [11]. These algorithms are used for single-objective optimization but MO variants of all have been developed, with MO evolutionary approaches being the most widely used [5, 7].

In the field of MO optimization the Alliance Algorithm (AA) is a relatively new single-objective optimization algorithm that has been applied successfully to NP-complete problems such as the Knapsack Problem [19], electrical energetic problems [3], mathematical functions [20], and artificial intelligence and robotics problems [22]. These promising results motivated the development of a MO variant [21], the performance of which has been compared with NSGA-II [8] and SPEA 2 [26]. That study [21] revealed a certain complementarity because the three approaches offered superior performance for different classes of problems. In this paper a new version of the MOAA is presented and applied to the problem of airfoil shape optimization for supersonic flow. This version has been developed in order to overcome several limitations of the previous version and to improve the overall performance.

The central goal of this work is to optimize the profile of a NACA0012 airfoil (a standard subsonic airfoil, see [1]) for supersonic flow. The flow conditions are an inlet Mach number of 1.5 and an angle of attack of 4° at a Reynolds number of 6.5×10^6. These conditions are representative of cruise conditions for a supersonic aircraft. Both NSGA-II and MOAA are utilized for this problem to provide a good basis of comparison.

The remainder of this paper is structured as follows: Sect. 2 and 3 discuss the CFD and optimization methodology, Sect. 4 describes how the new version of the MOAA works; Sect. 5 introduces the indicators and statistical tests used for the evaluation of the algorithms; Sect. 6 reports on the

GECCO'13, July 6-10, 2013, Amsterdam, The Netherlands.

MOAA's performance on this problem, comparing it with that of NSGA-II, and discusses the results.

2. METHODOLOGY

All flow simulations undertaken during this study are carried out by solving the compressible Euler equations using the SU^2 [23] open source flow solver. The 2D compressible Euler equations in conservation form can be written as:

$$\frac{\partial \mathbf{U}}{\partial t} + \frac{\partial \mathbf{F}_i}{\partial x_i} = 0 \tag{1}$$

$$U = \begin{bmatrix} \rho \\ \rho v_i \\ \rho E \end{bmatrix}, F_i = \begin{bmatrix} \rho v_i \\ \rho v_i v_j + p\delta_{ij} \\ \rho E v_i + p v_i \end{bmatrix}, (i = 1, 2) \tag{2}$$

where ρ is the density, p the pressure, E the internal energy, v_i the velocity component in direction i and δ_{ij} is the Kronecker delta. In order to close the above equations, we assume that the fluid is a perfect gas, and thus the pressure can be written as:

$$p = (\gamma - 1)\,\rho \left\{ E - \frac{1}{2}(v_1 \cdot v_2) \right\} \tag{3}$$

where γ is the ratio of specific heat capacities. Within the solver the above equations are discretized through a standard edge-based approach on an unstructured mesh using a finite volume method. A standard dual grid, constructed using a medial-dual vertex scheme, is used to evaluate the convective fluxes at the midpoint of an edge. The convective fluxes in the above equations are integrated using the classical Jameson-Turkel-Schmidt scheme (see [15]), which is a central, multi-stage Runge-Kutta scheme [4]. This scheme employs a higher-order artificial dissipation, which is computed using the differences in the higher-order Laplacians of connecting nodes and the difference in the lower-order conserved variables on connecting nodes. A pressure switch is used to blend these two levels of dissipation and for triggering lower-order dissipation next to shock waves [23]. The unstructured baseline NACA0012 computational mesh is shown in Fig. 1. It has been appropriately non-dimensionalized. It consists of an inviscid wall boundary on the airfoil surface and a far-field boundary at the inlet and outlet.

3. OPTIMIZATION FRAMEWORK

In addition to the CFD subroutine, there are two other key components that need to be integrated into the overall optimization loop. These are the airfoil surface perturbation method and the subsequent mesh deformation technique. These are discussed below.

3.1 Surface Perturbation

A total of eight points (shown in Figure 1) are used to vary the airfoil profile at x-coordinates of [0.2, 0.4, 0.6, 0.8] on both the upper and lower surfaces. Each point was permitted a ± 0.01 maximum deviation in the y-direction. These bounds are chosen such that top and bottom surfaces do not overlap. We employ Hicks-Henne bump functions [12] for shape modification. These functions can be added to the original airfoil geometry to modify the shape. They are expressed as a finite sum of basis functions of the form:

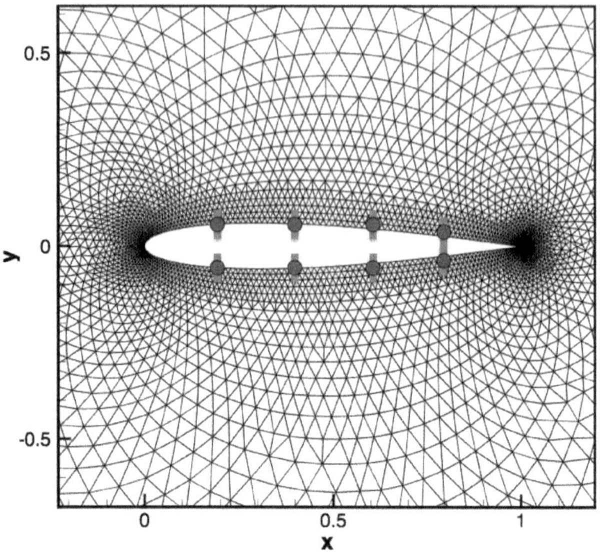

Figure 1: Close up of the NACA0012 unstructured mesh. Red lines show the maximum permissible deviation of points along each surface (±0.01). The blue dots show the points used for Hicks-Henne shape deformation.

$$\triangle y = \sum_{i=1}^{N} a_i f_i(x) \tag{4}$$

where $\triangle y$ is the total deformation, N is the number of bump functions and a_i is the design variable step. The basis functions are given to be:

$$f_i(x) = sin^3(\pi x^{e_i}), e_i = \frac{log(1/2)}{log(x_i)} \tag{5}$$

where the x values vary from 0 to 1.

3.2 Mesh Deformation

Once a new airfoil has been generated, the original mesh (see Figure 1) must be appropriately deformed. A torsional spring analogy[10] is used as the grid deformation technique. It consists of defining a stiffness matrix that connects two ends of a mesh edge, and then subsequently imposes an equilibrium condition at each mesh node. The overall system of equations is solved iteratively using a conjugate gradient method with Jacobi preconditioning [23]. Both the surface perturbation and mesh deformation capabilities are available in SU^2.

Integrating the surface perturbation and mesh deformation techniques along with the optimization algorithm, we have the following workflow:

1. The optimizer outputs y-displacement values for each of the eight points;
2. A new airfoil based on Hicks-Henne functions is generated;
3. The original mesh is deformed to contour to the new airfoil;

4. Compressible Euler equations are solved on the new mesh.

Steps 1–4 are repeated for each function evaluation of the optimizer. For our supersonic airfoil problem, the objective functions guiding the optimizer are given as $min\{C_d, -C_l\}$; that is, we want to minimize the drag coefficient whilst maximizing the lift coefficient. Details of the new version of the MOAA optimizer used in this study are provided below.

4. ALGORITHM

The MOAA is a metaheuristic optimization algorithm inspired by the metaphorical idea of a number of tribes struggling to conquer an environment that offers resources that enable them to survive. The tribes are characterized by two features: the skills and resources necessary for survival. Tribes try to improve skills by forming alliances, which are also characterized by the skills and resources needed, but these now depend on the tribes within the alliance. The two main search elements of the algorithm are the formation of alliances and the creation of new tribes. One MOAA cycle ends when the strongest possible alliances of existing tribes have been created. The algorithm then begins a new cycle starting with new tribes whose creation is influenced by the previous strongest alliances.

4.1 The Main Entities

Two main entities play important roles in the MOAA: tribes and alliances. A tribe t is a tuple (x_t, s_t, r_t, a_t) composed of:

- a point in the solution space x_t;
- a set of skills $s_t = [s_{t,1}, s_{t,2}, \dots, s_{t,N_S}]$ dependent on the values of the N_S objective functions S_i evaluated at x_t:

$$s_{t,i} = S_i(x_t) \quad \forall\ i = 1, \dots, N_S \tag{6}$$

- a set of resource demands $r_t = [r_{t,1}, \dots, r_{t,N_R}]$ dependent on the values of the N_R constraint functions:

$$r_{t,i} = R_i(x_t) \quad \forall\ i = 1, \dots, N_R \tag{7}$$

- an alliance vector a_t containing the IDs of the tribes allied to tribe t. Initially an alliance is composed of just one tribe, thus $a_t(1) = ID_t$.

An alliance is a mutually disjoint partition of tribes. The tribes within an alliance perform actions as a unique entity. Each alliance a forms a new point x_a in the solution space defined by the tribes in the alliance. The sets of skills s_a and resource demands r_a of the alliance consist of the objective and constraint functions S and R evaluated at x_a.

4.2 Algorithm Steps

The procedure followed by the MOAA can be divided into several steps which can be performed differently according to the problem at hand and user preference. A detailed description of the previous version of the algorithm can be found in [21].

4.2.1 Solution Generation

In the MOAA's first cycle the tribes (solutions) are chosen randomly (with a uniform distribution):

$$x_{t,i} = U(L_i, H_i) \quad \forall\ i = 1, \dots, P \tag{8}$$

where $x_{t,i}$ is the ith component of tribe t, L_i and H_i are respectively the lower and upper bounds on the ith variable, and P is the total number of variables.

In subsequent cycles, new solutions are sampled from a normal distribution with defined mean and standard deviation σ as follows:

$$\begin{aligned} &\text{If } p_1 \le P_1: && x_t = b_r \\ &\text{If } p_1 > P_1 \wedge p_2 \le P_2: && x_{t,i} = N(b_{r,i}, \sigma) \\ &\text{If } p_1 > P_1 \wedge p_2 > P_2: && x_{t,i} = b_{r,i} \end{aligned} \tag{9}$$

Here: p_1 and p_2 are random variables between 0 and 1, P_1 and P_2 are probability factors between 0 and 1; r is a random integer between 1 and N_P, the number of Pareto-optimal (PO) solutions found; $b_{r,i}$ is the normalized ith variable of the rth PO solution found.

One of the PO solutions found is chosen randomly and normalized; with probability P_1, a new solution is simply a copy of this PO solution; otherwise, with probability P_2, the variables are modified, on an individual basis, with a normal distribution with standard deviation σ around the chosen point, or, with probability $1 - P_2$, they assume the same values as those of the chosen point. This cycle is repeated until N tribes have been generated.

An important feature of this new version of the MOAA is the adaptive nature of σ: this parameter adaptively decreases in order to produce high diversity at the beginning of the optimization and low diversity at the end. This mechanism enhances the initial exploration of the solution space and the final convergence of the solutions already found. This task is accomplished with the following equations:

$$\begin{aligned} \sigma_{factor} &= \frac{\sigma_{end}}{\sigma_{init}}^{\left(\frac{E_c}{E_{tot}}\right)} \\ \sigma &= \sigma \cdot \sigma_{factor} \end{aligned} \tag{10}$$

Here: σ_{init} is the initial value of σ; σ_{end} is the final value of σ; E_c is number of function evaluations from the previous cycle; E_{tot} is the total number of function evaluations. The value of σ, starting with an initial value, is multiplied every cycle by σ_{factor} in order to approximately reach the final value. The value of σ is not updated if the size of the previous Pareto front is larger than the current Pareto front in order to prevent convergence in a few restricted areas. This adaptative process allows a gradual transition from global search to local search.

4.2.2 Token Phase and Ally Choice

In this phase an alliance/tribe (A/T) is chosen randomly and given the chance to forge an alliance by being given a token. Meanwhile all the other A/Ts wait their turn. The A/T t with the token chooses another tribe to become an ally, thus forming a new alliance.

4.2.3 Verification

In this phase an alliance (a point in solution space x_a) is created. In this case, x_a is made up of components drawn from the tribes within the alliance: given an alliance of N_a tribes, each component of x_a has a $1/N_a$ probability of being equal to the corresponding component of any tribe in the alliance. There is an additional probability P_3 that the component is then modified as per the following equations:

$$\begin{aligned} & c = U_d(1, N_a) \\ & \text{If } p_3 \leq P_3 : x_{a,i} = N(x_{c,i}, \sigma_{alliance} \cdot d_{tribes,i}) \\ & \text{Else} : x_{a,i} = x_{c,i} \end{aligned} \quad (11)$$

Here: c is the index of the chosen tribe within the alliance; $U_d(1, N_a)$ is the discrete uniform distribution between 1 and N_a; $x_{a,i}$ is the value of the ith component of the alliance; $x_{c,i}$ is the value of the ith component of the chosen tribe; $\sigma_{alliance}$ is a constant factor; $d_{tribes,i}$ is the distance between the highest and lowest values of variable i of the tribes within the alliance. This operation is repeated until all the components of x_a are defined. As the standard deviation for the creation of an alliance depends on the distance between the highest and lowest values of the corresponding variable among the tribes within the alliance, the standard deviation for an alliance of tribes that are close together is small (local search) and for tribes that are far apart it is large (global search). Generally at the start of an optimization the tribes within an alliance are far apart and then they start to come closer together. This behavior can be viewed as an initial global search followed by progressively more localized search.

The new alliance will only be confirmed if at least one skill in s_a of x_a is better than one skill in s_{t_1} of the solution representing the A/T with the token x_{t_1} and one skill in s_{t_2} of the tribe chosen to become an ally.

The resource function $R(x)$ plays no role here because the CFD problem tackled in this particular study is unconstrained.

4.2.4 Alliance and Data Structure Update

There are two possible outcomes from the Verification Phase: the chosen tribe joins the entity with the token forming a new alliance, or the tribe does not join and the new alliance is not confirmed. Next there is an update of the data structures necessary for the low level system to function, such as the necessity to provide a unique ID to the created alliances. The cycle termination conditions are also checked. The cycle finishes when each A/T has tried to form a new alliance with every other tribe and remains unchanged (because there is no advantage in changing). If this condition is not met, the algorithm returns to the Token Phase.

4.2.5 Selection of the Strongest Alliances and Termination

At the end of the interactions between tribes, many alliances will have been formed but only the strongest A/Ts will conquer the environment. Therefore the A/Ts selected are the non-dominated points in objective space. These correspond to the best solutions to the problem found thus far. They can be used as the input to another MOAA cycle or, if the algorithm has ended, they represent the final results.

There is a limit n to the number of best solutions saved in the archive of PO solutions. If the number of non-dominated solutions exceeds this, then all the solutions with at least one neighbor within a neighborhood distance d (in objective space) are eliminated. The initial value of d is 0 and then changes adaptively as follows:

$$\begin{aligned} \alpha &= \frac{N_f \cdot range_{tot}}{E_{tot}} \\ d &= d + \alpha \cdot \frac{n_p - n}{n} \end{aligned} \quad (12)$$

Here: N_f is a constant factor; E_{tot} is the total number of solution evaluations; $range_{tot}$ is the Euclidean distance in objective space between the maximum and minimum values of the PO solutions; n_p is the current number of PO solutions. This formulation takes into account that the reality that the rates of convergence have to depend on the number of function evaluations that can be afforded: slower convergence is possible if many function evaluations are possible; faster convergence is necessary with few function evaluations. Moreover it also depends on the actual ranges of the Pareto front: larger ranges require faster rates in order that the number of accepted solutions in the archive does not explode; conversely, smaller ranges require slower rates. In this way a balance around n is struck between the new PO solutions found by the algorithm every cycle and the solutions removed from the archive of PO solutions.

The MOAA is terminated when a specified limit E_{tot} on the number of solution evaluations is reached. The output of the algorithm is then the best solutions and the Pareto front found.

4.2.6 Extended Archive

Another innovation of this new version of the MOAA is the use of an Extended Archive. The archive with the PO solutions records only the non-dominated solutions, not considering many solutions that could help maintain diversity among solutions and the convergence of the algorithm. This issue is addressed by allowing other solutions to join the archive in the following way:

- For each dimension in objective space, the PO solutions and the solutions found in the cycle are sorted by increasing objective values.
- The distance (the difference in objective values for the relevant objective) between consecutive PO solutions is calculated as is the distance between the last PO solution (that with the worst objective value) and the solution from the current cycle with the worst value of that objective, in order to include the edge of the function.
- If the distance between two solutions is greater than the mean distance multiplied by a factor (discussed below), then non-dominated sorting of the solutions from the current cycle within that particular range is done and the non-dominated solutions from this group are added to the archive.

The factor changes adaptively increasing over time because the gaps between the solutions become smaller reaching similar values: increasing the value only large gaps (in comparison with the average) will be taken into consideration. The factor Af_i for objective i starts with value of 1 and is then updated by adding the number of the new entries to the archive $sol_{new,i}$ resulting from this process divided by the number of solutions already in the archive n_p.

$$Af_i = Af_i + \frac{sol_{new,i}}{n_p} \quad (13)$$

This number n_p is updated only at the end of the process, thus the same value is used for all objectives. Using this method, the factor is updated only if there are gaps that have been filled with some solutions from the current cycle: if many solutions are added, then many gaps have been filled and the factor's value can be increased faster. Furthermore, the factor update is closely related to the number of solutions in the archive: if there are few solutions then the number of possible gaps between them is small and the factor's value can increase faster; conversely, if there are many solutions, there many possible gaps and the factor's value has to increase slowly in order to fill them all.

5. INDICATORS AND STATISTICAL TEST

The performance measures chosen to evaluate the algorithms are the *epsilon indicator* [27] and *hypervolume indicator* [18] provided in the PISA package [2]. The epsilon indicator [27] makes use of the Pareto-dominance concept and measures, given a reference set of points (ideally the true Pareto front, if available), the minimum amount ϵ necessary to translate all the points of the found Pareto front to weakly dominate the reference set. The hypervolume indicator [18] calculates the difference between the hypervolume of the space dominated by the found Pareto front and the hypervolume of the space dominated by a reference set (again, ideally the true Pareto front). This indicator needs a reference point which is dominated by all the found points in order to bound the hypervolume.

The statistical test chosen for the evaluation of results is the Mann-Whitney test, provided in the PISA package [2]. This is a non-parametric rank-based test that can be used to compare two independent sets of sampled data. It outputs p-values that estimate the probability of rejecting the null hypothesis of the study question when that hypothesis is true. Here the p-values can be interpreted as the probability that MOAA is superior to NSGA-II only by chance.

6. RESULTS

Both MOAA and NSGA-II were tested with 300, 600 and 1000 function evaluations — the comparatively small number of evaluations reflects the computational cost of the CFD-based evaluations. Each test was repeated 20 times. The parameters used for NSGA-II are specified in [8]. The MOAA parameters used are shown in Table 1. These have already proven their effectiveness with standard benchmark functions such as the ZDT [25] and DTLZ [9] families. Thus, these values are general and have not been overfitted to the current problem. Although some of these parameters need further investigation to find better general values and provide appropriate justifications, there are some exceptions:

- The number of tribes N is a number between 5 and 10, in order to allow sufficient algorithm cycles.
- The initial standard deviation σ_{init} is 0.3 because a normal distribution with this standard deviation behaves approximately like a uniform distribution (global search).
- The final standard deviation σ_{end} needs to be in the range 0.01–0.001 in order to allow local searches.
- The total number of PO solutions archived and output can be chosen by the user.

The PO solutions found in each of the 20 runs for all three tests are shown in Fig. 2, while the PO solutions amongst all 20 runs are shown in Fig. 3. It is clear that for the 600 and 1000 evaluation tests many MOAA solutions dominate the NSGA-II solutions, showing better convergence. Another key point to note is that for all tests the Pareto front obtained by the MOAA is wider, thus identifying more airfoils with lower drag and higher lift coefficients.

Results from each of the 20 runs were used to compute the mean and standard deviation of the epsilon and hypervolume indicators along with their corresponding p-values. Lower values of these metrics are indicative of better performance. The reference set for these comparisons was composed of the PO solutions found by both algorithms.

Table 2 shows the mean and standard deviation of the epsilon indicator. Comparable performance for both algorithms is observed for 300 function evaluations. However, for the other two cases, MOAA yields lower mean values.

Hypervolume indicator metrics are shown in Table 3. Here too, mean values for the latter two tests are lower for MOAA. On the other hand, standard deviation values exhibited by NSGA-II are lower for both the epsilon and hypervolume indicators for 600 and 1000 evaluations.

To quantify the efficacy of these two metrics in characterizing their relative success, we compute the p-values obtained with the Mann-Whitney statistical test. Lower p-values indicate that one algorithm is better than the other. These values are shown in Table 4. In this case we compute the probability that MOAA provides a better set of PO solutions. While it is unclear which algorithm performs better for 300 function evaluations, from the table we can infer that for 600 and 1000 evaluations MOAA has a higher probability of obtaining lower epsilon and hypervolume indicators. Thus, for higher function evaluations for this problem, it may be concluded that MOAA outperforms NSGA-II.

Table 1: Parameters of MOAA

Parameter	Value	Description
N	6	Number of tribes
P_1	0.5	Probability 1 for creation of tribes
P_2	0.2	Probability 2 for creation of tribes
σ_{init}	0.3	Initial standard deviation
σ_{end}	0.01	Final standard deviation
P_3	2/V	Probability for creation of alliances
σ_a	0.1	Std for creation of alliances
N_{tot}	100	Total number of PO solutions
N_f	10	Factor for evaluation neighborhood

Table 2: Comparison with Epsilon Indicator

N. Eval	MOAA		NSGA-II	
	Mean	Std	Mean	Std
300	0.2942	0.0957	0.3009	0.0965
600	0.2249	0.0878	0.2647	0.0617
1000	0.1642	0.0953	0.1997	0.0926

Table 3: Comparison with Hypervolume Indicator

N. Eval	MOAA		NSGA-II	
	Mean	Std	Mean	Std
300	0.2092	0.0874	0.2080	0.0640
600	0.1096	0.0453	0.1265	0.0269
1000	0.0804	0.0470	0.1105	0.0270

Table 4: Mann-Whitney Statistical Test

N. Eval	p-value (MOAA better than NSGA-II)	
	Epsilon	Hypervolume
300	0.3524	0.4249
600	0.0880	0.0615
1000	0.0720	0.0043

7. OPTIMIZED AIRFOILS

The MOAA optimization study yielded two optimized airfoils: one with maximum lift and one with minimum drag. Viscous computations on these two airfoils were carried out using SU^2. This involves solving the Reynolds averaged Navier-Stokes (RANS) equations with a Spalart–Allmaras turbulence model for closure. The main motivation for this was to obtain better estimates of the lift and drag coefficients, and to see if Euler estimates were accurate. Table 5 compares these lift and drag coefficient values obtained from both Euler and RANS computations for the optimized airfoils with the baseline NACA0012. From the data, it is evident that MOAA is able to produce two airfoils with significantly better performance metrics compared to the baseline NACA0012. The maximum lift coefficient has been increased by 36%, while the drag coefficient has been reduced by 25%. We also note a slight offset in both lift and drag coefficients between Euler and RANS computations. This is expected as the latter includes a viscous drag component of force. Since the airfoil is at a non-zero angle of attack, a component of this drag is resolved in both lift and drag directions. On the whole, Euler computations do provide sufficient numerical accuracy for the purposes of our optimization problem.

Table 5: Airfoil optimization results

Airfoil	Euler		RANS	
	C_l	C_d	C_l	C_d
NACA0012	0.2163	0.1105	0.1837	0.1140
Optimized C_l	0.2550	0.1036	0.2494	0.1096
Optimized C_d	0.2249	0.0810	0.2031	0.0856

The key point to note from Table 5 is that the MOAA is successful in yielding two optimized airfoils. Figure 4 shows the airfoil profiles for the two optimized geometries compared to the baseline. For the optimized C_d case, the thickness of the chord has been visibly reduced, thereby reducing the profile drag. For the optimized C_l case, increased camber on the lower surface is observed. This results in a larger pressure differential between upper and lower surfaces, which increases the overall lift. Figures 5 to 7 show Mach number contours (generated from RANS) for the baseline NACA0012 and the optimized C_d and C_l cases. From the figures it is lucid that the bow shock at the leading edge is stronger for the maximum C_l airfoil, this is indicative of greater shock induced losses. This is also reflected in the relatively high value of C_d for this airfoil. For the minimum C_d airfoil, the bow shock is comparably weaker (see Figure 6), particularly on the lower airfoil surface.

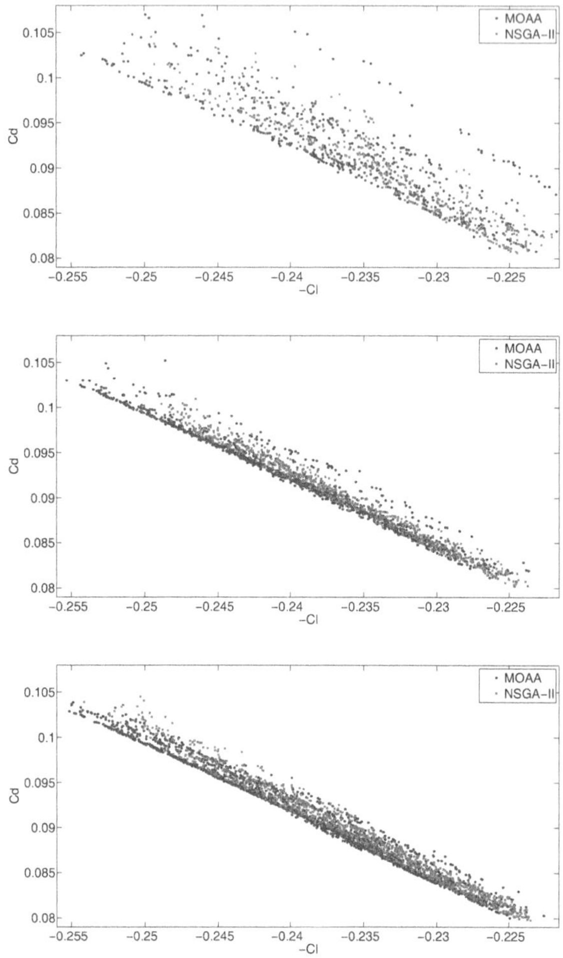

Figure 2: Comparison of the results from 20 runs in the three tests

8. CONCLUSIONS

In this paper a new version of MOAA has been introduced. This new version adds new features and uses improved variation operators which enhance the overall performance allowing it to solve complex problems with many local minima. The algorithm was applied to the optimization of a standard subsonic airfoil, to maximize C_l and minimize C_d, whilst being subjected to fully supersonic flow conditions. The results were compared with those given by NSGA-II. The following are some of the key conclusions of this study:

1. MOAA yielded comparable results with NSGA-II for 300 function evaluations for the airfoil optimization problem. For 600 and 1000 function evaluations the p-values for the epsilon and hypervolume indicators were in favor of MOAA, thereby demonstrating MOAA's efficacy on runs with higher numbers of function evaluations.

2. The overall width of the Pareto-optimal set found by MOAA was greater, in particular the algorithm provided airfoils with higher C_l values when compared with NSGA-II

3. The optimized airfoils showed an improvement in comparison to the baseline version.

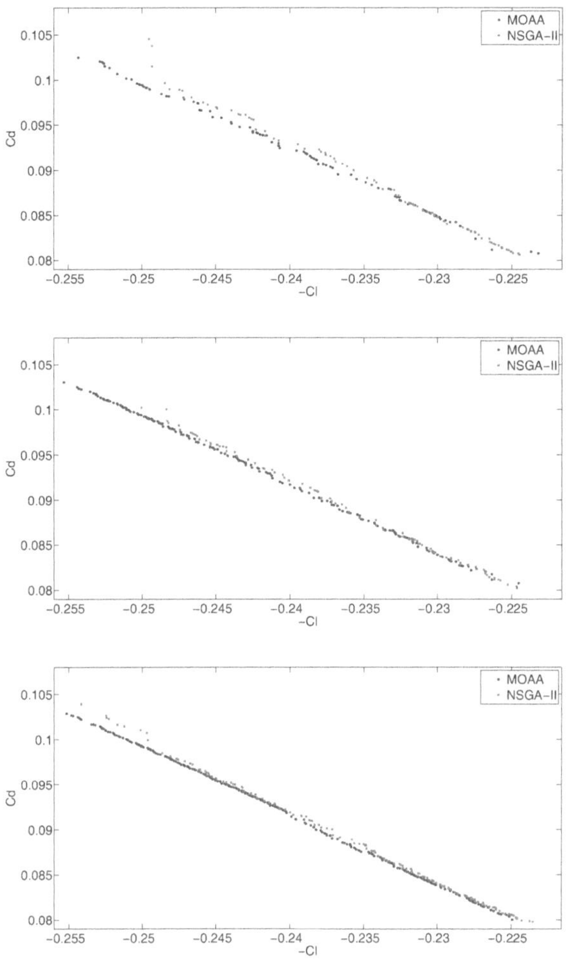

Figure 3: Comparison of the non-dominated solutions found in both tests

In the future, the MOAA will be compared to other well-known algorithms for more complex problems in order to understand the benefits and the limitations of this approach. We seek to explore problems with constraints and greater number of design variables with larger parameter bounds.

9. REFERENCES

[1] I. Abbott and A. Von Doenhoff. *Theory of Wing Sections, Including a Summary of Airfoil Data.* Dover Publications, New York, 1999.

[2] S. Bleuler, M. Laumanns, L. Thiele, and E. Zitzler. PISA—A platform and programming language independent interface for search algorithms. In *Conference on Evolutionary Multi-Criterion Optimization (EMO 2003)*, 2003.

[3] V. Calderaro, V. Galdi, V. Lattarulo, and P. Siano. A new algorithm for steady state load-shedding strategy. In *12th International Conference on Optimization of Electrical and Electronic Equipment (OPTIM)*, pages 48–53, 2010.

[4] T. Chung. *Computational Fluid Dynamics.* Cambridge University Press, Cambridge, 1st edition, 2002.

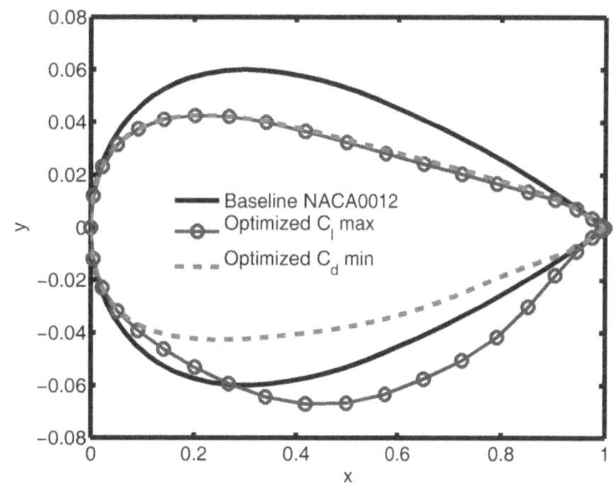

Figure 4: Profiles of the three airfoils - baseline NACA0012, C_l optimum and C_d optimum

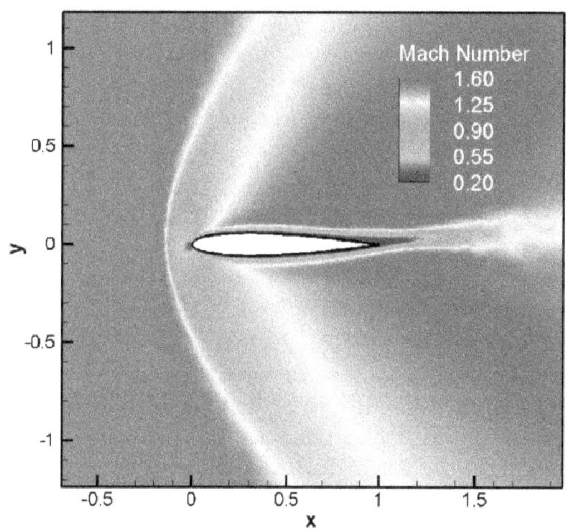

Figure 5: Mach number contours for baseline NACA0012

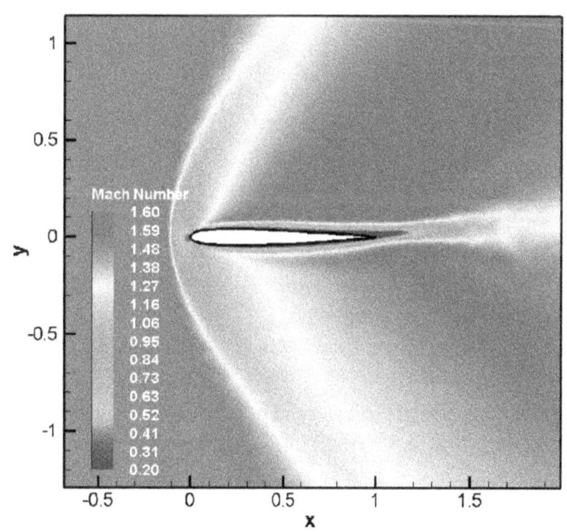

Figure 6: Mach number contours for optimized C_d minimum airfoil

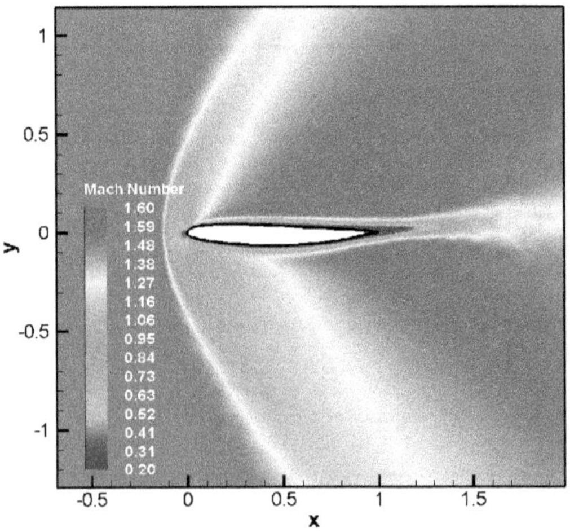

Figure 7: Mach number contours for optimized C_l maximum airfoil

[5] C. A. Coello Coello, G. B. Lamont, and D. A. V. Veldhuizen. *Evolutionary Algorithms for Solving Multi-Objective Problems (Genetic and Evolutionary Computation)*. Springer-Verlag, Secaucus, NJ, USA, 2006.

[6] A. Colorni, M. Dorigo, and V. Maniezzo. Distributed optimization by ant colonies. In *European Conference on Artificial Life*, 1991.

[7] K. Deb. *Multi-Objective Optimization Using Evolutionary Algorithms*. Wiley, Chichester, UK, 1 edition, June 2001.

[8] K. Deb, A. Pratap, S. Agarwal, and T. Meyarivan. A fast and elitist multiobjective genetic algorithm: NSGA-II. *IEEE Transactions on Evolutionary Computation*, 6:182–197, 2002.

[9] K. Deb, L. Thiele, M. Laumanns, and E. Zitzler. Scalable test problems for evolutionary multi-objective optimization. Technical report, Computer Engineering and Networks Laboratory (TIK), Swiss Federal Institute of Technology (ETH, 2001.

[10] C. Farhat, C. Degand, B. Koobus, and M. Lesoinne. Torsional springs for two-dimensional dynamic unstructured fluid meshes. *CMAME*, 163(1):231–245, 1998.

[11] F. Glover and M. Laguna. *Tabu Search*. Kluwer Academic Publishers, Boston, MA, USA, 1993.

[12] R. M. Hicks and P. A. Henne. Wing design by numerical optimization. *Journal of Aircraft*, 15(7):407–412, 1978.

[13] J. H. Holland. *Adaptation in Natural and Artificial Systems: An Introductory Analysis with Applications to Biology, Control and Artificial Intelligence*. MIT Press, Cambridge, MA, USA, 1992.

[14] R. Hui, A. Jameson, and Q. Wang. Adjoint-based aerodynamic optimization of supersonic biplane airfoils. *Journal of Aircraft*, 49(3):802–814, 2012.

[15] A. Jameson, W. Schmidt, and E. Turkel. Numerical solution of the euler equations by finite volume methods using runge-kutta time-stepping schemes. In *14th AIAA Fluid and Plasma Dynamic Conference*, jun. 1981.

[16] J. Kennedy and R. Eberhart. Particle swarm optimization. In *Neural Networks, 1995. Proceedings., IEEE International Conference on*, volume 4, pages 1942–1948, Aug. 1995.

[17] S. Kirkpatrick, C. D. Gelatt, and M. P. Vecchi. Optimization by simulated annealing. *Science*, 220(4598):671–680, 1983.

[18] J. Knowles, L. Thiele, and E. Zitzler. A Tutorial on the Performance Assessment of Stochastic Multiobjective Optimizers. TIK Report 214, Computer Engineering and Networks Laboratory (TIK), ETH Zurich, Feb. 2006.

[19] V. Lattarulo. Application of an innovative optimization algorithm for the management of energy resources. BSc thesis, University of Salerno, 2009.

[20] V. Lattarulo. Optimization of biped robot behaviors by 'alliance algorithm'. Master's thesis, University of Hertfordshire, 2011.

[21] V. Lattarulo and G. T. Parks. A preliminary study of a new multi-objective optimization algorithm. In *International Conference on Evolutionary Computation (CEC)*, 2012.

[22] V. Lattarulo and S. G. van Dijk. Application of the "Alliance Algorithm" to energy constrained gait optimization. In *15th Annual RoboCup International Symposium*, Istanbul, Turkey, 2011.

[23] F. Palacios, M. Colonno, A. Aranake, A. Campos, S. Copeland, T. Economon, A. Lonkar, T. Lukaczyk, T. Taylor, and J. Alonso. Stanford university unstructured (su2): An open-source integrated computational environment for multi-physics simulation and design. In *51st AIAA Aerospace Sciences Meeting and Exhibit*, jan. 2013.

[24] R. Storn and K. Price. Differential evolution - a simple and efficient heuristic for global optimization over continuous spaces. *J. of Global Optimization*, 11(4):341–359, Dec. 1997.

[25] E. Zitzler, K. Deb, and L. Thiele. Comparison of multiobjective evolutionary algorithms: Empirical results. *Evol. Comput.*, 8:173–195, June 2000.

[26] E. Zitzler, M. Laumanns, and L. Thiele. SPEA2: Improving the strength pareto evolutionary algorithm for multiobjective optimization. In *Evolutionary Methods for Design Optimization and Control with Applications to Industrial Problems*, pages 95–100, 2001.

[27] E. Zitzler, L. Thiele, M. Laumanns, C. M. Fonseca, and V. Grunert da Fonseca. Performance assessment of multiobjective optimizers: An analysis and review. *IEEE Transactions on Evolutionary Computation*, 7(2):117–132, 2003.

On the Impact of Streaming Interface Heuristics on GP Trading Agents: An FX Benchmarking Study

Alexander Loginov
Faculty of Computer Science
Dalhousie University
Halifax, NS. Canada
a.loginov@yahoo.ca

Malcolm I. Heywood
Faculty of Computer Science
Dalhousie University
Halifax, NS. Canada
mheywood@cs.dal.ca

ABSTRACT

Most research into frameworks for evolving trading agents emphasize aspects associated with the evolution of technical indicators and decision trees / rules. One of the factors that drives the development of such frameworks is the non-stationary, streaming nature of the task. However, it is the heuristics used to interface the evolutionary framework to the streaming data which potentially have most impact on the quality of the resulting trading agents. We demonstrate that including a validation partition has a significant impact on determining the overall success of the trading agents. Moreover, rather than conduct evolution on a continuous basis, only retraining when changes in trading quality are detected also yields significant advantages. Neither of these heuristics are widely recognized by research in evolving trading agent frameworks, although both are relatively easy to add to current frameworks. Benchmarking over a 3 year period of the EURUSD foreign exchange supports these findings.

Categories and Subject Descriptors

I.2.6 [**Learning**]: Parameter Learning

General Terms

Algorithms, Experimentation, Performance

Keywords

Foreign Exchange Trading; Streaming data; Dynamic environments; Symbiosis; Genetic Programming

1. INTRODUCTION

As per any application of machine learning in general to a task currently performed by humans, there are potentially a wide range of application specific decisions that play a significant role in determining the success of the resulting application. From the perspective of foreign exchange (FX) currency trading the initial data is described in terms of a sequence of trades. The trades are summarized with respect to a trading interval, typically in terms of the following attributes: opening, closing, highest and lowest price. Traders will construct rules to summarize a trading strategy. FX trading frequently make use of Stop–Loss or "S/L" thresholds in which an order to buy or sell is defined in terms of the market reaching a specific price. Moreover, trading rules are typically designed in terms of a combination of technical indicators (TI). The TI attempts to describe properties of the market that are useful for decision making in general. Such TI are estimated over a historical window of previous data relative to the current decision point, t.

Most research has concentrated on the application of evolutionary computation (EC) to the optimization of a priori technical indicators (TI) and decision trees (DT), Section 2. Conversely, less emphasis is placed on the contribution of parameters associated with interfacing the proposed EC to the application. For example, evolving trading agents in general assumes an online as opposed to offline application of EC. The data describing the trading environment is a continuous stream of a non-stationary nature. It is therefore not realistic to assume that solutions are evolved offline and then deployed. Instead, some heuristic needs to be adopted to either facilitate continuous evolution or detect changes in the stream and then retrain. In the case of continuous evolution a natural tradeoff between exploration and exploitation exists, whereas under change detection a poor choice of metric might result in missing important retraining events.

This research introduces a common framework for symbiotically coevolving TI and DT under representations appropriate for each task: hereafter FXGP (Section 3). A benchmarking study to quantify the significance of parameterizations pertinent to interfacing the FXGP trading agents to the stream represents the central contribution of this research. In particular, we are interested in the relative contribution of continuous coevolution versus change detection in supporting the development of effective trading agents. Secondary parameters are also considered such as support for a validation partition *during* application to the stream and the significance of evolving thresholds specific to the FX task (Section 4). We conclude that including a validation partition is of paramount importance. Change detection combined with population reinitialization is recommended to explicitly retrain trading agents as this appears to be more effective at avoiding carrying over unwanted model bias when a stream is non-stationary. Conversely, the current norm is to continuously evolve a population of trading

GECCO'13, July 6–10, 2013, Amsterdam, The Netherlands.

agents without reinitialization. This is shown to result in significant bias, thus lack the capacity to react appropriately to the non-stationary nature of the task.

2. BACKGROUND

Previous research has been reported with respect to the evolution of technical indicators (TI) alone e.g., [5]. One of the goals of evolving TI independently is to provide parameterizations for basic statistics such as moving averages, that are particularly appropriate for the data in question [14]. More recently separate TI were evolved for buying and selling [6]. Several authors have evolved trading rules or decision trees (DT) relative to a set of a priori selected TI e.g., [3], [7]. One of the most well known instances of GP in this context is 'EDDIE' [12]; the resulting IF–THEN rules are sampled by a human trader to determine which to use. Most recently, systems have been proposed to first evolve parameters for a fixed set of TI with the identification of DT e.g., [8]. To do so, a representation is assumed in which all of the information for the TI and DT appear in the same genome. We consider this problematic as both components need to be correct for an individual to be successful. Instead we assume a recent framework in which TI and DT are explicitly coevolved in two independent populations [11].

In general, authors have placed a lot of effort on designing fitness functions to penalize losses as well as reward profit [2], [8]. This also has implications for the potential robustness of the resulting trading agent as a whole. An alternative / complementary approach is to make use of verification data to curtail a training cycle, or early stopping [13]. Also of widespread utility is the use of some form of continuous training, where this is in recognition of the non-stationary nature of the task. For example, a 'rolling window' approach might be adopted [8] in which a sequence of data (or window) is used for training (N_t) and the champion individual deployed as the trading agent for the next δ data points. On reaching the end of the trading period the training window of N_t is realigned with the end of trading and training recommences using the content of the current population. Questions potentially arise regarding the number of generations to perform [2]. This is related to the degree of non-stationary (or appropriateness of any model bias) associated with the transition between training and trading periods. Indeed other authors have adopted training at *every* sliding window location [15]. In this work we compare reinitialization and retraining w.r.t. training criteria versus the typically assumed approach of continuous evolution.

3. FXGP ALGORITHM

Following the preamble established by the Introduction and Background (Sections 1 and 2) we will assume a framework capable of evolving both unique TI and DT. Specifically, the FXGP framework will be followed [11].[1] In the case of the TI, the desire is to support the evolution of properties pertinent to capturing temporal features e.g., parameterization of sliding windows over which basic statistics are estimated [14]; whereas the role of the DT is to combine an arbitrary number of uniquely parameterized TI into a trading rule. Thus, the DT assumes a comparatively straightforward representation: a sequence of conditional statements based on references to the TI population.

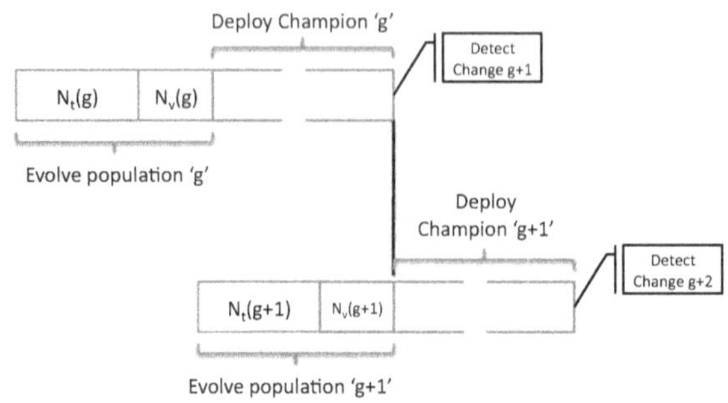

Figure 1: Identifying a new champion trading agent through change detection. g represents the count of independent cycles of evolution. Evolution is conducted relative to the most recent sample of training, $N_t(g)$ and validation data $N_v(g)$ from the stream.

Naturally, it is not possible to establish the fitness of the TI population independently of the DT population. Indeed it is only at the DT population that a direct measure of fitness can be established. Hence, FXGP *coevolves* DT and TI populations together under a symbiotic partnership where such schemes have previously been demonstrated for evolving teams of programs in genetic programming [10, 4].

The second aspect of the task domain to be addressed – and focus of this research – is the non-stationary nature of trading. That is to say, a champion individual evolved relative to a historical partition of trading data will only be effective for some duration of the future trading interval. Previous work proposed to employ *trading criteria* to define when a retraining cycle should be called [11]. Thus, a historical period of N_t records is used to construct a TI–DT population of trading agents, and a sequential period of N_v records is used to validate the champion TI–DT individual (Figure 1). The champion individual is allowed to trade until the trading criteria indicates that the champion individual is no longer effective i.e., change detection. The entire content of the TI and DT populations is then replaced with a corresponding new population of randomly initialized individuals. Retraining would then take place with training and validation partitions re-aligned with the point at which the trading criteria identified the failure (Figure 1).

3.1 Training

3.1.1 Representation

Individuals of the **TI population** assume a linear GP representation (e.g., [1]) with instruction set summarized by Table 1. Moreover, each TI has a header defining the basic TI properties: type, scale, period, shift (Table 2). The TI scale serves to detect useless TI and is checked after initialization. The TI initialization is repeated until the TI defines an outcome characterized by the scale type (see last paragraph of this sub-section).

TI programs assume a register level transfer language (Table 1). Thus, $R[x]$ denotes the content of register x, $R[y]$ de-

[1]This was previously demonstrated on three FX pairs [11]. However, no consideration was given to the impact of different schemes for interfacing with the stream, which is the focus of this research.

Table 1: TI functions. Note the three forms of division

Function	Definition
Addition	$R[x] \leftarrow R[x] + R[y]$
Subtraction	$R[x] \leftarrow R[x] - R[y]$
Multiplication	$R[x] \leftarrow R[x] \times R[y]$
Square root	$R[x] \leftarrow \sqrt{R[y]}$
Division	$R[x] \leftarrow R[x] \div R[y]$
Invert	$R[x] \leftarrow 1 \div R[x]$
Divide-by-2	$R[x] \leftarrow R[x] \div 2$

Table 2: TI parameters. Estimated relative to the current hour t of trading.

Parameter	Description
TI type	Weighted Moving Average (WMA), Moving Average (MA) or Value
TI scale	Defines a TI that crosses 0 or TI that crosses price
Period n	Number n of hours in a price history to calculate MA or WMA
Shift m	Price m hours back

notes either: register y content; a price, or; a price m hours back in (relative) time. Register $R[0]$ is assumed to contain the TI result after executing a TI program. The MA type of TI is calculated as (1) whereas the WMA type of TI is calculated as (2), where V_j is a TI price value from the trading data.

$$MA_i = \frac{\sum_{j=1}^{n} V_j}{n} \quad (1)$$

$$WMA_i = \frac{\sum_{j=1}^{n} \frac{V_j}{j+1}}{\sum_{k=1}^{n} \frac{1}{k+1}} \quad (2)$$

The **DT population** is initialized to a fixed size. A DT header declares the following information: DT *score* in pips[2], number of trades and a size of a Stop / Loss (S/L) order in pips. S/L is therefore an example of a task specific threshold which could potentially be evolved. The score and number of trades are initialized with 0; whereas the S/L can be initialized in one of two ways: 1) the S/L is initialized with a randomly selected value between the minimum (s_{min}) and maximum (s_{max}). 2) S/L is initialized with a maximum S/L size. The maximum and minimum S/L are currency pair specific and will be defined in Section 4. Likewise the benchmarking study will consider the degree of utility for each scheme as an experimental parameter.

A DT consists of a variable number of nodes. Each node consists of a conditional statement with either single or dual antecedent tests of the form:

- *if*($X_i > Y_i$) *then else*
- *if*(($X_i > Y_i$) *and* ($X_{i+m} < Y_{i+m}$)) *then else*

where X_i and Y_i can be 0, price or a TI. The *then* and *else* statements reference either: the next node or one of the trading signals: buy, sell or stay. Thus, a DT population is randomly generated with respect to X_i and Y_i scales; albeit under the following constraints:

1. if X_i is 0, then Y_i must also be a TI which crosses 0 and can not be a price or a TI which crosses the price, or;
2. if X_i is price, then Y_i can be also a price or a TI which crosses the price, and can not be 0 or a TI which crosses 0.

Note in the case of a dual antecedent clause, X_{i+m} and Y_{i+m} represent the value of X_i or Y_i respectively, albeit m samples back in (relative) time. FXGP can generate additional TI during DT population initialization if the TI population does not have a TI capable of satisfying the DT initialization constraints. Thus, the DT population size is fixed whereas the TI population size may vary.

3.1.2 Fitness and Selection

The DT fitness is defined as a score in pips over the training records. When TI and DT populations are initialized, FXGP simulates the trading activity for each DT over the training records and stores the score and the number of trades in the DT header. The number of trades is used to penalize the DT score for too high or low a frequency of trading. Moreover, if a DT generates only *buy* or *sell* signals its score is discarded and the DT targeted for replacement. The subset of DT individuals with lowest scores are explicitly identified for replacement cf., a breeder model of selection / replacement. Thus, a fixed percentage or *gap* size of the DT population is replaced per generation. All variation is asexual, thus following parent selection, cloning and variation takes place where either the DT or TI component of a clone can be varied. Following DT selection, any TI individual that no longer receive a DT index are considered ineffective and are also deleted; thus another factor contributing to a variable size TI population.

3.1.3 Mutation

FXGP uses mutation to produce offspring. Only the size of S/L and one DT node or one linked TI can be mutated in each cloned DT. FXGP randomly selects a parent DT, clones it and then (if enabled) mutates the size of S/L of the offspring with probability p_{sl}. After that the target for mutation (TI or node) is selected based on the probability of mutation p_{ti}. A DT mutation is performed by applying one of the following actions: 1) Generate a new conditional function; 2) Increment / decrement shift parameter m; 3) Generate new X_i and Y_i; 4) Switch X_i and Y_i; 5) Switch content of *then* and *else* clauses; 6) Insert new *then* clause content, or; 7) Insert new *else* clause content.

Likewise a mutated TI is first cloned to avoid interfering with other DT employing the same TI. The following parameters and functions of a TI can be mutated: 1) TI type; 2) Period (n); 3) Shift (m); 4) Generate a new function; 5) Delete a function, or; 6) Insert a function, where function insertion or deletion is performed with respect to the TI program size limits (Table 3). Training stops when the specified number of generations (T_{max}) was reached or when the best score in the DT population plateaus for a fixed number of generations, t_{flt} (Table 3). Thereafter a validation cycle is initiated.

[2]'pips' or 'ticks' are the smallest price movement in a currency. In EURUSD, a move of 0.0001 is one pip.

3.2 Validation

The validation process is used to check the quality of the DT–TI population and to select the best DT–TI agent for trading. To do so, FXGP checks the score of every tree in a DT population and if the DT score is greater than $\alpha_v \times$ *best score* it tests the DT. If DT is active the tested tree's counter is incremented. When all DT have been evaluated, FXGP checks the number of the tested DT. If it is greater than $P_{size} - P_{gap}$ then the DT (and referenced TI) with best score on validation assume the role of 'champion' and employed for trading. Otherwise the TI and DT populations are reinitialized and the entire training procedure is restarted i.e., rather than invest more generations in a population which fails under validation we choose to reinitialize and restart the training cycle.

3.3 Trading and Retraining criteria

During FX trading, the following three trading quality criteria are monitored and used to trigger retraining from an entirely new population pair of TI–DT populations:

- The magnitude of a decline in account value as measured from peak to subsequent trough. This is generally referred to as the *drawdown* and characterized in terms of a minimum (d_{min}) and maximum (d_{max}) number of pips;
- A maximum number of consecutive *losses* (n_{loss}); and
- A maximum number of consecutive hours *without trading* activity (n_{nt}).

The basic goal is to characterize when the trading conditions are deemed to represent a 'significant' difference from that of the previous training period. When any quality criteria are exceeded, FXGP stops trading, reinitializes the TI and DT populations and restarts the training-and-validation cycle (Figure 1). Content of the training and validation partitions is taken relative to the point 't' at which the trading quality criteria interrupted trading. Once a new TI–DT champion is identified trading resumes at the point trading was interrupted.

4. RESULTS

The following empirical study assumes FXGP as described in Section 3 as the underlying framework for coevolving TI–DT trading agents. Our interest is in the relative contribution of:

- Criteria based re-triggering of the retraining event (Section 3.3) versus the widely assumed case of continuously evolved trading agents (Section 4.1).
- Significance of including a validation partition. FXGP assumes that the champion individual is identified by a validation partition. However, this also implies that the most recent data is not available for training. We will consider the inclusion and non-inclusion of the validation partition.
- Degree of support for evolving market specific thresholds. In this case we consider two different forms of S/L thresholds (Section 3.1.1). Either a fixed threshold ($s_l = 0$) or thresholds evolved over a market specific spread interval ($s_l = 0.2$).

In the following we develop the framework for continuous re-evolution and then establish the common parameterization assumed throughout the benchmarking study. The specifics of the data source are then characterized. The results of the benchmarking study are then detailed. In all cases we are interested in performance across multiple runs; thus we report the distribution of results rather than a single best case. This latter point is particularly important because it is not known at the start of trading how effective a strategy might be.

4.1 Framework for continuous re-evolution

One of the unique characteristics of FXGP is that retraining is only ever performed when a negative change in trading behaviour is detected (Section 3.3). Conversely, the norm is to perform some form of continuous evolution e.g., [2], [8]. With this in mind, we assume the following framework for a 'rolling window' approach to evolution [8]. The TI–DT individuals are evolved as per FXGP with respect to training and validation partitions N_t and N_v respectively. Trading is then performed for a fixed duration (δ) using the champion trading agent (Figure 2). The caveat to this is that in the case of an open trade by the end of the period, trading is allowed to continue until all open trades are closed, resulting in potential variation in the trading period. After the δ trading period has elapsed, then the training and validation partitions are realigned with the end of the trading period (Figure 2) and the TI–DT populations are either:

1. Utilized as if evolution progressed from the last generation. Any new content assumes the bias established by the pervious cycle of evolution. This scheme reflects the intent of recent practice (e.g., [2], [8]) and hereafter will be referred to as continuous evolution or **ContEv**. Such a scheme naturally reflects a bias towards exploiting previously evolved policies. We also note that current practice is not to employ a separate validation partition to choose a champion trading agent for deployment. Indeed, under continuous evolution, benchmarking revealed that it was not possible to employ the validation criteria from Section 3.2 to deploy a validation partition. Determining the specific source of this remains a topic for future research;
2. Completely reinitialized before a new training–validation cycle begins. This means that any previously evolved individuals are replaced with an entirely new population as per the initial cycle of evolution. This represents a natural alternate case that emphasizes exploration and is similar to the approach adopted in [15]. Hereafter this will be referred to as stepwise evolution or **StepEv**. Unlike continuous evolution, benchmarking did not reveal any problems with the inclusion of a validation partition for stepwise evolution.

4.2 Source Data

The historical rates for EURUSD (1 hour resolution) were obtained from the Forex Historical Data repository.[3] Each 24 hour period therefore typically consists of 24 samples. Sampling at the rate of one hour intervals is conducted to reduce the impact of "trading noise" [9]. We concentrate on

[3]`http://fxhistoricaldata.com/EURUSD/`

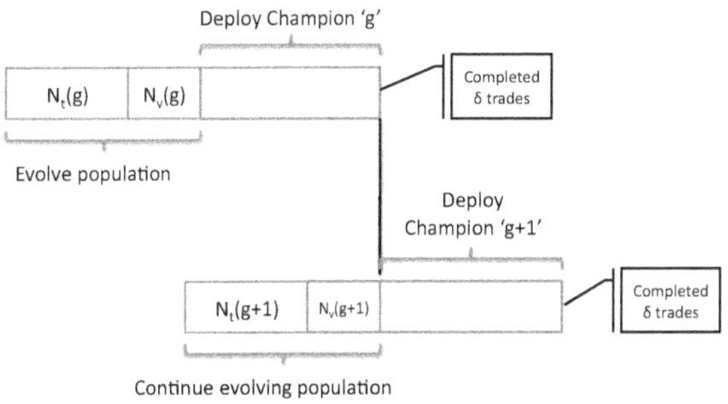

Figure 2: Identifying a new champion trading agent through rolling window. g represents the count of cycles of evolution relative to population content at cycle $g-1$. Trading is performed for a fixed number of cycles (δ) before a new cycle of evolution is performed.

Table 3: FXGP parameters

Parameter	Value
Training period (N_t)	1,000
Validation period (N_v)	500
Probability of TI mutation (p_{ti})	0.5
Max. training generations (T_{max})	1,000
DT population size (P_{size})	100
# DT replaced per generation (P_{gap})	25
Max. nodes (instr.) per DT (TI)	6
Max (Min) Stop/Loss (s_{max}, s_{min})	$(5, 100)$
Validation criteria (Section 3.2)	
Proportion with feasible trade (α_v)	0.95
Plateau detection threshold (t_{flt})	200
Retraining criteria (Section 3.3)	
Max (Min) Drawdown in pips	$(200, 400)$
Max. consecutive losses (n_{loss})	3
Max. consecutive inactive trades (n_{nt})	72

the most widely traded currency pair EURO-to-USD for the three year period July 2009 to November 2012 (or $\approx 17,860$ hrs). Data is described in terms of the following fields: Pair, Date, Time, bid price Open (Open), bid price Low (Low), bid price High (High) and bid price Close (Close).

4.3 Parameterization

Parameters for FXGP are separated into three sets: 1) generic parameters for sizing population, generations and frequency of operator application, 2) those for validation (Section 3.2), and 3) those for characterizing change detection (Section 3.3). All three sets of parameters are summarized in Table 3. Naturally, no claims are made regarding their optimization. Several parameters are then associated with the case of continuous and stepwise evolution of trading agents, Section 4.1. Specifically, the size of the fixed length trading period is varied over three independent experiments: $\delta \in \{120, 500, 1500\}$ or approximately 1 week, 1 month, 3 months. This reflects the lack of support for being able to dynamically trigger retraining. Hereafter these will be identified as *ContEv or StepEv xxx*, where *xxx* denotes the trading period duration. Naturally, all trading agents assume common $N_t = 1,000$ and $N_v \in \{0, 500\}$ parameterizations. Finally, we will also have a baseline TI–DT model in which no retraining is performed after the initial cycle of training. Hereafter this will be referred to as *Static*.

In total there are four frameworks: FXGP, StepEv (stepwise evolution), ContEv (continuous evolution; representing current practice) and Static. FXGP follows the single parameterization of Table 3. StepEv (or ContEv) replace and retrain (or update relative to current population content) after a fixed length trading period, δ, hence the "retraining criteria" of Section 3.3 is replaced by the approach of Section 4.1. As indicated above three different durations for the trading period are considered relative to fixed size training and validation periods. ContEv will only be deployed in a single configuration, on account of the approach to deploying validation partitions from Section 3.2 not selecting champion individuals. However, this also represents the most frequent scenario in which ContEv is deployed e.g., [2], [8]. For FXGP and StepEv we enable and disable validation ($N_v \in \{0, 500\}$) or support evolution of S/L thresholds or not. In the latter case, S/L is either fixed at 100 pips or evolved. This results in 23 experiments, each run over 100 initializations simulating trading activity for the EURUSD currency pair over the *trading period* from January 2, 2010 to November 30, 2012.[4]

4.4 Benchmarking results

Table 4 provides a high level summary of all 23 experiments. The table order reflects the median score in pips over the trading period as collected over all 100 runs. Naturally, there is a close correlation between median score and the percentage of runs that were profitable. Several general trends are apparent:

- Retaining population content between cycles of retraining (ContEv) appears to be detrimental to providing new trading agents capable of reacting to the next cycle of trading. However, neither ContEv nor StepEv appear to match the effectiveness of FXGP (dynamically identifying retraining intervals).

- Both FXGP and StepEv (the latter for trading periods of 1 to 4 weeks) have a strong preference for including the validation partition. Interestingly for the longer trading period under StepEv ($\delta = 1500$) there was no benefit in including a validation partition.

- Enabling the evolution of Stop / Loss thresholds did not result in a general pattern of preference for or against its inclusion. However, it does appear to be useful w.r.t. ordering FXGP.

- In the case of the lengths of trading considered with StepEv and ContEv – $\delta \in \{120, 500, 1500\}$ – the longest trading period was most effective with ContEv, but least effective with StepEv. Further research would be necessary to obtain a clearer picture of the dynamics behind this.

[4]Note that the first population is evolved using data starting from July 2009 in order to support a Jan 2010 start to trading.

- It is possible that any configuration can result in profitable (unprofitable) runs (see 'min' and 'max' columns of Table 4). However, in most cases at least 25% of runs are unprofitable (1st quartile). Given that it is not a priori possible to determine which runs will be profitable over the investment period, this means that it is very important to characterize performance over multiple runs. If only best case runs are considered, then even the static configuration is 'profitable'.
- Training once at the beginning of the three year period and then assuming that the resulting champion individual will be effective clearly does not work. This illustrates that the FX trading task is essentially non-stationary. Naturally, the use of a validation partition is irrelevant as 1 month of validation data is not sufficient for characterizing the following three years of trading when the underlying process is non-stationary.

In the case of the best configured framework – FXGP with validation partition and non-zero S/L threshold – we also plot the trading curves in pips and USD over the total trading period (Figure 3). The USD account assumes an initial balance of \$100,000 and a leverage of 1:100. One pip is worth 0.0001 USD and buying or selling actions are limited to 2% of the account balance.[5] These curves reflect the corresponding best, worst and median scores from Table 4. By way of comparison, investing in a mutual fund over exactly the same period could result in yearly rate of return of 3.95% on the same initial investment (\$100,000); or a gain of \$11,947 by the end of the 3 year period.[6] However, to obtain such a result the mutual fund was selected post investment i.e., once the three year investment is complete; whereas most mutual funds failed to match this level of return. Conversely, even the typical performance of FXGP in Figure 3 better this return.

Figure 4 illustrates the distribution in the ultimate trading outcome for the best configuration from Table 4 i.e., FXGP, StepEv, ContEv and Static as indicated by the †symbol. The FXGP cases (with validation) were the only solutions with 1st, 2nd (median) and 3rd quartile investments that were non-negative. Thus, at least 75% of the runs returned profitable training strategies. Conversely, trading agents evolved under any other approach failed to reach this degree of repeatability. Moreover, this was not achieved at a loss of median or 3rd quartile profitability. Table 5 confirms the degree of independence in the distributions as a student T-test. FXGP is in the worst case independent at the 95 percentile (w.r.t. StepEv) and more than a 99 percentile in the case of ContEv (as typically used when deploying evolutionary trading agents) and Static.

Finally, with respect to FXGP (with validation) we can also assess the frequency of training re-triggering. Figure 5 summarizes the trading interval between the re-triggering of training. The spread of the box plot (internal to the violin) reflects that variation in re-triggering does appear with a median of $\approx$ 200 hours, but a 1st / 3rd quartile spread of $[+140, -80]$; thus indicating that significant tuning of the retraining period is occurring.

[5] http://www.investopedia.com/articles/forex/07/forex_leverage.asp

[6] RBC Global asset management. https://services.rbcgam.com/portfolio-tools/public/investment-performance/

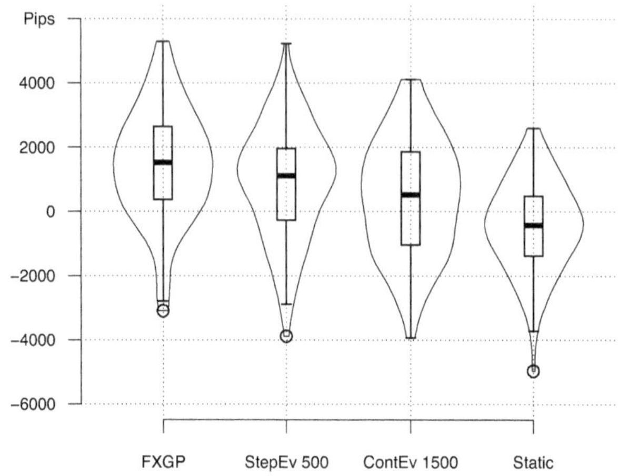

Figure 4: Comparison of 'pips' distribution associated with trading strategies from first ranked FXGP, StepEv, ContEv and Static parameterizations from Table 4. 100 runs per distribution.

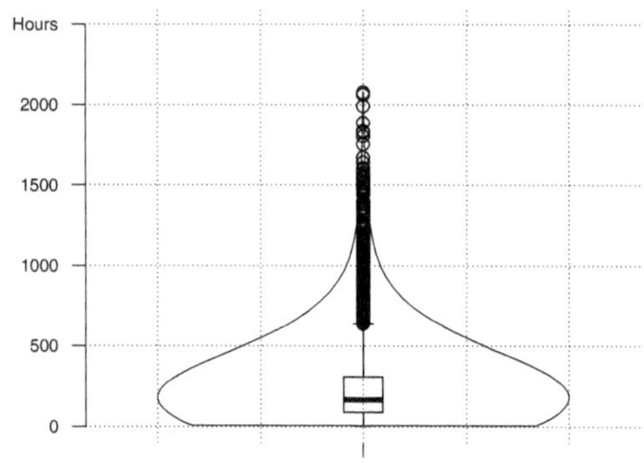

Figure 5: Distribution of intervals between re-triggering of FXGP training. Statistic collected across all 100 runs.

Table 5: *p-values* for pairwise Student T-test of FXGP versus StepEv, ContEv and Static identified by †in Table 4.

FXGP vs.StepEv	FXGP vs.ContEv	FXGP vs.Static
0.0332	6.112×10^{-5}	4.448×10^{-13}

Table 4: Result ranking w.r.t. average pips. †cases illustrated in Figure 4.

Algorithm	Validation (N_v) (500 / 0)	Stop / Loss (p_{sl}) (0.2 / 0)	Num. Profitable runs (%)	Score (pips) min	1st quartile	median	3rd quartile	max
FXGP†	500	0.2	82	-3087.9	383.375	1522.5	2639.525	5298.6
FXGP	500	0	79	-2924.2	296.425	1447	2580.9	5086.1
StepEv 500†	500	0	73	-3879.1	-234.85	1118.3	1947.15	5231.8
StepEv 120	500	0.2	73	-2722.9	-89.3	995.85	1862.975	4403.1
StepEv 500	500	0.2	73	-3200.9	-33.55	922.75	2167.825	4902.1
FXGP	0	0.2	60	-4377.5	-746.05	671.4	1792.35	4682.8
StepEv 120	0	0.2	63	-3659.0	-717.775	580.35	1663.275	3959.7
StepEv 120	500	0	66	-3438.4	-433.05	550.45	1630.375	5795.5
ContEv 1500†	0	0.2	61	-3920.9	-1020.875	534.55	1852.025	4115.7
StepEv 1500	0	0.2	58	-3167.4	-852.825	365.55	1460.3	3624.0
StepEv 1500	0	0	55	-4017.5	-1373.3	302.65	1482.425	3715.8
StepEv 500	0	0	53	-4558.4	-1150.65	169	1275.2	4454.3
ContEv 500	0	0.2	53	-3205.8	-739.5	122.45	1136.85	3553.8
FXGP	0	0	53	-3841.7	-1029.8	66.65	1123.15	4763.9
StepEv 500	0	0.2	52	-3855.6	-938.95	59.2	1416.925	4695.4
StepEv 1500	500	0	50	-4205.9	-1205.95	55.35	1019.05	4049.9
ContEv 120	0	0.2	52	-4135.8	-1099.925	15.3	1372.625	3908.2
StepEv 120	0	0	49	-3051.7	-1194.75	-48.2	1013.55	4043.4
StepEv 1500	500	0.2	45	-4490.8	-1202.225	-68.95	1129.95	4086.9
Static†	0	0.2	38	-4960.9	-1358.375	-421.25	467.7	2602.1
Static	0	0	37	-3775.7	-1531.55	-668.3	780.65	3631.3
Static	500	0.2	23	-5733.7	-2031.125	-804.55	-144.1	3166.5
Static	500	0	23	-5911.1	-2347.125	-1161.7	-109.775	3844.3

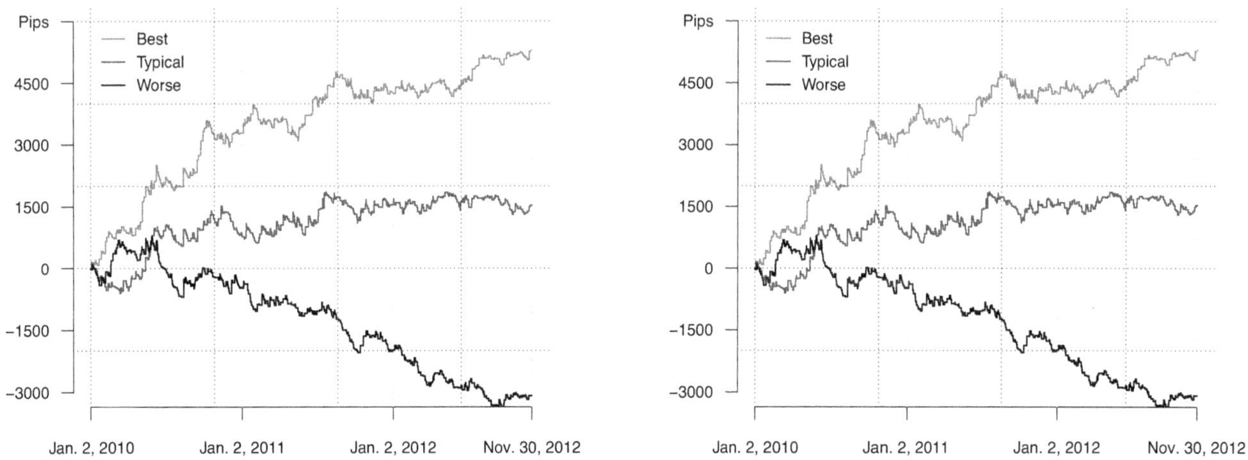

(a) pips

(b) USD

Figure 3: Trading profiles for (a) pips and (b) USD using best configured trading agent: FXGP with validation partition and S/L.

5. CONCLUSION

A benchmarking study is performed to assess the relative value of:

- Selecting a champion trading individual from an independent validation sample of data before deploying as a trader;
- Dynamic re-triggering versus continuous evolution of trading agents;
- Incorporating the evolution of task specific thresholds.

Validation of traders before deployment appears to be of central significance. A previous study pertaining to the use of early stopping criterion in financial applications [13] was not performed relative to streaming data (batch offline learning relative to static training and test partitions was employed). However, the authors did indicate that they believed that care was necessary when determining the criterion for applying early stopping. In this research, the very poor performance of the trader evolved under offline 'Static' training conditions verifies that the task was indeed non-stationary. It was also apparent that using trading criteria to re-trigger training was more effective than 'fixing' retraining at the end of each trading period as in continuous or stepwise evolution. Current practice is to assume the case of training on a continuous basis at the end of each trading period without the use of validation e.g., [2], [8]. This is certainly better than assuming 'static' offline deployment, but appears to be less effective than enforcing a fixed rate of *retraining* from an entirely reinitialized population (StepEv). Conversely, retraining at every sliding window location has been considered [15], but naturally incurs a computational overhead. Introducing retraining criteria provides a potential middle ground.

Part of the reason we see for continuous evolution to fare so badly in this context is that diversity is being compromised. In the monograph of Dempsey *et al.* [2], Chapter 2, various factors are identified as being of particular importance when constructing frameworks to operate on non-stationary domains. One of these was the maintenance of diversity. However, when evolution is performed on a continuous basis (ContEv), there is a natural bias towards exploitation rather than exploration. We do not see continuous evolution as fundamentally limited in this respect, but it certainly appears that the trading domain requires more emphasis to be placed on maintaining diversity than currently appears to be the case. Both of the frameworks that explicitly reset population content before retraining (StepEv and FXGP) avoided this pathology. In summary, rather than assume a specific interface between EC and trading data, the authors suggest that several schemes should be considered in which different exploration / exploitation tradeoffs are explicitly represented.

Acknowledgements

The authors acknowledge support from NSERC and MITACS grant programs.

6. REFERENCES

[1] M. Brameier and W. Banzhaf. *Linear Genetic Programming*. Springer, 2007.

[2] I. Dempsey, M. O'Neill, and B. A. *Foundations in Grammatical Evolution for Dynamic Environments*, volume 194 of *Studies in Computational Intelligence*. Springer, 2009.

[3] M. A. Dempster and C. M. Jones. A real-time adaptive trading system using genetic programming. *Quantitative Finance*, 1:397–413, 2001.

[4] J. A. Doucette, A. R. McIntyre, P. Lichodzijewski, and M. I. Heywood. Symbiotic coevolutionary genetic programming. *Genetic Programming and Evolvable Machines*, 13(1):71–101, 2012.

[5] P. Fernandez-Blanco, D. Bodas-Sagi, F. Soltero, and J. Hidalgo. Technical market indicators optimization using evolutionary algorithms. In *ACM Conference Companion on Genetic and Evolutionary Computation*, pages 1851–1858, 2008.

[6] A. Hirabayashi, C. Aranha, and H. Iba. Optimization of the trading rule in foreign exchange using genetic algorithm. In *ACM Conference on Genetic and Evolutionary Computation*, pages 1529–1536, 2009.

[7] A. Hryshko and T. Downs. An implementation of genetic algorithms as a basis for a trading system on the foreign exchange market. In *IEEE Congress on Evolutionary Computation*, pages 1695–1701, 2003.

[8] H. Iba and C. C. Aranha. *Practical applications of evolutionary computation to financial engineering*, volume 11 of *Adaptation, Learning, and Optimization*. Springer, 2012.

[9] Investopedia, accessed Sept, 2012. `http://www.investopedia.com/terms/n/noise.asp#axzz27d0d2rid`.

[10] P. Lichodzijewski and M. I. Heywood. Symbiosis, complexification and simplicity under GP. In *ACM Genetic and Evolutionary Computation Conference*, pages 853–860, 2010.

[11] A. Loginov and M. I. Heywood. On the utility of trading criteria based retraining in Forex markets. In *EvoApplications*, LNCS, to appear, 2013.

[12] E. P. K. Tsang and J. Li. Eddie for financial forecasting. In S. H. Chen, editor, *Genetic Algorithms and Genetic Programming in Computational Finance*, pages 161–174. Kluwer Academic, 2002.

[13] C. Tuite, A. Agapitos, M. O'Neill, and A. Brabazon. A preliminary investigation of overfitting in evolutionary driven model induction: Implications for financial trading. In *EvoApplications: Part II*, volume 6625 of *LNCS*, pages 120–130, 2011.

[14] N. Wagner, Z. Michalewicz, M. Khouja, and R. R. McGregor. Time series forecasting for dynamic environments: The DyFor genetic program model. *IEEE Transactions on Evolutionary Computation*, 11(4):433–452, 2007.

[15] G. Wilson and W. Banzhaf. Interday and intraday stock trading using PAM GP and linear GP. In A. Brabazon, O'Neill, and D. G. Maringer, editors, *Natural Computing in Computational Finance 3*, volume 293 of *SCI*, pages 191–212. Springer, 2010.

Vehicular Mobility Model Optimization Using Cooperative Coevolutionary Genetic Algorithms

Sune S. Nielsen
CSC Research Unit,
University of Luxembourg
6, rue Coudenhove-Kalergi
L-1359 Luxembourg
sune.nielsen@uni.lu

Grégoire Danoy
CSC Research Unit,
University of Luxembourg
6, rue Coudenhove-Kalergi
L-1359 Luxembourg
gregoire.danoy@uni.lu

Pascal Bouvry
CSC Research Unit,
University of Luxembourg
6, rue Coudenhove-Kalergi
L-1359 Luxembourg
pascal.bouvry@uni.lu

ABSTRACT

A key factor for accurate vehicular ad hoc networks (VANET) simulation is the quality of its underlying mobility model. VehILux is a recent vehicular mobility model that generates traces using traffic volume counts and real-world map data. This model uses probabilistic attraction points which values require optimization to provide realistic traces. Previous sensitivity analysis and application of genetic algorithms (GAs) on the Luxembourg problem instance have outlined this model's limitations. In this article, we first propose an extension of the model using a higher number of auto-generated attraction points. Then its decomposition on the Luxembourg instance using geographical information is proposed as a way to break epistatic links and hence make its optimization using cooperative coevolutionary genetic algorithms (CCGAs) more efficient. Experimental results demonstrate the significant realism increase brought by both the VehILux model enhancements and the CCGA compared to the generational and cellular GAs.

Categories and Subject Descriptors

G.1.6 [**Numerical Analysis**]: Optimization; I.2.8 [**Artificial Intelligence**]: Problem Solving, Control Methods, and Search—*Heuristic methods*; D.2.8 [**Software engineering**]: Metrics—*Performance measures*

Keywords

Simulation optimization; Transportation; Coevolution; Genetic algorithms

1. INTRODUCTION

The emergence of *vehicular ad hoc networks* (VANETs) has opened the door to new *intelligent transportation systems* (ITS) that aim at improving driving safety, infotainment and traffic efficiency. Many research challenges have to be faced, such as the development of new protocols, communication algorithms and applications. In order to develop and experiment VANET dedicated solutions, simulation is a must because of technical, cost and reproducibility constraints. Therefore, realistic simulation at both network and mobility levels are required. Previous works indeed demonstrated that the accuracy of the mobility greatly impacts the network connectivity and performance [6]. In this paper we focus on mobility models which aim is to generate traffic traces specifying each vehicles' origin, destination and route between these.

Mobility models can be classified as trace-based, survey-based or simulation-based. In the first class, traces are obtained from GPS data (e.g.[1]). However they do not represent regular traffic as they are limited to commercial vehicles (e.g. taxis or buses) and cannot be modified to generate phenomena like accidents. The second class, survey-based models, permits to generate traces at the macroscopic level, which is of limited interest for VANET applications. Finally the last class, simulator based-traces, focuses on micro-mobility, i.e. movement is considered at the vehicle level (acceleration, braking, etc.). A recent trend in this field is to combine real-world information such as maps, and statistical data together with microscopic simulation [9, 15].

In this work we focus on the last class, and more precisely on VehILux [11], a simulation-based model that exploits real-world information: geographical map and traffic counts in the considered area. To generate traces from these traffic counts, VehILux relies on a set of probabilistic geographical attraction points to determine destinations. In previous works on the VehILux model for Luxembourg [10], the authors analyzed the model through sensitivity analysis and later optimized VehILux probabilities using three different genetic algorithms (GAs), i.e. a generational GA, a steady-state GA and a cellular GA in [14]. These permitted to outline some limitations of the original VehILux model and previous GAs application: (1) the strong interdependencies between the model parameters, (2) the limited accuracy implied by the low number of attraction areas and (3) the lack of problem knowledge exploitation in the GAs.

This article therefore proposes an extension to the VehILux mobility model, through a more fine grained control over attraction areas of the map. In addition a decomposition of the modified model is defined, in which areas are geographically separated into so-called slices. The performance of a *cooperative coevolutionary GA* (CCGA) exploiting this decomposition is then compared to the GAs used in the previous work.

The remainder of this article is organized as follows. The next section presents the works related to VehILux usage, analysis and optimization. Then the original VehILux model and the proposed modifications are described in section 3. Section 4 presents the evolutionary approach used for optimizing VehILux original and modified models. Sections 5 and 6 respectively describe the experimental setup and contains the analysis of the obtained results. Finally section 7 contains our conclusions and perspectives.

2. RELATED WORKS

The work presented in this article relies on some previous vehicular mobility model development, analysis and optimization, and more precisely on the *VehILux* model [11].

VehILux is a survey-based mobility model that exploits two real-world data sources i.e. a geographical map and traffic counts from the considered geographical area, with the advantage being that such data is widely available and complete (e.g. [3]). In order to obtain mobility traces from this static data, origins, destinations and routes connecting them are generated using the concept of *repulsion* and *attraction* points. The former constitute typical origin points on the map, while the latter represent popular final destinations. The different attraction points are selected using a probabilistic model, i.e. each of them is assigned with a probability of being chosen as a destination.

These probabilities highly influence the accuracy, and therefore realism, of VehILux. In order to quantify this phenomenon, a sensitivity analysis of the model parameters was conducted using FAST99 and Morris approaches in [10]. On the considered instance, i.e. Luxembourg, it was shown that one of the parameters, the inner traffic ratio, has a predominant impact on the fitness, and that all parameters in general have strong interactions. This means that first order effects of parameters are relatively small compared to their combined effect in the model. Furthermore it was shown that the effect of parameter changes is subject to large amount of noise and that no obvious conclusions could be made on 'good' probability ranges, except for one (the inner traffic ratio).

Finding the best set of probabilities of VehILux for a given problem instance (i.e. a geographical area and its corresponding traffic counts) is a hard task and has been modeled as an optimization problem in [14]. The performance of three GAs - generational, steady-state and cellular - was compared on the same Luxembourg instance. The sensitivity analysis results were used to reduce the range of possible values for some variables (i.e. the inner traffic ratio). The results obtained with these metaheuristics have demonstrated the limitations of the original VehILux model. Indeed, all algorithms converged to some low quality solutions, i.e. the delta between the real counts and the counts obtained from the generated traces remains high.

Finally, in [8] the authors proposed to further enhance the realism of VehILux traces with of a new route assignment algorithm, i.e. the Gawron's algorithm [7]. To this end, the best VehILux traces previously obtained using GAs have been used in the SUMO microscopic traffic simulator [5]. This permitted to outline another limitation of the Vehilux model, as in realistic road conditions the simulator is unable to reproduce all the theoretical traffic due to road network

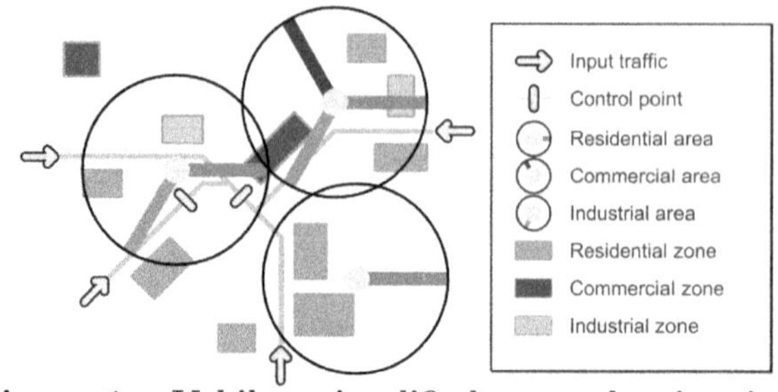

Figure 1: Vehilux simplified map showing input flows, control points, areas and zones.

congestion. One of the reasons is the limited number of attraction areas of VehILux that constrains the generation of traces to a limited set of routes.

The objective of this work is therefore to improve VehILux accuracy by proposing a new route assignment model that uses a larger number of attraction areas and further optimize its parameters through the exploitation of its decomposition capabilities with cooperative coevolutionary GAs.

3. PROBLEM DESCRIPTION

This section describes the problem of flow generation in general and how it was solved in the original VehILux work. Then the improvements of the current work to the model itself and how it is fitted specifically to a coevolutionary algorithm is described.

3.1 VehILux Original Model

The VehILux mobility model relies solely on traffic volume counts and geographical map data. The instance considered in this paper consists of a geographical map of Luxembourg city with its surrounding region as well as real traffic volume counts collected every hour in 28 locations within the region.

Entering points are selected from the 15 locations positioned at the edge of the map, as the problem instance addressed is concerned with commuting hours. These points and their volume counts are used as to initiate the flow of vehicles into the model, referred to as *outer traffic*, while the remaining 13 count locations positioned towards the center of the region are used to validate the quality of the generated traffic flows. In addition to the outer traffic, a certain portion of the traffic is generated inside the map, referred to as *inner traffic*.

From the geographical map data, information about the different zones in the region can be derived, and is used to predict the destinations of the vehicles. This is done by making a destination distribution model for the vehicles by assigning to each zone a probability of being chosen as a destination for a vehicle.

Route assignment concerns the selection of a destination zone for each origin and the selection of a route between the origin-destination pair. The selection of a destination is based on the notion of *zone types* and *attractivity areas* where possible types are *commercial*, *residential* and *industrial*. Each zone type is assigned with an overall global probability of being selected as a destination type, noted P_T where $T \in \{R, C, I\}$ is the zone type. However, zones of the same type can exist in several locations spread over the map where some locations are more popular than others and should hence be associated with a higher selection probability. This property is modeled by the concept of *attractivity areas*, which can cover any smaller or bigger part of the map and are defined independently for each zone-type.

Every zone location is associated with a specifically defined attractivity area, and if not, at least with a default attractivity area.

In Fig. 1 the concept is shown in a simplified example. The top right circular attractivity area contains zones of all three types, as shown by the three wheel spokes which denotes three overlapping areas with the same center and radius. Top left, a commercial zone is shown that is not covered by any specific area, therefore this zone will belong to the default commercial area of the map.

We define $P()$ and $S()$ as probability- and surface-functions respectively, and the probability $P(z)$ of the selected zone z becomes:

$$P(z) = P_T \times P(z.a) \times \frac{S(z)}{S(z.a)}, \tag{1}$$

where $P(z.a)$ and $S(z.a)$ are respectively the probability and surface of the attractivity area $z.a$ to which the zone z was assigned. These probabilities are essentially what we have to tune in order to generate realistic flows with the model.

As mentioned, a fraction of the flow is also generated inside the map. This generation is controlled by the parameter *inner traffic ratio* which is the probability of a trace having its origin located in a random residential zone within the map instead of in an input flow location on the edge of the map. When a destination has been chosen for a given origin, the route between the origin-destination pair is generated using Dijkstra's shortest path algorithm. Speed limits and traffic lights on roads are used to adjust the weight of each road in the generation process.

3.2 Model Modifications

To further enhance the quality of the produced flow, a number of modifications have been implemented and later tested.

3.2.1 Time-frame Reduction

The originally proposed VehILux model instance tackled the entire interval from midnight and 11 one-hour time slots ahead. An attempt to better match the real-life traffic was to look only at the traffic flow of three time-slots, covering peak-commuting hours from 6AM to 9AM. This is motivated by the idea that achieving optimal settings in different time slots would require different model parameters for each time slot. Another motivation is that the simulation is quite CPU-intensive and proportional to the number of vehicles injected into the model. Therefore by reducing the time-frame to 3 hours, we can optimize the model in a little more than one third of the time. The two instances of the model are called the *3-hour*- and *11-hour*-instances respectively.

3.2.2 Additional attractivity areas

The original VehILux instance considered fewer rather large attractivity areas situated around and the center of the map almost covering the city-center. In an attempt to enhance the model performance, we replace the original attractivity areas by many smaller areas placed systematically to cover the city-center as well. This is done by placing areas of the three types, residential commercial and industrial on the map in a grid covering the central region. When doing this an area is only placed if there is actually a zone of the same type within its circumference. This can be seen in Fig. 2, which represents the real Luxembourg instance tackled in our experiments. Some attractivity areas have up to three radial spokes representing the types of zones within the area, and on the other hand blank positions are found where there are no zones. If a zone is situated within the circumference of two or more overlapping attractivity areas, it is simply assigned to the first placed area.

This modification alone should in theory provide grounds for generating much better flows closer to real-life measurements with the drawback being an important increase of model variables to tune. Our expectations are that a coevolutionary algorithm will cope well with this large amount of variables.

3.2.3 Geographical Model Decomposition

In addition to generating attractivity areas systematically, we also group them depending on the geographical location on the map. In Fig. 2 this group assignment is shown by the numeric labels in the center of areas. We group attractivity areas by slicing the map, and the three slice borders or cuts are also seen in the figure.

We expect that optimising an attractivity area probability will have larger impact on the generated flow within its slice, and hence control points in the slice, rather than in other slices.

The main reason for this separation into groups is that eventually, each group of areas will be optimized in their own separate sub-population of a coevolutionary genetic algorithm, as described by Potter in [12]. In [13] Potter describes the ideal case where a problem can be decomposed into independent subcomponents. Here each sub-component could be solved independently without regards to the others. On the contrary when changing interdependent subcomponents it can be described as a "deforming" or "warping" of the fitness landscapes associated with each of the other subcomponents, which is to be avoided.

In addition to grouping the auto-generated attractivity areas by their slice location, the *default* attractivity areas are also divided by slice. The original VehILux model instance had three default areas, one per zone-type essentially containing all zones around the city center. To achieve as much independence between the slices as possible, these areas are also split into a total of 9 areas: three default areas per slice which are then optimized by the sub-population assigned to the slice.

4. METHODOLOGY

In this work, we compare the performance of three different GAs that rely on different population structures (panmictic, cellular and islands) in order to optimize VehILux original and modified models. We present in sections 4.2 to 4.3 the three algorithms used: generational GA, cellular GA and coevolutionary GA. Then the objective function is defined in 4.4, followed by the solution encoding an normalization in 4.5 and 4.6 respectively.

4.1 Generational GA

Generational GAs (genGAs) are a type of panmictic algorithm, i.e. individuals are grouped into a single structure-

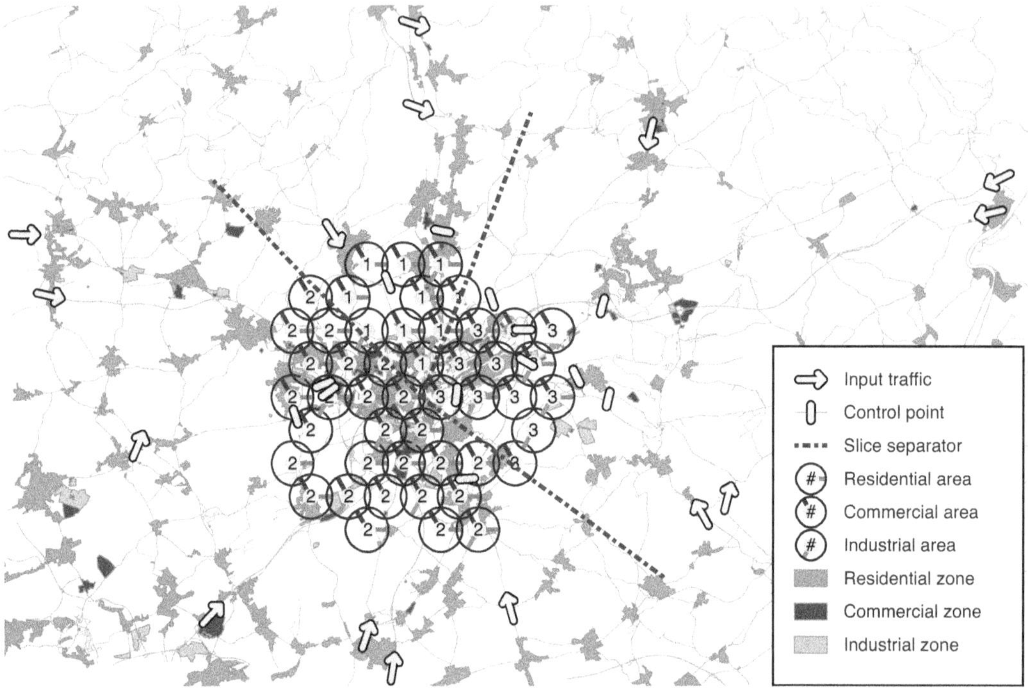

Figure 2: Real Vehilux map of Luxembourg with 102 auto-generated attractivity areas and its decomposition.

Algorithm 1 Pseudo-code of a canonical genGA

```
1: proc Evolve(genga)      // Parameters of the algorithm in 'genga'
2: GenerateInitialPopulation(genga.pop);
3: Evaluation(genga.pop);
4: while ! StopCondition() do
5:    for i←0 to genga.popSize do
6:       parents ← Selection(genga.pop);
7:       offspring ← Recombination(genga.Pc,parents);
8:       offspring ← Mutation(genga.Pm,offspring);
9:       Evaluation(offspring);
10:      Add(auxiliary_pop,offspring);
11:   end for
12:   genga.pop ← auxiliary_pop;
13: end while
14: end proc Evolve
```

less population also referred to as panmixia. Individuals can thus mate with any other individual in the population.

The genGA is a (μ, λ)-GA, where the newly generated individuals are placed in an auxiliary population which will replace the current population when it is completely filled, i.e., when the number of newly generated solutions is equal to the size of this auxiliary population. In our case, the sizes of both the auxiliary and the current population is the same ($\mu = \lambda$).

Algorithm 1 presents the pseudo-code of the generational GA. The population is first randomly initialized (line 2). Each generated individual is then evaluated using the fitness function defined for the tackled problem (line 3). The genetic loop then starts in line 4 until some predefined termination condition is met, e.g. a number of fitness function evaluations. "Parent" individuals are selected using some stochastic selection operator to construct the mating pool (line 6). Genetic variation is then ensured by the crossover (also called recombination) and mutation operators, both applied with some probability, which permit to visit other

Algorithm 2 Pseudocode for a canonical cGA

```
1: proc Evolve(cga)      //Algorithm parameters in 'cga'
2: while ! StopCondition() do
3:    for individual ← 1 to cga.popSize do
4:       n_list←Get_Neighborhood(cga,position(individual));
5:       parents←Selection(n_list);
6:       offspring←Recombination(cga.Pc,parents);
7:       offspring←Mutation(cga.Pm,offspring);
8:       Evaluation(offspring);
9:       Add(position(individual),offspring,cga);
10:   end for
11: end while
12: end proc Steps_Up;
```

search space regions (line 7 and 8). The obtained offspring is then evaluated and inserted into the auxiliary population (line 9 and 10). The offspring population will become the current one once full (line 12).

4.2 Cellular Genetic Algorithm

Cellular genetic algorithms (cGAs) [4] are a kind of GA with a structured population in which individuals are spread in a two dimensional toroidal mesh, and they are only allowed to interact with their neighbors.

A canonical cGA follows the pseudo-code included in Algorithm 2. In this basic cGA, the population is usually structured in a regular grid of d dimensions ($d = 1, 2, 3$), and a neighborhood is defined on it. The algorithm iteratively considers as current each individual in the grid (line 3), and individuals may only interact with individuals belonging to their neighborhood (line 4), so parents are chosen among the neighbors (line 5) with a given criterion. Crossover and mutation operators are applied to the individuals in lines 6 and 7, with probabilities P_c and P_m, respectively. Afterwards, the algorithm computes the fitness value of the new offspring individual (or individuals) (line 8), and inserts it (or one of them) instead of the current individual in the population

Algorithm 3 Pseudocode of the CCGA

```
1: gen = 0
2: for all species_s do
3:    Pop_s(gen) = randomly initialized population
4:    evaluate fitness of each individual in Pop_s(gen)
5: end for
6: while termination condition = false do
7:    gen = gen + 1
8:    for all species_s do
9:       select Pop_s(gen) from Pop_s(gen − 1) based on fitness
10:      apply genetic operators to Pop_s(gen)
11:      evaluate fitness of each individual in Pop_s(gen)
12:   end for
13: end while
```

(line 9) following a given replacement policy. This loop is repeated until a termination condition is met (line 2).

4.3 Cooperative Coevolutionary GA

In addition to the cellular model, another common way for structuring the population of GAs consists of splitting the whole population into several subpopulations. Each subpopulation independently evolves a GA, and exchange some information among them during the run. We study in this paper an algorithm following this model, namely CCGA, a cooperative coevolutionary GA. Instead of considering a population of similar individuals representing a global solution, like classical genetic algorithms, CCGA considers the coevolution of subpopulations of individuals representing specific parts of the global solution.

The CCGA considered here is based on the model proposed by Potter and DeJong [12], in which a number of subpopulations explore different decompositions of the problem. CCGA involves several species independently evolving with a GA a subset of the global solution vector. In order to evaluate complete solutions on the global problem, all subpopulations need to cooperate by exchanging representatives of their respective subpopulations.

A pseudocode of CCGA is provided in Algorithm 3). In the initial generation *(t=0)* individuals from a given subpopulation are matched with randomly chosen individuals from all other subpopulations. A fitness for each individual is evaluated, and the best individual in each subpopulation is found. The process of *cooperative coevolution* starts form the next generation *(t=1)*. For this purpose, in each generation a cycle of operations is repeated in a round-robin fashion. Only one current subpopulation is active in a cycle, while the other subpopulations are frozen. All individuals from the active subpopulation are matched with the best values of frozen subpopulations. When the evolutionary process is completed, a composition of the best individuals from each subpopulation represents a solution of a problem.

Two ways of evaluating the fitness of an individual, referred to as credit assignment 1 and 2 (CCGA-1, CCGA-2), are considered in this work. CCGA-1 evaluates an individual with the best individual of the other subpopulations, as presented in Algorithm 3. CCGA-2 additionally evaluates the individual with a random individual from each other subpopulation and the best fitness among the two obtained is kept. In this work however, the CCGAs are not frozen in turn, but evolve in parallel and exchange individuals at the beginning of each generation.

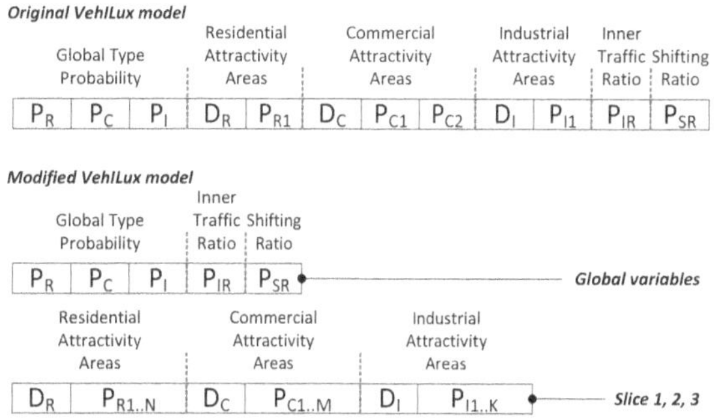

Figure 3: Individual encoding of original and modified model.

4.4 Objective function

As mentioned, the 13 of the 28 real-life traffic count locations positioned closer to the center of the region are reserved to validate the flow generated by the model. The quality of this flow is evaluated by comparing the generated traffic counts with real traffic volume counts at the control points.

The evaluation or fitness function F is the following:

$$F = \sum_{c=1}^{C} \sum_{t=1}^{T} |r_c(t) - c_c(t)|\,, \qquad (2)$$

where $r_c(t)$ is the real traffic volume count at control point c in time slot t, $c_c(t)$ is the number of vehicles at control point c derived from the generated traffic flows in time slot t, C is the number of control points and T is the number of time slots. The smaller this sum of absolute differences between the real traffic volume counts and the estimated ones is, the better the model estimated the real flow.

Traffic flows are generated independently for each one hour time slot t and control point c, i.e. $c_c(t)$, as real traffic count data are typically collected on per hour basis. However, there is no precise departure time related to each origin-destination pair, except the 60 minutes slots (e.g. vehicle i departs from point a to point b between 9 and 10AM). Such a function is proposed in [10]. It assumes that a vehicle passes through a control point at the same hour as it initiates the trip. This is not always true as the vehicle may pass through the control point in the next hour. To include this "delay" effect, a *shifting ratio* parameter is introduced, which defines the ratio of vehicles whose trips are scheduled to start in time slot t, but will pass through the control point in the slot $t+1$. The estimated number of vehicles that pass through control point c within time slot t ($c(t)$) is calculated as follows:

$$c_c(t) = p_c(t) \times (1 - \alpha) + p_c(t-1) \times \alpha, \qquad (3)$$

where $p_c(t)$ is the number of all vehicles generated in time slot t that pass through control point c, $p_c(t-1)$ is the number of vehicles generated in time slot $t-1$ that pass through control point c in time slot t, and α is the shifting ratio.

4.5 Solution Encoding

Fig. 3 shows how the parameters of the model are encoded in the original and modified model respectively. Global zone probabilities are noted P_T where $T \in \{R, C, I\}$ denotes the zone type. Default attractivity areas probabilities are noted D_T and remaining conventional areas are noted P_{Ti} where i is the index. In the modified version, the global parameters are assigned to the first sub-population and the remaining three sub-populations are responsible for optimizing only attractivity areas within their corresponding slice.

4.6 Solution Normalization

As the destination distribution model works by selecting destinations based on their probability, one important requirement is that the sum of all zone probabilities per type are 1. Therefore the probabilities of a slice are normalized according to the total surface of the zones in that slice compared to total surface of all zones. With $P()$ and $S()$ again being the probability- and surface-function respectively, the probability $P(a)$ of each area a in a slice $\mathcal{S}$ of the map $\mathcal{M}$ is normalized as follows:

$$\forall a \in \mathcal{S}, P'(a) = \frac{P(a)}{P(\mathcal{S})} \times \frac{S(\mathcal{S})}{S(\mathcal{M})}. \quad (4)$$

5. EXPERIMENTAL SETUP

This section presents the parameters of the genetic algorithms and problem instances used in our experiments. These are summarized in Table 1 .

5.1 Algorithms Parameters

Three different GAs have been used to tackle the optimization of the VehILux mobility model, a generational GA, a cellular GA and two coevolutionary GAs (CCGA-1 and CCGA-2). The genGA uses a single population of 100 individuals, the cGA a 10×10 population and the CCGAs 4 subpopulations of 25 individuals each. For all algorithms, the termination condition was limited to 8000 fitness function evaluations, due to the computationally heavy fitness evaluation. The recombination operator (the single point crossover—SPX) was used with the probability $p_c = 1.0$. The uniform mutation operator was applied with the probability $p_m = \frac{1}{chrom\_length}$. The binary tournament was used for the selection of the two parents except for the cGA where one parent is the central individual. Other cGA specific parameters are the neighborhood, we used C9 (9 closest individuals measured in Manhattan distance), and the replacement strategy. Finally, all the obtained results are averaged over 30 independent runs.

5.2 Problem Instances Parameters

In order to evaluate the VehILux mobility model, simulations have been based on a detailed map of Luxembourg from OpenStreetMap [2]. The considered area surface is 1700 square kilometers (47×36 kilometers). Traffic volume counts from 28 locations were obtained from [3]. 15 locations were selected as entering points and 13 as control points (see Fig. 2). For each control point, values corresponding to each hour were taken. Two different instances have been tackled, the 12 hours that was used in [14] to optimize the original VehILux model, and a new smaller instance of only 3 hours. During this period, i.e. morning hours, most of the travel involves commuting, therefore, the entering points are selected from the locations positioned at the edges of the map. Three zone types are defined: *residential*, *commercial* and *industrial*. Information about the number, position and surface of these zones was extracted from the OpenStreetMap.

Table 1: Algorithms and VehILux parameters

Genetic Algorithms	Population size	100 (genGA) 10 x 10 (cGA) 4 x 25 (CCGA)
	Termination Condition	8000 function evaluations
	Number of runs	30
	Selection	Binary tournament (BT) BT + Center individual (cGA)
	Neighborhood	C9 (cGA)
	Replacement Strategy	replace if better (cGA)
	Crossover operator	SPX, p_c=1.0
	Mutation operator	Uniform, $p_m = \frac{1}{chrom\_length}$
VehILux	Simulation area	1700 km^2 (47 x 36 km)
	Number of entering points	15
	Number of control points	13
	Simulated time periods	12AM–11AM (11 time slots) 6AM–9AM (3 time slots)

6. NUMERICAL RESULTS

In this section we present the results of our experiments and demonstrate the performance increase obtained thanks to the proposed modifications of the model. The results are discussed and compared for four different algorithms: GenGA, cGA, CCGA-1 and CCGA-2. We included CCGA-2 because of its increased explorative characteristics, in order to estimate its performance on the more challenging 11−hour instances. For each experiment with CCGA-1 and CCGA-2 on the modified model, we included experiments where the attractivity areas to sub-populations are randomly assigned (CCGA-1 shfl and CCGA-2 shfl). The objective is to evaluate the advantage of the problem decomposition based on geographical information.

Experimental results are summarized in Tables 2 and 3 showing best and average fitness with standard deviation for all algorithms. Additionally, for each problem instance, the overall best result and best average fitness among the algorithms is shown in bold font. Statistical confidence in our comparisons is assessed by performing the Wilcoxon test [16]. Finally convergence plots are presented in Fig. 4 to 7.

6.1 The 11-hour Instance

We start out by showing the results of the 11−hour instance, with convergence plots in Fig. 4 and 5 which is also the scenario used in previous works. A first straightforward conclusion is that the modified model is significantly better: in general almost 4000 points with a standard deviation 20 times less - regardless of the algorithm used.

When looking at the original model with 12 alleles we notice that the best result and best convergence is achieved with the CCGA-1, but that the best average is achieved with a regular GenGA. However, based on the Wilcoxon test, statistical confidence in this difference is only true between GenGA and CCGA-2. The latter being also significantly worse than the CCGA-1.

For the 107 alleles in the modified model, the coevolutionary algorithms seem to have an advantage in general, here Wilcoxon indicates that the CCGAs are both significantly better than all other GAs. The CCGA-1 algorithm is again superior in convergence and final result, but the explorative features of CCGA-2 almost allows it to catch up towards the 8000th evaluation.

Table 2: Summary of results for the 11-hour model

	Algorithm	*Bestfitness*	*Avg.fitness*
Modified model	GenGA	10602	$10803.000_{\pm 129.813}$
	cGA	10426	$10838.367_{\pm 157.585}$
	CCGA-1	**10320**	$\mathbf{10716.533}_{\pm 280.271}$
	CCGA-2	10419	$10722.333_{\pm 251.953}$
	CCGA-1 shfl	10415	$11024.667_{\pm 429.214}$
	CCGA-2 shfl	10558	$11072.933_{\pm 332.150}$
Org. model	GenGA	14330	$\mathbf{14427.667}_{\pm 55.079}$
	cGA	14326	$14441.500_{\pm 76.905}$
	CCGA-1	**14250**	$14431.833_{\pm 106.041}$
	CCGA-2	14312	$14484.833_{\pm 96.905}$

Table 3: Summary of results for the 3-hour model

	Algorithm	*Bestfitness*	*Avg.fitness*
Modified model	GenGA	3007	$3272.367_{\pm 136.323}$
	cGA	2961	$3207.500_{\pm 109.123}$
	CCGA-1	**2884**	$\mathbf{3189.700}_{\pm 145.070}$
	CCGA-2	2927	$3227.200_{\pm 138.607}$
	CCGA-1 shfl	3006	$3303.900_{\pm 158.914}$
	CCGA-2 shfl	3007	$3330.200_{\pm 210.293}$
Org. model	GenGA	4869	$4954.633_{\pm 43.615}$
	cGA	4865	$4950.800_{\pm 53.351}$
	CCGA-1	**4848**	$\mathbf{4933.067}_{\pm 86.745}$
	CCGA-2	4864	$4990.733_{\pm 99.371}$

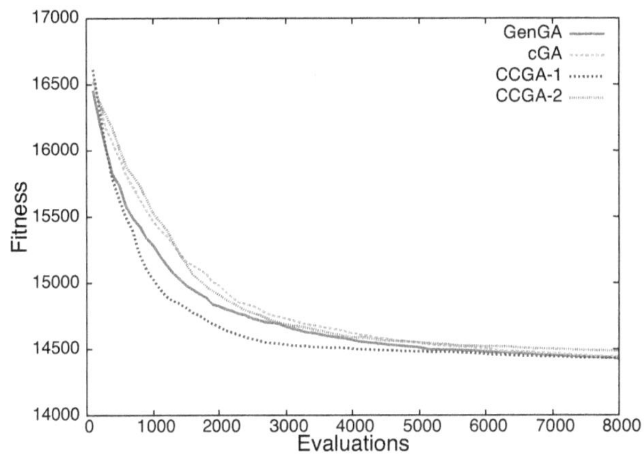

Figure 4: Convergence of the 11–hour original model.

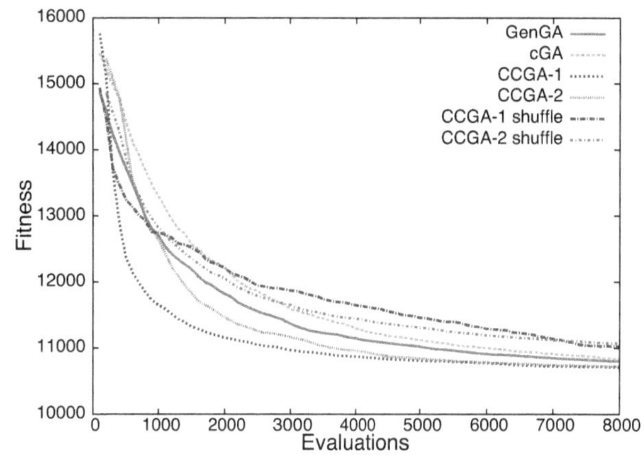

Figure 5: Convergence of the 11–hour modified model.

6.2 The 3-hour Instance

Table 3 shows the same experimental results as in Table 2, for the shorter 3–hour time-frame and with corresponding convergence plots in Fig. 6 and 7. The Wilcoxon tests indicate less difference amongst the algorithms in the modified model, and the only significant conclusion is that CCGA-1 is significantly better than GenGA. CCGA-1 still provides the overall best solution with 2884. We expect this is due to the less complex nature of the problem with a reduced number of time slots.

On the original model however, CCGA-1 is significantly better than all other algorithms, even CCGA-2 according to the Wilcoxon tests. In terms of initial convergence and best results achieved, the CCGA-1 is dominating in both original and standard models with 3– and 11–hour instances.

6.3 Comparing 3h- and 11h- Instances

To compare the best results achieved in the 3– and 11–hour instances better, we calculate the ratio of the best found individuals of the two models to the total flow injected into the model. The total number of vehicles injected for 3– and 11– hour instances respectively are 17342 and 46121. This results in the ratios 16,63% and 22,38% for the best found results of 2884 and 10320. Clearly the shorter time-frame allows the algorithms to fit the flow better.

6.4 Shuffled vs. grouped sub-populations

Another important aspect to study was the effect of grouping attractivity areas and assign them to sub-populations based on their geographic location in the model, i.e. model knowledge based decomposition. For both 3– and 11–hour instances we observe noticeable worse results when the sub-populations are shuffled. Considering the average fitness, the shuffled model represents the worst results for both instances, which is also the case for the best found solutions, except the 3–hour model where it represents the *2nd* worst. Overall the average performance of the CCGA-1 algorithm becomes 3.58% and 2.88% worse for the 3– and 11–hour shuffled models respectively and Wilcoxon tests indicate that the shuffled CCGA-1 is significantly worse than any non-shuffled version. Further the experiments with shuffled variables, have the highest variation in their final results indicating that some decompositions have been very unfavorable. These observations all underline the advantage of the proposed decomposition of the model into geographically determined slices each optimized by their respective coevolutionary sub-population.

7. CONCLUSIONS AND PERSPECTIVES

In this paper we presented a number of changes to the VehILux mobility model to firstly make the model more suitable for optimization with a Cooperative Coevolutionary Genetic Algorithm (CCGA), secondly to increase the solution quality in general. To reduce epistatic links among coevolving sub-populations, model knowledge is used to decompose the variables and group them according to geographical locations in the model. This effort was shown to have significant impact when comparing the same experiments to a randomized decomposition. By shuffling members of the sub-populations the performance of the CCGA-1 algorithm

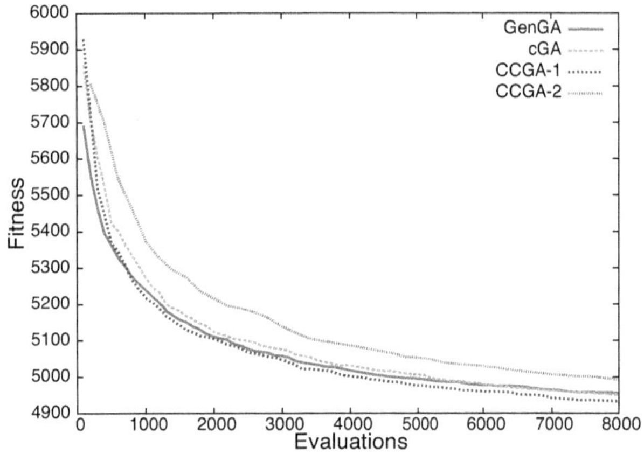

Figure 6: Convergence of the 3−hour original model.

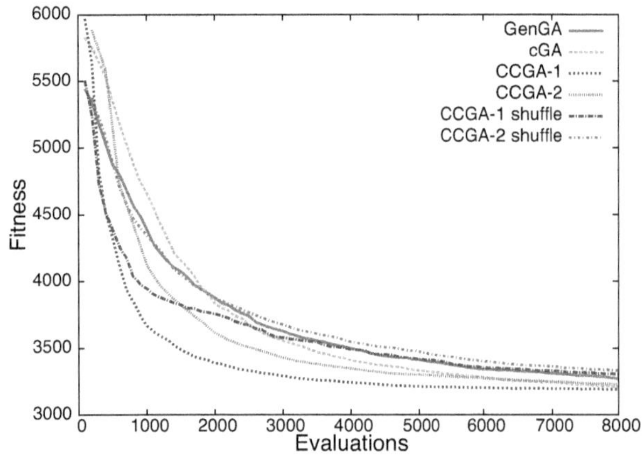

Figure 7: Convergence of the 3− hour modified model.

on average becomes 3.58% and 2.88% worse for the 3− and 11−hour models, with an additional increase in deviation of results indicating bad worst-case performances. As the Wilcoxon tests further confirm that results are statistically significantly better applying the intelligent decomposition by means of model knowledge, we succeeded in reaching the goal set for this work.

By optimizing the model for a shorter time-span, we also reduced the mismatch compared to the total flow from 22, 38% to 16, 63%. The modified model with added attractivity areas was able to decrease the mismatch in flow compared to the original model by 40.5% and 27.6% for the 3− and 11−hour instances respectively.

Future work will be focused on proposing an adaptive control of the mobility models simulation precision from the algorithm's point of view. Finally the newly generated traces will be used in the SUMO microscopic simulator and compared to the original model accuracy.

8. ACKNOWLEDGMENTS

This work has been funded by the UL-EvoPerf project. Sune S. Nielsen acknowledges the support of the National Research Fund of Luxembourg (FNR), with the AFR contract no. 1356145. Experiments presented in this paper were carried out using the HPC facility of the University of Luxembourg.

9. REFERENCES

[1] The cabspotting project. http://cabspotting.org/.

[2] OpenStreetMap project. http://www.openstreetmap.org/.

[3] Traffic volume counts in Luxembourg, Luxembourg ministry of transportation, [online]. http://www.pch.public.lu/trafic/comptage/index.html.

[4] E. Alba and B. Dorronsoro. *Cellular Genetic Algorithms.* Operations Research/Compuer Science Interfaces. Springer-Verlag Heidelberg, 2008.

[5] M. Behrisch, L. Bieker, J. Erdmann, and D. Krajzewicz. SUMO - Simulation of Urban MObility: An Overview. In *Proc. 3rd International Conference on Advances in System Simulation, SIMUL*, pages 63–68, Spain, 2011.

[6] T. Camp, J. Boleng, and V. Davies. A survey of mobility models for ad hoc network research. *Wireless Communications and Mobile Computing*, 2(5):483–502, 2002.

[7] C. Gawron. An iterative algorithm to determine the dynamic user equilibrium in a traffic simulation model. *International Journal of Modern Physics C*, 9(3):393–407, 1998.

[8] A. Grzybek, G. Danoy, and P. Bouvry. Generation of realistic traces for vehicular mobility simulations. In *Proceedings of the second ACM international symposium on Design and analysis of intelligent vehicular networks and applications*, DIVANet '12, pages 131–138, New York, NY, USA, 2012. ACM.

[9] V. Naumov, R. Baumann, and T. Gross. An evaluation of inter-vehicle ad hoc networks based on realistic vehicular traces. In *7th ACM international symposium on Mobile ad hoc networking and computing*, MobiHoc '06, pages 108–119, 2006.

[10] Y. Pigné, G. Danoy, and P. Bouvry. Sensitivity analysis for a realistic vehicular mobility model. In *ACM international symposium on Design and analysis of intelligent vehicular networks and applications (DIVANet 2011)*, pages 31–38. ACM, 2011.

[11] Y. Pigné, G. Danoy, and P. Bouvry. A vehicular mobility model based on real traffic counting data. In *Proc. 3rd International Workshop on Communication Technologies for Vehicles (Nets4Cars 2011)*, volume 6596, pages 131–142. Springer, LNCS, 2011.

[12] M. Potter and K. De Jong. A cooperative coevolutionary approach to function optimization. In *Parallel Problem Solving from Nature (PPSN III)*, pages 249–257. Springer, 1994.

[13] M. A. Potter. *The design and analysis of a computational model of cooperative coevolution.* PhD thesis, 1997.

[14] M. Seredynski, G. Danoy, M. Tabatabaei, P. Bouvry, and Y. Pigné. Generation of realistic mobility for vanets using genetic algorithms. In *IEEE Congress on Evolutionary Computation*, pages 1–8. IEEE, 2012.

[15] S. Uppoor and M. Fiore. Large-scale urban vehicular mobility for networking research. In O. Altintas, W. Chen, and G. J. Heijenk, editors, *VNC*, pages 62–69. IEEE, 2011.

[16] F. Wilcoxon. Individual comparisons by ranking methods. *Biometrics Bulletin*, 1(6):80–83, 1945.

Hybrid POMDP based Evolutionary Adaptive Framework for Efficient Visual Tracking Algorithms

Yan Shen
Inha University
yeon651@gmail.com

Sarang Khim
Inha University
sarang.khim@gmail.com

Won Jun Sung
Inha University
memorise8@gmail.com

Sungjin Hong
Inha University
sjhong0117@gmail.com

Phill Kyu Rhee
Inha University
pkrhee@inha.ac.kr

ABSTRACT

This paper presents an evolutionary and adaptive framework for efficient visual tracking based on a hybrid POMDP formulation. The main focus is to guarantee visual tracking performance under varying environments without strongly-controlled situations or high-cost devices. The performance optimization is formulated as a dynamic adaptation of the system control parameters, i.e., threshold and adjusting parameters in a visual tracking algorithm, based on the hybrid of offline and online POMDPs. The hybrid POMDP allows the agent to construct world-belief models under uncertain environments in offline, and focus on the optimization of the system control parameters over the current world model in real-time. Since the visual tracking should satisfy strict real-time constraints, we restrict our attention to simpler and faster approaches instead of exploring the belief space of each world model directly. The hybrid POMDP is thus solved by an evolutionary adaptive framework employing the GA (Genetic Algorithm) and real-time Q-learning approaches in the optimally reachable genotype and phenotype spaces, respectively. Experiments were carried out extensively in the area of eye tracking using videos of various structures and qualities, and yielded very encouraging results. The framework can achieve an optimal performance by balancing the tracking accuracy and real-time constraints.

Categories and Subject Descriptors

D.I.4 [IMAGE PROCESING AND COMPUTER VISION]: Scene Analysis – *tracking.*

Keywords

Visual tracking, genotype, phenotype, GA, real-time Q-learning

1. INTRODUCTION

Visual tracking algorithm deals with the problem of object motion estimation. Even though many successful and accurate object tracking approaches have been proposed in recent years [1], they frequently encounters serious performance degradations, i.e., cannot observe the object of interest well [2] since image appearances are sensitive to the changes in objects and environments such as object scales and shapes, illuminations, background clutters and occlusions. The challenge is to handle the sensitivities[3] since fixed object appearances and illuminations and static backgrounds cannot be assumed in most cases. The problem of the appearance uncertainty was tackled by adaptive template tracking approaches, generative model, environment model, adaptive discriminative trackers, and TLD framework [4]. Adaptation on the changes in appearances or observational models, however, is not straightforward since a search space of tracking algorithm optimization is intractable in general.

Intuitive rationale of our optimization framework of adaptive visual tracking based on the *POMDP* is that the agent aims to decide the state representing best system control parameters to optimize tracking performance relying on environments. The agent must struggle with the uncertainty under varying environments. Since the image quality information is only partially observable, the system control parameters are determined by the trial-and-errors relying upon experience and domain knowledge. Solving the uncertainty in visual tracking can be modeled as a sequential decision problem of system control parameters using *Markov* Decision Processes (*MDPs*) [5]. The agent can optimize a visual tracking algorithm more efficiently by adjusting the system control parameters based on its past actions and observations. If the agent can keep track of all the histories, the performance of the visual tracking algorithm can be optimized, but solving the uncertainty in this way is a very time-consuming and impractical for realistic applications.

Recently, some hybrid approaches combining the offline and online methods have been studied as effective and promising solutions for large-scale *POMDPs* [6], [8], [9], [10]. The offline algorithm explores the entire belief space with rough precision and the online algorithm searches on limited horizons with high precision retaining real-time constraints. Approaches balancing the offline and online policy computations are found in [11]. The policy approximation in the *POMDPs* can be either a single model based on a posterior belief or multiple models based on the concept of model-uncertainty [12]. In [13], a single model is derived from the posterior belief and followed that model's optimal policy for a fixed period. The multiple model sampling and action selection based on a vote or a stochastic forward search can be found in [14]. The full model-uncertainty *POMDP* approach is studied in [15].

In this paper, an evolutionary and adaptive framework for efficient visual tracking is formulated as a domain-specific *POMDP* by taking advantage of the hybrid of offline and online *POMDP* formulation. The hybrid *POMDP* approach provides a rich and efficient framework to overcome the limitations of the state-of-the-art for the visual tracking in stochastic partially observable domains due to varying environments without strongly-controlled situations or high-cost devices. The performance optimization of visual tracking is formulated as a dynamic adaptation of the system control parameters, i.e., thresholds and adjusting parameters. The hybrid *POMDP* allows to construct world-belief models which have an important role in improving the scalability under varying environments in offline, and to optimize the system control parameters of the visual tracking algorithm in online. The computational advantages become clear since the huge search space is localized in the offline learning, and only the focused space of the current world belief model is explored in online. However, searching directly over a local belief space is still intractable and requires strict real-time constraints.

The hybrid POMDP is discussed in Section 2. In Section 3, the evolutionary adaptive framework for efficient visual tracking algorithms is presented. The genotype and phenotype leaning algorithms are discussed for solving the hybrid POMDP in Section 4. The computational experiments and the main results are discussed in Section 5 and 6, and the conclusion and the future direction are discussed in Section 7.

2. HYBRID POMDP

This section presents the hybrid *POMDP* that solves the optimization problem of the visual tracking as the sequential decision process of the system control parameters influenced by the uncertainty from environments. The state space of the hybrid *POMDP* is defined as the joint space of the system control space and the image-quality space. The agent can solve the uncertainty by deciding which action is beneficial. However, the tracking can hardly be solved in real-time using a standard *POMDP* approach since the belief space B grows exponentially with the number of states |S|. Instead of search the belief space directly, the joint space of probability distributions of the state transitions, observations, and rewards determine a world-belief model. It is used to localize the search space using the prior domain knowledge of the visual tracking uncertainty. The state of standard *POMDPs* are observed in a single model. Unlike standard *POMDP*s, the transition dynamics of the hybrid *POMDP* can concentrate on local states relying on the current *world-belief* model. The proposed method might be less accurate in the tracking owing to the additional approximation, but the computational advantage for satisfying real-time constraints is obvious.

The hybrid *POMDP* is formulated as a tuple $\{S, A, O, T, \Omega, R, \gamma\}$. The state space is defined as the joint of two heterogeneous spaces: i) the system control parameter space of the visual tracking, and ii) the image-quality space influenced from varying environments. The state space S has a finite set of joint states that are not observable completely. Each state has factors that allow us to encode the aspects of the system control parameters and input image-quality. The joint state can also provide for efficient learning and inference with less effort since training data can be aggregated for more relevant aspects of the environment. Formally, the state space is a joint set of the system control space X from the visual tracking algorithm and image-quality space Y from the environment. That is, $S = X \times Y$ with $X = \{X_1, \ldots, X_L\}$ and $Y = \{Y_1, \ldots, Y_M\}$ are the sets of random variables in the system control space and image-quality space, respectively. The domain of possible values for a random variable X_i is denoted by D_i, and that for a random variable Y_j is denoted by E_j. A system control state is defined by assigning a value to each variable X_i, denoted by $x = \{X_1 = x_1, \ldots, X_L = x_L\}$ where $x_i \in D_i$, where X_i denotes a threshold value or a system parameter in the visual tracking algorithm. Similarly, an image-quality state is defined by assigning a value to each variable Y_j, denoted by $y = \{Y_1 = y_1, \ldots, Y_M = y_M\}$ where $y_j \in E_j$. Image-quality space Y represents an image-quality measure affected by environment. The image-quality state is represented by the factors, e.g., Y_1 as lighting direction, Y_2 as brightness, Y_3 as contrast, Y_4 as spectral composition, and Y_5 as camera angle. The state S in the joint space S is denoted by

$$s = \{(\{x_i\}_{i=1}^{L}, \{y_j\}_{i=1}^{M}) \mid x_i \in D_i, y_j \in E_j\} \quad (1)$$

where each dimension of $s \in S$ is a scalar that represents some aspect of the agent's environment. Note that the agent can change the system control parameters in the visual tracking algorithm, but cannot change the image-quality. Obviously, the image-quality is not computable or it is at least intractable using the state-of-the-art technology. Since the true value of the image-quality is only partially observable, the joint state s is also partially observable even though the exact system control parameters are observable by the agent.

Action space A is defined as a finite set of actions available at each state, and $a \in A(s_t)$ indicates an movement in the state space S, which indicates a decision of adjusting the thresholds/system parameters of the visual tracking algorithm at time-step t. Let $a_t = [\varsigma_{t,1}, \ldots, \varsigma_{t,L}]$ be an action at time-step t, where $\varsigma_{t,j}$ is $-d_1$, 0, or $+d_2$ meaning that the decrement of d units, stationary, the increment of d units in the ith normalized index of the system control parameter at time-step t.

The transition probability function T models the uncertainty on the future state of the visual tracking algorithm, and is assumed to satisfy the *Markov* property. Given the joint state of the current system parameter state and an image-quality state $s = (x, y)$ and an action a, it specifies the probability of moving from s and to a next state s'. The state transition probability function, $T: S \times A \times S \mapsto [0,1]$ defines a probability distribution over the next state s':

$$\begin{aligned} T_S(s, a, s') &= P(s_{t+1} = s' \mid s_t = s, a_t = a) \\ &= P(x_{t+1} = x', y_{t+1} = y' \mid x_t = x, y_t = y, a_t = a) \\ &= P(x_{t+1} = x' \mid x_t = x, a_t = a) \cdot P(y_{t+1} = y' \mid y_t = y) \quad (2) \end{aligned}$$

where $\Sigma_{s' \in S} T(s, a, s') = 1$.

The image-quality states are *latent variables* since they are not directly observed but are rather indirectly from other variables that are observed. We approximate the image-quality states by the image-quality labels. An image-quality label, denoted by ϕ is measured by the image-quality analysis methods [18], [19]. Observation o is defined over the observation space O is the joint space of the system performance space and the image-quality label space, i.e., $O = \{\tau, \upsilon, \phi\}$ where τ , υ and ϕ are the observations of the tracking accuracy, speed, and image-quality label, respectively. Observation probability function, $\Omega : S \times A \times O \mapsto [0,1]$ defines a probability distribution over the observation, and is given as follows:

$$\Omega(s', a, o') = P(o'_\tau, o'_\upsilon, o'_\varphi \mid o_\tau, o_\upsilon, o_\varphi, a_t = a) \qquad (3)$$
$$= P(o'_\tau \mid a)\ P(o'_\upsilon \mid a)\ P(o'_\varphi \mid a)$$

The reward is defined as the function $R : S \times A \rightarrow \ \xi$ using current state s and taken action a denoted by $r = R(s,a)$. It indicates the immediate payoffs incurred by an action. The reward function is measured by the normalized tracking performance, i.e., $r = \lambda_1 \tau + \lambda_2 \upsilon$ where λ_1 and λ_2 are normalization parameters.

Discount factor $\gamma \in (0,1]$ a discount rate used for balancing a tradeoff between short-term and long-term reward. It is interpreted that a reward received (k +1) time-steps later is only worth γ^k times, if it were obtained immediately. Using the reward function and discounted factor, the objective of the hybrid *POMDP* is defined to maximize a measure of the cumulative reward at time-step t, called *discounted expected reward*, in the long-term. i.e., $E\{\sum_{k=1}^{\infty} \gamma^k r_{t+k+1}\}$.

3. THE EVOLUTIONARY ADAPTIVE FRAMEWORK

Most visual tracking algorithms have system control parameters that are sensitive to varying environments. The adaptation of visual tracking algorithm is resolved by adjusting the system control parameters depending upon the environments, observations, and rewards. In this section we will discuss the framework architecture of the evolutionary adaptation and the world-belief models.

3.1 Framework architecture

Image distortions due to varying environments are the primary sources of uncertainty in visual tracking systems. The uncertainty is reduced dramatically if the image distortions are exactly computed directly by analyzing lighting direction, brightness, contrast, pose, viewing angle, and spectral composition. Unfortunately, it cannot be represented in a closed form except extremely simple and controlled environments. Instead of the direct analysis, the uncertainty is tackled by the hybrid POMDP based evolutionary adaptive framework consists of the image-quality analysis, visual tracking algorithm, and evolutionary adaptive modules (see figure 1). The image-quality module gets the image sequence and determines an image-quality label that constitutes the joint space of the world belief models and the system control parameters. The agent learns world-belief models using the *GA* (the genotype evolution) in offline using collected data, and processes the online learning and adaptation using the real-time *Q*-learning approach (the phenotype adaptation). The visual tracking algorithm gets the system control parameters decided by the evolutionary adaptive module and performs the visual tracking mission.

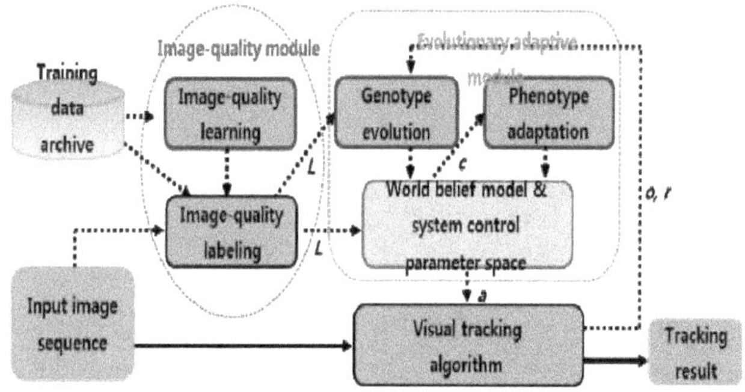

Figure 1. Flow diagram of the visual tracking system using the proposed evolutionary adaptive framework where *a* denotes action, *o* observation, *r* reward, *c* world-belief model, and *L* image-quality label.

3.2 World-belief models

The hybrid *POMDP* carries out both the offline learning in the world-belief space where the online learning for the states relying on the current world-belief model. Limiting the cardinalities of the sets *S*, *A*, *O*, and *R*, the hybrid *POMDP* allows sufficient constraints on the distributions on transition, observation, and reward. The offline learning computes world-belief models in the joint space defined by $WM = T \times \Omega \times R$. Figure 2 shows the difference between the standard *POMDP* and the proposed hybrid *POMDP*.

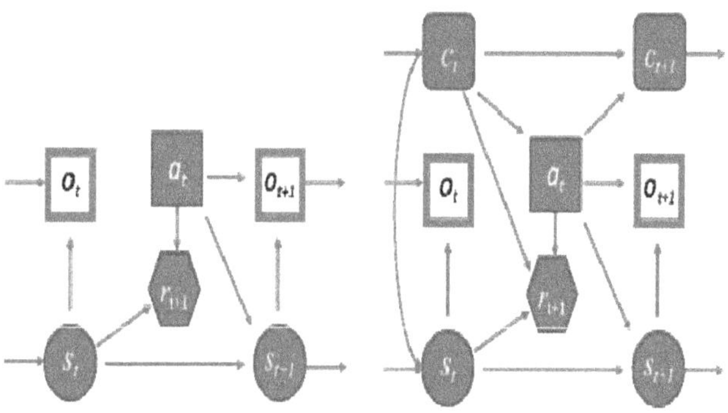

Figure 2. (Left): Standard *POMDP*: (Right): Hybrid *POMDP*.

While the actions are controlled by single world model in a standard *POMDP*, the transition dynamics in the hybrid *POMDP* are affected by both the current state and the current world-belief model. Assuming that the transition dynamics are stationary, the hybrid *POMDP* is converted into multiple world-belief models each of which has a local belief space with the underlying *MDP*. The agent takes advantage of its history of all the interactions with the environment to allow *Markovian* analysis with respect to all partial observations. Formally, let random variables *A*, *O*, and *R* be associated with probability the distributions T, Ω. and R, respectively. Let $A_0, A_1, ..., A_{N-1}$ be a random i.i.d. data set from T, $O_1, O_2, ..., O_N$ from Ω , and $R_0, R_1, ..., R_{N-1}$ from R. For actions $A_0 = a_0, A_1 = a_1, \cdots, A_{N-1} = a_{N-1}$, we have observations $O_1 = o_1, O_2 = o_2, \cdots, O_N = o_N$ and rewards $R_1 = r_1, R_2 = r_2, \cdots, R_N = r_N$, respectively. The collected training data for world-belief model c over WM space is then denoted as $h = \{(a_0, o_1, r_1), (a_1, o_2, r_2), \ldots, (a_{n-1}, o_n, r_n)\}$. The whole training data for all world-belief models is denoted as $H = \bigcup_{c \in WM} \{h\}$. Let $b_{WM}(c)$ denote a world-belief over world-belief model c, and it is approximated as follow [15]:

$$b_{WM}(c) \approx w(c) = \sum w_i \delta(c_i, c) \tag{5}$$

where $\delta(c_i, \cdot)$ is a delta function of world-belief model c_i and w_i indicates the weight associated with c_i. Both the world-belief model and states are partially observable, and the joint belief is factored as

$$b(s, c \mid h) = b_c(s) b_{WM}(c) \tag{6}$$

where $b_c(s) = b(s \mid c, h)$ and is determined by the belief update. The hybrid *POMDP* finds the optimal policy π^* that maximizes the expected discounted return over the infinite horizon. A world-belief $b_{WM}(c)$ has the set of beliefs $b_c(s)$ over states, and the optimal action is decided using the *Bellman* equation:

$$\begin{aligned} V^*(b_{WM}, \{b_c\}) &= \max_{a \in A} Q^*(b_{WM}, \{b_c\}, a) \\ Q^*(b_{WM}, \{b_c\}, a) &= \sum_{c \in WM} b_{WM}(c) R(b_c \\ &+ \sum_{c \in WM} b_{WM}(c) \gamma \sum_{o \in O} P(o \mid b_c(s), a, c) V^*(b_{WM}(a, o), \{b_c(a, o)\} \end{aligned} \tag{7}$$

where $\{b_c\}$ denotes the set of beliefs $b_c(s)$ for all $s \in S$ in $c \in WM$, $Q(b_{WM}, \{b_c\}, a)$ is interpreted as the value of taking action a with a belief over $\{b_c\}$, and $R(b_c(s), a)$ is $\sum_{s \in S} b_c(s) R(s, a)$.

If new random variables a, o, and r are available, the posterior is calculated over each world-belief model and the best world-belief model for the random variables can be determined using *MAP* classification rule. We have, however, a dilemma in that the random variables cannot be calculated before a world-belief model is determined. The dilemma is resolved by approximating a world-belief model based on the joint space of the system control space and image-quality space (Eq. (1)), the world-belief model is computed by

$$P(c \mid (x, \varphi)) = \frac{p((x, \varphi) \mid c, h^{(x,\varphi)}) P(c)}{\sum_{c \in WM} p((x, \varphi) \mid c, h^{(x,\varphi)}) P(c)} \tag{8a}$$

$$\hat{c}_{MAP} = \arg\max_{c \in WM} p((x, \varphi) \mid c, h^{(x,\varphi)}) P(c) \tag{8b}$$

where $h^{(x,\phi)} = \{(x_1, \phi_0), (x_2, \phi_1), \ldots, (x_n, \phi_{n-1})\}$. Note that the dynamics of the feature space of image-quality observations which can be thought as the extension of the clustered state model [14]. The local belief space of the underlying *MDP* is then defined as follows:

$$S_c = \{(\{X_i = x_i\}_{i=1}^L, \{Y_j = y_j\}_{i=1}^M) \mid x_i \in D_{c,i}, y_j \in E_{c,j}\} \tag{9}$$

where $S = \bigcup_{c \in WM} S_c$, $D_j = \bigcup_{c \in WM} D$ and $E_j = \bigcup_{c \in WM} E_{c,j}$. Let the whole value domain of image-quality labels be denoted by $D(\phi)$ and the image-quality label domain of a world-belief model c be denoted by $D(\phi_c)$. The local state s in S_c is denoted by

$$s = \{(x_i, \phi_c) \mid x_i \in D_{c,i}, \phi_c \in D(\phi_c)\}_{i=1}^L \tag{10}$$

where $D(\varphi) = \bigcup_{c \in WM} D(\varphi_c)$. Note that the search space of the underlying *MDP* for each world-belief model can provide more effective in computation by focusing on the local belief space. Furthermore, in a well-defined world-belief mode, we can assume that the factor of the image quality be homogeneous. The state space of well-defined world-belief models can be approximated by the underlying *MDP*:

$$S_c = \{(\{X_i = x_i\}_{i=1}^L \mid x_i \in D_{c,i}\} \tag{11}$$

Now, the optimization of the hybrid *POMDP* is divided into the offline learning for world-belief models calculation and the online learning for a local policy calculation. The hybrid *POMDP* determines the current world-belief model which was constructed by the offline learning, and finds a best policy in the local belief space. The advantage is obvious in that the online learning only considers the local belief space of the current world-belief model. This allows the agent to concentrate on a small set of belief states.

4. THE GENOTYPE AND PHENOTYPE LEANING

4.1 Genotype evolution

The genotype evolution for the adaptive system control parameters is carried out the *GA* approach. The *GA* evolves the genetic codes in the genotype control space constituted from the algorithm structure and its associated thresholds/parameters to optimize the performance of the visual tracking algorithm. The *GA* finds an appropriate genotype scheme, i.e., a genetic code representing an optimal visual tracking for the current world-belief model. Since environment changes are not fully predictable by the *GA* for each world-belief model, the real-time *Q*-learning algorithm, the role of which is an approximation of the online *POMDP*, is employed to seek a precise phenotype manifestation of visual tracking algorithm. The genotype control space of the *GA* is not the same as the phenotype space of the real-time *Q*-learning algorithm, but they are interrelated through the performance optimization in a real world environment.

We discuss how to encode the variation of the visual tracking algorithm into a genetic code so that the genotype control space is efficiently explored for offline optimization. The genotype of the tracking algorithm is denoted by genetic codes, each of which represents an algorithm structure and thresholds/parameters, and thus an optimal visual tracking algorithm that has evolved for each world model is denoted by a genetic code. We explain the encoding process by the simple eye tracking algorithm the structure of which consists of four substructures of the preprocessing, feature extraction, partial *Hough* transform, and *Kalman* filter prediction. The preprocessing is performed by the histogram equalization denoted by *HE*, and the feature extraction by the binarization (*BN*). Finally, the tracking is performed by the partial *Hough* transform (*PHT*) and *Kalman* filter (*KF*). The more details can be found in [17] Let X_{BN} be a parameter generator (random variable), i.e., the threshold value in the binarization substructure with domain D_{BN}, let X_{PHT1} be that of the partial *Hough* transform substructure with domain D_{PHT1}, and so on. The whole possible ensemble of the eye tracking algorithm is then described as follows [17].

$$\Psi = \Psi_{PRE}(HE)) >> \Psi_{FE}(BN(X_{BN}) >> \Psi_{PHT}(PHT(X_{PHT1}, X_{PHT2}, X_{PHT3}, X_{PHT4})) >> \Psi_{KF}(KF(X_{KF1}, X_{KF2})) \quad (12)$$

where Ψ_{PRE}, Ψ_{EE}, Ψ_{PHT}, and Ψ_{KF} denote the algorithm substructures of the preprocessing, feature extraction, partial *Hough* transform, and *Kalman* filter, respectively, and '>>' denotes a serial processing relation between algorithm substructures. Then, the system control parameter space of the eye tracking algorithm is represented by random variables and their domains

$$S^{\Psi}_{Genotype} = (X_{BN}, X_{PHT1}, X_{PHT2}, X_{PHT3}, X_{PHT4}, X_{KF1}, X_{KF2}) \quad (13)$$

where $X_{BN} \in D_{BN}$, $X_{PHT1} \in D_{PHT1}$, and so on. Note that the optimal adaptation of the eye tracking is reduced to the optimization of the system control parameters.

Note that the optimal adaptation of the eye tracking is reduced to the optimization of the system control parameters. Note that the optimal adaptation of the eye tracking is reduced to the optimization of the system control parameters. Genotype encoding format of the eye tracking algorithm in the genotype control space is illustrated in Table 1 [17].

Table 1. An illustration of the genotype encoding format of the proposed eye tracking system and the parameter value domains

	Partial Hough transform				Kalman filter	
X	X_{PHT1}	X_{PHT2}	X_{PHT3}	X_{PHT4}	X_{KF1}	X_{KF21}
No. of bits	4	4	4	4	4	4

Let x_A be a threshold (parameter) of an action unit A. The *pivot* x_A^{Pivot} is defined as the central value of a threshold range of x_A in the phenotype control space. Let $x_{A\min}$ and $x_{A\max}$ denote the minimum and the maximum threshold values of x_A, respectively. The interval of the threshold pivots between adjacent bit vector, $x_{A\alpha}$ is calculated by [17]

$$x_{A\alpha} = \frac{x_{A\max} - x_{A\min}}{2^{\beta} - 1} \quad (13)$$

where β is the number of bits representing x_A (see Table 1). The pivots of the action unit A are derived by adding $\theta_{A\alpha}$ starting from $x_{A\min}$ up to $x_{A\max}$. $x_{BN\min}$ and $x_{BN\max}$ are between 10 and 85 in gray level experimentally.

4.2 Phenotype learning- Solving local belief by real-time Q-Learning

Given a world-belief model, *Q*-learning maintains the *Q*-table which backs up the estimate of the optimal *Q*-values for each feasible state-action pair rather than that of the optimal evaluation function. The *Q*-table for world-belief model *c* is initialized using the collected training data. Q-learning can provide optimal actions by evaluating action–value Q(s, a) to generate sate-action relations. The action-value update is performed by the one-step Q-learning is given as follows [7].

$$Q_{t+1}(s,a) = Q_t(s,a) + \alpha[r_{t+1} + \gamma \max_{a'} Q_t(s',a') - Q_t(s,a)] \quad (14)$$

where s_i' is the next state, i.e., $s_i' = T(s_i, a_u)$.

5. EXPERIMENTS

Extensive experiments show that the hybrid *POMDP* based evolutionary adaptive framework can explore and exploit large search spaces of states and observations efficiently for the visual tracking in real-time performance. Experimental metrics used here are the interval tracking confidence, precision, recall, harmonic mean, and average execution speed. The combination of the offline and online learning is investigated using the variety types of image sequences in properties and structures by exploring various focusing parameters. We also find that the hybrid *POMDP* can take advantage of less data and time to adaptation for optimal performance than a standard single model approach. The experiments have been carried out extensively using *Pentium* 4 with 3 GHz and *Logitech* C910 Web camera.

Given image sequence $V = (I_1, I_2, \ldots, I_N)$, let $X = (x_1, x_2, \ldots, x_N)$ and $Y = (y_1, y_2, \ldots, y_N)$ be the sequences of the ground truth area and tracked area of a target object, respectively. Let ϑ_t denote the proportion of the overlapped to the union of x_t and y_t at the time-step t. If ϑ_t is greater than a matching threshold m, it is defined as a successful tracking in image frame I_t [4]. Formally, the success of visual tracking at time-step t is defined using the constraint of the the matching threshold m as follows:

$$f(x_t, y_t, m) = \begin{cases} 1 & \text{if } \vartheta_t \geq m \\ 0 & \textit{Otherwise} \end{cases} \quad (15)$$

The matching threshold *m* is normally set to equal and greater than 0.5 [4], and we set *m* as 0.6 in the eye tracking experiments considering more strict matching constraints. The *interval tracking confidence* (*ITC*) at the time step *t* is then defined as the mean of successfully tracked adjacent frames between time-steps $t-u$ and $t+u$ as follows:

$$ITC(X,Y,t,m) = \frac{\sum_{k=t-u}^{k=t+u} f(x_k, y_k, m)}{\sum_{k=t-u}^{k=t+u} \|x_k\|} \quad (16)$$

where interval parameter *u* denotes the number of frames in the left or right half of the interval, and used for the smoothness control of the *ITC* curve; $\| x_k \|$ is "1" if there exists a tracking object in frame I_k and it is defined "0" if the tracking object cannot be found in the frame due to a heavy noise. The precision, recall, and harmonic means are also evaluated in our experiments which are based on the evaluation method from information retrieval research [4], [16].

The videos used for the experiments are gathered with varying image-quality in terms of the lighting condition, eye movement speed and pose (see Figure 3). Ten volunteers joined in the test video gathering, and each person recoded eight different types of videos, which has around 1,200 image frames, and thus approximately 140,000 image frames are used. The halves of the videos are used for the offline learning, and the remaining half were used for the test of online eye tracking performance.

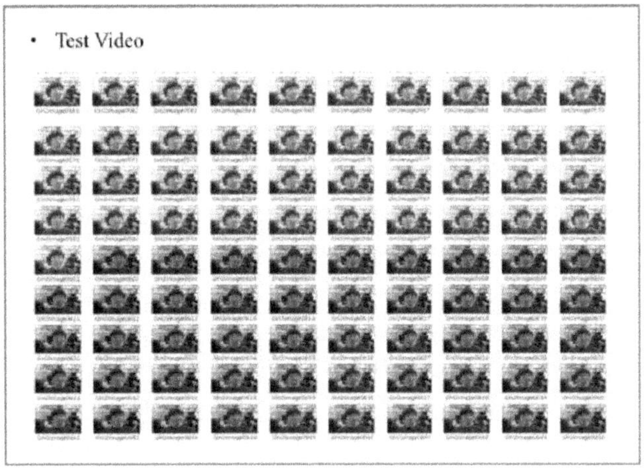

(a)

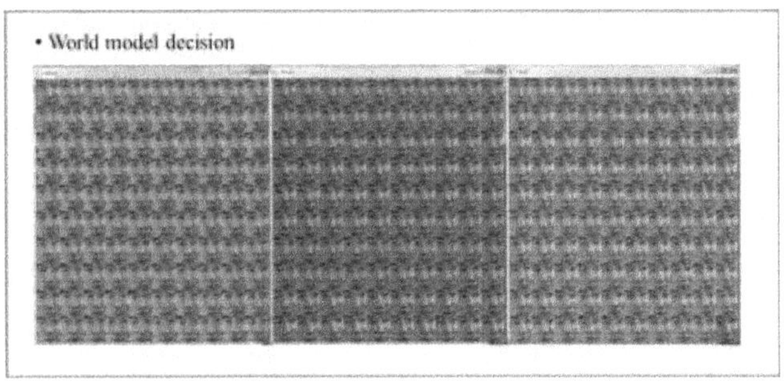

(b)

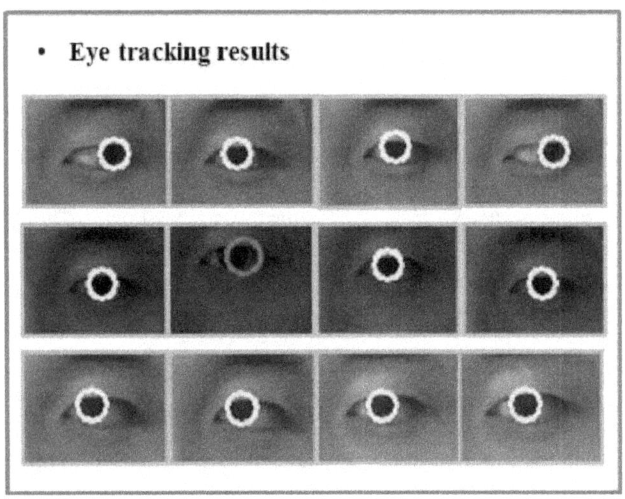

(C)

Figure 3. (a) is illustration of test videos with varying image quality in terms of illumination, eye movement, and face movement and (b) is three-world model decision and (C) part of eye tracking result.

We created five videos characterized as follows: Video 1 includes images with good quality of illumination in the first third of the video, moderate quality of illumination in the second third, and bad quality of illumination in the last third, and face and eye movements are moderate speed in the first third of video, fast speed in the second third, and slow in the last third. Video 2(see Figure 3) includes good quality of illumination, slow face movement, and slow, moderate, fast pose movement. Video 3 has the combination of bad, moderate, bad, moderate quality of illumination, fast, moderate, fast, slow face movement speed and fast, moderate, fast, moderate eye movement of image sequence. Video 4 has images with bad quality of illumination with fast, moderate, moderate face movement and moderate, fast, moderate eye movement. Video 5 has the combination of bad, moderate, good, bad quality of illumination, moderate, slow, fast, slow face movement and fast, slow, moderate, slow face movement of image sequence.

6. Experimental Results

The interval tracking confidence, precision, recall, harmonic mean and execution speed are investigated on the properties and structure types in a variety of image sequences by setting various focusing parameters such as state value horizons and the different world belief models. The initial values and value domains of each system control parameter are determined experimentally. Larger parameter domains are expected to give higher performance, but they usually require more computation overhead. The execution speed is managed not to be decreased much so that too many frames are not skipped considering the continue variation assumption of image-quality. Owing to the shortage of computation resources in our lab, the experiments focused on the adaptation functionalities of the feature extraction in terms of the binarization threshold and the four partial *Hough* transform parameters which mainly affect the tracking performance. Figure 4 shows the comparision of the tracking perfortmance of different world models. One can notice that the five-world model performs the best when the illumination environment changes a lot and single-model performs best when the illumination environment are keep consistency.

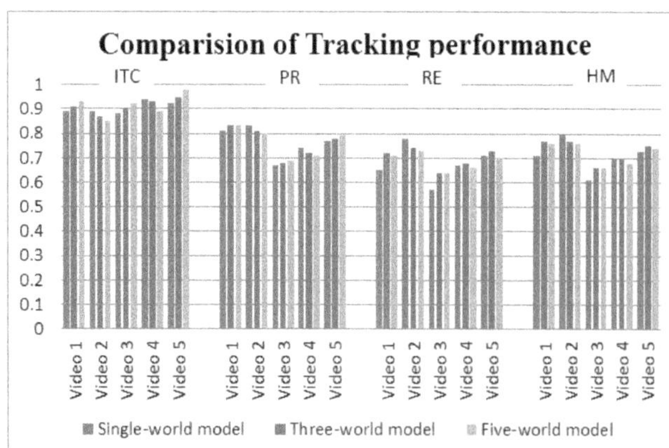

Figure 4. Comparision of the tracking perfortmance of different world models in terms of ITC, PR, RE, and HM indicate the interval tracking confidence, precision, recall, and harmonic mean, respectively, for image sequences with various properties and structure types.

We examined the trade-off the performance and computation overhead by adjusting the maximum number of Q-leaning steps per an image frame. Figure 5 shows the trade-off between the interval tracking confidence and the real-time computation overhead with changing the computation time constraints. The performance improvement can be found with increment of computation overheads. The balancing between the system accuracy and computing time is very attractive for the tackling increasingly large domains.

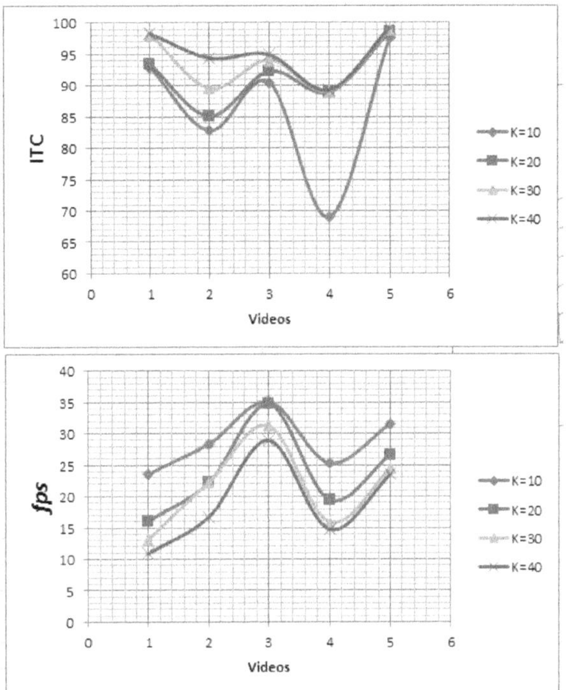

Figure 5. Comparision of the tracking performance with different computation time constraints in the five-world model.

* The real-time Q-learning parameters are set to ε=0.15, α=0.2, γ=0.95 and δ=20; ITC indicates the average tracking rate and K indicates the real-time Q-leaning with maximum k time-steps per frame. *fps* indicates the processed frames per second.

7. Concluding Remarks

We presented a hybrid *POMDP* based evolutionary and interactive framework for efficient visual tracking algorithms without strongly-controlled situations or high-cost devices. The hybrid *POMDP* approach allows for formulate a rich and efficient framework to overcome the limitations of the state-of-the-art technology for the visual tracking in stochastic partially observable domains due to varying environments. The real-time optimization of the visual tracking is tackled by combining the offline and online *POMDP*s based on flexible world-belief model approach instead of a single world model approach. The hybrid *POMDP* allows to construct world-belief models under varying environments in offline, and to optimize the system control parameters of visual tracking algorithms in online. Since searching directly over local belief space is still intractable, the hybrid *POMDP* is solved in the optimally reachable genotype and phenotype spaces, respectively, using the *GA* and real-time *Q*-learning approaches. The *GA* creates genetic codes using a collected training image set, and the real-time *Q*-learning algorithm organizes an evolved genetic code into a reactive phenotype that optimizes a visual tracking algorithm in real-time performance. The real-time *Q*-learning algorithm defines its states based on a genetic code which determines the domains of visual tracking thresholds/parameters in a phenotype control space and mainly performs interactive learning and adaptation in real-time. The proposed method is to optimize the performance under changing environments by managing the uncertainty into tractable hybrid spaces of the thresholds/parameters of visual tracking algorithms. The combination of the offline and online learning allows the variety types of image sequences in properties and structures by exploring various focusing parameters and can balance the tracking accuracy and the real-time requirements. We showed that the proposed framework can improve the visual tracking performance by searching the limited belief space, and focusing on right horizons. The proposed framework is readily extended to general vision system such as human robot interaction, smart space, and visual surveillance and even more complex systems by taking advantage of the combination synergy of the evolutionary offline learning and real-time *Q*-learning.

8. ACKNOWLEDGEMENT

This work was supported by an Inha University research grant. And following are results of a study on the "Leaders in Industry-university Cooperation" Project, supported by the Ministry of Education, Science & Technology and Inha University.

9. REFERENCES

[1] Yilmaz, O. Javed, and M. Shah, "Object tracking: A survey," ACM Computing Surveys, Vol. 38, No. 4, 2006.

[2] B.Leibe, et. al., "Coupled object detection and tracking from static cameras and moving vehicles," IEEE Trans. PAMI, 2008, 30, (10), pp. 1683–1698.

[3] X. Liu, et.al., "Adaptive Object Tracking by Learning Hybrid Template Online," IEEE Trans. on Circuits and Systems for Video Technology, Vol. 21, No. 11, Nov. 2011, pp.1588-1598.

[4] Z. Kadal, et.al., "Tracking-Learning-Detection," IEEE Trans on PAMI, Vol. 34, No. 7, July 2012, pp. 1409-1422.

[5] R. S. Sutton and A. G. Barto, Reinforcement Learning: An Introduction. Cambridge, MA: MIT Press, 1998.

[6] S. Ross, et.al., "Online Planning Algorithms for POMDPs," Journal of Artificial Intelligence Research 32, 2008, pp. 663-704.

[7] A. Barto, et.al., "Learning to act using real-time dynamic programming," AIJ, Vol. 72, 1995, pp. 81-138.

[8] S. Ross and B. Chaib-draa et.al., "Aems: An anytime online search algorithm for approximate policy refinement in large POMDPs," In Proceedings of the 20th International Joint Conference on Artificial Intelligence (IJCAI-07), 2007, pp. 2592-2598.

[9] S. Paquet, et.al., "Hybrid POMDP algorithms," Proceedings of The Workshop on Multi-Agent Sequential Decision Making in Uncertain Domains, 2006.

[10] S. Ross, et.al., "Theoretical analysis of heuristic search methods for online POMDPs," Advances in Neural Information Processing Systems, 2008.

[11] T. Wang, et.al., "Bayesian sparse sampling for on-line reward optimization," Proceedings of the 22nd international conference on Machine Learning, 2005, pp. 956-963.

[12] F. Doshi-Velez, et.al., "Reinforcement learning with limited reinforcement: Using Bayes risk for active learning in POMDPs," Artificial Intelligence, 2012, pp.187-188.

[13] M. Strens, "A Bayesian framework for reinforcement learning," International Conference in Machine Learning, 2000.

[14] F. Doshi-Velez, "The infinite partially observable Markov decision process," Advances in Neural Information Processing Systems, 22, 2009, pp. 477-485.

[15] P. Poupart and N. Vlassis, "Model-based Bayesian reinforcement learning in partially observable domains," ISAIM, 2008.

[16] C. Wolf and J.-M. Jolion, "Object count/area graphs for the evaluation of object detection and segmentation algorithms," International Journal of Document Analysis (2006) 8(4): 280–296.

[17] Y. Shen, et.al., "Evolutionary Adaptive Eye Tracking for Low-cost HCI Applications," Submitted to JEI.

[18] H. Sellahewa and S. A. Jassim, "Image-Quality-Based Adaptive Face Recognition," IEEE Trans. on Instrumentation and Measurement, Vol. 59, No. 4, April 2010, pp. 805-813.

[19] Q. Li and Z. Wang, "Reduced-Reference Image Quality Assessment Using Divisive Normalization-Based Image Representation," IEEE Journal of Selected Topic in Signal Processing, Vol. 3, No. 2, Apr. 2009, pp. 202-211.

Minimising Longest Path Length in Communication Satellite Payloads via Metaheuristics

Apostolos Stathakis
Interdisciplinary Centre for Security, Reliability and Trust
University of Luxembourg
Luxembourg
apostolos.stathakis@uni.lu

Grégoire Danoy
CSC Research Unit
University of Luxembourg
Luxembourg
gregoire.danoy@uni.lu

Julien Schleich
CSC Research Unit
University of Luxembourg
Luxembourg
julien.schleich@uni.lu

Pascal Bouvry
CSC Research Unit
University of Luxembourg
Luxembourg
pascal.bouvry@uni.lu

Gianluigi Morelli
SES Engineering
Betzdorf
Luxembourg
gianluigi.morelli@ses.com

ABSTRACT

The size and complexity of communication satellite payloads have been increasing very quickly over the last years and their configuration / reconfiguration have become very difficult problems. In this work, we propose to compare the efficiency of three well-known metaheuristic methods to solve an initial configuration problem, which objective is to minimise the length of the longest channel path. Experiments are conducted on real-world problem instances with realistic operational constraints (e.g., a maximum computation time of 10 minutes) and Wilcoxon test is used to determine with statistical confidence what technique is more suitable and what are its limitations. The results of this work will serve as an initial step in our research to design hybrid approaches to push even further the solving capabilities, i.e., tackling bigger payloads and more channels to activate.

Categories and Subject Descriptors

G.1.6 [**Numerical Analysis**]: Optimization; I.2.8 [**Artificial Intelligence**]: Problem Solving, Control Methods, and Search—*Heuristic methods*; D.2.8 [**Software engineering**]: Metrics—*Performance measures*

Keywords

Metaheuristics; Communication satellite; Payload optimisation

1. INTRODUCTION

The payload system of a telecommunication satellite is in charge of receiving and filtering the uplink signals, applying frequency conversion, signal amplification and retransmitting those signals on the downlink. In order to fulfil these missions, satellite payloads are composed of various components, such as amplifiers and channel filters, dedicated to the retransmission of signals. These components are interconnected via a large set of switches in charge of relaying a signal from a component to another. These sets of switches, also known as switch matrices, can be configured, i.e., the position of each switch can be changed remotely. By doing so, the topology of the potential paths changes, i.e., new links are activated while some others are not accessible anymore. This functionality allows the service provider to choose an initial configuration for the routing of the signals, and it also permits to reconfigure the payload depending on new communication needs and on mechanical or electronic failures.

To meet the modern requirements, payloads are becoming bigger, i.e., more switches, more channels and amplifiers. Consequently, the current operational process consisting of manual configurations with experienced engineers is quickly reaching its limits. Indeed, in this context, the manual approach has become time consuming, difficult, and prone to error. As a consequence, software-based solutions are needed to find optimal or near-optimal initial configurations and reconfigurations.

Commercial software solutions already exist for the optimisation of satellite payloads configuration. However, they suffer from various drawbacks from the point of view of the satellite operator. First, their closed APIs do not allow efficient integrations in company workflows. Second, they do not propose to incorporate custom satellite operator constraints or objectives and thus they are characterised by their lack of flexibility.

For all these reasons, in a previous work, Stathakis *et al.* proposed to model real-world requirements with the Integer Linear Programming (ILP) methodology. This model was validated on real-world instances of satellite payloads with the help of the commercial solver CPLEX [1]. Although the results were satisfying for small instances, this approach did not scale for bigger instances with numerous channels to activate.

As a consequence, in this paper we propose to relax the optimality constraint by solving various sizes of instances with well-known metaheuristic methods: a simple Genetic Algorithm (sGA), a cellular GA (cGA) and the Particle Swarm Optimisation (PSO) technique. Our main objective is to determine which method is the most suitable to efficiently solve our problem within a 10 minutes operational constraint.

The remainder of this paper is organised as follows. The next section provides a state of the art on commercial and academic techniques to solve the considered problem. Section 3 proposes a formalisation of the payload optimisation problem and Section 4 provides details concerning the methodology. Section 5 introduces and motivates the parameters of the experiments while Section 6 summarises and analyses the obtained numerical results. Finally, the last section concludes our work and provides some perspectives.

2. RELATED WORKS

The satellites communications market is increasing and rapidly evolving. Satellite operators aim, apart from providing the maximum possible capacity, to reach certain levels of flexibility in satellites, in order to meet modern requirements and adapt to market evolutions. Different levels of flexibility on communication satellites have been categorised in [4]. They concern among others flexibility at the orbit level (allowing the same mission to be achieved from different orbit locations), flexibility at the frequency plan (allowing to modify number of channels and their bandwidth), and flexibility at the routing level.

At this latter level, channel routing flexibility and redundancy are provided by large switch matrices used in todays satellites. As a consequence though, the increasing size makes the manual management of payload configuration and reconfiguration a difficult and time-consuming process for engineers. Commercial software packages exist to deal with this problem, like SmartRings [6] and TRECS [11]. Details concerning their algorithms and the models they use however are not accessible due to commercial restrictions. SmartRings uses a recursive search to compute all possible payload configurations. The algorithm is controlled with the use of constraint and optimisation parameters like the number of switches used or the number of interrupted paths. In the concern of TRECS, the software finds all feasible solutions, while rejecting the non-feasible ones, and generates the corresponding set of satellite commands for the engineers to reconfigure the payload. The main drawbacks of these commercial tools though, is the lack of flexibility for new potential operational constraints and objectives. Besides, they use a black-box solver that can not be changed or customised based on the problem that has to be solved, and most importantly they cannot be easily integrated in companies workflows.

On the academic side, few works have been proposed for the considered problem. In [7] a recursive algorithm was proposed to perform a breadth-first-search (BFS) in order to find all feasible paths that connect channels to amplifiers. Experiments showed the efficiency of the proposed method on a small switch network. For larger problems the BFS algorithm is limited due to its time complexity as every vertex and every edge will be explored in the worst case.

However, since this operation is time critical, enumerating all feasible solutions in current and future communication satellites payloads with a much larger number of switches, channels and amplifiers might be time consuming or even intractable. In addition, the set of all feasible solutions can be very large and will contain a lot of solutions that would never be chosen by the engineers due to their bad quality. This would generate huge losses of time and as a consequence, it is more suitable to find the best solutions based on well-defined objective functions.

In this vein, Stathakis *et al.* [9] proposed and validated an Integer Linear Programming optimisation model (ILP) for large payloads. This model allows the optimisation of specific objectives like the number of switch changes or the number of switches used in the new configuration. Besides, it is flexible as it allows to deal with different failures or switch types. In [10], the authors proposed and validated an extension of their mathematical model focusing on the minimisation of the number of channel interruptions for the reconfiguration problem. However, the experimental results obtained in these two papers [9, 10] showed that not all instances could be solved exactly within a realistic operational time constraint of 10 minutes. This is mainly due to the intrinsic nature of the considered exact approach that returns the optimal solution when found and nothing if it could not make it on time.

To overcome this limitation, in this work, we propose to apply and compare different population based metaheuristics in order to generate valid solutions within the same 10 minutes constraint. First, we develop a method to use metaheuristics for the telecommunication satellites payload configuration problem, that can be adapted for any objective that interests the satellite operator, and in a second time we evaluate their performances within a strict time limit focusing on minimising the length of the longest channel path.

3. PROBLEM DESCRIPTION

The general problem of payload reconfiguration can be divided in three related subproblems. The first one is the *initial configuration problem*, which consists in finding an optimal payload configuration for connecting an initial set of channels in an empty payload (i.e., without any pre-connected channel path that carries service). The second case is the *reconfiguration problem*, which occurs when there exists a set of pre-connected channel paths carrying services and some additional channels must be activated. The third problem is the *restoration problem*, which arises when a set of channels is already connected and one or more failures occur in amplifiers or switches. In this case, the channels affected by the failures have to be rerouted through a different path.

All the aforementioned subproblems have some common operational objectives which are important for payload engineers. For example, the number of switch changes has to be minimised, as changing the position of a switch may cause its permanent failure. Interruptions on the established channel paths have to be minimised since they impact the quality of service provided to customers. Finally, the length of the longest channel path is another important objective that has to be minimised. Long paths imply high attenuation and may cause restrictions on future reconfiguration process. In this work we deal with the initial configuration problem and we focus on minimising the longest path length. It is an objective of high interest for the satellite operators

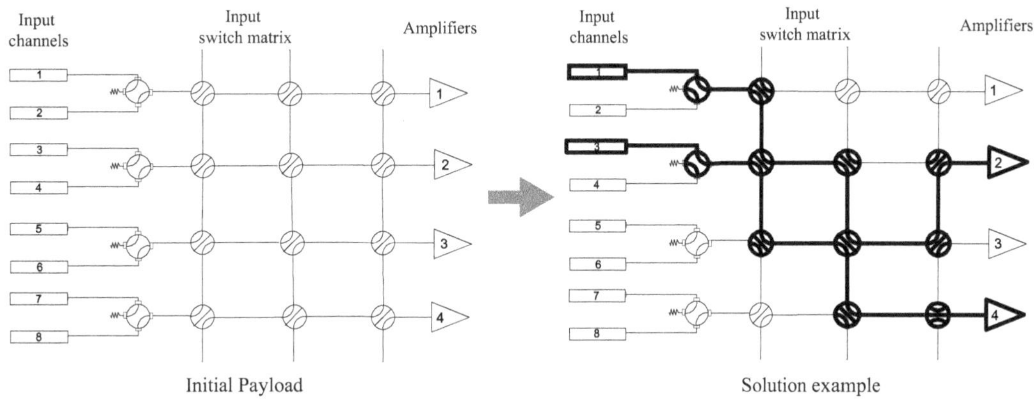

Figure 1: Simplified initial payload instance and example of a solution that connects channels 1 and 3 to amplifiers 2 and 4

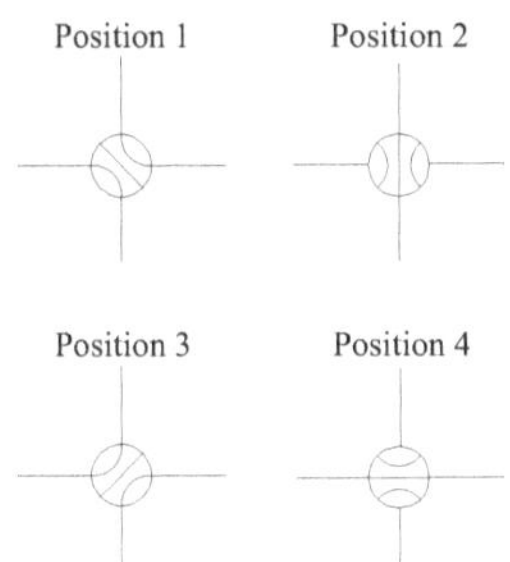

Figure 2: Positions of the R-type switch

and as can be seen in the numerical results section is a difficult objective to be solved with an exact approach within the strict operational time limit.

More precisely, given a set of channels to connect, the initial payload configuration problem consists in finding the positions of the switches that permit to establish the path from each channel to its amplifier. A simplified payload switch matrix example with 16 switches of R and C type is shown in Fig.1. The input signals are crossing the switch matrix and are guided for amplification to an appropriate amplifier. The routing of signals in the payload is achieved through reconfigurable switches organised in the switch matrix. Different types of switches may be used and each one has different positions allowing different paths. The four possible positions of an R-type switch are shown in Fig.2, whereas the C-type switch has only 2 possible positions. For example, one solution for connecting channel 1 to amplifier 2 and channel 3 to amplifier 4 is shown in Fig.1. In this case, channel 1 follows a path of 7 switch crossings and channel 3 follows a path with 6 switch crossings, i.e., number of switches used in the path.

4. METHODOLOGY

In order to overcome the limitations encountered with the exact approach, in this work we propose to study the performance of three different population-based metaheuristics, i.e., a panmictic GA, a structured GA and a swarm-based optimisation algorithm.

This section presents a detailed description of the three metaheuristics in sections 4.1 to 4.3. The solution encoding is then described in section 4.4 followed by details on the fitness function and its evaluation in section 4.5.

4.1 Generational GA

Generational GAs (genGAs) are a type of panmictic algorithm, i.e., individuals are grouped into a single structureless population also referred to as panmixia. Individuals can thus mate with any other individual in the population. The genGA is a (μ, λ)-GA, where the newly generated individuals are placed in an auxiliary population which will replace the current population when it is completely filled, i.e., when the number of newly generated solutions is equal to the size of this auxiliary population. In our case, the size of both the auxiliary and the current population is the same ($\mu = \lambda$).

Algorithm 1 Pseudo-code of a canonical genGA

```
1: proc Evolve(genga)      // Parameters of the algorithm in 'genga'
2:   GenerateInitialPopulation(genga.pop);
3:   Evaluation(genga.pop);
4:   while ! StopCondition() do
5:     for i←0 to genga.popSize do
6:       parents ← Selection(genga.pop);
7:       offspring ← Recombination(genga.Pc,parents);
8:       offspring ← Mutation(genga.Pm,offspring);
9:       Evaluation(offspring);
10:      Add(auxiliary_pop,offspring);
11:    end for
12:    genga.pop ← auxiliary_pop;
13:  end while
14: end proc Evolve
```

Algorithm 1 presents the pseudo-code of the generational EA. The population is first randomly initialised (line 2). Each generated individual is then evaluated using the fitness function defined for the tackled problem (line 3). The genetic loop then starts in line 4 until some predefined termination condition is met, e.g., a number of fitness function evaluations. "Parent" individuals are selected using some stochastic selection operator to construct the mating pool (line 6). Genetic variation is then ensured by the crossover (also called recombination) and mutation operators, both applied with some probability, which permit to visit other

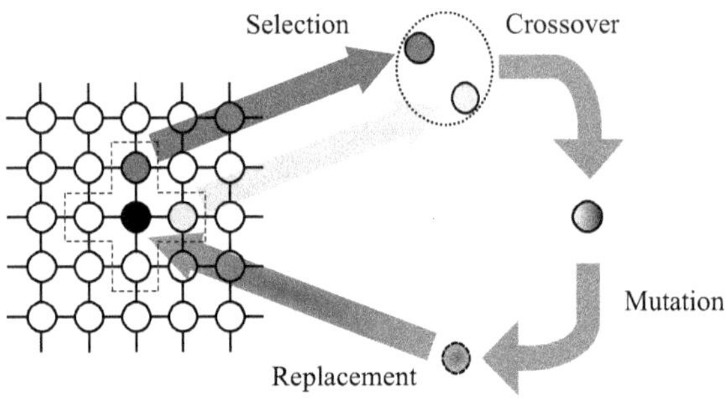

Figure 3: cGA reproduction cycle with 5×5 population and L5 neighborhood.

search space regions (line 7 and 8). The obtained offspring is then evaluated and inserted into the auxiliary population (line 9 and 10). The offspring population will become the current one once full (line 12).

4.2 Cellular GA

Contrary to panmictic GAs like the generational GA, the cellular genetic algorithm (cGA) [3] uses a structured population. Individuals are spread in a two dimensional toroidal mesh and are only allowed to interact with their neighbors. An illustration of the cGA breeding loop is presented in Fig. 3 with individuals arranged on a 5X5 toroidal grid and the neighborhood of the center individual, linear 5, is presented as dashed lines.

A canonical cGA follows the pseudo-code presented in Algorithm 2. The population is usually structured in a regular grid of d dimensions ($d = 1, 2, 3$), and a neighborhood is defined on it. The algorithm iteratively considers as current each individual in the grid (line 5), and individuals may only interact with individuals belonging to their neighborhood (line 6), so parents are chosen among the neighbors (line 7) with a given criterion. Crossover and mutation operators are applied to the individuals in lines 8 and 9, with probabilities P_c and P_m, respectively. Afterwards, the algorithm computes the fitness value of the new offspring individual (or individuals) (line 10), and inserts it (or one of them) instead of the current individual in the population (line 11) following a given replacement policy. This loop is repeated until a termination condition is met (line 4).

Algorithm 2 Pseudocode for a canonical cGA

```
1: proc Evolve(cga)     //Algorithm parameters in 'cga'
2: GenerateInitialPopulation(cga.pop);
3: Evaluation(cga.pop);
4: while ! StopCondition() do
5:    for individual ← 1 to cga.popSize do
6:       n_list←Get_Neighborhood(cga,position(individual));
7:       parents←Selection(n_list);
8:       offspring←Recombination(cga.Pc,parents);
9:       offspring←Mutation(cga.Pm,offspring);
10:      Evaluation(offspring);
11:      Add(position(individual),offspring,cga);
12:   end for
13: end while
14: end proc Steps_Up;
```

4.3 Particle Swarm Optimisation

Particle swarm optimisation [8] is a population based metaheuristic based on the social behaviors observed in nature (e.g., fish shoal). Solutions are represented as swarms that evolve and look for a good solution to the problem without central authority. Each swarm evolution is conditioned by the swarm's best position (pbest) and its neighbors best position (lbest).

A pseudo-code of a PSO is presented in Algorithm 3. The swarm, i.e., population of particles, is initialized randomly (line 2) and evaluated (line 3). Then each particle's new velocity $v(t)$ is calculated (line 6) based on the two social factors using the following equation:

$$v(t) = \omega \times v(t-1) + c_1 \times \rho_1 \times (pbest - x(t-1)) + c_2 \times \rho_2 \times (lbest - x(t-1)), \quad (1)$$

with ω the inertia weight, c_1 and c_2 the learning factors, ρ_1 and ρ_2 two random variables in [0,1] . The position of the particle is updated (line 7) using $x(t) = x(t-1) + v(t)$ and its new fitness calculated (line 8). Each particle then updates it lbest (line 9) and the lbest is updated once the whole swarm has moved (line 11).

Originally introduced for continuous optimisation, PSO variants were proposed to tackle combinatorial problems, like the one considered in this work. In our case a particle is associated with an n-dimensional binary vector (cf. section 4.4), we thus used a binary PSO. To update the position of the particle a sigmoid function $Sig(v_{id})$ is used to transform the velocities values v_i into the [0, 1] interval, defined as:

$$Sig(v_{id}) = \frac{1}{1 + exp(-v_{id})} \quad (2)$$

where v_{id} is the velocity for particle i at dimension d. A random number is generated in the same range and if the generated number is less than $Sig(v_{id})$ the position of the particle at the corresponding dimension is set to 1, otherwise it is set to 0.

Algorithm 3 Pseudocode for a PSO

```
1: proc Evolve(pso)
2: GenerateInitialSwarm(swarm);
3: Evaluation(swarm);
4: while ! StopCondition() do
5:    for particle ← 1 to swarm.size do
6:       velocity ← UpdateVelocity(particle)
7:       particle ← UpdatePosition(particle)
8:       Evaluation(particle)
9:       UpdatepBest()
10:   end for
11:   UpdategBest()
12: end while
13: end proc Steps_Up;
```

4.4 Solution Encoding

When using such metaheuristics, the selection of solution encoding is important as it drives the choice of the operators and therefore the search space exploration. In the proposed model of the payload configuration problem, a solution is the set of each switch position. We use a binary encoding where a switch position is encoded using two bits since a switch has 4 possible positions (see Fig. 2). The binary vector is thus of size $2 * n$ with n the number of switches in the payload.

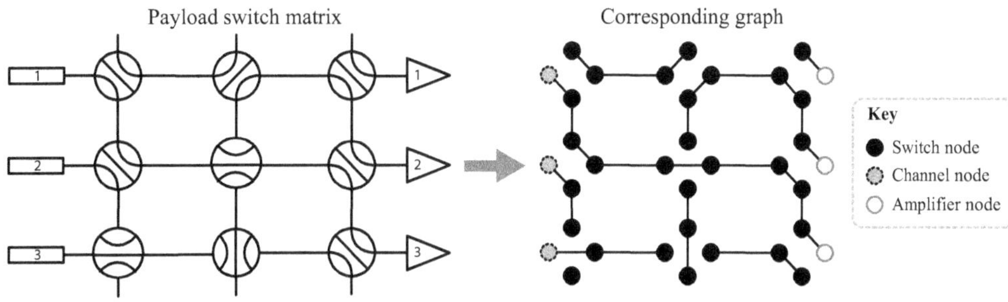

Figure 5: Example of payload representation as a graph

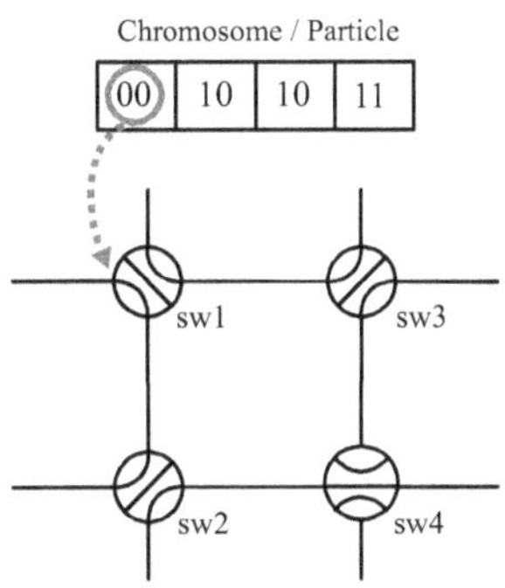

Figure 4: Solution encoding example.

A simple solution example with 4 switches is presented in Fig. 4, where the first two bits (circled) encode the position of switch 1 (sw_1), i.e., "00" corresponds to position 1. Then sw_2 is in position 2 with "10", etc.

4.5 Objective Function

The objective of this work is to find the best set of switch positions that (1) creates a path between each selected channel and an amplifier and (2) minimises the size of the longest created path. In order to assign a fitness value to the candidate solutions, we propose the following objective function:

$$F = r_c + \frac{lpl}{100} \tag{3}$$

where r_c is the number of selected channels that have not been connected to an amplifier and lpl is the longest path length, i.e., the number of switches used in this path. The real length of the path could not be used because this information is not made available and it cannot be deduced from the payload schemas since they do not reflect the real hardware design. Dividing lpl by 100 (the maximum switch matrix size we consider is 100) permits to penalise unsatisfactory solutions proportionally to the number of channels that remain to be connected. Using F we thus consider a minimisation problem.

In order to evaluate the fitness F of a solution, we create its corresponding payload graph. In this graph, each switch is represented as four vertices, one per switch ports, and edges between these vertices are created depending on the switch position. Edges between switches are statically defined. Edges between the nodes of a switch are defined based on its position. A unique partitioned graph is thus created per possible combination of positions. If a connected component of the graph includes a channel vertex and an amplifier vertex then the path is valid. A solution is thus valid if it exists such a connected component for each selected channel. Due to the payload design, a valid connected component can only represent a unique path from channel to amplifier. Its length is thus equal to its total number of switches.

A simple example of the payload transformation into a graph is presented in Figure 5. In the original payload channel 1 is connected to amplifier 3, therefore in the corresponding graph it exists a connected component that contains channel 1 and amplifier 3 vertices. This path uses five switches, its length is thus five.

5. EXPERIMENTAL SETUP

In this section we provide details on the three metaheursitics configuration and on the payload problem instances we have considered in our experiments.

5.1 Algorithms Parameters

Table 1 presents the parameters used for the GAs and the PSO. All algorithms have a total of 49 individuals/particles and a termination condition of 10 min, which is an operational constraint from the satellite operator. Two-point crossover with probability p_c=0.8, bit-flip mutation with $p_m = \frac{1}{chrom\_length}$ and an elitism strategy have been used. The two parent individuals are selected using binary tournament for the genGA while one parent is the current individual for the cGA. The neighbourhood of the cGA is L5 (5 closest individuals measured in Manhattan distance). For the PSO, the neighbourhood size is 2 and the inertia weight linearly decreases in a range from 0.9 to 0.4. Finally the two learning factors have an equal importance, i.e., $c_1 = c_2 = 2$. The three algorithms have been implemented using the ParadisEO framework v1.3 [5].

The mathematical model used in the exact approach is a variant of the ILP model presented in [9] adapted to the minimisation of the length of the longest channel path. One of the fastest non-commercial mixed integer programming (MIP) solver, SCIP (Solving Constraint Integer Programs) [2], was used.

5.2 Problem Instances Parameters

Experiments were performed on payload instances of 50 and 100 switches. For the small size payload, we have considered four different instance sizes from 8, 13, 18 and up to the maximum of 23 channels to connect. The total number of amplifiers is also 23. For the large size payload, we have considered three instances with 25, 30 up to the maximum of 35 channels to connect. The total number of amplifiers is also 35. For each payload instance size, 30 different sets of

Table 1: Parameters used for the genGA, cGA and PSO

	Population/Swarm size	49, 7 × 7 (cGA)
	Term. condition	10 minutes
genGA, cGA	Selection	Binary tournament (BT), Current indiv. + BT (cGA)
	Neighborhood	L5 (cGA)
	Crossover	DPX, p_c=0.8
	Mutation	bit flip, $p_m = \frac{1}{chrom\_length}$
	Replacement strategy	Replace if better (cGA)
	Elitism	1 individual
PSO	Neighborhood size	2
	Inertia weight	Linear decrease [0.9, 0.4]
	Learning factors	$c_1 = c_2 = 2.0$

channels to connect have been randomly generated. Indeed, due to the payload design, two random sets of channels of the same size will have a different complexity and solution quality.

6. NUMERICAL RESULTS

In this section, we review the performances of the different metaheuristics we used with the parameters detailed in Section 5 to solve our problem. Statistical confidence in our comparisons is assessed by performing the Wilcoxon test [12]. In a first part, we compare the results obtained by the exact approach to the chosen metaheuristics, i.e., sGA, cGA and PSO. The second part reviews the results obtained for the three tested methods on the small instances of payloads, i.e., 50 switches. The third subsection compares the numerical results for the big instances and presents the limits of all the different techniques. Finally, the last subsection proposes a summary of the aggregated experience for our problem.

6.1 Comparison with Exact Methods

The hit-rate of our exact approach, i.e., the percentage of solved instances in 10 minutes, decreases extremely fast with the number of channels to connect (see Table 2). These results have been obtained for the small payload instances (50 switches). Very encouraging results have been obtained for sGA and cGA as their hit-rate remains very high. In the case of metaheuristics, hit-rate stands for the percentage of instances where all channels have been connected. PSO exhibits very poor performances and thus cannot be considered a useful alternative to exact methods for this particular problem. It seems that the exact solver was able to cut efficiently in the solutions space in order to find the optimal solution very quickly while PSO's exploration process got stuck on invalid local optimum.

As previously mentioned, sGA and cGA are characterised by very high hit-rate but the quality of their solutions needs to be also checked with respect to those of the exact approach. To this end, we propose Table 3. This table is summarising results obtained only for the instances that have been solved by the exact approach. For these particular instances, Table 3 considers both the average of the 30 individual runs of each solved instance and the best runs of each instance. The results of both sGA and cGA are quite promising, as both the average and the best runs are very close to the optimal values obtained by the exact approach.

Table 2: Comparison with exact method - hit-rate

Channels	Exact	sGA	cGA	PSO
8	90 %	100 %	100 %	99.444 %
13	26.6 %	99.888 %	100 %	6.55 %
18	10 %	99.888 %	100 %	0 %
23	0 %	83.333 %	86.111 %	0 %

When considering only the best runs, we can notice that in some cases, the metaheuristics have found all the optimal solutions.

These results comforts us in our choice to use metaheuristics to cope with our problem, as we obtain a huge increase of the hit-rate while the degradation of the fitness is almost negligible compared to the exact approach.

6.2 Small Instances

The small instances consist of payloads composed of 50 interconnected switches. Intuitively, the complexity of the problem increases with the number of channels to activate. Indeed, if there are less channels to activate there should be more flexibility in the payload matrix to reach amplifiers without blocking other signals. Results displayed in Table 4 empirically confirm this trend. Indeed, all three techniques are decreasing in their capability to find valid solutions (hit-rate) in the given 10 minutes limits when the number of channels to activate increases.

PSO is undoubtedly not adapted to this problem as its hit-rate results decreases dramatically quick to finally reach 0 % for 23 channels to activate. On the contrary, the other two approaches are performing well with slight performance differences. Indeed, although cGA is able to find more valid solutions than sGA, the difference between both methods is quite small, i.e., 99.88 % (sGA) vs 100.0 % (cGA) for 18 channels and 83.0 % (sGA) vs 88.22 % (cGA) for 23 channels.

The fitness (see Table 4) results are similar to what can be observed with the hit-rate. Indeed, cGA is always providing the best results, sometimes ex-æquo with the other techniques. This is true for the average and the standard deviation, and as a consequence comfort us in the idea that cGA is the current best solution for the small instances. Moreover, when the number of channels increases, PSO obtains very bad results very quickly. We also observe a strong correlation between the complexity of the problem and the fitness value. This is logical as the hit-rate is lower for more complex problems and thus the fitness value is more often higher than 1 thus mechanically increasing the average fitness value.

In order to obtain statistical confidence, we apply the Wilcoxon test to all pairs of methods, i.e., sGA vs cGA, sGA vs PSO and cGA vs PSO. Although cGA obtained better results than sGA, this was not detected as statistically significant. As a consequence, we focused solely on representing ranking relations between the couple sGA, cGA on one side and PSO on the other side. Wilcoxon test unanimously states that PSO proposes significantly worse results (with 95% confidence) than both sGA and cGA for 13, 18 and 23 channels to activate, which is represented in Table 4 with a light grey background for PSO results.

Table 3: Comparison with exact method - fitness

	Channels	Exact		sGA		cGA		PSO	
Avg	8	0.001892	±0.000566	0.001938	±0.000643	0.001932	±0.000634	0.001924	±0.000618
	13	0.002500	±0.000534	0.002600	±0.000658	0.002562	±0.000603	0.048400	±0.209
	18	0.002660	±0.000577	0.003160	±0.000851	0.003140	±0.000954	1.569000	±0.670
Best	8	0.001892	±0.000566	0.001923	±0.000627	0.001923	±0.000627	0.001923	±0.000627
	13	0.002500	±0.000534	0.002500	±0.000534	0.002500	±0.000534	0.002500	±0.000534
	18	0.002660	±0.000577	0.003000	±0.001	0.003000	±0.001	0.337000	±0.578

Table 4: Fitness and hit-rate results

#S	#Ch	sGA			cGA			PSO		
		fitness		hit-rate	fitness		hit-rate	fitness		hit-rate
50	8	0.0019	±0.0005	100.0 %	0.0019	±0.0005	100.0 %	0.0019	±0.0005	100.0 %
	13	0.0032	±0.0006	100.0 %	0.0031	±0.0006	100.0 %	0.2830	±0.4514	72.11 %
	18	0.0040	±0.0333	99.88 %	0.0030	±0.0008	100.0 %	1.8830	±0.8752	5.0 %
	23	0.1750	±0.3754	83.0 %	0.1230	±0.3221	88.22 %	4.4070	±0.7108	0.0 %
100	25	0.068	±0.2613	94.11 %	0.072	±0.2627	93.66 %	-		-
	30	0.332	±0.6003	73.77 %	0.298	±0.5932	77.33 %	-		-
	35	2.251	±1.0475	3.666 %	2.130	±1.0262	3.777 %	-		-

6.3 Big Instances

The big instances consist of payloads composed of 100 interconnected switches. For these instances, we chose to focus on the most promising methods and thus discarded PSO. As a consequence, we focus on comparing sGA with cGA. Detailed results can be found in Table 4. The hit-rate is again highly influenced by the complexity of the problem, which is here mainly related to the number of channels to activate. For the big instances, the hit-rate is relatively high except for the extreme case of 35 channels where a bit less than 4 % of the experiments were successful. This indicates that we are very close to the maximum size of problem that can be dealt within the 10 min constraint. In the bigger instances, cGA is not the best technique for all problem sizes. Indeed, when 25 channels should be activated, sGA finds valid solutions for 94.1 % of the payloads while cGA solves only 93.66 % of them. However, when the problems become more complex to solve, cGA obtains better results concerning the hit-rate, i.e., 77.33 % vs 73.77 % for 30 channels and 3.777 % vs 3.666 % for 35 channels.

This highly increasing complexity can also be observed in the quality of the solutions via the fitness. Intuitively, the easier the problem, the more time you have to explore the solution space and thus, the higher is the quality of the final best solution. On the contrary, it is highly probable that for the biggest instances, for which less than 4 % of the payloads have a valid solutions, the fitness results will be significantly less good. sGA surprisingly provides better solutions than cGA for the instances with 25 channels to activate, i.e., 0.068 vs 0.072. These very good results are however not repeated for the more complex instances. Indeed, cGA obtains better solutions for 30 resp. 35 switches to activate, i.e., 0.298 vs 0.332 resp. 2.130 vs 2.251.

We applied the Wilcoxon tests for all pairwise comparisons. For 25 channels to activate, cGA provides significantly less good solutions than sGA. In Table 4, this is represented with a light grey background for cGA results. When 30 channels need to be activated, cGA is this time proposing significantly better solutions than sGA (represented with a dark grey background for cGA). Finally, for the biggest instance, i.e., 35 channels to activate, even if cGA provided better results, the Wilcoxon test cannot state if a technique is significantly better than the other, thus no specific background.

6.4 Summary

These experiments allowed us to obtain valuable insights on the suitability of the tested techniques for our problem. We now know that PSO is not suitable for our problem with the presented parameters settings. We observed that the time-limit is not responsible for its poor results. Indeed, preliminary analyses seem to suggest that PSO converges very quickly and get stuck quite regularly in invalid solutions. It is thus not impossible that fine-tuning some of its parameters, e.g., those in charge of the learning process, may drastically change its performances. However, this was not in the scope of this study and we tried to conduct it in the fairest way possible by applying standard parameter values to all of the methods.

Concerning the two other methods, cGA seems to be more efficient than sGA, for both the average fitness and its standard deviation, and the hit-rate. This could be explained by the fact that sGA may converge prematurely in some local optimum whereas in the case of cGA though, this is prevented thanks to the isolation by distance effect provided by the use of a structured population. This is of course not true for 100 switches and 25 channels to activate but that is the only exception and even in this case the performance difference between both method is not very important.

7. CONCLUSIONS AND PERSPECTIVES

In this work, we proposed a method to use metaheuristics for minimising the length of the longest channel path in communication satellites payloads. We compared the efficiency of three well-known metaheuristic methods , i.e., a simple Genetic Algorithm (sGA), a cellular GA (cGA) and the Particle Swarm Optimisation (PSO) technique, to solve a specific payload problem, i.e., minimising the longest path length. We proved the suitability of sGA and cGA compared to the state of the art exact approach.

Our experimental results clearly disqualify PSO for its very poor performances for both hit-rate and fitness, although both are correlated. cGA proposes the best solutions in most of the considered cases and will thus be considered for further experiments.

As a next step in our research, we plan in a first time to enhance the performances under the time constraint by fine-tuning the parameters of cGA and performing a sensibility analysis. If this is still not enough to perform on the most challenging instances, we will propose hybridisation schemes for cGA, such as including a problem specific local search mechanism. Finally, for the sake of flexibility, we plan to work on multi-objective techniques in order to propose panels of solutions to the deciders of the satellite company.

Acknowledgement

A. Stathakis acknowledges the support of the National Research Fund of Luxembourg (FNR), with the AFR contract no. 1346481. Experiments presented in this paper were carried out using the HPC facility of the University of Luxembourg.

8. REFERENCES

[1] Ibm ilog cplex. http://www.ilog.com/products/cplex/.

[2] T. Achterberg. SCIP - a framework to integrate constraint and mixed integer programming. Technical Report 04-19, Zuse Institute Berlin, 2004.

[3] E. Alba and B. Dorronsoro. *Cellular Genetic Algorithms*. Operations Research/Compuer Science Interfaces. Springer-Verlag Heidelberg, 2008.

[4] C. Balty, J.-D. Gayrard, and P. Agnieray. Communication satellites to enter a new age of flexibility. *Acta Astronautica*, 65(1-2):75 – 81, 2009.

[5] S. Cahon, N. Melab, and E.-G. Talbi. Paradiseo: A framework for the reusable design of parallel and distributed metaheuristics. *Journal of Heuristics*, 10(3):357–380, May 2004.

[6] J. Chaumon, J. Gil, T. Beech, and G. Garcia. Smartrings: advanced tool for communications satellite payload reconfiguration. In *Aerospace Conference, 2006 IEEE*, page 11 pp., 2006.

[7] S. Gulgonul, E. Koklukaya, I. Erturk, and A. Y. Tesneli. Communication satellite payload redundancy reconfiguration. In *Satellite Telecommunications (ESTEL), 2012 IEEE First AESS European Conference on*, pages 1 –4, oct. 2012.

[8] J. Kennedy and R. Eberhart. Particle swarm optimization. In *Neural Networks, 1995. Proceedings., IEEE International Conference on*, volume 4, pages 1942–1948 vol.4. IEEE, Nov. 1995.

[9] A. Stathakis, G. Danoy, P. Bouvry, and G. Morelli. Satellite payload reconfiguration optimisation: An ilp model. In J.-S. Pan, S.-M. Chen, and N. T. Nguyen, editors, *ACIIDS (2)*, volume 7197 of *Lecture Notes in Computer Science*, pages 311–320. Springer, 2012.

[10] A. Stathakis, G. Danoy, T. Veneziano, J. Schleich, and P. Bouvry. Optimising satellite payload reconfiguration: An ilp approach for minimising channel interruptions. In *2nd ESA Workshop on Advanced Flexible Telecom Payloads*, pages 1–8. European Space Agency, 2012.

[11] TRECS. Transponder reconfiguration system [online]. http://www.integ.com/TRECS.html.

[12] F. Wilcoxon. Individual Comparisons by Ranking Methods. *Biometrics Bulletin*, 1(6):80–83, 1945.

Red Swarm: Smart Mobility in Cities with EAs

Daniel H. Stolfi, Enrique Alba
LCC, University of Malaga
ETSI Informática, Campus de Teatinos
29071, Málaga, Spain
{dhstolfi,eat}@lcc.uma.es

ABSTRACT

This work presents an original approach to regulate traffic by using an on-line system controlled by an EA. Our proposal uses computational spots with WiFi connectivity located at traffic lights (the Red Swarm), which are used to suggest alternative individual routes to vehicles. An evolutionary algorithm is also proposed in order to find a configuration for the Red Swarm spots which reduces the travel time of the vehicles and also prevents traffic jams. We solve real scenarios in the city of Malaga (Spain), thus enriching the OpenStreetMap info by adding traffic lights, sensors, routes and vehicle flows. The result is then imported into the SUMO traffic simulator to be used as a method for calculating the fitness of solutions. Our results are competitive compared to the common solutions from experts in terms of travel and stop time, and also with respect to other similar proposals but with the added value of solving a real, big instance.

Categories and Subject Descriptors

I.6.3 [**Simulation and Modeling**]: Applications

Keywords

Application, evolutionary algorithm, road traffic, smart city, smart mobility, WiFi connections

1. INTRODUCTION

Nowadays, cities are evolving quickly. Most citizens are living in, using the services of, or thinking about moving to big cities, which is a new source of complex problems. Smart Cities is a world initiative leading to better exploit on of the resources in a city in order to offer higher level services to people. Smart cities are related to sensing the city's status and acting in new intelligent ways at different levels: people, government, cars, transport, communications, energy, buildings, neighborhoods, resource storage, etc.

One of the headlines of the strategy Europe 2020 is the reduction of greenhouse gas emissions by at least 20% compared to 1990 levels, an increment of the share of renewable energy sources in the final energy consumption to 20%, and a 20% increase in energy efficiency [1].

We believe that proposals like the one described here are directly related to the strategy Europe 2020 as well as to the smart cities initiative because we focus on the reduction of travel times, fuel consumption, and CO_2 emissions. We do so by reducing traffic jams so that the daily life of citizens in a smartcity improves.

To do this, we take advantage of the existent infrastructure in cities, such as traffic lights, open WiFi network, etc., in order to deploy several spots as a part of a collective system, called Red Swarm, each one placed in junctions with traffic lights and with the purpose of redirecting traffic based on each vehicle's destination. New routes are constructed with paths between Red Swarm spots, which relieve congested roads by distributing vehicles in alternative itineraries. Drivers are informed of the reroute proposed by using an On Board Unit (OBU) installed inside the vehicle which communicates with the infrastructure (V2I - car or smartphone to Red Swarm spot), by using the electronic panels placed around the city, or by using a portable device such as a smartphone or tablet.

Traffic optimization has always been a healthy line of research; now, even more so, with the utilization of ICT. There are solutions that focus on adjusting the traffic light cycles by using Particle Swarm Optimization (PSO) [4], or by using a Genetic Algorithm (GA) and a Cellular Automaton (CA) based traffic simulator [9], or by using optical information systems to calculate the size of the jam at the affected junction [7]. However, they do not modify the route of vehicles in advance, allowing drivers to make intelligent decisions as they move around the city.

In [3], bus lanes are opened when an additional traffic demand is recognized and in [5], a solution based on virtual police agents which are aware of the traffic conditions in their vicinity is presented. The former, only adds new lanes to existing roads and does not reroute vehicles while the later changes routes based on local information.

Recently, an approach which uses periodically emitted beacons to analyze the current traffic state via VANETs [6] was presented. It depends on V2V communications and the number of vehicles emitting beacons. Our proposal does not rely on the number of vehicles with a communication device to reroute them (off-line), although it is necessary to tell the driver of the suggested new route to follow.

The rest of this paper is organized as follows. In the next section we introduce the System Architecture proposed in-

GECCO'13, July 6–10, 2013, Amsterdam, The Netherlands.

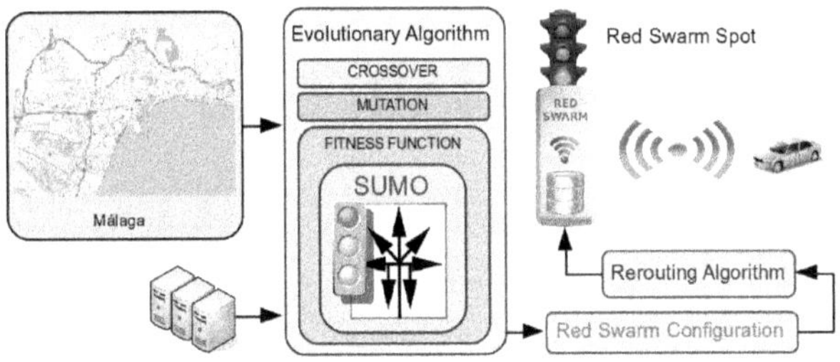

Figure 1: Component Schema of Red Swarm.

cluding the Evolutionary Algorithm and the steps taken to define its parameters and also the Rerouting Algorithm used in each Red Swarm spot. Section 3 presents the optimization results as well as the comparative between the experts' solution and the Red Swarm one, and finally in Section 4 conclusions and future work are given.

2. SYSTEM ARCHITECTURE

Our proposal, Red Swarm, is a computational system which consists of:

1. Several Red Swarm spots distributed throughout the city, installed at traffic lights which were chosen with the aim of redirecting the traffic efficiently.
2. The Evolutionary Algorithm which obtains the configuration of each spot.
3. The Rerouting Algorithm which suggests alternative routes based on the configuration of the system, so that drivers can take one of these routes when they enter the zone covered by a spot (WiFi)

In order to evaluate a configuration for the system we used the traffic simulator SUMO (Simulator of Urban Mobility) [2] in conjunction with TraCI (Traffic Control Interface) [10, 11]. SUMO is a microscopic traffic simulator which uses a microscopic model of discrete time and continuous space. Each moving vehicle implements the car-following model developed by Stefan Krauß in [8]. TraCI is an API which allows an external source (the Rerouting Algorithm in our case) to control SUMO as well as to obtain the state of the simulation and change it properly.

Figure 1 presents a schema with the components of Red Swarm. It shows the relation between the Evolutionary Algorithm, the map of the city, the simulator SUMO, and the configuration of the Red Swarm spots at design time. During execution time, the Rerouting Algorithm reads data from the configuration while it exchanges information with vehicles by using the Red Swarm spots. Each spot runs the same rerouting algorithm but only uses the configuration portion related to its own sensors.

2.1 Real Scenario

The scenario chosen is an area of the city of Malaga (in Spain) which is well-known for suffering traffic congestion at peak times, and it represents a typical challenge found in most European cities (non linear streets). The area is bordered to the north by Carretería Street, to the east by Gutemberg Street, to the west by the Guadalmedina River, and to the south by the Mediterranean Sea. In Figure 2

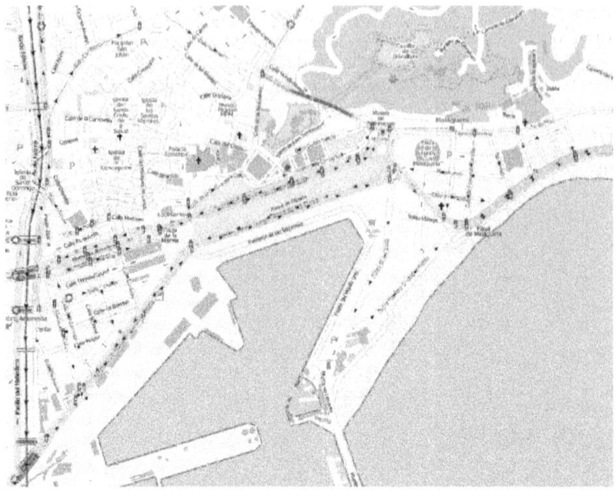

Figure 2: Malaga scenario for our smart mobility proposal.

we show the map of the zone chosen, obtained from the OpenStreetMap Project.

This zone contains eight inputs and eight outputs which represent real streets of the urban area. As we stated before, we used SUMO in order to simulate this vehicular environment by importing it from the project OpenStreetMap. This technique could be applied to any other middle-sized city in the world with little effort.

In order to implement the real model in SUMO, we had to divide each Red Swarm spot into a number of sensors which detect vehicles as they enter the area covered by the radio link of the spot. The real system could have sensors freely located or the detection could even be estimated off-line by the traffic municipal service.

Then, we defined all possible journeys between inputs and outputs from the zone in which vehicles follow the fastest path. As a result, we had 64 itineraries available. Furthermore, we defined four different kinds of vehicles (sedan, van, wagon, and transport), which are presented in Table 1 with the purpose of analyzing a truly general scenario.

Table 1: Type and characteristics of vehicles.

Type	Arriving prob.	MaxSpd. (Km/h)	Accel. (m/s^2)	Decel. (m/s^2)	Length (m)
sedan	0.50	160	0.9	5.0	3.8
van	0.25	100	0.8	4.5	4.2
wagon	0.15	50	0.7	4.0	4.3
transport	0.10	40	0.6	3.5	4.5

Finally, a problem instance was defined by different distributions of vehicle types, arriving time, arriving points and destinations (flows). In the experiments conducted we worked with three different instances. They were called *Sim1*, *Sim2*, and *Sim3*.

2.2 Evolutionary Algorithm

As this is a very complex problem, the technique developed for obtaining a configuration for the group of spots placed in the scenario was based on an Evolutionary Algorithm. By using it we were able to explore the solution space, looking to improve the current traffic flow in the city.

2.2.1 Representation

The structure defined, which contains the configuration of each input to a Red Swarm spot (sensors) and the destinations of the vehicles, is illustrated in Figure 3.

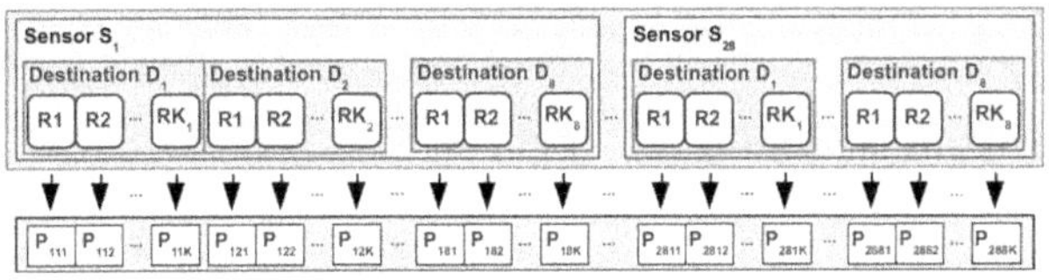

Figure 3: Problem representation.

If we look at the sensor S_1 for example, it contains all the possible destinations defined for the city (D_1 to D_8), and each destination contains all the probabilities for all the routes which start in S_1. For the routes of D_1 in S_1, there are RK_1 different paths, some of them to the rest of sensors and others to D_1 itself. Therefore, for the routes of D_2 in S_1, there are RK_2 different paths, and so on. Consequently, the solution vector contains all the probabilities associated with routes from sensors to other sensors and from sensors to destinations, arranged in blocks. In the scenario described, the solution vector is made up of 1119 probabilities values, which denotes the extreme complexity of this problem.

As presented in Equation 1, the result of the summation of the probabilities for the routes inside a destination block have to be equal to 1.0. Note that the subindex N identifies the sensor, the subindex M identifies the destination, and the subindex $R_i, i \in [1-K_{N,M}]$ identifies the different $K_{N,M}$ routes starting with the sensor S_N and belonging to the destination block D_M.

$$\begin{aligned} P_{S_N D_M} &= P_{N,M,R_1} + \cdots + P_{N,M,R_{K_{N,M}}} \\ &= \sum_{i=1}^{K_{N,M}} P_{N,M,R_i} = 1.0 \end{aligned} \quad (1)$$

2.2.2 Fitness Function

In order to evaluate each individual, we define the fitness function presented in Equation 2 which is done by the addition of three terms.

$$F = \alpha_1(N - n_{trips}) + \alpha_2 \frac{\sum t_{trip}}{N} + \alpha_3 \frac{\sum t_{delay}}{N} \quad (2)$$

The first one represents the penalization for the vehicles which are still in the city when the simulation is over. There, N is the total number of vehicles in the scenario (800 in this case), n_{trips} is the number of vehicles which complete their trip during the simulation, and α_1 is the weight of this term in the fitness function.

The second term represents the average travel time for the vehicles which complete the journey, being t_{trip} the travel time of each one. The third term is the average time spent by each vehicle waiting to enter the area because of red lights or traffic jams. This time is called t_{delay} in the equation.

Finally, α_2 and α_3 are the weights applied to the average travel time and to the average delay time, respectively. All values involved in the calculation of the fitness function are obtained from the results of the simulation run in SUMO when it is configured with the Red Swarm spots or with the experts' algorithm.

2.2.3 Recombination Operator

We propose two different recombination operators: Sensor Recombination and Destination Recombination. The first one consists of a two-point recombination which selects a range of sensors and their configurations from two individuals and exchanges them. As a consequence, the offspring obtained preserve part of their original sensor configuration and get a new configuration for only some of them, as depicted in Figure 4. Additionally, the initial position and the range of sensors are randomly chosen. Note that all the random selections made by the operators (recombination and mutation) are based on the uniform distribution implemented by the pseudo-random number generator included in the programming language, Python.

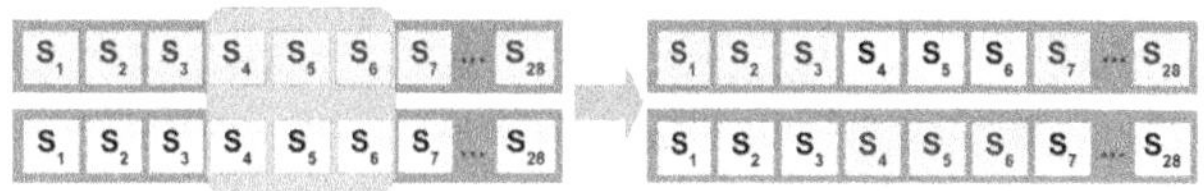

Figure 4: Sensor Crossover.

The second one, the Destination Crossover, preserves the configuration of the sensors along the routes that are being crossed, the exact opposite of what the other operator does. This behavior keeps the routes of each destination block unaltered after the crossing operation. Therefore, the offspring will be composed by complete routes obtained from both parents after the recombination.

2.2.4 Mutation Operators

We also propose several mutation operators. Each operator makes changes to the probabilities of the routes for sensors and destinations so that vehicles would take different routes when the Red Swarm spots are configured with different individuals. In this approach, we assigned probabilities equal to either 0 or 1, keeping only one route active in a destination block.

The ADOS operator (All Destinations - One Sensor) modifies the probabilities for all routes and all destinations in one sensor. Note that the sensor is randomly chosen, as depicted in Figure 6(a), where all routes for all destinations in S_2 are modified (shown in dark). This operator makes a number of changes to the status vector but it only affects one sensor.

The MDOS operator (Multiple Destination - One Sensor) changes all the routes for a few destination blocks in one sensor. The sensor and the destination blocks are randomly selected. As Figure 6(b) shows, this operator on average modifies fewer routes than the previous one but more than the next one. In this example, routes of blocks D_2 and D_8 in S_2 are modified. The destination blocks whose routes are changed are shown in a dark color.

The next operator, called ODOS (One Destination - One Sensor), makes the least number of changes of the status vector with respect to ADOS and MDOS. It selects only a random sensor and a random destination block and changes the routes associated with them. In Figure 6(c), we can observe that S_2 and D_2 have been selected as the target of the mutation operator.

The last two operators, ASMD (All Sensors - Multiple Destinations) and ASOD (All Sensors - One Destination),

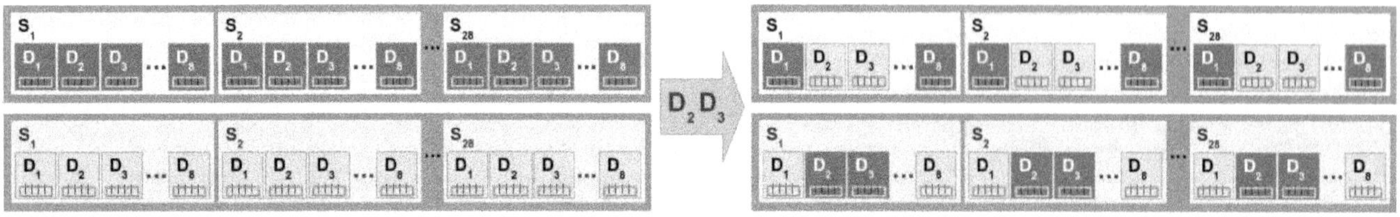

Figure 5: Destination Crossover.

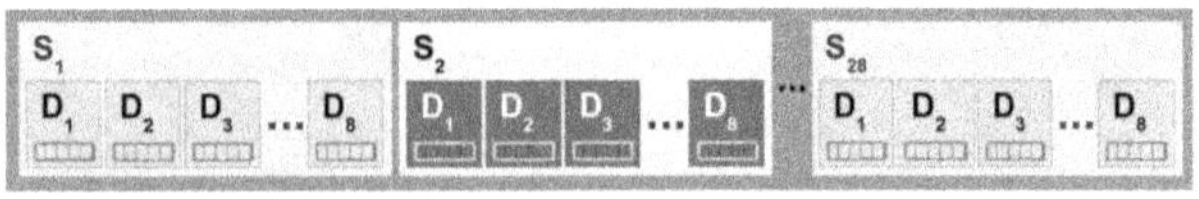

(a) ADOS: All Destinations - One Sensor

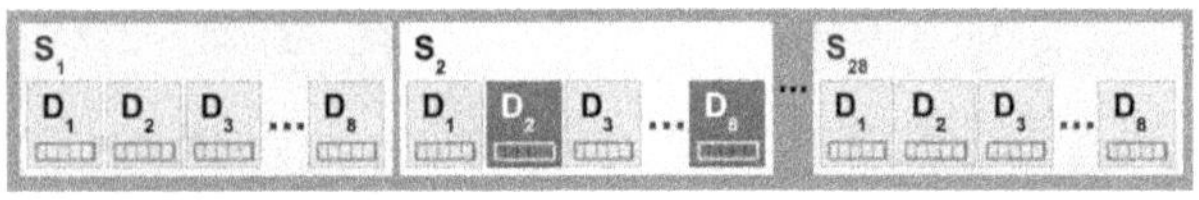

(b) MDOS: Multiple Destination - One Sensor

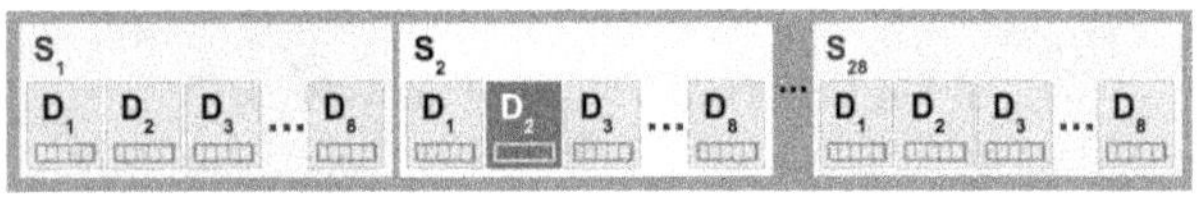

(c) ODOS: One Destination - One Sensor

(d) ASMD: All Sensors - Multiple Destinations

(e) ASOD: All Sensors - One Destination

Figure 6: Mutation Operators.

make changes to each flow individually. In the example presented in Figure 6(d) we can see how the routes in D_2 and D_8 are modified in all sensors, while in Figure 6(e), only D_2 is modified in all the sensors. Note that the selection of the destination blocks is made according to a uniform distribution of probability as in the rest of the operators.

2.2.5 *Parameterization*

First of all we need to evaluate the instances to know how long it takes for vehicles to complete their itineraries, and obtain a fitness value for each one in order to compare them with the solutions that we later calculate.

We worked with three different simulations called *EXP1*, *EXP2*, and *EXP3*, corresponding with the simulations in which routes are defined by using the experts' algorithm, run in the scenarios *sim1*, *sim2* and *sim3* respectively.

As stated before, we assigned 100 vehicles to each one of the eight flows to obtain the values presented in Table 2. Vehicles arrived in the scenario in the first 100 seconds and after 1500 seconds all the vehicles had left the city, as depicted in Figure 7. Based on this value, we set the maximum simulation time to 1800 seconds (30 minutes), in order not to excessively penalize solutions which last for more than the longest time spent in the EXPx simulations, but which could have a lower than average travel time.

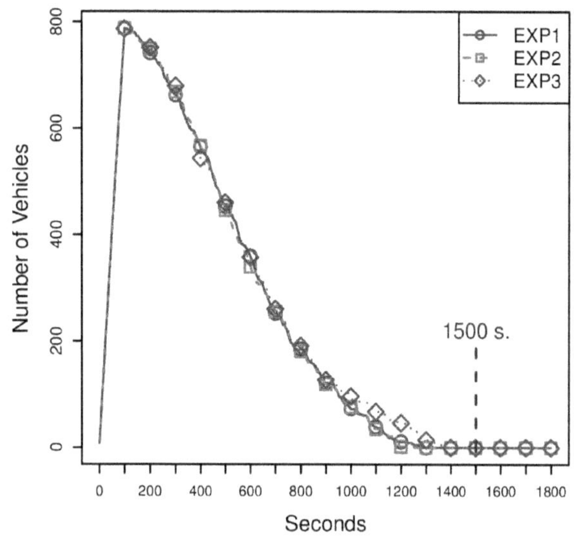

Figure 7: Vehicles in the city during the first 1800 seconds.

Table 2: Results produced by the experts' algorithm.

Metric	EXP1	EXP2	EXP3
# Trips Completed	800	800	800
Simulation Time (s)	1283	1253	1385
Minimum Fitness	532.9	530.8	549.0

The parameters for the Evolutionary Algorithm implemented are presented in Table 3. We worked with a population of ten individuals and in each new generation, two new descendants were created (crossover probability equal to 1.00), in order to implement a (10+2)-EA algorithm. Then, three in four descendants were mutated (mutation probability equal to 0.75) to provide genetic variety and finally, the new generation was updated following an elitist strategy. The algorithm was executed for 5000 generations to achieve each solution.

Additionally, α_1 was set to 900 (half of the simulation time), and α_2 and α_3 were set to one. By using these values, we penalized vehicles which did not finish their itinerary (α_1) and therefore were still stuck on their journey through the city when the simulation ended. Moreover, we assigned the

Table 3: Parameters of the Evolutionary Algorithm.

Simulation Time (s)	1800
Population Size	10
Offspring Size	2
Crossover Probability	1.00
Mutation Probability	0.75
Number of Generations	5000
$(\alpha_1, \alpha_2, \alpha_3)$	(900, 1, 1)

same weight to the travel time (α_2) and to the delay time (α_3) because they are equally important for us.

Once the algorithm had been configured, we evaluated the proposed operators. The results are reported in Table 4.

Table 4: Evaluation of operators.

Operators	Avg.	StdDev.	Min.	Conver.
Sensor: ADOS	3557.9	11403.5	555.8	93.8%
Sensor: MDOS	5057.4	9660.2	551.1	93.8%
Sensor: ODOS	6732.9	16455.4	548.4	81.3%
Sensor: ADOS-ODOS	1066.2	2901.1	**512.7**	94.6%
Sensor: ADOS-MDOS	1329.6	2908.2	516.0	**100.0%**
Dest.: ADOS	2347.5	6744.8	548.0	**100.0%**
Dest.: ODOS	**803.5**	**700.8**	555.9	**100.0%**
Dest.: ASMD	36199.5	18174.6	13309.0	87.5%
Dest.: ASOD	5273.9	16606.8	576.2	**100.0%**
Dest.: ADOS-ODOS	906.9	1758.6	518.8	90.0%
Dest.: ASMD-ASOD	5101.2	11110.6	591.9	43.3%

Note that we also tested combined mutation operators within the algorithm because they allowed us to get better results by using a faster mutation operator at the beginning of the execution, and then switching to a slower one when the fitness of the best individual is lower than a threshold. The value of the threshold was empirically set to 1000.

Based on the data in Table 4 we selected the Sensor Crossover as the recombination operator, while for the mutation operators we decided to start with ADOS and later change to ODOS. This combination was selected because it produced the best minimum value in spite of the fact that the average and the convergence percentage (Conver.) were not the best of the comparative.

Using the first mutation operator (ADOS) we quickly explore the data space. Then, when all the vehicles have finished their itineraries within the simulation time (which makes the best fitness of the population fall below the threshold value), we switch to the second one (ODOS).

By using the ODOS mutation, the search space is carefully explored by mutating only the probability of the routes included in just one destination block in one sensor. This only affects a small proportion of the Red Swarm spots, allowing the improvement of the solution in small steps.

2.3 Rerouting Algorithm

When a vehicle enters the simulation, SUMO assigns one of the eight destinations available as well as the corresponding route to it. Later, when the vehicle enters the coverage area of the Red Swarm spot (in the simulation it is detected by a sensor), the Rerouting Algorithm presented in Algorithm 1, is executed.

Algorithm 1 Rerouting Algorithm.

```
procedure REROUTING(vehicle)
    currentRoad ← getRoad(vehicle)
    if isDestination(currentRoad) then
        newroute ← currentRoad
    else
        routes ← getDestinationRoutes(currentRoad)
        if routes = [] then
            routes ← getSensorRoutes(currentRoad)
            newroute ← getRouteByProbability(routes)
        end if
    end if
    setNewRoute(newroute, vehicle)
end procedure
```

First, the current road is obtained from the vehicle and the destination is checked because if the vehicle is on the last road of its itinerary, no rerouting is done. Otherwise, all the routes from the current road to the destination of the vehicle are obtained from the configuration.

Then, if there are no routes to the destination (it is not reachable from the current position), the algorithm will obtain all routes from the current road to the rest of sensors.

Next, one of the routes from the current road to another road containing a sensor is chosen taking into account the probability stored in the configuration.

Finally, the route of the vehicle is changed to the new one and the process ends.

2.4 Experimental Settings

To optimize each traffic distribution we carried out 35 independent runs on the cluster belonging to the NEO (Networking and Emerging Optimization) group, consisting of 16 nodes, each equipped with an Intel Core2 uad CPU (9400) @ 2.66GHz and 3.5 GB of RAM, running GNU/-Linux 3.2.0-34. By using this hardware, each new generation took about 15 seconds to be calculated, and each execution of the algorithm lasted about 22 hours, having spent about 9 days of computation on the whole optimization process.

3. ANALYSIS OF RESULTS

Table 5 presents the number of trips completed (# Trips Comp.), the total simulation time (Total Time), and the minimum fitness value (Min. Fitness) for the scenarios which are routed according to experts' criteria implemented in SUMO. These results were achieved by optimizing the three scenarios separately.

Table 5: Comparison between the experts' algorithm and Red Swarm.

Metric	Experts' algorithm			Red Swarm		
	Sim1	*Sim2*	*Sim3*	*Sim1*	*Sim2*	*Sim3*
# Trips Comp.	800	800	800	800	800	800
Total Time (s)	1283	1253	1385	**1154**	**1201**	**1194**
Min. Fitness	532.9	530.8	549.0	**512.7**	**530.2**	**513.0**

With this data, we conducted the robustness test by applying the three best available solutions (belonging to the three traffic distributions) to the other simulations in order to discover which one was the most robust. That is, *Sim1* was simulated with the configuration of the solutions *sol2* and *sol3*; *Sim2*, with the configuration of *sol1* and *sol3*; and finally, *Sim3*, with *sol1* and *sol2*.

Table 6 demonstrates the improvement of using *sol1* to configure the second simulation instead of using *sol2*. Although *sol3* is a better configuration than *sol1* for *Sim3*, the average value achieved by *sol1* is the best of the three. These results encouraged us to select *sol1* as the most robust solution to configure the Red Swarm spots.

Table 6: Minimum fitnesses obtained from the robustness test.

	Red Swarm			Expert
	sol1	*sol2*	*sol3*	
Sim1	**512.7**	552.2	546.9	532.9
Sim2	**523.5**	530.1	555.4	530.8
Sim3	533.3	546.4	**513.0**	549.0
Average	**523.2**	542.9	538.4	537.6

In tables 7 and 8 we present the best results achieved with the aim of optimizing the traffic in the city center of Malaga. The average values of waiting time and travel time for all Red Swarm simulations are lower than the experts' solution. There are values such us the initial delay and route length which were not improved by our Red Swarm system, especially the latter as it is not included in the fitness function. Initial delays are higher (avg. 2.3%) mainly due to the traffic lights situated near the input streets where the vehicles arriving still need to be rerouted by a Red Swarm spot. Route lengths are also longer (avg. 5.3%) because we were rerouting vehicles via roads which are not part of the best path selected by the experts.

However, we achieved a maximum improvement of 20.2% in the average waiting time and 5.3% in the average travel time. So, it seems that experts just take into consideration the traveled distance, while the time is much better if we want to consider the comfort of reduced waiting at traffic lights and at traffic jams, and the reduced gas emissions thanks to this (continuous driving).

The distribution of the results is demonstrated in Figure 8 where the improvement achieved is presented in four box plots. Note that waiting times and travel times present lower values for R-S than the experts' solution.

Furthermore, we compare the total time needed by the vehicles to leave the city when we increment the number of arrivals in each input, in steps of 80 vehicles (ten per input). Figure 9 indicates how the Red Swarm system is actually an effective solution when the number of vehicles is higher than a certain value. So, when the number of vehicles in the area being studied is above 360 (400, 540) the utilization of our Red Swarm is profitable for the city. This number of cars is of course realistic for this part of the city (many more in general), thus explaining why the town hall is currently interested in a prototype.

Finally, we compare our proposal with the best configuration obtained from the execution against the RANDOM algorithm, which randomly looks for solutions during a time equivalent to that spent by the Evolutionary Algorithm we used. The results obtained by using a random search show a highly negative impact on the quality of solutions: cars are not advised of useful routes to their destinations. Many vehicles even remain in the system at the end of the period studied (63 vehicles for *Sim1*, 90 for *Sim2*, and 152 for *Sim3*). The reader might be thinking why we are reporting the behavior of a pure random algorithm: the reason is to perform a sanity check on the validity of our EA. It is

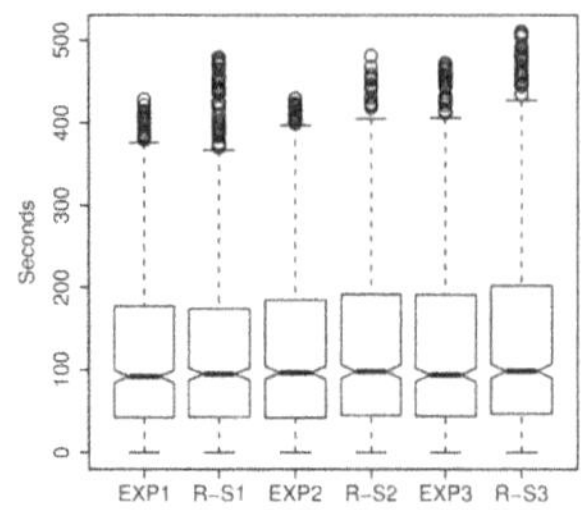

(a) Initial delay

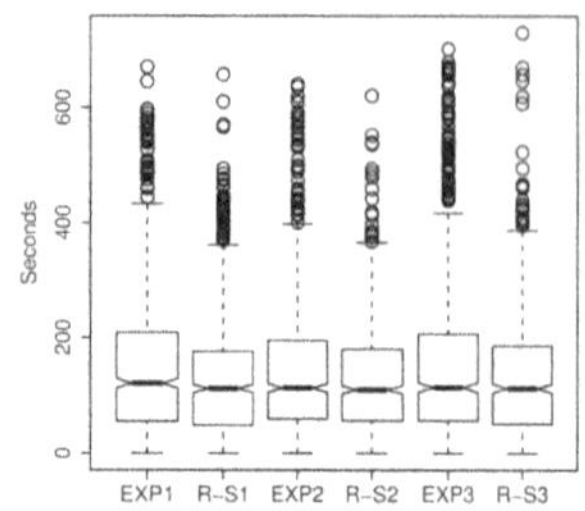

(b) Waiting time

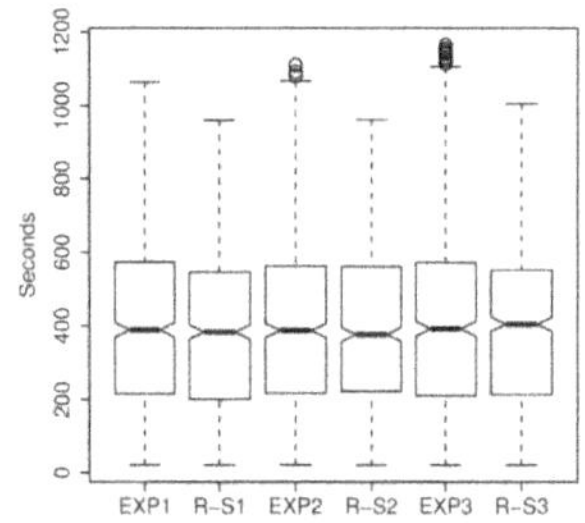

(c) Travel time

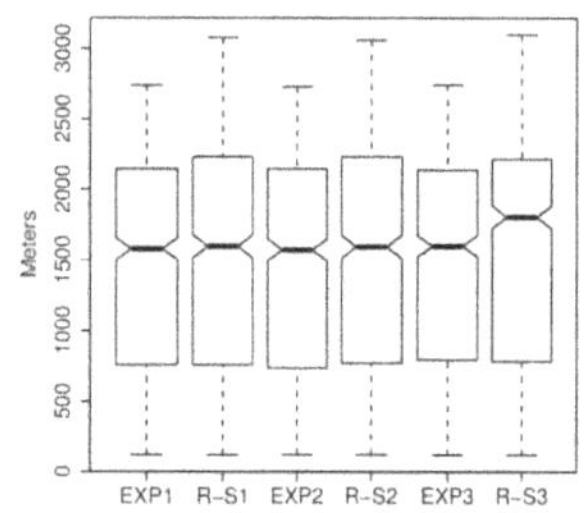

(d) Route length

Figure 8: Box plot representation of the distribution of the results for the experts' solution (EXP) and the Red Swarm (R-S).

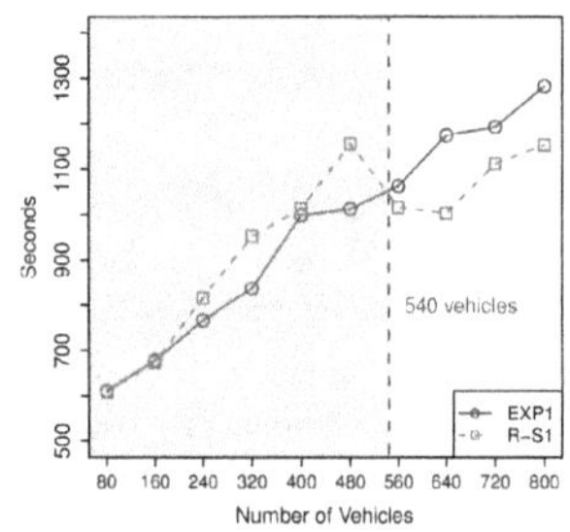

(a) *Sim1*

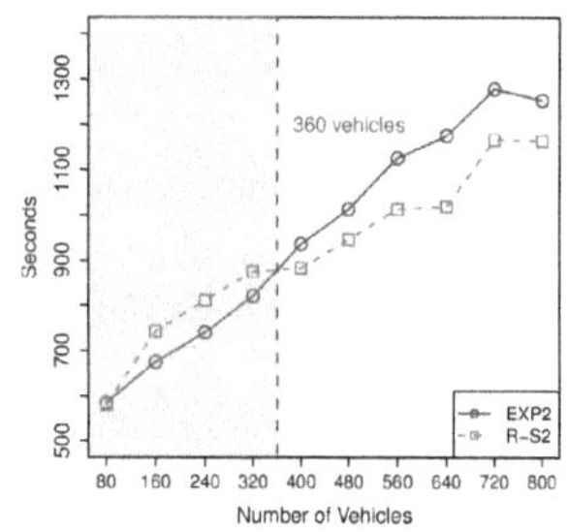

(b) *Sim2*

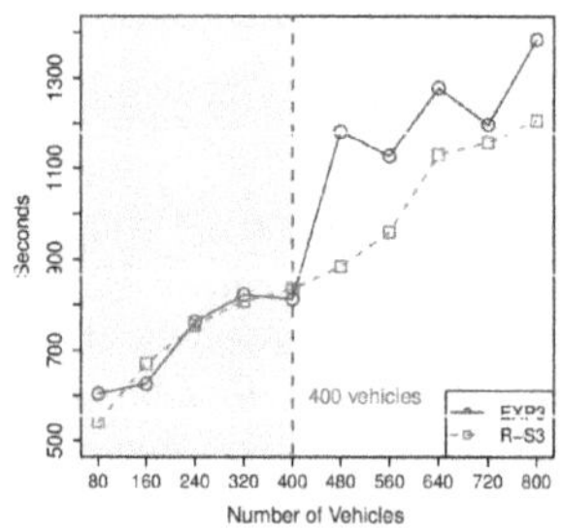

(c) *Sim3*

Figure 9: Exit Time vs Number of Vehicles. Note that the vertical line indicates the lowest number of vehicles, from which the optimization is effective.

Table 7: Metrics of experts' solution, Red Swarm, and RANDOM.

Metric	Experts' solution			Red Swarm			RANDOM		
	Sim1	*Sim2*	*Sim3*	*Sim1*	*Sim2*	*Sim3*	*Sim1*	*Sim2*	*Sim3*
# Trips Completed	800	800	800	800	800	800	737	710	648
Total Time (s)	1283	1253	1385	**1154**	**1164**	**1206**	1800	1800	1800
Minimum Fitness	532.9	530.8	549.0	**512.7**	**523.5**	**533.3**	57459.5	81797.6	137547.3

Table 8: Results of experts' solution and Red Swarm.

	Metric	Experts' algorithm			Red Swarm			Rate
		Avg.	StdDev.	Median	Avg.	StdDev.	Median	(Avg.)
sim1	Initial delay (s)	**123.0**	103.1	92.0	123.4	104.1	95.0	0.3%
	Waiting time (s)	151.8	130.3	121.0	**128.6**	106.4	112.0	-18.0%
	Travel time (s)	409.9	237.8	389.5	**389.2**	214.2	383.5	-5.3%
	Route length (m)	**1491.4**	767.6	1577.1	1565.4	853.6	1595.5	4.7%
sim2	Initial delay (s)	**124.7**	102.5	96.5	127.8	104.8	98.0	2.4%
	Waiting time (s)	146.3	127.4	113.0	**129.1**	98.1	110.0	-13.3%
	Travel time (s)	406.1	234.1	388.0	**395.7**	213.8	377.0	-2.6%
	Route length (m)	**1477.7**	777.9	1570.2	1566.3	845.9	1593.0	5.7%
sim3	Initial delay (s)	**127.0**	107.3	94.0	132.7	111.2	98.5	4.3%
	Waiting time (s)	161.2	153.3	114.0	**134.1**	110.9	112.5	-20.2%
	Travel time (s)	422.0	260.3	392.5	**400.6**	213.7	405.0	-5.3%
	Route length (m)	**1506.9**	753.9	1598.0	1594.8	834.3	1803.9	5.5%

quite common for researchers to not carry out such a sanity check, reporting results of algorithms that can be beaten by random search. We simply do not want this to happen here, and that is why we include its numerical results.

Data from the RANDOM executions are presented in Table 7. While in Figure 10 the graphs of the number of vehicles in the city vs. the total time for the three executions are illustrated.

The main reason for such a poor performance of RANDOM is that there were a number of vehicles moving in circles around the city because the Red Swarm spots did not reroute them properly towards their destination due to a suboptimal configuration.

In Figure 11 we show two photorealistic snapshots exported from SUMO to Google Earth™. The first one shows the path followed by a vehicle routed by the experts' algorithm and the second one presents the new route set by the Red Swarm spot placed at the junction in the center of the figure. This behavior is repeated each time a vehicle arrives in the surrounding area of a Red Swarm spot and the new route will depend on the destination of each vehicle as well as the configuration of the spot.

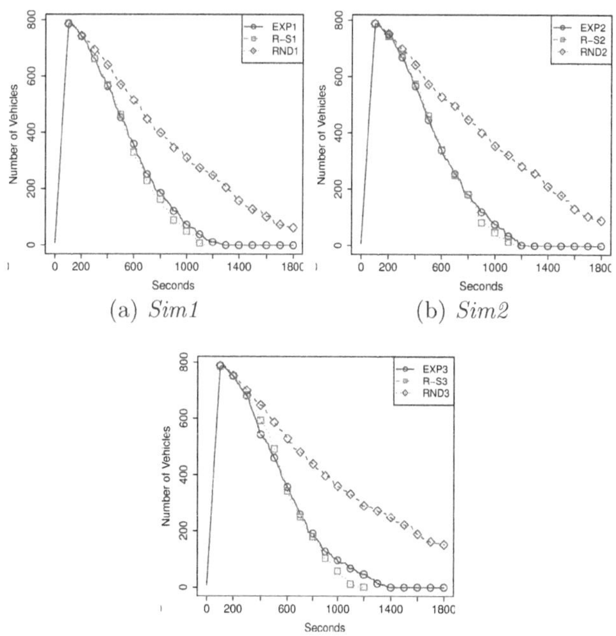

(a) *Sim1* (b) *Sim2* (c) *Sim3*

Figure 10: Traffic Density for experts' algorithm (EXP), RANDOM (RND), and Red Swarm (R-S).

4. CONCLUSIONS

In this paper, we have presented an innovative approach for preventing traffic jams. The results confirm that road traffic can be improved by using our proposal, especially in high density conditions (e.g. peak times, construction, accidents reducing the available streets, etc.). Although the average travel time was only 5.3% better than the solution of the experts, we lowered the waiting time of the vehicles by 20.2%. That means that drivers are wasting less time (about 23 second less on average) waiting at a red light and in each traffic jam.

As a matter for future work, we plan to expand the size of the analyzed region as well as include a larger number of

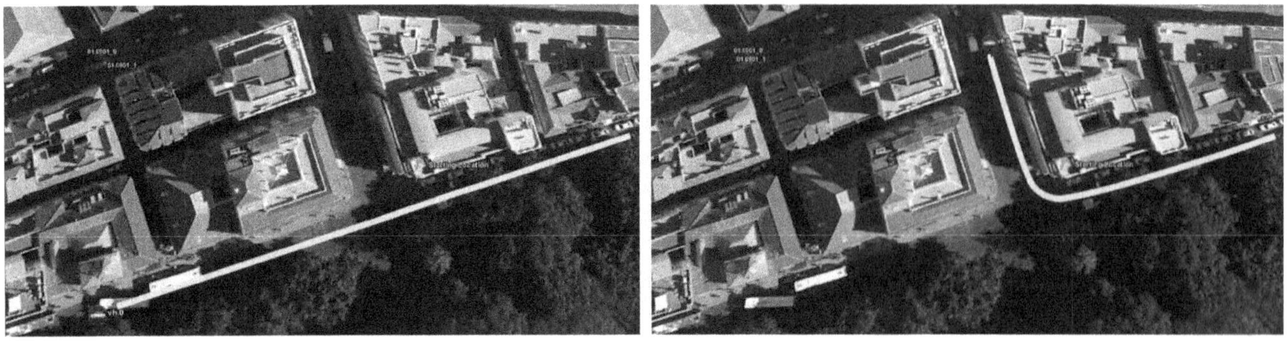

Figure 11: Route computed by experts' algorithm vs. route computed using Red Swarm.

Red Swarm spots which will also provide more alternative routes between each other.

For preliminary results for our future work, we have tested Red Swarm in 30 extra scenarios, different from the ones analyzed here. Our proposal not only has worked in all these scenarios but has also outperformed the experts' solution in 20 of them (66.7%).

Red Swarm will not only provide alternative routes for every single car in the city, but will also be able to collect information from the cars (in an anonymous way) permitting local authorities to better know the on-line and historical data of the city to actually help the evolution to a modern smart city.

We are also working on reducing green house emissions. As road traffic is one of the main sources of pollution, in future work we will include metrics of pollutant emissions and fuel consumption as SUMO implements them.

5. ACKNOWLEDGMENTS

Authors acknowledge funds from the Ministry of Economy and Competitiveness and FEDER under contract TIN2011-28194 (roadME `http://roadme.lcc.uma.es`).

6. REFERENCES

[1] Communication From the Commission - Europe 2020. Technical report, 2010. A strategy for smart, sustainable and inclusive growth.

[2] M. Behrisch, L. Bieker, J. Erdmann, and D. Krajzewicz. SUMO - Simulation of Urban MObility: An Overview. In *SIMUL 2011, The Third International Conference on Advances in System Simulation*, pages 63–68, October 2011.

[3] L. Bieker and D. Krajzewicz. Evaluation of opening bus lanes for private traffic triggered via V2X communication. In *Integrated and Sustainable Transportation System (FISTS), 2011 IEEE Forum on*, pages 48–53. IEEE, 2011.

[4] J. Garcia-Nieto, E. Alba, and A. Olivera. Enhancing the urban road traffic with Swarm Intelligence: A case study of Córdoba city downtown. In *Intelligent Systems Design and Applications (ISDA), 2011 11th International Conference on*, pages 368–373. IEEE, 2011.

[5] A. Gomez, G. Diaz, and K. Boussetta. How Virtual Police Agents can help in the traffic guidance? In *Wireless Communications and Networking Conference Workshops (WCNCW), 2012 IEEE*, pages 360–364. IEEE, 2012.

[6] F. Knorr, D. Baselt, M. Schreckenberg, and M. Mauve. Reducing Traffic Jams via VANETs. *Vehicular Technology, IEEE Transactions on*, 61(8):3490–3498, oct. 2012.

[7] D. Krajzewicz, E. Brockfeld, J. Mikat, J. Ringel, C. Rössel, W. Tuchscheerer, P. Wagner, and R. Wösler. Simulation of modern traffic lights control systems using the open source traffic simulation SUMO. In *Proceedings of the 3rd industrial simulation conference*, pages 299–302, 2005.

[8] S. Krauß. *Microscopic modeling of traffic flow: Investigation of collision free vehicle dynamics.* PhD thesis, Universitat zu Koln., 1998.

[9] J. Sánchez, M. Galán, and E. Rubio. Applying a traffic lights evolutionary optimization technique to a real case: "Las Ramblas" area in Santa Cruz de Tenerife. *Evolutionary Computation, IEEE Transactions on*, 12(1):25–40, 2008.

[10] A. Wegener, H. Hellbrück, C. Wewetzer, and A. Lubke. VANET Simulation Environment with Feedback Loop and its Application to Traffic Light Assistance. In *GLOBECOM Workshops, 2008 IEEE*, pages 1–7. IEEE, 2008.

[11] A. Wegener, M. Piórkowski, M. Raya, H. Hellbrück, S. Fischer, and J. Hubaux. TraCI: an interface for coupling road traffic and network simulators. In *Proceedings of the 11th communications and networking simulation symposium*, pages 155–163. ACM, 2008.

Fast and Effective Multi-Objective Optimisation of Wind Turbine Placement

Raymond Tran, Junhua Wu, Christopher Denison
Thomas Ackling, Markus Wagner, Frank Neumann

Evolutionary Computation Group
The University of Adelaide
Adelaide, SA 5005, Australia

ABSTRACT

The single-objective yield optimisation of wind turbine placements on a given area of land is already a challenging optimization problem. In this article, we tackle the multi-objective variant of this problem: we are taking into account the wake effects that are produced by the different turbines on the wind farm, while optimising the energy yield, the necessary area, and the cable length needed to connect all turbines.

One key step contribution in order to make the optimisation computationally feasible is that we employ problem-specific variation operators. Furthermore, we use a recently presented caching-technique to speed-up the computation time needed to assess a given wind farm layout. The resulting approach allows the multi-objective optimisation of large real-world scenarios within a single night on a standard computer.

Categories and Subject Descriptors

I.2.8 [**Artificial Intelligence**]: Problem Solving, Control Methods, and Search—*Heuristic Methods*

General Terms

Algorithms, Performance

Keywords

Wind Power, Wind Farm Layout, Multi-Objective Optimisation

GECCO'13, July 6–10, 2013, Amsterdam, The Netherlands.

1. INTRODUCTION

Wind power is an increasingly important source of growth within the global renewable energy market. Global cumulative production capacity is forecast to increase to almost 500 Gigawatts by 2016. This is more than double the figure recorded in 2011 [6]. *Wind turbine placement optimisation* is the process of determining the placement of wind turbines in Wind farms. This enables wind farm installations to maximise their cost-effectiveness, thereby increasing their competitiveness in the renewable energy market. In the single-objective yield optimisation of wind turbine placements, the wind turbines are placed within a specified land or offshore area, such that the output power is maximised.

In this paper, we demonstrate the multi-objective variant of the Wind Turbine Placement problem. Three different objective combinations are considered: output power and the area of the convex hull, output power and the total distance of the minimum spanning tree, and a combination of output power, convex hull area and minimum spanning tree. An improved version of the implementation of the wind turbine placement model [10] presented in [15] is used to evaluate the power output of the wind farm layouts. We use the multi-objective evolutionary algorithms NSGA-II [3], SPEA2 [20] and IBEA [19] to produce a number of different wind turbine layouts. These algorithms are combined with the problem-specific variation operators that are presented in the paper.

1.1 Related work

The optimal siting of wind turbines on a given area of land is a complex optimisation problem that is hard to solve by exact methods. The decision space is non-linear with respect to how sited turbines interact, when considering wake loss and energy capture. Several bio-inspired computation techniques such as evolutionary algorithms [5, 7] and particle swarm optimisation [9] have been used for the optimisation.

The different approaches for the single-objective wind farm layout problem are summarized in [12]. For example, Wan et al. [16–18] use cell-based approaches and compare different bio-inspired algorithms, each applied to the same set of wind farm models and parameters. An alternative to cell placement was explored in [10]: each turbine's location is a decision variable pair of real-valued, spatial (x,y) coordinates. In that paper a simple evolution strategy (ES) is used to optimise very small wind farms. In general, an ES is effective because it is easily parallelised and it self-adapts the extent to which it perturbs decision variables when generating a new potential solution. A more powerful ES called CMA-ES has been used for the same problem in [14]. Despite being computationally expensive, it allows for the effective optimisation of huge layouts for up to 1000 turbines. Recently, a random local search was presented that combines a problem-specific operator with an asymptotic speed-up of the computation time of the wake effects [15]. The resulting algorithm can effectively optimise huge layouts overnight, instead of requiring weeks on specialised computing servers.

Difficulties such as the expensive wake effects computation carry over from the single-objective problem to the multi-objective problem, which we see as one reason why the latter came up just recently (see, e.g. [2, 11, 13]). Common investigated objectives are the maximization of energy yield, the minimization of land cost, and the minimization of environmental impact. However, very often the results leave room for improvements, either because simplified wake models (to make the optimisation computationally feasible), or because the optimisation algorithms are not adjusted to the real-world scenarios. In [13] a first step was taken to combine a general purpose multi-objective algorithm with problem-specific repair strategies, while using the Park wake model for the energy yield computations. In contrast to their work, we employ problem-specific variation operators right from the beginning, investigate different optimisation algorithms and more scenarios, we use a faster wake calculation, and the cable length costs are added as an additional objective.

We proceed as follows. In Section 2, we formally introduce the multi-objective wind turbine placement problem and the different objectives that are subject to our investigations. New variation operators such as mutation and crossover for this highly constrained optimisation problem are described in Section 3. We report on our experimental investigations with popular evolutionary multi-objective optimisation algorithms in Section 4 and finish with some concluding remarks.

2. PRELIMINARIES

In the following, we outline the different objectives and constraints that we considered for the wind farm optimisation.

Let $X = \{x_1, \ldots, x_n\}$ and $Y = \{y_1, \ldots, y_n\}$ be a set of x and y coordinates of n wind turbines in the plane. The goal is to find a set of coordinates such that the energy output of the whole wind farm is maximised. At the same time, the total length of the cable necessary to interconnect the turbines, as well as the area necessary for the wind farm, should be minimised. Furthermore, the layout has to respect certain constraints. Each of the aforementioned attributes is set to the solution as a separate objective.

2.1 Energy Yield Prediction

2.1.1 *Energy Output*

The overall energy output of the wind farm varies depending on the chosen coordinates, because we have to take the wake effects into account. We consider the Park wake model, as it is a trade-off between highly simplifying wake models and computationally extremely expensive simulations based on fluid-dynamics. In this model, the wake effects on a turbine i change the wind resources available to it along different directions by reducing the *scale* parameter c of the Weibull distribution estimated for the entire farm, which is also called the free-stream wind resource. This wind resource is dependent on its location and the location of the rest of the turbines. Hence, we have a scale parameter c_i for each turbine i: its computation is complex and involves wind velocity deficits $Vdef_j$ that the turbine i experiences due to the influence of other

Algorithm 1: Procedure for evaluation of wake effects due to the Park model [10]

Given $\{X, Y\}$ as turbine locations, turbine thrust coefficient C_T, rotor diameter R, landscape-specific wake spreading factor κ ;

$a = 1 - \sqrt{1 - C_T}, b = \kappa/R, u \Leftarrow$ unit step function, $o = (x_i - x_j)cos\theta + (y_i - y_j)sin\theta$;

$d_{i,j} = \|o\|, \alpha = tan^{-1}\kappa$;

for $i = 1$ *to number of turbines* **do**

  for $\theta = 0^0$ *to* 360^0 **do**

    for $j = 1$ *to n-1 and* $j \neq i$ **do**

      $\delta_{i,j} = cos^{-1}\left(\frac{o + R/\kappa}{\sqrt{(x_i - x_j + \frac{R}{\kappa}cos\theta)^2 + (y_i - y_j + \frac{R}{\kappa}sin\theta)^2}}\right)$;

      $Vdef_{(i,j)} = u(\delta_{i,j} - \alpha)\frac{a}{(1+bd_{i,j})^2}$;

    $Vdef_i^\theta = \sqrt{\sum_j (Vdef_{(i,j)}^\theta)^2}$;

    $c_i(\theta) = c_i(\theta) \times (1 - Vdef_i)$;

turbines $j, j \neq i$ (see Algorithm 1). We refer the reader to [10] for a detailed presentation on the computation of this parameter when considering wake effects in the Park wake model. In short, the expected energy output η of the whole wind farm is given by

$$E^{farm}[\eta] = \sum_i \int_\theta P(\theta) \int_v p(v(\theta), c_i(\theta, X, Y), k(\theta))\beta^i(v).$$

Here, v is the wind speed, and the function $\beta^i(v)$ defines the power curve for turbine i. Wind speed v however is a random variable with a Weibull distribution, $p(v(\theta), c_i(\theta, X, Y), k(\theta))$, which is estimated from wind resource data and considers the wake effect using X and Y. This distribution is also a function of the wind direction, θ which varies from $0^0 - 360^0$. Note that the *shape parameter* of the Weibull distribution is not influenced by the Wake effects here. In addition, wind flows from a certain direction with some probability $P(\theta)$.

2.1.2 *Constraints and Assumptions*

Following recent literature (see [10, 13–15]), we have the following constraints placed on our optimization function. The first one enforces an upper bound on the area of the farm. This constraint ensures that we can only place a turbine i within a certain area, which is a realistic constraint for most layout problems. For a rectangular farm with length l and width w this constraint is satisfied *iff*

$$0 \leq x_i \leq l \text{ and } 0 \leq y_i \leq w, 1 \leq i \leq n.$$

Because turbines can be damaged through turbulences when they are located too close to each other, the second constraint regulates the spatial proximity. It is satisfied *iff*

$$\sqrt{(x_i - x_j)^2 + (y_i - y_j)^2} \geq M \cdot R, 1 \leq i \neq j \leq n$$

where R is the rotor radius and M is a proximity factor usually decided ahead of the optimization based on the make and model of the turbines used. We use $M = 8$ based on the industry standard.

In addition to the above constraints, we assume that all turbines have the same power curves (approximated as piecewise linear functions) and that the same wind resource spans the entire farm.[1] Note that the assumptions can be revised in a very straight forward manner to generate more realistic scenarios.

[1]To increase accuracy, these resources can be estimated for different parts in the farm.

2.2 Euclidean Minimum Spanning Tree

The Euclidean Minimum Spanning Tree is used to calculate the minimum length of cable required to connect all wind turbines in a specific wind farm configuration. It is computed by first constructing the complete graph on the set of points that represent the wind turbines and edge costs given by the Euclidean distance between any pair of turbines. The minimum spanning tree for this graph is computed and used as an objective representing the costs of the cable length. Figure 1 displays a wind turbine layout, as well as the minimum spanning tree, represented by the lines joining each wind turbine. All turbines are encompassed by a rectangular land area, represented by the dashed line.

2.3 (Cost of the) Convex Hull

For the purposes of our experiment, the cost of the convex hull is defined as the area contained by the set of points forming the convex hull. This value is the minimum land area that is required for a wind farm layout. We compute the convex hull using Graham's scan algorithm [8]. Figure 1 displays a wind turbine layout, as well as the area (cost) of the convex hull, shaded in grey. Provided that this shape is a non-intersecting polygon with n vertices, the area can be calculated as follows [1]:

$$A = \frac{1}{2}\sum_{i=0}^{n-1}(x_i y_{i+1} - x_{i+1} y_i).$$

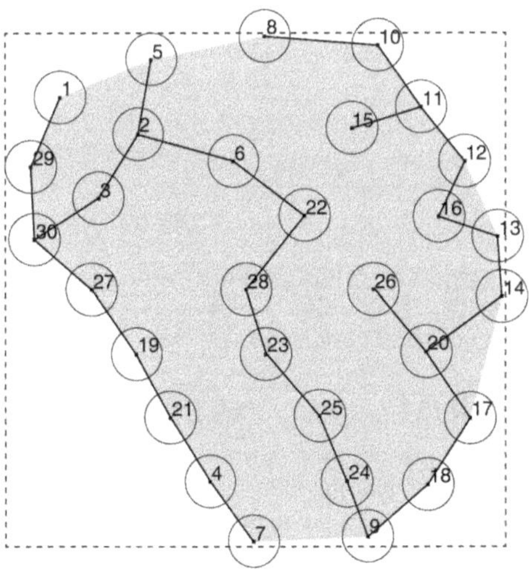

Figure 1: An example wind turbine layout. The shaded area represents the area of the convex hull. The lines signify the edges of the Euclidean Minimum Spanning Tree, or cables. The circles visualise the minimum safety distance imposed by the proximity constraint.

3. VARIATION OPERATORS FOR TURBINE PLACEMENT

In this section, we outline our framework and the problem-specific variation operators for the multi-objective wind turbine placement problem. As the problem is highly constrained due to a large number of turbines and the given safety margin around each turbine, our operators have to ensure that feasible placements are produced.

3.1 Movement Mutation

Mutation operators should do local changes to the current solution, i.e. the placement of the turbines on the given area of land. Our mutation operator called *Movement Mutation* (see Algorithm 2) moves a randomly selected specified proportion of the turbines in a given solution.

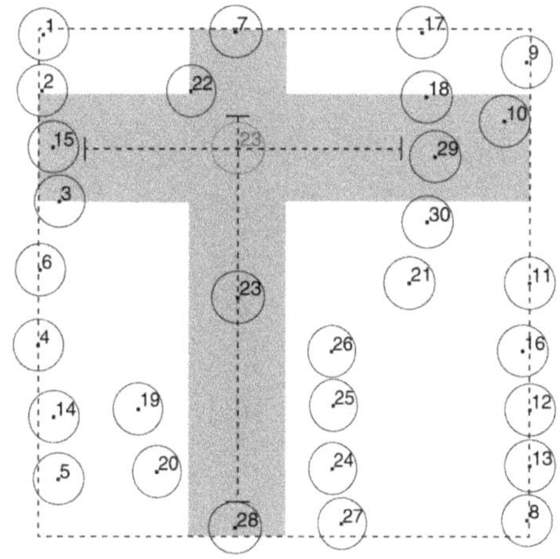

Figure 2: An instance of a Movement Mutation operation. The old and new positions of turbine 23 are shown, as well as the investigated area.

The distance and direction of the movement is determined randomly, subject to constraints.

In order to ensure that the solution remains feasible, the maximum distance that the wind turbine can move in each direction is computed. This is done by inspecting a designated area surrounding the x- and y-axis of the movement. In the inspection area, wind turbines whose rotor safety margins are found to overlap, restrict the constraints of movement for the selected turbine. The designated area is determined as two times the 38.5 metre margin of safety, emanating in each direction perpendicular from the axis of travel. In order to achieve a feasible placement after the movement of the turbines, the movement ranges M_v and M_h are computed based on the neighbouring turbines in the placement. By doing this it is guaranteed that a *Movement Mutation* operation does not produce an infeasible child individual.

Figure 2 depicts a single instance of a Movement Mutation operation. In this instance, a wind turbine (23) is randomly selected and moved directly south. The dotted lines represent the constraints of movement for the selected wind turbine. The shaded region represents the area that is inspected for overlapping wind turbines. The location of the turbine prior to the mutation is shown in grey. Note that the movements of turbine 23 are restricted by neighbouring turbines whose safety margins encroach upon the inspection area. The location of the turbine following the mutation is shown in black.

Provided that the algorithm of Movement Mutation (Algorithm 2) is based on a single loop of simple calculation, the time complexity of it can be determined as $O(n)$, in which n is the number of turbines in a solution.

3.2 Block Swap Crossover

Block Swap Crossover is designed to implant a randomly selected *block* from each of two parents to produce two children, each with a varying degree of information from each parent. A block is a rectangular area on the wind farm that is encompassed by the boundary of the entire wind farm. The first child uses the first parent as a basis. A block is randomly selected from the second parent for copying to the first child. Subsequently, the bounds of this block are expanded beyond the proximity constraint of every turbine by the value of twice the rotor radius (38.5 metres). This is to maintain

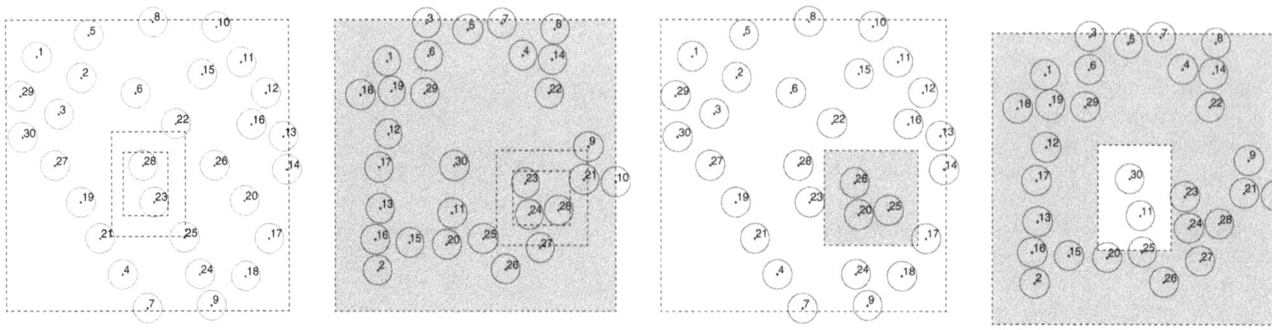

(a) The first parent turbine layout, prior to Block Swap Crossover. **(b)** The second parent turbine layout, prior to Block Swap Crossover. **(c)** The first Block Swap Crossover child. **(d)** The second Block Swap Crossover child.

Figure 3: Example: Block Swap Crossover.

Algorithm 2: Movement Mutation

1 Given P as selected parent with turbine locations $\{X, Y\}$;
2 Assuming turbine $t = \{x, y\}$ is selected for movement, $t \in P$, $x \in X$ and $y \in Y$;
3 Let S = safety distance;
4 Set M_h as horizontal movement range of t, M_v as vertical movement range of t;
5 **foreach** $t' = \{x', y'\} : (y - S < y' < y + S)$ **do**
6   **if** *x' is nearest to x on positive direction;*
7   **then**
8   Save x' to x_p;
9   **if** *x' is nearest to x on negative direction;*
10   **then**
11   Save x' to x_n;
12 M_h ranges from $x_p - S$ to $x_n + S$;
13 Redo the lines 5–12 to get of M_v;
14 **return** $t^n = \{x^n, y\} : (x^n \in M_h)$ or $t^n = \{x, y^n\} : (y^n \in M_v)$;

a margin of safety between the turbines in the copied block and the turbines outside these bounds. This boundary is then used in the child to determine the area that is replaced by the turbine information from the second parent. The above process is repeated for the second child, which uses the second parent as a basis, and copies information from the first parent.

The turbine position copying process is straightforward, provided that the destination area to be replaced in the child contains a lesser or equal number of turbines compared to the parent. In the event that this is not the case, a new boundary is randomly selected until this condition is satisfied. If in the event that a suitable block is not found for copying to create a child, its respective parent is returned as a result of the operation. This indicates that the crossover operation has failed. The turbines within the destination area are rearranged to the same configuration as the source area in the parent. If the number of turbines in the destination area matches the source, the operation ends. Otherwise, turbines are randomly selected from outside the child's destination area and moved into the destination area as substitutes. This ensures that the number of turbines is equivalent in both the source and destination.

Figures 3a and 3b show the configuration of the first and second parents, as well as the source area selected for copying. In Figures 3c and 3d, each child is shown, following the copying operation. The shaded areas represent information that is obtained from the second parent. White areas represent information from the first parent.

Algorithm 3: Block Swap Crossover

Given P_1 and P_2 are selected parents with turbine locations;
for $i = 0$ *to* T **do**
    Randomly generate a rectangular area A_1 in wind farm area;
    The turbines in P_1 are divided into two subsets, I_1 for the turbines inside A_1 and O_1 for the ones outside of A_1;
    Modify A_1 to A_1' in which each edge keeps a safety distance to nearest turbine in I_1;
    Apply A_1' on P_2 to get I_2 and O_2;
    if $|I_2| \geq |I_1|$ **then**
        Move $n = |I_2| - |I_1|$ turbines from O_1 into I_1;
        Set turbine locations in I_1 as in I_2;
        Return P_1 as child number 1;
    else
        continue;
Apply the above on P_2 to get child number 2;

The time complexity of the crossover operator is similar to the mutation operator. As it is also using a single loop (Algorithm 3), the complexity can be determined as $O(n)$.

4. EXPERIMENTAL INVESTIGATIONS

In this section, we describe our experimental setup and report on the results of different popular evolutionary multi-objective algorithms using our new variation operators for the multi-objective wind turbine placement problem.

4.1 Experimental Setup

We are solving the multi-objective wind turbine placement problems using popular multi-objective evolutionary algorithms together with the variation operator described in the previous section. For the basis of our experiments, the evolutionary multi-objective algorithms IBEA [19], NSGA-II [3], and SPEA2 [20] and their implementation in the jMetal framework [4] are utilised. The *BinaryTournament2* selection operator of NSGA-II is used for all experiments. In contrast to a pure binary tournament, this selection operator checks whether one solution dominates the other, before comparing the corresponding fitness values.

To evaluate our algorithm's performance we used wind *Scenario 2* defined in [10]. *Scenario 2* is rather complex, and the prevailing wind direction covers a broad sector of about 105°. The wind intensity per direction is given by Weibull distributions in both cases, which results in non-zero probabilities for wind coming from any direction. Therefore, one has to optimize the layout to work with minimum wake loss along all the wind directions.

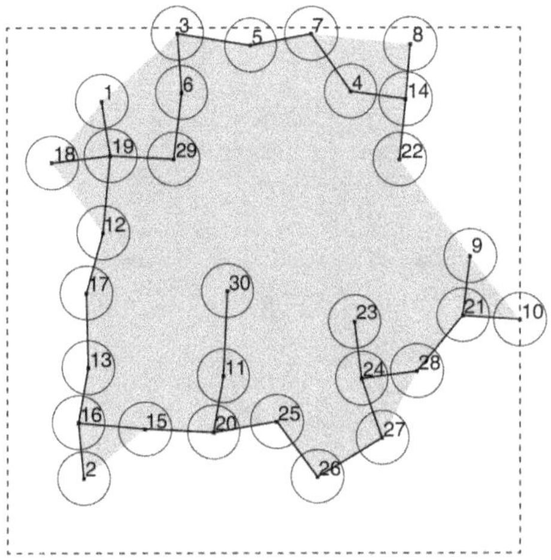

Figure 4: A *packed* 30 turbine configuration from an NSGA-II triple-objective experiment. It yields a total power output of 2.03×10^5 kW, with a convex hull area of 5.47 km^2 and a minimum spanning tree length of 10.7 km.

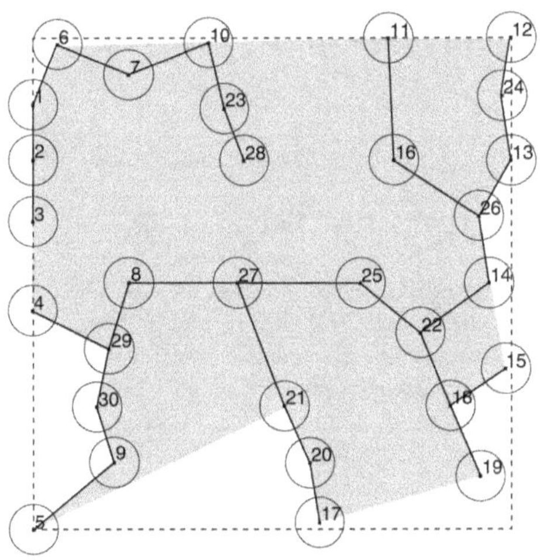

Figure 5: A *distributed* 30 turbine configuration from an NSGA-II triple-objective experiment. It yields a total power output of 2.31×10^5 kW, with a convex hull area of 8.55 km^2 and minimum spanning tree length of 14.1 km.

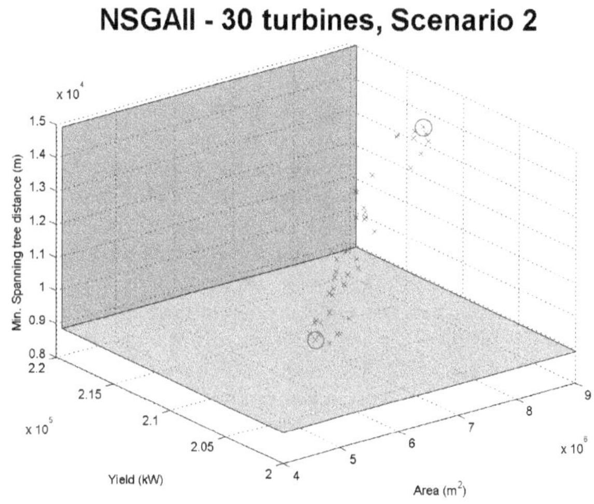

Figure 6: The locations of the packed and distributed turbine configurations on the Pareto frontier.

Lastly, we use the turbine rotor radius $R = 38.5m$ for the proximity constraints.

Based on the wind scenario, we can compute the expected yield that we then use as one objective in our optimisation. For the other objectives, the Euclidean minimum spanning tree and the convex hull area, more details are available in Sections 2.2 and 2.3 respectively.

In the experiments, we applied the multi-objective optimisation algorithms NSGA-II, SPEA2 and IBEA using our operators. In each simulation instance, a population size of 50 is utilised, over 20,000 generations, and its runtime is less than 15 minutes. The Movement mutation operator is applied with a probability of $p_m = 0.7$ in each iteration and it moves in each mutation step 5% of the turbines. The Block Swap crossover operator is applied with a probability of $p_c = 0.3$.[2] These parameter values are used for all three multi-objective algorithms, and for the following objective combinations:

1. maximising the power output (yield) and minimising the area of the convex hull,
2. maximising the power output (yield) and minimising the total distance of the minimum spanning tree, and
3. a combination of power, convex hull area and minimum spanning tree.

Each variation on the algorithm and objective combinations is repeated 10 times in order to build a point cloud. The land area is restricted to 3×3 km^2 in the experiments involving 30, 50, and 70 turbines. In the case of the 200 turbines, the land is restricted to 10×10 km^2. As a consequence of this fixed area, the set-ups have different qualities. For example, the algorithms can pack the 30 turbines tightly as well as distribute them over a large area, whereas even the tightest 70 turbine layouts will cover a significant portion of the available land area already. The scenario involving 200 turbines is computationally expensive due to the increasing costs of the wake computations. It allows us to compare our approach with the single-objective algorithms listed in [15] and the multi-objective approach outlined in [18] respectively.

4.2 Experimental Results

Figure 6 displays a 3D point cloud that represents the Pareto frontier over 10 runs of an experiment using the NSGA-II algorithm. The total footprint of the wind farm is shown in the x-axis. Yield, or power output of the wind farm is shown in the y-axis. The z-axis represents the total distance of the Euclidean minimum spanning tree formed by all wind turbines. The surfaces shown in the plot represent the feasible bounds of the experiment. The red surface represents the maximum feasible yield of a 30 turbine wind farm, without wake loss. This theoretical maximum is calculated using formula 22 in [10]. The green surface represents the minimum feasible value of the minimum spanning tree, taking into account the turbine rotor radius proximity constraints. This value is calculated as follows:

$$L = (n - 1) \times 8.0 \times 38.5$$

[2]Both values were chosen based on initial testing.

where n is the number of turbines in the wind farm.

The two extremes of the Pareto frontier are highlighted in Figure 6. The lower left focuses on minimising the footprint in the packed configuration. The upper right is an optimisation for maximum power.

Figures 4 and 5 draw comparisons between a "packed" turbine layout and a "distributed" turbine layout. In the former layout, we try to deliver a layout that yields the most power, while at the same time providing a compact footprint and reducing the length of cabling required to connect each wind turbine. In Figure 5, an attempt is made to make best use of the 3×3 km land area available for use. In this instance, we are simply concerned with optimising the yield without regard to cable length or footprint.

We summarise all experiments on the 200 turbine scenario in Figure 7. It is observed that IBEA has a tendency to select solutions with a minimal spanning tree distance and convex hull area. This is in contrast with NSGA-II and SPEA2 that both achieve an apparently greater spread. This is likely due to IBEA's lack of diversity preservation techniques [19]. The greater spread of NSGA-II and SPEA2 may be considered computationally wasteful, as a wind farm builder may generally prefer smaller EMSTs and smaller convex hulls. This is covered adequately by IBEA, as clearly shown in the Yield versus Convex hull area and Yield versus Minimum spanning tree distance plots. In addition, IBEA's layouts for small EMSTs and smaller convex hulls have a significantly higher energy yield. Therefore, due to its bias, IBEA seems to be the most adequate algorithm for the multi-objective optimisation of wind farm layout, given our scenarios.

It is interesting to see how our approach compares to existing ones. Firstly, we achieve virtually the same maximum energy yield as the best-performing single-objective optimisation algorithm listed in [15]. Secondly, we achieve maximum energy yields that are about 10% better than the results achieved by the approach outlined in [18]. We see both as strong indicators that our approach with the problem-specific variation operators enable the fast and efficient multi-objective optimisation of wind farm layouts.

To compare the performances of the different multi-objective algorithms, we use the hypervolume indicator. Before we compute the hypervolumes, we normalize objective values to the following ranges:

1. 30 turbines: area 5km^2 – 9km^2, yield $200,000$kW – $215,000$kW, spanning tree length 8,5km – 16km
2. 50 turbines: area 7km^2 – 9km^2, yield $320,000$kW – $340,000$kW, spanning tree length 15km – 21km
3. 70 turbines: area 8km^2 – 9km^2, yield $430,000$kW – $460,000$kW, spanning tree length 21km – 25km
4. 200 turbines: area 10km^2 – 100km^2, yield $1,000,000$kW – $1,440,000$kW, spanning tree length 60km – 150km

The results are listed in Table 1. Interestingly, IBEA's performance varies significantly for 30 and 50 turbines. However, it clearly outperforms the other two algorithms for 70 turbines. On 200 turbines, IBEA achieves the highest hypervolume values, and with very little performance variation.

5. CONCLUSIONS

Wind energy plays an increasing role in the energy supply worldwide. We have investigated the problem of placing wind turbines on a given area of land using different conflicting objective functions. We designed new variation operators for the wind turbine

n Turbines	IBEA	NSGA-II	SPEA2
30	$0.1382_{0.126}$	$0.2230_{0.018}$	$\mathbf{0.2654}_{0.024}$
50	$0.1179_{0.116}$	$0.2079_{0.018}$	$\mathbf{0.2358}_{0.018}$
70	$\mathbf{0.3421}_{0.075}$	$0.2119_{0.023}$	$0.2403_{0.021}$
200	$\mathbf{0.5380}_{0.001}$	$0.4060_{0.012}$	$0.3589_{0.020}$

Table 1: Comparison of mean 3D hypervolume indicator values. The corresponding standard deviations are listed in subscript, and the best performing algorithm (according to the hypervolume value) is highlighted in boldface.

placement problem and have shown that state-of-the-art evolutionary multi-objective algorithms are very effective for the multi-objective wind turbine placement problem when using these operators. The quality of our results is confirmed by the lower bounds given for the cost of a minimum spanning tree and the maximum achievable energy which is very close to the one obtained in the single-objective approach of [15].

It is interesting to see how far the optimiser can improve upon the initial grid-based layouts, as the energy yield increases by about 6% and the EMST length reduces by about 40%. These improvements can translate into significant capital expenditure savings when setting up the wind farm, and into millions of additional dollars of income per year during the lifetime of the wind farm.

References

[1] P. Bourke. Calculating the area and centroid of a polygon, 1988.

[2] S. Şişbot, O. Turgut, M. Tunç, and U. Çamdali. Optimal positioning of wind turbines on Gökçeada using multi-objective genetic algorithm. *Wind Energy*, 13(4):297–306, 2010.

[3] K. Deb, A. Pratap, S. Agrawal, and T. Meyarivan. A fast and elitist multiobjective genetic algorithm: NSGA-II. *IEEE Trans. Evolutionary Computation*, 6(2):182–197, 2002.

[4] J. J. Durillo, A. J. Nebro, and E. Alba. The jMetal framework for multi-objective optimization: Design and architecture. In *Proc. Congress on Evolutionary Computation (CEC '10)*, pages 4138–4325. IEEE Press, 2010.

[5] A. Eiben and J. Smith. *Introduction to Evolutionary Computing*. Springer, 2007.

[6] Global Wind Energy Council. Global Statistics – Market Forecast 2012–2016, 2012. http://tinyurl.com/gwec12.

[7] D. E. Goldberg. *Genetic Algorithms in Search, Optimization and Machine Learning*. MIT Press, Cambridge, MA, USA, 1989.

[8] R. Graham. An efficient algorith for determining the convex hull of a finite planar set. *Information processing letters*, 1(4): 132–133, 1972.

[9] J. Kennedy, R. C. Eberhart, and Y. Shi. *Swarm Intelligence*. Morgan Kauffman, 2001.

[10] A. Kusiak and Z. Song. Design of wind farm layout for maximum wind energy capture. *Renewable Energy*, 35(3):685–694, 2010.

[11] W. Y. Kwong, P. Y. Zhang, D. Romero, J. Moran, M. Morgenroth, and C. Amon. Wind farm layout optimisation considering energy generation and noise propagation. In *Proc. International Design Engineering Technical Conferences & Computers and Information in Engineering Conference (IDETC/CIE '12)*, pages 1–10, 2012.

[12] P.-E. Rethore. State of the art in wind farm layout optimization. *Wind Energy Research*, page 179, 2010.

[13] K. Veeramachaneni, M. Wagner, U.-M. O'Reilly, and F. Neumann. Optimizing energy output and layout costs for large

wind farms using particle swarm optimization. In *Proc. Congress on Evolutionary Computation (CEC '12)*, pages 1–7, 2012.

[14] M. Wagner, K. Veeramachaneni, F. Neumann, and U.-M. O'Reilly. Optimizing the layout of 1000 wind turbines. In *European Wind Energy Association Annual Event*, 2011.

[15] M. Wagner, J. Day, and F. Neumann. A fast and effective local search algorithm for optimizing the placement of wind turbines. *Renewable Energy*, 51(0):64–70, 2013.

[16] C. Wan, J. Wang, G. Yang, X. Li, and X. Zhang. Optimal micro-siting of wind turbines by genetic algorithms based on improved wind and turbine models. In *Conference on Decision and Control*, pages 5092–5096, 2009.

[17] C. Wan, J. Wang, G. Yang, X. Li, and X. Zhang. Optimal siting of wind turbines using real coded genetic algorithms. *European Wind Energy Association Conference and Exhibition*, 2009.

[18] C. Wan, J. Wang, G. Yang, and X. Zhang. Optimal micro-siting of wind farms by particle swarm optimization. In *Advances in Swarm Intelligence*, volume 6145 of *Lecture Notes in Computer Science*, pages 198–205. Springer, 2010.

[19] E. Zitzler and S. Künzli. Indicator-based selection in multiobjective search. In *Proc. 8th International Conference Parallel Problem Solving from Nature (PPSN VIII)*, volume 3242 of *LNCS*, pages 832–842. Springer, 2004.

[20] E. Zitzler, M. Laumanns, and L. Thiele. SPEA2: Improving the strength Pareto evolutionary algorithm for multiobjective optimization. In *Proc. Evolutionary Methods for Design, Optimisation and Control with Application to Industrial Problems (EUROGEN '01)*, pages 95–100, 2002.

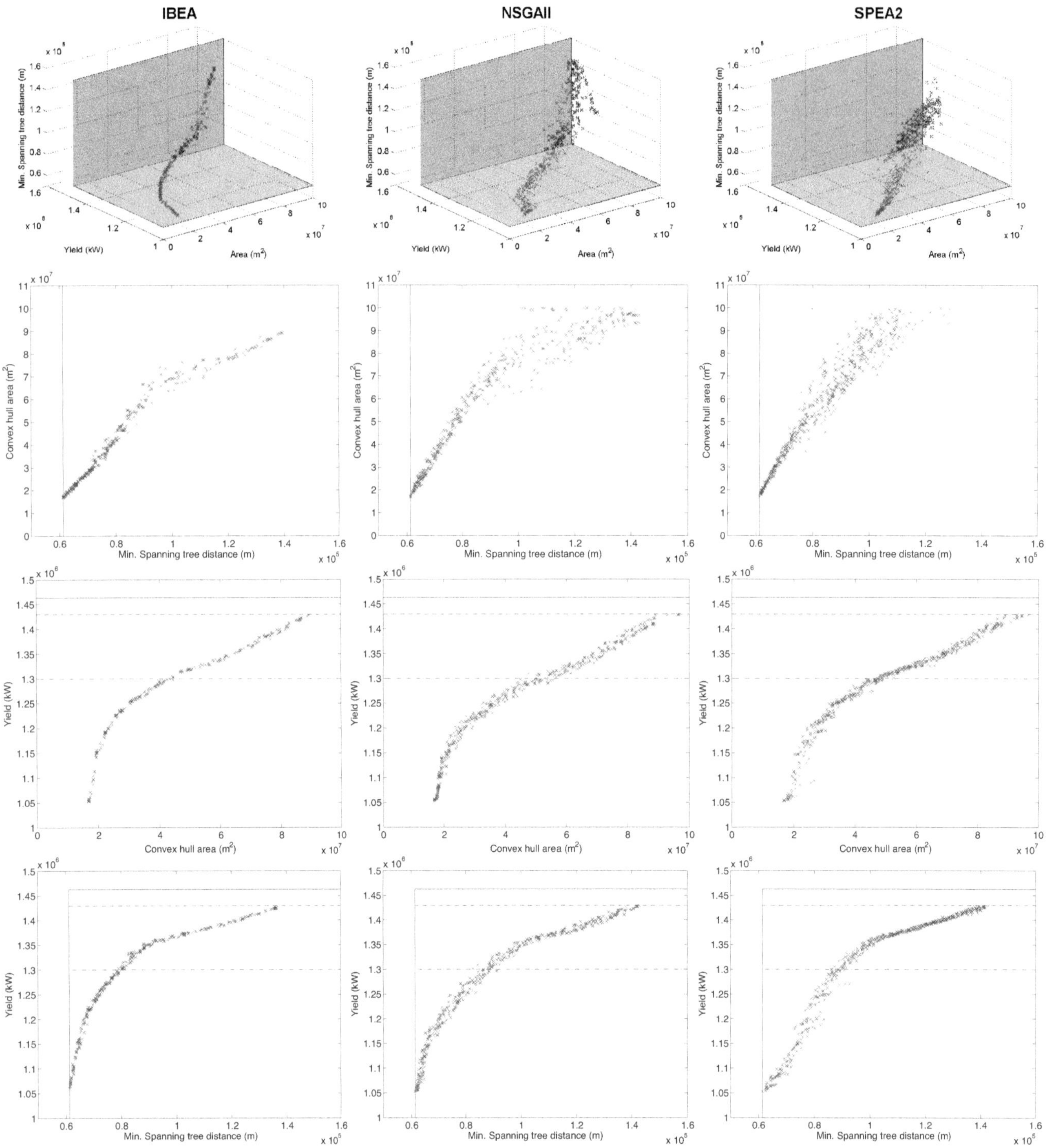

Figure 7: Point clouds depicting the Pareto frontiers for 10 runs - Scenario 2, 200 turbines. Where applicable, we show the theoretical limits (red=maximum yield, green=minimum spanning tree length) as coloured surfaces or as solid lines. The dashed lines show a yield of $1.43 \cdot 10^6$kW and $1.30 \cdot 10^6$kW. These are the averages achieved by the best-performing single-objective optimisation algorithm listed in [15] and the result achieved by the approach outlined in [18] respectively.

Differential Evolution Based Human Body Pose Estimation from Point Clouds

Roberto Ugolotti
Dept. of Information Engineering
University of Parma, Italy
rob_ugo@ce.unipr.it

Stefano Cagnoni
Dept. of Information Engineering
University of Parma, Italy
cagnoni@ce.unipr.it

ABSTRACT

This paper describes a method to estimate the body pose of a human from the point cloud obtained from a depth sensor. It uses Differential Evolution to find the best match between a candidate pose, represented by an instance of a 42-parameter articulated model of a human, and the point cloud. The results, compared to other four state-of-the art methods on a publicly available dataset, show that the method has good ability to estimate the pose of a person and to track him in video sequences.

The entire method, from Differential Evolution to fitness computation, is run on nVIDIA GPUs. Thanks to its massively parallel implementation in CUDA-C, it produces pose estimates in real time.

Categories and Subject Descriptors

I.5.4 [**Pattern Recognition**]: Applications—*Computer Vision*; I.2.10 [**Artificial Intelligence**]: Vision and Scene Understanding

Keywords

Body Pose Estimation, GPGPU programming, Parallel Computing, Differential Evolution

1. INTRODUCTION

Markerless body pose estimation is an important task in computer vision. The possible applications of such a task are countless: some common examples are human-computer interaction, gaming and medical assistance.

The research in body pose estimation has recently made significant progress, thanks to the present wide availability of low-cost systems able to compute depth maps, such as the Kinect by Microsoft. The availability of depth maps can limit the effects of some of the problems that hamper human pose estimation in images, because they simplify some tasks, like background subtraction, while totally solving others, like depth estimation.

In spite of the great effort made over the years [12], there is still much room for improving performance in terms of quality and precision. Amongst the main problems that must be tackled, one can definitely include the huge variability of the human body shape and appearance, possible partial occlusions, and the complexity of the problem of maximizing a matching function having high dimensionality and a large number of local optima.

Evolutionary algorithms (EAs) [7] can be very effective in tackling this problem. Their main weakness is that they need a large number of evaluations to reach good results; luckily, they are intrinsically parallel, since all members of the population interact very little with one another. In this regard, several parallel implementations based on commodity Graphic Processing Units (GPUs) have been developed recently [6, 13]. The recent expansion of general-purpose computing on graphics processing units (GPGPU) has been significantly stimulated by the release of CUDA (Compute Unified Device Architecture), a parallel computing framework by nVIDIA [16] which allows C code to be executed exploiting the parallelism of that company's GPUs.

In this paper, we propose a data-driven method that estimates a human's posture. The input data are organized as a point cloud that can be acquired from a depth sensor, like a Microsoft Kinect or a time-of-flight camera. The main goal of this approach is to minimize the distance, or maximize the similarity, between a generic model of the human body and the cloud of points, by means of an optimization process. We chose Differential Evolution [21], since it is one of the most successful EAs in dealing with highly multimodal functions.

To the best of our knowledge, this is the first approach to body pose estimation based completely on evolutionary computation that is able to run in real time. Our method does not make any assumptions on the nature of the point cloud under consideration and, thanks to the very general structure of the model, can be adapted for dealing with any shape other than a human body. Moreover, even without including a proper tracking system, our method is able to follow a subject's movements robustly.

The remainder of the paper is organized as follows: section 2 offers a brief overview of the most relevant methods related to ours, including those to which we have compared our approach. Sections 3 and 4 present the model we use and our algorithm, followed by the description of its parallel implementation in section 5. Some experimental results and concluding remarks are finally reported in sections 6 and 7, respectively.

2. BACKGROUND

The problem under consideration has been tackled very frequently in the last decade using many different approaches. In this section we briefly recall the main attempts to solve this problem using evolutionary techniques.

Our work is mainly inspired by [9, 14], where Particle Swarm Optimization (PSO) is used to minimize the difference between the images obtained from a multi-camera system and the projection of the model onto such images. In [20], a two-dimensional model-based tracking is performed using the Probability Evolutionary Algorithm, a method inspired by the Estimation of Distribution Algorithm. In [10], Krzeszowski et al use a Particle Filter embedding PSO to shift the particles toward more promising configurations of the human model. Similar approaches are presented in [18] and in [24], where Scatter Search is used instead of PSO. In [25], the authors use PCA to reduce the dimensionality of the problem, which is tackled using an ad-hoc Hierarchical Annealed Genetic Algorithm. Akhtar et al [1] employ the Bat Algorithm to maximize the similarity between the projection of the model and an image, using some features (silhouette, gradient, etc.) of the image itself. An approach similar to the one presented in this paper can be found in [11], which introduces a three-dimensional model that is matched to a point cloud using a co-evolutionary algorithm. In the latter, the model is matched to a small subset of the cloud to reduce computational cost.

It is important to notice that none of these algorithms work in real time.

2.1 Reference methods used for comparison

In Section 6, the results obtained by our method are compared to the ones obtained by these four approaches:

- Ganapathi et al [8] use coarse-to-fine hill climbing to optimize the kinematic chain that composes the skeleton. This procedure relies upon a set of previously trained patch classifiers to detect body parts. The classification results are propagated through the kinematic chain to recover from problems caused by noisy data and fast movements;

- Baak et al [2] extract a feature set from a point cloud using a variant of Dijkstra's algorithm. This set is then compared to a reference database of poses, to extract the most similar one, and to the pose computed in the previous frame. These two hypotheses of pose are then optimized locally and a late-fusion voting approach combines them to yield the final pose;

- Ye et al [23] match the point cloud with a set of precaptured motion exemplars to generate a body configuration estimation, as well as a semantic labeling of the input. The initial estimation is then refined by directly fitting the body configuration to the observation;

- Taylor et al [22] apply a regression forest (trained on over 300000 examples) on each pixel of the image. Each leaf node in the forest contains a distribution over the coordinates of their human model. The maximum-likelihood node in the forest is taken as the base model used for subsequent optimization.

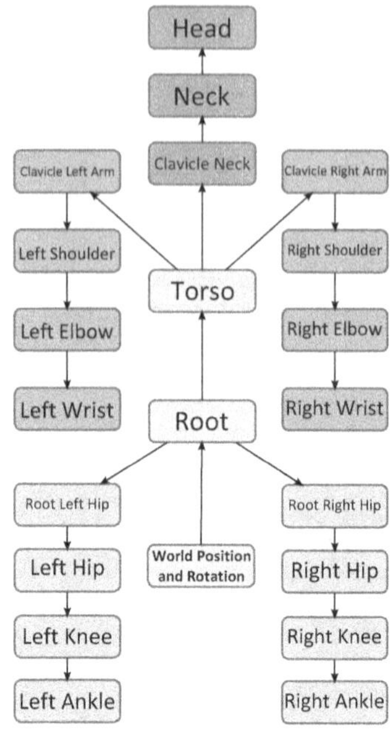

Figure 1: Kinematic chains used to describe the human model.

2.2 Differential Evolution

Differential Evolution (DE) has recently been shown to be one of the most successful EAs for global continuous optimization [5]. DE perturbs the members of the current population with the scaled differences of randomly selected and distinct individuals. Every element of the population acts as a parent vector, for which a donor vector is created. In the basic version of DE, the donor vector for the ith parent (X_i) is generated by combining three random distinct elements X_{r1}, X_{r2} and X_{r3}. The donor vector V_i is calculated as:

$$V_i = X_{r1} + F \cdot (X_{r2} - X_{r3})$$

where F (scale factor) is a parameter that strongly influences DE's performances and typically lies in the interval [0.4, 1]. After this mutation, every parent-donor pair generates one child (trial vector) by means of a crossover operation. Two kinds of crossover are typically used: binomial (uniform) and exponential. Crossover is applied with a certain probability Cr (crossover rate). Then, the trial vector is evaluated and its fitness is compared to its parent's: the better survives while the other is discarded. In the last years several mutation and crossover operators have been presented, and DE has been successfully applied to many different tasks [4].

In this paper we have used the GPU-based implementation of DE described in [15]. Other parallel implementations of DE can be found in [6, 19].

3. THE MODEL

This section introduces the three-dimensional model we have used. It can be separated into three different, albeit related, components.

3.1 Skeleton

The skeleton is defined a tree whose nodes are 4×4 transformations. Each node represents the relative position and

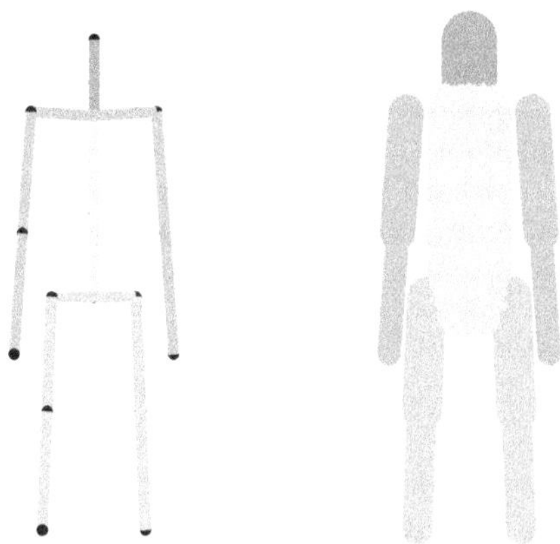

Figure 2: On the left, the skeleton of the model. The colors of the joints reflect the ones used in Figure 1. This is the base position of the model in the first frame. On the right, the base mesh generated by the skeleton.

orientation of a joint with respect to its parent node. A joint (root) corresponding to the pelvis is the top of the hierarchy. Five different kinematic chains are linked to it to describe the entire body. Figure 1 describes the kinematic model used for the skeleton, shown in Figure 2. The distances between two joints are based on the size of a standard model and are tuned according to the evolution of the *Dimensions* parameter vector (see Section 3.2). Since the anatomical limits of the human body do not allow some rotations (for instance, an elbow can rotate only around one axis), the degrees of freedom of the whole skeleton are only 29.

3.2 Dimensions

Dimensions is a vector of 7 parameters that define the actual size of the mesh. The reference model is defined as an average-height man, and these scaling parameters affect the distances between the joints as well as the thickness of the mesh built around them. These parameters are used as multipliers of the standard mesh, i.e., when they are equal to 1, the reference model is used as is; instead, when they are larger than 1 the model is taller/fatter than the standard and, when they are smaller than 1 the model is shorter/thinner. The range of values that these parameters can assume is large enough to allow the model to fit people of very different size and shapes, from children to tall men. Even if, in a video sequence, the actual size of the model can be computed in the first few frames and then kept constant, we chose to perform this calibration task on every frame, to check the consistency of the model during processing.

3.3 Mesh

The actual mesh (see Figure 2, right) is composed of 11 cylinder-spheres [3], whose positions depend on the location of the skeleton's joints and whose widths depend on the *Dimensions* parameters. Two of them are used to describe the torso, one represents the head, while the remaining eight stand for the arms and the legs.

In conclusion, the total number of parameters subjected to DE optimization is 29 angles + 7 scale factors + 6 values that represent the position and orientation of the model with respect to the world reference system, for a total of 42 parameters. The model is intrinsically hierarchical, and this feature is also exploited during optimization. In fact, the optimization is not performed all in one step, but is split into several steps, in each of which only some parameters of the model are optimized. In this way, one high-dimensional problem can be seen as N low-dimensional problems, at the cost of performing N different and consecutive optimization processes. After one optimization step ends, its resulting parameters are frozen and the next step considers them as constants. This choice has been made after some tests made clear that tackling the pose estimation problem in a single step led to large errors, particularly in the first frames of the sequences.

We tested several different sequences of tasks, of which the one that obtained the best trade-off between precision and speed is composed of four steps which optimize, respectively:

1. Global position and rotation in space of the person and dimensions of the body;

2. Global rotation of body, torso and head, and (again) dimensions of the body. This repetition can solve some critical situation. For instance, in some cases, in the first step the arms are identified as part of the torso; thus, allowing the size of the body to be modified also in this step can take it back to its correct shape;

3. Rotation and sizes of the legs;

4. Rotation and sizes of the arms.

4. ALGORITHM

The fitness of a candidate solution is proportional to the sum of the distances of all points in the cloud from the mesh. For each point in the cloud, the distance from each cylinder that composes the mesh is calculated using the method presented by Barbier et al. in [3]. This method has been chosen due to the very light computation needed to calculate the distance between a solid and a point. Its major drawback is that it works only with solids of revolution, so the mesh must be composed of shapes of this subclass. The only significant difference from Barbier's method is that such a method takes into account the distance between a point and a filled solid, so that, if the point is inside the solid, the distance is considered to be equal to 0. In our case, instead, we consider the distance between the point and the solid's surface, imposing that the mesh matches the point cloud and does not only enclose it.

The shortest distance (d_i) from each point i to the closest part of the mesh is then modified according to this simple equation:

$$d'_i = \begin{cases} {d_i}^{\alpha} & \text{if } d_i \leq \beta \\ \beta^{\alpha} & \text{otherwise} \end{cases}$$

The two parameters α and β affect the precision of the localization. A value of $\alpha > 1$ can be used to induce the model not to care too much about small details, but to be more focused on reaching all parts of the body (particularly hands and feet) while a value of $\alpha < 1$ induce the model to refine good solutions. β can be seen as the distance beyond which a point does not affect the pose estimate anymore. In this way, the behavior of the model becomes more robust with respect to outliers that are unlikely to be part of the body. The final fitness is then calculated as the sum of all d' terms.

This approach fits really well the GPGPU computing paradigm because the fitness of each point of the cloud can be computed in parallel and then added up only at the end. Moreover, using a population-based algorithm like DE, all candidate solutions can be evaluated in parallel, introducing a second level of parallelism that allows us to reach real-time performances.

An element of the DE population that describes a possible pose of the person is defined by a 42-dimensional array:

$$\begin{aligned} P_i &= \{ Pos_x, Pos_y, Pos_z, GR_x, GR_y, GR_z, \\ &\quad R_1, \dots, R_{29}, D_1, \dots, D_7\} \end{aligned}$$

where the parameters Pos and GR define the global position and rotation of the person in space, R are the rotations of the joints according to the scheme previously defined and D are the size modifiers described in section 3.2.

To track a person during the video sequence, the DE particles are not initialized randomly anywhere in the search space (like in the original algorithm) but their possible starting positions are constrained within a neighborhood of the best position found in the last frame. In other words, a neighborhood around the last best position is set, and all initial particles position are generated within it, and then allowed to move around the entire search space. In the first frame, where no previous position estimate exists, this is replaced by a standard standing position (see Figure 2) in front of the camera.

The optimization stops when either one of these two conditions is met:

- 100 generations;
- 5 generations without improving the best solution (10 for the first frame, to help the initial localization of the subject).

Doing so, we can run the optimization for a time sufficient to obtain good results, without wasting time when no better solutions can be found.

5. PARALLEL IMPLEMENTATION

The GPU-based implementation of DE has been introduced in [15] and is based on the CUDA environment by nVIDIA.

CUDA permits the development of routines (called *kernels*), that can be executed in parallel by N different CUDA threads on the GPU, following the Single Instruction Multiple Thread model. The performance of CUDA code mainly depends on the thread configuration and memory access schemes used. All methods used in this work try to exploit fast-access local memory instead of slower global memory as much as possible. CUDA threads are grouped in blocks. There is a limit to the number of threads per block, since all threads of a block are expected to reside on the same processor core and must share the limited memory resources of that core. In turn, blocks are organized into grid of blocks. Threads that do not reside within the same block do not share any fast-access memory.

Like all EAs, Differential Evolution is easily parallelizable, since very little information is shared among the population, and only few interactions among the particles occur. In [15], all steps of DE are implemented as two kernels. The former generates trial particles (using one thread per dimension) while the latter evaluates the fitness and performs selection; this is repeated until a stopping criterion is met. The most significant difference introduced in the implementation we are considering is the independent implementation of fitness evaluation because, due to its complexity, it needs a different number and distribution of threads than the rest of the DE algorithm, and it is not possible to share its configuration with the other phases of the procedure as happens when simpler functions are optimized. The final architecture is then composed of 5 different kernels, as shown in Figure 3. The first and the last are properly related to the DE algorithm, while the other three kernels are the actual implementation of the pose estimation method which leads to the final fitness evaluation:

- "Compute Skeleton" reads all DE trial particles in parallel and uses them to generate the location of the skeleton joints. Despite the hierarchical structure of the model, all joints can be computed in parallel in order to save time. A joint that depends on other joint locations, must go back to the root of the hierarchy and compute the chain;
- "Compute Mesh" generates the positions of the cylinders that compose the mesh using the joint locations and size modifiers;
- "Evaluate Fitness" computes, for each point, the distance from the closest part of the mesh and adds them up to obtain the final fitness. This is by far the most computationally expensive part of the algorithm because the number of points in a cloud is too high, which prevents the GPU from computing an individual within the same CUDA block, as for the other kernels. So, every individual must be split into several blocks, slowing down the performance of the algorithm. In fact, we tested several different block-thread configurations verifying that faster results can be obtained using a single thread to compute more points sequentially, instead of computing all points in parallel.

A CPU-based version of this body pose estimation method has not been implemented, so it is not possible to give an estimate of the speedup obtained by implementing it on a GPU. A good yardstick is presented in [14], where an approach similar to the one presented here could reduce the processing time by more than 25 times.

6. RESULTS

In order to prove that our algorithm behaves correctly, we tested it on two publicly available datasets:

- The videos that compose the first dataset (Cornell [1]) are acquired using Microsoft Kinect and comprise everyday actions (like cooking, talking on the phone,

[1] http://pr.cs.cornell.edu/humanactivities

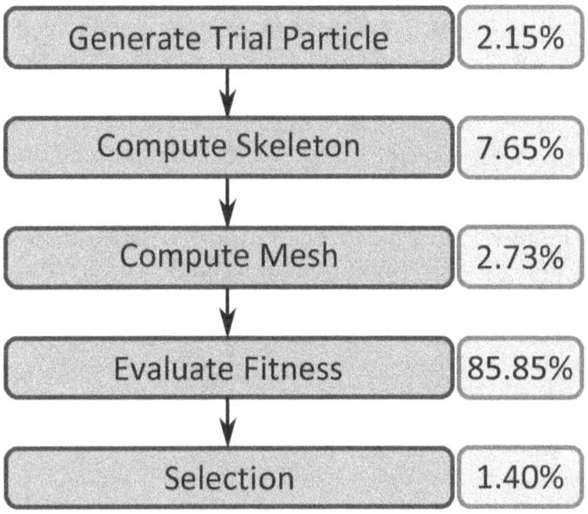

Figure 3: Block diagram of the CUDA Kernels. These five steps are iterated 100 times, or stopped when improvement seems no longer possible. On the right we report the percentage of time spent on every kernel during optimization. The total does not add up to exactly 100% because initialization and result retrieval are not included.

- wearing contact lenses ...) performed by four different subjects. These operations sometimes involve interactions with other objects, like tables or whiteboards. In the tests presented in this paper, we excluded the sequences featuring these interactions;
- The second test set (Stanford [8]) is composed of 28 sequences collected using a Swissranger SR4000 Time-of-Flight camera, which was set to record full-frame infrared intensity images and depth at a resolution of 176×144 pixels. During the acquisition, the subject was wearing markers, whose location can be used as ground truth to assess the precision of the pose estimation. This dataset has also been used in [2, 8, 22, 23], which allows us to compare our results with the ones reported therein.

All tests were performed on a PC equipped with a 64-bit Intel(R) Core^{TM} i7 CPU running at 3.40GHz using CUDA v. 4.2 on a nVidia GeForce GTX680 graphics card with 1536 CUDA cores, 2GB of DDR memory and compute capability 3.0 [16].

The DE parameters were $Cr = 0.9$, $F = 0.9$, population size of 24, binomial crossover and DE/RAND/1 mutation.

6.1 Tests on the Cornell Dataset

Since the Cornell dataset does not provide a "ground truth", we compare the skeleton obtained by our body pose estimation method with the skeleton provided by the OpenNI framework [17].

Figure 4 shows the average distance, computed in 10 independent runs on 12 different sequences, between the joints of our skeleton and the one generated by OpenNI. Since the two skeletons do not share the same model, only the corresponding joints related to head, neck, shoulders, elbows, wrists, knees and ankles are taken into consideration. In any case, results from OpenNI cannot be considered as a perfect "ground truth" and a visual inspection would confirm that,

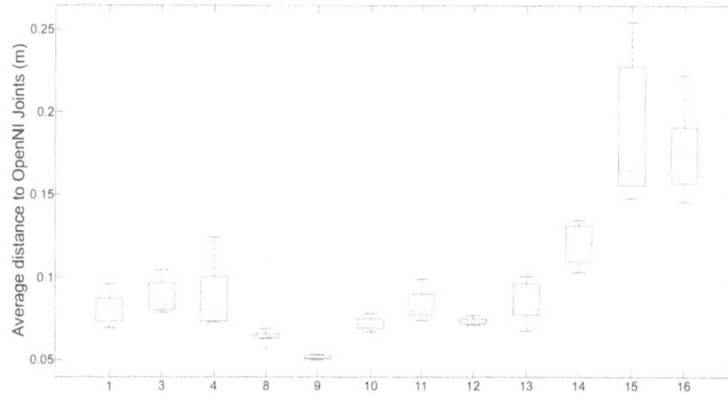

Figure 4: Comparison over the Cornell Dataset in terms of distances between joint locations of our skeleton and the ones provided by OpenNI. 10 independent runs for each sequence. The sequences used are the ones referred in the dataset as *data1*

in some frames, this reference body pose estimation is less precise than ours (some examples are provided in Figure 5).

Taking into consideration that we are not only estimating the pose of the subject, but also his body shape, a good test is to observe how the estimated model's height changes during the process. Figure 6 shows the average height (indicated by the sum of the lengths of the sequence of segments that connect the head with the ankle passing through neck, torso, root, hip and knee joints) of the model through all frames of all repetitions of the analysis of the first sequence. Except a few outliers, these result are sufficiently stable: the average height is 1.412 m with a standard deviation of 7.73 mm.

6.2 Stanford Dataset

For the evaluation of Stanford Dataset, we ran every sequence 10 times, and the average results (compared to the other four approaches) are presented in Figure 7. The sequences of the Stanford Dataset are approximately sorted by difficulty. While in the first ones the subject performs only small movements, in the last ones the movements are more complicated (including a 360° rotation and a tennis service). It can be seen that our method is one of the worst

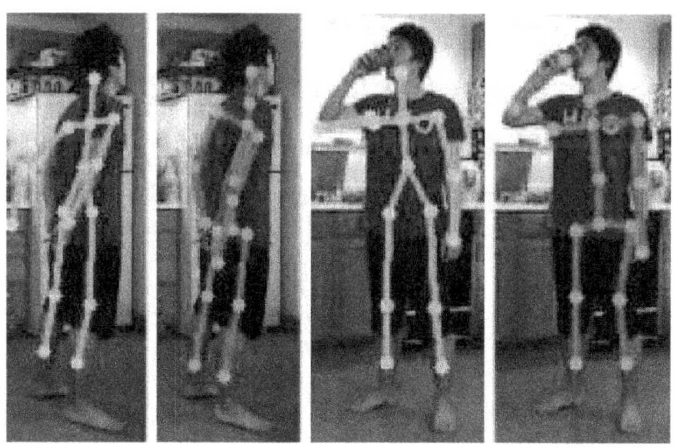

Figure 5: Some frames in which OpenNI's pose estimation (green skeleton, in 1st and 3rd image) is less accurate than our method's (red skeleton, 2nd and 4th image).

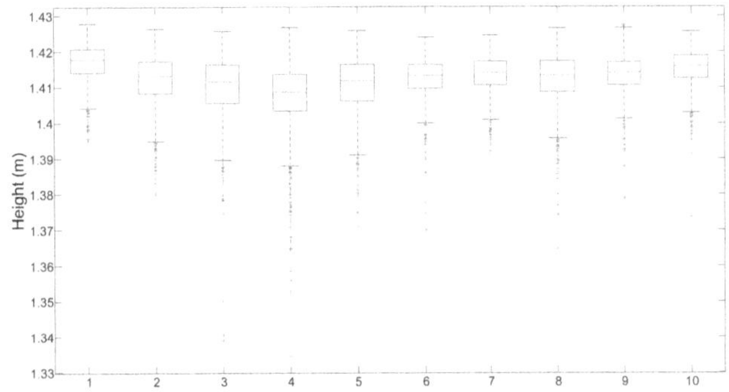

Figure 6: Distribution of the model's height in 10 independent runs of the first sequence of the Cornell Dataset.

performing on the simpler sequences (probably due to our mesh definition, since a cylinder is not a perfect approximation of an arm or of a leg) while, when processing the most complicated ones, results are comparable to the state-of-the art, showing that our method has good generalization properties and good tracking results. The bad performance on the first sequences could be improved using a more complex model (e.g. a triangular mesh), at the cost of an increase of the computational burden. This is left as future work.

Figure 8 uses boxplots to describe the distribution of the results over the 10 repetitions on each sequence. As can be observed, in the easiest sequences the variance is very small, while in some of the others it is much higher. These sequences feature sudden movements which cause the model to lose track of the subject, causing large estimation errors when this happens.

Regarding computation time, the complete hierarchical optimization takes an average of 114.7 ms (standard deviation of 5.5 ms) for the first frame, and 43.9 ms (standard deviation of 3.4 ms) for the other frames, allowing one to process a video sequence at a rate which is higher than 20 frames per second, considering that for 99% of the times, the processing time is below 53 ms.

7. CONCLUSIONS AND FUTURE DEVELOPMENTS

We have proposed an evolutionary method for estimating the body pose and the shape of a human in a video sequence. Our method does not use any other information than the point cloud generated by a depth sensor. Nevertheless, it is able to obtain good results in inferring the human pose and constantly tracking a subject in a video sequence. This is proved by a comparison with other state-of-the-art techniques. To the best of our knowledge, this is the first system performing human body pose estimation exclusively based on evolutionary computation that is capable of real time performances.

Our system can be improved as regards both speed and accuracy. Regarding speed, we will try to add a further level of parallelization. In the present implementation, each point is compared sequentially with the 11 elements of the model, while this step could be computed in parallel leading to a significant reduction of the time required. Regarding accuracy, the first step will be a systematic comparison of different evolutionary techniques as well as the automatic optimization of the parameters which regulate their behaviour. Finally, a significant increase in accuracy may be obtained introducing a classification step, as employed in several of the methods we have discussed in Section 2.

Acknowledgments

Roberto Ugolotti is funded by Fondazione Cariparma and Compagnia di San Paolo. The authors would like to thank the authors of the public datasets used in the tests and Youssef Nashed, Luca Mussi and Špela Ivekovič for sharing their knowledge and the basic procedures on which this work is based and for their inspiring comments.

8. REFERENCES

[1] S. Akhtar, A. Ahmad, and E. Abdel-Rahman. A metaheuristic bat-inspired algorithm for full body human pose estimation. In *Proc. Ninth Conference on Computer and Robot Vision (CRV)*, pages 369 –375, 2012.

[2] A. Baak, M. Müller, G. Bharaj, H.-P. Seidel, and C. Theobalt. A data-driven approach for real-time full body pose reconstruction from a depth camera. In *Proc. IEEE 13th International Conference on Computer Vision (ICCV)*, pages 1092–1099, 2011.

[3] A. Barbier Accary and E. Galin. Fast distance computation between a point and cylinders, cones, line-swept-spheres and cone-spheres. *Journal of Graphics Tools*, 9(2):11–19, 2004.

[4] U. K. Chakraborty. *Advances in Differential Evolution*. Springer, 1st edition, 2008.

[5] S. Das and P. Suganthan. Differential evolution: A survey of the state-of-the-art. *IEEE Transactions on Evolutionary Computation*, 15(1):4–31, 2011.

[6] L. de Veronese and R. Krohling. Differential evolution algorithm on the GPU with C-CUDA. In *Proc. IEEE Congress on Evolutionary Computation (CEC)*, pages 1–7, 2010.

[7] A. E. Eiben and J. E. Smith. *Introduction to Evolutionary Computing*. Springer Verlag, 2003.

[8] V. Ganapathi, C. Plagemann, S. Thrun, and D. Koller. Real time motion capture using a single time-of-flight camera. In *IEEE Conf. on Computer Vision and Pattern Recognition (CVPR)*, 2010.

[9] S. Ivekovic, E. Trucco, and Y. R. Petillot. Human body pose estimation with particle swarm optimisation. *Evolutionary Computation*, 16(4):509–528, 2008.

[10] T. Krzeszowski, B. Kwolek, and K. Wojciechowski. Articulated body motion tracking by combined particle swarm optimization and particle filtering. In L. Bolc, R. Tadeusiewicz, L. Chmielewski, and K. Wojciechowski, editors, *Computer Vision and Graphics*, volume 6374 of *Lecture Notes in Computer Science*, pages 147–154. Springer Berlin Heidelberg, 2010.

[11] D. L. Ly, A. Saxena, and H. Lipson. Co-evolutionary predictors for kinematic pose inference from RGBD images. In *Proc. of the 14th international conference on Genetic and evolutionary computation conference*, GECCO, pages 967–974. ACM, 2012.

[12] T. B. Moeslund, A. Hilton, and V. Kruger. A survey of advances in vision-based human motion capture

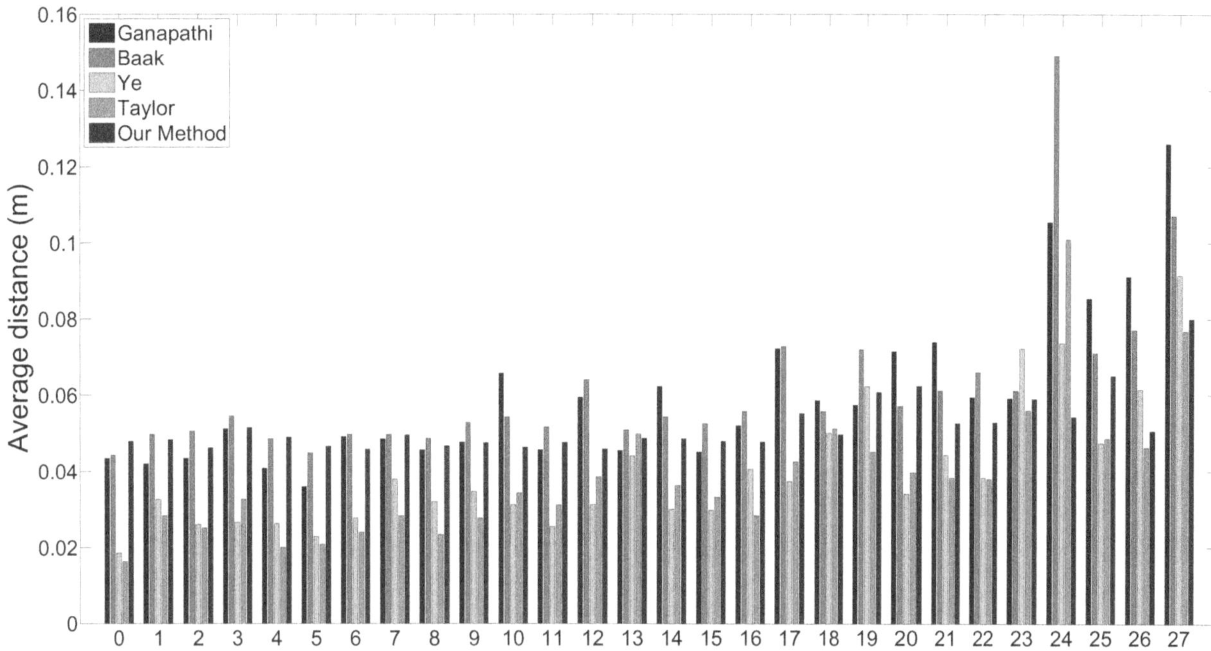

Figure 7: Comparison on the Stanford Dataset. Our results represent the average distance over all markers on all frames of the sequence over 10 independent runs.

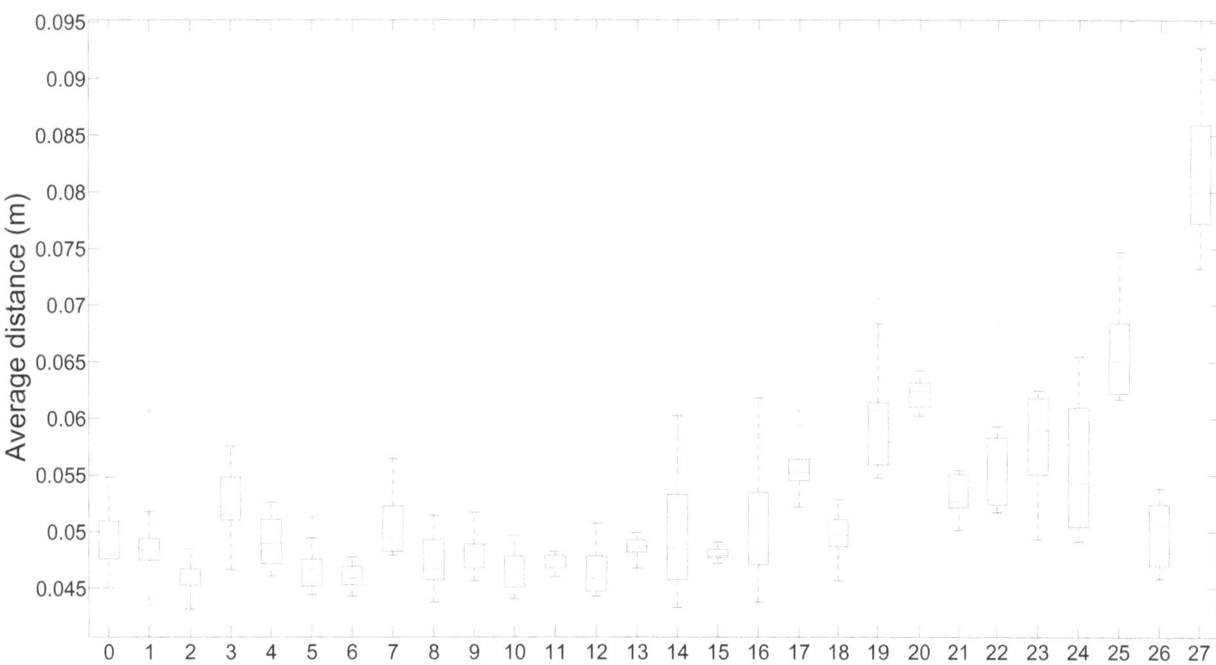

Figure 8: Boxplots summarizing the results over 10 repetitions on the Stanford Dataset.

and analysis. *Computer Vision and Image Understanding*, 104(2 - 3):90 – 126, 2006.

[13] L. Mussi, F. Daolio, and S. Cagnoni. Evaluation of parallel particle swarm optimization algorithms within the CUDA architecture. *Information Sciences*, 181(20):4642–4657, 2011.

[14] L. Mussi, Š. Ivekovič, and S. Cagnoni. Markerless articulated human body tracking from multi-view video with GPU-PSO. In G. Tempesti, A. M. Tyrrell, and J. F. Miller, editors, *Evolvable Systems: From Biology to Hardware - 9th International Conference, ICES 2010 York, UK*, number 6274 in Lecture Notes in Computer Science, pages 195–207, 2010.

[15] Y. Nashed, P. Mesejo, R. Ugolotti, J. Dubois-Lacoste, and S. Cagnoni. A comparative study of three GPU-based metaheuristics. In *Parallel Problem Solving from Nature - PPSN XII*, volume 7492 of *Lecture Notes in Computer Science*, pages 398–407. Springer, 2012.

[16] nVIDIA Corporation. *nVIDIA CUDA Programming Guide v. 4.2*, 2011.

[17] OpenNI organization. *OpenNI User Guide*, November 2010.

[18] J. Pantrigo, A. Sanchez, A. Montemayor, and A. Duarte. Multi-dimensional visual tracking using scatter search particle filter. *Pattern Recognition Letters*, 29(8):1160 – 1174, 2008.

[19] A. K. Qin, F. Raimondo, F. Forbes, and Y. S. Ong. An improved CUDA-based implementation of differential evolution on GPU. In *Proc. of the fourteenth international conference on Genetic and evolutionary computation conference*, GECCO, pages 991–998, 2012.

[20] S. Shen, M. Tong, H. Deng, Y. Liu, X. Wu, K. Wakabayashi, and H. Koike. Model based human motion tracking using probability evolutionary algorithm. *Pattern Recognition Letters*, 29(13):1877–1886, Oct. 2008.

[21] R. Storn and K. Price. Differential evolution- a simple and efficient adaptive scheme for global optimization over continuous spaces. Technical report, International Computer Science Institute, 1995.

[22] J. Taylor, J. Shotton, T. Sharp, and A. Fitzgibbon. The vitruvian manifold: inferring dense correspondences for one-shot human pose estimation. In *IEEE Conference on Computer Vision and Pattern Recognition (CVPR)*, pages 103 –110, 2012.

[23] M. Ye, X. Wang, R. Yang, L. Ren, and M. Pollefeys. Accurate 3D pose estimation from a single depth image. In *IEEE International Conference on Computer Vision (ICCV)*, pages 731 –738, 2011.

[24] X. Zhang, W. Hu, X. Wang, Y. Kong, N. Xie, H. Wang, H. Ling, and S. Maybank. A swarm intelligence based searching strategy for articulated 3D human body tracking. In *IEEE Conference on Computer Vision and Pattern Recognition Workshops (CVPRW)*, pages 45 –50, june 2010.

[25] X. Zhao and Y. Liu. Generative tracking of 3D human motion by hierarchical annealed genetic algorithm. *Pattern Recognition*, 41(8):2470 – 2483, 2008.

A Multi-Objective Approach to Evolving Platooning Strategies in Intelligent Transportation Systems

Willem van Willigen
VU University Amsterdam &
TNO The Hague
De Boelelaan 1081a
1081 HV Amsterdam, NL
w.h.van.willigen@vu.nl

Evert Haasdijk
VU University Amsterdam
De Boelelaan 1081a
1081 HV Amsterdam, NL
e.haasdijk@vu.nl

Leon Kester
TNO The Hague
Oude Waalsdorperweg 63
2597 AK Den Haag, NL
leon.kester@tno.nl

ABSTRACT

The research in this paper is inspired by a vision of intelligent vehicles that autonomously move along motorways: they join and leave trains of vehicles (platoons), overtake other vehicles, etc. We propose a multi-objective evolutionary algorithm based on NEAT and SPEA2 that evolves high-level controllers for such intelligent vehicles. The algorithm yields a set of solutions that each embody their own prioritisation of various user requirements such as speed, comfort or fuel economy. This contrasts with the current practice in researching such controllers, where user preferences are summarised in a single number that the controller development process then optimises.

Proof-of-concept experiments show that evolved controllers substantially outperform a widely used human behavioural model. We show that it is possible to evolve a set of vehicle controllers that correspond with different prioritisations of user preferences, giving the driver, on the road, the power to decide which preferences to emphasise.

Categories and Subject Descriptors

I.2.8 [**Artificial Intelligence**]: Problem Solving, Control Methods, and Search—*Heuristic methods*

General Terms

Algorithms, Performance, Reliability

Keywords

Intelligent Transportation Systems, Multi-Objective Optimisation, Platooning, Neuro-Evolution

Track

Real World Applications (RWA)

GECCO'13, July 6–10, 2013, Amsterdam, The Netherlands.

1. INTRODUCTION

In Europe's major cities, the average driver loses as much as 60 to 70 hours per year in traffic jams,[1] the cause of tremendous environmental and socio-economical impact. Vehicle manufacturers are introducing Adaptive Cruise Control (ACC) to help combat this issue. ACC allows the driver to set the desired distance to the preceding vehicle. The ACC system measures the vehicle's relative distance and velocity through radar and adjusts speed accordingly. Such automated maintenance of distance is hoped to increase the uniformity of traffic flows and so better utilise road capacity.

Cooperative Adaptive Cruise Control (CACC) is a major development in recent research on Intelligent Transportation Systems (ITS) that takes this automated control to the next level by adding direct communication between vehicles (see Figure 1). This enables the vehicles to directly communicate about their current velocity, position and acceleration and so removes some of the uncertainty and delays that relying only on radar measurements implies. Directly communicating such accurate state information allows vehicles to drive much closer to each other without compromising safety. This opens up the possibility of *platooning*: trains of vehicles that drive very close to each other at (near) equal speed, and therein lies one of the big selling points of CACC. It enables platoons to be *string stable*: changes in acceleration or deceleration are reduced by the following vehicles instead of amplified. This property is expected to greatly improve the throughput of vehicles on highways, because it is exactly the amplification of acceleration and deceleration that causes many traffic jams[2].

CACC will become available in the near future. Vehicles will be equipped with a simple button that turns the CACC mode on and off again. With the system turned on, the vehicle will then, for instance, search for the nearest platoon available to join and (almost) automatically drive along in the platoon until the driver decides to take matters into her own hands and turn CACC off again. Such CACC systems do not yet take into account the preferences of specific drivers. Some drivers like to drive fast, while others prefer fuel economy and care less about speed. Ride comfort is

[1] Wall Street Journal, November 3, 2010: `http://blogs.wsj.com/brussels/2010/11/03/europes-traffic-jam-capitals`

[2] See `http://www.drivenbyhelmond.nl/en/projecten/tno-doet-onderzoek-naar-spookfiles/`

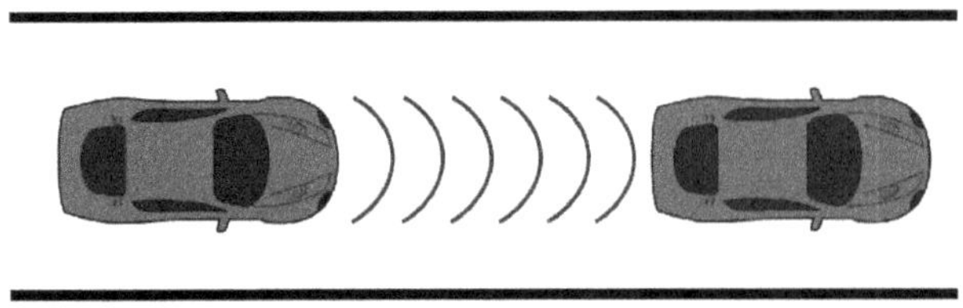

(a) ACC scenario - vehicles have an on-board radar that detects information about the preceding vehicle.

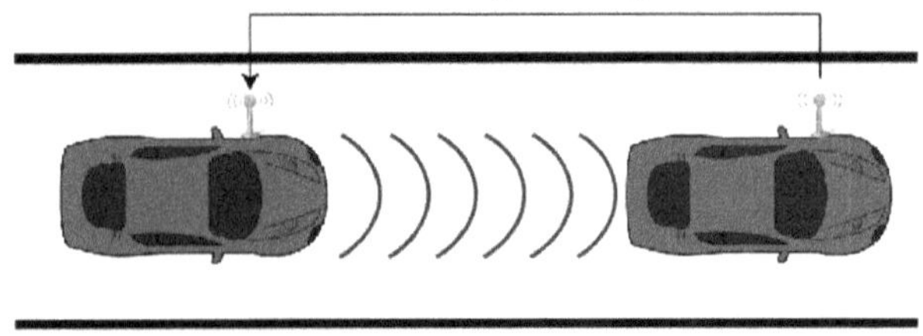

(b) CACC scenario - vehicles also have a radio unit on-board, to communicate directly with nearby vehicles (not only with the preceding vehicle).

Figure 1: A schematic representation of the difference between ACC and CACC.

also a consideration that can be measured in number of lane changes, changes in velocity, etc.

We envision a system where the driver can enter her preferences into the system at real time. Setting preferences corresponds with selecting a high-level vehicle controller. These controllers choose actions (e.g., joining, leaving or creating platoons, changing lanes or simply driving on) based on a number of input variables such as acceleration, velocity, and distance to preceding vehicle. This vision is at odds with most current research into controller development because of the way driver preferences are typically taken into account: the preferences are all summarised into one single metric (e.g. a weighted average) that is then optimised.

We propose to use multi-objective evolutionary algorithms as an approach to develop controllers without having to summarise the separate preference metrics into a single number. This approach yields a number of pareto-optimal controllers that each reflect their own prioritisation of preference measures. Some may be fast but less comfortable, others may be very comfortable but slow, yet others may strike another balance between the user preferences. Such a selection of controllers would enable a user to set the relative importance of fuel economy, speed, lane changes, etc. The controller that best approximates the current prioritisation of preferences is then activated and vehicle progresses as the user has requested. Thus, we seek the benefit of evolutionary multi-objective optimisation of autonomous vehicle controllers not so much in *better* control (although that would of course not be disregarded), but more in the fact that it would yield multiple controllers with varying emphasis on the different user preferences and so allow the user to select and change the appropriate vehicle behaviour while driving. The method we propose employs NEAT, a well-known algorithm for neuro-evolution [13] and combines it with the Pareto Strength approach as found in the SPEA2 evolutionary algorithm [19]. It is in itself not a new multi-objective evolutionary algorithm, but an easy way for multi-objectivation of an otherwise single-objective evolutionary algorithm.

As a proof-of-concept, we conduct a number of simulated experiments in which we evolve controllers to optimise both speed and comfort as twin objectives.

Our first research question is whether our NEAT-Pareto Strength (NEAT-PS) approach does indeed yield a useful set of controllers that embody different prioritisations of these objectives. Secondly, we hypothesise that the evolved controllers, by virtue of their platooning behaviour, yield better speed as well as comfort compared to a benchmark controller based on the Intelligent Driver Model (IDM) [15] in combination with the MOBIL lane changing model [14]. These two models are commonly used to model human drivers in traffic flow modelling.

In previous work [17], we presented preliminary results that showed the potential of this technology. In this paper, we present a more thorough investigation of the technique. By modifying the inputs and outputs of the neural network controller of the vehicles, and by increasing the number of fitness evaluations per individual, we managed to get a much better performance of the algorithm. The resulting pareto front clearly distinguishes between the two objectives. Furthermore, we validated the results by re-running the pareto-optimal solutions, and these validation reruns lie within range of the original pareto-optimal solutions, indicating that these pareto-optimal controllers perform consistently.

2. RELATED WORK

While ACC systems are currently being adopted in consumer vehicles, research and development into cruise control focuses on enabling more and better cooperation between ACC systems, yielding CACC systems. Van Arem *et al.* [16] describe the effect of CACC on traffic flow. They conclude that, when the penetration level of CACC-equipped vehicles is high enough ($> 60\%$), traffic stability and throughput is improved. In Yang *et al.* [18], a communication protocol is proposed in order to make a cooperative collision warning system on highways.

The main suggested application area of CACC technology these days is platooning. Broggi *et al.* [2] and Kanellakopoulos [9] both use image recognition techniques in combination with sensors to autonomously enable platooning. However, current technology has improved significantly since then, and nowadays direct radio communication between vehicles is used to enable platooning.

Naus *et al.* [11] thoroughly investigate the issue of string stability in platooning, with both ACC and CACC controllers. Their method includes several factors of delay in communication.

In [8], an extensive architecture is given for a layered multi-agent CACC architecture. The authors use this architecture to implement both centralised platoons (in which there is a coordinating platoon leader) and decentralised platoons (in which all vehicles operate as equals). Khan *et al.* [10] present different platoon (in their paper, convoy) forming strategies, based on a utility value of a platoon.

There has not been much work yet on the development of platooning *strategies*, where the vehicles have to decide while driving if and when they should be platooning. In the SARTRE project (Safe Road Trains for the Environment) [1], platoons are defined as trains of road vehicles of which the front one is a trained platoon driver. This project has implemented basic platooning strategies, also in real vehicles, but these strategies are only defined at the action level, where for example the join and leave actions are defined, but not at a higher level, where a strategy for driving on the highway is defined.

The multi-objective driving strategies domain has been investigated by Dovgan *et al.* [4, 5]. They use the NSGA-II multi-objective evolutionary algorithm to determine driving strategies that optimise travel time and fuel economy. Other vehicles are not taken into account in this work, only the vehicle's own state space and route state space. Platooning is not an application that is taken into account.

In the domain of human driver modelling, several well-known models exist, such as the simple yet elegant Intelligent Driver Model [15] and the older Gipps model [7].

Neuro-evolution is a form of machine learning that uses evolutionary algorithms to train artificial neural networks. There are many methods for neuro-evolution, with NEAT [13] and its extension HyperNEAT [6] as fairly recent notable developments.

There are also many multi-objective evolutionary algorithms; two well-known state-of-the-art approaches are SPEA2 [19] and NSGA-II [3]. SPEA2 calculates a single scalar fitness value based on the number of other individuals an individual dominates –the pareto *strength*– which is then used for parent and survivor selection. NSGA-II uses a pareto ranking mechanism, also based on the dominance relation, but doesn't attach specific fitness values, making it harder to reconcile with NEAT's standard selection and niching mechanisms.

3. ALGORITHM

NEAT [13] is a popular state-of-the-art algorithm for evolving neural networks which also optimises the network topologies. Thus, we conveniently don't have to decide on a topology for the neural network beforehand. This also allows for the algorithm to propose functionally quite different neural networks. To achieve this, it employs a clever method of speciation of the neural network topologies, taking into account specific sub-structures within the topology. The neural networks compete primarily with individuals within their own niches instead of with individuals of the entire population. This technique makes it easier to protect innovations within the topologies.

To achieve our vision, it is essential to take multiple objectives into account. The original NEAT algorithm, however, does not support multiple objectives. Therefore, we extend the NEAT algorithm to allow for multi-objective optimisation. We incorporated the Pareto Strength approach from SPEA2 into NEAT to create NEAT-PS. The advantage of the Pareto Strength is that it computes a *single* fitness value for each individual, based on the values of all objective functions, making it very straightforward to augment the NEAT algorithm with multi-objective capabilities.

Our proof of concept implementation uses two objectives: travel time and comfort. These objectives are somewhat incompatible, so controllers must prioritise the objectives in varying ways: some are fast but less comfortable, others are slower but much more comfortable. Controllers with varying prioritisations would allow the driver to balance the preferences as she wants at any time. Some users prefer speed, others prefer comfort, and this varies with their circumstances. By allowing the driver to switch between alternative controllers (by prioritising objectives) while driving, we allow for changes in driving behaviour to match the current preferences of the person behind the wheel.

The basis of the Pareto Strength evaluation is the domination relation:

$$i \succ j \iff \forall o \in O : o_i \succeq o_j \wedge i \neq j \tag{1}$$

In this formula, the $\succeq$ relation between objectives only specifies that objective o_i is equal or *better* than objective o_j, without saying whether the objective is maximised or minimised. In our specific experiments, we are minimising both objectives.

After calculating each objective function's value for all individuals, we calculate the Pareto Strength values for each individual i in population P as described in [19]:

$$S(i) = |\{j | j \in P \wedge i \succ j\}| \tag{2}$$

where $|\cdot|$ is the cardinality of a set, and $\succ$ is the dominance relation. Now we can calculate the raw fitness values of each individual i by summing the strengths of the individuals j that dominate i:

$$R(i) = \sum_{j \in P, j \succ i} S(j) \tag{3}$$

The final fitness value for an individual that we feed into the regular NEAT algorithm is then given by:

$$F(i) = \frac{10000}{1 + R(i)} \tag{4}$$

From these formulae, it follows that if an individual is not dominated, its raw fitness value is 0, and the final fitness value has the maximum value of 10,000. This evaluation creates a single fitness value that reflects multiple fitness metrics, and we can straighforwardly plug these results into the standard NEAT algorithm[3] to complete NEAT-PS.

4. EXPERIMENTAL SET-UP

Our experimental set-up consists of two main parts: the vehicle simulator in which we tested our controllers, and NEAT-PS which evolves the vehicle controllers based on the feedback it obtains from the simulator. This setup is schematically depicted in Figure 2.

We used Movsim[4], an open-source vehicle simulator that implements the Intelligent Driver Model (IDM) and MOBIL, which are respectively the longitudinal (determining minimum headway and consequent speed adjustments) model and lane changing model that form a benchmark in our experiments. Movsim is primarily a microscopic simulator of traffic, whereas we want to use higher-level actions as input for the vehicle (such as creating, joining and leaving a platoon). Therefore we had to extend the functionality of the simulator to provide these higher-level actions. In the original simulator, each vehicle can only use a single longitudinal controller and this controller decides on every timestep what the acceleration of the vehicle should be.

We extended the simulator so that each vehicle can use many controllers; a decision making process (such as a neural network) on a more abstract level selects the next action

[3]We used the NEAT4j implementation, `http://neat4j.sourceforge.net`

[4]Movsim, `http://www.movsim.org`

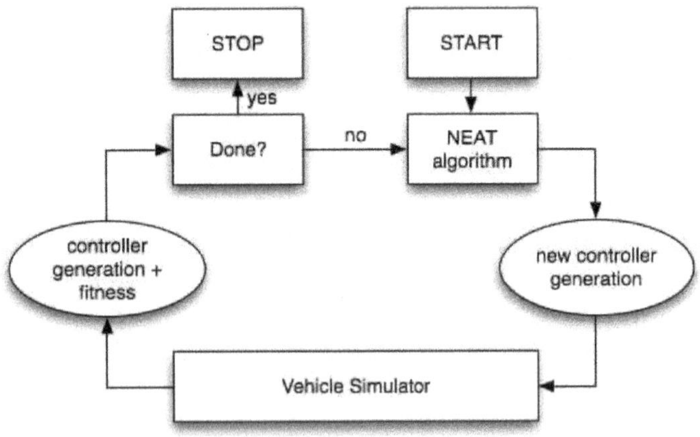

Figure 2: Graphical representation of our simulation loop. The NEAT algorithm generates a new population of controllers. Each member of a new generation of vehicle controllers is then evaluated by the vehicle simulation. The simulator assigns the fitness values (the pareto strengths) to the controllers for NEAT to use in its parent and survivor operators. The loop is repeated for a preset number of generations.

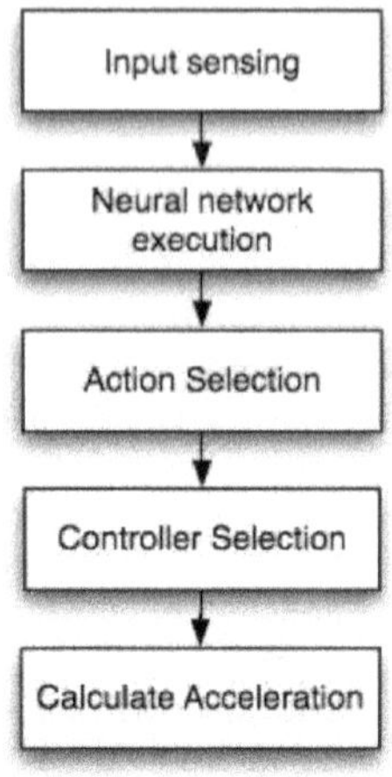

Figure 3: The five-layered architecture of our vehicle controllers. In the original simulation settings, the three layers in the middle are missing, thus calculating the acceleration directly based on the input variables.

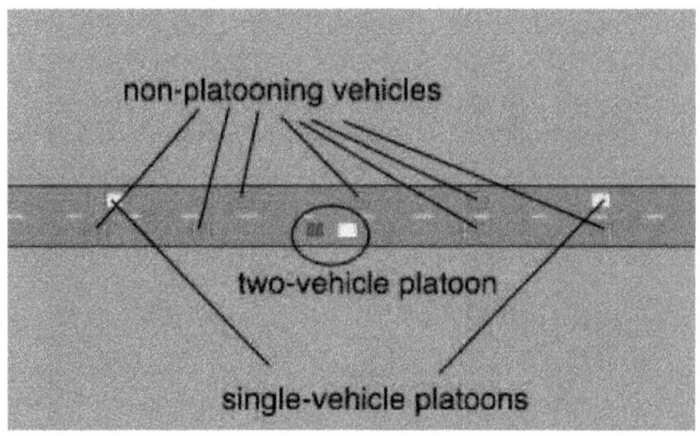

Figure 4: An example of a two-vehicle platoon. Note that the distance between the two platooning vehicles is much smaller than the distance between the non-platooning vehicles.

of the vehicle based on the current state of the vehicle. To execute the selected action the vehicle decides on the appropriate longitudinal controller for that moment. For example, when joining a platoon, the vehicle first has to drive towards the platoon using a specific longitudinal controller that facilitates this. Then, when the vehicle has approached the platoon, it may have to change to the correct lane. Other vehicles may have to make space for the joining vehicle. All these processes correspond with different longitudinal controllers. Figure 3 schematically shows the extra functionality of the simulator. The original Movsim implementation directly links inputs to acceleration; we introduce three intermediate layers to facilitate behaviours on a more abstract level.

The higher level actions implement realistic platooning behaviour, where vehicles on the highway drive very close to the preceding vehicles while copying the preceding vehicle's speed and acceleration. The intricacies of the platooning control, such as sensing, information fusing and communication models are not taken into account in this simulation: these issues should be solved at the lower levels of the system. They are not within the scope of this work, and we assume these technologies to be working correctly and without error.

Figures 4 and 5 show two example screen shots of the simulation. Note that these are very zoomed-in screen shots and therefore only show a very small part of the total simulation.

4.1 Controller

By default, the vehicles in our simulation drive according to the Intelligent Driver Model (IDM), and the MOBIL lane changing model. Additionally, our vehicles can execute actions, each triggering other versions of longitudinal controllers.

Create Platoon If the vehicle is currently not part of a platoon, it creates a new platoon. The IDM longitudinal model remains active, and the lane changing model is turned off (in our simulation, platoons cannot change lanes). The vehicle that creates the platoon automatically becomes the platoon leader – the foremost vehicle in the platoon.

Join Platoon Front If the vehicle is currently not part of a platoon, it tries to join a nearby platoon. This action checks if there is a platoon directly in front of the vehicle. If so, the vehicle drives up to the last vehicle in that platoon, and changes its longitudinal model to CACC, which copies the velocity and acceleration of the preceding vehicle.

Join Platoon Side This action joins a platoon that is directly next to the vehicle. First, the vehicle checks if there is a platoon on its side, and if so, the platoon makes way for the vehicle to join. As soon as there's enough space for this, the vehicle switches lanes and joins the platoon by switching to the CACC longitudinal model.

Leave Platoon If the vehicle is part of a platoon, the vehicle leaves the platoon, and starts driving using the

IDM and MOBIL models again. Immediately, more headway time is created. Additionally, if the vehicle that leaves the platoon was driving somewhere in the middle of the platoon, the platoon is split into two parts, being the sub-platoon in front of the vehicle and the sub-platoon behind the vehicle. If the leaving vehicle was platoon leader, this role is transferred to the second vehicle in the platoon. If the leaving vehicle was the only vehicle in the platoon, the platoon is disbanded. When a vehicle leaves the highway, it also leaves the platoon.

Change Lane If possible, the vehicle changes lanes. Our simulation currently consists of two lanes, so this action does not need a parameter telling which lane to change to.

Do Nothing The vehicle longitudinal controller remains unchanged.

In our current scenario, the vehicles drive completely autonomously and according to the decisions of the neural network. However, we believe that human drivers should be able to override any given action that the neural network comes up with, or to turn off the system altogether.

4.2 Neural Network

NEAT-PS evolves the neural network that selects from the six actions listed above. The network inputs and outputs are depicted in Figure 6, listing the following input variables for a vehicle c:

- Headway time of vehicle to preceding vehicle: The distance to the preceding vehicle divided by the velocity of c;
- Fraction of front platoon speed and desired velocity: The speed of the platoon in front of c (if there is one) divided by c's desired velocity;
- Fraction of side platoon speed and desired velocity: The speed of the platoon on the side of c (if there is one) divided by c's desired velocity;
- Fraction of desired velocity: The current velocity of c divided by its desired velocity;

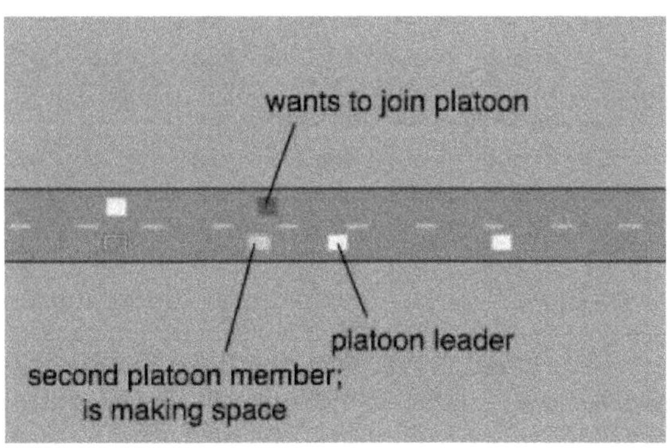

Figure 5: A join scenario. The light-blue vehicle was already part of the platoon, and the dark blue vehicle wants to join. After the light-blue vehicle has made sufficient space, the blue vehicle will change lanes and be part of the platoon.

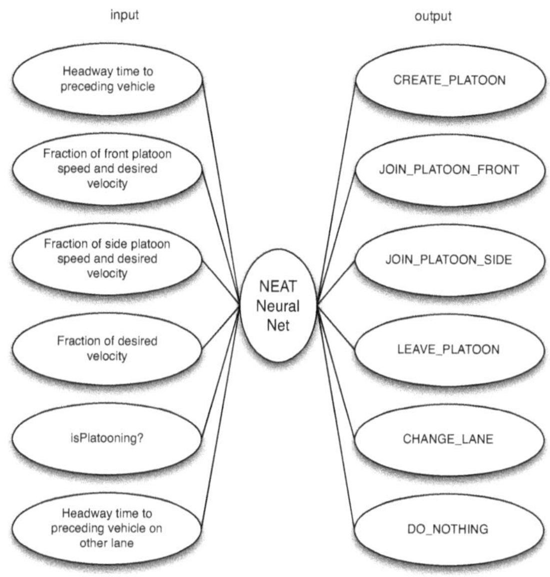

Figure 6: The input and output layers of the neural network controller of the vehicles. The inputs are observables from the simulation, and the outputs are the actions that need to be performed (if possible). The neural network layers in between the input and output layers are evolved by NEAT.

- isPlatooning?: The current platooning status of c;
- Headway time to preceding vehicle on other lane: the distance to the first preceding vehicle on the other lane divided by c's velocity.

The input variables can easily be modified or extended with other variables, but it has to be kept in mind that the vehicle should be able to register these variables autonomously and on a real-time basis. The values of the input variables are normalised to $[0, 1]$ (except those inputs that are a fraction of the desired speed, those can be greater than 1) to make them more amenable as inputs for the neural network.

The six output variables select from the actions that we have defined in our simulation: the controller simply picks the action with the highest corresponding output value.

4.3 Evaluation Criteria

The experiments described in this paper serve primarily as a proof-of-concept, and we limit ourselves to using two objectives:

Comfort As a measure of the comfort of a ride, we take the number of times a vehicle changes lanes during a ride, assuming that fewer lane changes indicates a more comfortable ride.

Speed Our second objective in this study is speed, simply measured as the time it takes a vehicle to complete the stretch of motorway in our simulation.

To evaluate each controller, we simulate a 10 km, two-lane stretch of road with 3000 vehicles entering per hour, all running that particular neural network. Each vehicle has a desired speed of 30m/s. Their initial speeds differ by a random amount up to 5m/s from the desired speed.

Each vehicle evaluates the neural network every 5 seconds, and executes the action that the neural network proposes. The vehicle only executes the action if it is possible. For example, the vehicle will not change lanes if this would result in a crash. If an action is not executable, the vehicle will simply remain using the longitudinal controller it was already using, waiting another 5 seconds before re-evaluating the neural network.

We run this simulation for 10 minutes of simulation time (i.e. ca. 500 vehicles enter the stretch of road), after which we measure the mean number of lane changes of the vehicles and the mean travel times of the vehicles that completed the 10km stretch. These measurements are then used to calculate the controller's Pareto Strength as described above.

In this setting, we ran 50 repeats of 50 generations each with population size 50. From the 50 final generations that obtained from these runs, we extract the combined pareto-optimal solutions.

To assess the quality of the evolved neural net controllers, we also performed 100 repeats of a benchmark experiment where the vehicles are controlled using only the IDM behavioural model.

Table 1 summarises the experimental settings. All code for the experiments can be found on the author's ResearchGate page[5].

Table 1: Experimental Setup

Setting	Value
Road length	10km
Vehicle inflow	3000veh/hr
Desired speed	approx. 30m/s
Max deceleration	-3m/s^2
Simulation time	10 minutes
Timestep size	0.20 seconds
Neural Network Evaluations	Every 5 seconds
Neural Network inputs	6
Neural Network outputs	6
Population Size	50
Fitness Evaluations per individual	10
Generations	50
Repeats	50
Benchmark runs	100
Validation runs	100

5. RESULTS & ANALYSIS

Figures 7 and 8 show the pareto-optimal solutions resulting from the 50 repeats of the NEAT-PS experiment. This

[5]https://www.researchgate.net/profile/WH_Van_Willigen/

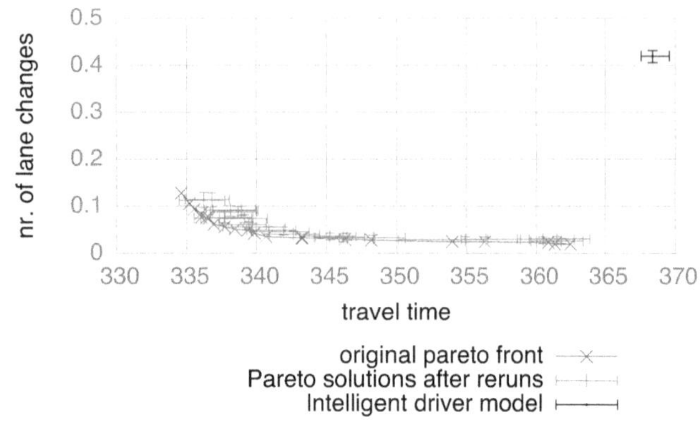

Figure 7: All experimental results. The original pareto front is show by '×' signs. The crossed error bars show the medians and quartile performance of the validation reruns. The crossed error bars in the top right show the IDM results. This controller clearly performs much worse than the evolved controllers.

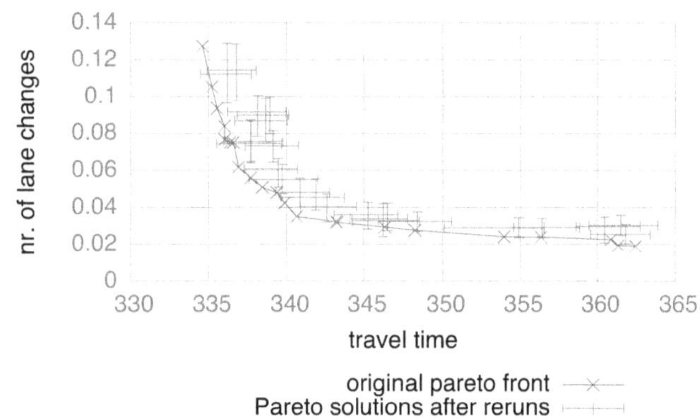

Figure 8: The experimental results, excluding the IDM results, for clarity reasons.

selection consists of the non-dominated controllers from the union of the non-dominated controllers per run. The '×' ticks indicate the performance in travel time and comfort for each of these controllers, averaged over 10 runs as explained in Section 4.3. In these plots, the x-axis shows the travel time in seconds, the y-axis the level of comfort measured as the mean number of lane changes over the 10km stretch.

The controllers are evenly spread along the pareto front; if these controllers were to be implemented (putting aside the issue of any reality gap for the moment), the user would indeed be offered a range of choices to strike a balance between speed and comfort.

Figure 7 also shows median and quartile performance on both objectives for 100 trials with different random seeds with the benchmark IDM controller. Because this controller performs at quite a different level from the solved controllers, Figure 8 shows the results for the NEAT-PS solutions in more detail.

When we compare the results of the evolved controllers with those of the benchmark IDM controller, it is clear that all the pareto-optimal controllers perform substantially better on both objectives.

To validate the stability of performance of the solutions on the final combined pareto front, we subsequently ran a further 100 trials with different random seeds for each of these solutions. The crossed error bars in Figures 7 and 8 show the median and upper and lower quartile performance from these validation runs. While these rerun results lie close to the original pareto front, they are, in all cases worse than the performance measured during evolution.

This difference is highlighted in Figure 9, which shows the results from the 100 reruns for a randomly selected pareto-optimal controller. The crossed error bars are close to the highlighted average performance during evolution. We think that the reason for this skewed expectation of performance is due to the way in which we combine the evaluation results during evolution – by taking the mean value of ten trials. A more sophisticated comparison of performance distribution, for instance by redefining the domination relationship as 'being significantly better' (with some α), might alleviate this problem. This approach is advocated in [12] for comparing multi-objective evolutionary algorithm runs. Alternatively, more consistent performance may be achieved by adding consistency as an additional objective. It must be noted that this consistency objective should not be an explicit objective for the user, but rather an implicit objective for the algorithm itself.

6. CONCLUSIONS & FUTURE WORK

We described our vision of a future in which vehicles on highways can drive autonomously using Cooperative Adaptive Cruise Control. With CACC technology, vehicles are able to form trains of vehicles that drive very close to one another, also known as platoons. We performed proof-of-concept experiments that show that multi-objective evolutionary algorithms can evolve a number of controllers that embody a variety of prioritisations of ride qualities like speed, comfort and fuel economy. Such a combination of controllers will, in our vision, allow the driver to emphasise different qualities based on her preference and needs in real time.

The experiments described in this study serve primarily as a proof-of-concept, and therefore we limited ourselves two objectives: speed and comfort. These two objectives are easily extended with more objectives, such as fuel economy (when a vehicle is platooning, it consumes less fuel than otherwise), or further measures for comfort (e.g. the variability of speed of the vehicle). We plan to consider such additional objectives in future work.

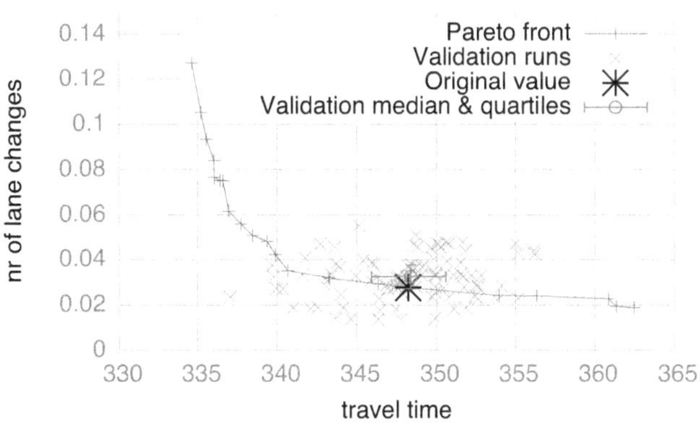

Figure 9: Original performance with raw and summarised validation results.

The evolved controllers outperform the benchmark IDM controller substantially. The IDM is a widely used model of human driver behaviour; we conclude that automatic driving as we envisage will substantially increase travel speed as well as ride comfort.

These preliminary results are very promising, but our conclusions need to be confirmed by more extensive experimentation, both in terms of complexity and number of experiments. Work to this end is underway.

The concept of evolving many pareto-optimal controllers represents a significant improvement from the current practice of optimising a weighted average of objectives to obtain a single controller that prioritises ride qualities as the developer deems appropriate. The consequent freedom of choice for drivers to select controller behaviour as they see fit will greatly benefit acceptance of CACC technology.

These results open up possibilities for substantial further research. Firstly, we plan to do experiments with more objectives, such as fuel economy, and other ways of measuring comfort in a vehicle. Secondly, we will include stability of the controller as an explicit objective in the NEAT algorithm.

Another track of future work includes tests with heterogeneous vehicles. In our current work, we tested a particular neural network by letting all vehicles in a simulation use the same network. The question remains whether these networks remain their performance when other vehicles have completely different controllers or even human drivers on board.

7. REFERENCES

[1] C. Bergenhem, Q. Huang, A. Benmimoun, and T. Robinson. Challenges of platooning on public motorways. In *17th World Congress on Intelligent Transport Systems*, 2010.

[2] A. Broggi, M. Bertozzi, A. Fascioli, C. G. L. Bianco, and A. Piazzi. Visual perception of obstacles and vehicles for platooning. *IEEE TRANS. INTELL. TRANSPORT. SYS*, 1(3):164–176, 2000.

[3] K. Deb, A. Pratap, S. Agarwal, and T. Meyarivan. A fast and elitist multiobjective genetic algorithm: Nsga-ii. *Evolutionary Computation, IEEE Transactions on*, 6(2):182–197, apr 2002.

[4] E. Dovgan, M. Gams, and B. Filipič. A multiobjective optimization algorithm for discovering driving strategies. In N. Krasnogor et al., editors, *GECCO '11: Proceedings of the 13th annual conference on Genetic and evolutionary computation*, pages 751–754, Dublin, Ireland, 12-16 July 2011. ACM.

[5] E. Dovgan, T. Tušar, M. Javorski, and B. Filipič. Discovering comfortable driving strategies using simulation-based multiobjective optimization. *Informatica*, (36):319–326, 2012.

[6] J. Gauci and K. Stanley. Generating large-scale neural networks through discovering geometric regularities. In *Proceedings of the 9th annual conference on Genetic and evolutionary computation*, GECCO '07, pages 997–1004, New York, NY, USA, 2007. ACM.

[7] P. Gipps. A behavioural car-following model for computer simulation. *Transportation Research Part B: Methodological*, 15(2):105 - 111, 1981.

[8] S. Hallé. Automated highway systems: Platoons of vehicles viewed as a multiagent system. Master's thesis, Université Laval, Québec, 2005.

[9] I. Kanellakopoulos, P. Nelson, and O. Stafsudd. Intelligent sensors and control for commercial vehicle automation. *Annual Reviews in Control*, 23:117 – 124, 1999.

[10] M. Khan, D. Turgut, and L. Bölöni. A study of collaborative influence mechanisms for highway convoy driving. In *Proceedings of International Workshop on Agents in Traffic and Transportation (ATT08), in conjunction with the Seventh Joint Conference on Autonomous and Multi-Agent Systems (AAMAS 2008)*, pages 46–53, May 2008.

[11] G. Naus, R. Vugts, J. Ploeg, M. van de Molengraft, and M. Steinbuch. String-stable cacc design and experimental validation: A frequency-domain approach. *Vehicular Technology, IEEE Transactions on*, 59(9):4268 –4279, 2010.

[12] S. Smit and A. E. Eiben. Multi-problem parameter tuning using bonesa. In J. Hao, P. Legrand, P. Collet, N. Monmarché, E. Lutton, and M. Schoenauer, editors, *Artificial Evolution*, pages 222–233, 2011.

[13] K. O. Stanley and R. Miikkulainen. Evolving neural networks through augmenting topologies. *Evolutionary Computation*, 10(2):99–127, Mar. 2002.

[14] M. Treiber and D. Helbing. Realistische mikrosimulation von strassenverkehr mit einem einfachen modell. In D. Tavangarian and R. Gruetzner, editors, *16. Symposium Simulationstechnik ASIM 2002*, pages 514–520, 2002.

[15] M. Treiber, A. Hennecke, and D. Helbing. Congested traffic states in empirical observations and microscopic simulations. *Phys. Rev. E*, 62:1805–1824, Aug 2000.

[16] B. van Arem, C. van Driel, and R. Visser. The impact of cooperative adaptive cruise control on traffic-flow characteristics. *Intelligent Transportation Systems, IEEE Transactions on*, 7(4):429 –436, 2006.

[17] W. van Willigen, E. Haasdijk, and L. Kester. Evolving intelligent vehicle control using multi-objective neat. In *2013 IEEE Symposium Series on Computational Intelligence*, 2013. To Appear.

[18] X. Yang, J. Liu, F. Zhao, and N. H̀. Vaidya. A vehicle-to-vehicle communication protocol for cooperative collision warning. *Mobile and Ubiquitous Systems, Annual International Conference on*, 0:114–123, 2004.

[19] E. Zitzler, M. Laumanns, and L. Thiele. SPEA2: Improving the strength pareto evolutionary algorithm for multiobjective optimization. In K. Giannakoglou, D. Tsahalis, J. Periaux, K. Papaliliou, and T. Fogarty, editors, *Evolutionary Methods for Design, Optimisation and Control with Application to Industrial Problems. Proceedings of the EUROGEN2001 Conference, Athens, Greece, September 19-21, 2001*, pages 95–100, Barcelona, Spain, 2002. International Center for Numerical Methods in Engineering (CIMNE).

MOEA/D assisted by RBF Networks for Expensive Multi-Objective Optimization Problems

Saúl Zapotecas Martínez
CINVESTAV-IPN (EVOCINV)
Departamento de Computación
México, D.F. 07360, MEXICO
saul.zapotecas@gmail.com

Carlos A. Coello Coello
CINVESTAV-IPN (EVOCINV)
Departamento de Computación
México, D.F. 07360, MEXICO
ccoello@cs.cinvestav.mx

ABSTRACT

The development of multi-objective evolutionary algorithms assisted by surrogate models has increased in the last few years. However, in real-world applications, the high modality and dimensionality that functions have, often causes problems to such models. In fact, if the Pareto optimal set of a multi-objective optimization problem is located in a search space in which the surrogate model is not able to shape the corresponding region, the search could be misinformed and thus converge to wrong regions. Because of this, a considerable amount of research has focused on improving the prediction of the surrogate models by adding the new solutions to the training set and retraining the model. However, when the size of the training set increases, the training complexity can significantly increase. In this paper, we present a surrogate model which maintains the size of the training set, and in which the prediction of the function is improved by using radial basis function networks in a cooperative way. Preliminary results indicate that our proposed approach can produce good quality results when it is restricted to performing only 200, 1,000 and 5,000 fitness function evaluations. Our proposed approach is validated using a set of standard test problems and an airfoil design problem.

Categories and Subject Descriptors

I.2.8 [**Computing Methodologies**]: Artificial Intelligence—*Problem Solving, Control Methods, and Search.*

Keywords

Multi-objective optimization, expensive optimization, RBF neural networks.

1. INTRODUCTION

Multi-Objective Evolutionary algorithms (MOEAs) have been successfully adopted to solve multi-objective optimization problems (MOPs) in a wide variety of engineering and scientific problems [1]. However, in real-world applications is common to find objective functions which are very expensive to evaluate (in terms of computational time). This has considerably limited the use of evolutionary techniques to these types of problems. In recent years, several researchers have developed different strategies for reducing the computational time (measured in terms of the number of fitness function evaluations) that a MOEA requires to solve a determined problem. From such strategies, the use of surrogate models has been one of the most common techniques adopted to solve complex problems. In the specialized literature, several authors have reported the use of surrogate models for dealing with MOPs—see for example [11, 4, 6, 16, 19] among others. However, the features of some problems, such as high modality and dimensionality, often present major obstacles to surrogate models. Therefore, if the Pareto optimal set of a MOP is located in a search space in which the surrogate model is not able to shape the corresponding region, the search could be misinformed and converge to wrong regions. Because of this, an important number of researchers have tried to improve the prediction of surrogate models by adding new solutions to the training set and then retraining the surrogate model at each iteration of the MOEA, see for example [19, 16]. However, as the training set gets larger, the complexity of the training also increases.

In this paper, we present an algorithm based on the well-known MOEA/D [18] which is assisted by radial basis function (RBF) networks. The proposed approach uses a static size for the training set and the function prediction of the surrogate model is improved by using a set of RBF networks in a cooperative way. With this, the computational complexity (measured in terms of computational time) is not dependent on the size of the training set, being limited only to the number of decision variables that the MOP has. The main goal of this paper is to contribute to the state-of-the-art regarding MOEAs assisted by surrogate models, which we believe is of interest in a wide variety of real-world problems (given the wide applicability of MOEAs [1]). We show in this paper that cooperative RBF networks can significantly reduce the number of fitness function evaluations that are required to produce reasonably good approximations of MOPs of different complexity.

The remainder of this paper is organized as follows. In Section 2, we present the basic concepts to understand the rest of the paper. In Section 3, we describe in detail our proposed approach. In Section 4, the test problems adopted to validate our approach are described. In Section 5, we show and discuss the results obtained by our proposed approach.

GECCO'13, July 6–10, 2013, Amsterdam, The Netherlands.

Finally, in Section 6, we provide our conclusions and some possible paths for future research.

2. BASIC CONCEPTS

2.1 Multi-Objective Optimization

Without loss of generality we will assume only minimization problems. Thus, a nonlinear multi-objective optimization problem can be formulated as:

$$\min_{\mathbf{x}\in\Omega} \quad \mathbf{F}(\mathbf{x}) \tag{1}$$

where Ω defines the decision variable space and $\mathbf{F}:\Omega\rightarrow\mathbb{R}^k$ defines the vector of objective functions $\mathbf{F}(\mathbf{x}) = (f_1(\mathbf{x}),\ldots, f_k(\mathbf{x}))^T$, such that $f_i:\mathbb{R}^n\rightarrow\mathbb{R}$ is a nonlinear function. In order to describe the concept of optimality in which we are interested, the following definitions are introduced [10]:

DEFINITION 1. *Let* $\mathbf{x},\mathbf{y}\in\Omega$, *we say that* $\mathbf{x}$ dominates $\mathbf{y}$ *(denoted by* $\mathbf{x}\prec\mathbf{y}$*) if and only if,* $f_i(\mathbf{x})\leq f_i(\mathbf{y})$ *and* $\mathbf{F}(\mathbf{x})\neq\mathbf{F}(\mathbf{y})$.

DEFINITION 2. *Let* $\mathbf{x}^\star\in\Omega$, *we say that* $\mathbf{x}^\star$ *is a* Pareto optimal *solution, if there is no other solution* $\mathbf{y}\in\Omega$ *such that* $\mathbf{y}\prec\mathbf{x}^\star$.

DEFINITION 3. *The* Pareto optimal set PS *is defined by:* $PS=\{\mathbf{x}\in\Omega|\mathbf{x}$ is Pareto optimal solution$\}$, *and the* Pareto optimal front PF *is defined as:* $PF=\{\mathbf{F}(\mathbf{x})|\mathbf{x}\in PS\}$.

2.2 Radial Basis Function Networks

Radial Basis Function (RBF) networks are a feed-forward kind of neural network, which are commonly represented with three layers: an input layer with n nodes, a hidden layer with h nonlinear RBFs (or neurons), and an output node φ. The function value in a RBF depends on the distance from each point $\mathbf{x}$ to the origin, i.e. $g(\mathbf{x}) = g(||\mathbf{x}||)$. This function value can be generalized to distances from some other point $\mathbf{c}_j$, commonly called *center* of the basis function, that is:

$$g(\mathbf{x},\mathbf{c}_j) = g(||\mathbf{x}-\mathbf{c}_j||)$$

The output $\varphi:\mathbb{R}^n\mapsto\mathbb{R}$ of the network is defined as:

$$\varphi(\mathbf{x}) = \sum_{j=1}^{h} w_j g(||\mathbf{x}-\mathbf{c}_j||) \tag{2}$$

where h is the number of neurons in the hidden layer, $\mathbf{c}_j$ is the center vector for the jth neuron, and w_j's are the weights of the linear output neuron. In its basic form, all inputs are connected to each hidden neuron. The norm is typically taken to be the Euclidean distance and the basis function g or kernel is taken to be Gaussian, although other basis functions are also possible (see for example those shown in Table 1).

RBF networks can be used to interpolate a function $f:\mathbb{R}^n\mapsto\mathbb{R}$ when the values of that function are known on a finite number of points: $f(\mathbf{x}_i) = y_i, i = 1\ldots,N$. Taking into account the h centers $\mathbf{c}_j$'s ($j=1,\ldots,h$) and evaluating the values of the basis functions at the points $\mathbf{x}_i$, i.e., $\phi_{ij} = g(||\mathbf{c}_j-\mathbf{x}_i||,\sigma_j)$ the weights can be solved from the equation:

$$\begin{pmatrix} \phi_{11} & \phi_{12} & \cdots & \phi_{1m} \\ \phi_{21} & \phi_{22} & \cdots & \phi_{2m} \\ \vdots & & \ddots & \vdots \\ \phi_{N1} & \phi_{N2} & \cdots & \phi_{Nm} \end{pmatrix} \begin{pmatrix} w_1 \\ w_2 \\ \vdots \\ w_m \end{pmatrix} = \begin{pmatrix} y_1 \\ y_2 \\ \vdots \\ y_N \end{pmatrix} \tag{3}$$

Table 1: Kernels for a RBF neural network, where $r = ||\mathbf{x}-\mathbf{c}_i||$

Kernel	Description
Cubic	$g(r) = r^3$
Thin Plate Spline	$g(r) = r^2\ln(r)$
Gaussian	$g(r,\sigma) = \exp(-r^2/2\sigma^2)$
Multi-quadratic	$g(r,\sigma) = \sqrt{r^2+\sigma^2}$
Inverse multi-quadratic	$g(r,\sigma) = \sqrt{r^2+\sigma^2}$

Therefore, the weights w_i's can be solved by simple linear algebra, using the least squares method, that is:

$$\mathbf{w} = (\mathbf{\Phi}^T\mathbf{\Phi})^{-1}\mathbf{\Phi}^T\mathbf{y} \tag{4}$$

The parameter σ_j of the kernels (Gaussian, multi-quadratic and inverse multi-quadratic) determines the amplitude of each basis function and it can be adjusted to improve the model accuracy.

3. OUR PROPOSED APPROACH

3.1 MOP Decomposition

A Pareto optimal solution to a MOP, under some assumptions, is an optimal solution of a scalar optimization problem in which the objective is an aggregation of all the objective functions f_i's. Therefore, an approximation of the Pareto optimal front can be decomposed into a number of scalar objective optimization subproblems. Several approaches have been proposed for decomposing a MOP into multiple single-objective optimization subproblems [10]. In the following, we describe an approach based on the normal boundary intersection (NBI) [2] method, which is referred to in this work.

3.1.1 Penalty Boundary Intersection Approach

The Penalty Boundary Intersection (PBI) approach proposed by Zhang and Li [18], uses a weight vector $\mathbf{w}$ and a penalty value θ for minimizing both the distance to the utopian vector d_1 and the direction error to the weight vector d_2 from the solution $\mathbf{F}(\mathbf{x})$. The optimization problem can be stated as:

$$\text{Minimize:} \quad g(\mathbf{x}|\mathbf{w},\mathbf{z}^\star) = d_1 + \theta d_2 \tag{5}$$

where

$$d_1 = \frac{||(\mathbf{F}(\mathbf{x})-\mathbf{z}^\star)^T\mathbf{w}||}{||\mathbf{w}||} \text{ and } d_2 = \left|\left|(\mathbf{F}(\mathbf{x})-\mathbf{z}^\star) - d_1\frac{\mathbf{w}}{||\mathbf{w}||}\right|\right|$$

such that $\mathbf{x}\in\Omega$ and $\mathbf{z}^\star = (z_1,\ldots,z_k)^T$, such that: $z_i = \min\{f_i(\mathbf{x})|\mathbf{x}\in\Omega\}$.

Therefore, a good representation of the Pareto front can be obtained by solving a set of problems defined by a well-distributed set of weight vectors. This is the main idea behind current decomposition-based MOEAs, see e.g. [18, 17].

3.2 General Framework

Our proposed MOEA/D assisted by Radial Basis Functions (MOEA/D-RBF) decomposes the MOP (1) into N single-objective optimization problems. MOEA/D-RBF uses a well-distributed set of N weight vectors $W=\{\mathbf{w}_1,\ldots,\mathbf{w}_N\}$ to define a set of single-objective optimization subproblems by using the PBI approach. Each subproblem is solved by MOEA/D, which is assisted by a surrogate model based on RBF networks. For a better understanding of the proposed

Algorithm 1: General framework of MOEA/D-RBF

Input:
$W = \{\mathbf{w}_i, \dots, \mathbf{w}_N\}$: A well-distributed set of weight vectors.
N_t: The number of points in the initial training set.
E_{max}: The maximum number of evaluations allowed in MOEA/D-RBF.
Output:
A: An approximation to the PF.

begin
- **Initialization:** Generate a set $T_{set} = \{\mathbf{x}_1, \dots, \mathbf{x}_{N_t}\}$ of N_t points such that $\mathbf{x}_i \in \Omega$ $(i = 1, \dots N_t)$, by using an experimental design method. Evaluate the **F**-functions values of these points. Set A as the set of nondominated solutions found in T_{set}. Set $n_{eval} = N_t$. Generate a population $\hat{P} = \{\mathbf{x}_1, \dots, \mathbf{x}_N\}$ of N individuals such that $\mathbf{x}_i \in \Omega$ $(i = 1, \dots N)$, by using an experimental design method. $stopping\_criterion = FALSE$. For details of this step see **Section 3.3**.
- **while** ($stopping\_criterion == FALSE$) **do**
  - **Model Building:** Using the **F**-function values of the points in T_{set}, build the predictive surrogate model by using different RBF networks. Calculate the weights for each RBF network according to its training error in T_{set}. For details of this step see **Section 3.4**.
  - **Evaluate $\hat{P}$:** Evaluate the population $\hat{P}$ using the surrogate model.
  - **Find an approximation to PF:** By using MOEA/D, the surrogate model and the population $\hat{P}$, obtain $\hat{P}^\star = \{\hat{\mathbf{x}}_i, \dots, \hat{\mathbf{x}}_{N_t}\}$, where $\hat{P}^\star$ is an approximation to PF, see **Section 3.5**.
  - **Select points for updating T_{set}:** By using the selection scheme, select a set of solutions from $\hat{P}^\star$ to be evaluated and included in the training set T_{set}. Update A using the selected solutions. For each evaluated solution, set $n_{eval} = n_{eval} + 1$. **If** $n_{eval} < E_{max}$ **then** $stopping\_criterion = TRUE$. For a detailed description of this step see **Section 3.6**.
  - **Update population $\hat{P}$:** Update the population $\hat{P}$ according to the updating scheme, see **Section 3.7**.
- **end**
- **return** A;

end

approach, Algorithm 1 shows the general framework of the proposed MOEA/D-RBF. In the following sections, we describe in detail the components of our MOEA/D-RBF which are outlined in Algorithm 1.

3.3 Initialization

Initially, a training set $T_{set} = \{\mathbf{x}_i, \dots, \mathbf{x}_{N_t}\}$ of N_t well-spread solutions is generated. For this task, we employed the Latin hypercube sampling method [9]. The set of solutions T_{set} is evaluated by using the real fitness function. The number of current fitness function evaluations n_{eval} is initially set as $n_{eval} = N_t$. MOEA/D-RBF uses an external archive A to store the nondominated solutions found so far in the evolutionary process. This archive is initialized with the nondominated solutions found in T_{set}. At the beginning, a population $\hat{P} = \{\mathbf{x}_i, \dots, \mathbf{x}_N\}$ of N solutions is generated by employing the Latin hypercube sampling method. The stopping criterion considered in MOEA/D-RBF is the number of fitness function evaluations and, therefore, the stopping criterion is initially set as false, i.e. $stopping\_criterion = FALSE$.

3.4 Building the Model

As previously indicated, we use a surrogate model based on RBF networks. In order to improve the prediction of the surrogate model, the Gaussian, the multi-quadratic and the inverse multi-quadratic kernels are used in a cooperative way

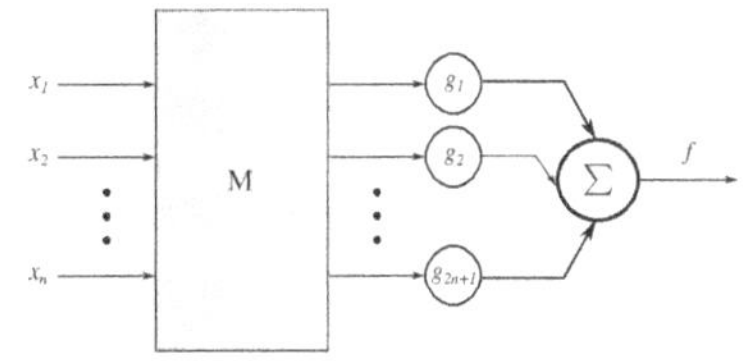

Figure 1: Network representation of Kolmogorov's theorem

for obtaining the approximated value of a solution. In the following sections, we describe the necessary components for building the surrogate model.

3.4.1 Hidden Nodes

The hidden nodes in an RBF network play an important role in the performance of the RBF network. In general, there is no method available for estimating the number of hidden nodes in an RBF network. However, it has been suggested in [5, 13] that Kolmogorov's theorem [7] concerning the realization of arbitrary multivariate functions, provides theoretical support for neural networks that implement such functions.

THEOREM 1 (KOLMOGOROV [7]). *A continuous real-valued function defined as $f : [0,1]^n \mapsto \mathbb{R}$, $n \geq 2$, can be represented in the form:*

$$f(x_1, \dots, x_n) = \sum_{j=1}^{2n+1} g_j \left(\sum_{i=1}^{n} \phi_{ij}(x_i) \right) \tag{6}$$

where the g_j's are properly chosen continuous functions of one variable, and the ϕ_{ij}'s are continuous monotonically increasing functions independent of f.

The basic idea in Kolmogorov's theorem is captured in the network architecture of Figure 1, where a universal transformation M maps $\mathbb{R}^n$ into several uni-dimensional transformations. The theorem states that one can express a continuous multivariate function on a compact set in terms of sums and compositions of a finite number of single variable functions. Motivated by this idea, the surrogate model built here, uses $2n + 1$ hidden nodes (where n is the number of decision variables of the MOP). Considering T_{set} as the training set of N_t solutions used by the surrogate model, the centers of the $2n + 1$ basis functions are defined by using the well-known k-means algorithm [8] on the training set T_{set} (with $k = 2n + 1$). This criterion establishes that the cardinality of T_{set} should be greater than $2n + 1$, i.e., $2n + 1 < N_t$.

3.4.2 Building the surrogate model

The high modality and dimensionality of some real-world functions, often produce problems to surrogate models. When the surrogate model is not able to properly shape the region of the search space in which the Pareto set is located, then the search may be biased towards inappropriate regions. In order to improve the function prediction, MOEA/D-RBF uses different kernels for building different RBF networks. Each RBF network provides different shape of the search space and all of them provide information to predict the value of an arbitrary solution. Here, three different kernels are adopted: Gaussian, multi-quadratic and inverse multi-quadratic; these kernels are chosen because they possess the parameter σ which can be adjusted to improve the model accuracy, see Table 1. Note however that other types of kernels can also be adopted, although the use of more kernels could significantly increase the training time. In the following description, we consider the case with one single output node, i.e. with a single function. Note however, that this model can be generalized for more than one function.

Let $T_{set} = \{\mathbf{x}_1, \ldots, \mathbf{x}_{N_t}\}$ be the set of N_t solutions evaluated with the real fitness function. Let h be the number of hidden nodes (or basis functions) considered in the RBF network. Let $\mathbf{c}_j$ and σ_j ($j = 1, \ldots, m$) be the center and the amplitude of each basis function, respectively. The training of the RBF network for a determined kernel K consists in finding the weight vector $\mathbf{w} = (w_1, \ldots, w_m)^T$ such that it solves equation (4). Each parameter σ_j of each basis function is initially defined by the standard deviation of the solutions contained in each cluster obtained by the k-means algorithm (with mean $\mathbf{c}_j$).

Once the weight vector $\mathbf{w}$ is obtained, the model accuracy is improved by adjusting the vector of parameters $\sigma = (\sigma_1, \ldots, \sigma_m)^T$. Since the value of the adopted kernel depends of σ_j, from equation (3), the training error on the training set T_{set}, can be written as:

$$\psi(\sigma) = ||\mathbf{\Phi}\mathbf{w} - \mathbf{y}|| \quad (7)$$

where $\mathbf{y} = (y_1, \ldots, y_{Nt})^T$ is the vector of the real function values for each solution $\mathbf{x}_i \in T_{set}$, i.e., $y_i = f(\mathbf{x}_i)$. $\mathbf{\Phi}$ is the matrix which contains the evaluations of each point $\mathbf{x}_i \in T_{set}$ for each basis function, i.e., $\phi_{ij} = g(||\mathbf{c}_j - \mathbf{x}_i||, \sigma_j)$, for $i = 1, \ldots, N_t$ and $j = 1, \ldots, h$.

The parameters σ_j are then adjusted by using the Differential Evolution (DE) algorithm [14], whose objective is to minimize the training error defined in equation (7). Once the σ_j parameters are adjusted, the prediction function for a determined kernel K of a solution $\mathbf{x} \in \Omega$ can be calculated by:

$$\hat{\varphi}_K(\mathbf{x}) = \sum_{j=1}^{h} w_j \cdot g(||\mathbf{x} - \mathbf{c}_j||, \sigma_j) \quad (8)$$

3.4.3 Cooperative surrogate models and Function Prediction

Once the three RBF networks are built, each of them using the three above mentioned kernels, the prediction of the function is carried out. Let $\varphi_{GK}(\mathbf{x}), \varphi_{MK}(\mathbf{x})$ and $\varphi_{IMK}(\mathbf{x})$ be the predicted value given by RBF networks using the Gaussian, multi-quadratic and inverse multi-quadratic kernel, respectively. These three RBF networks cooperate by providing information of the search space that they model. Therefore, the function prediction $\hat{f}$ for an arbitrary $\mathbf{x} \in \Omega$ is defined by:

$$\hat{f}(\mathbf{x}) = \lambda_1 \cdot \varphi_{GK}(\mathbf{x}) + \lambda_2 \cdot \varphi_{MK}(\mathbf{x}) + \lambda_3 \cdot \varphi_{IMK}(\mathbf{x}) \quad (9)$$

where $\mathbf{\Lambda} = (\lambda_1, \lambda_2, \lambda_3)^T$ is a weight vector, i.e. $\lambda_i \geq 0$ and $\sum_{i=1}^{3} \lambda_i = 1$. Therefore, the weight for each predicted value needs to be calculated.

Let T_{set} be the knowledge set for training the different RBF networks. The weight vector $\mathbf{\Lambda}$ is then calculated by:

$$\lambda_i = \frac{\alpha_i}{|T_{set}|}, i = 1, 2, 3 \quad (10)$$

where α_i is the number of solutions in T_{set} with the lowest prediction error for the ith RBF network (Gaussian, multi-quadratic and inverse multi-quadratic, respectively).

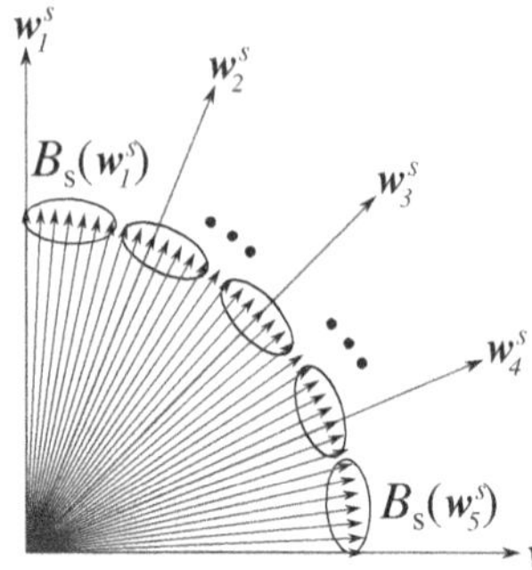

Figure 2: Association of weight vectors from W to W_s. The vectors in blue represent the projection of W set, while the vectors in red represent the projection of W_s set. This association defines the neighborhoods $B_s(\mathbf{w}_1^s)$ to $B_s(\mathbf{w}_5^s)$

3.5 Finding an Approximation to PF

MOEA/D-RBF approximates solutions to the PF by using the well-known MOEA/D [18]. The search is conducted by the set of weight vectors $W = \{\mathbf{w}_1, \ldots, \mathbf{w}_N\}$. MOEA/D searches the solutions to each scalar problem defined by each weight vector $\mathbf{w}_i \in W$. The evolutionary process of MOEA/D is performed during a determined number of generations by employing the prediction function defined in equation (9). The final population denoted as $\hat{P}^\star$ is then reported as an approximation to PF.

3.6 Selecting Points to Evaluate

Let $W = \{\mathbf{w}_1, \ldots, \mathbf{w}_N\}$ be the well-distributed set of weight vectors used by MOEA/D. Let $\hat{P}^\star$ be the approximation to PF obtained by MOEA/D. Let $W_s = \{\mathbf{w}_1^s, \ldots, \mathbf{w}_{N_s}^s\}$ be a well-distributed set of weight vectors, such that $|W_s| < |W|$. For each $\mathbf{w}_i^s \in W_s$, we define $B_s(\mathbf{w}_i^s) = \{\mathbf{w}_1, \ldots, \mathbf{w}_{N_a}\}$, such that $\mathbf{w}_1, \ldots, \mathbf{w}_{N_a} \in W$ are the $N_a = \lfloor \frac{N}{N_s} \rfloor$ closest weight vectors from W to $\mathbf{w}_i^s$. With that, an association of weight vectors from W to W_s is defined. This association defines a set of neighborhoods $B_s(\mathbf{w}_i^s)$ which are distributed along the whole set of weight vectors W, see Figure 2. Once the neighborhoods $B_s(\mathbf{w}_i^s)$ have been defined, a set of solutions is selected to be included in the training set T_{set}, according to the next description.

3.6.1 Selecting Points to be Evaluated using the Real Fitness Function

A set $S = \{\mathbf{x}_1, \ldots, \mathbf{w}_{N_s}\}$ of N_s solutions taken from $\hat{P}$ is chosen to be evaluated using the real fitness function. Each solution in S is selected such that it minimizes the problem defined by a weight vector $\mathbf{w}_j \in B_s(\mathbf{w}_i^s)$, where $i = 1, \ldots, N_s$ and $j = 1, \ldots N_a$.

At each call of the selection procedure, the weight vector $\mathbf{w}_j$ is selected by sweeping the set of weight vectors in $B_s(\mathbf{w}_i^s)$ in a cyclic way, i.e., once the last weight vector is selected, the next one is picked up from the beginning. Since the neighborhoods $B_s(\mathbf{w}_i^s)$ are distributed along the whole weight set W, the selection of solutions in each neighborhood should obtain spread solutions along the PF. No solution in S should be duplicated. If this is the case, the repeated solution should be removed from S. For each new evaluated solution, we set $n_{eval} = n_{eval} + 1$, if $n_{eval} \geq E_{max}$ then we set *stopping_criterion* $= TRUE$, where n_{eval} and E_{max} are the current and the maximum number of fitness function evaluations, respectively.

3.6.2 Updating the Training Set and the External Archive

The maximum number of solutions in the training set T_{set} is defined by the parameter N_t. The updating of T_{set} is carried out by defining a well-distributed set of N_t weight vectors $W_t = \{\mathbf{w}_1^t, \ldots, \mathbf{w}_{N_t}^t\}$. Therefore, the best N_t different solutions from $T = \{T_{set} \cup S\}$, such that they minimize the subproblems defined by each weight vector $\mathbf{w}_i^t \in W_t$, are used to update T_{set}. If after updating the training set, any solution $\mathbf{s}_j \in S$ was not selected to be included in T_{set}, then, it is added by replacing the closest solution (in the objective space) in T_s. With this, all solutions in S are included in T_{set} and the model can be improved even if it has been misinformed formerly.

The external archive A contains the nodominated solutions found along the search. For each $\mathbf{s}_j \in S$, the external archive is updated by removing from A all the solutions dominated by $\mathbf{s}_j$, and then, $\mathbf{s}_j$ is stored in A if no solutions in A dominate $\mathbf{s}_i$.

3.7 Updating the Population

Once the external archive is updated, the population $\hat{P}$ is also updated for the next iteration of MOEA/D. Considering the external archive A as the set of nondominated solutions found by MOEA/D-RBF, the population $\hat{P}$ of N solutions is updated according to the following description.

Let $\mathbf{m}$ and σ be the average and standard deviation of the solutions contained in A. Then, new bounds in the search space are defined according to:

$$\begin{array}{rcl} \mathbf{L}_{bound} & = & \mathbf{m} - \sigma \\ \mathbf{U}_{bound} & = & \mathbf{m} + \sigma \end{array} \tag{11}$$

where $\mathbf{L}_{bound}$ and $\mathbf{U}_{bound}$ are the vectors which define the lower and upper bounds of the new search space, respectively.

Once the new bounds have been defined, a well-distributed set Q of $N - |A|$ solutions is generated by means of the Latin hypercube sampling method [9] in the new search space. The population $\hat{P}$ is then redefined by the union of Q and A, that is $\hat{P} = \{Q \cup A\}$.

4. TEST PROBLEMS

4.1 Standard Test Problems

In order to assess the performance of our proposed approach (MOEA/D-RBF), we compare its results with respect to those obtained by the original MOEA/D [18] and by MOEA/D-EGO [19], which uses surrogates (based on the Gaussian stochastic process model). We adopted the Zitzler-Deb-Thiele (ZDT) test problems [20] except for ZDT5 (which is a discrete problem). The detailed description of such problems can be found in [20]. In order to evaluate the capabilities of MOEA/D-RBF when dealing with computationally expensive problems, we also tested its performance using a real-world problem, as a case study. Next, we describe the airfoil problem which was adopted to validate our proposed approach.

4.2 Airfoil Shape Optimization: A case study

Our case study consists of the multi-objective optimization of an airfoil shape problem adapted from [15] (called here MOPRW). This problem corresponds to the airfoil shape optimization of a standard-class glider, aiming to obtain an optimum performance for a sailplane.

4.2.1 Problem Statement

Two conflicting objective functions are defined in terms of a sailplane average weight and operating conditions [15]. They are defined as:

i) Minimize: C_D/C_L
s.t. $C_L = 0.63$, $Re = 2.04 \cdot 10^6$, $M = 0.12$

ii) Minimize: $C_D/C_L^{3/2}$
s.t. $C_L = 1.05$, $Re = 1.29 \cdot 10^6$, $M = 0.08$

where C_D/C_L and $C_D/C_L^{3/2}$ correspond to the inverse of the glider's gliding ratio and sink rate, respectively. Both are important performance measures for this aerodynamic optimization problem. C_D and C_L are the drag and lift coefficients.

The aim is to maximize the gliding ratio (C_L/C_D) for objective (i), while minimizing the sink rate in objective (ii). Each of these objectives is evaluated at different prescribed flight conditions, given in terms of Mach and Reynolds numbers. The aim of solving this MOP is to find a better airfoil shape, which improves a reference design.

4.2.2 Geometry Parametrization

In the present case study, the PARSEC airfoil representation [12] was adopted. Fig. 3 illustrates the 11 basic parameters used for this representation: r_{le} leading edge radius, X_{up}/X_{lo} location of maximum thickness for upper/lower surfaces, Z_{up}/Z_{lo} maximum thickness for upper/lower surfaces, Z_{xxup}/Z_{xxlo} curvature for upper/lower surfaces, at maximum thickness locations, Z_{te} trailing edge coordinate, ΔZ_{te} trailing edge thickness, α_{te} trailing edge direction, and β_{te} trailing edge wedge angle.

For the present case study, the modified PARSEC geometry representation adopted here allows us to define independently the leading edge radius, both for upper and lower surfaces. Thus, a total of 12 decision variables are used. Their allowable ranges are defined in Table 2.

Table 2: Parameter ranges for our modified PARSEC airfoil representation

Design Variable	Lower Bound	Upper Bound
r_{leup}	0.0085	0.0126
r_{lelo}	0.0020	0.0040
α_{te}	7.0000	10.0000
β_{te}	10.0000	14.0000
Z_{te}	-0.0060	-0.0030
ΔZ_{te}	0.0025	0.0050
X_{up}	0.4100	0.4600
Z_{up}	0.1100	0.1300
Z_{xxup}	-0.9000	-0.7000
X_{lo}	0.2000	0.2600
Z_{lo}	-0.0230	-0.0150
Z_{xxlo}	0.0500	0.2000

The PARSEC airfoil geometry representation uses a linear combination of shape functions for defining the upper and

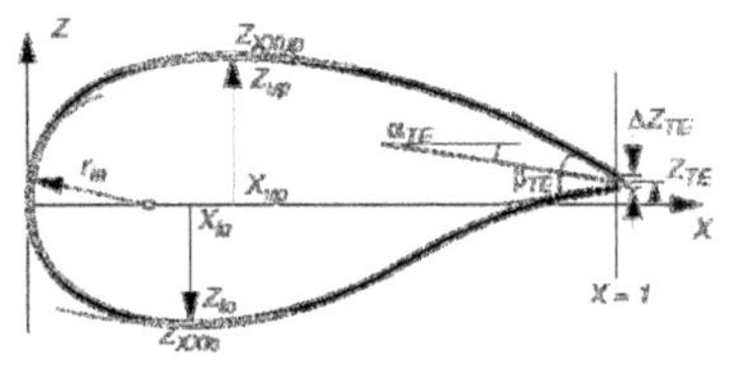

Figure 3: PARSEC airfoil parametrization.

lower surfaces. These linear combinations are given by:

$$Z_{upper} = \sum_{n=1}^{6} a_n x^{\frac{n-1}{2}}, \quad Z_{lower} = \sum_{n=1}^{6} b_n x^{\frac{n-1}{2}} \qquad (12)$$

In the above equations, the coefficients a_n, and b_n are determined as functions of the 12 described geometric parameters, by solving two systems of linear equations, one for each surface. It is important to note that the geometric parameters r_{leup}/r_{lelo}, X_{up}/X_{lo}, Z_{up}/Z_{lo}, Z_{xxup}/Z_{xxlo}, Z_{te}, ΔZ_{te}, α_{te}, and β_{te} are the actual design variables in the optimization process, and that the coefficients a_n, b_n serve as intermediate variables for interpolating the airfoil's coordinates, which are used by the CFD solver (we used the Xfoil CFD code [3]) for its discretization process.

5. COMPARISON OF RESULTS

5.1 Performance Measure

In order to evaluate the performance of our proposed approach, we compared its results with respect to those obtained by MOEA/D and MOEA/D-EGO. For comparing these algorithms, we adopted the I_H^- performance measure which is described below.

5.1.1 I_H^- metric

The Hypervolume (I_H) performance measure was proposed by Zitzler [21]. This performance measure is Pareto compliant [22] and quantifies the approximation of nondominated solutions to the Pareto optimal front. The hypervolume corresponds to the non-overlapped volume of all the hypercubes formed by a reference point **r** (given by the user) and each solution p in the Pareto set approximation (P). It is mathematically defined as:

$$I_H(P) = \Lambda \left(\bigcup_{\mathbf{p} \in P} \{\mathbf{x} | \mathbf{p} \prec \mathbf{x} \prec \mathbf{r}\} \right)$$

where Λ denotes the Lebesgue measure and $\mathbf{r} \in \mathbb{R}^k$ denotes a reference vector being dominated by all valid candidate solutions in P. The I_H^- performance measure is then defined as:

$$I_H^-(P^\star, P) = I_H(P^\star) - I_H(P)$$

where $I_H(P^\star)$ is the hypervolume between the Pareto optimal front $P^\star$ and a reference point **r**. I_H^- assesses both convergence and spread of the Pareto front. A low I_H^- value, indicates that our approximation P is close to PF and has a good spread towards the extreme portions of the Pareto front.

In our experiments, as in [19], we select 500 evenly distributed points on the Pareto optimal front PF and let these points be $P^\star$ for each standard test problem. Since the Pareto optimal front of the the airfoil shape problem is unknown, only the I_H performance measure is used. In this case, obtaining a high I_H value, indicates that our approximation P is close to PF.

5.2 Experimental Setup

As indicated before, the proposed approach is compared with respect to MOEA/D and MOEA/D-EGO. For each MOP, 30 independent runs were performed with each algorithm. As in [19], the number of decision variables is set to be eight for the ZDT benchmark. Each algorithm was restricted to 200 fitness function evaluations and the results of MOEA/D-EGO were directly taken from [19].

For the airfoil design problem, the search was restricted to 5,000 fitness function evaluations. Since the computational complexity of the model building in MOEA/D-EGO increases with the number of training points, MOEA/D-EGO becomes impractical as the number of fitness function evaluations increases, see [19]. Because of this, the comparison of results in the airfoil design problem is carried out only between MOEA/D and MOEA/D-RBF. In addition, we also show the results obtained by MOEA/D-RBF and MOEA/D using 30 and 10 decision variables for the ZDT test problems, as it was suggested by Zitzler et al. [20]. Since the difficulty to solve the ZDT test problems increases with respect to the number of decision variables, the search for these algorithms was restricted to 1,000 fitness function evaluations.

The parameters used for both MOEA/D and MOEA/D-RBF, were set as in [18], since there is empirical evidence that indicates that these are the most appropriate parameters for solving the ZDT test suite—see [18]. The weight vectors for the algorithms were generated as in [18], i.e., the setting of N and $W = \{\mathbf{w}_1, \ldots, \mathbf{w}_N\}$ is controlled by a parameter H. More precisely, $\mathbf{w}_1, \ldots, \mathbf{w}_N$ are all the weight vectors in which each individual weight takes a value from

$$\left\{ \frac{0}{H}, \frac{1}{H}, \ldots, \frac{H}{H} \right\}.$$

Therefore, the number of such vectors in W is given by $N = C_{H+k-1}^{k-1}$, where k is the number of objective functions.

For all the MOPs, MOEA/D was tested with $H = 99$, i.e. $N = 100$ weight vectors. For MOEA/D-RBF (and for MOEA/D-EGO) $H = 299$, i.e. 300 weight vectors. The set W_t was generated with $H = 10n - 1$, therefore $N_t = 10n$ weight vectors (which define the cardinality of the training set), where n is the number of decision variables of the MOP. The set W_s uses $H = 9$, i.e. $N_s = 10$ weight vectors. For adjusting the parameter σ in the model building, the DE/rand/1/bin strategy was adopted. The parameters for DE were set to: $CR = 0.5, F = 1$, a population size 20 and the number of generations was restricted to 50 generations. The execution of the algorithms was carried out on a computer with a 2.66GHz processor and 4GB in RAM.

As indicated before, the algorithms were evaluated using the I_H^- and the I_H metrics. The results obtained are summarized in Tables 3–5. These tables display both the *average* and the standard deviation (σ) of the I_H^- and I_H indicators for each MOP, respectively. The reference vector **r** used for computing the performance measures, for each MOP, is shown in each table of results. For an easier interpretation, the best results are presented in **boldface** for each test problem adopted.

Table 3: Results of the I_H^- performance measure for MOEA/D-RBF, MOEA/D-EGO and MOEA/D, using eight decision variables

MOP	MOEA/D-RBF *average* (σ)	MOEA/D-EGO *average* (σ)	MOEA/D *average* (σ)	reference vector (r)
ZDT1	**0.009170** (0.000890)	0.067200 (0.080100)	17.209529 (3.310987)	$(10, 10)^T$
ZDT2	**0.009703** (0.001520)	0.019800 (0.003500)	26.223664 (3.945007)	$(10, 10)^T$
ZDT3	**0.115358** (0.898476)	0.117800 (0.070700)	41.218250 (7.307372)	$(20, 20)^T$
ZDT4	**1681.548786** (469.374655)	1709.520000 (593.510000)	1749.365260 (436.261557)	$(50, 50)^T$
ZDT6	1.690381 (2.006687)	**0.100000** (0.100900)	68.134088 (2.672056)	$(10, 10)^T$

Table 4: Results of the I_H^- performance measure for MOEA/D-RBF and MOEA/D, using 30 and 10 decision variables, respectively

MOP	MOEA/D-RBF *average* (σ)	MOEA/D *average* (σ)	reference vector (r)
ZDT1	**0.004831** (0.000382)	9.758961 (1.235485)	$(5, 5)^T$
ZDT2	**0.006654** (0.000744)	14.040807 (1.806522)	$(5, 5)^T$
ZDT3	**2.298589** (0.952347)	11.029210 (1.526359)	$(5, 5)^T$
ZDT4	1828.493909 (382.604894)	**575.670683** (185.030230)	$(50, 50)^T$
ZDT6	**1.244183** (0.996797)	22.057469 (2.385873)	$(5, 5)^T$

5.3 Results and Discussion

5.3.1 ZDT Test Problems

Table 3 shows the results obtained for the I_H performance measure when the algorithms are tested on the ZDT test problems using eight decision variables. From this table, it can be clearly seen that the best results were obtained by MOEA/D-RBF and MOEA/D-EGO. With respect to MOEA/D-RBF and MOEA/D-EGO, it is possible to see that MOEA/D-RBF obtained better results than those obtained by MOEA/D-EGO in most of the adopted MOPs. The exception was ZDT6 where MOEA/D-EGO was significantly better than MOEA/D-RBF. However, this does not mean that the performance of MOEA/D-RBF is bad. The average CPU times of 30 independent runs performed by MOEA/D-RBF oscillate between 15 and 16 seconds for each ZDT test problem. According to studies by Zhang et al. [19] MOEA/D-EGO (using the Fuzzy C means method) employed between 936 and 1,260 seconds for solving ZDT1 and ZDT2, respectively. From such studies and the one reported here, we conclude that MOEA/D-RBF is much faster than MOEA/D-EGO, when solving the ZDT test problems using eight decision variables.

In Table 4, we show the results obtained by MOEA/D-RBF and the original MOEA/D in the ZDT test problems using 30 and 10 decision variables, respectively (for a detailed description see [20]). From this table it is possible to see that MOEA/D-RBF obtained a better approximation to PF than the one achieved by MOEA/D in most of the test problems adopted. This comparison was performed in order to show the effectiveness of our proposed MOEA/D-RBF in terms of the quality of the solutions that it reached with respect to the solutions obtained by MOEA/D. As we can see, MOEA/D-RBF significantly outperformed MOEA/D in most of the ZDT test problems. The exception was ZDT4 which is a multi-frontal MOP which evidently causes difficulties to the surrogate model proposed here.

5.3.2 Airfoil Design Problem

According to Table 5, we can see that MOEA/D-RBF obtained better hypervolume values than MOEA/D. Figure 4 shows the convergence graph for the I_H performance measure. From this graph, we can see that the results obtained by MOEA/D with 5,000 fitness function evaluations were achieved by our MOEA/D-RBF using a lower number of fitness function evaluations (only 1,250 evaluations, on average). MOEA/D employed, on average, 5,050 seconds to achieve the value reported in Table 5 in the I_H performance measure, while our MOEA/D-RBF required 2,000 seconds to achieve a similar value. Thus, we argue that our proposed MOEA/D-RBF is a good choice for dealing with computationally expensive MOPs. The approximations to the Pareto front for this problem is presented in Figure 5, which corresponds to the set of nondominated solutions found by each algorithm in the run with the value nearest to the mean value of the I_H performance measure.

Table 5: Results of the I_H performance measure for MOEA/D-RBF and MOEA/D for the airfoil design problem

MOP	MOEA/D-RBF *average* (σ)	MOEA/D *average* (σ)	reference vector (r)
MOPRW1	**2.493786e-07** (6.483342e-09)	2.149916e-07 (2.446593e-08)	$(0.007610, 0.005236)^T$

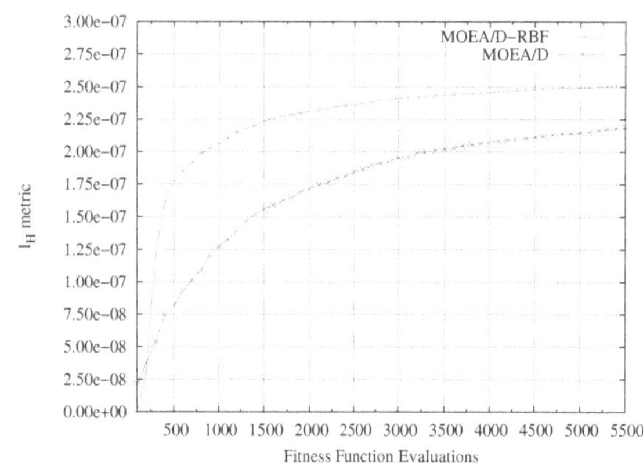

Figure 4: I_H convergence graph for the airfoil design problem

6. CONCLUSIONS AND FUTURE WORK

We have proposed here a version of MOEA/D which is assisted by cooperative RBF networks, with the aim of improving the prediction of the function value. The RBF networks employed here, use different kernels in order to have different shapes of the fitness landscape. With that, each RBF network provides information which is used to improve the value of the objective function. According to

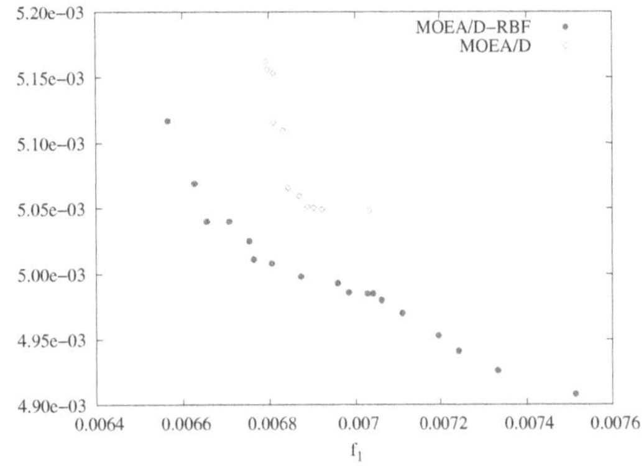

Figure 5: Approximation to PF given by MOEA/D-RBF and MOEA/D for the airfoil design problem

the results reported here, our proposed MOEA/D-RBF is able to outperform both to the original MOEA/D and to MOEA/D-EGO (which is a version of MOEA/D that also adopts surrogates) when performs only 200 and 1,000 fitness function evaluations. We also validated our proposed approach with a real-world computationally expensive multi-objective optimization problem: airfoil design. In this case, our proposed MOEA/D-RBF was able to reduce by more than half the CPU time required by MOEA/D to achieve a certain I_H value. This illustrates the potential of our proposed approach for solving computationally expensive multi-objective problems.

As part of our future work, we plan to use our approach in problems having three or more objectives. Also, we pretend to couple to our approach a local search mechanism, so that, while MOEA/D-RBF obtains candidate solutions to be evaluated with the real fitness function, the local search refines these solutions, thus accelerating the convergence towards the true Pareto front. Finally, we are also interested in testing our approach with more real-world problems having more decision variables, and that is indeed part of our ongoing research.

Acknowledgments

The first author acknowledges support from CONACyT to pursue graduate studies at the Computer Science Department of CINVESTAV-IPN. The second author acknowledges support from CONACyT project no. 103570.

7. REFERENCES

[1] C. A. Coello Coello, G. B. Lamont, and D. A. Van Veldhuizen. *Evolutionary Algorithms for Solving Multi-Objective Problems*. Springer, New York, second edition, September 2007. ISBN 978-0-387-33254-3.

[2] I. Das and J. E. Dennis. Normal-boundary intersection: a new method for generating Pareto optimal points in multicriteria optimization problems. *SIAM Journal on Optimization*, 8(3):631–657, 1998.

[3] M. Drela. XFOIL: An Analysis and Design System for Low Reynolds Number Aerodynamics. In *Conference on Low Reynolds Number Aerodynamics*, University Of Notre Dame, IN, June 1989.

[4] M. T. M. Emmerich, K. Giannakoglou, and B. Naujoks. Single- and multiobjective evolutionary optimization assisted by gaussian random field metamodels. *IEEE Transactions on Evolutionary Computation*, 10(4):421–439, 2006.

[5] R. Hecht-Nielsen. Kolmogorov's mapping neural network existence theorem. In *Proceedings of IEEE First Annual International Conference on Neural Networks*, volume 3, pages 11–14, 1987.

[6] J. Knowles. Parego: A hybrid algorithm with on-line landscape approximation for expensive multiobjective optimization problems. *IEEE Transactions on Evolutionary Computation*, 10(1):50–66, January 2006.

[7] A. K. Kolmogorov. On the representation of continuous functions of several variables by superposition of continuous functions of one variable and addition. *Doklady Akademii Nauk SSSR*, 114:369–373, 1957.

[8] J. B. MacQueen. Some Methods for Classification and Analysis of Multivariate Observations. In *Proceedings of the fifth Berkeley Symposium on Mathematical Statistics and Probability*, volume 1, pages 281–297. University of California Press, 1967.

[9] M. D. McKay, R. J. Beckman, and W. J. Conover. A comparison of three methods for selecting values of input variables in the analysis of output from a computer code. *Technometrics*, 21(2):239–245, 1979.

[10] K. Miettinen. *Nonlinear Multiobjective Optimization.* Kluwer Academic Publishers, Boston, Massachuisetts, 1999.

[11] Y. S. Ong, P. B. Nair, and A. J. Keane. Evolutionary optimization of computationally expensive problems via surrogate modeling. *AIAA Journal*, 41(4):687–696, 2003.

[12] H. Sobieczky. Parametric Airfoils and Wings. In K. Fuji and G. S. Dulikravich, editors, *Notes on Numerical Fluid Mechanics, Vol.. 68*, pages 71–88, Wiesbaden, 1998. Vieweg Verlag.

[13] D. A. Sprecher. A universal mapping for kolmogorov's superposition theorem. *Neural Netw.*, 6(8):1089–1094, January 1993.

[14] R. M. Storn and K. V. Price. Differential Evolution - a simple and efficient adaptive scheme for global optimization over continuous spaces. Technical Report TR-95-012, ICSI, Berkeley, CA, March 1995.

[15] A. Szöllös, M. Smíd, and J. Hájek. Aerodynamic optimization via multi-objective micro-genetic algorithm with range adaptation, knowledge-based reinitialization, crowding and epsilon-dominance. *Advances in Engineering Software*, 40(6):419–430, 2009.

[16] S. Zapotecas Martínez and C. A. Coello Coello. A Memetic Algorithm with Non Gradient-Based Local Search Assisted by a Meta-Model. In *PPSN XI*, volume 6238, pages 576–585. Springer. Lecture Notes in Computer Science, September 2010.

[17] S. Zapotecas Martínez and C. A. Coello Coello. A Multi-objective Particle Swarm Optimizer Based on Decomposition. In *GECCO'2011*, pages 69–76, Dublin, Ireland, July 2011. ACM Press.

[18] Q. Zhang and H. Li. MOEA/D: A Multiobjective Evolutionary Algorithm Based on Decomposition. *IEEE Transactions on Evolutionary Computation*, 11(6):712–731, December 2007.

[19] Q. Zhang, W. Liu, E. Tsang, and B. Virginas. Expensive Multiobjective Optimization by MOEA/D with Gaussian Process Model. *Evolutionary Computation, IEEE Transactions on*, 14(3):456 –474, june 2010.

[20] E. Zitzler, K. Deb, and L. Thiele. Comparison of Multiobjective Evolutionary Algorithms: Empirical Results. *Evolutionary Computation*, 8(2):173–195, Summer 2000.

[21] E. Zitzler and L. Thiele. Multiobjective Optimization Using Evolutionary Algorithms—A Comparative Study. In A. E. Eiben, editor, *PPSN V*, pages 292–301, Amsterdam, September 1998. Springer-Verlag.

[22] E. Zitzler, L. Thiele, M. Laumanns, C. M. Fonseca, and V. G. da Fonseca. Performance Assessment of Multiobjective Optimizers: An Analysis and Review. *IEEE Transactions on Evolutionary Computation*, 7(2):117–132, April 2003.

A Grammatical Evolution Approach for Software Effort Estimation

Rodrigo C. Barros
Institute of Mathematical Sciences and Computing
University of São Paulo
São Carlos, SP, Brazil
rcbarros@icmc.usp.br

Márcio P. Basgalupp
Institute of Science and Technology
Federal University of SP
S. J. dos Campos, SP, Brazil
basgalupp@unifesp.br

Ricardo Cerri
Institute of Mathematical Sciences and Computing
University of São Paulo
São Carlos, SP, Brazil
cerri@icmc.usp.br

Tiago S. da Silva
Institute of Mathematical Sciences and Computing
University of São Paulo
São Carlos, SP, Brazil
tiago.silva@icmc.usp.br

André C. P. L. F. de Carvalho
Institute of Mathematical Sciences and Computing
University of São Paulo
São Carlos, SP, Brazil
andre@icmc.usp.br

ABSTRACT

Software effort estimation is an important task within software engineering. It is widely used for planning and monitoring software project development as a means to deliver the product on time and within budget. Several approaches for generating predictive models from collected metrics have been proposed throughout the years. Machine learning algorithms, in particular, have been widely-employed to this task, bearing in mind their capability of providing accurate predictive models for the analysis of project stakeholders. In this paper, we propose a grammatical evolution approach for software metrics estimation. Our novel algorithm, namely SEEGE, is empirically evaluated on public project data sets, and we compare its performance with state-of-the-art machine learning algorithms such as support vector machines for regression and artificial neural networks, and also to popular linear regression. Results show that SEEGE outperforms the other algorithms considering three different evaluation measures, clearly indicating its effectiveness for the effort estimation task.

Categories and Subject Descriptors

I.2.m.c [**Artificial Intelligence**]: Miscellaneous—*Evolutionary computing and genetic algorithms*; D.2.8 [**Software Engineering**]: Metrics/Measurement

Keywords

Grammatical Evolution, Software Effort Estimation, Software Metrics, Genetic Programming, Evolutionary Algorithms

1. INTRODUCTION

Properly estimating the effort required to develop (or maintain) software is of great importance. Effort estimation supports project management in scheduling resources and evaluating risk factors. Either over or underestimation of software effort can result in troublesome scenarios. For instance, underestimation leads to schedule and budget overruns, which are recurrent causes of project cancellation. Overestimation, on the other hand, leads to loss of competitiveness and waste of resources, and it may ultimately prevent the company of securing a contract due to the excessive calculated costs.

The need for accurate effort estimates has motivated the investigation of many different strategies for generating predictive models in an efficient and effective fashion. An increasing number of *machine learning* approaches have been proposed and/or applied to predict software development (or maintenance) effort. Examples include case-based reasoning [10,17,20], artificial neural networks [5,6,19], decision trees [2, 12, 15], Bayesian networks [26, 29], support vector machines for regression [11, 27], genetic programming [23, 31], and evolutionary algorithms in general [3, 4].

The idea of exploiting evolutionary algorithms (EAs) for software effort estimation is based on the assumption that effort estimation can be formulated as an optimization problem [31], in which the EA strives for the predictive model that globally optimizes a given evaluation criterion — usually a measure of predictive performance. Given that the most popular technique for estimating software effort[1] is linear regression [22], it is fair to say that genetic programming (GP) is an obvious choice of EA for estimating effort, bear-

[1]The work of Jorgensen and Shepperd [22] actually refers to software cost estimation, though it is well-known that cost and effort are directly related, and that effort is usually preferred in academic studies due to confidentiality reasons.

ing in mind its straightforward application to evolve mathematical functions. Both traditional GP [8,14] and grammar-based (or grammar-guided) GP [33] have been successfully applied to software effort estimation, with promising results being reported.

In this work, we further exploit the use of EAs for software effort estimation. We propose a new *grammatical evolution* approach for software effort estimation called SEEGE (Software Effort Estimation with Grammatical Evolution). To the best of our knowledge, this is the first work to propose a grammatical evolution algorithm for software effort estimation. We believe grammatical evolution combines the advantages of grammar-based GP — flexibility and ability of incorporating prior knowledge — with the advantages of genetic algorithms — simplicity of breeding operations over vectors. In addition, grammatical evolution allows for neutral mutations, the so-called degenerative genetic code [28].

This paper is organized as follows. Section 2 presents work related to our approach. Section 3 details SEEGE, our novel grammatical evolution algorithm for software effort estimation. Section 4 describes the methodology we followed to set up the experiments, whereas Section 5 depicts the performance analysis of SEEGE in public effort data sets. Finally, we end this paper with our conclusions and future work directions in Section 6.

2. RELATED WORK

Several studies in the literature have exploited traditional GP for software effort estimation [1,8,9,16,23,31]. Burgess and Lefley [8] critically evaluate the potential of GP for effort estimation. They compare GP with previously published approaches, in terms of accuracy and ease of use. They show evidence that GP can offer significant improvements in accuracy, though they comment on the numerous parameters that need to be set.

Lefley and Shepperd [23] evaluate various statistical and machine learning techniques, including a GP tool, in the context of effort estimation. The main hypothesis tested was whether GP could significantly produce a better estimate of effort taking into account a public data set. They conclude that sophisticated estimation techniques such as artificial neural networks and GP provide better fitting models, though they require extra effort in design, whereas a simple linear regression approach can still provide useful estimates.

Tsakonas and Dounias [1] also employ GP in order to produce mathematical expressions that are highly accurate and can be used for estimating the development effort by revealing relationships between the project's features and the required work. According to the authors, their system was proved capable to produce results that not only carry higher regression accuracy as compared to those found in literature, but also are interpretable mathematical formulas, easy to be used by project managers.

Ferrucci et al. [16] carry out an empirical analysis to provide an insight on the use of GP for effort estimation, and in particular to analyze how the estimation accuracy of GP is affected by the use of different fitness functions. They experiment with different fitness functions based on widely recognized indicators used to evaluate the accuracy of the estimates and combinations of them.

Chavoya et al. [9] make use of GP with the goal of estimating the effort required in the development of short-scale projects. They compare it with the results obtained from a neural network and linear regression. Accuracy results from the model obtained with GP suggest that it could be used to estimate software development effort of short-scale projects when these projects are developed in a disciplined manner within a development-controlled environment.

Sarro et al. [31] also aim at getting an insight on the effects of using different measures as fitness function in a GP for effort estimation. In their study, they analyzed the performance of five different evaluation criteria — MMRE, Pred(.25), MdMRE, MEMRE and MdEMRE.

Only the work of Shan et al. [33] attempts on employing a grammar-based genetic programming approach (GGGP) for effort estimation. They conclude that GGGP performs better than linear regression in all aspects.

To the best of our knowledge, this is the first work to propose a grammatical evolution (GE) approach for software effort estimation. GE is a reasonably recent evolutionary algorithm that presents some interesting advantages over GP and other EAs: it combines the flexibility of grammar-based approaches with the simplicity of evolving linear strings. Hence, it inherits the advantages of GGGP and genetic algorithms, while taking advantage of neutral mutations [28]. We present our approach in detail in the next section.

3. SOFTWARE EFFORT ESTIMATION WITH GRAMMATICAL EVOLUTION

Software Effort Estimation with Grammatical Evolution (SEEGE) is a grammar-based Evolutionary Algorithm (EA) aimed at estimating software effort. As it is grammar-based, it differs from traditional EAs in the use of a grammar G in the evolutionary process. The grammar G defines a language L whose terms are the functions and terminals. A grammar can be represented by a four-tuple $G = \{N, T, P, S\}$, where N is the set of non-terminals, T is the terminal set, P is the set of production rules and S is the start symbol. The elements in P are responsible for deriving the language L by combining elements from sets N and T. The well-known Chomsky hierarchy classifies the types of grammars in four levels, from 0 to 3. Level 2, context-free grammars (CFG), are the most commonly used in grammar-based EAs [7,25,34].

Figure 1 presents a CFG grammar, written in the well-known Backus-Naur form (BNF), and an example of a derivation tree. For deriving the tree in 1(b), the following production rules were executed: <start> $\Rightarrow^{1}$ <exp> $\Rightarrow^{2}$ <exp><op><exp> $\Rightarrow^{5}$ <var><op><exp> $\Rightarrow^{12}$ x<op><exp> $\Rightarrow^{6}$ x+<exp> $\Rightarrow^{3}$ x+(<expr>) $\Rightarrow^{4}$ x+(<coef>*<var>) $\Rightarrow^{10}$ x+(a*<var>) $\Rightarrow^{13}$ x+(a*y).

In grammar-based GP, the individual that undergoes evolution is the derivation tree presented in Figure 1(b). Therefore, genotype and phenotype are both represented by the derivation tree. Grammatical Evolution (GE) differs from grammar-based GP in the sense that genotype and phenotype have different encoding structures. The genotype is represented as a linear string of bits and/or integers of variable size. The phenotype, which is the structure that defines fitness, is represented by the derivation tree. Hence, a mapping from genotype to phenotype is required in a GE algorithm. The mapping process to decode the string chromosomes into derivation trees is called *genotype-phenotype mapping* (GPM). Some allegedly benefits of this approach are the unconstrained search of the genotype while ensur-

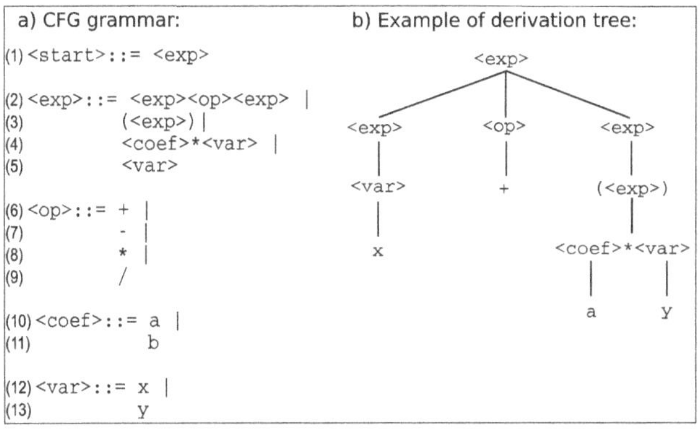

Figure 1: (a) CFG grammar for deriving expressions. (b) An example of tree derived from the grammar in (a). The derived expression was $x + (a \times y)$.

ing phenotype validity, and enhancing genetic diversity by allowing mutations which are neutral with respect to the phenotype (various genotypes can represent the same phenotype). Figure 2 depicts the *grammatical evolution* scheme.

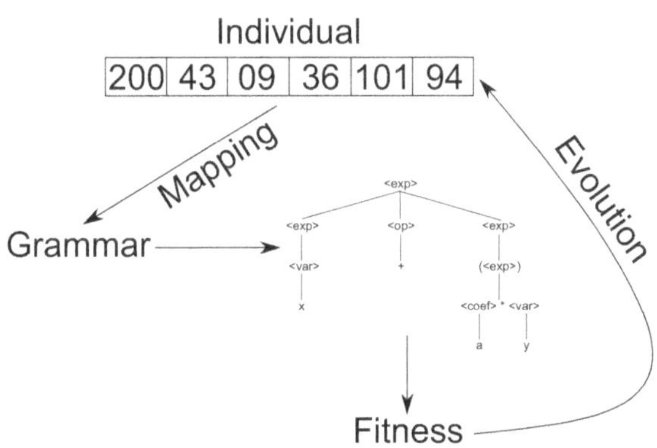

Figure 2: Grammatical evolution scheme.

3.1 Grammar and Genotype-Phenotype Mapping

SEEGE employs the GPM process proposed by Ryan et al. [30], in which codons are used to decide which choice to take when a non-terminal has more than one outcome. In molecular biology, a codon is a triplet of nucleic acids which encodes one amino acid. Its analogue in our case is a bit sequence of b bits, each encoding a symbol of the program. The genotype, thus, is a binary string consisting of n codons. Just like in a nucleotide sequence, where different codons can encode one amino acid, it is desirable that several codons get mapped into the same symbol (many-to-one mapping) in order to allow different genotypes to represent the same phenotype. Each codon is coded as a 8-bit sequence, and a chromosome consists of a variable number of codons. A 8-bit codon represents an integer value, which is used in a GPM function to choose the appropriate production rule from the grammar.

The GPM function is given by: (codon integer value) `MOD` (number of rules for the current non-terminal), where `MOD` is the modulus operation (it returns the remainder of the division of one number by another).

As an example of the GE approach, suppose we want to map the individual depicted in Figure 2 [200, 43, 09, 36, 101, 94] (already decoded from binary to integer) into a derivation tree, and consider that we are using the grammar shown in Figure 1. The GPM function in GE starts reading the string from left to right. The first integer is 200, and the grammar starts with the non-terminal `<exp>`. This non-terminal has 4 production rules associated to it (each element separate by "|"). The computation of the `MOD` operation — `MOD`(200, 4) — results in index 0. Considering that each non-terminal has n production rules associated to it, and that they are indexed from 0 to $n-1$, the selected production rule derives the non-terminal `<exp><op><exp>`. Next, we derive the leftmost non-terminal <exp> by mapping the next integer from the sequence (43) through the `MOD` function, resulting in index 3. The selected production rule derives the non-terminal `<var>`. Following this procedure, integer 9 results in index 1, which points to terminal x. Integer 36 is used to select the production rule in the `<op>` non-terminal. It results in index 0, selecting terminal $+$. Next, integer 101 applied to the non-terminal `<exp>` results in index 1, selecting non-terminal (`<exp>`). Then, integer 94 results in index 2, selecting non-terminal `<coef>`$*$`<var>`. At this moment, an important function from GE called wrapping is invoked, because the string has run out of codons before the derivation tree is complete. Wrapping works by returning the pointer to the beginning of the codons string, so codons can be re-utilized. In this example, 200 is once again evaluated, this time regarding non-terminal `<coef>`. It results in index 0, which means that terminal a is selected. The final non-terminal to be derived is `<var>`. The next integer to be read is 43, which results in index 1 and the posterior selection of terminal y. The derivation tree is completed, even though the second "scanning" over the codons has ended in the middle of the string.

To estimate software effort, we implemented two different grammars in SEEGE (see Figure 3). Grammar (a) is a simplified version of grammar (b). In both grammars, `<coef>` is a number (ephemeral random constant) that has its value randomly drawn from a uniform distribution — $U(0,1)$ generates real numbers between 0 and 1, whereas $U(0,100)$ generates integer numbers between 0 and 100 — and `<var>` is a predictive attribute of the training data set (chosen randomly from the set of predictive attributes). Note that grammar (b) allows if-then-else rules to be derived, enhancing the search-space of the resulting mathematical function.

3.2 Evolution

In the beginning of the evolutionary process, the individuals of the population are randomly initialized. They have variable length, with a minimum of five codons each, and a chance of 85% that new codons will be added to the individual. Hence, the process of adding codons finishes when the 85% probability is not fulfilled. Recall that each codon is comprised of 1 byte (8 bits), which is randomly generated.

To evolve the current generation of individuals, the following mutually-exclusive genetic operations can be performed: crossover, mutation, and duplication. Crossover has a chance of 90% of being performed, and both duplication and mutation have a chance of 5% of being applied.

```
<start>::= <exp>

<exp>::= <exp><op><exp> | <coef><op><var> |
         <op2><exp> | <coef> | <var>

<op>::=  + | - | * | /

<op2>::= sin | cos | log

<coef>::= U(0,1)

<var>::=  Predictive Attribute
```

(a) A simplified context-free grammar for effort estimation.

```
<start>::= <exp>

<exp>::= <exp><op><exp> | <coef><op><var> |
         <op2><exp> | <coef> | <var> |
         if<bool>then<exp>else<exp>

<op>::=  + | - | * | /

<op2>::= sin | cos | log

<bool>::= <exp><op3><exp>

<op3>::= > | < | >= | <= | = | !=

<coef>::= U(0,1) | U(0,100)

<var>::=  Predictive Attribute
```

(b) A more detailed context-free grammar for effort estimation.

Figure 3: Grammars used in SEEGE.

These operations are executed until all individuals of the new population are generated.

For crossover to be performed, two individuals are chosen via tournament selection (default tournament size of 7). After the individuals are selected, they are truncated, which means that the codons that are not used to generate the derivation tree are removed. The truncated individuals then take part in a standard one-point crossover operation, generating two children. In the duplication process, one individual is also selected using tournament selection, and it is also truncated to eliminate codons that are not used to generate a derivation tree. Then, two codons of the individual are randomly selected, and all codons located between these two selected codons are copied to the end of the individual. Regarding mutation, it requires one individual to be selected via tournament selection. This individual is then traversed codon by codon, where each codon has a 10% probability of having its value replaced by a randomly-generated 8-bit value. The three operators are illustrated in Figure 4.

Most papers that propose EAs for software effort estimation employ either the mean square error (MSE) or the mean magnitude of the relative error (MMRE) as fitness functions [31]. In the current version of SEEGE, we follow the literature and also employ the MSE error measure:

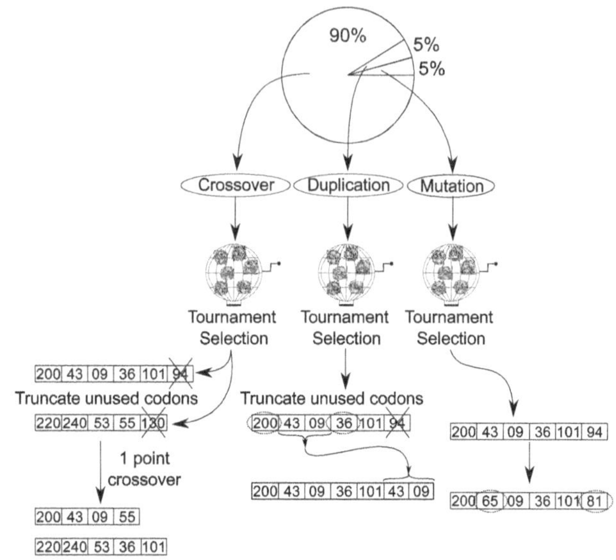

Figure 4: SEEGE evolutionary operators.

$$MSE = \frac{1}{N}\sum_{i=1}^{N}(y_i - \hat{y}_i)^2 \tag{1}$$

where y_i is the actual effort, $\hat{y}_i$ is the predicted effort value, and N is the number of objects in the data set.

4. EXPERIMENTAL PLAN

In this section, we present the methodology we employ for evaluating the performance of SEEGE in software effort data sets. In Section 4.1, we describe the data sets that we employ during the experiments, whereas in Section 4.2 we detail the algorithms that are used as baselines for SEEGE. Finally, Section 4.3 depicts the statistical tests we make use for providing some reassurance about the validity of the comparison results.

4.1 Data Sets

The empirical analysis presented in this paper is based on 10 different data sets from the PRedictOr Models In Software Engineering (PROMISE) Repository [32]. They are: albrecht, china, coc81, coc81lnh, cocomo-sdr, cocomo-nasa, desharnais, kemerer, maxwell, and nasa93. Table 1 provides some details about these data sets.

4.2 Algorithms, Parameters, and Evaluation

In order to assess the relative performance of SEEGE, we compare it to state-of-the-art machine learning algorithms, namely support vector machines for regression (SVM-Regression) and artificial neural networks (ANN). In addition, we compare it to traditional least-square linear regression, which is frequently employed for software effort estimation [22].

The implementations of the baseline methods are those found within the Weka Machine Learning Toolkit [18], namely: SMOreg (SVM-Regression), MultilayerPerceptron (ANN), and LinearRegression (Linear Regression).

SEEGE was implemented within the ECJ framework of evolutionary computation [24]. Bearing in mind that we

Table 1: Summary of the 10 effort data sets.

Data Set	#projects	#features	min Effort	max Effort	μ Effort	σ Effort	Description
albrecht	24	7	0.5	105.2	21.88	28.42	Data from 24 applications developed by IBM.
china	499	17	26	54620	3921.05	6480.86	No description available.
coc81	63	20	5.9	11400	683.53	1821.51	Data from COCOMO data analysis of 63 projects.
coc81lnh	63	71	5.9	11400	683.32	1821.58	Data from COCOMO data analysis of 63 projects with effort multipliers expressed as "low,medium,hight".
cocomo-sdr	12	134	1	22	5.73	6.84	Data from a Turkish Software Industry.
cocomonasa-v1	60	56	8.4	3240	406.41	656.97	Data from 60 NASA projects from 1980s and 1990s.
desharnais	81	11	546	23940	5046.31	4418.77	Data from a Canadian software house in the late 1980s.
kemerer	15	6	23.2	1107.31	219.247	263.06	Data from large business applications.
maxwell	62	27	583	63694	8223.21	10499.90	Data from one of the biggest commercial banks in Finland.
nasa93	93	124	8.4	8211	1135.93	1135.93	Data from 93 NASA projects from 1971 to 1987.

have proposed two grammars for SEEGE, we name its two versions as *SEEGE-a* and *SEEGE-b*, where SEEGE-a is the implementation of SEEGE with the grammar presented in Figure 3(a), and SEEGE-b is the implementation of SEEGE with the grammar presented in Figure 3(b).

The baseline methods were executed with their default parameter values, which are usually a combination of values that work well across a wide variety of data sets. In order to keep the comparison as fair as possible, we did not attempt to optimize the parameters of SEEGE. The list of configurable parameters of SEEGE is presented in Table 2.

Since SEEGE is a non-deterministic method, we execute it 10 different times varying the random seed of the stochastic operations. For evaluating the performance of both SEEGE and baseline methods, we employ a 10-fold cross-validation procedure, in which we collect the following evaluation measures: root mean square error (RMSE), which is simply the root of MSE; mean absolute error (MAE), and mean magnitude of the relative error (MMRE):

$$MAE = \frac{1}{N}\sum_{i=1}^{N} |\hat{y}_i - y_i| \quad (2)$$

$$MMRE = \frac{1}{N}\sum_{i=1}^{N} \frac{|\hat{y}_i - y_i|}{y_i} \quad (3)$$

Table 2: Configurable SEEGE parameters.

Parameter	Value
Initialization Probability	85%
Number of Individuals	1000
Minimum Individual Size	5
Number of Generations	100
Crossover Probability	90%
Duplication Probability	5%
Mutation Probability	5%
Mutation per Codon Probability	10%
Tournament Size	7
Elite	10

4.3 Statistical Analysis

To evaluate the statistical significance of the experimental results, we present the results of statistical tests by following the approach proposed by Demšar [13]. In brief, this approach seeks to compare multiple algorithms on multiple data sets, and it is based on the use of the Friedman test with a corresponding post-hoc test. The Friedman test is a non-parametric counterpart of ANOVA, as follows. Let R_i^j be the rank of the jth of k algorithms on the ith of N data sets. The Friedman test compares the average ranks of algorithms, $R_j = \frac{1}{N}\sum_i R_i^j$. The Friedman statistic, given by:

$$\chi_F^2 = \frac{12N}{k(k+1)}\left[\sum_j R_j^2 - \frac{k(k+1)^2}{4}\right] \quad (4)$$

is distributed according to χ_F^2 with $k-1$ degrees of freedom, when N and k are large enough.

Iman and Davenport [21] showed that Friedman's χ_F^2 is undesirably conservative and derived an adjusted statistic:

$$F_f = \frac{(N-1)\times\chi_F^2}{N\times(k-1)-\chi_F^2} \quad (5)$$

which is distributed according to the F-distribution with $k-1$ and $(k-1)(N-1)$ degrees of freedom.

If the null hypothesis of similar performances is rejected, we proceed with the Nemenyi post-hoc test for pairwise comparisons. The performance of two classifiers is significantly different if their corresponding average ranks differ by at least the critical difference

$$CD = q_\alpha\sqrt{\frac{k(k+1)}{6N}} \quad (6)$$

where critical values q_α are based on the Studentized range statistic divided by $\sqrt{2}$.

5. RESULTS AND DISCUSSION

Table 3 shows the RMSE values for Linear Regression, ANN, SVM-Regression, and both SEEGE versions (SEEGE-a and SEEGE-b). It illustrates the average RMSE over the 10-fold cross-validation runs and the standard deviation of the RMSE obtained in those runs (best absolute values in bold). It is possible to see that SEEGE generates the model with the lowest error values for all data sets. SEEGE-a provides the best model for seven data sets, whereas SEEGE-b achieves it in the remaining three.

To evaluate the statistical significance of the RMSE results, we calculated the average Friedman rank for Linear

Table 3: RMSE values of Linear Regression, ANN, SVM-Regression, and SEEGE.

Data Set	Linear Regression	ANN	SVM-Regression	SEEGE-a	SEEGE-b
albrecht	12.23 ± 11.20	11.50 ± 8.92	11.73 ± 10.11	**2.41 ± 4.81**	2.87 ± 4.92
china	775.06 ± 502.78	991.86 ± 599.01	720.92 ± 581.80	**544.34 ± 133.71**	597.55 ± 148.91
coc81	1359.14 ± 1184.96	815.88 ± 1143.77	758.13 ± 1325.62	**375.58 ± 173.83**	386.39 ± 227.29
coc81lnh	1081.15 ± 1530.09	1143.03 ± 1494.28	2422.65 ± 1169.92	453.40 ± 341.74	**428.35 ± 197.11**
cocomo-sdr	7.66 ± 6.05	9.93 ± 4.94	8.75 ± 6.97	0.66 ± 2.01	**0.57 ± 1.68**
cocomonasa-v1	545.96 ± 421.03	303.35 ± 334.83	481.73 ± 468.43	**81.45 ± 62.95**	112.90 ± 80.27
desharnais	2921.27 ± 1199.51	6045.28 ± 3728.47	2828.75 ± 1235.14	**1551.03 ± 412.06**	1755.36 ± 408.50
kemerer	183.05 ± 162.60	178.52 ± 203.75	91.65 ± 156.25	25.58 ± 55.70	**24.30 ± 48.96**
maxwell	6160.94 ± 3709.70	5952.22 ± 2604.27	5758.57 ± 3117.25	**2391.53 ± 1119.28**	2746.10 ± 1065.49
nasa93	819.01 ± 864.54	1336.17 ± 990.01	1384.26 ± 921.77	**347.55 ± 138.35**	444.10 ± 125.45
Average Rank	4.2	4.1	3.7	1.3	1.7

Table 4: MAE values of Linear Regression, ANN, SVM-Regression, and SEEGE.

Data Set	Linear Regression	ANN	SVM-Regression	SEEGE-a	SEEGE-b
albrecht	10.69 ± 9.20	10.30 ± 7.86	10.50 ± 8.26	**2.09 ± 4.15**	2.51 ± 4.42
china	351.31 ± 109.85	474.27 ± 166.24	270.54 ± 119.03	**293.31 ± 46.25**	307.68 ± 53.50
coc81	1078.00 ± 804.84	553.69 ± 753.86	523.14 ± 863.54	**243.87 ± 96.78**	270.83 ± 149.07
coc81lnh	892.00 ± 1025.29	832.00 ± 1019.81	1987.11 ± 770.11	**292.54 ± 195.10**	310.54 ± 143.92
cocomo-sdr	7.48 ± 6.11	9.74 ± 5.00	8.61 ± 6.96	0.66 ± 2.00	**0.57 ± 1.67**
cocomonasa-v1	437.08 ± 297.18	234.79 ± 259.85	385.62 ± 411.86	**61.26 ± 42.91**	85.98 ± 58.11
desharnais	2277.29 ± 908.01	4387.11 ± 2717.91	2235.54 ± 1035.25	**1209.47 ± 279.83**	1420.81 ± 329.92
kemerer	167.69 ± 133.60	168.36 ± 193.84	78.61 ± 128.21	23.16 ± 50.92	**21.29 ± 41.78**
maxwell	4642.71 ± 2545.82	4250.80 ± 1727.51	4190.51 ± 1875.96	**1858.02 ± 768.23**	2177.90 ± 805.25
nasa93	560.13 ± 511.89	1020.66 ± 694.63	1054.89 ± 722.09	**252.81 ± 90.40**	319.10 ± 91.19
Average Rank	4.2	4.1	3.5	1.3	1.9

Regression, ANN, SVM-Regression, SEEGE-a, and SEEGE-b: 4.2, 4.1, 3.7, 1.3 and 1.7, respectively. The average rank clearly suggests that both versions of SEEGE outperform the baseline methods regarding RMSE. The calculation of Iman's F statistic resulted in $F_f = 30.47$. Critical value of $F(k-1, (k-1)(n-1)) = F(4, 36)$ for $\alpha = 0.05$ is 2.63. Since $F_f > F_{0.05}(4, 36)$ $(30.47 > 2.63)$, the null-hypothesis is rejected. We proceed with a post-hoc Nemenyi test to find which method provides better results in a pairwise fashion. The critical difference $CD = 1.93$. The differences between the average rank of SEEGE-a and the rank of the baseline methods – Linear Regression, ANN, and SVM-Regression – are 2.90, 2.8, and 2.4, respectively. The difference between SEEGE-b and the baseline methods are: 2.5, 2.4, and 2.0, respectively. Given that every difference is greater than CD, we can argue that the performance of SEEGE is significantly better than Linear Regression, ANN, and SVM-Regression with statistical significance, regarding RMSE.

Table 4 shows the MAE values for Linear Regression, ANN, SVM-Regression, SEEGE-a, and SEEGE-b. Results show once again that SEEGE generates the best models for all data sets. In eight data sets SEEGE-a generated the best model, whereas SEEGE-b did the same for two data sets. Regarding the statistical analysis, the computed value of $F_f = 21$. Since $F_f > F_{0.05}(4, 36)$ $(21 > 2.63)$, the null-hypothesis is rejected. The differences between the average rank of SEEGE-a and the baseline methods – Linear Regression, ANN, and SVM-Regression – are 2.9, 2.8 and 2.2, respectively. The differences between the average rank of SEEGE-b and the baseline methods are 2.3, 2.2, and 1.6. Note that only the difference between SEEGE-b and SVM-Regression (1.6) is not greater than CD (1.93).

Finally, Table 5 shows the MMRE values for all methods. Results show that SEEGE generates the best model in nine out of ten data sets: SEEGE-a is the best method in seven data sets and SEEGE-b in two. SVM-Regression generates the best model for the china data set, whereas the remaining methods do not provide the best model for any data set.

The average rank for Linear Regression, ANN, SVM-Regression, SEEGE-a, and SEEGE-b are: 4.0, 4.2, 3.6, 1.4, and 1.8, respectively. It clearly suggests that SEEGE is the best performing method regarding MMRE. The calculation of Iman's F statistic results in $F_f = 19.13$. Since $F_f > F_{0.05}(4, 36)$ $(19.13 > 2.63)$, the null-hypothesis is rejected.

The differences between the average rank of SEEGE-a and the baseline methods (Linear Regression, ANN, and SVM-Regression) are 2.6, 2.8, and 2.2, respectively. Also, the differences between SEEGE-b and the baselines are 2.2, 2.4, and 1.8, respectively. Once again, with the exception of the difference between SEEGE-b and SVM-Regression, all the others are greater than CD, which indicates that the performance of SEEEGE is significantly better than Linear Regression, ANN, and SVM-Regression regarding MMRE with a significance level of $\alpha = 0.05$.

The statistical analysis previously presented clearly shows that the models generated by SEEGE outperform well-known methods such as Linear Regression, ANN, and SVM-Regression regarding their predictive performance in terms of three distinct evaluation measures, namely: RMSE, MAE, and MMRE.

It is interesting to notice that SEEGE-a often outperforms SEEGE-b, though the grammar employed in SEEGE-b offers many more choices for building mathematical models than SEEGE-a (*i.e.*, it allows `if-then-else` rules and integer constants). We believe SEEGE-b may have been slightly affected by *overfitting* — when the model over-learns the training data and fails to properly generalize to unseen data. Nevertheless, there were data sets in which SEEGE-b was indeed the best option, which means that some data sets require more complex functions than others. This was clearly the case of the cocomo-sdr and kemerer data sets, in which

Table 5: MMRE values of Linear Regression, ANN, SVM-Regression, and SEEGE.

Data Set	Linear Regression	ANN	SVM-Regression	SEEGE-a	SEEGE-b
albrecht	1.15 ± 1.73	1.69 ± 2.98	1.62 ± 2.48	$\mathbf{0.24 \pm 0.54}$	0.29 ± 0.49
china	0.24 ± 0.10	0.32 ± 0.08	$\mathbf{0.10 \pm 0.04}$	0.11 ± 0.02	0.11 ± 0.02
coc81	20.56 ± 18.47	4.51 ± 2.96	6.59 ± 6.22	$\mathbf{1.06 \pm 0.49}$	2.34 ± 1.45
coc81lnh	18.94 ± 14.67	9.08 ± 7.21	44.04 ± 34.46	$\mathbf{1.23 \pm 1.03}$	3.53 ± 3.69
cocomo-sdr	2.34 ± 2.39	3.03 ± 2.36	2.91 ± 3.12	0.19 ± 0.57	$\mathbf{0.15 \pm 0.45}$
cocomonasa-v1	5.34 ± 4.53	0.93 ± 0.69	1.74 ± 1.75	$\mathbf{0.25 \pm 0.10}$	0.54 ± 0.29
desharnais	0.66 ± 0.26	1.33 ± 0.87	0.58 ± 0.24	$\mathbf{0.37 \pm 0.09}$	0.47 ± 0.10
kemerer	1.16 ± 0.92	1.23 ± 1.38	0.36 ± 0.41	0.18 ± 0.36	$\mathbf{0.13 \pm 0.20}$
maxwell	1.46 ± 1.73	0.95 ± 0.63	1.07 ± 0.94	$\mathbf{0.35 \pm 0.10}$	0.44 ± 0.10
nasa93	4.19 ± 3.42	6.48 ± 5.76	5.83 ± 4.61	$\mathbf{1.03 \pm 0.52}$	1.64 ± 1.24
Average Rank	4.0	4.2	3.6	1.4	1.8

SEEGE-b consistently provided the best models regardless of the evaluation measure. For exemplifying this behavior, consider the following model generated by SEEGE-b for a particular training fold of the cocomo-sdr data:

IF $(0.63 + x_{132}) > (0.63/x_{17})$
THEN effort $= x_0$
ELSE effort $= cos(x_{121}/(sin(x_{13}) - (-5 - x_{13})))$

Albeit its high complexity, the above model was required so SEEGE-b could achieve its good results in cocomo-sdr. The thin line between accurate modeling and data overfitting has to be carefully explored. When in doubt, we recommend the user to choose the less-complex model, since the comprehensibility of simple models increases the confidence of the project manager in the prediction of effort for new projects to be developed.

We also highlight that SEEGE is capable of producing comprehensible models (much the same as linear regression), whereas ANN and SVM-Regression are "black box" approaches that do not offer any insight on the predictions that are provided. A comprehensible model allows the stakeholder to create new hypotheses regarding the available data, and also visually inspect whether the predictive model produces a logical output — *e.g.*, more requirement documents and adjusted function points necessarily mean more effort. By careful inspecting the generated model, the project manager can detect possible errors in the model that are a result of a poor data collection process, and then act towards improving the data collection and pre-processing.

6. CONCLUSIONS

In this paper, we proposed a new grammatical evolution (GE) algorithm called SEEGE (Software Effort Estimation with Grammatical Evolution). To the best of our knowledge, this was the first work to develop a GE approach for software effort estimation. GE is the state-of-the-art in grammar-based evolutionary computation, since it combines the flexibility of grammar-based approaches with the simplicity and efficiency of linear-string genetic operators.

We implemented two different grammars for SEEGE, and we evaluated its performance through three different evaluation measures, namely RMSE, MAE, and MMRE. The experiments were conducted taking into account 10 public software effort data sets from the PROMISE repository [32]. For comparison purposes, we analyzed the performance of SEEGE against state-of-the-art machine learning algorithms such as SVMs for regression and artificial neural networks. Also, we compared SEEGE with least-square linear regression, which is a widely-employed technique for software effort estimation [22].

Results indicated that SEEGE clearly outperforms the baseline methods with statistical significance, according to the protocol recommended by Demšar [13]. In addition, they indicated that in most cases, a simpler grammar is preferred over a more detailed one. Overly-complex models were shown to be useful only in two out of the ten data sets employed in this study.

As future work, we plan to perform a deeper analysis on the causes of overfitting in order to develop a strategy that can detect it during evolution, and act accordingly. A multi-objective fitness function that takes into account model complexity could be developed to mitigate this problem.

Acknowledgments

The authors would like to thank Fundação de Amparo à Pesquisa do Estado de São Paulo (FAPESP), Brazil, for funding this research.

7. REFERENCES

[1] T. A. and D. G. Deriving models for software project effort estimation by means of genetic programming. In *KDIR 2009 - 1st International Conference on Knowledge Discovery and Information Retrieval*, 2009.

[2] R. C. Barros, D. D. Ruiz, N. N. Tenorio Jr., M. P. Basgalupp, and K. Becker. Issues on estimating software metrics in a large software operation. In *Proceedings of the 32nd Annual IEEE Software Engineering Workshop*, SEW '08, pages 152–160, Washington, DC, USA, 2008. IEEE Computer Society.

[3] M. P. Basgalupp, R. C. Barros, T. S. da Silva, and A. C. P. L. F. de Carvalho. Software effort prediction: A hyper-heuristic decision-tree based approach. In *Proceedings of the 28th Annual ACM Symposium on Applied Computing (SAC 2013)*, 2013.

[4] M. P. Basgalupp, R. C. Barros, and D. D. Ruiz. Predicting software maintenance effort through evolutionary-based decision trees. In *Proceedings of the 27th Annual ACM Symposium on Applied Computing*, pages 1209–1214, New York, NY, USA, 2012. ACM.

[5] S. Berlin, T. Raz, C. Glezer, and M. Zviran. Comparison of estimation methods of cost and duration in it projects. *Inf. Softw. Technol.*, 51(4):738–748, Apr. 2009.

[6] P. L. Braga, A. L. I. Oliveira, and S. R. L. Meira. Software effort estimation using machine learning

techniques with robust confidence intervals. In *Proceedings of the 19th IEEE International Conference on Tools with Artificial Intelligence - Volume 01*, ICTAI '07, pages 181–185, Washington, DC, USA, 2007. IEEE Computer Society.

[7] P. Bruhn and A. Geyer-Schulz. Genetic programming over context-free languages with linear constraints for the knapsack problem: first results. *Evolutionary Computation*, 10(1):51–74, Mar. 2002.

[8] C. J. Burgess and M. Lefley. Can genetic programming improve software effort estimation? a comparative evaluation. *Information and Software Technology*, 43(14):863 – 873, 2001.

[9] A. Chavoya, C. Lopez-Martin, and M. E. M.-C. a. Applying genetic programming for estimating software development effort of short-scale projects. In *Eighth International Conference on Information Technology: New Generations*. IEEE Computer Society, 2011.

[10] N.-H. Chiu and S.-J. Huang. The adjusted analogy-based software effort estimation based on similarity distances. *J. Syst. Softw.*, 80(4):628–640, Apr. 2007.

[11] A. Corazza, S. Di Martino, F. Ferrucci, C. Gravino, F. Sarro, and E. Mendes. How effective is Tabu search to configure support vector regression for effort estimation? In *Proceedings of the 6th International Conference on Predictive Models in Software Engineering*, PROMISE '10, pages 4:1–4:10, New York, NY, USA, 2010. ACM.

[12] G. Costagliola, S. Di Martino, F. Ferrucci, C. Gravino, G. Tortora, and G. Vitiello. Effort estimation modeling techniques: a case study for web applications. In *Proceedings of the 6th International Conference on Web engineering*, ICWE '06, pages 9–16, New York, NY, USA, 2006. ACM.

[13] J. Demšar. Statistical Comparisons of Classifiers over Multiple Data Sets. *Journal of Machine Learning Research*, 7:1–30, 2006.

[14] J. J. Dolado. On the Problem of the Software Cost Function. *Information and Software Technology*, 43(1):61–72, 1 Jan. 2001.

[15] M. O. Elish. Improved estimation of software project effort using multiple additive regression trees. *Expert Syst. Appl.*, 36(7):10774–10778, Sept. 2009.

[16] F. Ferrucci, C. Gravino, R. Oliveto, and F. Sarro. Genetic programming for effort estimation: An analysis of the impact of different fitness functions. In *Search Based Software Engineering (SSBSE), 2010 Second International Symposium on*. IEEE Computer Society, 2010.

[17] G. R. Finnie, G. E. Wittig, and J.-M. Desharnais. A comparison of software effort estimation techniques: using function points with neural networks, case-based reasoning and regression models. *J. Syst. Softw.*, 39(3):281–289, Dec. 1997.

[18] M. Hall, E. Frank, G. Holmes, B. Pfahringer, P. Reutemann, and I. Witten. The WEKA Data Mining Software: An Update. *SIGKDD Explorations*, 11(1), 2009.

[19] A. Heiat. Comparison of artificial neural network and regression models for estimating software development effort. *Information and Software Technology*, 44(15):911 – 922, 2002.

[20] S.-J. Huang and N.-H. Chiu. Optimization of analogy weights by genetic algorithm for software effort estimation. *Information and Software Technology*, 48(11):1034 – 1045, 2006.

[21] R. Iman and J. Davenport. Approximations of the critical region of the friedman statistic. *Communications in Statistics*, pages 571–595, 1980.

[22] M. Jorgensen and M. Shepperd. A systematic review of software development cost estimation studies. *IEEE Trans. Softw. Eng.*, 33(1):33–53, Jan. 2007.

[23] M. Lefley and M. J. Shepperd. Using genetic programming to improve software effort estimation based on general data sets. *Genetic and Evolutionary Computation GECCO2003*, 2724(1):2477–2487, 2003.

[24] S. Luke. ECJ 20: A Java evolutionary computation library. http://cs.gmu.edu/~eclab/projects/ecj/, 2004.

[25] R. M. MacCallum. Introducing a perl genetic programming system - and can meta-evolution solve the bloat problem? In *Proceedings of the 6th European conference on Genetic programming*, EuroGP'03, pages 364–373, Berlin, Heidelberg, 2003. Springer-Verlag.

[26] E. Mendes and N. Mosley. Bayesian network models for web effort prediction: A comparative study. *IEEE Trans. Softw. Eng.*, 34(6):723–737, Nov. 2008.

[27] A. L. Oliveira. Estimation of software project effort with support vector regression. *Neurocomputing*, 69(13–15):1749 – 1753, 2006.

[28] M. O'Neill and C. Ryan. Grammatical evolution. *IEEE Transactions on Evolutionary Computation*, 5(4):349 –358, aug 2001.

[29] P. Pendharkar, G. Subramanian, and J. Rodger. A probabilistic model for predicting software development effort. *IEEE Trans. Softw. Eng.*, 31(7):615 – 624, july 2005.

[30] C. Ryan, J. Collins, J. Collins, and M. O'Neill. Grammatical evolution: Evolving programs for an arbitrary language. In *Proceedings of the First European Workshop on Genetic Programming*, pages 83–95. Springer-Verlag, 1998.

[31] F. Sarro, F. Ferrucci, and C. Gravino. Single and multi objective genetic programming for software development effort estimation. In *Proceedings of the 27th Annual ACM Symposium on Applied Computing*, SAC '12. ACM, 2012.

[32] J. Sayyad Shirabad and T. Menzies. The PROMISE Repository of Software Engineering Databases. School of Information Technology and Engineering, University of Ottawa, Canada, 2005.

[33] Y. Shan, R. I. Mckay, C. J. Lokan, and D. Essam. Software project effort estimation using genetic programming. In *Proceedings of International Conference on Communications Circuits and Systems*, pages 1108–1112. Press, 2002.

[34] I. Tanev and K. Shimohara. On role of implicit interaction and explicit communications in emergence of social behavior in continuous predators-prey pursuit problem. In *Proceedings of GECCO'03*, pages 74–85, 2003.

Testing of Precision Agricultural Networks for Adversary-Induced Problems

Karel P. Bergmann and Jörg Denzinger
University of Calgary
2500 University Dr. NW
Calgary, Canada
{bergmann,denzinge}@cpsc.ucalgary.ca

ABSTRACT

We present incremental adaptive corrective learning as a method to test ad-hoc wireless network protocols and applications. This learning method allows for the evolution of complex, variable-length, cooperative behaviour patterns for adversarial agents acting in such networks. We used the method to test precision agriculture sensor networks for vulnerabilities which could be exploited by attackers to significantly increase power consumption within the network. Our technique was able to find behaviours which increased power consumption by at least a factor of 3.6 for a node in each of the tested scenarios.

Categories and Subject Descriptors

D.2.5 [**Testing Tools**]: Security; I.2.8 [**Heuristic Methods**]: Security; C.4 [**Performance attributes**]: Security

General Terms

Security

Keywords

Non-functional Testing, Security, Mobile Ad-hoc Networks

1. INTRODUCTION

The testing of complex adaptive systems for emergent misbehaviours is poorly supported by current software engineering techniques. Wireless ad-hoc networks are an example of such systems where the complex interplay of protocols causes a potential for such emergent misbehaviours and their open nature allows for adversaries to exploit these vulnerabilities in ways which may be detrimental to the functioning of the network. The importance of testing for emergent misbehaviours in wireless ad-hoc networks is underlined by the somewhat regular discovery of vulnerabilities in commonly used protocol stacks, such as those described in [5]. In wireless ad-hoc networks, many protocols are combined in order to support the communication activities required by the network users. Additionally, the unsecured nature of the transmission medium in a wireless network renders it particularly vulnerable to an adversary controlling their own wireless nodes, which through participation in the network can eavesdrop and inject traffic into the network.

In this paper we describe a method of testing wireless ad-hoc networks for emergent misbehaviours we call *incremental adaptive corrective learning*. Our approach models the tested network along with wireless *attack nodes* controlled by the adversary as a multi-agent system and uses learning of cooperative behaviour, similar to [4] and [2]. Incremental adaptive corrective learning is an evolutionary learning method which substantially extends the traditional genetic algorithm in order to generate suitable movement and communication patterns for the attack nodes. Generating suitable behaviours for attack agents requires a complex learning process, as movement behaviours facilitate reception of injected traffic by the tested network, and any communications which are injected or modified by attack nodes must still conform to all of the network protocols in use (as far as nodes within the tested network can independently verify) in order to bring about emergent misbehaviours which may be of interest to software testers.

The behaviours of the attack nodes induce behaviours within the entire wireless ad-hoc network, and some of these behaviours are detrimental to the effective and efficient function of the network. Incremental adaptive corrective learning coordinates learning between the attack nodes by alternating between learning phases which focus on a newly introduced attack node and all attack nodes together, thus allowing the newly introduced node to integrate into the pre-existing attack sequence, and then improving upon the attack sequence with all of the attack nodes. As attack node behaviour changes, overall network behaviour changes as well. Incremental adaptive corrective learning accounts for these behavioural changes and corrects the learning system's view of overall network behaviour. Together with an appropriate fitness function, these two properties of our approach allow the learner to optimize attack node behaviour in order to maximize certain emergent misbehaviours within the network.

Precision agriculture ([1]) is an emerging application of wireless ad-hoc networks, where a wireless network is used to monitor growing conditions within an area used for crop cultivation. This information can be used by actuator nodes within the agriculture network to correct growing conditions when necessary. Due to the emerging nature of this applica-

GECCO'13, July 6–10, 2013, Amsterdam, The Netherlands.

tion area, aspects of network deployment, such as security have yet to be properly considered, making agriculture networks possible targets for attack by adversaries. We instantiated our testing approach with the goal of testing agriculture network deployments for emergent misbehaviours inherent to their topologies and protocol choices. The goal of precision agriculture networks is to reduce the manpower required to maintain a cultivation area. We deployed our learning system with the goal of maximizing power consumption within the agricultural network, thus negating the benefit of using such a network by increasing the frequency with which batteries would need to be replaced, or risking unacceptable growing conditions. Attack node behaviours which maximize network power consumption could then be analyzed by protocol designers, or system deployment specialists in order to adjust protocol algorithms and parameters to mitigate the effectiveness of the attacks. If such techniques were deployed during system development, it could greatly reduce the probability of deploying networks with exploitable vulnerabilities.

In our experiments, we applied our testing system to five different precision agriculture network scenarios. Across all nodes in all networks we were able to raise power consumption by an average factor of 3.56. In each test network at least one node can be consistently induced to consume at least 3.6 times the amount of power it would normally consume. In one of the test networks one wireless node can be induced to consume 9.4 times the power it would regularly consume. During these experiments, our testing system learned behaviours for attack nodes which exploited a number of worst-case communication scenarios for the protocols in use in order to bring about the increases in energy consumption exhibited in the tested networks.

2. TESTING NETWORK PROTOCOLS

We will first provide some basics of ad-hoc networks and network protocols, and then introduce the components of our testing approach.

2.1 Ad-hoc Networks and Network Protocols

A wireless ad-hoc network is a collection of potentially mobile wireless nodes within a geographic area. These networks are called ad-hoc because they lack any pre-determined configuration of connections. When a node attempts to communicate with another, the broadcast will be received by all wireless nodes which are within range. In the simplest case, the target of the communication is within this range and the communication has been completed. In the other case the wireless nodes discover a route to the intended recipient in order to pass along the message.

The communication techniques used by the wireless nodes within an ad hoc network are dictated by the *network protocols* in use, which must be agreed upon in advance by the nodes participating in the network. Typically, a number of different network protocols are used in conjunction to create a functional network. Protocols are often *layered* and each protocol is responsible for providing a different network service.

A typical network protocol consists of a number of different *packet* types, each with a number of *fields*. The use of some protocols commits the network nodes to obligations central to the functioning of the protocol. Such obligations include the inclusion of network nodes within a routing table, or responding to the receipt of a packet with some other type of packet - these obligations can spread through a network, generating a lot of traffic from one initial transmission. Network packets often contain packets from higher-level protocols as their payloads. Our testing approach shows how a combination of network protocols, together with a network configuration can be tested for emergent misbehaviours by inserting *attack agents* and evolving behaviour patterns for them. The attack agents are allowed to violate some of the commitments imposed by the protocols.

2.2 Testing Networks using MAS

A general definition of an agent, that we will use is the following, is as a tuple $Ag = (Sit, Act, Dat, f_{Ag})$ where Sit is a set of situations in which Ag can find itself, Act is the set of actions which can be undertaken by Ag, and Dat is the set of possible value combinations for Ag's internal data fields. Then $f_{Ag} : Sit \times Dat \mapsto Act$ is the decision function of Ag which produces an action given an agent's current situation and the contents of its internal data fields. A multi-agent system $Mult$ is then $Mult = (A, Env)$ where A is a set of agents which interact within an environment, Env. For this work, agents can be customer agents or attack agents. Customer agents are agents which are part of the network being tested, while attack agents are those inserted into the network by the genetic learner in order to test the customer agent network.

We can further instantiate the elements of an Ag as follows: Sit consists of an agent's current position within Env, together with any network packets arriving at the given point in time and the local environmental conditions.

$Act = Mov \cup Comm$, where Mov is the set of possible movement-related actions for an agent. An element of Mov is either of the form $spos$ or $v = (t, head, vel)$ where $spos$ is a starting position for the agent. Within a *movement change action* (v), $t \in \mathbb{R}, 0 \leq t \leq t_{max}$ is a time index ranging from 0 to a maximum duration, $head \in \mathbb{N}, 0 \leq head \leq 359$ is a direction heading and $vel \in \mathbb{R}, 0 \leq vel \leq vel_{max}$ is a velocity between 0 m/s and a maximum allowable velocity.

$Comm$ is the set of possible communication actions agents may make and is dependent on the protocols being used in the network. Preliminarily we can define an element of $Comm$ to be of one of five different forms: $c \in Comm = s|in|p|d|m$, where $s = (t, dest, data)$ is a *data initiation* action, indicating that the agent should initiate the procedure necessary to send $data$ to $dest$ at time index t. $in = (t, target)$ represents an *insertion action* where the agent in question should insert the packet specified in $target$ into the network at time t. The use of a given protocol may entail the commitment of network nodes to send packets in order to forward data, or to aid in the discovery of routing information. A p (protocol) action represents an action resulting from one of these network-induced commitments. A protocol action appears as $p = (t, target)$ where $target$ is the network-induced message sent at t. *Drop actions*, $d = (t, template)$, indicate to an agent that it should ignore a protocol-induced commitment of the form $template$, which should be sent at t. Finally, *modification actions*, $m = (t, t_{actual}, template, target)$, indicate to an agent that a protocol-induced packet, $template$, normally sent at t should be modified by replacing it with $target$ and sending it at t_{actual}. The use of t_{actual} allows an agent to delay the sending of the packet.

Dat consists of all of the network packets which have been received by an agent so far, historic environmental conditions and the agent's *action sequence*. The action sequence of agent j appears as $AS^j = (spos^j, a_1^j, \ldots, a_{l_j}^j)$, where $spos^j$ is the agent's starting position within Env and each of the a_k^j are elements of Act.

Finally, f_{Ag} maps an element of Sit and an element of Dat to an element of Act. This mapping is complex in nature and relies on the agent's *actions sequence* in conjunction with the network protocols in use and the environmental conditions. This process is fully described in Section 2.4 for attack agents. The procedure required for a customer agent is the same, however, since the customer agents must behave according to protocols, the m, d and in actions are not allowed in their action sequences.

2.3 Individuals

In order to define an individual within our GA, we must first define a *scenario*. A scenario fully specifies the configuration of the wireless ad-hoc network that is to be tested. So, a scenario, S, is defined as $S = (geo, t_{max}, vel_{max}, M, C)$ where geo defines the geographical setting in which agents (nodes) may interact, send messages and move, i.e. Env. The time allotted for agent interactions is t_{max} and the maximum speed with which agents are allowed to move is vel_{max}. M is the set of protocols that are used in the network. C is a set of *customer agents*, each of which represents a wireless node within the network, $C = \{Ag_{cust}^1, Ag_{cust}^2, \ldots, Ag_{cust}^m\}$, where the behaviour of each Ag_{cust}^i is dictated by the protocols indicated in M and AS_{cust}^i, the agent's *action sequence*.

The GA introduces *attack agents* into the scenario using incremental adaptive corrective learning, which is described in Section 2.5. The goal of the attack agents is to disrupt the activities of customer agents through learned movements and communication activities which may, or may not conform to the protocols defined in M. This *attack scenario* now consists of a scenario, and a set of attack agents. The behaviours of the attack agents make up the mutable part of the attack scenario, and these behaviours are what is evolved by the genetic learner. In our approach, an individual Ind consists of a set of *action sequences*, $Ind = \{AS_{att}^1, AS_{att}^2, \ldots, AS_{att}^n\}$. Each action sequence, AS_{att}^i corresponds to an attack agent Ag_{att}^i whose behaviour can be derived from AS_{att}^i when combined with a scenario, as shown in Section 2.4.

2.4 Simulating an Individual

The process of simulating an individual is a complex procedure. Recall that an individual includes a set of action sequences, each belonging to an attack agent. A new individual that never was simulated before may contain actions that in S_{Ind} (the attack scenario corresponding to Ind) may not be valid, and other actions may be missing due to the manner in which Ind was created during the learning process. These inaccuracies need to be repaired (*corrected*) and we accomplish this repair during the simulation of S_{Ind}.

During the simulation process of S_{Ind}, each agent in S_{Ind} is positioned at its starting position. Each action in the action sequences of the agents in the attack scenario is already labeled with the time index at which it is to be performed. As the simulation progresses, each action in S_{Ind} is performed until the simulation terminates. Consider Ag_{att}^j and assume that $a_1^j, \ldots, a_{i-1}^j$ have already been performed and that the time index for performing a_i^j has arrived. Additionally, assume that no protocol-induced commitment needs to be fulfilled at that time. In the case $a_i^j \in Mov$, the agent simply performs a_i^j and AS_{att}^j remains unchanged. The simulator reverses an agent's direction of travel should it hit the interaction space's boundary. In the case $a_i^j \in Comm$ there are a number of sub-cases. If a_i^j is of the form s, then Ag_{att}^j starts the execution of the action according to the protocols in place and AS_{att}^j remains unchanged. If a_i^j is of the form in, then Ag_{att}^j transmits the packet indicated in in and AS_{att}^j remains unchanged. If a_i^j is of the form m or d then AS_{att}^j needs to be repaired. In these cases, where there is no protocol-induced commitment to fulfill, there is no packet to modify or drop, and a_i^j is removed from AS_{att}^j in order to reflect the reality of S_{Ind}. The final case is where a_i^j is a p action. In this case, a_i^j is an artifact from a parent individual which is no longer required. a_i^j is removed from AS_{att}^j, Ag_{att}^j moves ahead to a_{i+1}^j and the simulation continues.

The second major case exists when it comes time to perform a_i^j and there is a protocol-induced commitment to fulfill (in the form of sending a packet). If $a_i^j \in Mov$, then as before Ag_{att}^j performs a_i^j, but then also performs the protocol-induced commitment. The protocol-induced commitment is inserted into AS_{att}^j as a_{i+1}^j as a p action. Ag_{att}^j then moves ahead to a_{i+2}^j in AS_{att}^j and the simulation continues. The p actions are not really necessary in order to simulate an individual, however we use them for two reasons. Firstly, the addition of p actions in the situations described here results in a complete sequence of the actions taken by the agents in S_{Ind} so that aspects of the network's performance can be measured by the fitness functions. Secondly, the p actions provide targets for genetic operators which introduce d and m actions into AS_{att}^j. Many potential genetic operators introduce d actions, or m actions, and one way to accomplish this is to identify a p action and replace it with a corresponding d or m action.

Next we consider the cases where $a_i^j \in Comm$ and there is a protocol-induced commitment for Ag_{att}^j to fulfill. In the cases where a_i^j is of the form in or s, then Ag_{att}^j performs a_i^j and then the protocol-induced action is inserted into AS_{att}^j as a_{i+1}^j, Ag_{att}^j moves ahead to a_{i+2}^j (if it exists) and the simulation continues. In the case where a_i^j is a m or d action, our approach requires that Ag_{att}^j checks to see if the packet listed in the *template* area of a_i^j *matches* the protocol-induced action that Ag_{att}^j is required to take. This matching simply involves Ag_{att}^j checking to see if the packets in a_i^j's template area and the protocol-induced action are of the same type, and that their fields contain the same information. If the packets match, then the protocol-induced commitment is not fulfilled, and instead a_i^j is performed. In the case where a_i^j is of the form m or d and the current protocol-induced commitment does not match the template in a_i^j, then there has been a change in the network's behaviour that caused a_i^j to be invalid. a_i^j is replaced in AS_{att}^j with a p action corresponding to the actual protocol-induced commitment (which Ag_{att}^j fulfills) and the simulation continues. Finally, we have the case where a_i^j is a p action. If a_i^j is a p action and the network-induced commitment matches the template area of a_i^j, then Ag_{att}^j simply fulfills the commitment and the simulation continues. If the network-induced commitment doesn't match the template area of a_i^j, then a_i^j is replaced with a new p action reflecting the actual protocol-induced commitment required of Ag_{att}^{j}, which is fulfilled.

The final major case to consider is that the simulation of S_{Ind} reaches a point where Ag_{att}^{j} has a new network-induced commitment to fulfill but AS_{att}^{j} has no element a_i^j at the current time index. In this case Ag_{att}^{j} examines AS_{att}^{j} in order to find a_{ins}^{j} and a_{ins+1}^{j}, where the time index of a_{ins}^{j} is earlier than the current time index and a_{ins+1}^{j}'s time index is greater than the current time index. A new p action corresponding to the network-induced commitment is created and inserted into AS_{att}^{j} between a_{ins}^{j} and a_{ins+1}^{j}.

This simulation process highlights the key difference between customer and attack agents. Although this procedure is followed when simulating either type of agent, in, m and d actions are only present in attack agents. These actions can only be introduced by genetic operators, which operate solely on attack agents. The in, m and d actions represent *communication misbehaviours*, which cannot be present in customer agents because nodes in the customer network must follow the protocols being tested.

2.5 Incremental Adaptive Corrective Learning

Our learning approach uses a form of learning we call *incremental adaptive corrective learning.* The *corrective* part of this process concerns the realization of the actions that agents take during a scenario and was described in Section 2.4. The *incremental adaptive* part of this process concerns how attack agents are introduced into scenarios, and is described below.

Due to the very large search spaces, our genetic learner uses a technique which first introduces a small number of attack agents (2) to a scenario, with no communication misbehaviours to start with. An entire population of such individuals is generated, where the only differentiating characteristics between the individuals are the starting positions of the introduced attack agents. This population is then subjected to a first *general learning phase*, GL_1. During GL_1 the genetic learner moves through ng_{GL_1} generations of learning. ng_{GL_1} is a system parameter which indicates the maximum number of generations that GL_1 should continue for. GL_1 may terminate before ng_{GL_1} generations are completed if no learning progress is made for n_{Stall} generations.

During each generation of learning, the current pool of individuals is evaluated using a fitness function. The n_{surv} individuals with the best fitness are allowed to remain within the population, while the rest of the individuals are discarded. The population is then restored to its previous size (n_{pop}). For each individual required, some of the retained individuals are selected and a genetic operator is applied to them to create the new individual. Since our approach can utilize an unlimited number of genetic operators (hundreds in this application), we utilize a form of reinforcement learning based on [6] in order to choose operators which may produce high-fitness individuals with higher probability. When the population is restored to its previous size, the generation is complete. In the general learning phases, genetic operators may modify any of the attack agents which make up the individuals.

When this first general learning phase is complete, the number of attack agents present in the individuals is *incremented*, in that another attack agent is introduced into each of the individuals with a pseudo-randomly selected start position. The genetic learner now enters an *adaptive learning phase*, AL_1. In the adaptive learning phase an *explicit targeting parameter* is used to ensure that genetic operators only modify the newly introduced attack agent. Using this technique, the newly introduced attack agent is integrated into the activities of the original attack agents in such a way that it minimally disturbs the previously existing attack scenario. The new attack agent *adapts* to the attack technique of the original attack agents over the course of ng_{AL_1} generations. This adaptive learning phase may terminate before ng_{AL_1} generations if no progress (increase in maximal fitness) is made for n_{Stall} generations. In our approach, the learning process alternates between general and adaptive learning phases until n_{maxA} agents have been introduced.

As has been described, attack agents are introduced into individuals with empty action sequences (save for a start position). These action sequences grow in two ways: When the individuals are simulated for the first time, their action sequences will be augmented with p actions, which in turn provide targets for the application mutation operators which introduce m and d actions. The second way is through the application of genetic operators which introduce, in, s and m actions from $Comm$ as well as actions from Mov. As the learning process proceeds the action sequences of the attack agents become more complex.

2.6 Evaluation of Individuals

In order to facilitate the repeated evaluation of individuals, it was necessary to construct a simulator which could be used to simulate a given attack scenario (S_{Ind}) and produce log files ($log(S_{Ind})$) from which the efficiency of the customer agent network could be measured. Such a simulator was constructed using the OMNet++ framework [12] and is utilized in the evaluation phase of the genetic learner. Each individual is combined with the scenario being tested, simulated and a fitness function F is then applied to the log files produced. If using this testing approach during system development, it would be necessary to produce code which is compatible with both the target architecture and the simulator in use to ensure additional errors are not introduced while converting the test code from the target environment to the testing environment.

We need to measure different aspects of a simulation, represented as sub-functions $f_0, f_1, \ldots, f_n$ which can be aggregated into F. A continuous range must be defined for each f_i, $f_i(log(S_{Ind})) \in [low_i \ldots high_i]$, where Ind is an individual. Additionally, for each f_i a goal point $g_i \in [low_i \ldots high_i]$ is defined where g_i is the optimization goal the genetic learner is to strive towards for f_i. When considered together, the ranges of $f_0, f_1 \ldots f_n$ define an n-dimensional *fitness space* and $g_0, g_1 \ldots g_n$ define an n-tuple which represents a *goal point* within that space. When an individual Ind needs to be evaluated, F is defined as $F(Ind) = dist((f_0(log(S_{Ind})),$ $f_1(log(S_{Ind})), \ldots, f_n(log(S_{Ind}))), (g_0, g_1, \ldots, g_n))$, where $dist$ is the Euclidean distance formula. Thus, $F(Ind)$ is the Euclidean distance between the goal point and the point constructed by evaluating the individual in question with each of the f_i. Given a number of individuals, the individual with the smallest F value is the most fit as it is most proximal to the goal point.

2.7 Genetic Operators

Since $Act = Mov \cup Comm$, we need genetic operators which apply to movement actions, and some which apply to communication actions. Movement-related operators are generic to the testing of all mobile networks and can be described here. Communication-based genetic operators are however specific to the protocol suite in use and are further detailed in Section 3.4.

2.7.1 Movement Operators

An attack agent's movement pattern is modified by movement operators which can change an agent's start position, and introduce, remove and modify movement actions within the agent's action sequence. Initial position modification operators replace the initial position of an attack agent, $spos$, with a new initial position $spos'$, which is generated to fall randomly within geo. An element of Mov, v, takes the form $v = (t, head, vel)$. Movement modification operators have been created which modify each of the fields of v. Introduction operators pseudo randomly generate elements of Mov which fall within geo, t_{max} and vel_{max}. Elimination operators randomly select an element of Mov from an action sequence and remove it. Intra-individual operators exist which *transplant* movement actions from the action sequence of one attack agent within an attack scenario to that of another. Finally, inter-individual movement operators exist which transplant elements of Mov from an agent in one individual to the action sequence of an attack agent in a different individual.

2.7.2 Communication Operators

The communication operators are dependent on the protocols defined in the scenario. Each communication action made by an attack agent is a nested structure of packets, each with its own fields. Each of these fields represent targets for genetic operators and we supply the learner with operators which mutate each field in several ways. We introduce operators which remove and add communication actions in their entirety. Import operators are supplied, which move communication actions between agents within an individual, or from different individuals. These modifications to an attack agent's communication behaviour are reflected in an attack agent's action sequence and may cause changes in the overall behaviour of the network.

3. TESTING OF PRECISION AGRICULTURE NETWORKS

In this section we apply our approach from the last section to the area of precision agriculture [1]. After introducing this area, we provide instantiations of all of the concepts presented in the previous section.

3.1 Precision Agriculture

Precision agriculture networks use wireless sensor networks in order to monitor growing conditions during the cultivation of crops. Actuators can be introduced into such a network so that the network can take corrective action when the monitored growing conditions become unacceptable. The use of a precision agriculture network can greatly decrease the amount of manual labor required to tend a large growing area, thus greatly reducing the operating cost for the grower.

Precision agriculture networks are not without their drawbacks, however. As with most wireless nodes, the sensor nodes in a precision agriculture network must function with limited computing and memory resources in order to maintain the financial feasibility of the approach as well as to deal with very limited power availability. Power must be provided to these nodes through a replaceable battery as electrical hookups are not available at arbitrary locations in a growing field. It is possible that some solar power could be harvested by the nodes of the network, but the battery remains essential so that nodes can remain active during the night and over potentially extended overcast periods.

This sensitivity to power utilization is a key vulnerability of precision agriculture networks - nodes should be as power efficient as possible in order to increase their duty cycle. If power consumption is increased to the point that wireless nodes would have to be serviced often, then it reduces the benefit of implementing the network, as manual labor will once more be required to service the nodes. If one were to neglect to service the nodes in a precision agriculture network, then the network would be unable to reliably maintain the desired environmental conditions for the crops. An adversary being capable of disabling a precision agriculture network, for even a short period of time could have a disastrous effect on a grower engaged in the cultivation of highly sensitive crops.

3.2 Individuals

As described in Section 2.3, we define a scenario as $S = (geo, t_{max}, vel_{max}, M, C)$. In the case of our precision agriculture application, we define $geo = (x_{max}, y_{max})$, so the geography of the interaction space is defined as a rectangular area x_{max} X y_{max} meters in area. Any location within this area can be addressed as (x, y) where $x \in \mathbb{R}, 0 \leq x \leq x_{max}$ and $y \in \mathbb{R}, 0 \leq y \leq y_{max}$. t_{max} is set to 100 simulated time units, and vel_{max} is set to 10 m/sec. The wireless configuration used in the precision agriculture networks, M, consists of the Internet Protocol (IP) [10], the User Datagram Protocol (UDP) [9], Ad-hoc On-demand Distance Vector Algorithm (AODV) for message routing [8] and an improvised agriculture network application layer protocol (IAP) which we define below. Lower level protocols are not modeled in this application.

The genetic learner was applied to the identification of adversary-induced vulnerabilities in a precision agriculture network with actuators that is responsible for the irrigation of theoretical vineyards using IAP. IAP requires a number of immobile network nodes, where one node N_m, the master node, is positioned somewhere in the network. The vineyard is then divided into irrigation zones. Each irrigation zone consists of a number of sensor nodes, $\{N_s^1, N_s^2, \ldots, N_s^k\}$ and one N_a actuator node. It is assumed that the theoretical vineyards occur in arid regions where irrigation is required. The simulated moisture content of the soil decreases over time, until the irrigation system is activated, at which time it increases by a set level.

In IAP, at each time interval, the sensor nodes within an irrigation zone monitor the soil's simulated moisture content. When the moisture content falls below a threshold value, the sensor node relays the irrigation zone identification number to N_m. Upon receipt of this *watering request* N_m relays a message to the N_a responsible for irrigating the irrigation zone in question. When an N_a receives the *water-*

ing trigger from N_m, it triggers the actuator controlling the irrigation system and the simulated moisture content of the soil in the irrigation zone rises.

With M defined, we can further specify the form of the *dest*, *template* and *target* fields present in the communication actions. Since the protocols in use include IP, the *dest* present in actions takes the form of an IP address. *template* and *target* both represent a complete transmission which may appear in the network and both take the form $(IP, UDP, Payload)$ where IP is a complete listing of the fields present in the IP packet enclosing the rest of the transmission. UDP is a listing of the fields present in the UDP packet encapsulated within IP and $Payload$ is a listing of the fields present in the payload packet. $Payload$ can appear as any of the payload packet types which are allowed in the network, these include the *watering trigger* and *watering request* packets from IAP, as well as the packets defined in AODV: *route error*, *route request*, *route reply*, and *hello*.

We can define Sit as the current state of the IP, UDP, AODV and IAP protocols for that agent in conjunction with the agent's role in the IAP network (N_m, N_s, N_a, or none for attack agents), the simulated moisture content it is sensing and its current energy level.

As described in Section 2.5, we use a number of parameters to coordinate the learning process. The parameters ng_{GL} and ng_{AL} were set to 50 generations, and n_{Stall} is set to 10 generations. n_{pop} is set to 30 individuals and n_{surv} is set to 10 individuals.

3.3 Evaluation of Individuals

Through experimentation we arrived at 5 fitness sub-functions, each with range [0, 10000] which are combined into a single fitness measure using the method in Section 2.6. The genetic learner attempts to maximize all of these functions. The goal points are all set to 10000. f_{pc} measures the power consumption of the tested network by counting the number of transmissions made. f_{pd} measures how the power consumption is distributed over the course of the simulation. f_{no} counts the number of nodes in the tested network which have exhausted their power supplies before the end of the simulation. f_{lw} counts the number of sensor nodes which end the simulation with moisture levels below the acceptable threshold. f_{uw} measures how long each sensor node registers a moisture level below the lowest level measured in the network with no attack agents present. The last 4 fitness measures were found to help steer the learner towards the worst possible outcome in our experiments.

3.4 Genetic Operators

The genetic operators relating to Mov were discussed earlier and the genetic operators relating to $Comm$ are discussed below, as they are intimately dependent on M. Due to space constraints, it is impossible to discuss all of the genetic operators utilized in detail, however a summary will be provided.

A typical Internet protocol packet has 13 fields in addition to a payload. For most of these fields we provide a genetic operator which changes the value of that field to another value which is relevant in the network in question and another operator which inserts a completely random value. Two other families of IP operators are utilized: IP supports a process referred to as packet fragmentation, where an IP packet can be subdivided into an arbitrary number of smaller packets. Genetic operators were created to fragment IP packets, de-fragment IP packets, as well as manipulate the nature of the packet fragmentation. These manipulations include the insertion of extra fragments, the non-transmission of some of the fragments and manipulations of the fields which IP uses to identify the order of the fragments. Additionally, since all network traffic in this application is encapsulated in IP packets, genetic operators were introduced to arbitrarily alter the timing of the sending of an IP packet (and its payload).

UDP is a simple transport layer protocol whose packets encapsulate application layer information, and are encapsulated by IP packets. A UDP datagram consists of 4 fields in addition to the application-layer payload and we have introduced a pair of genetic operators to operate on each of these fields, one replacing a value with a likely network-relevant value, the other replacing a value with a random value.

Payload packets in our networks include the watering request and watering trigger messages described as part of the IAP protocol discussed earlier. Genetic operators were developed to alter each of the fields of these simple messages. The AODV routing protocol is used to determine how messages must travel through the network in order to reach their intended recipients. The AODV protocol consists of a large system of protocol commitments and a number of different packet types. As with the other protocols discussed above, genetic operators are introduced which operate on each of the fields of each of the different AODV packets. In addition to these simple field-manipulation operators, genetic operators exist which invent payload packets of all of these different types and send them into the network. Since each protocol-induced transmission produced by an agent results in a p action which contains a complete listing of the above-mentioned fields, that p action is a potential target for the application of any genetic operator which manipulates one or more of those fields, in addition to genetic operators which drop, fragment or manipulate the timing of that p action.

4. EXPERIMENTS

We applied our learning system to five different test networks. The network scenarios were allowed to run for 100 simulated time units, and the learning process would continue until 7 attack agents were introduced into the scenario. Each customer agent was allotted double the power required to run the most power consumptive node in that customer network (with no attackers present). When this power supply was exhausted, the node would cease to function, requiring the network to adjust in order to continue functioning. For each test network, due to the existence of many random factors, the genetic learner was allowed 10 runs. If during those runs a node in the tested network ran completely out of power before the 100 simulated time units, the power consumption for that node was prorated linearly by the proportion of time remaining in the simulation after all of the node's power had been exhausted. That is, it was assumed that if attack agents could exhaust the power of the network node, then that average power consumption rate could continue to the end of the 100 simulated time units if the network node was provided more power to utilize. The baseline power consumption is expressed as the average number of transmissions per node in the customer agent network with no attack agents present. The power consumption factor of a node is the ratio of power consumed by the node

Table 1: Genetic Learning Results

Network	Baseline	Av. Fac	Min. Fac	Max. Fac
1	64.9	3.9	2.0	4.5
2	67.6	2.6	1.2	3.7
3	86.1	3.4	1.2	4.7
4	67.7	3.6	1.7	4.6
5	159.2	3.8	1.4	9.4

Figure 1: Test Network 5

with evolved attackers present to power consumed by the node with no attackers present, averaged over the 10 runs. The average power consumption factor is then the average of the power consumption factors. The maximum power consumption factor is the highest power consumption factor of the nodes within a given network, averaged over the 10 runs. The minimum power consumption factor is the lowest power consumption factor of the nodes within the network, averaged over the 10 runs. The results of our experiments are shown in Table 1.

The first test network consists of nine wireless nodes, including the single master node and two irrigation zones, each consisting of one irrigation node and three sensor nodes. The two irrigation zones are positioned sufficiently close together that multiple routes are possible between the irrigation nodes and the master node. In all of the test networks the transmission range of the wireless nodes is only sufficient to reach immediately adjacent nodes. As can be seen in Table 1, the average node power consumption can be increased by application of our learning system by a factor of 3.9. An outlying sensor node is the most easily exploited, showing average power consumption increased by a factor of 4.5. The master node seems to be the most difficult to exploit as attack agents are only able to increase average power consumption by a factor of 2.0. The second, third and forth test networks were other small networks with varying topologies. The final network is large and shown in Figure 1. It consists of eight different irrigation zones with many different topologies. Each irrigation zone contains between 1 and 5 sensor nodes (shown as circles), with a total of 21 sensor nodes (shown as stars) present in the customer network. The master node is shown as a square.

In all cases the master node was the most difficult to exploit by the attack agents. We hypothesize that this may be due to the fact that using the AODV routing protocol and IAP, the master node is never responsible for passing messages on behalf of other nodes. The master node simply receives watering requests and dispenses watering triggers, other nodes act as intermediaries for the master node, but not vise-versa. The most easily exploited nodes appear to be those which lie on a large number of routes between sensor and actuator nodes and the master nodes. Traffic injected by attack agents at many points in the networks must pass through these nodes, resulting in higher power consumption at those points.

Perhaps more interesting than the degree of increased power consumption induced by the attack agents within the tested networks are the behaviours learned by the test system in order to bring about the increases. Our approach allows attack agents to utilize communication misbehaviours in order to induce sub-optimal network performance. In many cases, the increased power drain was caused without the attack agents utilizing excess amounts of energy themselves, but rather through the application of targeted manipulations within a small group of packets. The corruption of routing information was a common target for the learner: the manipulation of AODV routing packets was used in order to cause problems for IAP. In some instances an attack agent would transmit AODV route error messages while masquerading as the IAP master node, this would result in all of the nodes in the tested network being required by AODV to rebroadcast the error so that all routing tables could be adjusted. Since many of the sensor nodes would subsequently need to send watering requests to the master node in order to have their irrigation zones watered, they would have to repeat the energy consumptive route discovery process in order to get a valid route to the master node. In other instances the attack nodes would cause underwatering in irrigation zones by broadcasting AODV Hello messages while masquerading as the master node, causing watering requests to be mis-forwarded and thus go unanswered. In some cases the learner would identify cooperative behaviours for attack agents to confuse the tested network. One example of such behaviour is a stationary attack agent periodically initiating route discovery for a highly mobile attack agent. The mobility of the intended destination node would cause route error messages to be propagated through the network as stale routes were identified, and then the expensive route discovery process would be repeated when a route to that node was rerequested, although no data was ever sent across the identified routes. In another case, a number of attack agents would transmit route error messages for random nodes into the network, requiring the route errors to be propagated through the entire network.

Attack agents made use of communication misbehaviours at different protocol levels. IP protocol numbers and UDP port numbers were manipulated to cause packets to be dropped by the destination node, or the next hop on an active route. These techniques cause data (IAP packets) to go undelivered and can be difficult to diagnose as the attack agent induces a legitimate node within the tested network to drop the packet. A similar example is an attack agent on an active route decrementing the IP ttl field of a packet before forwarding it, causing a subsequent node to discard the packet.

Finally, some learned behaviours didn't involve any communication misbehaviours at all, but rather involve unexpected uses of the tested network. An example is the cooperative behaviour between two attack agents which position themselves across the widest part of the tested network and start communicating, utilizing the tested network to forward their packets. The positioning of the attack agents required many of the legitimate nodes to forward the data packets and additional power was consumed by AODV discovering routes across the tested network in order to establish the communication session.

5. RELATED WORK

Search-based software engineering [15] is an active research area, and evolutionary learning has been applied to the testing of software systems. As detailed in [7], evolutionary algorithms have been applied to many areas of testing as far as they concern development of software. The non-functional testing of software systems has been addressed using evolutionary methods, but has been limited to execution time testing [13] of software. Until lately little has been published on the testing of complex systems using evolutionary learning. Our approach demonstrates a black-box approach to the non-functional testing of complex adaptive computer systems, more specifically wireless ad-hoc networks using an automated, evolutionary method.

Of the work published recently, a few pieces of work focus on security-related testing. KleeNet, [11] attempts to discover bugs in wireless sensor network protocol stacks and network configurations in an automated manner, however the network misbehaviours are not adversary generated, and are limited to packet loss, duplication and corruption - a subset of the types of network misbehaviours which can be applied in our test system. These anomalies were generated randomly and are not learned behaviours, precluding the possibility of the system finding additional, more effective misbehaviours to test the network with.

In [3] a different approach is taken in the application of evolutionary learning to protocol verification. Here BAN security protocols are constructed using genetic algorithms with constraints that ensure their correctness and security.

In [14] evolutionary algorithms are used to search for network topologies which result in poor network performance when the network is subjected to automatically generated traffic. Although this work identifies topologies which cause poor network performance, the protocols used by the network are not tested, in that no communication misbehaviours are allowed. Network nodes are static where network nodes in our test system can be mobile.

In [4] a learner was used to find vulnerabilities in harbour patrol policies and in [2] a learner was used to devise behaviours for units in a multi-player game in order to evaluate AI players. In both cases learning algorithms are used to construct cooperative behaviours for adversarial agents in order to detect emergent misbehaviours, but neither applies the technique to computer networks.

6. CONCLUSION AND FUTURE WORK

We have described a general framework for the testing of network protocols and topologies for adversary-induced emergent misbehaviour. The testing framework made use of our incremental-adaptive corrective learning in order to coordinate the learning process, structure the method by which adversarial agents are introduced into the tested networks and structure the method by which the behaviours of these adversarial agents are learned.

We instantiated our testing framework with the goal of testing sensor networks with actuators deployed in precision agriculture applications. In all five of the test networks, our method was able to identify ways of increasing power consumption by at least one node in the network by a factor of 3.6, and in some cases much more.

Our testing approach is very general and could be applied to any number of other applications of wireless ad-hoc networks as future work. An additional area of future work is to examine the impact of the tested networks actively using security mechanisms such as cryptography and more secure network protocols to protect themselves.

7. REFERENCES

[1] A. Baggio. Wireless sensor networks in precision agriculture. In *Proc. REALWSN 2005*, 2005. `http://www.sics.se/realwsn05/papers/baggio05wireless.pdf`, As seen Oct. 10 2012.

[2] M. Blackadar and J. Denzinger. Behavior learning-based testing of starcraft competition entries. *Proc. AIIDE 2011*, 116–121, 2011.

[3] J. A. Clark and J. L. Jacob. Protocols are programs too: the meta-heuristic search for security protocols. *Information and Software Technology*, 43:891–904, 2001.

[4] T. Flanagan, C. Thornton, and J. Denzinger. Testing harbour patrol and interception policies using particle-swarm-based learning of cooperative behavior. *Proc. CISDA'09*, 215–222, 2009.

[5] Y.-C. Hu, A. Perrig, and D. Johnson. Wormhole attacks in wireless networks. *Selected Areas in Communications, IEEE Journal on*, 24(2):370 – 380, feb. 2006.

[6] C. Jacob. *Illustrating Evolutionary Computation with Mathematica*. Morgan Kaufmann Publishers, 2001, 427–430.

[7] P. McMinn. Search-based software test data generation: A survey. *Software Testing Verification and Reliability*, 14:105–156, 2004.

[8] C. Perkins, E. Belding-Royer, and S. Das. Ad hoc On-Demand Distance Vector (AODV) Routing. RFC 3561 (Experimental), July 2003.

[9] J. Postel. User Datagram Protocol. RFC 768 (Standard), Aug. 1980.

[10] J. Postel. Internet Protocol. RFC 791 (Standard), Sept. 1981.

[11] R. Sasnauskas, O. Landsiedel, M. H. Alizai, C. Weise, S. Kowalewski, and K. Wehrle. Kleenet: discovering insidious interaction bugs in wireless sensor networks before deployment. *Proc. IPSN'10*, 186–196, 2010.

[12] A. Varga. The OMNeT++ Discrete Event Simulation System. *Proc. ESM2001*, 319–324, 2001.

[13] J. Wegener and M. Grochtmann. Verifying timing constraints of real-time systems by means of evolutionary testing. *Real-Time Systems*, 15(3):275–298, 1998.

[14] M. Woehrle. Search-based stress testing of wireless network protocol stacks. *Proc. ICST'12*, 794–803, 2012.

[15] Y. Zhang. Repository of publications on search based software engineering. `http://crestweb.cs.ucl.ac.uk/resources/sbse_repository/repository.html`. As seen Oct. 10 2012.

Cost-aware Pareto Optimal Test Suite Minimisation for Service-centric Systems

Mustafa Bozkurt
University College London
CREST, Dept. of Computer Science, UK
mustafa.bozkurt.10@ucl.ac.uk

ABSTRACT

Runtime testing cost caused by service invocations is considered as one of the major limitations in Service-centric System Testing (ScST). Unfortunately, most of the existing work cannot achieve cost reduction at runtime as they perform offline testing. In this paper, we introduce a novel cost-aware pareto optimal test suite minimisation approach for ScST aimed at reducing runtime testing cost. In experimental analysis, the proposed approach achieved reductions between 69% and 98.6% in monetary cost of service invocations while retaining test suite coverage. The results also provided evidence for the effectiveness of the selected algorithm HNSGA-II over the two commonly used algorithms: Greedy and NSGA-II.

Categories and Subject Descriptors

D.2.5 [**Software Engineering**]: Testing and Debugging—*Testing tools*

General Terms

Testing, Minimisation, Service-centric Systems

Keywords

SOA, web services, service-centric systems testing, multi-objective genetic algorithms, test suite minimisation

1 Introduction

In testing of software systems, one common problem that many testers face is the problem of cost. Cost of a test suite is often associated with the time it takes to complete its execution. However, with the introduction of services, the classical understanding of the term 'testing cost' has started to gain new dimensions, such as monetary cost of service invocations during testing [4].

According to literature, one of the limitations of Service-centric System(s) Testing (ScST) is the cost associated with invoking services [3, 4, 6]. The cost of invoking services during testing is a major problem at composition level. Increased test frequency for ScS exacerbates the severity of the issues regarding testing cost in ScST. Testing cost is identified as a challenge due to three side effects that might be caused by the increased frequency of testing. These are:

1. The monetary cost of invoking service during runtime testing.
2. Service disruptions that might be caused by extensive testing.
3. Effects of testing in some systems, such as stock-exchange systems, where each usage of the service requires a business transaction, that carries with it a monetary cost.

Solutions aimed at reducing the cost of testing in ScST, such as simulated testing and stub/mock services have previously been proposed [11, 12, 13, 14, 15, 16]. However, these approaches do not eliminate the need for runtime testing (testing with real services).

One widely studied solution aimed at reducing runtime testing cost is test suite minimisation [22]. The purpose of test suite minimisation is to reduce testing cost through removing redundant test cases. In test suite minimisation, there are concerns such as retaining coverage, test suite effectiveness or fault detection capability, execution time and resource usage, such as memory. According to the literature, problems with multiple competing and conflicting concerns can be investigated using pareto optimal optimisation approaches [9].

A tester is often faced with making decisions based on multiple test criteria during runtime testing. This is due to the fact that, in many situations, it is not expected that the tester aims to achieve a single goal during the testing process. Achieving a high coverage is often regarded as a major goal in testing [18, 20]. However, achieving high coverage can be expensive and expecting to achieve 100% coverage might not be realistic when testing complex systems.

The cost of a test suite is one of the most important criteria, since a tester wants to get maximum value (e.g. number of branches covered) from the execution of a test suite [9]. In the literature, the cost of a test suite is often associated with the time it takes to execute it [22]. As mentioned, with the introduction of web services, service compositions and online APIs, the concept of monetary cost of testing is starting to gain acceptance in software testing literature.

The reliability (also referred to as quality) of a test suite is also an important concern. A test suite with high reliability might reduce the cost of testing in two ways:

1. *Human-oracle cost reduction* due to the tester's trust in the test input source. If the test data used in testing has a high reliability, the tester will not need to inspect all test inputs for errors such as invalidity and conformance to input requirements (e.g. input format).

2. *Avoiding extra testing cost* caused by erroneous test inputs. The extra cost in this case occurs due to service invocations with invalid test data during the execution and the investigation of the unexpected test results that might occur as a result of invalid inputs.

For instance, consider the case of U.S. ZIP codes. Zip codes can be decommissioned or new ones might be assigned to new areas over time. As a result, during testing of an ScS that requires ZIP codes as input, only valid codes must be used. In this scenario, if the ZIP codes (used in testing) are generated from unreliable services, then the test suite's reliability will be low, which means the test suite might include decommissioned or invalid ZIP codes. It is safe to assume that testing with decommissioned ZIP codes can be classified as unnecessary execution (except if the tester is performing robustness testing), which is likely to produce false positives. The results from our experimental studies for ZIP codes (discussed in Section 5) provided evidence for the correctness of this assumption. The problem with false positives is that they might cause the tester to invest time in investigating the reasons for unexpected output(s).

In order to avoid the side effects of extensive runtime testing, a test suite minimisation approach could be used to remove 'redundant' test cases; those which merely cover previously covered features. On the other hand, to avoid side effects of a low reliability test suite, the selected approach must be able to manage multiple objectives. Thus, we propose to adapt the multi-objective test suite minimisation approach of Yoo and Harman [22] to ScST with the objectives, such as cost of service invocation, branch coverage and test suite reliability.

In this paper, we introduce a pareto optimal, multi-objective test suite minimisation approach to ScST aiming at reducing runtime testing cost. The advantages of the proposed application of multi-objective test suite minimisation for ScS are:

1. Reduced cost in runtime testing through test suite minimisation.
2. Its ability to discover trade-offs between cost of test runs and system coverage.
3. Its ability to discover more reliable test suite subsets without increasing the cost and affecting the coverage.

The rest of this paper is organised as follows. Section 2 discuses existing work in the fields of test cost reduction and test suite minimisation. Section 3 briefly introduces the concept test suite minimisation and explains the proposed multi-objective test suite minimisation approach for ScST. Section 4 presents our case studies, research questions and our method of investigation. Section 5 presents the results from our experiments and answers the research questions. Section 6 concludes the paper.

2 Related Work

The concept of cost awareness in test suite selection, minimisation and prioritisation for both traditional systems and ScS studied in the existing work [22]. As mentioned, most of these approaches consider cost as the time it takes to execute a test suite. Although, test suite execution time is a valid concern in ScST (also addressed [23]) the actual cost of service invocation which is a major limitation in ScST, gained more attention due to its greater impact.

The existing work targeting ScS that can help with cost reduction are focused on two main topics; simulated testing and generation of replacement services which includes stub, mock and other services aimed at replacing the invoked services. The approaches using simulated testing [11, 12, 14, 15] has the potential benefit of reducing testing cost by testing the correctness of a service composition offline. The approaches aimed at generating replacement services [12, 13, 16, 24] can directly reduce the testing by avoiding calls to the actual services during testing. Even though these approaches can potentially reduce testing cost they do not eliminate the need for runtime testing. Runtime testing is unavoidable for ScS due to the required testing for integration, interoperability and quality of service. Unfortunately, the mentioned approaches fail to help at runtime testing.

The only existing approach that can help with runtime cost reduction is proposed by Hou et al. [10]. The approach is aimed at avoiding extra cost that might occur due to high number service invocations during testing. The proposed prioritisation is based on the quota-based service usage payment plan (a detailed explanation for prominent payment plans is provided in Section 3.3). The approach optimises test case execution times and order around the tester's service usage quota. This approach can be very useful for avoiding extra cost, however it fails in two respects. First, the approach is only applicable to quota-based payment plans and second, the approach does not consider redundant test cases which can be safely considered as extra testing cost.

The approach presented in this paper addresses two of the concerns that was not addressed by the earlier work by using pareto optimality. First, the approach not only help reducing the testing cost but also provides grater flexibility to the tester by allowing the tester to choose a suitable test suite based on the cost/coverage/reliability trade-offs. Second, the approach is formulated for all prominent payment plans thus it can be applied to most of the existing ScS.

3 Multi-Objective Minimisation for Service-centric Systems

In this section, we explain the concept of test suite minimisation, our approach and present our objective functions.

3.1 Test Suite Minimisation and HNSGA-II

Test suite minimisation (or test suite reduction) techniques aim to reduce the size of a test suite by eliminating redundant test cases [22]. Test suite minimisation is considered as a hitting set (or set cover) problem which is an NP-complete problem.

Due to the test suite reduction problem (which is a minimal set cover problem) being NP-complete, the use of heuristics is proposed by many researchers [22]. According to the literature, another well known solution to the set cover problem is the greedy approximation. Yoo and Harman [21] proposed a solution (using an algorithm called 'HSNGA-II') which combines these two solutions into a pareto optimal test suite minimisation approach.

HNSGA-II is a variant of the standard NSGA-II and it may be more effective in multi-objective minimisation problems compared to NSGA-II. HNSGA-II combines the effectiveness of greedy algorithm for set cover problems with NSGA-II's global search. Results from the execution of additional greedy algorithm are added to the initial population of NSGA-II in order to create an initial population with better solutions compared to a 'random only' population. The goal in using a better initial population is to guide NSGA-II to a better approximation to the optimal pareto front. This process can be especially beneficial in problems with very large search spaces.

Algorithm 1 2-objective Additional Greedy Algorithm

```
Require: Test suite S
DEFINE current fitness, coverage, test suite S' := ∅
while not stopping rule do
    current fitness := 0
    for all test cases in S do
        if test case T is not in S' then
            coverage := coverage score of S' (Cov_S')
            ADD T to S'
            new fitness := (Cov_S' − coverage) / (cost of S')
            if new fitness is better than current fitness then
                current fitness := new fitness
                MARK T as selected
            end if
        end if
        REMOVE T from S'
    end for
    if no test case is selected then
        END
    else
        ADD selected test case to S'
    end if
end while
```

3.2 Proposed Approach

Our approach consists of two stages: test suite artefact calculation and multi-objective minimisation. After test suite generation, our approach requires the calculation of three measurements in order to apply multi-objective approaches. These are coverage, reliability and execution cost of each test case.

The reliability score of a test case is based on the reliability of its inputs. The reliability of each input is calculated using the formulation we described in our previous work [2, 3]. Previously, we introduced the concept of service-centric test data generation addressing the issues of automation in realistic test data generation [2]. The proposed solution called ATAM composes existing services to generate the required realistic test data. ATAM also calculates the reliability of each generated realistic input based on the services used in the input generation process. Details of our formulation for the input reliability score is available in an earlier paper [3].

Unlike reliability, execution cost and branch coverage cannot be acquired from an external source. The easiest way of acquiring this information is by executing the whole test suite. Unfortunately, performing a runtime execution for the whole test suite in order to measure its artefacts will increase the overall cost of testing which is an unacceptable side effect for an approach that aims to reduce testing cost. In order to avoid this cost, we propose the use of simulated testing using mock/stub services. Using stub/mock services will allow us to measure branch coverage and service invocation information for each test case without incurring additional costs.

Service invocation costs can occur in several ways (based on the type of contract agreed between the provider and the integrator). Two of the most prominent payment plans used at present are: pay per-use and invocation quota-based plans. As a result, two different cost calculation functions are introduced. Details of these two payment plans and the cost calculation associated with them are discussed in Section 3.3.

After completing stub/mock service generation, a simulated run for the test suite is performed in order to measure testing artefacts for each test case. These measured values then used in the optimisation process to determine the pareto optimal sets of test cases.

In order to adapt Yoo and Harman's minimisation approach to ScST, we modified the original greedy algorithm by replacing its objective functions with the objective functions from our approach. We used the following algorithms for the 2-objective and the 3-objective optimisation scenarios. The additional algorithm for 2-objective optimisation (described in Algorithm 1) uses the cost and coverage calculation algorithms discussed in Section 3.3.

The 3-objective additional algorithm considers an additional objective, reliability. In this algorithm, the objectives coverage, cost and reliability are combined into a single objective using the weighted-sum model. In our experiments, both coverage and reliability objectives were given equal weights.

As mentioned, HNSGA-II uses the results from the greedy algorithm runs as an initial population. In the second stage of our approach, we run the greedy algorithm and feed its results to NSGA-II to produce the pareto front. The generated front enables the tester to investigate the trade-offs between the measured testing artefacts. In the cases where the size of resulting set from greedy algorithm is less than the required population size for NSGA-II, we compensate for this shortcoming by adding randomly generated solutions to the greedy results.

3.3 Objective Functions

Branch coverage is calculated as the percentage of branches of ScS under test covered by the given test suite. In our approach, we considered coverage as an objective rather than a constraint, in order to allow the tester to explore all the possible solutions on the pareto optimal front. The following objective function is used for branch coverage since our aim is to maximise the coverage of the test suite.

$$Maximize \quad \frac{\text{branches covered by test suite}}{\text{total number of branches}} \tag{1}$$

The objective function for the cost is not as straightforward as branch coverage because it has multiple options for service invocation cost. Several different payment plans might exist for service usage. However, we considered only the two prominent ones: pay per-use and quota-based payment plans.

Pay per-use plan: In this case, the integrator is charged for each service invocation individually. The total cost of executing a test case is calculated as the total cost of services invoked by the test case and is formulated as:

$$cs(tc_m) = \sum_{i=1}^{n} X_{S_i} * C_{S_i}$$

where n is the number of services invoked by executing the test case tc_m, S_i is the ith executed service, C_{S_i} is the cost of invoking service S_i and X_{S_i} is the number of times service S_i invoked by this test case.

The objective function for pay-per use plan is formulated as:

$$Minimise \quad \sum_{i=1}^{k} cs(tc_i) \tag{2}$$

where k is the total number of test cases and $cs(tc_i)$ is the total cost of executing the ith test case in the test suite.

Quota-based plan: In this case, the integrator pays a subscription fee for a number of service invocations within a period of time (such as monthly or annually). In our scenario, we presume that all the services used in the composition are selected from a single provider and a total invocation quota applies to all services rather than an individual quota for each service. The objective function for this plan is formulated as:

$$Minimise \text{ number of services invocations.} \tag{3}$$

Generating test data using ATAM also enables the use of another test case artefact: reliability. Reliability of a test case is based on the reliability of its inputs. Reliability of a test input is calculated by ATAM as the combined reliability of the data sources used in generation of this input. The reliability calculation and data source selection in ATAM are discussed in an earlier work [3].

Each test case might include a combination of inputs generated using ATAM and user generated inputs. In the case of user generated inputs we consider the input to be 100% reliable and for ATAM generated inputs the reliability score is provided by ATAM. The reason behind considering the tester input as 100% reliable is our assumption of the tester's likely verification of the input data before test execution. Since we do not modify the tester inputs and use them as they are, we did not foresee any reason for having variations in the reliability score of the tester generated data.

In light of these possible cases, a reliability function covering these two cases is formulated as:

$$rf(in_x) = \begin{cases} 1.0 & \text{if } in_x \text{ is user generated} \\ \text{ATAM score} & \text{if } in_x \text{ is generated using ATAM} \end{cases}$$

where $rf(in_x)$ is the reliability score of the input in_x.

The reliability score of each test case is calculated as the average reliability of its inputs, and is formulated as:

$$rel(tc_m) = \frac{1}{y}\sum_{i=1}^{y} rf(in_i)$$

where y is the number of test inputs and $rf(in_i)$ is the reliability of the ith input (in_i) of the test case tc_m.

Reliability of a test suite is calculated as the average reliability of its test cases. Since our aim is to increase the reliability of the test suite, the objective function for test suite reliability is formulated as:

$$Maximise \ \frac{1}{z}\sum_{i=1}^{z} rel(tc_i) \tag{4}$$

where z is the number of test cases in the test suite and $rel(tc_i)$ is the reliability of the ith test case (tc_i) in the test suite.

4 Empirical Studies

In this section, we introduce the case studies we used in our experiments, present the research questions we asked and explain our method of investigation.

4.1 Case Study

In order to evaluate our approach, we selected two case studies with different characteristics. The reason behind this selection is to observe the effectiveness of our approach in different scenarios by providing results that might challenge the findings from the other case study. We included a brief description of the case studies in this section due to space constraints. However, a more detailed explanation including the details of the test cases used in the experiments (the web services used in generating them, their cost and their reliability) and workflows of the case studies are available as a technical report [1].

The first case study (CS1) is an example code used as a benchmark for applications/approaches that aim to achieve branch coverage called 'Complex'. Complex is a artificial test object with complex branching conditions and loops [19]. However, in its original form, Complex is not an ScS. In order to evaluate our approach, we transformed Complex into an ScS by replacing all mathematical, relational and logical operators with service calls. We choose an existing calculator web service [5] to replace the 4 mathematical operators: addition, subtraction, division and multiplication. For the other five operators, we implemented a web service providing the required services.

The second case study (CS2) is a synthetically created shipping workflow that combines the functionality of a number of available online services [8, 17]. In order to make CS2 as realistic as possible, the shipping service invokes a combination of existing real-world web services and other synthetically created services. We were required to use synthetic services in order to simulate the functions of existing services that we have restricted access to.

4.2 Research Questions

We ask the following three questions:

RQ1 Can multi-objective test suite minimisation reduce the testing cost by finding optimal test suite subset(s) for ScST?

RQ2 Is using a test suite with low reliability (containing invalid inputs) likely to generate false positives which might increase the testing cost?

RQ3 Can HNSGA-II algorithm discover dominating solutions compared to NSGA-II and the additional greedy algorithm in our problem?

4.3 Representation and Genetic Operators

To implement and evaluate our approach, we used the popular ECJ framework [7] which provides a built-in NSGA-II algorithm. We used a single population with a size of 2000 and set the number of generations to 100. After some tuning, we found that the ideal parameters that provide the most diverse solutions for our problem are: 5% mutation probability for each gene and single-point crossover with 90% crossover probability.

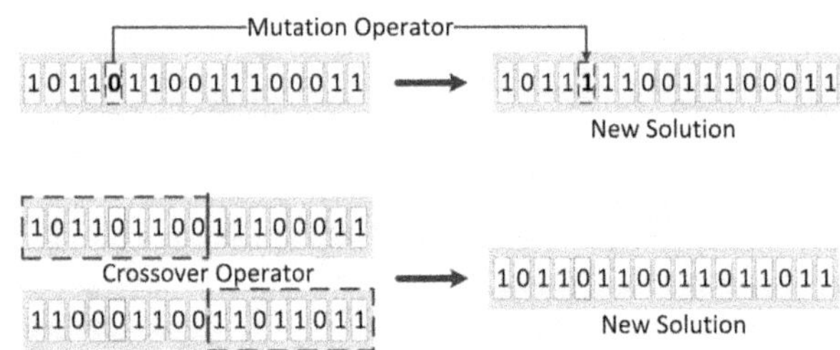

Figure 1: Illustration of the mutation operator and the crossover operators.

We represented test suite subsets as bit vectors (as depicted in Figure 1), where each bit in the vector represents a test case. The bits that are set to 'true' represent the test cases that are to be included in the subset. The mutation operator generates a new solution by modifying the value of a bit element in the vector. The crossover operator produces a new solution by combining two solutions into a new solution as depicted in Figure 1.

4.4 Method of Investigation

In order to answer RQ1, we applied our minimisation technique to both of the case studies. Initially, we tried to randomly generate a test suite that achieves 100% branch coverage for each case study. However, we experienced two issues while using random test generation. It was found to be ineffective in achieving full coverage in CS2 and many of the generated test cases cover exactly the same branches as another test case (equivalent test cases). For CS1 the test suite reached 100% coverage after 1000 test cases and for CS2, test cases covering 3 of the branches (where two ZIP codes of the same city are required) could not be randomly generated within several thousand tries. As a result, we manually generated 4 test cases that cover the uncovered branches in CS2 and applied a simple test case reduction technique to eliminate equivalent test cases.

The resulting test suite sizes were 50 test cases for CS1 and 100 test cases for CS2. The details of both test cases are presented in Table 1. We applied our approach to both of the test suites and measured the minimisation rates achieved by our approach for two different respects: reduction in the number of test cases and reduction in the test cost for both payment models.

Experiment	Test Suite Size	Coverage	Number of Service invocations	Cost
CS1	50	100%	29760	$1302.90
CS2	100	100%	693	$ 212.45

Table 1: Details of the test suites generated for CS1 and CS2.

The main reason for seeking the answer to RQ2 is to investigate our assumption that there is a need for reliable test suite. In order to answer RQ2, we measured the false positives occurred during testing of the four weather information services. In this scenario, a false positive occurs when one of the four services returns a negative response to the given ZIP code which is identified as 'invalid' by USPS service.

In order to answer RQ3, we evaluated the generated pareto fronts from two different aspects. First, we ran greedy, NSGA-II and HNSGA-II[1] with all possible combinations of configurations (both payment plans and both number of objectives) in our approach for both case studies and performed a domination analysis to compare the performance of the algorithms. We also measured the distances between discovered pareto fronts to give us a better understanding of the differences between the fronts. The distance metric we used (Υ) is calculated as the minimum Euclidean distance between two sets of solutions. In this part of the experiment, we used the pareto front generated by HNSGA-II as a reference front and measured the distance of the pareto front generated by NSGA-II to it.

5 Results and Analysis

In this section, we present the results from our experiments, provide answers to the research questions and discuss the threats to the validity of the results from experiments we conducted.

5.1 Results

We analysed the results of test suite reduction after the application of our approach to the initial test suites for both case studies in three different aspects. The first aspect is the reduction in number of test cases while retaining the branch coverage of the subject. As presented in Table 2, our approach achieved 84% reduction in the number of test cases for CS1 and 68% reduction for CS2.

Experiment	Number of Test Cases		
	Test Suite	Our approach	Reduction
CS1	50	8	84%
CS2	100	32	68%

Table 2: Reduction in the number of test cases with the application of our approach. The results from our approach are the minimum number of test cases from the initial test suite that provide 100% branch coverage.

During the experiments, we also found that only 12% of the test cases for CS1 and 34% of the test cases for CS2 in the initial test suites found out to be equivalent test cases. This is an important finding that justifies the diversity of the initial test suites, it also provides evidence for the effectiveness of our approach, since the reduction rates are higher than the equivalent test case rates.

Experiment	Cost (contract based)		
	Test Suite	Our approach	Reduction
CS1	29760	415	98.6%
CS2	693	197	72%

Table 3: Reduction in the number of service invocations with the application of our approach. The number for test suite represents the number of service invocations performed by executing the initial test suite. The results from our approach are the minimum number of invocations necessary to achieve 100% branch coverage.

The second aspect is the reduction in the number of service invocations. This aspect relates to the testing cost when using a contract-based payment plan. Our approach in this case targeted for finding the minimum number of service invocations required to achieve 100% branch coverage. As presented in Table 3, our approach found a solution that reduces the number of invocations from 29760 to 415 for CS1 achieving 98.6% reduction while retaining the branch coverage of the test suite. As for CS2, our approach achieved a 72% reduction in the number of service invocations.

Experiment	Cost (per-use based)		
	Test Suite	Our approach	Reduction
CS1	$1302.90	$19.86	98.5%
CS2	$212.45	$65.99	69%

Table 4: Reduction in the number of service invocations with the application of our approach. The number for test suite represents the number of service invocations performed by executing the initial test suite. The results from our approach are the minimum number of invocations necessary to achieve 100% branch coverage.

The third aspect is the reduction in the monetary cost of testing. This aspect relates to the testing cost when using a per-use payment plan. Our approach in this scenario seeks to find the set of test cases with the least expensive execution cost and achieves 100% branch coverage. As presented in Table 4, our approach found a solution that reduces the total cost of testing from $1302.90 to $19.86 for CS1 achieving 98.5% reduction while retaining the branch coverage of the test suite. As for CS2, our approach achieved a 69% reduction in the total cost of testing.

[1]We ran NSGA-II and HNSGA-II for 10 times in order to statistically evaluate their performance.

Expecting similar reduction rates for contract-based plans and per-use plans on the same ScS might be a natural assumption. However, the results from Table 3 and Table 4 suggest that this assumption might not hold in all cases. According to the results, in the case of CS1, the difference between the reduction rates is minor. However, for CS2 the difference is significantly higher.

In order to answer **RQ2**, we investigated the false positives generated by the 727 ZIP codes which are identified as invalid by the USPS web service. We tested all the weather services with invalid ZIP codes in order to observe whether they cause a false positive. In this scenario, a false positive occurs when a service does not return a weather information for an invalid ZIP code.

Service	False Positives	FP Rate	Error Rate
NOOA.gov	232	0.32	0.035
Myweather2.com	1	0.0014	0.013
CYDNE.com	493	0.68	0.101
Weatherbug.com	196	0.27	0.046

Table 5: The list of false positives caused by erroneous test inputs. In this scenario, a false positive occurs when one of the four services return a negative response to the given ZIP code which is identified as 'invalid' by USPS service. Values in 'FP rate' column represent the false positive generation rate for invalid inputs. The values in 'Error rate' column represent the erroneous output generation rates for the test cases in the test suite.

As it is presented in Table 5, there is a big variance in the number of false positives generated by the weather services. We believe this variance might be caused by weather services having ZIP code databases (or using an external ZIP code service) from different sources. For example, 'MyWeather2' service might be using a database which is very similar to the service (Webservicesx) we used in generating the ZIP codes. However, for the other weather services, we observed a much higher false positive rate. For example, for the 'NOAA' service, the tester needs to check the test results for 232 ZIP codes and verify each of these ZIP codes if they used this test suite.

There is also another interesting result observed in Table 5: an invalid ZIP code is more likely to generate a false positive than a valid one to cause an erroneous output. For all services except one, the false positive rate is much higher than error rate.

One other important finding we need to discuss in this analysis is that none of the services generated the all 727 false positives we expected to observe. Only 561 of the invalid ZIP codes caused a false positive and for the remainder of the codes the weather services returned a valid response. We believe this is a further indication that supports our claim regarding weather services not using up-to-date ZIP code databases/services.

The results from the domination analysis (presented in Table 6) revealed results that conform with the analysis of Yoo and Harman [21]. Our first finding came from the results of CS1 that NSGA-II might outperform HNSGA-II where additional greedy algorithm cannot outperform NSGA-II (as depicted in Figure 2, 4 and 5). We believe this is due to HSNGA-II starting with a good initial population, leading it to discover solutions around this set whereas NSGA-II explored a larger space using random population. However, as can be observed in Figure 4 and 5, the majority of the solutions discovered by both algorithms are the same.

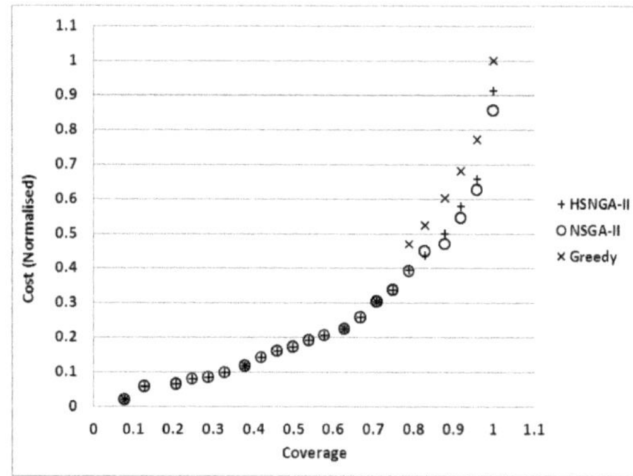

Figure 2: Pareto fronts discovered from the 2 objective optimisation of CS1 with per-use payment plan.

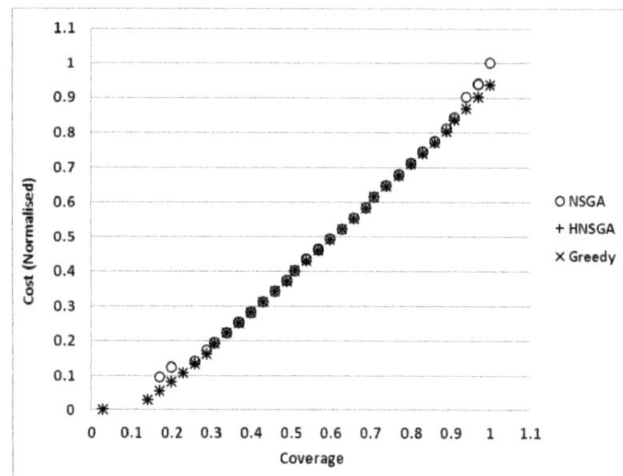

Figure 3: Pareto fronts discovered from the 2 objective optimisation of CS2 with per-use payment plan.

On the other hand, the results of CS2 provide evidence for the improvements HNSGA-II can provide for problems in which greedy outperforms NSGA-II. The results from both 2- and 3-objective runs indicate that HNSGA-II outperforms NSGA-II by a high margin (as depicted in Figure 3, 6 and 7). For example, on average, 68% of the discovered solutions with 2 objectives for CS2 (contract-based plan) dominate NSGA-II and the domination rate goes up to 89% for the same scenario with 3 objectives. A similar trend was also observed for other configurations of CS2.

Experiment	Contract					Per Use				
	n	HNSGA-II		NSGA-II		n	HNSGA-II		NSGA-II	
		Avg.	σ	Avg.	σ		Avg.	σ	Avg.	σ
CS1 (2 obj.)	23.0	0.5	0.67	1.5	1.43	23.0	0.1	0.3	1.0	1.48
CS2 (2 obj.)	32.7	22.2	1.89	0.3	0.46	32.3	25.1	2.98	0	0
CS1 (3 obj.)	201.8	14.8	3.68	25.1	7.88	204.6	15.8	4.29	23.6	4.03
CS2 (3 obj.)	238.9	212	6.03	1.0	1.18	241	209	10.14	0.7	0.71

Table 6: Results from our domination analysis. The column 'n' represents the average size of the discovered pareto fronts. 'Avg.' column for each algorithm represents the average number of dominating solutions discovered by the algorithm. The results lead to two important findings that NSGA-II and HNSGA-II's performances are similar for problems in which greedy algorithm does not outperform NSGA-II (such as CS1). However, for problems (such as CS2) where greedy outperforms NSGA-II, HNSGA-II outperforms NSGA-II.

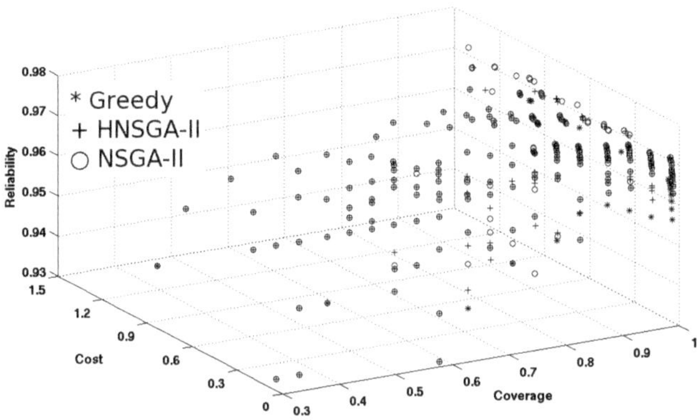

Figure 4: 3 objective optimisation for CS1 with per-use payment plan.

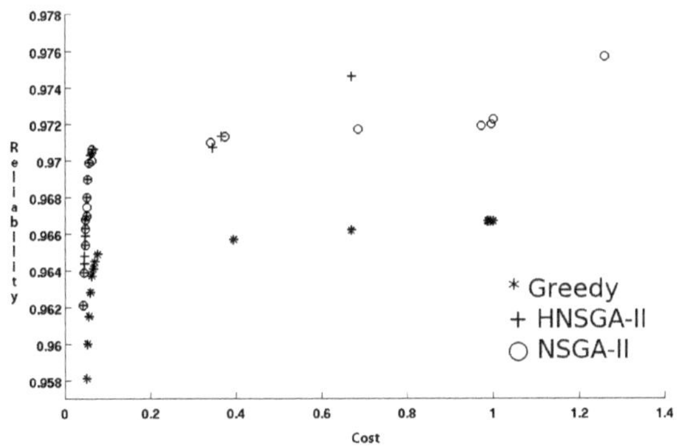

Figure 5: Projected view of Figure 4 focusing on the solutions with 100% coverage score.

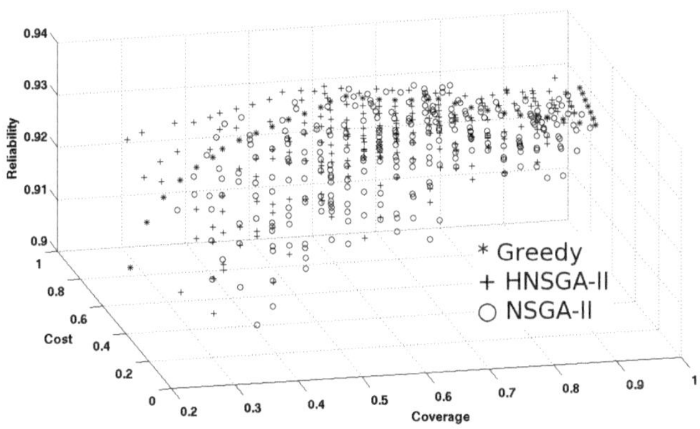

Figure 6: 3 objective optimisation for CS2 with per-use payment plan

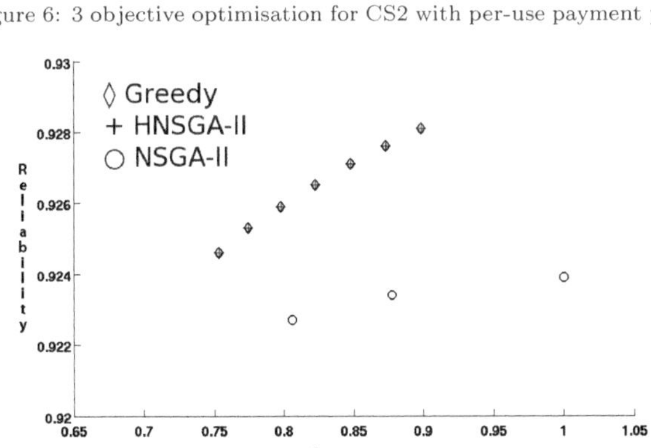

Figure 7: Projected view of Figure 6 focusing on the solutions with 100% coverage score.

Difference between the generated pareto fronts are presented in Table 6. Before the analysis our assumption was that the higher the number of dominant solutions, the higher the distance between the pareto fronts must be. The results provide evidence for the fact that for problems in which NSGA-II outperforms greedy, NSGA-II discovers solutions further from HNSGA-II. This can be observed in Figure 4 and 5, where NSGA-II discovered solutions (especially around 100% coverage) that are far from the solutions discovered by HNSGA-II.

Experiment	Contract		Per-use	
	Avg.	σ	Avg.	σ
CS1 (2 objectives)	0.6999	0.71219	0.0353	0.05036
CS2 (2 objectives)	5.4224	1.83578	0.9128	0.24409
CS1 (3 objectives)	4.5524	2.28092	0.07	0.08572
CS2 (3 objectives)	1.521	0.42198	0.4014	0.11026

Table 6: The average distances between the pareto fronts generated by both algorithms. Both algorithms are run 10 times and the average Euclidean distance between pareto fronts are measured using the distance metric Υ.

The results provide evidence for the effectiveness of HSNGA-II over both NSGA-II and greedy algorithm. For example, results from Figure 7 clearly indicate that HNSGA-II can match greedy's performance for problems in which greedy discovers a pareto front close to optimum front and can outperform NSGA-II. On the other hand, results from Figure 5 indicate that for problems in which greedy can outperform NSGA-II, HNSGA-II also can outperform greedy by matching NSGA-II's performance.

Unfortunately, due to space constraints we included only the figures from 'per-use' payment plan. We observed a similar trend when using 'contract-based' plan for both case studies. A more comprehensive presentation of our experimental results is available as a technical report [1].

5.2 Answers to Research Questions

The results from our experiments provide evidence for the effectiveness of our approach in testing cost reduction using multi-objective algorithms and answered **RQ1**. For both case studies, our approach achieved high reduction rates, with up to 84% reduction in the size of test suite and up to 99% reduction in the testing cost (for both payment plans) while retaining the coverage of the initial test suite.

With regards to **RQ2**, the results provide evidence for the fact that invalid inputs have a significant possibility of generating a false positive which might increase the testing cost in ScST. The observed false positive generation rates during the experiments were high (varying between 27% to 68%) for all the services we analysed except for one where the rate was 0.0014. The results also suggest that an invalid input is more likely to cause a false positive than the possibility of a realistic input causing an erroneous output in ScST.

As for **RQ3**, the results provide evidence for the fact that HNSGA-II performance is highly related to the performance of greedy algorithm. Since HNSGA-II executes the same NSGA-II algorithm for problems in which NSGA-II outperforms greedy (such as CS1), it performs similarly to NSGA-II. However, for the problems in which greedy outperforms NSGA-II, we observe the real benefit of HNSGA-II. The evidence for this claim came from the results of CS2, for both payment plans greedy discovered a very good set of solutions and HNSGA-II could not discover better results and resulted with the same pareto front. The advantage of using HNSGA-II is that it can match the performance of the best performing algorithm (out of the two) in any scenario, while outperforming the other one.

5.3 Threats to Validity

The most important external threat which might limit the general applicability of the proposed approach is the test subjects representing real-world scenarios. Although the ScS used in our experiments are synthetic examples, they are implemented merely to orchestrate the selected existing web services. Thus, these synthetic workflows definitely represent one of the possible orchestrations of these aforementioned services. Another concern might be the realism of the artefacts that are used in the experiments: reliability scores and service invocation costs. In order to make the case studies as realistic as possible, reliability and cost values used in the experiments are obtained from existing real-world services that are publicly available.

The most important internal threat which might have affected the results obtained is the accuracy of the instrumentation code. This code is used in measuring coverage, reliability and cost of test cases used in the experiments. Correctness of the instrumentation was verified using the coverage measurement plug-in provided by Netbeans IDE and manual inspection. Another factor that might have affected the obtained reliability scores is our use of USPS as the ground truth for ZIP code validation. We believe that USPS must use one of the most up-to-date ZIP code databases since it is one of the government bodies that is responsible for address standardisation in the U.S.

6 Conclusion

In this paper, we introduced a solution aimed at reducing runtime testing cost in ScST by using multi-objective optimisation, and presented an experimental study that investigated the effectiveness of proposed approach. We also investigated the HNSGA-II algorithm by comparing its performance against the two algorithms that are commonly used in test suite minimisation (NSGA-II and greedy). The experimental results provided evidence for the applicability and the effectiveness of the proposed approach. The results also affirmed the benefits of using HNSGA-II over NSGA-II in certain problems.

7 References

[1] M. Bozkurt, "Cost-cognisant test suite reduction for service-centric systems," University College London, Tech. Rep. RN/13/04, 2013.

[2] M. Bozkurt and M. Harman, "Automatically generating realistic test input from web services," in *SOSE '11*. Irvine, CA, USA: IEEE Computer Society, 2011, pp. 13–24.

[3] M. Bozkurt and M. Harman, "Optimised realistic test input generation using web services," in *SSBSE 2012*, vol. 7515. Riva Del Garda, Italy: Springer Berlin / Heidelberg, 2012, pp. 105–120.

[4] M. Bozkurt, M. Harman, and Y. Hassoun, "Testing & verification in service-oriented architecture: A survey," *STVR*, 2012, To Appear.

[5] Calculator web service. [Online]. Available: http://www.html2xml.nl/Services/Calculator/Version1/Calculator.asmx?WSDL

[6] G. Canfora and M. Di Penta, "Service-oriented architectures testing: A survey," in *Software Engineering*, ser. Lecture Notes in Computer Science. Springer, 2009, vol. 5413/2009, pp. 78–105.

[7] ECJ 20. [Online]. Available: http://cs.gmu.edu/~eclab/projects/ecj/

[8] FedEx Rate Calculator. [Online]. Available: https://www.fedex.com/ratefinder/home?cc=US&language=en&locId=express

[9] M. Harman, "Making the case for MORTO: Multi objective regression test optimization," in *Regression 2011*, Berlin, Germany, 2011.

[10] S.-S. Hou, L. Zhang, T. Xie, and J.-S. Sun, "Quota-constrained test-case prioritization for regression testing of service-centric systems," in *ICSM '08*. Beijing, China: IEEE, 2008, pp. 257–266.

[11] S. Ilieva, V. Pavlov, and I. Manova, "A composable framework for test automation of service-based applications," in *QUATIC '10*. Oporto, Portugal: IEEE Computer Society, 2010, pp. 286–291.

[12] Z. Li, W. Sun, Z. B. Jiang, and X. Zhang, "BPEL4WS unit testing: framework and implementation," in *ICWS '05*. Orlando, FL, USA: IEEE Computer Society, 2005, pp. 103–110 vol.1.

[13] S. Mani, V. S. Sinha, S. Sinha, P. Dhoolia, D. Mukherjee, and S. Chakraborty, "Efficient testing of service-oriented applications using semantic service stubs," in *ICWS '09*. Los Angeles, CA, USA: IEEE Computer Society, 2009, pp. 197–204.

[14] P. Mayer and D. Lübke, "Towards a BPEL unit testing framework," in *TAV-WEB '06*. Portland, Maine, USA: ACM, 2006, pp. 33–42.

[15] M. Palomo-Duarte, A. García-Domínguez, I. Medina-Bulo, A. Álvarez Ayllón, and J. Santacruz, "Takuan: A tool for ws-bpel composition testing using dynamic invariant generation." in *ICWE '10*, Vienna, Austria, 2010, pp. 531–534.

[16] H. Reza and D. Van Gilst, "A framework for testing RESTful web services," in *ITNG '10*. Las Vegas, NV, USA: IEEE Computer Society, 2010, pp. 216–221.

[17] Shipping Calculator. [Online]. Available: http://www.unitedstateszipcodes.org/shipping-calculator/

[18] S. Thummalapenta, T. Xie, N. Tillmann, J. de Halleux, and Z. Su, "Synthesizing method sequences for high-coverage testing," in *OOPSLA '11*. New York, NY, USA: ACM, 2011, pp. 189–206.

[19] J. Wegener, A. Baresel, and H. Sthamer, "Evolutionary test environment for automatic structural testing," *Information and Software Technology*, vol. 43, no. 14, pp. 841 – 854, 2001.

[20] X. Xiao, "Problem identification for structural test generation: First step towards cooperative developer testing," in *ICSE '11*, 2011.

[21] S. Yoo and M. Harman, "Using hybrid algorithm for pareto effcient multi-objective test suite minimisation," *Journal of Systems Software*, vol. 83, no. 4, pp. 689–701, 2010.

[22] S. Yoo and M. Harman, "Regression testing minimisation, selection and prioritisation: A survey," *STVR*, vol. 22, no. 2, pp. 67–120, 2012.

[23] L. Zhang, S.-S. Hou, C. Guo, T. Xie, and H. Mei, "Time-aware test-case prioritization using integer linear programming," in *ISSTA '09*. New York, NY, USA: ACM, 2009, pp. 213–224.

[24] H. Zhu, "A framework for service-oriented testing of web services," in *COMPSAC '06*, vol. 2. Chicago, IL, USA: IEEE Computer Society, 2006, pp. 145–150.

Test Suite Generation with Memetic Algorithms

Gordon Fraser
University of Sheffield
Dep. of Computer Science
211 Regent Court, Portobello,
S1 4DP, Sheffield
gordon.fraser@sheffield.ac.uk

Andrea Arcuri
Certus Software V&V Center
Simula Research Laboratory
P.O. Box 134, 1325 Lysaker,
Norway
arcuri@simula.no

Phil McMinn
University of Sheffield
Dep. of Computer Science
211 Regent Court, Portobello,
S1 4DP, Sheffield
p.mcminn@sheffield.ac.uk

ABSTRACT

Genetic Algorithms have been successfully applied to the generation of unit tests for classes, and are well suited to create complex objects through sequences of method calls. However, because the neighborhood in the search space for method sequences is huge, even supposedly simple optimizations on primitive variables (e.g., numbers and strings) can be ineffective or unsuccessful. To overcome this problem, we extend the global search applied in the EvoSuite test generation tool with local search on the individual statements of method sequences. In contrast to previous work on local search, we also consider complex datatypes including strings and arrays. A rigorous experimental methodology has been applied to properly evaluate these new local search operators. In our experiments on a set of open source classes of different kinds (e.g., numerical applications and text processing), the resulting test data generation technique increased branch coverage by up to 32% on average over the normal Genetic Algorithm.

Categories and Subject Descriptors

I.2.8 [**Artificial Intelligence**]: Problem Solving, Control Methods, and Search;
D.2.5 [**Software Engineering**]: Testing and Debugging

General Terms

Algorithms, Experimentation, Reliability

Keywords

EvoSuite, Search-based Software Engineering, Object-oriented, Evolutionary Testing

1. INTRODUCTION

Software testing is one of the most important techniques applied to improve software quality. When there is no automated test oracle available, as for example is often the case in white-box testing, test generation techniques aim to produce small test suites with high code coverage, such that these test suites can be analyzed by the developer in feasible time. In the case of object-oriented classes, test cases amount to sequences of method calls, and search-based testing [18] has been demonstrated to be an effective solution as it can handle not only optimizations on primitive datatypes, but also on complex data structures and sequences of method calls. The use of search-based techniques for optimizing entire test suites towards high branch coverage for classes [10] has been shown to be a successful technique for this purpose. Empirical experiments have shown that it is practically usable on a wide range of programs [9].

```
class Foo {                          Foo foo = new Foo();
  boolean bar(String s) {            String s = "test";
    if(s.equals("bar"))              foo.bar(s);
      // target
  }
}
```

Figure 1: Example class and test case: In theory, four edits of s can lead to the target branch being covered. However, with a Genetic Algorithm where each statement of the test is mutated with a certain probability (e.g., 1/3 when there are three statements) one would have to be really lucky: If the test is part of a test suite (size 10) of a Genetic Algorithm (population 50) and we only assume a character range of 128, then even if we ignore all the complexities of Genetic Algorithms, we would still need on average at least $50 \times 4 \times 1/(\frac{1}{10} \times \frac{1}{3} \times \frac{1}{128}) = 768{,}000$ fitness evaluations before covering the target branch.

When an individual of the search is a test suite consisting of a variable number of test cases, each of which is a sequence of method calls of variable length, then the neighborhood in the search space is simply huge: Here, a neighbor is not only defined by the next successive value for primitive types, but also as all the possible calls that can be inserted on existing objects and all the possible changes that can be performed on the sequences of method calls. If somewhere in such a test suite there is an individual primitive value that needs to be optimized, then the probability of it being mutated during the search with a Genetic Algorithm is low, and so the optimization towards the targets dependent on this value can take long. The urgency of this problem becomes even more apparent when one also considers string variables as primitives, where again the neighborhood is huge. Consider

GECCO'13, July 6–10, 2013, Amsterdam, The Netherlands.

the example test case in Figure 1: Even under very strong simplifications, with a "basic" Genetic Algorithm we would need an average of at least 768,000 costly fitness evaluations (i.e., test executions) to cover the target branch. If the budget is limited, then indeed the approach might fail to cover such goals.

To overcome this problem, we extend the Genetic Algorithm used in the whole test suite generation approach to a Memetic Algorithm: At regular intervals, the search inspects the primitive variables and tries to apply local search to improve them. Although these extensions are intuitively useful and tempting, they add additional parameters to the already large parameter space. In fact, misusing these techniques can even lead to worse results, and so we conducted a detailed study to find the best parameter settings. In detail, the contributions of this paper are:

Memetic algorithm for test suite optimization: We present a novel approach to integrate local search on primitive values in a global search for test suites.

Local search for complex values: We extend the notion of local search as commonly performed on numerical inputs to string inputs, arrays, and objects.

Sensitivity analysis: We have implemented the approach as an extension to the EvoSuite tool [10], and analyze the effects of the different parameters involved in the local search, and determine the best configuration.

Evaluation: We evaluate our approach on a set of 16 open source classes, and compare the results to the standard search-based approach that does not include local search.

2. BACKGROUND

Search-based testing applies meta-heuristic search techniques to the task of test data generation [18].

2.1 Local Search Algorithms

With *local* search algorithms [2] one only considers the neighborhood of a candidate solution. For example, a hill climbing search is usually started with a random solution, of which all neighbors are evaluated with respect to their fitness for the search objective. The search then continues on either the first neighbor that has improved the fitness, or the best neighbor, and again considers its neighborhood. The search can easily get stuck in local optima, which is typically overcome by restarting the search with new random values. A popular version of hill climbing often used in test data generation is Korel's Alternating Variable Method [7,16].

The Alternative Variable Method (AVM) is a local search technique similar to hill climbing, and was introduced by Korel [16]. The AVM considers each input variable of an optimization function in isolation, and tries to optimize it locally. Initially, variables are set to random values. Then, AVM starts with exploratory moves on the first variable. For example, in the case of an integer an exploratory move consists of adding a delta of $+1$ or -1. If the exploratory move was successful (i.e., the fitness improved), then the search accelerates movement with pattern moves. For example, in the case of an integer, the search would next try $+2$, then $+4$, etc. Once the next step of the pattern search does not improve the fitness any further, the search goes back to exploratory moves on this variable. If successful, pattern search is again applied in the direction of the exploratory move. Once no further optimization of the variable is possible, the search moves on to the next variable. If no variable can be improved the search restarts at another randomly chosen location to overcome local optima.

2.2 Global Search Algorithms

In contrast, *global* search algorithms try to overcome local optima in order to find more globally optimal solutions. Harman and McMinn [14] recently determined that global search is more effective than local search, but less efficient, as it is more costly.

With evolutionary testing, one of the most commonly applied global search algorithms is a *Genetic Algorithm* (GA). A GA tries to imitate the natural processes of evolution: An initial population of usually randomly produced candidate solutions is evolved using search operators that resemble natural processes. Selection of parents for reproduction is based on their fitness (survival of the fittest). Reproduction is performed using crossover and mutation with certain probabilities. With each iteration of the GA, the fitness of the population improves, until either an optimal solution has been found, or some other stopping condition has been met (e.g. maximum time or number of fitness evaluations). In evolutionary testing, the population would for example consist of test cases, and the fitness estimates how close a candidate solution is to satisfying a coverage goal. The initial population is usually generated randomly, i.e., a fixed number of random input values is generated. The operators used in the evolution of this initial population depend on the chosen representation.

A fitness function guides the search in choosing individuals for reproduction, gradually improving the fitness values with each generation until a solution is found. For example, to generate tests for branch coverage, a common fitness function [18] integrates the *approach level* (number of unsatisfied control dependencies) and the *branch distance* (estimation of how close the deviating condition is to evaluating as desired). Such search techniques have not only been applied in the context of primitive datatypes, but also to test object-oriented software using method sequences [11,21].

2.3 Memetic Algorithms

A Memetic Algorithm (MA) hybridizes global and local search. The use of MAs for test generation was originally proposed by Wang and Jeng [22] in the context of test generation for procedural code. Arcuri [5] combined a GA with hill climbing to form a MA when generating unit tests for container classes. Harman and McMinn [14] analyzed the effects of global and local search, and concluded that MAs achieve better performance than global search and local search. Baresi et al. [6] also use a hybrid evolutionary search in their TestFul test generation tool, where at the global search level a single test case aims to maximize coverage, while at the local search level the optimization targets individual branch conditions.

3. WHOLE TEST SUITE GENERATION

In whole test suite generation, the optimization target is not to produce a test that reaches one particular coverage goal, but it is to produce a complete test suite that maximizes coverage, while minimizing the size at the same time.

3.1 Representation

An individual of the search is a *test suite*, which is represented as a set T of test cases t_i. Given $|T| = n$, we have

$T = \{t_1, t_2, \ldots, t_n\}$. A test case is a sequence of statements $t = \langle s_1, s_2, \ldots, s_l \rangle$ of length l. The length of a test suite is defined as the sum of the lengths of its test cases, i.e., $length(T) = \sum_{t \in T} l_t$.

There are several different types of statements in a test case: *Primitive statements* define primitive values, such as Booleans, integers, or Strings; *Constructor statements* invoke constructors to produce new values; *Method statements* invoke methods on existing objects, using existing objects as parameters; *Field statements* retrieve values from public members of existing objects; *Array statements* define arrays; *Assignment statements* assign values to array indexes or public member fields of existing objects. Each of these statements defines a new variable, with the exception of void method calls and assignment statements. Variables used as parameters of constructor and method calls and as source objects for field assignments or retrievals need to be already defined by the point at which they are used in the sequence.

Crossover of test suites means that offspring recombine subsets from parent test suites. For example, for two selected parents P_1 and P_2, a random value α is chosen from [0,1], and on one hand, the first offspring O_1 will contain the first $\alpha|P_1|$ test cases from the first parent, followed by the last $(1 - \alpha)|P_2|$ test cases from the second parent. On the other hand, the second offspring O_2 will contain the first $\alpha|P_2|$ test cases from the second parent, followed by the last $(1 - \alpha)|P_1|$ test cases from the first parent.

Mutation of test suites means that test cases are inserted, deleted, or changed. With probability σ, a test case is added. If it is added, then a second test case is added with probability σ^2, and so on until the ith test case is not added (which happens with probability $1 - \sigma^i$). Each test case is changed with probability $1/|T|$. There are many different options to change a test case: One can delete or alter existing statements, or insert new statements. We perform each of these three operations with probability $1/3$; on average, only one of them is applied, although with probability $(1/3)^3$ all of them are applied. When removing statements from a test it is important that this operation must ensure that all dependencies are satisfied. Inserting statements into a test case means inserting method calls on existing calls, or adding new calls on the class under test. For details on the mutation operators we refer to [10].

3.2 Fitness Function

In this paper, we consider branch coverage as the optimization target, although the approach can be applied to any coverage criterion that can be expressed with a fitness function. Typically, fitness functions for other coverage criteria are based on the branch coverage fitness function. Branch coverage requires that for every conditional statement in the code there is at least one test that makes it evaluate to true, and one that makes it evaluate to false. For this, we can use a standard metric used in search-based testing, the *branch distance*.

For every branch, the branch distance estimates how close that branch was to evaluating to true or to false. For example, if we have the branch $x == 17$, and a concrete test case where x has the value 10, then the branch distance to make this branch true would be $17 - 10 = 7$, while the branch distance to making this branch false is 0. To achieve branch coverage in whole test suite generation, the fitness function tries to optimize the sum of all normalized, minimal branch distances to 0 – if for each branch there exists a test such that the execution leads to a branch distance of 0, then all branches have been covered.

3.3 Search Guidance on Strings

The fitness function in whole test suite generation is based on branch distances. EvoSuite works directly on Java bytecode, where except for reference comparisons, the branching instructions are all based on numerical values. Comparisons on strings first map to Boolean values, which are then used in further computations; e.g., a source code branch like `if(string1.equals(string2))` consists of a method call on `String.equals` followed by a comparison of the Boolean return value with `true`. To offer guidance on string based branches we replace calls to the `String.equals` method with a custom method that returns a distance measurement [17]. The branching conditions comparing the Boolean with `true` thus have to be changed to check whether this distance measurement is greater than 0 or not (i.e., `== true` is changed to `== 0`, and `== false` is changed to `> 0`). The distance measurement itself depends on the search operators used; for example, if the search operators support inserts, changes, and deletions, then the Levenshtein distance measurement can be used. This transformation is an instance of *testability transformation* [12], which is commonly applied to improve the guidance offered by the search landscape of programs.

Search operators for string values have initially been proposed by Alshraideh and Bottaci [1]. Based on our distance measurement, when a primitive statement defining a string value is mutated, each of the following is applied with probability 1/3 (i.e., with probability $(1/3)^3$ all are applied):

Deletion: Every character in the string is deleted with probability $1/n$, where n is the length of the string. Thus, on average, one character is deleted.

Change: Every character in the string is changed with probability $1/n$; if it is changed, then it is replaced with a random character.

Insertion: With probability $\alpha = 0.5$, a random character is inserted at a random position p within the string. If a character was inserted, then another character is inserted with probability α^2, and so on, until no more characters are inserted.

4. APPLYING MEMETIC ALGORITHMS

The whole test suite generation presented in the previous section is a global optimization technique, which means that we are trying to optimize an entire candidate solution towards the global optimum (maximum coverage). Search operations in global search can lead to large jumps in the search space. In contrast, local search explores the immediate neighborhood. For example, if we have a test suite consisting of X test cases of average length L, then the probability of mutating one particular primitive value in there is $\frac{1}{X} \times \frac{1}{L}$. However, evolving a primitive value to a target value may require many steps, and so global search can easily exceed the search budget before finding a solution. This is a problem that local search can overcome.

4.1 Local Search on Method Call Sequences

The aim of the local search is to optimize the values in one particular test case of a test suite. When local search is applied to a test case, EvoSuite iterates over its sequence of statements from the last to the first, and for each statement applies a local search dependent on the type of the statement. Local search is performed for the following types of statements: primitive statements, method statements, constructor statements, field statements and array statements.

4.1.1 *Primitive Statements*

Booleans and Enumerations: For Boolean variables the only option is to flip the value. For enumerations, an exploratory move consists of replacing the enum value with any other value, and if the exploratory move was successful, we iterate over all enumeration values.

Integer Datatypes: For integer variables (which includes all flavors such as `byte`, `short`, `char`, `int`, `long`) the possible exploratory moves are $+1$ and -1. The exploratory move decides the direction of the pattern move. If an exploratory move to $+1$ was successful, then with every iteration I of the pattern search we add $\delta = 2^I$ to the variable. If $+1$ was not successful, -1 is used as exploratory move, and if successful, subsequently δ is subtracted.

Floating Point Datatypes: For floating point variables (`float`, `double`) we use the same approach as originally defined by Harman and McMinn [13] for handling floating point numbers with the AVM. Exploratory moves are performed for a range of precision values p, where the precision ranges from 0–7 for `float` variables, and from 0–15 for `double` values. Exploratory moves are applied using $\delta = 2^I \times dir \times 10^{-p}$. Here dir denotes either $+1$ or -1, and I is the number of the iteration, which is 0 during exploratory moves. If an exploratory move was successful, then pattern moves are made by increasing I when calculating δ.

Strings: For string variables, exploratory moves are slightly more complicated: To determine if local search on a string variable is necessary, we first apply n random mutations on the string[1]. These mutations are the same as described in Section 3.3. If any of the n probing mutations changed the fitness, then we know that the string has some effect on it, regardless of whether the change resulted in an improvement or not. As discussed in Section 3.3, string values affect the fitness through a range of Boolean conditions that are used in branches; these conditions are transformed such that the branch distance also gives guidance on strings. If the probing on a string showed that it affects the fitness, then we apply a systematic local search on the string. The operations on the string must reflect the distance estimation applied on string comparisons:

Deletion: First, every single character is removed and the fitness value is checked. If the fitness did not improve, the character is kept in the string.

Change: Second, every single character is replaced with every possible other character; for practical reasons, we restrict the search to ASCII characters. If a replacement is successful, we move to the next character. If a character was not successfully replaced, the original character stays in place.

Insertion: Third, we insert new characters. Because the fitness evaluation requires test execution, trying to insert every possible character at every possible position would be too expensive – yet this is what would be required when using the standard Levenshtein distance (edit distance) as distance metric. Consequently, we only attempt to insert characters at the front and the back, and adapt the distance function for strings accordingly.

The distance function for two strings $s1$ and $s2$ used during the search is (c.f. [15]):

$$\text{distance}(s1,s2) = |\text{length}(s1) - \text{length}(s2)| + \sum_{i=0}^{\min(\text{length}(s1),\text{length}(s2))} \text{distance}(s1[i],s2[i])$$

4.1.2 *Array Statements*

Local search on arrays concerns the length of an array and the values assigned to the slots of the array. To allow efficient search on the array length, the first step of the local search is to try to remove assignments to array slots. For an array of length n, we first try to remove the assignment at slot $n-1$. If the fitness value remains unchanged, we try to remove the assignment at slot $n-2$, and so on, until we find the highest index n' for which an assignment positively contributes to the fitness value. Then, we apply a regular integer-based local search on the length value of the array, making sure the length does not get smaller than $n'+1$. Once the search has found the best length, we expand the test case with assignments to all slots of the array which are not already assigned in the test case (such assignments may be deleted as part of the regular search). Then, on each assignment to the array we perform a local search, depending on the component type of the array.

4.1.3 *Reference Type Statements*

Statements related to reference values (method statement, constructor statement, field statement) do not allow traditional local search in terms of primitive values. The neighborhood of a complex type in a sequence of calls is huge (e.g., all possible calls on an object with all possible parameter combinations, etc.), such that exhaustive search is not a viable option. Therefore, we apply randomized hill climbing on such statements. This local search consists of repeatedly applying random mutations to the statement, and it is stopped if there are R consecutive mutations that did not improve the fitness (in our experiments, $R = 10$).

We use the following mutations for this randomized hill climbing:

- Replace the statement with a random call returning the same type.
- Replace a parameter (for method and constructor statements) or the receiving object (for field and method statements) with any other value of the same type available in the test case.
- If the call creates a non-primitive object, add a random method call on the object after the statement.

The fitness function described in Section 3 requires that every branch is executed twice, such that there is at least one run we can optimize towards executing the branch to one direction, without losing the other direction. If during local search we determine that there is a branch that is only executed once, as a further optimization we duplicate its test case within the test suite.

4.2 Memetic Algorithm

Given the ability to perform local search on the individuals of a global optimization there is the question of how

[1]In theory, static analysis could also be used to determine when a string is a data dependency of one of the target branches; however, as the method sequences may use many different classes that are not known ahead of time, this is non-trivial.

Table 1: Case Study Classes

"Branches" is the number of branches reported by EvoSuite; "LOC" refers to the number of non-commenting source code lines reported by JavaNCSS (*http://www.kclee.de/clemens/java/javancss*).

Project	Class	LOC	Branches
Roops	IntArrayWithoutExceptions	64	43
Roops	LinearWithoutOverflow	223	93
Roops	FloatArithmetic	68	49
Roops	IA.WithArrayParameters	30	29
SCS	Cookie	18	13
SCS	DateParse	32	39
SCS	Stemmer	345	344
SCS	Ordered4	11	29
NanoXML	XMLElement	661	310
Commons CLI	CommandLine	87	45
JDOM	Attribute	138	65
Commons Codec	DoubleMetaphone	579	504
java.util	ArrayList	151	70
NCS	Bessj	80	29
Commons Math	FastFourierTransformer	290	135
Joda Time	DateTimeFormat	356	434

to integrate these techniques. Often, MAs are implemented such that individuals can perform Lamarckian or Baldwinian learning immediately after reproduction [20]. This, however, raises the questions of how often to apply the individual learning, on which individuals it should be applied, and how long it should be done. Because local search can be very expensive, we would like to direct the learning towards the better individuals of the population, such that newly generated genetic material is more likely to directly contribute towards the solution.

In EvoSuite, local search is applied at regular intervals; the rate at which it is applied is the first parameter of local search. When local search is applied, we iterate over the population ranked by their fitness, such that the first individual to be improved is the best individual of the search, then the second best, and so on. Thus, as a second parameter, there is a search budget for this local search.

5. EVALUATION

The presented techniques depend on a number of parameters, and so evaluation needs to be carefully done with respect to these. We therefore aim to empirically answer the following three research questions:

RQ1: Does local search improve the performance of whole test suite generation?

RQ2: Which parameter combination gives the best results?

RQ3: How do the results vary based on the available search budget?

5.1 Experimental Setup

To answer the research questions, we first need to decide for how long and how often to run local search in the MA; these are the two parameters discussed in Section 4.2. Because how often we apply local search depends on the number X of generations, how much local search is actually done is dependent on the population size. Consequently, we also had to consider the population size when designing the experiments. We also considered seeding from bytecode [8] as a further parameter to experiment with, as we expected it to have a large impact on the performance in the cases in which local search is successful (and this is confirmed in the experiments). In total, we had four different parameters to experiment with.

For our evaluation, we used the classes already used in previous experiments [4], but had to exclude those on which EvoSuite trivially achieves 100% coverage. In the choice of a variegated set of classes to experiment with, we tried to strike a balance among the different kinds of classes. To this end, beside classes coming from the case study in [4], we also included four benchmark classes on integer and floating point calculations from the Roops[2] benchmark suite for object-oriented testing, This results in a total of 16 classes, of which some characteristics are given in Table 1.

The use of only 16 classes was necessitated by the complex evaluation setup. In this paper, we study the effects of four different parameters. For population size, local search budget and rate we considered five different values, i.e., $\{5, 25, 50, 75, 100\}$, and for seeding two (on/off). We also included further configurations without local search (i.e., the default GA in EvoSuite), but still considering the different combinations of population size and seeding.

On each class, for each parameter, we ran EvoSuite 30 times with different random seeds to take into account their random nature. In each run, the stopping criterion was a 10 minute timeout. Thus, in total the experiments took $((2 \times 5^3) + (2 \times 5)) \times (30 \times 10 \times 16)/(60 \times 24) = 866$ days of computational time, which required the use of a cluster of computers. During these runs, EvoSuite was configured using the optimal configuration determined in our previous experiments on tuning [4].

5.2 Results

For both the cases in which seeding was used and not, we analyzed the 125 configurations using MA, and chose the one that resulted with highest average coverage over the 16 classes in the case study. The same is done for the basic GA, i.e., we evaluated which configuration of the population size gave best results. We call these four configurations (two for MA, and two for GA) "tuned". Table 2 shows the comparison between the tuned MA and tuned GA configuration based on whether seeding was used.

To evaluate the statistical and practical differences among the different settings, we followed the guidelines in [3]. Statistical difference is evaluated with a two-tailed Mann-Whitney U-test, whereas the magnitude of improvement is quantified with the Vargha-Delaney standardized effect size $\hat{A}_{12}$.

Results in Table 2 answer **RQ1** by clearly showing, with high statistical confidence, that the MA outperforms the standard GA in many, but not all, cases. For classes such as `Cookie`, improvements are as high as a $87 - 55 = 32\%$ average coverage difference (when seeding is not used).

> **RQ1:** *The MA achieved up to a 32% higher branch coverage than the standard GA.*

One thing that is clearly visible in Table 2 is that seeding, as expected [8], leads to higher results. On one hand, when seeding is not used, the difference in average coverage between the MA and the GA is $86 - 79 = 7\%$. On the other hand, when seeding is used, the difference is $89 - 88 = 1\%$. At a first look, such an improvement might be considered low. But the statistics in Table 2 points out a relatively high average 0.61 effect size, with four classes having a strong statistical difference. This is not in contrast with the 1% difference in the raw values of the achieved coverage. What the

[2] http://code.google.com/p/roops/

Table 2: Comparison of average coverage obtained by the tuned MA and by the tuned GA. Effect sizes ($\hat{A}_{12}$) with statistically significant difference at 0.05 level are shown in bold. Data are divided based on whether seeding was used or not.

Case Study	Without Seeding			With Seeding		
	MA	GA	$\hat{A}_{12}$	MA	GA	$\hat{A}_{12}$
roops.core.bv32.arr.noex.IntArrayWithoutExceptions	0.90	0.86	**0.91**	0.92	0.92	0.57
roops.core.bv32.linear.noex.gods.LinearWithoutOverflow	0.98	0.74	**1.00**	0.98	0.92	**1.00**
roops.extended.bv32.floats.FloatArithmetic	0.65	0.49	**1.00**	0.86	0.86	0.50
scs.Cookie	0.87	0.55	**0.94**	0.95	0.95	0.52
scs.DateParse	0.87	0.69	**1.00**	1.00	1.00	0.50
net.n3.nanoxml.XMLElement	0.98	0.98	0.52	0.98	0.98	0.54
org.apache.commons.cli.CommandLine	0.98	0.98	0.50	0.97	0.97	0.49
org.jdom.Attribute	0.84	0.79	**0.99**	0.86	0.86	0.57
org.apache.commons.codec.language.DoubleMetaphone	0.75	0.71	**0.98**	0.84	0.82	**0.76**
java2.util2.ArrayList	0.94	0.94	0.48	0.94	0.94	0.50
scs.Stemmer	0.72	0.73	0.47	0.74	0.72	**0.77**
ncs.Bessj	0.97	0.96	**0.57**	0.97	0.97	0.50
org.apache.commons.math.transform.FastFourierTransformer	0.63	0.62	0.42	0.62	0.63	0.53
org.joda.time.format.DateTimeFormat	0.81	0.74	**1.00**	0.83	0.77	**1.00**
scs.Ordered4	0.97	0.95	0.61	0.95	0.95	0.46
roops.extended.bv32.arr.noex.IntArrayWithoutExceptionsWithArrayParameters	0.90	0.90	0.50	0.90	0.90	0.50
Average	0.86	0.79	0.74	0.89	0.88	0.61

data in Table 2 suggest is that, when seeding is employed, there are still some branches that are not covered with the GA, and so require the local search of the MA to be reached.

To answer **RQ2** we can look at the configuration that gave the best result on average. This configuration uses an MA algorithm with seeding, small population size (five individuals), low rate of local search (every 75 generations), and a small budget of five fitness evaluations for local search. In other words, on average the best result is achieved using local search infrequently and with a low budget. This is surprising, and in Table 2 we see that the results change significantly between individual classes. This suggests that the benefit of local search is highly dependent on the problem at hand. For example, in a class with many string inputs, much of the budget may be devoted to local search, even if the input strings have no effect on code coverage levels. Although we do see an improvement, even on average, this clearly points out the need for parameter control—in order to adaptively change the local search configuration to the class under test and current state of the search.

At any rate, one problem with parameter tuning is that, given a large set of experiments from which we choose the best configuration, such a configuration could be too specific for the employed case study [4]. This is a common problem that in Machine Learning is called *overfitting* [19].

To reduce the threats of this possible issue, we applied a k-fold cross validation on our case study (for more details, see for example [19]). Briefly, we divided the case study in $k = 16$ groups, chose the best configuration out of the 250 on $k-1$ groups (training), and calculated its performance on the remaining group (validation). This process is then repeated k times, each time using a different group for the validation. Then, the average of these k performance values on the validation groups is used as an estimate of actual performance of tuning on the entire case study (the "tuned" configuration) when applied on other new classes (i.e., does the tuning process overfit the data?).

The obtained estimate for best MA configuration was 0.89, which is the same as the average value 0.89 in Table 2. Therefore, the best parameter configuration we found is not overfitted to the case study examples.

> **RQ2**: *The best configuration is the MA with small population size and local search applied infrequently with small search budget.*

The time spent for test data generation (i.e., the testing budget) is perhaps the only parameter that practitioners would need to set. For a successful technology transfer from academic research to industrial practice, the internal details (i.e., how often and how long to run local search inside EvoSuite) of a tool should be hidden from the users, and thus this choice should be made before the tools are released to the public. However, usually the best parameter configuration is strongly related to the testing budget [4].

To answer **RQ3**, we studied the performance of the tuned MA and the tuned GA at different time intervals. In particular, during the execution of EvoSuite, for all the configurations we kept track of the best solution found so far at every minute (for both the GA and the MA). With all these data, at every minute we also calculated the "best" MA configuration (out of 250) and the "best" GA (out of 10) at that particular point in time. By definition, the performance of the "tuned" MA is equal or lower than the one of the "best" MA. Recall that "tuned" is the configuration that gives the "best" results at 10 minutes.

From a practical stand point, it is important to study whether the "tuned" MA is stable compared to the "best" MA. In other words, if we tune a configuration considering a 10 minute timeout, are we still going to get good results (compared to the "best" MA and GA) if the practitioner decides to stop the search beforehand? Or was 10 minutes just a lucky choice? Figure 2 answers these questions by showing that, already from three minutes on, "tuned" performs very similar to the "best" configuration. Furthermore, regardless of the time, there is always a large gap between the "tuned" MA and GA.

Figure 2 shows the results averaged on all 16 classes in the case study. Thanks to the relatively small number of classes, in Figure 3 we can show the time analysis for each class

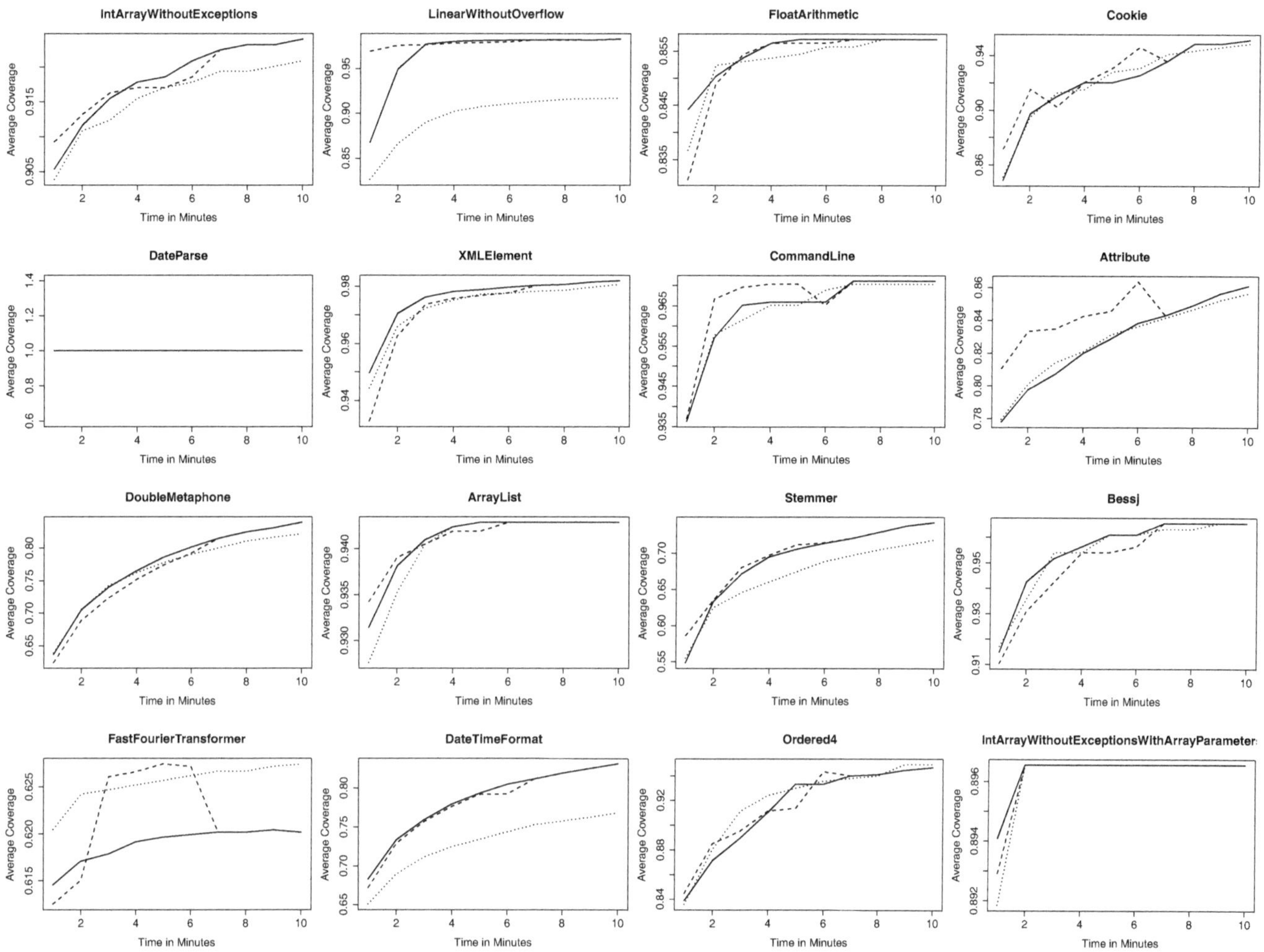

Figure 3: For each class in the case study, average coverage at different points in time for the "best" GA (dotted line), "best" MA (dashed line) and "tuned" MA at 10 minutes (solid line).

individually. The results provide interesting further insight by showing very different behaviors among classes. This stresses the importance of a rigorous empirical procedure when testing techniques are analyzed.

A peculiar result in Figure 3 is that, for the best MA, the performance is not monotonically increasing through time (as it is in Figure 2). This is particularly evident for the class `FastFourierTransformer`. The reason is that, at each point (minute) in time, we are considering the configuration with highest coverage averaged over all the 16 classes. Although on average the performance improves monotonically (Figure 2), on single classes in isolation everything could in theory happen (Figure 3).

> **RQ3**: *The best configuration only differs for small search budgets, and is consistent across higher budgets.*

6. THREATS TO VALIDITY

This paper compares the whole test suite generation approach based on a Genetic Algorithm to a hybrid version that uses a Memetic Algorithm with local search. Threats to *construct validity* are on how the performance of a testing technique is defined. We measured the performance in terms of branch coverage. However, in practice we might not want a much larger test suite if the achieved coverage is only slightly higher. Furthermore, this performance measure does not take into account how difficult it will be to manually evaluate the test cases and to add assert statements (i.e., to check the correctness of the outputs).

Threats to *internal validity* might come from how the empirical study was carried out. To reduce the probability of having faults in our testing framework, it has been carefully tested. But it is well known that testing alone cannot prove the absence of defects. Furthermore, randomized algorithms are affected by chance. To cope with this problem, we ran each experiment 30 times, and we followed rigorous statistical procedures to evaluate their results.

There is also the threat to *external validity* regarding the generalization to other types of software, which is common for any empirical analysis. Because of the large number of experiments required, we only used 16 classes for our evaluation. To make claims on generalization we will need to conduct further studies on representative sets of classes.

7. CONCLUSIONS

Whole test suite generation has been shown to be effective at producing test suites with high coverage for object-oriented classes. However, as mutations on any particular

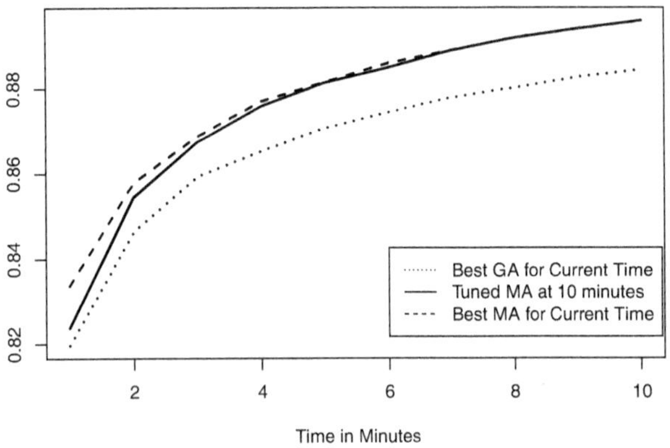

Figure 2: Average coverage at different points in time for the "best" GA (at each minute interval), the MA tuned at 10 minutes, and "best" MA configuration at each minute interval.

statement in a test suite of sequences of method calls have a low probability of occurring, it is not necessarily efficient. To overcome this problem, we have defined a set of local search operators, and extended the Genetic Algorithm used in the EvoSuite test generation tool to a Memetic Algorithm. Experiments on a set of case study classes have demonstrated that this approach results in higher coverage given a fixed search budget. We have observed that the effect is very dependent on the class on which test generation is applied, which makes it difficult to find an optimal parameter configuration. It will therefore be important for future work to make the local search *adaptive*, such that local search operators that lead to success on a particular problem instance are applied more frequently than those that are not.

For more information about EvoSuite please visit:

`http://www.evosuite.org/`

Acknowledgments. This project has been funded by a Google Focused Research Award on "Test Amplification", the Norwegian Research Council, and the EPSRC project "RE-COST" (EP/I010386).

8. REFERENCES

[1] M. Alshraideh and L. Bottaci. Search-based software test data generation for string data using program-specific search operators. *Software Testing, Verification, and Reliability*, 16(3):175–203, 2006.

[2] A. Arcuri. Theoretical analysis of local search in software testing. In *Symposium on Stochastic Algorithms, Foundations and Applications (SAGA)*, pages 156–168, 2009.

[3] A. Arcuri and L. Briand. A hitchhiker's guide to statistical tests for assessing randomized algorithms in software engineering. *Software Testing, Verification and Reliability (STVR)*, 2012. (to appear).

[4] A. Arcuri and G. Fraser. On parameter tuning in search based software engineering. In *International Symposium on Search Based Software Engineering (SSBSE)*, pages 33–47, 2011.

[5] A. Arcuri and X. Yao. A memetic algorithm for test data generation of object-oriented software. In *IEEE Congress on Evolutionary Computation (CEC)*, pages 2048–2055, 2007.

[6] L. Baresi, P. L. Lanzi, and M. Miraz. Testful: an evolutionary test approach for java. In *IEEE Int. Conference on Software Testing, Verification and Validation (ICST)*, pages 185–194, 2010.

[7] R. Ferguson and B. Korel. The chaining approach for software test data generation. *ACM Transactions on Software Engineering and Methodology*, 5(1):63–86, 1996.

[8] G. Fraser and A. Arcuri. The seed is strong: Seeding strategies in search-based software testing. In *IEEE Int. Conference on Software Testing, Verification and Validation (ICST)*, pages 121–130, 2012.

[9] G. Fraser and A. Arcuri. Sound empirical evidence in software testing. In *ACM/IEEE International Conference on Software Engineering (ICSE)*, pages 178–188, 2012.

[10] G. Fraser and A. Arcuri. Whole test suite generation. *IEEE Transactions on Software Engineering*, 39(2):276–291, 2013.

[11] G. Fraser and A. Zeller. Mutation-driven generation of unit tests and oracles. *IEEE Transactions on Software Engineering (TSE)*, 28(2):278–292, 2012.

[12] M. Harman, L. Hu, R. Hierons, J. Wegener, H. Sthamer, A. Baresel, and M. Roper. Testability transformation. *IEEE Transactions on Software Engineering*, 30(1):3–16, 2004.

[13] M. Harman and P. McMinn. A theoretical & empirical analysis of evolutionary testing and hill climbing for structural test data generation. In *ACM Int. Symposium on Software Testing and Analysis (ISSTA)*, pages 73–83, 2007.

[14] M. Harman and P. McMinn. A theoretical and empirical study of search based testing: Local, global and hybrid search. *IEEE Transactions on Software Engineering (TSE)*, 36(2):226–247, 2010.

[15] G. Kapfhammer, P. McMinn, and C. J. Wright. Search-based testing of relational schema integrity constraints across multiple database management systems. In *IEEE Int. Conference on Software Testing, Verification and Validation (ICST)*. IEEE, 2013.

[16] B. Korel. Automated software test data generation. *IEEE Transactions on Software Engineering*, pages 870–879, 1990.

[17] Y. Li and G. Fraser. Bytecode testability transformation. In *Search Based Software Engineering*, volume 6956 of *Lecture Notes in Computer Science*, pages 237–251. Springer, 2011.

[18] P. McMinn. Search-based software test data generation: A survey. *Software Testing, Verification and Reliability*, 14(2):105–156, 2004.

[19] T. Mitchell. *Machine Learning*. McGraw Hill, 1997.

[20] P. Moscato. On evolution, search, optimization, genetic algorithms and martial arts: Towards memetic algorithms. *Caltech Concurrent Computation Program, C3P Report 826*, 1989.

[21] P. Tonella. Evolutionary testing of classes. In *ACM Int. Symposium on Software Testing and Analysis (ISSTA)*, pages 119–128, 2004.

[22] H.-C. Wang and B. Jeng. Structural testing using memetic algorithm. In *Proceedings of the Second Taiwan Conference on Software Engineering*, 2006.

A Theoretical Runtime and Empirical Analysis of Different Alternating Variable Searches for Search-Based Testing

Joseph Kempka
Dept. of Computer Science
University of Sheffield
Sheffield S1 4DP, UK

Phil McMinn
Dept. of Computer Science
University of Sheffield
Sheffield S1 4DP, UK

Dirk Sudholt
Dept. of Computer Science
University of Sheffield
Sheffield S1 4DP, UK

ABSTRACT

The Alternating Variable Method (AVM) has been shown to be a surprisingly effective and efficient means of generating branch-covering inputs for procedural programs. However, there has been little work that has sought to analyse the technique and further improve its performance. This paper proposes two new local searches that may be used in conjunction with the AVM, Geometric and Lattice Search. A theoretical runtime analysis shows that under certain conditions, the use of these searches is proven to outperform the original AVM. These theoretical results are confirmed by an empirical study with four programs, which shows that increases of speed of over 50% are possible in practice.

Categories and Subject Descriptors

F.2.2 [**Analysis of Algorithms and Problem Complexity**]: Non-numerical Algorithms and Problems

Keywords

Search-based software engineering, test data generation, local search, runtime analysis, theory

1. INTRODUCTION

First proposed by Korel [8], the *Alternating Variable Method* (AVM) is a simple local search strategy has been shown to be surprisingly effective for covering branches of procedural programs. In a recent empirical study by Harman and McMinn with a range of C programs, the AVM was able to cover the majority of branches faster than a Genetic Algorithm [6]. This suggests that the underlying fitness landscape for covering individual program branches is relatively simple most of the time, with more "heavy-weight" population-based approaches like Genetic Algorithms only required in a minority of cases [11]. Despite this, there has been relatively little work devoted to analysing and improving the performance of the AVM technique.

The AVM can be regarded as a general framework in which a local search strategy is applied to each individual input vector variable in turn. In this paper, we view the local search strategy to be a component of the overall framework that may be substituted for another. The original AVM applied an accelerated hill climb that we refer to as *Iterated Pattern Search* (IPS), where "exploratory" moves in a direction of fitness improvement are proceeded by larger "pattern" steps in the same direction. In this paper, we propose to replace IPS with two new approaches for exploring individual dimensions of the input vector—*Geometric Search* and *Lattice Search*. Geometric and Lattice Search are elimination searches that are able to find the optimum of a one dimensional function that is unimodal on a given interval. They work by comparing the fitness values of two points at predetermined positions, using the result to select a new but smaller sub-range. The algorithm iterates until it is left with one point. Whereas Geometric Search splits the range in two by comparing the middle two positions, Lattice Search compares points that are offset by Fibonacci numbers.

We examine all three variants of the AVM theoretically and empirically. While prior theoretical runtime analyses of the original AVM with IPS involved specific programs and branches [1, 2], we furnish a more general result, proving that for all unimodal functions Geometric and Lattice Search are faster than IPS, when used in the framework of AVM. In a more general sense, Geometric and Lattice Search converge faster to local optima than IPS. These theoretical results are complemented by an empirical study on open source programs. On most branches our new local searches perform significantly better than IPS. This includes unimodal landscapes, in agreement with our theory, as well as non-unimodal ones, where the assumptions of our theory are not met. This indicates that faster convergence to local optima is beneficial on a broad range of instances. The only departure from this pattern was found for one complex landscape of a type for which—as observed in prior studies [6, 11]—a Genetic Algorithm is significantly better than AVM.

The contributions of this paper are therefore as follows:

1. Two new input variable search strategies for use with the AVM, *Geometric Search* and *Lattice Search* (Section 5).
2. A theoretical runtime analysis of the AVM with Geometric and Lattice Search, with extended results for the original AVM approach employing IPS (Section 4). Geometric and Lattice Search are proved to have faster runtimes for unimodal fitness landscapes (Sections 5.1 and 5.2).
3. An empirical analysis of the AVM, comparing IPS, Geometric and Lattice Search on four programs, including unimodal and non-unimodal functions, complementing our theoretical results on unimodal functions and providing additional evidence that our local searches also speed up search on non-unimodal functions, possibly due to their faster convergence to local optima (Section 6).

We begin by giving important background to search-based testing, the AVM, as well as introducing theoretical runtime analysis.

GECCO'13, July 6–10, 2013, Amsterdam, The Netherlands.

2. BACKGROUND

2.1 Representation and Fitness Function

The fitness function for covering individual program branches is a multivariate function $mf(\vec{x}) \rightarrow \mathbb{R}$, that takes an input vector $\vec{x} = [\, x_1 \; x_2 \; \cdots \; x_n \,]$, i.e. an ordered list of arguments that are passed to a procedure. In this paper, we assume $\vec{x}$ can be modelled as a sequence of integers (i.e., floating point values are permissible so long as a finite precision is used). The fitness function measures how "close" an input vector was to executing a target branch. It is minimised by the search, with a zero value indicating an input that covers the branch. The fitness function has two components. The *approach level* relates to the decision points in the program appearing en route to reaching the target branch. In terms of the program's control dependence graph, the approach level is equal to the number of nodes unexecuted by $\vec{x}$ on which the branch is transitively control dependent. The *branch distance* is computed from the values of variables at predicates where control flow diverged from the target branch. As an example, the branch distance of the predicate $x_1 = x_2$, is given by the formula $|x_1 - x_2|$ (see the survey paper by McMinn [12] for a full list of rules and formulas). Because the maximum branch distance is not known, the normalization function $norm(d(\vec{x})) = 1 - 1.001^{-d(\vec{x})}$ is used, where $d(\vec{x})$ is the raw branch distance and $norm(d(\vec{x}))$ is the normalized branch distance. The full fitness value is computed by normalizing the branch distance and adding it to the approach level, i.e. $mf(\vec{x}) = l(\vec{x}) + norm(d(\vec{x}))$ [18].

2.2 The Alternating Variable Method (AVM)

The AVM can be viewed as a general framework that proceeds from a random starting point in the search space, and works by calling a local search function on each element of the input vector in turn. That is, while the local search is performing "moves" on one component of the vector, the values for all other dimensions remain fixed. If, during this search, a fitness of zero is found, the AVM terminates with the branch-covering input. If, however, a local optimum is reached, the AVM advances to the next element. If fitness cannot be improved after cycling through all elements, the AVM restarts from another randomly-generated input, continuing the search for a branch-covering input until the number of fitness function evaluations exceeds a predefined maximum.

Algorithm 1 describes the AVM framework more formally. The algorithm transforms the multivariate fitness function *mf* into a one dimensional projection f (line 4). The function f is equivalent to evaluating *mf* with an input vector where all components except x_i are set to constants and x_i is substituted by the free parameter x. The function f is passed to a local search algorithm called **local_search**, along with x_i, the starting point for the search. The fitness function keeps track of the number of fitness evaluations, maintaining a mapping of previously evaluated vectors to their corresponding fitness values. Once a branching-covering input vector is found, or when the number of evaluations exceeds the maximum (i.e., the search has failed), an exception is raised to terminate the search (not shown in our algorithms for space and simplicity).

Algorithm 1 The AVM Framework

```
1:  while true do
2:      let x⃗ := random(), i = 1, c = 0
3:      while c < size(x⃗) do
4:          let f : mf ↦ mf((x⃗ \ x_i) ∪ {x})
5:          let x⃗' := local_search(f, x_i)
6:          if mf(x⃗') < mf(x⃗) then
7:              let x⃗ := x⃗', c := 0
8:          else
9:              let c := c + 1
10:         let i := i mod (size(x⃗)) + 1
```

2.3 Runtime Analysis

Runtime analysis has established itself as a leading theory in randomised search heuristics, with many new results in the last 10–15 years [16, 3]. Problems studied in search-based software engineering include computing input-output sequences [9, 10], test input generation [2], and project scheduling [14].

Arcuri, Lehre, and Yao [2] were the first to present an runtime analysis of search-based input generation. They focussed on the triangle classification problem, which involves three integer variables describing side lengths of a potential triangle. The task is to classify the input as a scalene, equilateral, or isosceles triangle, or not representing a triangle. Their analysis was limited to the time for covering the *equilateral* branch of the problem. If the range contains n numbers, the expected time of random search is $\Theta(n^2)$. Hill climbing needs expected time $\Theta(n)$, i. e., in every iteration a single variable is increased or decreased by 1. For the AVM they proved an upper bound of $O((\log n)^2)$ and a weaker lower bound of $\Omega(\log n)$ [2].

Later on, Arcuri [1] extended the analysis of the AVM to all branches of the triangle classification problem, showing that the expected running time is bounded from above by $O((\log n)^2)$ on all branches. Branches with many global optima only need $O(\log n)$ time. In this paper we extend his results by proving an upper bound of $O((\log n)^2)$ for *all* strictly unimodal functions (and functions with further global optima).

3. PRELIMINARIES

A function f is called *strictly unimodal* if it only has a single local optimum. If f is to be minimised (the case of maximisation is symmetric) this means that

$$f(\ell_1) > f(\ell_2) > f(\text{opt}) < f(r_1) < f(r_2)$$

for all $\ell_1 < \ell_2 < \text{opt} < r_1 < r_2$, where opt is the global minimum of f. In other words, if D is the domain of f, f is strictly decreasing on $D \cap (-\infty, \text{opt}]$ and strictly increasing on $D \cap [\text{opt}, \infty)$.

We consider the running time of local searches used within the framework of AVM. Thereby we count the number of function evaluations or fitness evaluations made by local search until an optimum is found for the first time. The motivation for considering fitness evaluations is that such an evaluation is the most costly operation as it involves simulating the program. In some cases we count *unique fitness evaluations*, i. e., the number of *different* search points evaluated. This reflects the fact that it is easy to cache past evaluations, so evaluating the same point twice only incurs insignificant additional cost.

In our analyses we consider minimising a function $f \colon D \rightarrow \mathbb{R}$ for a finite domain $D \subset \mathbb{Z}$. For ease of presentation, we assume $f(x) = \infty$ for all $x \notin D$. This includes settings where f is the branch distance before or after normalisation. The precise choice of a normalisation function is irrelevant in our work; all local searches analysed in this work only use information about the ranks of search points. So every strictly increasing normalisation function leads to the same sequences of search points queried and hence the same performance.

In previous work [1, 2] the authors derived performance results with regard to the size n of the domain, e. g., $\{1, \ldots, n\}$ or $\{-n/2 + 1, \ldots, n/2\}$. Here we consider the initial distance d to the optimum instead, as this distance governs the running time of all local searches considered in this work. As $d \leq n$ upper running time bounds using d are generally stronger than those using n.

4. ANALYSIS OF THE ORIGINAL AVM

4.1 Original AVM with IPS

The original AVM due to Korel [8] uses the following local search, shown in Algorithm 2, that we name *Iterated Pattern Search* (IPS). Starting at x, IPS first evaluates points $x-1$ and $x+1$ to identify a gradient. Unless x is a local optimum, it then performs a so-called pattern search, moving in the direction of decreasing f-values. The step size doubles with each step, so when the gradient is towards increasing indices IPS traverses the points

$$x, x+1, x+1+2, x+1+2+4, \dots, x+1+2+4+\dots+2^j.$$

Since $\sum_{i=0}^{j} 2^j = 2^{j+1}-1$ this sequence is equal to

$$x, x+2^1-1, x+2^2-1, x+2^3-1, \dots, x+2^{j+1}-1.$$

Pattern search stops if the next point does not improve the fitness, which happens on unimodal functions when the optimum is being overshot. This process is iterated; that is, IPS then starts another exploration. If the function is unimodal, IPS gets close to the optimum over time. However, this line search can be relatively slow. The reason is that IPS accelerates during exploration, but after overshooting the optimum IPS starts from scratch.

Algorithm 2 Iterated Pattern Search, starting at $x \in D$

```
while true do
    if f(x − 1) ≥ f(x) and f(x + 1) ≥ f(x) return x
    if f(x − 1) < f(x + 1) then let k := −1 else let k := 1
    while f(x + k) < f(x) do
        let x := x + k, k := 2k
```

4.2 Upper Bound for Original AVM

We start our investigations with Iterated Pattern Search, the local search used in the original AVM [8]. An upper bound $O(\log^2 n)$ (for domain size n) was proven for AVM with IPS in [2], for the special case that there is a linear relationship between the function value and the distance to the optimum. The following statement holds for arbitrary strictly unimodal functions.

THEOREM 1. *Consider iterated pattern search on a strictly unimodal function f where d denotes the initial distance from the starting point to the optimum. Then IPS finds an optimum after querying at most $4 + 8\log d + (\log d)^2$ values. This also holds for functions f that result from a strictly unimodal function f' and assigning function values* $\arg\min(f')$ *to further points.*

The last statement implies that we get an upper bound of order $O((\log d)^2)$ for many further common functions. Examples are functions where opt is a global optimum and all points $x > \text{opt}$ or $x < \text{opt}$ are global optima as well. In particular, all functions considered in Arcuri's work [1] are covered by this statement. However, for functions with many global optima the upper bound may not be tight [1].

Proof of Theorem 1. We allow the algorithm to traverse points outside of D, but assume that all $x' \notin D$ are worse than all $x \in D$.

We consider *passes* of IPS, corresponding to one iteration of the outer while loop in Algorithm 2: a pass starts with an exploratory search examining the two neighbouring solutions of the current point (index ± 1). It then performs a pattern search, doubling the distance travelled in each step. Note that a pass starting with the optimum makes exactly 3 queries. If a pass queries points up to a distance of $\sum_{j=0}^{i} 2^j = 2^{i+1}-1$ from the initial value, it queries $i+3$ values.

Without loss of generality assume that the current position is 0 and the optimum is at d. If $d = 1$ we need 4 queries, hence we assume in the following that $d \geq 2$. We claim that within at most 2 passes the distance to the optimum has been reduced to at most $\lfloor d/2 \rfloor$. Let i be the unique integer such that $2^i - 1 \leq d < 2^{i+1}-1$. Note that pattern search queries $2^i - 1$ and $2^{i+1}-1$ as the points are strictly improving in $[0, 2^i - 1]$. We consider two cases. First assume that $2^i - 1$ is better than $2^{i+1}-1$. Then pattern search stops at $2^i - 1$ and since $d \leq 2^{i+1} - 2$ the new distance to the optimum is at most $\lfloor d/2 \rfloor$. The number of queries made is at most $i+3$, and since $d \geq 2^i - 1 \geq 2^{i-1}$ this is at most $\lfloor \log d \rfloor + 4$.

Now consider the case that $2^i - 1$ is worse than $2^{i+1}-1$. This implies $2^i \leq d \leq 2^{i+1}-2$. Then pattern search will query $2^{i+2}-1$ and stop at $2^{i+1}-1$ as $2^{i+2}-1$ is worse than $2^{i+1}-1$. The second pass will traverse positions $2^{i+1}-2^1, 2^{i+1}-2^2, 2^{i+1}-2^3 \dots$. Since by unimodality all points in $[0, 2^i]$ are increasingly better, pattern search will stop at some $2^{i+1}-2^j$ with $0 \leq j \leq i$. As the optimum must be within $[\max(2^i, 2^{i+1}-2^{j+1}), 2^{i+1}-2^{j-1}]$, and the new current point is $2^{i+1}-2^j$, the distance between the current point and the optimum has decreased to at most 2^j for $j < i$ and 2^{i-1} for $j = i$. In both cases the new distance is bounded by $\lfloor d/2 \rfloor$.

In the worst case, we need one pass querying up to $i+4$ values, and a second pass querying up to $i+3$ points. The total is $2i + 7 \leq 2\lfloor \log d \rfloor + 7$ as $d \geq 2^i$.

The total number of queries made, $T(d)$, is then subject to the following recurrence: $T(0) = 3$, $T(1) = 4$, and $T(d) \leq 2\lfloor \log d \rfloor + 7 + T(\lfloor d/2 \rfloor)$ for $d > 1$. Due to all floor functions, we get the same recurrence for $T(d)$ as for $T(2^{\lfloor \log d \rfloor})$. Solving the latter gives

$$\begin{aligned} T(d) &\leq \sum_{k=1}^{\lfloor \log d \rfloor} (2k+7) + T(1) \\ &\leq 7\lfloor \log d \rfloor + 2 \cdot \frac{\lfloor \log d \rfloor (\lfloor \log d \rfloor + 1)}{2} + T(1) \\ &\leq 4 + 8\log d + (\log d)^2. \end{aligned}$$

The last remark of the statement holds true since adding further global optima can only decrease the expected time until some global optimum is found. □

4.3 Original AVM is Slow in the Worst Case

The following result shows that the lower bound from Theorem 1 is asymptotically tight. Both bounds together show that the worst-case running time of IPS is of order $\Theta((\log d)^2)$, when initial points up to distance d are allowed.

THEOREM 2. *Consider iterated pattern search minimising an arbitrary unimodal function f. If there are feasible starting points with distances $0, 1, \dots, d$ to the optimum, the worst case number of unique fitness evaluations is at least*

$$\frac{(\log d)^2}{10} - O(\log d).$$

Proof. We can assume w. l. o. g. that the optimum is at position 0. If the domain D is bounded on one side, we consider an extended function f' where the domain is $\mathbb{Z}$ and $f(x) = \infty$ for all $x \notin D$.

Define $T_s(\ell, r)$ as the number of different search points evaluated when IPS starts in s, counting evaluations from the set $\{\ell, \dots, r\}$ only. If $s \notin D$ we let $T_s(\ell, r) := \infty$. Let $T(\ell, r) := \min\{T_\ell(\ell, r), T_r(\ell, r)\}$ be the fastest time starting from ℓ or r.

Define $\ell_0 = r_0 = 0$ and $T(\ell_0, r_0) = 1$. Assume we have $\ell_i \leq 0 \leq r_i$ for some $i \in \mathbb{N}_0$, such that ℓ_i and r_i are not both outside f's domain. Let $\Delta_i := 2^{\lfloor \log(r_i - \ell_i) \rfloor + 1}$ for $i \in \mathbb{N}$ and $\Delta_0 := 1$ be the smallest power of 2 such that $\Delta_i > r_i - \ell_i$.

We define new points ℓ_{i+1}, r_{i+1} according to the following case distinction. First assume $f(\ell_i) > f(r_i)$, which implies $f(x) > f(r_i)$ for all $x \leq \ell_i$. It also implies that r_i exists. Let $r_{i+1} := r_i + \Delta_i - 1$ and $\ell_{i+1} := r_i - 2\Delta_i + 1$. If IPS starts at r_{i+1}, it will sample points at

$$r_{i+1}, r_{i+1} - (2^1 - 1), \ldots, r_{i+1} - (2^{\log(\Delta_i)} - 1) = r_i, r_i - \Delta_i$$

and since the fitness improves in every step but the last one, IPS will stop at r_i and restart exploration from there. All points but $r_i - \Delta_i$ are guaranteed to exist and are contained in $\{\ell_{i+1}, \ldots, r_{i+1}\}$; so IPS evaluates $\Delta_i + 1$ different search points from that set before restarting exploration. From r_i IPS needs time at least $T(\ell_i, r_i) - 1$ since so far IPS has evaluated a single search point from the set $\{\ell_i, \ldots, r_i\}$, namely r_i. We thus have established the recurrence

$$T_{\ell_{i+1}}(\ell_{i+1}, r_{i+1}) \geq \Delta_i + T(\ell_i, r_i). \tag{1}$$

Similarly, if ℓ_{i+1} exists and IPS starts from there, it will sample points at

$$\ell_{i+1}, \ell_{i+1}+2^1-1, \ldots, \ell_{i+1}+2^{\log(\Delta_i)}-1 = r_i-\Delta_i, r_i, r_i+2\Delta_i.$$

The fitness improves in each step but the last one, and so IPS will stop at r_i and start exploration from there. Not counting the evaluation of $r_i + 2\Delta_i$, IPS evaluates $\Delta_i + 2$ search points, hence as above we get

$$T_{r_{i+1}}(\ell_{i+1}, r_{i+1}) \geq \Delta_i + T(\ell_i, r_i) + 1. \tag{2}$$

Putting (1) and (2) together, we have shown

$$T(\ell_{i+1}, r_{i+1}) \geq \Delta_i + T(\ell_i, r_i).$$

This also holds when $\ell_{i+1} \notin D$ as then $T_{\ell_{i+1}}(\ell_i, r_i) = \infty$. The case $f(\ell_i) < f(r_i)$ is symmetric, and if $f(\ell_i) = f(r_i)$ we also get the same recurrence as IPS stops at r_i as in the case $f(\ell_i) > f(r_i)$ when starting from ℓ_{i+1} and IPS stops at ℓ_i as on the other case when starting from r_{i+1}.

It follows that

$$T(\ell_i, r_i) \geq \sum_{j=1}^{i-1} \Delta_j + T(\ell_0, r_0) \geq 1 + \sum_{j=1}^{i-1} \log(r_j - \ell_j).$$

Note that for $i \geq 1$ the difference $r_{i+1} - \ell_{i+1}$ does not depend on whether $f(\ell_i) > f(r_i)$ or not, hence w. l. o. g. we use the definition of ℓ_{i+1}, r_{i+1} from the case $f(\ell_i) > f(r_i)$. Along with $\Delta_i \geq r_i - \ell_i + 1$ we get

$$r_{i+1} - \ell_{i+1} = r_i + \Delta_i - 1 - (r_i - 2\Delta_i + 1) = 3\Delta_i - 2 > 3(r_i - \ell_i).$$

Expanding and using $\ell_1 - r_1 = 2$ yields

$$r_{i+1} - \ell_{i+1} > 2 \cdot 3^i.$$

Thus,

$$\begin{aligned} T(\ell_i, r_i) &\geq 1 + \sum_{j=1}^{i-1} \log(2 \cdot 3^{j-1}) \\ &= i + \sum_{j=0}^{i-2} \log(3^j) \\ &= i + \log(3) \cdot \frac{(i-2)(i-1)}{2} > \frac{\log(3)}{2} \cdot i^2 - O(i). \end{aligned}$$

It is easy to verify by induction that $r_i \leq 7^{i-1}$ and $|\ell_i| \leq 7^{i-1}$ for all $i \in \mathbb{N}$. Putting $i := \lfloor \log_7(d) \rfloor + 1$ then gives a lower bound of

$$\frac{\log(3)}{2} \cdot (\log_7(2))^2 \cdot (\log d)^2 - O(\log d) > \frac{(\log d)^2}{10} - O(\log d).$$

□

4.4 Original AVM is Slow on Average

The bad worst-case performance of IPS is not simply due to few unlucky choices of the initial point. In fact, most starting points lead to a running time of order $\Theta((\log d)^2)$. For the specific function $f(x) = |x|$ we show that when the target is chosen such that the distance between starting point and target is uniform in some interval, then we still get a lower bound of order $(\log d)^2$.

Note that $f(x) = |x|$ is quite an easy function as points closer to the optimum 0 are better than points that are further away from it. This encourages IPS to stop at the closest point to the optimum traversed in a pattern search, but we still get a time of $\Omega((\log d)^2)$.

THEOREM 3. *Consider iterated pattern search minimising the function $f(x) = |x|$ such that the target is chosen uniformly at random from $\{-2^i, \ldots, 2^i - 1\}$, for some $i \in \mathbb{N}_0$. The expected number of unique fitness evaluations is at least $\frac{i^2}{6}$.*

Proof. Let $T(i)$ denote the expected number of different search points queried when the target is chosen uniformly at random from $\{-2^i, \ldots, 2^i - 1\}$. The claim $T(i) \geq i^2/6$ is trivial for $i = 0$ and $i = 1$.

If IPS starts at some value $x < 0$ (the case $x > 0$ is symmetric), IPS will start a pattern search exploring points with higher indices, querying points at $x_1 := x + 2^0, x_2 := x + 2^0 + 2^1, x_3 := x + 2^0 + 2^1 + 2^2$, etc. (We do not count a potential evaluation of the point at $x - 1$ since it might not be in the domain of feasible search points.) Let $x_j := x + \sum_{\ell=0}^{j-1} 2^\ell = x + 2^j - 1$ for $1 \leq j \leq i$ be the first search point queried where $x_j \geq 0$. Now IPS will stop pattern search and continue with either x_{j-1} or x_j, depending on which is better. If x_j is better, IPS will also query x_{j+1}; but as this might be out of range, we do not count a potential evaluation of x_{j+1}.

Due to the fitness function used, the point with the smaller absolute value from either x_{j-1} or x_j is better. Note that their index difference is $x_j - x_{j-1} = 2^{j-1}$, so $x_j \in \{0, \ldots, 2^{j-1} - 1\}$. If $x_j \in \{0, \ldots, 2^{j-2} - 1\}$, x_j is better than x_{j-1}, and IPS starts another pass at $\{0, \ldots, 2^{j-2} - 1\}$. Otherwise, x_{j-1} is better and IPS will start another pass at $\{-2^{j-2}, -2^{j-2} + 1, \ldots, -1\}$. All these positions are attained with the same probability, hence we are in the same setting as described in the statement, with $j - 2$ in place of i.

The probability of stopping at x_j being the first point where $x_j \geq 0$ ($x_j \leq 0$ when starting at $x > 0$), for $1 \leq j \leq i$, is $2 \cdot 2^{j-1}/2^{i+1} = 2^{j-i-1}$ as there are $x_j - x_{j-1} = 2^{j-1}$ positions for x where this happens when $x < 0$ and the same holds for $x > 0$. Recall that all initial positions are chosen uniformly at random, and there are 2^{i+1} feasible positions.

While getting to x_j IPS has queried at least $j + 1$ mutually different points $x, x_1, \ldots, x_j$. Then the remaining time is at least $T(j - 2) - 1$; the reason for subtracting 1 is that we have already queried x_j. Defining $T(-1) := 0$, we have established the following recurrence

$$\begin{aligned} T(i) &\geq \sum_{j=1}^{i} 2^{j-i-1} \cdot (j + 1 + T(j-2) - 1) \\ &= \sum_{j=1}^{i} j \cdot 2^{j-i-1} + \sum_{j=1}^{i} 2^{j-i-1} \cdot T(j-2) \\ &= \sum_{j=0}^{i-1} (j+1) \cdot 2^{j-i} + \sum_{j=0}^{i-2} 2^{j-i+1} \cdot T(j) \\ &= i - 1 + 2^{-i} + \sum_{j=0}^{i-2} 2^{j-i+1} \cdot T(j) \end{aligned}$$

having used $\sum_{j=0}^{i-1} (j+1) \cdot 2^{j-i} = i - 1 + 2^{-i}$.

Assume for an induction that $T(j) \geq j^2/6$ all $0 \leq j < i$. Then

$$\begin{aligned} T(i) &\geq i - 1 + 2^{-i} + \sum_{j=0}^{i-1} 2^{j-i} \cdot \frac{j^2}{6} \\ &= i - 1 + 2^{-i} + \frac{1}{6} \cdot \sum_{j=0}^{i-1} 2^{j-i} \cdot j^2 \\ &= i - 1 + 2^{-i} + \frac{1}{6} \cdot (-4i + 6 + i^2 - 6 \cdot 2^{-i}) \\ &= \frac{i^2}{6} + \frac{i}{3} \end{aligned}$$

which implies the claim. □

5. NEW LOCAL SEARCHES FOR THE AVM

We now show that other local searches used in the framework provided by AVM only require $\Theta(\log d)$ evaluations instead of $\Theta((\log d)^2)$. This yields significant speedups over AVM's original local search method IPS, if the initial distance d to the optimum is not very small.

Our results formally only hold for unimodal functions, but they also indicate more generally that our new local searches converge faster to local optima. The reason is that the basin of attraction around a local optimum has the properties of a unimodal function. So, our analysis is partly applicable in a much wider context; exploring this further is left for future work.

5.1 AVM with Geometric Search

We propose more clever local searches that locate the optimum of a unimodal function more efficiently after the first exploration. The following *Geometric Search* uses a variant of binary search. The idea is to perform a pattern search, and then to use binary search to home in on the target. We will see that then the optimum of any unimodal function is found in time logarithmic in the initial distance. We call it "Geometric Search" since the initial pattern search is performed with a geometric sequence of numbers.

Algorithm 3 Geometric search, starting at $x \in D$

if $f(x-1) \geq f(x)$ **and** $f(x+1) \geq f(x)$ **return** x
if $f(x-1) < f(x+1)$ **then let** $k := -1$ **else let** $k := 1$
while $f(x+k) < f(x)$ **do**
  let $x := x + k$, $k := 2k$
let $\ell := \min(x - k/2, x + k)$, $r := \max(x - k/2, x + k)$
while $\ell \neq r$ **do**
  if $f(\lfloor(\ell+r)/2\rfloor) < f(\lfloor(\ell+r)/2\rfloor + 1)$ **then**
    $r := \lfloor(\ell+r)/2\rfloor$
  else
    $\ell := \lfloor(\ell+r)/2\rfloor + 1$
return ℓ

Geometric Search uses the same "geometric" pattern search as IPS, but afterwards uses a variant of binary search to narrow down the optimum. Thereby we are using that if pattern search queries search points x_{j-1}, x_j, x_{j+1}, stopping at x_j, we know that $f(x_{j-1}) > f(x_j) \leq f(x_{j+1})$. This implies that, if f is unimodal, the global minimum must lie in the set $\{x_{j-1}, \ldots, x_{j+1}\}$.

THEOREM 4. *Consider a one-dimensional search on a unimodal function where* d *denotes the initial distance from the starting point to the optimum. Then Geometric Search finds an optimum after querying at most* $3 \log d + 5$ *search points.*

Proof. Let i be such that $2^i \leq d < 2^{i+1}$. By the same arguments as in the proof of Theorem 1 pattern search stops at either $2^i - 1$ or $2^{i+1} - 1$ after querying at most $i + 3$ points. We pessimistically assume that it stops at $2^{i+1} - 1$, which results in the algorithm putting $\ell := 2^i - 1$ and $r := 2^{i+2} - 1$. We claim that each iteration of binary search updates ℓ, r towards ℓ', r' such that $r' - \ell' \leq \lfloor(r - \ell)/2\rfloor$. If $r' = \lfloor(\ell + r)/2\rfloor$ we have

$$r' - \ell' = \left\lfloor \frac{\ell + r}{2} \right\rfloor - \ell = \left\lfloor \frac{r - \ell}{2} \right\rfloor.$$

Otherwise, $\ell' = \lfloor \frac{\ell+r}{2} \rfloor + 1$ and using $-\lfloor x \rfloor - 1 \leq \lfloor -x \rfloor$ for $x \in \mathbb{R}$ we get

$$r' - \ell' = r - \left\lfloor \frac{\ell + r}{2} \right\rfloor - 1 \leq r + \left\lfloor -\frac{\ell + r}{2} \right\rfloor = \left\lfloor \frac{r - \ell}{2} \right\rfloor.$$

Initially $r - \ell < 2^{i+2}$, and due to the floor functions we get the same recurrence as for 2^{i+1}. Two queries are needed to replace the current distance by its floored half, ending at 0 with no further queries. Hence we need an additional amount of $2i + 2$ queries, leading to a total of $3i + 5 \leq 3 \log d + 5$ queries. □

5.2 AVM with Lattice Search

Lattice Search [15] is a refinement of Fibonacci Search [7] for integer domains. It can find the minimum of a unimodal function on a domain of integers $\{1, \ldots, F_n - 1\}$ using $n - 2$ function evaluations [15, page 190], where F_n is the n-th Fibonacci number: $F_1 = 1, F_2 = 1$, and $F_{n+2} = F_n + F_{n+1}$ for $n \in \mathbb{N}$ (Monahan [15, page 190] uses the definition $F_0 = 1, F_1 = 1, F_2 = 2 \ldots$). Search points are evaluated according to Fibonacci numbers in such a way that only one new search points needs to be evaluated in each iteration. This makes Lattice Search faster than Geometric Search.

Our local search using Lattice Search is as follows.

Algorithm 4 Lattice search, starting at $x \in D$

if $f(x-1) \geq f(x)$ **and** $f(x+1) \geq f(x)$ **return** x
if $f(x-1) < f(x+1)$ **then let** $k := -1$ **else let** $k := 1$
while $f(x+k) < f(x)$ **do**
  let $x := x + k$, $k := 2k$
let $\ell := \min(x - k/2, x + k)$, $r := \max(x - k/2, x + k)$
let $n := \min\{n \mid F_n \geq r - l + 2\}$
while $n \neq 3$ **do**
  if $\ell + F_{n-1} - 1 \leq r$ **and** $f(\ell + F_{n-2} - 1) \geq f(\ell + F_{n-1} - 1)$ **then**
    let $\ell := \ell + F_{n-2}$
  let $n := n - 1$
return ℓ

Note that the initial pattern search is done in a geometric fashion, i.e., increasing the step size geometrically as in IPS and Geometric Search. There is a related search technique called *Fibonaccian Searching* [4] (not to be confused with Fibonacci Search) where pattern search is done by means of Fibonacci numbers. The reason that we are using geometric pattern search is that it is generally faster.

Lattice Search further improves the leading constant preceding the $\log d$ term; using Fibonacci numbers to search for the optimum in the interval identified by pattern search is more efficient than the binary search used in our Geometric Search procedure.

THEOREM 5. *Consider a one-dimensional search on a unimodal function where* d *denotes the initial distance from the starting point to the optimum. Then Lattice Search finds an optimum after querying at most* $2.45 \log d + O(1)$ *search points.*

Due to space restrictions, we omit the proof. It follows from previous arguments, the analysis of Lattice Search [15, page 190] and rewriting the following closed formula for Fibonacci numbers:

$$F_n = \frac{(1+\sqrt{5})^n - (1-\sqrt{5})^n}{2^n \cdot \sqrt{5}}.$$

6. EMPIRICAL EXPERIMENTS

We now provide an empirical comparison of AVM using our different local searches to complement our theoretical results. We first show results on a simple function, designed to provide empirically confirmation of our proofs on a unimodal function, and actual differences in performance in practice. However, real-world programs are not so straightforward, involving fitness landscapes of varying shapes. Therefore, following an initial simple experiment, we continue onto performing experiments with four real-world programs.

6.1 Experiments with "is_zero" ($f(x) = |x|$)

We first study a simple and illustrative problem with just a single variable, as shown in the following program below:

```
void is_zero(int x) {
  if (x == 0) { /* TARGET BRANCH */ }
}
```

The goal is to find an input x that is equal to zero. The approach level is zero (since the branch is always reached), and the branch distance is $norm(|x|)$. Because our local searches do not rely on comparing absolute values, but instead their corresponding ranks, this problem is equivalent to minimizing the fitness function $f(x) = |x|$ (where the branch distance is not normalised) as analysed in Theorem 3.

Studying this simple program allows us to isolate the impact of the range and the initial distance d from the optimum on the running time of AVM. Our theoretical results show that, when the starting point is chosen uniformly at random from a set $\{-d, \ldots, d-1\}$ for d a power of 2, AVM with IPS will take $\Theta((\log d)^2)$ steps whereas AVM with Geometric Search or Lattice Search will succeed in only $\Theta(\log d)$ steps.

The performance of IPS, Geometric and Lattice in optimising the objective function, $f(x) = |x|$ was measured over the following ranges $[-d, d-1]$, where $d \in \{1, 2, 4, 8, \ldots 2^{31}\}$. For each range 100 runs of each local search were performed and the number of fitness evaluations to find the global optimum at 0 was counted. In each run the starting position, x_1 was chosen uniformly at random from the corresponding range (including boundaries).

For each range the runtime distributions of the local searches were compared in a pairwise manner using the Mann-Whitney U test. In addition to p-values, the non-parametric Vargha-Delaney statistic $\hat{A}_{12}$ [17], which is computed from mean ranks, is reported as a measure of effect size. It is possible to interpret $\hat{A}_{12}$ as the probability that a run of the first search algorithm takes a larger number of fitness evaluations compared to that of the second search algorithm. The implication is that if $\hat{A}_{12} < 0.5$, then the first local search performs better overall whereas the opposite is true if $\hat{A}_{12} > 0.5$. Also, depending whether the absolute difference: $|\hat{A}_{12} - 0.5|$ is > 0.21, > 0.14, > 0.06 or ≤ 0.06, the corresponding effect size can be divided into the following categories: large, medium, small and negligible.

The results show that for all ranges where $d \geq 2048$, IPS is worse than Geometric ($p \leq 0.0054$ and $\hat{A}_{12} \geq 0.61$) and also worse than Lattice ($p \leq 4.1 \cdot 10^{-8}$ and $\hat{A}_{12} \geq 0.72$). It was also found that for the same ranges Geometric is worse than Lattice ($p \leq 7.9 \cdot 10^{-8}$ and $\hat{A}_{12} \geq 0.72$).

Figure 1 shows how the average performance of each local search scales with increasing domain size. Here the variable, i is related to the logarithm of the distance, i. e. $i = \log_2(d)$.

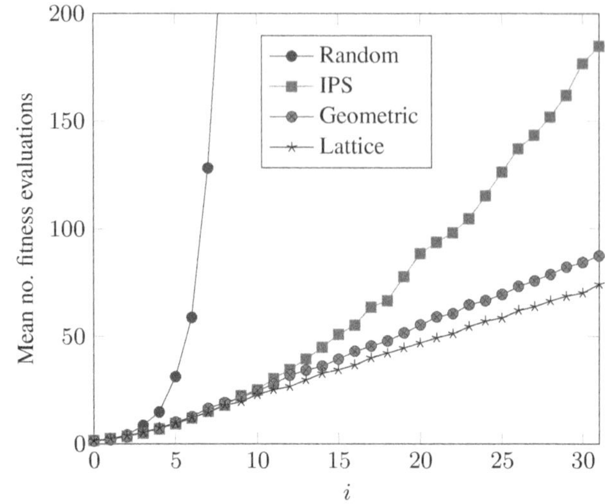

Figure 1: Mean number of fitness evaluations for optimising $f(x) = |x|$ with various local searches. The domain is chosen as $\{-2^i, \ldots, 2^i - 1\}$ for $i \in \{0, \ldots, 31\}$.

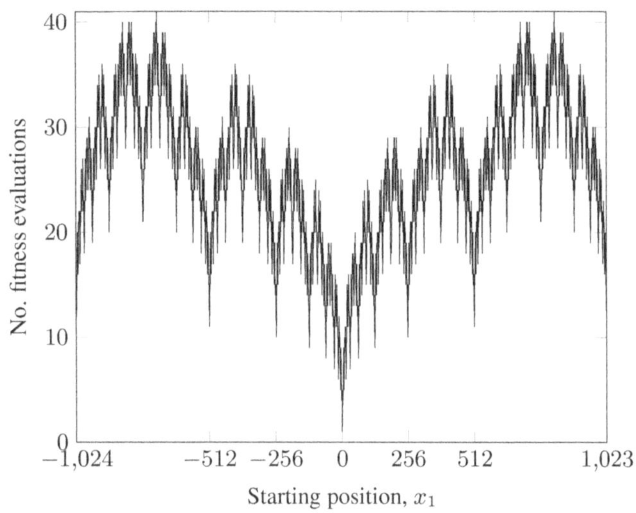

Figure 2: Number of fitness evaluations for optimising $f(x) = |x|$ with IPS for each starting position, $x_1 \in [-1024, 1023]$.

The empirical results agree with our theoretical results as one can clearly see a different scaling behaviour between IPS and our two new local searches, Geometric and Lattice. For small d the performance is similar, but as d grows the differences become obvious.

A second order polynomial was fit to the average running times of IPS using a weighted non-linear regression and then the χ^2 test was used to assess the goodness of fit. The equation of the fitted curve is as follows: $T(i) = 1.5189 + 0.717115 \cdot i + 0.169623 \cdot i^2$, where T is the mean number of fitness evaluations. Note that the leading constant 0.169623 almost exactly matches the constant $1/6 = 0.166666\ldots$ from Theorem 3. For the fit, the obtained value of χ^2 is 27.6887 and the number of degrees of freedom is $32 - 3 = 29$. Since $P(\chi^2 > 27.6887) = 0.5345$, it suggested that the fit is of high quality and explains the experimental results very well.

In Figure 2 we additionally show how the performance of iterated pattern search depends on the precise choice of the starting point. The performance is symmetric around 0 (modulo tiny differences in tie-breaking) and the pattern looks like a fractal structure.

This reflects the recursive nature of IPS, which also became visible in the recurrence arguments used in our proofs from Section 4. In accordance with our average-case analysis from Theorem 3, many starting points lead to rather high running times.

6.2 Experiments with Real-World Test Objects

In order to compare the performance of the local searches in a practical setting, we implemented our new AVM searches into and conducted our experiments with the IGUANA toolset [13], and selected four test objects, details of which are shown in Table 1. Each test object is written in C, and its source code was automatically instrumented by IGUANA for the purposes of collecting fitness information. The *clip_to_circle* function is from the graphical front-end of the *SPICE* electronic circuit simulator. The functions *gimp_rgb_to_hsv_int* and *gimp_hsv_to_rgb_int* are colour space converters from the *GIMP* image editor. Finally, *validate_card* is an implementation of the Luhn algorithm for checking 16 digit credit card numbers. Each test object consists of nested control structures in the form of *if* statements, *switch* statements and loops. IGUANA creates a pair of true and false branches when it detects that control flow diverges in the source code of a C function. Because there can be multiple pairs of branches in a single test object, each pair is labelled numerically.

In the experiments each local search was applied to each branch and the number of unique fitness evaluations needed to cover each branch was counted. This process was repeated 100 times with a different seed being used to initialize the random number generator in each run. For practical reasons the maximum number of fitness evaluations to cover any one branch was capped at 100,000. For each branch pairwise comparisons of the runtime distributions corresponding to different local searches were performed using the Mann-Whitney U test. The results including raw p-values and non-parametric effect sizes, $\hat{A}_{12}$, are shown in Table 2.

Only branches where random search performed notably worse than at least one of the local searches (i. e. $p < 0.05$ (significant) and $\hat{A}_{12} > 0.56$ (at least small effect size)) are considered. The purpose of filtering was to remove branches that are covered easily by any search as there is no reason to design a better algorithm for these branches. Similarly, there were 11 branches which were either infeasible (i. e. no inputs from the input domain execute it) or so hard that none of the tested algorithms found an optimum. In total, 24 out of 82 branches satisfied the selection criteria.

We used a sampling approach to investigate how many fitness landscapes presented to a local searcher are unimodal (details are omitted due to a lack of space). Across all branches listed in Table 2, 13% of landscapes were strictly unimodal and 62% had a similar property: all local optima were also global optima. Only 25% of all sampled settings contained local optima, which were not globally optimal; almost all of these belonged to *SPICE*.

For 14 out of the 24 branches, both Geometric and Lattice perform better than IPS. There were in total 16 branches where Geometric or Lattice were significantly better than IPS, and on 12 of these the effect size was medium or large. In a similar way it is observed that Lattice generally outperforms Geometric, however the effect sizes for such comparisons are typically smaller. Another important result is that the difference in runtime performance between two local search algorithms varies according to the specific branch. On some branches all local searches appear to perform equally well, whereas on other branches one local search is clearly better than another.

The largest improvements were observed with the *clip_to_circle* function (from the *SPICE* project). For the other functions, however, branches were covered relatively quickly regardless of the local search used, leading to a difference of only one or two evaluations on average. This is likely due to their function's small input domain size (see Table 1). While results for these functions were significant, the difference in runtime from a practical standpoint is almost negligible. There are also branches where significant differences between the runtime distributions of local searches exist but the calculated effect sizes are marginally small. Because no correction was made for multiple comparisons, it is likely that a few of the "less significant" results are false positives.

Table 1: Details of the test objects used in the experiments

Function name	No. of branches	Inputs and Ranges
clip_to_circle	42	$\{x_1 \ldots x_7\} \in [-2^{31}, 2^{31} - 1]$
gimp_rgb_to_hsv_int	14	$\{x_1 \ldots x_3\} \in [0, 255]$
gimp_hsv_to_rgb_int	16	$x_1 \in [0, 360], \{x_2, x_3\} \in [0, 255]$
validate_card	10	$\{x_1 \ldots x_{16}\} \in [0, 9]$

Furthermore, there is one branch (namely branch 14T of the *gimp_rgb_to_hsv_int* test object) in which IPS performs far better than both Geometric and Lattice. It is clear that this branch is difficult to cover because it was the only branch in all test cases which local searches failed to cover within the allowed number of fitness evaluations. The success rates for this branch are 0% for Random, 93% for IPS, 6% for Geometric and 2% for Lattice. Additional experiments with 10 runs per search and without a limitation on the maximum number of fitness evaluations gave the median number of fitness evaluations to achieve coverage of this branch to be $923,862$ for Geometric and $539,127.5$ for Lattice. We observed that all searches frequently resorted to restarting, with Geometric and Lattice only able to hit the target when a restart produces a solution with at least 2 out of 3 variables already optimised by chance. We found that the fitness landscape of the branch contains several plateaux, and IPS seems to perform better on this branch because it has a higher tendency to explore these plateaux. Further investigations with this branch and the Wegener Genetic Algorithm [6, 18] revealed the GA was much more efficient at finding a solution, requiring only $4,795$ evaluations as a mean average (median = 4633.5), compared to approximately $31,000$ for the AVM with IPS. This is a significant result ($p = 7.9 \times 10^{-18}$), with a large effect size ($\hat{A}_{12} = 0.85$). This result fits with those from previous studies in search-based test input generation, where the AVM works most efficiently for simple fitness landscapes with "obvious" optima, whereas diversifying GAs are more efficient at navigating less smooth landscapes generated by more difficult branches [6].

6.3 Threats to Validity

We briefly consider some threats to validity associated with our study. From the point of view of *external threats*, the test objects in our experiments may not generalise in practice, however, care was taken to select them from real-world open source examples. These examples go beyond the bounds of our theory, but still show positive results in the majority of cases. From the point of view of *internal threats*, possible errors come from our implementation of the techniques. However, as shown with the simple and controlled `is_zero` example, empirical results closely matched those expected from our theoretical observations. Furthermore we used non-parametric statistical tests to analyse our results, i.e. the Mann-Whitney U test and the Vargha-Delaney $\hat{A}_{12}$ statistic, both of which do not have assumptions regarding normality of the sample means, avoiding a further potential source of error from our analysis.

7. CONCLUSIONS AND FUTURE WORK

We have analysed the performance of the original AVM incorporating Iterated Pattern Search (IPS), proposing to replace the

Table 2: Results of test case experiments. The p-values formatted in bold indicate significance at the 0.05 level. Similarly, effect sizes that are large, medium, small and negligible are distinguished by bold, underlined, italic and normal formatting respectively.

Function	Branch	Median no. of fitness evaluations IPS	Geometric	Lattice	IPS v Geometric p-value	$\hat{A}_{12}$	IPS v Lattice p-value	$\hat{A}_{12}$	Geometric v Lattice p-value	$\hat{A}_{12}$
clip_to_circle	7F	401.5	181.0	150.5	$\mathbf{1.1 \times 10^{-12}}$	**0.79**	$\mathbf{5.1 \times 10^{-17}}$	**0.84**	$\mathbf{5.8 \times 10^{-6}}$	0.69
	10F	408.0	184.0	155.5	$\mathbf{3.0 \times 10^{-11}}$	**0.77**	$\mathbf{3.0 \times 10^{-19}}$	**0.87**	$\mathbf{3.0 \times 10^{-9}}$	**0.74**
	55T	1515.0	1296.0	1098.0	$\mathbf{2.4 \times 10^{-2}}$	*0.59*	$\mathbf{4.1 \times 10^{-3}}$	*0.62*	4.2×10^{-1}	0.53
	55F	552.5	303.5	271.0	$\mathbf{9.9 \times 10^{-9}}$	**0.73**	$\mathbf{6.1 \times 10^{-11}}$	**0.77**	1.6×10^{-1}	0.56
	57F	550.5	361.0	295.0	$\mathbf{1.5 \times 10^{-5}}$	0.68	$\mathbf{9.1 \times 10^{-10}}$	**0.75**	$\mathbf{1.7 \times 10^{-2}}$	*0.60*
	61T	484.5	267.5	209.0	$\mathbf{3.5 \times 10^{-10}}$	**0.76**	$\mathbf{1.8 \times 10^{-12}}$	**0.79**	6.9×10^{-2}	*0.57*
	66T	544.0	287.0	288.0	$\mathbf{2.2 \times 10^{-5}}$	0.67	$\mathbf{3.6 \times 10^{-6}}$	0.69	7.7×10^{-1}	0.51
	68T	2455.0	1535.5	1307.5	$\mathbf{1.4 \times 10^{-3}}$	*0.63*	$\mathbf{5.4 \times 10^{-6}}$	0.69	2.0×10^{-1}	0.55
	68F	833.0	422.5	423.0	$\mathbf{1.9 \times 10^{-5}}$	0.68	$\mathbf{2.0 \times 10^{-5}}$	0.67	7.3×10^{-1}	0.49
	70F	710.5	523.0	427.0	$\mathbf{2.8 \times 10^{-2}}$	*0.59*	$\mathbf{1.7 \times 10^{-4}}$	0.65	9.2×10^{-2}	*0.57*
	74T	736.0	450.5	343.0	$\mathbf{9.0 \times 10^{-4}}$	*0.64*	$\mathbf{4.2 \times 10^{-6}}$	0.69	9.6×10^{-2}	*0.57*
gimp_rgb_to_hsv_int	14T	31779.0	>100000.0	>100000.0	$\mathbf{2.2 \times 10^{-31}}$	**0.05**	$\mathbf{2.7 \times 10^{-34}}$	**0.04**	1.5×10^{-1}	0.48
	17T	36.0	34.5	33.0	5.1×10^{-1}	0.53	2.2×10^{-1}	0.55	3.4×10^{-1}	0.54
gimp_hsv_to_rgb_int	4T	21.5	23.0	19.0	8.5×10^{-1}	0.49	$\mathbf{3.2 \times 10^{-4}}$	0.65	$\mathbf{6.4 \times 10^{-10}}$	**0.75**
	11T	21.0	22.0	16.0	4.8×10^{-1}	0.53	$\mathbf{1.3 \times 10^{-11}}$	**0.78**	$\mathbf{2.2 \times 10^{-17}}$	**0.85**
validate_card	5F	6.0	5.0	5.0	6.2×10^{-1}	0.52	5.9×10^{-1}	0.52	9.3×10^{-1}	0.50
	7T	6.5	6.0	6.0	1.7×10^{-1}	0.56	5.5×10^{-1}	0.52	4.8×10^{-1}	0.47
	7F	6.0	5.0	6.0	$\mathbf{2.7 \times 10^{-2}}$	*0.59*	4.9×10^{-1}	0.53	1.5×10^{-1}	0.44
	9T	6.5	5.5	5.5	$\mathbf{9.7 \times 10^{-3}}$	*0.61*	6.1×10^{-1}	0.52	8.1×10^{-2}	*0.43*
	9F	7.0	5.0	5.0	$\mathbf{2.7 \times 10^{-4}}$	0.65	$\mathbf{4.0 \times 10^{-3}}$	*0.62*	4.5×10^{-1}	0.47
	11T	6.0	5.5	6.0	9.6×10^{-1}	0.50	8.7×10^{-1}	0.49	6.8×10^{-1}	0.48
	11F	5.0	6.0	6.0	4.2×10^{-1}	0.47	1.1×10^{-1}	*0.44*	5.5×10^{-1}	0.48
	14T	13.0	13.0	13.5	9.5×10^{-1}	0.50	2.7×10^{-1}	0.46	2.0×10^{-1}	0.45
	14F	7.0	6.0	6.0	1.5×10^{-1}	0.56	1.0×10^{0}	0.50	2.0×10^{-1}	0.45

latter with faster local searches, Geometric and Lattice Search. On strictly unimodal functions, these searches provably need less time than IPS. IPS requires time $\Theta((\log d)^2)$ while our new searches need time $\Theta(\log d)$, where d is the initial distance to the optimum. These theoretical results were confirmed with empirical experiments optimising the easy function $f(x) = |x|$.

We further empirically analysed Geometric and Lattice Search on test objects that gave rise to unimodal as well as multimodal functions. For multimodal functions there are no non-trivial performance guarantees for any local search; our experiments therefore extend the realm of what can be proven theoretically. Considering branches where any variant of AVM performed significantly better than random search, we found that both Geometric and Lattice performed better than IPS on a majority of branches. There was only one particular branch where IPS performed better (probably due to its better exploration). However, this branch was handled more efficiently by a Genetic Algorithm, as is generally the case for more complex landscapes. Local searches excel in simple conditions, and our paper instead concentrates on improving the AVM for these cases, which have been shown in the test input generation literature to be very common for procedural C programs [6].

With respect to applying the results of our paper, it is not clear what the fitness landscape looks like in advance of test input generation in practice. While further research is required to investigate this problem, our new local searches for the AVM may be used to further improve results with Memetic Algorithms (MAs) [5, 6], which combine diversifying GA searches with intensifying local search algorithms. Such an approach was found to provide the "best of both worlds" for test input generation in Harman and McMinn's study [6]. Thus, further work is needed to investigate the performance of our new local searches with the AVM when integrated into an MA.

Acknowledgement. This work is funded in part by the EPSRC project "RE-COST" (grant no. EP/I010386).

8. REFERENCES

[1] A. Arcuri. Full theoretical runtime analysis of alternating variable method on the triangle classification problem. In *SSBSE*, 2009.

[2] A. Arcuri, P. K. Lehre, and X. Yao. Theoretical runtime analyses of search algorithms on the test data generation for the triangle classification problem. In *SBST*, 2008.

[3] A. Auger and B. Doerr, editors. *Theory of Randomized Search Heuristics – Foundations and Recent Developments*. Number 1 in Series on Theoretical Computer Science. World Scientific, 2011.

[4] D. E. Ferguson. Fibonaccian searching. *Comm. of the ACM*, 3(12), 1960.

[5] G. Fraser, A. Arcuri, and P. McMinn. Test suite generation with memetic algorithms. In *GECCO*, 2013.

[6] M. Harman and P. McMinn. A theoretical and empirical study of search based testing: Local, global and hybrid search. *IEEE Trans. Soft. Eng.*, 36(2).

[7] J. Kiefer. Sequential minimax search for a maximum. *Amer. Math. Soc.*, 4, 1953.

[8] B. Korel. Automated software test data generation. *IEEE Trans. on Soft. Eng.*, 16(8), 1990.

[9] P. K. Lehre and X. Yao. Crossover can be constructive when computing unique input-output sequences. *Soft Computing*, 15, 2011.

[10] P. K. Lehre and X. Yao. Runtime analysis of the (1+1) EA on computing unique input output sequences. *Information Sciences*, 2013. (To appear).

[11] P. McMinn. An identification of program factors that impact crossover performance in evolutionary test input generation for the branch coverage of C programs. *Inf. and Soft. Tech.*, 55(1).

[12] P. McMinn. Search-based software test data generation: A survey. *Software Testing, Verification and Reliability*, 14(2).

[13] P. McMinn. IGUANA: Input generation using automated novel algorithms. a plug and play research tool. Technical Report CS-07-14, Uni. Sheffield, 2007.

[14] L. L. Minku, D. Sudholt, and X. Yao. Evolutionary algorithms for the project scheduling problem: Runtime analysis and improved design. In *GECCO*, 2012.

[15] J. F. Monahan. *Numerical Methods of Statistics*. Cam. Univ. Press, 2nd edition, 2011.

[16] F. Neumann and C. Witt. *Bioinspired Computation in Combinatorial Optimization – Algorithms and Their Computational Complexity*. Springer, 2010.

[17] A. Vargha and H. D. Delaney. A Critique and Improvement of the CL Common Language Effect Size Statistics of McGraw and Wong. *Journal on Educational and Behavioral Statistics*, 25(2), 2000.

[18] J. Wegener, A. Baresel, and H. Sthamer. Evolutionary test environment for automatic structural testing. *Inf. and Soft. Tech.*, 43(14), 2001.

Search-based Model Merging

Marouane Kessentini, Wafa Werda
Computer Science Department
Missouri University of Science and Technology
Rolla, USA
{ marouanek, werdaw}@mst.edu

Philip Langer, Manuel Wimmer
Business Informatics Group
Vienna University of Technology
Vienna, Austria
{langer,wimmer}@big.tuwien.ac.at

ABSTRACT
In Model-Driven Engineering (MDE) adequate means for collaborative modeling among multiple team members is crucial for large projects. To this end, several approaches exist to identify the operations applied in parallel, to detect conflicts among them, as well as to construct a merged model by incorporating all non-conflicting operations. Conflicts often denote situations where the application of one operation disables the applicability of another operation. Whether one operation disables the other, however, often depends on their application order. To obtain a merged model that maximizes the combined effect of all parallel operations, we propose an automated approach for finding the optimal merging sequence that maximizes the number of successfully applied operations. Therefore, we adapted and used a heuristic search algorithm to explore the huge search space of all possible operation sequences. The validation results on merging various versions of real-world models confirm that our approach finds operation sequences that successfully incorporate a high number of conflicting operations, which are otherwise not reflected in the merge by current approaches.

Categories and Subject Descriptors
D.2.9 [**Software Management**]: Software development

Keywords
Search-based software engineering, model-driven software engineering, model evolution, genetic algorithm.

1. INTRODUCTION
Nowadays, software systems are complex and large; therefore, Model-Driven Engineering (MDE) [24] is applied increasingly to cope with the complexity of software systems by raising the level of abstraction. To address the size of software systems, teams of developers have to cooperate and work in parallel on software models. Thus, techniques to support building models collaboratively are highly required.

When models are changed in parallel, they have to be merged eventually to obtain a consolidated model. Therefore, several approaches have been proposed for detecting the operations that have been applied in parallel by developers. Once the applied operations are available, conflict detection algorithms are used to identify pairs of operations that interfere with each other (cf. [16] for a survey on model versioning approaches). In this regard, a conflict denotes a pair of operations, whereas one operation masks the effect of the other (i.e., they do not commute) or one operation disables the applicability of the other. An example for the former is a pair of parallel operations that update the same feature in the model with different values. The latter case is at hand if one operation's preconditions are not valid anymore after applying the operations of the other developer. Such a scenario frequently occurs if composite operations, e.g., model refactorings [4, 28], are applied, because they have potentially complex preconditions that may easily be invalidated by parallel operations.

For resolving conflicts, empirical studies [27] showed that users prefer to work with a tentative merged model acting as a basis for reasoning about possible conflict resolutions, instead of working with the list of operations in terms of choosing to reject one or the other conflicting operation for creating a merged model. A few approaches respect this preference and produce a merged model by applying all non-conflicting operations; conflicting operations are omitted. However, especially in case of a large number of conflicts, many operations are not merged with this strategy, leading to a tentative merged model that lacks in reflecting the *maximal combined effect of the parallel operations*.

With this paper, we address this issue by proposing a method for producing a tentative merged model that reflects the maximum combined effect of the parallel operations by also considering conflicting operations. As mentioned already, an important kind of conflict denotes pairs of operations where one operation disables the applicability of the other. Whether one operation disables the other, however, often depends on the order in which they are applied. Thus, we aim at computing an operation sequence that minimizes the number of disabled operations among all parallel operations, including the conflicting ones. To cope with the huge number of possible operation sequences, a heuristic method is used to explore the space of possible solutions. To this end, we propose to consider model merging as an optimization problem. Our approach takes as input the initial model and the revised ones (i.e., the different parallel versions) and a list of the applied operations, which is computed as described in previous work [25, 26], and generates as output a sequence of operations that minimizes the number of disabled operations. Therefore, we use and adapt genetic algorithm as global heuristic search, which is a powerful heuristic search optimization method inspired by the Darwinian theory of evolution [5].

The remainder of this paper is structured as follows. Section 2 provides the background of model merging and demonstrates the challenges addressed in this paper based on a motivating example. In Section 3, we give an overview of our proposal and explain how we adapted the genetic algorithm to find optimal operation sequences. Section 4 discusses the results

GECCO'13, July 6–10, 2013, Amsterdam, The Netherlands

of the evaluation of our approach. After surveying related work in Section 5, we conclude with some future work in Section 6.

2. MODEL MERGING *CHALLENGES*

In this section, we define briefly the context and concepts of model merging required for this paper. Then we describe the challenges addressed in this paper based on a motivating example.

2.1 Background on Model Merging

In general, two kinds of merge approaches can be distinguished [15]. First, *state-based* merge approaches aim at merging two model versions by combining their model elements into one merged model. Second, *operation-based* merge approaches in contrast do not reason about the models' states, but consider recorded change histories and apply the combination of the parallel histories to the common initial version to compute the merged version.

For both approaches, the notion of conflict is essential, because when having two parallel evolutions of one model, not all changes may be combined to compute one unique merged model. Basically, we can distinguish between two kinds of conflicts. First, two operations are conflicting if one operation *masks* the effect of the other operation in the merged version: e.g., for update/update conflicts, the latter update in the change sequence applied on the model is effective, while the former update is lost. Thus, such conflicting operations are not confluent: different operation sequences result in different models. Second, a conflict also occurs if one operation *disables* the applicability of the other. Every operation has specific preconditions, e.g., an update of an element can only be performed when the element still exists; otherwise a delete/update conflict is raised.

Operation-based merge approaches [17] usually consider besides atomic operations (i.e, additions, deletions, and updates), also *composite operations*, such as *model refactorings*, which consist of a set of atomic operations and additional potentially more complex preconditions. For instance, in the case of model refactorings, certain conditions have to be fulfilled before a refactoring is applicable in order to preserve the semantics of a model after the refactoring has been applied. While in the change history produced by one single developer, the preconditions of the operations are clearly fulfilled, this is not guaranteed when two change histories from two different developers are combined. But this is exactly what is required to perform operation-based merging with the goal of maximizing the combined effect of the parallel operations.

A pure phasing-based approach is in general not solving this problem. For instance, applying first the change history of developer A and afterwards the change history of developer B, only the applicability of the operations of developer A is maximized. But there may be better solutions by intermingling the change histories of developer A and B. Considering all possible permutations of two change histories, we end up with a complexity of $n!$ (where n is the amount of all applied changes of both developers). Considering the length of change histories in practice, using an enumeration based approach is not feasible.

2.2 Motivating Example

For making the problem statement more concrete, we make use of a motivating example. The starting point is the UML class diagram shown in Figure 1. This version of a person management system has been subject to parallel evolution by two developers who concurrently applied a set of atomic and composite changes.

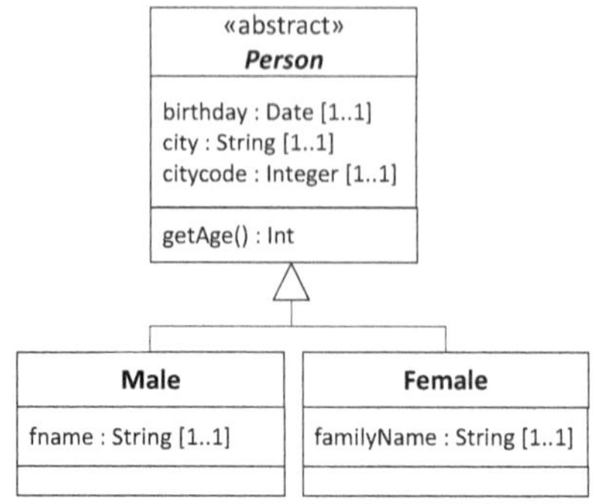

Figure 1: Initial Model v_0.

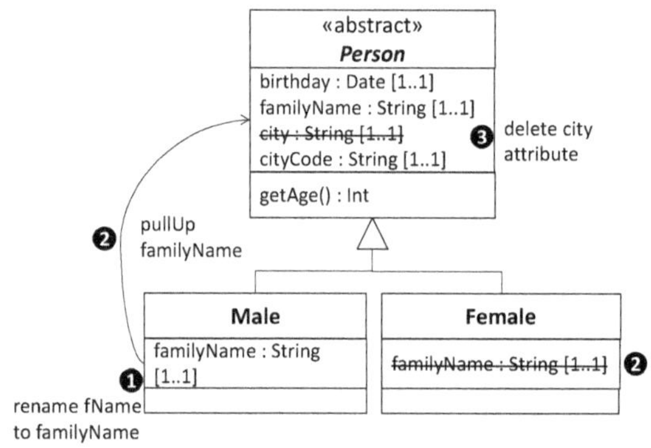

Figure 2: Revised Model v_{1a}.

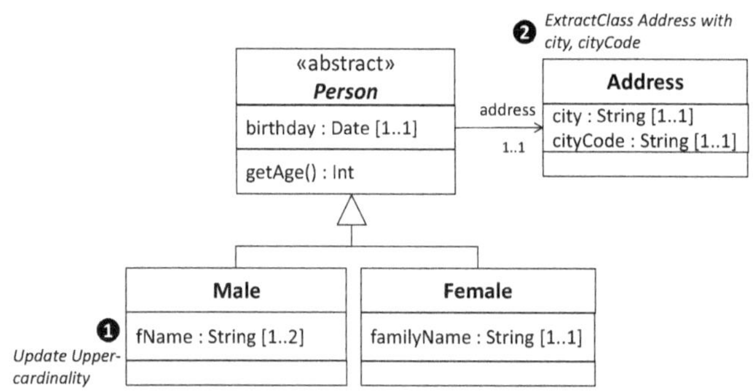

Figure 3: Revised Model v_{1b}.

Developer *A* is first renaming the *fname* attribute of class *Male* to *familyName* in order to apply the *PullUpAttribute* refactoring in a second step: the *familyName* attribute of class *Male* is moved to the class *Person* and the *familyName* attribute of class *Female* is deleted. This refactoring is represented by one composite operation which contains both atomic operations. The precondition of this refactoring is clearly fulfilled: both subclasses of class *Person* have the *familyName* attribute with the same property values, i.e., same data type and multiplicities. Finally, developer A deletes the *city* attribute of class *Person*, because she identifies that this attribute is redundant, as the information is already covered by *cityCode* attribute. The resulting model incorporating all mentioned changes is shown in Figure 2.

Developer *B* changes the upper bound cardinality of the *fName* attribute of class *Male* from one to two, and subsequently, applies the *ExtractClass* refactoring to create an explicit class for the address information. Again, this refactoring is represented by a composite operation consisting of several atomic operations. The resulting model is depicted in Figure 3.

Now a naive operation-based merge approach may apply the operations of developer *A* to the initial model, and subsequently, on this intermediate version, the changes of developer *B*. However, in this sequence, the *ExtractClass* refactoring is not applicable anymore, because the *city* attribute is already missing. Starting with the operations of developer *B* and continuing with the changes of developer *A*, also leads to one disabled operation: the *fName* attribute of class *Male* can be renamed to *familyName*, but the *PullUpAttribute* refactoring cannot be executed, because the *familyName* attributes in both subclasses have different cardinalities. Thus, the precondition of the refactoring is not fulfilled, and consequently, the operation cannot be applied.

Now the question arises whether there are more appropriate solutions in terms of sequences of operations that enable constructing a merged model that maximizes the combined effect of both developers. In our example, 118 different operation sequences have to be considered in addition to the previous two. In fact, solutions exist that allow for applying *all operations successfully* in our example by intermingling the operations of developer *A* and *B*. For instance, executing the *ExtractClass* refactoring, deleting the *cityName* attribute, renaming the *fName* attribute to *lastName*, executing the *PullUpAttribute* refactoring, and finally, setting the upper bound cardinality represents one operation sequence that is fully applicable. For five changes, an enumeration based approach is applicable, but when doubling the changes, we already have to explore 3.6 million combinations because *n!* solutions exist where *n* is the number of changes. Thus, in the next section a more scalable approach to solve this problem is presented.

3. FINDING THE BEST REFACTORING SEQUENCE FOR MODEL MERGING

We now describe our proposal and how we consider merging different model versions as an optimization problem. We start by giving an overview of our approach and provide subsequently a more detailed description on how we adapted and used the genetic algorithm, including the representation of refactorings and refactoring sequences, as well as the fitness function.[1]

3.1 Overview

The goal of our approach is to construct a tentative merged model that maximizes the (at least partial) combined effect of the parallel operations. Therefore, we use a mono-objective optimization algorithm to compute an optimal sequence of merging operations in terms of minimizing the number of refactorings that are disabled by preceding operations.

The general structure of our approach is sketched in Figure 4. The search-based process takes as inputs the sequences of operations that have been applied concurrently to a model by an arbitrary number of developers. These sequences can be detected using operation detection algorithms presented in previous work [25, 26]. Note that these sequences may also be obtained alternatively by tools that record operations directly in the modeling editor. The sequences are composed of operation applications, thereby each entry in a sequence states the operation type as well as the elements on which it has been applied. Having these sequences[2] at hand, we may now combine them into one common sequence of operations and compute the number of disabled operations. Therefore, we use composite operation specifications that contain explicitly specified preconditions in combination with a condition evaluation engine [12] to verify whether the preconditions of each operation in a sequence are fulfilled in a certain state of a model after the preceding operations in the sequence have been applied. If we determine an operation with invalid preconditions in a certain state of the model, we consider this operation to be disabled in the respective operation sequence.

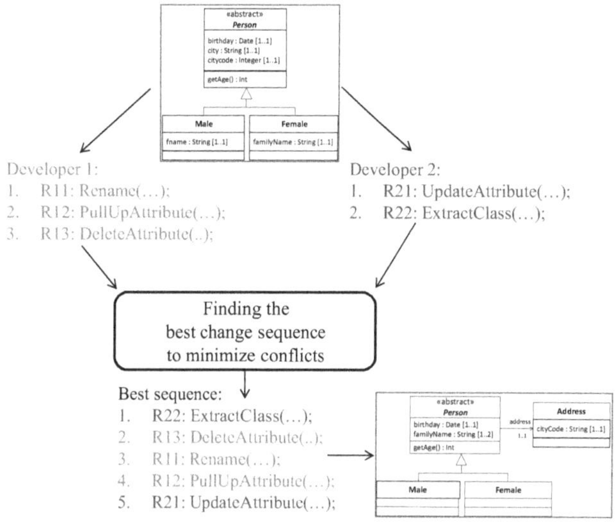

Figure 4: Finding the Best Operation Sequence.

The process of generating a solution can be viewed as the mechanism that finds the best order among all possible operation sequences that minimizes the number of disabled operations. The size of the search space is determined not only by the number of operations applied by the different developers on the same model, but also by the order in which they are applied. Due to the large number of possible refactoring sequences, we considered refactoring merging as an optimization problem. In the next subsection, we describe the adaptation of genetic algorithm to our problem domain.

3.2 Adaptation of the Genetic Algorithm

3.2.1 Genetic Algorithm

By using genetic algorithm (GA), the basic idea is to explore the search space by creating a population of candidate solutions, also called individuals, and evolve them towards an optimal solution for a specific problem.

In GA, a solution can be represented as a vector. Each dimension of this vector must contain symbols that are appropriate for the specific problem. Each individual of the population is evaluated by a fitness function that determines a quantitative measure of its ability to solve the specific problem.

The exploration of the search space is achieved by evolving candidate solutions using selection and genetic operators, such as crossover and mutation. The selection operator chooses the fittest individuals of the current population that are allowed to transmit

[1] In the following, we focus on refactorings, but the presented techniques apply for all kinds of changes in general.

[2] Please note that the length of the operation sequences of the different developers may vary as shown in Figure 4.

their features to new individuals by undergoing crossover and mutation. The crossover operator ensures generation of new children based on parent individuals and allows the transmission of the features of the best fitted parent individuals to new individuals. This is usually achieved by replacing randomly selected dimensions of one parent individual with randomly chosen dimensions from another parent individual to obtain one child. A second child is obtained by inverting parents. Finally, the mutation operator is applied, with a probability that is inversely proportional to its fitness value, to modify some randomly selected nodes in a single individual. The mutation operator introduces diversity into the population and allows escaping local optima found during the search.

Once selection, mutation, and crossover have been applied according to given probabilities, individuals of the newly created generation are evaluated using the fitness function. This process is repeated iteratively until a stopping criterion is met. This criterion usually corresponds to a fixed number of generations. The final result (the best solution found) is the fittest individual produced along all generations.

To adopt GA for solving the problem of finding an operation sequence that maximizes the combined effect of all concurrent operations, we start by constructing an initial GA population that represents possible operation sequences. Then, the main GA fragment explores the search space by constructing new individuals by reordering the operations using the aforementioned crossover and mutation operators, whereas promoting the individual with the best fitness; that is, the operation sequences with the lowest number of disabled operations. The process terminates when the termination criterion (maximum iteration number) is met, and returns the best sequence of operations.

3.2.2 Genetic Algorithm for Model Merging

In the following, we discuss how we adapted the genetic algorithm to solve the model merging problem. Therefore, we present the representation of operation sequences and the applied fitness function to evaluate the quality of operation sequences.

3.2.2.1 Generation of a Population

To represent a candidate solution (individual), we use a vector containing all operations that have been applied by the developers in parallel, whereas each item in the vector represents a single operation (with links to the elements to which it is applied) and the order of operations in this vector represents the sequence in which the operations are applied. Please note that some operations can be eliminated in case they are equivalent; that is, two developers applied the same operation to the same model elements. Thus, we exclude duplicates. Consequently, all vectors, each representing one candidate solution, have the same number of dimensions that corresponds to the number of all parallel operations applied by all developers.

Figure 5 depicts a possible population of operation sequences for the running example introduced above, whereas R^{**} refers to the label of the respective refactoring introduced in Figure 4. For instance, the solutions represented in Figure 5 are composed of five dimensions corresponding to five operations proposed by two different developers. All the solutions have the same length, but they constitute a different order.

Population of solutions

R21	R11	R22	R12	R13
R11	R21	R12	R22	R13
.....				
R22	R11	R12	R13	R22

Figure 5: A Population of Operation Sequences.

The proposed algorithm first generates a population randomly from the list of all operations. Second, crossover and mutation operators are used to generate new populations in the next iterations as explained in the following.

3.2.2.2 Generating New Populations

We used the principle of the Roulette wheel [5] to select individuals for mutation and crossover. The probability to select an individual for crossover and mutation is directly proportional to its relative fitness in the population. In each iteration, we select *population_size / 2* individuals from the population pop_i to form population pop_{i+1}. These (*population_size / 2*) selected individuals will "give birth" to another (*population_size / 2*) new individuals using a crossover operator. Therefore, two parent individuals are selected, and a sub-vector is picked on each one. Then, the crossover operator swaps the dimensions and their relative sub-vector from one parent to the other. When applying the crossover, we ensure that the length of the vector remains the same. The crossover operator allows creating two offspring p'_1 and p'_2 from the two selected parents p_1 and p_2. It is defined as follows: a random position, k, is selected. The first k operations of p_1 become the first k elements of p'_1. Similarly, the first k operations of p_2 become the first k operations of p'_2.

The mutation operator can be applied to pairs of dimensions selected randomly. Given a selected solution, the mutation operator first randomly selects one or many pairs of dimensions of the vector. Then, for each selected pair, the dimensions are swapped.

3.2.2.3 Evaluating Generated Solutions

The quality of an individual is computed based on the quality of its represented operation sequence. In each operation sequence, different operations may be disabled after certain preceding operations have been applied. Thus, the quality of a solution is determined with respect to the number of disabled operations within a certain operation sequence. In other words, the best solution is the one that minimizes the number of disabled operations, obtained by applying the respective operation sequence to the initial model.

The evaluation of an individual is formalized in terms of a mathematical function called fitness function. The fitness function quantifies the quality of the proposed solution. The goal is to define an efficient and simple—in the sense that it is not computationally expensive—fitness function in order to reduce the computational complexity. This function should evaluate the number of disabled operations. Therefore, we use previously developed tools to specify composite operations including their preconditions in combination with an engine for evaluating the conditions in a certain model state (cf. [12] for details). As evaluating conditions can be rather expensive, we only compute whether one operation in a sequence disables another for each possible *pair-wise combination* of operations in advance, instead of checking the preconditions of each operation with the combined effect of every operation that precedes the operation in the sequence. Please note that this might miss to detect some disabled operations in certain scenarios: the preconditions of an operation might be valid with each *single* preceding operation, but the preceding operations *in combination* might still invalidate the preconditions of the subsequent operations. As this is a rather rare case, we left this issue as a topic of future work.

The information on which operation in a sequence disables the other is represented in terms of a matrix $n \times n$ where n is the number of operations applied originally by the different developers in total (after eliminating duplicates). Each item in this matrix represents a combination of two operations and holds a value of either 0 or 1: if an operation i disables the operation j then, the item (i,j) in the matrix takes the value 1, otherwise it takes 0. Based on this matrix, we may determine easily the number of disabled operations for a specific operation sequence by summing up all values in the matrix.

To illustrate the fitness function, we consider one solution (cf. Figure 6) from our running example to evaluate. Since 5 operations have been applied in parallel, the computed matrix has a size of 5 × 5. To determine the number of disabled operations for the given sequence, we iterate over the operations of the sequence and sum the values of the matrix at the items representing current operation (row) and all operations that are after that operation in the sequence (column). For the example, the fitness function is $f_i = 2$.

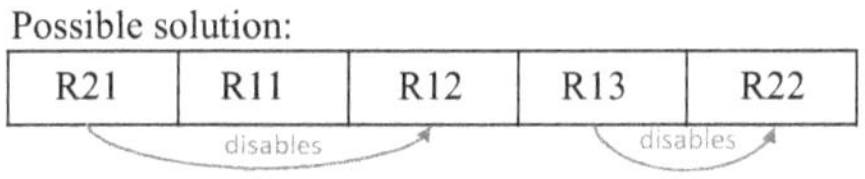

	R11	R12	R13	R21	R22
R11	-	0	0	0	0
R12	0	-	0	0	0
R13	0	0	-	0	1
R21	0	1	0	-	0
R22	0	0	0	0	-

Figure 6: An Illustration of the Fitness Function.

4. EVALUATION

To evaluate our proposal, we conducted experiments on six real-world models. We present first the objectives of this exploratory study and then we describe and discuss the obtained results. For replication purposes, the experimentation material can be downloaded from [7].

4.1 Research Questions and Experimental Setting

The study was conducted to quantitatively assess the performance of our approach when applied to real-world scenarios. Thereby, we aimed at answering the following research questions (RQ).

RQ1. *To what extent can the proposed approach reduce the number of disabled operations?*

RQ2. *To what extent the best merging solutions make sense semantically?*

To answer RQ1 and RQ2, we used a corpus containing an extensive evolution of multiple open source systems. Furthermore, we compared our results to those produced without taking into consideration the order of operations. We also investigated manually the semantics of merged models after applying the best solution generated by our algorithm. In the following, we describe details about our experiments' setting.

We chose to analyze the extensive evolution of three Ecore metamodels coming from the Graphical Modeling Framework (GMF) [8], an open source project for generating graphical modeling editors. We considered the evolution from GMF's release 1.0 over 2.0 to release 2.1 covering a period of two years. For achieving a broader data basis, we analyzed the revisions of three models, namely the Graphical Definition Metamodel (GMF Graph), the Generator Metamodel (GMF Gen), and the Mappings Metamodel (GMF Map). Therefore, the respective metamodel versions had to be extracted from GMF's version control system and, subsequently, manually analyzed to determine the actually applied operations between successive metamodel versions. In addition to GMF, we used model fragments extracted from three open source projects: GanttProject (Gantt for short) [9], JHotDraw [10], and Xerces-J [11]. We considered the evolution across three versions of Gantt (v1.7, v1.8, and v1.9.10), three versions of JHotDraw (v5.1, 5.2, and 5.3) and four versions of Xerxes-J (v1.4.4, v2.5.0, v2.6.0, and v2.6.1). Table 1 summarizes for each model evolution scenario the number of applied refactorings, as well as the number of model elements for the smallest and largest model version.

Additionally, we had to specify all operation types (i.e., their comprised atomic operations and preconditions) that have been applied across all versions leading to 38 different types of operations. The evolution of the analyzed models provides a relatively large set of revisions containing overall 401 different applications of the operation types as shown in Table 1.

Due to the lack of existing parallel revision histories that we could have used for evaluating our approach, we *emulate parallel evolution* by dividing the applied operations from the single revisions into parallel sequences of operations manually and asked five graduate students to additionally modify different model fragments of these open source systems in order to cause disabled operations in the considered evolutions.

To assess the accuracy of our approach, we evaluate manually the number of conflicts (NC), i.e., number of disabled operations of the best operation sequence found by our approach, as well as the correctness of the found operation sequences.

Automatic correctness (AC) consists of comparing the suggested operation order to the expected one, operation by operation. AC method has the advantage of being automatic and objective. However, since different possibilities exist to avoid disabled operations, AC could reject a good solution because it yields different operation sequences from the original one. To account for those situations, we also use manual correctness (MC) for evaluating the correctness of the proposed sequence, again operation by operation. When calculating MC, we verify whether the proposed operation sequence preserves the semantics of the design (and not only avoids disabled operations).

Table 1: Number of Refactoring Operations.

Model	*Number of refactorings*	*Number of elements (min, max)*
GMF Map	14	367, 428
GMF Graph	36	277,310
GMF Gen	112	883,1295
GanttProject	72	451, 572
Xerces-J	86	1698,1732
JHotDraw	81	985, 1457

We compared our results with: *(i)* a randomly generated order (random search), *(ii)* a traditional technique where internal sequence is not considered (we apply operations originally applied by developer 1 then developer 2, etc.), and *(iii)* another local search algorithm (Simulated Annealing) [6].

We used the AC and NC scores for the comparison. The different scores (AC, MC, and NC) are calculated as an average of 30 runs to ensure the stability of the results. In addition, the comparison between SA, random search and GA is also based on an average of 30 runs.

4.2 Results and Discussions

Table 2 summarizes our findings over an average of 30 runs. In general, using our search-based approach, we were able to reduce the number of conflicts. For instance, in JHotDraw only 11 disabled operations are detected after executing the optimal operation sequence. However, 37 disabled operations are detected by executing the operations as they appear without altering the internal order provided by different developers. Thus, we reduced the number of disabled operations by 70% (1 - 11/37). Similar results are obtained on remaining open-source systems where the number of conflicts is reduced by 63% (1 - 3/8), 69% (1 - 5/16), 68% (1 - 16/49), 43% (1 - 19/33), 59% (1 - 12/29) for GMF Map, GMF Graph, GMF Gen, GanttProject, and Xerces-J, respectively. Thus, we conclude that our proposal reduces significantly the number of disabled operations.

Table 2: Number of Disabled Operations (NC).

Systems	Number of disabled operations (with heuristic search)	Number of disabled operations (without heuristic search)
GMF Map	3	8
GMF Graph	5	16
GMF Gen	16	49
GanttProject	19	33
Xerces-J	12	29
JHotDraw	11	37

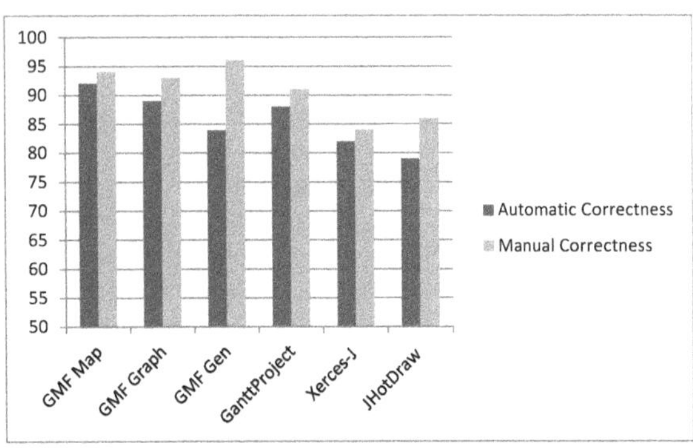

Figure 7: AC and MC Scores for the Case Studies.

Figure 7 illustrates the AC and MC scores on the different models. For the automatic precision, we compared the generated operation order to the expected (original) one provided manually by a group of five developers. The AC was more than 80% for all the various models. The lower AC score was found in JHotDraw. JHotDraw was extensively modified within only one large revision comprising 27 refactoring operations that will potentially lead to disabled operations when divided and applied in parallel. Thus, the evolution of this model is a very representative mixture of different scenarios for the application of operations leading to many disabled operations (as described in Table 2). However, our approach finds approximately the best order of operations to avoid disabled ones with an acceptable score (more than 80%) even if the number of all operations and disabled ones is large.

Similar to JHotDraw, Xerces-J versions were extensively revised leading to a huge list of operations. This can explain also the AC obtained by our approach (82%). The remaining models contain less model elements and revisions, thus AC scores were higher with more than 85%. For instance, the evolution of GMF Map contained four revisions, having in each revision a maximum number of three refactoring operations. Using our approach, we could find almost a very similar order to the reference one. We noticed that our technique does not have a bias towards the types of operations since most of them were used in the suggested solutions.

With regards to MC, the score for all the six models were improved since we found interesting operation order alternatives that deviate from the reference ones proposed by the experts: for all the six models, we obtained approximately more than 85% as MC, e.g., for GMF Graph 94% and for GMF Gen 96%. When we manually analyzed the results, we found that many disabled operations can be avoided in different manners and sometimes changing the order of some operations does not affect the number of disabled operations. In the context of this experiment, we conclude that our technique was able to find the best order of merging operations that reduces the disabled ones.

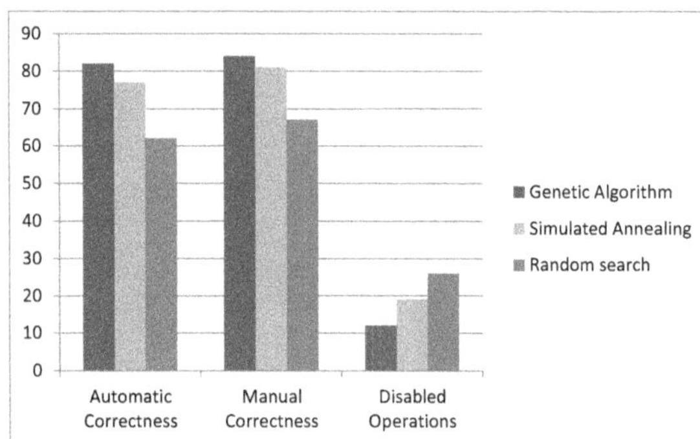

Figure 8: Comparison: Genetic Algorithm, Simulated Annealing, and Random Search for XercesJ.

In Figure 8, we compared our genetic algorithm (GA) results with a random search (without the use of change operators) and a local search algorithm, namely simulated annealing (SA). The local search starts from only one solution (instead of a population of solutions) generated randomly and then refined using mutation in the next iterations. The AC, MC, and NC scores for SA were also acceptable. However, GA performs better than SA in the case of Xerces-J, because Xerces-J exhibits a larger model and a larger list of applied refactorings, and GA usually provides better results than SA in scenarios having a larger search space.

The correctness results might vary depending on the operation sequence which is randomly generated, though guided by a meta-heuristic. To ensure that our results are relatively stable, we compared the results of multiple executions of GA as shown in Figure 9. We consequently believe that our technique is stable, since the AC and MC precision scores are approximately the same for several executions.

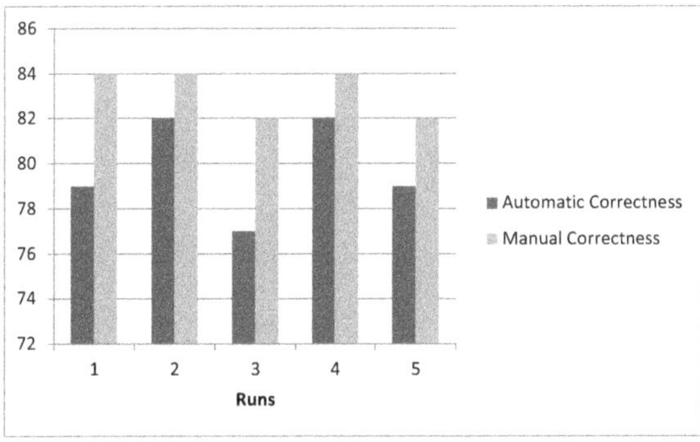

Figure 9: AC and MC Scores for Multiple Executions (5 runs).

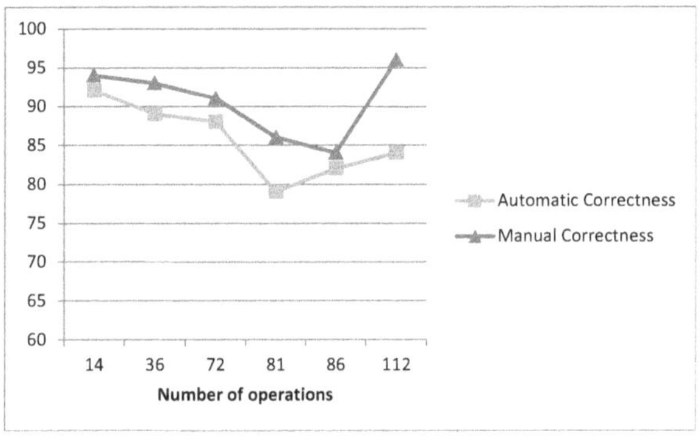

Figure 10: AC and MC in Comparison to Number of Operations.

Figure 10 analyzes the correlation between the number of operations and the correctness values. More precisely, we sort AC and MC based on the number of refactorings for each open source system described in Table 1. From this data, we conclude that AC and MC are not necessarily affected negatively by a larger number of refactorings. For example, MC even increases from 85% to 96% when the number of refactorings increases from 86 to 112. Thus, we can conclude that our proposal shows a good scalability and is not affected negatively by the number of refactorings. However, when the number of operations increases, it does not necessarily mean that the number of disabled operations does.

5. RELATED WORK

With respect to the contribution of this paper, namely to integrate two parallel operation histories into one operation sequence that maximizes the number of successfully applied operations, related work dates back to the early 1990ies. Before that time, merging has been mostly achieved based on the states of the artifacts under version control [23]. The origin work on operation-based merging has been published by Lippe [14]. He pointed out several advantages of operation-based merging over purely state-based merging and contributed the important notion of frontier set. The frontier set, including frontier points, is an indicator how far one can merge two sequences of changes. One goal is to shift the frontier points as far away from the original model version as possible to maximize the applicability of the performed operations. One way to shift the frontier points is to reorder the atomic operations, i.e., to apply all non-conflicting atomic operations before the conflicting ones. What we have contributed with our search-based approach is a mechanism to minimize the critical points in the merge process where users have to be involved, even when composite operations, such as refactorings, have been applied.

Operation-based merging has been heavily applied in asynchronous collaborative graphical editing. Edwards [13] has defined several strategies for combining two operation sequences into one sequence. The strategies range from fully automatic merging by computing each possible sequence of non-conflicting changes to interactive merging allowing the user to decide how each change of a conflicting change pair should be incorporated in the finally merged model. Ignat and Norrie [15] have compared an operation-based approach and a state-based approach for merging change logs of collaborative graphical editors. They distinguish "real" conflicts from resolvable conflicts. The latter may be resolved by finding an appropriate order to incorporate the changes to the finally merged model. For finding the appropriate order, priority lists for change types have to be defined.

With the advent of MDE, the research topic collaborative modeling is gaining momentum. Several state-based approaches for model versioning have been proposed (cf. [16, 23] for an overview), as well as a few operation-based approaches. Koegel et al. [18] record changes in modeling editors and provide conflict detection for two sequences of recorded changes. They also support composite changes, but only consider how these operations are build up from atomic changes while explicit preconditions are disregarded. If they detect that a composite change is in conflict with an atomic change, they let the user decide which one to take. Similarly, Barret et al. [19] discuss pushing the frontier points as far as possible by incorporating all non-conflicting changes to produce a merged model and then let again the user decide which change of a conflict pair to prioritize. Other operation-based approaches for models have been presented in [20, 22], but no dedicated reordering strategies have been discussed. In [21], the authors mention that finding an appropriate sequence for unifying the changes of two parallel change sets is an optimization problem, but they based their approach on manual conflict resolution during the merge process.

In summary, reasoning on arbitrary application orders of the operations to unify (including composite changes) to find the order that is maximizing the successful application of the operations is not considered by existing operation-based merge approaches. State-of-the-art approaches mostly reside on a two-phase process: first, they apply the non-conflicting changes and then let the user select the change to be prioritized out of two conflicting changes. In contrast, our approach explores arbitrary sequences and the result is the most applicable sequence of operations found by the genetic algorithm. Thus, we are able to minimize the critical and labor-intensive tasks involving user interaction in the merge process going beyond existing state-of-the-art approaches.

Our proposal is part of the search-based software engineering (SBSE) contributions [29]. SBSE uses search-based approaches to solve optimization problems in software engineering. Based on surveys proposed by Harman et al. [29, 30], our work represents the first attempt to treat the problem of model merging as a combinatorial optimization problem.

6. CONCLUSION

This paper proposes a novel approach for merging parallel versions of models by finding the best operation sequence. Such a sequence is very useful in model versioning to find a tentative merge, as a basis for subsequently resolving the remaining conflicts manually. Therefore, a merged model is necessary that maximizes the combined effect of all operations that have been applied by multiple developers in parallel to the same model. This is achieved by finding an optimal (potentially intermingled) order of operations that minimizes the number of disabled operations. As the search space in terms of all possible sequences of operations is potentially huge, we consider the merging process as an optimization problem.

We evaluated our proposal with six real-world models extracted from different open source systems. The experiment results indicate clearly that the number of disabled operations is reduced significantly in comparison to the number of disabled operations without taking into consideration the different possible operation orders. We further evaluated successfully that the computed operation sequences lead to correct models in terms of their semantics in most of the considered cases.

Although our approach has been evaluated with real-world models with a reasonable number of applied operations, we are working now on larger models and with larger list of operations applied in parallel. This is necessary to investigate more deeply the applicability of the approach in practice, but also to study the performance of approach when dealing with very large models. Moreover, we plan to investigate an empirical study to compare with other search-based algorithms. More generally, we plan to extend this work by fixing detected conflicts since this work focus only on minimizing the number of disabled operations.

7. REFERENCES

[1] D. Dig, K. Manzoor, R. E. Johnson, T. N. Nguyen. Effective Software Merging in the Presence of Object-Oriented Refactorings. *IEEE Transactions on Software Engineering,* 34(3):321-335, 2008.

[2] T. Ekman, U. Asklund. Refactoring-aware Versioning in Eclipse. *Electronic Notes in Theoretical Computer Science* 107:57-69, 2004.

[3] M. Koegel, M. Herrmannsdoerfer, Y. Li, J. Helming, D. Joern. Comparing State- and Operation-based Change Tracking on Models. In *Proceedings of EDOC,* 2010.

[4] M. Fowler, K. Beck, J. Brant, W. Opdyke, and D. Roberts. Refactoring – Improving the Design of Existing Code. 1st ed. Addison-Wesley, 1999.

[5] J. R. Koza. Genetic Programming: On the Programming of Computers by Means of Natural Selection. *MIT Press*, Cambridge, 1992.

[6] S. Kirkpatrick, C. D. Jr. Gelatt, M. P. Vecchi. Optimization by simulated annealing. *Sciences,* 220(4598):671–680, 1983.

[7] http://web.mst.edu/~marouanek/gecco13/merging

[8] www.eclipse.org/gmf

[9] http://www.ganttproject.biz

[10] http://www.jhotdraw.org

[11] http://xerces.apache.org/xerces-j

[12] P. Langer. Adaptable Model Versioning based on Model Transformation By Demonstration. *PhD Thesis, Vienna University of Technology*, 2011.

[13] W. K. Edwards: Flexible Conflict Detection and Management in Collaborative Applications. In *Proceedings of Symposium on User Interface Software and Technology*, pages 139-148, 1997.

[14] E. Lippe, N. van Oosterom. Operation-based merging. In *Proceedings of SDE*, pages 78-87, 1992.

[15] C. Ignat and M. C. Norrie. Operation-based versus State-based Merging in Asynchronous Graphical Collaborative Editing. In *Workshop on Collaborative Editing,* 2004.

[16] P. Brosch, G. Kappel, P. Langer, M. Seidl, K. Wieland, M. Wimmer: An Introduction to Model Versioning. In *Proceedings of SFM,* 2012.

[17] P. Brosch, P. Langer, M. Seidl, K. Wieland, M. Wimmer, G. Kappel. The Past, Present, and Future of Model Versioning; *Emerging Technologies for the Evolution and Maintenance of Software Models*, IGI Global, 2011.

[18] M. Koegel, H. Naughton, J. Helming, M. Herrmannsdoerfer. Collaborative model merging. In *OOPSLA Companion,* 2010.

[19] S. Barrett, P. Chalin, G. Butler. Table-Driven Detection and Resolution of Operation-Based Merge Conflicts with Mirador. In *Proceedings of ECMFA,* 2011.

[20] C. Schneider, A. Zündorf, J. Niere. CoObRA - a small step for development tools to collaborative environments. In *Workshop on Directions in Software Engineering Environments,* 2004.

[21] M. Schmidt, S. Wenzel, T. Kehrer, U. Kelter. History-based Merging of Models. In *Workshop on Comparison and Versioning of Software Models*, 2009.

[22] A. Mougenot, X. Blanc, M. Gervais. D-Praxis: A Peer-to-Peer Collaborative Model Editing Framework. In Proceedings of *DAIS,* 2009.

[23] T. Mens. A State-of-the-Art Survey on Software Merging. *IEEE Transactions on Software Engineering*, 28(5):449-462, 2002.

[24] J. Bézivin. On the Unification Power of Models. *Software and Systems Modeling,* 4(2):171-188, (2005).

[25] A. ben Fadhel, M. Kessentini, P. Langer, M. Wimmer. Search-based Detection of High-level Model Changes. In *Proceedings of ICSM*, 2012.

[26] P. Langer, M. Wimmer, P. Brosch, M. Herrmannsdoerfer, M. Seidl, K. Wieland, G. Kappel. A Posteriori Operation Detection in Evolving Software Models. *Journal of Systems and Software*, 86(2):551-566, 2013.

[27] K. Wieland, P. Langer, M. Seidl, M. Wimmer, G. Kappel. Turning Conflicts into Collaboration - Concurrent Modeling in the Early Phases of Software Development. *Computer Supported Cooperative Work*, 22(2-3):181-240, 2013.

[28] G. Sunyé, D. Pollet, Y. Le Traon, J. M. Jézéquel. Refactoring UML Models. In *Proceedings of UML*, 2001.

[29] M. Harman. The current state and future of search based software engineering. In *Proceedings of ICSE*, 2007.

[30] M. Harman, S. A. Mansouri, Y. Zhang. Search-based software engineering: Trends, techniques and applications. *ACM Computing Surveys* 45(1):Article11, 2012.

The Use of Development History in Software Refactoring Using a Multi-Objective Evolutionary Algorithm

Ali Ouni[1,2], Marouane Kessentini[2], Houari Sahraoui[1], Mohamed Salah Hamdi[3]

[1]DIRO, Université de Montréal, Canada
{ouniali, sahraouh}@iro.umontreal.ca

[2]CS, Missouri University of Science and Technology, USA
marouanek@mst.edu

[3]IT Department, Ahmed Ben Mohamed Military College, Qatar
mshamdi@yahoo.com

ABSTRACT

One of the widely used techniques for evolving software systems is refactoring, a maintenance activity that improves design structure while preserving the external behavior. Exploring past maintenance and development history can be an effective way of finding refactoring opportunities. Code elements which undergo changes in the past, at approximately the same time, bear a good probability for being semantically related. Moreover, these elements that experienced a huge number of refactoring in the past have a good chance for refactoring in the future. In addition, the development history can be used to propose new refactoring solutions in similar contexts. In this paper, we propose a multi-objective optimization-based approach to find the best sequence of refactorings that minimizes the number of bad-smells, and maximizes the use of development history and semantic coherence. To this end, we use the non-dominated sorting genetic algorithm (NSGA-II) to find the best trade-off between these three objectives. We report the results of our experiments using different large open source projects.

Categories and Subject Descriptors

D.2.7 [**Software Engineering**]: Software – *Restructuring, reverse engineering, and reengineering*

General Terms

Measurement, Performance, Design, Experimentation

Keywords

Search-based Software Engineering, Refactoring, Semantics, Code Change, Design Defects

1. INTRODUCTION

Software undergoes continuous change, through which new features are added, bugs are fixed, and quality is improved during software development lifecycle. To support these activities, many tools emerged to manage source code such as concurrent versions system (CVS), and subversion (SVN) [23] where all documentation, configuration, and code-changes are archived and called "software development history".

Software-development history can be used to ease maintenance activities. One of the widely-used activities is *refactoring* which improves design structure without affecting its overall behavior. In general, to apply refactoring, we need to identify 1) *where* a program should be refactored and 2) *which* refactorings to apply [6] [22]. Automating the refactoring suggestion task is essential and very useful to help software developers in improving the quality of their code such as reusability, maintainability, flexibility, and understandability, etc.

Recently, search-based approaches have been applied to automate software refactoring [10] [5] [3] [4]. Most of these work formulated refactoring as a single-objective optimization problem, in which the main goal is to improve code quality while preserving the behavior (see for example, [1] [4] [10] [12]). In some other work, other objectives are also evaluated such as reducing the effort (number of code changes) [2], preserving semantic coherence [5], and improving quality metrics. However, sometimes structural and semantic information is not enough to generate efficient refactoring.

The use of development history can be an efficient solution to propose refactoring. Code fragments that are modified over the past in the same period are semantically connected (same feature). Furthermore, fragments that are extensively refactored in the past have a good probability for refactoring in the future. Moreover, the code to refactor can be similar to some patterns that can be found in the development history thus developers can easily adapt them. However, despite its importance, the history of code changes has not been explicitly investigated/used to suggest new refactorings. Existing approaches including recent work [2] [5] [1] suggests refactorings without considering software-development history.

In this paper, we propose a multi-objective optimization-based approach to find the best sequence of refactorings that minimizes the number of bad-smells, preserves the semantic coherence, and maximizes the consistence with development history. To this end, we use the non-dominated sorting genetic algorithm (NSGA-II) [8] to find the best trade-off between these three objectives. After generating refactoring solutions, we evaluate first if similar changes were applied in previous versions of the code fragments that will be refactored by the generated solution. Then, we check if a large number of changes were performed in the past on the code fragments to modify, and if the refactored code elements are, in general, modified at, approximately the same time or not (co-changed). In addition, we use a combination of quality metrics to detect bad-smells [2] and two techniques are combined to estimate the semantics proximity between classes when moving elements between them (dependencies between classes extracted from call graphs and vocabulary similarity) [5]. Thus, three objectives are considered in our NSGA-II adaptation: minimizing the number of bad-smells, maximizing the semantic coherence and maximizing the use of development history information.

Our approach is evaluated on two large open source systems, and aimed at investigating to what extent can the use of code changes history improve the automation of code refactoring. We also evaluate the performance of our proposal by comparing it to existing contributions, random search and a single-objective algorithm without the use of the development history.

Thus, the paper presents the following research questions.

RQ1: To what extent the reuse of software development history can improve the results of refactoring suggestion compared to work that do not use them?

RQ2: How do the proposed multi-objective approach performs compared to random search, mono-objective approach and some existing work [1], [3], [2], and [15]?

The rest of this paper is structured as follows. Section 2 is dedicated to the background needed to understand our approach. In Section 3, we give an overview of our proposal and we describe how the historical code changes are used to guide the search-based refactoring. Then, in Section 4, we explain how we adapted the non-dominated sorting genetic algorithm to find "good" refactoring strategies. Section 5 presents and discusses the evaluation results. The related work in search-based refactoring and mining software version archives is outlined in Section 6. We conclude and suggest future research directions in Section 7.

2. BACKGROUND AND PROBLEM STATEMENT

To better understand our contribution, we start, in this section, by giving the definitions of important concepts. Then, we detail the specific problems that are addressed by our approach.

2.1 Background

Refactoring is a well-known technique frequently used during the whole software development cycle to improve software quality. Fowler [6] defines it as "A change made to the internal structure of software to make it easier to understand and cheaper to modify without changing its observable behavior". One motivation is to reorganize classes, fields and methods in order to improve the software design and to facilitate future extensions. This reorganization is used to improve different aspects of software-quality: reusability, maintainability, complexity, etc. [22]. To apply refactoring, a software developer should identify where a program should be refactored and which refactorings to apply. In this paper, we identify refactoring solutions for the problem of correcting design defects that are detected in the source code. Hence, to detect design defects, we used detection rules, *i.e.*, combination of software metrics/thresholds, as an indicator for the presence of design defects [2]. We consider that these defects are already detected using defects detection rules [2], and we need to find what are the suitable refactoring operations to fix them.

Bad-smells, also called design defects, anomalies, design flaws, or anti-patterns [7] [6], refer to design situations that adversely affect the development of software, which mainly results of bad programming practices. As stated by Fenton and Pfleeger [7], bad-smells are unlikely to cause failures directly, but may do it indirectly. In general, they make a system difficult to maintain, to change and to evolve, which may, in turn, introduce bugs. They should be systematically found, and fixed all along the software lifecycle. The most well-known examples of bad-smells are the *blob* [6] which can be found in designs where one large class monopolizes the behavior of a large part of the system and other related classes primarily encapsulate data. For example, to correct the blob defect many refactorings can be used to reduce the number of functionalities in a specific class, such as moving methods and/or extracting a class.

2.2 Problem statement

Various techniques are proposed to automate the refactoring process [5] [2] [3] [1] [12]. Most of these techniques are based on structural information using a set of quality metrics. The structural information is used to ensure that applied refactorings improve some quality metrics such as the number of methods/attributes per class. However, this is not enough to confirm that a refactoring makes sense and preserves the design semantic coherence. We need to preserve the rationale behind why and how code elements are grouped and connected.

To solve this issue, semantic measures are used to evaluate refactoring suggestions such as those based on coupling and cohesion or information retrieval techniques (e.g. cosine similarity of the used vocabulary) [5]. However, these semantic measures depend heavily on the meaning of code elements name/identifier (e.g., name of methods, name of classes, etc.). Indeed, due to some time-constraints, developers select meaningless names for classes, methods, or fields (not clearly related to the functionalities). Thus, it is risky to only use techniques such as cosine similarity to find a semantic approximation between code fragments. In addition, when applying a refactoring like move method between two classes many target classes can have the same values of coupling and cohesion with the source class. To make the situation worse, it is also possible that the different target classes have the same structure.

Past maintenance and development history can be used to determine refactoring opportunities. Many aspects can help to improve the automation of refactoring: 1) code elements which undergo changes in the past, at approximately the same time, are in general semantically dependent, 2) code elements changed many times in the past have a good probability to be "badly-designed", 3) the development history can be used to propose new refactoring solutions in similar contexts. Recently, only the third aspect has been used by existing work [15].

2.3 Motivating scenario

To illustrate some of the above-mentioned issues, Figure 1 shows a concrete example extracted from Xerces-J [25], a well-known open-source family of software packages for parsing and manipulating XML.

We considered a design fragment that contains three classes *XIncludeHandler*, *ValidatorHandlerImpl*, and *XIncludeTextReader*. Using the detection rules [2], the class *XIncludeHandler* is detected as a blob (i.e., a large class that monopolizes the behavior of a large part of the system). One possible refactoring solution to improve the design quality is to move some methods and fields from this class to other classes in the program. In this way, we will reduce the number of functionalities implemented in the blob class *XIncludeHandler*. A refactoring is proposed to move the method *checkNotation*() from the defected class *XIncludeHandler* to another suitable class in a way that we preserve the semantic coherence of the original program. Based on semantic and structural information [5] many other target classes are possible including *ValidatorHandlerImpl* and *XIncludeTextReader*. However, these two classes have approximately the same structure that can be formalized using quality metrics (e.g., number of methods, number of attributes, etc.). In addition, they are semantically close to *XIncludeHandler* using vocabulary-based measures, cohesion and coupling [5].

Based on the development change history found using CVS, the class *XIncludeHandler* has been never changed together with *ValidatorHandlerImpl* in any commit (code revision). However, we recorded that it has changed with the class *XIncludeTextReader* in more than 14 commits. As such, moving methods and/or attributes from the class *XIncludeHandler* to the class *XIncludeTextReader* has a higher correctness probability, and it is likely to be semantically coherent. Therefore, in this paper our hypothesis is that development change history is a valuable complement to semantic and structural information [5] to preserve the semantic coherence when applying refactoring.

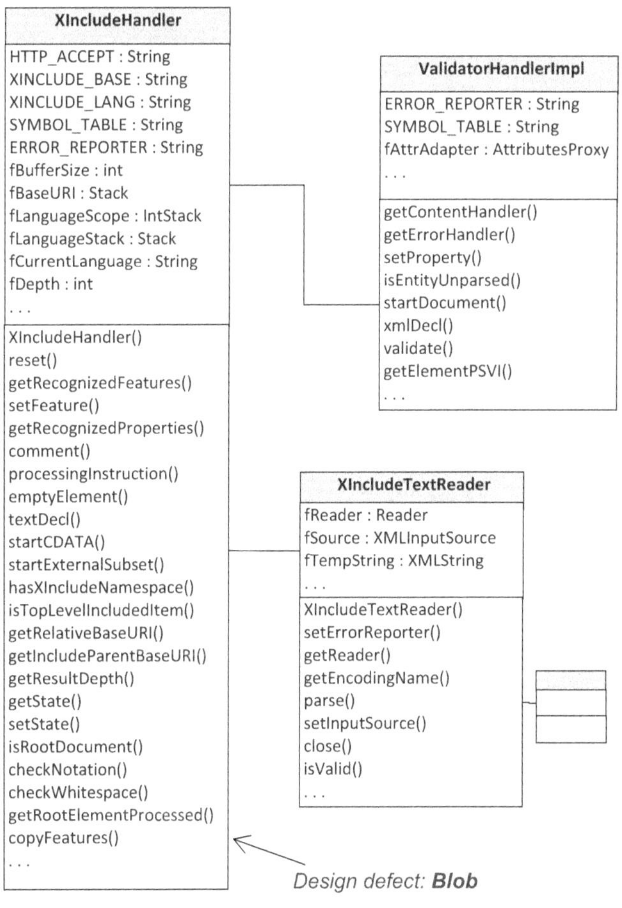

Figure 1. Design fragment extracted from Xerces-J v2.7.0

3. APPROACH OVERVIEW

The process of finding refactoring solutions, *i.e.*, sequence of refactoring operations, to correct bad-smells consist of exploring a huge search space. In fact, the search space is determined not only by the number of possible refactoring combinations, but also by the order in which they are applied. Thus, a heuristic-based optimization method is used to generate refactoring solutions. We have three objectives to optimize: 1) maximize quality improvement (bad-smells correction), 2) minimize the number of semantic errors, and 3) maximize the re-use with/of the development history. To this end, we consider the refactoring as a multi-objective optimization problem instead of a single-objective one. We propose an adaptation of the non-dominated sorting genetic algorithm (NSGA-II) [8]. This algorithm and its adaptation to the refactoring problem are described in section 4.

The search-based optimization process takes as inputs, a source code with defects, bad-smells detection rules [2], a set of possible refactoring operations, software version archive (*e.g.*, change log in CVS), recorded refactorings applied in the past, and a call graph for the whole program. As output, our approach recommends set of refactoring solutions. A solution consists of a sequence of refactoring operations that should be applied to correct the input code.

4. MULTI-OBJECTIVE SEARCH BASED REFACTORING

This section is dedicated to the description of our approach design. We describe how we encoded the optimization problem for the refactoring suggestion using NSGA-II.

4.1 NSGA-II overview

The basic idea of NSGA-II [8] is to make a population of candidate solutions evolve toward the near-optimal solution in order to solve a multi-objective optimization problem. NSGA-II is designed to find a set of optimal solutions, called non-dominated solutions, also Pareto set. A non-dominated solution is the one which provides a suitable compromise between all objectives without degrading any of them. As described in Algorithm 1, the first step in NSGA-II is to create randomly a population P_0 of individuals encoded using a specific representation. Then, a child population Q_0 is generated from the population of parents P_0 using genetic operators such as crossover and mutation. Both populations are merged into an initial population R_0 of size N, and a subset of individuals is selected, based on the dominance principle and crowding distance [8] to create the next generation. This process will be repeated until reaching the last iteration according to stop criteria.

while *stopping criteria not reached* **do**
  $R_t = P_t \cup Q_t$;
  F = fast-non-dominated-sort (R_t);
  $P_{t+1} = \emptyset$ and i=1;
  while $|P_{t+1}| + |F_i| \leq N$ **do**
    Apply crowding-distance-assignment(F_i);
    $P_{t+1} = P_{t+1} \cup F_i$;
    $i = i+1$;
  end
  $Sort(F_i, \prec n)$;
  $P_{t+1} = P_{t+1} \cup F_i[1 : (N\text{-}|P_{t+1}|)]$;
  Q_{t+1} = create-new-pop(P_{t+1});
  $t = t+1$;
end

Algorithm 1: High-level pseudo-code of NSGA-II

4.2 NSGA-II adaptation

This section describes how NSGA-II [8] can be used for the refactoring suggestion problem. In general, to apply NSGA-II to a specific problem, the following elements have to be defined: representation of the individuals, evaluation of individuals using a fitness function for each objective to optimize, selection of the individuals to transmit from one generation to another, creation of new individuals using genetic operators (crossover and mutation) to explore the search space, and generation of a new population.

4.2.1 Solution representation

To represent a candidate solution (individual), we used a vector representation. Each vector's dimension represents a refactoring operation. When created, the order of applying these refactorings corresponds to their positions in the vector. In addition, for each refactoring, a set of controlling parameters are randomly picked from the program to be refactored as illustrated in Table 1.

Ref	Refactorings	Controlling parameters
MM	Move Method	(source class, target class, method)
MF	Move Field	(source class, target class, field)
PUF	Pull Up Field	(source class, target class, field)
PUM	Pull Up Method	(source class, target class, method)
PDF	Push Down Field	(source class, target class, field)
PDM	Push Down Method	(source class, target class, method)
IC	Inline Class	(source class, target class)
IM	Inline Method	(source class, source method, target class, target method)
EM	Extract Method	(source class, source method, target class, extracted method)
EC	Extract Class	(source class, new class)

Table 1. Refactorings and its controlling parameters

An example of a solution is given in Figure 2. For short, we use abbreviations, e.g. MM for move method refactoring, EC for extract class (see Table 1). Of course, for each of these refactorings we specify pre- and post-conditions that are already studied in [11] to ensure the feasibility of applying these refactoring.

MM	MF	PUF	IM	EC	MF

Figure 2. Representation of an NSGA-II individual

4.2.2 Fitness functions

After creating a solution, it should be evaluated using fitness function to ensure its ability to solve the problem under consideration. The solution proposed in this paper is based on studying how to preserve the way how code elements are semantically grouped and connected together when refactorings are decided automatically, and how to use the development change history to automate refactoring suggestion. Semantic preservation is captured by different heuristics/measures that could be integrated into existing refactoring approaches to help preserving semantic coherence.

Since we have three objectives, we define three different fitness functions:

1) *Quality fitness function* that calculates the ratio of the number of corrected design defects (bad-smells) over the initial number of defects using detection rules [2].

2) S*emantic fitness function* that corresponds to the weighted sum of semantic measures [5]: vocabulary similarity (cosine similarity), and structural dependency (shared method calls and shared field access) used to approximate the semantic proximity between modified code elements. Hence, the semantic fitness function of a refactoring solution corresponds to the average of the semantic measure for each refactoring operation in the vector.

3) History of changes' fitness function that calculates an average of three measures: a) similarity with previous refactorings applied to similar code fragments, b) number of changes applied in the past to the same code elements to modify, and c) a score that characterizes the co-change of elements that will be refactored.

The first two fitness functions are studied before in [5] thus we are focusing in this paper on the third fitness function.

Recently, research has been carried out to mining software version repositories [20] [18] [16]. One of the important issues is to detect and interpret groups of software entities that change together. These co-change relationships have been used for different purposes: to identify hidden architectural dependencies [20], to point developers to possible places that need change [16], or to use them for software clustering [18]. Detecting historical co-change is mostly based on mining versioning systems such as CVS and in identifying pairs of changed entities. Entities are usually files and the change is determined through observing additions or deletions of lines of code. In the past decades, many CVS archives of open-source and industrial systems are freely available, e.g., via SourceForge.net.

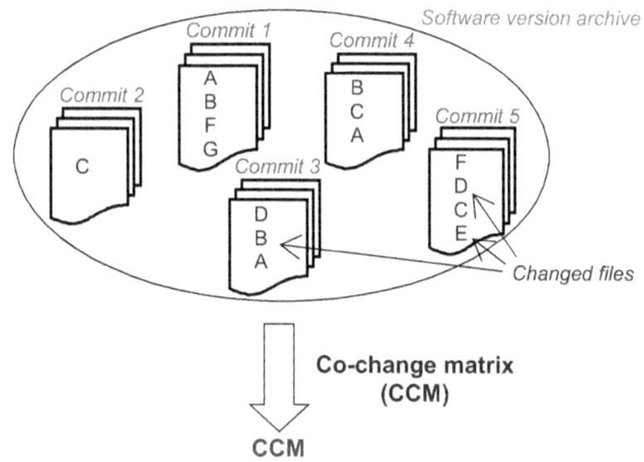

	A	B	C	D	E	F	G
A	3	3	1	1	0	1	1
B	3	3	1	1	0	1	1
C	1	1	3	1	1	1	0
D	1	1	1	2	1	1	0
E	0	0	1	1	1	1	0
F	1	1	1	1	1	2	1
G	1	1	0	0	0	1	1

Figure 3. Co-changes Matrix

We analyze CVS archives to identify which classes have been changed together at the same time. To this end, we use only source code files to extract co-change; however, other non-useful files (e.g., documentation, configuration files, etc.) are filtered out. We consider, that when a source code file has been changed then each class in this file is changed (almost only one or two classes per file are implemented in actual systems). Each commit/revision contains a lot of information such as the file name, the commit/revision number, the developer who performed the commit, the log message, and the timestamp of the check-in. Co-change can be easily detected by mining version archives, and is less expensive than program analysis (coupling, cohesion, etc.) [21]. We depict in Figure 3 an example of how to detect the co-change between classes through different commits from version history archives to generate a co-change matrix CCM. $CCM_{i,j}$ represented how many times the class *i* have been changed at the same time with class *j* (co-change). For example, we can observe that almost when the class A change, the class B change also. This reveals that the implementations and semantics of these two classes are strongly related. Therefore, moving code elements (methods/attributes) between them is likely to be semantically coherent since many changes have been manually performed between them in the past by software developers.

The second measure, *history_measure_2,* used in the history-based fitness function is the number of changes applied during the past to the same code elements to modify. If this number is high then we can conclude that this is a good indication that this code fragment is badly designed, thus represents a refactoring opportunity. This second measure is defined as:

$$history\_measure2(RO_i) = \sum_{i=1}^{n} t(e) \quad (1)$$

where *t(e)* is the number of times that the code element(s) *e* was refactored in the past and *n* is the size of the list of possible refactoring operations.

The third measure of the history-based fitness function is defined to maximize/encourage the use of new refactorings that are similar to those applied to same code fragments in the past. To calculate the similarity score between a proposed refactoring operation and different recorded/collected code changes, we use the following fitness function:

$$history\_measure3(RO) = \sum_{i=1}^{n} w * s \quad (2)$$

where *RO* is a suggested refactoring operation, *n* is the size of the list of recorded refactorings applied in the past, *s* is the number of times that a similar refactoring type has been applied in the past to the same code fragment/element and *w* is a refactoring weight (defined manually) that calculates the similarities between refactoring types if an exact matching cannot be found with the base of recorded refactoring.

4.2.3 Selection

To guide the selection process, NSGA-II sorts the population using the dominance principle and uses a comparison operator based on a calculation of the crowding distance [8] to select potential individuals to construct a new population P_{t+1}. Then, to generate an offspring population Q_{t+1}, the selection of individuals that will undergo the crossover and mutation operators in our adaption of NSGA-II is based on the Stochastic Universal Sampling algorithm [26].

4.2.4 Crossover and Mutation

To better explore the search space, the crossover and mutation operators are defined. As illustrated in Figure 4, both operators are fairly simple. For crossover, we use a single-point crossover, and the mutation operator simply picks at random some positions in the vector and replaces them by other refactoring operations.

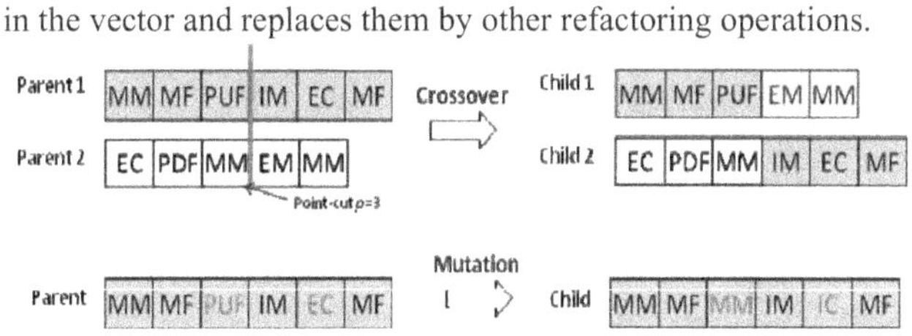

Figure 4. Crossover and mutation operators

5. VALIDATION

To evaluate the efficiency of our approach for generating good refactorings, we conducted experiments based on two large open-source systems to answer our two research questions described in section 1. We start by describing the designed our experiments. Then, we describe and discuss the obtained results.

5.1 Setup

We designed our experiments to address the above-mentioned two research questions. We apply our approach on two large open-source java projects JFreeChart [24] and Xerces-J [25]. JFreeChart is a powerful and flexible Java library for generating charts. Xerces-J is a family of software packages for parsing XML. Both programs and their change history are available through SourceForge.net. Table 2 provides some descriptive statistics about these two programs. To collect refactorings applied in previous versions, we use Ref-Finder [27], an Eclipse plug-in designed to detect refactorings between two program versions.

Systems	# classes	# defects	KLOC	# revision commits
Xerces v2.7.0	991	66	240	7493
JFreeChart v1.0.9	521	57	170	2009

Table 2. Program statistics

To answer **RQ1**, we validate manually the proposed refactoring operations to fix design defects. To this end, we calculate the defect correction ratio (DCR) given by Equation (3). It corresponds to the number of defects that are corrected after applying the suggested refactoring solution.

$$DCR = \frac{\#\,\text{corrected defects}}{\#\,\text{defects before applying refactorings}} \quad (3)$$

Then, we manually inspect the semantic correctness of the proposed refactoring operations for each studied system. We applied the proposed refactoring operations using ECLIPSE [28] and we check the semantic coherence of the modified code fragments. To this end, we define the metric refactoring precision (RP) that corresponds to the number of meaningful refactoring operations, in terms of semantic coherence, over the total number of suggested ones. RP is given by Equation (4).

$$RP = \frac{\#\,\text{coherent refactorings}}{\#\,\text{proposed refactorings}} \quad (4)$$

In our experiments, we calculate an average of the two-above mentioned scores over 30 runs to ensure the stability of our results.

In addition, to evaluate the efficiency of our approach, we compared our results to those produced by four existing contributions [3], [1], [2] and [15]. In [3], Harman et al. proposed a multi-objective approach that uses two quality metrics to improve (coupling between objects, and standard deviation of methods per class) after applying the refactorings sequence. In [1], a single-objective genetic algorithm is used to correct defects by finding the best refactoring sequence that reduces the number of defects. In [2], NSGA-II is used to find refactoring solutions to correct defects with low code modification/adaptation effort. And, in [15], a new objective is integrated to maximize the reuse of good refactorings applied to similar contexts. In all contributions, the development history is not used explicitly. We evaluate if our refactoring solutions produces more coherent changes than those proposed by [3], [1], [2] and [15] while having similar quality improvement.

To answer **RQ2**, we assessed the performance of the multi-objective algorithm NSGA-II compared to a random search, and a genetic algorithm where one fitness function is used (an average of the three objective scores).

Due to the stochastic nature of the algorithms/approaches we are studying, each time we execute an algorithm we can get slightly different results. To cater for this issue and to make inferential statistical claims, our experimental study is performed based on 31 independent simulation runs for each algorithm/technique studied. Wolcoxon rank sum test is applied between NSGA-II and each of the other algorithms/techniques (Kessentini et al., Ouni et al, MOGA, and Random Search) in terms of DCR with a 99% confidence level (α = 1%). Our tests shows that the obtained results are statistically significant with p-value<0.01 and not due to chance.

5.2 Results and Discussions

As described in Table 3, the majority of suggested refactorings by our approach improve significantly the code quality with acceptable correction scores compared to both other existing work. In addition, we preserve the semantics much better than all other approaches. For JFreeChart, 197 of the 210 proposed refactoring operations (94%) do not generate semantic incoherence. This score is higher than the one of the other approaches having respectively only 86%, 66%, 62% and 77% as RP scores. Thus, our multi-objective approach reduces the number of semantic incoherencies when applying refactoring operations. In the same time, after applying the proposed refactoring operations, we found that more than 86% (49/57) of detected defects were fixed. The corrected defects were of different types (blob, spaghetti code, and functional decomposition [2]). The majority of non-fixed defects are related to the blob type. This type of defect usually requires a large number of refactoring operations and is then very difficult to correct. This score is comparable to the correction score of other existing approaches that do not use development history (89%). Thus, the slight loss in the defect-correction ratio is largely compensated by the significant improvement of the semantic coherence.

Systems	Approach	Algorithm	DCR	RP
JFreeChart v1.10.2	***Our approach***	***NSGA-II***	***86% (49|57)***	***94% (197|210)***
	Ouni et al. '13 [15]	NSGA-II	82% (47|57)	86% (202|234)
	Harman et al. '07 [3]	Pareto opt.	N.A	66% (192|289)
	Kessentini et al. '11 [1]	GA	89% (51/57)	62% (147|236)
	Ouni et al. '12 [2]	NSGA-II	84% (48/57)	77% (157|203)
Xerces-J v2.7.0	***Our approach***	***NSGA-II***	***80% (53|66)***	***96% (282|294)***
	Ouni et al. '13 [15]	NSGA-II	79% (52|66)	93% (219|236)
	Harman et al. '07 [3]	Pareto opt.	N.A	63% (251|396)
	Kessentini et al. '11 [1]	GA	88% (58/66)	69% (212|304)
	Ouni et al. '12 [2]	NSGA-II	83% (55/66)	81% (186|228)

Table 3. Refactoring results

We also had similar results for Xerces-J. The majority of defects were corrected (80%), and most of the proposed refactoring sequences (96%) are coherent semantically. When comparing with previous work, Kessentini et al. performs slightly better for the number of corrected defects than NSGA-II (88%). However, for the refactoring precision, strategies proposed by our approach require less manual adaptation than those of Kessentini et al. Indeed, the majority of refactoring operations proposed by NSGA-II does not need programmer intervention to solve semantic incoherencies that are introduced when applying them. 89% of proposed refactorings by our approach for Xerces-J are correct, whereas Kessentini et al., Harman et al. and Ouni et al. proposes respectively 69%, and 63%, 93% and 81% of good refactorings.

In conclusion, our approach produces good refactoring suggestions both from the point of views of defect-correction ratio and semantic coherence using the development change history.

In addition, we compare the refactoring results with and without use of development history. As illustrated in Figure 5, when only the quality fitness function is used, just 61% of proposed refactorings are semantically coherent for JFreeChart (only 69% for Xerces). Indeed, when the semantics is considered (vocabulary and structural information), the RP is improved, but it is still less than 81% for JFreeChart and 89% for Xerces. However, when the development history is considered, the majority of the proposed refactorings are semantically coherent, and we obtained 96% of RP for Xerces and 94% for JFreeChart.

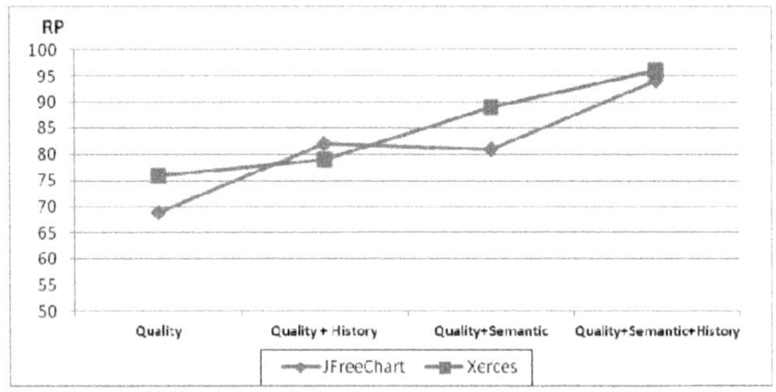

Figure 5. Impact of the use of development history on refactoring suggestion

To answer RQ2, for evaluating the efficiency of NSGA-II and justifying the need to use multi-objective algorithms, we compared the performance of our proposal to a random search and mono-objective algorithms. In a random search, the change operators (crossover and mutations) are not used, and populations are generated randomly and evaluated using the two fitness functions. In our mono-objective adaptation, we considered a single fitness function, which is the average score of the three objectives using genetic algorithm. Since in our NSGA-II adaptation we select a single solution without giving more importance to some objectives, we give equal weights for each fitness function value. As shown by Figure 6, NSGA-II outperforms significantly comparing to random-search and mono-objective algorithms in terms of corrected design defects and semantics preservation. For instance, in Gantt-Project NSGA-II has approximately the double of random/mono-objective RP and DCR scores.

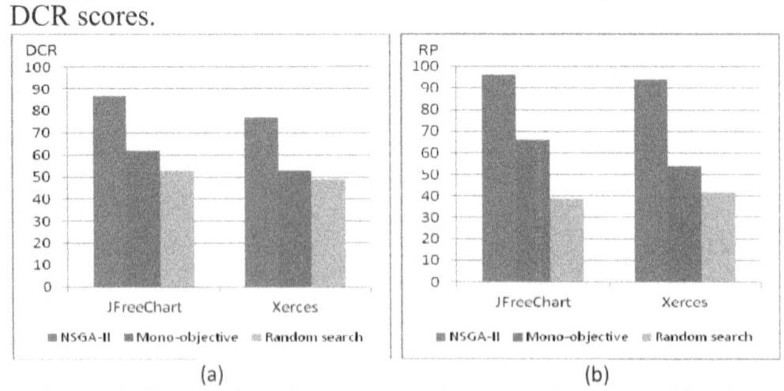

Figure 6. Comparison between random search, mono-objective, and multi-objective algorithms for refactoring suggestions: (a) Quality (DCR) and (b) Semantics preservation (RP).

Another element that should be considered when comparing the results of the three algorithms is that NSGA-II does not produce a single solution like GA, but a set of optimal solutions (non-dominated solutions). The maintainer can choose a solution from them depending on his preferences in terms of compromise. However, at least for our evaluation, we need to select only one solution. To this end and in order to fully automate our approach, we propose to extract and suggest only one best solution from the returned set of solutions. In our case, the ideal solution has the best value of quality (equals to 1), of semantic coherence (equals to 1), and of change history reuse. Hence, we select the nearest solution to the ideal one in terms of Euclidian distance.

Finally, it is important to contrast the results of multiple executions. Over 31 independent simulation runs on JFreeChart, the average value of RP, DCR, development history reuse (collected refactorings) and execution time for finding the optimal refactoring solution with a number of iterations (stopping criteria) fixed to 8000 was respectively 94.86%, 86,83%, and 43min25s as shown in Figure 7. The standard deviation values was lower than 1, except for development history reuse (2.32). This indicates that our approach is reasonably scalable from the performance standpoint. Moreover, we evaluate the impact of the number of suggested refactorings on the RP, development history reuse, and DCR scores in 31 different executions. The best RP and DCR scores are also obtained with higher number of suggested refactorings. Thus, we could conclude that our approach is scalable from the performance standpoint, especially that quality improvements is not related in general to real-time applications where time-constraints are very important. In addition, the results accuracy is not affected by the number of suggested refactorings.

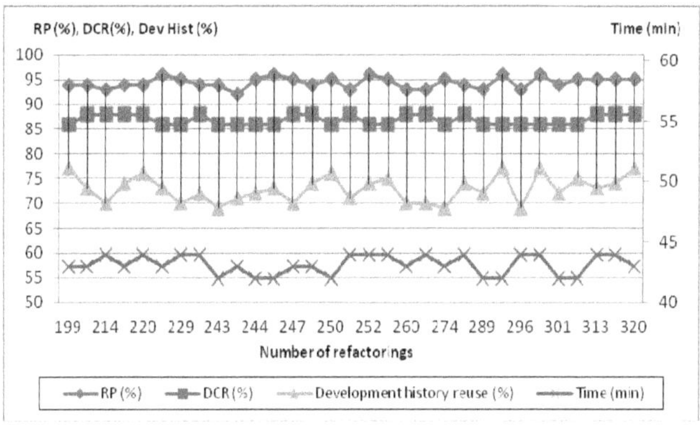

Figure 7. Impact of the number of refactorings on multiple executions on JFreeChart.

6. RELATED WORK

In this section, we review and discuss related work on the use of search-based refactoring, and the use of change history for several purposes in software engineering. We start by search-based refactoring that can be classified into two main categories: mono and multi-objective optimization approaches.

In the first category, the majority of existing works combine several metrics in a single fitness function to find the best sequence of refactorings. Seng et al. [4] have proposed a single-objective optimization based on genetic algorithm (GA) to suggest a list of refactorings that maximizes a weighted sum of some quality metrics (coupling, cohesion, complexity, and stability). Similarly, O'Keeffe et al. [10] have used different local search-based techniques such as hill climbing and simulated annealing, to provide automated refactoring support. Eleven weighted object-oriented design metrics have been used to evaluate the quality improvements. In [12], Qayum et al. considered the problem of refactoring scheduling as a graph transformation problem. They expressed refactorings as a search for an optimal path, using Ant colony optimization, in the graph where nodes and edges represent respectively refactoring candidates and dependencies between them. However, the use of graphs does not consider the domain semantics of the program and its runtime behavior. In [1], Kessentini et al. have proposed a single-objective combinatorial optimization using genetic algorithm to find the best sequence of refactoring operations that improve the quality of the code by minimizing as much as possible the number of design defects detected on the source code.

In the second category, Harman et al. [3] have proposed a multi-objective approach using Pareto optimality that combines two quality metrics, CBO (coupling between objects) and SDMPC (standard deviation of methods per class), in two separate fitness functions. The approach is designed to find a good sequence of move method refactorings that should provide the best compromise between CBO and SDMPC to improve software quality. In addition, a multi-objective optimization approach [2] has been proposed to find the best sequence of refactorings using NSGA-II. This approach is based on two fitness functions: quality and effort. The quality corresponds to the number of corrected defects that are detected on the initial program, and the effort fitness function corresponds on the code modification/adaptation score. This approach recommends a sequence of refactorings that provide the best tradeoff between quality and effort. Recently, Ouni et al. [5] have proposed a new multi-objective refactoring to find the best compromise between quality improvement and semantic coherence using two heuristics related to the vocabulary similarity and structural coupling. Later, in [15], the authors have integrated a new objective to maximize the reuse of good refactorings applied to similar contexts to propose new refactoring solutions. Ó Cinnéide et al. [14] have proposed a search-based refactoring to conduct an empirical investigation to assess some structural metrics and to explore relationships between them. To this end, they have used a variety of search techniques (Pareto-optimal search, semi-random search) guided by a set of cohesion metrics.

Thus, the vast majority of existing search-based software engineering approaches focused only on the program structure improvements. However, the main limitation is that the semantics preservation is not considered in the search process. Moreover, suggesting new refactorings should not be made independently to previous changes and maintenance/development history. This is one of the most relevant limitations on search-based refactoring approaches, which do not consider how the software has been changed and evolved and how software elements are impacted by these changes.

In addition, data extraction from development history/repository is very well covered. Research has been carried out to detect and interpret groups of software entities that change together. These co-change relationships have been used for different purposes. Zimmermann et al. [16] have used historical changes to point developers to possible places that need change. In addition historical common code changes are used to cluster software artifacts [17] [18], to predict source code changes by mining change history [21] [16], to identify hidden architectural dependencies [20] or to use them as change predictors [19]. In addition, recently, co-change has been used in several empirical studies in software engineering. However, in the best of our knowledge, until now, the development change history is not used to suggest refactorings.

7. CONCLUSION

In this paper, we presented a novel search-based approach to improve the automation of refactoring. We used software-development history, combined with structural and semantic information, to improve the precision and efficiency of new refactoring suggestions. We start by generating some solutions that represent a combination of refactoring operations to apply. A fitness function combines three objectives: maximizing design quality, semantic coherence and the re-use of the history of changes. To find the best trade-off between these objectives a NSGA-II algorithm is used. Our study shows that our technique outperforms state-of-the-art techniques where a maximum of two objectives is used.

The proposed approach was tested on open-source systems, and the results are promising. However, one of the main limitations of our work is how to deal with systems that did not have a history of applied refactorings. To solve this issue part of future work is to use collected refactorings from different systems and calculates a similarity with not only the refactoring type but also the context.

Acknowledgement

This publication was made possible by NPRP grant # [09-1205-2-470] from the Qatar National Research Fund (a member of Qatar Foundation). The statements made herein are solely the responsibility of the author[s].

8. REFERENCES

[1] M. Kessentini, W. Kessentini, H. Sahraoui, M. Boukadoum, and A. Ouni. Design Defects Detection and Correction by Example. In Proc. of the *19th IEEE Int. Conf. on Program Comprehension (ICPC)*, pp. 81-90, Kingston, Canada, 2011.

[2] A. Ouni, M. Kessentini, H. Sahraoui and M. Boukadoum. Maintainability Defects Detection and Correction: A Multi-Objective Approach. *Journal of Autmated Software Engineering*, Springer, 2012.

[3] M. Harman, and L. Tratt. Pareto optimal search based refactoring at the design level. In *Proceedings of the Genetic and Evolutionary Computation Conference* (GECCO'07), 1106-1113, 2007.

[4] O. Seng, J. Stammel, and D. Burkhart, Search-based determination of refactorings for improving the class structure of object-oriented systems, In *Proceedings of the Genetic and Evolutionary Computation Conference* (GECCO'06), 1909-1916, 2006.

[5] A. Ouni, M. Kessentini, H. Sahraoui and M. S. Hamdi. Search-based Refactoring: Towards Semantics Preservation. In *Proceedings of the 28th IEEE International Conference on Software Maintenance* (ICSM), Italy, september 2012.

[6] M. Fowler, K. Beck, J. Brant, W. Opdyke, and D. Roberts. Refactoring – Improving the Design of Existing Code, 1st ed. Addison-Wesley, June 1999.

[7] N. Fenton and S. L. Pfleeger. Software Metrics: A Rigorous and Practical Approach, 2nd ed. London, UK: International Thomson Computer Press, 1997.

[8] K. Deb, A. Pratap, S. Agarwal, and T. Meyarivan. A fast and elitist multiobjective genetic algorithm: NSGA-II, *IEEE Trans. Evol. Comput.*, vol. 6, pp. 182–197, Apr. 2002.

[9] http://www.refactoring.com/catalog/

[10] M. O'Keeffe, and M. O. Cinnéide. Search-based Refactoring for Software Maintenance. *Journal of Systems and Software*, 81(4), 502–516, 2006.

[11] W. F. Opdyke, Refactoring: A Program Restructuring Aid in Designing Object-Oriented Application Frameworks, Ph.D. thesis, University of Illinois at Urbana-Champaign, 1992.

[12] F. Qayum, and R. Heckel. Local search-based refactoring as graph transformation. *Proceedings of 1st Int. Symposium on Search Based Software Engineering*, 2009; 43–46.

[13] R. Heckel, Algebraic graph transformations with application conditions, M.S. thesis, TU Berlin, 1995.

[14] M. Ó Cinnéide, L. Tratt, M. Harman, S. Counsell, and I. H. Moghadam, Experimental Assessment of Software Metrics Using Automated Refactoring, *Proc. Empirical Software Engineering and Management* (ESEM), pages 49-58, 2012.

[15] A. Ouni, M. Kessentini and H. Sahraoui, Search-based Refactoring Using Recorded Code Changes, in *Proc of the 17th European Conference on Software Maintenance and Reengineering* (CSMR), Genova, Italy, march 5-8, 2013.

[16] T. Zimmermann, P. Weißgerber, S. Diehl, and A. Zeller. Mining version histories to guide software changes. In *Proc. 26th International Conference on Software Engineering* (ICSE), Edinburgh, Scotland, May 2004.

[17] T. Gîrba, S. Ducasse, A. Kuhn, R. Marinescu, and R. Daniel. Using Concept Analysis to Detect Co-Change Patterns. In *Proceedings of International Workshop on Principles of Software Evolution* (IWPSE), 2007.

[18] D. Beyer, and A. Noack. Clustering Software Artifacts Based on Frequent Common Changes. *Proceedings of the 13th International Workshop on Program Comprehension*, 2005.

[19] A. Hassan and R. Holt. Predicting change propagation in software systems. In *Proceedings 20th Int. Conference on Software Maintenance* (ICSM'04), pp. 284–293, 2004.

[20] H. Gall, K. Hajek, and M. Jazayeri. Detection of logical coupling based on product release history. *Int. Proc. of Conf. on Soft. Maintenance* (ICSM), pages 190–198, Los Alamitos CA, 1998.

[21] T.T. Ying, G. C. Murphy, R. Ng, and M. C. Chu-Carroll. Predicting source code changes by mining change history. *IEEE Transactions on Soft. Eng.* (TSE), Vol 30, No. 9, 2004.

[22] T. Mens, T. Tourwé: A Survey of Software Refactoring. IEEE Trans. Software Eng. 30(2), pp. 126-139, 2004.

[23] P. Cederqvist. Version Management with CVS, Dec. 2003. www.cvshome.org/docs/manual/

[24] http://www.jfree.org/jfreechart/

[25] http://xerces.apache.org/

[26] John R. Koza. 1992. *Genetic Programming: On the Programming of Computers by Means of Natural Selection*. MIT Press, Cambridge, MA, USA.

[27] K. Prete, N. Rachatasumrit, N. Sudan, M. Kim. Template-based reconstruction of complex refactorings. in *Proc. of the Int. Conf. on Software Maintenance* (ICSM), 2010.

[28] http://www.eclipse.org/

A Scenario-based Robust Model for the Next Release Problem

Matheus Paixão
State University of Ceará
1700 Avenida Paranjana
Fortaleza, Brazil
mhepaixao@gmail.com

Jerffeson Souza
State University of Ceará
1700 Avenida Paranjana
Fortaleza, Brazil
jerffeson.souza@uece.br

ABSTRACT

The next release problem is a significant task in the iterative and incremental software development model, involving the selection of a set of requirements to be included in the next software release. Given the dynamic environment in which modern software development occurs, the uncertainties related to the input variables considered in this problem should be taken into account. In this context, this paper proposes a novel formulation to the next release problem based on scenarios and considering the robust optimization framework, which enables the production of robust solutions. In order to measure the "price of robustness", several experiments were designed and executed over artificial and real-world instances. All experimental results are consistent to show that the penalization with regard to solution quality due to robustness is relatively small, which qualifies the proposed model to be applied even in large-scale real-world software projects.

Categories and Subject Descriptors

D.2.1 [**Software Engineering**]: Requirements Specifications—*Methodologies*

General Terms

Algorithms, Measurement, Reliability

Keywords

Next Release Problem, Robust Optimization, Search Based Software Engineering

1. INTRODUCTION

In an iterative and incremental software development process, a stable and executable version of the product delivered to the clients is called release. Despite bringing many benefits, this development model embodies more complexity to the project management, including the problem of selecting a set of requirements to be added to the software as part of the next release, which has become known as the Next Release Problem (NRP). The NRP was first modeled as an optimization problem by Bagnall et al. [1]. In this model, each client has an importance to the organization. The goal is to select a subset of clients which will have their requirements added to the next release, so that the sum of their importance is maximized. The total cost required to satisfy the clients is subject to a predefined bound, which must be respected. A variation of this model was proposed by Akker et al. [17], where each requirement has an importance value, which estimates its revenue. The objective here is to select a subset of requirements such that the total revenue is maximal and the available capacity is respected.

In order to employ an optimization technique to solve the Next Release Problem, it is necessary to obtain the values of importance and cost for each requirement. For instance, the requirement importance could be indicated by the clients and the cost determined by the development team. In both cases, these values are obtained based on estimates, which can be significantly hard to make due to the dynamic environment in which software development occurs. In the work by Harker et al. [8], requirements are classified in six types. Among those types, five are classified as *changing* and only one as *stable*, which stresses the evolving nature of requirements. In this context, requirement's importance and cost are among those features that can change after the initial requirements engineering phase. Indeed, the high level of uncertainty related to the variables of the next release problem generates a fairly complicated context, as pointed out by Zhang, Finkelstein and Harman in [22]:

> "Software engineering problems are typically 'messy' problems in which the available information is often incomplete, sometimes vague and almost always subject to a high degree of change (including unforeseen change). Requirements change frequently, and small changes in the initial stages often lead to large changes to the solutions, affecting the solution complexity and making the results of these initial stages potentially fragile."

More details about the impact caused by requirements' changes during the release development can be seen in the sensitivity analyses presented in [9]. Therefore, it seems reasonable that the uncertainties related to requirement's importance and cost should be considered when solving the next release problem through an optimization technique.

The robust optimization is an operational research framework that identifies and quantifies uncertainties in optimization problems [4]. It started to gain more visibility after [16]

GECCO'13, July 6–10, 2013, Amsterdam, The Netherlands.

and [2]. This optimization design technique admits that some problem aspects are uncertain. From this assumption, it builds up models which seek robust solutions, i.e., even with noisy input data, it produces good quality solutions while still fulfilling all constraints. Robust optimization has been successfully applied in several engineering disciplines including, but not limited to, production [12], aeronautical [5], electronic [14], mechanical [13], chemical [18] and metallurgical engineering [6].

Accordingly, the robust optimization framework can aid the proposition of original optimization models to the NRP, which could deal with the uncertainties present in this problem, allowing for the production of robust solutions. However, as can be assumed, this desired robustness will necessarily be accompanied by some loss in solution quality, which needs to be contemplated. This measure of loss has been called in the robust optimization literature as the "price of robustness" [3].

Therefore, motivated by this context, this paper aims at answering the following research questions:

- RQ_1: How to model the Next Release Problem as an optimization problem considering the uncertainties related to its input variables in order to allow for the production of robust solutions?
- RQ_2: What is the "price of robustness" for the proposed Next Release Problem model? In other words, how much would be lost with regard to solution quality in order to gain robustness?

Most of the works in the SBSE literature do not directly consider the uncertainties related to the input variables, which is also the case for the next release problem. However, as one of the exceptions, the work in [21] proposed a model considering the possibility of change in the requirement's importance. In this work, each requirement received an importance value called "today value" and it was assumed that this value, in some moment after the release development, would change to a certain "future value". The approach, therefore, seeks to balance the company's today and future needs by considering these two requirement values, along with the release total cost, via a multiobjective formulation.

In fact, the original and main contribution of this paper lies in the proposal of a novel formulation to the next release problem, considering the robust optimization framework, which was formally defined by Beyer et. al [4]. This new NRP model will allow the production of robust solutions by taking into account the uncertainties related to its input variables.

The remaining of this paper is organized as follows: Section 2 presents the proposed robust NRP formulation. Section 3 exhibits and examines the experiments designed to evaluate the proposed formulation. Finally, Section 4 concludes the paper and points out some future research directions.

2. A ROBUST NEXT RELEASE PROBLEM FORMULATION

Given a set of requirements $R = \{r_1, r_2, \dots, r_N\}$, the requirement r_i importance value and cost are represented by v_i and c_i, respectively. A basic Next Release Problem formulation is presented next:

$$\text{maximize} \sum_{i=1}^{N} v_i x_i \tag{1}$$

$$\text{subject to} \sum_{i=1}^{N} c_i x_i \leq b \tag{2}$$

where b is the release budget. The decision variable is a vector $X = \{x_1, x_2, \dots, x_N\}$, where $x_i = 1$ indicates that requirement r_i is included in the next release and $x_i = 0$ otherwise.

As pointed out in [8], the occurrence of certain events can change the requirements' importance values during the release development. Therefore, this type of uncertainty seems adequate to be quantified in a discrete and probabilistic way, using the robust optimization concept of scenarios [20]. A scenario can be defined as a set of values which represent different contexts due to the occurrence of certain events. Thus, one can formally define a set of scenarios $S = \{s_1, s_2, \dots, s_M\}$, where each scenario is represented by $s_i \subset S | s_i = \{v_1^s, v_2^s, \dots, v_N^s\}$, with v_i^s expressing the importance of requirement r_i in scenario s. The range a requirement's importance value can vary is discrete and depends on the set of scenarios S. In the assignment of these possible values, one should consider the probability of those events actually taking place. For each scenario s, it is defined an occurrence probability p_s, with $\sum_{i=1}^{M} p_s = 1$. Thus, the requirement's importance v_i in the proposed robust model is defined as:

$$v_i = \sum_{s=1}^{M} v_i^s p_s \tag{3}$$

The above requirement's importance can be looked at as a generalization of the importance in the basic NRP formulation. In fact, by considering a single scenario t, with a probability $p_t = 1$, the requirement's importance will be the same as the one in Equation 1.

The uncertainty related to the cost of the requirements is intrinsically distinct. In this case, it seems unreasonable to expect one to raise a set of scenarios based on certain events, since those costs usually vary independently and this change may not be discrete. Thus, in this paper, the uncertainty related to cost will be quantified in a deterministic and continuous fashion, as follows. Besides the requirement's cost c_i, it is defined a value $\hat{c}_i$ indicating the maximum expected cost variation. This variation is then used to generate lower and upper bounds to the cost c_i, so that $c_i - \hat{c}_i \leq c_i \leq c_i + \hat{c}_i$. For more information about uncertainties quantification strategies, see [4].

Therefore, a possible robust formulation for the release total cost is as follows:

$$\sum_{i=1}^{N} c_i x_i + \sum_{i=1}^{N} \hat{c}_i x_i \tag{4}$$

In the above case, besides the sum of all requirements' costs selected to the next release, the total release cost will also consider the sum of all respective cost variations $\hat{c}_i$. This approach will guarantee that, even in the worst case, when all selected requirements will cost their upper bounds (given by $c_i + \hat{c}_i$), the release budget will be satisfied. This, clearly, represents a very conservative approach, since it assumes that all cost estimates will be missed by the maximum amount. However, in real software development projects, different development teams have divergent estimating skills, usually related to the team's experience. To consider this assumption in order to generate a more realist model, it is defined a control parameter Γ [3], which indicates the expected level of failure in the cost estimations. This way, in the situation where the team estimates are historically 30% incorrect, in a project with 50 requirements, the control parameter would be $\Gamma = 15$, indicating that there is an expectation that 15 requirements will have real costs different from those that were originally predicted.

Using this new control parameter, the release total cost in the robust model proposed in this paper is computed as:

$$\sum_{i=1}^{N} c_i x_i + max_{W \subseteq R, |W| \leq \Gamma} \sum_{i \in W} \hat{c}_i x_i \tag{5}$$

The release total cost is composed by the sum of the cost estimates c_i and a second factor, which was added to guarantee a certain robustness level controlled by Γ, as explained next. Considering that there is an expectation that Γ requirements will have costs that were wrongfully predicted, the proposed formulation will seek a subset $W \subseteq R$ with cardinality $|W| \leq \Gamma$, where the sum of cost variations $\hat{c}_i$ is maximum. In other words, since there is no way to know in advance which requirements may have erroneous cost estimates, the model guarantees that, even if the development team misses the costs of the requirements with highest variations, the solution will still be valid.

Once again, it is straightforward to reach the basic NRP model or the conservative approach. Using $\Gamma = 0$, it is assumed that the team won't miss a single cost estimate. In this case, the total release cost proposed in Equation 5 will be the same as described in Equation 2. In addition, all cost variations will be taken into account when $\Gamma = N$, which carries the proposed formulation back to the conservative approach materialized by Equation 4. Finally, it is noteworthy that it is also possible to return to the basic formulation by setting all cost variations $\hat{c}_i$ to 0.

Therefore, the proposed robust Next Release Problem formulation is formally described as:

$$\text{maximize} \sum_{i=1}^{N} \sum_{s=1}^{M} v_i^s p_s x_i$$

$$\text{subject to} \sum_{i=1}^{N} c_i x_i + max_{W \subseteq R, |W| \leq \Gamma} \sum_{i \in W} \hat{c}_i x_i \leq b$$

where, $x_i \in \{0, 1\}$

R is the set of requirements

N is the number of requirements

M is the number of scenarios

p_s is the scenario s occurrence probability

v_i^s is the value of requirement r_i in scenario s

c_i is the cost of requirement r_i

$\hat{c}_i$ is the expected cost variation of r_i

Γ is the robustness control parameter

b is the release budget

Hence, the above formulation is a robust optimization model for the next release problem which considers the uncertainties related to the input variables of this relevant problem which, therefore, answers the research question RQ_1.

3. EXPERIMENTAL EVALUATION

In order to answer the research question RQ_2, that is, what is the "price of robustness" for the next release problem as modeled in this paper, a set of three experiments were performed, as described next:

- **Experiment A:** The first experiment aims at evaluating the "price of robustness" when the proposed model is applied to artificial instances of varying sizes.

- **Experiment B:** In this second experiment, different approaches for setting the cost variations $\hat{c}_i$ were considered. This experiment was designed to discover any relationship between the cost variations and the "price of robustness".

- **Experiment C:** Finally, the model is applied to several realistic instances based on real-world software projects, in order to evaluate whether its behaviour is similar when using synthetic data.

The experiments are presented in sections 3.1, 3.2 and 3.3, with their respective settings, results and analyses.

In order to permit the full replication of all experiments, all artificial and real-world instances are make available at the paper supporting webpage - `http://www.larces.uece.br/~jeff/rnrp/` -, which also contains all results that have to be omitted from this paper due to space constraints.

3.1 Experiment A

As mentioned earlier, an increased level of solution robustness should naturally generate some loss in the solution quality. In this first experiment, the proposed robust model has been applied to a set of artificial instances in order to measure the "price of robustness" for the proposed formulation. The goal is to estimate how much is lost with regard to fitness value as there is an increase in robustness.

3.1.1 Settings

The artificial instance set is composed of 7 randomly generated instances. Each instance has 3 scenarios and each requirement's importance value v_i^s can assume an integer between 1 and 10. The cost c_i also varies from 1 to 10. The cost variation $\hat{c}_i$ is set to 10% of the respective cost. To ensure that it is impossible to include all requirements in the next release, the release budget is set to 70% of the sum of all requirements' costs. The instances were generated with different numbers of requirements, ranging from 50 to 200. In this paper, the artificial instance name is in the format I_S_R, where R is the number of requirements. The instance I_S_100, for example, has 100 requirements.

In the experiments, the metaheuristics Simulated Annealing and Genetic Algorithm were considered, as described next:

- **Simulated Annealing**: algorithm for solving ordinary optimization problems, based on the thermodynamics' annealing process [11].

- **Genetic Algorithm**: widely known evolutionary algorithm, already applied in many optimization problems and inspired by the Darwin's natural selection theory [10].

Each algorithm configuration was empirically obtained, after several preliminary experiments over different instances. The final configurations are described next:

Simulated Annealing. Initial and final temperatures were set to 100 and 10^{-3}, respectively. Cooling rate equals to 0.9995. At each iteration, N (number of requirements) neighbour solutions are evaluated. A neighbour solution is defined as a solution that can be produced from the original one with one requirement addition or removal.

Genetic Algorithm. Population with N individuals. The initial population is randomly generated and composed by feasible individuals. Crossover probability is set to 0.9, using one point crossover. Mutation is performed for each requirement with a $1/(10.N)$ probability, consisting of a single requirement inclusion/exclusion. Both crossover and mutation might generate invalid individuals. Therefore, a repairing method was designed, randomly removing requirements from the individual until the solution becomes feasible. The implementation employs elitism, with 20% of the best individuals in the population being automatically included in the next generation. The algorithm returns the best individual after 10000 generations.

Since the metaheuristics are non deterministic approaches, each algorithm was executed 10 times for each instance, to obtain fitness value averages and standard deviations.

In order to measure the "price of robustness", it is considered a 'reduction factor' [3], which indicates the percentage of loss in fitness value due to robustness. Thus, assuming α_k as the fitness value average for $\Gamma = k.N$, the 'reduction factor' δ_k is calculated as follows:

$$\delta_k = 100 \times (1 - \frac{\alpha_k}{\alpha_0}) \qquad (6)$$

Therefore, in order to evaluate how the control parameter Γ impacts the solution quality, each instance was solved using different robustness levels, varying Γ from 0 to N.

Table 1: Simulated Annealing results, regarding the fitness values when increasing the solution robustness

Instance	Γ				
	0	$0.25N$	$0.5N$	$0.75N$	N
LS_50	231.08 ± 2.84	227.69 ± 3.04	225.37 ± 4.47	223.34 ± 2.62	222.82 ± 3.70
LS_70	297.72 ± 1.90	293.06 ± 4.30	287.74 ± 4.46	288.58 ± 3.84	288.76 ± 4.67
LS_100	371.18 ± 4.41	365.05 ± 4.63	360.54 ± 3.82	358.01 ± 3.46	358.44 ± 3.14
LS_120	474.34 ± 3.94	466.75 ± 5.93	461.73 ± 4.06	460.86 ± 3.28	461.43 ± 4.96
LS_150	594.52 ± 6.60	590.07 ± 9.85	580.74 ± 7.60	579.12 ± 5.17	578.07 ± 5.80
LS_170	666.63 ± 6.57	663.54 ± 8.67	659.98 ± 6.05	652.80 ± 6.91	652.57 ± 6.09
LS_200	731.95 ± 9.43	725.51 ± 5.68	724.45 ± 9.13	717.19 ± 6.54	720.67 ± 6.63

Table 2: Genetic Algorithm results, regarding the fitness values when increasing the solution robustness

Instance	Γ				
	0	$0.25N$	$0.5N$	$0.75N$	N
LS_50	256.93 ± 0.00	250.77 ± 0.42	247.11 ± 0.20	246.27 ± 0.00	246.27 ± 0.00
LS_70	342.39 ± 0.22	333.23 ± 0.52	327.73 ± 0.68	326.34 ± 0.40	326.37 ± 0.34
LS_100	450.20 ± 0.46	439.98 ± 0.50	434.01 ± 0.71	431.79 ± 0.20	431.63 ± 0.46
LS_120	581.46 ± 0.40	568.39 ± 0.46	561.38 ± 0.45	558.29 ± 0.51	558.47 ± 0.49
LS_150	740.09 ± 0.41	720.90 ± 0.58	709.85 ± 0.62	706.44 ± 0.26	705.97 ± 0.51
LS_170	850.20 ± 0.32	828.74 ± 0.65	816.51 ± 0.39	812.51 ± 0.65	812.50 ± 0.53
LS_200	948.62 ± 0.76	923.69 ± 0.65	910.62 ± 0.42	905.28 ± 0.68	904.48 ± 0.47

3.1.2 Results and Analyses

Table 1 presents the fitness values computed by the Simulated Annealing, while Table 2 presents the results produced by the Genetic Algorithm, considering different levels of robustness. As expected, as there is a gain in robustness, the fitness value decreases. For both metaheuristics, a similar behavior was observed in that regard.

In average, the GA performed better than SA. Furthermore, the GA's standard deviations were significantly smaller than those obtained from SA.

Interestingly, the decrease in fitness value is smoother then linear. For instance, with $\Gamma = 0.5N$, the loss in fitness value is only insignificantly higher when compared with the previous robustness level $\Gamma = 0.25N$, representing around 1% in average. These results indicate that a significant gain in robustness can be obtained with very little loss in solution quality. To highlight that behavior, Figure 1 presents the fitness values computed for the instance LS_70, both by the Simulated Annealing and the Genetic Algorithm. It is noteworthy the significantly small fitness loss after Γ is set to half the number of requirements. This feature is present in both algorithms, but seems less visible in SA due to its higher fitness variation.

Table 3 presents the reduction factors computed by the Simulated Annealing and Table 4 the results found by the Genetic Algorithm. In general, the fitness value loss is considerably small. Considering all instances, it is possible to obtain a 50% robustness level ($\Gamma = 0.5N$) by losing, in average, only 2.24% and 3.88% in fitness value, for the SA and GA respectively. In the worst case ($\Gamma = N$), where the development team is expected to miss all cost estimates, the SA loses only 2.73% and the GA gives up 4.37% in solution quality, in average.

Figure 2 highlights, for instance LS_120, the reduction factors computed by the two algorithms. For most Γ values, the GA's reduction factor is higher than SA's. In addition, as can be seen, a maximum of almost 4% reduction in solution quality is reached, even for maximum robustness levels.

The interesting results described above partially answer RQ_2 and clearly show that the proposed robust next release problem formulation can help protecting against the uncer-

Figure 1: Fitness values comparison between SA and GA for the instance I_S_70

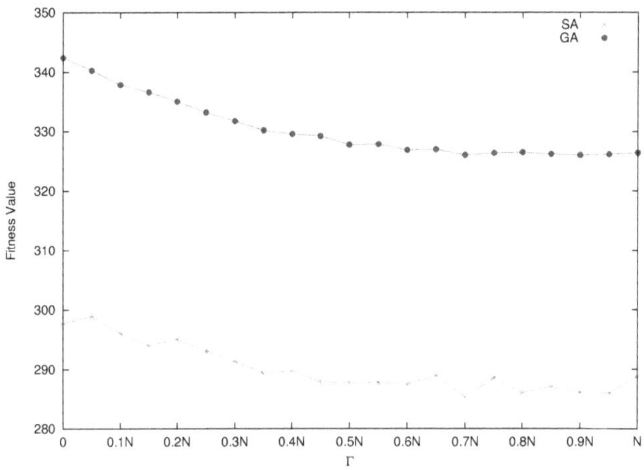

Table 3: Simulated Annealing results, regarding the reduction factor when increasing the solution robustness

Instance	Γ				
	$0.25N$	$0.5N$	$0.75N$	$0.9N$	N
I_S_50	1.46	2.47	3.35	3.47	3.57
I_S_70	1.56	3.35	3.07	3.90	3.01
I_S_100	1.65	2.87	3.55	3.47	3.43
I_S_120	1.60	2.66	2.84	2.70	2.72
I_S_150	0.75	2.32	2.59	3.02	2.77
I_S_170	0.46	1.00	2.07	1.27	2.11
I_S_200	0.88	1.02	2.02	1.53	1.54

tainties related to the input variables with little penalization with respect to solution quality.

3.2 Experiment B

As stated earlier, the cost variations $\hat{c}_i$ were set to represent 10% of the respective cost c_i. In practice, these variations may be estimated in different ways. Hence, in this experiment, the "price of robustness" is computed with different approaches for estimating the $\hat{c}_i$ values.

3.2.1 *Settings*

Basically the same artificial instances, described in the previous section, were used in this second experiment. The single difference relies on the strategy employed to produce the expected cost variations. This way, besides varying the percentage from 10% to 50% of the original cost, a random approach was also introduced, where each requirement's cost variation $\hat{c}_i$ is independently generated as a random number between 0 and 50% of c_i.

The Simulated Annealing and Genetic Algorithm were configured exactly as described in the previous section.

3.2.2 *Results and Analyses*

Figure 3 presents the particular reduction factors computed by the Simulated Annealing while Figure 4 presents the Genetic Algorithm's results, both for the instance I_S_120. As can be noticed and as expected, the higher the cost variation, the higher the reduction factor. However, this growth

Table 4: Genetic Algorithm results, regarding the reduction factor when increasing the solution robustness

Instance	Γ				
	$0.25N$	$0.5N$	$0.75N$	$0.9N$	N
I_S_50	2.40	3.82	4.15	4.20	4.15
I_S_70	2.68	4.28	4.69	4.79	4.68
I_S_100	2.27	3.60	4.09	4.17	4.13
I_S_120	2.25	3.45	3.99	3.93	3.95
I_S_150	2.59	4.09	4.55	4.60	4.61
I_S_170	2.52	3.96	4.43	4.44	4.43
I_S_200	2.63	4.01	4.57	4.68	4.65

Figure 2: Reduction factor comparison between SA an GA for the instance I_S_120

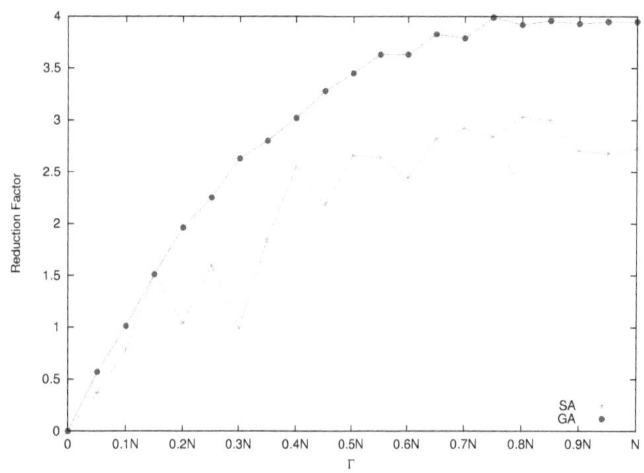

is not linear and even with significantly high variations, it is still possible to reach significant robustness levels with little loss in fitness value. As an illustrative example, considering the expected cost variation to be half of the requirement's original cost ($\hat{c}_i = 50\%$ of c_i), a 100% robustness level can be achievable by sacrificing only around 17% in fitness value. Still according to the results, a variation increase tends to close the gap between the SA and GA reduction factors, with SA losing more fitness value than GA in some cases.

In Figure 5 are presented the reduction factors computed by the GA with different variation values for the instance I_S_170. Comparing with instance I_S_120, the results are clearly similar. For others instances, the results are also very much alike, but due to space constraints, they have been omitted from this paper.

Thereby, the "price of robustness" of the proposed model remains interestingly low even when considering different strategies for generating the cost variations.

3.3 Experiment C

This experiment aims at evaluating the "price of robustness" of the proposed robust model in real-world instances, which are described next.

3.3.1 *Settings*

The real-world instances used in this experiment were adapted from the work by Xuan et al. [19]. In his paper, Xuan extracted the instances to the next release problem

Figure 3: Simulated Annealing price of robustness with different cost variation approaches for the instance I_S_120

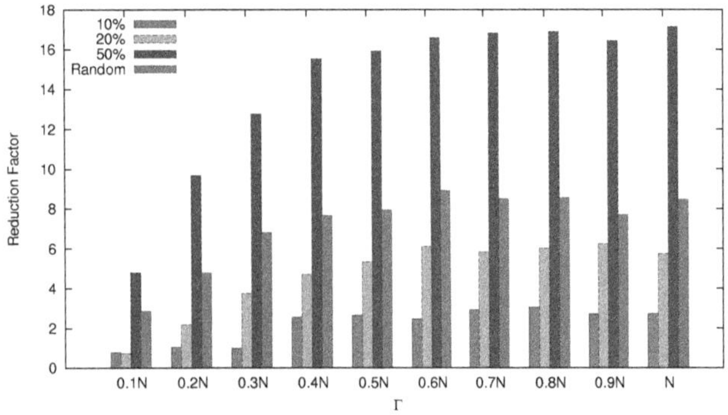

Figure 4: Genetic Algorithm price of robustness with different cost variation approaches for the instance I_S_120

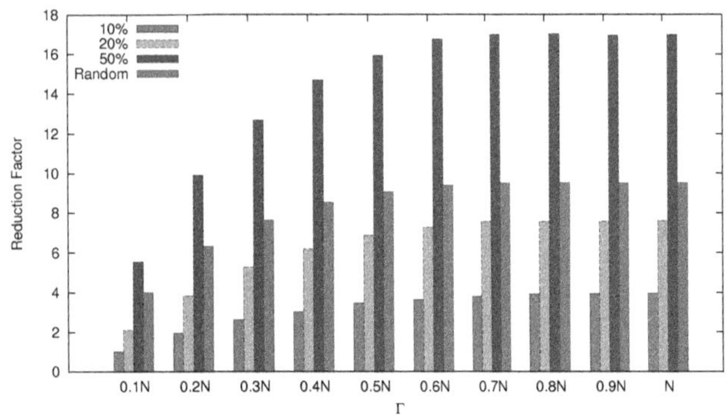

from bug repositories of three big open source projects, including Eclipse (a java integrated development environment) [7] and Mozilla (a set of web applications) [15].

A bug repository is a forum where users (end users, developers, testers, etc) can report bugs related to the project. Each bug is then considered as a requirement. In this forum, one bug report may be commented by many users. The requirement's importance value is then calculated as the number of users that commented on that particular bug report. In addition, the bug severity is mapped to the requirement's cost. Both the requirement's importance and cost are normalized to fall into the 1 to 10 interval. In all cases, each instance was considered to have only one scenario t (with a probability $p_t = 1$).

Three instances, composed by the most important requirements, were extracted from each bug repository. The instances contain 50, 120 and 200 requirements, respectively. The real-world instance names are in the format I_Re_P_R, where P represents the project (E for Eclipse and M for Mozilla) and R is the number of requirements. The instance I_Re_E_120, for example, was generated from the eclipse bug repository and has 120 requirements.

Since the Genetic Algorithm has systematically produced better solutions in previous experiments both regarding fitness values and standard deviation, only this metaheuristic

Figure 5: Genetic Algorithm price of robustness with different cost variation approaches for the instance I_S_170

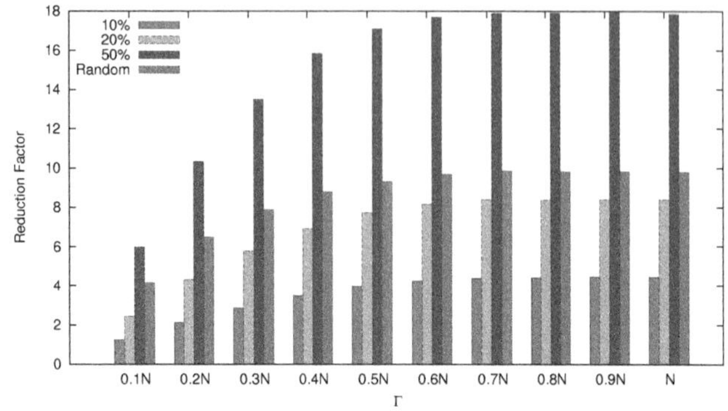

was considered in this experiment. Its configuration is the same as described previously.

3.3.2 Results and Analyses

Table 5 presents the results for fitness value found by the Genetic Algorithm for each real-world instance, with the requirement's cost variation set to 10% of the original cost. As can be seen, the model behaves nearly the same for artificial and real-world instances, which helps validating all results obtained in Experiment A. Once again, for $\Gamma = 0.5N$, the fitness value decrease becomes minimum when compared with previous robustness levels, even for the instances with 200 requirements.

Table 5: Genetic Algorithm fitness values results for the realistic instance set and standard deviation set to 10% of the cost

Instance	Γ				
	0	$0.25N$	$0.5N$	$0.75N$	N
I_Re_E_50	163.36 ± 0.82	159.09 ± 0.00	155.45 ± 0.00	155.18 ± 0.82	155.45 ± 0.00
I_Re_E_120	339.82 ± 0.68	332.09 ± 1.08	323.45 ± 0.68	322.27 ± 0.45	321.91 ± 0.27
I_Re_E_200	513.55 ± 1.25	500.18 ± 1.21	487.27 ± 1.00	484.73 ± 0.98	484.36 ± 1.67
I_Re_M_50	195.79 ± 0.98	192.14 ± 0.00	187.43 ± 0.65	186.71 ± 0.57	186.64 ± 0.46
I_Re_M_120	361.71 ± 1.40	354.57 ± 1.73	347.21 ± 2.01	344.00 ± 1.16	344.00 ± 1.51
I_Re_M_200	497.21 ± 0.50	486.07 ± 1.02	475.64 ± 0.50	472.14 ± 0.55	472.36 ± 0.85

Regarding reductions factor, Table 6 presents these results for each real-world instance. As mentioned earlier, even in the large real-world instances, the fitness value reduction after $\Gamma = 0.5N$ is very small. As an example, the results over real-world instances show that it is possible to reach a 100% robustness level losing only 5.12% of the fitness value, in average.

Figure 6 presents the reduction factor computed by the Genetic Algorithm for the instance I_Re_E_120 with different cost variation approaches. In Figure 7 are presented the same results for instance I_Re_E_200.

The reduction factors of both real-world instances are very

Table 6: Reduction factors computed by the Genetic Algorithm for the realistic instance set and standard deviation set to 10% of the cost

Instance	Γ				
	0.25	$0.5N$	$0.75N$	$0.9N$	N
I_Re_E_50	2.62	4.84	5.01	5.23	4.84
I_Re_E_120	2.27	4.82	5.16	5.22	5.27
I_Re_E_200	2.60	5.12	5.61	5.52	5.68
I_Re_M_50	1.86	4.27	4.63	4.63	4.67
I_Re_M_120	2.27	4.82	5.16	5.22	5.27
I_Re_M_200	2.24	4.34	5.04	5.09	5.00

Figure 6: Genetic Algorithm price of robustness with different cost variation approaches for the real-world instance I_Re_E_120

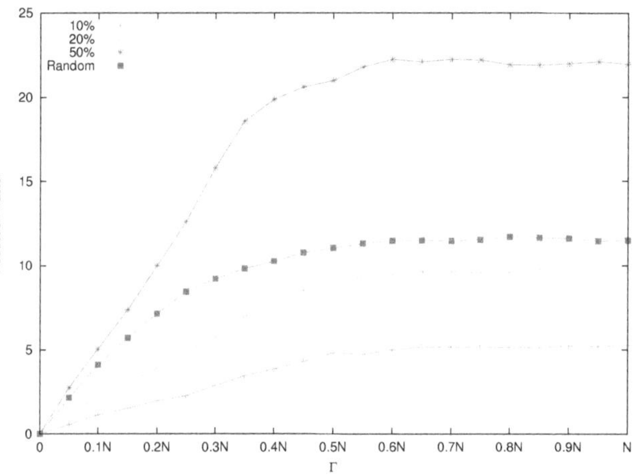

similar, akin to the behavior found in the artificial instances. For the Mozilla real-world instance I_Re_M_120, the results are also very consistent, as can be seen in Figure 8.

In conclusion, all results reported in this experiment are consistent to show that the behavior of the proposed robust formulation, regarding its "price of robustness", are similar to those found over artificial instances. That is, the penalization due to robustness is very small, which qualifies the proposed approach to be considered in real software projects.

Finally, the results obtained in the three experiments help answering RQ_2, pointing out to the ability of the model to produce robust solution with significantly small loss in quality.

3.4 Threats to Validity

The aspects that could affect the validity of the experimental results described in this paper are:

1. Relatively small number, size and diversity of instances: Even though the paper considers 7 artificial and 6 real-world instances, a higher number of instances would, clearly, produce more reliable results.

2. Parameterization of algorithms: In the experiments, the values for the algorithms' parameters were empirically calculated through a simplified experimental process. A more comprehensive parameterization process would be beneficial to the validity of the reported results.

Figure 7: Genetic Algorithm price of robustness with different cost variation approaches for the real-world instance I_Re_E_200

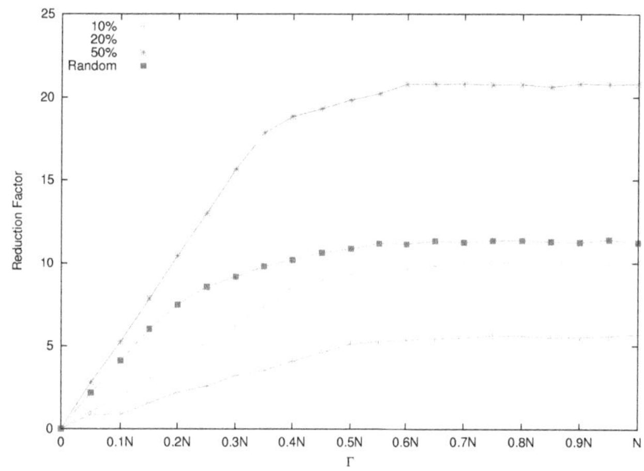

Figure 8: Genetic Algorithm price of robustness with different cost variation approaches for the real-world instance I_Re_M_120

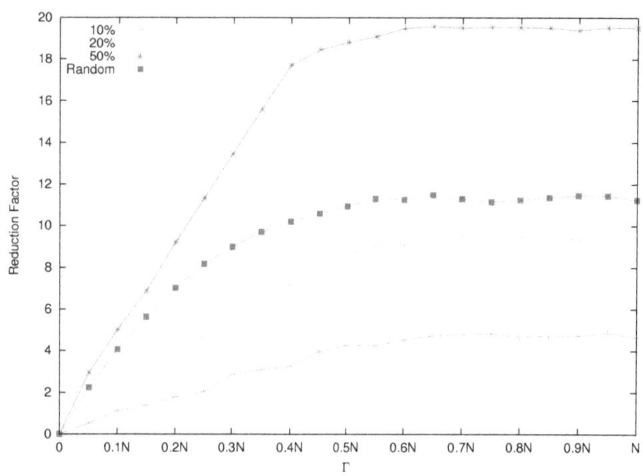

4. CONCLUSION AND FUTURE WORKS

The next release problem is an important task in the iterative and incremental software development model. For this problem, optimization models have been proposed to search for solutions based on estimates of requirements' importance and cost. However, such estimates may turn out to be erroneous, which can invalidate the search process.

This paper proposed an original robust formulation, based on scenarios, for the next release problem, which takes into account the uncertainties present in the input variables. In the proposed model, the uncertainties related to the requirement's importance were modeled in a discrete way using the concept of scenarios. Differently, the uncertainties regarding requirement's cost were treated in a continuous way by considering the expected cost variation for each requirement, along with a control parameter which allows for the adjustment of the desired level of robustness based on the development team estimating history.

The proposed robust model was applied to both artificial and real-world instances extracted from bug repositories of two large open source software projects (Eclipse and Mozilla). In order to evaluate the "price of robustness" for the proposed model, three sets of replicable experiments were designed, executed and analysed.

The first experiment was applied over artificial instances, using a cost variation set to 10% of the original requirement's cost. As a result, it was demonstrated that the gain in robustness was obtained with a loss in fitness value consistently and significantly small for all instances. Furthermore, results showed a nearly constant decrease in fitness value when the robustness control parameter was calibrated to at least half the number of requirements. In the second experiment, the "price of robustness" was computed for the artificial instances with different cost variation approaches. As expected, the higher the cost variation, the higher the fitness value loss. Nonetheless, even with high variations, it was still possible to achieve high robustness levels by losing only a small fitness fraction. The last experiment applied the robust model to a set of real-world instances. The results were nearly the same as for the artificial instances.

Accordingly, all results indicate that the proposed formulation can be employed to produce robust solutions with very little loss with regard to quality, even in large-scale real-world projects.

Since this is the first work to employ the robust optimization framework, in the search based software engineering field, a natural future research direction points out to the application of this framework to other requirements engineering problems, as well as to other software engineering problems subject to uncertainties. In addition, specifically related to the next release problem, other experiments could be proposed to evaluate the "price of robustness" under different numbers of scenarios and different release budgets. Finally, it seems also interesting to consider other metaheuristics, such as ant colony optimization or particle swarm optimization, as well as exact techniques, to evaluate whether different behaviors can be found.

5. REFERENCES

[1] A. Bagnall, V. Rayward-Smith, and I. Whittley. The next release problem. *Information and Software Technology*, 43(14):883–890, 2001.

[2] D. Bai, T. Carpenter, and J. Mulvey. Making a case for robust optimization models. *Management science*, 43(7):895–907, 1997.

[3] D. Bertsimas and M. Sim. The price of robustness. *Operations research*, 52(1):35–53, 2004.

[4] H. Beyer and B. Sendhoff. Robust optimization–a comprehensive survey. *Computer methods in applied mechanics and engineering*, 196(33):3190–3218, 2007.

[5] X. Du, Y. Wang, and W. Chen. Methods for robust multidisciplinary design. *AIAA*, 1785:1–10, 2000.

[6] G. Dulikravich and I. Egorov-Yegorov. Robust optimization of concentrations of alloying elements in steel for maximum temperature, strength, time-to-rupture and minimum cost and weight. *ECCOMAS–Computational Methods for Coupled Problems in Science and Engineering*, pages 25–28, 2005.

[7] Eclipse. http://www.eclipse.org/, January, 2013.

[8] S. Harker, K. Eason, and J. Dobson. The change and evolution of requirements as a challenge to the practice of software engineering. In *Requirements Engineering, 1993., Proceedings of IEEE International Symposium on*, pages 266–272. IEEE, 1993.

[9] M. Harman, J. Krinke, J. Ren, and S. Yoo. Search based data sensitivity analysis applied to requirement engineering. In *Proceedings of the 11th Annual conference on Genetic and evolutionary computation*, pages 1681–1688. ACM, 2009.

[10] H. Holland John. Adaptation in natural and artificial systems: an introductory analysis with applications to biology, control, and artificial intelligence. *USA: University of Michigan*, 1975.

[11] S. Kirkpatrick, M. Vecchi, et al. Optimization by simmulated annealing. *science*, 220(4598):671–680, 1983.

[12] S. Leung, S. Tsang, W. Ng, and Y. Wu. A robust optimization model for multi-site production planning problem in an uncertain environment. *European Journal of Operational Research*, 181(1):224–238, 2007.

[13] M. Li and S. Azarm. Multiobjective collaborative robust optimization with interval uncertainty and interdisciplinary uncertainty propagation. *Journal of mechanical design*, 130(8), 2008.

[14] S. Malcolm and S. Zenios. Robust optimization for power systems capacity expansion under uncertainty. *Journal of the operational research society*, pages 1040–1049, 1994.

[15] Mozilla. http://www.mozilla.org/, January, 2013.

[16] J. Mulvey, R. Vanderbei, and S. Zenios. Robust optimization of large-scale systems. *Operations research*, 43(2):264–281, 1995.

[17] J. Van den Akker, S. Brinkkemper, G. Diepen, and J. Versendaal. Determination of the next release of a software product: an approach using integer linear programming. In *Proceeding of the 11th International Workshop on Requirements Engineering: Foundation for Software Quality (REFSQ 2005)*, pages 119–124, 2005.

[18] J. Wang and G. Rong. Robust optimization model for crude oil scheduling under uncertainty. *Industrial & Engineering Chemistry Research*, 49(4):1737–1748, 2009.

[19] J. Xuan, H. Jiang, Z. Ren, and Z. Luo. Solving the large scale next release problem with a backbone-based multilevel algorithm. *Software Engineering, IEEE Transactions on*, 38(5):1195 –1212, sept.-oct. 2012.

[20] G. Yu. On the max-min 0-1 knapsack problem with robust optimization applications. *Operations Research*, 44(2):407–415, 1996.

[21] Y. Zhang, E. Alba, J. Durillo, S. Eldh, and M. Harman. Today/future importance analysis. In *ACM Genetic and Evolutionary Computation COnference (GECCO 2010)*, pages 1357–1364, 2010.

[22] Y. Zhang, A. Finkelstein, and M. Harman. Search based requirements optimisation: Existing work and challenges. *Requirements Engineering: Foundation for Software Quality*, pages 88–94, 2008.

The Optimisation of Stochastic Grammars to Enable Cost-Effective Probabilistic Structural Testing

Simon Poulding
Dept. of Computer Science
University of York
York YO10 5GH, UK
smp@cs.york.ac.uk

Robert Alexander
Dept. of Computer Science
University of York
York YO10 5GH, UK
rda@cs.york.ac.uk

John A. Clark
Dept. of Computer Science
University of York
York YO10 5GH, UK
jac@cs.york.ac.uk

Mark J. Hadley
Dept. of Computer Science
University of York
York YO10 5GH, UK
mjh130@york.ac.uk

ABSTRACT

The effectiveness of probabilistic structural testing depends on the characteristics of the probability distribution from which test inputs are sampled at random. Metaheuristic search has been shown to be a practical method of optimising the characteristics of such distributions. However, the applicability of the existing search-based algorithm is limited by the requirement that the software's inputs must be a fixed number of numeric values.

In this paper we relax this limitation by means of a new representation for the probability distribution. The representation is based on stochastic context-free grammars but incorporates two novel extensions: conditional production weights and the aggregation of terminal symbols representing numeric values.

We demonstrate that an algorithm which combines the new representation with hill-climbing search is able to efficiently derive probability distributions suitable for testing software with structurally-complex input domains.

Categories and Subject Descriptors

D.2.5 [**Software Engineering**]: Testing and Debugging; F.4.2 [**Mathematical Logic and Formal Languages**]: Grammars and Other Rewriting Systems; G.1.6 [**Numerical Analysis**]: Optimization

Keywords

Software Verification; Search-Based Software Engineering; Structural Testing; Statistical Testing; Stochastic Context-Free Grammars

GECCO'13, July 6–10, 2013, Amsterdam, The Netherlands.
Copyright 2013 ACM 978-1-4503-1963-8/13/07 ...$15.00.

1. INTRODUCTION

The term 'statistical testing' has a number of meanings in the context of software verification, but refers here to a form of probabilistic structural testing described by Thévenod-Fosse and Waeselynck [12, 13, 14]. The strategy is to randomly sample test inputs from an input profile (a probability distribution over the input domain) having a particular property: that every structural element in the software-under-test is exercised as frequently as possible by the sampled inputs.

Statistical testing is, potentially, a very effective testing strategy. As for deterministic forms of structural testing, the codes's structure provides guidance as how the testing effort should be applied in order to detect faults throughout software. But statistical testing additionally shares the benefits of other probabilistic methods of generating test inputs. In particular, it is easy to generate inputs for tests sets of any chosen size by repeatedly sampling from the input profile. This flexibility in the test set size enables the most effective use to be made of the available testing time and resources. Thévenod-Fosse and Waeselynck demonstrated empirically that the combination of structural guidance and flexible test size enables statistical testing to be more effective at detecting faults than both uniform random testing and deterministic structural testing [12].

However, a significant barrier to the use of statistical testing is the cost of finding a suitable input profile: it is difficult to derive a probability distribution over the software's input domain that induces an effective distribution over the software's structural elements.

In our previous work, we demonstrated a cost-effective search-based algorithm for deriving suitable input profiles [9, 10]. The algorithm represented candidate input profiles as a Bayesian network and therefore had a significant limitation: it could be applied only to software for which inputs consisted of a fixed number of numeric values. In this paper, we propose a grammar-based representation that overcomes this limitation.

The contributions we make are:

1. A new representation for input profiles that is capable

of generating structurally-complex test inputs. The complexity may arise from constraints on the validity of the input, a mixture of categorical and numeric data, and the use of variable-length sequences. The new representation is based on stochastic context-free grammars, but incorporates two novel extensions. Firstly, conditional production weights introduce a limited form of context-sensitivity and enable the representation of more subtle probability distributions than would normally be possible. Secondly, terminal symbols representing numeric values are aggregated so as to reduce the size of the representation and thereby facilitate its optimisation using search. (Section 3.1)

2. A search method that may be applied to the grammar-based representation in order to derive input profiles suitable for statistical testing. (Section 3.3)

3. A demonstration of the cost-effectiveness of a search algorithm using three diverse software examples, and empirical evidence that the two novel extensions to the grammar facilitate the derivation of input profiles. (Section 4)

2. BACKGROUND

2.1 Statistical Testing

Statistical testing requires that the input profile—the probability distribution over the input domain of the software-under-test (SUT) from which inputs are sampled—satisfies an adequacy criterion. The criterion is expressed in terms of a set, $\mathcal{C}$, of coverage elements such as structural elements of the SUT's source code or functional elements of the SUT's specification. For each coverage element, $c_i \in \mathcal{C}$, let p_i be the probability that the coverage element is exercised by a single input chosen at random from the given input profile, and p be the minimum of the p_i. The adequacy criterion requires that p (which we refer to as the *minimum coverage probability*) be as large as possible.

The rationale for this criterion is efficient coverage of the structural elements. Let Q be the probability that every coverage element is exercised by at least one test case in the test set. The relationship between Q, p, and the test size N is given by (adapting a result given in [13]):

$$Q = 1 - (1 - p)^N \tag{1}$$

For effective testing, Q should have a value close as possible to 1 in order to cover as much of the software as possible. Maximising the minimum coverage probability enables either (a) an increase in Q for a given test set size (which will improve the fault-detecting ability); or (b) a reduction in the test size (and thus the testing costs) while maintaining an acceptable value of Q.

To construct input profiles with suitably high minimum coverage probabilities, both static and dynamic techniques are described in the literature.

Gouraud and Denise describe a static technique which assigns weights to edges in the SUT's control-flow graph in order to sample execution paths in a manner that satisfies the statistical testing adequacy criterion [5, 2]. However, computationally expensive constraint-solving (similar to that used in symbolic execution) is required to derive test inputs which exercise the sampled paths, and many of sampled paths are infeasible in practice. Both these factors limit the scalability of the technique.

Thévenod-Fosse and Waeselynck describe a dynamic technique [13, 14]. The minimum coverage probability of a candidate input profile is estimated by executing an instrumented version of the SUT with inputs sampled from the profile. The results are used to guide the manual adjustment of the profile, and the process repeated until a suitable value of the minimum coverage probability is attained. However, Thévenod-Fosse and Waeselynck speculate that this technique is unlikely to be practical for large SUTs in its manual form.

2.2 Deriving Input Profiles Using Search

In our previous work, we demonstrated that metaheuristic search can automate the dynamic technique of Thévenod-Fosse and Waeselynck, and thereby reduce the cost of deriving suitable input profiles for statistical testing [9].

We made the assumption that inputs to the SUT were a fixed number of integer or real-valued arguments. This assumption enabled input profiles to be represented as Bayesian networks: directed acyclic graphs in which nodes correspond to input arguments, and edges describe conditional dependence between arguments. The conditional distributions at each node were represented by partitioning the domain of the input vector component into bins and assigning a probability to each bin.

To derive input profiles using this Bayesian network representation, we use random mutation hill-climbing to optimise the edges between nodes, the number and size of bins at a node, and the probabilities assigned to each bin.

In subsequent work, we demonstrated an enhancement to the search algorithm that improved performance by a factor of five for some SUTs [10]. The enhancement—described as 'direction mutation'—used additional information obtained from executing the instrumented SUT to bias the mutation operators to parts of the candidate input profile that exercised the coverage element(s) having the lowest coverage probability.

Although this work has shown that metaheuristic search is an effective and cost-efficient approach to deriving input profiles, the assumption of inputs being a fixed number of numeric values limits the SUTs to which this approach may be applied. It is this limitation we seek to remove using the new reprentation described in this paper.

3. PROPOSED SEARCH ALGORITHM

3.1 Representation

3.1.1 Stochastic Context-Free Grammars

Formal grammars define a language of *strings*: sequences of symbols drawn from a set of *terminal* symbols. The grammar restricts valid strings to be a subset of all possible sequences of terminals by means of production rules: only strings that can be constructed by the application of the grammar's production rules are valid. The productions of context free-grammars, on which our representation is based, have the form:

```
V → X1 X2 ...Xn
```

where `V` is one of an additional set of symbols called *variables*, and the `Xi` are either variable symbols or terminals.

The generation a valid string from the grammar begins with a string consisting of a single copy of the designated 'starting' variable symbol, usually denoted `S`. Generation proceeds by considering the leftmost variable in the current string. A production is chosen which has the this variable on the left-hand side, and the variable is replaced in the string with the symbols on the right-hand side of the production rule. The process of replacing variables continues until the string contains no variable symbols.

As an example, consider the following context-free grammar for defining simple arithmetic expressions. (For clarity, we surround terminal symbols in this and subsequent grammars by single quotes. We also use the standard notation of concatenating productions with same left-hand side variable, separating the alternative right-hand sides using vertical bars: `X` $\rightarrow$ `Y | Z` is equivalent to the two productions `X` $\rightarrow$ `Y` and `X` $\rightarrow$ `Z`.)

```
   S → Expr
Expr → Num | Expr Op Expr
 Num → '0' | '1' | '2' | '3' | '4' | '5'
  Op → '+' | '-' | '*' | '/'
```

This grammar generates valid strings such as `'4 + 3 * 5'`, but does not generate invalid strings such as `'- 3 1'`.

In a stochastic context-free grammar (SCFG), each production is additionally annotated by a weight. During string generation, if more than one production could be applied, the weights are interpreted as a probability distribution and one of the productions is chosen at random according to distribution.

When used as a representation for input profiles, the grammar productions define the valid inputs to the SUT, and the weights are used to define the probability distribution over the inputs, i.e. an input profile. (We note, however, that some types of input structures cannot be represented using context-free grammars.)

3.1.2 Conditional Weights

Context-free grammars are so-called because the set of productions that may be applied to a variable does not change depending on the symbols occurring before or after the variable in the string during the generation process; this is a consequence of only a single variable being permitted on the left-hand side of production rules.

The context-free property simplifies the grammar representation, but limits the types of input profiles that may be represented using the weights of a SCFG. Consider again the example grammar for generating simple arithmetic expressions. If an optimal input profile must avoid too many divide-by-zero arithmetic operations (i.e. the substring `'/ 0'`), the only mechanism available to do this is to assign a low weight to the production `Op` $\rightarrow$ `'/'`, or to the production `Num` $\rightarrow$ `'0'`. However such weights would also reduce the probability of otherwise desirable substrings such as `'/ 2'` and `'+ 0'`.

To overcome this limitation, we enhance the standard form of SCFGs by introducing conditional weights for the productions. A 'child' variable may be identified as having one or more 'parent' variables (the set of which may include the child variable itself) on which it is dependent. The distribution of weights over the productions for the child variable are then conditionally dependent on which productions were most recently applied to the parent variables.

For example, we may identify the variable `Num` in our example grammar as being dependent on the variable `Op`. The weights over the 6 productions for `Num` are then conditionally dependent on which production was most recently applied to `Op`. In effect, there are 5 (potentially different) distributions of weights over the productions of `Num`: one for each of the 4 possible productions of `Op`, plus a further distribution that is used if no production has yet been applied to `Op`.

The conditional dependency of weights extends the types of input profiles that may be represented by introducing a limited form of context-sensitivity (but only in the weights; the grammar itself remains context-free). It would, for example, enable divide-by-zero errors to be avoided more accurately by setting the weight of `Num` $\rightarrow$ `'0'` to a low value *only* in the conditional distribution used when the most recent production applied to `Op` was `Op` $\rightarrow$ `'/'`, but retaining a normal weight for `Num` $\rightarrow$ `'0'` for all the other productions of `Op`.

The conditional dependency between variables—which parents are related to which child variables—is discovered by the search algorithm; it does not need to be specified *a priori*.

3.1.3 Aggregation of Numeric Terminals

Some variables in the grammar may be used to represent a numeric range. For example, the variable `Num` in the example grammar above represents an integer in the range $[0, 5]$. When the cardinality of the range is small, it is feasible to use a separate production for each possible value in the range. However, for much larger ranges, such an approach would create an excessive number of productions and associated weights: it is unlikely that it would be practical to optimise such a large representation using search.

To accommodate large numeric ranges, we propose a further extension to the standard form of SCFGs. Variables representing numeric ranges are identified as special type that we term 'binned variables'. Rather than specifying a production for each possible value in the range, the range is instead partitioned into a small number of bins.

For example, if the variable `Num` instead represented the range $[-32768, 32767]$, it might be partitioned into three bins (of different sizes) as follows:

$$\texttt{Num} \rightarrow [-32768, -2480] \mid [-2479, 238] \mid [239, 32767]$$

When one of these three productions is chosen during the generation of a string from the grammar, the output is not the bin, but a value picked at random from a uniform distribution across the bin. For example, if the production `Num` $\rightarrow [-2479, 238]$ is applied, then the output is an integer between -2479 and 238.

By aggregating a potentially large number of terminals into a much smaller number of bins, the size of the representation is reduced; we speculate that this will improve the practicality of the search process.

The number and lengths of bins need not specified *a priori*: the search process attempts to derive a suitable partitioning.

3.2 Fitness Metric

The fitness metric is an estimate of the minimum coverage probability induced by the candidate input profile. It is evaluated by sampling a number (K) of inputs from the stochastic grammar, and executing an instrumented version of the SUT with the inputs. For each coverage element c_i, the estimated coverage probability, p_i, is the proportion of the K inputs that exercised the element one (or more) times. The lowest value of p_i across all the coverage elements is an estimate of the minimum coverage probability.

Since the sample of inputs is of finite size, the fitness metric is an estimate and may sometimes be higher than the 'true' value for the candidate input profile. In this situation, the input profile may be retained in error over many iterations of the search. In our previous work, we were able to minimise this effect by continuing to evaluate the current input profile (for up to μ_{eval} hill-climbing iterations), and re-calculating a more accurate estimate of fitness from the accumulated instrumentation data.

3.3 Search Method

There is some correspondence between the new grammar-based representation and the previous Bayesian network representation. For this reason, we propose a hill-climbing search similar to that described in [10].

3.3.1 Random Mutation Hill-Climbing

The search begins from an random input profile constructing by randomising the weights, conditional dependencies between variables, and number and size of bins in the grammar. A limit (μ_{prnt}) may be specified for the number of parent variables any one variable may be conditionally dependent on, and on the number of bins that a binned variable may have (μ_{bins}): both the initial random profile and neighbours created by mutation respect these limits.

At each iteration of the hill-climb, a small number (λ) of neighbours to the current input profile are created by applying one of the following mutation operators:

M_{prb} increases or decreases a single production weight by a factor ρ_{prb};

M_{add} adds a conditional dependency between two variables;

M_{rem} removes a conditional dependency;

M_{len} increases or decreases the length of one bin by a factor ρ_{len};

M_{spl} splits a bin into two new bins;

M_{joi} joins two adjacent bins.

Each mutation operator M_{x} has an associated weight, w_{x}: operators with higher weights are more likely to be applied when creating a neighbour.

The neighbours are evaluated, and if the fittest neighbour is fitter than the current input profile, the neighbour becomes the current profile in the next iteration.

3.3.2 Directed Mutation

We incorporate an enhancement to the search method that we describe as 'directed mutation'. (This enhancement was discussed in section 2.2 above, and is explained in detail in our previous work [10].) When the fitness of the current input profile is evaluated, data is maintained as to which productions gave rise to inputs that exercised the coverage element(s) with the minimum coverage probability. The weights (and bins, if a binned variable) associated with these productions are then mutated with a higher likelihood when creating neighbours of the current input profile.

Directed mutation is implemented by grouping the mutation operators into three groups:

G_{edge} operators that modify conditional dependencies: M_{add} and M_{rem};

G_{bins} operators that modify production weights and bin terminals directly: M_{len}, M_{spl}, M_{joi}, and M_{prb};

G_{drct} consists of the same weight- and bin-modifying operators as G_{bins}, but applies them *only* to production weights and bins that contributed strings that exercised the element(s) with the lowest coverage probability.

Each group G_{x} has associated weight W_{x}. When choosing a mutation operator to apply, a group is first chosen at random according to the group weights, and then a mutation operator is chosen at random from that group according to the mutation operator weights. The group weights control the 'strength' of directed mutation effect.

If the minimum coverage probability is zero, one or more coverage elements must have been exercised by none of the sampled inputs and so there is no data available with which to apply directed mutation. In this situation, the algorithm foregoes the local mutation operators described above and constructs entirely random neighbours (in the same way as initial random profile). The motivation is to rapidly explore the search space in order to find a region where the minimum coverage probability is non-zero and directed mutation will be effective.

4. EMPIRICAL DEMONSTRATION

4.1 Objectives

The objectives of the empirical work described in this section are:

1. To demonstrate that proposed search algorithm is able to derive input profiles suitable for testing software taking structurally-complex inputs.

2. To assess whether the two extensions to the standard form of stochastic context-free grammars—conditional production weights and the aggregation of numeric terminals—facilitate the search algorithm.

4.2 Software Under Test

4.2.1 circBuff

`circBuff` is the implementation of a circular buffer container in the BOOST C++ library, version 1.50. The testing objective is coverage of branches in the public methods of the public interface class of the container. (We omit the copy constructor and assignment operator in order to avoid a step-change in the complexity of the grammar since these methods take a further container object as a parameter.) The number of branches to be covered is 78. The public methods of the class constitute approximately 700 lines of code, but not all methods include branched code.

Since the container object maintains state between method calls, it is not sufficient for the test case to be a single method call. Instead, we consider a test input to be a sequence of method calls and we use the grammar shown in Figure 1 to create such inputs. The grammar defines a valid structure for the sequence of method calls: a constructor, method calls to the constructed object that fill the buffer, method calls

```
               S → Constructor FillMethods Methods 'destructor'
     Constructor → 'circular_buffer[0]' BufferCapacity
                 | 'circular_buffer[1]' BufferCapacity BufferSize
     FillMethods → FillMethod FillMethods | FillMethod
      FillMethod → 'push_front' | 'push_back'
         Methods → Method Methods | Method
          Method → 'push_front' | 'push_back'
                 | 'linearize' | rotate' IteratorPos
                 | 'set_capacity' BufferCapacity
                 | 'resize' BufferSize
                 | 'rset_capacity' BufferCapacity
                 | 'rresize' BufferSize
                 | 'insert[0]' IteratorPos
                 | 'insert[1]' IteratorPos Number
                 | 'rinsert' IteratorPos | 'erase[0]' IteratorPos
                 | 'erase[1]' IteratorPos IteratorPos
                 | 'rerase[0]' IteratorPos
                 | 'rerase[1]' IteratorPos IteratorPos
                 | 'pop_front' | 'pop_back'
                 | 'front' | 'back' | 'operator[]' Number
  BufferCapacity → [0,9]
      BufferSize → [0,9]
     IteratorPos → [0,9]
          Number → [0,9]
```

Figure 1: The grammar defining inputs to `circBuff`

```
                  S → EpuckCluster ObjClusters
       EpuckCluster → EpuckClustAzimuth EpuckClustDist Epucks
             Epucks → Epuck
              Epuck → EpuckAzimuth EpuckDist EpuckAngle
         ObjCluster → ObjClustAzimuth ObjClustDist Objects
        ObjClusters → ObjCluster | ObjCluster ObjClusters
            Objects → Object | Object Objects
             Object → Obstacle | Patch
           Obstacle → ObstAzimuth ObstDist ObstRadius
              Patch → PatchAzimuth PatchDist PatchRadius
  EpuckClustAzimuth → [0,359]
     EpuckClustDist → [0,199]
       EpuckAzimuth → [0,0]
          EpuckDist → [0,0]
         EpuckAngle → [0,359]
    ObjClustAzimuth → [0,359]
       ObjClustDist → [400,599]
        ObstAzimuth → [0,359]
           ObstDist → [0,99]
         ObstRadius → [10,99]
       PatchAzimuth → [0,359]
          PatchDist → [0,99]
        PatchRadius → [10,99]
```

Figure 2: The grammar defining inputs to `epuck`.

that operate on the buffer, and finally a call to the destructor. Terminals, such as `'push_front'`, specify method calls. (The suffices of the form `[n]` distinguish between overloaded methods.) Parameters to method calls are represented by the four binned variables at the end of the grammar. Recursion in the grammar enables the generation of variable-length sequences of method calls.

The strings generated by the grammar are interpreted by a test harness and applied to an instrumented version of the container class. The object returned by a call to a constructor method is stored by the harness and subsequent method calls are made to that object.

4.2.2 *epuck*

'E-pucks' are small, relatively cheap robots used in robotics research. The SUT `epuck` is controller code that forms part of a lightweight simulator for e-puck robots written in C by Paul O'Dowd of the University of Bristol. Features supported by the simulator include infra-red proximity detection, communication between robots, the placement and detection of coded patches on the floor, and the placement of static obstacles in the environment.

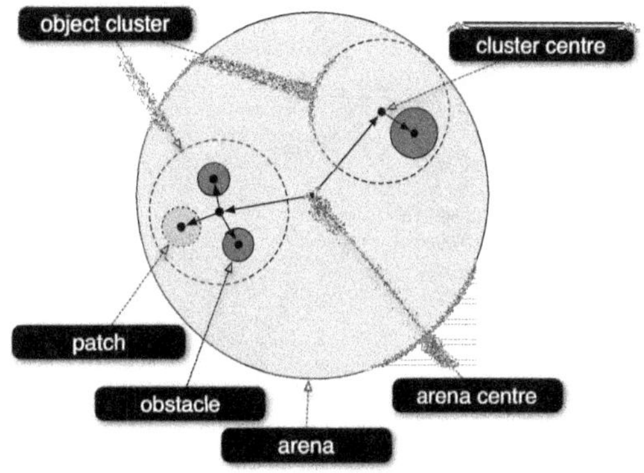

Figure 3: The mission environment specified in terms of object clusters.

The controller code has two significant conditional statements: the first tests whether an obstacle is nearby and if so, directs the robot to take avoidance; the second tests for the presence of coded 'food' patches on the floor and if so, attempts to maintain position over the patch. The testing objective is to exercise the four branches from these two conditional statements during a short 'mission' lasting the equivalent of 10 seconds in the simulation.

A test input is a configuration of the robot's environment in which the mission occurs, consisting of fixed circular arena and a number of obstacles and patches.

The configuration is described by the grammar listed in Figure 2, which defines obstacles and patches in terms of groups we call object clusters. An example of two clusters is shown in Figure 3. The objects in the cluster—obstacles and patches—are defined using distances and angles from centre of the cluster.

The recursion in the grammar permits different numbers of object clusters, each with different numbers of obstacles and patches, to be generated. Binned variables are used to generate the positions of clusters, obstacles, patches, and e-pucks; and the radii of obstacles and patches.

Strings generated by the grammar are interpreted by a test harness and used to configure the simulated environment. To avoid unrealistic environments, only the first three obstacles and first three patches are configured. Similarly, only the first e-puck specified by the generated string is added to the arena.

The controller code itself consists of 53 lines of code, but the testing process requires the code to be executed as part of the much larger simulator. The mission duration of 10 seconds is equivalent to 500 time steps in the simulation. While the real-world elapsed time for each simulated mission is much less than a second, this is nevertheless much longer than the execution of time of the other two SUTs used in this empirical work.

4.2.3 *tcas*

The previous Bayesian network representation could be applied only to SUTs with inputs consisting of a fixed number of numeric arguments. In order to demonstrate that the new grammar-based representation is also practical for

```
S → A1 A2 A3 A4 A5 A6 A7 A8 A9 A10 A11 A12
A1 → [0,39999]
A2 → [0,1]
A3 → [0,1]
A4 → [0,39999]
A5 → [0,4999]
A6 → [0,39999]
A7 → [0,3]
A8 → [0,39999]
A9 → [0,39999]
A10 → [0,2]
A11 → [1,2]
A12 → [0,1]
```

Figure 4: The grammar defining inputs to `tcas`.

SUTs with this simpler form of input domains, we include a common example from the testing literature: the Traffic Collision Avoidance System (TCAS) used by commercial aircraft. The code was provided by the Software-artifact Infrastructure Repository [3].

The SUT takes 12 integer arguments, and thus the grammar consists only of 12 binned variables—one for each argument across the valid range of the argument—plus the start variable (Figure 4). This simple grammar always processes each variable exactly once and always in the same order. For this (and similar) grammars, the fixed generation order enables the search space to be reduced by restricting the conditional dependencies between variables: the parent variable must be processed earlier than child, otherwise the dependency would have no effect.

The testing objective is coverage of all reachable 62 conditions (atomic Boolean predicates) in both conditional and assignment statements.

4.3 Empirical Method

The empirical demonstration compares four variants of the algorithm implemented in C++:

1. The standard hill-climbing algorithm as described in section 3.
2. A variant in which conditional production weights are prohibited (by setting the parameter μ_{prnt} to 0).
3. A variant in which the range of a numeric variable is not partitioned into bins (by setting the parameter μ_{bins} to 1).
4. An equivalent form of random search: instead of creating neighbours by application of a single mutation operator, an entirely random profile is generated (in the same way that the initial random profile is constructed).

For each variant and for each SUT, 16 trials—each using a different seed to the pseudo-random number generator—were run. Each trial executed on a single CPU core. The clock speed of, and memory accessible to, the cores were typical of a desktop PC. The trials ran for 20,000 iterations for `circBuff` and `tcas`, taking on average of 14 minutes and 1.5 minutes per trial, respectively. Each execution of `epuck` during fitness evaluation takes much longer than the other two SUTs, so the algorithm trials ran for a fewer number of iterations: 400 iterations, taking on average of 22 minutes per trial.

During each trial, the fitness (the estimated minimum coverage probability) of the best input profile found so far

Parameter	Description	Setting
K	evaluation sample size	302
λ	neighbourhood sample size	9
ρ_{prb}	production weight mutation factor	54.002
ρ_{len}	bin length mutation factor	2.755
W_{bins}	G_{bins} group weight	1000
W_{edge}	G_{edge} group weight	144
W_{drct}	G_{drct} group weight	10584
w_{rem}	M_{rem} mutation weight	1000
w_{add}	M_{add} mutation weight	689
w_{prb}	M_{prb} mutation weight	1000
w_{joi}	M_{joi} mutation weight	886
w_{spl}	M_{spl} mutation weight	1159
w_{len}	M_{len} mutation weight	1028
μ_{prnt}	max. parent variables per child	1
μ_{bins}	max. terminal bins per variable	$2\sqrt{\lvert\mathcal{C}\rvert}$
μ_{eval}	max. evaluations per profile	10

Table 1: The algorithm parameter settings. (The parameters are described in section 3.3. The expression $|\mathcal{C}|$ denotes the number of coverage elements.)

was recorded in order to assess the trajectory taken by the search. (The fitness of the *best* profile so far is not necessarily the same as that of the *current* profile owing to the re-evaluation mechanism described in section 3.3.)

The remaining algorithm parameter settings are listed in Table 1. The settings were re-purposed from the result of tuning the older Bayesian network algorithm to a different set of SUTs [8]. In order to reduce the threat to validity of using a single set of parameter settings, the parameters were not tuned to new grammar representation nor to the new SUTs under consideration here.

4.4 Results

The results are summarised in Figure 5 for each of three SUTs. The graphs illustrate the trajectory of the search by plotting the average fitness, calculated as the mean across all 16 trials of the algorithm variant, at each iteration of the algorithm. The fitness plotted is the estimated minimum coverage probability of the best profile found so far, and so this value is the fitness of the input profile that would have been returned by the search algorithm if it had been stopped at that iteration. The 95% confidence intervals, indicated by error bars at regular intervals along the trajectory, were calculated by bootstrap resampling.

We choose to summarise the results as trajectories to ensure that any conclusions we draw are reliable and not an artefact of a particular point at which we might choose to stop the algorithm.

The raw data from the algorithm trials is available at: `http://www.cs.york.ac.uk/~smp/supplemental/`.

4.5 Discussion

For all three SUTs, the hill-climbing algorithm (solid line trajectories) derives input profiles with the highest minimum coverage probability. (For `epuck`, there is no statistically significant difference between this algorithm and the variant that does not use conditional production weights: the error bars overlap across the entire trajectories.) As discussed in section 2.1, profiles with the highest minimum coverage probability will be the most cost-effective when used for statistical testing. We are not aware of any analysis in the literature of the best possible value of the minimum coverage probability for these SUTs against which we may compare

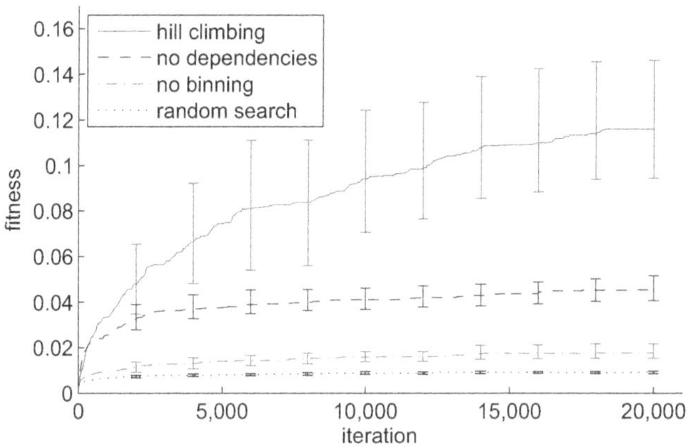

(a) circBuff

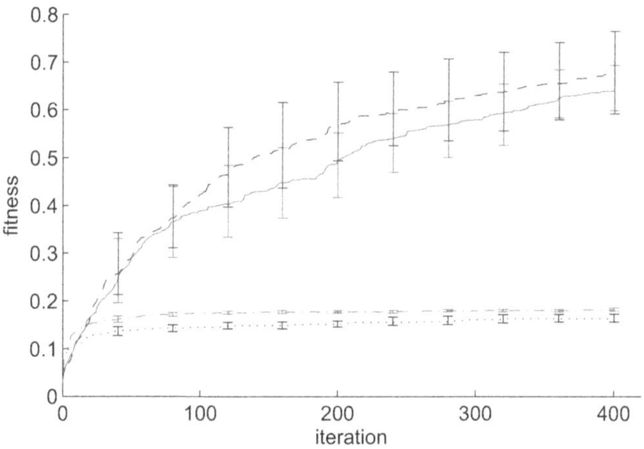

(b) epuck

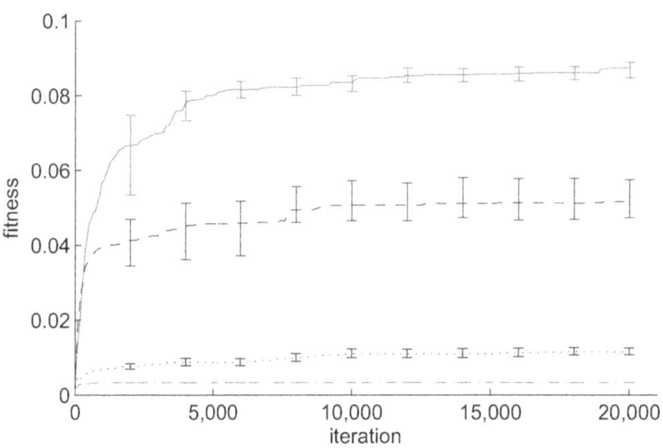

(c) tcas

Figure 5: Trajectories for the four search algorithms. The solid line plots the mean fitness of the best profile found to date at each iteration for the algorithm using the standard hill-climbing search method; the dashed line is the variant that omits any dependencies between variables; the dash-dot line is the variant that omits binning; and the dotted line is the algorithm using random search. The error bars show the 95% confidence interval; for clarity, they are plotted only at regular intervals.

these results. However, by applying equation (1), we note that *all* the coverage elements will be covered (with a probability, Q, of 0.99) using test set sizes of 38 for `circBuff`, 5 for `epuck`, and 51 for `tcas`. (At such a high value of Q, such test sets will often exercise every coverage element more than once.) These relatively small test sizes demonstrate that the search algorithm is effective at deriving input profiles.

For both `circBuff` and `tcas`, the algorithm variant that does not use conditionally dependent weights (dashed trajectories) derives profiles with a lower fitness than the standard hill-climbing algorithm. This difference is statistically significant across a wide range of iterations (the error bars do not overlap). We conclude that the novel extension of conditional production weights facilitates the search algorithm.

For all three SUTs, the algorithm variant that does not partition numeric variables into bins (dash-dot trajectories) derives profiles with a much lower fitness than the standard hill-climbing algorithm, and the difference is statistically significant. This is only partial evidence in support of aggregating numeric terminals. We do not produce empirical evidence in this paper for the other part of the argument: that if each numeric range were represented by separate terminals for each possible value, then the search space would be impractically large. Instead, we argue merely that for SUTs taking many thousands of different numeric inputs (such as `tcas`), this is a reasonable assumption.

Finally, for all three SUTs, random search (dotted trajectories) derives profiles with a much lower fitness than the hill-climbing algorithm. This result provides a check that the task of deriving input profiles for these SUTs is not a trivial search problem.

5. RELATED WORK

The use of grammars to generate test inputs is an established practice known as *grammar-based testing*. It is motivated by the need to generate test data for SUTs for which the nature of valid inputs is highly-constrained. For example, grammar-based testing can be used to generate test inputs—source code—for compilers and interpreters [7, 4]. Inputs consisting of random sequences of characters would be almost always raise errors in the lexer or parser phases of a compiler; the code of subsequent compilation phases would remain untested. A grammar, however, ensures the construction of semantically correct source code, enabling the compiler functionality to be fully tested.

In many cases, the grammar is deterministic and input data is generated by bounded-exhaustive enumeration: all valid language strings are generated up to a chosen size-related bound. However, a few techniques sampled inputs at random from stochastic grammars. Applications of this probabilistic approach include: testing of hardware arithmetic circuits in simulation [6]; differential testing of compilers [7]; and testing the bytecode verifier in Java Virtual Machine implementations [11]. In all these examples, the grammar's production weights were manipulated manually to achieve desirable properties in the randomly-sampled test inputs.

In this paper we have demonstrated the use of automated search—rather than manual manipulation—to adjust the weights of a stochastic grammar for this purpose; the desirable property in our case being a high value of the minimum coverage probability. In this respect, our approach is most similar to the recent work of Beyene and Andrews [1].

Although Beyene and Andrews' approach is not framed explicitly in the context of statistical testing, it achieves similar objectives. Grammars for structured HTML and XML inputs are converted to stochastic data generation programs, and the weights in the generation programs are optimised by metaheuristic search for high coverage of the SUTs.

Our proposed search algorithm differs from Beyene and Andrew's technique in two notable aspects.

Firstly, we use a grammar representation that incorporates two novel extensions: conditional production weights and the aggregation of numeric terminal symbols. Our empirical results show that these extensions enable the search algorithm to derive input profiles with significantly better minimum coverage probability.

Secondly, the adequacy criterion in Beyene and Andrew's experiments was statement coverage: between 50% and 73% of the statements were covered using large test sets of size 1000. Our empirical demonstration uses the much stronger adequacy criteria of branch and condition coverage. Moreover, we calculated above that we are able to (effectively) guarantee that 100% of the coverage elements would be exercised using *much* smaller test sets. (Since the SUTs used in the empirical work of this paper are not the same as those used by Beyene and Andrews, a more rigorous comparison of the two approaches is not currently possible.)

6. CONCLUSION

In this paper we proposed a novel grammar-based representation for input profiles, and demonstrated a search algorithm using this representation that is capable of efficiently deriving input profiles suitable for statistical testing. The grammar-based representation enables the algorithm to be applied to a wide range of software, in particular software with structurally-complex inputs. For three real-world examples, the algorithm took only a few minutes to derive suitable input profiles using computing resources equivalent of a desktop PC. Since the approach is automated and uses readily-available, affordable computing resources, the costs associated with deriving input profiles for statistical testing are reduced.

The new representation extends stochastic context-free grammars through the use conditional production weights and aggregating numeric terminal symbols in bins. The empirical results provide evidence that both of these novel extensions facilitate the search process.

The grammar-based representation and associated search algorithm provide a generic mechanism for describing and optimising probability distributions over the input domain of a SUT: they could be applied to the problems other than statistical testing for which the objective is to induce a particular probability distribution over the executed software. For example, the objective could be to exercise particular parts of the software that have been neglected by earlier testing; to focus on components that have a history of faulty behaviour; or to explore non-functional properties such as execution time.

As future work, we are investigating the use of stochastic grammars that are more flexible than context-free grammars and will facilitate the representation of input profiles for a yet wider range of SUTs.

Acknowledgments

This research was funded by the MOD Centre for Defence Enterprise and EPSRC grant EP/J017515/1, DAASE: Dynamic Adaptive Automated Software Engineering. The authors would like to thank Paul O'Dowd of the University of Bristol for providing the e-puck simulator code.

7. REFERENCES

[1] M. Beyene and J. Andrews. Generating string test data for code coverage. In *Proc. IEEE Int'l Conf.. on Software Testing, Verification and Validation (ICST 2012)*, pages 270–279, 2012.

[2] A. Denise, M.-C. Gaudel, and S.-D. Gouraud. A generic method for statistical testing. Technical Report 1386, Laboratoire de Recherche en Informatique (LRI), CNRS - Univ. de Paris Sud, 2004.

[3] H. Do, S. Elbaum, and G. Rothermel. Supporting controlled experimentation with testing techniques: An infrastructure and its potential impact. *Empirical Software Engineering*, 10(4):405–435, 2005.

[4] P. Godefroid, A. Kiezun, and M. Y. Levin. Grammar-based whitebox fuzzing. In *Proc. ACM SIGPLAN Conf. on Programming Language Design and Implementation (PLDI 2008)*, pages 206–215, 2008.

[5] S.-D. Gouraud, A. Denise, M.-C. Gaudel, and B. Marre. A new way of automating statistical testing methods. In *Proc. IEEE Int'l Conf. on Automated Software Eng.*, 2001.

[6] P. Maurer. Generating test data with enhanced context-free grammars. *IEEE Software*, 7(4):50 –55, July 1990.

[7] W. M. McKeeman. Differential testing for software. *Digital Technical Journal*, 10(1):100–107, 1998.

[8] S. Poulding. *The Use of Automated Search in Deriving Software Testing Strategies*. PhD thesis, Dept. Computer Science, University of York, (in review).

[9] S. Poulding and J. A. Clark. Efficient software verification: Statistical testing using automated search. *IEEE Trans. Software Eng.*, 36(6):763–777, 2010.

[10] S. Poulding, J. A. Clark, and H. Waeselynck. A principled evaluation of the effect of directed mutation on search-based statistical testing. In *Proc. 4th Intl. Workshop on Search-Based Software Testing (SBST 2011)*, pages 184–193, 2011.

[11] E. G. Sirer and B. N. Bershad. Using production grammars in software testing. *SIGPLAN Not.*, 35(1):1–13, Dec. 1999.

[12] P. Thévenod-Fosse and H. Waeselynck. An investigation of statistical software testing. *J. Software Testing, Verification and Reliability*, 1(2):5–26, 1991.

[13] P. Thévenod-Fosse and H. Waeselynck. Statemate applied to statistical testing. In *Proc. Int'l Symp. Software Testing and Analysis (ISSTA'93)*, pages 99–109, 1993.

[14] P. Thévenod-Fosse, H. Waeselynck, and Y. Crouzet. Software statistical testing. Technical Report 95178, Laboratoire d'Analyse et d'Architecture des Systèmes du CNRS (LAAS), 1995.

A Comparison of Two Memetic Algorithms for Software Class Modelling

Jim Smith
Department of Computer Science and Creative Technologies
University of the West of England
Bristol, UK
james.smith@uwe.ac.uk

Christopher Simons
Department of Computer Science and Creative Technologies
University of the West of England
Bristol, UK
chris.simons@uwe.ac.uk

ABSTRACT

Recent research has demonstrated that the problem of class modelling within early cycle object orientated software engineering can be successfully tackled by posing it as a search problem to be tackled with meta-heuristics. This "Search Based Software Engineering" approach has been illustrated using both Evolutionary Algorithms and Ant Colony Optimisation to perform the underlying search. Each has been shown to display strengths and weaknesses - both in terms of how easily "standard" algorithms can be applied to the domain, and of optimisation performance. This paper extends that work by considering the effect of incorporating Local Search. Specifically we examine the hypothesis that within a memetic framework the choice of global search heuristic does not significantly affect search performance, freeing the decision to be made on other more subjective factors.

Results show that in fact the use of local search is not always beneficial to the Ant Colony Algorithm, whereas for the Evolutionary Algorithm with order based recombination it is highly effective at improving both the quality and speed of optimisation. Across a range of parameter settings ACO found its best solutions earlier than EAs, but those solutions were of lower quality than those found by EAs. For both algorithms we demonstrated that the number of constraints present, which relates to the number of classes created, has a far bigger impact on solution quality and time than the size of the problem in terms of numbers of attributes and methods.

Categories and Subject Descriptors

I.2.8 [**Artificial Intelligence**]: Problem Solving, Control Methods, and Search—*Evolutionary Algorithms, Ant Colony Optimisation, Memetic Algorithms*; D.2.3 [**Software Engineering**]: Design Tools and Techniques—*Search Based Software Engineering, Class Modelling*

GECCO'13, July 6–10, 2013, Amsterdam, The Netherlands.

Keywords

Search-Based Software Engineering, Evolutionary Algorithms, Ant Colony Optimisation, Memetic Algorithms

1. INTRODUCTION

Recent research has demonstrated that the task of class modelling within early cycle object orientated software engineering can be successfully tackled by posing it as a search problem. This task has also been referred to as the Class Responsibility Assignment Problem. For the sake of brevity we will hereafter refer to it as "class modelling", with the restriction to the context of the early stages of the development life cycle being taken as read. The "Search Based Software Engineering" (SBSE) approach to class modelling has been illustrated using both Evolutionary Algorithms (EA) and Ant Colony Optimisation (ACO) to perform the underlying search. Each has been shown to display strengths and weaknesses - both in terms of how easily "standard" algorithms can be applied to the domain, and of optimisation performance. Interestingly both of these population based methods have been shown to outperform methods based on a single improving solution.

It has been shown on a wide range of problems that the incorporation of local search as a mechanism for refining and improving candidate solutions can improve both the effectiveness (quality of solutions found) and efficiency (number of solutions examined) of population-based search heuristics [6]. This paper extends work on early-stage SBSE by considering the effect of incorporating Local Search. Specifically we examine the hypothesis that within a memetic framework the choice of global search heuristic does not significantly affect search performance.

Our contention is that because of its complex, subjective nature, ultimately class modelling should be tackled via interactive search, albeit augmented with a surrogate fitness function to prevent user fatigue. Therefore ideally the choice of search method should consider the ease with which it can support users' input into the search process via actions such as "freezing" parts of designs. These considerations are orthogonal to the comparative search performance, so understanding the latter is vital before we can disregard it.

Simons and Smith [13, 14] have compared ACO and EAs as the basis for meta-heuristic search for class models, concluding that performance issues aside, there are practical reasons why one might prefer to use constructive heuristics such as ACO. For example, in an ACO "freezing" of partial solutions can be simply achieved via direct changes to the pheromone table, whereas in an EA it would necessitate manipulation of the recombination and mutation operators on-the-fly. Some attempts have been made in this direction by interleaving phases of human manipulation and evolutionary adaptation [17]. Regardless of the mechanisms underpinning the search, clearly algorithmic simplicity cannot be a substitute for poor performance. Therefore this paper addresses the following questions:

- Is there a difference in the performance of global search meta-heuristics when applied to class modelling? If so, on what sort of problems and why?
- Does the addition of Local Search to create Memetic Algorithms improve performance, and if so is there still a difference in performance arising from the use of different global search heuristics?

To answer these questions the rest of the paper is organised as follows: Section 2 provides a brief background to previous research in this problem domain. Section 3 describes the chosen representation and the meta-heuristics considered. Section 4 describes the experimental methodology used. Section 5 describes and analyses the results obtained. To conclude the paper, Section 6 summarises the findings and their implications for Search based Software Engineering in general, and early stage class modelling in particular.

2. BACKGROUND

Search-Based Software Engineering (SBSE) is now a well-established discipline, wherein search has been applied across the range of the software development lifecycle [18]. Historically, comparatively little research focus has been directed to the upstream stages of the software design, although this is recently being addressed, typically using metrics relating to coupling and cohesion to guide meta-heuristic search of design spaces such as the object-oriented modelling of design classes. Bowman *et al.* used a multi-objective EA to produce designs optimising a number of pre-specified metrics [1]. Simons and Parmee [12, 11] applied interactive EAs, using linear regression to learn a surrogate fitness model that combined coupling with a number of "elegance metrics" to approximate users' subjective preferences.

Working slightly later in the development life-cycle, Sievi-Korte *et al.* used a memetic algorithm based on an EA [9], and Vathsavayi *et al.* interleaved human and evolutionary adaptation of the usage of patterns [17].

However, as the name of the SBSE field suggests, potentially any search algorithm could be used, although in practice research effort has also tended to concentrate on Evolutionary Algorithms. As Harmann [4] noted:

> We must be wary of the unquestioning adoption of evolutionary algorithms merely because they are popular and widely applicable or because, historically, other re- searchers have adopted them for SBSE problems; none of these are scientific motivations for adoption.

Simons and Smith compared the use of ACOs and EAs for this problem [13, 14], concluding that given sufficient computational budget, global search via EAs was more effective at finding high quality solutions than that using ACO. When the computational budget was reduced (as for example is often the case in interactive search) the situation was reversed. However, with both algorithms, and both representations examined, a major issue was dealing with the constraint that a valid class model should contain at least one attribute and at least one method. Those papers used penalty functions (all invalid models were given zero fitness) and the use of random regeneration of invalid solutions. Dealing more efficiently with this constraint would necessitate either a significant adaptation of the underlying global search heuristics, or the provision of a "repair" mechanism. A well designed Local Search algorithm that systematically examined the effect of moving elements between classes provides a simple way of providing the latter, and also of improving valid solutions, hence part of the motivation of this paper.

3. REPRESENTATION AND ALGORITHMS

This section briefly overviews the way in which class modelling is posed as a search problem, and the three search algorithms used in this paper.

3.1 Representation

The creation of class models can be thought of as a process of grouping elements (attributes and methods) into classes, so that every class contains at least one element of each type. In order to map readily onto freely available ACO source code, we borrow a representation commonly used for Vehicle Routing Problem. A solution is considered to be a permutation of a set of items, comprising the design elements plus "end-of-class" markers. If a problems has a attributes, and m methods to be grouped into c classes, the representation is then a permutation of size $a+m+c-1$. The value of the ith position is taken to denote the element that occurs in the ith place in the tour, where the attributes are numbered from 1 to a, the methods from $a+1$ to $a+m$ and the "end-of-class" markers from $a+m+1$ to $a+m+c-1$. When the representation of a solution is decoded to give the candidate class model, a simple array $class = \{1, \ldots, c\}^{a+m}$ is constructed whose j^{th} element gives the class (from 1 to c) of element j using the numbering scheme above for attributes and methods.

3.2 Evolutionary Algorithm

The EA chosen is a standard generational genetic algorithm. Parents are chosen by deterministic binary tournaments, and elitism implemented so that the incumbent best solution is kept if not improved - replacing the least fit of the newly created offspring. We examined the use of both Edge Recombination and Order-Based Crossover. We do not provide a full algorithmic description of the EA as this is a well known algorithm with many descriptions online. Full details of the operators used can be found in e.g. [3].

There is now a significant body of evidence in favour of the use of self-adaptive mutation rates (see e.g. [7]), and also that for permutation based problems the "best" choice of mutation operator is not only problem, or even instance-specific, but in fact relates to the current state of the search problem [5, 8]. The operators we used were *Swap*, *Insert* and *Invert* operators. Following one of the schemes proposed in [8] each individual contained a single gene encoded for the mutation probability, and we adopted the following method for mutation:

- With probability 0.2 the encoded value for mutation rate was changed to a new value, selected uniformly at random from the fixed set of allowed values.

- This value was then multiplied by the representation length l, and the *floor* operator applied determine the number of mutations to apply.

- One of the three mutation operators was then selected at random, and applied the number of times determined in the previous step.

A fixed set of ten mutation rates was used, defined in terms of the representation length l as $1/l \cdot \{0.001, 0.002, 0.01, 0.02, 0.1, 0.2, 1, 2, MIN(0.25l, 5), MIN(0.25l, 10)\}$.

A range of population sizes were used as detailed below.

3.3 Ant Colony Algorithm

Following some preliminary experimentation and guided by the findings reported in [13, 14] we applied a $MAX-MIN$ ACO [16]. We here provide a brief description, considering the problem where the ACO is search a least-cost path through a set of nodes - for example the TSP. Full details may be found in Stuetzle's papers referenced above.

The ACO maintains a $l \times l$ "pheromone matrix" M, which reflects the search history, and a $l \times l$ matrix H of heuristic information, which between them define the probability distribution function for the generation of new solutions. In each iteration N ants are each placed at random at a starting node $i : 1 \leq i \leq l$ and independently construct tours as follows:

- At each node, the ant creates a list S of all the as-yet unvisited nodes, the heuristic and pheromone values associated with the relevant links.

- It then makes a selection from the list where the probability of moving from node i to node j is given by:

$$P_{move}(ij) = \begin{cases} \frac{M_{ij}^{\alpha} \cdot H_{ij}^{\beta}}{\sum_{j \neq i, j \in S} M_{ij}^{\alpha} \cdot H_{ij}^{\beta}} & j \in S \\ 0 & \text{otherwise.} \end{cases} \quad (1)$$

After each ant has constructed a full solution its fitness f is measured. If *best* denotes the least cost path for generation t, and $\{ij\} \in best$ taken to mean that edge ij is traversed in that path, then the pheromone matrix M is updated at the end of each generation according to:

$$M_{ij}^{t+1} = \begin{cases} (1-\rho) \cdot M_{ij}^{t} + 1/f_{best} & \{ij\} \in best \\ (1-\rho) \cdot M_{ij}^{t} & \text{otherwise.} \end{cases} \quad (2)$$

The key factors which distinguish the MAX-MIN ACO variants are that the pheromone matrix M is initialised to its maximum value, is only updated with the information from the best ant per generation, and that the pheromone levels are truncated to lie within a pre-specified range to avoid over saturation.

Preliminary experimentation revealed that the default recommended settings appeared to provide robust performance, with the exception that the influence of "heuristic information" was removed by setting the parameter $\beta = 0.0$. The rest of the relevant parameters were: $\alpha = 1$ (exponent of pheromone used to calculate next-node probabilities), $\rho = 0.02$ (pheromone decay rate).

We would like to gratefully thank the authors and maintainers for the public provision of the ACOTSP package version 1.02 [15]. The original code was modified to call the same fitness function designed for the EA for this application (see below) and the new Local Search algorithm implemented as described in the next section. Different numbers of ants were used as described below.

3.4 Local Search Algorithm

A single-step greedy local search algorithm was implemented following the algorithm described in Figure 1. The move operator considered moves one element to a different class. The only moves considered are those that create valid solutions, and where the "receiving" class has an attribute (or method) that is used by (uses) the incoming method (attribute). This last condition does not assure that the fitness of the neighbour is superior to that of the incumbent, but rules out evaluating some of the least fit neighbours - at least in terms of coupling.

```
BEGIN
  /* given a starting solution i */
  set f_i = calculate_fitness(i) ;
  set set of possible moves S = {} ;
  Decode i into a set of classes C;

  /* Build up a list of possible moves  */
  FOR EACH  class c ∈ C DO
    IF (c contains more than one method) THEN
      FOR EACH  method m ∈ c DO
        FOR EACH class k ∈ C, k ≠ c DO
          IF m uses an attribute in k THEN
          set S = S ∪ {m, k};
          FI
        OD
      OD
    FI
    IF (c contains more than one attribute) THEN
      FOR EACH  attribute a ∈ c DO
        FOR EACH class k ≠ c DO
          IF k contains a method that uses a THEN
          set S = S ∪ {a, k};
          FI
        OD
      OD
    FI
  OD

  /* Greedy search over the possible valid moves */
  Randomise Order of S;
  set improved = FALSE;
  WHILE ( S ≠ {} AND improved = FALSE ) DO
    take next possible move from S;
    apply move to create new solution j;
    set f_j = calculate_fitness(j);
    IF ( f(j) < f(i)) THEN
      set i = j;
      set improved = True;
    FI
    ELSE
      remove move from S;
    ESLE
  OD
END
```

Figure 1: Pseudocode of the Local Search algorithm

4. METHODOLOGY

4.1 Fitness and Performance Metrics

For the initial experiments the fitness function used was based on the Coupling Between Objects measure. Based on the Use Cases provided in the documentation for the problems, and the numbering scheme outlined above, a $l \times l$ table U was constructed with:

$$U_{ij} = \begin{cases} 1 & i \leq a, a < j \leq a+m, \text{ method } j \text{ uses attribute } i \\ 0 & \text{otherwise.} \end{cases}$$

The coupling-related fitness (to be minimised) is then defined as the percentage of all uses that are "out of class":

$$f_{CBO} = 100 \cdot \frac{\sum_i \sum_{j,class(j) \neq class(i)} U_{ij}}{\sum_i \sum_{j'} U_{ij}} \quad (3)$$

It is well known that optimising merely to reduce coupling tends to produce so-called "god" classes [2] - that is to say designs in which most attributes and methods are grouped in a single class. In practice software designers deprecate this "anti-pattern", as it tends to lead to low cohesion (amongst other problems). Several authors have pursued the concept of"design elegance" (in this and other fields) and a few metrics have recently been proposed that directly reflect design symmetry in terms of the distribution of attributes and methods [11].

One readily calculable metric which has been shown to correlate strongly with users' recorded feelings of "elegance" is the *Numbers Among Classes* (NAC): the arithmetic mean of the standard deviation of the numbers of attributes and methods among the classes of a design. This was truncated to the range [0, 6] and a fitness to be minimised calculated as:

$$f_{NAC} = \frac{100}{6} * \left(\frac{\sigma_{m_c}}{2} + \frac{\sigma_{a_c}}{2}\right) \quad (4)$$

where m_c and a_c denote the numbers of method and attributes in class c. The lower this value, the more symmetrical the appearance of attributes and methods among the classes in the design, hence it tends to counterbalance the effect of the CBO metric. Thus in the second set of experiments we considered a combined fitness to minimise:

$$f_{comb} = 0.5 * (f_{CBO} + f_{NAC}) \quad (5)$$

Given that ultimately we are concerned with the use of these search heuristics embedded in an interactive design tool, and that we do not know a "optimal" fitness for each instance, we have chosen performance metrics for the search heuristics that reflect the speed and reliability of the ability to find good solutions. Each time a candidate solution is evaluated (whether in local or global search) a counter is incremented, and for each run on each problem we note the best solution discovered, and after how many evaluations that occurred. Algorithms are then compared according to Mean Best Fitness (MBF) and AES (the mean number of evaluations to find the best solution discovered).

For reasons of space and clarity we present the results graphically in the form of plots of mean performance over each algorithm-instance and number of individuals N. SPSS v20 was used to carry out a one-way Analysis of Variance with dependant variables MBF and AES and fixed factors instance, N, and algorithm, followed by post-hoc testing for significant differences using Tukey's HSD test.

Regardless of metric, we often present rankings in the format $A < \{B, C\} < D$, which should be taken to mean that the values for A are significantly lower with more than 95% confidence than those for B, C and D. B is lower, but not significantly so that C, and D is significantly higher than A, B and C.

Table 1: Number of classes, Coupling (fCBO) and size-symmetry (fNAC) of Manual Software Designs

Name	Classes	F_{CBO}	F_{NAC}
CBS	5	15.4	13.69
GDP	5	29.7	43.2
SC	16	45.2	25.33

4.2 Problem Instances

To aid comparison with other published works, we used the three software design problems detailed in [10] which span a range of size and complexities. The first (CBS) is a generalized abstraction of a Cinema Booking System, with 16 attributes, 15 methods and 39 method/attribute uses. The second (GDP) is a university system for student records with 43 attributes, 12 methods and 121 method/attribute uses. The third (SC) is based on an industrial case study for booking cruise holidays with 52 attributes, 30 methods and 126 method/attribute uses. The previous authors provide results for manual designs which we reproduce in Table 1 with kind permission.

Both of the representations chosen permit models with variable numbers of classes to be present, since"end-of-class" markers could be adjacent in a permutation. In this paper, to facilitate easy comparisons with the results produced manually (which for the SC represented several hours work) we imposed the condition that evolved designs should contain the same number of classes as the manual ones. Candidate solutions for the CBS and GDP problems are therefore required to have 5 classes. Noting that the higher numbers of classes in the SC problem will mean that a large proportion of candidate solutions will violate the constraint of at least one attribute and method per class, we have created three different versions of the SC problem to try and tease apart the effect of size and constraint violation. These use 5, 10, and 16 classes, and are denoted SC5, SC10 and SC16 respectively in the results below.

4.3 Algorithm Parameters

The parameters specific to the ACO and EA are listed above. We ran experiments with 25, 50 and 100 individuals (i.e. members of the EA population, or ants respectively). The algorithm are hereafter referred to as *aco*, *aco-LS*, *EAer*, *EAerLS*, *EAor* and *EAorLS* where the lower case letters after "EA" denote the recombination operator used and the suffix *LS* denotes the memetic version. Each algorithm was run fifty times on each problem instance, with each run allowed to make 100,000 calls to the evaluation function.

5. RESULTS

5.1 Minimising f_{CBO}

Figure 2 shows a comparison of the mean best fitness per

run, separated by algorithm, problem instance, and number of individuals. The statistical analysis for MBF reveals ranking: $EAorLS < EAor < \{EAer, acoLS, EAerLS\} < \{acoLS, EAerLS, aco\}$. The obvious conclusion from this is that overall the Order based crossover is preferable to Edge Recombination, and that apart from EA using order crossover, the addition of Local Search does not provide a significant improvement in the MBF performance for coupling-based fitness.

A visual comparison of the results for SC5, SC10 and sC16 appears to confirm our hypothesis that it is the level of constraints, rather than necessarily the sheer scale of the problem, which causes a deterioration in the search process. Looking at the mean values for each algorithm there is a clear pattern that the best coupling achieved increases as the number of classes required increases. Intuitively this makes sense - if we optimise a design with c classes solely according to coupling, the system tends to produce 1 god class and $c-1$ much smaller classes with only one or two methods and attributes in each. If we increase c, then there can necessarily be fewer elements in the god class and so the design almost certainly has more coupling. However it is notable that the EA variants also show an increase in the variability - for example the confidence intervals for SC16 are far larger than for the other instances, and considering this problem alone the performance of all algorithms is not statistically significantly different. In other words, the ACOs are less affected by constraints, but at the expense of missing the occasional discovery of good solutions which characterises the EAs, especially $EAor$ and $EAorLs$.

Analysing MBF by Instance reveals the significantly different subgroups are: $CBS < SC5 < \{GDP, SC10\} < SC16$. Analysing the results by N revealed that the algorithms with 25 individuals gave the best performance, and $N = 50, = 100$ were not significantly different.

Analysis of the number of evaluations taken to find the best per run is illuminating. Figure 3 shows the mean number of evaluations per run after which the best individual was located. This reveals that this happens sooner for aco and $acoLS$, and that whereas the addition of local search speeds the discovery of good solutions for the $EAor$ (except on SC5) it delays the process for $EAer$. This is backed up by the statistical analysis, which discriminates different subsets in the increasing order as : $\{acoLS, aco\} < EAorLs < EAor < ERer < EAerLS$.

Analysis by instance shows $\{CBS, GDP\} < SC5 < SC10 < SC16$. This completes the picture we observed above - that increasing the number of attributes and methods, and hence the representation length does not necessarily increase the effectiveness of search (MBF) but does decrease its efficiency (AES). On the other hand, introducing constraints by requiring more classes impacts on both measures. Analysis by N shows the pattern $25 < 50 < 100$.

5.2 Minimising f_{comb}

Figures 4 and 5 show the MBF and AES performance for the fitness function combining coupling and elegance, measured by f_{CBO} and f_{NAC} respectively. These show a very similar pattern of behaviour to above. The overall ranking by MBF is $\{EAorLs, EAor\} < \{EAer, EAerLS\} < acoLs < aco$, so for these fitness landscapes the addition of Local Search aids the aco algorithm. The ranking by AES is $\{acoLS, aco\} < EAorLS < EAor < EAer < EAerLS$.

Analysing the performance on individual instances separately reveals that according to the combined metric, the ACO algorithms are worse on every problem.

Again, results for $ERor$ and $EAorLS$, particularly with larger population sizes, clearly show that the benefit in terms of both speed and quality for both fitness functions is more noticeable as the number of constraints increases. This supports our hypothesis that Local Search can act as a type of repair function for infeasible solutions.

5.3 Further experiments with ACO

The results above clearly show that for both fitness functions the ACO algorithms do not find as good solutions, but they find their best solutions much earlier in the run than their EA counterparts. One obvious reason could be that is due to premature convergence, especially as the MAX-MIN algorithm used only updates the pheromone trail with information from the best ant per iteration. To examine this we re-ran the ACO experiments using both higher ($\rho = 0.2$)and lower ($\rho = 0.002$) rates of evaporation, than its default value of 0.02. The MBF results with both values were statistically significantly worse than those with $\rho = 0.02$, and the time taken to find the best solutions was not significantly different either.

Another possibility is that the problem arise because the values returned by out fitness functions lie in the range 0-100, typically 20-30, which is far lower than the values typically seen in TSP problems for which the software is designed. This would mean that quantities of pheromone added to links on the best ants trail was relatively large, causing the pheromone matrix to "converge" fairly quickly to a set of values which represent a single path. This can be addressed in two ways - either by scaling the rate at which pheromones are laid down, or by using an exponent of less than one when calculating the probability of selecting different links during path construction. Accordingly we ran experiments with $\rho = 0.2$ and $\alpha = 0.7$. These similarly failed to produce improvements in the performance relative to EAs.

Since both the ACO and the EA use exactly the same code (indeed are compiled against the same files) to implement the Local Search and the fitness functions, it would appear that we can rule out implementation errors. There is extensive literature reporting the successful and competitive use of ACO for permutation-type problems. The final reason for the relatively poor performance of the many different parameterisations of MAX-MIN ACO tried would thus appear to be that the algorithm is designed to make extensive use of heuristic information, which was not available for these experiment as we wished to make a fair comparison with the EAs.

6. CONCLUSIONS

The results presented above show that in fact the use of local search is usually, but not always beneficial to the Ant Colony Algorithm, whereas for the Evolutionary Algorithm using an order based recombination it is highly effective at improving both the quality and speed of optimisation. Across a range of parameter settings ACO found its best solutions earlier than EAs, but those solutions were of lower quality than those found by EAs.

For both algorithms we demonstrated that the number of constraints present, which relates to the number of classes

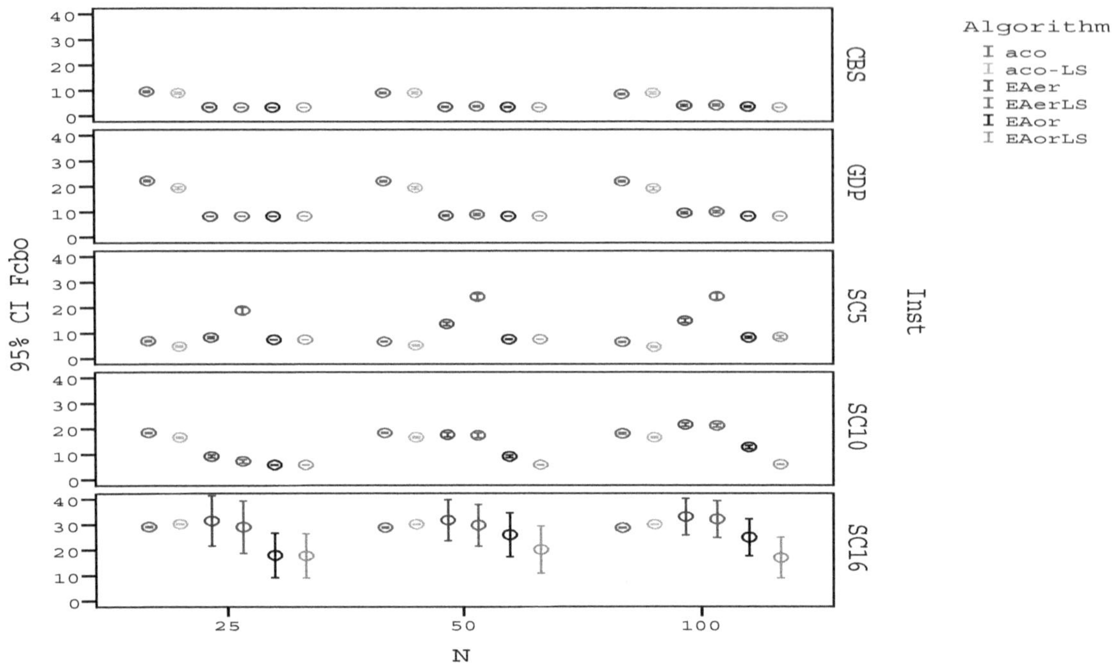

Figure 2: Comparison of Mean Best F_{cbo} values analysed by algorithm, instance and N

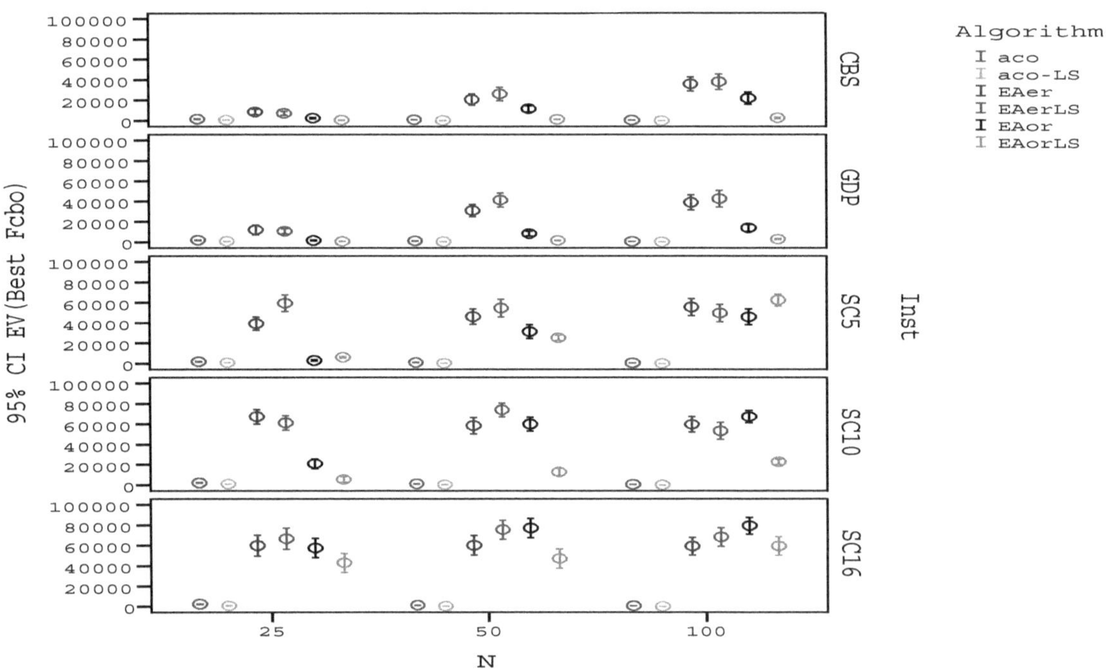

Figure 3: Comparison of Number of Evaluations after which Best F_{cbo} value per run was discovered analysed by algorithm, instance and N

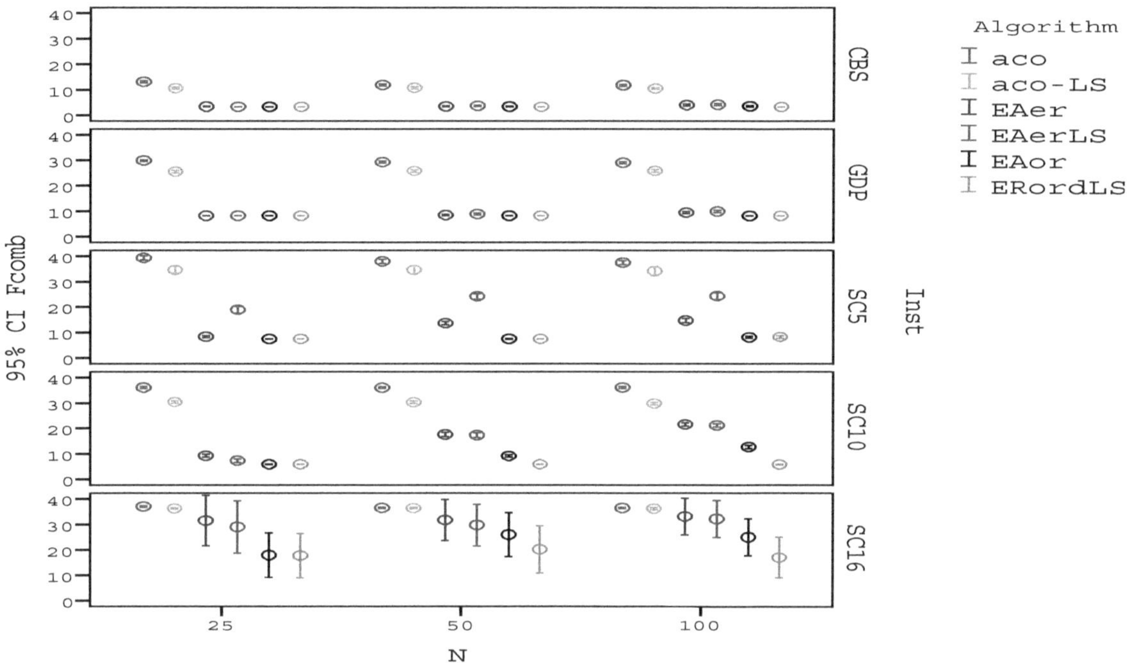

Figure 4: Comparison of Mean Best F_{comb} values analysed by algorithm, instance and N

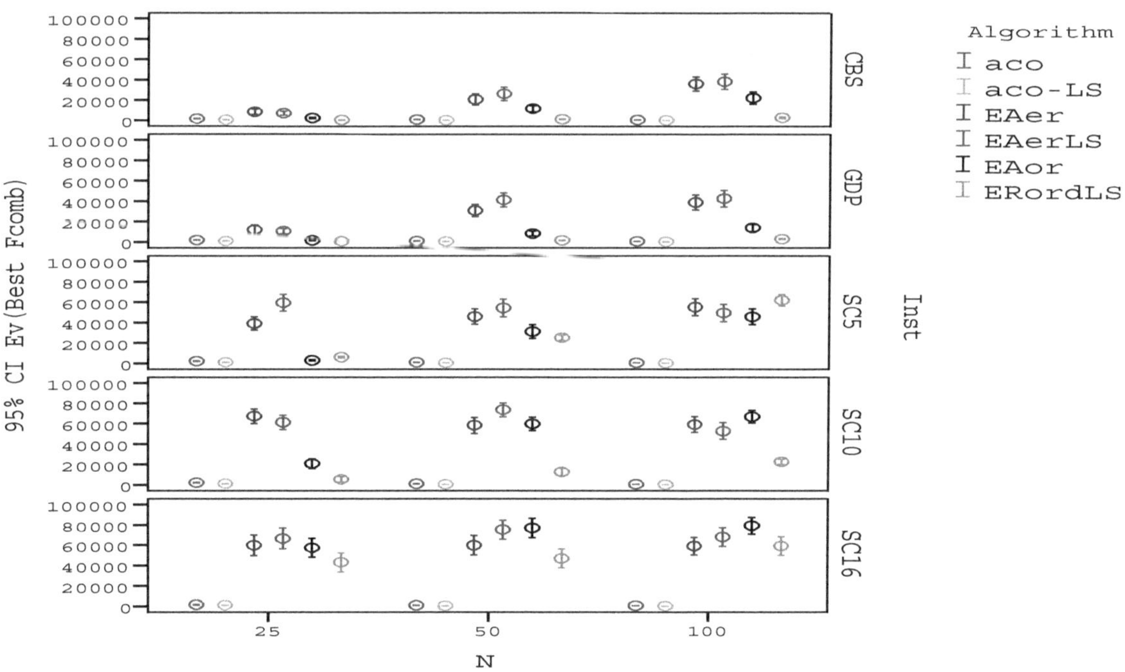

Figure 5: Comparison of Number of Evaluations after which Best F_{comb} value per run was discovered analysed by algorithm, instance and N

created, has a far bigger impact on solution quality and time than the size of the problem in terms of numbers of attributes and methods.

The analysis of the different parameters for the ACO also revealed that the reason for the relatively poor performance probably lies with its reliance on heuristic information to complement that stored in the pheromone matrix. In this paper we chose not to use such information, since it was not available to the Evolutionary Algorithm, but it would be relative straightforward to construct the equivalent of a distance matrix H (see Eq.1). A simple method would be to measure distance via use patterns - for example setting $H_{ij} = 1$ if method i used attribute j, $H_{ij} = 2$ if methods i and j shared a common attribute k, or if attributes i and j were both used by method k, and so on.

The original hypothesis of this paper was that the addition of Local Search to create memetic algorithms would to a large extent reduce the impact of the choice of global search heuristic. Certainly for the single-step local search method used here, the results conclusively disprove that hypothesis. While this is a shame from the perspective of easily incorporating user-provided hints etc, the reliance that we have exposed on heuristic information for the ACO algorithm does at least point a way forward.

7. REFERENCES

[1] M. Bowman, L. C. Briand, and Y. Labiche. Solving the Class Responsibility Assignment Problem in Object-Oriented Analysis with Multi-Objective Genetic Algorithms. *IEEE Transactions on Software Engineering*, 36(6):817–837, Nov. 2010.

[2] W. Brown, R. Malveau, H. McCormick, and T. Mowbray. *Anti-Patterns: Refactoring Software, Architectures, and Projects in Crisis*. Wiley, 1998.

[3] A. E. Eiben and J. E. Smith. *Introduction to evolutionary computing*. Springer: Heidelberg, Berlin, New York, 2003.

[4] M. Harman. Software Engineering Meets Evolutionary Computation. *Computer*, 44(10):31–39, 2011.

[5] N. Krasnogor and J. Smith. Emergence of profitable search strategies based on a simple inheritance mechanism. *Proceedings of the Genetic and Evolutionary Computation Conference, GECCO-2001*, pages 432–439, 2001.

[6] N. Krasnogor and J. Smith. Competent memetic algorithms: model, taxonomy and design issues'. *IEEE Transactions on Evolutionary Computation*, 9:474–488, 2005.

[7] S. Meyer-Nieberg and H.-G. Beyer. Self-adaptation in evolutionary algorithms. In F. G. Lobo, C. F. Lima, and Z. Michalewicz, editors, *Parameter Setting in Evolutionary Algorithms*, volume 54 of *Studies in Computational Intelligence*, pages 47–75. Springer, 2007.

[8] M. Serpell and J. Smith. Self-Adaption of Mutation Operator and Probability for Permutation Representations in Genetic Algorithms. *Evolutionary Computation*, 18(3):1–24, Feb. 2010.

[9] O. Sievi-Korte, E. Mäkinen, and T. Poranen. Simulated Annealing for Aiding Genetic Algorithm in Software Architecture Synthesis. Technical Report D-2010-019, Department of Computer Sciences, University of Tampere, Jan. 2010.

[10] C. Simons. Case study specifications, available at http://www.cems.uwe.ac.uk/~clsimons/casestudies.

[11] C. Simons and I. Parmee. Elegant object-oriented software design via interactive, evolutionary computation. *Systems, Man, and Cybernetics, Part C: Applications and Reviews, IEEE Transactions on*, 42(6):1797–1805, 2012.

[12] C. Simons, I. Parmee, and R. Gwynllyw. Interactive, Evolutionary Search in Upstream Object-Oriented Class Design. *Software Engineering, IEEE Transactions on*, 36(6):798–816, 2010.

[13] C. Simons and J. Smith. A Comparison of Evolutionary Algorithms and Ant Colony Optimization for Interactive Software Design. In *Proceedings of the 4 th Symposium on Search Based-Software Engineering*, page 37, 2012.

[14] C. L. Simons and J. E. Smith. A Comparison of Meta-heuristic Search for Interactive Software Design. *arXiv preprint arXiv:1211.3371, accepted for publication in the journal Soft Computing*, pages 1–32, Oct. 2013.

[15] T. Stuetzle. Acotsp, version 1.2, available at http://www.aco-metaheuristic.org/aco-code.

[16] T. Stuetzle and H. H. Hoos. Max-min ant system. *Future Generation Computer Systems*, 16(8):889–914, 2000.

[17] S. Vathsavayi, H. Hadaytullah, and K. Koskimies. Interleaving human and search-based software architecture design. *Proceedings of the Estonian Academy of Sciences*, 62(1):16, 2013.

[18] Y. Zhang. Repository of publications on search-based software engineering.

Minimizing Test Suites in Software Product Lines Using Weight-based Genetic Algorithms

Shuai Wang
Certus Software V&V Center
Simula Research Laboratory
Dept of Informatics, University of Oslo
P.O. Box 134, Lysaker, Norway
shuai@simula.no

Shaukat Ali
Certus Software V&V Center
Simula Research Laboratory
P.O. Box 134, Lysaker, Norway
shaukat@simula.no

Arnaud Gotlieb
Certus Software V&V Center
Simula Research Laboratory
P.O. Box 134, Lysaker, Norway
arnaud@simula.no

ABSTRACT

Test minimization techniques aim at identifying and eliminating redundant test cases from test suites in order to reduce the total number of test cases to execute, thereby improving the efficiency of testing. In the context of software product line, we can save effort and cost in the selection and minimization of test cases for testing a specific product by modeling the product line. However, minimizing the test suite for a product requires addressing two potential issues: 1) the minimized test suite may not cover all test requirements compared with the original suite; 2) the minimized test suite may have less fault revealing capability than the original suite. In this paper, we apply weight-based Genetic Algorithms (GAs) to minimize the test suite for testing a product, while preserving fault detection capability and testing coverage of the original test suite. The challenge behind is to define an appropriate fitness function, which is able to preserve the coverage of complex testing criteria (e.g., Combinatorial Interaction Testing criterion). Based on the defined fitness function, we have empirically evaluated three different weight-based GAs on an industrial case study provided by Cisco Systems, Inc. Norway. We also presented our results of applying the three weight-based GAs on five existing case studies from the literature. Based on these case studies, we conclude that among the three weight-based GAs, Random-Weighted GA (RWGA) achieved significantly better performance than the other ones.

Categories and Subject Descriptors

D.2.5 [**Software Engineering**]: Testing and Debugging

I.2.8 [**Artificial Intelligence**]: Problem Solving, Control Methods, and Search

General Terms

Algorithms, Performance, Experimentation, Verification

Keywords

Test minimization, feature pairwise coverage, fault detection capability, weight-based GAs

GECCO'13, July 6–10, 2013, Amsterdam, The Netherlands.

1. INTRODUCTION

Software Product Line Engineering (SPLE) is becoming a cost-effective way to develop similar products by exploiting and managing commonalities and variabilities among a large number of products [1][2]. SPLE has shown promising benefits in both academia and industry such as reducing development time and costs, speeding up product time-to-market and improving the quality of products of a product line family [2].

For testing a product line, in the current practice of industry (e.g., based on our experience of working with Cisco Systems, Inc. Norway), a test suite is typically developed to test the whole product line and the test suite will be modified as new products come into play or the current products need to be improved [1][3]. However, as the number of products increases, the number of test cases for testing the product line will also increase. Therefore, it becomes practically impossible to execute all the test cases of the product line due to limited available time and resources for each new product. It is therefore essential to seek a solution to minimize test suites for a specific product efficiently before execution to reduce the cost of testing [3].

Based on our collaboration with Cisco, a methodology has been proposed to support automated test case selection using Feature Model (FM) and Component Family Model (CFM) [4][5]. This methodology captures the commonalties and variabilities of a product line using a FM and the domain knowledge of test experts using a CFM. However, after carefully studying the results, we observed there still exist redundant test cases in the selected test suite and eliminating these redundant test cases can reduce the execution cost of testing (test minimization). Moreover, there are two potential risks for test minimization, i.e., the minimized test suite might not cover all testing functionalities (i.e., test requirements) and have lower fault detection capability than the original test suite. Therefore, we are facing a challenge, in our industrial context, to minimize the test suite for testing a product, whereas at the same time achieving high fault detection capability and functionality coverage. However, the current practice of reducing the number of test cases is manual and not systematic, which often decreases the functionality coverage and fault detection capability in addition to being time consuming as we observed in our previous work [4].

Based on the above-mentioned challenges, the problem we are targeting is a multi-objective optimization problem and multi-objective Genetic Algorithms (GAs) are known for solving such a problem [6]. Moreover, Weight-based GAs suits our context well since our goal is to minimize the test suite for testing a product, while keeping high feature pairwise coverage of testing and fault detection capability, i.e., we aim at balancing all the proposed objectives and achieving them best together. Therefore, in this paper, we propose an application of weight-based Genetic Algorithms (GAs) to minimize test suites for a product. More specifically, we first formally define the above-mentioned issues as three objectives: Test Minimization Percentage (*TMP*), Feature Pairwise Coverage (*FPC*) and Fault Detection Capability (*FDC*), and propose objective functions for them. Second, a fitness function is defined, based on these objectives to guide the search towards an optimal solution. Third, we present an industrial case study and five other case studies from SPLOT (http://www.splot-research.org/) to evaluate three different weight-based GAs (i.e., Weight–Based Genetic Algorithm (WBGA), Weight-Based Genetic Algorithm for Multi-objective Optimization (WBGA-MO), Random-Weighted Genetic Algorithm (RWGA)) based on the proposed fitness function. Random Search (RS) is used as the baseline to evaluate the performance of the selected weight-based GAs. Last, based on the obtained results and analysis, we propose a guideline for future practitioners to solve test minimization problems using weight-based GAs.

The contributions of this paper are: 1) Definition of a fitness function based on the three objectives; 2) Empirical evaluation of the three weight-based GAs by comparing them with RS, based on an industrial case study and five case studies from SPLOT.

The rest of paper is organized as follows: Section 2 provides a briefly introduction of the existing methodology for test case selection and the weight-based GAs we applied. Section 3 presents a formal representation of the problem, definitions and functions for all the three objectives followed by fitness function used by all the algorithms. In Section 4, empirical evaluation based on an industrial case study and five other case studies are presented. Section 5 discusses threats to validity and related work is presented in Section 6. Section 7 concludes the paper.

2. BACKGROUND

In this section, we briefly present our existing methodology for test case selection based on FM and CFM in the context of product line (Section 2.1) followed by related description of selected weight-based GAs (Section 2.2).

2.1 Test Case Selection based on FM and CFM

Feature modeling is a hierarchical modeling approach for capturing commonalities and variabilities in product line [2][7]. By modeling a product line with Feature Model (FM), various products can be configured through feature selection in a systematic way. A component family model (CFM) is used to represent how products are assembled and generated in a product line by modeling relations among software architectural elements [8]. It has a hierarchical structure including items such as *components* and *parts*. Meanwhile, *restrictions* play a key role, which are used to specify relations between features in FM and components/parts in CFM. Via *restrictions*, a specific product can be configured automatically from a valid selected feature model in a product line.

In our previous work [4][5], we proposed a systematic and automated methodology using a Feature Model for Testing (FM_T) to capture commonalities and variabilities of a product line and a Component Family Model for Testing (CFM_T) to capture the overall structure of test cases in the repository. With our methodology, a test engineer does not need to manually go through the repository to select a relevant set of test cases for a new product. Instead, a test engineer only needs to select a set of relevant features using FM_T at a higher level of abstraction for a product and a set of relevant test cases will be selected automatically. In addition, we developed a tool named as Import Plugin and Transformation (IPT) to support this automated test case selection methodology and it has been applied in Cisco Systems, Norway.

2.2 Description of Selected Weight-based GAs

Genetic Algorithms (GAs) are inspired by the Darwinian evolution theory, which are well known to address complex problems in Search-Based Software Engineering (SBSE) [9]. When applying GA, a population of individuals (i.e., candidate solutions) is evolved through a series of generations, where reproducing individuals evolve through crossover and mutation operators. Meanwhile, GAs are often compared with the techniques based on random search (RS) when applying to determine whether the complexity is warranted to address a specific SBSE problem. The use of the GAs may only be justified if it performs significantly better than, for instance, RS. To use a GA, a fitness function needs to be defined to evaluate the quality of a candidate solution (i.e., an element in the search space). The fitness function is problem dependent, and proper care needs to be taken for developing adequate fitness functions. The fitness function will be used to guide the search toward fitter solutions. Below, we provide a brief description of the weight-based GAs that we used in this paper, i.e., Weight–Based Genetic Algorithm (WBGA), Weight-Based Genetic Algorithm for Multi-objective Optimization (WBGA-MO), and Random-Weighted Genetic Algorithm (RWGA).

The working theory of these three weight-based GAs is to assign a particular weight to each objective function for converting the multi-objective problem to a single objective problem with a scalar objective function [6]. The difference of these algorithms can be summarized as the different mechanisms of assigning weights for each objective, which is shown in Table 1.

Table 1 Mechanisms of Assigning Weights for the Three Weight-based GAs

Algorithms	Mechanisms of Assigning Weights
WBGA	Predefined fixed weights
WBGA-MO	Weights in weight pool
RWGA	Randomly normalized weights

As shown in Table 1, WBGA assigns fixed weights for each objective defined for each objective before, which can be provided by users based on the domain knowledge and expertise. The same weight for each objective is used during all generations of the algorithm. WBGA-MO uses a weight pool including a set of predefined weights and each solution can choose weights for each objective randomly during running. The assigned weight for each objective changes during each generation, but is still limited from ones existing in the weight pool. Notice that such weight pool can also be provided by users. As for RWGA, different normalized weights are assigned randomly for each objective at each generation, i.e., it is not required to assign particular weights before and weights for each objective are assigned dynamically during running.

Based on the above discussions, these algorithms can be classified as *fixed-weight* algorithms and *dynamic-weight* algorithms according to their assigning ways of weights. Therefore, WBGA and WBGA-MO can be classified into *fixed-weight* algorithms and RWGA can be classified into *dynamic-weight* algorithms.

3. PROBLEM REPRESENTATION AND FITNESS FUNCTION

To guide the search towards an optimal solution using weight-based GAs, it is essential to define a fitness function, as is the case for any search algorithm. Our goal is to find a minimum subset of test cases to test a product in a product line from the entire set of test cases available for the product line. At the same time, we also want to achieve high feature pairwise coverage and fault detection capability. In Section 3.1, we first present formal representation of the search problem. Second, we define three objectives and related functions, i.e., *TMP*, *FPC* and *FDC* in Section 3.2 followed by the definition of the fitness function in Section 3.3.

3.1 Problem Representation

Suppose a product line P has a set of products $P = \{p_1, p_2, p_3 \dots p_{np}\}$, where np is the number of products in P. Moreover, P can be represented as a feature model with a set of features $F = \{f_1, f_2, f_3 \dots f_{nf}\}$ [2][5], where nf is the number of features (i.e., functionalities need to be tested for P). To test P, there is a test suite $TS = \{t_1, t_2, t_3 \dots t_{nt}\}$ comprising of a large number of test cases (nt). A specific product p_i in P, where $1 \le i \le np$, can be represented as a subset of F : $F_{p_i} = \{f_1', f_2', f_3' \dots f_{nf_{p_i}}'\}$, where f_i' can be any feature in F ($f_i' \in F$) and nf_{p_i} is the number of features used to represent the product p_i ($1 \le nf_{p_i} \le nf$). To test p_i, based on [4], there is a subset of the test suite TS: $TS_{p_i} = \{t_1', t_2', t_3' \dots t_{nt_{p_i}}'\}$ comprising nt_{p_i} test cases, where t_i' can be any test case in TS ($t_i' \in TS$) and $1 \le nt_{p_i} \le nt$. Based on TS_{p_i} for p_i, there is a set of potential solutions $S_{p_i} = \{s_{p_i1}, s_{p_i2}, s_{p_i3} \dots s_{ns_{p_i}}\}$, where ns_{p_i} is the total number of solutions for testing p_i, which can be measured as $2^{nt_{p_i}} - 1$. As the number of test cases increases, the potential solutions increase exponentially. Suppose we have 1000 test cases to test the product line P and using the methodology proposed by [4], 100 test cases are obtained to test the product p_i. Then there will be $2^{100} - 1$ potential solutions for testing p_i, which is a huge solution space. Each solution s_i in S_{p_i} is comprised of nt_{s_i} test cases from TS_{p_i}: $\{t_{s_i1}', t_{s_i2}', t_{s_i3}' \dots t_{nt_{s_i}}'\}$, where $1 \le nt_{s_i} \le nt_{p_i}$ and has a certain FPC_{s_i} and FDC_{s_i}, which are measured as described in the next section.

Based on the above discussion, the detailed problem can be represented as:

Problem: Search for a solution s_k (s_k is comprised by $\left\{t_{s_k1}', t_{s_k2}', t_{s_k3}' \dots t_{nt_{s_k}}'\right\}$ from TS_{p_i}, where $1 \le nt_{s_k} \le nt_{p_i}$) from S_{p_i} for testing the product p_i to achieve 1) high TM_{s_k} (i.e., less number of test cases); 2) high FPC_{s_k}; 3) high FDC_{s_k}.

3.2 Definitions and Functions for Three Objectives

In this section, based on the above-mentioned problem, we provide mathematical definitions and functions for these three objectives required to achieve test minimization.

3.2.1 Test Minimization Percentage (TMP)

TMP is used to measure the amount of reduction in the number of test cases and is calculated as follows.

$$TMP_{s_k} = \left(1 - \frac{nt_{s_k}}{nt_{p_i}}\right) * 100\%$$

As discussed in section 3.1, nt_{s_k} is the number of test cases for the solution s_k, where $1 \le nt_{s_k} \le nt_{p_i}$. nt_{p_i} is the number of test cases in the test suite for testing product p_i. *TMP* value ranges from 0 to 1 and a higher value of *TMP* represents higher test minimization.

3.2.2 Feature Pairwise Coverage (FPC)

FPC is used to measure how much pairwise coverage can be achieved by a chosen solution [10][11]. We chose this type of coverage based on our domain knowledge, discussion with test engineers, and history data about faults because a higher percentage of detected faults are mainly due to the interactions between features. *FPC* is designed to compute the capability of covering feature pairs by a chosen solution, which is computed as below:

$$FPC_{s_k} = \frac{Num\_FP_{s_k}}{Num\_FP_{p_i}} * 100\%$$

$Num\_FP_{s_k}$ is the number of feature pairs covered in the test cases for the solution s_k, which can be measured as follows.

$$Num\_FP_{s_k} = \sum_{i=1}^{nt_{s_k}} Num\_FP_{tc_i}$$

nt_{s_k} is the number of test cases for the solution s_k, where $1 \le nt_{s_k} \le nt_{p_i}$. $Num\_FP_{tc_i}$ is the number of unduplicated feature pairs covered by the test case i (tc_i). The feature pairs covered by tc_i can be computed as: $Num\_FP_{tc_i} = C^2_{size\,(F_{tc_i})}$. $size\,(F_{tc_i})$ is the number of features tested by test case tc_i. For instance, test case tc_i is used to test three features. Then the feature pairs covered by test case i are C_3^2 = 3*2/2 = 3. Notice that if some feature pairs are repeated ones compared with the feature pairs covered by the previous test cases, repeated pairs will be removed when computing $Num\_FP_{s_k}$.

$Num\_FP_{p_i}$ is all number of feature pairs for testing the product p_i which can be measured as: $Num\_FP_{p_i} = C^2_{\text{size}\left(F_{p_i}\right)} = nt_{p_i} * (nt_{p_i} - 1)/2$. F_{p_i} is the set of features representing the product p_i including nt_{p_i} features. For instance, if p_i is represented by ten features, all feature pairs covered by the product are C_{10}^2= 10*9/2 = 45. Note that *FPC* is calculated for a chosen test solution and ranges from 0 to 1 and a higher value of *FPC* shows higher feature pairwise coverage.

3.2.3 Fault Detection Capability (FDC)

FDC measures the fault detection capability of a selected test solution for a product. In out context, fault detection refers to the success rate of a test case in a given time, e.g., a week or a month. In our context, a test case is defined as a *success* if it can detect faults in a given time and as a *fail* if it does not detect any fault. The success rate of a test case can be measured as below.

$$SucR_{tc_i} = \frac{NumSuc_{tc_i}}{NumSuc_{tc_i} + NumFail_{tc_i}}$$

$SucR_{tc_i}$ is the success rate of execution for test case i during the given time (in our case, the given time is per week);

$NumSuc_{tc_i}$ is the number of *success* executions for the given test case i during the given time;

$NumFail_{tc_i}$ is the number of *fail* executions for the given test case i during the given time.

For instance, a test case is usually executed 1000 times per week in Cisco. So if a test case executes successfully for 800 times in the given week, the fault detection capability for the test case is 800/1000 = 0.8. Similarly, for a test solution including a set of test cases for a specific product, the fault detection capability can be measured as below.

$$FDC_{s_k} = \frac{\sum_{i=1}^{nt_{s_k}} SucR_{tc_i}}{nt_{s_k}}$$

nt_{s_k} is the number of test cases for the solution s_k, where $1 \leq nt_{s_k} \leq nt_{p_i}$. Note that *FDC* value also ranges from 0 to 1 and a higher value of *FDC* represents higher fault detection capability.

3.3 Fitness Function

In this stage, *TMP*, *FPC*, and *FDC* have been defined and can be computed through the mathematical formulas. To ease computation of the fitness function, the values for all the three objectives have been normalized by the above-proposed formulas, which range from 0 to 1. We adopted a fitness function for weight-based GAs presented in [6][12], and is defined as follows:

$$min\, Fitness\_F = 1 - (w_1 * TMP + w_2 * FPC + w_3 * FDC)$$

w_1, w_2 and w_3 are a set of assigned weights to *TMP*, *FPC* and *FDC* respectively, and they need to satisfy the constraint: $w_1 + w_2 + w_3 = 1$. Using this way, multi-objective optimization problem is converted to a single objective problem with a scalar objective function, which is a classical approach and is efficient to be solved using GAs [6]. Notice that different set of weights can represent distinct testing preferences. For instance, if *TMP* is considered as the most important objective, w_1 can be assigned the highest weight, such as 0.6. In practice, w_1, w_2 and w_3 must be identified in a more systematic way such as by a thorough domain analysis followed by a comprehensive questionnaire. In our context, we obtained two sets of values of w_1, w_2 and w_3 via domain analysis and discussion with test engineers of Cisco, i.e., w_1 = 1/3, w_2 = = 1/3, w_3 = 1/3 and w_1 = 0.2, w_2 = 0.4, w_3 = 0.4.

In this paper, three different weight-based GAs are used, which are the commonly used GAs based on weight theory, i.e., WBGA, WBGA-MO, and RWGA. We have used two sets of weights for WBGA which are: WBGA_W$_1$ (W$_1$ = (1/3, 1/3, 1/3)), WBGA_W$_2$ (W$_2$ = (0.2, 0.4, 0.4). As for WBGA-MO, we create weight pool using these two sets of weights for different objectives.

4. CASE STUDIES AND EMPIRICAL EVALUATION

In this section, first we present an industrial case study and five other case studies and then an empirical evaluation of various weight-based GAs is presented.

4.1 Case Studies

We evaluated our fitness function using one industrial case study and five case studies from the literature.

4.1.1 Industrial Case Study

Our industrial case study is provided by Cisco and is part of a large project on model-based testing of a Video Conferencing System (VCS) product line called Saturn [13]. The Saturn product line comprises of several VCSs such as C20, C40, and C60. The Saturn product line has more than 2000 test cases and for each product (e.g., C20), only a subset of all test cases is needed.

We chose four products C20, C40, C60 and C90 from Saturn. Based on our domain analysis, there are 169 features in Saturn and each product includes a subset of all features. Meanwhile, each feature can be tested by at least one test case (usually more than one). Table 2 shows more details about this. For instance, C20 contains 17 features (i.e., testing functionalities) and 138 test cases are used to test these features. Each test case tc_i has a success rate for execution ($SucR_{tc_i}$). In general, for Saturn, each feature is associated with 5-10 test cases; each test case is associated with 1-5 features and the fault detection capability ranges from 50% to 95%.

Table 2 Four Products in Saturn

Product	#Features	# Test Cases
C20	17	138
C40	25	167
C60	32	192
C90	43	239

4.1.2 Other Case Studies

Our other case studies are of five other products from different product lines from SPLOT (http://www.splot-research.org/). Each product line is represented by a feature model and each product includes a subset of all features [14]. Meanwhile, all test cases for testing the product line can be represented by a component family model and a subset of test cases can be obtained automatically for testing a specific product as discussed in [4]. For other five products represented by different sets of features from SPLOT as shown in Table 3. Here, we follow the similar phenomenon observed from Saturn and assume that each feature can be tested by 5-10 test cases, each test case can be used to test 1-5 features and the success rate (*SucR*) for each test case ranges from 50% to 95%.

Table 3 Five Case Studies from SPLOT

Name	Author	Description	#Features
Car Software System	Chr Wol	Simple model of a car's software product line	18
ATM Software	TCN	A feature model for ATM software	29
DELL Laptop/Notebook Computers	Moises Branco	A feature model describes the features of DELL Laptop/Notebook Products	46
SmartHome	Conejero	Adaptation of the original feature models for the SmartHome system used by AMPLE project as case study	59
J2EE web architecture	Reinout Korbee	A feature model for web architectures	77

4.2 Empirical Evaluation

This section discusses experiment design, execution, and analysis of the evaluation based on the guidelines reported in [15][16].

4.2.1 Experiment Design

The goal of our experiments is to assess the effectiveness of weight-based GAs for test minimization and at the same time achieving high feature pairwise coverage and fault detection capability.

4.2.1.1 *Research Questions*

From this experiment, we want to answer the following research questions:

RQ1: Are weight-based GAs effective to solve test minimization problem in our context?

RQ2: How do the weight-based GAs (WBGA, WBGA-MO, RWGA) compare to RS and among WBGA, WBGA-MO, RWGA, which one fares best in solving test minimization problem?

4.2.1.2 *Experiment Settings*

In our experiments, we compared three weight-based multi-objective GAs and RS, i.e., WGBA with two set of fixed weights based on the domain knowledge and expertise (WBGA_W_1 (W_1 = (1/3, 1/3, 1/3)), WBGA_W_2 (W_2 = (0.2, 0.4, 0.4)), WBGA-MO and RWGA. For all of them, we used a standard one-point crossover with a rate of 0.9 and mutation of a variable is done with the standard probability 1/n, where n is the number of variables. Meanwhile, the size of population and maximum number of fitness evaluation are set as 100 and 2000, respectively. Finally, RS was used as the comparison baseline to assess the difficulty of the addressed minimization problems [16]. Notice that different settings may lead to different performance for genetic algorithms, but standard settings usually perform well [15].

Moreover, a set of threshold values for *TMP*, *FPC*, and *FDC* are selected that show the minimum acceptable values for a particular context in our experiments. Note that these thresholds are set through the domain analysis and discussion with test engineers and a test manager at Cisco, and history data about test execution. In the context of our industrial case study, these thresholds values are: *TMP*:=0.8; *FPC*:=0.8; and *FDC*:=0.85.

4.2.1.3 *Statistical* Tests

To compare the obtained result and given thresholds, the Vargha and Delaney statistics and Mann-Whitney U test are used based on the guidelines for reporting statistical tests for randomized algorithms presented in [15].

- $\hat{A}_{12}$: The Vargha and Delaney statistics is used to calculate $\hat{A}_{12}$, which is a non-parametric effect size measure [15]. In our context, given performance measure $F = 1-(w_1 * TMP + w_2 * FPC + w_3 * FDC)$, $\hat{A}_{12}$ is used to compare the probability of yielding higher performance value *F* for two algorithms *A* and *B*. If $\hat{A}_{12}$ is equal to 0.5, the two algorithms are equivalent. If $\hat{A}_{12}$ is greater than 0.5, it means the first algorithm *A* has higher chances of obtaining higher *F* value than *B*.
- ***p*-value**: The non-parametric U-test (The Mann-Whitney U test) is used to calculate *p*-value for deciding whether there is a significant difference between two algorithms. We chose the significance level of 0.05, which means there is a significant difference if *p*-value is less than 0.05.

Based on the above description, we define that algorithm *A* has better performance than algorithm *B*, if the $\hat{A}_{12}$ value is greater than 0.5. Moreover, algorithm *A* has significantly better performance than algorithm *B*, if the $\hat{A}_{12}$ value is greater than 0.5 and *p*-value is less than 0.05.

4.2.2 *Experiment Execution*

According to the guidelines in [15], each algorithm is run for 1000 times to account for random variations inherited in search algorithms and is essential to increase the power of statistical tests that further improves the confidence on the results. We let WBGA_W_1, WBGA_W_2, WBGA-MO, RWGA and RS run up to 2000 fitness generations each time and collected the optimal solution including the final value of fitness function. We ran our experiments on a PC with Intel Core i7 2.3GHz with 4 GB of RAM, running Microsoft Windows 7 operating system.

4.2.3 *Results and Analysis*

In this section, we discuss and analyze the obtained results for the individual research question followed by an overall discussion. Note that Table 4 and Table 5 are shown in the last page of paper as landscape to save the space.

4.2.3.1 *Results and Analysis for Research Question 1*

Table 4 shows the results, when the performance of search algorithms is compared with the threshold values for our industrial case study and five case studies from SPLOT. In Table 4, we did one sample Mann Whitney test since we compared the obtained results from different algorithms with one set of fixed values for *TMP*, *FPC* and *FDC*.

Based on the obtained results, we can answer RQ1 as follows:

RWGA has higher probability to obtain better results when compared with the given thresholds. In other words, RWGA has higher probability to be adapted when required since most of $\hat{A}_{12}$ values are greater than 0.5 and there is no significant difference (all *p*-values are greater than 0.05) when comparing with the given thresholds as shown in Table 4.

In a way, the results obtained by WBGA-MO are almost equivalent to the given thresholds since most of $\hat{A}_{12}$ values are close to 0.5. Meanwhile, there are no significant difference between the results of WBGA-MO and the given thresholds (all *p*-values are greater than 0.05) as shown in Table 4.

For WBGA_W_1 and WBGA_W_2, the results do not stay stable. For some products, $\hat{A}_{12}$ values are close to 0.5, for other products, $\hat{A}_{12}$ values are much less than 0.5 (the given thresholds have much higher probability to be used). Meanwhile, for some products, there is no significant difference when compared with the given thresholds and there is a significant difference with the thresholds for other products as shown in Table 4. Since the only difference between WBGA_W_1 and WBGA_W_2 is the sets of weights, different weights can result in total different results when using WBGA. So providing reasonable weights before using WBGA is essential to obtain expected results.

Based on the results, we can see that RS always has less probability to be used in practice when compared with the given thresholds since all $\hat{A}_{12}$ values are less than 0.5 and there are significant differences when comparing with the given thresholds since *p*-values are less than 0.05 as shown in Table 4.

In general, weight-based GAs can assist to achieve the given thresholds. Given different weights, using WBGA can obtain total different results. So assigning a reasonable set of weights before using WBGA plays a key role to gain expected results. Notice that the obtained results by WBGA-MO and RWGA are more stable than WBGA, which is because WBGA-MO and RWGA are less dependent on a certain set of weights. Especially, since there is no need to provide weights before using, the obtained results by RWGA are more stable than WBGA-MO.

4.2.3.2 Results and Analysis for Research Question 2

Table 5 shows the results when different algorithms are compared for the Saturn products and five other products. According to the combination theory, 10 (C_5^2 = 5*4/2) pairs are compared.

Based on the obtained results, we can answer *RQ2* as follows:

Firstly, as shown in Table 5, we compared the performance of various algorithms with RS. When WBGA_W_1 is compared with RS, the $\hat{A}_{12}$ values are all greater than 0.5 and the *p*-values are mostly less than 0.05 (8 out of 9 in four VCS products and five other case studies). For the comparison of WBGA_W_2 and RS, the $\hat{A}_{12}$ values are mostly greater than 0.5 (8 out of 9 in four VCS products and five other case studies) and the *p*-values are all less than 0.05. When comparing WBGA-MO with RS, the $\hat{A}_{12}$ values are all greater than 0.5 and the *p*-values are all less than 0.05. Finally, when RWGA is compared with RS, the $\hat{A}_{12}$ values are all greater than 0.5 and the *p*-values are all less than 0.05. Based on the above results, we can conclude that weight-based GAs have significantly better performance than RS.

Now we discuss the results, when various weight-based GAs are compared. Firstly, when WBGA_W_1 is compared with RWGA, Table 5 shows that the $\hat{A}_{12}$ values are all less than 0.5 and the *p*-values are mostly less than 0.05 (8 out of 9 in four VCS products and five other case studies); secondly, comparing WBGA_W_2 with RWGA, the $\hat{A}_{12}$ values are all less than 0.5 and the *p*-values are also mostly less than 0.05 (8 out of 9 in four VCS products and five other case studies); thirdly, comparing WBGA-MO with RWGA, the $\hat{A}_{12}$ values are all less than 0.5 and the *p*-values are all less than 0.05. Based on the above results, we concluded that RWGA has significantly better performance than WBGA_W_1, WBGA_W_2 and WBGA-MO.

Finally, WBGA_W_1, WBGA_W_2 and WBGA-MO were compared. Since both WBGA_W_1 and WBGA_W_2 belong to WBGA, we studied them together and compare WBGA and WBGA-MO. Based on the obtained results as shown in Table 5, for the $\widehat{A}_{12}$ values, 10 out of 18 are less than 0.5 and 8 out of 18 are greater than 0.5 in four VCS products and five other case studies, and for the *p*-values, 4 out of 18 are less than 0.05 and 14 out of 18 are greater than 0.05. Based on the results, we can conclude that WBGA-MO has better performance than WBGA, but not significantly.

4.2.3.3 Overall Discussion

Based on the above-mentioned discussions when using weight-based GAs, different sets of weights (e.g., w_1, w_2 and w_3) can be provided depending on the testing requirements. So domain knowledge and thorough discussions with users is required before assigning weights.

Moreover, based on the obtained results and analysis, RWGA has the best performance among the three weight-based GAs and RS. The main reason is that RWGA assigns weights dynamically during search and thus the search is guided towards the best weights to achieve threshold values for *TMP*, *FPC* and *FDC*.

In particular, when testing requirements are not clear in practice, i.e., it is impossible to provide reasonable weights for *TMP, FPC* and *FDC*. We suggest using RWGA to minimize test suites for products since it assigns weights dynamically. In the context of VCS testing, after running RWGA 1000 times, based on the empirical evaluation, the best set of weights that obtains the best results of fitness function is w_1 = 0.24 for *TMP*, w_2 = 0.44 for *FPC* and w_3 = 0.32 for *FDC* respectively.

5. THREATS TO VALIDITY

To reduce *construct validity* threats, we used the same stopping criteria for all algorithms, i.e., number of fitness evaluations. We ran each algorithm for 2000 evaluations to seek the best solution for test minimization. This criterion is a comparable measure across all the algorithms since each iteration requires updating the obtained solution and comparing the computed value of fitness function.

A possible threat to *internal validity* is that we have experimented with only one configuration setting for the GA parameters. However, these settings are in accordance with the common guidelines in the literature and our previous experience on testing problems. Parameter tuning can improve the performance of GAs, although default parameters often provide reasonable results [15].

We ran our experiments on an industrial case study to seek the best solution to minimize test suites for testing a product. To reduce *external validity* threats (i.e., our results might not be applicable to other empirical studies), five other case studies from SPLOT were adapted using the same criteria, i.e., each feature can be tested by 5-10 test cases, each test case can be used to test 1-5 features and success rate for each test case ranges from 50% to 95%. In this way, the results obtained by the industrial case study and five other case studies should be more persuasive.

The most probable conclusion validity threat in experiments involving randomized algorithms is due to random variations. To address it, we repeated experiments 1000 times to reduce the possibility that the results were obtained by chance. Furthermore, to determine the probability of yielding higher performance by different algorithms, we measured the effect size using $\hat{A}_{12}$ by Vargha and Delaney statistics test. We chose Vargha and Delaney statistics test since it is appropriate for non-parametric effect size measure, which match our situation [15]. Meanwhile, we performed Mann-Whitney U test to determine the statistical significance of the results.

Finally, as already discussed in Section 4, our practical set of weights obtained by empirical evaluation may not be applicable to all product line testing. Therefore, in every specific product line needs to be tested, a different set of weights might be obtained when using RWGA. However, for some specific product line similar to VCS product line, the proposed set of weights could be adapted directly.

6. RELATED WORK

Software product line testing is a relatively new, but intense field of research since product line engineering has shown significant benefits in both academia and industry [1][17][18].

In [1], McGregor presented a set of activities, which can be used to address testing individual assets (e.g., verification of consistency between requirements and specifications) and testing artifacts (e.g., test-case derivation and test suite design) that represent complete products in the context of product line. In [17], based on a relational model capturing variability in product line, Cohen defined a family of cumulative coverage criteria to collect test coverage information, which was also used to map with existing combinatorial testing approaches for supporting product line testing. In [18], Muccini proposed associating regression testing with product line by comparing code execution with the architectural design, which can be used as guidelines for adapting existing techniques for regression testing to product line testing. However, most of these works are only proposals and only provide guidelines without specific testing process, which are not systematic. In our previous work [4], an methodology was presented to obtain a set of test cases for testing a specific product automatically by modeling software product line using feature model and test case structure using component family model, which is more related with test selection and there are still redundant test cases in the obtained test suite for a specific product through more investigation.

As for test minimization in regression testing, various types of minimizing techniques are proposed in the literatures [19]. In [20], Chen and Lau proposed GE and GRE heuristics to perform test minimization, which are thought as the variation of the greedy algorithms. In [21], Tallam and Gupta proposed an improved greedy algorithm called *the delayed greedy* approach based on the Formal Concept Analysis of the relation between test cases and testing requirements. In [22], Jeffrey and Gupta extended GE and GRE by introducing a secondary set of test requirements to determine whether a test case is redundant for test minimization. Although the number of techniques for regression test minimization is huge [19], there is no enough evidence to prove that these techniques still work well if being adapted in the context of product line.

In particular, Shin and Mark [23] proposed to use search-based algorithms (i.e., Fast Non-dominated Sorting Genetic Algorithm (NSGA II)) for multi-objective test case selection (e.g., code coverage, fault detection history, execution time) in regression testing, which is similar with our two objectives (i.e., *FPC* and *FDC*). However, our context is product line and we minimized the test suite obtained by our proposed test case selection methodology in [4] for testing a product. Moreover, we defined one additional objective (i.e., *TMP* to measure the minimization percentage of the minimized test suite as compared with the original test suite based on our industrial problem. In addition, we compared different weight-based GAs and RS, which was not addressed in [23].

7. CONCLUSION AND FUTURE WORK

In this paper, we proposed an application of weight-based GAs to minimize the test suite for testing a product at the same time achieving high feature pairwise coverage and fault detection capability in the context of software product line. We formally defined three objectives (i.e., Test Minimization Percentage (*TMP*), Feature Pairwise Coverage (*FPC*) and Fault Detection Capability (*FDC*)), followed by the definition of a fitness function (based on the objectives) to guide three different weight-based Genetic Algorithms (GAs): Weight-Based Genetic Algorithm (WBGA), Weight-Based Genetic Algorithm for Multi-objective Optimization (WBGA-MO), Random-Weighted Genetic Algorithm (RWGA).

We evaluated our fitness function based on an industrial case study and five other case studies from the literature using the three weight-based GAs. Given a set of thresholds, these three weight-based GAs and Random Search (RS) were evaluated and a comparison among them was conducted.

Results show that RWGA and WBGA-MO achieved the given thresholds, WBGA achieved the given thresholds in some products and failed in others, and RS hardly achieved the given thresholds. Among all of these algorithms, RWGA has the best performance, and WBGA-MO and WBGA are almost equivalent, both of which have better performance than RS.

In the future, we plan to conduct more case studies using the proposed application of weight-based GAs. Moreover, we want to investigate the quality of the minimized test suite as compared with the test suite selected by test engineers manually to assess whether the weight-based GAs are human competitive. Meanwhile, we will also evaluate the proposed fitness function using Pareto-based multi-objective GAs, such as Fast Non-dominated Sorting Genetic Algorithm (NSGA II), to validate whether better results can be obtained as compared to weight-based GAs.

ACKNOWLEDGMENTS

The work reported in this paper is funded by the Norwegian Research Council under the research-based innovation scheme (SFI) in the Certus Center hosted by Simula Research Laboratory. We would like to thank Marius Christian Liaaen (Cisco Systems, Inc. Norway) for providing us the detailed case study and thorough discussion.

8. REFERENCES

[1] J. McGregor. Testing a Software Product Line. Technical Report CMU/SEI-2001-TR-022. Software Engineering Institute, Carnegie Mellon University, Pittsburgh, Pennsylvania. 2001. http://www.sei.cmu.edu/library/abstracts/reports/01tr022.cfm

[2] D. Benavides, S. Segura, and A. R. Cortés. Automated analysis of feature models 20 years later: A literature review. *Information Systems*. (35), 615–636. 2010.

[3] T. Chen, and M. Lau. Dividing strategies for the optimization of a test suite. *Information Processing Letters*. 60(3), pp. 135–141. 1996.

[4] S. Wang, A. Gotlieb, M. Liaaen, and L. C. Briand. Automatic selection of test execution plans from a Video Conference System Product Line. In *Proceedings of the ACM MODELS Workshop VARiability for You (VARY' 12)*, pp. 30-35. 2012.

[5] S. Wang, A. Gotlieb, S. Ali, M. Liaaen. Automated Selection of Test Cases using Feature Model: An Industrial Case Study. Technical Report (2012-20), Simula Research Laboratory. 2012.

[6] A. Konak, D. W. Coit, and A. E. Smith. Multi-objective optimization using genetic algorithms: A tutorial. *Reliability Engineering & System Safety*. 91(9), pp. 992-1007. 2007.

[7] K. Czarnecki, C. Kim, and K. Kalleberg. Feature models are views on ontologies. In *Proceedings of International Software Product Line Conference*, pp. 41–51. 2006.

[8] Pure systems GmbH. Variant management with pure::variants. Technical white paper. Available from http://web.pure- systems.com, 2006.

[9] M. Harman, S. A. Mansouri, and Y. Zhang. Search based software engineering: A comprehensive analysis and review of trends techniques and applications. Technical Report TR-09-032009. King's College, London. 2009.

[10] K. C. Tai, and Y. Lei. A Test-Generation Strategy for Pairwise Testing. *IEEE Trans. of Software Engineering*. 28(1), pp. 109 - 111. 2002.

[11] R. Kuhn, Y. Lei, and R. Kacker. Practical combinatorial testing: Beyond pairwise. *IT Professional*. 10(3), pp. 19-23. 2008.

[12] T. Murata, T. Ishibuchi, and H. Tanaka. Multi-objective genetic algorithm and its applications to flowshop scheduling. *Comput Ind Eng*. 30(4), pp. 957–968. 1996.

[13] Cisco Systems. Cisco telepresence codec c90. Data sheet. 2010. Available from http://www.cisco.com.

[14] D. Benavides. On the Automated Analysis of Software Product Lines Using Feature Models. Doctoral Thesis. Universidad de Sevilla. 2007.

[15] A. Arcuri, and L. C. Briand. A Practical Guide for Using Statistical Tests to Assess Randomized Algorithms in Software Engineering. In *Proceedings of the International Conference on Software Engineering*. pp. 21-28. 2011.

[16] S. Ali, L. C. Briand, H. Hemmati, and R. K. Panesar-Walawege. A Systematic Review of the Application and Empirical Investigation of Search-Based Test Case Generation. *IEEE Trans on Software Engineering*, 36(6), pp. 742-762. 2010.

[17] M. B. Cohen, M. B. Dwyer, and J. Shi. Coverage and Adequacy in Software Product Line Testing. In *Proceedings ACM ISSTA Workshop on Role of Software Architecture for Testing and Analysis*. pp. 53-63. 2006.

[18] H. Muccini, and A. Van Der Hoek. Towards Testing Product Line Architectures. *Electronic Notes in Theoretical Computer Science*. 82(6), pp. 99-109. 2003.

[19] S. Yoo, and M. Harman. Regression test minimization, selection and prioritization: a survey. *Software Testing, Verification, and Reliability*; 22(2), pp. 67-120. 2012.

[20] T. Y. Chen, and M. F. Lau. Dividing strategies for the optimization of a test suite. *Information Processing Letters*. 60(3), pp. 135–141. 1996.

[21] S. Tallam, and N. Gupta. A concept analysis inspired greedy algorithm for test suite minimization. *SIGSOFT Software Engineering Notes*. 31(1), 35–42. 2006.

[22] D. Jeffrey, and N. Gupta. Test suite reduction with selective redundancy. In *Proceedings of the International Conference on Software Maintenance*. pp. 549-558. 2005.

[23] S. Yoo, and M. Harman. Pareto Efficient Multi-Objective Test Case Selection. In *Proceedings of the international symposium on Software testing and analysis (ISSTA)*. pp. 140-150.2007.

Table 4 Results for Comparing Different Algorithms with the Given Thresholds*

PA	C20		C40		C60		C90		S1		S2		S3		S4		S5	
	A	p	A	p	A	p	A	p	A	p	A	p	A	p	A	p	A	p
C1	0.34	**0.04**	0.29	**0.03**	0.22	**0.01**	0.41	**0.08**	0.41	**0.08**	0.34	**0.04**	0.55	0.16	0.44	0.24	0.23	**0.01**
C2	0.42	**0.06**	0.51	**0.04**	0.54	**0.09**	0.45	0.33	0.37	**0.04**	0.29	**0.02**	0.43	0.44	0.38	**0.09**	0.35	0.12
C3	0.55	0.23	0.48	0.19	0.61	0.12	0.38	**0.06**	0.44	**0.05**	0.41	0.22	0.64	**0.08**	0.46	0.15	0.39	**0.07**
C4	0.71	0.35	0.62	0.22	0.67	0.46	0.66	0.18	0.53	0.26	0.49	0.60	0.59	**0.07**	0.57	0.45	0.45	0.32
C5	0.39	**0.01**	0.42	**0.01**	0.22	**0.01**	0.18	**0.03**	0.28	**0.02**	0.22	**0.01**	0.41	0.29	0.32	**0.01**	0.29	**0.05**

*PA: Pair of algorithms, A: $\hat{A}_{12}$, p: *p*-value
S1: Car Software System, S2: ATM Software, S3: DELL Laptop/Notebook Computers, S4: SmartHome, S5: J2EE web architecture.
C1: WBGA_W$_1$ vs. Thresholds, C2: WBGA_W$_2$ vs. Thresholds, C3: WBGA-MO vs. Thresholds, C4: RWGA vs. Thresholds, C5: RS vs. Thresholds.
All *p*-values less than 0.05 are identified as bold.

Table 5 Results for Comparing Different Algorithms*

PA	C20		C40		C60		C90		S1		S2		S3		S4		S5	
	A	p	A	p	A	p	A	p	A	p	A	p	A	p	A	p	A	p
C6	0.48	0.15	0.52	0.25	0.41	0.51	0.55	0.10	0.51	0.61	0.55	0.59	0.47	0.15	0.43	0.35	0.49	0.25
C7	0.38	0.35	0.48	**0.03**	0.47	0.57	0.52	0.72	0.48	0.09	0.41	0.15	0.39	0.35	0.52	0.12	0.54	0.12
C8	0.33	**0.02**	0.45	0.42	0.22	**0.01**	0.29	**0.03**	0.29	**0.02**	0.31	**0.03**	0.22	**0.01**	0.27	**0.01**	0.33	**0.04**
C9	0.62	**0.06**	0.70	**0.01**	0.55	0.14	0.66	**0.02**	0.62	**0.02**	0.69	**0.04**	0.73	**0.01**	0.57	**0.02**	0.78	**0.01**
C10	0.51	0.15	0.44	0.61	0.39	0.09	0.53	0.52	0.44	0.52	0.51	0.35	0.57	0.09	0.46	0.27	0.55	0.16
C11	0.31	**0.03**	0.49	**0.05**	0.32	**0.02**	0.42	0.42	0.21	**0.02**	0.33	0.05	0.18	**0.01**	0.26	**0.02**	0.22	**0.03**
C12	0.69	**0.01**	0.58	**0.02**	0.62	**0.01**	0.48	**0.04**	0.55	**0.04**	0.64	**0.01**	0.51	0.05	0.73	**0.01**	0.59	**0.02**
C13	0.37	0.16	0.31	**0.03**	0.29	**0.01**	0.27	**0.01**	0.49	0.19	0.38	**0.03**	0.29	**0.01**	0.32	**0.02**	0.41	**0.01**
C14	0.59	**0.01**	0.65	**0.01**	0.61	**0.01**	0.56	**0.01**	0.68	**0.02**	0.59	**0.02**	0.62	**0.02**	0.71	**0.01**	0.56	**0.03**
C15	0.74	**0.02**	0.69	**0.01**	0.77	**0.03**	0.62	**0.02**	0.81	**0.02**	0.67	**0.01**	0.74	**0.01**	0.89	**0.01**	0.65	**0.02**

*C6: WBGA_W$_1$ vs. WBGA_W$_2$, C7: WBGA_W$_1$ vs. WBGA-MO, C8: WBGA_W$_1$ vs. RWGA, C9: WBGA_W$_1$ vs. RS, C10: WBGA_W$_2$ vs. WBGA-MO, C11: WBGA_W$_2$ vs. RWGA, C12: WBGA_W$_2$ vs. RS, C13: WBGA -MO vs. RWGA, C14: WBGA-MO vs. RS, C15: RWGA vs. RS.
All *p*-values less than 0.05 are identified as bold.

Entropy-based Adaptive Range Parameter Control for Evolutionary Algorithms

Aldeida Aleti
Faculty of Information Technology
Monash University, Australia
aldeida.aleti@monash.edu

Irene Moser
Faculty of Information and Communication Technologies
Swinburne University of Technology, Australia
imoser@swin.edu.au

ABSTRACT

Evolutionary Algorithms are equipped with a range of adjustable parameters, such as crossover and mutation rates which significantly influence the performance of the algorithm. Practitioners usually do not have the knowledge and time to investigate the ideal parameter values before the optimisation process. Furthermore, different parameter values may be optimal for different problems, and even problem instances. In this work, we present a parameter control method which adjusts parameter values during the optimisation process using the algorithm's performance as feedback. The approach is particularly effective with continuous parameter intervals, which are adapted dynamically. Successful parameter ranges are identified using an entropy-based clusterer, a method which outperforms state-of-the-art parameter control algorithms.

Categories and Subject Descriptors

I.2.8 [**Artificial Intelligence**]: Problem Solving, Control Methods, and Search—*Heuristic methods*

General Terms

Algorithms

Keywords

Evolutionary algorithms, optimisation, adaptive parameter control

1. INTRODUCTION

Evolutionary Algorithms (EAs) have successfully been employed to solve a range of hard optimisation problems [1, 2, 30, 17, 23, 28]. In recent years, it has been acknowledged that the success of these algorithms depends on the numerous parameters that these algorithms have [19, 14, 32, 6], which make the optimisation procedure flexible and efficient for any kind of problem, regardless of the search space difficulty.

Unfortunately, the settings of the parameter values are known to be problem-specific [31], often even specific to the problem instance at hand [5, 39, 38], and greatly affect the performance of the algorithm [32, 6, 25, 15]. In cases where the number of parameters and their plausible value ranges are high, investigating all possible combinations of parameter values can itself be an attempt to solve a combinatorially complex problem [8, 44, 7, 33]. It has also been empirically and theoretically demonstrated that different parameter settings may be required for different optimisation stages of a problem instance [6, 5, 39, 38, 10, 40], and therefore should vary during the search process for best algorithm performance [5, 39, 38].

To address the problem of parameterising Evolutionary Algorithms, adaptive parameter control [41, 16, 11, 12, 20, 21, 22, 26] emerged as a new line of thought. Instead of exploring parameter settings before using an EA, in adaptive parameter control parameters are adjusted during the optimisation process. More specifically, properties of an EA run (such as the quality of the solutions produced) are monitored and the change in the properties is used as a signal to change parameter values.

One of the difficult issues faced in adaptive parameter control methods is the choice for real-valued parameter assignments, such as the mutation rate and the crossover rate. Usually, adaptive parameter control methods [43, 10, 21, 16, 42, 41, 3] discretise the choices for parameter assignments and sample parameter values from the preselected ranges. Insight from existing research [5] shows that initial discretisation can be problematic. As the ranges are fixed, they remain sub-optimal throughout the optimisation process.

Confirming this view, Adaptive Range Parameter Selection (ARPS) [4] was introduced, which uses adaptive value ranges that change dynamically during the optimisation process. ARPS outperforms state-of-the-art adaptive parameter control methods, such as Probability Matching (PM) [41], Adaptive Pursuit (AP) [41], Dynamic Multi-Armed Bandit (DMAB) [16] and Predictive Parameter Control (PPC) [3]. However, it was observed that high-performing ranges were sometimes absorbed into very large intervals, making it difficult for the algorithm to re-establish small, promising areas within the range.

With the goal of handling real-valued parameter assignments effectively, we introduce a new adaptive parameter control approach which uses an entropy-based measure to discretise parameter value ranges. At every iteration, feed-

GECCO'13, July 6–10, 2013, Amsterdam, The Netherlands.

back from the search is used to cluster parameter values into successful and unsuccessful groups. The outcome from the clustering process is employed to cut the parameter range into two sub-ranges such that the class information entropy is minimised. Results from the experimental validation of the approach show that the Entropy-based Adaptive Range Parameter Control (EARPC) outperforms state-of-the-art methods.

2. BACKGROUND

2.1 Evolutionary Algorithms

Generally speaking, Evolutionary Algorithms maintain a population of solutions that evolves by means of the mutation operator, the crossover operator, the selection procedure, and the replacement procedure. The objective is to search the solution space in order to optimise some quality function(s). The optimisation process starts with a set of solutions as initial population, which can be randomly generated, created by applying heuristic rules (e.g. greedy algorithm), or provided by an expert. After the initialisation, EA evolves the population using the crossover, mutation and selection operators. The crossover and mutation operators are applied according to predefined crossover and mutation rates. These operators are applied to specific solutions, which are selected according to the selection procedures. The new individuals (offspring) created by the genetic operators are added to the population. The replacement procedure selects the solutions that will survive in the next generation and removes as many individuals as required to maintain the prescribed population size.

Before using an EA for optimisation, a number of algorithm parameters have to be adjusted, such as the population size, offspring number, selection procedure, mutation rate and crossover rate. A comprehensive overview of the research in various parameters of Evolutionary Algorithms is presented by Eiben and Schut [14].

2.2 Adaptive Parameter Control

Formally, given a set $\{v_1, ..., v_n\}$ of n algorithm parameters, where each parameter v_i has $\{v_{i1}, ..., v_{im}\}$ values that can be discrete numbers or intervals of continuous numbers, parameter control has the task of deriving the optimal next value v_{ij} to optimise the influence of v_i on the performance of the algorithm. As an example, when the mutation rate v_1 is dynamically adjusted by considering 4 intervals ($m = 4$), v_{12} stands for a mutation rate sampled from the second interval. In the discrete case of optimising the type of mutation operator v_2, v_{22} stands for the second operator.

The majority of the adaptive parameter control methods found in the literature [11, 12, 20, 21, 22, 26] belong to the class of probability matching techniques, in which the probability of applying a parameter value is proportional to the quality of that parameter value.

The earliest approaches [21, 20] tended to 'lose' value ranges if the feedback from the algorithm was not in their favour in the initial phases of the process. In later work, a minimum selection probability p_{min} is introduced [21], to ensure that under-performing parameter values did not disappear during the optimisation, in case they were beneficial in the later stages of the search.

These probability matching techniques [11, 12, 20, 21, 22, 26, 18] were based on the notion of selecting parameter values in proportion to their previous performances. One of the more recent and mature examples of probability matching is the work by Igel and Kreutz [21]. Their Equation 1 for calculating the selection probability for each parameter value incorporates the maintenance of a minimum probability of selection.

$$p'_t(v_{ij}) = p_{min} + (1 - mp_{min})\frac{p_t(v_{ij})}{\sum_{r=1}^{m} p_t(v_{ir})} \quad (1)$$

where m is the number of possible values for parameter v_i. Probability matching has been criticised for the loose correlation between the reward allocations and the differences in performance with vastly superior values receiving a marginal increase in selection probability.

Adaptive Pursuit (AP) [41] was conceived as an attempt to address this issue, ensuring that clearly superior values are rewarded with a maximum probability of choice. Even though every parameter value is selected from time to time, in practice the Adaptive Pursuit algorithm spends a number of iterations before responding to a change of best parameter value.

Dynamic Multi-Armed Bandit (DMAB) [16] addresses the problem by completely recalculating the probabilities when a change in the effects distribution is detected by using a change detection test, in this case the statistical Page-Hinkley (PH) test. The PH test checks whether the quality of the parameter values has changed. When a change is detected, the algorithm is restarted. As a result, DMAB can quickly identify the new best parameter value without being slowed down by old information.

Adaptive Range Parameter Selection (ARPS) [4] is the first attempt at adapting real-valued parameter ranges. The ARPS algorithm discretises continuous-valued parameters by partitioning its ranges into two equal intervals. At every iteration, the best-performing interval is subdivided by splitting it in the middle. At the same time, the worst-performing interval is merged with the worse-performing of its neighbours. The selection probabilities of the split intervals are initially the same, the merged interval maintains the neighbour's probability of selection.

Refining the most successful parameter areas into narrower intervals, the probability of choosing particular values increases. Merging badly performing parameters decreases their probability of selection. An analysis of the mutation/crossover ranges [4] revealed that ARPS sometimes absorbs high-performing intervals into very large ranges as a result of short-term underperformance. The merged ranges are usually very large and it takes many iterations for an absorbed sub-range to re-establish itself. This behaviour almost certainly affects the performance of the search. Therefore, an improved approach to maintaining parameter value intervals is the subject of this investigation.

3. ENTROPY-BASED ADAPTIVE RANGE PARAMETER CONTROL

At every iteration of an EA run, the chosen parameter values are employed to create different solutions, which are evaluated using the fitness function(s). The output from the evaluation process provides valuable information for the adaptive parameter control, since it can be used to assess the effect of the parameter values on the performance of the optimisation algorithm. The feedback from the search is used to approximate the cause of the change in the quality of the solutions and assign a quality to parameter values, denoted as $q(v_{ij})$. The quality of the parameter values is used to select the next parameter assignments, which are employed to create the next generation of solution(s).

In this framework, the feedback from the algorithm tends to fluctuate, and very good parameter ranges occasionally receive poor feedback, leading to the problem of the loss of a range as a result of merging when ARPS is used. Entropy-based Adaptive Range Parameter Control (EARPC) clusters the values of a parameter by performance and subdivides the intervals according to the clustering. Since the process is repeated at every iteration, disadvantaging a well-performing interval has no effect beyond the subsequent iteration.

The EARPC algorithm consists of two major steps; in the first step, it uses K-means clustering to determine how best to subdivide the values into two groups. K-means clustering starts with an initial random centre point for each group. All other points are allocated to the group whose centre is closer to them.

As we are clustering the parameter values based on their performance in the algorithm $q(v_{ij})$, the performance feedback used for controlling the parameters is used. Once all points have been allocated to one of the clusters, the mean of the values of each group is calculated. The point which is closest to this group mean becomes the new centre, and all other points are reallocated according to their distances to the new means. The algorithm stops when the centres no longer change.

The second step uses these clusters as a basis to define the range boundaries for the groups. The k-means method expects the k to be determined from the outset. Therefore, in this work, we assume $k = 2$ intervals. At the end of the k-means clustering algorithm, we obtain 2 clusters.

3.1 Adaptation of Parameter Interval Boundaries

From k-means clustering, we obtain two clusters of parameter values, grouped according to their distances to the clusters' centre points. When we align the parameter values along the axis of the actual parameter values, the members of the groups are likely interspersed. If c_1 denotes a member of cluster 1 and c_2 a member of cluster 2, an ordering according to the parameter values may present itself as '$c_1, c_1, c_2, c_1, c_2, c_1, c_1, c_2, c_2, c_1, c_2$'. The algorithm uses this sequence to determine the interval boundaries. The ideal boundary is located where the class entropy, calculated by Eq. 2, is minimal.

Let parameter value k partition range of parameter v_i representing values between $[min, max)$ into two intervals: v_{i1} representing values in the range $[min, k]$ and v_{i2} denoting values in the range $[k, max)$. To obtain the minimal entropy, we calculate all entropy values arising from placing k between each of the adjacent pairs in the sequence $c_1, c_1, c_2, c_1, c_2, ...$

$$e(v_{i1}) = -\frac{|c_1(v_{i1})|}{|c_x(v_{i1})|}log_2\frac{|c_1(v_{i1})|}{|c_x(v_{i1})|} - \frac{|c_2(v_{i1})|}{|c_x(v_{i1})|}log_2\frac{|c_2(v_{i1})|}{|c_x(v_{i1})|}$$

The calculation of the class entropy has to be repeated for each interval v_{ij}. In each case, it calculates the number of 'matching' cluster members (c_1 for interval v_{i1}) in one interval as a proportion of all samples located in that interval ($c_x(v_{i1})$) and subsequently the proportion of non-matching cluster members (c_2 for interval v_{i1}) of all samples in that cluster. The overall class information entropy when a range v_{ij} is partitioned at the cut-point k into two new ranges v_{i1} and v_{i2} is calculated as the weighted average of the class entropies of the sub-ranges. This constitutes the *class information entropy* and is computed as follows:

Algorithm 1 Entropy-based Adaptive Range Parameter Control.

```
procedure EARPC(v_i, clusters)
    CLUSTER(v_i, clusters)
    minEntropy = MAX(Integer)
    for all parameters v_i, i ∈ n do
        for all parameter values v_ij, j ∈ m do
            E(j|v_i) =INFOENTROPY(v_i1, v_i2, j)
            if E(j|v_i) < minEntropy then
                minEntropy = E(j|v_i)
                cutPoint = j
            end if
        end for
        ADJUSTRANGE(cutPoint,v_i)
    end for
end procedure

procedure CLUSTER(v_i, clusters)
    while True do
        oldC = newC
        for all parameter values v_ij, j ∈ m do
            for all cluster center newC[k] do
                if ED(v_ij, newC[k]) < mD) then
                    cl[j] = k
                end if
            end for
        end for
        for s = 0; s < clusters; s + + do
            for r = 0; r < m; r + + do
                if cl[r] = s then vec[s] = v_ir
                end if
            end for
            newC[j]= CALCULATECENTER(vec)
        end for
        if newC = oldC then return
        end if
    end while
end procedure

procedure INFOENTROPY(v_i1, v_i2, k)
    e(v_i1) = -|c1(v_i1)|/|cx(v_i1)| log2 |c1(v_i1)|/|cx(v_i1)| - |c2(v_i1)|/|cx(v_i1)| log2 |c2(v_i1)|/|cx(v_i1)|
    e(v_i2) = -|c1(v_i2)|/|cx(v_i2)| log2 |c1(v_i2)|/|cx(v_i2)| - |c2(v_i2)|/|cx(v_i2)| log2 |c2(v_i2)|/|cx(v_i2)|
    E(k|v_i) = |cx(v_i1)|/|cx(v_i)| e(v_i1) + |cx(v_i2)|/|cx(v_i)| e(v_i2)
    return E(k|v_i)
end procedure

procedure ADJUSTRANGE(cutPoint,v_i)
    v_i1(min) = v_i(min)
    v_i1(max) = cutPoint
    v_i2(min) = cutPoint+ MINFLOAT( )
    v_i2(max) = v_i(max)
end procedure
```

$$\mathcal{E}(k|\upsilon_i) = \frac{|c_x(\upsilon_{i1})|}{|c_x(\upsilon_i)|}e(\upsilon_{i1}) + \frac{|c_x(\upsilon_{i2})|}{|c_x(\upsilon_i)|}e(\upsilon_{i2}) \tag{2}$$

The best cut-point k is the one that minimises the *class information entropy* $\mathcal{E}(k|\upsilon_i)$. The method employs the cut-point k to partition the parameter range into two sub-ranges. These two intervals are employed to select the parameter values for the next iteration. The selection of parameter values is proportional to the average quality of the parameter values in each range. Let $p(\upsilon_{ij})$ denote the selection probability of parameter range υ_{ij} and $q(\upsilon_{ij})$ the combined quality of the members of the interval. The mean quality of the intervals is calculated according to Eq. 3, regardless of cluster membership.

$$q(\upsilon_{ij}) = \frac{1}{|c_x(\upsilon_{ij})|} \sum_{c_x \in \upsilon_{ij}} q(c_x) \tag{3}$$

The probability of sampling from a range $p(\upsilon_{ij})$ is derived from the combined quality of its members $q(\upsilon_{ij})$, normalised by the summed qualities of all intervals. The main steps of EARPC are given in Algorithm 1.

4. EXPERIMENTS

Evolutionary Algorithms are not expected to deliver exact and repeatable results, but to provide good approximate solutions where exact approaches cannot be devised. Hence, results concerning the performance of approximate algorithms such as EAs, are usually reported as mean values over repeated trials.

To obtain a fair comparison, the generally accepted approach is to allow the same number of function evaluations for each trial [36]. Therefore, for the current comparison, all algorithms trials were repeated 30 times for each optimisation scheme, for 30 000 function evaluations. These values were decided after running the algorithm once for every problem and choosing the value where the quality of the solutions seemed to not improve any further. Nevertheless there are indications that all algorithms still make small but steady improvements after these numbers of evaluations.

4.1 Benchmark Problems

According to Lin et al. [37], differences in performance among approximate algorithms are more likely to be detected statistically if all algorithmic approaches solve the same problem instances. Along this line, different instances of two problems were chosen: the generally accepted Quadratic Assessment Problem (QAP), which was especially designed for testing EAs, and the component deployment problem, which is a real world problem in the Software Engineering domain.

The problems were chosen due to their dissimilarity, which enables a more informed judgement as to the portability of the approach when applied to an EA. Both problems are NP-hard, which makes them difficult to be solved by an exact algorithm and justifies the use of Evolutionary Algorithms to optimise them.

4.1.1 Quadratic Assignment Problem

The Quadratic Assignment Problem (QAP) was first introduced by Koopmans and Beckmann [24], who used this mathematical model to solve the problem of assigning economical activities to resources. In QAP, n facilities have to be allocated to n locations, such that the total cost is minimised and every resource has only one economical activity.

The total cost is calculated as the flow between the facilities multiplied by the costs for placing the facilities at their respective locations. QAP is considered to be a very challenging combinatorial optimisation problem. More formally, the problem is modelled with two $n \times n$, representing the cost and the flow. The aim is to assign n utilities to n locations with minimal cost. The candidate assignments are evaluated according to equation 4.

$$C = \sum_{ij}^{n} B_{ij} \cdot u_{ij} + \sum_{ij,k,l} C_{ij,k,l} \cdot u_{ik} \cdot u_{jl} \tag{4}$$

where

- n is the number of facilities and locations.
- B_{ik} is the cost of assigning utility i to location k
- $C_{ij,k,l}$ is the cost of the flow between neighbouring utilities (given utility i is assigned to location k and utility j is assigned to location l
- u_{ik} is 1 if utility i is assigned to location k, 0 otherwise

QAP does not allow for multiple assignments to the same location, hence solutions are subject to the following constraints:

$$\sum_{j=1}^{n} u_{ij} = 1, \sum_{i=1}^{n} u_{ij} = 1, u_{ij} \in \{0,1\}, i,j = \{1,2,...,n\}$$

QAP is a well-known problem and instances of considerable difficulty have been made available as benchmarks. It is a single-objective problem with one objective function that lends itself as quality feedback for the performance assessment of the parameter values.

4.1.2 Component Deployment Problem

One of the practical applications of Evolutionary Algorithms is the component deployment problem in embedded systems [1], relevant e.g. for the automotive industry. An existing hardware topology is used to run software components which form the basis of the increasingly sophisticated functionality of contemporary cars. The quality of the overall system depends on the choice of hardware unit to host a particular software component [34].

The quality of the system is commonly measured in terms of non-functional attributes such as safety, reliability and performance. We model the embedded system as a set of software components and a set of hardware hosts. Formally, let $C = \{c_1, c_2, ..., c_n\}$, where $n \in N$, denote the set of software components. The parameters for the software architecture are as follows:

- Communication frequency $f : C \times C \to \mathbb{R}$.
- Data size $ds : C \times C \to \mathbb{N}$.
- Estimated time for a single execution $ext : C \to \mathbb{N}$.

Let $H = \{h_1, h_2, ..., h_m\}$, where $m \in M$, denote the set of hardware resources. The parameters for the hardware architecture are as follows:

- Data rate $dr : H \times H \to \mathbb{N}$.
- Network reliability $r : H \times H \to \mathbb{R}$.
- Network delay $nd : H \times H \to \mathbb{N}$.
- Processing speed $ps : H \to \mathbb{R}$.

The deployment problem is then defined as $D = \{d \mid d : H \rightarrow C_{sub}\}$, where $C_{sub} = \{c_0, c_1, ..., c_j\} \subset C$, and D is the set of all functions assigning hardware resources to components. Note that, since C and H are finite, D is also finite, and represents the set of all deployment candidates.

The deployment problem has many quality-related aspects and is therefore always modelled as a multi-objective problem. Data Transmission Reliability (DTR) follows the definition of Malek [27]. Reliability of the data transmission is a crucial quality attribute in a real-time embedded system, where important decisions are taken based on the data transmitted through the communication links.

$$f_{DTR}(d) = \sum_{i=1}^{n}\sum_{j=1}^{n} f(c_i, c_j) \cdot r(d(c_i), d(c_j)) \qquad (5)$$

In embedded systems with their constrained hardware resources, repeated transmissions between software components are discouraged. The Communication Overhead (CO) [29] objective attempts to enforce minimal data communication for a given set of components and system parameters, calculated as follows:

$$f_{CO}(d) = \sum_{i=1}^{n}\sum_{j=1}^{n} f(c_i, c_j) \cdot nd(d(c_i), d(c_j)) + \\ + \sum_{i=1}^{n}\sum_{j=1}^{n} \frac{f(c_i, c_j) \cdot ds(c_i, c_j)}{dr(d(c_i), d(c_j)) \cdot r(d(c_i), d(c_j))} \qquad (6)$$

The scheduling length (SL) describes the average time for a hardware unit (i.e. ECU) to complete the round-robin processing of all its assigned components. ST is given by

$$f_{SL}(d) = \frac{1}{m} \cdot \sum_{j=1}^{m} \left(\frac{\sum_{c \in C_{h_j}} ext(c)}{ps(h_j)} \right). \qquad (7)$$

where m is the number of components deployed in h_j and C_{h_j} is the set of components deployed to host h_j.

4.2 Experimental Settings

QAP as an assignment problem with constraints maps n tasks to n resources. Hence the solution representation is a simple array which describes the numbered locations and the values of the array represent the items. Multipoint crossover swaps the assignments between solutions. The mutation operator changes the assigned item of a single location. As we are solving the QAP, singularity of item occurrence is mandatory the genetic operators are specialised to create valid solutions.

A variety of instances with descriptions of properties are available in QAPLIB collection [9]. The instances Taixxxc, like Tai256c, occur in the generation of grey patterns. The distances of Skoxxxf problems are rectangular and the entries in flow matrices are pseudorandom numbers. Similarly, the distance matrices of Wilxxx and Thoxxx problems, such as Wil100 and Tho150 are rectangular.

The industrial problem of software deployment uses an EA with a specialised solution encoding which maps each hardware unit to one or more software components. The crossover operator combines the allocation lists of two solutions' locations (hardware units) and subsequently divides them again into two child solutions avoiding duplication. The mutation operator exchanges the host allocations of two randomly chosen components. The problem definition does not allow for duplication, and a repair operation follows the crossover/mutation move. Also, the component deployment problem is multiobjective in nature and requires a more specialised approach. One of the state-of-the-art multiobjective EA implementations is NSGA-II, devised by Deb et al. [13]. The component deployment problem (CDP) instance used for the benefit of these experiments is the H36C51, composed of 36 hardware units and 51 software components.

The crossover and mutation rates, used for the benefit of these experiments, are probably the most conspicuous control parameters to optimise in stochastic optimisation [14]. Based on preliminary exploration, a range of $0.01 - 0.5$ was adopted for the mutation rate and the interval $0.6 - 1.0$ was used for the crossover operator.

In the case of QAP, the quality feedback for the parameter values is based on the fitness values returned by the objective function. The multiobjective nature of the deployment problem necessitates the combination of the fitness values from all three objective functions into a single unary measure of solution quality. The most conspicuous choice for this feedback is the hypervolume indicator, which has been described as the most reliable unary measure of solution quality in multiobjective space [45].

5. RESULTS

The means and standard deviations of the 30 trials from the different optimisation schemes listed in Table 1 clearly indicate a significant difference between the result groups of EARPC and the benchmarks. The mean performance of EARPC is consistently above the averages of the benchmark approaches. The standard deviation of EARPC is relatively high in the Quadratic Assignment Problem, but lower than the respective values of the other parameter control strategies in the component deployment problem.

As EARPC consistently outperforms the four other parameter control schemes, we employ the Kolmogorov-Smirnov (KS) non-parametric test [35] to check for a statistical difference. The 30 results of the repeated trials for each of the problem instances were submitted to the KS analysis. EARPC was compared to the other four adaptive parameter control schemes, with a null hypothesis of an insignificant difference between the performances (EARPC vs. ARPS, EARPC vs. DMAB, EARPC vs. AP and EARPC vs. PM). The results of the tests are shown in Table 2.

All KS tests, used for establishing that there is no difference between independent datasets under the assumption that they are not normally distributed, result in a rejection of the null hypothesis with a minimum d-value of 0.36 at a 97% confidence level. Hence we conclude that the superior performance of EARPC is statistically significant.

The gap between result qualities widens in favour of the EARPC as the problem size increases. The biggest Quadratic Assignment Problem of dimension n=256 (TAI256c) is clearly solved to better quality using EARPC, as it is more complex than the smaller QAP instances.

In EARPC, the intervals of crossover and mutation rates over 230 iterations are depicted in Figures 1 and 2. The problem optimised for the benefit of this experiment is the QAP problem instance TAI256c. At the beginning of the optimisation process, all intervals are equal. The selection of the parameter values is based on the assigned probabilities

Table 1: The means and standard deviations of fitness functions for the 30 runs of each problem instance using different parameter control schemes.

Problem	Instance	Mean				
		PM	AP	DMAB	ARPS	EARPC
QAP	Tho150	9154000	9157000	9197000	9141000	**9053000**
	Wil100	287100	286800	287600	286100	**285500**
	Sko100	164716	164875	164990	164681	**164139**
	Tai256c	47450000	47490000	47750000	47410000	**46820000**
CDP	H36C51	12239	12147	12405	12128	**11854**
		Standard Deviation				
Problem	Instance	PM	AP	DMAB	ARPS	EARPC
QAP	Tho150	36173.41	33358.02	41541.24	29024.92	47453.43
	Wil100	784.2973	634.0923	745.9012	523.1157	686.7064
	Sko100f	619.2552	613.1455	686.2719	872.4846	573.6736
	Tai256c	261879.1	314044	293074.2	269008.5	166171.3
CDP	H36C51	447.5069	344.8195	432.7907	423.8407	289.714

Table 2: The Kolmogorov-Smirnov test values of fitness functions for the 30 runs of each problem instance using different parameter control schemes.

		Kolmogorov-Smirnov test							
Problem	Instance	EARPC vs. PM		EARPC vs. AP		EARPC vs. DMAB		EARPC vs. ARPS	
		d	p	d	p	d	p	d	p
QAP	Tho150	0.8065	< 0.01	0.8387	< 0.01	0.9032	< 0.01	0.7742	< 0.01
	Wil100	0.8065	< 0.01	0.8065	< 0.01	0.9032	< 0.01	0.9355	< 0.01
	Sko100f	0.4667	< 0.01	0.5333	< 0.01	0.6	< 0.01	0.3667	0.03
	Tai256c	0.871	< 0.01	0.9355	< 0.01	0.9677	< 0.01	0.9677	< 0.01
CDP	H36C51	0.4	0.01	0.4333	< 0.01	0.5	< 0.01	0.3667	0.03

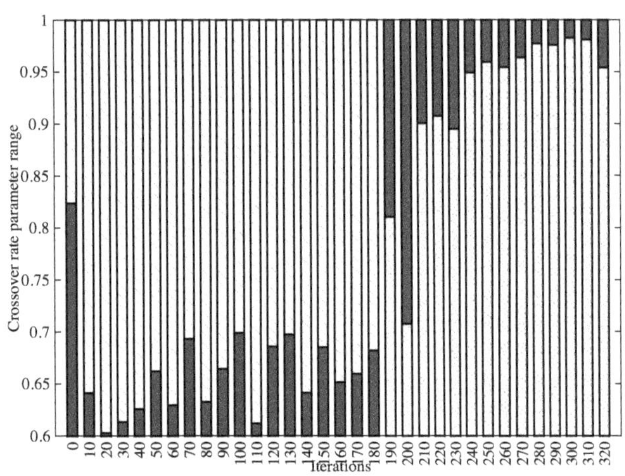

Figure 1: Adaptation of the range of crossover rate.

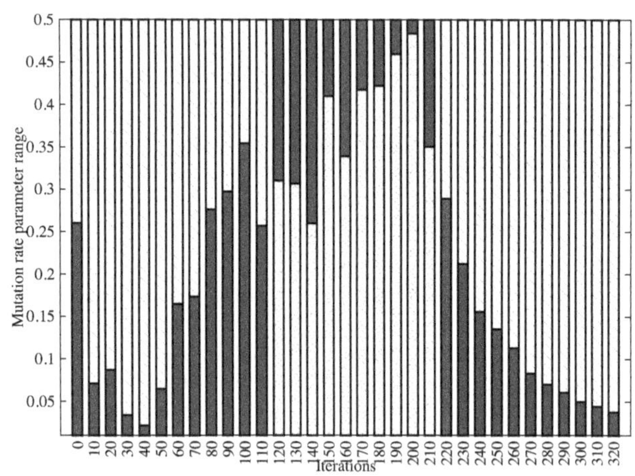

Figure 2: Adaptation of the range of mutation rate.

calculated using Equation 3. The probability of sampling from a range $p(v_{ij})$ is derived from the combined quality of its members $q(v_{ij})$, normalised by the summed qualities of all intervals. The higher the quality of the values in an interval, the more samples are taken from that interval.

In Figures 1 and 2, the most successful intervals are depicted with darker shade. We can clearly see that the behaviour of the entropy-based adaptive range parameter value selection is different for different parameters. The intervals of crossover rate develop quite differently compared to mutation rate. Higher crossover rates are more successful towards the end which runs somewhat contrary to popular opinion that crossover rates should decrease with iterations so as not to disturb solutions with high quality. On the other hand, the algorithm favours high mutation rates only in the middle of the optimisation process, and low rates at the beginning and at the end.

It can further be observed that high quality parameter values, both in mutation and crossover rates, are usually refined into narrower intervals compared to badly performing parameter values. This indicates that well performing values are usually diffuse into small regions of the parameter range and will be selected more frequently.

One might argue that although parameter configuration seems to be a very important factor of any algorithm, the parameter space is considerably smaller than the search space of all relevant NP-hard problems and the number of parameters is relatively small. So contrary to NP-hard optimisation problems, where 'solving by hand' is entirely inappropriate, 'choosing parameters by hand' is possible.

However, the use of parameter values that remain constant over the optimisation process has been observed in previous studies to achieve suboptimal results. This was also demonstrated by the analysis of parameter ranges during the optimisation process. Parameters of an EA can have different optimal values at different stages of the search. Thus, when an optimisation algorithm is tuned prior to the optimisation process, the selected parameters at the end of this process are not necessarily optimal.

This suggests that controlling parameters dynamically during the optimisation process is likely to lead to better outcomes. Hence, the proposed method of adapting parameters during the optimisation process is a more suitable option for the parameter configuration process. Furthermore, by reducing the number of parameters that need to be set in Evolutionary Algorithms, the transfer of these algorithms into industrial settings, where practitioners do not have any knowledge about EA parameters is facilitated.

6. CONCLUSION

The adaptive parameter control method introduced in this paper configures Evolutionary Algorithms during the optimisation process for optimal performance. According to our knowledge, the best-performing approaches with the same functionality are AP, PM, DMAB and ARPS. The new approach clearly outperforms the other parameter control methods.

The adaptation of parameter value ranges increases the sampling accuracy, which can explain the superior performance of EARPC compared to other approaches. Through using EARPC, we observed that different parameter intervals were optimal for different stages of the optimisation process. Furthermore, the ranges of the crossover rate developed quite differently compared to the mutation rate. Higher crossover rates were more successful towards the end of the optimisation process, whereas the opposite was observed for mutation rates.

To conclude the adaptive parameter control strategy presented in this paper, within its acknowledged limitations, is an effective method for adjusting parameters of Evolutionary Algorithms. In the future we intend to investigate algorithms for multi-interval partitioning, which we believe may improve the accuracy of interval boundaries and produce better algorithm performance.

7. REFERENCES

[1] A. Aleti, S. Björnander, L. Grunske, and I. Meedeniya. ArcheOpterix: An extendable tool for architecture optimization ofAADL models. In *Model-based Methodologies for Pervasive and Embedded Software (MOMPES)*, pages 61–71. ACM and IEEE Digital Libraries, 2009.

[2] A. Aleti, L. Grunske, I. Meedeniya, and I. Moser. Let the ants deploy your software - an ACO based deployment optimisation strategy. In *ASE*, pages 505–509. IEEE Computer Society, 2009.

[3] A. Aleti and I. Moser. Predictive parameter control. In *13th Annual Genetic and Evolutionary Computation Conference, GECCO 2011, Proceedings, Dublin, Ireland, July 12-16, 2011*, pages 561–568, 2011.

[4] A. Aleti, I. Moser, and S. Mostaghim. Adaptive range parameter control. In *Proceedings of the 2012 IEEE Congress on Evolutionary Computation*, pages 2405–2412, 2012.

[5] T. Bäck. The interaction of mutation rate, selection, and self-adaptation within a genetic algorithm. In *Parallel Problem Solving from Nature 2,PPSN-II*, pages 87–96. Elsevier, 1992.

[6] T. Bäck, A. E. Eiben, and N. A. L. van der Vaart. An empirical study on gas without parameters. In *Parallel Problem Solving from Nature - PPSN VI (6th PPSN'2000)*, volume 1917 of *Lecture Notes in Computer Science (LNCS)*, pages 315–324. Springer-Verlag (New York), 2000.

[7] T. Bartz-Beielstein, C. Lasarczyk, and M. Preuss. Sequential parameter optimization. In *IEEE Congress on Evolutionary Computation*, pages 773–780. IEEE, 2005.

[8] M. Birattari, T. Stützle, L. Paquete, and K. Varrentrapp. A racing algorithm for configuring metaheuristics. In *GECCO 2002: Proceedings of the Genetic and Evolutionary Computation Conference*, pages 11–18. Morgan Kaufmann Publishers, 2002.

[9] R. E. Burkard, S. Karisch, and F. Rendl. Qaplib-a quadratic assignment problem library. *European Journal of Operational Research*, 55(1):115–119, 1991.

[10] J. Cervantes and C. R. Stephens. Limitations of existing mutation rate heuristics and how a rank GA overcomes them. *IEEE Trans. Evolutionary Computation*, 13(2):369–397, 2009.

[11] D. Corne, M. J. Oates, and D. B. Kell. On fitness distributions and expected fitness gain of mutation rates in parallel evolutionary algorithms. In *Parallel Problem Solving from Nature - PPSN VII (7th PPSN'02)*, volume 2439 of *Lecture Notes in Computer Science (LNCS)*, pages 132–141. Springer-Verlag, 2002.

[12] L. Davis. Adapting operator probabilities in genetic algorithms. In *Proceedings of the Third International Conference on Genetic Algorithms*, pages 70–79. Morgan Kaufman, 1989.

[13] K. Deb, A. Pratap, S. Agarwal, and T. Meyarivan. A fast and elitist multiobjective genetic algorithm:NSGA-II. *IEEE-Evolutionary Computation*, 6:182–197, 2002.

[14] A. E. Eiben and M. C. Schut. New ways to calibrate evolutionary algorithms. In P. Siarry and Z. Michalewicz, editors, *Advances in Metaheuristics for Hard Optimization*, Natural Computing Series, pages 153–177. Springer, 2008.

[15] A. E. Eiben and S. K. Smit. Parameter tuning for configuring and analyzing evolutionary algorithms. *Swarm and Evolutionary Computation*, 1(1):19–31, 2011.

[16] Á. Fialho, M. Schoenauer, and M. Sebag. Analysis of adaptive operator selection techniques on the royal road and long k-path problems. In *Proceedings of the 11th Annual conference on Genetic and evolutionary computation*, pages 779–786. ACM, 2009.

[17] J. Fredriksson, K. Sandström, and MikaelÅkerholm. Optimizing resource usage in component-based real-time systems. In *Component-Based Software Engineering*, volume 3489 of *LNCS*, pages 49–65. Springer, 2005.

[18] M. Giger, D. Keller, and P. Ermanni. Aorcea - an adaptive operator rate controlled evolutionary algorithm. *Computers and Structures*, 85(19-20):1547 – 1561, 2007.

[19] D. E. Goldberg. *Genetic Algorithms in Search, Optimization and Machine Learning.* Addison-Wesley, 1989.

[20] T.-P. Hong, H.-S. Wang, and W.-C. Chen. Simultaneously applying multiple mutation operators in genetic algorithms. *Journal of Heuristics*, 6(4):439–455, 2000.

[21] C. Igel and M. Kreutz. Operator adaptation in evolutionary computation and its application to structure optimization of neural networks. *Neurocomputing*, 55(1-2):347–361, 2003.

[22] B. A. Julstrom. What have you done for me lately? Adapting operator probabilities in a steady-state genetic algorithm. In *Proceedings of the Sixth International Conference on Genetic Algorithms*, pages 81–87, San Francisco, CA, 1995. Morgan Kaufmann.

[23] T. Kichkaylo and V. Karamcheti. Optimal resource-aware deployment planning for component-based distributed applications. In *HPDC:High Performance Distributed Computing*, pages 150–159. IEEE Computer Society, 2004.

[24] T. C. Koopmans and M. J. Beckmann. Assignment problems and the location of economic activities. *Econometrica*, 25:53–76, 1957.

[25] F. G. Lobo. Idealized dynamic population sizing for uniformly scaled problems. In *13th Annual Genetic and Evolutionary Computation Conference, Proceedings*, pages 917–924. ACM, 2011.

[26] F. G. Lobo and D. E. Goldberg. Decision making in a hybrid genetic algorithm. In *Proceedings of the Congress on Evolutionary Computation*, pages 121–125. IEEE Press, 1997.

[27] S. Malek. *A User-Centric Approach for Improving a Distributed Software System's Deployment Architecture.* PhD thesis, Faculty of the graduate schools, University of Southern California, 2007.

[28] S. Malek, M. Mikic-Rakic, and N. Medvidovic. A decentralized redeployment algorithm for improving the availability of distributed systems. In *Comp. Dep.*, volume 3798 of *LNCS*, pages 99–114. Springer, 2005.

[29] N. Medvidovic and S. Malek. Software deployment architecture and quality-of-service in pervasive environments. In *Workshop on the Engineering of Software Services for Pervasive Environements, ESSPE*, pages 47–51. ACM, 2007.

[30] I. Meedeniya, B. Buhnova, A. Aleti, and L. Grunske. Reliability-Driven Deployment Optimization for Embedded Systems. *Journal of Systems and Software*, 2011.

[31] Z. Michalewicz and D. B. Fogel. *How to solve it: modern heuristics.* Springer-Verlag, 2004.

[32] Z. Michalewicz and M. Schmidt. Parameter control in practice. In F. G. Lobo, C. F. Lima, and Z. Michalewicz, editors, *Parameter Setting in Evolutionary Algorithms*, volume 54 of *Studies in Computational Intelligence*, pages 277–294. Springer, 2007.

[33] V. Nannen and A. E. Eiben. Relevance estimation and value calibration of evolutionary algorithm parameters. In M. M. Veloso, editor, *IJCAI'07, Proceedings of the 20th International Joint Conference on Artificial Intelligence*, pages 975–980, 2007.

[34] Y. Papadopoulos and C. Grante. Evolving car designs using model-based automated safety analysis and optimisation techniques. *The Journal of Systems and Software*, 76(1):77–89, 2005.

[35] A. N. Pettitt and M. A. Stephens. The kolmogorov-smirnov goodness-of-fit statistic with discrete and grouped data. *Technometrics*, 19(2):205–210, 1977.

[36] R. L. Rardin and R. Uzsoy. Experimental evaluation of heuristic optimization algorithms:A tutorial. *Journal of Heuristics*, 7(3):261–304, 2001.

[37] R. L. RardinBenjamin W. Lin. A short convergence proof for a class of ant colony optimization algorithms. *Management Science*, 25:1258–1271, 1980.

[38] J. Smith and T. C. Fogarty. Self adaptation of mutation rates in a steady state genetic algorithm. In *International Conference on Evolutionary Computation*, pages 318–323, 1996.

[39] C. R. Stephens, I. G. Olmedo, J. M. Vargas, and H. Waelbroeck. Self-adaptation in evolving systems. *Artificial Life*, 4(2):183–201, 1998.

[40] D. Thierens. Adaptive mutation rate control schemes in genetic algorithms. In *Proceedings of the 2002 Congress on Evolutionary Computation CEC2002*, pages 980–985. IEEE Press, 2002.

[41] D. Thierens. An adaptive pursuit strategy for allocating operator probabilities. In H.-G. Beyer and U.-M. O'Reilly, editors, *Genetic and Evolutionary Computation Conference, GECCO 2005*, pages 1539–1546. ACM, 2005.

[42] D. Thierens. Adaptive strategies for operator allocation. In *Parameter Setting in Evolutionary Algorithms*, volume 54 of *Studies in Computational Intelligence*, pages 77–90. Springer, 2007.

[43] Y.-Y. Wong, K.-H. Lee, K.-S. Leung, and C.-W. Ho. A novel approach in parameter adaptation and diversity maintenance for genetic algorithms. *Soft Computing*, 7(8):506–515, 2003.

[44] B. Yuan and M. Gallagher. Statistical racing techniques for improved empirical evaluation of evolutionary algorithms. In *Parallel Problem Solving from Nature - PPSN VIII*, volume 3242 of *LNCS*, pages 172–181. Springer-Verlag, 2004.

[45] E. Zitzler, L. Thiele, M. Laumanns, C. M. Fonseca, and da V. G. Fonseca. Performance assessment of multiobjective optimizers: an analysis and review. *IEEE Tran. on Evolutionary Comp.*, 7:117–132, 2003.

Non Stationary Operator Selection with Island Models

Caner Candan
LERIA - Université d'Angers
Angers, France
caner.candan@univ-angers.fr

Adrien Goëffon
LERIA - Université d'Angers
Angers, France
adrien.goeffon@univ-angers.fr

Frédéric Lardeux
LERIA - Université d'Angers
Angers, France
frederic.lardeux@univ-angers.fr

Frédéric Saubion
LERIA - Université d'Angers
Angers, France
frederic.saubion@univ-angers.fr

ABSTRACT

The purpose of adaptive operator selection is to choose dynamically the most suitable variation operator of an evolutionary algorithm at each iteration of the search process. These variation operators are applied on individuals of a population which evolves, according to an evolutionary process, in order to find an optimal solution. Of course the efficiency of an operator may change during the search and therefore its application should be precisely controlled. In this paper, we use dynamic island models as operator selection mechanisms. A sub-population is associated to each operators and individuals are allowed to migrate from one sub-population to another one. In order to evaluate the performance of this adaptive selection mechanism, we propose an abstract operator representation using fitness improvement distributions that allow us to define non stationary operators with mutual interactions. Our purpose is to show that the adaptive selection is able to identify not only good operators but also suitable sequences of operators.

Categories and Subject Descriptors

I.2.8 [**Artificial Intelligence**]: Problem Solving, Control Methods, and Search

Keywords

Island Models, Adaptive Operator Selection

1. INTRODUCTION

Basically, an evolutionary algorithm (EA) manages a population of individuals that encode possible configurations of the problem, in order to optimize a given fitness function. The individuals evolve by means of variation operators and selection processes. Although the efficiency of EAs is well-established on numerous optimization problems, their performance and robustness depend on the correct setting of its components by means of parameters. Parameter setting in EA has been extensively studied [LLM07]. According to usual taxonomies [EMSS07], we distinguish parameter tuning (off-line setting before solving) from parameter control (on-line setting during solving). Of course, different type of parameters can be considered: solving components (e.g., the selection process or the variation operators) or numerical parameters that modify the behavior of a given EA (e.g., the population size or the application rates of the variation operators). Most of the time, these parameters have strong interactions and it is very difficult to forecast how they will affect the performance of the EA. We focus here on the use of variation operators in population based algorithms: i.e., choosing at each iteration of the search process which variation operator should be applied.

Automatic tuning tools [NE07, HHKS09] have been developed to search for good parameters values in the parameters' space, which is defined as the crossproduct of the possible values of the parameters values and the possible instances of the problem. Specific heuristics are used in order to sample efficiently the possible values of parameters that are expected to have a significant impact on the performance. Another possible approach for parameter setting is to control the value of the parameters during the search. Adaptive operator selection (AOS) [Fia10] consists in providing an adaptive mechanism for selecting dynamically the suitable variation operator to apply on individuals at each iteration of the EA process. Recent approaches [FCSS08, MLS10] have proposed such adaptive mechanisms for general EAs with possibly many variation operators, whose behavior may be unknown. However, as suggested by the *No Free Lunch* theorems [WM97], it is difficult to anticipate the performance of an algorithm on any instances of a wide class of problems without preliminary experiment or learning process. Note that control could be consider as a dynamic tuning process: once the search has been achieved, the parameters values obtained by the control process can be synthesized and used for future runs. Of course, this dynamic approach allows the user to retrieve information on the temporal changes of the parameters' values.

In [CGLS12], we propose to use island models as an AOS mechanism. Island models [WRH98] provide a natural abstraction for dividing the population into several subsets, distributed on islands. An independent EA is run on each of these islands. Individuals are allowed to migrate from one island to another one in order to insure information sharing during the resolution and maintain some diversity on each island thanks to incoming individuals. In order to use island models as an AOS method, the main principle consists in distributing each operator on a different island. A dynamic migration policy between the islands is used in order to move at each step the individuals to the most promising operators, i.e. supposed to have the best current utility[1].

Given an EA, it can be really difficult to assess the utility of the operators on real problems since it may depend on the individual but also on the previously applied operators. Problem-specific operators are often required (e.g., k-opt exchanges for the travelling salesman problems), which makes difficult comparisons between different problems. Suitable and reliable criteria must be defined as well as methods for recording and using their values. Therefore, artificial scenarios have been proposed in order to focus on the management of the operators. These scenarios may serve as a methodological basis for assessing the benefit of AOS procedures [Thi05, CFSS08]. The main idea is to use reward distributions to simulate the utility of operators — a reward corresponds to the current effect of the operator on the population. As mentioned above, the utility of the operators is likely to change along the solving process and thus these distributions are permuted regularly among the operators. In this paper, we also focus on such non stationary operators. We propose to induce more interaction between the operator by using distributions that change according to the history of the search, i.e. the operators that have been applied before. In particular, when managing the balance between exploration and exploitation in an EA, it is clear that intensification operators can only be used until they reach a minimal optimum, while similarly diversification operators cannot diversify the search forever. Roughly speaking, an intensification (resp. diversification) operator may clearly become less and less efficient as long as it is used. Similar situations certainly occur in presence of several operators who share the same search purpose and who have thus strong interactions. Our purpose is to assess the AOS mechanism based on island models is able to identify precisely operators whose efficiency may vary continuously and also sequences of such suitable operators.

2. ISLAND MODELS

Based on the main principles of EAs, island models consider a set of sub-populations, clustered on islands, which are evolving independently during some search steps and interacting periodically. This model provides an improved management of diversity and simplify the parallel implementation of EAs. Island models have mostly been used in a static way, with individuals that migrate from islands to islands according to a fixed predefined policy. Nevertheless, dynamic regulation policies allow the model to increase or decrease the migration probabilities during the evolutionary process according to the impact of previous migrations between islands.

In the remaining of this paper, we are interested in solving general optimization problems. An optimization problem is a pair $(f, \mathcal{S})$ where $\mathcal{S}$ is a search space whose elements represent potential solutions of the problem and $f : \mathcal{S} \to \mathbb{R}$ is a fitness function that associates a value. An optimal solution (maximization problem) is an element $s^* \in \mathcal{S}$ such that $\forall s \in \mathcal{S}, s \neq s^*, f(s^*) \geq f(s)$.

2.1 Basic Notions

An island model can be defined by the following elements:

- Dimensions: a size n, a set of islands $\mathcal{I} = \{i_1, \ldots, i_n\}$, a set of algorithms $\mathcal{A} = \{A_1, \ldots, A_n\}$, a set of populations $\mathcal{P} = \{P_1, \ldots, P_n\}$, each P_i is a subset of $\mathcal{S}$. Each population P_k is assigned to island i_k. Each algorithm A_k is assigned to island i_k.
- A topology: an undirected graph $(\mathcal{I}, V)$ where $V \subseteq \mathcal{I}^2$ is a set of edges between islands of $\mathcal{I}$.
- A migration[2] policy: a squared matrix M of size n, such that $M(i, j) \in [0, 1]$ represents the probability for an individual to migrate from island i to island j. This matrix is supposed to be coherent with the topology, i.e., $\forall (i, j) \in \mathcal{I}^2 \setminus V, M(i, j) = 0$.

Different choices can be made for the topology: complete graph, ring... Note that a node (i, i) in the graph will be used if one wants to allow individuals to have the possibility to stay on the same island. A basic island model algorithm can be defined as algorithm 1, where $A_i(P_i)$ is the population obtained after applying a basic iteration of algorithm A_i on population P_i. *best* is a function that computes the best individual of a set with regards to the objective function f. The stop condition corresponds to a limited number of iterations or the fact that an optimal solution has been found in the total population $\bigcup_{k \in 1..n} P_k$ (if the optimal bound is known). Note that the size of this global population is fixed along the process but the size of each P_k changes constantly according to the migrations.

```
input : a migration matrix M,
        a set of islands I = {i_1, ..., i_n},
        a set of algorithms A = {A_1, ..., A_n},
        a set of populations P = {P_1, ..., P_n},
        an optimization problem (S, f)
output: a solution s*
while not stop condition do
    for i ← 1 to n do
        P_i ← A_i(P_i);
        for s ∈ P_i do
            generate a random number rand;
            if ∃(i, j) ∈ V and rand < M(i, j) then
                P_j ← P_j ∪ {s};
                P_i ← P_i \ {s};
    s* ← best(∪_i(P_i));
```

Algorithm 1: Basic Island Model

2.2 Dynamic Migration Policy

Dynamic island models use migration policy that evolves during the search. Each island is equipped with two main processes that define how its population evolves and how the migration policy is controlled.

[1]The utility of an operator corresponds to its expected effect for the next steps of the solving process. Other terms can be found in the literature, e.g. efficiency or impact.

[2]Note that alternative island models use migration policies where migration probabilities depend on the characteristics of the individuals [SJ05].

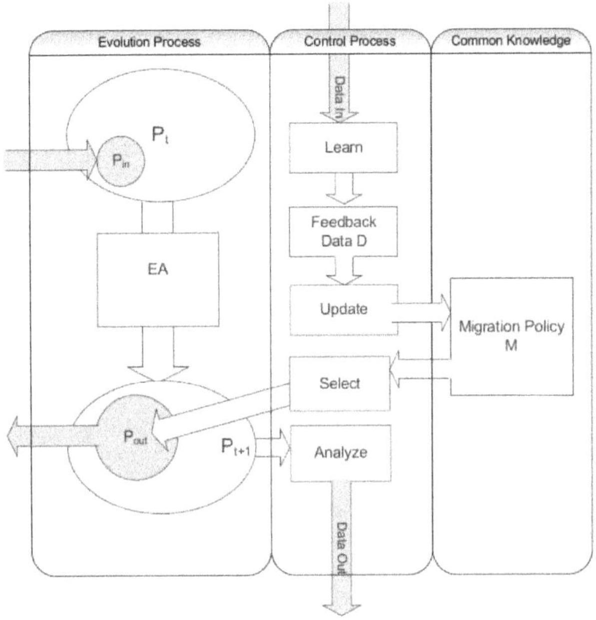

Figure 1: General Mechanism for an Island in a Dynamic Model

Figure 1 highlights that the migration policy is modified during the run according to incoming feedback received from other islands. This feedback allows the island to know how its individuals have been improved on other islands. The basic learning principle consists in sending more individuals to island that have been able to improve them significantly and less to islands that are currently less efficient for these individuals. To avoid brutal changes, these effects may be evaluated on a time sliding window. The *selection* component uses the migration matrix M to select the individuals that are sent to other islands. Of course, some individuals may stay on the same island. The *analyze* component aims to evaluate the improvements of the individuals after the EA has been applied. It sends this feedback information to the island these individuals were originated from. According to the previous notations, we define the following basic processes and data structures:

- A data matrix D is a square matrix of size n. $D(i, j)$ evaluates the improvement obtained by individuals of island i when they are processed on island j.
- An algorithm $A \in \mathcal{A}$ is a process that computes a new population P_{t+1} from a given population P_t by applying an evolution process.
- $learn(D, D_{in})$ is a process that modifies D according to information received in D_{in}. In fact this process can be seen as an operation $D \leftarrow D \oplus D_{in}$, which should be defined according to the problem.
- $update(M, D)$ is a process that modifies the migration matrix M according to the data matrix D.
- $select(P, M, j)$ is a process that selects a sets of individuals from the current population of the island P to be sent to another island j according to migration matrix M.
- $analyze(P)$ is a process that evaluates the improvement obtained in island i by individuals from island k during the last iteration of the algorithm $(D_{out}(k, i)$.

3. ADAPTIVE OPERATOR SELECTION

3.1 Operator Selection Mechanisms

Let us consider n operators $\{o_1, \ldots, o_n\}$ and associate an estimated utility $u_{i,t}$ of operator o_i at time t. The probability of selecting operator o_i at time t is $s_{i,t}$. In a static setting, one could of course use a predefined fixed roulette wheel selection $(s_1, \ldots, s_n)$, i.e. $s_{i,t}$ is constant during the execution of the algorithm. Note that these values can be determined by a tuning process. It is easy to check that a static roulette selection can be simulated in the island model. Given $r = (s_1, \ldots, s_n)$, we define a static transition matrix M whose n rows are all equal to r. Clearly $rM = r$ (r is a steady state vector, achieving just the expected application rates of the operators).

Contrary to a static tuning of the operator application rates, adaptive operator selection consists in selecting the next operator to apply at time $t+1$ by adapting the selection probability during the search. The utility has to be reevaluated at each time, classically using a formula $u_{i,t+1} = (1-\alpha)u_{i,t} + \alpha r_t$ where r_t is the reward associated to the application of operator i (immediate utility) and α is a coefficient that controls the balance between past and immediate utility, as in classic reinforcement learning techniques [SB98]. A classic mechanism is the probability matching selection rule:

$s_{i,t+1} = p_{min} + (1 - n.p_{min})\frac{u_{i,t+1}}{\Sigma_{k=1}^{n} u_{k,t+1}}$

where a non negative p_{min} insures a non zero selection probability for all operators.

This selection rules are known to have drawbacks[3] and an alternative selection rule has been proposed in [Thi05], called adaptive pursuit (AP), that distinguishes the best current operator from the others:

$$\begin{cases} s_{i^*,t+1} = s_{i^*,t} + \beta(p_{max} - s_{i^*,t}) \\ s_{i,t+1} = s_{i,t} + \beta(p_{min} - s_{i,t}) \end{cases}$$

where $i^* = \text{argmax}\{u_{i,t}, i = 1..n\}$, $p_{max} = 1 - (n-1)p_{min}$ and β is a parameter to adjust balance of this winner-take-all strategy.

3.2 Island Models as Adaptive Operator Selection Mechanisms

The generic model can easily be instantiated in order to manage classical evolutionary algorithms like genetic, memetic or population-based local search algorithms. We describe the specialization of this scheme for the management of operators. Each island i is equipped with a particular operator o_i and has the following specifications:

- The learning process is very simple here since we just keep the last performance (time window of size 1), i.e. $[D \oplus D_{in}](i, j) = D(i, j)$.
- The algorithm A_i applies the operator o_i assigned to this island on every individuals of the population P_i: $A_i(P_i) = \{o_i(s) | s \in P_i\}$.

[3]The proportional selection gives more importance to operators that have a good average behavior compared to operator that can be very efficient but less frequently.

- The $analyze(P)$ process computes the feedback information and sends it to each island (including its own). We may consider for instance the following functions:

  Mean $D_{out}(k,i) = \frac{\Sigma_{s \in P_i[k]} f(s)}{|P_i[k]|}$

  Max $D_{out}(k,i) = \max_{s \in P_i[k]}(f(s))$

  where $P_i[k] = \{s \in P_i | s \text{ comes from island } k\}$

- The *update* process uses the data matrix D (i.e., the feedback from other island) in order to modify the migration matrix. Of course, only the line corresponding to island i is modified. We compute an intermediate reward vector R. We propose to use an intensification strategy: only the island where individuals of i have obtained the best improvement is rewarded (note that there could be several such best islands).

$$R(k) = \begin{cases} \frac{1}{|B|} & \text{if } k \in B, \\ 0 & \text{otherwise,} \end{cases}$$

$$\text{with } B = \operatorname*{argmax}_k D(i,k)$$

then the migration matrix is updated as:

$M(i,k) = (1-\beta)(\alpha.M(i,k) + (1-\alpha)R(k)) + \beta N(k)$

where N is a stochastic vector such that $||N|| = 1$. The parameter α represents the importance of the knowledge accumulated during the last migrations (inertia or exploitation) and β is the amount of noise, which is necessary to explore alternative search space areas by means of individuals. The influence of these parameters has been studied in [CGLS12].

3.3 AOS as a Multi-Armed Bandits Problem

The initial multi-armed bandit problem was introduced in the context of the design of experiments by [Rob52]. It was formulated as the maximization of the total gain of a gambler who could make n tosses with two coins A and B with a gain of 1 for each head but nothing for tails. The biases of the coins are unknown. This problem is known as the *Two-armed Bandit* and has been extended to multi-armed bandit by Rodman [Rod78].

Let us consider K arms and an infinite sequence $\vec{x_1}, \vec{x_2}, \ldots$ of vectors $\vec{x}(t) = (x_1(t), \ldots, x_K(t))$, where $x_i(t) \in [0,1]$ is the reward obtained if the arm i is chosen at step t. At step $t+1$, the gambler only knows the rewards $x_{i_1}, \ldots, x_{i_t}$ obtained from the sequence $i_1, \ldots, i_t$, where $i_j \in \{1, \ldots, K\}$. A strategy is thus a sequence $I_1, \ldots, I_T$ with $I_j : (\{1, \ldots, K\} \times [0,1])^{j-1} \rightarrow \{1, \ldots, K\}$ whose cumulated reward is $R_S(T) = \Sigma_{t=1}^T x_{i_t}(t)$.

Optimal strategies have been initially proposed [Fel62, Git79] for this problem. Later, Auer [Aue02] has proposed to use this problem to manage the compromise between exploration and exploitation in optimization algorithms. The operator selection problem can be expressed as a multi-armed bandit problem [CFSS08]. An operator is associated to each arm. The rewards are the fitness improvements that are successively obtained. Upper bound confidence functions can be used to solve the associated bandit problem. The UCB1 [ACBF02] is defined as:

$$r_{j,t} + \sqrt{\frac{2 \log \Sigma_k n_{k,t}}{n_{j,t}}}$$

where $r_{j,t}$ is the average reward for arm j at iteration t and $n_{j,t}$ denote the number of times the jth arm has been played. The arm that maximizes the previous expression is chosen for being played at iteration $t+1$. Here, the reward distribution of the operator are likely to change according to the state of the search. Therefore dynamic multi-armed bandit has to be considered and UCB have to be revised [CFSS08]. A standard test – known as Page Hinkley – for the change hypothesis is used. The resulting DMAB selection algorithm is thus based on UCB1 with a dynamic restart mechanism that is driven by a Page Hinkley test. Of course one has to consider carefully performance measures in order to assess the utility of the operators [MFS+09]. Note that some hyper-heuristic approaches also use learning techniques (e.g., Markov chains in [MK11]) to learn good transitions between heuristics and attempt to model the best sequence of heuristics to apply.

4. USING NON STATIONARY OPERATORS

Most of the operators used in EAs have a behavior that depends on the individuals on which they are applied or, more generally, on the current state of the search. Therefore, it is likely that their impact on the exploration/exploitation balance will change over time. Moreover, the impact of an operator may also depend on the operators that have been previously applied on the individuals. In this case, the operator selection mechanism should be able to identify suitable sequences of operators instead of focusing only on the next operator to apply or on proportion of applications of each operators.

In the following abstract problem definition, operators will be represented by simple fitness improvements functions whose values may depend on the history of the individual. The history of an individual is the sequence of islands this individual has been on during the last t iterations of the algorithm.

Our purpose is to propose an abstract view of EAs in order to focus more on the operators than on the problem. Therefore, we will consider abstract operators that are independent from the genotypic description of the elements of the search space in order to be able to compute optimal or sub-optimal policies and to validate the properties of our AOS model against these policies.

A basic steady state process can be simulated by a tuple $(P_0, \mathcal{O}, \Omega, \sigma, \iota)$, including:

- an initial population $P_0 \subseteq 2^{\mathcal{S}}$.
- a set of variation operators $\mathcal{O}$ whose elements are relations $o \subseteq \mathcal{S} \times \mathcal{S}$. In practice, most operators cannot be expressed as functions $o : \mathcal{S} \rightarrow \mathcal{S}$ due to their non deterministic and stochastic nature. Therefore let us note $s \rightarrow_o s'$ the fact that $(s, s') \in o$.
- an operator selection function $\Omega : \mathbb{N} \rightarrow \mathcal{O}$ that select operator to apply at each iteration of the algorithm.
- a selection function $\sigma : 2^{\mathcal{S}} \rightarrow \mathcal{S}$ and an insertion function $\iota : 2^{\mathcal{S}} \times \mathcal{S} \rightarrow 2^{\mathcal{S}}$.

An execution of $A \equiv (P_0, \mathcal{O}, \Omega, \sigma, \iota)$ is thus a sequence $P_0, \ldots, P_T$, such that[4]

- $\forall 1 \leq i \leq T, P_i \subseteq 2^{\mathcal{S}}$,
- $\forall 0 \leq i \leq T-1, P_{i+1} = \iota(P_i, s)$ with $\sigma(P_i) \rightarrow_o s$ and $o = \Omega(i)$,
- T is the maximal number of allowed iteration.

We consider here fixed size populations, i.e., $\forall 1 \leq i \leq T, |P_i| = |P_0| = N$. Our purpose is to highlight on the operators during the search. Given the execution of an algorithm $P_0, \ldots, P_n$, we define a sequence $P_0^{\mathcal{O}}, \ldots, P_n^{\mathcal{O}}$, such that:

- $\forall 1 \leq i \leq T, P_i^{\mathcal{O}} \subseteq \mathcal{S} \times \mathcal{O}^*$, where $\mathcal{O}^*$ denotes the set of words constructed using operators in $\mathcal{O}$. An element of $P_i^{\mathcal{O}}$ is just a pair $(s, o_1 \ldots o_i)$ where s is an element of P_0 and $o_1 \ldots o_i$ is a sequence of operators that have been applied on it during the execution of the algorithm.
- $P_0^{\mathcal{O}} = \{\{(s, \epsilon) | s \in P_0\}\}$ is a multiset built with element of P_0 such that no operator has been applied on it yet.
- $\forall 1 \leq i \leq T, \Pi(P_i^{\mathcal{O}}) \supseteq P_i$, where $\Pi(P_i^{\mathcal{O}}) \equiv \{s' \in \mathcal{S} | (s, o_1 \ldots o_i) \in P_i^{\mathcal{O}}, s \rightarrow_{o_1} .. \rightarrow_{o_i} s'\}$

Due to the non-determinism of the operators, given a sequence of populations obtained by an algorithm $P_0, \ldots, P_n$ we cannot associate a unique sequence $P_0^{\mathcal{O}}, \ldots, P_n^{\mathcal{O}}$ as defined above (in fact $\forall 1 \leq i \leq T, \Pi(P_i^{\mathcal{O}}) \supseteq P_i$). In order to provide a general model for studying operators behavior, we abstract operators and individual according to the notion of fitness.

Given the execution of an algorithm $P_0, \ldots, P_T$, we associate a sequence $P_0^f, \ldots, P_T^f$, with $P_i^f \in \mathbb{R}^N$ and such that $\forall 1 \leq i \leq T, \forall s \in P_i, \exists v \in P_i^f, v = f(s)$. Therefore, we may now better link operators applications and successive populations. We define thus a relation $P_i \equiv_f P_i^{\mathcal{O}}$ if and only if there exists P_i^f, $\forall s \in P_i, \exists v \in P_i^f, v = f(s)$ and $\forall s \in \Pi(P_i^{\mathcal{O}}), \exists v \in P_i^f, v = f(s)$. At this stage, we do not need to consider the selection and insertion functions.

Operators can be abstracted by fitness improvements, given by a probabilistic distribution of their value. For maximization problem $(f, \mathcal{S})$, the effect of operators can be defined according to the evaluation function f. Given an element $s \in \mathcal{S}$, the variation of fitness f induced by an operator o is given as $\delta_f^o(s) = \frac{f(o(s)) - f(s)}{f(s)}$.

Abstracting operator by distributions has been investigated in [Thi05] where uniform distribution are associated to each operator in different overlapping intervals of values. Other distributions have been proposed in [CFSS08] with the Boolean and the outliers models. In these models, each operator o is associated a distribution (p_o, δ_o), i.e., $\forall s \in S, P(\delta_f^o(s) = \delta_o) = p_0 \wedge P(\delta_f^o(s) = 0) = (1 - p_0)$. The value of p_0 and δ_o are adjusted to insure some properties concerning the ordering of the operators according to expected rewards.

In these works, the distributions are fixed during a given number of iteration — epoch — and then are reassigned to operators according to a permutation. The utility of the operator is thus non stationary during the execution of the algorithm and the AOS mechanism has to discover the best operator to apply during each epoch.

Similarly, our purpose is to have operators whose behavior changes during the solving process in order to simulate real situation. We want to consider more continuous changes in the distributions. We consider possible interactions between the operators, i.e. the utility of an operator depends on the previously used operators on the same individual. Operators corresponds to fitness improvements functions whose values depend on the history of the initial individuals (i.e., the way it has been processed during solving). The idea is to provide a model where the utility of an operator decreases proportionally to its use. In such model, the AOS mechanism must not detect the best operator during an epoch but rather identify suitable sequences of operators.

Given an operator o with a distribution (p_o, δ_o), we extend our new operator to elements of $P_i^{\mathcal{O}}$ as a distribution $(p_o, \delta_o(1 - Occ(\omega, o)))$ with $Occ(\omega, o) = \frac{|\{i \in 1, \ldots, |\omega|, \omega_i = o\}|}{|\omega|}$ (i.e., proportion of operator o in ω). In practice, one has to choose the distribution but also a sliding window for recording not ω but only a subsequence of the operators that have been previously applied.

5. EXPERIMENTAL RESULTS

This section focuses on the capacity of the dynamic island model to detect a suitable scheduling of non stationary operators which maximizes the objective function. Two experiments have been conducted for observing the behavior of the model: the first one with equivalent operators and the second one with different operators.

5.1 Behavior with equivalent operators

We consider 3 equivalent operators associated to 3 islands and a population of 300 individuals uniformly distributed on each island. The parameters α and β of the *update* function (3.2) are respectively set to the default values 0.8 and 0.01. Each individual corresponds to $(s, |\omega|)$ (remind that we focus only on the fitness values, see Section 4) with a sliding window of length $|\omega| = 10$ in order to record the last visited islands. The fitness value of initial individuals is 0. Operators have similar distribution parameters $(p_o, \delta_o) = (1, 0.5)$. In this context, an expected application of the operators for an individual is to distribute them equitably in the window.

Representing simultaneously the evolution of all migration probabilities leads to unreadable figure. Nevertheless we systematically observe a fast stabilization of the model with a migration policy which simulate a ring topology, i.e. which follows a Hamiltonian circuit. Thus, in figure 2, we choose to only represent the sum of probabilities (in percent) corresponding to the two possible circuits (0,1,2) and (0,2,1).

In this figure, which represents a given run, one can observe a fast stabilization of the model with migrations corresponding to a circuit (0,1,2). Due to noise (parameter β), perturbations may appear at any time (for instance here between migrations 6000 and 8000) before stabilizing on a (possibly different) circuit.

Similar experiments were made with more than 3 islands and lead to same observations. For instance, figure 3 provides the complete graph representation of the migration probabilities between 10 islands, each having the same char-

[4]We must mention here that the P_i are indeed multisets of elements of $\mathcal{S}$. Nevertheless, in the following we will use the classic set notations in order to simplify the reading.

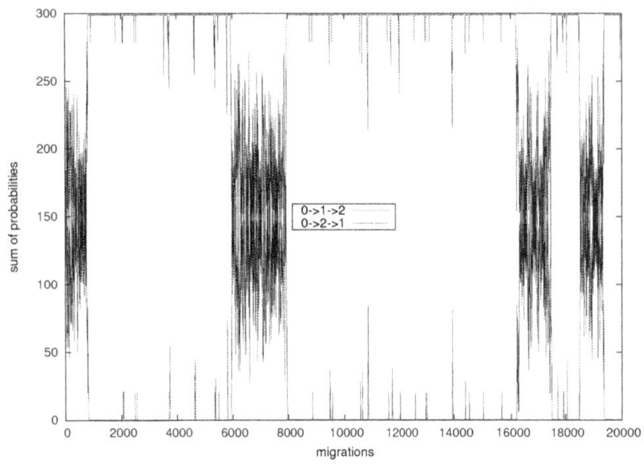

Figure 2: Stabilization periods on ring topology.

acteristics than in the previous experiment. As we have already mentioned, it is not possible to represent the evolution of the probabilities of migration but we developed a graphic application in order to observe the behavior of the model during the search. Figure 3 shows that a 10 islands circuit is found. More precisely, this figure corresponds to a state of the search in term of migration probabilities (represented by arrows). The animation shows an alternation between short perturbations periods and large stabilisation periods (with different circuits).

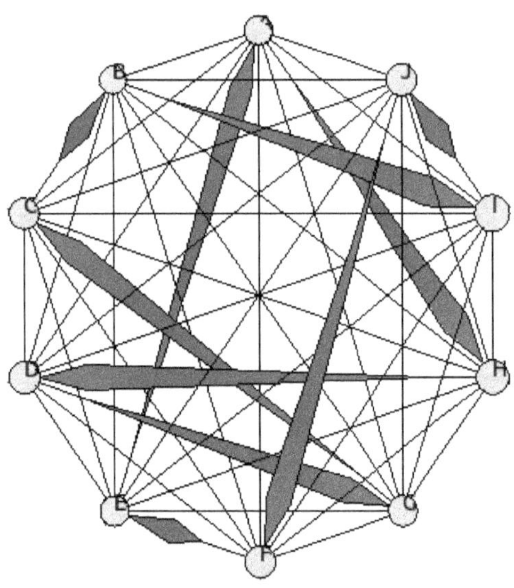

Figure 3: Circuit for 10 islands.

All experiments with equivalent operators show the ability of the dynamic island model to adapt its search strategy in order to make the search more efficient.

5.2 Comparison with other methods

Experiments with equivalent operators highlight the impact on migrations of non stationary operators. Now, we extend these experiments to a more general case with different operators. We first compare our model to simple roulette wheel selection mechanisms.

5.2.1 Island Models vs.Roulette Wheel Selection

Let us use 6 different sets of operators for our experiments with the next distribution parameters (with sliding window size equal to 10):

- set1: {(0.3,0.2), (0.8,0.2), (0.5,0.5), (0.1,0.9)}
- set2: {(0.7,0.7), (0.3,0.1), (0.8,0.1), (0.1,0.4), (0.8,0.9)}
- set3: {(0.9,0.1), (0.3,0.3), (0.2,0.7), (0.1,0.1), (0.6,0.3), (0.8,0.7)}
- set4: {(0.1,0.6), (0.5,0.7), (0.3,0.8), (0.4,0.6), (0.9,0.7), (0.2,0.3), (0.6,0.6)}
- set5: {(0.4,0.2), (0.6,0.1), (0.5,0.8), (0.7,0.3), (0.8,0.8), (0.1,0.1), (0.2,0.3), (0.9,0.6)}
- set6: {(0.1,0.9), (0.2,0.8), (0.3,0.7), (0.4,0.6), (0.5,0.5), (0.6,0.4), (0.7,0.3), (0.8,0.2), (0.9,0.1)}

The dynamic island model parameters are similar to those of the previous section. To assess the ability of the dynamic island model to well perform with different operators, we will compare its efficiency with other selection mechanisms: two different roulette and adaptive pursuit methods (see section 3.1).

- The *uniform roulette* is obtained using the island model defined in section 2 with $\alpha = 1$, $\beta = 0$ and an initial migration matrix M such that $\forall (i,j) \in \mathcal{I}^2, M(i,j) = 1/9$.
- The *tuned roulette* only differ on the initial migration matrix, which is initialized with probabilities given by an off-line tuning process. In our case, after a dynamic island model process, the average operators application rates are used to initialize the static migration matrix lines.

Table 1 shows results obtained by the 3 algorithms in term of average, standard deviation and best final value for 100 individuals and 2000 migrations.

We indicate in bold methods that are not statistically outperformed by any other one (w.r.t. Mann-Whitney test). One can observe that both tuned roulette and dynamic island model obtain the best results. However, remind that the tuned roulette requires first a dynamic island model run to set its value.

5.2.2 Island Models vs.Other AOS

Comparisons must also be performed with the AOS methods described in section 3.1. We consider here several possible scenarios in order to highlight the properties of the different methods. The scenarios are again defined by their corresponding sets of abstract operators. The length of the windows to compute the variation of fitness is still 10. We consider:

- A scenario with identical operators $s_1 \equiv \{(1, 0.5), (1, 0.5), (1, 0.5)\}$
- Two scenarios with three different operators. $s_2 \equiv \{(0.9, 1), (0.5, 4), (0.2, 9)\}$ where operators have close expected values and $s_3 \equiv \{(0.9, 10), (0.5, 10), (0.2, 1)\}$ where these expected values are more different.

Set	Nb op.	Uniform Roulette			Tuned Roulette			Dynamic Island Model		
		avg	sd	best	avg	sd	best	avg	sd	best
set1	4	210.4	7.0	227.3	140.1	5.7	155.1	**235.7**	6.1	245.1
set2	5	134.6	10.0	164.2	598.2	10.2	628.8	**624.3**	9.8	658.4
set3	6	296.5	12.0	323.0	344.5	8.2	367.7	**369.6**	8.1	378.3
set4	7	475.4	12.1	512.8	**592.0**	10.7	625.1	**610.0**	10.7	636.4
set5	8	438.2	11.4	479.4	**680.6**	10.5	710.3	**711.1**	9.5	733.2
set6	9	326.1	9.5	355.0	**359.9**	10.0	391.4	**361.8**	9.8	394.4

Table 1: DIM vs. RW on different sets of operators.

- Two scenarios with a larger number of operators and roughly two types of operators: good ones and bad ones. $s_4 \equiv \{(0.9,5),(0.2,10),(0.1,1),(0.1,1),(0.1,1)\}$ and $s_5 \equiv \{(0.9,5),(0.4,7),(0.3,8),(0.2,10),(0.2,1),(0.2,1),(0.1,1),(0.1,1),(0.1,1),(0.1,1)\}$.

The following AOS are used:

- OR is a *myopic* oracle that knows the values of the operators and the last applied operators in order to select the operator with the best expected value according to the variation of fitness. Note that this oracle does not compute the optimal solution for a given number of iterations since it does not take into account future operator applications.
- U is a uniform selection rule.
- ARW is a probability matching selection rule (adaptive roulette wheel). The minimal probability p_{min} is set to 0.01.
- DIM is our dynamic island model. The values of the parameters are $\alpha = 0.8$ and $\beta = 0.1$ except for s_2 where a very small number of individual requires a higher noise rate $\beta = 0.35$ to get acceptable results.
- AP is the adaptive pursuit method. The values of the parameters are $p_{min} = 0.1$ and $\beta = 0.8$.
- UCB uses the upper confidence bound UCB1
- $DMAB$ is the dynamic selection based on UCB1 with the Page Hinkley test. This method requires several parameters for the test. Note that, while the parameters values are quite intuitive for scenarios based on epoch as in [CFSS08], they are more difficult to set here and sometimes, $DMAB$ behaves worse or is equivalent to UCB. A deeper study of the parameter tuning should be conducted.

All these methods have been implemented in the same Scilab framework[5], each method is run 20 times with 1000 iterations each (i.e., 1000 applications of operators). For DIM the total number of individuals is denoted as *nbind*. The results correspond to the average value (rounded for sake of readability) and the (rounded) standard deviation obtained:

- by the best individuals of the *nbind* individuals of each run for DIM
- by the *nbind* best scores obtained over (20.*nbind*) runs for the other methods.

Note that our criteria do not favour DIM.

On table 2 we may remark that if U get good results as on s_1 then almost all methods are equivalent. AP provides good results for s_1 where indeed all operators are the same. Scenario s_2 shows that again, since the operators have close expected values, U obtains good results. Here, DIM requires a higher noise rate to balance the very few number of individuals. Keeping the same number of operators but inserting an operator that is clearly less efficient than the other ones is more difficult to detect for ARW. Of course U does not work well anymore. Note that increasing the number of individuals improves the results of DIM while increasing the number of runs has not necessarily an huge impact for all other methods, while the result computation favours these methods. This is especially clear for s_5. UCB and $DMAB$ are really efficient until the scenarios become larger. Even if it requires a sufficient number of individuals, DIM seems reliable and is able to improve its results if more computing resources are available. Note that more work should be done concerning the parameters of the methods. Moreover, additional criteria could be taken into account for assessing the utility of operators – e.g., entropy of the sub-populations or execution – in order to better manage the balance between intensification and diversification.

6. CONCLUSION

In this paper, the utility of non stationary operators is simulated by variable fitness improvement distributions. Contrary to previous artificial scenarios, the utility decreases proportionally to the previous applications of the operators and corresponds to situations where a single best operator cannot be used forever or for a sufficiently long number of iterations — e.g., always enforcing intensification. Adaptive operator selection aims thus at detecting suitable sequences of operators rather than identifying the best operator for a given epoch. In this context dynamic island models provide good results and can be used as an interesting alternative operator selection mechanism.

Acknowledgements : We are indebted to the anonymous referees for their valuable comments and suggestions. We also want to thank our students M. Dalle and Y. Hay for having provided the graphic interface for Figure 3. This work is partially supported by the Pays de la Loire Region (France) within the LigeRO project.

[5]http://www.scilab.org/

Set	Nb op.	Nb ind	OR		DIM		DMAB		ARW		U		AP		UCB	
			avg	sd	avg	sd	avg	sd	avg	sd	avg	sd	avg	sd	avg	sd
s_1	3	300	151	0	152	2	126	0	151	0	152	0	165	0	126	0
s_2	3	9	511	7	472	15	491	10	478	10	505	1	490	11	498	11
s_3	3	18	1477	12	1536	19	1533	25	1458	18	1482	19	1588	19	1588	30
s_3	3	99	1501	9	1604	13	1603	38	1489	11	1503	16	1629	13	1658	21
s_4	5	50	712	9	712	15	732	17	688	11	682	11	693	12	742	20
s_5	10	100	1301	15	1004	16	1082	29	1067	30	966	15	1030	13	1098	19
s_5	10	1000	1339	10	1226	15	1128	20	1141	16	998	9	1070	17	1138	19

Table 2: Results obtained with different AOS approaches on different sets of operators.

7. REFERENCES

[ACBF02] P. Auer, N. Cesa-Bianchi, and P. Fischer. Finite-time analysis of the multiarmed bandit problem. *Machine Learning*, 47(2-3):235–256, 2002.

[Aue02] P. Auer. Using confidence bounds for exploitation-exploration trade-offs. *Journal of Machine Learning Research*, 3:397–422, 2002.

[CFSS08] L. Da Costa, Á. Fialho, M. Schoenauer, and M. Sebag. Adaptive operator selection with dynamic multi-armed bandits. In *Genetic and Evolutionary Computation Conference, GECCO 2008, Proceedings, Atlanta, GA, USA, July 12-16, 2008*, pages 913–920. ACM, 2008.

[CGLS12] C. Candan, A. Goëffon, F. Lardeux, and F. Saubion. A dynamic island model for adaptive operator selection. In *Genetic and Evolutionary Computation Conference (GECCO'12)*, pages 1253–1260, 2012.

[EMSS07] A. E. Eiben, Zbigniew Michalewicz, Marc Schoenauer, and J. E. Smith. Parameter control in evolutionary algorithms. In *Parameter Setting in Evolutionary Algorithms*, pages 19–46. 2007.

[FCSS08] Á. Fialho, L. Da Costa, M. Schoenauer, and M. Sebag. Extreme value based adaptive operator selection. In *Parallel Problem Solving from Nature - PPSN X, 10th International Conference, Proceedings*, volume 5199 of *Lecture Notes in Computer Science*, pages 175–184. Springer, 2008.

[Fel62] D. Feldman. Contributions to the "two-armed bandit" problem. *The Annals of Mathematical Statistics*, 33(3):847–856, 1962.

[Fia10] Á. Fialho. *Adaptive Operator Selection for Optimization.* PhD thesis, Université Paris-Sud 11, Orsay, France, December 2010.

[Git79] J. C. Gittins. Bandit processes and dynamic allocation indices. *Journal of the Royal Statistical Society. Series B (Methodological)*, 41(2):148–177, 1979.

[HHKS09] F. Hutter, H. Hoos, K.Leyton-Brown, and T. Stützle. ParamILS: an automatic algorithm configuration framework. *J. Artif. Int. Res.*, 36(1):267–306, September 2009.

[LLM07] F. Lobo, C. Lima, and Z. Michalewicz, editors. *Parameter Setting in Evolutionary Algorithms*, volume 54 of *Studies in Computational Intelligence*. Springer, 2007.

[MFS+09] J. Maturana, A. Fialho, F. Saubion, M. Schoenauer, and M. Sebag. Compass and dynamic multi-armed bandits for adaptive operator selection. In *Proc. of IEEE Congress on Evolutionary Computation CEC*, pages 365–372. IEEE, 2009.

[MK11] K. McClymont and E. Keedwell. Markov chain hyper-heuristic (mchh): an online selective hyper-heuristic for multi-objective continuous problems. In *Proceedings of the 13th annual conference on Genetic and evolutionary computation*, GECCO '11, pages 2003–2010, New York, NY, USA, 2011. ACM.

[MLS10] J. Maturana, F. Lardeux, and F. Saubion. Autonomous operator management for evolutionary algorithms. *J. Heuristics*, 16(6):881–909, 2010.

[NE07] V. Nannen and A. E. Eiben. Relevance estimation and value calibration of evolutionary algorithm parameters. In *IJCAI 2007, Proceedings of the 20th International Joint Conference on Artificial Intelligence*, pages 975–980, 2007.

[Rob52] H. Robbins. Some aspects of the sequential desing of experiments. *Bulletin Amrican Mathematical Society*, (55):527–535, 1952.

[Rod78] L. Rodman. On the many-armed bandit problem. *The Annals of Probability*, 6(3):491–498, 1978.

[SB98] R. Sutton and A. Barto. *Reinforcement Learning: An Introduction.* MIT Press, 1998.

[SJ05] Z. Skolicki and K. De Jong. The influence of migration sizes and intervals on island models. In *GECCO*, pages 1295–1302, 2005.

[Thi05] D. Thierens. An adaptive pursuit strategy for allocating operator probabilities. In *Genetic and Evolutionary Computation Conference, GECCO*, pages 1539–1546. ACM, 2005.

[WM97] D. Wolpert and W. Macready. No free lunch theorems for optimization. *IEEE Trans. Evolutionary Computation*, 1(1):67–82, 1997.

[WRH98] D. Whitley, S. Rana, and R. Heckendorn. The island model genetic algorithm: On separability, population size and convergence. *Journal of Computing and Information Technology*, 7:33–47, 1998.

Sustainable Cooperative Coevolution with a Multi-Armed Bandit

François-Michel De Rainville*, Michèle Sebag†, Christian Gagné*, Marc Schoenauer†, and Denis Laurendeau*

*Laboratoire de vision et systèmes numériques
Département de génie électrique et de génie informatique
Université Laval, Québec (Québec), Canada G1V 0A6
francois-michel.de-rainville.1@ulaval.ca,
{christian.gagne,denis.laurendeau}@gel.ulaval.ca

†Équipe TAO, CNRS – INRIA – LRI
Université Paris-Sud
F-91405 Orsay Cedex, France
michele.sebag@lri.fr,
marc.schoenauer@inria.fr

ABSTRACT

This paper proposes a self-adaptation mechanism to manage the resources allocated to the different species comprising a cooperative coevolutionary algorithm. The proposed approach relies on a dynamic extension to the well-known multi-armed bandit framework. At each iteration, the dynamic multi-armed bandit makes a decision on which species to evolve for a generation, using the history of progress made by the different species to guide the decisions. We show experimentally, on a benchmark and a real-world problem, that evolving the different populations at different paces allows not only to identify solutions more rapidly, but also improves the capacity of cooperative coevolution to solve more complex problems.

Categories and Subject Descriptors

I.2.8 [**Artificial Intelligence**]: Problem Solving, Control Methods, and Search—*heuristic methods*

Keywords

Cooperative Coevolution, Multi-Armed Bandit, Credit Assignment, Adaptivity

1. INTRODUCTION

Coevolutionary algorithms [2, 10] are extending traditional evolutionary algorithms by making use of several subpopulations of individuals, often designated as species, and evaluating the fitness of the individuals jointly with individuals from other species. Cooperative coevolutionary algorithms [14] exploit modularity to decompose a problem into multiple interacting subcomponents, in a divide-and-conquer fashion. It is a paradigm where subcomponents not only emerge naturally from the evolution, but also cooperate to solve much more complex problems than those that can be tackled using standard single-species genetic algorithms. Examples of successful applications of cooperative coevolution include ensemble pattern classification [8], multi-agent learning [12], and sensor placement [5], among others.

Fair competition between the subcomponent populations has been introduced in the original algorithms. Indeed, each population can run for an arbitrary number of generations before the other populations provide new cooperating individuals. Potter and De Jong [14] present an asynchronous evolution of the populations, although only few have reported making their optimization in an asynchronous manner. However, for situations where the natural decomposition of the problem yields subproblems of varying difficulty, it is natural to assign a different number of generations to each subpopulation. The issue is then to determine how the generations should be allocated to each species.

That issue can be formulated as a decision problem where we need to determine which population should be evolved at each time step, in order to maximize the global progress of the coevolutionary algorithm. The multi-armed bandit framework [9, 11], widely studied in the context of game theory, strives at proposing actions maximizing the expected reward while acquiring more knowledge on the decision process. In our context, it is thus a natural and promising avenue to follow for an automatic subpopulation selection mechanism. Therefore, we propose to apply a dynamic multi-armed bandit to allocate more computational time to the most promising species in order to sustain the coevolution. For this purpose, we also present an efficient strategy to evaluate the rewards, in order to balance the evolution between the species, as this is a non-stationary decision process.

The structure of the paper is as follows. First, in Sec. 2 and 3, we discuss the important concepts involved in cooperative coevolution and multi-armed bandits, respectively. Then, we present our framework for the selection of the most promising population in Sec. 4. Next, we present experiments with our framework in Sec. 5 on an artificial problem and a real-world scenario on sensor placement. Finally, we conclude the paper on the contributions of this article and possible future work in Sec. 6.

2. COOPERATIVE COEVOLUTION

Cooperative coevolution has been proposed by Potter and De Jong [14] to exploit the modularity of a problem, similarly to the rules in Learning Classifier Systems and subroutines in Genetic Programming. In this paradigm, each subpopulation, the so-called species, represents a subcomponent of a solution, and a complete solution is obtained by combining a representative of each species. Each individual is assigned a fitness equal to the reward of the complete solution in which it participates. The number of species can change along the evolutionary process, new species being introduced when the evolution stagnates and species being removed when their best individual does not contribute enough to the complete solution. Potter and De Jong also propose to evolve the species asynchronously, which would allow to allocate more time to some species. To the authors knowledge, no work has been made to adjust the effort on each species to sustain the cooperative optimization. However, multiple avenues have been explored to improve the original algorithm, some are presented in this section.

A multiple interactions scheme for the cooperative coevolution has been studied by Wiegand [17] to increase the convergence of the algorithm, but it has been shown to generate subcomponents that are over-generalizing to fit to a multitude of collaborators. Furthermore, Bucci and Pollack [3] proposed a modification of the original cooperative coevolutionary algorithm by replacing the selection mechanism with a new one based on Pareto dominance. However, establishing the Pareto dominance among the individuals of each species requires a tremendous number of fitness evaluations when the population size or the number of populations increases. In fact, it requires $O(nm^{k-1})$ evaluations, where n is the number of individuals in the evaluated species, m is the number of individuals in each population with whom each individual is evaluated (required for evaluating Pareto dominance), and k is the number of populations. Such solution is not always possible for real world problems and thus other avenues need to be explored.

Panait et al. [13] biased the coevolutionary process by augmenting the fitness of an individual with an estimate of its best possible reward if it was evaluated with its optimal collaborators. The problem is now how to find the optimal collaborators for an individual in a non trivial problem. The authors propose to pair the individuals with the most successful collaborators found yet; or with collaborators that have cooperated well with structurally similar individuals; among other ideas. To our knowledge, none of these options have been tested nor compared with their proposed method when the optimal collaborators are known, making this solution unapproachable for real world problems.

Wu and Banzhaf [18] introduced a hierarchical decomposition of the problem domain. Cooperation among the individuals of the population is rendered by "groups" that are evolved in the framework. Groups provide a collaborating mechanism by assembling different individuals together into a solution which can be evaluated. In their algorithm, individuals and groups have their own fitness, which is shared by all individuals in a sharing radius to preserve diversity in the populations. Their technique exploits the uniqueness of the contribution of each subcomponent in a group to avoid carrying "free riders" that would have the same effect as bloat in Genetic Programming. Such uniqueness measures might not always be available for real world problems.

Albeit the promising enhancements to the original algorithm, this work is based on the standard cooperative coevolution of Potter and De Jong [14], for its simplicity, its

1 initialize $\mathfrak{P} \leftarrow \{\mathfrak{S}_i, i = 1, \ldots, n\}$
2 choose $\mathfrak{R} \leftarrow \{\text{select\_random}(\mathfrak{S}_i), i = 1, \ldots, n\}$
3 **while** $\neg$*stop* **do**
4   **foreach** *species* $\mathfrak{S}_i \in \mathfrak{P}$ **do**
5         $\mathfrak{S}_i \leftarrow \text{apply\_variations}(\mathfrak{S}_i)$
6         $\text{evaluate}(\mathfrak{S}_i, \mathfrak{R} \backslash \mathbf{r}_i)$
7         $\mathfrak{S}_i \leftarrow \text{select}(\mathfrak{S}_i)$
8     $\mathfrak{R} \leftarrow \{\text{select\_best}(\mathfrak{S}_i), i = 1, \ldots, n\}$
9   **if** *improvement* $< T_{\text{i}}$ **then**
10   remove species with *contribution* $< T_{\text{c}}$
11         $\mathfrak{R} \leftarrow \mathfrak{R} \backslash \mathfrak{R}^-$
12   add a new species $\mathfrak{P} \leftarrow \mathfrak{P} \cup \{\mathfrak{S}'\}$
13         $\mathfrak{R} \leftarrow \mathfrak{R} \cup \{\text{select\_random}(\mathfrak{S}')\}$

Algorithm 1: Cooperative co-evolution.

general applicability to any problems, and its ease of implementation. The pseudo-code is presented in Algo. 1. First, a population $\mathfrak{P}$ of n species $\mathfrak{S}_i$ is initialized randomly and one representative $\mathbf{r}_i$ of each species is placed in the representative set $\mathfrak{R}$. Then, lines 4 to 7 show how each species is evolved independently of the others and how interaction through evaluations is achieved. More specifically, on line 6, the evaluation of the individuals of a species is made in collaboration with the representatives of the other species, thus excluding the representative of the current species from set $\mathfrak{R}$ ($\mathfrak{R} \backslash \mathbf{r}_i$). The inner loop, beginning at line 4, is a classical genetic algorithm, which can be replaced by any other evolutionary algorithm. At each ecosystem generation, i.e. the outer loop beginning at line 3, the representatives are updated with the best individual of each species for the next generation. Then, the improvement of the evolution is verified at line 9. If the solution fitness, given by all representatives, has not improved over the last I generations by more than a given threshold T_{i}, then the system is considered as stagnating. In this situation, unproductive species that contribute less than a threshold T_{c} are removed from the population [1] – their representatives ($\mathfrak{R}^-$) are also removed from $\mathfrak{R}$ – and one new species is added to the population. The evolution continues until the termination criterion is reached.

3. MULTI-ARMED BANDIT

Multi-Armed Bandits (MAB), introduced by Robbins [15], are used to model the exploration-exploitation trade-off faced by an agent that takes actions in a given environment for which rewards are issued. In this setting, the agent has two opposite goals, which are: 1) to gain more knowledge about the environment and the rewards obtained (exploration), and 2) to exploit its current knowledge on the actions in order to maximize its immediate reward (exploitation). The standard MAB problem consists in a set of k arms, each arm representing a possible action. A fixed and unknown reward probability distribution $r_i \in [0, 1]$ is associated to each arm. At each time step of the problem, the agent selects an arm and receives a reward according to the corresponding reward probability.

Auer et al. [1] proposed the Upper Confidence Bound (UCB) algorithm, which has been demonstrated to achieve

[1] Newer species are removed first and the contribution is recalculated after each removal.

Input: arm index i, window of rewards $\mathbf{w}$
Output: credit q
sort lexicographically $\mathbf{w}$ according to rewards (best first), and ages in case of ties (newer first)
$q \leftarrow y \leftarrow 0$
forall the *ranks* $r \in [1 \cdots |\mathbf{w}|]$ **do**
    $\rho, j \leftarrow w_r$
    $\rho \leftarrow d^{(r-1)}(|\mathbf{w}| - (r-1))$
    if $i = j$ **then**
        $y \leftarrow y + \rho$
    else
        $q \leftarrow q + y\rho$

Algorithm 2: Area under the curve credit assignment.

1 $\mathbf{n} \leftarrow [0 \cdots 0], \mathbf{q} \leftarrow [0 \cdots 0], \mathbf{w} \leftarrow []$
2 **while** $\neg$*stop* **do**
3   **if** $\exists n_i \in \mathbf{n} : n_i = 0$ **then**
4         $arm \leftarrow \text{select\_random}(\{i | n_i = 0\})$
5   **else**
6         $arm \leftarrow \arg\max_i \left(q_i + C\sqrt{\frac{2\log\sum_{j=1}^{n} n_j}{n_i}} \right)$
7   apply selected *arm* and retrieve *reward*
8     $\mathbf{w} \leftarrow [(reward, arm)\ \mathbf{w}]$
9   **if** $|\mathbf{w}| > W$ **then**
10         $\mathbf{w} \leftarrow [w_i \in \mathbf{w}, i = 0, \ldots, W-1]$
11     $\mathbf{n} \leftarrow [\text{count}(i, \mathbf{w}), i = 1, \ldots, n]$
12     $\mathbf{q} \leftarrow [\text{auc}(i, \mathbf{w}), i = 1, \ldots, n]$

Algorithm 3: Multi-armed bandit selection.

asymptotically the optimal regret rate in the classical MAB case of independent and stationary reward probability distributions. This means that this algorithm strives at finding the best arm as fast as possible, while trying the other arms at an exponentially decreasing frequency. In an environment involving coevolutionary algorithms, none of the independent and stationary reward distribution assumptions are respected. Indeed, the quality of solutions in a species strongly depends on the solutions of the other species, which also makes the probability distributions non-stationary.

Da Costa et al. [4] proposed a dynamic MAB combining the principles of the UCB and the Page-Hinkley statistics for restarting the method. This bandit was used to automatically select variation operators during the course of an evolutionary algorithm, with promising results. Fialho et al. [6] refined this dynamic MAB in order to improve the robustness and invariance to monotonic transformations. They added a rank-based credit assignment scheme based on the Area Under the Curve (AUC) measure, commonly used in machine learning.

Fialho et al. [6] AUC dynamic MAB has been used as a basic species selection mechanism for the current work. We slightly modified the credit assignment by not taking into account the ties in the ranked rewards, since our reward model is binary ($\rho \in \{0, 1\}$) instead of continuous (see Sec. 4). The order of appearance of the rewards is thus taken into consideration, as a more recent reward obtains a higher credit than an equal but older one. Algo. 2 presents the credit assignment scheme, with $d \in [0, 1]$ being the decay factor proposed in [6] and $\mathbf{w} = [w_1 \cdots w_n]$ contains the tuples rewards, index obtained by the arms in the last n iterations.

The selection mechanism of the MAB is the same as the one proposed in [6], it is presented in Algo. 3. First, the number of times each k arm is selected $\mathbf{n} = [n_1 \cdots n_k]$, the credit each arm obtained so far $\mathbf{q} = [q_1 \cdots q_k]$, and the window of rewards $\mathbf{w}$ are all initialized. Then, we iterate over each selection step until the decision process ends. At first, if one or more arms have never been selected, we select randomly among these. Otherwise, we select an arm using the UCB formula, where C is a parameter to control exploration. Next, we apply the selected arm and retrieve the reward. A tuple made of the arm index and the reward is prepended to the window of rewards, from which the oldest tuple is removed if we have reached the maximum window size W. Finally, the number of times each arm is selected is updated according to the window and the credit is given by the AUC (Algo. 2) of each arm.

4. SELECTING SPECIES

The main idea at the source of the proposed algorithm is very simple. Instead of evolving every population at each generation, as presented in Sec. 2, we want to choose the most promising population to evolve with the dynamic MAB described in Sec. 3. This strategy has two major goals: it allows sustainable coevolution of the multiple subpopulations while balancing the global evolution resources allocated to each population, as they are not appearing in the evolution at the same time given the species addition and removal mechanisms used.

The evolution process starts similarly to the original algorithm. A number of species are initialized and one individual in each of them is selected as representative. The MAB is initialized with one arm associated with each species in the coevolution. Then, line 4 of Algo. 1 becomes lines 3 to 6 of Algo. 3, where the MAB selects the index i of the species to be evolved. The application of variation operators, evaluation, and selection of $\mathfrak{S}_i$ remain the same. Later, the best individual of $\mathfrak{S}_i$ replaces the previous representative of species i in $\mathfrak{R}$. The bandit is rewarded for the progress made by the representatives on the problem, and the rest of the iteration of Algo. 3 is run to complete the bandit update. The reward scheme will be detailed in the following Sec. 4.1. Finally, the cooperative process continues with the improvement verification of the standard algorithm (lines 9 to 13 of Algo. 1). The improvement length is set to the value in the original algorithm times the number of species, since we evolve only one species on each generation. The arms in the bandit are adjusted for each addition and removal of a species in the coevolution, as detailed later in Sec. 4.2.

4.1 Reward

Properly rewarding the selected arm is a crucial element that should be carefully designed to ensure success. The choice of the reward must encourage exploitation of the best arm while still allowing exploration of the other arms. The concept used in our case is borrowed from an assumption made in the original UCB, contrary to what is presented by Fialho et al. [6]. The reward given to the bandit is binary. An arm is assigned a reward of 1 if the fitness of the selected species representative is better than the one at the previous iteration, and 0 otherwise.

We argue that this reward method is the best that we can use in the context of population selection in cooperative coevolution compared to the direct and delta fitness assignment of Fialho et al. [6]. On the one hand, the direct fitness allocation suffers when the bandit is updated with a new fitness that caused a loss – if this fitness is still better than any other in the window that caused a gain, the arm will receive a higher credit for that loss than the other arm for its gain. This drawback has been addressed in the delta fitness assignment. On the other hand, this previous reward attribution is handicapped by the "log convergence" of optimization algorithms. The difference of fitness between consecutive iterations should decrease logarithmically with time. Sorting the delta fitness results in older data being privileged over new ones, which is counter intuitive as the current state of cooperation is probably closer to the next state than any older one. The Boolean reward allotment benefits from the properties of both assignments without their drawbacks, which explains its choice for the proposed method.

4.2 Adding and Removing Arms

As species are added and removed from the evolution, the number of arms must change. Instead of entirely restarting the bandit, we simply modify its internal state. When adding a species, we add entries in both the number of times each arm has been selected and the credit each arm received so far, that is $\mathbf{n} \leftarrow [n_1 \ \cdots \ n_k \ 0]$ and $\mathbf{q} \leftarrow [q_1 \ \cdots \ q_k \ 0]$. This procedure forces the bandit to select the newly introduced species a couple of times, giving it a chance to find a suitable niche without being bumped out of the coevolution.

Removing an arm is conducted in a similar manner to the addition, with entries corresponding to the removed species in $\mathbf{n}$ and $\mathbf{q}$ being removed, leaving them with $k - 1$ values each. For the window of reward $\mathbf{w}$, we remove all entries in which the removed species (indexed l) is involved, $\mathbf{w} \leftarrow [\forall(reward, arm) \in \mathbf{w} | arm \neq l]$.

5. EXPERIMENTS

The proposed algorithm (CCEA-MAB) is tested and compared against the original cooperative coevolution (CCEA) of Potter and De Jong [14] on a string covering benchmark and a sensor placement problem.

5.1 String Covering

The binary string covering problem, introduced in [7] and used by [14, 16, 18], benchmarks cooperative evolutionary algorithms. The problem consists in matching a number of strings in a test set $\mathcal{T}$ with strings in a match set $\mathcal{M}$, where $\mathcal{T}$ is generally much larger than $\mathcal{M}$. Thus, the strings in the match set must generalize the patterns in the target set to obtain an optimal cover. The match strength $s(\mathbf{x}, \mathbf{y})$ between two strings $\mathbf{x}$ and $\mathbf{y}$ is defined by the number of bits at the same position and of the same value that the two strings share. The strength of a match set $S(\mathcal{M}, \mathcal{T})$ is the average maximum match strength its strings has against the target set,

$$S(\mathcal{M}, \mathcal{T}) = \frac{1}{|\mathcal{T}|} \sum_{\mathbf{t}_i \in \mathcal{T}} \max_{\mathbf{m}_j \in \mathcal{M}} s(\mathbf{m}_j, \mathbf{t}_i).$$

The cooperative algorithm evolves a match set that is evaluated against the fixed test set. A number of arrangements of the fixed and variable bits is predetermined, these arrangements are called schemata. The test set consists of an equal number of each schemata where the variable bits have been replaced by randomly chosen binary values. In all experiments each set strings are 64 bits long.

Parameter	CCEA	CCEA-MAB
Species Size	50	50
Initial Number of Species	1	1
Crossover Rate	0.6	0.6
Mutation Rate	1.0	1.0
Flip Bit Rate	1/64	1/64
Tournament Size	3	3
Window Size (W)	–	50
Decay Factor (d)	–	1.0
Exploration Factor (C)	–	1.0
Improvement Length (I)	5	5
Improvement Threshold (T_i)	0.5	0.5
Extinction Threshold (T_e)	5.0	5.0

Table 1: Parameters used in the experiments.

The representation used for this problem is a 64 bits string. We use a two-point crossover and a flip bit mutation to generate the offspring, each variation operator being applied with a certain probability. The fitness of an individual is given by the match strength of the group it forms with the representatives of the other species. Tournament selection is used to select individuals in each species. The contribution of a species is computed by the number of times its representative has the best cover for a target string.

Four versions of the string covering problem are used to assess each property of the cooperative evolutionary algorithm of Potter and De Jong [14]. While the two first tests gauge the ability of the algorithm to locate and cover multiple niches, and to evolve the appropriate level of generality, we are more interested in the capacity of adaptation to a changing number of species and the ability to evolve the right number of species. The parameters of the algorithms are shown in Tab. 1. The parameters concerning the evolutionary algorithms and the coevolutionary process are set similar to what is presented in Potter and De Jong [14, pp. 10 and 17] and those for the bandit are set accordingly to the conclusions made by Fialho et al. [6].

5.1.1 *Adaptation During the Evolution*

The capability of adaptation of our version of the coevolutionary algorithm is crucial. As more time is allocated to more promising species, other species must still have enough time to adapt their representatives to the addition of new species. This test allows the ability of specialization of the species over time to be measured as more and more species are added to the evolution.

For this experiment, the evolution is not in charge of adding or removing species, allowing to focus solely on the adaptation property of the algorithm. Starting with a single species, a new species is added at each 100 generations until there is the same number of species as schemata to be matched. At the end of the evolution all schemata should be covered. Three scenarios have been designed.

Scenario 1 is similar to the one used by Potter and De Jong, where a 30 element target set is generated from the three following schemata, each containing 32 fixed bits and 32 variable bits.

```
1##1###1###11111##1##1111#1##1###1#1111##111111##1#11#1#11######
1##1###1###11111##1##1000#0##0###0#0000##000000##0#00#0#00######
0##0###0###00000##0##0000#0##0###0#0000##001111##1#11#1#11######
```

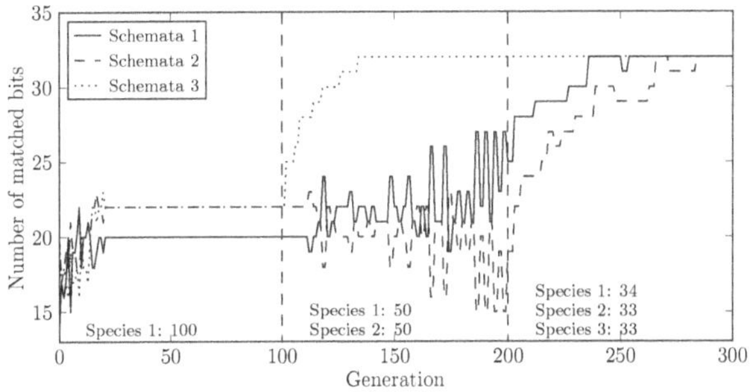

(a) CCEA

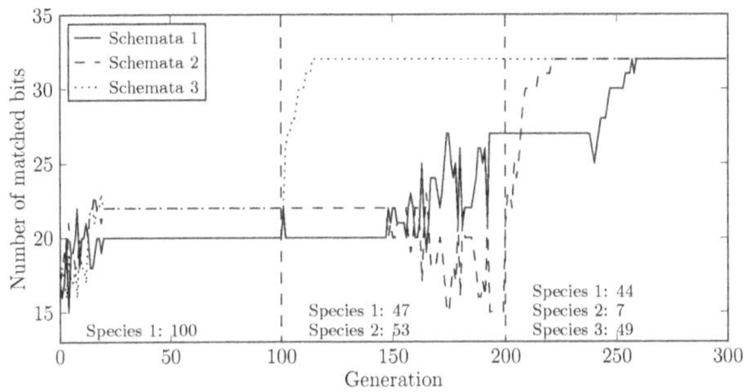

(b) CCEA-MAB

Figure 1: Maximum number of matched bits by a single match string on each schemata in scenario 1 with the number of times each species is evolved.

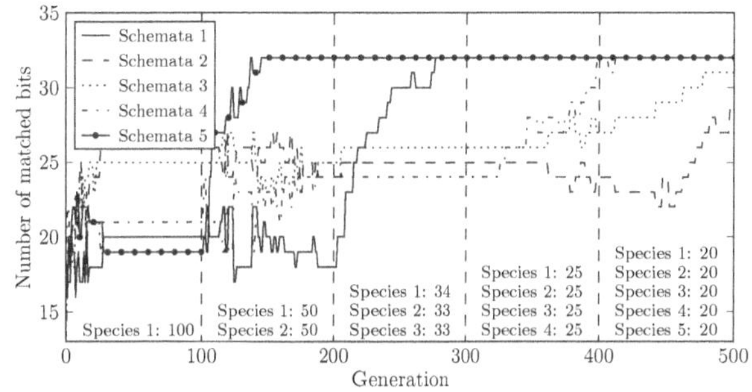

(a) CCEA

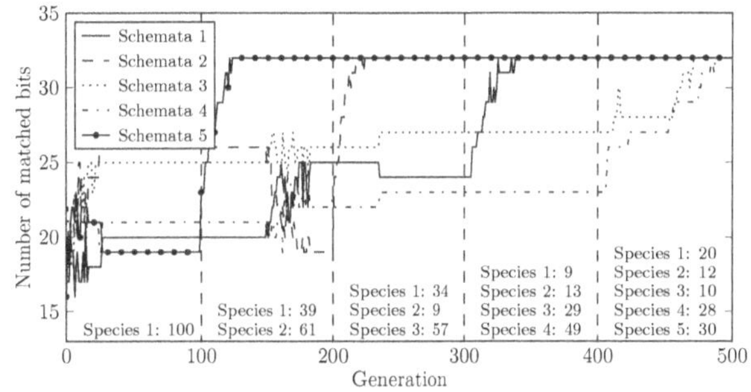

(b) CCEA-MAB

Figure 2: Maximum number of matched bits by a single match string on each schemata in scenario 21 with the number of times each species is evolved.

Scenario 2 is similar to the first one, with a 30 element target set. Five schemata are generated randomly to produce the target set, using the same noise pattern (variable bits) as in scenario 1, while the fixed bits correspond to those of a random integer uniformly chosen in $[0, 2^{32} - 1]$.

Scenario 3 is composed of a 50 element target set generated from five schemata, with a varying number of variable bits. For each schema, we first draw uniformly from $[16, 48]$ the number of variable bits (v) used. Then, the fixed bits are generated using the binary representation of a number taken uniformly in $[0, 2^{64-v} - 1]$. Finally, the variable and fixed bits are shuffled together to form a 64-bit schema.

It should be stressed that for all scenarios, all runs of CCEA and CCEA-MAB are carried out in pairs, with the same target set used for each pair of runs. This allows a fair comparison between the methods.

On 100 runs for scenario 1, the original and the MAB-driven algorithms find the optimal string cover on all occasions. A typical run is shown in Fig. 1, where the match strength against each schemata is presented. Fig. 1(b) clearly illustrates the allocation to the promising species right after generation 100 and 200 where the slope of the number of bits matched is generally steeper for CCEA-MAB. We also notice that once a species has converged to a schemata, time is allocated to adjust the other species, if there can be a reward, as exposed by the difference between the number of times each species is evolved in CCEA-MAB. In the third part of Fig. 1(b), we observe that species 2, which has converged to schemata 3, is chosen by the bandit only 7 times over the 100 last generations while the two other species for which convergence is still possible are chosen 44 and 49 times. This process saves much effort since the progress made by evolving a species is not interrupted by evolving another less promising or already converged one.

For the second scenario with five schemata, CCEA finds the optimal cover in only 22% of the experiments, while CCEA-MAB succeeds 71% of the time. Fig. 2 exposes a typical run with this configuration. We see that the two algorithms have mostly the same behaviour for the first couple of phases, but when the fourth and fifth species are introduced, alternating between the species in a round-robin fashion does not leave enough generations to the important species to converge to a niche, as seen in Fig. 2(a). The greater number of generations offered to the promising populations by CCEA-MAB in the fourth and fifth phases greatly helps to find an optimal coverage (Fig. 2(b)).

The experiments with scenario 3 show a success rate of 83% for CCEA and 88% for CCEA-MAB. While this appears to be contradictory with the previous experiment, we find that the large amount of time allocated between the introduction of new species (100 generations) greatly helps CCEA while not affecting the MAB version much. In fact, just reducing the number of generations allocated per species introduction to 75 reduces the number of perfect coverages found by CCEA to 10% and those found by CCEA-MAB to 33%, conserving its superiority observed previously.

5.1.2 *Finding the Appropriate Number of Species*

In this problem, the coevolutionary algorithm aims not only at evolving the perfect cover for a given target set, but also strives at finding the optimal number of species for that problem. For this test, we expect the MAB version of the coevolutionary algorithm to perform much better, with less species removed of their inability to identify a suitable niche in the allocated time. This test is the closest one to a real world problem where we do not know how many species

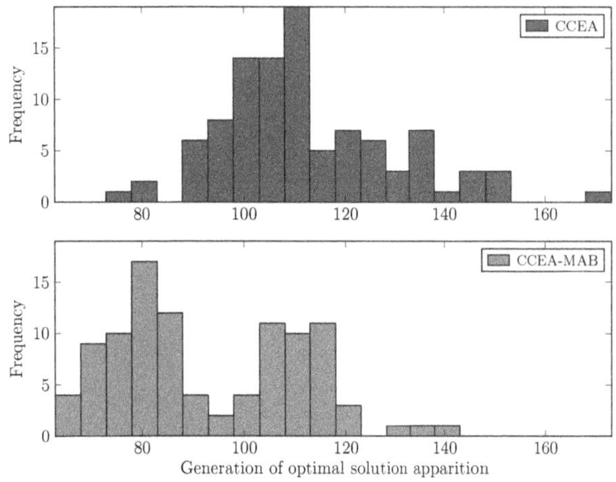

Figure 3: First hit generation histogram for scenario 1.

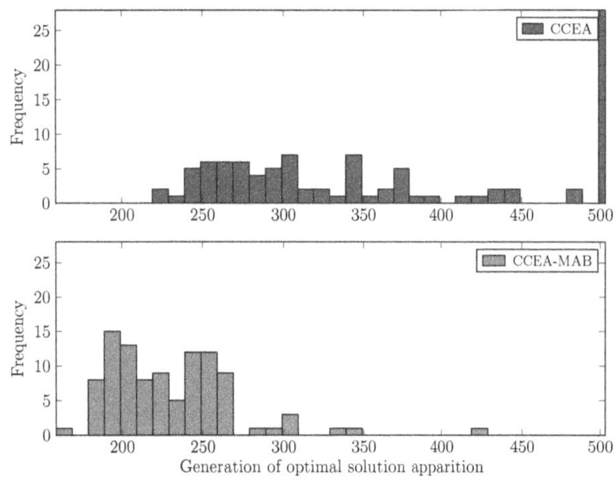

Figure 4: First hit generation histogram for scenario 2.

will be required, nor the time we should allocate after the addition of a species for the algorithm to stabilize.

For this experiment, the complete algorithms presented in Sec. 2 and 4 are used. The coevolution must concurrently determine the appropriate number of species, a niche for all those species, and the optimal coverage for the problem. Again starting with a single species, the cooperative coevolution mechanisms will be used to add and remove species. The evolution is run until the algorithm finds the perfect coverage or 500 generations have passed. We will use the same three scenarios as in the adaptation experiment.

Fig. 3 shows the generation at which the perfect coverage was found for scenario 1. The average first hit generation is 111.9 for CCEA and 92.5 for CCEA-MAB. A Wilcoxon signed test reveals that the two algorithms are different with a significance level of 99.9%.

The first hit generation histogram for scenario 2 is shown in Fig. 4. The average convergence time for CCEA, excluding those exceeding the 500 generations allocated, is 315.0 generations, while it is 229.7 generations for CCEA-MAB. A Wilcoxon signed test indicates that the two algorithms are different at a significance level of 99.9%. We also notice that CCEA-MAB does find the optimal coverage on all of the 100 runs, while CCEA does not converge in more than 25% of the experiments. Fig. 5 presents the run with the

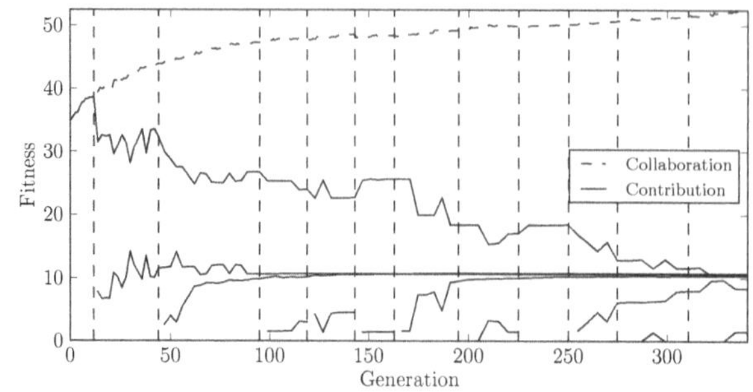

(a) CCEA

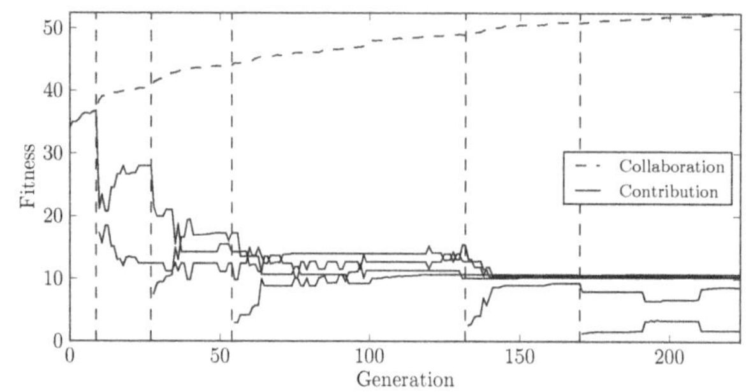

(b) CCEA-MAB

Figure 5: Collaboration (match set fitness) and contribution (fitness of each species independently) for scenario 2.

median first hit time for each algorithm. The contribution of the different species is shown with the continuous lines and the collaboration fitness is presented with the dashed line. This clearly illustrates that CCEA consumes much more species than CCEA-MAB. In fact, it takes 12 species and approximately 350 generations for CCEA to have the right elements to entirely cover the target set, while only 6 species and less than 250 generations are required for CCEA-MAB. This clearly shows that allocating more steps to the promising species allows them to find suitable niches and support global improvements in the optimization, while the original algorithm would have removed those species at the outset.

Finally, the first hit generation histogram for scenario 3 is shown in Fig. 6. The average convergence time for CCEA and CCEA-MAB on this experiment, excluding those exceeding the 500 generations allocated, are respectively 313.8 and 245.6 generations. The runs that have not converged represent more than 50% of the trials for CCEA and only 11% of the runs for CCEA-MAB. Again, the Wilcoxon signed test indicates that the two algorithms are different at a significance level of 99.9% in this configuration. Fig. 7 exposes the same problem as in the previous scenario, showing the runs corresponding to the median first hit time of each algorithm. We see that in CCEA, an enormous amount of evaluations are wasted on species immediately removed after their introduction. However, these species should have helped the algorithm to increase its collaboration fitness. This problem is not present in CCEA-MAB as it allocated enough resources to the promising species.

5.2 Sensor Placement

The string covering problem exposed the properties of our new algorithm. This section will illustrate how this algorithm performs on a more complex case. As shown by

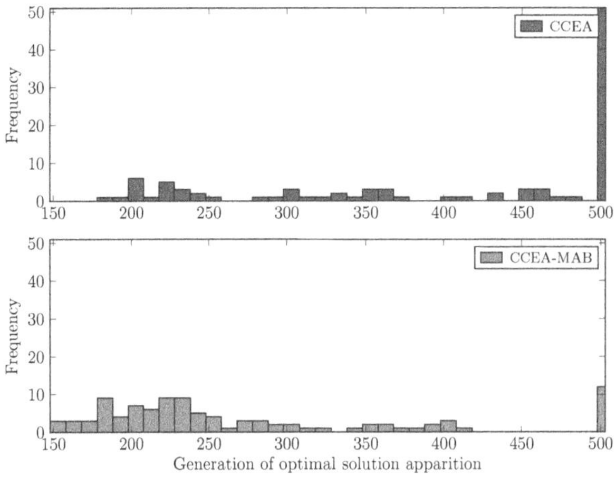

Figure 6: First hit generation histogram for scenario 3.

De Rainville et al. [5], cooperative coevolutionary algorithms apply well to the sensor placement optimization. We will study the effect of selecting the species to evolve on each generation on a similar scenario.

The sensor placement problem we face is to optimize the position of a group of sensors (i.e. directional cameras) so that an entire section of an environment is seen. The required number of sensors is unknown, thus the adaptation of the number of species in the evolution is essential. The representation used to tackle this problem is a real-valued vector representing the position and orientations of a sensor. Each species will evolve a single sensor and cooperation between species will produce multiple sensor solutions. We use a simulated binary crossover and a Gaussian mutation as variation operators. Selection between the individuals of a species is achieved by a tournament. The visibility of a sensor is computed by the integral of its resolution on the surface it senses. For space reasons, the details on computing a sensor visibility cannot be entirely exposed here.

The collaboration between species is evaluated by computing the complete visibility attained with all representatives. The fitness is the difference between the visibility required for the environment and the visibility given by the group of sensors. Fig. 8 shows the different visibility concepts implied in the sensor placement problem. In this figure, the environment desired view is determined by the resolution an omnidirectional camera would have of the environment if it was positioned on the dot. The visibility of a sensor is computed using the same process, a sensor placed at position "x" and oriented as shown by the arrow sees the thick dashed line. The fitness is the integral of the difference between the required visibility and the visibility of the sensor. Finally, a species contribution is computed as the difference of fitness the group of representatives would have with and without the individual from that species.

Experiments have been conducted for the environment of Fig. 8. The desired field of view is 360° while the sensors field of view is 45°, which results in a theoretical optimal solution with 8 sensors. We stopped the evolution for both techniques when a suitable coverage had been achieved, namely an error less than 10^4. The average first hit generation and average resulting number of sensors, for 10 independent runs, are shown in Tab. 2. A Mann-Whitney-Wilcoxon test reveals that the two algorithms are different with a significance level

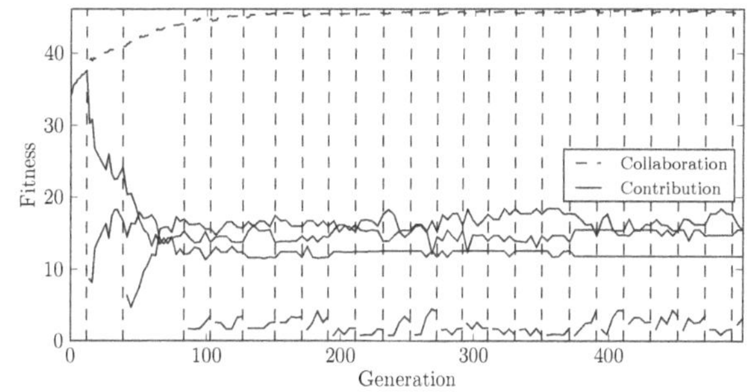

(a) CCEA

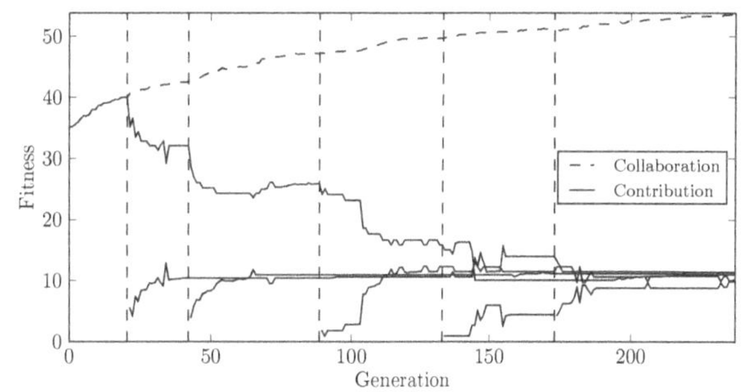

(b) CCEA-MAB

Figure 7: Collaboration (match set fitness) and contribution (fitness of each species independently) for scenario 3.

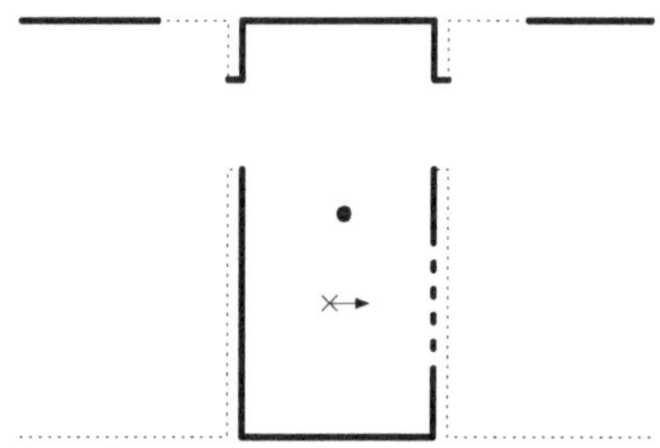

Figure 8: The environment used for the real world experiments. The desired view and the sensor view are shown respectively by the thick continuous and thick dashed lines.

of 99.9%. This clearly shows that the MAB maintained the focus of the optimization on the important sensors, and thus the algorithm converged more rapidly to a suitable solution. Fig. 9 shows the evolution of the collaboration fitness during the median run for both algorithms. As mentioned in the previous section, when many species are present, the MAB greatly increases the convergence of the algorithm because it allocates resources to the preferred population and offers some stability to the new species. Moreover, tuning the extinction threshold would force the algorithm to reach a better position for each sensor and not use the extra sensors, but it would also require more computational time to identify that solution. In addition, a fixed length real valued genetic algorithm has been run for several experiments with different number of sensors without success at producing any suitable solution even with carefully tuned parameters.

6. CONCLUSION

This paper presented an efficient way to automatically control the resources allocated to the cooperative popula-

Algorithm	First Hit Gen.	# Sensors
CCEA	429.4	8.8
CCEA-MAB	283.7	8.8

Table 2: Results for the second environment.

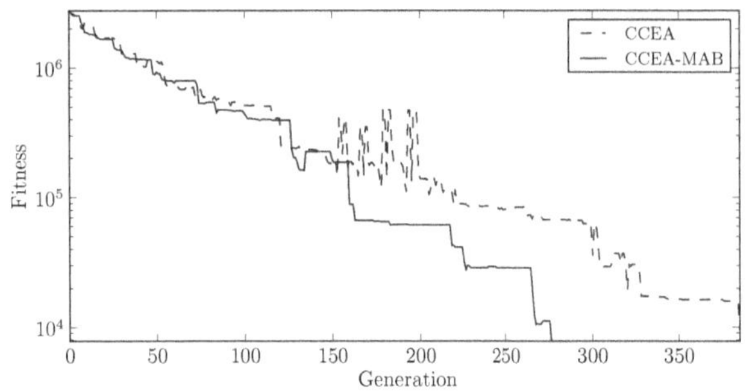

Figure 9: Fitness progress on the sensor problem.

tions in coevolution in order to sustain co-adaptation. Our technique exploits the complete potential of every species and learns when to select another species due to our multi-armed bandit. Our technique also alleviates the burden of precisely choosing the improvement length, as the allocation of the resources to the population is conducted automatically. Finally, we introduced a mechanism that responds to the difficulty of each problem by allocating the computing resources to the subpopulations which will sustain evolution. The string covering benchmark and the sensor placement problem clearly illustrate that our method helps the algorithm to converge more rapidly to a suitable solution in situations where the original algorithm struggles to keep up with the problem.

This work can be extended in a number of ways. First, different multi-armed bandits exist and much work has been carried out to solve combinatorial problems with these learners. It would be interesting to incorporate the dynamic technique in these bandits and use them in our algorithm as they do not make the independence assumption between the populations. Second, preliminary results show that the population selection technique can be applied efficiently to other types of coevolution such as competitive coevolution. In this case, the bandit would balance the progress made by both competitors so that one does not entirely dominate the other. Third, the bandit technique would also be promising in multi-population algorithms to invest resources in the most promising areas of the search space.

Acknowledgements

This work has been funded by the FRQNT (Québec) and NSERC (Canada). The authors wish to thank Annette Schwerdtfeger for proofreading the manuscript.

7. REFERENCES

[1] P. Auer, N. Cesa-Bianchi, and P. Fischer. Finite-time analysis of the multi-armed bandit problem. *Machine Learning*, 47(2–3):235, 256 2002.

[2] R. Axelrod. The evolution of strategies in the iterated prisoner's dilemma. In L. Davis, editor, *Genetic algorithms and simulated annealing*, pages 32–41. Pitman Publishing, 1987.

[3] A. Bucci and J. B. Pollack. On identifying global optima in cooperative coevolution. In *Proceedings of the Genetic and Evolutionary Computation Conference*, pages 539–544, 2005.

[4] L. Da Costa, Á. Fialho, M. Schoenauer, and M. Sebag. Adaptive operator selection with dynamic multi-armed bandits. In *Proceedings of the Genetic and Evolutionary Computation Conference*, pages 913–920, 2008.

[5] F.-M. De Rainville, C. Gagné, and D. Laurendeau. Co-adapting mobile sensor networks to maximize coverage in dynamic environments. In *Proceedings of the Genetic and Evolutionary Computation Conference Companion*, pages 1409–1410, 2012.

[6] Á. Fialho, M. Schoenauer, and M. Sebag. Toward comparison-based adaptive operator selection. In *Proceedings of the Genetic and Evolutionary Computation Conference*, pages 767–774, 2010.

[7] S. Forrest, B. Javornik, R. E. Smith, and A. S. Perelson. Using genetic algorithms to explore pattern recognition in the immune system. *Evol. Comput.*, 1(3):191–211, 1993.

[8] N. García-Pedrajas, C. Hervás-Martínez, and D. Ortiz-Boyer. Cooperative coevolution of artificial neural network ensembles for pattern classification. *Trans. Evolut. Comput.*, 9(3):271–302, 2005.

[9] J.C. Gittins. Bandit processes and dynamic allocation indices. *J. R. Statist. Soc.*, 41(2):148–177, 1979.

[10] W. D. Hillis. Co-evolving parasites improves simulated evolution as an optimization procedure. *Physica D: Nonlinear Phenomena*, 42(1–3):228–234, 1990.

[11] T. Lai and H. Robbins. Asymptotically efficient adaptive allocation rules. *Adv. Appl. Math.*, 6(1):4–22, 1985.

[12] L. Panait and S. Luke. Cooperative multi-agent learning: The state of the art. *Auton. Agent Multi Agent Syst.*, 11:387–434, 2005.

[13] L. Panait, S. Luke, and R. P. Wiegand. Biasing coevolution search for optimal multiagent behavior. *Trans. Evolut. Comput.*, 10(6):629–645, 2006.

[14] M. A. Potter and K. A. De Jong. Cooperative coevolution : An architecture for evolving co-adapted subcomponents. *Evol. Comput.*, 8(1):1–29, 2001.

[15] H. Robbins. Some aspects of the sequential design of experiments. *Bull. Amer. Math. Soc.*, 58(5):527–535, 1952.

[16] R. E. Smith, S. Forrest, and A. S. Perelson. Searching for diverse, cooperative populations with genetic algorithms. *Evol. Comput.*, 1(2):127–149, 1993.

[17] R. P. Wiegand. *An Analysis of Cooperative Coevolutionary Algorithms*. PhD thesis, George Mason University, 2003.

[18] S. X. Wu and W. Banzhaf. A hierarchical cooperative evolutionary algorithm. In *Proceedings of the Genetic and Evolutionary Computation Conference*, pages 233–240, 2010.

The Importance of the Learning Conditions in Hyper-Heuristics

Nuno Lourenço
CISUC, Department of Informatics Engineering
University of Coimbra, 3030 Coimbra, Portugal
naml@dei.uc.pt

Francisco B. Pereira
[1]CISUC, Department of Informatics Engineering
University of Coimbra, 3030 Coimbra, Portugal
[2]ISEC, Quinta da Nora, 3030 Coimbra, Portugal
xico@dei.uc.pt

Ernesto Costa
CISUC, Department of Informatics Engineering
University of Coimbra, 3030 Coimbra, Portugal
ernesto@dei.uc.pt

ABSTRACT

Evolutionary Algorithms are problem solvers inspired by nature. The effectiveness of these methods on a specific task usually depends on a non trivial manual crafting of their main components and settings. Hyper-Heuristics is a recent area of research that aims to overcome this limitation by advocating the automation of the optimization algorithm design task. In this paper, we describe a Grammatical Evolution framework to automatically design evolutionary algorithms to solve the knapsack problem. We focus our attention on the evaluation of solutions that are iteratively generated by the Hyper-Heuristic. When learning optimization strategies, the hyper-method must evaluate promising candidates by executing them. However, running an evolutionary algorithm is an expensive task and the computational budget assigned to the evaluation of solutions must be limited. We present a detailed study that analyses the effect of the learning conditions on the optimization strategies evolved by the Hyper-Heuristic framework. Results show that the computational budget allocation impacts the structure and quality of the learned architectures. We also present experimental results showing that the best learned strategies are competitive with state-of-the-art hand designed algorithms in unseen instances of the knapsack problem.

Categories and Subject Descriptors

I.2.8 [**Artificial Intelligence**]: Problem Solving, Control Methods, and Search—*Heuristic Methods*

Keywords

Evolutionary Algorithms, Hyper-Heuristics, Automatic Evolution

1. INTRODUCTION

Evolutionary Algorithms (EAs) are computational problem solvers loosely inspired by the principles of natural selection posit by Darwin. Over time, they have been successfully applied to complex problems, i.e., those that do not have an analytical solution or are computationally intractable, in areas like optimization, learning or design. When solving a particular problem, EAs usually require a carefully adjustment of some of its parameters and components. This might be a difficult task requiring specific skills, and it is typically performed off-line, by hand, even though there are EA variants that have a limited self-adaptation capacity.

The automatic adaptation of EAs to a specific problem is a promising way to replace specialized manual adjustments. In the last years, several proposals have been made that perform the autonomous evolution of bio-inspired approaches, namely Particle Swarm Optimization [9], Ant Colony Optimization [14] and Evolutionary Algorithms [3, 4]. Hyper-Heuristics (HH) are an emerging framework to accomplish this task. In general, this term identifies architectures where problem-solving methods search a set of possible heuristics, i.e., high level heuristics choose low level heuristics [12].

There are two main groups of HH. One seeks for the best sequence of low-level heuristics, chosen from a predetermined set of methods usually applied to solve the specific problem under consideration. The second group aims at generating or constructing new heuristics. In this case, the HH framework automatically learns the low-level algorithm needed to solve the problem at hand. Learning feedback is obtained by executing each solution candidate over one, or several, simple instances of the problem one aims to solve. Genetic Programming (GP) is a EA branch that searches the space of programs for effective algorithmic strategies. For that reason, it has been increasingly adopted as an HH. In concrete, the Grammatical Evolution (GE) [6, 7] variant has been successfully used in recent works [1, 4, 14], as it allows for a straightforward enforcement of semantic and syntactic restrictions.

GE based HH incurs on a learning process with a high computational effort, as the quality of each generated strategy must be estimated by applying it to an optimization situation. This leads to the appearance of two contradictory forces that must be balanced. On the one hand, the off-line learning should not take too long, which implies relying on small instances and adopting parameters (e.g., population size, number of iterations) that minimize the computational overhead. On the other hand, the adoption of excessively simple conditions might compromise results, hindering differences between competing strategies and potentially leading to an inaccurate assessment of the quality of evolved solutions. The experiments described in this paper aim to contribute to a better understanding of the impact of the learning conditions in the evolved strategies and to identify useful guidelines that help to define better HH. With this goal in mind, we present a GE based HH for evolving complete EAs that are effective in solving different instances of the 0-1 Knapsack Problem. Additionally, we will investigate the generalization ability of the best evolved EAs by applying then to unseen instances of the problem.

The paper is structured as follows: Section 2 describes the framework used. Section 3 introduces the experimental setup and presents an empirical study on the influence of the learning conditions on the structure of the evolved EAs. Section 4 compares the effectiveness of EAs evolved under different conditions by applying them to unseen instances of the knapsack problem. Finally, Section 5 gathers the main conclusions and suggests directions for future work.

2. THE HYPER-HEURISTIC FRAMEWORK

In this section we present a brief overview of recent research from the HH area that rely on GP approaches to evolve problem solving strategies. Next we describe the grammar used in our work.

2.1 Related Work

Several efforts have been reported in the literature to automatically evolve nature-inspired algorithms. In [13], Tavares et al. adopted GP to evolve a population of mapping functions between the genotype and the phenotype. Experimental results showed that GP finds mapping functions that can obtain results as good as the ones that are designed by hand.

In [3], Dioşan et al. adopted a two-level architecture to evolve full-fledged EAs. At a higher level, an EA with fixed settings is used, while, at the lower level, a solution is produced in the form of a sequence of genetic operations and corresponding parameters. Best solutions evolved are next used to solve specific optimization problems. The results presented confirm that it is possible to evolve EAs that perform similarly to the ones used for comparison.

In [9], Poli et al. evolved, using GP, the equation that controls the movement of particles in a Particle Swarm Optimization. Experimental results showed that the evolved strategy could effectively solve some selected problems.

In [8], Pappa et al. proposed a Grammar-Based GP (GBGP) framework to learn data mining algorithms. The evolved algorithms are competitive with state of art human-designed methods for data discovery. Recently, Burke et al. [1] presented a GE approach to evolve heuristics for the bin packing problem. The experimental analysis of the work focused on the quality, efficiency and consistency of the evolved heuristics. Best evolved heuristics were able to satisfy all these features.

In [14], Tavares et al. proposed a GE framework to evolve Ant Colony Optimization Algorithms to the Traveling Salesman Problem. Finally, Lourenço et al. [4] proposed a GE based HH to evolve full-featured EAs. The results showed that the proposed architecture is able to evolve effective algorithms for the problem considered in that study.

$$
\begin{array}{rlr}
< expr > ::= & < expr >< op >< expr > & (0)\\
 & |(< expr >< op >< expr >) & (1)\\
 & |< var > & (2)\\
< op > ::= & + & (0)\\
 & |- & (1)\\
< var > ::= & x & (0)\\
 & |y & (1)
\end{array}
$$

Figure 1: Example grammar

2.2 Grammatical Evolution

GE is a branch of GP and a form of GBGP. In GE, a linear genome representation is used, typically a binary string, and there is a clear separation between the genotype and the phenotype. The mapping genotype-phenotype is done by a grammar. The grammar can contain domain knowledge and the search engine is independent of the evaluation mechanism. For these reasons, a GE system is general and flexible [7]. The grammars used by GE are context-free. A context-free grammar is defined by a tuple $G = (N, T, S, P)$, where N is a non-empty set of non terminal symbols, T is a non-empty set of terminal symbols, S is an element of N called axiom, and P is a set of production rules of the form $A ::= \alpha$, with $A \in N$ and $\alpha \in (N \cup T)^*$ (see Fig. 1 for an example). Note that N and T are disjoint. A grammar G defines a language $L(G)$, that is the set of all sequences of terminal symbols that can be derived from the axiom, also called words, that is $L(G) = \{w : S \stackrel{*}{\Rightarrow} w, w \in T^*\}$.

GE performs the genotype to phenotype mapping in successive steps. The initial binary linear sequence (i.e., the genome) is first transcribed onto a sequence of integers, each one called a *codon*. Then, the sequence of codons is used to decide which production of the grammar is used to construct a derivation tree from the axiom. Finally, the phenotype, i.e., an executable program, is extracted from the derivation tree. As an example, consider that we have the grammar exemplified in Fig. 1. In the beginning, the genome is transcribed into a string of integers and we start with a syntactical form equal to the axiom $< expr >$. The objective is to rewrite the axiom and one must choose which of the three options is selected. The first integer from the string is divided by the number of options for $< expr >$. The remainder of that operation will indicate the option to be used. In the example, if the integer is 153 then $153\%3 = 0$ and the axiom will be rewritten as $< expr >< op >< expr >$. Then the decoding proceeds by reading the second integer and apply the same method to the leftmost non-terminal of the derivation. This process is iterated, until there are no more non-terminals to rewrite. If the decoding process runs out of integers, a wrapping mechanism is used, i.e., the process goes back to the beginning of the string. The existence of redundancy is also worth noting, for different integers may correspond to the same alternative due to the nature of the operation remainder. In the example above, the integers $3, 27, 153$, all codify for the same production alternative for $< expr >$. GE has been applied with success to different problems (for details see [6, 7]).

2.3 Grammar Definition

Our HH framework relies on GE to learn full-fledged EAs. We must then define a grammar whose words are EAs, i.e., the grammar must allow the generation of a complete algorithm, defining both its main components and its settings. In the present work, we rely on the grammar presented in Fig. 2, where $<$ *start* $>$ plays the role of the axiom. The grammar enforces a sequential construction of components, thereby modeling the overall structure of the evolved algorithms. The grammar implicitly describes algorithmic components, such as selection, variation operators and replacement strategy; likewise, it also specifies parameters including the number of individuals in the initial population, the number of offspring created at each generation and the probability of applying variation operators. An inspection of the right hand side of the first production clarifies how we constrain the general structure of the evolved solutions: first, parameters *mu* and *lambda* are specified, corresponding to the number of individuals in the initial population and number of offspring created at each generation, respectively. Both values are defined in proportion to the maximum population size granted to the algorithm. Afterwards, a cycle iterates over a predetermined sequence of typical EA operations: evaluation, selection, variation and replacement. The grammar defines alternatives for each component, thus allowing the GE to learn the most suitable combination for a given situation. It is worth noting that the grammar allows the generation of solutions without some components (option ϵ denotes the empty string). In addition, several recombination and mutation operators can simultaneously appear in the same EA.

```
⟨start⟩ ::= mu = ⟨proportion⟩
        lambda = ⟨proportion⟩
        while(not termination condition) do
        evaluate
        ⟨selection⟩
        ⟨variation⟩
        ⟨replacement⟩
        end while

⟨proportion⟩ ::= 0.25
        | 0.5
        | 0.75
        | 1.0

⟨selection⟩ ::= RouleteWheel()
        | SUS()
        | Rank()
        | Tournament(⟨t-size⟩)
        | ϵ

⟨t-size⟩ ::= ⟨integer-const⟩

⟨integer-const⟩ ::= randominteger()

⟨variation⟩ ::= ⟨operator⟩
        | ⟨operator⟩ ⟨variation⟩

⟨operator⟩ ::= ⟨recombination⟩
        | ⟨mutation⟩

⟨recombination⟩ ::= SinglePointXover(⟨prob-recombination⟩)
        | NPointXover(⟨prob-recombination⟩,⟨integer-const⟩)
        | UniformXover(⟨prob-recombination⟩)
        | ϵ

⟨mutation⟩ ::= PointMutation(⟨prob-mutation⟩)
        | BinarySwapMutation(⟨prob-mutation⟩)
        | ϵ

⟨prob-recombination⟩ ::= 0.5
        | 0.7
        | 0.9
        | 1.0
        | ⟨random-per⟩

⟨prob-mutation⟩ ::= 1.0 / n
        | 2.0 / n
        | 5.0 / n
        | 10.0 / n
        | ⟨random-per⟩

⟨random-per⟩ ::= random01()

⟨replacement⟩ ::= Generational()
        | RankReplacement()
        | RankReplacementNoDup()
        | Elitist(⟨random-per⟩)
        | ϵ
```

Figure 2: Grammar used to evolve EAs

3. LEARNING EVOLUTIONARY ALGORITHMS

Experiments described in this section aim to gain insight on how the learning conditions determine the overall structure of the evolved strategies. The settings of the GE adopted for all the tests are presented in Table 1 [7].

The quality of the strategies generated by the GE is directly related to their optimization ability. In our framework, we apply each learned algorithm to a predetermined problem instance and consider that its fitness corresponds to the quality of the best solution found. Evaluating a GE population is then a computationally intensive task. To prevent the learning process from taking an excessive amount of time, we rely on the following conditions to estimate the quality of evolved strategies: i) one single instance of moderate size is used to assign fitness; ii) only one run is performed; iii) the number of evaluations is kept low. To investigate how these design options impact the quality and structure of the solutions learned by the GE, we present learning results obtained with different conditions. In concrete, this paper focuses on the length of the run used to assign fitness and also on how the number of evaluations is split between generations and population size. We consider 4 settings, detailed in Table 2.

3.1 The 0-1 Knapsack Problem

The combinatorial optimization *0-1 Knapsack Problem* (KP) was selected as the testbed for our experiments. It can be described as follows: given a set of n items, each of which with some profit p and some weight w, how should a

Table 1: Parameters of the GE Framework

Parameter	Value
One Point Crossover Probability	0.9
Bit Flip Mutation	0.01
Codon Duplication Probability	0.01
Codon Pruning Probability	0.01
Population Size	100
Selection	Tournament with size equal 3
Replacement	Steady State
Codon Size	8
Number of Wraps	3
Codons in the initial population	10-16
Generations	50
Runs	30

subset of items be selected to maximize the profit while keeping the sum of the weights bounded to a maximum capacity C? In all instances adopted in our study, the knapsack capacity was set to half of the sum of the weights of all items. A standard binary representation is adopted and evaluation considers a linear penalty function to punish invalid solutions [5].

3.2 Learning Results

Table 2: Evaluation Learning Settings

Setting	Population size	Number of Generations	Evaluations
1	20	100	2000
2	20	250	5000
3	50	100	5000
4	50	250	12500

Table 3: GE Learning Results

Setting	Mean Best Fitness (MBF)	Best Hits
1	38961.94 ($\pm$73.73)	0 / 30
2	39084.77 ($\pm$12.23)	29 / 30
3	39087.00 ($\pm$00.00)	30 / 30
4	39087.00 ($\pm$00.00)	30 / 30

The KP instance selected to evaluate learned EAs is composed by $n = 100$ items, in which the profit of the optimal solution is 39087. Table 3 summarizes the results of the off-line learning step. For each setting, column MBF displays the mean of the best strategies found in the 30 runs performed by the GE and the corresponding standard deviation (in brackets). Last column (Best Hits) presents the number of runs where the GE evolved strategies that were able to discover the optimal solution of the selected instance. The chart from Fig. 3 displays the evolution of MBF, for all settings, along the 50 GE generations. These results show that the framework gradually learns better optimization strategies. Moreover, the outcomes in the Table 3 reveal that evolved EAs are able to discover the optimum or near-optimum solutions. Results obtained with setting 1 are an exception to this general rule. The low number of evaluations granted to each EA to solve the KP instance (between 16% and 40% of the computational budget granted by the other settings) prevents the discovery of the highest quality solutions. Note that this does not necessarily imply that the GE with setting 1 is unable to find good optimization strategies. Learning is also occurring with setting 1 (see the corresponding line in Fig. 3) and the optimization ability of the best strategies evolved in this scenario will be accessed in the next section.

A detailed inspection reveals that different learning conditions (as defined by the 4 settings previously described) impact the structure of the evolved algorithms. For all settings, we selected the best EA learned in each run and created charts that measure the frequency of appearance of the main components (the numerical settings are not considered in this analysis). Fig. 4 contains 3 panels that group the components by type: panels a), b) and c) display selection options, replacement options and variation operators, respectively. Unlike selection and replacement, components in panel c) are not exclusive. Virtually all best learned strategies rely on RankReplacementNoDup, a replacement mechanism based on the rank of the solutions with elimination of duplicates. This is true for all settings and is in accordance with the literature that states that this mechanism outperforms all other considered replacement components [10]. In what concerns selection, there is not a clear winner, although roulette wheel and rank mechanisms are slightly prevalent.

Interesting patterns arise in the selection of variation operators. For all settings, uniform crossover and binary swap mutation achieve the highest percentage, suggesting a clear advantage over the other alternatives when exploring the search space of the KP instance selected for learning. However, a close inspection of panel c) reveals a remarkable difference between settings 2 and 3. In spite of both having the same computational budget (5000 evaluations to estimate the quality of each EA), the mutation operator is frequently disregarded in the best strategies learned with setting 3. This may be explained by examining how the computational budget is allocated. In setting 2, a low population size (20 individuals) is iterated for a considerably high number of generations (250), which might lead to premature convergence. In these conditions the mutation operator plays a crucial role in diversity maintenance, thus avoiding convergence. On the contrary, setting 3 has a higher population size (50 individuals) coupled with a lower number of generations (100). Convergence is hardly a problem and, given the moderate size of the KP instance, the EA can probably rely just on uniform crossover to perform an appropriate sampling of the search space. Therefore, it is not surprising that many EAs learned with setting 3 prefer to not include mutation.

To confirm this hypothesis, we ran an additional set of experiments, with a slightly modified grammar, that only allows the appearance of a single variation operator in each evolved structure. This way, the hyper-heuristic has to select the most suitable operator (either crossover or mutation) to include in the optimization strategy, given specific learning conditions. We repeated the experiments for all four settings presented in Table 2. Fig. 5 displays the frequency of appearance of the variation operators using the modified grammar. An overview of the chart confirms our claims. Strategies evaluated with low population size (settings 1 and 2) need to incorporate mutation operators to prevent premature convergence. When the population size is high and the number of generations is low (setting 3), all the EA needs is crossover. Finally, setting 4 grants the EA a considerable computational budget to run. This allows the appearance of strategies that can either rely on crossover or mutation. It is worth notice that, in the experiments performed with the modified grammar, binary swap mutation is completely absent from the best learned solutions. This is probably related to the fact that this operator alone cannot modify the number of items in the knapsack, thereby preventing a full exploration of the search space.

Results presented in Figs. 4 and 5 reveal that different EA architectures emerge when different learning conditions are adopted. A complete understanding of the whole process is still in progress (e.g., the size or hardness of the instance selected to evaluate learned strategies might also play a relevant role), but it is, nevertheless, a relevant contribution to a better understanding of the impact of learning conditions adopted by a hyper-heuristics framework. To complete this section, in Algorithms T1, T2, T3 and T4 we present the best evolved algorithm for each one the settings, labelled according to the scenario where they were discovered. In agreement with the previous analysis, they share the same replacement method and tend to rely on different selection strategies. In what concerns the variation operators, T1, T2 and T4 include both crossover and mutation, whereas T3 relies solely on crossover.

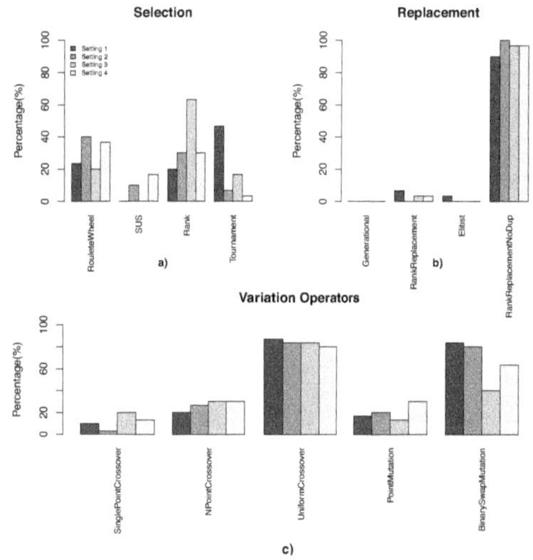

Figure 4: Frequency of components in the best evolved solutions: panels a), b) and c) display selection, replacement and variation operators, respectively.

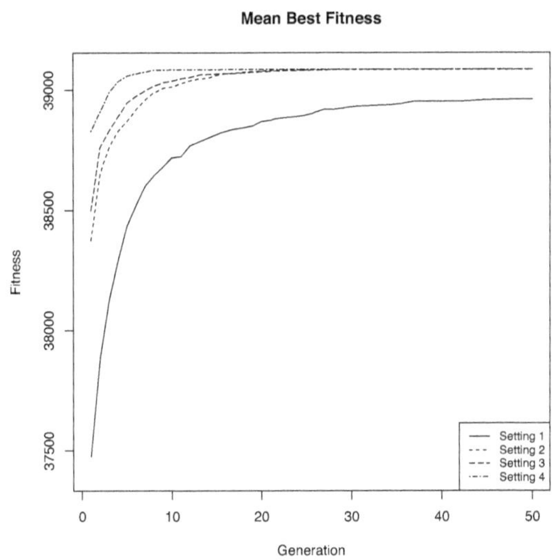

Figure 3: Evolution of GE MBF in the 4 Learning Settings

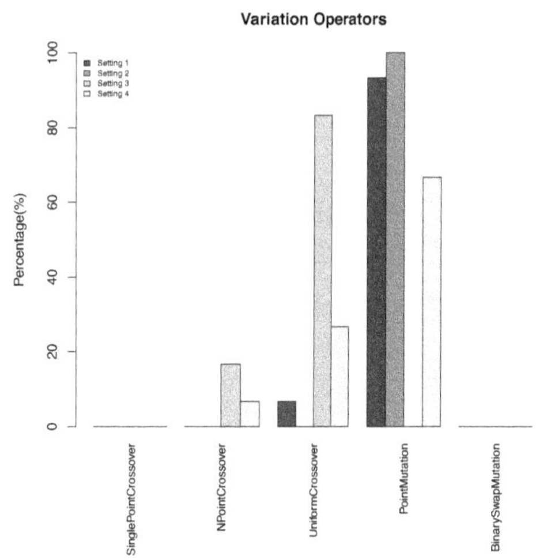

Figure 5: Frequency of components in the best evolved solutions with just one variation operator.

4. VALIDATION OF THE LEARNED EVOLUTIONARY ALGORITHMS

We present now a set of experiments to analyze how the 4 best evolved algorithms (T1, T2, T3, T4) behave in KP instances that are different from the one used in learning. Such study will help to gain insight into the optimization performance differences that may eventually arise between strategies learned in different conditions. Also, we will verify if the evolved EAs generalize well to unseen instances and are competitive with hand design approaches regularly applied to the KP. Three hand-designed algorithms (HEA1, HEA2, HEA3), based on proposals that appeared in the literature [2, 5, 11], were considered in this study. All hand-designed methods adopt the RankReplacementNoDup replacement mechanism and tournament selection with tourney size 3. They differ in the variation operators and/or corresponding rate of application, as detailed in Table 4. The EAs were applied to different KP instances, with a number of items ranging between 500 and 1000. Due to space limitations we present results obtained with just two instances (details in Table 5), although the same optimization trend is visible for other situations. To mimic the training conditions, we created four different validation scenarios in which we varied the population size and number of generations. The settings are detailed in Table 6. All EAs were applied to the two KP instances with each one of these settings. In every optimization scenario, 30 runs were performed and the best solution found was recorded.

The last two columns of Table 7 contain the optimization results, obtained in each one of the validation instances.

Algorithm T1

```
mu = 1.0
lambda = 1.0
while not termination condition do
    evaluate
    Tournament(11)
    UniformCrossover(1.0)
    BinarySwapMutation(1.0 / n)
    RankReplacementNoDup()
end while
```

Algorithm T2

```
mu = 0.5
lambda = 1.0
while not termination condition do
    evaluate
    RouleteWheel()
    UniformCrossover(0.9)
    BinarySwapMutation(2.0 / n)
    RankReplacementNoDup()
end while
```

Algorithm T3

```
mu = 1.0
lambda = 1.0
while not termination condition do
    evaluate
    Rank()
    UniformCrossover(1.0)
    RankReplacementNoDup()
end while
```

Algorithm T4

```
mu = 1.0
lambda = 1.0
while not termination condition do
    evaluate
    RouleteWheel()
    BinarySwapMutation(1.0 / n)
    UniformCrossover(0.9)
    RankReplacementNoDup()
end while
```

Table 4: Hand-designed EAs: Variation operators and rate of application.

ID	Variation Operator	Rate
HEA1	SinglePointCrossover	0.9
	PointMutation	1 / n
HEA2	UniformCrossover	0.9
	PointMutation	1 / n
HEA3	UniformCrossover	0.9
	BinarySwapMutation	1 / n

Values represent the MBF deviation from the optimum (in percentage). A brief perusal of the Table reveals that, in general, the learned EAs perform well across the different scenarios (as determined by the combination of a given instance and setting), suggesting that they are able to generalize, beyond the specific situation used for learning. Results also show that the effectiveness of the learned EAs is comparable to the hand-designed approaches, confirming that the GE framework was able to learn meaningful combinations of components and settings.

Despite the good general behavior of the evolved strategies, there are some differences in performance that require a detailed analysis. For the remainder of this section we concentrate on results obtained with validation instance 2 (the one with the higher number of items) and will investigate how a specific learning setting influences the generalization ability of evolved optimization strategies. The analysis is supported by a Friedman's ANOVA test that checks for statistical differences in the means obtained by the EAs considered in this study. When differences are detected, the *post-hoc* Wilcoxon Signed Rank Test, with Bonferroni correction, is applied to perform the pairwise comparisons. In both tests we used a significance level $\alpha = 0.05$.

Fig. 6 presents the MBF box plot distribution of the 7 EAs (both evolved and hand-designed). Four panels, corresponding to each one of the validation scenarios, are displayed.

Table 5: KP instances used for validation.

Instance	Parameters: Items (n)	Best Solution
1	500	169350
2	1000	333460

Table 6: Validation settings.

Setting	Population size	Number of Generations	Evaluations
1	50	100	5000
2	50	400	20000
3	100	200	20000
4	100	5000	500000

Clearly, the performance of evolved algorithms depends on the settings adopted for the optimization. Even though differences are not always statistically significant, T1 achieves the highest MBF in setting 1, T2 is the best method in setting 2, T3 outperforms all other approaches in setting 3, and T4 is the best in setting 4. This confirms that evolved strategies contain specific features that allow them to excel in situations similar to those found during learning.

Results from Table 8 help to further clarify the relative performance of learned strategies. Considering the MBFs attained, we performed a full set of pairwise comparisons between evolved methods and present a graphical overview: A $+++$ sign indicates that the algorithm in the row is statistically better than the one in the column, and that the effect size is large ($r \geq 0.5$). As an example, T1 clearly outperforms T3 in setting 2. A $++$ sign indicates that there are statistical differences, and that the effect size is medium ($0.3 \leq r < 0.5$), whereas a $+$ identifies a significant difference with a small effect size ($0.1 \leq r < 0.3$). A - signals scenarios where the algorithm in the row is worst than the one in the column. Finally, a $\sim$ indicates that no statistical differences between the algorithms were found.

If we count the number of comparisons where a given EA outperforms another learning strategy, we can see that this

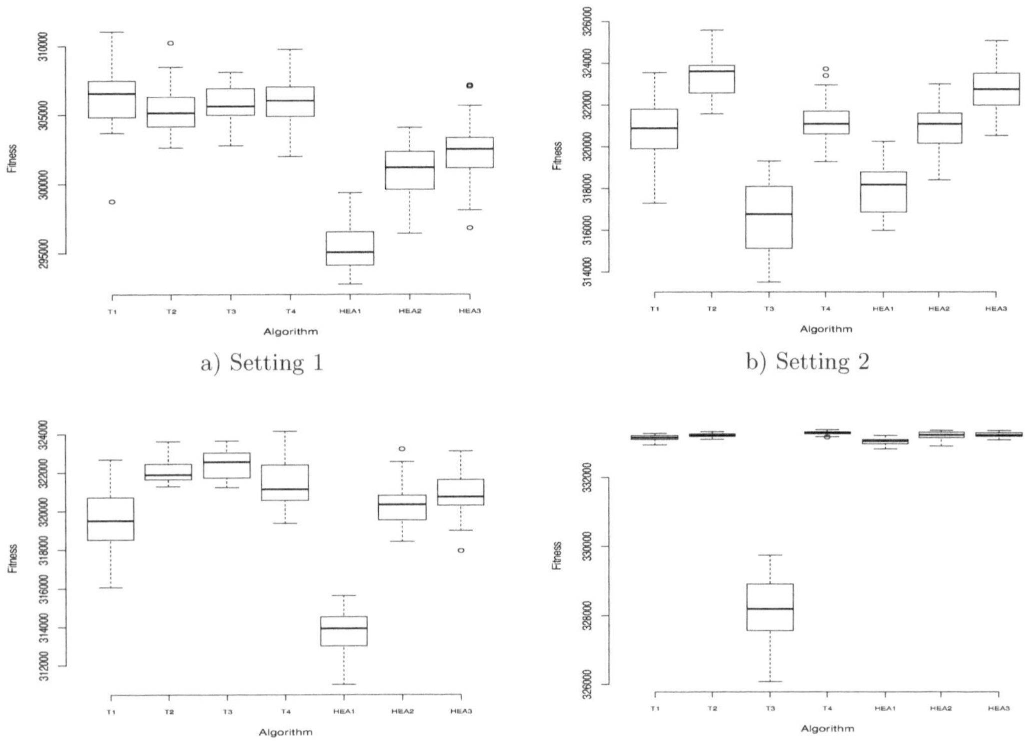

a) Setting 1

b) Setting 2

c) Setting 3

d) Setting 4

Figure 6: Box plot distribution of the MBF obtained by different EAs in the validation instance 2. Each panel corresponds to a given scenario as described in Table 6.

happens in 3 occasions for T1 and T3, 6 times for T4 and 7 times for T2. Moreover, the optimization advantage exhibited by T1 and T3 tends to be concentrated in settings that are similar to those they found during off-line learning. On the contrary, T2 and T4 maintain a reasonable effectiveness in unseen conditions. It seems then that these last two EAs have an increased robustness, which allows them to adapt to different optimization scenarios. On the contrary, T1 and T3 are brittle and tend to have a poor performance when the optimization conditions differ from those found during learning (see the position of some of the T1 and T3 box plots in Fig. 6). These outcomes allow us to conclude that the number of generations used to assign fitness in the off-line learning step is more important than the population size. The evolved strategies must be executed for a reasonable number of generations, in order to obtain an accurate estimate of their optimization ability. Finally it is worth noting that learning settings 2 and 4 were able to evolve algorithms with comparable effectiveness and robustness, even though setting 2 only needs 40% of the computational budget to evaluate candidates (when compared to setting 4).

5. CONCLUSIONS

GE is being increasingly adopted as the meta search method inside a HH framework. In this paper we analyzed a set of experiments to gain insight into the influence that learning conditions play in the effectiveness and robustness of evolved strategies. The 0-1 KP was selected as the target problem. Different off-line learning settings were defined, in what concerns the population size and the number of generations used to estimate the fitness of solutions evolved by the GE. The HH framework was executed in the different learning scenarios and the best evolved strategies were subsequently applied to unseen and larger KP instances. In the validation step, alternative optimization scenarios, with similar features to those adopted in the learning step, were considered. As a rule, evolved strategies obtained extremely good results in scenarios similar to those that they found during learning, showing that they contain features that are particularly suited for a specific environment. However, learning settings that allow the execution of a higher number of generations to estimate the fitness of solutions generated by the GE, allow the discovery of strategies with enhanced robustness. This is a relevant guideline for designing GE based HH, as it helps to distribute the existing computational budget for evaluating solutions.

The study presented here raises important research questions. In the near future we will investigate other learning design options, such as the adoption of a single or several training instances with different properties, to analyze how this impacts the quality and robustness of the evolved strategies. Also, the analysis must be expanded to other problems, in order to understand if the guidelines suggested in this paper can also be generalized to other optimization situations.

Table 7: Optimization results of the best learned EAs and hand-designed algorithms. The values depicted represent the MBF deviation from the optimum (in percentage).

Setting	Algorithm	Instance 1	Instance 2
1	T1	5.6	8.2
	T2	5.4	8.4
	T3	5.6	8.3
	T4	5.5	8.2
	HEA1	7.8	11.4
	HEA2	6.2	9.8
	HEA3	5.8	9.3
2	T1	1.8	3.8
	T2	1.4	3.0
	T3	2.9	5.0
	T4	1.7	3.7
	HEA1	2.3	4.7
	HEA2	1.7	3.9
	HEA3	1.4	3.2
3	T1	2.0	4.2
	T2	1.6	3.4
	T3	1.7	3.3
	T4	1.8	3.6
	HEA1	3.0	5.9
	HEA2	1.7	3.9
	HEA3	1.8	3.7
4	T1	0.0	0.1
	T2	0.0	0.1
	T3	0.8	1.6
	T4	0.0	0.1
	HEA1	0.1	0.1
	HEA2	0.0	0.1
	HEA3	0.0	0.1

Table 8: Statistical analysis between the learned architectures using the Wilcoxon Signed Rank Test ($\alpha = 0.05$).

	Settings	Alg. T1	Alg. T2	Alg. T3	Alg. T4
Alg. T1	1		+++	~	~
	2		-	+++	~
	3		-	-	-
	4		-	+++	-
Alg. T2	1	-		~	-
	2	+++		+++	+++
	3	+++		-	++
	4	+++		+++	-
Alg. T3	1	~	~		~
	2	-	-		-
	3	+++	++		+++
	4	-	-		-
Alg. T4	1	~	+	~	
	2	~	-	+++	
	3	+++	-	-	
	4	+++	+++	+++	

6. ACKNOWLEDGMENTS

This work was partially supported by Fundação para a Ciência e Tecnologia (FCT), Portugal, under the grant SFRH/BD/79649/2011.

7. REFERENCES

[1] E. Burke, M. Hyde, and G. Kendall. Grammatical evolution of local search heuristics. *IEEE Transactions on Evolutionary Computation*, 16(3):406–4127, 2012.

[2] P.C. Chu and J.E. Beasley. A genetic algorithm for the multidimensional knapsack problem. *Journal of Heuristics*, 4:63–86, 1998.

[3] L. Dioşan and M. Oltean. Evolutionary design of Evolutionary Algorithms. *Genetic Programming and Evolvable Machines*, 10(3):263–306, 2009.

[4] Nuno Lourenço, Francisco Pereira, and Ernesto Costa. Evolving evolutionary algorithms. In *Proceedings of the fourteenth international conference on Genetic and evolutionary computation conference companion*, GECCO '12, pages 51–58, New York, NY, USA, 2012. ACM.

[5] Z. Michalewicz. *Genetic Algorithms + Data Structures = Evolution Programs (3rd ed.)*. Springer-Verlag, London, UK, UK, 1996.

[6] M. O'Neill. Grammatical evolution. *IEEE Transactions on Evolutionary Computation*, 5(4), 2001.

[7] M. O'Neill and C. Ryan. *Grammatical Evolution: Evolutionary Automatic Programming in an Arbitrary Language*. Kluwer Academic Publishers, Norwell, MA, USA, 2003.

[8] G. L. Pappa and A. Freitas. *Automating the Design of Data Mining Algorithms: An Evolutionary Computation Approach*. Springer Publishing Company, Incorporated, 1st edition, 2009.

[9] R. Poli, C. Di Chio, and W. B. Langdon. Exploring extended particle swarms: a genetic programming approach. In *Proceedings of the 2005 conference on Genetic and evolutionary computation*, GECCO '05, pages 169–176, New York, NY, USA, 2005. ACM.

[10] G. R. Raidl. On the importance of phenotypic duplicate elimination in decoder-based evolutionary algorithms. In *Late Breaking Papers at the 1999 Genetic and Evolutionary Computation Conference*, pages 204–211, 1999.

[11] G R Raidl and J Gottlieb. Empirical analysis of locality, heritability and heuristic bias in evolutionary algorithms: A case study for the multidimensional knapsack problem. *Evolutionary computation*, 13(4):441–475, 2005.

[12] P. Ross. Hyper-heuristics. In Edmund K. Burke and Graham Kendall, editors, *Search Methodologies: introductory tutorials in optimization and decision support techniques*, chapter 17, pages 529–556. Springer US, 2005.

[13] J. Tavares, P. Machado, A. Cardoso, F. B. Pereira, and E. Costa. On the evolution of evolutionary algorithms. In Maarten Keijzer, Una-May OReilly, Simon Lucas, Ernesto Costa, and Terence Soule, editors, *Genetic Programming*, volume 3003 of *Lecture Notes in Computer Science*, pages 389–398. Springer Berlin / Heidelberg, 2004.

[14] J. Tavares and F. B. Pereira. Automatic design of ant algorithms with grammatical evolution. In *Proceedings of the 15th European conference on Genetic programming*, 2012.

Is the Meta-EA a Viable Optimization Method?

Sean Luke
Department of Computer Science
George Mason University
Washington, DC
sean@cs.gmu.edu

AKM Khaled Ahsan Talukder
Department of Computer Science
George Mason University
Washington, DC
atalukde@cs.gmu.edu

ABSTRACT

Meta-evolutionary algorithms have long been proposed as an approach to automatically discover good parameter settings to use in later optimization runs. In this paper we instead ask whether a meta-evolutionary algorithm makes sense as an optimizer in its own right. That is, we're not interested in the resulting parameter settings, but only in the final result. As it so happens, this use of meta-EAs make sense in the context of large numbers of parallel runs, particularly in massive distributed scenarios. A primary issue facing meta-EAs is the stochastic nature of the meta-level fitness function. We consider whether this poses a challenge to establishing a gradient in the meta-level search space, and to what degree multiple tests are helpful in smoothing the noise. We discuss the nature of the meta-level search space and its impact on local optima, then examine the degree to which exploitation can be applied. We find that meta-EAs perform well as optimizers, and very surprisingly that they do best with only a single test. More exploitation appears to reduce performance, but only slightly.

Categories and Subject Descriptors

I.2.m [**Artificial Intelligence**]: Miscellaneous—*Evolutionary Computation*

Keywords

Meta-Evolutionary Algorithms; Parallel Algorithms

1. INTRODUCTION

A meta-optimization algorithm iteratively improves the parameter settings of a second optimization algorithm, assessesing their quality or fitness by using them to run the second algorithm and examining its performance. The method is related to the general family of hyperheuristics [31]. Since the 1970s [8, 27] this idea has been proposed as a mechanism for automating the tuning process of evolutionary algorithms and other metaheuristics.

GECCO'13, July 6–10, 2013, Amsterdam, The Netherlands.

The traditional reasoning behind meta-optimization goes like this: an experimenter typically performs up-front parameter tuning of an optimization algorithm, and this is essentially a crude form of hill-climbing. Why not take him out of the loop? If one were going to do a large number of optimization runs with the same parameters, it might be helpful to automatically find good parameter settings first.

This philosophy leads to the notion of meta-optimization with the goal of finding an optimal set of *parameter settings* to put to use at some point in the future. We think this is the primary impetus behind much meta-optimization research. But there is an alternative reason to perform meta-optimization: as an optimization algorithm in its own right. Here, the goal would be to directly find an optimal *solution.* At first glance one might be bewildered by this: after all, meta-optimization is extraordinarily expensive. Surely all those cycles could be put to better use? But we think this second use of meta-optimization in fact has a definite niche in massively parallel optimization.

In this paper we study meta-optimization with the goal of an optimal solution. In our study, both levels of optimization are EAs (hence a *meta-EA*), and we use them in the context of optimizing thousands of runs on a supercomputer cluster.

Scenario. Imagine that an experimenter has a difficult-to-optimize function and has decided to tackle it by doing some (very large) N runs and returning the best result. This is hardly an uncommon scenario: depending on the problem it is often a preferred approach over other forms of parallelism, such as island models or distributed evaluation.

In fact, there are some parallel architectures for which the maximum of N runs is the most attractive option. One example: Parabon Computing produces a variant of the ECJ evolutionary toolkit [26] called *Origin,* which runs on their *Frontier* massively parallel platform.[1] Parabon contracts with organizations to install software on their PCs which makes them available as computational units to Frontier when not being used otherwise. This makes up to millions of PCs available as computational units. But because of security concerns inherent in contracting for PCs, jobs running on Frontier PCs are sandboxed and are not permitted to communicate with other PCs. This lack of intercommunication means that island models do communication through the master server, which is unattractive because communication to the master is slow. Furthermore, this slow communication with the master server means that distributed evaluation is infeasible unless the evaluation time is very high per-individual, or we

[1] http://www.parabon.com/

are doing opportunistic evolution [34]. But Frontier is an excellent target for massively parallel runs.

If the experimenter has settled on doing N runs, he must decide two things. First, he must determine how many *evaluations* each of these runs will perform. Second, he must decide on the details of his optimization procedure: he may have to choose an optimization procedure among many; or just select parameter settings for a procedure if he has already decided on which one to use.

The first decision (number of evaluations) is something that the experimenter must make himself: he cannot delegate it to an optimizer. But the second decision (algorithmic details) can be delegated. If he is fortunate, the experimenter may already have a general idea of the good range for parameter settings through previous experience or the suggestions of the research literature. But he is unlikely to know the *precise* best parameter settings for this particular problem. He can take a stab at some parameter setting for all N runs, or perhaps try random settings within the range. In any case, it would be helpful if the algorithm optimized to good-performing settings mid-run, given the high cost of the run itself.

Let us consider using a meta-EA to optimize these run settings. We divide the N total runs into G generations of P runs each. We create a population of P individuals consisting of parameter settings, and test them on parallel machines. We set the fitness of an individual to the best-so-far fitness from a run using its parameters. We use an evolutionary algorithm to produce a second generation of P individuals, and repeat up to G times.

The primary challenge this approach faces is the stochasticity of the fitness assessment. Parameter settings are not assigned a deterministic fitness, but rather a fitness based on the vagaries of the underlying evolutionary algorithm which used that parameter setting. The high stochasticity of evolutionary algorithms leads to a high degree of noise in the meta-EA's fitness function, which in turn can make it difficult for the meta-EA to establish a gradient to optimize. The obvious way to deal with this is to assess each parameter setting using some T number of tests and taking the mean or median best-of-run performance as its fitness. As T increases, the noise ideally reduces, but at the high cost of eating into the optimization: after all, the total budget is $N = T \times G \times P$. Either G or P, or both, must be reduced if $T > 1$. If T is prohibitively high, more intelligent statistical methods may be used to reduce the total number of tests [33].

It is also not clear whether, ignoring noise, the meta-level parameter-setting fitness landscape is complex. Will a hill-climber suffice? Is the space complex enough to require a nontrivial global optimization algorithm, and if so, what should be the parameters for *that* algorithm? Is it, so to speak, "turtles all the way down"?

2. PREVIOUS WORK

The history of parameter-setting in evolutionary algorithms is a very long one and has garnered a large amount of literature [15]. Because of its importance, the question of whether an parameter setting could be *automated* has been provoking the research community for several decades, at least since the study of adaptive or self-adaptive parameter tuning in the first evolution strategies.

The earliest investigations into *meta-level* parameter optimization were probably [8, 27]. However, these methods didn't use an evolutionary algorithm per se at the meta level, but rather a kind of pattern-learning technique similar to that of [4]. Later this general idea of meta-level control of optimization was extended to the notion of the meta-EA: an evolutionary algorithm to optimize one or more other evolutionary algorithms [16, 18].

Meta-evolutionary algorithms are related to the family of *hyperheuristics* [10, 13, 31] The difference between the two is soft. While meta-EAs focus on optimizing parameters to an evolutionary algorithm, hyperheuristics instead usually try to select from a set of prespecified algorithms, along with optimizing their parameters.

The existing meta-optimization literature is largely concentrated on finding the optimal parameter settings for the underlying optimization algorithm, for example [25, 29, 32]. There is debate as to whether this is an effective method. In [9], it was reported that the parameters discovered can be unimpressive. However [22] reported substantial and consistent performance improvements in parameter settings for a variety of (non-EA) algorithms.

An obvious choice to test a meta-optimization algorithm is a massively parallel model, as the problem's inherent properties demand it. Early examples of parallel meta-EAs include [1, 2, 23], which essentially describe a master-slave model with asynchronous evolution where the primary goal of the investigation is to discover optimal parameter settings to achieve "maximum convergence velocity". There are also a number of implementations of parallel models focusing on different aspects of meta-optimization. For example, in [7] the main goal was to find the optimal parameter settings for the One-Max problem to compare with expected theoretical results. In [3], the authors investigated how parallel hyperheuristics (rather than meta-EAs) could be utilized to find an algorithm along with its optimal parameters to solve difficult numerical optimization problems. Similar analyses may be found in [28]. In our work we presume a fixed budget, but [5] has examined how to perform meta-optimization with a flexible budget.

The parameter-level fitness landscape of a meta-EA is noisy. However inferring the shape of the parameter landscape is critical to successful meta-optimization. Investigations into the stochastic parameter landscapes may be found in [17]. In [21], the authors build a gaussian process model to deal with stochasticity. In this paper we examine using multiple tests to filter noise, a notion further examined in [33].

3. METHOD

Our basic approach is a straightforward meta-EA applied in a parallel setting. A meta-EA has two levels of evolutionary algorithms. At the *meta level*, individuals are parameter settings. To test a meta-individual, we run some T *lower level* evolutionary runs using that individual's parameter settings. We then extract the T best-fitness-of-run results from each run and set the fitness of the meta-individual to their mean. Though we use the mean of the best-fitness-of-run results as fitness values at the meta level, this is not how we track the performance of the meta-level algorithm. For that, we are interested in the best result discovered so far by *any* lower-level evolutionary run.

The meta-EA is parallelized on a computer cluster using S = 128 slave processors and one master processor. The master runs the meta-level evolutionary algorithm. To test a meta-individual a single time, we assign a slave processor to run a lower-level evolutionary algorithm using its parameters.

Thus to assess the fitness of a meta-level individual, slave processors are employed T times in total. The evolutionary computation system we used was ECJ [26].

Though we applied various evolutionary methods at the lower-level, we always used a variant of the $(\mu + \lambda)$ evolutionary strategy at the meta-level, as follows. After fitness assessment, the fittest μ individuals were directly copied to the next generation. The remainder of the population was then filled with $P - \mu$ children, each produced by uniformly randomly selecting among the μ elites, then applying mutation. Though the population size varied in size (due to T), we kept the fraction of μ roughly constant by setting $\mu = \max(\lfloor P/8 \rfloor, 1)$, except in Experiment 3. Since the meta-level fitness function was noisy, elites were always re-assessed for fitness at each generation.

Much of the complexity of a meta-EA lies in how it represents meta-individuals. In our experiments, meta-level genomes were fixed-length vectors of parameter settings, where each parameter was of one of the following types:

- *Floating-point values.* For example, the parameter "mutation probability" might have values from 0.0 to 1.0. Values were initialized randomly within legal bounds. Mutation occurred with a per-gene probability of 0.25, using Gaussian convolution with $\sigma = 0.25$ except where indicated. The algorithm repeatedly tried to find a convolution which would result in a value within bounds.
- *Ordered integer values.* For example, the parameter "number of generations" might have values from 1 to 64. Values were initialized randomly within legal bounds. Mutation occurred with a per-gene probability of 0.25, using an integer random walk of probability w. The random walk was a loop: each iteration either 1 or -1 was added to the gene value, and then with probability $1 - w$ the loop was exited.
- *Ordered set values.* These were strings with a specific order among them. For example, the parameter "population size" might have values of "32", "64", "128", "256", or "512". These values were treated as ordered integer values, namely 0, 1, 2, 3, and 4 respectively.
- *Unordered set values.* These were strings with no order among them. For example, the parameter "crossover type" might have values of "one-point", "two-point", and "uniform". These values were treated as integers (in this example, 0, 1, 2), and were initialized randomly within legal bounds (0–2). Mutation occurred with a per-gene probability of 0.25, and simply randomized the gene value. Boolean values were considered unordered sets consisting of the strings "true" and "false".

4. BENCHMARK PROBLEMS

To examine the generality of the technique across various optimization methods, we tested it on three different kinds of evolutionary algorithms (GA, ES, and DE) at the lower-level, each using a different objective function.

The objective functions were chosen for three qualities. First, they are reasonably difficult, so as to make multiple parallel runs reasonable. In no case would we expect the optimum to be discovered. Second, like many objective functions, they are sensitive to different evolutionary parameter settings, making them amenable to meta-evolution. And third but far from least, they are fairly fast. This third characteristic was crucial given the 14.2 million evolutionary runs performed. The three benchmark problems were:

A Genetic Algorithm (GA) applied to the Leading-Ones Blocks Problem. Leading-Ones Blocks is a stairstep variation of the Leading-Ones problem with tunable difficulty. Leading-Ones Blocks takes a boolean vector, and a tuning parameter b, then counts the number of successive strings of 1s of length b in the vector, starting from the beginning, until the first 0 is encountered. If b is small the problem is trivial, but if b is large the problem can be prohibitively difficult. We may formally define Leading-Ones Blocks as:

$$f(x_1, ..., x_n) = \left\lfloor \frac{1}{b} \sum_{i=1}^{n} \prod_{j=1}^{i} x_j \right\rfloor$$

We set the genome size to 400, and b to 20, meaning that the optimal fitness was 50 (higher is better).

The genetic algorithm worked as follows. Initial individuals were generated randomly, rejecting duplicate individuals. After fitness evaluation, given a population size P and a proportion $0.0 \le e \le 1.0$ of elites, some number $\lfloor e \times P \rfloor$ of elites were directly copied to the next generation. The remainder of the next generation population was filled by iteratively selecting parents in pairs, crossing them over, and mutating them. An evolutionary run lasted for 65,536 fitness evaluations.

At the meta-level, we optimized the following parameters:

- *Population Size (P): 32, 64, 128, 256, 512, 1024, 2048* Since the evaluations were fixed, this in turn would affect the generation size (2048, 1024, 512, 256, 128, 64, or 32 respectively). At the meta-level, these values were treated as ordered set values.
- *Elitism Proportion (e): [0.0...1.0]*
- *Tournament Size (t): [1.0...20.0]* Note that this is a floating-point number. With probability $t - \lfloor t \rfloor$ we select with tournament size $\lceil t \rceil$, else with tournament size $\lfloor t \rfloor$.
- *Per-gene Mutation Probability: [0.0...1.0]* Mutation was done by flipping the gene's bit.
- *Crossover Type: one-point, two-point, uniform* One-point crossover, two-point crossover, or uniform crossover with a per-gene probability c. At the meta-level, these were unordered set values.
- *Per-gene Crossover Probability: [0.0...0.5]* This was only relevant to uniform crossover.

A (μ, λ) Evolution Strategy (ES) applied to the Rotated Griewank Problem. The *non*-rotated Griewank problem is floating-point and ranges with $x_i \in [-600, 600]$:

$$f(x_1, ..., x_n) = 1 + \frac{1}{4000}\left(\sum_{i=1}^{n} x_i^2\right) + \prod_{i=1}^{n} \cos\left(\frac{x_i}{\sqrt{i}}\right)$$

Let $\vec{x} = \langle x_1, ..., x_n \rangle$. We rotated Griewank with a rotation matrix M, generated randomly once per lower-level evolutionary run, which defined a revised fitness function $r(\vec{x}) = f(M\vec{x})$. M was produced using Gram-Schmidt orthonormalization, following the procedure described in [19]. The genome size was 100. Lower fitness values were better.

The (μ, λ) ES worked as follows. We defined a population size λ and a specified proportion $0.0 \le m \le 1.0$ of parents, where μ was then set to $\max(\lfloor m\lambda \rfloor, 1)$. Initial individuals were created by randomizing each gene uniformly from [0.0...1.0], not permitting duplicate individuals. After fitness evaluation, we gathered the μ best members of the population as parents. Each parent generated λ/μ children via mutation, which were then added to the next-generation population. An evolutionary run would last for no more than 16,384 fitness evaluations.

At the meta-level, we optimized the following parameters:

- *Population Size (λ): 2, 4, 8, 16, 32, 64, 128, 256, 512, 1024, 2048* Since the evaluations were fixed, this in turn would affect the generation size (8192, 4096, 2048, 1024, 512, 256, 128, 64, 32, 16, or 8 respectively). At the meta-level, these were ordered set values.
- *m (μ as a Proportion of λ): [0.0...0.5]*
- *Per-gene Mutation Probability: [0.0...1.0]*
- *Mutation Type: Reset, Gaussian, Polynomial* At the meta-level, these were unordered set values. Reset mutation simply randomized the gene. Gaussian mutation added random gaussian noise of standard deviation σ to the gene until the result. Polynomial mutation applied random noise to the gene under the polynomial distribution of index value i. Two variants of polynomial mutation were used as described next.
- *Alternative Polynomial Version: true, false* We know of at least four different versions of polynomial mutation in the literature. ECJ provides two of these variants, which it calls the "standard" variant, as defined in [11], and the "alternative" variant, as defined in [12]. At the meta-level, these were unordered set values.
- *Polynomial Distribution Index (i): [0...40] (integers)* This was only relevant to polynomial mutation.
- *Gaussian Standard Deviation (σ): [0.0...1.0]* This was only relevant to gaussian mutation.

Both Gaussian and Polynomial Mutation can produce results outside of valid gene bounds. In both cases we would retry up to 100 times to find a valid in-bounds mutation, after which the gene would remain un-mutated.

Differential Evolution (DE) applied to the Lennard-Jones Problem. Here the goal is to find the global minimum of a potential energy function over a cluster of atoms which depends on their relative positions [36]. The potential energy E of a Lennard-Jones cluster is calculated as:

$$E = 4\epsilon \sum_i \sum_{j>i} \left[\left(\frac{\sigma}{r_{ij}}\right)^{12} - \left(\frac{\sigma}{r_{ij}}\right)^{6} \right]$$

r_{ij} is the Euclidian distance between atoms i and j respectively. We define atom positions in three dimensions, and so $r_{ij} = \sqrt{(i_x - j_x)^2 + (i_y - j_y)^2 + (i_z - j_z)^2}$. The genome has three numbers (x, y, z) for each atom, hence $i_x, i_y, i_z, j_x, j_y, j_z, k_x, k_y, k_z, \ldots$ etc. Like much of the literature [6], we set the ϵ and σ constants to 1.

We performed standard Differential Evolution (DE) with three common DE breeding operators: DE/rand/1/bin, DE/best/1/bin, and DE/rand/1/either-or. Differential Evolution is too complex a technique to describe fully here: instead, consult [30]. We deviated from DE tradition in one respect: we guaranteed that the operators produced children within valid gene bounds. We did this by trying up to 5 times to generate a valid child; otherwise we simply copied its primary parent instead. An evolutionary run would last for no more than 65,536 fitness evaluations.

At the meta-level, we optimized the following parameters:

- *Population Size (P): 32, 64, 128, 256, 512, 1024, 2048* Since the evaluations were fixed, this in turn would affect the generation size (2048, 1024, 512, 256, 128, 64, or 32 respectively). At the meta-level, these were ordered set values.
- *Breeding Operator: DE/rand/1/bin, DE/best/1/bin, DE/rand/1/either-or* At the meta-level, these were unordered set values.
- *Per-gene DE Crossover Probability (C_r): [0.0...1.0]* A standard DE parameter.
- *DE Mutation Scale Factor (FNOISE): [0.0...0.05]* A standard DE parameter used only by the DE/best/1/bin operator. FNOISE's range is so small that we modified its meta-level standard deviation, setting $\sigma = 0.001$.
- *DE Either-Or Probability (PF): [0.0...1.0]* This is a standard DE parameter used only by the DE/rand/1/either-or operator.

5. FIRST EXPERIMENT

We began by asking: how many tests per meta-level fitness evaluation are worthwhile? Let us assume that we had S processors at our disposal and were permitted to run each for some E evolutionary runs, for a total budget of $N = E \times S$ runs. In this arrangement, if we applied a single test per meta-level fitness evaluation, our population size P would be constrained to be $\ge S$. We chose the obvious setting ($P = S = 128$).

To examine the effect of tests, we must decide how increasing tests will impact on the budget. Tests could reduce the population size, or the number of generations, or both. For this experiment we chose to reduce the population size. Thus given T tests per meta-level fitness evaluation, $P \times T = S$ (= 128). This also determines the number of generations G in our meta-level algorithm, specifically, $G = E$.

We tried 1, 2, 4, 8, and 16 tests, with corresponding meta-level population sizes of 128, 64, 32, 16, and 8, and μ values of 16, 8, 4, 2, and 1 respectively. We performed 50 independent runs of each test size, and also performed 50 runs of entirely random search at the meta-level, where the parameter settings tried were randomly chosen from among their legal gene values. Random search provided our lower bound for comparison. Finally, we identified the single most successful parameter setting discovered from all meta-level runs, and performed 50 meta-level runs using just that parameter setting. This setting provided us with an approximate upper-bound. In all cases, meta-level runs lasted 64 generations, totaling 8192 fitness evaluations (hence lower-level evolutionary runs) per meta-level run.

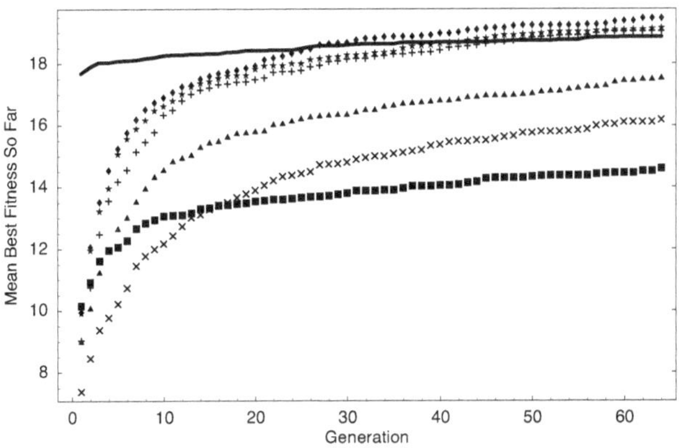

Figure 1: Meta-level mean best-fitness-so-far for the Leading-Ones-Blocks problem (GA, maximization). ♦ 1 Test ★ 2 Tests + 4 Tests ▲ 8 Tests × 16 Tests ■ Random Search — Best Discovered Setting

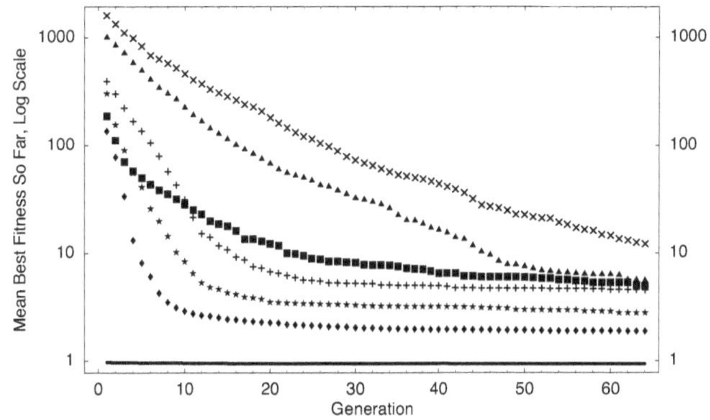

Figure 2: Meta-level mean best-fitness-so-far for the Rotated Griewank problem (ES, minimization). Log_{10} scale shown. ♦ 1 Test ★ 2 Tests + 4 Tests ▲ 8 Tests × 16 Tests ■ Random Search — Best Discovered Setting

	1 Test	*2 Tests*	*4 Tests*	*8 Tests*	*16 Tests*
> Random	**~1.0**	**~1.0**	**~1.0**	**0.9999**	**0.9999**
< Best	**0.9996**(>)	0.9399(>)	0.6979(>)	**0.9993**	**~1.0**
< 1 Test	——	0.8271	0.9524	**0.9999**	**~1.0**

Table 1: P-values of differences between methods on the GA Leading Ones Blocks problem. Bold values indicate statistically significant results. > means "is better than" and < means "is worse than". (<) means that the result is not better (the default) but in fact worse. Likewise (>) means that the result is not worse (the default) but in fact better.

	1 Test	*2 Tests*	*4 Tests*	*8 Tests*	*16 Tests*
> Random	**~1.0**	**~1.0**	**0.9999**	**0.9999**(<)	0.5774(<)
< Best	**~1.0**	**~1.0**	**~1.0**	**~1.0**	**~1.0**
< 1 Test	——	0.9979	**0.9999**	**0.9999**	**~1.0**

Table 2: P-values of differences between methods on the ES Rotated Griewank problem. Bold values indicate statistically significant results. > means "is better than" and < means "is worse than". (<) means that the result is not better (the default) but in fact worse. Likewise (>) means that the result is not worse (the default) but in fact better.

Results. We verified statistical significance using a nonparametric ranked two-tailed T-test. Experiments in the paper total to 67 comparisons, so we used a Bonferroni correction, adjusting the p value from 0.95 to 0.99925.

The results are shown in Figures 1 through 3. Additionally, Tables 1 through 3 show the p-values for comparison between various numbers of tests and three different runs: "Random" (random search), "Best" (the fittest parameter settings discovered in any run), and "1 Test" (since 1-Test was the best performing). As can be seen from the tables, comparisons generally produced quite high p-values. In many cases the p-value was "~1.0", meaning that the two compared distributions were disjoint when their samples were ranked.

Conclusions. How many tests was a good trade-off between noisy fitness and population size? The answer was very surprising: **1 test!** More tests yielded worse performance.

With a few exceptions, the multi-test runs were bounded between random runs and the best-of-all-runs parameter setting. In all cases, 1-, 2-, and 4-test arrangements proved statistically significantly superior to doing random runs. This confirmed our hypothesis that if you didn't really know what settings to use for a difficult problem, a meta-EA would probably be a better option to simply trying arbitrary settings within reasonable ranges.

In fact in several cases 1- and 2-test arrangements were statistically superior to the best-of-all-runs setting! This seemingly impossible event is easily explained: the best-of-all-runs setting is strongly susceptible to being a random outlier, and in practice it may actually underperform other top-ranked settings in the average. We believe that this provides more evidence for the claim made in [9]: that doing meta-evolution to produce an optimal parameter setting (as opposed to a final result) may not produce particularly good results due to such lucky outliers.

6. SECOND EXPERIMENT

In the first experiment, we examined trading off tests for population size. Another approach is to trade off tests for generations. However, if the meta-level evolutionary algorithm is slow to converge to a decent set of parameters, we imagined that cutting generations short could have a detrimental impact on the meta-evolutionary algorithm.

To test this, we once again used $S = 128$ processors, and fixed the population size $P = S = 128$. We varied the number of meta-level tests T per fitness assessment to 1, 2, 4, 8, and 16. To maintain a constant number of evaluations, we also varied the meta-level number of generations G to 64, 32, 16, 8, and 4 respectively. Thus more tests per individual resulted in fewer generations at the meta-level.

We restricted ourselves to the DE Lennard-Jones problem. While we included random search as a lower bound for reference, we did not include an upper bound, as we had already compared with it: we were more interested in how fewer generations impacted on performance. Besides P, T,

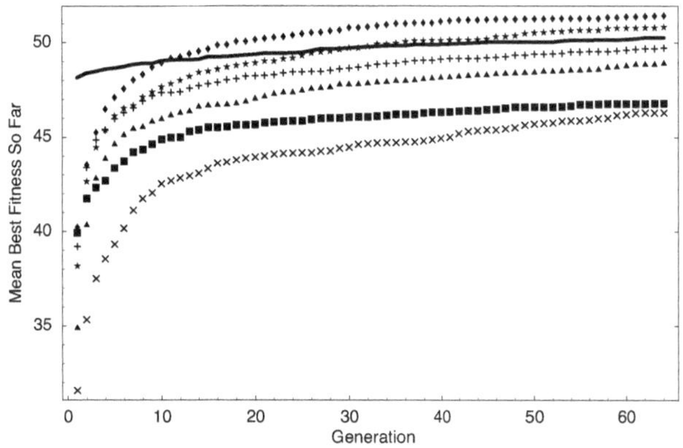

Figure 3: **Meta-level mean best-fitness-so-far for the Lennard-Jones problem (DE, maximization). ♦ 1 Test ★ 2 Tests + 4 Tests ▲ 8 Tests × 16 Tests ■ Random Search — Best Discovered Setting**

	1 Test	*2 Tests*	*4 Tests*	*8 Tests*	*16 Tests*
> Random	**~1.0**	**~1.0**	**0.9999**	**0.9999**(<)	0.9544(<)
< Best	**0.9999(>)**	**0.9990(>)**	0.275	0.9006	**~1.0**
< 1 Test	——	**0.9997**	**0.9999**	**0.9999**	**~1.0**

Table 3: P-values of differences between methods on the DE Lennard-Jones problem. Bold values indicate statistically significant results. > means "is better than" and < means "is worse than". (<) means that the result is not better (the default) but in fact worse. Likewise (>) means that the result is not worse (the default) but in fact better.

and G, we used the same meta-level parameters and number of runs as in the first experiment.

Results. We again verified statistical significance using a nonparametric ranked two-tailed T-test with a Bonferroni correction, adjusting the p value to 0.99925. The results are shown in Figure 4 and summarized in Table 4.

Conclusions. Once again, results worsened monotonically with increasing tests. In all cases, T tests was statistically significantly better than $> 2T$ tests, and to random search.[2] Again we have no reason to suggest using anything other than a single test!

7. A DIGRESSION

At this point it's worth discussing the nature of the space of parameters in an evolutionary algorithm and its impact on local optima. In the parameter optimization literature, the classical presentation of parameters has been as a vector of values. But in fact these parameters may be better thought of as a *tree*. The reason for this is because the presence of a certain parameter A will demand the existence of another

[2]We informally let this experiment run to twice as many generations to see if this effect diminished. It does. The results were still monotonic, but the p-values dropped below significance except for 1 > 4 and all > Random Search. We think this suggests that the benefits of the meta-EA might lie largely in the first 32 or so generations.

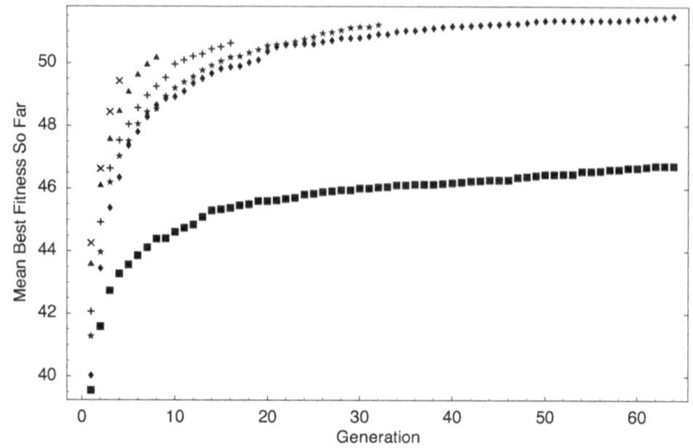

Figure 4: Meta-level mean best-fitness-so-far for the Lennard-Jones problem (DE, maximization) with generations traded for tests. ♦ 1 Test ★ 2 Tests + 4 Tests ▲ 8 Tests × 16 Tests ■ Random Search

	2 Tests	*4 Tests*	*8 Tests*	*16 Tests*	*Random Search*
< 1 Test	0.9157	**0.9999**	**0.9999**	**0.9999**	**~1.0**
< 2 Tests	——	0.9775	**0.9999**	**0.9999**	**~1.0**
< 4 Tests	——	——	0.9430	**0.9999**	**~1.0**
< 8 Tests	——	——	——	0.9807	**~1.0**
< 16 Tests	——	——	——	——	**0.9999**

Table 4: P-values of differences between different numbers of tests on the DE Lennard-Jones problem. Bold values indicate statistically significant results. < means "is worse than".

parameter B; or the absence of A will make B moot. For example, there's no reason to have a "per-gene crossover probability" parameter unless the "crossover type" parameter has been set to "uniform". Additionally, the same parameter may have different values in different contexts in the same evolutionary algorithm. This is particularly common when parameters define the breeding pipeline for the algorithm. For example, consider a pipeline where tournament selection feeds into polynomial mutation, which provides one child for uniform crossover, the other child being provided by *another* tournament selection (with a different tournament size). Such a parameter tree might look like:

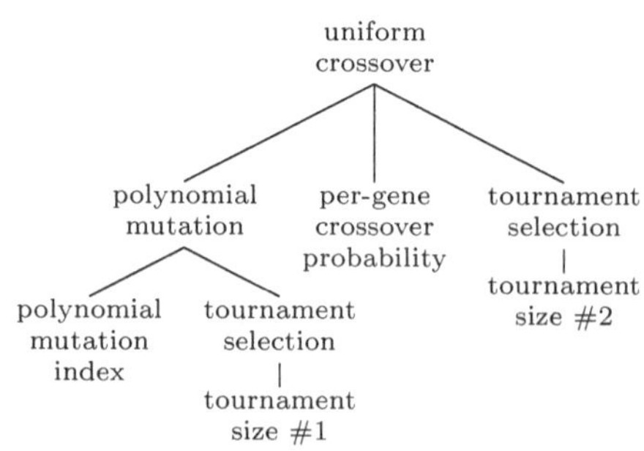

This tree structure is, we believe, a major reason why many evolutionary computation implementations define their parameters using a hierarchical rather than flat namespace.

We will not here attempt the daunting task of evolving tree-structured parameters, but we bring this up to point out that, when flattened into vectors, the naturally tree-

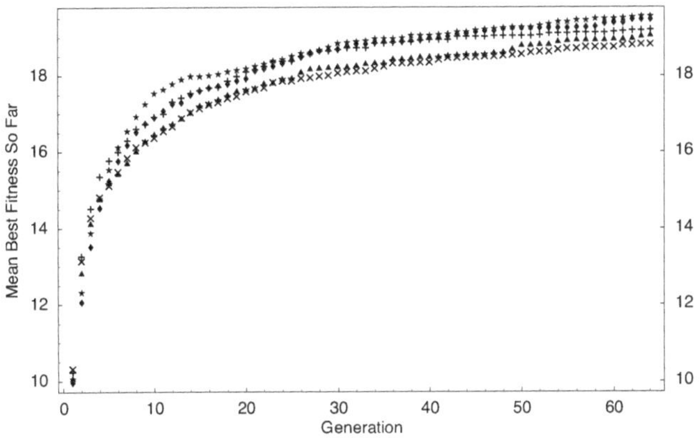

Figure 5: Meta-level mean best-fitness-so-far for the Leading Ones Blocks Problem (GA, maximization), with various levels of μ. ♦ $\mu = 16$ ★ $\mu = 8$ + $\mu = 4$ ▲ $\mu = 2$ × $\mu = 1$ Note that "♦ $\mu = 16$" is the same as "♦ 1 Test" from Figure 1.

	$\mu = 8$	$\mu = 4$	$\mu = 2$	$\mu = 1$
< $\mu = 16$	0.7424(>)	0.9799	**0.9998**	**0.9993**
< $\mu = 8$	——	0.7085	0.9925	0.9708
< $\mu = 4$	——	——	0.9490	0.8135
< $\mu = 2$	——	——	——	0.4470

Table 5: P-values of differences between different levels of meta-level μ on the GA Leading Ones Blocks problem. Bold values indicate statistically significant results. < means "is worse than". (>) means that the result is not worse (the default) but is in fact better. Note that "$\mu = 16$" is the same as "1 Test" from Table 1.

structured parameter space produces genes with a very high degree of epistasis, as some parameters are only active if other parameter are set to the right values.[3]

Our benchmark problems exhibited this several times: the GA's per-gene mutation probability; ES's alternative polynomial version, polynomial distribution index, and gaussian standard deviation; and DE's FNOISE and PF parameters. Such epistasis is one source of "weak" local optima in the parameter space. For example, uniform mutation with the right probability setting might be globally optimal, but if the genome is saddled with a poor per-gene probability setting, one- or two-point crossover will perform better. We have observed the meta-EA getting trapped in such local optima.

8. THIRD EXPERIMENT

We know that each of the parameter spaces has *at least* a few local optima due to the high epistasis among the parameters. Further, the space is quite noisy. However we still supposed that the underlying space was fundamentally simpler in nature than the complex test functions we chose. If so, it might be susceptible to a more exploitative hill-climber than the 1-Test result, which had used a population size of 128 and $\mu = 16$. We could adjust exploitation by changing the selection pressure, or the mutation rate, or both. Because the parameter genes are heterogeneous it is not simple to vary their mutation rates in a principled fashion, but we can easily change the selection pressure, in the form of μ. We compared 1-Test at $\mu = 16$ against the same approach at $\mu = 8, 4, 2$, clear down to 1, the most exploitative. We selected the GA Leading Ones Blocks benchmark as our target problem as it had the fewest parameters (1) in epistasis.

Results. We again verified statistical significance using a nonparametric ranked two-tailed T-test with a Bonferroni correction, adjusting the p value from 0.95 to 0.99925.

The results are shown in Figure 5, and Table 5 shows the p-values for comparison between various sizes of μ.

Conclusions. We had supposed that, assuming the space was relatively simple, a more exploitative technique would perform better. But the trend seems to be the opposite: as u decreases, so does performance. This could be either due to a more complex space than we had expected, or (we think more likely) the high noise in the function. Even so, the difference is surprisingly small, and only $\mu = 16$ is statistically significantly different from $\mu = 2$ and $\mu = 1$.

9. CONCLUSIONS AND FUTURE WORK

The goal of much meta-evolutionary algorithm research has been to find optimal parameters: but we have identified a common situation, in massively parallel computing, where a meta-evolutionary algorithm is helpful to find an optimal solution directly.

One commonly assumed problem with meta-EAs is their noisy fitness functions. We tested the approach on three benchmark problems and varying numbers of tests to reduce the noise, and found that in fact no noise reduction works best. We also noted that meta-EAs have high epistasis between certain genes because of the nature of the parameter search space in modern evolutionary algorithms. This will produce certain known local optima, but despite this we presumed that the meta-EA search space is generally simpler than the underlying lower-level EA search space. Under this assumption, we tested whether a more exploitative approach might perform better, but found that in fact the opposite was true, thus suggesting that the search space may hold more surprises yet.

As future work, we hope to perform a full sweep of the meta-level search space, though we have so far found ourselves stymied by the noise and sheer number of evaluations involved. Additionally, we would like to extend our analysis of the search space to ask whether meta-meta-EAs and meta-meta-metaEAs etc. continue to face complex spaces (a question also asked, but not answered, in [24]). That is, whether the meta-EA scenario really is, to use the famous phrase, "turtles all the way down".

10. ACKNOWLEDGMENTS

This work was funded by NSF Grant 0916870.

11. REFERENCES

[1] B. Adenso-Diaz and M. Laguna. Fine-tuning of algorithms using fractional experimental designs and local search. *Oper. Res.*, 54(1):99–114, Jan. 2006.

[2] T. Bäck. Parallel optimization of evolutionary algorithms. In *PPSN*, pages 418–427, 1994.

[3] Genetic programming is the obvious way to evolve tree-structured parameters. But we are not aware of an attempt to tackle entire parameter sets with GP, though there is work in using GP to adapt new breeding operators [14, 35, 20], usually through co-evolution.

[3] M. Biazzini, B. Banhelyi, A. Montresor, and M. Jelasity. Distributed hyper-heuristics for real parameter optimization. In *GECCO*, pages 1339–1346, 2009.

[4] W. W. Bledsoe and I. Browning. Pattern recognition and reading by machine. In *Eastern Joint IRE-AIEE-ACM Computer Conference*, pages 225–232, 1959.

[5] J. Branke and J. A. Elomari. Meta-optimization for parameter tuning with a flexible computing budget. In *GECCO*, pages 1245–1252, 2012.

[6] J. Brest, S. Greiner, B. Boskovic, M. Mernik, and V. Zumer. Self-adapting control parameters in differential evolution: A comparative study on numerical benchmark problems. *IEEE Transactions on Evolutionary Computation*, 10(6):646–657, 2006.

[7] C. Candan, A. Goeffon, F. Lardeux, and F. Saubion. A dynamic island model for adaptive operator selection. In *GECCO*, pages 1253–1260, 2012.

[8] D. J. Cavicchio, Jr. *Adaptive Search Using Simulated Evolution.* PhD thesis, Computer and Communication Sciences Department, University of Michigan, 1970.

[9] J. Clune, S. Goings, B. Punch, and E. Goodman. Investigations in meta-GAs: panaceas or pipe dreams? In *GECCO*, pages 235–241, 2005.

[10] P. I. Cowling, G. Kendall, and E. Soubeiga. A hyperheuristic approach to scheduling a sales summit. In *Third International Conference on Practice and Theory of Automated Timetabling*, pages 176–190, 2001.

[11] K. Deb. *Multi-objective optimization using evolutionary algorithms.* Wiley, 2001.

[12] K. Deb and S. Agrawal. A niched-penalty approach for constraint handling in genetic algorithms. In *International Conference on Artificial Neural Networks and Genetic Algorithms (ICANNGA)*, pages 235–243, 1999.

[13] J. Denzinger, M. Fuchs, and M. Fuchs. High performance atp systems by combining several ai methods. In *International Joint Conference on Artificial Intelligence (IJCAI)*, pages 102–107, 1997.

[14] B. Edmonds. Meta-genetic programming: Co-evolving the operators of variation. *Turkish Journal of Electrical Engineering and Computer Sciences*, 9:13–29, 2001.

[15] A. Eiben, R. Hinterding, and Z. Michalewicz. Parameter control in evolutionary algorithms. *Evolutionary Computation, IEEE Transactions on*, 3(2):124–141, 1999.

[16] D. Fogel, L. Fogel, and J. Atmar. Meta-evolutionary programming. In *Asilomar Conference on Signals, Systems and Computers*, volume 1, pages 540–545, 1991.

[17] O. Francois and C. Lavergne. Design of evolutionary algorithms: A statistical perspective. *IEEE Transactions on Evolutionary Computation*, 5(2):129–148, 2001.

[18] J. Grefenstette. Optimization of control parameters for genetic algorithms. *Systems, Man and Cybernetics, IEEE Transactions on*, 16(1):122–128, 1986.

[19] N. Hansen and A. Ostermeier. Completely derandomized self-adaptation in evolution strategies. *Evolutionary Computation*, 9(2):159–195, 2001.

[20] K. Harrington, L. Spector, J. Pollack, and U.-M. O'Reilly. Autoconstructive evolution for structural problems. In *Workshop for the Automated Design of Algorithms, GECCO*, 2012.

[21] F. Hutter, H. H. Hoos, K. Leyton-Brown, and K. P. Murphy. An experimental investigation of model-based parameter optimisation: SPO and beyond. In *GECCO*, pages 271–278, 2009.

[22] F. Hutter, H. H. Hoos, K. Leyton-Brown, and T. Stützle. ParamILS: an automatic algorithm configuration framework. *J. Artif. Int. Res.*, 36(1):267–306, Sept. 2009.

[23] D. Izzo, M. Rucinski, and C. Ampatzis. Parallel global optimisation meta-heuristics using an asynchronous island-model. In *CEC*, pages 2301–2308, 2009.

[24] K. D. Jong. Parameter Setting in EAs: a 30 Year Perspective. In F. G. Lobo, C. F. Lima, and Z. Michalewicz, editors, *Parameter Setting in Evolutionary Algorithms*, pages 1–18. Springer, 2007.

[25] A. J. Keane. Genetic algorithm optimization of multi-peak problems: studies in convergence and robustness. *Artificial Intelligence in Engineering*, 9(2):75–83, 1995.

[26] S. Luke. ECJ 20: An Evolutionary Computation Library in Java. Open source software. Available at http://cs.gmu.edu/~eclab/projects/ecj/, 2012.

[27] R. Mercer and J. Sampson. Adaptive search using a reproductive metaplan. *Kybernetes*, 7:215–228, 1978.

[28] D. Ouelhadj, S. Petrovic, and E. Ozcan. A multi-level search framework for asynchronous cooperation of multiple hyper-heuristics. In *GECCO Late-Breaking Papers*, pages 2193–2196, 2009.

[29] M. E. H. Pedersen and A. J. Chipperfield. Simplifying particle swarm optimization. *Applied Soft Computing*, 10(2):618–628, 2010.

[30] K. Price, R. Storn, and J. Lampinen. *Differential Evolution: A Practical Approach to Global Optimization.* Springer, 2005.

[31] P. Ross. Hyper-heuristics. In E. K. Burke and G. Kendall, editors, *Search Methodologies*, pages 529–556. Springer, 2005.

[32] S. Smit and A. Eiben. Comparing parameter tuning methods for evolutionary algorithms. In *CEC*, pages 399–406, 2009.

[33] F. Stonedahl and S. H. Stonedahl. Heuristics for sampling repetitions in noisy landscapes with fitness caching. In *GECCO*, pages 273–280, 2010.

[34] K. Sullivan, S. Luke, C. Larock, S. Cier, and S. Armentrout. Opportunistic evolution: efficient evolutionary computation on large-scale computational grids. In *GECCO Conference Companion*, pages 2227–2232, 2008.

[35] A. Teller. Evolving programmers: The co-evolution of intelligent recombination operators. In *Advances in Genetic Programming 2*, pages 45–68, 1996.

[36] D. J. Wales and J. P. K. Doye. Global optimization by basin-hopping and the lowest energy structures of Lennard-Jones clusters containing up to 110 atoms. *Journal of Physical Chemistry A*, 101(28):5111–5116, 1997.

Novelty and Interestingness Measures for Design-space Exploration

Edgar Reehuis
Natural Computing Group
LIACS, Leiden University
Niels Bohrweg 1, 2333 CA
Leiden, The Netherlands
ereehuis@liacs.nl

Markus Olhofer
Honda Research Institute
Europe
Carl-Legien-Straße 30
63073 Offenbach/M, Germany
markus.olhofer@honda-ri.de

Michael Emmerich
Natural Computing Group
LIACS, Leiden University
Niels Bohrweg 1, 2333 CA
Leiden, The Netherlands
emmerich@liacs.nl

Bernhard Sendhoff
Honda Research Institute
Europe
Carl-Legien-Straße 30
63073 Offenbach/M, Germany
bernhard.sendhoff@honda-ri.de

Thomas Bäck
Natural Computing Group
LIACS, Leiden University
Niels Bohrweg 1, 2333 CA
Leiden, The Netherlands
baeck@liacs.nl

ABSTRACT

Measures of novelty and interestingness are frequently encountered in the context of developmental robotics, being derived from human psychology. This work addresses these measures from the viewpoint of enhancing design-space exploration in black-box optimization. We provide a unifying notational and naming scheme with the intent of facilitating comparison, implementation, and application in the domain of design optimization. Initial analysis shows a promising interestingness measure for being tried on real-world design problems.

Categories and Subject Descriptors

I.2.8 [**Computing Methodologies**]: ARTIFICIAL INTELLIGENCE—*Problem Solving, Control Methods, and Search*

Keywords

Novelty, interestingness, surrogate model, exploration measure

1. INTRODUCTION

The idea of using *novelty* and *interestingness* of possible actions or solutions as an indication of what to try or where to explore next is widespread in *neuro-control* and *reinforcement learning* [19, 20, 3, 12, 6, 14, 13, 1, 7, 10]. In lesser extent, it is being proposed for design-space exploration in *black-box optimization* [5, 18, 2, 17].

Novelty of an observation, action, or solution, is a subjective notion in the sense that it depends on *similarity* to what was encountered before, and on the *state* of the agent, approach, or model used in *determining* this similarity. Easily modeled and frequently occurring solutions quickly lose their novelty, while solutions that are subject to *noise* always remain novel [6]. For efficient learning or modeling of a solution space, those solutions are selected at each time step that improve the understanding or model of the solution space most: An *interesting* solution has sufficient (not too simple, boring) but not too extreme (beyond understandable, for instance, again, noise) novelty [20]. Thus in learning, not the most novel but the most interesting solutions are to be selected (see Fig. 1).

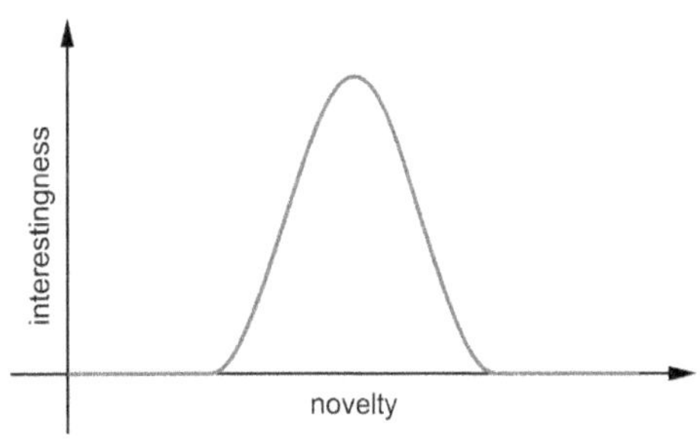

Figure 1: *Wundt's Curve.* Interestingness shown as a function of novelty. Image courtesy of Graziano et al. [6].

This paper provides an overview of novelty and interestingness expressions from the perspective of design-space exploration by unifying the expressions in notation, and proposing adjustments with this application in mind where necessary. A division is made between similarity-derived, distance-based novelty, and learning-based novelty related to fitting a surrogate model (in [6] referred to as *coherence* and *compression*, respectively). Note that the surrogate model is *not* intended here for reducing the number of used quality function evaluations, but for expressing the understanding, locally, of the quality landscape during optimization.

We aim for an exploration measure to focus on irregular areas in the search space, but eventually steer clear from regions with excessive noise. The first aspect is tested for in a preliminary experimental setup involving a low-dimensional artificial test function. A comparison is made in selecting on the exploration measures only, quality is not involved, while the reviewed measures are intended, in a later stage, to be employed as additional selection criterion in quality-based search, either in parallel to quality (e.g., [5, 18, 17]) or in an alternating fashion (e.g., [2]). Learning-based novelty should inherently focus on areas with higher variance in quality as these are more difficult to model, while distance-based novelty will only do this if supplied with a distance formulation that is derived from quality.

Following, Section 2 continues with an overview of novelty measures, and Section 3 with interestingness measures, after which the experiments are described in Section 4, of which the outcome and outlook are discussed in Section 5.

2. NOVELTY

To determine a *candidate solution*'s distinctiveness or *novelty* from the knowledge gathered on the design space during design-space exploration, an appropriate representation of the available knowledge is required such that new solutions can be compared to it. Here the notion of a candidate solution is based on an iterative search method that generates multiple candidates in each iteration, of which it selects a certain number to proceed into the next iteration. Possible representations of the available knowledge include an archive containing all sampled solutions, and a surrogate model that learns a mapping between different characteristics of a solution, for instance from the solution vector in the search space to the quality value that becomes available after evaluation.

2.1 Distance-based Novelty

In distance-based novelty a candidate solution is compared to an archive of earlier sampled solutions, and its difference to the most resembling solutions from this archive serves as novelty expression, determined with respect to a *domain-specific distance measure*. For the search spaces considered the solutions are real-valued vectors, therefore a generally-applicable distance formulation is the Euclidean distance between the solution vectors.

Sparseness

Lehman and Stanley [10] propose *sparseness* (Sp) as distance-based novelty measure: A candidate solution $\mathbf{x}$ is compared to the solutions $\mathbf{q}$ from the union of a *partial* archive S of earlier sampled solutions (that is, solutions $\mathbf{x}$ for which the quality value $f(\mathbf{x})$ was determined) and the set X of current candidate solutions excluding $\mathbf{x}$, to determine its closest k neighbors based on a domain-specific distance measure $\mathrm{d}(\mathbf{x}, \mathbf{q})$,

$$\operatorname*{arg\,min}_{\{\mathbf{q}_1,\ldots,\mathbf{q}_k\} \subseteq Q} \sum_{i=1}^{k} \mathrm{d}(\mathbf{x}, \mathbf{q}_i), \tag{1}$$

$$Q = \{\mathbf{q} \mid (\mathbf{q}, f(\mathbf{q})) \in S\} \cup X \setminus \{\mathbf{x}\}. \tag{2}$$

The sparseness of $\mathbf{x}$ is then taken as the average distance to these closest k solutions,

$$\mathrm{Sp}(\mathbf{x}) = \frac{1}{k} \sum_{i=1}^{k} \mathrm{d}(\mathbf{x}, \mathbf{q}_i). \tag{3}$$

Settings for the following parameters are required [10]:

- Number of closest solutions k: a value of 15 is used by Lehman and Stanley for varying problems;
- Dynamic archive-inclusion threshold $\mathrm{Sp}_{\mathrm{min}}$: only solutions with sparseness that exceeds this threshold are added to the archive. After some initial setting (we use 1.0), $\mathrm{Sp}_{\mathrm{min}}$ is lowered by 5% if $\frac{1}{100}$-part of the sampling budget was used and no solutions were added; it is increased by 20% if $\frac{1}{100}$-part of the sampling budget was used and more than 4 solutions were added;
- Each sampled solution has an unconditional 0.1% chance to be added to the archive.

Uniqueness

Seeking to reduce the complexity and the number of parameters involved, we reformulate sparseness as the *uniqueness* (Un) of a solution, that is, the minimum distance occurring to a solution $\mathbf{q}$ from an archive S containing *all* sampled solutions (also used by Hester and Stone [7]),

$$\mathrm{Un}(\mathbf{x}) = \min_{\mathbf{q}, (\mathbf{q}, f(\mathbf{q})) \in S} \mathrm{d}(\mathbf{x}, \mathbf{q}). \tag{4}$$

In expressing uniqueness there is no difference in novelty score in case the *closest solution* $\mathbf{q}$ has no similar counterparts in the archive, compared to when the closest solution is part of a group of similar archived solutions. However, as all sampled solutions are added to the archive, this effect is of less consequence than it would be in a sparseness scheme with $k = 1$ as the chance for a solution of being included in the archive there depends heavily on the moment during the search that it is generated. Furthermore, the unconditional archive leads to a higher computational load than the partial archive in sparseness, but the archive size is of course bounded by the number of allowed to be sampled solutions.

2.2 Learning-based Novelty

In learning-based novelty the error that a surrogate model makes or is likely to make in its prediction for a candidate solution serves as novelty expression [5, 14, 3]. This way the distinctiveness from available knowledge is represented as the *generalization performance* that the surrogate model trained on the available knowledge has in approximating the to-be-learned mapping for an unseen solution.

Prediction Error

For a surrogate model that approximates a mapping from solution vectors $\mathbf{x}$ to quality-function values $f(\mathbf{x})$, the *prediction error* (PE) is calculated as the absolute difference between the model's predicted quality value $\hat{f}(\mathbf{x})$ and the actual outcome $f(\mathbf{x})$ of evaluating $\mathbf{x}$ by the quality function,

$$\mathrm{PE}(\mathbf{x}) = \left| \hat{f}(\mathbf{x}) - f(\mathbf{x}) \right|. \tag{5}$$

Dispersion in Predictions

Since PE depends on the local variation in the outcome of the quality function (i.e., its ruggedness) and on the spatial

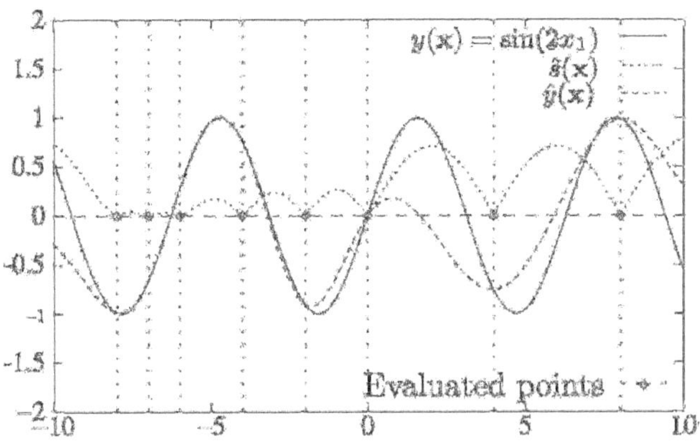

Figure 2: *Predictive Variance.* Quality function $y(\mathbf{x})$, predictive mean $\hat{y}(\mathbf{x})$, and predictive variance $\mathrm{PV}(\mathbf{x}) = \hat{s}^2(\mathbf{x})$ for the one-dimensional function $y(\mathbf{x}) = \sin(2x_1)$. Predictive variance depends on the spatial distribution of the sample points. Image courtesy of Emmerich [4].

distribution of the sampled solutions used in training the surrogate model, PE can be estimated by training an ensemble of multiple surrogate models [11] and measuring the *dispersion in predictions* (DP) for a candidate solution [17, 7]. DP is assumed to provide a similar ordering between candidate solutions as ranking them on their actual PE would, without the requirement of evaluating candidate solutions on quality beforehand; formally, for any two solutions $\mathbf{x}_1, \mathbf{x}_2$ it is assumed that

$$\mathrm{PE}(\mathbf{x}_1) < \mathrm{PE}(\mathbf{x}_2) \Rightarrow \mathrm{DP}(\mathbf{x}_1) < \mathrm{DP}(\mathbf{x}_2). \quad (6)$$

For calculating DP we make use of the *interquartile range* (IQR, the difference between the third and first quartile of the values, which is a robust statistic in the sense that it is not prone to outliers) between the quality value predictions of the different models,

$$\mathrm{DP}(\mathbf{x}) = \mathrm{IQR}(\hat{f}_1(\mathbf{x}), \ldots, \hat{f}_{\dim(\hat{\mathbf{f}})}(\mathbf{x})), \quad (7)$$

where $\dim(\hat{\mathbf{f}})$ equals the number of surrogate models used in parallel. DP requires surrogate models with potentially differing outcomes, either a combination of different modeling techniques or multiple instances of a technique that may vary in prediction outcome when differently initialized in presence of limited training data.

Predictive Variance

In using *Gaussian Process modeling* (GP) and *Kriging* methods for surrogate modeling, next to the predicted value $\hat{f}(\mathbf{x})$ (*predictive mean*) an estimate of the associated prediction error formulated as *predictive variance* (PV) is readily available for a point $\mathbf{x}$ [15, 9],

$$\mathrm{PV}(\mathbf{x}) = \sigma^2(\mathbf{x}) \text{ [GP]} \mathrel{\hat{=}} s^2(\mathbf{x}) = \mathrm{MSE}(\mathbf{x}) \text{ [Kriging]}, \quad (8)$$

assuming the actual quality value $f(\mathbf{x})$ to be a realization of $\mathcal{N}\left(\hat{f}(\mathbf{x}), \sqrt{\mathrm{PV}(\mathbf{x})}\right)$.

Schaul et al. [18] present PV as a criterion for design-space exploration[1], indirectly, through showing a direct relationship from PV to what they term *expected information gain*,

$$\Psi(\mathbf{x}) = \frac{1}{2}\log \mathrm{PV}(\mathbf{x}) - \frac{1}{2}\log \sigma^2_{\text{noise}}, \quad (9)$$

where the noise variance σ^2_{noise} [15] is constant, and thus holds that $\mathrm{PV}(\mathbf{x}_1) < \mathrm{PV}(\mathbf{x}_2) \Leftrightarrow \Psi(\mathbf{x}_1) < \Psi(\mathbf{x}_2)$ for any two solutions $\mathbf{x}_1, \mathbf{x}_2$.

Although PV depends on the ruggedness of the quality landscape, *relatively* PV depends only on the distribution of the sample points used in training because of the assumption that this ruggedness is uniform in each region of the input space (*stationarity assumption*), see Fig. 2. PV could be adjusted to depend on local ruggedness, like PE and DP, by using a *non-stationary* variant of GP or Kriging [22], or by re-training the surrogate for each solution $\mathbf{x}$ for which PV is to be assessed using its closest neighbors only from the available training data.

3. INTERESTINGNESS

The learning-based novelty of a solution is expressed as the prediction error in that point made by a surrogate model approximating the mapping of solution vectors to, e.g., the quality-function landscape. In selecting on learning-based novelty, solutions with maximum error are promoted. However, should notoriously hard regions exist in the design space that are effectively impossible to model, e.g., because of non-stationary noise or high non-stationary uncertainty, these are ideally detected and avoided.

Instead of directly selecting on the prediction error that the latest state of the surrogate model gave rise to, we can compare the modeling error at different moments in time during the learning process. The *interestingness* of a solution is formulated as the *learning progress* in the region that the solution lies in, serving as a way of omitting regions that cannot be modeled, that is, in which the surrogate model's performance does not improve over time. In selecting on interestingness those solutions are picked that improve or are expected to improve the surrogate model's approximation of the to-be-learned mapping most by including them in model training, after sampling them (i.e., evaluating them on quality).

3.1 Interestingness Measures

The interestingness measures are all based on *determining* or *estimating* the learning progress that a candidate solution will induce *after* including it in model training. In defining the interestingness measures, the following notation will be used:

- t is the current position in time; time is viewed as passing *discretely*, each iteration of the iterative search method defining a single time step and initializing at $t = 0$;
- $\mathbf{x}_{i,t}$ is a candidate solution from the set X_t of all candidate solution vectors at time t, with $1 \leq i \leq |X_t|$; X_t contains the solutions that are candidate *at* time t, *not* all previous candidates up to time t;

[1]We view PV as an expression of learning-based novelty, and not like Schaul et al. of interestingness (see Section 3), as PV does not include a(n) (implicit) mechanism for dealing with regions of the design space that, effectively, cannot be modeled.

- $\mathcal{R}(\mathbf{x}_{i,t})$ is the region in the design space in which $\mathbf{x}_{i,t}$ lies (for a definition, see Section 3.2);
- $\mathbf{s}_{j,t} = (\mathbf{x}, f(\mathbf{x}))$ is a solution sampled at time t, that is, for which quality value $f(\mathbf{x})$ was determined;
- $S_t = \bigcup_j \{\mathbf{s}_{j,t}\}$ is the set of all solutions sampled at time t; not necessarily all candidate solutions at time t are sampled: In interestingness based on PE, S_t equals $\{(\mathbf{x}_{i,t}, f(\mathbf{x}_{i,t})) \mid 1 \leq i \leq |X_t|\}$, but in using DP and PV, S_t is based on a subset of X_t;
- $\mathcal{M}(T)$ is a surrogate model that approximates the mapping from solution vectors $\mathbf{x}$ to quality values $f(\mathbf{x})$, and that is trained on tuples of solutions with quality values in the supplied training set T;
- $T_t = \bigcup_{k=0}^{t-1} S_k$ is the training data available for $\mathcal{M}$ at time t, containing tuples of all earlier sampled solutions with accompanying quality values;
- V_t is the test set for determining the performance of $\mathcal{M}$ at time t; in case of PE, V_t needs to contain tuples of solution vectors with accompanying quality values $(\mathbf{v}, f(\mathbf{v}))$, in case of DP and PV the quality component is not required and can be replaced by 0 for solutions for which it is not available;
- $\mathrm{ME}(\mathbf{v}, \mathcal{M})$ is the modeling error that $\mathcal{M}$ gives rise to for a solution $(\mathbf{v}, f(\mathbf{v})) \in V_t$ at time t; it is either determined as $\mathrm{PE}(\mathbf{v})$, or approximated as $\mathrm{DP}(\mathbf{v})$ or $\mathrm{PV}(\mathbf{v})$;
- $\mathrm{Err}(\mathcal{R}, \mathcal{M}, V)$ is the *regional error value* for region $\mathcal{R}$ that is derived from the modeling errors $\mathrm{ME}(\mathbf{v}, \mathcal{M})$ for solutions $\mathbf{v} \in V_t$; an approach for determining regional error values is given in Section 3.2.

Before we can describe the interestingness measures, a definition of the observed learning progress in a region $\mathcal{R}$ at time u is required. It is calculated as the discrete-time derivative of the regional error $\mathrm{Err}(\mathcal{R}, \mathcal{M}, V)$, taken as the decrease of the error from time $u - \tau$ to time u,

$$\mathrm{LP}(\mathcal{R}, u) = \mathrm{Err}(\mathcal{R}, \mathcal{M}(T_{u-\tau}), V_{u-\tau}) - \mathrm{Err}(\mathcal{R}, \mathcal{M}(T_u), V_u). \tag{10}$$

To determine the performance of surrogate model $\mathcal{M}(T_u)$, at each time step u the set S_u of new solutions sampled *at* time u serves as test set V_u. Now, importantly, Eq. (10) provides the learning progress observed in region $\mathcal{R}$ at time u, depending on the modeling errors observed in the candidate solutions $\mathbf{x}_{i,u}$, since $V_u = S_u \subseteq \{(\mathbf{x}_{i,u}, f(\mathbf{x}_{i,u})) \mid 1 \leq i \leq |X_u|\}$. However, in order to determine the learning progress that a solution that is candidate at time u itself *induces*, we have to be *one time step in the future*! The model has to be re-trained, now including the candidate solution, and then tested again in the same region.

Therefore, if we want to know the learning progress that a candidate solution at time t will have given rise to at time $t + 1$, we perform the following steps:

1. We are at time $t + 1$ and in the region that candidate solution $\mathbf{x}_{i,t}$ defines, we determine the previous regional error based on the modeling errors that the model at time t (taking $\tau = 1$) showed for the set S_t of solutions sampled at time t,
$$\mathrm{Err}\left(\mathcal{R}(\mathbf{x}_{i,t}), \mathcal{M}(T_t), V_t = S_t\right); \tag{11}$$
2. We then re-train the model on the union of the training set used at time t *and* the candidate solution $\mathbf{x}_{i,t}$, which needs to have been sampled, and again determine the error in region $\mathcal{R}(\mathbf{x}_{i,t})$, now defined as
$$\mathrm{Err}(\mathcal{R}(\mathbf{x}_{i,t}), \mathcal{M}(\, T_t \cup \{(\mathbf{x}_{i,t}, f(\mathbf{x}_{i,t}))\} \,), V_{t+1} = \, S_{t+1} \,), \tag{12}$$
thus, the regional error at time $t + 1$ is based on the modeling errors observed in the newly sampled solutions S_{t+1};
3. By subtracting the regional error at time t and $t + 1$ according to Eq. (10), we obtain the learning progress that $\mathbf{x}_{i,t}$ has induced.

Actual Learning Progress
Schmidhuber [19, 13, 14] follows the steps laid out above, but at time t already re-trains the model, for *each* candidate solution $\mathbf{x}_{i,t}$, thus generating $|X_t|$ temporary[2] models to be able to express each candidate's interestingness. The requirement of being one time step in the future rises from the fact that a set of newly sampled solutions S_{t+1} is to be used in evaluating the updated model. This is however circumvented by evaluating the updated model on the *same* test set again, namely the solutions sampled at time t. We term this measure *actual learning progress* (ALP),

$$\begin{aligned}\mathrm{ALP}(\mathcal{R}(\mathbf{x}_{i,t})) = \; & \underbrace{\mathrm{Err}\left(\mathcal{R}(\mathbf{x}_{i,t}), \mathcal{M}(T_t), V_t = S_t\right)}_{\text{error in region } \mathcal{R}(\mathbf{x}_{i,t}) \text{ \underline{before} training on } \mathbf{x}_{i,t}} - \\ & \underbrace{\mathrm{Err}\left(\mathcal{R}(\mathbf{x}_{i,t}), \mathcal{M}(\, T_t \cup \{(\mathbf{x}_{i,t}, f(\mathbf{x}_{i,t}))\} \,), V_{t+1} = \, S_t \,\right)}_{\text{error in region } \mathcal{R}(\mathbf{x}_{i,t}) \text{ \underline{after} training on } \mathbf{x}_{i,t}}.\end{aligned} \tag{13}$$

Previous Learning Progress
Oudeyer et al. [14, 13] propose for each region $\mathcal{R}$ to adopt the learning progress $\mathrm{LP}(\mathcal{R}, \theta_{\mathcal{R}})$ that was realized at the last time step $\theta_{\mathcal{R}}$ that a solution was sampled in that region. For the used regional error value definition (see Section 3.2) holds that at time t for all regions $\theta_{\mathcal{R}}$ equals t.

The *previous learning progress* (PLP) measure indicates for a region whether it has been possible to better approximate the to-be-learned mapping there between samplings, and should thereby detect regions in which the surrogate model does not improve. For a candidate $\mathbf{x}_{i,t}$, PLP is taken as the learning progress that *was* realized in the region $\mathcal{R}(\mathbf{x}_{i,t})$ that it defines, at time t (candidate $\mathbf{x}_{i,t}$ itself induces learning progress at time $t + 1$),

$$\begin{aligned}\mathrm{PLP}(\mathcal{R}(\mathbf{x}_{i,t})) \; = \; & \mathrm{LP}(\mathcal{R}(\mathbf{x}_{i,t}), \, t \,) = \\ & \underbrace{\mathrm{Err}\left(\mathcal{R}(\mathbf{x}_{i,t}), \mathcal{M}(T_{t-\tau}), V_{t-\tau} = S_{t-\tau}\right)}_{\text{error in region } \mathcal{R}(\mathbf{x}_{i,t}) \text{ at time \underline{$t-\tau$}}} - \\ & \underbrace{\mathrm{Err}\left(\mathcal{R}(\mathbf{x}_{i,t}), \mathcal{M}(T_t), V_t = S_t\right)}_{\text{error in region } \mathcal{R}(\mathbf{x}_{i,t}) \text{ at time \underline{t}}}.\end{aligned} \tag{14}$$

Note that in combination with the used region definition, the discriminative power between candidate solutions $\mathbf{x}_{i,t}$ is limited to the difference in regional error values that arises from the *distance* between the defined regions $\mathcal{R}(\mathbf{x}_{i,t})$.

[2]It could be argued that only $|X_t| - 1$ models are temporary as the model of the best-ranked candidate can be preserved, but this does not hold in case multiple candidates are selected to proceed to the next iteration.

Previous Competence Change

Next to promoting high learning progress, reflecting that the model is capable of improving its mapping in a certain region, Baranes and Oudeyer [1] suggest valuing *negative* learning progress as this could point at deterioration in a region in which improvement was shown earlier. That region should be focused on again for verifying the fact of (not) being able to improve there. *Previous competence change* (PCC) is like PLP based on the most-recent learning progress shown in a region, but taking the absolute value,

$$\begin{aligned}\mathrm{PCC}(\mathcal{R}(\mathbf{x}_{i,t})) &= |\mathrm{PLP}(\mathcal{R}(\mathbf{x}_{i,t}))| = \\ &|\underbrace{\mathrm{Err}\left(\mathcal{R}(\mathbf{x}_{i,t}), \mathcal{M}(T_{t-\tau}), V_{t-\tau} = S_{t-\tau}\right)}_{\text{error in region } \mathcal{R}(\mathbf{x}_{i,t}) \text{ at time } \underline{t-\tau}} - \\ &\underbrace{\mathrm{Err}\left(\mathcal{R}(\mathbf{x}_{i,t}), \mathcal{M}(T_t), V_t = S_t\right)}_{\text{error in region } \mathcal{R}(\mathbf{x}_{i,t}) \text{ at time } \underline{t}}|. \end{aligned} \quad (15)$$

Reducible Error

Yet another approach is valuing *only* negative PLP. Luciw et al. [12] aim for error maximization like in selecting on learning-based novelty directly, but account for regions that cannot be modeled by subtracting the *irreducible* error, that is, the error in the region at an earlier time step, from the novelty score, resulting in the *reducible error* (RE),

$$\begin{aligned}\mathrm{RE}(\mathcal{R}(\mathbf{x}_{i,t})) &= -\,\mathrm{PLP}(\mathcal{R}(\mathbf{x}_{i,t})) = \\ &\underbrace{\mathrm{Err}(\mathcal{R}(\mathbf{x}_{i,t}), \mathcal{M}(T_t), V_t = S_t)}_{\underline{\text{current}} \text{ error in } \mathcal{R}(\mathbf{x}_{i,t}), \text{ at time } \underline{t}} - \\ &\underbrace{\mathrm{Err}(\mathcal{R}(\mathbf{x}_{i,t}), \mathcal{M}(T_{t-\tau}), V_{t-\tau} = S_{t-\tau})}_{\underline{\text{irreducible}} \text{ error in } \mathcal{R}(\mathbf{x}_{i,t}), \text{ at time } \underline{t-\tau}}. \end{aligned} \quad (16)$$

Regions with a high error in the past but a lower error now, *exactly* those that are promoted by PLP, get a *negative* reducible error! They have shown (relatively) high learning progress, meaning that the model was improved there *already*, and therefore the model is now expected to be improved more in regions that featured *low* or *negative* learning progress.

The irreducible error has to be initialized to a low value for *new* regions that have not been visited yet for the principle to work (in the used regional error calculation this is accounted for, as regions that have not been sampled closely yet get errors near zero). A region will then feature *high reducible error* upon first sampling: High *current* error, and low past, *irreducible* error. In *unlearnable* regions the current error will remain high, making that the past error becomes high as well after repeated sampling, resulting in a *low reducible error*.

3.2 Regional Error Value

Most of the interestingness measures in Section 3.1 are intended to be calculated by comparing regional error *averages* $< \mathrm{Err}(\mathcal{R}, \mathcal{M}, V) >$ over two time *periods* [14, 1, 12], instead of regional error values $\mathrm{Err}(\mathcal{R}, \mathcal{M}, V)$ at two singular time steps. First we lay out an approach that derives regional error values from the modeling errors that occurred in the test points, then we give an overview of different ways of obtaining two distinct regional error averages.

Instead of exclusively assigning test points $\mathbf{v}$ to regions, the influence of a test point's modeling error $\mathrm{ME}(\mathbf{v}, \mathcal{M})$ is determined based on the probability density function of the

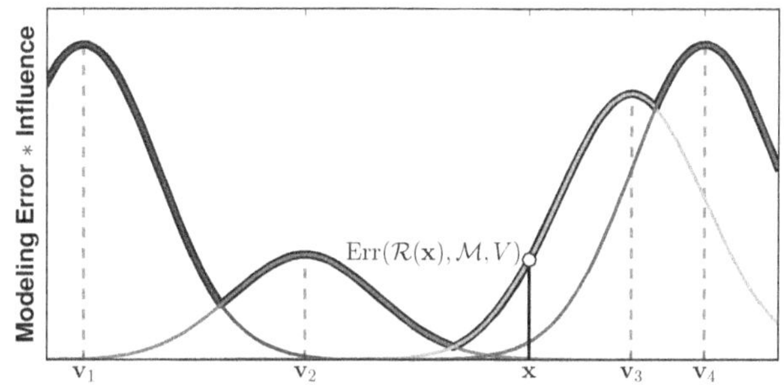

Figure 3: *Regional Error Value.* The regional error $\mathrm{Err}(\mathcal{R}(\mathbf{x}), \mathcal{M}, V)$ in region $\mathcal{R}(\mathbf{x})$, defined by the position of x, is calculated as the maximum of the modeling errors in test points $\mathbf{v}_1, \mathbf{v}_2, \mathbf{v}_3, \mathbf{v}_4$ times their normally-distributed influence.

standard normal distribution $\mathcal{N}(\mathbf{v}, \mathbf{I})$ around $\mathbf{v}$. Hence, perhaps a bit contradictory, a region $\mathcal{R}(\mathbf{x})$ is defined merely by the position of $\mathbf{x}$ that indicates the influence of the test point's modeling errors. The regional error value is calculated as the *maximum* of the modeling errors $\mathrm{ME}(\mathbf{v}, \mathcal{M})$ in points $\mathbf{v}$ from the test set V, times each point's influence (see Fig. 3),

$$\mathrm{Err}(\mathcal{R}(\mathbf{x}), \mathcal{M}, V) = \max_{\mathbf{v} \in V} \left(\mathrm{ME}(\mathbf{v}, \mathcal{M}) \cdot \mathrm{pdf}_{\mathcal{N}(\mathbf{v}, \mathbf{I})}(\mathbf{x}) \right), \quad (17)$$

where

$$\mathrm{pdf}_{\mathcal{N}(\boldsymbol{\mu}, \mathbf{I})}(\mathbf{x}) = (2\pi)^{-\frac{1}{2}|\boldsymbol{\mu}|} \cdot \exp(-\tfrac{1}{2}(\mathbf{x} - \boldsymbol{\mu})' \mathbf{I} (\mathbf{x} - \boldsymbol{\mu})). \quad (18)$$

The result is that *all* regions get an error value at each time step for which training data is available, anywhere in the search space, and if no training data is available at time u, $\mathrm{Err}(\mathcal{R},\ \mathcal{M}(T_u = \emptyset),\ V_u)$ is set to 0.

Singular Errors

The first option for obtaining regional error averages at time steps u and $u - \tau$ is simply adopting the non-averaged, singular error values at those time steps,

$$< \mathrm{Err}(\mathcal{R}, \mathcal{M}(T_u), V_u) >= \mathrm{Err}(\mathcal{R}, \mathcal{M}(T_u), V_u), \quad (19)$$

where the test sets V_u and $V_{u-\tau}$ are defined by the used interestingness measure.

Separated Averages

Oudeyer et al. [14] propose calculating the mean error over two time periods with window size w that lie τ time steps apart. The mean errors, over periods ending in time step u and in $u - \tau$, are calculated as follows,

$$< \mathrm{Err}(\mathcal{R}, \mathcal{M}(T_u), V_u) >= \frac{1}{w} \sum_{k=0}^{w-1} \mathrm{Err}(\mathcal{R}, \mathcal{M}(T_{u-k}), V_{u-k}). \quad (20)$$

Based on [14] we use $w = \min\left(15, \lfloor \frac{1}{2} \cdot u \rfloor\right)$ and $\tau = \min(25, u - w)$, where w and τ grow until the listed values are possible.

Adjacent Averages

In [1] Baranes and Oudeyer propose a simplification of this scheme by assigning the $2 \cdot w$ most recent time steps to the two error averages, taking $w = \lfloor \frac{1}{2} \cdot \min(40, u) \rfloor$ and $\tau = w$.

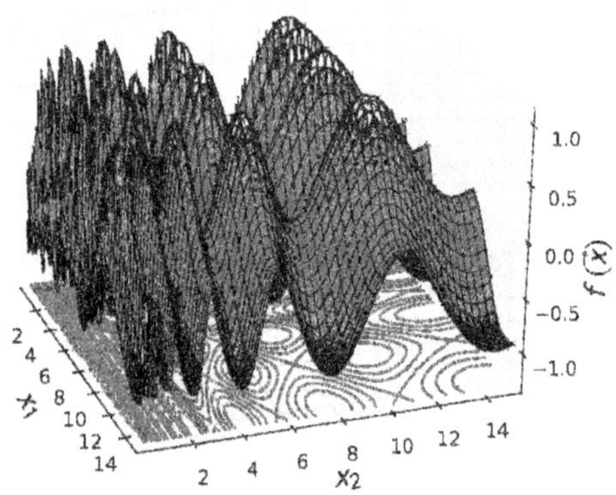

Figure 4: *Sine Non-stationary Variance.* Test function featuring exponentially increasing variance in its function landscape for input variables approaching zero.

Short-term/Long-term Memory

Luciw et al. [12] use *exponential smoothing* to obtain error averages in the form of two error *memories*, one with a slower forgetting rate (Mem_{long}) than the other ($\text{Mem}_{\text{short}}$),

$$\begin{aligned}\text{Mem}_{\text{long}}(\mathcal{R},u) &= (1-\eta_{\text{long}})\cdot\text{Mem}_{\text{long}}(\mathcal{R},u-1)+\\ &\quad \eta_{\text{long}}\cdot\text{Err}(\mathcal{R},\mathcal{M}(T_u),V_u),\\ \text{Mem}_{\text{short}}(\mathcal{R},u) &= (1-\eta_{\text{short}})\cdot\text{Mem}_{\text{short}}(\mathcal{R},u-1)+\\ &\quad \eta_{\text{short}}\cdot\text{Err}(\mathcal{R},\mathcal{M}(T_u),V_u),\end{aligned} \tag{21}$$

using $\eta_{\text{long}} = 0.1$ for forgetting slowly, and $\eta_{\text{short}} = 0.2$ for forgetting quicker. $\text{Mem}_{\text{long}}(\mathcal{R},u)$ is used as the regional error average at time $u-\tau$, and $\text{Mem}_{\text{short}}(\mathcal{R},u)$ is used as regional error average at time u.

4. EXPERIMENTS

We analyze the described novelty and interestingness measures on a two-dimensional instance of the *Sine Non-stationary Variance* (SineNSV) test function [21] (see Fig. 4),

$$f(\mathbf{x}) = -\frac{1}{n}\sum_{i=1}^{n}\sin(10\cdot\ln(x_i)). \tag{22}$$

Within the used search domain $[0.05,15]^{n=2}$ SineNSV has 181 global extrema, occurring in exponentially increasing frequency when moving toward the (0.05, 0.05)-corner.

As we want exploration to focus more on areas featuring higher variance in quality, we determine the *sample Pearson correlation coefficient* between SineNSV's distribution of extrema, and the placement of sample points in the search space that the used exploration measure gives rise to. The search space is per dimension equally divided in 10 intervals, leading to 100 boxes and hence two ordered sets of 100 values, expressing either the number of extrema or sampled points per box, between which the correlation is determined.

In the test runs we select on exploration measure only, the quality function is not (directly) involved. The used iterative search method has to be able to cope with the dynamic search landscape that changes in each iteration, therefore we use a relatively simple isotropic Evolution Strategy that has a single stepsize per individual that is self-adapted through mutation with learning rate $\tau = \frac{1}{\sqrt{2n}}$, population sizes of (2, 14), uses no recombination, and that is allowed to run for 500 generations. We initialize in the (15, 15)-corner of the search space with an initial stepsize of $14.95\cdot10^{-3}$. For constraint handling we employ a transformation function $\text{T}_{[0.05,15]}(x_i)$ [16] that reflects the object variables x_1, x_2 back at a constraint boundary, or, if the distance to the boundary is larger than 14.95, results in uniform-random placement in feasible space.

For the learning-based novelty measures we use two types of surrogate models: Feed-forward neural networks (FFNN) for PE and DP (using a *vertical* ensemble of 10 instances), and Kriging for PV. We emulate a *global* surrogate model using a *horizontal* ensemble (of, in case of DP, vertical ensembles) of *local* models trained using a sliding window of 5 generations of sample data [17], permanently retaining each 5th model. The novelty score is evaluated on all stored models and the *lowest* of the outcomes is adopted.

The FFNN have linear outputs and a hidden layer of 10 sigmoidally-activated nodes, a bias node, and are trained using improved Rprop [8] for a maximum of 10 epochs from initial connections weights in $[-0.1, 0.1]$. They are fully connected, including direct connections from input to output nodes. All data is used for training, no validation set is used. Ordinary Kriging is employed, fitted through CLF-maximization by tuning the θ_i in $[10^{-10}, 10^2]$ and the p_i in $[1, 2]$ (power-exponential multiparameter kernel), and allowing the λ to vary in $[-10, 0]$. Fitting is done using Differential Evolution with population size 50, for 50 generations, followed by a Hill Climber phase.

All techniques and measures have been implemented using the Shark Machine Learning Library v2.3.3[3].

4.1 Results

The outcome of the experiments is summarized in Fig. 5. A selection of 10 interestingness and error calculation combinations was tested for PE, and 3 combinations for DP and PV. In terms of quality evaluations, the PE-based measures used a count of 6987, DP and PV-based 999, while Sp and Un did not require quality evaluations with their solution-vector-based distance measure.

First of all, judging by the median scores, apparently none of the measures reliably focuses on regions with higher variance in quality. Furthermore, there is not one measure that significantly outperforms the others when it comes to the used performance measure. However, these scores do not fully capture the difference in sampling behavior between the different measures (see Fig. 6). Sp and Un sample everywhere with similar density, while PE, DP, and PV get stuck, even in a relatively simple part of the search space. This is surmised to be due to interaction with stepsize adaptation: Regions with higher novelty become invisible due to the limited search horizon induced by a small step size. ALP and PLP interestingness show uniform sampling as well, while PCC (basically alternation between PLP and RE) and especially RE show clear spatial separation between samples over time. Furthermore, RE based on DP does not perform worse than its PE counterparts, while only using 1/7th of the number of quality evaluations.

[3]`http://shark-project.sourceforge.net`

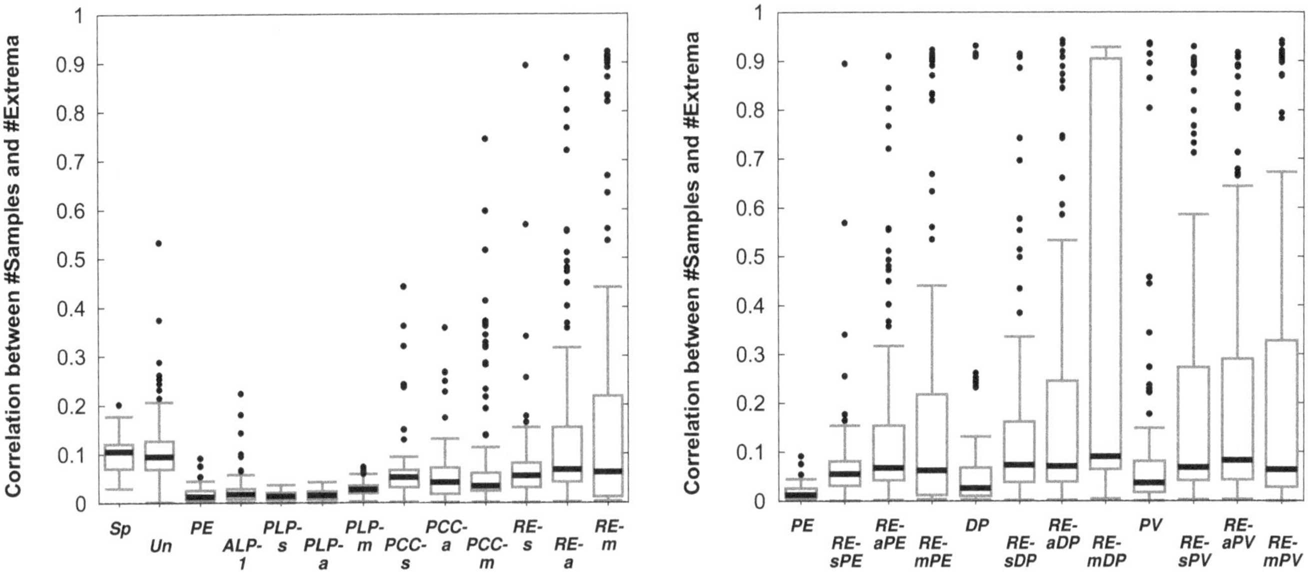

Figure 5: *Results on Sine Non-stationary Variance.* Per exploration measure, the correlation score between the distribution of the solutions sampled during a single run and the distribution of the test function's extrema is determined. The box plots summarize the scores over 100 runs per method, showing the statistics over 100 single-run scores. The *left* figure shows a comparison between distance-based novelty, PE, and interestingness based on PE. The *right* figure shows a comparison between PE, DP, and PV, and interestingness measure RE based on each of these. Used error calculation is indicated by 1 (singular), s (separated), a (adjacent), m (memory).

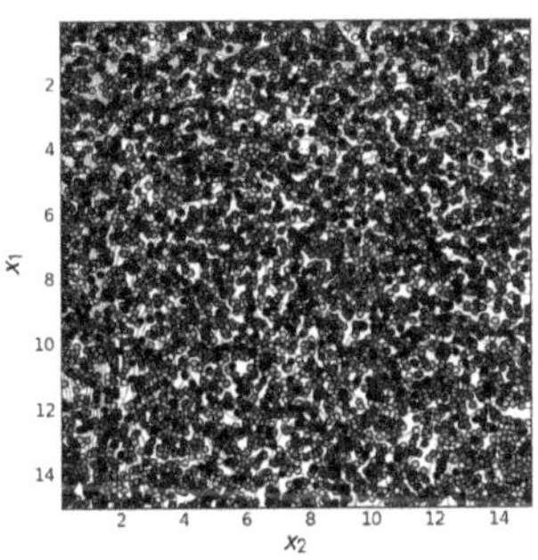

(a) Sp 0.118

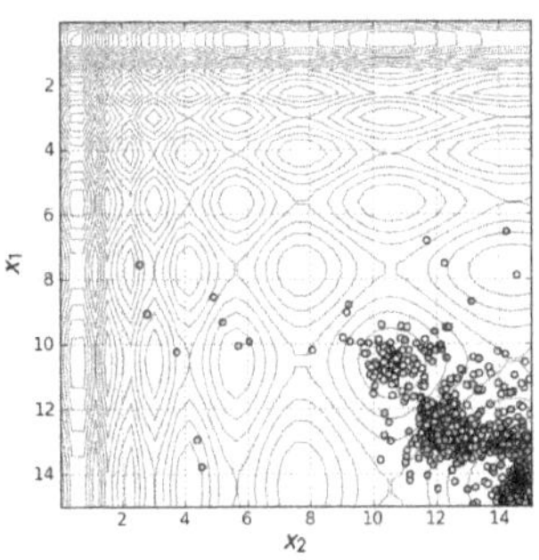

(b) PE 0.017

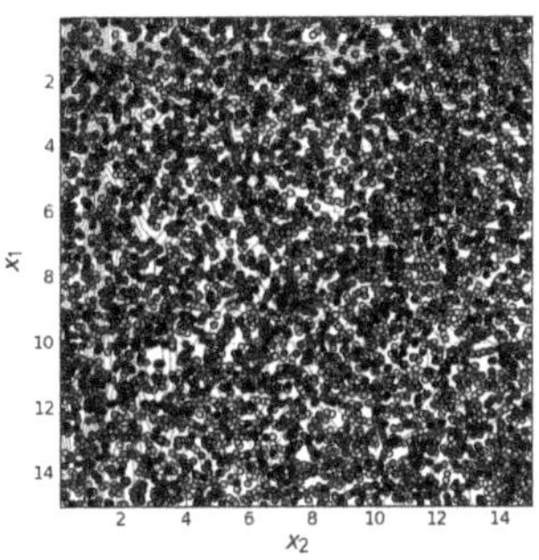

(c) ALP-1 (PE) 0.018

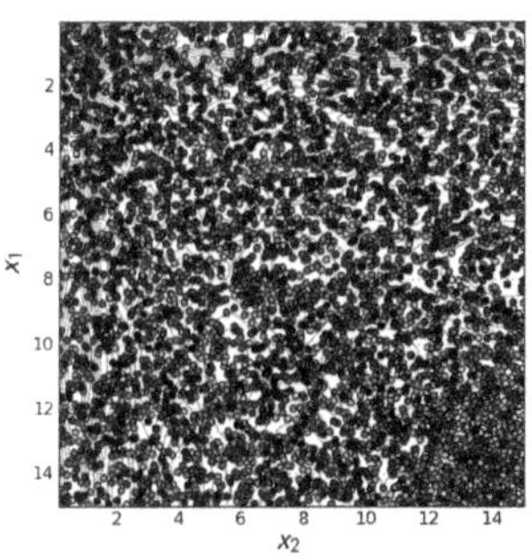

(d) PLP-m (PE) 0.030

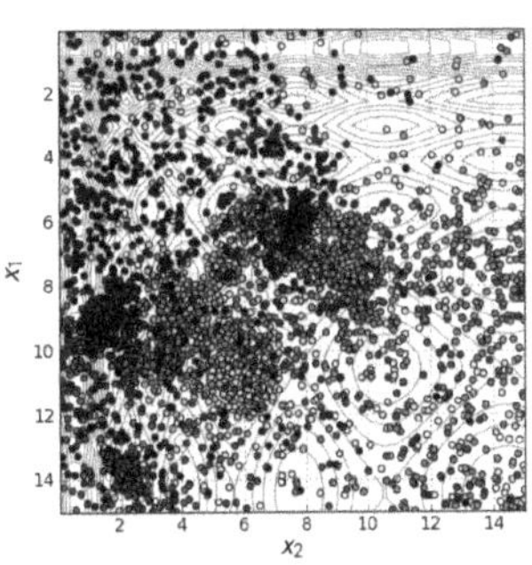

(e) PCC-s (PE) 0.051

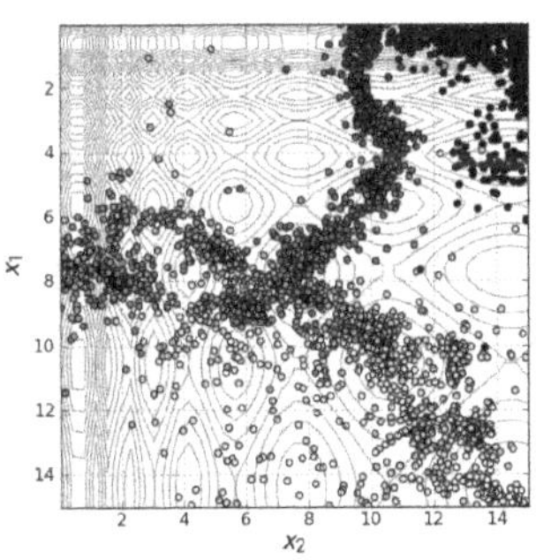

(f) RE-s (PE) 0.056

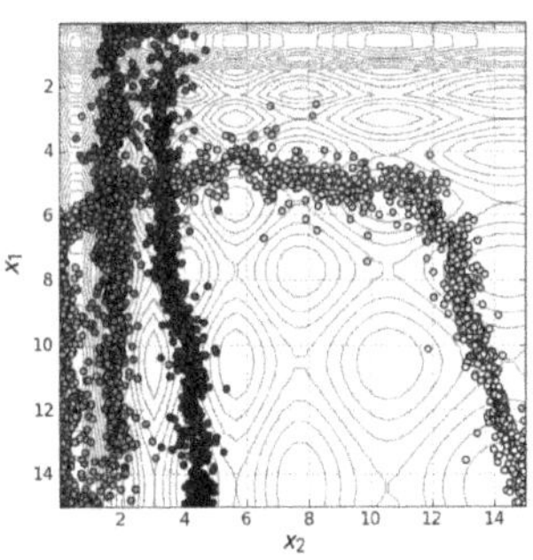

(g) RE-m (DP) 0.104

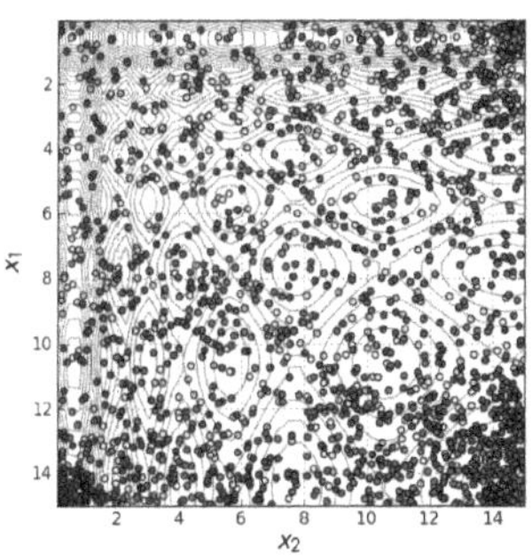

(h) RE-a (PV) 0.092

Figure 6: *Sampling Behavior on Sine Non-stationary Variance.* Per selected exploration measure, a temporal plot is shown of all solutions generated by a single run with median *correlation between samples and extrema*-score (dark: lastly sampled solutions, bright: firstly sampled solutions).

5. DISCUSSION

This paper primarily provides an overview of novelty and interestingness measures, grouped together, described in unifying notation, and adapted to be applied in design-space exploration by proposing a regional error calculation scheme. While the view on how to maximize learning progress differs strongly between authors, it turns out that the mathematical formulations of their interestingness measures are nevertheless highly related.

Secondarily, for verification and initial analysis, the described measures are tested on a low-dimensional test case of a quality landscape with exponentially increasing non-stationary variance. As performance measure the focus of the methods on areas with higher number of extrema is evaluated. In the tested setup, none of the methods is sufficient for focusing on locally higher variance. Even though areas with high variance are more difficult to model, the interestingness measures do not generate more samples there. This is either inherent to their formulation, or could be due to insufficient complexity in the used test case.

On the other hand, interestingness expressed as reducible error (RE) shows clearly directed sampling in the search space. Furthermore, RE based on dispersion in predictions (DP) performs similarly to its prediction error (PE) counterpart at much lower evaluation count.

Further study is required to determine the behavior of the different measures in the presence of non-stationary noise and in higher-dimensional test cases, including real-world design problems. They are to be integrated in quality-based search, requiring appropriate schemes of combining quality and exploration measure. Moreover, in real-world scenarios the strength of distance-based novelty is better captured through the use of a problem-specific distance measure, on which the regional error calculation could be based as well.

6. ACKNOWLEDGMENTS

The authors thank Giles Endicott for providing the used Kriging implementation.

7. REFERENCES

[1] A. Baranes and P.-Y. Oudeyer. Active Learning of Inverse Models with Intrinsically Motivated Goal Exploration in Robots. *Robotics and Autonomous Systems*, 61(1):49–73, 2013.

[2] G. Cuccu, F. Gomez, and T. Glasmachers. Novelty-Based Restarts for Evolution Strategies. In *CEC 2011*, pages 158–163. IEEE, 2011.

[3] G. Cuccu, M. Luciw, J. Schmidhuber, and F. Gomez. Intrinsically Motivated NeuroEvolution for Vision-Based Reinforcement Learning. In *ICDL 2011*. IEEE, 2011.

[4] M. Emmerich. *Single- and Multi-objective Evolutionary Design Optimization Assisted by Gaussian Random Field Metamodels*. PhD thesis, Department of Computer Science, TU Dortmund, Germany, 2005.

[5] L. Graening, N. Aulig, and M. Olhofer. Towards Directed Open-ended Search by a Novelty Guided Evolution Strategy. In R. Schaefer et al., editor, *PPSN XI, LNCS, vol. 6239*, pages 71–80. Springer, 2010.

[6] V. Graziano, T. Glasmachers, T. Schaul, L. Pape, G. Cuccu, J. Leitner, and J. Schmidhuber. Artificial curiosity for autonomous space exploration. *Acta Futura*, 4:41–51, 2011.

[7] T. Hester and P. Stone. Intrinsically Motivated Model Learning for a Developing Curious Agent. In *ICDL 2012*. IEEE, 2012.

[8] C. Igel and M. Hüsken. Empirical evaluation of the improved Rprop learning algorithms. *Neurocomputing*, 50:105–123, 2003.

[9] D. Jones, M. Schonlau, and W. Welch. Efficient Global Optimization of Expensive Black-Box Functions. *Journal of Global Optimization*, 13(4):455–492, 1998.

[10] J. Lehman and K. Stanley. Abandoning Objectives: Evolution through the Search for Novelty Alone. *Evolutionary Computation*, 19(2):189–223, 2011.

[11] D. Lim, Y. Jin, Y.-S. Ong, and B. Sendhoff. Generalizing Surrogate-Assisted Evolutionary Computation. *IEEE Transactions on Evolutionary Computation*, 14(3):329–355, 2010.

[12] M. Luciw, V. Graziano, M. Ring, and J. Schmidhuber. Artificial Curiosity with Planning for Autonomous Perceptual and Cognitive Development. In *ICDL 2011*. IEEE, 2011.

[13] P.-Y. Oudeyer and F. Kaplan. What is intrinsic motivation? A typology of computational approaches. *Frontiers in Neurorobotics*, 1(6):1–14, 2007.

[14] P.-Y. Oudeyer, F. Kaplan, and V. Hafner. Intrinsic Motivation Systems for Autonomous Mental Development. *IEEE Transactions on Evolutionary Computation*, 11(2):265–286, 2007.

[15] C. Rasmussen and C. Williams. *Gaussian Processes for Machine Learning*. MIT, 2006.

[16] E. Reehuis and T. Bäck. Mixed-Integer Evolution Strategy Using Multiobjective Selection Applied to Warehouse Design Optimization. In J. Branke et al., editor, *GECCO'10*, pages 1187–1194. ACM, 2010.

[17] E. Reehuis, J. Kruisselbrink, M. Olhofer, L. Graening, B. Sendhoff, and T. Bäck. Model-guided Evolution Strategies for Dynamically Balancing Exploration and Exploitation. In J.-K. Hao et al., editor, *Artificial Evolution 2011, EA 2011*, pages 306–317, 2011.

[18] T. Schaul, Y. Sun, D. Wierstra, F. Gomez, and J. Schmidhuber. Curiosity-driven Optimization. In *CEC 2011*, pages 1343–1349. IEEE, 2011.

[19] J. Schmidhuber. Curious Model-Building Control Systems. In *1991 International Joint Conference on Neural Networks, IJCNN'91*, pages 1458–1463. IEEE, 1991.

[20] J. Schmidhuber. What's interesting? Technical Report IDSIA-35-97, IDSIA, Lugano, Switzerland, 1997.

[21] O. Shir, M. Emmerich, and T. Bäck. Adaptive Niche Radii and Niche Shapes Approaches for Niching with the CMA-ES. *Evolutionary Computation*, 18(1):97–126, 2010.

[22] Y. Xiong, W. Chen, D. Apley, and X. Ding. A non-stationary covariance-based Kriging method for metamodelling in engineering design. *Numerical Methods in Engineering*, 71(6):733–756, 2007.

Generating Single and Multiple Cooperative Heuristics for the One Dimensional Bin Packing Problem Using a Single Node Genetic Programming Island Model

Kevin Sim
Institute for Informatics and Digital Innovation
Edinburgh Napier University
Edinburgh, Scotland, UK
k.sim@napier.ac.uk

Emma Hart
Institute for Informatics and Digital Innovation
Edinburgh Napier University
Edinburgh, Scotland, UK
e.hart@napier.ac.uk

ABSTRACT

Novel deterministic heuristics are generated using Single Node Genetic Programming for application to the One Dimensional Bin Packing Problem. First a single deterministic heuristic was evolved that minimised the total number of bins used when applied to a set of 685 training instances. Following this, a set of heuristics were evolved using a form of cooperative co-evolution that collectively minimise the number of bins used across the same set of problems. Results on an unseen test set comprising a further 685 problem instances show that the single evolved heuristic outperforms existing deterministic heuristics described in the literature. The collection of heuristics evolved by cooperative co-evolution outperforms any of the single heuristics, including the newly generated ones.

Categories and Subject Descriptors

Computing methodologies [**Machine learning**]: Machine learning algorithms

Keywords

Hyper-Heuristics; One Dimensional Bin Packing Algorithms; Single Node Genetic Programming

1. INTRODUCTION

This paper introduces a system for generating both discrete and cooperative heuristics for application to the 1D Bin Packing Problem (BPP). A compact form of Genetic Programming (GP) named Single Node Genetic Programming (SNGP) [16, 15] is used as a generative hyper-heuristic (HH) to create novel deterministic heuristics. The motivation for the research lies with the premise that selective HH can exploit the abilities of different heuristics by selecting the one that is best suited for each problem instance. Also generative HH can be used to generate single heuristics which exhibit superior performance than similar human designed heuristics and can be used to produce collections of heuristics that collectively maximise the potential of selective HH. The papers contribution is two fold. Single heuristics capable of outperforming a range of well researched deterministic heuristics are generated by combining features extracted from those heuristics. Secondly an island model[19] is adapted to use multiple SNGP implementations to generate diverse sets of heuristics which collectively outperform any of the single heuristics when used in isolation. Both approaches are trained and evaluated using equal divisions of a large set of 1370 benchmark problem instances sourced from the literature[11, 22]. The heuristics generated outperform 6 well researched human-designed deterministic heuristics in terms of both the number of optimum solutions found in the test set, and the total number of bins required to solve all instances.

2. ONE DIMENSIONAL BIN PACKING

The one dimensional bin packing problem (BPP) is a well researched NP-hard problem [13] which has been tackled using exact procedures[22], deterministic heuristics[13], biologically inspired metaheuristics [11, 18] and HH [20, 1, 21, 5, 24]. The objective is to find the optimal number of bins, $OPT(bins)$, of fixed capacity c required to accommodate a set of n items, $J = \{\omega_1 \dots \omega_n\}$ with weights $\omega_j : j \in \{1 \dots n\}$ falling in the range $1 \leq \omega_j \leq c$ whilst enforcing the constraint that the sum of weights in any bin does not exceed the bin capacity c. For any instance $OPT(bins)$ must lie between the lower and upper bounds shown in Equation 1 with the upper bound occurring when all items are greater than half the bin capacity and the lower bound achieved when the total free space summed across all bins is less than the capacity of one bin.

$$\lceil (\sum_{j=1}^{n} \omega_j) \div c \rceil \leq OPT(bins) \leq n \qquad (1)$$

Metaheuristics, such as Genetic Algorithms (GA) [11] and Ant Colony Optimisation [18], have been successfully used to solve the BPP. However they are often complex hybrid procedures incorporating both stochastic global search and highly optimised local search mechanisms tailored to the benchmark problem instances they are designed to solve. Metaheuristics have been criticised as being costly in terms of the time and the level of expertise required to develop and adapt them for real world applications.

HH, introduced in the following section, aim to address many of the issues surrounding the complexities associated with applying metaheuristics by finding "good enough - soon enough - cheap enough" [2] methods for solving problem instances of widely varying characteristics.

3. HYPER-HEURISTICS

The term hyper-heuristics (HH) first appeared in relation to combinatorial optimisation problems in [6] although the term was first coined in [9] to describe an amalgamation of artificial intelligence techniques in the domain of automated theorem proving. However, the *concept* can be traced back to the 1960's when Fisher & Thompson [12] used machine learning techniques to select combinations of simple heuristics to produce solutions to local job-shop scheduling problems. Originally described as *"heuristics to select heuristics"* [2] the field has evolved to encompass techniques including *"heuristics to generate heuristics"* using GP to create new heuristics from constituent component parts [4, 5]. All HH, no matter the approach, have the commonality that they search over a landscape defined by a set of heuristics, or their component parts, for a procedure to solve a problem rather than searching directly over the space defined by the problem itself. A more concise review can be found in [2, 3].

HH have been applied to the BPP previously not only in the 1D form investigated here but also in its 2D and 3D varieties. Ross et al.[21], developed a HH that introduced the notion of describing the state of a problem instance according to the percentage of items that fall into 4 pre-defined "natural" categories relating to item size, given as a ratio of the bin capacity. A Michigan style Learning Classifier System (LCS) was used to evolve a set of rules mapping problem states to suitable heuristics. Each iteration the chosen heuristic packs a single bin with the potential of a filler process being invoked that attempts to fill a partially filled bin further. The remaining items are then reclassified using the new problem state resulting in the application of a sequence of heuristics for solving each instance.

In [24] the authors built on the work presented in [21] by training a k-nearest neighbour classification algorithm to predict which from a set of four deterministic heuristics would perform best on a large set of benchmark problem instances. Rather than utilising the pre-determined "natural" characteristics used in [21] a genetic algorithm was used to evolve an undetermined quantity of characteristics. The characteristics evolved were expressed as variable sized ranges of the bin capacity and were shown to improve the accuracy when predicting the best heuristic for an instance.

Both HH described above can be characterised as *heuristics to select heuristics* using the classification schema set out in [4]. In contrast the approaches taken in [1, 5] fall into the class of *heuristics to generate heuristics* where GP techniques were employed as a means of automating the design of *on-line* heuristics for the BPP. In both of these studies a small number of 1D BPP benchmark instances were used to evaluate the performance of the heuristics generated. The research presented here is evaluated against a far larger set of problem instances which in conjunction with the fact that the heuristics generated are off-line heuristics means that no direct comparison can be made. In order to evaluate the approach taken here the results obtained are compared to a range of off-line heuristics sourced from the literature. It should be noted that these include a hand crafted heuristic (ADJD) created for a previous study [24] in order to address the poor performance of the other heuristics used on problem instances where the average item size is small when measured as a ratio of the bin capacity.

Heuristics are generated using a compact form of GP, described in Section 5, to evolve both single and innovatively a *set* of cooperative *off-line* heuristics which collectively cover more of the problem search space.

In [1, 5] the heuristics evolved directly decide which bin to pack an item into given the state of any partially packed bins and the characteristics of the next item presented. In contrast the heuristics evolved here indirectly pack items, one bin at a time, by means of a *side effect* of the heuristic. The result of executing a heuristic is not used explicitly to decide whether to pack an item; rather, the value returned determines whether the packing process currently running should terminate or continue. As a consequence of executing a heuristic certain terminal nodes may be invoked which may cause one more more items to be packed into the current bin; an outcome described in the literature as a "side effect".

4. BENCHMARKS

Six deterministic heuristics and five sets of benchmark problem instances were sourced from the literature and used to evaluate the heuristics evolved here. Three of the data sets totalling 1210 instances were introduced in [22] and have optimal solutions that vary from the lower bound given by Equation 1. All optimal solutions are known and have been solved since their introduction [23]. A further 2 data sets comprising 160 problem instances were taken from [11]. All but one have optimal solutions at the lower bound [14]. For the remainder of this paper the term "optimal" refers to the solutions described within these publications. The complete set of 1370 benchmark instances were split into equal sized *training* and *test* sets with the test set comprising of every 2nd instance. This ensured an even distribution of instances from each of the data sets and from each of the subsets that were generated using discrete parameter combinations. The reader is directed to the original publication for a description of how these problem instances were generated.

Six deterministic heuristics, described below, are used for comparison. All but one are off-line algorithms. The exception is the Sum of Squares (SS) algorithm [7, 8] which is designed as an on-line algorithm but used here as a deterministic off-line heuristic. All heuristics described here, are presented with each problem instance's items pre-sorted in descending order of size.

- *First Fit Descending* (FFD) packs each item into the first bin that will accommodate it. If no bin is available a new bin is opened. All bins remain open for the duration of the procedure.

- *Djang and Finch* [10] (DJD) packs items into a bin until it is at least one third full. The set of up to three items which best fills the remaining space is then found with preference given to sets with the lowest cardinality. The bin is then closed and the procedure repeats using a new bin.

- *DJD more Tuples* (DJT) [21]. DJT works as for DJD but considers sets of up to five items after the bin is filled more than one third full.

- *Adaptive DJD* (ADJD) [24] packs items into a bin until the *free space* is less than or equal to three times the average size of the remaining items. It then operates like DJD looking for the set of up to three items of lowest cardinality that best fills the remaining space.

- Best Fit Descending (BFD) works as for FFD but packs each item into the bin with the least free space which will accommodate it.

- Sum of Squares (SS) [7, 8] is an on-line bin packing heuristic which puts items into bins such as to minimise the number of bins with equal free space. It is included here as a deterministic off-line heuristic with items presented in descending order of size.

It is interesting to note that SS solves 79 of the 80 instances in Falkenauer's Triplet set when presented with the items in the order that they are published. When the order of items was shuffled randomly, SS failed to find any optimal solution for any of the 80 problem instances. When SS was applied to the 685 problem instances in the test set with the items presented in the order that they are published it finds 421 optimal solutions using 61231 bins. When items are pre-sorted in descending order of size it finds 383 optimal solutions using a total of 61369 bins. When items were shuffled randomly 100 times. SS finds on average 97 optimal solutions using an average of 63282 bins.

5. SNGP

Single Node Genetic Programming was introduced by Jackson in [16] and applied to 3 problems amenable to being solved using dynamic programming, namely 6 multiplexer, even-parity and symbolic regression. SNGP differs from the conventional GP model introduced by Koza [17] in a number of key respects.

- Each individual node may be the starting point for evaluation, not only the top most node.

- Nodes may have any number of parent nodes (including none and duplicates) allowing for network structures other than *trees* to be formed.

- The only evolutionary operator used is mutation which is employed as a hill climber with the mutation undone if no improvement is achieved.

Figure 1 shows two partial SNGP structures with any nodes not connected to the current top node omitted for clarity. The standard tree structure on the left show how the DJD heuristic could be represented using the nodes outlined in Table 1. The right side of the diagram highlights a key difference between SNGP and conventional GP; that individual nodes are permitted to have multiple parent nodes. In keeping with the terminology used in the literature each node is considered as an individual in a population. Each node can be the starting point for evaluation making each a unique heuristic. As described later, each SNGP structure contains exactly 1 of each of the available terminal nodes and a predefined number of randomly selected terminal nodes. These may be disconnected during the mutation process. When evaluating a node only it and those nodes connected recursively as child nodes need to be considered. Evaluation of the population may either be carried out by averaging the

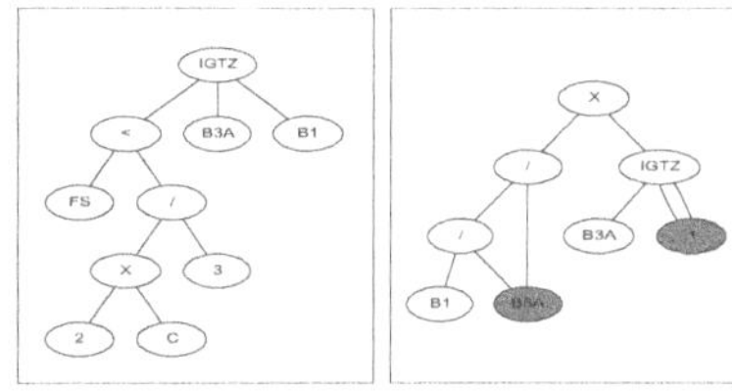

Figure 1: Two examples of partial SNGP structures with any unused nodes hidden.

fitness of all nodes or by considering the node with the best fitness in isolation. The second elitist measure is adopted here.

One of the advantages of SNGP is in its efficiency as all nodes do not need to be re-evaluated after each mutation. However this only holds for problems where the numerical output of an evolved program is used to explicitly make some decision. Jackson carried out a further investigation of SNGP in [15] where its effectiveness on problems where the solution is obtained as a *side effect* was explored. For this class of problem executing the program does not yield a result which determines an appropriate action but causes a side effect such as producing a transition between adjacent positions in a maze. Three such problems were tackled using SNGP; the Santa Fe artificial ant problem, a maze navigation task and third problem where the objective was to generate a program capable of parsing arithmetic and logical expressions. SNGP was shown to be an effective approach for tackling this class of problem. The results presented showed significant improvement to those obtained using conventional GP. SNGP operates as follows.

1. Each terminal node $T \in \{t_1, \dots t_r\}$ is added once and given an integer identification number ranging from 1 $\dots r$.

2. A number, n, of function nodes are selected at random from the set of all function nodes $F \in \{f_1, \dots, f_s\}$ and given an identification number ranging from $r+1$, $\dots r+n$. Function nodes may be duplicated or omitted from the SNGP structure.

3. Each function node has its child nodes assigned at random from the set of all nodes with a lower id to prevent any recursive loops.

4. A single mutation operator is used which selects a function node at random and reassign one of its edges to point at a node chosen randomly from the set of all nodes with a lower identification number.

5. If no node from the new mutated network proves more effective on the training problems then the network is reverted to its previous state.

Steps 4 and 5 are repeated until the stopping criteria is met which for both experiments described in Section 7 was after 500 generations. In the two HH studies, described in Section 3, the value output from the evolved program was used to directly decide where to pack the next item. The system presented here differs in that the process of evaluating a terminal node may cause items to be packed into the current bin.

In order to ensure that all heuristics terminate, even when no items are packed, a wrapper, described by Algorithm 1, is used to encompass the node being evaluated. The wrapper is responsible for determining when to open a new bin based on both the value returned by the heuristic and the state of the solution currently being constructed. The nodes selected for use in this study, described in Table 1, were identified by decomposing the heuristics outlined in Section 4.

Table 1: Nodes Used

Function Nodes	
/	Protected divide. Returns -1 if the denominator is 0 otherwise the result of dividing the first operand by the second is returned
>	Returns 1 if the first operand is greater than the second or -1 otherwise
IGTZ	Is Greater Than Zero: If the first operand evaluates as greater than zero then the result of evaluating the second operand is returned. Otherwise the result of evaluating the third operand is returned
<	Returns 1 if the first operand is less than the second or -1 otherwise
X	Returns the product of two operands
Terminal Nodes	
B1	Packs the single largest item into the current bin returning 1 if successful or -1 otherwise
B2	Packs the largest combination of exactly 2 items into the current bin returning 1 if successful or -1 otherwise
B2A	Packs the largest combination of up to 2 items into the current bin giving preference to sets of lower cardinality. Returns 1 if successful or -1 otherwise
B3A	As for B2A but considers sets of up to 3 items
B5A	As for B2A but considers sets of up to 5 items
C	Returns the bin capacity
FS	Returns the free space in the current bin
INT	Returns a constant integer value randomly initialised from $\in [-1, 1, 2, 3, 4, 5]$
W1	Packs the smallest item into the current bin returning 1 if successful or -1 otherwise

Algorithm 1 SNGP Node Wrapper

Require: $I \in \{i_1, i_2, ..., i_n\}$ {The set of items to be packed}
Require: $B = \emptyset$ {The set of bins which is initially empty}
  repeat
    add a new bin b to B
    repeat
      $I' = I$
      $result = evaluate(Node)$ {This may cause items from I to be packed into the current bin b}
    until $result < 0$ **or** $I = \emptyset$ **or** $I = I'$
    if $I = I'$ **and** $I \neq \emptyset$ **then**
      pack each remaining item in a new bin
    end if
  until $I = \emptyset$

SNGP was chosen as a methodology after trials using conventional GP were unsuccessful due to the network structures suffering from bloat. SNGP eliminates this undesirable trait due to its use of a single mutation operator. With no crossover employed there is no mechanism to allow the structures generated to grow beyond their initial size. SNGP also allows for more complex programs (using the same number of nodes) to emerge than would be possible using GP which restricts the topology of networks to tree structures.

HH search for a suitable procedure for solving a problem instance rather than directly searching for a solution. The research presented incorporates an island model with multiple instances of SNGP to generate sets of heuristics which collectively cover this search space better than any single heuristic. The system is explained in the following section.

6. ISLAND MODEL

6.1 Description

The model used here is adapted from [19] where the authors used a novel approach for evolving "interacting coadapted subcomponents". The authors distinguish their model from other approaches, such as Learning Classifier systems which the authors describe as *competitive* rather than *cooperative.* The model is evaluated on a simple bit string pattern matching task before being applied to the more complex task of evolving weights for a cascading neural network. The bit string pattern matching task involves finding a *match set* of N binary strings which match as well as possible a much larger *target set* of K bit strings. The target set is generated at random using either 2, 4 or 8 disparate masks. The objective is to generate a set of either 2, 4 or 8 matching strings. For example if 2 masks are used, ####1111 and 1111#### (where# represents a random binary value), then the objective of is to generate two strings which between them match as many of the bits in this set as possible. The model allows the number of islands to emerge as a property of the system making the technique amenable in situations where the number of cooperating subcomponents is not known *a priori.* A matching string is evaluated by averaging the number of bits in the same position with the same value over the complete target set. Islands are removed if their contribution is deemed negligible and are added when the fitness of the system stagnates.

The system described in the following section evolves a set of complimentary heuristics which cover different portions of the heuristic search space and collectively outperform any of the individual constituent heuristics.

6.2 Implementation

Figure 2 illustrates the utility of combining heuristics. Non-overlapping areas describe those instances for which a heuristic uses fewer bins than any other. Heuristic H2 gives no contribution and could be eliminated as it is fully enclosed by H1. The island model described was adapted to use multiple instances of SNGP rather than GAs. Each node in an island's network structure is evaluated by measuring its ability to cooperate with the best nodes taken from each of the the other islands. The process of co-evolving heuristics is described by Algorithm 2 and conceptualised by Figure 3. Note that only partial SNGP structures are depicted due to space restrictions. The fitness value attributed to a heuristic (node) is designed to reflect its ability to cooperate with the best nodes from each of the other islands.

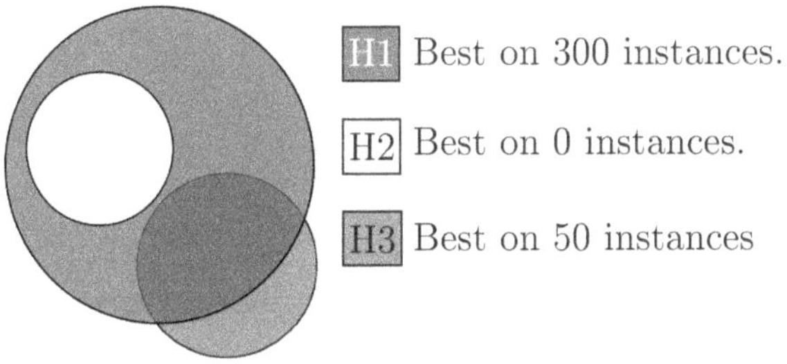

Figure 2: The Venn diagram conceptualises how a set of heuristics collectively improve upon their individual abilities to solve a set of problem instances.

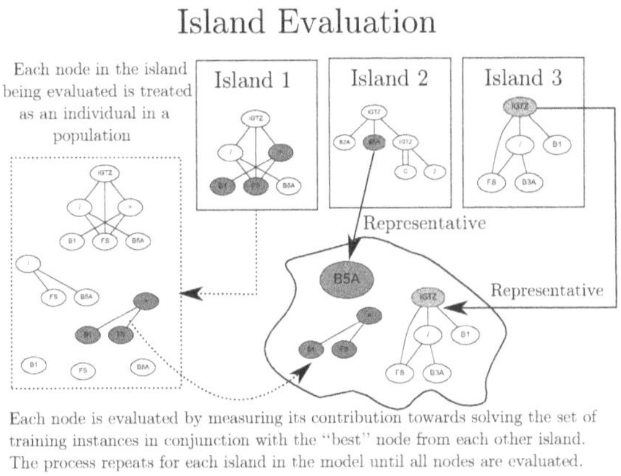

Figure 3: Measuring an Islands Contribution to the Ecosystem.

Fitness is calculated using Equations 2, 3 and 4 and is simply the sum of the number of bins fewer required by the heuristic in comparison to the best result achieved by any of the other islands best heuristics. Only problem instances where the heuristic being evaluated uses less bins than any of the other islands best heuristics are used for the fitness metric's calculation.

$$fitness_{ij} = \sum_{k=1}^{p} \Delta bins_{ijk} \tag{2}$$

where $fitness_{ij}$ is the fitness of $island_i$ $node_j$ evaluated across all training problem instances $k = 1, \ldots, p$

$$\Delta bins_{ijk} = \begin{cases} best_p - bins_{ijk} & \text{:if } bins_{ijk} < best_p \\ 0 & \text{:otherwise} \end{cases} \tag{3}$$

where $\Delta bins_{ijk}$ is the difference in the number of bins used to solve problem instance k using island i node j and the best result obtained using the other islands given by $best_p$

$$best_p = \min\left(best_{i_{bins_p}}\right) \; \forall i \in \{1, \ldots, n\} : i \neq x \tag{4}$$

where x is the id of the island being evaluated, $best_{i_{bins_p}}$ is the number of bins required to pack problem p using the node with the best fitness from island i and n is the number of islands in the ecosystem. Each island is evaluated in turn. The diagram shows how each of the six nodes from island 1 (along with their successor nodes) that constitute the 6 *heuristics* are decomposed. Each node from the island being evaluated is placed into a set of nodes containing one representative from each of the other islands. The node selected as a representative from each of the other islands is that which was awarded the highest fitness score during the previous iteration. All nodes in an island have their fitness value recalculated after the island is mutated as follows.

Algorithm 2 Island Model Pseudo-Code

```
add one Island to the empty set of Islands
bestBins = Integer.MaxValue
repeat
  if bestBins is unimproved for 20 generations then
    for all Island ∈ Islands do
      Remove Island
      if total number of bins > bestBins then
        reinstate Island
      end if
    end for
    add new island
    evaluate all nodes in new island
    set all of the new islands nodes fitnesses
  end if
  bestBins = evaluateBins()
  for all Island ∈ Islands do
    mutate(island)
    evaluate all nodes in mutated island
    set all nodes fitnesses in mutated island
    if evaluateBins() ≥ bestBins then
      revert Island to previous state before mutation
    else
      bestBins = evaluateBins()
    end if
  end for
until 500 generations have elapsed
```

- Each of the 685 training problem instances are solved using each of the the representatives from the other islands.
- If the node being evaluated is able to solve any of the same instances using fewer bins then the improvement in the number of bins is added to its fitness score.
- Only problem instances where an improvement is seen are used for determining a node's fitness.
- Once all nodes in an island have been evaluated the collective ability of the ecosystem is evaluated by measuring the total number of bins required to pack all training instances when the best node from each island is applied greedily to all training instances.
- If the total number of bins required increases from the value obtained during the last iteration then the mutation is undone and the island is reverted to its previous state.

This process then repeats with the other islands.

7. EXPERIMENTS AND RESULTS

Two sets of experiments were conducted using the set of training instances and then evaluated on the unseen test instances outlined in Section 4. Both experiments were conducted using the island model outlined previously with the first experiment restricted to using a single island.

The objective of the first experiment was to generate a single heuristic which minimised the cumulative number of bins required when applied to all 685 problems in the test set. The second experiment used the island model described previously to co-evolve a set of cooperative heuristics which when applied greedily to the test set were able to collectively outperform any of the individual constituent heuristics.

Both experiments were executed 30 times and each terminated after 500 iterations. The results presented here only show the first 250-260 generations as no improvement was observed after this point. In all cases the SNGP structures were initialised as described in Section 5 using 12 randomly selected function nodes. The software was implemented in Java and executed on a high performance cluster comprising of 18 servers each equipped with dual, quad-core cpu's with 16Gb ram running Fedora 12.

The results of the first experiments are summarised in Table 2 which shows for comparison the number of problem instances that were solved optimally by each of the six deterministic heuristics described in Section 4. The number of extra bins more than the optimal of 60257 required by each heuristic when applied to the same set of instances is also given. The table also gives the results obtained by treating each terminal node as an individual heuristics. This highlights the benefits of using SNGP to evolve heuristics which are composed of combinations of nodes used in the terminal set. It is interesting to note that by encompassing the nodes in a *wrapper* that continues to execute the heuristic until no more items are packed even the simple terminal nodes when used in isolation can outperform the human designed heuristics.

Table 2: Comparison between 6 deterministic heuristics, the terminal nodes that cause a *side effect* and the best generated heuristic (HGEN) on the test set of problem instances.

Heuristic	Optimal Solutions	Extra Bins
FFD	393	1088
DJD	356	1216
DJT	**430**	**451**
ADJD	336	679
BFD	394	1087
SS	383	1112
Terminal Node	Optimal Solutions	Extra Bins
B1	393	1088
B2	308	3250
B2A	**432**	944
B3A	303	764
B5A	332	**692**
W1	31	16761
Generated Heuristic	Optimal Solutions	Extra Bins
HGEN	**518**	**257**

Figures 4 and 5 show statistical results for single heuristic generation taken over 30 runs. The box plots illustrate how 25 of the 30 runs evolve in less than 250 generations to give the same results using both the number of instances solved and the total number of bins required as metrics. For those 5 runs where the results deviated from the best the deviation was minimal. Using a Mann-Whitney rank sum test to compare the best human designed heuristic (DJT) to the best evolved heuristic using the number of bins required as a metric offers little insight into the obvious improvement in the results due to the fact that both heuristics generate solutions which require an equal number of bins for many of the problem instances. However if Falkenauer's fitness function [11] is used as a metric then the one-tailed and two-tailed P values obtained show the results to be highly significant measuring at 5.48×10^{-5} and 10.96×10^{-5} respectively. Two of the best heuristics generated are shown in Figure 6.

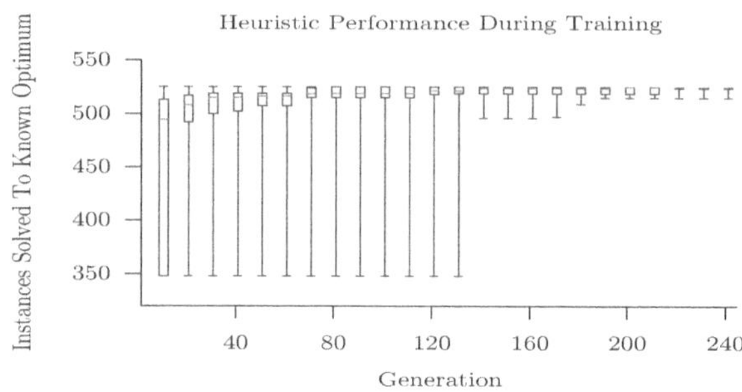

Figure 4: Single heuristic performance over 30 runs using the number of training problem instances solved using the known optimal number of bins as a metric

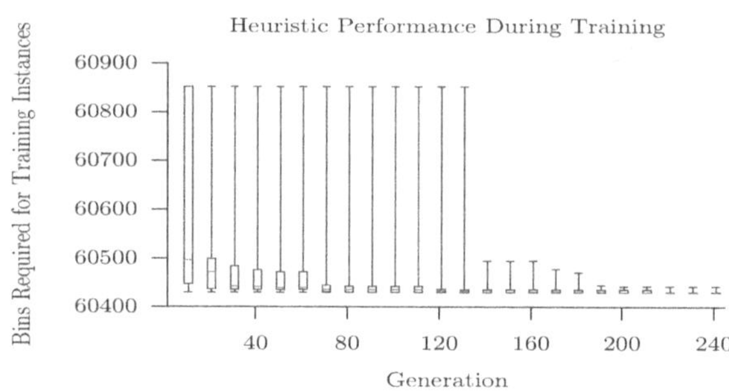

Figure 5: Single heuristic performance over 30 runs using the total number of bins required to pack all training instances as a metric

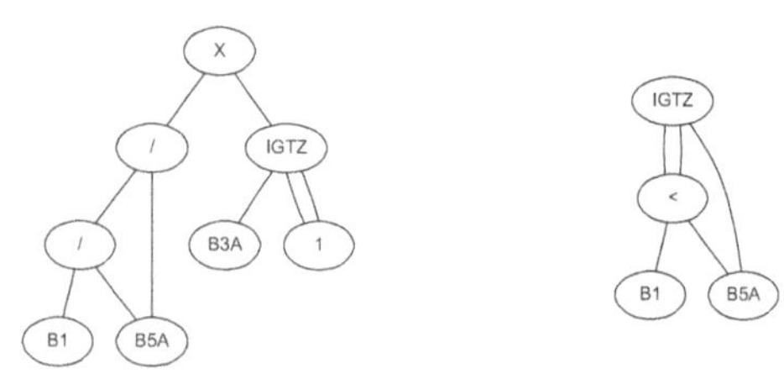

Figure 6: Two of the single heuristics evolved.

The results of the second experiment, designed to generate a set of cooperative heuristics which when applied greedily to the training problems collectively minimise the number of bins required, are shown in Table 3 The number of heuristics evolved is an emergent property of the system and is not predefined. All heuristics contribute towards the combined improvement. The number of optimal solutions found and the number of bins utilised by each new heuristic are shown. These results are contrasted with the 6 heuristics described in Section 4

Table 3: Comparison between 6 man made heuristics and 6 generated heuristics on 685 test problems

Heuristic	Optimal Solutions	Extra Bins
FFD	393	1088
DJD	356	1216
DJT	430	451
ADJD	336	679
BFD	394	1087
SS	383	1112
Combined	**544**	**186**
H1	332	692
H2	476	820
H3	465	363
H4	420	500
H5	267	850
H6	471	409
Combined	**559**	**159**

The table also shows the total number of problems solved and the number of extra bins than the optimal required by each collection of heuristics if applied in a *greedy* manner. It is clear that the evolved heuristics outperform the human designed ones in terms of both metrics used. In order to provide a further comparison, the best heuristics obtained from each experiment were used to solve a much larger set set of 15830 problem instances (available from `http://www.soc.napier.ac.uk/~cs378/bpp/`). The best single evolved heuristic used 7.8% fewer extra bins than were required by ADJD which was the best human designed heuristic on these problems. ADJD used 18541 extra bins that the known optimal of 1,362,542. The set of six cooperative heuristics collectively required 21% fewer extra bins (15070) than the optimal number than were needed when greedily applying the best of the man made heuristics.

Figures 7 and 8 show the performance of the island model during training. The darkest line at the top of Figure 7 and the bottom of Figure 8 show the results obtained if the heuristics are applied greedily to each instance. The other plots on each graph show the results obtained on the training set by each of the individual constituent heuristics evolved by the system.

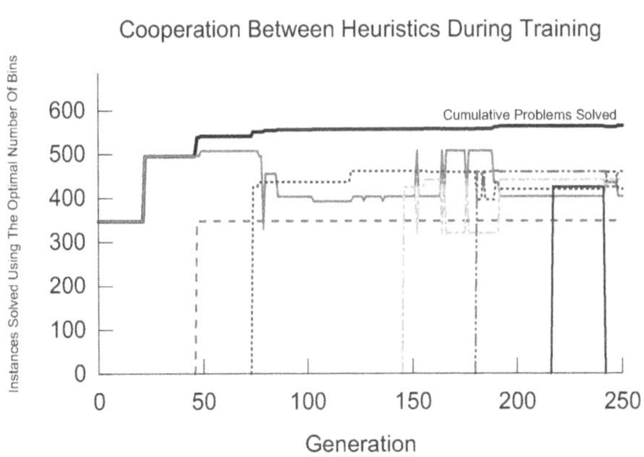

Figure 7: Number of problems solved individually and cumulatively from 685 problem instances used during training

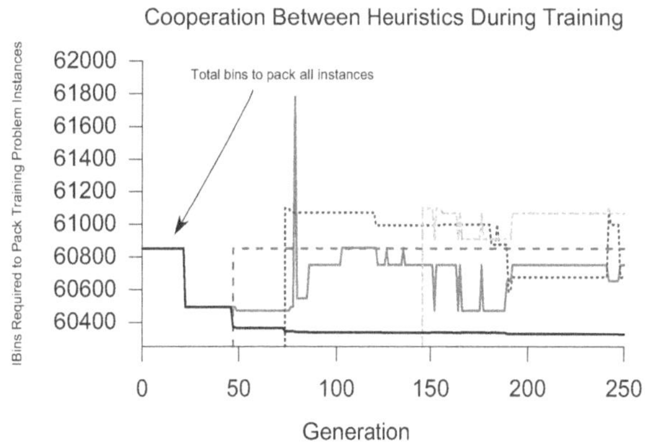

Figure 8: Number of bins used individually and collectively during training.

Figure 9 depicts one of the best sets of 6 heuristics evolved during this experiment which is the set used to obtain the results shown here. Although the results shown are for one individual run, as was the case with the first experiment nearly all of the 30 runs conducted converged to produce identical results which are omitted to increase clarity (27 out of the 30 runs conducted produced sets of heuristics which gave the same results when evaluated using both metrics).

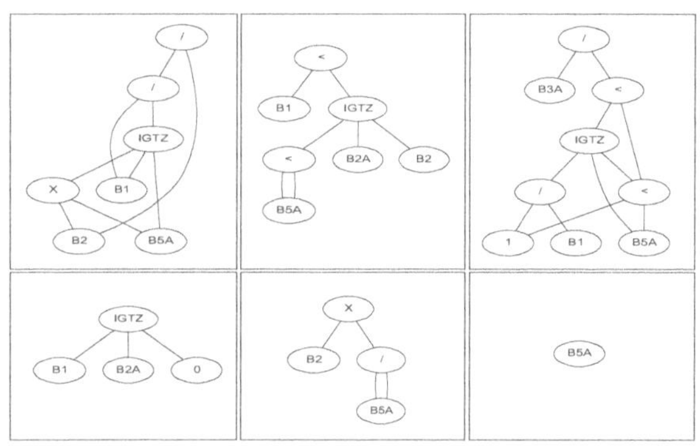

Figure 9: An evolved set of cooperative heuristics with unused nodes omitted for clarity.

8. CONCLUSIONS AND FUTURE WORK

Single heuristics were generated that outperformed a selection of well researched deterministic heuristics when used to solve a large set of 685 problem instances frequently used as benchmark instances in the literature. Furthermore an island model was added which used a form of cooperative co-evolution to generate a *set* of novel heuristics that interact cooperatively to collectively minimise the number of bins used across the same set of problem instances.

The approach is novel both in its use of SNGP to find new heuristics, and in its use of cooperative co-evolution to find sets of heuristics. The results attained highlight the utility of using HH to combine simple deterministic heuristics in order to exploit their combined strength. It is intended to expand the approach taken here by incorporating a heuristic selection strategy. This would create a HH which falls into both HH categories; "heuristics to select heuristics" and "heuristics to generate heuristics".

9. REFERENCES

[1] E. Burke, M. Hyde, and G. Kendall. Evolving bin packing heuristics with genetic programming. In *Parallel Problem Solving from Nature - PPSN IX*, volume 4193 of *Lecture Notes in Computer Science*, pages 860–869. Springer Berlin / Heidelberg, 2006.

[2] E. Burke, G. Kendall, J. Newall, E. Hart, P. Ross, and S. Schulenburg. Hyper-heuristics: An emerging direction in modern search technology. In *Handbook of Metaheuristics*, International Series in Operations Research & Management Science, chapter 16, pages 457–474. Kluwer, 2003.

[3] E. K. Burke, M. Hyde, G. Kendall, G. Ochoa, E. Özcan, and R. Qu. Hyper-heuristics: A survey of the state of the art. *School of Computer Science and Information Technology, University of Nottingham, Computer Science Technical Report No. NOTTCS-TR-SUB-0906241418-2747.*, 2010.

[4] E. K. Burke, M. Hyde, G. Kendall, G. Ochoa, E. Özcan, and J. R. Woodward. A classification of hyper-heuristic approaches. In M. Gendreau and J.-Y. Potvin, editors, *Handbook of Metaheuristics*, volume 146 of *International Series in Operations Research & Management Science*, pages 449–468. Springer US, 2010.

[5] E. K. Burke, M. R. Hyde, G. Kendall, and J. Woodward. Automating the packing heuristic design process with genetic programming. *Evol. Comput.*, 20(1):63–89, Mar. 2012.

[6] P. I. Cowling, G. Kendall, and E. Soubeiga. A hyperheuristic approach to scheduling a sales summit. In *Selected papers from the Third International Conference on Practice and Theory of Automated Timetabling III*, PATAT '00, pages 176–190. Springer-Verlag, London, UK, 2000.

[7] J. Csirik, D. S. Johnson, C. Kenyon, J. B. Orlin, P. W. Shor, and R. R. Weber. On the sum-of-squares algorithm for bin packing. *J. ACM*, 53(1):1–65, Jan. 2006.

[8] J. Csirik, D. S. Johnson, C. Kenyon, P. W. Shor, and R. R. Weber. A self organizing bin packing heuristic. In *Selected papers from the International Workshop on Algorithm Engineering and Experimentation*, ALENEX '99, pages 246–265, London, UK, UK, 1999. Springer-Verlag.

[9] J. Denzinger and M. Fuchs. High performance atp systems by combining several ai methods. In *Proceedings Fifteenth International Joint Conference on Artificial Intelligence (IJCAI 97)*, pages 102–107. Morgan Kaufmann, 1997.

[10] P. A. Djang and P. R. Finch. Solving one dimensional bin packing problems, 1998.

[11] E. Falkenauer. A hybrid grouping genetic algorithm for bin packing. *Journal of Heuristics*, 2:5–30, 1996.

[12] H. Fisher and G. L. Thompson. Probabilistic learning combinations of local job-shop scheduling rules. In J. Muth and G. L. Thompson, editors, *Industrial Scheduling*, pages 225–251. Prentice Hall, Englewood Cliffs, New Jersey, 1963.

[13] M. R. Garey and D. S. Johnson. *Computers and intractability : a guide to the theory of NP-completeness*. A Series of books in the mathematical sciences. W.H. Freeman, San Francisco, 1979.

[14] I. P. Gent. Heuristic solution of open bin packing problems. *Journal of Heuristics*, 3(4):299–304, 1998.

[15] D. Jackson. A new, node-focused model for genetic programming. In A. Moraglio, S. Silva, K. Krawiec, P. Machado, and C. Cotta, editors, *Genetic Programming*, volume 7244 of *Lecture Notes in Computer Science*, pages 49–60. Springer Berlin Heidelberg, 2012.

[16] D. Jackson. Single node genetic programming on problems with side effects. In C. Coello, V. Cutello, K. Deb, S. Forrest, G. Nicosia, and M. Pavone, editors, *Parallel Problem Solving from Nature - PPSN XII*, volume 7491 of *Lecture Notes in Computer Science*, pages 327–336. Springer Berlin Heidelberg, 2012.

[17] J. R. Koza. *Genetic Programming: On the Programming of Computers by Means of Natural Selection.* MIT Press, Cambridge, MA, USA, 1992.

[18] J. Levine and F. Ducatelle. Ant colony optimization and local search for bin packing and cutting stock problems. *The Journal of the Operational Research Society*, 55(7):705–716, 2004.

[19] M. A. Potter and K. A. De Jong. Cooperative coevolution: An architecture for evolving coadapted subcomponents. *Evol. Comput.*, 8:1–29, 2000.

[20] P. Ross, J. Marín-Blázquez, S. Schulenburg, and E. Hart. Learning a procedure that can solve hard bin-packing problems: A new ga-based approach to hyper-heuristics. In E. Cantú-Paz, J. Foster, K. Deb, L. Davis, R. Roy, U.-M. Oï£¡Reilly, H.-G. Beyer, R. Standish, G. Kendall, S. Wilson, M. Harman, J. Wegener, D. Dasgupta, M. Potter, A. Schultz, K. Dowsland, N. Jonoska, and J. Miller, editors, *Genetic and Evolutionary Computation GECCO 2003*, volume 2724 of *Lecture Notes in Computer Science*, pages 215–215. Springer Berlin / Heidelberg, 2003.

[21] P. Ross, S. Schulenburg, J. G. Marín-Blázquez, and E. Hart. Hyper-heuristics: Learning to combine simple heuristics in bin-packing problems. In *Proceedings of the Genetic and Evolutionary Computation Conference*, GECCO '02, pages 942–948, San Francisco, CA, USA, 2002. Morgan Kaufmann Publishers Inc.

[22] A. Scholl, R. Klein, and C. Jürgens. Bison: a fast hybrid procedure for exactly solving the one-dimensional bin packing problem. *Comput. Oper. Res.*, 24(7):627–645, 1997.

[23] P. Schwerin and G. Wäscher. The bin-packing problem: A problem generator and some numerical experiments with ffd packing and mtp. *International Transactions in Operational Research*, 4(5-6):377–389, 1997.

[24] K. Sim, E. Hart, and B. Paechter. A hyper-heuristic classifier for one dimensional bin packing problems: Improving classification accuracy by attribute evolution. In C. Coello, V. Cutello, K. Deb, S. Forrest, G. Nicosia, and M. Pavone, editors, *Parallel Problem Solving from Nature - PPSN XII*, volume 7492 of *Lecture Notes in Computer Science*, pages 348–357. Springer Berlin Heidelberg, 2012.

An Analysis of Post-selection in Automatic Configuration

Zi Yuan*
School of Information Systems, Singapore Management University, Singapore
zhiyuan@smu.edu.sg

Thomas Stützle
IRIDIA, CoDE, Université Libre de Bruxelles (ULB), Brussels, Belgium
stuetzle@ulb.ac.be

Marco A. Montes de Oca
Dept. of Mathematical Sciences, University of Delaware, Newark, DE, USA
mmontes@math.udel.edu

Hoong Chuin Lau
School of Information Systems, Singapore Management University, Singapore
hclau@smu.edu.sg

Mauro Birattari
IRIDIA, CoDE, Université Libre de Bruxelles (ULB), Brussels, Belgium
mbiro@ulb.ac.be

ABSTRACT

Automated algorithm configuration methods have proven to be instrumental in deriving high-performing algorithms and such methods are increasingly often used to configure evolutionary algorithms. One major challenge in devising automatic algorithm configuration techniques is to handle the inherent stochasticity in the configuration problems. This article analyses a post-selection mechanism that can also be used for this task. The central idea of the post-selection mechanism is to generate in a first phase a set of high-quality candidate algorithm configurations and then to select in a second phase from this candidate set the (statistically) best configuration. Our analysis of this mechanism indicates its high potential and suggests that it may be helpful to improve automatic algorithm configuration methods.

Categories and Subject Descriptors

[**Computing Methodologies**]: Artificial Intelligence-Search Methodologies

Keywords

Automatic Algorithm Configuration, Post-selection, Search

1. INTRODUCTION

The performance of many optimization algorithms depends on their parameter settings. Obtaining high performance requires that the parameters are appropriately set. In the last few years, it has been shown that the offline configuration of algorithm parameters can effectively been done by automatic algorithm configuration techniques such as ParamILS [15], F-Race [7] and iterated racing approaches [8], gender-based genetic algorithm [2], or model-based search approaches [12]. These aforementioned methods can be applied to general configuration tasks that include the setting of categorical, ordinal and numerical algorithm parameters. If only numerical parameters require to be determined, these methods remain applicable but they may be sidelined by methods from numerical optimization [21], estimation of distribution algorithms [17] or methods based on classical experimental designs such as CALIBRA [1]. Whatever the configuration task, these methods not only free humans from a tedious, manual trial-and-error process, but they often result in parameter configurations that substantially improve over default configurations proposed by the algorithm's designers.

In this paper, we focus on offline configuration [6], i.e. on finding a good parameter configuration before the algorithm is actually applied, a typical situation in algorithm design. The task in offline configuration is to identify an algorithm parameter configuration based on a set of training instances, such that the best-found configuration performs well on future, unseen problem instances. Offline configuration involves two sub-tasks, namely generation and evaluation. The first sub-task, the generation of candidate algorithm configurations, is typically done by search algorithms including, e.g. direct search methods [15, 8], model-based search methods [5, 14, 12], or modern continuous optimizers [21], etc. The second sub-task requires evaluating candidate algorithm configurations and at some point selecting the one with the best evaluation. This second sub-task is stochastic due to two main sources of randomness [6]: first, the algorithm to be configured may be a stochastic algorithm—this is always the case if randomized decisions are taken during the algorithm execution; second, the stochasticity due to estimating algorithm performance of candidate algorithm configurations by different training instances—these instances may be seen as drawn from some random distribution of problem instances. Most work on configuration problem fo-

*The main part of the research was carried out while Zhi Yuan was with IRIDIA, CoDE, Université Libre de Bruxelles, Brussels, Belgium.

GECCO'13, July 6–10, 2013, Amsterdam, The Netherlands.

cuses on the first sub-task, while the second sub-task is less discussed and studied.

In this paper, we extend the analysis of post-selection [21], which is a promising mechanism designed to address the second sub-task in the offline configuration, the evaluation and selection of candidate configurations. The basic idea of the post-selection mechanism is to divide the configuration process into two phases: in the initial elite qualification phase, a number of elite algorithm configurations are identified; then, in the subsequent elite selection phase, the best of these elite algorithm configurations is carefully selected using, for example, a racing method. Initial results [21] indicated that with a careful elite selection in the final phase, the post-selection mechanism allows to use a more coarse evaluation of the candidate configurations in the elite qualification phase (that is, evaluating most of the candidate configurations on less training instances) As a result, more candidate configurations may be generated and, thus, potentially better configurations may be found. In the empirical study in this paper, we extend the analysis of the post-selection method in [21] to (i) study the impact of the maximum number of algorithm runs (called configuration budget) on the con gurator performance; (ii) examine the impact of using a very small number of training instances in the elite qualification phase; (iii) consider more search methods for generating the elite candidate configurations; (iv) empirically investigate some new settings of post-selection and derive a new high-performing configurator for setting numerical parameters.

The article is structured as follows. Section 2 reviews automatic algorithm configuration and Section 3 describes the experimental setup. Section 4 studies post-selection before we compare our post-selection configurators to iterated F-Race and ParamILS in Sections 5 and 6, respectively.

2. CONFIGURATION ALGORITHMS

A *configuration algorithm* (or *configurator*) typically combines a *search* method that generates candidate algorithm configurations and a mechanism for handling stochasticity through evaluating the configurations and selecting the most promising. In this article, we examine post-selection, a recent mechanism for combining search and evaluation methods. Here, we introduce briefly the search methods and the evaluation methods we consider for comparisons.

2.1 Black-box search methods

A *search* mechanism in a configurator iteratively generates candidate algorithm configurations. In this article, the algorithm to be configured use mainly numerical parameters, in which case we refer to the configuration problem also as tuning problem. For these numerical parameters, including continuous or quasi-continuous (e.g. integer, for which rounding may be applied) parameters, we consider the following (black-box) continuous optimizers as search methods:

Bound Optimization BY Quadratic Approximation (BOBYQA). BOBY A [18] is a model-based trust-region continuous optimizer that iteratively builds and refines a quadratic model based on which the trial points are sampled.

Covariance Matrix Adaptation Evolution Strategy (CMA-ES). CMA-ES [9] is a (μ, λ)-evolutionary strategy. It iteratively samples candidate solutions from a multivariate Gaussian distribution, with a sample mean as a linear combination of μ elite parents and a covariance matrix automatically adapted based on the search trajectory.

Mesh Adaptive Direct Search (MADS). MADS [3] is an extension of generalized pattern search algorithms. It is a mesh-based search method that systematically adapts the mesh coarseness, search radius, and search direction.

For discrete parameter configurations, an iterated local search method underlying ParamILS is considered in Sec. 6.

2.2 Evaluation method

Configurators typically have a limited *evaluation budget* B, which can be a maximum number of times the algorithm to be configured can be run on training instances. The evaluation method needs to determine how good candidate configurations are and select the one that performs best. How to allocate the available budget for evaluation is an important topic in the study of configuration algorithms, since on one side the evaluation budget is limited due to the high computational cost of each evaluation, but on the other side the evaluation error of a candidate reduces with the number of evaluations. A good compromise is to allocate more budget to promising candidates, so that they can be evaluated more carefully. The evaluation methods considered in this article include:

Repeated evaluation. It evaluates each candidate configuration by the same, fixed number of algorithm runs.

Racing. A *racing* method [16, 7, 6] evaluates candidate configurations instance by instance and eliminates inferior ones as soon as statistical evidence is gathered against them. Thus, better candidate also receive more evaluations. Racing methods differ in the statistical tests that are used to detect inferior candidates; e.g., F-Race adopts the Friedman and its post-hoc tests, and t-Race uses Student's t-test.

Intensification. *Intensification* mechanisms are used in methods such as FocusedILS [15], SPO+ [14], ROAR or SMAC [12]. It is used to compare a newly generated configuration to the incumbent, i.e. the best configuration found so far, and eliminate a new configuration as soon as it is worse than the incumbent in the sequence of instances the incumbent was already evaluated on; if a new candidate is not eliminated, its number of evaluations increases by, e.g. one, and compares with the incumbent again, until it reaches the same number of evaluations as the incumbent, then a new incumbent is determined.

2.3 Combination of search and evaluation

Given a search method and an evaluation method, a configurator essentially consists of an efficient, non-trivial combination of the two. We discuss two possibilities below, the second being the mechanism studied here.

Iterated selection. Iterated selection we call the approach where two distinctive phases are iterated: first new candidate configurations are generated, and then evaluated by an evaluation method, possibly updating the incumbent. Most of the established configurators are based on some form of iterated selection, including SPO [5] and SPO+ [14], iterated racing techniques such as iterated F-Race [4, 8], MADS/F-Race [22], and CMA-ES/F-Race [21], or FocusedILS [15]. These methods include the incumbent from iteration to iteration. Some of them consider using an intensification mechanism to preserve the incumbent (e.g. FocusedILS and SPO+). The possible drawbacks of iterated selection are that an incumbent may be lost if no specific mechanism

Algorithm 1 Post-selection

Phase 1: elite qualification. Run configurator and collect the best configurations as *elite* configurations. Each elite configuration θ_e is stored in Θ_e. A budget of R_n ($n = |\Theta_e|$) depending on the number of elite configurations is reserved for Phase 2. Go to Phase 2 when the budget for qualification phase finishes.

Phase 2: elite selection. Use an evaluation method, e.g. racing, to select the best θ^* from Θ_e.

Table 1: The range of $\mathcal{MMAS}$ parameters.

param.	α	β	ρ	m
range	$[0.0, 5.0]$	$[0.0, 10.0]$	$[0.0, 1.00]$	$[1, 1200]$
param.	γ	nn	q_0	
range	$[0.01, 5.00]$	$[5, 100]$	$[0.0, 1.0]$	

for incumbent preservation is used, while if an incumbent preservation mechanism is used, it may be too aggressive in eliminating potentially promising new candidates, leading to stagnation as observed occasionally in FocusedILS [15].

Post-selection. The basic idea of the post-selection mechanism is to divide the configuration process into two phases: a first elite *qualification* phase and a second elite *selection* phase. During the qualification phase, a number of elite configurations are identified by running a configurator. These elite configurations can be collected by, for example, enforcing quick convergence of the configurator and then taking the best configuration in each independent restart. Alternatively, different configurators may be run simultaneously and the best configurations returned by various configurators may be qualified as elites. In the elite selection phase, an evaluation method is applied to select the best from these elite configurations. See Algo. 1 for a summary of the post-selection mechanism. A number of configurators are devised following the post-selection approach and investigated in the following sections. We also compare post-selection configurators to iterated racing techniques and FocusedILS.

3. EXPERIMENTAL SETUP

In this article, we focus on one configuration domain, where the algorithm to be configured is $\mathcal{MAX}$–$\mathcal{MIN}$ Ant System ($\mathcal{MMAS}$) [20] applied to the traveling salesman problem (TSP). The numerical parameters in $\mathcal{MMAS}$ that are considered in this study include: α and β, the relative importance of pheromone trail and heuristic information; ρ, the proportion of the pheromone evaporated after each iteration; m, the number of ants; γ, which controls the gap between the minimum and maximum pheromone trail limits in $\mathcal{MMAS}$; nn, the size of the nearest neighbor candidate list in the solution construction; and q_0, the probability with which an ant selects deterministically the best possible choice at each construction step. The range of the values considered for these parameters is listed in Table 1. In the configuration process, each search algorithm generates the parameter space with a precision of two significant digits.

From these seven numerical parameters we extracted a number of *case studies*, where a subset of parameters is to be set while the others assume their default values. More in detail, we extracted three case studies for $d \in \{2, 3, 4, 5, 6\}$ parameters to be set, resulting in $3 \times 5 = 15$ case studies. These case studies are listed in Table 2.

Table 2: The 15 case studies of configuring 2 to 6 parameters (each with 3 case studies) of $\mathcal{MMAS}$.

n.param.	case 1	case 2	case 3
2	$\alpha\ \beta$;	$\rho\ m$;	$\gamma\ nn$;
3	$\alpha\ \beta\ m$;	$\beta\ \rho\ nn$;	$\rho\ \gamma\ nn$;
4	$\alpha\ \beta\ \rho\ m$;	$\alpha\ \beta\ \gamma\ nn$;	$\rho\ m\ \gamma\ nn$;
5	$\alpha\ \beta\ \rho\ m\ nn$;	$\alpha\ \beta\ \rho\ m\ \gamma$;	$\alpha\ \beta\ m\ \gamma\ nn$;
6	$\alpha\ \beta\ \rho\ m\ \gamma\ nn$;	$\alpha\ \beta\ \rho\ m\ \gamma\ q_0$;	$\alpha\ \beta\ \rho\ m\ nn\ q_0$;

The instances are uniformly randomly distributed Euclidean TSP instances. Two sets of instances are considered in this article: the homogeneous (`hom`) set consists of uni-size instances of 750 nodes, 1 000 instances for the training phase, and 300 for the testing phase; the heterogeneous (`het`) set consists of instances ranging from 100 nodes to 1 200 nodes, 900 instances for training and 300 for testing. The computation time for $\mathcal{MMAS}$ is 5 seconds. The $\mathcal{MMAS}$ implementation is based on the ACOTSP software [19] with minor extensions to allow the usage of the parameter γ.

In each case study, seven *budget levels* are considered. The minimum level of the configuration budget is chosen to be $B_1 = 5\cdot(2d+2)$, which results in a budget $B_1 = 30$ when $d = 2$ and in a budget $B_1 = 70$ for $d = 6$. The other six levels of the configuration budget are $B_i = 2^{i-1}\cdot B_1, i = 2, 3, 4, 5, 6, 7$, which doubles the budget for each next level. Each budget level of each case study is considered as one *test domain*, resulting, thus, in $7 \times 15 = 105$ test domains. For each test domain, 10 trials were run. To reduce experimental variance, in each trial, the same random order of training instances is used for running each configurator, and each instance is evaluated with a common random seed. The instance order and random seed change from trial to trial. In each trial, an archive is used in order to prevent the same parameter configuration being evaluated twice on the same instance; in such case, the evaluation is read from the archive without consuming configuration budget.

When comparing testing results, we suppose every testing instance, large or small, is of the same importance. Therefore, in each test domain, we perform a standardized z-score normalization of the performance of configurations on each testing instance, such that for any given instance, the distribution of performance over tested configurations has mean zero and variance one. Whenever ranking results are presented, each rank is based on the mean value of the normalized performance in one test domain. Whenever results of statistical tests are reported in the following, we use Wilcoxon's signed-rank test with $\alpha = 0.05$, and with Holm's method in case of multiple comparison.

4. STOCHASTICITY HANDLING USING POST-SELECTION

In this section, we examine the impact post-selection has on the performance and the behavior of various search methods with which it is combined. Before the presentations of these details, we concisely show that, in general, there exist interactions between the budget level and settings of the

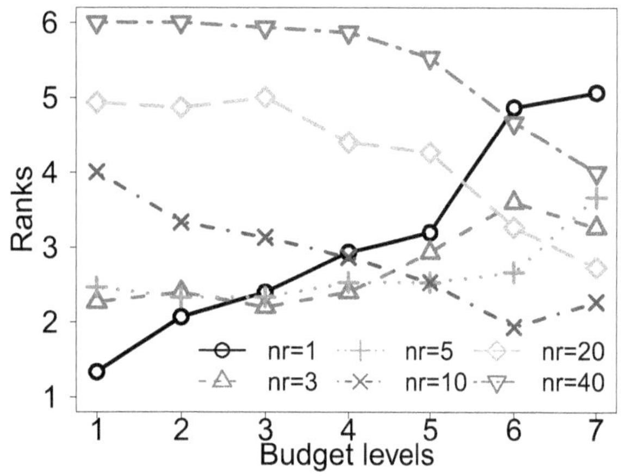

Figure 1: Average ranks of six nr settings ($nr \in \{1, 3, 5, 10, 20, 40\}$) for repeated evaluation over seven budget levels across 15 case studies of $\mathcal{MM}$AS.

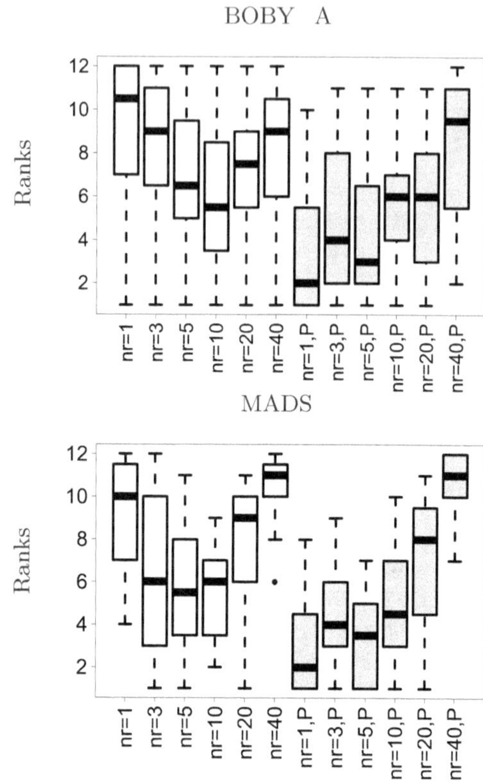

Figure 2: The rank distribution of 12 settings: repeated evaluation without post-selection (the left six light-blue box-plots in each plot) or with post-selection (the right six yellow box-plots dubbed with "P"), using $nr \in \{1, 3, 5, 10, 20, 40\}$. BOBYQA (top) and MADS (bottom) are tested on eight case studies, each with budget levels from B_4 to B_7.

evaluation method used. This sheds also some light on side-advantages of the post-selection mechanism, namely to make the configurator more robust to specific parameter settings for the evaluation method.

4.1 Repeated evaluation

The simplest evaluation method is probably repeated evaluation, where each candidate configuration is evaluated nr times. We consider here values of $nr \in \{1, 3, 5, 10, 20, 40\}$ and evaluate their performance on the 105 test domains. To illustrate the trade-offs incurred between the setting of nr and different configuration budgets, we use a uniform random search (we observed similar behavior with other search methods). Fig. 1 shows the average ranks of the six settings of nr. The relative performance of different nr settings depends strongly on the configuration budget: while for the lowest budget levels B_1 and B_2 the setting of $nr = 1$ appears to be best, the performance of low nr settings downgrades as the configuration budget increases. The clearest example is the setting $nr = 1$, which is the best for B_1 and B_2 but becomes the worst for the two highest budgets B_6 and B_7. On the contrary, large nr settings are the worst for low budgets but they improve as the configuration budget increases. Similar trade-offs were also observed in [13].

4.2 Effectiveness of Post-selection

For the experiments with post-selection, we adopted whenever possible the settings used in [21]: The budget reserved for elite selection phase is set to

$$R_n = \begin{cases} 2 \cdot n^2 & \text{if } n < 10 \\ 20 \cdot n & \text{if } n \geqslant 10 \end{cases} \tag{1}$$

and the first Friedman test starts at $f_n = \min\{n + 2, 10\}$-th instance, where n is the number of candidates for the elite selection. The first line in Equation 1 extends [21] to ensure reasonable settings for the low budget levels. In post-selection, the default is that only restart-best configurations qualify as candidates for the elite selection, where a restart-best solution is the best solution in one independent restart of the algorithm–restarts are triggered by convergence of the algorithm. Finally, each configuration generated in the elite qualification phase is evaluated by nr same instances.

We present results with the search methods BOBY A and MADS with either repeated evaluation or post-selection. Each search method is restarted when it stagnates. Stagnation can be detected, for example, if the search radius drops to less than the degree of significant digits (two in this work). In earlier work [21], post-selection was studied with nr ranging from 5 to 40, and it was shown that post-selection is effective when nr is small. Here, we explore smaller settings of nr equal to one and three on a subset of the test domains on the four high budget levels from B_4 to B_7 and taken from eight of the case studies and the homogeneous instance set. The box-plots for the ranking of each of the explored settings are given in Figure 2.

Considering the versions without post-selection (left six boxes in each plot), the best setting of nr appears to be 5 or 10, in accordance to what was observed in the previous section for uniform random sampling. However, for the versions with post-selection (right six yellow boxes dubbed with "P" for post-selection), the best setting is $nr = 1$, resulting in the best ranking improving also over the *a posterior* best settings of nr for BOBY A and MADS without post-selection. Hence, the overall best performance with post-selection is obtained when during the run of the search method each candidate configuration is evaluated on one same instance.

Saving evaluations allows to evaluate more configurations and to obtain more restart-best configurations, which then are evaluated more carefully in the elite selection phase.

4.3 Advanced settings of post-selection

Next, we extended the study in Sec. 4.2 by considering also the low budget levels B_1, B_2, and B_3. Here, we empirically examine several advanced settings of post-selection, including nr setting (Sec. 4.3.1), alternating instances (Sec. 4.3.2, dubbed A in Figure 3), early qualification (Sec. 4.3.3, dubbed E in Figure 3), and iterated selection hybrid (Sec. 4.3.4, dubbed IS in Figure 3).

4.3.1 nr setting

As high nr settings perform poorly with post-selection (see Fig. 2), here we consider only values of $nr \in \{1, 3, 5\}$. In Fig. 3(a-d), it can generally be observed that the best post-selection configurator in each plot uses $nr = 1$. Considering the curves identified by "$nr = 1, P$", "$nr = 3, P$", and "$nr = 5, P$" in Fig. 3(a-d), $nr = 1$ ranks either best or very well, and $nr = 3, 5$ rank slightly better only in the smallest budget levels of BOBY A-based configurators (Fig. 3(a,b)) and in high budget levels of CMA-ES-based configurators (Fig. 3(d)). The reason for the latter is further discussed and addressed in Sec. 4.3.3.

4.3.2 Alternating instances

Note that in our basic setting each configurator restart uses the same instances (or the same instance if $nr = 1$) and only in the final elite selection phase different instances would be used. This may lead to poor results especially on instance sets where instances are heterogeneous (as in our **het** set—for this instance set good $\mathcal{MM}$AS settings are known to depend on instance size).

Here we consider a different variant, where we use *alternating instances* instead of fixed instances; hence, each elite configuration is qualified through nr different instances. We compared this approach empirically with the basic post-selection using fixed instances, taking BOBY A as case study across 105 test domains of configuring $\mathcal{MM}$AS in both homogeneous instance set (**hom**, see Fig. 3(a)) and the heterogeneous instance set (**het**, see Fig. 3(b)). As $nr = 1$ is the best nr setting for post-selection, we compared directly $nr = 1$ fixed instance ("$nr = 1, P$" in Fig. 3(a, b)) with alternating instances ("$nr = 1, P, A$'). In **hom**, using alternating instance performs as well as using a same, fixed instance and no statistically significant difference was detected (p-value 0.3). However, in **het**, using alternating instances leads to significant improvement. We included also $nr = 3$ alternating instances ("$nr = 3, P, A$") for **het**; it again performs significantly better than using $nr = 3$ same instances ("$nr = 3, P$"), but significantly worse than $nr = 1$ with alternating instance. To sum up, using alternating instances results in better performance, especially when the target instance set is heterogeneous.

4.3.3 Early qualification

CMA-ES is the only of the three search methods, where the setting $nr = 1$ does not perform as well as $nr > 1$ especially for higher budget levels (see Fig. 3(d)). One reason is probably that CMA-ES is slower than MADS and BOBY A to converge and restart and in our basic setting only restart-best configurations qualify for the elite selection. However, one may obtain more configurations for post-selection by qualifying configurations earlier, as done, e.g., by picking all iteration-best configurations instead of only the restart-best. Besides, as suggested in Sec. 4.3.2 for BOBY A, each iteration may use *alternating* instances for evaluation. This new setting "$nr = 1, P, A, E$" (E for *early qualification*) of CMA-ES configurator is shown in Fig. 3(d) to be the significantly best-performing configurator on all budget levels.

4.3.4 Iterated selection with post-selection

Instead of using a fixed number of nr instances, one may apply iterated selection during the elite qualification phase. Such examples include MADS/F-Race [21, 22] and CMA-ES/F-Race [21], where F-Race is not only used in the elite selection phase to select the best of the elite configurations, but also used within each iteration of the search method in the elite qualification phase to select the best among the incumbent and newly-generated configurations.[1] Besides, our CMA-ES/F-Race applies also the idea of *early qualification* (Sec. 4.3.3), i.e. both iteration-best and restart-best configurations are qualified as elites. However, this interesting hybrid, either MADS/F-Race ("IS, P" in Fig. 3(c)) or CMA-ES/F-Race ("IS, P, E" in Fig. 3(d)), does not perform well compared with the other post-selection variants derived in this work. MADS/F-Race is significantly outperformed by post-selection with $nr \leq 5$, despite the better performance of MADS/F-Race over MADS with fixed nr evaluations without post-selection [22]. CMA-ES/F-Race is also significantly outperformed by post-selection CMA-ES with one alternating instance and early qualification.

5. POST-SELECTION VS. I/F-RACE

We compare the best post-selection configurators with I/F-Race, a state-of-the-art iterated selection configurator [8]. Additionally, we compare also to U/F-Race, which generates configurations uniformly at random and then selects the best by F-Race. As the best post-selection configurators we select the best setting for each of the three search methods found in Sec. 4.3, including BOBY A with one alternating instances ("$nr = 1, P, A$" in Fig. 3(a,b)), CMA-ES with one alternating instance and early qualification ("$nr = 1, P, A, E$" in Fig. 3(d)) and MADS with $nr = 1$ ("$nr = 1, P$" in Fig. 3(c), only shown in **hom**).

Fig. 4 shows the comparison of these configurators in dependence of the budget level (top row) and the number of parameters to be configured (bottom row) on the homogeneous (left column) and the heterogeneous instance set (right column). The clear winner is the CMA-ES configurator: it significantly outperforms all other configurators in almost every budget level and every number of parameters being configured. BOBY A generally performs well in case studies with 2, 3, or 4 parameters being configured, but its performance declines in case studies with 5 or 6 parameters, as shown in Fig. 4(c) and Fig. 4(d). I/F-Race is only applicable in the four high budget levels due to its default parameter settings, and it is outperformed by CMA-ES. MADS is not considered in the experiments of **het** due to its unsatisfactory performance in **hom**. All the above-mentioned configurators outperform U/F-Race.

[1]Note that in BOBY A, each configuration has to be evaluated on the same number of instances due to the way its quadratic model is built; therefore, F-Race cannot be combined with BOBY A in the iterated selection manner.

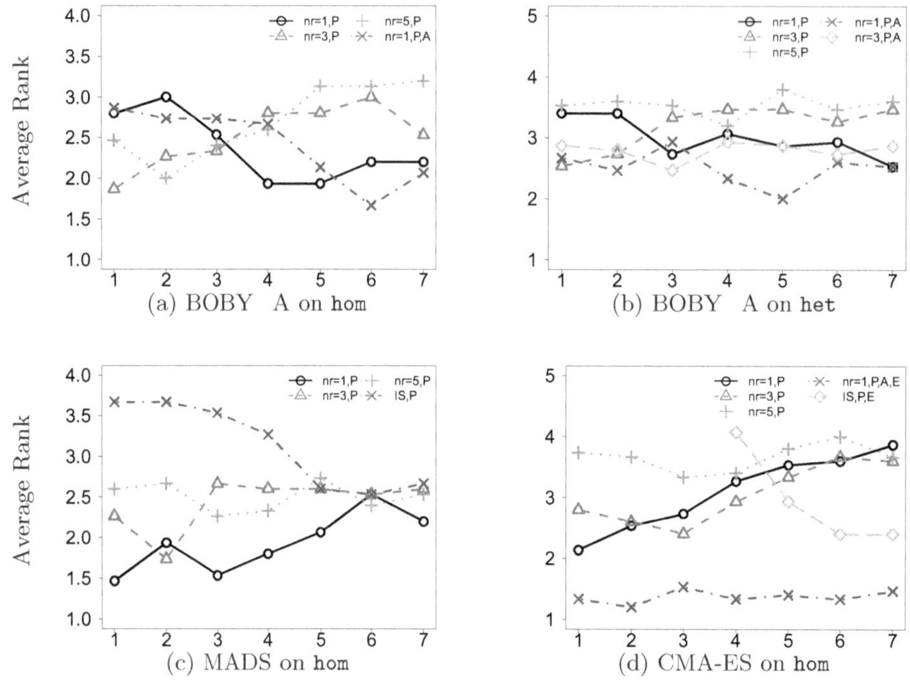

Figure 3: Average ranks of different settings for post-selection. These settings include nr values (Sec. 4.3.1), "P" for post-selection (Algo. 1), "A" for alternating instances (Sec. 4.3.2), "E" for early qualification (Sec. 4.3.3), or "IS" for iterated selection hybrid (Sec. 4.3.4). This study is done using three search methods as testbed, BOBYQA, MADS, and CMA-ES, and each setting is tested on seven budget levels (shown in the X-axis) for 15 case studies of $\mathcal{MM}$AS with either homogeneous (`hom`) or heterogeneous (`het`) instance sets.

6. POST-SELECTION IN PARAMILS

For a final set of experiments we introduce post-selection into ParamILS with the goal of comparing it to the *intensification* mechanism used in FocusedILS. We adopted the version 2.3.5 of ParamILS [11], kept the search mechanism (ILS), and adapted its *intensification* mechanism into a post-selection mechanism in a straightforward manner. Since the best setting of post-selection found in Sec. 4.2 is using $nr = 1$, alternating instance, BasicILS(1) is adopted for the elite qualification phase of post-selection. The main question then is how to define configurations that qualify as elite. In this study, only the best configuration found in each restart is qualified. We adopted three restart schemes.

Natural restart. We restart ParamILS either when it is naturally restarted as triggered by the parameter $p_{restart}$ (set to 0.01 by default) or when the search falls into a local optimum and perturbation starts. Post-selection ParamILS with natural restart is denoted as `PPn`.

Fixed early restart. We enforce ParamILS to restart earlier so as to qualify more elites. The simplest way to enforce early restart is to restrict the maximum number of evaluation B_r for each run to a small value. Considering that each ParamILS run evaluates 10 uniformly random initial configurations before starting ILS, $B_r = 30$ appears to be a setting that allows reasonable exploitation while keeping reasonably frequent restarts. This version is denoted as `PP30`.

Incremental early restart. Besides fixing B_r, we also consider incrementing B_r by 10 from restart to restart, i.e. let $B_r = 10$ in the first restart, increment B_r to 20 in the second restart, $B_r = 30$ in the third, etc. Post-selection ParamILS with incremental early restart is denoted as `PPi`.

We compared FocusedILS with the three versions of post-selection ParamILS, `PPn`, `PP30`, and `PPi` on the six case studies of $\mathcal{MM}$AS with five or six parameters to be configured. Both homogeneous and heterogeneous instance sets are considered. Since ParamILS handles only discrete parameters, each parameter of our case studies is discretized into 10 equidistant values. ParamILS does not support standardized z-score normalization, and so we adopted the *mean* algorithm performance as the objective measure. Accordingly, the post-selection applies a t-Race without adjustment for multiple comparisons [6] instead of F-Race.

The results are presented in Fig. 5. They show that post-selection with early restart, especially `PP30`, is clearly the best configurator in budget levels B_1 to B_6. FocusedILS performs better than `PP30` only in the highest budget level B_7. `PPn` doesn't perform very well as expected, since it usually takes around 100 to 400 evaluations to reach a natural restart; this leads to very few elite configurations, which greatly worsens the impact of post-selection. Enforcing early restart in `PP30` and `PPi` proves to be a more successful setting of post-selection than natural restart. However, frequent restart may weaken the exploitation ability in finding promising configurations during the elite qualification phase. A better approach than enforcing early restart is to use *early qualification* as done for CMA-ES in Sec. 4.3.3, qualifying elite configurations without interrupting the search procedure. However, we leave this possibility for future research.

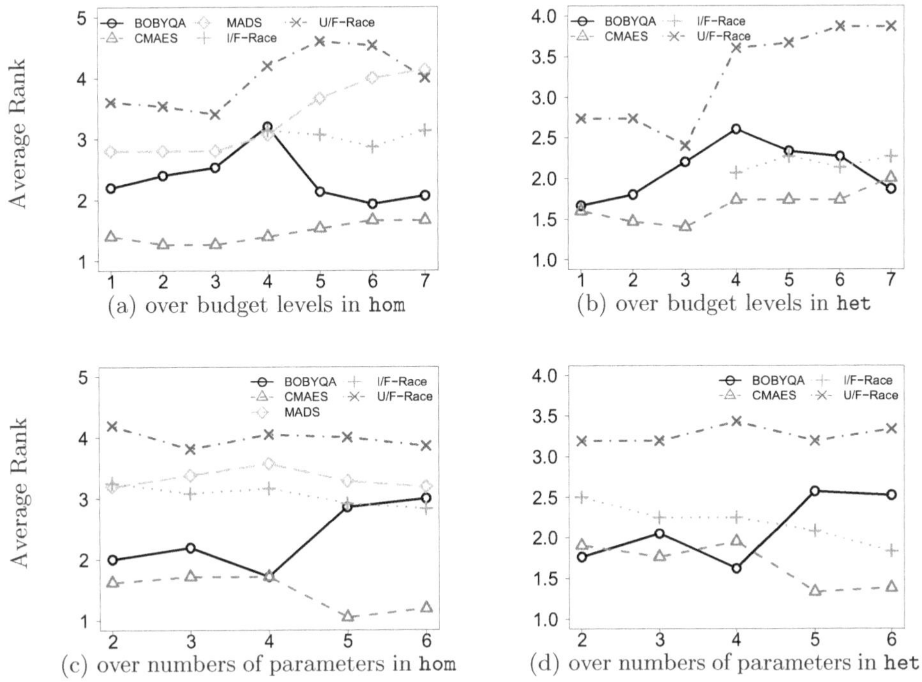

Figure 4: Comparison of best post-selection configurators with I/F-Race U/F-Race for configuring 15 case studies of $\mathcal{MM}$AS with either homogeneous (hom) or heterogeneous (het) instance sets.

7. DISCUSSION AND CONCLUSIONS

Post-selection adopts two distinct phases in the automatic algorithm configuration process. In the elite qualification phase, a number of elite configurations are identified, for example, by independent runs of some algorithm configurator. The subsequent elite selection phase tries to identify then the best of these elite configurations, for example, by a racing method. In this paper, we have examined in more detail such a post-selection mechanism, proposed earlier in [21], using the example application of algorithm configurators for setting numerical parameters of $\mathcal{MAX}$–$\mathcal{MIN}$ Ant System applied to the traveling salesperson problem (TSP). Our analysis of post-selection showed that it is enough to evaluate candidate configurations on rather few instances during the elite qualification stage. In our case studies only one instance was even enough, but we expect that on other configuration tasks with more heterogeneous instances than in the TSP a larger number of instances in the elite qualification stage may be better. If the configurator in the elite qualification phase cannot gather many elite configurations, enforcing early restarts or an *early qualification* mechanism, as proposed in this paper, may be useful. Overall, our results showed that post-selection is a promising approach that should receive further attention. In addition, we identified a post-selection CMA-ES configurator with alternating instances and early qualification, as a high-performing configurator for setting numerical parameters.

In future work, we plan to test the effectiveness of post-selection on other configuration tasks with more parameters and to explore complementing other configuration methods with post-selection. The fact that with post-selection, each run of automatic algorithm configuration method in the elite qualification stage may use few same instances, makes post-selection also applicable to model-based search methods such as SPO, which cannot easily be enhanced by iterated selection methods that evaluate candidate configurations with different numbers of instances (see BOBY A in Sec. 4.3.4 as an example). Furthermore, post-selection can be seen as a form of stochasticity handling and it may also be useful for optimization problems with noise, e.g., it may be integrated into deterministic algorithms for optimizing noisy functions such as those of the black-box optimization benchmarking workshop series [10]. The positive results obtained with post-selection in this paper indicate that the directions outlined above are promising ideas to pursue.

Acknowledgments

This work was supported by the META-X project, an *Action de Recherche Concertée* funded by the Scientific Research Directorate of the French Community of Belgium and support from the FRFC project "*Méthodes de recherche hybrides pour la résolution de problèmes complexes*". This research and its results have also received funding from the COMEX project within the Interuniversity Attraction Poles Programme of the Belgian Science Policy Office. Zhi Yuan, Mauro Birattari, and Thomas Stützle acknowledge support from the Belgian F.R.S.-FNRS. Zhi Yuan also acknowledges support by the Singapore National Research Foundation under its International Research Centre @ Singapore Funding Initiative and administered by the IDM Programme Office.

8. REFERENCES

[1] B. Adenso-Díaz and M. Laguna. Fine-tuning of algorithms using fractional experimental designs and local search. *Operations Research*, 54(1):99–114, 2006.

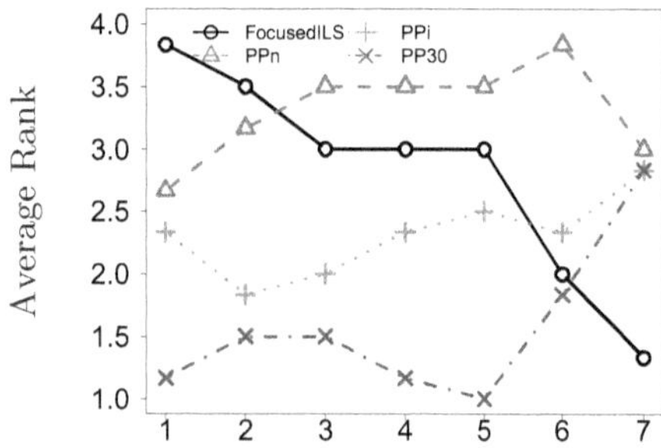

(a) homogeneous instances

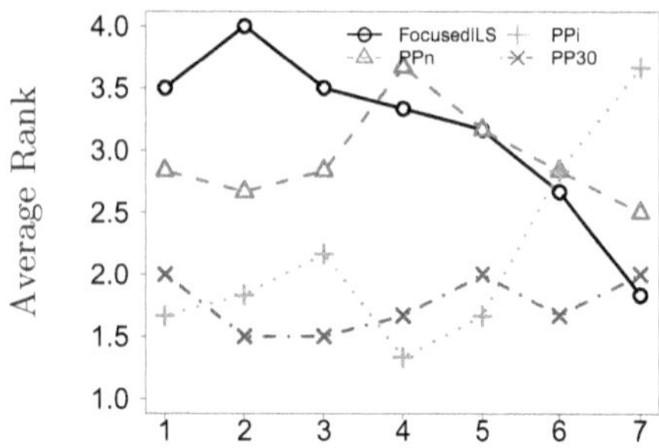

(b) heterogeneous instances

Figure 5: Average ranks of four ParamILS-based configurators over seven budget levels for configuring six case studies of $\mathcal{MM}$AS with either (a) homogeneous or (b) heterogeneous instance set. The four ParamILS versions include FocusedILS, and post-selection variants PPn, PP30, and PPi.

[2] C. Ansótegui, M. Sellmann, and K. Tierney. A gender-based genetic algorithm for the automatic configuration of solvers. In I. P. Gent, editor, *CP 2009*, volume 5732 of *LNCS*, pages 142–157. Springer, Heidelberg, Germany, 2009.

[3] C. Audet and J. J. E. Dennis. Mesh adaptive direct search algorithms for constrained optimization. *SIAM Journal on Optimization*, 17(1):188–217, 2006.

[4] P. Balaprakash, M. Birattari, and T. Stützle. Improvement strategies for the F-Race algorithm: Sampling design and iterative refinement. In T. Bartz-Beielstein et al., editors, *HM'2007*, volume 4771 of *LNCS*, pages 108–122. Springer, Heidelberg, Germany, 2007.

[5] T. Bartz-Beielstein, C. Lasarczyk, and M. Preuss. Sequential parameter optimization. In *CEC 2005*, pages 773–780. IEEE, 2005.

[6] M. Birattari. *Tuning Metaheuristics: A machine learning perspective.* Springer, Berlin, Germany, 2009.

[7] M. Birattari, T. Stützle, L. Paquete, and K. Varrentrapp. A racing algorithm for configuring metaheuristics. In W. B. Langdon et al., editors, *GECCO 2002*, pages 11–18. Morgan Kaufmann Publishers, San Francisco, CA, 2002.

[8] M. Birattari, Z. Yuan, P. Balaprakash, and T. Stützle. F-Race and iterated F-Race: An overview. In T. Bartz-Beielstein et al., editors, *Experimental Methods for the Analysis of Optimization Algorithms*, pages 311–336. Springer, Berlin, Germany, 2010.

[9] N. Hansen. The CMA evolution strategy: a comparing review. In J. Lozano et al., editors, *Towards a new evolutionary computation*, volume 192 of *Studies in Fuzziness and Soft Computing*, pages 75–102. Springer, Berlin, Germany, 2006.

[10] N. Hansen, S. Finck, R. Ros, and A. Auger. Real-parameter black-box optimization benchmarking 2009: Noisy functions definitions. Technical Report RR-6869, INRIA, 2009.

[11] F. Hutter. Software ParamILS. `http://www.cs.ubc.ca/labs/beta/Projects/ParamILS`, 2010.

[12] F. Hutter, H. Hoos, and K. Leyton-Brown. Sequential model-based optimization for general algorithm configuration. In *Proc. LION 2011. Volume 6683 of LNCS*, pages 507–523. Springer, 2011.

[13] F. Hutter, H. Hoos, and K. Leyton-Brown. Tradeoffs in the empirical evaluation of competing algorithm designs. *Annals of Mathematics and Artificial Intelligence*, 60(1):65–89, 2010.

[14] F. Hutter, H. H. Hoos, K. Leyton-Brown, and K. P. Murphy. An experimental investigation of model-based parameter optimisation: SPO and beyond. In F. Rothlauf, editor, *GECCO 2009*, pages 271–278. ACM press, New York, 2009.

[15] F. Hutter, H. H. Hoos, K. Leyton-Brown, and T. Stützle. ParamILS: An automatic algorithm configuration framework. *Journal of Artificial Intelligence Research*, 36:267–306, 2009.

[16] O. Maron and A. W. Moore. Hoeffding races: Accelerating model selection search for classification and function approximation. In J. D. Cowan et al., editors, *Advances in Neural Information Processing Systems*, volume 6, pages 59–66. Morgan Kaufmann Publishers, San Francisco, USA, 1994.

[17] V. Nannen and A. E. Eiben. Relevance estimation and value calibration of evolutionary algorithm parameters. In *Proc. of IJCAI 2007*, pages 975–980. AAAI Press/IJCAI, Menlo Park, CA, 2007.

[18] M. J. D. Powell. The BOBY A algorithm for bound constrained optimization without derivatives. Technical Report NA2009/06, Department of Applied Mathematics and Theoretical Physics, University of Cambridge, Cambridge, UK, 2009.

[19] T. Stützle. Software ACOTSP. `http://iridia.ulb.ac.be/~mdorigo/ACO/aco-code/public-software.html`, 2002.

[20] T. Stützle and H. H. Hoos. $\mathcal{MAX}$–$\mathcal{MIN}$ ant system. *Future Generation Computer Systems*, 16(8):889–914, 2000.

[21] Z. Yuan, M. Montes de Oca, M. Birattari, and T. Stützle. Continuous optimization algorithms for tuning real and integer parameters of swarm intelligence algorithms. *Swarm Intelligence*, 6(1):49–75, 2012.

[22] Z. Yuan, T. Stützle, and M. Birattari. MADS/F-Race: mesh adaptive direct search meets F-race. In M. Ali et al., editors, *Proceedings of IEA-AIE 2010*, volume 6096 of *LNAI*, pages 41–50. Springer Verlag, Heidelberg, Germany, 2010.

S-Race: A Multi-Objective Racing Algorithm

Tiantian Zhang
University of Central Florida
4000 Central Florida Blvd.
Orlando, FL, 32816
zhangtt@knights.ucf.edu

Michael Georgiopoulos
University of Central Florida
4000 Central Florida Blvd.
Orlando, FL, 32816
michaelg@ucf.edu

Georgios C. Anagnostopoulos
Florida Institute of Technology
150 W. University Blvd
Melbourne, FL 32901
georgio@fit.edu

ABSTRACT

This paper presents a multi-objective racing algorithm, S-Race, which efficiently addresses multi-objective model selection problems in the sense of Pareto optimality. As a racing algorithm, S-Race attempts to eliminate candidate models as soon as there is sufficient statistical evidence of their inferiority relative to other models with respect to all objectives. This approach is followed in the interest of controlling the computational effort. S-Race adopts a non-parametric sign test to identify pair-wise domination relationship between models. Meanwhile, Holm's Step-Down method is employed to control the overall family-wise error rate of simultaneous hypotheses testing during the race. Experimental results involving the selection of superior Support Vector Machine classifiers according to 2 and 3 performance criteria indicate that S-Race is an efficient and effective algorithm for automatic model selection, when compared to a brute-force, multi-objective selection approach.

Categories and Subject Descriptors

G.3 [**Probability and Statistics**]: Statistical Computing; I.2.8 [**Artificial Intelligence**]: Problem Solving, Control Methods, and Search—*Heuristic methods*; G.1.6 [**Numerical Analysis**]: Optimization

General Terms

Algorithms, Experimentation

Keywords

Racing Algorithm, Model Selection, Multi-objective Optimization

1. INTRODUCTION

Model selection is an important aspect of Machine Learning (ML). Aside from its traditional meaning, occasionally a "model" could also refer to any algorithm or learning strategy. Given an ensemble of candidate models, each model's performance is assessed on a common set of test instances and, eventually, based on their performance on the aforementioned test, a single champion model or a subset of the ensemble is identified as the best for the given ML task. Typically, the larger the cardinality of the test instance set, the more confidence can be bestowed on the final choice(s). However, as the number of test instances and models to be compared increases, model selection becomes a time-consuming task. For a candidate pool of size M and a validation set of size V, the computational complexity of comparing all models at once on the entire set, an approach we will refer to as Brute-Force Approach (BFA), is obviously an increasing function of M and V. Therefore, much research in model selection focuses on how to perform this selection process faster. Recent attempts lie in the areas of experimental design methods, local search approaches, and evolutionary computation algorithms [1, 17].

Alternatively, one may be willing to trade off some computational complexity for a somewhat reduced, but still acceptable, likelihood that the models obtained from a suitably-modified selection process are indeed the ones that outperform the rest of the ensemble, when the assessment is based on all the test instances. This very notion forms the main premise of Racing Algorithms (RAs), which have been widely used in parameter tuning [3], automatic model configuration [18], algorithm development [10] and industrial applications [2, 6].

RAs are iterative procedures that start off with a set of competing candidate models (*ensemble*). At each step of the racing, when sufficient statistical evidence is gathered, those candidates who perform poorly are eliminated. The aforementioned evidence revolves around a single criterion of model optimality (optimization objective) that depends on the ML task at hand, *e.g.* recognition accuracy, likelihood, mean-squared error, etc. The goal of RAs is to automatically detect under-performing models and exclude them from further consideration as early as possible during the race in order to save on computations. The first RA was proposed in [20] and its performance comparison instrument is based on Hoeffding's inequality to estimate a confidence interval for the true expected error of each model from a sequence of observed prediction errors. The so-called Hoeffding Racing is non-parametric, however, it is less effective, when all candidate models perform comparably. To address this issue, A. W. Moore proposed a pristine RA, BRACE, based on Bayesian statistics in [23]. In BRACE, the sample errors are assumed to be Gaussianly distributed and the sample mean and variance are estimated via Maximum Likelihood

Estimation. BRACE is demonstrated to be faster than Hoeffding Racing in eliminating under-performing candidates. Later, another RA based on Bernstein's inequality was proposed in [22]. In Bernstein Racing, both the range and the variance information are used in confidence interval calculations. The empirical Bernstein bound quickly becomes much tighter than Hoeffding's bound, when the sample size increases. Furthermore in [3], in an attempt to combine the advantages of both Hoeffding Racing and BRACE, F-Race was developed based on Friedman's test. F-Race features a non-parametric statistical test and it employs block design. Later on, an extended version of F-Race, I/F-Race (Iterated F-Race) [4] was suggested. Other instances of RAs include A-Race based on ANOVA analysis [29], tn-Race based on paired t-test without any correction for multiple tests [3], tb-Race based on paired t-tests with Bonferroni correction [3] and racing based on Welch's t-test [16].

So far, all existing RAs consider a single measure of goodness, in order to refine an ensemble of candidate models. Hence, we will refer to them as Single-Objective Racing Algorithms (Single-Objective RAs). However, in real-life problems, model selection often involves employing more than one quantifiable selection criterion. For example, as less complex models (*e.g.* with fewer parameters) may exhibit better generalization performance (or, plainly, be preferred to) than more complex ones. Model complexity could or should be considered in addition to prediction accuracy. Furthermore, in a Multi-Task Learning context, models with multiple outputs are considered to simultaneously serve more than one tasks (each output is dedicated to a specific task). In such a scenario, the performance quality for each task is linked to a different objective function and the model selection problem becomes one of multi-objective nature. Obviously, one could scalarize in some fashion the relevant multi-objective selection problem by considering a single scalar measure that is a function of all task objectives, *e.g.* a conic linear combination of the objective functions, or a quality indicator. For instance, in [18] and [19], the author employed I/F-Race in combination with unary quality indicators. However, the disadvantages of such an approach are many [15]: (i) in the case of a conic combination of objectives, non-convex parts of the problem's Pareto front (set of non-dominated models) cannot be examined, (ii) the scalarized objective function cannot fully represent the trade-off relation between different objectives, especially for conflicting objectives, and (iii) the optimal model based on the scalarized objective doesn't provide any insight into the multi-objective selection problem. Ideally, if all objectives were considered simultaneously, a relevant selection process would return a set of non-dominated models, which would allow the decision maker to assess the nature of trade-offs between objectives prior to selecting one or more suitable models. We will refer to such selection problems as Multi-Objective Model Selection (MOMS), which means selecting models with multi-objectives based on Pareto optimality. To the best of our knowledge, RAs for MOMS (MORAs) have not yet been pursued in the relevant literature.

This paper aspires to propose a novel Multi-Objective RA procedure, namely *S-Race*. Its purpose is to yield the subset of the candidate ensemble, whose models are non-dominated in the Pareto sense with respect to the remainder of the ensemble, when all objectives are taken into account simultaneously. Being a RA, the S-Race procedure attempts to eliminate candidate models as soon as there is sufficient statistical evidence of their inferiority relative to other models in the race with respect to all objectives. Furthermore, via a tunable parameter, it is able to trade off computational effort with likelihood of producing a final pool of best candidates containing exactly the ones obtained from a brute-force MOMS procedure.

Section 2 of this paper describes the S-Race procedure. At the highest level, the step-wise racing algorithm employs testing the significance of simultaneous dominance relationships that may be observed between families of candidate models. Strong Type I control of these simultaneous formal tests is achieved by the Holm's Step-Down procedure. At a lower level, dominance relationships between individual pairs of models are inferred based on the Sign Test for matched-pair comparisons.

In order to characterize the efficiency and effectiveness of S-Race in practical ML settings, a MOMS problem involving an ensemble of Support Vector Machines (SVMs) is considered in Section 3. The ensemble is trained on a variety of 2- and 3-class recognition problems and the recognition accuracy for each class is regarded as an individual objective. S-Race is compared to a multi-objective BFA, which would be the typical choice for identifying the set of non-dominated models within the ensemble. The experimental results demonstrate that S-Race is able to identify the optimal set with relatively small effort. Finally, Section 4 summarizes our work and ends with a few closing remarks.

2. S-RACE DESCRIPTION

Throughout the paper, we will assume that the merit of a candidate model C participating in the ensemble is measured by a set of L real-valued objective functions $\{f_i\}_{i=1,\ldots,L}$, whose values $f_i(C)$, we'll assume, are stochastic in nature. Without loss of generality, we will assume that the functions f_i represent different costs/losses, so that models with low $f_i(C)$'s are preferred. $\mathbf{f}(C) \triangleq [f_1(C)\ f_2(C)\ \ldots\ f_L(C)]$ will stand for the *performance vector* associated with model C. In the sequel, we will say that model C dominates model C' and denote this fact as $C \succ C'$, when $\mathbf{f}(C)$ is preferred over $\mathbf{f}(C')$ in the Pareto sense , *i.e.*, if and only if

$$\begin{aligned} & f_i(C) \leqslant f_i(C') \quad \forall\, i \in \{1, 2, \cdots, L\} \\ & \text{and } \exists\, j \in \{1, 2, \cdots, L\} \mid f_j(C) < f_j(C') \end{aligned} \tag{1}$$

When we mentioned earlier that MOMS procedures should return the subset of the candidate ensemble that consists of non-dominated models, we implied a dominance in the Pareto sense as just described. The aforementioned subset is also referred to as Pareto front or Pareto optimal subset in the Multi-Objective Optimization literature [8].

2.1 Framework of S-Race

The framework of S-Race follows the typical procedure of a RA and is depicted in Table 1. Assume we have a pool of m candidate models, $\{C_1, C_2, \ldots, C_m\}$, at the beginning of racing. At each step during the racing, each model's performance is assessed on a *batch* (usually one or several test instances from the validation set) and is represented as a performance vector, of which each element refers to one measurement of goodness. Subsequently, a statistical test is performed to establish whether there is significant difference in performance between the members of the pool. As statistical evidence accumulates with each step, certain differences in performance become statistically significant and the under-performing models are excluded from the race. As we assume a multi-objective setting, when comparing a pair of candidates, what needs to be established is a statistically significant Pareto dominance between them. The models to be excluded are those, whose performances are dominated by the corresponding performances of at least one other model in the racing pool. At the end of the race, we expect the final pool to contain the entire or most of the Pareto-optimal models depending on how much computational effort one is willing to trade off.

Step 1	Randomly select a batch and test on all remaining models.
Step 2	Evaluate the performances of each model based on this batch.
Step 3	Identify statistically significant dominance relationships between compared models.
Step 4	Remove all dominated models from race.
Step 5	Go to Step 1, if available batches are not exhausted or more than one model is left.

Table 1: General Framework of S-Race

2.2 Statistical Inference of Dominance

Pareto dominance of one model over another cannot be established with absolute certainty based on limited observations, especially when the objective functions involved are of stochastic nature. A formal test of hypothesis needs to be employed in order to infer such a relationship with a certain Type I probability of error (falsely inferring dominance). Furthermore, in order to preserve the range of the proposed algorithm's applicability, no distributional assumptions, whether marginal or joint, will be made about the objective function values. Thus, the test would be robust, even when the sample distributions of performances corresponding to different models differ significantly. This desideratum implies the exclusion of any parametric tests. Moreover, among non-parametric tests, it is desirable to use the ones that are based on paired observations, when compared to tests that do not use paired observations. This is also known as *blocking design*; it effectively reduces the variability caused by differences between batches and yields tests with lower Type II error (falsely inferring absence of dominance).

In order to establish dominance between a pair of candidate models, S-Race employes the Sign Test (ST) for matched pairs [21]. Let's assume two candidate models, C_i and C_j, whose performances have been evaluated on a validation set. Moreover, assume that the experimental evidence so far shows that C_i's performance vector dominates that of C_j, which is established in the following manner: if n_{ij} are the number of instances that C_i's performance vector dominates the performance vector of C_j and n_{ji} is similarly defined, then we have observed that $n_{ij} > n_{ji}$. Let N_{ij} and N_{ji} stand for the random variables corresponding to n_{ij} and n_{ji} respectively. Also, let $S \triangleq N_{ij} + N_{ji}$ and its observed value $s \triangleq n_{ij} + n_{ji}$. If we define $p \triangleq P(N_{ij} = 1|S = 1)$, then the ST's null hypothesis H_o is $p = \frac{1}{2}$ and its alternative hypothesis H_a is $p > \frac{1}{2}$. Additionally, since $N_{ij}|S = s \sim \text{Binomial}\left(s, \frac{1}{2}\right)$, a p-value (observed significance level) of the ST is given as

$$\pi(n_{ij}, n_{ji}) \triangleq \frac{1}{2^s} \sum_{k=n_{ij}}^{s} \binom{s}{k} \quad (2)$$

Therefore, the ST rejects H_o and concludes that $C_i \succ C_j$, when $\pi(n_{ij}, n_{ji}) < \alpha$, where α is the desired significance level (maximum Type I error). A large difference $n_{ij} - n_{ji}$ supports the belief that the probability of the event $C_i \succ C_j$ is high[1].

When the ensemble of candidates is large, which is not unusual in ML practice, considering only pair-wise STs for a given significance level may lead to an increased number of false rejections by chance and, therefore, useful models may be excluded from further consideration. This is especially critical in the early stages of the race, where the entire ensemble partakes in the race. To guard against such false rejections, S-Race employs multiple hypothesis testing of dominance relationships whenever warranted. On the other hand, in order for the multiple testing procedure not to be overly conservative, a testing approach that controls the Family-Wise Error Rate (FWER) [11] is applied[2]. The FWER amounts to the probability of falsely rejecting one ore more null hypotheses (termed *false discoveries*), and is the Type I error for the set (termed *family*) of simultaneously compared models; in S-Race's setting, it reflects the probability of falsely inferring a dominance relationship between one or more pairs of candidate models. There are various FWER controlling procedures found in the literature [26]. In S-Race, Holm's Step-Down procedure [12] is adopted. An outline of the procedure is illustrated in Table 2.

	Given a predefined maximum FWER α, a family of m tests of hypothesis and their corresponding p-values:
Step 1	Order the m p-values in ascending order as $\pi_{(1)} \leq \pi_{(2)} \leq \cdots \leq \pi_{(m)}$
Step 2	Find the smallest $k = k_o$ such that $\pi_{(k_o)} > \frac{\alpha}{m+1-k_o}$
Step 3	Reject the null hypotheses of the tests with p-values $\pi_{(k)}, k < k_o$; if $k_o = 1$, reject none; if no such k_o, reject all.

Table 2: Holm's Step-Down procedure

Holm's procedure is a step-down version of Bonferroni's method. Since it's a closed testing procedure, it controls the FWER in a strong sense, *i.e.*, it guarantees that the FWER will not exceed a user-specified threshold. In addition, it makes no assumptions on the normality or independence of the test statistics involved [13].

[1]The notions laid out here are closely related to the concept of *probabilistic dominance* presented in [27, 14].

[2]Applying a procedure that controls the False Discovery Rate (FDR) would be another option. However, such procedures offer only loose control over Type I error rates.

2.3 S-Race Specifics

A description of the whole S-Race procedure is illustrated in Algorithm 1. During a single step of the race, first, the performance vectors of all candidates currently in the pool are evaluated on the given batch. Note that batches are randomly sampled from the validation set without replacement. Next, the previously-defined quantities n_{ij} $(i \neq j)$ are computed for every pair of candidates and families of simultaneous tests are identified. Within the same family, the p-values $\pi(n_{ij}, n_{ji})$ are computed as in Equation (2). In Algorithm 1, Holms($\cdot, \cdot$) implements the Holm's Step-Down procedure, which, for a set of p-values, returns the set of model indices, which were found to be dominated by other candidates in the pool for a FWER not exceeding α. Subsequently, these models are removed from the pool. Eventually, the race terminates, when the available batches are exhausted, or when there is only one candidate model left in the pool. Note that in Algorithm 1, $|\cdot|$ stands for the cardinality of its argument and $\setminus$ denotes set difference.

Algorithm 1 S-Race Pseudo-code

```
Initialize Pool ← {C_1, C_2, ··· , C_m} (m ≥ 2)
repeat
  Randomly sample a batch from the validation set.
  Evaluate all the remaining models on the batch
  for each model C_i ∈ Pool do
    P_values ← ∅
    for each model C_j ∈ Pool \ {C_j} do
      P_values ← P_values ∪ {π(n_ij, n_ji)}
    end for
    Pool ← Pool \ {C_k}, where k ∈ Holms(P_values, α)
  end for
until validation batches exhausted or |Pool| = 1
return Pool
```

As we will show next, it is possible to strongly control the Type I error of the whole race in the following sense: we can choose α in order to guarantee a minimum probability Δ that no Type I errors will occur during the race. As suggested in Section 2.2, the overall probability of making even one Type I error within each family of hypotheses testing (*i.e.*, the FWER) is controlled by Holm's procedure:

$$Pr\{\text{at least one Type I error within a family}\} \leq \alpha \quad (3)$$

Let M be the size of the original candidate pool. At each step, it is not difficult to see that the maximum number of families that may be simultaneously tested is $M-1$. According to the disjunctive probability inequality, which states that $Pr\{\mathcal{A} \cup \mathcal{B}\} \leq Pr\{\mathcal{A}\} + Pr\{\mathcal{B}\}$ for any measurable sets $\mathcal{A}$ and $\mathcal{B}$, we have that

$$\begin{aligned} &Pr\{\text{at least one Type I error during a step}\} \\ &\leq (M-1)\alpha \end{aligned} \quad (4)$$

Let's assume that the S-Race will perform at most B steps, which are equal to the number of available batches. Again, due to the disjunctive probability inequality, we obtain that

$$\begin{aligned} &Pr\{\text{at least one Type I error during race}\} \\ &\leq B(M-1)\alpha \end{aligned} \quad (5)$$

or, equivalently

$$\begin{aligned} \Delta &\equiv Pr\{\text{no Type I errors during race}\} \\ &\geq 1 - B(M-1)\alpha \end{aligned} \quad (6)$$

In other words, we established the following connection between α and Δ:

$$\alpha \leq \frac{1-\Delta}{B(M-1)} \quad (7)$$

Therefore, if one desires to control via Δ the probability of a non-dominated model being incorrectly retired at any point during the race, Equation (7) determines the maximum value of α to be used for the simultaneous tests within any family. Notice that the bound provided in Equation (7) is exceedingly loose, since during the racing procedure, the number of models in the pool is non-increasing from one step to another. Actually, the lower bound for Δ displayed in Equation (6) is only attained in the extreme case, where the race never retires/abandons any model.

One can observe that, the larger the value of Δ, the smaller the maximum FWER α allowed during simultaneous testing within families, which raises the standards of the necessary evidence to infer pair-wise dominance relationships. Hence, abandonment of under-performing models only occurs in much later stages of the race, if ever. In the extreme case, when $\Delta = 1$ and, therefore, $\alpha = 0$, no dominance relationships are virtually ever discovered and none of the candidate models in the ensemble are ever retired. On the other hand, the larger the size of the pool at any given step, the more computations are required during that step. Therefore, the value of Δ should be carefully selected, so as to maintain the balance between obtaining a final ensemble that matches as close as possible to the one obtained from a BFA, while regulating the computational effort exerted during the race.

3. EXPERIMENTS

In this section, we illustrate the performance of S-Race by selecting among an initial pool of SVMs [7] based on their performance on a set of recognition problems. Descriptions of the corresponding datasets are provided in Table 3. For all problems, LIBSVM [5] was used to train these models using a variety of settings and kernel functions. For each problem/dataset, the MOMS formulation was as follows: the performance vector of each model consisted of the percentage of misclassified samples per class. Obviously, smaller misclassification percentages are preferred and Pareto dominance was defined accordingly.

3.1 Experimental Setting

For all the experiments, we used an initial pool of $M = 50$ models. SVMs were formed using a variety of kernel types and kernel parameters and, subsequently, were trained using different regularization parameter values C. At the beginning, 50 sets of SVM parameter settings were randomly selected from the settings depicted in Table 4. In this paper, we only adopt a random sampling design for model initialization. Other sampling strategies, such as full factorial design, are not considered here, because the goal of the experiment is to demonstrate that S-Race is able to identify the same Pareto-optimal models as a BFA would, but in a shorter time, regardless of the particular choice of initial models. Each dataset is randomly divided into two non-overlapping

name	Train #	Val #	Class #	Atr #	Source
a1a	1605	10318	2	123	[24]
a2a	2265	10098	2	123	[24]
a3a	3185	9792	2	123	[24]
acoustic(1)	2872	3969	2	50	[9]
connect-4(1)	6401	13676	2	126	[24]
MiniBooNE	2815	4961	2	50	[24]
protein(1)	3509	2728	2	357	[28]
mushrooms	1626	1620	2	112	[24]
w1a	2477	15757	2	300	[25]
acoustic(2)	2464	2464	3	50	[9]
combined	2464	2464	3	100	[9]
protein(2)	1915	2209	3	357	[28]
seismic	2465	2465	3	50	[9]
connect-4(2)	5632	5632	3	126	[24]
dna	600	1186	3	180	[24]

Table 3: Selected Datasets

sets: training set and validation set. After initialization, 50 SVM classifiers with corresponding parameters are trained. The value of Δ was allowed to vary, in order to illustrate its influence on the race outcomes; we chose values for it from the discrete set $\{0.7, 0.8, 0.9, 0.999\}$. At each step of the race, a batch was randomly selected from the validation set without replacement. In all experiments, a batch consisted of a single labeled sample from each class. The corresponding performance vectors of all retained models were recorded after classification. Therefore, after k steps, each candidate model was associated with k two-dimensional or three-dimensional vectors. S-Race was then applied and dominated models, with a certain confidence, were removed from the race. This process was repeated at each step until all batches were exhausted or the pool was left with a sole model. The final ensemble of models was deemed as the Pareto-optimal models identified by the racing procedure.

parameter	range
C	$0.001 \sim 50$
kernel type	$K_{poly}(x_i, x_j) = (a(x_i \cdot x_j) + b)^c$ $K_{rad}(x_i, x_j) = exp(-\gamma\|\|x_i - x_j\|\|^2)$ $K_{sig}(x_i, x_j) = tanh(\gamma(x_i \cdot x_j) + d)$
a	$1 \sim 10$
b	$0 \sim 5$
c	$1 \sim 5$
γ	$\gamma = q^t$, where $q \in (1, 9), t \in (-9, 9)$
d	$-0.1 \sim 0$

Table 4: SVM Parameter Description

3.2 Performance Metrics

Let $\mathcal{P}_{BFA}$ be the final ensemble obtained via a BFA, which amounts to running the S-Race on a single batch that contains all available validation samples. Similarly, let $\mathcal{P}_{SR}$ be the final ensemble obtained from the S-Race. Note that, in an ideal scenario, we would like to have $\mathcal{P}_{SR} = \mathcal{P}_{BFA}$ at a much less computational cost than a BFA. In our experimental analysis, we considered two quantities to evaluate the quality of $\mathcal{P}_{SR}$. These were the *retention* R and the *excess* E values, which are defined as shown next:

$$R = \frac{|\mathcal{P}_{SR} \cap \mathcal{P}_{BFA}|}{|\mathcal{P}_{BFA}|} \quad (8)$$

$$E = \frac{|\mathcal{P}_{SR} \setminus \mathcal{P}_{BFA}|}{|\mathcal{P}_{SR}|} = 1 - \frac{|\mathcal{P}_{SR} \cap \mathcal{P}_{BFA}|}{|\mathcal{P}_{SR}|} \quad (9)$$

As their names somewhat imply, R measures S-Race's ability to retain models obtained via the BFA. On the other hand, E measures S-Race's ability to correctly identify dominated models that do not appear in $\mathcal{P}_{BFA}$. Equivalently, E quantifies the proportion of models in $\mathcal{P}_{SR}$ that are not present in $\mathcal{P}_{BFA}$.

From Section 2.3 we can see that Δ implicitly controls R, while E is loosely related to the probability of making Type II errors during the S-Race, which is a quantity beyond the algorithm's control. Optimally, the S-Race should behave like the BFA and, therefore, exhibit $R = 1$ and $E = 0$. However, in practice, one would be content, if S-Race exhibited high R and low E values for a given computational gain.

Apart from R and E, which focus on the quality of S-Race's final ensemble, we also consider a measure T of S-Race's computational effort. It is defined as the ratio of total running time of the S-Race over the running time of the BFA, which, as we mentioned earlier, is equivalent to performing the S-Race on a single batch containing the entire validation set.

If the S-Race involves L objectives and a validation set of size V, then it is not difficult to show that the S-Race's computational complexity does not exceed an order of $O(LV\overline{M} + V\overline{M^2 \log M} + V^2\overline{M^2})$. In the previous expression, $\overline{M}$ is the average number of models competing in the race over its entire duration; the remaining averages involving M are similarly defined. For BFA, these averages are just equal to M, $M^2 \log M$ and M^2 respectively, where M is the size of the initial candidate pool. Given these facts, we expect the S-Race to have a lower running time than the BFA, because we expect to see the pool size to gradually decrease, since dominated models will be retired as the race progresses. Obviously, this implies that the values of the aforementioned averages will be much smaller than the corresponding expressions for the BFA, *i.e.*, $\overline{M} < M$, etc. This fact is also witnessed in our experiments.

3.3 Results

To illustrate the efficiency of S-Race in the SVM MOMS tasks that involve the 2-class recognition problems, the retention, excess, computational effort (relative to BFA) and BFA's final ensemble size $|\mathcal{P}_{BFA}|$ are reported in Table 5. Note that the values being reported are averages over 30, while the initial pool size was $M = 50$ for all experiments.

We first observe that, in all cases, the computational effort of S-Race is less than the one of the BFA, since in all cases $T < 1$. As a matter of fact, for $\Delta < 0.999$, S-Race typically spent less than 30% of the time it took the BFA to identify its set of non-dominated models. In general, smaller Δ values lead to more computation savings. That's because smaller Δ leads to larger α, which makes the rejection of null hypothesis easier, and, thus, more models are labeled as dominated models and are removed. As we can see, when Δ approaches 1, the computational cost of S-Race increases sharply in most cases, since S-Race hardly performs any rejections for an α value close to 0.

Dataset		Δ			
		0.7	0.8	0.9	0.999
a1a	R	1	1	1	0.99
	E	0.11	0.10	0.09	0
	T	0.20	0.20	0.20	0.31
	$\lvert\mathcal{P}_{BFA}\rvert$	8.07	8.17	8.37	10.87
a2a	R	1	1	1	1
	E	0.20	0.18	0.14	0
	T	0.17	0.17	0.17	0.26
	$\lvert\mathcal{P}_{BFA}\rvert$	6.40	6.57	6.90	8.60
a3a	R	1	1	1	1
	E	0.18	0.16	0.14	0
	T	0.21	0.21	0.22	0.32
	$\lvert\mathcal{P}_{BFA}\rvert$	7.80	8.03	8.17	10.77
acoustic (1)	R	1	1	1	1
	E	0.22	0.18	0.18	0
	T	0.11	0.11	0.12	0.20
	$\lvert\mathcal{P}_{BFA}\rvert$	3.93	4.13	4.23	8.57
connect-4 (1)	R	0.94	0.94	0.96	0.96
	E	0.18	0.16	0.10	0
	T	0.18	0.19	0.19	0.29
	$\lvert\mathcal{P}_{BFA}\rvert$	7.37	7.67	8.27	10.17
MiniBooNE	R	1	1	1	1
	E	0.41	0.41	0.40	0
	T	0.14	0.15	0.16	0.24
	$\lvert\mathcal{P}_{BFA}\rvert$	4.90	5.27	5.6	22.00
protein (1)	R	1	1	1	0.99
	E	0.56	0.56	0.54	0
	T	0.32	0.32	0.33	0.44
	$\lvert\mathcal{P}_{BFA}\rvert$	5.03	5.13	5.77	19.03
mushrooms	R	0.97	0.97	0.99	0.99
	E	0.15	0.15	0.18	0
	T	0.08	0.08	0.08	0.17
	$\lvert\mathcal{P}_{BFA}\rvert$	2.17	2.2	2.2	4.73
w1a	R	1	1	1	0.95
	E	0.20	0.22	0.20	0
	T	0.28	0.29	0.30	0.63
	$\lvert\mathcal{P}_{BFA}\rvert$	2.97	2.97	3.07	9.43

Table 5: S-Race on 2-objective problems: Average Retention R, Excess E, computational effort T relative to BFA and final BFA ensemble size $|\mathcal{P}_{BFA}|$ for varying Δ values

Regarding the retention (R) values, one observes that they are all close to 1 regardless of the values of Δ, which implies that Pareto-optimal models chosen by the BFA are all retained by the race. In cases, where S-Race did not achieve a retention value of 1 (for instance, for the *connect-4(1)* and *mushrooms* datasets), it is obvious that the R increases as expected with increasing value of Δ.

Regarding excess (E), the obtained values are typically less than 25%, but there are cases, such as the *protein(1)* dataset, where E is around 0.5; this means that about half of the final models returned by the S-Race were dominated models according to the BFA. However, with increasing Δ, E values decrease. This is expected, since, when Δ is large, fewer models will be removed and the size of the Pareto-optimal models produced by the BFA is large. When Δ is extremely close to 1, all E values are 0.

The corresponding results for the 3-class recognition problems are depicted in Table 6. In this case, $L = 3$ and, intuitively, we expect larger final ensembles being reported by the BFA and S-Race, as more non-dominated models will most likely be found. For this setting, the observations regarding the 3 metrics are similar to the ones made for the 2-class recognition problems. Apart from the case of *connect-4(2)*, whose retention values improve with increasing Δ, retention values for the remaining problems are fixed at 1. Typical E values seem to be slightly higher, which can be attributed to the increased number L of objectives, which, in turn, implies the existence of more non-dominated final models. The same reason seems to be behind the elevated values of T.

Dataset		Δ			
		0.7	0.8	0.9	0.999
acoustic (2)	R	1	1	1	0.99
	E	0.40	0.40	0.40	0
	T	0.26	0.27	0.28	0.47
	$\lvert\mathcal{P}_{BFA}\rvert$	3.53	3.60	4.10	18.60
combined	R	1	1	1	0.99
	E	0.30	0.31	0.30	0
	T	0.19	0.19	0.20	0.37
	$\lvert\mathcal{P}_{BFA}\rvert$	3.17	3.20	3.47	16.03
protein (2)	R	1	1	1	1
	E	0.11	0.08	0.07	0
	T	0.53	0.53	0.54	0.78
	$\lvert\mathcal{P}_{BFA}\rvert$	18.27	18.87	19.17	25.83
seismic	R	1	1	1	1
	E	0.30	0.26	0.25	0
	T	0.24	0.24	0.25	0.46
	$\lvert\mathcal{P}_{BFA}\rvert$	4.40	4.70	5.00	22.47
connect-4 (2)	R	0.95	0.95	0.98	0.99
	E	0.13	0.11	0.11	0
	T	0.20	0.20	0.21	0.42
	$\lvert\mathcal{P}_{BFA}\rvert$	1.43	1.50	1.50	3.20
dna	R	1	1	1	1
	E	0.30	0.27	0.23	0
	T	0.31	0.32	0.33	0.50
	$\lvert\mathcal{P}_{BFA}\rvert$	7.00	7.33	7.90	14.80

Table 6: S-Race on 3-objective problems: Average Retention R, Excess E, computational effort T relative to BFA and final BFA ensemble size $|\mathcal{P}_{BFA}|$ for varying Δ values

Finally, we ought to comment on the variability of the E and R values obtained in the previous sets of experiments. It was observed that E's variability, as measured by standard deviation, depends on the specific experiment, but, in general, was relative high; a typical value encountered was 0.25. However, it also typically decreased, in most cases to 0.0, with increasing Δ. The opposite effect holds for R. Also, R's standard deviation was a magnitude smaller than the one of E for high Δ values, but, usually, it was 0.0. These effects are less of a surprise given the fact that S-Race strongly controls the probability of Type-I errors, which, in turn, is intimately connected to R, but far less to E.

To allow for better insight in how S-Race performs its task, in Figure 1 we show how the metrics R, E and T vary during the course of the race for the 2-class recognition problem connected to the *a2a* dataset. Along with the aforementioned metrics, we also report the proportion P of initial candidate models still racing at each step of the race. Note that the results reported are averages over 30 runs.

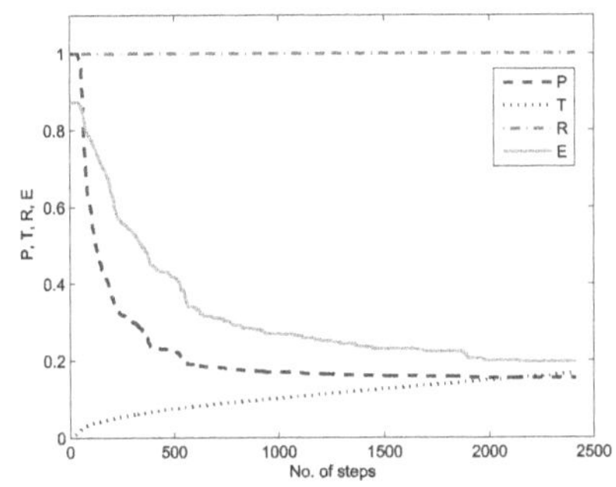

(a) $\Delta = 0.7$

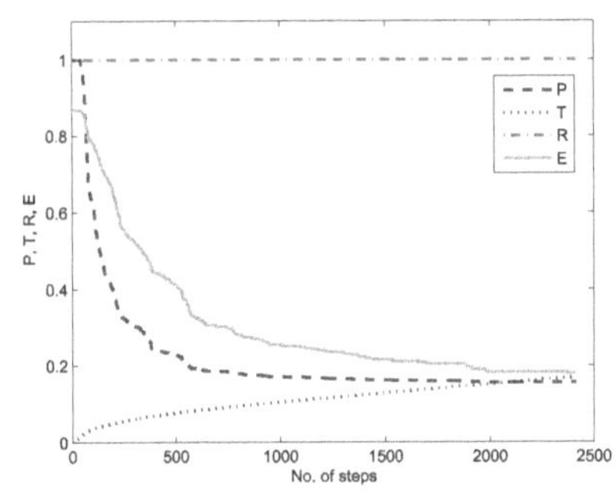

(b) $\Delta = 0.8$

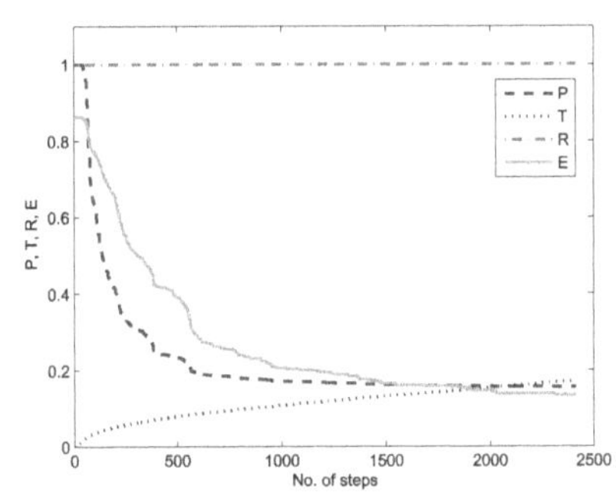

(c) $\Delta = 0.9$

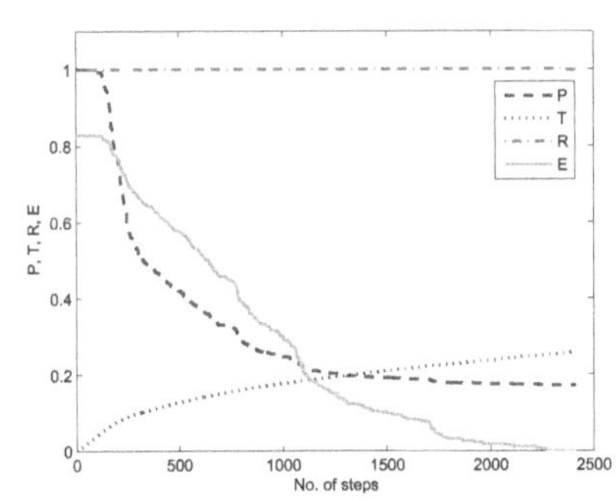

(d) $\Delta = 0.999$

Figure 1: *a2a* dataset: Averages of retention R, excess E, computational effort T relative to BFA and proportion P of initial candidate models still racing vs. S-Race steps.

From the figure it can be observed that retention values remain fixed at 1 during the course of the race as expected given the corresponding result of R for this dataset in Table 5. Obviously, the values P decrease as the race proceeds eliminating dominated models through its course. The decrease is sharp during the first 200 steps and continues becoming smaller until it levels off after 2000 steps. This implies that S-Race is able to greatly save on computations after the early stages of racing. This is also reflected in the T curves, which remain uniformly below 1. The E curve follows a similar predictable trend according to the P curve. As Δ increases, we witness a faster decreases in E values that result in lower final E values. For Δ close to 1, as expected, the computational effort of the S-Race increases noticeably.

4. CONCLUSIONS

In this paper, we presented S-Race, which is a racing algorithm for Multi-Objective Model Selection (MOMS). Such problems are encountered often in machine learning contexts, such as multi-task learning, where model selection needs to be based on a model's merit according to more than one criterion/objective. Unlike other approaches that have appeared previously in the literature, S-Race addresses MOMS problems in the proper sense of Pareto-optimality. Being a typical Racing Algorithm (RA), S-Race attempts to identify dominated models early on in the race, in order to retire them and save on computations. As S-Race assumes stochastic objectives, it relies on the non-parametric Sign Test to establish dominance relationships between pairs of models. Furthermore, it employs Holm's Step-Down procedure to test many pair-wise dominance relationships simultaneously. We showed that S-Race allows for strong control of Type I errors, *i.e.*, wrongly retiring models, which should have been retained in the race.

The ultimate purpose of S-Race is to produce, ideally, the same final ensemble of non-dominated models as a Brute-Force Approach (BFA) would yield, *i.e.*, an approach that identifies non-dominated models in one sweep using the entire set of available validation samples, but at a fraction of computational cost. We showcased the efficiency of S-Race in a series of MOMS experiments involving ensembles of Support Vector Machines (SVMs) that were trained for 2- and 3-class recognition problems. The results showed that S-Race is able to report, most of the time, the same non-dominated models as BFA would do, while at the same time exhibiting significant computational savings. However, it also tends to yield additional models that the BFA would find as being dominated by other members of the ensemble. As the desired maximum Type I error decreases, these excess models seize to appear in S-Race's final ensemble. At the same time, though, the computational savings decline. On balance, our experimental results imply that S-Race typically offers cogent computational advantages in exchange for relatively small discrepancies in the set of Pareto-optimal models as inferred by the BFA.

5. ACKNOWLEDGMENTS

T. Zhang acknowledges partial support from National Science Foundation (NSF) grants No. 1200566 and No. 0525429. Moreover, M. Georgiopoulos acknowledges partial support from NSF grants No. 0525429, No. 0963146, No. 1200566 and No. 1161228. Any opinions, findings, and conclusions or recommendations expressed in this material are those of the authors and do not necessarily reflect the views of the NSF. Finally, the authors would like to thank the anonymous reviewers of this manuscript for their time and helpful comments.

6. REFERENCES

[1] B. Adenso-Díaz and M. Laguna. Fine-tuning of algorithms using fractional experimental designs and local search. *Operations Research*, 54:99–114, 2006.

[2] S. Becker, J. Gottlieb, and T. Stützle. Applications of racing algorithms: An industrial perspective. In *Lecture Notes in Computer Science*, volume 3871, chapter Artificial Evolution, pages 271–283. Springer, 2005.

[3] M. Birattari, T. Stützle, L. Paquete, and K. Varrentrapp. A racing algorithm for configuring metaheuristics. In *GECCO'02 Proceedings of the Genetic and Evolutionary Computation Conference*, pages 11–18, 2002.

[4] M. Birattari, Z. Yuan, P. Balaprakash, and T. Stützle. F-race and iterated f-race: An overview. Technical report, IRIDIA, 2011.

[5] C.-C. Chang and C.-J. Lin. LIBSVM: A library for support vector machines. *ACM Transactions on Intelligent Systems and Technology*, 2:1-27, 2011.

[6] M. Chiarandini, M. Birattari, K. Socha, and O. Rossi-doria. An effective hybrid algorithm for university course timetabling. *J Sched*, 9:403–432, 2006.

[7] C. Cortes and V. N. Vapnik. Support-vector networks. *Machine Learning*, 20:273–297, 1995.

[8] K. Deb. *Multi-Objective Optimization Using Evolutionary Algorithms*. John Wiley & Sons, 2009.

[9] M. Duarte and Y. H. Hu. Vehicle classification in distributed sensor networks. *Journal of Parallel and Distributed Computing*, 64:826–838, 2004.

[10] V. Heidrich-Meisner and C. Igel. Hoeffding and bernstein races for selecting policies in evolutionary direct policy search. In *ICML '09 Proceedings of the 26th Annual International Conference on Machine Learning*, pages 401–408, 2009.

[11] Y. Hochberg and A. Tamhane. *Multiple Comparison Procedures*. New York: Wiley, 1987.

[12] S. Holm. A simple sequentially rejective multiple test procedure. *Scandinavian Journal of Statistics*, 2:65–70, 1979.

[13] M. Horn and C. W. Dunnett. Power and sample size comparisons of stepwise fwe and fdr controlling test procedures in the normal many-one case. *Recent Developments in Multiple Comparison Procedures*, 47:48–64, 2004.

[14] E. J. Hughes. Evolutionary multi-objective ranking with uncertainty and noise. *Evolutionary Multi-criterion Optimization*, 1999:329–343, 2001.

[15] Y. Jin. Pareto-based multiobjective machine learning: An overview and case studies. *IEEE Transactions on Systems, Man and Cybernetics, Part C: APplications and Reviews*, 38:397–415, 2008.

[16] H. Leather, M. O. Boyle, and B. Worton. Raced profiles: Efficient selection of competing compiler optimizations. In *roceedings of the 2009 ACM SIGPLAN/SIGBED conference on Languages, compilers, and tools for embedded systems*, pages 50–59, 2009.

[17] S. Lessmann, R. Stahlbock, and S. Crone. Genetic algorithms for support vector machine model selection. In *IJCNN '06. International Joint Conference on Neural Networks*, pages 3063–3069, 2006.

[18] M. Lopez-Ibanez and T. Stützle. Automatic configuration of multi-objective aco algorithms. In *Proceedings of 7th International Conference, ANTS 2010, Brussels, Belgium, September 8-10, 2010.*, pages 95–106, 2010.

[19] M. Lopez-Ibanez and T. Stützle. Automatically improving the anytime behaviour of optimisation algorithms. Technical report, IRIDIA, 2012.

[20] O. Maron and A. Moore. Hoeffding races: Accelerating model selection search for classification and function approximation. *Advances in Neural Information Processing Systems*, 6:59–66, 1994.

[21] W. Mendenhall, D. D. Wackerly, and R. L. Scheaffer. *Mathematical Statistics with Applications*, chapter Nonparametric statistics, pages 674–679. PWS-Kent, 1989.

[22] V. Mnih and C. Szepesvari. Empirical bernstein stopping. In *Proceedings of the 25th International Conference on Machine Learning*, 2008.

[23] A. W. Moore. Efficient algorithms for minimizing cross validation error. In *Proceedings of the Eleventh International Conference on Machine Learning*, pages 190–198, 1994.

[24] D. J. Newman, S. Hettich, C. L. Blake, and C. J. Merz. UCI repository of machine learning databases, 1998.

[25] J. C. Platt. *Advances in Kernel Methods - Support Vector Learning*, chapter Fast training of support vector machines using sequential minimal optimization. MIT Press, 1998.

[26] A. C. Tamhane. Multiple comparisons. In E. S. Ghosh and C. R. Rao, editors, *Handbook of Statistics*, pages 587–630. Elsevier Science, 1996.

[27] J. Teich. Pareto-front exploration with uncertain objectives. *Evolutionary Multi-criterion Optimization*, 1999:314–328, 2001.

[28] J.-Y. Wang. Application of support vector machines in bioinformatics. Master's thesis, National Taiwan University, 2002.

[29] B. Yuan and M. Gallagher. Statistical racing techniques for improved empirical evaluation of evolutionary algorithms. In *Parallel Problem Solving from Nature - PPSN VIII, 8th International Conference*, pages 172–181, 2004.

Can Quantitative and Population Genetics Help us Understand Evolutionary Computation?

Nick Barton
Institute Science and Technology Austria
Am Campus, 1
Klosterneuburg, Austria
nick.barton@ist.ac.at

Tiago Paixão
Institute Science and Technology Austria
Am Campus, 1
Klosterneuburg, Austria
tiago.paixao@ist.ac.at

ABSTRACT

Even though both population and quantitative genetics, and evolutionary computation, deal with the same questions, they have developed largely independently of each other. I review key results from each field, emphasising those that apply independently of the (usually unknown) relation between genotype and phenotype. The infinitesimal model provides a simple framework for predicting the response of complex traits to selection, which in biology has proved remarkably successful. This allows one to choose the schedule of population sizes and selection intensities that will maximise the response to selection, given that the total number of individuals realised, $C = \sum_t N_t$, is constrained. This argument shows that for an additive trait (i.e., determined by the sum of effects of the genes), the optimum population size and the maximum possible response (i.e., the total change in trait mean) are both proportional to $\sqrt{C}$.

Categories and Subject Descriptors

F.2.2 [**Analysis of Algorithms and Problem Complexity**]: Nonnumerical Algorithms and Problems

General Terms

Theory

Keywords

Theory, Genetic algorithms, Selection, Speedup technique, Working principles of evolutionary computing, Population genetics

1. INTRODUCTION

Evolutionary biology began with Darwin's development of the idea of natural selection, by analogy with the artificial selection of domesticated plants and animals. The rediscovery of Mendelian genetics in 1900 led to its eventual synthesis with Darwinian selection; by the 1930s, the population genetics developed by Fisher, Haldane and Wright provided a sophisticated quantitative theory of evolution [32]. Following the elucidation of the physical basis of heredity in the 1960s, Kimura applied stochastic population genetics to the evolution of DNA sequence [16]. In parallel, quantitative genetics, developed in the practical context of plant and animal breeding, provided a statistical description of the evolution of complex traits that is largely independent of the genetic details.

It was realised very early that selection provides a powerful and general algorithm for designing complex systems: indeed, this was the central problem which Darwin set out to explain. Fisher [7] presented a simple geometrical model for optimisation in multiple dimensions, which has been widely applied in recent years [28]. Wright [42] introduced the metaphor of the "adaptive landscape", and the theory of a "shifting balance", to understand how evolution might avoid being trapped at local optima. Kimura [16] estimated the amount of information that could be accumulated by selection ($\sim 10^8$ bits since the Cambrian). Digital computers were first used to simulate evolving populations in the 1950's, and the idea that such simulations could be used to solve computational problems was taken up soon after [9]. This has led to diverse approaches to evolutionary computation: genetic algorithms, genetic programming, artificial life, and so on. Population geneticists also used computer simulation extensively, yet there has been remarkably little interaction between these parallel developments.

Why have the fields developed almost independently? Evolutionary biology is concerned with many issues that are not directly relevant to computation: tracing the actual history of species and genes, understanding the genetic basis of phenotypic variation and the processes that maintain it, understanding the origin of new species, and so on. Yet, natural selection plays a special role as the sole cause of adaptation, and understanding how selection leads to complex adaptation is central to both evolutionary biology and evolutionary computation.

An important difference between the fields is that evolutionary biologists are resistant to ideas that evolution is in any sense optimal, leading to "progress", or to any necessary increase in complexity (though, see [37]). This is largely a reaction against naive ideas that evolution acts "for the good of the species" (see [41]). Thus, rather than asking what genetic system would be most effective, we ask what in fact evolves - which may in extreme cases even lead to extinction (e.g. [8]). Another difference is that in evolutionary

GECCO'13, July 6–10, 2013, Amsterdam, The Netherlands.

computation, we are free to make up arbitrary rules - retaining the fittest individuals indefinitely, allowing sex between more than two individuals, and changing parameters at will. Nevertheless, actual algorithms tend to use the same basic processes, and as we shall see, diverse implementations are often equivalent. The lack of communication between evolutionary biology and evolutionary computation may simply reflect the human tendency to form separate communities; indeed, both fields are fragmented into many subfields, grouped around different journals and conferences. The arguments set out here suggest that recombination between fields as well as subfields would be beneficial.

Evolutionary biology and evolutionary computation share the same fundamental questions, and can learn much from each other. First, how effective can selection be? Thinking on the largest scale, were $\sim$ 4,000 million years (Myr) needed for the present complexity of life to evolve? Could we have evolved in 400 Myr, or in 40 Myr? What limits the ability of selection to evolve and maintain complex organisms and complex algorithms? On a smaller scale, how should we optimise a selection scheme, given constraints on the number of organisms and their reproductive capacity, or on the number of computations? Second, does the genetic system evolve to be evolvable? In evolutionary biology, a long-standing question has been whether mutation and recombination are maintained because these processes produce the variation that is essential for adaptation; such questions are close to the parallel questions in evolutionary computation, of what are the optimal rates of mutation and cross-over, and how can they be chosen. A harder question - which has only recently received sustained attention in biology - concerns the relation between genotype and phenotype [20]. In evolutionary computation, it is clear that the way an algorithm is coded is crucial. It is extraordinary that the development and behaviour of a complex organism can be coded by relatively little information (at most 6×10^9 bits in the human genome, for example), and that organisms are robust to random changes in this code.

2. A COMMON FRAMEWORK

The basic theoretical framework is common to both fields. A genotype is represented by a linear sequence that represents a DNA molecule or a bit string. In real organisms, each nucleotide can take one of four values $\{A, T, G, C\}$, but this is most often approximated by $\{0, 1\}$, since there are usually at most two variants per site. Blocks of sequence can be represented by multiple discrete values (termed *alleles*) or by a continuous value. Nevertheless, for most cases a bit string $\underline{X}$ suffices.

Selection acts through the fitness of each individual; we take the fitness of an individual to be the number of offspring it produces after one discrete generation, W, or its rate of reproduction in continuous time, r. A full stochastic model would require the distribution of fitness of each genotype. However, when selection is weak, all that matters is the expected fitness; the variance in fitness determines the rate of random fluctuation, and can be taken to be the same for all genotypes. We write the expected fitness of genotype $\underline{X}$ as $W(\underline{X})$ or $r(\underline{X})$, in discrete or continuous time. In evolutionary computation, "fitness" often refers to some measure that is to be optimised, and reproduction is some function of this measure. We will keep to the population genetic usage, referring to such measures as fitness components, $\omega(\underline{X})$. Often, we also need to consider a set of *traits*, whose expected value is an arbitrary function of genotype, $\underline{z}(\underline{X})$, and which in turn determine the fitness components, $\underline{\omega}(\underline{z})$; traits can be arbitrary functions of genotype. To give a concrete example, a cow can be described by a set of traits (milk yield, growth rate, lifespan, etc), and these depend in a complex way on both genotype and environment. These traits in turn determine some selection index, ω, which the farmer uses to determine which cows will breed: for example, those below some threshold all have zero fitness (note that there are complex issues concerning the way we average over variation at each level, which we ignore). Population genetic terms and notation are summarised in Table 1 of the accompanying paper (Paixão and Barton, 2013).

Crucially, in both the real and the virtual worlds, the relation between phenotype (i.e., the traits, z) and genotype, $\underline{X}$, is unknown. It can be determined for any particular $\underline{X}$ by rearing an organism, or by carrying out a computation, both being expensive. We take this realisation of the organism or algorithm to determine the cost of the breeding program. Of course, in a computer we directly observe the code, and in biology, it is now feasible to determine the entire genome of an organism. However, observing the phenotype of even a very large number of individual genotypes does not tell us which sites cause differences in phenotype, or how they interact: this fundamental problem frustrates large-scale genome-wide association studies aimed at finding the variants that cause human disease. In plant and animal breeding, it is not at all clear how much knowing the full genome sequence helps.

The basic processes of selection, mutation, recombination and random sampling are common to both fields. (Migration between distinct populations may also be important, but is not considered here). In evolutionary computation, any kind of mutation or recombination can be invented, but also in biology, there can be arbitrary errors and rearrangements in copying the DNA sequence.

Provided that the composition of a population changes slowly, evolution can be approximated as being continuous in time, with the details of each process being absorbed into a single parameter - the selection coefficient, s, the rate of random sampling fluctuations, $1/N_e$, the rate of mutation, μ, and so on. As we shall see, the evolution of allele frequencies at individual loci may be slow, even when selection on the overall phenotype is strong. The outcome depends on the ratios between these rates ($N_e s$, $N_e \mu$, etc.); this gives population genetics a remarkable generality, which carries over to describe the idiosyncrasies of genetic algorithms.

Under this continuous time approximation, the distribution of states of the population follows a diffusion equation that depends on the mean and variance of change between generations: there is a precise analogy between the stochastic evolution of a population, and the diffusion of a molecule. In physics, we may deal with an actual collection of molecules, whereas in population genetics, we must imagine an abstract probability distribution across possible states of a single population; however, the mathematical description is the same. (The diffusion approximation developed independently in physics and population genetics, both tracing back originally to a model for share prices; [5]). Kimura [17] developed the diffusion approximation and applied it to molecular evolution; it is intimately connected with the coalescent process that describes the evolution of genealogical relations between sampled genes.

Even where the diffusion equation cannot be solved, it plays a key role in justifying the use of scaled parameter combinations, and allowing extrapolation from simulations of small populations over short times out to very large populations over long times. Moreover, it provides a precise connection with statistical physics, which rests on the same mathematical foundation.

2.1 Some key results

Although any model can in principle be solved numerically, we seek general analytical results that aid our intuitive understanding. The main difficulty is in dealing with arbitrary interactions in the nonlinear relation between genotype and phenotype, $z(\underline{X})$. Nevertheless, there are some general results, summarised in Table 1. Most of these results apply with arbitrary interactions; exceptions are the three results for genetic load are derived assuming no interaction, but which extend to allow some forms of interaction.

It is surprising that few results have been transferred between the fields, or independently re-derived. Perhaps the most prominent theoretical concept in evolutionary computation is Holland's [14] idea of "schema", which correspond in population genetics to the *average excess* of a combination of alleles; Livnat et al.'s [22] coefficients of "mixability" are closely related, and correspond to *average effects* - a regression of trait values onto the allelic values. Attention has been drawn to Wright's "shifting balance" theory, but only in a qualitative way [27, 39]. The strongest connection between evolutionary biology and evolutionary computation has been made by Mühlenbein and Mahnig [24], who use the *breeder's equation* to make a deterministic analysis of genetic algorithms; they emphasise the independent evolution of allele frequencies, which will be the focus of this note. Several statistical physicists have included the effect of random sampling on evolving populations; Prügel-Bennet [33] describes a maximum-entropy approximation for trait evolution, whilst [4, 38] independently derive the stationary distribution in the limit where populations are close to fixation for a single type. These results are closely related to Wright's [43] more general formula for the stationary distribution of allele frequencies [2, 3].

2.2 Evolution as hill-climbing

We will focus on how selection can most efficiently accumulate favourable alleles, viewing evolution as a hill-climbing algorithm. This needs some justification, since the central problem in optimisation is often seen quite differently: how to find the best solution, without being trapped at local peaks. These different viewpoints were at the heart of the long dispute between Fisher and Wright [31]. Fisher's view was that although "adaptive valleys" obviously exist, populations may never cross them: there may always be ways by which fitness can increase, especially since in nature, the adaptive landscape changes with the environment. The metaphor of an adaptive landscape may be misleading when visualised in two dimensions: if there are enough degrees of freedom, progress may always be possible in some direction. If the landscape were in fact so rugged that populations are trapped within a few steps, then any search algorithm would be frustrated: values of individuals already tested must carry some information about untested individuals, otherwise search might as well be random.

It is important to understand that there are distinct versions of the adaptive landscape: it may refer to individuals or to populations, and it may refer to genotypes or to traits. The first distinction is between the fitness of an individual, considered as a function of its genotype or traits ($W(\underline{X})$ or $W(\underline{z})$), and the mean fitness of a population, considered as a function of its allele frequencies, or trait means $\left(\bar{W}(\underline{p})\right.$ or $\left.\bar{W}\left(\underline{\underline{z}}\right)\right)$; Wright used these without distinction [32]. However, it is the latter that leads to a quantitative theory: selection moves populations through allele frequency or trait space at a rate proportional to the gradient of mean fitness, and (provided that genes are well shuffled by recombination) the stationary distribution is proportional to $\bar{W}^{2N_e}$ [43].

The second distinction is between the adaptive landscape in allele frequency space versus trait space. We will assume a smooth relation between fitness and traits, and ask how efficiently selection can push a population towards the locally fittest trait combination. However, even if there is a single peak in trait space, there may be multiple peaks in genotype space: even in the simplest case where traits are additive (i.e., $z = \sum_i \alpha_i X_i$), many combinations of + and - alleles can give the optimal phenotype. However, populations cannot evolve between different combinations by selection alone, because mixed populations will produce sub-optimal genotypes by recombination. Despite this microscopic ruggedness of the landscape, low rates of mutation and random sampling can allow populations to evolve smoothly and predictably at the phenotypic level [3].

Note that in a large sexual population, if the individual-level landscape has multiple peaks, then so will the population-level version - provided that we consider allele-frequency space: if all single-step changes from the locally fittest genotype are deleterious, then none can invade from low frequency, and a fitter *combination* of alleles will be broken up by recombination. In contrast, an asexual population can move towards a higher peak provided that the mutation rate is high enough that fitter combinations, involving multiple changes, are generated. A similar smoothing occurs in a sexual population, when we consider the evolution of phenotypic traits: the mean fitness of a population $\left(\bar{W}\left(\underline{\underline{z}}\right)\right)$ is a smoothed version of the individual-level landscape (W(z)), so that if the genetic variance is high enough, adaptive valleys may be smoothed out [19].

2.3 Evolution of allele frequencies

In the following, we assume that alleles are well shuffled (i.e., in *linkage equilibrium*), so that the composition of a population is described by its allele frequencies. This is a good approximation for natural populations if recombination is faster than other processes, and indeed, applies to most outcrossing sexual species. In simulations, it can be imposed by constructing individuals locus by locus, from the list of allele frequencies; this is a kind of mass mating, in which all the genomes in the population take part, rather than just two at a time [24]. In a breeding program, the same result could be obtained by allowing several generations of reproduction in the absence of selection.

The prevalence of sexual reproduction suggests that natural selection acts most efficiently in this limit of complete shuffling. However, it has taken a substantial theoretical ef-

Population genetics			
Breeder's equation	$\Delta\bar{z} = \frac{V_a}{V_p} S$	V_a : additive variance V_p : total variance S : change in $\bar{z}$ due to selection	[23]
Wright's gradient formula	$\Delta\bar{z} = V_a \frac{\partial \log(\bar{W})}{\partial \bar{z}}$		[21, 43]
Secondary theorem of natural selection	$\Delta\bar{z} = \text{cov}\left(\frac{W}{\bar{W}}, z\right)$		[30, 35]
Mutation load	$\frac{\Delta\bar{W}}{\bar{W}} \sim -U$	U: total rate of deleterious mutation	[10, 25]
Substitution load	$\sum_t \Delta\log\left(\bar{W}\right) \sim -\log\left(\frac{1}{p_0}\right)$	p_0 : initial allele frequency	[11]
Drift load	$\frac{\Delta\bar{W}}{\bar{W}} \sim -\frac{d}{2N_e}$	d : #of degrees of freedom N_e : effective population size	[18]
Wright's distribution	$\left(\prod_i p_i^{4N_e\mu-1} q_i^{4N_e\nu-1}\right) \bar{W}^{2N_e}$	μ, ν: rate of mutation away from alleles P, Q	[43]
Statistical physics			
Fitness flux	$\left\langle e^{-N_e\Phi+\Delta\mathcal{H}}\right\rangle = 1$	Φ : net fitness flux $\Delta\mathcal{H}$: change in log likelihood	[15, 26]
Maximum entropy	$\frac{\partial}{\partial t}\langle \underline{A}\rangle \sim \underline{B}.(\underline{\alpha} - \underline{\alpha}^*)$		[3]
Evolutionary computation			
Schema theorem	$E\left[\frac{g_{t+1}[H]}{g_t[H]}\right] \geq \frac{W_t[H]}{\bar{W}_t}(1-\pi)$	$g_t[H]$: frequency of H at time t π : probability that H is broken up	[14]
Drift analysis			[12]

Table 1: Summarises key results from the various fields, in schematic form. The first three lines give alternative formulae for the change in trait mean, $\Delta\bar{z}$, due to selection and reproduction, ignoring random fluctuations. The next three lines give the net reduction in mean fitness (i.e., the *genetic load*) due to deleterious mutations at total rate U, due to substitution of an allele that was initially at frequency p_0, and due to random sampling (termed *drift* in population genetics). The final formula drawn from population genetics gives the stationary distribution of allele frequencies under mutation, selection and random sampling. The first result from statistical physics relates the change in log likelihood, $\Delta\mathcal{H}$, to the net *fitness flux*, Φ, a measure of the total selection acting along an arbitrary path. The next result approximates the change in expectation of arbitrary traits, A, under selection on those traits α; α^* is the selection that would maintain the current $\langle \mathbf{A}\rangle$, and B is a generalised additive genetic covariance. The penultimate result sets a bound on the change in frequency of a combination of alleles (or *schema*), H, given by the product of its relative fitness and its chance of surviving recombination and mutation, $1-\pi$. Finally, *drift analysis* sets bounds on the number of computations (or *runtime*) needed to reach some desired region of search space.

fort to show exactly why this is so, and how it leads to the selection of higher rates of recombination. Essentially, recombination is favoured because it breaks up negative associations between favourable alleles (++−, −++ etc.), which mask the effects of each individual allele. Thus, in the presence of negative associations, recombination increases the additive genetic variance that drives the response to selection. An allele that increases recombination is at an immediate disadvantage, because it breaks up favourable gene combinations, but gains a long-term advantage, because it is associated with increased additive variance [1]. The key issue, then, is why there should tend to be negative associations among alleles. Such associations may be generated by selection, but this requires a delicate choice of parameters, for which there is little evidence. More generally, random drift interacts with directional selection to generate negative associations: in the simplest case, different favourable mutations almost always arise separately, and so must be brought together by recombination. This is known as the Hill-Robertson effect [13]; when a large number of loci are selected, it is more significant than epistatic interactions, even in large populations [29]. This justifies our focus on well-shuffled populations.

2.4 The infinitesimal model

Here, we focus on the *infinitesimal model*, introduced by Fisher [6]. This has been developed as the foundation of animal breeding, yet has received relatively little attention within population genetics. It allows a remarkably general analysis of the performance of genetic algorithms, without requiring detailed knowledge of the complex relation between genotype and phenotype.

At the phenotypic level, the infinitesimal model is easily defined, Unrelated parents produce offspring with trait values that are normally distributed around the mean of the parents, with fixed variance $\frac{V_0}{2}$. If individuals mate randomly, and all have the same fitness, then the population rapidly tends to a normal distribution with variance V_0: random mating reduces the variance twofold in each generation, but this is compensated by the release of genetic variance within families (i.e., $V_{t+1} = \frac{V_t}{2} + \frac{V_0}{2}$). Selection can produce arbitrary distortions in the trait distribution, but these rapidly dissipate, so that in the long term, only the mean changes, the variance remaining constant.

If parents are related, sharing a fraction F of their genes *identical by descent*, the within-family variance is reduced by a factor $(1-F)$; in a population of size N, $(1-F)$ decreases by a factor $\left(1-\frac{1}{N}\right)$ per generation. Mutation adds a constant variance V_m per generation, and so at an equilibrium between mutation, random sampling, and sexual reproduction, the trait variance equilibrates at $N\,V_m$.

This simple phenotypic model can be justified in the limit of a very large number of unlinked loci, n,with additive effects. The within-family variance is generated by recombination, at a rate proportional to the number of heterozygous loci, which is in turn proportional to $(1-F)$. Selection on each locus is weak $\left(s \sim \frac{1}{n}\right)$, and so only changes the genetic variance over timescales of $\sim n$ generations. Short - term changes in the distribution are due to correlations between loci (*linkage disequilibria*), and so dissipate rapidly in the absence of genetic linkage. Here, we assume that the population is well shuffled (i.e., in *linkage equilibrium*), so that the distribution is close to Gaussian; this is a good approximation even with quite strong selection, and can be imposed directly in a genetic algorithm.

The infinitesimal model leads immediately to a simple prediction for the total response to selection - that is, the total change in the expected trait mean [34]. Genetic variance dissipates at a rate $1-\frac{1}{N}$, and so the total genetic variance, summed over generations, is $V_1 N$. Since the change in mean (i.e., the *selection response*) is proportional to V_t in each generation, the total change is just $\sum_{t=1}^{\infty} \Delta\bar{z}_t = N\Delta\bar{z}_1$. Robertson [34] gave an alternative derivation of this result, based on the probability $u(a,p)$ that an allele with effect a and with frequency p will ultimately be fixed in the population. The total change in the trait mean must be $\sum_{t=1}^{\infty} \Delta\bar{z}_t = \sum_i a_i\left(u\left(a_i, p_i\right) - p_i\right)$, where the sum on the right is over all loci, i. If the effect of an allele, a, is weak, then $u = p + N\beta\, a\, p(1-p) + O\left(a^2\right)$, where $\beta = \partial W/\partial z$ [34]. This immediately gives $\sum_{t=1}^{\infty} \Delta\bar{z}_t = N\beta\sum_i a_i^2 p_i\left(1-p_i\right) = N_e\beta \mathrm{V}_1 = N\Delta\bar{z}_1$. This shows that under the infinitesimal model, the change in the mean is due to the cumulative effect of small perturbations to the distribution of allele frequencies at each locus. This simple additive approximation predicts the selection response over 50 generations remarkably well, for a wide range of traits and organisms (Figure 1, from [40]). This suggests that the infinitesimal model may also give a good approximation to arbitrary genetic algorithms, where the relation between genotype and traits, $z(\underline{X})$, is far from additive.

Robertson's derivation suggests a generalisation to arbitrary relations between genotype and phenotype. If traits depend on a large number of loci, then strong selection on the traits may only slightly perturb the underlying distribution of allele frequencies from its neutral trajectory. Moreover, this perturbation depends only on the marginal effect of the allele - that is, its additive effect on the trait. In the short term, the mean changes at a rate proportional to the additive variance, which itself stays approximately constant. In the longer term, the additive effects change as the genetic background changes, in an unpredictable way that depends on how genes interact. However, it may still be possible to optimise the selection scheme, using purely "local" information.

2.5 Optimising the selection response

How can we optimise the net response to selection, for a given total number of individuals? For simplicity, we neglect mutation, and assume that the mean changes solely by selection on the initial pool of variation. We begin by assuming *truncation selection* on an additive trait, z, choosing the best θ of individuals out of N $(0 < \theta < 1)$. In order to

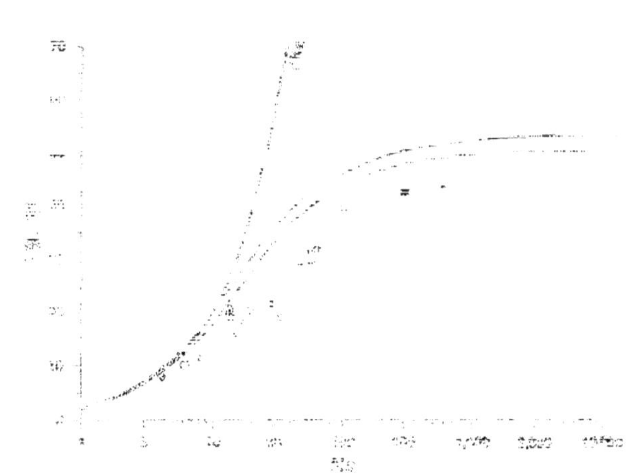

Figure 1: The ratio between the change in mean over 50 generations, and the change in the first generation (R_{50}/R_1), plotted against effective population size, N_e. Symbols represent the outcome of independent selection experiments in maize, mouse and Drosophila. The upper curve (labeled $2N_e$) is Robertson's [34]) prediction for the ultimate response, $R_\infty = 2N_e R_1$, whilst the lower curve is the prediction for the response at 50 generations, from the same infinitesimal model. The middle curve is the prediction including a contribution from mutation, $V_m = 0.001V_g$, which makes little difference over this short timescale. The observed responses are about 10-20% below the prediction, probably reflecting the effect of selection on alleles of large effect; however, the overall relationship fits surprisingly well, given that the selected traits are unlikely to have an additive genetic basis. From Figure 4 in [40].

select a fraction θ from a normal distribution, those more than x standard deviations above the mean must be chosen; $\theta = \frac{1}{2}\mathrm{erfc}\left[\frac{x}{\sqrt{2}}\right]$, where erfc[]is the integral of a Gaussian. The direct effect of selection is to change the mean by $S = i(\theta)\sqrt{V}$, where V is the variance of the trait, and where $i = \frac{e^{-\frac{x^2}{2}}}{\theta\sqrt{2\pi}}$. Throughout, we assume that there is no non-genetic variance.

The problem is to choose the optimal N_i, θ_i, given the constraint $C = \sum_{t=1}^{\infty} N_t$. We will see that the maximum possible response has the form $A\sqrt{V_1 C_1}$, where A is to be determined. With this *ansatz*, we must trade an immediate gain of $i\left(\theta_1\right)\sqrt{V_1}$ against a future gain of:

$$A\sqrt{\left(C_1 - N_1\right) V_1\left(1 - \frac{1}{N_1\theta_1}\right)}$$

Note that the loss of variance depends on the number of *selected* individuals, $N_1\theta$, whereas the cost is counted as the total number of individuals, $C_1 = \sum_{t=1}^{\infty} N_t$. Assume that $C_t, N_t\theta_t$ are large, so that $C_t \gg N_t$, $N_t\theta_t \gg 1$. Then, the optimal scheme is $N_1 = \sqrt{C/\theta_1}$, $A = -2i'\theta_1^{3/2}$. The same argument applies throughout the process, and so gives the full schedule of N_t, θ_t. We see immediately that the optimal θ is the same throughout, but that the optimal N_t

decreases with the remaining number of individuals, $\sqrt{C_t}$. Approximating change as continuous in time, this implies that $\partial C/\partial t = -N = -\sqrt{C/\theta}$, so that $C = \left(\sqrt{C_1} - \frac{t}{2\sqrt{\theta}}\right)^2$, with selection ending at time $t_{\max} = 2\sqrt{C_1\theta}$. Integrating over time, we have:

$$A\sqrt{V_1C_1} = i\sqrt{V_1}\int_0^{2\sqrt{C_1\theta}} \exp\left(-\int_0^t \frac{d\tau}{2\sqrt{C_\tau/\theta}}\right) dt = \frac{2i\sqrt{V_1C_1\theta}}{1+\theta}$$

This confirms the ansatz, and implies $A = \frac{2i\sqrt{\theta}}{1+\theta}$. Combining this with the criterion for optimising θ, $A = -2i'\theta^{3/2}$, we find $\theta = 0.391$, $A = 0.883$. For comparison, if we select with constant N, θ for time $\frac{C}{N}$, then the response is $i\sqrt{V_1}\int_0^{C/N} \exp\left(-\frac{t}{N\theta}\right) dt = 2N\theta\, i\sqrt{V_1}\left(1 - \exp\left(-\frac{T}{2N\theta}\right)\right)$. The optimal solution is now when $\theta = 0.270$, $N = 1.213\sqrt{C}$, $T = \frac{\sqrt{C}}{1.213} = \frac{N}{1.471}$, and the net response is $0.574\sqrt{V_1C_1}$ - rather less than with the optimal schedule, in which N falls over time, and the total response is $0.883\sqrt{V_1C_1}$. These values agree with Robertson's analysis of this problem [36].

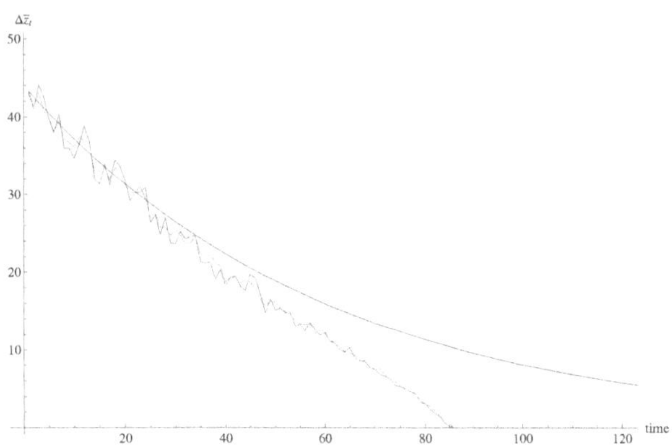

Figure 2: The decrease in the rate of response to truncation selection over time. The blue curve shows the change in mean in successive generations, averaged over 5 replicates. The red curve shows the predicted change, $\iota[\theta]\sqrt{V_t}$, which is proportional to the standard deviation of the trait. The upper smooth curve shows the predicted rate of decay of the standard deviation, $\sqrt{(1-1/N)^t} \sim e^{-t/(2N)}$. The area under the blue curve gives the total selection response, whilst the area under the smooth curve gives the prediction based on the infinitesimal model. There are N=30 selected individuals, each with 10^4 selected loci with equal additive effects, α=1. In each generation, N/θ=111 individuals are generated; the fraction selected is θ=0.27. Initial allele frequencies are drawn from a beta distribution with mean p_0=0.5, and variance $F\,p_0q_0$, $F = 0.5$.

These arguments are illustrated by simulations of truncation selection on an additive trait, based on 10^4 loci of equal effect, α=1, and starting with average allele frequency 0.5 - and hence a trait mean $\sum_{i=1}^n \alpha_i\, p_i = \frac{n}{2}$. Figure 2 shows an example with $N = 30$ selected individuals, showing how the standard deviation initially decreases as $\sqrt{(1-1/N)^t}$, but then falls away more rapidly than predicted by the infinitesimal model, as selection fixes favourable alleles. In any generation, the change in mean is very close to the prediction, $\iota\sqrt{V_t}$. The area under these jagged curves gives the total response to selection, which is somewhat less than the infinitesimal prediction, shown by the area under the smooth curve. Figure 3 shows that the infinitesimal model predicts the ultimate response quite well for N$\leq$30; in larger populations, selection is more effective at eliminating variation relative to sampling, and so the infinitesimal prediction is much to high. This must necessarily be so, because the ultimate response approaches the maximum possible, $\frac{n}{2}$, as N increases. Figure 4 shows the optimal choice of N,and the maximum possible response, given the constraint that the total number of individuals realised is $C = N\,T$ (and using constant N, θ for simplicity). This fits the predictions $\hat{N} = 1.213\sqrt{CV_0}$, $\hat{R} = 0.574\sqrt{C}$ well for $N \leq 50$; for larger values of C, $\hat{N}$ is larger and $\hat{R}$ is smaller, because selection as well as sampling eliminate variation.

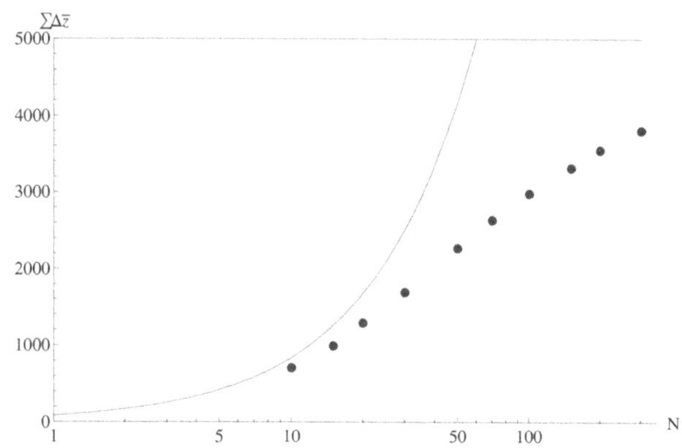

Figure 3: Points show the ultimate response to selection, $\sum_{t=1}^{\infty}\Delta\bar{z}_t$, plotted against the number of selected individuals, N; other parameters are as in Figure 2. The upper flat line shows the maximum possible change, $\frac{n}{2} = 5000$, and the curve shows the prediction based on the infinitesimal model, $2N\,\Delta\bar{z}_1$.

3. CONCLUSIONS

This note has outlined how quantitative genetics can predict the response of a population to selection on a trait, without any detailed knowledge of the genetic basis of that trait: the assumption is essentially that selection is spread over so many loci that the distribution of allele frequencies at each is hardly perturbed. In biology, this very simple model, which assumes additive effects, is remarkably successful in predicting the short-term evolution of traits that are clearly not additive (e.g. Figure 1). Figure 3 shows that the ultimate change due to selection on an additive trait - made without making any assumption whatever about the number of loci involved, the distribution of allele frequencies, or the distribution of allelic effects - is predicted well for small population sizes, provided that the number of loci is large. It overestimates the response for larger population sizes, essentially because the population approaches the global optimum, which sets an upper bound on the response. One might object that in evolutionary computation, one is interested in precisely this regime. However, local predictions for the response over some tens of generations, may allow optimisation of the selection scheme. In biology, artificial selection of domesticated plants and animals has been remarkable, even though it is very far from producing an ultimate "global optimal" (whatever that might mean).

Figure 4: The optimal population size, $\hat{N}$, and the corresponding maximum possible selection response, $\hat{R} = \left(\sum_{t=1}^{T} \Delta \bar{z}_t\right)_{\max}$, plotted against the total number of individuals realised, $C = TN/\theta$. These values are calculated by interpolation from the simulation results summarised in Figure 3. The straight lines show the theoretical predictions, $\hat{N} = 1.213\sqrt{CV_0}$, $\hat{R} = 0.574\sqrt{C}$.

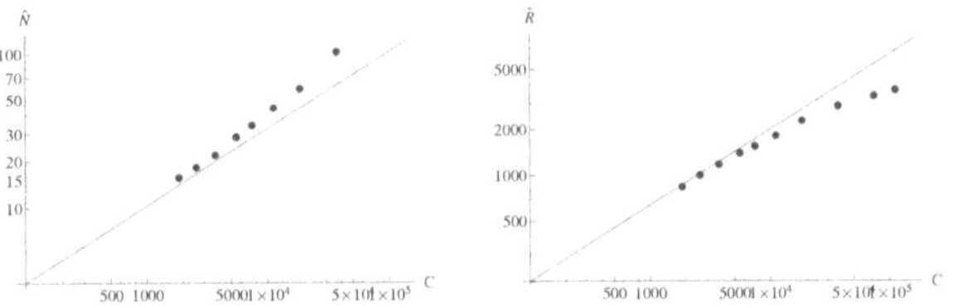

There is clearly much more to be done in applying quantitative genetic methods to improving evolutionary algorithms: most obviously, in finding the range of non-additive models for which these methods are sufficient approximations. Mutation should also be incorporated, and here one must take account of the effect of mutation in degrading the mean, as well as increasing the variance. An intriguing possibility is to use the regression of mean and variance of trait values on the number of mutations in the realised individuals, to estimate the optimal mutation rate.

4. ACKNOWLEDGMENTS

The authors would like to thank the reviewers for their helpful comments. This work was supported by ERC Advanced Grant ERC-2009-AdG-250152 SELECTIONINFORMATION.

5. REFERENCES

[1] N. H. Barton. A general model for the evolution of recombination. *Genetical Research*, 65(2):123–144, 1995.

[2] N. H. Barton and J. Coe. On the application of statistical physics to evolutionary biology. *Journal of Theoretical Biology*, 259(2):317–324, 2009.

[3] N. H. Barton and H. P. de Vladar. Statistical mechanics and the evolution of polygenic quantitative traits. *Genetics*, 181(3):997–1011, 2009.

[4] J. Berg, S. Willmann, and M. Lassig. Adaptive evolution of transcription factor binding sites. *BMC Evolutionary Biology*, 4(1):42, 2004.

[5] M. Davis and A. Etheridge. *Louis Bachelier's Theory of Speculation: The Origins of Modern Finance.* Princeton University Press, 2006.

[6] R. A. Fisher. The correlation between relatives on the supposition of mendelian inheritance. *Proceeding of the Royal Society of Edinburgh*, 52:399–433, 1918.

[7] R. A. Fisher. *The Genetical Theory of Natural Selection.* Clarendon Press, Oxford, 1930.

[8] D. B. Fogel, editor. *Evolutionary Computation: The Fossil Record.* Wiley-IEEE Press, 1 edition, 1998.

[9] P. J. Gerrish, A. Colato, A. S. Perelson, and P. D. Sniegowski. Complete genetic linkage can subvert natural selection. *PNAS*, 104(15):6266–6271, 2007.

[10] J. B. S. Haldane. The effect of variation of fitness. *The American Naturalist*, 71(735):337–349, 1937.

[11] J. B. S. Haldane. The cost of selection. *J. Genet.*, 55:511–524, 1957.

[12] J. He and X. Yao. A study of drift analysis for estimating computation time of evolutionary algorithms. *Natural Computing*, 3(1):21–35, 2004.

[13] W. Hill and A. Robertson. Effect of linkage on limits to artificial selection. *Genet. Res.*, 8(3):269–294, 1966.

[14] J. H. Holland. *Adaptation in natural and artificial systems: an introductory analysis with applications to biology, control, and artificial intelligence.* University of Michigan Press, 1975.

[15] C. Jarzynski. Nonequilibrium equality for free energy differences. *Phys. Rev. Lett.*, 78(14):2690–2693, 1997.

[16] M. Kimura. Natural selection as the process of accumulating genetic information in adaptive evolution. *Genetical Research*, 2(01):127–140, 1961.

[17] M. Kimura. *The Neutral Theory of Molecular Evolution.* Cambridge University Press, 1985.

[18] M. Kimura and T. Ohta. Genetic loads at a polymorphic locus which is maintained by frequency-dependent selection. *Genet. Res.*, 16(2):145–150, 1970.

[19] M. Kirkpatrick. Quantum evolution and punctuated equilibria in continuous genetic characters. *American Naturalist*, 119(6):833–848, 1982.

[20] M. Kirschner and J. Gerhart. Evolvability. *Proceeding of the Natianal Academy of Sciences U.S.A.*, 95(15):8420 –8427, 1998.

[21] R. Lande. Natural selection and random genetic drift in phenotypic evolution. *Evolution*, 30(2):314–334, 1976.

[22] A. Livnat, C. Papadimitriou, N. Pippenger, and M. W. Feldman. Sex, mixability, and modularity. *PNAS*, 107(4):1452–1457, 2010.

[23] J. Lush. *Animal Breeding Plans.* Iowa State University Press, 1956.

[24] H. Mühlenbeim and T. Mahnig. Evolutionary computation and beyond. In Y. Uesaka, P. Kanerva, and H. Asoh, editors, *Foundations of Real World Intelligence*, pages 123–187. University of Chicago Press, 2001.

[25] H. Muller. Our load of mutations. *Am. J. Hum. Genet.*, 2(2):111–176, 1950.

[26] V. Mustonen and M. Laessig. Fitness flux and ubiquity of adaptive evolution. *Proc. Natl. Acad. Sci. U. S. A.*, 107(9):4248–4251, 2010.

[27] F. Oppacher and M. Wineberg. Reconstructing the shifting balance theory in a GA: taking sewall wright seriously. In *Proceedings of the 2000 Congress on Evolutionary Computation, 2000*, volume 1, pages 219–226 vol.1, 2000.

[28] H. A. Orr. The population genetics of adaptation: The distribution of factors fixed during adaptive evolution. *Evolution*, 52(4):935–949, 1998.

[29] S. P. Otto and N. H. Barton. Selection for recombination in small populations. *Evolution*, 55(10):1921–1931, 2001.

[30] G. R. Price. Selection and covariance. *Nature*, 227(5257):520–521, 1970.

[31] W. B. Provine. *Sewall Wright and Evolutionary Biology*. University Of Chicago Press, 1989.

[32] W. B. Provine. *The Origins of Theoretical Population Genetics*. University Of Chicago Press, 1 edition, 2001.

[33] A. Prügel-Bennett. Modelling evolving populations. *Journal of Theoretical Biology*, 185:81–95, 1996.

[34] A. Robertson. A theory of limits in artificial selection. *Proc. Biol. Sci.*, 153:234–249, 1960.

[35] A. Robertson. A mathematical model of culling process in dairy cattle. *Animal Production*, 8:95–108, 1966.

[36] A. Robertson. Some optimum problems in individual selection. *Theoretical Population Biology*, 1(1):120–127, 1970.

[37] M. Ruse. *Monad to Man: The Concept of Progress in Evolutionary Biology*. Harvard University Press, first edition, 1997.

[38] G. Sella, A. E. Hirsh, and S. A. Levin. The application of statistical physics to evolutionary biology. *Proceedings of the National Academy of Sciences of the United States of America*, 102(27):9541–9546, 2005.

[39] Y. Toquenaga and M. J. Wade. Sewall wright meets artificial life: the origin and maintenance of evolutionary novelty. *Trends in Ecology & Evolution*, 11(11):478–482, 1996.

[40] K. E. Weber and L. T. Diggins. Increased selection response in larger populations. II. selection for ethanol vapor resistance in drosophila melanogaster at two population sizes. *Genetics*, 125(3):585–597, 1990.

[41] G. C. Williams. *Adaptation and Natural Selection: A Critique of Some Current Evolutionary Thought.* Princeton University Press, 1996.

[42] S. Wright. Evolution in mendelian populations. *Genetics*, 16(2):97–159, 1931.

[43] S. Wright. The distribution of gene frequencies in populations. *Proc Natl Acad Sci U S A*, 23(6):307–320, 1937.

A Method to Derive Fixed Budget Results From Expected Optimisation Times

Benjamin Doerr
Max Planck Institute for Informatics
Saarbrücken, Germany
doerr@mpi-inf.mpg.de

Thomas Jansen
Dep. of Computer Science
Aberystwyth University
Aberystwyth, SY23 3DB, UK
t.jansen@aber.ac.uk

Carsten Witt
DTU Compute
Technical University of Denmark
2800 Kgs. Lyngby, Denmark
cawi@dtu.dk

Christine Zarges
School of Computer Science
University of Birmingham
Birmingham B15 2TT, UK
c.zarges@bham.ac.uk

ABSTRACT

At last year's GECCO a novel perspective for theoretical performance analysis of evolutionary algorithms and other randomised search heuristics was introduced that concentrates on the expected function value after a pre-defined number of steps, called budget. This is significantly different from the common perspective where the expected optimisation time is analysed. While there is a huge body of work and a large collection of tools for the analysis of the expected optimisation time the new fixed budget perspective introduces new analytical challenges. Here it is shown how results on the expected optimisation time that are strengthened by deviation bounds can be systematically turned into fixed budget results. We demonstrate our approach by considering the (1+1) EA on LeadingOnes and significantly improving previous results. We prove that deviating from the expected time by an additive term of $\omega\left(n^{3/2}\right)$ happens only with probability $o(1)$. This is turned into tight bounds on the function value using the inverse function. We use three, increasingly strong or general approaches to proving the deviation bounds, namely via Chebyshev's inequality, via Chernoff bounds for geometric random variables, and via variable drift analysis.

Categories and Subject Descriptors

F.2.2 [**Analysis of Algorithms and Problem Complexity**]: Nonnumerical Algorithms and Problems

General Terms

Algorithms, Design, Performance, Theory

Keywords

runtime analysis, fixed budget computation, tail bounds, (1+1) EA, LeadingOnes

1. INTRODUCTION

Evolutionary algorithms (like all randomised search heuristics) are applied to find solutions for difficult problems in situations where no good problem-specific algorithms are available. They are incomplete optimisers in the sense that it is not guaranteed that an optimal solution is found in any given run of finite length. The general hope is that they find sufficiently good solutions in reasonable time. Note that even if an optimal solution is found the user has usually no way of knowing this. In stark contrast to this way of applying evolutionary algorithms their theoretical analysis often concentrates on the expected optimisation time [1]. For this scenario many results and analytical methods are known, for typical example problems [9] as well as for combinatorial optimisation problems [12]. This analytical perspective has contributed to the gap between between theory and practice in the field.

Addressing this problem Jansen and Zarges [10] have introduced a novel perspective, called fixed budget computations. They suggest to consider the function value that has been achieved after a fixed number b of function evaluations. This perspective is similar to the consideration of best-so-far curves, a popular way of evaluating the performance of evolutionary algorithms in empirical studies [16]. In [10], two particularly simple randomised search heuristics, random local search and the (1+1) EA, are considered for two well-known example functions, OneMax and LeadingOnes. The analysis is rather long and complicated and does not lead to tight bounds in most cases. One of the conclusions and observed open problems is the need for the development of novel analytical methods to facilitate analysis in the fixed budget scenario. We address this need here.

We present a method that allows one to turn results on the expected time needed to reach a specific function value into a fixed budget result provided that the original result is accompanied with tail bounds. Using commonly available results on the expected time three major steps are involved.

First, the results on the expected optimisation time need to be generalised into results on the expected time needed to reach a solution of a pre-specified quality. This can usually easily be done. Second, the results need to be accompanied by tail bounds for the probability to deviate from the expected times. We present three concrete examples for doing this for LeadingOnes, based on Chebyshev's inequality, based on a rarely used Chernoff bound for sums of geometric random variables, and based on variable drift analysis. Using Chebyshev's inequality we prove that the probability to deviate from the expected time to reach a leading 1-bits on LeadingOnes by an additive term of d is bounded above by $O(n^3/d^2)$ where n is the number of bits. The exact result allows for concrete statements for rather small values of n. Via Chernoff bounds for sums of independent geometric random variables, we can reduce the above error probability to a much stronger $\exp\left(-\Theta(d^2/n^3)\right)$, however giving weaker bounds for concrete small values of d^2/n^3. Both the Chebyshev and the Chernoff approach exploit the particular knowledge of the distribution of the random variables describing the runtime of the algorithm. Since such knowledge may often not be present, we also develop a proof of concept for a more universal approach to obtain tail bounds from variable drift analysis. This allows us to bound the error probability by $\exp\left(-\Omega\left(d/n^{3/2+\epsilon}\right)\right)$, which is still exponentially small if $d = \Omega\left(n^{3/2+2\epsilon}\right)$.

In the next section we formally define the notions, algorithm, and function. Section 3 introduces our approach via the inverse function of the expected optimisation time. This is followed by our results obtained using Chebyshev's inequality (Section 5), Chernoff bounds (Section 6), and variable drift analysis (Section 7). We conclude with a comparison of our bounds with the previous results in Section 8.

2. FRAMEWORK AND DEFINITIONS

Our main contribution is a general method to derive fixed budget results from results about the expected optimisation time. We demonstrate the approach using a specific simple evolutionary algorithm, the (1+1) EA, and a specific well-known example function, LO (often called LeadingOnes). This addresses an open problem posed by Jansen and Zarges [10] when introducing the fixed budget perspective.

We concentrate on the simplest evolutionary algorithm, the (1+1) EA. It is similar to random local search since it also has a population of size only 1, creates one new search point in each generation and deterministically replaces the current population with the new search point if this is of at least equal fitness. It differs from random local search since the new search point is not selected from a neighbourhood but generated by means of standard bit mutations. This difference can make the two algorithms perform very differently [6]. Specifically in the fixed budget framework this difference can complicate the analysis drastically [10].

ALGORITHM 1. *(1+1) Evolutionary Algo. ((1+1) EA)*
1. $t := 0$; *Select* $x_t \in \{0,1\}^n$. *Evaluate* $f(x_t)$.
2. *While* $t+1 < b$ *do*
3. $\quad t := t+1$
4. $\quad y := x_{t-1}$. *For each* $i \in \{1,2,\ldots,n\}$ *with probability* $1/n$ *flip i-th bit in* y.
5. $\quad$ *Evaluate* $f(y)$.
6. $\quad$ *If* $f(y) \geq f(x_{t-1})$ *then* $x_t := y$ *else* $x_t := x_{t-1}$.

The example function we consider yields as function value the number of leading one bits counted from left to right. Its formal definition is given below.

DEFINITION 2. *The function* LO: $\{0,1\}^n \to \mathbb{R}$ *is defined by* $\mathrm{LO}(x) = \sum_{i=1}^{n} \prod_{j=1}^{i} x[j]$.

It has been long known that the expected optimisation time of the (1+1) EA on LO is $\Theta(n^2)$ and that the expectation is sharply concentrated [7]. Böttcher et al. [2] determined the exact expected optimisation time of the (1+1) EA on LO (even for arbitrary mutation probabilities). We will build on their results in Section 3.

We adopt the fixed budget perspective and analyse the function value that can be achieved with b function evaluations. For the (1+1) EA, this means we are interested in $f(x_b)$. Since $f(x_b)$ is a random variable we are interested in its expectation $\mathrm{E}(f(x_b))$ as well as properties of its distribution, e. g., bounds on the probabilities to achieve at least or at most a given function value.

3. FIXED-BUDGET RESULTS VS. OPTIMISATION TIMES

We want to obtain results on the function value after b function evaluations, $f(x_b)$ for the (1+1) EA. Theoretical analysis usually concentrates on the time needed for optimisation. It has been pointed out [9] that it is not difficult to generalise this to optimisation goals other than exact optimisation. The same methods used for analysing the expected optimisation time can still be applied without any change.

Consider $T_{A,f}(a)$, the number of function evaluations some specific algorithm A needs to reach function value a for some specific fitness function f. Formally,

$$T_{A,f}(a) = \min\{t \mid f(x_t) \geq a\}.$$

If the algorithm A is deterministic then the inverse function $T_{A,f}^{-1}(b)$ yields the function value reached after b function evaluations have been made. However, we are dealing with randomised search heuristics and $T_{A,f}(a)$ is a random variable. Note that if we consider the expected number of function evaluations needed to reach function value a, $\mathrm{E}(T_{A,f}(a))$, its inverse function does *not* necessarily coincide with the expected function value after b function evaluations as the following tiny example shows.

Consider an algorithm A and a function f where $f(x_0) = 0$ with probability 1. For $t > 0$, it is defined as follows. If $f(x_{t-1}) = 0$ then $f(x_t) = 1$ with probability 1/2 and $f(x_t) = 0$ otherwise. If $f(x_{t-1}) = 1$ then also $f(x_t) = 1$ with probability 1. Clearly, $\mathrm{E}(T_{A,f}(0)) = 0$ and $\mathrm{E}(T_{A,f}(1)) = 2$ holds. For the expected function value we have $\mathrm{E}(f(x_b)) = \Pr(f(x_b) = 1) = 1 - (1/2)^b$. We notice two things. First, the inverse function $\mathrm{E}_{T_{A,f}}^{-1}(b)$ of $\mathrm{E}(T_{A,f}(a))$ is only defined for $b \in \{0,2\}$. Second, if we consider $\mathrm{E}_{T_{A,f}}^{-1}(2) = 1$, we see that this is different from $\mathrm{E}(f(x_2)) = 1 - (1/2)^2$.

Things are different if we have bounds on the time needed. Suppose we know an "upper tail" function $t_u(a)$ such that $\Pr(T_{A,f}(a) \geq t_u(a)) \leq p_u$. Then $\Pr\left(f(x_b) \leq t_u^{-1}(b)\right) \leq p_u$ holds. Analogously, if we know a "lower tail" $t_l(a)$ s. t. $\Pr(T_{A,f}(a) \leq t_l(a)) \leq p_l$ then $\Pr\left(f(x_b) \geq t_l^{-1}(b)\right) \leq p_l$.

Bounds for the probability of $T_{A,f}(a)$ being above or below some values are typically derived as bounds that $T_{A,f}(a)$

deviates from its expected value $\mathrm{E}(T_{A,f}(a))$. Since the fixed budget perspective requires results to be as tight as possible we are interested in determining the expectation $\mathrm{E}(T_{A,f}(a))$ as exactly as we can and derive bounds for the probability to deviate from it that are as sharp as possible. For our work here we start with analysing $T_{(1+1)\text{ EA,LO}}(a)$, in the following abbreviated as $T(a)$, exactly.

4. EXACT OPTIMISATION TIME FOR LO

We use the precise analysis by Böttcher et al. [2] as starting point. Let A_i denote the random number of mutations needed to increase the function value from i to something larger. Böttcher et al. [2] prove that $\mathrm{E}(A_i) = 1/((1-p_i)^i p_i)$ holds (Lemma 2 and Theorem 1 in [2]) where p_i denotes the mutation probability. We consider the case of a constant mutation probability of $1/n$ so this simplifies to $\mathrm{E}(A_i) = n/(1-1/n)^i$. They carry on determining the expected number of mutations until the function value is increased from i to n (Lemma 3 and Theorem 2 in [2]). This is easily generalised to the expected number of mutations needed to increase the function value from i to at least j. If $B_{i,j}$ denotes the random number of mutations needed we have

$$\mathrm{E}(B_{i,j}) = \mathrm{E}(A_i) + \frac{1}{2}\sum_{k=i+1}^{j-1}\mathrm{E}(A_k).$$

From this, we now derive an expression for $\mathrm{E}(T(a))$. If $\mathrm{LO}(x_0) \geq a$, the expected number of mutations is 0. Hence,

$$\begin{aligned}\mathrm{E}(T(a)) &= \sum_{i=0}^{a-1}\Pr(\mathrm{LO}(x_0)=i)\cdot\mathrm{E}(B_{i,a})\\ &= \sum_{i=0}^{a-1}\left(\frac{1}{2}\right)^{i+1}\cdot\left(\mathrm{E}(A_i)+\frac{1}{2}\sum_{j=i+1}^{a-1}\mathrm{E}(A_j)\right) = \frac{1}{2}\sum_{i=0}^{a-1}\mathrm{E}(A_i)\end{aligned}$$

holds.

From $\mathrm{E}(A_i) = n/\left(1-1/n\right)^i$, we derive

$$\mathrm{E}(T(a)) = \frac{n^2-n}{2}\cdot\left(\left(1+\frac{1}{n-1}\right)^a - 1\right).$$

Note that our approach via the inverse function of $\mathrm{E}(T(a))$ makes only sense for budgets $b \leq \mathrm{E}(T(n))$. Larger budgets are beyond the domain of $\mathrm{E}(T(a))$ so that its inverse function does not yield useful values. Therefore, we work with budgets $b \leq \mathrm{E}(T(n))$ in the following.

For the expected function values some results are known [10]. We cite the results here and show how our methods help to improve over them in the following.

THEOREM 3 (THEOREM 8 FROM [10]). *Let the budget $b = (1-\beta)n^2/\alpha(n)$ for any β with $(1/2)+\beta' < \beta < 1$ where β' is a positive constant and $\alpha(n) = \omega(1)$, $\alpha(n) \geq 1$.* $\mathrm{E}(\mathrm{LO}(x_b)) = 1 + (2b/n) - O(b/(n\alpha(n))) = 1 + (2b/n) - o(b/n)$.

THEOREM 4 (THEOREM 9 FROM [10]). *Let the budget $b = cn^2$ for any constant c with $0 < c < 1/2$.*
$\Pr\left(ce^{-c}\left(1+e^{-ce^{-ce^{-c}}}\right) \leq \frac{\mathrm{LO}(x_b)}{n} \leq c\left(1+e^{-ce^{-c}}\right)\right) = 1-o(1)$.

Note that Theorem 3 is already tight but only holds for budgets $b = o(n^2)$. For budgets $b = \Theta(n^2)$ we have bounds in Theorem 4 but these are not tight.

Since our focus in this work are results more precise than merely computing expectations, we shall discuss the actual random variables now. To this aim, we regard a modified optimisation process. It is identical to the one of the (1+1) EA optimising LO with a random initial search point apart from the fact that the mutation operator does not flip bits with index higher than the current LO value plus one. Since in both processes these bits are independent and uniformly distributed in $\{0,1\}$, both processes are equivalent in the sense that the random search point at any time t is equally distributed in both processes. In particular, all statements on runtimes and fitnesses reached after certain times hold for both processes.

For this reason, let us now analyse the runtime of the modified process. Denote by $x = (x[1],\ldots,x[n])$ the random initial search point. Since in the modified process bits higher than the LO value plus one never change, we observe that to gain a fitness level of at least a exactly those fitness levels i have to be left that satisfy $i < a$ and $x[i] = 0$. The waiting time to leave the ith level again is a geometric random variable A_i with success probability $q_i := (1-1/n)^i/n$. Consequently, when conditioning on x, the time $T(a)$ needed to reach a fitness level of a or higher is $\sum_{i\in\{j\in[a-1]\mid x[j]=0\}} A_i$. Since the $x[j]$ are independent and uniformly distributed in $\{0,1\}$, we have the following.

LEMMA 5. *Let $a \in \{0,\ldots,n\}$. The random time $T(a)$ taken by the (1+1) EA started with a random search point to find a solution with* LO *value at least a can be written as*

$$T(a) = \sum_{i=1}^{a-1} X_i A_i,$$

where the X_i are uniformly distributed in $\{0,1\}$, the A_i are geometric random variables with parameter $q_i = (1-1/n)^i/n$, and all X_i and A_i are mutually independent.

5. BOUNDS WITH THE CHEBYSHEV INEQUALITY

We have demonstrated in Section 3 that knowledge of $\mathrm{E}(T_{A,f}(a))$ and its inverse function is not sufficient to compute $\mathrm{E}(f(x_b))$. Therefore, we want to derive bounds for the event that $T(a)$ deviates from its expectation. The simplest way of doing this would be Markov's inequality [3]. However, since this only delivers bounds for deviations by at least constant factors ($\Pr(T(v) \geq c\mathrm{E}(T(a))) \leq 1/c$) it is too weak for our purposes. Chebyshev's inequality [3] is of similar generality like Markov's inequality but delivers much tighter bounds. However, it requires to have at least bounds on the variance of the random variable.

THEOREM 6. *For any $d = \omega\left(n^{3/2}\right)$ and $b \leq \mathrm{E}(T(n))$ the following holds:* $\Pr\left(\mathrm{LO}(x_b) = n\ln\left(1+2b/n^2\right) \pm \Theta(d/n)\right) = 1-o(1)$.

PROOF. We use $\mathrm{E}(T(a))$ from Lemma 5. Since A_i is geometrically distributed with parameter $q_i = (1-1/n)^i/n$, $\mathrm{E}(A_i) = 1/q_i$ and $\mathrm{Var}\left(A_i\right) = 1/q_i^2 - 1/q_i$ are well-known. Consequently, we compute

$$\begin{aligned}\mathrm{E}\left(A_i^2\right) &= \mathrm{Var}\left(A_i\right) + \mathrm{E}(A_i)^2 = 2/q_i^2 - 1/q_i\\ \mathrm{E}\left((X_iA_i)^2\right) &= \mathrm{E}\left(X_iA_i^2\right) = (1/2)\mathrm{E}\left(A_i^2\right) = 1/q_i^2 - 1/(2q_i)\\ \mathrm{E}(X_iA_i) &= (1/2)\mathrm{E}(A_i) = 1/(2q_i)\end{aligned}$$

$$\begin{aligned}\mathrm{Var}(X_iA_i) &= \mathrm{E}((X_iA_i)^2) - \mathrm{E}(X_iA_i)^2 \\ &= 1/q_i^2 - 1/(2q_i) - 1/(4q_i^2) \\ &= (3/4)(1/q_i^2) - (1/2)(1/q_i).\end{aligned}$$

Since the (X_iA_i) are independent, we have $\mathrm{Var}(T(a)) = \sum_{i=0}^{a-1} \mathrm{Var}(X_iA_i)$, which after a somewhat lengthy and tedious calculation gives $\mathrm{Var}(T(a)) = n^3 \cdot (3/8)\big((1+1/(n-1))^{2a-1} - 1\big) - \Theta(n^2)$. By Chebyshev's inequality, this yields

$$\Pr(|T(a) - \mathrm{E}(T(a))| \geq d_a) \leq \frac{3\left((1+1/(n-1))^{2a-1} - 1\right) \cdot n^3}{8d_a^2}$$

so that for any $d_a = \omega\left(n^{3/2}\right)$ we have for the expected time upper and lower bounds

$$\frac{n^2-n}{2} \cdot \left(\left(1+\frac{1}{n-1}\right)^a - 1\right) \pm d_a$$

that hold with probability converging to 1, i. e., $1 - o(1)$.

To obtain bounds on the expected function value we need to compute the inverse function. If we use for d_a some d independent of a we obtain

$$\Pr\left(\frac{\ln\left((n^2-n)\,/\,(n^2-n+2b-2d)\right)}{\ln(1-1/n)} \leq \mathrm{LO}(x_b) \leq \frac{\ln\left((n^2-n)\,/\,(n^2-n+2b+2d)\right)}{\ln(1-1/n)}\right) = 1 - o(1)$$

for any $d = \omega\left(n^{3/2}\right)$. If n is not very small we have $\ln(1 - 1/n) \approx -1/n$ (since for $x \approx 0$ we have $e^x \approx 1+x$), so that we obtain $\Pr\left(\mathrm{LO}(x_b) = n\ln\left(1 + (2b)\,/\,(n^2-n) \pm \Theta(d/n^2)\right)\right) = 1 - o(1)$ for any $d = \omega\left(n^{3/2}\right)$. We observe that $2b/(n^2 - n) = (2b/n^2) + O(b/n^3)$ holds and we can replace $2b/(n^2-n)$ by $2b/n^2$: The introduced error is $O(b/n^3) = O(1/n)$ and subsumed in $\Theta(d/n^2)$. To simplify further to $\ln\left(1+2b/n^2\right) \pm\Theta(d/n^2)$ we first observe that we can restrict our interest to $d = O(n^2)$. For larger values of d the error term $O(d/n^2)$ dominates and the theorem's statement becomes trivial. With $d = O(n^2)$ we have $1 + (2b/n^2) \pm \Theta(d/n^2) = \Theta(1)$ and the claim follows by applying the Taylor expansion of the natural logarithm. □

6. USING CHERNOFF BOUNDS FOR SUMS OF GEOMETRIC RANDOM VARIABLES

The bounds on the optimisation time derived in the previous section hold with probability $1 - O(n^3/d^2)$. Note that the error term is a polynomial in d, which is due to Chebyshev's inequality. However, it has already been proven using Chernoff bounds that the actual optimisation time of the (1+1) EA on LO is within the interval $[c_1n^2, c_2n^2]$ for two constants c_1, c_2 with probability $1 - 2^{-\Omega(n)}$ [7], i. e., with probability exponentially close to 1. Hence, we could hope for much stronger tail bounds than proved by Chebyshev's inequality.

Unfortunately, the result from [7] is too weak for our purposes since it only bounds the probability of deviations $d = \Omega(n^2)$ from the expectation. As pointed out in the previous section, meaningful fixed-budget results are only obtained if we bound the probability of deviations $d = o(n^2)$, i. e., deviations by a lower-order term.

In this section, we solve this problem and prove that the actual runtime deviates from the expected one by an additive term of d only with probability $\exp(-\Theta(d^2/n^3))$. A main difficulty here is that the independent random variables X_iA_i have an unbounded range. This forbids a straightforward application of classic Chernoff bounds. To overcome this, we use a seemingly lesser known Chernoff bound for sums of independent random variables having a geometric distribution, which is due to Scheideler [15] (see [3, Section 1.4.4] for an elementary proof of a similar result for identically distributed geometric random variables). It takes some more work to handle the fact that the X_iA_i are not truly geometric random variables. To this aim, we regard the conditional expectations $\mathrm{E}(T(a)|X_1,\ldots,X_n)$. All this leads to the following result.

THEOREM 7. *For all $d \leq 2n^2$, the probability that $T(a)$ deviates from its expectation of $(1/2)(n^2-n)((1+1/(n-1))^a - 1)$ by at least d, is at most $4\exp(-d^2/(20e^2n^3))$.*

To prove this result, let $a \in [n]$. Let $X_1,\ldots,X_n$ and $A_1,\ldots,A_n$ be as in Lemma 5. Write $X = (X_1,\ldots,X_n)$. Assume that all these random variables are defined over a common probability space Ω. Let $T = \sum_{i=0}^{a-1} X_iA_i$ be a random variable describing the distribution of $T(a)$.

The conditional expectation $\mathrm{E}(T|X)$ is a random variable defined over Ω by $\mathrm{E}(T|X)(\omega) = \mathrm{E}(T|X = X(\omega)) = \sum_{\omega' \in X^{-1}(X(\omega))}(\Pr(\omega')/\Pr(X^{-1}(\omega)))T(\omega')$. A simple application of the triangle inequality gives

$$|T - \mathrm{E}(T)| \leq |T - \mathrm{E}(T|X)| + |\mathrm{E}(T|X) - \mathrm{E}(T)|.$$

Consequently, we have

$$\Pr(|T - \mathrm{E}(T)| \geq 2d) \leq \Pr(|T - \mathrm{E}(T|X)| \geq d) + \Pr(|\mathrm{E}(T|X) - \mathrm{E}(T)| \geq d) \quad (1)$$

for all d. We show that both terms are small when $d = \omega(n^{3/2})$.

Tail Bounds for $|T - \mathrm{E}(T|X)|$ via Chernoff Bounds for Geometric Random Variables. By law of total probability, we have $\Pr(|T-\mathrm{E}(T|X)| \geq d) = \sum_{x\in\{0,1\}^n} \Pr(X = x)\Pr(|T - \mathrm{E}(T)| \geq d \mid X = x)$. Let us condition on $X = x$. Let $S = \{i \in \{0,\ldots,a-1\} \mid x_i = 1\}$. Then $T = \sum_{i\in S} A_i$ is a sum of independent geometric random variables and $\mathrm{E}(T) = \sum_{i\in S}\mathrm{E}(A_i)$ is its expectation. We use the following Chernoff bound for sums of such random variables due to Scheideler [15, Theorem 3.38].

THEOREM 8. *Let $Y_1, Y_2, \ldots, Y_s$ be independent, geometrically distributed random variables with parameters q_1, q_2, $\ldots$, $q_s \in (0,1)$. Let $q = \min\{q_i \mid i \in \{1,\ldots,s\}\}$. Let $Y := \sum_{i=1}^s Y_i$ and $\mu = \mathrm{E}(Y)$.*

(a) For all $\delta > 0$,

$$\Pr(Y \geq (1+\delta)\mu) \leq (1+\delta\mu q/s)^s \exp(-\delta\mu q).$$

(b) For all $\delta \in [0,1]$,

$$\Pr(Y \leq (1-\delta)\mu) \leq \exp(-\delta^2\mu q/2).$$

We apply this theorem to $A_i, i \in S$, to $q = \min\{q_i \mid i \in S\}$, and $d \le n^2$. Note that thus $d \le n/q$. Using (i) that $(1+c/s)^s$ for all $c \ge 0$ is increasing in s, (ii) the estimate $(1+\delta)/\exp(\delta) \le (1+\delta)/(1+\delta+\delta^2/2) = 1-(\delta^2/2)/(1+\delta+\delta^2/2) \le 1-\delta^2/5 \le \exp(-\delta^2/5)$ valid for all $\delta \in [0,1]$, and (iii) finally $q \ge 1/en$, we compute

$$\begin{aligned}\Pr(T \ge \mathrm{E}(T)+d) &\le (1+dq/s)^s \exp(-dq)\\ &\le (1+dq/n)^n \exp(-dq/n)^n \le \exp(-(dq/n)^2/5)^n\\ &\le \exp(-d^2/(5e^2n^3)).\end{aligned}$$

For the lower tail, still conditioning on $X = x$ and using $\mu \le \frac{e-1}{2}n^2$, we compute

$$\begin{aligned}\Pr(T \le \mathrm{E}(T)-d) &\le \exp(-d^2q/(2\mu))\\ &\le \exp(-d^2/(e(e-1)n^3)).\end{aligned}$$

Consequently, conditional on $X = x$, we have $\Pr(|T - \mathrm{E}(T)| \ge d) \le 2\exp(-d^2/(5e^2n^3))$, which is independent of x. Therefore,

$$\begin{aligned}&\Pr(|T-\mathrm{E}(T|X)| \ge d)\\ &= \sum_{x\in\{0,1\}^n} \Pr(X=x)\Pr(|T-\mathrm{E}(T)| \ge d \mid X=x)\\ &\le \sum_{x\in\{0,1\}^n} 2^{-n}2\exp(-d^2/(5e^2n^3))\\ &= 2\exp(-d^2/(5e^2n^3)). \qquad (2)\end{aligned}$$

Tail Bounds for $|\mathbf{E}(T|X) - \mathbf{E}(T)|$. Note that the random variable $\mathrm{E}(T|X)$ by definition only depends on $X_1, \ldots, X_n$. We have $\mathrm{E}(T|X) - \mathrm{E}(T) = \sum_{i=0}^{a-1}(X_i - 1/2)\mathrm{E}(A_i)$. Here, the $(X_i - 1/2)$ are independent random variables uniformly distributed in $\{-1/2, +1/2\}$ and the $\mathrm{E}(A_i)$ simply are number of order $\Theta(n)$. Hence $\mathrm{E}(T|X) - \mathrm{E}(T)$ is a sum of independent random variables each with expectation zero and range at most $\mathrm{E}(A_{n-1}) \le en$. Hence a standard Chernoff bound (like Theorem 1.11 of [3]) for all $d \ge 0$ yields

$$\begin{aligned}\Pr(|\mathrm{E}(T|X)-\mathrm{E}(T)| \ge d) &\le 2\exp(-2d^2/(a(en)^2))\\ &\le 2\exp(2d^2/(en^3)). \qquad (3)\end{aligned}$$

From (1) to (3), Theorem 7 immediately follows.

Notes. We stated Theorem 7 only for $d \le 2n^2$, which is enough to obtain an exponential failure probability. Larger d seem therefore not too interesting. They could be handled, though, easily by exploiting $(1+\delta)/\exp(\delta) = \exp(-\delta(1-o(1)))$ in the estimates for the upper tail bounds for the sums of geometric random variables. We did not try to optimise the constant in the $\exp(-\Theta(d^2/n^3))$ term.

7. USING DRIFT ANALYSIS WITH TAIL BOUNDS

The results from the previous two sections heavily rely on knowing the precise distribution of the random variable describing the runtime (Lemma 5). Such an exact description is usually not available. It is therefore worth investigating whether sharp tail bounds can be obtained by other, potentially more general, methods. We show that drift analysis, which has become the key method for the runtime analysis of randomised search heuristics, is suitable as well for our purposes. As a proof of concept, we derive in Theorem 9 sharp tail bounds on the optimisation time of the (1+1) EA on LO, with deviations in lower-order terms only, using drift analysis combined with the exponential-moment method (which was only recently introduced to the runtime analysis of evolutionary algorithms in [4]). Although this result is weaker than the one obtained in the previous section, two advantages in other respects can be identified: (1) the method does not need the discussed characterisation of runtime and (2) it can also be used if the (1+1) EA is initialised with a fixed starting point (instead of a uniform one).

Theorem 9. *The time for the (1+1) EA to reach a LO-value of at least a, where $0 < a \le n - \log n$, is bounded from above by*

$$\frac{n^2-n}{2}\left(\left(1+\frac{1}{n-1}\right)^a - 1\right)\left(1+O(\tfrac{1}{\sqrt{n}})\right) + d$$

with probability at least $1 - e^{-dn^{-3/2-\epsilon}}$ and from below by

$$\frac{n^2-n}{2}\left(\left(1+\frac{1}{n-1}\right)^a - \left(1+\frac{1}{n-1}\right)^{\sqrt{n}}\right)\left(1-O(\tfrac{1}{\sqrt{n}})\right) - d$$

with probability at least $1 - e^{-dn^{-3/2-\epsilon}+O(\log n)} - 2^{-\Omega(\sqrt{n})}$ for an arbitrarily small constant $\epsilon > 0$ and any $d > 0$.

Before we prove the theorem, we look into its consequences for the function value at time b. As long as the following bounds do not exceed $n - \log n$, we obtain

$$\Pr\left(\frac{\ln\left((n^2-n)\,/\,(n^2-n+2b-2d-o(d))\right)}{\ln(1-1/n)} \le \mathrm{LO}(x_b) \le \frac{\ln\left((n^2-n)\,/\,(n^2-n+2b+2d+o(d))\right)}{\ln(1-1/n)}\right) = 1 - 2^{-\Omega(n^\epsilon)}$$

for any $d = \Omega(n^{3/2+\epsilon})$, where ϵ is an arbitrarily small constant. This is slighly weaker than the bound from the previous section since Theorem 7 only requires $d = \omega(n^{3/2})$.

To prove Theorem 9, we use Lehre's [11] proof of the variable drift theorem and combine it with ideas implicit in Hajek's [8] paper on drift analysis, including the exponential-moment method. We start by defining some notation.

Definition 10. *Let x_t denote the current search point of the (1+1) EA at time t. Its distance to the target a is defined by $d(x_t) := \max\{0, a - \mathrm{LO}(x_t)\}$.*

Given a search point x_t of distance $d(x_t) > 0$, we denote by $\delta(x_t) := d(x_t) - d(x_{t+1})$ the decrease in distance in the next step. Slightly abusing notation, we also write $\delta(i) := i - d(x_{t+1} \mid d(x_t) = i)$ for the decrease in distance if $d(x_t) = i$.

We now bound the drift $\mathrm{E}(\delta(i))$ (assuming a random x_t satisfying $d(x_t) = i$, but omitting this in the expectation for the sake of readability). At a later point of time, a potential function based on $\delta(i)$ will be defined, and drift analysis will be carried out with respect to that potential function.

Lemma 11. *For all $i > 0$, $\mathrm{E}(\delta(i)) = (2 - 2^{-n+a-i+1}) \cdot (1-1/n)^{a-i} \cdot (1/n)$.*

Proof. The leftmost zero-bit is at position $a - i + 1$. To increase the LO-value (it cannot decrease), it is necessary to flip this bit and not to flip the first $a - i$ bits, which is reflected by the last two terms in the lemma. The first term is due to the expected number of free-rider bits. Note that there can be between 0 and $n - a + i - 1$ such bits. By the usual argumentation using a geometric distribution, the expected number of free riders in an improving step equals

$$\sum_{k=0}^{n-a+i-1} k \cdot \left(\frac{1}{2}\right)^{\min\{n-a+i-1,k+1\}} = 1 - 2^{-n+a-i+1},$$

hence the expected progress in an improving step is $2 - 2^{-n+a-i+1}$. □

We now turn to the potential function, which is obtained from the drift $\delta(i)$ in a similar way as in the proof of the variable drift theorem (cf. [14]).

Definition 12. *Given a search point x_t, its potential is defined by $g(x_t) := \sum_{k=1}^{d(x_t)} 1/\mathrm{E}(\delta(k))$. We also write $g(i) := g(x_t \mid d(x_t) = i)$ for the potential at distance i. The random change of the potential is defined by $\Delta_t := g(x_t) - g(x_{t+1})$. We also write $\Delta_t(i) := g(i) - g(x_{t+1} \mid d(x_t) = i)$.*

The drift $\mathrm{E}(\Delta_t)$ of the potential (more precisely, we mean $\mathrm{E}(\Delta_t \mid x_0, \dots, x_t)$, which is the same as $\mathrm{E}(\Delta_t \mid x_t)$ since we are dealing with a Markov chain) is crucial in the following. Note that $\mathrm{E}(\delta(i))$ is non-decreasing in i. Hence, as in the proof of the variable drift theorem, we can obtain $\mathrm{E}(\Delta_t) \geq 1$. We make this now explicit and prove an upper bound as well.

Lemma 13. *If $i > 0$ then $\mathrm{E}(\Delta_t(i)) \geq 1$. If $i > 0$ and $a \leq n - \log n$ then $\mathrm{E}(\Delta_t(i)) = 1 + O(1/\sqrt{n})$.*

Proof. By Lemma 11, $\mathrm{E}(\delta(i))$ is decreasing in its argument. Hence, if $\delta(i) = j$, we get $\Delta_t = g(i) - g(i-j) = \sum_{k=0}^{j-1} \frac{1}{\mathrm{E}(\delta(i-k))} \geq \sum_{k=0}^{j-1} \frac{1}{\mathrm{E}(\delta(i))} = j \cdot \frac{1}{\mathrm{E}(\delta(i))}$. This implies $\mathrm{E}(\Delta_t) \geq \sum_{j=1}^{i} \frac{j}{\mathrm{E}(\delta(i))} \cdot \Pr(\delta(i) = j) = \frac{\mathrm{E}(\delta(i))}{\mathrm{E}(\delta(i))}$, which proves the lower bound.

For the upper bound, we study the distribution of $\delta(i)$. Using ideas from the proof of Lemma 11, we get $\Pr(\delta(i) = j) \leq (1 - 1/n)^{a-i}(1/n)2^{-j}$. As $a \leq n - \log n$, we get $\mathrm{E}(\delta(i)) = (2 - O(1/n)) \cdot (1 - 1/n)^{a-i} \cdot (1/n)$ from Lemma 11. In the remainder of this proof, we omit the $-O(1/n)$ term in all calculations involving $\mathrm{E}(\delta(\cdot))$. It is clear that this only can introduce an additive error of $O(1/n)$.

We bound the change of potential, given $\delta(i) = j$. Then

$$\begin{aligned} &g(i) - g(i-j) \\ &= \sum_{k=0}^{j-1} \frac{1}{\mathrm{E}(\delta(i-k))} = \frac{n}{2}\left(1 - \frac{1}{n}\right)^{i-a} \sum_{k=0}^{j-1} \left(1 - \frac{1}{n}\right)^{-k} \\ &= \frac{1}{\mathrm{E}(\delta(i))} \cdot \frac{\left(1-\frac{1}{n}\right)^{-j} - 1}{\left(1-\frac{1}{n}\right)^{-1} - 1} = \frac{(n-1)\left(1 + \frac{1}{n-1}\right)^{j} - (n-1)}{\mathrm{E}(\delta(i))} \\ &\leq \frac{(n-1)\left(1 + \frac{j}{n-1} + \left(\frac{j}{n-1}\right)^2\right) - (n-1)}{\mathrm{E}(\delta(i))}, \end{aligned}$$

where the last inequality used $(1+x)^y \leq e^{xy} \leq 1 + (xy) + (xy)^2$ for $0 \leq xy \leq 1$.

Simplifying the last bound and putting everything together, we get

$$\mathrm{E}(\Delta_t) \leq \sum_{j=1}^{i} \Pr(\delta(i) = j) \cdot \frac{j + \frac{j^2}{n-1}}{\mathrm{E}(\delta(i))}.$$

If $j < \sqrt{n}$, then $j + j^2/(n-1) = j(1 + O(1/\sqrt{n}))$. If $j \geq \sqrt{n}$, then $\Pr(\delta(i) = j) \cdot j^2/(\mathrm{E}(\delta(i))) = 2^{-\Omega(\sqrt{n})}$. Altogether, $\mathrm{E}(\Delta_t) = 1 + O(1/\sqrt{n})$ follows. □

We now bound the value of the potential function depending on the distance. As a by-product from additive drift analysis (using the result from Lemma 13), a bound on $g(a)$ is also a bound on the expected time to reach at least the target value a.

Lemma 14. *For all $i \geq 0$ and $a \leq n - \log n$, it holds*

$$g(i) \leq \frac{n^2 - n}{2}((1 - 1/n)^{-a} - (1 - 1/n)^{-a+i})(1 + O(1/n))$$

and

$$g(i) \geq \frac{n^2 - n}{2}((1 - 1/n)^{-a} - (1 - 1/n)^{-a+i}).$$

The proof of the lemma is elementary and has been omitted due to space restrictions.

Recall that our aim is to show tail bounds. To this end, we consider the moment-generating function of the drift. The following statement (where we again omit the condition "$\mid x_t$" for readability) bounds the moment-generating function of the negated and unnegated drift away from 1.

Lemma 15. *If $\lambda = n^{-3/2-\epsilon}$ for an arbitrarily small constant $\epsilon > 0$ and $g(x_t) > 0$, then there is a constant $c > 0$ such that $\mathrm{E}(e^{-\lambda\Delta_t}) \leq 1 - \lambda(1 - cn^{-1/2})$ and $\mathrm{E}(e^{\lambda\Delta_t}) \leq 1 + \lambda(1 + cn^{-1/2})$.*

Proof. We start with the bound on $\mathrm{E}(e^{-\lambda\Delta_t})$. From Lemma 11, we get $\mathrm{E}(\delta(i)) \geq 1/(en)$ for any $i > 0$, which implies $g(i + j) - g(i) \leq ejn$ for any $j > 0$. Moreover, similarly as argued before, the probability of decreasing the distance (i. e., increasing the LO-value) by at least j is at most $2^{-j+1}/n$ as $j - 1$ free-riders and a flip of the leftmost zero-bit are necessary. Hence, $\Pr(\Delta_t \geq ejn) \leq 2^{-j+1}/n$. We use this exponential decay to bound the higher-order moments of Δ_t. More precisely, similarly as in the proof of the simplified drift theorem [13], we get

$$\mathrm{E}\left(e^{-\lambda\Delta_t}\right) \leq 1 - \lambda + \sum_{k=2}^{\infty} \frac{\lambda^k \mathrm{E}(|\Delta_t|^k)}{k!},$$

where we have used that $\mathrm{E}(\Delta_t) \geq 1$ (Lemma 13). The sum for $k \geq 2$ is at most

$$\sum_{k=2}^{\infty} \frac{\lambda^k}{k!} \sum_{j=0}^{n} (e(j+1)n)^k \Pr(\Delta_t^k \geq (ejn)^k)$$

as Δ_t does not take on negative values and the maximum change of distance is at most n.

Now, for any k, the inner sum is at most

$$\sum_{j=0}^{n} (e(j+1)n)^k \frac{2^{-j+1}}{n} = \frac{2 \cdot (en)^k}{n} \sum_{j=0}^{n} (j+1)^k 2^{-j}.$$

To bound the sum over j, we distinguish several cases. If k is constant then obviously $\sum_{j=0}^{n}(j+1)^k 2^{-j} = O(1)$. If $k \leq n^{1/2+\epsilon/3}$, then $\sum_{j=0}^{n}(j+1)^k 2^{-j} = O(n^{(1/2+2\epsilon/3)k})$ as $2^{-j} = o(j^{-n^{1/2+\epsilon/3}})$ for $j \geq n^{1/2+2\epsilon/3}$. Otherwise, we use the trivial bound $\sum_{j=0}^{n}(j+1)^k 2^{-j} = O(n^k)$. This, along with our choice $\lambda = n^{-3/2-\epsilon}$, bounds the outer sum by

$$\sum_{k=2}^{6/\epsilon} \frac{C^k n^{-(1/2+\epsilon)k}}{nk!} + \sum_{k=6/\epsilon+1}^{n^{1/2+\epsilon/3}} \frac{C^k n^{-(1/2+\epsilon)k}}{nk!} n^{(1/2+2\epsilon/3)k}$$

$$+\sum_{k=n^{1/2+\epsilon/3}+1}^{\infty}\frac{C^k n^{-(1/2+\epsilon)k}n^k}{nk!}$$

$$\leq O(n^{-2-\epsilon})+\sum_{k=n^{1/2+\epsilon/3}+1}^{\infty}\frac{C^k n^{(1/2-\epsilon)k}}{n^{(1/2+\epsilon/3)k}}\leq\frac{c}{n^{2+\epsilon}}=\frac{c\lambda}{\sqrt{n}}$$

for constants $C, c > 0$ since $k! \geq (k/e)^k$.

The bound on $\mathrm{E}(e^{\lambda\Delta_t})$ is obtained in a very similar way. We have $\mathrm{E}(e^{\lambda\Delta_t}) = 1 + \lambda\mathrm{E}(\Delta_t) + \sum_{k=2}^{\infty}\frac{\lambda^k\mathrm{E}((\Delta_t)^k)}{k!}$. Using Lemma 13, we get $\mathrm{E}(\Delta_t) = 1 + O(1/\sqrt{n})$. The higher-order moments are bounded as before, such that $\mathrm{E}(\Delta_t) = 1 + \lambda(1 + c/\sqrt{n})$ follows by choosing c large enough. □

With the previous bound on the moment-generating function, the proof of the desired tail bounds will mostly be applications of Markov's inequality.

PROOF OF THEOREM 9. Let T denote the random time until the distance from the target a is reduced to 0. We start with the upper tail. For any $t > 0$, we have

$$\Pr(T > t) = \Pr(g(x_t) \geq g(1)) = \Pr(e^{\lambda g(x_t)} \geq e^{\lambda g(1)})$$
$$\leq \mathrm{E}(e^{\lambda g(x_t)} \mid x_0)$$

where the inequality uses Markov's inequality along with $e^{\lambda g(1)} \geq 1$. Now,

$$\mathrm{E}(e^{\lambda g(x_t)} \mid x_0) = \mathrm{E}\Big(e^{\lambda g(x_{t-1})}\cdot\mathrm{E}(e^{-\lambda\Delta_{t-1}} \mid x_{t-1}) \mid x_0\Big)$$
$$= e^{\lambda g(x_0)}\cdot\prod_{s=0}^{t-1}\mathrm{E}(e^{-\lambda\Delta_s} \mid x_s),$$

where the last equality follows inductively (note that this does not assume independence of the Δ_s). Using Lemma 15, our bound is no larger than

$$e^{\lambda g(x_0)}\cdot(1-\lambda(1-cn^{-1/2}))^t \leq e^{\lambda g(x_0)}e^{-t\lambda(1-cn^{-1/2})},$$

which, using Lemma 14 with $i = a$, is at most

$$e^{\lambda((n^2-n)/2)((1-1/n)^{-a}-1)(1+O(1/n))-t\lambda(1-cn^{-1/2})}.$$

As $(1-cn^{-1/2})(1+2cn^{-1/2}) \geq 1$, plugging in $t := ((n^2 - n)/2)((1-1/n)^{-a}-1)(1+C/n)(1+2cn^{-1/2})+d$ for some sufficiently large constant C finally yields

$$\Pr(T > t) \leq e^{-\lambda d} = e^{-dn^{-3/2-\epsilon}}.$$

Noting that $(1+O(1/n))(1+2cn^{-1/2}) = 1+O(n^{-1/2})$ and $(1-1/n)^{-1} = 1+1/(n-1)$, the first statement of the theorem follows.

The second statement, the lower tail, is proved similarly. By a union bound,

$$\Pr(T < t) \leq \sum_{s=0}^{t-1}\Pr(g(x_s) = 0).$$

Since $g(x_s) = 0$ is equivalent to $e^{-\lambda g(x_s)} \geq e^{-\lambda 0} = 1$, we get $\Pr(e^{-\lambda g(x_s)} \geq 1) \leq \mathrm{E}(e^{-\lambda g(x_s)})$ from Markov's inequality. Now, $\mathrm{E}(e^{-\lambda g(x_s)}) = e^{-\lambda g(x_0)}\cdot\prod_{r=0}^{s-1}\mathrm{E}(e^{\lambda\Delta_r} \mid x_r)$. By Lemma 15, this is no larger than $e^{-\lambda g(x_0)}\cdot e^{s\lambda(1+cn^{-1/2})}$. Due to random initialisation, $\Pr(d(x_0) \leq a-\sqrt{n}) = 1-2^{-\Omega(\sqrt{n})}$. From Lemma 14, we get $g(x_0) \geq ((n^2-n)/2)((1-1/n)^{-a} - (1-1/n)^{-\sqrt{n}})$ in this case. Let $t := ((n^2-n)/2)((1-1/n)^{-a}-(1-1/n)^{-\sqrt{n}})(1-2cn^{-1/2})-d$ for some sufficiently large constant c. Then for all $s \leq t$, $\Pr(g(x_s) = 0) \leq e^{-\lambda d}$. Now the lower tail follows by the above union bound over $t \leq en^2$ steps. □

8. CONCLUSIONS

We have presented a general method to derive results on the function value after a pre-specified number of function evaluations, called budget. Our method starts with results on the expected runtime (to find a solution of a given quality) that come with tail bounds and turn these into fixed-budget results by means of the inverse function. The method has the advantage of allowing for the re-use of a large body of existing work.

We have tested our method on a simple test case, the (1+1) EA on LO. The (1+1) EA was one of two algorithms considered in the original paper introducing fixed budget computations [10] and is more realistic than random local search, the other of the two algorithms. We have been able to improve over the bounds from [10] considerably. In Section 5 we use Chebyshev's inequality to derive tail bounds (a method that, as Doerr [3] points out, was rarely used in the theory of randomised search heuristics; this may change now). In Section 6 we provide asymptotically much stronger results using Chernoff bounds. Both methods strongly rely on properties of LO. In Section 7 we also prove strong tail bounds now using an implicit variable drift theorem with tail bounds. We are currently working on an explicit version of such a theorem, which is expected to be very useful to obtain further fixed-budget results. The asymptotic nature of the much more involved proofs from this section make it difficult, however, to derive numerical statements for concrete values of n. Numerical bounds based on Theorem 7 are also not strong enough for the values of n we consider. Therefore, when we compare our bounds with the ones from [10] we do so only with the results from Section 5.

We depict the bounds from Theorem 4 from [10] with our result from Theorem 6 for $n \in \{200, 1000, 5000, 10000\}$ and plot the bounds in Figure 1. Our bounds are derived numerically using an exact expression for the variance $\mathrm{Var}(T(a))$ in Chebyshev's inequality. We choose d_a in such a way that the function value stays between the upper and lower bound with at least 90% probability.

Remember that the bounds from [10] only make a statement for budgets $b < n^2/2$. Therefore, the corresponding curves in Figure 1 stop at this point. Our bounds allow for statements for the whole range of budgets up to the expected optimisation time. For large values of n our bounds are clearly much better. For smaller values of n and rather small budgets this is not necessarily the case (see, e.g., the curves for $n = 200$ and $b \leq 11000$ in Figure 1). Note, however, that the bounds from [10] are asymptotic and it is not clear that they are actually valid for such small values of n. We see that our bounds are not only much sharper asymptotically but also allow for concrete (numerical) statements for concrete values of n and b.

The presentation of our method allows for a wealth of new results in the fixed budget framework. This requires revisiting existing results on expected optimisation times, generalising them to results on the expected time needed to find results of a pre-defined quality (i.e., results on the expected approximation time), and strengthening them by adding tail bounds to the statements on the expected times. While general tools for this are available (see, e.g., the drift

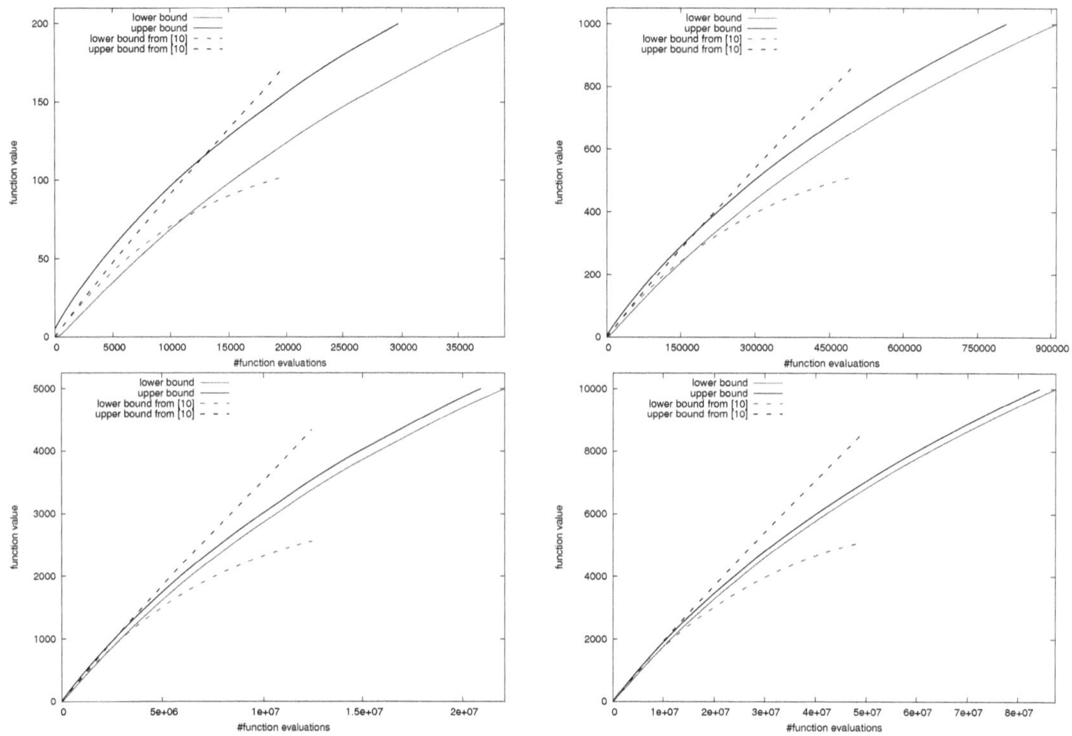

Figure 1: Bounds from Theorem 4 from [10] and Theorem 6 for $n = 200$ (top left), $n = 1000$ (top right), $n = 5000$ (bottom left) and $n = 10000$ (bottom right). The function value $\mathrm{LO}(x_t)$ stays between the upper and lower bound with at least 90% probability.

theorem with tail bounds by Doerr and Goldberg [5]) it has not often been done in the past. We expect to see the need for more tools to allow for the derivation of such tail bounds and a renewed interest in the development of such analytical methods. We hope that this line of research proves to be motivating and intriguing for theoreticians and delivers results that will be of interest to practitioners.

9. REFERENCES

[1] A. Auger and B. Doerr, editors. *Theory of Randomized Search Heuristics*. World Scientific, 2011.

[2] S. Böttcher, B. Doerr, and F. Neumann. Optimal fixed and adaptive mutation rates for the LeadingOnes problem. In *Proc. of the 11th Int'l Conf. on Parallel Problem Solving From Nature (PPSN 2010)*, pages 1–10. Springer, 2010. LNCS 6238.

[3] B. Doerr. Analyzing randomized search heuristics: Tools from probability theory. In Auger and Doerr [1], pages 1–20.

[4] B. Doerr, M. Fouz, and C. Witt. Sharp bounds by probability-generating functions and variable drift. In *Proc. of the Genetic and Evolutionary Comp. Conf. (GECCO 2011)*, pages 2083–2090. ACM Press, 2011.

[5] B. Doerr and L. Goldberg. Drift analysis with tail bounds. In *Proc. of the 11th Int'l Conf. on Parallel Problem Solving From Nature (PPSN 2010)*, pages 174–183. Springer, 2010. LNCS 6238.

[6] B. Doerr, T. Jansen, and C. Klein. Comparing global and local mutations on bit strings. In *Proc. of the Genetic and Evolutionary Comp. Conf. (GECCO 2008)*, pages 929–936. ACM Press, 2008.

[7] S. Droste, T. Jansen, and I. Wegener. On the analysis of the (1+1) evolutionary algorithm. *Theoretical Comp. Science*, 276(1–2):51–81, 2002.

[8] B. Hajek. Hitting and occupation time bounds implied by drift analysis with applications. *Advances in Applied Probability*, 14:502–525, 1982.

[9] T. Jansen. *Analyzing Evolutionary Algorithms. The Computer Science Perspective.* Springer, 2013.

[10] T. Jansen and C. Zarges. Fixed budget computations: A different perspective on run time analysis. In *Proc. of the Genetic and Evolutionary Comp. Conf. (GECCO 2012)*, pages 1325–1332. ACM Press, 2012.

[11] P. K. Lehre. Drift analysis (tutorial). In *Companion to GECCO 2012*, pages 1239–1258. ACM Press, 2012.

[12] F. Neumann and C. Witt. *Bioinspired Computation in Combinatorial Optimization.* Springer, 2010.

[13] P. S. Oliveto and C. Witt. Simplified drift analysis for proving lower bounds in evolutionary computation. *Algorithmica*, 59(3):369–386, 2011. Erratum in `http://arxiv.org/abs/1211.7184`.

[14] J. E. Rowe and D. Sudholt. The choice of the offspring population size in the $(1, \lambda)$ EA. In *Proc. of the Genetic and Evolutionary Comp. Conf. (GECCO 2012)*, pages 1349–1356. ACM Press, 2012.

[15] C. Scheideler. *Probabilistic Methods for Coordination Problems*, volume 78 of *HNI-Verlagsschriftenreihe.* University of Paderborn, 2000. Habilitation thesis. Available at: `www.cs.jhu.edu/~scheideler/papers/habil.ps.gz`.

[16] N. P. Troutman, B. E. Eskridge, and D. F. Hougen. Is "best-so-far" a good algorithmic performance metric? In *Proc. of the Genetic and Evolutionary Comp. Conf. (GECCO 2008)*, pages 1147–1148. ACM Press, 2008.

How the $(1 + \lambda)$ Evolutionary Algorithm Optimizes Linear Functions

Benjamin Doerr
Max-Planck-Institut für Informatik
66123 Saarbrücken, Germany
doerr@mpi-inf.mpg.de

Marvin Künnemann
Max-Planck-Institut für Informatik
66123 Saarbrücken, Germany
marvin@mpi-inf.mpg.de

ABSTRACT

We analyze how the $(1 + \lambda)$ evolutionary algorithm (EA) optimizes linear pseudo-Boolean functions. We prove that it finds the optimum of any linear function within an expected number of $O(\frac{1}{\lambda} n \log n + n)$ iterations. We also show that this bound is sharp for some functions, e.g., the binary value function. Hence unlike for the $(1 + 1)$ EA, for the $(1 + \lambda)$ EA different linear functions may have run-times of different asymptotic order. The proof of our upper bound heavily relies on a number of classic and recent drift analysis methods. In particular, we show how to analyze a process displaying different types of drifts in different phases. Our work corrects a wrongfully claimed better asymptotic runtime in an earlier work [12].

Categories and Subject Descriptors

F.2.2 [**Theory of Computation**]: Analysis of Algorithms and Problem Complexity—*Nonnumerical Algorithms and Problems*

Keywords

Theory; runtime analysis; population-based EA

1. INTRODUCTION

If there is one single problem that was most influential on the theory of evolutionary computation, then clearly it is the innocent question of how simple evolutionary algorithms optimize linear pseudo-Boolean functions, that is, functions $f : \{0,1\}^n \to \mathbb{R}; x \mapsto \sum_{i=1}^n w_i x_i$ with $w_1, \ldots, w_n \in \mathbb{R}$. While easy to state, this problem is surprisingly difficult and already for the simple (1+1) evolutionary algorithm (EA) was subject to a sequence of works [9, 10, 13, 14, 15, 17, 6, 5, 3, 2, 18, 30, 7, 4, 31]. More importantly, the quest for understanding this linear functions problem led to a large number of strong analysis tools like artificial fitness functions [10], additive drift analysis [13], average drift [17], multiplicative drift [6] and adaptive drift [3] (see Section 3 for an explanation of these terms). These techniques subsequently were heavily used and gave rise to a number of remarkable results in different areas, e.g., to the ICARIS 2011 best paper award winner [21] analyzing an immune inspired B-cell algorithm for the vertex cover problem.

In this work, we significantly extend this line of research and analyze how the $(1 + \lambda)$ EA solves the linear functions problem. We prove a sharp upper bound on the runtime for arbitrary linear functions. This is the first time a sharp runtime analysis for a population-based EA for the linear functions problem is given (note that the only previous work in this direction is not correct, see the discussion below).

1.1 Optimizing Linear Functions

Rigorously analyzing how evolutionary algorithms solve optimization problems, and supporting this understanding with mathematical proofs, is one of the main goals in the theory of evolutionary computation. The hope is that a deeper understanding tells us which problems are tractable with evolutionary methods, what particular methods are best suited to solve a particular problem, how to choose the parameters of these methods in the right way, and what computational efforts to expect.

Unfortunately, even for simple evolutionary algorithms and very simple optimization problems such an understanding is surprisingly hard to obtain. For example, the innocent-looking question how the $(1+1)$ EA finds the minimum of a pseudo-Boolean linear function $f : \{0,1\}^n \to \mathbb{R}, x \mapsto \sum_{i=1}^n w_i x_i$ with positive coefficients $w_1, \ldots, w_n$ kept the field busy for around 15 years. It seems obvious that any reasonable randomized search heuristic should easily find the unique optimum $x^* = (0, \ldots, 0)$, since flipping any 1-bit into a 0-bit strictly improves the objective value. Unfortunately, if the w_i are not all equal, mutations may be accepted that increase the number of 1-bits (namely if the gain from flipping fewer 1-bits to 0-bits is larger than the loss from flipping more bits in the other direction). Consequently, it is easy to prove that *randomized local search (RLS)* (flipping only single bits) finds the optimum of any linear function in $n \ln n + O(n)$ iterations. However, the analogous bound of $en \ln n + O(n)$ for the $(1 + 1)$ EA was only proven last year in Witt's remarkable STACS paper [30], ending series of works [9, 10, 13, 14, 15, 17, 6, 5, 3, 2, 18, 7, 4, 31] from various research groups over the last 15 years. See the extended version [31] of Witt's paper for a detailed account of the history of this problem.

One noteworthy consequence of Witt's result is that the

GECCO'13, July 6–10, 2013, Amsterdam, The Netherlands.

$(1+1)$ EA finds *all* linear functions (with non-zero coefficients) equally easy to optimize (ignoring lower order terms). This follows from the lower bound [7] of $en \ln n - O(n)$ shown for the particular linear function of ONEMAX together with the general result [1] that ONEMAX has the shortest optimization time among all linear functions (when using the $(1+1)$ EA).

1.2 Population-based EA

While the linear functions problem for the $(1+1)$ EA is now well-understood and, moreover, many tight or near-tight analyses for combinatorial optimization problems like minimum spanning trees or shortest paths exists (see the book [23]), our understanding of population-based EA, even simple ones like the $(\mu+1)$ EA or the $(1+\lambda)$ EA, is comparably weak.

What among the few runtime analyses on population-based EA comes closest to our work is the paper by Jansen, De Jong, and Wegener [20]. Among other results, they determine the asymptotic optimization times of the $(1+\lambda)$ EA on the classic test functions ONEMAX and LEADINGONES. While for the LEADINGONES function an optimization time of $\Theta(\frac{1}{\lambda}n^2+n)$ generations is not too difficult to show, the optimization behavior of the simple linear function ONEMAX : $\{0,1\}^n \to \mathbb{R}; x \mapsto \sum_{i=1}^n x_i$ is already surprisingly rich. For all $\lambda = O(\log n \log\log n / \log\log\log n)$, only $O(\frac{1}{\lambda}\log n)$ generations are needed. Hence for these λ, a *linear speed-up* is observed. For larger values of λ, a linear speed-up provably does not exist, that is, $\omega(\frac{1}{\lambda} n \log n)$ generations are necessary. Note that these results are far from trivial, in fact, their proofs span several pages in [20]. Similar analyses on how the $(\mu+1)$ EA solves the ONEMAX problem, also technically highly demanding, have been conducted by Storch [27] and Witt [29]; results on how the $(1,\lambda)$ EA optimizes ONEMAX were given by Jägersküpper and Storch [19] as well as Rowe and Sudholt [26].

There are some more results on runtimes of population-based EAs on artificial functions and a few scattered results on combinatorial optimization problems [24, 22], but the overall impression remains that our understanding of population-based EAs is much inferior to the one of simpler randomized search heuristics.

1.3 Our Result

Our main result is that the $(1+\lambda)$ EA with population size $\lambda = O(n^{1-\varepsilon})$ finds the optimum of any linear function in $O(\frac{1}{\lambda} n \log(n) + n)$ generations. This bound is larger than the one [20] for the ONEMAX function. This is with good reason. We show that our bound is sharp for the linear function BINVAL : $\{0,1\}^n \to \mathbb{R}; x \mapsto \sum_{i=1}^n x_i 2^{i-1}$. Consequently, not all linear functions have the same asymptotic runtime. We find this quite surprising—recall that for the $(1+1)$ EA, all linear functions not only have the same asymptotic runtime of $O(n \log n)$, but even are all in $en\ln(n) \pm \Theta(n)$.

Our result also shows that the point when larger populations cease to yield a linear speed-up, for general linear functions can be smaller than for ONEMAX. There, this turning point, also called cut-off point, was shown to be $\Theta(\log n \log\log n / \log\log\log n)$, whereas our result shows that it can be as low as $\Theta(\log n)$ for certain linear functions.

Given that both the analyses of how the $(1+1)$ EA optimizes linear functions and work [20] on how the $(1+\lambda)$ EA optimizes ONEMAX are quite technical, it is no surprise that to prove our results we need a number of non-trivial tools, mostly from the drift analysis world. A particular difficulty we face is that the $(1+\lambda)$ EA, when optimizing a linear function, first makes a constant progress (both in terms of the Hamming distance to the optimum and in terms of the potential function we use for the drift analysis), but later makes progress proportional to the distance from the optimum. Hence the first phase calls for the additive drift theorem of He and Yao [13], the second phase for the multiplicative one [6]. Using either theorem for both phases necessarily would not give sharp results. Unfortunately, we cannot simply use one analysis after the other—while in the second phase we observe an expected multiplicative drift, it is well possible that mutations are accepted that bring us back into the range of additive drift. Hence we cannot guarantee a multiplicative drift for the whole remaining process as required to apply the multiplicative drift theorem.

We solve this difficulty as follows. We easily see that the additive and multiplicative regime overlap. Once in the multiplicative regime, we may use an additive negative drift theorem [25] to show that the probability of leaving the multiplicative range is small. Hence the expected number of times we revert to the purely additive regime is small, and Wald's equation allows us to bound the total time spent. We are optimistic that this technique will find more applications in the near future.

1.4 Relation with He's Analysis [12]

In the discussion above, we omitted a paper [12] that appeared at CEC 2010. The reason is that its main claim is not correct, as we noticed when performing this research.

In [12], also the linear functions problem for the $(1+\lambda)$ EA is analyzed. An upper bound of $O(\frac{1}{\lambda} n \log n + n\frac{\log\log\lambda}{\log\lambda})$ is claimed to hold for all linear functions. For λ being asymptotically larger than logarithmic in n, this contradicts our lower bound of $\Omega(n)$ for the BINVAL linear function (see Section 6). Consequently, [12] also obtains the too optimistic cut-off point that a linear speed-up only ceases to exist for $\lambda = \omega(\log n \log\log n / \log\log\log n)$.

We are sorry to have to point out this mistake in [12], because it is truly a courageous work. Note that at that time, neither multiplicative nor adaptive drift was known. Consequently, an extremely complicated potential function had to be invented, which allows to analyze an inherently non-additive process via the additive drift theorem. This might be the cause for the problem, and also the reason why no reviewer found the mistake.

2. PRELIMINARIES AND NOTATION

In this work, we will be solely regarding one evolutionary algorithm called $(1+\lambda)$ *evolutionary algorithm* ($(1+\lambda)$ EA), and use it to *minimize* pseudo-Boolean functions $f : \{0,1\}^n \to \mathbb{R}$.

This algorithm keeps a population $P = \{x\}$ of size one only. Initially, this one member is chosen uniformly at random from the search space $\{0,1\}^n$ of all length-n bit strings.

In one iteration, exactly λ offspring $x^{(1)}, \ldots, x^{(\lambda)}$ of x are generated independently via standard bit-mutation with mutation probability $1/n$. That is, for all $i \in [\lambda] := \{1, \ldots, \lambda\}$ independently, we have that $x^{(i)}$ satisfies the following: For all bit positions $k \in [n]$ independently, we have $\Pr(x_k^{(i)} = x_k) = 1 - 1/n$ and $\Pr(x_k^{(i)} = 1 - x_k) = 1/n$.

If the best of these offspring is as good as x, it replaces x in the population. More precisely, we choose x^* uniformly at random from the multi-set $\{x^{(i)} \mid i \in [\lambda] \wedge \forall j \in [\lambda] : f(x^{(j)}) \geq f(x^{(i)})\}$ of offspring having the best f-value. If x^* is at least as good as x, then we set $x := x^*$. Recall that we minimize f.

This loop is iterated until a suitable termination criterion is satisfied. Since in this theoretical investigation we aim at understanding how many iterations it takes to find an optimal solution, we do not specify a termination criterion here.

The usual measure for the performance of an evolutionary algorithm is its *optimization time*, which is the number T_f of f-evaluations the algorithm performs until an optimal solution is found. Note that for the $(1+\lambda)$ EA, this is at most λ times the number of iterations ("generations") performed (plus one, to be precise and include the evaluation of the initial individual). For convenience, in this work we shall mainly talk about the number of generations until an optimum is found. Note also that T_f is a random variable, since we regard a randomized algorithm.

Algorithm 1: The $(1+\lambda)$ Evolutionary Algorithm for minimizing pseudo-Boolean functions $f\colon \{0,1\}^n \to \mathbb{R}$.

choose $x \in \{0,1\}^n$ uniformly at random;
for $t = 0$ **to** ∞ **do**
  create $x^{(1)}, \dots, x^{(\lambda)} \in \{0,1\}^n$ independently, each by flipping each bit of x with probability $1/n$;
  choose x^* uniformly at random from the multi-set $\{x^{(i)} \mid i \in [\lambda] \wedge \forall j \in [\lambda] : f(x^{(j)}) \geq f(x^{(i)})\}$;
  if $f(x^*) \leq f(x)$ **then**
    $x := x^*$

We shall analyze how the $(1+\lambda)$ EA optimizes *linear* pseudo-Boolean functions, that is, functions $f : \{0,1\}^n \to \mathbb{R}; x \mapsto f(x) := \sum_{i=1}^n w_i x_i$, where $w_1, \dots, w_n$ are arbitrary real-valued coefficients. It is easy to see (consult [10] if in doubt) that in the analysis of upper bounds of the optimization time of the (1+1) EA on linear functions we may assume without loss of generality that the weights w_i are all positive and in increasing order, that is, we have $0 < w_1 \leq \cdots \leq w_n$. Naturally, the same is true for the $(1+\lambda)$ EA. Hence in the following we assume

$$0 < w_1 \leq \cdots \leq w_n.$$

Unfortunately, due to lack of space, the full proofs of several lemmas in Sections 4 and 5 have to be deferred to an extended version of this paper.

3. DRIFT ANALYSIS

Our work heavily uses a method known as drift analysis. To ease reading, we collect in this section the results we shall use.

In a nut-shell, drift analysis comprises a number of methods that allow to translate information of the expected progress of a randomized process into information on the expected time the process needs to reach a particular goal. In evolutionary algorithms, an easy example could be the following: We let the $(1+1)$ EA optimize the LeadingOnes test function. Denote by X_t the fitness of the population after the t-th iteration. Then it is easy to see that we have an expected progress of $E[X_{t+1} - X_t \mid X_t < n] \geq 1/(en)$. Drift analysis can translate this information into the bound that the first time T such that $X_T = n$, that is, an optimal solution is found, satisfies $E[T] < en^2$. Such an approach, already for the much more difficult linear functions problem, was first in the theory of evolutionary computation conducted by He and Yao in their seminal paper [13].

Usually the random process will be more complicated than simply regarding the fitness of the individual (or its fitness difference to the optimum). Choosing the right measure for the progress of an EA is usually tricky. Let us remark that the idea of tracking not the fitness, but some potential function ("artificial fitness function") was first used without explicit drift methods in [10].

The drift theorem first used in the analysis of evolutionary computation is the *additive drift* theorem of He and Yao [13, 15]. It is strongest when we have a similar progress throughout the whole random process. Due to symmetry in terms of upper and lower bounds, it often allows to prove sharp bounds.

Lemma 1. *(Additive drift theorem). Let $S \subseteq \mathbb{R}$ be a finite set of positive numbers and let $\{X_t\}_{t\in\mathbb{N}}$ be a sequence of random variables over $S \cup \{0\}$. Let T be the random variable that denotes the first point in time $t \in \mathbb{N}$ for which $X_t = 0$.*

Upper bound. *Suppose that there exists a real number $\delta > 0$ such that for all $t \geq 0$, we have $E[X_t - X_{t+1} \mid T > t] \geq \delta$. Then*

$$E[T \mid X_0] \leq \frac{X_0}{\delta}.$$

Lower bound. *Suppose that there exists a real number $\delta > 0$ such that for all $t \geq 0$, we have $E[X_t - X_{t+1} \mid T > t] \leq \delta$. Then*

$$E[T \mid X_0] \geq \frac{X_0}{\delta}.$$

Often, the progress is not constant, but stronger when further from the optimum. In such situations, the following multiplicative drift theorem can be the right tool. Note that it not only gives a bound on the expected hitting time, but also admits large deviation bounds. The concept of multiplicative drift was first used in [6, 7], the large deviation bound was found shortly thereafter [3, 4].

Lemma 2. *(Multiplicative drift theorem). Let $S \subseteq \mathbb{R}$ be a finite set of positive numbers with minimum $s_{\min}$. Let $\{X_t\}_{t\in\mathbb{N}}$ be a sequence of random variables over $S \cup \{0\}$. Let T be the random variable that denotes the first point time $t \in \mathbb{N}$ for which $X_t = 0$. Suppose there exists a real number $\delta > 0$ such that*

$$E[X_t - X_{t+1} \mid X_t = s] \geq \delta s$$

holds for all $s \in S$ with $\Pr[X_t = s] > 0$. Then for all $s_0 \in S$ and $t \geq 0$ with $\Pr[X_0 = s_0] > 0$, we have

$$E[T \mid X_0 = s_0] \leq \frac{1 + \ln(s_0/s_{\min})}{\delta}.$$

Moreover, we have $\Pr[T > (\ln(X_0/s_{\min}) + r)/\delta] \leq e^{-r}$ for all $r > 0$.

All theorems above deal with the situation that the target is in the direction the drift is pointing to. Sometimes, we need to prove that the probability that we reach a target that is in the opposite direction of the drift is very small. A *negative drift* theorem as introduced in [25] would yield such results. In private communication with the authors of [25] we learned that their proof contains a small mistake, but that the following version is correct.

LEMMA 3. *(Negative drift theorem with scaling). Let $X_t, t \geq 0$ be the random variables describing a stochastic process over some discrete state space $S \subseteq \mathbb{R}$. Let $S_t := \{(x_0, \dots, x_t) \in S^t \mid \Pr[X_0 = x_0, \dots, X_t = x_t] > 0\}$. Suppose there exist an interval $[a, b]$ in the state space, and, possibly depending on $\ell := b - a$, a bound $\varepsilon := \varepsilon(\ell) > 0$ and a scaling factor $1 \leq r := r(\ell) \leq \min\{\varepsilon^2\ell, \sqrt{\varepsilon\ell/(132\log(\varepsilon\ell)}$ such that for all $t \geq 0$ the following two conditions hold:*

1. *For all $(x_0, \dots, x_t) \in S_t$ with $a < x_t < b$, we have $\mathrm{E}[X_t - X_{t+1} \mid X_0 = x_0, \dots, X_t = x_t] \geq \varepsilon(\ell)$*
2. *For all $(x_0, \dots, x_t) \in S_t$ with $x_t < b$, we have that $\Pr[|X_t - X_{t+1}| \geq jr \mid X_0 = x_0, \dots, X_t = x_t] \leq e^{-j}$ for all $j \in \mathbb{N}_0$,*

For the first hitting time $T^* := \min\{t \geq 0 : X_t \geq b\}$ it then holds

$$\Pr\left[T^* \leq e^{\varepsilon\ell/(132r^2)} \mid X_0 \leq a\right] = O\left(e^{-\varepsilon\ell/(132r^2)}\right).$$

Before the work [2], all drift analyses in the field of evolutionary computation used the same way of measuring progress ("universal potential function") for all instances of the problem under considerations (e.g., the same potential function for all linear functions). Using a different potential function for each linear function, which is called *adaptive drift analysis*, was used in [2] to obtain results on higher mutation probabilities, which provably cannot be shown via universal potential functions. The same is true for Witt's [30, 31] sharp analysis for the linear functions problem.

We finally state a result strongly connected to drift analysis. Wald's equation [28] allows to bound the expectation of a sum of random variables, where the range of summation is also controlled by a random variable (a so-called stopping time). Wald's equation is usually stated for all random variables in the sum to be equally distributed. We shall need the following slight extension, which avoids the notion of stopping times and is analogous to a lower-bound version used in [16]. We, however, do not require the random variables $X_1, X_2, \dots$ to be bounded.

LEMMA 4. *Let T be a random variable with bounded expectation and let $X_1, X_2, \dots$ be non-negative random variables with $\mathrm{E}[X_i \mid T \geq i] \leq C$. Then*

$$\mathrm{E}\left[\sum_{i=1}^{T} X_i\right] \leq \mathrm{E}[T] \cdot C.$$

PROOF. We compute

$$\begin{aligned}
\mathrm{E}\left[\sum_{i=1}^{T} X_i\right] &= \sum_{i=1}^{\infty} \mathrm{E}[I_{T\geq i} X_i] \\
&= \sum_{i=1}^{\infty} \Pr[T \geq i]\mathrm{E}[X_i \mid T \geq i] \\
&\leq C\sum_{i=1}^{\infty} \Pr[T \geq i] = \mathrm{E}[T] \cdot C.
\end{aligned}$$

The transformation in the first line is legal, since the series $\sum_{i=1}^{\infty} \mathrm{E}[I_{T\geq i} X_i]$ converges absolutely, which follows from $\mathrm{E}[T] < \infty$. □

Note that when all X_i, conditioned on $T \geq i$, have equal expectation C, then we actually have equality: $\mathrm{E}\left[\sum_{i=1}^{T} X_i\right] = \mathrm{E}[T] \cdot C$. In this case, Wald's equation may also be used to conduct a drift analysis. If X_i is the progress made in iteration i, then $d := \sum_{i=1}^{T} X_i$ is simply the distance from the initial population to the optimum and the time to get there satisfies $\mathrm{E}[T] = d/C$. A similar application of Wald's equation for the analysis of evolutionary algorithms can be found in [10].

4. OUTLINE OF THE ANALYSIS

Our main theorem provides an upper bound on the optimization time of the $(1+\lambda)$ EA on arbitrary linear functions, both in expectation and with high probability.

THEOREM 5. *Let $f(x) = \sum_{i=1}^{n} w_i x_i$ with $0 < w_1 \leq \dots \leq w_n$ be any linear function on bit strings with positive bit weights. Let $\lambda : \mathbb{N} \to \mathbb{N}$ be an arbitrary function with $c < \lambda(n) = O(n^{1-\varepsilon})$ for some constant c and any $\varepsilon > 0$. Then the $(1 + \lambda)$ EA optimizes f in an expected number of*

$$O\left(\frac{n \log n}{\lambda(n)} + n\right)$$

iterations. Furthermore, for each $s > 0$ there is a constant $C(s)$ such that the probability that the optimum is not found within $C(s)(\frac{1}{\lambda(n)} n \log n + n)$ iterations can be bounded by $O(n^{-s})$.

The proof of this theorem relies on analyzing two overlapping phases of the optimization process. In the beginning of the process, in each optimization step an individual with a strictly better fitness is found with constant probability. In this first phase, the gain of creating several offsprings in parallel does not scale linearly with $\lambda(n)$. Later in the process, when the current individual is already close to the optimum value, the probability of finding a strictly better individual decreases, which allows a speed-up asymptotically linear in $\lambda(n)$.

In the rest of the section, let $\lambda := \lambda(n)$ be given as in the statement of the theorem. We define phase 1 as active, if the current individual x has at least $\theta_2 := \gamma_2 n/\lambda$ one-bits, i.e., ONEMAX$(x) \geq \theta_2$, for some $\gamma_2 > 0$. Phase 2 becomes active, if ONEMAX$(x) < \theta_1 := \gamma_1 n/\lambda$ for some $\gamma_1 > \gamma_2$. The constants $0 < \gamma_2 < \gamma_1$ can be chosen arbitrarily. We say that an individual x lies above or below some threshold θ, if its number of one-bits ONEMAX(x) is at least or at most θ, respectively. We pessimistically assume that the starting individual lies above θ_1 and the process needs to traverse both phases to get to the optimum.

In Section 5, we will prove that phase 1 can be traversed in $O(n)$ generations both in expectation (by use of the additive drift theorem) and with high probability (by use of suitable martingales and the Azuma-Hoeffding inequality).

LEMMA 6. *Let $x \in \{0, 1\}^n$. The expected number of generations until the $(1 + \lambda)$ EA hits the first element below θ_2 when starting with x can be bounded by $O(n)$. The probability that it fails to do so in cn steps is at most $e^{-\Omega(n^{c'})}$ for some constants $c, c' > 0$.*

In contrast to the first phase, phase 2 provides a drift towards the optimum that lies within a $\Omega(\lambda)$-factor of the drift of the (1+1) EA. Using the multiplicative drift theorem, we obtain an expected number of $O(\frac{1}{\lambda}n\log n)$ iterations to find the optimum, under the condition that the process does not leave phase 2. Large deviation bounds follow immediately from the use of multiplicative drift.

LEMMA 7. *The expected number of generations until the $(1+\lambda)$ EA hits the optimum 0^n under the condition that phase 2 stays active throughout the process is bounded by $O(\frac{1}{\lambda}n\log n)$. For each $s>0$, the probability that it fails to find the optimum value in $\frac{c(s)}{\lambda}n\log n$ steps under this condition is bounded by n^{-s} for some constant $c(s)$.*

The lemma above needs to ensure that the drift guarantee of phase 2 applies to all individuals observed throughout the process. It is however possible, although very unlikely, that the process returns to above θ_1. By use of a negative drift theorem, we can bound the probability of this event.

LEMMA 8. *The probability to ever return above θ_1 with the $(1+\lambda)$ EA starting at some individual below θ_2 can be bounded by $e^{-\Omega(n^{s'})}$ for some $s'>0$.*

PROOF SKETCH. The negative drift theorem ensures that with high probability, the process does not return above θ_1 starting below θ_2 in an exponential number of steps t. The expected number of generations until the optimum is found while phase 2 is active is only polynomial. Hence already Markov's inequality ensures that the process, conditioned on not returning above θ_1 in t steps, finds an optimum almost surely in t steps and can never return above θ_1. □

As an immediate collorary of the previous three lemmas, we bound the optimization time with high probability. Let $s>0$ be arbitrary and choose c sufficiently large. The probability of not finding the optimum value in $c(\frac{1}{\lambda}n\log n+n)$ steps can be bounded by the sum of the probabilities of (i) not finding the first element below θ_2 in cn steps, of (ii) returning to an element above θ_1 again, and of (iii) not finding the optimum value in $\frac{c}{\lambda}n\log n$ although never returning above θ_1. It is thus bounded by $e^{-\Omega(n^{c'})}+n^{-s}+e^{-\Omega(n^{s'})}=O(n^{-s})$.

To bound the expected number of generations to find the optimum, split the optimization process into stages. In each stage, the $(1+\lambda)$ EA starts with an individual (typically above θ_1), traverses phase 1 to below θ_2 and then either returns to above θ_1 and enters the next stage or finds the optimum and stops the process. One can show that the number of stages N and the times T_i defined as the time spent in stage i satisfy the conditions for Lemma 4. Note that $\mathrm{E}[T_i]\le O(\frac{1}{\lambda}n\log n+n)$. This allows to bound the expected number of generations by

$$\mathrm{E}\left[\sum_{i=1}^{N}T_i\right]\le \mathrm{E}[N]\cdot O\left(\frac{n\log n}{\lambda}+n\right)=O\left(\frac{n\log n}{\lambda}+n\right),$$

using Lemmas 6, 7 and 8.

We believe that our analysis can be refined to show a stronger upper bound for special classes of linear functions. In particular, for bounded coefficients we expect to obtain the same bound that was proven in [20] for ONEMAX. For this, an approach using variable drift for the first phase or, alternatively, splitting the first phase again into two phases with different drift guarantees seem appropriate. The statement of the drift in Section 5.1 (Lemma 10) aims to provide a general way to perform such an analysis.

5. BOUNDING THE DRIFT

An essential aspect in drift analysis is to choose a suitable potential function to measure the progress of the random process towards the optimum value. We rely on the following potential function that has proven useful to give tight bounds on the optimization time of the (1+1)-EA on linear functions [30]. For $x\in\{0,1\}^n$, define $g(x):=\sum_{i=1}^n g_i x_i$ with

$$g_i:=\left(1+\frac{1}{n-1}\right)^{\min\{j\le i|w_j=w_i\}-1}.$$

Note that the weights $g_1,\dots,g_n$ of the potential function are non-decreasing as are the bit weights $w_1,\dots,w_n$. Furthermore, bits of equal weight receive the same weight in g. Note also that $1\le g_i\le(1+1/(n-1))^{n-1}\le e$ and thus $g(x)\le en$ for all $x\in\{0,1\}^n$.

The *drift* $\Delta(x)$ of an optimization step with parent individual x is defined by $\Delta(x)=g(x)-g(x^*)$ if $f(x^*)\le f(x)$ and $\Delta(x)=0$ otherwise.

Let a parent individual $x\in\{0,1\}^n\setminus\{0^n\}$ be given. In the following, we aim at bounding the bit-flip probabilities in the winner individual x^*. For the $(1+\lambda)$ EA, this is more intricate than for the (1+1) EA, since the bits of the winner individual are not independently flipped with probability $1/n$, but result from choosing the offspring with the best fitness. This distribution even depends on the fitness function. However, for a very general class of events, we show how to bound the conditional bit-flip probability of a zero-bit of x in x^*.

For the statement of this class of events, let an index $1\le j\le n$ with $x_j=0$ be given. Let $y^{(1)},\dots,y^{(\lambda)}\in\{0,1\}^n$ be a realization of the offspring individuals, in which the winner individual $y^*:=\operatorname{argmin}_{z=y^{(1)},\dots,y^{(\lambda)}}f(z)$ has the j-th bit set to one, i.e., $y_j^*=1$. Let m be the first index with $f(y^{(m)})=f(y^*)$. We define an injective map $M:(y^{(1)},\dots,y^{(\lambda)})\mapsto(\bar{y}^{(1)},\dots,\bar{y}^{(\lambda)})$ by

$$\bar{y}^{(i)}=y^{(i)}\text{ for }i\neq m,\quad \bar{y}_{j'}^{(m)}=y_{j'}^{(m)}\text{ for }j'\neq j,\quad \bar{y}_j^{(m)}=0.$$

We say that an event $\mathcal{E}$ is *zero-flip closed* if for any realization $y^{(1)},\dots,y^{(\lambda)}$ with $y_j^*=1$, $(y^{(1)},\dots,y^{(\lambda)})\in\mathcal{E}$ implies that $(\bar{y}^{(1)},\dots,\bar{y}^{(\lambda)})\in\mathcal{E}$.

LEMMA 9. *Let j be such that $x_j=0$ and $\mathcal{E}$ be a zero-flip closed event. Then $\Pr[x_j^*=1\mid\mathcal{E}]\le 1/n$.*

5.1 Phase 1

We outline the proof of Lemma 6. By conducting a careful case analysis in the spirit of [7] and [30], and exploiting Lemma 9, a suitable bound on the drift in phase 1 can be obtained. Let E_ℓ denote the event that exactly ℓ of the one-bits of x flip in the winner individual x^*.

LEMMA 10. *Let $x\in\{0,1\}^n$ be such that $\Pr[f(x^{(i)})<f(x)]\ge\frac{c_1}{\lambda}$. Then $\mathrm{E}[\Delta(x)]\ge\Omega(F(x))$ and $F(x)\ge\Omega(1)$, where $F(x)=\sum_{\ell=0}^n\Pr[E_\ell\mid f(x^*)\le f(x)]\ell$ is the expected number of flipped one-bits of x in an accepted winner individual x^*.*

Note that it is possible that $F(x)$, and thus the bound on $\mathrm{E}[\Delta(x)]$, heavily depends on the specific linear function to be minimized.

Using this, we can prove Lemma 6. Let the $(1+\lambda)$ EA start at an arbitrary individual $x \in \{0,1\}^n$. The hitting time of the first element below θ_2 is bounded by zero if $\textsc{OneMax}(x) \leq \theta_2 = \frac{\gamma_2 n}{\lambda}$ already holds. Otherwise, the constant drift guarantee of the previous lemma holds, since

$$\begin{aligned}\Pr[f(x^{(i)}) < f(x)] &\geq \sum_{j,x_j=1} \frac{1}{n}\left(1-\frac{1}{n}\right)^{n-1} \\ &\geq \frac{\textsc{OneMax}(x)}{ne} \geq \frac{\gamma_2}{\lambda e}.\end{aligned}$$

Since throughout the phase we have a constant positive drift D, the additive drift theorem (Lemma 1) ensures that the expected hitting time of the first element below threshold is bounded by $g(x)/D \leq en/D$ independent of the starting individual x.

We outline how to show that the linear time bound also holds with high probability. An obstacle to overcome is that, although a constant drift is guaranteed throughout phase 1, the random variables representing the drift in a fixed number of rounds B are not independent and can get as large as $\Omega(n)$ in the absolute value. Hence, Chernoff bounds do not seem to suffice here. However, it is possible to bound the absolute value of the drift throughout B optimization steps with high probability and define a martingale on a process that is conditioned on experiencing only small drifts in each direction. Applying the Azuma-Hoeffding inequality to bound the deviation from the martingale's expectation, the time spent in phase 1 can be bounded with high probability.

5.2 Phase 2

This subsection is dedicated to proving Lemma 7. In phase 2, the probability of making progress towards the optimum is small. Hence, the parallel mutations can be regarded as repetitions of a Bernoulli trial with small success probability; the expected gain scales favourably with λ. The following lemma makes this claim formal and shows a multiplicative drift that is larger than corresponding bounds for the $(1+1)$ EA by a factor of $\Omega(\lambda)$.

LEMMA 11. *Let $x \in \{0,1\}^n$ be such that $\Pr[f(x^{(i)}) < f(x)] \leq \frac{c_2}{\lambda}$, let $\lambda > e^{c_2+1}$ and let n be large enough. Then*

$$\mathrm{E}[\Delta(x)] \geq \frac{\lambda g(x)}{e^{c_2+1}n}.$$

To prove Lemma 7, start with any individual $x \in \{0,1\}^n$ below θ_2. Observe that we condition on $\textsc{OneMax}(x) \leq \theta_1 = \frac{\gamma_1 n}{\lambda}$ throughout the process, hence all encountered parent individuals satisfy

$$\Pr[f(x^{(i)}) < f(x)] \leq \sum_{j,x_j=1} \Pr[x_j^{(i)} = 0] = \frac{\textsc{OneMax}(x)}{n} \leq \frac{\gamma_1}{\lambda}.$$

Consequently, the drift guarantee of the previous lemma applies and we conclude using the multiplicative drift theorem (Lemma 2) and the facts that $g(x) \geq 1$ for all $x \in \{0,1\}^n \setminus \{0^n\}$ and $g(x) \leq e\textsc{OneMax}(n)$ that the expected hitting time of the optimum value, conditioned on not returning above θ_1, is bounded by

$$\frac{e^{\gamma_1+1}n}{\lambda}(1+\ln(en/\lambda)) = O\left(\frac{n\log(n)}{\lambda}\right).$$

By choosing $r := s\log n$ and a sufficiently large c, the multiplicative drift theorem also directly satisfies the corresponding tail bound.

6. LOWER BOUNDS

In this section, we prove our lower bound showing that for all $\lambda \leq n$, the expected number of generations needed to optimize the linear function $\textsc{BinVal} : \{0,1\}^n \to \mathbb{R}; x \mapsto \sum_{i=1}^n x_i 2^{i-1}$ is at least $\Omega(n)$.

THEOREM 12. *(Lower Bound for* BINVAL*). For the $(1+\lambda)$-EA with $\lambda \in O(n)$, the expected number of iterations performed on* BINVAL *to find the optimum is lower bounded by $\Omega(n)$.*

This result has some important consequences. (i) It shows that the stronger upper bound claimed in [12] cannot be true. (ii) It shows that our general upper bound cannot be improved (note that a lower bound of $\Omega(\frac{1}{\lambda}n\log n)$ generations follows from the standard argument that in $o(\frac{1}{\lambda}n\log n)$ generations, at least $\omega(1)$ of the bit positions originally not equal to zero (recall that we minimize!) will never have been flipped (for a more formal proof, see Theorem 3 in [20]). (iii) Our result also shows that, surprisingly and very differently from what we know from the $(1+1)$ EA, the optimization time of different linear functions varies significantly (recall that [20] proved that $O(n\frac{\log\log\log n}{\log\log n})$ iterations suffice for the $(1+\lambda)$ EA to find the optimum of ONEMAX when λ equals the cut-off point $\log n\frac{\log\log n}{\log\log\log n}$. In the setting of estimation of distribution algorithms, it was already observed in [8] that different linear functions can have different optimization times.

There is a not too difficult explanation for the different optimization behaviors of ONEMAX and BINVAL. When λ is large, say equal to n, then a simple balls-into-bins argument [11] shows that with high probability there is an offspring with $\Theta(\log n/\log\log n)$ bits flipped. If the parent has a ONEMAX value of $n/2$, with constant probability the number of bits flipping from one to zero is by $\Theta(\sqrt{\log n/\log\log n})$ larger than the number of bits flipping in the other direction. Consequently, we have an expected gain of $\Theta(\sqrt{\log n/\log\log n})$ in this situation (see [20] for arguments why also for smaller ONEMAX values a non-constant improvement is likely).

When optimizing BINVAL instead of ONEMAX, of course, we will also create offspring being by $\Theta(\sqrt{\log n/\log\log n})$ closer to the optimum (in terms of the Hamming distance). However, since the winner individual is mostly decided by the most-valuable flipping bit, such an individual has only a minimal advantage in becoming the winner individual. We make this precise in the following proof. We first show that throughout the optimization process, there is at most a constant drift; we then apply the additive drift theorem.

LEMMA 13. *Let $x \in \{0,1\}^n$ be arbitrary. Consider optimizing $f =$* BINVAL *with $\lambda \in O(n)$, then the drift of the x satisfies $\mathrm{E}[\Delta(x)] \leq O(1)$.*

PROOF. We model the process of determining the winner individual of the λ offspring of x by successively revealing the bit at position $1 \leq i \leq n$, from the highest-weighted to the lowest-weighted bit, in the offspring individuals. Analyze the set W_i of potential winner individuals after sampling the bits $n, n-1, \ldots, i$ in all offspring individuals. For BinVal, once $x^{(i)}$ strictly dominates $x^{(j)}$ in the highest-weighted bits, $f(x^{(i)}) > f(x^{(j)})$ follows.

We count the expected number of flipped one-bits F of x in the winner individual x^*. The probability of a one-bit of x to flip in x^* is $1/n$ as soon as the winner individual is uniquely determined. To analyze the process before the winner is determined, we compute the probability that the winner individual stays undetermined if the count of flipped one-bits of x in the winner is increased. This is the complementary event to having exactly one potential winner individual flip a bit under the condition that at least one of them lets it flip. More formally, for $i \in I$ and $k \geq 2$,

$$\Pr\left[|W_i| = 1 \,\middle|\, \begin{array}{l} |W_{i+1}| = k \text{ and} \\ \exists j \in W_{i+1} : x_i^{(j)} = 0 \end{array}\right] = \frac{\frac{k}{n}\left(1-\frac{1}{n}\right)^{k-1}}{1-\left(1-\frac{1}{n}\right)^k} =: p_k.$$

Note that p_k is decreasing in k. Hence, we can pessimistically assume that $|W_i| = \cdots = |W_{n+1}| = \lambda$ until a winner is uniquely determined, i.e., $|W_j| = 1$ for some j. Also, we disregard all zero-bits of x, since by revealing these bits, the number of potential winners can only decrease and the number of flipped one-bits is left unchanged. If all potential winner individuals leave a one-bit of x unchanged, then the number of flipped one-bits keeps its value as well. Consequently, the number of flipped one-bits until a unique winner is found can be upper bounded by a geometrically distributed random variable X with success probability p_λ. Once the winner is determined, we flip the remaining at most $n-1$ bits with probability $1/n$. This yields,

$$\begin{aligned} F(x) &\leq \mathrm{E}[X] + (n-1)\cdot\frac{1}{n} \leq \frac{1-\left(1-\frac{1}{n}\right)^\lambda}{\frac{\lambda}{n}\left(1-\frac{1}{n}\right)^{\lambda-1}} + 1 \\ &= \frac{n}{\lambda}\left(\left(1+\frac{1}{n-1}\right)^{\lambda-1} - \left(1-\frac{1}{n}\right)\right) + 1 \\ &\leq \frac{n}{\lambda}\left(e^{\frac{\lambda-1}{n-1}} - 1\right) + 1 + \frac{1}{\lambda} = O(1), \end{aligned}$$

for $\lambda \in O(n)$. Consequently, the bound $\mathrm{E}[\Delta(x)] \leq eF(x)$ establishes the claim. □

7. EXPERIMENTS

Asymptotic analyses in general, while explaining the growth behaviour for very large problem sizes, bear the possibility to hide phenomena in the range for practical problem sizes. To illustrate that even for small n the predicted results are reflected in practical observations and to provide further evidence for our results, we conducted an empirical investigation. We implemented the $(1+\lambda)$ EA in C++, using the GNU Scientific Library to generate pseudo-random numbers.

The results in Figure 1 depict the number of iterations performed to hit the optimum, averaged over 10,000 runs, of the $(1+\lambda)$ EA on OneMax and BinVal for $\lambda = \lceil \log_2(n) \rceil$ and $\lambda = n$, respectively. The empirical standard deviation for any depicted value does not exceed a value of 140 and stays within 47 percent of the mean. The plot indicates that for $\lambda = \lceil \log_2(n) \rceil$, the expected logarithmic speed-up is obtained for both OneMax and BinVal; however, the slope of the functions differs. Observe that jumps in the function value occur near powers of two due to the rounding of the logarithm. The corresponding values for $\lambda = n$ give insight into the performance far above the cut-off point. BinVal, as predicted by Theorem 12, does not profit from the larger value of λ in terms of asymptotic growth. OneMax, however, shows a sublinear growth and deviates heavily from the optimization time of BinVal.

8. ACKNOWLEDGEMENTS

We thank the anonymous reviewers for helpful remarks and Karl Bringmann for pointing out the short proof of Lemma 4.

9. REFERENCES

[1] B. Doerr, M. Fouz, and C. Witt. Quasirandom evolutionary algorithms. In *GECCO '10: Proc. of the 12th Ann. Genetic and Evolutionary Computation Conf.*, pages 1457–1464. ACM, 2010.

[2] B. Doerr and L. A. Goldberg. Adaptive drift analysis. In *PPSN '10: Proc. of the 11th Int. Conf. on Parallel Problem Solving from Nature*, pages 32–41, 2010.

[3] B. Doerr and L. A. Goldberg. Drift analysis with tail bounds. In *PPSN '10: Proc. of the 11th Int. Conf. on Parallel Problem Solving from Nature*, pages 174–183. Springer, 2010.

[4] B. Doerr and L. A. Goldberg. Adaptive drift analysis. *Algorithmica*, 65:224–250, 2013.

[5] B. Doerr, D. Johannsen, and C. Winzen. Drift analysis and linear functions revisited. In *CEC '10: Proc. of the 2010 IEEE Cong. on Evolutionary Computation*, pages 1967–1974. IEEE, 2010.

[6] B. Doerr, D. Johannsen, and C. Winzen. Multiplicative drift analysis. In *GECCO '10: Proc. of the 12th Ann. Genetic and Evolutionary Computation Conf.*, pages 1449–1456. ACM, 2010.

[7] B. Doerr, D. Johannsen, and C. Winzen. Multiplicative drift analysis. *Algorithmica*, 64:673–697, 2012.

[8] S. Droste. A rigorous analysis of the compact genetic algorithm for linear functions. *Natural Computing*, 5(3):257–283, 2006.

[9] S. Droste, T. Jansen, and I. Wegener. A rigorous complexity analysis of the (1+1) evolutionary algorithm for linear functions with Boolean inputs. In *CEC'98: Proc. of the 1998 IEEE Cong. on Evolutionary Computation*, pages 499–504. IEEE, 1998.

[10] S. Droste, T. Jansen, and I. Wegener. On the analysis of the (1+1) evolutionary algorithm. *Theoretical Computer Science*, 276:51–81, 2002.

[11] G. H. Gonnet. Expected length of the longest probe sequence in hash code searching. *J. ACM*, 28:289–304, 1981.

[12] J. He. A note on the first hitting time of $(1+\lambda)$ evolutionary algorithm for linear functions with Boolean inputs. In *CEC '10: Proc. of the 2010 IEEE Cong. on Evolutionary Computation*, pages 1–6. IEEE, 2010.

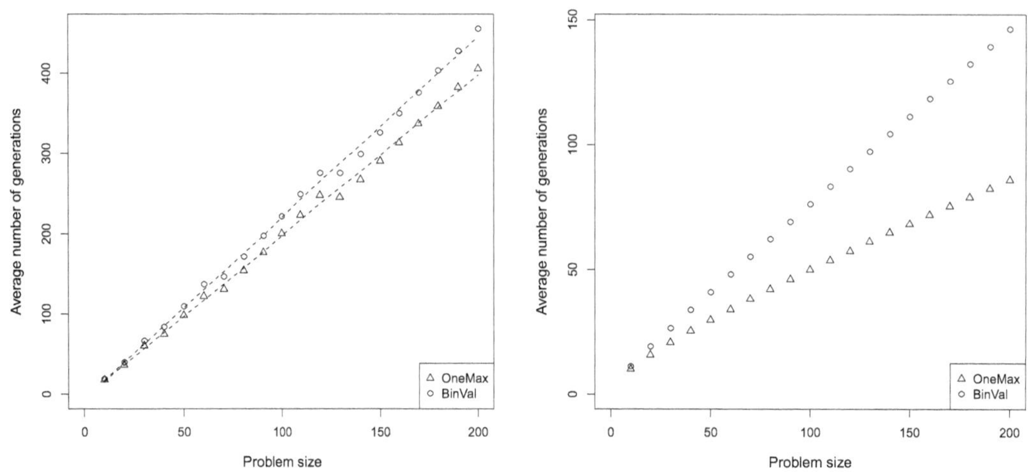

Figure 1: Number of generations performed by the $(1+\lambda)$ EA on OneMax and BinVal for $\lambda = \lceil \log_2(n) \rceil$ (left, together with regression lines) and $\lambda = n$ (right).

[13] J. He and X. Yao. Drift analysis and average time complexity of evolutionary algorithms. *Artificial Intelligence*, 127:51–81, 2001.

[14] J. He and X. Yao. Erratum to: drift analysis and average time complexity of evolutionary algorithms [artificial intelligence 127 (2001) 57–85]. *Artificial Intelligence*, 140:245–248, 2002.

[15] J. He and X. Yao. A study of drift analysis for estimating computation time of evolutionary algorithms. *Natural Computing*, 3:21–35, 2004.

[16] J. Jägersküpper. Algorithmic analysis of a basic evolutionary algorithm for continuous optimization. *Theoretical Computer Science*, 379(3):329–347, 2007.

[17] J. Jägersküpper. A blend of Markov-chain and drift analysis. In *PPSN '08: Proc. of the 10th Int. Conf. on Parallel Problem Solving from Nature*, pages 41–51. Springer, 2008.

[18] J. Jägersküpper. Combining Markov-chain analysis and drift analysis—the (1+1) evolutionary algorithm on linear functions reloaded. *Algorithmica*, 59:409–424, 2011.

[19] J. Jägersküpper and T. Storch. When the plus strategy outperforms the comma strategy and when not. In *FOCI '07: Proc. of the IEEE Symp. on Foundations of Computational Intelligence*, pages 25–32. IEEE, 2007.

[20] T. Jansen, K. A. D. Jong, and I. Wegener. On the choice of the offspring population size in evolutionary algorithms. *Evolutionary Computation*, 13:413–440, 2005.

[21] T. Jansen, P. S. Oliveto, and C. Zarges. On the analysis of the immune-inspired B-cell algorithm for the vertex cover problem. In *ICARIS'11: Proc. of the 10th International Conference on Artificial Immune Systems*, pages 117–131. Springer, 2011.

[22] F. Neumann and I. Wegener. Randomized local search, evolutionary algorithms, and the minimum spanning tree problem. *Theoretical Computer Science*, 378:32–40, 2007.

[23] F. Neumann and C. Witt. *Bioinspired Computation in Combinatorial Optimization*. Springer, 2010.

[24] P. S. Oliveto, J. He, and X. Yao. Analysis of population-based evolutionary algorithms for the vertex cover problem. In *CEC'08: Proc. of the 2008 IEEE Cong. on Evolutionary Computation*, pages 1563–1570, 2008.

[25] P. S. Oliveto and C. Witt. On the analysis of the simple genetic algorithm. In *GECCO '12: Proc. of the 14th Ann. Genetic and Evolutionary Computation Conf.*, pages 1341–1348, 2012.

[26] J. E. Rowe and D. Sudholt. The choice of the offspring population size in the (1,λ) EA. In *GECCO '12: Proc. of the 14th Ann. Genetic and Evolutionary Computation Conf.*, pages 1349–1356. ACM, 2012.

[27] T. Storch. On the choice of the parent population size. *Evolutionary Computation*, 16:557–578, 2008.

[28] A. Wald. On cumulative sums of random variables. *Annals of Mathematical Statistics*, 15:283–296, 1944.

[29] C. Witt. Runtime analysis of the $(\mu + 1)$ EA on simple pseudo-Boolean functions. *Evolutionary Computation*, 14:65–86, 2006.

[30] C. Witt. Optimizing linear functions with randomized search heuristics - the robustness of mutation. In *STACS '12: Proc. of the 29th Ann. Symp. on Theoretical Aspects of Computer Science*, pages 420–431, 2012.

[31] C. Witt. Tight bounds on the optimization time of a randomized search heuristic on linear functions. *Combinatorics, Probability and Computing*, in press, available online:DOI: http://dx.doi.org/10.1017/S0963548312000600. Preprint available at http://arxiv.org/abs/1108.4386.

NP-Completeness and the Coevolution of Exact Set Covers

Jeffrey Horn
Northern Michigan University
1401 Presque Isle Avenue
Marquette, Michigan, 49855 USA
www: cs.nmu.edu/~jeffhorn
jhorn@nmu.edu

ABSTRACT

Recent success with a simple type of coevolution, *resource defined fitness sharing* (RFS), involving only pairwise interactions among species, has inspired some static analysis of the *species interaction matrix*. Under the assumption of equilibrium (w.r.t. selection), the matrix yields a set of linear equations. If there exists a subset of species that exactly cover the resources, then its characteristic population vector is a solution to the equilibrium equations. And if the matrix is non-singular, a solution to the equilibrium equations specifies an exact cover of the resources. This polynomial-time reduction of exact cover problems to linear equations is used in this paper to transform certain exact cover NP-complete problems to certain linear equation NP-complete problems: 0-1 Integer Programming, Minimum Weight Positive Solution to Linear Equations. While most of these problems are known to be in NP-complete, our new proof technique introduces a practical, polynomial-time heuristic algorithm for solving large instances of them.

Categories and Subject Descriptors

G.1.6 [**Mathematics of Computing**]: Optimization—*global optimization, stochastic programming*; I.2.8 [**Artificial Intelligence**]: Problem Solving, Control Methods, and Search—*heuristic methods*

General Terms

Algorithms, Theory

Keywords

genetic algorithm, evolutionary algorithm, evolutionary computation, coevolution, cooperative coevolution, niching, niches, speciation, species, sharing, fitness sharing, resource-defined fitness sharing, NP-completeness, exact cover, XC, X3C,tiling, shape nesting, integer programming, MWSLE

GECCO'13, July 6–10, 2013, Amsterdam, The Netherlands.

1. INTRODUCTION

A recently introduced coevolution algorithm, *Resource-defined Fitness Sharing* (RFS), has had empirical success [8, 6] on the practical problems of shape nesting and packing [2, 10]. RFS also appears to be simple enough to allow for unusual progress in theoretical analysis of coevolution. In particular, empirical studies show RFS is an effective algorithm for coevolving shape nestings that form exact covers [7]. At the same time, static analysis of RFS has resulted in proofs that equilibrium states of RFS evolution correspond to unique exact covers for the problem at hand. In this paper we connect these proofs to the theory of NP-completeness.

2. BACKGROUND

2.1 Resource defined Fitness Sharing (RFS)

2.1.1 *RFS Originally Applied to Shape Nesting*

The RFS algorithm has had success at *shape nesting* problems [8, 6], in which the goal is to nest as many copies of the same shape onto a substrate, without overlaps, as possible (e.g., as in Figure 1). RFS treats each shape placement as an individual in the evolving population whose fitness is equal to its coverage of the substrate (i.e., resource) penalized by overlap with other individual shape placements in the population. In this way the selection operator can be seen to be driving the population towards a set of non-overlapping individuals that cover the substrate. These individuals can be considered to be covering (or "containing") subsets of the set of resources in the substrate. Since RFS uses coverage information only, it is really trying to solve a set covering problem. An exact nesting corresponds to an exact cover. It was noticed early on [7] that RFS consistently converges on exact nestings when they are present in the initial population (e.g., as in Figure 2).

2.1.2 *A New Focus on Exact Cover Problems*

Since this paper is concerned with RFS for finding exact covers, we clearly define that term here. Let S be a set of subsets $s_j, j \in \{1, 2, ..., |S|\}$ (possibly intersecting) of the finite resources (discrete or continuous) to be covered. Let X be the set of all elements in the subsets s_j, that is $X = \cup S$. The s_j might be considered agents that *cover* some of the resources in X. The *exact cover problem* is to find the smallest set of disjoint s_j whose union is X. We further restrict our analysis to subsets s_j of identical size: $\forall j : |s_j| = r$ for some finite, positive, rational r. Despite this restriction,

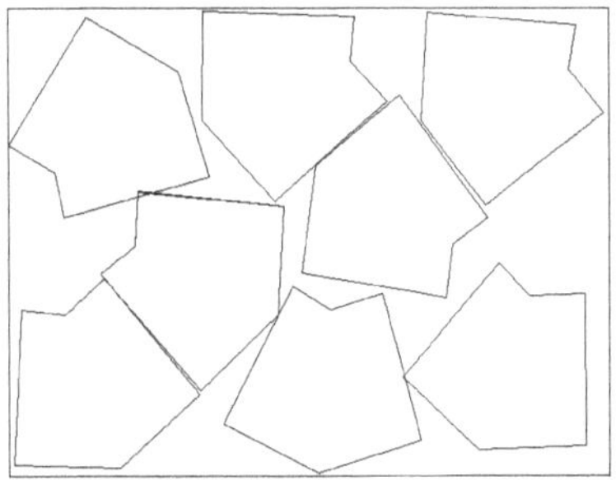

Figure 1: A nesting of identical shapes by RFS.

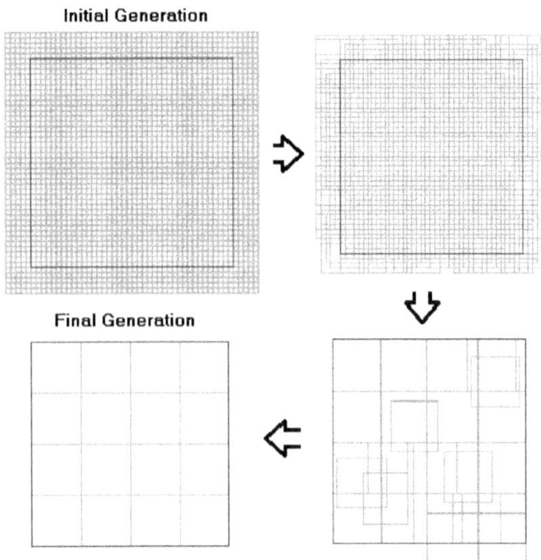

Figure 2: The evolution of a "perfect nesting" corresponding to an exact cover of the large square substrate by sixteen of the smaller squares, found by RFS. (For this particular problem, all shapes were axis-aligned; no rotations allowed.)

the problem of *exact cover by equally-sized subsets* (XrC) remains NP-complete (see section 3.2).

2.1.3 The RFS Algorithm

RFS works by applying proportionate selection to the *shared fitnesses* [4, 1] of the individuals in the population. The shared fitness calculation implements simple coevolution by reducing the fitness of individuals in proportion to the amount of overlap they have with other individuals. Specifically, RFS shared fitness $f_{sh}(x) = (\sum_{y \in P} f_{x,y})^{-1}$, where x is an individual in the population P and $f_{x,y}$ is the pairwise overlap in "coverage" between individuals x and y in P. (Figure 3 illustrates the terms r and $f_{x,y}$ as areas in a 2D shape nesting problem.) The denominator is the cumulative pairwise overlap between x and other individuals in P, thus simulating sharing of finite resources with competitors in the population. The summation in the denominator of $f_{sh}(x)$ is known as the *niche count* for x.

In our model p_x is the proportion of the population that are copies of individual x. We call this set of copies a *species*. Thus the species u maps to a unique chromosome, and is represented in population P by p_u exact copies. Let $S(P)$

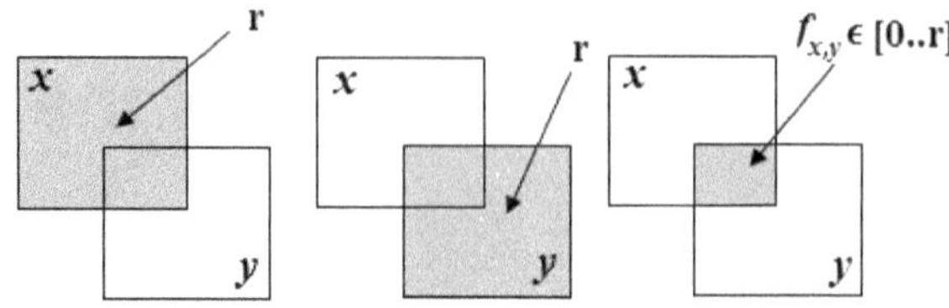

Figure 3: For shape nesting, $f_{x,y}$ is the area of overlap between two identical shapes of area r, thus $f_{x,y}$ varies from 0 to r. In our analysis we set $r = 1$.

designate $Species(P)$, and be the set of unique species (.i.e., chromosomes) in population P. Let u and v vary over the species (that is, unique chromosomes) in population P so that $\sum_{u \in S(P)} p_u = 1$, and we can express shared fitness as $f_{sh}(u) = (\sum_{v \in S(P)} p_v * f_{u,v})^{-1}$.

Then the RFS algorithm analyzed in this paper (and by Horn in [5]) consists of the following steps[1].

1. INITIALIZE:
   (a) Generate initial set of species (unique chromosomes) S;
   (b) $\forall u, v \in S$: calculate pairwise intersection[2] and store as $f_{u,v} := \frac{|u \cap v|}{|u|}$;
   (c) $\forall s \in S : p_s := \frac{1}{|S|}$; // Uniform distribution across all species, initially.
2. LOOP: while (termination condition[3] is false) do
   (a) $\forall u \in S$: Evaluate and store shared fitnesses as $f_{sh}(u) := (\sum_{\forall v \in S} p_v * f_{u,v})^{-1}$;
   (b) Calculate and store average shared fitness as $\overline{f_{sh}} := \sum_{\forall u \in S}(p_u * f_{sh}(u))$;
   (c) Calculate next generation species proportions p' as $\forall u \in S : p'_u := p_u * \frac{f_{sh}(u)}{\overline{f_{sh}}}$; // This implements proportionate selection, using shared fitnesses.
   (d) Move to next generation by updating species proportions as $\forall u \in S : p_u := p'_u$;
3. END LOOP.

We note that the algorithm presented is deterministic under the assumption of exact representation of population proportions (i.e., with arbitrary precision). There are no discovery operators such as recombination or mutation. All genetic diversity is generated in the creation of the initial population P_0. Randomness might be used to create the initial set of species $S(P_0)$, but subsequent generations are created deterministically from the previous generation solely via proportionate selection. Under proportionate selection, if we assume arbitrarily high precision for computing and storing

[1]RFS applied to shape nesting is covered under US Patent No. 7181702.

[2]Note normalization of $f_{u,v}$ so that all intersection magnitudes are between zero and one.

[3]Some possible termination conditions include: `population distribution appears to be at equilibrium`, or `an exact cover has been found` (perhaps formed by the K most populous species), or `maximum computational limits have been reached`.

species proportions, no species will ever go extinct. At an extreme, a species s that has consistently below average shared fitness ($f_{sh}(s) < \overline{f_{sh}}$) will asymptotically approach extinction: $\lim_{t\to\infty} p_s = 0$. Thus $S(P_0) = S(P_1) = S(P_2) = ...$ In the rest of this paper we let $S = S(P_0)$ represent this fixed set of species present in all populations throughout a run of the RFS algorithm.

2.1.4 *Special Properties of Overlap Terms $f_{u,v}$ in Exact Covers*

We define two useful properties of species overlap when there exists a set of species forming an exact cover E (where E is the set of species in the exact cover) with $E \subseteq S$.

Property I: $\forall u, v \in E$: *Minimum* $u \leftrightarrow v$ *Competition*

$$f_{u,v} = 0$$

Property II: $\forall w \notin E$ *Maximum* $E \leftrightarrow w$ *Competition*

$$\sum_{u\in E} f_{u,w} = 1$$

We assume here that all species have a coverage of exactly one (that is, we normalize species coverage to one: $r = 1$). Property I states that if species u and v are members of E, then u and v do not overlap in coverage. Under Property II any species w not in E is completely *covered* by the species in E, which means the sum of all the overlaps of species in E with w is equal to w's total coverage (one).

2.2 A Static Analysis of Niching Equilibrium

We assume that selection using RFS shared fitnesses will drive the population to an equilibrium in which all shared fitnesses are equal. We define this population distribution as the *equilibrium population* and solve for it by setting all shared fitnesses to be equal to each other: $\forall(u, v \in S(P))$: $f_{sh}(u) = f_{sh}(v)$. Since the shared fitnesses are calculated by taking the inverse of their *niche counts*, we can simply set all the niche counts equal to each other to compute equilibrium. In particular we can write the equilibrium equations as a set of linear equations, each representing the summation in the denominator of the shared fitness formula: for a species u, we get the equation $\sum_{v\in S(P)} f_{u,v}\, p_v = C'$, where C' is some constant for all the niche counts, thus enforcing the requirement that all niche counts be the same at equilibrium. Solving this set of linear equations for the population vector $\vec{p}^*$ allowed Horn to show that under certain conditions the solution $\vec{p}^*$ identifies an exact cover [5]. Early in the next section we rederive that result more directly.

3. NEW RESULTS

Here we present a simpler proof (than the original proof by Horn in [5]) that the problem of finding an exact cover by equally sized sets is equivalent to solving a set of linear equations (at least when the interaction matrix is non-singular). We then use this proof to build polynomial-time transformations of NP-complete exact cover problems to specific systems of linear equations.

3.1 A More Direct Proof That XrC Reduces to Linear Equations

We first recast Horn's *species interaction matrix* $\mathbf{M}_{RFS}$ (2008) as a *set intersection matrix*. We then recompute Horn's niching equilibirum matrix equations and use these to show how XrC reduces directly to a system of linear equations, without having to partially solve these equations as Horn did in [5].

3.1.1 *New Terminology: Species → Sets*

First we shift our terminology from ecosystems to set theory. Thus instead of species in the population we will have a set S of subsets s_j whose union is X, the set of all elements, thus: $S = \{s_1, s_2, ..., s_{|S|}\}$, and $X = \cup S = \cup_{j=1}^{|S|} s_j$. The RFS requirement that all shapes be the same can be relaxed here (since we are generalizing from shapes to sets) to the requirement that all subsets have the same size[4] (or cardinality): $|s_j| = r$, $\forall j \in (1..|S|)$, where r is some positive rational number. To allow for exact covers, we assume that $|X|$ is some multiple K of the subset size r: $|X| = rK$, where integer $K \geq 3$.

For this analysis we assume that the fixed subset size (cardinality) r is normalized to one ($r = 1$). This will simplify our notation and analysis without sacrificing generality of our results.

Following [5], we use the *species interaction matrix* $\mathbf{M}_{RFS}$ to hold the overlaps among species' coverages, or in our case the size of subset intersections. Thus matrix entry $f_{i,j} = |s_i \cap s_j|$, for $i, j \in [1..|S|]$. Next we assume[5] that there exists at least one exact cover in S. We choose[6] such an exact cover E and without loss of generality we assume that the K subsets in E ($|E| = K$) are listed first in the matrix $\mathbf{M}_{RFS}$. This means that subsets $s_1, s_2, ..., s_K$ form an exact cover of S, that is $E = \{s_1, s_2, s_3, ..., s_K\}$. (The other subsets $s_{K+1}, s_{K+2}, ..., s_{|S|}$, which might or might not contain another exact cover, we will call the $\overline{E}$ *subsets*, since they do not belong to E.)

It is interesting to consider a partition of this matrix, shown in Equation 1. The upper left submatrix consists of all interactions (intersections) solely among the species (sets) of E, $s_1, s_2, ..., s_K$. The lower right submatrix contains all interactions (intersections) solely between pairs of $\overline{E}$ species (sets) $s_{K+1}, s_{K+2}, ..., s_{|S|}$. The lower left and upper right submatrices are transposes of each other and define the interactions (intersections) between each E and each $\overline{E}$ species (set).

We note that this square matrix is symmetric about the main diagonal, since niche overlap is a symmetric relationship: $f_{i,j} = f_{j,i}$. We further note that the entries on the main diagonal are all 1, since $\forall i : f_{i,i} = 1$. And we recall Property I: $f_{i,j} = f_{j,i} = 0, \forall(i, j$ such that $i, j \leq K \wedge i \neq j)$, which holds for the upper left submatrix, among the members of E. Thus $\mathbf{M}_{RFS}$ can be re-written as shown in Equation 2. This upper left submatrix is an identity matrix, thanks to Property I. Furthermore, because of Property II, the sum of each column (row) in the upper right (lower left) submatrix is equal to one: $\forall(i > K) : \sum_{j=1}^{K} f_{j,i} = \sum_{j=1}^{K} f_{i,j} = 1)$.

[4]Our analysis applies to finite sets s_j, whether they are discrete or continuous: $|s_j|$ means *cardinality* if s_j is discrete, and it means *size* if s_j is continuous.

[5]The case of no exact cover in S is handled in sections 3.3 (last paragraph) and 3.4.2, where we show that if S has no exact cover, then there is no solution to the derived integer programming problem based on $\mathbf{M}_{RFS}$ (Section 3.3), nor a solution to the derived minimum weight solution to linear equations problem based on $\mathbf{M}_{RFS}$ (Section 3.4.2).

[6]If there are multiple exact covers, we arbitrarily choose one.

$$\mathbf{M}_{RFS} = \left[\begin{array}{cccc|cccc} f_{1,1} & f_{1,2} & \cdots & f_{1,K} & f_{1,K+1} & f_{1,K+2} & \cdots & f_{1,|S|} \\ f_{2,1} & f_{2,2} & \cdots & f_{2,K} & f_{2,K+1} & f_{2,K+2} & \cdots & f_{2,|S|} \\ \vdots & \vdots & \ddots & \vdots & \vdots & \vdots & \ddots & \vdots \\ f_{K,1} & f_{K,2} & \cdots & f_{K,K} & f_{K,K+1} & f_{K,K+2} & \cdots & f_{K,|S|} \\ \hline f_{K+1,1} & f_{K+1,2} & \cdots & f_{K+1,K} & f_{K+1,K+1} & f_{K+1,K+2} & \cdots & f_{K+1,|S|} \\ f_{K+2,1} & f_{K+2,2} & \cdots & f_{K+2,K} & f_{K+2,K+1} & f_{K+2,K+2} & \cdots & f_{K+2,|S|} \\ \vdots & \vdots & \ddots & \vdots & \vdots & \vdots & \ddots & \vdots \\ f_{|S|,1} & f_{|S|,2} & \cdots & f_{|S|,K} & f_{|S|,K+1} & f_{|S|,K+2} & \cdots & f_{|S|,|S|} \end{array}\right] \tag{1}$$

$$\mathbf{M}_{RFS} = \left[\begin{array}{cccc|cccc} 1 & 0 & \cdots & 0 & f_{1,K+1} & f_{1,K+2} & \cdots & f_{1,|S|} \\ 0 & 1 & \cdots & 0 & f_{2,K+1} & f_{2,K+2} & \cdots & f_{2,|S|} \\ \vdots & \vdots & \ddots & \vdots & \vdots & \vdots & \ddots & \vdots \\ 0 & 0 & \cdots & 1 & f_{K,K+1} & f_{K,K+2} & \cdots & f_{K,|S|} \\ \hline f_{K+1,1} & f_{K+1,2} & \cdots & f_{K+1,K} & 1 & f_{K+1,K+2} & \cdots & f_{K+1,|S|} \\ f_{K+2,1} & f_{K+2,2} & \cdots & f_{K+2,K} & f_{K+2,K+1} & 1 & \cdots & f_{K+2,|S|} \\ \vdots & \vdots & \ddots & \vdots & \vdots & \vdots & \ddots & \vdots \\ f_{|S|,1} & f_{|S|,2} & \cdots & f_{|S|,K} & f_{|S|,K+1} & f_{|S|,K+2} & \cdots & 1 \end{array}\right]. \tag{2}$$

$$\left[\begin{array}{cccc|cccc} 1 & 0 & \cdots & 0 & f_{1,K+1} & f_{1,K+2} & \cdots & f_{1,|S|} \\ 0 & 1 & \cdots & 0 & f_{2,K+1} & f_{2,K+2} & \cdots & f_{2,|S|} \\ \vdots & \vdots & \ddots & \vdots & \vdots & \vdots & \ddots & \vdots \\ 0 & 0 & \cdots & 1 & f_{K,K+1} & f_{K,K+2} & \cdots & f_{K,|S|} \\ \hline f_{K+1,1} & f_{K+1,2} & \cdots & f_{K+1,K} & 1 & f_{K+1,K+2} & \cdots & f_{K+1,|S|} \\ f_{K+2,1} & f_{K+2,2} & \cdots & f_{K+2,K} & f_{K+2,K+1} & 1 & \cdots & f_{K+2,|S|} \\ \vdots & \vdots & \ddots & \vdots & \vdots & \vdots & \ddots & \vdots \\ f_{|S|,1} & f_{|S|,2} & \cdots & f_{|S|,K} & f_{|S|,K+1} & f_{|S|,K+2} & \cdots & 1 \end{array}\right] \left[\begin{array}{c} p_1 \\ p_2 \\ \vdots \\ p_K \\ \hline p_{K+1} \\ p_{K+2} \\ \vdots \\ p_{|S|} \end{array}\right] = \left[\begin{array}{c} C' \\ C' \\ \vdots \\ C' \\ \hline C' \\ C' \\ \vdots \\ C' \end{array}\right] \tag{3}$$

$$\left[\begin{array}{cccc|cccc} 1 & 0 & \cdots & 0 & f_{1,K+1} & f_{1,K+2} & \cdots & f_{1,|S|} \\ 0 & 1 & \cdots & 0 & f_{2,K+1} & f_{2,K+2} & \cdots & f_{2,|S|} \\ \vdots & \vdots & \ddots & \vdots & \vdots & \vdots & \ddots & \vdots \\ 0 & 0 & \cdots & 1 & f_{K,K+1} & f_{K,K+2} & \cdots & f_{K,|S|} \\ \hline f_{K+1,1} & f_{K+1,2} & \cdots & f_{K+1,K} & 1 & f_{K+1,K+2} & \cdots & f_{K+1,|S|} \\ f_{K+2,1} & f_{K+2,2} & \cdots & f_{K+2,K} & f_{K+2,K+1} & 1 & \cdots & f_{K+2,|S|} \\ \vdots & \vdots & \ddots & \vdots & \vdots & \vdots & \ddots & \vdots \\ f_{|S|,1} & f_{|S|,2} & \cdots & f_{|S|,K} & f_{|S|,K+1} & f_{|S|,K+2} & \cdots & 1 \end{array}\right] \left[\begin{array}{c} y_1 \\ y_2 \\ \vdots \\ y_K \\ \hline y_{K+1} \\ y_{K+2} \\ \vdots \\ y_{|S|} \end{array}\right] = \left[\begin{array}{c} 1 \\ 1 \\ \vdots \\ 1 \\ \hline 1 \\ 1 \\ \vdots \\ 1 \end{array}\right] \tag{4}$$

$$\left[\begin{array}{cccc|cccc} 1 & 0 & \cdots & 0 & f_{1,K+1} & f_{1,K+2} & \cdots & f_{1,|S|} \\ 0 & 1 & \cdots & 0 & f_{2,K+1} & f_{2,K+2} & \cdots & f_{2,|S|} \\ \vdots & \vdots & \ddots & \vdots & \vdots & \vdots & \ddots & \vdots \\ 0 & 0 & \cdots & 1 & f_{K,K+1} & f_{K,K+2} & \cdots & f_{K,|S|} \\ \hline f_{K+1,1} & f_{K+1,2} & \cdots & f_{K+1,K} & 1 & f_{K+1,K+2} & \cdots & f_{K+1,|S|} \\ f_{K+2,1} & f_{K+2,2} & \cdots & f_{K+2,K} & f_{K+2,K+1} & 1 & \cdots & f_{K+2,|S|} \\ \vdots & \vdots & \ddots & \vdots & \vdots & \vdots & \ddots & \vdots \\ f_{|S|,1} & f_{|S|,2} & \cdots & f_{|S|,K} & f_{|S|,K+1} & f_{|S|,K+2} & \cdots & 1 \end{array}\right] \left[\begin{array}{c} 1 \\ 1 \\ \vdots \\ 1 \\ \hline 0 \\ 0 \\ \vdots \\ 0 \end{array}\right] = \left[\begin{array}{c} 1 \\ 1 \\ \vdots \\ 1 \\ \hline 1 \\ 1 \\ \vdots \\ 1 \end{array}\right] \tag{5}$$

3.1.2 Niching Equilibrium Equations

At niching equilibrium [5], $\mathbf{M}_{RFS} \cdot \vec{p} = \vec{C}'$, where $\vec{p}$ is a vector of proportions of each species $s \in S(P)$ and $\vec{C}'$ is a constant vector for some constant C', as in Equation 3. That is, at niching equilibrium, the niche count for every species is the same $(= C')$. Furthermore we know what this constant should be: if at equilibrium we expect to have the entire population evenly divided among, and only among, the K exact cover species, then $C' = 1/K$, (the *equilibrium niche count.*) Multiplying both sides of the equilibrium equation above by K gives us $\mathbf{M}_{RFS} \cdot (K\vec{p}) = \vec{1}$. We introduce a new solution vector $\vec{y}$, where $y_i = Kp_i$ and $0 \leq y_i \leq K, \forall i \in (1..|S|)$. Thus $\mathbf{M}_{RFS} \cdot \vec{y} = \vec{1}$, as in Equation 4.

We note that if there exists an exact cover solution, it must consist of exactly K subsets/species which we can arbitrarily designate as $s_1, s_2, ..., s_K$. The characteristic vector $\vec{y}^* = (1, 1, ...1, 0, 0, ...0)$ consisting of K ones and $|S| - K$ zeroes, must be a solution of Equation 4, as shown in Equation 5. Clearly the first K rows involve multiplying the identity matrix by the identity vector. The remaining $|S| - K$ rows yield equations of the form $\sum_{j=1}^{K} f_{i,j} = 1$ for the ith row where $i = K + 1$ to $|S|$. These equations are all true by Property II of exact covers.

Thus we have shown that for any exact cover problem in which the subsets s_i are of equal size, if the interaction matrix (that is, matrix of pairwise set intersection magnitudes) $\mathbf{M}_{RFS}$ is non-singular, then an exact cover, or its non-existence, can be computed by solving the set of linear equations $\mathbf{M}_{RFS} \cdot \vec{y} = \vec{1}$. Note solving a set of linear equations can be done in time polynomial in the number of equations and the number of unknowns (which in this case are both $|S|$), if all the coefficients are rational (thus our restriction of r in XrC to the non-negative rational numbers).

3.2 XrC is in NP-complete (X3C $\propto$ XrC)

We note that the proof above applies to *exact cover by equally sized sets*, XrC (meaning "exact cover by sets of size r, where r is any rational, non-negative number). We now need to make clear that XrC is in NP-complete.

We proceed from Garey and Johnson's result for *exact cover by 3-sets*, X3C, which is problem SP2 from their classic text [3]. Garey and Johnson prove that X3C is in NP-complete. We simply note that 3 is a non-negative rational number, so any instance of X3C is an instance of XrC. Thus we have reduced a known NP-complete problem, X3C, to XrC in polynomial time. Therefore XrC is also in NP-complete. Furthermore any algorithm for solving XrC is immediately applicable, with no additional cost, to X3C. Finally, any reduction of XrC to another problem Q (e.g., next two sections, 3.3 and 3.4) can be immediately used to reduce X3C to Q as well.

3.3 XrC $\propto$ 0-1 Integer Programming

We reduce XrC to Karp's 0-1 Integer Programming as decribed under problem 2 of [9] (p. 94): *Given an integer matrix $\vec{C}$ and integer vector $\vec{d}$, does there exist a 0-1 vector $\vec{x}$ such that $\vec{C} \cdot \vec{x} = \vec{d}$?*

We transform $\mathbf{M}_{RFS}$ into an integer valued matrix, $\mathbf{M'}_{RFS}$ by a series of multiplications, since $\mathbf{M}_{RFS}$ has only rational coefficients (therefore each can be written as a ratio of two integers). These same multiplications must also be applied to the right side of the linear equations of course (which is vector $\vec{d}$ in the 0-1 integer programming problem above, and vector $\vec{1}$ in our formulation of XrC earlier) yielding a new right-hand-side vector $\vec{d}'$. The transformed linear problem is then $\mathbf{M'}_{RFS} \cdot \vec{y} = \vec{d}'$ for $\vec{y}$, with both $\mathbf{M'}_{RFS}$ and d' integer-valued.

Next we recall the "simplex constraint" that requires our solution vector of population proportions $\vec{p}$ to lie in the unit simplex of dimension $|S|$: $\sum_{i=1}^{|S|} p_i = 1$, which after multiplication of both sides by K give us an additional equation for our linear system involving the solution vector $\vec{y}$: $\sum_{i=1}^{|S|} y_i = K$. (This recalled equation means that any 0-1 solution for $\vec{y}$ must include exactly K ones and $|S| - K$ zeroes.)

If an exact cover exists, then its **characteristic vector** (a 0-1 vector with ones corresponding to the members of the exact cover and zeroes corresponding to members of $\overline{E}$) would be a solution to the 0-1 Integer Programming problem described above, which is $\mathbf{M}'_{RFS} \cdot \vec{y} = \vec{d}'$ plus the equation $\sum_{i=1}^{|S|} y_i = K$. This must be so since we showed earlier that the characteristic vector of an exact cover solution would be a solution to the original equations, $\mathbf{M}_{RFS} \cdot \vec{y} = \vec{1}$, and all we have done to modify the original equations is to multiply both sides by the same integers, which does not alter the solution(s) to the equations. Furthermore, an exact cover solution must have exactly K ones in its characterstic vector since we defined the XrC problem as having a total size (that is, $| \cup S|$) of Kr, needing exactly K r-sized subsets to cover $| \cup S|$.

Conversely, a solution to the 0-1 Integer Programming problem described above must be the characterstic vector of an exact cover to the original XrC problem. First we note again that since multiplication of both sides of an equation by the same factor does not alter the solutions of that equation, the 0-1 solution to $\mathbf{M'}_{RFS} \cdot \vec{y} = \vec{d}'$ must also be a solution to $\mathbf{M}_{RFS} \cdot \vec{y} = \vec{1}$. Note that for each non-zero element of the solution vector $\vec{y}$, that is for each i such that $y_i = 1$, we have $f_{i,i}\, y_i = 1$, since $f_{i,i} = 1$. Therefore all other terms $f_{i,j}\, y_j$ $(i \neq j)$, in the row corresponding to the equation $\sum_{j=1}^{|S|} f_{i,j}\, y_j = 1$, must have either $f_{i,j} = 0$ or $y_j = 0$. (Recall that the matrix $\mathbf{M}_{RFS}$ is non-negative.) Thus there is no overlap $(f_{i,j} = 0)$ between non-zero elements y_i. If there are K non-overlapping subsets, these must form an exact cover for the original XrC problem, by definition of an exact cover.

3.4 XrC $\propto$ MWPSLE

The set of equations $\{\mathbf{M}_{RFS} \cdot \vec{y} = \vec{1}\} \cup \{\sum_{i=1}^{|S|} y_i = K\}$ can also be used in a polynomial time transformation of XrC to a constrained version of the well-known NP-complete problem *Minimum Weight Solution to Linear Equations* (MWSLE), as defined in Garey and Johnson's 1979 text [3] on the theory of NP-completeness:

> [MP5] **MINIMUM WEIGHT SOLUTION TO LINEAR EQUATIONS**
> INSTANCE: Finite set X of pairs $(\vec{x}, b)$, where $\vec{x}$ is an m-tuple of integers and b is an integer, and a positive integer $K \leq m$.
> QUESTION: Is there an m-tuple $\vec{y}$ with rational entries such that $\vec{y}$ has at most K non-zero entries and such that $\vec{x} \cdot \vec{y} = b$ for all $(\vec{x}, b) \in X$?
> *Reference:* [Garey and Johnson, ———]. Transformation from X3C.

The additional constraint on MWSLE in the current paper is the requirement that the non-zero "weights" (i.e., coefficients) in the solution vector $\vec{y}^*$ must be positive (that is, all components must be non-negative). On the CS theory web blog site `cstheory.stackexchange.com` the poster "Esteve" names this constrained version of MWSLE the *Minimum Weight Positive Solution to Linear Equations* (MWPSLE) [11].

3.4.1 XrC solution ⇒ MWPSLE solution

We assume the existence of an exact cover solution to the given XrC problem. We show that the characteristic vector for that solution, $\vec{y}^*$ (where $y_i^* = 1$ if subset s_i is in the exact cover and is zero otherwise), is also a solution to the MWPSLE problem formed by the reduction described above, which yields the equations given by $\mathbf{M}_{RFS} \cdot \vec{y} = \vec{1}$ along with the one equation $\sum_{i=1}^{|S|} y_i = K$.

First we recall that an exact cover E for a set S of subsets s_j all of size $|s_j| = r$ must have $K = |S|/r$ members. So the characteristic vector $\vec{y}^*$ of E must have exactly K positive components with the rest of the components equal to zero, thus satisfying the MWPSLE's requirement that the solution have at most K positive weights. Furthermore we note that K ones sum to K, thus satisfying the "extra equation" in our reduction of XrC to MWPSLE.

To show that $\vec{y}^*$ solves the MWPSLE of the transformation, we look at each equation in $\mathbf{M}_{RFS} \cdot \vec{y} = \vec{1}$ and note that we can drop all of the terms $f_{i,j}\, y_j^*$ for which $s_j \notin E$ (and for which therefore $y_j^* = 0$). We are left with the equations $\sum_{j:s_j \in E} f_{i,j}\, y_j^* = 1$, one such equation for each $i = 1..|S|$. But we know that $f_{i,j} = 0$ for i and j such that $(s_i, s_j \in E) \wedge (i \neq j)$ (zero intersection among distinct exact cover members), and so we can drop those terms from the summations. Let us partition what is left. For those equations (rows)i corresponding to members of E (that is $s_i \in E$), we have only one term left on the left hand side: $f_{i,i}\, y_i^*$, and since $f_{i,i} = 1$ and $y_i^* = 1$, then their product is one and that equation is satisfied. For the other partition, which contains the equations (rows) corresponding to the $|S| - K$ subsets that are NOT in E, the remaining terms in the left hand side summations are $\sum_{j:s_j \in E} f_{i,j}\, y_j^*$. Since $y_j^* = 1$ for all j with $s_j \in E$, then these sums reduce to just $\sum_{j:s_j \in E} f_{i,j}$, where $s_i \in \overline{E}$. By Property II of an exact cover, these sum to one, thus satisfying the equations for the subsets that are not in the E.

Thus all equations in the transformed MWPSLE are satisfied by the characteristic vector of an exact cover solution to XrC.

3.4.2 XrC solution ⇐ MWPSLE solution

We assume the existence of a solution $\vec{y}^*$ to the MWPSLE problem obtained by the above reduction for the given XrC problem. We show that this solution vector must be the characteristic vector for an exact cover for the set of subsets S in the original XrC problem.

First we show that the positive solution components y_i^* must each equal one. Note that for each of the positive components y_i^*, the ith equation in $\mathbf{M}_{RFS} \cdot \vec{y} = \vec{1}$, contains the term $f_{i,i}\, y_i^*$ in the left hand side summation $\sum_{j=1}^{|S|} f_{i,j}\, y_j^*$. Since $f_{i,i} = 1$ and since y_i^* is positive, this term must contribute to the sum on the left side of its equation. Recall that the right side of the equation is the value one, and that all coefficients of the matrix and solution vector are non-negative. Therefore $y_i^* \leq 1$. Recalling that the K positive components y_i^* must sum to K, clearly all positive components y_i^* must equal one exactly.

Next we show that for any two distinct positive solution components y_i^* and y_j^* $(i \neq j)$ the corresponding matix coefficients $f_{i,j}$ and $f_{j,i}$ must be zero: $\forall i, j : (y_i^* = y_j^* = 1 \wedge i \neq j \rightarrow f_{i,j} = f_{j,i} = 0)$. Proof by contradiction: If $f_{i,j}$ were not zero, then it would be positive and would add to the total of the left hand side summation of both equations i and j (that is, rows i and j). But since both y_i^* and y_j^* equal one, the left hand sides of equations i and j will then exceed one, and those equations would not be satisfied, contradicting our premise that $\vec{y}^*$ solves the MWPSLE. So $f_{i,j}$ (and $f_{j,i}$) must be zero in this case.

Thus the K positive components of $\vec{y}^*$ correspond to K subsets s that do not intersect. Since the K subsets are all of size r their union must be of size rK. Since $|X| = rK$, the subsets selected by $\vec{y}^*$ must be an exact cover of S.

4. COMPARISON WITH PAST RESULTS

In this paper we have introduced polynomial time reductions of exact cover problems to different types of linear equation solving, providing proofs of NP-completeness for the targets of the reductions. But others (e.g., Garey and Johnson (1979)) have already claimed similar transformations of exact cover problems to linear problems. How different and significant are our transformations? In this section we examine the "obvious reduction" of exact cover to linear equations, and show a significant difference between this technique and ours.

4.1 Garey and Johnson's Unpublished Reduction

In our search for similar reductions, we came across only Garey and Johnson's 1979 proof of the NP-completeness of Minimum Weight Solution to Linear Equations (MWSLE) by transformation from Exact Cover by 3 Sets (X3C). In the text of the book Garey and Johnson do not actually provide the proof. Instead, in their statement of the problem (see quote 3.4 above) in their list of proven NP-complete problems, they have a reference to "[Garey and Johnson, ——]." This citation is the very common (in their 1979 text) "unpublished results." A brief email from Dr. Johnson confirms the unpublished status of this transformation [Johnson, personal communication, November 2012]. It seems likely that the transformation of X3C to MWSLE was left out because of obviousness. There is a simple and direct transformation, which is suggested in a 2010 post by Warren Schudy on the authoritative web site *cstheory.stackexchange.com*[11]. Below is our version of this direct (and heretofore unpublished) transformation of X3C to MWSLE.

4.2 X3C ∝ MWSLE

First we change Garey and Johnson's notation slightly, substituting our own symbols S and s_i for a set S of subsets $s_i, i = 1, 2, ..., |S|$ of elements $x_j, j = 1, 2, ..., |X|$ from the set $X = \cup S$, in place of their C and c_i for a collection C of sets c_i, also drawn from the element set X. We form the subset membership matrix $\mathbf{M}_{SM}$:

$$\begin{array}{c|cccc} & s_1 & s_2 & \cdots & s_{|S|} \\ \hline x_1 & m_{1,1} & m_{1,2} & \cdots & m_{1,|S|} \\ x_2 & m_{2,1} & m_{2,2} & \cdots & m_{2,|S|} \\ \vdots & \vdots & \vdots & \ddots & \vdots \\ x_{|X|} & m_{|X|,1} & m_{|X|,2} & \cdots & m_{|X|,|S|} \end{array} = \mathbf{M}_{SM} \tag{6}$$

$$\text{where } m_{i,j} = \begin{cases} 1 & \text{if } x_i \in s_j \\ 0 & \text{otherwise} \end{cases}$$

where the coefficients are the values of the membership function $m_{i,j}$. Thus column j is the characteristic vector for subset s_j.

The rest of the reduction is essentially the same as our earlier reduction, but substituting the 0-1 matrix $\mathbf{M}_{SM}$ for $\mathbf{M}_{RFS}$. We form the same equation, mutiplying our matrix by the solution vector $\vec{y}$ and solving for it when this product equals the ones vector, as in the equation $\mathbf{M}_{SM} \cdot \vec{y} = \vec{1}$:

$$\begin{bmatrix} m_{1,1} & m_{1,2} & \cdots & m_{1,|S|} \\ m_{2,1} & m_{2,2} & \cdots & m_{2,|S|} \\ \vdots & \vdots & \ddots & \vdots \\ m_{|X|,1} & m_{|X|,2} & \cdots & m_{|X|,|S|} \end{bmatrix} \begin{bmatrix} y_1 \\ y_2 \\ \vdots \\ y_{|S|} \end{bmatrix} = \begin{bmatrix} 1 \\ 1 \\ \vdots \\ 1 \end{bmatrix}. \tag{7}$$

Just as in our earlier reduction, here an exact cover solution to the original X3C problem corresponds to the characteristic vector of S that picks out exactly the subsets s_j that are members of the exact cover: $(s_j \in E) \leftrightarrow (y_j^* = 1)$. With this transformation we can finish the proof that there exists an exact cover for the set S if and only if there exists a solution to the corresponding set of linear equations (7) with at most K non-zero entries.

4.2.1 X3C solution ⇒ MWSLE solution

Assume an exact cover solution E. Then the characteristic vector $\vec{y}^*$ of this exact cover solves the equation set 7. To see this, note that every member s_j of E has a solution vector component $y_j^* = 1$. When the matrix and solution vector are multiplied, we get $|X|$ equations of the form $\sum_{j=1}^{|S|} m_{i,j}\, y_j^* = 1$, for all $i \in (1..|X|)$. For each of these equations, all of the terms $m_{i,j}\, y_j^*$ for which s_j is not in the exact cover are zero since y_j^* must be zero. Furthermore for the terms where s_j is in the exact cover (and hence $y_j^* = 1$) there can be ONLY ONE value of j for which $m_{i,j}$ is one, since by definition of *exact cover* each element x_j can only appear once in the exact cover. Therefore there is only one term $m_{i,j}\, y_j^*$ whose value is one, on the left hand side of each of the equations. All other terms are zero. Thus each of the left hand sides sum to one, satisfying the $|X|$ equations of 7. Finally, since there are exactly K members of the exact cover, the last equation of our MWSLE formulation is satisfied: $\vec{1} \cdot \vec{y}^* = K$ (the components of the solution sum to K).

4.2.2 X3C solution ⇐ MWSLE solution

Assume a solution $\vec{y}^*$ to the MWSLE corresponding to the X3C problem, which means that $K = |X|/3$ (we require that $|X|$ be divisible by three). We show that $\vec{y}^*$ must be the characteristic vector of an exact cover of S. First we note that every equation in the set of equations 7 must have at least one positive term in the summed terms on the left hand side, $\sum_{j=1}^{|S|} m_{i,j}\, y_j^*$ (for the equation corresponding to row i and hence element x_i), since the right hand side is positive one. For a term $m_{i,j}\, y_j^*$ to be positive, the matrix coefficient $m_{i,j}$ must be one which means that element $x_i \in s_j$. Recalling that X3C requires that all subsets are of size three, $|s_j| = 3$ for all $j \in (1..|S|)$, it follows that each of the subsets selected by $\vec{y}^*$ (i.e., all s_j such that $y_j^* = 1$) have exactly THREE matrix coeficients $m_{i,j}$ equal to one, and that there are at most $K = |X|/3$ subsets selected by $\vec{y}^*$, it follows that each such selected subset s_j must "cover" (i.e., include) exactly three distinct equations (or rows, or elements) of the total of $|X|$ such equations (or rows, or elements). Thus the subsets selected by $\vec{y}^*$ must be distinct subsets that include all elements of X. Hence these subsets form an exact cover. (Visually, looking down each column of the selected subsets, each has exactly three ones. Each row must be "covered" by one of these. Since there are at most $|X|/3$ subsets to cover $|X|$ rows, with each covering at most three rows, then there can be no overlap in row coverage.)

Furthemore, it follows that every element x_i is covered by exactly one of the non-zero coefficients (i.e., subsets) in $\vec{y}^*$. Therefore that coefficient (and therefore all of the non-zero coefficients y_j^*) MUST be equal to one, so that the left hand side of each row equation will sum to one. So we have shown that $\vec{y}^*$ must not only have non-zero coefficients for each s_j in an exact cover of the X3C problem, but also that those non-zero coefficients must be ones so that $\vec{y}^*$ must be the characteristic vector of an exact cover solution.

4.3 X3C $\propto$ MWPSLE

The result of the previous section actually proves a bit more than was claimed by Garey and Johnson (1979). Not only does the proof transform X3C to MWSLE, but it also transforms X3C to MWPSLE. Thus the proof technique outlined in the previous section is indeed an alternative reduction of X3C to MWPSLE. (We noted earlier that our reduction of XrC to MWPSLE could be trivially extended to reduce X3C to MWPSLE, since X3C is trivially reduced to XrC: X3C $\propto$ XrC $\propto$ MWPSLE). However this point has not been made in the literature (that is, a proof of MWPSLE's membership in NP-complete via a reduction from X3C), other than a version posted to a web site [11].

4.4 Analysis: M_{RFS} versus M_{SM}

Both our new transformation and the older, unpublished, "obvious" transformation make use of "interaction matrices" to reduce exact cover by equally sized sets to a set of linear equations. But in the case of the assumed Garey and Johnson transformation, the matrix $\mathbf{M}_{SM}$ represents interactions between the subsets and the elements of the domain. Specifically, a set membership matrix is used. In our transformation, the matrix $\mathbf{M}_{RFS}$ represents interactions among the subsets themselves, making no explicit use of the elements of the domain. Specifically, a set intersection matrix is used. While this fundamental difference in the approaches might have some deep implications for theoretical study, space constraints limit us here to a discussion of some practical implications.

4.5 Analysis: Practical Implications

Practitioners might actually use these transformations to solve some large instances of exact cover problems by computing solutions to the associated linear equations, so we consider the two different matrices derived earlier. The matrix $\mathbf{M}_{SM}$ is of size $|X|$ by $|S|$ while the size of matrix $\mathbf{M}_{RFS}$ is $|S|$ by $|S|$. This means that as $|X|$ grows larger, holding $|S|$ constant, $\mathbf{M}_{SM}$ grows while $\mathbf{M}_{RFS}$ stays the same size. In fact, the $\mathbf{M}_{RFS}$ approach can handle arbitrarily large domains $|X|$ while the solution time for $\mathbf{M}_{SM}$ grows polynomially in $|X|$. $\mathbf{M}_{RFS}$ can even handle continuous sets.

An example of this size difference between the two matrices $\mathbf{M}_{RFS}$ and $\mathbf{M}_{SM}$ can be found in approaching the shape nesting problem introduced earlier in this paper in Figure 2. While only sixteen of the small squares are needed to exactly cover the larger square, as seen in the lower left of the figure, a total of 1600 different small squares (species) were generated for the initial population, shown in the upper left of the figure. For these experiments from [7] and [5], the 2D space was discretized into a grid such that the small squares measured 10 units on a side while the larger square measured 40 units on a side. $40 * 40 = 1600$ squares (species) were generated for the initial generation, one for each possible location covering or partially covering the large square. Of these 1600, $30 * 30 = 900$ are completely contained within the large square. (The other 700 small squares extend partially outside the large square and can be immediately discarded from consideration for exact cover membership.)

As an alternative to running RFS evolution, we might simply generate the interaction matrix, either $\mathbf{M}_{RFS}$ or $\mathbf{M}_{SM}$, and directly solve the associated system of linear equations to find the exact cover. But note that $\mathbf{M}_{RFS}$ for this problem would be of size 900 by $900 = 810,000$ (to hold all pair-wise intersections among the 900 candidate species). The matrix $\mathbf{M}_{SM}$, on the other hand, would be of size 900 by$1600 = 1,440,000$ since it would have to indicate whether or not each of the 40 by $40 = 1600$ discretized area elements within the large square is covered by each of the 900 small squares. This difference would only grow larger if the resolution of the discretization were increased. In addition, computing set membership for each element might be significantly more expensive than computing the magnitude of pairwise intersections.

Another consideration is the type of problem knowledge available. $\mathbf{M}_{RFS}$ only requires knowledge of pair-wise set intersections, not set membership information. (On the other hand, set intersections might be expensive to compute, while set membership information is readily available.)

Another consideration is matrix singularity. Recall that if the matrix is non-singular we are guarranteed a solution to the exact cover problem instance. It might be the case that for some problem instances the associated $\mathbf{M}_{RFS}$ is non-singular while $\mathbf{M}_{SM}$ is singular, or vice versa.

A final observation which might be of practical import for those pursuing the theory of coevolutionary algorithms is the fact that a very different approach to solving a classical problem in computational theory came from a simple analysis of a simple algorithm for coevolution. Who knows what algorithms, techniques, models, reductions, and transformations will come from more complex systems of coevolution and/or more sophisticated analyses of them?

5. ACKNOWLEDGMENTS

Dr. Horn was supported by a sabbatical award from Northern Michigan University.

6. REFERENCES

[1] K. Deb and D. E. Goldberg. An investigation of niche and species formation in genetic function optimization. In J. D. Schaffer, editor, *Proceedings of the Third International Conference on Genetic Algorithms*, pages 42–50. Morgan Kaufman, San Mateo, CA, 1989.

[2] R. Dighe and M. J. Jakiela. Solving pattern nesting problems with genetic algorithms: employing task decomposition and contact detection between adjacent pieces. *Evolutionary Computation*, 3(3):239–266, 1996.

[3] M. R. Garey and D. S. Johnson. *Computers and Intractability*. W. H. Freeman and Company, New York, 1979.

[4] D. E. Goldberg and J. Richardson. Genetic algorithms with sharing for multimodal function optimization. In J. Grefenstette, editor, *Proceedings of the Second International Conference on Genetic Algorithms*, pages 41–49. Lawrence Erlbaum Associates, 1987.

[5] J. Horn. Optimal nesting of species for exact cover of resources: Many against many. In G. Rudolph, T. Jansen, and N. Beume, editors, *Parallel Problem Solving From Nature - PPSN X, Lecture Notes in Computer Science*, volume 5199, pages 438–448. Springer, 2008

[6] J. Horn. Pure co-evolution for shape nesting. In J. Filipe and J.Kacprzyk, editors, *International Joint Conference on Computational Intelligence 2010: Proceedings of the International Conference on Evolutionary Computation*, pages 255–260. SciTePress, Portugal, October 2010.

[7] J. Horn. Resource-based fitness sharing. In J.J. Merelo Guervós, P. Adamidis, H.-G. Beyer, J.-L.Fernández-Villacañas, and H.-P. Schwefel, editors,*Parallel Problem Solving From Nature - PPSN VII, Lecture Notes in Computer Science*, volume 2439, pages 381–390. Springer, Berlin, Germany, 2002.

[8] J. Horn. Coevolving species for shape nesting. In J. D. Schaffer, editor, *The 2005 IEEE Congress on Evolutionary Computation (IEEE CEC 2005)*, pages 1800–1807. IEEE Press, Piscataway, NJ, 2005.

[9] R. M. Karp. Reducibility among combinatorial problems. In R. E. M. J. W. Thatcher, editor, *Complexity of Computer Computations*, pages 85–103. Plenum Press, New York, 1972.

[10] G. Kendall. *Applying Meta-Heuristic Algorithms to the Nesting Problem Utilising the No Fit Polygon*. PhD thesis, University of Nottingham, 2000.

[11] W. Schudy. Is that particular case of the 'minimum weight solution to linear equations' [problem] still np-complete? In *cc.complexity theory*, http://cstheory.stackexchange.com/a/3721, 2010.

Runtime Analysis of Ant Colony Optimization on Dynamic Shortest Path Problems

Andrei Lissovoi
DTU Compute, Technical University of Denmark
Kgs. Lyngby, Denmark

Carsten Witt
DTU Compute, Technical University of Denmark
Kongens Lyngby, Denmark

ABSTRACT

A simple ACO algorithm called λ-MMAS for dynamic variants of the single-destination shortest paths problem is studied by rigorous runtime analyses. Building upon previous results for the special case of 1-MMAS, it is studied to what extent an enlarged colony using λ ants per vertex helps in tracking an oscillating optimum. It is shown that easy cases of oscillations can be tracked by a constant number of ants. However, the paper also identifies more involved oscillations that with overwhelming probability cannot be tracked with any polynomial-size colony. Finally, parameters of dynamic shortest-path problems which make the optimum difficult to track are discussed. Experiments illustrate theoretical findings and conjectures.

Categories and Subject Descriptors

F.2 [**Theory of Computation**]: Analysis of Algorithms and Problem Complexity

General Terms

Theory, Algorithms

Keywords

Ant Colony Optimization, Shortest Paths, Dynamic Problems, Runtime Analysis

1. INTRODUCTION

Ant colony optimization (ACO) is a class of nature-inspired algorithms that is mostly used to solve combinatorial optimization problems. In recent years, runtime analysis of nature-inspired algorithms has advanced considerably [2, 12]. Even though the majority of results still apply to simple evolutionary algorithms, a lot of progress has also been made in the analysis of ACO. With respect to problems from combinatorial optimization, which is the classical domain of application for ACO, there are results on shortest paths [1, 18], minimum spanning trees [11], minimum cuts [7] and the traveling salesperson problem [20, 9].

Real-world optimization problems are not always static in nature. Often problem and goal of optimization are dynamic, i. e., they change over time. In these cases, it is important to find a solution that is "good" with respect to the current goal of optimization. Nature-inspired algorithms are often considered to be "robust" optimizers which can adapt to such dynamic problems if the underlying optimal solution does not change too quickly or extremely. In particular, many applications of evolutionary algorithms on dynamic problems are reported in the literature [13].

In this paper, we are concerned with ACO on dynamic problems. Our aim is to understand, using rigorous runtime analyses, the conditions under which ACO algorithms are able to track the optimum of a dynamically changing problem. Such runtime analyses are motivated by related theoretical studies of evolutionary algorithms for dynamic problems [16, 6, 4]. We have chosen the single-destination shortest path problem (SDSP) as object of our analysis as this is probably the combinatorial optimization problem that ACO has been understood best on. There are even runtime analyses of ACO on stochastic optimization problems [19, 3, 5], which, together with dynamic problems, can be subsumed under the term "optimization under uncertainty". However, methods for the analysis of stochastic optimization problems are not directly applicable to dynamic problems.

So far, there is only a single runtime analysis of ACO on dynamic problems. Kötzing and Molter [8] compare a simple ACO algorithm and a simple evolutionary algorithm on a dynamic pseudo-boolean problem and show that the ACO algorithm can outperform the evolutionary one. To the best of our knowledge, our work is the first runtime analysis of ACO on a dynamic combinatorial optimization problem.

Our findings can be summarized as follows. A simple ACO algorithm based on the Max-Min Ant System [17] is studied on dynamic shortest path problems with increasing amount of dynamics. First it is analyzed how long it takes the system to adapt of a one-time modification of the graph. It is proved that two extreme cases can happen: only a single pheromone value or all pheromone values might need to be updated to adapt. Upper and lower bounds on the time required are proved. Then periodic changes are studied. Examples are shown where the changes exhibit enough locality for the system to track them reliably by updating independent components. Interestingly, this is possible by increasing the size of the ant colony moderately. The utility of a population for tracking problems was studied in evolutionary computation by Jansen and Schellbach [6], but our result seems the first of this kind in the runtime analysis of ACO. Finally, an example is given where the problem changes globally, which makes it very unlikely that changes can be tracked quickly. Experiments supplement the theoretical findings, and we discuss properties of the dynamics that are related to the difficulty of the tracking problem.

The paper is structured as follows. Section 2 introduces notation and the algorithm λ-MMAS, which generalizes previously studied MMAS by introducing a larger population. Section 3 proves polynomial lower and upper bounds on the time for the system to adapt to one-time changes. Periodic changes with locality are studied in Section 4 and polynomial upper bounds are proved, given that a larger colony is used. Section 5 describes a globally changing example that is conjectured to be difficult to track. Experiments are described in Section 6. We finish with some conclusions.

2. PRELIMINARIES

The λ-MMAS algorithm (Algorithm 1) is a generalized version of the $\text{MMAS}_{\text{SDSP}}$ analyzed on shortest path problems in [18], where the generalization is due to a use of a population (see [10] for a related algorithm in pseudo-boolean optimization). The algorithm allows for negative weights, but requires that all cycles in the graph are of strictly positive weight.

Every iteration of the algorithm starts λ ants at each vertex, and each ant constructs a simple path through the graph, following arcs randomly with probability proportional to their pheromone values until it reaches the destination vertex t, or until it reaches a vertex from which no arcs lead to a vertex that has not already been visited. For each vertex v, the best-so-far path x_v^* is updated to the path of least weight of the λ paths constructed from v in the current iteration and the previous x_v^* path, and is then used to update the pheromone values on arcs leaving v.

The algorithm needs to start at least one ant at each vertex, even if the goal is to find the shortest path between a specific pair of vertices, in order to ensure that the shortest paths can be found in expected polynomial time. The issue is illustrated in [18] using the graph shown in Figure 1: if the weight on the (r,t) arc is $n = |V|$ and all other arcs have unit weights, the vertex r is avoided by the s-t shortest path. An ant started at s will, with probability $1 - 2^{-n/2}$, make no more than $n/2$ steps towards t before visiting r. Subsequent iterations will only accept a path that makes additional steps towards t if it reaches t, which occurs with probability at most $2^{-n/2}$; discovery, acceptance, and pheromone updates based on paths that take even less steps towards t before visiting r will only decrease the probability of reaching t without visiting r over time.

Three parameters affect the behavior of the algorithm: the evaporation rate ρ controls the speed with which the pheromone values are updated, while the pheromone bounds $\tau_{\min}$ and $\tau_{\max}$ control how likely an ant is to deviate from a pheromone trail, balancing exploration with the ability to follow reinforced paths. Typically, the pheromone bounds are chosen based on Δ, the maximum vertex out-degree, and ℓ, the maximum number of arcs in any shortest path in the graph; the standard choice is

$$\tau_{\min} = 1/(\Delta\ell) \qquad \tau_{\max} = 1 - \tau_{\min}$$

where $n = |V|$ can be used in place of Δ or ℓ if either value is unknown. This choice of pheromone bounds allows an ant to follow a path of $\ell - 1$ arcs with probability at least $1/e$ if the pheromone values along the path are all equal to $\tau_{\max}$.

Algorithm 1 The λ-MMAS algorithm on a directed graph $G = (V, \mathcal{A})$, with pheromone bounds $\tau_{\min}$ and $\tau_{\max}$, and evaporation rate ρ, where $t \in V$ is the destination vertex.

```
Initialize τ_a ← 1/deg⁺(v) for all a = (v, v') ∈ A
for i ← 1, 2, ... do
    for each v ∈ V do
        for j = 1, 2, ..., λ do
            Let x_{v,j} be a new path starting at v
            p ← v, S ← {(p, v') ∈ A | v' ∉ x_{v,j}}
            while S is not empty and p ≠ t do
                Pick arc a = (p, h') from S with probability:
                    p_a = τ_a / Σ_{s∈S} τ_s
                Append a to x_{v,j}
                p ← h', S ← {(p, v') ∈ A | v' ∉ x_{v,j}}
        x_v ← arg min_{x_{v,j}} f(x_{v,j})
        if i = 1 or f(x_v) < f(x_v*) then
            x_v* ← x_v
    for each a = (v, v') ∈ A do
        τ_a ← { min(τ_max, (1 − ρ)τ_a + ρ)   if a ∈ x_v*
              { max(τ_min, (1 − ρ)τ_a)       otherwise
```

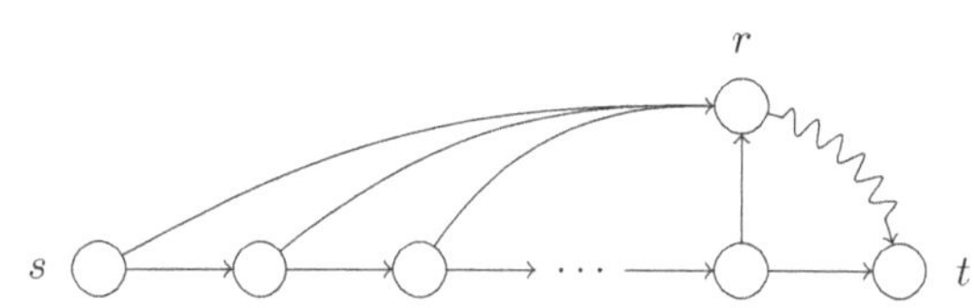

Figure 1: An example graph; the weight on the (r,t) arc affects whether the vertex r is visited or avoided by the shortest paths to t.

The following lemma is heavily used to study the probabilistic pheromone model, and is proved in [18].

LEMMA 1. *The sum of pheromone values on all outgoing arcs from any vertex is at most 2.*

As a consequence of Lemma 1, the probability that an ant will follow any specific outgoing arc from a vertex is at least $\tau_{\min}/2$.

When the first shortest path from vertex v is constructed by an ant, it will be used as the best-so-far path x_v^* in every subsequent pheromone update. The following Lemma from [1] bounds the freezing time – the number of iterations of reinforcing a single arc before the pheromone values reach the pheromone bounds, at which point they will remain unchanged by subsequent pheromone updates until a new best-so-far path, using a different arc to leave v, is discovered. The freezing time is also a bound on the number of iterations between the discovery of a shortest path and the pheromone value on its first arc reaching $\tau_{\max}$.

LEMMA 2. *If x_v^* is unchanged for $\ln(\tau_{max}/\tau_{min})/\rho$ iterations, the pheromone value on the first arc of x_v^* is τ_{max}.*

PROOF. Consider the effect of $\ln(\tau_{\max}/\tau_{\min})/\rho$ pheromone updates on the pheromone value on an arc. It is easy to see that that this number of pheromone updates is sufficient to reduce a pheromone value from $\tau_{\max}$ to $\tau_{\min}$:

$$\tau_{\max} \cdot (1-\rho)^{\ln(\tau_{\max}/\tau_{\min})/\rho} \leq \tau_{\max} \cdot e^{-\ln(\tau_{\max}/\tau_{\min})} = \tau_{\min}$$

Consider two pheromone values, initially set to $\tau_{\max}$ and $\tau_{\min}$; while the first evaporates, the second is reinforced. The sum of the two values is initially 1, and remains 1 as multiplying both values by $(1-\rho)$ is exactly balanced by adding ρ to the second value. Thus the number of iterations required to increase a pheromone value from $\tau_{\min}$ to $\tau_{\max}$ is equal to the number of iterations required to reduce it from $\tau_{\max}$ to $\tau_{\min}$.

As those are the greatest possible changes to a pheromone value, $\ln(\tau_{\max}/\tau_{\min})/\rho$ iterations of reinforcing any single arc will raise its pheromone value to $\tau_{\max}$, while also reducing the pheromone values on other arcs exiting its source vertex to $\tau_{\min}$. □

The next section examines how λ-MMAS is able to handle a one-time change to the weight function, and motivates using $\lambda > 1$ ants to reduce the expected number of iterations needed to discover the shortest paths after a one-time change. Following sections illustrate the benefits and limitations of pheromone memory in a setting where the weight function is changed more frequently: it allows a relatively small number of ants to keep track of shortest paths if the differences between the weight functions are relatively minor, but requires a super-polynomial number of ants if the changes are more significant.

3. A ONE-TIME CHANGE

If the oscillation is sufficiently slow, λ-MMAS may be able to rediscover and re-freeze all of the shortest paths before the next change to the weight function occurs. If this is the case, the process can be treated as a series of one-time modifications to the weight function, with each modification followed by a number iterations during which λ-MMAS rediscovers the shortest paths, and a number of iterations during which the pheromones are frozen to favor the shortest paths, resulting in each ant having at least a constant probability of constructing the shortest path from its starting vertex.

The expected number of iterations λ-MMAS needs to discover the shortest paths of the new weight function depends both on how similar these shortest paths are to those of the previous weight function, and on the maximum number of arcs in any shortest path in the graph using the new weight function. The more similar the shortest paths, the fewer pheromone values need to be changed; and the fewer arcs in the longest shortest path, the more shortest paths can be discovered in parallel.

The proof of the following theorem is based on the analysis in [18]. The presentation here is simplified; a finer analysis in [18] demonstrates that it is not necessary to wait for the full freezing time, removing the log factor from the freezing time component of the expected number of iterations.

THEOREM 3. *With high probability, λ-MMAS (for $\lambda = 1$) will after $O(\ell^*/\tau_{min} + \ell\ln(\tau_{max}/\tau_{min})/\rho)$ iterations have discovered all shortest paths after a one-time change to the weight function given that such shortest paths are unique, where $\ell^* = \max(\ell, \log n)$ and ℓ is the maximum number of arcs in any shortest path to t in the new graph. This is also the expected number of iterations before all the shortest paths are re-discovered after the weight function is altered.*

PROOF. Consider an arbitrary vertex v: the shortest path from v to t has at most $\ell \leq \ell^*$ arcs. λ-MMAS can discover the shortest path from v to t by constructing all of its subpaths (ending at t) in the order of increasing number of arcs. This allows shortest paths to be discovered by only constructing subpaths with one arc with a sub-$\tau_{\max}$ pheromone value at a time, waiting for the pheromones to freeze, and repeating the process for the next subpath.

Let p_{path} be the probability that a specific ant constructs a specific k-arc path containing a single sub-$\tau_{\max}$ arc. In order to discover the v-t shortest path, at most ℓ^* subpaths, all with $k \leq \ell^*$, need to be constructed (and frozen). Assuming the pheromone values on the shorter subpaths are frozen at $\tau_{\max}$, the probability of discovering a new shortest path in this fashion is at least p_{path}:

$$p_{\text{path}} \geq \frac{\tau_{\min}}{2} \cdot {p_{\max}}^{k-1} \geq \frac{\tau_{\min}}{2e}$$

where $p_{\max}$ is the probability that an ant selects an arc with pheromone value $\tau_{\max}$ at an arbitrary vertex; recall that the pheromone bounds are chosen so as to ensure that ${p_{\max}}^{\ell-1} \geq 1/e$.

The number of the desired subpaths discovered in this fashion can be bounded using a Chernoff bound: if every considered iteration is able to discover the next subpath with probability p_{path}, the ℓ^* desired subpaths are discovered in $t = 10e\ell^*/\tau_{\min}$ iterations with high probability. Let N_t be the number of subpath discoveries in t iterations, then $\mu = E(N_t) = t \cdot p_{\text{path}} \geq 5\ell^*$ (treating N_t as binomially distributed), and apply the Chernoff bound:

$$\begin{aligned} P(N_t < \ell^*) &= P(N_t < (1-4/5)\cdot\mu) \\ &< e^{-5\ell^*\cdot(4/5)^2/3} = O\left(n^{-16/15}\right) \end{aligned}$$

inserting $\ell^* \geq \log n$ in the last step.

At most $\ell\ln(\tau_{\max}/\tau_{\min})/\rho$ additional iterations are required to freeze the pheromone values after each discovery to preserve the $p_{\min}$ lower bound on the probability of discovering the next subpath in each iteration. Thus a shortest path from an arbitrary v to t is discovered in at most $10e\ell^*/\tau_{\min} + \ell\ln(\tau_{\max}/\tau_{\min})/\rho$ iterations with high probability. Shortest paths from all of the n vertices in the graph are also found with high probability, which can be shown by applying a union bound:

$$\begin{aligned} P(\min_{v\in V} N_t \geq \ell^*) &\geq 1-(1-P(N_t < \ell^*))^n \\ &\geq 1 - nP(N_t < \ell^*) \\ &= 1 - O\left(n^{-1/15}\right) \end{aligned}$$

Treating this as a success probability in a geometric distribution, it is clear that, in expectation, no more than $O(1)$ phases of $10\ell^*/\tau_{\min} + \ell\ln(\tau_{\max}/\tau_{\min})/\rho$ iterations each are required. Thus, the expected number of iterations before all shortest paths are rediscovered after the weight function changed is $O(\ell^*/\tau_{\min} + \ell\ln(\tau_{\max}/\tau_{\min})/\rho)$. □

As remarked in [18], the unique shortest paths constraint can be dropped at the cost of introducing a $\log n$ factor to the first component of the bound, by requiring in the analysis that all shortest paths of length i are found and frozen before λ-MMAS is considered to have a change to discover a shortest path of length $i+1$; the expected time until all shortest paths of a particular length are found (given that all shorter paths have been found and frozen) is dominated by the coupon collector problem, and is therefore $O(\log n/\tau_{\min})$; in total, there are no more than ℓ^* such phases.

To illustrate the potential effects of a one time change, consider the graph in Figure 1 and the weight functions w_1 and w_2 shown below; the shortest paths of w_1 visit r immediately, while w_2 avoids r if possible:

$$w_1(\alpha) = \begin{cases} -1 & \text{if } \alpha = (r,t) \\ 1 & \text{otherwise} \end{cases} \qquad w_2(\alpha) = \begin{cases} n & \text{if } \alpha = (r,t) \\ 1 & \text{otherwise} \end{cases}$$

If the pheromone values are frozen to the shortest paths using w_1, λ-MMAS will require a large number of iterations to rediscover all of the shortest paths when the weight function is changed to w_2. The proof of the following lower bound is also inspired by a related result in [18], which allows for even finer bounds, but considers a uniform initialization of pheromone values, which is not given after λ-MMAS has frozen the pheromones to favor specific shortest paths.

THEOREM 4. *One-time changes to the weight function may require an expected $\Omega(\ell/\tau_{min})$ iterations for λ-MMAS (for $\lambda = 1$ and $\rho = 1$) to discover all shortest paths, where ℓ is the maximum number of arcs in any shortest path to t in the new graph.*

PROOF. Given the high evaporation rate ($\rho = 1$), after the first iteration, all pheromone values are at the pheromone bounds, and switch between those instantly whenever new shortest paths are discovered by λ-MMAS. Assume for a moment that the optimization proceeds as in the proof of Theorem 3: only shortest paths with a single non-$\tau_{\max}$ arc are discovered until shortest paths from all vertices have been found.

The probability that the next subpath (with only one non-$\tau_{\max}$ arc) is discovered in a single iteration is at most $\tau_{\min}$. Let T_i be the number of iterations between the discoveries of subpaths $i-1$ and i; assuming that the graph is non-trivial, i.e. $\Delta \geq 2$ and hence $\tau_{\min} \leq 1/2$, the probability that the next subpath is not discovered for at least $1/(2\tau_{\min})$ iterations is:

$$\begin{aligned} P(T_i > 1/(2\tau_{\min})) &\geq (1-\tau_{\min})^{1/(2\tau_{\min})} \\ &= \sqrt{(1-\tau_{\min})^{1/\tau_{\min}}} \geq 0.5 \end{aligned}$$

When the weight function is changed to w_2, the entire ℓ-arc longest shortest path needs to be rediscovered, changing the pheromone values on the outgoing arcs from each of the ℓ non-trivial vertices. Let N be the number of subpaths for which $T_i > 1/(2\tau_{\min})$, and $\mu = E(N) \geq \ell/2$. A Chernoff bound shows that at least a quarter of the subpaths will require more than $1/(2\tau_{\min})$ iterations each with overwhelming probability:

$$\begin{aligned} P(N \geq \ell/4) &= 1 - P(N < (1-1/2)\mu) \\ &> 1 - e^{-\mu/2^2/3} \geq 1 - e^{-\ell/24} \end{aligned}$$

Thus, if no shortest paths with more than one non-$\tau_{\max}$ arc are discovered, $\Omega(\ell/\tau_{\min})$ iterations are required with overwhelming probability.

How likely is λ-MMAS not to find any shortest paths with more than one non-$\tau_{\max}$ arc? The probability p_f of discovering such a path is greatest at the beginning of the process, when shortest paths with 2, 3, ..., ℓ non-$\tau_{\max}$ arcs can be discovered; and the probability that no such paths are found for $1/\tau_{\min}{}^2$ iterations is at least a constant:

$$p_f \leq \tau_{\min}{}^2 \sum_{i=2}^{\ell} \tau_{\min}{}^{i-2} < 2 \cdot \tau_{\min}{}^2$$

$$(1-p_f)^{1/\tau_{\min}{}^2} \geq 1/16$$

assuming $\tau_{\min} \leq 1/2$ as before.

Thus, with at least constant probability, λ-MMAS does not discover any shortest paths with more than one non-$\tau_{\max}$ arc in $1/\tau_{\min}{}^2 \geq \ell/\tau_{\min}$ iterations, and $\Omega(\ell/\tau_{\min})$ iterations are required to rediscover the shortest paths with overwhelming probability if only subpaths with a single non-$\tau_{\max}$ arc are discovered. Therefore, the expected number of iterations before the shortest paths are rediscovered by λ-MMAS (with $\lambda = 1$ and $\rho = 1$) after switching from w_1 to w_2 is $\Omega(\ell/\tau_{\max})$. □

Conversely, there also exist combinations of weight functions for which the shortest paths may be rediscovered relatively quickly – for example, switching from w_2 to w_1 on the graph of Figure 1 is easier than the alternative, as a low $\ell = 2$ value reduces the interdependency between shortest paths, allowing them to be discovered in parallel without requiring ants to select more than one non-$\tau_{\max}$ arc at a time. Additionally, changing the weight of the (r,t) arc to values been the extremes considered in w_1 and w_2 would change only some of the shortest paths, reducing the amount of pheromone values that need to be updated.

These analyses suggest that λ-MMAS spends most of the iterations *waiting* to discover the next subpath. The expected number of iterations can be reduced by increasing the number of ants simulated in each iteration, as expanded upon in Theorem 5. This seems to be the first runtime result on the use of an enlarged colony in ACO for combinatorial optimization.

THEOREM 5. *Using $\lambda = 2e/\tau_{min}$ ants allows discovery of new shortest paths in expected constant time, allowing shortest paths to be rediscovered in $O(\ell + \ell \ln(\tau_{max}/\tau_{min})/\rho)$ iterations.*

PROOF. The probability that a single ant will construct a specific path with only one non-$\tau_{\max}$ arc is at least $\tau_{\min}/2e$, so the probability that at least one of λ ants constructs it is at least p_c:

$$p_c \geq 1 - (1 - \tau_{\min}/2e)^{2e/\tau_{\min}} \geq 1 - 1/e$$

Shortest paths up to ℓ arcs long may therefore be discovered using the same mechanism as in Theorem 3, with each subpath taking an expected $e/(e-1) = O(1)$ iterations to discover, and $\ln(\tau_{\max}/\tau_{\min})/\rho$ additional iterations to freeze (as the freezing rate is unaffected by the increased number of ants simulated in each iteration). The total number of iterations required to rediscover and freeze all shortest paths is, per linearity of expectation, at most $O(\ell + \ell \ln(\tau_{\max}/\tau_{\min})/\rho)$. □

While increasing the number of ants simulated does not reduce the amount of work performed by the algorithm, it does allow the work to be parallelized to a greater extent, as each ant in an iteration can be simulated independently of others, only needing to compare the fitness values of the constructed paths at the end of the iteration.

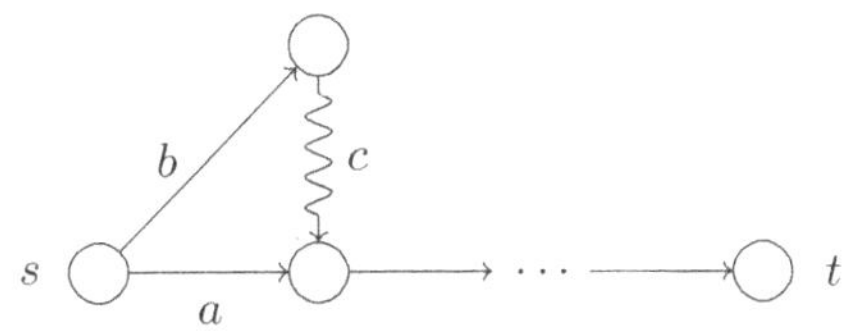

Figure 2: Changing the weight of arc c controls which of the a and b arcs is on the shortest path from s to t.

The theorems presented in this section used ℓ, the maximum number of arcs in any shortest path to t, to bound the complexity of rediscovering the shortest paths after a weight function change. In the examples considered so far, this has been accurate; though there are graphs where it is an overestimation (see e.g. Figure 2). More precise bounds could instead consider, for each shortest path, the number of vertices along the path at which an ant would have opportunity to deviate from the shortest path, and for which the shortest path was altered by the weight function change.

4. PERIODIC LOCAL CHANGES

If the weight functions change more frequently than the expected number of iterations required to rediscover and refreeze the shortest paths after each change, the process can no longer be treated as a series of recoveries from one-time changes. In the extreme case, the weight functions may change in *every* iteration of λ-MMAS. If the shortest paths derived from weight functions are sufficiently similar, tracking the shortest paths may still be possible.

This section considers oscillation between two similar functions on the graph in Figure 2, where although the longest shortest path has at least $n-2$ arcs, the shortest paths are only changed at a single vertex, and the simulated ants only have the opportunity to deviate from the shortest path at a single vertex.

$$w_1(\alpha) = \begin{cases} 1 & \text{if } \alpha = c \\ 0 & \text{otherwise} \end{cases} \quad w_2(\alpha) = \begin{cases} -1 & \text{if } \alpha = c \\ 0 & \text{otherwise} \end{cases}$$

In this situation, it is possible for λ-MMAS to use relatively few ants and still maintain the ability to correctly identify the shortest path in each iteration with at least constant probability for a super-polynomial number of iterations.

LEMMA 6. *Starting $\lambda = 4$ ants at each vertex is sufficient to ensure that if the weight functions w_1 and w_2 alternate every iteration, and the evaporation rate satisfies $\rho \in o(1/\log n)$, the pheromone values on outgoing arcs from s remain in the $[0.3, 0.7]$ range for a super-polynomial number of iterations with respect to n with a probability super-polynomially close to 1.*

PROOF. Let $\tau'_t = \min(\tau_t(a), \tau_t(b))$ be the minimum of the pheromone values on the arcs a and b after iteration t. Consider the effect of two sequential pheromone updates on τ'_t:

$$-\rho < \tau'_{t+2} - \tau'_t < 2\rho \qquad (1)$$

as evaporation may at most reduce the smaller value by $\rho/2$ (as $\tau_t(a)+\tau_t(b) = 1$, and hence $\tau'_t \leq 1/2$), and reinforcement may at most increase the smaller value by ρ.

If the arc with the smaller pheromone value τ'_t is only reinforced in the second of two pheromone updates, the effect is:

$$\tau'_{t+2} - \tau'_t \geq \tau'_t(1-\rho)^2 + \rho - \tau'_t \geq \rho - 2\rho\tau'_t \qquad (2)$$

It is convenient to scale the minimum pheromone values, such that a constant number of pheromone updates alter the scaled values by at most a constant:

$$g(\tau_t) = \min(\tau_t(a), \tau_t(b))/\rho$$

Consider the expected change $\Delta_t(\tau'_t) = g(\tau_{t+2}) - g(\tau_t)$ of these scaled values two pheromone updates after an update that favored reinforcing the arc with the τ'_t pheromone value. For a lower bound, assume that the τ'_t arc is never reinforced during the next iteration (when it is not on the shortest path), and let p_f be the probability that it is also not reinforced during the iteration after the next (when it is on the shortest path), which yields:

$$\begin{aligned} E(\Delta_t(\tau'_t)) &> (1-p_f)\cdot(1-2\tau'_t) + p_f\cdot(-1) \\ &= 1 - 2p_f(1-\tau'_t) - 2\tau'_t \end{aligned}$$

by applying g to the bounds in (1) and (2). For the weight functions w_1 and w_2, $p_f \leq (1-\tau'_t(1-\rho))^\lambda$. The drift is at least 0.02 when $0.3 \leq \tau'_t \leq 0.4$, $\lambda = 4$, and $\rho \leq 0.05$.

The simplified drift theorem [15, 14] can then be applied to the scaled values when the pheromones are within this region, treating two iterations of λ-MMAS as a single step in a Markov process over the scaled values, with steps aligned in such a way that the arc with the minimum pheromone value was always favored last.

The drift is greater than 0.02 within a region specified by $a = (3/10)/\rho$ and $b = (4/10)/\rho$. Notably, the length of the drift region may need to be reduced by the equivalent of a single pheromone update to ensure that the last pheromone update favored reinforcing the τ'_t arc, so the length of the drift region is $\ell \geq b - a - 1 = \omega(\log n)$. This region then satisfies the first requirement of the simplified drift theorem.

As a consequence of (1), the process cannot make large changes to the scaled values in a single iteration. The second requirement of the simplified drift theorem is satisfied by setting $r(\ell) = 4$ and $\delta = 1$:

$$P(|\Delta_t| \geq j) \leq \frac{r(\ell)}{(1+\delta)^j} = 2^{2-j}$$

as $P(|\Delta_t| > 2) = 0$, and the right side of the inequality is at least 1 for $j \leq 2$.

Then, per the simplified drift theorem, there exists a constant c^* such that with probability $1-2^{-\omega(\log n)}$, the Markov process first reaches a state $X_t \leq a$ (and hence first encounters a $\tau'_t \leq 3/10$) after at least $2^{c^*\omega(\log n)}$ iterations. □

Given that the pheromone values remain within this range for a super-polynomial number of iterations, the probability that the correct shortest path x^*_s is constructed also remains bounded for a super-polynomial number of iterations.

A more detailed analysis than the approximations used in Lemma 6 is needed to show whether $\lambda = 3$ ants are also sufficient. This setting is revisited as part of an experiment in Section 6.

THEOREM 7. *When the weight function on the graph of Figure 2 alternates between w_1 and w_2 every iteration, λ-MMAS with $\lambda = 4$ ants and evaporation rate $\rho \in o(1/\log n)$*

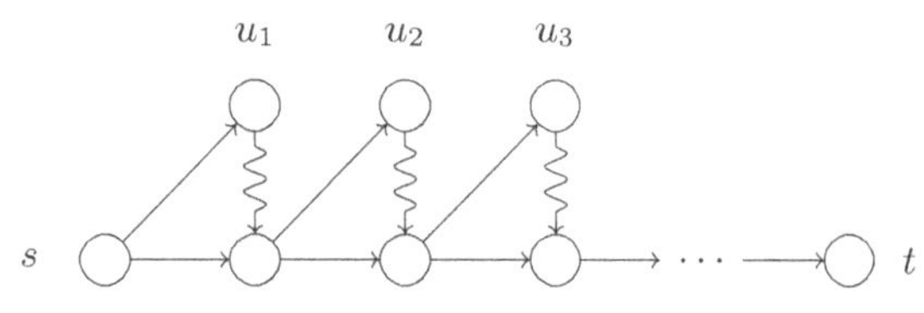

Figure 3: Multiple oscillating triangles on the path from s to t.

will with probability super-polynomially close to 1 be able to find the correct s-t shortest path with at least a constant probability in each iteration for any polynomial number of iterations.

PROOF. Let $\tau'_t = \min(\tau_t(a), \tau_t(b))$ after iteration t; then, the probability that x^*_s is correct is at least the probability of any ant constructing a path through the arc with pheromone value τ'. As long as τ'_t is at least a constant, e.g. 0.3, this probability is also at least a constant:

$$P(x^*_s \text{ is correct} \mid \tau'_t \geq 0.3) \geq 1 - (1 - 0.3)^4 = 0.7599$$

Per Lemma 6, $\tau'_t \geq 0.3$ for a super-polynomial number of iterations with probability super-polynomially close to 1, which proves the theorem. □

The proof relies on a special property of the considered weight functions: only the choice made at s affects whether the ant constructs a correct shortest path to t. If the weight function or graph were changed to require the ants to follow a pheromone-reinforced path after leaving s, $\lambda = 4$ ants may be insufficient to ensure a positive drift. Using the usual pheromone bounds, the probability of an ant successfully following any pheromone-reinforced path is at least $1/e$, so the failure probability can be adjusted accordingly:

$$p_f \leq (1 - \tau'_t(1 - \rho) \cdot 1/e)^\lambda$$

With this adjustment, $\lambda = 12$ ants are sufficient to ensure that the drift is greater than 0.003 for the same constraints on τ'_t and ρ as were used in Lemma 6.

5. PERIODIC GLOBAL CHANGES

Using pheromones as an implicit memory, λ-MMAS is able to reliably construct shortest paths even with a constant number of ants when the oscillating weight functions only make slight alterations to the shortest paths in the graph. In this section, we consider an oscillation between two weight functions where the shortest paths at many vertices change, and there are many opportunities for an ant to deviate from the shortest path.

Suppose that there are k oscillating triangles on the path from s to t, as illustrated in Figure 3. The weight functions w_1 and w_2 can be extended such that the shortest path using w_1 avoids all of the vertices $u_1, \ldots, u_k$, while w_2 favors visiting all of those vertices. Let U be the set of arcs leaving the u_i vertices; the extended weight functions are then:

$$w_1(\alpha) = \begin{cases} 1 & \text{if } \alpha \in U \\ 0 & \text{otherwise} \end{cases} \qquad w_2(\alpha) = \begin{cases} -1 & \text{if } \alpha \in U \\ 0 & \text{otherwise} \end{cases}$$

When k is large, i.e. $k \in \omega(\log n)$, ensuring that the correct shortest path from s to t is constructed with at least constant probability in each iteration requires starting a super-polynomial number of ants at each vertex.

THEOREM 8. *On the graph of Figure 3, λ-MMAS with $\rho \leq 0.5 - \Omega(1)$ requires $\lambda = 2^{\Omega(k)}$ ants to be started at each vertex, where k is the number of oscillating triangles in the graph, in order to have at least a constant probability of constructing the shortest path from s in every iteration when the weight function is swapped between w_1 and w_2 in every iteration.*

PROOF. Consider the pheromone state in an iteration of λ-MMAS. Classify triangle i as *favorable* with respect to the current weight function if the pheromone value on the correct shortest path arc from s_i is at least 0.5. If less than $k/2$ triangles are favorable, constructing the shortest path from s requires a number of ants that is exponential with respect to k, as at least some ant has to make the correct choice of outgoing arc in all of at least $k/2$ unfavorable triangles. Let p_s be the probability that one of the λ ants started at s constructs the correct shortest path, p_k be the probability that a particular ant correctly navigates the $k/2$ unfavorable triangles, and $p_1 \leq 0.5$ be the probability that a particular ant correctly navigates a specific unfavorable triangle, then

$$p_s \leq 1 - (1 - p_k)^\lambda \leq 1 - (1 - (0.5)^{k/2})^\lambda \leq \lambda \cdot 2^{-k/2}$$

To ensure that p_s is at least a constant, at least $2^{\Omega(k)}$ ants must be started from s.

If more than half the triangles are favorable in the current iteration, an exponential number of ants will be required to construct the shortest paths from s in the next iteration. Let $\tau \geq 0.5$ be the pheromone value on the correct shortest path arc in a triangle in the current iteration; then $1 - \tau$ is the pheromone value on the other arc in the same triangle. In the next iteration, that other arc will be on the shortest path, and its pheromone value will be at most $0.5 + \rho$. As long as ρ is upper-bounded by a constant less than 0.5, the derivation of p_s can be repeated using $p_1 \leq 0.5 + \rho$ to show that an exponential number of ants must be started from s in the next iteration.

Thus, at least every second iteration requires λ to be exponential with respect to the number of triangles in order for λ-MMAS to have a constant probability of at least one ant constructing the shortest path from s to t. □

A closer analysis may be able to show that in expectation, no more than some constant fraction of the triangles will favor a specific weight function. This would mean that an exponential number of ants is required in every iteration (rather than at least every second iteration as concluded in the proof of Theorem 8) to ensure a constant probability of the correct s-t shortest path being constructed in an arbitrary iteration.

In general, the smaller the evaporation rate, the less effect the first iteration has on the pheromone values, reducing the amount of bias towards w_1 introduced at the start of the optimization process. A smaller λ has a similar effect: ants started further away from t may not be able to find the full shortest path, which reduces the probability that the w_1-favored arc is reinforced. Subsequent iterations will, due to drift, reduce the bias introduced by the asymmetry at the start of the process; i. e. if more triangles favor w_1 than w_2, in expectation more w_1-favoring triangles will be reinforced towards w_2 during a w_2 iteration than w_2-favoring triangles towards w_1 during a w_1 iteration.

In any case, the example illustrates the nature of the difficulty: the pheromone memory isn't capable of separating

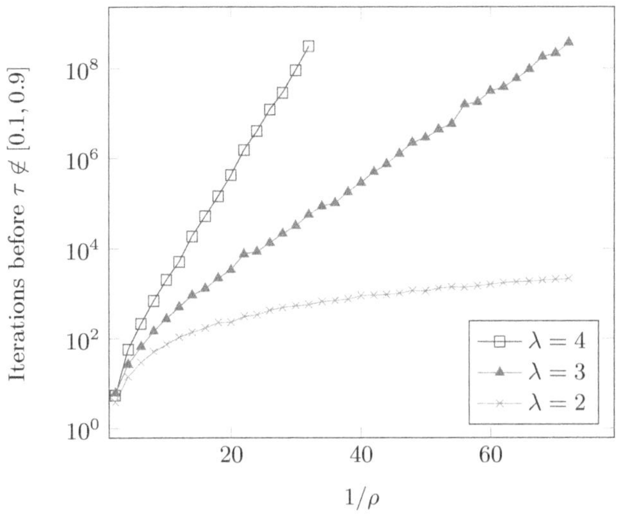

Figure 4: Single triangle; number of iterations before pheromone values on the triangle were about to freeze for the first time.

the two weight functions, and thus does not scale well if the differences between the weight functions extend over multiple vertices.

6. EXPERIMENTS

To illustrate the behavior of λ-MMAS in settings introduced in previous sections, a number of simulations were performed.

In the local changes setting with a single triangle, λ-MMAS with $2 \leq \lambda \leq 4$ ants started at each vertex was simulated with different evaporation rates, recording the first iteration at which the pheromone values on the triangle exited the $[1/10, 9/10]$ range (i. e. were about to freeze) for the first time. Figure 4 shows the average number of iterations over at least 60 simulations. While it seems the $\lambda = 2$ curve is concave, which suggests that $\lambda = 2$ ants are not sufficient to prevent pheromones from freezing for a superpolynomial number of iterations, it seems that $\lambda = 3$ ants may be sufficient to achieve this.

In the global changes setting with $k = 200$ triangles in series, λ-MMAS was simulated with $\lambda = 6$ and $\rho = 1/50$. The number of triangles with pheromone values outside the $[1/4, 3/4]$ range was recorded; Figure 5 displays these results, averaged over 660 simulations, collated by which weight function the triangles outside the pheromone range were favoring. Notably, the number of triangles favoring either weight function increases at approximately equal rates, and eventually stabilizes, keeping approximately a third of the triangles in the graph within the $[1/4, 3/4]$ pheromone range.

Figure 6 presents the same metric in the global changes setting with the evaporation rate set to $\rho = 1$ to maximize the impact of the first iteration. Somewhat surprisingly, even with this extreme evaporation rate, the ratio between the number triangles frozen to favor w_1 and w_2 is initially only 3:2. As suggested in Section 5, the ratio decreases gradually over time, illustrating that the impact of the initial bias is counteracted, rather than compounded, by subsequent iterations.

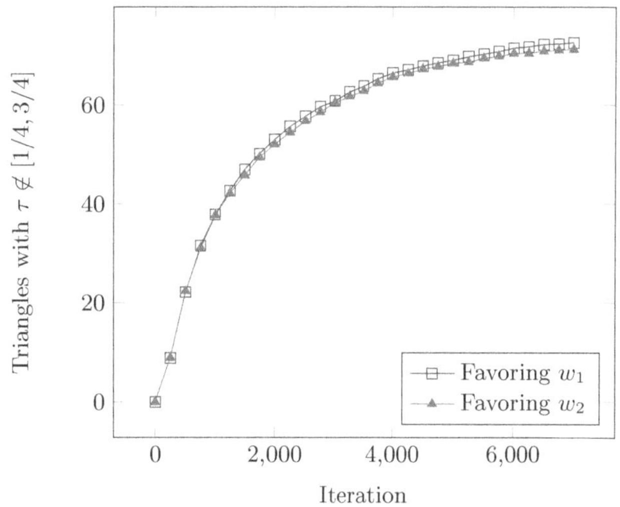

Figure 5: 200 triangles in series; average over 660 runs; $\rho = 1/50$.

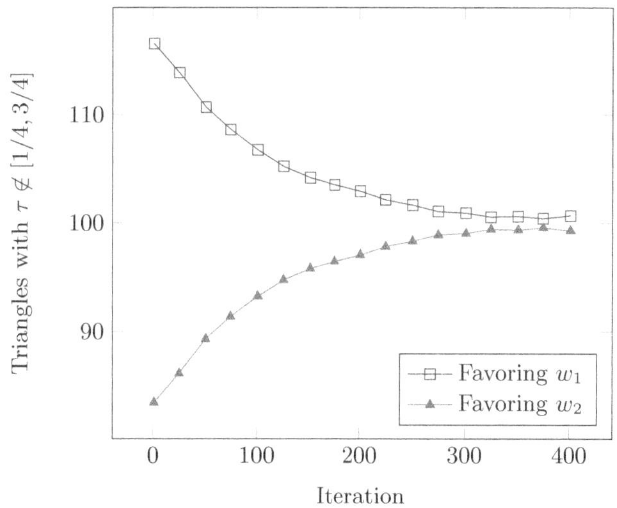

Figure 6: 200 triangles in series; average over 550 runs; $\rho = 1$.

The number of triangles favoring w_1 in Figures 5 and 6 is consistently greater than the number of triangles favoring w_2. This is an artifact of always recording the number of triangles after an iteration using the w_1 weight function.

7. CONCLUSIONS

We have studied a simple ACO algorithm called λ-MMAS for dynamic variants of the single-destination shortest paths problem. Building upon previous results for the special case of 1-MMAS, it was studied to what extent an enlarged colony using λ ants per vertex helps in tracking an oscillating optimum. We showed that λ-MMAS, even with constant number of ants per vertex, can deal with dynamic shortest paths problems where the shortest paths are changed infrequently (by rediscovering the shortest paths before the next change occurs), or changed rapidly between a small set of possible similar solutions (by keeping the pheromone values close to 1/2 for the affected arcs). However, we also identified an example where a fast oscillation between two weight functions that are sufficiently different is so hard to track that a super-polynomial number of ants is needed. Furthermore, we have discussed properties of the dynamics that make the problem hard. Experiments show that the theoretical results are also valid for small problem dimensions and illustrate effects that are not yet visible in theorems.

8. FUTURE WORK

In the future, the performance of λ-MMAS in settings with more complex weight function changes could be analyzed – for instance, generalizing results to slightly slower oscillations, oscillations between more than two weight functions, or using a less regular schedule than was considered here. Having different components of the graph oscillate at different frequencies could also pose an interesting challenge to ACO algorithms, one that could potentially be addressed by maintaining several sets of pheromones updated using different evaporation rates.

9. REFERENCES

[1] N. Attiratanasunthron and J. Fakcharoenphol. A running time analysis of an ant colony optimization algorithm for shortest paths in directed acyclic graphs. *Information Processing Letters*, 105(3):88–92, 2008.

[2] Anne Auger and Benjamin Doerr, editors. *Theory of Randomized Seach Heuristics–Foundations and Recent Developments*. World Scientific, 2011.

[3] Benjamin Doerr, Ashish Hota, and Timo Kötzing. Ants easily solve stochastic shortest path problems. In *Proc. of the Genetic and Evolutionary Computation Conference (GECCO 2012)*, pages 17–24. ACM Press, 2012.

[4] Stefan Droste. Analysis of the (1+1) EA for a dynamically bitwise changing OneMax. In *Proc. of the Genetic and Evolutionary Computation Conference (GECCO 2003)*, pages 909–921. Springer, 2003.

[5] Matthias Feldmann and Timo Kötzing. Optimizing expected path lengths with ant colony optimization using fitness proportional update. In *Proc. of Foundations of Genetic Algorithms (FOGA 2013)*. ACM Press. To appear.

[6] Thomas Jansen and Ulf Schellbach. Theoretical analysis of a mutation-based evolutionary algorithm for a tracking problem in the lattice. In *Proc. of the Genetic and Evolutionary Computation Conference (GECCO 2005)*, pages 841–848. ACM Press, 2005.

[7] Timo Kötzing, Per Kristian Lehre, Frank Neumann, and Pietro Simone Oliveto. Ant colony optimization and the minimum cut problem. In *Proc. of the Genetic and Evolutionary Computation Conference (GECCO 2010)*, pages 1393–1400. ACM Press, 2010.

[8] Timo Kötzing and Hendrik Molter. ACO beats EA on a dynamic pseudo-boolean function. In *Proc. of Parallel Problem Solving from Nature (PPSN 2012)*, pages 113–122. Springer, 2012.

[9] Timo Kötzing, Frank Neumann, Heiko Röglin, and Carsten Witt. Theoretical analysis of two ACO approaches for the traveling salesman problem. *Swarm Intelligence*, 6(1):1–21, 2012.

[10] Frank Neumann, Dirk Sudholt, and Carsten Witt. A few ants are enough: ACO with iteration-best update. In *Proc. of the Genetic and Evolutionary Computation Conference (GECCO 2010)*, pages 63–70, 2010.

[11] Frank Neumann and Carsten Witt. Ant colony optimization and the minimum spanning tree problem. *Theoretical Computer Science*, 411(25):2406–2413, 2010.

[12] Frank Neumann and Carsten Witt. *Bioinspired Computation in Combinatorial Optimization – Algorithms and Their Computational Complexity*. Springer, 2010.

[13] Trung Thanh Nguyen, Shengxiang Yang, and Jürgen Branke. Evolutionary dynamic optimization: A survey of the state of the art. *Swarm and Evolutionary Computation*, 6:1–24, 2012.

[14] P. S. Oliveto and Carsten Witt. Erratum: Simplified drift analysis for proving lower bounds in evolutionary computation. *arXiv:1211.7184*, 2012. http://arxiv.org/abs/1211.7184.

[15] Pietro S. Oliveto and Carsten Witt. Simplified drift analysis for proving lower bounds in evolutionary computation. *Algorithmica*, 59(3):369–386, 2011.

[16] Philipp Rohlfshagen, Per Kristian Lehre, and Xin Yao. Dynamic evolutionary optimisation: An analysis of frequency and magnitude of change. In *Proc. of the Genetic and Evolutionary Computation Conference (GECCO 2009)*, pages 1713–1720. ACM Press, 2009.

[17] Thomas Stützle and Holger H. Hoos. MAX-MIN ant system. *Future Generation Computer Systems*, 16(8):889–914, 2000.

[18] Dirk Sudholt and Christian Thyssen. Running time analysis of ant colony optimization for shortest path problems. *Journal of Discrete Algorithms*, 10:165–180, 2012.

[19] Dirk Sudholt and Christian Thyssen. A simple ant colony optimizer for stochastic shortest path problems. *Algorithmica*, 64(4):643–672, 2012.

[20] Yuren Zhou. Runtime analysis of an ant colony optimization algorithm for TSP instances. *IEEE Transactions on Evolutionary Computation*, 13(5):1083–1092, 2009.

Population Size Matters: Rigorous Runtime Results for Maximizing the Hypervolume Indicator

Anh Quang Nguyen
Evolutionary Computation Group
School of Computer Science
The University of Adelaide
Adelaide, SA 5005, Australia

Andrew M. Sutton
Department of Computer Science
Colorado State University
Fort Collins, CO 80523, USA

Frank Neumann
Evolutionary Computation Group
School of Computer Science
The University of Adelaide
Adelaide, SA 5005, Australia

ABSTRACT

Using the hypervolume indicator to guide the search of evolutionary multi-objective algorithms has become very popular in recent years. We contribute to the theoretical understanding of these algorithms by carrying out rigorous runtime analyses. We consider multi-objective variants of the problems OneMax and LeadingOnes called OneMinMax and LOTZ, respectively, and investigate hypervolume-based algorithms with population sizes that do not allow coverage of the entire Pareto front. Our results show that LOTZ is easier to optimize than OneMinMax for hypervolume-based evolutionary multi-objective algorithms which is contrary to the results on their single-objective variants and the well-studied (1+1) EA.

Categories and Subject Descriptors

F.2 [**Theory of Computation**]: Analysis of Algorithms and Problem Complexity

General Terms

Theory, Algorithms, Performance

Keywords

Multi-objective Optimization, Theory, Runtime Analysis

1. INTRODUCTION

Evolutionary algorithms have become very popular for handling problems in multi-objective optimization [11, 10]. They seem to be well suited for these types of problems since, in multi-objective optimization, the goal is to compute a set of solutions that represent the trade-offs with respect to the given objective functions. Evolutionary multi-objective algorithms aim to compute a set of such trade-offs by iteratively evolving a population of solutions into a reasonable collection that represents a good set of trade-offs with respect to the given objective functions.

Hypervolume-based evolutionary algorithms have become very popular in recent years for multi-objective optimization [17, 12, 5, 2]. These algorithms work with a fixed population size of μ and try to maximize the volume of space that is covered by the μ objective vectors corresponding to each individual of the population.

Despite their popularity, it is difficult to understand from a theoretical point of view how hypervolume-based evolutionary algorithms work. Many studies in recent years have concentrated on the optimal hypervolume distribution for a wide range of problems, or the cost of computing or approximating the value of the hypervolume indicator for a given set of μ points [6, 7]. These studies tackled the difficult task of determining the configuration of the optimal distribution of the μ individuals without considering the computational costs to reach this goal. Other studies relate the optimal hypervolume distribution to the best achievable approximation ratio when using μ solutions to cover the Pareto front [4, 8].

In this paper, we want to put forward the theoretical understanding of the optimization process of hypervolume-based evolutionary algorithms. We do this by carrying out rigorous runtime analyses of hypervolume-based evolutionary algorithms and point out, using popular example functions, when and why they are able to achieve an optimal hypervolume distribution in expected polynomial time. On the other hand, we show that even on very simple problems, hypervolume-based algorithms can have significant difficulties achieving the optimal configuration if the population size is not set correctly.

To our knowledge, the only article on the runtime analysis of hypervolume-based algorithms is the article by Brockhoff et al. [9]. We push forward the runtime analysis of hypervolume-based evolutionary algorithms by studying the algorithm called $(\mu+1)$ SIBEA introduced in [9] in order to extend these initial investigations.

We start by analyzing the OneMinMax problem introduced in [13], which is the multi-objective version of the famous OneMax problem. We show that as long as μ is large enough to cover the entire Pareto front, $(\mu+1)$ SIBEA computes the whole Pareto front in expected polynomial time. Furthermore, we point out that a smaller population size might lead to plateaus that are hard to leave in polynomial time. In particular, we show that there exists an initial population of size $\mu = O(\sqrt{n})$ such that the optimization time of $(\mu + 1)$ SIBEA is exponential with probability very close to 1.

After having investigated OneMinMax, we turn our attention to the multi-objective problem LOTZ introduced in [15]. Extending the investigations of [9], we show that $(\mu+1)$ SIBEA optimizes LOTZ in expected polynomial time if $\mu \leq n/3$. This shows that LOTZ is easier to optimize than OneMinMax by $(\mu+1)$ SIBEA for small μ.

The outline of the paper is as follows. In Section 2, we introduce the framework that is subject to our investigations. Section 3, studies the behavior of $(\mu+1)$ SIBEA on OneMinMax and these studies are extended to LOTZ in Section 4. We finish with some concluding remarks.

2. PRELIMINARIES

Let $\mathcal{X}$ be a finite domain. In multi-objective optimization, we work with a vector-valued fitness function $f : \mathcal{X} \to \mathbb{R}^m$ where $m \in \mathbb{N}$ and the fitness of an element $x \in \mathcal{X}$ is given by the vector $f(x) = (f_1(x), \dots, f_m(x))$. Assuming we want to maximize each function f_i, we say $f(x) \geq f(x')$ if and only if $f_i(x) \geq f_i(x')$ for $x, x' \in \mathcal{X}$ and all $i \in \{1, \dots, m\}$. We say a solution x dominates a solution x' if $f(x) \geq f(x')$ and $f(x) \neq f(x')$.

For a fitness function $f : \mathcal{X} \to \mathbb{R}^m$, we define

$$\mathscr{P} = \{x \in \mathcal{X} : f(x) \geq f(x') \implies f(x) = f(x'), \forall x' \in \mathcal{X}\}$$

as the Pareto set of f. We sometimes call a point $x \in \mathscr{P}$ *Pareto optimal.*

The *hypervolume indicator* is a set measure that identifies a set of elements in $\mathbb{R}^m$ (corresponding to images of elements in $\mathcal{X}$) with the volume of the dominated portion of the objective space. In particular, given a reference point $r \in \mathbb{R}^m$, the hypervolume indicator is defined on a set $A \subset \mathcal{X}$ as

$$I_H(A) = \lambda\left(\bigcup_{a \in A} [f_1(a), r_1] \times [f_2(a), r_2] \times \cdots \times [f_m(a), r_m]\right)$$

where $\lambda(S)$ denotes the Lebesgue measure of a set S and $[f_1(a), r_1] \times [f_2(a), r_2] \times \cdots \times [f_m(a), r_m]$ is the orthotope with $f(a)$ and r in opposite corners.

We define the *extreme points* of a problem as

$$\{x \in \mathscr{P}, \exists i \in \{1, \dots, m\} : f_i(x) \geq f_i(x'), \forall x' \in \mathcal{X}\}.$$

The extreme points are the points in $\mathscr{P}$ that maximize at least one objective function.

We study variants of $(\mu+1)$ SIBEA algorithm introduced by Brockhoff et al. [9] outlined in Algorithm 1. A *trace* is

Algorithm 1: $(\mu+1)$ SIBEA.

```
Start with an initial population P^(1) consisting of μ
elements from X.
repeat forever
    Select x from P^(t) u.a.r.;
    x' ← mutate(x);
    P'^(t) ← P^(t) ∪ {x'};
    foreach x ∈ P'^(t) do
        d(x; P'^(t)) ← I_H(P'^(t)) − I_H(P'^(t) \ {x});
    z ← arg min_{x∈P'^(t)} d(x; P'^(t)) with ties broken u.a.r.;
    P^(t+1) ← P'^(t) \ {z};
```

an infinite stochastic sequence of μ-multisets

$$\left(P^{(1)}, P^{(2)}, \dots, P^{(t)}, \dots\right)$$

where $P^{(t)}$ denotes the population visited by $(\mu+1)$ SIBEA in iteration t.

It will often be convenient to discuss how the properties of individual solutions change during the construction of an intermediate population $P'^{(t)}$ from a population $P^{(t)}$ in iteration t. To facilitate such discussion, we will employ the following notation scheme. We denote as x' the offspring produced by applying mutation to some individual in $P^{(t)}$. For each $x_i \in P^{(t)}$ we denote $x'_i \in P'^{(t)} \setminus \{x'\}$ to denote the same solution in the intermediate population directly after a mutation, but before undergoing truncation selection.

We are ultimately interested in the *optimization time* of $(\mu+1)$ SIBEA, which is the random variable

$$T = \inf\{t \in \mathbb{N} : I_H(P^{(t)}) \text{ is maximal over } \mu\text{-multisets}\}.$$

In the following sections, we will derive asymptotic bounds for the expectation of T.

Given a population P, we define the hypervolume *contribution* of an individual $x \in P$ (with respect to P) as

$$d(x; P) = I_H(P) - I_H(P \setminus \{x\}).$$

Hence, $d(x; P)$ represents the volume of space that the point $x \in P$ uniquely contributes to the total hypervolume covered by the population P. When the population is clear from context, we will denote the contribution of x simply as $d(x)$.

In this paper, we will consider multi-objective problems over length-n binary strings, that is $\mathcal{X} = \{0,1\}^n$. For a point $x \in \{0,1\}^n$, we will use square brackets to address individual elements of the bitstring, that is $x = (x[1], x[2], \dots, x[n])$ so that $x[i] \in \{0,1\}$ denotes the i-th bit in the string x. The mutation operator that we consider differs slightly from the variants of $(\mu+1)$ SIBEA initially proposed by [9]. In particular, we will study only a local, single-point mutation operator, in which a single bit, chosen uniformly at random, is flipped at each mutation step. In this way, the algorithms we consider are more similar to indicator-based randomized local search. The mutation operator we study is defined formally as follows.

Function mutate(x)

```
x' ← x;
Choose i ∈ {1, ..., n} u.a.r.;
x'[i] ← 1 − x'[i];
return x';
```

In the case of bicriteria optimization, we will be interested in the dynamics of the intervals between points on one fitness function, say f_1. To do so, we label a population P with respect to its ordering on f_1, that is $P = \{x_1, x_2, \dots, x_\mu\}$ such that $f_1(x_i) \leq f_1(x_{i+1})$. We define the following function that measures the intervals defined by the projection of points onto the f_1 axis (see Figure 1).

$$\iota(x_i) = \begin{cases} f_1(x_i) - f_1(x_{i-1}) & i > 1; \\ f_1(x_i) + 1 & i = 1. \end{cases}$$

3. ONEMINMAX

The OneMinMax problem, originally introduced by Giel and Lehre [13], is defined as the bicriteria optimization problem over the set of binary strings as $f : \{0,1\}^n \to \mathbb{N} \times \mathbb{N}$

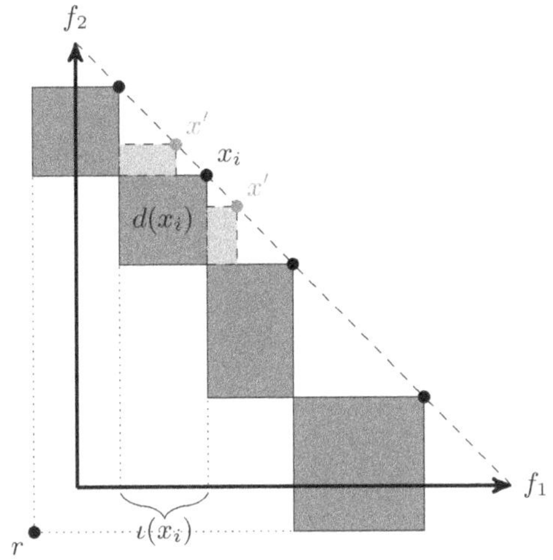

Figure 1: Shaded areas denote contribution $d(x_i)$ of each individual x_i to the hypervolume indicator.

with

$$f(x) = (f_1(x), f_2(x)) \quad \text{with}$$
$$f_1(x) = \text{OneMin}(x) = n - \text{OneMax}(x) \quad \text{and}$$
$$f_2(x) = \text{OneMax}(x) = \sum_{i=1}^{n} x[i].$$

The goal is to maximize both objectives. In OneMinMax, every solution belongs to $\mathscr{P}$. Denoting as $f[\mathscr{P}]$ the image of $\mathscr{P}$ under f in objective space, it is clear that $|f[\mathscr{P}]| = n+1$, since each string with k ones ($n-k$ zeros) is mapped to a unique, non-dominated point in objective space. We define the reference point to be $r = (-n, -n)$ such that the extreme points always have the highest contributions. We are interested in the expected time for $(\mu+1)$ SIBEA to arrange the population on the Pareto front so that the hypervolume indicator is maximized.

Theorem 1. *Choosing $\mu \geq n+1$, the expected optimization time of $(\mu+1)$ SIBEA on* OneMinMax *is $O(\mu n \log n)$*

Proof. Since every solution belongs to $\mathscr{P}$ and $\mu \geq n+1$, solutions are never lost during a run. The algorithm reaches the optimal hypervolume when the population covers the whole Pareto front. In the case of OneMinMax, a population P covers the whole Pareto front when, for every $i \in \{0, 1, \ldots, n\}$, there exists an $x \in P$ such that $\text{OneMax}(x) = i$ and $\text{OneMin}(x) = n - i$. Thus it suffices to bound the expected time it takes for $(\mu+1)$ SIBEA to generate all missing values for OneMax.

Suppose t is a generation in which $I_H(P^{(t)})$ is suboptimal. In such a generation, the Pareto front is not yet covered. Hence, there exists at least one individual $x \in P^{(t)}$ such that at least one of the following is true.

1. $\nexists x' \in P^{(t)}, \text{OneMax}(x') = \text{OneMax}(x) + 1.$
2. $\nexists x' \in P^{(t)}, \text{OneMax}(x') = \text{OneMax}(x) - 1.$

It is thus possible to gain a missing OneMax value by mutating x by flipping either a one bit or a zero bit. Without loss of generality, suppose there are no solutions $x' \in P^{(t)}$ with $\text{OneMax}(x') = \text{OneMax}(x) + 1$ and $\text{OneMax}(x) < n$ (otherwise, a symmetric argument holds for $\text{OneMax}(x') = \text{OneMax}(x) - 1$ and $\text{OneMax}(x) > 0$). In this case, a mutation operation creates a new Pareto optimal solution if x is selected for mutation, and one of the zero bits in x is flipped to produce a new solution x'' where $\text{OneMax}(x'') = \text{OneMax}(x')$.

The probability of this event is at least $\text{OneMin}(x)/(\mu n) = (n - \text{OneMax}(x))/(\mu n)$. The total expected waiting time to generate all missing OneMax values is thus bounded by

$$\sum_{i=0}^{n} \frac{\mu n}{n-i} = \mu n \sum_{i=0}^{n} \frac{1}{i} = O(\mu n \log n).$$

The same argument holds in the case of missing values for $\text{OneMax}(x) - 1$, and the claimed bound on the expected time to cover the Pareto front follows. □

Theorem 1 shows that, so long as the population is sufficiently large, the optimization time of $(\mu+1)$ SIBEA on OneMinMax is bounded by a polynomial in μ and n. We now show that, if the population size is too small, the optimization time can become exponential in n.

On OneMinMax for strings of length n, a population P is distributed along the line $x + y = n$ in the xy-plane. We label the population $P = \{x_1, x_2, \ldots, x_\mu\}$ such that $\text{OneMin}(x_i) \leq \text{OneMin}(x_{i+1})$. We now show that, after a polynomially-bounded number of iterations of $(\mu+1)$ SIBEA, the population contains the extreme points $(00\cdots0)$ and $(11\cdots1)$.

Lemma 1. *Choosing $\mu \geq 2$, the expected time until the two extreme points are contained in the population is $O(\mu n \log n)$.*

Proof. In OneMinMax, the two extreme points are the points $(11\cdots1)$ and $(00\cdots0)$. In every iteration during the run of $(\mu+1)$ SIBEA, the value corresponding to the highest OneMax value in the population never decreases (since removing this point results in a population with a strictly smaller hypervolume indicator value).

In iteration t, the individual $x \in P^{(t)}$ with the highest OneMax value is selected with probability $1/\mu$, and a zero bit is selected with probability k/n where k is the number of zero bits in x. The highest OneMax value can be increased at most n times until $(11\cdots1)$ enters the population. A symmetric argument holds for the OneMin value, and the expected time to until both extreme points enter the population is upper bounded by:

$$2\sum_{k=1}^{n} \left(\frac{1}{\mu}\frac{k}{n}\right)^{-1} = 2\mu n \sum_{k=1}^{n} \frac{1}{k} = O(\mu n \log n).$$

□

Without loss of generality, in order to simplify the analysis we will assume for the remainder of the paper that n is divisible by $\mu - 1$. We remark here that our results still hold in the case that $\mu - 1$ does not divide n evenly, but this requires some extra attention to technical details.

The *optimal μ-distribution* for a Pareto front $\mathscr{P}$ is the set of μ points on the front that maximize the hypervolume indicator. The following theorem is due to Auger et al. [3, Theorem 7].

Theorem 2. *If the Pareto front is a (connected) line, the optimal μ-distribution with respect to the hypervolume indicator is such that the distance is the same between all neighboring solutions.*

In other words, assuming $2 < \mu < n+1$ and $\mu - 1$ divides n evenly, in the optimal μ-distribution, the intervals $\iota(x_i) = \iota(x_j) = n/(\mu - 1)$ for all $i, j \in \{2, \ldots, \mu\}$.

Since OneMinMax has a linear front, the conditions for the theorem are satisfied.

Proposition 1. *Let x' be produced from x_i by flipping a single bit. Then either*

$$d(x') = \text{OneMin}(x_{i+1}) - \text{OneMin}(x_i) - 1 = \iota(x_{i+1}) - 1, \quad \textit{or},$$
$$d(x') = \text{OneMin}(x_i) - \text{OneMin}(x_{i-1}) - 1 = \iota(x_i) - 1.$$

For example, see Figure 1.

Proposition 2. *The contribution of a solution x_i is calculated by*

$$d(x_i) = (\text{OneMin}(x_i) - \text{OneMin}(x_{i-1})) \times (\text{OneMax}(x_{i+1}) - \text{OneMax}(x_i)),$$

and since $\text{OneMax}(x_i) = n - \text{OneMin}(x_i)$,

$$d(x_i) = \iota(x_i)\iota(x_{i+1}).$$

Lemma 2. *Given a population $P^{(t)}$ on* OneMinMax, *$(\mu + 1)$ SIBEA can produce an offspring that strictly improves $I_H(P^{(t)})$ if and only if one of the following conditions is satisfied:*

1. *There exists a solution $x_i \in P^{(t)}$ such that $|\iota(x_i) - \iota(x_{i+1})| \geq 2$*
2. *There exist two solutions $x_i, x_j \in P^{(t)}$ such that $\iota(x_i) > d(x_j) + 1$*

PROOF. For the first condition, without loss of generality, assume that $\iota(x_{i+1}) = \iota(x_i)+k$ for $k \geq 2$. In order for a strict improvement to occur, a new solution x' can be generated by flipping a one bit in x_i to a zero. We calculate the new intervals in the intermediate population $P'^{(t)} \leftarrow P^{(t)} \cup \{x'\}$ as $\iota(x'_i) = \iota(x_i)$, $\iota(x') = 1^*$, and $\iota(x'_{i+1}) = \iota(x_{i+1}) - 1$. It follows that $d(x'_i) = \iota(x'_i) = \iota(x_i) < \iota(x_i) + k - 1 = \iota(x_{i+1}) - 1 = d(x')$. Hence replacing x'_i with x' results in a strictly higher hypervolume indicator.

For the second condition, assume that there are two solutions x_i, x_j such that $\iota(x_i) > d(x_j) + 1$. Let x' be a new solution produced by mutating x_i or x_{i-1}. According to Proposition 1, $d(x') = \text{OneMin}(x_i) - \text{OneMin}(x_{i-1}) - 1 = \iota(x_i) - 1 > d(x_j)$.

Therefore, if one of the above conditions is satisfied, there always exists a solution z in the intermediate population such that

$$I_H(P^{(t+1)} \leftarrow P'^{(t)} \setminus \{x'\}) < I_H(P^{(t+1)} \leftarrow P'^{(t)} \setminus \{z\})$$

On the other hand, suppose none of the above conditions hold. In this case, for all solutions $x_i, x_j \in P^{(t)}$, $|\iota(x_i) - \iota(i+1)| \leq 1$ and $\iota(x_i) \leq d(x_j) + 1$. Assume that a solution $x_k \in P^{(t)}$ is selected for mutation and let x' be the new solution obtained by mutating x_k. Again, by Proposition 1, either $d(x') = \text{OneMin}(x_{k+1}) - \text{OneMin}(x_k) - 1$ or $d(x') = \text{OneMin}(x_k) - \text{OneMin}(x_{k-1}) - 1$ and we make the following case distinction.

Case 1. If $d(x') = \text{OneMin}(x_{k+1}) - \text{OneMin}(x_k) - 1 = \iota(x_{k+1}) - 1$, then only the value of $\iota(x_{k+1})$ changes, which leads to $d(x'_k) = \iota(x_k)$, $d(x'_{k+1}) = (\iota(x_{k+1}) - 1) \times \iota(x_{k+2})$ while the contribution of other solutions in the population remain the same. Obviously, $d(x') \leq d(x'_{k+1})$ and $d(x') \leq d(x'_k)$ from the first counter conditions. Furthermore, based on the second counter condition, $d(x') \leq d(x'_j)$ for all $j \neq k$ and $j \neq k + 1$.

Case 2. If $d(x') = \text{OneMin}(x_k) - \text{OneMin}(x_{k-1}) - 1 = \iota(x_k) - 1$, then only the value of $\iota(x_k)$ changes, which leads to $d(x'_k) = \iota(x_{k+1})$, $d(x'_{k-1}) = (\iota(x_k) - 1) \times \iota(x_{k-1})$ while the contribution of other solutions in the population remain the same. Using a similar argument, $d(x') \leq d(x'_j)$ for all $1 \leq j \leq \mu$

Therefore, if none of the conditions are satisfied, for all solutions x_j in the population,

$$I_H(P^{(t+1)} \leftarrow P'^{(t)} \setminus \{x_j\}) \leq I_H(P^{(t+1)} \leftarrow P'^{(t)} \setminus \{x'\}).$$

This completes the proof. □

We define an initial population P^w in which (1) $\mu = \sqrt{n}+1$, (2) the extreme points already exist in P^w, and (3) the intervals are as follows.

$$\iota(x_i) = \begin{cases} 1 & \text{if } i = 1; \\ \sqrt{n} + 1 & \text{if } i = 2; \\ \sqrt{n} - 1 & \text{if } i = \mu; \\ \sqrt{n} & \text{otherwise.} \end{cases}$$

The set of intervals of P^w with respect to OneMin are illustrated below.

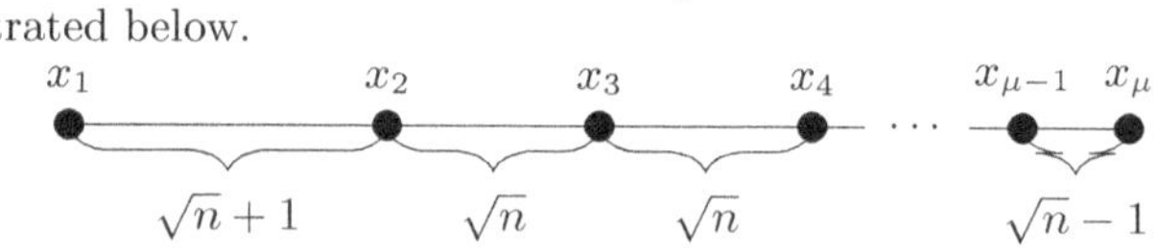

In the next part, we will show that, with probability approaching one exponentially fast, $(\mu + 1)$ SIBEA requires exponential time to reach the optimal population state from P^w.

Theorem 3. *Starting with the initial population P^w where $\mu = \sqrt{n}+1$, the expected optimization time of $(\mu+1)$ SIBEA on* OneMinMax *is exponential with probability $1 - e^{-\Omega(n)}$.*

PROOF. By Theorem 2, the population is optimal when $\iota(x_i) = \sqrt{n}$ for all $x_i \in P^{(t)}$.

During the run, we call an interval *large* if $\iota(x_i) = \sqrt{n}+1$. Similarly, we call the interval *small* if $\iota(x_i) = \sqrt{n}-1$. At the beginning of the above configuration, the interval belonging to x_2 is large, and the interval belonging to x_μ is small.

In this configuration, an offspring is only accepted if it results in moving the large interval or the small interval in either direction by flipping one of the bits in the solutions that bound the intervals.

No other mutation will be accepted since it would result in an offspring with a strictly smaller contribution. To reach the optimum, the large interval and the small interval must meet, i.e., $\iota(x_i) = \sqrt{n} + 1$ and $\iota(x_{i+1}) = \sqrt{n} - 1$ for some $i \in \{2, \ldots, \mu\}$. From this state, only a single mutation is possible to reach the optimum.

Let T be the random variable corresponding to the optimization time of $(\mu + 1)$ SIBEA . We consider the position of the large and small intervals during all times $t < T$. Let

---

[*]Note that here we are abusing the ι notation slightly. The $\mu+1$ intervals in the intermediate population should be understood in terms of their relative positions along the f_1-axis. This may be different than their canonical subscripts due to the addition of x'.

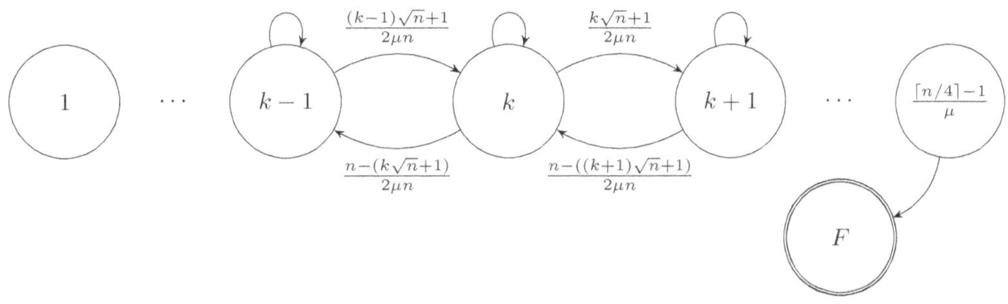

Figure 2: Markov chain for interval dynamics for $(\mu+1)$ SIBEA on OneMinMax.

$a = a(t)$ be the index at time t such that $\iota(x_a) = \sqrt{n}+1$ and let $b = b(t)$ be the index at time t such that $\iota(x_{b+1}) = \sqrt{n}-1$. The optimal solution is only reachable from the state in which $a = b$. Before this occurs, at least one of the following conditions must hold at some time $t < T$. (1) $\text{OneMin}(x_a) \geq \frac{n}{4}$, or (2) $\text{OneMin}(x_b) \leq \frac{n}{4}$.

We now prove that either of these conditions only occur after exponential time with probability approaching one exponentially fast. For the first condition, note that probability of a mutation that moves the large interval to the right is $\text{OneMin}(x_a)/(2\mu n)$. Here, $1/\mu$ is the probability of choosing the correct individual, x_a from the population, $\text{OneMin}(x_a)/n$ is the probability of flipping one of zero bits in the current solution and $1/2$ is the probability of keeping the new solution.

Meanwhile, the probability of moving the large interval to the left (if possible) is $\text{OneMax}(x_{a-1})/(2\mu n)$ where $1/\mu$ is the probability of choosing the correct solution x_{a-1} from the population, $\text{OneMax}(x_{a-1})/n$ is the probability of flipping one of the one bits in the current solution and $1/2$ is the probability of keeping the new solution.

Let X^t be the set of variables describing a Markov process over a finite state space $S = \{1, 2, \ldots, (\lceil n/4\rceil - 1)/\mu\} \cup F$ where the k-th state corresponds to the event in which $\text{OneMin}(x_{a(t)}) = k\sqrt{n}+1$, that is, the large interval has moved into position k. The chain is absorbed into a final accepting state F if the small interval meets it (we later show this also takes exponential time). Letting T denote the time when the intervals first meet, for all $0 \leq t < T$, $X^{t+1} - X^t \in \{-1, 0, 1\}$. Using the above transition probabilities (illustrated in Figure 2), for all $0 < t < T$ and $1 \leq X^t \leq (\lceil n/4\rceil - 1)/\mu$,

$$P(X^{t+1} - X^t = -1 \mid X^t) \geq \delta \cdot P(X^{t+1} - X^t = 1 \mid X^t),$$

where $\delta \geq (n - n/4)/(n/4) = 3$. By the Local Gambler's Ruin Theorem [14], the time until $a(t)$ is large enough so that $\text{OneMin}(x_{a(t)}) \geq n/4$ conditioned on the event that it has not yet met the small interval is at least $\delta^{1/3\cdot(1-1/(4\mu))\cdot n} \geq 3^{\Omega(n)}$ with probability $1 - e^{-\Omega(n)}$.

A symmetric argument shows that, with high probability, it requires exponential time for $b(t)$ to reach $\text{OneMin}(x_{b(t)}) \leq n/4$. Since both conditions require exponential time with probability $1 - e^{-\Omega(n)}$, the claim follows. □

4. LOTZ

The *leading ones, trailing zeros* (LOTZ) problem is a bi-criteria optimization problem over binary strings first introduced by Laumanns et al. [15], defined as $\text{LOTZ} : \{0,1\}^n \to \mathbb{N}^2$ where

$$\text{LOTZ}(x) = (f_1(x), f_2(x)) \qquad \text{with}$$

$$f_1(x) = \text{LO}(x) = \sum_{i=1}^{n}\prod_{j=1}^{i} x[j], \qquad \text{and,}$$

$$f_2(x) = \text{TZ}(x) = \sum_{i=1}^{n}\prod_{j=i}^{n}(1 - x[j]).$$

Similar to OneMinMax, we set the reference point as $r = (-n, -n)$ and label the population $P = \{x_1, x_2, \ldots, x_\mu\}$ such that $\text{LO}(x_i) \leq \text{LO}(x_{i+1})$.

Since the Pareto front of LOTZ is linear, Theorem 2 holds. Moreover, as long as all points are on the Pareto front, Propositions 1 and 2 hold (using the requisite objective function) and Lemma 2 carries over to LOTZ as well. The following theorem follows directly from Brockhoff, Friedrich and Neumann [9, Theorem 2].

Theorem 4. *Choosing $\mu \geq n+1$, the expected optimization time of $(\mu+1)$ SIBEA on* LOTZ *is $O(\mu n^2)$*

Though the proof of Theorem 4 is carried out for a more general version of $(\mu+1)$ SIBEA, the claim holds also for our choice of mutation operator, which is only slightly easier to control.

Theorem 5. *Let $1 < \mu < n+1$. The expected time for $(\mu+1)$ SIBEA to reach a population that contains only Pareto optimal solutions and solutions for the objective vectors $(n, 0)$ and $(0, n)$ is $O(\mu^2 n^2)$*

PROOF. In any point $x \notin \mathscr{P}$, a 0 must appear before a 1 in x. Thus, $x = 1^a 0\{0,1\}^b 1 0^c$ for $a, b, c \geq 0$. A mutation is only accepted if the 0 in position $a+1$ is flipped, or the 1 in position $a+b+2$ is flipped. In either case, the resulting offspring must have a strictly higher LO (TZ) value (respectively), so the highest LO (TZ) value in the population never decreases.

Let $x \in P^{(t)}$ be the point in the population with the highest LO value in iteration t. The probability that x is selected for mutation, and the correct bit is flipped to increase the LO value is bounded below by $1/(\mu n)$. This event can occur a maximum of n times until the extreme point with the highest LO value is in the population. It follows that the expected time until the extreme point with the highest LO value is $O(\mu n^2)$. A symmetric argument holds for the extreme point with the highest TZ value. Thus the expected time until both extreme points are in the population is $O(\mu n^2)$.

During the runtime of the algorithm, the count of Pareto optimal solutions in the population never decreases since each accepted mutation on a non-Pareto optimal solution will generate an offspring that either dominates or is dominated by its parent. The number of Pareto optimal solutions can increase when there exists a dominated solution in the population, or the new Pareto optimal solution dominates one of the non-Pareto, non-dominated solutions.

In the first case, where there is at least a dominated solution, there exists a point $x \in P^{(t)} \cap \mathscr{P}$ with a Hamming neighbor x' such that $x' \in \mathscr{P}$ but $x' \notin P^{(t)}$. The probability of creating x' by applying a mutation to x is $1/(\mu n)$. Such a mutation must increase the number of Pareto optimal solutions in the population by one.

In the second case, where there is no dominated solution in the population, a new Pareto optimal solution that satisfies the previous conditions can be obtained by moving a non-dominated solution toward the Pareto front. A non-dominated solution can be moved closer to the Pareto front by first selecting it for mutation and then mutating the correct bit. This event occurs with probability $1/(\mu n)$. Since there are at most n bits that need to be flipped, the expected time to increase the number of Pareto optimal solutions in the population is $O(\mu n^2)$. Hence, the expected waiting time until all μ individuals are Pareto optimal is bounded above by $O(\mu^2 n^2)$ and the claimed bound follows. □

We now consider some conditions on a given population that imply the existence of mutations that can improve the hypervolume indicator.

Theorem 6. *Let $1 < \mu < \frac{n}{3}$ and let $P^{(t)}$ be the population in iteration t of $(\mu+1)$ SIBEA on* LOTZ. *If $P^{(t)} \subseteq \mathscr{P}$ and there is no single mutation that results in a population with a strictly higher hypervolume indicator, then $\iota(x_i) \geq 2$ for all $x_i \in P^{(t)}$.*

PROOF. Since $1 < \mu < \frac{n}{3}$, if $P^{(t)}$ is optimal, then for all $x \in P^{(t)}$, $\iota(x) \geq 3$. Suppose $P^{(t)}$ is not optimal. If there exists a solution $x_i \in P^{(t)}$ such that $\iota(x_i) = 1$, then there must also be a solution x_j where $\iota(x_j) \geq 4$. If a strict improvement cannot be made in a single mutation, then the first condition of Lemma 2 tells us that $|\iota(x_i) - \iota(x_{i+1})| \leq 1$, which implies that $0 \leq \iota(x_{i+1}) \leq 2$ (recall here that Lemma 2 carries over to LOTZ when all points in the population are in $\mathscr{P}$). Therefore, $d(x_i) = \iota(x_i) \times \iota(x_{i+1}) \leq 2 < \iota(x_j) - 1$, and the second condition of Lemma 2 is satisfied. This contradicts the assumption that no improving mutation is possible. □

We define a *neutral move* to be the transformation of a population $P^{(t)}$ via mutation and selection to a population $P^{(t+1)}$ such that $I_H(P^{(t)}) = I_H(P^{(t+1)})$.

Lemma 3. *Let $1 < \mu < \frac{n}{3}$ and let $P^{(t)}$ be the population in iteration t of $(\mu+1)$ SIBEA on* LOTZ. *If $P^{(t)} \subseteq \mathscr{P}$ and there exists a solution $x_k \in P^{(t)}$ such that $\iota(x_k) = 1$, then using only neutral moves, it is not possible for the population to enter a state in which a strict improvement cannot occur in one mutation.*

PROOF. Suppose for contradiction that it is possible for a neutral move to result in a population $P^{(t+1)}$ from which a strict improvement cannot occur. By Theorem 6, for all $x_i \in P^{(t+1)}$, $\iota(x_i) \geq 2$. This means that to produce $P^{(t+1)}$, either x'_k or x'_{k-1} must be removed from the intermediate population $P'^{(t)}$. Furthermore, when a solution in $P^{(t)}$ is mutated to produce the intermediate population, two new intervals are produced with at least one of them equal to 1. The only configuration in which two unit intervals can be removed from the intermediate population is when the unit intervals are adjacent on the Pareto front and the solution between them is subsequently removed. Thus to produce such an intermediate population, it follows that x_k, x_{k+1} or x_{k-1} must be mutated.

In the first case, when x_k is mutated, let x' be the new solution. We have $\iota(x') = 1$, $\iota(x'_{k+1}) = \iota(x_{k+1}) - 1 \geq 1$ so that $d(x'_k) = 1 \leq d(x')$. Because this is a neutral move, $d(x') = d(x'_k) = 1$, which means $\iota(x'_{k+1}) = 1 = \iota(x') = \iota(x'_k)$.

In the second case, without loss of generality, assume that x_{k-1} is mutated to produce a new solution x'. Using the same argument, $d(x') = d(x'_{k-1}) = 1$, which implies that $\iota(x_{k-1}) = 2$ and after mutation, $\iota(x'_k) = \iota(x'_{k-1}) = \iota(x') = 1$.

Thus, as long as there is a solution x_k in $P^{(t)}$ such that $\iota(x_k) = 1$, any neutral move produces a new population $P^{(t+1)}$ such that there must exist some $x_i \in P^{(t+1)}$ with $\iota(x_i) = 1$. However, by the contrapositive of Theorem 6, a strict improvement is possible in $P^{(t+1)}$. □

If no strict improvement is possible, then $(\mu+1)$ SIBEA working on LOTZ is on a plateau. To analyze the behavior in this situation, we will appeal to a result from the theory of random walks on graphs. The cover time of a random walk on a graph is the number of steps in the walk until each vertex has been visited at least once. The following theorem is a well-known result due to Aleliunas, Karp, Lipton, Lovász, and Rackoff [1] and stated, for instance, in [16, Theorem 4.6].

Theorem 7. *Given an undirected, connected graph $G = (V, E)$ with n vertices and m edges, the cover time of a random walk on G is bounded above by $2|E|(|V|-1)$.*

Lemma 4. *Let $1 < \mu < \frac{n}{3}$ and let $P^{(t)}$ be the population in iteration t of $(\mu+1)$ SIBEA on* LOTZ. *If $P^{(t)} \subseteq \mathscr{P}$ and no strict improvement is possible, then the expected time until $(\mu+1)$ SIBEA leaves the plateau and achieves a strict improvement is $O(\mu^3 n)$.*

PROOF. Suppose no strict improvement is possible from $P^{(t)}$. By Lemma 2, $\iota(x_i) \leq d(x_j) + 1$ for all $2 \leq i, j \leq \mu$. In this situation, the solutions in the population need to be shifted around in order for a strict improvement to be possible. In this case, $(\mu+1)$ SIBEA must move first along a plateau before encountering an improving move.

By Theorem 6, for all $x_i \in P^{(t)}$, we have $\iota(x_i) \geq 2$, which implies $d(x_i) \geq 4$. If there exist two solutions $x_i, x_j \in P^{(t)}$ such that $\iota(x_i) = d(x_j) + 1 \geq 5$, a strict improvement can be made after a single neutral move. In this neutral move, either x_i or x_{i-1} is selected from the population with probability $1/\mu$ and a correct bit is flipped with probability $1/n$ to generate a new solution x' with contribution $d(x') = \iota(x_i) - 1 \geq 4$. Since there is at least one solution $x'' \in P^{(t)}$ that has the same contribution as x', it follows that x' replaces x'' to create population $P^{(t+1)}$ with probability at least $1/2$.

If this mutation is accepted, it is not possible for a subsequent mutation to revert to the previous population state.

This is because a single mutation always results in two new intervals in which at least one of them is equal to one. Since we supposed that $P^{(t)}$ had no such interval, the claim follows. Moreover, after this step, there are two adjacent intervals with values 1 and $\iota(x_i) - 1$ in the population, and a mutation that strictly improves the hypervolume indicator is possible. Again, such a mutation occurs with probability $1/(\mu n)$. Finally, we point out that after this initial step, by Lemma 3, it is not possible to enter a state in which a strict improvement is impossible. Summing up the expected time for both correct steps to occur, the expected waiting time for a strict improvement to occur in this case is $O(\mu n)$.

Otherwise, we have $\iota(x_i) < d(x_j) + 1$ for all $1 < i, j \leq \mu$. Let x_i, x_j with $i < j$ be the two closest solutions such that $|\iota(x_i) - \iota(x_j)| \geq 2$. The following two conditions are guaranteed. (1) $\iota(x_{i+1}) = \iota(x_{i+2}) = \cdots = \iota(x_{j-1}) = (\iota(x_i) + \iota(x_j))/2 = \alpha$. Without loss of generality, assume that $\iota(x_i) < \iota(x_j)$, for a solution x_k $(i < k < j)$, if $\iota(x_k) > \alpha$ or $\iota(x_k) < \alpha$ then x_k, x_j and x_i, x_k become the closest solutions accordingly. (2) $|\iota(x_i) - \iota(x_j)| = 2$. Otherwise, $|\iota(x_i) - \iota(x_j)| > 2$ implies that $|\iota(x_i) - \alpha| = |\iota(x_j) - \alpha| > 2$. This contradicts the supposition that x_i and x_j are the closest solutions that satisfy the condition.

According to Lemma 2, in order for a strict improvement to be possible, $\iota(x_i)$ and $\iota(x_j)$ must meet, implying that $j = i + 1$. In one step, the distance between x_i and x_j can be changed by either moving x_i and x_j closer or further. The probability of moving x_i toward x_j is $1/(2\mu n)$. Here, the probability 1/2 comes from the fact that after flipping a correct bit, there are at most two solutions in the population with the same contribution. Similarly, the probability of moving x_i further away from x_j is $1/(2\mu n)$, because we need only to flip the correct bit in the correct individual and maintain it in the population. Finally, by the same argument, the probability of moving x_j toward (further from) x_i is $1/(2\mu n)$. It follows that the probability that x_i and x_j are moved closer (further) is $2/(2\mu n) = 1/(\mu n)$.

After x_i and x_j become adjacent on the Pareto front, a strict improvement can be performed with probability $1/(\mu n)$. The process of shifting the distance between x_i and x_j is illustrated in the Markov chain in Figure 3. In this Markov chain, there are $\mu + 1$ states that each correspond to the distance between x_i and x_j, and a final absorbing state reachable from the zero-distance state that corresponds to an improving move.

Excluding transition probabilities that are zero, the structure of the state transition graph is a simple path. Furthermore, the transition probabilities between neighboring states in the path (excluding the absorbing state) are all equal to $1/(\mu n)$. It suffices to bound the expected time to absorption of this Markov chain. The expected time to leave any state is $\mu n/2$ and the transition probabilities to a predecessor or successor on the path are equivalent. Thus, the expected absorption time of the Markov chain is at most a factor of $\mu n/2$ slower than the cover time of an unbiased random walk on an undirected path with $\mu + 2$ vertices. The claimed bound then follows from Theorem 7. $\square$

Finally, we can state the main theorem for LOTZ which shows that the maximum hypervolume is obtained in expected polynomial time if $1 < \mu < \frac{n}{3}$ holds.

Theorem 8. *Choosing $1 < \mu < \frac{n}{3}$, the expected optimization time of $(\mu + 1)$ SIBEA on* LOTZ *is $O(\mu^3 n^3)$.*

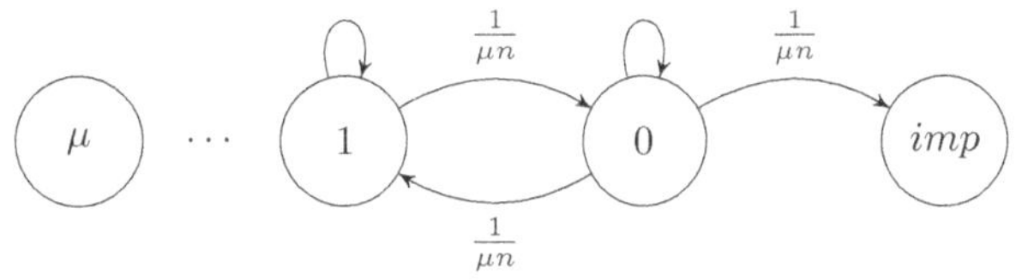

Figure 3: Markov chain for interval dynamics for $(\mu + 1)$ SIBEA on LOTZ**.**

PROOF. If a strict improvement is possible, the expected waiting time until the algorithm discovers that improvement is bounded by $O(\mu n)$. There are at most $O(n^2)$ strict improvements, which implies that the algorithm needs at most $O(\mu n^3)$ to reach the maximum population hypervolume, as long as the algorithm never visits a state from which there are no strict improvements.

On the other hand, if the algorithm reaches a state from which a strict improvement is not possible, it must then deal with a plateau. In this case, by Lemma 4, the waiting time until the algorithm leaves the plateau and discovers a strict improvement is $O(\mu^3 n)$. The total number of improvements with respect to the hypervolume is $O(n^2)$, which implies that $(\mu + 1)$ SIBEA spends at most $O(\mu^3 n^3)$ steps in such situations.

Taking the maximum of the expected times spent in the two different situations, the expected optimization time of $(\mu + 1)$ SIBEA on LOTZ is $O(\mu^3 n^3)$ if $1 < \mu < n/3$. $\square$

5. CONCLUSIONS

We have contributed to the theoretical understanding of hypervolume-based evolutionary algorithms and have developed rigorous results on the runtime of these algorithms. Our results specifically show that LOTZ is easy to optimize for a wide range of μ. Furthermore, we have shown that even simple problems such as OneMinMax can lead to plateaus that are hard to leave for $(\mu + 1)$ SIBEA . This implies that the optimization time of this algorithm becomes exponential when starting with such a worst-case initial population.

Although our analyses provide new insights and cover important values of μ, it would be very desirable to have similar results for all possible values of μ.

6. REFERENCES

[1] Romas Aleliunas, Richard M. Karp, Richard J. Lipton, László Lovász, and Charles Rackoff. Random walks, universal traversal sequences, and the complexity of maze problems. In *FOCS*, pages 218–223. IEEE, 1979.

[2] Anne Auger, Johannes Bader, Dimo Brockhoff, and Eckart Zitzler. Investigating and exploiting the bias of the weighted hypervolume to articulate user preferences. In *Proc. 11th annual Conference on Genetic and Evolutionary Computation (GECCO '09)*, pages 563–570. ACM Press, 2009.

[3] Anne Auger, Johannes Bader, Dimo Brockhoff, and Eckart Zitzler. Hypervolume-based multiobjective optimization: Theoretical foundations and practical implications. *Theoretical Computer Science*, 425:75–103, 2012.

[4] Rudolf Berghammer, Tobias Friedrich, and Frank Neumann. Convergence of set-based multi-objective

optimization, indicators and deteriorative cycles. *Theoretical Computer Science*, 456:2–17, 2012.

[5] Nicola Beume, Boris Naujoks, and Michael T. M. Emmerich. SMS-EMOA: Multiobjective selection based on dominated hypervolume. *European Journal of Operational Research*, 181:1653–1669, 2007.

[6] Karl Bringmann and Tobias Friedrich. Approximating the volume of unions and intersections of high-dimensional geometric objects. *Computational Geometry: Theory and Applications*, 43:601–610, 2010.

[7] Karl Bringmann and Tobias Friedrich. Approximation quality of the hypervolume indicator. *Artif. Intell.*, 195:265–290, 2013.

[8] Dimo Brockhoff. Optimal μ-distributions for the hypervolume indicator for problems with linear bi-objective fronts: Exact and exhaustive results. In *Proc. 8th International Conference on Simulated Evolution And Learning (SEAL '10)*, volume 6457 of *LNCS*, pages 24–34, 2010.

[9] Dimo Brockhoff, Tobias Friedrich, and Frank Neumann. Analyzing hypervolume indicator based algorithms. In Günter Rudolph, Thomas Jansen, Simon M. Lucas, Carlo Poloni, and Nicola Beume, editors, *Parallel Problem Solving from Nature–PPSN X*, volume 5199 of *Lecture Notes in Computer Science*, pages 651–660. Springer, 2008.

[10] C. A. Coello Coello, D. A. Van Veldhuizen, and G. B. Lamont. *Evolutionary Algorithms for Solving Multi-Objective Problems.* Kluwer Academic Publishers, New York, 2002.

[11] K. Deb. *Multi-objective optimization using evolutionary algorithms.* Wiley, Chichester, UK, 2001.

[12] Michael T. M. Emmerich, Nicola Beume, and Boris Naujoks. An EMO algorithm using the hypervolume measure as selection criterion. In *Proc. Third International Conference on Evolutionary Multi-Criterion Optimization (EMO '05)*, pages 62–76. Springer, 2005.

[13] Oliver Giel and Per Kristian Lehre. On the effect of populations in evolutionary multi-objective optimisation. *Evolutionary Computation*, 18(3):335–356, 2010.

[14] Edda Happ, Daniel Johannsen, Christian Klein, and Frank Neumann. Rigorous analyses of fitness-proportional selection for optimizing linear functions. In Conor Ryan and Maarten Keijzer, editors, *GECCO*, pages 953–960. ACM, 2008.

[15] Marco Laumanns, Lothar Thiele, and Eckart Zitzler. Running time analysis of multiobjective evolutionary algorithms on pseudo-boolean functions. *IEEE Trans. Evolutionary Computation*, 8(2):170–182, 2004.

[16] Frank Neumann and Carsten Witt. *Bioinspired Computation in Combinatorial Optimization – Algorithms and Their Computational Complexity.* Springer, 2010.

[17] Eckart Zitzler and Simon Künzli. Indicator-based selection in multiobjective search. In *Proc. 8th International Conference Parallel Problem Solving from Nature (PPSN VIII)*, volume 3242 of *LNCS*, pages 832–842. Springer, 2004.

Improved Runtime Analysis of the Simple Genetic Algorithm

Pietro S. Oliveto*
School of Computer Science
University of Birmingham
United Kingdom
p.s.oliveto@cs.bham.ac.uk

Carsten Witt
DTU Compute
Technical University of Denmark
Denmark
cawi@dtu.dk

ABSTRACT

A runtime analysis of the Simple Genetic Algorithm (**SGA**) for the ONEMAX problem has recently been presented proving that the algorithm requires exponential time with overwhelming probability. This paper presents an improved analysis which overcomes some limitations of our previous one. Firstly, the new result holds for population sizes up to $\mu \leq n^{1/4-\varepsilon}$ which is an improvement up to a power of 2 larger. Secondly, we present a technique to bound the diversity of the population that does not require a bound on its bandwidth. Apart from allowing a stronger result, we believe this is a major improvement towards the reusability of the techniques in future systematic analyses of GAs. Finally, we consider the more natural **SGA** using selection with replacement rather than without replacement although the results hold for both algorithmic versions. Experiments are presented to explore the limits of the new and previous mathematical techniques.

Categories and Subject Descriptors

F.2.0 [**Theory of Computation**]: Analysis of Algorithms and Problem Complexity

Keywords

Simple Genetic Algorithm, Crossover, Runtime Analysis

1. INTRODUCTION

For many years it has been a challenge to analyze the time complexity of Genetic Algorithms (GAs) using stochastic selection together with crossover and mutation. A first step towards a systematic analysis of GAs has been recently presented through a runtime analysis of the *Simple Genetic Algorithm* (**SGA**) for ONEMAX in our previous work [17]. The main result is the proof that the **SGA** has exponential runtime with overwhelming probability for population sizes up to $\mu \leq n^{1/8-\varepsilon}$ for some arbitrary small constant ε and problem size n.

The main novelties of the work were two. On one hand, a rigorous proof that the **SGA** cannot optimize ONEMAX in polynomial time was provided (1). The inefficient hillclimbing performance of the **SGA** due to the loss of selection pressure was well known in the Evolutionary Computation (EC) community since the algorithm has been well studied in literature. In fact, Goldberg [5] reports experimental results in his seminal book showing the loss of selection pressure of the algorithm and suggesting fitness scaling mechanisms to solve the problem. Nevertheless a rigorous proof was yet not available. On the other hand, the major driving force was the obtainment of a first basis of mathematical techniques towards systematic runtime analyses of GAs using at the same time mutation, crossover and stochastic selection (2). Undoubtedly significant progress has been achieved in recent years in the runtime analysis of EAs [1]. Nowadays, the performance of simple EAs can be analyzed on well-known combinatorial optimization problems [14]. Furthermore, major advances have been achieved in the analysis of population-based EAs with stochastic selection through techniques such as the *simplified negative-drift theorem* [16], the *negative drift in populations* theorem [9] and the *fitness levels for non-elitist populations* technique [10]. However, these techniques cannot be directly applied to the analyses of more realistic GAs incorporating a crossover operator. Several results were indeed available proving that crossover is useful [7, 20, 15, 2, 8, 12, 19], but they rely heavily on elitist selection operators. Moreover, mostly only upper bounds on the running time of crossover-based algorithms were available.

In this paper we present an improved runtime analysis of the **SGA** as a first step towards overcoming the limitations of our previous analysis. The first limitation was the bound on the population size $\mu = O(n^{1/8-\varepsilon})$ for the results to hold. The analysis presented here allows population sizes up to a power of 2 larger. Another significant limitation was the necessity for a bound on the so-called *bandwidth* of the population from which a measure on the diversity of the population was derived. The bandwidth was defined as $h - \ell$ where h is the best ONEMAX value in a population and ℓ the worst ONEMAX value, while diversity s was defined as the number of *non-converged* bit positions, that is both bit values are taken by individuals of the population. The whole analysis depended on the fact that if the diversity of the population is

*P.S. Oliveto was supported by EPSRC under grant N. EP/H028900/1

GECCO'13, July 6–10, 2013, Amsterdam, The Netherlands.

sufficiently low, then the behavior of fitness proportional selection is very close to that of uniform selection. The crucial observation to derive a bound on the diversity s was that $h - \ell \leq s$, i.e., the bandwidth cannot be larger than the number of non-converged bits. However, the achievement of a bound on the bandwidth for not too small population sizes μ is a non-trivial task. Furthermore, the bandwidth is heavily dependent on the problem at hand which seriously limits the generality and reusability of the technique. In this paper we present a new technique to bound the diversity of the population that does not require a bound on its bandwidth. Apart from allowing a stronger runtime result, we believe that this constitutes a major improvement towards the reusability of the presented technique in future analyses of the **SGA**.

Roughly speaking, in our previous work we measured the number of one-bits that individuals of the population have at a given position i in the bitstring with a random variable X_t^i and showed that, if the population size is not too large, X_t^i has a very similar behavior to that of a martingale (i.e., the expected value of the random variable remains the same from one step to the next). This enabled us to define a potential function $Y_t^i := (X_t^i - \mu/2)^2$ exhibiting a positive drift (i.e., the bits converge). However, for larger population sizes the positive drift does not necessarily hold since the X_t^i-process starts to resemble a submartingale (i.e., the expected value of the random variable can increase from one step to the next) and the Y_t^i-process might drift towards 0 even if the X_t^i-process increases. The proof strategy presented herein defines a different potential function Y_t^i such that a positive drift can be proved even if the underlying X_t^i-process closely resembles a submartingale. This allows the proof of exponential runtime up to population sizes $\mu \leq n^{1/4-\varepsilon}$. From the analysis an intuition can be derived that for larger populations (i.e., $\mu = \Omega(\sqrt{n})$) the bit positions no longer converge sufficiently disabling the effectiveness of the mathematical techniques presented herein and in our previous work [17]. To this end, in aid of future research, we present some experiments showing how the diversity increases rapidly when the population size reaches values around $\mu = c\sqrt{n}$ for various constants $c > 0$.

The final improvement compared to our previous work [17] is a slight variation in the algorithm. We change the selection operator to select individuals from the population *with replacement* rather than *without replacement*. We feel that the chosen selection operator is the more natural variant, hence redefined the algorithm. In any case, since the probability of choosing an individual for selection twice is $O(1/\mu)$, this does not really affect the analysis. The results in the paper would also hold for the variant in [17], as could that variant also be used in this paper.

The rest of the paper is structured as follows. In Section 2 we discuss previous related work, define the **SGA** precisely and outline the new proof strategy in greater detail. In Section 3.1 we discuss the submartingale property of the random variable X_t^i and present a lower bound on the drift of the new potential function Y_t^i. Using the drift we derive an upper bound on the time for many bits to "almost converge" (i.e., to achieve low diversity) in Section 3.2. Finally in Section 3.3, we can apply the machinery from [17] to prove exponential time for the **SGA** with population sizes up to $\mu \leq n^{1/4-\varepsilon}$. The experiments focusing on understanding at what population size the diversity starts increasing rapidly are presented in the Conclusions together with final remarks. Due to space restrictions, the proofs of Section 3.3 that are essentially the same as those in [17] and some proofs of helper results have been omitted.

2. ALGORITHM AND PROOF STRATEGY

The results that will be presented herein are a continuation of previous work. Happ et al. performed the first runtime analysis of fitness proportional selection (f.p.s.) by considering only one individual and bitwise mutation [6]. This work was extended by Neumann et al. to consider arbitrary population sizes again on a mutation-only EA [13]. In particular, it was proved that the runtime of an EA using f.p.s. and bitwise mutation for OneMax is exponential with overwhelming probability (w. o. p.) whatever the polynomial population size. Also if the population is not too large (i.e., logarithmic in the problem size), then the algorithm cannot optimize any function with unique optimum in polynomial time w. o. p. Finally, in [17] we presented the first analysis of the complete **SGA** for OneMax using selection without replacement and proving exponential runtime for population sizes up to $\mu \leq n^{1/8-\varepsilon}$ for some arbitrary small constant ε and problem size n. The well-known **SGA** with the more natural selection with replacement is displayed in Figure 1.

Algorithm (SGA) [5]

1. Create a parent population P consisting of μ randomly chosen individuals;
2. $C := \emptyset$.
3. While $|C| < \mu$ do
    - **Fitness proportional selection:** Select two individuals x' and x'' from P according to fitness-proportional selection with replacement.
    - **Uniform crossover:** Create an offspring x by setting each bit $x(i) = x'(i)$ with probability 1/2 and $x(i) = x''(i)$ otherwise, for $1 \leq i \leq n$.
    - **Standard Bit Mutation:** Flip each bit $x(i)$ of x with probability $1/n$, for $1 \leq i \leq n$.
    - $C := C \cup \{x\}$.
4. Set $P := C$ and go to 2.

Figure 1: The Simple GA

In the following we outline the improved proof strategy.

Let X_t denote the number of individuals with a one-bit at position 1 (the same analysis applies to all other positions) at time t. The old analysis in [17] started out with an idealized process, where individuals were selected uniformly. In this case, $\mathrm{E}[X_{t+1} \mid X_t] = X_t$, i.e., the process is a martingale. This implied that the process $Y_t := (X_t - \mu/2)^2$ was exhibiting positive drift $\mathrm{E}[Y_{t+1} - Y_t \mid X_t] = \mathrm{Var}[X_t]$. The variable drift theorem could be used that a Y-value of $(\mu/2)^2$ was obtained after an expected number $O(\mu \log \mu)$ steps, which meant that all individuals either had a one-bit or a zero-bit at position 1 then. The bit is called *converged* then and this property was used to bound the effect of crossover.

Furthermore, the old analysis exploited that the actual process, where fitness-proportional instead of uniform selection is used, is very close to the idealized process under strong assumptions, including the bound $\mu = O(n^{1/8-\varepsilon})$.

Then the X_t were so close to a martingale that Y_t still was drifting towards its maximum value. However, for larger μ the following problem occurs: the actual process (if mutation is ignored) is a submartingale, i. e., $\mathrm{E}[X_{t+1} \mid X_t] \geq X_t$, i. e., there is positive drift $\mathrm{E}[X_{t+1} - X_t \mid X_t] > 0$. Unless the strong assumptions were made, the drift of the X_t-process was too strong to maintain positive drift of the Y_t-process. For instance, if $X_t = \mu/4$, then the positive drift of the X_t-process towards the "middle" $\mu/2$ could imply a negative drift of the Y_t-process.

We can overcome this difficulty to some extent by redefining $Y_t := X_t^2$. Our aim is to show that the Y_t-process has a drift that can be bounded from below by a useful value (whereas the drift of the X_t-process is not necessarily strong enough). The expected first hitting time for either 0 or at least $\mu^2(1 - O(1/n))^2$, i. e., the expected time for the bit to "almost" converge, will be bounded by $O(\mu \log^2 \mu + n^{\varepsilon/16})$. As long as $\mu = O(n^{1/4-\varepsilon})$, many almost converged bits will hinder the process from reaching the optimum. On the way towards this bound, we need:

1. a formal proof that the X_t-process resembles a submartingale (Lemma 2),
2. a lower bound on the drift of the Y_t-process (Lemma 3),
3. an application of the variable drift theorem (Lemma 6). Here the additional difficutly arises that the drift is not monotone in the distance to the optimum, which is required by the standard version of the variable drift theorem. Fortunately, there is a more recent generalization of the variable drift theorem in Feldmann and Kötzing [3] that can be adapted to our case. In order to apply it, some technical conditions have to be verified, e. g., that the maximum jump size of the Y_t-process is bounded (Lemma 8).

With the new convergence analysis, we can apply the machinery from our previous work [17]. Roughly speaking, a potential function collapsing the whole population into a single value is defined and a drift away from the optimum is proven, given that there is a sufficient number of converged bits; see Section 3.3.

3. DETAILED THEORETICAL ANALYSIS

3.1 "Submartingale" Property and Drift

We analyze the X_t-process and find out that $\mathrm{E}[X_{t+1} \mid X_t] \geq X_t(1 - 2/n)$, see Lemma 2. If the term $-2/n$ (which is due to mutation) was not present, this would characterize the process as a submartingale. As $\mu = o(n)$ and $X_t \leq \mu$, the term $-2/n$ is not significant, which intuitively means that the process still resembles a submartingale. To prove the desired property, we need a helper result.

LEMMA 1. *Consider the random population of the* **SGA** *on* ONEMAX *at an arbitrary point of time. Let k be the number of individuals with a one-bit at position 1. Then an application of the fitness-proportional selection operator will select such an individual with probability at least k/μ.*

PROOF. Let a random population $P = (x_1, \dots, x_\mu)$ at the considered point in time be given, ordered in an arbitrary but fixed way. Let p_i, where $1 \leq i \leq \mu$, be the probability of x_i having a one-bit at position 1. Furthermore, let s_i be the probability of fitness-proportional selection selecting x_i.

For arbitrary $i, j \in \{1, \dots, \mu\}$, we claim $p_i \geq p_j \iff f(x_i) \geq f(x_j) \iff s_i \geq s_j$. To see this, note that conditioning on a certain number r of one-bits in an individual means that each position is 1 with probability r/n. This is a consequence of the unbiased variation operators [11]. Hence, $p_i = f(x_i)/n \geq f(x_j)/n = p_j$ if and only if $f(x_i) \geq f(x_j)$. The equivalence $f(x_i) \geq f(x_j) \iff s_i \geq s_j$ is immediate.

Consequently, if the individuals are listed according to decreasing fitness $f(x_1) \geq \dots \geq f(x_\mu)$, we obtain $p_1 \geq \dots \geq p_\mu$ and $s_1 \geq \dots \geq s_\mu$. Let p^* by the probability of selecting an individual with a one-bit at position 1 in a single selection trial, which is the probability we have to bound in the lemma. By definition, $p^* = s_1 p_1 + \dots + s_\mu p_\mu$. Since the s_i form a probability distribution, Chebyshev's sum inequality yields $p^* \geq (p_1 + \dots + p_\mu)/\mu$. Conditioning on that the number of one-bits at position 1 equals k, we have $p_1 + \dots + p_\mu = k$ and the lemma follows. □

LEMMA 2. *The random variable X_{t+1} is the sum of μ independent Bernoulli trials with common success probability p, where $p \geq 1/n$ if $X_t = 0$, $p \geq X_t/\mu$ if $X_t \leq \mu/2$, and $p \geq (X_t/\mu)(1 - 2/n)$ otherwise. Moreover, $\mathrm{E}[X_{t+1} \mid X_t] \geq X_t(1 - 2/n)$ and $\mathrm{E}[X_{t+1} \mid X_t = 0] \geq 1 - e^{-\mu/n}$.*

PROOF. We consider the creation of a single individual. For it to have a one-bit (at position 1), either the result of crossover must be a one-bit and mutation must not flip it, or the result of crossover must be a zero-bit and mutation must flip it. The result of crossover is a one-bit for sure if both parents have a one-bit, and it is a one-bit with probability 1/2 if the parents differ at the position (which happens if the first parent has a one and the second a zero or the other way round). Let s be the probability of fitness-proportional choosing an individual with a one-bit. We get

$$
\begin{aligned}
p &= s(1-s)\frac{1}{2}\left(1 - \frac{1}{n}\right) + (1-s)s\frac{1}{2}\left(1 - \frac{1}{n}\right) + s^2\left(1 - \frac{1}{n}\right) \\
&\quad + s(1-s)\frac{1}{2}\frac{1}{n} + (1-s)s\frac{1}{2}\frac{1}{n} + (1-s)^2\frac{1}{n} \\
&= s(1-s) + s^2 - \frac{1}{n}(s^2 - (1-s)^2) = s - \frac{2s-1}{n}.
\end{aligned}
$$

The last expression is $1/n$ if $s = 0$. It is monotone increasing in s and bounded from below by s if $s \leq 1/2$. Moreover, $s \geq X_t/\mu$ by Lemma 1. Together, if $X_t/\mu \leq 1/2$, then $p \geq X_t/\mu - (2X_t\mu - 1)/n \geq X_t/\mu$. Otherwise, we estimate $p \geq s - 1/n \geq X_t/\mu - 1/n \geq X_t/\mu(1 - 2/n)$. This proves the statement on p.

The bound on $\mathrm{E}[X_{t+1} \mid X_t]$ follows immediately from the bound on p since the number of trials equals μ. If $X_t = 0$, then $X_{t+1} \geq 1$ if at least one out of μ trials with success probability $1/n$ is a success. The probability is $1 - (1 - 1/n)^\mu \geq 1 - e^{-\mu/n}$, which proves the bound on $\mathrm{E}[X_{t+1} \mid X_t = 0]$. □

Now we consider the new process $Y_t = X_t^2$ with the aim to prove that it drifts. Later, this drift will allow us to bound the time for bits to converge.

LEMMA 3. *For $t \geq 0$ it holds $\mathrm{E}[X_{t+1}^2 - X_t^2 \mid X_t] \geq \mathrm{E}[(X_{t+1} - (X_t - 2/n))^2 \mid X_t] - 4X_t/n \geq \mathrm{E}[(X_{t+1} - \mathrm{E}[X_{t+1} \mid X_t])^2 \cdot \mathbb{1}\{X_{t+1} \geq \mathrm{E}[X_{t+1} \mid X_t]\} \mid X_t] - 4X_t/n$. Finally, $\mathrm{E}[X_{t+1}^2 - X_t^2 \mid X_t = 0] \geq 1 - e^{-\mu/n}$.*

PROOF. The conditional expectation on $X_t = 0$ follows immediately from Lemma 2. We now study the second inequality in the first statement of the lemma. Using Lemma 2, $X_{t+1} \geq E[X_{t+1} \mid X_t]$ implies $X_{t+1} \geq X_t - 2/n$, so that the expression $X_{t+1} - (X_t - 2/n)$ to be squared is non-negative if the indicator function is non-zero. Using Lemma 2 again, we obtain $X_{t+1} - (X_t - 2/n) \geq X_{t+1} - E[X_{t+1} \mid X_t]$ and the desired inquality follows.

The first inequality follows from this by elementary manipulations. More precisely,

$$
\begin{aligned}
&E[(X_{t+1} - (X_t - 2/n))^2] \\
&\quad = E[X_{t+1}^2] - E[2X_{t+1}(X_t - 2/n) + (X_t - 2/n)^2] \\
&\quad \leq E[X_{t+1}^2] - E[2(X_t - 2/n)^2 - (X_t - 2/n)^2] \\
&\quad \leq E[X_{t+1}^2] - E[X_t^2] + 4X_t/n,
\end{aligned}
$$

where the first estimation used Lemma 2 again. □

The aim is now to show in Lemma 5 that X_{t+1} with constant probability exceeds its expectation by a considerable amount, which, together with Lemma 3, will allow us to bound the drift of the Y-process (Lemma 6). To show the deviation, we make use of the following well-known result from probability theory [4] and use it later in Lemma 5.

LEMMA 4 (BERRY-ESSEEN INEQU.). *Let $X_1, \dots, X_\mu$ be independent, identically distributed random variables with $E[X_i] = 0$, $E[X_i^2] = \sigma^2 > 0$, and $E[|X_i|^3] = \rho < \infty$ for $1 \leq i \leq \mu$. Then there is a constant $C > 0$ such that the cumulative distribution function (cdf.) F_Y of $Y := (X_1 + \dots + X_\mu)/(\sigma\sqrt{\mu})$ satisfies*

$$|F_Y(x) - \Phi(x)| \leq \frac{C\rho}{\sigma^3\sqrt{\mu}}$$

for all $x \in \mathbb{R}$ (where $\Phi(x)$ denotes the cdf. of the standard normal distribution).

LEMMA 5. *Let X be the sum of μ independent Bernoulli trials with success probability at least r/μ each, for some $r \in [0, \mu]$. Let $\ell := \min\{r, \mu - r\}$. Then*

$$\text{Prob}[X \geq r + \sqrt{\ell/2}] = \Omega(1).$$

PROOF. Within this proof, we let X_i denote the $\{0,1\}$-random variable corresponding to the i-th trial, $1 \leq i \leq \mu$. In order to apply Lemma 4, we pessimistically assume that all X_i have success probability exactly r/μ. We introduce $X_i' := X_i - r/\mu$ and note that $E[X_i'] = \frac{r}{\mu} - \frac{r}{\mu} = 0$ and

$$
\begin{aligned}
\sigma^2 := E[X_i'^2] &= \frac{r}{\mu}\left(1 - \frac{r}{\mu}\right)^2 + \left(1 - \frac{r}{\mu}\right)\left(-\frac{r}{\mu}\right)^2 \\
&= \frac{r}{\mu}\left(1 - \frac{r}{\mu}\right) \\
\rho := E[|X_i'|^3] &= \frac{r}{\mu}\left(1 - \frac{r}{\mu}\right)^3 + \left(1 - \frac{r}{\mu}\right)\left(\frac{r}{\mu}\right)^3 \\
&\leq \frac{r}{\mu}\left(1 - \frac{r}{\mu}\right).
\end{aligned}
$$

Consider the random variable Y as defined in Lemma 4 and note that $\sigma\sqrt{\mu} = \sqrt{r(\mu - r)/\mu} \geq \sqrt{\min\{r, \mu - r\}/2}$. Hence, $X \geq r + \sqrt{\ell/2} = E[X] + \sqrt{\ell/2}$ is implied by $Y \geq E[Y] + 1$. The lemma yields

$$
\begin{aligned}
\text{Prob}[Y \leq E[Y] + 1] &\leq \Phi(1) + \frac{C\rho}{\sigma^3\sqrt{\mu}} \\
&\leq \Phi(1) + \frac{C\sqrt{\mu}}{\sqrt{\mu(\mu - r)}} \leq \Phi(1) + \frac{2C}{\sqrt{\ell}}.
\end{aligned}
$$

If ℓ is greater than a sufficiently large constant, then the last bound is less than 1 and the theorem is proved in this case. Otherwise, we have $\ell = O(1)$ and distinguish between two subcases. If $r \geq \mu/2$, we obtain $\text{Prob}[X = \mu] \geq (1 - \ell/\mu)^\mu = \Omega(1)$. Otherwise, we note that $\text{Prob}[X = s] \geq \binom{\mu}{s}(\ell/\mu)^s(1 - \ell/\mu)^s = \Omega(1)$ for any constant $s \geq 0$. Hence, $\text{Prob}[X \geq r + \sqrt{\ell/2}] = \Omega(1)$ in any case. □

We can now bound the drift of the Y-process.

LEMMA 6. *For $t \geq 0$, $E[Y_{t+1} - Y_t \mid X_t] = \Omega(\min\{X_t, \mu - X_t\}) - 4X_t/n$. There is a constant $c > 0$ s. t. $E[Y_{t+1} - Y_t \mid X_t] = \Omega(\min\{X_t, \mu - X_t\})$ if $X_t \leq \mu(1 - c/n)$ for sufficiently large n. Finally, $E[Y_{t+1} - Y_t \mid X_t = 0] \geq 1 - e^{-\mu/n}$.*

PROOF. Recall that $Y_t = X_t^2$ for all $t \geq 0$. According to Lemma 2, X_{t+1} stochastically dominates $\text{Bin}(\mu, (X_t/\mu)(1 - 2/n))$. Moreover, according to Lemma 3, it is sufficient to establish a deviation of X_{t+1} above its mean in order to bound the drift of the Y-process. Applying Lemma 5 with $r = X_t(1 - 2/n)$, the event

$$X_{t+1} \geq E[X_{t+1}] + \sqrt{\frac{\min\{X_t(1 - 2/n), \mu - X_t(1 - 2/n)\}}{2}}$$

occurs with probability at least c' for some constant $c' > 0$ and sufficiently large n. Hence,

$$
\begin{aligned}
&E[(X_{t+1} - E[X_{t+1} \mid X_t])^2 \cdot \mathbb{1}\{X_{t+1} \geq E[X_{t+1} \mid X_t]\} \mid X_t] \\
&\quad \geq (c'/2)\min\{X_t, \mu - X_t\}
\end{aligned}
$$

for sufficiently large n, such that an application of Lemma 3 completes the proof of the first statement in the lemma.

A sufficient condition for the second statement to follow from the first one is given by $4X_t/n \leq (c'/4)\min\{X_t, \mu - X_t\}$. For sufficiently large n, $4X_t/n \leq X_t$ is satisfied. The condition $4X_t/n \leq (c'/4)(\mu - X_t)$ is equivalent to $X_t \leq \mu/(1 + 16/(c'n))$, and the last expression is at most $\mu(1 - 16/(c'n))$. Hence, the second statement is obtained with $c := 16/c'$. The third statement from the theorem is just a reformulation of the last statement from Lemma 2. □

So far, we have established a positive drift of the Y-process as long as $X_t \leq \mu(1 - c/n)$. This drift is dependent on X_t. Unlike the analysis in [17], the drift is not monotone in X_t. Therefore, the standard variant of the variable drift theorem (see [18] for the most recent version) cannot be applied. We use the following generalization (building upon [3]) instead.

LEMMA 7 (EXTENDING [3]). *Let $(Z_t)_{t\geq 0}$, be a stochastic process over $\{0\} \cup [z_{\min}, \infty)$, where $z_{\min} > 0$. Suppose there exists two functions $h, d\colon [z_{\min}, \infty) \to \mathbb{R}^+$, where h is integrable, and a constant $c \geq 1$ such that for all $t \geq 0$*

(1) $E[Z_t - Z_{t+1} \mid Z_0, \dots, Z_t \cap Z_t \geq z_{\min}] \geq h(Z_t)$,

(2) $\frac{E[(Z_{t+1} - Z_t) \cdot \mathbb{1}\{Z_{t+1} > Z_t\} \mid Z_t \geq z_{\min}]}{E[(Z_t - Z_{t+1}) \cdot \mathbb{1}\{Z_{t+1} < Z_t\} \mid Z_t \geq z_{\min}]} \leq \frac{1}{2c^2}$,

(3) $|Z_t - Z_{t+1}| \leq d(Z_t)$ *if* $Z_t \geq z_{\min}$,

(4) for all $x, y \geq z_{\min}$ with $x \leq y \leq x + \min\{d(x), d(y)\}$, it holds $h(x) \leq ch(y)$.

Then it holds for the first hitting time $T := \min\{t \mid Z_t = 0\}$ that

$$E[T \mid Z_0] \leq 2c\left(\frac{z_{\min}}{h(z_{\min})} + \int_{z_{\min}}^{Z_0} \frac{1}{h(x)}\,\mathrm{d}x\right).$$

We will apply the previous lemma w. r. t. the process $Z_t := \mu^2 - Y_t = \mu^2 - X_t^2$, where the aim is to minimize the Z-value. According to Lemma 6, we get

$$\mathrm{E}[Z_t - Z_{t+1} \mid X_t] = \Omega(\min\{\sqrt{\mu^2 - Z_t}, \mu - \sqrt{\mu^2 - Z_t}\})$$

if $1 \leq X_t \leq \mu(1-c/n)$ and $\mathrm{E}[Z_t - Z_{t+1} \mid X_t = 0] \geq 1 - e^{-\mu/n}$.

Loosely speaking, the drift is a parabolic function with a maximum at $Z_t = 3\mu^2/4$. In particular, it is monotone increasing in Z_t only if $Z_t < 3\mu^2/4$. In order to apply Lemma 7, we need a bound on the maximum change of the process and the ratio of positive and negative drift. From now on, let us assume that $p \leq (X_t/\mu)(1 + 2/n)$ (which, proven along the lines of Lemma 2, holds for the **SGA** with uniform selection, whose individuals are distributed symmetrically around $n/2$; fitness-proportional selection only increases the probability of X_t converging to μ). This gives rise to the following lemma.

LEMMA 8. *Let $\mu = o(n)$ and $n^{\varepsilon/16} \leq X_t \leq \mu - n^{\varepsilon/16}$. Then $\mathrm{Prob}[|X_{t+1} - X_t| \geq (X_t)^{2/3}] = e^{-\Omega(n^{\varepsilon/48})}$. Moreover, $\frac{\mathrm{E}[(Z_t - Z_{t+1})\cdot \mathbb{1}\{Z_{t+1} < Z_t\} \mid X_t]}{\mathrm{E}[(Z_{t+1} - Z_t)\cdot \mathbb{1}\{Z_{t+1} > Z_t\} \mid X_t]} = 1 - \Omega(1)$.*

PROOF. The first statement follows from Chernoff bounds with $\delta = X_t^{-1/3}$ and using that $\mathrm{E}[X_{t+1} \mid X_t] \geq X_t(1 - 2/n) \geq X_t - 1/2$ as well as $\mathrm{E}[X_{t+1} \mid X_t] \leq X_t(1 + 2/n) \leq X_t + 1/2$ for n large enough.

For the second statement, we first assume $X_t \leq \mu/2$ and observe that $\mathrm{E}[(Z_t - Z_{t+1}) \cdot \mathbb{1}\{Z_{t+1} < Z_t\} \mid X_t] - \mathrm{E}[(Z_{t+1} - Z_t) \cdot \mathbb{1}\{Z_{t+1} > Z_t\} \mid X_t] = \Omega(X_t)$ according to Lemma 6. Moreover, by analogous calculations to Lemma 5, we get $\mathrm{E}[(Z_{t+1} - Z_t) \cdot \mathbb{1}\{Z_{t+1} > Z_t\} \mid X_t] = O(X_t)$. Combining the two observations, we obtain $\mathrm{E}[(Z_{t+1} - Z_t) \cdot \mathbb{1}\{Z_{t+1} < Z_t\} \mid X_t]/\mathrm{E}[(Z_t - Z_{t+1}) \cdot \mathbb{1}\{Z_{t+1} < Z_t\} \mid X_t] = 1 + \Omega(1)$. The case $X_t \geq \mu/2$ is proved analogously with X_t replaced by $\mu - X_t$. □

Taking everything together, we can bound the time for a bit to converge.

LEMMA 9. *Let $\mu = o(n)$. Then the expected time for an arbitrary bit position to reach either 0 or at least $\mu(1 - O(1/n))$ one-bits is $O(\mu \log^2 n + n^{\varepsilon/16})$.*

PROOF. We analyze the Z-process defined above. Throughout this lemma, we assume $\mathrm{Prob}[|X_{t+1} - X_t| \leq (X_t)^{2/3}]$ for a period of $\Theta(\mu \ln^2 n)$ steps. As $\mu = o(n)$, we obtain from Lemma 8 a failure probability of $o(n)\cdot e^{-\Omega(n^{\varepsilon/48})} = e^{-\Omega(n^{\varepsilon/48})}$. Moreover, as the maximum change of the Z-process is μ^2, the jumps of larger size can contribute only $\mu^2 n^{-\Omega(n^{\varepsilon/48})}$ to the drift $\mathrm{E}[Z_t - Z_{t+1} \mid X_t]$. Hence, the assumption can reduce the drift by only $e^{-\Omega(n^{\varepsilon/48})}$.

The aim is to apply Lemma 7 on the Z-process (if $n^{\varepsilon/16} \leq X_t \leq \mu - n^{\varepsilon/16}$ and using trivial estimations otherwise). Since Lemma 6 does not yield a bound on the drift if $X_t > \mu(1 - c/n)$, we stop our considerations in this case. Now, in the analysis of the Z-process the drift from Lemma 6 is assumed to hold also for $X_t > \mu(1 - c/n)$. Let us now consider the first point in time T such that $Z_t = 0 \vee Z_t = \mu^2$. This is not less than the first point in time T' such that $X_t = 0 \vee X_t > \mu(1 - c/n)$.

We define $h(z) := C\min\{\sqrt{\mu^2 - x}, \mu - \sqrt{\mu^2 - x}\}$ for some sufficiently small constant C. Note that $h(Z_{t+1}) \leq h(Z_t)$ if $Z_{t+1} \leq Z_t \leq 3\mu^2/4$ and $h(Z_{t+1}) \leq (1 + x^{-1/3})h(Z_t)$ otherwise (assuming the maximum jump size in both cases). Hence, in conjunction with Lemma 8, we can satisfy Lemma 7 with $c = 1 + n^{-\varepsilon/48}$ (since $X_t \geq n^{\varepsilon/16}$), $d(x) = x^{2/3}$ and a minimum positive Z-value of $z_{\min} := \mu^2 - (\mu - 1)^2 = 2\mu - 1$ to get

$$E[T \mid Z_0] \leq 2c\left(\frac{z_{\min}}{h(z_{\min})} + \int_{z_{\min}}^{Z_0} \frac{1}{h(z)}\,\mathrm{d}z\right) \leq (\ln n)\cdot$$
$$\left(\frac{2\mu}{\Omega(1)} + \int_{2\mu-1}^{3\mu^2/4} \frac{O(1)}{\mu - \sqrt{\mu^2 - z}}\,\mathrm{d}z + \int_{3\mu^2/4}^{\mu^2-1} \frac{O(1)}{\sqrt{\mu^2 - z}}\,\mathrm{d}z\right)$$
$$= O(\mu \log n) + O(\ln n)\cdot\left(\left[\mu\ln(z) + 2\sqrt{\mu^2 - z}\right.\right.$$
$$\left.\left. + \mu\ln\left(\frac{\mu - \sqrt{\mu^2 - z}}{\mu + \sqrt{\mu^2 - z}}\right)\right]_{2\mu-1}^{3\mu^2/4} + \left[-2\sqrt{\mu^2 - z}\right]_{3\mu^2/4}^{\mu^2-1}\right).$$

The first integral evaluates to $O(\mu \log \mu)$ and the second one to $O(\mu)$. Since $\mu = o(n)$, the first hitting time for either 0 or at least $\mu(1 - c/n)$ is altogether $O(\mu \log^2 n)$. □

Note that unlike the analysis in [17], the previous lemma does not need a bound on the bandwidth of the population (i. e., the difference of best and worst individual). This constitutes a significant improvement in the sense that it might be used independently in future analyses of the **SGA**.

The results we have worked out so far will allow to prove that the **SGA** is inefficient if $\mu \leq n^{1/4-\varepsilon}$. We note that then $\mu(1 - O(1/n)) > \mu - 1/2$ if n is large enough. Hence, due to integrality of the X_t-value, Lemma 9 actually gives a bound on the time for a bit to converge *completely*, i. e., for all individuals to either have a one or a zero at the bit position. We would like to know when all bits are converged for the first time. This is finally answered by the following lemma, which is very similar to Lemma 10 in [17].

LEMMA 10. *The expected number of generations for an arbitrary bit position i in the population of the **SGA** with $\mu \leq n^{1/4-\varepsilon}$ to converge is $O(\mu \log^2 n)$. With probability at least $1 - 2^{-\Omega(n^{\varepsilon/16}/\log n)}$, after $O(\mu n^{\varepsilon/8})$ generations all bit positions have been converged at least once.*

We can now apply the machinery from [17].

3.2 Low Diversity

As in [17], we denote by s the number of bit positions that are not converged, which means that both bit values are taken by individuals in the population. The number of non-converged positions is a simple measure of diversity; for simplicity s is also called *the diversity* hereinafter. We study this measure since crossover does not have any effect on bit positions that are converged. Lemma 10 contains a statement for a single bit. We need to prove that almost all positions will be converged at any time w. o. p.; in other words, the diversity s is bounded. Throughout this section, we assume that $\mu \leq n^{1/4-\varepsilon}$ for some constant $\varepsilon > 0$.

To actually bound the diversity, we consider time phases of $T = \mu n^{\varepsilon/8}$ generations. In the first phase, diversity will collapse, and this will be maintained for the following phases. The following lemma equals Lemma 11 in [17].

LEMMA 11. *Consider the* **SGA** *at some generation* t, *where* $t \geq \mu n^{\varepsilon/8}$ *and* $t \leq 2^{n^{\varepsilon/18}}$. *Then* $s = O(\mu^2 n^{\varepsilon/8})$ *at generation* t *with probability* $1 - 2^{-\Omega(n^{\varepsilon/17})}$.

Roughly speaking, this means that the number of non-converged positions is $O(n^{1/2-15\varepsilon/8})$ for an exponential number of generations. In more simple terms, we have $s = O(n^{1/2-\varepsilon})$, which will be essential in the following.

Finally, in the very first generations before bits have converged, we use the following rough estimate of the progress. The lemma is the same as Lemma 5 in [17].

LEMMA 12. *With probability at least* $1-e^{-\Omega(n^{2\varepsilon})}$ *the maximum progress achieved by the crossover operator in one step is* $n^{1/2+\varepsilon}$. *With probability at least* $1-e^{-\Omega(n^{2\varepsilon})}$ *the maximum progress achieved by a crossover and mutation step is* $2n^{1/2+\varepsilon}$. *The maximum progress per generation is bounded in the same way if* $\mu = poly(n)$.

3.3 Drift of Best and Worst Fitness Values

In this section, the whole population is proved to drift towards the center of the boolean hypercube, which results in exponential optimization time. In the analysis, we consider the quantities h (the best ONEMAX-value of a population), and ℓ (the worst ONEMAX-value). Obviously, if $h < n$ then the optimum has not been found. The rest of this section is, up to minor adjustements reflecting the new bound on μ, basically a copy of Section 3.2 in [17].

The aim is to bound h and ℓ in a drift analysis using a so-called potential function. Similarly as in [13], the potential of an individual x is defined by $g(x) := e^{\kappa \text{ONEMAX}(x)}$ for some $\kappa := \kappa(n)$ to be chosen later, and $g(X) := \sum_{i=1}^{\mu} g(x_i)$ for every population $X := \{x_1, \dots, x_\mu\}$ (note that populations are multisets). Let us consider a current population X_t (note that X_t has been redefined) at generation t and the process of creating the next population X_{t+1} at generation $t+1$ (dropping the time indices unless there is risk of confusion). This process consists of μ consecutive operations choosing two parent individuals, crossing them over and mutating the result. Let P_i and Q_i be the two random parent individuals in the i-th operation (at generation t), $1 \leq i \leq \mu$, and let K_i be the random offspring. The next lemma notes an important observation on the ONEMAX-value of the offspring.

Hereinafter, $\Delta^{(\mathrm{m})}(j)$ denotes the random change in ONEMAX-value when applying standard bit mutation to an individual with j one-bits, $B(a,b)$ denotes a random variable following the binomial distribution with parameters a and b, and $H(\cdot,\cdot)$ denotes the Hamming distance.

LEMMA 13. *It holds that*

$$|K_i| = \frac{|P_i| + |Q_i| + 2C(P_i,Q_i)}{2} + \Delta^{(\mathrm{m})}(|P_i|/2 + |Q_i|/2 + C(P_i,Q_i)),$$

where $C(P_i,Q_i) \sim B(H(P_i,Q_i),1/2) - H(P_i,Q_i)/2$. *Moreover,*

$$|K_i| = \frac{|P_i| + 2C(P_i,Q_i) + 2\Delta^*(|P_i| + C(P_i,Q_i))}{2} + \frac{|Q_i| + 2C(P_i,Q_i) + 2\Delta^*(|Q_i| + C(P_i,Q_i))}{2},$$

where $\Delta^*(j) := B(n/2 - j/2, 1/n) - B(j/2, 1/n)$ *is the random increase in one-bits given that each bit in a string of length* $n/2$ *with* $j/2$ *one-bits is flipped with probability* $1/n$, *i. e., half the standard mutation probability.*

Due to linearity of expectation and $\mathrm{E}[C(P_i,Q_i)] = 0$, we have $\mathrm{E}[\Delta^*(|P_i|+C(P_i,Q_i))] = 1/2-|P_i|/n$, and analogously for Q_i. This results in $\mathrm{E}[|K_i|] = (|P_i|/2 + (1/2 - |P_i|/n)) + (|Q_i|/2 + (1/2 - |Q_i|/n))$. In other words, the random K_i depends on the random P_i and Q_i, whereas $\mathrm{E}[|K_i|]$ only depends on $|P_i|$ and $|Q_i|$, each of which has weight $1/2$. Considering $\mathrm{E}[|K_i|]$, we see that one operation is "split" into two analogous terms, whose values are determined by $|P_i|$ and $|Q_i|$, respectively.

However, the random potential of the offspring is given by $e^{\kappa|K_i|}$, and we have to bound $\mathrm{E}[e^{\kappa|K_i|}]$. We will see below that $\mathrm{E}[e^{\kappa|K_i|}]$ is not too different from $e^{\mathrm{E}[|K_i|]}$ for small κ. Actually, we will also "split" an operation into two terms that "basically" only depend on P_i and Q_i, respectively.

LEMMA 14.

$$e^{\kappa|K_i|} \leq \frac{e^{\kappa(|P_i|+2C(P_i,Q_i)+2\Delta^*(|P_i|+C(P_i,Q_i)))}}{2} + \frac{e^{\kappa(|Q_i|+2C(P_i,Q_i)+2\Delta^*(|Q_i|+C(P_i,Q_i)))}}{2}.$$

Both terms on the right-hand side have in common that they depend on the random $C(P_i,Q_i)$. The influence of $C(P_i,Q_i)$ will be neglegible for sufficiently small κ, as the following lemma shows.

LEMMA 15. *Let* $s = H(P_i,Q_i) \geq 1$. *If* $|P_i| \geq (1+c)(n/2)$ *for some arbitrarily small constant* $c > 0$ *and* $s \leq (c/4)n$ *then choosing* $\kappa \leq \frac{c}{20s}$ *yields*

$$\mathrm{E}[e^{\kappa(2C(P_i,Q_i)+2\Delta^*(|P_i|+C(P_i,Q_i)))}] \leq 1 - \Omega(\kappa).$$

If the assumption on $|P_i|$ *is dropped and* c *is small enough then* $\mathrm{E}[e^{\kappa(2C(P_i,Q_i)+2\Delta^*(|P_i|+C(P_i,Q_i)))}] \leq 1 + O(\kappa)$.

Our aim is to bound $\mathrm{E}[g(X_{t+1}) - g(X_t) \mid X_t]$. Let S_i denote the number of times that individual $x_i := x_i^{(t)}$ is chosen as first or second parent in a crossover operation during the μ operations. We consider the other random parent $y_i(j)$ in the j-th operation choosing x_i and study the potential of their random offspring $K(x_i, y_i(j))$ (created by a crossover-mutation sequence). We get

$$g(X_{t+1}) = \frac{1}{2}\sum_{i=1}^{\mu}\sum_{j=1}^{S_i} e^{\kappa|K(x_i,y_i(j))|},$$

where the factor $1/2$ accounts for the fact that the double sum counts each offspring twice, namely once for each parent. Using Lemma 14, we get

$$\begin{aligned} &g(X_{t+1}) \\ &\leq \frac{1}{2}\sum_{i=1}^{\mu}\sum_{j=1}^{S_i}\Bigg(\frac{e^{\kappa(|x_i|+2C(x_i,y_i(j))+2\Delta^*(|x_i|+C(x_i,y_i(j))))}}{2} \\ &\quad + \frac{e^{\kappa(|y_i(j)|+2C(x_i,y_i(j))+2\Delta^*(|y_i(j)|+C(x_i,y_i(j))))}}{2}\Bigg) \\ &= \sum_{i=1}^{\mu}\sum_{j=1}^{S_i}\frac{e^{\kappa(|x_i|+2C(x_i,y_i(j))+2\Delta^*(|x_i|+C(x_i,y_i(j))))}}{2}, \end{aligned}$$

where the equality holds since each second term in the big parentheses also appears as first term for another index i, more precisely when i indexes the individual called "$y_i(j)$".

Now let x_i' denote the worst case from the random $y_i(j)$, more precisely the one that makes the offspring potential stochastically largest. Since crossover and mutation work independently of selection, we get the following bound on the potential of the offspring population:

$$\mathrm{E}[g(X_{t+1}) \mid X_t] \leq \sum_{i=1}^{\mu} \mathrm{E}[S_i] \cdot \frac{\mathrm{E}[e^{\kappa(|x_i|+2C(x_i,x_i')+2\Delta^*(|x_i|+C(x_i,x_i')))}]}{2}. \quad (1)$$

The following simple lemma bounds $\mathrm{E}[S_i]$.

LEMMA 16. $\mathrm{E}[S_i] \leq 2h/\ell$.

More effort is needed to bound the second expectation in the right-hand side of (1). If $g(X_t)$ is large, then the following lemma will help us to obtain a negative drift. Hereinafter, a sufficiently small constant $c > 0$ and the choice $\kappa := c/(20s)$ are fixed.

LEMMA 17. *Suppose that* $s \leq n^{1/2-\varepsilon}$ *and* $\mu = poly(n)$. *If* $g(X) \geq e^{\kappa(1+2c)n/2}$, *then there is a non-empty set* $X^* \subset X$ *of individuals* $x \in X$ *satisfying* $|x| \geq (1+c)n/2$. *Moreover,* $g(X) = (1 + 2^{-\Omega(n^{1/2+\varepsilon})}) \sum_{x \in X^*} g(x)$.

From now on, also $s = O(n^{1/2-\varepsilon})$ is assumed (which, as already noted, follows from Lemma 11 for $\mu \leq n^{1/4-\varepsilon}$). The next lemma states a multiplicative drift of the potential away from large values, assuming some minimum value of the worst individual.

LEMMA 18. *If* $g(X_t) \geq e^{\kappa(1+2c)n/2}$ *and* $\ell \geq n/10$, *then* $\mathrm{E}[g(X_{t+1}) \mid X_t] \leq (1 - \Omega(\kappa)) \cdot g(X_t)$.

We will apply the following simplified negative-drift theorem with slightly weaker third condition than in [17].

THEOREM 1 (SIMPLIFIED DRIFT WITH SCALING 2013). *Let* X_t, $t \geq 0$, *be real-valued random variables describing a stochastic process over some state space. Suppose there exist an interval* $[a,b] \subseteq \mathbb{R}$ *and, possibly depending on* $\ell := b-a$, *a drift bound* $\varepsilon := \varepsilon(\ell) > 0$ *as well as a scaling factor* $r := r(\ell)$ *such that for all* $t \geq 0$ *the following three conditions hold:*

1. $\mathrm{E}[X_{t+1} - X_t \mid X_0, \ldots, X_t \wedge a < X_t < b] \geq \varepsilon$,
2. $\mathrm{Prob}[|X_{t+1} - X_t| \geq jr \mid X_0, \ldots, X_t \wedge a < X_t] \leq e^{-j}$ *for* $j \in \mathbb{N}_0$,
3. $1 \leq r^2 \leq \varepsilon\ell/(132\log(r/\varepsilon))$.

Then for the first hitting time $T^* := \min\{t \geq 0\colon X_t \leq a \mid X_0, \ldots, X_t \wedge X_0 \geq b\}$ *it holds that* $\mathrm{Prob}[T^* \leq e^{\varepsilon\ell/(132r^2)}] = O(e^{-\varepsilon\ell/(132r^2)})$.

The bound from Lemma 18 results in following lemma, which says that the population is "centered" in the middle of the hypercube for an exponential number of generations, assuming that the diversity is bounded.

LEMMA 19. *Assuming* $s \leq n^{1/4-\varepsilon}$ *the whole time, all populations up to generation* $2^{c'n^{2\varepsilon}}$, *for some constant* $c' > 0$, *satisfy* $\ell \geq (1-c)n/2$ *and* $h \leq (1+c)n/2$ *with probability* $1 - 2^{-\Omega(n^{2\varepsilon})}$, *where* $c > 0$ *is an arbitrarily small constant.*

Figure 2: Conv. bits vs n. of gens and $\mu = (1/6)\sqrt{n}, \sqrt{n}, 3\sqrt{n}, 6\sqrt{n}$ respect. for $n = 2^{12}$ and $n = 2^{14}$.

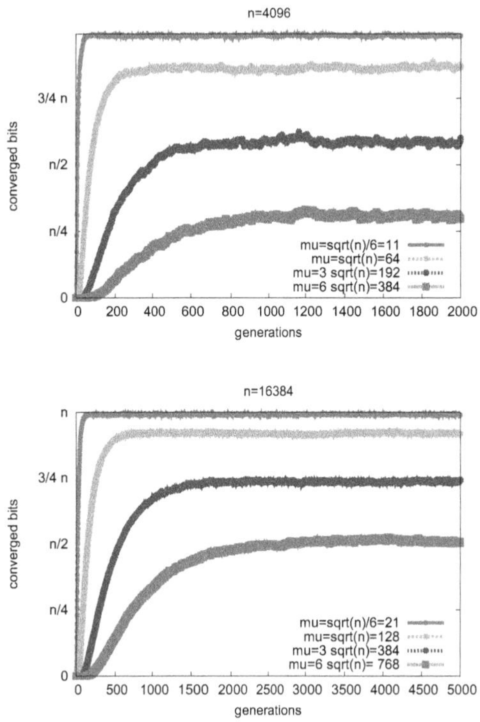

As proved in the previous subsection, we indeed have $s \leq n^{1/4-\varepsilon}$ for an exponential number of generations w. o. p. In each generation there is a probability of only $2^{-\Omega(n^{2\varepsilon})} + 2^{-\Omega(n^{\varepsilon/17})}$ (the latter error term stems from Lemma 11) that one of our assumptions (low diversity and $\ell \geq n/10$) is not satisfied. Since the sum of the failure probabilities within $2^{n^{\varepsilon/18}}$ generations is still $2^{-\Omega(n^{\varepsilon/17})}$, we have proved the following main result.

THEOREM 2. *Let* $\mu \leq n^{1/4-\varepsilon}$ *for an arbitrarily small constant* $\varepsilon > 0$. *Then with probability* $1 - 2^{-\Omega(n^{\varepsilon/17})}$, *the* **SGA** *on* ONEMAX *does not create individuals with more than* $(1+c)n/2$ *or less than* $(1-c)n/2$ *one-bits, where* $c > 0$ *is an arbitrarily small constant, within the first* $2^{n^{\varepsilon/18}}$ *generations. In particular it does not reach the optimum then.*

4. CONCLUSIONS

An improved analysis of the **SGA** for ONEMAX has been presented. Through new combinations and extensions of state-of-the art techniques for the analysis we have bounded the diversity of the population up to $\mu \leq n^{1/4-\varepsilon}$ without requiring a bound on its bandwidth. This generality will very likely allow to re-use the new techniques in future analyses of the **SGA**.

Our analysis requires that, at each generation, a large number of the bits in the population are converged. In particular, Lemma 11 bounds the fraction of non-converged bits by $o(1)$ only if $\mu = o(n^{1/2})$. We only managed to show a result for $\mu = O(n^{1/4-\varepsilon})$ since the proof of Lemma 18 requires $\kappa = \omega(s/n)$, while $\kappa = O(1/s)$. This means that $s = o(n^{1/2})$

Figure 3: Conv. bits vs n. of gens and $\mu = (1/6)\sqrt{n}, \sqrt{n}, 3\sqrt{n}, 6\sqrt{n}$ respect. for $n = 2^{15}$ and $n = 2^{16}$.

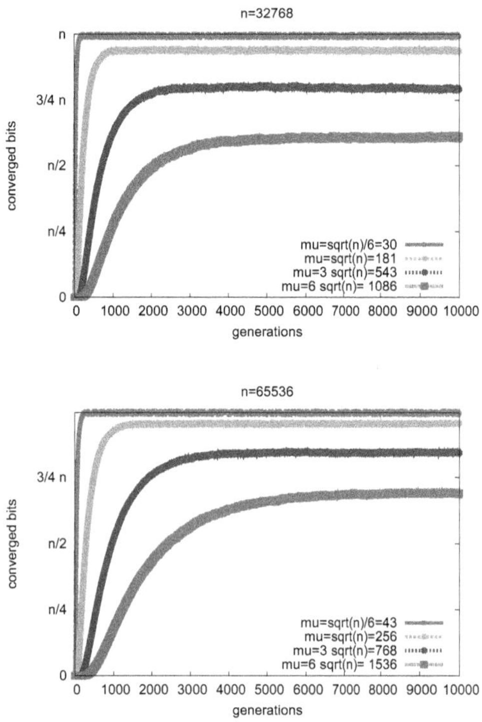

is required, and by Lemma 11 we get $\mu = O(\sqrt{s}) = o(n^{1/4})$. It is an open problem to remove the requirement $\kappa = \omega(s/n)$.

We perform some preliminary experiments to further look into the number of converged bits during runs of the algorithm. We consider exponentially growing problem sizes n, concentrate the population size around $\mu = c \cdot \sqrt{n}$ with $c = 1/6, 1, 3, 6$ and plot the number of converged bits at each generation. The figures show how, for the considered problem sizes, the number of converged bits indeed drops around $\mu = O(n^{1/2})$. In particular, for $\mu = \sqrt{n}/6$ the number of converged bits would be sufficient for Lemma 11 to hold, while for $c \geq 1$ the number of converged bits would not be sufficient. Nevertheless as n grows we can also see that, if the time for bits to converge after initialization increases quickly, also the number of converged bits increases for a fixed population size μ. Hence, we cannot rule out the possibility that for sufficiently large n a sufficient number of bits converge unless we perform more extensive experiments with more computation power which we leave for future work. In any case, if $\mu = \omega(n^{1/2})$, completely different techniques might be needed.

5. REFERENCES

[1] A. Auger and B. Doerr, editors. *Theory of Randomized Seach Heuristics–Foundations and Recent Developments*. World Scientific, 2011.

[2] B. Doerr, D. Johannsen, T. Kötzing, F. Neumann, and M. Theile. More effective crossover operators for the all-pairs shortest path problem. In *Proc. of PPSN '10*, pages 184–193, 2010.

[3] M. Feldmann and T. Kötzing. Optimizing expected path lengths with ant colony optimization using fitness proportional update. In *Proc. of FOGA '13*, to appear, 2013.

[4] W. Feller. *An Introduction to Probability Theory and Its Applications*, volume 2. Wiley, 1971.

[5] D. E. Goldberg. *Genetic Algorithms in Search, Optimization and machine learning*. Addison-Wesley, 1989.

[6] E. Happ, D. Johannsen, C. Klein, and F. Neumann. Rigorous analyses of fitness-proportional selection for optimizing linear functions. In *Proc. of GECCO '08*, pages 953–960, 2008.

[7] T. Jansen and I. Wegener. Real royal road functions: where crossover provably is essential. *Discrete Applied Mathematics*, 149(1-3):111–125, 2005.

[8] T. Kötzing, D. Sudholt, and M. Theile. How crossover helps in pseudo-boolean optimization. In *Proc. of GECCO '11*, pages 989–996, 2011.

[9] P. K. Lehre. Negative drift in populations. In *Proc. of PPSN '10, Part I*, pages 244–253, 2010.

[10] P. K. Lehre. Fitness-levels for non-elitist populations. In *Proc. of GECCO '11*, pages 2075–2082, 2011.

[11] P. K. Lehre and C. Witt. Black-box search by unbiased variation. *Algorithmica*, 64(4):623–642, 2012.

[12] F. Neumann, P. S. Oliveto, G. Rudolph, and D. Sudholt. On the effectiveness of crossover for migration in parallel evolutionary algorithms. In *Proc. of GECCO '11*, pages 1587–1594, 2011.

[13] F. Neumann, P. S. Oliveto, and C. Witt. Theoretical analysis of fitness-proportional selection: Landscapes and efficiency. In *Proc. of GECCO '09*, pages 835–842, 2009.

[14] F. Neumann and C. Witt. *Bioinspired Computation in Combinatorial Optimization – Algorithms and Their Computational Complexity*. Springer, 2010.

[15] P. S. Oliveto, J. He, and X. Yao. Analysis of population-based evolutionary algorithms for the vertex cover problem. In *Proc. of CEC '08*, pages 1563–1570, 2008.

[16] P. S. Oliveto and C. Witt. Simplified drift analysis for proving lower bounds in evolutionary computation. *Algorithmica*, 59(3):369–386, 2011.

[17] P. S. Oliveto and C. Witt. On the analysis of the simple genetic algorithm. In *Proc. of GECCO '12*, pages 1341–1348, 2012.

[18] J. E. Rowe and D. Sudholt. The choice of the offspring population size in the (1,λ) EA. In *Proc. of GECCO '12*, pages 1349–1356, 2012.

[19] D. Sudholt. Crossover speeds up building-block assembly. In *Proc. of GECCO '12*, pages 689–702, 2012.

[20] R. A. Watson and T. Jansen. A building-block royal road where crossover is provably essential. In *Proc. of GECCO '07*, pages 1452–1459, 2007.

Particle Swarm Optimization Almost Surely Finds Local Optima

Manuel Schmitt Rolf Wanka
Department of Computer Science, University of Erlangen-Nuremberg, Germany
{manuel.schmitt, rolf.wanka}@cs.fau.de

ABSTRACT

Particle swarm optimization (PSO) is a popular nature-inspired meta-heuristic for solving continuous optimization problems. Although this technique is widely used, up to now only some partial aspects of the method have been formally investigated. In particular, while it is well-studied how to let the swarm converge to a single point in the search space, no general theoretical statements about this point or on the best position any particle has found have been known. For a very general class of objective functions, we provide for the first time results about the quality of the solution found. We show that a slightly adapted PSO almost surely finds a local optimum by investigating the newly defined *potential* of the swarm. The potential drops when the swarm approaches the point of convergence, but increases if the swarm remains close to a point that is not a local optimum, meaning that the swarm charges potential and continues its movement.

Categories and Subject Descriptors

I.2.8 [**Artificial Intelligence**]: Problem Solving, Control Methods, and Search—*heuristic methods*

General Terms

Algorithms, Performance, Theory

Keywords

Particle swarm optimization, quality of solution, fitness landscapes

1. INTRODUCTION

Background. Particle swarm optimization (PSO), introduced by Kennedy and Eberhart [10, 4], is a very popular meta-heuristic for solving continuous optimization problems. It is inspired by the social interaction of individuals living together in groups and supporting and cooperating with each other. Fields of very successful application are, among many others, Biomedical Image Processing [18], Geosciences [12], and Materials Science [14], to name just a few, where the continuous objective function on a multi-dimensional domain is not given in a closed form, but by a "black box." The popularity of the PSO framework in these scientific communities is due to the fact that it on the one hand can be realized and, if necessary, adapted to further needs easily, but on the other hand shows in experiments good performance results with respect to the quality of the obtained solution and the speed needed to obtain it. By adapting its parameters, users may in real-world applications easily and successfully control the swarm's behavior with respect to "exploration" ("searching where no one has searched before") and "exploitation" ("searching around a good position"). A thorough discussion of PSO can be found in [13].

To be precise, let an objective function $f : \mathbb{R}^D \to \mathbb{R}$ on a D-dimensional domain be given that (w.l.o.g.) has to be minimized. A population of *particles*, each consisting of a position (the candidate for a solution), a velocity and a local attractor, moves through the search space $\mathbb{R}^D$. The local attractor of a particle is the best position with respect to f this particle has encountered so far. The population in motion is the *swarm*. In contrast to evolutionary algorithms, the individuals of the swarm cooperate by sharing information about the search space via the global attractor, which is the best position any particle has found so far. The particles move in time-discrete iterations. The movement of a particle is governed by so-called movement equations that depend on both the particle's velocity and its two attractors and on some additional fixed parameters (for details, see Sec. 2).

Although this method is widely used in real-world applications, there has unfortunately not been any formal analysis explaining more than only partial aspects of the algorithm. A theoretical analysis of the particles' trajectories can be found in [2]. A discussion of runtime aspects is presented in [19]. For the case of a bounded high-dimensional search space, theoretical work about the initial behavior of the particle swarm is presented in [5, 6]. Some guidelines for the choice of the fixed parameters that control the impact of the current velocity and the attractors on the updated velocity of a particle can be found in [16, 8], where the authors prove that under certain conditions about the parameters the swarm provably converges. However, mathematical properties of the limit, i.e., the quality of the solution, are unknown. Van den Bergh/Engelbrecht [17] substantially modify the movement equations, enabling the particles to count the number of times they improve the global attrac-

GECCO'13, July 6–10, 2013, Amsterdam, The Netherlands.

tor and use that information. Empirical evidence for the capability of their method to find local optima on common benchmarks is given.

Closest to our work, Lehre/Witt [11] modify the movement equations by adding in *every* step a small random perturbation to the velocity. Their detailed analysis for one specific, simple, one-dimensional objective function shows that their modified PSO finds this function's unique optimum. But it is not clear how to apply this special analysis to higher dimensional search spaces and larger classes of functions.

An overview of known theoretical results about PSO can be found in [20].

New results. Up to now, every formal analysis providing results about the quality of the best search point obtained by the particle swarm has been restricted to a very special class of objective functions. In this paper, we provide the first *general* mathematical analysis of the quality of the global attractor when it is considered as a solution for objective functions from a very general class $\mathcal{F}$ of functions (see Def. 2 below) and therefore of the quality of the algorithm's return value. Informally, functions in $\mathcal{F}$ resemble (if restricted to 3-dimensional pictures) an (everted) island. On its almost arbitrary surface, the lowest point has to be found. The sea around the island is of no interest. We introduce the new approach of defining the *potential* Φ of the particle swarm that changes after every step. Φ covers two properties of the swarm: It tends to zero if the particles converge, but it increases if the whole swarm stays close to a search point that is no local minimum. In the latter case, the swarm charges potential and resumes its movement. As a consequence, we prove an emergent property of PSO for $\mathcal{F}$, namely that in the one-dimensional case the swarm almost surely (in the well-defined probabilistic sense) finds a local optimum. For the general D-dimensional case, we slightly modify the classical PSO and prove that this adapted swarm almost surely finds a local optimum. Necessity of such a modification is constituted in [15], where we report on significant experiments that show that even on the very simple sphere function the swarm does not necessarily converge towards the only local optimum at the center. Note that our analysis carries over to presumably all variants of PSO developed so far. One would expect such strong results to hold only for a very small class of objective functions. Indeed, we need some restrictions, but as it turns out the class $\mathcal{F}$ of objective functions for which our results hold is much more general than, e.g., the subset of the class of unimodal functions that is considered in [7] in the context of restricted $(1+1)$ evolutionary algorithms.

2. ANALYSIS OF THE CLASSICAL PSO ALGORITHM

First we present the model we are going to use for our analysis of the PSO algorithm. The model describes the positions of the particles, the velocities and the global and local attractors as real-valued stochastic processes. Furthermore, we define in Def. 5 the potential of the swarm which depends on the state of the particles and will be a measure for their movement. A swarm with high potential is more likely to reach search points far away from the current global attractor, while a swarm with potential approaching 0 is converging. (The basic mathematical tools from probability theory we need for our analysis can be found in, e.g., [3].)

Definition 1 (Classical PSO Process) *A swarm $\mathcal{S}$ of N particles moves through the D-dimensional search space $\mathbb{R}^D$. Let $f : \mathbb{R}^D \to \mathbb{R}$ be the objective function. For $\mathcal{S}$, we define the stochastic process $(S_t)_{t\in\mathbb{N}_0} = ((X_t, V_t, L_t, G_t))_{t\in\mathbb{N}_0} = ((X_0, V_0, L_0, G_0), (X_1, V_1, L_1, G_1), \ldots)$, consisting of*

- $X_t = (X_t^{n,d})_{1\le n\le N, 1\le d\le D}$ *(d-th coordinate of the* position *of particle n after step t),*
- $V_t = (V_t^{n,d})_{1\le n\le N, 1\le d\le D}$ *(d-th coordinate of the* velocity *of particle n after step t),*
- $L_t = (L_t^{n,d})_{1\le n\le N, 1\le d\le D}$ *(d-th coordinate of the* local attractor *of particle n after step t),*
- $G_t = (G_t^{n,d})_{1\le n\le N, 1\le d\le D}$*, (d-th coordinate of the* global attractor *before the t-th step of particle n).*

We will write X_t^n for the vector $(X_t^{n,1}, ..., X_t^{n,D})$ (analogously, V_t^n, L_t^n, G_t^n) and X_t^d for the vector $(X_t^{1,d}, ..., X_t^{N,d})$ (analogously, V_t^d, L_t^d, G_t^d). Furthermore $\tilde{G}_t^{n,d}$ denotes the d-th coordinate of the global attractor after *the t-th step of particle n, i.e., $\tilde{G}_t^{n,d} = G_t^{n+1,d}$ if $n < N$, and $\tilde{G}_t^{N,d} = G_{t+1}^{1,d}$. With a given distribution for (X_0, V_0) and the values $G_0^1 := \operatorname{argmin}_{1\le n\le N}\{f(X_0^n)\}$ and $L_0 := X_0$, $S_{t+1} = (X_{t+1}, V_{t+1}, L_{t+1}, G_{t+1})$ is determined by the following recursive equations that are called the* movement equations*:*

- $G_t^{n+1} = \operatorname{argmin}\{f(L_t^n), f(G_t^n)\}$ *for* $t \ge 0$, $1 \le n \le N-1$,
- $G_{t+1}^1 = \operatorname{argmin}\{f(L_t^N), f(G_t^N)\}$ *for* $t \ge 0$,
- $V_{t+1}^{n,d} = \chi \cdot V_t^{n,d} + c_1 \cdot r_t^{n,d} \cdot (L_t^{n,d} - X_t^{n,d}) + c_2 \cdot s_t^{n,d} \cdot (G_{t+1}^{n,d} - X_t^{n,d})$ *for* $t \ge 0$,
- $X_{t+1}^{n,d} = X_t^{n,d} + V_{t+1}^{n,d}$ *for* $t \ge 0$,
- $L_{t+1}^n = \operatorname{argmin}\{f(X_{t+1}^n), f(L_t^n)\}$.

In case of a tie when applying argmin*, the new value prevails, i.e., whenever a particle finds a search point with value equal to the one of its local attractor, this point becomes the new local attractor. If additionally the value is equal to the one of the global attractor, this one is also updated. Here, χ, c_1 and c_2 are some positive constants called the* fixed parameters *of $\mathcal{S}$, and $r_t^{n,d}$, $s_t^{n,d}$ are uniformly distributed over $[0, 1]$ and all independent.*

If after the t-th step the process is stopped, the *solution* found by $\mathcal{S}$ so far is $\tilde{G}_t^N$.

Basically, this definition describes the common movement equations with two specifications: If a particle visits a point with the same objective value as its local attractor or the global attractor, then the attractor is updated to the new point. And the global attractor is updated after every step of a single particle, not only after every iteration of the whole swarm. Another common variant of PSO only updates the global attractor after every iteration of the whole swarm, however, due to our choice the information shared between the particles is as recent as possible.

PSO is designed to handle any objective function. But for the rest of this paper, we consider only objective functions from the set $\mathcal{F}$ defined below.

Definition 2 *Let $f : \mathbb{R}^D \to \mathbb{R}$ be a function. $f \in \mathcal{F}$ iff*

(i) there is a compact set $K \subset \mathbb{R}^D$ with positive Lebesgue measure, such that $P(X_0^n) \in K = 1$ for every n and $\{x \in \mathbb{R}^D \mid f(x) \leq \sup_K f\}$ (the island) is bounded;

(ii) f is continuous and has a continuous derivative.

Restriction (i) states that there is a compact set K such that for all $x \in K$, the set of all search points y as least as good as x, i. e., all y with $f(y) \leq f(x)$, is a bounded set. Since the particles are initialized inside K and since $f(G_t^n)$ is nonincreasing in t, (i) ensures that the possible area for the global attractor is limited if the positions of all particles are initialized inside of K (being on any point of the island is better than being in the sea). If for example $\lim_{|x|\to\infty} f(x) = \infty$ or if f has compact support and is negative on K, (i) is already satisfied. E. g., common benchmark functions like the sphere function $f(x) = \sum_{i=1}^{D} x_i^2$ or the Rosenbrock function $f(x) = \sum_{i=1}^{D-1}((1 - x_i)^2 + 100 \cdot (x_{i+1} - x_i^2)^2)$ are in $\mathcal{F}$. On functions that violate (i), the swarm might move forever because either they do not necessarily have a local optimum like $f(x) = x$ or they have an optimum, but improvements can be made arbitrary far away from it, like, e. g. in the case of the function $f(x) = x^2/(x^4 + 1)$, where $x = 0$ is the only local and the global optimum, but if the particles are far away from 0, they tend to further increase the distance because f converges to 0 as $|x|$ approaches ∞. Under such circumstances, convergence cannot be expected and it is necessary to restrict the function class in order to avoid this. However, (ii) might be the only true restriction.

From Def. 1 it follows that $(S_t)_{t\in\mathbb{N}}$ has the strong Markov property. Another interesting property of this stochastic process that follows immediately from the movement equations is the following:

Observation 1 *Let $\mathcal{S}$ be a swarm and $((X_t, V_t, L_t, G_t))_{t\in\mathbb{N}_0}$ its corresponding stochastic process. Let $\mathcal{L}^k$ denote the k-dimensional Lebesgue measure, $\mathcal{L}[Y]$ the distribution of a random variable Y and "$\ll$" (just in this observation) absolute continuity between two distributions. Assuming $\mathcal{L}[(X_0, V_0)] \ll \mathcal{L}^{2\cdot N\cdot D}$, it follows $\mathcal{L}[(X_t, V_t)] \ll \mathcal{L}^{2\cdot N\cdot D}$ for every $t \geq 0$. If $X_t^n \neq G_t^n$ for every n, then for every $t' > t$, $\mathcal{L}[(X_{t'}, V_{t'}) \mid S_t] \ll \mathcal{L}^{2\cdot N\cdot D}$ almost surely*[1].

If the positions and velocities of the initial population are distributed in some natural way, e. g., uniformly at random over K, Obs. 1 states that the swarm has similar restrictions as a process consisting only of variables that are sampled u. a. r. in the sense that events with probability 0 in the latter case also have probability 0 in the first case. If the function contains no plateaus, we cannot expect the swarm to ever hit a local optimum since the probability to hit that particular point by just sampling is zero and so is the probability for hitting it with the swarm. Another consequence is that no point in $\mathbb{R}^D$ is visited more than once because that would not happen under uniform sampling since $\mathbb{R}^D$ is not enumerable. This implies that the well-studied equilibrium when every particle is at the global attractor and has velocity 0 is a state that the process may converge to but that will never be reached. Therefore we give a definition of the kind of convergent behavior that can be expected.

Definition 3 (Convergence) *Swarm $\mathcal{S}$* converges *if there almost surely is a point z such that the following two conditions hold:*

1. *$\lim_{t\to\infty} V_t = 0$ (the movement of the particles tends to zero),*
2. *$\lim_{t\to\infty} X_t^n = z$ for each $n \in \{1, \ldots, N\}$ (every particle moves towards z).*

A consequence of the above conditions is that for every $n \in \{1, \ldots, N\}$ $\lim_{t\to\infty} G_t^n = z$ almost surely and $\lim_{t\to\infty} L_t^n = z$ almost surely. Although the convergence analysis in the literature ([8]) usually makes the assumption that at least the global attractor is constant forever, a prerequisite that because of Observation 1 we cannot assume, the generalization of the convergence proof from [8], showing that their results still hold under the weaker assumption of only the convergence of the attractors, is straight-forward.

We want to prove more, namely, that under the stated assumptions about f the swarm is able to find a local minimum. Here, the notion of the potential of a swarm comes into play. Roughly speaking, as long as the swarm has potential high enough to overcome the distance to at least one local minimum, the probability to find it within a few steps is still positive. A problem occurs when the value of the potential is too low for the swarm to overcome the distance to the next optimum by only a small number of steps. In other words, if f is monotonically decreasing in some direction and on an area that is large in comparison to the potential of the swarm, the particles must be able to "run down the hill," i. e., they must be able to surpass every distance as long as f decreases. The following definition formally describes the situation of a swarm while it is "running down the hill" and will lead to the definition of the potential.

Definition 4 (Running Particle Swarm) *Let $d_0 \leq D$ be an arbitrary dimension. We call $\mathcal{S}$ positively running in direction d_0, if the following two properties hold: First, $G_t^{n,d_0} = \max_{1\leq i\leq N}\{X_{t'}^{i,d_0}\}$ for $t' = t$ if $i < n$ and $t' = t - 1$ otherwise. Second, $L_t^n = X_t^n$ for every n. In other words, while the swarm is running, each particle updates its local attractor at every step and the global attractor is always the local attractor with greatest value in the d_0-th dimension. If the global attractor is always the position with smallest d_0-value instead, we call the swarm negatively running in direction d_0.*

Note that while a particle swarm is positively running, every particle has positive velocity in direction d_0, in terms: $V_t^{n,d_0} > 0$. If the swarm is negatively running in direction d_0, then $V_t^{n,d_0} < 0$. Intuitively one may think of running as the behavior a swarm shows when it moves through an area that is monotone in one dimension and changes in any other dimension are insignificant.

For our analysis, we now define the potential of $\mathcal{S}$.

Definition 5 (Potential) *For $a > 0$, the potential of swarm $\mathcal{S}$ in dimension d right before the t-th step of particle n is $\Phi_t^{n,d}$ and its potential in dimension d after the t-th step of*

[1]Let $(\Omega, \mathcal{A}, P)$ be a probability space. An event $E \in \mathcal{A}$ happens almost surely iff $P(E) = 1$.

particle n is $\tilde{\Phi}_t^{n,d}$ with

$$\Phi_t^{n,d} := \sqrt{\sum_{n'=1}^{N}\left(a\cdot|V_{t-1}^{n',d}| + |G_t^{n,d} - X_{t-1}^{n',d}|\right)},$$

$$\tilde{\Phi}_t^{n,d} := \sqrt{\sum_{n'=1}^{N}\left(a\cdot|V_t^{n',d}| + |\tilde{G}_t^{n,d} - X_t^{n',d}|\right)}.$$

Basically, the potential Φ is an extension of the physical interpretation of the particle swarm model. If the particles move faster and get farther away from their global attractor, the potential increases. If the swarm converges, the potential tends towards 0. However, for technical reasons explained later, we need the additional parameter a and the square root. Note that general tendencies towards 0 or ∞ are invariant under different choices of a.

Example 1 *Consider a 1-dimensional particle swarm and the objective function $f(x) = -x$. Assume that the velocities of the particles are all positive. Then the swarm is positively running in direction 1 from 0 until ∞. It is obvious that the position with the greatest x-value leads to the smallest value of $f(x)$ and therefore becomes the global attractor. It remains to prove that the velocity of every particle stays positive. Given the old velocity $V_t^{n,1}$, the new velocity $V_{t+1}^{n,1}$ is a positive linear combination of the three components $V_t^{n,1}$, $G_t^{n,1} - X_t^{n,1}$ and $L_t^{n,1} - X_t^{n,1}$. The value for $V_t^{n,1}$ is positive by assumption, $G_t^{n,1} - X_t^{n,1}$ and $L_t^{n,1} - X_t^{n,1}$ are non-negative since $G_t^{n,1} \geq L_t^{n,1} \geq X_t^{n,1}$. Therefore, the velocity stays positive and the swarm will stay positively running forever. In that situation, a good behavior would be increasing (or at least non-decreasing) Φ.*

Informally speaking, if a swarm $\mathcal{S}$ has a too little potential Φ left to make it to the next local minimum, it is necessary that Φ increases after $\mathcal{S}$ has become running, and so Φ enables the swarm to overcome every distance. The following lemma is the central technical observation of our work and makes a statement about how to choose the parameters to make sure that a running swarm has an increasing potential.

Lemma 1 (Running to Infinity Lemma) *For certain parameters N, χ, c_1, c_2 and the swarm $\mathcal{S}$ positively (negatively, resp.) running in direction d_0, $V_t^{n,d_0} + X_t^{n,d_0}$ ($-V_t^{n,d_0} - X_t^{n,d_0}$, resp.) tends to ∞ for every n almost surely. In particular, the swarm leaves every bounded set $B \subset \mathbb{R}^D$ almost surely.*

PROOF. W.l.o.g., assume that the swarm is positively running. The main idea of this proof is to show that on expectation the potential significantly increases after every iteration of the particle swarm. More precisely, we want to show that $\mathrm{E}[1/\Phi_t^{n,d_0}] \xrightarrow{t\to\infty} 0$, which is equivalent to $1/\Phi_t^{n,d_0} \xrightarrow{t\to\infty} 0$ almost surely and therefore $\Phi_t^{n,d_0} \xrightarrow{t\to\infty} \infty$ almost surely. Our strategy to prove the convergence of $\mathrm{E}[1/\Phi_t^{n,d_0}]$ is to prove that for $\Phi_t^{n,d_0} \neq 0$ the bound $\mathrm{E}[\Phi_t^{n,d_0}/\Phi_{t+1}^{n,d_0} \mid S_t] \leq q$ holds for some fixed $q < 1$ almost surely (due to Lemma 1, the case $\Phi_t^{n,d_0} = 0$ for some t has probability 0). We bound $\mathrm{E}[\Phi_t^{n,d_0}/\Phi_{t+1}^{n,d_0} \mid S_t]$ for our concrete choice of the potential from Def. 5. Although there are better choices for the definition of a potential leading to larger areas of parameters that match our requirements, for our existence proof this one is sufficient.

We need to determine the values for N, χ, c_1 and c_2, for which the potential fulfills

$$\mathrm{E}\left[\Phi_t^{n,d_0}/\Phi_{t+1}^{n,d_0} \mid S_t\right] \leq q \tag{1}$$

for a $q < 1$. In other words, during one iteration of all particles, we want the reciprocal of the potential to decrease on expectation by at least a factor of q. Since the contributions of the different particles to the whole potential might differ arbitrarily much, we can not expect that every step of a single particle decreases the potential of the swarm by a constant factor. More reasonable and sufficient for our purpose is to prove that the expectation during each step of a single particle is bounded from above by 1 and that there is at least one particle (e.g., the one with the largest contribution to the potential) with an expected decrease of the term bounded from above by q. Therefore we now focus only on the movement of one single particle n. If we can verify $\mathrm{E}[\Phi_t^{n,d_0}/\tilde{\Phi}_t^{n,d_0}] \leq 1$ for every n and $\mathrm{E}[\Phi_t^{n,d_0}/\tilde{\Phi}_t^{n,d_0}] \leq q$ for at least one n, that would imply (1). We show the calculation only for $n = 1$ since the situation is symmetric and we want to avoid too much mess with the indices.

$$\mathrm{E}\left[\frac{\Phi_{t+1}^{1,d_0}}{\tilde{\Phi}_{t+1}^{1,d_0}} \mid S_t\right] = \mathrm{E}\left[\sqrt{\frac{a\cdot V_t^{1,d_0} + N\cdot G_{t+1}^{1,d_0} - X_t^{1,d_0} + R}{a\cdot V_{t+1}^{1,d_0} + N\cdot \tilde{G}_{t+1}^{1,d_0} - X_{t+1}^{1,d_0} + R}} \mid S_t\right]$$

where we substituted R for $\sum_{n=2}^{N} a\cdot V_t^{n,d_0} - X_t^{n,d_0}$, describing the state of the other particles that did not move.

Now there are two cases. In the first case, the position of particle 1 is the global attractor, i.e., $G_{t+1}^{1,d_0} = X_t^{1,d_0}$. Then its move is deterministic and its new position will be the new global attractor. In this case, we obtain:

$$\mathrm{E}\left[\frac{\Phi_{t+1}^{1,d_0}}{\tilde{\Phi}_{t+1}^{1,d_0}} \mid S_t\right] = \mathrm{E}\left[\sqrt{\frac{a\cdot V_t^{1,d_0} + (N-1)\cdot G_{t+1}^{1,d_0} + R}{a\cdot V_{t+1}^{1,d_0} + (N-1)\cdot \tilde{G}_{t+1}^{1,d_0} + R}} \mid S_t\right]$$

$$= \sqrt{\frac{a\cdot V_t^{1,d_0} + (N-1)\cdot G_{t+1}^{1,d_0} + R}{a\cdot\chi\cdot V_t^{1,d_0} + (N-1)\cdot\left(G_{t+1}^{1,d_0} + \chi\cdot V_t^{1,d_0}\right) + R}}$$

$$= \sqrt{\frac{a\cdot V_t^{1,d_0} + (N-1)\cdot G_{t+1}^{1,d_0} + R}{(a+N-1)\cdot\chi\cdot V_t^{1,d_0} + (N-1)\cdot G_{t+1}^{1,d_0} + R}},$$

which is less than 1 for every possible V_t^{1,d_0} and every possible R if and only if $a < (a + N - 1)\cdot\chi$. Given that, we can furthermore find the desired bound of a $q < 1$, if $(N-1)\cdot\tilde{G}_{t+1}^{1,d_0} + R < \mathrm{const}\cdot V_t^{1,d_0}$ for some constant. That is the case, if, e.g., particle 1 has the largest value of $a\cdot V + (G - X)$ among all particles of the swarm and therefore makes the largest contribution to the potential.

The second case when $G_{t+1}^{1,d_0} > X_t^{1,d_0}$ is more difficult. Since the potential is invariant under translation, we can assume $X_t^{1,d_0} = 0$. Furthermore, w.l.o.g., we set $G_{t+1}^{1,d_0} = 1$. Otherwise we could scale $\hat{\Phi}_t^1$ and $\tilde{L}_t^1$ by the factor $1/G_{t+1}^{1,d_0}$ and replace $V_t^{1,d_0}/G_{t+1}^{1,d_0}$ by V_t^{1,d_0} and $R/G_{t+1}^{1,d_0}$ by R which does not change the result since we need to bound the term for every positive V_{t-1}^{1,d_0} and every $R > -(N-1)\cdot G_{t+1}^{1,d_0}$. We

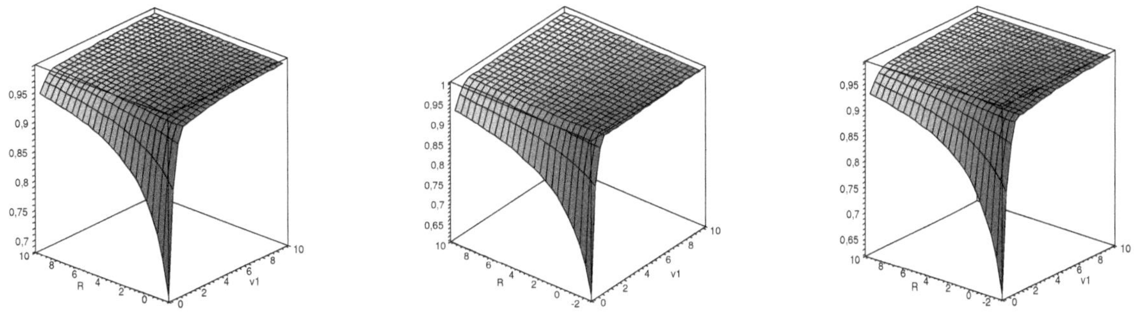

(a) $\chi = 0.729$, $c_2 = 1.49$, $N = 2$, $a = 2.69$ [2]

(b) $\chi = 0.729$, $c_2 = 1.3 \cdot \chi$, $N = 3$, $a = 5.38$ [1]

(c) $\chi = 0.6$, $c_2 = 1.7$, $N = 3$, $a = 2.98$ [16]

Figure 1: The integral $I(\chi, c_2, N, a)$ for different parameter choices

obtain:

$$
\begin{aligned}
&\mathrm{E}\left[\frac{\Phi_{t+1}^{1,d_0}}{\tilde{\Phi}_{t+1}^{1,d_0}} \mid S_t\right] \\
&= \mathrm{E}\left[\sqrt{\frac{a \cdot V_t^{1,d_0} + N \cdot G_{t+1}^{1,d_0} - X_t^{1,d_0} + R}{a \cdot V_{t+1}^{1,d_0} + N \cdot \tilde{G}_{t+1}^{1,d_0} - X_{t+1}^{1,d_0} + R}} \mid S_t\right] \\
&= \mathrm{E}\left[\sqrt{\frac{a \cdot V_t^{1,d_0} + N + R}{a \cdot V_{t+1}^{1,d_0} + N \cdot \tilde{G}_{t+1}^{1,d_0} - X_{t+1}^{1,d_0} + R}} \mid S_t\right]
\end{aligned}
$$

Now we insert the movement equations from Def. 1

$$
\begin{aligned}
&= \mathrm{E}\left[\left(\frac{a \cdot V_t^{1,d_0} + N + R}{(a-1) \cdot \left(\chi \cdot V_t^{1,d_0} + c_2 \cdot s_t^{1,d_0}\right) + N \cdot \max\left\{1, \chi \cdot V_t^{1,d_0} + c_2 \cdot s_t^{1,d_0}\right\} + R}\right)^{1/2} \mid S_t\right] \\
&= \int_0^1 \left(\frac{a \cdot V_t^{1,d_0} + N + R}{(a-1) \cdot \left(\chi \cdot V_t^{1,d_0} + c_2 \cdot s\right) + N \cdot \max\left\{1, \chi \cdot V_t^{1,d_0} + c_2 \cdot s\right\} + R}\right)^{1/2} ds \\
&=: I(\chi, c_2, N, a)
\end{aligned}
$$

Here we make use of the square root in our potential! The integral $I(\chi, c_2, N, a)$ is a function containing a case distinction (because of the max) and square root terms. So, the desired bound can be shown by tedious, but straight-forward calculation, after eliminating the square roots, a polynomial remains. If we had left out the square root in the definition of the potential, the result of the integral would have contained logarithmic terms that can not be handled that easily. We plotted the integral (see Fig. 1) for three different choices of the parameters, so one can easily verify that for the typical parameter sets found in the literature and a good choice of a, only two or three particles are sufficient to keep the value always less than 1 and that under the assumption that particle 1 makes the largest contribution to the potential, one can find an upper bound $\hat{q} < 1$. That finishes the proof. □

In Fig. 2, one can see the borderlines between choices for c_2 and χ that satisfy the conditions of Lemma 1 and those that do not. The parameters that satisfy both Lemma 1 and convergence requirements will be referred to as good parameters. Note that in [11], the authors have shown the existence of "bad" parameters that allow stagnation on arbitrary search points with positive probability. They have proven that for $N = 1$, all choices of parameters are bad, so a swarm with good parameters needs at least two particles. From here on we assume the parameters to be good.

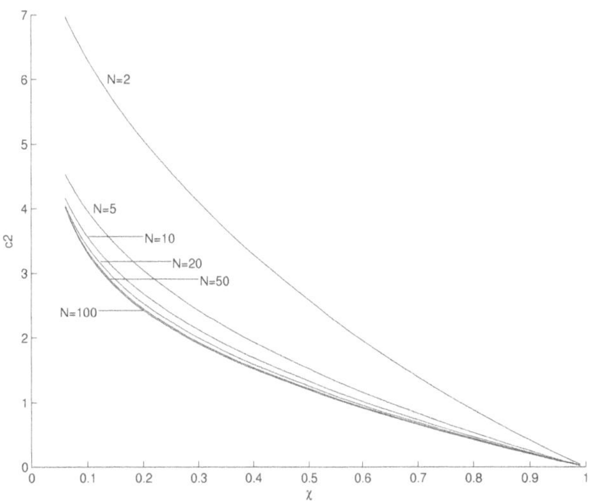

Figure 2: Borders between the too low values for c_2 and χ and the ones large enough to satisfy the requirements in Lemma 1 for some swarm sizes N.

Lemma 1 says that, given the parameters are good, a swarm that moves into the right direction can overcome every distance and increase its potential, no matter how small it was in the beginning. In other words: The equilibrium when all attractors and particles are on the same point and every velocity is zero is not stable because arbitrary small changes of an attractor, a position or a velocity can be sufficient to lead the swarm far away from this equilibrium, as long as there is a direction with decreasing value of the fitness function.

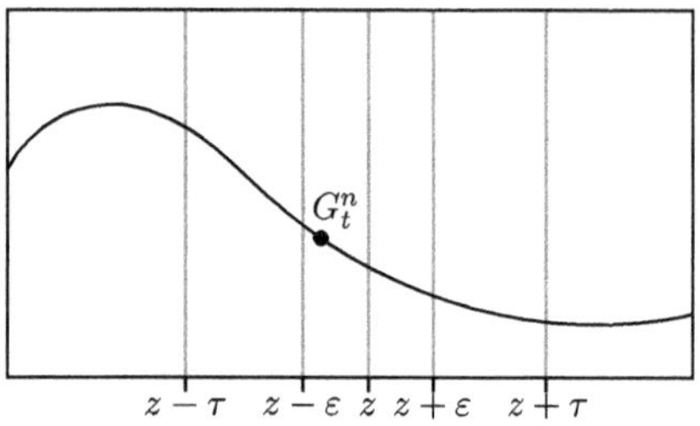

Figure 3: Fitness function f monotonic on $B_\tau(z)$, global attractor in ε-neighborhood of z

Theorem 1 *If $D = 1$, then every accumulation point of $(G_t^n)_{n=1,\dots,N;t\in\mathbb{N}}$ is a local minimum of f almost surely.*

PROOF. Assume for contradiction, that there is an accumulation point $z \in \mathbb{R}$ such that (w.l.o.g.) f is monotonically decreasing on $B_\tau(z) = (z-\tau, z+\tau)$ for some $\tau > 0$. Since z is an accumulation point, for every $\varepsilon > 0$ G_t^n is inside the neighborhood $B_\varepsilon(z) = (z-\varepsilon, z+\varepsilon)$ of z infinitely often. Fig. 3 gives a visualization of the described situation. For no n and no t, G_t^n enters $[z, z+\tau]$ because otherwise it could never again get closer to z since $f(G_t^n)$ is decreasing with t. Let for some n_0 and some t_0 be $G_{t_0}^{n_0} \in B_\varepsilon(z)$. Now we consider two cases: The first case is that there is at least one particle n (maybe n_0 itself) that has position outside of $B_\tau(z)$, i.e., if the swarm has large potential, this will happen with positive probability. The set $M := \{x \in \mathbb{R}^D \mid f(x-\varepsilon) > f(x) > f(z)\}$, which is the set of all search points that improve the global attractor without abandoning z as an accumulation point, can be made arbitrary small by choosing ε small. So we can assume that with positive probability $M \setminus B_\tau(z)$ will not be hit by particle n_0 within the next iteration. The only situation violating this assumption is when a particle has position and local attractor close to $G_t^{n_0}$ and a velocity greater than τ and pointing towards a point in M, because the influence of the random terms in the movement equation for its next move will be small unless another particle updates the global attractor before. However, for this situation to occur a very specific value of the velocity is necessary, so it will with positive and actually comparatively high probability not happen.

Now we will outline a sequence of iterations that leads particle n to $[z, z+\tau]$. In the worst case, particle n has a large velocity compared to the distances to the local and global attractor. However, after the first constant number of iterations this is no longer the case because this huge velocity will lead the particle far away from the attractors, so it points away from $G_t^{n_0}$ and can therefore be consumed. How many iterations this takes depends on the parameters of the swarm. When a state is reached where the velocity of particle n is much smaller than the distance to the attractors, the global attractor in particular, it is easy to see that the probability for hitting $[z, z+\tau]$ within the next constant number of iterations is positive. I.e., assuming $c_2 > 1$, one decreases the velocity between 0 and $\tau/(3\cdot\chi)$. Then, with $r_t^n \le \tau/(3\cdot c_1\cdot(L_t^n - X_t^n))$ and $s_t^n \in [1/c_2 + (z - G_{t+1}^n)/(c_2\cdot(G_{t+1}^n - X_t^n)), 1/c_2 + \tau/(3\cdot c_2\cdot(G_{t+1}^n - X_t^n))]$, the next step leads to $[z, z+\tau]$. If $c_2 < 1$, the argument is similar, one needs just more iterations. Note that the probability for the described sequence is constant and therefore the probability for this sequence to happen never within the infinite number of times when the global attractor is within an ε from z is 0.

It remains to cover the case when no particle has position outside of $B_\tau(z)$, so assume the potential is low enough such that all particles will stay inside $B_\tau(z)$ forever, which means that the local attractors are inside $B_\tau(z)$ as well. That is the point were Lemma 1 becomes useful. Since f is monotonic on $B_\tau(z)$, the local and the global attractor are always greater or equal to the current position of the particle. Therefore the velocities will with probability 1 all become positive after a finite number of iterations and stay positive. It follows that each particle will exceed its local attractor almost surely after a finite number of iterations. Let t_1 be the time when the last particle has exceeded its local attractor. Then the swarm is positively running from t_1 to t_2 with t_2 being the time when the first particle surpasses a local minimum and therefore leaves or has already left $B_\tau(z)$. With Lemma 1, this will happen after a finite number of iterations almost surely. So, z is no accumulation point of G_t^n. □

Corollary 1 *If $D = 1$, then $f(G_t^n)$ converges towards the value of a local minimum. Particularly, if no two local minima have the same value, then G_t^n converges towards a local minimum. If the swarm converges towards a point $z \in \mathbb{R}$, then z is a local minimum.*

PROOF. The first statement follows directly from Thm. 1. From Def. 2 it follows that the sequence of the global attractors over the time is bounded and therefore has at least one accumulation point. If there is more than one accumulation point, then f has the same value on each of them because f is continuous. Due to Thm. 1 every accumulation point is a local minimum, so if there are no two local minima with the same value, there is only one accumulation point that therefore is the limit of G_t^n. That proves the second statement. The third statement again is a direct consequence of Thm. 1 because convergence of the swarm implies convergence of G_t^n. □

3. MODIFIED PSO ALGORITHM

Now the question arises how much of the results from the 1-dimensional PSO can be transferred to the general case. Unfortunately, the stated result is not true in a D-dimensional situation with $D > 1$. The main problem is the following: Assume that the whole swarm is close to a point that allows improvements neither in positive not in negative changes of the first coordinate. Furthermore let the swarm have high potential in the first and low potential in any other dimension. Then an improvement of the global attractor is still possible and will indeed happen infinitely often, but it is very unlikely and between two updates are many iterations without an update. The reason is that any improvement in some of the dimensions 2, ..., D is voided by the much larger worsening in dimension 1. In the meantime, the swarm tends to converge and therefore continuously looses potential and never gets running. A small and simple modification of the PSO algorithm avoids that problem by enabling the swarm to rebalance the potentials in the different dimensions:

Definition 6 (Modified PSO) *For some arbitrary small but fixed $\delta > 0$, we define the modified PSO via the same equations as the classic PSO in Def. 1, only modifying the* *third equation to*

$$V_{t+1}^{n,d} = \begin{cases} (2 \cdot r_t^{n,d} - 1) \cdot \delta, \\ \quad \text{if } \forall\, d' \in \{1, ..., D\} : |V_t^{n,d'}| + |G_{t+1}^{n,d'} - X_t^{n,d'}| < \delta, \\ \\ \chi \cdot V_t^{n,d} + c_1 \cdot r_t^{n,d} \cdot (L_t^{n,d} - X_t^{n,d}) \\ \qquad + c_2 \cdot s_t^{n,d} \cdot (G_{t+1}^{n,d} - X_t^{n,d}), \\ \quad \text{otherwise.} \end{cases}$$

Whenever the first case applies, we call the step forced.

In words: As soon as for one particle the sum of the velocity and the distance between the position and the global attractor are below the bound of δ in every single dimension, the updated velocity of this particle is drawn u. a. r. from the interval $[-\delta, \delta]$. Note the similarity between this condition and the definition of the potential. Indeed, we could have used the condition $\Phi_{t+1}^{n,d} < \delta$ (with some fixed a) instead, but we decided to keep the modification as simple and independent from the terms occurring in the analysis as possible. Now the potential can no longer converge to 0 while staying unbalanced because if it decreases below a certain bound, we randomly assign a value to the velocity which on expectation has an absolute value of $\delta/2$.

This modified PSO is similar to the Noisy PSO proposed by Lehre and Witt in [11] where they generally add a random perturbation drawn u. a. r. from $[-\delta/2, \delta/2]$ for some small δ and prove that their swarm is able to find a local optimum. However, their analysis is restricted to one specific 1-dimensional fitness function.

In case of our modified PSO, we consider the change from the classic PSO as comparatively simple. The main difference to previous approaches (e. g., [17]) is that the PSO uses the modification not as its engine. Rather, we will see that the number of forced steps is small and if the swarm is not already within an δ-neighborhood of a local optimum, after some forced steps the potential increases and the swarm switches back to classical steps, a behavior we also observed experimentally [15].

Note that we sacrifice the convergence of the swarm in order to increase the quality of the solution, since the potential cannot approach 0 anymore. Instead, we can only expect the global attractor to converge.

Theorem 2 *Using the modified PSO algorithm, every accumulation point of G_t^n is a local minimum of f almost surely.*

PROOF. Assume, for contradiction, that there is some accumulation point z of G_t^n that is no local minimum. Then, in any neighborhood of z and therefore in particular in $B_\delta(z)$, there is a point $x_0 \in B_\delta(z)$ with $f(x_0) < f(z)$. Since f is continuous, x_0 has some neighborhood $B_\tau(x_0)$, such that $f(x) < f(z)$ for every $x \in B_\tau(x_0)$. Fig. 4 gives an overview over the situation.

The set $B_\tau(x_0)$ plays the role of the interval $(z, z+\tau)$ from the proof of Thm. 1. Now we investigate what happens when G_t^n enters $B_\varepsilon(z)$. This will for each $\varepsilon > 0$ happen infinitely often because z is an accumulation point. Like in the first case of the proof of Thm. 1, one can explicitely construct a sequence of iterations, leading a particle into $B_\tau(x_0)$ if the potential is sufficiently high. However, due to the modification of the movement equation, the potential cannot converge to 0 anymore, so the second case from the proof of 1 is unnecessary here. □

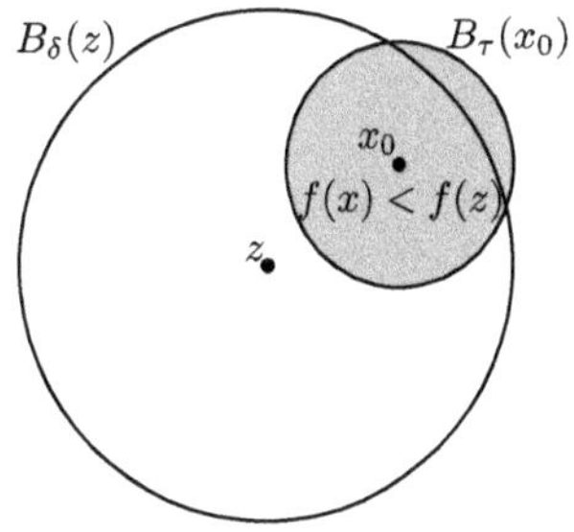

Figure 4: Every point x_0 with $f(x_0) < f(z)$ has a neighborhood $B_\tau(x_0)$, such that $f(x) < f(z)$ for $x \in B_\tau(x_0)$

This result is not surprising because in the modified PSO random perturbations occur when the swarm tends to converge and it is easy to see that small random perturbations can optimize any continuous function (but with a very poor runtime). Note that the proof of Thm. 2 does neither make use of f having a continuous derivative nor of Lemma 1. To supplement this result, we need to prove a statement about how often the modification actually applies. It is obvious that for δ chosen too large, every step of the particles could be forced. The case of δ being small with respect to the structure of the function is the interesting one. On the other hand, if the distance of a particle and a local optimum is smaller than δ, presumably all upcoming steps will be forced because there is no room for further improvements. But one can show that, given the swarm is sufficiently far away from the closest local optimum, the forced steps only balance the potentials between the different dimensions and enable the swarm to become running. In particular, consider the following situation: Let for some dimension d_0 and some $c \gg 1$ be $\frac{\partial f}{\partial d_0} < 0$ on a $(c \cdot \delta)$-neighborhood of the current global attractor and let the swarm have low potential, i. e., every particle has in every dimension potential of order δ. Instead of only being driven by the random perturbation, we would like the swarm to become running in direction d_0, increasing the potential in that direction, so the velocity updates can be done according to the classical case again.

Theorem 3 *In the situation described above, the probability for the swarm to become running within a constant number of iterations is positive and independent of δ.*

PROOF. We will explicitely describe a possible sequence of iterations enabling the swarm to become running. First, the particles decrease their distance to the global attractor in every single dimension to at most $\delta \cdot \epsilon/2$ with $\varepsilon \ll 1$ and a velocity of absolute value less than $\delta \cdot (1 - \varepsilon/2)$, such that the local attractor is updated for all particles except the one whose local attractor is equal to the global attractor. If the current global attractor G_t^n is no local maximum, this can be done because every local attractor has a function value worse than the global attractor and since f is continuous, so the function values of f approach $f(G_t^n)$ when x approaches G_t^n. The case of G_t^n being a local maximum has probability 0. Then the next step of each particle is forced. In the next iteration, the velocity of every particle gets smaller than $\delta \cdot \varepsilon/2$ in each dimension except d_0. In dimension d_0, one particle obtains velocity greater than $\delta \cdot (1+\varepsilon)/2$, such that it gets to a search point that is in dimension d_0 more than $\delta/2$ and in any other dimension at most $\varepsilon \cdot \delta$ away from the previous global attractor. For ε sufficiently small, this particle will update the global attractor since f has a positive partial derivative in dimension d_0. Every other particle obtains in d_0 a velocity less than $-\delta\cdot(1+\varepsilon)/2$, making sure that its new position and the new global attractor after that step differ by more than δ. So the next step will not be forced and the potentials have order $\sqrt{\delta}$ in dimension d_0 and only $\sqrt{\delta\cdot\epsilon}$ in every other dimension. So for ε sufficiently small with respect to the function f, the swarm will become running and therefore the steps will actually become unforced. □

The behavior of the modified PSO is the same as of the classic PSO, except that due to the modification the particles can overcome "corners," i. e., if the global attractor stagnates because the potential of wrong dimensions is too high and the potential of dimensions where the function value can be decreased is too low, the modification helps to balance the potentials of the different dimensions. The "blind" algorithm that just randomly checks a point around the previous best solution with range δ would of course find a local minimum but the running time would tend towards ∞ if δ approaches 0.

4. CONCLUSION

This paper focuses on the capability of a particle swarm to find a local minimum. The PSO algorithm is analyzed under this aspect and it is pointed out why the swarm might not always find a local minimum, namely the swarm gets stuck if the differences of the potentials between the dimensions are too large. A suggestion to modify the algorithm by randomly assigning a small velocity when the potential of a particle falls below a certain bound is suggested. It is proven that this modification together with some new parameter selection guidelines enables the swarm to find a local minimum for a large class of objective functions. Additionally, it is shown that the modification does not take over the swarm, it just corrects the direction before the classic movement equations are applied again.

Acknowledgement

We would like to thank Berthold Vöcking for useful advice on an earlier version of the paper, and the anonymous referees for their valuable remarks.

5. REFERENCES

[1] A. Carlisle and G. Dozier. An off-the-shelf PSO. In *Proc. Particle Swarm Optimization Workshop*, pages 1–6, 2001.

[2] M. Clerc and J. Kennedy. The particle swarm – explosion, stability, and convergence in a multidimensional complex space. *IEEE Transactions on Evolutionary Computation*, 6:58–73, 2002.

[3] R. Durrett. *Probability: Theory and Examples.* Cambridge Series in Statistical and Probabilistic Mathematics. Cambridge University Press, 2010.

[4] R. C. Eberhart and J. Kennedy. A new optimizer using particle swarm theory. In *Proc. 6th International Symposium on Micro Machine and Human Science*, pages 39–43, 1995.

[5] S. Helwig. *Particle Swarms for Constrained Optimization.* PhD thesis, Department of Computer Science, University of Erlangen-Nuremberg, 2010. urn:nbn:de:bvb:29-opus-19334.

[6] S. Helwig and R. Wanka. Theoretical analysis of initial particle swarm behavior. In *Proc. 10th Int. Conf. on Parallel Problem Solving from Nature (PPSN)*, pages 889–898, 2008.

[7] J. Jägersküpper. Analysis of a simple evolutionary algorithm for minimization in Euclidean spaces. *Theoretical Comput. Sci.*, 379:329–347, 2007.

[8] M. Jiang, Y. P. Luo, and S. Y. Yang. Particle swarm optimization – stochastic trajectory analysis and parameter selection. In F. T. S. Chan and M. K. Tiwari, editors, *Swarm Intelligence – Focus on Ant and Particle Swarm Optimization*, pages 179–198. 2007. Corrected version of [9].

[9] M. Jiang, Y. P. Luo, and S. Y. Yang. Stochastic convergence analysis and parameter selection of the standard particle swarm optimization algorithm. *Inf. Process. Lett.*, 102:8–16, 2007. Corrected by [8].

[10] J. Kennedy and R. C. Eberhart. Particle swarm optimization. In *Proc. IEEE International Conference on Neural Networks*, volume 4, pages 1942–1948, 1995.

[11] P. K. Lehre and C. Witt. Finite first hitting time versus stochastic convergence in particle swarm optimisation, 2011. arXiv:1105.5540.

[12] J. E. Onwunalu and L. J. Durlofsky. Application of a particle swarm optimization algorithm for determining optimum well location and type. *Computational Geosciences*, 14:183–198, 2010.

[13] B. K. Panigrahi, Y. Shi, and M.-H. Lim, editors. *Handbook of Swarm Intelligence — Concepts, Principles and Applications.* Springer, 2011.

[14] K. Ramanathan, V. M. Periasamy, M. Pushpavanam, and U. Natarajan. Particle swarm optimisation of hardness in nickel diamond electro composites. *Archives of Computational Materials Science and Surface Engineering*, 1:232–236, 2009.

[15] M. Schmitt and R. Wanka. Particles prefer walking along the axes: Experimental insights into the behavior of a particle swarm. In *Proc. Genetic and Evolutionary Computation Conference (GECCO)*, 2013. Full version arXiv:1303.6145.

[16] I. C. Trelea. The particle swarm optimization algorithm: Convergence analysis and parameter selection. *Inf. Process. Lett.*, 85:317–325, 2003.

[17] F. van den Bergh and A. P. Engelbrecht. A new locally convergent particle swarm optimiser. In *Proc. IEEE Int. Conf. on Systems, Man and Cybernetics (SMC)*, volume 3, pages 94–99, 2002.

[18] M. P. Wachowiak, R. Smolíková, Y. Zheng, J. M. Zurada, and A. S. Elmaghraby. An approach to multimodal biomedical image registration utilizing particle swarm optimization. *IEEE Transactions on Evolutionary Computation*, 8:289–301, 2004.

[19] C. Witt. Why standard particle swarm optimisers elude a theoretical runtime analysis. In *Proc. 10th ACM SIGEVO Workshop on Foundations of Genetic Algorithms (FOGA)*, pages 13–20, 2009.

[20] C. Witt. Theory of particle swarm optimization. In A. Auger and B. Doerr, editors, *Theory of Randomized Search Heuristics*, chapter 7, pages 197–223. World Scientific Publishing, 2011.

Author Index

www.ingramcontent.com/pod-product-compliance
Lightning Source LLC
LaVergne TN
LVHW080105011026
849160LV00013B/1035
* 9 7 8 1 4 5 0 3 2 7 0 1 5 *